THE
UNIVERSAL JEWISH
ENCYCLOPEDIA

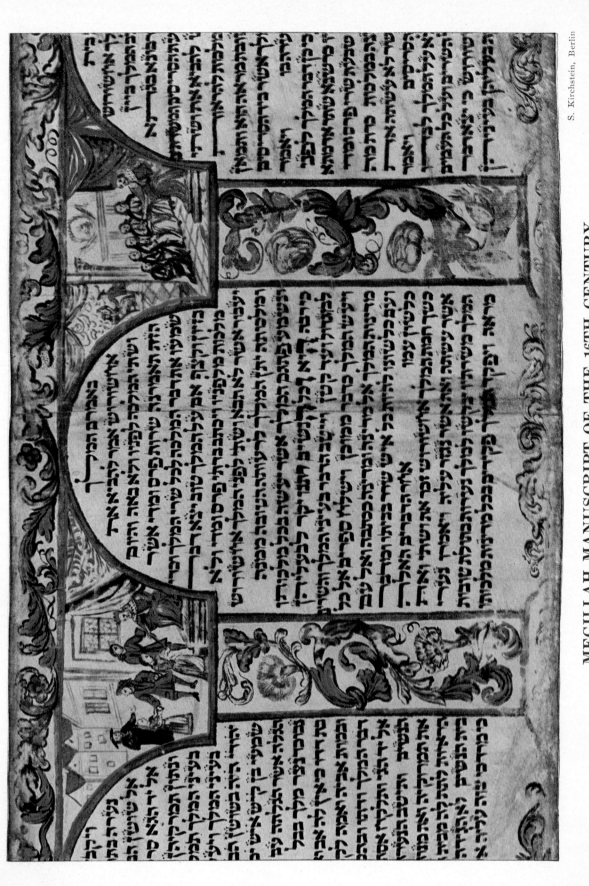

MEGILLAH MANUSCRIPT OF THE 16TH CENTURY

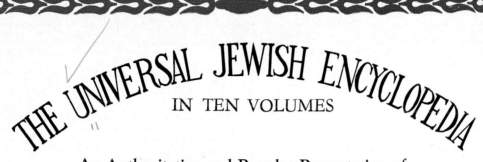

THE UNIVERSAL JEWISH ENCYCLOPEDIA

IN TEN VOLUMES

An Authoritative and Popular Presentation of Jews and Judaism Since the Earliest Times

EDITED BY

ISAAC LANDMAN

Rabbi of Congregation Beth Elohim, Brooklyn, New York
Founder and Director of the Academy for Adult Jewish Education

In Collaboration with the Following
BOARD OF EDITORS:

EXECUTIVE AND LITERARY EDITOR
Louis Rittenberg, American Editor, *London Jewish Chronicle;* formerly Editor, *The American Hebrew*

AMERICANA: A. S. W. Rosenbach, President, American Jewish Historical Society

ANGLO-JUDAICA: Paul Goodman, Historian and Author, London

ARCHAEOLOGY: William F. Albright, Professor, Semitic Languages, Johns Hopkins

ART: Clifton Harby Levy, Rabbi, Author and Journalist

BIBLE: Julian Morgenstern, President and Professor of Bible and Semitic Languages, Hebrew Union College

ETHICS: Louis L. Mann, Rabbi of Temple Sinai, Chicago; Lecturer, Oriental Languages and Literature, University of Chicago

HISTORY: Ismar Elbogen, Research Professor, Jewish Theological Seminary, Hebrew Union College, Jewish Institute of Religion, and Dropsie College

Abraham A. Neuman, President and Professor of History, Dropsie College

JEWISH LITERATURE: Joshua Bloch, Chief, Jewish Division, N. Y. Public Library

LITURGY: Solomon B. Freehof, Rabbi of Congregation Rodef Shalom, Pittsburgh; formerly Professor of Liturgy, Hebrew Union College

PHILOSOPHY: Leo Strauss, Associate Professor, Political Science, Graduate Faculty of Political and Social Science, New School for Social Research

RABBINICS: Louis Finkelstein, President and Professor of Theology, Jewish Theological Seminary of America

SOCIAL INSTITUTIONS: Maurice J. Karpf, Formerly President, Faculty, and Professor, Social Technology, Graduate School for Social Work, New York; Executive Director, Federation of Jewish Welfare Organizations and Jewish Community Council, Los Angeles

THEOLOGY: Samuel S. Cohon, Professor of Theology, Hebrew Union College

REVISION EDITOR: Abraham Shinedling, Rabbi, Linguist and Reviewer

DIRECTOR OF RESEARCH
Simon Cohen, D.D., Former Instructor at the Hebrew Union College School for Teachers

★

VOLUME 7

THE UNIVERSAL JEWISH ENCYCLOPEDIA, INC., NEW YORK

The United States Work Projects Administration for the City of New York (Official Project No. 465-97-3-39) cooperated with the editors of this work to the extent of providing scholarly employment for a highly specialized group of clergymen, professors and college graduates, in order that they might maintain their skills by working in fields as near as possible to those in which they had been trained. The Works Progress Administration, however, takes no responsibility whatever for the final form of the articles in the preparation of which this group participated, or for any opinions or judgments expressed by editors of the Encyclopedia.

In accordance with the provisions of the Works Projects Administration, the research material compiled by WPA workers will be deposited in the New York Public Library, where it will be available to the public.

Acknowledgment

The editors make grateful acknowledgment of the assistance rendered to this work by the United States Work Projects Administration in supplying research workers to compile material from authoritative sources in the fields of biography, ancient and medieval history and literature, translators in several languages, and bibliographers.

The final shaping of the articles—including syntax, style and any expressions of opinion or judgments—is solely the responsibility of the editors and contributors, not of any of the workers furnished by the Works Progress Administration.

MADE IN THE UNITED STATES OF AMERICA

SPECIAL CONTRIBUTORS TO VOLUME SEVEN

WILLIAM F. ALBRIGHT, Baltimore
Professor of Semitic Languages, Johns Hopkins University

GRIGORY ARONSON, New York
Yiddish and Russian Writer

ISAAC L. ASOFSKY, New York
Executive, Jewish Social Service Association

SAMUEL ATLAS, London
Author and Lecturer

JULIUS BAB, New York
Dramatic Critic and Author

FRITZ BAER, Jerusalem
Professor of History, Hebrew University

MAJER SAMUEL BALABAN, Warsaw
Historian and Educator

SOLOMON BALSAM, Brooklyn
Journalist

BERNARD J. BAMBERGER, Albany
Rabbi, Temple Beth Emeth

FRITZ BAMBERGER, Chicago
Instructor of Philosophy, College of Jewish Studies

JOSEPH L. BARON, Milwaukee
Author, and Rabbi, Congregation Emanu-El-B'nai Jeshurun

NATHAN CARO BELTH, New York
Director of Public Relations, Army and Navy Service Division, Jewish Welfare Board

EPHRAIM I. BENNETT, New York
Writer

DAVID BERENT, Lewiston, Me.
Rabbi, Congregation Beth Jacob

SOL BERNSTEIN, New York
Research Worker

MARTIN BIRNBAUM, Westport, Conn.
Art Critic

EUGENE BLACHSCHLEGER, Montgomery, Ala.
Rabbi, Temple Beth-Or

JOSHUA BLOCH, New York
Chief, Jewish Division, New York Public Library

ABRAHAM JAKOB BRAWER, Jerusalem
Historian, Cartographer and Author

MOSES BRIND, New York
Poet and Journalist

LOUIS CASSEL, Mobile, Ala.
Rabbi, Ahavas Chesed Congregation

UMBERTO CASSUTO, Rome
Rabbi and Historian

MARCUS COHN, Basel, Switzerland
Jurist

FERDINAND DANZIGER, New York
Research Worker

GABRIEL DAVIDSON, New York
General Manager, Jewish Agricultural Society

M. DLUZNOWSKI, New York
Journalist

WALTER DUCAT, New York
Research Worker

ALEXANDER M. DUSHKIN, New York
Director, Jewish Education Committee

MARGARET T. EDELHEIM, New York
Editor, "Ort Economic Bulletin"

DAVID MAX EICHHORN, Tallahassee, Fla.
Rabbi, Temple Israel

ALFRED EINSTEIN, Northampton, Mass.
Professor of Music, Smith College

ISMAR ELBOGEN, New York
Research Professor, Jewish Theological Seminary, Hebrew Union College, Jewish Institute of Religion, and Dropsie College

FRANK EPSTEIN, New York
General Secretary, Federation of Lithuanian Jews

EZEKIEL MOSES EZEKIEL (deceased)
Former Professor in Hebrew and Semitics, University of Bombay

ADOLPH J. FEINBERG, Hammond, Ind.
Rabbi, Temple Beth-El

WALTER J. FISCHEL, Jerusalem
Fellow, Institute of Oriental Studies, Hebrew University

MOSES Z. R. FRANK, New York
Journalist

CLARENCE I. FREED, New York
Writer and Linguist

HUGO FUCHS, Buenos Aires
Rabbi and Author

JOSEPH GAER, Washington, D. C.
Author and Editor; Consultant to the Departments of Agriculture and the Treasury

SERGE GELEBIAN, New York
Research Worker

MOSES GINSBURGER, Strasbourg, France
Author, Librarian and Professor

JOSEPH GITIN, Butte, Mont.
Rabbi, Congregation B'nai Israel

ABRAHAM Z. GOLDBERG (deceased)
Former Writer and Editor

MILTON W. GOLDBERGER, Memphis, Tenn.
Editor, "The Hebrew Watchman"

PAUL GOODMAN, London
Historian and Author

BESS GORDON, New York
Research Worker

HIRSCH LOEB GORDON, New York
Writer and Critic

L. ELLIOT GRAFMAN, Long Beach, Cal.
Rabbi, Temple Israel

ALAN S. GREEN, Troy, N. Y.
Rabbi, Temple B'rith Sholom

JULIUS H. GREENSTONE, Philadelphia
Principal, Gratz College

WILLIAM GROPPER, New York
Painter and Cartoonist

MAURICE GROSSMAN, Miami, Fla.
Executive Director, Y.M.H.A.

ALFRED GROTTE, Breslau, Germany
Specialist on Synagogal Architecture

MAX GRUNWALD, Jerusalem
Rabbi and Author

JULIUS GUTTMANN, Jerusalem
Professor of Philosophy, Hebrew University

HERMAN HAILPERIN, Pittsburgh
Rabbi, Congregation Tree of Life

HARRY HANSEN, New York
Literary and Dramatic Critic, "New York World Telegram"

ISRAEL HARBURG, Lynn, Mass.
Rabbi, Temple Beth El

GEORG HERLITZ, Jerusalem
Director, Central Archive of the Jewish Agency

LIONEL HILL, New York
Poet

ABRAHAM HORVITZ, Madison, Wis.
Rabbi, Congregation Agudas Achim

MOSES HYAMSON, New York
Professor of Codes, Jewish Theological Seminary of America

DAVID S. JACOBSON, San Antonio, Texas
Rabbi, Temple Beth-El

JULIUS JARECKI, Berlin
Scholar

MAX JOSEPH, Jerusalem
Rabbi and Author

HENRY E. KAGAN, Mount Vernon, N. Y.
Rabbi, Sinai Temple

FRITZ KAHN, Palestine
Physician and Author

HANS KALISCH, Berlin
Attorney

SCHIMA KAUFMAN, Washington, D. C.
Biographer

RUDOLF KAYSER, New York
Author

SOLOMON KERSTEIN, New York
Publicity Director, Mizrachi Movement

BRUNO KIRSCHNER, Jerusalem
Co-editor, "Jüdisches Lexikon"

SAMUEL KLEIN (deceased)
Former Ordinary Professor of Historical Geography, Hebrew University

REBEKAH KOHUT, New York
Author

SAMUEL KRAUSS, Cambridge, England
Professor and Author

SAMUEL KREITER, New York
Research Worker

ALEXANDER KRISTIANPOLLER, Jerusalem
Librarian and Author

CORLISS LAMONT, New York
Author

JUDA LEO LANDAU, Johannesburg, South Africa
Chief Rabbi, Federated Synagogues of the Witwatersrand

PAUL LAZARUS, Wiesbaden, Germany
Rabbi

ALGERNON LEE, New York
Writer

ARTHUR J. LELYVELD, Omaha, Neb.
Rabbi, Temple Israel

JACOB LESTSCHINSKY, New York
Director, Department of Economics and Statistics, Institute of Jewish Affairs, New York

RUDOLF LESZYNSKY, Tel-Aviv
Orientalist and Historian

IRVING M. LEVEY, Brockton, Mass.
Rabbi, Temple Israel

SAMUEL J. LEVINSON, Brooklyn
Rabbi, Temple Beth Emeth

FELIX A. LEVY, Chicago
Rabbi, Congregation Emanuel

LOUIS LEWIN, Breslau, Germany
Rabbi and Historian

SALOMON HUGO LIEBEN, Prague
Historian

Continued on next page

SPECIAL CONTRIBUTORS TO VOLUME SEVEN

Continued from preceding page

Max A. Luria, Brooklyn
Professor of Romance Languages, Brooklyn College

Edgar F. Magnin, Los Angeles
Rabbi, Congregation B'nai B'rith

Joseph Marcus, Haverstraw, N. Y.
Rabbi

Harry S. Margolis, St. Paul, Minn.
Rabbi, Mount Zion Hebrew Congregation

Adam Margoshes, New York
Editorial Assistant

Isaak Markon, Ramsgate, England
Professor and Librarian

David F. Markus, Constantinople
Rabbi

Harry H. Mayer, Kansas City, Mo.
Rabbi, Temple B'nai Jehudah

Joseph Meisl, Jerusalem
Former General Secretary, Berlin Jewish Community

Saul Mézan, Sofia, Bulgaria
Bulgarian Jewish Leader and Author

Ella McKenna, Friend Mielziner, Truro, Mass.
Biographer

Simon Miller, Yonkers, N. Y.
Research Aide

Robert A. Millikan, Pasadena, Cal.
Physicist

Albert G. Minda, Minneapolis, Minn.
Rabbi, Temple Israel

Jacob S. Minkin, New York
Rabbi and Author

Henry Montor, New York
Executive Director, United Palestine Appeal

Leopold Moses, Palestine
Museum Curator and Author

Moses Moskowitz, New York
Secretary, Committee on Peace Studies, American Jewish Committee

Simon Mowshowitz, New York
Research Worker

Leon Nemoy, New Haven, Conn.
Curator, Hebrew and Arabic Literature, Yale University

Siegbert Neufeld, Leipzig, Germany
Rabbi and Historian

Abraham A. Neuman, Philadelphia
President, Dropsie College

Nathan A. Pelcovits, New York
Instructor, Department of Government, College of the City of New York

Francis D. Perkins, New York
Music Editor, "New York Herald Tribune"

Eugene Pessen (deceased)
Former Librarian

David Philipson, Cincinnati
Rabbi Emeritus, Bene Israel Congregation

Chris Phoskos, New York
Research Worker

David de Sola Pool, New York
Rabbi, Spanish and Portuguese Synagogue Shearith Israel

Arthur Posner, Jerusalem
Rabbi and Author

Bernard Postal, Washington, D. C.
Director, Public Relations, B'nai B'rith

Samuel Rabinowitz, New York
Research Worker

Samuel Rappaport, Vienna
Rabbi and Author

Joseph Rauch, Louisville, Ky.
Rabbi, Congregation Adath Israel

Charles Recht, New York
Author and Poet

Victor E. Reichert, Cincinnati
Rabbi, Bene Israel Congregation

Nathan Ricardo, New York
Journalist

Paul Rieger (deceased)
Former Rabbi

Louis Rosenberg, Winnipeg
Agricultural Economist and Author

Ludwig A. Rosenthal (deceased)
Former Rabbi

Newman H. Rosenthal, Melbourne, Australia
Communal Leader

Charles A. Rubenstein, New York
Rabbi and Author

Ira E. Sanders, Little Rock, Ark.
Rabbi, Congregation B'nai Israel

Aron Sandler, Palestine
Physician

Nicholas Sargologos, New York
Research Worker

Israel Schapiro, Washington, D. C.
Librarian, Semitics Division, Library of Congress

Henrietta Schmerler (deceased)
Research Worker

Chaim Schneid, Palestine
Educator

Karl Schwarz, Palestine
Art Historian, Former Custodian of the Art Collection, Berlin Jewish Community

Simon Segal, New York
Member, Research Institute for Peace Studies of the American Jewish Committee

Leo Shpall, New York
Journalist

Abraham Shusterman, Baltimore
Rabbi, Har Sinai Congregation

Mendel Silber, New Orleans, La.
Rabbi, Gates of Prayer Congregation

Lou H. Silberman, Jr., Cincinnati
Rabbi, Hebrew Union College

Leon Julius Silberstrom, Palestine
Chemist

Henry P. Silverman, Kingston, Jamaica
Rabbi, United Congregation of Israelites

Solomon L. Skoss, Philadelphia
Professor of Arabic, Dropsie College

Philip Slomovitz, Detroit
Editor, "Jewish News"

Joshua Starr, New York
Managing Editor, "Jewish Social Studies"

William Stein, Tarrytown, N. Y.
Professor and Historian

Meier Steinglass, New York
Journalist

J. W. F. Stoppelman, New York
Editor, "Netherlands News"

Mark Sullivan, New York
Journalist and Commentator

Alphons Summit, New York
Writer

Sidney S. Tedesche, Brooklyn
Rabbi, Union Temple

Felix A. Theilhaber, Palestine
Physician

Schulim Abi Todos (deceased)
Former Librarian and Educator

Louis Untermeyer, New York
Author and Editor

Benjamin Veit, New York
Former Assistant Superintendent in charge of Junior High Schools

Aaron Walden, Monticello, N. Y.
Rabbi, Jewish Community Center of Monticello, Inc.

Bruno Walter, New York
Conductor

Joseph Warren, Lowell, Mass.
Rabbi, Temple Beth El

Herbert Weinstock, New York
Musical Historian

Robert Weltsch, Jerusalem
Editor

M. Donald Whyte, New York
Former Director, Whyte Gallery, Washington, D. C.

Max Wiener, Cincinnati
Lecturer in Rabbinics, Hebrew Union College

Jonah B. Wise, New York
Rabbi, Central Synagogue

Siegfried Wolff (deceased)
Former Attorney and Author

George B. Wright, New York
Research Worker

Leah R. C. Yoffie, Chapel Hill, N. C.
Educator and Folklorist

Israel Zoller, Trieste
Rabbi and Former Professor

Rules Governing Transliterations, Citations, Spelling of Proper Names, and Abbreviations

THE following general rules will aid the reader in consulting these pages:

TRANSLITERATION. In transliterating from languages that do not employ the Roman alphabet, our aim has been to approximate the phonetic sound of the words for the benefit of the reader who does not understand such languages. It is assumed that the scholar will have no trouble recognizing the words in any case, while the lay reader is apt to be confused by special distinguishing signs.

In the case of Hebrew and Yiddish, transliteration has been preferred throughout, the only exceptions being instances where reproduction of the Hebrew letters may be essential to the comprehension of the article.

Hebrew has been transliterated in accordance with the rules adopted by the Joint Committee of the Jewish Theological Seminary of America, the Hebrew Union College, Central Conference of American Rabbis, and National Council for Jewish Education. We have, however, made two exceptions: *ch* instead of *kh*, to represent the aspirate Kaf, and *tz* instead of *z,* to represent Tzade. In addition, Hebrew words have been transliterated in their entirety, without the use of hyphens, while a reduplication of letters has been reduced to a minimum. (See chart on pp. 202-3 for the transliteration of consonants. For vowels see Volume 10).

Yiddish is transliterated (phonetically) with special care to distinguish its spelling from that of German. Thus *sh* is used instead of *sch,* and *fun* instead of *von.*

SPELLING OF NAMES. In all instances where the individual signs his name in Roman letters, the name is spelled precisely as he himself gives it, e.g. Chaim, Jakob, Zacharias. If, however, the person wrote in Hebrew, Russian or Yiddish, the name is recorded according to our rules of transliteration—unless it happens to be Biblical. In the latter event, the spelling adopted by the Jewish Publication Society of America is the criterion followed.

CITATIONS. When given in English, citations from the Bible conform to the version published by the Jewish Publication Society of America. The number before the colon indicates the chapter; the number following, the verse (*Gen.* I:8-10; *Isa.* 23:14).

Tractates of the Babylonian Talmud are given by their names, by page and column, according to standard usage (*Taan.* 30a). The Palestinian Talmud is indicated by prefixing Yer. (Yerushalmi); page and column are designated according to the Krotoschin edition. But chapter and Halachah are cited for the guidance of readers who have no access to this edition (*Yer. B.B.* 5:2, 15b). Mishnah citations give chapter and verse in the same form as citations from the Bible.

In citing the Midrash, we use the more readily understandable form of Midrash Genesis, Midrash Exodus, etc., rather than Hebrew terms that require explanation (Bereshith Rabbah, Shemoth Rabbah, etc.). Classical works of Jewish literature are cited, wherever possible, by standard editions and pages.

LITERATURE. The bibliography, or literature, given at the end of articles is furnished primarily to enable the interested reader to learn more about any given subject than space limits of the article permit. It is authoritative throughout, yet no complete bibliography has been attempted since many of the sources contain no more than has been adduced in the article itself, while others, especially of foreign tongue, may tend to confuse rather than help.

Standard reference sources, such as encyclopedias, *Konversationslexika,* biographical collections and literary catalogues, are ordinarily omitted on the assumption that the student will consult them automatically when in need of collateral data. Preference has been given to reference works in English. Books and periodicals have not been included where investigation has shown that they are not easily available to the reader.

TITLES: In determining titles for the articles, care has been taken to choose such names and terms as are likely to be most familiar to those consulting our pages. Individuals of the modern era are entered under their family names. For the ancient and medieval periods, where the usual form is A ben (or ibn) B, the listing will be found under the first name, e.g. Aaron ben Elijah. Where, however, ben or ibn is part of the family name (as in the case of Ben Zeeb, or Ibn Tibbon), the person in question is listed under the family name, e.g., Ibn Tibbon, Judah—not Judah ibn Tibbon.

The general order of arrangement of titles embodying names follows: (1) single names, e.g. Abraham; (2) titles containing the name of the individual, e.g. Abraham, Apocalypse of; (3) titles representing individuals listed by their first names, e.g. Abraham bar Hiyya Hanasi; (4) titles listed by family names, e.g. Abraham, Abraham. The words *of* and *the* are disregarded, but not *bar, ben* or *ibn.*

CROSS REFERENCES. Special care has been taken to assist the reader by extensive cross-references, so that information desired may be obtained with the least amount of effort.

The *See also* paragraphs at the conclusion of articles (always present in general subjects) will aid the reader in securing additional details on the subjects under examination or on kindred topics.

ABBREVIATIONS. Essential abbreviations employed throughout the encyclopedia include—b. (born), d. (died), cent. (century), ed. (edition), edit. (edited by), trans. (translated by). A list of abbreviations pertaining to the Biblical references follows:

BIBLE

Gen.	Genesis
Ex.	Exodus
Lev.	Leviticus
Num.	Numbers
Deut.	Deuteronomy
Josh.	Joshua
I Sam.	I Samuel
II Sam.	II Samuel
Isa.	Isaiah
Jer.	Jeremiah
Ezek.	Ezekiel
Ob.	Obadiah
Hab.	Habakkuk
Zeph.	Zephaniah
Zech.	Zechariah
Mal.	Malachi
Ps.	Psalms
Prov.	Proverbs
Lam.	Lamentations
Eccl.	Ecclesiastes
Neh.	Nehemiah
I Chron.	I Chronicles
II Chron.	II Chronicles

NEW TESTAMENT

Matt.	Matthew
Rom.	Romans
Cor.	Corinthians
Gal.	Galatians
Eph.	Ephesians
Phil.	Philippians
Col.	Colossians
Thess.	Thessalonians
Tim.	Timothy
Philem.	Philemon
Heb.	Hebrews
Rev.	Revelation

TALMUD

A. Z.	Abodah Zarah
Arach.	Arachin
B. B.	Baba Bathra
B. K.	Baba Kamma
B. M.	Baba Metzia
Bech.	Bechoroth
Ber.	Berachoth
Betz.	Betzah
Bik.	Bikkurim
Eduy.	Eduyoth
Erub.	Erubin
Git.	Gittin
Hag.	Hagigah
Hal.	Hallah
Hor.	Horayoth
Hul.	Hullin
Ker.	Kerithoth
Keth.	Kethuboth
Kid.	Kiddushin
Kin.	Kinnim
M. K.	Moed Katan
M. S.	Maaser Sheni
Maas.	Maaseroth
Mach.	Machshirin
Mash.	Mashkin
Mak.	Makkoth
Meg.	Megillah
Meil.	Meilah
Men.	Menahoth
Mid.	Middoth
Ned.	Nedarim
Neg.	Negaim
Nez.	Nezikin
Nid.	Niddah
Ohal.	Ohaloth
Pes.	Pesahim
R. H.	Rosh Hashanah
Sab.	Sabbath
San.	Sanhedrin
Shebi.	Shebiith
Shebu.	Shebuoth
Shek.	Shekalim
Suk.	Sukkah
T. Y.	Tebul Yom
Taan.	Taanith
Tem.	Temurah
Toh.	Toharoth
Uktz.	Uktzin
Yad.	Yadaim
Yeb.	Yebamoth
Zebah.	Zebahim

This volume is
dedicated to the
noble memory of

Portrait by Mark S. Joffe

JACOB HENRY SCHIFF
(1847-1920)

Philanthropist and communal
leader, whose life linked the cultures of Europe and America, and
whose philanthropy, freely and
impartially extended, translated
the creed of Judaism into action

LEVITAN, ISAAC ILYITCH, painter, b. Kibarty, near Wirballen, Russia, 1861; d. Moscow, Russia, 1900. He studied under Savrasov and at the Moscow Art School. His *Autumn Day in Sokolniki,* painted at the age of nineteen, attracted wide attention. He belonged at first to the Society of Wandering Exhibitions, an association of independent artists who had broken away from academic constraint, and later to Mir Is-kusstva (The World of Art), a congenial group whose appreciation was beneficial to the development of his particular genius.

Striving after new media of expression, Levitan sought indefatigably to improve his technique. Painting his subjects over and over again, he succeeded in expressing what he saw in Russian landscape: its quiet charm, its melancholy. His influence on other painters was marked, and he was considered the father of Russian landscape painting. His painting, *The Needy,* was awarded first prize at the Amateur Exhibition in 1892; and his *Isle in the Government of Novgorod, Spring* and *Autumn* won a silver medal at the Paris World Exhibition. He was appointed member and director of the Division of Landscape Painting of the Moscow Art Academy, and was given supervision of instruction at the Moscow Art School.

A great number of his tableaux are in the Tretyakov collection at Moscow, others at the Russian Museum of Leningrad.

Lit.: Thieme, U., and Becker, F., *Allgemeines Lexikon der bildenden Künstler,* vol. 23, p. 165; Benois, Alexandre, *The Russian School of Painting* (1916) 160; *Israel, La Rassegna Mensile,* vol. 6 (1931) 293-300.

Solomon Levitan

Isaac Ilyitch Levitan

LEVITAN, SOLOMON, state treasurer of Wisconsin, b. Prussia, 1862; d. Madison, Wis., 1940. Educated at the Yeshivas of Slobodka, Kovno, and Vilna, Levitan came to the United States in 1880. He peddled in Maryland, Pennsylvania, and Wisconsin, and became the owner of several stores in the latter state. He was an organizer of the Commercial National Bank, Madison (1907), served as president from 1914 to 1926, and as chairman of its board of directors from 1927 to his death. He was also chairman of the board of the Madison Trust Company from 1926 on, and president of the People's Investment Co.

A colorful figure in Wisconsin commercial and political affairs, Levitan was widely known as "Uncle Sol," and once stood for election as lieutenant-governor of the state. He was a delegate to several Republican national conventions, and in 1922 was elected State Treasurer of Wisconsin, serving five consecutive terms to 1932. He was returned to that office again for another term in 1936, running on the Progressive ticket. He was treasurer of the Board of Regents of the University of Wisconsin and of the State Normal Schools of Wisconsin.

Lit.: American Hebrew, Dec. 7, 1924, p. 144; *Jewish Advocate* (Boston), July, Aug., 1938, p. 1; *New York Times,* Feb. 28, 1940.

LEVITES, according to the Bible, the descendants of Levi and members of that tribe which had no portion in the inheritance of Canaan. The eponymous ancestor was the third son of Jacob by Leah, and apart from this biographical fact only two others are mentioned, i.e. the episode of Shechem (*Gen.* 34) and the blessing of Jacob (*Gen.* 49:5-7). In both the latter

Levi is coupled with his elder brother Simeon; in the last reference they are cursed to be "scattered in Israel." Simeon as a tribe was dispersed, and probably never existed as a separate geographical unit. Its inheritance which a later generation assigned to it actually belonged to Judah (cf. *Josh.* 19:1-9 with 15:26-32, 42; *I Chron.* 4:28-33; *I Sam.* 27:6; 30:30; *II Sam.* 24:7; cf. also *I Kings* 19:3). In the Blessing of Moses no mention is made of Simeon. Levi ceased to exist, if ever it was such, as a secular tribe, and was reconstructed on a sacerdotal basis, according to the views of some scholars.

Others doubt even the priestly origin of the tribe of Levi. Because its members had neither a common ethnic nor a geographic bond, claiming descent from Moses, because of the close association between Simeon and Levi, and because the scene of Moses' greatest exploits was in and around Sinai, Elias Auerbach thinks that Levi must have occupied the extreme south of Palestine near Simeon's reputed territory (cf. *Judges* 1:17; *Josh.* 19:1-9). Moses' activity was centered around the oasis of Kadesh, the northern end of the Sinai peninsula, hence, says this scholar, one must look for the habitat of the Moses (descendant of Levi) clan in this region. Auerbach would explain the name as a cognate or borrowed form of l-w-' (feminine, l-w-'-t), a word found in the inscriptions of the Minean oasis *El Ola* and which means priest. This etymology is not quite satisfactory, although it does not conflict necessarily with the more plausible derivation from a Hebrew root which means "attached to" (that is, to the service of God or the sanctuary). The account of the history and development of the Levites depends upon the critical views of the writer and the chronological order of the documents of the Pentateuch accepted by the particular critic, hence the following description would not be endorsed by some students.

According to *Deut.* 33:9 (the Blessing of Moses), a Levite is one who devotes himself to the service of the Lord, who interprets the oracle and who teaches Israel Torah. Verse 9 perhaps refers to the incident of the Golden Calf (*Ex.* 32:25-29), according to which story the Levites, for their zeal in slaying the idolators, were "consecrated" to the Lord; thus Moses' own kinsmen became the bearers of the priesthood. There is no mention, however, of a priestly tribe, and perhaps in both these passages, certainly in *Deuteronomy*, Levi may mean simply a consecrated person without any patronymic significance. Thus the origin of the priesthood would be voluntary, and the priesthood would be recruited from all geographic and tribal divisions. This seems to be borne out by *Judges* 17:7-13, which refers to a young man of Beth-lehem in Judah, who was a Levite and found a "job" with Micah as officiating minister of the latter's "private chapel." In *Judges* 19:1 we find a Levite sojourning on the farther side of the hill country of Ephraim. *Deut.* 14:27 certainly portrays a pre-Josianic or even a pre-kingdom condition where the Levite depends upon the bounty of his neighbors, before there was a priestly caste with its perquisites and its fixed sanctuaries and steady positions for the ministrant. Similarly, *Deut.* 26, which contains a very ancient liturgical formula—a dialogue between priest and offrant at any sacred place ("which the Lord shall choose," according to verse 2) in which the part

of the layman is far more important than that of the priest—points to a fluid state of affairs in which (verse 3) there is no priestly caste. The sacrificer eats his offering himself, and the Levite (verse 11) shares with the stranger. In the tithing in verse 12 the priest has no share. The chapter presupposes a distinction between Levite and priest, both of whom, according to the oldest narrative, descended from Moses. *Deut.* 26 probably reflects a time, certainly pre-Josianic, when the priests of the provincial sanctuaries moved around from one holy place to another (verse 3). *Deut.* 18 prescribes the portion of the priests and the Levites, verse 5 revealing that the former have become a caste, while verse 6 shows that the itinerant Levite still receives consideration.

If we accept this theory of the origin of the Levites rather than that which makes the Levites members of a blood clan, the development took place as follows: The first-born among the shepherds was sanctified to the service of the Lord. This was much easier in the nomadic state because of economic reasons, while in the sedentary state of society—agricultural—the first-born was redeemed with money or its equivalent in goods. These Kedeshim, or sanctified ones, sometimes found a berth in a private or public holy place, and once he was so fortunately situated, it would be hard to dislodge the occupant from his office. Certainly a community could more easily support from its bounty these holy men who were occasionally recruited from anywhere or who pledged their lives to God's ministry than it could make provision for a whole tribe, as was done for the stranger and orphan. Once the early Levite was placed, he would try to hand on his living to his son, particularly when the nomadic period was over. Thus there could easily arise a professional class that would forget its own origin, and insist on its prerogatives as over against the newcomer, the free lance or the volunteer. The former would gravitate to found a guild, which, however, could not entirely prevent the rise of itinerant Levites because of the force of custom and tradition. Jeroboam at a later period (*I Kings* 12:31) would hardly have appointed laymen as priests in the face of a different accepted usage.

The Levites then were hardly a tribe or even a caste, although they would in the course of time become one and claim a common family bond, doubly sacred because the descent went back to Moses, himself perhaps an original "holy" person. The early story certainly makes Moses the first-born and knows nothing of his brother Aaron. When the latter appears he does so as rival and opponent (*Num.* 12; *Ex.* 32). God has to remind Moses that he has a brother—evidently a later version.

The individual priests mentioned in the early historical books were therefore descendants of Moses: the house of Eli at Shiloh and that of Gershom at Dan. Perhaps the genealogies are of a later date that accepted the fact of the connection of a Levite tribe and priesthood and provided a family tree as proof of its priestly prerogative. David, who reorganized the priesthood, had protected Abiathar, chief priest of Nob, a descendant of Eli and therefore of Moses, and took him as his priest because Abiathar possessed the ephod (*I Sam.* 23:9; 30:7). When later the priest sided with

*The Levites marching through the wilderness, carrying the sacred utensils of the Tabernacle. From Fürst's
"Pracht-Bibel"*

Adonijah, he was banished, and the house of Zadok (*I Kings* 2:26-27, 35), of unknown origin but, according to *I Chron.* 5:27-41, of Gibeon, received the official priesthood. Zadok claimed descent from Aaron, and Moses is thus supplanted as the legitimate ancestor of the priests and the way is prepared for making him a simple Levite and the forbear of the Levites. A later account, *Ex.* 28, after the fact, explains this separation as having occurred at the time of the construction of the Tabernacle, when God commanded Moses to take Aaron and his sons for the priestly office, while the more menial tasks were given to the rest of the tribe of Levi (*Num.* 1:47-54; 4:4-16, 22-28, 29-33). The Levites dare not approach the sacred objects (*Num.* 4:19), hence may not act in an officiating capacity. This is not in accord with the facts as we know them of Israel's earliest history, but is a later explanation.

In *I Chron.* 23 the lowly status of the Levites due to David's organization of the Temple service is confirmed (cf. also chaps. 25 and 26). Zadok founded the hierarchy of the Aaronite priesthood and made it preeminent. When the break came between Judah and Israel, and, later, when the former alone remained, this preeminence was naturally enhanced. In this period the priests of Judah were called Levitical priests, down to the reformation of Josiah, because their colleagues of the Northern Kingdom could not claim descent from Levi, a guild entrance qualification fostered by the dominant priestly families. When, finally, the central sanctuary was firmly established and became the nation's fane, the complete subordination of Levite to priest was effected. The wandering Levites, if there were any, or the priests and Levites of erstwhile local sanctuaries or of so called non-Aaronidic stock were absorbed by the Jerusalem group and relegated to an inferior rank. *Ezek.* 44:9-16 shows how this was done, his words indicating that before the Exile even foreigners and "outcast" Levites, i.e. volunteers, had performed priestly functions.

The Levites of the later Temple period killed and prepared the animals for sacrifice, had charge of the music, probably kept the Torah or Torahs and did teaching and other less dignified chores. According to *Neh.* 7:43-45, the Levites who came back with Nehemiah from the Exile numbered 360; according to *Ezra* 2:40-42, they numbered 341, and were later joined by thirty-eight more, a proof, thinks Auerbach, of the unattractiveness of their office. (Even today the proportion of Levi's to Cohen's is 1 to 3.) These figures, in comparison with the 4,289 priests who returned from the Exile, show the falsity of the claim that the priests are the descendants of Aaron while the Levites stem from the remainder of their ancestral tribe.

Whether the Levites were all of one blood kinship as the Bible indicates, and as some authorities accept, or whether, following Eduard Meyer, Menes, and Gershman, they were recruited from any tribe, they were supported solely by the community and had no full civil rights. As *Judges* 17:7-9 shows, the Levite in early times was a *ger* (stranger, sojourner), and although at a later period Abiathar might possess land (*I Kings* 2:26), the group never was the social or economic equal of the Israelite yeomen. At the time of Josiah the priests became an upper estate and the Levites continued as a "sacred" class less so than the sacerdotal group. One theory has it that it was the Levites who guarded monotheism in its purity and safeguarded the tradition, very often against their superiors' will, and that rabbinic Judaism or Pharisaism developed out of the religious thought and idealism of these menial and minor servants of the Lord.

The support of the Levites throughout their official career came from the offerings which they received. *Deut.* 14:28-29 describes the Levites' portion as taken from the third year tithe. *Num.* 18:21-32 states that the whole tribe (including priests) gets a yearly tithe, of which they give a tenth to the sanctuary. *Neh.* 10:38-40 corroborates the latter.

The Levite cities in *Josh.* 21 are a later fiction, as close scrutiny must reveal. Some of the towns mentioned, Gibeon, Shechem, Gezer, Aijalon, Taanach and Nahalal, did not even belong to ancient Israel. Similarly, the division in *Josh.* 21:11, like that in *Num.* 35:5, is in the realm of the ideal rather than of the actual.

Levi and Levites in Hellenistic Literature. The Levites and Levi are idealized in Hellenistic literature. The Shechem episode is glorified and the tribe's right to the priesthood is exalted, both harking back to the exceptional merit of the ancestor. More or less extended references are found in the *Fragment of a Zadokite Work* (edit. Solomon Schechter) and in the *Testament of Levi*. The *Book of Jubilees* (chaps. 30 and 31), the *Testament of Naphtali* (chap. 5) and the *Testament of Judah* (chap. 25) all contain Midrashic material, evoked by the similarity of the Maccabean war to Levi's campaign against Shechem. The Levite material is made into eschatology (*Testament of Reuben* 6; *Testament of Judah* 21); only Philo mentions the Levites' steadfastness at the incident of the Golden Calf (*Life of Moses* II, 173). The Levites as Temple servants, below the priestly class, are mentioned in Josephus, *Antiquities*, book 3, chap. 11). In *Antiquities*, book 13, chap. 3, the same author tells of the presence of Levites in the Egyptian temple of Onias. *Tobit* 1:7 speaks of the tithe of the Levites. Philo and Josephus speak of the watches in the Temple service as well as their other offices pretty much in agreement with Bible and Mishnah. Some of the Haggadic material in this literature has its counterpart in rabbinic sources.

Levites in the Halachah. The latter deals mainly with the part which the Levites played in the Temple service. Every Levite must serve (*Sifre* to *Num.* 18:23). The Levite requires five years' preparation (*Hul.* 24a); minors might only sing (*Arach.* 2:6), and the Levite serves from his thirtieth to his fiftieth year (*Hul.* 29a). The twenty-four divisions and orders of the servitors

are explained in *Taan.* 27a and in *Mishneh Torah, Hilchoth Kele Hamikdash* 3:9. The Levites acted as treasurers, bookkeepers, and the like for the Temple, and were under stringent supervision. Their song service consisted in choral accompaniment of the community sacrifice (*korban tzibbur*). The choir was comprised of at least twelve men (*Arach.* 2:6); the accompanying orchestra might include others. They sang various psalms (*Mid.* 7:4); to Sabbath Musaf (Additional Service) they sang *Deut.* 32; to the evening offering, *Ex.* 15 (cf. *R. H.* 31a). There are long discussions in the Talmud as to those to whom the tithes belong, whether to the priests or to the Levites, the former being generally favored.

Most of the legislation for the priesthood applies to the Levites, for example the exemption of the firstborn from redemption and the laws regarding family purity.

In the reading of the Torah, the Kohen (priest) is called first, and the Levite second. The Levites still wash the hands of the priests before these go up to the altar to recite the ancient threefold priestly benediction (*birkath hakohanim*). This practice is not ancient, but is due to Cabalistic influence.

FELIX A. LEVY.

Lit.: Auerbach, Elias, *Wüste und Gelobtes Land;* idem, article "Levi," *Encyclopaedia Judaica,* vol. 10 (1934) cols. 833-37; Wellhausen, J., *Prolegomena;* Meyer, Eduard, *Die Israeliten und ihre Nachbarstämme* (1906); Menes, *Die vorexilischen Gesetze; International Critical Commentary;* Abidob, *Nethiboth Bibekoreth Hamikra;* Steinberger, Leo, *Der Bedeutungswechsel des Wortes Levit* (1935); Kaufman, Ezekiel, "The Levites and the Priests of the Bamoth," *Klausner Anniversary Book* (1937) 79-86.

LEVITICUS, the third book of the Torah (Pentateuch). The name suggests that the book deals with "Levitical" matters. This has to be taken generally as meaning priestly matters, the Levites being referred to only occasionally. The rabbinical name *Torath Kohanim* ("Law of the Priests") expresses the same idea. The customary Hebrew title is *Vayikra*. Leviticus has twenty-seven chapters with 859 verses, and is the shortest book of the Pentateuch. It is divided into ten portions for Sabbatical reading.

The contents of Leviticus are almost entirely legislative. Chaps. 1 to 7 contain laws of sacrifice; chaps. 8 to 10 the installation of the priests; chaps. 11 to 15 laws of purity; chap. 16 the annual Day of Atonement; chaps. 17 to 26 laws of holiness; chap. 27 a supplement on vows and tithes.

The sacrifices, for which detailed rules are given in chaps. 1 to 7, are burnt-offerings, meal-offerings, peace-offerings, sin-offerings, and guilt-offerings.

The consecration of Aaron and his four sons as priests, described in chaps. 8 to 10, lasted seven days. On the eighth day they officiated for the first time. Aaron blessed the people and the glory of God appeared. But the ceremony came to a tragic end, as two of Aaron's sons, Nadab and Abihu, suddenly died when they offered "strange" fire.

The laws of purity in chaps. 11 to 15 regulate which animals may be eaten. They set forth that certain facts make a person unclean, such as touching the carcasses of unclean animals, childbirth, leprosy, natural secretions. Conditions, sacrifices, and other ceremonies are prescribed for the ending of this uncleanliness.

The sixteenth chapter is used for reading on the Day of Atonement.

The laws of holiness in chaps. 17 to 26 demand not only certain ceremonies and abstention from defilement, but also obedience to the highest moral requirements. Israel's watchword has to be, "Ye shall be holy; for I the Lord your God am holy" (19:1). Among the prohibitions is that of eating blood. This gave origin to the ritual method of slaughtering animals, the Shehitah. Chap. 18 prohibits various acts of unchastity and marriage between near relations. The same prohibitions are repeated in chap. 20; others are added, and heavy penalties are instituted for all of them. Chap. 19 is the climax of the book, containing laws of humanity and charity both to the Israelite and to the stranger. It is a counterpart to the Decalogue. It contains the words, "Thou shalt love thy neighbour as thyself," and, "Thou shalt love him [the stranger] as thyself; for ye were strangers in the land of Egypt." Chaps. 21 and 22 contain laws on priests and offerings; both have to be without blemish. Chap. 23 orders the holy seasons. Chap. 24 brings laws on the lamps and the shewbread in the tent of meeting, and laws on blasphemy, manslaughter, and injuries to a person. Chap. 25 institutes laws of great social consequence: the Sabbatical year and the year of Jubilee, with redemption of land property and slaves. Chap. 26 is a concluding exhortation (tochahah), promising with great vigor blessings for obedience and calamities for disobedience.

Christianity has never had much use for Leviticus because of its legal character. Christian orthodoxy used it as typical and prophetic of Jesus' sacrifice of his life. Yet Judaism has always held Leviticus in high regard, because it is the basis for the greater part of Jewish religious law. Sacrifices and ritual purity dominated the life and thoughts of the Jewish people until the destruction of the Second Temple to a degree which can not be overestimated. Other ceremonial institutions of Leviticus are still observed today by Orthodox and Conservative Jews, such as the dietary laws and those on ritual bathing. The moral prescriptions of Leviticus were and still are of the greatest influence, stressing the holiness of the home, charity, justice, all duties to fellow men, and the sanctification of God's name (Kiddush Hashem), and liberating men from brutality and bestiality. Many Jewish virtues can be traced back to this book, which was often used for acquainting children with the Scriptures. Because of this appreciation, Leviticus has been commented on not only by the great Jewish commentators of medieval times, but by many modern Jewish scholars as well (Hartwig Wessely, Malbim, David Hoffmann, Joseph H. Hertz). A new commentary by B. Jacob was in preparation in 1942.

For the critical view of Leviticus, see BIBLE CRITICISM; HOLINESS CODE; PRIESTLY CODE.

ERNEST I. JACOB.

Lit.: The commentaries by Driver and White (1906), MaKlaren (1906), B. Baentsch (1903), A. Bertholet (1901), von Hummelauer (1897), David Hoffmann (1905-6); Jacob, B., Die Thora Moses (1912).

LEVITICUS RABBAH, see MIDRASH LEVITICUS.

LEVITZKI, MISCHA, pianist, b. Kremenchug, Russia, 1898; d. New York city, 1941. He came to the United States in his eighth year, and from 1906 until 1911 he studied at the Institute of Musical Art in New York with Stojowski. Following this, he was a pupil of Dohnányi at the Berlin Hochschule, twice winning the Mendelssohn Prize for piano playing. In 1914 he made his concert debut in Berlin. A projected European tour was interrupted by the outbreak of the first World War, whereupon he returned to the United States and made his premier American appearance in New York in 1916. Since that time, Levitzki made more than twenty tours of the United States, and circled the globe several times.

Levitzki's playing was marked by brilliance, artistic finish, and technical fluency. He was perhaps at his best in the works of Chopin and Liszt. He also composed a ballet, songs, and many pieces for the piano, in addition to making transcriptions for the violin which appear in the repertoire of many concert artists.

LEVONTIN, ZALMAN DAVID, one of the first pioneers of Jewish colonization in Palestine, b. Orsha, Russia, 1856; d. Tel-Aviv, Palestine, 1940. In 1882 he founded the first Chovevei Zion colony, Rishon Le Zion, near Jaffa. He was a director of the Jewish Colonial Trust in London, and from 1901 to 1924 manager of the Anglo-Palestine Company in Jaffa. His autobiography, Leeretz Abothenu (1924), is a valuable contribution to the history and criticism of Palestinian colonization.

Lit.: Levontin, Zalman David, Leeretz Abothenu (1924); Anglo-Palestine Company, An Account of its Work.

LÉVY, a family of French publishers.

MICHEL LÉVY (b. Pfalzburg, 1821; d. Paris, 1875), the youngest son of a poor family, was the real founder of the great publishing house. Originally he intended to become an actor. He was a friend of a girl equally poor and unknown, who was later the celebrated actress Rachel. But Michel Lévy did not follow Rachel's career. He went to Paris and founded, in 1836, at the age of fifteen, a small bookshop specializing in dramatic literature. In 1846 Lévy invited his brothers Calmann and Nathan to participate in his business. The brothers accepted, but Nathan retired in 1850. The Brothers Lévy acquired, in 1848, the ownership of the dramatic paper L'Entr'acte which strengthened Michel Lévy's connections with French playwrights. They founded the Bibliothèque dramatique, the Théâtre contemporain illustré, the Bibliothèque contemporaine, and, in 1854, the Collection Michel Lévy. Of all the book series initiated by Michel Lévy, the Collection Michel Lévy was the greatest success. The Lévy's were able to sell new books of renowned authors at a selling-price of one franc.

In 1856, the Brothers Goncourt remarked in their journal that "Michel Lévy has become the Augustus of men who live by writing." On the other hand, Ernest Renan said in his Souvenirs: "Michel Lévy must have been created by a special decree of divine providence to be my publisher." Like Renan, almost all the great celebrities of French literature of the middle of the 19th cent. were Michel Lévy's authors, such as Guizot, Tocqueville, Lamartine, Victor Hugo,

Count D'Haussonville, the duke of Broglie, and the duke of Aumale, son of king Louis Philippe, in so far as he was not forced to publish his works abroad. All these authors were opposed to Napoleon III and Michel Lévy was forced to bear the consequences during Napoleon's reign.

After Michel's death, CALMANN LÉVY (b. Pfalzburg, 1819; d. Paris, 1891) directed the publishing house under his own name. Calmann Lévy was a worthy successor of his brother. Renan acclaimed him as "truly one of the tribe of those who struggle for justice." Calmann Lévy was deeply interested in the works of his authors. He discovered the importance of Anatole France, who was then completely unknown. According to Ludovic Halévy, he was "young until his last hour." Calmann's sons, Paul, Gaston and Georges Lévy, continued the direction of the Calmann Lévy editions.   HUGO BIEBER.

Lit.: Renan, Ernest, Souvenirs; idem, Feuilles détachées; France, Anatole, La vie littéraire, vol. 4; Goncourt, Edmond de, Journal des Goncourt; Halévy, Ludovic, Journal; Archives Israélites, May, 1875.

LEVY, AARON, American merchant and land speculator, b. Amsterdam, Holland, 1742; d. Philadelphia, 1815. He emigrated to America about 1760 and came to Northumberland, Pa., where he engaged in trading with the Indians, speculating in real estate and furnishing supplies to the colony. He won recognition as a pioneer of Northumberland County, his name appearing in 1778 as a signer of a document wherein the state was asked to protect the petitioners against inroads of the British and the Indians. In the directory of 1780 he is listed as a shopkeeper in Lancaster, Pa., where he was in business with Joseph Simon. The Pennsylvania State Archives frequently refer to him and also contain copies of several letters that Aaron Levy wrote or had addressed to him.

It is not generally known that Aaron Levy, during the Revolutionary War, loaned a large sum of money to the Continental Congress and that this money was never fully repaid. This loan was made through Robert Morris, with whom Levy had substantial business transactions. Through his connections with John Nicholson, Levy furnished supplies to the regular army. In the books of Robert Morris, at the time of his bankruptcy, there is an item which states that "he (Aaron Levy) is entitled to credits that will bring a balance in his favor, exclusive of Bonds and Notes which he holds." But, due to the loss or destruction of Levy's papers, including land and loan office certificates, the exact amount of the loan which Levy made to the government could not be determined.

Aaron Levy was one of the greatest real estate operators of his time in the United States. He is recorded to have owned immense tracts in nearly every county of Pennsylvania. But he is chiefly remembered as the founder of the town of Aaronsburg (or Aaronsburgh), the first town in the United States founded by and named after a Jew. On May 23, 1786, he issued a public notice, declaring that "he hath laid out a town, called Aaronsburgh, very pleasantly situated, in that beautiful, healthy and fertile settlement, called Penn's Valley."

At the outset of his career Aaron Levy became acquainted with the Gratzes and Ettings of Philadelphia, and appears to have had intimate relations with various members of these families. He moved to Philadelphia in 1782, and was one of the original members of Congregation Mickve Israel.

Lit.: Publications of the American Jewish Historical Society, No. 2 (1894) 157-63; No. 9 (1901) 34-35; No. 30 (1926) 83-85; Wiernik, Peter, History of the Jews in America (1931) 95; American Jewish Year Book, vol. 28 (1926-27) 216-17; Morais, H. S., The Jews of Philadelphia (1894) 50; Ellis and Evans, History of Lancaster County, 369-70; London, Hannah R., Portraits of Jews, 30-31.

LEVY, AARON, American army officer, b. New York city, 1771; d. New York city, 1852. He was paymaster in the 6th Regiment of Infantry as early as 1800. Appointed an auctioneer in 1807, he became a member of the firm of Isaac Moses and Sons. The War of 1812 recalled him into army service as captain and paymaster in the 9th Regiment of the First Brigade of the New York State Artillery, which garrisoned the northern battery of New York for three months. He was made a first major in 1815, and a lieutenant colonel in the year following.

Levy retired from the service in December, 1819, after twenty years of military activity. He was a prominent member of Congregation Shearith Israel in New York, and son-in-law of Isaac Moses, the merchant who advanced 3,000 pounds sterling for the patriot cause. Levy left a diary, dated from 1805 to 1834. He was highly esteemed in the community at large.

Lit.: Publications of the American Jewish Historical Society, No. 4 (1896) 210; No. 6 (1897) 132; No. 26 (1918) 177-78; No. 27 (1920) 168, 336-44.

LEVY, AARON JEFFERSON, judge, b. New York city, 1881. He was educated at the Cooper Union School of Science in New York city and at the New York University Law School (LL.B., 1902). In addition to practising law (1903-14), he engaged actively in local politics as a member of the Democratic Party. In 1908 he was elected to the New York State Assembly and reelected annually six successive times. During his tenure in this office he was chairman of the committee on judiciary in 1911 and majority leader in 1913. He was chairman of the New York State Widows' Compensation Commission in 1914 and 1915.

In 1913 Levy was elected municipal judge of the Second Judicial District. In 1923 he was elected justice of the First Judicial District of the New York State Supreme Court for a fourteen-year term, and was reelected in 1937. He presided over the joint commission trying Judge Cohalan of the Supreme Court. Levy was active in Jewish community work, and was president of the Hebrew National Orphan Home and of the Israel Home for the Aged.

LÉVY, ALFRED, chief rabbi of France, b. Lunéville, France, 1840; d. Paris, 1919. He was educated at the College of Lunéville and at the Paris Rabbinical Seminary. After serving as rabbi at Dijon, Lunéville, and Lyon (1867-80), he was appointed chief rabbi of the Central Consistory of the Israelites of France (1908), which dignity he held until his death.

Lévy wrote "Les Israélites de la Franche-Comté au 14ᵉ siècle" (Archives Israélites, 1869); "Les Juifs du duché de Bourgogne au Moyen-âge" (ibid., 1869); Le deuil et les cérémonies funèbres chez les israélites

(1879); *Notice sur les israélites du duché de Lorraine* (1885); *Notice sur les israélites de Lyon* (1894); *Les doctrines d'Israel, recueil de sermons* (1896). He also translated into French the *Tahkemoni,* the chief work of Judah al-Harizi, 13th cent. Spanish-Jewish author. He was named Chevalier of the Legion of Honor in 1888. In 1932 a street was named after him in Lunéville.

Lit.: L'Univers Israélite, June 22, 1914; July 25, 1919; Aug. 1 and 8, 1919; *Archives Israélites,* June 21, 1917; July 31, 1919.

LÉVY, ALPHONSE, artist, b. Marmoutiers, Alsace, 1843; d. Algeria, 1918. He studied under Gérôme in Paris and first exhibited at the Salon of 1874. Combining the eye of the caricaturist for line with the vision of the artist for expression, he found the models for his art in the country Jews of his native Alsace, remnants of a past world of unsophisticated piety. His scale of artistic presentation ranged from the next-to-caricature to drawings of such intense beauty as *Week of Mourning,* which won him the surname of "Millet of the Jews." A great number of his drawings and lithographs exhibited in 1903 were purchased by the Luxembourg Museum and for the Collection of Etchings of the Bibliothèque Nationale. In 1904 he undertook a series of sketches of Jewish life in Algeria.

Lévy also did a series of etchings from the period of the French Commune which he signed by the pseudonym Saib. Wellknown are his illustrations to Sacher Masoch's Jewish stories (1889). In 1900 he won a prize at the International Exhibition.

Lit.: Archives Israélites, vol. 78-80 (1918); *Ost und West,* 1905, cols. 317-20; Wininger, S., *Grosse Jüdische National-Biographie,* vol. 3 (1928) 65-66; Benézit, *Dictionnaire des peintres.*

LÉVY, ARMAND, mathematician and mineralogist, b. Paris, 1794; d. Paris, 1841. The son of a Jewish father and a Catholic mother, he received his education at the Lycée Henri IV and entered the École Normale in 1812, where he tutored in mathematics from 1814 to 1815. Due to the restoration of the Bourbons, he had to leave his position and went to England, where he supported himself as a teacher of mathematics. From 1820 to 1827 he prepared a descriptive catalogue of Heuland's collection of minerals, during which time he won the high esteem of the great mineralogists Wollaston and Brewster. In 1827 he was recommended as professor of mathematics at the University of London, but was rejected because of his French nationality; later he had the same experience in Brussels because of his Jewish origin. However, he was appointed lecturer at the University of Brussels, serving from 1828 to 1830, and in the latter year became a member of the Academy of Sciences and Fine Arts of Brussels. The July Revolution made it possible for him to return to France in the same year; he was made professor of mineralogy at the Collège Charlemagne and maître de conférences at the École Normale. Lévy was a gifted and versatile scholar who described several new minerals, one of which, "Levyn," was named after him by Brewster. He was an editor of the *Encyclopaedia Britannica* and published works on power systems, on the definition of specific weights and on surfaces of the second order. He contributed to *Annals of Philosophy, Philosophical Magazine,* Quételet's *Correspondence Mathématique* and to the transactions of the Academy of Sciences, Paris.

Lit.: Académie Royale de Belgique, 1843-45, pp. 138-43; *Société Française de Minéralogie Bulletin,* vols. 42-43, pp. 122-34.

LÉVY, ARTHUR, historian, b. Nancy, France, 1847; d. Paris, 1931. He attracted the attention of historians everywhere by publishing (1893) *Napoléon intime.* He not only discovered many unknown documents bearing on Napoleon's life, but professed also fervent worship of the emperor, portraying him as a good, grateful and kindly man. Lévy's arguments were disputed but generally recognized as "learned and sincere." In 1902, Lévy essayed the still more formidable task, of proving the greatest of conquerors a lover of peace, by the publication of *Napoléon et la paix.* This work aroused even more violent controversy, but the German historian Max Lenz shared Lévy's opinion, and the greatest French authorities, such as Sorel and Madelin, adopted it with modifications. So did Leslie Hore-Belisha, former British minister of war.

Lévy also published (1917) a description of the state of the soul of Paris during the first months of the first World War: *1914 août-septembre à Paris.* In 1926 he dealt with the geographical service of the French army during the War in *Les coulisses de la guerre.* In the same year, Lévy published *Histoires intimes des temps du premier empire,* and in 1929 a biography of G. J. Ouvrard, *Un grand profiteur de guerre.*

Lit.: Gooch, G. P., *History and Historians in the 19th Century* (1935).

LEVY, ASSER (ASSER LEVY VAN SWELLEM), first American Jewish citizen, and champion of civil and religious liberty among early settlers in New Amsterdam (New York city); d. 1681. His full name, Asser Levy Van Swellem, indicates that the family came originally from Schwelm, Westphalia. The date of his birth is unknown. He landed in old New York in September, 1654, having come as one of a band of twenty-three Jewish refugees who set sail from Brazil and reached the Dutch settlement by way of the West Indies.

On landing at New Amsterdam, Levy owned practically nothing—the ship's captain having taken the little he had to defray the cost of his passage. But neither poverty nor the uncertainty of his condition had power to discourage the heart of the Jewish pioneer. For a year or two he supported himself by manual labor. But he soon turned to trade and business as well. He was a butcher, tavern-keeper, dealer in real estate, business agent and general trader. Before long he became prominent and influential, his business connections bringing him in touch with the leading burghers of the Dutch colony and with settlers up the Hudson River as far as Albany.

About a year after his arrival Asser Levy began to make his presence felt and known. In a petition, dated November 5, 1655, he asked for the right to stand guard like other burghers or else to be relieved from paying the heavy tax imposed on Jews in lieu thereof.

His petition was refused and he was told that he could leave the community if dissatisfied. But the authorities failed to reckon with Asser Levy, who appealed the case until he finally won. It was due to his courage and persistency that the Jewish settlers in New Amsterdam were admitted to full citizenship rights.

Levy was probably the first Jewish landowner in North America. In 1661 he purchased property in Albany and acquired a piece of land on South William Street in New York. He also bought two lots which became the site for the first synagogue in the city. By the time of the British occupation (1664), Asser Levy was a man of wealth and the only Jew deemed prominent enough to be called upon to swear allegiance to the new government. Although frequently engaged in litigation in which he was the plaintiff, insisting on his rights, he impressed Jews and non-Jews alike with his integrity. Because of his friendly relations with his Christian neighbors, Levy was several times named the executor of their wills. In 1671 he gave money to the Lutherans for the building of their first church in New York.

While he stood on friendly terms with Christians, Levy appears to have been an observant Jew. When he was sworn in as a licensed butcher in 1660, he asked to be excused from killing hogs because his religion forbade it; and he took the oath which the Jews were accustomed to take. About 1678 he built a public slaughter house, so that "all persons should have liberty to kill and hang therein meat."

Levy died intestate about the year 1681. The place of his burial is unknown, and there is no trace of Levy's having left any children, although an Asser Levy, who may have been a son, appears on the record. But he was survived by his wife, Maria Levy, who in April, 1682, was appointed the administratrix of his estate, the complete inventory of which shows him to have been the richest Jew in the colony. The grounds and buildings left by Asser Levy within the city of New York were appraised at £218, whereas the slaughter-house outside the gate of the city was valued at £1,800. In those days he was considered among the wealthiest inhabitants of the settlement. But his fame rests upon the fact that he was the first champion of Jewish rights among the early American colonies.

CLARENCE I. FREED.

Lit.: Publications of the American Jewish Historical Society, No. 8 (1900) 9-23; American Hebrew, Sept. 30, 1921, p. 474; ibid., Sept. 10, 1926, p. 492.

LÉVY, AUGUSTE-MICHEL, geologist and mineralogist, b. Paris, 1844; d. Paris, 1911. After completing his studies at the École Polytechnique and the École des Mines, he took part after 1876 in, and became director in 1887 of, the geologic survey of France. His was the greatest contribution to the detailed geologic map which was prepared as a result of this scientific enterprise. As professor at the Collège de France, he distinguished himself for his researches on eruptive rocks, their origin and microscopic structure.

He was president of the Société Française de Minéralogie in 1894, was elected a member of the Academy of Sciences in 1896, and honorary member of the London Mineralogical Society in 1898. He became Inspector General of Mines in 1907, and was made an officer of the Legion of Honor. He took an active part in Jewish affairs, and in 1892 was elected to the Consistory in Paris.

In addition to a number of minor works, Lévy published: Mémoires sur les divers modes de structure des roches éruptives étudiées au microscope (1876); Mémoires pour servir à l'explication de la carte géologique détaillée de la France (1879); Étude sur la détermination des feldspaths dans les plaques minces (1894-96); Contribution à l'étude des magmas chimiques (1903); with F. Fouqué as co-author: Minéralogie micrographique (1879) and Synthèse des minéraux et des roches (1882); Mission d'Andalousie (first part, Bergeron co-author, 1884; second part, F. Fouqué co-author, 1887); with Alfred Lacroix as co-author: Les minéraux des roches (1888).

Lit.: Gauthier, "Éloge de A. M. Lévy," in Publications de l'Académie des Sciences, 1911; Mineralogical Magazine, vol. 16 (1911-13) 248; Archives Israélites, vol. 72, Sept. 28, 1911; Société Française de Minéralogie, Bulletin, 1914, vol. 37, pp. 196-215.

LÉVY, BÉLA, jurist, b. 1873. He received his degree of Doctor of Law as well as his lawyer's diploma from the University of Budapest, and taught law at the Commercial Academy from 1899 to 1904. Subsequently he was a member of the national board of Hungarian Juridical Examiners.

His published volumes include A magyar szabadalmi jog rendszere (1898); A kereskedelmi jog elhatárolásának kérdése (1900); Az ipari mintáról szóló törvénytervezet bírálata (1902); A szabadalmi törvény előadói tervezete (Z. Kósa co-author; 1909); A biztosítási jelzálog kérdéséhez (1916); A szabadalmi törvényjavaslat előadói tervezete (1917); A mérlegjog törvényhozási problémái (1930), which deal with the problems of commercial law in general and of legislation governing patents, trade samples, foreclosure and balance sheets in particular. Lévy also contributed the article on the Hungarian code of commercial law for Handelsgesetze des Erdballs (Borchard edit.), a dictionary of commercial law.

LEVY, BENJAMIN, early English financier and Jewish communal leader, b. probably in Hamburg or Altona, Germany, about 1650; d. London, 1704. Levy seems to have settled in England about 1670. His letters of denization were granted him in 1689; in 1697 Levy was one of the twelve Jews admitted to the Exchange. Prior to his official admittance he had held the special standing of a "Jew-broker." Levy was also said to have been an important figure in the reorganization of the East India Company in 1698.

For many years Levy was a member of the Sephardic community, though of Ashkenazic parentage, and served as a Yahid in the Spanish and Portuguese congregation. As the Ashkenazic community grew, however, Levy became active in organizing it into a separate group. The Ashkenazic synagogue was established in 1692; in 1696 Levy is known to have purchased a cemetery for the community. After Levy's death leadership was assumed by Moses Hart, his cousin.

Lit.: Wolf, Lucien, "Notes on Benjamin Levy," Jewish Chronicle (London), Aug. 7, 1903, p. 18.

LEVY, BENJAMIN, American merchant, b. New York city, about 1720. He was one of the signers of the Non-Importation Agreement of 1765, aimed at the repeal of the British Stamp Act. As a young man, he moved to Philadelphia with his brother Samson Levy, who was also a signer of the Non-Importation Agreement and a founder of the City Dancing Assembly.

Levy appears to have been one of the contributors to the Pennsylvania Hospital, founded in 1751. Together with David Franks and other Philadelphia merchants, he signed the petition to the Governor and the Council of Pennsylvania for the building of a new road to facilitate the marketing of food products. Moving to Philadelphia in 1773, he opened a store which sold liquors, spices, drugs, foodstuffs and general drygoods. He corresponded with Major Horatio Gates, later a general in the Revolutionary Army, and was friendly also with Robert Morris, one of the signers of the Declaration of Independence.

In 1776 Congress appointed Levy one of the authorized signers of bills of credit. In 1780, he was listed as the owner of considerable property in Philadelphia. As late as 1793, he appears to have lived at Baltimore and drawn up a contract on behalf of Nathan Levy, his father-in-law, in connection with certain rights of burial within the Spruce Street Cemetery of Philadelphia. The date and circumstances of Levy's death are unknown. He was the grandfather of the famous Commodore Uriah P. Levy.

Lit.: American Hebrew, vol. 119, pp. 495, 530; Publications of the American Jewish Historical Society, No. 1 (1892) 21-22, 60, 86; No. 5 (1897) 198; No. 23 (1915) 58-59.

LÉVY, CALMANN, see LÉVY (family of publishers).

LEVY, CHAPMAN, colonel and lawyer, b. Camden, S. C., 1787; d. Camden, Miss., 1850. He was admitted to the bar in South Carolina in 1806. Later he represented the district of Kershaw in the State Legislature (1829-33, 1836-38), and also served in the State Senate. Levy was a member of the Nullification Convention in 1832, voting against nullification. He earned his military title during the War of 1812.

Lit.: Elzas, Barnett, The Jews of South Carolina (1905).

LEVY, CLIFTON HARBY, rabbi and writer, b. New Orleans, La., 1867. He traced his American ancestry back to 1740. Levy graduated from the University of Cincinnati (A.B., 1887), was ordained rabbi at the Hebrew Union College and occupied his first pulpit in New York city (1890). Levy was superintendent of classes for immigrant children under the Baron de Hirsch Fund, believed to have been the first organized effort at Americanization. He was rabbi at Lancaster, Pa. (1892-94), and at Baltimore (1894-96), where he opened the first Jewish kindergarten in a religious school; there he launched also the movement to establish the first United Hebrew Charities in Baltimore, in addition to editing The Jewish Comment.

Levy was founder and rabbi until 1919 of Tremont Temple, New York city. Simultaneously and thenceforward he contributed to numerous periodicals and newspapers on archeological and Biblical subjects. He prepared the text and captions for Tissot's Old Testament illustrations and published Life of Guynemer (1918; adapted from the French); Judaism Applied to Life (1925); The Ant People (from the German; 1927);

The Bible in Art (1936). In New York city he organized the Centre of Jewish Science (1924), emphasizing the spiritual values of Judaism. In 1936 he issued Ten Constructive Commandments, stressing affirmative injunctions as contrasted with the negative. He was made art editor (1939) of this encyclopedia. In 1942 he was editor of The Bible in Pictures, a five-year project for religious schools, illustrating the Scriptures.

LEVY, SIR DANIEL, Australian jurist and statesman, b. London, 1873; d. Sydney, Australia, 1937. He was educated at Sydney University, where his brilliant scholarship won him many honors. He received the highest rating in the Junior University public examination and the Hordern Prize of one hundred pounds. He also received the highest rating in the Senior University public examination and the John West Gold Medal. At matriculation in 1890 he was awarded scholarships in classics, mathematics, and modern languages. In 1893 he received his B.A. degree with first class honors and the gold medal in classics. In 1895 he got his LL.B. degree, again with honors. He was admitted to the bar the same year.

The next two years he was associated with Justice Henry Emanuel Cohen of the Supreme Court of New South Wales. From 1901 to 1917 he represented Darlinghurst in the New South Wales Legislative Assembly, and from 1917 to 1927 he represented Sydney. From 1927 until his death, ten years later, he was the member for Paddington. He was chairman of committees of the New South Wales Parliament from 1917 to 1919, and speaker of that body from 1919 to 1925. He was the speaker of the Legislative Assembly from 1927 to 1937, and was knighted in 1929.

Levy was an active community worker in both Jewish and general circles. He was a fellow of the senate of Sydney University, president of the trustees of the Public Library of New South Wales, director of the Sydney Hospital, and director of the New South Wales Benevolent Society. He was the editor of The Australian Hebrew and honorary secretary to the Shakespeare Society of New South Wales, as well as author of many articles on law reform.

LEVY, ELLIS, Jamaican public official, b. Kingston, 1870. He was a magistrate in Kingston, and served on the legislative council by the appointment of the governor. He was for several years a director of the United Congregation of Israelites, vice-president and president of the Jamaica Chamber of Commerce, and a member of the directorate of the Daily Gleaner and of numerous important business enterprises. In 1939 he was appointed a member of the government Sugar Control Board and was awarded the King's Commemoration Medal.

Lit.: Who's Who and Why in Jamaica, 1939-40; Daily Gleaner, Sept. 13, 1934.

LEVY, EMIL, expert in the Romance languages, b. Hamburg, Germany, 1855; d. Freiburg, Germany, 1918. He was one of the most prominent experts on the Provençal Middle Ages. In 1883 he obtained a fellowship at the University of Freiburg. Four years later his study, Poésies religieuses provençales et françaises, was published. His main work is the Provençal supplément dictionnaire (8 vols., 1892-1925). It last volume was published after Levy's death and edited by Appel.

In consequence of this important publication the Diez prize was bestowed on Levy. He also edited the *Petit dictionnaire provençal-français* (1900).

LEVY, FELIX ALEXANDER, rabbi, b. New York city, 1884. He was educated at the College of the City of New York (A.B., 1904), and pursued post-graduate studies at Columbia University and the Jewish Theological Seminary of America in 1904 and 1905. He later attended the Hebrew Union College, where he was ordained rabbi in 1907, and the University of Chicago, where he received his Ph.D. degree in 1917. In 1939 he was awarded an honorary D.D. degree by the Hebrew Union College.

Levy was rabbi (1907-8) of Brith Kodesh Congregation, Rochester, N. Y. In 1908 he was called to Emanuel Congregation, Chicago, where he was still serving in 1942. During this time he was active in Jewish religious and educational affairs. He was a lecturer for the Jewish Chautauqua Society and associate editor of the *B'nai B'rith News.* In 1917 and 1918 he served in France as a member of the Jewish Welfare Board. He was a member of the board of governors of the Hebrew Union College, chairman of the board of the College of Jewish Studies, and a member of the board of Jewish education. He was a member of the executive board of the Zionist Organization of America, and over a number of years served as secretary, vice-president, and president of the Central Conference of American Rabbis. He was president of the Liberal Ministers' Association, and vice-president of the League Against War and Fascism.

Levy was also the author of several books, including: *Royal Dynastic Obelisks* (1917); *Moses Mendelssohn's Ideals of Religion* (1929); *The Task of Reform Judaism* (1930); *Judaism and Modern Thought* (1931); *God and Reform Judaism* (1935); *Judaism* and *Marriage.* He was also a contributor to *The Reform Advocate; B'nai B'rith News, Hebrew Union College Monthly,* and *The Sentinel.*

LEVY, FERDINAND, American soldier, b. Milwaukee, Wis., 1843; d. New York city, 1923. He was the son of Simon Levy, who served in the Civil War as colonel of a New York regiment. Ferdinand Levy came to New York at the age of fifteen. He was one of the first to volunteer at the outbreak of the Civil War, participated in many important engagements and rose to the rank of captain.

Upon his return to civil life he became a leader in the Democratic Party, serving as a delegate to numerous conventions and as a member of the Tammany Hall general committee. He was elected alderman-at-large in 1872 and coroner in 1882 and 1885. Levy later served as register and commissioner of taxes and assessments of the city and county of New York. He was active in a number of Jewish organizations, and in 1888 was elected grand master of the Order Sons of Benjamin. He was for a time commander of the Steinwehr Post of the Grand Army of the Republic, likewise president of the Jewish Immigration Society, and of the Association of Jewish Veterans.

Lit.: Wolf, Simon, *The American Jew as Patriot, Soldier and Citizen* (1895) 275-76; *Publications of the American Jewish Historical Society,* No. 17 (1909) 217.

LEVY, FLORENCE NIGHTINGALE, art organizer and author, b. New York city, 1870. She was educated at the National Academy of Design and at the Louvre in Paris. In 1898 Miss Levy founded the *American Art Annual,* which she published until 1919. She was the founder of the first art weekly, *The New York Art Bulletin.* Her *Art in New York* had six editions between its first appearance in 1916 and 1939. *Art Education in New York* was published in 1938. Miss Levy was also the author of numerous studies on art education and industrial art for the Metropolitan Museum of Art, the Bureau of Education in Washington and the Federated Council of Art Education. In 1927 she was made executive secretary of the Arts Council, which post she still occupied in 1942.

LÉVY, GUSTAVE, etcher and engraver, b. Toul, France, 1819; d. Paris, 1894. He was a pupil of Galle and Cogniet, and first exhibited at the Salon of 1844. He engraved a large number of classical works—such as those of Raphael, Annibale Carracci, Philippe de Champagne and Greuze—in the manner of Edelink, Dutch copperplate engraver of the 17th cent. He also engraved numerous portraits by his contemporary, the painter Winterhalter, as well as the portraits of the two chief rabbis Lazard Isidor and Zadoc Kahn. He won a medal of honor in 1894. He was vice-president of the French Society of Engravers, and was made a knight of the Legion of Honor in 1892.

The Museum of Toul has several of Lévy's engravings in addition to his drawing of *Head of Medusa.* His last engraving, after Raphael's *Fair Gardener,* is framed on his tombstone in Montmartre.

LEVY, HAYMAN, American Colonial merchant and fur trader, b. Hannover, Germany, 1721; d. New York city, 1789. He was one of the leading merchants in New York and the largest fur trader among the colonists, a trade which he entered in 1760, dealing chiefly with the Indians. There are entries in his books to show that he employed John Jacob Astor to beat furs at $1.00 a day. He failed in business in 1768 because of England's restrictive policy on Colonial trade, but he succeeded in paying off his creditors with interest. In the great New York fire of 1776 Levy's extensive real estate was destroyed; yet he was able to continue in business until his death.

Levy was one of the signers, in 1770, of a resolution to make more stringent the Non-Importation Act of 1765; his name is sometimes mistaken for that of Hyman Levy, Jr., who affixed his signature to the Non-Importation Act itself. The similarity in names accounts for the confusion. Hayman Levy moved to Philadelphia when the British occupied New York during the Revolutionary War. He was one of the founders of Congregation Mikve Israel in Philadelphia, and served on the first board of trustees of the congregation. Returning to New York in 1784, he helped to reorganize Congregation Shearith Israel of that city.

Lit.: Daly, Charles P., *The Settlement of the Jews in North America* (1893) 52-54; *Publications of the American Jewish Historical Society,* No. 4 (1896) 210-11; No. 26 (1918) 237; No. 27 (1920) 168.

LÉVY, HENRI-LÉOPOLD, painter, b. Nancy, France, 1840; d. Paris, 1904. He studied at the École des Beaux Arts, and was a pupil of Picot, Cabanel and Fromentin. Of the romantic school of Delacroix, he took his subjects chiefly from Greek antiquity, the Bible and holy legends, making his debut at the Salon of 1865 with his *Hecuba Finding the Body of her Son Polydorus on the Shore,* which was awarded a medal. Other medals were won by him at the Salons of 1867 and 1869; his *Deucalion and Pyrrha,* at the International Exhibition of 1900, was awarded a gold medal.

Lévy painted murals, portraying the life of St. Denis, for the church of St. Merri in Paris, and one for the Panthéon, *The Coronation of Charlemagne* (1869). In 1872 he was made a Chevalier of the Legion of Honor. His most famous painting, *Hebrew Captive Weeping over the Ruins of Jerusalem* (1869), is at the museum of Nancy. The city of Dijon owns a series of his *Great Men of Burgundy.* Other paintings of his are in the possession of the Musée du Luxembourg, Paris.

LEVY, HERMANN, economist, b. Berlin, 1881. In 1905 he became an instructor at the University of Halle, and continued his teaching at the University of Commerce in Mannheim in 1907. In 1910 he was appointed assistant professor at the University of Heidelberg, and in 1921 he became professor at the University of Technology in Berlin-Charlottenburg. His field is research on the normalizing of European economic conditions.

Levy's publications on this problem are: *Die Not der englischen Landwirte zur Zeit der hohen Getreidezölle* (1902); *Entstehung und Rückgang der landwirtschaftlichen Grossbetriebe in England* (1904); *Die Stahlindustrie der Vereinigten Staaten von Amerika* (1905); *Ausfuhrzölle* (1907); *Monopele, Kartelle und Truste* (1909); *Large and Small Holdings* (1911); *Vorratswirtschaft und Volkswirtschaft* (1915); *Soziologische Studie über das englische Volk* (1920); *Die englische Wirtschaft* (1922); *Die Vereinigten Staaten als Wirtschaftsmacht* (1923); *Die Grundlagen der Weltwirtschaft* (1924); *Volkscharakter und Wirtschaft* (1927). In addition, he published literary sketches and short stories, such as: *Orchideen* (1911); *Die stille Frau* (1912); *Die Frau im Traum* (1913); *Der Weg zur Einsamkeit* (1922); *Cyris and Gaselis* (1923).

LEVY, I. MONTEFIORE, lawyer and communal worker, b. New York city, 1883. He took his law degree in 1904 at New York University, and entered practice in New York city. Beginning with 1910, Levy became active in civic and Jewish communal affairs. His first civic post was as commissioner on the New York city Board of Education, where he served from 1910 to 1916, and was responsible for the resolution which permitted married women to continue teaching. Levy also occupied various executive posts with the Democratic party. He served also on several model housing commissions and committees. The New York County Lawyers Association has frequently chosen him for special tasks; in 1942 he was secretary of its committee on public relations and a member of the committee on professional ethics. Among Levy's Jewish activities in 1942 were his presidency of the New York Guild for the Jewish Blind and of the seventh Zionist district in Manhattan.

LEVY, ISAAC, merchant and trader, b. New York city, early in the 18th cent.; time and place of death unknown. He was naturalized under the act of 1740, and remained in New York until 1752, when he moved to London. In 1754, while in London, Levy purchased a half-interest in some inland property off the coast of Georgia from one Bosworth. This purchase subsequently involved him in considerable litigation. In 1756 Levy set sail for America in order to develop his property, which included a coal mine, but the outbreak of the war with France seriously interfered with his plans.

As soon as Levy learned of a proposed sale of his property by Bosworth, he took steps to obtain legal redress. His case was one of the few of sufficient importance to warrant an appeal directly to the king in Council. Levy presented a memorial or petition to the king (1759), setting forth his grievances. The case came up several times before the Privy Council. No Georgia lawyer could be secured to take up the case, the governor of Georgia being himself involved. On his return to England in 1764, Levy set about to employ the best legal talent available to push his case before the crown; but he received no redress, and they referred him back to the courts of Georgia.

In presenting his arguments, Levy predicted the future uses of coal in America to replace wood as fuel. His last petition being denied, Levy was forced to give up the fight. In December, 1768, he was in Philadelphia, and in October of the following year in Boston. Thereafter he disappeared from public view.

Lit.: Friedenwald, Herbert, "Isaac Levy's Claim to Property in Georgia," *Publications of the American Jewish Historical Society,* No. 9 (1901) 57-62.

LÉVY, ISAAC, rabbi, b. Marmoutier, Alsace, 1835; d. Paris, 1912. He was a pupil of his grandfather, Rabbi J. Haguenau of Marmoutier, and graduated from the rabbinical school of Metz at the age of twenty-two. After being rabbi from 1850 at Verdun, where he was editor of *Le foyer israélite* (1863-64), rabbi at Lunéville from 1865 and chief rabbi at Colmar from 1869, he left Alsace, which was becoming a part of Germany, in 1872. His farewell sermon, attended by many Christians, was an ardent profession of French patriotism, while his *Alsatiana échos patriotiques de la chaire israélite* (1873) testified to his love for Alsace. The French government created for him the chief rabbinate of Vesoul; in 1887 he was called as chief rabbi to Bordeaux, and was subsequently made honorary chief rabbi of Gironde. In 1912 he was induced to retire, and died several weeks later.

Lévy was considered one of the leading liberals of the French synagogue. He published *La Synagogue et M. Renan* (two editions, 1863), an answer to the author of *The Life of Jesus; Isaïe, ou le travail* (2nd ed., 1866); and *Défense du Judaisme* (1867). His *Heures de recueillement* (1898) was a prayer-book for Sabbath and holidays, and his *Prières en français* (2 vols., 1907-8) a general prayer-book in French. He wrote also several books for the instruction and edification of Jewish youth, among which *Histoire sainte* (15th ed., 1925) has become a classic.

LEVY, JACOB, rabbi and lexicographer, b. Dobrzyca, Posen, 1819; d. Breslau, Germany, 1892. His Talmud instructors were his father and Akiba Eger. Levy was a graduate of the Matthias Gymnasium in

Jacob Levy

Breslau, of Breslau University, and of the University of Halle (1845). He was rabbi of Rosenberg, Silesia, until 1850, when he moved back to Breslau, primarily because he wanted to live in an intellectual center. He was appointed associate rabbi of the Breslau community in 1857, and instructor at the Mara-Salomon Leipziger Stiftung in 1878, a position which he retained for the rest of his life. In recognition of his work the Prussian University granted him in 1875 the title of Königlicher Professor. Levy's rabbinic lexicographic work was compiled by modern scientific methods which contributed considerably to rousing the interest of Christian scholars in rabbinical literature. His most important work was *Neuhebräisches und Chaldäisches Wörterbuch über die Talmudim und Midraschim* (4 vols., Leipzig, 1876-89), which was revised by Lazarus Goldschmidt in 1923 to 1924 and is still a standard work. His other work was *Chaldäisches Wörterbuch über die Targumim* (1865-88).

Lit.: Heppner-Herzberg, *Aus Vergangenheit und Gegenwart der Juden und der jüdischen Gemeinden in den Posener Landen* (1909) 315, 373; Goldschmidt, Lazarus, "Vorwort" to *Neuhebräisches und Chaldäisches Wörterbuch über die Talmudim und Midraschim* (1924).

LEVY, JEFFERSON MONROE, American Congressman and lawyer, b. New York city, 1852; d. New York city, 1924. He was the nephew of the famous Commodore Uriah P. Levy, and became the owner of Monticello, the former home of Thomas Jefferson, near Charlottesville, Va., which he bequeathed to his sister, Mrs. A. L. Mayhoff, and which was later purchased by the Thomas Jefferson Memorial Association. He graduated from New York University Law School in 1873. A member of Congress from 1899 to 1901 and from 1911 to 1915, he was a leader of the "Gold Democrats" in the Fifty-Sixth Congress, and originated and introduced the Reserve Bank Bill in the Sixty-Second and Sixty-Third Congresses; he also obtained an increase in wages for postal clerks. He helped found the Democratic Club of New York. As his ancestors landed in America in 1662, he was a member of the Sons of the Revolution and the Society of the War of 1812.

Lit.: Wiernik, Peter, *History of the Jews in America,* 241; *American Jewish Year Book,* 1904-5, p. 138; *Biographical Dictionary of the American Congress* (1928) 1221.

LEVY, JONAS PHILLIPS, United States naval commander and merchant, b. Philadelphia, 1807; d. New York city, 1883. He was the brother of Uriah P. Levy and the father of Jefferson M. Levy. During the Mexican War he commanded the United States steamer *America* and was active in the transportation of United States troops to Vera Cruz. On the surrender of that port he was appointed its captain by General Winfield Scott. In 1850 the Mexican Congress granted him the exclusive privilege of making a road from New York to San Francisco which would pass through Mexico; nothing came of it, however.

Levy endeared himself to the Peruvian government and was granted the freedom of that country for his services to its navy. His arrival in Washington, D. C., in 1852, immediately stirred new life in the handful of Jews already settled there. Under his leadership they secured from Congress a charter for the formation of the Washington Hebrew Congregation, of which Levy was first president. He was also active on the Board of Delegates of American Israelites. Levy played a prominent role in the movement set afoot, in 1854, in connection with the treaty between Switzerland and the United States, to prevent discrimination against the Jews by Switzerland. Evidence of this is found in his correspondence with the Honorable Lewis Cass, Secretary of State under President James Buchanan. After a sojourn of seven years in Washington, Levy moved to New York.

Lit.: Publications of the American Jewish Historical Society, No. 11 (1903) 17-46; No. 26 (1918) 213-18; No. 27 (1920) 507; Morais, H. S., *The Jews of Philadelphia* (1894) 471.

LEVY, JOSEPH BENJAMIN, cantor, b. Kiel, Germany, 1870. In 1895 he became first cantor of the Börneplatz synagogue in Frankfort, and in 1924 he was elected president of the German cantors' association. In 1939 he emigrated to the United States, settling in New York city. Levy's writings include: *Shaare Tefillah* (1906), a prayer-book which went through sixteen editions; *Denkmäler des jüdischen Geistes* (with Benjamin May, 1912); an edition of *Psalms* with translations by famous German writers (with Benjamin May, 1915); *Das Vincenz-Lied* (1916), a metrical translation into modern German, with notes; *Der Frankfurter Kantor* (1920), a collection of south German synagogal melodies; *Sabbathgesänge* (with Frank Rothschild, 1920); *Shaare Hayim* (1925), a Hebrew textbook.

LEVY, JOSEPH (J.) LEONARD, rabbi, b. London, 1865; d. Pittsburgh, 1917. He received his A.B. degree from the University of London in 1884, and a year later accepted the position of rabbi at the Bristol Hebrew Congregation. In 1889 he came to the United States. Levy was rabbi of B'nai Israel Congregation, Sacramento, Cal. (1889-93), associate rabbi of Keneseth Israel Reform Congregation, Philadelphia (1893-1901), and, from 1901 until his death, rabbi of Temple Rodeph Sholom, Pittsburgh. In 1898 he was elected chaplain

Lucien Lévy

of "Keegan's Brigade," with which he served in the Spanish American War. Levy organized a number of religious and charitable societies in Philadelphia. He was a noted pulpit orator and lectured throughout the United States and abroad. He wrote *A Book of Prayer* (1902); *The Jew's Beliefs* (1903); *Nineteenth Century Prophets* (1907); *Founders of Faiths* (1908); and translated the tractate *Rosh Hashanah* of the Babylonian Talmud (1895).

LEVY, JOSEPH MOSES, publisher, b. London, 1812; d. Ramsgate, England, 1888. He was educated at Bruce Castle school, and engaged in his youth in commercial pursuits. He purchased, in 1854, a printing establishment connected with the *Sunday Times,* whose chief proprietor Levy became, conducting the paper for a year. In 1855, the Newspaper Stamp Act was repealed by the British government. This measure inaugurated a new epoch in the history of the British press. But very few men were aware of its importance, and Levy was perhaps the only man in England who grasped the new possibilities of the newspaper's affairs and who acted immediately in order to create a new type of newspaper. Circumstances favored Levy's enterprising spirit. In June, 1855, a Colonel Sleigh founded a two-penny daily, entitled *Daily Telegraph and Courier.* But Sleigh was soon heavily indebted and forced to give up. Levy took the paper, and on September 17, 1855, he started it under the title of *The Daily Telegraph* as a one-penny newspaper, devoting all his money to the enterprise. By June, 1856, the new proprietor had secured a daily sale of 27,000 copies.

In 1860 Levy bought the *Morning Chronicle* to remove a possible rival to the *Daily Telegraph,* which, in 1870, was acknowledged to have the largest circulation of any daily paper in the world. Levy's success, as he stated himself in the *Daily Telegraph* in 1856, was complete, although he had combined against his paper "the entire metropolitan, and a large section of the provincial press." Levy had recognized that a new public awaited a penny paper able to satisfy the well-to-do middle classes. But the *Daily Telegraph,* although it inclined toward flamboyance, adopted a schol-

arly style and provided its readers with excellent reading. Levy's paper supported Gladstone for many years, but combatted him on the Home Rule issue. Levy started a collection for the starving people of Lancashire during the crisis of 1862, and a similar collection for the people of Paris beleaguered in 1870. In 1873 he financed George Smith's expedition for excavations in the area of Nineveh. Together with the New York *Herald,* he financed Stanley's African expedition (1875-77), and in 1884 he supported Sir H. H. Johnston's exploration of the Kilimanjaro. At all times Levy was proud of his Jewish origin. He declined to change his family name as his brother and his son did. T. H. S. Escott said in his *Masters of English Journalism* that it is largely due to Levy's family "that popular journalism has organized itself as an honorable and prosperous profession."

Lit.: Yates, Edmond, *Recollections* (1884); Sala, George Augustus, *Life and Adventures* (1895); Jones, Kennedy, *Fleet Street and Downing Street* (1920); Escott, T. H. S., *Masters of English Journalism* (1911); Bourne, Fox, *History of the Newspaper Press.*

LEVY, JULIUS, merchant and philanthropist, b. Baltimore, 1868; d. Baltimore, 1926. He entered business with his father in what became one of the largest straw hat factories in the country, and helped make Baltimore a leading city in this field. He participated in the erection of the Jewish Educational Alliance Building and the Betsy Levy Home for Orphans in Baltimore. Levy was likewise active in the movement leading to the establishment of the Baltimore Museum of Art. He was president of many Jewish organizations, founder of the Baltimore Jewish College, and a leading member of the Chizuk Amunah Congregation.

Lit.: Publications of the American Jewish Historical Society, No. 31 (1928) 281.

LEVY, LOUIS EDWARD, photo-chemist, inventor and editor, b. Pilsen, Bohemia, 1846; d. Philadelphia, 1919. He came to the United States with his parents at the age of eight, and was educated in Detroit. His work in the photo-engraving field led to the invention of a new process, called "Levytype," in 1875, and to the establishment of the Levytype Company in Baltimore. In 1877 the business moved to Philadelphia, where Levy continued his improvements in typography, receiving many medals and awards.

Levy was also a contributor to various technical journals, and from 1887 to 1890 was the publisher and editor of the Philadelphia *Evening Herald,* a daily, and of the *Mercury,* a Sunday paper. He was the author of *The Russian Jewish Refugees in America* (1895) and *Business, Money and Credit* (1896). He remained an active member of the Philadelphia Jewish community, and was particularly concerned with the possibilities of Jewish immigration to the United States. He was the editor and publisher of *The Jewish Year* (1895).

LÉVY, LUCIEN, mathematician, b. Paris, 1853; d. Paris, 1912. He was a graduate of the École Polytechnique. His career as an educator began at Rennes, where he taught mathematics; he subsequently taught at the Lycée Louis-le-Grand (1880-85), and was director of scientific studies at the Collège Sainte-Barbe (1885-90), where he reorganized instruction with notable success. In 1890 he was appointed examiner of admission to the École Polytechnique, and professor at the House of Education of the Legion of Honor, St. Denis. He was promoted at the École Polytechnique as examiner of graduates in mechanics in 1910, a post which, due to impaired health which led to his death in 1912, he could not fill.

Lévy's monograph "Sur quelques équations aux dérivées partielles du second ordre," in the *Journal de l'École Polytechnique,* and his *Sur les systèmes des surfaces triplement orthogonaux* (1896), which was crowned by the Belgian Academy, suggested further potential important contributions to the science of mathematics. He also contributed to the *Bulletin de la Société Mathématique* several articles on the theory of electricity, and on geometrical and physical optics. He was, however, very devoted to his duties as an educator and, in addition to several textbooks for secondary schools, published two works on applied mathematics: *Précis élémentaire de la théorie des fonctions elliptiques* (Eugène Rouche, co-author) and *Analyse infinitésimale à l'usage des ingénieurs* (1900-2). The French edition of the *Mathematical Encyclopedia* contains his article on geometric elements utilized by mechanics.

From 1910 to 1911, Lévy was president of the Mathematics Society of France. He was an officer of the Legion of Honor.

Lit.: *Nouvelles annales de mathématique,* vol. 72 (1913) 355-63; *Revue Scientifique,* vol. 50 (1912) 186; *Catalogue des livres imprimés de la Bibliothèque Nationale,* vol. 97, p. 306.

LÉVY, MAURICE, physicist, b. Ribeauville (Rappoltsweiler), Alsace, France, 1838; d. Paris, 1910. He became a civil engineer in 1858. Engaged in the practical problems of transportation on water during eight years in the provinces, he settled in Paris in 1872; he directed transportation on the Seine and Marne rivers, becoming inspector-general in 1894. This experience was translated into theoretical works on hydrodynamics: *L'hydrodynamique moderne et l'hypothèse des actions à distance* (1890); *Leçons sur la théorie des marées* (1898).

Lévy filled a number of distinguished educational posts, being professor of applied mechanics at the École Centrale des Arts et Manufactures from 1875; instructor of mechanics at the École Polytechnique (1862-83); and of analytical and celestial mechanics at the Collège de France (1885-1909). In 1883 he became a member of the Academy of Sciences. The capacity and versatility of his mind were further revealed in numerous articles contributed to *Nouvelles annales de mathématique* and *Génie civil* on various fields of theoretical research underlying transportation and construction, such as kinetics, analytical mechanics and geometry, spiral surfaces, power of resistance of materials, theory of heat and of elasticity. His standard work in the field of applied statistics was *La statique graphique et ses applications aux constructions* (4 vols. and four atlases; 3rd ed., 1907-26).

Lit.: Necrology by E. Picard in the *Comptes Rendus* of the Paris Academy of Sciences, vol. 151; *La Grande Encyclopédie,* vol. 22, p. 148.

LEVY, MAX, inventor of half-tone screens and other devices, b. Detroit, 1857; d. Allenhurst, N. J.,

Maurice Lévy

1926. He was the brother of Louis Edward Levy. With comparatively little formal schooling to his credit, Levy first became apprenticed to an architect in Detroit, during which period (1871-75) he also studied drawing. When Louis Edward Levy established his photo-engraving business in Baltimore (1875), Max Levy went with him and until 1887 made line drawings that were to be used in black-and-white reproduction. The possibility of half-tone reproductions occupied him, however, and in 1887, despite difficulties, he set about working out a practicable half-tone screen.

Max Levy

The task was completed the same year, and the screen was an immediate and world-wide success. From 1887 until his retirement in 1921, Levy headed the firm he had established for the manufacture of these screens. His work received the highest award at every world's fair and exposition between 1887 and the year of the inventor's death. Levy was also awarded the John Scott Medal of the Franklin Institute. The Smithsonian Institute in Washington and other science museums maintain a permanent exposition of the Levy half-tone screen processes.

Other scientific fields attracted Levy's attention. In 1902 he helped to design and build, for use as his laboratory, the first reinforced concrete structure in Philadelphia. During the first World War (1914-18) Levy was commissioned by the United States government to make various precision instruments for military and medical use. Among these were gun-sights, binocular sights and haemacytometers, or blood-counting chambers. Levy's production of the haemacytometers, which had previously been imported from Germany, attained a degree of perfection beyond that demanded by government standards. Levy also constructed a machine to make diffraction gratings for use in spectrum analysis, ruling ten to 30,000 lines on an inch of specular metal, which he compounded.

LÉVY, MICHEL, see LÉVY, FAMILY OF PUBLISHERS.

LEVY, MORITZ ABRAHAM, orientalist, b. Altona, Germany, 1817; d. Breslau, Germany, 1872. During a period of thirty years he served as religious teacher in Breslau. In connection with his educational activity he wrote *Die biblische Geschichte nach den Worten der heiligen Schrift der israelitischen Jugend erzählt* (3rd ed., 1870) and *Systematisch geordnetes Spruchbuch als Leitfaden für den jüdischen Religionsunterricht* (1867). Levy's chief work was devoted to Semitic paleography and epigraphy. Levy wrote also popular historical works, such as *Don Joseph Nasi, Herzog von Naxos* (1859). In 1865 he received the title of professor in Prussia.

LEVY, MOSES, judge, b. Philadelphia, 1757; d. Philadelphia, 1826. He was the son of Samson Levy, a Philadelphia merchant, and the nephew of Benjamin Levy. Moses Levy was graduated from the University of Pennsylvania in 1776 and admitted to the bar two years later. From 1802 to 1822 he was recorder of Philadelphia, and for the following three years he presided as judge of the district court for the city and county of Philadelphia. He served also, at one time, as a member of the Pennsylvania Legislature, and was for twenty-four years a trustee of the University of Pennsylvania.

As counsel in many important cases and because of his brilliant record as judge, Levy was esteemed by his associates of the Philadelphia bench and bar. He appears also to have been a man of property, for he sold a house on Chestnut Street for $10,000 to the Bank of North America, the first bank in the United States.

Lit.: Morais, H. S., *The Jews of Philadelphia* (1894) 38-41, 409-11, 431; *Publications of the American Jewish Historical Society,* No. 9 (1901) 35; No. 19 (1910) 121; No. 20 (1911) 121-22.

LEVY, NATHAN, merchant, b. New York city, 1704; d. Philadelphia, 1753. He was the son of Moses

Moses Levy. From a painting by Rembrandt Peale. From Hannah R. London's "Portraits of Jews"

Levy (1665-1728) of New York, and a brother of Benjamin and Samson Levy. His name appeared frequently on the roster of Congregation Shearith Israel in New York in connection with its early activities. Levy moved to Philadelphia after 1730, entering a business partnership with David Franks under the firm name of Levy and Franks. They were joint owners of several ships registered at the Port of Philadelphia, and their advertisements in the *Pennsylvania Gazette* offered medicines, European goods, and general merchandise for sale.

Levy secured the first grant of land for Jewish burial purposes, a plot thirty feet square, on September 25, 1740. He had it fenced in and was later forced to have it enclosed by a brick wall to guard against desecration. The *Pennsylvania Gazette* of September, 1751, contained an advertisement by Levy, offering a reward of twenty shillings for the arrest and conviction of persons who "fired several shots against the fence of the Jews' burying ground." In 1752 Levy purchased an additional lot, thirty feet wide and sixty feet in depth, for burial purposes.

Lit.: Morais, H. S., *The Jews of Philadelphia* (1894) 200-2; *Publications of the American Jewish Historical Society,* No. 1 (1892) 20-22; No. 4 (1896) 193-96; No. 5 (1897) 203-4; No. 6 (1897) 108; No. 23 (1915) 158-59; No. 26 (1918) 235-36.

LEVY, NEWMAN, attorney and author, b. New York city, 1888. He was educated at New York University, taking his B.A. degree in 1910 and his LL.B. degree in 1911. Levy was assistant district attorney of New York from 1916 to 1919. When the first World War threatened America, Levy entered the United States Army School of Aeronautics; during the War he served in the Aviation Corps and learned to fly "very badly."

Levy had been writing ever since his college days, but it was not until after the War that he made his first bid for attention as a professional author. That bid was not accepted, and his *Twelve Hundred a Year* (1920), a collaboration with Edna Ferber, never reached the audiences it was intended to arouse. He also wrote plays with Montague Glass and Howard

Dietz. Three years later, Levy published *Opera Guyed* (1923), a work received with instant applause and which has become a classic of its kind. In a surprising light verse, something like the English W. S. Gilbert, and even more like the American Guy Wetmore Carryl, Levy took the libretti of the most popular operas and retold them in uproarious burlesques. The rhythms were intricate; the rhymes were the envy of his contemporaries; the phrasing was broad yet, somehow, exact. Anthologists ransacked its pages; the selection *Thais,* among others, was reprinted countless times.

Two other volumes of miscellaneous light verse followed: *Gay But Wistful* (1925) and *Saturday to Monday* (1930). The chuckles were there, though the brilliance was lacking. If they failed to attain the popularity of Levy's first collection of wayward rhymes, they are not without charm, high spirits, and the dexterity characteristic of this author. After ten years, Levy satisfied his admirers with the sequel that they had often demanded: *Theatre Guyed* (1933). It was in every way worthy of its notable predecessor. Ranging from Shakespeare to Eugene O'Neill, Levy used a style that was both brisk and bravura to caricature (and, sometimes, to satirize) the drama. Nothing of the kind —not even in *Opera Guyed*—surpassed the extraordinary effects of neatness and levity achieved in *Othello* and *The Merchant of Venice.* Much of Levy's verse appeared originally in the columns conducted by Franklin P. Adams (F. P. A.) in metropolitan newspapers.

During the 1930's, Levy temporarily abandoned the law and spent a short time in Hollywood, where he did some script writing for the motion pictures. He also wrote many sketches for the radio and was chief editor of the "Information Please" program. After 1938 most of his time was spent working with the American Jewish Committee in the fight on anti-Semitism.   LOUIS UNTERMEYER.

LÉVY, PAUL, mathematician, b. Paris, 1886. A son of Lucien Lévy, he studied at the École Polytechnique and at the École Supérieure des Mines (1904-10). He served in the French Army as captain of artillery during the first World War.

Lévy was appointed professor of analysis at the École Polytechnique in 1920; he occupied the chair of analysis in the École Nationale Supérieure d'Aéronautique from 1930 on and that of mathematical and mechanical analysis at the École Supérieure des Mines from 1925 on. He was named chief inspector of mines and made an officer of the Legion of Honor. He was president of the Mathematical Society of France.

In 1941 he was one of the few Jews who, for distinguished scientific service, were exempted from the anti-Jewish statutes and continued to teach at the École Polytechnique, transferred, in 1940, to Lyon and at the École Supérieure des Mines at Paris. He declined an invitation to the United States.

His major published works, two of which won awards from the Academy of Sciences, include: *Sur les équations différentielles définissant des fonctions de lignes* (1911); *Leçons d'analyse fonctionelle* (1922); *Leçons de calcul des probabilités* (1925); *Cours d'analyse de l'École Polytechnique* (2 vols., 1930-31). His minor works, numbering fifty-four, between 1910 and 1937, were published in the *Journal de l'École Polytechnique* and mathematical journals in France.

LÉVY, RAPHAEL-GEORGES, economist, b. Paris, 1853; d. Paris, 1933. Lévy came from a Jewish family of farmers residing in Alsace. His father, a teacher of German, had migrated to Paris and had been appointed by Napoleon III instructor of the prince impérial. Then he had become the first professor of the German language at the École de Guerre and general inspector of public education.

Raphael-Georges Lévy entered the Banque de Paris et des Pays-Bas, and represented it at St. Petersburg, Berlin, London and Constantinople. Returning to France, Lévy became director of the Compagnie Française des Mines d'Or and vice-president of the Crédit Mobilier. Paul Painlevé, who was minister and a friend of Lévy, appointed him vice-president of the Association Économique Franco-Chinoise and an Anglo-French committee preparing the Channel tunnel.

In 1891 Lévy was appointed professor at the École Libre des Sciences Politiques, continuing his profession of banking. In 1913 he was appointed member of the Académie des Sciences Morales et Politiques. In 1914, after the outbreak of the first World War, Lévy transformed his mansion into a military hospital which he supported at his own expense until 1919. In 1920 Lévy was elected a member of the French Senate. He retired from this post in 1927 for reasons of health.

Lévy was a highly esteemed public speaker who represented the French Academy as well as the French Senate on several important occasions, such as at the funerals of Cardinal Mercier and of Léon Bourgeois. The peculiar value of his writings is based upon the combination of practical experiences acquired in business and theoretical clearness displayed by Lévy in every line of his works. Lévy attracted international attention in 1886 by his study *La conversion des rentes.* In 1896 he threw light upon the economic constitution of France by his study *La diffusion de la fortune mobilière en France.* In 1911 he published his standard work, *Banques d'émission et trésors publics,* and in 1921 he condensed his experiences and theories in *L'initiation financière.* Lévy considered free competition the essential condition of any sound development in national and international affairs. In 1920 he defended the French point of view concerning the treaty of Versailles in *Peace and Justice.* Poincaré said that Lévy was "better informed than any one else on the great European questions and on the true financial conditions of the countries of the Old World."

Lit.: Marlio, Louis, in *Revue des travaux de l'académie des sciences morales et politiques* (1935).

LEVY, RUDOLF, painter, b. Stettin, Germany, 1875. He studied in Munich from 1897 to 1903, then went to Paris, where he studied with Matisse and remained until the outbreak of the first World War. After the War he lived in Munich and Düsseldorf, but in 1921 moved to Berlin, where he remained for many years. Levy was a leader of the German impressionist movement and, although during his sojourn in Paris he was noted mostly for his café wit and personality, subsequent exhibitions proved him to be an outstanding painter who specialized in still lifes and portraits. His work is represented in the museums of Hamburg, Düsseldorf, Ulm and Pittsburgh. Levy was last heard of in the United States between 1935 and 1937; his whereabouts thereafter are unknown.

Lit.: Mende, Dietrich, "Rudolf Levy," *Jahrbuch der jungen Kunst,* 1923, pp. 155-58; Scheffler, Karl, "Rudolf Levy," *Kunst und Künstler,* 1922, pp. 371-77; *Kunst und Dekoration,* vol. 56, pp. 81-83.

LEVY, SAMSON (Junior), lawyer, brother of Moses, b. Philadelphia, 1761; d. Philadelphia, 1831. He studied law with his brother, and was admitted to the bar in 1787. By his wit and eloquence he became one of the best known attorneys in the city and a favorite among his colleagues of the bench and bar. Many amusing anecdotes are recalled of his erratic conduct in the handling of cases. But despite his peculiarities, or perhaps because of them, Levy enjoyed a lucrative practice, earning from $6,000 to $7,000 annually. He became a convert to the Protestant Episcopal Church. He was one of the incorporators of the Pennsylvania Academy of Fine Arts. Levy's portrait was engraved, in 1802, by Charles B. J. Fevret de St. Mémin, noted French artist, who included Levy in his portrait collection of distinguished Americans.

Lit.: Morais, H. S., *The Jews of Philadelphia* (1894) 39-42, 411, 446; Markens, I., *The Hebrews in America* (1888) 12; *Publications of the American Jewish Historical Society,* No. 6 (1887) 154; No. 9 (1901) 35; No. 19 (1910) 120-21.

LEVY, SAMUEL, lawyer and public official, b. New York city, 1876. He studied at the College of the City of New York (B.S., 1894) and New York Law School (LL.B., 1896). In 1929 he was appointed a member of the Board of Education of New York city to fill an unexpired term, and served until 1931. In that year, when the office of the borough president of Manhattan became vacant, Levy was chosen by the board of aldermen to complete the term. He was elected borough president for the full term of four years in 1933.

Levy was a leader in many Jewish communal activities. He was chairman of the committee that raised the funds for the building now occupied (1942) by the Rabbi Isaac Elchanan Theological Seminary and Yeshiva College, and became chairman of the College Council. He was also chairman of the building committee of Beth Israel Hospital, and was vice-president of the Lebanon Hospital Association. In 1934 he was granted an honorary degree (LL.D.) by Yeshiva College.

LEVY, SAMUEL DAVID, judge, b. New York city, 1860; d. New York city, 1940. He studied at New York University Law School (LL.B., 1880), and was admitted to the bar of New York in the following year. He served as counsel without fee to the United Hebrew Charities of the City of New York and to children charged with an offense, particularly those arraigned for the first time. He was appointed a city magistrate in 1912 and, in 1916, a justice of the Court of Special Sessions, assigned to the Children's Court. In 1923, and again in 1934, he was reappointed, and served in the capacity of a judge of the Children's Court and the Domestic Relations Court (which, in 1933, combined the functions of the Children's Court and the Family Court) until 1935, when he retired.

Levy was president of the Hebrew Sheltering Guardian Society for nine years (1896-1905) and vice-president for twenty-five (1905-30). As an officer of the society,

Samson Levy, Jr. From an engraved portrait (1802) by Charles B. J. Fevret de St. Mémin

he was instrumental in the adoption of the cottage plan of caring for the orphans in its charge. He helped establish the Jewish Protectory and Hawthorne School at Hawthorne, N. Y. He was also chairman of the New York committee of the National Jewish Hospital for Consumptives in Denver.

He is the author of a number of monographs on child psychology, particularly with respect to delinquency.

LEVY, URIAH PHILLIPS, United States naval officer, b. Philadelphia, 1792; d. New York city, 1862. He was the son of Michael and Rachel (Phillips) Levy, and a grandson of Jonas Phillips, a patriot soldier of the Revolution. Levy shipped as a cabin-boy on a coasting vessel at the age of ten. In 1806 he was apprenticed to a shipowner, in whose craft he sailed for four years, except during nine months spent at a Philadelphia naval school in the study of navigation. His term of apprenticeship being ended, Levy shipped as first mate of a brig carrying sundry provisions. In 1811 he was master of a schooner, *George Washington,* in which he bought a one-third share. Before the age of twenty he had passed through every grade of the service, from cabin-boy to captain.

While master of the *George Washington,* Levy was left stranded on a remote island, his crew having mutinied and deserted him. Compelled to serve in a British sloop, whose captain tried to enlist him into the British navy, Levy refused the offer and made his way back to the United States. The War of 1812 having just started, Levy volunteered his services and received an appointment as assistant sailing master to the brig *Argus,* which had been ordered to run the British blockade and carry William Crawford, the American envoy, safely to a landing in France. That duty done, the *Argus* went on a cruise and destroyed twenty-one enemy ships, Levy being assigned to board and destroy the prizes. In an attack upon a large British warship Levy met with defeat; he was, however, thereafter taken prisoner and held for sixteen months until peace was declared.

Upon his return to the United States, Levy continued in the service. He received various commissions, one for the suppression of piracy in the Gulf of Mexico and another for the extermination of the slave trade along Honduras Bay. Levy had thrilling adventures in foreign lands. He was frequently involved in difficulties, possibly enhanced by the anti-Jewish sentiment among his opponents. He fought a duel which resulted in the death of his adversary. Levy suffered court-martial on several occasions.

He also met with disappointments. After the United States Navy had promoted him from a lieutenancy to the rank of captain, in 1844, he was retired from active service for more than ten years. It was only after a special, legislatively-established court of inquiry (in proceedings in which Benjamin F. Butler, a leader of the New York bar, represented him), rendered a judgment in his favor (1854) that he secured reinstatement, and was given command of a ship anew. The evidence indicated that he had been demoted in large degree because of anti-Semitic prejudice, and the testimony and his defense were printed. He subsequently rose to the highest rank and was justly entitled to be styled commodore, although that office had not yet been officially established.

Levy triumphed over many obstacles by virtue of his courage and strength of character. A staunch admirer of Thomas Jefferson, he purchased the statesman's Monticello home and left it and most of his estate to the government, to maintain there an agricultural school for orphaned children of naval officers, but the will was invalidated on technical grounds in the leading case of Levy vs. Levy 33 N. Y. 97. In 1833 he donated a fine bronze statue of Jefferson to the United States government—now on view at the Capitol in Washington. When the Civil War broke out, Levy manifested his public spirit by subscribing liberally to the war loan. At the time of his death, he is said to have been the highest ranking naval officer in the service. His remains rest in Cypress Hills cemetery, and the inscription on his tombstone states that he was the father of the law for the abolition of corporal punishment in the American Navy.

CLARENCE I. FREED.

Lit.: Wolf, Simon, in *American Jewish Year Book,* 1902-3, pp. 42-45; *American Israelite,* Jan. 20, 1898; *Century Magazine,* 1899, pp. 796-800; Wiernik, Peter, *History of the Jews in America,* 238-41; *Publications of the American Jewish Historical Society,* No. 3 (1895) 40; No. 17 (1909) 1581; No. 26 (1918) 194-95.

LEVY, WILLIAM AUERBACH, *see* AUERBACH-LEVY, WILLIAM.

LEVY, WILLIAM MALLORY, American Congressman, b. Isle of Wight, Va., 1827; d. Saratoga, N. Y., 1882. He graduated from William and Mary College, Williamsburg, Va., in 1844, served in the Mexican War as second lieutenant in Company F, First Regiment Virginia Volunteers, then studied law, was admitted to the bar in 1851, and commenced practice in Norfolk, Va. He moved to Natchitoches, La., in 1852, and continued the practice of law. He served as a member of the state house of representatives (1859-61); as presidential elector on the Democratic ticket of Douglas

Uriah P. Levy

and Johnson in 1860; in the Confederate Army during the Civil War, where he was commissioned captain of Company A, Second Louisiana Infantry (1861); and subsequently as a major in the Adjutant General's Department.

Levy was elected a Representative from Louisiana on the Democratic ticket to the Forty-fourth Congress (1875-77). He was a member of the state constitutional convention in 1879, and was appointed associate justice of the State Supreme Court in 1879, serving until his death.

Lit.: Biographical Dictionary of the American Congress (1928) 1222.

LÉVY-BRUHL, LUCIEN, philosopher and sociologist, b. Paris, 1857; d. Paris, 1939. From 1899 on he was professor at the Sorbonne, and in 1917 he became a member of the Académie des Sciences Morales et Politiques. He was also a member of the Institut Français and editor of the *Revue philosophique de la France et de l'étranger.*

After the death of Émile Durkheim, Lévy-Bruhl became the leading French social philosopher. He started with works on the history of philosophy and wrote books on Jacobi, on German philosophy since Leibnitz, on modern French philosophy, and on Auguste Comte, whose philosophical and sociological ideas had greatly influenced him. As a follower of Comte's positivism, Lévy-Bruhl represents a philosophy of social realism. He employed methods similar to those of the natural sciences, aiming to establish moral and social laws similar to natural laws. In this attitude he was a strict opponent of metaphysical morals. He saw analogies between the social, moral and physical developments of man. The task of sociology, he held, is to rediscover the successive stages through which various social and cultural phenomena passed during their historical development.

Lévy-Bruhl became the first sociologist who successfully used the comparative methods of biology, combining them with social and historical investigation. He stressed the close link between ethics and sociology, a problem with which he dealt in his book *La morale et la science des moeurs* (Paris, 1903; English trans., Elizabeth Lee, *Ethics and Moral Science,* London, 1905). By his combined methods Lévy-Bruhl succeeded in revealing the existence of a "primitive mentality" as a certain type of thinking, feeling and social behavior. This type believes in supernatural forces, is essentially mystic and opposed to all analytical and abstract thinking. "The whole life of the 'primitive,' from birth to death, and even beyond, bathes, so to speak, in the supernatural," he contended.

In numerous books, which made his name famous the world over, Lévy-Bruhl dealt with the qualities and characteristics of primitivism. In 1910 *Les fonctions mentales dans les sociétés inférieures* (English trans., Lilian A. Clare, *How Natives Think*, London, 1926) was published; in 1922 *La mentalité primitive* (English version known as *Primitive Mentality*, New York, 1923); in 1927 *L'âme primitive* (English text entitled *The Soul of the Primitive*, New York, 1928); in 1931 *Le surnaturel et la nature dans la mentalité primitive* (translated as *Primitives and the Supernatural*, New York, 1935); and in 1935 *La mythologie primitive*. These penetrating studies are among the most important applications of modern sociological ideas and methods to the prehistoric realm.   RUDOLF KAYSER.

Lit.: Chang-Li, Chang, *La morale et le sociologisme de M. Lucien Lévy-Bruhl* (1937).

LEVY-RATHENAU, JOSEFINE, social worker and leader of women's movements, b. Berlin, 1877; d. Berlin, 1921. During her youth she came under the influence of the well-known social worker Alice Salomon, and eventually developed a point of view which preferred prevention to cure in relation to social ills. Her interests were soon directed toward the need for reconstructing the vocational stratification of German women. In 1900, the same year in which she married Dr. Max Levy, she founded a club of working women.

From 1910 to 1920 she edited *Frauenberuf und Erwerb,* a periodical of vocational information. In 1911 and 1912 she established a bureau of vocational guidance for women in Berlin; later this served as a model for boys' vocational guidance institutions. During the last year of her life she was a city councillor for Berlin. Josefine Levy-Rathenau was the author of *Die deutsche Frau im Beruf* (1912). Although without direct connections in the German Jewish community, she persistently fought the anti-Semitic movements which arose in Germany after the first World War.

Lit.: Ernst, Johanna, *Josefine Levy-Rathenau und die Berufsberatung* (1922); Levy, Max, *Josefine Levy-Rathenau zum Gedächtnis* (1921).

LEVY-ULLMAN, HENRY, jurist, b. Paris, 1870. At first a practising lawyer, in 1899 he was invited to teach civil law at the University of Montpellier; he subsequently taught the same subject at the Universities of Lille and Paris (from 1916 on). He took an active part in the French administration, serving as chief of cabinet of the ministry of labor and social security, of the ministry of public works, and of the ministry of justice (1924-26). Levy-Ullman was vice-president of the International Academy of Comparative Law at The Hague.

LEVYSOHN, ARTHUR, journalist and editor, b. Grünberg, Silesia, Germany, 1841; d. Meran, Italy, 1908. He was baptized at an early age. He learned the elements of journalism from his father, who was the editor of the local weekly, and about 1860 went to

Fanny Lewald

Paris as a foreign correspondent. He returned to Germany before the outbreak of the Franco-Prussian War (1870-71) and published the semi-official organ of the German headquarters during the siege of Paris. In 1871 Levysohn became foreign editor of the *Neues Wiener Tagblatt,* but was expelled by the government in 1875 for his political views. He then joined the editorial staff of the *Berliner Tageblatt* and founded two weeklies, *Deutsches Montagsblatt* (1877) and *Deutsche Lesehalle* (1880), both of which were incorporated into the *Tageblatt* in 1882, when Levysohn became its chief editor.

Levysohn not only made many improvements in the affairs of the newspaper but also made it a political mouthpiece. He followed no party, but advocated the union of all the German liberal groups. He attacked the protectionism of Bismarck on the one hand, and such liberal leaders as Lasker and Eugen Richter. He retired from active editorship in 1906.

LEWALD, FANNY, author, b. Königsberg, Germany, 1811; d. Dresden, Germany, 1889. She embraced Christianity in 1828 at the instigation of her teacher. In Berlin she met Rahel Varnhagen in 1832 and other literary people of renown. In 1849 she wrote her novel *Prinz Louis Ferdinand* (3 vols.). An earlier novel, *Clementine* (1842), condemned conventional marriage. In 1854 she married the esthete Adolph Stahr. She described her journeys in keenly observant travel letters. Her autobiographical works include *Erinnerungen aus dem Jahre 48* (1850) and *Zwölf Bilder aus dem Leben* (1888). Her battle cry, "For and against women" (1870), served the cause of woman's emancipation. She was a pioneer among writers of the modern fiction dealing realistically with feminine subjects, of which the most important was *Die Familie Darner.*

THEODOR LEWALD (b. Berlin, 1860), German public official, was the nephew of Fanny Lewald. He was half-Jewish, and was baptized. From 1904 to 1905 he was commissioner of the German empire at the St. Louis World's Fair, and in 1919 to 1920 state secretary to the Ministry of Home Affairs during the republican regime. In 1919 he was appointed president of the Reichsausschuss für Leibesübungen. In 1920 Lewald, who was actively interested in athletics, founded the German University for Gymnastics in Berlin. In 1921 to 1922 he acted as German plenipotentiary in the negotiations for the settlement of the Upper Silesia boundary dispute between Germany and Poland, and held the same position in the negotiations in 1923 to 1924 (the "Wiener Abkommen" with Poland) and in 1925 to 1927 (the German-Polish Commercial Treaty). In 1936 he served as commissioner of the German empire for the Olympic Games held in Berlin, after which he retired from the German Civil Service.

Lit.: Lewald, Fanny, *Meine Lebensgeschichte* (6 vols., 1861-63).

LEWALD, JOHANN KARL AUGUST, author, b. Königsberg, Germany, 1792; d. Munich, Germany, 1871. Lewald, a cousin of Fanny Lewald's father, was baptized in a Protestant church in his childhood. He began to study at the University of Königsberg, but was forced to interrupt his studies after his father's death, and entered a business. In 1813 Lewald volunteered in the Prussian army and was wounded. Having recovered, Lewald made the acquaintance of the Russian general Von Rosen, and became the general's secretary in the headquarters of Field-Marshal Barclay de Tolly. From 1815 to 1824, Lewald was actor and dramatist at Breslau, Brünn, Vienna, Nuremberg and Bamberg. From 1824 to 1831 he resided in Hamburg. There he became a friend of Heinrich Heine, who met him later in Paris and dedicated to Lewald his "Briefe über die französische Bühne."

In 1826 Lewald published his first book, a history of music. In 1831 he went to Paris, but the Asiatic cholera made him flee to Germany. From 1834 to 1846 Lewald resided at Stuttgart and there edited the liberal periodical *Europa.* Then he went to Vienna, which he left in 1848, deterred by the revolution. In 1849 Lewald became stage-manager of the royal theatre at Stuttgart, and edited there the conservative *Deutsche Chronik.* In 1852 he was converted to Catholicism. In 1863 he retired from office.

During the years 1831 to 1846 Lewald published more than fifty books, mostly of entertaining character, which he disavowed when he became converted to Catholicism. Formerly a sympathizer of liberal "Young Germany," Lewald became afraid of any revolutionary movement, and he stiffened his resistance to liberalism after 1848 as he was growing older. His last novels, *Clarinette, Der Insurgent,* and *Anna,* published in 1863, 1865 and 1868, followed in the footsteps of the Catholic convert, Countess Hahn-Hahn, the adversary of Fanny Lewald. His autobiography, *Aquarelle aus meinem Leben,* had been composed in 1837, before his conversion, and was enlarged by later editions. Another autobiography, written after his conversion to Catholicism, was published in Rosenthal's *Konvertitenbilder,* vol. 1.

LEWANDA, JUDAH LÖB (LEO), writer, b. Minsk, Russia, 1835; d. Leningrad, 1887. He graduated from the rabbinical school at Vilna (1854), became instructor in the government school in Minsk and was later appointed advisor on Jewish affairs to the governor of Vilna. Here he wrote textbooks and

Louis Lewandowski

participated in the work of the Vilna commission for Jewish affairs. Lewanda began to write at an early age, contributing to numerous Jewish periodicals in Russia, such as *Rassvyet* and *Zion.* His stories, novels and articles dealt with various aspects of Jewish life and its problems. He was a strong advocate of the Russification of the Jews, but he gradually changed as a result of his disappointment with the younger Jewish generation, and after the pogroms of 1881 he joined the Hibbath Zion movement. The city library in Tel-Aviv bears his name. His better known works include: *Goriatshoye Vremya* (A Hot Time; 1871-73), dealing with the Polish insurrection; *Ocherki Proshlovo* (1875), sketches from Jewish life; a novel on the life of Abraham Esofowicz (*Voskhod,* 1885 and 1887).

LEWANDOWSKI, LOUIS, cantor and composer, b. Wreschen, Posen, 1823; d. Berlin, 1894. The son of a Talmudic scholar and linguist, the young Louis, with his four brothers, accompanied his father when the latter, as was often the case, was chosen to chant the Musaf (Additional) Service on the high holidays as well as on other auspicious occasions. At the age of twelve, having suffered the loss of his mother, he took leave of his father and went to Berlin, where he joined the choir of Cantor Asher Lion, and entered the Gymnasium, spending his free hours studying the violin and the piano. Through his teacher of Hebrew, Salomon Plessner, an introduction to Alexander Mendelssohn (grandson of Moses Mendelssohn) was arranged. In the musical atmosphere of the latter's home, he decided in favor of a musical career. Courses in music at the University of Berlin were followed by his admission (as the first Jew) into the Academy of Arts, where he soon distinguished himself as a talented musician and was awarded prizes in excellence. Here he produced a cantata for solo, chorus, and orchestra, also a symphony which was awarded the plaudits of his teachers.

A tragic interlude interrupted his rapid progress. His physical strength giving way, a four-year retirement and cessation from all work was ordered by his doctors. Thanks to the devotion of his sister Rosalie, his recuperation slowly but surely came about, and in 1844 he was invited by the Berlin Jewish community to organize a choir and serve as its director.

Before inaugurating his duties, Lewandowski was sent by his community to Vienna to acquaint himself with the service introduced there by Salomon Sulzer. Unfortunately, upon his return, he found Asher Lion looking with disfavor upon the Sulzer style of service. With the engagement, however, of Cantor Abraham J. Lichtenstein, an ideal team, such as later in Odessa with Minkowsky and Nowakowsky, was born for the elevation of the synagogue service. Lewandowski, the great musician, and Lichtenstein, the fine singer and authority on traditional liturgical music, complemented each other, and the foundation of an esthetic, musical and dignified service was laid.

Although his excellent harmonizations and masterful contrapuntal treatments of the traditional melodies in his volumes *Todah Vezimrah* were sufficient to assure him everlasting fame, it was his competent treatment of the recitatives for cantor and his melodious two-part arrangements in his *Kol Rinah Uthefillah* that found immediate favor with cantors and choirmasters throughout Europe.

His activities were by no means limited to choir instruction and composition. Many well-known cantors received their instruction from him at the Teachers' Institute in Berlin. Also as teacher of music in the congregational religious school for children, he had the task of bringing order and beauty into the hitherto confused subject of songs for children.

He was honored by the Prussian government and by local and distant communities on the occasions of his twenty-fifth and fiftieth jubilees.   MAX WOHLBERG.

Lit.: Friedman, A., *Die synagogale Musik* (1904); idem, *Lebensbilder berühmter Kantoren,* vols. 1 and 2 (1921).

LEWI, ISIDOR, journalist, b. Albany, N. Y., 1850; d. New York city, 1938. The son of Dr. Joseph Lewi, he was educated at the Albany Academy. First engaged in mercantile work, he went into journalism in 1870 as a contributor to *The American Israelite.* He joined the staff of the New York *Tribune* in 1892, following years of service on the Albany *Argus* and the Albany *Morning Express.* Before he retired from active service on the New York *Tribune* shortly after the beginning of the first World War, Lewi had covered the Chicago fire of 1871, served as a *Tribune* correspondent in Cuba during the Spanish-American War, and sent dispatches from Vienna on the mobilization of the Austrian Army at the outbreak of the World War. At one time he served as press agent for Mark Twain and for General Lew Wallace, producer of *Ben Hur.* On the New York *Tribune,* Lewi served as reporter, special writer, Sunday editor, war correspondent and editorial writer.

As a boy, Lewi saw President Abraham Lincoln at Albany on his way from Springfield to be inaugurated for the first time. After that, he personally saw every president from Lincoln to Franklin D. Roosevelt, with the exception of President Warren G. Harding.

Active in Jewish circles, Lewi contributed to many Jewish magazines and periodicals. He was the author of *Isaac Mayer Wise and Emanu-el* (New York, 1930), a biographical and historical work. Always active at Temple Emanu-el, Lewi was present at the dedication of the Temple building at 43rd Street and Fifth Avenue on September 11, 1868, as well as being present at the last service of the Temple on July 23, 1927, before it was torn down prior to the building of a new Temple at Fifth Avenue and 65th Street.

EMITA PENINNAH WOLFF MAY LEWI (b. La Guayra, Venezuela, 1851; d. New York city, 1931), wife first of Lewis May and then of Isidor Lewi, was active in communal work. She helped found the Emanu-el Sisterhood, the Hebrew Technical School for Girls, and the Mount Sinai Training School for Nurses.

LEWI, JOSEPH, physician, b. Radnitz, Bohemia, 1820; d. Albany, N. Y., 1897. He was educated at the Universities of Prague and Vienna (M.D., 1846). In 1846 he was appointed assistant at the Vienna Lying-in Hospital, and in 1847 he started practising medicine in Radnitz. The following year he was involved in the revolution and fled to the United States.

For almost fifty years Lewi was known in Albany medical circles as an ideal general practitioner, modest, learned, and competent. He was president of the Albany County Medical Society and senior censor of the New York State Medical Society. In 1863, at the time of the Civil War, he was one of the forty-three Albany citizens who founded the Albany Union League. During the same period he served on a commission to examine surgeons for the volunteer army. He was on the board of public instruction for twelve years.

He was the father of thirteen children who distinguished themselves in medicine, journalism, and other fields of public service.

LEWI, MAURICE, J., physician, b. Albany, N. Y., 1857. The son of Joseph Lewi, he studied journalism under Leo Altmeyer and medicine at the Albany Medical School (M.D., 1887). Later he did postgraduate work abroad at the Universities of Heidelberg and Vienna.

He had a varied career in many branches of the medical field. He was house physician of Albany Hospital, surgeon of the fire department, coroner's physician, county physician, instructor at the Albany Medical College, and professor of medical jurisprudence at the Albany Law School. Later he was medical consultant of the H. A. Metz Laboratories, and medical director of the American Union Insurance Company.

Lewi was a pioneer in the field of podiatry and a leader in the move to separate the power of awarding diplomas from that of granting licenses to practise. He was largely responsible for the laws of 1890 and 1893 that created the New York State Board of Medical Examiners, and he served as secretary of that body from 1892 to 1913. In 1913 he resigned in order to become the president of the first Institute of Podiatry in New York city, which had been made possible by the law he had helped frame in 1912, providing for the regulation of chiropody by the State Board of Medical Examiners. Theretofore no medical school had taught podiatry as a separate subject and the science had progressed but slowly. He was still president of the Institute in 1942.

Lewi edited several books on podiatry which are recognized as authoritative references in the field: *Text Book of Chiropody* (1914); *Surgery, With Special Reference to Podiatry* (1917); *Practical Podiatry* (1918); *Foot Orthopaedics* (1927).

LEWIN, JUDAH LÖB (known as Jehalel, from the initials of his name), Hebrew poet and journalist, b. Minsk, Russia, 1845; d. Kiev, Russia, 1925. In the last decades of the 19th cent. he influenced to a high degree the Hebrew-reading public and the Jewish intelligentsia in Eastern Europe.

Three epochs may be distinguished in Lewin's literary activity, which at the same time characterize the process of development of modern Russian Jewry: 1. At first he took up the struggle against backwardness and conservative fanaticism, after the manner of the Haskalah (enlightenment). 2. In the 1870's, Lewin became one of the first advocates of Socialism and historical materialism in Hebrew literature. He was one of the permanent contributors to the first Socialist Hebrew periodical, *Ha'emeth,* published by Aaron Samuel Libermann, with whom he carried on a lively correspondence. In this epoch he represented the standpoint that the Jewish question forms a part of the general social question and will find its solution together with that. The social poems of Lewin ("Ebed Abadim," "Kishron Hamaaseh" and others) brought him great popularity; in modern Hebrew literature they are numbered among the strongest protests against the capitalistic order of society. 3. In the 1880's Lewin arrived at a national consciousness as the result of the Jewish pogroms, since he himself had experienced one of them with all the horrible details in Kiev. Lewin now recognized the necessity of a Jewish emigration; he at first wished to see such a movement take place to America, but then turned to the Hibbath Zion movement and founded in Kiev, together with Max Mandelstamm, a society for the colonization of Palestine, which allied itself with the Odessa Committee.

He wrote an autobiography, *Zikkaron Basefer* (1910).

Lit.: Fichman, Jacob, in *Hashiloah,* vol. 45, Nos. 5-6; Bernstein, S., in *Zukunft* (New York), vol. 12 (1925).

LEWIN, KURT, educator and psychologist, b. Mogilno, province of Posen, Germany, 1890. He studied psychology at the University of Berlin, where he obtained the Ph.D. degree. In 1921 he became a lecturer (Privatdozent) and in 1927 professor of psychology at that university. He was co-editor of the philosophical journal *Symposion.* In 1933 he left Germany for the United States where, in 1934, he became acting professor at Cornell University, Ithaca, N. Y. From 1936 on he was professor of child psychology at the University of Iowa.

Lewin was one of the foremost representatives of "Gestalt theory." He used the experimental methods of the natural sciences in approaching the workings of the mind. In 1922 he wrote *Der Begriff der Genese in Physik, Biologie und Entwicklungsgeschichte,* an attempt to see identical laws governing different branches of science. By employing a mathematical

setup of "space" he introduced the concept of "topology" into psychology in his book *Principles of Topological Psychology* (1936). Other books representative of Lewin's psychology were *A Dynamic Theory of Personality* (1935); *The Conceptual Representation and Measurement of Psychological Forces* (1938); and *Studies in Topological and Vector Psychology:* part 1, *Formalization and Progress* (1940); part 2, *Frustration and Regression* (1941; results of joint researches under the direction of Lewin at the Iowa Child Welfare Station).

Lewin also approached problems of social psychology. He directed comparative experiments at Iowa University on children subjected to the influence of democratic, dictatorial and anarchistic governments. In 1942 he participated in the seminars of that university on interreligious relations. His articles, "Psycho-Sociological Problems of a Minority Group," in *Character and Personality* (1935), and "Self-Hatred among Jews," in the *Contemporary Jewish Record* (1941), dealt with special Jewish problems.

He was co-editor of a series of monographs entitled *Contributions to Psychological Theory.*

Toni Oelsner.

LEWIN, LOUIS, pharmacologist, b. Tuchel, Russia, 1850; d. Berlin, 1929. He received his M.D. degree from the University of Berlin, worked for two years at the laboratories of Voit and Pettenkofer at Munich, then became connected with the University of Berlin, being gradually advanced from his initial position of assistant to the Pharmacological Institute to that of an associate professor. In 1919 he was named honorary professor at the Technical School of Berlin.

Lewin was one of the most eminent contributors to modern pharmacology. The vast amount of investigations and experiments which he carried on throughout his long life were dedicated chiefly to poisons, and their main trends were the extensive study of narcotics and snake venoms; poisoning in factory work and its prevention; the treatment of lepra and febrile diseases, and that of chronic morphinism. He also studied poisoning by gases such as hydrocyanic acid, potassium cyanide, benzol, nitrous fumes, trinitrotoluol and others. One of the plants whose toxic quality he discovered was named anhalonium Lewinii after him. To this work, conducted at the clinic and in the laboratory, correspond over 200 publications in periodicals and in book form, many of which mark important progress in the science of medicine. His great cumulative works on toxicology, some of which were translated into other languages, are: *Die Nebenwirkungen der Arzneimittel* (1881; several editions); *Die Wirkungen von Arzneimitteln auf das Auge; Lehrbuch der Toxikologie* (4th ed., 1928); *Die Gifte der Weltgeschichte* (1920).

Lewin was an active member of the Berlin Jewish community and represented the conservative group in the communal assembly. His unwillingness to renounce his faith barred, until the end of his brilliant scientific career, his appointment to full professorship. He often worked under great handicaps; much of his work was carried on in his small apartment to which physicians and students from all over flocked. At the age of seventy-eight he was investigating banisterin,

Elhanan Löb Lewinsky

a drug used in the treatment of senile paralysis, when he was paralyzed himself. He died within the year.

Lit.: Macht, D. I., *Louis Lewin*, Reprint from *Annals of Medical History*, New Series, vol. 3, No. 2, p. 179.

LEWIN, PHILIP, surgeon, b. Chicago, 1888. He was educated at the University of Chicago (B.S., 1909) and at Rush Medical College (M.D., 1911). He later pursued post-graduate studies at the Sorbonne in Paris, France. He did important research work on the surgical treatment of diseases of the bones and joints. For many years he served as professor at the Cook County Graduate School of Medicine and as associate professor of orthopedic surgery at Northwestern University Medical School; he still held both posts in 1942. He also served as consultant to the Chicago Health Department, was a member of the medical advisory committee of Warm Springs, Ga., and of Governor Henry Horner's Commission on infantile paralysis.

Lewin wrote many articles on orthopedic surgery and allied subjects for medical journals, and was the author of several books, including: *A Text Book on Orthopedic Surgery for Nurses* (1928); *Fractures and Dislocations* (1937); *The Foot and Ankle*: *Their Injuries, Diseases, Deformities and Disabilities* (1940; 2nd. ed., 1941); *Infantile Paralysis, Anterior Poliomyelitis* (1941).

LEWINSKY, ELHANAN LÖB (pseudonym, Rabbi Karob), Hebrew and Yiddish writer, b. Podberesye, Lithuania, 1857; d. Odessa, Russia, 1910. As a student at the University of Kharkov he joined the Bilu movement and went with a group of colonists to Palestine, but had to return because of an eye infection. In 1888 he became lessee of a farm and in 1895 manager of Carmel, the Palestinian wine company, at Odessa. At the same time he contributed to *Hamelitz* and other Hebrew periodicals. His feuilletons were distinguished by wit, joy of life, and a limpid style. He participated actively in Zionist and Hebrew movements, and helped found the Ivriah language organization and the Moriah publishing company. He edited the Yiddish periodical *Gut Morgen* at Odessa toward the end of his life. His collected works were published after his death in three volumes under the editorship of Joseph Klausner. Among the best known of them are his Utopia, *Massa Leeretz Yisrael Bishenath Tath Leelef Hashishi* (Odessa, 1893; Berlin, 1922; Yiddish trans., M. Kleinmann), and the series "Mahshaboth Umaasim" (*Hashiloah*) and "Hazon Haruhoth" (*Luah Ahiasaf*, 1894-1904).

LEWINSOHN, ISAAC BÄR, *see* LEVINSOHN, ISAAC BAER.

LEWINSOHN, RICHARD (pseudonym, **Morus**), physician, economist, writer and journalist, b. Berlin, 1894. He first studied medicine, later economics, and graduated in both fields. His brilliant written essays and articles were printed mostly in the *Vossische Zeitung* and in *Die Weltbühne*. Besides, he wrote apologetic articles for Jewish periodicals in Germany. He was editor in chief of the financial and business section of the *Vossische Zeitung* from 1926 to 1933 and foreign correspondent for this well-known liberal paper. Lewinsohn wrote: *Sozialismus und Bevölkerungspolitik* (1922); *Die Umschichtung der europäischen Vermögen* (1925); *Jüdische Weltfinanz?* (1926); *Wie sie gross und reich wurden* (1927); *Der Mann im Dunkel, Sir Basil Zaharoff* (1929; translated into French, Italian, Swedish, Greek, Polish and Czech); *Das Geld in der Politik* (1930); *Die Welt aus den Fugen, Amerika in der Krise* (1932).

LEWIS, SIR GEORGE HENRY, barrister, b. Holborn, England, 1833; d. London, 1911. He was educated at University College, London, and was admitted as a solicitor in 1856. He was often brought to public attention because of his work in sensational cases. His action as barrister for Parnell against the *Times* meant not only a triumph for Parnell and his party but also a position of great prominence for Lewis. During the last decade of his life Lewis had more financial cases than any other lawyer in London. In 1895 he was knighted and in 1902 was made a baronet.

Lit.: Men and Women of the Times; Burke's *Peerage, Baronetage and Knighthood* (1903).

LEWIS, HARRY EMERSON, judge, b. New York city, 1880. He was admitted to the bar of New York in 1901. In 1915 he was appointed a county judge of Kings County (Brooklyn); during that year he presided over one of the longest and most involved trials in the history of the state, that of a former comptroller of the city of New York and later president of the bankrupt Union Bank, who was accused of perjury in his report on the condition of the bank. In April of the following year Lewis was appointed district attorney of Kings County, and in November was elected for the balance of the term; he was reelected in 1921.

As district attorney Lewis leaped into prominence when he disclosed that the wire-tapping facilities of the police department were being used in an investigation relative to the Catholic Charities. This resulted in the indictment of both the commissioner of charities and of the attorney for the investigating body. In 1919 Lewis investigated and succeeded in indicting those to blame

Harry Emerson Lewis

William M. Lewis

for the famous Malbone Street subway disaster; he personally prosecuted and convicted the notorious bandits Chapman and Hanby. In 1921 Lewis was elected to the New York Supreme Court, and in 1935 was reelected for a second term, upon the joint nomination of the two major political parties. In 1931 he was designated by Governor Franklin D. Roosevelt to preside in the extraordinary terms of the Supreme Court in cases involving certain bank scandals in Manhattan and Brooklyn.

Elected a delegate-at-large to the New York Constitutional Convention of 1937, Lewis was made chairman of the Bill of Rights Committee. His proposal to make wire-tapping legal by court order was adopted despite objection upon the ground that the national authorities were opposed to it. Lewis' stand was vindicated by national authorities after the outbreak of the war in 1941, when J. Edgar Hoover and Attorney General Francis Biddle suggested the necessity for the interception of telegraph and telephone wires. Lewis was instrumental in amending the state constitution to provide that "no person shall be denied the equal protection of the laws of this state or any subdivision thereof. No person shall, because of race, color, creed or religion, be subjected to any discrimination in his civil rights by any other person or by any firm, corporation, or institution, or by the state or any agency or subdivision of the state" (Article 1, section 11, Bill of Rights).

Lewis has served as a member of the Appellate Term of the Supreme Court since 1929, and is one of the presiding judges of that court, for which he wrote a number of opinions involving important questions of law.

LEWIS, HARRY SAMUEL, rabbi, b. London, 1863; d. New York city, 1940. He was educated at

King's College School (1877-81) and Cambridge University (A.B., 1884; M.A., 1896). In 1931 he received a doctorate in Jewish theology from the Jewish Institute of Religion.

He was editor of *The Jewish Standard* in London from 1887 to 1889. From 1900 to 1906 he was a member of the Stepney borough council. He was a founder of the Jewish Religious Union. From 1908 to 1913 he was rabbi of the Manchester Congregation of British Jews. Lewis migrated to the United States in 1913 and served as New York city prison chaplain for twenty years. From 1922 until his death he was chaplain and associate professor of Hebrew at the Jewish Institute of Religion.

Lewis wrote several books on Jewish subjects, including: *Targum on Isaiah* (in Hebrew, 1889), *The Jew in London* (1901); *Liberal Judaism and Social Service* (1916); *Emmanuel of Rome* (1935).

LEWIS, LEOPOLD DAVIS, playwright, b. London, 1828; d. London, 1890. He was educated at King's College School and in 1850 became a solicitor. Until 1875 Lewis practised law. But in 1871 he had turned to the drama with an adaptation of Erckmann-Chatrian's *Le juif polonais*, which was produced by Sir Henry Irving as *The Bells*. Among Lewis' other plays were *Wandering Jew* (1873); *Give a Dog a Bad Name* (1876); and *Foundlings* (1881). For a short time in 1868 he was co-editor of a monthly, *The Mask*. In 1880 a three-volume collection of his stories was issued as *A Peal of Merry Bells*.

LEWIS, WILLIAM M., judge, b. Poneviez, Lithuania, 1884; d. Philadelphia, 1939. He came to the United States in 1896, and two years later took up residence in Philadelphia. For many years of his youth he sold newspapers at the very corner of City Hall where later he was to have his judicial offices. He was educated at the University of Pennsylvania and admitted to the bar in 1905. In 1914 he was elected to the city council and served for six years. He was appointed a judge of the municipal court in 1922, was elected for a full term of ten years in 1923, and was reelected in 1933. That year, in a secret poll conducted by the Philadelphia Bar Association, he was given the highest percentage of approval of any sitting judge.

Lewis was vitally interested in the Zionist movement and was regarded as one of its leaders in the United States. He was a national vice-president of the Zionist Organization of America, national chairman of the United Palestine Appeal (1927-28), and was named a Zionist member of the council of the Jewish Agency in 1929. He was likewise active in other communal activities, serving as a director of the Federation of Jewish Charities and of the Jewish Publication Society, a member of the board of overseers of Gratz College, president of the Associated Talmud Torahs of Philadelphia, chairman of the Philadelphia Labor Board, and grand master of the Brith Sholom fraternal society for three consecutive terms.

Lit.: American Jewish Year Book, vol. 41 (1939-40) 67-73.

LEWISOHN, ADOLPH, philanthropist, b. Hamburg, Germany, 1849; d. Saranac Lake, N. Y., 1938. He came to the United States in 1867, to join his brothers Julius and Leonard. Their business interests soon centered on mining, and it was especially in copper mines—located both in the United States and other countries—that the Lewisohn fortune, devoted generously to educational and philanthropic purposes, was made. The greater part of the Lewisohn contributions to public welfare began with the second decade of the 20th cent. Civic institutions and undertakings of particular Jewish significance shared in the $2,000,000 Lewisohn distributed.

Through his brother Leonard, Lewisohn developed an interest in the Hebrew Sheltering Guardian Society, and it was under his presidency, a post he retained for more than thirty years until his death, and largely through his efforts, that the model cottage home of the society was opened in Pleasantville, N. Y., in 1912. The following year Lewisohn announced a gift which subsequently became identified with one of the major features of New York city's musical life—the Stadium of the College of the City of New York. The amphitheatre was dedicated in 1915, and three years later the first of the summer orchestral concerts was held there. From attracting audiences that did not total more than 5,000 the first year, the Lewisohn Stadium concerts, by 1942, were annually giving a long series of concerts that sometimes attracted 23,000 on a single night. Lewisohn was from the inception of the summer concerts a leading supporter of their budget. He had also, in 1913, turned over to City College his valuable German library of 1,500 volumes.

Among the Lewisohn benefactions of substantial size were: $300,000 to Columbia University for a school of mines building; $300,000 to Mount Sinai Hospital and pathological laboratory, New York; $140,000 to the Hebrew Technical School for Girls, a non-sectarian institution; $50,000 to the Jewish Protectory; $30,000 for an ophthalmology fellowship in Wilmer Institute, Johns Hopkins University, and $25,000 to the Scientific Foundation in Hamburg. Lewisohn was one of the

Adolph Lewisohn

founders of the Federation for the Support of Jewish Philanthropic Societies in New York and during his lifetime contributed approximately $200,000 to it. His son, Samuel A. (treated separately), followed in his footsteps in communal and civic pursuits.

Lewisohn added an intellectual interest in the problems of philanthropy to his own benefactions. His concern for the cause of child welfare made him a pioneer in the treatment of child care problems in America. His interest in prison reform brought him the presidency of the National Committee on Prisons and Prison Labor, which post he held until his death. On his seventieth birthday, the committee presented him with $30,000 to be used in prison work. Lewisohn fought for fair wages for prison labor and for the improvement of hygienic conditions in penal institutions. In 1924, Lewisohn was largely responsible for the founding of the American ORT, which provided trade and agricultural training for European Jews. He was also an art collector, both for himself and on behalf of museums. The Brooklyn Museum was the recipient of most of his gifts. In 1941 the Adolph Lewisohn house, a gift of the Lewisohn family, was dedicated as a social center by the College of the City of New York.   NATHAN RICARDO.

Lit.: American Hebrew, May 22, 1925, p. 87; Nov. 12, 1926, p. 24; May 24, 1929, p. 32; Boston Evening Transcript, Dec. 31, 1924; New York Times, Aug. 18, 1938, p. 1.

LEWISOHN, LEONARD, merchant, b. Hamburg, Germany, 1847; d. London, 1902. He came to New York city in 1865 and became a subordinate in his father's store, taking full charge of the business in the following year, and founding the firm of Lewisohn Brothers, pioneers in the development of extensive copper-mines throughout the United States. In later years he devoted his energies and efforts to interests other than business, and was active in the reorganization of the Jewish Theological Seminary of America, becoming one of its incorporators as well as one of the founders of its endowment fund. He was for many years one of the leaders in New York Jewish communal affairs. He was the elder brother of Adolph Lewisohn.

Lit.: *American Hebrew,* vol. 70 (1902) 485; *Publications of the American Jewish Historical Society,* No. 11 (1903) 199.

LEWISOHN, LUDWIG, novelist, critic and lecturer, b. Berlin, 1882. His parents brought him to the United States in 1890. He holds the degrees of B.A. and M.A. (1901) and Litt.D. (1914) from the College of Charleston, S. C.; also a master's degree from Columbia University. Lewisohn records that he began writing when he was only ten, composing German prose and poetry. He described his family in *Upstream* as feeling "that they were Germans first and Jews afterwards. They were not disloyal to their race nor did they seek to hide it. But they had assimilated, in a deep sense, Aryan ways of thought and feeling."

The Lewisohn family came to South Carolina in 1890, where, in Charleston, Ludwig received his lower education at a school built by the Baptist Congregation. In those days "he accepted Jesus as my personal Saviour and cultivated, with vivid faith, the habit of prayer in which I persisted for many years." But the deep faith he then knew was that of "the primitive Church," a faith which he transferred with equal passion to the lore and ritual of the Jews, which he was not to know until manhood. He was under twenty when he had his first vivid intimacy with problems as they affected Jews in the United States. He had lived the Christian life but found that when he wanted a good teaching position he was excluded because he was a Jew. "So long as there is discrimination, there is exile," he concluded.

Lewisohn's life until 1910 was that of a literary craftsman on the periphery of an adequate livelihood. An editorial writer, reviewer and poet, he tried his hand at every literary job, always hoping that his mind would be free for the larger work which he contemplated. For a year he taught German at the University of Wisconsin, and from 1911 until 1919 he was professor of German at Ohio State University.

His first novel, *The Broken Snare,* appeared in 1908. It was a mature novel for its time. It was the period of the early work of Sinclair Lewis and Theodore Dreiser, with both of whom he was friendly. It was a novel of love with a theme which was to recur in all the subsequent novels of Lewisohn, sometimes with greater passion, sometimes with greater bitterness.

During the first World War, Lewisohn could not understand the bitterness toward Germany. If he left for a sabbatical year, it was to avoid exclusion from the university. For five years, until 1924, he was on the editorial staff of *The Nation,* continuing the criticism of the theatre and the analysis of current writing that were to make his name one of the luminous tokens in a richly creative era in American literature.

Until 1934 he sought escape in Europe from the dry forms that were beginning to encrust American economic and political society. For two decades he lifted his voice to demand the preservation of Jewish tradition. He became the first great American literary spokesman for the Zionist movement, imparting to it the glow of his style and the conviction of his spirit. Through his mind and writings filtered the culture of his age, refined by the uniquely Jewish tinge which he imparted. One of the serenest novels in American letters, one of the finest distillations of the Puritan inheritance, is *The Golden Vase,* written in 1931.

Lewisohn, in evaluating his literary productivity, ranked first *The Case of Mr. Crump* (Paris, 1926); then his *The Last Days of Shylock* (1931); *The Golden Vase* (1932); *For Ever Wilt Thou Love* (1939); *The Island Within* (1928); *Stephen Escott* (1930). In his non-fiction, he placed *The Permanent Horizon* (1934) and *Expression in America* (1933) first. He felt that *Upstream* (1922) and *Mid-Channel* (1929), books which projected his name on a universal canvas, were merely intervals between his other writings, pages from his diary but not necessarily the apex of his achievement. His range of gifts is revealed in *The Romantic,* a book of short stories issued in 1931; in two plays; in prolific literary and theatrical criticism, philosophic and social studies, such as *Israel* (1925) and *The Answer* (1939); and in numerous anthologies, such as *German Style* (1910), *Creative America* (1933) and *Rebirth* (1935). Through the experience with which he was most familiar, Lewisohn distilled the universal spirit. He made American letters greater by his own enlargement of its treasures and by the broader horizon which he achieved for it through his magnificent translations of many of the great writers and dramatists of Europe. Through him America became acquainted with Hauptmann, Sudermann, Latzko, Wassermann, Werfel and others. In 1942 he wrote *Renegade,* a tale of 18th cent. Paris.

In the career of Ludwig Lewisohn is to be found the full cycle of experience of the Jewish people in the first two generations of the 20th cent. The pendulum of his life, which started with one far edge of faint association with problems as they affect Jews in America, swung slowly and then sharply to the opposite extreme, so that he became the symbol of Jews preoccupied with the problem of existence and not merely with the methods of living.   HENRY MONTOR.

(See illustration in vol. 1, p. 268.)

Lit.: Gillis, Adolph, *Ludwig Lewisohn: The Artist and His Message* (1933); *Jewish Tribune,* Aug. 7, 1925, p. 8; Oct. 16, 1925, p. 1; Jan. 1, 1926, p. 22; Nov. 23, 1928, p. 1; *Opinion,* May, 1933, p. 30; Jan., 1934, p. 31; Oct., 1934, p. 13; May, 1937, pp. 19-20; Aug., 1939, pp. 23-24; *Jewish Social Studies,* vol. 2, No. 1 (Jan., 1940) 85-91.

LEWISOHN, RICHARD, physician, b. Hamburg, Germany, 1875. He was educated at the Universities of Berlin, Strasbourg, Breslau, and Freiburg (M.D., 1899). He was an assistant at the Jewish Hospital in Hamburg from 1900 to 1902, and an instructor in pathology at Frankfort from 1902 to 1904. The following two years he served as a surgeon at the clinic of Heidelberg. He settled in the United States in 1906, became a surgeon at Mount Sinai Hospital and a consulting surgeon at the Home for Aged and Infirm Hebrews and at the Hebrew Orphan Asylum.

Lewisohn did important research on blood transfusion, and in 1915 he discovered a new and greatly simplified method of transfusion, the citrate method, that revolutionized the science of that operation. In 1919 he proved that very large transfusions strained the heart, sometimes fatally. In 1923 he discovered that

chills after transfusions can be reduced by bloodtests
and other precautions, and ten years later he and
Dr. Nathan Rosenthal demonstrated that post-trans-
fusion chills can be completely eliminated by the use
of solutions prepared with triple-distilled water. He
later conducted research in ulcers, and in 1938 he
found that subcutaneous injections of concentrated
spleen extract on mouse sarcoma prevented further
growth of the tumor.

He was the author of many articles on the surgery
of blood transfusions and the treatment of ulcers for
European and American medical journals.

LEWISOHN, SAM ADOLPH, communal worker
and philanthropist, b. New York city, 1884. The son
of Adolph Lewisohn, he was graduated from Princeton University in 1904 and took his law degree at
Columbia University in 1907. Later he was admitted
to the New York bar and also became affiliated with
the banking and mining interests of the family.
Lewisohn has been notably concerned with the problems of unemployment, penal reform, and child welfare. He was made a member of the Federal advisory
council of the United States Employment Service and
has acted on various unemployment and labor commissions. He has served on state and national committees and commissions on parole and penal reform.
Among Lewisohn's interests in Jewish communal life
have been his trusteeship of the New York Association
for Jewish Children and that of the Federation for
the Support of Jewish Philanthropic Societies. In 1940
he served as Greater New York chairman for the
United Jewish Appeal. He was a trustee, as well, of
the New York Foundation.

Marking his devotion to the popularization of art,
Lewisohn was vice-president and trustee of the Museum
of Modern Art and a trustee of the governing committee of the New York Museum. *Painters and Personality* (1937) is a full-length volume containing
Lewisohn's ostensibly lay opinions on artists and their
work, but actually indicating not only the presence
of emotional appreciation but of authoritative knowledge. Lewisohn was also the author of *The New
Leadership in Industry* (1926).

LEWISTON, a city in the southern part of the
state of Maine. Its population of 35,598 (1940 census)
includes about 1,100 Jews.

In the 1860's, several Jews settled in Lewiston; among
these, Ehrenfried, Greenberg, and I. Isaacson. The
three became successful merchants and I. Isaacson was
also a member of the board of trade, the city council,
and the state legislature.

A number of the immigrants who left Europe, particularly Russia, in the 1880's and the 1890's made
their way as peddlers into Maine from Boston and
and New York city; a few settled in Lewiston. Among
these, and other settlers during this period, were
Herman Isaac Berman, Max Berman, Jacob Bronstein,
Michael Brownstein, Samuel Epstein, H. M. Lempert,
Max Mendelson, Myer Rosenbloom, Allen Ross, Abraham Shapiro, and Abraham Singer. Between 1900
and 1910, the Jewish community of Lewiston grew
from about thirty-five families to about 150. Many
of the new settlers came directly from Russia to relatives and friends in Lewiston.

Sam Adolph Lewisohn

In 1895 a hall on one of the main streets served
as the religious and social center of the community.
By 1907 Congregation Beth Jacob was organized, but
it was not until 1925 that a synagogue was built. In
this Conservative services are held (1942). Morris
Sprince was rabbi until 1910; a Rabbi Gray served from
1910 until 1930; Ralph B. Hershon was rabbi from
1937 to 1940; and from 1940 on, David Berent. Israel
Gerber, from 1941 on, was an instructor in the religious school conducted by the congregation. The
rabbi and the choir of the synagogue conduct a bi-
weekly broadcast over radio station WCOU.

In 1895 the Jewish community of Lewiston acquired
a cemetery within the city limits.

Together with Jewish residents of the neighboring
city of Auburn, the Zionists of Lewiston form a district of the Zionist Organization of America. There
is also a branch of the Hadassah in Lewiston and of the
Pioneer Women's Organization (Women's Organization for the Pioneer Women of Palestine).

The local B'nai B'rith Lodge is known as the Twin
City Lodge and draws its membership from both
Lewiston and Auburn. The Young People's League
of the United Synagogue of America has a local
branch.

Among the Jewish residents of Lewiston who were
elected to state or municipal office are: I. Isaacson,
member of the city council (1918-20) and representative in the state legislature (1920-2); Samuel Epstein,
member of the board of health (1910-22); Benjamin
Louis Berman, state attorney for Androscoggin County
(1921-22; 1924-26) and county probate judge (1929-
33); his brother, David Victor Berman, corporation
counsel (1930-31); Milton Wheeler, corporation counsel (1938); and Harris Isaacson, recorder of the Municipal Court (1937-40). The following held the post of
city physician: Henry Sprince (1937); Morris E. Goldman (1938); Irving Shallette (1939); and Abraham
Mandalstam (1941). Benjamin Louis Berman was

also chairman of the Republican County Committee and a state committeeman of the Republican Party. Oscar Goldman was chairman of the Lewiston Republican City Committee.   DAVID BERENT.

LEWITE, LEON, Zionist leader, b. Warsaw, Poland, 1878. His father, Joseph Lewite, a prosperous merchant, had been an early adherent of the Zionist cause. Leon Lewite began his Zionist activities when he was still a student at the University of Leipzig. On his return to Poland he aided in founding the Russian Zionist organ, *Rassvyet.* During the first World War he resided in Moscow, where he was elected president of the Zionist organization; at the end of the War, he returned to Warsaw, where he was several times president of the Zionist Organization of Poland. He played a large part in persuading thousands of Polish Jews of means to go to Palestine and establish industries there. In 1925 he aided in organizing the Polish-Palestine Chamber of Commerce and Industry (Izba Handlowo-Przemyslowa Polsko-Palestynska) and was its president until 1939; he was founder and chairman of the Polish-Palestine Bank at Warsaw. From 1932 to 1939 he and Joseph Thon were the editors of the only Jewish magazine in Polish which was devoted to economic affairs, *Palestyna i Bliski Wschod* (Palestine and the Near East). In 1939 he emigrated to Palestine, settling in Tel-Aviv.

LEWITH, HENRY F., founder of Be Kind to Animals Week, b. Charleston, S. C., 1876, d. Charleston, 1926. His only schooling was at the Arts and Crafts School in Charleston. For more than eighteen years he was a proofreader for the *News and Courier* in that city, and likewise worked as a linotype operator, retiring to devote himself exclusively to humane education activity.

There is no telling when he first conceived the slogan "Be Kind to Animals," and the idea of a week's observance, which has since become so famous. Lewith flooded the mails with letters to persons who he thought would be interested, but until Dr. Francis H. Rowley, president of the American Humane Education Association, heard of his plans, he was regarded as a crank. At the annual meeting of the Association in April, 1914, a resolution was approved inaugurating a Be Kind to Animals Week. Lewith immediately went to work to popularize the idea, and it was as a result of his initiative and energy that the Week became a national institution. He spent all his time and all his resources on the project. A master showman, he staged national contests, issued special newspaper supplements and made dozens of cities humane-conscious. At one time, when he had gigantic oil-cloth signs painted with his slogans, and hung them on the fronts of all the important buildings in Charleston, he conceived the idea of putting one on the Capitol in Washington, and sent out a new batch of letters seeking influence to negotiate his ambitious coup.

Lewith always remained in the background, and refused to have his name associated with the many contests and promotional programs which he originated and financed. In this connection, Dr. Rowley, writing of the nationwide observance of Be Kind to Animals Week, once observed: "The man who suggested it, whose persistency and zeal never flagged, who is he?

He will not let us tell his name. Let this suffice: he is a Jew with a heart so Christian and so full of the milk of human kindness that his gifts are steadily flowing out to minister not only to defenseless animals but to the orphans and friendless." Lewith's collie dog, Beauty, gained national popularity when his master bought a number of Liberty Bonds during the first World War and registered them in the animal's name. The dog's picture was reproduced millions of times in connection with humane publicity.

In scores of cities throughout the United States he placed marble drinking fountains for horses. All the funds for his activities came from his meagre savings and from a small estate inherited from his father, and which he devoted exclusively to this work. A kindred spirit and associate of his was Jacob S. Raisin, rabbi of Congregation Beth Elohim of Charleston.

Lit.: Alpert, Carl, "The Animal's Best Friend," *Buffalo Jewish Review,* April 11, 1941; *Our Dumb Animals,* Oct., 1926.

LEWKOWITSCH, JULIUS, chemist, b. Ostrovo, Silesia, Germany, 1857; d. Chamonix, France, 1913. He was educated at the Berlin Agricultural High School and at the University of Heidelberg. In 1888 he became naturalized as a British subject, and he lived and worked in London until the time of his death.

He did important research in stereo-chemistry, but his special field was the chemistry of fats and oils. He was recognized in scientific circles as the foremost contemporary authority on this subject. As director of the London Research Institute he developed the industrial technology of fats and oils to a previously unattainable level of usefulness and efficiency. His outstanding contribution was a book, *Chemical Technology and Analysis of Oils, Fats, and Waxes* (5th ed., rewritten and enlarged, 3 vols., 1913-15). This work embodied the findings of years of experimentation and is still regarded as the standard reference work in its field.

LEWY, ISRAEL, Talmud scholar and teacher, b. Inowrazlaw, Germany, 1841; d. Breslau, Germany, 1917. He studied at the Jewish Theological Seminary at Breslau (1864-69), became instructor in Talmud in 1872 at the newly founded Hochschule für die Wissenschaft des Judentums in Berlin, and in 1883 he was called to the Breslau seminary, where he remained as seminary rabbi until his death. Stimulated by Zacharias Frankel to a critical study of the Talmud, Lewy extended the method of his teacher and gave new direction to the critical study of the Talmud. He combined a profound knowledge of the Talmud with a keen and impassionate critical spirit and scientific thoroughness. His *Fragmente aus der Mischna des Abba Saul* (1876), *Ein Wort über die Mechilta des Rabbi Simon* (1889), and his *Einleitung zur Interpretation des palästinischen Talmud-Traktats Nesikin* (1895) contain methodological distinctions and analyses which are fundamental for an examination of the Mishnah, Midrash and Talmud. His last published works were his interpretations of the Palestinian Talmud tractate *Nezikin* (1-6; 1895-1914). On the occasion of his seventieth birthday his pupils, among whom were men such as Adolf Büchler, S. Horovitz, Immanuel Löw and Solomon Schechter, and his friends, dedicated to him a volume entitled *Festschrift zu Israel Lewys siebzigsten Geburtstag*, which was published by Marcus Brann and Ismar Elbogen.

LEWY, JULIUS, professor of Semitic languages and history of the Near East, b. Berlin, 1895. He studied at the Universities of Leipzig and Berlin, and received his Ph.D. degree in Berlin in 1921. The following year Lewy became an instructor in Semitics and history of the ancient Near East at the University of Giessen. In 1927 he was made assitant professor, and also founded a lectureship for post-Biblical Judaism at the University. Lewy was made a professor in 1930, the first Jew to be so appointed. He was also director of the Oriental Seminary at the University and at the same time curator of the Hilprecht collection of Babylonian antiquities at the University of Jena.

Lewy was ousted from his posts in Germany in 1933, as the result of the Nazi persecutions. For one year he lectured in Assyriology at the Sorbonne in Paris and then came to the United States, where he was still living in 1942. During this period he was for two years visiting professor in Semitics at Johns Hopkins University, for a time visiting professor in oriental history at both the Jewish Theological Seminary of America in New York and the University of Cincinnati, and (1936-40) visiting professor in Semitic languages and Bible at the Hebrew Union College. He was made full professor at the Hebrew Union College in 1940, and in 1942 still held this post.

Lewy's main research was on the interpretation of the so-called *Kültepetexte;* the results of these efforts were published in 1926, 1929 and 1930 to 1935, the latest in collaboration with Georg Eisser. In addition, Lewy wrote: *Untersuchungen zur akkadischen Grammatik* (1924); *Forschungen zur alten Geschichte Vorderasiens* (1925); *Zur Chronologie der Könige von Israel und Juda* (1927); *Keilschriftentexte aus Kleinasien* (1932); and *Tablettes Cappadociennes* (3 vols.,

Israel Lewy

1935-37). Lewy was also, from 1928 to 1933, editor of *Mitteilungen der vorderasiatisch-ägyptischen Gesellschaft,* founder and editor of *Arbeiten aus dem orientalischen Seminar der Universität Giessen* (1928-33), and founder and editor of *Texte und Materialien der Frau Professor Hilprecht Collection of Babylonian Antiquities* (1930-34).

From 1913 to 1918 Lewy served in the German army and was awarded German and Turkish decorations. His wife, HILDEGARD LEWY, is also an orientalist.

LEX TALIONIS, see RETALIATION, LAW OF.

LEXICOGRAPHY, HEBREW. The rudimentary attempts at explanation of the derivation of some words and especially names, found in the Bible, can hardly be termed lexicological. However, there are occasional lexicological observations in the Talmudic and Midrashic literature, such as the statement of Resh Lakish that the Hebrew particle *ki* has four significations: "if (when)," "perhaps (lest)," "but," and "because" (*R.H.* 3a and elsewhere), a rule which became the basis of many Biblical interpretations and Halachic decisions; or the occasional use of Vav in the meaning of *or*, as in the verse "And he that curseth his father and (or) his mother" (*Mechilta* to *Ex.* 21:17). Several lists of synonyms are given in *Aboth de Rabbi Nathan* (34, 37 and 39) and elsewhere, such as ten synonyms for *idols*, ten for *prophet*, ten for *gladness*, and the like. This led Stern (*Liber Responsium*, Vienna, 1870, Appendix, p. 55) to believe that the Talmudic authorities must have compiled for their use alphabetical glossaries and lists of synonyms, such glossaries having been perhaps employed by the Aramaic interpreters of the Bible, the *Methurgemanim*. However, we possess no reference to such compilations.

The earliest lexicographical work in Hebrew literature, to which we have definite reference, was written by the Gaon Zemah ben Paltoy of Pumbeditha (last quarter of the 9th cent.) under the title of *Aruch.* It was a dictionary of difficult words of the Talmud, and it is known only through quotations by Nathan ben Jehiel, as it is no longer extant. A few decades later,

Julius Lewy

in 902 to 903, Saadia Gaon wrote the first dictionary of the Bible, known as *Agron*. It was divided into two parts, the first part containing a concise Hebrew-Arabic dictionary; the second was a rhyming dictionary, i. e. the words were alphabetically arranged according to their final letters to facilitate the making of rhymes. Of this dictionary a part of the introduction and only an eight-leaf fascicle of the first part, which begins in the middle of the letter Kaf and ends in the middle of the letter Samech, have been preserved. The vocabulary contains also some words from the Mishnah and Targum; when the word is of rare occurrence its form as found in the Bible is added to the root and translated. The renditions in most instances agree with Saadia's version of the Bible, although not invariably so. Another little lexicographical work of Saadia is his *Explanation of the Seventy Isolated Words* (in Arabic). This list actually contains ninety hapax legomena and other rare Hebrew and Aramaic words in the Bible, which he explains by way of analogy with similar expressions in the Talmud and Midrash.

The first lexicographical work devoted to comparative Semitic philology was written by Judah ibn Koraish of Tahort, North Africa, a contemporary of Saadia. The work was written in Arabic in the form of an epistle addressed to the Jews of Fez, Morocco, urging them not to neglect the reading of the Targum to the Torah in their synagogues. It is divided into three parts, each alphabetically arranged; the first part comprises comparisons of Hebrew words with their cognates in Aramaic, unfortunately the letters Lamed to part of Tav being missing here; the second deals with comparisons with the late Hebrew of the Mishnah and Talmud; the third treats of the relation of Hebrew to Arabic both lexicographically and grammatically, followed by a selection of comparisons with foreign and Berber dialects. Ibn Koraish alludes also to a dictionary which he had previously written that included a study of the interchange of the letters of the entire alphabet, but it is no longer extant and there is no other reference to it. A younger contemporary of his, Dunash ibn Tamim of Kairwan, is mentioned as having written a treatise on the lexical comparison of Hebrew with Arabic, which has not reached us. Very little is known about it, just a few quotations and references in works by later authors.

The first comprehensive Hebrew-Arabic dictionary of the Bible, *Kitāb Jāmi' al-Alfāz* (Book of Collection of Words), was written by the Karaite David ben Abraham Alfasi (of Fez), who flourished in the second half of the 10th cent. The work is complete in its scope, as it embraces both the Hebrew and Aramaic vocabulary of the Bible as well as proper names, omitted by other early lexicographers. The general introduction explains the plan of the dictionary, then treats of the formation of Hebrew stems, which the author divides into four classes: (1) one-consonantal, (2) bi-consonantal, (3) tri-consonantal, and (4) four-consonantal. The dictionary proper is divided into twenty-two parts, each part beginning with an introductory discussion of the grammatical uses of the particular letter. Although a Karaite, the author does not hesitate to make use of the Targum and rabbinic literature. In his method of identification and interpretation of

Hebrew and Aramaic roots he applies the principle of interchange or transposition of consonants and of comparisons with their cognates in the Aramaic and Arabic languages as well as with post-Biblical Hebrew. David ben Abraham wrote his dictionary in two versions, a longer and a shorter one; the former was abridged and revised in the beginning of the 11th cent. by Ali, son of the Karaite exegete Yefet ben Ali. His compendium was in turn epitomized about the middle of the 11th cent. by the Rabbinite authority Ali ben Israel, and some decades later by the Karaite exegete Ali ben Sulaiman.

With Menahem ben Saruk, probably a contemporary of David ben Abraham, Hebrew lexicography begins its career in Spain. His dictionary *Mahbereth Menahem*, written in Hebrew, embodies the Hebrew and Aramaic vocabulary of the Bible, although it is not as comprehensive as that of David ben Abraham. Also he recognizes one-consonantal and bi-consonantal stems in Hebrew, but he is emphatically against comparisons with Arabic. Menahem's dictionary became the standard reference work among the Jews in Christian countries generations after it became antiquated in its native Spain (where it was superseded by the works of Judah Hayyuj and Jonah ibn Janah), and it is frequently quoted by Rashi and others. This work was severely criticized by his contemporary Dunash ibn Labrat, who had a better insight into the formation of Hebrew roots; this criticism evoked a rejoinder from Menahem's pupils and also from Jacob Tam, Rashi's grandson, in the 12th cent.

A younger contemporary of Menahem was Machir ben Judah (b. Metz), a brother of Gershom (Meor Hagolah). His dictionary, known as *Alfa Beta de Rabbi Machir,* no longer extant, is frequently cited by Rashi, by his two grandsons Samuel ben Meir and Jacob Tam, and by other authorities. It evidently was an alphabetical glossary of mostly difficult expressions in the Talmud, although Rashi also quotes this work in the interpretation of *botnim* (*Gen.* 43:11).

At the beginning of the 11th cent., Judah Hayyuj of Fez (but for many years a resident of Cordova), rightly considered the father of modern Hebrew philology, discovered the tri-consonantal system of Hebrew roots. His Arabic works on weak and geminative verbs mark a turning point in the scientific treatment of Hebrew grammar and lexicography alike. They were twice translated into Hebrew, by Moses ibn Gikatilla in the 11th cent. and by Abraham ibn Ezra in the 12th cent.

One of the foremost Hebrew philologists of the Middle Ages, Jonah ibn Janah, a native of Cordova and a physician by profession (first half of the 11th cent.), brought to a brilliant conclusion what Hayyuj had begun. His chief contribution to Hebrew lexicography is the *Book of Roots,* written in Arabic, which is the first Hebrew dictionary based on the tri-consonantal theory. It includes all Hebrew roots of the Bible, omitting the Aramaic vocabulary and personal names. After an introduction in which the method of determining the roots of words and of arrangement of the work are discussed in detail, the dictionary proper is divided into twenty-two parts, in accordance with the letters of the Hebrew alphabet. The various forms of the roots are thoroughly discussed and fully illustrated by well chosen quotations from the Bible, with special attention to the independent Hebrew particles, the many uses of which are amply explained. In his elucidations of roots he draws freely upon comparisons with their cognates in the Arabic and Aramaic languages and the late Hebrew of the Mishnah and Talmud. Ibn Janah takes for granted that all who use his dictionary are familiar also with Hayyuj's works on weak and geminative verbs; accordingly, he omits the discussion of such verbs, referring the reader to these works as well as to his own treatises in which he supplemented Hayyuj. The great importance of the dictionary was forthwith recognized, and no less than three Hebrew translations of it were undertaken in the 12th cent., of which the only complete one, that of Judah ibn Tibbon (1171), has been preserved. It has likewise become the basis of similar lexicographical works through the centuries, down to Gesenius in the beginning of the 19th cent.

Ibn Janah's contemporary and able opponent, the statesman Samuel Hanagid of Granada, similarly made many very important contributions to Hebrew lexicography, judging from the few preserved fragments of his Arabic treatise *The Book of Self-Sufficiency*, edited by Kokowzoff. Mention should also be made here of "the Grammarian from Jerusalem," the Karaite Abu'l-Faraj Harun ibn al-Faraj, an older contemporary of Ibn Janah, whose extensive philological treatise in Arabic, *The Comprehensive*, contained two parts devoted to Hebrew and Aramaic lexicography. To the same period belongs the Gaon Hai, author of *The Book of Comprising* (in Arabic), a dictionary of probably difficult words in the Bible and the Talmud, of which a small fragment is found in the Leningrad Library. A special characteristic of the last two named works is that the tri-consonantal roots are treated so that all the roots formed by various combinations through transposition of the three consonants are grouped together. A few decades later Abraham the Babylonian wrote in Hebrew a small treatise of lexicographical character, based on the system prevalent before Hayyuj.

In the second half of the 11th cent. there were two famous Bible exegetes in Spain—Moses ibn Gikatilla and Judah ibn Balaam, who were also authors of small lexicographical treatises, the former having written a study of *The Masculine and Feminine* genders in nouns and the latter treatises on *Homonyms, Particles,* and *Denominative Verbs*. At the end of the 11th cent. Isaac ibn Barun wrote in Arabic the very significant work *The Book of Comparison between the Hebrew and Arabic Languages,* which embodies much important lexicographical material, when he compares the vocabulary of the two languages. About the same period Nathan ben Jehiel of Rome wrote the famous lexicographical work *Aruch,* the earliest comprehensive dictionary of the Talmud, Targum, and Midrash that has come down to us. For his work he utilized the earlier *Aruch* of the Gaon Zemah ben Paltoy, no longer extant. In his philological theories Nathan, the same as Rashi and his other contemporaries in Christian Europe, follows Menahem ben Saruk and the corrections of Dunash ibn Labrat. This dictionary has enjoyed great popularity through the centuries; it appeared in many additions, abridgements, and revisions

with several additions and corrections, down to its modern monumental revision by Alexander Kohut under the title *Aruch Hashalem (Aruch Completum)* in eight volumes (1878-92; 2nd ed., 1926). In 1143 Menahem ben Solomon, also of Rome, wrote a manual for the study of the Bible, known as *Eben Bohan* (Testing Stone), of which the main part is a dictionary. The work is based on Menahem ben Saruk and Dunash ibn Labrat, revised and supplemented by the author's own observations.

About two decades later Solomon ibn Parhon, a native of Spain who settled in Salerno, Italy, and a pupil of Judah Halevi and Abraham ibn Ezra, wrote a dictionary of the Bible (preceded by a brief grammar), bearing the title *Mahbereth Hearuch*. It is a very lucid and concise revision of Ibn Janah's dictionary, with additions from Hayyuj's treatises and lexicological and exegetical comments of his own. In 1150 Joseph Kimhi of Narbonne wrote the *Sefer Hagalui,* which contains much lexical material in addition to critical observations of Menahem ben Saruk. But of far greater importance for Hebrew lexicography is the dictionary of his younger son David (b. 1160), *Sefer Hashorashim* (Book of Roots). It is patterned after Ibn Janah's dictionary, but it is more systematic and thoroughgoing in the derivation of the roots. Not seldom he gives the meaning of words in the Romanic vernacular of his day, the same as Rashi is wont to do. He frequently refers to older authorities, but especially so to his father, Joseph Kimhi, in whose name he cites numerous interpretations. David Kimhi's dictionary was for centuries the standard reference work of students of the Bible, superseding all previous lexicographical works. A contemporary of his (end of the 12th cent.) was Moses ben Isaac of England, who wrote the dictionary *Sefer Hashoham,* preceded by a brief grammatical introduction. Its chief characteristic is that the strong, weak, and quadriliteral verbs are grouped separately, then follow the nouns, particles, and numerals.

With David Kimhi closes a 300-year period of very fruitful activity in the field of Hebrew philology and lexicography both in the Near East and Western Europe. Henceforth fewer scholars occupied themselves with this field, and those who did were engaged in various phases of this science and in new departures from the beaten track. So Tanhum of Jerusalem (second half of the 13th cent.) wrote in Arabic a large dictionary, *The Adequate Guide,* with the primary aim of explaining the late Hebrew idiom of the *Mishneh Torah* of Maimonides, but he also includes much of the vocabulary of the Mishnah. A contemporary of his, Abraham ben Isaac Bedaresi (i.e. from Béziers), wrote an extensive treatise on Hebrew synonyms, *Hothem Tochnith (Ezek. 28:12).* It is very comprehensive and often profusely illustrated by quotations from the Bible. Some decades earlier flourished in Germany its first Hebrew lexicographer, Shimshon by name. In his dictionary, where the words are often translated into German, he still follows Menahem ben Saruk and Dunash ibn Labrat, although he frequently cites also Solomon ibn Parhon.

Next in order is a remarkable lexicographical work written, of all places, in Urgenj, Khiva (in Russian Turkestan), in 1339. It is the Hebrew-Persian dictionary *Sefer Hamelitzah* of Solomon ben Samuel, which embodies the vocabularies of the Bible, the Targum, and the Talmudic and Midrashic literature. Occasionally he elucidates the significations of the words by rendering them into Arabic, Turkish, or even the Romanic idiom (mostly Italian), which he probably borrowed from Nathan ben Jehiel's *Aruch* and Rashi, whom he cites as "Solomon the Frenchman" (*Hatzarfathi*). This work has the distinction of being the only comprehensive Hebrew-Persian dictionary that has been fully preserved, and is, according to Bacher, one of the most interesting Jewish literary monuments that we possess (*Hebräisch-persisches Wörterbuch*, pp. 1-2). To the first half of the 14th cent. belong Joseph ibn Kaspi, the author of the dictionary *Sharsheroth Kesef* (Silver Chains), where he endeavors to apply the science of logic to lexicography, and Joseph ben David Hayevani, whose work *Menorath Hamaor* (Lamp of Light) comprises a dictionary with a grammatical introduction.

About the middle of the 15th cent. Joseph ben Judah Sarco wrote the dictionary *Baal Halashon* (*Eccl.* 10:11). A few decades later Solomon ben Abraham of Urbino wrote the comprehensive dictionary of synonyms *Ohel Moed*, where the most frequently used words, with all their synonyms grouped with them, are arranged in alphabetical order. In 1468 Saadia ibn Danan of Granada completed his Hebrew-Arabic dictionary, where he frequently cites earlier authorities and draws freely on comparisons of Hebrew with Arabic and Aramaic. Mention should be made here also of the Hebrew-Italian-Arabic glossary of the Bible *Makre Dardeke* (Children's Teacher), which appeared in Naples in 1488, but was probably written much earlier and attributed to a certain Jehiel. Together with the Italian are grouped also French and Provençal renditions, especially those found in Rashi's commentary and Kimhi's dictionary. It thus represents the first polyglot glossary of the Bible, which could be conveniently used by Jews sojourning in European countries.

The beginning of the 16th cent. marks a turning point in the history of Hebrew lexicography with the entrance of Christian scholars into this field. Johann Reuchlin's *Rudimenta Linguae Hebraicae* (1506) comprises an elementary Hebrew grammar and dictionary, patterned after Kimhi, and is the first written by a Christian. A younger contemporary of his, Elijah Levita, who was born in Germany but settled at an early age in Italy, wrote a selected glossary of post-Biblical literature, *Tishbi*, and a dictionary of the Targum, *Methurgeman*, in addition to glosses to Kimhi's dictionary. One of his most distinguished pupils, Sebastian Münster, made important contributions to Hebrew and Aramaic lexicography in his *Dictionarium Chaldaichum* (Basel, 1527) and his Hebrew-Latin-Greek *Dictionarium Trilingue* (Basel, 1530), which enjoyed several editions.

A number of other lexicographical works appeared in the 16th and 17th centuries. Among the more important ones are: the Hebrew-Italian dictionary *Galuth Yehudah* of Judah Leon of Modena (Venice, 1612); Johann Buxtorf the Elder's *Lexicon Chaldaicum, Talmudicum et Rabbinicum*, edited by Buxtorf the Younger (Basel, 1639); Edmund Castell's *Lexicon Heptaglotton Hebraicum, Chaldaicum, Syriacum, Samaritanum,* *Aethiopicum, Arabicum, et Persicum* (London, 1669). In the 18th cent. there were distinguished orientalists and Biblical scholars who made important contributions to Hebrew lexicography, such as the eminent Dutch scholar Albert Schultens (d. 1750), who wrote several treatises in this field, with special attention to comparisons of Hebrew with Arabic, and Michaelis (d. 1791), who wrote an important supplement to Hebrew lexicons. These scholars applied their broad knowledge of Semitic languages in their lexicographical studies.

In the beginning of the 19th cent. Ben Zeeb wrote his *Otzar Hashorashim* (1807), which became quite popular among the Jews for some decades. However, the father of modern Hebrew lexicography may be rightly considered Wilhelm Gesenius (1786-1842). The first edition of his dictionary under the title *Hebräisches-Deutsches Handwörterbuch über die Schriften des Alten Testaments* appeared in Leipzig in 1810; since then it passed through many editions and revisions and became the standard reference work for Biblical philology. Its last, the 17th edition by Buhl, in collaboration with other eminent scholars, bearing the title *Hebräisches und Aramäisches Handwörterbuch über das Alte Testament* (Leipzig, 1922), summarizes the results of brilliant and painstaking research in Hebrew and Semitic philology up to his time. The *Thesaurus Philologicus Criticus Linguae Hebraeae et Chaldaeae Veteris Testamenti* (Leipzig, 1829-58) of Gesenius was finished after his death by Roediger. It is a monument to the author's tireless industry and thoroughness as well as to his sound knowledge. Robinson's English translation of Gesenius's dictionary (Latin ed., 1833) appeared in 1836, and was subsequently edited and revised several times. A thorough revision of it under the title of *A Hebrew and English Lexicon of the Old Testament*, edited by Brown, Driver, and Briggs, appeared at Oxford in 1906.

Of other important modern lexicographical works may be mentioned here the following: Fürst, *Hebräisches und Chaldäisches Handwörterbuch über das Alte Testament* (3rd ed., Leipzig, 1876), translated into English by Davidson (1885); Siegfried and Stade, *Hebräisches Wörterbuch zum Alten Testament* (1892-93), where the etymology of words was almost entirely excluded, and König, *Hebräisches und Aramäisches Wörterbuch zum Alten Testament* (2nd and 3rd ed., Leipzig, 1922). Of post-Biblical Hebrew and Aramaic: Levy, Jacob, *Neuhebräisches und Chaldäisches Wörterbuch über die Talmudim und Midraschim*, with additions by Fleischer (1876-89; 2nd ed., 1924); idem, *Chaldäisches Wörterbuch über die Targumim* (1881); Kohut, Alexander, *Aruch Completum* (1878-92; 2nd ed., 1926); and Jastrow, Marcus, *A Dictionary of the Targumin, the Talmud Babli and Yerushalmi, and the Midrashic Literature* (1903; 2nd ed., 1926). Important contributions to Hebrew lexicography were made also by Bondi, Lagarde, Barth, Ehrlich, Perles, Nöldeke, Krauss, and others. Dalman's *Aramäisch-Neuhebräisches Handwörterbuch* (1901; 2nd ed., 1922) is a very concise manual, to which is appended Händler's useful *Lexicon der Abbreviaturen*. Several dictionaries were published in pre-revolutionary Russia, such as those of Finn, Steinberg, Kahan, and others. Of lexicographical works which include also the modern Hebrew idiom, in addition to the Biblical and post-

Josef and Rosina Lhevinne

Biblical Hebrew, the more important ones are: Ramberg (and Salkind), *Millon Ibri* (Lexicon of the Hebrew Language; Warsaw 1924 et seq.), with explanations in Hebrew and translations in German, English, Polish, and Russian; Grasovski, *Millon Hasafah Haibrith* (Tel-Aviv, 1935-37); but by far the most important work in this field is Eliezer ben Jehudah's monumental *Thesaurus Totius Hebraitatis,* of which ten volumes were published (some posthumously) by 1940. It embodies the entire Hebrew vocabulary of the Bible, Talmud and Midrash, liturgy, medieval and modern Hebrew literature up to the present time, translated into German, French, and English, fully illustrated with copious quotations, and provided with explanatory notes.   SOLOMON L. SKOSS.

Lit.: Berliner, *Beiträge zur hebräischen Grammatik im Talmud und Midrasch* (1879); Bacher, *Hebräische Sprachwissenschaft vom 10. zum 16. Jahrhundert* (1892); idem, "Anfänge der hebräischen Grammatik, *Zeitschrift der Deutschen Morgenländischen Gesellschaft,* vol. 49 (1895) 1-65, 335-92 (and separately); Steinschneider, M., *Die arabische Literatur der Juden* (1902); Hirschfeld, *Literary History of Hebrew Grammarians and Lexicographers* (1926; to be used cautiously); Skoss, Solomon L., "Fragments of Unpublished Philological Fragments of Saadia Gaon," *Jewish Quarterly Review,* New Series, vol. 23, p. 329 et seq.; idem, *The Hebrew-Arabic Dictionary of the Bible of David b. Abraham al-Fasi,* vol. 1 (1936), Introduction.

LEYELESS, A. (b. 1889), pseudonym of Aaron Glanz (correct spelling), *see* GLANCZ, AARON.

LHEVINNE, JOSEF, pianist, b. Moscow, Russia, 1874. He made his concert debut in Moscow (1888) while still a student at the Moscow Conservatory. After graduating, he toured Russia extensively, then entered a second period of study, this time with Anton Rubinstein. In 1902 he accepted a teaching position in Tiflis, subsequently holding other teaching posts in Berlin and Moscow. In 1905 he went to the United States, making his American debut in January of the following year. This concert was so successful that he was immediately given a contract for 150 concerts throughout the country. Tours in America and Europe followed, during which Lhevinne impressed himself on the music world as one of the great pianists of the time. Extraordinary technique was combined with astute musicianship; in certain works—by Chopin and Tschaikowsky—he was regarded as unexcelled.

In 1899 Lhevinne married a young and gifted pianist, who renounced her own career to devote herself to the welfare of her husband. However, husband and wife soon began playing together on two pianos and were so enthusiastically praised by friends that they decided to become a professional team. Since their first public appearance in 1899, Josef and Rosina Lhevinne have given two-piano recitals in every major city of Europe and America. In 1939 the fortieth anniversary of the two-piano partnership of the Lhevinnes was celebrated with a festive concert at Carnegie Hall.

Both Josef and Rosina Lhevinne distinguished themselves as teachers of the piano. They were members of the Juilliard Graduate School in New York.

LIADY, SHNEOR ZALMAN OF, *see* SHNEOR ZALMAN BEN BARUCH OF LADI,

LIBATION, *see* SACRIFICE; YAYIN NESECH.

LIBAU (LIEPAJA), city in Latvia, on the Baltic Sea; in 1940 it had about 8,100 Jews, or about 14 per cent of the population. Jews were not allowed to live there until the end of the 18th cent., but the Jewish population grew steadily after the province of Courland was under Russian rule. By the end of the 19th cent. its number was 9,700, but after that the government sought to reduce the Jewish population when the city became a military harbor. In 1941 Latvia was invaded by the German armies; most of the Jews fled before the occupation; the rest were ordered to leave Libau.

LIBERMAN, HYMAN, communal worker and philanthropist, b. Poland, 1853; d. Cape Town, South Africa, 1923. He emigrated to South Africa after a brief sojourn in England, and settled at Cape Town in 1873. He made a hobby of public service, and achieved an enviable record in this direction. For fifteen years he was a member of the Cape Town city council. He was elected mayor of Cape Town on three successive occasions, the first Jew to be so honored. He proved to be a capable chairman of a committee that dealt with the welfare of the 20,000 refugees who filled Cape Town during the Anglo-Boer war of 1899 to 1902. During his lifetime he served on the committees of many Cape Town institutions.

Liberman was also active in Jewish affairs. Elected treasurer of the Cape Town Hebrew Congregation in 1897, he continued as warden in the office of president or treasurer, with a short interval, for twenty years.

He bequeathed generous sums to many Jewish and non-Jewish institutions, the local university and hospital, and the Corporation of the City of Cape Town. The Liberman Institute, a center of learning and social intercourse, situated in the poorer quarter of Cape Town, was established as a result of his benevolence. Again, when it was found impossible to complete the National Art Gallery in Cape Town for lack of funds, the trustees dedicated a large portion of his bequests to the building of the fine central hall. After its completion this wing was dedicated by J. H. Hofmeyer, then Minister of the Interior. Liberman's death was mourned by the entire community of Cape Town.

S. A. ROCHLIN.

Lit.: Cape Times, June 23, 1923, p. 11; South African Jewish Chronicle, July 6 and 13, 1923; South African Jewish Year Book (1929) 63; Laidler, P. W., The Growth and Government of Cape Town (1939) 428, 434.

LIBERMANN, AARON SAMUEL, Hebrew writer and Socialist organizer, b. Luna, Russia, about 1845; d. Syracuse, N. Y., 1880. He studied first to be a rabbi, in 1868 conducted a private school, and in 1869 went to St. Petersburg to enter the Institute of Technology. Here he became interested in the Socialist movement. Denounced to the authorities, he fled to London in 1875, where he published the first Socialist proclamation in Hebrew, Al Shelume Bahure Yisrael; smuggled into Russia, this pamphlet created a deep impression among rabbinical students and Hebrew writers. In 1876 Libermann organized the first Jewish socialist organization in London, as well as a union of workingmen. In 1877 he moved to Vienna, where he and L. Zuckermann published the first Socialist periodical in Hebrew, Haemeth; only two issues appeared.

Here he took the name Arthur Freeman. In 1878 he was arrested, handed over to the Prussian authorities, and sentenced to serve nine months in jail. At the expiration of the sentence he went to London, and then to the United States, where he died by suicide.

Libermann's writings include: Shmerl un Berl; Maase Satan; Massath Hanefesh; Toafoth Habikkoreth Vehadimyon Latikkun Olam Al Pi Melachah, a study of Utopias. A complete edition of his works was issued at Tel-Aviv in 1928.

LIBERMANN, ELIEZER, early leader of the Reform Movement in Judaism; he lived in the first half of the 19th cent., but the exact place and date of his birth and death are unknown. In one of his books he claims to be the son of Wolf, chief rabbi of Hagenau, but no such individual is known; according to other sources, he came from Hungary. He was for some time the religious leader of the Hungarian Jewish community of Humenne. He became acquainted with Israel Jacobson and other leaders of the Reform Movement, and on their behalf traveled through Europe and collected rabbinical opinions favoring the introduction of an organ and German prayers into the services, as was done in the Hamburg Temple; these he published in his Noga Hatzedek (Light of Righteousness; Dessau, 1818). About the same time he wrote a book defending reforms in the services, Or Nogah (Shining Light). The assertion made by Graetz and other historians that Libermann was later baptized is erroneous, and probably is due to a confusion of Libermann with the convert Jacob Libermann, the son of the rabbi of Zabern.

LIBERTY. Biblical Conception. The institutions of ancient Israel, as portrayed in the Bible, imply an underlying conception of personal and national liberty, though not, perhaps, in the developed form which the French Revolution introduced into modern civilization.

The idea of personal liberty appears especially in the legal codes of the Pentateuch. The Ten Commandments, pivotal point of the entire legislation, are based on the premise that the regimen of good society depends just as much upon respect for the rights of man as for the service of God. Along with injunctions against idolatry and blasphemy, the Decalogue therefore includes prohibitions against destroying a man's life (murder), home (adultery), reputation (false witness) or property (theft and covetousness).

The same principle also obtains in the laws regulating labor. Out of a sense of inalienable human rights, ancient Israel had no such institution as slavery. What today is translated by this term was, in fact, little more than employment, for while it is true that the employee did not enjoy full civil rights, it is equally true that he was not a slave, in the modern connotation of the word. Indeed, the whole point of the Hebrew law was to assert the rights of the worker, and to prevent service from degenerating into servitude.

Thus, in what scholars regard as an earlier code, which is placed significantly immediately after the Ten Commandments (Ex. 21:2 et seq.), the existence of basic human rights is taken for granted. A Hebrew servant may not be held for more than six years, except by his own will (Ex. 21:2, 6). His life is protected, and he may not be beaten to death (verse 20). If he be disabled by chastisement, he is entitled to release (verses 26 and 27). He is included in the law of Sabbath rest (*Ex.* 20:10). A maid servant taken into concubinage likewise possesses inalienable rights. If her master find her distasteful, he is bound to permit her ransom, and may not dispose of her by selling her outside of the community of her people. If he take another as his mistress, he is still obliged to support her, and may not deny her connubial rights (*Ex.* 21:8-11).

The law in *Deuteronomy,* assigned by scholars to the Deuteronomic Code (about 650 B.C.E.), goes even further in its recognition of human rights. As against the earlier law, it enjoins the release of female as well as male servants in the seventh year, and it insists that the manumitted employee must be given severance pay, to help him to a new start in life (*Deut.* 15:12-13). Moreover, in contrast to the earlier Semitic law of Hammurabi (sections 15-20), it forbids the deliverance of a runaway to his master (*Deut.* 23:15). The Deuteronomic Code also introduces another element into the ancient Israelitic conception of liberty. It turns the national experience of bondage in Egypt into a moral and legal reason for respecting the liberty of workers and strangers (*Deut.* 15:15; 16:12; 24:18, 22). Even the institution of the Sabbath rest, enjoined in the Ten Commandments, is interpreted in the light of this idea (*Deut.* 5:15).

Other Pentateuchal laws are likewise based upon respect for fundamental human rights, and among these the inviolability of the person takes high place. Kidnapping is therefore a capital offense (*Ex.* 21:16), while rape of an unbetrothed virgin entails not only compensation to her father for his consequent commercial loss, but also protection for the girl herself by indissoluble marriage in order to offset the interference with her person (*Ex.* 22:28-29). Indeed, the fact that the Hebrew term for "to rape" means properly "to humiliate" shows that the offense was viewed not only from the standpoint of material damage but also of infringement of inherent human liberty and dignity.

Not infrequently, Israel's growing sense of human rights and dignity—the embryonic form of the libertarian concept—led to the abolition of earlier Semitic institutions, and set standards of morality which have continued to the present day. Cases in point are those of harlotry and witchcraft, both of which were interdicted (*Deut.* 23:17; *Ex.* 22:18; *Lev.* 20:6). These were closely associated, throughout the Ancient Near East, with religious practices (cf. *Hosea* 4:14), and it is therefore not improbable that the prohibition was originally designed as no more than a measure against apostasy. In course of time, however, it came to assume a moral complexion, the harlot then being denounced not as an idolatress but as one who wrought a social mischief by undermining human dignity and the inviolability of the person. The gruesome narrative in *Judges* 19, apparently written in the 9th cent. B.C.E., shows the development of this attitude, while it is significant that the Pentateuchal codes, dated by modern critics some two centuries later, include the prohibitions among sexual, and not among ritual, laws.

When one comes to consider Biblical ideas concerning *national* liberty, he treads upon more treacherous ground, for here the evolution of libertarian and democratic conceptions was colored also by other considerations. The standard example of national liberty in the Bible is the rejection, in the earlier period, of human kingship. The Biblical attitude is summed up in two noteworthy episodes. The first is that of the making of the Covenant between God and Israel at Sinai. This is pictured on essentially democratic lines. The Covenant, which constitutes the charter of Israel's nationhood, is not imposed by superior power, through the agency of any one authority, but is offered to and accepted by *the whole people collectively:* "And Moses took the book of the covenant, and read in the hearing of the people, and they said, All that the Lord hath spoken will we do, and be obedient" (*Ex.* 24:7). The second episode is that of Gideon's refusal to become king of Israel, or to allow his family to be turned into a dynastic household. God, he avers, is the only true king (*Judges* 8:22-23).

Both of these episodes might appear at first sight to evidence the emergence in Israel of a growing sense of democracy—a principal ingredient in the modern complex of liberty. Such a construction, however, would be but a half-truth, for the fact is that they are inspired more by a sense of theocracy than of democracy. While one should certainly recognize the germs of libertarianism in the idea that the whole of Israel had to accept God before they could be claimed as His people, in the case of Gideon the primary factor seems to lie in the conflict between dynastic and charismatic theories of kingship, and to be but little connected with notions of democracy or national self-determination. Gideon refuses the establishment of a hereditary monarchy, not because he believes in republicanism, but because he adheres to the traditional view that the criterion of kingship must be divine inspiration and election, and not accident of birth. It is therefore a mistake to cite this incident as evidence of libertarian attitudes in Israel.

Up to this point, the main ingredients of the libertarian philosophy in Israel were recognition of individual human rights and the dim foregleams of national democracy. With the Babylonian Exile, however, another important element was added—that of independence. The political eclipse of the nation led to an aspiration after deliverance and national freedom. Exilic and post-Exilic literature is full of this note, and in the thought of Deutero-Isaiah the redemption and salvation of Israel comes to be blended with dreams of a golden age of universal freedom and liberty.

Just as in the 20th cent. the political and military struggle of the nations takes on the epic complexion of a fight between order and chaos, light and darkness, civilization and barbarism, so in that age, Israel's deliverance becomes but a symptom of a new world order of liberty for all the constrained. If Israel is to be the focus of the golden age (*Isa.* 60), this is merely because the universal has not yet been entirely divorced from the local. But the germs of this divorce are there. It is significant that, to use Hebrew terms, the emphasis tends constantly to shift from *ge'ulah,* which is merely *release,* or *redemption,* to *yeshu'ah,* which means etymologically something like *expansiveness,* and which envisages a *state* of salvation, rather than an *act* or *process* of deliverance.

In other words, the full conception of liberty is coming to birth. The idea comes out especially in the

The Liberty Bell (Philadelphia) which contains the Biblical inscription: "Proclaim liberty throughout all the land, unto all the inhabitants thereof"

imagery of these Exilic and post-Exilic writers. In Babylon, there was an annual New Year pantomime portraying the victory of order (Marduk) over chaos (Tiamat). A Jewish writer takes up this picture and expands it into a symbol of a future victory of Yahveh over the dragon of confusion (*Isa.* 26:1), prior to ushering in a new world-order.

Post-Biblical Conception. Jewish thought after the close of the Bible era added the two remaining constituents of the modern ideal of liberty, namely, tolerance and responsibility. The Diaspora had tended to break down the exclusiveness of Jewish religious thought and to force upon the best minds the notion that spiritual issues are universal and cannot be poured into a nationalist mode. Thus, the writer of the apocryphal *II Esdras* (*4 Ezra*) sees all men, and not Israel alone, standing in need of salvation, and therefore injects into his writing a note of religious liberty and toleration, viewing the whole of mankind as partners in a single spiritual struggle. In something of the same vein, Philo of Alexandria (20 B.C.E. to 40 C.E.) identifies Judaism with righteousness, by which alone the redemption of the soul struggling for freedom can be brought about (*De Sacrificio Abelis et Cain,* edit. Cohn-Wendland, section 120 et seq.).

Thus, the gradual evaporation of national exclusive-

ness as the mainspring of Judaism prepared the way for a realization of the fact that all men everywhere are struggling for freedom from the shackles of humanity. The emergent sense of universal human liberty therefore injects into the complex its modern ingredient of mutual tolerance. After a time, this comes to be an accepted tenet. Josephus states categorically (*Antiquities,* book 4, chap. 8, section 10) that it is against Jewish tradition to criticize the institutions of other nations, and forbidden to mock or blaspheme their gods, while at a much later age the *Yoreh Deah* (148 and 178) embodies the principle of religious liberty in the assertion that Judaism sanctions no interference with other persons' religious institutions.

Side by side, however, with this developing sense of general human liberty there emerges the doctrine that liberty is restricted and conditioned, and that it is not mere license. Jewish thinkers, from the 2nd cent. C.E. onwards, never tire of pointing out that the true definition of liberty is free acceptance of the Torah. The point is finely stated in the saying attributed in *Aboth* 6:2 to Joshua ben Levi. "Say not," says this sage, "that the Law was *haruth,* graven, upon the tablets. Say rather that it was *heruth,* freedom, embodied in the tablets; for no man is free but he who occupies himself in the Torah." The same sentiment is expressed also in the Talmud (*A.Z.* 5b): "Only he is master of himself who lives for God and men; he is free from the power of sorrow, free from the yoke of the oppressor, free from the limitations of mortality." This, in Jewish thought, is the ultimate freedom.

The Hasidim gave it a mystical twist. To them this freedom involves ascetic retreat from the world of the here below and immergence in the unlimited spirit of the divine. But to the Jew at large, freedom and liberty are merely other names for what human life would be if it were led in accordance with the Torah. Acceptance of the yoke of the Torah is the *sine qua non* of liberty, and the best description of the free man is that which is given in the Orthodox daily morning service, but the point of which is so often misrendered:

All of them take their stand in the high places of the world, and in reverence all give expression to that which is spoken by God, the source of all life and the King of the world. All are beloved, all are pure, all are mighty men . . . all of them take upon themselves the yoke of the kingdom of heaven, one from another, and give sanction to one another to evince the holiness of their Creator.

Jewish Origins of American Liberty. American ideas of liberty are in a measure indebted to earlier Jewish thinking. In 1636 the Plymouth Colony expressly drew up its constitution on the basis of the system introduced by Nehemiah after the Return from the Babylonian Exile (*Neh.* 9 and 10). In 1647, the Massachusetts Colony declared its adherence to Mosaic principles in framing its code of laws. The same was done in Connecticut in 1650, and in New Haven in 1655. In the words of the historian Lecky (*Rationalism in Europe*, vol. 2, p. 168): "The Hebraic mortar cemented the foundations of American Democracy."

The famous Liberty Bell contains an inscription taken from *Lev.* 25:10: "Proclaim liberty throughout all the land, unto all the inhabitants thereof."

American Jews have participated fully in all movements for the assertion of liberty. In April, 1935, they joined with Protestants and Catholics in urging the authorities not to place curbs upon civil liberties, while shortly after the first World War the Reform rabbinate was active in pressing for the release of political prisoners. The La Follette Committee on Civil Liberties was appointed, in 1935, 1936 and 1937, largely through the efforts of the Reform rabbis, in concert with the Federal Council of Churches and the National Catholic Welfare Council. All Jewish groups have also participated in demanding legislation against lynching.

Emma Lazarus' sonnet "The New Colossus," written on the occasion of the erection of the Statue of Liberty in New York Harbor in 1886, was later chosen to be inscribed on a bronze tablet which was placed inside the pedestal of the statue in May, 1903.

THEODOR H. GASTER.

LIBIN, SOLOMON (pseudonym, Israel Hurewitz), Yiddish short-story writer and dramatist, b. Gorki, Mohilev, Russia, 1872. His father instructed him in traditional Jewish learning, while his older brother tutored him in his secular studies. At the age of twenty he emigrated to London, where he lived seven months in great privation, after which he left for New York city; there he spent many years as a worker in a sweatshop. This latter experience he has employed as material for short stories, of which he has written several thousand, portraying with stark realism the life of immigrant workers and ghastly sweatshop conditions. His attitude is well-defined in these autobiographical lines: "This is a life which has been thoroughly merged with my own. My muse was born in the dreary sweatshop, beside the Singer machine where I first heard her anguished outcry: my muse was nurtured in the dark tenement graves." His short stories place Libin among the pioneers of artistic Yiddish prose writing and, together with Jacob Gordin and Leon Kobrin, he belongs to the school of social naturalism. His subjective approach and sentimentalism are of a lyric quality; his true-to-life descriptions are essentially objective, for they are well-documented. In toto his stories, most of which have appeared in the *Forward,* have furnished an effective and authentic portrayal of an epoch in Jewish history in the United States since the 1890's.

These qualities are well blended with the humorous and have found expression in Libin's more than fifty plays. His four-act drama, *Gebrochene Hertzer* (Broken Hearts; 1903), the most successful, was staged in the United States and in Europe, and was made into a film in 1926, with Maurice Schwartz and Lila Lee in the leading roles. He also wrote *Gotts Shtroff* (God's Punishment; 1909), a drama of family life, and published the following books: *Yiddishe Skitzn* (Jewish Sketches; 1902); *Geklibene Skitzn* (Selected Sketches; 1910); *Geklibene Shriftn* (Selected Writings; 2 vols., 1912); *Gezamelte Werk* (Collected Works; 4 vols., 1915-16); *Dertzeilungen, Skitzn un Felietonen* (Short Stories, Sketches and Feuilletons; 1934).

N. B. MINKOFF.

Lit.: Libin, S., "Materialn far Mein Biografie," *Geklibene Shriftn* (1912) 3-10; Baal-Machshoves, in *Shriftn,* vol. 3; Gorin, B., in *Geschichte fun Yiddishn Teatr*, vol. 2, pp. 208-10; Weinstein, B., in *Fertzik Yor in der Yiddisher Arbeter Bavegung,* pp. 159-61; Rogoff, H., in *Nine Yiddish Writers* (1931); Niger, S., in *Zukunft*, Feb., 1935.

LIBMAN, EMANUEL, physician, b. New York city, 1872. He was educated at the College of the City of New York (A.B., 1891) and the Columbia University College of Physicians and Surgeons (M.D., 1894). He pursued post-graduate studies at the Universities of Berlin, Vienna, Graz, Munich, and Prague (1896-97).

Libman was house physician at Mount Sinai Hospital from 1894 to 1896, associate physician from 1904 to 1912, attending physician from 1912 to 1925, and in 1925 he became consulting physician, a post he still held in 1942. In 1909 he was appointed professor in clinical medicine at the Columbia University College of Physicians and Surgeons. He was president of the New York Pathological Society in 1908, and served as chairman of the executive committee of the American committee for the development of the medical department of the Hebrew University of Jerusalem.

Libman was noted as an original research worker in the fields of bacteriology, pathology, and clinical medicine. His most important experiment was an investigation of the varying sensitivity to pain and the invention of a method to test the intensity of the individual's reaction to pain. He found that the examiner could determine the strength of the painful feeling by hold-ing his thumb over the patient's styloid process. He also did important work on subacute bacterial endocar-ditis (Libman's Disease), which he was the first to recognize as a separate pathological entity.

He wrote numerous articles for medical journals, most of which were collected in a three-volume book, *Contributions to the Medical Sciences,* and published in 1932 by his friends and pupils as a tribute on his sixtieth anniversary.

LIBRARIES, JEWISH. Jewish libraries exist either as independent collections of books (owned by private persons or in congregations, societies and scientific institutions) or as Hebraic or Judaic departments at general libraries (state libraries, community libraries, university libraries, and monastic libraries).

1. Independent Collections. Most of the public Jewish libraries were originally private collections, and even by far the greatest part of the state and university libraries received their Hebrew books from private possession. It is not easy to determine when the first Jewish libraries arose, but it was probably in the early Middle Ages. They were formed at first, as was natural, at Jewish institutions of learning and in syna-gogues. The Middle Ages were, on the whole, not favorable to the formation of Jewish libraries, since the Jews were constantly subjected to persecutions and the collectors often had to change their place of residence. Nevertheless, there were even then great private collections, for instance that of Samuel Hanagid in Granada, that of Judah ibn Tibbon in Southern France, and that of Judah Mosconi in Bulgaria.

The invention of printing and the better and more regulated conditions of the Jews in Italy, Turkey, and later in Holland furthered the collecting of books. Thus great private book collections were formed in Italy (for example, those of Menahem Volterra, Mena-hem Azariah da Fano, Elijah Levita in Rome, and Abtalion de Modena in Ferrara), in Turkey (Isaac Roman in Constantinople, David Vital in Patras, Sam-uel Benveniste in Salonika), and finally in Holland (Raphael d'Aguilar, Samuel Abbas, Manasseh ben Israel, and Scaliger in Leyden). The Renaissance and the Reformation awakened among Christians an interest in the Hebrew language. Some of them became zealous collectors of Hebrew books, as for instance the German humanist Johann Reuchlin, and another humanist of Germany, Albert Widmanstadt (1506-57), whose li-brary became the nucleus of the Hebrew department of the Munich State Library. In addition to these, there were the two Buxtorfs, father and son, in Basel. In the 17th cent. the great collection of David Oppen-heimer in Prague, which passed into the possession of the Bodleian Library at Oxford in 1829, was famous. In Germany there were the great collections of books of Nathan Abraham Schweriner (18th cent.) and of the banker Daniel Itzig.

Gradually there arose also in synagogues and Ye-shivas great collections of books; among them that in the Crimea and that in Fostat, near Cairo, Egypt (the Genizah), have attained great fame. In Western and Central Europe, as a rule, congregational and seminary libraries originated from the synagogal collections. Of the specially Jewish libraries of the present day, the

Emanuel Libman

most valuable in Europe is that of Jews' College, in London, containing in 1941 about 38,000 volumes and 600 manuscripts. It consists principally of the private collections of Michael Joseph, Leopold Zunz, Solomon J. Halberstamm, A. L. Green, and Moses Montefiore. The library of the Alliance Israélite Universelle in Paris, too, contains over 25,000 volumes and 200 manu-scripts. It owes its existence to the gifts of Baron Lionel Rothschild and the legacies of Isador Loeb, Bernhard Lazare, and Salomon Munk. In the United States there are two important Jewish libraries, i.e. in the Hebrew Union College, in Cincinnati, and in the Jewish Theological Seminary of New York; the latter is the most important Jewish library.

The Montezinos library in the Ets-Haim theological seminary in Amsterdam (containing 20,000 books and 1,000 old pamphlets) and that of the Landesrabbiner-schule in Budapest (containing about 30,000 volumes) are very valuable. In Germany the public libraries are of later date, and for this reason contain very few old or rare books. The library of the Jewish Theological Seminary in Breslau, with 25,000 books and many manuscripts, forms an exception. It consists in part of the private collections of L. Saraval (Trieste) and Bernhard Beer (Dresden). The Hochschule für die Wissenschaft des Judentums in Berlin had over 60,000 volumes in 1941. Furthermore, a large number of community libraries—for instance in Berlin, with about 50,000 books and pamphlets, in Breslau, Frankfort, Dresden, Cologne, and in Hannover—were formed in Germany, and these proved of great value for the Jewish education of the members of the communities. The same was true of the library of the Vienna Jewish community. The same purpose of providing for popu-lar education is aimed at by the many societal and communal libraries in Russia and Poland (for instance, the library in the Tlomackie Synagogue in Warsaw and the Straschun Library in Vilna). They have been of inestimable value in maintaining Judaism. Among the private libraries which still existed in 1942 are that of David Sassoon in London and that of Salmann Schocken in Zwickau. The extraordinarily valuable

An artist's conception of the ancient Talmudic library

private library of Baron David Günzburg was acquired after his death by the National Library in Jerusalem, but in 1942 was still in Moscow; this noted collection contains over 1,000 manuscripts and about 10,000 books, of which more than half are Hebrew.

An entirely different character is manifested by the Jewish National and University Library in Jerusalem. This library, founded in 1896, is today (1942) the greatest collection of Jewish books. It contains, besides Jewish books, numerous scientific and belletristic works on non-Jewish content in all cultured languages, and serves principally as a University library. It owes its existence and rapid growth to the desire of the Jewish people to create a cultural center in Palestine. For this reason it is not the endowment of one or of several philanthropists, nor did it come into existence due to the support of a rich institution or of a wealthy state, but, like many other institutions of the Jews in Palestine, it was built up by the whole of Jewry. The cost of its maintenance is borne by the Keren Hayesod (Jewish Foundation Fund) and the Hebrew University, Jerusalem. The library was founded in 1896 by Dr. Joseph Chasanovich in Bialystok, and was joined to the small society book collection, Beth Midrash Abarbanel, founded in 1892. With tireless energy Chasanovich collected books and funds for the library, and by 1910, due to his self-sacrifice and industry, it numbered several tens of thousands of volumes, among them numerous bibliographical rarities. The medieval and late rabbinical Hebrew literature was well represented there. For many years this library was managed by the Jerusalem B'nai B'rith Lodge, and was not open to the public. For this reason, it was decided, at the Eleventh Zionist Congress held at Vienna in 1913, to create a new library for the University, and Prof. Heinrich Loewe of Berlin undertook its organization.

In the various Jewish centers book-collecting points were established, and greater consignments were sent to Jerusalem. After the World War, in the summer of 1920, both libraries were taken over by the Zionist Organization and combined, and the management was entrusted to Hugo Bergmann, formerly of the Prague University Library. In the summer of 1920 this library had 32,000 volumes, of which 13,000 were Hebraica and 4,800 Judaica; in January, 1923: 60,000 volumes; in the summer of 1925: 100,000 volumes, of which 25,000 were Hebraica and more than 12,000 Judaica; in 1942: 400,000 volumes. It receives, besides, over 600 current periodicals; its yearly increase in the most recent period was about 25,000 volumes.

This rapid development is due in the first place to considerable gifts of books from Jewish sources, such as legacies, gifts of individuals, publishing houses and institutions, then to very liberal donations of several European governments, and finally to purchases made with the help of funds specially designated for this purpose. The careful work of collecting is done by numerous societies specially founded for this purpose, and the Gesellschaft der Freunde der Jerusalem-Bibliothek (Society of the Friends of the Jerusalem Library), founded in 1914, served as a model for them. Among the larger private gifts may be mentioned the Plaskov Library, that of Dr. Feinberg (Kovno), those of Hermann Schapira and Frederic Mocatta before the War, and the libraries of Popper-Lynceus (legacy), E. Chamitzer, J. Davud (London), E. Hertz and E. S. Rosenthal (New York), of Mrs. E. A. Gordon, a Christian woman (Kyoto, Japan), of Oscar Straus and many others after the War. Of Jewish corporations which furthered the formation of these libraries, the Union of Jewish Physicians in New York deserves special mention. Important collections of books were donated by the French, Spanish, Netherlands, Italian and Russian governments, by the League of Nations, and also by the Prussian Department of Education. Among those acquired by purchase are the very valuable libraries of Ignaz Goldziher, Theodor Gomperz, Samuel Poznanski, G. Itelson, A. von Hye-Glunek (an Austrian jurist), and Prof. Felix Klein (Göttingen), but the most important of all is the library of Baron David Günzburg, which, however, has not yet come into the possession of the National Library. Furthermore, several valuable archives were incorporated into the library, among them the archives of the Chovevei Zion in London and Odessa, the archives of the Bene Moshe, those of the Jewish Territorial Association, and parts of the archives of the Jewish Ministry in the Ukraine (1918-20). The autograph collection contains, among other things, a valuable collection by Abraham Schwadron as well as numerous manuscripts and letters of modern Jewish poets and savants.

Since 1924 the library has been publishing a bibliographical periodical, *Kiryath Sefer,* which gives detailed reports concerning the condition of the book collections and the new acquisitions of the library. The library building was erected (1930) from the David Wolffsohn fund, which was designated for that purpose.

The Shaare Zion library in Tel-Aviv, founded about the same time as the National Library and bearing the name Lewandas, has the character of a city library.

It contains more than 20,000 volumes, among others the legacy left by Ahad Haam, and the greater portion of the duplicates of the Jerusalem Library. The organization of the Jewish Workers of Palestine (Histadruth Haobedim) has a library of 50,000 volumes with about 100 branches.

2. Jewish Departments of General Libraries. The formation of Hebrew departments in general libraries is of much earlier date, and extends in part as far back as the 16th cent. The most extensive collection is to be found in England, in the Oxford University Library, the Bibliotheca Bodleiana. As far back as 1693 the Hebrew department was of considerable size, and the purchase of the David Oppenheimer and the Michael libraries in 1829 made it the most complete and valuable collection of that time. It contains about 3,000 manuscripts and 30,000 books. The British Museum in London in 1759 had only one Hebrew book, a first edition of the Talmud; in the same year Solomon da Costa, an immigrant Jew from Holland, presented a collection of 180 books of rabbinics. It now possesses more than 20,000 Hebrew books, eighty incunabula, and 2,700 manuscripts. It includes the libraries of Giuseppe Almanzi, Moses Gaster, and M. W. Schapira (among them numerous Yemenite manuscripts). It possesses also a part of the things found in the Genizah of the synagogue in Cairo. The greater part of the things found, the Taylor-Schechter collection, was given to the University Library in Cambridge, which today has the greatest number of Hebrew manuscripts. The Jewish Library of University College in London comprises several thousand volumes formerly in the possession of Frederic Mocatta and Hermann Gollancz (especially Anglo-Judaica).

France: The Paris National Library, even as far back as the 14th cent., contained Hebrew manuscripts which were found in the house of a Jew who had been driven out of the city. It has about 1,500 Hebrew manuscripts and numerous books, which are not, as in England, placed in a special department, but are arranged in various other departments according to subjects. For the most part, they come from the collections of Christian savants.

Italy: The Italian libraries are especially rich in old manuscripts. Of enormous scientific value is the Hebrew department of the library in Parma, which contains over 2,000 Hebrew manuscripts. They belonged mainly to the Christian Hebraist G. B. de Rossi, who left 1,377 manuscripts to the library. The Vatican has hundreds of valuable Hebrew manuscripts.

Russia: The Hebrew department of the State Library in Leningrad possesses a very valuable collection of manuscripts, among them very many old ones found in the East, for the first discoveries from the Genizahs were brought thither. A large portion of the manuscripts was obtained from Abraham Firkovich, including numerous Samaritan and Karaitic ones. Besides these, this library contains more than 15,000 Hebrew books and many Judaica, for the most part in the Russian language. Of equal importance is the Hebrew department of the Asiatic Museum in Leningrad. It consists in the main of the Friedland Library, the most important private library of the 19th cent., which was built up by Leo Friedland out of individual smaller private libraries by means of an enormous expenditure of work and financial sacrifices and was presented to the Asiatic Museum in 1892.

Poland: The Ossolinski Public Library in Lvov contains valuable material relating to the history of the Jews in Poland.

The Netherlands: The Amsterdam University Library obtained possession of the great private collection of L. Rosenthal at Hannover, with many rare specimens. The Akademie der Wissenschaften in Leyden has more than 15,000 Hebrew books, and many valuable manuscripts.

Austria: The Vienna National Library has several hundred Hebrew manuscripts. Its collection of books is not particularly important.

Hungary: David Kaufman's important collection of books has been taken over by the Akademie der Wissenschaften in Budapest.

Germany: The German libraries are comparatively poor in Hebrew books and manuscripts. The Munich State Library, with several hundred manuscripts, of which a great portion comes from Albert Widmanstadt, is the largest in this respect. The Prussian State Library in Berlin contains only a few thousand volumes of Hebraica as well as 300 manuscripts. More important is the Hebrew division of the Municipal Library in Frankfort, containing very valuable rabbinical works and numerous incunabula. Among other collections, it took over the libraries of Abraham Merzbacher and Abraham Berliner. The Hebrew manuscripts of the Hamburg Municipal Library (now in the Hamburg State and University Library) are of great scientific value.

The numerous moderate-sized and smaller collection in other European libraries can not be mentioned here, although each of them has a certain importance for learning. The catalogues of the individual collections were compiled, in the course of the last century, with great scholarliness and skill by Jewish savants, and contain very valuable biographical material. Up to the present the Spanish and Portuguese libraries were treated very superficially, and it was only recently that work was done on them in greater measure with respect to Hebrew books. It is probable that they, too, contain great bibliographical treasures.

It should be noted, however, that the foregoing facts and figures about European libraries are given on the basis of the latest available reports that are reliable. Since 1938 in particular the Nazi authorities in Germany have been in position to seize or destroy numerous collections of Jewish books and there is no certainty as to what may have befallen them during the Second World War. There have been reports that libraries at Vienna, Vilna, Frankfort and other places have been destroyed; there have been other reports that Jewish collections have been transferred to Munich for the use of the departments of anti-Semitism and of genealogy.

3. Collections of Jewish Literature in the United States: After the huge immigration from Eastern European countries in the closing decades of the 19th century, numerous institutions of Jewish education and learning were founded in the United States, and collections of Hebraica and Judaica began to be

A glimpse of the Semitic division of the Library of Congress at Washington, D. C.

Reading room of the erstwhile Warburg Library at Hamburg, the contents of which were transferred to London soon after the advent of Nazi rule in Germany

Main library building of the Hebrew Union College at Cincinnati

assembled. In 1942 the United States possessed the largest collections of this material in the world.

Library of the Jewish Theological Seminary of America, New York city. Librarian: Dr. Alexander Marx. Starting with 5,000 books when the Seminary was reorganized in 1902, the Library has expanded rapidly. In 1941 it possessed about 121,000 books and 7,800 manuscripts, some of which date back to the 9th cent. In recent years it acquired thousands of priceless works. With the acquisition of the Elkan N. Adler Collection its group of manuscripts became the most notable in the world. It is rich also in incunabula, 16th cent. books, and rare specimens of Oriental and Russian presses. It has one of the best collections of vellum; its Haggadah Collection numbers more than 1,000 different editions. In addition to the acquisition of the Adler Collection, the Library has come into the possession, among others, of the books of Halberstam, Steinschneider, Kautzsch, Schechter and Sulzberger. In October, 1930, the new Jacob H. Schiff Memorial Library was dedicated.

Library of the Hebrew Union College, Cincinnati, Ohio. Among its librarians were Siegmund Mannheimer, Max Schloessinger and Adolph S. Oko. In 1942 the librarian was Walter E. Rothman, the first alumnus of the college to serve in that capacity. It contained in 1941 about 85,000 Hebrew, Yiddish and Judaic books, and over 2,500 manuscripts. In addition to the yearly regular accessions, the Library has incorporated special collections such as those of Eduard Birnbaum, cantor of Königsberg, Germany (mainly music), Louis Grossmann (education), L. C. Karpinski (Palestiniana), Israel Solomons (Anglo-Judaica), and S. Rehfisch (Pirke Aboth). In May, 1931, the new Library of the Hebrew Union College was dedicated.

Jewish Division of the New York Public Library. Chief of the Division: Dr. Joshua Bloch. In November, 1897, Jacob H. Schiff offered a Jewish Collection, and Abraham S. Freidus (d. 1923) was placed in charge. The Division is noted for its large collections of modern Hebrew and Yiddish works and periodicals. To the Schiff Collection were added the Bank Collection which embraces the Mandelstamm Library and the Isaac Myer Collection. It possesses a modest collection of Hebrew and Yiddish manuscripts, including an illuminated manuscript of the Hebrew Scriptures of the 13th cent. and a beautiful manuscript of the Samaritan Pentateuch of the same age. Its collection of Hebrew incunabula contains fine specimens of early Hebrew printing and includes a vellum copy of the earliest Hebrew printed book, the *Arba Turim* (Pieve di Sacco, 1475). It is rich in all branches of Judaica, and the entire collection of Jewish books in the New York Public Library covers all aspects of the subject it represents. The aim of the Jewish Division is to bring together and maintain a collection of material which is to embrace as far as possible all branches of the encyclopedic knowledge pertaining to the Jews, their life and their lore. All fields of Jewish learning and thought, ancient and modern, are adequately represented. The collection consists of material in many languages, and includes a wide range of subjects, sacred and secular.

Semitic Division of the Library of Congress, Washington, D. C. Chief of the Division: Dr. Israel Schapiro. This comprises Hebraica, Yiddish, Judaica, Arabica and other cognate languages, also vernaculars such as Judeo-Arabic, Judeo-Persian, and Judeo-Spanish (generally known as Ladino). The Division was organized in 1913. The nucleus was a collection of Hebraica of over 10,000 volumes brought together by Ephraim Deinard and presented by Jacob H. Schiff in 1912. A supplementary collection of over 4,000 volumes bought from the same collector was presented by Schiff in 1914. In 1917 and 1921 the Library bought from the same collector two additional collections amounting to about 6,000 volumes. With the material since acquired by purchase, gift and copyright, the number of Hebrew books in the Library of Congress was in 1942 around 40,000 volumes. The material covers all fields of old and new Hebrew literature, containing also a number of manuscripts and incunabula, and numerous rare books of the 16th and 17th centuries. The Yiddish Collection numbers over 8,000 volumes, among which are found the best representative works printed in this country and abroad. Judaica in all European languages are likewise well represented.

Library of the Dropsie College for Hebrew and Cognate Learning, Philadelphia, Pa. Librarian: Dr. Joseph Reider. Its collections of Hebraica and Judaica numbered in 1942 about 46,000 volumes. Incorporated are the libraries of Isaac Leeser, Joshua I. Cohen, Eduard Glaser, and selected books from the libraries of Judge Mayer Sulzberger and Henry Malter. The Library contains also Oriental manuscripts, incunabula and 450 fragments from the Cairo Genizah in Hebrew and Arabic.

Jewish collections are now being built up by the Jewish Institute of Religion and the Yeshiva College, both of New York city, and by the Rabbinical College of Chicago, Ill., the recently established Jewish institutions of learning in the United States.

Notable Jewish collections are found also in the libraries of several leading universities. New York Universty possesses the Anton de Lagarde collection rich in Hebrew and Aramaic texts. Columbia University received from Temple Emanu-El as a gift its Almanzi Collection of 5,000 volumes, containing some manuscripts and incunabula; a Yiddish collection of distinction, numbering about 3,000 books and pamphlets which Professor Leo Wiener brought together on a visit to Russia, is located in the Harvard University Library; while Yale University Library had as a nucleus for its Jewish Collection the Alexander Kohut library of 4,500 books (of which 1,700 are in Hebrew) which his son, George Alexander Kohut, established as a memorial in 1915. Adolf Sutro left his collection of over 200,000 items of books and manuscripts to the city of San Francisco, which then established the Sutro Library. In 1930 Lucius N. Littauer gave to Harvard University a collection of 12,000 volumes (the Nathan Littauer Library); in the same year a collection of 3,000 volumes in honor of Judge Julian W. Mack was presented to the same library. The Abraham I. Schechter collection of Hebraica and Judaica was (1942) the property of the University of Texas. In 1940 the College of the City of New York received the 7,500 volume library of Dr. Israel Davidson, presented by his wife after his death; this was formally dedicated in 1942.

ISRAEL SCHAPIRO.

The most important catalogues of the larger libraries:

Place	Library	Collection	Compiled by	Year of Publication
Amsterdam	University Library (Rosenthaliana)	Books	Roest	1875
		Books	L. Hirschel and M. S. Hillesum	1936–
Berlin	State Library	Manuscripts	M. Steinschneider	1878-97
Bologna	University Library	Manuscripts	L. Modona	1889
Bologna	University Library	Incunabula	L. Modona	1890
Breslau	Jewish Theological Seminary	Books		
		Manuscripts	B. Zuckermann	1876
		Beer's Legacy (Books)	B. Zuckermann	1876
			G. Wolf	1863
Budapest	Akademie der Wissenschaften	D. Kaufmann Collection	M. Weiss	1906
Cambridge	University Library	Manuscripts	S. M. Schiller-Szinnessy	1876
Cambridge	Girton College	Books and Manuscripts	H. Loewe	1915
Cambridge	Trinity College	Manuscripts	H. Loewe	1926
Cincinnati	Hebrew Union College	Books	Adolph S. Oko	Yearly Reports
Florence	Mediceo-Laurenziana Library	Manuscripts	Umberto Cassuto	1912
		Incunabula	Umberto Cassuto	1908-9
Frankfort	City Library	Merzbacher Legacy	R. N. Rabinowitz	1889
Frankfort	City Library	Incunabula	A. Freimann	1920
		Books	F. K. Ebrard	1902
		Books	A. Freimann	1932–
Hamburg	City Library	Manuscripts	M. Steinschneider	1878
Leyden	Akademie der Wissenschaften	Manuscripts	M. Steinschneider	1858
Leghorn (Livorno)	Talmud Torah	Books and Manuscripts	Bernheimer	1915
Leningrad	Asiatic Museum	Manuscripts	A. Neubauer	1866
	Asiatic Museum	Books	S. Wiener	1893–
	State Library	Manuscripts	Harkavy	1875-84
London	Jews' College	Manuscripts	A. Neubauer	1886
			H. Hirschfeld	1905
London	British Museum	Manuscripts	G. Margoliouth	1903, 1905, 1912
		Books	Zedner	1867
			Van Straalen (Supplement)	1894
Mantua	Library of the Jewish Community	Manuscripts	M. Mortara	1872
Modena	City Library	Manuscripts	S. Jona	1883
Munich	State Library	Manuscripts	M. Steinschneider	1875; 2nd ed., 1895
New York	Public Library	Books	Joshua Bloch	Yearly Reports
New York	Jewish Theological Seminary	Sulzbacher's Legacy	E. Deinard	1896
		E. Adler's Collection	E. N. Adler	1921
Oxford	Bodleian Library	Manuscripts	A. Neubauer	1886-1906
		Books	M. Steinschneider	1852-60
		Books	A. E. Cowley	1929
Paris	National Library	Manuscripts	S. Munk and Zotenberg	1866
			M. Steinschneider (Supplement)	1903
			M. Schwab (Supplement)	1912
Paris	Alliance Israélite Universelle	Manuscripts and Books		
Parma	University Library	Manuscripts	De Rossi	1803
			Perreau (Supplement)	1880
Philadelphia	Dropsie College	Manuscripts	B. Halper	1924
Rome	Bibliotheca Vaticana	Manuscripts	Assemani	1756
			Mai (Supplement)	1831
Rome	Bibliotheca Casanatensis	Manuscripts	Sacerdote	1897
Turin	Athenaeum	Manuscripts	B. Peyron	1878-80
Upsala	University Library	Manuscripts	Zettersteen	1900
Vienna	National Library	Manuscripts	A. Z. Schwarz	1925
Vilna	Straschun Library	Books		1889
Vienna	Jewish Community Library	Books	Wachstein	1911-14
Washington	Library of Congress	Books	Israel Schapiro	Yearly Reports

The Jewish Council and Beth Din (rabbinical tribunal) at Tripoli in Libya

LIBYA, North African territory between Egypt and Tunisia, comprising the provinces of Cirenaica and Tripolitania; in 1912 it came under Italian sovereignty. Although the name of Libya was frequently used in ancient times, its origin and meaning remain obscure. It derives apparently from the name ("Lbw") of one of the populations of Cirenaica, as was revealed by the discovery of ancient Egyptian inscriptions. In the Bible they are mentioned as the "Lehabim" (*Gen.* 10:13; cf. *I Chron.* 1:11; in both these passages Lehabim is probably equivalent to Ludim). In later periods the name Libya served to indicate larger extensions and even the whole of North Africa.

Contacts between Libya and Palestine were established in early times. Cirenaica, the eastern peninsula of Libya, attracted Jewish traders and settlers long before the destruction of the First Temple (586 B.C.E.). In 320 B.C.E. Ptolemy I of Egypt established Jewish military strongholds in upper Libya, peopled mostly by captives brought from Palestine. These Jewish garrisons enjoyed a large amount of autonomy; they defended the cause of Ptolemy against the Greeks of the Pentapolis.

During the period of persecutions by Antiochus IV (Epiphanes) of Syria (2nd cent. B.C.E.), many Pharisees established themselves at Cyrene. Jason, a local author, compiled in classic Greek a historical description of the Jewish people from the persecutions suffered under the Seleucids to the insurrection of Judah Maccabee. *II Maccabees* is only an extract from Jason's work.

In 74 B.C.E. the Jews of Cyrene, who were living an organized and autonomous life, felt strong enough to resist by military force the occupation of the country by the Romans. After the destruction of Jewish independence in Palestine, Jonathan the Zealot gathered a force of 2,000 Jews and sought to stir up the Jewish military garrisons against the Romans. He was captured by the prefect Catullus' legionnaires. Thousands of Jews of Cirenaica were killed and their goods confiscated. In 115 the Jews of Cyrene renewed their revolt against the Roman authorities; it lasted for over two years. The Roman general Marcus Turbo finally suppressed this revolt, and during the severe and cruel reprisals which followed, the Jewish population of Cirenaica was almost entirely annihilated. Only small nuclei escaped destruction, finding refuge among the Berber populations in the interior parts of the country.

In Tripolitania the major Jewish settlements were in the three principal cities of that region, i.e. Sabratha, Oea and Leptis Magna. Many Jewish families came thither at the time of the persecution of Antiochus Epiphanes. The tradition which attributes the origin of many Jewish nuclei in Tripolitania to the prisoners brought thither by Titus is widespread among the Jews of the interior, particularly among the troglodytes of Tigrinna and of Jebel Garian.

Under the dynasty of the Fatimids (969-1171) there was in Tripoli a Jewish population of about 800 persons. Subsequent migrations from neighboring African states considerably increased this number. The influx of Spanish Jews, when the territory was wrested from its Spanish rulers, contributed toward the raising of the material and moral level of the Libyan Jewish communities.

The conquest of Tripolitania by Sultan Suleiman the Magnificent in 1551 opened new and better prospects for those Jews. While the Jews of the major centers could devote themselves to their preferred and skilled trades as goldsmiths and silversmiths, and lived in relative security, those of the interior were always exposed to the fanaticism and jealousy of the Arabs and had to endure serious privations.

In 1705 the Jews of Tripolitania faced grave danger when the bey of Tunis besieged Tripoli and threatened to exterminate the Jews in that city once his troops succeeded in taking it. The outbreak of a sudden plague which decimated his troops prevented him from entering Tripoli and executing his threat. The 24th of Tebet was declared to be a "Purim Kidebuni" (false Purim), to commemorate the deliverance of the Tripoli community from certain destruction. That community was again exposed to grave danger and persecution when, on July 30, 1793, the corsair Ali Bourghel and his men entered the city of Tripoli. For nearly a year and a half the Jews of Tripoli and of the interior were tortured, pillaged and humiliated by the troops of Ali Bourghel. On January 19, 1795, Ahmed Karamanli Pasha succeeding in reestablishing the rule of his family over Tripolitania. The local rabbis instituted the 29th of Tebet as another Purim, the "Purim Bourghel."

A view of the Jewish quarter of Tripoli in Libya. Photographs on pp. 44 and 45 reproduced by courtesy of David Kleinlerer

In 1850, at the time when Benjamin II visited Tripoli, there were about 1,000 Jewish families there.

The Jews of Libya suffered greatly from the Italo-Turkish war operations of 1911 to 1912, which were conducted mainly in the coastal cities of Libya, where the Jewish population is predominant. The attitude of the Italian occupants toward those Jewish nuclei in the years which followed their conquest of Libya was fair, although there occurred frequent episodes of violence and discrimination against the Jews on the part of the Italian colonists who were brought to Libya in increasing numbers.

In view of the fierce resistance of the Arab population to the new Italian rulers, which in Cirenaica assumed the aspect of an open revolt, the first governors of Libya, and particularly Count Giuseppe Volpi, sought, for opportunistic reasons, to gain the sympathy and loyalty of the local Jews, acceding to their religious and social needs. On April 22, 1928, King Victor Emmanuel III, during his first official visit to Libya, attended the inauguration of a new Jewish synagogue, situated in the Al Hara quarter of Tripoli, and visited other Jewish communities of the Libyan colony.

According to the census of 1931, there were 21,508 Jews in Tripolitania and 3,595 in Cirenaica. About 3,000 Jewish children attended the general public schools, while more than half of this number were pupils in the Talmud Torahs. According to data furnished by the official Agenzia dell'Italia e dell'Impero, the Jewish population of Libya increased in the years following the census of 1931, and on June 30, 1937, reached the total of 29,166, of whom 74.2 per cent were in the province of Tripoli, 12.2 per cent in that of Benghazi, and the remaining 10.9 per cent and 2.7 per cent in the provinces of Misurata and Derna, respectively. The birth rate of the Jews of Libya exceeds their mortality rate by 20 per thousand.

The condition of the Jewish population of Libya took a definite turn for the worse since the Italian government initiated a strongly accentuated policy of favoring the Arabs and of seeking to ingratiate itself with them. The Fascist organ of Libya, the *L'Avvenire di Tripoli,* frequently published anti-Semitic material and began a systematic campaign of incitement against the Jews. In January, 1937, a decree was issued by the governor of Libya, Marshal Italo Balbo, that the Jewish shops situated in the European quarters of Tripoli and Benghazi were to be kept open on Saturdays and Jewish holidays. The protests of the elders and rabbis of the Jewish communities of those cities were of no avail. The Jews were determined, however, not to desecrate the Sabbath. Balbo ordered five Jewish merchants who had disobeyed his decree to be flogged in a public square of Tripoli. Thousands of Arabs were driven by the police to attend the flogging, as the public spectacle was designed to persuade them that the Fascist government was a "friend of the Moslems." The intervention of the president of the Union of Jewish Communities of Italy, Felice Ravenna, who strove to have the drastic order cancelled, brought no result.

On March 14, 1938, Benito Mussolini, at the end of his Libyan trip, during which he proclaimed himself the "protector of Islam," visited also the Jewish quarter Al Hara in Tripoli. At that time he assured the chief rabbi, Aldo Lattes, that the Italian government would always respect the religious traditions and rights of the Jewish population. In spite of that, however, the Jews of Libya began to feel the entire brunt of the newly proclaimed racial anti-Semitic policy. The Maccabi athletic organizations of Tripoli and Benghazi were excluded from the Libyan Sports Federation. The Ben Yehouda cultural organization of Tripoli was closed. The Jews were not allowed to have their businesses in the European quarters of the principal cities. Thousands of young Jews were sent to build fortifications and defense posts at the borders of Egypt and Tunisia.

Italy's entrance into the second World War, on June 10, 1940, gravely endangered the very existence of the Jewish nuclei of Libya, which became one of the most hotly contested battlefronts of the war. During the first British occupation of Benghazi, in the spring of 1941, a few hundred Jews succeeded in reaching Egypt and Palestine. The bombardments and alternate occupations of the city virtually ruined the important and relatively prosperous Jewish community there. The same fate befell the Jewish groups in Tobruk (175 in all), Bardia (45), Derna (293), Barce (248) and other small Jewish groups along the Cyrene coast. The Al Hara (Jewish quarter) of Tripoli, located near the port installations, suffered heavily from British bombardment.

See also: AFRICA; BENGHAZI; CYRENE; TRIPOLI.

DAVIDE KLEINLERER.

Lit.: Feraud, L. Charles, *Annales tripolitaines* (1927); Bergna, P. Costanzo, *Tripoli dal 1510 al 1850* (1925); Cohen, M., and Moreno, M., *Gli Ebrei in Libia* (published under the auspices of the Italian minister of colonies); Slouschz, Nahum, *Travels in North Africa* (1927); Tully, Richard, *Tripoli au xviii-ième siècle* (1922); *Encyclopaedia Judaica*, vol. 10 (1934), cols. 939-40, where additional literature is given.

LICHT, MICHAEL (MICHI), Yiddish poet, b. Plisk, Volhynia, Russia, 1893. Until the age of twenty he lived in Bielozorka, at the home of his aunt and uncle who guided his early education (in traditional Jewish learning, as well as in secular studies). His poem, *Dem Feter Shaye un der Mume Pesye* (For My Uncle Shaye, and My Aunt Pesye), dedicated to these simple people, is among the finest modern Yiddish sentimental lyrics written in folk manner.

In 1913 Licht emigrated to the United States, where he studied literature, history, sociology and philosophy at the College of the City of New York and at the New School for Social Studies.

He began to write in Russian at the age of eight. His English poems and translations (signed Sonin or M. Licht Sonin) were published in the *Call* (1915 and 1916), in the *Pagan* (1918 and 1919), the *Playboy* (No. 3, 1919), and some of his verse was included in the *Second Pagan Anthology* (1919).

Licht made his debut in Yiddish with a short story in the *Tog* (1916) of New York. His poems have been published in such periodicals as *Onheib, Feder, In Sich, Shriftn, Loglen* (which he edited together with Jacob Glatstein), *Kultur* (Chicago), *Undzer Buch, Unzug* (Toronto), *Neie Zeit, New Yorker Vochnblatt, Kern* (1925 and 1926), (edited in collaboration with N. B. Minkoff), and *Bodn*. His first book of verse, *Egoemen* (Egoems, 1922), is distinguished by sensitivity, lucidity and purity of expression. His second book, *Vazon* (Flower-Pot; 1928), is more lyrical, although herein personal, intimate motives are more abstruse, sublimated by a classical mastery of form. *Protzesies un Andere Lieder* (Processions and Other Poems; 1932) depicts the recondite adventures of modern man's spiritual self, his concepts and his aspirations, influenced by his 20th cent. environment. His poem "Der Vint" (The Wind), included in this volume, apotheosizes the modern soul.

Licht's *Fragmentn,* published in *Bodn* (1934-37), is part of a larger work in poetry and prose, purporting to describe "the particular biography of a certain attitude of our (Jewish) present times." Licht has published also critical essays and experimental short stories. His contribution to Yiddish poetry has been unique; while his style is ultra-modern and innovational, his expression is rigidly disciplined, modifying the starkly sentimental by the intellectual. His highly polished language is rich in folk idioms and manner.

Lit.: Minkoff, N. B., in *Undzer Buch*, Sept.-Oct., 1926, reprinted separately as *Sistem un Relativkeit in Poezie: Vegn Michl Licht* (1927); Marmor, K., in *Freiheit*, April 19, 1927; Olgin, M., in *Hamer*, Sept., 1926.

LICHTENAUER, JOSEPH MORTIMER, painter, b. New York city, 1876. He was educated at the Arts Students League (1895-98) and studied art in France and Italy for the next five years. He made a special study of the decorative arts of the great palaces of Europe, and the baroque influence was visible in his subsequent work, particularly in his murals, first exhibited in the Paris Salon. After that he showed his pictures all over the United States. He was commissioned to paint murals for Washington Irving High School in New York city and for the Schubert, Adelphi, and Wallach theatres. His work is represented in the collections of the Metropolitan Museum of Art of New York city, the Brooklyn Museum, and the Smithsonian Institute in Washington, D. C.

Lichtenauer was awarded the president's prize for mural sketches of the New York Architectural League in 1903 and 1907. In 1937 he received a bronze medal at the Paris Exposition.

LICHTENBERG, ALEXANDER VON, urologist and surgeon, b. Budapest, 1880. He received his M.D. degree from the University of Budapest in 1902, and worked at the surgery clinics of Czerny and Narath at Heidelberg (1902-8) and of Madelung at Strasbourg (1908-18), becoming instructor at the University of Strasbourg in 1910. In 1922 he became associate professor at the University of Berlin, and established a section for urological surgery at the Hedwig Hospital there. He was founder and editor of the *Zeitschrift für urologische Chirurgie* up to 1936, and edited the *Jahresberichte für Urologie* up to 1933 and the *Handbuch der Urologie* (1929), in which were published his monographs "Allgemeine urologische Diagnostik und Symptomatologie" and "Allgemeine Röntgen-Diagnostik." Uroselectan, a dye invented by him, made the kidney, its pelvis and all urinary organs stand out clearly in X-ray pictures and thus facilitated diagnosis and operation. He also published, in addition to numerous minor works, *Über die Kreislaufstörung bei der Peritonitis und über die Kochsalz-Suprarenin Therapie* (1909). After 1936 he lived in Budapest.

LICHTENBERG, EMIL, conductor, b. Budapest, 1874. He studied at the Music Academy of Budapest. After short periods of conducting at Cologne and Prague, he joined the staff of the Budapest Opera in 1902, and was its conductor from 1907 to 1925. He formed several choral societies at Budapest, and in 1908 he founded the Budapest Chorus and Orchestra Association for the performance of oratorios and kindred compositions. From 1925 on Lichtenberg devoted himself entirely to the conducting of this chorus and orchestra, presenting from year to year the finest compositions by masters of the 17th and 18th centuries, which he often accompanied with spoken interpretations.

Lichtenberg also published several volumes of musical analyses, dealing notably with Brahms' *Requiem;* Haydn's *Creation;* Bach's *Matthew Passion;* Beethoven's *Missa Solemnis;* Berlioz' *Damnation of Faust;* Wagner's *Nibelungen;* Wagner's *Parsifal.* He also wrote *A fuga művészete* (The Art of the Fugue). In 1932 the title of chief government councillor was bestowed upon him by Regent Nicholas Horthy. Lichtenberg embraced Christianity.

LICHTENSTADTER, ILSE, orientalist, b. Hamburg, Germany. She specialized in Arabic literature and the Islamic religion, and received doctor's degrees from the Universities of Frankfort (1931) and Oxford (1937). She was the first woman to be elected a member of the New York Oriental Club (1939). Her writings include: "Das Nasîb der altarabischen Qasîde" (*Islamica,* vol. 5, 1931); *Women in the Aiyâm al-'Arab* (London, 1935); articles in the *Encyclopaedia of Islam;* "Muhammad ibn Habîb and His Kitâb al-Muhabar" (*Journal of the Royal Asiatic Society,* London, 1939); "Some References to Jews in Early Arabic Poetry" (*Proceedings of the American Academy for Jewish Research,* 1940). She also edited Muhammad ibn Habib's *Kitâb al-Muhabar* (Hyderabad, 1942).

LICHTENSTEIN, FERENC LAJOS, Hungarian patriot and editor, b. Szigetvár, Hungary, 1828; place and date of death unknown. As a young man of twenty, and as a Jew deprived of civil rights, he won the confidence of Lajos Kossuth, and acted as a special courier for the leader of the Hungarian revolution of 1848 to 1849. On one occasion he was made bearer of Kossuth's command to the self-willed General Artur Görgey to join forces and cooperate with General Dembinszky. Lichtenstein delivered the message with such authority that the infuriated army chief wanted to

have him shot, and only the intervention of Görgey's adjutant saved Lichtenstein's life. Subsequently, he received a diplomatic mission.

After the capitulation of the Hungarian army, he was made a political prisoner, but managed to escape. He expatriated himself and engaged in journalism abroad. His extradition was demanded by the Austrian government, but it was refused.

In 1863, when the Magyars had placated the central Austrian government, he returned to Hungary. There he took part in the founding of the Land Credit Institute, edited a trilingual bulletin, *Pester Correspondenz,* and an economic publication, *Ungarischer Aktionär.* He was also active in Hungarian freemasonry.

LICHTENSTEIN, GASTON, historian, b. Tarboro, N. C., 1879. He studied at the University of Cincinnati (1897-1900) and the Hebrew Union College (B.H.L., 1899).

Lichtenstein initiated the movement that led to the erection (1922-29) in Richmond, Va., of a statue to Matthew Fontaine Maury (1806-73), the hydrographer. Lichtenstein was historian of the Stonewall Jackson Camp of the Sons of Confederate Veterans who, under his inspiration, launched a movement for the erection of a monument, in Richmond, in memory of Judah P. Benjamin. This project was still in progress in 1942.

Lichtenstein was the author of: *The History of the Jews of Richmond from 1769 to 1917* (1917, with Herbert T. Ezekiel, including a section on the Jews of Richmond in the first World War added in 1920); *From Richmond to North Cape* (1922; travel in Scandinavia and Germany); and a number of historical articles, two collections of which were published as *George Washington's Lost Birthday* (1924) and *Thomas Jefferson as War Governor* (1925). An early article, *Early History of Tarboro, North Carolina,* was published in 1908. Lichtenstein also edited a narrative of the first World War, compiled from original records, entitled *Repatriation of Prisoners of War from Siberia* (1924).

LICHTENSTEIN, HILLEL, rabbi, b. Vágvecse, Hungary, 1815; d. Kolomea, Galicia, 1891. He was a disciple of Rabbi Moses Sofer (Hatham Sofer) of Pozsony (Pressburg) who advocated complete seclusion of the Jews from the surrounding world as the only means of preserving Judaism. With all the force of his remarkable personality, Lichtenstein fought for this principle against the rising new generations that were eager to receive the boon of emancipation held out by a willing government in exchange for formal innovations, among which adoption of the Magyar vernacular was foremost.

Lichtenstein served as rabbi at Szentmargit in 1850; in the following year he moved to Nagyvárad and later to Szentmargit, where he lived until 1865, when he was installed as rabbi of Szikszó. During these years he traveled about the country, agitating the communities with his oratory against any change in synagogal rites and against contact with reformers. He preached in Yiddish and violently opposed the use of German in the synagogues of Western Hungary, or of Hungarian, which some rabbis had introduced in the pulpits of Central Hungary. It was especially the liberalizing project of the Hungarian Rabbinical Seminary, endorsed by the government, which prompted him to action of wide scope. He convoked the synod of Nagymihály (1865) where seventy-one rabbis passed a *pesak beth din* (decision of the synod) outlawing all changes in synagogal rites and customs as well as preaching in German. A delegation of rabbis was sent to Francis Joseph I, protesting against the establishment of the seminary as an influence destructive of positive Judaism. In 1867 Lichtenstein was called to the rabbinate of Kolomea, Galicia, but he continued to correspond with the irreconcilable rabbis of Hungary and exerted great influence on the dissident Orthodox group at the National Jewish Congress (1868-69).

Contrary to his teacher, the Hatham Sofer, Lichtenstein had mystical tendencies. He was a great admirer of Rabbi Hayim Halberstam, the miracle worker of New Sandec. In the observance of the law he went beyond all practised standards of piety; he kept domestic animals in order to fulfill Biblical commands enjoined upon Jews of antiquity engaged in agriculture (the redeeming of the first-born of an ass, *Ex.* 13:13; giving the first fleece of the sheep to the priest, or Kohen, *Deut.* 18:4). He conducted a Yeshiva at Kolomea, and his homiletical interpretations of the Torah were published in *Makre Dardeke* (Lemberg, 1888-99); his responsa and letters addressed to Hungarian rabbis, in the volume *Beth Hillel*, were published after his death (Szatmár, 1908). His sermons, collected in the volumes *Maskil el Dal* (Ungvár 1863-69); *Shire Maskil* (Lemberg, 1877); as well as his works *El Haadarim* (Pressburg, 1864); *Abkath Rachel* (Lemberg, 1883-85); *Eth Laasoth* (Lemberg, 1873), impassioned pamphlets against Reform, attained several editions. By personal example and through his writings, Lichtenstein remained a powerful influence in Hungarian Orthodoxy, which continued to isolate itself from those modern methods from which Orthodoxy itself had benefited in most other countries.

His biography was written by his disciple Zebi Hirsh Heller, entitled *Beth Hillel* (Munkács, 1893).

ANNA BETTELHEIM.

Lit.: Venetianer, Lajos, *A zsidóság szervezete az európai államokban;* Ujvári, P., *Magyar Zsidó Lexikon;* Bettelheim, Samu, "Das Buch Nehemia," published serially in *Jüdisches Familienblatt* (1930).

LICHTENSTEIN, ISAAC, painter and Yiddish art critic, b. near Warsaw, Poland, 1888. He was educated in a public school. From 1906 on he studied painting at Cracow, Rome, Florence, and Munich. He made several visits to Palestine, and resided in Jerusalem for a number of years. During the first World War Lichtenstein lived in the United States. In 1918 he volunteered in the Jewish Legion and served in Palestine. At the close of the War he took up residence in London, then in Poland, and for a number of years he made his home in Paris. Later he settled in the United States, where he was still a resident in 1942.

Lichtenstein's paintings were exhibited in Lodz, Warsaw, Vilna, Paris and New York. His art depicts many moods, but mostly the piquant and the unusual. He had a deep sense of the pathetic, the grotesque and the humorous. Although Lichtenstein's influence has been many-faceted, he belongs to the Paris school

of painting. His critical essays on art (in Yiddish) have appeared in the *Zukunft, Shriftn, Onheib, Renesans* (London), and in *Literarishe Bletter.* His memoirs of the Jewish Legion in Palestine were published in *Haint* (Warsaw).

In 1941 he illustrated a pastoral by H. Gold, *A Moid Mit a Tzepl* (Girl With a Pigtail), thus reviving the Machmadim Farlag which from its very beginning in 1912 devoted its endeavors to the artistic illustration of Yiddish books. His *Jerusalem,* a portfolio of ten images, was issued by the same publishing house.

Lit.: Broderson, M., in *Literarishe Bletter,* No. 39; Jan-Topass, *Isaac Lichtenstein* (1928); Taylor, B. D., in *Manchester Guardian,* Jan. 14, 1924.

LICHTENSTEIN, JOY, insurance executive, b. San Francisco, 1874. He was educated at the University of California (1897-1901). From 1894 to 1906 he was assistant librarian at the San Francisco Public Library.

In 1906 he was general agent of the American Bonding Company of Baltimore. Later he became secretary of the Pacific Coast Casualty Company and then manager of the Globe Indemnity Company. He was soon recognized as one of the outstanding men in the insurance field of the West. He became vice-president of the Hartford Accident and Indemnity Company, Pacific Department (1924), and manager of the Hartford Fire Insurance Company, Pacific Department (1924); he still held both posts in 1942.

Lichtenstein was chairman of the Pacific coast committee of the National Board of Fire Underwriters, vice-chairman of the National Automobile Underwriters Association, and chairman of the department of public relations of the Board of Fire Underwriters of the Pacific. He was also consulting professor of insurance at Leland Stanford University.

LICHTENSTEIN, LEON, mathematician, b. Warsaw, Poland, 1878; d. Leipzig, Germany, 1933. He studied at the University of Berlin and became a lecturer at the Technical High School of Berlin-Charlottenburg in 1910, was appointed professor of mathematics at the University of Münster (1920) and ordinary professor at the University of Leipzig (1922), where he taught until his death in 1933. His special field of activity was astronomical mathematics. He published, among other works: *Astronomie und Mathematik in ihrer Wechselwirkung* (1921); *Mathematische Probleme in der Theorie der Figur der Himmelskörper* (1923); *Grundlagen der Hydromechanik* (1929). He edited the periodical *Mathematische Zeitschrift* from 1918 on, and the *Jahrbuch über die Fortschritte der Mathematik* from 1911 to 1927.

LICHTENSTEIN, MORRIS, rabbi and founder of the Jewish Science Movement, b. in a village near Memel, Lithuania, 1889; d. New York city, 1938. His parents had intended him for the rabbinate, and he began his studies at a very early age, attending the Yeshiva of Bialystok and receiving rabbinical ordination (Semichah) at the age of seventeen. However, instead of immediately following a rabbinical career, he decided to take up secular studies, and in 1907 came to the United States for that purpose. He resided first in Galveston, then in Minneapolis, where he attended the high school, and then continued his education at the University of Cincinnati and the

Morris Lichtenstein

Hebrew Union College (A.B., 1916; Rabbi, 1916). He subsequently received the M.A. degree from Columbia University.

From 1916 to 1922 Lichtenstein served as rabbi in congregations in New York state and at Athens, Ga. As early as his student years, however, he had been deeply grieved about the spread of the Christian Science movement among Jews, and noted that while Jewish leaders and rabbis had opposed it in words, no constructive effort had been made to deflect this tendency. He gave thought and time to the problem of launching a counter-movement, and in 1922 left his pulpit and went to New York city, where he organized the Society of Jewish Science. His earliest services were held in one of the rooms of the Young Women's Hebrew Association. The movement initiated by him grew from a mere handful to a large organization. After Lichtenstein's death the leadership was taken over by his wife, Tehilla Lichtenstein, a daughter of Rabbi Hayim Hirschensohn. Lichtenstein wrote a number of books dealing with Jewish Science, notably *Jewish Science and Health* (1925).

LICHTENSTEIN, WALTER, banker, b. Brunswick, Germany, 1880. He was brought to the United States at the age of two and was educated at New York University (Ph.B., 1899) and Harvard University (A.B., 1900; M.A., 1901; Ph.D., 1907).

Before he entered the banking business, Lichtenstein engaged in various literary pursuits. He was editor of the *New International Encyclopedia* (1902-3) and curator of the Hohenzollern collection at Harvard (1905-6; 1908-19). He was librarian and professor at Northwestern University (1908-19). In 1908 he translated into German Coolidge's *The United States as a World Power.* He was co-editor (1912) with Samuel Jackson of Zwingli's Latin and German works.

In 1918 Lichtenstein entered the service of the First National Bank of Chicago as foreign trade adviser; from 1921 to 1933 he was its executive secretary, and from 1933 on vice-president. He was secretary (1921-28) of the economic policy commission of the American Bankers Association. Lichtenstein placed his financial talents at the service of the government in 1926, when he became secretary of the national advisory council of the Federal Reserve System, a position which he still occupied in 1942. In 1929 he was general secretary of the organization committee for the Bank for International Settlements at Baden-Baden, Germany. He was an official delegate of the United States government at the telecommunication conference at Madrid, Spain, in 1932.

LICHTHEIM, LUDWIG, physician, b. Breslau, Germany, 1845; d. Bern, Switzerland, 1928. He studied at Breslau, Zurich and Berlin. In 1876 he became an instructor at the University of Breslau, after having served for several years as an assistant at the clinics for internal and surgical medicine of that city. Having embraced Christianity at an early stage of his life, he was promoted, in due recognition of his merit, to assistant professorship at Jena in 1877, to full professorship at Bern in 1878 and to full professorship at Königsberg in 1888, where he was also chief of the medical clinic. After his retirement in 1912 he lived at Bern.

Lichtheim published classical works on hydremia and hydremic oedema, and on the atelectasis of the lungs. Of great importance were his contributions to neurology on the various kinds of aphasia (the subcortical sensoric aphasia is called "Lichtheim's disease") and on tumors of the brain and of the spinal cord. He also published notable results of his investigations into paroxysmal tachycardia, progressive atrophy of the muscles and meningitis. He was co-founder of the *Deutsche Zeitschrift für Nervenheilkunde.*

LICHTHEIM, RICHARD, Zionist, b. Berlin, 1885. He studied at the Universities of Berlin and Freiburg. From 1911 to 1913 Lichtheim was editor of *Die Welt,* the Zionist central organ, in Berlin. In 1913 he was made diplomatic representative of the Zionist Organization in Constantinople, but returned later to Germany and from 1917 to 1920 was president of the German Zionist Federation. Lichtheim came to London in 1920, to serve as president of the organization department of the Zionist Executive. But three years later he joined Vladimir Jabotinsky's revisionist movement. He eventually returned to the World Zionist Organization. In 1939 he was made chief of the World Zionist office in Geneva, which post he still held in 1942.

LIDZBARSKI, MARK, philologist, b. Plock, Poland, 1868; d. Göttingen, Germany, 1928. He became instructor of oriental languages at the University of Kiel in 1896, associate professor at Greifswald in 1907 and associate professor in Göttingen in 1917. His field of scholarly work was the definition and collection of Semitic inscriptions of all kinds on monuments, tombstones, seals, weights, and the like; he also wrote several works on the origin of the Semitic script. All these subjects he treated comprehensively in his great work *Handbuch der nordsemitischen Epigraphik* (1898). He published a periodical, *Ephemeris,* dedicated to epigraphic investigations (vol. 1, 1900-2; vol. 2, 1903-7; vol. 3, 1909-15). He wrote also *Die Neuaramäischen Handschriften der Königlichen Bibliothek zu Berlin* (Weimar, 1896), and *Das Johannesbuch der Mandäer* (1905-15). His reminiscences were published in *Auf rauhem Wege* (1927). Lidzbarski was baptized.

LIEBEN, ADOLF, chemist, b. Prague, 1836; d. Vienna, 1914. When a young boy, he had Moritz

Hartmann for a private tutor. He studied chemistry at Vienna, Heidelberg and Paris. At Heidelberg he worked in the laboratory of Bunsen. He was professor of chemistry at the University of Palermo from 1862 on, in Turin from 1867 on, and in Prague after 1871. In 1875 he was appointed professor of general and pharmacological chemistry in Vienna.

He performed many important experiments, especially in the field of organic chemistry. From his investigations on the synthesis of alcohols, he obtained a series ranging from methyl alcohol to hexyl alcohol. The iodoform reaction for ethyl alcohol, used in urinalysis, goes by his name. Other research of his led to the discovery of chloro-acetals and dichloro-ethers, and to the determination of chelidonic acid. He also investigated the processes of plant assimilation. In addition to the published volumes *Über die Einwirkung schwacher Affinitäten auf Aldehyd* (1861); *Jodbenzol* (1869); and *Festes Benzolchlorid* (1875); he contributed scientific papers written by him in German, French and Italian, all of which languages he mastered, to the publications of the Academies of Vienna and Paris, of the German Chemical Society, of Berlin, and to *Gazetta Chimica Italiana*, of Palermo.

Lieben was a member of the Austrian Upper Chamber. In 1922 a monument was erected in his honor in the arcade of the University of Vienna.

RICHARD LIEBEN, a brother of Adolf Lieben, published, in collaboration with Rudolf Auspitz, *Über die Theorie des Preises* (1889), a disquisition on the theory of price which was translated into French and Japanese.

Lit.: "Dr. Adolf Lieben," *Nature,* vol. 93 (1914) 534.

LIEBEN, KOPPELMAN, communal leader and author, b. Prague, Bohemia, 1811; d. Prague, 1892. He was a member of the Jewish community board and of the Assembly of Notables in Prague. A great bibliophile, he accumulated a notable library which he willed to the Prague Jewish community. He was author of a book which contained one hundred brief biographies of prominent people (1890), and of *Gal Ed,* a work on the inscriptions of the Old Prague Israelite cemetery (1856).

LIEBEN, ROBERT VON, physicist and inventor, b. Vienna, 1878; d. Vienna, 1913. His father was knighted for services as vice-governor of the Austro-Hungarian state bank. He was a nephew of Adolf Lieben. He did not graduate from the secondary school (Realschule) which he attended at Vienna but, after some practical experience at the Siemens-Schuckert electrical plant at Nuremberg, Germany, he was a guest student at the University of Vienna. In 1899 he went to Göttingen, Germany, where he worked at the Institute for Physical Chemistry and was inspired to serious research by the great Walter Nernst.

At various periods of his life, Lieben operated a laboratory and a telephone plant of his own. He was interested in mechanics; his improved model of the Wright airplane was accepted by the Austro-Hungarian army. He constructed an electrolytical phonograph, and his research on the polarization of X-rays resulted in the granting of a patent on cathode rays for the amplifying of alternating currents in long distance telephone and wireless (1906). In 1910 he obtained

a patent for his standard invention, an archetype of the modern amplifying tube, with a grid inserted between the cathode and anode (Eugen Reisz and Siegmund Strauss co-inventors), which made possible modern radio technique, talking pictures and television.

Lieben died of cancer at the age of thirty-five. He had dissociated himself from the Jewish community and professed no religion. A commemorative tablet with his portrait in bas relief, inserted in the front wall of the Vienna radio building (RAVAG), was removed by the National Socialist regime after March, 1938. An Austrian stamp was issued in his memory, and the original model of his amplifying tube was in the Vienna Technical Museum.

Lit.: Poggendorff, J. C., *Biographisch-literarisches Handwörterbuch zur Geschichte der exacten Wissenschaften;* Bettelheim, A., *Neue Österreichische Biographie,* vol. 6; Hoffmannsthal, Hugo von, "Robert Lieben, Naturforscher und Erfinder," *Die prosaischen Schriften gesammelt,* vol. 3 (1920) 48; Nernst, W., "Zur Erinnerung an Robert von Lieben," *Telefunken Zeitung,* vol. 6 (1923).

LIEBEN, SOLOMON HUGO, historian, b. Prague, Bohemia, 1881. He taught religion in the Prague Mittelschule. In 1906 he founded the Prague Jewish Museum, of which he became the director. He devoted himself to the study of the history of the Jews in Prague, writing many books on the subject. His works include: *Handschriftliches zur Geschichte der Juden in Prag* (Frankfort, 2 vols.); *Rabbi Eleasar Fleckeles* (Frankfort); *Der hebräische Buchdruck in Prag im 16. Jahrhundert* (Prague, 1927); *David Oppenheim* (Frankfort, 1928); *Die Ramschakchronik* (Prague, 1929).

LIEBERMAN, CHAIM (HERMAN), Yiddish journalist, critic and essayist, b. Kolk, Volhynia, Russia, 1889. His early education was acquired at the Heder and at a progressive Hebrew school. In 1905 he emigrated to the United States, where he continued his education at the College of the City of New York (1907-10) and at Columbia College (B.A., 1926). He pursued graduate studies in literature, philosophy and psychology at Columbia University.

He was among the first to formulate the principles of the progressive Yiddish schools in the United States, especially in his books *Dos Problem fun der Yiddisher Dertziung in Amerike* (1914; revised ed., 1916); *Die Yiddishe Ertziung in Amerike* and *Die Yiddishe Religion in der Natzional-Radikaler Dertziung* (1915).

Lieberman was a founder of the Yiddish Teachers' Seminary and for many years on its teaching staff. His career as a journalist began in the *Yiddishes Tageblatt.* Later he wrote for the *Zeit,* official organ of the Poale Zion movement. In 1922 he visited Germany, where he devoted two years to the study of German philosophy and literature. There he published his first volume of literary essays, *Dichter un Veltn* (Poets and Worlds), which contains the first lengthy study ever written on Yehoash, also an attack upon Chaim Zhitlowsky's theory of "biological nationalism." This book reveals the most characteristic features of Lieberman's writing. His style of criticism is impressionistic: each analysis qualified by an intuitive appreciation of the work under study. His other critical works are: *Ernst Toller—Die Tragedie fun a Zuchndn Geist* (Ernst Toller—the Tragedy of a Searching Spirit; 1924);

Elias Lieberman

Literarishe Siluetn (1927); *Eugene O'Neill, an Amerikaner Dramaturg* (1930); *Biecher un Shreiber* (1933).

Upon his return to New York in 1924, Lieberman became a staff member of the *Forward*. In 1929 he left for a year's visit to Paris and Palestine. Because of the wide range of his interests and the fervor of his style, he was regarded as an outstanding Yiddish pamphleteer. Among his works of this genre are: *Sheidim in Moskve* (Devils in Moscow; 1937); *Chaim Zhitlowsky un S. Niger,—A Debate in Zeks Briev* (1937); *In Kampf far Yiddisher Dertziung* (1941). Some of his essays on current topics are lyric in quality, registering both protest and despair. Among these are: *In Tol fun Toit* (In the Valley of Death; 1938); *Oib Ich Vel Es Dir Fargesn, England* (If I Should Forget Thee, England; 1939). His essay on the history of Yiddish literature (in English) is included in *Great Literatures of Small Peoples* (Columbia University Courses of Literature; 1929). Lieberman's volume, *Fun die Tiefenishn* (Out of the Depths; 1942), is written in prose-poetry and describes the tragedy of the Jews since the Nazis' rise to power.   N. B. MINKOFF.

Lit.: Lieberman, H., *Die Shtimme fun Tol* (1940); Weinper, Z., *Portretn fun Yiddishe Shreiber*, vol. 1 (1933); Bickel, S., *In Sich un Arum Sich* (1936) 153-57; Zhitlowsky, Chaim, *Gezamlte Shriftn*, vol. 10.

LIEBERMAN, ELIAS, author and educator, b. St. Petersburg (Leningrad), Russia, 1883. He was brought to the United States in 1891, and was educated in New York city, receiving his A.B. degree from the College of the City of New York in 1903, his A.M. degree from New York University in 1906, and his Ph.D. degree from the same university in 1911. Lieberman entered the New York city school system as a teacher in 1903; in 1918 he became head of the department of English at Bushwick High School, and in 1924 he was made principal of Thomas Jefferson High School. In 1940 he was named associate superintendent of schools by the New York city Board of Education. During much of his active teaching career Lieberman also gave special courses in poetry appreciation and writing. From 1921 until 1940 he was a lecturer in poetry writing at the College of the City of New York, and from 1924 to 1933 he taught poetry appreciation at Hunter College and Brooklyn College.

Both his vocation and avocation, his work as educator and his work as author, must be considered in evaluating Lieberman's contribution to American life and letters. His chief concern as teacher and educational administrator was the humanizing of the pedagogic process. Thomas Jefferson High School, of which he was principal from 1924 to 1940, was a busy bee-hive of activity in which every one of the 7,500 students found a useful place and an individualized program of instruction. His own interest in writing led Lieberman to organize special courses for the training of gifted children in Creative Literary Expression. Again and again his students were the recipients of prizes, particularly for poetry, in New York city as well as in national contests. For many years in succession the school newspaper, *The Liberty Bell,* and the literary magazine, *The Jeffersonian,* were rated by the judges of the Columbia Interscholastic Press Contest either as medalists or first place winners. Training for social usefulness was the chief goal set for his school by Lieberman during his service as principal.

Lieberman's work as a poet falls into two classifications: poems in which he enunciates not only his own Americanism but the basic loyalty to American ideals of all foreign-born men and women; poems in which he appraises the passing scenes and the diverse characters of the city life he knows so well. His "I am an American," first published in *Everybody's Magazine* in 1916, and his "Credo" brought him national recognition. Both poems were widely anthologized, recited and included as poems for study in school curricula throughout the country. The first was also incorporated into the *Congressional Record* of pre-War proceedings. Much of his work in *Paved Streets* (1918); *Hand Organ Man* (1930); and *Man in the Shadows* (1939) falls into the second category. It plumbs the sorrows and uncovers the joys of ordinary living in a metropolitan environment. For him, as for all genuine poets, nothing is commonplace. Although Lieberman was prolific and versatile in the writing of short stories, magazine articles, editorials and plays as well, and although many of these productions received major recognition, it is by his best poetry that he deserves to be remembered. Among Lieberman's other work was *The Awakening of Narradin,* a play written in collaboration with Gustav Blum (1916), and *The Stranger,* a novel translated and adapted from the Yiddish of Perez Hirschbein. He also edited many textbooks on literature for school use. In 1917 and 1918 he was editor of *Puck;* from 1916 to 1932 he was literary editor of *The American Hebrew.* His interest in Jewish affairs has been felt largely in cultural spheres. He was responsible for the introduction of Hebrew into the curriculum of Thomas Jefferson High School.
                                    LIONEL HILL,

LIEBERMAN, HERMAN, lawyer, statesman, and labor leader, b. Drohobycz, Galicia, 1870; d. London, 1941. He graduated from the University of Cracow. From his earliest youth, Lieberman participated in the Polish independence and socialist movements. He became one of the prominent Polish lawyers and leader of the Socialist Party in Galicia. He represented the party in the Austrian Parliament, where he was considered one of the most gifted speakers. He was a member of the Polish Parliament from 1919 to 1930, and one of the authors of the Polish democratic constitution of 1921.

Following the coup d'état of Marshal Joseph Pilsudski in 1926, Lieberman became a leader of the parliamentary opposition against the regime. Together with other opposition leaders, Lieberman was arrested and incarcerated in the Brest-Litovsk fortress. After his release, he left the country and refused to return as long as Pilsudski or his followers were in power. After the Nazi occupation of Poland in 1939, Lieberman was appointed by the Polish government-in-exile to the Polish National Council, and soon after was elected its vice-president. Following the collapse of France in June, 1940, he went to London together with other Polish leaders.

Upon reorganization of the government-in-exile on September 4, 1941, Lieberman was appointed minister of justice. He was the first Jewish member of a Polish Cabinet. Throughout his life Lieberman identified himself with the Polish independence and socialist movements, and took little if any interest in Jewish affairs. Indeed, for some time prior to his death, he seemed inclined toward Catholicism. In one of his last articles, he advocated a synthesis between socialism and Christianity.   SIMON SEGAL.

Lit.: Ilustrowana Encyklopedja Trzaski, vol. 3; *New York Times,* Oct. 22, 1941; *Robotnik Polski* (New York), Oct. 26, 1941; *Who's Who of the Allied Governments* (edit. Joel Cang, London, 1941).

LIEBERMAN, SAUL, Hebraist, b. Motili, near Pinsk, Russia, 1898. He studied at the Yeshiva of Slobodka and at the University of Kiev. For a while he was a student of medicine. He left Russia for Palestine after the first World War and continued his studies at the Hebrew University (M.A., 1932). He lectured on the Talmud at the Hebrew University until 1935, when he was appointed Dean of the Harry Fischel Institute for Talmudic Studies in Jerusalem.

Lieberman came to the United States in 1940 as a visiting professor at the Jewish Theological Seminary of America. In 1941 he was awarded the honorary degree of Doctor of Hebrew Letters by the seminary and was appointed professor of Palestinian Literature and Institutions. His published works include: *Talmudah Shel Keserin* (1931; Talmud of Caesarea); a commentary on the Palestinian Talmud based on its literal meaning (*Hayerushalmi Kifeshuto,* 1935); an edition of Moses Samuel Zukermandel's edition of the Tosefta (1937); a new edition of *Midrash Deuteronomy* (*Debarim Rabbah,* 1940) based on the Oxford manuscript, a version current among the medieval Jewish schools in Spain and quite unlike the texts of other editions. In 1939 Lieberman published *Shekiin,* in which he recovered long forgotten Jewish legends and traditions from Karaite and non-Jewish and anti-Jewish

Carl Liebermann

works in Greek and Latin by the Church Fathers, and in 1942, *Greek in Jewish Palestine,* a study of the use of Greek in the Palestinian Talmud and the Palestinian Midrashim and of the influence of Hellenistic thought, including a discussion of Greek and Latin proverbs in rabbinic literature.

LIEBERMANN, CARL, chemist, b. Berlin, 1842; d. Berlin, 1914. He was the son of the textile manufacturer Benjamin Liebermann. Together with Graebe, he made a study of alizarin and determined its constitution. Shortly thereafter (1869) he succeeded in the synthesis of alizarin from anthracene, through which the first natural dye was artificially produced. In 1869 Liebermann became an instructor in the Industrial Academy and at the University of Berlin. Upon the departure of Baeyer, Liebermann became his successor as professor at the Industrial Academy, which was changed in 1884 into the Technical School. He also devoted himself further to the investigation of dyes and of naphthalene and of alkaloids, and similar researches.

Lit.: Berichte der Deutschen Chemischen Gesellschaft, vol. 48, p. 4; vol. 51, p. 1135; Festschrift for the celebration of the fiftieth anniversary of the Deutsche Chemische Gesellschaft (1918) 96.

LIEBERMANN, CHARLES H., physician and surgeon, b. Riga, Latvia (then Russia), 1813; d. Washington, D. C., 1886. His father was a military surgeon. He studied at the Universities of Dorpat and Berlin (M.D., 1838). He came to the United States in 1840 and settled in Washington. In that year he performed the first operation for strabismus in the United States. He became a leading oculist and was one of the founders of the medical department of the University of Georgetown. He was professor of surgery there from 1849 to 1853 and again from 1857 to 1861; in 1861 he was elected professor emeritus. He was president of the Medical Society of the District of Columbia (1865-68). Liebermann was called in when Abraham Lincoln was dying and was one of the nine doctors at his deathbed. His portrait is among those in Alonzo Chappel's painting, *The Last Hours of Lincoln* (1867).

Liebermann did not belong to any Jewish organization and it is not certain that he was a Jew. However, according to Isaac Markens ("Lincoln and the Jews," *Publications of the American Jewish Historical Society*, No. 17, 1909, p. 150), neighbors of Liebermann in Washington were "of the impression that he was a Jew."

LIEBERMANN, FELIX, historian, brother of Max, b. Berlin, 1851; d. Berlin, 1925. Liebermann entered, in 1869, a banking house at Berlin, and in 1870 he went to Manchester, England, representing a German exporting firm. In 1872 he returned to Germany, and began to study history at the University of Göttingen, from which he was graduated in 1875. From 1882 to 1888 Liebermann was an esteemed collaborator on the *Monumenta Germaniae Historica;* then he was charged by the Bavarian Academy of Sciences with the edition of the sources of Anglo-Saxon law. Liebermann's edition of *Die Gesetze der Angelsachsen* (3 vols., 1898-1916) laid new and firmer foundations for the study of the earliest English jurisprudence. Maitland acknowledged that "no foreign scholar rendered more substantial service to the study of Anglo-Saxon law and history."

In 1900, the Jewish Historical Society of England published Liebermann's study on *King Alfred and the Mosaic Law*. During the first World War, Liebermann courageously opposed German professors who deprecated England and its historical tradition. In 1920 he published a study, *Beowulf,* which broached a new theory as to the origin of that poem. Liebermann never received an official appointment. But Cambridge gave him an honorary doctorate in 1896, and Oxford in 1909. He was a member of the academies of Munich, Göttingen and London, and of the Royal Historical Society. He was also curator of the Zunz-Stiftung and of the Auerbach'sche Waisenhaus in Berlin.

LIEBERMANN, LEÓ, DE SZENTLŐRINC, biochemist and educator, b. Debrecen, Hungary, 1852; d. Budapest, 1926. He studied at the University of Vienna, and became adjunct professor of medical chemistry at the University of Innsbruck, Austria, in 1875. In 1878 he lectured on chemistry and subsequently on legal medicine and criminal chemistry at the University of Budapest. He organized the state's experimental laboratory of chemistry. In 1902 he was appointed full professor of public hygiene at the University of Budapest; in 1908 he was made dean of the medical faculty. Other honors bestowed on him for opening new branches of science were Hungarian nobility, in 1908, and the title of royal court councillor. Liebermann embraced Christianity. He published works on general and bio-chemistry, on the chemistry of hygiene and of legal medicine.

Leó Liebermann, Jr., de Szentlőring, his son (b. Budapest, 1882; d. Budapest, 1938), was an oculist. In 1914 he became assistant professor, in 1924 associate professor, of ophthalmology at the University of Budapest. He was also oculist-in-chief at the municipal hospital, president of the Association of Hungarian Ophthalmologists from 1928 to 1932, and a member of the National Board of Health of Hungary. In 1930 he received the title of health councillor-in-chief. Brought up in the Christian faith, Liebermann was driven to suicide in December, 1938, by a feeling of shame and humiliation over the Nuremberg-inspired anti-Jewish bill then before the Hungarian Lower Chamber.

Tódor Liebermann de Szentlőring, otologist, (b. Budapest, 1891), was an army surgeon in the first World War and, after serving in university clinics of otology at Budapest and at Pécs, Hungary, he was physician-in-chief of otology in two municipal hospitals in the Hungarian capital. He published, in addition to several contributions to journals of otology, a volume on the pathology and therapy of ear, nose and throat diseases. He was brought up in the Christian faith.

LIEBERMANN, MAX, painter and etcher, b. Berlin, 1847; d. Berlin, 1935. Although the son of a well-to-do cotton merchant, he chose painting as his career. He studied first in Berlin, and in 1869 went to Weimar to work under Ferdinand Pauwel. While here he painted *Women Plucking Geese,* one of his great paintings. Liebermann came to Paris in 1873, and two years later made his first visit to Holland, to which he returned many times. From 1878 to 1884 he lived mostly in Munich, and after that in Berlin, where he became a professor in the Prussian Academy of Art in 1898.

The position held by Liebermann in Germany up to the time of his death was not unlike that of Sargent in England and America. No one contested his supremacy as the leading German Impressionist, and even after he resigned (1933) his honorary presidency of the Prussian Academy of Arts as a protest against the Nazi regime, one of his brilliant self-portraits hung in a place of honor at the Art Museum of Hamburg.

Karl Steffeck, his first teacher in Berlin, kept preaching the doctrine "Draw what you see," and Liebermann was a realist from the very start. The walls of his villa on the shore of the Wannsee were lined with the work of Menzel and Degas, two great realists whom he idolized. When Liebermann was on the threshold of his career, it was the custom of German painters to spend a great deal of time in Italy, but after only a cursory glance at the country, he realized that its romance and traditions had little significance for him. For a number of years he showed regularly at the Paris Salon, and he was the first German to win official recognition in Paris after the Franco-Prussian War. Munkácsy, the celebrated Hungarian painter, who was his companion in France, introduced him to the revolutionary leaders of the Parisian world of art, and in Holland he fell under the influence of his coreligionist, Jozef Israels. Very soon he followed the example of his Dutch friend and began to translate the lives of the humble onto his canvases with rare sensibility.

Liebermann, however (unlike Israels, Millet and Meunier), made no effort to arouse sympathy for the patient laboring classes. He was a seeker after simple truth, and there was already an austere accent in his early canvases, depicting scenes in the Jewish hospitals of Amsterdam and its ghetto. His uncompromising vision reported what he saw without any sentimentality. Nor was he seeking novelty. He once

Max Liebermann

said, "If while studying nature, you deliberately look for something merely new, you may find something which the world will hail as original, but you will not find *originality*, which is the hallmark of genius." The curse of 20th cent. artistic life and a sad commentary on its artistic poverty is this mad search for mere superficial novelty. Genuine novelty in art is nothing more than a profound new artist on the horizon, revealing his reactions and his hitherto unknown soul. In accordance with such doctrines, Liebermann strove to express himself with authority, simplicity and clarity. He was in full sympathy with the French Impressionists who were just coming into their own, and when he returned to Germany his works almost created a scandal. Munich had no patience with a man who claimed to be an artist, and who was nevertheless interested in ignoble subjects like peasants working in potato fields, or wrinkled old women watching their goats. Liebermann ignored such academic points of view. The independence of Manet and Courbet and the experiments of Monet and Pissarro had fired his enthusiasm, and his published monographs on Degas (1922) and Israels are not only tributes to the artists he discusses but apologias and explanations of his own art.

Despite similarity between his subject matter and that of other artists of his time, it must not be supposed that he was guilty of imitation. All these men had submitted to careful academic training and they arrived at their uncanny precision and style only after long experience and diligent practice. When, in 1884, Liebermann took up residence in Berlin, he opened the windows of the dingy Academy and let in fresh air and sunlight. He replaced German pseudo-Gothic and romanticism with real nationalism and a German "école du plein air." He had little use for the old Prussian discipline, and as a substitute he introduced spontaneity and impressionism. He despised modish-

ness, and even if he respected a new fashionable figure like Cézanne, he warned the student that it was silly to convert the Grünewald into a Provençal forest.

Liebermann's own fluid, nervous technique, peculiarly suited to dry points and lithographs, became a standard of excellence, and his long gallery of portraits of contemporaries like Richard Strauss, Rudolf Virchow, von Hindenburg, Georg Brandes, Gerhart Hauptmann and Warburg are notable for their realistic vigor and almost brutal clearness.

As president of the Academy Liebermann became the artistic symbol of his beloved Berlin with all its intelligence, and no act the Nazis committed can remove him from one of the high pedestals of German art. His presidency of the Academy was achieved only in 1920. Before the first World War, Kaiser Wilhelm II had vetoed even Liebermann's election to the Berlin Academy. He retained his presidency of the Prussian Academy until 1928, at which time he was made honorary president. Liebermann had also been awarded the Gold Medal of Prussia for his services to art, and von Hindenburg granted him the eagle plaque, the highest civil decoration offered by republican Germany.

Among Liebermann's best known paintings were *The Old Men's Home in Amsterdam*, which won the gold medal at the Paris Salon of 1881; *The Courtyard of the Orphanage in Amsterdam; Cobbler Shop* (1882); *Dutch Orphan Girls* (1887); *Flax Spinners* (1889); *Women With Goats* (1892). A memorial exhibition of his work was held in the Jüdisches Museum in Berlin in 1936. Another memorial exhibition was held in New York City in 1940.   MARTIN BIRNBAUM.

Lit.: Huneker, James Gibbons, *Ivory Apes and Peacocks* (1915) 173-87; Hancke, Erich, *Max Liebermann, sein Leben und seine Werke* (1914); Friedländer, Max J., *Max Liebermann* (1924); Galliner, Arthur, *Max Liebermann, der Künstler und Führer* (1927); Ostwald, Hans Otto, *Das Liebermann Buch* (1930); *Menorah*, vol. 5 (1927) 441-72.

LIEBERT, ARTHUR (originally, **Levy**), philosopher, b. Berlin 1878. In 1910 he became secretary of the Kant-Gesellschaft, which he directed until 1933. In 1915 Liebert became lecturer at the commercial academy of Berlin and in 1925 lecturer at the University of Berlin. When the Nazis came into power, Liebert became professor at the University of Belgrade, but in 1938 the government of Yugoslavia was forced by Nazi pressure to dismiss Liebert, who went to England. From 1937 Liebert edited the annual *Philosophia*.

Liebert first followed Neo-Kantianism and Hermann Cohen's philosophical position, but later tried to combine the Kantian point of view with those of Plato and Hegel. He remained, however, an ardent defender of idealism. Among the numerous works which Liebert published, the most important are: *Das Problem der Geltung* (1914); *Die geistige Krise der Gegenwart* (1923); *Geist und Welt der Dialektik* (1929); *Erkenntnistheorie* (1932); *Die Krise des Idealismus* (1936); *Liberalismus* (1938). According to Liebert, idealism involves individual freedom, criticism of life, evaluating interpretation of reality, synthetical, systematic and universal spirit. He also stresses the connection between the cultural crisis of the present age and the lack of clearness and ethical foundation in modern philosophy.

LIEBLING, GEORG, pianist and teacher, b. Berlin, 1865. He studied the piano with Kullak and Franz

Liszt, and composition with Urban and Dorn. After many highly successful concert tours of Europe, he was appointed court pianist to the Duke of Coburg (1890). He founded his own music school in Berlin in 1894, and from 1898 to 1908 was professor of the piano at the Guildhall School of Music in London. After 1908, he directed his own music school in Munich. In 1931 he received an honorary musical doctorate from the University of Southern California. His *Great Mass* was performed in Los Angeles in 1931. He composed also several operas, two violin concertos, *Concerto Eroico* for piano and orchestra, several symphonic suites, symphonic poems, and various works for piano and chamber music ensembles. In 1942 he lived in retirement in Hollywood, Cal.

Lit.: Braun, G., *Hofpianist G. Liebling* (1896).

LIEBMANN, JOST or **JOBST (Jodocus)**, court jeweler of the Great Elector of Brandenburg and of his son Frederick III (King Frederick I of Prussia), b. Göttingen, 1640; d. Berlin, 1702. Liebmann, who had no money, was sent by his relatives to Danzig to buy for their account cheap pearls of a special kind to be used for women's robes. He thus acquired knowledge of jewelry and a fortune of 800 or 900 thalers. He then resided at Hannover, Halberstadt and Hildesheim, where he was the partner of Hayim von Hameln, husband of Glückel von Hameln. Meanwhile, Liebmann became engaged to Esther Schulhof, widow of Aaron Israel of Königsberg, who had been the Great Elector's court Jew and died after his bankruptcy. In 1677 Esther provided Liebmann with a letter of safeconduct for Berlin, and Liebmann married her.

Esther Liebmann is said to have been a beautiful, intelligent and ambitious woman who was an intimate friend of the Great Elector's son Frederick. Warned by her first husband's ruin, she did not allow Liebmann to become a court Jew and to conduct daring transactions. She insisted that Liebmann confine his activity to the jewelry business, and, owing to her influence, Liebmann was appointed court jeweler in 1678. Liebmann provided the Great Elector with presents for

princes and ambassadors which were used as political gifts and bribes at that time. Some of Liebmann's jeweler's works became far-famed. In 1684, Liebmann was exempted from the Leibzoll (body-tax) and from all the other customs.

The Great Elector did his utmost to facilitate Liebmann's business matters. He paid Liebmann mainly with the receipts from the taxes paid by the Jews of Brandenburg. At the end of the Great Elector's reign, almost all Jewish tax-receipts came into Liebmann's cash-box. Liebmann became the wealthiest man in Berlin, and gained an esteemed and favorable position.

The Great Elector, notwithstanding the opposition of his diet, granted Liebmann the privilege of opening a private synagogue, the Liebmann Schul, in 1684. Liebmann also was authorized to interfere with Jewish affairs everywhere in Brandenburg. He utilized his influence for installing his relatives in the office of rabbi or elders of several Jewish communities. He appointed his son-in-law, Aaron Benjamin Wolf, rabbi of his private synagogue, and his sons Isaac and Jost Liebmann, Jr., elders of the Jewish community of Berlin. Liebmann successfully supported the petition of the Jews of Cleves for the repeal of the increase of their taxes.

Under the reign of the Great Elector's successor Frederick, Liebmann's position and influence increased even more. Liebmann had lent to Frederick before his father's death more than 50,000 thalers. He lent him more than 200,000 thalers during the following years. The receipts from taxes paid by Jews became inadequate to meet Frederick's indebtedness to Liebmann. In 1699, Liebmann offered to support a quarter of all poor newcomers in Berlin, mainly Jews. Liebmann therefore was exempted from all local taxes.

Although Liebmann's wife prevented him from engaging in the banking business, she obtained for herself, in 1700, the privilege of coining money. After Liebmann's death, his widow entered into a fierce conflict with Marcus Magnus, the confidant of the crown prince, later King Frederick William I. Their quarrel divided the Jewish community of Berlin. Esther Liebmann was the chief of the partisans of the reigning king; her adversaries put their trust in his successor. For years, Esther Liebmann bitterly opposed the new community synagogue planned for Berlin by Marcus Magnus, but a public synagogue was built in 1712.

After the death of King Frederick, his successor, Frederick William I, arrested Esther Liebmann, in 1713, accusing her of having abused his father's "passion." The inquiry was ended after ten weeks. Esther Liebmann sacrificed three tons of gold (300,000 thalers) and she was graciously rehabilitated. She remained a very wealthy woman. But she was hurt by the change of affairs, and died in 1714.

Her son, Jost Liebmann Jr., protected by King Frederick William I, had large business dealings. He was an enemy of Veitel Heine Ephraim, and died in 1747. The composer Giacomo Meyerbeer and his brothers, the poets Michael and Wilhelm Beer, are among Jost Liebmann's descendants.

Hugo Bieber.

Lit.: Geiger, Ludwig, *Geschichte der Juden in Berlin* (1876); Stern, Selma, *Der preussische Staat und die Juden* (1925); Rachel and Wallisch, *Berliner Grosskaufleute und Kapitalisten*, vol. 2 (1938).

Georg Liebling

LIEBMANN, OTTO, philosopher, b. Loewenberg, Silesia, 1840; d. Jena, Germany, 1912. He was lecturer at the University of Tübingen in 1865, professor at the University of Strasbourg in 1872, and at the University of Jena from 1882 on. During the Franco-Prussian War (1870), Liebmann was in the German army which beleaguered Paris, and he published anonymously *Vier Monate vor Paris* (1871), expressing strongly patriotic sentiments.

Liebmann was one of the main initiators of Neo-Kantianism in German philosophy. Publishing *Zurück zu Kant* (1865), he combatted post-Kantian metaphysics just as vigorously as empiricism, sensualism and materialism. In *Analysis der Wirklichkeit* (1896), he endeavored to demonstrate the dependence of empirical sciences upon non-empirical foundations. He developed his views in *Gedanken und Tatsachen* (1882-1904) and in several special monographs, particularly in *Die Klimax der Theorien*. According to Liebmann, philosophy is no mere science, or theory, but an ethical tendency to elevate life. The special aim of Liebmann's philosophical works is to reconcile mechanistic and teleological points of view. He was fond of expressing philosophical thoughts in poetic form. His poems were collected (1899) under the title *Weltwanderung*.

Lit.: Kant-Studien (1912).

LIEBMANN, PINCHAS, painter, b. Schwerin, Germany, 1777; d. Hamburg, Germany, 1832. He attended the Art Academy of Copenhagen from 1797 to 1805, was awarded two silver medals in 1807 and 1809, and a golden one in 1816, and settled in that city as a miniaturist. In 1822 he moved to Gothenburg, Sweden, where he executed some oil portraits of Jewish merchants. Two years later he went to Hamburg, his last residence. His miniature portrait of J. G. Wingvist, stamp-office chief, is in the Gothenburg Museum.

Lit.: Lemberger, E., Die Bildnisminiatur in Skandinavien, vol. 2 (1912) 116, 120, 172.

LIEBREICH, OSCAR MATTHIAS EUGEN, pharmacologist, b. Königsberg, Germany, 1839; d. Berlin, 1908. He was a younger brother of Richard Liebreich. In 1869 instructor, in 1872 professor and director of the Institute of Pharmacology at the University of Berlin, he discovered the narcotic effect of chloral hydrate; he also introduced the use of butyl chloral hydrate and ethyl chloride as anesthetics, and that of strychnine as an antidote to chloral hydrate. Investigating the chemical substance of the brain, he established the presence of protagon. He determined that neurin was distinct from cholin, and thoroughly investigated the effects of the former in addition to those of cresol, formaldehyde and methyl violet. He discovered the healing effects of lanolin and obtained lanolin paste from sheep wool, also introduced the use of platiniridium cannulas for the hypodermic syringe. The scope of his research embraced pure chemistry, pharmacology, hygiene and balneology.

From 1887 on, Liebreich edited *Therapeutische Monatsblätter*. He published *Medizinisches Rezepttaschenbuch* (Langgard, co-author, 1884) and *Enzyklopädie der Therapie* (1895). He founded the Balneologische Gesellschaft. In 1891 he was named Geheimer Medizinalrat. Liebreich accepted the Christian faith.

Oscar Liebreich

Lit.: Berichte der Deutschen Chemischen Gesellschaft, vol. 41, p. 4801; *Jahrbuch der Chemie,* vol. 18 (1908) 121; *Jahrbuch der organischen Chemie,* vol. 2 (1908) 421.

LIEBREICH, RICHARD, ophthalmologist, brother of Oscar, b. Königsberg, Germany, 1830; d. Paris, 1917. He lived in the classical age of ophthalmology, to which he made significant contributions. Beginning his career as an assistant to Donders and Graefe, he left Berlin in 1862 and established himself in Paris, where he presented scientific papers to the International Congresses of Ophthalmology in 1862 and 1867. From 1870 on he lived in London, where he became a lecturer and clinicist at St. Thomas Hospital. He gave up much of his private practice in 1895, and devoted himself to the study of classic art.

Liebreich worked mainly on anomalies of accommodation and refraction, on the hygiene of eyes of school children, and on squint and cataract operations, and constructed an ophthalmoscope which is still widely used today. He also published the first atlas of ophthalmoscopy (1863; 3rd ed., 1885).

LIEFMANN, ROBERT, economist, b. Hamburg, Germany, 1878. He was lecturer at the University of Giessen (1900), and became professor at Freiburg in 1904, retiring in 1933. Liefmann proceeded from a thorough examination of great industrial and financial enterprises, especially their combinations, conventions and trusts. His standard work, *Kartelle, Konzerne und Trusts* (1905; 8th ed., 1930), was translated into English in 1932. He dealt with holding companies in *Beteiligungs- und Finanzierungsgesellschaften* (1909; 4th ed., 1923), and summarized his experiences in *Die Unternehmungsformen* in 1912.

Subsequently Liefmann devoted himself to the founding of a new general theory of economics which he explained in *Grundsätze der Volkswirtschaftslehre* (1917-20). Charging his predecessors with having confounded production with economics, Liefmann stressed mainly the problems of trade and price. As for the theory of price and value, he was opposed to the classical economists as well as to Karl Marx. In 1924 Liefmann pub-

Heinz Liepmann

land, particularly in the case of the Emek, which—as he foresaw—would determine land values in Palestine. With Julius Simon and Robert Szold, he submitted a report, in 1920, which urged that the funds of the Jewish National Fund and the Palestine Foundation Fund be used entirely for colonization and settlement, leaving social and cultural activities to the Palestine population itself. Because his program of land acquisition was not adopted, de Lieme resigned from his executive posts in the World Zionist Organization, but remained within the ranks of the movement itself. His final break with the movement came in 1938, in protest against the acceptance by the Zionist Congress of the partition of Palestine as a principle.

Lit.: Report of the Reorganization Commission (1921); *Minutes of the Twelfth Zionist Congress*; Sokolow, Nahum, *History of Zionism*, vol. 2 (1919) 49; Schloessinger, Max, "A Tribute to Nehemia de Lieme," *New Palestine*, July 18, 1941, pp. 10-11.

LIEPMANN, HEINZ, author, b. Hamburg, Germany, 1905. He was educated at the Universities of Hamburg and Frankfort and in Paris. Liepmann first came to the United States in 1920, as a stowaway. Later, however, he returned for longer stays, and in 1937, following an escape from a Nazi concentration camp in Germany, he came to the United States to settle. His *Wanderers in the Mist* won the Harper prize in 1930 as the best European novel of the year. Among his other books were *Murder Made in Germany* (1934); *Nights of an Old Child*, autobiographical sketches not originally intended for publication (1937); and *Poison in the Air* (1938). In 1942 Liepmann was living and writing in the United States.

LIEPMANN, HUGO, psychiatrist and neurologist, b. Berlin, 1863; d. Berlin, 1925. His original study was philosophy, but he soon found himself more interested in the infant science of psychology. In 1911 he became instructor and in 1918 professor at the University of Berlin, a post he held until his death. In 1919 he was awarded the title of honorary professor. From 1911 to 1919 he was director of the lunatic asylum at Herzberg.

Liepmann was a pioneer in the investigation of the physical bases of psychic states. His most important research was on the inequality of the two halves of the brain and its effects on deaf-muteness. He also studied the mechanism of the inferiority complex. He was the author of *Über Ideenflucht* (1904); *Über Störungen des Apraxiegebietes* (1905); and *Drei Aufsätze aus dem Apraxiegebiet* (1908). He wrote also numerous articles on brain anatomy, psychopathology and related subjects for medical journals.

Lit.: Biographisches Lexikon hervorragender Ärzte, vol. 2, p. 915.

LIEPMANN, MORITZ, criminologist, b. Danzig, East Prussia, 1869; d. Hamburg, Germany, 1928. Liepmann was baptized in his early youth. He was educated at the Universities of Jena (LL.B., 1891) and Halle (Ph.D., 1896). In 1897 he became an instructor in criminal law at the University of Halle.

From 1910 to 1919 Liepmann was professor at the University of Kiel, in 1919 at the University of Hamburg, and also a judge of the latter city; he held both positions until his death. He was actively interested in reforming the methods of punishing and rehabilitating

lished *Geschichte und Kritik des Sozialismus*, asserting that Marx was no "critic" of political economics but relied upon Ricardo. Liefmann likewise disputed Marx's conception of capital. Liefmann's views aroused heated controversy among most of the important German economists. But many of his original adversaries ultimately adopted, avowedly or tacitly, with more or less modification, some of Liefmann's major ideas.

Liefmann also contributed to the history of American settlement in the 17th and 18th centuries by his study on *Die kommunistischen Gemeinden in Nordamerika* (1922).

Lit.: Klug, Oskar, *Robert Liefmanns Gesetz des Ausgleichs der Grenzerträge* (1929); Schaefer, Georg, *Robert Liefmanns Begriff des Ertrages* (1933).

LIEME, NEHEMIA DE, Zionist leader, b. The Hague, Holland, 1882; d. The Hague, 1940. Although possessing little formal education, de Lieme learned the banking business, and at the age of twenty-two founded the Workmen's Insurance Bank in The Hague. He was managing director of this bank until his death.

De Lieme became a Zionist at the time of the Eighth Zionist Congress, held at The Hague in 1907. In 1909 he became president of the Dutch Zionist Federation, and was many times reelected. His first association with the Jewish National Fund, which was thereafter to hold his main interest, was during the first World War, when he became a member of its executive committee. In 1919 the main office of the Fund was moved to The Hague, and de Lieme was made its director.

Specializing in land problems, de Lieme became an advocate of the acquisition of large tracts of land in Palestine, both for agricultural and urban settlement. He fought, however, against paying high prices for criminals, and he was a leader in the movement for the abolition of the death penalty.

His books include: *Einleitung in das Strafrecht* (1900); *Reform des deutschen Strafrechts* (1921); *Kommunistenprozesse* (1928).

LIFE (Hebrew, *hayim*). Life is regarded by the Bible as coming directly from God. It was He Who breathed life into the clay of the first man, and Who creates all living things on earth. In this way the Bible expresses its belief that life is holy and divine, and is granted to man as a favor from God. Hence long life is considered often to be a reward for the proper fulfillment of God's commandments, as in the Fifth Commandment, where it is the reward for the honoring of parents. Again, the choice between good and evil is described as the choice between life and death (*Deut.* 30:19). Life is good and desirable; accordingly, in most of the passages of the Bible it is felt that the wicked will be punished by an untimely death. Only in a few passages, as in *Ecclesiastes* and *Job,* is there the idea that life may carry misfortunes that are unrelated to good or evil conduct.

The rabbinical view of life is not uniform. There is less of the joyous optimism of the Bible, and more of a considered pessimism. According to *Erub.* 13b, the rabbis definitely debated whether it was better or not never to have been born. Life is described as fleeting, full of unfulfilled wishes, and but the antechamber of the life of the soul. Yet there is no conscious rejection of life on earth, as appeared among some ascetic sects. Life is still desirable, still valuable; accordingly, the preservation of life is still the most important of considerations. The Sabbath law may be broken if danger of life is involved; save for the three cardinal sins of idolatry, murder and immorality, offenses against the law are regarded as venial if they are necessary to preserve one's life.

The attitude of the Jews of the Middle Ages toward life was conditioned by their environment. In times of persecution, they sought to flee earthly life, and directed their religious practice toward bringing about the future salvation and the better life of the world to come. This otherworldliness disappeared in better times; and as the situation of the Jews began to improve in the 18th cent., there was a return to the Biblical joy in life, which expressed itself in the cultural reawakening of the Jews.

See also: DANGER TO LIFE; OPTIMISM.

LIFE OF ADAM AND EVE, *see* ADAM, BOOKS OF.

LIFSCHITZ, MALKAH (pseudonym, Esther; known also as Frumkin, from the name of her first husband), Yiddish writer, b. Minsk, Russia, 1880. In 1901 she became a member of the "Bund," in which she wielded strong influence after the Russian Revolution of 1905. She participated in the so-called language-war between Hebrew and Yiddish, and was an outstanding champion of Yiddishism. After having been repeatedly arrested, she was exiled to Siberia during the first World War until 1917. At first she allied herself with the Mensheviki, but in 1919 joined the Communists, and was active in the liquidation of the "Bund" in Russia. In 1942 she was one of the leading Jewish Communists of Russia, and a member of the editorial staff of the Yiddish Communist organ, the *Emes,* and of the

editorial group which was then issuing the works of Lenin in Yiddish.

LIFSHITZ, JOSHUA MORDECAI (YESHUE MORDCHE), Yiddish lexicographer, b. probably Berdichev, Russia, 1822 (or 1824); d. Berdichev, 1878. Although his early education was traditional and Orthodox, he acquired a thorough secular education in Vienna, where he studied mathematics, physics and chemistry. From Vienna he transferred his laboratory equipment to Berdichev and, according to one version, he was blinded for a year as the result of an unsuccessful experiment which he carried on in his Berdichev laboratory.

Notwithstanding his knowledge of Hebrew, Russian, German and French, his ardent democratic spirit and the influence of the social ideas of the folkists (Narodniki) provoked his bitter opposition to those Maskilim who were protagonists either of Hebrew or of Russian. It was Lifshitz's firm conviction that Yiddish must be accepted as the only vehicle by which the Jewish masses can be reached and educated. Thus he made vain attempts to obtain permission from the czarist government for the publication of a newspaper in Yiddish.

His essay, "Die Fier Klassn," published in *Kol-Mevassar,* Nos. 21-23 (1862) and in *Die Daitch-Yiddishe Brik,* No. 31 (1867), set forth the basic principles of the modern Yiddishist cultural movement, which came into being some fifty years later. Thus he has earned the name father of modern Yiddishism. Furthermore, he is credited by some as having influenced Mendele Mocher Sforim to abandon writing in Hebrew and to turn to Yiddish. It was through Lifshitz's initiative as well that the Yiddish daily, *Kol-Mevasser* (edited by Tzederboim), came into being in 1862. This newspaper ushered in a new era in the Yiddish press and literature. In No. 9 of this daily, Lifshitz published a rhymed dialogue, which was called "Yudl un Yehudis," denoting the Jewish people and their language: Yiddish. The ideas expounded in this dialogue, as well as in "Die Fier Klassn," were then considered very daring, almost revolutionary, for he defined Yiddish as the mother tongue and declared it to be the only means of teaching the people. Defying those who would Hebraize, Germanize, Russify, or Polonize the masses, he accused the Maskilim of maintaining a superficial attitude toward culture and concluded that the only means left for "humanizing the Jews" was Yiddish.

Lifshitz did not content himself with propagandizing his ideas of Yiddish, but sought as well to broaden the scope of the language in order that it might become the suitable bridge between the European and Jewish cultures. With this practical aim in view, he compiled a German-Yiddish dictionary (completed in 1867, but never published); a Russian-Yiddish dictionary (published in 1869); and a Yiddish-Russian dictionary (1876). These dictionaries continue to be regarded as source books for Yiddish lexicography and linguistics. They include an almost complete vocabulary of Volhynian Yiddish; the author has noted (in the Russian-Yiddish dictionary) the gender of each noun and introduced the first system of Yiddish phonetical spelling.

Lifshitz published also a series of popular scientific

articles, written in dialogue form: *Dos Falgezetz* (The Law of Gravity), *Vie der Roich Kimt Ahin* (What Becomes of Smoke; 1864); *Chmare un Pare* (Clouds and Vapor); *Geld* (Money; 1869).

He was one of the first Jewish socialists and the central figure of the early socialist circles in Berdichev. His hatred of the czarist government is expressed in a satire, *Die Hintishe Komedie.*   N. B. MINKOFF.

Lit.: Reisen, Z., in *Bicher-Velt*, No. 1-2 (1923); idem, in *Grammatik fun der Yiddisher Shprach*, vol. 1, pp. 119-23; Berkowitch, M., in *Zukunft*, June, 1924; Kahan, A., in *Zeitschrift*, vol. 1 (1926) 255-56; Shtif, N., in *Literarishe Bletter*, Aug. 17 and 24, 1928.

LIGETI, MIKLÓS, sculptor, b. Budapest, 1871. He studied at the Industrial Art School of Budapest, at the Academy of Vienna, and at Julian's at Paris. He exhibited for the first time in Budapest in 1892, and his *Crab Fisher* won the award of the city of Budapest in 1893. One of his first works, the statue of *Anonymus* (unknown medieval chronicler), an impressive imaginative work of art, was erected in a Budapest park and was officially called to the attention of every school child in the metropolis.

Ligeti's ingenious technique of carving portrait busts in colored marble won him the patronage of aristocracy. He was also commissioned to do such statues as *Francis Joseph I* (at Fehértemplom, Hungary), *Empress-Queen Elizabeth* (at Szeged), and *Crown Prince Rudolf* (at Budapest). His statues of *Lajos Kossuth* and *István Széchenyi* were erected at Visonta-Csoknya. Subsequently he did the portrait busts of the leaders of the Austro-Hungarian army of the first World War (in the Heeres-Museum, Vienna, and the Hadi muzeum, Budapest); of King Charles of Austria-Hungary (marble); of the painter Pál Szinyei-Merse (marble); of Regent Nicholas Horthy (bronze); and of the Archduke Joseph (bronze). In 1935 he created the War Memorial of the Hungarian Artillery (bronze), and in 1937 the statue of the American general Bandholtz, who was a member of the Allied military mission at Budapest in 1919.

Several of Ligeti's marble groups are in the possession of the Museum of Fine Arts of Budapest, such as *The Tree of Knowledge; Adam and Eve; Love; The Burying of Christ.* The latter subject has been treated by Ligeti also in a grey marble relief adorning the frontispiece of the Terézvárosi Catholic church at Budapest. Other statues and compositions of Ligeti's making are in the park of the Royal Palace, in the building of parliament, and outside of the Adria Palace of Budapest.

Ligeti's works include also several beautiful tomb memorials and colored ceramics inspired by folk tales. Some of his works are included in sculpture collections at Vienna, Rome, Lausanne, Munich and Paris. He was recipient of gold medals at Munich (1905), Torino (1907), London (1908) and Budapest (1922, 1933 and 1935); of many decorations, and of the title of state councillor-in-chief (1936). Ligeti was brought up in the Jewish faith, but later embraced Christianity.

LIGHT. Light is universally regarded in Jewish literature as the source and symbol of good. It was the first creation of God, day and night being created on the first day, whereas the luminaries, the sun, moon and stars, were not brought into existence until the fourth. This goes back to a conception in which there is an original, primeval light, of which the heavenly bodies are only the intermediaries. Light is used in a figurative sense of knowledge, redemption, truth and divinity. Israel is to be a light—that is, an educator—to the nations; the people who walk in darkness await the light of redemption; the commandment is a lamp in that it is true. Light is so intimately connected with God that Moses was said to have acquired a face of dazzling brilliancy during his stay on Mount Sinai to receive the revelation (*Ex.* 34:29-35). The eschatological visions of the future often contain the detail of an increase of light; thus the light of the sun is to be sevenfold, and that of the moon equal to the present sun (*Isa.* 30:26). In many cases there is a connection between light and life itself, and the life of the individual is symbolized as a lamp (*Job* 18:5 and frequently).

In apocryphal and rabbinic literature light is frequently represented as wisdom and as the garment of God. The first man and woman were clothed in light and lost their radiance only after their disobedience. This divine light will be the share of the righteous in the world to come. As wisdom was increasingly identified with Torah, the latter was also symbolized by light. Similarly, light came to symbolize not only law, but the soul, as in the Yahrzeit light.

LIGHT, PERPETUAL, *see* PERPETUAL LIGHT.

LIGHTNING (*barak*). Lightning, which occurs with unusual violence in Palestine, was regarded in the Bible as the manifestation of the divinity, and especially of its fierce wrath. For this reason it was figuratively called an arrow and regarded as the weapon with which God destroyed His enemies (*Ps.* 144:6); there is also a reference to the "lightning," or "glittering point" of the sword (*Job* 20:25). The name Barak was frequent among the Hebrews; the most famous man to bear it was the leader of the confederate tribes in their battle against Sisera, in the period of the judges (*Judges* 4 and 5); cf. the name of the Carthaginian general Hamilcar Barca. We also find such place names in Palestine as Bene-berak and Barkai. The priests in the Second Temple used to watch for the first gleam of the morning star, which they called *barkai* (*Yoma* 3:1).

The origin of the term was no doubt a mythological one; later generations no longer understood the original meaning of the word, hence the explanations given for it in the Talmud are unsatisfactory. The rabbis commanded that one should say the benediction "Blessed art Thou, O Lord our God, King of the universe, Whose power and Whose might fill the world," on beholding the phenomena of comets, earthquakes, thunder, lightning and storms (*Ber.* 9:2). The next verse in the Mishnah, however, prescribes the benediction, "Who made the works of creation," for one who beholds mountains, seas, streams and deserts. The rabbis of Babylonia were of the opinion that the latter benediction was to be recited also over the first group of phenomena, including lightning. This interpretation was disputed by the Posekim and again in the *Shulhan Aruch*. However, Jewish prayer-books still have the rubric that the first of these two bless-

Silver hanging lamp in the synagogue at Kriegs-haber, Bavaria

ings is to be pronounced on hearing thunder, as this is the more violent manifestation, while the second is to be said on seeing lightning, comets, towering mountains or dreadful deserts.

LIGHTS. Lights are employed in a number of instances in Jewish ritual observances. The Tabernacle had a perpetual fire burning upon the altar and was illuminated by the golden seven-branched candlestick (Menorah); similarly, the synagogue has the perpetual light (Ner Tamid) above the Ark and Menorahs as part of its illumination. The Sabbath eve, the eight days of Hanukah and the close of the [Sabbath Habdalah] are all observed by the use of lights; in the time of the Second Temple the Feast of the Water-Drawing was observed in a torchlight procession. A special light is kindled over the body of one who has died, and a similar light (Yahrzeit light) is lit on each anniversary of the death.

In many cases the act of lighting such lights (*hadlakah*) is a ceremony in itself. When a new synagogue is dedicated, the perpetual light is kindled by the oldest member of the congregation. In the home the Sabbath lights are kindled by the wife, who generally spreads out a white cloth, places two candlesticks upon them and spreads out her hands to the light before reciting the blessing. The same is done on the eve of the Jewish holidays. At Hanukah the lights are kindled and the blessing pronounced by any or all of the family; in the Habdalah service, a taper is kindled by the father. The blessing that accompanies the kindling of the light usually contains the phrase "Who hast commanded us to kindle the light of . . ." (*'asher . . . tzivvanu lehadlik ner shel . . .*), accompanied by the name of the festival.

A custom which has prevailed down to modern times has been that of kindling on the eve of Yom Kippur a special candle which burns for twenty-four hours. The Hasidim commemorate the anniversary of the death of their saints by kindling many lights; such anniversaries

are often observed by means of solemn processions with lights to the graves. The material burned as light has varied in the course of the ages; oil lights have been replaced in turn by candles, and in modern times, even by gas or electricity. In many Reform Jewish synagogues, where there are memorial tablets for the deceased, provision is made for an electric light to burn by the side of a name on the anniversary of the death when the mourners come to recite Kaddish.

Jewish legends often have stories of miraculous lights, which are represented as burning far beyond expectation or by unknown means. The earliest of these stories is that of the miraculous light at the time when the Temple was rededicated after the victory of the Maccabees, which burned for eight days on one day's oil. Other legends tell of a light in the home of Jehiel of Paris that burned for eight days at a time, and of another owned by Solomon Luria that always remained kindled, although it held fuel for only an hour, as long as he was "learning." Hasidic legends tell also of miraculous lights or flames which accompany the devout in the course of their ecstatic prayers or studies.

SIMON COHEN.

LIGHTS, FEAST OF, *see* HANUKAH.

LIGUE POUR LA DÉFENSE DES DROITS DE L'HOMME ET DU CITOYEN, an organization founded in Paris in 1898 for the protection of human rights everywhere. The immediate occasion for its formation was the Dreyfus Case in France. Nonsectarian in character, the Ligue grew rapidly and had as many as 200,000 members. It was leftist in politics, played an important part in the creation of the Popular Front, and was among the first to combat Fascism and Nazism. It made notable efforts against anti-Semitism; thus in 1918 it called a meeting, in its own offices, with Roumanian representatives to discuss the situation of the Jews in Roumania.

Its last president (since 1926) was the noted Jewish leader and author Victor Basch, professor at the Sorbonne; the last secretary, Emil Kahn, was also a Jew and a writer. However, the fact that these officers were Jews did not prevent the league from growing in scope and power up to 1940. After the fall of France

Hanging lamp in the synagogue at Worms

in that year and the coming into power of the Pétain regime, the Ligue had to cease its activities; its building at Paris was occupied by the Germans.

LIKKUTE ZEBI, a prayer-book arranged and published by the printer Hirsch (Zebi) ben Hayim, much beloved in pious circles. The name has a double meaning; literally it is the "collection of Zebi"; but since the Biblical word *tzebi* means also "pride," "beauty," the title can be taken in the sense of the "beautiful collection." The book was first published in Fürth in 1737; a third edition appeared in 1757. It was soon reprinted in Sulzbach, Lunéville, Metz, and Amsterdam, and still enjoys great popularity in Eastern Europe. It contains penitential prayers and petitions to be said during the penitential period from the month of Elul to Sukkoth. Its contents include many selections from the Mishnah, Talmud, Posekim literature, and responsa of pious men, including the famous Rabbi Jonah Gerondi, and it is intended to bring about a pious frame of mind and to promote repentance. S. Baer issued a sterling revision of the book at Rödelheim in 1856.

LILIEN, EPHRAIM MOSES, artist, b. Drohobycz, Galicia, 1874; d. Badenweiler, Germany, 1925. In 1895 Lilien became one of the first illustrators for the Munich *Jugend,* and later for the *Süddeutscher Postillon.* In 1898 he settled in Berlin, where he made illustrations for various periodicals and books. He was a master of black and white drawings and etchings, to which he was able to give a plastic expressiveness by a skillful use of a minimum of lines, which gives his work a three-dimensional aspect. He made numerous sketches of Jews in his travels through Russia,

Ephraim Moses Lilien

Switzerland and the Orient. He was an ardent Zionist, and was one of the founders of the Democratic fraction at the Fifth Zionist Congress (1901), which advocated a stronger emphasis on the cultural motif in Zionism. For a year he taught at the Bezalel School in Jerusalem. Among the books which he illustrated were: Börries von Münchhausen's *Juda* (1902); Morris Rosenfeld's *Songs of the Ghetto* (1904); Gabriele D'Annunzio's poems (1904); E. A. Regner's edition of the *Song of Songs* (1905); vols. 1, 6 and 7 of Westermann's edition of the Bible (1908-12).

Lit.: Zweig, Stefan, introduction to *E. M. Lilien, Sein Werk* (1903); Brieger, L., *E. M. Lilien* (1922).

LILIENBLUM, MOSES LEIB (abbreviated as **MaLaL**), Hebrew writer, b. Keidany, Russia, 1843; d. Odessa, Russia, 1910. At the age of nine he was well versed in the teachings of the Talmud. From 1864 to 1869 he taught at a Yeshiva in Vilkomir. During these years he studied the literature of the current Hebrew Haskalah, especially the anti-Talmudic writings of Joshua Schorr and Mordecai Aaron Günzburg. He also conducted a small library, for which he was denounced as a heretic by the town Orthodox, although, being conservative at that time, he excluded anti-religious books from it. His troubles multiplied after publishing in *Hamelitz* a series of articles called "Orehoth Hatalmud" and "Nosafoth Leorehoth Hatalmud" in which he proposed to create a new *Shulhan Aruch* in the spirit of the age. He underwent bitter persecution as a result of these, and was almost in peril of his life.

Lilienblum fled to Odessa in 1869 and began to contribute to *Hashahar,* his first allegorical-satirical poem, "Kehal Refaim" (A Community of the Shades), being published in 1870. In this poem he ridicules the people who held office in their lifetime by describing how they come before the judgment of God in the hereafter. In Odessa Lilienblum became acquainted with Abraham Krochmal, son of the philosopher Nachman Krochmal, who bewildered him with his critical studies of the Bible and free-thinking ideas.

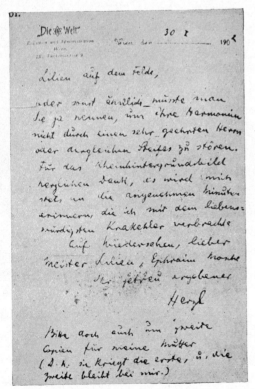

Facsimile of a letter of Theodor Herzl addressed to Ephraim Moses Lilen

Moses Leib Lilienblum

A new period in Lilienblum's life began with his reading of Pissarev's works and Tchernishevski's socialist novel, *Tchto Delat?* (What is to be Done?). The products of this period were "Olam Hatohu" (World of Chaos) and *Hatoth Neurim* (The Sins of Youth; 1876), dealing with the struggles of his soul and of many like him, in the 1860's; the work shows a positive attitude toward the realities of life and ridicules the value of historical research.

In 1874 he returned to Vilkomir, where he intended to prepare himself for admittance into a university, but had to abandon his plans for financial reasons. Here he published *Hakol* (The Voice) and its supplement *Asefath Hachamim* (Assembly of the Wise), dealing with the problem of capital and labor. "Mishnath Elisha ben Abuyah," a parody in the style of the Mishnah, may be regarded as the best of these articles.

Under the influence of the pogroms of 1880 to 1881, Lilienblum's entire philosophy changed and he became the champion of the Hibbath Zion movement and later of political Zionism. At the end of 1883 he was appointed secretary of the Chovevei Zion organization. Upon obtaining a permit from the Russian government to settle in Palestine, he was appointed secretary of the Hebrath Hayishub (Settlement Company; 1899). In 1894 the Chovevei Zion celebrated Lilienblum's fiftieth birthday. In 1902 he participated in the Zionist convention at Minsk as representative of the Odessa Committee.

Lilienblum also wrote in Yiddish the historical drama, *Zerubobel* (1888), and many propagandistic articles which he published in the *Yiddishes Folksblat* and in the *Yiddisher Vecker,* of which he was co-author. Other later works of Lilienblum include "Bikkoreth Kol Shire Gordon," in *Melitz Ehad Mini Elef* (St. Petersburg, 1894); *Derech Laabor Golim* (Warsaw, 1899), a history of the Hibbath Zion movement; *Derech Teshubah* (The Way of Repentance), describing the transition from the period of enlightenment to that of national reawakening. He was also editor of various Hebrew publications, such as *Kavvereth* (Odessa, 1890) and *Luah Ahiasaf.*

The essays and articles of Lilienblum are mostly of a publicistic nature, and are marked by soberness of mind and a lucid style. His works left a great impression upon his contemporaries and contributed much to raising the standard of Hebrew literature. Four volumes of his writings were collected and published by Joseph Klausner (Cracow and Odessa, 1910-13).   MOSES BRIND.

Lit.: Spiegel, S., *Hebrew Reborn* (1930) 199-205; Aaron, B., *Lilienblum, the Zionist* (1912); Epstein, L., *Mosheh Leib Lilienblum* (1935); Simon, L., *M. L. Lilienblum* (1912); Lachower, F., *Toledoth Hasifruth Haibrith Hahadashah,* vol. 2, pp. 201-10.

LILIENTHAL, DAVID ELI, lawyer and public official, b. Morton, Ill., 1899. He received his A.B. degree from De Pauw University, in Indiana, in 1920, and his law degree from Harvard in 1923. After being admitted to the Illinois bar that same year, he opened a law office in Chicago. Lilienthal remained in private practice until 1931, when he was made a member of the Wisconsin Public Service Commission. In 1933 he left this post to become the director of the Tennessee Valley Authority. The following year Lilienthal was admitted also to the Tennessee bar. In 1941, President Franklin D. Roosevelt made him chairman of the Tennessee Valley Authority, which position he still held in 1942. Lilienthal has written articles for various legal magazines, and from 1926 to 1931 was also the editor of *Public Utilities and Carriers Service.*

LILIENTHAL, HOWARD, surgeon, b. Albany, N. Y., 1861. He was educated at Harvard University (A.B., 1883) and the Harvard University Medical School (M.D., 1887). He was with the McLean Asylum in Boston in 1886, and lectured on surgery at the New York Polyclinic Medical School and Hospital in 1888. He became surgeon at Mount Sinai Hospital in 1892 and consulting surgeon in 1924; in 1909 he became surgeon and later consulting surgeon at Bellevue Hospital. In 1917 he was appointed professor of clinical surgery at the Cornell University Medical College.

Lilienthal was commissioned as a first lieutenant in the Medical Reserve Corps in 1911 and as a major in 1917; in 1918 he was promoted to the rank of lieutenant-colonel. He saw active service at the front, and in 1921 was cited for the Distinguished Service Medal. He was a prolific author on surgical subjects. He was an advisory editor of the *Journal of Thoracic Surgery* and, in addition to over 300 articles for medical journals, he wrote several books, including *Imperative Surgery* (1900) and *Thoracic Surgery* (1925).

LILIENTHAL, MAX (MENAHEM), rabbi and educator, b. Munich, Germany, 1815; d. Cincinnati, 1882. In 1840 he was called to the principalship of the newly opened Jewish school in Riga. When Uvarov, the Russian minister of public instruction, took up the question of a general educational reform through the establishment of modern Jewish schools, he called Lilienthal to St. Petersburg as an expert intermediator between the government and the Jews. Lilienthal was commissioned to negotiate with German scholars with regard to the engaging of foreign teachers, and to work out plans for the reform of the Jewish schools

in collaboration with Nissan Rosenthal in Vilna. However, with the exception of a small group which was
continually growing smaller, all the Russian Jews
were opposed to Lilienthal; the Orthodox and the
Hasidim from principle, although he believed that he
could dispose them favorably through diplomatic negotiations; the Maskilim (enlighteners) opposed him
because they felt that he had neglected them. The
opposition to him increased to such an extent that he
was subjected to a personal insult on the occasion of
his visit to Minsk.

Lilienthal believed that headway could be made
against this opposition through energetic measures.
Uvarov, however, rejected this proposal, and took no
further action aside from connecting the reform most
intimately with the name of the emperor by means
of the ukase of June 22, 1842. In addition, a committee
of outstanding Jewish representatives was to be formed
at Lilienthal's proposal, and Lilienthal himself was
to travel throughout the Pale of Settlement in order
to spread propaganda for secular education. Although
he met with much favor in some communities, notably
in Odessa, where he was offered the rabbinical position,
in the end his efforts proved entirely unsuccessful.
His manifesto to the Jews, *Maggid Yeshuah,* aroused
against him the progressive groups, whose interpreter,
Mordecai Aaron Günzburg, wrote a reply, *Maggid
Emeth* (1843). Lilienthal participated in the work
of the Commission on Jewish Reform (May to August, 1843), which sponsored the issuing of the ukase
of November 3, 1844.

In 1845 Lilienthal left Russia and came to New
York city, where he served as rabbi of several congregations until 1850. He then established a private
school for boys, over which he presided until 1855,
when he became rabbi of Bene Israel Congregation
in Cincinnati, where he served until his death. He
was active in local educational affairs, serving as a
member of the Cincinnati Board of Education and
of the board of directors of the University of Cincinnati. He served for some time as associate editor
of the *American Israelite* and its German supplement,
Die Deborah. He was one of the foremost sponsors
of the Union of American Hebrew Congregations
(1873) and of the Hebrew Union College (1875). He
wrote *Freiheit, Frühling und Liebe,* and described his
Russian experiences in the *Allgemeine Zeitung des
Judentums* (1855), in the *Jüdisches Volksblatt* (1856,
No. 36) and in the *American Israelite* (vols. 1 and 2).

Lilienthal's brother, Samuel, settled in New York
city and was a noted physician. His son, Jesse W. (b.
Haverstraw, N. Y., 1856; d. San Francisco, 1919), was
a prominent lawyer and financier in California. His
other sons, Albert (d. 1910), Philip Nettre (d. 1908),
and the latter's son, Joseph L., also achieved distinction.   DAVID PHILIPSON.

Lit.: Philipson, David, *Max Lilienthal, His Life and
Writings* (1915); idem, "Max Lilienthal in Russia," *He-
brew Union College Annual,* vol. 12-13 (1937-38) 825-39;
Raisin, Jacob S., *The Haskalah Movement in Russia* (1913);
Kahana, David, in *Hashiloah,* vol. 27, p. 320.

LILIENTHAL, SIEGFRIED, art critic (pseudonym, Fritz Stahl), b. Rosenberg, Western Prussia,
1864; d. Berlin, 1928. For many years he wrote art
criticism in the *Berliner Tageblatt.* His point of view

was rather conservative, although he was neither dogmatic nor opportunistic. Even his adversaries acknowledged his sincerity and good intentions. In 1907 he
published a study on Jozef Israels as Jewish artist.

Lilienthal was interested also in making scientific
comparisons of the portraits of great personalities in
order to appraise their true significance. Hence he
wrote *Wie sah Goethe aus?* (1904), *Wie sah Bismarck
aus?* (1905) and *Wie sah Rembrandt aus?* (1924). He
published (1928) also monographs on the artistic tradition of such cities as Paris and Rome.

LILITH, a female demon in Jewish folklore. The
name is the Hebraized form of the often mentioned,
powerful Babylonian demon Lilitu, who, with her
two associates, her husband Lilu and his maidservant,
Ardat Lile, were probably storm-spirits. In later rabbinic tradition Lilith, by a false derivation from the
Hebrew word *layelah* ("night"), was reinterpreted as
a demon of the night and came to play a most important role, particularly as the demon who caused sex
dreams and nightly emissions by men, and robbed newborn children and their mothers of their lives, particularly during the first seven days of birth. In Talmudic tradition Lilith was conceived of as having con-
sorted with Adam during the period of his separation
from Eve after the expulsion from Eden, and as having
borne to him numerous demoniac progeny. Another
explanation was that Lilith was the first wife of Adam,
made like him from the dust of the earth; they did
not suit one another, however, and Lilith fled, vowing
vengeance. She was overtaken by three angels, but
refused to return; hence she endeavors to kill the
children of Eve, but can, according to the superstition,
be stopped by the presence of an amulet bearing the
names of the three angels who had halted her in her
flight.

LIMA, see PERU.

LIMAN VON SANDERS, OTTO, German gen-
eral, b. Schwessin, near Stolp, Prussia, 1855; d. Munich,
1929. He was half-Jewish by descent, his father and
grandfather having been baptized Jews. He entered the
German army in 1874 and rose through the ranks until
1913, when he was ennobled and made head of the
German military mission in Constantinople. In August,
1914, he became the commander of the First Turkish
Army and later of the Second as well. The appointment
was annulled because of Russian protests, but Liman
von Sanders remained in Turkey as inspector of Turkish troops. After Turkey entered the War, he commanded the Fifth Turkish Army and won the title of
"lion of Gallipoli" for his successful defense of that
position against the British and French forces from
February, 1915, to January, 1916. In 1918 he succeeded
Von der Goltz as commander of the Turkish army in
Palestine, which was defeated by Allenby in 1918; by a
peculiar twist of fate the half-Jew Liman von Sanders
fought to prevent, and the non-Jew Allenby to bring
about, the fulfillment of the British promise to make
Palestine a Jewish homeland. After the War Liman
von Sanders returned to Germany, where he wrote a
book on his experiences in Turkey, *Fünf Jahre Türkei*
(1920; English trans., *Five Years in Turkey,* 1928).

LINCOLN, capital of the state of Nebraska; it had a Jewish community of 1,200 out of a total population of 81,984 (census of 1940).

In 1856 settlers were first attracted to the site of Lincoln by the salt springs. The settlement, known as Lancaster, consisted of five or six houses when it was selected for the state capital in 1867. It was renamed Lincoln (1869). Moses Oppenheimer and his wife, who had been living in Nebraska City and settled in Lincoln in 1868, were the first Jewish settlers. Their son, Joseph R. Oppenheimer, was born in 1873—the first Jewish child born there.

In 1869, Moses' brother, Isaac Oppenheimer, Isaac's wife, Rose, and their two sons, Jacob and Sol, settled in Lincoln. Louis Poska, who was born in Poland, came to Lincoln from Burlington, Iowa, in 1869 or 1870. His brother, Charles, came directly from Poland in 1874. About the same time one Stine and his wife, with an adult son, Morris, left Louisville, Ky., for Lincoln. Stine was a Shohet and served as such the Jews of Lincoln and Omaha. Other settlers at that time were Ed Cerf, David May, Will and Louis Meyer, Morris Adler, H. Levy, Peretz Polsky, and his two sisters. One of them, Anna Polsky, and Louis Poska were married by Stine in 1877—the first Jewish wedding in Lincoln. Their son, Albert Poska, enlisted in the United States Army during the Spanish-American War and returned from the Philippines an invalid to die at the age of twenty (1899).

Other settlers in Lincoln in the late 1870's were Isaac Cahn, Aaron Katzenstein, Leopold Barr, M. Z. Newmark, Isaac Friend, Cohn and Block (in the dry goods business together), David, Isaac, and Charles Wise, Julius Pepperburg, Moses Ackerman, Ed Gugenheim, M. N. Acht, Harry Blum, Alex Poska, his wife and four children, Morris Polsky, his sister, Sarah, and their mother, Libbie. Of later settlers, Louis I. Bogen, who came to Lincoln in 1903, was the first Jewish physician. His wife, who had been Jennie Logasa, was the first Jewess to teach in the schools of Lincoln.

Congregation B'nai Jeshurun (Reform) was organized in 1884. A temple was built in 1893 but the congregation, because of the hard times, could not hire a rabbi. Leo M. Franklin, who was a rabbi in Omaha, came to Lincoln every other Sunday evening to conduct services. It was not until 1906 that Congregation B'nai had its own rabbi. Israel I. Mattuck served for two years; in 1908 he was succeeded by Frederick Braun, who also served for two years. Gustave Lowenstein was rabbi from 1910 to 1911; Jacob Singer served as rabbi from 1912 to 1923; Solomon E. Starrels from 1923 to 1928; and Jacob J. Ogle from 1928 on. He was still serving in that capacity in 1942. A new temple was completed in 1924. The congregation controls and uses Mount Lebanon cemetery.

The Orthodox congregation, Tifereth Israel, was organized in 1886. Among its rabbis have been: Albert Mandelbaum (1921-22); Herman Eisenberg (1924-26), its first Conservative rabbi); Theodore Shabshelowitz (1926-27); and the incumbent in 1942, Harry Jolt (1928-   ). In 1913 the congregation erected a synagogue. Tifereth Israel uses the Bnai Yehuda cemetery.

There were several charitable organizations in Lin-

coln, but their work was finally taken over by the Jewish Welfare Federation, organized in 1931.

There is a B'nai B'rith lodge in Lincoln. It was organized in 1887 by Carl Brandeis of Omaha. Other organizations in Lincoln in 1942 were branches of Senior (1924) and Junior (1929) Hadassah, and a branch of the Workmen's Circle (1910).

In 1942 Rabbi Harry Jolt was counselor of the Hillel Foundation at the University of Nebraska in Lincoln.

HARRY JOLT.

LINCOLN, county town of Lincolnshire, England, with a population of 63,080 (1941). The city was one of the principal centers of the English Jews before the Expulsion in 1290. First attested in *Pipe Rolls* of 1159, they appear to have settled in the Brauncegate, or St. Martin's Parish, a site now occupied by Steep Hill. The principal record of Lincoln Jewry is furnished by a collection of Hebrew deeds (*shetaroth*), preserved in the British Museum and in the Chapter House of Westminster Abbey. These were published in 1888 by Myer D. Davis, in connection with the Anglo-Jewish Historical Exhibition. From them it appears that during the 13th cent. several important properties in the county, including estates belonging to Newhouse Abbey and to Bullington Priory, in Wyckford, were pledged with local Jewish money-lenders. The most prominent of the latter were Aaron of Lincoln (about 1125-86), who at one time controlled the plate of Lincoln Minster, and a certain Leo, described in a tallage list of Henry III as among the six wealthiest men in England. Other leading Jews of the period were Benedict (Berachiah), son of Isaac, Aaron's brothers Senior and Benedict, and his sons, Elias, Abraham and Vives (Hayim).

The control of non-Jewish holdings exercised by the Jewish financiers provoked several outbreaks against the community. The first of these occurred during the reign of Richard I (1189-99), but on that occasion the Jews escaped annihilation by seeking refuge in Lincoln Castle, whither they were granted access by the local Bishop Hugh. In 1220, however, the Jewish quarter was again raided, and two members of the community, Moses de Ballio and Sarah, wife of Deulecresse (Gedaliah), were done to death. Thirty-five years later (1255), Lincoln Jewry was the victim of a blood accusation, in which it was alleged that a local youth named Hugh, slain by them for ritual purposes, had miraculously denounced his murderers from the bottom of a well, into which they had thrown his body. (The story, to which there are many parallels in anti-Semitic folklore, forms the subject of Chaucer's "Prioress's Tale" in the *Canterbury Tales*.) Finally, in 1266, the barons, seeking to destroy the records of their indebtedness, organized a systematic attack upon the houses of Lincoln Jews. This, however, did not achieve their entire elimination, for records of escheats made in connection with the Expulsion, some twenty-four years later, list at least sixty-six Jewish householders in the city.

Since the Expulsion there has been no formal community of Jews in Lincoln. In 1940, however, the city became one of the centers of evacuation from the bombed metropolis of London, and a small congregation was established.

Among the antiquities of Lincoln are the two stone

Abraham Lincoln

houses originally owned by Aaron, the money-lender, and by Balasset, the daughter of Benedict. The latter was executed, in 1287, for clipping coins.

Lit.: Davis, M. D., "Hebrew Deeds of English Jews before 1290," *Publications of the Anglo-Jewish Historical Exhibition,* No. 2 (1888) 287-311; Roth, Cecil, *Medieval Lincoln Jewry and the Synagogue;* Jacobs, Joseph, *The Jews of Angevin England* (1893); idem, "Little St. Hugh of Lincoln," *The Jewish Historical Society of England, Transactions,* vol. 1 (1893) 89-135; idem, "Aaron of Lincoln," *ibid.,* vol. 3 (1899) 157-79; Haes, Frank, "Lincoln, 1898," *ibid.,* vol. 3 (1899) 180-86; see also the illustrations in the article ENGLAND, vol. 4, p. 115.

LINCOLN, ABRAHAM, sixteenth president of the United States, b. on a farm in Kentucky, 1809; d. Washington, D. C., 1865. Following a childhood spent on farms and several small towns in Kentucky and Indiana, Lincoln removed to Salem, Ill., in 1831, and became its representative in the state legislature in 1834. In 1837, he resided at Springfield, Ill., engaged in law practice, and became active in Whig politics, served a single term in Congress (1847-49), and became a recognized leader of the new Republican Party when the Kansas-Nebraska Act opened the western territories to slavery. Champion of the forces opposed to the extension of slavery and committed to the maintenance of the Union, Lincoln was elected president in 1860 and reelected in 1864, by which time he had established his position as the Great Emancipator and the successful leader of the Union forces. During this period his biography is coincident with the history of his country.

Imbued with a humane and liberal spirit, Lincoln knew no distinctions of race or creed in his friendships and official actions. He counted several Jews among his close friends, while an even larger number of them became his ardent admirers and staunch supporters. Of a deeply religious nature despite the fact that he was affiliated with no church, Lincoln's Biblical training, which had a profound effect on his life and literary style, led him to an acceptance of ethical standards of justice in close harmony with Jewish doctrine.

The remarkable resemblance of Lincoln's beliefs to those of Hillel and of his life to that of Moses has been noted by his biographer, Emanuel Hertz.

Documentary evidence of Lincoln's contacts with Jews before he became president is scarce, but Emanuel Hertz suggested that Lincoln undoubtedly came into contact with the Jewish pioneers of the Middle West. Of the Jewish residents of Illinois in pre-Civil War days, Julius Hammersborough of Springfield and Henry Rice of Jacksonville knew Lincoln well. Hammersborough was closely acquainted with the Lincoln family, was a frequent caller at the White House during Lincoln's incumbency, and was named one of the committee of Springfield citizens which accompanied Lincoln's remains in the funeral procession from Washington. Jews figured among Lincoln's most ardent political admirers. Two of them, Moritz Pinner of Missouri and Lewis N. Dembitz of Kentucky, were delegates to the Republican convention of 1860 which nominated Lincoln, and another, Maier Hirsch of Oregon, was a delegate to the convention of 1864 which renominated him. Two electoral votes were cast for Lincoln by Jews, one in the election of 1860 by Sigismund Kaufmann of New York, another in 1864 by Abraham J. Dittenhoefer, also of New York. Among Lincoln's friends were also Henry Greenebaum and Abraham Kohn of Chicago. Kohn, city clerk of Chicago, a merchant of some education, well-versed in Hebrew literature and described by the Democratic press as "one of the blackest Republicans and Abolitionists," was so impressed by his meeting with Lincoln in 1860 and by the latter's Biblical qualities that he came to regard him as the Moses destined to free the slaves. When the president-elect departed for Washington, he received from Kohn a silk flag of the Union inscribed with the Hebrew characters of the third to the ninth verses of the first chapter of *Joshua,* ending with the exhortation "be strong and of good courage; be not afraid, neither be thou dismayed; for the Lord thy God is with thee whithersoever thou goest."

Lincoln's most intimate personal and political Jewish friend, however, was Abraham Jonas, a leading lawyer and politician of Quincy, Ill., their friendship dating back to the birth of the Whig party in 1834 and lasting until Jonas' death in 1864. Jonas served in the state legislatures of Kentucky (1828-33) and Illinois (1842), was prominent in Whig politics and became an influential leader in the new Republican party. He was closely identified with Lincoln in Illinois Republican politics, served with him as a presidential elector on the Fremont ticket in 1856, and was among the first to suggest Lincoln as presidential timber. Whenever he visited Quincy, Lincoln spent much of his time in Jonas' company and did his work in the offices of the law firm of Jonas and Asbury. That many of Lincoln's biographers have failed to mention Jonas is particularly surprising in view of the fact that Lincoln, in a confidential letter of July 21, 1860, appealed to Jonas to scotch the rumors then current about Lincoln's supposed affiliation with the Know Nothing party.

Lincoln reappointed Jonas to the postmastership at Quincy on April 29, 1861, a post which he had held from 1849 to 1852. During the Civil War, Lincoln maintained contact with his Quincy friend, and when Jonas was on his deathbed in 1864, the president issued an order for the parole of his son, Charles H. Jonas, a prisoner of war as a Confederate soldier, to visit his dying father. Despite the fact that four of Jonas' sons served in the Confederate army, while only one, Edward, served with the Union forces as major of an Illinois regiment, Lincoln not only maintained his close friendship with Jonas, but also, according to Benjamin F. Jonas, "Mr. Lincoln always asked after us when he saw any one from New Orleans during the war."

The election of Lincoln in 1860 was generally welcomed by the Jewish community, and during the war years many Jewish citizens who had previously been his political opponents came to support him as president, many of them becoming his admirers to the point of adoration. A great number of Jewish citizens and their leaders came into contact with the president on official and personal business, and some came to know him well. At the time of his election, political sentiment among Jews was divided and both rabbis and laymen took an active interest in political affairs. Arrayed with Lincoln's party and prominent among the abolitionists were Rabbi David Einhorn, publisher of the German-language monthly *Sinai* devoted to the anti-slavery movement; Rabbi Samuel M. Isaacs, of New York, publisher of the *Jewish Messenger,* who favored Lincoln's policy for preservation of the Union; Rabbi Sabato Morais, of Philadelphia; Rabbi Liebman Adler, of Chicago, who sent his only son to serve in the ranks of an Illinois regiment; Dr. Abraham B. Arnold, of Baltimore, member of the Republican State Executive Committee; Philip J. Joachimsen who, as assistant district attorney of New York, secured the first conviction for slave-trading; and, prominent among the abolitionists, Michael Heilprin.

On the other side was a not insignificant proportion of Jewish leaders such as Rabbi Morris J. Raphall, of New York, and Leander Ker, of Missouri. Rabbi Raphall, like Rabbi Isaac Mayer Wise, who at first did not look upon Lincoln with favor, later came to support him and sent his son to serve in the Union forces. Before Lincoln assumed the presidency, Wise was one of the Jewish leaders who thought Lincoln too belligerent in speech. On January 13, 1861, the *Israelite,* a weekly edited by Wise, wrote that it was "not so much the election of Lincoln in itself that threatened the destruction of the Union as the speeches of Lincoln and his colleagues on the irrepressible conflict doctrine." Carl Sandburg, in *The War Years* (vol. 1, p. 39), notes that when Lincoln, in an impromptu speech at Lafayette, Ind., remarked to his audience that "still we are bound together in Christianity, civilization, and patriotism," Jewish citizens protested, wishing to know when the United States was exclusively bound to Christianity as against other religions. The *Israelite,* conceding the possibility that Lincoln used the term loosely to signify

religion, took occasion to remark that he had not yet learned the precise use of words. When Lincoln used similar phrasing in his first inaugural address and again in his General Order Respecting the Observation of the Sabbath Day in the Army and Navy (November 15, 1862), several Jewish citizens protested. B. Behrend, of Narrowsburg, N. Y., the father of a Jewish soldier in the Union army, sent a long address to the president pointing out that "thousands in the army who celebrate another day as Sunday should be allowed to celebrate that day which they think is the right day according to their consciences." Whether or not such protests had any effect, it is perhaps significant that Lincoln's famous Proclamation for a National Fast Day (March 30, 1863), which refers to the divine basis of human action, is free from any sectarian implications.

Lincoln's administration was marked by several incidents affecting Jews as a group, of which two assumed noteworthy proportions: the appointment of a Jewish chaplain and Grant's General Order expelling Jews as a class from his military department in 1862. The Jewish chaplain question grew out of the refusal of Secretary of War Simon Cameron, in the fall of 1861, to grant the application of the Reverend Dr. Arnold Fischel for appointment as chaplain of the Cameron Dragoons, a New York regiment with a large percentage of Jews, because by Act of Congress it was provided that chaplains must be ministers of some Christian denomination. Agitation for a modification of the law to permit appointment of Jewish chaplains became widespread and was supported by newspapers in New York and Baltimore.

The Board of Delegates of American Israelites took up the matter in November, and on December 6, 1861, appointed Rabbi Fischel to supervise the general spiritual welfare of the Israelites in the camps and military hospitals attached to the Department of the Potomac. Two days later the Board of Delegates wrote to President Lincoln, asking him "to designate properly qualified Israelites to be attached as chaplains to the hospitals in the several military departments." At the same time, they petitioned Congress for modification of the law, protesting that it constituted "prejudicial discrimination against a patriotic class of citizens on account of their religious belief." The president declared his intention of recommending to Congress modification in the law to meet Jewish needs, and on December 14th, wrote to Fischel promising that "I shall try to have a new law broad enough to cover what is desired by you in behalf of the Israelites." Following the presentation of petitions to Congress and the adoption of the cause by many Christians, Congress on March 12, 1862, amended the law so as to authorize the employment of brigade chaplains "one or more of which shall be of the Catholic, Protestant or Jewish religion."

Angered by the repeated violations of the Northern blockade by cotton traders, some of whom were Jews, Major-General Ulysses S. Grant hastily, as he later admitted, singled out the Jews among them in several orders issued in November and December, 1862, culminating in the General Order No. 11 (December 17th), which stated that "the Jews, as a class, violating every regulation of trade established by the Treasury Department and also department orders, are hereby expelled from the department within twenty-four hours from the receipt of this order." This occurrence and the reaction to it caused, according to the New York *Times*, "one of the deepest sensations of the war." Agitation for the immediate revocation of the discriminatory order spread throughout the Jewish communities of the North. Cincinnati and Paducah, Ky., which were directly affected by Grant's action, became the storm centers for these protests. Rabbi Isaac Mayer Wise, in the *Israelite*, demanded the recall of the order, while Captain Ferdinand Levy of Company H., Battalion New York Volunteers, wrote to the *Jewish Messenger* urging that the president compel General Grant to apologize or retire from service.

While the Jews of Cincinnati were trying to reach the president, the leading Jewish merchants of Paducah wrote to him on December 29, 1862, pointing out that the order for the expulsion of all Jews without distinction was an insult to "the undersigned good and loyal citizens of the United States and residents of this town," and that the execution of this the "grossest violation of the Constitution" would place the Jewish families of the town "as outlaws before the world." The injustice of singling out the Jews and of condemning them "as a class" for the faults of a few was emphasized, and immediate revocation of the order urged. To back up this letter, Paducah sent Cesar Kaskel, one of the signers of the appeal and vice-president of the Paducah Union League Club, armed with letters from Rabbi Max Lilienthal and Daniel Wolf, prominent Cincinnati merchant, to Washington, which he reached on January 3, 1863, and immediately sought audience with the president.

Lincoln heard the case and remarked, "And so the children of Israel were driven from the happy land of Canaan?" Kaskel, entering into the spirit of it, replied: "Yes, and that is why they have come unto Father Abraham's bosom, seeking protection." "And this protection they shall have," Lincoln promised, seating himself at a table to write the order to General Halleck, general-in-chief of the Northern armies, revoking Grant's Order No. 11. Due to some delay, the revocation was not issued until January 7th. In explaining the president's action to Grant, Halleck wrote that Lincoln deemed it necessary to revoke the order "as it in terms proscribed an entire religious class, some of whom are fighting in our ranks."

Before the results of Kaskel's mission became known, Rabbis Wise and Lilienthal, accompanied by Edgar M. Johnson, a Cincinnati lawyer, Martin Bijur, of Louisville, and Abraham Goldsmith, of Paducah, had gone to Washington. When the order was revoked, they visited Lincoln to express the gratitude of the Jewish community. Lincoln expressed his surprise that such an order should have been issued, and added: "I don't like to see a class or nationality condemned on account of a few sinners." The president convinced his audience that he had no prejudice against any nationality and especially none against Israelites. Similarly, the assistant secretary of war, P. J. Watson, writing to the Board of Delegates on January 16, 1863, acknowledging its expression of gratitude for the prompt revocation of Grant's order, stated: "No discrimination against any class of our people, of native or foreign birth, on ac-

Heroic bronze statue of Abraham Lincoln designed by the American artist Max Kalish (on ladder) for the city of Cleveland

count of their religious belief, can receive the sanction of this Department."

Among the Jews whom Lincoln came to know in Washington were Adolphus S. Solomons, of the publishing and printing firm of Philip and Solomons, which for many years did government printing; Joseph Seligman, of the New York banking firm, who was frequently called in for consultation on financial questions and who placed many issues of government bonds abroad in the days when Union credit was low; and Simon Wolf, who has told the story of his meetings with Lincoln in *The Presidents I Have Known From 1860 to 1918*.

Of Lincoln's relations with Jewish soldiers and officers in the Civil War little is known, although several incidents have been related which reflect on his character as a man of justice and compassion. Isaac Markens relates several instances of pardons granted to Jewish soldiers convicted of infringing army regulations and others where Lincoln refused to interfere with sentences handed down by the military authorities. Most distinctive is the story told by Simon Wolf of his intercession for a Jewish soldier who had been condemned to death for desertion when, unable to obtain furlough, he left camp without permission to visit his dying mother. At first Lincoln refused to countermand the sentence. Wolf pointed out that this was really not a case of desertion as the soldier had acted out of filial devotion, not out of disloyalty to the flag. Lincoln issued the pardon and, according to Wolf, "that American citizen of Jewish faith led the forlorn hope with the flag of his country in his hands at the battle of Cold Harbor and was shot to death fighting heroically for the country of his birth." When Lincoln, months later, heard what had become of the young soldier, he was visibly moved and exclaimed: "I thank God for having done what I did."

Of Lincoln's other Jewish contacts, most interesting evidence is afforded by the letter written to Secretary of War Edwin M. Stanton by the president on January 25, 1865, about two cases affecting Jews:

"About Jews, I wish you would give Dr. Zacharie a pass to go to Savannah, remain a week and return, bringing with him, if he wishes, his father and sisters or any of them . . . I promised him long ago that he should be allowed this whenever Savannah should fall into our hands. Blumenberg, at Baltimore, I think he should have a hearing—He has suffered for us and served us well—had the rope around his neck for being our friend—raised troops—fought, and been wounded—He should not be dismissed in a way that disgraces and ruins him without a hearing—"

Dr. Issachar Zacharie, referred to in the letter, was a young English Jew, a skillful chiropodist, who attended Lincoln and members of his cabinet. Dr. Zacharie was instrumental in securing the release of Goodman L. Mordecai of South Carolina, arrested in Washington because of his activities on behalf of the Confederacy, and extravagant claims of his influence with Lincoln were current, the anti-administration New York *World* of September 24, 1864, hinting that "there must be a reason for this remarkable intimacy between an obscure toe-nail trimmer and the Chief Executive of a great nation." There is no evidence of any such influence or intimacy, cordial professional relations and Lincoln's well-known good nature being sufficient to explain the favor done for Zacharie.

Major Leopold Blumenberg, the other person mentioned, had helped to organize the fifth regiment, Maryland Volunteers, served near Hampton Roads and, having been wounded in the battle of Antietam, was appointed provost-marshal of the third Maryland District. Subsequently cleared of the charges which caused his dismissal, he was promoted by President Andrew Johnson to the rank of brevet brigadier-general of the United States Volunteers.

In the demonstrations of public grief which followed Lincoln's death, Jews everywhere were prominent, the first eulogies in fact being preached in the synagogues of the United States on the Jewish Sabbath day of his death, April 15th. In the synagogue Shearith Israel of New York, the rabbi recited the Hashkabah (Sephardic prayer for the dead), the first time that this prayer had been said for one not professing the Jewish faith. Special funeral services were held in synagogues throughout the country during the week following his death, and the sermons then preached testify to the profound sense of loss felt by Jews upon Lincoln's passing and their immediate appreciation of his great character. These sermons, as well as subsequent eulogies and addresses on Lincoln delivered by Jewish religious leaders and laymen, were collected by Emanuel Hertz and published in 1927 under the title *Abraham Lincoln: The Tribute of the Synagogue.*

NATHAN A. PELCOVITS.

Lit.: Markens, Isaac, "Lincoln and the Jews," *Publications of the American Jewish Historical Society*, No. 17 (1909) 109-65; Hertz, Emanuel, "Lincoln's Jewish Contacts," *The Magazine of History*, No. 38, vol. 40, No. 1 (1930) 26-37; idem, *Abraham Lincoln: The Tribute of the Synagogue* (1927); Wolf, Simon, *The Presidents I Have Known from 1860 to 1918*, pp. 4-49; Van Dorn Stern, Philip, *The Life and Writings of Abraham Lincoln* (1940) 613-14.

The Canard Regarding Lincoln's Murderer. Abraham Lincoln was assassinated on the 14th of April, 1865, by John Wilkes Booth, actor, son of the famous actor Junius Brutus Booth, and brother of Edwin Booth. It has been alleged that the murderer and his family were of Jewish descent. The journalist G. A. Townsend, author of a small book entitled *Life, Crime and Capture of J. W. Booth,* was first to publish this opinion. His book appeared a fortnight after Lincoln's murder. All representations pertaining to the Jewish origin of the Booths seem to derive from the report of a Unitarian clergyman who claimed to have met Junius Brutus Booth, who told him about being of Jewish origin. But old Junius was a very odd man, fanatically devoted to all religions—Catholic, Mohammedan, Buddhist, and Jewish. His son Edwin wrote about his father: "When he acted Shylock in the evening, he was a Jew all day long."

In all likelihood Junius Brutus had said something to the minister which he thus misunderstood. It is noteworthy that the clergyman published this story more than twenty years after he had met Booth. Indeed, there is not the slightest evidence that the family was of Jewish origin. Junius B. Booth's grandfather, John Booth, was a Christian goldsmith in London. Asia Booth, sister of Edwin and John, married the actor Clarke, and wrote a number of books about the famous members of her family. She recorded the fact that many of the ancestors of the Booth family are buried in the yard of the ancient Church of St. John of Jerusalem at Clerkenwell, England. Hence there can be no doubt that the Booth family was of Christian origin.

JULIUS BAB.

LINDAU, PAUL, author, b. Magdeburg, Germany, 1839; d. Berlin, 1919. The son of a baptized Jew, Lindau was sponsored by Joseph Lehmann. He went to Paris in 1855 and studied French journalism until 1860. In 1863 he became editor of the *Düsseldorfer Zeitung,* and was on friendly terms with Ferdinand Lassalle, whom he rendered important services. From 1866 to 1869 Lindau edited the *Elberfelder Zeitung.* In 1872 he founded the weekly *Die Gegenwart* which he edited until 1881, supported by Eduard Lasker, Ludwig Bamberger and other celebrities of that time. In 1877, he founded the monthly *Nord und Süd,* to which the leading professors of Germany contributed.

From 1895 to 1899 Lindau was stage-manager of the Duke of Meiningen's Hoftheater. From 1900 to 1903 he directed the Deutsches Theater in Berlin, then became dramaturge of the Royal Schauspielhaus in Berlin until 1918. During the 1870's and 1880's Lindau was esteemed, feared and fought as "the literary pope of Germany." He established his literary position by critical essays, *Literarische Rücksichtslosigkeiten,* published in 1870. He satirized Richard Wagner by his *Nüchterne Briefe aus Bayreuth* in 1876, and by his *Bayreuther Briefe vom reinen Toren* in 1883. Many of his dramatic works met with great applause, especially *Maria und Magdalena* (1872), *Ein Erfolg* (1874), and *Gräfin Lea* (1879).

In *Gräfin Lea,* Lindau combatted anti-Semitism. As a dramatist, he drew on French models, especially Dumas and Sardou. He wrote also novels and stories, the best-known of which was *Der Zug nach dem Westen,* published in 1886. At the end of the 1880's Lindau was violently opposed by the naturalistic movement, and was finally defeated. None of his works found lasting fame.

Lindau married David Kalisch's daughter Anna, who later married the French author Jules Case. At the end of his life, Lindau met with great success in publishing his drama, *Vorspiele auf dem Theater* (1915), and his memoirs, *Nur Erinnerungen* (1917).

LINDAU, RUDOLF, diplomat and author, b. Gardelegen, Germany, 1829; d. Paris, 1912. He was the brother of Paul Lindau. He studied at the Universities of Berlin, Paris and Montpellier, was secretary of Barthélemy Saint-Hilaire, and contributed to the *Revue des deux mondes,* to the *Journal des débats,* and to the *Nouvelle biographie générale.*

In 1860 the Swiss government sent Lindau to Japan, and he effected the first commercial treaty between Switzerland and Japan. As consul of Switzerland, he resided in Japan until 1869. In 1863 he published *Voyage autour du Japon,* and in 1864 he founded the *Japan Times* at Yokohama. He also visited China and the United States. Returning to Europe, Lindau participated in the campaign of 1870 as secretary of Prince August of Württemberg. Lindau's report, *Die preussische Garde im Feldzug 1870-71,* is generally esteemed as the best description of that war written by a German author. It was his first attempt in German, for he had previously written in either French or English.

After the Franco-Prussian War, Lindau was attached to the German Embassy at Paris. In 1878 Bismarck appointed him councillor in the Foreign Office at Berlin. He was an intimate friend of Bismarck and his family until Bismarck's dismissal.

In 1892 Lindau became representative of Germany in the administration of the Dette Ottomane at Constantinople. He retired from office ten years later. At an advanced age, Lindau became a novelist, writing in French, English and German. His *Peines perdues* was published in 1881; *The Philosophical Pendulum and other stories* in 1883; *Gordon Baldwin* in 1887; *Robert Ashton* in 1879; and *Türkische Geschichten* in 1897.

As a novelist, Lindau was one of the first followers of Turgenev, but his art of developing personal originality was on a high level.

Lit.: Bieber, Hugo, *Der Kampf um die Tradition* (1928); Brauer, A. von, *Im Dienst Bismarcks* (1936); Raschdau, Ludwig, *Unter Bismarck und Caprivi* (1939).

LINDEN, a city in the state of New Jersey, about ten miles south of Newark; its population of 24,115 (1940 census) includes about 2,200 Jews. It has three Orthodox congregations: Anshe Chesed (organized about 1913); Ahvis Achem; and Agudath Achim. Morris Baicofsky was rabbi of Anshe Chesed from 1920 on, and was still serving as such and as head of the Talmud Torah of the congregation in 1941. In 1941 Louis Tabachnik was rabbi of Ahvis Achem,

and Yale Goldberg head of the Talmud Torah conducted by Agudath Achim.

There are a number of other Jewish organizations in Linden. These include the Progress Club, a branch of the Zionist Organization of America, a group of the Hadassah, two Hebrew free loan associations, and several benevolent societies.

Charles Kasper was one of the first Jewish councilmen of Linden. Abraham Weinberg was also a councilman. Julius Kalish was a member of the city council (1941). Lewis Winetsky, before becoming city attorney in 1934, was president of the common council; in 1941 he was still serving as city attorney. His predecessor was Philip Cohen (1930-34). Louis Levine was a member of the board of education; he was succeeded by Francis Schwartz, and the latter by Emanuel Margulies, still serving in this capacity in 1941. When Linden was still a township, William E. Reibel was the police judge. Louis Rakin is at present (1941) serving as police court judge.   LEWIS WINETSKY.

LINDERER, ROBERT, writer and theatre manager, b. Erfurt, Germany, 1824; d. Berlin, 1886. When he was two years old, the family moved to Berlin. His father, a dentist, decided that Robert also should become a dentist and sent him to the Friedrichswerder Gymnasium in preparation for the university. But the father's sudden death (1840) put an end to Robert's study, since the means left by the father were not sufficient to enable his many children to attend higher schools of learning. So Robert became a printer and made his living by printing until 1861. From this point on he turned wholly to writing. In 1866 he became joint owner of the R. Frankesche Theateragentur and of its official theatre magazine, called *Neue Schaubühne.*

In 1886 the performance of *Unsere Marine,* a musical, made his name famous all over Germany, since its eleventh scene started with a patriotic poem *Stolz weht die Flagge schwarz weiss rot,* which became one of the most popular patriotic songs during the first World War, and which was sung in Germany as late as 1942. The music was written by a non-Jew, Eugen Friedrich Richard Thiele. *Unsere Marine* is a satirical play, like all the other plays by Linderer, such as: *Promenadenbekanntschaften* (1864); four books to plays with music: *Ra-Ta-Tschin,* a Chinese burlesque with songs and ballet (1850); *Zankteufelchen* (1885); *Der schönste Mann im Regiment* (1886); and *Neptun oder der Verräter in Gips,* performed in 1888 after his death. In addition to satirical lyric and prose writings, Linderer published *Humoresken* (1846); *Lichtbilder* (1847); *Freie Lieder* (2 vols., 1848); *Brennesseln* (1850); *Hochzeits- und Tischreden* (1862); *Jubelreigen* (1863); *Humoristische Ein- und Ausfälle* (1879); and *Berlin, wie es leibt und lebt* (1880).

LINDHEIM, IRMA L., Zionist worker, b. New York city, 1886. She studied at Columbia University and the Jewish Institute of Religion. From 1908 to 1912 she was director of the Federation of Child Study, for the five years following was a social worker at Lebanon Hospital, and during the first World War was with the Motor Corps Service of America.

Her Zionist service has included two years as chairman of the seventh district in New York of the Zionist

Organization (1919-21); two years as national vice president of the Z. O. A. (1926-28); two years as national president of Hadassah (1926-28); and a term as national vice-chairman of the United Palestine Appeal (1933). In the latter year she took up permanent residence in Palestine, and engaged in colonization work in Mishmar Haemek, a collective agricultural colony. On several occasions she returned to the United States to lecture in behalf of the Jewish National Fund, Hadassah, the Z. O. A., the League for Labor Palestine, the Histadruth, Hashomer Hatzair and the Jewish Welfare Board. In 1942 she was in the United States in behalf of Zionist youth activity, and participated in the formation of the American Zionist Youth Commission. She wrote *Palestine, the Immortal Adventure* (1928), as well as innumerable articles in Zionist publications.

LINDO, DAVID, experimental chemist, b. Island of Jersey, 1833; d. Jamaica, British West Indies, 1889. He began experimenting at any early age, fitting up his own laboratory without any aid. He introduced many chemical reagents, such as the test for albumen, nitrates and nitrites. He also did original research in the chemical production of pure glass, and showed how impurities could be eliminated in the course of manufacture. He was regarded as the finest chemist in the West Indies. His method, together with Sladding's, for determining the total nitrogen in fertilizers was adopted by the United States government and is known in textbooks as the Lindo-Sladding Method.

Lit.: Lindo, Alicia, in *Publications of the American Jewish Historical Society,* No. 23 (1915) 37-43.

LINDO, ELIAS HAYIM, Anglo-Jewish historian, b. 1783; d. London, 1865. About 1835 he emigrated to England from the island of St. Thomas, where he had been one of the leading merchants and president of the congregation.

In England, in addition to his business activities, he devoted himself to literary productions. In 1838 he published a *Jewish Calendar for Sixty-four Years;* this includes a comprehensive chronological table of Jewish history. A translation of Manasseh ben Israel's *Conciliator* appeared in 1842. He traveled to the Iberian Peninsula in order to obtain material from original sources for his book *History of the Jews in Spain and Portugal,* published in 1848. Lindo made translations in manuscript of several valuable Hebrew, Spanish and Portuguese works.

He was an active member of the London Spanish and Portuguese congregations.

LINDO, MOSES, merchant, b. probably in England, about 1712; d. Charleston, S. C., 1774. Little is known about his early life. He was a London dealer in indigo, and came to the colony of South Carolina in 1756 to carry on his trade. He was convinced of the superiority of Carolinian over French indigo and invested the sum of 120,000 pounds in his business.

Lindo soon came to be recognized as the leading indigo exporter of the colony; at that time indigo was next to the largest industry in South Carolina, second only to rice. In 1762 he was appointed surveyor and inspector-general of indigo for the Carolinas, a position he held until he resigned in 1772. He was interested in indigo from the scientific as well as financial point of view, and in 1763 his description of his

chemical researches was printed in the *Transactions of the British Royal Society* under the title "An account of a new dye from the berries of a weed in South Carolina."

Though more is known about Lindo's years in South Carolina than about his previous life, there have been several errors prevalent in historical writings about his true position in the colony. Elzas definitely proved, in *The Jews of South Carolina,* that Lindo was never a soldier, a planter, or a slave-holder, as stated by earlier historians.

Lit.: Huhner, Leon, *The Jews of South Carolina Prior to 1800;* Elzas, Barnett A., *The Jews of South Carolina* (1905) 47-67.

LINETZKI, ISAAC JOEL, satirist, b. Winnica, Russia, 1839; d. Odessa, 1915. His acquaintance with the Maskilim of his town made him desire to acquire secular learning, which he obtained with the greatest secrecy. His father, a religious fanatic, suspecting him of heresy, married him off at the age of fourteen to a bride of twelve. Further oppression drove him to Odessa (1858), where he studied for the rabbinate. His literary career began at Zhitomir in 1862.

His first Hebrew article appeared in *Hamelitz* in 1865, and his first Yiddish story, the remarkable "A Polisher Yingel" (A Polish Boy), appeared in *Kol Mebasser.* The success of the latter was instantaneous. In 1869 his satirical poems appeared under the title *Der beiser Marshalik.* In this work he spared neither the Hasidim nor the aristocrats and forcibly criticized all the negative phases of Jewish life. In Lemberg in 1875 he met his childhood friend, Abraham Goldfaden; the two conducted a newspaper, *Yisrolek,* which lasted for only twenty issues. He then returned to Odessa, where he issued a "practical calendar," a series of "Linetzki's writings" and numerous booklets under the general title, *Amerika zu Eretz Yisroel,* in which he championed political nationalism. He also wrote a geography of Palestine, translated into Yiddish works of Lessing, Graetz and others, as well as the prayer-book, and wrote *Der Vorem in Chrein,* a sequel to "A Polisher Yingel."

Linetzki's literary career was no less tragic than had been his early youth. For while he was the most famous Yiddish writer of his day, he was almost completely forgotten by the end of the century. He had survived his own writing by a whole generation, and the new reading public no longer considered his works timely, nor could his ever-rebellious and bitter spirit appeal to them. Nevertheless, this remarkable literary personality well deserves to be known as one of the pioneers of modern Yiddish literature, for (1) he was the first Maskilim-writer who enjoyed a direct approach to the great numbers of the Jewish masses; (2) his "A Polisher Yingel" was the surest and deadliest weapon by means of which the Haskalah had stormed the camp of its enemy, Hasidism; and (3) he had dared to take a positive and democratic stand toward Yiddish, regarding the language not only as purely utilitarian but as a literary vehicle superseding Hebrew. "Only in *zhargon* (Yiddish) can the spirit and the characteristics of the unhappy Jewish people be reflected."

His language was vigorous and inventive, his style simple, direct and dynamic. Those of his passages which are exclusively devoted to description (rather

Paul Link

than to an exposition of his Haskalah ideas) reveal a passionate artist whose lucidity and depth hold the reader spellbound. His portrayals are often infused with pathos or rendered grotesque by his own peculiar high-lighting.

Because of his tendency to write fleeting descriptions, Linetzki may be said to be the forerunner of modern Yiddish impressionism. Likewise he is the forerunner of Yiddish expressionism, because of his dynamic and spasmodic depictions.

Lit.: For an extensive bibliographical list, see Reisen, Z., *Lexikon fun der Yiddisher Literatur, Presse un Filologie*, vol. 2 (1927). In addition, see Granovsky, R., in *Pinkes*, vols. 1-2 (1927); vol. 3 (1928); Shalit, M., in *Fun Yor Tzu Yor*, No. 4 (Warsaw, 1929); Shtif, N., in *Die Eltere Yiddishe Literatur* (1929); Litvak, A., in *Literatur un Kampf* (1933); Niger, S., in *Zukunft*, Oct., 1939; Minkoff, N. B., in *Freie Arbeter Shtimme*, May 3 and 10, 1940.

LINK, PAUL, textile expert, b. Sahy, Czechoslovakia, 1903. He was educated at the Textile Academy of Vienna, Austria (1921) and at Leeds University in England (diploma in textile industries, 1925). In 1931 he was awarded the Leeds University scholarship. He emigrated to Argentina in 1925 to become professor of industries at the Industrial College of Buenos Aires, and in 1934 he became adviser on wool to that country's Ministry of Agriculture; he still held both posts in 1942. As an expert on wool he was an important figure in the commercial circles of Argentina, where sheep raising is one of the major industries.

Link was interested in Jewish affairs and was a member of the International Order of B'nai B'rith and of the executive board of the Zionist Federation of Argentina.

Link wrote several books in Spanish and English, including: *Lanares y lanas de la Republica Argentina* (1933); *Sheep Breeding and Wool Production in the Argentine Republic* (1934); *Evolución del Judaismo* (1934); *Patagonia y Tierra del Fuego* (1936); *Ovinos* (1937). He was correspondent of several technical and Jewish journals and a contributor to this encyclopedia.

LINZ, capital of Upper Austria, situated on the Danube river about eighty miles west of Vienna; in 1937 it had over 100,000 inhabitants, including about 1,500 Jews. The city was an important trading center, and Jews settled there at least as early as the 12th cent. The first definite evidence of their presence comes from about 1300, when their communal life was already active and they were considered to be old settlers. They suffered persecutions in the 14th cent. and there was an accusation of host desecration in 1338; in 1349, on the other hand, they escaped attacks because of the Black Death and took in refugees from other stricken Jewish communities. In 1396 all the Jews of the city were thrown into prison and escaped only with the loss of their possessions and the payment of a ransom; in 1426 they were expelled, probably as a result of the host desecration charge at Enns; their synagogue was turned into a church.

In the next centuries Jews visited Linz only for the purpose of trading, and after the expulsion of all the Jews from Austria (1573) Jews came thither from Bohemia and Moravia for the annual fairs, where they traded in jewels, grains, clothes, spices, feathers and horses. They were first officially permitted to settle permanently again in Linz in the middle of the 19th cent., and from then on the community grew rapidly. A cemetery was laid out, a synagogue built, and various rabbis served the community, among them being Adolf Kurrein (1876-83) and his son Victor (from 1923 on).

Linz has a special interest as being the place where Adolf Hitler attended school and had some of his first contacts with Jews. In spite of the fact that the city was a center of German racialism, it had apparently no effect on him, and in fact his family at that time had a Jewish physician. However, after the Nazi seizure of Austria in 1938, the Linz community was not spared, and one of the first acts of the new regime was to expel all the Jews of the city.

Lit.: Kurrein, Victor, "Die Juden in Linz," *Festschrift anlässlich des 50-jährigen Bestandes des Linzer Tempels* (1927).

LION. Lions were frequent and abundant in the Near East through the entire ancient period. The Assyrian kings reserved them for their sport of hunting, and depicted such scenes on their monuments; the classical stories frequently allude to combats between their heroes and ferocious lions. It is not surprising, therefore, that the Bible should contain frequent references to the "king of beasts," which was ever a danger to the lives and the domestic animals of the inhabitants of Palestine.

The Bible writers characterize the lion as being notable for beauty, strength, courage and ferocity. Its haunts are in the woods, the caves in the mountains, the thickets, the deserts, and the lush jungle of the Jordan valley. *Ezek.* 19, with its parable of the lion as representing the royal family, gives a complete picture of the life of the lion from its rearing as a cub to its final capture. Yet while the lions of Palestine are frequently mentioned as attacking flocks and killing people, they were less formidable beasts than those of Africa, as shepherds sometimes were able to attack them with sling and staff and even rescue "two legs, or a piece of an ear" of an animal (*I Sam.* 17:34-36; *Amos* 3:12). One of Samson's feats was that of killing a lion with his bare hands (*Judges* 14:5-6); Benaiah, one of David's heroes, won renown by killing a lion in a pit on a snowy day (*II Sam.* 23:20). On the other hand, lions

Jacques Lipchitz

terrorized the colonists whom the Assyrians settled in Palestine (*II Kings* 17:25-26). The lions mentioned as being kept in a den by the king of Persia (*Dan.* 6:8) were probably kept to be released for hunting.

Since the Bible considers the lion as the symbol of majesty and strength, it frequently compares its heroes—such as Judah, Gad, Dan, Saul and Jonathan, and even God himself—to lions. In the *Psalms* the lion symbolizes the powerful and rich oppressors of the poor. Judas Maccabeus is compared to a lion roaring for prey (*1 Macc.* 3:4).

Rabbinical literature distinguished seven names for the lion: *gur,* "cub"; *kefir,* "young lion"; *'ari or 'aryeh,* "adult lion"; *shahal,* "a lion advanced in age and strength"; *shahatz,* "a lion in full vigor"; *labi,* "old lion"; *layish,* "a lion decrepit with old age." Since lions were used in gladiatorial combats, Jews were forbidden to sell them to the heathen. There are numerous fables similar to those of Aesop in which the lion figures, and the word "lion" is often used as a symbol for scholars.

Since the lion was the symbol of Judah (*Gen.* 49:9), it became a frequent Jewish symbol in the Middle Ages and after. Persons named Judah often adopted additional personal names or family names based on words for lion. Among these are Ari, Aryeh, Leo, Leon, Löwe and its variants Löw, Loew, Loewe, Loewi and the like, and Lion and Lyon.

LION, FLORA, painter, b. London. She studied at the Royal Academy in London and later with Jean Paul Laurens in Paris. Miss Lion has exhibited at the Royal Academy shows since 1900, and also at salons throughout Europe. Although her work included also studies and prints, her reputation was built to a large extent on her portraiture. Many of England's leading personages have sat for her, including Queen Elizabeth, of whom she made a portrait in 1940. Miss Lion's work has been purchased by the Tate Gallery, which has a portrait of her mother, and also by the British Museum Print Room and the Imperial War Museum. She painted two murals for Great Westminster House.

LIPCHITZ, JACQUES, sculptor, b. Druskieniki, Poland, 1891. He studied first in Vilna and came to Paris in 1909, where he attended the École des Beaux-Arts and the Académie Julian. This was the height of the cubist period, and the first influences to which Lipchitz was subjected were those approaching the abstract in art. His own interpretative powers, however, adopted the cubist method as a departure. Soon after the first exhibition of his work was held in Paris in 1912, Lipchitz became known as one of the outstanding representatives of the modernist trend. Showing regularly at the Salon des Indépendants and the Tuileries thereafter, Lipchitz continued to work out his own technique of simplifying form, and came away from the cubist to a clearer line of plastic continuity. With Lipchitz, the method frequently achieves a liveliness which the abstract approach does not usually have; his *Sailor* (1914) already displayed this capacity in its freedom and swagger. Later, as his subject matter included deeper concepts, his individuality, which Élie Faure described as an "escape from the tyranny of formula in order to find beneath it the true tradition," manifested itself in occasionally more abstract, but unquestionably increasing power.

Lipchitz, who became a French citizen in 1924, remained a member of the artists' colony there until 1941, living in a house near Paris. He came to the United States in 1941, and in 1942 was living in New York city. His work is represented, in the United States, in the Barnes Foundation in Philadelphia, the Museum of Modern Art, the Richmond, Va., museum and in many private collections.

Lit.: Raynal, Maurice, *Jacques Lipchitz* (1920); George, Waldemar, *Jacques Lipchitz* (1929); *Documents,* 1930, No. 1, pp. 17-24; *Amour de l'Art,* 1921, pp. 255-58; 1926, pp. 299-302; Medgyes, Ladislas, "The Sculpture of Jacques Lipchitz," *American Hebrew,* Feb. 22, 1924, p. 441.

LIPINER, SIEGFRIED, author, b. Yaroslav, Galicia, 1856; d. Vienna, 1903. Under great hardships caused by poverty he studied in Leipzig, Strasbourg and Vienna. His drama, *Der entfesselte Prometheus* (1876), his epic, *Renatus* (1878), and his philosophical work, *Buch der Freude* (1880), caused a literary sensation, and he was awarded the Austrian State Literature Prize. In 1881 he was appointed librarian to the Austrian Senate; this provided him a steady income so that he could devote himself to literary work. But the high hopes aroused by his three books went unfulfilled. He confined himself to translating works of prominent Czech and Polish authors and poets, among them Adam Mickiewicz, whom he introduced to the German public. Lipiner was converted to Christianity.

Lit.: Scherer, Wilhelm, *Kleine Schriften,* vol. 2 (1893).

LIPKIN, ISRAEL, Talmudist and moralist, known frequently as Rabbi Israel Salanter, chief exponent of the "Musar" (moralist) movement in the 19th cent., b. Zhagory, Kovno, Lithuania, 1810; d. Königsberg, Germany, 1883. As a child he gave promise of unusual intellectual endowments and exhibited a precocious ethical sense. He received Talmudic instruction from Rabbi Hirsch Broda (Braude), and was initiated into the mysteries of "Musar" by Joseph Zundel. In 1840 he was called to Vilna as head of the Ramailes Yeshiva, but owing to personal differences with Rabbi Mordecai Meltzer, he resigned in favor of his rival and established

Jacob Goodale Lipman

his own Yeshiva at Zarechye, a suburb of Vilna. He also founded societies for the propagation of ethical principles which he had evolved.

Lipkin exhorted his enthusiastic disciples to strive to attain moral elevation by means of self-renunciation and mental discipline. He endeavored to make virtuous behavior an instinctive matter. In order to counteract the effects of the Haskalah (enlightenment), Lipkin tried various ways of diffusing Talmudic knowledge, but with little success. He aided the publication of such ethical works as the *Mesillath Yesharim* of Moses Hayim Luzzatto, the *Heshbon Hanefesh* of Mendel Levin and the *Goren Nachon* of Solomon ibn Gabirol. In 1861 he founded and edited, in Memel, the rabbinical weekly *Hatebunah,* which contained also his own contributions; only twelve issues appeared.

When, in 1884, the Russian government founded the first rabbinical seminary, Lipkin declined, for religious reasons, the position as supervisor. Owing to his austerity and rigorous self-discipline he became afflicted with a nervous disorder which manifested itself in 1857, when he moved to Germany for psychiatric treatment. Lipkin left behind no large work. Desultory essays of his were published by his disciples and were incorporated into *Eben Yisrael* (Warsaw, 1883) and *Etz Peri* (Vilna, 1880).

Lit.: Rosenfeld, S., *Israel Salanter* (Hebrew; 1911); Maggid and Steinschneider, *Ir Vilna,* p. 128 et seq.; Fünn, S. J., *Keneseth Yisrael,* p. 697; Weinberg, in *Yeshurun,* 1920, pp. 595-605; 1921, pp. 52-61, 162-68.

LIPMAN, CLARA, actress, *see* MANN, LOUIS.

LIPMAN, JACOB GOODALE, soil chemist and bacteriologist, b. Friedrichstadt, Russia, 1874; d. New Brunswick, N. J., 1939. His parents were living in Moscow when the Russian government expelled the Jews from the city, and he came to the United States in 1888. His father bought a farm in New Jersey, and Jacob studied at the Baron de Hirsch Agricultural School at Woodbine (1894). Supporting himself, at first, by doing chores for neighboring farmers, he continued his studies at Rutgers College (B.S., 1898) and Cornell University (M.A., 1900; Ph.D., 1903).

Lipman was an assistant chemist from 1898 to 1899 at the New Jersey State Agricultural Experiment Station, New Brunswick, N. J. He was soon (1901) soil chemist and bacteriologist at the station and, from 1911 on, director. He also taught at the New Jersey State College of Agriculture of Rutgers University: instructor in agricultural chemistry from 1902 to 1906; assistant professor from 1906 to 1907; associate professor of agriculture from 1907 to 1910; professor of soil fertility and bacteriology—the first department of its kind in the United States—from 1910 to 1913; professor of agriculture from 1913 on and, from 1915 until his death, dean of the faculty of agriculture.

His work was chiefly devoted to increasing the yield of the soil, and his studies, for the most part, turned upon the action of bacteria in maintaining and increasing fertility. He was the author of *Bacteria in Relation to Country Life* (1908) and *Laboratory Guide of Soil Bacteriology* (1912). He was the founder and editor-in-chief of *Soil Science,* and associate editor of the *Annales des Sciences Agronomiques,* the *Archiv für Pflanzenbau,* and the *Pennsylvania Farmer.*

He was the delegate of the United States government to a number of international conferences concerned with problems of agriculture. He was president of the First International Congress of Soil Science, held at Washington, D. C., in 1927, and chairman of the American delegation to the third congress at Oxford, England, in 1935. He received a number of awards; these include: a prize in 1928 of $1,250, presented by the American Society for Agronomy because of his contributions to the field of nitrogen research (he gave the money to the trustees of Rutgers University to form the nucleus of an endowment for research in soil science); in 1934, the Chandler Medal, presented by Columbia University for his work in agricultural chemistry. Rutgers College conferred an honorary degree (D.Sc.) upon him in 1923, and the Catholic University of Santiago, Chile, another honorary degree in 1930.

Lipman was a director of the Jewish Agricultural Society. In 1928 he was a member of the commission of experts that made a survey of Palestine to study its possibilities for settlement by Jews, and in the following year he became one of the non-Zionist members of the Jewish Agency.

CHARLES BERNARD LIPMAN, plant physiologist (b. Moscow, 1883), was a younger brother of Jacob Goodale Lipman. He was brought to the United States in 1889. He studied at Rutgers College (B.S., 1904; M.S., 1909), the University of Wisconsin (M.S., 1909), and the University of California (Ph.D., 1910). He was Goewey fellow at the Univerity of California from 1908 to 1909, and from then on was on the staff of the university: instructor in soil bacteriology (1909), assistant professor of soils (1910), associate professor (1912), professor of soil chemistry and bacteriology (1913-21), professor of plant nutrition (1921-25), and, from 1925 on, professor of plant physiology. From 1923 on, he was dean of the graduate division.

Lipman was associate editor of *Soil Science, Journal of Bacteriology,* and *Plant Physiology.* He wrote numerous articles on bacteriology and plant physiology for scientific journals.

In 1934 he was awarded the honorary degree of Doctor of Science by Rutgers University.

CHARLES REZNIKOFF.

LIPMANN, OTTO, psychologist and expert in vocational guidance, b. Breslau, Germany, 1880; d. Berlin, 1933. From 1906 to 1916 he was co-director, and from 1916 to his death director, of the Institut für Angewandte Psychologie, and from 1907 to his death he and William Stern were editors of the institute's publication. The two editors also issued, from 1918 on, *Schriften zur Berufseignung und des Wirtschafts-lebens* and *Annalen der Betriebswissenschaft und Arbeitsforschung.* Lipmann was secretary of the Arbeitsausschuss der deutschen Wirtschaftsenquete from 1926 to 1930.

His most important writings are: *Grundriss der Psychologie für Juristen* (1908; 3rd ed., 1925); *Grundriss der Psychologie für Pädagogen* (1909); *Psychische Geschlechtsunterschiede* (1917; 2nd ed., 1919); *Psychologische Berufsberatung* (1917; 2nd ed., 1919); *Psychologie für Lehrer* (1920); *Psychologie und Schule* (1920); *Berufseignung, Berufswahl, Berufsberatung* (1922); *Das Arbeitszeitproblem* (1924); *Unfallursachen und Unfallverhütung* (1925); *Grundriss der Arbeitswissenschaft* (1926).

LIPMANN-MÜHLHAUSEN, YOMTOB BEN SOLOMON, apologete who lived in Prague and its vicinity in the 14th and 15th centuries. He was judge (Dayan) and possibly head of the Yeshiva at Prague; it is probable that he also resided for a time at Lindau in Bavaria and at Cracow. He was not only a rabbinical authority, but was well acquainted with the Bible, knew Latin, and possessed a secular education unusual for his time. In 1399 Lipmann-Mühlhausen and a number of other Jews were arrested because of the charges of an apostate Peter (Pesah) to the effect that the Jews were blaspheming against the Christian religion. He was called upon to defend the Jews against these charges, and did so with skill and adroitness; nevertheless, all the other Jews were condemned to the stake.

Lipmann-Mühlhausen, as the result of this and other controversies, composed (probably between 1401 and 1405) his great apologetic work, *Sefer Hanitzahon* (Book of Victory). In this he attacks the main Christian doctrines, as well as the Karaite doctrines, paying especial attention to refuting Christian interpretations of individual passages from the Bible. It is characterized by acute discussion and keen humor, and shows a thorough knowledge of the New Testament. The book caused a great sensation among the Christians, and induced the bishop of Brandenburg, Stephan Bodecker, and other Christian scholars to publish counter-arguments. An incomplete edition was published by Hakspan (Altdorf and Nuremberg, 1644), and more complete versions from 1709 on; it was translated several times into Latin.

Lipmann-Mühlhausen wrote also a Cabalistic book on the alphabet, printed with the *Baruch Sheamar* of Samson ben Eliezer (Shklov, 1804), a commentary on the *Shir Hayihud* poem in the liturgy, printed in the Siddur of Naphtali Treves (1560), and various responsa. He is identified with a Tabyomi who wrote various Cabalistic works, and Wagenseil attributes to

him a *Zichron Sefer Hanitzahon,* a refutation of Christianity, which he printed in his *Tela Ignea Satanae* (Freiburg, 1681) with a Latin translation.

Lit.: Kaufmann, I., *Rabbi Yomtob Lipmann Mühlhausen* (Hebrew; 1927).

LIPPE, KARPEL (Nathan Pethahiah), Roumanian Jewish leader and author, b. Stanislawów, Galicia, 1830; d. near Vienna, 1915. He served as physician in Jassy, Roumania, from 1860 on, became a Zionist, and took an active part in the struggles of the Roumanian Jews for emancipation. As early as the 1870's he advocated Jewish colonization in Palestine. He then joined the Hibbath Zion movement and founded Hibbath Zion societies in almost all the cities of Roumania.

In 1882 he participated in the establishment of two Roumanian colonies in Palestine, Zichron Yaakov and Rosh Pinah, and at the Kattowitz Conference in 1884 he represented the Roumanian Chovevei Zion. Lippe was founder of the first Hebrew school in Jassy and co-founder of the Ohole Shem Society for Hebrew literature. One of the first to join the political Zionism movement, he opened the first Basel Zionist Congress, and thereafter, despite his advanced age, he continued as an active worker of the Zionist movement in Roumania. At the beginning of the first World War Lippe fled from Przemysl to Vienna. The best-known of his works are: *Dareche Harefuah* (1869); *Causeries historiques* (1869); *Der Talmud* (1873); *Die Essäer als Maurer* (1875); *Die gerichtliche Medizin in der biblisch-talmudischen Gesetzgebung* (1910).

LIPPMANN, EDMUND OSKAR VON, chemical analyst and historian, b. Vienna, 1857. He was educated at the Vienna Gymnasium and in the chemical division of the Technical High School of Zurich, Switzerland, where he studied under George Lunge. He later attended the University of Heidelberg, and received the degree of doctor of chemistry in 1878.

From 1878 to 1881 Lippmann worked as assistant chemist at the Maschinenbauanstalt at Brunswick. He served as director of the sugar refinery at Duisburg on the Rhine from 1881 to 1884, and held the same position at Rositz from 1884 to 1889. His main contributions to industrial chemistry were made at Halle, where he was director of the largest sugar refinery in Germany from 1889 until he retired in 1926. During this period he developed the process of sugar refining to a remarkably high degree of efficiency, using charcoal for the first time.

He received the title of professor from Halle University in 1901, but resigned in 1923 because of the pressure of outside work. In 1926 his retirement from industrial activity at last permitted him to accept the standing invitation to become honorary professor of historical chemistry, a position which he occupied until the anti-Semitic regime came into power in 1933. Important as his research in chemical analysis was, it was as historian of chemistry that he achieved most notably. In 1927 a *Festschrift* was published in his honor by the Berlin Academy of Sciences, and he was awarded the Academy's highest distinction, the Leibnitz medal.

Lippmann was a remarkably prolific author, noted for the literary distinction of his works as well as for brilliant reasoning and wide learning. He published

Gabriel Lippmann. From a sketch by Ivan Sors

hundreds of papers and dozens of books on all phases of chemistry and chemical history. His most significant work is *Entstehung und Ausbreitung der Alchemie* (2 vols., 1919 and 1931); it contains the only comprehensive survey of the origins and philosophical premises of alchemy. Among his other works are: *Geschichte des Zuckers seit den Ältesten Zeiten* (1890; 2nd ed., 1929); *Rohstoffe, Erzeugnisse und Hilfsprodukte der Zuckerfabrikation* (1900; 8th ed., 1934); *Abhandlungen und Vorträge zur Geschichte der Naturwissenschaften* (2 vols., 1906 and 1913); *Geschichte des Wismuts* (1930); *Erzeugung und Lebenskraft* (1933).

He was deprived of his titles and honors by the Nazi government which took office in 1933, and shortly thereafter he emigrated to London. Advanced age stimulated rather than retarded his mental faculties, and he was still engaged in his work early in 1942.

Lit.: Partington, J. R., "Edmund Oskar von Lippmann," *Osiris*, vol. 3, pp. 5-21.

LIPPMANN, EDUARD, chemist, b. Prague, Bohemia, 1842; d. Vienna, 1919. He studied at the Vienna Gymnasium, at the University of Leipzig and at the University of Heidelberg (Ph.D., 1864). He later pursued post-graduate studies at the Sorbonne in Paris.

In 1868 Lippmann became an instructor at the University of Vienna. Four years later he was appointed a teacher of chemistry at the technical high school of Brünn. From 1877 to 1881 he was professor of analytic chemistry at the Vienna Commercial Academy. In 1875 he became professor in chemistry at the University of Vienna and head of the university's third chemical institute; he held both positions until his death.

He did important research, primarily in the field of organic chemistry. Perhaps his most important work was his experimentation in the preparation of homologues of quinine.

Lippmann wrote many articles on chemical subjects for European scientific journals.

Lit.: Eisenberg, *Das geistige Wien*, vol. 2 (1895).

LIPPMANN, FRIEDRICH, historian of art, b. Prague, Bohemia, 1838; d. Berlin, 1903. He studied in Prague and in Berlin, and was a director of the Berlin Collection of Engravings from 1876 until 1903. His publications embodied authentic researches on engraving and woodcarving, each of his books being issued in several editions. The best-known are: *Zeichnungen von Albrecht Dürer in Nachbildungen* (issued as a standard publication with catalogue in 7 vols. from 1883 to 1927; after Lippmann's death the non-Jew Friedrich Winkler continued this publication); *Zeichnungen von Boticelli zu Dantes Göttlicher Komödie* (1884-87, and thereafter published in many editions, including one with smaller plates in 1896); *Der italienische Holzschnitt im 15. Jahrhundert* (1885). His great work, *Zeichnungen von Rembrandt Harmensz van Rhyn,* was published in ten volumes (the first volumes were published in Berlin and London from 1888 to 1892, the next in The Hague in 1900 and 1901, and the last in Leipzig in 1903; the work was completed by Hofstade de Groot).

In 1893 the first edition of *Der Kupferstich, Handbuch der königlichen Museen zu Berlin* was published. This handbook of engraving, carefully checked over by the directors of the Berlin Collection of Engravings whenever a new edition was made (sixth edition in 1926), was generally regarded as reliable. It includes a survey of the history of the art of engraving and instructions in the technique of engraving, also a bibliography of engraving. In 1895 he edited and introduced a collection of Lucas Cranach facsimiles printed by the Reichsdruckerei in Berlin under the title of *Lucas Cranach, Sammlung von Nachbildungen seiner vorzüglichsten Holzschnitte und seiner Stiche.*

LIPPMANN, GABRIEL, physicist and Nobel Prize winner, b. Hollerich, Luxembourg, 1845; d. Le Havre, France, 1921. Educated at the École Normale in Paris and at the University of Heidelberg, he studied at the laboratory of the celebrated Helmholtz in Berlin in 1874, and in the following year received the D.Sc. degree from the Sorbonne at Paris.

Lippmann became professor of physical mathematics at the Sorbonne in 1883, and of experimental physics in 1885. He was recognized as one of the most important physicists of his day. In 1886 he was honored by election to the Académie des Sciences, and in 1908 he was awarded the Nobel Prize for physics.

Lippmann's outstanding contribution was the invention of the process of color photography in 1891, and he later developed the process to a higher degree of perfection. He also did important research in the physics of surface tension, and invented the capillary electrometer which is a very useful instrument in experiments in physical chemistry.

Lippmann wrote many articles on physics for European and American scientific journals, and was author of two textbooks, *Cours de thermodynamique* (1886) and *Cours d'acoustique et d'optique* (1888).

LIPPMANN, WALTER, author, b. New York city, 1889. He was an outstanding writer on public affairs—questions of government, the organization of society, the trend of the world—at a time when these subjects engaged the public mind as never before since the French Revolution, and on a broader scale, because

Walter Lippmann

of increase in the proportion of the public who could read. The period saw two formidable attempts at new conceptions of society—Communism in Russia, National Socialism in Italy and Germany. By the attempts of these to establish themselves throughout the world—by their bitter conflict with each other, by the attacks of both on the existing order, by the defense of the older order, and a world war arising in part out of conflict among the three—by all this, human society was in ferment everywhere; throughout the world, the very foundations of government rocked.

Through more than a decade of this, among writers dealing with the principles involved and the questions that arose, Lippmann's was at all times one of the three or four voices most widely listened to in America. Part of the time he was practically alone in eminence—by any test composed of scholarship, precision of thought, and lucidity of expression—the number of his readers larger, his influence greater, than any other.

When Lippmann came to this place in American life, in the early 1930's, he was a little over forty years old. His background, and the experience and training which had equipped him, were at once wide and various, and at the same time remarkably focused to form the type of mind for which the times called.

His academic education, completed in 1910 at Harvard (A.B., 1909), had emphasized philosophy—during his final year he was associated with a distinguished professor of that subject, George Santayana. In politics, at this period of his life, his leaning was toward the Socialism of that day; he helped found a Harvard Socialist Club; after graduation he served for a few months as secretary to a Socialist mayor of Schenectady (George R. Lunn). For vocation, his bent was writing. For a short time (1911) he worked as an assistant to a famous journalistic radical, Lincoln Steffens, in investi-

gations (for *Everybody's Magazine*) into political and commercial corruption in large cities, a field of magazine writing widely approved at the time as "muckraking." By an adventitious circumstance during this period—a summer vacation spent with a man who was making the first English translation of Sigmund Freud's work on psychology—Lippmann became familiar with a science important to the understanding of man and society.

Out of what his mind had accumulated at the age of twenty-three, Lippmann wrote a book, *A Preface to Politics,* described as a "searching out of the . . . motives and impulses that underlie human action in the political field." The book brought Lippmann into contact with Theodore Roosevelt, then forming a new political party, the Progressives, designed to adapt politics and government to changes that had come into the world of business and economics. Lippmann's book brought him into contact also with the founders of a journal of opinion, *The New Republic,* an organ of liberalism, as liberalism was then understood; Lippmann became an associate editor (1914). Through this connection Lippmann came into contact with President Woodrow Wilson, then busy at once with reforms in the United States and with the problems emerging upon him from the first World War in Europe. Lippmann was now deep in the welter of querying about government and society, a commotion which the generation of 1915 felt was great.

After the United States entered the first World War, in 1917, Lippmann, as an assistant to Secretary of War Newton D. Baker, was in charge of the relations between the War Department and representatives of the workmen engaged in building cantonments. Later, as secretary of the organization directed by Edward M. House, he helped prepare material for the guidance of the American delegation to the Paris Peace Conference; he was with the delegation at Paris. (In the meantime, he had been commissioned a captain in the United States Army intelligence service in 1918 and attached to the general staff of the American Expeditionary Force in France.) In 1919 he resumed his connection with *The New Republic.* He was also a correspondent of the Manchester *Guardian* (1920). In 1921 he became an editorial writer on the New York *Morning World*—its editorial page was the best in the country. In 1923 he was appointed chief editorial writer and in 1929 editor. After seven years of this, and with his previous experiences, Lippmann was rich in knowledge of public questions, a master of lucid expression.

In 1931 came one of those combinations of circumstances in which the public circumstances affect the course of history, and their impacts on individuals often determine human destiny. In America, a decade of fabulous prosperity had recently ended in calamitous collapse, causing violent disruptions in every area of life, public and private—business, finance, politics, personal situations. Whether as an incident of this, or merely as a coincidence, the *Morning World* ceased publication. That left Lippmann foot-loose. He was asked by the New York *Herald-Tribune* to become a columnist. That the leading Republican newspaper of the country took on the former editor of the leading Democratic paper arrested public interest, and called attention to the flux of the times. It gave Lippmann a strong spring-board of momentum. The title chosen for his column, "Today and Tomorrow," had a connotation of prophecy, suggested light on coming developments. And it was light on the future that America was desperately trying to find.

Millions of men had been jolted loose from their business connections, had lost much or all that composed their material footing in the world, were adrift economically, spiritually bewildered. The older school of American business said that the depression had to run its course to the bottom, and these were echoed by some of the more orthodox economists in colleges. From abroad, and from some sources at home, came suggestions that America ought to, or would be obliged to, adopt one of the forms of planned society recently arisen in Europe. From hundreds of sources came proposals of panacea—fiat money, "technocracy."

To a people thus distracted, Lippmann wrote three times a week, in the New York *Herald-Tribune* and in the local papers of more than a hundred other cities and towns (by 1942, about 170), in which his writing was syndicated. Reading him became part of the morning or evening ritual of millions. The people were almost frantically hungry for guidance. In their confusion they would have gulped guidance from almost anyone who gave it with a manner of assurance—many did accept guidance from such. But what they got from Lippmann was always dictated by disinterestedness and conscience. If those who read his interpretations did not always get the whole answer, always they got light and they found a direction pointed, a direction based on sound principle, and fruit of the reflection of a first-class mind. Always he gave light and understanding. Always he was lucid—that word was used about him more than any other. It was as if the jumbled facts and principles of a confused situation were poured into a smooth-running intellectual machine, were by that brought into order, and emerged as a product that could be understood. Never did he make any effort to be popular or seek merely to entertain. He used no devices for achieving a specious effectiveness. He seemed less a journalist making the most of his career than a scholar who used journalism as a means of getting his thought before the people. Austerely, but lucidly, as the decade went on, he wrote about aspects of the complex controversy that engulfed the world—between individualism and collectivism in the economic field; and in government, between centralized power for the sake of desirable efficiency, and parliamentary power for the sake of preserved freedom. To the problems arising out of that conflict, Lippmann devoted a sustained high level of sound thought and clear expression.

The publications of Lippmann, besides a *Preface to Politics* (1913), include: *Drift and Mastery* (1914); *The Stakes of Diplomacy* (1915); *The Political Scene* (1919); *Liberty and the News* (1920); *Public Opinion* (1922); *The Phantom Public* (1925); *Men of Destiny* (1927); *American Inquisitors* (1928); *A Preface to Morals* (1929); *The United States in World Affairs* (1931, 1932, and 1933; with William O. Scroggs); *Interpretations* (1932); *Interpretations* (1933-35); *The Method of Freedom* (1934); *The New Imperative* (1935); *The Good Society* (1937); *Some Notes on War and Peace* (1940).

Lippmann was made an officer of the Legion of Honor and elected a member of the National Institute of Arts and Letters and of the American Academy of Arts and Letters. From 1933 to 1939 he was a member of the board of overseers of Harvard University. He was awarded honorary degrees by a number of universities and colleges, including Amherst College, Columbia University, Dartmouth College, George Washington University, the University of California, the University of Michigan, and the University of Wisconsin.   MARK SULLIVAN.

Lit.: Drake, William A., in *American Hebrew*, Dec. 5, 1924; *American Magazine*, Sept., 1932, p. 16; *Nation*, May 25, 1940; *Time*, Sept. 27, 1937, pp. 45-48; Howe, Quincy, *The News and How to Understand It* (1940); *Current Biography* (1940) 508-10.

LIPPOLD (Yomtob ben Judah Hakohen), mintmaster of Elector Joachim II of Brandenburg, b. Prague, at the beginning of the 16th cent.; d. 1573. He and his family were granted the right of residence in Berlin in 1550, and in 1556 all the Jews in Brandenburg were handed over by the elector to "our trusty and well-beloved Jew Lippold," who was authorized to examine the documents of all Jews and to collect the special taxes imposed upon the Jews. At the same time he conducted a small pawnbroking business. He won favor with the elector, who appointed him mintmaster in 1565; but he was hated by Christians and Jews alike because of his haughty conduct and brutal ways. The Jews of Brandenburg made a complaint against him to the elector, and the Jewish communities of Posen, Cracow and Prague placed him under the ban. However, Lippold's position remained unchallenged until Joachim II suddenly died in 1571. His successor, Johann Georg, arrested Lippold and tried him on a charge of malfeasance in office; of this he was acquitted, since all that could be proved against him was a few petty debts. Immediately afterwards he was accused of witchcraft and of having poisoned the late elector; he was put to the torture, and a "confession" extorted from him. He was broken on the wheel and quartered on January 28, 1573; his wife and children took refuge in Vienna, and the German emperor later forced the elector to restore a thousand talers of Lippold's confiscated estate.

Lit.: Ackermann, Aron, *Münzmeister Lippold* (1910); Heise, W., *Die Juden in der Mark Brandenburg* (1932); Kohut, George A., "Lippold the Court Jew," *Menorah Journal*, vol. 15 (1893) 175-85.

LIPSCHITZ, LEOPOLD, rabbi and communal leader, b. Hagyalja-Mád, Hungary, 1837; d. Budapest, 1904. He studied at the Yeshiva of his father, Isaac Nathan Lipschitz, who had married a granddaughter of Eleazar Löw, known as Shemen Rokeah, and had succeeded him in the rabbinate of Abaujszántó. Lipschitz acquired also a secular education of wide scope. He was active in the centralized organization of the Orthodox Jewish community of Hungary, and served as an official at the Orthodox chancery. He served as rabbi in Abaujszántó from 1874 to 1890, when he was appointed president of the Orthodox chancery. In that capacity he was the head of Hungarian Orthodoxy for more than a decade. He did much to bring Orthodox Jewry into the civic community of Hungary, mediating between government and the Orthodox community. He was not prejudiced against Zionism, which at the end of the 19th cent. filled the students of the Pozsony Yeshiva with new enthusiasm, as long as it went hand in hand with the study and observance of the Torah. The *Jüdisches Tagblatt,* organ of Orthodox Jewry in Hungary, published reports of the fourth Zionist Congress, and in 1900 the Orthodox congregation of Pozsony authorized appeals for the Jewish National Fund to be made in the synagogue.

In 1882 Lipschitz collected testimonials by the greatest non-Jewish contemporary theologians on the blood accusation, which he published under the title *Christliche Zeugnisse gegen die Blutbeschuldigung* and which influenced public opinion on the blood accusation of Tiszaeszlár, then on trial before a court of law. His collection of responsa is still unpublished. In 1896 he was made a knight of the order of Francis Joseph.

LIPSCHITZ, RUDOLF OTTO SIGISMUND, mathematician, b. Königsberg, East Prussia, Germany, 1832; d. Bonn, Germany, 1903. He was educated at the University of Königsberg (Ph.D., 1853). He became Privatdozent at the University of Bonn in 1857, and assistant professor of mathematics at the University of Breslau in 1862. In 1864 he was appointed professor at the University of Bonn, a post which he held until his death.

Lipschitz conducted his most important research in the theory of functions and in advanced analytics. His discoveries in this field are embodied in his principal work, *Lehrbuch der Analysis* (2 vols., 1877-80). His other books include: *Wissenschaft und Staat* (1874); *Die Bedeutung der theoretischen Mechanik* (1876); *Untersuchungen über die Summen von Quadraten* (1886). He wrote many articles on both pure and applied mathematics for scientific journals.

LIPSCHITZ, WERNER, pharmacologist, b. Berlin, 1892. He studied at the Universities of Berlin and Frankfort, and became a lecturer at the University of Frankfort in 1920. In 1924 he was appointed assistant professor and in 1926 professor of the University of Frankfort; later he became head of the pharmacological institute of that university. In 1933 he left Frankfort for Istanbul, since he was forced to give up his position at a German university as a Jew. His researches on the osmotic changes of the blood, effects of poison, and cellular respiration, and also on the pharmacology of inflammations, were published in numerous scientific articles in periodicals.

LIPSCHÜTZ, ALEJANDRO, physician, b. Riga, Russia, 1883. He studied at the Universities of Berlin, Zurich, and Göttingen (M.D., 1907). After a post as physician in an asylum for epileptics in Switzerland (1908) and another as assistant in the departments of pharmacology and physiology of the Universities of Göttingen, Bonn, and Bern, he became an instructor (Privatdozent) of physiology in the University of Bern (1915-19). In 1919, he was appointed professor of physiology and head of the department at the University of Dorpat, Estonia, and served as such until 1926. From 1938 on he was director of the department of experimental medicine of the National Health Service of Chile.

The publications of Lipschütz include: *Warum wir sterben* (Stuttgart, 1914; translated into Russian, 1925, and Spanish, 1930, as well as into other languages); *The Internal Secretions of the Sex Glands* (Cambridge and Baltimore, 1924; translated into Spanish, Madrid, 1928); *La autonomía del corazón* (Madrid, 1930); *La trasplantación ovárica* (Madrid, 1930; translated into German, Leipzig and Budapest, 1930); *Indoamericanismo y raza india* (1937); *El médico y la medicina experimental* (1939); *Ciencia y universidad* (1939).

LIPSCHÜTZ, ELIEZER MEIR, educator, b. Stryj, Galicia, 1879. He settled in Palestine in 1909 and until 1914 taught at the teachers' seminary of the Hilfsverein der Deutschen Juden in Jerusalem. He was a teacher and later director of the Ezra Hebrew teachers' seminary there until 1917, when he was expelled by the Turks. In 1921, after his return, he founded and became director of the Mizrahi teachers' seminary in Jerusalem, where he was still serving in 1942. He was active in the work of the Vaad Halashon in Palestine. In addition to essays in Hebrew and Yiddish periodicals, he wrote: *Rashi* (Warsaw, 1912); *Hamishnah* (also in German translation, 1914 and 1919); *S. J. Agnon* (1925); and a collection of essays, *Vom lebendigen Hebräisch* (Berlin, 1920).

Lit.: Nonsen, J., in *Hashiloah,* vol. 28, pp. 455-61; Gorion, Micah Joseph bin (Micah Joseph Berdyczewski), *Bisede Sefer,* vol. 3, pp. 30-32.

LIPSCHÜTZ, ISRAEL BEN GEDALIAH, rabbi and author, b. 1782; d. Danzig, 1860. He was the son of Gedaliah Lipschütz (1746-1826), who was rabbi in Emden and various other Eastern German communities, and the grandson of Israel ben Eliezer Lipschütz, 18th cent. German rabbi and author. Lipschütz served as rabbi in the communities of Wronke, Dessau, Colmar and finally in Danzig, whither he came in 1837 and where he remained until his death. His major work was the Mishnah commentary *Tifereth Yisrael,* which was distinguished for its clarity and systematic arrangement and remained a source of Talmudic study even in the 20th cent. His introductions and appendices, which included consideration of problems of his day, are of special value. Lipschütz also left commentaries on the Pentateuch, sermons, glossaries to Maimonides and the *Shulhan Aruch,* responsa, and a will, which was published in 1861, and which contained twenty-eight paragraphs of moral and ascetic precepts. His own life was marked by asceticism and prolonged fasts, which won the respect of the Jews of his period.

LIPSCHÜTZ, JACOB HALEVI, Orthodox Jewish writer and opponent of the Haskalah, b. Vilkomir, province of Kovno, Lithuania, 1838; d. Kovno, 1921. In 1870 he went to Kovno, where he became secretary of Rabbi Isaac Elhanan Spektor and conducted his world-wide correspondence. Here, too, he founded a center for combatting the Maskilim, who called him Lishkah Shehorah ("the black chamber"). Lipschütz was the author of the following works: *Dibre Shalom Veemeth* (Words of Peace and Truth; Warsaw, 1884), a collection of articles opposing the project of founding a modern rabbinical seminary; a biography of Isaac Elhanan Spektor, *Toledoth Yitzhak* (1897); extensive memoirs, which his son Notel published under the title of *Zichron Yaakob* (1925-31), containing much interesting material for the understanding of the con-

Louis Lipsky

flict waged in those days by the Orthodox against the protagonists of enlightenment.

LIPSITCH, I. IRVING, social worker, b. Tilsit, Germany, 1884; d. Los Angeles, 1935. He was educated at New York University and the Jewish Theological Seminary of America. He represented the United Hebrew Charities and HIAS at Ellis Island from 1906 to 1914, was general manager of HIAS for the following two years, was manager of the B'nai B'rith employment bureau in New York, and served as superintendent of social service of the Federation of Jewish Charities in San Francisco from 1916 to 1925. He was also a member of the national executive committee of the Zionist Organization of America. At the time of his death he was director of the Federation of Jewish Welfare Organizations in Los Angeles.

LIPSKY, LOUIS, author and Zionist leader, b. Rochester, N. Y., 1876. For a period of more than three decades Lipsky has participated actively in the work of the Zionist Organization of America, the World Zionist Organization and the American Jewish Congress, each of which he aided by writing, speaking, organizing and administering. Lipsky entered Jewish public life through the field of journalism. After editing an English Jewish weekly in Rochester, he was, from 1899 to 1914, managing editor of the *American Hebrew* in New York city. From 1910 to 1913 he was on the staff of the New York *Telegraph,* writing on the theatre and contributing fiction, play reviews and book reviews. For some two years during that time he wrote an article weekly for the Sunday issue of the *Morning Telegraph.*

He also wrote for the *Reader Magazine,* which was edited at that time by Louis Howe, with Sinclair Lewis as his associate. His articles appeared in the New York *Press* on Sundays, and in the *Associated Magazine,* which was the Sunday supplement edition of a nation-wide chain of newspapers, including the New York *Tribune.* He also edited an English page for the *Jewish Daily Herald,* of which Michael Mintz was publisher.

He established the *Maccabaean* as a monthly official organ of the Zionist Organization of America in 1899, and was its managing editor from the first issue, with but brief intervals, until 1913. He continued to edit the paper with the assistance of Meyer Weisgal until 1918, when the *Maccabaean* was transformed into the weekly, *The New Palestine,* as the official organ of the Zionist Organization of America.

Lipsky held a variety of posts in the Zionist movement, first as editor of the *Maccabaean,* then as member of the Zionist Organization of America Executive Committee, and then as chairman of the Executive Committee, following Israel Friedlaender in 1912. He continued as chairman of the Executive Committee until the amalgamated Zionist Organization of America was formed, when he became secretary for organization, retaining that post until 1921, when he became successively general secretary, chairman, and in 1925 president of the Zionist Organization of America. He held that post until 1930.

In his capacity as chairman of the Executive Committee of the Federation of American Zionists, he helped to create the organization committee for an American Jewish Congress in 1913, and represented the Federation in that organization committee until the Boston Zionist convention in 1915, and was subsequently active in the elections for the American Jewish Congress. He was the floor leader of the Zionists at the preliminary conference and also at the first session of the Congress. He was active in the American Jewish Congress in varying periods after the first World War until 1934, when he became one of the vice-presidents and subsequently the only vice-president of the American Jewish Congress. He was largely responsible for the organization of the World Jewish Congress. In 1942 he was chairman of the Governing Council of the American Jewish Congress, and participated in the editing of the *Congress Weekly.*

The first Zionist Congress he attended was that at Vienna in 1913, and thereafter he attended all Zionist Congresses, with the exception of the one in Geneva in 1939. From 1921 on, he attended all meetings of the Actions Committee, which were held in various parts of Europe, including one session held in Palestine.

Lipsky has been recognized as the foremost theoretician of the Zionist movement in America. His editorials in *The New Palestine* and his public statements became the pattern by which Zionist policy in America was formulated. Throughout his Zionist service he was closely associated with Chaim Weizmann, and shared with him in the founding of the Palestine Foundation Fund (Keren Hayesod) in America. He supported Weizmann fully in his efforts to establish the enlarged Jewish Agency, which culminated in its formation at Geneva in 1929. His exceptional style and logical simplicity made his formulations of Zionist program famous throughout the Zionist world, to which he became familiar as the first American Jew who had identified his career completely with the strengthening and the building of the Zionist movement in America.

Having become president of the Eastern Life Insurance Company of New York in 1930, Lipsky devoted himself to the development of that organization into an important agency in the field, but simultanneously continued his active participation in all Jewish and Zionist affairs. In 1942 his offices included the following: national chairman of the Palestine Foundation Fund; vice-president of the Zionist Organization of America; national co-chairman of the United Palestine Appeal; national co-chairman of the United Jewish Appeal; chairman of the Governing council of the American Jewish Congress.

In 1927, on the occasion of Lipsky's fiftieth birthday, his two-volume *Stories of Jewish Life* was published, containing selections from his works.

HENRY MONTOR.

Lit.: Jewish Tribune, Nov. 6, 1925, p. 4; *ibid.,* June 29, 1928, p. 26; American Hebrew, June 7, 1935, p. 89; June 14, 1935, p. 109; Dec. 4, 1936, p. 612.

LIPSNER, BENJAMIN BERL, air mail pioneer, b. Chicago, 1888. During the first World War, as an aeronautical engineer, he was in charge of an army school in airplane construction and maintenance for army pilots; his rank was that of captain. Army mail was transported by airplane, and Lipsner, in 1917, began to gather data with respect to the cost of establishing and maintaining air mail service. After a year's study, he compiled and issued the first official bulletin of the Post Office on the subject.

In 1918 Lipsner was appointed the first superintendent of the Post Office's new air mail division, which was to use army pursuit planes. In two months he established the route between New York and Chicago, and planned new routes, while organizing a trained civilian personnel. He devised electrically heated clothes for the pilots. During his administration there was not a single fatal accident in his division. But in the very year of his appointment Lipsner resigned in protest against what he believed the unnecessary expenditure of large sums for the purchase of special planes for mail transport and because of the hiring of ill-trained pilots.

In 1931 Lipsner was appointed by the mayor of Chicago to regulate flying in that area.

Lit.: Rittenberg, Louis, "An Aerial Pathfinder," *The American Hebrew,* June 7, 1929, pp. 96, 128; idem, "An Airmail Pathfinder," *ibid.,* Sept. 18, 1931, pp. 380, 396.

LIPSON, EPHRAIM, economist and historian, b. Sheffield, England, 1888. He was educated at Cambridge University, and taught history at Oxford from 1910 to 1931. Lipson was the author of many books written from an economist's viewpoint; among them were: *The Economic History of England* (3 vols., 1915-31); *Europe in the 19th Century* (1916); *The History of the English Woolen and Worsted Industries; Increased Production* (1921); *Europe 1914-39* (1940). He was also a contributor to various scholarly journals, and was the first editor of the *Economic History Review,* retaining the post until 1934. Lipson was on the committee of the Jewish Historical Society of England.

LIPTAI, IMRE, journalist and playwright, b. Miskolc, Hungary, 1876; d. Budapest, 1927. After graduating from secondary school he became a journalist at Szeged. In 1907 he went to Budapest where, from 1910 to 1919, he was responsible editor of the daily newspaper *Pesti Napló.* In the years preceding his death in 1927 he was connected with the evening paper *8-Órai Ujság.*

Liptai also wrote for the stage, and cultivated various dramatic genres. His drama *Sarkantyu* (Spurs), written in collaboration with Andor Gábor, was performed by the state National Theatre at Budapest in 1911. The subject for his play *Eresz alatt* (Under the Eaves), was taken from the life of the peasants, while his comedies *Rossz pénz nem vész el* (A Bad Penny Turns Up), *Pesti asszony* (Budapest Girl; 1921); *A jó fiu* (Good Boy) and *Vörös ember* (Red-Haired Man; farce comedy; Gábor Drégely, co-author) satirized Budapest society life. Liptai also contributed farce comedies and sketches for the cabarets, and published six one-act plays under the title *Kegyelmes Uram* (Your Excellency).

LIPTON, see COLONIES, AGRICULTURAL (under CANADA).

LIPTOVSKÝ SVÄTÝ MIKULÁŠ, city in Slovakia. Under the Magyar name of Liptószentmiklós, it was the capital of Liptó county in Hungary until the dismemberment of the Austro-Hungarian monarchy in 1919. From 1918 to 1939 it was incorporated into the Czechoslovak republic, and since 1939 it has belonged to the German-controlled state of Slovakia. The Jewish community of Liptovský Svätý Mikuláš was founded in 1728, but there were sporadic Jewish settlements in the city before that. The noble family of Okolicsányi bestowed its protection upon the Jews, and subsidized the building of a synagogue, in 1731, with a large sum. As the community gradually developed, the synagogue had to be enlarged in 1770 and 1818. A new synagogue, erected in 1846, was destroyed by fire and restored, on two occasions, in 1878 and 1906. The community also had a Beth Hamidrash (house of study). Its first rabbi was Mose Hacohen (called Moreh Zedek), who founded a Talmud Torah in 1756. In 1776 Rabbi Judah Löb Kunitz (1773-1812) founded a Yeshiva, where subsequently Rabbi Eleazar Löw, the famed Shemen Rokeah, taught from 1821 to 1830. The Yeshiva was in existence up to 1860, the year when Rabbi Issachar Ber Sinai, author of *Minhath Oni,* died.

The community maintained a high school of its own which it subsequently had to discontinue for lack of funds, and retained only its elementary school. It had also a library and an archive which was valuable as a source for the history of the community written by Emil Hercog, *A zsidók története Liptószentmiklóson* (1894). Such widely known figures as the theologian Wilhelm Bacher and the German publisher Samuel Fischer stemmed from this community.

Under the Czechoslovak republic, several new charitable institutions sprang up in addition to those in existence before, and Zionism inspired the founding of various cultural and sports associations.

During the years 1940 to 1941 the community was hit by professional and trade restrictions imposed upon the Jews of Slovakia, to whom also residence in the cities was interdicted.

LIPTZIN, SOLOMON, literary scholar, b. Satanov, Russia, 1901. He came to the United States at the age of nine. He was educated at the College of the City of New York (A.B., 1921) and at Columbia University (M.A., 1922; Ph.D., 1924). In 1923 he was appointed assistant professor of German and of comparative literature at the College of the City of New York, which position he still held in 1942.

Liptzin was especially interested in the romantic movement in the German literature of the 19th cent. and its relationship to the contemporary movement in English letters. He wrote several books on these subjects, including: *Shelley in Germany* (1924); *The Weavers in German Literature* (1926); *Lyric Pioneers of Modern Germany* (1928); *Heine* (1928); *From Novalis to Nietzsche* (1929); *Richard Beer-Hofmann* (1936); *A Historical Survey of German Literature* (1936). He wrote also numerous articles for scholarly journals.

Liptzin was actively interested in Jewish and particularly Zionist affairs. He was a member of the Yiddish Scientific Institute and president of the Jewish State Party of America.

LISBON, capital of Portugal. It is more than probable that Lisbon, with its extremely favorable location, attracted Jews during the rule of the Romans and Visigoths. When Henriques Alfonso (1130-85) reconquered the South from the Saracens, he found Jews at Lisbon. Because Alfonso made the city the capital of Portugal, the Jewish population increased to such an extent that it surpassed the communities of Evora and Santarem, which had been more important at an earlier period. The Jews established there in the course of time four "Judarias" (Jewish streets), while each of forty cities of Portugal had merely one Jewish quarter. The oldest Judaria was called "de Pedeira," where in 1260 Ibn Yahya built the first synagogue known to us, at his own expense. The most important Jewish district was the Judaria de Conceilção. At the beginning of the 15th cent. the Judaria Nova was established, and about fifty years later the Judaria near the Pedro Gate.

Portugal was the first country of Europe to organize its Jewry, and Lisbon became its center. Beginning with the reign of Alfonso III (1246-79) the chief rabbi resided here with his staff, controlling the religious and social life of the Jews of the seven provinces.

Among the Jews of Lisbon all kinds of urban occupations were to be found, including those of tailor, shoemaker, mason, smith, carpenter and shopkeeper. Jewish merchants controlled almost the entire commerce of the country by buying the products of the peasants and providing them with what they needed. Through the increasing traffic between Northern Africa and the European west coast the Jews became wealthy; they built magnificent houses and wore expensive clothing. This and the influence of the Jewish physicians, astronomers and taxfarmers at the royal court aroused the enmity of the clergy and the populace. Their repeated complaints that the Jews did not observe the canonical rules of living within the Judarias, of wearing the distinctive Jewish badge and of restricted social intercourse between Jews and Christians do not seem to have changed the generally favorable position of the Jews. The kings needed their economic activity and appreciated their Jewish advisers in the fight for the

A Bible manuscript, dated 1229, from the Lisbon collection at Cervera

independence of the country against the Spaniards and in the campaigns against the Moors. The warnings of such men as Solomon ibn Yahya against luxury and arrogance and the complaints over indifference to the Jewish religion and Jewish studies were not heeded. It is surprising that the birthplace of Isaac Abravanel had no intellectual life of importance comparable to that displayed in several Jewish centers in Spain. For the Abravanel family came from Seville, and scholars such as Joseph Vecinho and Abraham Zacuto lived here as Spanish refugees; only the Ibn Yahya family produced several remarkable scholars.

For about two centuries the situation of the Jews remained favorable on the whole. The first unmistakable sign of insecurity surprised them in 1373, when the invading Castilian army plundered the Jewish quarter at Lisbon and murdered several Jews. After the death of Dom Ferdinand of Portugal (1385) the people, incited by the clergy, forced the removal of the hated Jewish taxfarmers, who were regarded as responsible for the heavy taxes. Riots menaced the existence of all the Jews of Lisbon until the new king João, assisted by his English allies, was able to protect them. But they could not be restored to their previous position. However, when his son Duarte tried to stop economic relations between Jews and Christians, the Jews of Lisbon were strong enough to enforce an investigation.

Under Alfonso V the Jews' position improved, since he needed them in his struggle against the landed classes. But the attitude of the populace remained hostile. In 1449, during the absence of the king, riots broke out at Lisbon, and when the Jews defended themselves several of them were killed. The king punished the culprits, but he could not root out the antagonism. Thus, in 1460, the Cortes of Lisbon voluntarily imposed a tax upon itself on condition that no Jews be allowed to contribute. However, neither these nor similar events seem to have disturbed the feeling of security among the Jews at Lisbon. In 1485 the learned Eliezer Toledano established a printing office which produced, among other important works, the commentary of the Pentateuch by Moses ben Nahman. This establishment and another printing office at the neighboring mountain town of Leiria might be attributed to the increasing influx of Spanish refugees who were settled there without difficulties.

When, in 1492, most of the 100,000 Jewish refugees expelled from Spain came to Lisbon, a severe pestilence broke out. The refugees were considered responsible for it, and were therefore obliged to dwell outside of the city. Only a few craftsmen and the leader of the Castilian Jews, Samuel Naya, and an outstanding physician, Samuel Judan, were exempted from this measure. When, in consequence of the marriage of João II with Isabella of Spain in 1497, all Jews, the remnant of the Spanish refugees as well as the Portuguese Jews, were confronted with the alternative of becoming Christians or of leaving the country, those who decided to remain faithful to Judaism had to gather at Lisbon for departure. About 20,000 preferred exile. They were brought to the castle of Os Estaos, previously inhabited by foreign ambassadors and afterwards the seat of the Inquisitional tribunal. All means were employed to convert them by force. Some gave in, some managed to flee, and the rest were tortured most cruelly. Simon Maimi, the last great rabbi, died as a martyr.

When Emanuel and João II promised not to disturb the converted Jews in their religious practices, they did this in order to retain the Jews as an invaluable and irreplaceable factor in the economic life of his country. The Jewish bankers of Lisbon were indeed just beginning to make the capital not only the port of entry to Europe of the products of the East and West Indies, but also the point of distribution. They were extending their businesses beyond Portugal by setting up branch houses abroad. The Mendes family, for instance, had as their customers the emperor Charles V and Francis I, king of France.

The fact that nearly all the Portuguese Jews had been forced to adopt Christianity distinguished them essentially from the Spanish Marranos, for the latter were deprived of the strongminded who had preferred exile to conversion. Thus the New Christians were able to develop a separate existence; they even had a secret synagogue at Lisbon. But the populace did not relent in its hatred. When, in 1503, a famine threatened, the New Christians were regarded as guilty because of their deceitfulness. An uprising against them at Lisbon could be suppressed only with difficulty.

In 1506 New Christians who had celebrated the Passover and had been surprised and imprisoned were released after two days. This mildness and a tactless utterance by a Marrano on the occasion of a supposed miracle produced a terrible massacre which raged for three days and in the course of which more than 2,000 Jews were killed. The king, seeing his purpose crossed,

punished the ringleaders rigorously and even restricted the autonomy of Lisbon. He extended religious tolerance for another twenty years and gave the Marranos permission to emigrate. For nearly half a century the Marranos managed to avert establishment of the Inquisition. The first auto da fé took place on September 20, 1540. The tribunal at Lisbon far outdistanced those of Evora and Porto in its cruelty and zeal; the archives of Lisbon contain over 40,000 reports of Inquisitional cases down to 1780. Curiously enough, at the middle of the 17th cent., under the Primate of Portugal, a conspiracy against the more progressive government was supported by the Marranos, actuated by a promise of a cessation of the persecutions. The plot was discovered, and some of the leaders were executed. Toward the end of the same century the custom was established of bringing all sentenced Marranos of Portugal to Lisbon to be executed there. Marquis Pombal, the great liberal reformer, struck the first blow against the Inquisition when he ordered, in 1752, that all sentences had to be confirmed by the government. When, in 1755, the earthquake laid nearly the whole city in ruins, the Palace of the Inquisition was destroyed and its seat transferred to Evora. In 1771 Pombal ordered the burning of the registers of the New Christian families, and made intermarriages between them and the old Christians obligatory.

After the Treaty of Utrecht in 1713, Jews from Gibraltar returned to Lisbon as British subjects, joined soon by those from London, mostly descendants of the Portuguese fugitives. In 1801 they rented a small portion of ground for a cemetery and built a small synagogue. During the Napoleonic wars and the terrible famine of 1810 Jewish commercial houses, especially the important firms of Moses Levy Aboab and Manuel Cardozo, helped the government import food. In 1813 a Jewish community was established under the leadership of Rabbi Abraham Dabello; its name, "Gate of Heaven," is the same as that of the Sephardic community at London, indicating their close connection. In 1821 the deputy José Ferraro proposed to the Cortes a law recalling all Jews to Portugal. But the constitution of 1826 did not state whether a Portuguese had the right to belong to any other than to the Catholic religion.

When Levy Bensabbat, who had started the important exportation of cork, participated in the struggle against the autocratic King Miguel and was arrested, he owed his liberty solely to the English consul, who protected him. The official recognition of the Jewish community of Lisbon took place in 1868, but even then only as a colony, and the new synagogue was not permitted to display any external sign, despite the fact that Ashkenazim, who had joined the Sephardim in the last decades of the 19th cent., had backed the government as bankers in its desperate financial troubles and had repeatedly negotiated foreign loans. Finally, during the revolution of 1910, the Jews received equal rights.

After the first World War the Jewish community, about 2,000 persons in number, owned three synagogues, a library, a school and the usual charity institutions. It became of special importance for the return to Judaism of the Marranos of the northern provinces whose existence it made known to the Jewish world. During the second World War (from 1939 on), Lisbon, after the collapse of France, became, as in 1497, practically the sole port of escape for Jewish refugees. On an average, about 4,000 fugitives were at all times in Lisbon, awaiting their American visas.

WILLIAM STEIN.

Lit.: Kayserling, Moritz, *Geschichte der Juden in Portugal* (1867); D'Azevedo, I. L., *Historia dos Cristãos Novos Portugueses* (1921); Schwarz, Samuel, *Os Cristãos-Novos em Portugal no século XX* (1925); Graetz, H., *History of the Jews,* vol. 4 (1927) 374-77, 485-90; vol. 5 (1927) 32, 91; Mendes dos Remedios, *Os judeos em Portugal* (1895); Roth, Cecil, *The History of the Marranos* (1932).

LISBONNE, French Jewish family whose members played an important part in the political history of modern France.

EUGÈNE LISBONNE (b. Nyons [Drôme], 1818; d. Montpellier, 1891) became public prosecutor at Béziers in 1848. Opposed to Napoleon III, Lisbonne was deported to Algeria immediately after the coup d'état of December, 1851. The amnesty of 1863 brought Lisbonne back to France, but he continued to oppose Napoleon's government. In 1870, Lisbonne was appointed prefect of the department of Le Hérault by the government of national defense. Lisbonne was one of the most ardent leaders of the republican party in its struggle against monarchic reaction. He violently resisted President MacMahon's action of May 16, 1877. Later on Lisbonne was elected president of the bar of Montpellier.

ÉMILE-JOSEPH LISBONNE (b. Nyons, 1875), son of Eugène Lisbonne, became assistant public prosecutor of the Seine department in 1919. He was vice-president of the executive committee of the Radical-Socialist party, and was elected senator in 1924. He was a member of one of the cabinets of Camille Chautemps. Lisbonne was a firm supporter of the Front Populaire. He was defeated in the election of 1936. Closely connected with Lucien Lévy-Brühl, Lisbonne always defended humanitarian interests, combatting anti-Semitism and summoning his French coreligionists to help persecuted Jews of other nations. In September, 1941, Lisbonne was placed under administrative internment.

RENÉ LISBONNE, son of Émile-Joseph Lisbonne, was director of the Félix Alcan publishing house at Paris, and edited scientific serial publications and periodicals.

Other members of the Lisbonne family were:

JOCHANAN LISBONNE, who in 1821 supported the petition of the Jews of the former Comtat Venaissin for exemption from the payment of the debts contracted by the government of the Comtat.

SOLIMAN LISBONNE, who was president of the Alliance Israélite Universelle at Bordeaux in the 1860's and a friend of Adolphe Crémieux.

ÉLISSA LISBONNE, who in 1865 published *Étude sur la religion d'Israël.*

ÉMILE ÉLIACINTH LISBONNE, who in 1888 published *Le canal des deux mers,* supporting the agitation for the construction of a canal between the Atlantic and the Mediterranean, and in 1890 a study, *La navigation maritime.*

MAXIME LISBONNE (b. Paris, 1839; d. Paris, 1905). At the age of sixteen, Lisbonne left his family and became a sailor. He was a French soldier in the Crimean War and participated in several French colonial wars. In 1870, Lisbonne was an officer of the National Guard of Paris, and excelled in the battles of Issy and Vaugirard. Then he was a leader of the Commune. While defending a barricade against the troops of the French government, he was wounded, captured and twice sentenced to death by different tribunals. In 1872 his punishment was commuted to life imprisonment. After the amnesty of 1880, Lisbonne went to Paris and directed the Bouffes-du-Nord theatre. He was also director of several cabarets at Paris. In 1884 he edited the *Revue Maratiste.*

LISSA (Polish, Leszno), industrial city in the Polish province of Poznan. It had, in 1931, a population of some 20,000, of whom about 300 were Jews. Originally a village on the estate of the powerful Leszczýnski family, it was made a city by Count Raphael Leszczýnski in 1547 and became of great importance during the Reformation as a haven for religious refugees. Jews received formal permission to settle there after 1580. The first privilege granted to them is dated 1626, and the oldest extant tombstone bears the date 1667. They lived in a separate quarter in the northwestern part of the city with their own constitution and powers of administration, which extended even to their having their own night-watchman. Engaging in various handicrafts, such as tailoring, fur-making and embroidery, some of their guilds had their own rabbis and synagogues. There was also a flourishing trade which extended as far as Moscow and the Turkish border and, in Western Europe, to Leipzig and Berlin. Lissa sent most of Poland's visitors to the Leipzig fairs. The Jews of Lissa, however, had a tragic history in that the ghetto was destroyed by fire several times, notably in the Swedish wars in the 17th cent. Besides, the city changed hands several times (it belonged to Prussia from 1793 to 1807 and from 1815 to 1919). Its Jewish population which, in its most prosperous days, between 1750 and 1790, numbered from 4,000 to 5,000, decreased to about 300 in the post-first World War period.

Lissa was a great center of Talmudic learning, and the "wise men of Lissa" formed a renowned intellectual body. At the beginning of the 18th cent. the Jewish community of Lissa exercised a sort of leadership among the communities of Greater Poland, and in 1751 it could boast of containing the "chief synagogue of Greater Poland." At the end of the 18th cent. Rabbi Akiba Eger the Younger taught in Lissa and married the daughter of a wealthy Jewish citizen. Jacob Lissa, the "Lissaer Rab," a recognized codifier, lived in Lissa from 1809 to 1821. Among the famous men who were born in Lissa were Raphael Kosch (1803-72), the first vice-president of the Prussian National Assembly and a champion of Jewish rights, and Ludwig Kalisch (1814-82), a progressive writer who took part in the revolution of 1848 and later lived in Paris and London as a political refugee.

Situated near the German-Polish frontier, Lissa was one of the first places to be occupied by the German army in September, 1939.

Lit.: Lewin, Louis, *Geschichte der Juden in Lissa* (1904); *Encyklopedja Powszechna Ultima Thule,* vol. 6 (1934) 445.

LISSA, JACOB, *see* Jacob ben Jacob Moses of Lissa.

LISSAUER, ERNST, poet, b. Berlin, 1882; d. Vienna, 1937. In a rather deplorable way he became famous through his "Hassgesang gegen England," which appeared at the beginning of the first World War and was then the most popular poem in Germany. But even before this he had written notable poems, first a small volume, *Der Acker,* containing epigrammatical verse, and then, in a rhapsodic manner, hymns entitled *Der Strom.* Here and in later lyric volumes he developed a highly personal and particular style to express his veneration for nature, history and art. Other works of his were the Moses drama *Der Weg des Gewaltigen,* and *Das Weib des Jephtha.* Lissauer's dramatic efforts were not successful. But he was an eminent editor of lyric anthologies and a gifted critic of literature. Two of his works on literary criticism are *Festlicher Werktag* and *Von der Sendung des Dichters.* After the first World War he went to Austria, which he loved very much and about which he wrote many beautiful essays.

LIST, EMANUEL, opera singer, b. Vienna, 1891. As a boy he served as chorister at the Theater-an-der-Wien in Vienna, later singing small parts in opera productions. Following this, he toured Europe with a vocal quartet, and accepted recital engagements in England, Australia, and New Zealand. After coming to the United States, he was coached by Josiah Zuro. For a brief period he sang in several leading motion picture theatres in New York. In 1922 he returned to Europe, sang for Felix Weingartner, and was engaged for the Volksoper in Vienna. Thence he went to the Berlin State Opera, remaining there for ten years, and achieving a formidable reputation in operas by Wagner and Richard Strauss.

In 1933 List made his American debut in opera at the Metropolitan Opera House in New York city. Since then, he has been a permanent member of the Metropolitan, specializing in leading bass roles in the Wagnerian repertory. He has also achieved note on the American concert stage in recitals of *Lieder.* In February, 1938, List cancelled his participation in the Salzburg music festival, at which he had sung for several summers, because of political and racial discrimination by the newly formed Austrian government. After the Nazi occupation of Austria, List established his home in the United States and applied for American citizenship. In 1939 he sang in Wagner, Mozart and Strauss operas at the Colon Theatre, in Buenos Aires, Argentina, in a three-month engagement.

LITERATURE. Jewish literature may be defined as those products of the pen which are written by Jews and primarily for Jews. Thus the Hebrew Bible, though it has become part of the cultural heritage of the world, is actually the first collection of Jewish literature; on the other hand, much of the literature produced by Jewish writers in modern times, being intended for the general public, is not Jewish literature as such, but the Jewish contribution to world literature.

Jewish literature is unique in that it is confined neither to a single language nor to a geographical area. It is not a unit, but rather a complex of many currents which interact upon one another. It is written in a number of languages, in countries of varying degrees of culture, and for different groups within Jewry. Jewish literature, then, may be roughly classified as follows:

A. By Language:
   1. Hebrew Literature
   2. Yiddish Literature (including Judeo-German)
   3. Aramaic Literature of the Jews
   4. Arabic Literature of the Jews
   5. Jewish Literature in Jewish Dialects (Judeo-Spanish, Judeo-Persian, and the like)
   6. Jewish Literature in the Vernaculars of Various Countries.

B. Chronologically:
  I. Ancient Times
   1. Bible (including the Apocrypha)
   2. Hellenistic Literature
   3. Talmud
   4. Midrash
  II. Middle Ages
   5. Grammar and Lexicography
   6. Bible Exegesis
   7. Rabbinic Literature (Commentaries and Codes)
   8. Responsa
   9. Philosophy and Theology
   10. Liturgy and Liturgical Poetry
   11. History, Geography and Travel
   12. Scientific
   13. Secular Prose and Poetry
   14. Ethical Literature
   15. Cabala
   16. Polemics and Apologetics
  III. Modern Times
   17. Literature of Jewish Scholarship
   18. Modern Presentations of Judaism
   19. Modern Secular Prose and Poetry

These separate phases of Jewish literature, as well as the Jewish contribution to world literature, are treated in the articles that follow and in a number of others scattered through the encyclopedia, such as: Apologists and Apologetics; Arabic Literature of the Jews; Aramaic Literature of the Jews; Bible; Bible Exegesis; Historiography; Midrash; Philosophy, Jewish; Responsa; Science of Judaism; Travelers and Travel Literature.   Isaac Landman.

LITERATURE, ANONYMOUS. In common with the literature of other early peoples, the literature of ancient Israel was largely, if not wholly, anonymous. The name of no author appears in many of the books of the Bible, such as *Judges, Samuel, Kings, Job, Ruth, Lamentations and Chronicles,* although the Talmudic rabbis, it is true, did ascribe authors to every Biblical book (*B.B.* 14b-15a). In similar fashion, much of the Apocryphal (such as *Judith* and *1 Maccabees*), apocalyptic (for instance, *Jubilees*), Midrashic and Talmudic literature is anonymous. Most of the Gaonic and rabbinic literature appeared under the name of the author or under a pen name; this is true also of the literature produced in the Spanish period. However, some of the earlier Cabalistic writings (such as *Sefer Yezirah, Book of Raziel, Shiur Komah*) were published without the author's name.

In the modern period, the literature of the Hasidim is the only outstanding type which was produced anonymously. That literature consists of collections of legends, tales of marvels, biographies of miracle workers and books of mystical and ethical instruction. In the Judeo-German literature, moreover, we find published anonymously chapbooks (Maaseh books), as well as books for private prayers (Tehinnoth) especially designed for the use of women. On the other hand, the Hebrew and Yiddish writers of the Haskalah (enlightenment) period almost always published their writings in their own names or over a pseudonym. Some of the more important anonymous writings in modern Hebrew literature are: *Gebuloth Eretz,* an abridged geography of the world (Berlin, 1821); *Shulhan Aruch Eben Shethiyah,* a Purim parody (1862); *Galuth Sefarad,* a novel of Jewish life in Spain, translated from the Russian (Vilna, 1860); *Hed Harim,* Hebrew translations from noted European poets (Berdichev, 1891); *Toledoth Alexander,* published by Rabbi Israel Halevi and the Mekitze Nirdamim society (Berlin, 1887); numerous polemics against the Hasidim, such as *Maamar Shebet Legev Kesilim, Yalkut Haroim* and *Sheber Posheim;* collections of tombstone inscriptions, open letters, appeals, topical poems and stories more or less historical (Maasiyoth), and of letters. Anonymity was used generally as a cloak for those who, because of political, religious or personal reasons, did not want to father their own creations; and this will explain why, since the latter part of the 19th cent., it has generally fallen into desuetude.

Lit.: The only comprehensive source book of Jewish anonymous literature is Saul Chajes' *Otzar Biddui Hashem* (or *Thesaurus pseudonymorum, quae in literatura hebraica et judaeo-germanica inveniuntur;* Vienna, 1933). *Jewish Encyclopedia,* vol. 1, p. 613 et seq., gives a list of over 300 Hebrew anonymous works published before 1875. See also Fürst, Julius, *Bibliotheca Judaica;* Benjakob, I. A., *Otzar Hasefarim.*

LITERATURE, BIBLE IN, see BIBLE IN LITERATURE.

LITERATURE, CHILDREN'S, see YOUTH.

LITERATURE, DEVOTIONAL. By devotional literature is meant, in the broadest sense, all writings which have for their purpose the expression of prayer to God; in a narrower sense, the term is confined to those writings, outside of the prayer-book and the formal ritual, which contain prayers intended for the use of the individual. In Judaism there has never been a clearcut distinction between private and public prayer. The Jewish liturgy was intended to be recited by the entire congregation as individuals, and not merely read to them; hence prayers originally composed by and for individuals were again and again introduced into the public services and became a fixed part of the Jewish daily and festival devotions.

This close connection between public and private prayer appears in the *Psalms,* the earliest prayers in Judaism, assigned by Bible scholars, for the most part, to the period of the Second Temple which saw the rise of the synagogue. Many of the psalms are written in the first person singular, and it is still a moot question whether they were intended for individual or public devotion. The prayers in the Apocrypha, although placed in a historical setting, are couched in such general terms as to suggest that they were intended to serve as models for the petitions of individuals. The New Testament (*Matt.* 6:9-13) contains the so-called Lord's Prayer, in itself an assemblage of phrases drawn from current Jewish devotions to form a complete model for private devotion.

The Talmudic rabbis who began the task of establishing a definite liturgy for the worship of the synagogue were careful not to let it become a rigid formula. Eliezer ben Hyrcanus (2nd cent. C.E.) declared that one can not pray truly if he makes his prayer a "fixed task"; and the Palestinian teachers explain this saying as meaning that one should add spontaneous prayers to the standard petitions. Thus, if one were sick, he should add his personal petitions to the benediction which speaks of God as the Healer of the sick; if he desired prosperity, he should add his personal request to the benediction which asks God to bless the year (*Yer. Ber.* iv, 8a; *A.Z.* 8a). The Talmud records numerous individual prayers on the part of the rabbis of the period (*Ber.* 16b-17a), many of which, such as the "O God, keep my tongue from evil" (*'elohai netzor*) and "The soul, O God, which thou hast given unto me" (*'elohai neshamah*), have become a part of the Jewish prayer-book. The Talmudic and Midrashic literature is full of such sample prayers, interspersed among legalistic, ethical and ritualistic literature.

The composition of individual prayers continued through the Gaonic and Arabic periods. Individual prayers are mentioned in the *Seder Rab Amram,* the *Mahzor Vitry* and other early prayer-books; prayers by such famous rabbis as Saadia, Bahya ibn Pakuda, Maimonides, Nahmanides and Jonah Gerondi were preserved for the use of future generations. The manuscripts found in the Cairo Genizah and elsewhere contain hundreds of individual prayers in Hebrew and Aramaic, although it is impossible to know whether these were intended for the use of individuals or were merely for the purpose of preserving the finest prayer productions of inspired individuals.

It was at least as early as the 12th cent. that collections of prayers for individual devotion began to be made and circulated. The movement apparently arose in Central Europe, where there was a distinct trend among Jews toward mysticism as opposed to the rationalism of those countries further west. The moralists Judah Hehasid of Regensburg and his disciple Eleazar Rokeah of Worms composed numerous prayers in Hebrew that were distributed in books under such names as *Tefilloth Rabbi Yehudah Hehasid* and *Yoreh Hattaim.* Other collections of this or a similar nature were Samuel David Ottolenghi's *Keriah Neemanah,* Zebi ben Hayim's *Likkute Tzebi,* Aaron Berechiah of Modena's *Maabar Yaabok* and Joseph Jedidiah Carmi's *Kenaf Renanim.* Many of the prayers dealt with individual problems and perils, such as the crossing of seas, times of epidemics, and similar occasions of peril; others were to be recited on visiting cemeteries.

The spread of the Cabala among the Jews in the latter part of the Middle Ages, together with the times of distress that helped turn the Jews to mysticism, greatly increased the amount of devotional literature. On the one hand, the perils to which the Jews were being constantly exposed led them to supplicate God with personal petitions; on the other, the Cabala stressed the importance of prayer and its effectiveness in bringing about redemption. Numerous new prayers, intended to inculcate devotion on the part of the worshipper and to put him in the proper frame of mind to utter the standard prayers of the liturgy, found their way into the prayer-book. In the 16th cent. there was a sudden development of Tehinnoth, books of private prayer written in the Judeo-German vernacular. While these Tehinnoth were intended primarily for women, there is evidence that men were expected to use them as well; thus there are prayers to be recited by a man asking for prosperity in business or while he is fasting. The prayers reflect the life of the Jews of the period, for they ask for deliverance from enemies and from false accusations. Nevertheless, it was largely for women that this literature was created, and it is significant of the new attitude toward women which arose in that age, an attitude which felt that they too must now pray as well as men. From the same period comes the beginning of Judeo-German expositions of the Bible (Teitsch-Humesh) which, as they were intended for the reading of women who attended the services in the synagogues, but who could not read and were not required to read the Hebrew prayers, may also be considered a part of devotional literature.

As the Jews of Europe began to acquire the use of the vernacular, new devotional literature, again especially for women, began to be written in European languages. The first of such books in German was Joshua Heschel Miro's *Gebetbuch für gebildete Frauenzimmer* (1833); there was one in Dutch as early as 1853, and various Hungarian prayers for the same purpose were written by Immanuel Löw, M. Stern and A. Kiss. Fanny Neuda's *Stunden der Andacht* (1859) was very popular among German Jewish women, and was brought by them to America, where it was translated into English (New York, 1866). There are a number of books of private devotion in English. Among the individual productions of this sort are Ascher's *Book of Life,* Cohen's *Prayers for Family Use,* Montagu's *Prayers for Jewish Working Girls* and Annie Josephine Levi's *Meditations of the Heart.* In modern times rabbis have issued various books of devotion, for instance, Gustav Gottheil (*Sun and Shield*), Chief Rabbi Joseph H. Hertz (*A Book of Jewish Thoughts*) and Herbert S. Goldstein (*Home Service*). The Central Conference of American Rabbis has issued a book of private devotions, *Blessings and Praise,* and has added a group of private prayers to the *Union Prayer Book.* There are also a number of small pamphlets of various origins, containing prayers which are recited by individuals on visiting the graves of parents and other relatives.

See also: HAGGADAH, PASSOVER; LITURGY; PIYUT; PRAYER-BOOK.   SIMON COHEN.

Lit.: Dembitz, L. N., *Jewish Services* (1898); Steinschneider, M., *Jewish Literature* (1857), sections 19 and 28; Eisenstein, J. D., in *Jewish Encyclopedia,* vol. 4, pp. 550-52; Freehof, S. B., "Devotional Literature in the Vernacular," *Central Conference of American Rabbis Year Book,* vol. 33 (1923) 375-424; Schechter, S., *Studies in Judaism,* First Series (1896).

LITERATURE, ETHICAL. What the teachers of Israel accomplished from the close of the Bible canon to the end of the 19th cent. has been to a great extent, if not exclusively, the development and accentuation of Israel's ethical ideal. The Apocrypha, the Mishnah, the Talmud, the Midrash, the responsa, the works of the Geonim and the commentators—all that is connotated by Halachah and Haggadah—down to the 20th cent. in the persons of Moritz Lararus, Morris Joseph and Hermann Cohen, have had as their task the exposition of the moral law, of which the Bible, especially the Prophets, is the source.

It is significant that with the impetus given by Ezra, the scribe or teacher became the expounder of the law, when the Biblical canon was closed about 250 B.C.E. The Bible, the book of the Law, then became an open book for the Jewish laity.

In the period of the Second Commonwealth it was the Pharisees, later much contemned in the church and Christian literature, who laid the greatest emphasis on moral excellence in the nation and the individual.

In the Apocrypha, all the books included in it, *Tobit, Judith, Susanna, Sirach* and *IV Maccabees,* have in view the moral life, teaching the virtues of honoring the dead, the giving of alms, chastity, and the restraint of human passions. Far excelling these is *Aboth,* with its matchless presentation of moral precepts embracing every form and condition of human life. There Hillel is seen as the teacher par excellence of peace and lovingkindness.

The Mishnah, far from being a barren code of laws, was the earnest attempt of a long succession of great teachers to humanize the moral code and to inculcate the principles of righteous conduct, a whole treatise being devoted to that end. That was the purpose of the Halachah. It finds its complement in the Haggadah, which, in a more entertaining form, depicts the practical ways of a moral life.

The Talmud is not mere legalism but combines with religious laws—and by means of these laws—moral precepts touching not alone on individual and family life but on all social and civic relations. Such are also the Haggadic books, the *Pirke de Rabbi Eliezer* and *Tanna Debe Eliyahu.* As an illustration of the ethical teachings of the Talmud, two sayings may be cited: "He who curbs his anger, he who does good out of love, he who is cheerful under suffering—these are the friends of God." "The first question that will be put to us on the Judgment Day is: Have your dealings with your fellow men been honest dealings?"

In the Middle Ages the Jewish philosophers, though greatly occupied with theological speculation, continued on an even broader scale the course of ethical teaching. There are few works devoted exclusively to the teaching of morals, and it is often difficult in the great mass of medieval Jewish literature to see any delimitation, philosophy and ethics being inextricably combined. Of this Maimonides furnishes the most striking illustration. The *Moreh Nebuchim,* in which he endeavors to harmonize Judaism with Aristotelian philosophy, is in many respects also a guide of morals. Among the works in this period that specifically deal with practical ethics may be mentioned: *Tikkun Middath Hanefesh,* by Solomon ibn Gabirol; *Hoboth Halebaboth,* by Bahya ibn Pakuda;

and *Sefer Hasidim,* by Judah ben Samuel of Regensburg. Always the purpose is to evolve an ethical way of life elaborating on all phases of duty and in every sort of relation: duties to self, the family and the state; the imperativeness of business integrity, of truthfulness, of honor, of benevolence and the like.

Besides these works there are the ethical testaments and wills written by fathers for the moral edification of their children.

In the modern age, there is noticeable the same absence of strictly moral works in Jewish literature and the same intermingling of philosophy and ethics. No attempt is made to establish rules and principles in the many didactic works which this period produced. They are all practical guides, outlining the conduct of a pious Jew and emphasizing all the great virtues. Chief among these works are: *Shaare Teshubah,* by Jonah Gerondi; *Sefer Hayashar,* by Zerahiah Hayevani; *Sefer Hamiddoth,* by an unknown author; and *Sefer Hametzaref,* by Berechiah Hanakdan. The last book deals with personal refinements, showing the need of curbing the passions, of cultivating personal honor, of sympathetic regard for the poor and friendless, of putting into practice a spirit of justice and fair play.

From this period to the close of the 19th and the beginning of the 20th cent. Jewish ethical literature—in most cases, as before, interwoven with philosophy or theology—is abundant. There are to be noted the works of Solomon Formstecher, Samuel Hirsch, Solomon Schechter, Moritz Lazarus, Kaufmann Kohler, Abraham Geiger, Claude G. Montefiore, and Hermann Cohen, among others. Formstecher made the radical departure of divesting Judaism of all its particularistic forms, holding that the ceremonies had no value beyond serving to ennoble character. Israel, he maintained, must struggle to demonstrate to the world that men can live an ethical life. Samuel Hirsch found the greatest distinction between Judaism and paganism in the fact that Judaism has always proclaimed purity of morals, freedom, and love of fellowmen. In this he was joined by Ludwig Philippson and carried it to a point where Judaism almost loses its distinctive character. Koller, in *The Foundations of Jewish Ethics,* however, bases his work on tradition and historical development. CHARLES A. RUBENSTEIN.

LITERATURE, HEBREW. 1. From the Completion of the Talmud to the End of the Gaonic Period.
The men who gave the final touches to the literature of the Talmud closed a remarkable period in the history of Hebrew literature. They were known as the Saboraim, and while they added nothing essentially new to the Talmud, they edited and revised its text, transmitting their heritage to the Geonim who received it as the subject of study and instruction. The activities of these Geonim lasted from the latter part of the 6th cent. to the first half of the 11th, and during this period they were the recognized authorities in Judaism. They had much to do with the adaptation of the Talmud to the changing social conditions of the Jewry of their time, while by their improved educational methods they deeply influenced Jewish life and letters. Although many Gaonic writings have vanished, the discoveries in the Genizah have restored some of their literary products.

The centuries between the final redaction of the Talmud and the beginning of Jewish culture in the West form one of the most obscure epochs in the history of Hebrew literature. It was an age of decline; but although the Gaonic age did not bring forth a single monumental work in Hebrew literature, it produced such powerful religious movements as Karaism and Jewish mysticism, both of which left a definite impress upon Hebrew letters. It was this period that witnessed the first serious attempt to harmonize Hellenism with Talmudic Judaism. During these four centuries and a half the text of the Talmud was fixed; the Targumic and Midrashic works received their final redaction; and a beginning was made in the scientific study of the Hebrew language and in Jewish philosophy, as well as in various other branches of literature and science, which attained full development in a later period. Although poetry and philology, Targum and Midrash, mysticism and philosophy were all represented in the time of the Geonim, their output par excellence was Halachic, or legal, in character and purport. In their writings they limited their activities almost exclusively to the exposition and codification of the Talmud, and their actual literary production began only when they became the leaders of the Diaspora, so that they were consulted by Jewish communities for decisions on practical questions and for explanations of difficult Biblical and Talmudic passages. They left a legacy of replies to these inquiries which constitutes the most important branch of their literary endeavors and which deals with life in all its aspects, enabling one to penetrate into the study of the scholar as well as into the home of the every-day man.

The oldest work of the Gaonic period is the *Sheeltoth* (Questions) of Rabbi Aha of Shabha, of whom nothing is known except that he left Babylonia in the middle of the 8th cent. and settled in Palestine. With this work he endeavored to introduce the Babylonian Talmud to the Palestinians by extracting verbatim considerable portions of the Talmud, especially practical material dealing with the Biblical laws, these excerpts being arranged according to the weekly lessons from the Pentateuch. In 870 the Gaon Amram prepared a prayer-book which has become a great source of liturgical information, and about the same time Zemah ben Paltai compiled a lexicon of the Talmud.

One of the most prominent authors of the Gaonic period was Sherira Gaon, whose fame as a critical sage is based primarily upon a famous letter which he addressed in 980 to the scholars of Kairwan, Northern Africa, giving a valuable outline of the history of Jewish tradition. Another important work was the *Halachoth Gedoloth,* a compilation of laws attributed to various authors, although actually the work of Jehudai Gaon in the middle of the 8th cent., and recast by Simeon Kayyara in the first half of the 9th cent. It was the most important Halachic compendium of the Gaonic period, and was intended to be a guide for the student seeking Talmudic learning and to make it possible to decide cases according to law without traversing the entire "sea of the Talmud." Many of the writings of the Geonim have come down to us anonymously, but it is known that the later scholars of this period were far more productive than the earlier. Samuel ben Hophni (d. 1034) and Hai ben Sherira, the last of the Geonim (939-1038), were the authors of many works on Biblical, Talmudic, and other branches of Jewish literature. Hai was also a gifted poet.

The most important and original writer of Gaonic times was Saadia Gaon, whose writings served, in many respects, as models for certain of his successors, as well as for later scholars. Some of his works are lost to posterity, while others still await publication; but he is best known for his philosophical work *Emunoth Vedeoth* (Beliefs and Practices) and for his Arabic version of, and commentary on, the Bible. He was a many-faceted scholar whose introductions and methodological works tended toward a historic and critical understanding of the Talmud, while as a codifier he sought to arrange rabbinic law in a unified logical system.

The most characteristic branch of the literary activity of the Geonim is found in their "responsa," or replies to the technical questions addressed to them. The advice and guidance of these famous scholars were sought by Jews from all parts of the world on various matters religious and literary, and to all inquiries the Geonim sent responses in the form of letters, sometimes addressed to individual correspondents, sometimes to communities or groups of communities. Many of these documents, mostly legal in nature, have been collected and published, but many more are still in manuscript, particularly those which have come to light since the discovery of the Genizah. They represent the earliest specimens of "questions and answers" (*Sheeloth Uteshuboth*), a very characteristic branch of Hebrew writing, paralleled only by the responses made by Parsi scholars in India to their coreligionists in Persia; this type of literature has gone on in unbroken continuity down to the present time.

2. Karaite Literature. The activities of the Geonim in the 8th cent. brought about a religious and literary reaction when Anan ben David established a new sect —the Karaites—which produced a noteworthy literature of its own. Benjamin Nahavendi (9th cent.) was a famous Karaite author who wrote on Biblical and philosophical subjects. Abu'l-Faraj Harun (11th cent.) was known for his grammatical studies, and among the Karaites who distinguished themselves in controversies with the Geonim during the 9th and 10th centuries were Solomon ben Yeroham, Sahl ben Mazliah, Joseph Albasir, Hasun ben Mashiah, and Japheth Halevi. In the 11th cent. Judah Hadasi devoted himself to science, philosophy, and classical literature. His *Eshkol Hakofer* (Cluster of Henna Flowers) is an encyclopedic work dealing with Judaism, Christianity and Mohammedanism. By the end of the 12th cent., Karaism had exhausted its originality and fertility and, with the exception of Isaac Troki's *Hizzuk Emunah* (Strengthening of Faith), a bold defense of Judaism against Christianity (1593), it produced no important work after the 12th cent.

During the early years of the activity of the Geonim, Hebrew and Aramaic were the languages employed in their writings, but when, in course of time, Arabic became the lingua franca of the Jews, it replaced Hebrew to a larger extent in their works. The literature of the Karaites is in great part composed in Arabic, as is a goodly portion of the writings of their opponents,

the Geonim; yet Hebrew remained for all time the vehicle of devotional feeling among the Jews, and as such reigned supreme.

3. Philosophical and Theological Literature. Toward the end of the Gaonic period Judaism began to develop a wealth of literature dealing not only with theological problems, but, more especially, with philosophy in the wider sense of the term, with ethics, and with mysticism, this last trend finally attaining wide renown under the name of Cabala. As regards philosophy proper, Jewish speculation of this type is traceable to the Bible, for the Talmud contains no special treatise on philosophy, although it abounds in rabbinical enunciations on matters metaphysical. Systematic treatment of such problems appeared first among the Hellenistic Jews of Alexandria, who were strongly under the influence of Greek culture, of which philosophy was an integral part.

The philosophical movement in medieval Jewry arises from a desire to reconcile two apparently independent sources of truth—revelation and reason. Its origin is to be traced to the Arabs, among whom, after the rise of Mohammedanism, various schools of philosophy had come into being, both Jewish and Arab philosophers being interested primarily in religious problems in philosophy, although they were concerned also with other questions. The movement continued among the Jews until about the end of the 15th cent. A brilliant galaxy of distinguished names, with a long list of learned and profound works on metaphysical questions, testifies to the remarkable zeal with which Jewish minds devoted themselves to philosophy. Their influence on Judaism was profound. Some of them affected deeply the religious thinking of non-Jews.

Isaac Israeli, an eminent physician, was the author of *Sefer Hayesodoth* (Book of Elements) and *Sefer Hagebulim Vehareshumim* (Book of Definitions and Limits), although in neither of them did he concern himself with Judaism as a theological system, since he was chiefly a pioneer in directing the attention of the Jews to the science and philosophy of the Greeks, albeit in Arabic dress. Saadia Gaon was really the first to apply philosophical methods to the interpretation of Judaism, his *Emunoth Vedeoth,* already noted, having been written to prove that Jewish teachings are in harmony with reason and scientific thought. Belief in revelation, according to him, does not exclude independent search for knowledge. He was the author of an Arabic translation and of a commentary on the *Sefer Yetzirah* (Book of Creation), a mystical work of great antiquity, which he did not regard as a source for the theory of Judaism. A contemporary of his, the Karaite al-Kirkisani, dealt with the principal doctrines which one would seek in a Jewish philosophy of religion.

Solomon ibn Gabirol, the great poet, was equally famous as a philosopher. The diffusion of Neo-Platonism was due in great measure to the fact that his philosophical work enjoyed a wide popularity among Christians. Written in Arabic (probably under the title of *Yanbu al-Hayat*), the original of his *Mekor Hayim* (Fountain of Life) was lost, but its Latin version, the *Fons Vitae,* was diligently studied among the scholastics. The name of the Jewish writer, in process of translation from Arabic into Latin, came gradually to be changed out of all resemblance to what it actually was. From Ibn Gabirol it became Avencebrol, then Avincembron, and finally Avicebron, the designation by which the author of the *Fons Vitae* was known to the Christians of the Middle Ages. Until 1844, when Solomon Munk identified this author with Solomon ibn Gabirol, the *Fons Vitae* was thought to have been written by a Christian. Ibn Gabirol was the author also of an important ethical treatise, *Sefer Tikkun Hamiddoth* (*The Improvement of the Moral Qualities;* English trans., Stephen S. Wise), in which principles of ethics were treated independently of religious precepts, and in which he emphasizes the interdependence of physical and psychical elements in the determination of morality, anticipating to a certain extent the modern standpoint in this regard.

A highly popular treatise was the *Hoboth Halebaboth* (*The Duties of the Heart*), by Bahya ibn Pakuda, which represents an attempt to present Judaism as being essentially a great spiritual truth founded on reason, revelation and tradition. Although not formally a metaphysical treatise, it contains a compendium of religious philosophy, and in it the rich ethical content of Judaism is formulated into a system.

Judah Halevi, who was so eminent as a poet, also ranks high as a Jewish philosopher. In his *Kitab al-Khazari* (*Sefer Hakuzari*), couched in the form of a conversation between the inquiring king of the Khazars and the wise men to whom he turned for guidance, he offers a philosophic apology for Judaism, in which he endeavors to show that revealed religion is superior to natural religion. In addition to its philosophical teachings, the work distinctly reflects the poetic, profoundly religious, and warmly Jewish nationalistic sentiments characteristic of its author. In the first half of the 12th cent. Neo-Platonic philosophy among the Jews was represented by Abraham bar Hiyya, a follower of Ibn Gabirol and an eminent mathematician and astronomer, who wrote likewise on ethics and philosophy; other Jewish Neo-Platonists were: Moses ibn Ezra, author of the *Arugath Habosem* (Garden-Bed of Spices; original title, *Al Hadikah fi Maani al-Mujaz wal-Hakikah*), an Arabic treatise on philosophy; Joseph ibn Zaddik, whose *Olam Katan* (Microcosmos; original Arabic title probably *Al-Alam al-Saghir*) is preserved in Hebrew translation; and Abraham ibn Ezra, whose philosophical ideas are scattered throughout his writings.

Abraham ibn Daud, astronomer and historian, was an Aristotelian in philosophy, and sought, in his *Al-Akidah al Rafiyah* (Exalted Faith; Hebrew trans., *Emunah Ramah*), to show that true philosophy is an aid to revealed religion. The greatest Jewish thinker of the Middle Ages, however, was Moses Maimonides, who was likewise an Aristotelian in philosophy, but who was so important a figure in the history of Hebrew literature and thought as to overshadow many others of his own and of other eras in Jewish history. After his death controversies arose which led to a decline in the study of philosophy among the Jews during the 13th cent.; for although Joseph ibn Aknin wrote on philosophical questions, and although others dealt with similar problems, their work, for the most part, was destitute of originality. With the dawn of

the 14th cent., on the other hand, Aristotelianism was revived among the Jews, finding its most pronounced form in Levi ben Gershon (Gersonides), the author of the *Milhamoth Adonai* (The Wars of the Lord) and of other philosophical and scientific works which expressed more or less the same ideas as those of Maimonides. A contemporary of Levi ben Gershon was Jedaiah Bedaresi, who wrote a small treatise, *Behinath Olam* (Examination of the World), a philosophico-didactic contemplation of the world and human life which attained tremendous popularity among the Jews.

The reaction against the extreme philosophical position of Maimonides and his disciples was marked by the appearance of the *Or Adonai* (The Light of God), a profound philosophical work which sought to liberate Judaism from the bondage of Aristotelianism. Its author, Hasdai Crescas, endeavored to meet the philosophical weapons, and it is believed that his ideas influenced the thoughts of Spinoza, who was also a close student of Maimonides. In defense of the latter Simon Duran attacked Crescas in his *Magen Aboth* (Shield of the Fathers), although it was through the work of his pupil, Joseph Albo, that Crescas' ideas made themselves felt on later Jewish thought. In his *Sefer Haikkarim* (Book of Principles), which became extremely popular among the Jews because of its simple style, Albo reduced the absolutely essential principles of religion to three: the existence of God, revelation, and reward and punishment.

Several Jewish philosophical writers of merit flourished after Albo, although none possessed marked originality. Judah Messer Leon, Elijah Delmedigo, Isaac Arama and Isaac Abravanel are some of the outstanding names of the 15th and 16th centuries, but Jewish philosophy in the strict sense of the term came to an end, and even if books dealing with philosophical questions were still written, no great contributions were made.

4. Ethical and Didactic Literature. When one turns from philosophy to ethics, mention should be made of certain works of importance in addition to those already noted. Here belongs, for instance, the *Sefer Hasidim* (Book of the Pious), which enjoyed wide popularity in the Middle Ages and which, although attributed to Judah Hehasid (Judah the Pious), of whom very little is known, was, in reality, of composite authorship. It is a product of the Jewish spirit of the 13th cent., and embraces various elements— mystical, ethical and ceremonial—in certain parts displaying deep insight into the cravings of the human heart. Eleazar of Worms, a pupil of Judah Hehasid, was the author of the *Rokeah* (Spice Mixture), a popular book of similar character, while the *Sefer Middoth* (Book of Moral Qualities) was an anonymous ethical treatise written in Judeo-German, probably in the 15th cent. In its Hebrew recension it is known as *Orehoth Tzaddikim* (Paths of the Righteous), and in this form has gained greater popularity than in the Judeo-German original.

Compilations of moral teachings contained in earlier Jewish writings formed a favorite class of ethical works, the earliest and most highly esteemed of these being the *Menorath Hamaor* (Candlestick of Light) of Isaac Aboab, while the *Reshith Hochmah* (Beginning of

Wisdom) of Elijah ben Moses de Vidas was a collection of maxims on such topics as the love and fear of God, repentance, holiness and humility. Peculiarly Jewish were the ethical tracts written by Jewish moralists in the form of wills, these being private documents, not intended for publication, in which a father or a teacher left instructions on morality to his children or disciples. Some of them were very carefully composed, and practically constituted formal treatises on ethics. Of the purely devotional literature of Judaism, there is one other ethical book, extremely popular among the Jews, which deserves notice, the *Mesillath Yesharim* (The Highway of the Upright) by Moses Hayim Luzzatto, a dramatist and student of the Cabala.

5. The Shulhan Aruch. The ethical and religious literature of medieval Jewry, so far as practical life was concerned, was summed up in the *Shulhan Aruch* (Prepared Table) of Joseph Caro which, published in 1565, soon obtained a popularity denied to almost all previous works in which digests of Jewish ethics and ritual observances had been presented. The book, based on previous systematic codes, was the outcome of centuries of scholarship and became *the* code for all Jews who regulate their lives according to rabbinical law. It contains a full and complete statement of the rules governing all actions, from rising up in the morning to lying down at night, from the cradle to the grave, directions for prayer, principles for the observance of Sabbaths and festivals, dietary regulations, laws for marriage and divorce, for mourning and burial—all are included, and no phase of human life or experience is omitted. While the *Shulhan Aruch* brought system into the discordant opinions of rabbinical authorities as to Jewish law, it was the great bulwark of their conception of life. In its form and content the *Shulhan Aruch* was not an unworthy conclusion to a series of legal and ethical teachings which began with the Mishnah and continued to grow with the development of Jewish life in the Middle Ages.

6. Cabalistic Literature. Jewish mysticism, generally termed Cabala, developed as an esoteric system concerning God and the universe, and claims to have come down from a remote past, for the *Sefer Yetzirah* (Book of Creation), an early mystic text, was systematically studied even in the days of the Geonim, although at that time the subject attracted only small circles. It was not until the 13th cent. and onward that Cabala received a great impetus and enjoyed wide diffusion, when it gave rise to an extensive literature, written in a peculiar Aramaic dialect, and grouped around the *Zohar* (Brightness). This, despite its claim to be a product of great antiquity and to be the work of Simeon ben Yohai, who lived in the 2nd cent., is now assumed to have been written by Moses de Leon, although it probably underwent considerable revision. In spiritual beauty, in fancy, in daring imagery and depth of devotion the *Zohar* ranks among the great books of the world even if its style is difficult and involved. It is remarkable that the very period which produced the rationalism of Maimonides gave rise to the mysticism of Cabala, which evidently served at first as a protest against excessive intellectualism and rigidity in religion. A number of writers dealt with

the subject, among them Ezra, or Azriel, who in 1240 compiled a book called *Bahir* (Brilliancy) which, like other Cabalistic works, was at once regarded as a product of remote antiquity. Under Abraham Abulafia, in the 13th cent., the mystical movement among the Jews took practical shape, its votaries being much excited by stories of miracles performed and of the appearance of a new Messiah. It greatly influenced Jewish religious ceremonies and produced saintly souls, but it did not retain a high place in the realm of literature.

The *Zohar* became the secret textbook of students of Cabala, and practically every later product of Jewish mysticism was a commentary upon it. Although it thus absorbed all the earlier Cabalistic writings, such as the *Sefer Yetzirah,* the *Sefer Raziel* (Book of Raziel), and the *Othioth de Rabbi Akiba* (Alphabet of Rabbi Akiba), it inspired no works of originality, so that one need merely name a few of the outstanding Cabalists of post-Zohar days. The ideas of Isaac Luria were transmitted in the prolific writings of his faithful disciple Hayim Vital. Isaiah Horowitz was the author of a much admired ethical work, *Shene Luhoth Haberith* (The Two Tablets of the Covenant), and among other eminent contributors to the subject were Moses ben Jacob Cordovero, Nehemiah Hayun and Moses Hayim Luzzatto. The Jewish mystics were responsible for some of the most exquisite prayers and meditations which have found their way into medieval Hebrew literature, and the study of Cabala has not been confined to Jews alone, for it touched Christianity, and a host of Christian scholars have likewise devoted time and energy to it.

7. Medieval Hebrew Poetry. Medieval Hebrew poetry is mostly of a religious nature, for such verse always precedes that which is secular in character. With an essentially religious people like the Jews, who felt themselves oppressed by a sense of almost constant martyrdom, it was only natural that their longings and aspirations, their woes and hopes, should receive expression in religious songs which subsequently found their way into their liturgy.

Two distinct types of Piyut (liturgical poem) arose in Hebrew literature. The Kaliric Piyut, so named from its best representative, Eleazar Hakalir, was written in an involved style, containing many rare words and obscure allusions, and lacking all beauty of form. The other type, the Spanish Piyut, had these faults in less pronounced degree, and in the hands of some of its best representatives it became poetry of the finest type both in form and in thought. The Piyut had its birth in Palestine, where it slowly developed, during a period of several centuries, from the simple form of the older liturgy to the highly artificial diction and construction of the Kaliric type. Among the earliest of these poets were Eleazar Hakalir and Jannai, both of them Palestinians living prior to the 9th cent., and both of them fond of the use of alphabetical acrostics. Much of their work is didactic, endeavoring to teach the traditional explanations of the Bible and the ritual laws. Their compositions must have been voluminous, although some failed of survival to later ages.

It was in Spain that medieval Hebrew poetry attained its zenith in the 11th and 12th centuries. There, under Hasdai ibn Shaprut, Cordova became the home of Jewish culture and learning. There, too, lived so noted a Jewish man of letters as Dunash ibn Labrat, who is best known as a grammarian, but whose importance as a poet is considerable since he was the first to apply Arabic rules of meter to Hebrew poetry, although very few of his verses have survived. About half a century after Hasdai's death Samuel ibn Nagdela was the head of the Jewish community in Granada, and as such he became known as Nagid (The Prince). A profound student of rabbinical literature, he was the author of an introduction to the Talmud. He wrote also many hymns in the style of *Psalms* and *Proverbs*. Several songs on wine and love are likewise credited to him. When Samuel Hanagid died, in 1055, the golden age of Jewish literature in Spain was in sight with the coming of Solomon ibn Gabirol, Moses and Abraham ibn Ezra, and Judah Halevi. The Hebrew poetry of this period, although largely religious, embraced secular subjects as well. Moreover, it was pure in diction, melodious and graceful. The Hebrew poets loved nature in her gentler moods, and in their love songs they blended both piety and love.

One of the greatest of the poets and philosophers of this period was Solomon ibn Gabirol. Little is known of his life, but from his poems one learns that he was left an orphan and one gathers that his early life must have been unhappy since some of his poems give melancholy expression thereof. His verses, written in a Hebrew style characterized by simplicity and beauty, breathe a profound trust in God. Many of them have found a place in the Jewish prayer-book. One of the most beautiful of them is his *Kether Malchuth* (Royal Crown), a lengthy philosophical and ethical poem in rhymed prose, which describes the universe, sphere within sphere, and forms a glowing panegyric of the glory of God as manifested in the realm both of the material and of the spiritual. Here Ibn Gabirol poured forth his heart even more unreservedly than in his philosophical *Mekor Hayim,* or in his ethical *Sefer Tikkun Hamiddoth* or in his *Mibhar Hapeninim* (Choice of Pearls), a compilation from the wisdom of the past. Ibn Gabirol stood a little outside of and a great deal above the circle of the Hebrew poets who made this era famous. Many of them are now forgotten; they had their day of popularity, but their poems have not all survived. Solomon ibn Gabirol died in 1070. A legend has it that he was killed by a jealous Arab poet who buried his corpse under the roots of a fig-tree, which began forthwith to bear blossoms of surpassing beauty and an abundance of extraordinary sweet fruit. The whole city talked of the marvel, and when they dug beneath the tree in search of the cause, they found the body of the murdered poet, whereupon the slayer expiated his crime with his life.

Another master of Hebrew poetry was Moses ibn Ezra, who was born in the very year of Ibn Gabirol's death, but of whose life little is known. With him, as with Ibn Gabirol, philosophy and poetry went hand in hand. Many of his verses found a place in the liturgy of his people. His chief secular poem, *Tarshish* (The Topaz), in ten parts, containing 1,210 lines, tells of wine, love and song and vividly paints the beauties of country life. In his verse he bewails the loss of youth, finding the only consolation of age in its freedom from passion. His other poems are chiefly elegies on the death of scholars and praises of men whom he admired. There was another Ibn Ezra, Abraham, who became famous as a scientist, philosopher and exegete of the scriptural text, although he was also a poet, even if verse was obviously not his principal occupation. Admirable and lofty as are the sentiments expressed in his lines, and excellent though they are in form, they lack the imaginative element. His fame in Jewish annals rests primarily on his commentaries on the text of the Scriptures, in which he anticipated many of the results of modern criticism of the Bible, but he was equally renowned for his brilliant wit and for his many-sided learning.

The greatest of all medieval Hebrew poets was Judah Halevi. Although many had arisen before him and others were destined to arise after him, they were all his inferiors. Judah al-Harizi may be regarded as the last great representative of Hebrew verse in Spain, even if in spirit his poems differ entirely from those of his great predecessors. His chief work, the *Tahkemoni* (Wise One), was written in the form of the Arabic Makama, a species of spoken drama in rhyming prose in which two personages take part: the hero, who relates various episodes about himself, and the narrator, who acts as a chorus, drawing out the hero by his questions. Harizi's distinction lies in the ease with which he plays upon the Hebrew language, and, generally speaking, the stories which the *Tahkemoni* tells are in racy style, while its criticisms of men and things are shrewd and striking.

There were many other Hebrew poets, both in Spain and outside of that country, whose verse found a place in the liturgy of Israel, and from the 10th to the 18th centuries Germany, France and Italy could boast of distinguished representatives, some of whom expressed the fine devotional spirit with which mystics enriched the Jewish prayer-books. The close of the period of medieval Hebrew poetry was marked by a tendency toward secular subjects. The influence of classical models was felt at the time of the Renaissance, and then the Hebrew poets were joyous poets, so full of the gladness of life that their verse was condemned by pietists as too frivolous and too much disfigured by ill-timed levity. Immanuel ben Solomon of Rome was the most eminent figure in the group. A scholar well-versed in science and literature, he wrote various works in Hebrew and Italian, although his original composition was mostly in poetry. A contemporary, and perhaps a friend, of Dante, Immanuel was influenced by him, and was in sympathy with the contemporary social and intellectual life of Italy. He introduced the sonnet into Hebrew poetry, and alternate instead of single rhymes. In his *Mahberoth,* or collected poems, he intermingled satires, letters, prayers and dirges. His parodies, his clever allusions and puns and his equivocations were gems of diction. One of his poems, *Hatofeth Vehaeden* (Hell and Paradise), is a vision clearly modeled on Dante's *Divine Comedy,* although planned on Harizi's *Tahkemoni.* Love and wine were his frequent themes to such a degree that his songs were often described as sensuous and his satires as blasphemous. This, though, was due not to lack of reverence on his part, but rather to a desire to reconcile the ideals of Italian society of the period of the Renaissance with those of Judaism. Moses da Rieti, in his *Mikdash Meat* (Little Sanctuary), again imitated Dante. Italy remains famous in the history of medieval Hebrew poetry, primarily because of the abundance of secular compositions which it produced. Hebrew drama likewise had its most important representative in that land.

These represent in a measure the effects of the Renaissance on the literature of Israel in the Middle Ages. In other countries, the condition of the Jews was such that they were excluded from external influences; their literature as well as their lives suffered from restriction to the ghettos, many of which were erected both by the Jews themselves and by the governments of Europe.

8. Modern Hebrew Literature. The beginning of the 18th cent. marked the initiation of a revival in Hebrew literature. This revival, launched in Italy by Moses Hayim Luzzatto, author of *Migdal Oz* and *Layesharim Tehillah,* made Germany its center of social and educational influences. The period of the Meassefim, named after the periodical *Hameassef,* was then inaugurated. With Moses Mendelssohn as its foremost representative, it introduced rationalistic and cosmopolitan tendencies, so that the Hebrew literature of the time possessed all the dryness and lack of imagination and emotion characteristic of rationalism. Yet, despite its meagre literary output, this period made its impress upon the literature produced by the subsequent liberal Haskalah (Enlightenment) movement, in which the atmosphere of the Meassefim prevailed. With the last issue of the *Hameassef* (1797) modern Hebrew passed away from Germany, where the Reform Movement in Judaism, aided by a variety of other causes, effected an almost complete divorce between the Hebrew language and Jewry. The center of activity in Hebrew literature was now transferred to Galicia, and in the first quarter of the 19th cent., when Biblical criticism and historical investigation came to the fore, Nachman Krochmal and Solomon Judah Rapoport distinguished themselves as brilliant scholars in these fields of learning and lore. Their contemporary, Isaac Erter, whose stories and sketches were collected in his *Hatzofeh Lebeth Yisrael,* distinguished himself as a satirist. In like manner Joseph Perl, in his *Megalleh Temirin,* attacked the teachings and practices of Hasidism.

The middle of the 19th cent. saw Russia take the lead in Hebrew literature. Lithuania became the center of this activity. The Haskalah movement, in its opposition to traditional exclusiveness and in its insistence upon the value and necessity of modern education, found in the novel a new weapon more potent than criticism of rabbinism. It was in Lithuania, where the Hebrew novel was introduced as an effective vehicle for the cultivation of a new attitude toward life, that romanticism first entered Jewish literature. The embodiment of the romantic spirit in the poetry of the period was undoubtedly Micah Joseph Lebensohn, who reminds one of Keats in poetic fire, idyllic beauty and vividness of erotic emotion. He was the son

of Abraham Baer (Dob) Lebensohn, the first of the modern Hebrew poets in Russia, who, under the influence of Moses Hayim Luzzatto, wrote a drama in which he ridiculed superstition and the ways of Orthodoxy. The romanticist par excellence was Abraham Mapu, who was likewise the creator of the Hebrew novel. His novels *Ahabath Tziyyon* (Love of Zion), *Ashmath Shomeron* (Guilt of Samaria), and *Ayit Tzabua* (The Painted Hawk) are as popular today as they were when first published, if not more so. Although weak in his character-drawing, Mapu was very strong in his construction of plots and in the charm of his narrative. He had, moreover, some fine romantic descriptions of nature, coupled with praise and admiration for the idyllic life, together with a most remarkable ability to apply Biblical phraseology to his subject, so that he naturally exerted much influence upon the development of modern Hebrew literature.

When, at the beginning of the second half of the 19th cent., the effect of the Russian revolutionary movement began to assert itself in Jewish life and to penetrate Hebrew literature as well, the Haskalah movement engaged in various literary skirmishes in behalf of religious reforms. The zeal evinced by their intellectuals was, however, by no means shared by the masses, for the great majority of the Jews clung to their traditional life, opposed innovation, looked upon the "enlightened" with suspicion, and persecuted them whenever possible. Nevertheless, the Haskalah movement continued its activities.

Abraham Mapu, with his *Ayit Tzabua,* first introduced the conflict over the Haskalah movement into the novel. The story *Haaboth Vehabanim* (Fathers and Sons), by Shalom Jacob Abramowitsch, belongs to the same class. It closely resembles Mapu's *Ayit Tzabua.* While the latter describes Jewish life in Lithuania, Abramowitsch's novel dealt with Hasidic life in Volhynia. Both of them, however, together with a few others of their kind, were transitional, for full expression of the conflict of the Haskalah with religion was reserved for Reuben Asher Braudes. All the merits and faults of the Haskalah period may be seen in his *Hadath Vehahayim* (Religion and Life), but he was also the earliest to present the transition to a more modern epoch in his novel *Shete Haketzavoth* (The Two Extremes), the atmosphere of which is altogether different from that of his first romance. These, like his other stories, have the merit of reflecting the conflicts and ambitions of a whole period, as well as of showing some advance in precision of style, coordination of incident and distinctness of characterization.

The superficiality of the Haskalah movement was well satirized in the sketches of Mordecai David Brandstaetter, who so ably ridiculed the Hasidim, Judah Leon Gordon, the poet of the Haskalah era, and Abraham Baer Gottlober who, with many other writers, tried their hand at the short story. The achievement of this period in the domain of the novel and of the story was marked by a retrogression in appreciation of nature, although it gained in technique and in its endeavor to modernize Hebrew style.

The output of poetic writings and literary criticism in the Haskalah era was considerable, both in quantity and in quality. The poets show a marked decline from the passionate throbbing romanticism of Lebensohn to the first attempt, in that period, at an allegorical drama, the *Tifereth Libene Binah* (Glory for the Sons of Understanding) by Gottlober, whose literary activities were not confined to the lyric drama, since he was also the author of many poems, a few stories, and a couple of quasi-scientific works. It was at this time that the long narrative poem *Kehal Refaim* (The Congregation of the Dead) of Moses Leib Lilienblum appeared, and that the rather monotonous versifier Yehalel (Judah Loeb Lewin) revealed himself to Hebrew readers. The foremost poet of the Haskalah period was Judah Leon Gordon. Although he can not be described as the bard of hope, the prophetic comforter of his people, or the passionate preacher of a higher, nobler and more spiritual life, his influence on his contemporaries was remarkable. He was the typical expounder of the Haskalah—utilitarian, rationalistic and scathingly satirical, excelling all other Hebrew poets in this latter vein. Among the literary critics of the time, the outstanding names were those of Abraham Jacob Paperna and Abraham Uri Kovner, both of whom were active between 1864 and 1870.

A prominent figure in the Haskalah movement was Peretz (Peter) Smolenskin, a talented novelist, a sincere and most sympathetic essayist who soon won the admiration of his readers and became their spiritual guide. He was the forerunner of the movement of national revival in Jewry insofar as he believed that Hebrew should be cherished as a prime national factor. He was the first to introduce real tragedy into the Hebrew novel, giving character and individuality free scope to develop. Smolenskin exercised a deep influence upon contemporary and later writers, and left a strong impress upon Hebrew thought and letters.

Shortly before Smolenskin's death the beginning of anti-Semitic riots in Russia gave to the revival in East European Jewry an impetus which brought about a reaction against the Haskalah. Creating a Jewish national policy, this trend culminated in the so-called Hibbath Zion (Love of Zion) movement which so profoundly affected Jewish life that it automatically created a national and cultural atmosphere, inaugurated in Hebrew literature by three poets: Mordecai Zevi Manne, Menahem Mendel Dolitzki and Constantin Asher Schapiro. The first of these brought a new precept into Hebrew literature: art for art's sake, beauty for beauty's sake. The greatest number of his poems, and those of deepest interest, dealt with nature. He was the first to introduce the personal element into Hebrew verse, substituting self-centered individualistic emotion for the collective sentiment of the Maskilim, the adherents of the Haskalah movement. Dolitzki contributed little that was new to Hebrew literature, although, despite his lack of originality, he gave expression to the national aspirations. Schapiro, on the other hand, a convert to the Russian Orthodox Church, was a poet of extraordinary power and delicacy who contributed to Hebrew verse some of its finest passages and introduced some of its most original figures. He expressed a tenderness and an infinite yearning for the life of the ghetto and its

ideals. His verse is instinct with emotion and love for the Jewish people and for their sacred possessions. Naphtali Herz Imber sang of the return to Zion, and his "Hatikvah" has become a popular anthem among Jews everywhere.

The revival movement produced a powerful and able thinker of its own in Ahad Haam (Asher Ginzberg), who made his debut in Hebrew literature in 1889. The Hibbath Zion movement had overemphasized the economic and political significance of the rehabilitation of Palestine. In his *Lo Zeh Haderech* (This Is Not the Way) Ahad Haam urged that the settlement of the Jewish people in Palestine would never solve the problem of the Jews, but only of Judaism. He accordingly advocated the idea of making Palestine a center of Jewish culture. In his many essays he developed a rounded and consistent theory book of Zionism and of Judaism as a whole. Unlike his predecessors Krochmal, Luzzatto and Smolenskin, who likewise laid stress on the national side of Judaism, although as indissolubly connected with its religious side, Ahad Haam drew a marked distinction between Judaism as a religion and Judaism as a nationality. He asserted that the religion of Israel was the product of the national genius, and that the former was dependent upon the latter, not vice versa. Presenting this theory with forceful argument combined with virility and lucidity of style, he was bound to leave a marked impress upon the development of Hebrew literature and was a potent factor in the spiritual development of Jewish life. Aaron David Gordon laid the philosophical foundation for "the religion of labor" as practised nowadays by the Halutzim in Palestine.

Realism was introduced into Hebrew literature in 1891, when Ben Avigdor (Abraham Leib Schalkowitz) began to publish the *Sifre Agorah* (Penny Books), to which some of the most talented Hebrew writers contributed stories, sketches, and poems, the realism of which affected the literature as a whole. This series brought about the establishment of two well-known Hebrew publishing houses, Ahiasaf and Tushiyah, under the influence of Ahad Haam, who caused them to work for the promotion of Hebrew letters in every respect. His influence upon them began to penetrate the realms of fiction. Mordecai Z. Feierberg, who died at an early age, was one of the first to be filled with its spirit. His writings reveal a talent of considerable power, a note of yearning toward the great and noble, a soul quivering with emotion and idealism. In his *Lean?* (Whither?) he developed Ahad Haam's idea that complete harmony between the Jew and the man can be attained only in a Jewish center in Palestine. The problems with which he deals and the solution that he gives them are entirely in harmony with the spirit of Ahad Haam's theory of cultural Zionism.

The individualistic and symbolic spirit in Hebrew literature is due to the influence of the modern mystic movement known as Hasidism. Isaac Loeb Peretz ranks foremost as an author who was capable of depicting important psychological tendencies and whose fame transcended the limits of the language in which he wrote. Judah Steinberg, in whom individuals first found complete and varied representation in Hebrew fiction, began to compose late in life and died after a very short period of literary activity. Yet, he bequeathed to Hebrew literature a heritage considerable in bulk as well as in quality. The charm with which his characters are endowed is seldom to be found in modern Hebrew fiction, and the same statement holds good of his lucid, fluent and convincing style. He scarcely ever reshapes an old character to serve as a new creation, so that his works are filled with a wealth of individualities.

Turning now from prose, we find that poetry has made rapid strides in modern Hebrew literature. It produced a host of gifted writers of manysided verse. The most representative of modern Hebrew poets is Hayim Nahman Bialik who, with the exception of Judah Halevi, is perhaps the leading Jewish national bard. He inherited the pathetic idealism and the prophetic seriousness of his race. He stands out preeminently as the poet of his people's woe. The national hopes and aspirations of Jewry rarely find expression in his verse, in which the ideals of Ahad Haam and the influence of Judah Leon Gordon's style and form are traceable. None of the Hebrew poets has grasped and represented so well the spirit of the ghetto and its poetry as has Bialik, and none has shown such sympathy and such tenderness of feeling for its departing spirit. Next to Bialik stands Saul Tchernichovski, the first to introduce into Hebrew poetry an admiration for the Greek spirit of complete enjoyment of life. He is responsible also for a system of meter and rhyme hitherto unused in Hebrew. Jacob Cohen is an idealist, who displays originality of conception in some of his poems; Zalman Schneor is a writer who shows at times a gentle pessimistic vein. His verse is full of life and beauty; the rhythm has harmony and tunefulness; the imagery is rich, varied and striking, and the movement is quick and bold. His prose, too, is marked by life and beauty. These poets appeared almost simultaneously and launched out with vigor the Hebrew verse of the 20th cent. In the years immediately preceding the first World War and those that followed, the number of Hebrew poets increased rapidly. In Palestine and Poland, in the United States and other lands, young Hebrew poets contributed richly to the rapid growth of Hebrew verse. It is a remarkable fact that lyric poetry has been the strongest point of modern Hebrew literature, as of Hebrew literature in general, excelling all other branches in personal expression and artistic workmanship.

David Shimonowitz, a poet with a thorough knowledge of Palestine, endeavored in his verse to describe the charm of the sacred land, while Jacob Fichman, who is both poet and critic, shows a fine appreciation of the sublime and tender in life and literature. Jacob Steinberg's verse is pleasing but otherwise not yet clearly definable, while Isaac Katzenelsohn is the poet of the gladness of life. In his light and dainty songs, as in some of those by Bialik and Shneor, all is music and melody.

The various transformations brought about by the Zionist and other Jewish movements, and the influence of foreign literatures, affected the reshaping of contemporary Hebrew fiction, notably the novel and the short story. The latter is, in type, artistic in technique and generally psychologic in presentation, delineating the individual in a variety of moods and situations; at the same time it is marked by a minute, torturing self-analysis, by an impotence in the will of its heroes, and by an outlook upon life that is gloomy and despondent. Its creators are followers of the school of Micah Joseph Berdyczewski, whose point of view was influenced by the individualistic theories of Nietzsche. Together with Hillel Zeitlin he founded a theoretical and poetic basis for Hasidism in modern Hebrew literature. Among the short story writers mention may be made of Isaiah Domashevitzky (known as J. Bershadsky), Joseph Hayim Brenner, Uri Nisan Gnessin, G. Schofmann, Isaac Dob Berkowitz, S. Ben-Zion, realists of the first order; among the novelists such names may be cited as those of Abraham Aaron Kabak and Moses Smilansky. Special mention must be made of Samuel Joseph Agnon, a master of Hebrew style whose specialty is Hasidic folklore recast in modern fiction.

The first World War era produced a group of Hebrew writers who endeavored to portray the upheaval brought about in Jewish life in the aftermath of that war. Representative of that group are: Meir Smelansky, whose writings largely deal with the horrors of the pogroms in the Ukraine in 1919 to 1921; Hayim Hazaz and A. Steinman, whose characters are as a rule Jews who, though forcibly removed from Judaism, still retain enough of it not to become completely dejudaized; Asher Barash, who depicts Hasidic life with a wealth of detail; Avigdor Meiri (Feuerstein), who both as novelist and poet is wont to dwell on the horrors of war as he himself experienced them, and, like Uri Zebi Gruenberg, to lament and denounce the shortcomings of his people. J. Burla is the first of the Hebrew novelists to deal with the life of those native Palestinian Jews whose ancestors were among the exiles from Spain when they settled in the Holy Land.

Hebrew literature also has a number of authors who have made themselves known in various types of letters. The talent of David Frischman extended over the domains of the feuilleton, the short story, poetry and criticism. Brainin was considered the finest stylist, but his literary ideas and tastes were largely dictated by external influences, to such an extent as frequently to be rather misleading. Joseph Klausner is active in many fields—critical, historical, journalistic and scientific. He possesses marvelous erudition, as well as a certain amount of historic insight, although he exhibits scarcely any originality of thought. Fishel Lachower, too, is active in many fields. Hillel Zeitlin, gifted with a mystic soul, has made original contributions to almost every phase of modern Hebrew literature. The greatest Hebrew journalist, writing for his coreligionists in many languages, was Nahum Sokolow. Simon Bernfeld, though not always original, was a versatile and very prolific writer who more than any one of his contemporaries effectively employed the Hebrew language for the popularization of the results of modern Jewish learning.

David Neumark was a gifted and very learned writer of philosophical essays and the historian par excellence of Jewish philosophy. In his religious views he was a liberal, whereas Wolf Jawitz endeavored to represent the position of a nationalized orthodoxy. On the other hand, in the philosophical writings of Jacob Klatzkin one meets with a view of Jewish life based upon two single values: land and language.

The stormy tides of activity engulfing Palestine in the years intervening between the two world wars found repercussion in the dashing verse, often free, of many young poets. They are numerous and their verse is vigorous. Abraham Schlonsky sings of love for the soil, while Isaac Lamdan, in his dramatic poem *Masadah,* reechoes the religious fervor that animates the builders of Palestine. The joy in suffering for Palestine is expressed in the poetry of Judah Karni and in the lyrics of Mordecai Temkin and M. Z. Wolfovsky. The cross-currents of Palestinian Jewish life are likewise reflected in the prose of contemporary Hebrew writers. Such authors as Dob Kimhi, A. Reubeni and Judah Yaari have endeavored to deal with the intruding effect of Occidental life upon the hallowed traditions of Palestine. Nathan Bistritzky, Jacob Rabinowitz, S. Zemach and others, although their works vary in literary merit, have one thing in common: they deal with life in the remotest corners of Jewish settlements in Palestine. Many of the Hebrew writers residing in Palestine in the 1940's were recent arrivals in the country. Not all of them confine their activities to fiction and poetry alone; their interest lies in every sphere of literary endeavor. It is not altogether surprising to find that often the background of much of their creative work is laid in countries other than Palestine. In fact, some of the finest prose works written in Palestine reflect life and experience in other lands. The number of Hebrew essayists in Palestine is legion, and that of scholars now larger than in any other country at any given time.

The beginnings of modern Hebrew literature in the United States are traceable to the stubborn efforts of a few pioneers who, during the last decades of the 19th cent. and after, had come to that country with more or less established reputations as Hebrew writers. The large number of Hebrew periodical publications which have appeared intermittently in the United States since 1871 testify to the tenacious efforts to give the Hebrew language and literature a foothold on American soil. Menahem Mendel Dolicki, Naphtali Herz Imber and Isaac Rabinowitz are among the early poets. Gershom Rosenzweig, satirist, George Selikowitz, essayist, Alexander Kohut, lexicographer, Abraham Hayim Rosenberg, author of a great Biblical encyclopedia, Judah David Eisenstein, anthologist and editor of the *Otzar Yisrael,* Henry Gersoni, Ephraim Deinard, Moses Shinedling, Perez Wiernik, M. L. Rodkinson, Arnold B. Ehrlich, Abraham Baer Dobsewitch (Dobsevage), Z. Wolf Schur, M. Reicherson, A. S. Waldstein, Israel Davidson and the brothers Max and Jacob S. Raisin are among the pioneers of Hebrew literature in the United States.

The fact is that little progress was made in the field of creative Hebrew literature until the early years of the 20th cent. With the wave of immigrants from Russia there came then to the United States a goodly number of enthusiastic Hebraists. Soon they became the leaders in every movement for the advancement of Hebrew culture in America. With the

help of those who preceded them, and encouraged by the frequent visits of eminent Hebrew writers and leaders in Jewish cultural activities from Europe, a band of young writers began to make their contributions to modern Hebrew literature in the form of poems, novels, dramas and other prose writings in which they gave expression to their experiences and observations in the "new land." Abraham Soyer, Reuben Wallenrod, Harry Sakler and J. D. Berkowitz are among the gifted short story writers, while Simon Halkin, in addition to fine verse and keen criticism, is also a novelist. S. L. Blank, though drawing upon Jewish life in Bessarabia, is the author of several novels and a number of short stories. Johanan Twersky specializes in the biographical and historical novel.

Most of the Hebrew poets in the United States, such as A. S. Schwartz, Aaron A. Domnitz, Simon Ginsburg, Hillel Babli, Moses Brind, Moses Feinstein, A. Regelson, Abraham Z. Halevi, Gabriel Preil, Eisig Silberschlag, Aaron Zeitlin and Reuben Grossman (later in Palestine), have excelled in lyrical verse. Several leading poets have written great epics. In their eagerness to display the influence of America on their verse they have turned to Indian mythology and drawn from it abundantly for their poetry. It was Saul Tchernichovsky, who, by rendering into Hebrew Longfellow's *Hiawatha,* first introduced Indian life and legends into modern Hebrew literature. This inspired Benjamin Nahum Silkiner, perhaps the outstanding American Hebrew poet, to write his *Mul Ohel Timurah* (Opposite the Tent of Timura), an epic in which the struggle of an Indian tribe to maintain its existence is depicted. The example thus set was soon followed by Ephraim Lisitzki with a like epic, *Meduroth Doachoth* (Low Burning Fires). It deals with Indian life before the arrival of the Whites and of the struggle that ensued. Israel Efros, scholar and poet, likewise drew upon Indian lore for his *Wigwamim Shothekim* (Silent Wigwams). Without neglecting distinctly Jewish themes, these and other Hebrew poets in the United States have drawn upon native themes for their verse and given that country a durable place in modern Hebrew literature.

American Hebrew literature produced a host of essayists and journalists. In addition to the men of letters who had come to the United States with established reputations and some whose names have already been mentioned, Menahem Ribalow, an able editor and stimulating critic, Meyer Waxman, Joseph Reider, S. B. Maximon, A. Epstein, A. R. Malachi, A. Goldberg, Daniel Persky, Shalom Spiegel, M. Meisls, J. S. Frishberg, J. J. Wohl, Hirsh L. Gordon, Isaac Rivkind, Pinhos Churgin, S. Bernstein, J. Orsay, Chaim Tchernowitz, N. Touroff and others have given to Hebrew literature a wealth of learning and criticism in the form of substantial works and minor studies, the influence of which has touched Hebrew readers everywhere.

Brief as this survey of the swift development of modern Hebrew literature necessarily is, its outline of the salient features of its theme will at least reveal two facts of interest and importance: that much of the deepest life of the Jewish people is recorded in the tongue of their ancestors; and that, although it extends far into the past, Hebrew literature is being made today and every day, and bids fair to be made for many years to come.   JOSHUA BLOCH.

LITERATURE, JUDEO-GREEK, *see* JUDEO-GREEK.

LITERATURE, JUDEO-ITALIAN, *see* JUDEO-ITALIAN.

LITERATURE, JUDEO-PERSIAN. 1. Bible Translations. It was not until about 1900 that any of the Judeo-Persian literature was known in Europe, with the single exception of the translation of the Pentateuch by Jacob ben Joseph Tavus (Constantinople, 1546). Other manuscripts, chiefly translations of parts of the Bible, were discovered in the latter part of the 19th cent. It was not, however, until Elkan N. Adler brought back hundreds of manuscripts from his journey to Persia (now in the library of the Jewish Theological Seminary of America in New York city) that the full range and manysidedness of Judeo-Persian literature was properly appreciated. The first investigation of Judeo-Persian manuscripts, both in the collection of Adler and in various European libraries, was undertaken by Wilhelm Bacher. He made the first survey of Judeo-Persian literature (up to 1904), later supplemented by Walter J. Fischel (up to 1933). Simon Chacham (d. 1910), a Bokharan Jew living in Jerusalem, was one of the most active promoters and publishers of this literature; it was due to his efforts that a new Judeo-Persian translation of the Pentateuch was published (Jerusalem, 1901-8), as well as of the Prophets. Some parts of the Bible (*Psalms, Job, Proverbs, Song of Songs* and the Prophetic books) had been previously translated into Judeo-Persian and published by various editors. There were also translations of such extra-canonical books as *Tobit, Megillath Antiochus, Judith* and the apocryphal *Daniel,* preserved in various European libraries.

2. Dictionaries. The most noteworthy of the Bible commentaries and dictionaries in Judeo-Persian are the *Sefer Hamelitzah* of Solomon ben Samuel, written in Urgendj, Russian Turkestan, in 1339, the *Agron* of Moses ben Aaron of Shirwan, Persia, in the 15th cent., and the *Kitzur Sefer Millim* of Chwailchot (Jerusalem, 1907), a Hebrew-Russian-Persian dictionary. A linguistic guidebook is discussed below (section 6).

3. Traditional Literature. The Mishnaic tractate *Aboth,* containing the sayings of the Jewish sages, has been repeatedly translated into Judeo-Persian, as have the Mishnah tractate *Sabbath* and some parts of the *Zohar.* Selections from the writings of Maimonides and of Bahya's *Hoboth Halebaboth* in Judeo-Persian translation were used by Simon Tob Melamed of Meshed in his *Ruah Hayim* (Jerusalem, 1898). Rabbi Aminow translated parts of the *Shulhan Aruch* into Judeo-Persian under the title of *Likkute Dinim.* A Judeo-Persian Midrash on the Torah was written by Rahamim Melamed of Shiraz, under the title of *Sefer Zichron Rahamim* (Jerusalem, 1922).

In the field of liturgy, there are Judeo-Persian translations of prayer-books (Siddurim and Mahzorim), prayers and poems (Selihoth, Pizmonim) and of the Passover Haggadah; Mulla Mordecai Adler of Meshed was particularly active in this field, which was investigated by Elkan N. Adler. The synagogal poetry translated into Judeo-Persian includes the poems of Solomon ibn Gabirol ("Kether Malchuth" and "Azharoth"), of Judah Halevi ("Mi Chamocha") and of Israel Nadjara, these being the most popular. Numerous collections of Judeo-Persian song books, such as the *Yismah Yisrael* (Jerusalem, 1901), containing songs for various religious occasions, bear witness to the strong interest of the Persian-speaking Jews in religious poetry. But these Jews were interested also in secular Persian poetry, and there are preserved in libraries and collections numerous Hebrew transcriptions of the works of such classical Persian writers as Hafiz, Nizami and Saadi.

4. Maulana Shahin. In the poet Maulana Shahin of Shiraz (14th cent.) the Persian Jews can boast of a creative genius of their own who was a pioneer in Judeo-Persian poetry. Of his works there have survived a "Book of Moses" and a "Book of Genesis"—poetic paraphrases of the Torah, elaborated by the addition of Moslem legends and war epics—a Persian epic, based on *Esther,* and a "Book of Ezra" (edit. S. Chacham, Jerusalem, 1902-5). Shahin followed the form and meter of the Persian classics, especially Firdusi, but his subject matter is drawn mainly from the Hebrew Bible. In the 16th cent. another poet of Shiraz, Imrani, set out to continue the work of Shahin and produced a poetic elaboration of *Aboth* and of the Bible story from Joshua to Solomon, arranged in the form of a large-scale epic. Toward the end of the 17th cent. a Judeo-Persian school of poets flourished in Bokhara; their leader was Jussuf Jehudi, whose songs, poems and translations (the outstanding one of these is *Haft Braderan*) have, in part, survived.

5. Poetical Chronicles. The most notable Judeo-Persian work in this field is the *Kitab Anusi* of Babai ben Lutf and Babai ben Farhad of Kashan, which portrays the religious persecutions suffered by the Persian Jews in the 17th and 18th centuries under Shahs Abbas I and II (partly edit. W. Bacher). A poetical chronicle *Chudaidad,* written in the 18th cent. by Ibrahim Abul Kair (edit. C. Saleman, 1897), relates the martyrdom of a Bokharan Jew.

6. Historical Narratives. Judeo-Persian literature has been enriched by translations of historical Midrashim (*Targum Sheni, Megillath Antiochus, Eldad Hadani* and others) and of narratives from world literature. Among the latter are a part of Shakespeare's *Comedy of Errors* (Jerusalem, 1911), S. Friedberg's *Zichronoth Lebeth David* and many stories of the *Maasiyoth Niflaim* type. Abraham Mapu's *Ahabath Tziyyon,* translated into Judeo-Persian and published in two editions, helped arouse the love of Zion in the hearts of Persian-speaking Jews. The *Sefer Millim Shishah* of Solomon ben Pinchasoff (Jerusalem, 1909, 1912), a dictionary in six languages and a literary curiosity, has served the needs of the Persian-speaking Jews of Persia, Afghanistan, Bokhara and other countries, who emigrated to Palestine.

7. Printing Presses. Toward the end of the 19th cent. a printing press was established in Jerusalem to supply translations into Judeo-Persian of prayer-books and Jewish literature to meet the literary needs of the Persian-speaking Jews. After the first World War, this

A page from Joseph Caro's "Shulhan Hapanim," printed (1568) in Judeo-Spanish at Salonika. Reproduced by courtesy of the Jewish Theological Seminary of America

Title page of Miguel de Silveyra's "Poema Heroico," printed (1636) in Judeo-Spanish at Naples

Titelblad van „Het Pascha

Title page of "Het Pascha," a Dutch tragi-comedy by Joost van den Vondel, published anonymously in 1612

VREUGDE LOF en DANKBAARHÉYD
gecalebreerd by de
HOOGDUITSCHE JOODEN,
In der selver SYNAGOGUE ten dage dat
hare DOORLUCHTIGE en KONING-
LYKE HOOGHEDEN de HEERE
P R I N C E
en MEVROUWE de
P R I N C E S S E,
van ORANJE & NASSAU. &c. &c. &c.
Onse stad met hoogst derselver tegen
woordigheyd vereerd hebben.

TOT AMSTERDAM,
by JOSEPH, JACOB, & ABRAHAM
SALOMONS PROOPS.
GHY ZYT VEEL sCHOONDER DAN DE MEN-
SCHEN KINDEREN ; GENADE IS UYTGESTORT IN
UWE LIPPEN ; DAEROM HEEFT U GODT GEZEGENT
IN EUVVIGHEYT.   PSAL. XLV. 3.

Title page of a collection of Jewish prayers in Dutch (dated 1768) in honor of the royal family activity was removed to Teheran. Among the first products of the Hebrew press of that city were a text-book of Hebrew for the Jews of Iran, by Solomon Cohen (Teheran, 1918), a history of the Zionist movement by Assis Naim (Teheran, 1920), a Judeo-Persian periodical, *Hageulah,* and *Hahayyim* (1920). The most active individual in these efforts was Mullah Chaim More, whose three books, *Derech Hayim* (1921), *Gedulath Mordecai* (1924) and *Yede Eliyahu* (1927), were intended to transmit the religious and historical values of Jewish tradition to the younger generation.

In the 20th cent. some of the Persian Jews started to publish books in Persian characters, as well as in the Persian language. Among these is Suleiman Chajim, who has written a drama, *Jussuf and Suleicha,* and an English-Persian dictionary (Teheran, 1933 et seq.), regarded as one of the best in this field.

WALTER J. FISCHEL.

Lit.: Munk, S., *Notice sur R. Saadja* (1838); Kohut, A., *Kritische Beleuchtung der persischen Pentateuchüber-setzung des Jacob b. Joseph Tavus* (1871); Lagarde, P., *Persische Studien* (1884); Adler, Elkan N., *The Persian Jews, Their Books and Their Ritual* (1890); the writings of Wilhelm Bacher on the subject, listed in the bibliographies of his works by L. Blau (1910) and Dénes Friedman (1928); Friedberg, *Beth Eked Sefarim* (1928-32); Finkel, J., in *Jewish Quarterly Review* (1931) 353; Margoliouth, *ibid.,* vol. 15, p. 281; Saleman, C., *Judaeo-Persica* (1897); Levy, R., in *Jewish Studies in Memory of G. A. Kohut* (1935); Fischel, Walter J., "Zur jüdisch-persischen Literatur," *Monatsschrift für Geschichte und Wissenschaft des Judentums* (1933) 113; idem, "Eine jüdisch-persische Toledoth-Jeshu-Handschrift," *ibid.* (1934) 343.

LITERATURE, JUDEO-SPANISH.

The main divisions of Judeo-Spanish (Ladino) literature may be divided roughly into (1) religious writings, (2) works of an ethic-homiletic character, (3) poetry, (4) proverbs, and (5) plays.

A cursory examination of the whole field of Ladino literature will reveal that works of a religious nature predominate. Originality is lacking, however, even in this restricted category, for many of the works are only translations from the Hebrew. It seems rather paradoxical that the Ladino-speaking Jews, with a rich intellectual and literary heritage, should have made relatively few contributions to literature. Perhaps an explanation lies in the fact that the first emigrants to leave Spain in 1492 were largely individuals who belonged to the humbler classes. Beginning life in new lands with limited intellectual and material resources, and confronted by the necessity of earning a livelihood under difficult conditions, they must have had little or no opportunity for the cultivation of belles-lettres.

The gradual decline in the use and knowledge of Hebrew made necessary another linguistic medium to keep alive the religious practices of Judaism. This situation left only Spanish, which became for all practical purposes a liturgical language.

The first translation made into Ladino was that of a ritual employed in the slaughtering of animals, which was published in Constantinople in 1510. It was a part of the *Shulhan Aruch,* the standard code of Jewish law, and was given the title *Dinim de Sehita y Bedica* (from the Hebrew words *shehitah* and *bedikah*). Another book dealing with religious laws and ceremonies, and also based on Caro's code, was the *Shulhan Hapa-*

nim or *Mesa del alma* (Salonika, 1568). There are many Judeo-Spanish translations of the daily prayers and those used on the festivals. Several Ladino versions of the Passover Haggadah have been published in various parts of the Balkans.

The first Ladino translation of the Pentateuch, printed in Hebrew square characters, appeared in Constantinople in 1547. The various Judeo-Spanish versions of the Bible that followed were modeled largely on this translation. In 1568 there appeared in Salonika a Ladino version of the Pentateuch and the Prophets, but it can hardly be called an original translation since it is essentially a transcription in Hebrew characters of the Ferrara translation, which was printed in Roman characters and published in Italy in 1553.

In the field of ethics and homiletics, a prominent name is that of Moses Almosnino (about 1510-80). His *Hanhagath Hahayim,* or *Regimiento de la vida,* was published in Salonika in 1564. Written in Spanish, the book had an object which may be summarized in the author's own words: *. . . en el cual se contiene cuanto conviene para poder bien andar toda la jornada de la vida humana sin errar, comprendiendo en él toda la filosofía moral muy copiosamente* ("containing within it whatever is necessary to enable one to go through every day of mortal life without erring, and comprehending in it all moral philosophy in a most detailed form"). The language employed by Almosnino shows a correctness and purity of the Spanish language and style that could naturally be expected in a book written by a profound scholar some seventy years after the expulsion of the Jews from Spain.

The first Jewish system of ethics, *Al Hidayah ila Faraidi al Kulub* (Guide to the Duties of the Heart), written originally by Bahya ibn Pakuda in Arabic, was translated into Hebrew by Judah ibn Tibbon under the title *Hoboth Halebaboth.* It was again translated, this time into Ladino, by Joseph Formon, and published in 1713 under the title *Obligacion de los corazones.*

A book which has had a wide popular following is the *Meam Loez,* published in Constantinople in 1733. It is an encyclopedic commentary dealing with Jewish life in all its relations. Begun by Jacob Culi, it was continued after his death by Isaac Magreso and Isaac Behar Arguiti.

In the realm of poetry, the old Spanish ballads, or *romances,* are still preserved among the Ladino-speaking Jews. Some of these ballads, lost completely or in part in Spain, have remained alive in Judeo-Spanish tradition. Many, however, have been mutilated by the inclusion of foreign words or by modifications. These ballads were a source of inspiration, serving as models for many poems written in Ladino.

In 1732 Abraham Toledo published a rhymed story of Joseph under the title *Coplas de Joseph.* Judeo-Spanish has a wealth of *cantares, coplas* and *roscas,* which are sung or read during the Purim festival. Among these may be mentioned: *Cantares para alabar al Dío en la festividad de Purím* (Livorno, 1820); *Roscas de Purím* (Vienna, 1866); *Coplas nuevas de Purím* (Salonika, 1868). Among the modern poets worthy of mention are Rabbi Baruth Mitrany, David Florentin, Saadia Halevy, Abraham Cappon, M. Papo, Joseph Marcou Baruch, Mose David Gaon, Zeky Efendi Atias and Laura Papo.

Facsimile of a letter addressed by Moses Mendelssohn to Johann Gottfried Herder

Der Meßias

ein

Heldengedicht.

HALLE,
bey Carl Herrmann Hemmerde.
1749.

Title page of Klopstock's "Messias," printed in 1749

A

LETTER

CONCERNING

Toleration:

Humbly Submitted, &c.

LICENSED, *Octob.* 3. 1689.

LONDON,
Printed for *Awnsham Churchill,* at the *Black Swan* at *Amen-Corner.* 1689.

*Title page of John Locke's "Letter Concerning Tolera-
tion," published at London in 1689*

Although proverbs are a minor literary genre, Judeo-Spanish has not only preserved numerous proverbs brought from Spain, but has added many others taken from the countries in which the Ladino Jews settled. Many collections of these proverbs have been made.

Plays, notably French, have been translated into Ladino. Among the original compositions may be mentioned: *La familia misteriosa*, by Jacob Behar; *Capitán Dreyfus*, by Jacques Luria; *Abrabanel*, by Behor Azaria; *Los aguisadores*, by Abraham Cappon. Rabbi Sabetay J. Djaen has also contributed to the Judeo-Spanish stage.   Max A. Luria.

Lit.: Djaen, Sabetay J., "Sobre algunos escritores en ladino," *Judaica*, vol. 7 (1939) 40-43; Franco, M., *Essai sur l'histoire des Israélites de l'empire ottoman* (1897); Grünbaum, M., *Jüdisch-spanische Chrestomathie* (1896); Kayserling, M., *Biblioteca española-portugueza-judaica* (1890); Yaari, Abraham, *Catalogue of Judeo-Spanish Books in the Jewish National and University Library* (Hebrew; 1934).

LITERATURE, MODERN HEBREW (NEO-HEBREW), *see* Literature, Hebrew.

LITERATURE ON AND BY JEWS. I. Czech.

Jewish themes have been treated frequently in Czech literature ever since it first arose about the beginning of the 19th cent. That these treatments have not always been favorable is due to a large extent to the political background in Bohemia and Moravia, where there was a struggle between Czech nationalism and government efforts toward the Germanization of all groups in the Austro-Hungarian empire. Whereas the Czech writers naturally were on the side of the Czech revival, the Jews, who had received every improvement in their position from the government and who spoke German as their vernacular, were for the most part on the side of Germanization. This ranging on opposite sides is apparent in some of the presentations of Jews by Czech writers. It is nevertheless noteworthy that one of the leading early Czech poets, K. H. Mácha, made a Jewish girl the heroine of his short story "Cikáni" (Gypsy), as well as giving a sympathetic and favorable portrayal of the servant-girl Judith. On the other hand, the contemporary poet Jan Neruda (1834-91) took an unfriendly attitude toward the Jews in his pamphlet *Pro strach židovsky* (The Fear of Judaism).

Svatopluk Čech (1846-1908), who had had a Jewish friend as a schoolboy, sings of the passive heroism of the Jews in *Sny Palestinské* (Palestinian Dreams); he praises the suffering and accomplishments of the Jews in the past, in contrast to the actions of the Jewish traders of his own time. He describes the ghettos of Kutaj, Cracow and Constantinople on his *Dávné vzpomínky* (Old Memories) and *Kresby z cest* (Travel Pictures); he attacks Jewish usurers and peddlers in *Zastavená povaha* (The Disgraced Character) and *Věčný Žid* (The Eternal Jew). In contrast to him, Julius Zeyer (1841-1901), descended on his mother's side from one of the old Jewish families of Prague, presents a merchant of the ghetto of Prague as a heroic figure; he also wrote charming tales and legends derived from the Hebrew Bible. Of all the Czech poets, Jaroslav Vrchlicky (1853-1912) has the greatest number of Jewish themes; to these he devoted a hundred poems, two plays, two stories and a literary essay.

The most important of the legends is *Kříž Božětěchuv* (The Cross of Bozetech). His greatest accomplishment and contribution to Czech literature is his epic poem *Bar Kochba;* his most noted comedy in the field is *Rabínská moudrest* (The Wisdom of the Rabbi), a story of the great Prague rabbi, Löwe Judah ben Bezalel. Among other things, he translated into Czech Morris Rosenfeld's Yiddish *Songs of the Ghetto*.

J. S. Machár pictures, in his "Viennese Profiles" (Czech), a number of prominent Jews who lived in Vienna at the end of the 19th cent., and takes a strong stand against anti-Semitism. The Czech worker-poet Peter Bezruč, on the other hand, in his songs (such as *Slezké písně*, Silesian Songs), takes a hostile attitude against the "drinking Jews" and the Rothschilds in particular, and against all Jews in general. Viktor Dyk wrote a poem satirizing Jews, "Kohn and Bloch" (Czech), and introduces Jewish figures into two of his novels. Jewish characters are often depicted in the historical novels which form such an important part of Czech literature, as in the works of R. Khol, Karel de Wetter's *Zlatý Věk* (The Golden Age), F. J. Cecetka's *Židovka* (The Jewess), Karel Leger's *Suchý Čert* (The Lean Devil), J. D. Konrad's *Židovka Malkah* (The Jewess Malkah) and in the writings of Benjamín Klicka, Ignat Hermann and Rudolf Kronbauer.

Josef J. Kolár wrote a very popular play, *Pražský Žid* (The Jew of Prague), in which he depicts a Jew who helps the Czechs wherever he can. Josef Till's drama *Rasa* (Race) was performed in Slovakia during the post-War period. Alois Jirásek, writer of historical romances, reproduces Jewish legends, and describes a pogrom of the Middle Ages in his *Syn ohnicuv* (The Son of the Fire-Riders). His novel *Temno* (Darkness) presents the Jew Lazar Kisch, a man of goodness and self-denial. Arne Novák, in *Židovdké Hřbitovy* (Jewish Cemeteries), touchingly describes the sacrifices of Polish Jewish refugees in concentration camps. Dramas with Jewish characters include J. N. Štěpánek's *Čech a Němec* (The Czech and the German), which has as one of its characters a Jewish thief, and V. Kliepura's *Israelitka* (The Jewess) and *Popelka Varšavská* (The Cinderella of Warsaw). Jewish figures are treated in an unsympathetic manner in such pastoral novels as that of Josef Holeček, *Naši* (Our People), Johann Klecanda's great pastoral novel *Maloměstský apoštol* (The Small Town Apostle), and in the writings of Jan Herben.

Emil Vachek, in his psychological novel *Sup* (The Vulture), depicts an ideally gifted young Jewish man, but this is in contrast to other, less agreeable Jewish characters. Similarly, in Jan Vrba's novel, *Dum Otmara Loevyho* (The House of Otmar Löw), the hero is an exception, the other Jews being unheroic. On the other hand, Edvard Bass, in *Pán Goldschmidt na Cestách* (Mr. Goldschmidt's Travels), depicts a Jewish merchant as a splendid figure. The fortune and fate of another Jewish merchant are described by Vasclar Stech in the novel *Štěch Zlatého Roznu* (The Luck of the Golden Drink); in this novel Jewish characters are presented in a most favorable contrast to the Christian ones. One of the leading Czech poets of village tales, the kindly Karel Klostermann (1848-1923), wrote: "Do not despise the Jews and look down upon them, but admire their strangth, which helps them to endure and to grow, in spite of the disfavor of many centuries, in spite of their being scattered among many peoples." His novel *Srul,* in particular, presents a kind and sympathetic Jew.

Karl Čapek-Chod, a writer of the 19th cent., presented in his novel *Anton Vondrejec* the touching figure of an elderly Jewish ritual slaughterer, and in his *Dceruška Jajrova* (The Daughter of Jair) a Jewess who is one of the most beautiful characters in all Czech literature. Here one finds artistic realization of the spirit of reconciliation and democracy which was at the basis of the Czechoslovakian republic. Another noteworthy example of this spirit is the sketch *Naš Pan Fuechsl* (Our Mr. Fuechsl), written by Tomáš Garrigue Masaryk in his youth. He draws the characters from a Jewish peddler whom he knew in his youth, who by his goodness and trustworthiness taught him that a Jew could possess real nobility.

In the 20th cent. a number of Czech writers showed an interest in the development of the new Jewish center in Palestine. Especially significant is the diary of the geologist Petribok, who enthusiastically praises the work of the Jewish colonists, especially the pioneers (Halutzim). Viktor Musik describes Jewish hospitality in Palestine in glowing terms.

In addition to the authors of Jewish descent mentioned above, a number of others made contributions of various sorts to Czech literature. Max Lederer wrote stories of the ghetto and of the villages under the title *Za Zrežavelými dráty* (Behind Rusty Bars). Egon Hostovský edited several books, such as *Ghetto Vnich* (The Deep-Rooted Ghetto) and *Danajský dar* (The Gift of the Danaei). Robert Saudek wrote in his youth a one-act play, *Zidovštvi kluti* (Jewish Boys), and a well-known Czech poet of Jewish descent, Franz Gellner, wrote a group of stories set in Jewish scenes. The Zionist poet F. K. Gottlieb wrote *Cesta do Canáan* (The Way to Canaan). Friedrich Adler made an excellent translation of Vrchlicky's *Bar Kochba* into German; other Jews who translated Czech works into German include Paul Eisner, Rudolph Fuchs, and Otto Pick.   OSCAR FRANKL.

Lit.: Donath, Oscar, *Žide a Židovstvi v česke literatuře* (1923-30).

II. Dutch. On Jews. In the medieval literature of The Netherlands as well as that of the remainder of Christian Europe, the Jew is viewed as a member of a foreign and hostile faith. The Jew is represented in this literature as the symbol of the evil and diabolic. From the story of the Passion he is looked upon as the Christ-killer. The Dutch prototype for this point of view is the poem, *Van den Levene ons Heren,* written probably by a Brabant author about a century before the great persecutions of 1350 to 1370, and strongly anti-Jewish. Furthermore, the Jew is held to be in league with the devil as in the Theophilus legend, a variation of the Faust legend. Even in the short but sympathetic mention of Meester Abrion in the animal fable of Van den Vos Reinaerde (about 1250) there is a feeling of the supernatural and diabolical with which the Jew is surrounded. Moreover, the Jew not only is said to have crucified Jesus, but to continue this activity with images of Jesus and Mary; even the baptized Jew can not deny his basic nature (cf. the

Legends of Maerlant; Spieghel Historiael; annals of the Abbey of Kamerijk, about 1322; Chronicon Egmundanum; Spel van den Smet van Cambroen). The Jew is regarded as the desecrator of the host, as characterized in the historical song of the events of 1349 to 1350, the story of St. Gudula in Brussels as the cause of the pogrom of 1370, and by the chronicler Albert Snavelde of Zwolle; and blood is needed by him not for ritual purposes but for healing (cf. Bienboec, a Middle-Dutch version of the Liber Apum, and Thomas de Cantimpré). His conversion to Christianity serves the glorification of the faith, especially of the Virgin Mary. Finally, the Jew is ridiculed and contemned in the legends, didactic observations and wonder-tales especially because of his Messianic belief; as, for example, in the Ghent manuscript Caesarius of Heisterbach.

The problem of Jewish existence is treated in the historical works of Jacob van Maerlant (1235-1300) such as *Der Naturen Bloeme, Spieghel Historiael,* which is a history of the world until 1250, and *Rijmbijbel.* Der *Leken Spieghel* by Jan van Boendale of Brabant is more systematic and significant than the works of Maerlant. In the chapter, "Van den Joden ende van haren Wesen," he calls the Jews obstinate and asserts that even the writings of the Jews point to Jesus as the Messiah. Boendale is also the keen observer and narrator of the events in Brabant of 1349 to 1350 (*Brabantsche Geesten,* end of Book 5). A "Rederijkersspel" drama of the 16th cent. entitled *Van den ghedinghe tuschen eenen coopman ende eenen jode* describes a kind of Shylock a hundred years before Shakespeare. This literature not only reflected the attitude of the people toward the Jews but often gave the impetus for the hatred of the people toward the Jews.

The Renaissance was a turning point in the judgment of the Jews in Dutch literature. In spite of the social and cultural importance of the immigrant Portuguese Jews, they are not even mentioned in the many-sided Dutch literature of the Golden Age of the 17th cent. This was due perhaps to the fact that they lived within their own cultural and religious tradition and were looked upon as foreigners. But in Dutch painting as well as literature Jews are looked upon from a Biblical standpoint, through the eyes of the Bible, and they are shown in Old Testament garb. Joost van den Vondel (1587-1679), who is the poet laureate of all Dutch poets, dealt with Bible themes especially after his conversion to Catholicism. His Joseph trilogy particularly had great influence upon the people; other works worthy of mention are his earliest drama *Het Pascha ofte De Verlossinghe der Kinderen Israels,* in which the Jews play a heroic part; *Jephta, Adam in Ballingschap, Solomon, Samson,* and the two David dramas. His play *Joseph in Dotan* attained to great fame. Only to his youthful work, *Hierusalem verwoest,* did Vondel prefix a sonnet, "Aan de Joodsche Rabbinen"; it is quite clear from the sonnet what he thought of the Jewish reading public. In the works of the other classicists of the time, Hooft (1581-1647) and Breeroo (1585-1618), who describe Amsterdam life in detail, one seeks in vain for references to Jews. Only Calvinist theology in the 17th cent. took an interest in the ritual services and fate of the Jews. The works of Buxtorf and Basnage's *Histoire des Juifs*, in Dutch, were published in Holland too.

Typical of the Calvinist point of view is the *Historie der Jooden*, by Abraham Coster (1609). It is not so much a history of the Jews as of Jewish ritual, custom and doctrine. Its strong anti-Jewish tendency is not merely theoretical; it is replete with prejudice and charges against Jewish writings and Jews themselves. Coster used this work to agitate, as representative of the Calvinists before the Amsterdam council, against the construction of a synagogue. Henricus Groenewegen, too, emphasizes in his book, *De Verloessinge Israels uyt Zion, ofte de gewensche bekeeringe der Joden tegen het laatste der dagen* (Amsterdam, 1667), the obstinacy of the Jews who have renounced the redeemer, and he expects their conversion to Christianity on the Judgment Day. Jean de Labadie differs only in tone from the other Calvinist preachers in his *Ordeel der Liefde en gerechtigheyt over den gegenwoordigen toestandt der Joden*. Jean de Labadie, founder of the sect of the Labadists and exponent of a religio-philosophical freethought, preached sufferance and tolerance of those of different faith so that in more gentle manner Jews might be won to Christianity. The jurist, statesman and theologian Hugo de Groot (1583-1645) is not only the author of a plan for governing the "Jewish nation" (1615) in which he favored freedom for the Jewish religion but also limiting their number in Amsterdam to 300; he was also a theologian and exegete, and in his *Annotationes ad Vetus Testamentum* (3 vols., 1644) he made use of the assistance of Manasseh ben Israel. Concerning many Biblical precepts, for example the dietary laws of the Jews, he expressed remarkably modern opinions. Like Labadie, however, he does not deviate in principle from the Calvinist doctrine. He wrote the best modern apology for Christianity, *De veritate religionis Christianae* (1622); but in general he sponsored tolerance for all positive religions. Answering the inquiry of Stupecki in Lublin, he wrote against the ritual murder legend on December 12, 1636.

In the 17th cent., Dutch literary interest in the Jews was restricted to the theologians, and they looked upon their Jewish compatriots only as subjects for conversion. In the first quarter of the 18th cent. this changed. With the large immigration of German Jews, who were regarded by the Dutch citizenry not as believers in a non-Christian faith but as social enemies, the *smous* (usurer and deceiver) appears in popular literature for the first time, and is identified with the Jew and ridiculed in his own jargon. The antagonistic expression against the Jews began in Dutch literature about 1710 to 1720, the time of the widespread speculation mania which had also gripped the Jews. Ridicule of the Jews and of their language reached its peak in the caricature and satire *Het groote Tafereel van 1720;* in poems in the form of "landgezangen"; in the comedies and burlesques of Pieter Langendijk (1683-1756); in the periodic lampoons of one Hoefnagel and Jacob Campo Weyerman (1677-1747), in which the latter sharply attacked the Jewish clergy, the rabbis, just as he did not spare the Catholic clergy. Hoefnagel's infamous sheets of 1770 revealed such an evil anti-Semitism that they became a kind of 18th cent. *Stürmer*.

On an even lower cultural level is the popular chapbook literature which seeks to amuse the populace by satirizing and ridiculing the *smous*. Between 1731 and 1740 three volumes appeared, *De Gevange, de Gestrafte* and *de Doode Smous,* which Claus van Laar is supposed to have written. They contrast the deceitful and usurious Jew, the Shylock character, with the fine Christian merchant (cf. the list of chapbooks about Jews in Waller, F. G., *Catalogus van Nederlandsche en Vlaamsche Populaire Boeken,* The Hague, 1936, p. 521).

On the other hand, the period of the Enlightenment in the 18th cent., with its rationalistic viewpoint, diverged from the Calvinist theologians of the 17th cent. The Enlightenment was restricted in Holland to one group of the upper intellectual level, and found expression in the "Spectatoriale Geschriften" (journals). Justus van Effen (1684-1735), who set himself a cultural and didactic task, founded the first Dutch *Spectator* (1731-35), after the English model. He was not a friend of the Jews in its fullest sense, but he was more objective than his contemporaries in judging the charges against the Jews. In opposition to the Calvinists, he maintained that a distinction had to be made between the Jews of that day and those of sixteen centuries earlier. He censured the educated persons of his times who scorned and cursed the Jews. He emphasized that there were good persons among the Jews just as among the Christians, and that respectable and honest persons were to be found among the High German Jews as well as the Portuguese; but he turned sharply against the low morality prevailing among the Jewish rabble. He placed the responsibility for this condition upon the well-situated Jews who had not provided suitable education and moral instruction. Although Justus van Effen represented the point of view, typical of the period of Enlightenment, that education and evolution could improve mankind, he overlooked almost completely the social and economic causes of this condition of morality among the Jewish masses. The social and economic limitations were more correctly interpreted as the cause of the situation of the Jews in Holland by later journals such as *De Denker* (1764), *De Opmerker* (1778) and *De Koopman* (1768-76), and they indicated the need for Jewish economic and cultural emancipation.

After the emancipation of the Jews in Holland at the end of the 18th cent., the Jews still appeared in Dutch literature as a special class of the people, but in general they were not treated any worse than any other class. One of the moving and artistically perfect lyric poems of Antony C. W. Staring (1767-1840), the Dutch Béranger, is the oft-cited "De Israëlitische Looverhut," in which the poet gives expression to his profound respect and consideration for the Jewish tradition of the children of Abraham. Nicolaas Beets (Hildebrand, 1814-1903), for example, described the Jews of the middle class in his *Camera Obscura,* which has since become a classic and which painted a picture of Dutch middle class society with keen observation and priceless humor. Multatuli (E. Douwes Dekker, 1820-87) described, in *de Jodenbuurt te Amsterdam,* the Amsterdam ghetto as it must have been in the middle of the 19th cent. Aart van der Leeuw (1876-1931) published in his *Vluchtige Begroetingen* (1925) a short story of three Jews who are put to death because of a theft. The humorous writer and novelist Justus van Maurik (1846-1904), who wrote especially on subjects dealing with the life of the people of Amsterdam, mentioned the Jews favorably in some of his sketches; he wrote, among other things, a book called *Izak van den Dam.* The Flemish author August Vermeylen (b. 1872) wrote a symbolic narrative in his best-known work, *De wandelende Jood* (1906), in which he described the history of a human soul and its philosophy of life as follows: Ahasuerus and the Nazarene, Ahasuerus on the Way to Hell, Ahasuerus on the Way to Heaven, Ahasuerus among the Human Beings. Characteristic for Holland is also the fact that on July 27, 1936, an inter-denominational committee (Committee van Waakzaamheid) was founded which, despite the political convictions of its members, applied itself to the cultural combatting of National Socialism and published brochures against this cultural menace.

By Jews. The Portuguese Jews made their contribution to the golden age of Dutch literature even though they did not write in Dutch but in Spanish, Portuguese and Latin. One of the most outstanding of them is Manasseh ben Israel (1604-57), who may be characterized as a humanist because of his knowledge of various languages and literatures, his scientific connections with the Dutch humanists and his creative writings. In addition, the philosophers Uriel da Costa (1585-1640) and Spinoza (1632-77) must be mentioned. Spinoza's contemporary, the physician and philosopher Isaac Orobio de Castro (1620-87), strongly opposed Spinoza's teachings in his *Certamen Philosophicum,* in which he took a somewhat Kantian position. Numerous poets wrote in Spanish and dealt with Jewish themes; Jacob Israel Belmonte (d. 1629) was most prominent among them. Jacob Barocus translated several of the works of Lope de Vega. Thus the Spanish comedy gained popularity in Holland, and about 1750 the Portuguese Jews themselves began to produce Spanish dramas. Hebrew poetry flourished in 18th cent. Holland through the efforts of Isaac Cohen Belinfante (d. 1780) and David Franco Mendes (1730-92).

About this time the beginnings of the Enlightenment appear also among the Jews. The most important representative is Isaac de Pinto (1717-87). Most of his writings are on economic and social questions. He wrote polemics against Voltaire on the Jews, a book on the rebellion of the English colonies in America, and his most important work bears the title *Traité de la circulation et du crédit,* which Sombart called the *Song of Songs* of the system of public debt and property. He challenged materialism and the lack of faith of his times, and attacked especially Holbach's *Système de la Nature* (1770) by means of the most important proofs of dualism. The title of his work is *Précis des Arguments contre les Matérialistes avec de Nouvelles Réflexions sur la Nature de nos Connaissances, L'existence de Dieu, l'immatérialité et l'immortalité de l'Âme* (The Hague, 1774).

In 1791 an important work, *Geschiedenis der Kolonie van Suriname Behelzende derzelver opkomst, voortgang, burgerlyke en staatkundige gesteldheid, tegenwoordigen staat van koophandel, en eene volledige en naauwkeurige beschryving van het land, de zeden en gebruiken der ingezetenen. Geheel op nieuw samengesteld Door een gezelschap van Geleerde Joodsche Mannen Aldaar,* appeared in Amsterdam and Harlingen. Although it shows the influence of Christian Wilhelm Dohm, a number of whose letters to and from the Jewish community are incorporated into the introduction, it is largely the work of David de Is. C. Nassy, who at that time was a commissioner and representative of the Jewish community of Surinam. Nassy signed the dedication to this book on September 20, 1788. He also published a political, theological and moral letter on the Jews, favoring their equality. The High German Jews also made themselves felt in the period of the Enlightenment in Holland. Nathan Levy argued in the journal, *De Denker* (1764), for the economic emancipation of the Jews. Under the influence of the philosophy of the Enlightenment Hartog Ulman published (1769) two works of no great importance.

Most prominent in Dutch literature of the 19th cent. was Isaac da Costa (1789-1860), a descendant of the Portuguese Jewish community. He was under the lifelong influence of the versatile and admired poet and author, Willem Bilderdijk (1756-1831). Under his influence Da Costa became converted to the Reformed Church, but even after his baptism continued his adherence to his people. Filled with passion but of calm exterior, a "snow-capped volcano" according to Albert Pierson (1831-90), he became one of the protagonists of the Protestant "réveil" (reawakening) in which the spirit of romanticism attacked the barren dogmatism and deism of the 18th cent. His major work, *Bezwaren tegen den Geest der Eeuw* (1823), is directed against liberalism. For Isaac da Costa, being a poet meant to be withdrawn from the mundane; his poetry is not as varied as Bilderdijk's but is filled with insight and always serious and sublime. His *Tijdzangen* have become best known of all his poetry. In the splendid and colorful Biblical poem *Hagar* (1848) he depicts the mother of Ishmael as the representative of the Mohammedan religion and of its worldly power who, despite all her science, art and majesty, ultimately bows before Christ and withdraws into the tent of Abraham. Da Costa and his works are loved by some, but others sense in them something foreign to the Dutch spirit. Da Costa's friend, H. J. Koenen, wrote *Geschiedenis der Joden in Nederland* (Utrecht, 1843).

In the 1880's there was a renaissance of Dutch literature. Since 1885 the periodical *Nieuwe Gids,* has taken over the leadership. Among the leading Jewish spirits Herman Heijermans (1864-1924) must be mentioned first. He began with very naturalistic novels, such as *Trinette* (1893) and *Een Jodenstreek en Diamantstad* (1904). Under the nom de plume of Koos Habem he wrote *Kamertjeszonde* (1898); as Samuel Falkland he wrote feuilletons which were later published in thirteen little volumes under the title *Schetsen.* Until this time the theatre held second place in Dutch literature in the 19th cent. At the end of the century, however, there was a reawakening of realistic drama, no small part of which was due to Heijermans' dramatic works. His social dramas, *Ghetto* (1898), *Het Zevende Gebod* and others, show great technical skill and remarkable descriptive powers; they belong among the greatest triumphs of the Dutch stage. From Heijermans' last years come the two novels *Droomkoninkje* and *Vuurvlindertje.* Heijerman's most successful play was

Op Hoop van Zegen (1900), which was the only one to be made into a motion picture.

Israel Querido (1874-1932) was an artist of tremendous talent, phantasy, emotion and depth. He combined sharp contrasts and the most diverse subjects in his presentations with an extravagance of linguistic expression and images. He refused to be a realist and wanted to approach his subjects from a visionary attitude and feeling. He began with naturalistic dramas patterned after Zola. The world of the diamond workers from which he came he described in *Levensgang* (1901). The theme that Breeroo depicted in his Spanish Brabander became for the artist Querido the point of departure for a grandiose and rich description of life as a whole as he envisioned it in *De Jordaan*, a cycle of novels in four parts (1925). At the same time Querido wrote historical novels. His last work, *Het Volk Gods,* is an epic of Amsterdam (1932). He wrote two dramas for theatre, *Saul* and *David,* and published literary historical essays and theatre and music criticisms.

Jacob Israel de Haan (1881-1924) belonged to the younger generation, which found its organ of expression in Albert Verway's periodical *De Beweging.* He came from a rabbinical home, but in his youth turned away from traditional beliefs; for some years he was a Socialist, then a Zionist. Completely disillusioned, he finally returned to the faith of his childhood. He remained at heart always the broken restless spirit. This spiritual unrest and dissatisfaction found a place in his poetry. *Libertijnsche Liederen* appeared in 1914, and shortly thereafter his religious and nationalistic Jewish lyric, *Het joodsche Lied.* This work drew general attention to him, and he became recognized as a Jewish poet of large stature. From 1919 on, as a Zionist and as correspondent for the *Algemeen Handelsblad,* he lived in Palestine, where he was murdered in 1924. His sister was Carry van Bruggen (Carry Pit de Haan, 1881-1932). She was a writer of excessive sensibility but also of keen understanding, marked individuality and passionate humanity, and both in her life and works she evinces a constant vacillation between adaptation and independence. In her early works, first of all in her *In de Schaduw,* her adaptation to other realistic literature is evident. Later it was her task to portray and interpret her life experience directly. Her being a Jewess, together with her youthful reminiscences and her leaving the traditional Jewish home of her parents, is told in the novels *De Verlatene* (1910), one of the finest narratives of Dutch literature, and in *Het Joodje,* in *Avontuurtjes,* and in *Vier jaargetijden,* while the later clarification of these reminiscences finds its expression in *Het huisje aan de sloot* (1921). She portrays her direct past in keen psychological analysis in her *Een Coquette Vrouw* and under the name of "Justine Abbing" in her *Uit het leven van een denkende vrouw.* Her last novel, *Eva,* is a document of the emancipation of women in the 19th cent. While she visioned her life work in her philosophical book *Prometheus,* her talent consists in evaluating and utilizing her experiences rather than in speculation.

Annie Salomons (b. 1885), of Jewish descent, is the author of *Verzen (I en II), Nieuwe Verzen en Liederen,* and of short stories and novels. The novel *Een Meisje studentje* (1906) brought her fame. She was of considerable importance for her work in the women's movement. Under the pseudonym Ada Gerlo, she earned renown with her *Herinneringen van een onafhankelijke vrouw* (Remembrances of an Independent Woman).

Among the younger writers is Victor Emanuel van Vriesland (b. 1892). He wrote in *De Vrije Bladen,* which was founded in 1924. In 1929 he became literary critic for the *Nieuwe Rotterdamsche Courant,* and in 1937 edited *De Groene Amsterdammer.* His lyrics are suggestive of the Frenchman Valéry, and modern. His prose, like his poetry, is strongly intellectualistic. His best-known novel is *Het Afscheid van de Wereld in drie Dagen* (1926). In 1915 he published *De cultureele noodtoestand van het joodsche Volk,* and in 1939, at Amsterdam, *Spiegel van de Nederlandsche poezie door alle eeuwen.* Finally, he has made his mark also as a dramatist with *Der verlorene Sohn* (Leipzig, 1925) and *De Havenstad* (1933). Noteworthy among his poems are *Voorwaardelijk Uitzicht* (1929) and *Herhalingsoefeningen* (1935).

One of the most remarkable figures of modern Dutch poetry is Herman van den Bergh (b. 1897), typical representative of the periodical *Het Getij.* Furthermore, Siegfried Emanuel van Praag (b. 1899) must also be mentioned; he published studies in 1926 entitled *De Westjoden en hun Letterkunde sinds 1860,* and he has written short stories and novels, including the biographical studies *La Judith* (1930) and *Julie de l'Espinasse* (1934). Another poet worthy of mention is Sebastian Bonn (1881-1930), who published verses on social subjects in a volume entitled *Wat Zang en Melody* (1910) and later *Immortellen* (1912).

Important among writers of the younger generation is Maurits Dekker (b. 1896). His first book, *Doodenstad* (Town of the Dead), appeared in 1923. While doubtless of the realistic school, he paints word pictures with oriental richness of color and fantasy. In many of his novels there is subtle satire on middle class society and masterful delineation of character. His *Amsterdam* (1930), a kaleidoscopic picture, was an outstanding success, followed by such books of revolt as *Brood* (Bread; 1932); *Reflex* (1932); *De Menschen Meenen Het Goed* (People Mean Well; 1934), and others. His outstanding literary effort was a novel on the Russian pattern (published under the Russian pseudonym of Boris Robazki), *Waarom Ik Niet Krankzinnig Ben* (Why I am Not Mad; 1929). The critics, unaware that Dekker and Robazki were identical, praised this work, whereas they had found fault with all of Dekker's earlier books.

After the Nazis rose to power (1933) Dekker wrote many pamphlets against the Nazi movement. For one of these a Dutch court fined him 100 guilders on a charge of "having insulted the legal head of a friendly State." Subsequently Dekker wrote a novel on Nazi persecution of the Jews, purportedly taking place in a fictitious country but obviously portraying events in the Reich. This book, entitled *Mordje, de Jood* (Mordje, the Jew), was published only a few months before the Nazi invasion of the Netherlands (May, 1940). Dekker also wrote a number of radio plays, mainly for the V.A.R.A., Socialist broadcasting station of Holland.

In 1942 it was unascertainable whether Dekker was unharmed; he was known to be alive, in Amsterdam, at about the middle of 1941.   ADOLF KOBER.

Lit.: Barnouw, A. I., *Holland under Queen Wilhelmina* (1923) 256 et seq.; Brugmans, H., and Frank, A., *Geschiedenis der Joden in Nederland,* part 1 (1940) 105-56, 714-71; *Festschrift zu Simon Dubnows siebzigstem Geburtstag* (1930) 87-112; da Silva Rosa, J. S., *Geschiedenis der Portugeesche Joden te Amsterdam 1593-1925* (1925); Prinsen, F., *Handboek tot de Nederlandsche Letterkundige Geschiedenis* (3rd ed., 1928); Romein-Verschoor, Anna Helena Marga;.the, *De Nederlandsche Romanschrijfster na 1880* (1935) 108-20; Loewenstamm, A., "Hugo Grotius' Stellung zum Judentum," *Festschrift,* Jewish Theological Seminary, of Breslau, vol. 2 (1929) 295-302.

III. English. Even before Jews had set foot upon her soil, the literature of England was steeped in Hebraic traditions. Caedmon (d. 680), her earliest known Anglo-Saxon writer, had composed a metrical paraphrase of the Bible, and Archbishop Aelfric (d. 1005) had translated several portions of the Hebrew Bible.

Pre-Expulsion Jews came from Normandy, and spoke French. Moreover, their literary activity was devoted mainly to Biblical and rabbinic studies, for which Hebrew was the natural medium. Hence, there are no Jewish writers in the English literature of this period. There are, however, several references to Jews in the contemporary Chronicles. Thus, the notorious massacre at York, in 1190, is fully described by William of Newbury (1198), while Matthew of Paris (d. 1259) frequently mentions the Jews, reproducing in full the spirited protest of their leader, Master Elias, against the excessive tallage of 1253. He also records, with due reverence for current slanders, the alleged "ritual murder" of Hugh of Lincoln in 1255. The latter incident called forth a veritable spate of popular ballads in the Anglo-Norman and Scots dialects, many of which take pains to perpetuate the anti-Jewish libel. They have been collected and published in modern times by Michel (1834) and Childs (1882). Geoffrey Chaucer likewise alludes to the episode in his "Prioress' Tale" (about 1390), for although he lays the scene of his very similar story in "Asia, the great city," he concludes with an invocation to "young Hugh of Lincoln, slain also With cursed Jews, as it is notable, For it is but a little while ago." Jews also figure prominently in contemporary miracle and mystery plays, where they are invariably represented as the traducers of Christ or as greedy usurers. Typical of such productions is the Croxton *Sacrament,* which deals with an alleged Jewish plot to desecrate the host in 1356. William Langland (d. 1360), in his *Vision of Piers Plowman,* similarly castigates the Jews for being unproductive and "using usury," while John Gower (d. 1408) mentions them in comparable vein in his *Confessio Amantis* (Confession of a Lover). On the other hand, acquaintance with Jewish lore was not entirely lacking. Roger Bacon (d. 1292) composed a Hebrew grammar; while it was contended by Moses Gaster, in 1887, that the stories of Arthur and Merlin, as narrated by Geoffrey of Monmouth (d. 1154) and others, were indebted to the Biblical saga of David and to later Jewish legends about Solomon and Ashmodai.

In this pre-Expulsion era the Jews of England were forced to engage almost exclusively in usury. That, in fact, was the very purpose for which William the Conqueror had brought them from Normandy. Accordingly, the popular picture of a Jew was of a usurer, or, alternatively, a mendicant, eking out a precarious living by the sale of old clothes, and living largely on his wits. This view persisted as a literary convention throughout the Tudor period, when Jews themselves were not permitted permanent residence in the country. Moreover, a popular outcry, in the late 16th cent., against the malpractices of Christian moneylenders made it expedient to saddle this evil upon a tradition allegedly initiated by their Jewish forerunners. In 1568 Sir Thomas North, in his *Dial of Princes,* had classed together "drunkards, thieves, villains and Jews," while some ten years later a play called *The Jew* had portrayed to London audiences "the greediness of worldly choosers and bloody minds of usurers." The trial and execution, in 1594, of the Jewish physician Roderigo Lopez on a charge of conspiring to poison Queen Elizabeth added a further weapon to the arsenal of vilification, for Jews were now represented as potential poisoners. This is one of the basic motifs of Christopher Marlowe's *Rich Jew of Malta* (about 1596), the central figure of which, the infamous Barabas, not only acquires his wealth with the help of the Devil (Machiavel), but also describes himself as one who "walks abroad o'nights, and kills sick people groaning under walls." In the course of the action, not only does he poison all the inmates of a nunnery, but also his blackmailing slave and the latter's paramour. Similarly, in John Marston's *Malcontent* (1604), a character named Malevole boasts that he can poison people "no Jew, 'pothecary or politician better." The characterization of the Jew as a usurer receives its most notable expression in William Shakespeare's *Merchant of Venice* (1596), though it has been argued by several critics (Philipson, Stoll, Ward) that the playwright really intended to arouse sympathy for the tragic Shylock, or, alternatively, conceived him as an essentially *comic* character. Later writers of the period likewise depict the Jew as crafty and unscrupulous. In a play entitled *The Three English Brothers* (1607), the Jewish character is described as "a crucifying hangman trained in sin, One that would hang his brother for his skin," while in another, *A Challenge for Beauty* (1636), English Jews are said to sell their fathers and prostitute their wives for gain. Ben Jonson mentions them as dealers in old clothes in his *Every Woman in Her Humour* (1609), while in the *World Lost at Tennis* (1620), by Thomas Middleton and William Rowley, there is an interesting allusion to Jewish cobblers and tailors in Spitalfields, London.

By the middle of the 17th cent., public opinion had undergone a considerable change. The economic and diplomatic usefulness of the rich crypto-Jews who had trickled into the capital had impressed itself upon Cromwell and his associates, while the Puritanism which informed the Commonwealth tended to encourage a more liberal outlook. Moreover, the atmosphere was then charged with chiliastic ideas, and in religious circles this inspired the theory that contact should be established with the "remnant of Israel" so that it might be converted before the advent of the "great and awful day." Contemporary literature sounds this note repeatedly. It is, for example, the dominant motif of Leonard Busher's *Religious Peace* (1614; reprinted, 1644) and of Norwood's *Proposals for the Propagation of the Gospel* (1652), while the influence of general liberal thought is clearly to be seen in the writings of Hugh Peters (1647), John Sadler (1649), Henry Jessey (1653) and Thomas Barlow (1654), all of whom advocate the readmission of the Jews. There were, however, dissentient voices. John Speed, in his *History of Great Britain* (1650), wrote with marked antipathy against the Jews, while in 1656 William Prynne, a Puritan lawyer, in his famous *Short Demurrer to the Jews' long discontinued Remitter into England,* described them as "not fit for our land, nor yet for our dunghills." Similar, though less violent, was the view of the poet Abraham Cowley (1618-67).

With the growth of the Marrano community in London, interest in the Jews increased. John Selden (d. 1654) refers to them, in his *Table Talk,* as "thriving where'er they come. . . . None of them beg; they keep together." Samuel Pepys, the diarist, describes a visit to their synagogue, in 1663, on the occasion of Simhath Torah (The Rejoicing in the Law), and Samuel Butler (d. 1680) alludes, in his *Hudibras,* to the ceremonial annulment of vows in the Kol Nidre service of the Day of Atonement. Lastly, in 1689, the noted philosopher John Locke openly contends, in an anonymous *Letter,* that "neither pagan nor Mahomedan nor Jew ought to be excluded from the civil rights of the commonwealth because of their religion."

As for the Jews themselves, most of them were of Spanish or Portuguese origin, and therefore unable to write in English. Manasseh ben Israel's main works were composed abroad in Spanish or Latin, while the Haham David Nieto (1654-1728), foremost intellectual light of contemporary English Jewry, wrote in Hebrew or Spanish. Moreover, it must be remembered that during the greater part of this period Jews were obliged to lead a semi-clandestine existence.

The rapid increase of the Jewish community during the early part of the 18th cent. excited a variety of reactions among English men of letters. Purely academic interest was revealed in Thomas Madox' *History of the Exchequer of the Kings of England* (1711), in which an entire section was devoted to the medieval Exchequer of the Jews, and in D'Bloissiers Tovey's *Anglia Judaica* (1738). Both are still standard works. The leading literary figures of the day were divided in their attitude. Jonathan Swift, writing in *The Examiner* of April 12, 1711, feared the increase of the Jews and their possible alliance with Dissenters (cf. Pharaoh's fears of Israel in *Ex.* 1:9-10!), while in his *Reasons* for repealing the *Sacramental Test in Favour of Catholics* (1733) and in his poetic satire *On Dr. Rundle, Bishop of Ferry* (1733) he classed Jews with infidels and Turks. Daniel Defoe, in his *Roxana, or the Unfortunate Mistress* (1724), portrayed a "malicious" and "cursed" Jew who ultimately turns out to be an extortioner and a murderer; and in his *Life and Adventures of Mrs. Charles Davis* (1740), he alleged that Jews follow armies in order to buy up the loot. Alexander Pope (1688-1744) was scarcely less hostile, being responsible for a scurrilous screed describing how "certain eminent Jews" of 'Change Alley had forcibly converted and circumcised one Edmund Curll, a non-Jewish stationer of Fleet Street, London. Contemporary novelists also joined in this literary attack. Henry Fielding, in his *An Enquiry into the*

Causes of the Late Increase of Robbers (1743), charges Jews with being "fences," or receivers of stolen goods, while Tobias Smollet, in his *Adventures of Roderick Random* (1748), introduces a particular repulsive Jew in the character of one Isaac Rapine (perhaps a pun on Rabbin!).

The "Jew Bill" of 1753, by which resident Jews were granted the right to naturalization, opened the floodgates of literary violence and abuse. Wolf and Jacobs' *Bibliotheca Anglo-Judaica* (1888) lists no less than fifty-four anti-Jewish pamphlets and ballads, and the number can be increased. An interesting result of this hostility was the introduction of "Jewish gibberish" into the convention of the stage, Jewish characters being made to speak, usually with a lisp, in a fantastic, broken English. This device had already been employed, in 1749, in the virulent *Jewish Infirmary,* the central character of which was a monkey! That play, however, was never actually produced, and it was therefore left to John O'Keefe to initiate the tradition with his *The Young Quaker,* performed in 1783. One of the main characters of this piece is Shadrach Boaz, a Jewish moneylender who seeks to exact payment for a loan with the honor of a pretty Quakeress. Once inaugurated, this tradition maintained itself for well over a century, and even survives in contemporary burlesque. The tendency of wealthy Jews to seek civil status by conversion, after the repeal of the Naturalization Bill in 1754, also aroused adverse comment, especially after the defection of Sampson Gideon, the noted financier. Thus, Mrs. Hannah Cowley, in her *Belle's Stratagem* (1780), makes a pseudo-Jewish character observe, in answer to the question, "Where are your Joshuas and your Gideons, eh?" that "Some of us turn Christians, and by degrees, grow into all the privileges of Englishmen. In the second generation, we are patriots, rebels, courtiers and husbands." A more liberal note was struck, however, by Richard Cumberland (1732-1811), grandson of the illustrious Richard Bentley, who, in his *The Jew* (1793), first introduced a benevolent Israelite in the generous, if still eccentric, character of the philanthropic moneylender, Sheva.

Jews themselves contributed but little to contemporary letters. Their foremost representative was the industrious David Levi (1742-1801), originally a hatter, who not only translated the Sephardic liturgy, but also engaged in a spirited defense of Judaism against the attacks of Joseph Priestley (*Letters to the Jews,* 1787-89) and Thomas Paine. Others who may be mentioned are: the poetaster Moses Mendes (d. 1758), author of *The Chaplet, The Shepherd's Lottery,* and other works; the conchologist Emanuel Mendes da Costa (1717-91), and the mediocre Ralph Schomberg (1714-92), a physician, who might have done well to apply his surgeon's knife to some of his essays and poems. The close of the century, however, saw the entry of Jews into English literature proper, in the publication of Isaac Disraeli's *Curiosities of Literature* (1791) and *Romances* (1799).

Writers of the Romantic Age (1800-33), which ushered in the 19th cent., displayed little interest in contemporary Jewry, concentrating rather upon fanciful idealizations or upon ancient legends. Among the latter, the story of the Wandering Jew possessed an especial fascination. Not only was it the subject of

Caput I.

Im traurigen Monat November war's,
Die Tage wurden trüber,
Der Wind riß von den Bäumen das Laub,
Da reist' ich nach Deutschland hinüber.

Und als ich an die Grenze kam,
Da fühlt' ich ein stärkeres Klopfen
In meiner Brust, ich glaube sogar
Die Augen begunnen zu tropfen.

Und als ich die deutsche Sprache vernahm,
Da ward mir seltsam zumute;
Ich meinte nicht anders, als ob das Herz
Recht angenehm verblute.

Ein kleines Harfenmädchen sang.
Sie sang mit wahrem Gefühle
Und falscher Stimme, doch ward ich sehr
Gerühret von ihrem Spiele.

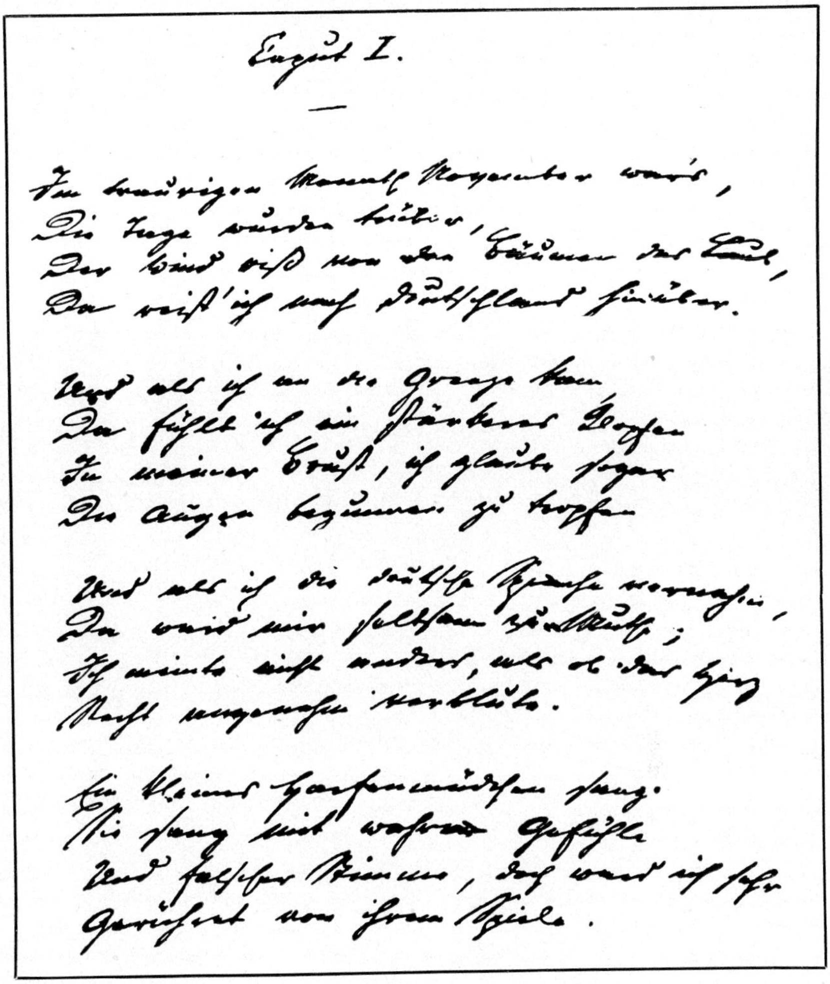

(Right) Facsimile of a page of manuscript from Heinrich Heine's "Deutschland, ein Wintermärchen"; (bottom, left) title page of a historical essay on Surinam by David de Israel Cohen Nassy, published in 1788; (bottom, right) title page of Henrik Wergeland's epic poem "Jodesagen," espousing the cause of the Jews of Norway, printed in 1841

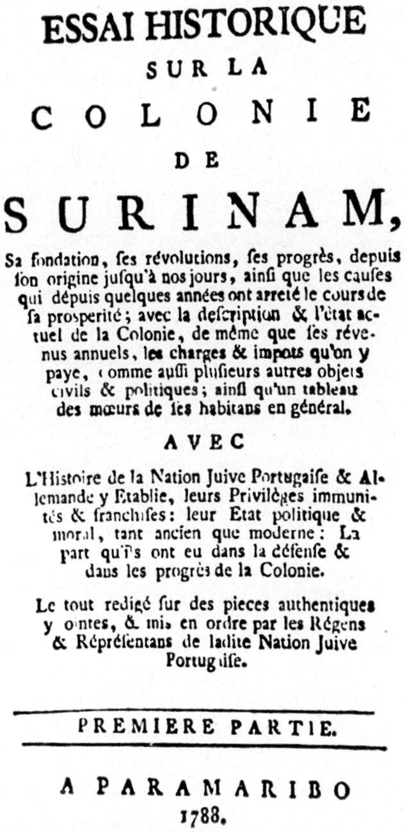

ESSAI HISTORIQUE
SUR LA
COLONIE
DE
SURINAM,

Sa fondation, ses révolutions, ses progrès, depuis son origine jusqu'à nos jours, ainsi que les causes qui depuis quelques années ont arreté le cours de sa prosperité; avec la description & l'état actuel de la Colonie, de même que ses revenus annuels, les charges & impots qu'on y paye, comme aussi plusieurs autres objets civils & politiques; ainsi qu'un tableau des mœurs de ses habitans en général.

AVEC

L'Histoire de la Nation Juive Portugaise & Allemande y Etablie, leurs Privilèges immunités & franchises: leur Etat politique & moral, tant ancien que moderne: La part qu'ils ont eu dans la défense & dans les progrès de la Colonie.

Le tout redigé sur des pieces authentiques y ointes, & mis en ordre par les Régens & Réprésentans de ladite Nation Juive Portugaise.

PREMIERE PARTIE.

A PARAMARIBO
1788.

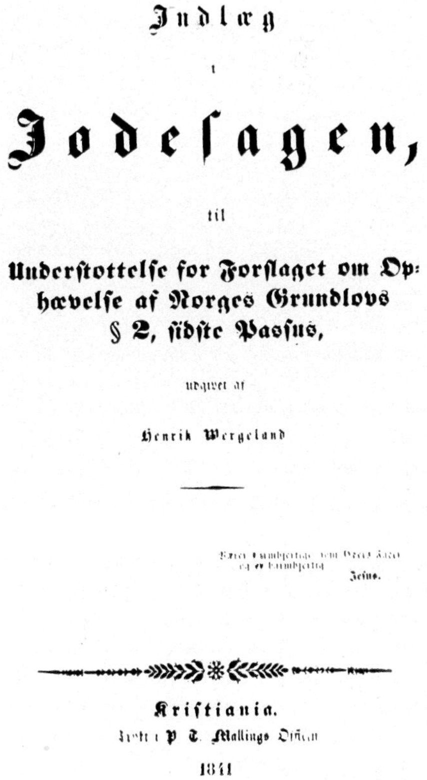

Indlæg
i
Jodesagen,
til
Understøttelse for Forslaget om Ophævelse af Norges Grundlovs § 2, sidste Passus,
udgivet af
Henrik Wergeland

Kristiania.
Trykt i P. T. Mallings Officin
1841

several dramatic productions, but it was also exploited by William Wordsworth in his *Song for the Wandering Jew* (1800), and by Percy Bysshe Shelley in the eighth canto of his *Queen Mab* (1812-13). Byron also turned his attention to Jewish themes, and in 1815 published a series of short poems on Biblical and Palestinian subjects under the title of *Hebrew Melodies.* These were later set to music by his friend Isaac Nathan (1792-1864), and were actually chanted in the services of the synagogue! Samuel Taylor Coleridge (1772-1834) was another who showed interest in Jewish lore, including versifications of three rabbinic tales in his work *The Friend.* There were, however, also hostile elements in contemporary literature. The poet George Crabbe painted a harsh picture of metropolitan Jewish life in his *The Borough* (1810), complaining that the Jews were loath to study and even to defend themselves. A series of novels by Maria Edgeworth, written between 1801 and 1811, likewise depicted Jews as unscrupulous usurers and cheats, or else as excessively mercenary. However, following a protest by an American Jewess, Rachel Mordecai, this writer changed her tone, and in 1816 published a novel, *Harrington,* describing how a young Christian, imbued in youth with anti-Jewish prejudices, gradually overcame them by experience. To the same period also belongs Sir Walter Scott's *Ivanhoe* (1819), with its sympathetic, if historically inaccurate, portrayal of Jewish life in York in 1194.

The middle years of the 19th cent. were occupied largely with the struggle for the emancipation of the Jews, and this also left its mark upon English literature. Apart from ephemeral tracts, scarcely pertinent to this survey, mention may be made of William Hazlitt's *Essay on the Emancipation of the Jews* (*The Tatler,* 1830) and of Thomas Babington Macaulay's *Civil Disabilities of the Jews* (*Edinburgh Review,* 1831), both of which were strongly in favor of the cause. The same period also saw the appearance of Dean Henry Milman's *History of the Jews* (1829) and of John E. Blunt's *Status of the Jews in England* (1830), both standard works.

The interest in Jews continued into the Early Victorian Age. It is best exemplified by the novels of Benjamin Disraeli. Especially noteworthy are: *Alroy* (1833), based on the story of the medieval adventurer Daud ibn Alruhi; *Coningsby* (1844), in which the author's political and religious philosophy is voiced through the Jew, Sidonia, probably based on Lionel de Rothschild; and *Tancred* (1847), which attempts, albeit in exaggerated terms, to assert the value of the Jewish heritage for modern civilization. Another side of the picture is painted, however, by Charles Dickens, whose *Oliver Twist* (1837) portrays, in the character of Fagin, the trainer of juvenile thieves, what is undoubtedly the most loathsome Jew of English fiction. Nevertheless, the novelist later made amends for this lapse by the introduction into *Our Mutual Friend* (1863) of the distinctly sympathetic character of the Jew, Riah.

Significant as a contemporary Jewish writer was the novelist Grace Aguilar (1816-47), a descendant of Portuguese Marranos, whose best-known work, *The Vale of Cedars* (published posthumously in 1850), deals with the sufferings of Jews in medieval Spain.

During the later half of the 19th cent. several famous English writers handled Jewish themes. Foremost among them was George Eliot, whose *Daniel Deronda* (1876) is supposed by some to have been based on the career of Colonel A. E. W. Goldsmid. The poet Robert Browning (1802-89), who was conversant with Hebrew, treats of Jewish subjects in "Holy Cross Day" (1855), "Rabbi Ben Ezra" (1864), "Filippo Baldinucci" (1876) and "Jochanan Hakkadosh" (1883), while his "Jocoseria" incorporates a few Talmudic tales. (It is interesting to note that Browning was one of the sponsors of the Anglo-Jewish Historical Exhibition of 1887.) Algernon Charles Swinburne wrote a powerful poem "On the Russian Persecution of the Jews" in 1882, while the playwright Arthur Wing Pinero introduced Jewish characters, not always sympathetically, in his *The Cabinet Minister* (1890) and *Letty* (1903).

Jewish writers of this period were occupied mainly with Jewish themes. Benjamin Farjeon (1833-1903) was a prolific novelist, whose *Salomon Isaacs* (1877) and *Aaron the Jew* (1894) dealt sympathetically with the new complexion of the Anglo-Jewish community. More successful in this *genre,* however, was Israel Zangwill (1864-1926), whose *Children of the Ghetto* (1892) made the first serious attempt to portray the life of East European immigrants in London's Whitechapel. *The King of the Schnorrers* (1894), *Dreamers of the Ghetto* (1898) and *Ghetto Comedies* (1906) were other works which secured for this author the rank of the greatest purely Jewish novelist of English literature. Samuel Gordon (1871-1927) was a lesser representative of the same school, his *Daughters of Shem* (1898) and *Sons of the Covenant* (1900) enjoying marked popularity. In poetry, mention may be made of the sisters Nina and Elsie Davis, and of Mrs. Henry Lucas and Helena Frank, all of whom produced pleasing verse renderings of Hebrew compositions.

The 20th cent. has thus far (1942) proved a fertile age for English literature, and both Jewish writers and Jewish subjects have been well represented. George Bernard Shaw (b. 1856) introduces Jewish characters in *The Doctor's Dilemma* and in *Man and Superman,* while in *Saint Joan* a nobleman is made to remark: "The Jew generally gives value. They make you pay, but they deliver the goods." The clash of racial and class allegiances between Jews and non-Jews is effectively portrayed in John Galsworthy's *Loyalties* (1922), which was filmed. Prominent Jewish writers have included: the poets Isaac Rosenberg (1890-1918) and Humbert Wolfe (1885-1941); Philip Guedalla (b. 1889), historian and essayist; Louis Golding (b. 1895), whose novel *Magnolia Street* (1932) depicted Jewish life in the Cheetham Hill section of Manchester; Siegfried Sassoon (b. 1886), poet, whose *Memoirs of a Fox-Hunting Man* (1928) was awarded the Hawthornden Prize; G. B. Stern (b. 1890), whose *The Matriarch, A Deputy was King, Mosaic* and *Shining and Free* sketched the lives of a Jewish family through successive generations in Vienna, Paris and London; Samuel L. Bensusan, novelist and travel-writer; Naomi Jacob, whose *Founder of the House* (1936) traced the early adventures of the well-known Gollancz family; and Lily Tobias, author of *The Nationalists* (1921), *My Mother's House* (1931) and the successful *Eunice Fleet* (1933), telling a tale of conscientious objection

stock wrote not only *Der Messias* but dramas based on material from the Hebrew Bible, such as *Adams Tod.* His less talented Swiss contemporary, Bodmer, wrote large epics such as *Noachide* and *Jacob und Josef.* But these motives only gained deep importance when Herder brought the Bible home to his contemporaries and made them aware of it as a national original poetry; as a result of this Goethe, in his epic *Faust,* could take the opening scene in heaven directly from the Biblical *Job.*

In the following generation the Bible stories furnished themes for the great dramatists such as Grillparzer (*Esther*), Hebbel (*Judith*) and Otto Ludwig (*Die Makkabäer*). The tradition has continued in more recent German drama with numerous dramas based on the Samson story, by Wedekind and others, Hauptmann's beautiful fragment, *Hirtenlied,* Walter Harlan's treatment of the story of Tamar, and Barlach's *Sintflut.* Rainer Maria Rilke used Biblical themes for many poems, and Thomas Mann has created a monumental three-volume Joseph epic. It is natural, moreover, that Biblical motives appear in the works of such modern German Jewish writers as Beer-Hofmann, Emil Bernhard Cohn, Max Brod, Stefan Zweig, Ernst Lissauer, and most important of all, Franz Werfel (*Hearken Unto the Voice*).

On the other hand, the contemporary Jew appeared in German literature of the pre-Reformation period only as a grotesque and peculiar minor character in mystery plays and in farces. It was not until the period of Enlightenment, in the 18th cent., that any attempt was made to show that the Jews were also human beings, as in Lessing's youthful work, *Die Juden.* A generation later the same author made a great, human and free Jew the hero of his classic work, *Nathan der Weise.*

In romanticism the figure of the Wandering Jew (Ahasuerus) becomes an important motive to represent the restlessness and homelessness of the soul. (The origin of this figure is obscure, but it certainly does not go back further than the 16th cent.) Achim von Arnim, at the beginning of the 18th cent., displayed in his *Halle und Jerusalem* a twin Jewish motive, a contrast between the suffering and pure soul of the eternal Jew and the soullessness of the limited commercial Jew. This double motive of the common and the noble Jew is characteristic of the German literature of the 19th cent. Pairs of such contrasted Jews appear in Gustav Freytag's *Soll und Haben,* Fritz Reuter's Plattdeutsch *Stromtid,* and in Gustav Meyrinck's *Golem.* In the once highly popular *Uriel Akosta* this dual motive also appears, although it is toned down into a conflict between orthodoxy and freedom of opinion. It is perhaps more significant that the great North German novelist Wilhelm Raabe gives an unfavorable presentation of a Jew in his youthful work, *Der Hungerpastor,* but has an agreeable and just presentation of the Jew in his later work, *Frau Salome.*

The great Austrian writer, Adalbert Stifter, made an African Jew the hero of his *Abdias;* but the character is one of phantastic primitive powers and reveals little that is characteristically Jewish. The Alemanic poet Hebel, in his *Rheinischer Hausfreund,* presented sympathetic and humane variations to old farces about the Jews; Chamisso described a Polish Jewish Maskil with sympathy. Finally Gerhart Hauptmann, the most important German author of a generation ago, frequently portrayed Jewish characters in his dramas and novels; his most interesting figure is Docter Boxer in *Der rote Hahn,* in all probability modeled after Hauptmann's brilliant brother-in-law and friend Moritz Heimann.

2. Jewish Authors in the German Language. During the first period of Jewish life in Germany, during which time they lived harmoniously and productively in the midst of the German people down to the catastrophic events of the 14th cent., only one Jewish author employing the German language has been recorded as having lived. This was the minnesinger Süsskind von Trimberg (about 1250-1300), whose portrait showing him wearing the pointed Jews' hat has been preserved in a manuscript. His songs, though otherwise substantially in the style of the time, reflect in some passages the peculiar fate of the Jewish people. During the following centuries, when Jewish cultural life was completely disrupted, the only possible German author of Jewish origin is the cleric Johannes Pauli (1455-1530), author of the once widely read *Schimpf und Ernst,* who may have been a secret Jew.

It was not until the period of Enlightenment in the 18th cent. that Jews really began to make contributions to German literature. Moses Mendelssohn, the leading spirit of the German Jews of that period, wrote important philosophical works; his *Phaedon* (1767) enjoyed a great influence. Other philosophical writers were Marcus Herz (1747-1803), Lazarus Bendavid (1762-1832) and the Polish Jew Solomon Maimon (1754-1809). There were a few who essayed to write poetry, such as Issachar Falkensohn Behr (1746-1817), who came from the Baltic regions and whose poems of a Polish Jew (1772) were criticized by the young Goethe in a manner that was not unfriendly but conveyed a justifiable regret for the completely conventional and un-Jewish character. A stronger personality was Moses Ephraim Kuh of Breslau (1731-90), whose passionate devotion to the newly opened field of German culture, together with his own overexertions, led to his insanity.

It was during the period of literary romanticism in Germany that Jewish influence became noticeable. Dorothea Mendelssohn, the baptized daughter of the philosopher, became the wife of Friedrich Schlegel, the leader of the romantics. The Berlin salons, created by her, by Henriette Herz and by Rahel Levin (1771-1833), became the center of German intellectual society, and aided in winning recognition for Goethe.

Among the Jewish poets of the period were a brother of Rahel, who wrote under the name of Ludwig Robert (1778-1832), and Michael Beer (1800-33), brother of the composer Meyerbeer and member of the noted Jewish banking house. Their weak and sentimental efforts were soon overshadowed by the rising and international fame of Heinrich Heine (1797-1858). Heine, the poet of the "Lorelei," for a long time the most popular German song, described himself as a disciple of romanticism, but his critical mind, which recognized the new social problems, presaged a new period in German literature. Heine and Karl Ludwig

Börne (1786-1837), whose interests were entirely political, became the leaders of the "Young Germany" movement, which, in the 1830's, provoked vehement discussions. Heine, however, later broke with Börne, preferring poetry to politics. He created magnificent ballads, was the first German writer to express the love for the sea, and was a master of topical satire and of ever-living phantasy. Up to the present day, more of his works have been set to music than of any other German writer. His *Buch der Lieder* gave him his greatest fame, but it may be that his ironic epic *Deutschland* and his *Atta Troll* will give him his greatest immortality. Heine had numerous imitators among Christians and Jews; the latter include the Austrian Moritz Hartmann (1821-72).

The next period, which had as its ideal that of middle-class education, found its most perfect representative in Berthold Auerbach (1812-82) who, though professing Judaism, expressed the thought that "religion must become education." He achieved great success with his tales of the Black Forest. Other representatives of this period were the half-Jew Paul Heyse (1830-1914), the dignified representative of German post-classicism and Nobel Prize Winner (1910); Julius Rodenberg (originally Levy; 1831-1914), founder and editor of the *Deutsche Rundschau;* Georg Ebers (1834-98), Egyptologist and writer of novels dealing with ancient times; and Fanny Lewald (1811-98), a prolific writer of novels. Austrian writers of the time included the lyric poetess Betty Paoli, and Hieronymus Lorm (Heinrich Landesmann) who, although deaf and blind, lived and wrote for more than eighty years (1821-1902). The only Jew who contributed to the popular Vienna plays of this period was Karlweis (1850-1901); in Berlin David Kalisch (1820-72) was one of the originators of the type of drama, and a little later Salingré and Louis Herrmann wrote successful local farces. Adolf L'Arronge (b. 1838) wrote popular plays of the same type; on the other hand, Lubliner, Blumenthal and Kadelburg gave their comedies more of an international character.

It was in the same period that Aaron Bernstein of Berlin began his versatile productivity and the Austrian Leopold Kompert began to write stories drawn from Jewish life. Karl Emil Franzos (1848-1904) gained renown through his *Juden von Barnow;* but an even greater service to literature was his vindication of the great German poet Georg Büchner, whose literary remains he edited a generation after his death. Similarly, Emil Kuh and Siegmund Engländer fought to obtain recognition for Friedrich Hebbel. Jewish critics of the period rendered good service in bringing before the public the merits of such writers as Anzengruber, Gerhart Hauptmann, Dehmel, Stefan George.

Jewish poets contributed comparatively little to the period of naturalism at the end of the 19th cent.; but they were important as the critics who led and who organized that movement. Especially noteworthy in this connection are Leo Berg and his society, "Durch"; Otto Brahm, director of the *Freie Bühne* and of the Deutsches Theater; Moritz Heimann, who was the guiding spirit in the publishing house of S. Fischer; the critics Arthur Eloesser and Alfred Kerr; Maximilian Harden who, like Theodor Wolf, later devoted himself entirely to the political field; and Fritz Mauth-

ner (1849-1923) who, after an eminently successful career as a writer, later devoted himself exclusively to his great philosophical work, *Kritik der Sprache.* Georg Hirschfeld, a disciple of Gerhart Hauptmann, made a deep impression as a dramatist with his first work, *Die Mütter.* Ludwig Fulda (1862-1938) shows little artistic independence in his many plays, but was important as the translator of Molière and Rostand. In fact, German Jews rendered outstanding services as translators during this period, bringing a knowledge of the works of the most important foreign authors to the German reading public. Thus Tolstoi was introduced by Löwenfeld; Ibsen, by Elias; Oscar Wilde, by Hedwig Lachmann and Max Meyerfeld; George Bernard Shaw, by Trebitsch; Verhaeren, by Stefan Zweig.

Felix Holländer, Georg Engel and Olga Wohlbrück hardly possess any substantial influence as Jewish novelists. On the other hand, Georg Herrmann (b. 1871), in his *Jettchen Gebert,* gave a remarkable description of Berlin Jewry in the Biedermeier period of the 19th cent. He also produced important documents for life in modern Berlin in such works as *Kubinke* and *Die Nacht des Doktor Herzfeld.*

The Viennese counterpart to Georg Herrmann is Arthur Schnitzler (1862-1931), who mirrored the upper class world of his native Vienna with the same basic tone of melancholy and skepticism which marked it at the close of the 19th cent. His novels and dramas reveal the beginning of the transition from naturalism to a new romanticism which doubts reality and takes refuge in the realms of fantasy. The most important interpreter of this new romanticism was the part-Jew Hugo von Hofmannsthal (1879-1929). Another member of this group was Richard Beer-Hofmann (b. 1866), who finds a barrier against the pessimism of his time in his consciously evolved Jewishness. The novelist Jakob Wassermann (1873-1924), a native of Franconia, felt at home in this Viennese milieu. Peter Altenberg (Richard Engländer; 1859-1919), who wrote unique lyrical aphorisms, lived in Vienna, as did Karl Kraus (1824-1936), editor of *Die Fackel,* who adopted a decidedly polemical attitude toward his environment.

The more recent Viennese writers included such Jews as Egon Friedell (1878-1938), humorist and cultural philosopher; the critics Willi Handl (1872-1920) and Alfred Polgar (b. 1875); the lyric poet and theatrical director Viertel; and the successful novelist and historian Stefan Zweig (1881-1942). There were also Felix Salten, the half-Jew Raoul Auernheimer, the Prague physician Hugo Salus and the short-lived and serious-minded Jakob Julius David. More important than all of these, however, was the Bohemian Jew Franz Kafka (1883-1924), whose psychologically subtle epic was edited by his compatriot Max Brod.

Among the group of authors headed by Stefan George who were largely responsible for the abandonment of naturalism by German writers at the beginning of the 20th cent. were the Jewish writers Karl Wolfskehl (b. 1869) and Friedrich Gundolf (originally Gundelfinger; 1880-1933), both of whom played an important part. Gundolf attained recognition less as a creative writer than as a historian of literature. His analytical work on Goethe remains a classic. He was overshadowed, however, after the first World War, by the epic biographies written by Emil Ludwig, who

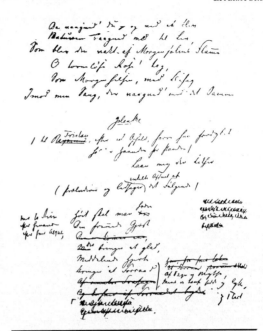

MEIR EZOFOWICZ.

POWIEŚĆ Z ŻYCIA ŻYDÓW.

PRZEZ

ELIZE ORZESZKOWĄ.

Z 26 ILLUSTRACYAMI M. ANDRIOLLEGO.

WARSZAWA.

NAKLAD I DRUK S. LEWENTALA.

1879.

SĘDZIOWIE

TRAGEDYA

NAPISAŁ STAN. WYSPIAŃSKI

(Top, left) Title page of "Meir Ezofowicz," by the Polish authoress Elize Orzeszkowa; (top, right) a page from the manuscript of Henrik Hertz' "Kong Renés Datter," a Danish play written in 1845; (bottom, right) title page of the Polish drama "Sedziowie," by Stanislaw Wyspianski; (below) the author's handwritten lines on the margin of a leaflet concerning Jakob Wassermann's "Etzel Andergast"

thereby created a new type of biographical description and whose books had the greatest success of all books written in German in the first half of the 20th cent.

A more significant poetic figure was that of Ernst Lissauer (1882-1936), the lyricist. After his somewhat unfortunate success in 1914 with his "Hassgesang gegen England," he created genuine poetry of rhythmic originality through his intense devotion to the German landscape and to German culture, and wrote excellent essays on artistic problems. A poetical force of prime importance was Alfred Mombert (b. 1872), the friend of Richard Dehmel, who in a flight of fancy, which he called himself "Asiatic" in origin, dissolved reality into lyric visions.

With Mombert and his related but weaker feminine counterpart, Else Lasker-Schüler (b. 1876), commences, in substance, the expressionism which dominated the last period of German literature. In this period appears Franz Werfel (b. 1890), the third greatest of the Jewish poets (after Heine and Mombert). His dramas deal with problems, his large-scale novels are not always of the greatest artistic purity, but in his lyrics there are echoes of a penetrating and lofty force. Alfred Wolffenstein and Martin Gumpert were also noted lyric poets of this period; the latter later evidenced his great talent through literary productions of an entirely different kind.

The expressionist drama which, after Max Brod, was developed particularly by Paul Kornfeld, was not long-enduring; the productions of Ernst Toller (1893-1939) show more of a noble spirit in politics than of a definite artistic talent. Carl Sternheim produced several successful satirical comedies, but fell later into a lamentable rigidity of style.

The successful Jewish novelists of the expressionist period include Bruno Frank, strong-minded follower of Thomas Mann, Lion Feuchtwanger of international renown, Robert Neumann, Arnold Zweig, and the gifted Alfred Neumann. The strongest and most unique force among them was probably Alfred Döblin who, after some remarkable attempts, succeeded in creating in his novel *Alexanderplatz* something like a new mystic realism.

Among those who, at the time that National Socialism destroyed all further development, seemed to be escaping the forms of expressionism to create a new form of psychically exalted realism was the dramatist Carl Zuckmayer (b. 1896), who was becoming a writer of importance. A half-Jew like Heyse and von Hofmannsthal, he demonstrated for the third time how the blending of Jewish and non-Jewish forces could prove to be particularly productive for German literature.   JULIUS BAB.

Lit.: Geiger, Ludwig, *Die deutsche Literatur und die Juden* (1910).

VI. Hungarian. 1. Jews in Hungarian Literature (1770-1919).

The Jew as a character first appears in Hungarian literature in the late 18th cent., when he is identified with the usurer of the classical comedy and ridiculed for his incorrect language. In this age, as in times to follow, prejudiced hatred of the Jews was a characteristic of second-rate minds, the great thinkers rising to a more elevated view of humanity. Mihály Vitéz Csokonai (1773-1805), great lyric poet, pointed out that the Jews were useful and branded as "uncouth Magyarism" the hatred of a different nationality. He made the first attempt at portraying the country Jew realistically in his play *Cultura*. Ferenc Kazinczy (1759-1831), performing a mission of humanism and of awakening national culture, blamed social disabilities for the shortcomings of the Jews. József Katona (1791-1830), Hungary's greatest tragic dramatist, took a sympathetic view of the Jews in his *Jeruzsálem pusztulása* (The Destruction of Jerusalem), wherein they defended their homeland and faith.

From 1838 to 1868 the intended emancipation of the Jews kept public opinion in a state of ferment. Mihály Stáncsics, in his *Pazardi* (Spendthrift; 1838), was the first to contrast the thrifty and industrious Jew with the extravagant non-Jewish country gentleman, a contrast which was to work great social changes in Hungary. András Fáy in *Salamon* (1838), Ede Szigligeti in his comedy *Zsidó* (The Jew; 1844), and Baron József Eötvös, champion of emancipation, in *A falu jegyzője* (The Village Notary; 1845), by emphasizing the shortcomings of the Jews, spoke for a change in their social status. Others, authors of lesser consequence (Ignác Nagy, 1815-54, and Lajos Kuthy, 1791-1830), rationalized their fear and objection to emancipation in depicting the Jews as usurers, thieves and parricides. Gáspár Bernát visualized the economically emancipated Jews invading and exploiting the cities; Károly Bérczy's novel, *Egy zsidó a XIII. században* (A 13th Cent. Jew), conjured up the shadow of Teka, the wealthy chamberlain of King Endre II, to give life and reality to the "Jewish peril." Baron Miklós Jósika (1794-1865), the Hungarian Walter Scott, began by portraying sinister Jews and noble hearted Jewesses, but the devotion of the Jews to the cause of the national revolution (1848-49) prompted him to create the realistic character of Icig Hirsch, the patriotic tavernkeeper (*Egy magyar család a forradalom alatt;* A Hungarian Family during the Revolution, 1871-72). Mór Jókai (1825-1904), one of the greatest narrative geniuses of all times, having fought in the revolution, depicted Jewish fellow-combatants or sympathizers in Salamon, the peddler, Ábrahám Rotheisel (*Rab Ráby*), Samu Pelikán and other characters. The main figure of his *Levente,* a drama about the migrating Magyars of the 9th cent., with Jahel, the (Khazar) Jewish daughter-in-law of the Magyar chieftain as heroine, pleads the brotherhood of all religions. Baron Zsigmond Kemény devoted a historical novel, *Rajongók* (Visionaries), to the Sabbatarians of the 16th and 17th centuries.

The post-revolutionary theatre, between 1858 and 1888, featured plays of village life and introduced realistic types of the country Jew instead of the former stereotyped one; the figures of the wheat broker, the moneylender who eventually tricks the country squire out of his land, the Jewish tenant and his dressed-up lady, the village shopkeeper who educates himself and dabbles in world politics, present a social history of the Jews in Hungary at that time. In its appraisal of these types the folk play was indebted somewhat to the Magyar folk song which looks upon the Jewish tavern- or shopkeeper as shrewd, resourceful and double dealing, but, realistically, takes these qualities for granted and bears him no especial ill-will.

Emancipation, when it came in 1867, immediately followed the political and economic liberties granted to Hungary by Austria. In order to avail itself fully of its economic emancipation from Austria, Hungary, which but for a small group of German burghers had no moneyed middle class, needed the Jews. The Jews, in two decades, built up the capitalistic system of Hungary practically without competition and rose to an economic power of the first magnitude. The history of the economic and social rise of the Jews was sketched in the rich Jew edging away from his poor friends (Beőthy, László, *Goldbach & Comp. fűszerkereskedése;* Goldbach & Co. Groceries, 1858); in the knighted Jew aspiring to matrimony with members of the aristocracy (Vadnai, Károly, *Téli estékre;* Winter Nights, 1862); in the snobbish Jewish lady who gains access to society through charity (Berczik, Árpád, *Jótékony célra;* For Charity, 1877). The two classes faced each other in the play of István Toldy, *Az uj emberek* (The New Men; 1874), which took sides with the industrious Jew and berated the happy-go-lucky gentry; in Kornél Ábrányi's novel *Régi és új nemesek* (Old and New Aristocrats; 1881); and in Emil Kazár's *Ösök és unokák* (Forebears and Scions; 1881). Dazzling Jewish careers that came to a sad end were told in Ignác Acsády's *Fridényi bank* (1882) and Lajos Tolnai's *Báróné ténsasszony* (Bourgeois Baroness; 1882). Kálmán Mikszáth's *Uj Zrinyiász* (New Epic; 1904) is a satire of Hungarian society changed by the forward thrust of the Jews. The second generation of emancipated Jews was the theme of Gergely Csiky's *Atlasz család* (The Atlas Family). Zoltán Ambrus' *Berzsenyi báró és családja* (Baron Berzsenyi and his Family; 1902) and Ferenc Herczeg's *Andor és András* (1911) offered gentle satires of Jewish good society. In his whimsically realistic stories Kálmán Mikszáth (1849-1910) depicted the funny manners, shrewdness and business consciousness of the country Jew as well as his fundamental decency and his kindly humor (*Szent Peter esernyője;* St. Peter's Umbrella, 1901).

2. Literature by Jews. The first Jewish note appeared in Hungarian literature with the Judaizing Sabbatarians (16th and 17th centuries), who produced a complete translation of *Psalms* and of the Hebrew prayer-book into Magyar, as well as the beginnings of religious poetry in that language. The first attempts at secular literature were made by Jews in newspapers in the German language (about 1820). The poets Moritz Gottlieb Saphir and Karl Beck wrote in German, and the dramatist Karoly Hugo also wrote his first works in German. All three embraced Christianity. Mór Szegfi, however, revealed himself a conscious Jew in his Magyar poem *Zsidó vagyok* (I am a Jew).

The history of Jewish contributions to Hungarian literature is that of a clash of two ideologies defined by historical development. József Kiss (1843-1924) was the first to receive wounds in this battle. Hailed as the great poet of the nation (1875), he had yet to understand that he did not belong to the gentry class and therefore was not entitled to those academic honors or positions which alone ensured economic security to a poet in a country with a small reading public. József Kiss, who in style and sentiment, adopted the national ideals, was followed in these tendencies by a number of Jewish poets, lyrical as Lajos Palágyi and Henrik Lenkei, and dramatic as Baron Lajos Dóczy. Plays of a "nationalistic" inspiration were also contributed to the repertory of the state theatre by György Ruttkay senior, Samu Fényes and Sándor Hevesi.

Another class of Jewish writers did not go back to accepted models of national literature but was formed in the school of journalism. Adolf Ágai (1836-1916) was the first and greatest of Hungarian feuilletonists. He also founded the comic magazine *Borsszem Jankó* (Jack Peppercorn), among whose popular characters the Jewish Salamon Seifensteiner spluttered forth his comments on current political events. This tradition of mild Jewish self-irony was subsequently carried on by the Hungarian cabaret which, predominantly a Jewish creation, remained a means of expressing public opinion in times when newspapers were withering under censorship. Journalism was also the school for the naturalist novelists Sándor Bródy (1863-1924); Ede Kabos (1864-1923); and Tamás Kóbor (b. 1867), the latter being the author of a series of novels depicting Jewish life in Budapest (*Ki a ghettóból;* Out of the Ghetto; *Hamupipőke őnagysága;* Miss Cinderella); and for the master of objective narration, Lajos Biró (b. 1880). A lyric, whimsical or satirical impressionism colored the novelettes and sketches of daily life contributed to the newspapers by Jenő Heltai (b. 1871), Ferenc Molnár (b. 1878), Frigyes Karinthy (1888-1938) and Ernő Szép (b. 1884). Out of these sketches grew the plays and novels of Heltai and Szép, pervaded by a warm humanism, smiling in the former, emotional in the latter; the novels and satires of Karinthy, cutting deeply into realities and appearances in search of a higher form of truth and perfection; the novelettes of Molnár, revealing him as the poet in prose of Budapest life, and his plays in which he often checked the hot springs of his humanism for the sake of a deft and brilliant handling of the dramatic situation.

These writers, who wrote for the new middle class that had sprung up in Budapest, about itself in its own language, also provided its theatre. Jews had a great part in sponsoring, directing and supplying plays for the Budapest comedy stage, Vigszinház, and several other theatres which were the starting place for such playwrights as Sándor Bródy, Ferenc Molnár, Menyhért Lengyel, Lajos Biró, László Bus-Fekete, Béla Szenes, László Lakatos, and Ernő Vajda, many of whom saw their plays subsequently produced on the stages and in the moving picture theatres of several continents. Otto Indig put to profit the smiling humanism of his masters in interpreting the Jewish problem in his comedy, *The Bride of Toroczkó.* Dezső Szomory had his historical dramas performed by the State National Theatre, which also produced the comedies of Sándor Hajó, Andor (Andreas) Latzkó and Géza Szilágyi.

The Jewish spirit, as it manifested itself in journalism, fiction and on the stage, was resented as foreign by official literary circles. The accusation which was hurled again and again at the Jewish authors was that of "cynicism," meant to characterize an abundant use of the intellect in seeing to the bottom of the individual's real motives. While Hungarians preferred great and simple constructive ideas, such as those of loyalty to national traditions, purity and idealism in love and family life, by means of which they wanted to hold together their country composed of many nationalities, the Jews, though great lovers of their country and passionately interested in its welfare, subconsciously did not work toward cementing the nation, but toward pushing humanity forward on the road of seeing itself without false illusion. Such tendencies were revealed by Ignotus (b. 1869) in his poems and essays, by Molnár, and by Karinthy, and, in a subsequent generation, by the self-lacerating Béla Zsolt (b. 1895) and Károly Pap.

The latent conflict between the two tendencies burst into a great literary battle when, in 1908, three Jewish critics, Hugo Ignotus, Ernő Osvát and Miksa Fenyő, founded the review Nyugat (West), the former two demanding, with the force of their erudition and initiative, due recognition for protagonists of contemporary literature who were for the most part non-Jewish. The main object of contention was the non-Jewish poet Endre Ady (1877-1919), who, during his lifetime, never received any encouragement except from Jews. To the Nyugat were attached the poets Géza Szilágyi, Anna Lesznai, Oszkár Gellért, Simon Kemény and Piroska Reichard, also Béla Balázs and Milán Füst, esoteric in their poetry and fiction, and Béla Révész, the novelist of the poor people. Apart from the Nyugat galaxy, Andor Peterdi, Zseni Várnai and Zoltán Somlyó attained high poetic standards.

The Jews were not only in the literary but also in the political vanguard, playing a great part in the progressive daily newspaper Világ (World), the journal of sociology Huszadik Század (Twentieth Century), the socialist daily newspaper Népszava, and, after the first World War, in the communist daily newspaper Vörös Ujság (Red News).

With their greater nervous sensitivity the Jews sensed the approaching social crisis in Europe of which the first World War was a symptom. They were eager to contribute to the solution of the problems, and when these solutions first failed (1919), they were blamed for the cataclysm and for the impossibility of stemming it. A large number of Jewish writers had to emigrate from Hungary, and "nationalistic" literature prepared for an exclusive rule of the field. New Jewish talent sprang up, however, some of them, like Mihály Földi and Renée Erdős, strongly inspired by Catholicism, yet both early in their careers contributing to the picture of Magyar Jewish society, Földi by his A Halasi-Hirsch fiu (The Halasi-Hirsch Boy) and Erdős by her novel Az új sarj (The New Scion; 1920). About this time were written Molnár's Andor (1918), the portrait of a degenerate Jewish young man; Biró's A bazini zsidók (The Jews of Bazin; 1921), carrying the message that Jews gained in moral strength by persecution; and Hatvany's somewhat autobiographical Zsiga a családban (in English, Bondy Jr.; 1931). Some Hungarian Jewish authors—though not the greatest—attained world fame by winning international novel competitions; they were Ferenc Körmendi, with his Escape to Life (1932), and Jolán Földes, with The Street of the Fishing Cat (1937). Special Jewish subjects were treated by Péter

Ujvári, Samu Fényes and Arnold Kiss; Illés Kacér (Khafrit) and Lajos Szabolcsi (A csillag fia, Bar Kochba) tried their hand at the Jewish historical novel; Lipót Kecskeméti's lives of prophets, Ézsajás (1935) and Jeremiás (1932), belong to Hungarian belles-lettres because of the extreme beauty and power of their language. In the early 1930's the Tábor publishing society was founded for the publication of books with Jewish interest, translations to a great extent. Poets with a Jewish source of inspiration were Emil Makai, Arnold Kiss and József Patai, who also translated the works of Hebrew and Yiddish poets. Among the younger lyricists were László Bródy, some of whose poetry was translated into Hebrew, Yiddish and English, Aladár Komlós, Béla Vihar, Endre Barát and Endre Sós. Return to Jewish sentiment and Jewish subjects was marked among poets and authors from 1938 on.

The greatest talent among the younger Jewish novelists was Béla Zsolt, who probed into the relationship of man to man, man to woman and Jew to non-Jew, denouncing the inadequacies of his Jewish contemporaries as a class with reckless self-exposure (It Ends in Marriage, 1931; Villámcsapás [Stroke of Lightning], 1937). This attitude, a reaction to being denied the love of the mother country, was even surpassed by Károly Pap, who indulged in passionate questioning of himself, of his parents and of his Jewish forebears (Zsidó sebek és bűnök; Jewish Wounds and Sins, 1935; Azarel, 1937).

Literary criticism produced such distinguished Jewish contributors as József Keszler, Géza Feleky, Antal Szerb, József Turóczi-Trostler, Aladár Komlós and Jenő Zsoldos, the latter specializing in the Jewish aspects of Hungarian literature. Ferenc Baumgarten, by means of a foundation bestowing annual literary awards and prizes, encouraged outstanding literary achievement. The roster of Jews who translated the best of Magyar poetry, drama and fiction into foreign languages and served as propagandists for the culture of their nation, would be a long one.

Béla Révész wrote a biography, Max Nordau (1941), about the Jew fighting against injustice; Rodion Markovics, author of a highly successful war story, published Reb Áncsli, whimsical Jewish stories and legends; the Jewish émigré was the subject of Kálmán Sándor's Kórház az őserdőben (Hospital in the Jungle); and the experience of the Jewish forced laborer was sung by the poet György Dénes. The literary Review Libanon was a forum for the representative Jewish authors of the time.

3. Jews in Hungarian Literature after 1919. The anti-Jewish sentiment which pervaded Magyar public life after 1919 was reserved for articles of publicism or literary criticism, but found very little expression in fiction or drama. Nothing to match in violence the Diary of an Outcast by Cecile Tormay, a pamphlet against Jewish participants in the revolutions of 1918 and 1919, was written in Hungarian. Dezső Szabó, in his Az elsodort falu (A Village Swept Away; 1919), blamed the Jews for the misery of the people but recognized that they were the only class in Hungary to create something. Zsigmond Móric analyzed the possibilities of the Jews' being assimilated by the gentry class in his Kivilágos kivirra-

datig (Until Dawn; 1926). The legendary figure of the eternal Jew, marked by the curse of cleverness and wickedness, was taken up in a modern form by Demeter Szeő in his *Zsidó vagyok* (I am a Jew; 1931). In other works criticism of the Jews was confined to exaggerating special Jewish mannerisms.

Great men and great authors always felt that Jews were just like other humans. When an anti-Jewish bill was first introduced into the Hungarian Parliament in 1938, practically all the great names in Hungarian letters and arts graced the protest which was presented against such a measure. Previously to 1938, an earnest spirit had begun to blossom forth as a result of the work of the enthusiastic, non-Jewish, sociographers. Jews were about to be relieved of the sole blame for social evils in Hungary when Hitlerite propaganda set in, throwing thought and conditions in Hungary into a new state of chaos.

Such attempts as that of Faluszinpad (Village Stage) to revive the figure of the Jewish usurer ruining an entire village (*Ártatlanok?;* Are they Innocent?, 1941) were offset by poets like Sándor Remenyik who pronounced himself against racial prejudice (*Petrovics itél;* Petrovics Is Judge), and identified himself with Jewish moral teaching (*Tépelődés a Sinai hegyen;* Meditation on Mount Sinai, 1941).

ANNA BETTELHEIM.

Lit.: Komlós, Aladár, "Irodalom, part 1, Költészet," *Magyar Zsidó Lexikon* (1929) 393-94; idem, *Irók és elvek* (1937); Zsoldos, Jenő, in *Magyar Zsidó Lexikon* (1929) 394-96, 983-86; idem, *A romantikus zsidószemlélet* (1935); Benedek, Marcell, *A modern magyar irodalom* (1924); Farkas, Gyula, *A "Fiatal Magyarország" kora* (1932); idem, *Die Entwicklung der ungarischen Literatur* (1934); Schöpflin, Aladár, *A magyar irodalom története a XX. században* (1937).

VII. Italian. 1. Jewish Motives in Italian Literature. Jewish characters and types began to appear in Italian literature at the end of the 19th cent. and the beginning of the 20th. After the fall of the last vestiges of the ghetto and with the progress of the civic emancipation of the Jews, contacts between Jews and non-Jews in Italy became more frequent and more close. The analysis of the state of mind of the Jew toward the new society into which he had entered as an equal, and particularly the problems arising out of mixed marriages, served as a background and found expression in various novels. The mental crises of conscience arising from mixed marriages were discussed in such novels as the *Il Monte Calvo* of the Jewish novelist Enrico Castelnuovo, the *La nave degli eroi* of Clarice Tartufari, the *Ebrei* of Mario Puccini, and in the *Jom Hakippurim* of the Jewish author Giuseppe Morpurgo, which deal with the love of young people of different religious faiths and the repercussions caused by the different environments of their families.

The problem of the "Jewish inferiority complex" is treated in the novel *Remo Maun, avvocato,* by Adriano Grego, in which the author seeks to analyze the torment of an assimilated Italian Jew who is torn between his Jewish consciousness and his desire to be fully identified as an Italian.

The rise of Nazism to power, the growing threat to the Jews, and the raising of the racial issue gave birth to a series of Italian novels centering around Jewish types. A German Jewess, Else Wolf, is the central figure in the novel *Lilith* of Salvatore Gotta, and in its sequel, *Il paradiso terrestre.* Alfredo Panzini used the background of a novel, *Viaggio con la giovane Ebrea,* as a pretext to publicize all the vulgar accusations against the Jews, such as their alleged plans for world dominion and their international solidarity; but he permits his Jewish character, Rosanna, to utter counterarguments and to defend her people against these accusations.

Two Italian novelists have used an Oriental background in introducing their Jewish characters. Guido Milanese, in *Kadish,* sympathetically describes his Jewish heroine Nora, who escaped a pogrom in Smyrna by fleeing to a Catholic monastery, but preferred to leave her secure refuge to share the danger of her coreligionists. The Jewish author Alfredo Segre, in his *Agenzia Abramo Lewis* (which won the Mondadori Prize), is rather pitiless in presenting and depicting a Levantine Jew, the owner of a suspected business agency in Cairo.

2. Italian Jewish Writers. Though small in number, the Jews of the Italian peninsula have made a noteworthy contribution to Italian letters, especially after 1870, when Italy became a united nation. Before that period there were a few Jews in the field of Italian letters, foremost of all Salomone Fiorentino (1743-1815), called "the Jewish Petrarch"; but as a whole the Jews, many of whom were still confined in ghettos, did not participate in Italian cultural life.

Once they were fully emancipated (1870) the Jews of Italy took an active part in the literary and social life of the Italian nation. They quickly adopted the Italian language and customs, and fused their own ideas with those of the non-Jews to such an extent that the work of Jewish authors can hardly be distinguished, in form, style and content, from that of non-Jewish writers.

Alberto Cantoni (1841-1904) introduced a form of writing that was not too frequent in Italian literature, that of humor, while in his philosophical approach to life and human personality he may be called a forerunner of Pirandello. In the same period Giuseppe Revere of Trieste won fame as a brilliant playwright. He was followed in the field of dramatic production by such other Jewish writers as Mario Morais, Oscar Bassano, Alberto Nunes Franco, and, foremost of all, Sabatino Lopez.

Lopez may be regarded as one of the most representative masters of the Italian "bourgeois" theatre of the last decades of the 19th and the beginning of the 20th cent. The background of his plays is that of the Italian middle class, and their success was due to the realistic delineation of characters and theatrical technique which they evinced. His most famous play was *La Signora Rosa,* which became a standard repertoire work. Lopez was considered one of the best literary and dramatic critics in Italy. Until 1938 he taught Italian literature at the Academy of Brera.

Ettore Schmitz (pseudonym, Italo Svevo) occupies a special place in Italian letters. He was hailed as the "Proust of Italy" for his keen analysis of life, as revealed in his *Coscienza di Zeno.* The same approach was manifest in the writings of Albert Moravia (originally Pincherle), one of the ablest writers of the younger generation. His first novel, *Gli Indifferenti,* published when he was twenty-two, received much attention because of its unusual analytic and corrosive style; his later works established his place in modern Italian literature.

Angiolo Orvieto (b. 1869) is a poet whose writings rank with the finest examples of Italian Renaissance poetry. Together with his brother Adolfo, he founded in Florence the noted literary publication, *Il Marzocco.* He was active in Jewish cultural life and an inspiration to Jewish youth. His poem "Il Vento di Sion" depicts a Hebrew poet of the 16th cent. who, living in the liberal Florence of the Medicean period, could love Italy and Florence on the one hand, and Zion as motherland on the other, with the same burning and unshakable love.

After the first World War two Italian Jewish writers gained wide popularity and enjoyed a sensational but brief fame: Guido da Verona and Pittigrilli (originally Segre). Their erotic writings, veiled by exoticism and modern romanticism, and conceived with a certain ingenuity, reached a circulation of millions of copies and were translated into various languages. The novelists Annie Vivanti and Ida Finzi (Haudee) won considerable attention and they hold a prominent place among Italian women writers.

Italian Jews have been prominent in literary criticism, where their influence has been inspiring and beneficent. Such writers as Enrico Rocca, Arturo Foa, Cesare Levi and Paolo Milano have contributed much to a better understanding of Italian creative literature.

In the field of historical research and studies, wide prominence has been gained by Samuele Romanin and Cesare Augusto Levi, who published valuable works on the history of Venice; Giacomo Lumbroso and his son, Alberto Lumbroso, one of the most renowned and authoritative historians of the Napoleonic epoch; Ermanno Loevinson, author of many studies relating to the epoch of the Risorgimento movement; and Alberto del Vecchio, director of the Archivio Storico Italiano.

In the large galaxy of Italian Jewish historians and commentators on Hebrew, Semitic and Biblical subjects the most outstanding are Professor Umberto Cassuto, author of the work *Gli Ebrei a Firenze nell'età del Rinascimento* (1918), which was awarded the prize of the Italian Academy dei Lincei (in 1942 Cassuto was at the Hebrew University, Jerusalem); and Professor Giorgio Levi della Vida (b. Venice, 1886); in 1942 he was at the University of Pennsylvania, in Philadelphia), among whose many notable works may be mentioned *Gli Ebrei: storia-religione-civiltà* (1924) and *Storia e religione nell'oriente semitico* (1924).

DAVID KLEINLERER.

VIII. Polish. 1. Jewish Motives in Polish Literature. Since the Poles and the Jews have been living side by side for centuries, and the number of Jews in Poland amounts to about 10 per cent of the entire population in recent times, it is natural that many writers in Polish should have discussed questions affecting the Jews. In the earliest period of Jewish settlement in Poland, the Jews were perforce a people apart from their non-Jewish neighbors. They were known to the latter only as being of different religion who came into contact with them as moneychanger,

trader, or business agent of the nobility. Thus in the earliest writings in Polish dealing with the Jew he is depicted in dark colors, as a usurer and as anti-Christ, that is, as the enemy of the Christian religion.

In the 18th and 19th centuries Jewish problems began to be discussed with a greater sympathy. The first partition of Poland in 1772 aroused a new sense of national responsibility, and for the first time Polish writers began to discuss whether Jews might not be granted a greater measure of rights. Among the writers who dealt with this question were Ignacy Krasicki, the greatest Polish poet of fairy tales, and Pater Stanislaw Staszic. At the end of the 18th cent. Poland lost its independence, but at the same time it began to develop a national Polish literature, in which the Jew was sometimes still presented as anti-Christ and usurer, but often as a fellow-citizen and as a fighter in the struggle to regain Poland's lost independence. During the insurrections of 1830 to 1831, 1861 to 1863, 1905 and 1914 to 1918, Jews fought shoulder to shoulder with their Christian fellow-citizens in behalf of Poland; this is reflected by the fact that the figures of such Jewish fighters for independence appear more and more in Polish literature, especially in works of fiction. The most prominent of these Jewish figures was that of Colonel Berek Joselowicz, whose exploits became the theme of numerous folk-songs.

In the second half of the 19th cent. the Polish Jews of Galicia and Prussia obtained full equality of rights, while those in Russian Poland began to participate in Polish culture. This situation is reflected in Polish literature. Foremost in the van of the liberals was Eliza Orzeszkowa, who envisioned a fraternization and mutual appreciation among all the various nationalities in Poland. She introduced a large number of Jewish characters into her novels, and devoted several to descriptions of Jewish life, the most famous being *Meir Esofowicz,* laid in the 19th cent., which shows a young Jew born into an Orthodox Jewish environment and finding his way through a thousand difficulties to European culture. In addition, the authoress wrote a pamphlet, *O Zydach i Kwestji Zydowskiej* (The Jews and the Jewish Problem).

Other writers of the period were not always so liberal in their attitude toward the Jews, and various views can be found in the Polish literature of the period. The writers who wrote on Jewish themes or discussed Jewish questions include Boleslaw Prus, Ignacy Kraszewski, M. Gawalewick *(Mechesi),* Gabriela Zapolska *(Zydziak, Antysemitnik, Matka Szwarzenkopf),* W. Lozinski, Klemens Junosza, Maria Rodziewicz, L. Rydel, Z. Kaczkowski and Z. Krasinski.

In the first decades of the 20th cent. the poet Stanislaw Wyspianski had a great influence on Polish intellectual life, and his work *Sedziowie* (The Judges) was much discussed. The most prominent Jewish figure he created was that of Rachela, a hyperintellectual and exalted girl, an example of wrongly applied assimilation.

When Poland regained its independence in 1919 and the nation was faced with new problems, the question of the Jews was again and again discussed and treated by Polish writers. It is true that the greater part of the Polish literature of this and the following period is definitely anti-Semitic. The well-known dramatist

Stefan Zeromski even went so far as to identify Jews and Bolsheviks, and the prominent Adolf Nowczynski attacked the Jews bitterly and declared that they were enemies of Polish culture. An exception was the historian Badouin de Courtenay, who demonstrated the important cultural contributions of the Jews to Poland. Among the other writers who either attacked or defended the Jews in this period were Teresa Lubienska, L. Grendyszynski, Maria Konopnicka, J. A. Swiecicki, Ludwik Kulczycki, Tadeusz Zubrzycki, Stefania Sempotowska and Jerzy Husarski.

2. Jewish Writers in the Polish Language. It was not until the Jews had been emancipated from the confines of the ghetto and had time to acquire the language and culture of Poland that they began to make contributions to Polish literature. The most prominent Polish poet, Adam Mickiewicz, had a Jewish mother, and expressed his deep sympathy for the Jews. Until comparatively recent times Polish Jewish authors wrote mostly in Hebrew or Yiddish.

In the 20th cent. there was no field of Polish literature in which Jews were not prominently represented. Wilhelm Feldmann, the greatest critic of literature in Poland and himself a Jew, stated that one-fifth of the Polish writers were Jews. One of the most famous of the latter was Juliusz Klaczko, historian of culture, whose "Florentine Nights" became famous in translation throughout Europe. Some of the prominent Jewish writers were baptized, but most remained loyal to their religion. Alfred Nossig, who did much for the literature and the language, was an exponent of Jewish nationalism. Julius Tuwim was regarded in the 20th cent. as undoubtedly the greatest living Polish poet although, as a Jew, he was not elected to the Academy of Sciences, while Joseph Wittlin, author of the novel *Salt of the Earth* (Polish), was regarded as the greatest living Polish writer of romances. Antoni Slonimski, a baptized Jew who is a grandson of the famous Rabbi Hayim Selig Slonimsky, is outstanding as a satiric dramatist.

The following is a list of other noted Polish Jewish writers in various fields:

Belles-Lettres and Lyric Drama: Aleksander Kraushar, Cezary Jellenta, Bronislawa Nuefeld, Leo Belmont, Ostap Ortwin, Jakob Apenszlak, Benedykt Hertz, J. Tugenhold, M. Bersohn, Felicya Arnsztajn, M. Garfein, Michael Muttermilch, D. Zglinski, M. Batucki, Jan Sten, Antoni Lange, L. Kampf, Maximilian Bienenstock, S. Lack, J. Kwiatek, Samuel Hirszhorn, Andrzej Marek (Marek Arnsztajn).

Research on Literature and Folk-Lore: Henryk Biegeleisen, Juliusz Kleiner, Leon Sternbach, Ludwik Zamenhof, Mateusz Mieses, Samuel Adalberg, Jakob Fajtatowicz, Leon Wiener, Wilhelm Berkelhammer, M. Kaufer, Gisela Reicher.

Humanistic Sciences: Edward Rittner, Josef Rosenblatt, Moses Allerhand, Rafael Taubenschlag, Tadeusz Nussbaum, Hilarowicz, J. B. Bloch, A. Kempner, Leopold Caro, Szymon Askenazy, Moses Schorr, Alex Balaban, Alfred Landau, Arie Tartakower, Ludwik Gumplowicz, Ludwik Fischel, Marceli Handelsman and Nathan Michael Gelber.   JOSEPH THON.

IX. Roumanian. 1. Jewish Motives in Roumanian Literature. Roumanian literature written in the modern Western European manner is of comparatively recent origin, coming into being about 1880. Since by far the greater number of Roumanians were illiterate, it reflected from the beginning the views and sentiments of the minority group of the reigning classes: old families of boyars, upper middle class and industrialists, and merchants and bankers, most of whom, due to their fear of competition and backwardness in culture, were violently anti-Semitic. As a result, from the beginning of the 19th cent. on, as soon as national consciousness was awakened, Roumanian writers and politicians started to foster anti-Semitism. Among them were the first Roumanian philosopher, Vasile Conta, and Vasile Alexandri, the chief author of the country in the period between 1850 and 1880; Alexandri depicted the Jews as leeches and parasites. Gheorghe Bengescu-Dabija ridiculed them for speaking in a specific Roumanian Jewish jargon.

The tradition of presenting Jews who speak bad Roumanian, with the implication that it is impossible for them to pronounce it correctly, has survived to the present day. A celebrated collector of popular anecdotes, Theodor Sperantza, has given a number which thus ridicule Jewish speech, though without malice. Jon Creanga, a gifted story teller of 1880 and after, described the Jewish population of northern Moldavia in an unfriendly manner. A similar romance of the same time is the *La Juivea* of Leon Negruzzi, now totally forgotten. In 1930 the talented Ionel Teodorian published a romance, *Medelenie,* in which there are Jewish characters who not only speak Roumanian poorly but are also dishonest and disgusting.

Other Roumanian writers did not present Jewish characters, but defamed them in political writings. Such were Bogdan Petriceicu-Hadjeu, who assailed the Jews bitterly, but left a tender portrait of his own Jewish grandmother; Mihail Eminescu, a fanatic Roumanian nationalist who uttered the wildest and most nonsensical anti-Semitic accusations; Bratescu-Voinesti, who expressed himself sympathetically toward all human suffering, yet later became one of the most ferocious anti-Semites.

There are, however, exceptions to the general rule of anti-Semitism in Roumanian literature. A number of important Roumanian authors had nothing to say against the Jews; others have presented them objectively; two or three have even depicted them favorably. Among these is Ion Carageale, the greatest Roumanian dramatic author, whose short story, "Faclia de Pasti" ("An Easter Candle"), depicts the fear of a Jewish tavernkeeper who, on the eve of Easter, sees approaching one who wants to murder him. This is not the traditional description of Jewish cowardliness. After the peasant revolution of 1907, Carageale published a pamphlet in which he took a stand against anti-Semitism. Mikhail Sadoveanu, regarded as the best modern Roumanian writer of romances, presented Jews objectively in his story of the Jewish girl in the ghetto of Pascani who loves a non-Jew. Liviu Rebreanu, in his story called "The Forest of the Hanged" (Roumanian), gives an equally objective picture of a Jewish soldier. Victor Crasescu, a writer of the second rank, wrote *The Jew* (Roumanian) one of the few romances definitely in favor of the Jews; he openly fights anti-Semitism and says, with truth, that the peasants themselves are not anti-Semitic.

2. Jewish Writers in Roumanian. There are numerous Jewish writers in all branches of literary activity in Roumania, although almost none of them has reached a very high rank. One of the most talented of the Jewish authors, Ronnetti-Roman, produced a highly successful play, *Manasse* (1903); this presents the contrast between the honest, traditionally minded Manasse and his niece Lelia, who wants to marry a Christian. The resulting conflict ends in a tragedy. Another noted character in the play is that of Zelig Sor, the poor, troubled Jew without definite occupation who manages nevertheless to be a keen observer and to preserve a certain gayety of spirit in his misery. Cilibi Moise (1812-70), a man with an inexhaustible comical vein, and a popular philosopher, produced an oral literature of proverbs and aphorisms that survived for decades and were carefully collected by the Roumanian Academy and by M. Schwarzfeld of Bucharest.

For the most part, Jews who wrote in Roumanian have made no careful attempts to depict Jewish life, with the exception of Ronnetti-Roman, mentioned above, and the young J. Peltz, whose *Calea Vacaresti* (1934) describes with humor life in the Jewish ghetto of Bucharest. Other Jewish writers have for the most part chosen general or Roumanian subjects. There is a rich literature against anti-Semitism, including a book of Ronnetti-Roman, *The Two Measures* (Roumanian).

Jews have contributed much to the cultural and intellectual life of Roumania. Philology, grammar and Roumanian folklore owe much to the creative works of Gaster, Saineancu, Tiktin and Candrea; of these the first was expelled from the country, the second expatriated himself because he could not become a Roumanian citizen, the third died in misery in Berlin, and the fourth, Candrea, author of the best dictionary of the Roumanian language, a gigantic work, could never attain a professorial position because he was a Jew. Adolf Stern (d. 1931) translated many foreign poets into Roumanian. A number of Roumanian Jews have been noted literary critics, including G. Dobrogeanu-Gherea, Henric Sanielivici, Barbu Lazareanu, Jon Trivale (d. 1916) and Aurelin Weiss. There are a number of noted Jewish lyric poets, such as A. Steuerman-Rodin, Wemtzeanu, Dominic A. Toma, and Adrien Verea; J. Ludo, J. Peltz and M. Sebastian are noted writers of romances.

Finally, Roumanian Jews have contributed to the cultural progress of the country through the Samitea, Saraga, Alcalay and Adeverul publishing houses which have disseminated the works of Roumanian authors, as well as translations of the great foreign writers.

X. Russian. 1. Jewish Motives in Russian Literature.

The subject of the Jew is a minor one in Russian literature. He appears occasionally in the pages of Pushkin, of Lermontov, and of their contemporaries and immediate successors as a conventional figure, often contemptible, sometimes sinister, rarely noble. The several unflattering caricatures of him drawn by Gogol are not without a touch of realism. Dostoevsky's *House of the Dead* (1862) contains a spiteful and inaccurate sketch of a Jew. Malice is exceeded only by contempt in the few attempts Leskov made to treat the subject. A rather humane attitude toward Jews is discernible only in Turgenev's later works. Tolstoy spoke out against anti-Semitism in his ethical writings, but Jews do not figure in his imaginative work. In the verse of Nekrasov, the civic poet of the 1860's and 1870's, as in the prose of Reshetnikov and Pisemsky, the Jew is excoriated as the vulgar upstart, the exploiter and the parasite, symbolizing as he does the inroads of capitalism into the primitive economy of the country. Saltykov, the master satirist, adds his voice to this thin chorus, yet he could also speak of the problems confronting the Jews with tolerance and good will. Krestovsky's novel, *Egyptian Darkness* (1889), with its two sequels, pictures Jewry ("the Kahal") as a monstrous menace to Christian civilization.

The authors—Chekhov, Korolenko, Gorky, Andreyev, Artzybashev, and Savinkov—who dealt with Jewish themes in the last two or three decades before the Russian Revolution were apt to present the Jew in more sympathetic colors. In fact, the prevalence of official anti-Semitism put them in a frame of mind in which they tended to idealize the Jew and sometimes to grow maudlin about him, though their pity and indignation sometimes thinly disguised an unacknowledged distaste. Kuprin, in his stories, and Chirikov, in his play, *Jews* (1904), came closest to a clear insight into the realities of ghetto life.

After 1917 the anti-Jewish note was sounded in the works of several émigrés, notably in those of General P. N. Krasnov, author of many shoddy novels. In one of them, translated into English under the title of *From Double Eagle to Red Flag* (1923), the Jews are blamed for the Bolshevik revolution. As for Soviet literature, the Jew does not often figure there, and when he does appear usually remains in the background. He is likely to be presented in a rather favorable light, and occasionally assumes heroic stature, as in Nikiforov's *Hoary Days* (1927) and particularly in Fadeyev's novel, translated into English as *The Nineteen* (1929), where young Levinson is depicted as one who triumphs over his physical and social disabilities to become the shining example of revolutionary courage, a leader of fighting men. In a more recent and more ambitious novel on which the same author was at work for a dozen years, he introduced a venomous sketch of a wealthy Jewish family, but the animus, one feels, is directed against the capitalist rather than the Jew. On the other hand, the anti-Semitic pattern occasionally emerges in a new setting. Thus, in Malashkin's *The Moon on the Right* (1927), one encounters once again the familiar type of the Jew as the unsavory parasitic alien.

2. Jewish Writers Using the Russian Language. It was in the 1860's that several budding authors, imbued with the spirit of the Haskalah movement, adopted the official language of the country as their medium of expression, while drawing their subject matter from the Jewish life in which they were rooted. These early Russian Jewish writers, notably Osip Rabinovich, Grigori Bogrov and Judah Levanda, wrote not so much for their own people, to whom Russian was alien, as for outsiders, and their feeble stories and novels were exercises in apologetics as well as denunciations of the evils of the ghetto way of life. Their successors, such as Ben-Ami (Mark Rabinovich), Naumov and Yaroshevsky, had a larger public and were less given to pleading the cause of their people, but their performance, too, lacked vigor and assurance. It did not have any organic connection with folk life, as did Yiddish literature, nor was it allied to the great tradition that nourished the neo-Hebrew revival.

In the 1880's and 1890's Frug's Russian verse, which echoed the sorrows and the rising nationalism of an oppressed people, enjoyed great popularity, but it is significant that Frug eventually began to write in the language of the masses and toward the end of his life (he died in 1916) he turned to Hebrew. Somewhat the same course was followed by Frug's more gifted contemporary, S. An-Ski (Solomon Rappaport). This novelist, playwright and great folklorist employed as his medium not only Russian but also, and perhaps to better advantage, Yiddish.

In the decade immediately preceding the first World War, Eisman's short stories and Yushkevich's more incisive tales and plays of the middle class and the underworld had a considerable vogue, offering the general public an interpretation of the Jewish scene.

The period which began with the revolution of 1917 has seen some additions to Russian Jewish literature. Matvey Roizman is perhaps the only writer who confines himself to Jewish subjects. In his novel, *Minus Six* (1928), which was translated into German, he drew a sordid picture of the middle class trying to adjust itself to new conditions. His next novel, *These Gentlemen* (1932), which depicts life in the agricultural settlements of the Crimea, was specifically an attack on anti-Semitism. An impressive study of that ancient disease as it manifested itself under Soviet conditions was made by Mikhail Kozahov in his tale, *The Man Who Prostrates Himself* (1929). The same author produced a novelette about a Jewish hotel-keeper in the manner of Yushkevich. Vera Inber often draws upon her experiences as a Jewess, and Babel has written several tense short stories about his own people, including some autobiographical pieces and a few plays, the setting of which is his native Odessa and the milieu the Jewish underworld. Andrey Sobol, in his early youth a Socialist-Zionist, wrote, in 1915, a novel on the tragedy of the Jewish revolutionist. He continued to write under the Soviet regime, but could not wholly accept the new order, and in 1926 committed suicide at the age of thirty-eight. Several other novelists of Jewish extraction introduced Jewish themes and characters into their work, although giving them a subordinate place.

In the main the authors enumerated above do not blink the uglier aspects of Jewish life and are singularly free from sentimentality; like the good Communists or fellow travelers that they are, they champion the poor and exhibit an anti-religious or at least anti-clerical bias. This holds true also of those who use verse as their medium. Edward Bagritzky (1895-1934), a child of the Odessa slums, has a poem in which he recalls with horror his early days and "the rusty Jews" among whom he lived, ending on a brusque note of repudiation of his origins. Yet in his major work, a play in verse (*The Lay of Opanas*), a Red Army commissar by the name of Joseph Cohen is represented as the embodiment of the spirit of the revolution. Among the early works of the talented Joseph Utkin, known chiefly as a writer of militant and patriotic lyrics, there is a

tale in verse about red-headed Motele, a tailor whom the revolution turns into a man. It is written in a kind of Judeo-Russian, with a considerable admixture of Yiddish words. The author pokes fun at his characters in a rather friendly fashion, and even the local rabbi does not come off too badly. Alexander Bezymensky is less good-natured. In one of his autobiographical poems he draws a cruel portrait of the petty trader who was his father, saying that history needed him only that he might beget Bolshevik sons.

Under the old regime a bare handful of authors of Jewish birth produced works which belong to the body of Russian literature proper. The facile verse of Nadson, the son of a converted Jew, was popular in the 1880's and 1890's; N. Minsky was one of the initiators of the modernist movement in Russian poetry; Vengeroff, Volynsky and Gershenzon did distinguished work in the field of criticism and history of literature. Since the Soviets have come into power, a much larger number of persons of Jewish stock have made important contributions to Russian letters. In depicting the heroic period of the revolution in the book translated into English under the title of *Red Cavalry*, sketches of Budenny's troops, Babel did pioneer work of enduring value. As novelists and playwrights, Ehrenburg, Kozakov, Boris Levin, Libedinsky, and Mikhail Slonimsky helped to write the social history of their country in imaginative terms. To this group belongs perhaps also Veniamin Kaverin, one of the more penetrating and thoughtful Soviet writers. Like most of those just mentioned, he deals chiefly with intellectuals. Victor Shklovsky, in addition to being the leader of the formalist school of literary criticism, is the author of a number of popular scenarios. A Jew, Ilya Ilf (1897-1937), was a member of the literary team which produced *The Little Golden Calf* (1931; English trans., 1932) and other successful novels in the humorous vein so rare in Soviet literature. Samuel Marshak occupies a prominent place among writers of juveniles. Men of Jewish descent are among the most notable Soviet poets. Such are: the acknowledged master, Boris Pasternak, a sophisticated and highly original craftsman; the above-mentioned Bagritzky, a more accessible and highly regarded lyricist; Ilya Selvinsky; a daring innovator in verse technique. Among those of lesser calibre are Svetlov, Jack Althausen and particularly Bezymensky, who is very popular, especially with the Communist youth. All these authors identify themselves completely with the country of their birth and neither the matter nor the manner of their work sets it apart from current Soviet literature.   Avrahm Yarmolinsky.

Lit.: *Yevreiskaya Entziklopedia*, vol. 13, pp. 639-43; Kunitz, Joshua, *Russian Literature and the Jew* (1929); Lvov-Rogachevsky, L., *Russko-Yevreiskaya Literatura* (1922).

XI. Scandinavian Languages. 1. Denmark. Of the three Scandinavian countries, Jews settled earliest in Denmark and Schleswig-Holstein, which, until its absorption by Prussia, belonged to the Danish crown. Denmark was also the first Scandinavian country to grant them equal rights. Therefore, Jews are much more represented in Danish literature than in the literature of either Norway or Sweden.

The father of the Danish stage, Ludvig Holberg (1684-1754), not only wrote a history of the Jews, but used them repeatedly as characters in his plays. He did not portray them favorably, as, according to his own words, he did not like Jews much. His plays in which Jews appear—always in a secondary role—are *Diderich Menschenskræk, Ulysses von Ithacia, Det arabiske Pulver* and *Den 11. Juni.*

Other Danish writers who followed in Holberg's steps also presented Jewish characters. But some of them showed Jews in a favorable light. Peter Andreas Heiberg (1758-1841), after several unpleasant Jewish characters, shows the magnanimity of a Jew in his play *Chinafarerne* (1792). Jens Baggesen (1764-1826), in his book *Labyrinthen* (1792), warmly takes the part of Jews. Denmark's great poet Adam Gottlob Oehlenschlaeger (1779-1850) also gives good and bad traits to his Jewish characters. Whereas in his poetic work *Alladin* (1805) Jews are described as greedy, in *Sct. Hans Aftenspil* (1802) he praises the filial devotion of a Jewish boy.

The next notable Danish writer in point of time is Hans Christian Andersen (1805-75), world-known for his fairy tales. In a story *Jödepigen* he praises the faithfulness of a Jewish servant, and in his novel *At være eller ikke være* (1857) his noble heroine is a Jewish woman who in the end, however, becomes converted. In his poem *Rabbi Meyer* Andersen tells of the rabbi's sorrows.

The time of rising assimilation is treated by Wilhelm Oestergaard (1852-1928) in his play *2den April* (1887). Here a Jewish girl marries a naval officer while her father keeps strictly to his faith. One of Denmark's leading writers, Henrik Pontoppidan (b. 1857), presents a number of varied Jewish characters in his novel *Lykkeper* (1904).

The earliest Jewish writer who established his place in Danish literature was Henrik (Heymann) Hertz (1797-1870). He was educated by the leading Danish Jewish economist and editor, Levin Mendel Nathanson. Hertz tried unsuccessfully to reconcile his Jewish birth and Danish upbringing by baptism (1832). Up to that year he published his works under pseudonyms. Among these are his plays *Hr. Borchardt og hans Familie* (1827) and *Kærlighed og Politi* (1827). In 1832 he published a didactic poem, "Nature and Art," and some comedies. His highest achievements were his drama *Svend Dyrings Hus* and the lyric work *Kong Réné's Datter.* Collections of lyric poems appeared successively in 1832, 1840, 1844. Hertz was regarded as one of the best poets of his time and, in his comedies, as one of the best portrayers of Copenhagen's bourgeois society.

Meïr Aaron Goldschmidt (1819-87), another Danish Jewish writer of merit, devoted himself to literature after a stormy career as a journalist. His first greater literary work, the novel *En Jöde,* shows spiritual contrasts between Jews and their non-Jewish surroundings. Other of his works which deal with Jewish problems are the plays *Rabbi Elieser* (1861) and *Rabbien og Ridderen* (1869). His novels which are based on Jewish themes are *Hjemlös* (1854), *Ravnen* (1867) and *Avromche Nattergal* (1871). He returns to the same questions in his memoirs *Livs-Erindringer og Resultater* (1877). The last, unfinished part of this work, entitled *Nemesis,* deals with ancient Egyptian mysticism, which ideas he had first mentioned in his work *En Skavank* (1867).

Hertz' role as portrayer of Copenhagen's society was taken up again by Poul Theodor Levin (1869-1929). His last book of this series was *Det hemmelige Land* (1926). Previously he had published *Den döde By* (1902), *Familien i Danmark* (1911), *Lykkens Veje* (1913), *Den lykkelige Mand* (1916), *Den stjaalne Glaede* (1917), *Hjem* (1919), *Sönnen* (1920) and *Löftet* (1922). Among his stage plays are *Antoinette* (1895) and *Sejr* (1899).

Among Danish Jewish writers of the late 19th and early 20th centuries are Simon Koch (b. 1871), Louis Levy (b. 1875) and Henri Nathansen (b. 1886). The latter's first work was a story, *Sommernat* (1899), which was followed by the novels *Den forbudne Frugt* (1901) and *Floden* (1902). During the following years Nathansen wrote a number of dramas. Of these, *Inden for Murene* (1912), which deals with Jewish family life and tradition, has had the most success in Denmark and abroad. A novel, *Af Hugos Liv* (4 parts, 1917), also treats a similar theme.

Levy began his literary career with a novel, *Breve fra Ensomheden* (1898). His next greater book was *Hjemkomst* (1907). Since 1917 he has published successively under the title *Börnerim* several volumes of poems. In cooperation with others he has written a number of plays, among them *H. C. Andersen (1934).* Koch's best works are the novels *Ung Krigsmand* (1903) and *Digteren* (1907). In 1921 he published his autobiography, *Den unge Erik.*

Georg (Morris Cohen) Brandes (1842-1927) was a noted Danish writer, but his works are not of a belletristic but of a critical nature.

2. Sweden. Compared with their role in Denmark, the role of the Jews in the literature of Sweden is meagre. In 1847 Pastor Karl Herman Lewin, himself of Jewish descent, pleaded in a long poem for the granting of equality to Jews. In 1800 the Swedish writer Lindgren had translated Richard Cumberland's successful, pro-Jewish play *The Jew* from the English. A Swedish novelist, Klas Livijn, during the anti-Jewish movement of the post-Napoleonic time, published an anti-Jewish farce which even his biographer Mortensen describes as "fantastic, raw and overdone."

The outstanding Swedish writer of Jewish blood is Oscar Levertin (1862-1906), a poet, essayist, literary historian, critic and university teacher. He dealt repeatedly with Jewish themes, although the Jewry he portrayed belonged to the past. Levertin started with naturalistic novels, but turned later against naturalism. In 1891 he published a confessional poem, using Jewish motifs, under the title *Legender och visor.* His last poetical work, *Kung Salomo och Morolf,* again made use of Oriental and Biblical subjects. His short stories, collected under the titles *Rococonoveller* and *Sista Noveller,* are regarded as outstanding examples of modern Swedish fiction. Among his essays are *Diktare och drömmare* (1898) and *Svenska Gestalter.*

The fiction writer Sophie Elkan, née Salomon (1853-1921), is best known for her historic novels, some of which were published under the pseudonym of Rust Roest. In 1889 she published a collection of stories, *Dur och moll,* which were followed by others. Her first novel was *Ricka flickor* (1893). However, the first real success came with her novel *John Hall* (1899). Her impressions of Palestine, which she visited in the company of Selma Lagerlöf, are laid down in *Drömmen om österlandet* (1901). From 1904 to 1906 she wrote her most important work, *Konungen, en sannsaga,* and its continuation, *I landsflygt.* These books, which deal with the life of Sweden's unhappy King Gustaf IV, were translated into English.

The Jewish painter and poet Ernst Abraham Josephson (1857-1906) is called "a romanticist in a realistic time." His mental power broke long before his physical strength. Josephson's literary achievements are three volumes of lyric poems, *Svarta Rosor* (1888), *Gula Rosor* (1896) and *Svarta rosor och gula* (1901).

3. Norway. Norway, where Jews were not generally admitted before 1851, and where the number of Jews in the 20th cent. was less than 2,000, has not produced any Jewish writer of note. On the other hand, one of Norway's greatest poets, Henrik Arnold Wergeland (1808-45), a non-Jew, devoted a great deal of his writings to Jews, in his endeavor to achieve equality for them. Whereas most of these writings are of a political or polemic nature, two are collections of poems: *Jöden* (1842), and *Jödinden, elleve blomstrende Tornkviste,* which he wrote on his deathbed. The effect which these poems had in Norway has been compared to the effect of *Uncle Tom's Cabin* in the United States.

The plea for Jewish equality was also supported by Adolf Rosenkilde's play *En Jöde in Mandal* (1849). The author was born in Denmark, but spent many years as an actor and writer in Norway. Anti-Semitism was attacked in the novel *Jödinden* (1892) by John Olaf Paulsen (1851-1924). The book's heroine is a Jewess who contracts an unhappy marriage with a nobleman.   ALPHONS SUMMIT.

Lit.: Granqvist, P. M. (Lazarus v. Rothschild), *Det svenska Israel* (1933); Valentin, H. M., *Judarnas Historia i Sverige* (1924); Balslev, B., *De danske Jöders Historie* (1932); *Tidskrift for Jödisk Historie og Literatur* (1923) 261-84; *American Hebrew,* July 19, 1929, p. 283 et seq.; May 23, 1930, p. 21 et seq.; Sept. 8, 1939, p. 39 et seq.

XII. Spanish. The attitude of non-Jewish Spanish writers toward Jews in the 16th and 17th centuries reflects the intolerance with which the church indoctrinated the Spanish people and their rulers during the Middle Ages. Expressive of this attitude is the comedia, not alone because it made the literary genius of Spain for two centuries most articulate, but also because it assumed the proportions of a great national literary movement.

It may be safely stated that the comedia, revealing whatever knowledge the writers possessed of the Jewish faith, customs, history, and tradition, is illustrative of the official attitude in Spain, as well in the period covered by the dramatist as in his own time. Previous to the expulsion only two writers may have come into actual contact with Jews: the author of the *Coplas de Mingo Revulgo* and the author of the *Celestina,* the former flourishing about twenty years, the latter ten years before the expulsion of 1492. After that no other writer, owing to the expulsion, had personal knowledge of professing Jews in Spain, with the exception of Cervantes, who became acquainted with Jewish fellow captives in Algiers.

In view of the fact that Jews in Spain, even if their religion was held damnable, had in the past mingled freely with the people—individual Jews often received royal favor—one would expect to find in the comedia a conspicuous part assigned to the Jew. That, however, is not the case, no doubt because the writers who were strictly accountable to the Inquisition would find little attraction in a class of people long since driven out, whose very name was anathema to the church. They, of course, must have known of Marranos. But if a Marrano were to be unfavorably depicted, prudence and tact permitting no other characterization because of the Church policy, the writer feared offending the very personages to whose favor or "protection" he aspired. He knew, as everyone else did, that there was a Jewish strain in families moving in the highest circles in court, in society, and even in the church. The only exception is found in Lope de Vega's *El Niño Inocente de la Guardia,* where a "ritual murder" is committed by Marranos. And it is a significant fact that although many comedias have for their *mise-en-scène* Moorish Spain, not one celebrated Jewish figure of that period is noted on the stage. Evidently, in accord with the policy of the church and the Inquisition, the comedia had to maintain a discreet silence in this regard.

In the comedia the attitude of the government is uniformly represented as inimical and condemnatory. The strongest terms of opprobrium are applied to the Jew: he is a menace to the state, the implacable enemy of the people. In the *Mingo revulgo,* the first dramatic effort at the close of the Middle Ages, King Henry IV is severely rebuked because he did not enforce anti-Jewish legislation with sufficient rigor. The same tone is noted in the *Celestina.* According to Lope, nothing ever deserved so much praise as Ferdinand and Isabella's edict of expulsion: Spain would henceforth be politically "secure" and spiritually "uncontaminated."

The material bearing on the social status of the Jew contains many interesting observations on his general appearance, his manners and customs, and his commercial pursuits. Jews have nearly always Biblical or typically Jewish names. Roman names are several times given to Jewesses. Names of conversos are always Spanish. Often no names are given, the characters being designated simply by "un judio," "dos judias," and the like. Jews wear the "bonete," a cap, the sombrero being worn only by the Spaniard. Cervantes describes a Jew with ear-locks (Peoth). The Semitic features are often emphasized. The Jewess is always portrayed as beautiful. In sharp contrast the Jew's personal appearance nearly always excites pity, it is so woebegone.

With the exception of Diamante's *La judia de toledo,* the comedia reveals the Jewish character as low and contemptible. In Lope's *Las paces de los reyes* Raquel is depicted as a wanton, whom her father urges to become the king's mistress, purely for profit. On the other hand, Diamante, dealing with the same theme, reveals Raquel as a medieval Esther and gives her father a most noble character. All other references in the comedia make the Jewish character more or less abhorrent. Torres Naharro makes the Jew a coward and a cheat; Tirso de Molina, a traitor; Alarcon, a creature wholly corrupt. As regards sex, Jews are not accused of immorality, except in one instance by Lope, who also accuses Jewesses of moral depravity. In trade the Jew is a pawnbroker, moneylender, or second-hand clothes dealer. Jews are also physicians.

In the matter of religious antagonism the comedia is prolific in animadversions on Jews and Judaism. Lope condemns Judaism as a "detestable heresy." Tirsa de Molina declares that a Jew accounts it great merit to kill a Christian. The *Celestina* views Jews as forever hated because of the crucifixion. That was also the view of the dramatist Juan del Encino. Another writer, Gil Vincente, says that Beelzebub is in league with Judaism and delights in its followers. On the other hand, Cervantes, in *Los baños de Argel* and in *La gran sultana,* refers almost admiringly to the religious loyalty of the Jew and to the pride he takes in his people and faith. Diamante writes in the same strain.

In the references to ancient history the comedia portrays no such figure—the Jew as an object of hatred and scorn. The writers had different material before them. Judas Maccabeus, for instance, could not be referred to other than as a hero; nor would a Herod, a friend of the masters of Rome, be treated with contempt. The bias developed by the church could hardly be made retroactive to a time when the church did not yet exist. Only Gaspar Aguilar, in *La gitana melancolica,* flagrantly violates historical truth when he says that during the siege of Jerusalem preparations were made for human sacrifice in the Temple.

It must be remembered that the liberalization of thought which arose in other parts of Europe in the 16th cent. and after found no echoes in Spain until long after the "golden age" of Spanish literature. Even at the close of the 17th cent. the spirit of Spanish writers was the same as that of the time of Ferdinand and Isabella. This may adequately explain the attitude of Spanish writers toward Jews.

CHARLES A. RUBENSTEIN.

Lit.: Amador de los Rios, José, *Études historiques . . . sur les juifs* (1861); Menendez y Pelayo, Marcelino, *Historia de los heteredoxos españoles* (3 vols., 1880); Merimée and Morley, *History of Spanish Literature* (1930); Rennert, Hugo A., *The Spanish Stage in the Time of Lope de Vega* (1909).

South America. The contributions of Jews to the literature of the various countries of South America is hard to appraise because of the amalgamation of the Jewish elements of the population into the surrounding life, particularly in those countries where the Jewish population has remained small. In a country like Argentina, however, with its Jewish population of 260,000, the integrated nature of the community makes identification easier, even in those instances where a writer deals entirely with secular subject matter.

One of the most serious novelists in Argentina is Max Dickmann (b. Buenos Aires, 1902), author of the Argentine trilogy, *Europe* (1930), *Madre América* (1935) and *Gente* (1936). *Madre América* was awarded the Buenos Aires municipal prize in literature. Dickmann's novels are non-Jewish in character, nor does he concern himself with social problems. His trilogy is a record of the struggle of man against nature, and of the life of the common people.

Samuel Eichelbaum (b. Dominguez, Argentina, 1894) is a dramatist. Two of his plays, *Tormento de Dios* (1930) and *Señorita* (1937), won the Buenos Aires municipal prize. He was also the author of two volumes of short stories. A play on a Jewish subject, *The Jew Aaron,* remained unproduced (1942), but whenever Eichelbaum touched on Jewish life in his prose, the result was less fortunate than in his other subjects, for Eichelbaum had no intimate knowledge of Jewish life.

Enrique Espinoza (Samuel Glusberg, b. 1898) is a critic and novelist who occasionally deals with Jewish subjects. Some of his stories, which depict Jewish scenes in the midst of Argentinian life, are candid reports of the intermingling of the two cultures and its occasional tragedy. He is the author of *La levita gris* (1924), a collection of Jewish stories; *Trinchera; Compañeros de viaje* (published in Chile in 1937); and *Chicos de España* (1937). He was also the editor of several literary reviews.

Perhaps the most outspokenly Jewish fiction in the vernacular of Argentina is *Los gauchos judíos* (1910), by Alberto Gerchunoff (b. Tultsin, Poland, 1884). The book describes the life of the Jewish settlers in the Argentinian prairies; it was translated into many languages, including Yiddish. Gerchunoff is the author of numerous other volumes of fiction, history and criticism, and though his affiliation is avowedly Jewish, his work is largely secular. Gerchunoff, who came to the Argentine as a child and was self-educated, was a professor of literature at the Colegio Nacional del Pilar of Buenos Aires (1915-18) and occupied many important editorial posts, including membership on the staff of *La Nación* (1908-).

A poet who handles both Jewish and general subjects is Carlos Moises Grunberg (b. Buenos Aires, 1903). His first volume of poems was *Las Cameras del rey* (1922). In *Mester de Judería* (1940) he derived the title from the name of the craftsmen who work within the walls of a ghetto; the title signifies his own erudite, almost esoteric approach to poetry, for he is less a lyricist than a scholar with a magnificent sense of the Spanish language. Grunberg also translated verse from other languages into Spanish, including Heine's "Judah Halevi."

Lassara Liaca (Lichovitzki) is an essayist and lyrical poet. Born in Buenos Aires, he is himself a product of the Jewish and Spanish cultural streams combined in the New World, and his poetry is a statement of both. He is the author of two volumes of poetry, both in Spanish, *A Bite of Bread* and *Bread of Buenos Aires.*

Rebecca Mactas is the author of a volume of short stories, *Los judíos de las Acacias,* which is a sad and sentimental description of Jewish life. She is also a translator, and introduced the work of Judah Halevi and Chaim Nachman Bialik to Spanish readers.

One of the most provocative of Argentinian Jewish writers is Cesar Tiempo (Israel Zeitlin), a dramatist and poet, who frequently undertakes the polemical defense of the Jews against attack. His own work, however, which presents Jewish characters, was accused by Jews of having an unfortunate effect on the attitude of the general public toward the Jews. *Pan Kriazho,* a play about a Jewish judge and his children, who are Argentina-born, and *I Am The Theatre,* a play about an actress who happened to be a Jew, were both the cause of displeasure. Tiempo's intentions, however, were not open to question; in all his work, as in his brochures about the Jews, he wished sincerely to create a salutary effect, although the mode of his approach did not always make it seem likely that he did.

Among other leading scholars, historians and translators who have added to the value of Argentinian literature in the 20th cent. are Alfred Cohn, José Liebermann, Alberto Palcos and Antonio Portnoy. Louis Karduner, L. Dujovne, S. M. Neuschlosz and A. Reznik are among the translators and literary historians who deal almost exclusively with Jewish subject matter in Spanish. There are several publishing houses that specialize in issuing material of Jewish interest in Spanish; among these are Israel, Hebraica, M. Gleizer, and Ateneo.

In other South American countries there are several creative writers of Jewish descent: Levi Fernandes Carneiro in Brazil; Fabio Lozano y Lozano, historian, and Juan Lozano y Lozano, a poet, of Colombia, where Jorge Isaacs (1837-95) was the author of the national classic, *Maria;* and Efraím Cardozo, a historian, of Paraguay. Elsewhere the stream lies more deeply buried in the welter of assimilation and ancient Marrano heritage.

With the European anti-Jewish influences of the 1930's, Jews as subject matter in literature written by non-Jews began to make their appearance, but mostly in journalism.   NATHAN RICARDO.

Lit.: Gerchunoff, Alberto, "Yiddisher Geist in der Spanisher Kultur," *Yubl-Buch* (Buenos Aires, 1940) 479-86; Boleslavski, L., "Yidden in der Spanish-Argentiner Literatur, Vissenshaft un Journalistik," *ibid.,* 487-506.

LITERATURE, YIDDISH. Table of Contents:

Yiddish literature does not present a uniform body of writing, but two distinct groups which have hardly any points of contact. The first is that which prevailed up to the end of the 18th cent. and was the folk literature of the Jews who lived according to tradition. The second, which did not rise so much from the first as alongside of it, was the quickly flourishing literature of that part of the Jewish people which had begun to secularize its life and to adopt modern European ways.

A. The Literature of Tradition. I. General. Little is known about the earliest period of Yiddish literature, since most of its products have been lost. Even as late as the first century after the invention of printing (about 1450) there are books which are known only by name and of which not one copy has survived. The earliest traces of Yiddish literature that have been preserved are glossaries to Bible commentaries, Halachic works and the like, which go back to the 12th cent. The oldest dated Yiddish manuscript, a single page devoted to folk medicine, is as late as 1396, whereas the oldest dated manuscript in Hebrew characters in Germany comes from the 13th cent.

This literature first arose in South Germany, whence it spread to other parts of Germany and thence to Austria, Poland, Lithuania, Hungary, Lombardy and the Netherlands. It appears in about equal quantity in the three chief regions, the west, Bohemia as far as Hungary, and the east, and it is not until the beginning of the 18th cent. that Germany takes a considerable lead. Furthermore, more than a third of all the works that appeared since the invention of printing are anonymous; thus their origin can not as a rule be determined. The places where they are printed are no help in this connection, as the authors frequently traveled about or had their works published far from their own homes. In the 16th cent. the chief places for such publication were South Germany (including Prague, Basel and Zurich), Poland (Cracow) and Lombardy (Mantua, Venice and Cremona). Subsequently the Lombard printshops disappeared, and were replaced by those in Amsterdam and other localities. As a result of the invention of printing, many of the older Yiddish works were revised or pirated; at the same time many new ones were given circulation. The oldest continuous printed text in Yiddish, except depositions of witnesses, is probably the "Bau-Lied" in the Prague Passover Haggadah (1527).

One can hardly speak of a literary development in this type of Yiddish literature. This can easily be seen from the fact that the same works were reprinted again and again, the only changes being to make the language more comprehensible to contemporaries. It was a religious literature, which sought to bring to its readers a closer knowledge of the Bible and other Jewish writings. There are some secular writings, not of very great importance, but a large part of these deal with matters of Jewish interest. Translations, commentaries and paraphrases form a large part of the literature, but in the 17th and 18th centuries half of the books are original productions.

During the first third of the 18th cent. the production of Yiddish literature reached its height; the period is marked by a number of new works in all fields, as many as in the entire 16th cent. Immediately afterwards there is a decided drop in Yiddish writing, and but few works appear—the tocsin of the approaching period of enlightenment and assimilation. By the 19th cent. Yiddish literature had practically disappeared in Western Europe, as all groups, even the Orthodox, had adopted the vernacular. A few ritual works, beloved by individuals, survived for a while, but eventually also passed out of use.

In Eastern Europe not much Yiddish literature was created in the 18th cent., but the literature itself did not disappear; the older works continued to be printed and circulated. In the last decades of the century a revival of Yiddish writing began; this was due to the growth of Hasidism and the reaction against the Haskalah. Hasidism continued the use of Yiddish, which had been strengthened by the earlier Cabalistic movements. Still later the growing movement back to traditionalism began to find a literary expression in Yiddish.

II. Divisions. 1. Glosses and Glossaries to the Bible. There have been Yiddish translations of difficult words in the Bible and traditional Jewish literature since the earliest period. Complete glossaries to parts of the Bible and such writings as those of Rashi appeared soon after, and were a favorite vehicle of instruction. The first of these to be spread in printed form was *Mirkeves Hamishneh Lekonkordansia,* later *Seifer shel Reb Anshel* (Cracow, 1534), the oldest printed work consisting mainly of Yiddish. The two books of Moses ben Issachar Sertlin, *Beer Mosheh* and *Lekah Tob* (Prague, 1605, 1604), containing both Hebrew and Yiddish glosses, were held in high esteem.

2. Bible Translations and Paraphrases. There are a number of manuscripts of Yiddish translations of parts of the Bible; the earliest come from the 13th cent., but it is probable that other earlier ones have been lost. The invention of printing gave a new means for instruction and learning, so it is not surprising that almost half the printed works which appeared in their first hundred years are of this type. Two translations of the Pentateuch appeared in 1544; the older was by the convert Paulus Aemilius and was printed in Augsburg, the other by the converts Michael Adam and Paulus Fagius. Moses Naphtali Bresch of Poland made a revision of the Augsburg translation, and added one of Rashi, to create the first purely Jewish printed Bible translation in Yiddish (Cremona, 1560; Basel, 1583). Elijah Levita's translation of *Psalms* had appeared a little earlier (Venice, 1545). Isaac Sulkes translated and interpreted *Song of Songs* (Cracow, 1579), and Rabbi Jacob Koppelman ben Samuel Bunem, the five Megilloth (Freiburg, 1584). An edition of *Isaiah* (Cracow, 1586) includes the commentary of David Kimhi and epitomes. Leib Mehler made a paraphrase of *Esther* (Cracow, 1590). The famous *Taitsch Humesh* of Isaac ben Samson, which contains extracts from Rashi and the Midrashim, appeared in Prague in 1608. Another favorite paraphrase was the *Taitsch Esrim Vearbe* of Hayim ben Nathan (Hanau, about 1625), a paraphrase of the books from *Joshua* to *Kings,* plus *Daniel, Ezra* and *Nehemiah.*

It was usual in these books to follow the translation of each verse or part of the verse with an explanatory or Midrashic supplement. A typical example of this is the *Seifer Hamaggid* of Jacob ben Isaac Ashkenazi, which comprises the Prophets and the Hagiographa (Prague, 1576?). His more popular *Tzeenah Ureenah,* or *Tzenne-Renne,* is not a translation, but a free Midrashic reworking of the Bible story. It was frequently revised and reprinted.

Complete Yiddish translations of the Bible first appeared in the 17th cent. from the hands of Jekuthiel Blitz (Amsterdam, 1676-79) and Joslin ben Alexander Witzenhausen (Amsterdam, 1679). The *Abir Yainkev* of Simeon Akiba Baer ben Joseph Henochs (Sulzbach, 1700) is a collection of Cabalistic Midrash on *Genesis;* a similar work is the *Nachles Tzvi,* or *Tatsch Zoier,* of Rabbi Selig, which is based on the *Zohar* and was popular down to modern times in various minor revisions. Menahem Man ben Solomon Amelander and

Leiser Redelheim made a completely new translation of the Bible under the title *Magishe Minhah* (Amsterdam, 1725), which became very popular. Other translations of parts of the Bible appeared from time to time in the next hundred years.

3. Reworkings of the Bible Story. The best-known of these are the *Shmul Buch* about the life of David, probably composed in the 14th cent. and extant in manuscripts of the 16th, and the *Melochim Buch* and *Esther Buch,* probably also from the 14th cent. The *Jüdische Stamm,* which recounts the sacrifice of Isaac, is ascribed to the 15th cent. Similar books were made on the basis of the Biblical *Joshua* and *Judges* (Moses ben Mordecai; Mantua, 1511), *Daniel* (Basel, 1557) and again *Judges* (Mantua, 1564).

4. Religious Poetry. Some of the earlier translations and reworkings of the Bible into Yiddish were couched in the form of verse, such as those of Rabbi Jacob Koppelman ben Samuel Bunem (the Megilloth), Moses Stendel (*Psalms*) and Abraham Schedel (*Ezekiel*). There were also a poetic reworking of *Midrash Vayosha* (end of the 17th cent.), the *Targum Sheni Lied* (Amsterdam, 1649) and Elhanan ben Issachar's rhymed translation of *Judith,* the *Soshanneke-bichl* (1702). A large number of translations of the hymns for the Sabbaths and holidays have been preserved in manuscript or in printed form, such as the *Simches-Tore-lied* of Rivka Tiktiner (d. 1550) and the Sabbath songs of Akiba Frankfort (Basel, 1590). The composers of such religious poetry included Taube Pan, Menahem Mendel Krochmal, Channe Ashkenaz, and the famous Levi Isaac of Berdichev (1740-1810).

5. Secular Poetry. There are numerous anonymous ballads the origin of which goes back for centuries. They depict passionate joy of life, the sufferings of individuals and the Jews as a whole, religious feelings and personal yearnings. Topical poems in Yiddish were great favorites. Elhanan ben Abraham Helen's *Vinz-Hans-Lied* (Hebrew and Yiddish, about 1616) depicts the Fettmilch riots in Frankfort. Other poems of this genre include *Kine al gezeires hakilles dekak Ukraine* (1648); *Horben Hagodl,* on the destruction of Ungarisch-Brod in 1683; *Ein Shein Nei Lied Fun Ofen* by Aaron ben Joseph (Prague, 1688); *Ain Nei Klog-Lied fun geiresh Tanhousn* by Seligman ben Isaac of Tannhausen (1721).

6. Plays and Stories. The favorite Yiddish drama was the Purim play, which appeared in numerous variations. The Ahashverosh play, another form of it, has been preserved in a manuscript of 1697. Other favorite subjects for drama were the story of Joseph and the conflict of David and Goliath; other plays deal with the sacrifice of Isaac, the Judgment of Solomon, Hannah and Peninah, Solomon and Asmodeus, and the stories of Agag and of the wicked city of Sodom.

The books of stories in the traditional period are mainly of a religious nature. One of the most famous of these is the *Maisse-Buch* (*Maaseh Book*), which contains a wealth of material from Talmudic, Midrashic, Cabalistic and other rabbinic sources as well as some non-Jewish stories; it was first printed toward the end of the 16th cent. Jonathan ben Nathan of Ofen wrote *Ein Nei Maisse-Buch* (Dyhernfurth, 1637), and the *Maisse Berie Vezimre* was printed in Prague about 1660. This branch of literature is richly represented; perhaps the best is the book of tales about the Hasidic rabbi, Nahman of Bratzlav, issued as *Sippire Masses* (1815), a collection of moral tales which combine all the various elements in Jewish thought up to and including the Hasidic movement.

7. Musar Literature. Of a similar nature is that group of Yiddish literature which is directed primarily to the cultivation of a moral life, though written in such a way as to be of interest and entertainment. It is significant that the earliest printed work which contains only Yiddish is a book of the Musar literature, the *Middes-Buch* (Isny, 1542), a reworking of the Hebrew *Orehoth Tzaddikim,* which was not published until 1581. There are a number of Yiddish translations and paraphrases of Hebrew Musar literature. The *Sefer Hayirah* of Jonah Gerondi was translated into Yiddish prose, probably by Michael Adam (Zurich, 1546), and in versified form as *Seifer Haye Olem* or *Buch des Eibigen Lebns* (Freiburg, 1583). Many of these books were intended primarily for women, such as *Ein Shein Froen Bichlein* of Benjamin Aaron ben Abraham Slonik (Cracow, 1577) and the *Menekes Rivka* of Rivka Tiktiner (Prague, 1609). Other noted Yiddish productions of the Musar literature include: *Sam Hahayim,* by Abraham Apteiker of Vladimir; the *Brantspiegel* of Moses ben Enoch Altschul of Prague (Basel, 1602); the versified *Tzuchtspigl* of Seligmann Ulm (Prague, 1610); the *Leb Tob* of Isaac ben Eliakim of Posen (first dated publication, Prague, 1620); the *Lev Hachomim* of Hayim ben Jacob Arbisch (end of the 17th cent.); while the Hebrew works, such as the *Kitzur Shene Luhoth Haberith, Menorath Hamaor, Kab Hayosher, Eben Bohan, Shebet Hamusar* and *Behinath Olam,* were frequently translated into Yiddish or given a Yiddish reworking. The Hasidic rabbi Baer of Liady wrote *Poikeiech Ivrim,* and the famous Maggid, Jacob Dubno ben Wolf Kranz, *Seifer Hamiddes* (1861). Hillel Lichtenstein is the author of a Musar book, *Seifer Es Laasses,* in which he makes a plea for Yiddish as an aid to religion (Lemberg, 1872); Israel Meir Kahan (Hafetz Hayim) wrote *Geder Olam, Nidhe Yisrael* and *Taharath Yisrael.*

8. Ritual and Devotional Works. Most of the ritual works in Yiddish are short, practical treatises explaining the proper observances and laws in various fields of the Halachah. Among these are the *Vaiber-Buch,* or *Seider Noshim,* of Samuel Schmelke ben Hayim (Prague, 1629), the *Seider Hanikker* of Judah Leib ben Ezekiel of Ostrog, the *Hilches Mile* of Naphtali ben Samuel Pappenheim (Amsterdam, 1652) and the *Minhogim* of Isaac Tyrnau (Amsterdam, 1662). The prayer-books are for the most part intended for the use of women, and are of two types. The first is that of translations of the Hebrew prayer-book, of which there are many in manuscript, the earliest preserved being from the 13th cent. The first printed translation of the Siddur was published by Joseph ben Yakar (Ichenhausen, 1544); this was followed by many others, including the favorite *Korban Minche.* The first printed translation of the Mahzor is probably that of Avigdor ben Moses of Eisenstadt (Cracow, 1571). The second form of prayer-book is that of the Tehinnoth, or books of private devotions in Yiddish. The first printed Tehinnoth appear to have been compiled by Abraham Apteiker. Aaron ben Samuel of Hergershausen wrote *Libliche tfille oder greftige arznei far guf un neshome* (1709). In the later period the Tehinnah *Shloishe Sheurim* of Sarah bath Mordecai (Sarah bath Tobim) of Satanów (probably at the beginning of the 19th cent.) became so popular that many imitations were published under its name.

9. Light Literature. In this are included the books of fables, such as the *Kuh-Buch* of Abraham ben Mattathias (Verona, 1555), which still exists, not in the original edition, but in a reprint or revision, and the *Seifer Mesholim* of Moses ben Leizer Wallich (Frankfort, 1687). The fox fables of Berechiah were put into Yiddish rhymes by Jacob Koppelman ben Samuel Bunem (Freiburg, 1588). Another group is that of the satiric poems, such as *Di Beshreibung fun Ashkenez un Polek* (Prague, about 1675) and *Ein Nei Klog-Lied. . . . ouf ein Meshores fun Frankfort* (1708). The bulk of this early Yiddish light literature as such is of non-Jewish origin. Jewish writers took over the medieval stories of chivalry and merely removed the Christian religious note. A number of such books were printed, the best known being *Kuenig Artus-Hof,* produced in the 14th cent., a reworking of the *Wigalois* of Wirnt von Gravenberg. *Die schöne Magelone* has been preserved in various forms, such as the *Maglene-Lied* (Prague, about 1650). The *Bove-Buch* of Elijah Levita (oldest extant publication, Prague, 1660) is derived from the Italian romance of Buovo d'Antona and gave its name to a whole series of similar novels. A second book of the same type, *Paris un Viene,* of which no title page has been preserved, is generally ascribed to Levita.

10. Historical Literature. This deserves to be mentioned, as it is written primarily to be read for entertainment. The *Josippon,* translated into Yiddish by Michael Adam (Zurich, 1546), was very popular. There were other translations from the Hebrew, including Ibn Verga's *Shebet Yehudah,* David Gans' chronicle, and Nathan Hannover's *Yeven Metzulah.* There are writings which describe contemporary events, such as the *Viener Gezeire* of Avigdor ben Moses of Eisenstadt (Cracow, 1609). A historical allegory, *Geshichtnis fun Reb Meier* (first separate edition, Fürth, 1694), purports to deal with the life of the composer of the liturgical poem *Akdamuth.* There are a few autobiographies in Yiddish, such as the memoirs of Glückel of Hameln and the diary of Aron Isak, the first Jew in Sweden (1802).

B. Modern Yiddish Literature. I. The Haskalah Literature. An entirely different picture is furnished by modern Yiddish literature which has progressed simultaneously with the traditional but never really developed out of it. Whereas traditional Yiddish literature was based on the essential religious spirit of the Jewish people in their separate environment, the Haskalah literature represented that portion of the people over whom the old religious life had begun to lose its hold, and who wished to change Jewish life to a more modern form. It represents a transition from the old Yiddish literature to the new flowering that took place in the second half of the 19th cent.

The Haskalah literature arose among the very groups who despised and hated the Yiddish language and regarded it as a sign of unenlightenment and degradation. The first Maskilim, or followers of the Haskalah, generally avoided it; a few, such as Isaac Euchel and Aron Halle Wolfson, employed it only for satiric purposes, contrasting the Yiddish of the elders with the literary German of the "enlightened." But Yiddish still survived in Eastern Europe among the masses, and the Maskilim were perforce compelled to employ it as a medium for spreading their ideas of modernization and culture. They often mishandled the instrument which they used, but they were, all unwittingly, the pioneers of the new Yiddish literature.

The Yiddish literature of the Haskalah is marked by didacticism and comparatively small artistic merit. The Kantian Mendel Levin Satanower (1741-1819) began to translate the Bible into contemporary Yiddish, so that a Bible translation is practically the beginning of modern Yiddish literature. Israel Axenfeld (1787-1866), who besought the aid of the Russian government in his fight against Hasidism, wielded a somewhat primitive, but effective pen. Isaac Baer Levinsohn (1788-1860), "the father of the Enlightenment," wrote a satire. The most talented author in the group was Solomon Ettinger (1799-1855); his sentimental poems and his comedy *Serkele* were the first works in this literature to possess a correct European form. Most of the Haskalah works had little circulation or influence. Abraham Baer Gottlober (1811-99), Judah Leon Gordon (1829-92), Michel Gordon (1823-90) and Isaac Joel Linetzki (1839-1916) wrote the usual satires. Abraham Mendel Mohr (1815-68) of Galicia published the first Yiddish periodical (*Catung,* that is, *Zeitung;* 1848). Eisik Meir Dick (1807-93) was a unique personality, of notable powers of observation and description. He wrote more than 400 little books, intended to educate the people, to free it from superstition and to improve it generally. His historical, realistic, sentimental and humorous stories and romances were very important for the cultural development of Lithuanian Jewry.

The middle and second half of the 19th cent. was the era of the Badhan writers, who composed poems of an original character in inns and similar places. Berl Broder-Margulies (1815-68) sang in simple fashion the wretched lot of those whom fate has disinherited. Wölwel (Wolf) Zbarazer Ehrenkranz (1819-82), a Haskalah Bohemian, developed some real lyric notes. Eliakim Zunser (1840-92) was another beloved Badhan. A similar character, though not exactly of the same group, was Abraham Goldfaden, like them an entertainer of the masses—superficial but powerful, who created a primitive stage that had a lowly artistic level but nevertheless became the cornerstone of the modern Yiddish stage.

II. The Flowering of Yiddish Literature. In the course of the 19th cent. the modernization of Jewish life extended to every greater circle and Europeanization had acquired the status of a tradition. This made possible the Europeanization of Yiddish literature and the rapid ascent to prominence of the three classicists—Mendele (Abramowitsch), Peretz and Sholem Alechem. The early decades of this new literature were marked by a secular idealism. In it are found the expression of the lyric and the dramatic, the tragic and the skeptic, the visions of the mystic and

the sharp decisions of the cool reasoner. All fields of writing are represented; but fiction and poetry arise earlier than drama. There is a wide variety of subjects: quiet suffering, intense passion, adventure, imaginary events, joy in existence, bitter *Weltschmerz,* loneliness, intrigues, memoirs, mass movements, national survival, the class war, nature, legends, the exotic, the Biblical, the symbolic. Only a few of the hundreds of modern Yiddish writers can be mentioned here.

The writers who inaugurated this new phase of Yiddish literature were all rooted in the Haskalah. They began their literary career in Hebrew and turned to Yiddish as a means of reaching the people.

Mendele Moicher Sforim (Shalom Jacob Abramowitsch; 1836-1917) is the first Yiddish writer, aside from Ettinger, who belongs to the realm of art. This does not mean that he rejected the Haskalah; on the contrary, the call to arms of enlightenment is found again and again in his epic depictions of a full and complete life of the people, with its lights and shadows, vivified by elements of dramatic tension and now and then illuminated by satiric flashes. He is the most important delineator of the life of East European Jewry in the 19th cent., a literary painter full of humor and full of sympathy. His portrayals of nature are always noteworthy and are made impressive when viewed through human and Jewish eyes. His form of expression is subjective; his characters see through his eyes and speak his language. He was a great artist in language and was the creator of the modern literary style for both Yiddish and Hebrew.

Isaac Loeb Peretz (1851-1915), the second creator of Yiddish literature, completely freed himself from the influence of the Haskalah. He passed through the stages of the naturalism expressed in miniatures of society, of skepticism, satire, intellectualism and masterly psychological analysis to attain the romanticism of Hasidism. Following the style of the folk tale and the legend, or using phantastic and symbolic forms, he depicts the lives of saintly Jews or the sheer ecstasy of the Hasidic soul. At last he reached the eternal study of the Jewish fate. He was a story-teller full of lyrical pathos and dramatic force, and a master of style; he is regarded as the founder of the language of the modern Yiddish intelligentsia.

Sholem Alechem (1859-1920), like the others, wrote on the basis of the Haskalah; but he shows no traces of it, and his earliest writings reveal no special tendency. Out of his creations there arises that sheer, bubbling laughter and that triumph over human sufferings that mark him among the world's greatest humorists. He depicts realistically and with a keen gift of observation; in many of his creations, such as Menahem Mendel, the representative of the activities of the Jewish *Luftmensch,* or the milk-dealer Tevye, the people's sage, he rises to symbolic heights. He embraces all classes and types of the life of the people, even the child, even the "world of Jewish animals," and presents it to the observer with a wealth of natural grace.

In addition to these three, there were a number of other writers, mostly of the next generation, who may be grouped as follows:

a) Lyric Poetry. Mark Warschawski (1848-1907)

sang simple songs in the style of folk poetry, and many of these have become veritable folk songs. Morris Wintschweski (b. 1856) championed the cause of Socialism in his poetry. Morris Rosenfeld (1862-1923) wrote social poems full of the pathos of suffering and of invective, national poems full of mourning and eternal faith, and poems of nature with melancholy tones. He is probably the first Yiddish lyricist who wrote individually and personally. Simon Samuel Frug (1860-1916) depicted nature in ringing verses, gave expression to national suffering in melancholy notes and at times indulged in satire. Hayim Tchemerinski (1862-1917) possessed a versatile talent and is best-known for his fables, with their strength of portrayal. Yehoash (Solomon Bloomgarden; 1871-1927) is regarded as the classic of the newer poetry. He was at the same time a poet of ideas and a painter, as well as a master of form who skilfully used all colors and tones. The rich creations of his profound nature include romantic ballads and popular legends, nature poems of cosmic feelings, Biblical and Talmudic themes together with satiric actuality, national poems and humorous verses, elegiac songs of love as well as philosophic poems and fables. He devoted the last decade of his life to a translation of the Bible. Abraham Liessen (b. 1872) writes of quiet longing as well as of the heroism of Jewish martyrs and social suffering. Hayim Nahman Bialik (1873-1934) produced both idylls and fiery denunciation. Abraham Reisen (b. 1875) sings of the sorrows of solitary souls, of love yearnings and of melancholy mourning. He also wrote naturalistic sketches, with a basis of quiet humor.

b) Fiction. Jacob Dinesohn (1865-1919), at first the complete Maskil, eventually wrote notable stories of a sentimental character. Mordecai Spektor (1858-1925) was a realistic depicter of environments and an exact observer. Judah Steinberg (1861-1908) wrote tales drawn from the life of the Hasidim. S. An-Ski (1863-1920) was a folklorist, the themes of whose works grew out of his collections of tales; his *Dybbuk* is credited with having produced the shift to mysticism. David Frischman (1865-1922) wrote not only feuilletons but also short stories with romantic and tender strokes. S. Libin (b. 1872), Israel Joseph Zevin (Tashrak; b. 1872) and David Nomberg (1876-1927) described the life of the Jewish immigrant in America. S. J. Onoychi (Zalman Isaac Aronsohn; b. 1876) is best-known through his Hasidic themes, but also described life in Jewish towns, the modern uncertain intellectual of Eastern Europe, and life and nature in Palestine. Jente Serdazki (b. 1879) devotes her pen to the mute tragedies of women and the yearning for happiness in love. Sholem Asch (b. 1880) is an epic writer of the historic scene, and has gained a place in modern English literature. Itsche Meir Wassenberg (b. 1881) depicts noble characters from the life of the people.

c) Drama. Jacob Gordin (1853-1909) raised the Yiddish theatre from its lowly estate; he wrote more than seventy plays and considerably elevated the taste of his audience. Leon Kobrin (b. 1872) followed in his footsteps, while David Pinski (b. 1872) has written problem plays dealing with individuals and the people that are the most important dramas of modern

Hebrew literature. Mark Arnstein (b. 1879) won fame through dramas and comedies. A. Waiter (Isaac Meir Devenishki; 1879-1919) gave expression to the spiritual unrest of the modern East European intelligentsia, and its desire for a complete Judaism. Perez Hirschbein (b. 1880) dealt successively with the realism of suffering, symbolic pieces, people's drama, the idyllic life of the Jewish farmer and the discussion of Jewish problems. Leib Bassein (Leon Elbe; 1879-1929) described immigrants who could not adapt themselves to American materialism; he wrote charming stories about children.   Salomo Birnbaum.

III. The Twentieth Century. 1. Introduction.

Yiddish literature of the 20th cent. has found its expression in a series of developments resulting directly from Jewish historic realities. Although it has enjoyed an independent life in each country in Europe and America, leading to diverse literatures, often diametrically opposed, it is noteworthy that it has everywhere exhibited the same general influences and tendencies. The latter may be conveniently classified into the following movements: impressionism (1906-17); expressionism (1917-25); traditionalism (1925-42).

The romanticism which tinged the new impressionism was already discernible in the 19th cent. period of realism, especially in the writings of three groups: Mendele Moicher Sforim, Sholem Aleichem and Isaac Loeb Peretz; David Pinski (who is in a category by himself); Abraham Reisen, H. D. Nomberg and Sholem Asch. Thus the "Massoes Binyomin Hashlishi" of Mendele has flashes of symbolism; Peretz' tales, *Folkstimleche Geshichtn,* and his Hasidic stories display pure romanticism; Sholem Aleichem's *Menachem Mendl* points to an impressionistic portraiture; Pinski's later symbolism of his "Berg Shteiger" was visible in his earlier works; Sholem Asch wrote idyllic descriptions of the small town. These romantic streaks reflect hopes and promises of a more brilliant future which were then stirring various Jewish groups—the rising labor movement with its dreams of freedom and social justice, the awakened national aspirations and hope in a national reconstruction. There was a similar tendency in the United States, where such poets as Wintchevsky, Morris Rosenfeld, David Edelstadt and Joseph Bovshover, and such prose writers as Leon Kobrin, Z. Libin, M. Adelshleger and Z. Levin, expressed not only burning despair, but great faith in the future. Abraham Liessin and Yehoash were also romanticists, each in his own fashion. The poets Yankev Adler, H. Rosenblatt, and Joel Slonim, and the novelist M. J. Haimovitch showed traces of romantic elements that characterized the impressionist poetry which succeeded them.

2. Impressionism.

Impressionism, a modern form of romanticism founded upon individualism and subjectivism and stressing a free and indirect method of expression, appeared in Yiddish literature simultaneously in three countries: in Russia (also part of Poland), in Galicia, and in the United States. In each it displayed the same psychological pattern and esthetic aspects. Each was influenced by contemporary impressionism in Europe; in Poland and Galicia, by the "Mloda Polska" group; in Russia, by the Russian symbolists; in both by German impressionism and its forerunner, the poet Heinrich Heine.

a. Russia. An additional factor in Russia was the romantic glow of revolutionary and nationalist movements and, to a lesser degree, the newly discovered urbanism of the proletarianized and nationally-conscious Jewish masses, from whom most of the writers came. The failure of the first Russian revolution (1905), which was drowned in the blood of the pogroms, led to nihilism and defeatist resignation, in place of glowing romanticism. Subjectivism was nurtured, creating that nebulous depth which quelled all vigor and replaced it by abstraction; the poets no longer described active expressions and feelings, but rather a yearning for these, or else merely moods.

Although many of the writers of that period began as realists, their realism was modified by a subjective approach. Thus Yoine Rosenfeld devoted much space to erotic and psychopathological analyses; Perez Hirschbein turned to symbolism; the novelist Lamed Shapiro stressed the extraordinary and the gruesome. Even I. M. Weissenberg, who introduced naturalism into modern Yiddish literature, expressed, especially in his stories of poverty-stricken Jews, earthy animal instincts, subjectivism and gross generalizations, which permitted the artist to paint everything in broad, sweeping strokes.

As in all European literature, Yiddish impressionism displayed a variety of nuances. David Einhorn, Z. Segalovitch, Menachem (Boraisha), B. Lapin, Daniel Charney, Leib Neidus, Mark Schweid and A. Almi (Sheps) among the poets; S. J. Onoychi (Zalman Isaac Aronsohn), Lipman-Levin, Joel Mastboim, I. Katzenelson, Z. Shneor, Moishe Taitch, the belated Nihilist Reb Mordchele (Tchemerinski), M. Stavsky, Hershele, Efraim Kaganovsky, Zvi Hirshkan, David Bergelson, Der Nistor, among the novelists and dramatists—each in his own way expressed the morbid mood resulting from unsuccessful revolution. A typical expression of this mood appears in A. Waiter's dramas, in which the repentant intellectual advocates a return to piety.

Thus Russian Yiddish impressionism vacillated between hope and despair, irresolution and dependence. Yet the Yiddish impressionists were not completely impotent; they remained on the whole social-minded, despite their defeatist attitude and their exaggerated individualistic tendencies. During this period there appeared S. Niger, who became the most prominent Jewish critic.

b. United States. The specific special factors in developing Yiddish impressionism in the United States were Jewish immigrant life in the new country, its incompatibility with its surroundings and all the resulting psychological complexities. The turmoil and chaos of the new life, its primitiveness, its economic and cultural poverty, the tragedy of being uprooted and transplanted—disappointed and even repelled the dazed romanticists and subjective esthetes. They felt lost, suddenly alone and superfluous in the great metropolis, New York. Their feeling of being strangers strengthened their defeatism and resignation, caused them to exaggerate their dejected individualism, and to retreat to a world of private illusions.

The weary, quiet flow of their poetry, the minor moods of joy and sorrow, are replete with a misty, diffused indefiniteness. Yet there are other forms of this subjectivism. An indirect method of expression and an exaggerated, intense subjectivism are found in all the poetry of that group known as "Die Yunge." The quick tempo and bluster of M. L. Halpern spring from the same exaggerated subjectivism as the excessive calm of Rolnik. The indefatigability and impetuous will of H. Leivick are no less subjective than the weary etherealness of Mani Leib, the romantic preciosity of Z. Landau, or the imagist resignation of R. Iceland. These poets created a new literary movement because, although their temperaments were different, their art approach and their methods were essentially alike.

The Yiddish impressionists in the United States can be roughly divided into two groups. The first are devoted to "art for art's sake," sensual, private, far removed from any problem that might be turned into thematic material; they include J. Rolnik, Zisho Landau, Mani Leib, R. Iceland, A. M. Dillon and the novelist A. Raboy. The second react to problems of immediate actuality; among them are M. L. Halpern, H. Leivick, and to some extent I. I. Schwartz and Moishe Nadir, as well as the novelist J. Opatoshu. Of the latter group, the novelist Dovid Ignatoff was the most active; he fought for the recognition of the "Yunge" and of their literary school in *Shriftn,* the chapbooks which he edited.

c. The Synthesists. The synthesists were a group of writers, not formally allied, but sufficiently alike in artistic concepts to form a group, which bridged the gap between impressionism and the later expressionism. Among them were M. Bassin, I. Berger, M. Perlmutter of the earlier period, and of the later, E. Auerbach, B. I. Bialistotsky, Naftoli Gross, Z. Weinper, A. Nissenson, R. Ludwig (in his earlier writings), Nochum Yud, I. I. Siegal and A. Lutzky. Although they discarded the "swooning romanticism" and "grey monotony" of the impressionists, they sought to express an other-worldliness in their poetry. The further these poets were removed from impressionism, the more weighty and concrete their art became, the less they stressed "sweet singing," the more they approached realism, social motives, and problems.

d. Galicia. The Galician impressionists did not have to endure the catastrophe of their counterparts in Russia, nor the uprooted immigrant life of those in the United States. They were better able to nurture their art on the folk idiom, to render their writing more abstract and idyllic; yet in general their poetry had a sadder note than that of their brother poets. Among the group known as "Young Galicia" were S. J. Imber, Yankev Mestel, M. Chmelnitzky and, later, Dovid Koenigsberg.

e. Achievements of the Impressionists. It was characteristic of the impressionists that they did not subordinate their art to social or utilitarian ends, but emphasized its esthetic purpose. Their search for new forms and the variety of their methods added subtleties to the language and refined Yiddish as an art vehicle. A wider range of themes and problems came into usage. The intensified subjectivism stimulated sensuality and the use of the ego motive.

This course of development stimulated the production of the novel and the drama. During this period the essay made great progress (Chaim Zhitlovsky,

David Frischman, Hillel Zeitlin, N. Birnbaum, N. Sirkin, B. Hoffman, A. Coralnik, Der Lebediker, Chaim Greenberg); literary and theatrical criticism flourished (Baal Machshoves, S. Niger, A. Mukdoni, Joel Enteen, B. Rivkin, Hillel Rogoff, Chaim Lieberman, Kalmen Marmor, M. Olgin, A. Almi, Z. Reisen, I. Schipper, J. Shatzky, I. Tzinberg); scientific analyses took their place in Yiddish literature (J. Lestschinsky, Ber Baranov, H. D. Hurvitz, L. Hersh, Itzchok Isaac Hurwitz, K. Fornberg), as also did philology and folklore (Z. Reisen, Z. Kalmanowitsch, N. Prilutzki and Judah A. Joffe).

3. Expressionism. The first World War and the Russian Revolution changed the entire outlook of Yiddish literature. The stability of the "old home," with its staid and steady ties, became a thing of the past, and was replaced by a new psychological approach, a new attitude toward one's-self and the world. A stranded and thwarted generation was endeavoring to find its bearings, to reestablish its identity upon a new foundation in the midst of chaos and destruction. The change manifested itself almost at the same time in the three countries where Yiddish literature persevered: in Poland (including Galicia), in Russia, and in the United States.

a. Poland. Utter disappointment in the world and unmitigated despair found expression in the works of the group known as "Chaliastre." The key-note of their works was "horror." Influenced by German expressionism and Russian cubo-futurism, they exalted heedless disruption and sought "the unknown" as a starting point from which to create a "new" and just world. This approach was especially evident in the work of those poets who lacked a firm foundation of cultural traditions: Uri Zvi Greenberg, Peretz Markish and Meilech Ravitch, whose chaotic verse scoffed at almost everything and jeered at esthetics and lyricism. Aaron Zeitlin was the one exception, for he had a heritage of culture and was deeply imbued with the classical traditions; this mystic poet sought to continue the past into the future, albeit according to expressionist concepts. The same tendency was found in the post-impressionist Moishe Kulbak, who later identified himself with Soviet Yiddish literature.

In prose an unadorned and deformed naturalism persisted. Primitiveness, brutality, abysmal darkness, prevailed in Oizer Warshavsky's novel, *Shmuglars,* in the short stories of A. M. Fuchs, in the works of S. Harontchik, as well as in the earlier novels of I. J. Singer.

Despite the most difficult conditions in Poland, such as the "zoological" anti-Semitism of the government and dire poverty and hunger, Yiddish expressionism maintained a constructive creativeness. Some of the older writers of the previous period, as well as younger writers who arrived upon the literary scene after the War, made significant contributions to Yiddish literature. Among them were: the poets and dramatists A. Zeitlin, Moishe Kulbak, M. Broderson, B. Horowitz, I. Shtern and Kadye Maladowsky; the novelists and short story writers I. J. Singer, I. I. Trunk, Alter Katzizne, J. Perle, A. Zeitlin, S. Berlinsky, M. Burshtein, I. Bashevis and H. L. Zhitnitzky; the literary historians and critics, the folklorists and philologists M. Weinreich, Max Erik, I. I. Trunk, Z. Reisen, Z.

Kalmanowitch, N. Maizel, M. Weichert, I. Rappaport, M. Shalit, S. Lehman and P. Graubard. The great activity of the publishing houses, the numerous and varied newspapers and magazines, were evidence of the pulsating and intensive literary life which persisted until it was crushed by the Nazi invasion.

b. Soviet Union. The four years of the first World War and the civil wars that followed in Russia brought devastation to the Jewish masses in Russia, especially in such battlegrounds as White Russia and the Ukraine. Under these conditions Yiddish literature completely abandoned both the impressionism of Bergelson and the primitive symbolism of Der Nistor. In their two chapbooks, which they called *Eigns,* these writers introduced a group of lyricists whose poetry definitely exhibited a new approach, such as prevailed in Soviet Yiddish literature until 1925 (when the Moscow magazine, *Shtrom,* ceased publication). This group of poets included Osher Shwartzman, Dovid Hofstein, Leib Kwitko, Peretz Markish, L. Reznik, the poet and critic I. Dobrushin, and the symbolic dramatist Benish Shteiman, who perished by a Denikin bomb.

Torn between the horrors of the bloody pogroms, which threatened completely to destroy the Jewish masses, and the revolutionary upheaval, which they hoped would bring salvation, this group struggled with esthetic, national and revolutionary ideals. Osher Shwartzman's voluntary enlistment in the Red Army, his oath ("And I shall not return again, not before I have heard the word of salvation, of complete salvation!"), and his tragic death upon the battlefield— all held a symbolic significance for the writers of this expressionist group. The chief themes of Soviet Yiddish literature of this period were the Civil War, the successful outcome of the October Revolution, and the pogrom disasters. In this optimistic atmosphere of faith in the Revolution, the course which Yiddish literature pursued was not from "horror" to disruption, as in Poland, but from "horror" to activism. This activism was clearly reflected in the works of Hofstein, Markish, Kwitko, Kushnirov, Reznik, E. Fininberg and Chashtchevatzky. Because of the instability of the period, its entire literature consisted of poetry.

c. United States. While the Yiddish writers of the United States were aware both of the catastrophic effects of the War and pogroms and of the promise of the Russian revolution, these were too far removed from them to affect them directly; they displayed neither the disruption of the Polish group nor the optimism of the Soviet writers. The keynote of expressionism in the United States was introspectivism or "Insichism" (so-called from the *In Sich* anthology and magazine, published in 1920). The refraction of the outer world through the prism of the individual (*sich*) contained both the "horrible" and the optimistic; it presented a complete view of life itself. The better to clarify the existing chaos of the period, these poets sought to express the world through a kaleidoscopic outlook. They traversed a course from chaos to a state of variegation, from a single phase to many facets, from direct description to significant allusions, suggestions or associations, from monotonous verse forms to free verse. Although their poetry had already revealed new ideas and a new content in previous years, the Insichists first appeared as a definite literary movement in 1920, when the above-mentioned anthology carried a manifesto signed by Y. Gladshtein, A. Leyeless and N. B. Minkoff, the editors; its contributors, besides these three, included M. Afranel, Al Gurye, Bernard Lewis, Ruven Ludwig and Yankev Stodolsky. Their magazine, *Insich,* which appeared intermittently for about twenty years, printed the verse of Anna Margolin, Michl Licht, B. Alkwit, Zilye Drapkin, S. Liev, Aaron Kurtz, and, later, A. Weissman. Somewhat in accord with the general tendencies of the introspectivists—either by direct influence or contact with their writings—were the following poets: E. Greenberg, Alef Katz, L. Feinberg, I. Goichberg, Esther Shumiatcher, A. Esselin, Mattes Deitch, Shloime Shwartz, L. Kalushiner, Leivi Goldberg. To this period, although not closely connected with any group, belong the novelists Boruch Glassman, Sh. Miller, L. Chanukoff, B. Ressler, and, quite remotely, B. Demblin.

d. Achievements of the Expressionists. Expressionism gave rise to the development of hitherto unexplored methods and forms, especially through its adoption of free verse (in the United States), of a rhythmic poetry and irregular lines (in Russia and Poland). The movement undoubtedly freed Yiddish literature, especially poetry, from stilted and stereotyped word associations; nor was any theme debarred as unacceptable. As a result of the newly introduced imagism and the use of nuances, subtle associations, references and allusions (especially in the case of the Insichists) their poetic lexicon gained new words, formations, phrases and cadences. Urbanism was underscored as a new art feeling. Their penetrating emotionalism did not merely express moods; it sought to delve deeper and analyze the basic feelings beneath. Their intensified search did not rest content with achieving a perceptual synthesis (the impression) but endeavored to analyze the entire range of the prismatic processes describing the inner life of the ego, as a reflection of the outer world. Although their methods and approach were subjective, they essayed to merge social and individual realities in an art synthesis.

4. **Traditionalism.** As the result of the efforts of the expressionists, some sort of stability was achieved despite the disruptive occurrences of the past and the still difficult problems of the present. A consolidation of social and of cultural forces had been achieved; the world-spectacle had assumed more definite and distinguishable contours. Yiddish writers attained greater profundity and maturity in their work. Yiddish literature began, as it were, to retrace its steps, to rediscover conservatism; this traditionalism was expressed not in the writings of those who newly arrived on the literary scene, but also in the evolution of the writers of earlier decades.

Traditionalism must not be construed as a return to petrified, dogmatically accepted concepts, but rather as a quest to go back to the fundamentals, to the stability and orderliness that existed long before the first World War. It might not be possible to restore that stability altogether, since the impress made by new experiences had been too great; but the will to be sound, moderate and concrete made itself felt in every achievement, in every literary success or failure. Almost every writer of the period, each in his own manner, in accordance with his own experiences or temperament, sought to revaluate a definite course of the past and to continue its traditional pattern. Though on the surface this tendency might seem to appear reactionary, it was in reality a step forward, for writers did not unconditionally accept the works of the past and their art concepts. The renewed interest in the past signified a rebirth of the old, modified by a modern coloring. Because of this dualism—conservative art concepts modified by new, though not too easily discernible, patterns—it is difficult to determine definite tendencies in this broader movement toward traditionalism. However, the movement may roughly be divided into the following: modern classicism, proletarianism, lyric realism, post-impressionism and neo-romanticism. It is not always easy to differentiate between these various tendencies, as some writers are under the simultaneous influence of several of these tendencies, while others fluctuate from one tendency to another.

Hitlerism was a strong factor in impelling writers to examine their heritage, to seek out some line of continuity. There were also characteristic modifications in each center, although the tendencies mentioned above appear in all. This is especially true of Yiddish literature in the Soviet Union. The rise of proletarianism, in turn, influenced authors living in other countries (the United States, Poland, Argentina, Canada, Lithuania, Mexico and Roumania) who were either leftist in politics or inclined toward realism. While Insichism exerted its influence upon "Yung Vilno" and many poets of other lands, post-impressionism manifested itself in Galicia and in the United States.

a. Soviet Union. When the magazine *Shtrom* ceased to appear (1925), its contributors divided into two groups. The one, that of the "October" writers, published *Nei Erd;* the other, represented by the Jewish seetion of Mopp (Moscow Association of Proletarian Writers), published *Oktiabr.* This latter group earnestly endeavored to free itself of its "bourgeois past" and to get "into stride." The two groups gradually disappeared as such and a new period of socialist realism and of folkism was ushered in. Yet the tendential differences of the two groups was still apparent. The *Nei Erd* group passed through a period of expressionism, or activism. Under the influence of the first revolutionary, and later of Soviet realism, they sought to discipline their artistic fervor, which had previously expressed agitation, national anguish and revolutionary pathos. Because of this their work reflected artistic contemplation and tended in style toward classical solidity, orderliness and sedateness. This proclivity toward classicism is discernible in the works of the most important Soviet Yiddish poet, David Hofstein. It gradually manifested itself in the later works of Peretz Markish, as well as in those of Kwitko, Reznik, S. Halkin, Z. Akselrod, S. Driz, Cholodenko, Choral and Chenkino.

This tendency to the sedate and the orderly led to the reappearance of Yiddish prose writing, which could not function during the previous years of turbulence. Such novelists as M. Daniel, Orland, D. Volkenstein, and Motte Lurye now came to the fore; to their number must be added the research writers and critics I. Dobrushin, Nochum Auslander, M. Wiener (especially during his earlier period), who were also poets, dramatists and novelists.

The more influential and official group of writers were organized in the Yiddish section of the General Soviet Association of Proletarian Writers. These were almost exclusively the proletarian and communist writers who had been reared during the years of the Revolution and had never experienced the painful adjustments of the earlier group. The Yiddish sections of Mopp (Moscow Association of Proletarian Writers), of Vussp (Ukrainian Association of Proletarian Writers) and Belapp (White Russian Association of Proletarian Writers) were part of the General Association. Mopp, however, included several pre-revolutionary writers. Its members included A. Kushnirov, S. Godiner, S. Persov, I. Yoffe (one of the oldest Yiddish workers' poets), A. Veviorke, M. Taitch (the former impressionist), S. Rossin, I. Rives, M. Chashtchevatzky, I. Robin, E. Gordon, N. Lurye, I. Lerman, B. Olevsky, I. Zeldin, N. Tchernis, Hartzman and Helmond.

Itzik Feffer, E. Fininberg, M. Alberton, A. Abtchuk, Shkarovsky, A. Kahan, Aronsky, M. Shapiro, Velednitzky, Chane Levin, Piatigorskaya, Pinchevsky, Kotliar, Sito, Shturman, Veinerman and the critics S. Zhukovsky, Mizhritizky and the late Henech Kozakevich, as well as Chaim Gildin, David Hofstein and Itzik Kipnis were at one time or another members of such sections of Vussp and Belapp.

Since White Russia did not become a center of Yiddish literature until after the October Revolution, almost none of its writers were pre-revolutionary. The Belapp group included such Yiddish writers as B. Orshansky, Izzi Charik, Dolgopolsky, M. Lifshitz, I. Gorelik, S. Gorelik, M. Taif, I. Goldman, Lasker, Vitenzon, Gordon, Kamenetzky, E. Kahan, A. Kahan, Maizel, Savikowsky, the critic Duneitz, and Uri Finkel. This exclusively proletarian stamp denoted neo-realism. Its groundwork had been laid by the social poets of the 1880's and 1890's, such as Vintchevsky, Edelstadt, Bovshover, and, in part, Morris Rosenfeld; the proletarian writers also imitated the direct approach, simplicity of phrase and idiom of Abraham Reisen. Their new realism displayed great optimism and a freedom of style, in contrast to the social poets of the past, although they had gained from the literary experience of their forerunners and had learned from them the use of revolutionary pathos.

With the advent of socialist realism, the sharp line of demarcation between the two groups of Yiddish Soviet writers disappeared. The chief point of interest was no longer style and image, but the building up of socialism. Up to the time of Hitler's invasion of Russia (1941) all Yiddish writers there were regarded as Soviet writers, labels and "isms" having vanished from the literary horizon.

b. Poland. There being no pressure from without, no party influence or political and social constraints, traditionalism in Poland followed various directions. Aaron Zeitlin, for instance, is the most important representative of the tendency toward neo-classicism, while Moishe Kulbak, another neo-classicist (who later became a Soviet writer), was inclined to imitate the impressionistic style of David Einhorn. I. I. Trunk, on the other hand, effected a synthesis of impressionism and modern classicism. I. J. Singer, after an early stage of expressionism, and I. Bashevis became neo-realists

with a semi-classic style. A cubo-constructivist was the poetess Dvoire Vogel.

Another group of writers stressed proletarianism. Their realistic form and style followed that of their Soviet compeers, but the optimism of the latter was replaced by a depiction of the intense horrors, the hunger and privation of the Polish Jewish masses, painted in morbid colors. Among this group were: the former expressionist Joseph Kirman, Kalmen Liss, Binem Heller, M. Shulstein, Kadie Molodorska, Rochl Korn, Ashendorf, Shudrich, Bomze, Shnaper, L. Olitzky, Boruch Olitzky, and Sh. Zaromb. Joseph Rubinstein's realism was essentially that of a painter rather than that of a proletarian writer.

The neo-romantic tendency had two trends: romanticism per se and religious romanticism. To the first trend belong: Moishe Shimell, Ptashkin, and M. L. Fuchs; to the second trend belong the former expressionist Israel Shtern, Israel Emiot, Chaim Semiatstzky, and J. Lehrer. The urge to return to religious poetry was indicated by Aaron Zeitlin.

"Yung Vilno" is the title given to a rather heterogenous body of writers. It is a school of writing in search of stability and discipline, displaying a variety of influences, of which Insichism seems to have been the strongest. The fact that these youthful writers have experienced from earliest childhood the grim and chaotic conditions of Polish Jewish life has left its impress upon their art. Among the "Yung Vilno" group are: Moishe Levin, Shimshen Kahan, Sh. Katcherginski (Ch. Shmerke), Chaim Grade, Peretz Miranski, A. Wogler, A. Suckever, and Leizer Wolf.

c. United States. The urge to rediscover the literary traditions of the past followed the same general course in the United States as in Poland; it took the directions of modern classicism, neo-impressionism and proletarianism. It is also noteworthy that religious and folkistic tendencies, which have persisted since Hitler's rise to power and are virtually a form of neo-romanticism, were evidenced in the work of artists having a natural predisposition to impressionism.

The tendency toward modern classicism was clearly indicated in 1925 by a group of writers some of whom had been directly associated with Insichism (for example, N. B. Minkoff), others of whom had been indirectly associated with it (such as Michl Licht) and still others who had never been Insichists (Hasye Cooperman). Their magazines, *1925, 1926, Kern, Insich* (of which they printed two issues in 1930) and even *Bodn* (which was published several years later), were evidence of a complete departure from Insichism, its clichés, its generalizations (the residual effects of impressionism) and its diffused and redundant style. While Insichist poetry had stressed personifications, the use of attributes and the allegory, these neo-classicists aspired to symbolism, its conciseness of form and its significant discipline. S. Liev, Aaron Kurtz (who later became one of the foremost proletarian writers), Yankev Stodolsky, and, for some time, I. A. Weissman, were identified with this movement.

A return to romanticism was evidenced in the works which were printed in the magazine *Feiln.* This tendency was represented by the poet and critic A. Tabachnik, by Abba Shtolzenberg, Meier Shtiker and others. Their verse reflected the impressionism of the "Yunge." While Tabachnik and Shtiker fused their impressionism with lyric realism, Shtolzenberg introduced the element of folklore. Eliezer Greenberg was somewhat influenced by Insichism, but gave it a realistic slant; while I. Teller, also adhering to this style of poetry, was inclined toward the use of psychologism. The magazine *Leim un Tzigl* introduced the following writers: Berish Weinshtein, I. L. Teller, and S. Maltz. Lyric realism is clearly discernible in the short stories of Chaim Pett, Metzker and Fershleiser.

The new realism is an integral part of proletarian writing in the Yiddish literature of the United States. These American members of the Yiddish "Proletpen" were strongly influenced by the Soviet Yiddish writers; they included such poets as Aaron Kurtz, A. Suhl, Martin Birnboim, I. Greenshpan, L. Miller, L. Dinski, D. Seltzer, Ber Green (A. Prince), B. Fenster, B. Friedman, Meinke Katz, I. E. Rontch, and Moishe Shifris, and the following prose writers: Leo Yurman, Chaver Paver, L. Chanukoff, Chaim Margoles-Davidson, Leib Sobrin, David Kasher, and S. Deiksel.

5. Other Countries. The general tendencies and movements of Yiddish literature, as evidenced in the larger centers of Poland, Russia and the United States, have left their impress also on the groups in other countries, which are briefly discussed below.

a. Roumania. The sentimental romanticism of such troubadours as Wölwel Zbarazer, of the Broder singers and of Abraham Goldfaden (founder of the Yiddish theatre) has reverberated in all the modern Roumanian writers, including the most recent, notwithstanding the changes that have evolved in several generations of poets and prose writers. At times a single writer represented an entire generation, as for instance the classical and folkistic poet and master of fables Eliezer Steinberg, the impressionist I. Gropper, and the expressionists Yankev Sternberg and Moishe Altman.

The direction toward traditionalism followed the courses of neo-romanticism and neo-realism. Mingling impressionistic tendencies with folkism and sentimental zest, neo-romanticism was reflected in the verse of Itsig Manger and of his followers, Chaim Robertson, Efraim Roitman, M. Freed and Simche Schwartz. Neo-realism was colored by the folk idiom and was directly affected by Yiddish Soviet literature. The Yiddish proletarian writers of Roumania include Motl Saktzier, Hertz Rivkin, Yosl Lerner, Hersh-Leib Karzhber, Yosef Trachtenberg, B. Shnabl, Kubi Vohl, Jehiel Shreibman and the young critic Yankl Yakir.

The essayist Shloime Bickl, who represents a synthesis of Jewish traditionalism and secular universalism, steered his course midway between expressionism and neo-classicism. Among the traditionalists must also be added the name of B. Tutchinsky, although he leans strongly toward impressionistic analysis.

b. Argentina. Yiddish literature has manifested some special trends due to specifically local problems, but has followed the same general pattern. Before the first World War it was realistic, though romantic in some respects, at the time when impressionism was in full sway in other centers of Yiddish literature. Its realism was not vigorous and was inspired by the style of the great writer of memoirs, Mordche Alperson, dean of organized Yiddish literature in Argentina.

Israel Helfman, Noyach Vital, Abba Kliger, Boruch Bendersky and M. Frumkin were primitive impressionists, quasi-realistic and sentimental. Moishe Pintchevsky, the most impetuous and energetic among Argentine writers, was an impressionist with a proclivity toward realism; he left later for the Soviet Union.

The second stage, from the close of the War to about 1930, exhibited the three phases of estheticism (a merging of impressionism with expressionism), proletarian placard-poetry and folkistic impressionism. Yankev Eisenstein, Yankev Streicher, Avrohom Moshkowitch, Avrohom Zeid, Shmuel Glazer (born in Argentina), L. Meilach, M. D. Gieser, H. Blaustein (later in the Soviet Union), Itchok Blumstein, Yankev Botoshansky, S. Rozhansky, H. Wolf, Z. Wasserzug, S. Freilach (Litman), A. Feierman, Avigdor Spritzer, N. Zucker, M. Meidanik, Yosef Rabinovitch, A. A. Fisher, I. L. Goldberg, A. Margolin, S. Granievich, B. Z. Feigin, Efraim Goldberg, Moishe Konstantinovsky, Menashe Konstantinovsky, the fable writer C. I. Farber, as well as S. Wasserman and Pinchos Bizberg, represent this second period.

The third period marks a return to stability; the stormy writers of the earlier period have assumed a quieter tempo, their mood is more sedate, often even despondent, and there are trends indicating a return to the traditional styles. Most of the writers of this period came to Argentina at an early age and thus had their entire careers in that country. Among this group are Berl Greenberg, S. Suskowitch, Moishe Koifman, Falik Lerner, Shmul Fiert, Zelig Mazur, B. Epstein and Yardenya Fein (the two last born in Argentina); those who began their careers in other countries include Avigdor Shpritzer, Kohos Kliger, Sore Birnboim, Shmuel Tzesler, Izi Shaffer, Mimi Pinzon, Avrohom Koval, Golde Krimer, A. I. Zakusky, F. Katovsky, Aaron Weitzman, Elye Verblun and Kalmen Farber.

It is interesting to note that in this most recent period Argentine Yiddish literature has been outstanding in its books for children.

c. Palestine. There is a small group of Yiddish authors among the dreamers and workers in the new Jewish center. They are an integral part of the work of reconstruction there, and their prose and poetry are devoted to its problems. Their writing is uniquely in harmony with Palestinian life, and they have described the spirit of the Halutzim. Nevertheless they display traces of the general tendencies, from expressionism to traditionalism. Among them are the poets Yosef Papiernikov, Arieh Shomri, Avrohom Lev, I. Z. Shargel and Yankev Shtal, and the prose writers S. Izban (later in New York city), A. Rives, I. Heiblum and L. Chein.

d. Mexico. Although the Jewish settlement in Mexico is very young, it has made great progress in Yiddish cultural endeavors. Besides its newspapers and literary magazines, it has produced books which are not only representative of the modern era, but also of the spirit of the environment, the very color and rhythm of Mexico. Among the best-known Yiddish writers in Mexico are the poets Yankev Glantz and Itzchok Berliner, the prose writers M. Korona and B. Rubinstein, and the critic and essayist Solomon Cahan (later in the United States).

This sketch of the history and progress of Yiddish literature from the earliest times to the present must necessarily touch only briefly on the work of hundreds of authors. The emphasis here has been on trends and groupings. Details of the subject matter and style of individual Yiddish writers will be found in their biographies.

N. B. MINKOFF.

Lit.: Niger, S., "New Trends in Post-War Yiddish Literature," *Jewish Social Studies,* vol. i, No. 3 (July, 1939) 337-58.

LITHUANIA, one of the succession states of the Russian Empire. Lithuanian independence was formally proclaimed on February 16, 1918. The definitive frontiers of the new state comprised the former Russian province of Kovno (Kaunas), the greater part of the province of Suwalki, parts of the provinces of Vilna (Vilnius) and Courland (Kurland), and the district of Memel. Within these territories (exclusive of the city of Vilna) there lived in 1897 close to 257,000 Jews, or 12.9 per cent of the total population. Emigration overseas and forced evacuations during the first World War reduced the number of Jews in that area by more than 100,000. According to the census of 1923 —the latest available official figures—the Jewish population numbered 153,743, or 7.6 per cent of the total population of 2,028,971. The majority of Jews lived in small towns. The largest Jewish communities were: Kaunas (25,044); Panevezys (6,845); Siauliai, or Shavli (5,335). Later estimates placed the number of Jews in Lithuania at the outbreak of the second World War in September, 1939, at about 155,000, exclusive of the Memel district, with an estimated Jewish population of 3,000.

Developments during the early years of Lithuanian independence augured well for the future of the Jews in the new republic. The memories of a common struggle against Czarist oppression, the intensive campaign carried on by Lithuanian Jews at home and abroad on behalf of the new state, as well as their defense of Lithuania's right to Vilna, seized by Poland in 1920, created an atmosphere of mutual confidence and understanding which was reflected in official policy. On August 5, 1919, the Lithuanian peace delegation in Paris, led by Professor Voldemaras, addressed a letter to the Committee of Jewish Delegations (Comité des Délégations Juives) in which the Jews were guaranteed proportional representation in the legislative bodies, full autonomy in their internal affairs, public legal recognition of their autonomous organs as well as their mother tongue and the right to a ministry of Jewish affairs in the cabinet. These rights were confirmed, in general terms, by the constitution of 1922, which guaranteed the rights of cultural autonomy to those of the national minorities which "formed a considerable proportion of the population." Thus, the Lithuanian government went beyond its international commitments to minorities contained in the Lithuanian declaration before the League of Nations on May 12, 1922.

Of all the minorities in Lithuania, the Jews alone succeeded in establishing a far-reaching autonomy based on local communities (Kehilloth) and a national council of these Kehilloth. A law promulgated on March 4, 1920, provided the legal basis for the existence of these communities. Its main characteristics were the establishment of a united Jewish community on a more than religious basis, which had charge of schooling, social work, health and the like, a democratic representation in the various communal bodies, and compulsory taxation of all Jews for the Jewish community. Although the law did not provide for a central body, the Jewish National Council, elected at the first National Assembly of Lithuanian Jews, received *de facto* recognition by the government.

All Lithuanian cabinets between December, 1918, and the middle of 1924 included a minister for Jewish affairs, although the constitution of 1922 failed to provide for such a ministry. The first Jewish minister was Dr. Wigodsky, who served in the first Lithuanian cabinet. He was succeeded, respectively, by Drs. M. Soloweitschik, J. Brutzkus and S. Rosenbaum. The last minister appointed without consultation of the Jewish community was Judge Friedman. Similarly, a cabinet decree of December 31, 1921, granted equality of status in the courts and administrative bodies to the languages of national minorities in localities where they constituted 20 per cent of the total population or over, which gave wide discretion to the use of Yiddish and Hebrew. The ministry of education included a special inspectorate for Jewish educational institutions.

The years 1919 to 1923 marked the high point in Jewish rights in Lithuania. In 1923 the Christian Democratic Party succeeded in obtaining a majority in the parliamentary elections and initiated an era of intense nationalism. Gradually the Jewish population lost many of the rights which it had won in 1919. The first Christian Democratic cabinet formed in 1924 no longer included a Jewish ministry, and thus established a precedent for the future. In the same year the government dissolved the Jewish National Council as well as the local Kehilloth as these existed since 1919 to 1920. By this act the government made the coordination of the Jewish community impossible and deprived it of the right to levy taxes. A law promulgated on June 4, 1924, restored the old Russian system of the strictly religous synagogue councils which, because of the protest of the Jewish population, were not elected until three years later. Thus Lithuania, one of the few states to grant national autonomy to the Jews, was the first to abolish the public legal character of the organization of the Jewish community. Under the pressure of circumstances, the early form of a united community was replaced by the creation of two central organizations: the Adath Israel for religious affairs, Ezra for social welfare activities.

The promise of parliamentary proportional representation made to the Jews in 1919 was never fulfilled. Whereas, in the first regular national elections to the second Sejm, the Jews were represented by seven deputies, in the elections of 1924, due to gerrymandering, they won only three seats. The same tendency obtained in the municipal elections, especially in the capital city of Kaunas, where a special election system reduced the proportion of Jews in the local administration. The position of the Yiddish language, too, declined. A persistent campaign, carried on in the summer of 1923 against Yiddish signs and placards and which continued for a year, culminated, on July 15, 1924, in orders issued by the provincial authorities forbidding signs and placards in Yiddish and in other minority languages. These orders were rescinded, but unofficially, two years later.

Of all the Jewish autonomous institutions, the Jewish school system alone was left intact. In 1923 there were 300 Hebrew and Yiddish elementary schools and twenty high schools throughout the country, and one teachers' seminary in Kaunas, with Hebrew as the predominating language of instruction. The school registration of 1924 to 1925 showed that 93 per cent of the Jewish children of school age attended Jewish public schools and that 78 per cent of all Jewish high school students were in Jewish high schools. In 1934 to 1935 only 79.6 per cent of the Jewish children of school age attended schools with Hebrew or Yiddish as the language of instruction. These schools were administered by the Tarbuth for the Zionists, the Yabneh for the Orthodox and the Folkslige for the Yiddishists. In addition, there were also several Yeshivas, including the renowned academies of Telz, Slobodka and Radin. All Jewish schools were maintained largely out of private funds as the state more and more curtailed its subsidies.

The internal political life of the Jews revolved mainly around the political groups and parties, including the various Zionist factions, the Agudath Israel and its several branches, the Mizrahi, and different labor groups. Lithuanian Jewry was known as culturally highly advanced, and was Hebraized to a very high degree. It supplied proportionately one of the highest percentages to the various pro-Palestine movements, especially the Halutz (pioneer) movement. Mostly of Orthodox and Zionist complexion, Lithuanian Jewry experienced little assimilation. Of the five daily Jewish newspapers in 1939, the *Yiddishe Shtimme* and *Hajntike Naies* were published by the Zionist Organization, *Dos Vort* by the People's Party, while the *Folksblatt* and *Oventblatt* were published under the auspices of the Jewish Education Association. Among the weeklies were the *Yiddishe Leben,* issued by the Youth Group of the Agudath Israel, and the non-partisan *Der Naie Veg.*

Among the various cultural institutions supported by the Jewish population may be mentioned the two theatres in Kaunas and a number of theatre groups in the provinces, and the Jewish Historical-Ethnographic Society in Lithuania.

The latest figures available regarding the occupational distribution of the Jews in Lithuania come from 1923. According to the census of that year, 6% of the Jewish population were engaged in agriculture. Of the Jews engaged in non-agricultural pursuits, less than one-third (31.9%) were in commerce, while almost one-fourth (22%) were in industry; the remainder were employed in public works (5.3%), communication and transportation (3%) and other occupations, including the liberal and learned professions, army, domestic service and unspecified (37%). Compared with their percentage of the population (7.6%) the Jews contributed over ten times their quota (77%) to commerce, three times their quota (21%) to industry, almost two and one-half times (18%) their quota to communication and transportation, and almost one-

quarter more (9%) than their quota to public works.

The economic situation of the Jews varied, naturally, with the rise or decline of the prosperity of the country. Nevertheless, the government-directed economic policy, beginning with the Agrarian Reform Law of 1924, frequently displayed anti-Jewish tendencies. The Compulsory Sunday Rest Law adopted in 1924 not only violated the guarantee of 1919 regarding the observance of the Sabbath, but also cut deeply into the economic position of the Jews. The growth of the cooperative movement, enjoying the aid of the government, undermined many Jewish commercial positions, especially in the smaller towns. On the other hand, with the growth of industry, the position of the Jews in this and in allied fields improved considerably. They also retained a strong foothold in the import trade, which to some extent compensated for their reduced position in the export trade. Insofar as public employment was concerned, the tendency was definitely towards the elimination of Jews.

As was the case in other Eastern European lands, the divergence in the social-economic character of the Jewish and non-Jewish populations in Lithuania was largely responsible for the rise of an anti-Semitic movement which boded ill for the future of the Jews. A new middle class was emerging, recruited mainly from the peasant population of the impoverished and overcrowded villages. This new class lent itself as a convenient instrument in the hands of the older commercial and professional classes of the non-Jewish population who exploited a natural process of urbanization to destroy the competition of Jews by means of anti-Semitism. In these circumstances anti-Semitism, too, was slowly but surely emerging as a political force. The most vociferous anti-Jewish group was the so-called Verslinkai Traders' and Artisans' Association. Under the pressure of Nazi propaganda, anti-Semitism threatened to assume a violent form. There was frequent talk in private as well as governmental circles of legislative measures directed against Jews and, in the case of the Society for the Prevention of Cruelty to Animals, these talks took concrete form in a proposal to abolish the Jewish form of ritual slaughtering of animals. On the whole, however, the government succeeded in stemming the tide of anti-Semitism and in preventing it from becoming a threat to the peace and security of the state.

The majority of the 3,000 Jews in the Memel district originated from Lithuania proper and composed the wealthiest Jewish community in the republic. With the rise of Nazism the Jews began to remove their business enterprises to Lithuania proper. This movement, however, was soon halted by the government lest it undermine the economy of the district. When the Nazis occupied Memel on March 15, 1939, many Jews had already left the city and the others opted for Lithuanian citizenship. Although they had suffered irreparably from the Nazi occupation, a number of Jews succeeded in salvaging a portion of their possessions through the German-Lithuanian agreement.

At the outbreak of the second World War, on September 1, 1939, Lithuania became one of the few countries of refuge for Jews and, after the military defeat of Poland, the last citadel of free Jewish life and culture in Eastern Europe. At the end of 1939

The Jewish quarter in Kaunas, Lithuania

the Polish Jewish refugees in Lithuania numbered 11,000, and included many notable rabbis and cultural and communal leaders who succeeded in establishing a Polish Jewry in exile by recreating many cultural institutions which were destroyed by the war in Poland. The appreciation of these facts charted the course of the Lithuanian-Jewish relations. On October 10, 1939, Lithuania and Russia ratified a mutual assistance pact under the terms of which the city and some of the region of Vilna were transferred to Lithuania. Thus this ancient city of Jewish learning had escaped for a brief period the fate of other cultural centers in Poland. Efforts were made to transplant Jewish institutions from Poland to Lithuania.

On June 15, 1940, Soviet Russian troops once again marched into the Baltic lands, this time to complete the occupation which they had begun in October, 1939. Lithuania, along with her sister states, was incorporated into the Soviet Union, and the Jews thenceforth shared the fate of their coreligionists in the rest of Russia.

In the early weeks of the Russo-German War, which broke out on June 22, 1941, Lithuania was conquered by the Nazi hordes, and the Jewish community met with the fate which befell their coreligionists in other parts of the continent occupied by the Nazis.

In May, 1942, reports of mass executions of Jews by Nazis in the Kaunas district reached the United States. In the five towns of Shavli, Troki, Novo-Vileika, Niemenchin and Eishyshok a total of 10,780 Jews were reported massacred by Nazi machine gunners, after they had been stripped of their clothing. In that month only 35,000 of the 70,000 Jews living in Vilna before the German occupation remained, and large numbers of Jews in the Kaunas ghetto were deported to ghettos and concentration camps outside of the city.

See also: POLAND; RUSSIA; VILNA.

MOSES MOSKOWITZ.

Lit.: "Review of the Year," *American Jewish Year Book,* vols. 32 (1930-31), 40 (1938-39), 41 (1939-40), 42 (1940-41); Kreppel, J., *Juden und Judentum von Heute* (1925); World Jewish Congress, *Rapports sur la situation des Juifs dans différents pays européens en 1938* (1939); Wischnitzer, Mark, *Die Juden in der Welt* (1935); Lazerson, Max M., "The Jewish Minorities in the Baltic Countries," *Jewish*

Social Studies, July, 1941; Macartney, C. A., *National States and National Minorities* (1934); *Yor Ein Yor Ois, Yorbuch Kalendar, 1939,* issued by the Jewish Historical-Ethnographic Society in Lithuania.

LITHUANIAN JEWS, FEDERATION OF, an organization founded in New York in 1937 for the purpose of bringing together Jews born in Lithuania and their descendants and of helping their brethren in the home country. The organization was first proposed by Frank Epstein, after a long visit in his home town in Lithuania; he succeeded in gathering around him, as founders, Dr. M. Sudarsky, B. L. Jaffe, Yuddle Mark, M. Chesler, H. Leibowitz, William Herman, D. Mathis, L. Smith, I. Krut, H. Fine, D. Levenson, and A. Shulman. The movement grew into a national organization with chapters not only in New York but also in Chicago, Cleveland, Detroit, Philadelphia, Boston and other cities, and including numerous *Landsmannschaften.* Large sums of money, as well as clothing and other supplies, have been sent to Lithuania in order to relieve the sufferings of the Jewish masses there, as well as to build and maintain nurseries, shelters, schools and homes for the aged.

In 1941 the officers of the organization were: Sidney Hillman, national honorary president; J. H. Jaffe, of New Jersey, vice-president; Elihu Fife, chairman of the board of directors; Frank Epstein, general secretary; Meyer M. Keilson, treasurer; Leon Shapiro, legal advisor.

FRANK EPSTEIN.

LITMAN, SIMON, economist, b. Odessa, Russia, 1873. He was educated at the Odessa Commercial College (A.B., 1892) and awarded honorary citizenship for his high scholarship. He came to the United States in 1893, but returned to Europe for a few years to continue his studies. He graduated from the École des Sciences Politiques of Paris in 1899, and in 1899 and 1900 he did post-graduate research at the University of Munich. In 1901 he received the degree of Doctor Juris Publici et Rerum Camerariarum from the University of Zurich.

In 1894 he served as an inspector and tabulator on the New York City Tenement House Commission,

Lucius N. Littauer

In 1902 he lectured at the École Russe des Hautes Études Sociales in Paris. He was an instructor in economics at the University of California from 1903 to 1908. From 1908 to 1910 he was associate in commerce at the University of Illinois, and in 1910 he became assistant professor of economics. In 1919 he was appointed professor, a position which he still held in 1942.

Litman was a prolific author. He wrote many articles on social and economic subjects, and a number of books, including: *Die Möglichkeit der Lohnfondstheorien* (1902); *Trade and Commerce* (1911); *Price Control in Great Britain and the United States* (1919); *Essentials of International Trade* (1923, revised ed., 1927). He was interested in Jewish affairs, and was a member of the American Jewish Historical Society.

LITTAUER, LUCIUS NATHAN, manufacturer, American Congressman, and philanthropist, b. Gloversville, N. Y., 1859. His father, a peddler, settled in Gloversville in 1850, when it was a village of only a hundred houses, and began to manufacture gloves. The son studied at Harvard University (A.B., 1878) and entered his father's business in 1878. In 1882 he succeeded his father as the owner.

Littauer was a member of Congress for five terms (1897-1907). When a bill, one of several attempting to restrict immigration, finally passed the House of Representatives in 1906, he succeeded in having an amendment adopted which admitted persons seeking refuge on religious or political grounds; the bill, however, did not become a law. Earlier, with Jacob H. Schiff, he brought the plight of the Roumanian Jews to the attention of Secretary of State John Hay who, as a result, issued a note (1902) to the signatories of the Treaty of Berlin denouncing the Roumanian treatment of the Jews.

But Littauer is famous chiefly for his philanthropies. In 1929 he gave more than a million dollars to the trustees of the Lucius N. Littauer Foundation in New York city for the welfare of mankind by aiding research in the causes, cure, and prevention of pneumonia and cancer, by helping Jewish communal activities, and by promoting better understanding among all men. By 1942 his gifts to this foundation amounted to more than three million dollars. He was the donor of more than two million dollars to Harvard University in 1935 for the establishment of its Graduate School of Public Administration, which offers training in public service. His interest in good government also led him to help in the endowment of the Graduate Faculty of Political and Social Science at the New School for Social Research in New York city.

He made many large gifts to hospitals and medical schools. For example: in 1926 he established the Nathan Littauer Stiftung, in memory of his father, in conjunction with the Jewish hospital of Breslau, Germany; in recognition of his gifts to the Saint Antoine hospital of Paris, France, he was awarded a medal of the department of hygiene and made a member of the Legion of Honor in 1929; he gave a new building in 1937 to the National Hospital for Speech Disorders (reorganized as the Lucius N. Littauer Institute for Speech Disorders) in New York city; at the end of 1941 he established a $250,000 research fund at the College of Medicine of New York University for fellowships in psychiatry and neurology.

Others of Littauer's gifts—of Jewish interest particularly—include: the establishment in 1925 of the Nathan Littauer professorship of Jewish literature and philosophy at Harvard University in honor of his father (Harry A. Wolfson was the first to hold the chair); the gift to Harvard in 1930 of 12,000 Hebrew books and manuscripts, collected by the Hebrew author and bibliophile, Ephraim Deinard, to which, in 1937, Littauer added more than 2,000 other rare Hebrew books; and the founding, in 1939, of the Institute of Interdenominational Studies at the Jewish Theological Seminary of America to promote a better understanding of Judaism among both Jews and Christians.

His native city of Gloversville was the object of many of Littauer's benefactions. In 1894 he built the Nathan Littauer Hospital in memory of his father, and his additions to the original building include the Harriet Littauer Home for Nurses in memory of his mother. In 1928 he built an extensive swimming pool for Gloversville. He also erected the Jewish Community Center Building, opened in 1930, and the American Legion Building. He gave the city of Fonda, N. Y., where one of his business enterprises was located, a recreation center in 1928. The citizens of Gloversville erected a statue of Littauer in 1929.

He was a regent of the University of the State of New York from 1912 to 1914. Hamilton College awarded him the honorary LL.D. degree. In 1937 the Jewish Theological Seminary of America awarded him an honorary degree (D.H.L.). In 1942 the Phi Epsilon Pi, national college social fraternity, conferred on him the national science award for making "the finest contribution to the essential Jewish life of America" in 1941.   CHARLES REZNIKOFF.

LITTEN, FRITZ JULIUS, professor of law, b. Elbing, Germany, 1873. Litten embraced Protestantism, and became lecturer at the University of Halle in 1903. In 1905 he was appointed professor of law at the University of Königsberg, and became an important personality, called "the uncrowned king of Eastern Prussia." He was a friend of the German crown prince, of Hindenburg, and of General von Blomberg. He was married to Irmgard Wüst, a descendant of a family of Protestant theologians, and had three sons who were intended for careers as teachers of law. But all of them frustrated their father's hopes.

The second son, HEINZ LITTEN (b. Königsberg, 1905), became a producer. The third son, REINHARD LITTEN (b. Königsberg, 1909), became an actor. But the eldest son, HANS LITTEN (b. Halle, 1903; d. in the Dachau concentration camp, 1938), troubled his father the most. He became a lawyer at Berlin and, from 1929 on, was prominent in conducting political trials. He pleaded the cause of many leftists, mostly communists. In May, 1931, he sued for damages on behalf of two workers who had been stabbed by Nazis of the ill-famed Storm Troop 33, then Adolf Hitler's favorites.

At Litten's request, Hitler was called as a witness and was cross-examined by Litten for two hours. Realizing Hitler's embarrassment, Litten drove him into making emphatic declarations, and then challenged him to square these declarations with contradictory declarations made by Hitler previously and with other declarations of Joseph Goebbels. This case stirred Hitler's wrath and his personal hatred of Litten. On the night of the Reichstag fire, Litten was arrested. In the concentration camp he was tortured. From the night of the Reichstag fire until her son's death in 1938, Litten's mother struggled desperately to ameliorate his fate. But all intervention on the part of friends was in vain. According to the National Socialist minister Freisler, "Hitler grew purple in the face when he heard Litten's name."

Lit.: Litten, Irmgard, *Beyond Tears* (1940).

LITTLE ROCK, capital of the State of Arkansas and seat of the oldest, largest and most important Jewish community in the State. The population of Greater Little Rock, according to the 1940 census, was 109,261, of whom some 1,850 (in 1942) were Jews, or slightly less than 2 per cent.

The earliest Jewish settlers, the brothers Jacob, Hyman and Levi Mitchell, who came from Cracow, Galicia, in 1838, established a commercial house in Little Rock. They were soon followed by the Hempnew family, Jonas Levy, the Ottenheimer brothers, and others. Prior to 1860 the number of permanent Jewish residents in Little Rock was small, although the first Jewish burial society was founded in that year. Most of the Jews in Little Rock fought on the side of the Confederacy during the Civil War. After the war the Jewish population began to increase; in 1905 it was about 1,000.

A Reform congregation was organized and incorporated in 1866 under the presidency of Morris Navra. In the following year it was chartered as Congregation B'nai Israel of Little Rock. A temple for the congregation was completed and dedicated on September 27, 1872, with Jacob Block as rabbi. In 1897 a new building was erected and dedicated. The following rabbis have served this congregation: J. B. Benson (1881-84); Joseph Stolz (1884-87); E.

Schreiber (1889-91); Charles A. Rubenstein (1891-97); Harry H. Mayer (1897-99); Louis Wolsey (1899-1907); Louis Witt (1907-19); James G. Heller (1919-20); Emanuel Jack (1921-25); Ira E. Sanders (1926--). In 1942 the congregation numbered 341 families.

Shortly after the Orthodox Congregation Agudas Achim was organized in 1907, the eminent Vilna scholar Samuel Katzenellenbogen was called to its pulpit. In 1942 the spiritual leader was Joseph N. Shapiro.

Many of the Jews of Little Rock occupied prominent positions in public life. Jonas Levy was mayor of the city (1860-65); Jacob Erb, county judge (1890-94); Jacob Trieber, United States attorney for the eastern district of Arkansas (1897-1900) and United States district judge for the same district (1900-27); Joe Loeb, city attorney (1904-6); Charles Jacobson, private secretary to Governor Jeff Davis (1901-7) and state senator (1911-15). Most of the Jews of the community of Little Rock are merchants and tradesmen, and there are a number of lawyers and doctors among them as well; they have been active in civic and communal organizations, Jewish as well as general.

IRA E. SANDERS.

Lit.: Jewish Encyclopedia, vol. 2, pp. 113-14; Linfield, Harry S., *The Communal Organization of the Jews in the United States* (1930).

LITURGY, a term derived from the Greek word *leitourgia,* "service," which was used figuratively for the service of God, and then for the prayers which are the most characteristic form of that service. Similarly, the Hebrew word *'abodah* first meant "service," then the Temple service; while the "service of the heart" (*'abodah shebaleb*) is defined as meaning prayer (*Taan.* 2a). The term "Jewish liturgy" has been in use since the 19th cent. to denote Jewish services in the various rituals that have given it a comparatively fixed form; it usually connotes congregational prayers although, as a matter of fact, there is little difference between these and the prayers to be said by the individual worshipper. The Jewish liturgy includes not only prayers but also readings from the Torah and the prophetical books (Haftarah), their interpretation, and a number of symbolic actions.

The times of day for the various Jewish prayers have been fixed as the result of different ideas; they are partly based on the visible daily changes of nature, partly derived from the sacrificial cult, and the two conceptions have been fused together. Thus there are three daily services: morning (Shaharith), afternoon (Minhah) and evening (Maarib). On Sabbaths, new moons and festivals, there is a fourth, known as the additional (Musaf) service; Yom Kippur, in addition to these, has the Neilah service concluding its liturgy.

The history of the early development of the liturgy is veiled in obscurity, since it is not until the Mishnaic period (about 200 B.C.E. to 200 C.E.) that there is any attempt to establish a definite form for Jewish prayers. *Psalms* refer to prayers in the morning and at night; *Dan.* 6:11 depicts Daniel as praying three times a day; the adaptation of the various services in the liturgy to the sacrificial services may not have been completed until after the destruction of the Second Temple (70 C.E.).

Every Jewish prayer service contains as its central portion the Tefillah, a series of benedictions and petitions. It is usually called Shemoneh Esreh, or Eighteen Benedictions, from the fact that it formerly contained eighteen prayers; later the number became nineteen. The first three benedictions are devoted to praise, the last three to thanksgiving and the intervening paragraphs are in the form of petitions. The morning service (Shaharith) and the evening service (Maarib) have also the Keriath Shema, or Reading of the Shema, which consists of the confession of faith, "Hear, O Israel: the Lord our God, the Lord is One" (*Deut.* 6:4), together with the prayers which precede and follow it. The Sabbath and festival services that are held in the daytime (as well as the weekday services on Mondays and Thursdays) contain readings from the Torah and the Prophets, which are fixed exactly in the various rituals. Finally, there is a regularly occurring prayer, the Kaddish, a prayer for the coming of the Kingdom of God and of peace upon earth, which is recited at every break in the service. It occurs principally in two forms: the full Kaddish (*kaddish shalem*), and the half Kaddish (*hatzi kaddish*), which consists of the first two paragraphs.

In addition to these basic prayers, there are a number of special prayers which vary according to the services, the time of the year and the particular occasion that is being observed. This makes the Jewish liturgy appear to be extraordinarily complicated; but in reality it is not, as the basic prayers are the same for all the days of the year, and the changes, which apply only to details, are the result of very logical conceptions.

The morning service (Shaharith) opens with a series of benedictions known as the Birchoth Shahar, which were originally intended for individual and occasional recital and not for congregational worship. They include selections from the Bible, the Mishnah (Ezehu Mekoman) and the Talmud (the thirteen hermeneutical rules of Rabbi Ishmael) which were placed there in order to afford every worshipper the opportunity of fulfilling the duty of daily study. Next come the Pesuke Dezimra, a series of selections from *Psalms,* which was likewise originally for individual use, and was incorporated into the congregational service at a comparatively late time. The fact that both these sections were originally private devotion is still reflected in the usage that a Minyan, or number of ten men necessary to be present for congregational worship, need not be on hand for this part of the service.

The congregational worship proper is introduced by the half Kaddish, and begins with the Keriath Shema group of prayers. This is followed by the Tefillah (Shemoneh Esreh), which is recited twice: first silently, then audibly. In the second reading the Sanctification ("Holy, holy, holy" and other prayers; the Hebrew term is Kedushah) and the Priestly Blessing (Birkath Kohanim; *Num.* 6:24-26). This is followed immediately by the Tahanun, or supplication prayer, at the end of which comes the full Kaddish; then come the Alenu prayer, a number of psalms and the "orphans' Kaddish" (*kaddish yathom*), which is recited especially by the mourners. On Mondays and Thursdays the Tahanun is lengthened by the addition

of the Vehu Rahum and other prayers, and it is followed by a short reading from the Torah, taken from the portion for the coming Sabbath.

The afternoon service (Minhah) begins with the Ashre (*Ps.* 145, preceded by 84:5 and 144:15). The half Kaddish is then followed by the Tefillah, recited twice, and by the Tahanun and the full Kaddish exactly as in the morning service. The evening service (Maarib) consists of the Keriath Shema prayers and the Tefillah; the latter is introduced by the half Kaddish, is not repeated, and is closed by the full Kaddish. The afternoon and evening services are usually combined, and there is a mourners' Kaddish at the end of the evening service. Many synagogues have another mourners' Kaddish at the end of the afternoon service as well. On Friday the Tahanun of the afternoon service is omitted because of the approach of the Sabbath.

Since about 1560 the entrance of the Sabbath has been ushered in by a series of prayers known as the Kabbalath Shabbath; there are several psalms and the Lechah Dodi hymn of Solomon Alkabetz, which hails the Sabbath as the bride. *Ps.* 92 and 93, which are recited immediately after, were made a part of the Sabbath evening service at a far earlier period. The Kabbalath Shabbath is followed by the Sabbath evening service proper, with the Keriath Shema and the Tefillah as on weekdays. However, the Tefillah consists of only seven benedictions, the three first and the three last of the Eighteen Benedictions, and there is a special middle benediction; hence this Tefillah is known as Tefillath Sheba. There is a sort of recapitulation of the Tefillah, closing with the Kiddush, or sanctification of the day with the cup of wine.

The Sabbath morning service has the same structure as the morning service for the weekdays, but there is an increase in the number of the Pesuke Dezimra. At the end of the service comes the reading of the Torah and of the Haftarah, special portions from each being designated for every Sabbath of the year. The removal and return of the scroll are accompanied by the recitation of psalms and other Scriptural verses. This is followed by the Ashre and the additional (Musaf) service, consisting of a special form of the Tefillath Sheba, a special form of the Kedushah, and several hymns, including the En Kelohenu. The Sabbath afternoon service adds the Kedushah Desidra after the Ashre; next comes a short reading from the Torah portion of the following week and the Tefillah. In the winter *Ps.* 104 (Barechi Nafshi) and *Ps.* 120 to 134 (Shir Hamaaloth) are recited; in summer a chapter from *Aboth* (Pirke Aboth, Sayings of the Fathers) is read each week. The evening service at the end of the Sabbath begins with *Ps.* 144 (Ledavid Baruch) and 67, and is closed by a number of Biblical passages and the Habdalah prayer that marks the end of the Sabbath; otherwise it has the usual content of the daily evening service.

This weekly cycle is subject to modification when one of the days coincides with the new moon, with the eight days of Hanukah, or with Purim. In such cases the Tahanun is omitted on the preceding evening and on the day itself, and a suitable insertion (Yaaleh Veyabo, on the new moon; Al Hanissim, on Hanukah and Purim) is made. On the new moon the morning service is followed by the Hallel (*Ps.* 113 to 118), a reading from the Torah, and the additional service. On the days of Hanukah there is a Hallel and the reading of the Torah, but no additional service; Purim has a reading from the Torah, but neither Hallel nor additional service. In addition, the Hanukah lights are kindled and appropriate hymns of praise are sung, while on Purim *Esther* (the Megillah) is read in the evening and in the morning.

On fast days there are slight expansions in the Tefillah; there is a reading from the Torah, which is repeated in the afternoon service and expanded by a Haftarah. The morning service of the Ninth of Ab (Tishah Beab) also has a Haftarah; in addition, *Lamentations* is read in the evening, while lamentation prayers (Kinoth) are recited, a few in the evening and a number in the morning.

The liturgy for the festivals generally modifies the weekday ritual in the same fashion as does that for the Sabbath. These festival services are very similar to those for the Sabbath, and have their own special portions from the Torah and Haftarahs from the Prophets; the only difference is that there is no reading of the Torah at the afternoon service. In addition, each festival has its own special ceremonies, a prayer in which its special nature is mentioned (Tefillath Hayom) and an addition to the service which is devoted to the idea to which the day is consecrated.

On Rosh Hashanah (New Year) there is the blowing of the Shofar, which takes place immediately after the reading from the Scriptures, before the additional service. Another special feature of this liturgy is that the Tefillah for the additional service has nine paragraphs, in contrast to the seven of the Sabbath and the other festivals, and that the fourth, fifth and sixth of these paragraphs are interrupted by the repetitions of the blowings of the Shofar.

During the Ten Penitential Days which run from Rosh Hashanah to Yom Kippur (Day of Atonement) inclusive, there are additional changes in the liturgy, since they are considered to be the season in which God decides as to the fate of all mortals during the coming year. There are changes in the prayers which salute Him as King, insertions in the Tefillah which contain petitions for the year that is to come, and the litany Abinu Malkenu, consisting of a number of brief invocations, is added at the end of both the morning service (just before the reading from the Torah) and the afternoon service. Selihoth, or penitential prayers, are recited before the morning service for some time before Rosh Hashanah; the Sephardim begin them as early as the first of Elul, but the Ashkenazim recite them only in the last week of Elul. The Hasidism begin the Selihoth service at midnight.

The evening service for Yom Kippur begins with the chanting of the Kol Nidre, proceeds through the usual evening service, and ends with Selihoth. In addition to the insertions customary for the ten Penitential Days, mentioned above, the Tefillah is changed by the addition of the confession of sins (Viddui) at the end. The morning service follows the basic form for the penitential days. During the Musaf there is a special section known as the Abodah, which describes the Temple service as performed by the high priest on Yom Kippur; during this service the congregants prostrate themselves three times. As on all fast days, there is a reading from the Torah and the Haftarah in the afternoon service. The conclusion of the service is formed by the Neilah, which has the same structure as the afternoon service except for a few changes in the text of the Tefillah. The service for Yom Kippur is continuous, and extends over an entire day, being interrupted only during the night; its end is signalized by the blowing of the Shofar.

Sukkoth (Feast of Booths) is the festival of the Lulab and the Hoshana prayers, and its service is featured by numerous processions around the synagogue, especially on the seventh day, Hoshana Rabbah. On Shemini Atzereth (Eighth Day of Assembly) there is a prayer for the rain (Tefillath Geshem) that is needed for the new seed; this prayer is recited in the additional service. On Simhath Torah there are processions around the synagogue with the scrolls of the Torah; in the morning there is an especially prolonged and solemn reading from the Torah and, as usual, a Haftarah. On the first day of Passover (Pesach) there is a prayer for the refreshing dew that is necessary for the fields and the gardens (Tefillath Tal), recited in the additional service. On Shabuoth (Feast of Weeks) the memory of the revelation from Sinai is revived.

On each of the above three pilgrimage festivals (Shalosh Regalim) the Hallel is recited, and one of the five scrolls (Megilloth) is read: *Ecclesiastes* on Shemini Atzereth, or on the preceding Sabbath; *Song of Songs,* on the seventh day of Passover, or on the preceding Sabbath; *Ruth,* on Shabuoth. In Eastern Europe and in the Conservative and Orthodox congregations in the United States there is a memorial service (Hazkarath Neshamoth) on the last day of all three pilgrimage festivals and on Yom Kippur; in Western Europe and in the Reform congregations this takes place only on Yom Kippur. (The 1940 edition of the *Union Prayer Book* makes provision for additional memorial services on the festivals, if the congregation desires it.) Another feature of these festivals is the recitation of the Priestly Blessing by the members of the priestly families (Kohanim) themselves, in a ceremony known as Duchenen. The Ashkenazim, strangely enough, omit this on the Sabbath, while the Sephardim and some Ashkenazic congregations (for instance, that of Frankfort, Germany) have it on Sabbaths as well as festivals. In Palestine, Syria and Egypt, the Kohanim recite the Priestly Blessing at every daily service.

The intervening days between the more important first and the last days of each festival are known as half-holidays (Hol Hamoed); there are four of these during Passover and five during Sukkoth. On these half-holidays the liturgy is similar to that for the new moon, with the insertion of the Hallel and the reading from the Torah, and inclusion of an additional service.

All these basic prayers are common to Jews all over the world; nearly all of them are already mentioned in the Talmud, with the text of which, except in a few insignificant details, they agree. Beginning with the 5th cent. C.E., however, the liturgy began to accept more and more of the Piyutim, or synagogal poetry; and the form of the liturgy began to vary,

The first consequence was merely a very simple expansion of the basic prayers, imperceptible additions which were generally accepted. Next, smooth reworkings of the traditional prayers were created; the Tefillah in particular was the favorite field for such poetic modifications. The golden age of the Piyutim came when permission was given to interrupt the basic prayers with poetic adornments. Whereas the basic prayers are distinguished by an exalted simplicity which lends them a classic value, the Piyutim are fanciful, emotional, and at times characterized by extravagance of words or a straining for effect.

The results of the insertion of the Piyutim were manifold. The liturgy was expanded to an extraordinary degree. The services for the festivals and certain special Sabbaths were given an appearance that was totally different from what they had been. The uniformity of the Jewish liturgy gave way to a variety of liturgies, since each country and its individual communities would choose the poetic material which pleased them and insert it into their own services. The scanty remains of the prayer-books of the period just before the invention of printing, remains which are still extant in manuscripts, afford a picture of the extraordinary abundance and multiplicity of the various liturgical rituals. This movement toward diversification was checked by the expulsion of the Jews from their medieval residences, as well as by the rise of printing, both of which had the effect of suppressing individual rituals and perpetuating the main types, thus making the liturgy more uniform.

After prayer-books began to be printed, there was a new series of expansions in the liturgy because of the rise of the Cabala, which stressed the importance of devotion and the necessity of preparing the mind of the worshipper to utter the basic prayers. As a result of the "practical Cabala" of Isaac Luria and his followers, numerous invocations and prayers for different occasions were inserted into the prayer-book. The Cabalists began to attribute special meanings to the positions of the letters of the Hebrew alphabet and to the Hebrew words, especially the name of God, and to underline the meaning of individual prayers in a fashion by means of special introductions or emphases. As a result, by the 18th cent. the Ashkenazic form of the liturgy, in particular, had become exceedingly lengthy by reason of the numerous Piyutim and Cabalistic prayers surrounding the basic benedictions.

In the 18th and 19th centuries this lengthy liturgy was fiercely assailed by the Hasidic Jews on the one hand and by the Reform Jews on the other. Both felt that the prayers had become too long and were merely recited by rote, but chose different methods to modify the liturgy according to their own ideas. The Hasidim changed to the Sephardic form of the liturgy, because it was simpler and not so heavily laden with Piyutim. The Reform Jews went further and made a radical operation upon the entire prayer-book. At first they shortened the forms of the prayers and omitted those parts which disagreed with their theology. The American group, as represented in the *Union Prayer Book,* recast the entire structure of the liturgy. They retained many of the basic prayers, but selected and rearranged them so as to conform to the ideas of their own congregations. In the Reform liturgy the additional service (Musaf) is entirely omitted and its contents are combined with the morning service; many new prayers in the vernacular are introduced; the Kaddish is preserved only as a mourners' prayer, and the Cabalistic insertions and nearly all the Piyutim are entirely eliminated.

The Jewish liturgy as outlined above was intended from the very beginning for public worship and was so organized. Originally the service was recited by a leader and the individuals participated only in certain responses, especially the Amens at the end of the benedictions. At a very early period, however, it became customary to require that individuals should recite the daily prayers. Hence many individuals read the prayers as private devotions, omitting such portions as the Kaddish, the Kedushah, and the reading from the Torah, which are reserved for public worship. According to Jewish law, the worshipper who does not understand Hebrew can recite his private prayers in any language that he understands.

In addition to the liturgy of the synagogue, there are liturgies for individual and home worship, such as grace at meals, the Passover Seder, and the blessings that are to recited on every occasion in life, such as weddings, funerals, circumcisions, the dedications of houses, and the like. Most Jewish prayer-books, therefore, contain not only the liturgy of public services, but also the liturgy of such private devotions.

See also: ABINU MALKENU; ABODAH; ABOTH; ABRAHAM (under 3. In the Liturgy); ADDITIONAL SERVICE; ADON OLAM; ADORATION; AFTERNOON SERVICE; AHABAH RABBAH; AKDAMUTH; AKEDAH; AL HANISSIM; ALENU; AMEN; AN'IM ZEMIROTH; ASHAMNU; ASHRE; AZHAROTH; BAMMEH MADLIKIN; BENEDICTIONS; CONFESSION; DEVOTION; DIVINE SERVICE; EIGHTEEN BENEDICTIONS; EL MALE RAHAMIM; EL MELECH YOSHEB; EL NORA ALILAH; ELI ZION; ELIJAH (under 3. In the Liturgy); EMETH VEYATZIB; EVENING SERVICE; FUNERAL; GEULLAH PRAYER; GRACE AT MEALS; GRAVES, VISITING OF; HABDALAH; HAFTARAH; HAGGADAH, PASSOVER; HALLEL; HALLELUJAH; HASHKIBENU; HEALING, PRAYERS FOR; HOLIDAYS; HOSHANA RABBAH; KABBALATH SHABBATH; KADDISH; KAVVANAH; KEDUSHAH; KIDDUSH; KOL NIDRE; LAMENTATIONS, LITURGICAL; LECHAH DODI; LIKKUTE ZEBI; LITERATURE, DEVOTIONAL; MAARIBIM; MAH TOBU; MAHZOR VITRY; MALCHUYOTH; MAOZ TZUR; MARRIAGE BENEDICTIONS; MEMORIAL SERVICE; MI CHAMOCHA; MINYAN; MORNING SERVICE; NEILAH; OFANNIM; OMNAM KEN; PIRKE SHIRAH; PIYUT; PIZMON; PRAYER; PRAYER FOR THE GOVERNMENT; PRAYER-BOOKS; PRAYERS, SPECIAL; PRIESTLY BLESSING; PSALMS, LITURGICAL; RITUALS; SABBATH SERVICE; SELIHOTH; SEVEN BENEDICTIONS; SHALOM ALECHEM; SHEMA; SHIR HAYIHUD; SHOCHEN AD; SHOFAROTH; SILLUK; TAHANUN; TEFILLAH; TORAH, READING OF; UNETHANNEH TOKEF; VECHOL MAAMINIM; VEHU RAHUM; VEYEETHAYU; YAALEH; YEKUM PURKAN; YIGDAL; YOTZEROTH; ZEMIROTH; ZICHRONOTH; ZULATH.   ISMAR ELBOGEN.

Lit.: Idelsohn, A. Z., *Jewish Liturgy* (1932); Dembitz, Lewis N., *Jewish Services* (1898); Abrahams, Israel, "Companion to the Authorised Daily Prayer Book," often published together with Singer, S., and Abrahams, I., *The Authorised Daily Prayer Book* (1922); Zunz, L., *Die Ritus des synagogalen Gottesdienstes;* Elbogen, I., *Der jüdische Gottesdienst in seiner geschichtlichen Entwicklung* (3rd ed., 1931); Munk, Elie, *Die Welt der Gebete* (1933).

Maxim M. Litvinoff, photographed at his desk in Moscow shortly before his return to the United States in 1941

Children's Services. Children's services developed in the 19th cent. among certain liberal groups in Germany because of the feeling that the official liturgy, intended primarily for adults, did not precisely meet the religious needs of children. The first such children's services were held at the Cassel synagogue and at the Jacobson School in Seesen in 1809, even before the beginnings of the Reform Movement. There were others in the private schools of M. H. Bock and Jeremias Heinemann at Berlin, in Josef Perl's school at Tarnopol, and in Austria. More developed in Vienna and in Germany toward the end of the 19th cent.

In the United States a number of children's services were developed by rabbis of the Reform wing, especially toward the end of the 19th and the beginning of the 20th centuries. The most elaborate book of this sort is Morris Lazaron's *Religious Service for the Jewish Youth;* Alvin S. Luchs has published four different children's services as well as special children's services for Rosh Hashanah and Yom Kippur. There are several children's services, mainly for the religious school, in the hymn book of Isaac S. Moses and the *Union Hymnal.* There are a large number of confirmation services which are widely used by congregations; David Philipson and A. J. Cohon have written services for harvest festivals held at the time of Sukkoth. Ferdinand M. Isserman has written a children's peace service, and Barnet A. Elzas and G. A. Rose have published children's liturgies for use in summer camps.

LITVAK, *see* PHRASES, POPULAR.

LITVINOFF, MAXIM MAXIMOVITCH, Russian statesman, b. Bialystok, Russia, 1876. The son of middle class parents (named Wallach), he was educated at the local high school. At eighteen he entered the czarist army. He joined the Kiev committee of the Russian Social Democratic Labor Party in 1899, was arrested and exiled in 1901; he escaped to Switzerland in 1902. He met Lenin in 1903. When the Party split (1903), Litvinoff identified himself with the Bolshevik wing. In 1905 he returned to St. Petersburg and collaborated with Maxim Gorky on the newspaper *Novaya Zhizn* (New Life), the first legally published Bolshevist organ in Russia. Soon forced to flee again, he went to France, and in 1908 to England, where he lived for ten years in comradeship with Lenin.

On January 4, 1918, Litvinoff was designated Soviet ambassador to Great Britain, and thus began his long career in diplomacy. He became assistant people's commissar for foreign affairs under Chicherin in 1921, acting commissar in 1928, and commissar in 1930, a post he held until May 3, 1939.

On November 6, 1941, Litvinoff was appointed ambassador to the United States and once again assistant commissar. From 1934 to 1941 he was a member of the Central Committee of the Communist Party of the Soviet Union. He was awarded the order of Lenin on his sixtieth birthday (1936) for "outstanding services in the struggle for peace."

The career of Litvinoff can not be separated from the history of Soviet foreign policy, for he was its most frequent and consistent spokesman for two decades. His first assignment in diplomacy soon ended with his arrest by the British government. He was released in exchange for Bruce Lockhart, and went to work in the Foreign Office in Moscow. In 1919 he negotiated a non-aggression pact with Estonia. He was then sent to Copenhagen to arrange an exchange of prisoners with Great Britain and other countries. While there he expressed the basic principles upon which his country's foreign policy was to rest in the coming years: "We know that Russia can not live alone, and we desire first of all a peaceful relationship with the other countries of the world. We believe, moreover, in self-determination and the right of every country to choose its own form of government."

The first task facing the Soviet Foreign Office was to break the cordon sanitaire of intervention, blockade, and non-recognition. By 1927 Chicherin and Litvinoff had won virtually universal de jure recognition of the Soviet regime, although open hostility and "incidents" continued. The United States remained apart, however, despite overtures by Litvinoff from Stockholm in 1918 and in Copenhagen the following year. When normal diplomatic relations were finally established between the two countries in 1933, after direct personal discussions between President Franklin D. Roosevelt and the Soviet foreign minister, the latter hailed the step as the final triumph of the principle that the "two systems" could co-exist in peace.

Once the Allied armies of intervention were defeated and withdrawn, the Soviet government began its campaign for disarmament as the surest way to guarantee world peace. Chicherin attempted to place the question of disarmament on the agenda of the Genoa conference in April, 1922, but without success. Equally fruitless was the disarmament conference of the Baltic states held in Moscow at the end of the same year, under the chairmanship of Litvinoff. Five years later came the dramatic proposal by Litvinoff at the Fourth Preparatory Disarmament Conference in Geneva of a fourteen-point program for the "complete abolition of all land, marine, and air forces." Two vigorous and biting speeches on March 19 and 22, 1928 (fifth session), received tremendous publicity and made Litvinoff a world figure overnight. The proposal was rejected, with only the representatives of Germany and Turkey speaking in its favor, and Litvinoff promptly introduced a plan for partial disarmament. Over his bitter protest, this second plan was denied a place on the agenda. Litvinoff then reported to his government that, though "we are bound to express our sincere disappointment and extreme regret over the outcome" of the Preparatory Disarmament Commission, "the fact that, whatever the results of the discussion, the Soviet government managed to get the idea of full and general disarmament brought forward for discussion in the international arena . . . for the first time in history, must be considered an enormous achievement and a historic task of the first importance."

A new phase in Soviet international relations began with the great depression, which reached its full force in Europe in 1931. The deterioration in European economic conditions, the rapid pace of Soviet industrialization, the accession of Hitler, and the imminence of a new world war made the Soviet Union a far more powerful factor than before and at the same time necessitated a new direction for its peace policy. Trade agreements and non-aggression pacts became more numerous; for example, at the World Economic Conference in London (1933), Litvinoff signed no

less than nine treaties. But non-aggression pacts were insufficient. Reasoning from the premise that "peace is indivisible," Litvinoff worked ceaselessly to achieve a system of collective security against aggression (not to be confused with the traditional bloc or concert of powers directed against another state or group of states). He argued that the united peace forces of the world could successfully discourage aggression; and, more than that, "not only will the danger of war be averted, but sooner or later the aggressor will have to ask to be included in the general system of collective security" (League of Nations address, September 28, 1936). The implementation he proposed as early as May, 1934, envisaged a network of regional or bilateral pacts of mutual assistance, modelled after the Franco-Soviet and Czech-Soviet pacts of May 2 and May 16, 1935, respectively. The text of the Franco-Soviet pact explicitly left the door open for the adherence of other countries, particularly of Germany.

Collective security was no "peace at any price" program. Litvinoff warned against a fascist peace; "we are against their dictating the terms of negotiation or paying them premiums for being so kind as to negotiate." Nor was it a departure from the principle of self-determination. "We, as a state," Litvinoff told the Eighth Congress of the Soviets on November 28, 1936, "are not concerned with the internal Fascist regime of this country or that." However, he added, "Fascism is not only a specific internal regime. . . . It represents at the same time preparation for aggression, preparation for war against other states."

The main arena of Litvinoff's struggle for collective security was the League of Nations, to which the Soviet Union was admitted in 1934. As crisis piled on crisis, it was Litvinoff who asked most vigorously and most consistently that the member nations fulfill their obligations under the League Covenant. He called for full sanctions against Italy in the Ethiopian War; he minced no words in condemning (1936-38) the so-called non-intervention policy in Spain; and he guaranteed direct Soviet military aid to Czechoslovakia. Even in the Munich days (1938) he still believed and said that the League was "strong enough by its collective action to avert or arrest aggression." The League was doomed by the other major powers, however. The Fascist peace which Litvinoff feared had come.

On April 1, 1938, United States Ambassador Joseph E. Davies reported to Secretary of State Cordell Hull that Litvinoff felt that "Soviet Russia must count on no outside aid . . . in the last analysis the Soviet Union was quite content, if the democracies pursued 'their course of present folly and indifference to international peace and justice' to rely upon itself." Munich decided the issue. Litvinoff's resignation on May 3, 1939, was the warning, as the resignation of a foreign minister is always the signal in Europe. The Nazi-Soviet non-aggression pact followed soon after.

A little less than two years later, with Hitler's surprise invasion of the Soviet Union on June 22, 1941, came the attack on his country which Litvinoff had sought to stave off during two decades of work.

Coincident with the formation of the anti-Axis alliance (1941) between Russia, England and the United

States, Litvinoff became Soviet ambassador to the United States. His appointment was generally welcomed by the American press as the coming of a statesman who, in the words of the *New York Times,* "has been from the outset of the Soviet regime, the uncompromising and outspoken advocate of collaboration with the Western democracies." As guest of honor at the annual dinner of the Overseas Press Club (New York, February 26, 1942), Litvinoff issued a call (broadcast by radio throughout the world) for the opening of a western front by the United Nations against the Nazi armies.

Litvinoff's reappearance upon the international scene was once more a signal, this time heralding an era of genuine world cooperation against the forces of aggression and tyranny, and of the Soviet Union's earnest desire to bring about an international system of collective security after the war.

CORLISS LAMONT.

Lit.: Litvinoff, Maxim, *Against Aggression: Speeches* (1939); idem, *The Bolshevik Revolution* (1920); idem, "Soviet International Economic Policy," *Current History,* vol. 34 (1931) 510-16; Davies, Joseph E., *Mission to Moscow* (1941); *The Soviet Union and Peace* (1929; with an introduction by Henri Barbusse); *Current Biography,* Dec., 1941, pp. 35-37; Reston, James B., "The Outspoken Mr. Litvinoff," *New York Times Magazine,* Jan. 18, 1942, pp. 15 and 28, *Bolshaya Entziklopedia* (1938).

LITWAK, A. (pseudonym), *see* HELFAND, HAYIM JACOB.

LITWAKOV, MOSES, Yiddish publicist, critic and editor, b. Tcherkas, Ukraine, Russia, 1875. Up to the age of seventeen he studied Talmud, and subsequently graduated from the Gymnasium. From 1902 to 1905 he studied in Paris.

Litwakov began his political and social career as a Zionist of Ahad Haam's ideology, and was a pioneer of proletarian (Poale Zion) Zionism. He participated in a number of that party's conferences, and contributed liberally to its press. During the first (abortive) Russian revolution (1905) he returned to Russia from abroad and sojourned in Vilna, where he edited the periodicals *Der Neier Veg, Unser Veg* and *Dos Vort,* and also wrote in Hebrew for *Hazeman.* He published the brochure *Der Zionismus und die Uganda Frage.* From 1908 on he was staff writer for the Russian newspaper *Kievskaya Mysyl,* under the pseudonym of M. Lirov. He contributed to the collective volumes *Fun Tzeit tzu Tzeit* (Kiev, 1911-12), was active in relief work during the first World War, and instituted the slogan "Help through work!"

Following the March revolution, he became associate editor of *Die Neie Tzeit,* published in Kiev, for which he wrote political articles. In 1919 he helped organize the Kultur Liga in Kiev, and was for a time member of its central committee. Soon after the annexation of the Ukraine by Soviet Russia, the expected split in the Socialist party occurred. As leader of its left wing ("Combund"), Litwakov induced his faction to join the "Comterband" (May, 1919). Thereafter he was the leading personality in the Jewish Communist section, and editor-in-chief of its official organ, *Der Emes,* published in Moscow. He was co-editor of Lenin's collected works in Yiddish.

From the very beginning of his career Litwakov had a definitive conception of proletarian territorialism, and was a consistent theoretician of Jewish spiritual revolution. He tenaciously combatted, in the name of the Jewish working class, the traditional Jewish ideology as well as the Hebraist and assimilationist tendencies and bourgeois Zionism. He visualized the historic aim of the Jewish revolutionary movement in: (1) democratization of Jewish society by transforming it from a well-to-do, Orthodox group into a compact entity; (2) secularization of Jewish traditional life; and (3) development of Jewish culture by fusing it with the life of the masses. This was to be accomplished through the medium of their language—Yiddish—in a manner consistent with the revolutionary interests of the working class.

Litwakov was among the first to apply the materialistic (Marxian) conception of history to Jewish literary-cultural phenomena. He was a vivid, influential critic in Soviet Russia who held the view that literature is a fitting instrument in the struggle for freedom and the abolition of classes. He was the leading sponsor of the Moscow Kammer theater, and wrote a book, about its inception and artistic growth, entitled *Finf Yor Meluchesher Yiddisher Kammer Teater, 1919-1924* (Moscow, 1924). Notable among his critical studies is *In Umru* (Unrest; vol. 1, Kiev, 1918; vol. 2, Moscow, 1926), a collection of interpretive articles written between 1906 and 1918.

SAMUEL KREITER.

Lit.: Reisen, Z., *Lexikon fun der Yiddisher Literatur, Presse un Filologie,* vol. 2 (1927) cols. 135-41; Latzki-Bertholdi, W., in *Bicher-Velt,* vol. 2 (1919) 26-30; Niger, S., "Kultur Revolutzionism," *Vilna Tog,* 1919, pp. 41-47; Gurstein, A., *Vegen Undser Kritik* (1924).

LIUBAVICHER, DER, *see* MENAHEM MENDEL OF LIUBAVICH.

LIUZZI, FERNANDO, composer and musicologist, b. Senigaglia, Italy, 1884; d. 1941. He studied in Bologna with Fano, Reger and Mottl, then was invited (1910) to lecture on composition at the famous Conservatory of Parma, where he remained until 1917. During the next decade he taught the same subject and the history of music at the Royal Conservatory in Florence. In 1927 Liuzzi assumed the chair of history of music at the University of Rome, lecturing at the same time at the Institute of Roman Studies and at the Summer University for Foreigners at Perugia.

In 1917 he composed a chamber opera for marionettes, *L'Angellin bel verde,* and some organ music. He devoted himself to research and transcriptions of little-known Italian medieval, chamber and liturgical music. His two-volume edition of transcriptions, *La lauda e i primordi della musica italiana,* which contains 135 unpublished melodies, mostly of the 13th and 14th centuries, and which appeared in 1935, is one of the most valuable works in this field. Of equal importance and value is his previous work, *L'espressione musicale del dramma liturgico* (Turin, 1929), which offers a penetrating analysis and study of Church liturgy, and reveals its new musical aspects. Liuzzi published many studies and essays on esthetics and the history of music, mostly of the medieval period. He contributed articles on musical subjects to the *Enciclopedia Italiana.* Dismissed from the University of Rome in October, 1939, as a result of anti-Semitic decrees, he came to the United States, where he lectured on subjects of musical esthetics through 1942.

LIVERIGHT, HORACE BRISBIN, book publisher and play producer, b. Osceola Mills, Pa., 1886; d. New York city, 1933. He was educated in the schools of Osceola and Philadelphia. Coming to New York city, he was first engaged as a bond salesman; later, in 1911, he entered the paper manufacturing business. But his interest in books and his friendship with people in literary circles resulted in the establishment of the firm of Boni and Liveright in 1917. Among other undertakings, the firm published a series of classics, modern and old, in a standard form that came to be known as the Modern Library Edition. Later Liveright organized the publishing firm under his own name and was instrumental in introducing many writers to the American public, among them Eugene O'Neill, Hendrick Willem van Loon, Ernest Hemingway, and Robinson Jeffers. In 1924 Liveright also entered the theatrical field as a producer, offering *The Firebrand*. Later he presented *Hamlet* in modern dress, and other plays. He retired from the publishing business in 1930. For his services to French literature, he was made an Officier d'Académie.

Lit.: The New Yorker, Oct. 10, 1925, pp. 9-10.

LIVERPOOL, prominent West Coast seaport on the River Mersey, Lancashire, England; in 1942 its Jewish population was estimated at 8,000 (0.9 per cent) out of a total of 855,000. Jewish settlement dates from the middle of the 18th cent., when Sephardic merchants from London having trade with Dublin, Ireland, remained for convenience in this western seaport. The nucleus of a congregation existed as early as 1790, but it was not until 1806, when the corporation of the city presented a plot of land in Seel Street, that a formal synagogue and community came into being. This synagogue, transferred in 1874 to its present location in Princes Road, was distinguished for the fact that it was the first Jewish house of worship in Britain in which sermons were delivered in English, the preacher being its first minister, Tobias Goodman. A rift in the community in 1838 resulted in the establishment, four years later, of a rival congregation, subsequently accommodated at premises in Hope Place. This synagogue remained in existence until 1937, when its members amalgamated with a later congregation and erected an edifice in Greenbank Drive.

The Liverpool Jewish community was, in 1942, the fourth largest in Great Britain. It possessed no fewer than twelve synagogues, and boasted a fairly complete network of educational and social institutions. A Liverpool Jewish Association and a Committee of Local Members of the Board of Deputies keep watchful eye over communal affairs, while religious interests are supervised by a district rabbi (Rabbi Iser Judah Unterman) and an Ecclesiastical Committee. There is also a Board of Shechita.

Social services are administered primarily by a Jewish Board of Guardians, established in 1875, and by a variety of smaller organizations, prominent among which are the Philanthropic Society, founded as early as 1811, the Ladies' Benevolent Society (1849), the Provident Society (1850) and the "Somech Noflim" Hebrew Distress Relief Society (1909).

The Great Synagogue on Grove Street, Liverpool

Cultural activities are concentrated in a Jewish literary society, a Hebrew center, and a number of synagogue guilds and minor organizations. There is also a Jewish students' society connected with the local university. Jewish education is provided for children by an educational institution and Talmud Torah schools, and for adults by a Talmudical college (Yeshivath Torath Hayyim, 1915) and a teachers' seminary. For the coordination of pedagogical activities, Liverpool Jews cooperate with neighboring communities in a Central Conference of Merseyside Jewish Educational Institutions. The Zionist movement is well represented, several local societies being

The Old Hebrew Synagogue on Princess Road, Liverpool

A room in the Jewish Museum of Livorno

Interior view of Temple Israel in Livorno

federated in a central Zionist Council, while branches of the Mizrahi and Revisionist wings are also active. Zion House serves as a general meeting-place for social and cultural activities. Lastly, the community enjoys the distinction of having established, in 1867, the first English branch of the Alliance Israélite Universelle, which later functioned as a branch of the Anglo-Jewish Association.

Liverpool Jewry has produced several noted personalities, among whom mention may be made especially of: Lionel D. Barnett, orientalist, formerly Keeper of Oriental Printed Books and Manuscripts in the British Museum; Bertram B. Benas, prominent Anglo-Jewish leader and legal expert; Henry Cohen, professor of medicine; Louis Rosenhead, professor of applied mathematics in the local university. Civic distinction has fallen to Jews in the persons of Louis S. Cohen (1846-1922), who was elected successively member of the city council (1895), mayor (1900) and alderman (1910), and to his son, Major Jack Brunel Cohen, who sat as Unionist member of Parliament for the local Fairfield division from 1923 to 1926. The Cohen family has been especially interested in the development of Liverpool University (founded 1903). A chair in dentistry was endowed, in 1920, by Louis S. Cohen, while the magnificent premises of the University Library were erected largely through the munificence of his son, Harold Leopold Cohen (1873-1936).

German air attacks on the city, in 1940 and 1941, inflicted serious losses on Jewish life and property. A local synagogue was subsequently dynamited because of the danger of its collapse. On the other hand, Zion House, which was spared, was immediately thrown open as a general refuge for the homeless.

Theodor H. Gaster.

Lit.: The Jewish Year Book (London, 1940); Jewish Chronicle (London), 1939 to 1941; Benas, Bertram B., Later Records of the Jews in Liverpool (1929).

LIVORNO (LEGHORN), Italian city on the Tyrrhenian sea, seat of a flourishing Sephardic Jewish community which owes its origin to the Livorno decree issued in 1590 by Ferdinand I, the grand duke of Tuscany. The purpose of this law was to make Livorno great and populous; accordingly it made the city a free port and opened its gates to the Marranos who were being persecuted in Portugal and to the Jews of all countries.

In 1591 the grand duke issued a letter-patent, solemnly confirmed in 1593, establishing the privileges to be granted to the Jews who had settled down in Pisa or Livorno (Livorno was at that time dependent on Pisa). These privileges, which were extended also to the baptized Jews, were extraordinarily extensive. The "Massari," or heads of the Jewish community, were given the power to exercise civil, and to a large extent even criminal jurisdiction. In addition, they had the right, not only to impose taxes upon the Jews of their community, but even to pass upon the request of Jews from other countries to settle there. In this way it was in their power to grant or refuse naturalization, since those Jews whose admission they accepted became forthwith subjects of Tuscany. The new arrivals, mostly from Spain, Portugal, North Africa and the Orient, were granted immunity for crimes which had been committed or debts which had been incurred in the time before this arrival; subsequently the condition as to crimes was abrogated, and later on that as to debts received limitations.

In 1597 the Jews of Livorno, on appealing to the grand duke, received his permission to separate from the community of Pisa and to form an autonomous community with their own "Massari." Numerous Sephardic and Levantine Jews streamed into Livorno because of the privileges granted to the Jews. There were 114 Jews in Livorno in 1601; 711 in 1622; 1,175 in 1642; and their number amounted to about 1,250 in 1692. In the first half of the 18th cent. it rose to 5,000; in the second half of the 18th cent. it was at

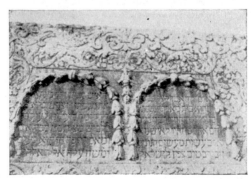

A tombstone (Renaissance period) in the Spanish Jewish cemetery in Livorno

Carved walnut bench (16th cent.) in the synagogue at Livorno

least 7,000 according to a conservative estimate, and another opinion placed it as high as 9,000.

The Jews lived voluntarily around the synagogue in a special quarter, but they were not shut up in a ghetto although such attempts were made after the death of Cosimo II in 1621. They had a significant share in the development of Livorno and in the prosperity of its commerce with all ports of the Mediterranean as well as of other seas. They also took up manufacturing, such as the making of soap (16th cent.), silk and woollen cloth (17th cent.), and articles made of coral (17th cent., and up to the present). After the end of the 18th cent. they dealt in marine insurance.

The by-laws of the community were several times revised in details (1637, 1642, 1667, 1690, 1693 and 1715), but the privileges always remained in force. In addition to the "Massari," five in number, who formed the executive board, there existed a council of fifty (later sixty), a sort of little parliament, which had the power to make resolutions. Under Cosimo III (1670-1726), some restrictions were imposed and proselytizing among the Moslem slaves and the Jewish population was undertaken. In 1686 a rabbinic student was converted to Christianity and took the name of Paolo Sebastiano Medici, under which he became known as preacher and author. The Jews were nevertheless protected from molestation. In 1739 Francis I withheld from the Inquisition the right to censor the books printed by Joseph Athias.

When the grand duchy fell to the house of Lorraine in 1737, the new dynasty confirmed the old privileges of the Jews. In 1751 there was a popular tumult against the Jews, who were charged with having shot at two Jews who had been baptized; but the police soon had the movement under control. In 1780 Grand Duke Peter Leopold stipulated that a representative of the Jews of Livorno had to take part in the city council of Livorno. The reactionary movements which wished to thwart the liberal reforms of Peter Leopold assumed in 1790 an anti-Jewish character in Livorno, but were soon quelled.

In 1808 the levelling French dominion abolished the Jewish privileges, yet the Jews of Livorno, who numbered nearly 4,900, received, after prolonged negotiations, the same rights as the Jews of Bordeaux. After the reinstallation of the grand duke of Lorraine in 1814, the privileges were for the most part restored. In 1859, after the end of the grand duchy and its union with Piedmont (which after 1861 formed a part of the Italian kingdom), the Jews were made

the equals of the other citizens. The free port was abolished in 1868. From that time on many Jews emigrated from Livorno, and the community significantly decreased. It numbered 3,500 in 1838; 4,205 in 1850; 4,542 in 1852; and about 2,500 in the period between 1929 and 1933.

The most important rabbis in Livorno were: in the 17th cent., David Nieto, Salomo Ezobi and Immanuel Frances; in the 18th cent., Joseph Ergas, Malachi Hakohen, Abraham Isaac Castello, Joseph Athias, and Hayim Joseph David Azulai; in the 19th cent., Elijah Benamozegh. The Hebraist David Castelli (d. 1901), and Sabato Morais, founder of the Jewish Theological Seminary of New York, and the dramatist Sabatino Lopez also came from Livorno. Among the numerous Jewish scholars of Livorno were: Solomon Ayllon, Benjamin Espinosa, Jacob Hagiz, Raphael Meldola, Jonah Nabon, Immanuel Hai Richi, Hezekiah da Silva, and Samuel Colombo Coën (chief rabbi in 1904).

The synagogue of Livorno, built in 1603, is one of the most beautiful buildings in the city. There was a Hebrew printing house belonging to Jedidiah Gabbai in Livorno from 1650 to 1658. In the 18th and 19th centuries a number of Hebrew printing houses were found there, and in the early 1930's it was the seat of the flourishing activity of the Belforte press, which supplied the Near East and Northern Africa with liturgical and Biblical books.

UMBERTO CASSUTO.

In the years following the first World War the Jewish community was considerably reduced owing to migration to the major Italian centers and to the continuous decline of the Livorno port traffic. Mixed marriages, particularly frequent among the upper class of the Jewish bourgeoisie, diminished still more the number and the strength of the community, once called the "Jerusalem of Italy." Chief Rabbi Alfredo Toaff sought to strengthen Jewish consciousness in his community by furthering cultural, religious and social activities there. Due to his initiative, Livorno was chosen, in 1925, the seat of the first Congress of Jewish Cultural Clubs in Italy. In 1927 he submitted to the council of the community a proposal to establish a Museum of the Jewish Community of Livorno which

Silver Rimmonim used in a Livorno synagogue

should contain and preserve the numerous precious relics, Jewish cult objects, manuscripts, Kethubahs and Sefer Torah of the monumental Jewish Temple of Livorno. The Museum was inaugurated in 1930, revealing many artistic riches and unusual documents and prints illustrating the history of the Livorno community.

In 1938, following the resignation of two members of the council of the Jewish community and the previous death of two others, a government commissar was assigned to administer the community affairs. As a result of the anti-Semitic decrees which barred Jewish pupils from the elementary and secondary schools, a Jewish high school was organized, in that autumn of 1938, under the direction of Professor Roberto Menasci, himself previously director of the board of education of the city of Livorno. The name of the "Piazza Elia Benamozegh" (after the famous rabbi and theologian) was changed, as a result of the Fascist decree ordering the removal of Jewish names from streets and piazzas of Italy. The Jewish population of Livorno at the beginning of 1942 was about 1,000.   DAVID KLEINLERER.

Lit.: Loevinson, Ermanno, *Le basi giuridiche della comunità israelitica di Livorno* (1937; reprint from *Bolletino storico livornese*, Year 1, No. 2, 1937); Jona, "Alcune notizie sulla communione e sulla vita degli Hebrei di Livorno," *Antologia ebraica* (1901) 10 et seq., 53 et seq.; Lattes and Toaff, *Gli studi ebraici a Livorno nel secolo XVIII.* (1909); Rignano, *La università israelitica di Livorno e le opere pie da essa amministrate* (1890); Sonnino, *Storia della tipografia ebraica a Livorno* (1912); Toaff, in *Vessillo israelitico*, vol. 61 (1913) 299-305; Vivoli, *Annali di Livorno* (1842-46); Pera, *Curiosità livornesi* (1888); idem, *Nuove curiosità livornesi* (1899); *Revue des études juives*, vol. 55, pp. 119-45; vol. 56, pp. 90-123; vol 91, pp. 1-27; Pardi, *Archivio storico italiano*, vol. 76, part 1 (1918) 1-96; Roth, Cecil, *A History of the Marranos* (1932); Graetz, H., *History of the Jews*, vol. 4 (1927) 672-73; vol. 5 (1927) 16, 161, 264.

LIVY, see ROMAN WRITERS ON JEWS.

LIVYATHAN, see LEVIATHAN.

LO ALECHEM, see PHRASES, POPULAR.

LOAN SOCIETIES, see COOPERATIVES.

LOANS. In the primitive agricultural economy of the Israelites, a loan was thought of primarily as an accommodation to a friend or acquaintance who was in need. This is clearly seen from *Ex.* 22:24, where the whole passage deals with kindness toward the poor man who has to ask for a loan and give his garment as a pledge. *Deut.* 23:20-21, which is regarded by Bible critics as the product of a time when more of the people were engaged in commerce, mentions the taking of interest, but with a limitation: "Unto a foreigner thou mayest lend upon interest; but unto thy brother thou shalt not lend upon interest." It is possible that by "foreigner" was meant any person, Jew or otherwise, who was not well known to the lender; but early interpretation equated "foreigner" and "non-Jew"; when the Christian church took over many of the laws of the Hebrew Bible, it similarly interpreted "foreigner" as meaning "non-Christian."

In the Talmud there is no question of loans at interest, so the subject is hardly touched upon. A

Title page of a book of Responsa of Rabbi David ibn Abi Zimra, printed in Livorno (1651)

loan was a debt, and therefore was annulled by the Sabbatical year; like other debts, it could avoid the provisions of the Sabbatical year by the use of the Prosbul. Talmudic law is more concerned with loans of animals and other property and the question of the responsibility of the borrower for loss or damage. A famous passage in the Mishnah (*B.M.* 5:1) discusses the prohibition of the various forms of interest known in the Bible as *neshech* (literally, "bite") and *tarbith* ("increase"). The former is interest as such, which is forbidden; the latter consists of transactions which may accrue to the profit of the lender, such as the loan of a quantity of grain, to be returned at a time when grain increases in value. The Talmudic rabbis tended to rule against such forms of gain upon loans. However, the necessities of commercial transactions in which there was need for credit led to the creation of a sort of partnership between debtor and creditor, whereby the creditor was to receive a certain sum over and above the money he had advanced; this was technically not interest, but his profit in the venture. This was regarded as legal only if a special document for the purpose was drawn up (*shetar 'iska*).

During the Middle Ages a peculiar situation developed which forced the Jews into the business of making loans on interest. On the one hand, the frequent persecutions compelled them to put their wealth into forms that could be easily carried about, such as money; on the other hand, since by church law Christians could not borrow money at interest from Christians and therefore could not borrow at all, they turned to borrow from the Jews at interest, since this was legal under Jewish law. Jews, however, still continued to lend to Jews without interest, and the institution of free loans has continued to modern times. However, in most countries of the western world, where a capitalistic economy has recognized the right of money to earn a wage for its use, these free loans are not a matter of business, but rather a form of benevolence.

See also: BAILMENTS; MONEY-LENDING; SOCIAL SERVICE.

LOANS, ELIJAH BEN MOSES, rabbi and Cabalist, b. Frankfort, Germany, 1555; d. Worms, Germany, 1636. He was a descendent of Rashi. He studied under Akiba Frankfort and Jacob Ginzberg in Frankfort, and later under Menahem Mendel at Cracow. He served as rabbi at Fulda (1600), Hanau (1612), Friedberg (1620), and Worms (1630), where he stayed until his death.

Loans was one of the leading Cabalistic scholars of his time, and many legends were woven around his personality. He was an extremely prolific author of commentaries on the books of the Bible and the *Zohar*. Among his works are: *Rinnath Dodim* (1600); *Michlol Yofi* (1695); *Vikkuah Yayin im Hamayim* (1757).

LOANS, JACOB BEN JEHIEL, physician and scholar, b. probably in Germany, date unknown; d. Linz, Germany, about 1506. For many years he was the personal physician of Emperor Frederick III, by whom he was knighted for faithful service. After the emperor's death in 1493 Loans enjoyed the favors of his successor, Maximilian. Through Jacob's influence one of his relatives, Joseph ben Gershom Loans (Josel of Rosheim), was appointed official representative of all the German Jews at the Diet.

The great humanist and Hebraist, Johann Reuchlin, met Loans at Linz in 1492, and the latter became his first teacher of Hebrew language and literature. Reuchlin thought very highly of Loans and mentioned him in his book, *De rudimentis hebraicis* (1506).

Loans lived at a time when the Jews endured great hardships and persecutions throughout Europe and especially in Germany, and his official honors and high personal connections were practically unique.

Lit.: Graetz, H., *History of the Jews*, vol. 4 (1927) 413-14, 435; Geiger, Ludwig, *Johann Reuchlin*, pp. 105-6.

LOANS, JOSEPH, see JOSEL OF ROSHEIM.

LÖB SORES (Sarah's son, Löb), Hasidic rabbi, d. Yaltushkov, province of Podolia, Russia, 1791. Of his life little is known that is not conjecture or legend. The place of his birth may have been Rovno in Russian Poland, where his mother lived at one time, and the date of his birth has been supposed to be about 1730.

He was a friend, and some say a disciple, of Baer (Dob) of Meseritz, who wrote of him—in a letter of introduction which Löb Sores carried about—that he was to be aided and believed and that he was of great help to Jews but just how could not be put in writing. He seemed to be in touch with persons of authority in the government, and wandered about from town to town. Sometimes he would open a poor little store that never seemed to do any business, so that it became a saying among the Ukrainian Jews about that kind of enterprise that it was "the store of Löb Sores."

Some thought that Löb Sores was a spy of the Austrian or Polish government, but the Hasidim preferred to believe that he was looking after the welfare of the thirty-six unknown men (Lamed Vav Zaddikim) who, according to Hasidic tradition, in each generation keep the world from destruction by their righteousness. His name became famous in Jewish folklore. The name itself, repeated three times, was thought to be a charm against lightning; he was believed to be able to travel with supernatural speed and to have the power of becoming invisible, a power which he is supposed to have used to beat Emperor Joseph II of Austria, whose changes in the laws relating to Jews were obnoxious to the Hasidim. The grave of Löb Sores became a place of pilgrimage.

Löb Sores preached no sermons, gathered no followers, and left no writings. The gist of his teaching, stressing conduct rather than mere learning, may be gathered from the two quotations in *The Hasidic Anthology* by Louis I. Newman (1934, in collaboration with Samuel Spitz): "The good man should himself be the Torah, and the people should be able to learn good conduct from observing him" (p. 8); "in his actions, in his speech, in his bearing, and in his fealty to the Lord, man must make manifest the Torah" (pp. 29-30).

Lit.: Horodezky, S. A., *Leaders of Hassidism* (1928) 53-54.

LÖBEL, JACOB, industrialist and communal leader, b. Bucharest, Roumania, 1828; d. Bucharest, 1867. In the course of his brief life he played an important role in Jewish life in Roumania. He stemmed from a family of wealthy merchants and, entering business at an early age, soon gained great success, being one of the many Roumanian Jews who, as bankers, industrialists and merchants, greatly contributed to the entry of Roumania, then an agrarian and feudal country, into modern European economy.

Löbel founded an important bank, the Banque de Roumanie, of which he was the head until his death. He was the first to introduce an insurance company into Roumania. By reason of his position as banker, he was able to enter into business relations with the boyars (nobles) and government officials, and took advantage thereof to intervene in favor of his persecuted coreligionists. He had access to the princely palace. The then reigning prince, Alexander Cuza (he ruled the country between 1859 and 1866), a liberal, was not hostile to the Jews. This was the time when (1860 to 1865), despite a strong anti-Semitic movement, there still existed in Roumania a vestige of liberalism, the heritage of the Revolution of 1848. Roumanian political leaders who still called themselves liberals—and who later embraced anti-Semitism—took a friendly interest in the Jews, whom they wished to guide toward progress. Löbel devoted all his efforts to this work, in collaboration with other prominent Jews. He had a definite aim: to induce the Jews to leave the ghetto and to enable them to acquire modern culture. Löbel, as president of the Jewish community of Bucharest, eager to put his theories into practice,

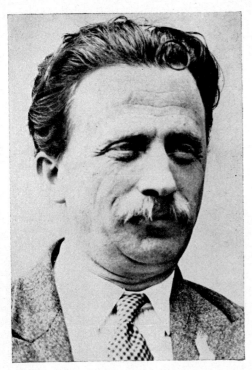

Berl Locker

LÖBISCH, ARYEH (known also as Aryeh-Leib Calahorra), martyr rabbi and preacher in Posen in the 18th cent., and descendant of the apothecary and martyr Mattithiah Calahorra. On the eve of the New Year's holiday of 1734, he and Rabbi Jacob Meir, together with a number of other Jews, were arrested on a blood accusation and imprisoned. Although cruelly tortured, he refused to renounce his religion. In mortal agony he was carried to his home, where he died in the autumn of 1736 as a result of the fiendish treatment. A commission of royal officials, appointed by King Augustus III to investigate the outrage, rendered a decision sentencing him to be burned at the stake; his body was exhumed for this purpose in 1737.

Lit.: Perles, *Geschichte der Juden in Posen* (1865) 82, 100-1; Dubnow, Simon, *Weltgeschichte des jüdischen Volkes,* vol. 7 (1928) 142; idem, *History of the Jews in Russia and Poland,* vol. 1 (1916) 174; Natonek, *Kether Shem Tob, Festgabe zum 25-jährigen Amtsjubiläum des Rabbiners Dr. Moritz Landsberg in Liegnitz* (1880).

LOBO, MOSES FINZI, journalist, b. Bridgetown, Barbados, West Indies, 1834; d. Philadelphia, 1904. He came to the United States at the age of eleven, and was educated in the public schools of Philadelphia. From 1859 to 1867 he worked for Henry Cohen, a stationery importer.

He was on the editorial staff of the *North American* and of the *Age,* and he was appointed head of the press bureau established at the Centennial Exhibition of 1876. For a time he served as private secretary to the superintendent of the Philadelphia Mint, but he resigned that post in order to devote his full time to literary and journalistic pursuits. He wrote grammatical works and several articles on the history of Pennsylvania. He also wrote numerous political tracts from the viewpoint of the radical Republicans. It is difficult to estimate his full importance because many of his writings were published anonymously.

Lobo was an Orthodox Jew, and in 1860 he joined Congregation Mickve Israel, with which he remained affiliated until his death.

LOCKER, BERL, Labor Zionist, b. Krivetz, Galicia, 1877. He studied at the German Gymnasium in Serat, Bucovina, then at the law school of the German University at Czernowitz. Locker began to write in 1902 for the *Yiddisher Arbeiter,* published in Lemberg; from 1911 to 1914 he was editor of the paper. In the meantime, too, he had been instrumental in organizing the Poale (Labor) Zionist party in Austria. During the period of the first World War (1914-18) Locker was for some time in the United States, where he was a contributor to Yiddish labor papers. In 1916, however, he organized and headed the Poale Zion offices in The Hague.

Locker remained with the right wing of the Poale Zion movement when it split in 1920. He became a member of the Zionist Executive and of the Jewish Agency in 1933. In 1942 he was living in London, where he was a member of the smaller administrative committee of the Jewish Agency. Locker was the author of several studies on Zionist problems, among them *The Jewish Labor Movement* (1920).

His wife, MALKA LOCKER, is known as a Yiddish poet, and is the author of several volumes of verse.

undertook the construction of a large modern temple and the erection of Roumanian Jewish schools. It is noteworthy that a number of Roumanian non-Jews were among those who contributed funds for this temple. One of the most prominent of these was Mihail Kogalniceanu, considered by Roumanians as their greatest statesman. But hardly had the temple been finished and was on the point of being dedicated when a violent anti-Semitic agitation broke out at Bucharest; on June 18, 1866, the populace, incited by anti-Semitic agitators, destroyed the temple.

Shortly thereafter, he sustained a still more crushing blow. His pregnant wife, Carolina, who, during the anti-Semitic agitation had fled for safety with her children to Brashov (a border city in Transylvania), died soon after reaching her destination (1866) from the fatigue and strain.

During his lifetime he had created several foundations which are still in existence. In 1823 he founded at Bucharest the "Jacob and Carolina Löbel" Roumanian school, the largest Jewish school in Roumania, which has educated tens of thousands of Jewish children. Always with the idea of spreading modern culture among the Jews, he established at Bucharest a fund for the assistance of poor Jewish students, and in the same city he formed a branch of the Alliance Israélite Universelle, making large contributions to Jewish social and welfare work in Paris.

Among the many prominent non-Jews who attended his funeral was Ion Bratianu, a former Carbonari (member of the famous secret political association which existed at the beginning and in the middle of the 19th cent. and whose aim was the establishment of democratic social republics), and later, for many years, premier of Roumania under whose government numerous laws were adopted against Jews.

LOCKSPEISER, EDWARD, writer on music, b. London, 1905. He was a student at the Royal College of Music in London, then a private pupil in composition of Nadia Boulanger in Paris. He contributed numerous critical and historical articles on music to the foremost music journals in France, England, and the United States. He was the author of a biography of Claude Debussy (New York, 1936), and the adapter into English of Henri Prunières' four-volume history of music (New York, 1939).

LOCUST, the insect most often referred to in the Bible. The locust has nine names in the Old Testament (some used collectively): *'arbeh* (interpreted as "the many" literally), the usual term; *gazam* (interpreted as "that which cuts off" literally); *geb, gob,* or *gobai* (interpreted as "that which collects or swarms" literally); *hagab* (interpreted as possibly meaning literally "that which hides the sky"); *hargol* (interpreted as "the swift runner" or "that which runs to right and left" literally); *hasil* (interpreted as "the devourer" literally); *sal'am* (interpreted as "the swallower" literally); *tzelatzal* (interpreted as "the whirring" or "buzzing one" literally); and *yelek* (interpreted literally as possibly related to the verbs meaning "to lick" and "to hasten").

The locust is a symbol of destruction in the Bible. Locusts were the eighth plague of the ten with which God afflicted the Egyptians (*Ex.* 10:12-20). The locust is used as a symbol of destruction by the Deuteronomist (*Deut.* 28:38, 42), by the Psalmist (*Ps.* 78:46), by Amos (*Amos* 1:7-2) and by Joel (*Joel* 1:4; 2:25), and by the authors of *I Kings* (*I Kings* 8:37) and *II Chronicles* (*II Chron.* 6:28; 7:13). The description in *Joel* (*Joel* 2:2-10) of an invading army is generally believed to picture a plague of locusts. In the New Testament, locusts are described as feeding upon men "which have not the seal of God in their foreheads" (*Rev.* 9:4).

The locust is also used in the Hebrew Bible as the symbol of a multitude (*Judges* 6:5; 7:12; *Jer.* 46:23; *Nahum* 3:15), of discipline without command (*Prov.* 30:27; perhaps *Joel* 2:7), of small stature (*Num.* 13:33), of weakness (*Ps.* 109:23; *Nahum* 3:17), and of insignificance (*Isa.* 40:22).

'Arbeh, sal'am, hargol, and *hagab* are among the "winged swarming things" which may be eaten by Israelites (*Lev.* 11:21-22). However, because of the difficulty of distinguishing the locusts that may be eaten from those forbidden, the rabbinical authorities of the Middle Ages forbade them all. According to the general interpretation, John the Baptist lived on locusts and wild honey (*Matt.* 3:4; *Mark* 1:6), but some authorities hold that carob pods or beans, which look like locusts, are meant. Locusts are used for food to this day in the Near East and are sold, it is said, in the markets of Baghdad and Damascus. But they are eaten only by the Bedouins, by the poor, if at all, and are fed to horses and camels.

Locusts are still one of the dread plagues of Palestine. At the beginning of 1928 they covered the plain of Jezreel. The English troops attacked them with flame throwers and, in a single district of Transjordania, collected 3,700 liters of locust eggs.

CHARLES REZNIKOFF.

LODOMERIA, *see* GALICIA.

LODZ, the second largest and one of the youngest cities in Poland. It was founded in the first half of the 18th cent., and in 1793 it was a village of 191 inhabitants, among them eleven Jews. It grew so rapidly that in 1939 Lodz had 650,000 inhabitants, including 250,000 Jews. The city is called the Polish Manchester because of its very large textile industry, in whose growth the Jews took the first and largest part.

The rapid growth of the Jewish population of Lodz may be illustrated by the following table:

YEAR	JEWISH POPULATION	PER CENT OF TOTAL POPULATION
1808	58	13.4
1827	397	14.0
1857	2,886	11.7
1897	98,386	31.8
1921	156,155	34.5

Until 1806 Lodz belonged to Prussia, and then, until 1915, it belonged to the Russian Empire. During the first World War it was occupied by the Germans, and after 1918 it was the industrial center of the republic of Poland.

The big textile industry was founded in 1823 by weavers from Silesia. But the first weavers were handworkers on handlooms. The first steam weaving looms were introduced in 1835. During this period the Jews had to live in a special Jewish quarter, the so-called Baluty. A large Jewish and non-Jewish immigration to Lodz started in the middle of the 19th cent., when the custom border between Russia and Russian Poland was abolished. Long before it was known in the United States the sweating system was well-known in Lodz, especially in one of its suburbs. Brzeziny was the center of the cheapest manufacturing labor in Poland.

Lodz, together with Warsaw and Bialystok, was the chief center of the Jewish proletariat. Although the Polish labor unions were not friendly toward the Jewish labor movement and toward the growing employment of the Jewish laboring masses, the number of Jewish workers steadily increased. The Jews of Lodz founded many weaving businesses, from the smallest shops to the biggest factories; thus, for instance, one-third of the production of Lodz and almost all commerce were concentrated in their hands. It is noteworthy that the Jews of Lodz founded textile industries in several other countries to which they emigrated since 1920, i.e. in Roumania and in Palestine, where they founded the first textile factory, "Lodzia." Statistics show that among the gainfully occupied Jews in Lodz there were 45 per cent of laborers, 10 per cent of employees, and 45 per cent of other employed persons, i.e. merchants, the intelligentsia and handicraftsmen.

The political, social and cultural life of the Jews in Lodz was most diversified. As in all parts of Poland, the three main political trends were represented in Lodz: the Orthodox, the Zionist and the Socialist movements. Lodz was particularly strong in its labor movement among the Orthodox Jews, the Poale Agudath Israel. In Lodz two Yiddish daily newspapers were published, the *Lodzer Tagblatt* and the *Lodzer Folksblatt.* Lodz was the center of the national Jewish high schools of Poland. Dr. Marcus Mordecai Braude, a progressive rabbi in Lodz for more than twenty-five years, and a senator in the Polish Sejm, was the president of this network, of which several standard schools were in Lodz itself. The largest manufacturers among the Jews were J. K. Poznanski (outstanding textile manufacturers of Eastern Europe), B. Dobranicki, Borys and Naum Etingom, Oskar (Usher) Kohn and J. Spektor. Several of them founded big hospitals and charitable institutions. From Lodz came the world-famous chess champion David Janowski. Lodz had among its Jewish residents such eminent Jewish painters and sculptors as Enrico (Henryk) Glicenstein, Samuel Hirszenberg, Leopold Pilichowski, and Arthur Szyk. The noted novelist David Frischman came from Lodz. The influential club of the Jewish intelligentsia had as its president Albert Thon. Lodz sent to every Polish parliament a Zionist deputy, among them Dr. Jerzy Rosenblatt, and an Orthodox deputy, Rabbi Halpern, later an Orthodox deputy named Mincberg. The spiritual leaders of Lodz included Rabbi Pinchas Hillel (d. 1823), Rabbi Ezekiel (d. 1851), Adolf M. Radin, Israel Jelsky and Marcus Mordecai Braude.

Lodz was invaded in the first days of September, 1939, by the Germans. Many Jews fled, but most of them remained. Some 50,000 of the Jewish population were forced to leave Lodz for Warsaw or Cracow, but the remainder, about 150,000, were driven to the narrow streets of the old Jewish ghetto. Lodz was the first city in Europe in which the Germans set up a ghetto (1939), under the supervision of the so-called "der Älteste der Juden in Lodz," Hayim Rumkowski, a well-known Jewish philanthropist. The Jews in the ghetto of Lodz were forced to perform labor services for the Germans. In 1941 some 20,000 were transferred to the munitions factories near Berlin. Early in 1942 the textile factories in Lodz, owned by J. K. Poznanski, were taken over by a German-Italian syndicate. In that year about 8,000 Jews living in the Lodz ghetto were employed in the textile factories of the city.   Joseph Thon.

LOEB, AUGUST BENJAMIN, financier and communal worker, b. Bechtheim, Germany, 1841; d. Ventnor, N. J., 1915. He came to the United States at the age of ten, and was educated in the public schools of Philadelphia. He and two brothers organized a corporation for the manufacture of tartaric acid preparations, one of the first of its kind in the country; he served as president of the corporation. He later entered the banking business, and in 1893 he became a director of the Finance Company of Pennsylvania. He was elected director of the Tradesmen's National Bank in 1896 and president in 1910, a position which he held until his death. He was also a director of the Real Estate Trust Company, the South Chester Tube Company, and the Philadelphia Rapid Transit Company.

Loeb contributed generously to both Jewish and general charities, and especially to the Jewish Hospital

Isidor Loeb

and Home for the Aged and Infirm of Philadelphia. He became treasurer of that organization in 1880, and later served as chairman of the executive committee and of the committee on investments. In 1864 he and his brothers endowed a room in the new building of the Home for Aged and Infirm Israelites in memory of their parents.

LOEB, HANAU WOLF, physician, b. Philadelphia, 1865; d. St. Louis, Mo., 1927. He was educated at the University of Missouri (A.B., 1883; A.M., 1886) and the College of Physicians and Surgeons of Columbia University (M.D., 1888). He practised medicine in St. Joseph, Mo., for two years, and then removed to St. Louis.

In 1905 he was elected president of the American Academy of Ophthalmology and Oto-Laryngology, and in 1909 he was a member of the House of Delegates of the American Medical Association. In 1890 he was one of the founders of the Marion-Sims Beaumont School of Medicine. He became professor of laryngology at the St. Louis University School of Medicine in 1904 and dean in 1913; he held these two posts until his death.

Loeb was one of the first to volunteer his services when the United States entered the first World War, and he was commissioned a major in the Medical Corps. In 1919 he was promoted to the rank of colonel. At this time he published *A Handbook on Military Surgery of the Ear, Nose and Throat*, recognized by the medical profession as standard work on the subject.

In 1924 he was elected president of the American Laryngological, Rhinological and Otological Society. He was also editor of the *Annals of Otology, Rhinology and Laryngology.*

Lit.: Kagan, S. R., *Jewish Contributions to Medicine in America* (1939) 274-75.

LOEB, ISIDOR, university dean, brother of Hanau Wolf Loeb, b. Roanoke, Mo., 1868. Loeb received his

Jacob M. Loeb

M.S. and LL.B. degrees from the University of Missouri in 1893, when he had already been a tutor in history there for a year. In 1895 he was made assistant professor and in 1899 professor of political science and public law. This post Loeb retained until 1925, although in 1899 and 1900 he studied at the University of Berlin and in 1901 received his Ph.D. degree from Columbia University. From 1910 to 1916 he was also dean of the university faculty, and from 1916 to 1925 dean of the faculty of business and public administration. During 1923 Loeb was acting president of the university. He was called to Washington University, in St. Louis, in 1925, to serve as dean of the faculty of business and public administration there. He was made emeritus in 1940.

Loeb was active in various civic posts, an outgrowth of his pragmatic application of the theoretical problems which he taught. He was a consulting expert for the state of Missouri in problems of taxation, a legal adviser in food administration (1917-18), and a member of the constitution commission in 1921. In 1942 he was serving as reemployment committeeman for the St. Louis county draft district and as special representative to the National Defense Medical Board. Loeb also occupied executive posts in secular and Jewish communal undertakings; among these were his presidency of the Jewish Federation of St. Louis (1934) and his membership on the board of directors of the National Refugee Council. He was co-founder and first secretary of the State Historical Society of Missouri, and (1931) president of the American Political Science Association.

The manifold activities in which Loeb participated, together with his scholastic standing, made him one of the most outstanding citizens of the state. He was author of: *Legal Property Relations of Married Parties* (1900); *Government in Missouri* (1912); *Syllabus of American Citizenship* (1920). He was co-editor of the

Journal, Missouri Constitutional Convention of 1875 (2 vols., 1920) and of *Debates, Missouri Constitutional Convention of 1875,* of which nine volumes appeared between 1935 and 1942. He received the honorary LL.D. degree from the University of Missouri (1933).

LOEB, ISIDORE, rabbi and historian, b. Sulznatt, Upper Alsace, 1839; d. Paris, 1892. He was educated in the Orthodox Jewish tradition by his father, Rabbi Seligmann Loeb. He later studied at the college of Rufach, the Lycée of Colmar, and the Séminaire Israélite de France in Paris (Rabbi, 1862).

He tutored for three years at Bayonne and Paris, and in 1865 he was called to serve as rabbi of the congregation of Saint Étienne. In 1869 he became secretary of the Alliance Israélite Universelle, a post which he held until his death; he collected the famous library of the Alliance, one of the world's most extensive libraries of Judaica. In 1878 Loeb succeeded Albert Cohn as professor of Jewish history at the Paris rabbinical seminary. Two years later he became one of the founders of the Société des Études Juives and the editor of its organ, the *Revue des études juives.*

Loeb was a prolific author of scholarly works on Jewish history, philosophy, and literature. His books include: *La situation des Israélites en Turquie, en Serbie, et en Roumanie* (1869); *Biographie d'Albert Cohn* (1878); *Les juifs de Russie* (1891).

LOEB, JACOB MORITZ, communal worker, b. Chicago, 1875. He was in the insurance business. From 1912 on, he was president of the Chicago Hebrew Institute (afterwards, The Jewish People's Institute).

In 1913 Loeb was appointed a member of the Chicago board of education, and held the office until 1922. He was president of the board from 1914 to 1917 and again from 1918 to 1919. He was instrumental in inaugurating military training in the public high schools of the city, and fought political influence in school affairs. With Harry A. Lipsky, another member of the board, he succeeded in having Hebrew made part of the high school curriculum, and he had public schools named after Theodor Herzl and Emil G. Hirsch.

Loeb was chairman of the drive in 1921 for the relief of Jewish war sufferers, and succeeded in almost doubling Chicago Jewry's quota of a million dollars. He originated the "foodless banquet" as a means of impressing his audience with the necessity which they were asked to relieve. He was chairman of other successful drives to raise money for local institutions (1922 and 1925), and was vice-president of the Jewish Welfare Board.

Lit.: Bregstone, Philip P., *Chicago and Its Jews* (1933) 169-74; *History of the Jews of Chicago* (1924; edited by Hyman L. Meites and published by the Jewish Historical Society of Illinois) 308, 310.

LOEB, JACQUES, biologist, b. Mayen, Germany, 1859; d. Hamilton, Bermuda, 1924. Loeb was the descendant of Portuguese Jews who had migrated to the Rhine provinces during the Inquisition. Both his parents died before he was sixteen, and Loeb went to work in a bank owned by an uncle of his in Berlin. He studied at the Askanisches Gymnasium

Jacques Loeb

in that city, and in 1880 entered the University of Berlin, planning to specialize in philosophy. Then his interest changed to science, and after periods of study at various German universities, he received his medical degree from the University of Strasbourg in 1884.

Between 1885 and 1891, when he came to the United States, Loeb was an assistant in physiology at the Universities of Würzburg and Strasbourg, and at the biological station in Naples. His first work was in brain physiology, which later elicited sarcastic comments from Loeb himself. At the end of his long career he was working with colloids, which he considered the basis of human life, and he pointed out the irony of the young scientist undertaking the study of man as a whole, while the experienced scientist was content to examine the simplest form in biological matter.

Loeb was called to Bryn Mawr, Pa., as an associate in biology in 1891. In the following year he went to the University of Chicago, where he eventually became a full professor and where he remained until 1910. In 1910 the Rockefeller Institute made Loeb the head of its division in general physiology, and under the auspices of this institution Loeb proceeded with the studies which had already won him international renown as well as opposition. Loeb discredited a theory of evolution which used words like "environment" and "adaptation" in a fashion he considered careless. Some of his experiments were directed toward proving that certain forms of life reacted instinctively in uniform ways to experiences which they could not previously have had; Loeb therefore considered part of the evolutionary argument invalidated. The components of environment, however, fascinated him, and in seeking to break down the larger term into its chemical constituents he reached his own materialistic philosophy. Loeb's theory of tropisms, presented in 1889, clarified his interpretation of the physical and chemical processes of life,

In 1899 the tropism theory was applied by Loeb to animals as well. That same year he made a successful experiment that brought him much more popular acclaim than he wanted, for Loeb knew the smallness of his accomplishment beside the greatness of the problem. By treating eggs of the sea-urchin with solutions of sugar and salt, he succeeded in fertilizing the eggs and thus presented an actual case of parthenogenesis. As his studies continued, Loeb offered additional evidence for his theory that all life is conditioned by chemical processes. The same chemicals, according to him, both created life and destroyed it, since the solutions with the aid of which he succeeded in fertilizing eggs artificially could also, in different proportions, dissolve a living cell. One of his discoveries was a saline solution which is used in restoration of living matter.

Loeb's experiments with marine life led to the establishment of a special laboratory in Bermuda, and it was while working there that he died. His published work ranged from scientific studies to lengthy presentations for more popular consumption. Among his books were: *Artificial Parthenogenesis and Fertilization* (1913); *The Dynamics of Living Matter* (1906); *Studies in General Physiology* (2 vols., 1905); *The Organism as a Whole* (1916); *Forced Movements, Tropisms and Animal Conduct* (1918); *Proteins and the Theory of Colloidal Behavior* (1922). He was the founder of the *Journal of General Physiology* (1918), and its co-editor until his death.

NATHAN RICARDO.

Lit.: De Kruif, Paul H., "Jacques Loeb," *American Mercury*, July, 1925, pp. 273-79; Osterhut, W. J. V., "Jacques Loeb," *Jacques Loeb Memorial Volume, The Journal of General Physiology* (1928); Harrow, Benjamin, "Some Notes on Jacques Loeb," *Menorah Journal*, Dec., 1925, pp. 620-23; *American Hebrew*, Feb. 15, 1924, p. 416; Kagan, S. R., *Jewish Contributions to Medicine in America* (1939) 328-31.

LOEB, JAMES, banker and classical scholar, b. New York city, 1867; d. Murnau, Bavaria, Germany, 1933. He was the son of Solomon Loeb and the brother of Morris Loeb. Loeb was graduated from Harvard University in 1888, and shortly thereafter entered the banking firm which his father had helped to establish—Kuhn, Loeb and Co. His cultural interests, however, outweighed his interests in banking, and in 1901 Loeb retired from the firm. About 1912 he gave up his residence in the United States, and spent most of the rest of his life in Murnau.

Before leaving the United States, Loeb had founded the Institute of Musical Art in New York, in memory of his mother, and had also given the Music Building to Harvard. After settling in Germany, he continued his benefactions in cultural fields on both sides of the ocean, although the first World War (1914-18) kept him, for its duration, devoted especially to the alleviation of war suffering in Bavaria. In 1912 Loeb established the Loeb Classical Library, as the result of an idea presented by Salomon Reinach (1858-1932), the archeologist and scholar. Through the Library, classical texts, with English translations facing each page, were offered to the world. Loeb was variously honored for the services which the Library performed in the presentation of classical

Leo Loeb

literature to larger sections of the population; Cambridge University gave him an honorary LL.D. degree in 1926.

Loeb was himself the translator of several studies on the classics, mostly from French into English. He was a member and trustee of archeological and other scientific societies in many countries, and endowed a lectureship in the Archaeological Institute of America. The University of Munich, in 1922, gave him an honorary Ph.D. degree in recognition of his efforts in relieving the War and post-War famine in the vicinity. With his brother Morris Loeb, he presented the Solomon and Betty Loeb Memorial Home for Convalescents in East View, N. Y. The terms of his will left $800,000 to Harvard College, $300,000 of which was to be used in establishing the Loeb Classical Library Foundation. The American School of Classical Studies in Athens received $500,000, as did also the Loeb Memorial Home.

Lit.: *American Hebrew*, June 2, 1933, p. 61.

LOEB, LEO, professor of comparative pathology, b. Mayen, Germany, 1869. He studied at the Universities of Heidelberg, Freiburg, Basel, Edinburgh, Berlin and Zurich from 1889 until 1896. In 1896 he received his M.D. degree from the University of Zurich. In 1900 he left Europe for the United States, and served as adjunct professor of pathology at the College of Physicians and Surgeons in Chicago for one year. In 1902 he was experimental pathologist of the New York State Pathological Laboratory in Buffalo. In 1903 he became research fellow at McGill University, Montreal. From 1903 to 1904 he was demonstrator, and from 1904 to 1910 assistant professor of experimental pathology in charge of laboratory at the University of Pennsylvania.

From 1910 to 1915 Loeb was the director of the Department of Pathology at the Barnard Free Skin and Cancer Hospital, in St. Louis. From 1915 to 1936 he was Edward Mallinckrodt Professor of Pathology at the University of Washington, and at the same time pathologist of the Barnes, St. Louis Children's,

and St. Louis Maternity hospitals. On January 1, 1937, he became professor emeritus of pathology and research professor of pathology at the University of Washington, and still held this position in 1942.

From 1908 to 1909 Loeb was a member of the editorial board of the *Folia Haematologica*, from 1908 to 1911 he served on the editorial board of the *Folia Serologica*, and after 1918 on the editorial board of the *Journal of Cancer Research*.

Among his published works are: *The Vernon of Heloderma* (1913); *Effect of Undernourishment on Mammalian Ovary and the Sexual Cycle*, and *Causes and Definition of Cancer*, both published in *Collected Papers from the Washington University School of Medicine* (1921); *Edema* (1923).

LOEB, LOUIS, painter, b. Cleveland, 1866; d. Canterbury, N. H., 1909. In the first decade of the 20th cent. Louis Loeb ranked, with the possible exception of Albert Sterner, as the most distinguished painter among American Jews. He felt the urge toward art in his earliest teens, and became apprentice to a lithographer in his native city. Before he was twenty he went to New York to study at the night schools of the Art Students League. Five years later, in 1890, he was in Paris, in the famous atelier of Gêrome. A painting of Loeb's was awarded a medal at the Paris Salon in 1897. Meanwhile, and for some years thereafter, he earned his more assured bread and butter through magazine illustrations. Of them it may be said that they far excelled the work of the great majority of contemporary illustrators by reason of their rich painting quality. But it was not until the early 1900's that Loeb came fully into his own. To that period belong his best-known canvases, among which *Temple of the Winds, The Breeze, The Joyous Life,* and *The Dawn* are preeminent.

Loeb was a very able and sympathetic portraitist, as his presentments of Israel Zangwill, Eleanor Robson and Jacob H. Schiff make manifest. Yet he will be remembered foremost for his landscape. In the *Temple of the Winds,* which won the Silver Medal at Buffalo's Pan-American Exposition, there is a feeling of ideality in the striving figures, a feeling of nobility in crags and sky that, quite apart from harmonious arrangement, give stirring appeal to the canvas. *The Dawn* is an idyllic landscape which would have done honor to the brush of Corot. By common consent of art critics it deserved the Webb Prize awarded it in 1903. Perhaps the loveliest of all of Loeb's paintings is *The Joyous Life.* Here a group of maidens form a rhythmic wave of human beauty amid the beauty of Nature.

Those who knew Loeb saw in the delicacy of his colors and the sensitiveness of his brushwork indications of the man himself. Reserved—even shy— thoughtful, modest, idealistic, Loeb was an artist who painted few canvases, not so much because he died comparatively young (in 1909, at the age of forty-three), but because he was non-commercial and ever strove to achieve his deep intent. Painstakingly he reached toward that beauty which appeals to the spirit as well as to the eye. In his masterpieces he attained it.   GEORGE S. HELLMAN.

LOEB, MORRIS, chemist and philanthropist, b. Cincinnati, 1867; d. New York city, 1912. He was the son of Solomon Loeb and the brother of James Loeb. After receiving his A.B. degree from Harvard University in 1883, Loeb studied chemistry at the Universities of Heidelberg, Leipzig and Berlin, receiving his Ph.D. degree in Berlin in 1887. He remained in Germany studying for another year, then returned to the United States, where he became assistant to Wolcott Gibbs at Newport, R. I. From 1899 to 1901 Loeb taught at Clark University; in 1891 he became professor of chemistry at New York University, which post he retained until 1910. From 1895 to 1906 he was also director of the chemical laboratory at New York University.

Loeb severed his university connections in 1910 to devote all his time to his private laboratory and to his philanthropic activities. Since before the turn of the 20th cent. he had been active, not only as a donor, but as a directive force, in many of the Jewish communal undertakings that marked the period of heavy immigration into the United States. He was among the first directors of the Jewish Agricultural and Industrial Aid Society, serving with the organization from 1900 to 1914. During this time he was especially concerned with the establishment of the Industrial Removal Office (1901) and with the various farm experiments supervised by the Society, such as the Jewish Agricultural Experiment Station in New Jersey. Loeb was also president of the Hebrew Technical Institute for many terms and a trustee of the Jewish Theological Seminary of America, in New York city, from its foundation. As part of his belief in the scientific treatment of social welfare, particularly in relation to immigration, Loeb established a Bureau of Statistics at his own expense. He was one of the founders of the American Jewish Committee and of the Educational Alliance. Shortly before Loeb's death Mayor William J. Gaynor of New York appointed him to the Board of Education.

Loeb wrote extensively for chemical journals, and devised some apparatus for experiments in chemistry. He aided the furthering of chemical studies in the United States, and was for a time president of the Chemists' Club.

See also HIRSCH FUND, BARON DE.

Lit.: American Chemical Journal, vol. 48 (1912) 547-48; Sulzberger, Cyrus L., "Morris Loeb," *Publications of the American Jewish Historical Society,* No. 22 (1914) 225-27; Joseph, Samuel, *History of the Baron de Hirsch Fund* (1935).

LOEB, MORITZ, journalist, b. Unkstein, Germany, 1812; d. Doylestown, Pa., 1887. After working for nine years for a newspaper in Lebanon, Pa., he bought, while still in his early twenties, an interest in *Der Morgenstern,* a weekly newspaper published in German at Doylestown, Pa. He was its editor—for nearly fifty years—until his retirement in 1885.

Loeb was at first a Whig and then a Republican. His influence with President Abraham Lincoln and the members of the Republican Party procured the exemption of the Mennonites from military service. Lincoln offered him the post of United States consul at Stuttgart, Germany, but he declined it. He wrote for Jewish periodicals as well as his own, and con-tributed fiction to the *Deborah,* edited in Cincinnati by Isaac M. Wise.

LOEB, ROBERT, pharmacologist, b. Chicago, 1895. He was educated at Harvard University (M.D., 1919). In 1928 he was appointed professor of medicine at the Columbia University College of Physicians and Surgeons, a post which he still held in 1942. In recognition of his contributions to medical science he was awarded the Stevens Triennial Prize of Columbia University in 1934.

Loeb was remarkable for his patience and industry in experimentation as well as for his brilliance. As early as 1918 he worked with G. Minot on the prevention of influenza. Later he specialized in diseases of metabolism. He and Jacques Loeb studied the effect of electrolytes on the solution and precipitation of casein and gelatine in 1921. He later made further experiments with electrolytes, and in 1933 he investigated electrolyte balance in adrenalectomized dogs. He wrote numerous articles on pharmacology and internal medicine for professional journals.

LOEB, ROBERT FREDERICK, professor of medicine, b. Chicago, 1895. He received his medical degree from Harvard University in 1919. In 1921 he joined the staff of the Presbyterian Hospital in New York city, and remained there until 1938. Loeb became associate medical director of the Neurological Institute in New York city in 1938, and in 1942 was still serving in that capacity. He was also, in 1942, associate professor of medicine at Columbia University, with which he had become affiliated in 1921.

LOEB, SOLOMON, banker and philanthropist, b. Germany, 1828; d. New York city, 1903. He came to the United States in 1849 and settled in Cincinnati, where he entered the dry goods business. In 1865 he moved to New York, and with Abraham Kuhn and Samuel Wolff established the banking firm of Kuhn, Loeb and Co. Through the marriage of two of Loeb's daughters to Jacob H. Schiff and Paul M. Warburg, the family interest in the firm was retained even after the retirement of Loeb's son, James Loeb (1901). Loeb was a contributor to numerous charities, and on the occasion of his seventieth birthday donated the Hebrew Charities Building to the New York community. His sons James and Morris established the Solomon and Betty Loeb Memorial Home for Convalescents in East View, N. Y., in 1906.

Lit.: American Hebrew, Dec. 18, 1903, p. 188; Adler, Cyrus, *Jacob H. Schiff, His Life and Letters* (1928).

LOEB, SOPHIE IRENE (née Simon), social worker and journalist, b. Russia, 1874; d. New York city, 1929. She was brought to the United States as a child and taken to McKeesport, Pa., where she attended school. In 1896 she married Anselm Loeb. In 1910 she became a feature writer for the New York *Evening World,* and during her visits to the slum neighborhoods of the city, on reporting assignments, she saw how badly state legislation was needed for the remedying of social injustices, particularly those affecting children. Her propaganda was partly responsible for the passing of the Widows' Pension Law of New York State in 1914, and she then started a national campaign toward the same end. Miss Loeb

Sophie Irene Loeb

sought to provide a continuance of home life for children who had been orphaned or who were for other reasons in danger of being institutionalized. She was a member of the New York State Commission for Widows' Pensions, and afterwards president of the Child Welfare Committee of America. Miss Loeb was one of the leaders at the First International Child Congress in 1926, and in 1927 she was a member of the social service section of the League of Nations engaged in framing an international code for the care of dependent and afflicted children. One of her campaigns resulted in the establishment of a penny-lunch system in the New York city public schools.

Miss Loeb was the first woman asked to serve as a mediator in a New York city strike (1917), when she settled a taxicab strike. She fostered a bill which permitted school buildings to be used for public forums, and was responsible for campaigns resulting in improved housing and sanitation conditions and in the elimination of fire hazards. Toward Jewish matters, Miss Loeb held a view which supported Orthodoxy against Reform religious movements; she believed that the spiritual values derived from the Orthodox teachings were a better educational basis for young people than other approaches to religious life, and attributed her own interest in social problems to her mother's orthodox instruction. She also came to regard a Jewish homeland in Palestine as an essential to the perpetuation of the ethical and spiritual values represented by the Jews. *Palestine Awake* (1926) was a compilation of her reports on a visit to that country. Among her other published works were *Epigrams of Eve* (1913) and *Everyman's Child* (1925). The city of McKeesport, Pa., where Miss Loeb spent her childhood, erected a monument in her honor, and in 1933 the Sophie Irene Loeb playground was opened on the East Side of New York.

LIBBY BENEDICT.

Lit.: Loeb, Sophie Irene, "The Great Mistake of the Jew!," *Jewish Tribune*, Sept. 23, 1927, pp. 14, 54; *ibid.*, May 29, 1925, p. 10; *American Hebrew*, Jan. 25, 1929, p. 402; *New York Times*, Jan. 19, 1929.

LOENING, German family of Jewish origin, founded by Zacharias Loewenthal, who assumed the name of Loening after his conversion to Protestantism in 1845. Loewenthal, who was born in Mannheim, studied at the University of Heidelberg and was graduated in 1833. As a student he became a friend of August Lewald and Karl Gutzkow. In 1835 Loewenthal founded a publishing house at Mannheim devoted to the tendencies of "Young Germany." However, immediately after publishing Gutzkow's novel *Wally,* Loewenthal was denounced by the corporation of German publishers, which demanded publicly that his publishing house be suppressed by the government because of the publisher's alleged "anti-Christianism." The governments of all the German states, united in the Bundestag at Frankfort, issued a general prohibition of the publications of all "Young German" authors, including Heine and Börne, and of all the publications of Loewenthal's firm. Loewenthal, financially ruined, went to France, but in 1845 returned to Germany, having changed his name and his religion, and founded the Literarische Verlagsanstalt Ruetten und Loening at Frankfort, which became one of the most important publishing houses in Germany. It was in a prosperous condition when the German Nazis seized it in 1933.

EDGAR LOENING (b. Paris, 1843; d. Halle, Germany, 1919), a son of Zacharias Loewenthal, became professor of constitutional and international law at the University of Dorpat in 1877. He was professor at the University of Rostock from 1883 on, and at the University of Halle from 1886 on. In 1901 he was appointed a member of the Prussian Upper House. He published *Geschichte des deutschen Kirchenrechts* (1878), *Lehrbuch des deutschen Verwaltungsrechts* (1884), and *Die Gemeindeverfassung des Urchristentums* (1888). In 1899 Loening published a study on the representative constitution, *Die Representativverfassung im 19. Jahrhundert.* He was co-editor of the *Handwörterbuch der Staatswissenschaften.*

RICHARD LOENING (b. Frankfort, 1848; d. Jena, 1903), another son of Zacharias Loewenthal, was professor of criminal law at the University of Jena from 1882 until his death. He was highly esteemed because of his juridical, historical and philosophical views, and was an authority on civil process law. In 1876 Loening dealt with the problem of breach of contract in his study *Der Vertragsbruch und seine Rechtsfolgen.* In 1903 he presented a thoroughgoing study of the problem of responsibility, from the juridical and philosophical points of view, in his *Geschichte der strafrechtlichen Zurechnungsfähigkeit.* Two other important works of his were *Die Wiederklage im Reichszivilprozess* (1881) and *Die strafrechtliche Haftung des verantwortlichen Redakteurs* (1889). In his lecture "Wurzel und Wesen des Rechts" (1901) Loening displayed his credo, which was opposed to the "imperative" as well as to the "positivist" theory of law. According to Loening, law has to harmonize social life by adjusting individual rights to collective rules.

OTTO LOENING (b. Dorpat, Estonia, 1880), first son of Edgar Loening, was professor of law at the University of Danzig and the first vice-president of the free city. He published several studies on the legis-

lation of medieval German towns and the constitution
of Danzig. He was retired from office in 1933.

HERMANN LOENING (b. Rostock, 1885), second son
of Edgar Loening, was co-editor of *Wirtschaft und
Recht,* and occupied important posts in German industrial organizations. Like his brother Otto, he was
compelled to retire from office in 1933 with the advent of the Nazis to power in Germany.

LILI LOENING, daughter of Zacharias Loewenthal,
married Otto von Gierke, one of the eminent jurists
in German history. Gierke, founder of the Genossen-
schaft, also helped create the Deutschnationale Volks-
partei which succeeded the conservative party in
1918. He tried constantly, but in vain, to wean his
party away from anti-Semitism. His six children
were in important positions when the Nazis came
to power and turned them out of office.

HUGO BIEBER.

LOESKE, LEOPOLD, botanist, b. Hohensalza,
Germany, 1865; d. Berlin, 1935. He was a recognized
expert on moss flora. Loeske was the type of
modest scholar who, hardly known to the public, was
so much the more esteemed by his colleagues. He published a great deal of the results of his researches in
botanical magazines, and became editor of the *Bryol-
ogische Zeitschrift* in 1916. His books included:
Moosflora des Harzes (1903); *Studien zur vergleichen-
den Morphologie und Systematik der Laubmoose*
(1910); *Die Laubmoose Europas* (vol. 1, 1914; vol.
2, 1930); *Monographie der europäischen Grimmiaceen*
(1930); *Bryologica Universalis* (in collaboration with
M. Fleischer; 1918).

LOEVE-VEIMARS, ADOLPH, French journalist, translator and diplomat, b. Paris, 1801; d. Paris,
1854. In 1814 Loeve-Veimar's parents, who were
German Jews, returned to Hamburg, their native
city, and Loeve-Veimars became a merchant's clerk.
But he was dissatisfied with his profession and with
life in Germany. By 1821 he had become converted
to Christianity and left Hamburg for Paris. At first
he earned his living in Paris by translating German
literature into French, but soon he began to publish
historical and literary studies. In 1824 he published a
history of the German vehmic courts, *Précis d'histoire
des tribunaux secrets dans le nord d'Allemagne,* in
1828 *Résumé de la littérature allemande,* from 1827
to 1830 *Scènes contemporaines et scènes historiques,*
and in 1833 *Népenthès,* a collection of stories and
critical essays.

Loeve-Veimars met with even greater acclaim
through his translation into French, beginning with
1829, of the tales of the German romantic poet E.
Th. Hoffmann, and, from 1831, of several works of
Heinrich Heine. Loeve-Veimars also rendered other
services to Heine, especially when the poet had to
write in French or to negotiate with French publishers. For Loeve-Veimars had, by 1830, become an
influential personage in French literature and society.

In 1830 he became literary editor and drama critic
of the newly founded newspaper *Le Temps,* and from
1833 on he was a regular contributor to the *Revue
des deux mondes* who attracted international attention by his articles on French statesmen and foreign
affairs. In 1835 he became a member of the board of

directors of the Grand Opera of Paris. In 1836 Louis
Adolphe Thiers, who was minister of foreign affairs
and esteemed Loeve-Veimars highly, sent him to Russia on a diplomatic mission. In the same year he
was appointed French consul at Baghdad. In 1849
he became consul in Caracas, Venezuela, and in 1853
returned to Paris to be informed of a more important
appointment at Lima, Peru. While preparing for his
departure for Peru, he died suddenly. Heine composed
an obituary notice on Loeve-Veimars, defending him
against his detractors but by no means concealing
some of the weak points of his old friend, whom he
liked because Loeve-Veimars disliked Hamburg's merchants as much as Heine himself did.

Lit.: Heine, Heinrich, *Loeve-Veimars* (1855); Janin,
Jules, in *Journal des Débats,* Nov. 20, 1854; Sainte-Beuve,
Premiers lundis, vol. 2; Véron, *Mémoires d'un bourgeois de
Paris,* vol. 3.

LOEVENHART, ARTHUR SOLOMON, pharmacologist, b. Lexington, Ky., 1878; d. Madison, Wis.,
1929. He was educated at Kentucky State University
(B.S., 1898; M.S., 1899) and at Johns Hopkins University (M.D., 1903). From 1903 to 1908 he served as
assistant and then associate professor of pharmacology
and physiological chemistry at Johns Hopkins University. In 1908 he became professor in pharmacology
and toxicology at the University of Wisconsin, a post
which he held until his death. He was chief pharmacologist and secretary of the research division of
the Chemical Warfare Service of the American University in 1918. From 1919 to 1921 he was president
of the Society for Pharmacology and Experimental
Therapeutics.

Loevenhart was one of the leading pharmacologists
of his day. His most important work was his research
on the relation of chemical composition to pharmacological action in antisyphilitic drugs. His experimentation in this field led to his being regarded by
many as the successor to Paul Ehrlich. He wrote
numerous articles on pharmacological subjects for
medical journals.

LOEVINGER, GUSTAVUS, judge, b. Neu Ulm,
Germany, 1881. He came to the United States at the
age of eight, and was educated in the public schools
of Mitchell, S. D., and at Dakota Wesleyan University
(A.B., 1903). Later he studied at the College of Law
of the University of Minnesota (LL.B., 1906). In
1932 he was awarded the honorary LL.D. degree by
Dakota Wesleyan University.

Immediately after his graduation from law school
Loevinger was employed as associate editor of *Current Law,* a periodical published at St. Paul, Minn. One
year later he resigned to engage in private law practice. In 1931 he was appointed judge of the District
Court of Ramsey County, Minn., by Governor Floyd
B. Olson. In the following year he was elected to the
same post, and was reelected in 1938.

Loevinger was actively interested in Jewish affairs.
He was one of the founders of the Jewish Literary
Society of the University of Minnesota, probably the
first Jewish literary society in any American university. He served as a director of the Jewish Home
for the Aged of the Northwest, a member of the
executive committee of the Zionist Organization of

America, a trustee of Mount Zion Congregation, a delegate to the first American Jewish Congress, and a delegate to the Keren Hayesod meeting in New York. He was a contributing editor of the Minneapolis *American Jewish World* for many years before he became a judge in 1931.

LOEVINSON, ERMANNO (HERMANN), historian, b. Berlin, 1863. In 1889 he went to Rome, where in 1891 he became a naturalized Italian citizen after being appointed keeper of the Archives, a post which he occupied until 1927. He also taught in the Roman State Lyceum. In 1927 he was made director of the Parma Royal State Archives, and held this position until 1930, when he was appointed superintendent and head administrator of the Bologna Archives.

Although his early work dealt with Westphalian history, his scholarly reputation rests chiefly on his contributions to Italian historiography. He wrote many articles, including several essays on the Jews of Italy, for such periodicals as the *Rassegna Storica del Risorgimento, Allgemeine Zeitung des Judentums, Ost und West, Monatsschrift für Geschichte und Wissenschaft des Judentums*, and *Nuova Antologia* (his "Camillo Cavour e gli Israeliti" was published in the latter in 1910). His *Roma Israelitica* (German; 1927), containing the author's reactions as a Jew wandering through the historic sites of Rome, is a spiritual and artistic guide to that ancient city.

Loevinson's other principal works were: *Beiträge zur Verfassungsgeschichte der westfälischen Reichsstiftsstädte* (1889); *Die Mindensche Chronik des Busso Watensted, eine Fälschung Paullinis* (1890); *Cristoforo Colombo nella letteratura tedesca* (1893); *Giuseppe Garibaldi e la sua legione nello stato romano (1848-49)* (3 vols., 1902-7); *Gli ufficiali del periodo napoleonico nello Stato Pontificale* (1914); *Gli ufficiali napoleonici parmensi* (1930); *La concession de banques de prêts aux juifs par les Papes des 16ième et 17ième siècles* (1934). In 1892 Loevinson translated into German Pasquale Villari's *La storia è una scienza?*

In 1938 Loevinson was dismissed from his position with the Bologna Archives as a result of the Italian anti-Jewish racial policy.

LOEW, ELEAZAR, *see* Löw, Eleazar.

LOEW, LOUIS, French jurist, b. Strasbourg, 1828; d. Paris, 1917. Converted to Protestantism in his early youth, Loew studied law at the University of Strasbourg, from which he was graduated in 1851. He was assistant public prosecutor at Strasbourg, and imperial public prosecutor at Altkirch and Mulhouse. In 1861 Loew became president of the court at Mulhouse, and in 1870 he assumed the same function at Le Havre. Having been attorney general at Paris for some years, Loew in 1894 became president of the criminal court at the French supreme court (cour de cassation).

By 1897 Loew had become involved in the struggle about the Dreyfus case. At first he was convinced of Dreyfus' guilt, and refused to hear any friend of Dreyfus. After reading the documents, however, he took personal charge of the appeal for revision of the

Gustavus Loevinger

trial, and directed the court's work. Revision of the Dreyfus case would surely have been thwarted if Loew had not displayed so much resolute courage and acuteness, or if another judge had presided over the criminal court. Loew was therefore violently attacked by such anti-revisionists as Rochefort and Cassagnac. He was calumniated by some of his own subordinates, even by his colleague Quesnay de Beaurepaire. The generals involved in the Dreyfus case were enraged at Loew because he was less credulous of their assertions than were the moderate or even the leftist ministers. Lebret, minister of justice in the Dupuy cabinet, hampered Loew as much as he could, and disavowed him publicly, but Loew continued his efforts and effected the admission of Madame Dreyfus' petition to review her husband's case (1899).

In 1903 Loew retired from office. He was honored by the president of the republic and appointed grand officier of the Légion d'honneur, but was the continual object of threats by the anti-Dreyfusards, who never forgave Loew for the service he had rendered the cause of Dreyfus.

Lit.: Reinach, Joseph, *Histoire de l'affaire Dreyfus* (1905).

LOEW, MARCUS, motion picture magnate, b. New York city, 1870; d. Glen Cove, N. Y., 1927. Beginning his career as a New York newsboy, he became one of the dominant factors in the motion picture business. Starting as the operator of penny arcades, the precursor of motion picture theatres, Loew concerned himself principally with the exhibition end of the business. While Zukor, Lasky, Selznick, and others devoted themselves to production, Loew built, operated and managed theatres. In 1919 he purchased the then dying Metro Pictures. Loew was forced into the production end of the motion picture industry because of the nation-wide fight between producers and exhibitors that threatened the Loew chain of theatres. As a precaution Loew decided to produce his own pictures.

The first production of Metro Pictures under Loew's ownership was *The Four Horsemen of the Apocalypse*, made at a cost of $640,000. The Blasco Ibañez picture grossed more than four million dollars in earnings. Before his death in 1927, Metro Pictures had become Metro-Goldwyn-Mayer, perhaps the most important producing firm in Hollywood at the time. Coincidental with this was the expansion of Loews Incorporated, with theatres throughout this country. Loew was decorated by the French government with the Legion of Honor for his promotion of French pictures. He was the head of the Gaumont chain of theatres throughout France. Besides *The Four Horsemen of the Apocalypse*, two of Loew's greatest pictures were *Ben Hur* and *The Big Parade*.

LOEWE, HEINRICH, historian and Zionist leader, b. Wanzleben, Germany, 1869. He was educated at the University of Berlin, where he worked as librarian. in 1891 he founded the society Hobebe Sefath Eber. The following year he founded the first Zionist organization in Germany, Jung-Israel, which later became the Berliner Zionistische Vereinigung. He also founded the Verein Jüdischer Studenten.

He was one of the leaders of the Zionist movement in the early days when it was little known and struggling for popular support. In 1893 and 1894 he edited the Zionist periodical *Jüdische Volkszeitung,* and in 1895 he founded the monthly *Zion,* which he edited for two years. He acted as editor of the *Jüdische Rundschau* from 1902 to 1908. He led the movement for a national Jewish library, and when the Hebrew University of Jerusalem was founded he organized the Verein der Freunde der Jerusalem-Bibliothek. In 1933 he emigrated to Palestine and became director of the municipal library of Tel-Aviv; he still held this position in 1942.

Loewe was a prolific author of books on Jewish history and folklore. He wrote also Zionist propaganda under the pseudonym of Heinrich Sachse. Among his works are: *Aus der Geschichte der Berliner Judenschaft* (1908); *Sprachen der Juden* (1911); *Die jüdisch-deutsche Sprache der Ostjuden* (1915); *Schelme und Narren mit jüdischen Kappen* (1920); *Reste von altem jüdischen Volkshumor* (1922); *Proselyten* (1926); *Geschichten von jüdischen Namen* (1929).

LOEWE, HERBERT MARTIN JAMES, orientalist, b. London, 1882; d. Cambridge, England, 1940. He was educated at St. Paul's School and at Queen's College, Cambridge. While holding the position of curator of Oriental manuscripts at the Cambridge University Library (1908-9, 1923-24, 1927), he compiled a catalogue of the Samaritan, Hebrew and Arabic-Hebrew manuscripts of the institution, and at other times catalogues of Mary Frere's manuscripts at Girton College (1916) and of Aldis Wright's manuscripts at Trinity College (1926). He was visiting lecturer in rabbinics at Cambridge in 1923 and again from 1926 to 1931, university lecturer in rabbinic Hebrew at Oxford, Maynard lecturer in Oriental languages at Exeter College, director of Oriental studies at St. Catharine's College, and Goldsmid lecturer in Hebrew at London University. During the first World War he was a lieutenant in the 11th South Staffs (1915) and head of munitions inspection at Alipore (1917).

His published works include: *Mediaeval Hebrew Minstrelsy* (1926); *Mediaeval Hebrew Poesy* (1927); *A Rabbinic Anthology* (1938); *Render unto Caesar* (Cambridge, 1940). He edited Abrahams and Stokes' *Starrs and Jewish Charters* (1933); *Essays,* by Harold Marcus Wiener; vol. 2 of *Judaism and Christianity,* with Claude G. Montefiore (1937), and contributed articles to the *Cambridge Mediaeval History,* to Hastings' *Encyclopaedia of Religions and Ethics,* and to the *Encyclopaedia Britannica.*

Lit.: Jewish Chronicle (London), Oct. 18, 1940, p. 5.

LOEWE, ISIDOR, *see* LOEWE, LUDWIG.

LOEWE, JOEL BEN JEHUDA (BRILL), Bible exegete and Hebrew grammarian, b. Berlin, 1760; d. Breslau, Germany, 1802. He studied in Berlin under Isaac Satanow, who represented the Moses Mendelssohn enlightenment movement, and himself became a protagonist of the movement. Mendelssohn's friendship for Loewe helped Loewe obtain the position as tutor in the home of David Friedländer. In 1891 Loewe became principal of the Wilhelma-Schule in Breslau, where he remained until his death.

In collaboration with Aaron Wolfsohn, Loewe edited *Hameassef* (1784-97), and in it published many of his own poems and essays. Besides helping Mendelssohn in the latter's compilation of Bible commentaries, Loewe wrote a Hebrew commentary and introduction to *Psalms* (1788), which was published in conjunction with the Mendelssohn translation of *Psalms.* Together with Wolfsohn, Loewe also published a commentary on *Song of Songs* as well as on other Biblical books. In his devotion to the poetry of the Bible Loewe practically produced a history of Biblical poetry. He was also the first to translate the Passover Haggadah into German (1785). His projected study of the elements of the Hebrew language (*Ammude Halashon*) did not get beyond the publication of the first volume (1794), and his hope of publishing a comprehensive Hebrew grammar was frustrated. Loewe was a contributor to Johann Gottfried Eichhorn's *Allgemeine Bibliothek der biblischen Literatur.*

Loewe was a participant in the movement to do away with rapid burial of the Jewish dead. He wrote personally to various Jewish burial societies (1794) urging longer waits between death and burial, and translated Marcus Herz's *Über die frühe Beerdigung der Juden* into Hebrew (1789).

Lit.: Freudenthal, "Die ersten Emanzipationsbestrebungen der Juden in Breslau," *Monatsschrift für Geschichte und Wissenschaft des Judentums,* vol. 37, pp. 37-38, 60-61.

LOEWE, LOUIS (ELIEZER HALEVI), orientalist, b. Zülz, Silesia, 1809; d. London, 1888. He was the son of Marcus Jacob Loewe, chief rabbi of Rosenberg, Silesia. Loewe studied under Rabbi Mordecai Benedict or Baneth and Rabbi Moses Sofer at Nikolsburg and Pozsony (Pressburg), receiving his theological diploma at Pozsony and his secular degree at Berlin, where he attended lectures by Schleiermacher, Neander and Hengstenberg. He was interested in oriental languages, and acquired a proficiency in thirty-nine tongues. In 1836 Loewe left Berlin for London, and was presented there to Augustus Frederick, duke of Sussex (1773-1843), a son of King George III. The duke, who became president of the Royal Society in 1838, was especially interested in the study of Hebrew and in the defense of the rights of the Jews. He grew fond of Loewe, whom he allowed to use his extensive and valuable private library. Like the duke of Sussex, the earl of Munster (son of King William IV and member of several learned societies) also protected Loewe, as did Admiral Sir Sidney Smith and other members of British aristocracy. But, as Lady Blessington said, "while Dr. Loewe is courted in society, he is left to his own resources."

Loewe explored the archives and libraries of Westminster, Oxford, Cambridge, and Paris. From 1837 to 1839 he traveled through Egypt, Nubia, Ethiopia, Syria, Palestine, Asia Minor and Greece. Passing Safed, he was robbed and tortured by the Druses. On his return to Europe, he studied for eight months in the library of the Vatican, protected by Cardinals Mezzofanti, Angelo Mai, and Lambruschini. At Rome, Loewe met Sir Moses Montefiore, who engaged him as interpreter and secretary. Loewe accompanied Sir Moses five times to Palestine, twice to Russia and to Turkey. He assisted Montefiore especially in his intervention (1840) in behalf of persecuted Jews of Damascus.

Having returned to London, Loewe became examiner for oriental languages to the Royal College of preceptors, and principal of Jews' College and of the Judith Lady Montefiore College at Ramsgate. He became the literary executor of Sir Moses Montefiore's will, and edited his *Diaries* in 1870. He translated some important hieroglyphs for Khedive Mehemet Ali Pasha, who sent a copy of Loewe's translation to King Frederick William IV of Prussia. Loewe published, in 1837, *The Origin of the Egyptian Language*, in which he sought to prove that this language was derived from Hebrew. He also edited the first *Dictionary of the Circassian Language* in 1857. He contributed various articles to the study of the topography of Palestine, and translated Isaac Baer Levinsohn's *Efes Damim* (No Blood) in 1841 and David Nieto's *Matteh Dan* (The Rod of Judgment) in 1842.

Lit.: *Celebrities of the Day*, April, 1881; Kurrein, Jessie, "Louis Loewe, ein Lebensbild," *Jahrbuch für Jüdische Geschichte und Literatur*, 1926.

LOEWE, LUDWIG, industrialist and German Reichstag deputy, b. Heiligenstadt, Thuringia, Germany, 1839; d. Berlin, 1886. Well educated by his father, who was a poor Jewish teacher, Loewe went to Berlin and entered a hardware shop, then dealt in machines and became a wealthy and esteemed merchant. In 1860 he was elected city councillor of Berlin. In 1876 he was elected a member of the Prussian Landtag, and in 1878 he was a member of the Reichstag. He was an adherent of the democratic party, and combatted Bismarck as well as Adolf Stöcker, who at that time was the leader of German anti-Semitism.

In 1869 Loewe founded the Ludwig Loewe Commanditgesellschaft auf Aktien für Fabrikation von Nähmaschinen. Before the factory was opened, in the spring of 1870, Loewe visited the United States in order to study American methods of production and business. His trade report of December 10, 1870, is one of the most important documents in the history of German industry. He was the first European industrialist to introduce American methods of production into his manufacturing plant, and is acknowledged by historians of German industry as "the champion and prototype of American industrialization in Germany." Loewe was the first European to recognize specialization, normalization and serial production as conditions of progress. He was also the first in Europe to stress the importance of scientific inquiry and of the education of workers for industrial improvement and competition. The high standard of modern German industry is due to Loewe's pioneering. His example encouraged other German industrialists to develop American methods. Before Loewe's time, German industry by no means excelled in organization. Notwithstanding his keen spirit of enterprise, Loewe was and remained a very cautious financier who was able to steer his business through periods of crisis and commercial depression. At all times he preferred quality to quantity, and had a strong sense of moral responsibility to his workers and country. He was opposed to protectionism, and combatted German militarism although he became one of the most important manufacturers of arms in Germany.

When Loewe realized that the German market was not capable of absorbing enough sewing machines, he began to make machine tools, and by 1872 commenced the production of rifles for the German army. He succeeded so well that the German minister of war overlooked his political opposition and favored his rifles. Loewe became the first manufacturer of rifles able to export his products on a large scale. After his death, his brother Isidor Loewe continued the direction of the Ludwig Loewe joint stock company.

IsIDOR LOEWE (b. Heiligenstadt, 1848; d. Berlin, 1910), industrialist and financier, was the younger brother of Ludwig Loewe. He entered the business in 1875, took over the factories after the latter's death and developed them into a large, worldwide-known concern. He was always his brother's best adviser, first as confidential clerk of the Ludwig Loewe Gesellschaft (1875-78), and later as its director. The cooperation between the two brothers during Ludwig's lifetime was ideal, since Ludwig was the technical expert and Isidor the organizer and financial expert.

After his brother's death, Isidor Loewe united the Ludwig Loewe Gesellschaft with the Waffenfabrik Mauser of Oberndorf (1887) so as to be able to manufacture the more than one million rifles ordered by the Prussian ministry of war and by Turkey. The fact that the Prussian ministry of war gave this order to a factory whose director and owner was a Jew led to the bringing of the anti-Semitic rector Hermann Ahlwardt to trial for his several articles on *Judenflinten* (Jews' Rifles; 1892). Ahlwardt accused Loewe of being a traitor to Germany and of having purposely used such poor materials for the manufacture of the rifles that they became more dangerous to their bearers than to the enemy. On December 2, 1892, Ahlwardt was sentenced to five months' imprisonment.

In 1890 Loewe merged the three largest German

munitions factories into the Waffen- und Maschinen-
fabrik A. G., which later cooperated with the Belgian
Fabrique National d'Armes de Guerre at Herstal.
Loewe's plant became the largest rifle-factory in the
world, which, from 1896 on, as the Deutsche Waffen-
und Munitionsfabriken A. G., supplied Germany,
Turkey, Russia, Spain, China, Argentina, Chile and
Brazil with arms. Loewe's great interest in electricity
led to collaboration with the Thomson-Houston Electric Co., of Boston (later the General Electric Co.),
in the founding of the Union Elektrizitäts-Gesellschaft
in Berlin (1892), which built the trolley-cars of many
German and Belgian cities. In 1903 this Union became
consolidated with the AEG. Thus the Ludwig Loewe
Gesellschaft was developed by Isidor Loewe into a
combination of three enterprises, electricity, machinery,
and the manufacture of arms. Furthermore, he established a car-foundry, which later was taken over by
the Daimler Gesellschaft, and sponsored the building of airplanes. The Technische Hochschule of Char-
lottenburg bestowed upon him the honorary degree of
doctor of engineering.   HUGO BIEBER.

Lit.: Wegeleben, Fritz, *Die Rationalisierung im deutschen Werkzeugmaschinenbau* (1924); Matschoss, Conrad,
and Schlesinger, Georg, *Geschichte der Ludwig Loewe & Co.
A. G.* (1930); Zielenziger, Kurt, *Juden in der deutschen
Wirtschaft* (1930).

LOEWE, MOSES SAMUEL, (pseudonym, Johann
Michael Siegfried Loewe), painter, b. Königsberg, East
Prussia, Germany, 1756; d. Berlin, 1831. He studied
in Berlin and in Dresden, traveled through Italy, and
in 1780 went to St. Petersburg, where he is said to
have portrayed Empress Catherine II. In 1784 he was
again a resident of Königsberg. One of the notable
portraits executed by him that year was a miniature of
Immanuel Kant, which was engraved several times. He
portrayed also the poet Kotzebue and Moses Mendelssohn. In 1795 Loewe moved to Berlin and started
the publication of *Portraits and Autobiographies of
Contemporaneous Scholars in Berlin,* a series which
was highly appreciated by Goethe. His experiments
with etching on copper (*mit Pinsel auf Kupfer zu
radieren*), proved to be a failure. The Berlin Collection of Engravings possesses etchings by Loewe.

LOEWE, VIKTOR, German historian and master
of the rolls, b. Laurahütte, Silesia, 1871; d. Breslau,
Germany, 1933. He studied at the Universities of
Vienna and Marburg, and was appointed to the
position of keeper of and adviser to the State Archives
in Breslau. His special field was German history of
the Middle Ages and modern times. His publications
are: *Organisation und Verwaltung der Wallensteinschen
Heere* (1895); *Behördenorganisationen unter Friedrich Wilhelm I.* (3 vols., 1898-1901; published together
with Schmoller and Krauske); *Bücherkunde der deutschen Geschichte* (1903; 5th ed., 1919); *Kritische
Bücherkunde der deutschen Bildung* (1912); *Preussische Staatsverträge unter Friedrich Wilhelm I* (1913);
Das deutsche Archivwesen (1921); *Ezechiel Spanheim,
ein Diplomat und Gelehrter* (1924). Loewe was editor
of the *Jahresberichte der deutschen Geschichte* from
1918 to 1926.

LOEWENBERG, JAKOB, poet and pedagogue,
b. Niederntudorf, Westphalia, Germany, 1856; d.

Hamburg, 1929. He was educated in the Jewish
schools of his native village and of Salzkotten, and in
1870 entered the seminary of the Marks-Haindorf
foundation at Münster. In 1873 he became teacher and
religious official at Padberg. His great pedagogic gifts
were highly esteemed by Jews and Catholics alike.
In 1875 he was teacher at Rendsburg. In 1876 he returned to Westphalia and was teacher in Geseke. In
1881 he went to London, where he served as private
tutor. After sojourning at Paris for six months,
he went to Heidelberg (1884) to study philology.

As a student, he was author of the song "Ich war
in Heidelberg Student," which became very popular
and was printed in the *Allgemeines Kommersbuch*. In
1886 he wrote his thesis, *Über Otways und Schillers
"Don Carlos,"* and was graduated with the Ph.D. degree. That same year he went to Hamburg, where
he taught modern subjects and sciences at the secondary school of the Calvinist congregation. In 1892
he was placed in charge of a private school for girls.
It was during this year that the cholera raged in
Hamburg, and Loewenberg was one of the first who,
indefatigably and at the risk of his own life, offered
his aid in combatting this dreadful epidemic to which
countless persons fell victims. His novel *In Gängen und
Höfen* (1893) relates his experiences during those
horrible days. At Hamburg Loewenberg soon won
the esteem of all progressive pedagogues as a master
of education. He was called "the conscience of Hamburg's teachers" by Fritz von Borstel.

Loewenberg was one of the first pedagogues, perhaps
the first, who collaborated systematically with the
parents of pupils. He summarized the results of his
pedagogical experiences in his *Geheime Miterzieher*
(1903) and *Aus der Welt des Kindes* (1910). Meanwhile, he gained recognition also as a poet. In 1889 he
edited the first collection of his lyrical poems, *Gedichte*.
In 1892 he published *Lieder eines Juden,* poems of protest against anti-Semitism and professing solidarity
with his coreligionists. An enlarged edition of this
book was published by Loewenberg in 1901 under the
title of *Aus jüdischer Seele.* In 1914 he published
Aus zwei Quellen, a novel dealing with the problems
of a German Jew whose consciousness is imbued with
Jewish and German traditions. Loewenberg did not
ignore the difficulties of his position, but he confessed:
"I have never felt any contradiction between German
and Jewish elements of my spirit." In 1824 he published a collection of stories, *Der gelbe Fleck.*

His last years were troubled by the rise of anti-
Semitism, which he combatted vigorously. At all times
Loewenberg was a German patriot and a firm adherent of Judaism, although he was not religious.
He was greatly interested in the cultural life of Hamburg, and in 1892 founded in that city the Literarische
Gesellschaft. He was an intimate friend of the German poets Liliencron, Dehmel and Falke, who were
grateful to him for the propaganda which he made
in their favor. Loewenberg published some of his
lectures under the title of *Deutsche Dichterabende* in
1905; a lyrical anthology, *Vom goldenen Überfluss* in
1902; a fairy-tale play, *Rübezahl;* and *Abendleuchten*
(1926), a collection of his poems.   HUGO BIEBER.

Lit.: Loewenberg, Ernst, "Jakob Loewenberg, Lebensbild eines deutschen Juden," *Jahrbuch für jüdische Ge-*

schichte und Literatur, vol. 29 (1931) 99-151; idem, edit., *Jakob Loewenberg, Auswahl aus seinen Schriften* (1937); Kruger, *Deutsches Literatur-Lexikon* (1914).

LOEWENBERG, JULIUS, geographer and author, b. Strzelno, Prussia, 1800; d. Berlin, 1893. He studied at the Talmudic school of Kleczewo, and at the University of Berlin, where he came in contact with the great geographer and naturalist, Alexander von Humboldt. Loewenberg was a prolific writer, remarkable for the beauty and clarity of his style as well as for the depth and range of his erudition. His works include: *Afrika* (1835); *Geschichte der Geographie* (1840); *Humboldts Reisen in Amerika und Asien* (1844); *Geschichte der geographischen Entdeckungen* (1882); *Das Weltbuch Sebastian Franck* (1893).

LOEWENFELD, THEODOR, lawyer, b. Munich, Germany, 1848; d. Munich, 1919. He was an authority on the history of Roman law and Roman civil law, and well-known for his studies on philosophy of law and German civil law. Loewenfeld studied in Munich, was a lawyer in the Bavarian capital until his death, an instructor at the University of Munich from 1877 to 1895, and honorary professor there from 1895 to 1919. For more than twelve years he was a member of the board of the association of lawyers in Munich. In 1912 he became privy counsellor of justice. Widely known are the following of his works: *Die selbständige actio de in rem verso* (1873); *Entgeltliche und unentgeltliche Rechtsgeschäfte* (1877); *Inästimabilität und Honorierung der artes liberales nach römischem Recht* (1883; published in honor of Johann Julius Wilhelm von Planck); *Kontraktbruch und Koalitionsrecht* (1891), a study in connection with the reform of the German trade law; *Koalitionsrecht und Strafrecht* (1899); the introduction and general presentation of *Personenrecht* in I. von Staudinger's famous commentary on the German civil code in eight editions from 1903 to 1912.

LOEWENHERZ, LEOPOLD, physicist and astronomer, b. Czarnikau, Posen, 1847; d. Berlin, 1892. He studied at the Realschule in Posen and at the University of Berlin (D.Sc., 1870). Immediately after he received his doctorate he was appointed instructor in physics. Loewenherz worked for many years as an assistant at the Berlin astronomical observatory, and in 1888 became director of the technical division of the Physikalisch-Technische Reichsanstalt, a post he held until his death. His most important scientific contributions were in the field of improved methods and instruments of physical measurements.

LOEWENSTEIN, ERNST, bacteriologist, b. Karlsbad, Czechoslovakia, 1878. He received his M.D. degree from the University of Prague. During the first World War he served as regimental physician in the Austro-Hungarian Army. From 1920 on he was professor of pathology at the University of Vienna, and from 1927 on director of the serum institute of the Federal State of Austria. He came to the United States in 1938, and was living at San Francisco in 1942.

In 1909 Loewenstein discovered a chemical method to render toxins non-toxic and to utilize them as harmless vaccines. His methods for immunization against diphtheria, lockjaw, tuberculosis in childhood, and other diseases caused by bacilli were widely used. Loewenstein also did special work in the tuberculosis department of the Vienna Serum Laboratory; in the years following the first World War tuberculosis was practically eradicated in that city.

His published books and approximately 200 papers in the field of bacteriology include such major works as *Tuberculosevorlesungen* (1920; Spanish trans., 1924); *Handbuch der gesamten Tuberkulosetherapie* (2 vols., 1923); *Tuberkelbazillämie in ihrer Auswirkung auf die Gesamtmedizin* (1936).

LOEWENSTEIN, KARL, political expert, b. Munich, Germany, 1891. He was educated at the Universities of Munich, Heidelberg, Paris and Berlin from 1910 to 1914. He became a referendary at Munich in 1914, and passed the bar examination as an assessor in 1917. He was admitted to the Munich bar in 1918, and received the LL.D. degree from the University of Munich in 1919. During the first World War he served in France with the German Infantry.

He practised law before the superior courts of Munich and the Bavarian Supreme Court from 1919 to 1933. During this time he acquired a reputation as one of the leading European experts on legal and political science. From 1931 to 1933 he was lecturer on international law and jurisprudence at the University of Munich.

In 1933 Loewenstein had to flee Germany because of the accession of the violently anti-Semitic Nazi government. From 1934 to 1936 he was associate professor of political science at Yale University. He was professor of comparative law at the University of Colorado in the summer of 1936. In the fall of 1936 he was appointed professor of political science at Amherst College, a position he still held in 1942.

In addition to many articles and essays for European and American journals of the social sciences, including one published at Montevideo, Loewenstein wrote a number of books in German and English, including: *Das Problem des Foederalismus in Grossbritannien* (1921); *Das heutige Verfassungsrecht des britischen Weltreichs* (1925); *Erscheinungsformen der Verfassungsänderung* (1931); *Untersuchung zum Artikel 76 der Verfassung des Deutschen Reiches* (1932); *Hitler's Germany, the Nazi Background to War* (1939).

LOEWENSTEIN VON OPOKA, NATHAN, lawyer and government official, b. Butschwitz, Moravia, 1859; d. Lemberg, Poland, 1929. He was the protagonist of a Jewish assimilation party which functioned in Galicia during the rule of the Austro-Hungarian Empire. Loewenstein's political activity started in the 1890's, when he became a member of the Lemberg community council; this post he held, through various regimes, until his death. In 1893 he was elected to the Galician Diet as a representative of the Chamber of Commerce of Brody; in 1908 he became the representative of the city of Lemberg in the Diet. An investigation into the condition of Galician Jews which Loewenstein sponsored in 1906 had no results.

Elected to the Vienna Senate in 1907, Loewenstein belonged to the Poland Club and continued his efforts for Jewish assimilation. His electoral district was the scene of bloodshed in 1911, when a dispute

Otto Loewi

arose between his followers and Jewish nationalists. The militia was called out, thirty-two persons were killed and more than a hundred wounded. Loewenstein resigned his post as a result of this affair, but was reelected by a large majority. Not until 1922, when the newly formed Polish state proved the complete failure of his assimilation policy, did Loewenstein retire entirely from public life. He had been ennobled by the emperor of Austria.

LOEWENTHAL, WILHELM, writer, publisher and hygienist, b. Rybnik, Silesia, 1850; d. Berlin, 1894. He studied medicine at the University of Berlin, and after receiving his M.D. degree he left for the Caucasus to do medical research. Back in Berlin he acquired the civil *Bürgerzeitung,* a well-known paper of those days. Besides this, he specialized in bacteriology and in school hygiene. He published a résumé, in 1887, entitled *Grundzüge einer Hygiene des Unterrichts.*

Loewenthal then left for Switzerland and became a lecturer, later professor, at the Universities of Geneva and Lausanne, where he pursued special research into the cholera bacillus. This brought him in close contact with Robert Koch. He continued his studies with Cornil in Paris, and later left for new research in other countries; in India, sponsored by the French government, he conducted practical experiments on how to resist cholera in Tonking.

Baron Maurice de Hirsch sent Loewenthal to Argentina to ascertain whether there were any possibilities for the resettlement of Russian Jews; this was the first step toward the famous ICA settlements there. Many years later he went back to Berlin and became co-partner of the Berliner Adressbuch Verlag. But Loewenthal did not cease his idealistic, humanitarian studies, taking an active part in the advancement of the feminist movement and serving as lecturer at the Humboldt-Academie in Berlin.

LOEWI, OTTO, pharmacologist and Nobel Prize winner, b. Frankfort, Germany, 1873. He studied at the Universities of Frankfort, Strasbourg and Munich, receiving his M.D. degree from the former in 1896. He conducted his first researches in pharmacology at the Pharmacological Institute in Strasbourg, later at the Chemical Institute of Martin Freund in Frankfort. Shortly thereafter, Professor Hofmeister of the Physical-Chemical Institute of the University of Strasbourg made him his assistant, but soon Loewi left Strasbourg again for Frankfort to join Professor Norden at the Städtisches Krankenhaus. In 1900 he was back again in Strasbourg as lecturer on pharmacology, in 1904 he became assistant professor at the University of Marburg, and in 1905 he was appointed associate professor at the University of Vienna; this position he held for four years, and in 1909 became associate professor at the University of Graz, Austria, where he taught until 1938. From 1938 to 1939 he served as Franqui professor at the University of Brussels.

On October 29, in 1936, Loewi together with his collaborator and close friend, Sir Henry Hallet Dale, received the Nobel Prize for medicine and physiology, awarded to them for research on the chemical transmission of nervous impulses. Experiments with the heart of a frog, begun in 1921, enabled Loewi to demonstrate the existence of a chemical substance which is produced by irritation of the vagus nerve and transmits the irritation to the cardiac muscle.

Loewi often visited the United States. He was Dunham lecturer at Harvard, guest lecturer at Yale, and also before the Harvey Society in New York. He was Ferrier lecturer at the Royal Society in London, but consistently refused appointments to American, German or Dutch universities, retaining his professorship at Graz. When, however, the Nazi purge of Austrian universities (March, 1938) subjected Loewi to "protective custody" and later forced him into exile, he settled permanently in the United States. In September, 1940, he was appointed research professor of pharmacology at New York University College of Medicine.

In addition to his researches, Loewi published many papers on metabolism, diabetes and heart diseases.

Professor Leon Asher, head of the Physiological Institute in Bern, Switzerland, endeavored to utilize the Loewi and Dale discoveries for the advancement of medical therapy.

Lit.: New York Times, Sept. 17, 1940.

LOEWIT, MORITZ, physician, b. Prague, 1851; d. Innsbruck, Austria, 1918. From 1876 to 1879 he was assistant in the first medical clinic and from 1880 on assistant lecturer at the Institute for Experimental Pathology of the German University in Prague. He became professor of general and experimental pathology in Innsbruck in 1887, and was for a time president of the Institute for Experimental Pathology at the University of Vienna. Loewit wrote *Studien zur Physiologie und Pathologie des Blutes und der Lymphe* (Jena, 1892) and *Vorlesungen über allgemeine Pathologie* (1897-1900).

Lit.: Wininger, S., *Grosse Jüdische National-Biographie,* vol. 4, p. 176.

LOEWY, ADOLF, physiologist, b. Berlin, 1862; d. Berlin, 1937. He was a student of Emil Du Bois-

Reymond and Hugo Kronecker. From 1895 to 1922 he lectured at the University of Berlin, practising medicine at the same time. His main researches aimed at the correlation of climate, altitude and blood circulation. He was elected director of the newly founded Schweizer Institut für Hochgebirgsklima und Tuberkuloseforschung in Davos in 1922. When he retired in 1933 it had already won a world wide reputation. Later on he lived and worked in Arosa, Switzerland, returning to Berlin shortly before he died. Loewy's principal works were: *Höhenklima und Bergwanderungen in ihrer Wirkung auf den Menschen* (1905); *Lehrbuch der Physiologie* (together with Nathan Zuntz; 1909); *Blutgase und Gaswechsel* (1910); *Seeklima and Seebäder* (1910). On his seventieth birthday (1932) he published *Physiologie des Höhenklimas,* and on his seventy-fifth birthday (1937) his *Pathology of the High Altitude Climate,* whose publication the Nazi government refused to permit, appeared at London in English.

LOEWY, ALBERT, rabbi and orientalist, b. Aussee, Moravia, 1816; d. London, 1908. During his student days he helped found Die Einheit Society in Vienna for the betterment of the condition of oppressed Jews, and in 1840 went to London to promote its aims. The scheme did not then materialize. In 1842, upon the dedication of the West London Synagogue of British Jews, he was appointed co-minister with the Reverend Marks, which position he filled for half a century. In 1871 he helped found the Anglo-Jewish Association, of which he served as secretary until 1889. He associated himself with many communal activities, especially of an educational nature. His erudition was evidenced by contributions to the Society of Hebrew Literature, of which he was one of the founders (1870) and by lectures before the Society of Biblical Archeology. As one of the few scholars with a knowledge of the Samaritan language, he catalogued for the Earl of Crawford the latter's rare collection of Samaritan literature (1872). To Loewy was entrusted the preparation of the catalogue of Hebraica and Judaica in the Guildhall Library (1890), for which he devised an unusual subject index. In 1893, in recognition of his researches, the University of St. Andrews conferred upon him the honorary LL.D. degree.

Lit.: *Jewish Chronicle* (London), Feb. 15, 1907; May 22, 1908; *Jewish World,* May 29, 1908.

LOEWY, ALFRED, mathematician, b. Rawicz, Posen, Germany, 1873; d. Freiburg, Germany, 1935. He studied in Breslau, Munich and Göttingen, received his doctor's degree in 1894, and became instructor at the University of Freiburg in 1897, assistant professor at this university in 1902, and associate professor in 1919. Loewy's first publication was *Über bilineare Formen* (1898). His main works were: *Versicherungsmathematik* (1903; 4th ed., 1924); *Lehrbuch der Algebra* (1915); *Mathematik des Geld- und Zahlungsverkehrs* (1920). Loewy's final publication, written after the Nazis forced him to retire, had the characteristic title *Zur Mathematik in Bibel und Talmud.* Besides his numerous essays in the *Mathematische Annalen, Mathematische Zeitschrift,* and *Transactions of the American Mathematical Society,* that on Jewish

Chronology in the *Annual Report of the German Mathematical Association* (vol. 26, 1918) is noteworthy. Loewy edited in 1924 the eleventh volume of the literary remains of the famous mathematician Karl Friedrich Gauss, wrote the article on life insurance in Alfred Manes' well-known *Versicherungslexikon* (1908-13), and was editor of the periodical *Composito Mathematica.* Throughout his life he was active in Jewish affairs, and became a member of the Badischer Oberrat der Israeliten in Karlsruhe in 1908.

LOEWY, EMANUEL, historian of art, b. Vienna, 1857; d. Vienna, 1938. He studied classical philology in Vienna and was a member of the Viennese archeological epigraphical seminary. In 1887 he became a lecturer at the University of Vienna. In 1889 he was appointed professor of classical archeology at the University of Rome, where he taught until 1914. During these years he also carried on researches in Greece and in Asia Minor. He founded the Museum of Plaster Casts of Classical Art in Rome, and was King Victor Emmanuel's adviser on the completion of his collection of coins. He was also a member of the papal academy and of the academies of science of Vienna, Athens, Stockholm and Oxford. He was made an honorary member by numerous scientific institutions all over the world. Having retained his Austrian citizenship, he was forced to leave Rome when Italy entered the first World War in 1915 and he had to abandon all his property there. He returned to Vienna and held a fellowship at the University of Vienna from 1918 to 1928. He specialized in classical Greece. His main published works were: *Inschriften der griechischen Bildhauer* (1883); *Untersuchungen zur griechischen Künstlergeschichte* (1883); *Lysip und seine Stellung in der griechischen Plastik* (1891); *Die griechische Plastik* (2 vols., 1911); *Stein and Erz in der statuarischen Kunst* (1915); *Neu-attische Kunst* (1922); *Polygnot* (2 vols., 1929); *Ursprünge der bildenden Kunst* (1930); *Zur Chronologie der frühgriechischen Kunst* (1932).

LOEWY, MAURICE, astronomer, b. Pressburg, 1833; d. Paris, 1907. He was educated at the University of Vienna and received his first astronomical training at the Imperial Observatory of Austria. From 1856 to 1859 Loewy was an assistant in the Vienna Observatory, but advancement to a professorship was impossible without his being baptized. Loewy went, instead, to Paris, where he had been offered an Observatory post. He remained here from 1860 until his death, becoming assistant director of the Paris Observatory in 1873 and director in 1896. In 1864 Loewy became a naturalized French citizen, and fought with the French armies at Paris during the Franco-Prussian war (1870).

Loewy's position as a leading astronomer was secured during his early years in Paris. In 1871 he devised a new form of equatorial, known as the equatorial coudé, which depends on reflecting mirrors for the transmission of light rays. Although the first instrument built from Loewy's plans was not completed until 1882, it soon became a standard for certain types of observation. Loewy also specialized in the simplification of orbit computation, studied the details of the meridial circle and determined the longitude of various European cities with new precision.

With the aid of the equatorial coudé, better photographs of the moon than had hitherto been possible were obtained. The *Atlas photographique de la lune* (1896), published in collaboration with Puiseaux, presented these improved studies. Among his other published works were: *Nouvelles méthodes pour la détermination des orbites des comètes* (1879); *Des eléments fondamentaux de l'astronomie* (1886); *De la constance de l'aberration et de la refraction* (1890). Loewy was for more than thirty years editor of *Connaissance de Temps* and was also the editor of *Annuaire du Bureau des Longitudes*. His equatorial coudé won the gold medal of the Royal Astronomical Society of Great Britain in 1889, and he was a corresponding member of the academies of St. Petersburg, Vienna, Berlin, Rome and Washington. He was made a member of the French Académie des Sciences in 1873, and in 1896, with his appointment as director of the Observatory, he was given a full professorship title.

Lit.: Poincare, Henri, "Maurice Loewy," *Bulletin Astronomique,* vol. 24, pp. 385-95; *Royal Astronomical Society Monthly Notices,* Feb., 1908, pp. 249-52; Kohut, Adolph, *Berühmte israelitische Männer und Frauen,* vol. 2 (1901) 247.

LÖFFLER, ALEXANDER, criminologist, b. Szentes, Hungary, 1866; d. Vienna, 1929. After receiving his LL.D. degree from the University of Vienna in 1889, he worked at the seminar of criminology conducted by Franz von Liszt at Halle. He became instructor (1896), assistant professor (1902) and associate professor (1903) of penal law and criminal procedure at the University of Vienna, after having served for five years in law courts. His inaugural thesis, *Schuldformen des Strafrechts* (vol. 1, 1895), was a critical survey of the evaluation of forms of guilt, which inspired other works in the same field. He founded the first journal of criminology in Austria, *Österreichische Zeitschrift für Strafrecht,* in which appeared (from 1910 to 1918) his views on bills before the Austrian Parliament pertaining to penal law, and his comparative criticism of decisions rendered by the Austrian supreme court. *Die strafrechtliche Behandlung Jugendlicher* (1908), on the reformatory treatment of juvenile delinquents, as well as his *Vergehen wider das Leben,* on attempted murder (in *Vergleichende Darstellung des deutschen und ausländischen Strafrechts,* Besonderer Teil, vol. 5, 1905), were considered his most significant contributions to criminology, in addition to minor writings on the questions of responsibility and self-defense. He edited several books of Austrian statutes.

As a criminologist, Löffler was a conservative and advocated the maintenance of capital punishment. After the first World War, as member of a commission to probe neglect of military duty, he made a report on events in the southwestern (Italian) theatre of war at the time of the armistice. He was no longer affiliated with Judaism.

Lit.: Deutsches biographisches Jahrbuch (1929), Totenliste; *Rektorwechsel Universität Wien* (1930/31) 25-27.

LOGOS (Greek for "word"), a theological concept found in the Judaism of the period of the Second Temple and in Christianity. It is most elaborately expressed in the opening verses of *John:* "In the beginning was the Word, and the Word was with God, and the Word was God. When he was in the beginning with God all things were created through him; without him came no created thing into being. In him was life, and the life was the light of men; and the light shone on in the darkness, and the darkness overcame it not."

The ideas underlying this concept of the Logos go back to the Biblical verse (*Ps.* 33:6): "By the word of the Lord were the heavens made." Many mystics of the period of the Second Temple interpreted this literally, especially since to them God was so spiritual and far removed from the world that it seemed impossible for Him to deal with it directly. They therefore involved the idea of a "word" (in Aramaic, *Memra* or *Dibbura*) which would be equivalent to the presence of God. In the Targums the word Memra is introduced in every instance in the Bible in which God is represented as talking to man, thus explaining away all the anthropomorphisms found in the text.

This "word" partook of the nature of God but was also a sort of emanation from Him, a messenger who carried out His commands, as in *Wisdom of Solomon* 18:15: "Thine all-powerful word leaped from heaven out of the royal throne, a stern warrior." According to a Talmudic passage, "The Holy One, Blessed be He, created the world by the *ma'amar* (*Mechilta, Beshallah* 10).

Logos means Word as *John* uses it, but it means also "reason." To philosophers of Persia, India, Egypt, Greece and Judea it expressed an attempt to find God by searching out the immanent logic and reason as well as cause of existence. Jewish philosophers tried to explain how it was that God could create the world out of nothing. They had met Greek philosophers after Alexander's conquest of the ancient world. These Greek philosophers were imbued with the Aristotelian philosophy that "out of nothing comes nothing."

They wanted to know how God, who was incorporeal and all spirit, could create material existence. Was it all only a "vision" of a reality which could in the last analysis exist only in the heavens above, a mere "pattern of that which was shown to Moses on Mt. Sinai," where God allowed him to look into heaven; or were material things actual reality?

The Greek schools of philosophy were looking for the "reason" of things and the causes as well as means of existence. They used the word Logos, and this Logos idea of Greek philosophy suited the harmonizing and allegorical interpretation of Philo, the Alexandrian Jewish philosopher, although it is improbable that he thought that the "Logos or Word became flesh."

It remained for John and the Christian theologians to accept this idea of the Creative Word as a part of God as well as apart from God to explain the relation of God, the Son, to God the Father, connected by the emanation of the Holy Ghost or Holy Spirit. Through this emanation, this word, the material world was created by the Spiritual Creator. The word not merely was with God but the word was God. He was with God in the very beginning and through him all existence came into being nor was there any existence that came into being apart from him.

This Christian idea of Logos that became flesh was

developed from Philo and the Alexandrian school. The Stoics believed in a sort of material pantheism in which the world of material nature is the sole reality. This soul of the world they called the Logos, or rational principle which they believed to be everywhere present as a more active and subtle kind of matter. The human soul, breath or spirit is part of this world soul, partaking of its rational qualities and finally becoming again part of the universal reason, wherein its individuality is lost.

In the Hellenistic literature, such as *Wisdom of Solomon,* both wisdom and Logos are mentioned. They are personified as a figure of speech rather than as a real personalization which is known as hypostasis.

Philo, when met by the acute questions of the Greek philosophers, was the foremost among those who tried to harmonize and syncretize the different conceptions of Hellenism and Judaism. He tried to adapt the Greek philosophical idea of Logos as the form principle, rational principle and creative principle to bridge the gap between God and matter. Philo influenced the Neo-Platonist ideas, by postulating a graduated scale of existence, connecting the two extremes of God and creation by a series of progressions, each one emanating from original perfection and falling away until they reach finite existence. Philo made this Logos idea, related to the Memra idea of the Targums, the bridge between the two alien strands of thought. It was not estranged from Jewish monotheism, and yet adequately described the divine activity in terms of Hellenic thought.

The creative Word of the Bible is the Memra of the Targum and the Logos of the Stoics and is also Philo's conception of God's relation to finite matter. Philo's conception of the Logos is therefore much more than " 'the principle of reason, informing the infinite variety of things, and so creating the World-Order.' " It is also "the divine dynamic, the energy and self-revelation of God." To Philo, God stood apart from the world in ineffable and unthinkable perfection, so He had to be connected with actual things by a series of lesser, but more intelligible forms, which are regarded, sometimes as Platonic ideas, sometimes from the standpoint of angels or messengers. These are somehow an offshoot from God's nature, without actually belonging to it as component parts. In other words, Philo's conception of the Logos of Greek philosophy was that the Logos was the mediator of God's revelation of Himself. Wherever God makes Himself manifest throughout the Bible, it was only through the Logos, the divine intelligence, reason or word that this was done. Materialization or personification of God was through the intermediary of the Logos which was the means of this Divine emanation.

In order to understand the Logos of Philo we have to realize the inescapable dilemma in which Philo finds himself. He has to accord to the Greek Logos "a semi-independent position beside the supreme God of Judea." He speaks of the Logos (1) as the agency by which God reveals Himself, in some measure to all men, in greater degree to chosen souls. The appearances recorded in the Old Testament are manifestations of the Logos, and the knowledge of God possessed by the great leaders and teachers of Israel is due to the same source; (2) as the agency whereby

man, enmeshed by illusion, lays hold of the higher spiritual life and, rising above his partial point of view, participates in the universal reason. The Logos is thus the means of redemption, those who realize its activity being "emancipated from the tyranny of circumstance into the freedom of the eternal."

The New Testament Gospel of *John* shows great dependence on Philo. The author of *John* recognizes, too, that a man shows his inner self and makes himself known to the world through speech, therefore God through the Logos or the Word expressed His will and power, His divine dynamic and creative energy. John goes further than Philo. Philo's Logos was an abstraction or semi-personification. John's Logos becomes fully personified or hypostasized. The Word became flesh, having subsisted from the very beginning of things as a distinct personality within the divine nature.

Then, too, John emphasizes the redemptive power of the Logos rather than its creative function, positing at the same time that "all things were made by Him." His interest is not in how the world came into being but rather in the means by which spiritual life residing in the Logos was communicated to men. To him Logos as Reason is secondary to Logos as Word, "the expression of the divine Will and Power and Purpose of life, love and light."   SIDNEY S. TEDESCHE.

Lit.: The articles and sections in the *Encyclopaedia Britannica; Jewish Encyclopedia;* Schürer, Emil, *Geschichte des jüdischen Volkes;* Rogers, *History of Philosophy;* Bacon, *Making of the New Testament.*

LÖHNER, FRITZ (pseudonym, Beda), author and librettist, b. Wildenschwert, Bohemia, 1883. His essays and satirical poems, in which he often opposed the idea of Jewish assimilation, were written for such papers as *Welt, Morgen* and *Muskete* in Vienna, for the *Hamburger Fremdenblatt,* for *Die Jugend* in Munich, and many others. The tenth edition of a collection of his epigrams and poems, *Getaufte und Baldgetaufte,* was published in 1909. Others of his anthologies are *Wie man sich trefft im Ampezzotal, Die Muse im Negligée* and *Israeliten und andere Antisemiten,* the latest printed in six editions. Löhner wrote the libretti of such well-known operettas as *Ball im Savoy, Die wilde Marie* and *Märchen im Grand Hotel,* and of the song "Ich hab mein Herz in Heidelberg verloren." More important, however, was his activity as vice-president of the Austrian Authors Society and as a member of the board of the Academic Society Kadimah in Vienna.

LÖHR, MAX RICHARD HERMANN, Protestant theologian, b. Stettin, Germany, 1864; d. Königsberg, Germany, 1931. From 1890 to 1892 he served as instructor in Old Testament exegesis at the University of Königsberg, and for the next seventeen years as associate professor at the University of Breslau. Löhr wrote extensively on various problems of ancient Hebrew religion and literature and on Biblical subjects. These works, which display an unprejudiced appreciation of the religious historical achievements of Judaism, include: an edition of the Syriac annotations of Bar Hebraeus to the Pauline epistles (Göttingen, 1889); *Die Klagelieder des Jeremias erklärt* (for Wilhelm Nowack's *Handkommentar zum Alten Testa-*

ment, 1894); *Der Missionsgedanke im Alten Testa-
mente* (Freiburg, 1896); *Geschichte des Volkes Israel*
(Strasbourg, 1900); *Untersuchungen zum Buche Amos*
(Giessen, 1901); *Volksleben im Lande der Bibel*
(1907); *Stellung des Weibes zu Jahwe-Religion und
Kult* (1908); *Einführung in das Alte Testament*
(1912); *Psalmen-Studien* (1922); *Zum Geist des Chas-
sidismus* (1925). He prepared the third edition of
O. Thenius' *Kommentar zu den Büchern Samuelis*
(Leipzig, 1898).

LOKSHEN KUGEL, *see* COOKING.

LOMBROSO, CESARE, psychiatrist and criminologist, b. Verona, Italy, 1835; d. Turin, Italy, 1909.
Scion of a prominent Italian Jewish family of scholars
and patriots, he showed even at an early age unusual
intellectual qualities and an interest in various fields
of research. At the age of fifteen he published two
works which denoted precocity and profound historical insight. His *Essay on the Study of the History
of the Roman Republic* and *Agriculture in ancient
Rome* attracted wide attention to the adolescent
scholar. At that time he studied also Semitic languages, literature and philology under the direction of
Professor Paolo Marzolo.

Induced, however, to take up the study of medicine,
Lombroso entered (1854) the faculty of medicine at
the University of Pavia, centering his interest on abnormal types of organic life. He continued his medical studies in Vienna, where he completed his work
on the causes of cretinism. In 1859 he joined the
Piedmontese army in the war against Austria, and
was decorated with two medals for gallantry. In 1862
he was invited to lecture on psychiatry at the University of Pavia, continuing there his inquiries which
he initiated on the anthropological character of various
regions of the Italian Peninsula; the results of these
researches were published in 1865 under the title
Studies on the Medical Geography of Italy. These inquiries offered him an excellent opportunity to study
a great number of criminals and to observe their
physical and psychic reactions, which led him to the
conclusion that there are discernible and definite signs
which distinguish a born criminal from a normal
human being. He also made the startling assertion
that pellagra, a disease then widespread in the northern provinces of Italy, was due to a poison contained
in maize mold. Since maize was the main food
product of the agricultural population of Italy, the
results of his researches aroused against him bitter
opposition on the part of the landlords. They conducted against Lombroso an unscrupulous campaign
of denunciation and calumny. He withstood these attacks with courage and integrity.

In 1875, after a brief period during which he served
as director of the lunatic asylum at Pesaro, Lombroso
began lecturing at the University of Turin on psychiatry and legal medicine. There he conducted and
completed his studies in the field of anthropology,
which found expression in his most famous work,
L'uomo delinquente, first published at Milan (1876).
Here Lombroso maintained that in most cases there
survive in the criminal, as a result of hereditary laws,
the physical and psychical traits of primitive man—
a theory which, due to its striking and revolutionary

Cesare Lombroso. From a sketch by Ivan Sors

character, aroused great controversy and provoked
numerous polemical works.

Although his positive and organic conception of
criminal man and delinquency were not generally accepted, the anthropological studies of Lombroso and
of his "School" contributed greatly to the progress of
legal medicine and to the enlarging of the scope of
criminal anthropology. Lombroso displayed faith in
the bases of his theory, and defended them vigorously in books, studies and lectures, as well as at the
international congresses of criminal anthropology. In
1890 he founded the Archives of Psychiatry, Penal
Sciences and Criminal Anthropology, which published
a number of studies by Italian and foreign scholars
contributing to the affirmation and diffusion of the
essential ideas and implications of the Lombrosian
theories and of the science of criminal anthropology.
Among other works of Lombroso's which aroused
wide interest were *Genio e follia* (1864), in which he
endeavored to show the affinity between genius and
psychic anormalcy; *L'uomo bianco e l'uomo di colore*
(1871), in which he came to the same conclusions as
those later developed by Charles Darwin; and *L'uomo
delinquente, la prostituta e la donna normale* (1893).
In 1894 he published a book on anti-Semitism and
science in which he sought to determine the atavistic
elements in Jew-baiters and in anti-Semitism.

In his latest years he devoted himself to the study
of spiritual phenomena, but his death prevented his
completion of a fuller study on this subject. Bound
by long and intimate friendship with Max Nordau, he
expressed to the latter his regret that he could not
personally attend the First Zionist Congress. Lombroso's funeral was arranged at the expense of the
Italian state, and the urn containing his ashes was
placed in the Italian Pantheon at the Monumental
Cemetery of Turin, where Cavour and many other
great sons of Italy are buried. In 1925 there was
erected in his native town, Verona, a monument

Gina Lombroso

situated on the Piazza Lombroso. Until the issuing of the decree of February, 1941, which changed the names of streets bearing names of Jews, there were in Italy a number of towns which had a street or a public place bearing the name of Lombroso.

DAVID KLEINLERER.

Lit.: Lombroso Ferrero, Gina, *Cesare Lombroso: Storia della vita e delle opere narrate dalla sua figlia* (1915); idem, in *Judeans* (Judean addresses selected, vol. 4, 1933); Theilhaber, Felix A., "Cesare Lombroso," *Menorah* (Vienna, 1932); Ferri, E., "Cesare Lombroso e la funzione sociale della scienza," *Rivista Italiana di Sociologia* (1909); Kurella, H., *Cesare Lombroso als Mensch und Forscher* (1910).

LOMBROSO, ENRICO, novelist and playwright, b. Verona, Italy, 1910. He began his literary career by contributing essays and short stories to Italian periodicals and literary magazines. In 1931 he became associate editor of *Il Messaggero* and later of *Il Giornale d'Italia* in Rome. His first play, *Amanti al lambico,* was awarded first prize in a national contest for a literary play promoted on the occasion of the celebration of Alighieri Dante's 700th anniversary. This and other plays were successfully performed on the Italian stage. His novel *Danzano i Satiri* was translated into French and Spanish. Active also as theatrical director, Lombroso staged, among other plays, *L'olimpiade* of Pergolesi, performed on the occasion of the bicentennial anniversary of the death of the famous Italian composer. After the introduction of the anti-Semitic measures in Italy in July, 1938, Lombroso traveled in Switzerland, France and England before coming to the United States in 1940.

LOMBROSO, GINA, author, biographer and sociologist, daughter of Cesare, b. Pavia, Italy, 1872. Like her father, she intended to follow medical studies, but after graduating from the Lyceum in her native town, she was prevented from following these studies as women were not, at that time, admitted to the faculties of medicine in Italy. She then entered the faculty of literature and philosophy at the University of Pavia, and received her doctor's degree

upon the presentation of an interesting and valuable study on saints in the Occidental and Oriental civilizations. Finally admitted to the study of medicine, she published *Degeneration or Evolution,* in which efforts were made to explain these phenomena mostly with reference to men's endeavors to adapt themselves to changing conditions of nature and environment.

In 1896, induced by grave consequences of the economic crisis in Italy, she published a thorough study on the effects and perils of the machine age, which aroused considerable interest. In 1901 she married Guglielmo Ferrero, noted historian and disciple of her father. After her father's death in 1909, she devoted herself to the posthumous publication of his works, collecting data, facts, and memories pertaining to his life, struggles and scholarly achievements. She published a two-volume biography of her father, which first appeared in Italian under the title *Cesare Lombroso: Storia della vita e delle opere narrate dalla sua figlia* (1915), and was later translated into various languages. She was engaged during the first World War in various social activities and in the work of progressive Italian women's organizations. In 1919 she published *L'anima della donna,* which was widely read and was translated into eighteen languages. The second volume and continuation of this work, dealing with women in life and in present society, met with the same wide and spontaneous success. In 1931 she visited the United States, where she lectured on social subjects and those dealing with women, on problems of anti-Semitism and on her father's life.

After the establishment of Fascism in Italy, she and her husband lived in Geneva, Switzerland, where she founded the publishing house Nuove Edizioni di Capolago, which printed works of noted Italian anti-Fascists and intellectuals in exile.

LEO FERRERO, the only son of Gina Lombroso Ferrero, who, in spite of his youth, had acquired a reputation as a brilliant writer and author of literary and philosophical essays, was killed in an automobile accident at New York city in 1933.

DAVID KLEINLERER.

LOMBROSO, PAOLA, feminist, social worker and psychologist, daughter of Cesare, b. Pavia, Italy, 1871. Her first works centered around child psychology and the improvement of the social and sanitary conditions of the Italian working class. In 1894 she published *Saggi di psicologia del bambino,* essays on the psychology of the child, with an introduction by her father. She married the Italian criminologist Professor Mario Carrara, and took part in his scientific work. In 1899 she published *Povera gente,* which was followed by other studies and books on the material and social needs of the poverty-stricken Italian population. As a result of her initiative there were created a large network of circulating libraries in the rural villages of Italy and asylums for tuberculous children. During the first World War she was actively engaged in alleviating the sufferings in the northern provinces of Italy which came under Austrian occupation; she was popularly known throughout Italy as "Donna Paola" and "Zia Mariu," and was hailed for her social, cultural and humanitarian activities. She was kept under surveillance and arrested several times

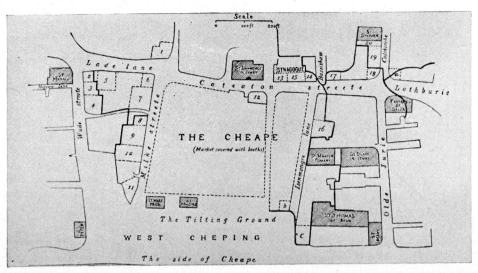

*Map of London Jewry in the year 1290. The numbered sites were owned by Jews. From Joseph Jacobs'
"Jewish Ideals"*

after the "March on Rome" and the assumption of power in Italy by the Fascist regime.

LOMBROSO, UGO, physiologist, son of Cesare, b. Turin, Italy, 1871. He began his scholarly career as assistant professor at the University of Turin, subsequently teaching physiology at various Italian universities, including those of Rome (1917-22), Messina (1919-22) and Palermo (1923-34). He was invited, in 1934, to assume the chair of physiology at the University of Genoa. As a result of the anti-Semitic legislation, he was dismissed, in October, 1938, from his professorship and had to resign from various Italian scientific bodies. Lombroso published numerous works, especially on the problems of metabolism, endocrinology and the digestive glands.

LONDON, capital of England, with a population (1941) of 8,204,000, of whom 234,000 (2.8 per cent) were Jews.

1. The Pre-Expulsion Period (about 1070 to 1290). Jews first settled in London in the latter half of the 11th cent., when they came from Rouen with William the Conqueror (reigned 1066-87). It is not, however, until the reign of Henry I (1100-35) that reference to their presence is noted. At that time they appear to have lived around the central market of West Cheap. A Jews' Street, situated in what is now Old Jewry, is mentioned, in 1115, in a list of lands held by the Dean and Chapter of St. Paul's, while from other records of the period it is learned that Jews occupied houses in the neighboring Milk Street, Wood Street, Cat Street and Colechurch Street.

Knowledge of this early community, however, is extremely meagre, depending on a bare half-dozen references over a period of more than a century. Like the rest of their brethren in England, they were the chattels of the king, and thus exempt from fealty to the barons. Regarded as aliens, and excluded from the guilds, they were free from taxation. Since, however, their primary function was to provide revenue for the crown, they were subject at all times to considerable and arbitrarily imposed tallages. Under

Henry I they were warrantized from the exchequer, and the constable of the Tower was invested with special jurisdiction to preserve the peace between them and their non-Jewish neighbors. For the settlement of internal disputes they were allowed their own tribunal (*Capitulum Judaeorum=Beth Din*), controlled by recognized "Masters of the Law." On the whole, they seem to have led a placid and undisturbed existence, although, in 1130, a collective fine of 2,000 pounds was inflicted on them for "killing a sick man" (evidently through inexpert medical attention), and six years later they suffered grievously as the result of a fire.

Privileges previously accorded were renewed by Henry's successor, Stephen (1135-54), while during the subsequent reign of Henry II (1154-89) and until the close of the 12th cent., London Jewry flourished both materially and spiritually. According to Solomon ibn Verga, writing in the 15th cent., by 1166 its number had increased to close to 2,000, and until 1177 it was still the primary center of the entire Anglo-Jewish population, all of the Jewish dead in the kingdom being required to be buried at its cemetery in Jewin Street.

On the cultural side, several distinguished Hebrew scholars in the community devoted themselves mainly to Masoretic and grammatical studies. Among them were Joseph ben Jacob Morel (Josce fil Copin), host of Abraham ibn Ezra in 1158 and 1166, who later paraphrased his guest's great commentary on the Bible; Moses ben Yomtob, author of a still extant work on punctuation (*Darche Hanikkud Vehaneginoth;* edit. Salomon Frensdorff, Hannover, 1847); and Elhanan ben Isaac (Deodatus the *episcopus*), who composed a now lost treatise on the mysteries of the calendar (*Sod Haibbur*). This scholastic activity was considerably increased in 1182 by the arrival of several noted French rabbinical scholars who had been expelled from the Ile de France by Philip Augustus.

With the accession of Richard I in 1189, London Jewry entered an eventful phase of its history. On the very day of the coronation (September 3rd), a massacre of Jews occurred in the city. Their houses were besieged by a fanatical rabble from 9 in the morning until sunset, and finally set afire. "The Jews," says the contemporary chronicler, William of Newbury, "were either roasted in their houses or, if they came out, received with swords." Some thirty men were put to death, among them the celebrated Tosafist, Jacob of Orleans. Richard, discountenancing the outrage, immediately issued an edict guaranteeing peace to the Jews. His attitude was, moreover, further confirmed, on March 22, 1190, when he granted a charter to Isaac, son of Josce, of London, assuring to the Jews the right "to reside in our land freely and honorably," to claim trial by their peers, to swear oaths on the Torah or the Hebrew Bible, to enjoy unmolested travel, and to be "quit of all customs and toll and prisage of wine."

With the reign of John (1199-1216), however, there began a period of unrelieved misery. King and barons were at loggerheads, and the Jews were the victims of both. In 1204 riots, encouraged by the barons, broke out in the London Jewry, and although the king formally protested to the mayor and the barons (June 22nd), the protest was actuated more by a desire to safeguard his own "property" than by any humanitarian considerations. In 1210 all the Jews of the kingdom were thrown into prison, against a fine of 60,000 marks (about $6,120,000). So heavy, indeed, was the affliction that many subsequently left the country, and in the following year (1211) a kind of Zionist conference met in London to plan a large-scale exodus to Palestine. Some 300 English and French Jews are said to have actually emigrated to the Holy Land, under the leadership of a certain Rabbi Meir. In 1215 the barons, revolting against John, again pillaged the London Jewry, removing tombstones from the cemetery in order to provide stones for the repair of Ludgate.

These hardships continued throughout the reign of Henry III (1216-72). In 1226 a tallage of 4,000 marks was imposed, and in 1230 one of 6,000 marks. In 1231 the main synagogue, situated in what is now Threadneedle Street, was given over to the Friars of St. Anthony, subsequently to become St. Anthony's Hospital, while two years later (1233) a special retreat for converts (Domus Conversorum) was established in New Street (now Chancery Lane), on a site occupied in the 20th cent. by the Record Office. The retreat for converts continued in existence until the reign of Charles II (1660-85).

In 1241 the London community sent its due quota of six delegates to the Jewish Parliament convened at Worcester, where a tallage of 10,000 marks was imposed. In 1259 it was mulcted in the further sum of 500 marks toward the expenses of Henry's passage to France. Four years later (1263) the barons were once more on the warpath. Archives containing evidence of their indebtedness to the Jews were systematically raided, and the London Jewry was sacked by the followers of Simon de Montfort. According to contemporary records, some 200 persons were killed, the rest being either forcibly baptized or imprisoned. In 1267 the Jews of the metropolis were among those who sought refuge in the Tower, and helped to defend it, against the Earl of Gloucester and the Disinherited. Their loyalty, however, availed them little. Four years later (1271), their synagogue at the northeast corner of Old Jewry was given over to the Friars de Sacca.

The accession of Edward I, in 1272, brought no remission of these sufferings. In 1278, six hundred and eighty London Jews were imprisoned in the Tower on charges of clipping coin, and 267 of them were subsequently hanged. Two years later, Jews were compelled to attend Dominican conversion services. In 1281 Bishop Peckham protested against the opening of a new synagogue, and in 1282 ordered closed all Jewish houses of worship in the metropolis. Finally, in 1290, when the Jews were expelled from the kingdom, more than twenty out of their 138 houses were confiscated by the crown.

Internal Life. Concerning the internal life of the pre-Expulsion community there is but scant information. At least four synagogues are mentioned in 13th cent. records. One of these, situated in Threadneedle Street, was given over to the Friars of St. Anthony in 1231. Another stood at the Gresham Street corner of Old Jewry and Lothbury, but was presented in 1271 to the Friars Penitentiar. A third was located on the site which subsequently became that of St. Stephen's Church, while a fourth was the predecessor of the famous St. Mary Colechurch, destroyed in the air raids of 1940. There was a cemetery in Jewin Street, near Cripplegate, and a high school (magna schola Judaeorum), owned by Abraham fil Rabi, was located in Iremonger Lane. A ritual bath (Mikveh) appears to have been attached to the synagogue in Gresham Street. It is also probable, though as yet unconfirmed, that the London Jews possessed their own hospital and recreation center.

The judicial administration of the community appears to have been in the hands of certain officials known as episcopi. The exact nature of their functions is disputed, but since three of them are mentioned at the same time, there is plausibility in the suggestion of Joseph Jacobs that they were dayyanim, or judges of the Beth Din (Capitulum Judaeorum). Known occupants of the position are: Deodatus (1168-78); Abraham; Deulesalt; and Vives (about 1194).

In addition to the local episcopi, English Jewry was supervised, during the 13th cent., by a series of presbyters. These were civil commissioners, attached to the Exchequer of the Jews. Five of the six known incumbents of this position were members of the London community: Jacob (1199); Josce (1209); Elias ben Moses (1243); Hagin ben Moses (1258); Cok Hagin, son of Deulacres (1281). Jacob, the first presbyter, is believed to have been the Jacob of London mentioned in a rabbinical source (Darche Mosheh to Orah Hayim 473) as having paraphrased the Passover Haggadah for the use of women and children. Josce is possibly to be identified with the Joseph Yehiel who was the donor of the famous "Bodleian bowl." Elias, who had previously served as an episcopus, and who was appointed as successor to Aaron of York, is especially noted for his spirited defense of the Jews against the exorbitant tallage of 1253. Four years later, however, he was indicted for trespass against the king and "the king of Almaigne" (Richard, Earl of Cornwall), and removed from office. Following his deposition, his brother Hagin (Hayim) was appointed, and after his death, in 1280, the office passed, allegedly through the intervention of Queen Eleanor, to his nephew Cok (Isaac) Hagin.

In so far as their manners and customs are concerned, London Jews appear to have been little distinguished from their coreligionists in the rest of the country, and to have retained, in general, their Norman way of life. Indeed, so close was their bond with France that Meir of Rothenburg (1215-93), in one of his responsa (Cremona ed., 1537, No. 117), actually described England and France as *one* country, from the Jewish point of view. The quarter in which they lived was called "the Jewry," in imitation of the "Juifverie" of Rouen. They bore names which were the French equivalents of Hebrew originals (such as Dieulecresse=Gamaliel, or Gedaliah; Vives=Hayyim), and used French as their vernacular. The school system, to judge from a contemporary manual, was cast upon the model of French Jewry, and in 1171 they joined their French and Rhenish brethren in observing the 20th of Sivan as a fast day in commemoration of the Jewish martyrs of Blois. In matters of synagogue ritual they appear to have followed the traditions of France, although they did draw up a prayer-book of their own. Thus, according to Leopold Zunz, they were called to the reading of the Torah bareheaded. On certain points, however, they maintained an independent line. It is recorded, for example, in the *Etz Hayim* of Jacob ben Judah Hazan (about 1287), himself a Londoner, that English Jews, in contrast to their coreligionists abroad, did not partake of food on Sabbath afternoons.

Economic Status. The economic status of the London Jews varied. Sir B. L. Abrahams contended that the majority of them were poor. On the other hand, there is evidence to suggest that they included several men of substance. Thus, in 1195 the community contributed no less than £478, seven shillings, fourpence, out of a total of 5,000 marks raised by Anglo-Jewry for the king's ransom. Similarly, in 1250 they paid nearly a third of the £1,000 tallage imposed on all the Jews of the kingdom, although they constituted no more than an eighth of their number. Moreover, no Jew was permitted to live in the city unless he could contribute to the tallage; therefore the problem of the destitute stranger scarcely existed.

Furthermore, many of the London Jews owned houses of exceptional grandeur, so much so that they were subsequently considered fitting residences for the nobility. Thus, during the reign of Richard I, the corner house in Iremonger Lane was purchased from a Jew by the Earl of Lancaster, while another, previously belonging to one Isaac of Norwich, was granted by John, in 1214, to the Earl of Derby. It was estimated by Jacobs, on the basis of contemporary records, that the average rental of the Jews' houses was three pounds (about $450 in modern value) per annum.

Against this evidence of wealth, however, must be set the enormous tallages imposed upon the Jews (amounting to about £5,000 annually for the entire Anglo-Jewish population) and the fact that the property of a Jew could be escheated at his death, if he could be shown to have committed any offense during his lifetime. The fabrication of false charges, involving such posthumous confiscation, was therefore a common practice. This, and the steady encroachment of the City Churches during the 13th cent., effected a marked westward drift on the part of London Jews, and by the time of the Expulsion (1290) scarcely any were left in the original Jewish quarter.

London Jews were frequently engaged in general professional life. A physician named Isaac is mentioned in 1192, while in the 13th cent. a Jew named Meir le Brun of Billingsgate was commissioned by the future Edward I to paint a picture of the Virgin for St. Mary-in-All-Hallows Church. The portrait was still in existence in the reign of Henry VIII (1509-47).

The scholastic level of the community was high, several rabbinic authorities being quoted in contemporary and later sources. Among these were Elhanan (Deodatus) ben Isaac of Dampierre, Joseph of Orleans, and Elijah Menahem of the 12th cent., and Rabbi Moses (Magister Mosse) of the 13th. The last-named appears to have been expert, especially, in culinary matters, and his recipe for the preparation of Haroseth is still extant. Abraham ibn Ezra, in his *Yesod Mora* (The Foundation of Religion), written in London in 1158, mentions these scholars, and a 13th cent. Hebrew Psalter, written in England and preserved, until recently, in the Lambeth Palace Library, London (Ms. 435), contains grammatical and other glosses dictated by an unnamed rabbi.

2. The "Middle Period" (1290-1656). It is now established that there were Jews in England in the period between the Expulsion (1290) and the Resettlement (1656). How many, however, were resident in London remains something of an enigma. The House of Converts, established in 1234, continued in existence, but the number of its inmates naturally dwindled. In 1305, when they probably included several who had chosen the path of least resistance at the time of the Expulsion, there were twenty-eight men and twenty-eight women. In 1330, however, there were only eight men and thirteen women. In 1450 there were but five inmates altogether, and in 1500 only four. Such Jews as still remained in the metropolis were obviously obliged to conceal their identity. Vivid indeed is the picture of their condition painted, in 1390, by the visiting Spanish Archbishop Paul de Burgos (1351-1435), himself a convert originally named Solomon Levi. The Jews, he says in his satirical *Purim Letter,* are unable to observe the holiday with traditional merriment, neither have they wine for the Kiddush and Habdalah ceremonies of the Sabbath.

The expulsion did not, however, preclude occasional visits to the country by distinguished foreign Jews. In 1409, for instance, one, Master Samson of Mirabeau, was summoned by the Lord Mayor, none other than the renowned Dick Whittington, to treat his ailing wife, the Lady Alice, while three years later (1412) another Jewish physician, Dr. David de Nigarelli of Lucca, attended King Henry IV.

By the end of the 15th cent. there appears to have been a marked infiltration of Jewish and Marrano refugees from Spain, the historian Amador de los Rios stating categorically that England was among the first countries to provide a haven for the exiles of 1492. To what extent they settled in London is, however, uncertain.

In 1531 Jewish influence actually appeared at court. Henry VIII, seeking a divorce from his first wife, Catherine of Aragon (1529), sought a way of circumventing Biblical restrictions, and appealed to various learned Jews abroad to interpret anew the "awkward" commandments of *Lev.* 18:16 and *Deut.* 25:5. A suitable and convenient opinion was rendered by one Mark Raphael of Venice, who was invited to London in this year, and subsequently became a royal favorite. Eleven years later (1542), a number of suspected Jews were arrested, but by the close of the century the Portuguese Marranos appeared to have gained a firm foothold and to have established a colony. Telltale names like Carvajal, de Lima and Alvarez occur in contemporary records, and a Dr. Hector Nunez, of Evora, established a practice in Mark Lane.

Even Queen Elizabeth herself was said to have been partial to the newcomers, affording hospitality in the country to a party of Marranos taken off a captured ship in 1590, and driving openly through the streets of London in the company of the beautiful Maria Nunez Rodrigues, one of the passengers. By 1592 the crypto-Jews had so far shaken off the shackles of the Inquisition as to attend divine services organized in his London home by Solomon Cormano, envoy of the Jewish Duke of Mitylene, Alvaro Mendes (Solomon aben Ayish). Two years later scandal stalked abroad. The physician Rodrigo Lopez (1525-94), who had settled in the city in 1559 and who had fallen out with his previous patient, the Earl of Essex, was implicated in plots for the invasion of Portugal in the Spanish interest, and on June 7th was hanged, drawn and quartered in the Tower on charges of conspiring to poison Queen Elizabeth. Other troubles, less personal in character, were soon to follow, for in 1609 the Portuguese Marranos, quarreling among themselves, were banished from the country.

English literature of the 16th cent. contains a number of scattered references to the presence of Jews. Shakespeare (1564-1616), whose plays were produced at the Globe Theatre, London, mentions them, always slightingly, in *Two Gentlemen of Verona* (1594-95), *A Midsummer Night's Dream* (1595-96), the first part of *Henry IV* (1597), *Much Ado about Nothing* (1598-99) and *Macbeth* (1606). A play of 1609, *Every Woman in Her Humour,* alludes to them as dealers in old clothes, while a pamphlet of 1625, entitled *The Wandering Jew Tells Fortunes to Englishmen,* asserts, in so many words, that "a store of Jews we have in England, a few in Court . . . many i' the city."

3. The Resettlement (1656-57). At the time of the Commonwealth (1649-60) there was living in London a small colony of some 200 crypto-Jews from Spain and Portugal. Many of these were merchants, importing large quantities of bullion and able, by reason of their widespread trade connections, to supply the Roundheads with valuable foreign intelligence. Chief of the group was Antonio Ferdinando Carvajal, a native of Fundão, Portugal, who had established himself in Leadenhall Street at some time between 1630 and 1635. Papers discovered by Lucien Wolf, in 1891, reveal that Carvajal was in receipt of regular bulletins from abroad from two agents named John Butler (alias Jacob Goltburgh) and John Somer. These appear to have been transmitted to Cromwell, and it was no doubt partly in recognition of this service that Carvajal and his two sons were naturalized in 1655. Similar assistance was rendered to the state by Manuel Martinez Dormido, a relative of Manasseh ben Israel, who received periodic reports from two intelligencers named David Nasy and Manuel Grasian. Other important figures of the London colony included the merchants Duarte Henriques, Henrique Jorge Mendes, a member of the famous banking family of Lisbon and Antwerp, and Simon de Caceres, a native of Hamburg, who submitted to the Protector a curious plan for the conquest of Chile, and who offered to raise a band of Jewish volunteers for the purpose.

In view of these and other services, Cromwell was prepared to turn a blind eye to the existence of the crypto-Jews, and they were even permitted to meet privately for worship in one another's houses. Their identity, however, was an open secret. "Touching Judaism," writes John Howel, in 1653, to his friend R. Lewis of Amsterdam, "some corners of our city smell as rank of it as yours doth there."

In course of time, their existence more or less secure, the little colony became more open in its religious allegiance, and although certain elements, among them Carvajal, appear to have preferred a more cautious policy, moves were set on foot to obtain formal recognition. These were at first tied up with efforts to secure admission to the country of exiled Jews from Spain and Portugal, and in 1654 the aforementioned Dormido petitioned the Protector to allow them "to be dwellers here with the same equalness and conveniences which your inland born subjects do enjoy." This petition was referred to a special sub-committee of the Council of State, but the latter reported adversely upon it. Thereupon, in 1655, Manasseh ben Israel (about 1604 to 1657), a rabbi and scholar of Amsterdam, who had previously been endeavoring to secure similar privileges for his coreligionists both from Cromwell himself and from Queen Christina of Sweden, came to London and, from an address in the Strand, forwarded to the Protector his famous *Humble Addresses on behalf of the Jewish Nation.* Manasseh asked for (1) admission and protection of Jews; (2) permission to found synagogues and practise the Jewish religion; (3) permission to open a cemetery outside the city; (4) permission to engage freely in trade; (5) appointment of a commissioner to meet new arrivals and swear them to loyalty; (6) sanction of a *beth din* (ecclesiastical tribunal) to settle internal disputes; and (7) repeal of any existent anti-Jewish laws.

Manasseh ben Israel was duly received in audience by Cromwell, and his request was likewise referred to the Council of State. On November 13, 1655, that body reported that, while it saw no legal bar to the admission and protection of Jews *as aliens,* it felt that the open practise of the Jewish religion must be conditional on giving no offense to Christians. Moreover, it denounced the granting of religious autonomy as constituting a potential threat to the Church, and remarked, in regard to the question of free trading, that "great prejudice is like to arise . . . which, besides other dangers, . . . we find very commonly suggested by the inhabitants of the city of London." This decision, while it constituted a virtual charter for the actual London colony, satisfied neither Cromwell nor Manasseh ben Israel. In the following month (December, 1655), a conference of notables was convened at Whitehall, but here again the old prejudices asserted themselves. While it was conceded that there were no legal grounds for refusing admission to Jews, the precise terms on which this should be done were the subject of considerable dispute. In the end, the conference was dismissed without definite result. From that time forward, however, the legal rights of resident Jews came to be taken for granted.

Emboldened by this degree of success, the colony seems to have decided to press its claims, though on a less ambitious basis, this time seeking no more than a legal recognition of its own existence and permission to establish a formal congregation. To this limited policy Carvajal and other influential members of the group were now prepared to lend their support, and on March 24, 1656, a further petition, asking for the right to build a synagogue and open a cemetery, was addressed to the Protector by Manasseh and six leaders of the colony (including Carvajal and Dormido). The chances of this petition were appreciably enhanced by the outcome of the Robles case in the following May. The war with Portugal having broken out, Antonio Rodrigues Robles, a wealthy crypto-Jew, was denounced as a Portuguese and therefore liable to confiscation of property. This charge was at once seen as a threat to the entire Marrano colony, and the defense therefore decided to make a test case of it, contending that the accused was neither a Portuguese nor a Spaniard, but a Jew, and thus immune from the law against "enemy aliens." The plea was accepted by the Privy Council, and by their ruling the status of the London group was at last legally stabilized.

Perhaps in consequence of this decision, the Protector appears to have reacted favorably to the petition of Manasseh and his colleagues. A document in the British Museum (B.M.Ms. 4223, f. 156) reveals that, toward the end of the year, permission was obtained, through one John Sandler, to build a synagogue, while in February, 1657, a burial ground at Mile End was leased in the names of Carvajal and Caceres, the first interment taking place in the following September. The synagogue in question was situated in Creechurch Lane, its first rabbi being Moses Athias, a cousin of Carvajal. The exact date of its dedication, usually assumed to be 1657, is not entirely certain. In December of that year, the Earl of Monmouth, writing to his "dear Nan," speaks of the *projected* establishment of two London synagogues. On the other hand, the diarist Samuel Pepys visited the synagogue in 1659, and a pamphlet published in 1660 alludes to its existence. A graphic account of its services is contained in a letter sent, in April, 1662, by one Reverend John Greenhalgh to his friend Thomas Crompton. A second synagogue, for the

nascent congregation of Ashkenazim, was opened at about the same time in Great St. Helens.

4. The Restoration Period (1660-64). The peaceful life of the London community was soon to be disturbed. In 1659, following the death of Oliver Cromwell in the previous year, a petition against the Jews, demanding their expulsion from the country and the confiscation of their property, was addressed to the new Protector by one Richard Baker, while a few months later, Thomas Violet, a City jeweler and the arch anti-Semite of his day, laid information against them before Mr. Justice Tyril. The judge counselling caution, in view of the unsettled state of public affairs, Violet sought to bolster his case by an unsuccessful attempt to plant spurious money upon Athias, the London rabbi. Balked in this device, he waited until the fall of the Commonwealth, in May, 1659, and then, within a few weeks, marched flamboyantly down Whitehall personally to deliver to the Lords in Council his notorious *Petition against the Jews*. As soon as Charles II was firmly restored to the throne, the Lord Mayor and Aldermen of London, apprehensive of commercial competition, waited upon him with a virtual endorsement of Violet's plea. The Jews, however, at once convened a meeting in the house of Maria Carvajal, widow of their now departed leader, and prepared a counter-petition. Both statements were considered by the Privy Council, on December 7th, and were referred by that body to the House of Commons. The Commons, however, took no definite action, so that the privileges previously accorded under Cromwell remained undisturbed.

The policy of the "merry monarch" was friendly toward the Jews, no less than nineteen of their number being naturalized by the end of 1661. This friendliness, which continued throughout the king's reign, was due partly to the presence of influential Jews at court, among them being Duarte da Silva, a merchant of Amsterdam, who had been brought to England in 1662 to administer the dowry of the king's bride, the Infanta Catherine of Braganza. It should be added, however, that da Silva subsequently fell from favor, and was imprisoned, when he refused to honor his master's premature drafts upon yet unpaid instalments of the marriage portion.

By 1663 the London community had grown both in numbers and affluence, and a radical reorganization was therefore undertaken. A meeting of September 3rd approved annual assessments on its members, and in the following April by-laws (*Ascamoth*) were drawn up, and Jacob Sasportas (1618-98), an eminent Dutch rabbi, who had accompanied Manasseh ben Israel on his mission to London, was summoned from Amsterdam as Haham, or ecclesiastical chief. At the same time, steps were taken to build a larger synagogue.

Once again, however, the even tenor of life was rudely interrupted. In 1664 the Earl of Berkshire and a certain Mr. Ricaut called on the officers of the congregation and told them that the king had verbally committed the Jews to their care, and that, failing payment of a substantial sum, their property would be seized. This clumsy attempt at extortion failed, however, to daunt such a man as Dormido, the then president, and he immediately reported the matter to the king. Charles thereupon took occasion to reply to the previous petition of the Jews against Violet by assuring them, on August 22, 1664, that they might "promise themselves the effects of such favor as formerly they enjoyed, so long as they demean themselves peaceably and quietly, with due obedience to His Majesty's laws and without scandal to his Government." This declaration, though scarcely an "Act of Toleration," as some have supposed it to be, is nevertheless the first unequivocal confirmation of Jewish rights after the Resettlement.

5. The Late Seventeenth Century (1666-1700). The Great Plague of 1665 frightened Haham Sasportas back to Amsterdam. Before he left, however, the community had been swept by rumors of the appearance of a Messiah in Smyrna. The Haham spared no efforts to expose the impostor, Sabbatai Zevi, but there can be no doubt that the heresy claimed many adherents among his congregants. One of the staunchest devotees of the fanatic was Benjamin Levi, beadle of the synagogue in Creechurch Lane. In December, 1665, Henry Oldenburgh, secretary of the Royal Society, wrote to Benedict Spinoza in Amsterdam asking his opinion on the matter, and remarking that "few in this place believe it, but many wish it." The following year, the popular excitement died down before the major disaster of the Great Fire of London. Actually, the conflagration seems to have skirted the Jewish quarter, and a curious tale told in the anti-Sabbatian work *Meoroth Zebi* (The Lights of Zevi) presupposes the undisturbed continuance, in 1666, of the regular communal machinery.

In 1667 the community participated, on appeal from Venice, in the ransoming of Jews captured aboard Turkish ships and sold into slavery by the Knights of Malta. "Wardens of the Captives" were appointed annually among the regular officers of the congregation, and it is interesting to note, in this connection, that even at the present day a prayer, partly in Spanish, is offered in the Kol Nidre service of the Sephardim of London on behalf of "all our brethren who are going on journeys by land or sea."

In 1670, after an interval of four years in which the community was without spiritual direction, Sasportas was succeeded by Joshua da Silva. Three years later, London Jews were favored with a further token of the king's friendliness when an indictment against them for technical breach of the Conventicle Act, restricting religious assemblies to five persons, was quashed by royal command. In 1680, however, following the conversion, allegedly for gain, of a Jewess named Eve Cohan, attempts were made by outraged Christian elements to confine the community to a ghetto. The project, however, failed to find support, and five years later, when an effort was made by one Thomas Beaumont to imprison thirty-seven London Jews for alleged infringement of the Elizabethan Act of Uniformity, King James II (1685-89) repeated the assurance of protection given by his predecessor in 1673. Meanwhile, Haham da Silva had died, and a successor had been appointed in 1680 in the person of Jacob Abendana, a noted scholar settled in Amsterdam. Abendana retired, however, after eight

years, his place being filled by Solomon Ayllon (1664-1728). Addicted to Sabbatian heresies, Ayllon was scarcely a success, and in 1701 he, too, retired, and assumed a rabbinical post in Amsterdam.

6. The Eighteenth Century. The new century opened auspiciously for London Jewry. In 1702 a larger synagogue (now scheduled as one of the City's ancient monuments) was consecrated in Bevis Marks, one of the main beams of the building being especially presented by Queen Anne (1702-14). The first Haham was no less eminent a personality than David Nieto (1654-1728), the famed scientist and philosopher, and around the synagogue there developed, during the succeeding fifty years, a complete network of philanthropic and educational institutions. In addition to the Medrash Etz Haim and the Gates of Hope School, founded already at the reorganization of the community in 1664, these included an Orphan Asylum (1703), a school for girls, established by Isaac da Costa Villareal (1730), a Marriage Portion Society (1736), a Hospital (1747) and a philanthropic society known as the Mahasim Tobim (1749).

In marked contrast to the wealth and organization of the Sephardim were the poverty, ignorance and chaos which prevailed among the Ashkenazim. These, driven westward by the persecutions in Eastern Europe, had begun to settle in London during the period of the Commonwealth. In 1692 they had established a small congregation in Broad Court, Mitre Square, Aldgate, and four years later, a burial ground in the East End of London had been purchased for them by Benjamin Levy, a wealthy financier. In 1722 a more commodious synagogue was erected in Duke's Place, Aldgate, the cost being defrayed by one Moses Hart, of Isleworth, whose brother Aaron Hart (Uri Phaibus Hamburger, 1670-1756) was appointed its first rabbi. The synagogue, rebuilt and enlarged in 1790 (mainly at the expense of Moses Hart's daughter, Judith Levy, "the Queen of Richmond Green"), subsequently became known as the Great Shool. In 1732 a Talmud Torah was established, and in 1745 an Initiation Society (which still functioned in 1942) came into existence.

The Ashkenazim, however, were not united. In 1704, as the result of internal dissensions, a rival congregation was founded by one Marcus Hamburger on his own premises in Fenchurch Street. This subsequently acquired its own burial ground in Hoxton (1707), and in 1736 built a new place of worship, known as the Hambro Synagogue. (The latter was later incorporated into the United Synagogue, but was closed in 1936.)

Although separated in matters of communal organization, both sections of the community united in all that pertained to the national welfare, their ready patriotism in supplying funds and men during the Jacobite uprising of 1745 helping in no small degree to secure passage of the Naturalization Bill of 1753. When, however, this measure was repealed in the following year, in consequence of popular agitation, the effect upon the Sephardim was disastrous. Several of its wealthier members, seeing in apostasy their only chance of social and civic advancement, renounced Judaism, or married out of the faith. Chief among them was Samson Gideon, the famous stockbroker, who subsequently became Lord Eardley of Spalding, the first person of Jewish birth to attain such rank in England. In 1746, after a Jewish Naturalization Bill for Ireland had been rejected by the Irish Parliament, a "Committee of Diligence" was formed to look after Jewish interests. At first confined to the Sephardim, it later embraced their Ashkenazic coreligionists, and ultimately (1836) developed into the Board of Deputies of British Jews.

While the increasing assimilationism of its members was causing secessions from the Sephardic community, religious persecution and war on the continent were steadily swelling the ranks of the Ashkenazim, and toward the close of the century they numbered between 12,000 and 15,000 persons. Most of them, however, were without resources, unskilled, and handicapped by the demands of their faith. The result was that they tended to drift into peddling and huckstering, and not infrequently came into conflict with the law. An attempt to relieve their plight, beyond the inadequate aid supplied by the meagre and undependable synagogue funds, was accordingly made by a few wealthier members of the community in 1779, when the Meshibath Nephesh, or Bread, Meat and Coal Charity (still active in 1942), was established. This, however, could scarcely cope with the problem, and later, through the efforts of the banker Benjamin Goldsmid (1755-1808), an Old Jews' Hospital was established at Mile End in 1806. (This was subsequently removed, in 1861, to Norwood, and later, in 1876, amalgamated with the Jews' Orphan Asylum.)

Meanwhile, a noticeable drift westward, coupled with seemingly inveterate disputes, led to the founding of new congregations. A "New Synagogue" was

Painting of the Tables of the Decalogue (ascribed to Aaron de Chavez), preserved in Bevis Marks, London

opened, in 1761, in the Bricklayers' Hall, Leadenhall Street, and another, in 1788, in Lauriston Road, Hackney. The westward drift also occasioned the establishment, in 1768, of a small Minyan in Bedford Row, but when neighbors complained of the noise created by the blowing of the Shofar, the devout worshippers moved (1797) to Denmark Court, Strand, subsequently to amalgamate with the Maiden Lane congregation and form the independent Western Synagogue.

The ecclesiastical direction of the Sephardim was entrusted, during the 18th cent., to the Hahamin David Nieto (1701-28), his son, Isaac Nieto (1733-41), Mosshe-Gomez de Mesquita (1741-48), and Moses Cohen d'Azevedo (1761-84), while that of the Ashkenazim was in the hands of the rabbis of the Great Synagogue. These were Aaron Hart (1709-56), Hart Lyon (1756-64) and David Tevele Schiff (1765-92).

The spiritual and cultural level of the community appears to have been low. Isaac Nieto, feeling himself cramped, resigned as Haham in 1741. Similarly, in 1764, Hart Lyon gave up the rabbinate of the Great Synagogue in disgust, complaining that he "had money, but no Jews," while the contemporary physician Meyer Löw Schomberg (1690-1761) complained that London Jews were unobservant, mercenary and corrupt. "Their God," he says, "is Mammon or the Nithsday Bank." Nevertheless, the community was not without its handful of scholars and devoted workers. Among these, high place should be given to David Levi (1742-1801), a self-educated hatter who translated the liturgy and defended Judaism against the attacks of Joseph Priestley; Michael Josephs (1763-1849), Hebraist; the brothers Benjamin and Abraham Goldsmid, founders of the Jews' Hospital; and Joshua Van Oven (1766-1838), one of the founders of the Jews' Free School.

Nor was the community inactive in the general life of the nation. Among its more prominent representatives mention may be made of Jose Cortissos (1656-1742), who came to England in 1712 and had previously served as contractor general for the allied forces of Great Britain, Portugal and Holland in the war against Spain; Jacob de Castro Sarmento (1691-1762), renowned physician and theologian; Moses Mendes (d. 1758), poetaster and author of musical

The Central Synagogue, London

comedies; Myer Leon (Leoni), opera singer and composer; Benjamin Goldsmid (1755-1808), banker and founder of the Naval Asylum; "Dutch Sam" (1775-1816) and Daniel Mendoza (1763-1836), pugilists; Mrs. Bland (1769-1810), actress and singer; and John Braham (1774-1856), tenor singer and composer.

There was also an interesting sprinkling of freaks and eccentrics. Chief among these were the quasi-mystic and Cabalist Haim Samuel de Falk (1708-82), known as "the Baal Shem of London"; Ephraim Lopez Pereira, Baron d'Aguilar (1739-1802), notorious miser, whose house at Colebrook Row, Islington, was popularly known as "Starvation Farm"; and Lord George Gordon (1750-93), the temperamental hero of the "No Popery" riots of 1780, who subsequently embraced Judaism. Reference may also be made to the beautiful and romantic Kitty da Costa Villareal (b. 1709) who, after the death of her first husband, married out of the faith and became the ancestress of Viscount Galway, who was governor general of New Zealand in 1942.

7. The Nineteenth Century. The history of London Jewry during the 19th cent. was conditioned by three major developments: (1) the struggle for civic and political emancipation; (2) the internal consolidation of the community; (3) the influx of Jewish refugees from Eastern Europe in the 1880's and 1890's.

During the first quarter of the century the Jewish population of London had increased to about 20,000. The vast majority were still concentrated in the East End, engaged as petty traders. The older element, however, consisting largely of the Sephardim, were slowly establishing themselves as persons of influence and standing in the commercial world, being occupied especially in trade with the West Indies and China. Jewish professional men were few, owing to the obstacles which stood in the way of education, for Jewish children were not yet admitted to the public schools, and Jews were debarred from the universities in consequence of the Christological oath imposed upon undergraduates. The first non-sectarian institution of higher education, University College, London, was not founded until 1826, and then largely through the efforts and support of Isaac Lyon Goldsmid (1778-1859).

It was against this social background that the struggle for emancipation commenced. The immediate stimulus was provided by the repeal, in 1828, of the Test and Corporation Acts and the granting of emancipation to Catholics in the following year. In this struggle the Jews of the metropolis won victory after victory, largely owing to the influence which their commercial usefulness commanded. In 1831 they were admitted as Freemen of the City, being thus enabled to engage in retail trade within its boundaries. In 1833 Francis Goldsmid (1808-78), a leading champion of the cause, was admitted to the bar, being the first English Jew to attain the right. He was permitted to take the required oath on the Old Testament. Two years later, David Salomons (1797-1873) was elected sheriff of London and Middlesex, a special Sheriff's Declaration Act (5 & 6 William IV, c. XXVIII) being passed to enable him to occupy that office without being obliged to take the oath

"on the true faith of a Christian." In 1837 Salomons was succeeded in this honor by Moses Montefiore (1784-1885), who was elected sheriff of London in 1837, appointed high sheriff of Kent in 1845, and created a baronet in 1846.

There were, however, setbacks in the struggle. Elected alderman in 1835, and reelected several years later, Salomons was not permitted to take his seat, because he refused to swear the usual Christian oath. Not until 1845 was a special Jewish Disabilities Removal Act (8 & 9 Victoria, c.LII) passed, substituting another form of declaration. The parliamentary battle, however, had still to be won. In 1847, and again in 1849, 1850 and 1852, Lionel de Rothschild, elected to the House of Commons, was debarred from taking his seat because of his insistence on omitting the Christian formula in the initial oath. The same thing happened, in 1851, when Salomons was elected, and it was not until the passing of the Jewish Relief Act (21 & 22 Victoria, c.XLIX) in 1858 that this disability was removed, while further legislation in 1866 (29 Victoria, c.XIX) and 1871 (34 & 35 Victoria, c.XLVIII) achieved the final political emancipation of the Jews. In 1855 Salomons was elected first Jewish Lord Mayor of London, and in 1869 he was created a baronet.

Meanwhile, the internal structure of the community was undergoing significant changes. Early in the century, the three Ashkenazic synagogues had agreed to pool resources in the matter of burials and other common services, and in 1804 a centralized Board of Shehitah was set up. Moreover, following adverse criticism of metropolitan Jewish life, a number of charitable institutions were established. Chief of these were two benefit societies, the Tents of Righteousness (1812) and the Lovers of Justice and Peace (1823), a Jewish Blind Society (1819), a Society for Relieving the Aged Needy of the Faith (1829), a Promoters of Charity Society (1840) and a Soup Kitchen for the Poor (1854). In addition, the Sephardim created a comprehensive Board of Guardians, in 1837, and the Ashkenazim followed suit in 1859. The latter body, in the 1930's, disbursed some £40,000 (about $200,000) annually in relief. Educational institutions were likewise called into being, such as the Westminster Jews' Free School (1811) and the Jews' Free School, Bell Lane, Spitalfields (1817). The latter was, in 1942, the largest Jewish day school in the world.

At the same time, however, the community was torn by internal schism. The westward drift of its wealthier members had led to a demand for the erection of a new synagogue to serve those who were now living at too great a distance from Bevis Marks. This demand, however, was consistently rejected by the conservative officers of the Sephardic congregation, more especially when it was coupled, in 1836, with an appeal for religious reforms which included the curtailment of the services, the abolition of the second days of festivals and the introduction of instrumental music. Dissatisfied with this seemingly diehard attitude, eighteen Sephardim, together with six Ashkenazim from the Duke's Place congregation, at length seceded and established themselves independently, in 1841, in Burton Street. Swept by the Reform tendencies then developing in Germany, the Reformers compiled their own prayer-book and appointed two min-

Exterior of the Great Synagogue at Duke's Place, London

isters in the persons of Professor D. W. Marks (1811-97) and Dr. Albert Loewy. The secession met with bitter opposition from the Orthodox section, and a formal ban (Herem) was pronounced against the Reformers by Solomon Herschell (1762-1842), then rabbi of the Great Synagogue. (Raphael Meldola had died in 1828, and the Sephardim were temporarily without a Haham.) This drastic measure, however, was strongly discountenanced within the parent synagogues, and in 1849 the ban was lifted. The congregation, however, was still considered un-Jewish, and was excluded from representation on the Board of Deputies. Moreover, it was forced to apply for special parliamentary recognition before marriages could be performed under its auspices.

Solomon Herschell was succeeded, in 1845, by Nathan Marcus Adler (1802-90), a grandnephew of David Schiff, who was brought over from Hannover. Adler concentrated his attention upon welding the community into a formal organization. At first he attempted to reconcile the Reformers, but in this he was unsuccessful, and in 1855 he established Jews' College for the training of ministers and rabbis. Adler, however, was thoroughly imbued with German ideas of a Jewish community. His main program was to unite the various Ashkenazic synagogues of London into a central federation under his own spiritual authority, and he endeavored, throughout his career in the metropolis, to elevate his position of rabbi of the Great Synagogue to that of chief rabbi of England. In 1870 he finally achieved this purpose when an association of the five London synagogues of the

Ashkenazim was formally recognized by Act of Parliament as the "United Synagogue."

From the first, this association became an institution of far-reaching influence in the community. It pursued a liberal policy in synagogal government, encouraged and assisted the establishment of local congregations, and carried on charitable work on behalf of the Jewish poor. The association, in 1942, comprised twenty-two constituent, thirteen district, nine associate and ten affiliated synagogues, and owned eight metropolitan cemeteries (four no longer used).

Efforts were made to develop also the cultural life of the community, an influential Association for the Diffusion of Religious Knowledge being initiated, in 1860, by Dayan Barnett Abrahams, who was then functioning as Ab Beth Din of the Sephardic congre-

Home of the Jewish Board of Guardians, London

Petticoat Lane (Middlesex Street), London

gation. An Anglo-Jewish press was also established. Two monthlies, *The Hebrew Intelligencer* (1823) and the *Hebrew Review* (1834-60), made their appearance, and in 1841 the weekly *Jewish Chronicle* was founded by David Meldola and Moses Angel. It celebrated its hundredth anniversary in 1941.

While the community was thus more securely establishing itself, it was faced with the problem of succoring an influx of destitute coreligionists from Central Europe, who settled chiefly in the East End. It was principally in their interest that the Board of Guardians was established in 1859. The influx was increased, during the 1880's and 1890's, by the pogroms in Russian and the Ukraine, as the result of which the numbers of the community were almost trebled, and the Ashkenazim became at last the dominant element in London Jewry. The immigration presented a serious challenge to the English labor market, and a special Russo-Jewish Committee was founded to assist in the repatriation of some of the refugees and the movement of others to the United States. Nevertheless, the vast majority remained.

This led to the development of a marked "Yiddish" element of the community. A Judeo-German newspaper, the *Londoner Israelit,* was established by Naphtali Levy in 1878, and this was succeeded later by a score of others, the most notable of which were the *Jewish Express* (defunct since 1934) and *Die Zeit.* A number of small synagogues grew up in the Whitechapel district, and in 1887, largely through the initiative of Samuel Montagu (the first Lord Swaythling), these were combined, in 1887, into a Federation of Synagogues. Starting with sixteen organizations, the Federation, in 1942, comprised fifty-six constituents, and owned two cemeteries, in North London and Rainham respectively. At the same time, efforts were made to avert dangers resulting from overcrowding by the establishment of several clubs for the younger people. Chief among these were the Leman Street Girls' Club (1886), the West Central Jewish Club (1892) and the Brady Street Clubs (1896). A number of friendly societies were also founded, the most important of them being the Order Achei Brith and Shield of Abraham (1888), the Grand Order of Israel and the Order of the Shield of David (1897), and the Manasseh ben Israel Friendly Society (1898).

The intellectual life of the community also prospered. Succeeding an earlier generation which had included such men as David de Sola (1796-1860), Hebraist; Emanuel Deutsch (1829-73), Semitist; Joseph Zedner (1804-71), Hebrew bibliographer; J. Waley (d. 1874), lawyer and economist; Numa Edward Hartog (1846-71), first Jewish Senior Wrangler of Oxford University; Asher Asher (1837-89); and Alfred E. Newman (1851-87), noted collector of Anglo-Judaica, there arose a remarkable coterie of scholars and cultural leaders. Most prominent among them were Solomon Schechter (1850-1915), Michael Friedlaender (1833-1911), principal of Jews' College, Hermann Gollancz (1852-1930), Joseph Jacobs (1854-1916), Lucien Wolf (1857-1930), Israel Abrahams (1858-1925), Asher Myers, Israel Zangwill (1864-1926), Isidore Spielman (1854-1925), Claude G. Montefiore (1858-1938), and Moses Gaster (1856-1939). An Anglo-Jewish Exhibition was held, in 1887, in Albert Hall, among the sponsors being several distinguished non-Jews, including the poet Robert Browning. In 1891 the Ancient Order of Maccabeans, an intellectual fraternity, was organized, and two years later the Jewish Historical Society of England came into being. The spiritual supervision of the Ashkenazim was entrusted to Nathan Marcus Adler (1845-90) and to his son Hermann Adler (1891-1911), while that of the Sephardim was in the hands of Benjamin Artom (1866-79) and Moses Gaster (1887-1918).

The interests of London Jews were not, however, confined to communal activities. No longer debarred by religious disabilities, many entered public life, often attaining to positions of eminence. Among those who held high civic or government office were: Sir Benjamin Philips (1811-89), elected Lord Mayor in 1865; Sir George Jessel (1824-83), appointed Solicitor-General in 1871 and Master of the Rolls in 1873; Nathaniel Mayer Rothschild (1840-1915), the first professing Jew to be raised to the peerage; Sir Julian Goldsmid (1838-96), made Deputy Chairman of Committees in the House of Commons in 1893; and Judah Peter Benjamin (1812-84), eminent jurist. In the year of the Diamond Jubilee of Queen Victoria (1897) the Lord Mayor was a Jew, Sir George Faudell-Philips.

The community also commanded sufficient influence at this period to organize protest meetings in the Mansion House against the Damascus blood libel of 1840 (July 3rd) and the Russian pogroms of 1882 (February 1st). A similar meeting to protest against

Signal corps of the Jewish Lads' Brigade, London

British notables at a festival observance (Jan., 1927) of the London Jewish Hospital. Among those shown were (l. to r.): Mrs. Charles Rothschild, David Lloyd George, Marchioness of Reading, James de Rothschild, Margaret Lloyd George, Marquis of Reading, and Mrs. James de Rothschild

the latter outrages was held in the Guildhall on December 10, 1890.

8. The Twentieth Century. The 20th cent. witnessed several notable developments in the history of London Jewry. Prominent among these was the introduction of the Liberal Jewish movement, mainly inspired by the theologian Claude G. Montefiore. Although bitterly opposed by the Orthodox section, the movement succeeded in appealing to the younger people and to many who would otherwise have remained distant from things Jewish. A sumptuous synagogue was erected in 1910 in St. Johns Wood.

There was also a marked advance in welfare services. A Jewish Institute, to serve as an educational and recreational center for East London Jewry, was established by the United Synagogue in 1905, and a large Jewish Hospital was erected in the same quarter. The Independent Order of B'nai B'rith, founded in New York city in 1843, established lodges in London, while

a useful Free Reading Room was opened in Whitechapel. A Jewish War Memorial, established in commemoration of British Jews who fell in the first World War, with headquarters at Woburn House, Woburn Square, W., developed into a communal center accommodating the offices of the Board of Deputies, United Synagogue, B'nai B'rith and other important bodies. Part of the building was occupied by Jews' College and by a museum of Jewish antiquities. Another war memorial, established by the Reform and Liberal Synagogues, took the form of a large East End settlement. Originally constructed in 1919, this was later enlarged and endowed by Bernhard Baron, the tobacco magnate and philanthropist. Another Jewish museum, the property of the Jewish Historical Society, was located in the Gustave Tuck theatre at University College. This was virtually an extension of the Mocatta Library and Museum, left to the Society by Frederic David Mocatta (1825-1904) and presented

Street demonstration in London: more than 40,000 Jews and non-Jews marched (July, 1933) in protest against anti-Semitic persecutions in Germany

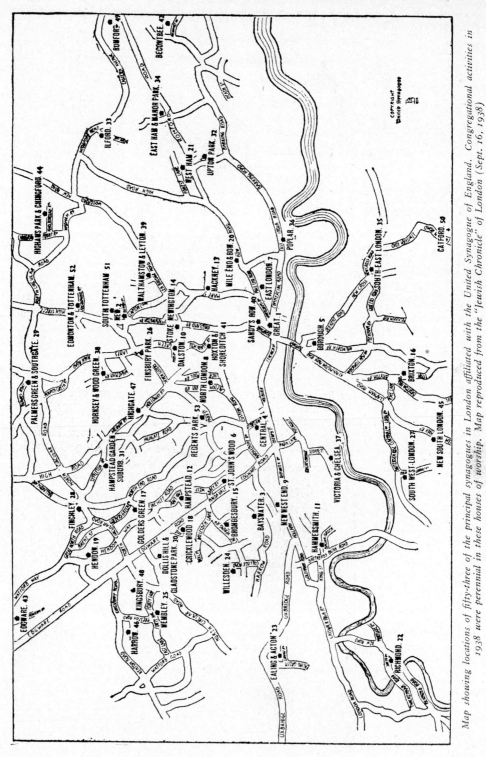

Map showing locations of fifty-three of the principal synagogues in London affiliated with the United Synagogue of England. Congregational activities in 1938 were perennial in these houses of worship. Map reproduced from the "Jewish Chronicle" of London (Sept. 16, 1938)

to the College in 1905. Other libraries of Jewish interest were those of Jews' College, containing some 38,000 volumes and manuscripts, and the Beth Hamedrash, administered by the United Synagogue. The British Museum also contained extensive Hebrew collections, based principally on the holdings of Solomon da Costa, H. I. Michael of Hamburg, Joseph Almanzi and Moses Gaster, while there was likewise

much of Jewish interest in the Salomons library of the Guildhall.

Shortly before the outbreak of the second World War, in 1939, London Jewry was gravely perturbed by a marked recrudescence of anti-Semitic feeling stimulated by Sir Oswald Mosley's blackshirted Union of British Fascists. Jews in the East End were terrorized, and sometimes beaten, while virulent attacks upon

Ruins of the ark in the Great Synagogue of London caused by air-raids in 1941. Reproduced by courtesy of "Hadassah News Letter," New York

them were made at open-air meetings. On September 7, 1936, a giant protest was organized, tens of thousands of Jews marching through the streets of London to a rally in Hyde Park. Nevertheless, the agitation continued, but on the following October 4th an effective demonstration was made by London's Jewish masses when some 250,000 persons blocked the route of a Fascist march through the East End. This action forced the hand of the commissioner of police to ban the march, and although traditional British conceptions of "free speech" provided further opportunity for blackshirt tactics, the eyes of the government had been opened to the menace, and shortly after the outbreak of the War the Fascists were officially banned and Sir Oswald Mosley detained.

The air raids over London in 1940 and 1941 profoundly affected Jewish life. On the one hand, there was a marked exodus to the country, leaving communal institutions devoid of funds and disrupting the cohesion of the community. On the other hand, very many Jewish buildings were hit by enemy action, eleven out of twenty-two constituents of the United Synagogue being damaged. The Great Synagogue and

the Western Synagogue were completely gutted during the night of May 10 to 11, 1941, while other buildings which were hit included the Mocatta Library and Museum, the offices of the Beth Din, the Jewish Institute, the Board of Guardians, the London Jewish Hospital, the Spanish and Portuguese Congregational Almshouses, the West Central Jewish Lads' Club, Woburn House, the Reform Synagogue, the Liberal Synagogue, the branch synagogue of the Sephardim in Lauderdale Road, W., and the offices of the *Jewish Chronicle*. Even cemeteries were not spared, bombs falling, among others, on the ancient burial ground of the Sephardim in Mile End.

Nor was it only communal buildings that suffered in the Blitz. Many hundreds of humble Jewish homes in the Whitechapel, Stepney and Bethnal Green districts were razed during a particularly savage attack on September 6 to 7, 1940. The resultant chaos, especially among those unable to follow directions given in English, was indescribable. Jewish relief agencies, and notably the welfare branch of the United Synagogue, worked heroically to bring succor. The older clubs and the Jews' Temporary Shelter (established 1885)

The Liberal Synagogue in London

opened their doors to the homeless, while the London Jewish Hospital, itself badly damaged, distinguished itself by bravely carrying on in the face of the havoc. Thousands of Jews rallied to the fire-fighting and other services, many earning commendation for especially heroic acts.

Moreover, in common with the rest of the population, the Jews of London refused to be daunted. When synagogues were destroyed, festival services were organized in underground shelters, and there was also a great deal of friendly interchange of accommodation among Jewish and Christian congregations. The Liberal Jewish Synagogue was accommodated in the premises of the famous Lord's Cricket Ground. Nevertheless, despite the courage with which this disaster was met, there can be no doubt that not only the material edifices but also the internal structure and cohesion of London Jewry were among the victims of the war.

See also ENGLAND. THEODOR H. GASTER.

Lit.: Jacobs, Joseph, *The Jews of Angevin England* (1893); idem, "London Jewry, 1290," *Publications of the Anglo-Jewish Historical Exhibition* (1888); Friedlaender, M., "Ibn Ezra in England," *The Jewish Historical Society of England, Transactions,* vol. 2 (1896) 47-60; Hyamson, A. M., "Jews in Tudor England," in *Essays in Jewish History,* Cecil Roth edit. (1934); Prynne, W., *A Short Demurrer* etc. (1855); Wolf, Lucien, "Resettlement of the Jews in England," *Jewish Chronicle,* 1888; idem, "Cromwell's Jewish Intelligencers," *ibid.,* 1891; idem, "The Jewry of the Restoration, 1660-1664," *ibid.,* 1902; Gaster, Moses, *History of the Ancient Synagogue of the Spanish and Portuguese Jews* (1901); Henriques, H. S. Q., *The Return of the Jews to England* (1905); Duschinsky, Charles, *The Rabbinate of the Great Synagogue, London, from 1756 to 1842* (1921); Adler, Elkan N., *London* (1930; Jewish Community Series); Hyamson, A. M., *A History of the Jews in England* (1907); Roth, Cecil, *History of the Jews in England* (1941); idem, edit., *Anglo-Jewish Letters* (1938); Adler, M., *Jews of Medieval England* (1939); *The Jewish Year Book* (London, 1940); *American Jewish Year Book,* vols. 42 and 43 (1940-41 and 1941-42), under "Review of the Year: Great Britain"; *Catalogue of the Anglo-Jewish Historical Exhibition* (1887). In addition, the *Transactions* and several separate volumes published by the Jewish Historical Society of England contain a rich store of indispensable material.

LONDON, MEYER, lawyer, labor leader, and Socialist member of the American Congress, b. province of Suvalki, Russia, 1871; d. New York city, 1926. He was the eldest son of Efraim London, a Talmudic scholar and small trader imbued with revolutionary ideas. His childhood and youth were passed in the province of Poltava, where he attended Hebrew school, afterward Russian school and Gymnasium. In 1888

A first-aid post in (Whitechapel) wartime London (1941). L. to r.: Dr. B. Cimbelman; Dr. J. Seidenberg, medical officer in charge; Dr. N. Pines. From an official photograph of the British Ministry of Information

Jewish participation in the defense of wartime London (1941). Photographs depict (top): City of London cadets, Bernhard Baron Company first Battalion Royal Fusiliers; (bottom) a first-aid post in Whitechapel; (right) a stirrup pump party in Whitechapel. From official photographs of the British Ministry of Information

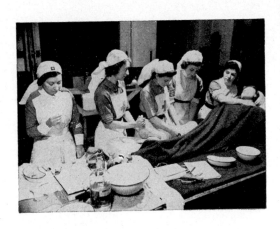

Meyer London

the father and his second son emigrated to New York, and the family followed in 1891. Here Meyer London maintained himself by tutoring and library work, studied law, and began practice in 1898.

As a lawyer London rendered invaluable service to trade unions, especially in the needle industry, and to related organizations, as well as to individual victims of injustice. He had few well-to-do clients and often served without fee; being also generous to a fault, with money as well as time, he died a poor man. For the unions he was not only legal adviser and advocate; he took a large part in shaping union policy, and his eloquence inspired their members in every strike or lockout. While still a law student London joined the Socialist Labor party; after the schism of 1899 he became a member of the new Socialist Party, to which he belonged as long as he lived. He was a charter member also of the Workmen's Circle (Arbeiter Ring), formed in 1906, and always prominent in its ranks. In 1896 he was nominated for the state legislature from a district in the Jewish East Side, and was a Socialist standard-bearer in almost every election year thereafter.

In 1914 London was elected to Congress—the first Socialist to sit in that body. Reelected in 1916, narrowly defeated (probably counted out) in 1918, he was returned once more in 1920; a brazen gerrymander of his district then made a Socialist victory impossible. Landmarks of his congressional career were his proposals for restoration of peace in Europe, in December, 1915 and December, 1917; his opposition to American entry into the war; his repeated proposals favoring unemployment insurance; his opposition to drastic anti-immigration laws, to the raising of tariff walls, and to reducing the income tax in the upper brackets; his fight for amnesty to political prisoners; his advocacy of a liberal maternity aid law; his support of the anti-lynching bill; his proposal of a law affecting coal mines which foreshadowed the much later Industrial Relations Act. London was proud of the achievements of the Jewish people and intensely

active in fighting every manifestation of anti-Semitism; yet although, properly speaking, he was not an assimilationist, he opposed the Jewish nationalist and Zionist movements. By yielding on this point he could undoubtedly have won the 1918 election, but he never compromised on what he regarded as questions of principle. In the long run the friends he lost came back to him.

Throughout his career, though London always had violent opponents, he had no enemies. Highly temperamental, untiring, audacious, in many aspects unpractical, he was a genuine idealist, a keen thinker, and a lovable and greatly loved man. Few even of his admirers realized the breadth of his cultural life. He read voraciously in six languages, not only in the fields of history, economics, and current affairs, but also in classic and contemporary literature. At the height of his powers London died by an automobile accident in June, 1926. Half a million people crowded the streets on his way to the grave.

ALGERNON LEE.

Lit.: Rogoff, Harry, *An East Side Epic; The Life and Work of Meyer London* (1930); works by Louis Lorwin, James Oneal and others on the history of unionism in the needle trades.

LONG BEACH, city in California, on the Pacific coast, south of Los Angeles. Its population, according to the 1940 census, was approximately 185,000, of whom some 2,500, or about 1.3 per cent, were Jews. The city developed, primarily as a beach resort, early in the 20th cent. Its Jewish community was not numerous enough for organization until 1921, when Temple Israel, a Reform congregation, was founded. Its rabbis have been: Julius Leibert (1924-28); Harvey B. Franklin (1928-38); L. Elliot Grafman (1938-). A new house of worship was dedicated in 1941.

Temple Sinai, Conservative, was organized in 1922. Its first rabbi was M. Friedlander (1922-28); among the other occupants of the pulpit have been Maurice Abramson (1935) and I. S. Ravetch (1936-).

The Jewish community of Long Beach had, in 1942, various local organizations, including a welfare fund, United Jewry, established in 1935. Its chairmen have been Nathan Nagel, I. E. Barker, Irving Schneider, I. S. Ravetch. There was also a B'nai B'rith lodge (founded 1920), which had several auxiliaries, and divisions of the Zionist Organization of America and of Hadassah. Because of its proximity to Los Angeles, Long Beach had no burial facilities of its own for the Jewish community.

With the onset of the war emergency in 1940, the town absorbed a large number of families brought there for defense industry work. Among the 40,000 to 50,000 families thus added to the population of Long Beach there were many Jews. The two rabbis of the community were both engaged in war work as chaplains. L. ELLIOT GRAFMAN.

LONG BRANCH, *see* NEW JERSEY.

LONG ISLAND, *see* NEW YORK (state).

LONGEVITY (in the Bible). In general, according to *Ps.* 90:10 (the so-called Psalm of Moses), seventy or eighty years is considered the period of a man's life. The word of God in *Gen.* 6:3 sets another

Henry Wadsworth Longfellow

standard: "Therefore shall his (man's) days be a hundred and twenty years." Finally we have the traditions of the extreme ages of the Biblical figures before the Flood (thus Methuselah 969, Adam 930, Enoch 365 years) and of the patriarchs (Abraham 175, Isaac 180, Jacob 147, Joseph 110 years). We find approximately the following system of ages for the various periods of the Biblical account:

From Adam to Noah	700—1,000 years
From Noah to Abraham	200— 600 years
At the time of the patriarchs	100— 200 years
At the time of the narrator	70— 80 years

Apparently the Biblical narrator wished to show that the God-fearing races of ancient times were long-lived, but that as man grew more wicked his life became shorter (cf. *Prov.* 10:27; *Isa.* 65:20). This corresponds fully with the idea frequently expressed in Biblical writings of the early post-Exilic period that the divine reward of righteousness is length of life on earth.

It is interesting to observe that the legendary kings of Babylonia, particularly those who reigned just after the flood, were said to have ruled for very long periods of years corresponding in general to the years of the long lives of the early Biblical generations. There appears also to be a distant relation between the names of those kings and the names of the ante-diluvian patriarchs in the Bible, so that possibly and in some indirect way the older Babylonian legends influenced the Biblical account (cf. Barton, G. A., *Archaeology and the Bible*, 1925, pp. 289-98).

See also LIFE.

LONGFELLOW, HENRY WADSWORTH, non-Jewish American poet, b. Portland, Me., 1807; d.

Cambridge, Mass., 1882. His paternal ancestor had emigrated to Massachusetts from Yorkshire, England, in 1676; on his mother's side he was a descendant of the Puritans John and Priscilla Alden. He spent many years as a professor of modern languages, first at Bowdoin (1829-35) and then at Harvard (1836-55). His verse was very popular, both in the United States and England: simplicity, hopeful sentimentality, and a romantic story well told were among the reasons. Of note, among his minor poems, are "The Skeleton in Armor," "The Wreck of the Hesperus," "The Village Blacksmith," and "Excelsior," all published in 1841, "My Lost Youth" (1855), and "The Children's Hour" (1863); among the longer poems, *Evangeline* (1847), *The Song of Hiawatha* (1855), and *The Courtship of Miles Standish* (1858).

While traveling in Europe, Longfellow called on Adah Isaacs Menken in Paris, during her last sickness, and wrote a poem in her album. He also met a Jew from Morocco, Israel Edrehi, "like an old Patriarch," who became The Spanish Jew, one of the guests in Longfellow's *Tales of a Wayside Inn* (1863). The description of The Spanish Jew is among the earliest friendly portraits of a Jew in American literature. He tells "The Legend of Rabbi Ben Levi" in which the rabbi gets the sword of the Angel of Death and returns it on the promise that, thereafter, angel and sword would be invisible. In the third part of the *Tales of a Wayside Inn* (1863), The Spanish Jew again tells a story of the Angel of Death ("Azrael"). In this tale, a Hindu guest of King Solomon, seeing the Angel of Death, begs the king to send him back to India; the king does so and is thanked by the Angel of Death who is bound for India to meet that very guest.

Earlier, Longfellow wrote "Sandalphon" (1858). This is based on a Talmudic legend of an angel (Sandalphon) who turns the prayers of mankind into flowers and weaves them into garlands. A friend found the legend in Corrodi's *Chiliasmus* and read it to Longfellow, who also examined J. P. Stehelin's *Traditions of the Jews*. Longfellow later wrote a tragedy in five acts on the struggle between Judaism and Hellenism, *Judas Maccabeus* (1872).

Best known, perhaps, of Longfellow's verse about Jews is his "The Jewish Cemetery at Newport," which he wrote in 1852 after visiting the place. Typical of an America that welcomed every refugee from political tyranny or religious persecution, he expresses his sympathy in the poem for those who fled from "Christian hate." Although the poet concludes that "the dead nations never rise again," yet he sees the Jews "trampled . . . as the sand" but "unshaken as the continent."

Lit.: *Publications of the American Jewish Historical Society*, No. 10 (1902) 170 (a reference to Longfellow's diary concerning his visit to the Jewish cemetery at Newport and an anecdote concerning Rabbi Isaac M. Wise and Longfellow's poem "Sandalphon"); *ibid.*, No. 12 (1904) 170 (a poem contributed to *The American Israelite* by Longfellow).

LONZANO, MENAHEM DA, Masoretic scholar, grammarian and poet, d. Jerusalem, after 1608. It has been conjectured that he was born in Italy, and he is known to have led a life of wandering about which there are only meagre and indefinite reports. It is plain that he was highly respected for his knowledge of the Masorah and Midrashic literature. He made collections of old texts, carefully studied the grammatical questions involved in their interpretation, and published the results of his labors in one large work, *Shete Yadoth* (Two Hands, Venice, 1618). This consists of two volumes, each divided into five parts, or "fingers." Some of these were published individually, such as: *Or Torah* (Light of the Law), Masoretic studies and emendations to the smaller Bible edition of Bomberg; *Maarich,* explanations of foreign words in the Talmud, Midrash and *Zohar;* expositions of difficult passages and the stories that he found in his manuscripts. The obscure Midrashim gathered by him, such as *Agadath Bereshith* and *Aboth de Rabbi Nathan,* were little regarded by his immediate successors and received proper attention only in the 19th cent.

Lonzano wrote liturgical poetry of a didactic and ethical character. He was considerably interested in instrumental music and religious songs, and was well acquainted with the folk songs of Spain, Turkey and Arabia. His other writings include: *Adi Zahab,* glosses to the *Lebush* of Mordecai Jaffe; *Imre Emeth,* glosses on the Cabalistic works of Ḥayim Vital; *Omer Man,* a commentary on the section "Idra Zuta" in the *Zohar;* glosses to the Palestinian Talmud (published in the edition of Warsaw, 1836).

Lit.: Jellinek, introduction to the *Maarich* (1853); Kaufmann, D., in *Jewish Quarterly Review,* vol. 8, p. 525; Luncz, *Jerusalem,* vol. 1, p. 115.

LOOKSTEIN, JOSEPH HYMAN, rabbi, b. Simyatich, Mohilev, Russia, 1902. He came to the United States at the age of eight. He was educated at Yeshiva College (Rabbi, 1926), the College of the City of New York (A.B., 1928), and Columbia University (M.A., 1929). He served as rabbi for the Kings Highway Jewish Center of Brooklyn, N. Y., in 1922 and 1923. In 1923 he was called to Congregation Kehilath Jeshurun of New York city as associate rabbi, and in 1926 he succeeded his wife's grandfather, Rabbi M. S. Margolies, as rabbi there; he still occupied that position in 1942.

During the term of his rabbinate Lookstein rose to national prominence as one of the outstanding younger leaders of the Orthodox Jewish religion in the United States. He became a director of Yeshiva College in 1930 and assistant professor in homiletics in 1932. In 1932 he also became principal of the Hebrew Teachers' Training School. In 1934 he was elected secretary of the Rabbinical Council of America, and in 1936 he was a delegate to the World Jewish Congress at Geneva, Switzerland. He also served as a member of the executive board of the Union of Orthodox Jewish Congregations, president of the United Aged Home of Palestine, vice-president of the Mizrahi Organization of America, and editor of the Orthodox monthly magazine, *Jewish Outlook.*

LOPÉS-DUBEC, a Sephardic Jewish family active in 18th and 19th cent. French Jewish affairs, particularly in Bordeaux. The first member of the family to gain prominence was Solomon Lopès-Dubec (d. 1837). In 1779 he is known to have been one of a delegation of Jews who were called on to determine the proper procedure in Jewish divorce proceedings. In 1788 he was a member of the committee chosen

by the Portuguese Jews of Bordeaux to present their claims for emancipation to Lamoignon-Malesherbes, the French prime minister. The demands were characterized by the insistence on the part of the Portuguese Jews that only they were entitled to emancipation, but that Jews from other parts of Europe were not. Although the Lopès-Dubec family was not as wealthy as the Gradis family, also of Bordeaux, to judge by records of contributions to communal funds, they were nevertheless active and helpful in communal problems. Lopès-Dubec was a member of the tribunal of commerce. He was also a deputy of the Bordeaux Jews to the Sanhedrin established by Napoleon.

BENJAMIN LOPÈS-DUBEC (date of death unknown) was the son of Solomon Lopès-Dubec. He was active politically and a member of the Bordeaux municipal government. In 1841 he was made a chevalier of the Legion of Honor.

CAMILLE LOPÈS-DUBEC (d. 1860) was the son of Benjamin Lopès-Dubec. He was first a member of the municipal council, and in 1848 was elected to the National Assembly for Bordeaux.

Lit.: Malvezin, Théophile, *Histoire des Juifs à Bordeaux* (1875); Detcheverry, Arnaud, *Histoire des Israélites de Bordeaux* (1850).

LOPEZ, AARON, one of the leading merchants in New England prior to the American Revolution and probably the most successful Jewish businessman of his time in the United States. Born in 1731 in Portugal, he emigrated with his wife and child to America and settled in Newport, R. I., in October, 1752. He was one of the first to recognize the commercial possibilities of Newport, with its fine harbor, and to utilize these advantages to the fullest extent. His business ventures extended to Africa and the Falkland Islands, besides embracing Europe and the West Indies.

In partnership with Jacob Rodriguez Rivera, his father-in-law, Lopez promoted the whaling and sperm oil industry and was largely instrumental in developing Newport's commercial prestige. He induced more than forty Jewish families to settle in Newport, thereby enlarging the Jewish community, which included men of intelligence, wealth and business enterprise. Lopez laid the cornerstone of the old Newport Synagogue in 1763.

At the outbreak of the American Revolution, Lopez himself owned thirty ships employed in foreign and domestic trade. His estate inventoried at about $100,000 and his mode of life reflected a man of considerable wealth. But his espousal of the American cause threatened the complete ruin of his immense fortune. For Lopez, while he was attempting to bring his possessions from the British-held island of Jamaica, lost nearly all his ships through capture by private armed vessels owned by inhabitants of the United States (American privateers). In 1777, when the British took possession of Newport, Lopez removed with his family to Leicester, Mass., accompanied by many of his Jewish townsmen. Although his losses were heavy, he still retained enough to enable him to erect a large mansion at Leicester, where he is said to have lived in state and given lavish entertainments. This mansion

A contemporary representation of Rodrigo Lopez, accused of conspiring to poison Queen Elizabeth

became later the Leicester Academy which Lopez founded.

After the British had evacuated Newport, Lopez set out for his former home; but, unfortunately, he met with an accident on the way, when he drove to the side of a treacherous pond to water his horses. His death occurred on May 28, 1782. His body, on being recovered, was interred in the old cemetery at Newport. According to a Newport historian, his untimely death was the greatest misfortune that had ever befallen their city. For many years thereafter the memory of Aaron Lopez was revered by his fellow townsmen of every denomination. In the annals of New England, as well as in American Jewish history, Aaron Lopez is distinguished as one of the pioneers who largely influenced America's commercial prosperity in respect to foreign trade. Various members of his family were more or less prominent during the Colonial period, but his figure overshadowed them all.

Lit.: Daly, Charles P., *The Settlement of the Jews in North America* (1893) 76-79, 82-83, 85-86; Gutstein, Morris A., *Aaron Lopez and Judah Touro* (1939); Wiernik, Peter, *History of the Jews in America* (1931) 73, 98-99; Wolf, Simon, *The American Jew as Patriot, Soldier and Citizen* (1895) 33; Mason, G. C., *Reminiscences of Newport;* Kohut, George A., *Ezra Stiles and the Jews* (1902); Washburn, *Historical Sketches of the Town of Leicester,* pp. 120-21, 124; *Publications of the American Jewish Historical Society,* No. 2 (1894) 101-12; No. 6 (1897) 72-74; No. 27 (1920), portrait on frontispiece; *Jewish Comment,* Nos. 23 and 25 (1905); a paper, still unpublished, read before the American Jewish Historical Society by J. Mark Jacobson in Dec., 1927, on Jewish merchants in Newport in pre-Revolutionary days, based in part on unpublished letters belonging to the American Jewish Historical Society and others in Rhode Island.

LOPEZ, RODRIGO (RUY), Queen Elizabeth's physician, b. probably in Portugal, about 1525; executed at Tyburn, London, 1594. He came to England, most likely from Antwerp, about 1559, and settled in London "to get his living by physike." Discarding the Catholicism that had been forced upon his family about sixty years before (1496), he joined the Church of England; but he was only nominally a member. Privately he was a Jew and was generally known as such.

Lopez soon gained a reputation as a careful and skillful physician. He was appointed house physician at St. Bartholomew's Hospital, the first physician to hold that post; elected a member of the College of Physicians, he was chosen (1571) to read the anatomy lecture, but declined the honor. In 1574, his name was high on Stowe's list of the leading physicians of London.

By 1584 Lopez had become the household physician of Robert Dudley, Earl of Leicester, a favorite of Queen Elizabeth. It was prudent for him, a Jew and an alien—and indeed for any physician those days—to enter the service of one of the great nobles in order to be able to claim, if need be, his protection. Unfortunately for Lopez, afterwards, it was said of Leicester by his many enemies that he removed those who stood in his way by poison, and some of that slander stuck to the physician.

Lopez became the chief physician of Queen Elizabeth in 1586. He belonged to—rather was patronized by—the Puritan party at court. Eager for war with Catholic Spain, at its head were Leicester (d. 1588), his stepson, the Earl of Essex, who succeeded his stepfather as the queen's favorite, and Sir Francis Walsingham, the queen's secretary of state.

The chief physician had a house in Holborn, London, near Gray's Inn Gate, which a thankful patient had given him; he had, by grant of the Queen, a monopoly for a time of the importation of aniseed and sumac; he was given the revenues of a parsonage to support his son at Winchester College; and, it is recorded, he was also presented by the queen with almost a shipload of papal indulgences that were being carried to the New World for sale at two reals apiece when captured by the English. But he was not well off. His position at court cost him in clothes and gratuities, no doubt, more than it earned; the great who were his patients probably did not pay small men gladly; and the queen herself was close-fisted. The monopoly of aniseed and sumac terminated in 1589 and he could not get it renewed; the gift of the papal indulgences, if not merely an instance of the English sense of humor, proved to be unprofitable when Lopez, with the help of an Italian banker resident in London, tried to market them in Spanish America.

Soon after his appointment as the queen's physician, if not before, Lopez was caught up by the plans and plots of the queen's ministers. It has been suggested that through his Marrano relatives in Antwerp, Leghorn, and Constantinople, he had a share in furnishing the information that led to the defeat of the Spanish Armada in 1588. His brother-in-law, Alvaro Mendez, Duke of Metilli, had succeeded to the influence of João Miquez (Mendez's relation, too) at the court of the Sultan and was the chief friend in Turkey of English policy. When Don Antonio (natural son of the Infante Luis and a Jewess, Violante Gomez), the claimant to the throne of Portugal after its conquest by Philip II of Spain, came to England, Lopez was the Portuguese Pretender's interpreter; and it was Lopez who urged Elizabeth to permit Don Antonio's attempted invasion of Portugal in 1589—which ended in a fiasco.

In Don Antonio's suite were, of course, spies for Spain. The Portuguese Pretender soon lost most of his wealth and much of his standing. Trying to leave England secretly, since Queen Elizabeth would no longer further his plans, he arranged through Manuel de Andrada, one of the ablest of his followers, for a ship to take him to Dieppe, from which he could continue his warfare against Philip of Spain. Andrada hired a Flemish skipper who was to go to Dunkirk instead and deliver Don Antonio to the Spaniards; but Andrada's letter to the Spanish ambassador in Paris, outlining the plot in cypher and invisible ink, was seized by Walsingham's spies at Dover. Andrada was arrested and turned over to his liege lord, Don Antonio, who sentenced him to be hanged.

While Andrada was waiting for death, Lopez began pleading with Elizabeth that the sentence be changed to banishment, and Andrada was set free. Before he left England, Lopez sent for him and, after reminding him how he (Lopez) had saved also 300 Spaniards from the gallows when they were captured on one of the galleons of the Armada—which Lopez had really done—he authorized Andrada to tell the Spanish ambassador in Paris that now, if ever, was the time to negotiate a peace with England, that Lopez was ready to act for Spain in beginning the negotiations, and that he would see to it that Andrada had a passport to return. In all this, no doubt, Lopez was acting for Walsingham, the secretary of state, in ferreting out the plans of the Spaniards—or, perhaps, in persuading them to relax their guard.

The Spaniards were willing to have another agent in England, for so they regarded Andrada, and they supplied him with a little money and a ring, in which were set a diamond and a ruby, for Lopez's daughter. In 1591 Andrada reached Havre and wrote to Lopez for the passport. But Walsingham was dead (d. 1590). It was Burghley who sent the passport and, since his spies on the continent had been watching Andrada, he was promptly arrested when he landed at Rye. He was turned over to the custody of Dr. Lopez, for, no doubt, Burghley knew, or was soon told, that the doctor had been acting for Walsingham. Lopez offered the ring, which Andrada brought, to the queen, but, quite unlike herself, she refused it.

Nothing came of the Andrada affair except that, when Lopez was charged with plotting for Spain, the story was added to the evidence against him. And Don Antonio and Lopez were no longer friendly, perhaps because Lopez had pleaded for Andrada, but more likely because Don Antonio, in return for the help of Lopez's powerful brother-in-law, Alvaro Mendez, was spreading a tale about him, malicious and untrue, saying that Mendez had become rich by cheating the government of Portugal. Lopez was now also hated by Essex, the favorite of Elizabeth. Once, when Lopez had been drinking with Don Antonio and another, the doctor told of a sickness that Essex had, for which Lopez had treated him—a sickness "which did disparage to the Earl's honour." Don Antonio had been quick to tell Essex of the physician's breach of confidence.

In 1593 the spies of Essex found out that Ferreira da Gama, a Portuguese living in Dr. Lopez's house in Holborn, had offered, or was ready to offer, to kill Don Antonio for the king of Spain. Ferreira da Gama was arrested and a watch set for all letters addressed to any Portuguese. Soon afterwards, Gomez d'Avila, a Portuguese who lived near Lopez in London, landed at Rye on the way back from Flanders. He had with him a letter addressed to an unknown Portuguese; the letter itself was not at all clear and

mentioned mysteriously "your Pearles" and "a little Muske and Amber, the which I am determined to buy." Gomez d'Avila also was imprisoned. At this time, a packet addressed to someone in Brussels was opened at Dover and in it were found two letters: one from Lopez to Ferreira da Gama with news of what was going on at court, and another letter from Ferreira da Gama to the Spanish secretary of state in Flanders.

Lopez, meanwhile, who knew nothing of the letters that had been seized or of the arrest of Gomez d'Avila, was trying to persuade the queen to set Ferreira da Gama free, suggesting that he would be just the substitute for Andrada in negotiating with Spain. As Gomez d'Avila was waiting in an antechamber of Essex House to be questioned by the Earl, the prisoner saw an acquaintance and begged him to tell Dr. Lopez that he had been arrested. The message was delivered—after it had been told to Essex. Gomez d'Avila, in fear of the rack, now confessed that he was a messenger between Ferreira da Gama, to whom the mysterious letter he had carried was really addressed, and someone called Tinoco, a Portuguese living in Brussels who was an agent of the Spanish secretary of state in Flanders. On his part, Ferreira da Gama, still in prison and ignorant of the arrest of the messenger, sent to a fellow Portuguese a letter begging him to warn Dr. Lopez not to let Gomez d'Avila come from Flanders; and, in answer, by means of a note hidden in a handkerchief, Dr. Lopez wrote—perhaps to set da Gama's mind at ease—that he had sent to Flanders several times to stop d'Avila and would spare no expense to do so. The note was intercepted; by his own writing, Lopez was in the plot.

Persuaded that he had been betrayed by Lopez, Ferreira da Gama was eager to save himself. Lopez, he said, had been an agent of Spain for a long time, and now he was plotting to have Don Antonio poisoned and his heir, Don Manuel, make his submission to Philip. Gomez d'Avila added to the story: a large sum was to be sent to Ferreira da Gama from Flanders with which to buy the allegiance of Don Manuel. In January (1594), a Portuguese appeared before the English consul at Calais and asked for a passport, claiming that he had discovered a plot against England and wished to disclose it to the queen herself. As soon as he had crossed the Channel, he was arrested; according to the letters from Spanish officials which he carried, he proved to be the Tinoco who had sent the mysterious letter about pearls, musk, and amber that Gomez d'Avila was carrying to Ferreira da Gama. The letters which Tinoco carried spoke, too, of Don Manuel's submission and of some other service for Spain, and Tinoco had, besides, bills of exchange for a large sum.

Essex believed that he now had enough evidence to arrest Lopez on the charge of conspiring with Spain: to murder Don Antonio, to secure the submission of Don Antonio's heir to Spain, and to cajole England into making peace. The frightened doctor was brought before Lord Burghley, Burghley's son, Robert Cecil, and Essex. The Cecils saw nothing whatever against Lopez; they knew of the Andrada affair and that Lopez had been dealing with the

Spaniards—but only "to cozen the King of Spain"; and the younger Cecil hurried to the queen to tell her that Essex had arrested her physician on the flimsiest evidence. When the favorite, his influence already dwindling, appeared next day, the queen scolded him, calling him, before Robert Cecil and another gentleman of the court, "a rash temperarious youth" for what he had done. Essex left the royal presence, flushed and furious, determined to prove Lopez guilty of "a most dangerous and desperate treason."

The earl had many agents and followers in London, many friends among the wits and writers. He himself was somewhat of a poet. Soon the inns of London, as well as Essex House, were loud with talk of how her Jewish physician had plotted to poison the Queen. Essex himself was to write to Anthony Bacon, brother of Francis, "The point of conspiracy was her majesty's death. The executioner should have been Doctor Lopez; the manner poison."

That there was no evidence—as yet—to involve Lopez, or anyone, in a plot against the queen herself did not matter; nor that it would be unlikely for any Jew to serve a country which all Jews, not without reason, hated and feared; and particularly unlikely for anyone who had been befriended and honored in England as Lopez had been for forty years to act so for any reward and at best an uncertain one. What mattered was that Lopez was a foreigner and a Jew, and that the English, intensely anti-Spanish, were ready to believe any tale of a Spanish plot. Indeed, their great ally, William the Silent, of Orange, had been assassinated by a poisoned bullet ten years before, and the Spanish government was still paying a pension to the family of the assassin. The clamor which arose among the people for Lopez's death was such that no one dared befriend him, certainly not the Cecils, whose policy, in their own affairs and in those of the nation, was always to be cautious.

Evidence to convict Lopez of plotting to poison the queen was easily supplied. Tinoco was ready to swear to anything Essex wanted if it would save his life. Ferreira da Gama was no better. At first Lopez insisted that all his dealings with Spain had been to gain information for England. Then, broken by his solitary confinement and fear of the rack, he stated that he had promised to poison the queen but had never intended to do so: he wished merely "to gull the King of Spain." He withdrew the statement, afterwards, but it was enough to hang him.

At the trial at Guildhall on February 28, 1594, the mysterious phrases in the letter Gomez d'Avila had carried were given a fantastic construction and held to show a plot to poison the queen. Lopez was called "vile Jew" throughout the trial. His enemy Essex sat on the commission that tried and condemned him. Lopez wrote again and again to the queen begging for his life, and she waited three months before signing the death warrant. Lopez's brother-in-law, the great Alvaro Mendez, interceded for him, pleading only for a reprieve until he could prove him innocent. Mendez's envoy, Judah Serfatim, was then in London, but he was answered by Waad, clerk of the Council, that "the discontent of the people was so great" that the request made could not be granted.

Sabatino Lopez

On the 7th of June, 1594, Lopez, Ferreira, and Tinoco were dragged upon hurdles to Tyburn and there hanged, disemboweled, and quartered. The great crowd that had come to see them die shrieked and howled at them. In a moment of quiet, Lopez tried to defend himself. "I love the queen," he cried out, "as I love Jesus Christ." Hearing a Jew speak so, the crowd roared with laughter.

In spite of the queen's reputation for parsimony, although by law she had the right to Lopez's property, she let his widow have it all, except the ring Philip had sent by Andrada. That she took and wore, it is said, until her death.

Francis Bacon (one of the commissioners) wrote an account of the trial, and it was circulated by the government throughout the land. As for the other writers of London, the anger of the people against the Jewish physician was something to be turned to profit. Marlowe's *Jew of Malta* (first acted in 1592) had a revival and was played twenty times that year. There are references to Lopez in other plays by Marlowe, Middleton, and Dekker, and Shakespeare's *Merchant of Venice* was said to have been written because of the trial. Richard Burbage, who first acted Shylock, wore a beard like that of Lopez.

More than 300 years after the execution of Lopez, the state papers of Philip's reign were made public. They show that Andrada's story, incredible as it was, was true, but that, although there was a pretence by Lopez at negotiating a peace, afterwards, and an offer to win over Don Antonio's heir, and, perhaps, even to have Don Antonio poisoned, there never had been a plot or offer to harm the queen by Lopez or the others who died with him.

CHARLES REZNIKOFF.

Lit.: Hume, Martin, "The So-Called Conspiracy of Dr. Ruy Lopez," *The Jewish Historical Society of England, Transactions*, vol. 6 (1912) 32-55; Kohler, Max J., "Dr. Rodrigo Lopez, Queen Elizabeth's Jewish Physician, and His Relations to America," *Publications of the American Jewish Historical Society*, No. 17 (1909) 9-25; Lee, Sidney, "The Original of Shylock," *Gentleman's Magazine*, Feb., 1880; idem, "Elizabethan England and the Jews," *Transactions of the New Shakespere Society* (1887-92); Wolf, Lucien, "Jews in Elizabethan England," *The Jewish Historical Society of England, Transactions*, vol. 11, pp. 1-91.

LOPEZ, SABATINO, playwright and theatrical critic, b. Livorno, Italy, 1867. He taught Italian literature in Genoa, and later at the Accademia di Brera in Milan. His first comedies at once revealed a talented playwright and won him the unanimous recognition of Italian critics. Among his theatrical plays, which depicted the life, problems and social surroundings of the Italian bourgeoisie, the best known are *La buona figliuola, Ninetta, Il Principe Azzurro* and *La Signora Rosa.* They were translated into foreign languages and acclaimed in France, Poland, Austria and South America. From 1911 to 1919 Lopez was president of the Italian Society of Authors. He wrote numerous articles and essays on the Italian theatre, mostly in the *Illustrazione Italiana,* and published his recollections about famous Italian actors in a book entitled *Gli ultimi zingari.* He took an active part in Jewish cultural and social life in Milan, and was president of the Zionist group.

LOPEZ-ROSA, MOSES DUARTE, physician and poet who lived in the 17th cent., b. Beja, Portugal. He lived for a time in Rome, then went to Amsterdam, where he reembraced Judaism publicly. He became a member and referee of the literary society Academia de los Floridos, founded in 1685 by Baron de Belmonte. Lopez-Rosa, an admirer of King Pedro II of Portugal and of his wife Maria Sophia, dedicated to them several sonnets and one longer poem, "Alientos de la verdad en los clarines de la fame" (Amsterdam, 1688). Several years later, when a son was born to the king, he composed another poem, "Elogios ao felice nacimiento de ser Infante de Portugal" (Amsterdam, 1691). He wrote several philosophical books and a volume of Spanish stories.

LOPEZ-ROSA, SIMON (called also Abraham Farrar el Viejo), physician and president of Beth Jacob, the oldest Sephardic congregation in Amsterdam, Holland, d. Amsterdam, 1618. He was not an Orthodox Jew, and many members of the community shared his liberal viewpoint. His criticism of the authority of the rabbis led to Rabbi Joel Serkes' recommendation that the congregation excommunicate him; although this step was not taken, his liberal sentiments led to the secession of part of the congregational members and the founding of a more pious congregation, Beth Israel. Lopez-Rosa headed the list of Marranos in Amsterdam who were denounced to the Lisbon Inquisition in 1617.

Lit.: Kayserling, M., in *Revue des études juives,* vol. 43, p. 275; idem, *Geschichte der Juden in Portugal* (1867) 319; *Jewish Encyclopedia,* vol. 8, p. 182.

LORANT, STEFAN, author and editor, b. Budapest, 1901. He was living in the United States in 1942. He studied at the Evangelical Gymnasium and the Commercial Academy of Budapest. He was editor, in turn, of *Das Magazin,* Leipzig (1925), *Bilder Courier,* Berlin (1926) and *Münchner Illustrierte Presse,* Munich (1927-33). In the latter capacity he was arrested in 1933 by Hitler's police. After being set free, he went to London and there published *I Was Hitler's Prisoner* (1935), a book describing early Nazi methods in getting rid of political opponents, which sold 400,000 copies. In London, Lorant founded and edited *Lilliput,* a pocket magazine (from 1937 on); he also edited *Picture Post* (from 1938 on). He visited the United States in 1940 to obtain material for a special United States issue of *Picture Post,* and in 1942 published in New York city *Lincoln, his Life in Photographs.*

LORD'S PRAYER, a series of petitions which is given this name because it was taught by Jesus as an example of the proper kind of prayer to be addressed to God. It is perhaps the most important prayer in the whole liturgy of the Christian faith. The composition of such a prayer by Jesus was not in itself a novelty, as private prayers of this type were not uncommon additions to the formal service in Judaism and a number have been recorded (*Tos. Ber.* 3:7; *Ber.* 16b et seq.; *Yer. Ber.* iv, 7d). The New Testament has two versions of the Lord's Prayer and two slightly varying accounts of its origin (*Matt.* 6; *Luke* 11). The version in *Luke,* on account of its brevity and inner construction, is thought to be the earlier, though that in *Matthew* in some places seems more faithful to an Aramaic original. The two versions given below are in the rendering of *The New Testament, An American Translation:*

Matt. 6:9-13

Our father in heaven
Your name be revered!
Your kingdom come!
Your will be done on earth as it is done in heaven.
Give us today bread for the day,
And forgive us our debts, as we have forgiven our debtors,
And do not subject us to temptations,
But save us from the evil one.
(In some manuscripts the doxology is added: For yours is the kingdom and the power and the glory, forever.)
Amen.

Luke 11:1-4

Father
Your name be revered!
Your kingdom come!
Give us each day our bread for the day,
and forgive us our sins, for we ourselves forgive anyone who wrongs us;
and do not subject us to temptation.

On the whole, with one or two possible exceptions, the Lord's Prayer may be said to have a Jewish tone. The first few verses resemble the opening phrases of the Kaddish prayer: "Magnified and sanctified be His great name in the world which He hath created according to His will. May He establish His kingdom during your life . . . even speedily and at a near time. . . ."

The opening words, "Our Father," are frequently found in the Jewish liturgy with or without the addition of the words "in heaven" (*I Chron.* 29:10; the fourth, fifth and sixth of the Eighteen Benedictions; the Abinu Malkenu prayer of the Penitential Days; *Ber.* 5:1; *Yoma* 8:9; *Sotah* 9:15; *Aboth* 5:20 and elsewhere). "Your name be revered" and the following verse are paralleled in the Kaddish and in the Kedushah. The two ideas of the hallowing of God's name and the coming of His kingdom are closely connected, as it was felt that the Messiah would come only when men would acknowledge the holiness of God. Jewish literature is full of expressions of hope for the speedy coming of this Messianic redemption, and the words proposed by Jesus were based on the lively expectation of the promised kingdom in that very age.

The next words, "Your will be done," are best understood in reference to this same Messianic hope; they are the expression of the trust that God will bring about His kingdom in His own time. In a later period, when the expected Messianic era did not arrive either in the lifetime of Jesus or in the first generations of the Christian church, the statement was first interpreted to refer to the second coming of Jesus (*Luke* 22:18) and then enlarged to include complete submission on the part of man to the will of God. This idea of submission is expressed frequently in Jewish literature, for instance in the prayer of Eliezer ben Hyrcanus recorded in the *Tosefta:* "Do Thy will in heaven above; grant tranquillity of spirit to those who fear Thee on earth (below) and do that which is good in Thy sight." Both Jewish and Christian statements echo *Ps.* 135:6.

The petition for daily bread which follows continues the Messianic thought. He who has faith and seeks the kingdom of God need have no fear for the day's sustenance or the morrow's. *Mechilta Vayassa* 3 (edit. Lauterbach, vol. 2, p. 103) reads: "Rabbi Eleazar (of Modin) used to say: He who has enough to eat for today and says, What shall I eat tomorrow? behold, he is of little faith." *Sotah* 48b records a similar dictum: "Rabbi Eliezer the Great declares: Whoever has a piece of bread in his basket and says, What shall I eat tomorrow? belongs only to those of little faith." The words "daily bread" are the *lehem hukki* ("mine allotted bread") of *Prov.* 30:8.

The next sentence offers some difficulties, since the versions differ as to whether it is "sins" or "debts" that are to be forgiven. The relation between the two clauses in each of the statements is open to various interpretations. They may mean either that men can not expect the pardon of God unless they extend the same pardon to man, or that the grace and mercy of God as expressed in forgiveness can certainly not be less than ordinary human mercy and forgiveness of fellow-humans.

The closest parallel to this idea is in *Sirach* 28:2: "Forgive thy neighbor the wrong he has done thee, and then thy sins will be pardoned when thou prayest." Another passage reads: "To whom is sin pardoned? To him who forgives iniquity" (*Derech Eretz Zuta* 8:3; *R.H.* 17a; cf. also *Mark* 11:25). On the whole, however, this idea of asking for forgiveness of God in return for forgiveness of man is foreign to Jewish liturgy. Thus the sixth of the Eighteen Benedictions and the service of the High Holy Days merely ask for forgiveness outright. The Lord's Prayer thus adds a new thought, possibly under the influence of the Christian doctrines of atonement and mediation.

The next phrase, "Do not subject us to" (more generally rendered, "Lead us not into") "temptation," is found in the Orthodox daily prayer-book as part of the morning prayers recited at the beginning of the daily service. The passage is taken from *Ber.* 60b and reads: "O lead us not into the power of sin or of transgression or iniquity or of temptation. . . ." This paragraph of supplication enumerates all possible sources of temptation, such as the evil inclination, bad companions, scorn and the like. In a similar prayer, recited in the evening, there is mentioned "Satan" or the "adversary," the "evil one" (or "evil," as more commonly rendered) from which the Lord's Prayer asks to be delivered. There is a similar statement in *Ber.* 16b, and the idea is frequent in Jewish prayers.

The closing doxology in *Matthew* ("Yours is the kingdom") is taken directly from *I Chron.* 29:11, which is used in the Orthodox Jewish liturgy at the time when the Scroll of the Torah is taken from the Ark. This doxology is not a general conclusion, but is connected with the prayer for forgiveness. Kohler believes that the Lord's Prayer as it now stands is an insertion in *Matthew,* and derived from *Didache* 8:2, and that the passage originally contained a saying identical with *Mark* 11:25, since the sequel in *Matt.* 6:14-15 is the same as *Mark* 11:26.

From the discussion above it can be seen that the Lord's Prayer owes much to Jewish thought. Many of its ideas are Jewish, and its phraseology closely resembles that uttered by Jewish teachers. But the choice and grouping of the phrases is original and the whole bears the mark of the special Christian theology. It therefore is a Christian rather than a Jewish prayer.   FELIX A. LEVY.

Lit.: Kohler, K., in *Jewish Encyclopedia,* vol. 8, pp. 183-84; Abrahams, I., *Studies in Pharisaism and the Gospels,* Second Series, p. 94 et seq.; Taylor, C., *Sayings of the Jewish Fathers;* Chase, F. H., "The Lord's Prayer in the Early Church," *Texts and Studies;* Montefiore, C. G., *Rabbinic Literature and Gospel Teachings;* idem, *The Synoptic Gospels;* Dalman, G., *The Words of Jesus.* For a somewhat different point of view, see Friedlander, Gerald, *The Jewish Sources of the Sermon on the Mount.*

LORIA, name of a prominent Jewish family whose origin goes back to the 14th cent. and which may perhaps be traced back to the town of Loria, near Bassano, in the Italian province of Vicenza. In Hebrew literature the name Loria has almost exclusively been changed into Luria, Lurje, Lurie, Lurja, and Lourié, and appears very seldom in its original form. A few well-known representatives of this name exist in Italy.

See also LURIA.

Lit.: Lourié, Anton, *Die Familie Lourié* (Luria) (1923); *Encyclopaedia Judaica,* vol. 10 (1934), cols. 1194-95.

LORIA, ACHILLE, economist and Italian senator, b. Mantua, Italy, 1857; d. Rome, 1936. He began his teaching and scholarly career at an early age, assuming the chair of political economy at the University of Siena when he was twenty-three. Ten years later, in 1891, Loria was transferred to the old University of Padua, where he taught until 1903. Thereafter, for nearly thirty years, he was professor of political economy at the University of Turin. In 1919 he was nominated a member of the Italian senate. From 1922 to 1928 he was managing editor of the economic and political publication *Echi e Commenti.* Loria was possessed of an acute and brilliant mind, and his studies on Marxism, capitalist society and the social and economic consequences of the first World War were recognized as of fundamental value and were translated into other languages. Among his best-known works are: *Analisi della proprietà capitalista* (vol. 22, 1889); *Verso la giustizia sociale* (vol. 2, 1920); *Karl Marx* (1924). At the age of seventy Loria published his memoirs under the title of *Ricordi di uno studente settuagenario* (1927).

LORIA, GINO, mathematician, b. Mantua, Italy, 1862. He taught advanced geometry at the University of Genoa, and published valuable works in the field of mathematics, the most noteworthy being: *Il passato e il presente delle principali teorie geometriche* (Turin, 1887); *Le scienze esatte nell'antica Grecia* (Modena, 1895); *Vorlesungen über darstellende Geometrie* (lectures given at the University of Leipzig, 1913); *Storia della geometria descrittiva* (Milan, 1921); *Storia delle matematiche* (Turin, 1928). Loria was a member of the Italian Accademia dei Lincei and of the Academy of Turin. He was awarded gold medals by the Academy of Madrid and the Institut de France.

LORIA, LAMBERTO, explorer, b. Alexandria, Egypt, 1855; d. Rome, 1913. He traveled through Australia and New Guinea, and described the results of his geographical and ethnographical researches in several works. He founded the ethnographical museum in Florence, and in 1911 equipped the department of Italian folk-customs in Rome.

LORIA, PROSPERO MOSÉ, philanthropist, b. Mantua, Italy, 1814; d. Milan, Italy, 1892. A successful merchant at Alexandria, Egypt, for many years, he returned in 1866 to his native land, where he devoted himself to social questions, especially the founding of colonies for workers. In 1884 he published a book advocating the organization of such colonies, but the public failed to support his proposal. He founded the Società Umanitaria in Milan, in which Count Dolfin Guerra was his co-worker, endowed several schools, and supported the association movement in Italy. Loria, who died before his work was finished, left his fortune of twenty million lire for the founding of an association for the aid of the needy.

Lit.: Boccardo, in *Nuova Enciclopedia Italiana;* Wininger, S., *Grosse Jüdische National-Biographie,* vol. 4, p. 188.

LORKI, JOSHUA (Geronimo de Santa Fé), *see* ARAGON; DISPUTATIONS.

LORM, HIERONYMUS (pseudonym), *see* LANDESMANN, HEINRICH.

LORRAINE. Table of Contents:

1. Expansion. The name Lorraine was applied to different territories at different periods. Originally it was the territory situated between the Scheldt, Rhine, Meuse and Saone rivers, allotted to Lothair III as his kingdom in a division of King Lothair I's Carolingian empire among his sons (855). In the treaty of Meersen (870) the larger, German-speaking section of the country, including the cities of Trèves, Metz, Aix-la-Chapelle and others, was annexed to the Eastern Frankish lands (Germany). Emperor Otto I gave Lorraine to his brother, Bruno, Archbishop of Cologne, and in 959 the territory was divided into Lower Lorraine, consisting of approximately what was known up to 1940 as The Netherlands, Belgium (not including Flanders), Luxembourg and the major part of Rhenish Prussia, and Upper Lorraine, corresponding to what was known in 1940 as Lorraine,

with the cities of Metz and Nancy and the bishoprics of Toul and Verdun. Any references in Hebrew literature to the persecution of Lorraine Jews by the Crusaders of 1096 and to the scholars and religious practices of Lorraine appear to pertain to the undivided duchy of Lorraine, especially the districts of Speyer, Worms and Mayence. This article will deal only with the history of the Jews in Upper Lorraine, including Metz, Nancy and the bishoprics of Toul and Verdun, a territory approximately covered by the departments of Meuse, Meurthe-et-Moselle and Moselle in 1940.

2. The Jews in the Middle Ages. There is definite evidence of the presence of Jews in the ancient episcopal city of Metz as early as the 9th cent. The persecution of Jews in 1096 originated in Lorraine, and twenty-two Jews were killed at Metz. There are references to the Jewish street, synagogue and Jewish cemetery of Metz dating from the first half of the 13th cent. Among those referred to as "the sages of Lorraine," Eliezer ben Samuel (about 1195), successor of Eliezer ben Nathan in the Mayence rabbinate and author of *Sefer Yereim;* David ben Samuel at Würzburg; and possibly also Gershom ben Judah and his brother Machir, came from Metz. Visiting Jews had to pay thirty deniers at Metz. At Nancy, which from the 12th cent. on was the capital of Lorraine, the presence of Jews is traced back to 1225; in 1286 they acquired a cemetery in the village of Laxou, near Nancy, which they possessed for the following 200 years.

Mention is made also of the Jews of the old episcopal cities of Toul and Verdun in the 13th cent. Jewish sources refer to the eminent Tosafist Eliezer of Toul (flourished in the first half of the 13th cent.) and to his brother Abraham of Toul. The Tosafoth (12th to 13th centuries) contain references to the city of Verdun. Jewish money-lenders resided also in the smaller towns of Lorraine, and they, like the Lombards, enjoyed the protection of the dukes of Lorraine. In the latter period of the Middle Ages they were persecuted and expelled, like their coreligionists in Germany. In 1322 Jews of Metz who were accused of having poisoned the wells and of having participated in the leper revolt were burned at the stake. In 1365 a fire, caused by a stroke of lightning, which destroyed also twenty-two houses in the Jewish quarter, served as an excuse for the expulsion of the Jews from Metz. The mention of an alleged act of host desecration and of the burning of a Jew in Metz at the time of Bishop Pierre of Luxembourg (1348-86) permits no definite conclusion as to the presence of Jews in Metz at the end of the 14th cent.

In 1410 some of the Jews expelled from France settled in the Duchy of Lorraine. In 1422 the bishop of Metz, Konrad Bayer of Boppard, granted the Jews the privilege of being merchants and pawnbrokers and of building synagogues, cemeteries, a slaughterhouse and dwelling houses within the confines of his secular territory. Verdun, too, expelled its Jews, and the representative of the chapter and city at the Council of Basel (1433) pleaded in vain for the readmission of the Jews to Verdun. In 1477 Duke René II of Lorraine expelled the Jews from the country on the pretext that they had shown themselves partial to Burgundy. From that time on Jews were allowed to stay in Lorraine only temporarily.

3. From 1552 to the French Revolution.

A new era began for the Jews of Lorraine when Henri II of France took possession of the bishoprics of Metz, Toul and Verdun (1552). On June 22, 1597, Charles III, Duke of Lorraine, anxious to foster commerce in his country, granted to a Jewish merchant, Gabriel Magginus of Tuscany, and to several other Jews who traveled with him a letter of patent for twenty-five years, authorizing him to trade in Levantine fabrics at Nancy, the capital, and other cities of Lorraine. In the early 17th cent. several Jewish families settled at Bourgaldorf; at this period, Jews resided also at Esdorf, Biesingen, Kriechingen, Wieblingen, Falkenberg, Genglingen and some other places. The French kings gave tokens of their benevolence toward the Jews by granting them the privileges of March 24, 1603, and October 18, 1605; these were subsequently confirmed by Louis XIII, Louis XIV and Louis XV.

Leopold Joseph Charles, who became ruler of the duchy in 1697, suspended for three years all debts owing to the Jews and reduced the rate of interest to 5 per cent. Heedless of the protestations of the clergy, Duke Leopold, in 1712, permitted several Jewish bankers to settle at Nancy. They acted as his agents for the ducal mint; among them, Samuel Levy, who had been rabbi of Upper and Lower Alsace from 1702 to 1709, played an important role as financier. From 1715 to 1716 he was tax collector-in-chief of the Duke of Lorraine; he was discharged subsequently, imprisoned in 1717 and ordered to leave the country in 1722. In 1717 the prohibition against the holding of services in public by the Jews of Nancy was made more stringent; in 1720 a decree against Jewish usurers was issued; in 1721 all Jews who had entered the country after January 1, 1680, were ordered to leave. The latter decree was alleviated by permitting sixty-nine families to reside in twenty-four places. In 1733, a total of 180 families were permitted to reside in Lorraine; this status was kept up until the French Revolution (1789).

The commerce of the Jews of Lorraine was limited by law, and their housing was restricted by a decree of 1753. During the reign of Stanislaus Leszczinsky, king of Poland, who was duke of Lorraine from 1736 to 1766, and especially after the union of Lorraine with France in 1766, the position of the Jews improved. Stanislaus granted two Jewish families the right of residence in Lunéville; in 1785 there were sixteen Jewish families residing there.

The Jews of Lorraine formed a single community directed by the rabbi of the province and a body of syndics. Matters of civil law among Jews were decided according to Jewish jurisprudence; the Jewish community of Lorraine was responsible as a body for the annual tax of 10,000 livres. About 1780 Jacob ben Isserl Schweich was rabbi at Nancy. There were about 180 Jewish families in Nancy in 1784. The best-known Jewish family in Nancy was that of Isaac Berr, who was appointed syndic of the Jewish communities of Lorraine by Stanislaus Leszczinsky. His noted son, Berr-Isaac Berr (1744-1828), became the champion of Jewish emancipation in France, was elected a member of the city council of Nancy in 1792, and in 1806 was granted permission to add the designation "de Turique" to his name. He was author of *Réflexions sur la régénération complète des Juifs en France* (Paris, 1806). His cousin, Jacob Berr, "maître en chirurgie à Nancy," later in Metz, interceded in behalf of the complete emancipation and assimilation of the Jews.

The Jews of the city and the district of Metz formed a distinct body. Permission to stay at Metz having been granted to three Jews in 1565, a Jewish community of twenty households was founded in 1595. Henceforth the community developed at a remarkable pace, favored by the "lettres patentes" of the French kings (for example, that of September 25, 1657). The following table illustrates its growth:

Year	Households (Families)	Persons
1595	20	120
1603	24	
1614	58	
1632	76	
1657	96	
1689	294	950 and 29 foreign Jews
1709	336	
1718	480	
1739	563	2,213
1788	415	1,865
1808		2,266

The Jews of Metz traded also at Verdun, but in 1744 they were denied admission to that city, and their efforts to have this prohibition revoked were still without results in 1748. They also maintained business relationships with Nancy, and the downfall of tax collector-in-chief Samuel Levy entailed heavy losses for them. Severe adversity for the Jews of Metz attended the blood accusation raised (1670) against one Raphael Levy of Bolchen. This resulted not only in the execution of an innocent man, but provoked further accusations.

From about the year 1650 on the Jewish community of Metz was consolidated, and in the following period attained to increased rank and importance. In addition to the synagogue and cemetery, it owned its own hospice and Talmud school. Eminent rabbis from Poland and Germany became its leaders. Its first rabbi was Isaac Levy (d. 1620), son of Lazar Levy. Rabbis of Metz in the 17th cent. include Moise Cohen Narol (1649-59), whose son, Tobiah Hakohen (b. Metz, 1653), was a noted physician and author of *Maaseh Tobiah;* Jonah Teomim Fraenkel (1660-69); Gerson Oulif Ashkenazi (1670-93). Those of the 18th cent. include Abraham Broda (1703-12), Jacob Reicher (1716-33), Jacob Joshua Falk (author of *Pene Yehoshua;* 1733-40), Jonathan Eybeschütz (1742-50), Lion Asser (author of *Shaagath Aryeh;* 1765-85) and Ury Phoebus Cahen (1793-1806). The rabbinical court, on the ground of the royal privileges, decided all civil disputes between Jews.

The taxes imposed upon the Jews of Metz were diverse and exorbitant. In addition to the usual imposts and levies, the Jews of Metz assumed new burdens after the blood accusation of 1670. They paid to the Duke of Brancas, son-in-law of the president of the parliament, and to the Countess de Fontaine, daughter of the royal governor, a very considerable yearly subsidy, which they discontinued after the deaths of the president of the parliament and of the governor. The beneficiaries, however, protested vigorously, and after much controversy a letter of patent issued on November 30, 1715, by Philip of Orleans (regent of France) guaranteed the Duke of Brancas and the Countess de Fontaine an annuity of forty livres from each Jewish family residing in the district of Metz. This tax amounted to 20,000 livres yearly. (Voltaire congratulated the countess on the occasion.) Although a ducal letter of July 9, 1718, made all the Jews residing in the district of Metz (pays Messin) responsible for this annual sum, the Jews of the city of Metz had to take loans à fond perdu in order to be able to raise it.

The repeated efforts of the Jews, in 1734, 1739, and 1743, to free themselves from the Brancas tax were fruitless. By 1789 they had contracted a debt of 42,000 livres and their liabilities for that year were 101,500 livres, according to one source, while another puts them at 140,000 livres. A liability of 450 livres was on each family. It was not until July 20, 1790, that the taxes for "residence, protection and tolerance," including the Brancas tax, were abolished by the Constituent Assembly. This did not, however, abolish the debts which the Jews had contracted on account of this tax and which were considered "a common debt of all the Jews of the flat land." The governor of the generality Metz de Pont had ordered, on December 24, 1789, that payment of the tax owing by the community of Metz should be enforced by foreclosure, if necessary, and that the Jews of the flat land should be equally responsible for the payment. Another order of payment was issued on July 1, 1790. When, on May 20, 1791, a temporary decree authorizing appeals against the tax register was issued, the Jews of Nancy were the first to protest to the Constituent Assembly that they had never belonged to the community of Metz. Further appeals against the assessment were made by the Jews of Diedenhofen, Pfalzburg, Saarburg, Burscheid and Mittelbronn. The matter was finally settled in 1802 by an equitable decision of the consuls. It was not until 1854, however, that the Jewish community of Metz paid up all its debts.

4. From 1789 to 1870. In 1785 the Royal Society of Sciences and Arts of Metz offered an award for the best essay on the question "Est-il des moyens de rendre les Juifs plus utiles et plus heureux en France?" (Are there ways of rendering the Jews of France more useful and happier?). Among nine essays submitted, seven were in favor of emancipation; the prize was divided between Abbé Grégoire, who subsequently espoused the emancipation of the Jews in the Constituent Assembly, Adolphe Thierry, a lawyer of Nancy, and Salkind Hurwitz, a native of Poland. These papers contributed to preparing public opinion for the emancipation of the Jews in France. The Jews were permitted to send deputies to the Constituent Assembly. In Nancy, Lunéville, Sarreguemines, Dieuze, Bouley, Bouzonville, Lixheim, Fénétrange and Schamburg, places which had a sufficient number of Jews, election meetings presided over by the syndics were held. On June 9, 1789, the elected Jewish deputies met at Nancy for the redaction of the "Cahiers de la Lorraine" (Lorraine Books). The French population

also submitted their cahiers. Several communities demanded that the Jews be expelled. The third estate of Bouley urged that they be forbidden to trade in grain. Certain rural communities, the clergy of Sarrebourg and Sarreguemines and the nobility of Vic supported a demand that the edict of 1784, the last legislative measure of the old regime with reference to the Alsatian Jews, imposing certain disabilities upon the Jews of Alsace, should be extended also to the Jews of Lorraine and of the three archbishoprics. A number of representatives of the third estate and of the ecclesiastical communities, and the nobility of Nancy and Darney sought to compel the Jews to conduct financial transactions before notaries. The third estate of Metz and Vic demanded that the Jews be rendered useful to the state; that of Dieuze recommended that they be made citizens and admitted to the trades. Like the Jews of Alsace, those of Lorraine and of the three archbishoprics asked for citizenship rights in September, 1789; their petition was submitted to the Constituent Assembly on October 14, 1789, by Berr-Isaac Berr of Nancy; his words were heard with sympathy and attention. The bishop of Nancy, La Fare, acknowledged in the Assembly the important services which the Jews had performed for Lorraine and especially for the city of Nancy; nevertheless, he spoke against the granting of the rights of citizenship to the Jews. Berr-Isaac Berr and Jacob Berr appealed to him in their letters of April 22 and 25, 1790. It was not until September 23, 1791, that citizenship was bestowed upon the Jews of Alsace, Lorraine and the three archbishoprics, on condition that they take an oath on the constitution.

During the Reign of Terror, the Jews were persecuted; in Nancy and Toul it was demanded that the usurers of the stock exchange be expelled. The free exercise of their religion was threatened; in Nancy the Jews had to deliver up their gold and silver ritual objects; in Metz the Torah scrolls were cast out of the synagogue; the synagogue of Lunéville was closed in 1794. The Jews soon adjusted themselves to the new conditions, as was shown by the report for 1801 to 1806 of the prefect of the department of Moselle. In this department, to which Metz and its district belonged, about 6,320 Jews were living in 1806.

In the Sanhedrin convened by Emperor Napoleon in 1807, the Lorraine Jews were represented by Berr-Isaac Berr and Moïse Lévy of Nancy, Mardoché Cahen, rabbi of Verdun, and Jacob Berr of Metz. The French laws of 1808 regulating the situation of the Jews applied naturally also to Lorraine, as did later also the cult constitution (ordinance of May 25, 1844), which was preceded by an earlier ordinance of February 18, 1831. Metz became the seat of the Lorraine consistory in 1808, and remained the center of Jewish life. The first chief rabbi of the consistory was Mayer Charleville. A rabbinical school (École Centrale Rabbinique) was established at Metz in 1829. In 1831 the French government began to provide funds for the school, and in 1859 it was transferred to Paris. Its first director was Lion Mayer Lambert (1787-1862). The Jews founded also technical schools for youths at Metz and Nancy in the 1820's.

Michel Berr (1780-1843), second son of Berr-Isaac Berr of Nancy, was the first Jewish attorney in

France; in 1807 he served as secretary of the Grand Sanhedrin, and was active in the writing of works on Judaism, general history, politics and literature. Lippmann Lippmann de Baccarat (d. Nancy, 1843), together with his two brothers, in December, 1806, took over the glass factory in Baccarat (Département of Meurthe et Moselle) which had been founded in 1765 by the archbishop of Metz. Although this transfer of ownership occurred at the most critical period in the factory's existence, Lippmann successfully managed it until 1815—in 1812 a total of 600 workers were employed in it—and thus performed notable patriotic service. Thereafter numerous Lorraine Jews rose to positions of honor and high rank in France.

5. From 1871 to 1918. When Lorraine was incorporated into the German Reich by virtue of the treaty of May 10, 1871, a great number of Lorraine Jews moved to France. In the German Reich the Lorraine Jews continued to enjoy equal rights; from 1871 to 1918 the Jews of Lorraine were recognized and subventioned by the state as a religious community like the Christian churches. When German rule came to an end in 1918, there were, in addition to the chief rabbinate, four rabbinates and fifty Jewish houses of worship in existence in Lorraine. The Jewish population of Lorraine was as follows:

YEAR	NUMBER OF JEWS			
1789	7,500 (city of Metz, 2,000; district of Metz, 1,500; province of Lorraine, about 4,000)			
1806 to 1811	10,896			
1871	8,646	in a total population of		464,316
1905	7,165	"	"	" 615,790
1910	7,015	"	"	" 655,211

As in other countries, the Jewish group decreased as against a steady increase of the general population.

6. From the Treaty of Versailles to 1940. After the return of Lorraine to France by the Treaty of Versailles on June 28, 1919, it was proved once more that the Jews of Lorraine were deeply attached to France, which did not discriminate between her citizens.

The disastrous effects of the Nazi regime in Germany soon became noticeable in Lorraine, not only as a result of the influx of refugees, but also through violent anti-Semitic propaganda incited and fostered by Germany in Alsace-Lorraine. As early as 1933 the city of Metz passed a law limiting the number of German-Jewish employees to 5 per cent of the total. In June, 1938, the French government was asked to investigate conditions in Alsace-Lorraine, which in many parts had assumed a frankly anti-Jewish character. In the same month a monument for 6,000 French and 2,000 British and American Jews, fallen in the first World War, was dedicated at Douaumont, near Verdun, with the highest authorities attending. Before the outbreak of the second World War, however, Nazi agitation had reached a climax.

7. After June 22, 1940. On June 22, 1940, France fell. The Jews of Alsace-Lorraine had to disappear from both public life and the professions. Soon their total expulsion began. If available figures are correct, 20,000 Jews of Alsace-Lorraine, among them the Jews of Metz and Nancy, were affected. They were allowed to take with them to unoccupied

France only hand luggage and from 500 to 1,000 francs per capita, and even this amount was reduced subsequently, so that the expelled arrived in the free zone stripped of every possession. In October, 1940, the synagogue of Nancy was transformed into a storehouse for fodder; another synagogue in Alsace-Lorraine was demolished to make room for a square for the holding of military parades. The above-mentioned soldiers' monument at Douaumont near Verdun was defaced and badly damaged by Nazis on August 16, 1940. On December 18, 1940, Jewish-owned property was distributed among "needy Germans." The Jewish welfare organizations found it difficult to keep up with the enormous tasks facing them. On August 15, 1940, the OSE assumed responsibility for 1,000 Jewish children from Alsace-Lorraine, and allotted an additional amount of 500,000 francs per month. The refugees from Alsace-Lorraine were admitted, according to a report of February 4, 1941, to North Africa, whence, at the same time, other Jews were ordered to leave.

ADOLF KOBER.

Lit.: American Jewish Year Book, vols. 36 to 42 (1936-42); vol. 22 (1919-20) 53-79; Contemporary Jewish Record, vols. 3 to 4 (1940-41); Anchel, Robert, Napoléon et les juifs (1928); Cahen, Abraham, "Le rabbinat de Metz pendant la période française (1567-1871)," Revue des études juives, vol. 7, pp. 103-16, 204-26; vol. 8, pp. 255-74; vol. 12, pp. 283-97; vol. 13, pp. 105-26; Dienemann, Max, "Die jüdischen Gemeinden in Elsass-Lothringen, 1871-1918," Zeitschrift für die Geschichte der Juden in Deutschland, vol. 7 (1937) 77-85; Clément, Roger, La condition des Juifs de Metz sous l'ancien régime (1903); Festschrift zum 70. Geburtstage Simon Dubnows (1930) 207-14; Encyclopaedia Judaica, vol. 10 (1934), col. 1131 (also the bibliography in the article Lothringen); Dubnow, Simon, Weltgeschichte des jüdischen Volkes, vols. 7 and 8 (1928); Gérardin, Edouard, Histoire de Lorraine, duchés, comtés, évêchés, depuis les origines jusqu'à la réunion des deux Duchés à la France (1766) (1925); Germania Judaica, vol. 1, part 1 (1917); vol. 1, part 2 (1934); Gross, Henri, Gallia Judaica (1897); Netter, N., Vingt siècles d'histoire d'une communauté juive (1938); idem, "Die Schuldennot der jüdischen Gemeinde Metz," Monatsschrift für Geschichte und Wissenschaft des Judentums, vol. 57 (1913) 591-611; vol. 58 (1914) 63-80; Pfister, C., Histoire de Nancy, vol. 3 (1908); Parisot, Robert, Histoire de Lorraine, 3 vols. and index volume (1919-24); Revue des études juives, vol. 1, p. 96; vol. 31, pp. 75, 88; vol. 44, p. 108; vol. 46, p. 277; vol. 50, p. 112 et seq.; vol. 51, pp. 280-302; vol. 52, pp. 272-81; vol. 53, pp. 270-72; vol. 89, pp. 79-85; vol. 90, p. 10; vol. 91, pp. 113-14; Sulamith, vol. 7, pp. 349-50; Yiddish Scientific Institute, section on the history of the Jews in France, Studies and Materials, edit. G. Tscherikower, 2 vols. (1942); Posener, S., "The Immediate Economic and Social Effects of the Emancipation of the Jews in France," Jewish Social Studies, vol. 1, No. 3 (July, 1939) 271-326.

LOS ANGELES, largest city on the Pacific Coast. Its population, according to the 1940 census, was 1,504,277; that of Los Angeles County was 2,785,277, of whom 100,000 were Jews. Most of the Jews came to Los Angeles from the Eastern and Middle Western states after 1920. While the Jewish inhabitants are scattered over the entire city and its environs, there are several dense centers of population, such as Boyle Heights, West Adams and the Beverly, Wilshire and Hollywood districts. Beverly Hills, a suburb, Hollywood and Santa Monica comprise the chief residential districts of many of the Jews who are affiliated in one way or another with the great motion picture industry. In addition to motion pictures, Jews are found in every walk of life. The needlework and furniture

Sinai Synagogue of Los Angeles

Alfred Newmark who was first president (1854-62) of Congregation B'nai B'rith, Los Angeles

industries grew tremendously in the 1930's, largely with the cooperation of Jews.

Los Angeles started as a little Spanish Mexican pueblo in 1781. At that time, and during the immediate years that followed, life centered about the Plaza. The first Jews settled here in 1849; the United States census of 1850 included six Jewish names. Among the early founders of Jewish life and institutions may be mentioned Herman Schlesinger, Baruch Marks, Hillard Loewenstein and Solomon Lazard. But it remained for Joseph Newmark in 1854 to officiate at the first religious services, in John Temple's adobe. Although Newmark was an ordained rabbi, he acted in the capacity of a volunteer layman, never having followed his religious calling professionally in the United States. In 1854 also the Hebrew Benevolent Society was founded by Jacob Elias, who became the first president. A tract of land was purchased and dedicated as a cemetery, which the Society cared for until, in January, 1891, under the leadership of Mrs. Maurice Kremer, the Home of Peace Society took charge of it and turned it over to Congregation B'nai Berith. In 1942 the cemetery was owned by Wilshire Boulevard Temple, and on its beautiful grounds stands the new Home of Peace Mausoleum, the first Jewish mausoleum in the country.

Congregation B'nai Berith was founded in 1862. Later it became Congregation B'nai B'rith, more popularly known as the Wilshire Boulevard Temple. Rabbi Abraham Wolf Edelman was the first elected spiritual leader, and Wolf Kalisher was the first president. Services were strictly Orthodox; most of the thirty-odd members were from Germany or France. Services were held at Arcadia or Stearn's Hall on North Los Angeles Street; later in Leck's Hall on Main Street between Second and Third; still later in Judge Ygnacio Sepulveda's court room.

In 1884 the congregation became less conservative, and Edelman, who was Orthodox, resigned. Emanuel Schreiber was next elected rabbi, and the Jastrow prayer-book was used. In 1888 the wearing of hats at services was abolished. Abraham Blum followed Schreiber in 1889; M. G. Solomon became rabbi in 1895, when the Union Prayer Book was adopted. In

1899 Sigmund Hecht became the spiritual leader. Until 1919, when he was retired for life as rabbi emeritus, the Jewish community made considerable progress. Hecht played an important part in the development of both Jewish and communal social, cultural and religious life of the city. In 1915 Edgar F. Magnin became associate rabbi, to succeed Hecht in 1919. Maxwell H. Dubin, made assistant to Magnin in 1925, and later associate rabbi, wrote textbooks for Jewish religious schools.

The cornerstone of the first synagogue building was laid in 1872, that of the second in 1896. In 1929 the cornerstone was laid of the Wilshire Boulevard Temple, which consists of three buildings of Renaissance architecture facing Wilshire, Hobart and Harvard Boulevards. Mural paintings by Hugo Ballin, depicting Jewish history and literature through the ages, were the gift of the Warner family. A famous old world collection of Jewish ceremonial objects, in the lobby, was the gift of Mr. and Mrs. Henry Weinberger.

There were more than forty-five synagogues in Los Angeles in 1942. Among the most prominent are Sinai (Rabbi Jacob Kohn); Temple Israel of Hollywood (Rabbi Morton Bauman); Beth Israel (Rabbi Simon A. Dolgin); Bethel (Rabbi N. I. Adelson); Western Jewish Institute (Rabbi S. M. Neches); Mogen David (Rabbi A. I. Maron); Fairfax Temple (Rabbi Sonderling); Etz Jacob (Rabbi Lupo); Congregation Talmud Torah (Rabbi Osher Zilberstein); the Community Synagogue (Rabbi Mayer Winkler); Temple B'nai Zion; Beth Jacob West Adams Hebrew Congregation (Orthodox); and the Spanish-Portuguese Temple Tifereth Israel, founded in 1920 by Rabbi David Tovi (its synagogue was dedicated in February, 1932).

Other cemeteries besides the Home of Peace Cemetery and Mausoleum are Agudath Achim, B'nai Israel, Mt. Zion, Beth David, Mt. Carmel and Beth Olom.

The Rabbinical Association of Southern California includes all duly ordained rabbis. Jacob Kohn and Edgar F. Magnin were presidents of the Board of Rabbis.

Los Angeles has many philanthropic organizations and institutions. The Federation of Jewish Welfare

Murals (by Hugo Ballin) depicting Jewish ceremonies in the Wilshire Boulevard Temple, Los Angeles

Ark (left) of the Wilshire Boulevard Temple, Los Angeles; (top) The Federation Building of Los Angeles

Organizations, organized in 1911, was first composed of seven societies. The constituent organizations in 1942 were: the Jewish Centers Association, the Jewish Social Service Bureau, the Julia Ann Singer Day Nursery, the Jewish Big Brothers Association, the Cedars of Lebanon Hospital, the Hamburger Home, for working girls, the Jewish Loan Fund, the Jewish Orphans' Home, the Los Angeles Convalescent Home.

The Federation has its own building. Its presidents since its inception have been George Mosbacher, Jay B. Jacobs, Marco R. Newmark, Milton Baruch and David Tannenbaum. Among the executive secretaries of the Federation were Dora Berres, Boris Bogen, I. Irving Lipsitch, Charles Schottland and Maurice S. Karpf, who was elected in 1942.

Los Angeles has, in addition, the Jewish Employment Bureau, the Jewish Loan Fund, the League for Assistance to Jewish Students, the Jewish Committee for Personal Service in State Institutions, the Mt. Sinai Hospital and Clinic, the Home for Wayfarers, the Jewish Home for the Aged, the Helping Hand, the Industrial Center for the Aged, the Hebrew Free Loan and the El Nido summer camp for girls. The Jewish Consumptive and Ex-Patients Home is a national institution, housing and caring for patients from all over the United States.

The Jewish Émigré Service Committee, with Ludwig Schiff as president, handles all the refugee problems in the county. Los Angeles also has well organized branches of the Jewish Welfare Board and the United Service Organizations, in which Jews play a prominent part.

The Council of Jewish Women plays an important role in the social, philanthropic and cultural life of the city. There is also a chapter of the United Order of True Sisters, and all the principal fraternities and sororities are represented in the local universities.

The Independent Order of B'nai B'rith started with Los Angeles Lodge No. 587. Sigmund G. Marshuts was the first president. In 1942 there were nineteen lodges in and around Los Angeles.

Los Angeles has a Jewish Community Council, composed of the representatives of more than 150 organizations. Its functions are to help unite the Jewish community as far as possible and to provide a forum for the discussion of important local, national and international Jewish problems. Judge Harry A. Hollzer has been president since its inception.

Los Angeles and Hollywood are the center of the motion picture industry. Many of the founders and producers are Jews, as well as a great number of actors, writers and musicians. The cinema brought to the vicinity a number of famous personages in the fields of acting, writing and music. Many of the Jews in the motion picture industry are actively identified with religious, philanthropic and cultural activities.

Since the earliest days Jews have played an important part in the development of Los Angeles and Southern California. Maurice Kremer in 1870 was a member of the school board and on the committee to erect the first Los Angeles high school. He was also authorized to overhaul and arrange documents in the Spanish archives, and in 1871 he discovered an original Proclamation of Peace between the United States and Mexico. Solomon Lazard was the first president of the original Chamber of Commerce; he assisted in the forming of the first water company and was one of the original directors.

Bernard Cohn, in 1888, was elected for a term to the City Council. David W. Edelman, son of the first rabbi, was a member of the Executive Committee of the Native Sons, and was active in the Democratic Party. Herman W. Frank was president of the Merchants and Manufacturers Association, and president of the Board of Education. Eugene Germain was the American consul in Zurich, Switzerland, and a Commissioner for California to the Paris Exposition. An outstanding figure in community life was Louis M. Cole, president of the Chamber of Commerce, potentate of the Shrine, and food administrator for Los Angeles and Southern California during the first World War. Harris Newmark was a member of the original Library Board as well as of the Board of the

Architect's design of the Cedars of Lebanon Hospital at Los Angeles

The Jewish Community Center of Los Angeles

The Spanish-Portuguese Temple Tifereth Israel

Associated Charities. M. H. Newmark was on the first Harbor Commission. Rabbi Sigmund Hecht served as a member of the Public Library Board.

Meyer Lissner organized the City Club, was chairman of the California Republican State Central Committee, president of the Board of Public Utilities of the City of Los Angeles, member of the California Industrial Accident Commission, and served on the United States Shipping Board. From time to time Los Angeles Jews served as members of the Board of the Chamber of Commerce. Among them were Ludwig Schiff and Henry W. Louis. Ben R. Meyer was, in 1942, treasurer of the Symphony Association and the Community Chest.

Jews have contributed much toward the development of music in Southern California. Among the conductors of the Los Angeles Symphony were Walter Rothwell, Artur Rodzinski and Otto Klemperer.

Among the judiciary may be mentioned the Honorable Harry A. Hollzer of the United States Court, Judge Edward Brand, Lester Roth, Isaac Pacht, Ben Scheinman, H. Leonard Kaufman and Leo Freund. Judge Hollzer was (1942) an officer of the United Service Organizations Board and active in many civic movements. Judge Scheinman was (1942) chairman of the Boy Scouts. Judge Pacht was chairman of the California State Prison Board.

A. M. Edelman was a member of the State Board of Architects for many years. On the Board of the Los Angeles Urban League were Maxwell H. Dubin, Morton Bauman and Marco R. Newmark, who was also president of the Southern California Historical Society. Marco and Irving Hellman have played an active part in civic affairs. Irving Hellman was chairman of the Los Angeles Board of Pensions Commissioners for many years. Solomon Kahn and Samuel Prager played an important part in Masonic circles, as did Daniel J. Brownstein and Louis Nordlinger.

On the faculties of the various universities in Southern California were, in 1942, a number of Jews prominent in their fields. Among them were Joseph Kaplan and Arthur Klein, physicists, and Arnold Schoenberg and Ernst Toch in the field of music.

The Zionist movement and all its affiliates had a large and active membership, as had Hadassah. A branch of the Friends of the Hebrew University in Jerusalem was established in 1941. Los Angeles had a number of Jewish labor unions. Among the Jewish periodicals published in Los Angeles were (1942) the *B'nai B'rith Messenger* and the *Jewish Voice;* the latter appeared in both Yiddish and English. There were a number of social clubs, including the Town Club and the Hillcrest Country Club. In earlier years the Concordia Club occupied an important place in the social life of the community.   EDGAR F. MAGNIN.

Lit.: Newmark, Harris, *Sixty Years in Southern California;* Workman, Boyle, *The City that Grew;* Graves, Jackson A., *Seventy Years in California;* Frank, Herman W., *Scrap Book of a Western Pioneer;* Files of the *B'nai B'rith Messenger,* especially written by Marco R. Newmark.

LOSINSKI, SAMUEL, historian, b. Bobruisk, Russia, 1874. He became instructor at the University of Leningrad in 1915, and was president of the Teachers' Association at the Jewish National University of Leningrad from 1919 to 1923. In 1924 he became teacher at the Pedagogical Institute in Leningrad. He wrote (in Russian): *History of the Second French Revolution* (1904); *History of Belgium and Holland in Modern Times* (1908); *Political Parties and the National Problem in Austria* (1907). Under his editorship a number of historical works were translated into Russian, including Ernest Renan's *History of the People of Israel* and Henry Charles Lea's *History of the Inquisition.* He was one of the editors of the *Yevreiskaya Entziklopedia.*

LOSONC, city in Nógrád county, Hungary. The Jewish community of Losonc-Tugár was founded in 1808. Previously the Jews carrying on trade with Losonc lived in the neighboring villages. Toward the end of the 18th cent. the aristocratic landlords of Szilassy granted permission to the Jewish family Wohl to settle on their estate in Tugár, a suburb of Losonc. The first rabbi of the congregation was Mose Hőgyész, and the second Simon Kohen, who distinguished himself by his patriotism in the national war of independence (1848-1849). Losonc was laid waste by the allied Austrian and Russian troops, and the rabbi had to flee to Alsókubin, a city in the mountains. Com-

Lot and his daughters. From a painting by Guido Reni in the National Gallery of London

munal life, suspended by the havoc of war, was re-vived, but later there was dissension between the advocates of the Reform and Orthodox trends. The community finally organized itself on the principle of

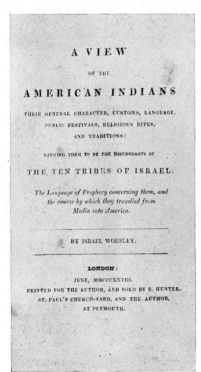

Title page of a book (1828) by Israel Worsley dealing with the American Indians as possible descendants of the "Lost Tribes"

moderate reform, and erected its first synagogue in 1863. A second synagogue was built in 1925.

In 1919 Losonc, under the name of Lučenec, was incorporated into the Czechoslovak republic. It was returned to Hungarian sovereignty in 1938. The community then numbered 2,200 members in a total population of 12,000. It maintained a small Yeshiva and a Talmud Torah. In both 1919 and 1938 the community suffered from the dislocation of the city from an established economic system. In 1938 it had to adjust itself to the added hardship of civic and work restrictions imposed upon Jews. In 1940 Arthur Reschofsky was rabbi of Losonc.

LOSS (Hebrew, *'abedah*). Jewish law is especially concerned with lost property, the return of which it considers one of the most important duties of every individual. The injunction to restore that which is lost, first mentioned in the Bible, is expanded into no less than four chapters in the Mishnah (*B.M.* 1 to 4), which deal with individual cases. Furthermore, there is a precedence in the seeking of lost property. Thus if both one and a stranger are seeking property which has been lost, it is self-understood that one may search for his own property before turning to assist the stranger. On the other hand, if the loss be that of one's father or teacher, their need receives primary attention. Wilful retention of an article which one finds when he knows that it belongs to another is considered equivalent to embezzlement and is punished accordingly.

See also: BAILMENTS; FINDING OF PROPERTY.

LOST TRIBES. Jewish legends more than once contain references to portions of the Israelite nation which became lost and which presumably will be

Lot and his wife and daughters flee from Sodom. From a painting by Peter Paul Rubens (1577-1640)

reunited with their brethren in the time of the Messianic redemption. These stories seem to have arisen out of attempts to expound certain obscure verses in the Bible as well as to explain the reason why the people of Israel still remained small in number.

Lot's flight and the destruction of Sodom, as depicted in the manuscript of a 13th cent. Psalter in the National Library, Paris

Thus, according to an account which appears in a number of Midrashic sources (especially *Pirke de Rabbi Eliezer* 48; *Midrash Vayosha* 54; *Sanh.* 92b), the tribe of Ephraim, or a large part of them, miscalculated by thirty years too soon the date of the promised deliverance of the Israelites from slavery in Egypt. They left the country and marched toward Palestine, but were defeated in battle by the Philistines, and hundreds of thousands of them were slain. Their bodies remained in the desert, unaffected by the elements, and a later rabbi claimed to have seen them; according to other accounts, however, they were the dead who were resurrected by Ezekiel (*Ezek.* 37). The story may be a dim reminiscence of the wars between Egypt and Canaan before the Israelite conquest: it is possibly connected with the references to Ephraim in *I Chron.* 7:21-22 and *Ps.* 78:9.

The second lost group was that of the descendants of Moses (Bene Mosheh) who, according to the interpretation of *Ex.* 32:10, were to be a great nation, as numerous as Israel (*Ber.* 7a and other places). According to legend, these descendants migrated in a body at the time of the destruction of the First Temple and took up their abode to the east, beyond the river Sambation. With them were associated the Rechabites, to whom Jeremiah (*Jer.* 35:18-19) had promised perpetuity. These legends are mentioned in the Koran and by Arabic writers, and are perhaps connected with the early Jews in Arabia, who did not observe all the later Jewish customs and could therefore be regarded as the descendants of Moses.

The most famous of all the lost tribes were the Ten Tribes of Israel, carried away by the Assyrians after the fall of Samaria (722 B.C.E.). Since there were numerous prophecies that they would return and be united to their brethren, there was a lively expectation that they might be found by diligent search, and every nation which appeared to have a trace of Jewish customs, from American Indians to Anglo-Saxons, was identified with these lost tribes.

See also: BENE MOSHEH; TRIBES, TEN LOST.

LOT, son of Haran and nephew of Abraham. According to the Bible account of him in connection with the story of Abraham in *Gen.* 11 to 19, he accompanied his grandfather Terah from Ur of the Chaldees to Haran, and his uncle Abraham on his journey to Canaan. The two separated because of a quarrel over pasturage, and Lot settled in Sodom. Warned by the angels of the approaching doom of the city, he took his wife and two of his daughters and fled in time; his wife disobeyed, looked back and was turned into a pillar of salt. Lot then resided in a remote cave in the mountains, where his daughters made him drunk and propagated by him the ancestors of the Moabites and Ammonites.

Lot is depicted in the story as rather weak and self-seeking by nature, but possessed of the virtue of hospitality. Bible scholars regard his story as a reminiscence of the relationship of the Israelites and the Moabite and Ammonite nations, who were their enemies and therefore given a shameful ancestry; while the story of Lot's wife is connected, probably, with some legend of the Dead Sea, the same legend that deals with the destruction of the wicked cities. The story of Lot's capture by the four kings (*Gen.* 14) and his rescue by Abraham is regarded by the critics as a very late addition to the text.

Rabbinic sources expand the Bible story, usually depicting Lot and his wife in an even more unfavorable light, as he is charged with being quarrelsome, lustful and avaricious. On the other hand, some sources represent him as praying to God all night to spare the people of Sodom.

LOTH, DAVID GOLDSMITH, author, b. St. Louis, 1899. He was the grandson of Solomon Sonnenschein, rabbi and author, and of Rosa Sonnenschein, who founded the *American Jewess.* His great-grandfather was Hirsch Bär Fassel (1802-83), noted Hungarian Reform rabbi and author. Loth received his degree in journalism from the University of Missouri in 1920, and was connected, in various writing capacities, with the New York *World* from 1920 to 1930. In 1931 he was one of the founders of the Majorca *Sun and Spanish Times,* which was the first newspaper to be published in English on Spanish soil. Loth returned to the United States in 1934. He served for a number of years on the staff of the New York *Times,* and in May, 1941, joined the staff of the United States Office of Inter-American Affairs.

The Brownings (1929) was the first of Loth's biographical studies, and was followed by *Lorenzo the Magnificent* (1929); *Charles II, Ruler and Rake* (1930); *Philip II, Master of the Armada* (1932); *Public Plunder* (1938); *Alexander Hamilton, Portrait of a Prodigy* (1939) and *Woodrow Wilson, the Fifteenth Point* (1941).

LOTH, MORITZ, early leader of Reform Judaism in the United States, and communal worker, b. Milotitz, province of Moravia, Austria, 1832; d. Cincinnati, 1913. He was a merchant. A devoted follower of Rabbi Isaac M. Wise, Loth, as president in 1872 of Bene Yeshurun Congregation (then occupying the Plum Street Temple), recommended the appointment of a committee to meet with committees from other congregations to form a union; he was the first president of the Union of American Hebrew Congregations from its inception in 1873 until 1889. From then on, until his death, he was a member of the executive board.

Since the primary object of the Union of American Hebrew Congregations had been the establishment of a Jewish theological school, Loth was active in furthering the beginnings of the Hebrew Union College (founded 1875), whose classes were held, at first, in the Plum Street Temple. He helped raise funds for the first building of the Hebrew Union College, dedicated in 1881.

LOTHAR, ERNST (pseudonym for Ernst Lothar Müller), author, b. Brünn, Moravia, 1890. He was living in New York city in 1942. Lothar studied law at the University of Vienna, and served at the Austrian ministry of commerce, whence he retired with the title of Hofrat. He then became associated with the *Neue Freie Presse* as a free lance author at first, subsequently becoming theatre critic and literary editor of that newspaper. When Max Reinhardt gave up the direction of the Josefstädter Theater, Lothar became his successor. He was president of the Association of Creative Artists of Austria. After the Nazi occupation of Vienna, he left for the United States, where he wrote novels and taught dramatic arts, but was no longer an adherent of the Jewish faith. He was a brother of the dramatist Hans Müller.

He was the author of several volumes of poetry, such as *Der ruhige Hain* (1910) and *Die Rast* (1913). His novels, written in German, include: *Der Feldherr* (1918); *Irrlicht der Welt* (1922); *Irrlicht des Geistes* (1922); *Der Hellseher* (1929). *A Woman Is Witness* (English version by Barrows Mussey, New York, 1941) dealt with the experiences of a woman in the Nazi world.

LOTHAR, RUDOLF (originally **Rudolf Spitzer**), author and playwright, b. Budapest, 1865. He was reported to be living in Switzerland in 1942. He studied law at the University of Vienna and Romance philology at those of Jena and Rostock, receiving his Ph.D. degree from the University of Heidelberg. From 1890 to 1907 he worked for the *Neue Freie Presse* at Vienna; in 1900 he founded the literary journal *Die Wage;* from 1907 to 1912 he was connected with the *Berliner Lokal-Anzeiger.* In 1912 he took over the direction of the *Komödienhaus,* Berlin; during the first World War he served at the German Embassy at Bern, and in 1920 he returned to Berlin. Again in Vienna in 1932, he became theatre critic of the *Neues Wiener Journal.*

Lothar traveled extensively; he is the author of several travel books, among them *Die Seele Spaniens* (1915) and one on Palestine, *Zwischen drei Welten.* He visited the United States and worked for the motion picture industry. Not all of his more than seventy stage plays have literary value, but such plays as *König Harlekin* (1900); *Die grosse Gemeinde* (L. Lipschitz, co-author; 1906); *Casanovas Sohn* (1920), which had over 3,000 performances; *Werwolf* (1921); and *Die Republik befiehlt* (F. Gottwald, co-author; 1926) well deserved the great success they had with the public. Lothar wrote the opera text for Eugene d'Albert's *Tiefland* (1904). In his later years he was a successful theatrical author under various Spanish and Italian pseudonyms. Among his essays, the one dealing with the Vienna Burgtheater is the most important. His novels include: *Der Golem* (1900); *Kurfürstendamm* (1910); *Der Herr von Berlin* (1911).

LOTMAR, PHILIPP, law professor, b. Frankfort, Germany, 1850; d. Bern, Switzerland, 1922. He studied Roman law, and in 1876 received the right to teach at the University of Munich. In 1888 he became associate professor at the University of Bern. He wrote: *Die Causa im römischen Recht* (1875); two lectures, *Das Recht, das mit uns geboren ist* and *Die Gerechtigkeit* (1889); *Der unmoralische Vertrag* (1896); *Der Arbeitsvertrag* (2 vols., 1902 and 1908), his major work, in which he laid the basis for the doctrine of labor law.

Lit.: Sinzheimer, Hugo, *Jüdische Klassiker der deutschen Rechtswissenschaft* (1938).

LOTS, FEAST OF, see PURIM.

LOUIS THE PIOUS, see GERMANY.

LOUIS, HENRY, mining engineer, b. London, 1855; d. Newcastle on Tyne, England, 1939. He was educated in London, then in Bavaria. After graduating from the Royal School of Mines, he went to Canada and later to the United States. He also engaged in mining in the Malay States, South Africa, Borneo and Spain. In 1890 he founded his own firm in Singapore.

Louis was made professor of mining at Armstrong College, Newcastle, in 1896, and occupied the post for twenty-seven years, after which he became professor emeritus. He held various executive and honorary positions with national and international mining organizations. In 1927 he was president of the Institute of Mining Engineers, and from 1929 to 1931 president of the Iron and Steel Institute. He was awarded the Bessemer Medal in 1932. Louis wrote numerous mining textbooks and studies on mineralogy.

LOUISIANA, a Southern state of the United States with a population of 2,363,880 (census of 1940), including about 16,000 Jews.

Jews were among the first settlers in Louisiana. In 1718, thirty-six years after the territory was claimed for France and named in honor of Louis XIV by La Salle (1682), in the very year that New Orleans was founded by the Sieur de Bienville, Jacob David, a shoemaker, and Romain David, a tailor, were among a company bound for a plantation near New Orleans. They landed about the first of the new year (1719). Among other immigrants who came in 1719 were Robert Jacobs and his wife and a soldier, Louis Solomons. What became of Jacob and Romain David and the others is unknown; they are not listed in the census of Louisiana which was taken in 1721.

In 1724, Bienville, governor of the province, issued his *Code Noir* (The Black Code), regulating slavery but including, among its first provisions, an order expelling Jews and prohibiting any religious worship except that of Roman Catholicism. This was to be the law under the French, and later under the Spanish, until 1803 when, by the Louisiana Purchase, the territory became part of the United States and was admitted to its religious freedom.

Before 1803, however, Jews, welcome or not, lived in the colony. There is a record of one, Pallachio, who was a trader in flour at New Orleans in the 1760's; Samuel Israel, a resident of New Orleans, Alexander Solomons, and Joseph Depalacios bought some land from the Chevalier de Monberault in 1765. When Judah Touro settled in New Orleans in 1802, he is said to have found other Jews in that city of 10,000 inhabitants, among these the son of Haym Salomon, Ezekiel (d. 1821), who was to become governor of the local branch of the Bank of the United States.

Jacob da Silva Solis, a merchant of New York, came to New Orleans on business about 1826. Not only was there no Jewish congregation in the city at the time but he had to bake his own Matzoth, and he began the organization of Congregation Shangari Chassed (later Touro Synagogue), chartered in 1828 —for almost forty years the only synagogue in the state. In 1936 there were twenty-one congregations with a membership of 13,464 in Louisiana (*Census of Religious Bodies, Jewish Congregations,* United States Bureau of the Census).

The largest Jewish community in the state is that of New Orleans, numbering 6,472 (1938), and the next largest is that of Shreveport, with about 2,200 Jews. Baton Rouge, Alexandria, and Monroe have Jewish communities of more than 500, and about forty other cities and towns have more than ten Jews each.

BATON ROUGE (population 34,719, census of 1940), the third largest city of the state and its capital, had in 1942 the third largest Jewish community, numbering about 600. The first Jewish communal organization in Baton Rouge was a cemetery association, founded in 1858; the first burial (1858) was that of Isaac Kahn, a young man who had died of yellow fever. The Hebrew Congregation of Baton Rouge was incorporated in 1859. However, the Jewish community was soon scattered by the Civil War. Congregation Shaare Chesed was founded in 1868 and formally organized in 1871. The congregation acquired in 1876 for a synagogue a building of red brick and cement that had been used as a church and school, but this was lost by litigation in 1883. In 1884 the congregation took the name of B'nai Israel, and in 1885 repurchased its former synagogue building. The Minhag America (Reform) had been adopted in 1879 when Isador Lewinhall was the rabbi. In 1942 Walter G. Peiser, whose service began in 1927, was rabbi. The congregation owns its cemetery, which includes the tract originally bought in 1858. In 1874 the Children's Hebrew Benevolent Society was organized, among other purposes, for the establishment of a Sunday school. The Jewish Welfare Fund was established in 1937. A B'nai B'rith lodge was organized in Baton Rouge as long ago as 1875.

ALEXANDRIA. Jews settled in Alexandria (population 27,066, census of 1940) as early as 1848. In 1854, when the corpse of "an unknown Jew" was brought into the town, they hastily raised a fund and bought a cemetery plot in which to bury the dead man. This was the beginning of the Hebrew Benevolent Association. In 1861 a congregation, Gemiluth Chassodim (Reform), was established. The old synagogue, built in 1870, was replaced by a new one in 1909. Marx Klein, whose service began in 1875, was the first resident rabbi. Leonard J. Rothstein was rabbi from 1907 to 1917. Albert G. Baum, whose service began in 1930, was rabbi in 1942. Gemiluth Chassodim had its own cemetery (originally established by the Hebrew Benevolent Association). A second congregation, B'nai Israel (Orthodox), was founded in 1913, and its new building was completed in 1932. Reuben Arenson, who served from 1913 to 1915, was the first resident rabbi. B'nai Israel conducted a school for daily instruction in Hebrew. The congregation owned a cemetery. In 1938, the Jewish Welfare Federation was organized to serve the neighboring places, such as Bunkie and Lecompte, as well as Alexandria. The Jewish community of Alexandria numbered almost 600 in 1942.

MONROE (population 28,309, census of 1940) had a Jewish community of about 525 members (1942). In 1868 a group that had been meeting in the home of Gottliebe King for religious services formed Congregation B'nai Israel (Reform). A synagogue was built in 1870, and a new synagogue of brick and terra cotta in 1915. The first resident rabbi was one Gluck. Israel Heinberg was rabbi for a number of years about the beginning of the 20th cent. Ferdinand K. Hirsch, whose service began in 1928, was rabbi in 1942. There is also a record of a Congregation Manasas at Monroe. In 1861 it purchased a tract of land for a cemetery, afterwards called the Hebrew Burying Ground and then Cemetery B'nai Israel; among those buried here is Louis Lock (d. 1916), a pioneer in the development of the Monroe gas fields. The United Jewish Charities of Northeast Louisiana was organized at Monroe in 1938; it serves also the communities of Bastrop, Ferriday, Lake Providence, Tallulah, and Winnsboro. The B'nai B'rith lodge was organized in 1882. The Unity Club, formed in 1904, became in 1913 the Young Men's Hebrew Association. Arnold Bernstein was mayor of Monroe for almost twenty years, from 1918 until his death in 1937.

LAKE CHARLES (population, 21,207, census of 1940) had a Jewish population of about 300 in 1942. Congregation Temple Sinai was formed in 1895. Services were Reform, conducted according to the Minhag America. In 1899 members of the congregation established Graceland Cemetery. The Lake Charles Hebrew Benevolent Association was organized in 1902 or 1903 to conduct the business connected with the erection of Temple Sinai; the new structure was built and dedicated in 1904. Camillus Angel was rabbi from 1935 to 1936. One of his predecessors was Rabbi Joshua Bloch, who later became chief of the Jewish Division in the New York Public Library. A B'nai B'rith lodge was established in Lake Charles in 1900.

LAFAYETTE (population, 19,210, census of 1940) had a Jewish community of about one hundred persons in 1942. Alexandre Mouton, an Acadian, who had been governor of the state (1843-46) and had presided at the Secession Convention of 1861, gave the Jews of Lafayette ground for a cemetery in 1869 and the site for a synagogue in 1881. The Menachim Aveilim cemetery, established in 1869, has a statue of Mouton. In 1883 Congregation Rodeph Sholom (Reform) built a synagogue on the site donated by Mouton. Emanuel Sternheim was rabbi of Congregation Rodeph Sholom at the time of his death in 1942.

CROWLEY (population 9,523, census of 1940), near Lafayette, with a Jewish community of about fifty in 1942, had a congregation, Emanu El (organized in 1902). In 1938, Congregation Emanu El merged with Rodeph Sholom of Lafayette. Other members of this congregation live in Rayne (population 4,974, census of 1940), with about twenty-five Jews. Jefferson D. Marks was mayor of Crowley in 1904.

NEW IBERIA (population, 13,747, census of 1940), like Lafayette, had in 1942 a Jewish population of somewhat more than one hundred persons. In 1870, if not earlier, Michell Heyman of New Iberia presented a scroll of the Law to his fellow Jews worshipping with him. Another of the Jews who were among the first to settle in New Iberia was Joseph Wise (1830-1902). Congregation Schangary Tefilot (Reform) was organized in 1897. A synagogue was built in 1904. The congregation was ministered to by Dr. Mendel Silber, of New Orleans, from 1915 to 1933.

BOGALUSA. Congregation Beth El (Orthodox) in Bogalusa (population 14,604, census of 1940) was chartered in 1922 and a synagogue was dedicated in 1925. The services are according to the Minhag Chassidim. Bogalusa had a Jewish population of about eighty (1942).

DONALDSONVILLE (population 3,889, census of 1940) had in 1942 about as many Jews as Bogalusa. Congregation Bikur Cholim was organized as early as 1856. The synagogue was dedicated in 1872. The congregation was reorganized in 1890, and in 1901 joined the Union of American Hebrew Congregations (Reform). There is a B'nai B'rith lodge in Donaldsonville, organized in 1902. There is a record of two Jewish mayors, Meyer Leman and David Israel, in the early 1880's.

MORGAN CITY (population 6,969, census of 1940) had Jewish residents before the Civil War. Shaarey Zedek (Reform) was founded in 1871, and the first synagogue was built in 1875. Leopold Loeb, who had come from Bavaria and had settled in Morgan City in 1860, was the cantor. The first resident rabbi, one Lewenstein, and his family died of the yellow fever in 1878. The synagogue was destroyed by fire in 1901 and another building was occupied for worship in the following year; a new synagogue was built in 1929. The congregation included about fifteen members living in Berwick, La., and was ministered to by Dr. Mendel Silber, of New Orleans, from 1915 to 1933. Morris E. Norman was mayor of Morgan City from 1924 to 1931. The Jewish population in 1942 was about sixty.

OPELOUSAS (population 8,980, census of 1940) had a Jewish community of about sixty in 1942. Congregation Gemiluth Chassodim was founded in 1877. In 1929 Temple Emanu El was built and the earlier organization became part of the new congregation. There has been a Jewish burial place, Hebrew Rest Cemetery, at Opelousas for many years. There was also a B'nai B'rith lodge in Opelousas for a while, but it is no longer in existence.

Other small Jewish communities in 1942 were: PLAQUEMINE (population 5,049, census of 1940), with about fifty-five Jews; NATCHITOCHES (population 6,812, census of 1940), with about fifty Jews; and BASTROP (population 6,626, census of 1940), with about forty Jews. In 1856 the Hebrew Benevolent Society of Plaquemine was incorporated for the purpose of building a temple and establishing a cemetery. Land for the cemetery was bought that year, and a hall was bought in 1860. Congregation Ohavi Sholom of Plaquemine was founded in 1878 and held regular services until 1932. The congregation was ministered to by Dr. Mendel Silber, of New Orleans, from 1915 to 1932. B'nai Israel Association was chartered in Natchitoches in 1871. The organization managed the Jewish cemetery and purchased a church in 1904 for a synagogue. Services were discontinued in 1924 for lack of members. In 1877 Congregation B'nai Sholom was organized in Bastrop. In the following year land for a cemetery was purchased. A brick synagogue was built in 1885. By 1923 the services of the congregation were discontinued, and in 1938 the synagogue was torn down.

Temple Sinai was organized in 1892 in ST. FRANCISVILLE (population 821, census of 1940). A synagogue was built in 1902. Max Raisin was the rabbi in 1904. Services were discontinued, however, the following year because of loss of members. In 1942 there were few Jews in St. Francisville.

In 1881 the Hebrew Foreign Mission Association of New Orleans, together with the Hebrew Immigrants' Aid Association, helped establish a cooperative agricultural colony of 173 Russian Jews (about sixty families) at Sicily Island (Catahoula Parish) in the Mississippi delta. The immigrants had a tract of several thousand acres but the settlers were discouraged by a flood of the Mississippi (1882) which swept over the tilled land and washed away houses and stock, and the colony did not last more than a year.

In 1915 the Jewish community of Shreveport, represented by Sidney Herold, brought suit to enjoin the reading of the Bible in the public schools as a violation of the state constitution. The suit was won, and established a precedent followed throughout the state.

Of the Jews of Louisiana who were soldiers, S. Cohen, as well as Judah Touro, fought in defense of New Orleans under General Andrew Jackson in the War of 1812. Adolphus Sterne, who came to Louisiana in 1828 when he was sixteen, formed a company of riflemen and led them as their captain to join the Texans in their war for freedom from Mexican rule (1835-36). Leon Dyer, quartermaster of the state militia, enlisted under General Tom Green and was a major in the same war. Albert Emanuel fought at San Jacinto (1836). Both Dyer and Emanuel fought afterwards in the Mexican War.

One hundred and fifty-three Jews from Louisiana are recorded as having served in the Confederate armies, but this list is not complete (Simon Wolf, for example, lists 224); of these, twenty-six were killed in action and twenty-eight were commissioned officers. Of the three Levy brothers who had joined the Dreux Battery as volunteers, Joseph, a lieutenant, was killed leading a charge at Shiloh, and Eugene was wounded at Petersburg. Attached to Fenner's Battery as a private was Benjamin F. Jonas, afterwards United States Senator from Louisiana, who was one of five brothers, three of whom fought in Mississippi units and one, as a Federal soldier, in an Illinois regiment. Isaac Levy of Pointe Coupee Parish, a staff officer, served through the war with a surgeon's discharge in his pocket. Colonel Edwin I. Kursheedt was in the 2nd Washington Artillery; S. M. Hyams, because of his bravery, rose to be a colonel. Colonel Leon R. Marks was killed at Vicksburg; Major Alexander Hart was wounded at Sharpsburg and again at Gettysburg; Lewis P. Lippman, enlisted as a private and promoted to captain for bravery, was killed at Fredericksburg; Captain J. C. Cohen was killed at Manassas; Captain Isaac L. Lyons was wounded at Malvern Hill; David C. Levy, Jr., promoted from private to lieutenant, was twice wounded and finally was killed at Malvern Hill; so was Lieutenant Henry Clay Marks.

It is noteworthy that of the seven Jews who at various times were members of the United States Senate, three came from Louisiana, namely: Judah P. Benjamin, who represented Louisiana in the United States Senate from 1853 to 1861; he was, afterwards, secretary of war for the Confederacy and secretary of state; Michael Hahn, who was governor of Louisiana, but resigned in 1865 to take a seat in the United States Senate; Benjamin F. Jonas, who had been a member of the state senate from 1872 to 1874, and was a United States senator from 1879 to 1885. There was also a United States Congressman, Adolph Meyer, who served from 1891 to 1908. Henry Michael Hyams, who had been a member of the state assembly from 1852 to 1854, was lieutenant governor of Louisiana from 1856 to 1860. Other members of the state legislature were: Mayer Hahn (senator, 1878-80), Leopold Caspori (senator, 1890-1900), Jules J. Fisher (senator, 1924-), Edwin Warren Moïse (1844-59; speaker of the House of Representatives, 1858; he was afterwards United States district attorney, 1859-61, chief justice of the Confederate state court of Louisiana, 1861-65, and attorney general of the state, 1865-66), William M. Levy (1858-60), Isaac Friedman (1905), Simon Leopold (1905), Nathan Strauss (1908), Bertram Weil, senator (1908), William Winter (1908), David B. Samuel (1912-16), F. J. Dreyfus (1914), Jules Dreyfus (1914), Abe Leopold (1914), Norman Bauer, speaker of the House (1942), George Joel Ginsberg (1928-32; chairman of a number of important committees and a member of the board of managers on behalf of the House of Representatives in prosecuting the impeachment of Governor Huey P. Long before the Senate in 1929), Edward Loeb, David Fink. Morris Marks, a Republican in Reconstruction days and an advocate of equal rights for negroes, was a judge in Ascension Parish in 1868 and was elected to the state senate in 1870 but never took his seat; he was appointed a collector of internal revenue in Louisiana by President Ulysses S. Grant in 1878.

Henry A. Lazarus was a member of the State Supreme Court (1880); Emile Godchaux, who was a member of the state board of education in 1908, sat on the Court of Appeal from 1909 to 1918; Max Dinkelspiel was a member of the Court of Appeal from 1919 to 1924; I. D. Moor was also a judge of that court. Monte M. Lemann, professor of law at Tulane University from 1910 on, was a member of the National Commission on Law Observance and Enforcement (Wickersham Commission) from 1929 to 1931. Charles Weinberger was a United States commissioner in 1917. The following were members of the Orleans Parish School Board: Dave Cohn (1888); John Kohn (1903-8); William M. Levy (1906-7); Edgar B. Stern (1912); Sol Wexler (vice-president, 1912; president, 1913-16); Harry Goodman (1927-28); Isaac S. Heller (1929-40). Lewis Arnheim was mayor of Vidalia from 1869 to 1871.

Louisiana had two Jewish periodicals in 1942: the *Jewish Ledger,* a weekly, established in 1895 and published at New Orleans; *The Jewish Journal,* established in 1937 and published at Shreveport.

See also: NEW ORLEANS; SHREVEPORT; BENJAMIN, JUDAH P.; TOURO, JUDAH.   MENDEL SILBER.

Lit.: The Louisiana Historical Records Survey, Work Projects Administration, *Inventory of the Church and Synagogue Archives of Louisiana: Jewish Congregations and Organizations* (1941); Wolf, Simon, *The American Jew as Patriot, Soldier, and Citizen* (1895; list of Jewish soldiers from Louisiana in the Confederate armies, pp. 190-99).

LOUISSON, CHARLES, New Zealand government official, b. London, 1854; d. Christchurch, New Zealand, 1924. Louisson went to the Antipodes in 1855, settling first in Victoria, Australia, then, in 1865, in New Zealand. Here he entered the brewery business with his brother, Alfred Louisson. Louisson was for ten years a city councillor, for many years a justice of the peace, and in 1888, 1889, 1898 and 1899 mayor of Christchurch. In 1888 he was commissioner for New Zealand at the Melbourne exhibition. Louisson was also for several years president of the Jewish Congregation of Christchurch.

LOUISVILLE, largest city in the state of Kentucky, with a population (1941) of 360,000, of whom some 14,000, or about 3 per cent, were Jews. Little authentic information about the earliest Jewish settlers is available, but the first arrivals seem to have been brothers named Heymann (Hyman), who came about 1814. The Louisville directory of 1834 mentions a Jewish Benevolent Society, and this date may be taken as the beginning of unbroken Jewish life in the city.

Congregation Adath Israel, established in 1836, was granted a State charter in 1843, and from that year on there ensued a steady growth in the Jewish population and in Jewish communal development. The first Adath Israel Temple was dedicated in 1849, and the cemetery in 1876. Among the rabbis who occupied the pulpit at Adath Israel were Emil G. Hirsch (1878-80) and Hyman G. Enelow (1901-12). Joseph Rauch, who succeeded Enelow, was still rabbi in 1942.

Congregation Beth Israel, organized in 1856, had originally been chartered in 1851 as the Polish House of Israel. It was the first Orthodox congregation in the city. Its first synagogue was dedicated in 1857. There were, in 1942, three Orthodox congregations in Louisville, of which the chief rabbi was Chaim

Ben Zion Notelewitz. There was also another Reform congregation besides Adath Israel, and one Conservative congregation. Among the other rabbis in the city were E. M. Bleiberg of Congregation Agudath Achim, Benjamin Brilliant and Charles Chaval, Orthodox, and Jacob J. Gettleman of Adath Jeshurun, Conservative.

Louisville in 1942 had a Jewish Welfare Federation, organized in 1908, and therefore one of the pioneer Federations in the country. It included all the Jewish philanthropic organizations of the city. The Louisville Conference of Jewish Organizations, founded in 1934, comprised every group of the Jewish population. It took official action on all matters touching Jewish problems and the raising of money for national and international Jewish needs, and was the Jewish public forum for vital Jewish questions. There was (1942) a Young Men's Hebrew Association in Louisville, a Jewish hospital, a Jewish children's home, a Hahnasath Orehim (aid to transients) and a Jewish country club. There were also branches of the Zionist Organization of America, the Hadassah, Mizrahi and the Jewish National Workers' Alliance.

The Jewish population has always been prominent and active in all the important affairs of the city, and individual Jews have achieved world-wide distinction. Louisville Jewry counted among its members Lewis N. Dembitz (1833-1907), Jewish savant and erudite jurist, who enriched Jewish learning as well as Kentucky jurisprudence; his nephew, Louis Dembitz Brandeis (1856-1941), Associate Justice of the Supreme Court of the United States and one of the great legal minds of his generation; and Simon Flexner, who made valuable contributions to medicine.

Among the best and most complete libraries concerning modern Palestine in general and the Zionist movement in particular was that in the library of the University of Louisville. This was a gift to the university from Brandeis. In the library were included pamphlets and original autographed editions not to be had elsewhere; it has been pronounced one of the most complete and rarest collections of books on the subject. This collection of Hebraica and Judaica was supplemented by a special fund made available by Congregation Adath Israel.

The University of Louisville had several Jews on its faculty. Armand Earl Cohen and Charles Siegel Frankel were associate professors at the School of Medicine, Sidney Isaac Kornhauser was professor of anatomy and executive secretary of the School of Medicine, and Sara Landau was associate professor in economics. Herman Gilbert Handmaker was professor of law at the university, a member of the Kentucky House of Representatives from 1928 to 1932, and assistant county attorney in 1933 and 1934. Robert A. Persky was also a member of the Kentucky House of Representatives (1933-35). David Alexander Sachs, Jr., was a teacher at the Jefferson School of Law. Grover Grauman Sales was departmental counsel for Louisville and special judge of the Jefferson County Circuit Court, and also a professor at the University of Louisville Law School. Among the other leading Jewish citizens of Louisville were Albert Y. Aronson, managing editor of the Louisville *Times,* and Blanche Beitman Ottenheimer, active in club work and honorary vice-president of the National Council of Jewish Women.   JOSEPH RAUCH.

Lit.: Publications of the American Jewish Historical Society, No. 1 (1892) 100; Selligman, Alfred, and Goldsmith, Charles, *History of Congregation Adath Israel of Kentucky* (1906).

LOURIE, DAVID ABRAHAM, judge, b. Lithuania, 1878, d. Boston, 1930. He arrived in the United States at the age of six, peddled newspapers on the streets of Boston, taught English to immigrants, and despite great economic handicaps put himself through school, graduating from Boston University Law School in 1899. He practised law until 1922, when he was appointed judge of the Municipal Court of Boston. In 1924 he was named by Governor Channing H. Cox a Justice of the Superior Court of Massachusetts, the first Jew to sit on that bench.

Lourie was active in civic and communal affairs, and was especially interested in the Zionist movement, serving as honorary vice-president of the Zionist Organization of America. He was a member of the Chelsea School Committee, president of the Home for Jewish Children, vice-chairman of the executive committee of the Federated Jewish Charities of Boston, honorary vice-president of the national Palestine Foundation Fund, member of the American Jewish Committee, delegate to the first American Jewish Congress, chairman of the Chelsea Board of Health and vice-president of the Bureau of Jewish Education in Boston.

Lit.: The Jewish Advocate, Oct. 16, 1924; *Jewish Daily Bulletin,* Jan. 21, 1930.

LOURIE, HARRY, South African merchant and communal leader, b. Libau, Latvia, 1875. He intended to study for the rabbinate, but under the influence of the Haskalah (enlightenment) movement decided to enter business instead and migrated to Johannesburg, South Africa, in 1895. Here he became one of the leading merchants in the country, supplying the jewelry, diamond and optical trades. His early training in Jewish culture, however, led him to maintain an increasingly active interest in Jewish educational and communal affairs.

In 1897 Lourie helped found and was the first treasurer of the Jewish Young Men's Friendly Association. He was on the committee of the Johannesburg Hebrew High School and honorary Hebrew examiner for several years after 1912. Later he was president of the South African Jewish Board of Education. From 1927 to 1928 he was a member of the executive of the South African Jewish Board of Deputies.

Affiliated with the Zionist movement from the inception of political Zionism, Lourie was a member of the executive of the South African Zionist Federation from 1919 on. He visited Palestine many times, and helped establish the South African Palestine Enterprise (Binyan) Co., in Haifa, as well as other investment concerns. Lourie was one of those responsible for establishing a chair in Hebrew at the Johannesburg University. For many years chairman of the South African Friends of the Hebrew University, he was made a member of the board of governors of the university in 1939. In 1942 he was living temporarily in the United States.

ARTHUR LOURIE (b. Johannesburg, 1903) was the eldest son of Harry Lourie. In 1942 he was living in New York city as secretary of the Emergency Committee for Palestine. Lourie was educated in Johannesburg and later studied at Harvard and Cambridge Universities on fellowships. Although he practised law for a short period, his activity in Zionist affairs brought him the offer of the political secretaryship of the Jewish Agency for Palestine, with headquarters in London. Lourie lived in London until 1940, when he came to the United States to assume his post with the Emergency Committee.

NORMAN LOURIE (b. Johannesburg, 1909) was the youngest son of Harry Lourie. He received his degree from the London School of Economics in 1929. While at the college, he was one of the founders of the Habonim movement, and in 1942 was still serving as its Manhig.   LIBBY BENEDICT.

LOUSADA, a family of Jewish origin that achieved prominence in various parts of Europe, England and the West Indies. The family separated into two groups during the Inquisition in Spain; one group remained in Spain as Neo-Christians, and the other went to Holland to resume the practice of Judaism. Of the Spanish group one member became the Duke de Lousada and Marquis di San Minato. From Holland members of the family emigrated to England and to Jamaica. Moseh Baruch Lousada, son of Isaac de Lousada, was one of the few Jews known to be living in London in 1640; in 1664 he was a member of a committee of Jews who exposed to Charles II an attempt to blackmail the Jews of England and thus forestalled probably tragic consequences. He was one of the first two Parnasim of the Sephardic congregation of his time, and in 1679 he was made a member of the Exchange. A family which spelled its name Louzada and showed the name Baruch frequently was important in 17th cent. Jewish life in Barbados.

In 1848 an Isaac de Lousada of Jamaica presented family papers to Queen Isabella of Spain and convinced her of his right to bear the old Lousada title. He was made Duke of Lousada and Losada, but was not permitted to live in Spain because of his Jewish faith. Of this branch of the family, many of whose members returned to England, there were also subsequently many departures into the Catholic faith, and except for a line descended from Moses Baruch Lousada, they have played no part in Jewish life. Julian G. Lousada (b. 1874) was president of the West London Synagogue and honorary solicitor of the Jewish Board of Guardians.

Lit.: da Costa, Isaac, Noble Families among the Sephardic Jews, pp. 108, 154; Wolf, Lucien, "Anglo-Jewish Families," *Essays in Anglo-Jewish History* (1934).

LOVE (*'ahabah*). The term "love" is used throughout Jewish literature not only for the ordinary sensual emotion, but also and far more frequently to express the highest and finest of relationships, the desire to serve, cherish, protect and bestow benefit upon the object of one's affections. Three types of love are represented as furnishing the motive power for all the finer things of life: the love of God for man, which is the supreme law of the universe; the love of man for God, which is the essence of religion; and the love of man for his family and fellow-humans, which furnishes the incentive to every social virtue. These three forms of love are not set apart; they are intimately connected and interwoven in Jewish thought, and stressed again and again as the highest of principles. They are not the only standards of human conduct; there are also truth, justice, hatred of evil and abhorrence of sin—but over them all love sets the highest standard. It is not surprising therefore that the rabbis uttered such expressions as "The world was created by divine love" and "The will of God is done through love."

The prophets of Israel took the sensual element with which the religion of their time was permeated and turned it into a lofty ideal. Hosea, followed by Jeremiah and Isaiah, portrayed the relationship between God and His people as one akin to the love of husband and wife, or father and child. *Deuteronomy* makes love the foundation of its code. The command, "Thou shalt love the Lord thy God with all thy heart, with all thy soul, and with all thy might" (*Deut.* 6:5), is an explanation of the words "those who love Me" in the Second Commandment (*Ex.* 20:6; *Deut.* 5:10). The admonitions to love God, to keep His statutes, and to obey His voice and His commands, recur again and again in the book (*Deut.* 11:1; 13:4; 19:9; 30:6, 16, 20); Joshua supplicates his people to "take diligent heed to do the commandment and the law . . . to love the Lord . . . and to walk in His ways" (*Josh.* 22:5; cf. *Deut.* 13:4).

Man's love for God is reciprocal to God's love for Israel, and above Israel, for all mankind. The Bible, however, tends to use the term "mercy," rather than "love," in this connection. It was the rabbis of the post-Biblical period who made especial use of the doctrine of divine love to explain the relationship of God to man. To quote but one instance, Akiba said (*Aboth* 3:18): "Beloved is man, for he was created in the image of God; but it was by a special love that it was made known to him that he was created in God's image."

The supreme test of man's love for God, however, is the love that he shows to his fellowmen. The Law of Holiness in *Lev.* 19, which starts out with the idea that man must imitate the holiness and purity of God, emphasizes a series of duties, all predicated upon the love of men for men. Just weights and balances, filial love, equal justice for rich and poor alike, regard for the weak, the halt and the blind, are the actions by which man fulfils the commandment "Thou shalt love thy neighbor as thyself" (*Lev.* 19:18), which Akiba of a later generation regarded as the supreme commandment of the Torah. Lest this doctrine of love be confined to one's actual neighbors and kinsmen, the chapter is careful to remind one that he must also love the stranger as himself (verse 34). The rabbis went still further and extended the idea of love to all humanity, to all "fellow-creatures." Thus the saying of Hillel (1st cent. C. E.) ran: "Be of the disciples of Aaron, loving peace, pursuing peace, loving one's fellow-creatures and bringing them near to the Law" (*Aboth* 1:12). When Hillel was asked to define the essence of the Law, he expressed it in terms of human feelings, not of reward or punishment: "What is hateful to thee, do not do to thy fellow," in other words, to deal with others as fairly and as lovingly as with one's self.

The Talmud states that the Torah begins with an act of love (creation) and ends with an act of love (the burial of Moses by God; *Sotah* 14a), an expression of the idea that love is the essence of the Law and its fulfillment. Thus Divine love and human love become the driving forces in Jewish law and morality; God loves the world and therefore bestows upon man life, freedom of will and the opportunity for perfection; man loves God and therefore serves Him by worship and obedience to the Divine Law that gives practical expression to the love of one's fellowmen. As Judah Abravanel put it, "Love links together the entire universe."

See also ALTRUISM; CHARITY; GOD; MERCY.

SAMUEL J. LEVINSON.

Lit.: Hastings, James, edit., *Dictionary of the Bible*, vol. 3, p. 153; idem, *Encyclopedia of Religion and Ethics*, vol. 8, p. 173; Hirsch, E. G., in *Jewish Encyclopedia*, vol. 6, pp. 21-22; Kohler, K., *ibid.*, vol. 8, pp. 188-90; Cohon, Samuel S., "Love, Human and Divine, in Post-Biblical Literature," *Central Conference of American Rabbis Year Book*, vol. 27 (1917) 244-300.

LOVE, GODDESS OF, *see* ASHERAH; ASTARTE; ISHTAR.

LOVE OF MANKIND, *see* ALTRUISM.

LOVE, WORKS OF, *see* ALTRUISM; CHARITY; PHILANTHROPY.

LOVEMAN, ROBERT, poet and author, b. Cleveland, 1864; d. Dalton, Ga., 1923. He was educated in the public schools of Dalton, and later in life he received an honorary A.M. degree from the University of Alabama. He also traveled and studied in Europe. Loveman wrote many articles on cultural and political subjects for American magazines. He was author of several books, which attained a wide popularity in their time. His works include: *Poems* (3 vols., 1889, 1893, 1897); *A Book of Verses* (1900); *The Gates of Silence, with Interludes of Song* (1903); *Songs from a Georgia Garden, and Echoes from the Gates of Silence* (1905); *The Blushful South and Hippocrene* (1909); *On the Way to Willowdale* (1912); *Sonnets of the Strife* (1917).

LOVENSTEIN, WILLIAM, public official, b. Henrico County, Va., 1840; d. Richmond, Va., 1896. A private in the Confederate Army, he was taken prisoner at Roanoke Island and afterwards exchanged. He served until the end of the Civil War, was a delegate to the State Legislature from Richmond (1869-79), and subsequently a member of the State Senate, of which he was president pro tem, the highest state office ever held in Virginia by a Jew. He was active in the affairs of Congregation Beth Ahabah and of the B'nai B'rith.

Lit.: Ezekiel, H. T., and Lichtenstein, G., *The History of the Jews of Richmond* (1917).

LOW, ALFRED MAURICE, journalist, b. London, 1860; d. London, 1929. He was educated at King's College, London, and for a time in Austria, where some of his relatives lived. In early manhood Low went to the United States, where he switched from architecture to politics. He became Washington correspondent of the Boston *Globe,* and was thus the first non-American Washington correspondent. In 1896 Low became Washington correspondent of the London *Daily Chronicle,* and a short time later assumed the same function for the London *Morning Post.* From 1896 on he was also a regular contributor to the *National Review,* of London. Sharing the views of its editor concerning Germany, Low was one of the earliest publicists who warned Britons and Americans of the increasing German threat. He contributed to most of the important magazines of the United States.

In 1900 Low was charged by the government of the United States with investigating British labor legislation for the United States Department of Labor, which had been founded shortly before that. In 1903 he investigated British trade unions for the same department. Low considered it the principal purpose of his activity to improve relations between Great Britain and the United States. During the first World War he applied himself to explaining the Allied cause to the American public. In 1901 he published the novel *The Supreme Surrender.* His later publications, until 1914, are devoted to the study of the United States; they include *Protection in the United States* (1904), *America at Home* (1908), and *The American People* (1908-11), a study of national psychology which attracted special attention in Europe and destroyed many prejudices. After the outbreak of the first World War, Low published *Great Britain and the War* (1914), *The Freedom of the Sea* (1915), *Blockade and Contraband,* and *The Law of Blockade* (1916). He combined his American and World War studies in a book entitled *Woodrow Wilson* (1918). He was knighted in 1922.

LÖW, DER HOHE RABBI, *see* Löwe Judah ben Bezalel.

LÖW, ELEAZAR (Eleazar ben Leb), rabbi, called Shemen Rokeah after his earliest work, b. Wodzislav, province of Kielce, Poland, 1758; d. Abaujszántó, Hungary, 1837. Both his father, Aryeh Leb, a merchant, and his mother were descendants of outstanding rabbinical scholars. He studied at the Yeshiva of his grandfather, Rabbi Phinehas Selig, author of *Atereth Paz,* in Lask, where he obtained his rabbinical diploma at the age of sixteen. Married to Yitta, a granddaughter of Rabbi Aryeh Leb of Amsterdam (Gur Aryeh), he became, at the age of seventeen, assessor and subsequently president of the rabbinical collegium in his native town. When he was twenty he was appointed rabbi at Piliza, near Cracow, where his fame as a judge of great learning and equity attracted litigants, and his reputation as a great teacher students in large numbers from far and near. At the age of thirty (1788) he published the first volume of his responsa, *Shemen Rokeah* (Precious Oil of the Apothecary). In their approbations, Rabbis Ezekiel Landau, of Prague, Meir Barby of Pressburg, and Jeremiah of Mattersdorf called him *Hagaon Hagadol.*

This first decade of fruitful teaching and study at Piliza was followed by a series of catastrophes. The fortune which his wife had brought him in marriage was lost through the disloyalty of a friend, and in 1792 his wife Yitta died. He remembered her in the preface to his work *Samma Dehayye* (Elixir of Life; 1796). His second wife was a daughter of Rabbi Isaac Abraham of Pintchov, author of *Kether Kehunah,* and a descendant of SHaCH (abbreviation for Sabbatai

Cohen). Poland was at that time beset by war at the hands of three powers that eventually divided the country among themselves. Piliza was incorporated into Russia, while the neighboring Cracow fell prey to Austria. In these years of trouble Eleazar completed his work which was to serve as a guide for further rabbinic decisions, *Torath Hesed* (The Law of Righteousness), on the norms and principles of the Talmud underlying Halachic decisions. The preface to this great work contains a pathetic confession: "I will be brief in my disquisition, for affliction besets me on all sides. The little I have been able to achieve is due to the mercy of the Creator (praised be He) and to heavenly assistance, for (on account of my numerous sins) my head is encompassed with sorrow and care, apart from the burden of the community." The community, indeed, was ruined by the disastrous wars; Rabbi Eleazar was deeply distressed that it could no longer maintain a great Yeshiva.

On a trip to Vienna, undertaken in order to have his books published there, he accepted the rabbinate of Triesch, Moravia, offered him by Mordecai Benét, the chief rabbi of that province. It was there that he adopted, according to the law, a family name and was called Eleazar Löw henceforth. The Yeshiva of this pious community attained its zenith under him. Triesch saw the publication of his *Shaare Hochmah* (Gates of Wisdom; 1807). In the preface to this work he explained its purpose, which was to acquaint his students with the method of the Talmud so that, instead of abstruse Pilpulistic hair-splitting and interpretation, they should acquire a useful instrument in establishing the true meaning of Talmudic teachings.

In 1812 he accepted the district rabbinate of Ronsperg, Bohemia (including the cities of Pilsen and Klattau), which had become vacant through the early death of his son-in-law, Rabbi Samuel Cohen. Ronsperg, a rabbinate of greater importance and more income than Triesch, afforded him an opportunity for carefree study, yet he resented the "new spirit" which was beginning to make inroads into these western regions. His community of Triesch, notwithstanding negotiations carried on in the meantime with Rabbi Akiba Eger, welcomed him again when he returned to it in 1815.

Urged by the Orthodox elements of Hamburg, he voiced, in 1819, his disapproval of the Temple movement, but resorted to persuasion rather than condemnation of his opponents. In the same year his Yeshiva was ruined once more by a great fire which laid Triesch waste and consumed most of his library, including the manuscript of his *Orehoth Mishpat* (Paths of Justice). This event and the Familiantengesetz of Moravia (prohibiting the marriage of Jews except for one single male in each family) induced the sixty-year-old master to accept an invitation from the community of Liptószentmiklós (Liptovsky Svätý Mikulaš), in Northern Hungary (1821). There he once more gathered about him not only numerous students but also the members of the community eager to study. Lessons of the week were summed up and discussed extensively on the Sabbath in the synagogue. Yet the spirit of the new day, proceeding victoriously on its way east, gave the rabbi much concern and induced him, in 1830, to continue teaching and writing at Abaujszántó, in the northeast of Hungary, where traditions had remained intact. There he wrote three more works, among them *Zichron Aharon*, in memory of his son Rabbi Aaron. In 1833 he lost most of his eyesight as the result of a stroke of lightning which came close to him. He continued teaching, aided by his astounding memory, until his death in 1837.

Löw was worshipped far and wide not only for his knowledge but also as a great judge who protected the poor and did not tolerate injustice. In his writings he strove for system and sound method in the study of the Talmud. For him, power of mind did not justify the pursuit of brilliancy and originality in the interpretation of detail; it was an instrument to be used humbly and purposefully in order to understand the teachings in their essence and purity. His spirit was carried far and wide over land and sea by his more than 2,000 students and, through his many sons and daughters, was handed down as a spiritual heritage to numerous rabbinic families in Hungary and elsewhere.

His published works are: *Shemen Rokeah*, responsa and notes (part 1, Novy-Dvor, 1788; part 2, Prague, 1802; part 3, Szinérváralja, 1909; new series, Cracow, 1902); *Samma Dehayye* (homilies; Warsaw, 1796); *Torath Hesed* (Vienna, 1800); an edition of *Mekah Umemkar* by Hai Gaon with notes, *Zer Zahab* (Vienna, 1800); *Shaare Hochmah* (Prague, 1807); "Zer Zahab" in *Ene Haedah*, comments on the Tosafoth of Rabbi Isaiah di Trani and on the notes of Ritba (Rabbi Yom Tob Ishbili) to *Kiddushin* (Prague, 1809); *Hiddushe Hilchoth Shemen Rokeah* (notes to the Talmudic tractates *Berachoth*, *Pesahim* and *Betzah* (Prague, 1812); *Yabin Shemuah* (homilies; Prague, 1814); *Shaare Deah* (notes to *Shulhan Aruch, Yoreh Deah;* Vienna, 1820; part 2, Zólkiew, 1828); *Zichron Aharon* and *Kontereth Hahazakah* (Book of [Legal] Presumptions; Lemberg, 1934); *Maaseh Rokeah*, an annotated edition of *Shulhan Aruch, Orah Hayim* (Lemberg, 1836-37). *Orehoth Mishpat*, his notes to all the other Talmudic tractates and to *Shulhan Aruch, Hoshen Mishpat*, which he rewrote after its destruction by fire, remained unpublished.

BENJAMIN ZEEB Löw, rabbi, called Shaare Torah after his main work (b. Wodzislav, 1777; d. Verbó, Hungary, 1851), was a son of Eleazar Löw. A pupil of his father's, he was rabbi at Rosprza, near Piotrków, and subsequently at Amshonov, in the province of Warsaw. At the age of seventeen he edited, in collaboration with Abraham Abush Tannenbaum, notes to the responsa of Rabbi Isaac Alfasi (Vienna, 1794). In 1812 he followed his father to Bohemia, becoming rabbi of Kolin (1812-26). In 1821 he published the first volume of his great work, *Shaare Torah* (Gates of the Law), on the basic principles of Halachah. The first part deals with the principle of *ne'emanuth*, or religious authenticity. In 1826 he followed his father to Hungary, becoming rabbi of Nagytapolcsány, and in 1836 of Verbó. The second part of *Shaare Torah*, on *hazakah*, or the different kinds of legal presumption, was published in the year of his death (Vienna, 1851); the third part on *rab*, or the principle of plurality, was published

by his son Jeremiah (Sátoraljaujhely, 1872), while the fourth part, on the testimony of single witnesses and the modalities of assumption or estimate (*umdana*), was still unpublished in 1942. He had hundreds of pupils, and was considered one of the keenest intellects among Talmudists of his time.

JEREMIAH Löw, rabbi (b. Kolin, Bohemia, 1812; d. Sátoraljaujhely, Hungary, 1874), was a son of Benjamin Zeeb Löw. He followed his father to Hungary in 1826 and became rabbi of Nagymagyar; he succeeded him in the rabbinate of Verbó (1851). He was subsequently rabbi of Sátoraljaujhely, and his Yeshiva was one of the largest in Hungary. He was surnamed Yirmeyahu Harif (Jeremiah the keenminded). As the recognized leader of Hungarian Orthodoxy, he was appointed, by the conference of Orthodox rabbis held at Nyiregyháza in 1864, speaker of a delegation which protested to Francis Joseph I against the establishment of a rabbinical seminary in Hungary. At the National Jewish Congress of 1868 to 1869, Löw vigorously opposed the Reformist majority, but he was also against the secession of the Orthodox whom he did not join, and thus became the originator of the status quo (the same status as before) communities. He did not, however, give them a strong central organization, and his son and successor, Eleazar Löw, in 1886 seceded from the main body of the Sátoraljaujhely community and formed an Orthodox congregation.

A pupil of the rationalistic, lucid school of thinking of his father and grandfather, Jeremiah Löw fought Hasidism, which had been established in Sátoraljaujhely by his predecessor, Rabbi Moses Teitelbaum. He corresponded with many rabbis of his time. *Dibre Yirmeyahu*, his notes to Maimonides' *Mishneh Torah*, was published after his death by his son (part 1, Sátoraljaujhely, 1875; part 2, Munkács, 1876). Other works of his remained unpublished.

His son Eleazar, after founding an Orthodox congregation at Sátoraljaujhely, was rabbi at Ungvár from 1887 until his death in 1918. His work *Pekudath Eleazar* was in turn published by his son Wolf Löw (d. 1935), author of *Anshe Hashem*.

ANNA BETTELHEIM.

Lit.: Münz, L., *Rabbi Eleasar, genannt Schemen Rokeach* (1895); Münz, J., *Stammtafel des Rabbi Eleasar Löw, genannt Schemen Rokeach* (1926); Gold, H., *Die Juden und Judengemeinden Mährens* (1929) 542; Wachstein, B., *Mafteah Hahespedim*, vol. 1 (1922) 10; vol. 2 (1927) 8; vol. 3 (1930) 15; Löwenstein, L., *Index approbationum*, Nos. 922 and 927; Singer, L., "Rabbi Eleasar Löw," *Judaica*, No. 21-22 (1937) 3.

LÖW, IMMANUEL, rabbi and savant, son of Lipót, b. Szeged, Hungary, 1854. Upon his ordination by the Lehranstalt für die Wissenschaft des Judentums of Berlin, in 1878, he succeeded to the rabbinate of Szeged, which had become vacant by the death of his father in 1875. As a rabbi he continued the tradition of his father, and was known as a great orator. A collection of one hundred of his sermons, *Száz beszéd,* was published in 1923. He commemorated the centenary of his congregation in 1885 by publishing, in collaboration with Zsigmond Kulinyi, a history of the community of Szeged, *A szegedi zsidók.* He also published a prayer-book for women in Mag-

Immanuel Löw

yar, as well as poetic translations of *Song of Songs* and of various psalms.

In 1920, in connection with the anti-Semitic counter-revolution in Hungary, he was kept in prison for several months. Upon the accusation of a journalist without reputation it was alleged that Löw had fostered the rule of the Soviets in Hungary; he was acquitted, there being no trace of evidence against him. In 1927 he was elected to the Upper Chamber of Parliament as representative of the "congressional" (as distinct from the Orthodox) Jewish community of Hungary, an incumbency which he held until 1940, when Jewish representation in the Hungarian Upper Chamber was abolished.

His fame rests upon his philological and archeological research. He received his Ph.D. degree in 1879 for a dissertation entitled *Aramäische Pflanzennamen*. This work of forty-nine pages was increased by further research, and a new edition appeared in 1881. It was followed by *Meleagros aus Gedera und die Flora aramaea* (1883). The young savant was later invited to collaborate on the *Hebräisches und aramäisches Wörterbuch über das alte Testament* (edit. Gesenius, 10th ed., 1886; 11th ed. 1890) and on the *Lexicon syriacum* (Brockelmann edit., 1895). He annotated Samuel Krauss' *Griechische und lateinische Lehnwörter im Talmud, Midrasch und Targum* (1899), and collaborated on his *Talmudische Archäologie* (1910-12).

His works on philology and archeology appeared in the journals of Jewish and Oriental sciences of several countries. He specialized in research on the fauna and flora in Bible, Talmud and rabbinic literature. His life's work was summed up in the four volumes of *Die Flora der Juden* (1924-34), a work arranged according to the botanical system and published with the aid of the Alexander Kohut Memorial Foundation. By the combined effort of the vast research of several decades in the fields of comparative linguistics, archeology and botany which he devoted to this work, Löw brought into the realm of tangible reality many references and incidents in Jewish literature. He facilitated the identification of the Palestine of today with the setting of Biblical and post-Biblical events, thus providing a link between knowledge of the past and the present.

The jubilee issue of the *Monatsschrift für Geschichte und Wissenschaft des Judentums* (January, 1934), published in honor of his eightieth birthday, was planned by George Alexander Kohut and Samuel Krauss. The Hebrew University of Jerusalem joined in the celebration. In 1941 he donated his library, consisting of over 6,000 rare books, to the Jewish community of Szeged.

Löw was a member of the Jewish Agency for Palestine, vice-president of the Hungarian Pro Palestina League, and life member of the Szeged city council. The Jewish Theological Seminary of America and the Jewish Institute of Religion conferred honorary doctorates upon him.   ANNA BETTELHEIM.

LÖW, LIPÓT (LEOPOLD), rabbi and savant, b. Czernahora, Moravia, 1811; d. Szeged, Hungary, 1875. He was descended from "Der Hohe Rabbi Löw" of Prague. In Löw's education, Jewish and secular trends ran parallel. In his native village he received instruction from a private tutor in Yiddish, and from the Catholic priest in the vernacular. Six years of intense study—spent at the Yeshivas of Trebitsch, Kismarton (Eisenstadt) and Leipnik (1824-30)—were fortified by five years at the Protestant Lyceum of Pozsony (Pressburg) and at the Universities of Pest and Vienna (1835-40). Löw spent the five years from 1830 to 1835 at Prossnitz as a student of Rabbi Löw Schwab, his future father-in-law. Studies of classical and modern languages, in addition to more modern training in Jewish theology during this period, prepared him for the extensive study of dogmatics, ethics, exegesis, natural history, archeology and orientalia which became the foundation for his later work on the study and interpretation of historical Judaism.

In 1840 Löw was elected rabbi of Nagykanizsa, Hungary, where he introduced the use of correct German instead of the time-hallowed Judeo-German, and founded schools where Hungarian, too, was taught. In 1844 he edited *Ben Chananja,* a journal of Jewish interest; in the same year he began agitating for emancipation and preaching in Magyar. In the *Pesti Hirlap,* the daily newspaper edited by Louis Kossuth, he demanded emancipation not dependent on the convocation of a Sanhedrin as proposed by Kossuth. He is also credited with having prevented, in 1848, the introduction of a Kossuth bill that sought to sanction mixed marriages with all the offspring to be raised in the Christian faith, and to place the Jews of Hungary under civil jurisdiction, and to dissolve the Jewish community as a political unit.

Löw's election to the rabbinate of Pápa, in 1846, brought into the limelight his conflict with Orthodox Jewry. Its representatives in the community of Pápa demanded that the authorities suspend a rabbi who had departed from law and custom, but they failed to carry their point in the courts of law. Löw taught

Hebrew at the Protestant College of Pápa and enjoyed friendly relations with Christian ministers. At the outbreak of the Magyar national revolution in 1848 he became a chaplain in the revolutionary army, and by his rousing speeches caused many to join. He and his father-in-law, Löw Schwab, then chief rabbi of Pest, were arrested in 1849 on charges of sedition; both were pardoned through the intervention of Löw's wife with an Austrian princess.

In 1850 Löw accepted a call as rabbi of Szeged, a community in a purely Magyar region which proved more receptive to his teachings. In his harmonious relationship with the congregation as well as with the non-Jewish notables and people of Szeged he devoted himself to constructive work in various directions: to a historical study of Judaism; to a vigorous defense of the Jews, in other channels, in the course of which he became one of the great figures of Hungarian national life.

In 1855 he published *Hamafteah,* an introduction to Biblical exegesis among the Jews. In 1858 he resumed publication of *Ben Chananja.* His opinions on matters of Jewish law, ritual and education were frequently sought by the courts, the government, other rabbis and communities. These views proved to be a shaping influence in the religious life of Hungarian Jewry. As is indicated also by the title of his first pamphlet, "Die Reform des rabbinischen Ritus auf rabbinischem Standpunkte" (preface to A. Chorin, *Yeled Zekunim,* 1839), he undertook the adjustment of tradition to contemporary life on rabbinic principles. He held that in the history of Halachah (law), individual rabbis claimed the authority to make decisions without submitting to the letter of the Talmud.

Resistance of the Orthodox caused him to abandon his blueprint for a reform of cult and law which he did not wish to impose upon the Jewish community before a change of inner attitude had been attained. He had combatted the Kossuth plan for a Sanhedrin, and abstained from attending the National Jewish Congress of 1868 to 1869, a government project, because he felt that a religious revival could not be dictated from without.

Löw's dauntless defense of the Jews and his convincing authority and erudition turned many an anti-Semite into an advocate of emancipation. His refusal to administer the Jewish oath, and his historical essay on the subject, *A zsidó eskü multja* (1868), resulted in the abolition of that derogatory practice.

Löw inaugurated many synagogues in Hungary, and his sermons preached on these as well as on more important occasions in Hungarian national life elevated him to a place among the eminent orators and patriots of the nation. He was a member of the city council of Szeged, served as member on all city committees and as spokesman for the city in numerous delegations and on public occasions. His death was declared a national loss, and on the occasion of the nation-wide celebration of the centenary of his birth a street was named after him at Szeged.

Löw was the first to write about the history of the Jews in Hungary. Among the works published in his lifetime, *Die graphischen Requisiten* (1870-71); *Die Lebensalter in der jüdischen Literatur* (1875); and the fragment of *Der synagogale Ritus* (1884),

which was planned to include also investigations on labor and means of transportation in Jewish antiquity, were the first major monographs on Jewish archeology. His minor writings were published by his son, Immanuel Löw, in five volumes, *Gesammelte Schriften* (1899-1900).   ANNA BETTELHEIM.

Lit.: Loew, William N., *Leopold Loew: a Biography* (1912); Eisler, Mátyás, "Löw Lipót," *Magyar Zsidó Szemle* (1911) 161-77; Hochmuth, A., *Leopold Löw als Theologe, Historiker und Publizist* (1871); *Magyar Zsidó Lexikon* (1929) 543; Bernstein, Béla, *Az 1848/49-iki magyar szabadsagharc és a zsidók* (1898) 148.

LÖW, MORITZ, astronomer and geodesist, b. Makó, Hungary, 1841; d. Gross-Lichterfelde, near Berlin, 1900. He studied at the Universities of Leipzig and Vienna from 1861 to 1864, and received his Ph.D. degree from the University of Pest in 1867. He became an assistant at the Leipzig observatory, and in 1883 departmental chief of the Prussian Geodetic Institute at Potsdam, with the title of professor.

In addition to a number of minor works which appeared in *Astronomische Nachrichten* from 1872 through 1881 and in 1889, Löw published the volumes *Détermination télégraphique de la différence de longitude Genève Strasbourg* (E. Plantamour, co-author; 1879); *Astronomisch- geodätische Ortsbestimmungen im Harz* (1882); *Polhöhe-bestimmungen im Harzgebiet, ausgeführt 1887-91* (1894 and 1898). He also edited the scientific publications of his section in *Veröffentlichungen des Geodätischen Instituts, Potsdam.*

Lit.: Wininger, S., *Grosse Jüdische National-Biographie; Biographisches Jahrbuch und deutscher Nekrolog,* vol. 5, col. 105; Poggendorff, J. C., *Biographisch-literarisches Handwörterbuch zur Geschichte der exacten Wissenschaften,* vol. 3, p. 825; vol. 4, p. 904; *Catalogue de la Bibliothèque Nationale,* vol. 100.

LOW, SIR SIDNEY, historian, b. Blackheath, England, 1857; d. London, 1932. He was the son of Maximillian Low, a Hungarian liberal who came to England following the failure of the Kossuth revolution (1848). Low was educated at Oxford and became a barrister at Inner Temple. From 1888 to 1897 he was the editor of the *St. James Gazette,* and during this period he is known to have given encouragement to many writers who later became famous, notably Rudyard Kipling and H. G. Wells. In 1904 Low was editor of the *Standard,* and during this year also were published the *Dictionary of English History,* which he had written in collaboration with F. S. Pulling, and *The Governance of England,* which Low wrote alone.

The Governance of England became a textbook for the study of English government, and established Low's reputation as an essentially conservative historian. During the royal visit to India in 1905 and 1906, Low was a special newspaper correspondent, and later toured many other parts of the world as a reporter. His style, adapted to newspaper use, was readable and informative, and he applied it in his many books as well. Among his other published works were: *A Vision of India* (1907); *Political History of the Reign of Queen Victoria* (1907); *De Quincey* (1911); *Egypt in Transition* (1914); *The Spirit of the*

Allied Nations (1915); *Italy in the War* (1916); *The Call of the East* (1921); *The British Constitution* (1928); *Indian States and Princes* (1929). In *The Spirit of the Allied Nations* Low pointed out that the problems of empire and the problem of nationality would have to be solved as a prerequisite to lasting peace. He pointed out that the will to existence and the will to power had to be harmonized with the demands of civilization. Low was knighted in 1918, when he was editor of the wireless service of the Ministry of Information. His niece Ivy Low, daughter of his brother Walter, married Maxim Litvinoff.

Lit.: Chapman-Huston, Desmond, *The Lost Historian* (1936).

LÖW, TIBOR, chief judge of the Hungarian Court of Appeals, b. Budapest, 1873; d. Budapest, 1942. He was a son of Tóbiás Löw and a grandson of Lipót Löw. After studying at the Universities of Budapest and Leipzig, he was admitted to the bar and also qualified as a judge; he received his first juridical appointment in 1899. In 1921 he was named chief judge of the Royal Tribunal of Budapest, in 1925 assistant judge, and subsequently chief judge at the Hungarian Court of Appeals. Retired from his juridical duties, he was appointed, in 1941, a member of the National Board of Hungarian Jewish Communities of Congressional Organization. He contributed articles to periodicals of law on problems of civil and credit law. His published work, *Das ungarische Handelsgesetz,* attained several editions.

LÖW, TÓBIÁS, Royal Hungarian deputy attorney general, son of Lipót, b. Nagykanizsa, Hungary, 1844; d. Budapest, 1880. After serving as a secretary at the Hungarian ministry of justice, he was appointed, at the age of twenty-six, deputy attorney general. He published, by commission of the ministry of justice, the Hungarian penal code of law with a full collection of precedents. In addition to translating into Hungarian several major works on jurisprudence, he published a volume on civil marriage, reedited *Magyarország közjoga* (The Common Law of Hungary) by Emil Pécsi, and edited, from 1870 on, *Magyar Igazságügy,* a journal of law. He died at the age of thirty-six.

LÖWE JUDAH BEN BEZALEL (known as Der Hohe Rabbi Löw and as the Maharal of Prague), famous rabbi, b. probably Posen, about 1525; d. Prague, 1609. From about 1553 to 1573 he was rabbi in Nikolsburg, Moravia; after that time, except for two short intervals in Moravia and Posen, he functioned in Prague, where he was finally recognized as the religious head of the community. The special achievements he accomplished in the community were the organization of the famous Prague Hebrah Kaddisha (burial society) and the establishment of a Talmudic Academy, the Klaus, which burned down in 1689 and was replaced by the later "Klaus synagogue." His pupils included such famous men as Yom Tob Lipmann Heller and David Gans, and he won expressions of honor and admiration from Solomon Luria, Meir of Lublin, Samuel Bacharach and others, who called him "the iron pillar that supports Israel," "our breath of life" and "the marvel of the age."

Statue of Löwe Judah ben Bezalel, known as Der Hohe Rabbi Löw

He was equally honored by non-Jews, and in particular was friendly with the astronomer Tycho Brahe. Through the instrumentality of the latter Löwe Judah had an audience with Emperor Rudolph II (February 16, 1592) which lasted for a long time; however, the subjects of their discussion were never revealed.

He wrote about fifteen works on rabbinic subjects, the most important of which is *Gur Aryeh* (Lion's Whelp; Prague, 1578), a supercommentary to Rashi on the Pentateuch. In all his writings and teachings he laid stress on understanding the simple and literal meaning of the passages studied; he opposed excess of casuistry (Pilpul) and was not too friendly to Cabala. He insisted that children should have a thorough grounding in Bible and Mishnah before they took up the Talmud, and he opposed the *Shulhan Aruch* as an authority, because this would lead to a neglect of the Talmudic sources from which so many of the laws were derived.

As was natural in view of the high esteem in which Löwe Judah was held by his contemporaries, legends clustered about his life. He was credited with being a miracle worker; thus he is said to have shown the emperor his far-off castle by television. The most famous story is that of the Golem which he created out of clay by the use of an amulet bearing the Name of God; every Friday evening he would remove the amulet from his creation in order that it might not profane the Sabbath by working, but once he forgot, and after that the Golem was laid away permanently and was believed to rest in the attic of the Prague synagogue. In later times, when the ghetto was torn down, a statue of Der Hohe Rabbi Löw, created by Ladislaus Saloun, was placed before the new city hall. The story of the rabbi and his friends, as well as of the Golem, has been used by numerous writers, such as Holitscher, Meyrink, Frischmann, Brod and Salus.

See also GOLEM.

Lit.: Hock, in Lieben, *Gal Ed* (1856), German section, p. 2 et seq. (Lieben and Rapoport also have articles on the subject in this volume); Grün, N., *Der Hohe Rabbi Löw* (1885); *Sippurim* (1883).

LOWE (LÖWE), ADOLF, economist and sociologist, b. Stuttgart, Germany, 1893. He was living in New York city in 1942. He studied at the Universities of Munich, Berlin and Tübingen, obtaining the J.D. degree. From 1914 to 1915 he served with the German Army in France. Having published *Arbeitslosigkeit und Kriminalität* (1914) and *Wirtschaftliche Demobilisation* (1916), he became, after the first World War, an adviser to the government of the Weimar Republic on matters of social legislation, reparations policy and national economy. He served at the Reich Ministries of Demobilization, Labor and Economic Affairs (1918-24) and at the International Conferences of Geneva (1921 and 1925) and Genoa (1922). While serving at the Reich Bureau of Statistics (1924-26) he founded the Institute for Business Cycles Research (Institut für Konjunkturforschung), Berlin (1925); from 1926 to 1930 he was a permanent expert assigned to the German Enquête Commission.

In 1930 he became professor of economic theory and sociology at the University of Kiel, where he had lectured from 1924; in 1931 he obtained the chair of political economy at the University of Frankfort. Deprived of it by the Nazi regime, he was Rockefeller fellow and honorary research fellow at the University of Manchester, England (1933-38); he taught at that university until 1940. On the occasion of his becoming a British subject he changed his name from Löwe to Lowe. From 1940 on he was a member of the Graduate Faculty of Political and Social Science, New York city.

Lowe belonged to the school of economists who developed after the first World War a new approach to economic problems. While still in Germany he elaborated ideas similar to those of the Keynesian school in Cambridge and of the economists of Sweden. At the same time he continued the tradition of the German social economists who emphasized the sociological approach to economics and the interconnection of social, historical and economic facts. An eminent educator, Lowe also developed the theory of the sociology of education.

His main works in English include: *Economics and Sociology* (1935); *The Price of Liberty* (1937); *The Universities in Transformation* (1940).

LOWE, ELIAS AVERY, paleographer, b. Kalvaria, Lithuania, 1879. He was educated at the College of the City of New York (1894-97) and at Cornell University (A.B., 1902). He later traveled in Europe and studied at the University of Halle and the University of Munich (Ph.D., 1907). He was a fellow at the American School of Rome, Italy, from 1908 to 1910. He occupied the post of Sandars reader at Cambridge University in 1914. In 1936 he was awarded an honarary D.Litt. degree by Oxford University.

In 1911 he became an associate in paleography at the Carnegie Institution at Washington, D.C. He was appointed lecturer in paleography at Oxford in 1913 and reader in 1927. In 1936 he became a professor at the Institute for Advanced Study at Princeton, N.J. He still held this position in 1942.

Lowe was one of the outstanding authorities on both classical and medieval Latin paleography. In addition to many articles for learned journals, he was the author of a number of books in several languages, including: *Die ältesten Kalendarien aus Monte Cassino* (1908); *Studia Palaeographia* (1910); *The Bobbia Missal* (1920); *"Handwriting" in the Legacy of the Middle Ages* (1926); *Codices Latini Antiquiores* (3 vols., 1934, 1935 and 1938).

LOWE, JAMES HENRY, publisher and author, b. Brighton, England, 1852. He was the author of *Tutorial Preparation for Mishnoh and Gemoro* (1926); *Rashi on Genesis* (1928); *Oriental Calendars* (1935 and 1936); and *Jewish Essentials* (1938). Lowe was the owner of the Hebrew Compendium Publishing Company, and had for a time served as managing secretary of the Jewish Colonial Trust. In 1942 he was living in London.

LOWELL, city in northern Massachusetts, with a population (1941) of 101,331, of whom approximately 2,500, or 2.5 per cent., were Jews. Although most of the Jews in Lowell arrived shortly after the Kishinev pogrom (1905) from the Lithuanian communities of Grodno, Vilna and Suwalk, the first ten Jewish families to settle in the city came between 1881 and 1893.

In the beginning, religious services were conducted in a small rented room; in 1889 the first Jewish congregation, Hevra Kehillath Jacob, was founded, and larger quarters were rented. Elias Wolfson served both as rabbi and Shohet for forty years. In 1906 Congregation Anshe S'fard was founded by Russian Jews, and later the Montefiore Society Synagogue by the Lithuanian Jews. In 1933 Elie Kahn, a graduate of the Volozhin Yeshiva, became rabbi of both Orthodox synagogues, and later was elected rabbi for life.

The Lowell Hebrew Community Center, combined with Temple Beth El (Conservative), was organized in 1927. Bernard H. Ziskind occupied the pulpit until 1929, and was succeeded by Joseph Warren (1930—).

The largest men's organization is the B'nai B'rith Lodge, organized in 1920 under the leadership of Benjamin S. Pouzzner (d. 1926), publisher and editor of the Lowell *Sunday Telegram*. Several divisions of Hadassah are affiliated with the Community Center. There is a Zionist district and a Poale Zion group. The Lowell Post of the Jewish War Veterans, organized in 1930, has a Ladies' Auxiliary, organized in 1939. Lowell also has a unit of the Workmen's Circle.

Various local charitable organizations, such as the Ladies' Helping Hand, the Gemilath Hasadim (relief) and the Hachnasath Orehim (aid to transients), have coordinated their fund-raising activities in a Jewish

Isaac Lowenberg

community chest. Significant contributions to overseas funds and national agencies are raised through the Lowell United Jewish Appeal.

There are two religious schools in Lowell, the Hebrew Free School (Orthodox), organized in 1910, and the other at the Lowell Hebrew Community Center (Conservative), organized in 1927. The city has two Jewish cemeteries, the older of which is maintained by the Israel Brotherhood and the second by Merrimack Lodge, Independent Order Brith Abraham.

For the most part, the Jews of the community are engaged in merchandising, manufacturing, and the free professions. Comparatively few have held public office of any kind. Bessie London Pouzzner succeeded her husband as publisher of the Lowell *Sunday Telegram*.   JOSEPH WARREN.

Lit.: *Illustrated History of Lowell and Vicinity* (1897) 740.

LOWENBERG, ISAAC, mayor, b. Hechingen, Hohenzollern, Germany, 1837; d. Natchez, Miss., 1888. He came to the United States at the age of seventeen. He worked and studied at Cincinnati and at Hamilton, Miss., until the Civil War broke out in 1861. He volunteered for the Union Army and served with the commissary department. After the war Lowenberg settled in Natchez, where he conducted a wholesale grocery business. He was one of the leaders of communal life and became very popular with all citizens, fostering the intellectual growth of the city. He was instrumental in routing the railroad through Natchez. In 1872 he was elected alderman, and acted as chairman of the finance committee for six years. He successfully ran for mayor in 1882, carrying every ward. He was unanimously reelected in 1884 and nominated again in 1886, though he refused to accept the office this time for reasons of health. In 1887 he was elected president of the National Bank of Natchez.

LÖWENFELD, RAPHAEL, writer and stage director, b. Posen, 1854; d. Berlin, 1910. He started his literary career as a journalist in Berlin and St.

Petersburg. In 1894 he founded the Schiller Theater in Berlin, the first theatre performing dramas of literary value for a popular audience and without any financial profit. This first Schiller Theater gave its performances in the old building of the Wallner Theater. In 1902 Löwenfeld rented the Friedrich Wilhelmstädtisches Theater in addition to the Schiller Theater. The success and reputation of these stages became so great that in 1907 he erected a new modern theatre building, the Schiller Theater in Berlin-Charlottenburg, which later was taken over by the Prussian state. The founding of the Schiller Theater made Löwenfeld an outstanding figure in the history of the popular theatre in Germany.

Besides his theatrical activities, Löwenfeld became noted as the champion in Germany of Leo Tolstoi. He translated and edited Tolstoi's works, first in eight volumes (1891-93), later (1910-11) in thirty-three volumes. In 1892 he published *Gespräche über und mit Tolstoi.*

LÖWENSTAMM, MAX (known also as Mordecai Löwenstamm), cantor and composer of synagogal music, b. Trebitsch, Moravia, 1814; d. Munich, Germany, 1881. After studying Hazanuth in Prague and Vienna, in the latter city under the noted cantor and composer Salomon Sulzer, Löwenstamm served as cantor in Prague (1840-42), as chief cantor of the New Temple in Pest (1842-47), and from 1847 on as chief cantor in Munich. As a result of his successful synthesis of the elements of Polish Jewish liturgical music with those of the Jewish liturgical music of Southern Germany, he acquired a great name in the history of modern synagogal music. His synagogal song book *Zemiroth Leel Hai* was published posthumously by his son Franz Josef Löwenstamm (1882; 2nd ed., 1900), and became a favorite with Jewish congregations.

Lit.: Friedmann, Aaron, *Lebensbilder berühmter Kantoren*, vol. 2, pp. 58-67.

LÖWENSTAMM, SAUL BEN ARYEH LÖB, rabbi and author, b. Rzeszow, Poland, 1717; d. Amsterdam, Holland, 1790. Until about 1747 Löwenstamm served as rabbi in Lokaczy, Volhynia, then went to Dubno as successor to his father-in-law Abraham ben Shalom ben Shachna Kahana. In 1755, when Löwenstamm's father, who had been rabbi of the Ashkenazic community of Amsterdam, died, Löwenstamm was called to take his place and remained there for the rest of his life. When the Council of Four Lands met in Jaroslaw in 1754, Löwenstamm was present as the representative of Volhynia.

Of his published works, *Binyan Ariel* is the best-known. It consists of two parts: notes to the Pentateuch and to the Megilloth, and notes to the Talmud. The book was first published in Amsterdam in 1788, and a new edition was issued in Lemberg in 1885. Löwenstamm's father established a school in Amsterdam which the son rebuilt in 1778.

LÖWENSTEIN, RUDOLF, poet, b. Breslau, Germany, 1819; d. Berlin, 1891. He was baptized at the age of nine. In the following year, after his father's death, Löwenstein went to Bunzlau and was educated there, in the orphan asylum, at the expense of King

Solomon Lowenstein

Frederick William III of Prussia. Despite the royal favor, Löwenstein adhered to liberalism. He studied philology and intended to become a teacher, but he turned to politics and became a journalist. His political poems, those expressing liberal opposition as well as national sentiment, were widely popular in Germany. Many of them grew into folk songs or soldiers' songs, such as the one about the chassepot in 1870, or students' songs, which were printed in the *Allgemeines Deutsches Kommersbuch*.

Löwenstein was also one of the best modern poets of children's songs. Many verses in his collection *Löwensteins Kindergarten* (1846) and of his *Kinderland* (1886) were set to music by Taubert and other composers, and illustrated by painters of the Düsseldorf school. In 1848 Löwenstein and David Kalisch founded the *Kladderadatsch,* whose actual director Löwenstein was until it abandoned liberalism in 1887. Löwenstein's satiric poems on Bismarck met with great applause, not the least on the part of Bismarck himself, who dealt with Löwenstein very courteously even when he persecuted him.

Although Löwenstein never concealed his liberalism, he was highly esteemed by conservative artists and learned men. He was a member of the club Der Tunnel, where political personages of all shades were united. In 1890 Löwenstein published a selection of his lyrical poems, *Aus bewegten Zeiten.*

Lit.: Hofmann, R., *Der Kladderadatsch und seine Leute* (1898).

LOWENSTEIN, SOLOMON, social service executive, b. Philadelphia, 1877; d. New York city, 1942. He received his B.A. degree from the University of Cincinnati in 1898, and his rabbinical degree from the Hebrew Union College in 1901.

Even prior to his completion of the rabbinical course, Lowenstein entered the social service field, then still in its early stages, when it was made up of sepa-

rately functioning groups looking little beyond simple charity. Lowenstein's first association with social work was as head worker in the Jewish Settlement in Cincinnati. Later, in 1901, he was made superintendent of the United Jewish Charities in Cincinnati. In 1904, with his coming to New York as assistant manager of the United Jewish Charities, Lowenstein arrived where his organizational talent was to make him one of the most significant figures in 20th cent. social service development. From 1905 to 1920 he was superintendent of the Hebrew Orphan Asylum, and in 1920 Lowenstein assumed the executive directorship of the Federation of Jewish Philanthropic Societies. For fifteen years he held this post, then he was made executive vice-president and remained in this position until his death.

Although, from 1920 on, Lowenstein was involved in almost every Jewish philanthropy of local, national and international scope, and was, besides, active in civic affairs, it was in the directorship of Federation that his influence was most telling. The period of his incumbency brought not only new viewpoints created by expansion and combinations in philanthropy, but acute needs produced by economic disaster and, finally, the entry of public service agencies into what had previously been the province of private endeavor. For all these changing conditions Lowenstein was prepared, not only with resilience, but with foresight. Expansion and systematization of philanthropy, under Lowenstein, was to take away the stigma of charity, but not to depersonalize relationships or freeze the humaneness which was its basis.

Lowenstein's other activities increased with the degeneration of world conditions after 1929. He was a member of the Temporary Emergency Relief Committee of New York State in 1934, and in 1936 was on the New York State Board of Social Welfare. He was chairman of the executive group of the New York city coordinating committee on unemployment in 1932 and also chairman of the Welfare Council committee on social service exchange. The advent of Hitlerism threw Lowenstein into international philanthropy, which he had already served, in 1918 to 1919, as deputy commissioner of the American Red Cross to Palestine; while there he served in a similar capacity with the American Jewish Joint Distribution Committee. He was chairman of the German Jewish Childrens' Aid (1934). Lowenstein was also a trustee of the American Jewish Committee and of the Joint Distribution Committee, vice-president of the American Friends of the Hebrew University, and occupied numerous other posts in social service and philanthropic activities. Among these were the presidency of the National Conference of Jewish Social Service in 1922, of the New York State Conference of Social Work in 1923, and of the New York City Conference of Social Work in 1932 to 1933. Lowenstein was also, in 1938, president of the National Conference of Social Work, an honor which had previously been achieved only by two other Jews, Julian W. Mack and Lillian D. Wald. Lowenstein received an honorary D.H.L. degree from the Hebrew Union College in 1926.

JONAH B. WISE.

Lit.: *New York Times,* Jan. 21, 1942, editorial page; *American Hebrew,* Nov. 20, 1931, p. 9; Jan. 30, 1942, p. 3.

LOWENTHAL, MARVIN, writer and lecturer, b. Bradford, Pa., 1890. He studied at the University of Wisconsin (A.B., 1915) and at Harvard (M.A., 1916). He was connected with *The Menorah Journal* from 1921 to 1930, first as associate editor and then as foreign editor. Before that he had been director of the Zionist Bureau of the Pacific Coast at San Francisco (1916-20); while foreign editor of *The Menorah Journal* he was European representative of the American Jewish Congress (1926-28) and secretary of the World Congress for International Peace Through Religion (1928-30).

Lowenthal is the author of the following: *A World Passed By* (1933; the history of the Jews and their culture traced by means of exhibits in museums and the sights and monuments of places in which they lived); *The Autobiography of Montaigne* (1935; excerpts from the writings of Montaigne arranged in chronological order); *The Jews of Germany* (1936; a history from the last quarter of the 3rd cent. to present times); and *Henrietta Szold: Life and Letters* (1942). Lowenthal also translated into English the memoirs of Glückel of Hameln (1932). His writing has—besides learning—humor and wit, lucidity and charm. He has lectured widely throughout the United States on aspects of Jewish history.

LÖWINGER, ADOLF, rabbi and folklorist, b. Tormos, Hungary, 1864; d. Szeged, Hungary, 1926. He received the Ph.D. degree from Budapest University in 1896, his dissertation being *Rabbi Eleazar Kalir nyelvezete* (The Diction of Rabbi Eleazar Kalir). Ordained in 1898, he was appointed in the same year rabbi at Szeged, an office which he held until his death. His works on Jewish folklore appeared in several journals and compilations. In addition, he published in German: *Der Traum in der jüdischen Litteratur* (1908); *Der Schatten in Bibel und Folklore der Juden* (1910); *Rechts und Links in Bibel und Tradition der Juden* (1916); *Der Himmel in nachbiblischer Auffassung* (1912); *Die Auferstehung in der jüdischen Tradition* (1923); *Der Windgeist Keteb* (1925).

LÖWINGER, SÁMUEL, scholar, b. Debrecen, Hungary, 1904. He was living in Budapest in 1942. He entered the high school course of the Rabbinical Seminary of Budapest in 1921 and distinguished himself as president of the Wilhelm Bacher Literary Club there. He was ordained rabbi after completing the course of theology at the Seminary, and after receiving his Ph.D. degree from the University of Budapest. In 1931 he became associate professor at the Rabbinical Seminary, lecturing on Talmud, Bible, Bible exegesis, Jewish history and the evaluation of its sources, as well as on Hebrew language. In the same year he became co-editor of the *Magyar Zsidó Szemle,* a Jewish scientific journal published in Magyar, and subsequently of *Hasocher,* a Hebrew publication of that journal.

Löwinger was a prolific author whose research embraced a wide range of problems in Hebrew philology, Jewish archeology and history. In an atmosphere of anti-Jewish measures, dictated by the philosophy then prevalent in Europe, he was not discouraged and became a leading influence in all Jewish scientific endeavors in Hungary. He was co-editor of the jubilee volumes published in honor of Lajos (Ludwig) Blau (1927) and Ede (Eduard) Mahler (1937), was secretary of the IMIT (Jewish Hungarian Literary Society), director of the Jewish Hungarian Free University from 1927 on, and librarian of the Rabbinical Seminary.

He published in book form: *Alphabetum Siracidis* (1926); *Farrisol Ábrahám* (1928); *Tractatio de punctis* (1929); *Die Handschriften-Sammlung des Professor Dr. Lajos Blau* (1929); *A zsidó vallás védői* (Defenders of the Jewish Faith; 1929); *Héber nyelvű kommentár Habakkuk könyvéhez* (Hebrew Commentary on the Book of Habakkuk; 1930); *Achikar* (1920); *Ibn Adreth Beth Hamajimja* (1930); *Két középkori héber grammatikáról* (Two Medieval Hebrew Grammars; 1931); *A halotthamvasztás zsidó szempontból* (Cremation from the Jewish Point of View; 1932); *Juda és Izrael királyainak kronológiája* (Chronology of the Kings of Judah and Israel; 1933); *Saar Hamajim* (1933). He also published in Hebrew, in the *Magyar Zsidó Szemle:* "The Unpublished Hebrew Tales of Berechiah Hanakdan" (1938); "Notes on the History of Hebrew Linguistics" (1938); and "New Variations of the Books 'Judith' and 'Susannah' in the Collection of Manuscripts of the Budapest Rabbinical Seminary" (1939). He contributed to the *Revue des études juives.*

LOWY, ALEXANDER, chemist, b. New York city, 1889; d. Pittsburgh, 1941. He was educated at Columbia University (B.S., 1911; M.A., 1912; Ph.D., 1915). In 1918 he was appointed professor of organic chemistry at the University of Pittsburgh, a position which he held until his death. Lowy was one of the outstanding experts on protective chemistry, and invented a method for the safeguarding of bank vaults. He also did important research on the improvement of dyestuffs. He served as vice-president of the American Electro-Chemical Society from 1930 to 1933 and again from 1939 to 1941.

Lowy wrote many articles on electro-chemistry and organic chemistry for scientific journals. He also wrote a book, *Organic Type Formulas, Organic Type Reactions, Coal Products Chart* (1922-24), and was co-author of several textbooks, including *Introduction to Organic Chemistry* (1924) and *A Laboratory Book of Organic Chemistry* (1926).

LOWY, ISRAEL, cantor, b. Glogau, Germany, 1773; d. Paris, 1832. As a young boy he showed remarkable musical talent, so that at the age of thirteen his appearances in Saxony, Bohemia, Moravia, and Bavaria as guest cantor were eagerly awaited by the respective Jewish communities. At twenty-six he was engaged as cantor in Fürth, where he studied the Hebrew, Italian and French languages. He also devoted a great deal of time to learning the piano, violin, and cello. To complement his musical education, he acquainted himself with the creations of Haydn, Mozart and other composers. His fame reached far and wide, so that the city fathers of Nuremberg, where at that time no Jews were allowed, permitted him to give six concerts with the accompaniment of his Meshorerim. His success was so great that Prince Josef Maximilian, later king of Bavaria, requested Lowy to sing the tenor part in a forthcoming presentation of Haydn's *Creation*. It is of historical interest to note the fact, date, and place of some of his concerts. A musical program was presented by a Jewish cantor to an appreciative purely Christian audience in 1799 in the city of Nuremberg. In 1806 he left Fürth for Paris but, concertizing on the way, he stayed for three years in Metz, and for eight years in Strasbourg. In 1816 he reached Paris, and in 1818 became Hazan of the great synagogue on the Rue Notre Dame de Nazarite. His singing was of such fine quality that the foremost composers then living in Paris, such as Paer, Rossini, Calma and Mme. Catalini, frequented his services. As a result of the great crowds storming the synagogue whenever he officiated, the Jewish Kehillah of Paris decided to build a larger synagogue, with an organ. This edifice was dedicated on March 5, 1822. Lowy was the first to introduce a modern four-part choir. Until his time liturgical music was sung by the traditional trio of Hazan, bass, and singer (boy soprano). Lowy passed away on January 7, 1832, a Sabbath, after conducting the morning service.

MAX WOHLBERG.

Lit.: Friedmann, Aaron, Lebensbilder berühmter Kantoren, vol. 2 (1921); Idelsohn, A. Z., "Song and Singers of the Synagogue in the Eighteenth Century," Hebrew Union College Annual, jubilee volume (1925) 397-424.

LÖWY, IZSÁK, industrialist, founder of the city of Ujpest in Hungary, b. Nagysurány, Nyitra county, Hungary, 1793; d. Ujpest, 1847. He received a traditional Jewish education and pursued with great zeal advanced Talmudic studies at the Yeshivas of Dunaszerdahely, Pozsony (Pressburg) and Trebitsch, Bohemia. In the latter city he studied also secular subjects. He succeeded his father in the leather business founded by him, but having met with difficulties in marketing his products in his native county of Nyitra due to anti-Jewish feeling, he tried to secure permission to settle in the capital of the country, Pest. The burghers of that city, however, did not allow the Jewish tradesman to settle, which circumstance, in 1835, caused Löwy to lease some uninhabited territory to the north of Pest from the landlords, the counts Károlyi.

The lease, in many ways, anticipated a spirit of liberalism which was not to prevail generally in Hungary until 1848. It provided for the foundation of a new town, to be called Ujpest (New Pest), and ensured the settlers autonomy and freedom of religion and of trade, with all members of the community to have equal rights. Soon other industries were attracted because of the lack of guild restrictions, and as the Jewish community grew, Löwy, in 1839, erected a synagogue at his own expense on ground donated by the landlords. He organized aid for, and gave generously himself to, needy settlers. For outstanding service to the community he was elected chief judge of the town (1840 and 1841). The city honored his memory by naming a street after him. However, the plate bearing Löwy's name was removed in the course of an outburst of anti-Semitism in 1941.

The city of Ujpest, which in 1940 had 67,400 inhabitants, with a Jewish community of 11,400, became an important Danubian port, a shipbuilding and industrial center of the first magnitude in Hungary. The greater part of its export industries, vital for the Hungarian trade balance, among them the plywood industry

which has grown from the firm founded by David Löwy, a son of Izsák, was established and run by Jews. David Löwy himself continued the efforts of his father on behalf of the city, providing projects for street car transportation and a bridge at Ujpest. See illustration in volume 5, p. 492.

Lit.: Magyar Zsido Lexikon (1929) 545; Wininger, S., Grosse Jüdische National-Biographie; Judaica, Nos. 3-4 (1934) 6-8.

LOZOVSKY, SOLOMON ABRAMOVICH (properly Solomon Abramovich Dridzo), vice-commissar for foreign affairs, b. Russia, 1878. His father was a poor Jewish teacher, and at the age of eleven Lozovsky was earning his living in his brother's shop and at a blacksmith's. At the outset of his political career, in 1900, he organized workmen's clubs among railroad workers in the stations of Paniutino and Lozovaia; it is from the latter place that he derived his party name Lozovsky which was to cover his identity when, in 1901, he joined the Russian Social Democratic Labor Party. Looking for a wider field of work, he had gone to St. Petersburg. It was for activities there that he served his first prison term (1903-4). The revolution of 1905 found him active in Kazan; as a result of its failure he was subjected to several arrests and trials; for more revolutionary activity in Kharkov (1908) he was being sent to Siberia when, on the way to exile, he escaped and made his way to Paris.

During the years 1909 to 1917 Lozovsky was a member of the Paris section of the Russian Social Democratic Labor Party, and during the first World War he edited several publications in Russian, among them Golos (The Voice) and Nasha Slovo (Our Word). He also joined the French Socialist Party and was elected secretary of the Hatters Trade Union and of the Bakers Cooperative. For trying to organize international political groups within the French Socialist Party and the French Trade Unions he was expelled from the Party and from France in 1917.

On his return to Russia (1917) he was chosen secretary of the All-Union Council of Trade Unions, subsequently becoming a member of its presidium. Having joined the left (Bolshevik) wing of the Social Democratic Labor Party in July, 1917, he was expelled for his marked and undaunted opposition on the question of the October Revolution and the Trade Unions, at the end of 1917, but accepted party policies and rejoined it in 1919. From 1918 to 1939 Lozovsky dedicated himself to the trade union organizations, being a member of the most important among them. He was instrumental in the organization, and became secretary, of the Red International of Trade Unions (Profintern) in 1921. As president of the Soviet delegation, he attended the All-China conference and the Pacific Trade Union Conference. From 1928 to 1933 he was editor-in-chief of The Red International of Labor Unions Magazine, a monthly publication in Russian, English, French and Spanish, to which he contributed articles on subjects ranging from the technique of trade-union organization to theoretical disquisitions on internationalism, of which he was strongly in favor. He also retained his earlier critical attitude in fearlessly advocating renewal from within if he found it necessary.

Numerous honors and titles were bestowed on Lozovsky, who became a member of the Central Executive Committee of the USSR, a candidate to the Comintern Presidium, was elected deputy by the Kirghiz Soviet Socialist Republic to the All-Russian Congress of the Soviets, and at the fifteenth, sixteenth and seventeenth congresses of the Communist Party of the Soviet Union was elected to candidacy in its Central Committee.

On June 9, 1939, Lozovsky was appointed vice-commissar for foreign affairs. In June, 1941, following the outbreak of the Russo-German war, he was made assistant director of the Soviet Foreign Information Bureau. Official press spokesman and editor of most of the communiqués in this capacity, Lozovsky applied to this important task his keen critical faculty and fearless view of things.   ANNA BETTELHEIM.

Lit.: Lenin, *Selected Works,* vol. 2, p. 632 (Russian ed., 1933); *Red International of Labor Unions,* vol. 1, p. 2, Nov., 1928; *New York Times,* March 1, 1940; June 29 and July 28, 1941; Aug. 10, 1941; *Time,* July 14, 1941, p. 23; Aug. 4, 1941, p. 18; *Bolshaya Entziklopedia* (1938).

LOZOWICK, LOUIS, artist, b. Ludvinovka, Russia, 1892. He came to the United States in 1906 and received his A.B. degree from Ohio State University in 1918. Prior to that he had studied at the National Academy of Design (1912-15), and later he attended the Sorbonne in Paris and the University of Berlin.

The paintings and graphic productions of Lozowick portray the dynamics of the machine age, industry, construction, bridges, steam-shovels, concrete-mixers, the scientific development of the 20th cent. His attitude conveys to the observer that machines save labor and should be a means to help man out of the dark ages. On the other hand, his work also levels a sharp critical note at those who abuse the machine to exploit labor and make robots of human beings. This is particularly noticeable in his industrial cities and the buildings that stand stark and bare, void of any human element.

In contrast to the industrial interpretations of mechanical forms, Lozowick executed a great number of lithographs and paintings of the human element, of men and women with tractors on the farms, peasants working and playing and dancing, and horsemen—evidently inspired by his many trips to the Soviet Union. With the growth of interest in the Soviet Union that characterized the intellectual life of the late 1920's and 1930's, Lozowick allied himself with those who looked for the source of new creative powers and inspiration in a country which claimed to have harnessed machine dynamics to the demands of human beings.

The art of Lozowick is derived from his studied, factual analysis; each line is put down by scientific logic and reason. Like an engineer and builder, he eliminates the non-essentials, simplifies the composition, and creates his forms and lines with a sharp, direct craftsmanship that is perfection.

Like his paintings and graphic art, Lozowick is well-known for his cultural and organizational contributions to society. He was, in 1942, among the few artists whose abundant knowledge of the history of art qualified them as outstanding lecturers and authoritative writers on their subjects. In his capacity as director and chairman of the American Artists Congress, the American Group, the American Artists School, and other art societies, Lozowick helped to direct, formulate and develop the advancement of American art and the understanding of European art as well.

He was the author of *Modern Russian Art* (1925) and, with Joseph Freeman and Joshua Kunitz, of *Voices of October* (1930). His work is represented in the permanent collections of some of the leading museums in the United States and abroad. He won the $1,000 Cleveland Print Club prize in 1931, and was the recipient of various other art prizes. In 1942 he was living in New York city. At that time he had to his credit more than 200 notable graphic works in addition to many oils, water colors and drawings. Some of these are owned by the Metropolitan Museum of Art, the Whitney Museum (New York) and numerous other collections.   WILLIAM GROPPER.

Lit.: Jahrbuch der jungen Kunst (1925) 312-15; *Jewish Tribune,* Sept. 19, 1930, p. 52; *Current Biography,* vol. 3 (1942), No. 4, pp. 40-42.

LUACH, LUAH (Hebrew word for calendar), *see* CALENDAR.

LUAH AHIASAF, LUAH ERETZ ISRAEL, *see* COMPILATIONS, LITERARY.

LUBARSCH, OTTO, pathologist, b. Berlin, 1860; d. Berlin, 1933. He was educated at the Universities of Leipzig, Heidelberg, Jena, Berlin, and Strasbourg (M.D., 1883). In 1899 he became director of the pathologic anatomical division of the Royal Hygiene Institute of Posen, and in 1913 a member of the faculty of the Institute's Academy. In 1917 he was appointed professor at the Academy for Practical Medicine in Düsseldorf. From 1917 to 1928 he served as professor of general pathology and pathological anatomy at the University of Berlin, and in 1928 he was honored with the title of professor emeritus.

He wrote hundreds of papers on medical subjects, and several books, including: *Über die Ursachen der angeborenen und erworbenen Immunität* (1890); *Zur Lehre von den Geschwülsten und Infektionskrankheiten* (1898); *Pathologische Anatomie und Krebsforschung* (1902); *Die Nierengewüchse* (1924).

Lubarsch was a brilliant and colorful personality, but somewhat erratic. After he embraced Christianity he frequently attacked the customs and religion of the Jews. He was a member of the intensely nationalistic Deutschnationaler Hochschullehrerverband, and in 1919 wrote a pamphlet, *In der Frage der Hochschulereform,* in which he expressed his anti-Jewish ideas.

LUBIN, ARTHUR, motion picture director, b. Los Angeles, 1898. He was educated at the Carnegie Institute of Technology, the Page Military Academy, and the San Diego School of Expression from 1915 to 1918. From 1917 to 1919 he acted in stock companies at San Diego, Cal. During the first World War he served as radio landsman for the United States Navy.

From 1920 to 1930 he acted in various stage plays and moving pictures in Los Angeles. In 1930 and 1931 he worked as a casting director for Crosbie Gaige. In 1931 he became a director for the Ray-Miner Corporation, a subsidiary of Paramount Pictures. After that he was a director for Monogram Pictures, Re-

David Lubin as he looked in 1922. From a painting by Olivia Rosetti Agresti

public Pictures, Universal Studios, and Warner Brothers First National Studios. Among his most successful pictures were *Honeymoon Limited* (1935), *Frisco Waterfront* (1935) and *I Cover the War* (1937).

Lubin also produced and directed several plays in Los Angeles, including *When the Bough Breaks* (1932), *The Man of Wax* (1933) and *The Green Bay Tree* (1934).

LUBIN, DAVID, agriculturist, b. Klodowa, Poland, 1848; d. Rome, Italy, 1919. He and his half-brother, Colonel Harris Weinstock, engaged in business in Sacramento, their store becoming famous as the first "one price" store west of the Mississippi. Through their commercial relations with the farmers in the surrounding country, Lubin soon sensed certain adverse economic conditions working great injustice on agriculturists. In 1885 he engaged in fruit-growing, and in the same year was active in the organization of the Fruit Growers Convention in San Francisco, from which came the impulse for the organization of the California Fruit Growers Exchange. This Exchange initiated a new chapter in the economic history of the West as well as in the marketing of farm produce. Lubin also conceived the great idea of financing the farmer through rural credit banks.

Lubin soon realized the need for equal protection as between industries and agriculture, and advocated that the tariff on imports affording protection to manufacturers and industrial laborers be offset by a bounty on exports to be granted to farmers in the form of a government subsidy to reduce the cost of ocean carriage from the shipping points to the foreign receiving markets. In 1884 Lubin's bounty idea was adopted by the Republican convention of California. The national issue to which this proposal gave rise was known as "Lubinism," and so great was the interest it aroused in 1896 and 1897 that fifty-five clergymen of Philadelphia formed a Lubin Club to support this movement. The plan was revived from time to time. Although the bounty idea was not carried out, several other suggestions that Lubin made at the same time had lasting effects.

He was responsible for many of the later developments in the parcel post service, working on the theory that the parcel post would facilitate cheap and direct connection between producer and consumer, and would thus be of service in farm marketing.

At this point Lubin transferred his attention to the project which absorbed the rest of his life and won him the name of being the first internationalist in agricultural statesmanship. He wished to organize a centralized international attack upon the problem of low prices of farm products, which, he argued, are determined by world conditions, low prices in certain countries causing low prices in other countries. Several years of study in San Francisco preceded Lubin's international campaign to strengthen the conservative element in democracy, the landowning farmer, for this was the ultimate goal of his endeavors. After an unsuccessful attempt to interest the United States, England, and France in the establishment of an international institute of agriculture, he succeeded in obtaining the assistance of King Victor Emanuel III of Italy. As a result, the delegations of forty governments met in Rome in 1905 and decided upon the establishment of the International Institute of Agriculture in Rome. Thus for the first time in the history of the world the nations were leagued for constructive economic and political effort.

Lubin's ideas went far beyond those which the Institute had thus far embodied, but it has, nevertheless, fulfilled a vital need in the field of agriculture and points the way to even more effective methods of world cooperation. The Institute, of which Lubin was head until his death in 1919, has become the clearing house for international statistics relating to farm products. On the twenty-fifth anniversary of its establishment the seventy countries now members of the Institute sent delegations to honor Lubin by making a pilgrimage to his tomb in Rome. The United States was not represented.

Lubin's gigantic practical achievements were fostered by the belief in the divine mission of Judaism, for he regarded the Jew as God's chosen vehicle for the "righteous" economic development of the world. After a trip to Palestine, undertaken in 1884, he published an article on the settlement of Jews in Palestine.

GABRIEL DAVIDSON.

Lit.: Agresti, *David Lubin: A Study in Practical Idealism* (1922); Hobson, *The International Institute of Agriculture* (1931) 3-33; *American Hebrew*, Oct. 10, 1930, p. 634; Stewart, in *The Illinois Agriculturist*, Oct., 1926; *The New York Times*, Oct. 5, 1930.

LUBIN, ISADOR, economist and government official, b. Worcester, Mass., 1896. He received his B.A. degree from Clark University in 1916. The following year he received his M.A. degree from the University of Missouri, and in 1926 his Ph.D. degree from Brookings Institution.

In 1918, after teaching economics for one year at the University of Missouri, Lubin became a statistician for the United States Food Administration; then he served as a special expert on the United States War Industries Board. From 1920 until 1928 Lubin devoted himself entirely to research and to the teaching of economics. But in 1928, when he became economic advisor to the senate committee on education and labor, Lubin reentered government service. Although he retained his teaching connections until 1933, his responsibilities with various government departments and committees increased fast after his reentry into the service.

Lubin became United States commissioner of labor statistics in 1933. The complicated gathering and interpretation of data relating to the industrial organization of the country were put in his charge. As the growing world crisis, after 1933, gave Lubin additional tasks, some of his work as commissioner had to be relegated to others in his department. The selection and training of competent assistants was a practice Lubin had mastered during his many years of teaching. Although, in 1942, he still held his position as commissioner in addition to the extra responsibilities he had been given, the department continued to function with all necessary precision.

After 1933 Lubin served as chairman of the labor advisory board of the Federal Emergency Administration of Public Works; he was a member of the Industrial Resources Committee, a member of the advisory committee to the Federal co-ordinator of railroads and of various other groups handling specific sections of the industrial life of the United States. In 1938 Lubin was appointed a member of the Temporary National Economic Committee, in which capacity he prepared the material for an outline of a suggested basic readjustment to changing economic conditions. Later, as special statistician to President Franklin Delano Roosevelt, Lubin became a member of the White House staff. He also served as advisor to the Office of Production Management, and was an aide to Harry Hopkins in the carrying out of the Lease-Lend program of assistance to the other countries fighting Germany and her allies.

During his years as teacher and in research, Lubin was assistant professor of economics at the University of Michigan (1920-22); from 1922 to 1924 he was with the Brookings Institution in Washington, and in 1924 he was associate professor of economics at the University of Missouri. Returning to the Brookings Institution the following year, Lubin remained a member of its staff until 1933.

Lubin was the author of *Miners' Wages and the Cost of Coal* (1924); *The Absorption of the Unemployed by American Industry* (1929); *The British Coal Dilemma* (1927) and, with A. C. C. Hill, Jr., *The British Attack on Unemployment* (1934). He also wrote for various economic journals. Lubin was a member of the board of directors of the National

Isador Lubin

Child Center (1932-) and chairman of the board from 1932 to 1935. He was vice-president of the American Statistical Association from 1938 to 1939. Among his Jewish communal activities were his presidency of the Intercollegiate Menorah Society from 1920 to 1922 and later his participation in the activities of the United Jewish Appeal. Lubin received an LL.D. from the University of Michigan in 1941 and an honorary LL.D. from Clark University the same year. In 1942 he was on leave of absence from his post as Commissioner of Labor Statistics and concentrating his efforts on his special statistical work for President Roosevelt. He was becoming known as the "government's best statistician," and his reports were evoking praise for their dependable and imaginative interpretations.

NATHAN RICARDO.

Lit.: *American Hebrew*, Dec. 4, 1936, p. 615; *Current Biography*, Oct. 1941.

LUBIN, SIMON JULIUS, merchant and communal worker, b. Sacramento, Cal., 1876; d. San Francisco, 1936. He received his education at Harvard University (A.B., 1903). He was the manager of the New York office of Weinstock, Lubin, and Company of Sacramento from 1904 to 1906. He acted as secretary of that corporation from 1906 to 1916 and as vice-president from 1916 to 1920. He was elected president in 1920, and continued in that capacity until his death.

Lubin's achievements as a communal worker were even more noteworthy than his industrial accomplishments. In 1913 he founded and became first president of the California State Commission of Immigration and Housing. In 1926 he founded and became president of the Sacramento Region Citizens Council, which fostered the economic, political, and social welfare of Northern California. Perhaps his most important social service work was done as head of the Labor

Ernst Lubitsch

Commission of California, which did much to alleviate the notorious poverty of the migratory workers.

In 1931 he took the initiative of calling a conference of United States and Latin American Pacific coast industrial interests, and was elected permanent president of the Institute founded at that time. Although a capitalist, he was a believer in economic liberalism and supported much of the social legislation of the Roosevelt administration. He was a member of the Republican Party, the American Association for Labor Legislation, the California Conference of Social Work, and the National Economic League.

LUBITSCH, ERNST, motion picture producer and director, b. Berlin, 1892. Educated at the Sophien Gymnasium, in 1910 he started his theatrical career as an actor in Max Reinhardt's stock company. He later became one of the most popular directors of dramatic and cinematic productions in Germany. In 1922 he came to the United States to direct Mary Pickford. That year he was employed by Warner Brothers as a director, and worked for that company for three years. From 1925 to 1927 he was with Metro-Goldwyn-Mayer, and in 1927 began directing for Famous-Players-Lasky. He was a managing director for Paramount in 1935 and 1936.

Lubitsch was one of the first to recognize motion pictures as an art medium rather than merely a popular amusement. He directed with a light touch, and his pictures were famous for their gaiety, wit, and sophistication. Among his best-known productions were *Passion* (1919), *Lady Windermere's Fan* (1925), *Old Heidelberg* (1927), *The Patriot* (1928), *Broken Lullaby* (1931), *Design for Living* (1933) and *Angel* (1937). Perhaps his most successful production was *Ninotchka* (1939), in which Greta Garbo appeared for the first time as a comédienne. In 1942 he produced *To Be or Not to Be,* a motion picture which, starring Jack Benny and Carole Lombard, was based on an original story written by Lubitsch in collaboration with Melchior Lengyel. Lubitsch was made a chevalier of the French Legion of Honor.

LUBLIN, city in Poland, founded in the 13th cent. Jews were not allowed to live within the limits of the city for a long time. Therefore they settled not far from the city, in a village known under the name of Piaski Zydowskie (Jewish sands). During the 14th and 15th centuries the city still had its *privilegium de non tolerandis Judaeis.* In 1523 King Sigismund I, the "Old," allowed Jews to settle in Lublin, which thereafter became one of the largest commercial centers of the republic of Poland.

The first Jew to be allowed to build a house in Lublin, even before 1523, was Josko (Joseph) the Jew, "the King's tenant," who built his house there in 1500. After he died his widow Golda renewed the personal privilege, asking for it and personally persuading King Sigismund. The Jews in Lublin had special covenants with the Christian inhabitants of the city, the so-called *pacta cum Judaeis inita.* The voivode (governor) and his deputy had jurisdiction over the Jews under the name of *iudices judaeorum.*

For a long time Lublin was the very center of Polish Jewry. Its rabbis had the titles of district rabbis and elders. One of the first was Rabbi Judah Aaron, whose jurisdiction was over the voivodeship of Lublin, Belz, and Chelm. One of his successors was the world-famous rabbi, Maharshal (Rabbi Solomon ben Jehiel Luria), scientist and Talmudist (b. Brest-Litovsk, 1510; d. Lublin, 1573). Another famous rabbi was "Maharam"; both of them gave their names to synagogues in Lublin. In Lublin was located the great Talmudic Yeshiva, the head of which, named by the king, bore the title "Rector of the Talmudic Academy" in Lublin.

Lublin was the center of the political and religious life during the sessions of the Parliament of Polish Jewry, the so-called Vaad Arba Aratzoth (Council of Four Lands). From the last quarter of the 16th cent. to the 18th cent. it was the highest authority in the religious, economic and juridical life of the Jews of Poland. The sessions of the Vaad were later transferred to Yaroslaw. One of its best-known presidents was Abraham Heilpern of Lublin in the 18th cent. Jewish physicians of Lublin were famous all over Poland, including Solomon Luria, Samuel ben Mattithyahu and Moses Montalto. In Padua there studied in the middle of the 17th cent. a Jewish doctor "Vitalis Felix Chajim Judaeus Polonus Lublinensis."

Many ritual murder trials against Jews took place in Lublin, and the elders of the Kehillah were forced to attend the cruel executions of their fellow Jews—always on a Saturday in front of the Maharshal Shul. In the 17th cent. the Jewish quarters of Lublin were destroyed during a war, and more than 2,000 Jews were killed during a pogrom. In the course of the Swedish wars under Kings Charles Gustav and Charles XII, the Jewish community suffered greatly. In 1761, after many ordeals, the Jews were expelled from the city of Lublin, and not until 1862, under the Russian government, were they allowed to return to the city.

The most famous rabbi during the 18th cent. was Reb Jacob Isaac Horowitz. Two of the leaders of the Polish Hasidic world during the first decades of the 19th cent. were Jacob Lubliner and his pupil Mendel of Kock.

From the partition of Poland to 1915 Lublin was

Interior of the Maharschal synagogue at Lublin

under Russian domination. The Jewish population was wealthy and was steadily growing in number. During the first World War Lublin was the seat (1915-18) of the Austrian governor general. Thenceforth Jewish life in the city flourished.

After 1918 Lublin was the seat of a Polish voivode. The Jewish population there was 50,000 out of a total population of 130,000. Lublin had several Jewish high schools and two Jewish daily newspapers. In 1925 the famous Yeshivath Hacheme Lublin, a kind of continuation of the century-old Talmudic academy, was founded; its first rector was Rabbi Shapiro, leader of the Orthodox Jews in Poland.

In September, 1939, Lublin was occupied by the German Nazis and made one of the four district towns of the government general. It was believed for a time that the Germans would transfer to the district of Lublin the entire Jewish population of the country temporarily dominated by the Nazis. In 1942 this process was still continuing, as the German authorities kept sending tens of thousands of Jews into this district. By an ironic coincidence, the Jews of Lublin, when forced to leave the city, were in 1942 concentrated in the same village, Piaski Zydowskie, where the Jews of Lublin used to live in the 14th cent.

JOSEPH THON.

Lit.: Contemporary Jewish Record, vol. 3 (1940) 119-33.

LUBLIN, MEIR BEN GEDALIAH, Talmudist, b. probably Lublin, Poland, about 1558; d. Lublin, 1616. He was head of the school at Lublin from 1582 to 1587, when he succeeded his father-in-law, Isaac Spira, as head of the academy in Cracow; in most of his responsa he signed himself "the son-in-law of the king, his majesty Rabbi Isaac." In 1595 he became rabbi of Lemberg (Lwów) and in 1613 of Lublin, where he spent his last years. His career was marked by dissensions with Simon Wolf Auerbach and Joshua Falk; but he had numerous followers, and among

his distinguished pupils were Joshua Heschel of Cracow and Isaiah Horovitz. He wrote numerous works on Talmudic subjects, some of which are still in manuscript; in these he did not hesitate to criticize the opinions of earlier authorities. His Talmudic notes (Hiddushim) are included in many editions of the Talmud; they were published individually under the title *Meir Ene Hachamim* (Enlightening the Eyes of the Wise; Venice, 1619). His son, Gedaliah, published 140 of his responsa in *Manhir Ene Hachamim* (Illuminating the Eyes of the Wise; Venice, 1618).

LUBLINER, DER, *see* JACOB ISAAC OF LUBLIN.

LUBLINER, HUGO, playwright, b. Breslau, Germany, 1846; d. Berlin, 1911. In 1865 he became director of a weaver's shop. By 1875 he began to write comedies, after having studied French models intensively, especially Scribe and Sardou. Lubliner sought to combine comic effects with psychological questions and social tendencies. He succeeded more than once in amusing his audience, but was never acknowledged by any literary critic when he touched on psychological or social matters. He scored his greatest successes through the plays *Der Frauenadvokat* (1875), *Die Frau ohne Geist* (1879) and *Ein Jourfix* (1882). Subsequently Lubliner endeavored to describe the civilization of Germany under the empire of William I in the novels *Ein Gläubiger des Glücks* (1886), *Die Frau von 19 Jahren* (1887) and *Der Roman eines anständigen Mädchens* (1899).

LUBLINER, LUDWIG (OSIAS), author and political leader, b. Warsaw, Poland, 1809; d. Brussels, Belgium, 1868. He was an active participant in the Polish uprising of 1831, and though he was made an ensign and awarded the silver cross for bravery at the battle of Paprotina, he had to flee the country to escape from the Russian police. Settling in Brussels, Lubliner took up the practice of law, but remained an important figure among the Polish émigrés and was one of the founders of the Demokratische Vereinigung, a liberalist European movement of the 1840's. Lubliner was particularly close to Joachim Lelewel (1786-1861), the Polish historian.

Lubliner fought against anti-Jewish tendencies among the Polish émigrés, and tried to impress on Poles and Jews alike the inseparability of equal rights for Jews and a democratic Polish republic. During the Polish rebellion of 1861 to 1863, Lubliner urged the Polish leaders to grant the Jews equal rights; on the other hand, he urged the Jews to take an active part in the rebellion, and to both groups he advocated the desirability of the assimilation of the Jews into Poland. He founded the "Alliance polonaise de toutes les croyances religieuses" as a movement to foster the union of all religious groups in an independent, democratic Poland. Among Lubliner's published works were *Des Juifs en Pologne* (1839) and *De la condition politique et civile des Juifs en Pologne,* and many historical and political studies in French and Polish.

LUBLINSKI, SAMUEL (SALLY), author and historian, b. Johannisburg, East Prussia, 1868; d. Weimar, Germany, 1910. He was a bookseller until, in 1895, he began to contribute to periodicals and devoted all his time to literature. He was a friend of the poet Ludwig Jacobowski, who influenced him in his views on German nationality and Judaism, as well as on the tendencies of modern literature and the application of evolution to history. Both endeavored to vindicate the cause of the German Jews, at the same time criticizing severely the questionable conduct of some Jews in Germany.

Like Jacobowski, Lublinski gained recognition as a literary critic because of the undoubted sincerity of his utterances. In 1899 and 1900, in his *Jüdische Charaktere bei Grillparzer, Hebbel und Otto Ludwig* and *Literatur und Gesellschaft im 19. Jahrhundert,* Lublinski published one of the first German attempts to present literary history from the sociological point of view. In 1904 Lublinski professed opposition to literary naturalism by publishing his *Die Bilanz der Moderne,* continued in 1908 by *Der Ausgang der Moderne.* While Lublinski, as literary critic, demanded modernization of classical tendencies, he wrote plays in consonance with his critical program. Other works of his were the tragedies *Der Imperator* (1900), *Kaiser und Kanzler* (1901), *Hannibal* (1902), *Peter von Russland* (1906), and *Gunther und Brunhilde* (1908). Meanwhile Lublinski became more and more absorbed in the history of religion. But his studies on the genesis of Christianity (1910) and Judaism (1903) are lacking in critical method and historical foundation, especially his attempt to prove that neither Jesus nor Paul actually existed. For a while Lublinski was an adherent of Zionism, but severed his relations with it after being severely criticized by Ahad Haam. His literary remains were published posthumously under the title *Nachgelassene Schriften* (1914).

LUBOSCHUTZ, LEA, violinist and teacher, b. Odessa, Russia, 1889. After studying at the Odessa School and the Moscow Conservatory, she toured Poland, Germany, and France in more than one hundred concerts, frequently appearing as soloist under Artur Nikisch. After an appearance in the United States she entered a competition held in Moscow among twenty leading European violinists, winning first prize. From 1921 to 1925 she was professor of violin in Berlin and Paris. Returning to the United States, she made her second American debut successfully. She has since toured the country extensively, sometimes in sonata recitals with Josef Hofmann. In 1927 she was appointed a member of the faculty of the Curtis Institute of Music, where she has since been conducting classes in violin playing.

PIERRE LUBOSCHUTZ (b. Odessa, 1894), her brother, has distinguished himself by virtue of his two-piano recitals with his wife, Genia Nemenoff. They made their first tour in 1936, and since then have established themselves as one of the leading two-piano teams in the United States.

LUCA, ABRAHAM AXELRAD, poet, author and editor, b. Barlad, Moldavia, Roumania, 1879. He made his literary debut with poems of a Jewish background in the Zionist weekly *Rasaritul* (The East), published at Jassy (1899-1901). These poems were collected in a volume called *Toward the East,* a preface being written by the Jewish lyric poet Rodion Steuerman, director of the *Rasaritul.* For some time Luca was principal of the Roumanian Jewish Ronetti-Romann School at Bucharest. Subsequently he edited

for many years the *Orizontul* (Horizon), a journal of popularized science which helped the Roumanian public to get acquainted with ideas and facts to which, previously, it had little access. When, in the Nazi era, the anti-Jewish movement in Roumania, under the auspices of the Iron Guard, grew in importance, Luca, with a view to disproving the anti-Semitic accusations, conducted a publicistic campaign in the *Curierul Israelit,* organ of the Union of Roumanian Jews, an organization whose aim was the safeguarding of the civic rights of the Jewish population. This gave Luca an opportunity to study, among other things, the attitude of Eminescu, greatest lyric poet of Roumania, on the Jewish problem.

Luca also translated into Roumanian the poems of Morris Rosenfeld. Like all other Jewish authors writing in Roumanian, he was reduced to complete inactivity by the ordinances and laws of the anti-Jewish Roumanian governments of the years 1937 to 1942 which forbade Jews to publish anything in Roumanian.

LUCAS, ALBERT, communal worker, b. England, 1859; d. Edgemere, L. I., 1923. He founded the Hebrew Benevolent Society of Staten Island in 1896 and took part in furthering other activities among the Jewish population. His paper "Religion in Education," read before the convention of the Union of Orthodox Congregations in 1903, brought forth an order from the New York Board of Education that no sectarian hymns be permitted in schools and that children should be excused from attending school on the holy days of their faith. Lucas was the first secretary of the Joint Distribution Committee and often represented it in foreign countries. He was also active in the Central Relief Committee.

Lit.: Jewish World, (London), July 12, 1923, p. 12.

LUCAS, LEOPOLD, rabbi and historian, b. Marburg, Germany, 1872. He became rabbi in Glogau, Germany, in 1899. As a result of his historical studies, he was appointed a member of the Byzantiological Society in Athens in 1911. He initiated the Gesellschaft zur Förderung der Wissenschaft des Judentums in Berlin, which finally was founded by Martin Philippson in 1902. Lucas wrote: *Geschichte der Stadt Tyrus zur Zeit der Kreuzzüge* (1895); "Judentaufen und Judaismus zur Zeit des Papstes Innocenz III. (in *Revue des études Juives*); and *Zur Geschichte der Juden im vierten Jahrhundert* (1910). In 1942 Lucas was living in retirement in Berlin.

LUCCA, capital of the province of Lucca, Tuscany (Central Italy), with thirty-six Jews out of a total population of 54,500 (1938). The city, which played a certain role in the early history of Christianity—St. Paulinus, a disciple of St. Peter, is said to have preached the Gospel there—never attained the importance of such neighboring cities as Pisa and Livorno in Jewish history. There is evidence of the possession of real estate (vineyards) near Lucca by Jews during the first half of the 11th cent. The city was also the seat of the famous Kalonymus family which, in the 9th or 10th cent., moved to Mayence, Germany, there establishing a dynasty of scholars and poets. Abraham ibn Ezra wrote his commentary on *Isaiah* during his stay in Lucca (1154-55); he also taught there. Benjamin of Tudela, who visited the city on his way to Rome (about 1165), recorded the existence of a settlement of forty Jews, and cited the names of three rabbis, David, Jacob and Samuel.

Angelo di Gaio, a Jew from Forli, was permitted to settle in Lucca in 1431. He opened a loan bank, but when King Sigismund, who passed through the city, imposed a tax of 1,500 gold florins on him, di Gaio left Lucca. Later other Jews were allowed to live in Lucca, where they had a synagogue and a cemetery. When a complaint was made against them, their privileges were confirmed by Pope Nicholas V, who annulled the constitutions of Clement V and the bishop of Lucca. David di Dattilo da Tivoli, son of the wealthiest banker of Florence, was a patron of philosophers and Cabalists, and had a bank in Lucca from 1477 to 1493.

About 1500 the Jews abandoned the city, where their residence was neither profitable nor secure, or they were driven out. Although some returned, Jews were in general not permitted to sojourn in the city for more than fifteen consecutive days. Records of May, 1728, give the names of Jews who had permission to enjoy extended residence in Lucca.

Heinrich Heine visited the baths of Lucca in 1828, and wrote *Die Bäder von Lucca* (1829) and *Die Stadt Lucca* (1830); the former contains his polemic against the homosexual anti-Semitic poet Count August von Platen.

LUCCA, PAULINE, world-famous soprano, niece of Samuel Benedict Lucka, b. Vienna, 1841; d. Vienna, 1908. After singing in the chorus of the Vienna Opera, she was engaged by the Olmütz Opera, where she sang leading roles following her debut in 1859. In 1860 she sang at the Prague Opera, where she was heard by Meyerbeer, who invited her to Berlin to create the principal soprano role of Selika in his opera *L'Africaine*. She was an instantaneous success in Berlin, and was engaged on a life contract. Beginning with 1863, she sang for nine seasons at Covent Garden, London, where she was a sensation. In 1872 she severed her connections with Berlin and came to the United States for a two-year tour.

Madame Lucca became a member of the Vienna Opera in 1874, remaining there for fifteen years. She also made a series of brilliant guest appearances in the leading opera houses of Europe. When she retired in 1874 she was made honorary member of the Vienna Opera. Her voice was extraordinary for its range and command of nuances. On the stage she was a magnetic figure, electrifying audiences not only with phenomenal vocal gifts but also with her personality, charm, and pronounced dramatic talents. Her repertory included about sixty roles.

LUCENA (Hebrew and Arabic, Alyasana), city in southern Spain, situated between Cordova and Granada. Although the exact number of its Jewish inhabitants has not been transmitted, it is known to have contained one of the largest Jewish communities in Spain. During the 9th cent. it was called the Jews' City, and no non-Jews were supposed to be living there.

The Ibn Daud and Abravanel families maintained that their ancestors had come to the neighborhood of Lucena at the time of Nebuchadrezzar's destruction of the First Temple. When the Moors conquered the region early in the 8th cent., the Jewish population of the city must already have been large and important. The community was in communication with the academies at Sura and Pumbeditha in Babylonia. Under the generally benevolent rule of the Moors, the Jews prospered and developed their own cultural center in Lucena. In 1089 Isaac Alfasi came thither to succeed Isaac ibn Ghayyat as head of the community, and to found the academy which he directed until his death. It seems likely that among Alfasi's pupils at Lucena was Judah Halevi, and that Halevi's elegy on Alfasi's death (1103) was composed as the result of their pupil-teacher relationship in the academy. During the rule of Alfasi the Lucena Jewish community flourished as never before; it was the outstanding community in Spain.

In 1066 a large number of Jews escaping from the persecutions at Granada found refuge in Lucena. But within a century the city was itself to be the victim of Islamic persecutions, during the conflict between the sects of the Almoravids and the Almohades. Yusuf ibn Teshufin, a prince of the Almoravids, tried to force Islam on the Jews of Lucena. Some of them feigned acceptance of the creed, but Yusuf was both bought off by the Jews and talked out of his intention by wiser Islamic counsellors. Later the Almohades took over the city, and in 1148 they closed the academy. From that time on until the expulsion of the Jews from Spain in 1492 Lucena waned in Jewish significance. The defeat of the Moors by the Christians hastened the disappearance of the community, and after the expulsion only Marranos and faithful neo-Christians were left in what had once been a center of Jewish culture.

Lit.: Graetz, H., *History of the Jews,* vol. 3 (1927); *Encyclopaedia Judaica,* vol. 10 (1934), cols. 1175-76.

LUCENA, ABRAHAM DE, one of the earliest Jewish residents of New York, d. about 1670. He came to New Amsterdam in February, 1655, probably one of the group of Dutch Jews who escaped from Brazil after the Portuguese occupation. He was an enterprising merchant who seems to have lost no time in establishing himself. In fact, he was involved in legal difficulties, on the ground of having kept his store open during the Sunday sermon, before a month was over—proving his ignorance of the local law. He soon became, however, an acknowledged spokesman of the little Jewish community, together with Asser Levy and a few others.

Lucena was one of three Jewish merchants who, in November, 1655, petitioned for the right to trade in South River, Fort Orange, and other outlying settlements. The following year his signature appeared on a petition to have a burial ground set aside for Jews —a request which seems to have been granted. He also pleaded for the right to hold real estate and for the right of citizenship, which he seems to have acquired in 1657. Jacob and Moses de Lucena, contemporaries of his in New Amsterdam, may have been his brothers; there is also some likelihood that he was an elder relative of Abraham Haim de Lucena (d. 1720), the second known minister of the Shearith

Israel Congregation. Another Abraham de Lucena, of a later date, was also prominent in the Jewish community of New York.

Lit.: Publications of the American Jewish Historical Society.

LUCERNE, see Switzerland.

LUCIFER, the rendering of the Vulgate for the Hebrew phrase *helal* ("day-star") in *Isa.* 14:12; the verse is rendered in the Authorized Version as: How art thou fallen from heaven, O Lucifer, son of the morning!" The passage in question is a song of derision over the downfall of a Babylonian king; the figure used may trace back to a Hebrew or Babylonian astral myth like the Greek story of Phaëthon, in which the day-star is cast out of heaven because of presumption. The term Lucifer is never used in Jewish legend; but Christian writers identified Lucifer with Satan who, according to the gospels (*Luke* 10:18), fell from heaven like lightning; accordingly, Lucifer became one of the terms for the devil in Christian theology.

LUCK, city in Volhynia, southeastern Poland, one of the oldest towns in the territory of Poland and Ukraine. There is ample evidence that in the 7th and 8th centuries Luck was inhabited as a fortress, surrounded by the river Styr. The name of the town was then Luczesk. During the following centuries the population of the city became a very mixed one. Lithuanians, Poles, Jews, Tatars, Armenians, Germans, Russians, and in the last centuries even Czechs, were among the peoples who lived in the city at the crossroads of history.

The Jewish community in Luck is among the oldest. There are traces of Jews in and around Luck as far back as the 10th cent. The Jews supposedly came to Luck from the East after the powerful Jewish state of the Khazars collapsed. In the beginning of the 13th cent. some 2,000 Karaites came to Luck and other Volhynian settlements. For many centuries Luck was the scene of quarrels between those known as the Rabbinite Jews and the Karaites.

The Jews of Luck were granted a charter of privileges by the grand duke of Lithuania, Witold I, in 1388. The Polish king Wladislaw Jagiello renewed this privilege in 1432, granting the Armenians and the Jews of Luck the same rights as those of Cracow and Lwów, with the exception of the right to collect custom duties, which the king reserved for himself.

During this century the Jewish community grew, and acquired great influence. The best proof of this is the meeting of European monarchs which took place (1429) in Luck. Among the monarchs who attended this event were the German emperor Sigismund of Luxembourg, the Polish king Wladislaw Jagiello, the Russian grand duke Wasyl of Moscow, Eric, king of Denmark, several Tatar Khans, and the duke of Wallachia. There were present also many cardinals, archbishops, bishops, and many lay personages. Among those invited to attend this meeting were the chief rabbi of the community of Luck and the Hacham (rabbi) of the Karaites.

In 1495 the Jewish community of Luck suffered a grave disaster in connection with the expulsion of the Jews of Lithuania, but they returned to the city in 1503. The Jews received new privileges under which the Jewish leaseholders and taxfarmers were subjected to the immediate jurisdiction of the king. During the Cossack uprising of Bogdan Chmielnicki in 1648 to 1649 the Jewish community suffered very great losses, together with the rest of the city's population. The famous Yeshiva of Luck was destroyed. The synagogue of Luck, which is known the world over, resisted destruction during this war, just as it resisted wars and fires in the course of modern times. This synagogue, probably built before the 13th cent., is an outstanding example of Jewish architecture and symbol of the thousand-year-old cultural life of the Jews in Poland. It has endured for more than eight centuries as an intellectual and religious fortress of the Polish Jews.

In 1791 Luck came under Russian domination, and remained so until the first World War (1914). In 1915 the Russian army, fighting its way back, organized a pogrom against the Jews of Luck. In 1918, when Luck was occupied by the Germans, the Ukrainian puppet Hetman Petlura, who was installed by the Germans, organized in Luck, and all through the Ukraine and Volhynia, bloody pogroms which cost the lives of hundreds of thousands of Jews.

Among the curiosities of Luck is the wooden synagogue of the Karaites, the so-called "Kenasa," with parchment Torah scrolls of the 15th, 16th and 17th centuries. Since 1918 Luck has been the district seat of the Polish voivode. The Jewish population amounted to some 25,000 out of a total of 35,000. Luck had an active Jewish nationalistic movement, several Hebrew high schools, and libraries.

In September, 1939, Luck was invaded by the Russians, and in June, 1941, it was occupied by the Nazis. A new ghetto was instituted in the centuries-old narrow streets of the Jewish quarter of Luck.

Among the outstanding Jewish scholars, rabbis and leaders of Luck were: in the 15th cent.: Shachna, Nowakowicz, Alkhn, Danilewicz, Enka and Momotliwy; in the 16th cent.: Szamach, Danilewicz, Nissan Kozka, Abraham Szachnowicz and M. Jesofowicz; in the 18th and 19th centuries: E. Getzel, Judah Zeeb ben Tobias (martyred in 1764), and the Maggid of Luck, Meir ben Hayim.   Joseph Thon.

LUCKA, SAMUEL BENEDICT, physician and author, b. Prague, Bohemia, 1803; d. Vienna, 1891. He received his education at the University of Vienna (M.D., 1833). In 1841 he settled in Marienbad, where he devoted his time, energy and medical skill and knowledge to the service of the poor. He founded the Jewish Hospital there and acted as managing physician without accepting any compensation. In 1873 he was named an honorary citizen of Marienbad.

One of the most prominent balneologists of his time, he wrote a number of medical works, including: *Der Kreuzbrunnen zu Marienbad* (1858); *Zur Orientierung in Marienbad* (1890); *Die Homöopathie* (1840).

Lucka was also a poet and dramatist. He belonged to the group of Bohemian authors who wrote in German; they favored Bohemian national independence but believed in the superiority of German cultural values. Among his friends and colleagues in this group were H. E. Ebert, W. Marseno, and Gottfried Schmelkes. Perhaps his most successful literary work was *Die Antisemiten und das Blutmärchen* (published under the pseudonym of Dr. S. J. Senex, 1887), a novel inspired by a then current anti-Semitic campaign.

Mathilda Lucka (b. Marienbad, Bohemia, 1844; d. Vienna, 1921), his daughter, acquired a reputation as a German translator of Scandinavian writers, including Brandes and Strindberg. She used the pseudonym Erich Holm.

LUDD, *see* Lydda.

LUDENDORFF, ERICH VON, *see* Anti-Semitism (under Germany).

LUDO, J., Roumanian writer, b. Jassy, Roumania, 1897. He was one of the most talented Jewish writers in Roumanian. In the 1930's he visited the United States, and after his return to Bucharest wrote a novel on the Jews of New York. It is a satirical piece of work, occasionally exaggerated in the description of the milieu and the Jewish types, but very much alive. Ludo also made several trips to Palestine, and did a great deal of work for Zionist publications, as a protagonist of ideas which are at the base of the Zionist ideology, but which he always treated from a personal and critical point of view. Part of Ludo's work in relation to Palestine was a book, *The Jordan Flows Into the Thames.*

But the greater portion of Ludo's literary achievement, all in Roumanian, is dedicated to the discussion of the Jewish question in Roumania. Gifted with powerful analytical ability, and fusing sarcasm, irony and humor in his critical approach, he has added beautiful and enduring pages to the record of polemics against anti-Semitism. The primary target of his attack was the old Roumanian anti-Semitic leader, A. C. Cuza, who maintained that Jews are unable to assimilate the language of their native countries or of the countries in which they live, and that they are incapable of producing anything of beauty or originality in literature, poetry and art. In *Two Great Poets— A. C. Cuza and Heinrich Heine,* Ludo, in addition to drawing a satirical parallel between Cuza—a versifier devoid of talent—and Heine, dissects the anti-Semitic theory of nationalism in art and proves its falsity. This study was of importance primarily in Roumania. But in a comprehensive book of almost 500 pages, *Around an Obsession: Presentations of a Jew to Roumanians of Good Faith* (1936), Ludo analyzes precisely the accusations made by Hitlerites and by Cuza. The book is spirited and replete with argument, and contains a study of the novel *Medelenii,* which had been very successful in Roumania. Written by a Roumanian Christian, Yonel Teodorian, the novel contains several Jewish characters, depicted as dishonest, and physically and morally repugnant.

For several years Ludo edited a weekly, *Adam,* published in Bucharest, and dedicated to the struggle against anti-Semitism. He was active in Jewish life in Roumania. Living in France during 1938 and 1939, Ludo worked on a study of Voltaire and the Jews, which, in 1942, was still in Paris in manuscript form.

Saniel Labin.

LUDOMIR, VIRGIN OF (Ludmirer Moyd), popular name of a mysterious Hasidic "woman-Zaddik" of the 19th cent., b. Ludomir, province of Volhynia, Russia, about 1815; d. Palestine, 1905. Her real name was Hannah Berbermacher (she was known also as Chane Rachel Werbermacher). She acquired an extensive knowledge of Haggadah and Midrash, and indulged in ecstatic praying. Soon the word spread that the daughter of Monesh Berbermacher was holy and worthy of the title of "Zaddik." She became engaged to a man whom she loved greatly, but her yearning for this man whom custom forbade her to see, and the death of her mother, led her to seek solitude and to retire from society.

After an illness during which, according to legend, she was translated to Heaven, where she received a new and very great soul, she broke her engagement, and began to live like a male, observing all the religious duties observed by Jewish men, such as praying in a Tallith and putting on the Tefillin. She built a house of prayer in which she preached to the people from an adjoining room. Multitudes made pilgrimages to her home because of her alleged miracles, and a special group of Hasidim gathered about her; these were known as the "Hasidim of the Maid of Ludomir." Prominent Zaddikim attempted to persuade her to marry; they were finally successful, and she married twice, in name only, but was soon divorced. After her marriage her popularity waned; toward the end of her life she went to Palestine, where she died.

Lit.: Horodezky, S. A., *Religiöse Strömungen im Judentum* (1920) 187-90; idem, *Hahasidim Vehahasiduth,* vol. 4, pp. 70-71; Gross, Joseph, in *Jewish Ledger,* Dec. 4, 1936.

LUDWIG, EMIL, author, b. Breslau, Germany, 1881. His grandfather and other members of his family were Silesian steel manufacturers; his father, Hermann Ludwig Cohn (see vol. 3, p. 260), was an eminent ophthalmologist and humanitarian on the faculty of the University of Breslau. When Ludwig was two years old his father, wishing to protect his children against the anti-Jewish bias then prevalent, established the family name as Ludwig, by a special royal decree (1883). The son was awarded the degree of doctor of jurisprudence at the university and, following his father's example, became interested in social health. Until the age of twenty-five he followed legal and mercantile pursuits.

Although Ludwig began writing plays and verses at fifteen, he did not attempt prose seriously until he was thirty. From 1907 on he traveled widely and lived only intermittently in Germany; he established his home on Lake Maggiore in 1907, leaving Germany at an early age "for no reason other than the lack of freedom." Before the first World War he went to London as the correspondent of a German newspaper.

Ludwig's first published writings were six plays, three of them achieving performances. Then followed a novel, *Diana* (1918), and its sequel, *Quiet Sea* (1919). In 1920 he published his first analytical study of a great intellectual, *Goethe,* and found the channel for his creative energies. It was the first full-length biography in the style, widely emulated since then, that preceded the English and French biographies, as well as those by other Germans. From

Emil Ludwig

that time on, in a succession of books, he published his analyses of great leaders, living and dead, supplementing his reading by personal interviews with his subjects, including Franklin D. Roosevelt, Benito Mussolini, Joseph Stalin, Thomas A. Edison, David Lloyd George, and many other leading figures.

Ludwig's literary reputation was greatly enhanced in Europe by the publication of *Goethe*, whom he regarded as his "only master" throughout his career. Of this book 120,000 copies were sold in Germany. But the book that won him wide popularity in the United States was *Napoleon*, issued abroad in 1926 and in America in 1927. So little known was Ludwig that several of his early books were bought by American publishers for nominal sums from European agents; thus *Napoleon* was sold in the United States for $1,000. In quick succession he now published books dealing with Bismarck, Wilhelm II, Lincoln, and Jesus. Later on he began interviewing living personalities for a series of interpretative portraits, some of which made a sensation. Chief among these, besides the leaders already mentioned, were Calvin Coolidge, Thomas G. Masaryk, Fridtjof Nansen, Aristide Briand, Eleutherios Venizelos, and Jane Addams. In 1923 Ludwig sought to introduce the former Kaiser Wilhelm II as a character in a play entitled *Bismarck's Dismissal*. The Kaiser, an exile in Holland, attempted to prevent production of the play, but Ludwig won the resulting lawsuit against Wilhelm and the play was performed more than 1,000 times throughout Germany.

In his method of sizing up both the mental and physical characteristics of his subjects Ludwig was in tune with modern methods of studying character, but despite the emphasis he gave to Wilhelm II's withered arm and President Roosevelt's fight with infantile paralysis (*Roosevelt,* 1937), he denied that he was in any way indebted to Freud, whose theory seemed to him "disastrous rather than educative." Describing himself as a painter of landscape and character, he refused to be identified with original research into documents but formed his estimates on the basis of studies already available, guided by his intuitive knowl-

edge of human behavior. Only in one instance, *Schliemann* (1931), did he write from original research made by him on the subject. He considered the public and private life of a man equally valuable to the interpreter and said "there are no uninteresting people." Some of his work has been criticized for its journalistic glibness. His interest in environment led him to write *The Nile* (1936), a successful study of the influence of a river on people.

With the intensification of nationalism and totalitarianism in Europe, Ludwig placed himself on the side of a rational world order in which imperialism and dictatorship were outlawed. Early in life he had been enrolled as a member of the Lutheran state church; when Walther Rathenau was murdered in 1922 he resigned officially as a protest and emphasized his Jewish birth, declaring: "This cold-blooded murder of a great Jew, who was my friend, made such a fearful impression on me that I decided to show before all Germany that I am a Jew too."

In 1932 he applied for citizenship in Switzerland, where he had lived virtually since his youth. His antagonism to the Nazi party led to the announcement, in 1933, that Ludwig's books—including his most popular, *Goethe*—would be burned publicly with those of Thomas Mann, Lion Feuchtwanger, Jakob Wassermann, Jack London, Upton Sinclair and many others; Ludwig, at the time in his Swiss home, said defiantly: "Remarque, my neighbor, and I attempt to hear over the radio the crackling of the flames and drink together the oldest Rhine wine." Subsequently he preserved within a single frame such of his honors as the French Légion d'Honneur, a certificate of honorary Swiss citizenship, an American honorary university degree, and a photograph of the burning of his books in Berlin. The confiscation of his funds by Germany led to a protest by Switzerland, and they were restored to him.

In 1934 Ludwig declared that "fate is preparing the final doom of nationalism," and "the ideal of world citizenship will tower above the waters of the final deluge." During a lecture tour of the United States (1936), he predicted the imminence of a world war. At the Congress of the P. E. N., an international organization of writers, in Edinburgh in 1934, he proposed that authors band together in formal protest against war-mongering and war, thus speaking in place of "the impotent League of Nations." At a session of the American Jewish Congress in New York in September, 1937, he urged recognition of the Jews as entitled to membership in the League.

After the outbreak of war in 1939, Ludwig continued to advocate a United States of Europe, without, however, developing any detailed economic and political proposals. In 1940 he published *Three Portraits,* studies of Mussolini, Stalin and Hitler, which contained a revision of his earlier estimate of Mussolini's character in *Talks with Mussolini* (1932). In the earlier book Ludwig reported Mussolini's praise of the Jews of Italy and his abhorrence of theories of racial purity; now Ludwig decided that Mussolini had found it expedient to yield to Hitler. He still saw a chance for Mussolini to rank as a statesman, but "if he plunges into his imitator's adventure, he will perish with him." In 1940 Ludwig returned to the United States to give s to work for the defense savings program foreign language groups. Following the at- Pearl Harbor in December, 1941, he under- a dollar-a-year job at Washington to conduct propaganda, writing, and broadcasting to the Germans in the United States.

Among Ludwig's other books of note were: a biography of Lincoln (1939); *July, 1914* (1929); *Leaders of Europe* (1934); *Hindenburg* (1935); *Cleopatra* (1937); *A New Holy Alliance* (1938); *Quartet* (1939); *Bolivar, the Life of an Idealist;* and *The Mediterranean* (1942). Ludwig was author also of *Gifts of Life: A Retrospect* (1931); *The Germans* (1941), and of several novels and plays. His play *Versailles* was produced in London in 1932. Ludwig also depicted with comprehension such outstanding controversial Jewish figures as Ferdinand Lassalle, as the great counterfoil of Bismarck, dealt with in the first part of the trilogy *Bismarck* (1929), and Walther Rathenau, in the book *Eight Etchings from Life* (1934).

Some of his works were translated into twenty-six languages. In 1942 there were twenty-five of these renditions in American libraries. The British-American edition of *Goethe* is fragmentary, containing only half the book, which exists in extenso in twelve other languages.   HARRY HANSEN.

Lit.: Ludwig, Emil, "A Portrait of My Father (Hermann Ludwig Cohn)," *Opinion,* vol. 8, No. 12 (Oct., 1938) 13-14; Graeber, I., "A Romantic Historian, the Career of the Eminent Writer of Biographies, Emil Ludwig," *Jewish Tribune,* Jan. 20, 1928, p. 1; Ludwig, Emil, "My Return to the Fold," *American Hebrew,* April 3, 1931, p. 527; *ibid.,* March 11, 1932, p. 436 (excerpts from his autobiography); "Herman Keyserling Snubs Ludwig for Book on Bismarck; Biographer Charges Anti-Semitism," *Jewish Tribune,* March 9, 1928, p. 19; Hansen, Niels, *Der Fall Emil Ludwig* (1930).

LUDWIG, MAXIMILIAN, actor, b. Breslau, Germany, 1847; d. Berlin, 1906. At first he played in various small theaters; later he gave performances at the Brunswick court theater, the Stadttheater of Breslau and the German Hoftheater in St. Petersburg. In 1870 he married the actress Anna Zipser, and in September, 1872, they were guest artists at the Berlin Schauspielhaus. Ludwig received immediate acclaim, and for thirty-four years, until his death, he played important roles there. He was equally versed in classical drama and in modern comedy.

LUDWIG, RUVEN, Yiddish poet, b. province of Kiev, the Ukraine, Russia, 1895; d. Los Angeles, 1926. Until the age of twelve he attended the Heder and received a traditional Jewish education. For the next three years he lived in Kiev and attended the Brodsky school; however, having no right to live there, he emigrated to the United States in 1910. Here he attended public schools and was quickly Americanized. His first published poem appeared in English in the socialist newspaper, *The Call.* During his last years Ludwig lived in California and Arizona, whose landscapes are ever-present in his poetry.

His first Yiddish poems were published in 1915. His verse appeared in the *Freie Arbeter Shtimme, Yiddishe Volk, Yiddisher Kempfer, Zukunft, Varheit, Tog, Unheib, Vort* and other publications. In 1919 he joined the "Insich" group of expressionist poets, who called themselves "Introspectivists." His free verse appeared

in their anthology of 1920, and he continued to be identified with their movement until the time of his death. Yet, paradoxically, the impressionist poets, known as the "Yunge," considered his poetry more akin to their own, and Zisho Landau included a significant number of Ludwig's poems in the anthology which he edited in 1918.

Ludwig's poetry was full of suggestive imagery. In the first period of his writing the element of individualism was prevalent. During his second period, while living in the west, he was influenced by the rhythms and motifs of Indian and American life. His themes became broader and less subjective, permeated by a mood of quiet resignation.

His collected poems were published posthumously by his widow and A. Leyeles (*Gesamelte Lieder,* New York, 1927).   N. B. MINKOFF.

Lit.: Glanz, A. (Leyeles), in *Tog,* Nov. 23, 1924, and Aug., 1926; Feinberg, L., in *Freiheit,* Aug., 1926; Leyeles, A., preface to Ludwig's *Gesamelte Lieder;* Weinper, Z., *Yiddishe Shriftshteler* (1933) 136-39.

LUEGER, KARL, see ANTI-SEMITISM (UNDER AUSTRIA).

LUGO, city in Italy. A Hebrew inscription from the grave of Moses Min Hapesachim, now kept in the city museum and dating from the year 1285, shows that Jews lived in Lugo at about that time. Otherwise nothing is known of a Jewish community then. In the 16th cent. Lugo was a center of Jewish learning, as the presence of rabbis like Samuel del Vecchio and Benjamin Raphael da Reggio proves. The censor Camillo Tagel lived there at the beginning of the 16th cent. Many Hebrew manuscripts were copied in Lugo in that period, of which the valuable Kaufmann manuscript of the Mishnah is especially noteworthy.

In 1598 Lugo came under papal jurisdiction, together with the Duchy of Ferrara, and in 1639 the Jews were compelled, by order of the pope, to live in the ghetto. The Jews of the neighboring towns of Bagnocavallo, Cotignola, Massa and Fusignano, in which the pope had forbidden the Jews to stay, concentrated in Lugo. The families of Finzi, Sinigaglia, and Del Vecchio, from which many rabbis came, were prominent in the 17th cent.

In 1796 the city was conquered and plundered by the French; the Jews especially suffered. After the withdrawal of the French forces the homes of the Jews were again pillaged by the peasants of the neighborhood who had been stirred up against the foreign intruders. But after the French had proclaimed the emancipation of the Jews, the gates of the ghetto fell, and in 1799 Moses Finzi, a Jew, was elected to the city council. Nevertheless, in the same year the homes of the Jews were again plundered by the populace upon the approach of the Austrian troops. A rabbi of Lugo, Solomon David del Vecchio, was a member of the Napoleonic Sanhedrin.

The reestablishment of the papal rulership in 1814 restored the former unfavorable position of the Jews. Therefore many Jewish families, especially those with property, emigrated, and thus the decline of the Jewish community began. After short periods of freedom in 1831 and from 1848 to 1849, the Jews of Lugo finally received equal civic rights in 1859 with the end of the papal rulership. In 1860 Lugo became a part of the kingdom of Sardinia, which in 1861 was incorporated into the new kingdom of Italy.

The Jewish community of Lugo continued to diminish, and in 1933 it numbered only twenty persons and was not organized. In the synagogue of Lugo beginning at that time services were held only on Yom Kippur. A Pinkas (record book) of the Jewish community of Lugo from the years 1621 to 1630 was, in 1942, in the British Museum (Codex 1141). The Pinkas of the Hebrah Kaddisha (burial society) of Lugo for 1618 to 1687 and the Death Matricule (Register of Deaths) for 1658 to 1824 were, in 1942, in the library of the Jewish Theological Seminary of America, in New York (Register 5689, p. 136 et seq.).

Prominent rabbis who lived in or came from Lugo in the 17th cent. included Solomon David ben Moses, Abraham ben Sabbatai Isaac Berechiah of Fano, Elhanan David Foà and Netanel Segrè; in the 18th cent., Sabbatai Elhanan ben Elisha and Solomon Moses.

After the promulgation, in 1930, of the new law governing Jewish communities in Italy, the small Jewish community of Lugo became a section of the community of Ferrara, where it was represented by Mario Forli (d. 1938). By 1942, as a result of the Italian Fascist anti-Semitic legislation and emigration overseas, the Lugo community was reduced to only a few families.   UMBERTO CASSUTO.

Lit.: Pesaro, "Cenni sulla comunità israelitica di Lugo," *Vessillo Israelitico*, vol. 29, pp. 234, 267, 298, 330, 360; vol. 30, p. 4; Krauss, Samuel, in *Monatsschrift für Geschichte und Wissenschaft des Judentums*, vol. 51, p. 460; Mortara, *Indice*; Della Torre, *Scritti sparsi*, vol. 2; *Revue des études juives*, vol. 16, p. 247; Margoliouth, *Catalogue of the British Museum*, vol. 3, p. 568 et seq.

LUGOJ (LUGOS), city in southwestern Transylvania, Roumania, with a Jewish population of 1,700 out of a total of 19,000. Up to the peace treaty of Trianon (1920) Lugoj, known as Lugos, in Krassó-Szörény county, formed a part of Hungary. The Jewish community was founded between 1780 and 1790 as an affiliate of the Jewish community of Makó, Hungary. In the beginning it was under the jurisdiction of the chief rabbi of the neighboring Bánát government district. In 1790 the Hebrah Kaddisha (burial society) of Lugos had 220 members. The elementary school founded in 1833 was still functioning a hundred years later, and during the first World War the Jewish community established in its building a hospital for wounded soldiers. The synagogue was built in 1842; the Talmud Torah, founded in 1903, had 160 students. Jews conducted large manufacturing industries.

Whereas from 1918 to 1938 the Jews of Lugoj were subjected mostly to cultural handicaps in that, contrary to minority rights, they were forced to adopt Roumanian as the language of instruction in their school, after 1938, under German Nazi influence, many were deprived of citizenship rights and suffered other serious disabilities and persecution.

LUIS DE TORRES, *see* AMERICAN CONTINENT; COLUMBUS, CHRISTOPHER.

LUKÁCS, GYÖRGY (GEORG), philosopher and esthete, b. Budapest, 1885. He was the son of a wealthy banker, and received his degrees of political sciences and doctor of philosophy University of Budapest. Before the first Wor he took part in the founding of the Thalia theat stage for the production of modern plays in Budapest. He also published such works of merit on esthetics as (in German) *Die Seele und die Form* (1911) and (in Hungarian) *A modern dráma fejlődésének története* (History of the Development of Modern Drama; 1912). He was appointed commissar of education in the Hungarian Republic of Soviets (1919), and after the downfall of that government emigrated to Vienna, and subsequently to Russia. During the 1920's he published (in German): *Die Theorie des Romans* (1920); *Geschichte und Klassenbewusstsein* (1923); *Lenin: Studien über den Zusammenhang seiner Gedanken* (1924); *Moses Hess und das Problem der idealistischen Dialektik* (1926); and (in French) *Après Trianon* (1927); *La Hongrie et la civilisation* (1929). He contributed to the Hungarian journal of literature and opinion *Uj Hang* (New Voice), published from 1938 on in Moscow.

Lukács' works reflect the development of revolutionary philosophy during two decades from militant revolutionism toward the rapprochement to the humanitarian ideal which is the core of democracy. In his earlier writings he was concerned with the philosophy of planned revolutionary action. Later he investigated the effect of rationalized industry upon the individual and his means of self-expression, such as philosophy, art and literature. He held that the rationalization and division of production led to the disintegration of the human personality. To him, the psychological trend of contemporary literature betrayed a deliberate shrinking from contact by fractionary modern personality with the complexity of the outer world. He considered Freud's *oeuvre* as a symptom of decadence. The salvation of mankind, according to him, will come from humanism as embodied in the writings of such novelists as Tolstoi, Gorki, Romain Rolland and Thomas and Heinrich Mann. He conceived the masses, unaffected by modern abstractions, as powerful reservoirs of humanism.

LUKAS (LUKÁCS), PAUL, film and stage actor, b. Budapest, 1895. He was living in New York city in 1942. The son of a Jewish father and a Christian mother, Lukas was brought up in the Christian faith. At the age of nineteen he served in the Austro-Hungarian army during the first World War; on being discharged because of wounds, he took up dramatic studies and soon appeared before the public at Kassa. In 1918 he was given a contract by the Vigszinház at Budapest, foremost privately owned stage of Hungary. He played leading roles in comedies and dramas by Shaw, Chekhov, Molnár, Lengyel and others.

In 1927 he received a contract from Paramount Famous Players-Lasky Corporation of Hollywood, and since that time appeared in a number of moving pictures, such as *The Vice Squad, Shopworn Angel, Strictly Dishonorable, Little Women, Dodsworth, The Lady Vanishes* and *Confessions of a Nazi Spy*. His insight into the rich variations which are produced in men's characters by the individual context of their fates enabled him to offer convincing interpretations.

Lulab delivered to the home, a regular custom in many lands

When, in 1937, after a decade of film acting, he appeared on Broadway as Dr. Rank in Ibsen's *A Doll's House,* his performance was hailed for its depth and complexity. His appearance in *The Watch on the Rhine,* in 1941, scored another great success and won him, among other honors, the Delia Austrian Medal of the Drama League for the most distinguished performance of the season.

LUKE, GOSPEL OF, *see* GOSPELS.

LULAB. The Lulab consists of four different species of plants, a citron ('*ethrog*), a palm-branch (*lulab*), three myrtle twigs, and two branches of the willows of the brook. These four plants are combined into a bunch and held in the hand at the Sukkoth festival, in accordance with the Biblical command (*Lev.* 23:40): "And ye shall take you on the first day the fruit of goodly trees, branches of palm-trees, and boughs of thick trees, and willows of the brook. . . ." Therefore, during the seven days of the festival of Sukkoth, with the exception of the Sabbath, these four plants, bound together, are held in the hand, while the one who prays over them pronounces the prescribed benediction '*al netilath lulab* ("to hold the Lulab in the hand"). Then the Lulab is waved in all directions. These wavings are intended to symbolize joyful gratitude for the manifold gifts offered by nature, and the supreme power of God in the world.

In order to be fit for use in worship, the plants which compose the Lulab must be fresh and in a perfect condition. Thus the tip of the palm-branch must not be broken off or split, and the point of the Ethrog must be whole. The myrtle and willow leaves must be as intact as possible. The Ethrog is held in the left hand during the prayer; the other three plants, joined into a bunch by means of wickerwork or rings of palm leaves, are taken into the right hand. The worship in the synagogue is rendered especially solemn at the Sukkoth festival by reason of the fact that the Lulab is taken into the hand also when the Hallel Psalms (*Ps.* 113 to 118) are sung, and at the end of the special prayers (Hoshanoth) solemn processions are made around the scrolls of the Torah, which are placed in the middle of the synagogue, at the reading desk. Many symbolical interpretations of the meaning of the combination of plants are found in the Haggadah; they are sometimes regarded as symbols of Israel and its social and religious organization, sometimes as symbols of the patriarchs and matriarchs and their virtues, and often also as a glorification of God and His exalted powers (*Midrash Lev.* 30).

LULLABIES, *see* FOLK SONGS.

LUMBROSO, BARON ABRAM, physician and Tunisian public official, b. Tunis, 1813; d. Florence, Italy, 1887. Lumbroso was a descendant of an eminent Sephardic family; his father, Isaac Vita Lumbroso, was for thirty years president of the Portuguese consistory of Tunis and for four years judge of its court of appeals. Lumbroso studied both in Florence and in Pisa, obtaining his M.D. degree from the University of Pisa in 1835. That same year he became personal physician to the Tunisian Bey, and afterward director of the state sanitary service.

In 1846 Lumbroso visited Paris with the Bey, and received from King Louis Philippe the Order of the Legion of Honor. For his self-sacrificing activities during the cholera epidemic he received the title of baron from King Victor Emanuel II of Italy. He was decorated also by the Sultan of Turkey with the Order of the Medjidie. Lumbroso founded several scientific institutions in Tunis, of one of which he was president, and distinguished himself by his philan-

Blessing of the Lulab in the synagogue. From a 19th cent. sketch

thropic acts as well as by his skill as a physician. Two of his published works were *Schizzo storico-scientifico sul colera asiatico che invase la reggenza di Tunisi nel 1849-1850* (1850) and *Lettere medico-statistiche sulla reggenza di Tunisi* (1850).

Lit.: Jewish Encyclopedia, vol. 8, p. 153; De Gubernatis, *Piccolo dizionario dei contemporanei;* Haberling, Hübotter, Vierordt, *Biographisches Lexikon hervorragender Ärzte*, vol. 3, 2nd ed. (1929) 865; *Resiconto sulle opere del Barone Dr. Abram Lumbroso* (1886).

LUMBROSO, ALBERTO EMMANUELE, historian, b. Turin, Italy, 1872. Although he studied law at the University of Rome, he was soon attracted by literary and historical studies, and became known through articles and studies devoted chiefly to the Napoleonic epoch. One of his initial major works was a bibliography of the Napoleonic period (1896). In the following year he published *Napoleone I e l'Inghilterra*, in which he analyzed the origin and economic consequences of the Continental blockade, and a bibliography of the Continental blockade. Of greatest importance among his later works, almost all of which center around Napoleon and his times, was his *Napoleone, la sua Corte e la sua famiglia* (Genoa, 1913). During the first World War Lumbroso served as military attaché in Greece. In his major historical work on the economic and diplomatic origin of the first World War (1927) he gave a broad analysis of the background of the European conflict. He was principal contributor to, and for some time editor-in-chief of, the *Revue Napoléonienne* in Paris.

LUMBROSO, BARON GIACOMO, historian and archeologist, son of Abram, b. Tunis, 1844; d. Rapello, Italy, 1925. He served as professor of ancient history at the Universities of Pisa, Palermo and Rome. He devoted himself to research on the Hellenistic civilization in ancient Egypt, investigating the papyri and other sources. Lumbroso published the results of his studies in such books as *Recherches sur l'Égypte sous les Lagides* (1870), *L'Egitto al tempo dei Greci e dei Romani* (1882) and *Raccoltà di lettere scritte in Egitto* (1907). His chief work, *Testi e commenti concernenti l'antica Alessandria*, in ten volumes, was never published.

LUMBROSO, JACOB, rabbi and physician who lived in Venice in the early years of the 17th cent. He published an edition of the Hebrew Bible with an introduction and Masoretic notes, which he called *Melo Kaf Nahath* (Venice, 1638-39), and wrote a Spanish glossary to difficult words in the Bible, *Heshek Shelomoh* (Venice, 1588). His supposed authorship of a Spanish refutation of Grotius' attacks on the Jews, *Sostenimiento de la Ley Divina*, is refuted by the fact that Lumbroso himself ascribed the work to Isaac Orobio.

LUMBROZO, JACOB (JOHN), physician and early American colonist, b. Lisbon, Portugal; d. Maryland, at the end of 1665 or the beginning of 1666. From the fact that he had a sister in Holland whom he mentions in his will (her name is illegible, except for an initial R) and that his wife Elizabeth, presumably a non-Jewess, bore an English name, it has been conjectured that he spent some time in Holland and England before coming to America. "Ye Jew doctor," as he was called, was the first known Jew to settle in the colony of Maryland, and a document of the time notes an event as occurring "soone after ye arryvall of ye Jew." The exact date of his settlement can not be determined; the earliest date in the records connected with him is January 24, 1656, when he presented to a planter a bill amounting to 400 pounds of tobacco, that being the ordinary currency of the time. It is probable, therefore, that he had been in the colony for at least some months previous. Lumbrozo not only practised his profession, but was an active trader and money-lender; between December 1, 1657, and December 1, 1658, he was rendered judgments or attachments on at least nine persons because of debts owing him.

At the beginning of 1658 Lumbrozo was arrested and charged with blaspheming against the Christian religion by a group of zealots from Virginia who had temporarily assumed control of the colony. The so-called Edict of Toleration, promulgated in the colony in 1649, applied only to orthodox Christians; Lumbrozo, as a Jew, was by his very belief subject under the law to imprisonment or death. He was saved only by the general amnesty proclaimed on March 3, 1659, when Richard Cromwell succeeded his father as Lord Protector of England.

During the eight remaining years of his life Lumbrozo continued to reside in the colony, but gradually gave up his medical practice in favor of land speculation. After 1661 he is invariably called "John" rather than "Jacob"; in 1662 he married a Christian woman, and in 1663 he took out letters of denization. Since, in the latter case, he had to take an oath "on the true faith of a Christian," it is probable that he at least outwardly conformed to the Christian religion. In 1665 he was granted the right to trade with Indians, and about the same time secured a land grant along Nangemy Creek which was known for some time as Lumbrozie's Discovery. His death seems to have been sudden, but no details are known; his only son, John, was born a month after his father's death.

One of the results of Lumbrozo's trial for blasphemy was that Jews avoided the colony of Maryland for nearly a century afterwards, not settling there until shortly before the Revolution.

Lit.: Hollander, J. H., in *Publications of the American Jewish Historical Society*, No. 1 (1892) 25-40; No. 2 (1894) 38-41; Hartogensis, B. H., in *Jewish Exponent*, Dec. 2, 1927.

LUMLEY, BENJAMIN, theatrical director, b. Canada, 1811; d. London, 1875. He was brought to England in his childhood by his father, and was educated at King Edward's School in Birmingham. He became a solicitor in London in 1832. From 1837 to 1842 he served as a parliamentary agent, and in 1838 he published *Parliamentary Practise on Passing Private Bills*, which is still the standard book on the subject.

From 1836 to 1841 he supervised the finances of Her Majesty's Theatre, and in 1841 became its manager. He remained in this position for eight years, and in that time he revolutionized the entire system of opera production. His most important innovation was the introduction of the star system. Among the well-known artists he employed were Grisi, Persiani,

Tamburini, and Jenny Lind. In 1849 quarrels with the stars and other factors forced him to retire from the management. He tried to recoup his fortunes in Paris in 1850 and again in London in 1856, but failed both times and was compelled to accept the receipts of two benefit performances held for him in 1863.

Lumley was the author of two scientific fantasies of the type which H. G. Wells later popularized, *Sirenia* (1862) and *Another World* (1873). He wrote also *Reminiscences* (1864).

LUNCZ, ABRAHAM MOSES, historian and geographer of Palestine, b. Kovno, Russia, 1854; d. Jerusalem, 1918. He was sent to Jerusalem at the age of fourteen, and was educated in the Orthodox Jewish tradition at the rabbinical school Etz Chayim. His studies brought him into contact with the Maskilim, and he accepted their doctrines of reform and enlightenment; therefore he had to leave the school in 1870. During the following years he traveled extensively through Palestine, writing newspaper articles on the physical and spiritual condition of the country. He went blind at the age of twenty-five, but this personal tragedy in no way diminished the enthusiasm or volume of his writings on Palestine. In 1902 he founded the Institute of the Blind, of which he was president until the time of his death.

Luncz was a pioneer in the study of everything that pertained to Palestine. He wrote books on that country's anthropology, archeology, history, geography, literature and sociology in Hebrew, Yiddish, German and English. He also edited many volumes on the same subjects. Among his own works were *Moreh Derech Beeretz Yisrael Vesuriah* (1891), *Durch Palestina* (Yiddish; 1895) and *Die jüdischen Kolonien Palästinas* (1902). Among the works which he edited were *Jerusalem, Jahrbuch zur Beförderung einer wissenschaftlich genauen Kenntnis des jetzigen und des alten Palästina* (German and Hebrew; 13 vols., 1882-1919), *Hameammer* (3 vols., 1905-19), and the tractates *Berachoth, Peah, Demai, Kilayim and Shebiith* of the Palestinian Talmud (1907-19).

The Jewish Society for the Exploration of Palestine dedicated a book to Luncz in 1928.

LUNEL, chief town in the department of Hérault, Southern France. Some historians maintain that Lunel was founded by Jews who came thither in the 1st cent., after the destruction of the Second Temple. Sidonius Apollinarius mentions a Jewish community existing in Lunel at the end of the 5th cent. There was a synagogue here in the 6th cent. The barons and bishops in general were well-disposed toward the Jews of Lunel and also to those of other localities, who many times found refuge and protection in Lunel, especially when they fled from the persecutions of the West Goths in the 6th and 7th centuries, and from the persecutions which took place in southeastern France in the 12th cent.

Lunel was not only an important commercial center, but also a great center of Jewish culture. Benjamin of Tudela, who visited Lunel in 1166, extolled the community of 300 members for being prosperous and educated, for energetically interceding in favor of their coreligionists in other lands, and for supporting the many foreign students who attended the famous acad-

emy of Lunel, which was therefore called "the dwelling place of the Torah" (*Itinerary,* vol. 1, p. 37). Maimonides also greatly esteemed the community; in one of his letters he declared: "Members of the congregation of Lunel and of the neighboring towns are the only ones who raise aloft the banner of Moses." Meir ben Todros Halevi Abulafia of Toledo (1180-1244) addressed a letter "to the wise men of Lunel" in which he sharply objected to Maimonides' theories. When Solomon ben Abraham of Montpellier banned the adherents of Maimonides, the community of Lunel opposed such obscurantism and, in cooperation with three other Provençal communities, retaliated by excommunicating him and his two disciples.

The inhabitants of Lunel took no part in the Albigensian wars, hence the Jews, who then enjoyed full rights, were left unmolested by the troops of Simon de Montfort in 1209 to 1213. Among those commissioned in 1286 to collect the taxes imposed upon the Jews by Philip the Fair was Solomon ben Isaac the "Nasi." In 1293 part of the revenues of Lunel was pawned by Rosselin, lord of Lunel, to a Jew called Thauros. The Jews' privileges continued to be respected when Lunel came under the rule of Philip the Fair; however, the expulsions of the Jews from France in 1306 and in 1321 to 1322 led to the extermination of this prosperous community, of which only the former synagogue in the Rue Alphonse Ménard and the cemetery remain.

But Lunel continued to live in the surnames and family names Yarhi and Hayarhi, which occurred frequently. The Hebraized name of this town was Jericho, also Bikath Jericho and Migdal Jericho, probably because the name Lunel was derived from the French *lune* ("moon") and was translated as *yerah* into Hebrew. Sages who were born or who resided in Lunel for a time therefore assumed the surname Yarhi. Among these were the Talmudist David Hayarhi, the liturgical poet Judah Hayarhi ben Levi, the sage Solomon ben Abba Mari, and the polemist Abba Mari ben Moses, chief anti-Maimunist, whose *Sefer Hayerah* clearly alludes to Lunel. Other famous sages who came from Lunel or lived there for a rather long time were: Judah ibn Tibbon (1120-90), translator and physician; Samuel ibn Tibbon (1160-1239), translator; Meshullam ben Jacob (d. 1170), who induced Judah ibn Tibbon to translate Bahya ibn Pakuda's *Duties of the Heart* into Hebrew, and his five learned sons Joseph, Isaac, Jacob, Aaron, and Asher, surnamed "the Rosh of Lunel"; Abraham ben David of Posquières (d. 1198); Abraham ben David of Lunel, at whose request Maimonides sent the *Moreh Nebuchim* to Lunel; Joseph ibn Plaut, in his day an important rabbi of Provence; Manoah of Lunel, commentator of Maimonides' *Mishneh Torah;* Meir ben Isaiah; Moses ben Jehudah of Béziers; Abraham ben Nathan, author of the famous ritual book *Hamanhig;* and Jonathan ben David Hakohen, "who stood at the head of the wise of Lunel."

NICHOLAS SARGOLOGOS.

Lit.: Graetz, H., *History of the Jews,* vol. 3 (1927) 396-98, 489-92, 524, 530; vol. 4 (1927) 33, 48, 55; Bédarrides, *Les juifs en France,* p. 102; Gross, H., *Gallia Judaica* (1897) 277-90; Dubnow, S., *Weltgeschichte des jüdischen Volkes,* vol. 4 (1926) 299, 332; Saige, *Les Juifs du Languedoc,* pp. 21, 39; Vaissette, *Histoire générale du Languedoc,* vol. 2, pp. 516-17; vol. 3, p. 499 et seq.; *Revue des études juives,* vol. 14, p. 172; Carmoly, E., *Histoire des médecins juifs* (1844); Millerot, *Histoire de la ville de Lunel;* Rouet, Abbé A., *Notice sur la ville de Lunel,* pp. 13-77; Zunz, Leopold, *Literaturgeschichte der synagogalen Poesie* (1865-67) 460; *Histoire littéraire de la France,* vol. 16, pp. 381-87; Renan, E., and Neubauer, A., *Les rabbins français* (1877) 431 et seq., 510-14; idem, *Les écrivains juifs-français* (1894) 401, 404 et seq.

LUNEL, ARMAND, author, b. Aix-en-Provence, France, 1892. He studied literature and philosophy, and became professor at the College of Monaco. In 1926 Lunel published his novel *Esther de Carpentras,* a historical picture describing the condition of the Jews in the ancient Comtat Venaissin. Darius Milhaud composed an opera on the basis of a libretto which dramatized Lunel's novel. The history of the Jews of the Comtat Venaissin, especially of Carpentras, continued to occupy Lunel's poetic fancy, which was nourished by his Jewish consciousness, his knowledge of Jewish and French history, and his genuine love of his Provençal country. Lunel's literary style developed into an original and attractive blend of the specific Provençal humor and Jewish wit and irony, of Provençal and Jewish folklore and creative imagination. These qualities distinguish his stories *Du temps des ghettos comtadins* (1932) and *Jérusalem à Carpentras.* Lunel also published the novel *Le balai du sorcier* (1935) and other novels and short stories.

LUNGE, GEORG, chemist, b. Breslau, Germany, 1839; d. Zurich, Switzerland, 1923. He was educated at the University of Breslau, and obtained his Ph.D. degree at the age of nineteen. He later continued his studies at the University of Heidelberg. In 1865 he went to England to work as a chemist for a coal-tar products factory. He founded and was first president of the Newcastle Chemical Society, which later became the Society of Chemical Industry.

He returned to Europe in 1876 and was appointed professor of technical chemistry at the Polytechnische Schule at Zurich, a post which he held until 1907, when he resigned. During this time he conducted his most important experiments and became famous as the outstanding technical analyst of his day. He perfected various chemical processes, introduced methyl orange as an indicator, and invented the nitrometer and the gasvolumeter. He also drew up tables of the specific gravities of hydrous solutions.

Lunge was an extremely prolific author of books and articles covering the entire field of technical chemistry. Among his major works are: *Handbuch der Sodaindustrie* (2 vols., 1879-80); *Die Industrie des Steinkohlenteers* (1882); *Chemisch-technische Untersuchungsmethoden* (4 vols., 1900-5); *Handbook of Technical Gas Analysis* (1912). He translated all his works into English.

LUNTESCHUTZ, JULES ISAAK, painter, b. Besançon, France, 1822; d. Frankfort, Germany, 1893. He studied at the École royale des Beaux Arts in Paris. In 1845 he moved to Frankfort. He was a welcome guest in the patrician homes of Frankfort, where he painted many ceilings and sofraportes. He preferred the historical style, but his main field was portraiture. Four times he painted Schopenhauer, who was a close friend. He himself was portrayed by Courbet, as also by Marées. Lunteschutz' style may be termed impressionistic. Some of his paintings were exhibited at the Germanic Museum in Nuremberg, at the Staedel Institute, and also at the Schopenhauer-Archiv in Frankfort. Lunteschutz translated into German Passavant's study on Raphael.

LURIA, widespread and frequent Jewish family name in Central and Eastern Europe and the United States; there are numerous by-forms, such as Loria, Lourie, Lurie and Lurje. A tradition traced the family back to the Mishnah teacher Johanan Hasandelar (2nd cent.), and at various times genealogical tables were even drawn up to trace the descent back that far. Thus there is in existence a table by Johanan Luria (15th cent.), contained in the *Hamikneh* of Josel of Rosheim; another, by Hananiah Solomon ben Aaron, was printed in *Hamaggid* (vol. 1, p. 178). The best-known is an old table, published in the *Maaloth Hayuhasin* of Ephraim Solomon Margolioth (Lemberg, 1900), in which the Italian and Polish line is carefully worked out.

It may be assumed with tolerable certainty, despite the fact that the accounts can be verified only in part, that the Luria family was descended from Solomon Spira (14th cent.), a descendant of Rashi. The most trustworthy genealogy is that of Abraham Epstein, *Mishpahath Luria* (Vienna, 1901). This seems to have been used by Anton Lourié, who published a private edition (Vienna, 1923) which included the German and Polish branches. The origin of the name is nevertheless uncertain, although it may come from the Italian town of Loria; the connection between the Italian Lurias and the other branches of the family has not been established. On the other hand, the early German branch can be traced to 1613, after which it continues in Poland. The first known bearer of the name was Anton Luria, who lived in Alsace in the 15th cent.; among the most famous were Josel of Rosheim, Jehiel ben Aaron of Brest-Litovsk, founder of the Polish line, and those given separate articles.

Lit.: Horodezky, S. A., in *Encyclopaedia Judaica,* vol. 10 (1934), cols. 1194-96.

LURIA, ISAAC, founder of the school of practical, or Lurian, Cabala, b. Jerusalem, 1534; d. Safed, Palestine, 1572. He is known also as Haari (generally abbreviated to Ari, "lion"), from the initials of the words *ha'elohi rabbi yitzhak,* "the divine rabbi Isaac," and is sometimes given the family name Ashkenazi, because his parents originated from Germany. His brief life is encrusted with layers of legend. No Cabalist authority of modern times enjoyed greater veneration, and to his followers he was the ideal of spirituality. This adoration was not altogether undeserved, for Luria's life was dedicated to the pursuit of the spiritual and his character was a saintly one.

Luria's father died when the son was but a child, and the latter was sent to Cairo, where he was brought up by a rich uncle. He became a Talmudic authority in his teens, and then passed over to the study of the recently published *Zohar.* When he was about twenty-two he became a hermit, and lived alone for the next thirteen years, visiting his family only on Sabbaths and speaking entirely in Hebrew. Long periods of seclusion and contemplation nurtured his fertile imagination, and he began to believe that he had communication with the prophet Elijah, who on numerous occasions explained to him the difficult passages in the *Zohar*. He also intimated that he was the forerunner of the Messiah; he believed that in his sleep his soul engaged in discourses with the ancient Talmudic sages in heaven. His disciples attributed to him supernatural knowledge, the power of performing miracles, the ability to exorcise demons, and a knowledge of the languages of the trees, birds and angels.

In 1569, in response to a "divine call," Luria journeyed to Palestine; he settled in Safed, then a center of Cabalistic study. He soon surrounded himself with a coterie of disciples and colleagues, including Solomon Alkabetz, Joseph Caro (who was apt to fall asleep when Luria expounded the mysteries of Cabala to him), Moses Cordovero, Luria's master, and Hayim Vital, Luria's Boswell. It is from Vital that a comprehensive account of the life and utterances of Luria is derived; for the latter wrote virtually nothing but three Sabbath hymns in the Aramaic language and a few other poems. When he was asked why he had written so little he replied to the effect that the abundance and profoundity of his thoughts rendered their recording impossible.

Vital, however, made a collection of all the available lecture notes written down by Luria's pupils. These notes thus assembled amounted to many volumes. Some were published, the most important collection being Vital's *Etz Hayim* (6 vols., Korzec, 1782), which furnishes the best presentation of Luria's Cabalistic views.

The pivotal points in the Lurian theoretical Cabala are the explanations of the Sefiroth, or organic vehicles of the Deity, and the Partzufim, or intermediaries. God Himself, as the En Sof ("The Endless"), was present everywhere before the creation of the world; but in order that the finite, whose existence and manifestation rest upon the merit of the infinite, might be brought into being, the En Sof had to contract or concentrate Himself, and from this contraction (*tzimtzum*) issued the infinite light. The concentration of this light produced a vacuum in its center which was surrounded by ten Sefiroth, or organic vehicles, vessels of the infinite realities in all their ramifications. Some of the infinite light, however, did manage to penetrate to the center. The inability of some of the Sefiroth to withstand the light necessitated their transformation into Partzufim, figures representing certain forces pervading life. While the light of the En Sof is a beneficent force, the lights of the broken Sefiroth or of those Sefiroth which are unable to endure the light are malevolent and the root of all evil. There are four worlds: emanation, creation, formation, and the physical world, in all of which these conflicting powers, forces, forms and degrees are functioning.

Luria regarded the creation of man "in the image of God" (*Gen.* 1) as a compelling reality. It was man's soul that united the infinite with the finite. Luria indulged in weird anthropological fancies, such as that when Adam was created all the souls destined for humanity were simultaneously created with all the organs of his body. Every human being is a "spark" (*nitzotz*) of Adam, and the quality of human souls is dependent upon the organ with which each is identified. When Adam sinned, the harmony previously existing among the various gradations of the souls was shattered, resulting in the debasement of the superior souls by contact with the inferior ones. This intrusion of inferiority Luria called Kelifoth ("shells"). The heathen world was the product of the inferior classes of souls, while the Jewish world issued from the superior souls. Nevertheless, because of the rupture in the harmony among the souls, the worst persons have some good in them and the best, some evil. The equilibrium or the ideal state (Olam Hatikkun) will be ushered in only with the advent of the Messiah. In the meanwhile, however, since man's soul, because of his imperfections, can not return to its origin, it is forced to migrate through various mundane objects such as human beings, animals and even inanimate objects. Luria would not kill even a worm because he believed that it carried someone's soul.

Luria believed that the whole world was teeming with spirits and he was reputed to be able to detect the souls residing or passing through a person. To his doctrine of the transmigration of souls Luria added that of Ibbur, or impregnation of the soul. Laxity in the observance of religious duties compelled the return of a departed soul to this world and its attachment to the soul of a living being for the purpose of purification. Even pure souls who had departed in death from the body would return in order to aid their weaker brethren, but only if they had some kinship in common, that is, if they issued from the same organ of Adam. The reason for the dispersion of the Jews, according to Luria, was that thereby the Jewish souls might elevate the non-Jewish souls.

Luria further held that every man bore in a mark upon his forehead the biography of his soul. Purification by union with a higher soul could be effected by mystical formulas and by the esoteric manipulation of numbers and letters. He invested every religious injunction and ceremony with mystic meaning; thus the Sabbath was the personification of God. Devotion in the recitation of prayers would have results in the celestial realms. In fact, perfunctory prayer was one of the greatest obstacles to the coming of the Messianic redemption. When a Jew prayed, he became a receptacle of divine light and a new agent for divine mercy. The mystical minutiae which Luria thus introduced were collected and systematized in a work called *Shulhan Aruch Shel Haari* (first published Cracow or Lublin, no date).

This absorption in mysticism popularized by Luria was destined to run riot and result in fantastic Messianic movements, culminating in that of Sabbatai Zevi. The form and content of Hasidism was also profoundly influenced by Lurian mysticism, particularly in regard to its belief in the efficacy of unrestrained emotion in prayer.

At first the notes of Luria's lectures were forbidden to be taken out of Palestine, under penalty of excommunication. Later, however, they were published in other countries, particularly in Italy, Germany, Holland and Poland.

The most important representatives of the Lurian

Cabala during the master's lifetime and afterwards were Israel Saruk, Moses Zacuto, Menahem Azariah da Fano, Nathan Spira, Abraham Azulai, Isaiah Horovitz and Moses Hayim Luzzatto. It is noteworthy that Luria's efforts to translate his principles into reality, by having his disciples and their families live in a group apart from society, proved a dismal failure, because of discord among their wives. However, the Lurian Cabala spread in various countries and proved lucrative to Luria's disciples: to Saruk in Italy, Horovitz in Germany, and Naphtali Frankfurter in Poland.

The hazardous theosophy of Luria is often a spiritualized anthropomorphism with its intimate corporeal description of the Godhead and its preoccupation with such irrational apparatus as mystical formulas, juggling with numbers, and excessive asceticism marked by frequent ablutions, fasting and vigils. A second Day of Atonement (Yom Kippur) was introduced on the seventh day of the joyous Sukkoth festival. The doctrine of the harmony of souls also produced baneful effects by increasing divorces to an alarming degree; petty mental differences were magnified and misinterpreted as being due to dissonant souls. Perhaps Luria recognized the dangers inherent in his views; according to Vital Luria, on his deathbed he urged his pupils to cease their studies as to marriages because the consequences, he feared, might be disastrous. Nevertheless, Luria did succeed in accentuating the importance of kindliness and righteousness and made religion a compelling and embracing force in the lives of his disciples. So highly did his pupils revere him that some of them, after his death, believed that his resurrection was imminent.

Among some of the works ascribed to Luria are the following: glosses to the tractates *Zebahim* and *Betzah,* no longer extant; *Sefer Hakavvanoth* (Venice, 1624), a mystical explanation of prayers; *Shulhan Aruch,* a mystical explanation of religious ceremonies; *Zohar Harakia* (Korzec, 1785), a commentary on the *Zohar.* He introduced also a prayer-book which in the main follows the Sephardic ritual but eliminates the Piyutim; this is widely used by Hasidic groups.

WALTER DUCAT.

Lit.: Bloch, P., *Die Kabbala auf dem Hohepunkte und ihre Meister* (1905); Ginsburg, C., *The Kabbalah* (1865); Horodezky, S. A., *Neuere mystisch-religiöse Strömungen unter den Juden in Polen* (1914); idem, in *Encyclopaedia Judaica,* vol. 10 (1934), cols. 1213-17; Schechter, S., *Studies in Judaism,* second series, pp. 251-80.

LURIA, MAX AARON, philologist, b. New York city, 1891. He was a great-great-grandson of the noted Cabalist Isaac Luria. Luria was educated at Columbia University (B.S., 1913, with special diploma for teaching French and Spanish; M.A., 1918; Ph.D., 1931). He taught English in Puerto Rico from 1910 to 1911, and French and mathematics at the Pleasantville (New York) Hebrew Sheltering Guardian Society School from 1912 to 1913. He taught Spanish at De Witt Clinton High School, New York city, from 1914 to 1917; was head of its Spanish department, from 1917 to 1924, and principal of its annex from 1924 to 1926. From 1926 to 1930, he was assistant professor of Spanish at the College of the City of New York, and became associate professor of Romance lan-

guages there in 1930. Four years later he was appointed to a full professorship in Romance languages at Brooklyn College, and still held this position in 1942. He served for one term as vice-president and then president of the New York chapter of the American Association of Teachers of Spanish.

Luria did notable research on the origins and development of Judeo-Spanish, the secular language of the Sephardic Jews, and made original contributions to the field of developing standards and measurements in Spanish. He wrote many articles on this and on other linguistic subjects, and the following books: *Correspondencia Comercial* (1917); *Lecturas Fáciles* (1916; with Lawrence A. Wilkins); *Lecturas Elementales* (1922); *Lectures Élémentaires* (1922; with Chankin); *Judeo-Spanish Dialects in New York City* (1930-31); *A Study of the Monastir Dialect of Judeo-Spanish* (1930; with extensive bibliography on Judeo-Spanish language and literature); *Judeo-Spanish Proverbs of the Monastir Dialect* (1933); *Correspondencia Comercial al Dia* (1941). He was also a contributor (1941-42) to this encyclopedia.

LURIA, SOLOMON BEN JEHIEL (known as **MaHaRSHaL,** from the initials of his title and name), Talmudist, b. Brest-Litovsk, Lithuania, 1510; d. Lublin, Poland, 1573. He received his Talmudic training from his grandfather, Rabbi Isaac Klauber of Posen, after which he became rabbi at Brest-Litovsk and founded a Yeshiva there. About 1550 he received a call to Ostrog, where he also founded a Yeshiva and was appointed by the government as district rabbi over Volhynia. In 1555 he moved to Lublin, where he spent his last years as director of the famous Yeshiva.

Luria was an intrepid seeker of the truth and of a stern, austere nature. He declaimed passionately against justice and hypocrisy, particularly on the part of the rabbis. This made him unpopular, but he won friends, for a synagogue in Lublin was called the Maharshal Shul, after him. His exposition of the Talmud was thorough and critical; he rejected the Pilpulistic methods of Jacob Pollak as well as the codifications of Joseph Caro and Moses Isserles. His chief service to Talmudic study was his endeavor to establish a correct Talmud text; the fruit of this was his *Yam Shel Shelomoh* (Sea of Solomon), a series of notes to seven tractates of the Talmud. Many of the corrections and variant readings assembled by Luria were incorporated into the first Amsterdam edition of the Talmud (17th cent.) and from there into later editions.

Luria denounced blind adherence to authority and did not shrink from attacking Maimonides and other codifiers when he believed that they were wrong. In general he was opposed to the systematic presentation of the laws in codes, holding that they did more harm than good. He was severely condemnatory of Cabala, attacking it in his *Menorath Zahab Tahor,* and he disliked philosophic speculations. His sole interest was the study of the Talmud, which he endeavored to render an exact science by careful determination of the text, stress upon a knowledge of grammar, and painstaking and exhaustive research.

His other works include: *Hochmath Shelomoh,* glosses to the Talmud; *Yerioth Shelomoh,* a commentary on Rashi; *Atereth Shelomoh,* a commentary on the

Shaare Durah of Isaac ben Meir; *Ammude Shelomoh,* a commentary on the *Sefer Mitzvoth Gadol* of Moses of Coucy; several Piyutim; responsa (Lublin, 1574-75).

Lit.: Hurwitz, Simon, *The Responsa of Solomon Luria* (1938); Horodezky, S. A., *Kerem Shelomoh* (1897).

LURIE, HARRY LAWRENCE, social worker, b. Goldingen, Latvia, 1892. He came to the United States at the age of six, and received his M.A. degree from the University of Michigan in 1922. From 1915 to 1920 Lurie was research director of the Associated Charities of Detroit, and from 1920 to 1922 director of relief and social service for that city's department of public welfare. While in Detroit he was also a lecturer in sociology at the Merrill-Palmer School. Lurie was made superintendent of the Jewish Social Service Bureau of Chicago in 1925, and remained there until 1930. For the last four years of this period he was on the faculty of the University of Chicago Graduate School of Social Service Administration, and in 1929 and 1930 a state public welfare commissioner for Illinois.

Lurie became director of the Bureau of Jewish Social Research in New York city in 1930. In 1935, when the organization became the Council of Jewish Federations and Welfare Funds, he was appointed executive director of the new organization. In 1942 he still held this post. Lurie also taught (1931) at the New York School of Social Work.

Lurie was especially active in promoting government relief and social security provisions. In 1930 he was made a member of the advisory committee of the United States Children's Bureau, and in 1940 a member of the Federal Family Security Committee. He was still serving on both committees in 1942. Lurie wrote many articles for social service periodicals, and became a member of the editorial board of the *Jewish Social Service Quarterly* in 1933.

LURJE, JOSEPH, educator and author, b. Pompiania, Lithuania, 1871; d. Jerusalem, 1937. He received his Ph.D. degree from the University of Berlin in 1896, and began his teaching career in Warsaw. In 1899 he became an editor of *Der Jud,* which was published in Warsaw. Lurje joined the staff of *Freind,* which was published in St. Petersburg, in 1903, and of *Das Yiddishe Folk* (Vilna) in 1906. A Zionist from his youth on, he attended the first Zionist Congress and many subsequent congresses. In 1907 he went to Palestine to teach at the Herzliah High School. From 1907 to 1911 he was head of the Palestine Teachers' Center. From 1919 to 1927 Lurje was director of the department of education for the Zionist Executive. Then he became supervisor of secondary schools, which post he held until 1933, when he was made director of education for the Jewish community of Palestine. Lurje occupied this position until his death.

LURYE, NOTE, Yiddish short story writer, b. Russia, 1907. He was reared in a Jewish agricultural colony, becoming first a worker, then a Comsomol (1922). He was a member of the Vuspp (Ukrainian Association of Proletarian Writers). In 1931 he completed his education at a Vuz (Institute for Higher Learning). Lurye made his literary debut in 1929,

when an excerpt from his novel, *Der Step Ruft* (The Steppe Calls), was published in *Emes.* The central theme of this work was the socialist reconstruction of the old Jewish agricultural colony, which was turned into a kolkhoz (collective farm), and the class struggle which ensued. Since he had a first-hand knowledge of farm-life and was a master of landscape description, his depiction of the Jewish farmers and of their mode of living is superb. Although the novel is realistic, there are traces of impressionism throughout. *Der Step Ruft* is one of the outstanding works of Yiddish proletarian prose written in the Soviet Union.

LURYE, NOYACH, Yiddish writer, b. Blanshe, district of Minsk, Russia, 1885. From 1905 to 1918 he was an active member of the Jewish Bund. He served in the Russian Army during Kerensky's regime, and in 1920 enlisted in the Red Army, partaking in the latter's march on Warsaw. He was also one of the active organizers of the Yiddish schools in the Soviet Union. Although Lurye embarked upon a literary career in 1911, it was not until after the Revolution that his works assumed maturity. He is best known by his long story, *Zavl Die Fies.* His most important work, *Brikn Brenen* (Bridges are Burning), is a collection of short stories and novelettes, most of which are devoted to episodes describing the civil war, the role of the Cheka in destroying nests of counter-revolutionaries, and the fiendish murder of the Jews by the Petlura and similar bands. Lurye is also author of a novel, *Hoichreider* (Loudspeaker; 1930).

Lit.: Reisen, Z., *Lexikon fun der Yiddisher Literatur, Presse un Filologie,* vol. 2, cols. 105-7.

LUSCHAN, FELIX VON, non-Jewish anthropologist, b. Vienna, 1854; d. Berlin, 1924. One of the leading anthropologists of his day, he served as professor of anthropology at the University of Berlin from 1900 to 1922 and as director of the Berlin Museum of Ethnology from 1904 until his death. In 1892 he formulated a theory of Jewish racial origin from a mixture of Semites, Aryan Amorites and Hittites. This theory had great vogue with Houston Stewart Chamberlain and other anti-Semites, but it was disproved by later investigations and disavowed by Luschan himself.

He was a tireless fighter against anti-Semitism and other forms of pseudo-scientific racism. In his Huxley memorial lecture in 1911 he stressed the fact that language, religion, nationality and race are quite distinct conceptions, although repeatedly confounded by the general public. In 1922 he published *Völker, Rassen, Sprachen,* in which he specifically discussed the Jewish question and denounced anti-Semitism. It was his contention in this book that science has shown that there is no race which is biologically inferior.

Luschan wrote voluminously on anthropological subjects. His works include: *Die Ausgrabungen von Sendschirli* (5 vols., 1893-1925); *Beiträge zur Anthropologie von Kreta, Rassen und Völker* (1908); *Die Altertümer von Benin* (1919).

Lit.: Zeitschrift für Ethnologie (1924).

LUSITANUS, ABRAHAM ZACUTUS, *see* ZACUTUS LUSITANUS, ABRAHAM.

LUSITANUS, AMATUS, *see* AMATUS LUSITANUS.

LUTHER, MARTIN, German religious reformer, b. Eisleben, Saxony, 1483; d. Eisleben, 1546. His attitude toward the Jews was decidedly friendly at the beginning of his career, but became pronouncedly hostile toward the end.

In the first period of his activity, from 1513 to 1535, Luther had little opportunity of coming into personal contact with Jews. His position with respect to them was that of the Christian theologian of his day. He was occupied with the idea of their conversion, which at the outset he regarded as altogether impossible of realization. However, when the Jews, inspired by hope that the convulsion within Christianity presaged the dawn of the Messianic era, began to concern themselves actively with Luther, and therefore took a more sympathetic stand toward him, there grew within him the conviction that it was the fault of the Catholic Church that the Jews had not yet been converted. He actually believed that the Jews would adopt his teaching collectively, and that the great work of their conversion would be bound up with his name. Out of this spirit was born his writing *That Jesus Christ was Born a Jew* (1523). Naturally, when his hopes failed of success, a reaction took place in his attitude toward the Jews, aggravated, no doubt, by a series of unpleasant experiences in his dealings with certain Jews, as well as by the rise of Judaizing sects among his own adherents. He was aroused also by the objections which had been raised by Jewish scholars to certain particulars in his translation of the Bible. Gradually Luther developed into a Jew-hater, who launched against them the coarsest of invectives and the most provoking of diatribes.

In two of his writings (*Concerning the Jews and Their Lies,* 1544, and *Concerning the Shem Hamforash,* 1544) he repeated the accusations directed against them by the apostates Anton Margaritha and Bernhard Ziegler. He demanded that the Christians burn the synagogues and destroy the houses of the Jews; that the princes subject the Jews to enforced labor; that their sacred writings be taken from them by force, and that they be forbidden to pray. He goaded the princes into banishing them, and the robber-knights into attacking them. Indeed, only four days before his death in 1546 at Eisleben he delivered a fiery sermon against the Jews and demanded their expulsion.

The reformer and crusader against religious prejudices was himself far removed from religious tolerance. He was party to the outrages perpetrated against the Jews by the Protestant princes and their subjects, which exceeded in violence even those committed by the Catholics. His dual nature, which demanded evangelical freedom, but at the same time took sides with the princes against the oppressed peasants, which admonished to humility and mercy, and yet declared the Ten Commandments to be invalidated, likewise failed to render justice to the People of the Book. Luther showed no understanding whatever of the morally elevating character of the Jewish religion.

Luther, despite a not too great knowledge of Hebrew, for which he had boundless admiration, translated the Bible into German and so gave impetus to knowledge of the Scripture, important for Protestantism, whose source of authority the Sacred Writ remains, as over against the Pope, or the Catholic Church's interpretation, which is final for the Roman Catholics. He refers unfavorably to the Jews in his commentary on *Psalms* 109. His use of Jewish exegesis was usually second hand.   WILLY COHN.

Lit.: Lewin, Reinhold, *Luthers Stellung zu den Juden* (*Neue Studien zur Geschichte der Theologie und Kirche,* N. Bonwetsch and R. Seeberg edit., part 10, 1911), where the older literature is listed which has been completely superseded by Lewin's work; Krauss, Samuel, "Luther und die Juden," *Der Jude,* vol. 2 (1917-18) 544; Dubnow, S., *Weltgeschichte des jüdischen Volkes,* vol. 6 (1927) 199 et seq., 210 et seq.; Graetz, H., *History of the Jews,* vol. 4 (1927) 467-75, 547-52.

LUTZKY, AARON (pseudonym of Aaron Zucker), Yiddish poet, b. Dimidovke, near Lutzk, Russia, 1893. He left the Heder at the age of twelve to study under a cantor in Lutzk. His father, a Hasid, disapproved of a cantor's career and sent him to the Yeshiva. Under his mother's influence he was also taught the violin.

At the age of fourteen Lutzky began to write poetry, which won the praise of Isaac Loeb Peretz. Upon the death of his father (1914), Lutzky emigrated to the United States, stopping on his way to visit Peretz in Warsaw. He made his literary debut in the *Yiddisher Tageblatt* with a poem called "Eider Aza Lebn Beser Shoin der Toit" (Death Would be Better Than a Life Like This). Shortly thereafter he was invited by Abraham Cahan to write for the *Forward,* signing his work *L.*

In 1918 he joined the American Expeditionary Forces. After returning from France at the close of the first World War, he resumed his writing, which was published in *Feder, In Sich, Groiser Kundes, Nei Yiddish, Kinder Zhurnal,* and others. His cycle *Fun a Toiter Velt* (Out of a Dead World) was written during this post-War period.

In 1921 Lutzky began to make concert appearances as an improviser, combining acting ability and musical talent with his poetic creativeness. His improvisations and interpretations were witty word pictures, sparkling with keen observation and the art of mimicry. His imaginative originality was modern in form, almost futuristic, although his improvisations often recall the minstrel or Badhan. Many of these, notably "Jazz," "Vasserfall," "Die Chasene," "Die Kapelye," and "Beim Rebns Tish," were published in the *Zukunft* (1922).

His published works include: *Nemt es, S'iz Gut far Eich* (Take It, 'Twill Do You Good; New York, 1928); *Umetik un Freilech* (Sad and Gay; New York, 1927); *Breishis-Inmitn* (Genesis-Midway; New York, 1932).

Lit.: Heller, H., in *Feder,* vol. 1 (1920); Niger, S., in *Zukunft,* May, 1928; Epstein, S., in *Freiheit,* Jan. 8, 1928; Britt, G., in *New York World-Telegram,* June 22, 1932; Rivkin, B., in *Zukunft,* June, July and Aug., 1935.

LUXEMBOURG (or **LUXEMBURG**), an independent grand duchy situated between the borders of Germany, Belgium and France, with a principal city of the same name. The rule of the country shifted with the tides of empire, the territory being successively under the rule of the Hapsburg dukes, Burgundy, Germany, Spain, Austria, France, the Netherlands and Belgium. In 1867, by agreement of the Powers, it was declared independent and perpetually neutral; it was occupied by the Germans from 1914 to 1918 and again in May, 1940.

The earliest document mentioning a Jew in Luxembourg is dated 1276. In July, 1349, Emperor Charles IV of Germany commanded the provosts, knights and judges and the city of Lützelburg-Luxembourg to protect the lives and possessions of the Jews against mobs in the time of the Black Death, but the city of Luxembourg as well as Echternach in Luxembourg are mentioned among the martyr cities of the year 1349. In 1370 the Jews were expelled from Brabant as well as from Luxembourg, and with this the first chapter of the history of the Jews in Luxembourg ends. From this period derive Jews' lane, Jews' cemetery, and Jews' gate, one of the gates of the fortified city (mentioned in 1348, 1356, 1376 and 1477).

After the union with Burgundy in 1443 the right of settlement and of abode in Luxembourg was apparently granted officially to Jews. During a persecution in 1470 the Jews found refuge in the citadel of Backfelsen. At the end of the 15th and the beginning of the 16th cent. Jews were living in the German part of the duchy, and paid a yearly tribute of two florins to the duke, since in a book of accounts of Grevenmachern (in Luxembourg) in 1519 to 1520 taxation of the Jews is mentioned. The surrender of the country to Spain in 1555 evidently deprived the few Jews who lived there of the right of residence. Henceforth, with few exceptions, Jews were excluded from continuous residence in Luxembourg until the French Revolution.

On the other hand, Jews for short periods were permitted to trade in Luxembourg, especially at cattle and horse-markets. They and the cattle were subject, however, to a bridge toll of four sols; and for a stay of twenty-four hours in the city, to two and a half sols. These taxes are certified in documents of 1664, 1673, 1683, 1685 and 1719. Orders of Philip V of September 6, 1703, and of Emperor Charles VI of September 20, 1720, confirmed these old tax rights over the Jews.

Jacob Bonné from Waldevisse (Lorraine) established himself with his cousin Zé and five other servants in Cobreville as guest of Count Berlosuys, chamberlain of the emperor, on April 16, 1788, in order to trade. The Cobreville officials, however, despite the edict of tolerance published in the Netherlands on May 9, 1782, succeeded in expelling Bonné from the castle. After the union of the city with France in 1795, a few Jewish families from Thionville and Metz established themselves there; they amounted in 1808 to approximately twenty-four persons, and in 1811 to seventy-five persons, who, in spite of all efforts could not be excepted from the "infamous" decree of Napoleon of March 17, 1808, which reintroduced restrictions on the Jews.

Under the French law the Jews of Luxembourg became citizens with equal rights and belonged to the consistory of Trèves. In 1815, after the union of Luxembourg with the Netherlands, they became united with the synagogue in Maastricht, and in 1830, because of Holland's separation from Belgium, the Jewish community as well as the duchy became independent. On January 12, 1899, the community of Luxembourg received the rights of incorporation. The new cemetery originated in 1884; the new synagogue in 1894. In the beginning of the 19th cent. there were organized Jewish communities also in Ettelbrück, Grevenmachern, Esch, and Medernach. In Esch a synagogue was built in 1899. Judaism, like the Christian denominations, were recognized by the state in Luxembourg; therefore the rabbis were, too. The first rabbi of the grand duchy was the religious philosopher Samuel Hirsch (1843-66); from 1863 to 1866 he was paid by the government. From Luxembourg he went to Philadelphia. His successor was the Frenchman Sopher, who came from Dijon (1866-70). He was followed by Isaak Blumenstein (1871-1903), who was chaplain in the German army in the Franco-Prussian War of (1870-71). Blumenstein's successor was his son-in-law, Samuel Fuchs. The last rabbi of the grand duchy was Robert Serebrenik.

In 1871 there were 525 Jews in Luxembourg out of a total population of 197,328. By 1927 there were 1,771 out of a total population of 285,524, and in 1935 there were 3,144 out of a total population of 296,-913. The large increase in the latter years was due to immigration from Germany; thus in 1935 as many as 2,274 Jews, or more than two-thirds, were of foreign birth. The Jews were distributed as follows: in the city of Luxembourg itself, 2,069; in Esch, 330; in Ettelbrück, 144; the remainder, 601, were scattered in fifty-five settlements. They participated in industry, trade and agriculture, and had factories for the manufacture of clothing, gloves and furniture. Only a few Jewish officials, the mayors of Hamm, Jules, Samson, and Paul Godchaux, are mentioned in the 19th and 20th centuries. After 1935 there were new arrivals from Germany and Austria; on the other hand, on November 11, 1939, when a German invasion of Luxembourg was feared, a number of Jews fled from Luxembourg to France.

In May, 1940, occurred the invasion of the German army, and on August 14, 1940, the Luxembourg constitution was abolished. On May 31, 1940, the registration of the Jews in Luxembourg began. The decree of September 7, 1940, forbade marriage and marital relations with "Aryans," and the registration of all property owned by Jews of Luxembourg as well as by Luxembourg Jews abroad was ordered. The term "Jew" was interpreted in the sense of the "Nuremberg Laws." Of the decrees dealing with the registration of Jewish-owned property, i.e. those of December 19, 1940, and February 7 and 18, 1941, the latter two ordered the confiscation of the property of Jews who had escaped or emigrated from the grand duchy. The decrees of December 23, 1940, and January 15, 1941, excluded Jews from the state subsidies granted to families with a large number of children. On December 3, 1940, Shehitah was prohibited. In August, 1941, it was announced that Luxembourg Jews would be treated in all respects like those in Germany.

On September 18, 1940, Rabbi Serebrenik received the order to have all Jews leave the land within two weeks, and to take with them not more than $30 in money and sixty pounds of baggage. Since execution of this order was impossible, hundreds of Jews were crowded into freight cars and shipped to the Portuguese border in November, 1940. Due to the joint efforts of the grand duchess of Luxembourg and of the Jewish

Rosa Luxemburg

relief organizations the refugees were permitted to remain in the vicinity of Lisbon; a few of these received steamship tickets.

The deportation of the Luxembourg Jews was decreed in October, 1941. The first group was transported in cattle cars to Poland. On October 26, 1941, more than 130 Jews from Luxembourg who had visas from the Dominican Republic reached the Spanish border. It was only when the American consul had given a written guarantee to the Spanish authorities, that these refugees would receive visas for the United States, that they were allowed to pass through Spain. According to a statement from Stockholm of December 17, 1941, about 250 Jews from Luxembourg, who were over sixty-five years old and had been allowed to stay in the country, were killed by lethal gas in an old cloister.

ADOLF KOBER.

Lit.: Anchel, Robert, *Napoléon et les juifs* (1928); Anders, I., *Le Grand-Duché de Luxembourg* (1919); *Contemporary Jewish Record*, vols. 3 and 4 (1940 and 1941); *Jewish Encyclopedia*, vol. 8, p. 219; Grand-Duché de Luxembourg, *Publications de l'office de statistique*, fascicule 69; *Résultats de recensement de la population du 31 Décembre, 1935*, vol. 1 (1938); *Revue des études juives*, vol. 7 (1883) 119; vol. 8 (1883) 206-22; vol. 90 (1931) 114-33; vol. 91 (1931) 46-51; van Wervede, N., *Kulturgeschichte des Luxemburger Landes*, vol. 2 (1924) 16-18; *American Jewish Year Book*, vol. 43 (1941-42) 175-76.

LUXEMBURG, ROSA, revolutionary, b. Zamost, Russia, 1871; assassinated, Berlin, 1919. As a student of a Gymnasium at Warsaw, she was active in the underground movement of Socialist youth. Upon her graduation at the age of fifteen, she worked in the illegal Polish party called "The Proletariat" and, in 1888, when this party was suppressed, fled to Switzerland in order to escape deportation to Siberia. She studied political economy and philosophy at the University of Zurich, where she obtained her Ph.D. degree in 1897, brilliantly defending her dissertation on industrial development in Poland and Russia. From 1892 on she played a leading role in the Social Democratic circle of Polish emigrants and helped set up their journal, *The Workers' Cause* (Polish), which, in 1893, delegated her to the Second International Congress held at Zurich.

In 1897 she went to Germany and obtained German citizenship by marrying the printer Georg Lübeck; the marriage was immediately dissolved. In 1898 she became editor of the *Sächsische Arbeiterzeitung,* and subsequently contributed a series of articles to the *Leipziger Volkszeitung,* which were later separately published as *Sozialreform oder Revolution?* (1899). She opposed Eduard Bernstein's doctrine of a revision of Marxism in favor of an evolutionary process of reform. She also opposed the Bolsheviks on questions of Russian revolution, party and party membership, always following her own convictions and not bowing to any authorities or majorities.

In 1905 she was in Warsaw and took part in the attempted revolution, for which she was arrested and given a one-year prison sentence; after three months she managed to escape and returned to Germany. Living in Berlin, she lectured at the Socialist college there and was renowned as the ablest orator and debater of the Socialist party.

During the years preceding the first World War she traveled the length and breadth of Germany, decrying militarism and war. She had served her first prison term in Germany in 1900; in 1904 she was arrested for lèse majesté and for one of her anti-war speeches, delivered at Frankfort, and was jailed again. Throughout the War she inveighed against the maltreatment of soldiers in the barracks, whereupon, in 1915, she was arrested and held in protective custody until the end of the War. In prison she wrote and translated many works, also organized the Spartakus-Bund (1916), out of which, on December 31, 1918, the Communist Party of Germany was born.

In November, 1918, she founded, together with Karl Liebknecht, the communist newspaper *Die rote Fahne.* It was her and Liebknecht's aim to carry through the German revolution to their goal of concentrating the power in the hands of the proletariat, a process which they believed to be the only alternative to reaction and militarism. After the *Putsch* of the Berlin Spartacists had been crushed, Rosa Luxemburg was arrested again (January 15, 1919) and, together with her fellow leader, Liebknecht, was murdered by the arresting officers on their way to Moabit prison. Her body was thrown into a canal and recovered later.

She wrote *Akkumulation des Kapitals* (1913) and *Die Krise der Sozialdemokratie* (pseudonym Junius; 1918). After her death her letters were published by Sophie Liebknecht and Luise Kautsky. Posthumously published were also: *Was die Epigonen aus der Marx'schen Theorie gemacht haben* (1921); *Die russische Revolution* (1922); *Einführung in die National-ökonomie; Militarismus, Krieg und Arbeiterklasse.*

ANNA BETTELHEIM.

Lit.: Monographs by Klara Zetkin (1919), Max Adler (1919), Karl Radek (1921), Karl Kautsky (1921) and Max Huchdorf (1930).

LUZ, 1. Canaanite name of the city known to the Israelites as Beth-el, because of Jacob's dream near there (*Gen.* 28:19). It seems to have retained that name until the time of the Israelite conquest.

2. city in the north of Palestine, founded in memory of the former by one of its inhabitants who was spared because he showed the invading Israelites the secret entrance into the city (*Judges* 1:22-26). Later legend invested the city with marvellous powers; Sennacherib and Nebuchadnezzar had been unable to conquer it, and no one who stayed within its walls could die, for the angel of death had no power there (*Sotah* 46a).

3. a bone of the spinal column, reputed to be indestructible; it is from this that the resurrection of the dead will take place (*Midrash Lev.* 18, which relates a discussion between Hadrian and Joshua). This belief was connected with *Ps.* 34:21, which was interpreted to mean, "there is one of his bones that can not be broken." In the Middle Ages non-Jewish scholars accepted the legend literally and spoke of the "Jews' bone" (*Judenknöchlein*), and attempted to identify it as the last vertebra of the spinal column or one of the sesamoid bones of the thumb.

LUZKI (also **LUTZKI** or **LUCKI**), **JOSEPH SOLOMON BEN MOSES,** Karaite scholar, b. Kokizow, near Lemberg, Galicia; d. Eupatoria, Crimea, 1844. He officiated as minister (Hazan) of the Karaite community of Eupatoria. He was a member of the Karaite delegation which successfully negotiated with Emperor Nicholas I for the exemption of Karaites from military conscription.

Among Luzki's works are: *Iggereth Teshuath Yisrael,* an account of the delegation's activity (Eupatoria, 1840); *Sefer Hahinnuch,* a schoolbook, printed with his Tatar translation of Benjamin Mussafia's poem *Zecher Rab* (Orta-Kiöi, 1831); *Tirath Kesef,* a commentary on the *Sefer Hamibhar* of Aaron ben Joseph the Elder (printed with the latter, Eupatoria, 1835). Several liturgical hymns from his pen were incorporated into the official Karaite prayer-book.

Lit.: Poznanski, S., *The Karaite Literary Opponents of Saadiah Gaon* (1908) 90; Mann, Jacob, *Texts and Studies,* vol. 2 (1935).

LUZKI (also **LUTZKI** or **LUCKI**), **SIMHAH ISAAC BEN MOSES,** Karaite author, a native of Lutzk, later resident in Chufut-Kale, Crimea, d. 1766. Luzki earned the sobriquet of "Microcosm" (*'Olam Tza'ir*) by his wide learning, which embraced not only Karaite literature and theology, but also rabbinic and Cabalistic writings. Of his numerous works only two have been printed: *Or Hahayyim,* a commentary on the *Etz Hayyim* of Aaron ben Elijah the Younger (printed with the latter, Eupatoria, 1847); *Orah Tzaddikim,* an abridgment of his *Ner Tzaddikim,* a bio-bibliography of Karaite literature (printed with Mordecai Kokizow's *Dod Mordechai,* Vienna, 1830). In spite of its errors and shortcomings, the *Orah Tzaddikim,* the earliest work of its kind, is still of considerable scientific value. Some of his liturgical hymns were incorporated and printed in the official Karaite prayer-book. His unpublished works extend over a wide variety of subjects, including theology, philosophy, law and mysticism.

Luigi Luzzatti

Luzki was also an industrious copyist of old Karaite manuscripts, thereby contributing toward the preservation of many old works which would have been otherwise irretrievably lost.

Lit.: Neubauer, A., *Aus der Petersburger Bibliothek* (1866) 82-87; Mann, Jacob, *Texts and Studies,* vol. 2 (1935).

LUZZATTI, LUIGI, Italian statesman and economist, b. Venice, 1841; d. Rome, 1927. He received a Hebrew education under the direction of his teacher, Mose Soave, and showed great interest in religious disciplines. At an early age, however, he turned to the study of economic problems and the pursuit of social reforms. He organized the gondolieri in his native Venice along cooperative lines, but, suspected by the Austrian police and threatened with arrest, he escaped to Milan. There he continued his studies of economic and social theories, centering his attention on cooperative societies, loans and saving banks (Banche Popolari). He became professor of political economy in 1863 at the Technical High School of Milan, a post which he held until 1866, when he was called to the chair of constitutional law at the University of Padua.

At the age of twenty-eight Luzzatti became general secretary of the ministry of agriculture, industry and commerce, a post equivalent to that of under-secretary of state and thereafter had a leading part in shaping Italy's economic and financial policies. He laid the foundations of Italy's tariff and customs legislation, and prepared and negotiated the principal commercial agreements between Italy and other countries during a half-century.

Elected in 1870 to the Italian Parliament, he was one of Italy's most inspired orators. His speeches were distinguished by their noble tone and magnificent form. He was called by Gabriele D'Annunzio "a Prophet in his own country."

In the years succeeding 1891 he was called five times to assume the portfolio of the treasury, was minister of finance and in 1910 minister of agriculture. Thanks to his sound economic policies and his financial ability, he considerably reduced the chronic deficits of the Italian treasury and even reestablished the parity of the Italian budget, saved the Banco di Napoli from bankruptcy, and conceived and carried out the difficult operation of conversion of the Italian public debt.

It was mainly due to his interest and intervention with King Victor Emmanuel III that David Lubin's project of creating an international institute of agriculture, presented in 1904 in Rome, finally materialized.

In 1908 there was conferred on Luzzatti the title of minister of state. In 1911 he became minister of the interior and prime minister, a position held for the first time by a Jew in the history of Italy. He furthered political cooperation between Italy and France and closer ties between Italy and other Latin nations. In the years preceding the first World War he used his prestige and political influence to defend Jewish rights in various countries of oppression, and intervened through diplomatic channels for the granting of civic rights to the Jews of Roumania, the "last slaves remaining in Europe," as he called them in his passionate appeals.

During the first World War Luzzatti became commissioner for the relief of the stricken populations of Northern Italy and of war refugees. He established the National Foundation for the Sons of Peasants Fallen in the War.

In 1921 he was nominated member of the Italian Senate. The next year, in April, 1922, at the International Conference in Genoa, he presented a plan for an international stabilization of all currencies.

Luzzatti was a sincere deist and made valuable studies of Christianity, Buddhism and other faiths and religious creeds. Although he had little outward relations with Judaism as a religion, he followed with deep and growing interest the development of Jewish achievements in Palestine, particularly in the field of cooperative societies. In 1921, at the age of eighty, he sent a moving message to the Jewish agricultural settlements in Palestine, extolling their work aimed at the redeeming of the ancient soil. He sent a message to Lord Balfour in 1925 in connection with the inauguration of the Hebrew University in Jerusalem. A collected edition of his numerous books, manuscripts, pamphlets and notes began to appear in 1924 under the title of *Opere di Luigi Luzzatti*. By 1942 two volumes had appeared: *Grandi Italiani: grandi sacrifizi per la patria* (1924); *Dio nella Libertà: studi sulle relazioni tra lo Stato e la Chiesa* (1926; English ed., *God in Freedom*, New York, 1930; a comprehensive work on religious liberty, edited by Max J. Kohler, with American supplementary chapters).

DAVID KLEINLERER.

Lit.: Biographical sketch by Dora Askowith in Luzzatti's *God in Freedom* (1930); *American Hebrew,* May 10, 1918, p. 5; April 1, 1927, p. 732; Tittoni, in *Nuova Antologia* (1927) 385 et seq.; Behar, J., *Luigi Luzzatti* (1928); vol. 1 of *Reminiscences* (Italian; 1931); Ghezzi, Cesare, "Luigi Luzzatti e il credito popolare," *Rivista bancaria,* vol. 18, No. 12 (Dec., 1937) 885-910; vol. 19, No. 1 (Jan., 1938) 1-27; No. 2 (Feb., 1938) 84-100; No. 3 (March, 1938) 145-61; *Jewish Tribune,* March 5, 1926, p. 8; Jan. 8, 1926, pp. 3, 19; April 8, 1927, p. 4; *American Hebrew,* April 1, 1927, p. 732; April 8, 1927, p. 753; April 15, 1932, p. 574.

LUZZATTO, BENEDETTO, physician and rabbi of the 17th cent. He was a pupil of Leon da Modena, who praised his Halachic learning. He wrote poems in Hebrew and Italian, including a sonnet in the latter language, an encomium of the astronomical treatise *Porto Astronomico,* written by his friend Immanuel Porto Rapa. He graduated from the University of Padua, and was physician and preacher in Venice and in Padua; in the latter city he is mentioned as being a member of the rabbinical collegium in 1669.

LUZZATTO, BENIAMINO, physician, b. Padua, Italy, 1850; d. Padua, 1893. He was the son of Samuel David Luzzatto, and came from a family of Italian scholars, their genealogy dating back to the 16th cent. Beniamino Luzzatto was a physician at the hospital in Padua, became a lecturer on pathology in 1876, and assistant professor and chief of the propaedeutic clinic of the University of Padua in 1882. He wrote various essays, among them works on chronic bronchopneumonia and tuberculosis, the systolic murmur of the apex of the heart, also *Embolia dell'arteria pulmonale* (Milan, 1880) and *Vado mecum di percussione* (Padua, 1882).

Lit.: Pagel, *Biographisches Lexikon;* Brann, in *S. D. Luzzatto, Ein Gedenkbuch* (1900).

LUZZATTO, EPHRAIM, physician and poet, brother of Isacco, b. San Daniele, Friuli, Italy, 1729; d. Lausanne, Switzerland, 1792. Upon graduation from the University of Padua in 1750, he practised for a time in Italy, traveled considerably, and finally settled in London (1762), where he served for almost thirty years as physician of the Hospital of the Portuguese Congregation. He possessed a natural talent for poetry, which he wrote in Italian and Hebrew and which dealt with nature, love and national themes.

A collection of his Hebrew poetry was published under the title of *Eleh Bene Haneurim* (London, 1768); a uniform edition was printed under the title of *Kol Shahal* (Berlin, 1796); a third edition was compiled and published by Meir Letteris (Vienna, 1839). He contributed selected poems to *Hameassef* (1784 and 1785 and later). Luzzatto is regarded as one of the forerunners of modern Hebrew poetry. His wish to rejoin his brother was not fulfilled, since he died in Lausanne on his trip back to Italy.

Lit.: Delitzsch, *Zur Geschichte der jüdischen Poesie* (1836) 92; Carmoly, E., in *Revue orientale,* vol. 1 (1841-44) 459; Klausner, Joseph, *Historiyah shel Hasifruth Haibrith Hahadashah* (1930) 262-71.

LUZZATTO, FILOSSENO, linguist and scholar, b. Trieste, Italy, 1829; d. Padua, Italy, 1854. He was the son of Samuel David Luzzatto, and his name is a translation of his father's work, *Oheb Ger* (Loving the Stranger). He was a precocious youth, mastered Sanskrit and many European and Semitic languages, and at the age of thirteen had deciphered the Hebrew epitaphs in the old Jewish cemetery in Padua. Although he died at a very early age, he wrote a number of important works, including: *Dell'Asia antica,* *occidentale e media* (Milan, 1847); *Le sanscritisme de la langue assyrienne* (1849); and several important studies, published in *Archives Israélites,* on such subjects as Hasdai ibn Shaprut, cuneiform inscriptions found in Persia, and the Falashas.

LUZZATTO, ISACCO (ISAAC), physician and poet, brother of Ephraim, b. San Daniele, Friuli, Italy, 1730; d. San Daniele, 1803. He received the degree of doctor of medicine from the University of Padua, together with his brother, in 1750, and returned to his birthplace to practice. When the Jews were expelled from San Daniele in 1777, he and his family were permitted to remain. He composed many Hebrew poems; a collection entitled *Toledoth Yitzhak* is still in manuscript at the British Museum and Oxford University. He translated Metastasio's poem "La Libertà a Nice" into Hebrew, and wrote *Massecheth Derech Eretz,* a satire on his townsmen in the form of a Talmudic parody.

Lit.: Luzzatto, *Autobiografia* (1882) 7 et seq.; Brann, "Die Familie Luzzatto," *S. D. Luzzatto, Ein Gedenkbuch* (1900); *Buschs Jahrbuch,* vol. 6 (1848); Grünwald, *Autobiographie S. D. Luzzatto,* p. 23 et seq.; Davidson, Israel, *Otzar Hashirah Vehapiyut,* pp. 52, 203.

LUZZATTO, JACOB BEN ISAAC, 16th cent. rabbi and author, b. probably Safed, Palestine; d. probably somewhere in Palestine. He is known to have spent his childhood in Safed but afterward found his way to European centers, living in Basel and (in all likelihood) in Posen and Cracow as well. Luzzatto was the author of *Kaftor Vaferah,* or *Yashresh Yaakob* (Basel, 1580; Amsterdam, 1790). The volume is a collection of various studies aimed at weakening the attacks of certain authors on the Haggadoth; Luzzatto's own approach was through a semi-mystical interpretation of chosen passages. Luzzatto was also the author of *Kehillath Yaakob* (Salonika, 1584) and the editor of Talmudic glossaries and of works by Elijah Vidas and Solomon Molcho.

LUZZATTO, MARCO, writer and translator, b. San Daniele, Friuli, Italy, 1720; d. Trieste, Italy, 1799. He translated from Spanish into Hebrew the *Fortaleza del Judaismo* of Abraham Ger da Cordova, under the title *Tzeriah Beth El* (cf. *Judges* 9:46); he made Italian versions of the *Conciliador* of Manasseh ben Israel and of the *Hizzuk Emunah* of Isaac Troki. Luzzatto compiled a Hebrew-Italian directory, and wrote many other minor works, including Hebrew poems.

Lit.: Morais, *Italian Hebrew Literature* (1926) 163 et seq.

LUZZATTO, MOSES HAYIM, mystic and Hebrew writer (known as RaMaHaL, from the initials of his name), b. Padua, Italy, 1707; d. Acco, Palestine, 1746. He came of a family wealthy and prominent in the annals of Italian Jewry. He received a good Hebrew education from the noted Isaiah Bassan(i) of his native city, learned Latin and probably knew Greek and French. He began his prolific literary activity at an early age, writing both in Hebrew and Aramaic, using the former for political, ethical and philosophic works and the latter most often for his Cabalistic effusions.

Title page of "Kaftor Vaferah" by Jacob ben Isaac Luzzatto

Luzzatto was typical of the great portion of learned Italian Jewry which still lived in the physical and spiritual ghetto of the Middle Ages. Unlike its northern counterparts, Italian Jewry was not so strongly affected by the legalism of the *Shulhan Aruch,* but was greatly influenced by the counter current of mysticism which swept over European Jewry in the 17th cent. and which was climaxed in the movement of the pseudo-Messiah Sabbatai Zevi. Despite the disappointment which followed this upsurge, many Jews, particularly in Italy, would not yield their Messianic hopes. Luzzatto belonged to this group. He combined in his person a strong visionary bent and a fine artistic and literary sensitivity. He was a Jew of the "Galuth" (exile) who would not, if he could, leave his exile until the redeemer appeared, and who lived in his own Jewish culture and milieu with little concession to the outward world. Like so many other "initiates" among the mystics, Luzzatto believed that he had a spiritual mentor who brought him into converse with Metatron, Adam, the Patriarchs, Moses, Elijah and Rabbi Hamnuna, and who confirmed his subject's Messianic pretensions.

Luzzatto has been called the father of modern Hebrew literature. He broke with the highly involved mode of writing of the Spanish period and breathed a spirit of purity and simplicity into his language. He was a literary genius, but was unrecognized for his remarkable gift of diction during his own time. He had no imitators and exerted no influence until a much later period. A century after Luzzatto's lifetime, Isaac Baer Levinsohn resumed where he had left off. At sixteen Luzzatto wrote an elegy on Isaac Vita Cantarini; at seventeen, *Leshon Limmudim,* a treatise on rhetoric dedicated to his teacher, Bassan. Another youthful attempt is his *Maase Shimshon,* in which he handles the Samson story with imagination and Biblical chastity of language, despite the artificiality and amateurishness of the poem. In honor of the wedding of his teacher's son he penned *Migdal Oz* (Tower of Strength), an allegorical drama after the Italian *Pastor Fido* of Battista Guarini; Luzzatto's work, however, is not a slavish imitation but contains many elements of originality.

But Luzzatto's heart was in the Cabala, the Lurian variety of the mystic doctrine. In it he studied day and night and he taught its tenets concerning God's will to others. He looked upon himself as the Messiah who was to liberate unfortunate Israel, and wrote a second *Zohar,* which is lost, but in which he gave expression to his hopes and thoughts. His own Italian confrères seem to have sympathized with him and took very little action against his "heresy." The rabbi of Altona, Germany, Moses Hagiz, who was the chief opponent of the Sabbatarian movement, heard indirectly of Luzzatto's works and saw in them the threat of the repetition of the old danger of Messianic frenzy. He persuaded his German colleagues to put Luzzatto's activities under the ban, to forbid writing in the (Aramaic) language of the *Zohar* and the reading of such writings. Bassan thereupon exacted a promise from his pupil to give up the study of Cabala and not to circulate his books without permission. Luzzatto gave his manuscripts into the custody of the Venetian rabbinate (1730).

He now turned to commerce and to the writing of some secular pieces; he married the daughter of Rabbi David Finzi of Mantua. He failed in business, and in the meantime his family had become so impoverished that it could not help him; he therefore turned for solace to his beloved Cabala, and again wrote mystic treatises in Hebrew. The Venetian rabbis felt impelled (some would say that the loss of the family fortunes and prestige made them bold where once they were timid) to excommunicate Luzzatto (1735). He then left Italy to go to Amsterdam, but at Frankfort, on his way thither, he was compelled to sign a confession of guilt and to promise not to study Cabala until he reached forty years of age. In Amsterdam he became a diamond cutter and a gem setter; in addition to following his trade he taught and prospered. He maintained a correspondence with his friends and followers in Italy. When Luzzatto was again accused of spreading his doctrines, Bassan sent the chest of manuscripts to Rabbi Jacob Popper of Frankfort, who burned a part and buried others.

In his fortieth year Luzzatto went to Palestine to devote himself to his favorite occupation of mystic contemplation and perhaps to realize his cherished Messianic ambition. He and his family died there shortly after their arrival (May 16, 1746). They were buried probably in Kfar Jassif, and not next to the tomb of Rabbi Akiba in Tiberias, as is popularly supposed.

Luzzatto was a voluminous writer. He wrote a number of liturgical pieces, including 150 psalms which he hoped might supersede the Psalter in the affections of the devout; most of this material is lost. A large amount of mystical, philosophical and other writings by him are extant in manuscript. He is best known today for his popular *Mesillath Yesharim* (Path of the Upright; Amsterdam, 1740), a pilgrim's progress through various stages leading to the goal of holiness. The book, despite its lack of originality of thought, is a handbook of piety and religious fervor, and has become a classic of the Musar (moralist) literature.   FELIX A. LEVY.

Lit.: Ginzburg, Simon, *The Life and Works of Moses Hayim Luzzatto* (1931), with additional literature, p. 146 et seq.; idem, *Rabbi Mosheh Hayim Luzzatto Ubene Doro;* Spiegel, S., *Hebrew Reborn* (1930); Abrahams, I., *By-Paths in Hebraic Bookland* (1920); the text and translation of *Mesillath Yesharim,* edited by Mordecai M. Kaplan (1936).

LUZZATTO, SAMUEL DAVID (abbreviation, ShaDaL), a founder of modern Jewish scholarship, defender of Orthodoxy, builder of Hebrew culture, and forerunner of Zionism, b. Trieste, Italy, 1800; d. Padua, Italy, 1865. Luzzatto's exceptional linguistic talents, as well as his life purpose, to fortify Orthodox Jewish belief and practice, appeared very early. At eight years of age, he looked upon himself as a "regenerator of my nation." The reading of the book of *Job* at this time prompted his decision to write a commentary on it. At eleven, he began the composition of a Hebrew grammar, and made various exegetical notes on the Torah. At thirteen, Luzzatto came to the conclusion that the vowel points and accents in the Torah were not written by Moses, a radical view for that day. At this time, also, he rejected the Cabala, and recognized that the *Zohar* could not have been written by Simeon ben Yohai because of its reference to the accents and vowel points, which, he asserted, were of post-Talmudic origin (elaborated in his *Vikkuah Al Hakabbalah,* 1852).

Forced to withdraw from school because of illness at thirteen, Luzzatto continued his education mainly on his own. He already possessed an excellent background in Hebrew, secular languages and sciences, gained in nine years of attendance at the Trieste Talmud Torah, where an eminent faculty, under Chief Rabbi Abraham Eliezer Halevi, encouraged both Jewish and secular learning. At fourteen, the death of his mother brought Luzzatto to a long trying period, in which he had to take care of the household for his little sister and his scholarly father, who barely eked out a living as a carpenter. Despite his father's insistence that he enter a trade, the son clung to his scholarly pursuits, winning ever-widening recognition with his poetry and his philological and exegetical writings. At twenty-one, he was called by the community leaders to translate the prayer-book into Italian.

Not until he was twenty-nine, however, did Luzzatto attain a position of security and recognition. In 1829 he was called by the eminent Rabbi Isaac Samuel Reggio to the faculty of the newly-established Rabbinical College at Padua, which Reggio had set up in sympathetic response to the governmental order that rabbinical students receive philosophical training. At this first modern rabbinical school in Europe Luzzatto taught a variety of subjects until his death in 1865.

Samuel David Luzzatto

Here, also, he prepared series of discourses on Jewish ethics, and on the history and religion of Israel, for the Jewish students at the University of Padua. These, as well as his historical lectures to rabbinical students, were published in several popular volumes in Italian. In vigorous scholarly pursuits Luzzatto found solace for his recurrent private sorrows: his first wife's long melancholia preceding her early death, the loss of his first-born son and spiritual heir, Filosseno, at the age of twenty-five, and that of his only daughter at eighteen.

Luzzatto's philosophy of religion was directed to the support of Orthodoxy and its harmonization with a free quest for truth. It centered about the following principle: whereas man must use his critical faculties to search out and gain logical support for certain aspects of religion, the fundamental bases of religion are not subject to analysis by reason. Reason can not disprove such phenomena as miracles, prophecy, the creation of the world and the existence of God, for first, rational investigation depends upon the perception of the senses, and these matters do not fall under our senses, and secondly, although some of these may seem to be out of accord with the "laws" of nature, there is no proof that the "laws" of nature could not have been different in other times. Thus, already in his *Torah Nidresheth*, begun in 1818, Luzzatto rationally limited the applicability of reason, and gave support to one who clings to faith because his heart impels him. (Mystic extremes such as Cabala, however, he rejected as foreign to true Judaism.)

The great purpose of religion, he maintained, is *goodness*, and not truth—for it is impossible to tell the "truth" about creation, for instance, to limited human intellects. All metaphysical researches he therefore condemned as "beyond the power of man,"

and philosophy as a whole as destructive of one's natural goodness and understanding.

Luzzatto condemned Maimonides for trying to unite the Torah and philosophy: "The God, impassive and unalterable, of philosophy is not, and will not be, that of religion." Judaism, he insisted, stands in opposition to rationalism, and especially to "atticism" (Greek philosophy). Its foundation is the belief, not simply in one God, but in the divine authorship of the Torah, which involves adherence to all beliefs and commandments contained therein. Its great objective, ethics, it pursues successfully by setting up, not a rational system of conduct—which can not work, since men act impulsively—but an emotional one, based upon compassion as its root, reenforced by a belief in divine retribution. Luzzatto attacked Spinoza for attempting to make reason the basis of ethics, and for so ignoring all but the intellect in man that he could see no God beyond the world and no freedom for man's will. Abraham ibn Ezra, likewise, met with Luzzatto's disfavor for pretending to be pious while hinting at sceptical and rationalistic conclusions.

Luzzatto's principle of applying "faith" to the realm of presuppositions and "reason" to the analysis of details is clearly manifested also in his exegetical contributions. No student sought wider bases in reason and knowledge. He was the first Jewish scholar to turn his attention to Syriac, which aided his analysis of the Aramaic Targum Onkelos (*Oheb Ger,* 1830). He was the first to attempt an Aramaic grammar. He revealed, likewise, a knowledge of the Samaritan tongue, and advanced the understanding of Hebrew synonyms. Thus fortified, he was the first Jew to amend the text of the Hebrew Bible, his proposed corrections winning wide acceptance. This, plus his daring denial of the Mosaic authorship of the Pentateuchal vowel points, shows the lengths to which a rational critical spirit carried him. Here, however, he stopped. "We certainly must not correct a single letter in the Torah," he insisted. And when he became aware that Geiger and Marcus Jost disbelieved in the early dating, hence Mosaic authorship, of the Torah, he censured them for undermining Judaism.

In his analysis of the book of *Isaiah,* Luzzatto combatted Krochmal, Rapoport, Gesenius and others who argued that another author must have written the latter part. The details of their evidence he countered entirely on their own grounds of modern criticism, explaining how differences in style and verbiage could have been employed by the same man. But beyond that, he insisted, what troubled the others was that they really did not believe in prophecy.

Luzzatto himself predicted that future generations would say of him: "Shadal made criticism compatible with belief; it alone satisfied the 'needs of the generation.'" In this spirit he prepared his Hebrew commentaries on the Pentateuch and *Isaiah,* his notes on *Jeremiah, Ezekiel, Proverbs,* and *Job,* and his Italian translations of the Torah and Haftarahs, *Isaiah* and *Job.*

"Hebrew is my passion, and the revival of its literature, the most beautiful dream of my whole life," wrote Luzzatto. His Hebrew poems, original and translations, won him early fame (*Kinnor Naim,* 1825; vol. 2, 1879). His contacts with old Hebraic collections in Italy enabled him to reveal and interpret many rare manuscripts for the advancement of the knowledge of Judaism. He aided Zunz in his studies of religious poetry, Steinschneider in his bibliographies, Rapoport in his portrayals of literary figures. He furthered historical understanding by publishing studies of old epitaphs (*Abne Zikkaron*, 1841). He opened up and interpreted the whole field of Jewish poetry in Spain's Golden Age by publishing the *Diwan* of Judah Halevi (1864), in whom he sensed a kindred spirit, and by copying from rare sources hundreds of poems for publication and analysis by Leopold Dukes, Geiger, and Michael Sachs. His detailed contributions to Jewish scholarship through many hundreds of personal letters, learned articles and notes, chiefly in Hebrew, cover all of Judaism. Through them Luzzatto sought to make Hebrew literature intelligible and appealing. Indeed, he assisted certain German Jewish scholars only on condition that they correspond with him in Hebrew.

Luzzatto's love for Hebrew was but part of his vigorous Jewish nationalism, whose basis he found in the Torah itself. For in his *Yesode Hatorah* he added to his oft-mentioned two great roots of the Torah—compassion and belief in retribution—a third: Israel's consciousness of divine election as bearer of the true belief to mankind. This the Torah furthers by commandments designed to keep Israel distinct from other nations, such as the dietary laws. In modern times, as well, Luzzatto insisted, unless Jews cling to their faithful observance of the Torah and to their belief in its divine origin, and reject "rationalism," Israel will disappear and be forgotten. Israel's welfare, he maintained, is not to be served by seeking emancipation—which might endanger Jewish observance—but by reviving its national feeling, its love of Jewish ideas, and its consciousness of its own dignity and capacity. Foreshadowing Zionist principles even further, he proposed that Palestine be worked and guarded by Jews, and that Jewish life and instruction be reestablished there, where they might be free "from all external compulsion."   ALAN S. GREEN.

Lit.: Waxman, M., *A History of Jewish Literature,* vol. 3 (1936) 389-99, 489-500; Morais, S., *Italian Hebrew Literature* (1926); Spiegel, S., *Hebrew Reborn* (1930); *Gedenkbuch zum hundertsten Geburtstag Luzzattos* (1900), especially the articles by W. Bacher, A. Berliner, S. Bernfeld, P. Bloch, M. Brann and M. Kayserling, comprising 109 pages, plus five pages of translations of Luzzatto's poetry; Klausner, J., *Historiyah shel Hasifruth Haibrith Hahadashah,* vol. 3 (1937) 40-121.

LUZZATTO, SIMONE (SIMHAH) BEN ISAAC, rabbi and author, b. Venice, Italy, 1583; d. Venice, 1663. He was a member of the rabbinical collegium at Venice, and took part in a dispute concerning the ritual bath (Mikveh) at Rovigo. He was an ardent champion of the rationalistic views of Maimonides and an opponent of Cabala. His views on the reconciliation of faith and science are set forth candidly in his parable *Socrate* (Venice, 1651), written in Italian. Luzzatto defended Judaism in several of his writings, the best known of which is his *Discorso circa il stato degli ebrei* (Venice, 1638). The argument is entirely practical and avoids the theological arguments of earlier apologetes; instead, he points out the contributions of the Jews to the well-being of the Venetian republic and that they are essentially law-abiding. He is said

David Lvovitch

to have written a work called *Debar Shemuel,* defending the Oral Law and refuting the claims of the Karaites; Jacob Aboab is known to have owned a copy of the work, but it is no longer extant. Luzzatto was not only an authority in rabbinics, but also a distinguished mathematician.

LVOVITCH, DAVID (DAVIDOVITCH) Jewish territorialist leader and communal worker, b. Russia, 1882. The son of the only Jewish representative in the local Duma, he studied engineering and economics in Munich, and law and economics at the University of St. Petersburg (graduated 1913). As a student he became interested in socialist Zionism. After thorough investigation, however, he came to the conclusion that Palestine was not a suitable country for Jewish colonization, and became a territorialist.

In 1905 he participated in the seventh Zionist Congress in Basel, at which the territorialists, headed by Israel Zangwill, left the congress on the Uganda issue, and became one of the co-founders of the Jewish Territorial Organization (ITO). When, later, the Portuguese government offered Angola to the Jews, he participated in the investigation.

His interest in both Jewish and Russian politics induced him to join the Russian Socialist Territorialist Party, S.S. (called the Socialist Zionist Party, according to its origin). In his political activities he became known as Davidovitch. The Party sent him to Odessa to head the S.S. organization there. He led the self-defense organization in Odessa during the 1905 pogroms.

After the pogroms had been stopped, Lvovitch left for Germany and participated in the International S.S. Conference in Leipzig, where he was elected a member of the Central Committee of his Party. At this conference he presented a resolution stating that neither territorialism nor Zionism results from ideological or from national or religious movements, but

A synagogue in Lwów

are mainly the answer to the need for emigration, which at that period averaged 200,000 a year from Russia and Galicia. This resolution was accepted and incorporated in the program of the Party.

In 1907 Lvovitch represented the Party at the International Socialist Congress at Stuttgart and advocated that emigration and colonization be included in the program of the International Socialist Movement.

In connection with his active interest in all emigration and colonization efforts, Lvovitch visited the United States in 1908 to help further the Galveston Plan inaugurated by Jacob H. Schiff.

During the first World War Lvovitch visited the United States several times with the special mission from Russian Jewry to inform American Jews about czarist anti-Jewish persecutions. Upon the outbreak of the revolution he returned to Russia and was elected a member of the Constitutional Assembly as the only representative of the Jews. In those years he became interested in the ORT movement, and in 1919 he and Leon Bramson were elected by the Russian ORT Central Committee as delegates to Central and Western Europe. In 1920 he organized the Polish ORT. In 1921 the World ORT Union was founded in Berlin, and Lvovitch was elected vice-president, a post he still held in 1942.

At the same time he settled in Berlin, where he engaged in the chemical business. He moved to France in 1932 and came to the United States in 1939, at the beginning of the second World War. During this period he devoted most of his time to ORT work, visiting many countries and organizing ORT institutions. In the United States, too, he helped spread the ORT idea and organization. In 1928 he visited Moscow and made an agreement with the Soviet government whereby the ORT was entitled to import machinery and implements for declassed Jews, free of duty. Almost two million dollars' worth of machinery was sent from relatives and friends in the United States and other countries to those Jews in need in Russia. This plan, which was conceived and carried out by Lvovitch, became known as "The Relatives' Constructive Help."

Lvovitch published many articles and pamphlets on Jewish and general economic problems, in which he remained faithful to his old idea: that only economic adjustment of the Jews, together with large-scale colonization, can lead to the solution of the Jewish problem.   MARGARET T. EDELHEIM.

LWÓW (in German, **Lemberg**), city in southeastern Poland, formerly the capital of Galicia, Austria. Lwów Jews were mentioned in the 13th cent., during the reign of the Ruthenian princes; in 1356 and 1364 the earliest recorded privileges were given them. The Jews originally resided at the southwestern corner of the city walls. The thoroughfare leading from the high castle to the low one was settled under the rule of Prince Leo by Ruthenians, Tatars and Jewish court merchants. It formed a suburb of Lwów wherein Mongolian refugees could find protection. After the annexation of Lwów (1340-49) to the Polish empire by Casimir III the Great (reigned 1333-70), the Jews of Lwów were given full equality, but the Jews of the suburb remained under the jurisdiction of the castle purveyor, with the right of appeal to the Starosta. The Jewish privileges were confirmed by Ladislaus of Oppeln and by Ludwig of Anjou. In 1387 the king of Poland and Lithuania, Wladyslaw Jagiello, sustained the privileges conferred by his queen, Jadwiga. His successor, Wladyslaw III, endorsed the Jews' commercial privileges and encouraged

Tombstones in the old Jewish cemetery of Lwów

the educational system as well as the beautification of the town, the improving of the water supply and method of irrigation, and the constructing of parks.

Prince Andreas Odrowaz incited mercenary troops to plunder and slaughter the Jews and schismatic Ruthenians, who found refuge in Lwów, which successfully resisted siege by the foe. In 1494 a conflagration destroyed the Jewish settlement, whereupon Johann Albrecht exempted the impoverished section from taxes for fifteen years; but three years later he issued an edict forbidding Jews, Armenians and Ruthenians to engage in commerce. Meanwhile, the Tatars and Turks continued to devastate the outskirts of the town. For purposes of fortification the ruins were blasted.

During the reign of Sigismund I, the Jewish commercial privileges were preserved, but their social status was degraded. The position of the Jews improved considerably after the accession of Sigismund August in 1548. Stefan Batory was benevolent to the Jews, and declined to recognize such accusations brought against them as that they defamed the sacraments or that they committed ritual murder. At the end of the 16th cent. a synagogue was erected. However, Sigismund III sanctioned expropriation of the building by the Jesuits, who transformed it into a church. When they discovered that it was unsuitable for their purposes, the Jesuits agreed to its redemption for 23,000 Polish gulden in 1608.

In 1616 a conflagration almost destroyed the entire Jewish section. In 1623 pestilence, starvation and fire took their toll. In 1624 the Jews were plundered by the Tatars. In 1625 a conflagration caused great damage.

The sufferings of the Jews of Lwów reached their maximum during the Chmielnicki revolt. In 1648, when the beleaguered town was unable to bear the food and water shortage, it delivered to Chmielnicki an exorbitant ransom to which mostly Jews contributed. Refugees had to be taken care of by the impoverished community. However, the Jews were rewarded with economic privileges after participating in the victory over Chmielnicki at Sokol. In 1655, when Chmielnicki besieged Lwów again, the municipal government refused to deliver the Jews and their property over to the relentless foe.

In 1664, owing to Jesuit agitation, the mob killed hundreds of Jews; the government, sympathizing with the Jews, indemnified them for their losses. Under Jan III Sobieski the Jewish community flourished. After his death the Jews suffered from rowdy soldiers. In 1703, when an explosion of the arsenal killed thirty-six persons, Jacob Joshua ben Zebi Hirsch, author of the *Pene Yehoshua,* was saved as if by a miracle.

In 1704 the Jews suffered as a result of the war between Charles XII of Sweden and Augustus II of Poland. When the former's soldiers entered the city, they were encouraged to kill and pillage Christians and Jews indiscriminately. A conflagration added to the misery of the Jews, who were forced to contribute to the ransom paid to the victor. After the evacuation by the Swedes various diseases wrought havoc.

In 1728 a blood accusation was brought against the Jews. In the same year the brothers Haim and Joshua Reizes (or Reizeles) were convicted and tortured to death for allegedly persuading a converted Jew to return to Judaism.

The Kahal of the suburb was united with that of the city proper by the Edict of Toleration of Emperor Joseph II in 1782. The community was retarded in its development by burdensome taxation and ransom contributions. However, with the colonization of eastern Poland, Lwów entered upon economic, religious and judicial relations with the nearby provinces. In 1765 its Jewish population numbered about 6,000; in 1825 it comprised only 4,000, and in 1931 it totalled about 100,000.

During the Polish period Lwów was the seat of the chief rabbinate of the Red Russian fellow-countrymen, and also of a Yeshiva in which scholars of great repute studied and labored. In the Austrian period the enlightenment (Haskalah) movement was transplanted thither; it found its staunchest adherents in Solomon Leib Rapoport, Nachman Krochmal (who lived in Zólkiew, near Lwów), Isaac Erter, Judah Löb Mieses, and, in the 1840's, Jacob Bodek, Mendel Mohr and Meir Letteris. In 1844 Abraham Kohn was called to Lwów as the first progressive rabbi; in 1846 the so-called German Temple was built. These innovations in the beginning met with the support of the government, which wished to "Germanize" the Jews. The Orthodox would not allow themselves to be intimidated, however, and in 1848 Abraham Kohn, together with his family, was poisoned by a fanatic.

SIMON MOWSHOWITZ.

Lwów became the first center of the Jewish national movement beginning with 1880. The young generation followed the call of Dr. Leon Pinsker and founded self-educational circles. Some ten years before Theodor Herzl published his *Judenstaat* there was a strong Zionist movement in Lwów and Eastern Galicia which corresponded with the Chovevei Zion and Bilu movements in Russia. This Zionist movement was embodied in the organization Syon (Zion) in Lwów, with branches all over Galicia. Its founders were young Orthodox Jews who emancipated themselves and later became the most outstanding leaders of Galician, Austrian and Polish Zionism, including Salamon Schiller, Abraham Korkis, Osias Thon, Adolph Stand, Gershon Zipper, David Schreiber and Markus Braude, and among the younger ones, Leon Reich, Henryk Rosmarin, Jakob Thon and Jakob Korkis. They laid the foundation for a strong Zionist organization in Lwów and in the whole of Galicia, which joined soon after he had taken the first steps toward Zionism.

In November, 1918, Lwów was the scene of a bloody struggle between Poles and Ukrainians. After the Poles occupied the Jewish quarter, the Jews, who declared themselves neutral in the struggle, became victims of a violent pogrom which caused the death of seventy-two persons and destroyed by fire a vast area inhabited by the Jews. The ruins of this pogrom lasted until 1939.

Lwów in 1919 was incorporated, together with Eastern Galicia, into Poland, after the Ukrainian government in Stanislawów had been defeated and expelled from the country. During the twenty years of the Polish government the Jews of Lwów fought for their national cultural and economic rights. They founded many educational institutions, professional schools, and Hebrew high schools and colleges. The main instrument of this political struggle was the Zionist organization and two daily newspapers, *Dos Yiddishe Togblatt,* founded in 1905 by Gershon Bader and later edited by Moses Frostig, Abraham Insler, Maikel Ringel and Fishel Rotenstreich, and the Polish daily *Chwila* (The Moment), founded in November, 1918, by Gershon Zipper, and edited and directed later as the main political organ by Leon Reich and Henryk Rosmarin. Lwów sent to the Polish Sejm, from 1922 on, only Zionist deputies: Dr. Leon Reich (until his death in 1929); Carol Eisenstein, leader of the Jewish merchants; Dr. Emil Sommerstein (until 1939); and, for a short period, Dr. Max Leser and Dr. Wolf. Dr. David Schreiber was a Jewish senator of Lwów to the Polish Senate. Reich and Sommerstein were for many years presidents of the Jewish Parliamentary Club.

The Jewish youth movement originated in Lwów under the form of the scout movement Zeire Zion and of the Hanoar Hatzioni and Hashomer Hatzair. Many of the rabbis of Lwów were famous, both Orthodox and progressive. Among the Orthodox were Rabbi Schmelkes, grandfather of the president of the Great Council of the World Agudah Organization and of the Sejm deputy Aron Lewin and great-grandfather of the young leader of the Agudah, Dr. Izaak Lewin (who in 1942 was in New York city); Rabbi Izaak Ziff, Rabbi Leib Braude, Dr. Yehezkiel Caro, Dr. Samuel Gutmann, Dr. Levi Freund, and Dr. Yehezkiel Lewin (another grandson of Rabbi Schmelkes).

In September, 1939, Lwów was occupied by the Russians and made the capital of the Soviet Republic of Western Ukraine. In July, 1941, Lwów was invaded by the German Nazis, who instituted a ghetto where more than 150,000 Jews of Lwów and Jewish refugees from other cities were, in 1942, living under extremely bad conditions.   JOSEPH THON.

Lit.: Caro, J., *Geschichte der Juden in Lemberg* (1894); Balaban, *Zydzi Lwowscy na przelomie 16 i 17 wieku* (1906); idem, *Dzieje Zydów w Galicji i w Rzeczypospolitej Krakowskiej* (1916); Balaban, *Zhist. Zydów w Polsce* (1920); Balaban, *Z wczorajsziego Lwowa* (1925-26); Prochaska, *Sejmik wiszenski wobec Zydów* (1920).

LYDDA (Hebrew, **Lod**; Arabic, **Ludd**), a town in Palestine, situated in the valley of Aijalon, to the southeast of Jaffa. Talmudic tradition had it that Lydda was established as a walled city at the time of Joshua; *1 Chron.* 8:12 states that it was founded by Shemer, a Benjamite, after the Babylonian exile (*Ezra* 2:33). The Samaritans conquered the region during the 4th cent. B.C.E. Julius Caesar returned it to Judea in the 1st cent. C.E., in recognition of the support given him by Antipater, father of Herod. During the Roman rule Lydda was the capital of one of the five toparchies established in the country, but in the unrest that preceded the destruction of the Second Temple Lydda seems to have been a center of anti-Roman activity. By surrendering to Vespasian, however, it was able to provide a haven for the scholars who had fled from Jerusalem.

Eliezer ben Hyrcanus had founded an academy in Lydda; it was to Lydda that he was brought for burial after his death in excommunication and loneliness. Akiba and others of his pupils taught at Lydda, and

during the reign of Hadrian the city seems to have been the seat of rabbinical assemblies, particularly those dealing with the required behavior of Jews in the face of Roman compulsion. Again, in the 4th cent., Lydda became the headquarters for revolt, and as a result was partly destroyed by the Romans. Although it had been known for its metropolitan atmosphere, Lydda then began to decline, until its reputation became that of a hovel of the impoverished. During the 4th cent. Lydda was known as a Christian center and the seat of a bishopric. It was declared to be the burial place of St. George; the church erected over his supposed tomb was destroyed by Saladin (12th cent.) and only partly rebuilt in more recent times. The name Diospolis, which had been given to Lydda during one of the Roman conquests, rapidly passed into disuse. Its Jewish population dwindled until Benjamin of Tudela (12th cent.) found only one Jew in the city—a dyer.

The situation of Lydda, on an important travel crossroads, had always contributed to its importance. With the disappearance of its cultural and religious activity, its geographical significance remained unchanged, and in the 20th cent. it was still an important railroad junction for travel through Palestine and into Egypt. In the late 1930's, out of a total population of less than 12,000, about thirty were Jews.

Lit.: De Haas, Jacob, *History of Palestine* (1934); Graetz, H., *History of the Jews,* vols. 1 and 2 (1927); *Encyclopedia of Islam,* vol. 3, part 1; Smith, G. A., *The Historical Geography of the Holy Land,* pp. 141, 160-65.

LYNN, city in Massachusetts having a population of 98,123 (census of 1940), including about 8,500 Jews. These population figures cover Lynn, Swampscott, Nahant, Saugus, and Marblehead—the area embraced by Greater Lynn.

The first and oldest organization in the city was the Hebrew Benevolent Society, formed in 1884. It was composed of ten families from Germany and from Lithuania. It was a fraternal organization whose aim was to provide the membership with burial grounds and sick benefits.

In 1900 the Jewish population of Lynn included about one hundred families. The Ahabat Shalom synagogue was organized in 1901. Its ritual was that of Lithuanian Orthodoxy. The rabbi in 1942 was Morris Landes. In 1903 the Anshe Sfard synagogue (Orthodox) was established by about thirty-five families who came from Ukraine. In 1904 the Beth Israel synagogue (Orthodox) was organized in West Lynn. Other Orthodox congregations included Hevra Thilim and B'nai Jacob. The community's foremost Talmudic scholar was (1942) Rabbi Benjamin Lipschutz, who was maintained by a private society, Agudas Horav.

The liberal element of Greater Lynn organized Temple Beth El (Reform) in 1927. It had (1942) a membership of 225 families, and was the largest Jewish congregation in Greater Lynn. The rabbi in 1942 was Israel Harburg.

There were, in 1942, a Hebrew school headed by Dr. Jacob Loewenbach and a community center under the supervision of William Pruss. The various Jewish labor groups met at their headquarters, which housed a Yiddish secular school. The outstanding organizations which provided for local relief were the Federated Jewish Charities, the Hebrew Sheltering Home and the

Free Loan Society. There were also a number of lodges and societies representing almost every Jewish national organization in the country. In 1940 all the local, national, and overseas Jewish philanthropies consolidated under the United Jewish Appeal with an annual budget of about $50,000.

There were in Lynn, in 1942, about 150 Jewish professionals represented in medicine, law, engineering, education and social work.   ISRAEL HARBURG.

LYON, city in southern France, in the Rhône department, with a population (1940) of about 580,000. Soon after the founding of the Roman colony of Lugdunum (43 B.C.E.) Herod Antipas, tetrarch of Galilee, was exiled to Lugdunum (later called Lyon) by Emperor Caius Caligula in 39. According to the legend, Jews from Palestine settled at Bordeaux, Arles and Lyon after the destruction of Jerusalem in 70; Salomon Reinach believes that the existence of a Christian community at Lyon in the 2nd cent. justifies the conclusion that Jews lived in Lyon in the same years. Lyon became the capital of Burgundy, and the Burgundian law of the 6th cent. adopted measures affecting the Jews; Lyon became also the see of an archbishop, and the church councils held in the archbishopric dealt with the Jews. On the basis of all these facts the presence of Jews at Lyon from the first Christian centuries on may be assumed.

The Jews of Lyon do not appear in the full light of history until the reign of Louis the Pious (814-40). The Jews David and Joseph and their coreligionists obtained a privilege from the emperor (before 825). They were granted personal safety, security in pecuniary matters, and exemption from duties and taxes. They enjoyed the king's protection, and were expected to serve him loyally. They were allowed to exchange their lawfully acquired property with whom they chose, to practise their religion freely, to give work to Christian employees except on Sundays and Christian holidays, and to buy foreign slaves and sell them within the empire. No one was allowed to baptize the foreign slaves of Jews without their permission. If a Christian brought a complaint against a Jew, he was obliged to produce three competent Christian witnesses and the same number of Jewish witnesses, while in the case of a complaint brought by a Jew against a Christian, the complaint had to have Christian witnesses in order to secure a conviction. When, in ascertaining the truth, difficulties arose, the duke was to aid in clearing up the case. Intricate disputes about slaves and property were to be deferred until the emperor was present. Jews could be punished with scourging in specified cases only. Attempted murder, or murder, of a Jew was punished by a fine of ten pounds of gold payable to the emperor.

As is learned from other sources, the Jews were permitted to build synagogues. A Christian "Magister Judeorum" (master of the Jews) appointed by the emperor had the duty of supervising the provisions concerning the Jews.

The Jews of Lyon resided in a street of the quarter of St. Paul under the hill de Fourvière. There were active relations between Jews and Christians. The latter partook of Jewish meals, gladly listened to Jewish sermons, celebrated the Sabbath, and were in the service of Jews, doing household work and cultivating Jewish-owned land.

The archbishop of Lyon, Agobard (813-40), and his successor, Amulo (841-52), made severe attacks on the influence and social position of the Jews. Agobard preached sermons full of hatred and repeatedly addressed written complaints to Louis the Pious (later collected under the title *De insolentia Judeorum*). The Jews, in turn, complained to the emperor of Agobard's actions. The emperor ordered his officials to protect the Jews from the attacks and fanaticism of the clergy. Consequently the anti-Jewish efforts of Agobard and Amulo remained fruitless for some time.

During the reign of the Capetians the position of the Jews became worse. About 1049 the Jews of Lyon were attacked, some were killed, and their property was seized and allotted to the cloister d'Ainay. The decree of the council of Lyon in 1245 exempting the Crusaders from the payment of interest to Jews and excluding Jews from all public offices and introducing the Jew badge had, of course, reference to the Jews in general. In 1250 Archbishop Philip of Savoy assigned to the Jews residences in the quarter of St. George; in 1251 they were expelled from the city, their homes looted and their property sold at auction for the benefit of the church. They moved to a suburb, but were expelled from there, too, in 1260. For a temporary stay at Lyon they had to pay twelve deniers each time.

However, they reappeared in the city very soon. Further expulsions took place in 1306 (the banishment of the Jews from France), 1322, 1346 and 1347; they were readmitted in 1315, 1328 and 1350. In 1312 the city of Lyon was attached to the crown of France. When King John the Good was taken prisoner by the English in 1360, the Jews of Lyon paid the ransom for him, at his request; in return, he granted them privileges which were repeatedly renewed for cash payments. In 1379 they were ordered to move to the right bank of the Rhône; a "Magister Judeorum" had to defend their rights as before. In 1391 they were granted a letter of patent by Charles VI; in 1392 they came under the archbishop's reign, so that they were presumably not directly affected by the general edict of expulsion against the Jews from France in 1394. In 1420, however, they were finally expelled from Lyon, after having been again ordered, in 1409, to wear the Jew badge. They settled chiefly in the neighboring towns of Burgundy and the Dauphiné, and from there they continued to frequent the markets of Lyon.

Little is known about the intellectual life of the Jews of Lyon in the Middle Ages. Considering the importance of the Lyon community, no doubt, Jewish savants of good reputation resided there. The *Mahzor Vitry* refers to a Rabbi Solomon who probably hailed from Lyon. Rabbenu Tam mentions, in the first half of the 12th cent., "les rabbins de Lyon et de Carpentras." However, at that time Lyon appears to have no longer had a leading part in the cultural life of the French Jews.

After the visit of Henry IV and Catherine de' Medici to Lyon in 1548, some Jewish merchants tried to settle there, but their attempt was promptly suppressed. In an Italian collection of rabbinical responsa of the 16th cent. (by Josua Fermi of Ancona) a financial dispute at Lyon between Emmanuel Pereyre and Rodrigue de Lyon is referred to. Under Louis XV a few Jews from Alsace and southern France appeared at Lyon. About the middle of the 18th cent. fifteen Jewish families lived there, and were granted a cemetery by the city of Lyon. In 1781 Elijah Rouget was named syndic (head) of the community.

From the French Revolution on the Jewish community of Lyon developed slowly but visibly. One of the victims of the many executions in Lyon during the French Revolution was the Jew Azariah Vidal (1793). In 1795 the community bought grounds for a cemetery at Guillotière. In October, 1810, the number of Jews in Lyon was 195, hailing from Alsace-Lorraine, Bordeaux, Avignon, Brabant, Westphalia and Poland. The total property of the Jews of Lyon at the time was valued at 512,000 francs. The prefect's opinion as to their honesty was not unfavorable. Lyon was then the only community of the department, and was under the control of the consistory of Marseille.

In the first half of the 19th cent. the Jewish community was headed by Isaac Helft, Isaac Cerf of Ricqlès, and Nordheim. In 1850 the communities of the départments of Rhône, Isère and Loire were united to form one district rabbinate; its rabbi was Jacques Weinberg (d. 1879), of Rappoltsweiler, who had his residence in Lyon. In 1851 the communities of these departments were united with those of the departments of Ain, Jura, Saône-et-Loire and Doubs into a consistorial district. Its representatives at the central consistory included Salomon Munk, Michel Alcan and Eugene Manuel, the poet. In 1864 the new synagogue at Quay Tilsit, one of the most beautiful in France, was consecrated; in 1868 an asylum for the aged was founded, and in 1870 new grounds for a cemetery adjacent to the old ones were acquired. Weinberg's successors were Alfred Lévy (from 1905 on chief rabbi of France), Abraham Bloch and Edgar Sèches. After the separation of church and state, the Association Cultuelle des Israélites de Lyon was founded, to which the communities of Grenoble, Chambery, Aix-les-Bains and other places belong.

The number of the Jews in Lyon was:

Year	Total Population	Number of Jews
1894		1,500
1904	466,767	1,500
1911	524,000	2,600
1928	570,000	2,000

In the ancient consistorial district of Lyon there lived, in 1926, a total of 3,500 Jews. There were several Jewish welfare organizations in Lyon and its district.

Jews were active in all branches of industry and trade in Lyon, which was one of the most important commercial and textile towns of the world, and one of the most important cultural and scientific research centers of France. The surname De Lyon was borne by Abraham De Lyon, who went from Portugal to the United States and introduced viticulture into Georgia in 1737.

After June 22, 1940, when France collapsed during the second World War, the Jews of Lyon, which formed a part of unoccupied France, were also affected by all exceptional laws. Attacks on Jews were made at Lyon in August, 1940, the same as in Vichy and Toulouse. On the other hand, in early September,

1941, the municipal authorities permitted the reopening of the Yeshiva, which had previously been attended mostly by refugee students. The principal of the school in 1942 was Rabbi Ehrman, a member of the executive of the World Agudah.   ADOLF KOBER.

Lit.: Anchel, Robert, Napoléon et les Juifs (1928); Aronius, Regesten (1902), nos. 82, 88, 89, 92, 94, 99, 107 and 557; Contemporary Jewish Record, vols. 3 and 4 (1940-41); Dubnow, S., Weltgeschichte des jüdischen Volkes, vol. 4 (1926); Encyclopaedia Judaica, vol. 10 (1934), cols. 1256-60, and the literature cited there; Gross, H., Gallia Judaica (1897) 306-7; Jewish Encyclopedia, vol. 8, pp. 228-31; Juster, J., Les Juifs dans l'empire romain, vol. 1 (1914) 185; Lévy, Alfred, Notice sur les Israélites de Lyon (1894); Revue des études juives, vol. 1, p. 247; Acta, vol. 1, p. lxxx; vol. 2, p. 144; vol. 3, p. 1132; vol. 5, p. 218; vol. 7, p. 2; vol. 30, pp. 137-38; vol. 51, p. 245 et seq.; vol. 56, pp. 141-42; vol. 48, p. 299; Tcherikower, The Jews in France, Jewish Scientific Institute (1942).

LYON, ABRAHAM DE, early American settler and vine-grower, one of the forty Jewish pioneers who settled in Savannah, Ga., in 1733, the same year that the colony was founded by Oglethorpe. Abraham De Lyon probably came from Portugal as a refugee from the Portuguese Inquisition. He appears to have brought with him a practical knowledge of viticulture in the cultivation of wine-producing fruits. To promote this industry De Lyon requested the trustees of the colony to lend him 200 pounds for three years without interest. The trustees dispatched their agent, Colonel William Stephens, to inspect the De Lyon plantation and render a report. Stephens was favorably impressed; he left a glowing account of the visit he made, on December 6, 1737, to the Jewish vine-grower's plantation. Upon Stephen's recommendation the trustees agreed to lend De Lyon the required sum; they sent the money to Oglethorpe to deliver to the borrower, who, unfortunately, received only a small part of it, Oglethorpe having decided to use the rest of the money for other purposes.

De Lyon was probably among the number of Jewish colonists of Savannah who removed to Charleston, S. C., in 1740, because of the illiberal policy of the Georgia trustees. But it is likely that he returned subsequently and spent the last years of his life in Savannah. De Lyon was the founder of a family which contributed to American progress.

Lit.: Publications of the American Jewish Historical Society, No. 1 (1892) 10-12; No. 10 (1902) 69-73, 79-80, 85-86; No. 12 (1904) 164; Jewish Encyclopedia, vol. 8, pp. 228-29.

LYON, ROBERT, journalist, b. London, 1810; d. New York city, 1858. He came to the United States in 1854 and engaged in business in New York city for five years. In 1849 he founded the Asmonean, of which he was publisher and editor until his death. This was one of the first Anglo-Jewish weeklies in the United States. During the same period he edited the Mercantile Journal, a trade organ. The Asmonean numbered Isaac M. Wise and other nationally famous Jewish figures among its contributors, but it never achieved the position of chief organ of American Jewish opinion which Lyon hoped for.

LYON-CAËN, CHARLES, jurist, b. Paris, 1843; d. Paris, 1935. His father, Jacob Lyon-Caën, was a tailor but keenly interested in literature and science, ready to spend all he could afford for the education of his children. Lyon-Caën was educated at the Institut Sainte Barbe, then entered his father's business. Some months later the father became aware that his son was anxious to study but too timid to utter his wishes, and sent him to the university. Lyon-Caën studied law, and was graduated as licencié in 1864, docteur en droit in 1866 and aggrégé in 1867, his thesis, *Partages d'ascendants,* attracting the attention of learned jurists.

In 1872 Lyon-Caën became professor of law at the Sorbonne, and remained in this post until 1919. During the war (1870-71) he excelled in the battles around Paris, especially at Montretout, as a member of the national guard. In 1884 he was elected member of the Institut de France. In 1893 he was elected permanent secretary of the French Academy, thus becoming the representative speaker of that world-renowned organization. In 1934 he was honored on the occasion of the fiftieth anniversary of his membership.

In 1885 Lyon-Caën joined with Louis Renault in publishing *Précis de droit commercial,* which became a classical textbook of French juridical literature, as well as his *Traité de droit commercial* (8 vols., 5th ed., 1921-36). Having edited, from 1877 on, the *Tableau des lois commerciales des principaux états de l'Europe et de l'Amérique,* Lyon-Caën became an international authority in commercial law. He enhanced his reputation through *Traité des sociétés commerciales* (1892). Meanwhile, he inaugurated a new branch of the science of law by publishing his *Droit international privé maritime* in 1883, and by numerous special inquiries and treatises he completed his new doctrine of civil maritime law. But he never became a mere specialist; he dealt with international law, maritime law, legislation of societies and industrial property. Lyon-Caën propounded the problem of uniting commercial and civil law. His conception of the law did not seek to restrict it to an abstract and isolated theory. He integrated the explanation of juridical facts and terms to the whole of social and economic life, and compared French legislation with that in force abroad. Lyon-Caën was president of the Société de législation comparée, of the Société d'études législatives, of the Académie de droit international, and of the juridic committee of the Banque de France. He was president or member of the disciplinary courts of the ministries of finance, justice, colonies and marine. He was also president or member of the directory of several Jewish organizations in France, and professed interest in Jewish history and in the conservation of the rights of the French Jews by his study on Abbé Grégoire.

Lit.: Académie des sciences morales et politiques, *Revue des travaux* (1937).

LYONS, ABRAHAM MONTAGU, member of the British Parliament, b. Lincoln, England, 1894. He was educated at Old Clee Grammar School in Lincolnshire, served in the army from 1914 to 1916, and in 1922 he was admitted to the bar. He was active in politics as a member of the Conservative Party. In 1929 he ran for Parliament from Clay Cross Division, Derbyshire, but was defeated. Lyons traveled extensively through many parts of the world, including the United States. He ran again in 1931, this time from East Leicester, and was elected. In 1942 he still represented East Leicester in Parliament. In 1933 he was honored with the title of King's Counsel. Lyons was interested also in Jewish affairs, and was a member of the Board of Deputies of British Jews.

LYONS, ALEXANDER, rabbi, b. Mobile, Ala., 1867; d. New York city, 1939. He received his rabbinical degree from the Hebrew Union College in 1891, and his B.L. degree at the University of Cincinnati the same year. Later, while living in New York, he received an M.A. and a Ph.D. degree from Columbia University. From 1891 to 1895 Lyons was rabbi of Temple Israel in Terre Haute, Ind., and from 1895 to 1901 he headed Congregation Beth Emeth of Albany, N. Y. In 1901 he was called to Temple Beth Elohim of Brooklyn, N. Y., where he served until his death.

Lyons was active in the promotion of good will between Christians and Jews, but believed that it should grow out of a serious fulfilment of obligations to the various religions rather than out of superficial fellowship. He wrote numerous articles to further the cause, and in 1920 founded and became editor of *The Supplement,* a monthly magazine devoted to interfaith understanding. In 1937 he collected a number of his essays in *Jew and Christian.*

Lyon also sought a more sententious interpretation of the role a house of worship must play in relation to the faith it represents. He did not belittle the desirability of the social aspects of churches and synagogues, but inveighed against giving these priority. He participated in general and Jewish social work, and was a member of the executive board of the Society for the Prevention of Crime, a member of the Brooklyn Library Board, and an honorary member of the Young Men's Christian Association. In 1907 he founded the Consumptives' Jewish Aid Society of Brooklyn.

Lyons was decorated by the French government in 1919 as a Chevalier of the Legion of Honor.

Lit.: Landman, Isaac, "Alexander Lyons," *Central Conference of American Rabbis Year Book,* vol. 49 (1939) 301-2.

LYONS, EMANUEL B., Jamaican public official and communal leader, b. London, 1807; d. Kingston, 1872. He came to Jamaica and entered the hardware business. For seven years a captain in the Kingston Foot Militia, he was extremely active in the Jewish community and in civic affairs. He was appointed a magistrate for Kingston, and was for several years president of the Kingston Ashkenazic Synagogue on Grange Street. A memorial service to his memory was held in the Scotch Kirke on Duke Street, which was attended by members of all denominations. The sermon of the minister was afterward published and sold, and the proceeds were devoted toward the memorial tablet erected in his memory in the chapel of the Elletson Road Jewish Cemetery.

Lit.: Files of *The Gleaner,* Jan. 16 and May 30, 1872.

LYONS, EUGENE, author, journalist and editor, b. Uzlian, Russia, 1898. Coming to the United States at the age of nine, he was later educated at the College of the City of New York and Columbia University. From 1919 to 1922 he worked as a reporter for the

Erie *Dispatch*, the New York *Financial American*, the Paris *Herald*, the Boston *Telegram* and other papers.

In 1922 Lyons was the editor of *Soviet Russia Pictorial*, and from 1923 to 1927 assistant director of the New York bureau of Tass, Soviet news agency. In 1927 he went to Moscow as a correspondent for the United Press, and stayed there in that capacity for seven years. Upon his return to the United States he wrote a book, *Assignment in Utopia* (1937), in which he described his disillusionment over what he considered the failure of the Soviet experiment. In 1939 Lyons became editor of the *American Mercury*, a post he still held in 1942. It was the opinion in liberal circles that, after his return from Russia, Lyons became obsessed with anti-communism.

He wrote many articles and editorials for magazines. He was also the author of several books on political subjects, including: *The Life and Death of Sacco and Vanzetti* (1927); *Moscow Carrousel* (1935); *The Red Decade* (1941). Among the books he edited were *Six Soviet Plays* (1936) and *We Cover the World* (1937).

LYONS, ISAAC, physician and surgeon-general during the Texas war for independence, b. Columbia, S. C., 1811; d. Charleston, S. C., 1837. In 1836 he was attached to the volunteer army commanded by Thomas Jefferson Green in the Texas war of independence. His salary was to have been $2,500 a year, but he died after three months of service.

    Lit.: Kagan, Solomon R., *Jewish Contributions to Medicine in America* (1939) 7-8, 44, 454, 485.

LYONS, ISRAEL, astronomer, mathematician and botanist, b. Cambridge, England, 1739; d. London, 1775. He was the son of Israel Lyons, who emigrated from Poland to England and died at Cambridge in 1770. The father settled down as a silversmith in Cambridge; however, he became known as a Hebrew scholar and a "teacher of the Hebrew tongue" at the University of Cambridge. The older Lyons wrote several books on Hebrew grammar.

These were the surroundings in which the more famous son was born. His first interest in mathematics was later on overshadowed by his studies of botany, to which he devoted his whole life. His initial work was entitled *Treatise on Fluxions* (Cambridge, 1758) and was dedicated to his master Dr. Smith of Trinity College. In 1763 there appeared *Fasciculus plantarum circa Cantabrigiam nascentium, quae post Raium observatae fuere.*

About the same time, his former pupil Joseph Banks, then president of the Royal Society in London, invited him to lecture at Oxford. He agreed, but soon returned to Cambridge. It was not until 1773 that he left his birthplace to accompany Captain Phipps, the later Lord Mulgrave, on his expedition to the North Pole, serving as chief astronomer.

After his return, Lyons married and settled in London, where he died almost a year later suffering from an illness caused by the hardships experienced during the Phipps expedition. His death interrupted his editing of papers of the famous astronomer Edmund Halley, then secretary of the Royal Society in London.

Lyons was a collaborator on the *Nautical Almanac* and author of the astronomical part of John Sealley's

Jacques Judah Lyons

Complete Geographical Dictionary. Maria Edgeworth portrayed him in her novel *Harrington*.

    Lit.: C.-V.-Zeitung, vol. 17, October 2, 1938.

LYONS, JACQUES JUDAH, rabbi, b. Paramaribo, Surinam, 1813; d. New York city, 1877. He was the son of Judah and Mary Lyons, who had emigrated to Surinam from Philadelphia. He was minister at Paramaribo from 1833 to 1837. In 1837 he came to the United States and accepted a call from Congregation Beth Shalom of Richmond, Va. Two years later he became minister of the Spanish-Portuguese Congregation Shearith Israel of New York city, a post he held until his death. During this time he vigorously defended the Orthodox Sephardic ritual against all attempts at reform.

Lyons was actively interested in all phases of Jewish affairs. He was one of the founders of the Jews' Hospital, which later became Mount Sinai Hospital. He also served as superintendent of the Polonies Talmud Torah School, president of the Hebra Hesed Veemet, and president of the Sampson-Simpson Theological Fund. In 1854 he and Abraham de Sola of Montreal, Quebec, compiled and published a Jewish calendar for a period of fifty years.

Perhaps his most important contribution was the collection of a vast library of American Judaica. He started collecting items in 1861, and acquired new material until his death. Many of the documents he discovered cast new light on hitherto obscure problems of American Jewish history, and in recognition of their value and as a tribute to the memory of Lyons they were published in two volumes by the American Jewish Historical Society (1903 and 1920).

    JULIUS JUDAH LYONS (b. New York city, 1843; d. San Diego, Cal., 1920), son of Jacques Judah Lyons, was a lawyer by profession. He was admitted to the bar of New York in 1866. He was one of the organizers, and a director, of The State Bank, the bank most patronized by the Jewish immigrants who settled on the East Side of New York city, and until 1909 he was its counsel. He was a judge advocate, with the rank of major, in the New York State National Guard.

Lyons was also a musician. He composed an opera, *The Lady or the Tiger,* which was produced by De Wolf Hopper's company, and he founded and for several years directed a large orchestra, The Metropolitan Amateur Orchestra. He was music editor of *The Daily News,* and wrote on music for the New York *Herald.*

For more than twenty years he was an officer and director of Jewish organizations in New York city, including Mount Sinai Hospital, of which he was secretary for ten years, the Montefiore Home for Chronic Invalids, and the Hebrew Technical Institute.

Lit.: Publications of the American Jewish Historical Society, No. 21 (1913) xxiii-xxvii; No. 27 (1920) 144-49.

LYONS, SIR JOSEPH, restaurateur, b. London; d. 1917. He spent his early adult years as an artist, but later entered the catering field and became the head of J. Lyons and Co., Ltd., the largest restaurateur and hotelier firm in England. Lyons was knighted in 1911.

LYRA, NICOLAS DE, French Franciscan monk, commentator of the Old and New Testaments—the "St. Jerome" of the later Middle Ages—b. 1270; d. 1349. He came originally from Lyre, in Normandy. He joined the Franciscan order about 1300. The first years of his calling were spent in Normandy; the rest of his life was lived in Paris mainly, where he taught as member of the theological faculty of the University of Paris. His most important work is his *Postillae Perpetuae,* a running commentary on the Bible.

Nicolas de Lyra is justly famous for his quotations from the Bible commentaries of Rashi (about 1040-1105), the most popular Jewish interpreter of the Bible. Just as Rashi had been concerned over the tendencies among the Jews to interpret the Bible too loosely and too lavishly, so Lyra, in his age, was concerned above all with getting at the sense of the Bible according to the minds of its authors. Lyra turned to Rashi's writings in addition to those of the Christian authorities, in order to get material which would elucidate the simple, literal and natural understanding of the Scriptures. He found certain difficulties in the Latin trans-

lation of the Old Testament. He realized that every language, including the Hebrew, had a *proprietas* ("special nature") and that it was necessary to know the original Hebrew and the Hebrew commentaries, especially those of Rashi, if the Old Testament was to be understood completely and accurately. He knew Hebrew, and he had Hebrew teachers who guided him and helped him with the reading of the rabbinic writings of the earlier and later Middle Ages.

Because Rashi's name appears as an authority on almost every page of Lyra's great work, some have called Lyra "Rashi's ape." Lyra had very great respect for Rashi, but he did not "ape" Rashi; he absorbed Rashi. Rashi was Lyra's *guide.* Lyra does not repeat as a disciple; he is too vigorously interested in his own Christian thinking; he wishes to be wholly honorable and to learn. Lyra is attracted to Rashi because Rashi's mental habits appealed to him.

Lyra draws upon Rashi (1) for word and sentence explanations; (2) for aid in correcting the Latin Bible on the basis of the Hebrew text; (3) for knowledge of Jewish religious practices and of Jewish law; (4) for correcting occasionally the interpretations of some of the Christian scholars; and (5) for many quotations from the Midrash and Talmud. On certain points Lyra feels that he knows enough to take issue with his master and to quote Talmud, Midrash and Targum outside of what Rashi gives him.

Whatever Rashi materials are found in the writings of Christian scholars, Catholic and Protestant, from the days of Luther down to our own times, have their original source, in the main, in the writings of Nicolas de Lyra.

Lyra wrote two special anti-Jewish polemical treatises, but these small tracts are "anti-Jewish," for the most part, in the *academic, scholastic* sense; they are really on the defensive side mainly, and they attempt to clarify the Christian religion for Christians as well as for Jews.   HERMAN HAILPERIN.

Lit.: Hailperin, H., in *Rashi Anniversary Volume* (1941) 115-47.

LYSIAS (Syrian general), *see* JUDAS MACCABEUS.

LYSIMACHUS OF ALEXANDRIA, *see* GREEK WRITERS ON JEWS.

M

MAABAR YABBOK, *see* AARON BERECHIAH BEN MOSES OF MODENA.

MAABAROTH, *see* COLONIES, AGRICULTURAL.

MAALE HA'HAMISHA, *see* COLONIES, AGRICULTURAL.

MAAMADOTH ("posts," "standing committees"), groups of laymen whose duty it was to attend the daily sacrifice in the Temple at Jerusalem. The origin of the custom is explained in *Taan.* 4:2 as being due to the feeling that as the offering is the gift of the people, the people should be present; and that since it was obviously impossible for them all to attend, they were represented by selected laymen from Jerusalem, who

were divided into twenty-four groups corresponding to the twenty-four divisions of the priesthood and who, like them, served for a week in turn. The custom is attributed to the early prophets, but probably arose in the time of the Second Temple. Later on the Jews outside of Jerusalem also divided themselves into twenty-four Maamadoth; but instead of going to the Temple in the assigned week, they would meet in their own cities or villages and read portions from the Torah and recite the prayers. The institution seems to have stopped after the destruction of the Second Temple, but it may have had its influence on the creation of a fixed liturgy.

In a figurative sense, the name Maamadoth is given to compilations from the Bible and Talmud for the purpose of prayer; they are still recited by many pious individuals, and are included in many Orthodox prayer-books.

MAAPILIM, see COLONIES, AGRICULTURAL.

MAARABOTH, see MAARIBIM.

MAARIB, see EVENING SERVICE.

MAARIBIM (called also Maaraboth), poetic insertions in the Evening Service (Maarib). There are such poems for all the festivals; in the Orient such verses are known even for the special Sabbaths. Every pause in the basic prayer for the eve of the festival receives a short poem. Thus there are two before the Shema (before *hama'arib 'arabim* and before *'oheb 'ammo yisra'el*) and four after it (at the end of *'emeth ve'emunah* and *mi chamocha* and before *ga'al yisra'el* and *hapores sukkath shalom*). Besides these six short poems, there is a longer one at the end of *'emeth ve'emunah*. The German ritual for the second evening of Passover presents a long passage of Halachic content before *hapores;* the other rituals have this prose insertion on the eve of the other festivals as well. The Maaribim do not occur in the German and Polish rituals for Rosh Hashanah and Yom Kippur, except in that of Worms. The Sephardic ritual has no Maaribim at all.

Lit.: Elbogen, Ismar, *Der jüdische Gottesdienst,* p. 212; Idelsohn, Abraham Zebi, *Jewish Liturgy* (1932) 40, 330-32; Davidson, I., *Otzar Hashirah Vehapiyut,* vol. 4 (1933) 493.

MAARSEN, ISAAC, theologian, chief rabbi of The Hague, b. Amsterdam, Holland, 1892. He was educated at Amsterdam University and the Netherlands Jewish Seminary; at the latter institute he was a lecturer from 1917 to 1918. From 1919 to 1925 he was a Dayan of the Amsterdam Rabbinical Council. In 1925 he became chief rabbi of The Hague.

Maarsen wrote many theological and historical essays, also anti-Reform pamphlets, commentaries on the Scriptures, and a critical edition of Rashi's commentaries on the prophets and Hagiographa, entitled *Parshandatha* (part 1, The Minor Prophets, Amsterdam, 1930; part 2, Isaiah, Jerusalem, 1933; part 3, Psalms, Jerusalem, 1936). This edition is based on several manuscripts, some of them now in the library of the Jewish Theological Seminary of America, in New York city. To the *Geschiedenis der Joden in Nederland* (History of the Jews in The Netherlands), the first volume of which was published in 1940, shortly before the German invasion, Maarsen contributed the chapter on Jews in science and literature up to 1795. His other works include: *Jodendom, Sabbath en Kalenderhervorming* (1930); *De Responsa als Bron voor de Geschiedenis der Joden in Nederland* (1933); a work on Maimonides (1935); a work on ethics (1935).

Lit.: European *Who's Who,* vol. 2; Brugmans, H., and Frank, A., *Geschiedenis der Joden in Nederland,* vol. 1 (1940), book 2, chap. 6.

MAAS, SIMON, wholesale merchant, b. Grosbockenheim, Bavaria, 1842; d. Selma, Ala., 1907. He came to the United States at the age of thirteen and, after living for a few years in the smaller towns of Alabama, settled in Selma. In 1887 he was elected mayor of the city without opposition, and served in

that office for two years. He was for many years president of the Mishkan Israel congregation.

Lit.: American Jewish Annual (1887).

MAASEH BERESHITH, see CABALA; CREATION; GNOSTICISM; MYSTICISM.

MAASEH BOOKS, see CHAP-BOOKS.

MAASEH MERKABAH, see CABALA; GNOSTICISM; MYSTICISM.

MAASER, see TITHE.

MAASER SHENI ("second tithe"), eighth tractate of Zeraim, the first division of the Mishnah, and consisting of five chapters. It deals with the second tithe which, according to the rabbinic interpretation of *Deut.* 14:22-27, was to be separated in the first, second, fourth and fifth years of the seven-year cycle. The owner was either to take a tenth of his agricultural produce to Jerusalem and eat it there, or else redeem it by substituting money which was used to purchase food to be eaten in Jerusalem. The tractate discusses the regulations about the second tithe and the money which may replace it, and lays down the law for the proper observance of the commandment to give this tithe. The fifth chapter discusses the law about the fruits of a tree, which may not be eaten before the fifth year of its bearing, the avowal required in *Deut.* 26:13, as well as certain innovations of John Hyrcanus.

The Tosefta to the tractate also has five chapters, but the material is somewhat differently arranged. There is an exposition of the tractate in the Palestinian Talmud, but not in the Babylonian.

MAASEROTH ("tithes"), seventh tractate of Zeraim, the first division of the Mishnah, and consisting of five chapters. It was known also as Maaser Rishon, "first tithe," in contrast to the following tractate, Maaser Sheni, "second tithe." Maaseroth deals with the tithes, which, according to the Torah (*Num.* 18:21-32), were to be set aside from certain forms of produce and given to the Levites. It is principally concerned with what agricultural products are subject to the tithe and at what season of their growth. A large section of the tractate is taken up with cases in which the purchaser of agricultural products may have to separate a tithe before he can eat them, as there is a suspicion that the tithes have not been previously separated by the farmers. The tractate ends with the enumeration of certain agricultural products that are exempt from the tithes.

There is a Tosefta to the tractate, of three chapters, and a corresponding tractate in the Palestinian Talmud, but not in the Babylonian.

MACALISTER, ROBERT ALEXANDER STEWART, non-Jewish archeologist, b. Dublin, Ireland, 1870. Commissioned by the Committee of the Palestine Exploration Fund, he directed excavations in various parts of Palestine from 1898 to 1909, and again in 1924. One of the explored mounds proved to represent the Biblical Mareshah; another was the Biblical Gezer. Macalister's discoveries are extremely valuable. His publications include: *Excavations in*

The mother of the Maccabees. From an engraving by Gustave Doré

which tells about the persecutions of the Jews under the Seleucidean kings, in the period from the beginning of the reign of Antiochus IV Epiphanes (175 B.C.E.) to the death of Simon, the last of the five Maccabean brothers (135). It was originally written in Hebrew, or possibly in Aramaic; Origen gives as the Hebrew title the obscure words σαρβηθ σαρβαναιελ, or something similar. Jerome claimed to have been well acquainted with the original. The fact that the book shows a good knowledge of Palestine warrants the conclusion that it was written by a Jew of that country. The closing verse speaks of a historical work on John Hyrcanus, who died in 104 B.C.E., hence the book was probably written after that date. However, the most likely time is before 63 B.C.E., since it knows of the Romans only as the friends of the Jews; hence the period between 100 and 70 B.C.E. is the most probable one. The translation is an excellent one. Josephus depended on it, and it is probably considerably earlier than his time.

The author was an excellent historian and the book a historical source of the first order. His sole prejudice was in favor of the Maccabees, whom he glorifies as the sole deliverers of Israel (5:55-62). Most of the attacks upon its credibility, such as those of Fabricius, have been proved unfounded. It is obviously based on good oral tradition, and to some extent on written testimony (cf. 9:22). It has certain errors and exaggerations, especially in regard to the numbers of the armies and the prisoners, and the speeches, prayers, and probably the letters and the documents are written by the author; but these are defects which were characteristic of the times.

Everything that takes place is explained as a natural occurrence; even the victory of the Maccabees is due to their courage and farsightedness, and not to a supernatural intervention of God. The main interest of the author is in the secular and national happenings. The book probably comes from circles favorable to the Hasmonean dynasty. The temperate and scientific presentation is adorned by reasonably short expressions of judgment and infrequent poetic passages, which are most likely citations, such as 7:17 (*Ps.* 79:2-3); cf. 1:26-27; 14:8 et seq., and the like. The whole is illuminated by a simple and profound religious spirit. The great age, one of the greatest in Jewish history, has found a worthy description; and Luther well said that the book was worthy of acceptance into the Biblical canon. Unfortunately, the time treated lay beyond the line that had been drawn for the Biblical literature, and so the Alexandrinians had to perform the service of preserving the book for posterity in the Septuagint.

II MACCABEES is a historical book of edification, differently constituted from I Maccabees. The history it relates in its fifteen chapters begins and ends at 'an earlier time than the other book; it starts with the reign of Seleucus IV, the predecessor of Antiochus Epiphanes, and ends with the death of Nicanor (from about 180 to 161 B.C.E.). The main body of the book is preceded by three sections by way of introduction: a) 1:1-9, an invitation of the "Jewish brethren in Jerusalem to the Jewish brethren in Egypt" to observe the festival of Hanukah; b) 1:10 to 2:18, a letter from Judas (Maccabeus?) and the elders of Jerusalem, to Aristobulus, the teacher of Ptolemy (probably the philosopher Aristobulus, the favorite of Ptolemy VI Philometor), also inviting the Egyptian Jews to introduce the observance of Hanukah, and referring to all sorts of legends about the Temple in Jerusalem. Between these two letters there is a date, 188 (or 180 or 148, equals 164 B.C.E.) of the Seleucidean Era; c) 2:19-32, the final and real introduction of the author, which declares that the book is an abridgment of the five-volume work of Jason of Cyrene, a statement which some have wrongly thought as being merely intended to deceive the reader.

The two (or three) introductory sections are considered by most interpreters to be spurious; however, Graetz (*Geschichte der Juden*, vol. 3, note 10) and Niesse consider them to be genuine. Apparently verses 1:7-10a come from Jason, and 1:1-6; 10 to 2:18 are an expansion by the author. There is still much doubt about the relation of 1:12-17 to chap. 9. Willrich thinks that chap. 9 comes from Jason, and 1:12-17 from the author; in any case, both reports are unhistorical.

The main work, like its model, was originally written in Greek. According to 15:17, 37, it was composed before Jerusalem was taken by Pompey in 63 B.C.E. Eduard Meyer places it around 125 B.C.E., but Willrich puts it between 70 and 73 C.E. It is generally assumed that Egypt was the place of its origin. The author writes a good Greek, with occasional rhetorical embellishments according to the prevailing mode. His thoughts, however, are not philosophical, but Essene or Pharisaic. Thus there is retribution, measure for measure, in 5:9 and other places; and resurrection is mentioned in 12:44 and 14:46. II Maccabees is the only book in the range of Biblical literature that speaks of prayers for the dead (12:42-44); it was therefore highly valued by the Catholic church.

The book generally tells less of the actual story than does I Maccabees, and sometimes gives particulars for which we are grateful and which appear to be creditable. These include the account of the times of Jason in chaps. 4 and 5, and such passages as 6:2; 13:3-8; and 14:1. Of course II Maccabees often reports as history obvious legends, miracles, and exaggeration of numbers; among the former are the accounts of the martyrdoms of Eleazar and of the mother and her seven sons. All this is in the style of the Hellenistic historians. To the writer edification

was more important than science, and religion of greater concern than political history; his highest pathos is given to the martyrs and not to the battles. To condemn the book, as so frequently happens, is one-sided. It is far more valuable as a historical source than was earlier assumed, although it was regarded also as a book of edification.

III MACCABEES is a story in seven chapters, which has nothing to do with the time of the Maccabees. It tells how Ptolemy IV Philopator (222-204 B.C.E.) wished to enter the Holy of Holies in the Temple of Jerusalem at the time when he conquered Palestine; as a result of the prayers of the people, he was crippled by a miracle. When he returned to Egypt, he took his revenge by robbing the Jews of their civil rights, since they were unwilling to worship Bacchus, and had many of them driven into an arena, where elephants, made mad by intoxication, were to trample them. However, a miracle took place, and the animals instead turned against their own drivers. This was sufficient to make the king experience a change of heart; he gave a meal to those who had been delivered, and permitted the Jews to punish 300 renegades with death. This story includes the legend of Heliodorus; the miracle about the elephants was reported by Josephus (*Against Apion* 2:5) about Ptolemy IX Physcon (146-117 B.C.E.); other features would fit the persecution of the Jews in Alexandria under Caligula. Hence the little book seems to have been written during the reign of the latter to encourage the Jews. In any case it must have been written before 70 C.E., before the Temple was destroyed. The whole has no value from the religious, historical, or esthetic point of view. Its style is full of bombast and exaggerations.

IV MACCABEES is a sermon about the "rulership of reason over the passions," explained by the examples of Joseph, David, Jacob, and Daniel. The main portion of the book is chaps. 4 to 17; chap. 18 contains supplements. It is formed by tales about Eleazar, the mother and her seven sons, and the martyrs of the Maccabean period. Freudenthal believes that it was given as a sermon, and probably at Hanukah. Grimm believed that it was intended only for reading. E. Norden (*Die Antike Kunstprosa,* 1898) holds that it is a diatribe, or scholastic polemical treatise. From the time of Eusebius on it has been ascribed to Josephus, under the title "On the Martyrdom of the Maccabees," but this is certainly false (Freudenthal, *Die Flavius Josephus beigelegte Schrift . . .*). It was originally written in Greek.

The author had received a training in philosophy, and his viewpoint is that of the Stoics. The method, style, and presentation of the book are in the manner of the current Greek rhetoric. The writer combines the Greek sense of beauty and talent for form with a spirited adherence to Judaism, at least in its Hellenistic and universalistic form. He considers the Torah identical with wisdom or reason. He knows nothing of resurrection, but probably believes in the requital of the soul beyond the grave. He takes for granted the freedom of the will. He attacks the Jews who despise the Law. Most interpreters believe that he was an Alexandrian. The time when the sermon arose is apparently the last decade before 66 C.E., since it

The Maccabiad held in Germany in 1937

Street streamers welcoming members of the Maccabis to the 2nd winter Maccabiad in Czechoslovakia

Members of the Maccabis greeted on the opening day of the Maccabiad in Germany (1937). Photographs by H. S. Sonnenfeld

says nothing of disturbances in Palestine, and on the other hand presupposes the *Wisdom of Solomon.* The book, with its thought of the suffering of the righteous, and with the strength in faith and hope of immortality that it preaches, is one of the most beautiful memorials of the union of the Greek and the Jewish spirit in world history.   HUGO FUCHS.

Lit.: Barton, G. A., and Abrahams, I., in *Jewish Encyclopedia,* vol. 8, pp. 239-44; the commentaries, especially Charles, R. H., *The Apocrypha and Pseudepigrapha of the Old Testament* (1913); Rawlinson to I and II Maccabees in Wace, *Apocrypha* (1888); Abrahams, I., in *Jewish Quarterly Review* (1896) 39-58; Freudenthal, *Die Flavius Josephus beigelegte Schrift* (1869); Fairweather, in Hastings, James, *Dictionary of the Bible,* vol. 3, pp. 187-96; Kahana, *The Book of Maccabees* (Hebrew).

MACCABI, name adopted by various Jewish athletic groups, most of them affiliated with the Maccabi World Union. The first Maccabi bodies were founded about the year 1895 in Berlin by Heinrich Loewe, in Constantinople, Bucharest and St. Petersburg. Earlier, it is indicated, there were as many as 10,000 Jewish members of the Deutsche Turnerschaft, and it was with the encouragement of Max Nordau and Max Mandelstamm that a Jüdische Turnerschaft was established. It was not until after the first World War, however, that the organization, with headquarters in Berlin, took on the aspect of a permanent international cooperative athletic movement. The headquarters were moved to London upon the Nazis' accession to power.

Prior to the outbreak of the second World War, the Maccabi World Union included thirty-eight international organizations with a membership estimated at 200,000. Member groups were located in practically every country in Europe, in Palestine, Turkey, Egypt, China, Australia, Brazil, Argentina and South Africa. In 1931 a Maccabi Association of America was founded, but it had a brief existence of only three or four years. In 1941 refugees and former members of the Maccabi groups in Austria, Czechoslovakia and Germany again founded an American Maccabi body, and launched an athletic program.

The primary objective of the Maccabi associations is to promote athletics among Jewish youth. The movement is also closely associated with Zionism and encourages Jewish culture, study of Hebrew, and Palestine work among its members. Stated objectives are: "The cultural and physical training of its members for responsible participation in all national tasks of the Jewish people and especially in the upbuilding of Eretz Israel." A close fraternal spirit exists among the members and between the various groups.

Perhaps the best-known Maccabi project has been the staging of the Maccabiads, or Jewish Olympics, in Palestine. The first attempt at international Maccabi games was made in Czechoslovakia in 1929, and in the following year the games were held in Antwerp, Belgium. In 1932 the first Maccabiad was held in Tel-Aviv, Palestine, with Jewish athletes from twenty-two countries participating. The brilliant affair was successfully repeated in 1935, and again there was an excellent representation of Jewish athletes from all parts of the world.

Dr. Selig Brodetsky was, in 1942, president of the Maccabi World Union, and Dr. W. Meisel was its secretary general.

MACHADO, a Portuguese Marrano family that came to the Americas from Lisbon toward the end of the 16th cent. The first mention of the name in official records is in the report of the trial of Jorge de Almeida by the Mexican Inquisition in 1600; Antonio Machado and his daughter Isobel, who were professing Catholics, were accused of secretly practising the rites of Judaism. Abraham de Machado, probably a member of the same family, lived in Martinique in 1680, and one M. Machado was a planter in Surinam in 1690.

The most important branch of the family stems from David Mendoza Machado. In 1732 he escaped from Lisbon when he was correctly suspected by the Inquisition of secret Judaism. He sailed to England and from there to the new colony of Georgia, where he arrived in 1733, a few months after Oglethorpe. Later that year he was called to New York city to serve as Hazan of the Spanish and Portuguese Congregation Shearith Israel, a post he held until his death. Among his eminent descendents were: Jonas Phillips, who fought in the American Revolution; his son Joseph, who fought in the War of 1812; Commodore Uriah P. Levy; Congressman Henry M. Phillips; Mordecai M. Noah; N. Taylor Phillips.

Lit.: Publications of the American Jewish Historical Society, No. 2 (1894) 45-62.

MACHANE YEHUDA, *see* COLONIES, AGRICULTURAL.

MACHIR BEN ABBA MARI, author of a commentary on the Bible. He is assumed to have lived in the Provence during the 14th cent. The work by which he is known, the *Yalkut Hamachiri,* is a compilation of Haggadic material on the books of *Isaiah, Jeremiah, Ezekiel,* the minor prophets, *Psalms, Proverbs* and *Job.* In the selection of subject matter, the *Yalkut Hamachiri* differs from the *Yalkut Shimeoni,* which treats of the entire Bible. There have been divergent opinions on whether Machir ben Abba Mari or the author of the *Yalkut Shimeoni* lived earlier. The accepted idea is that Machir lived at a later period, but that the *Yalkut Shimeoni* was unknown to him.

MACHNAYIM, *see* COLONIES, AGRICULTURAL.

MACHPELAH, the field and cave acquired by Abraham from the Hittite Ephron for use as a hereditary burial place (*Gen.* 23). However, by Machpelah is usually meant only the cave in which Abraham and Sarah, Isaac and Rebekah, and Jacob and Leah are supposed to be buried (Adam and Eve also, according to legend). It is mentioned also by Josephus and in the Talmud. The present sanctuary, which for centuries was accessible only to Mohammedans, is the restoration of a magnificent building erected by Herod the Great, to whose Idumean (Edomite) countrymen Machpelah was just as sacred as it was to the Jews. The external wall of large draughted stones is the finest extant Herodian masonry. The name Machpelah is interpreted in rabbinic literature as "double cave" (from the Hebrew stem *kafal,* "to double").

MACHSHIRIN ("predisposers to uncleanliness"), eighth tractate of Toharoth, the sixth division of the

Alfred Mack

David I. Macht

Mishnah, and consisting of six chapters. It deals with those liquids which, according to *Lev.* 11:38, when poured upon agricultural products, make them susceptible to uncleanliness. The tractate is sometimes called Mashkin, "liquids." It enumerates seven liquids to which the law applies: wine, honey, oil, milk, dew, blood and water, and discusses various varieties of each liquid, and under what conditions they bring about the susceptibility to uncleanliness. Thus the liquids must have been poured on the agricultural products by the owner himself, or have fallen upon them by reason of some action of which he approved. A section of the tractate deals with the differences in general regulations in Jewish law where the city is one of mixed population.

The Tosefta to the tractate has five chapters; there is no Gemara in either Talmud.

MACHT, DAVID ISRAEL, physician and experimental scientist, b. Moscow, 1882. He was brought to the United States at the age of eight. After graduating from Baltimore City College in 1899, Macht received his A.B. degree from Johns Hopkins University in 1902. Subsequently he studied at other colleges in the United States and Europe, and received his M.D. degree from Johns Hopkins in 1906.

In 1910 Macht was appointed instructor in medicine at Johns Hopkins, retaining this post until 1914. From 1912 to 1932 he was also a lecturer in pharmacology at the university. After 1932, however, Macht devoted himself to research and to his work as director of pharmacological research for the drug manufacturing firm of Hynson, Westcott and Dunning. He investigated the bio-physics of polarized light and of ultra-violet rays, drug absorption through various parts of the body, the therapeutic values of cobra venom and numerous other pharmacological problems. He was the discoverer of certain properties of benzyl esters which have been introduced in medical practice to take the place of opium. He also dis-

covered the local anesthetic properties of benzyl alcohol.

Macht was also expressly interested in various aspects of Jewish life in relation to pharmacology. He wrote a thesis, *The Holy Incense,* in which he maintained that every incense mentioned in the Bible had a scientific reason for its use, and he also defended the Jewish dietary laws on the basis of science. Among his other studies on Jewish subjects was a monograph on Maimonides (1906). Macht received an honorary D.H.L. degree in 1929 from Yeshiva College in New York city, where he was for a time visiting lecturer in physiology and in 1942 professor of general physiology. He also received a degree in law (1914) from the Hamilton College of Law in Baltimore.   CHARLES R. RUBENSTEIN.

Lit.: Jewish Tribune, Sept. 13, 1929, pp. 3-4; *American Hebrew,* Nov. 17, 1939, pp. 4, 17; Kagan, Solomon R., *Jewish Contributions to Medicine in America* (1939) 359-61, 753, 768.

MACHUZA, *see* MAHOZA.

MACHZOR, *see* PRAYER-BOOKS.

MACHZOR VITRY, *see* MAHZOR VITRY.

MACK, ALFRED, judge, b. Cincinnati, 1862. He was the son of Henry Mack, who was a state senator in the Ohio legislature from 1888 to 1890. He was educated at the Harvard University Law School (LL.B., 1883). He was a member of the law firm of Simrall and Mack from 1883 to 1892 and of the firm of Cohen, Mack, and Hurtig from 1894 to 1930. He was a director of the University of Cincinnati from 1919 to 1930.

From 1898 to 1907 Mack was a referee in bankruptcy cases. He was elected judge of the Court of Common Pleas of Hamilton County, Ohio, on the Republican ticket in 1930, and reelected in 1938; he was still serving in this position in 1942. In 1936 he was elected presiding judge for a term of one year.

Mack was actively interested in Jewish affairs. He

Julian W. Mack

was an honorary member of the board of governors of the Hebrew Union College, a member of B'nai B'rith, and a president of the congregation of the Isaac M. Wise Temple. During the first World War Mack was a member of the Legal Advisory Committee.

MACK, JULIAN WILLIAM, judge and Zionist leader, b. San Francisco, 1866. He received his LL.B. degree from Harvard in 1887, then did three years of post-graduate work at Harvard and at the Universities of Berlin and Leipzig. From 1895 to 1902 Mack was a professor of law at Northwestern University, and in 1902 he accepted a similar post at the University of Chicago. Although his active teaching terminated in 1911, when he was appointed to the United States Commerce Court, he was considered technically on leave from that time on.

Mack was a member of the Chicago Civil Service Commission in 1903. In 1903 he was elected judge of the Circuit Court of Cook County, Ill., and in 1909 he was reelected. In 1911 he was appointed to the United States Commerce Court, and two years later, when that court was abolished, he became United States Circuit Court judge. He sat in the United States Circuit Court of Appeals for the second, sixth, seventh and ninth circuits and in numerous district courts throughout the country. Mack served also as chairman of the section on compensation of soldiers and sailors and their dependents of the Committee of Labor of the Council of National Defense, a post to which he was appointed in 1917. He was an umpire on the National War Labor Board and a member of the board of inquiry on conscientious objectors, all during the first World War.

It was during the first World War that Mack's great interest in the Jewish people came to the fore, under conditions and circumstances very similar to those attending the emergence of Justice Louis D. Brandeis, with whom Mack was closely associated in Zionist activity. To his early contacts with such Zionist pioneers as Shemarya Levin, Aaron Aaronsohn and Henrietta Szold, who inducted him into the ideology of Jewish nationalism, he attributed his first interest in the Zionist Movement. As a result of his active interest he was elected president of the Zionist Organization of America in 1918, and served until the Cleveland convention of 1921. It was largely due to Mack's guidance and vision, in collaboration with Brandeis, that the Zionist movement in the United States gained immeasurably in membership and prestige while he was president.

An exponent of democracy in Jewish community life as well as in national affairs, Mack was an ardent supporter of the American Jewish Congress, and upon its formation in 1917 was elected its first president. During the difficult days of the Paris Peace Conference in 1919, when conflicting ideologies and philosophies among the various Jewish committees in attendance threatened to wreck all Jewish effort, it was his patience, judicial temperament and unfailing objectivity as first chairman of the Committee of Jewish Delegations which helped avoid open clashes. He was succeeded in that high post by Louis Marshall. The various minority rights clauses written into the constitutions of Central European countries were largely the result of the efforts of this Committee.

Up to 1942 Mack had served for seventeen years as an overseer of Harvard University. He was in that year president of the Palestine Endowment Fund, Inc., and the Alexander Kohut Memorial Foundation; chairman of the Board of Trustees of the Jewish Institute of Religion; member of the Board of Governors of the Hebrew University, Jerusalem. He was a member-at-large of the American Jewish Committee, honorary vice-president of the Zionist Organization of America, honorary vice-president of the Jewish Publication Society of America; honorary president of the World Jewish Congress; the American Economic Committee for Palestine; honorary chairman of the United Palestine Appeal and the United Jewish Appeal.

The full scope of Mack's many interests is indicated by the fact that he was first president of the national organization of the Y.M. and Y.W.H.A.'s in 1917, a director of the Jewish Charities of Chicago for nineteen years until 1911, president of the National Conference of Jewish Charities, vice-president and chairman of the board of Survey Associates, Inc., a member of the Immigrants' Protective League, and of many other organizations.

Impartial in controversy, liberal in outlook, Mack was not only a distinguished American judge and interpreter of law, but a notable figure on the Jewish scene as well. In 1941 a colony in Palestine, Ramath Ha'shophet, was named in his honor. It is adjacent to En Ha'shophet, the colony named for Justice Brandeis.

MORRIS ROTHENBERG.

MACK, WILLIAM JACOB, lawyer and judge advocate, b. Cincinnati, 1885. He received his law degree from the Harvard Law School in 1910 and was admitted to the Illinois bar the same year. In 1920 Mack came to Cleveland where, until 1924, he served as impartial chairman in labor disputes and was responsible for the establishment of an unemployment insurance plan in the local ladies' garment industry—one of the first such plans in the country.

Coming to New York city in 1930, Mack engaged in mediation and arbitration work in private industry and government agencies alike, acting for the National Labor Board, the National Labor Relations Board and the Labor Appeals Board of the Works Progress Administration. He was also commissioner of conciliation and arbitrator for the United States Department of Labor. During his service with the United States armies in France in the first World War, Mack was made major judge advocate and presiding judge of the General Court Martial at headquarters. He was awarded the Purple Heart Decoration and cited for exceptional service by General John J. Pershing.

Mack had been active in general social service during his residence in Chicago. He was also treasurer and director of the Jewish Aid Society of Chicago from 1912 to 1917, director of the Big Brothers for the same period and held other Jewish communal posts. In 1942 Mack was living in New York city and continuing his work in government and private arbitration.

MACKOWSKY, HANS, historian of arts, b. Berlin, 1871. He studied at Berlin and Freiburg from 1890 to 1893. In 1891 he published a volume of poems, *Ein Erdentag*. In 1894 he went to Italy, where he remained until 1896, studying Italian art. From 1897 to 1899 he was assistant at the Museum of Berlin, and from 1901 to 1903 lived at Florence. After returning to Berlin, Mackowsky lectured at popular high schools, and in 1912 became director of the Rauch Museum at Berlin. From 1914 to 1933 he was attached to the National Gallery of Berlin. The creation of a special gallery of portraits as a part of that institution is due to Mackowsky's initiative. He published the following monographs: *Verrocchio* (1901); *Michelangelo* (1908); *Paul Wallot* (the architect of the German Reichstag building; 1912); *Christian Daniel Rauch* (1916); *Johann Gottfried Schadow* (1927); *Schadows Graphik* (1935).

MADAGASCAR, a tropical island roughly about as large as the state of Texas, located in the Indian Ocean, off the eastern coast of Africa. A census taken in 1936 revealed a total of about 30,000 Europeans in a population of close to 4,000,000. According to Alfred Grandidier, French explorer and writer, the northern natives are partly descendants of a Jewish tribe which came to the island hundreds of years earlier. The rite of circumcision and observance of the Sabbath are found among these natives, who are of a Semitic type. The island has several times been under consideration as a possible center for the settlement of large numbers of European Jews. In 1926 the Polish Ambassador to France, Count Chlapowski, called upon Marcel Olivier, governor-general of Madagascar, then visiting Paris, and broached the subject of possible large-scale colonization of Poles on the island. Olivier discouraged such consideration on the grounds of climatic conditions unsuitable for Europeans, and the presence of malaria and other endemic diseases. In 1927 a Japanese commission

visited the island and after a thorough study dropped the project as a possible home for their co-nationals.

Nazi sources began recommending deportation of Jews from Europe to Madagascar as early as 1931. The Polish government sent a three-man commission to the island in 1937 with the understanding that the possibilities of enforced Jewish emigration from Poland were to be explored. Major Mieczyslav Lepecki headed the commission, which included also Leon Alter, director of the HICEM office in Warsaw, and Solomon Dyk, an agricultural engineer from Tel-Aviv. Though Major Lepecki reported that small-scale settlement in the highlands was possible, the other two were more discouraging. The local press also protested against the idea of settlement of Polish Jews. Early in 1937 French Colonial Minister Moutet likewise advanced a scheme for mass Jewish settlement there.

It has been agreed that the coastal lowlands are not suitable for habitation by white people, and some difference of opinion exists regarding the feasibility of small-scale settlement in the highlands. About 85 per cent of the natives suffer from malaria, and the death rate from this disease is high. Agricultural opportunities are poor and the climate is irregular.

During 1941 there were several reports from Nazi sources to the effect that in the event of a victory Hitler planned to deport a large number of Europe's Jews to the island.　　　　CARL ALPERT.

Lit.: Hevesi, Eugene, "Hitler's Plan for Madagascar," *Contemporary Jewish Record,* Aug., 1941; Olivier, Marcel, "Madagascar—Terre d'Asile?," *L'Illustration,* Feb. 19, 1938, pp. 197-98 (published in English in *Congress Bulletin,* March 18, 1938); *Jewish Chronicle* (London), July 23, 1937, pp. 9, 18; Dec. 31, 1937.

MADARASSY-BECK, family of outstanding Hungarian economists. An ancestor of the family, Mendel Beck, founded the Jewish community of Bácsalmás in 1773. In the third decade of the 19th cent., when Hungary organized its economic life independent of Austria, three brothers, Miksa, Nándor and Hugo Beck, rose to positions of distinction. In 1895 they were knighted and authorized to use the prefix "de Madaras." The German poet Karl Beck was also a scion of the family.

MIKSA DE MADARASSY-BECK, economist (b. Bácsmadaras, 1838; d. Budapest, 1924), made banking his career, and in 1870 was appointed director general of the Hungarian Discount and Exchange Bank which had been founded in the preceding year. Under his direction, the original capital stock of one-half million gulden was increased, within twenty-five years, to fifteen million gulden. He was instrumental in issuing and converting state loans and public utility bonds. The bank founded also armament industries as well as shipyards and took part in organizing Danubian and oceanic shipping. Miksa Beck de Madaras, who embraced the Catholic faith, was made a baronet in 1911.

MARCELL DE MADARASSY-BECK, economist (b. 1872), was a son of Miksa de Madarassy-Beck. He succeeded his father as president director general of the Hungarian Discount and Exchange Bank. He adopted Catholicism.

NÁNDOR DE MADARASSY-BECK, economist (b. Bácsmadaras, 1840; d. Budapest, 1909), began his career in Vienna, and in 1869 became director general of the Hungarian Hypothecary Credit Bank, founded in that year with a capital stock of one-half million gulden. By 1881 the capital stock had been raised to ten million gulden, and by extending land credits on a larger scale the bank greatly contributed toward modernizing agricultural productions in Hungary. Nándor Beck was able to secure foreign, especially French, capital. In 1899 he became president of the bank, succeeding Kálmán Széll, who was then appointed prime minister of Hungary. After Széll's resignation from the administration, Beck relinquished his post to him and retired. Knighted in 1895, he was also named chancellor of the court and made a baronet in 1906. He also embraced Catholicism.

GYULA DE MADARASSY-BECK, economist (b. Budapest, 1873), son of Nándor de Madarassy-Beck, succeeded his father in the presidency of the Hungarian Hypothecary Credit Bank after studying law and economics, and serving in various banks in Hungary and abroad. While he was still a student, his essay *A bankjegyügy elmélete* (Theory of the Bank Bill System) was awarded a prize. He wrote also *A városok hitelügye* (The Credit Problem of Municipalities). He was vice-president of the Hungaro-Italian Bank, president of the Hungarian Hall of Commerce, a deputy in the Hungarian Lower Chamber (spokesman of its committee on finance), and a member of the Austro-Hungarian delegation for dual governmental affairs. He adopted the Catholic faith. The authoress Lily Hatvany was his second wife.

See also: BECK, HUGO; BECK, KARL.

ANNA BETTELHEIM.

Lit.: Magyar Zsidó Lexikon, pp. 547-48; *Pallas Lexikon,* vols. 7 and 12; Kempelen, Béla, *Magyarországi zsidó és zsidóeredetü családok,* vol. 2, pp. 26-28.

MADISON, capital city of the state of Wisconsin, with a Jewish community of approximately 1,500 in a population of 67,477 (1940 census). The first Jewish settlers of Madison were immigrants from Germany, primarily from Bavaria, who, in 1856, founded Congregation Shaarei Shomayim. The Reverend Joseph Thuringer conducted the services in the synagogue erected in 1861. The members of the congregation were engaged in the retail clothing trade. As the second and third generation moved away from the community, the synagogue building was sold and the proceeds devoted to philanthropic causes. The minute book of the congregation (1856-1922) was presented to the American Jewish Historical Society by Miss Mathilda V. Cook (1939).

Russian immigrants, about 1900, founded Congregation Agudas Achim. The members of this congregation for the most part earned a livelihood from peddling. Their synagogue building was twice enlarged; a daily Hebrew school, a burial society and a free loan association were affiliated with the congregation. In 1934 Rabbi Abraham Horvitz, a graduate of the Jewish Theological Seminary of America and a Ph.D. from the University of Chicago, was called to the pulpit. He introduced the English sermon, late Friday night services and a modern Sunday school.

A Conservative congregation, Beth Jacob, was formed in 1928, and a Reform Temple was organized in 1939, with Dr. Manfred Swarsensky, formerly of Berlin, as spiritual leader.

Madison in 1942 had a Jewish Welfare Federation, a branch of the B'nai Brith, Hadassah, Council of Jewish Women, Zionist Organization and an Arbeiter Ring Shule. A Hillel foundation under the direction of Rabbi Max Kadushin served over 1,000 Jewish students at the University of Wisconsin.

Two Jewish citizens of Madison rose to prominence in the city and state. Samuel Klauber, president of Congregation Shaarei Shomayim, was a benefactor in many causes. His portrait, with the inscription "Pioneer Merchant," hangs in the Wisconsin Historical Museum. Solomon Levitan, an immigrant from Lithuania, was elected six times treasurer of the state, leading the ticket (see LEVITAN, SOLOMON, in this volume).

MADISON, JAMES, called "father of the Constitution" of the United States and the fourth president, b. Port Conway, Va., 1751; d. Montpelier (Orange County), Va., 1836. Upon graduation from the College of New Jersey (afterwards Princeton University) in 1771, he thought for a while of entering the ministry. He spent another year studying theology and Hebrew and continued these studies upon returning to Virginia. But whether or not he ever knew much Hebrew is problematic.

The principle of absolute religious liberty, now accepted without question by all Americans, was not established in the United States without a struggle, and in this Madison took a leading part. In 1776, as a young delegate to the constitutional convention of Virginia and a member of the committee drafting the constitution, he objected to the word "toleration" in a provision that all men should enjoy the fullest toleration in the exercise of religion, contending that liberty of worship was not a matter of grace but of right. And he succeeded in having the provision amended to read that "all men are equally entitled to the free exercise of religion, according to the dictates of conscience." But the provision, so amended, was not adopted.

Later, in 1784, after the state's support of the Episcopal Church in Virginia had been terminated and the growing influence of the French deists had frightened many, a movement to establish Christianity as the religion of the state—without limiting such support to any particular sect or persecuting any non-Christians—led to the introduction in the Virginia legislature of a resolution providing that the people of the commonwealth ought to pay a tax for the support of "the Christian religion, or of some Christian church, denomination or communion of Christians, or of some form of Christian worship." The resolution had been drafted by Patrick Henry and had the support of Richard Henry Lee, John Marshall, and others of like standing.

Jefferson would have led the opposition but he was in France. However, Madison, who had been elected a member of the House of Delegates, was his ardent disciple and able general. A bill, based on the resolution, passed its second reading; before its adoption, Madison succeeded in having the third reading postponed. In the meantime, an Episcopalian himself, he prepared a "memorial and remonstrance" against the

James Madison

bill to be circulated throughout the state. "Who does not see," it read, "that the same authority which can establish Christianity to the exclusion of all other religions may establish, with the same ease, any particular sect of Christians in exclusion of all other sects? . . . The proposed establishment is a departure from that generous policy, which, offering an asylum to the persecuted and oppressed of every nation and religion, promised a lustre to our country and an accession to the number of its citizens. . . Instead of holding forth an asylum to the persecuted, it is itself a signal of persecution. It degrades from the equal rank of citizens all those whose opinions in religion do not bend to the legislative authority. Distant as it may be, in its present form, from the Inquisition, it differs from it only in degree. The one is the first step, the other the last, in the career of intolerance."

Madison's appeal to the people of Virginia was successful. The Assembly, when it met again, not only abandoned the proposed assessment but, in 1785, passed the act which had been drawn by Jefferson and proposed six years before (1779) for the establishment of complete religious liberty. And of the first ten amendments to the Constitution of the United States, based upon those submitted by Madison to form a bill of rights, the first clause of the very first article as finally adopted in 1791 reads, "Congress shall make no law respecting an establishment of religion, or prohibiting the free exercise thereof."

Almost three decades afterwards, in reply to Mordecai M. Noah, who had sent a copy of his address at the dedication of the Mill Street synagogue in New York city, Madison, now an old man, wrote (1818) that he had "ever regarded the freedom of religious opinions and worship as equally belonging to every sect, and the secure enjoyment of it as the best human provision for bringing all, either into the same way of thinking, or into that mutual charity which is the only proper substitute."

Two years later (1820), acknowledging receipt of a copy of an address by Jacob De La Motta, delivered at the dedication of the synagogue of the Mickve Israel congregation in Savannah, Madison wrote De La Motta: "Among the features peculiar to the political system of the United States is the perfect equality of rights which it secures to every religious sect. And it is particularly pleasing to observe in the citizenship of such as have been most distrusted and oppressed elsewhere, a happy illustration of the safety and success of this experiment of a just and benignant policy. Equal laws, protecting equal rights, are found, as they ought to be presumed, the best guarantee of loyalty and love of country; as well as best calculated to cherish• that mutual respect and good will among citizens of every religious denomination which are necessary to social harmony, and most favorable to the advancement of truth."

Madison was an acquaintance of Haym Salomon. The latter's financial services to the cause of the American· Revolution included assisting needy members of Congress whose resources, those dark days, were cut off. He distinguished between loans to merchants who wished money for business and others, like Madison, who lacked money for their expenses while devoting themselves solely to the cause of liberty. From such, it seems, Salomon would take no interest. Of him, Madison (who was elected to Congress in 1780 and continued a member until 1783) wrote from Philadelphia to Edmund Randolph on August 27, 1782, "I cannot in any way make you more sensible of the importance of your kind attention to pecuniary remittances for me than by informing you that I have for some time been a pensioner on the favor of Haym Salomon, a Jew Broker," and again on September 30, 1782, "The kindness of our little friend in Front Street, near the coffee-house, is a fund that will preserve me from extremities, but I never resort to it without great mortification, as he obstinately rejects all recompense. The price of money is so usurious that he thinks it ought to be extorted from none but those who aim at profitable speculations. To a necessitous delegate, he gratuitously spares a supply out of his private stock."

During his presidency, Madison appointed a number of Jews to office. In 1814 he nominated John Hays, a friend of Lewis Cass and John C. Calhoun, for the post of collector for the Indian Territory, and the appointment was confirmed by the Senate. The year before Madison appointed Mordecai M. Noah consul general at Tunis and, in 1817, Joel Hart to be consul at Leith, Scotland.   CHARLES REZNIKOFF.

Lit.: Kohler, Max J., "Phases in the History of Religious Liberty in America, with Special Reference to the Jews," *Publications of the American Jewish Historical Society,* No. 11 (1903) 60-65.

MADRID, *see under* SPAIN.

MAFTIR, *see* HAFTARAH.

MAGDEBURG, the oldest Jewish settlement in East Germany. Emperor Otto I gave to the Moritz Monastery complete jurisdiction over the city in 965. According to the document, Jews as well as other merchants residing there were placed under the authority of the head of the monastery. After the founding of the archbishopric of Magdeburg, jurisdiction was transferred from the Mortiz Monastery to the

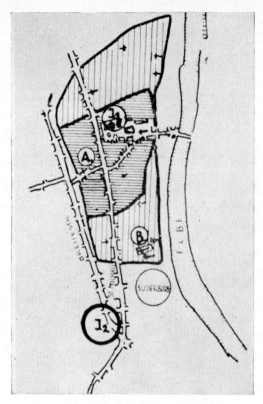

Map of the ancient Jewish quarter in Magdeburg

archbishop himself. The decrees of Emperor Otto II in 973 and in 978 to 979 state explicity that jurisdiction over merchants as well as other classes of residents in Magdeburg and its environs rested solely with the governor chosen by the archbishop. A Jewish traveler from some place in Arabia, Ibrahim ibn Jakub, came to the Slavic countries by way of Prague. In 965 or 973, as he himself tells, he visited, presumably on a political mission, the court of Emperor Otto I, which was probably in Magdeburg.

The story of Bishop Thietmar of Merseburg seems to indicate that relationship between the archbishop and Jews at that time was not bad. According to this story, Jews took active part in the mourning during the funeral procession of Archbishop Walthard of Magdeburg in 1012. It may be inferred from the decrees of Otto I that the Jews of Magdeburg lived in a merchants' settlement around the ancient market place of the old city. This fact is corroborated by a later document of 1315 according to which the Jews had previously lived in the Kleiderhof on the north side of the old market place. In addition, there existed a compact Jewish settlement, at least from the 14th cent. on, called Judendorf, in the Sudenburg near Magdeburg, which lay between the Berge Monastery and the city; it was also in the archbishop's domain.

The documents of 965 and 973 indicate that the occupation of the Jews in Magdeburg was mainly trading. The Crusade manifesto of 1199 directed to the archbishop is one of the numerous similar Crusade bulls in which Pope Innocent III warned the clergy of Germany and neighboring lands to support the Christians in the the Orient, and it may be inferred that the Jews of the archbishopric of Magdeburg also did financing. Proof of this is found in the fact that Abbot Herdolf of the Berge Monastery had to sell the great bell of the monastery church to the Jews in 1287 in order to pay debts. Especially effective and industrious as a financier was Jude Smol (Samuel), who was court Jew to Archbishop Dietrich from 1361 to 1367. He stood in high favor also with Archbishop Peter of Magdeburg who in his privilege to the Jews on April 21, 1372, favored especially the Jew Samuel and his family. Pope Gregory XI, in a letter dated June 14, 1372, chastises Archbishop Peter because he favored the Jew Samuel who in Salince had set up a synagogue in an old chapel.

The Jews in Magdeburg were not free of persecution. On Sukkoth, 1261, Archbishop Ruppert had the richer Jews arrested to compel them to pay him large ransoms (reportedly 100,000 silver marks). The Jews were expelled from Judendorf in 1301 because of a supposed desecration of an icon, but in 1309 they are found there again. At the time of the Black Death in 1349 the archbishop was not able to protect the Jews. Judendorf was plundered and the homes of Jews and their inhabitants burned. Rabbi Shalom became a martyr; a gravestone of the year 1356 also names a martyr. The large number of deaths in the city of Magdeburg in 1384 gave cause for renewed plundering of Judendorf and the Jews were driven away. But in 1385, by payments to the archbishop of the city (500 to 1,000 marks), they received permission again to live in the Judendorf. Archbishop Günther issued a protective letter in 1410 covering the Jews in the bishopric for four years, for which they had to pay forty silver marks.

The attempts of the archbishop to get money from the Jews in Magdeburg during the following years, however, were frustrated by the city. Despite the fact that the Jews had welcomed the archbishop of Saxony upon his assumption of office in 1476, he notified them in 1492 that their residence in the archbishopric was to end within nine months. By 1493, 1,400 Jews were supposed to leave the city. After the city had purchased the land belonging to the Jews, on August 11, 1493, Archbishop Ernest gave Judendorf to the city with the same freedoms and rights that the Jews had possessed. From then on Judendorf was called Mariendorf, and the synagogue, Marienkapella. The Jewish cemetery behind Buckau, which had been increased by purchases in 1312, was converted into a farm and in 1561 attached to the Berge Monastery.

There was little Jewish spiritual life in medieval Magdeburg, in comparison to cities in the west and in the south. Many documents of Isaac ben Moses Or Zarua and Rabbi Meir of Rothenburg provide information concerning internal Jewish affairs in Magdeburg about the middle of the 13th cent. The best-known scholar of the 13th cent. was Hezekiah, son of the learned Rabbi Jacob. It seems that his decisions and expositions are given in the *Lebush Mordecai,* in *Hayim Or Zarua* and in the *Haggahoth Maimoniyyoth;* his quotations make up a large part of the *Haggahoth Asheri.* Moreover, the following scholars are to be named: Shalom, Shabtai ben Samuel and Isaac of Magdeburg; the latter is mentioned by Jacob Mölln in the 15th cent.

Apparently between 1493 and 1705 no Jews were permitted to settle in Magdeburg. When Abraham Liebman, rabbi in the duchy of Magdeburg and the principality of Halberstadt, was named rabbi also of the principality of Minden and county of Ravensburg by the Elector Frederick III in 1692, it seems that Jews were living in the duchy of Magdeburg. Apparently this was the same Abraham Liebman to whom King Frederick I had granted permission to trade in 1704 despite the protest of the city and the attempt to hinder the settlement of the Jews within or outside the city.

On January 10, 1703, King Frederick I granted to the two sons, Moses and Levin, of the protected Jew David Samuel Bloch of Halberstadt, permission to settle in the Sudenburg. In 1715 King Frederick William I allowed Bloch's son-in-law, Levin Bauer, to live in the new city of Magdeburg. Elias Ruben Gumpertz was granted permission in 1719 to settle in the city of Magdeburg. The continuous protests of the city of Magdeburg resulted in a royal command in 1729 that the city of Magdeburg was to be cleansed of all Jews.

It is said—but there is no evidence—that in November, 1806, the representative of Magdeburg referred to the city's privilege of having no Jews, but that General Ney replied: "France knows only of Israelites, no Jews."

In 1807 Magdeburg was incorporated into the new Kingdom of Westphalia under the rule of Jerome Bonaparte, and it became chief city of the Elbe department. This changed completely the situation affecting the Jews. A decree of March 21, 1808, laid the foundation for a consistorial constitution. In every department syndics were to oversee the Jewish community. For the syndicated area of Magdeburg two syndics were appointed. This district included, in addition to the city of Magdeburg, also the cities of Stendal, Schoenebeck, Gommern, Neubalderberg, Gardelegen and Barby.

In 1807 there were two protected Jews in the city. Immigration from Alsace, Halberstadt, Anhalt and the duchy of Warsaw increased the number of Jews in Magdeburg in 1809 to eighty-four families, in 1810 to 225 persons and in 1811 to 288. In 1816 seventy-two members contributed 1,000 taler to the community; in 1823 seventy members contributed 840 taler, and in 1846 ninety-three members contributed 1,214 taler. In 1823 the syndics were replaced by a board of directors. City officials and the municipal council requested the provincial diet, on February 18, 1845, for equal rights for the Jews, and asked that it intercede with the king. In accordance with the Prussian law of July 23, 1847, the synagogal community of Magdeburg was organized on February 4, 1850. Its constitution was approved by the lord lieutenant of the province on October 11, 1856. To the synagogal community of the district of Magdeburg belonged all the Jews of Magdeburg, Neustadt, Sudenburg, Buckau and Gross-Ottersleben, as well as the Jewish inhabitants of those localities which might be added to the synagogal district of Magdeburg. On September 19, 1850, the festive cornerstone laying of a synagogue took place on a piece of land provided by the magistrate at low interest. Until 1851 the community had only a modest assembly room for public worship. The consecration of the synagogue took place on September 14, 1851. A new synagogue was consecrated on September 26, 1897, and the Joel prayer-book was introduced. The first rabbi of the community in the 19th cent. was Isaak Heilbronn, who took office on March 15, 1809. Cantor Moses Salomon succeeded him.

A new chapter in the history of the community of Magdeburg began when Ludwig Philippson became preacher and teacher in 1833, which office he filled for twenty-eight years. Philippson created in Magdeburg, in 1834, the first well-organized religious school in North Germany. Moreover, he founded the *Allgemeine Zeitung des Judentums* in 1837; between 1839 and 1854 he completed his great Biblical work and finally, in 1854, together with others, he founded the Institut zur Förderung der jüdischen Literatur. Philippson's activity not only brought great respect to the synagogal community of Magdeburg but was important for all Jewry. His successor was Mortiz Güdemann (1862-66), who later became chief rabbi of Vienna and an authority on Jewish cultural history. Then came Moritz Rahmer (1867-1904), who was not only rabbi but also editor of the *Predigtmagazin* (1874-94), *Israelitische Wochenschrift* (1878-94) and *Jüdisches Literaturblatt* (1873-1904). Georg Wilde (1906-39), famous for his sermons, was the last rabbi.

The cemetery of the community was located in the Sudenburg suburb after 1816. The Jewish societies of Magdeburg included the Israelitischer Frauenverein (1836-82), Chevra Kadisha (founded 1838; reorganized, 1882), Israelitischer Witwen und Waisenverein (founded 1871) and Mendelssohn Lodge I.O.B.B. (founded 1885). Magdeburg was the headquarters of the Synagogenverband of Saxony (founded 1898) and of the Verein jüdischer Lehrer in Mitteldeutschland (founded 1879). Magdeburg had also many local branches of the large organizations in Germany. The number of Jewish foundations indicates the active Jewish life of a middle-sized community which consisted in 1889 of 2,000 Jews, in 1913 of 1,843 (out of a total population of 279,629, or 6.9 per cent), and in 1934 of 1,600 (or 5 per cent of the total population).

The advent of the Nazi regime in Germany in 1933 brought destruction and annihilation also to the Jewish community of Magdeburg. ADOLF KOBER.

Lit.: Spanier, Moritz, "Über den Anteil der Juden—vorzugsweise der Magdeburger—an den Vaterlandskriegen," *Verwaltungsbericht des Vorstandes der Synagogen-Gemeinde zu Magdeburg* (1893); idem, *Geschichte der Juden in Magdeburg* (1923); Aronius, J., *Regesten* (1902), nos. 129, 133, 134, 149, 201, 240, 347, 372, 390, 455, 674, 678; *Germania Judaica*, vol. 1, part 2 (1934) 163-70; Güdemann, M., *Zur Geschichte der Juden in Magdeburg* (1866); Hertel, G., *Urkundenbuch der Stadt Magdeburg*, vol. 1 (1892); vol. 2 (1884); Lewinsky, A., "Der jüdische Hofbankier der Magdeburger Erzbischöfe im 14. Jahrhundert," *Monatsschrift für Geschichte und Wissenschaft des Judentums*, vol. 48 (1904) 457-60; *Statut der Synagogen-Gemeinde Magdeburg* (1857); *Synagogen- und Gebets-Ordnung für die Synagogen-Gemeinde Magdeburg*, 5628 (1867); *Verwaltungs-Bericht des Vorstandes der Synagogen-Gemeinde zu Magdeburg* (1890); Pinthus, in *Zeitschrift für die Geschichte der Juden in Deutschland*, vol. 2 (1930) 130, 201; Salfeld, S., *Das Martyrologium des Nürnberger Memorbuches* (1898) 247, 267; *Handbuch der jüdischen Gemeindeverwaltung und Wohlfahrtspflege* (1913); Kober, Adolf, *Grundbuch des Kölner Judenviertels* (1920) 10-11, 13.

MAGDIEL, *see* COLONIES, AGRICULTURAL.

MAGEN DAVID, *see* SHIELD OF DAVID.

MAGGID, a Hebrew word (plural, *maggidim*) originally meaning "narrator" or "relater," which is used in various significations.

1. As Preacher. From a very early period in Jewish history it was the custom to expand and to elucidate the Biblical text by means of sermons in which stories and moral lessons were embodied. Much of this material was preserved in the Midrash and subsequent Derushim (Derashoth) literature. During the Middle Ages, however, preaching declined, and became intellectual rather than inspirational. The Derashoth which the Polish rabbis used to deliver, at least twice a year (following tradition), on Shabbath Hagadol before Passover and on Shabbath Shubah before Yom Kippur, were, for the most part, strictly Halachic (legal) and strongly Pilpulistic (dialectic) in tone. Only at the end were they Haggadic, but it was considered proper to end them with a Messianic outlook; they were primarily intended to demonstrate the profound knowledge and penetration of the rabbi, and they were understood only by a few of the large audiences who came to hear them. As a result, the Jewish masses of Poland came to long for edifying lectures and for religious instruction which they could understand.

This need for popular preaching was filled by the Maggid, or popular preacher, who was attached to no synagogue, but would go about from place to place to give sermons. He was also known by the Hebrew title of Baal Darshan, in popular speech corrupted to Baldarsher. He usually possessed an extensive knowledge of Haggadic, Midrashic and moralist literature, from which he knew how to draw adroitly numerous sayings and teachings for his lectures. The Derashah (sermon) of the Maggid was always of a religious, moral and didactic tendency. It contained clever allegorical interpretations, words of comfort, and the hope for a better future for the Jewish people. It often contained stern admonitions and reproofs. This *Musar sagen* deeply stirred the listeners and often moved them to open sobs and tears. A Maggid who delivered such a sermon of admonition was called a Mochiah (plural Mochihim); according to a legend, even the famous Solomon Luria (MaHaRSHaL), of Lublin, would listen to such lectures with fear and trembling.

In order to heighten the effect of the Derashah the Polish Maggid would make use of the parable (*mashal*) from real life. Such parables, often ingenious and full of meaning, such as those of the Dubner Maggid (Jacob Kranz), soon became generally known, and are still current in the speech of the Jewish folk of Eastern Europe.

Eventually many Maggids acquired a permanent post with congregations. In many cities, the Maggid would deliver popular lectures, derived from the Bible and its commentaries, from the Midrash, *En Yaakob* and *Hoboth Halebaboth,* every evening after prayer, to a group assembled in the Beth Hamidrash or other place of prayer. He would deliver lectures to a larger audience on Sabbath afternoons or some suitable weekday evening. Many Maggids enjoyed the highest esteem and respect of contemporary Talmudists.

From time to time the Maggid would take trips to deliver his lectures in other cities. For these lectures he would receive money from his listeners. Many Maggids who either could not or would not find any fixed position led an uncertain wandering life and eked out a wretched existence by means of the gifts collected for them after their lecture. Their official title was always Maggid Mesharim ("preacher of uprightness").

The following were popular and famous Polish Maggids:

Zebi of Vaidaslac, who wrote *Asarah Lemeah* (Berlin, 1801) and *Eretz Zebi* (Prague, 1786).

Jacob Kranz, the Dubner Maggid, famous for his parables.

Ezekiel Feivel of Vilna, who flourished about 1800.

Abraham Hayim of Mohilev, author of *Path Lehem.*

Hayim ben Issachar Melamed, author of *Minhah Ketannah* (Amsterdam, 1759).

A special group of Maggids were the followers of the Musar movement founded by Israel Lipkin. One of the most famous of these Musar preachers in modern times was Moses Isaac (Darshan) of Kelmy, known as the Khelmer Maggid (1828-1900). For more than half a century he was an itinerant preacher in almost all the cities of Russian Poland. A typical modern Maggid was the Slutzker Maggid, Zebi Hirsch Dainow (1830-77), the preacher of the Haskalah who, when he became suspect among the Orthodox Jews of Russia, settled in London, and was highly esteemed there by the immigrant Russian and Polish Jews.

2. Among the Hasidim. Many of the Hasidic Zaddiks (saints) were also called Maggid, because they carried on the functions of Maggid in their native place. Many were and are known better by their Maggid title, which included the name of their locality, than by their own names. The most important of them were:

Dob Ber of Meseritz, disciple of Israel Baal Shem; he was called "the great Maggid" or the Meseritscher Maggid.

Isaac Maggid of Drohobycz, another pupil of the Baal Shem.

Jehiel Michel Maggid of Zloczow.

Solomon of Luck, Maggid in Sokal, and therefore called the Sikubler Maggid; he was a pupil of the "great Maggid."

Israel of Kozienice, known as the Kozienicer Maggid; he was the pupil of Levi Isaac of Berdichev.

The Zaddiks of Chernobyl include: Nahum, called Rabbi Nuchimtsche Chernobler; his son, called Rabbi Motale Chernobler and the Chernobler Maggid; the latter's two sons, Aaron and Abraham, the latter known as the Trisker Maggid.

3. As Rabbinical Judge. In towns where there was a special rabbinical court, its president occasionally bore the title of Maggid; but in order to indicate his judicial functions, the title was expanded to Maggid Mesharim Umoreh Tzedek ("preacher of uprightness and judge of righteousness"). Thus in Lemberg from 1702 to 1859 there were two such tribunals, the presiding judge of each of which was entitled Maggid. Joseph ben Meir Teumim, author of the commentary *Peri Megadim* on the *Shulhan Aruch,* was such a Maggid in Lemberg.

Solomon Kluger, one of the most widely recognized Talmudic authorities of the 19th cent., was so modest that he would not take the title of "rabbi," but was known solely as Maggid; he is generally referred to as the Brodyer Maggid.

4. Other Uses of the Term. According to Cabalistic teachers, one who leads a sanctified life will be rewarded by the appearance of an angel known as his Maggid, who makes prophecies to him about the future, reveals to him the secrets of the Torah, and gives him instructions as to his proper course in life. Joseph Caro believed that such a Maggid, whom he sometimes identified with the Mishnah itself, bestowed such teachings and prophecies upon him. Solomon Molcho and Moses Zacuto each believed that a personal Maggid attended them.

The father of the household, in his capacity as narrator of the Passover story and its accompanying miracles, is termed Maggid in tradition. Accordingly the word Maggid is used to describe the fifth of the fourteen sections of the Seder, the relation of the Passover story.

The Biblical books of the Prophets and Hagiographa used to be called Maggidim (plural of Maggid) on account of their didactic and moralizing contents. In many editions this word appears on the title page.   SAMUEL RAPPAPORT.

Lit.: Zunz, L., *Gottesdienstliche Vorträge;* Baeck, *Die Darshanim;* Horodezky, S. A., *Hahasiduth Vehahasidim;* Eisenstein, J. D., in *Jewish Encyclopedia,* vol. 8, pp. 252-54.

MAGGID, DAVID, writer, son of Hillel, b. Vilna, 1862. After completing his education at St. Petersburg, he became secretary to Samuel Joseph Fünn, whom he assisted in the writing of *Haotzar* and *Keneseth Yisrael.* From 1890 to 1897 he was a teacher at a Jewish Gymnasium; in 1918 he became librarian of the Jewish Oriental department of the state library in Leningrad. In 1921 he became also professor of the history of art at the Russian Institute, and in 1925 professor of Hebrew at the University of Leningrad, the first Jewish professor to hold this chair.

Maggid has written extensively for Russian Jewish journals. He was a contributor to the *Yevreiskaya Entziklopedia* and was editor of *Tzemah David* (1897) and of *Luah Hatehiah.* He wrote numerous scholarly articles in various languages. His works in Hebrew include *Toledoth Antokolski* (Warsaw, 1897); a monograph on Mordecai Aaron Günzburg, and a history of the Günzburg family; those in Russian deal with such subjects as Jewish dogma, Jewish liturgy and the Jews of the Caucasus. He also prepared a polyglot Bible in some forty languages and dialects.

MAGGID, HILLEL NOAH (known also as Hillel Steinschneider, from his occupation as lapidary), genealogist, b. Vilna, 1829; d. Vilna, 1903. He published genealogical and bibliographical articles in various Hebrew periodicals, the most notable of these being his biography of David Oppenheim (*Gan Perahim,* 1882) and historical notes on the past of the Lemberg Jewish community (*Anshe Hashem,* 1895). He collaborated with Samuel Joseph Fünn in his celebrated *Kiryah Neemanah,* the history of the Vilna Jewish community. Maggid's chief work, *Ir Vilna,* which he

began to publish in 1900, was never completed; it contains hundreds of biographies of important rabbis and personages, as well as material for the history of the Jews of Vilna and Lithuania.

Lit.: Ben Ami, in *Voskhod,* Nov., 1903.

MAGIC. Magic, or the alleged coercion of nature by occult means, was always discountenanced in Jewish teaching, since it challenged the omnipotence of God and usually involved adoption of heathen practices. Nevertheless, it represented an approach to the world which was common throughout the ancient Near East and which formed the basis of most early Semitic religions. The Israelites therefore inherited a great deal of magical lore from their forebears, while their entry into Canaan, on the one hand, and their exile in Babylonia, on the other, brought them into close contact with peoples among whom occult practices were a part of daily life. Similarly, during the later periods of Persian and Greek domination and, indeed, throughout their subsequent history, they not infrequently strayed upon the darkling paths of pagan sorcery.

I. Magic in the Bible. In early Semitic culture magic was associated especially with the service of the temple. Priests were also magicians, while priestesses and sacred harlots commonly practiced witchcraft. For this reason the legal codes of the Pentateuch place magic in the category of apostasy (*Lev.* 20:6, 27; *Deut.* 18:10-20) or unchastity (*Ex.* 22:18), sorcerers being liable to death by stoning. Similarly, the religious reformation of King Josiah of Judah, in 621 B.C.E., included the abolition of all vehicles of magic (*II Kings* 23:24), while the denunciation of sorcerers is a common feature of Old Testament prophesy (*Micah* 5:11; *Mal.* 3:5 and other passages).

Several types of magicians are mentioned in the Bible, but it is not always possible to identify the precise meaning of the technical terms employed. The following are the principal categories:

1. Sorcerer (Hebrew, *mechashef*). This is the generic term. The corresponding Assyrian word, *kishpu,* likewise possesses a purely general meaning. In Arabic and Ethiopic, however, *k-s-f* means "to cut," and this has suggested that the term originally denoted one who "shreds" herbs for magical brews.

2. Charmer (Hebrew, *hober heber*). Since the Hebrew verb *habar* properly means "to tie," this is thought to refer to the common practice of "tying magical knots." However, it may denote no more than "spellbinder."

3. Necromancer (Hebrew, *ba'al 'ob* or *sho'el 'ob*). The word *'ob* probably connects with the Arabic *a-w-b,* "return," in the sense of *revenant* (ghost). Closely connected with the *ba'al 'ob* (literally, "possessor of an *'ob''*) is the *yide'oni,* which probably denotes a "possessor of a familiar spirit."

4. One who obtains oracles (Hebrew, *kosem*). The corresponding Arabic term is used of drawing lots at a sanctuary, with headless arrows. The latter, inscribed with the possible alternative contemplated, are shaken in a quiver, and the one which first falls out is taken to express the divine oracle. A similar procedure is described in *Ezek.* 21:26.

5. Soothsayer (Hebrew, *me'onen*). This term probably means "crooner," crooning being characteristic of the Oriental soothsayer. Some, however, relate it to the Hebrew word *'anan,* "cloud," in the sense of "weather-maker."

6. Augurer (Hebrew, *menahesh*). This term is used in *Gen.* 44:5, 15 of the magical practice whereby omens are sought by observing the play of light in a cup of liquid. In Syriac the corresponding word denotes divination from natural phenomena.

The Bible contains several allusions to magical practices. Thus, the trial by ordeal, described in *Num.* 5:11-31, is based on a belief in the magical properties of water. The incident in *II Kings* 13:14-19, where Elisha instructs King Joash to divine his chances against Aram from the flight of arrows, has parallels among the Thompson River Indians and other primitive peoples, while Jeremiah's action in breaking a pot as a symbol of the imminent break-up of Judah (*Jer.* 19 to 20) can be shown, from Babylonian and Egyptian analogies, to have been a common magical practice. The anointing of shields before going into battle (*II Sam.* 1:21; *Isa.* 21:5) derives from the custom of smearing persons and weapons with animal fat in order to acquire added strength, while if the initial words of Deborah's war-song (*Judges* 5:1) be rendered "When men let grow their hair in Israel," this will allude to the magical idea—recurrent in the story of Samson—that hair is a "life-index," and may therefore not be cut in wartime. Lastly, the familiar verse, "They that sow in tears shall reap in joy" (*Ps.* 126:5), has now been shown to be a metaphor derived from the magical practice of weeping while sowing, in order to deceive noxious demons.

The Biblical saga embody a number of magical motifs, many of which recur in the folklore of other ancient and primitive peoples. Thus, Moses is provided with a wonder-working staff which can turn into a serpent, produce water from a rock, and, being uplifted, achieve the rout of the enemy. Similarly, Elijah can send or withhold rain (*I Kings* 17:1; 18:43-46), while the witch of Endor is able to evoke the dead.

It is not improbable that several of the religious institutions of early Israel were but sublimations of time-honored magical usages. To this category may well belong the Urim and Thummim of the high priest— two oracular pebbles carried in a pouch, as well as the bells on the hem of his robe—originally designed to scare demons. Phylacteries (*totafoth*), fringes (*tzitzith*) and inscriptions on doorposts (*mezuzoth*) are undoubtedly of the same order, the first named being, probably, a later substitution for original tattoo marks. It may also be observed that according to some scholars the very word Torah is of magical origin, originally denoting a sacred lot cast by the priestly soothsayers (cf. Hebrew *yarah,* "to cast lots").

II. Post-Biblical Magic. In the post-Biblical period Jewish magic became a reflex of contemporary pagan practices, developing into a bizarre amalgam of Persian, Greek, late Egyptian and Gnostic elements. Nevertheless, the Bible remained the pivotal point. Biblical verses were used as charms. Thus, *Gen.* 19:11, referring to the miraculous blinding of the men of Sodom, was recited to procure invisibility, while *Num.* 12:13, describing the healing of Miriam from leprosy, was used as an incantation against fever. Most sig-

nificant of such texts was *Ps.* 91, the contents of which marked it out as a suitable charm against evil spirits. Indeed, there is reason to believe that the "arrow that flieth by day" and the "pestilence that walketh in darkness," mentioned therein, are really appellations of demons.

To render them unintelligible to the demons themselves, Biblical verses were often disguised by permutations and substitutions of letters. The two principal methods employed were those of Notarikon and Gematria. In the former, initials were written instead of complete words, while in the latter the original letters were replaced by others adding up to the same numerical value. Frequently these queer permutations developed an independent existence, sometimes being taken as the names of angels, or standardized, like abracadabra, as technical terms of the black art. Permutations of divine names also possessed special virtue, while transcriptions of the ineffable Tetragrammaton YHVH occur frequently, even in Greek texts. Names of pagan deities and demons are also cited with particular relish. Thus, on inscribed bowls of the 7th cent. C.E., found at Nippur and used to trap demons, Babylonian and Persian demons are often named. Numbers likewise were held to hold magical properties, three, seven and nine being especial favorites.

If there was a magic of word and number, there was also one of script and sign. Mystical alphabets of Cabalistic origin were invented in order to render magical prescriptions more secret, while frequent use was made of zodiacal signs and of such geometrical devices as the pentagram ("the seal of Solomon") and the hexagram ("the shield of David"), the latter occurring as early as the 2nd cent. C.E. in the catacombs of Beth-shearim, Palestine. Even the arrangement of letters enhanced the potency of a written charm. Thus, to avert blindness, the word *Shabrir* (blindness) was written repeatedly in a descending triangle: *Shabriri, briri, riri, iri, ri,* while the disposition of letters in magic squares, or other special patterns, was also extremely common. These magical letters were used also in spoken manner, or incantations.

Magical qualities were assigned likewise to animate and inanimate objects. Thus, Jewish charms of the Gaonic period prescribe the fabrication of symbolic clay figures as a means of encompassing one's designs on an individual by the process known technically as *envoutement,* while bodily parts of animals are frequently mentioned as ingredients of magical brews, and human spittle was considered especially potent (*Tos. Sanh.* 12:9; 13:12). Elements and minerals were similarly endowed with magical qualities. Demons could not cross water, while iron was a kind of lightning-conductor against them. Salt was another magical medium, possessing both protective and destructive properties. In ancient Semitic times it was strewn over razed cities, and was taboo to Babylonian kings on certain days of the month, while in Jewish custom newborn children were rubbed with it, and in Palestine it is still offered to the dead and to departed saints. Precious stones had each its own peculiar "virtue." A 14th cent. manuscript in the library of the Jewish Theological Seminary of America prescribes ruby against miscarriage and inebriation of women, carbuncle for rejuvenation, turquoise as a prophylactic against falling, and onyx as a means of acquiring grace.

The successive stages of life were marked by magical procedure. Women in childbirth had to be protected from the child-stealing Lilith, and to this end a charm against her (called *Kimpettzettel = Kindbettzettel,* i.e. "childbirth-ticket") was suspended in the lying-in chamber. The prototypes of this familiar charm may be found already in Egypt and Assyria, while an interesting Canaanite example of it, of the 8th cent. B.C.E., has recently come to light at Arslan Tash in Mesopotamia. At marriages the custom of walking seven times around the bridegroom has magical significance, as has also that of breaking a glass, while the showering of the bridal couple with nuts (or confetti) was originally designed to forefend hovering demons. Pouring out water at death is also of magical import, while the custom of throwing dust or grass over the shoulder on leaving a graveyard was an ancient method of pelting demons.

Magic likewise obtrudes in more formal rituals. Thus, the custom of looking at the fingernails in the light of the Habdalah candle is probably connected with a well-known method of divination. The Tashlich ceremony, on the first day of the New Year (Rosh Hashanah), whereby sins are symbolically shaken out over running water, is of magical origin, while the quaint rite of Kapparah, on the eve of the Day of Atonement (Yom Kippur), when a hen is slain as a substitute for man, has a similar explanation. The beating of willow-branches on Hoshana Rabbah may be compared with the well-known European fertility-charm, the most striking example of which is that of the German *Ostersmacken,* or "Easter smacks," while the water-drawing ceremony current in Temple times during the Feast of Tabernacles (*Suk.* 4: 9-10) is a rain-charm whose history can be traced to Canaanite usages in the 16th cent. B.C.E. Other magical practices embodied in formal Jewish ritual include the custom of leaping thrice upon blessing the new moon, and abstention from marriage during the days of the Omer between Passover and the Feast of Weeks. The latter links up with a worldwide custom of observing a lenten period of mortification before harvest.

The development of Cabalistic philosophies, and the emergence of Hasidism in the late 18th cent., were two powerful forces in the preservation of magical tradition. Cabalistic and psuedo-Cabalistic formulae were introduced, for esoteric effect, into magical prescriptions, while the appearance of wonder-working Zaddikim in Eastern Europe stimulated belief in miraculous virtues and occult arts. Indeed, a brisk trade was transacted in the sale of magical recipes, and the slow corrosion of such quackery, reminiscent of the charlatan practices of Sabbatai Zebi and Jacob Frank, contributed largely to the later disrepute and collapse of the Hasidic movement.

In modern times, scientific progress has tended to eclipse the ancient belief in magic. Popular traditions, however, die hard. In Eastern Europe, faith in wonder-working Zaddikim still obtains among the older generation, and it is possible to see pious Jews in Polish cemeteries placing written requests on the tombs of departed rabbis. In the West, magic survives mainly in the form of such innocuous superstitions as the belief that "Friday the 13th" is unlucky, or the like. Specifically Jewish magic has largely died out. In the East End of London, however, Jewish children sometimes wear blue beads against the evil eye, while during the first World War (1914-18) Jewish soldiers were known occasionally to carry coins embossed with the divine Hebrew letter *He* (the initial of God). The tendency, especially common in the United States, to wear miniature Mezuzoth or Shield of David brooches as mascots represents, in terms of commercial exploitation, a last lingering survival of the magical tradition. It should be emphasized, however, that all such practices are regarded in Jewish teaching as aberrations, and in no way represent the true level of religious doctrine.

See also: AMULETS; CABALA; DEMONS; HASIDISM; LILITH; MIRACLES; TASHLICH; WATER.

THEODOR H. GASTER.

Lit.: Trachtenberg, J., *Jewish Magic and Superstition* (1939; the standard work, with comprehensive bibliography, pp. 315-32); Brecher, G., *Das Transcendentale, Magie und magische Heilarten im Talmud* (1850); Blau, L., *Das altjüdische Zauberwesen* (1898); Gaster, M., *The Sword of Moses* (1896); Jacob, B., *Im Namen Gottes* (1903); Lods, A., "Le rôle des idées magiques dans la mentalité israélite," *Old Testament Essays* (1926) 151-74; idem, "Magie hébraique et magie cananéen," *Revue de l'histoire des religions* (1927) 1-16; Budge, E. W., *Amulets and Superstitions* (1930), chap. 8 ("Hebrew Amulets") 212-38; Gaster, T. H., "A Canaanite Magical Text," *Orientalia* (1941) 41-76; idem, "Some Ancient Oriental Folklore," *Folk-Lore* (1938) 335-75; Driver, S. R., *Deuteronomy (International Critical Commentary,* 1895) 223-27; Montgomery, James A., *Aramaic Incantation Texts from Nippur* (1913).

MAGIC SQUARES, definite quadratic arrangements of numbers so that their total in any direction or diagonally is the same. There are more complicated forms, containing concentric minor squares within the larger one. The peculiarity involved in the repetition of totals resulted in magical significance being attributed to them. In the ancient Chinese civilization, in the Arabic world, where magic squares were known in the 10th cent., and in the Western world, to which they were introduced about the 14th cent., the occult interpretation is occasionally found.

In Jewish literature a magic square was first employed mathematically in the works of Abraham ibn Ezra. Later, magic squares in which Hebrew letters represented the numbers were used as amulets. Many of them had some connection with astrology; not only did the letters used spell out the name of one of the planets, but the other side of the amulet was decorated with a picture of the corresponding Greek divinity. Because of this mixture of influences it is not known whether the amulets originated with Jewish or Christian Cabalists.

Lit.: Ahrens, *Hebräische Amulette mit magischen Zahlenquadraten* (1918); Liharzik, *Das Quadrat als Grundlage aller Proportionalität;* Bischoff, *Praktische Kabbala.*

MAGIDOFF, JACOB, Yiddish journalist, b. Odessa, Russia, 1869. He came to New York city in 1886. Magidoff received his law degree in 1902 from the New York University Law School, and was admitted to the bar in 1904. In 1894 he had entered Yiddish newspaper work as associate editor of the *Arbeiter Zeitung;* from 1896 to 1899 he was city editor

Judah L. Magnes

of the *Abend Blatt*. Subsequently, after short periods of association with the *Jewish Daily News* and the *Abend Post,* Magidoff became city editor of the *Jewish Morning Journal* (1901). In 1926 he also became chief editorial writer of the paper. He relinquished the city editorship in 1935, but in 1942 he was still an editorial writer for the *Journal*.

MAGNES, JUDAH LEON, rabbi, community leader, and president of the Hebrew University in Jerusalem, b. San Francisco, 1877. He received his B.A. degree from the University of Cincinnati in 1898 and his rabbinical degree from the Hebrew Union College two years later. From 1900 to 1902 Magnes was in Europe, for the most part in Germany, where he did post-graduate work at both the University of Berlin and the University of Heidelberg. He received his Ph.D. degree from Heidelberg in 1902.

Returning to the United States in 1903, Magnes did not at once enter the active rabbinate but instead became librarian and instructor at the Hebrew Union College. In 1904 he was called to Brooklyn to occupy the pulpit of Temple Israel.

The first years of the 20th cent. were a period of great germination in American Jewish life. Although the impetus, both hopeful and tragic, came from Europe, the more sensitive spirits in American Jewish life responded quickly, and among them was Magnes. He became secretary of the Federation of American Zionists (1905-8), and in so doing he helped to bridge the schism in language and in ideology between the groups he represented and the growing masses of East European Jewry who spoke and read Yiddish. He was among the first to insist that in America

Zionism must be interpreted in conformity with the American environment rather than with the theories of national life prevailing in the European countries of origin.

Through his Zionist work, the Jewish masses came to know Magnes and he them. He identified himself still further with their needs and aspirations when he organized the protest meetings and made the relief appeals called forth by the Kishinev pogroms, and himself headed the protest parade.

His forthrightness and forensic abilities resulted in his being offered the influential pulpit of Temple Emanu-El in New York in 1908, at the suggestion of Louis Marshall. But his advocacy of the resumption of more traditional aspects of worship and custom brought about his resignation from that pulpit in 1910.

It was during his two years' incumbency at Emanu-El that Magnes succeeded in laying the ground for what might have become a unified Jewish community in New York City: the Kehillah. Magnes was its chairman during the entire period of its existence (1909-22). The comprehensive program of that short-lived Kehillah proved to be premature. But its Bureau of Jewish Education, which Magnes called into being in 1910, continued until 1941, and profoundly influenced the community organizations for Jewish education throughout the United States.

In the meantime, having left Temple Emanu-El, Magnes sought to carry out his personal adoption of more conservative Judaism by becoming rabbi of Congregation B'nai Jeshurun. A year later he organized the Society for the Advancement of Judaism, and was its leader until 1920. He helped found the Yiddish daily *Der Tog,* sponsored the Intercollegiate Menorah Society and promoted many other Jewish cultural institutions.

During the first World War (1914-18) Magnes was one of the prime movers in establishing the Joint Distribution Committee, and in 1916 headed the first commission that went to Europe to arrange for the distribution of American Jewish relief funds. But during the entire four years of the War, Magnes was subjected to a great deal of opposition and criticism because of his espousal of the pacifist cause. Despite the attacks made on him, he did not alter his position; not until twenty years later, when in 1939 Britain went to war against Nazi Germany, did Magnes relinquish the unflinchingly pacifist credo to which he had adhered his whole life.

With the end of the first World War and the development of Jewish activities in Palestine, Magnes was asked to undertake the organization of the Hebrew University. He secured the initial funds for its maintenance and laid the basis for its academic structure. When it was opened in 1925, Magnes became chancellor, and in 1935 he was made president of the university.

Living in Palestine, Magnes has continued to follow a path of political belief which has frequently clashed with majority opinion. He was from the very beginning outspoken in favor of cooperative activity with the Arab population rather than dependence on British protection. He disagreed with the official Zionist leadership by expressing doubts about the possibility of establishing a Jewish commonwealth

Eduard Magnus

that would be accepted peaceably by the Palestinian Arabs. His counter-suggestion was that "bi-national" parity be established in Palestine between Jews and Arabs, that agreement with them be reached on the rate of Jewish immigration, and that the country be made part of an Arab Federation in the Near East. He made several unsuccessful efforts to implement his plan of bringing together the moderate Arab spokesmen with the Zionist leadership in Palestine.

On the other hand, Magnes remained his old challenging self in other aspects of Jewish life, urging, for instance, that Jews the world over adopt the insignia of the yellow Magen David imposed on the Jews of Nazi-controlled countries, and thus turn it into a mark of honor. As head of the Hadassah Emergency Committee in Palestine, he was instrumental in maintaining the morale and well-being of the population and in putting the resources of the Hadassah Medical Organization and of the Hebrew University at the service of the British war effort.

ALEXANDER M. DUSHKIN.

Lit.: *American Hebrew*, July 9, 1937, pp. 5, 20; *Sefer Magnes* (sixtieth anniversary volume, 1938).

MAGNIN, EDGAR FOGEL, rabbi, b. San Francisco, 1890. He was educated at the University of Cincinnati (A.B., 1913) and at the Hebrew Union College (Rabbi, 1914). He served as rabbi of Temple Israel of Stockton, Cal., in 1914 and 1915. In 1915 he was called to the rabbinate of the Wilshire Boulevard Temple of Los Angeles, which position he still held in 1942. In 1934 he became lecturer in history at the University of Southern California. During part of this time he was president of the Los Angeles Rabbinical Association.

Magnin was a vitally active communal worker, interested in both Jewish and general affairs. He was a chairman of the local Jewish Welfare Board (its representative during the first World War), vice-president of the Cedars of Lebanon Hospital, director of the Los

Angeles chapter of the American Red Cross, and a member of the special citizens' committee of the advisory board of the Los Angeles Board of Education. Magnin was also a member of the advisory committee of the Los Angeles Philharmonic Orchestra Association and of the advisory board of the National Academy of American Literature. He has lectured over the Columbia and Mutual broadcasting systems.

MAGNUS, BARON ANTON IVAN VON, German diplomat, b. Berlin, 1821; d. Görlitz, Germany, 1882. He was a son of Friedrich Martin Magnus, whose original name was Meyer and who, converted to Protestantism, founded in Berlin the most important banking house in the Prussian capital until (after 1870) Bleichroeder, favored by Bismarck, surpassed it. The Magnus family was knighted in 1853, and made baronial in 1858. In the same year, Anton von Magnus became secretary of the Prussian legation at Brussels, and in 1863 he was appointed Prussian minister at The Hague. In 1865 he was chargé d'affaires at St. Petersburg, and there negotiated with Gorchakov about Russia's friendly attitude toward Prussia in the coming wars.

Magnus was married to Baroness Helene Brunow (1835-59), daughter of the Russian ambassador at London. Because of his intimate relations with his brothers Rudolf Martin (chief of the banking house) and Victor (British consul at Berlin), Magnus was better informed on international affairs than the average Prussian diplomat.

In 1867 Magnus became Prussian minister at Mexico, and interceded with Juarez for the unhappy emperor Maximilian. Although Magnus was unable to save Maximilian's life, his "excellent behavior" was acknowledged by King William of Prussia, Emperor Napoleon III and Empress Eugenie, who honored Magnus during his visit at Paris, and especially by Emperor Francis Joseph of Austria, who decorated him with the high order of the Iron Crown of the Lombards. During his stay at Vienna, Magnus contributed much to the reconciliation between Austria and Prussia. After 1870 he became minister at Stuttgart in order to eliminate the opposition of Southern Germany to the new state of things. In 1879 he was appointed German minister at Copenhagen, where he faced an equally difficult situation because Bismarck, immediately before Magnus's arrival at Copenhagen, shocked the feelings of the people of Denmark by repealing the stipulation of the treaty of Prague concerning the plebiscite in Northern Slesvig. Magnus was successful in his reconciliatory efforts. He even was more courteous than Bismarck tolerated, and in 1881 retired from office.

Lit.: *Die auswärtige Politik Preussens 1859-1870*, vols. 1 to 10; *Bismarck und die Schleswig-Holsteinsche Frage*; Felix Prinz Salm-Salm, *Queretaro* (1868); Corti, Cesare, *Maximilian and Charlotte of Mexico* (1928).

MAGNUS, EDUARD, painter and author, b. Berlin, 1799; d. Berlin, 1872. He studied medicine, philosophy and architecture at first, traveled in France, Italy, Spain, and England, and then devoted himself to painting. In 1837 he became a member and in 1844 a professor of the Berlin Academy of Arts. In his paintings, many of which are in the National Gallery of Berlin and in the Museum of Erfurt, he was in turn a Nazarene, a romantic, and a realist. He painted mainly portraits, among them those of the singer Jenny Lind, Madame Marie Jungken, Madame Albert Magnus, the composer Wilhelm Taubert, Thorwaldsen, Mendelssohn-Bartholdy, Adolf Menzel, and the members of the Prussian royal family. In addition to receiving several medals, he was decorated with the Order of Michael and the Order of the Eagle. Magnus wrote numerous articles for journals and periodicals, such brochures as: *Ein Wort über ein nationales Kunstmuseum* (Berlin, 1864); *Die Polychromie vom künstlerischen Standpunkt; Ein Vortrag über eine Anzahl befreundeter Künstler und Kunstverständiger* (Berlin, 1871).

Lit.: Bryan's *Dictionary of Painters and Engravers,* vol. 3 (1904) 269; Thieme, U., and Becker, F., *Allgemeines Lexikon der bildenden Künstler,* vol. 23, p. 565.

MAGNUS, HEINRICH GUSTAV, physicist and chemist, b. Berlin, 1802; d. Berlin, 1870. He was educated at Stockholm, where he studied under Berzelius, and at the University of Berlin, whence he graduated in 1827. From 1827 to 1833 he engaged mainly in chemical researches which resulted in the discovery of the first of the platino-ammonium compounds. He was appointed lecturer at the University of Berlin in 1831, assistant professor in 1834, and full professor in physics and technology in 1845, a post he held until his resignation in 1869. In 1840 he was elected a member of the Prussian Academy of Sciences.

During the period he taught at Berlin Magnus conducted many physical experiments. He studied the expansion of gases by heat (1841-44), electrolysis (1851), and the polarization of heat (1866-68). Perhaps his most important contribution was the discovery that projectiles subjected to rapid rotation are turned aside from their original direction by forces which act upon them cross-wise; this phenomenon, which was later used by Flexner in the operation of his rotors, is now known as the "Magnus effect." He described the results of his physical and chemical researches in many papers for scientific journals.

The Jewish descent of Magnus is generally assumed, but has not been definitely established.

Lit.: Helmholtz, *Rede zum Gedächtnis an Gustav Magnus* (1871); Hofmann, *Zur Erinnerung an Gustav Magnus* (1871).

MAGNUS, JULIUS, jurist, b. Berlin, 1867. He studied law, and became a reputable lawyer in Berlin. He contributed considerably to the knowledge of patent law, protection of design, and copyright. From 1919 to 1922 he was president of the general union of German lawyers, and from 1922 to 1933 editor of the *Juristische Wochenschrift.* He edited also *Tabellen zum internationalen Recht.* In 1932 Magnus published a study, *Die Notlage der Juristen,* which created a great sensation. He received honorary degrees from two universities, and was member of the directory of the Jewish community of Berlin and of the German union for the promotion of the Hebrew University, Jerusalem.

MAGNUS, LADY KATIE, authoress and communal worker, b. Portsmouth, England, 1844; d. London, 1924. The daughter of E. Emanuel, she married Sir Philip Magnus. She published many popular stories and historical tales, mainly for young readers, which met with great approval, especially her *Outlines of Jewish history* (1886; later edited by M. Friedlaender and Herbert M. Adler). This history begins with the Babylonian exile and ends with a brief record of Sir Moses Montefiore. The authoress intended to write as plainly as possible, and was highly successful in her manner of expressing enthusiasm for Jewish tradition without exaggeration. In 1901 she published *Jewish Portraits,* studies on Judah Halevi, Heinrich Heine, Manasseh ben Israel, Moses Mendelssohn, and on charity in the Talmudic period. This book, too, was highly esteemed by British readers, Jewish as well as non-Jewish, and was reedited after her death. She was connected with several committees of the Berkeley Street Synagogue at London, whose minister was Sir Philip Magnus for many years. She supported the Jewish Deaf and Dumb Home, and was treasurer of the Jewish Girls Club.

MAGNUS, LAURIE, journalist, author and publisher, son of Philip, b. London, 1872; d. London, 1933. Educated at St. Paul's School, London, and at Magdalen College, Oxford, Magnus began his career in 1896 as Berlin correspondent of the London *Morning Post,* subsequently becoming a writer of editorials. This position he retained for four years, serving at the same time as reviewer of French books for the *Sunday Times.* Upon his return to London in 1902, he became joint managing-director of George Routledge and Sons, publishers, and from 1901 to 1904 he was also educational editor for the firm of John Murray. Magnus' own writings during this period were devoted mainly to studies in English literature. His *Primer of Wordsworth* appeared in 1897, and was followed by *Introduction to Poetry* (1902), *How to Read English Literature* (1906) and *Documents Illustrating Elizabethan Poetry* (1906). In 1902, however, he entered the arena of Jewish politics with his anti-Zionist *Aspects of the Jewish Question,* and in 1907 his *Religio Laici Judaici* (Faith of a Jewish Layman) reiterated the view that Judaism is a religion, not a nationality. Throughout the rest of his career Magnus was prominently identified with this position. From its foundation in 1917 until its suspension fourteen years later, he was editor of the weekly *Jewish Guardian,* established by Claude G. Montefiore as an organ of anti-Zionism and Progressive Judaism, while in 1917 he took a leading part in the formation of the League of British Jews, and was one of the signatories of the famous *Times* letter of June 1st, protesting against Jewish nationalism.

During the first World War Magnus served as a major in the Royal Defence Corps, and was twice mentioned in dispatches. Returning to civilian life, he occupied several public offices both in the Jewish and general community. He was a warden of the West London (Reform) Synagogue, a member of the council of Jews' College, and sometime president of the Union of Jewish Literary Societies. From 1929 until his death he was chairman of the Girls' Public School Trust.

In addition to the works mentioned above, Magnus wrote: *The Third Great War in Relation to Modern History* (1917); *A General Sketch of European Litera-*

ture in the Centuries of Romance (1918); *The Jews in the Christian Era and their Contribution to its Civilization* (1930). The last-named is considered his *magnum opus*. He compiled the *Dictionary of European Literature,* and was joint-author with C. Headlam of *Prayers from the Poets* (1899) and *Flowers from the Cave* (1900).

Lit.: Calisch, Edward N., *The Jew in English Literature* (1909) 189; *Jewish Chronicle* (London), May 5, 1933.

MAGNUS, MARCUS (Mordecai ben Man Dessau), 18th cent. court Jew, b. Dessau, Germany; d. Berlin, 1736. He was court Jew to Crown Prince Frederick William I, and in this capacity served, from 1709 until his death, as chief elder of the Jewish community of Berlin. His duties were to protect the royal interests, and he had the right to control communal administration. Though the extent of his influence on the internal affairs of the Jewish community is questionable, he was the advocate of a united synagogue in Berlin and thereby came into conflict with several of the outstanding Jewish families of the city, who preferred the retention of family centers of prayer. A law-suit with the family of Jost Liebmann resulted from this dispute. The united synagogue group acquired ground on Heidereutergasse in 1711, but the Liebmann family, supported by King Frederick, succeeded in preventing the construction of the building. When King Frederick died, Magnus obtained permission (1713) to continue the work, and the synagogue was completed in 1714. It was still standing when the Nazi party assumed power in Germany in 1933.

MAGNUS, MEYER, communal worker, b. Berlin, 1809; d. Berlin, 1883. He was a son of the silk manufacturer Jacob Abraham Meyer, and became an important banker at Berlin. But in his early years Magnus restricted his commercial activity in order to devote his time to communal endeavor for the city and for the Jewish community of Berlin. He was municipal councillor and, from 1866 until his death, president of the Jewish community of Berlin. A friend of Abraham Geiger for many years, Magnus adhered to religious liberalism. In 1871 he protested energetically to the Evangelischer Ober-Kirchenrat whose manifesto had characterized conversion to Judaism as "return to old bondage." The pubic approved Magnus' protest and the Ober-Kirchenrat apologized to him.

When, in 1879, the anti-Semitic movement was started by Adolf Stöcker, Magnus immediately resolved to combat it. He intervened personally with the Prussian ministers of justice and interior, but the government remained evasive. It asserted that Magnus, in his capacity as president of the Jewish community of Berlin, was not entitled to represent the whole of German Jewry. Magnus then had recourse to the crownprince (later Emperor Frederick III), who was fond of him because of his efforts to aid disabled soldiers, Magnus being vice-president of the Victoria Nationale Invaliden-Stiftung whose president was the crown prince.

On January 15, 1880, Magnus had an audience with the crown prince after a meeting of the directorate of the Stiftung, and he answered the prince's question as to the situation in Germany by intimations about the

rise of anti-Semitism. The crown prince, in turn, told Magnus that anti-Semitism was "the disgrace of the century." Next day Magnus published that declaration in the *Nationalzeitung* and it caused a great sensation; Stöcker wrote, in a letter to his wife, that the Jews were unduly elated over the crown prince's attitude toward anti-Semitism. But after Magnus died, during the election contest of 1884, Stöcker publicly denied the truth of Magnus' declaration. The liberal deputy Schmidt-Elberfeld, in a lawsuit against Stöcker, produced legal evidence of the statement published by Magnus. In 1893, Stöcker once more attempted to repudiate it, in the Reichstag, by calling Magnus a liar. Magnus' sons, Rudolf, Paul and Ernst, protested in a memorial, addressed to the president of the Reichstag, supported by testimony on the part of Admiral Stosch, former minister of naval affairs, and Georg von Bunsen, both intimates of the late emperor. Magnus was fully vindicated in the ensuing Reichstag debate.

MAGNUS, SIR PHILIP, rabbi and educator, b. London, 1842; d. London, 1933. He was educated at University College, London, and at the University of London, graduated with first honors in arts and science, and continued his studies in Berlin from 1865 to 1866. On his return to London he became one of the ministers of the Berkeley Street Synagogue at London, and professor of mechanics at the Catholic University. In 1874 he published *Lectures on Elementary Mechanics,* a favorite textbook for many years.

In 1880 Magnus became secretary of the City and Guilds of London Institute for the Advancement of Technical Education, and member of the royal commission for technical education. In this capacity he visited the educational centers of most of Western Europe, and became one of the prime authorities on technical education. In 1886 he was knighted. In the same year he published *Industrial Education,* a model for many studies on the same problem by continental specialists.

During the years 1883 to 1885 Magnus was principal of the Finsbury Technical College. In 1890 he became member of the London School Board, in 1900 fellow of the Senate of London University, and from 1906 to 1922 he represented London University in Parliament. He was president of the Council of College Preceptors, and in 1927 vice-president of the Royal Society of Arts. In 1880 he retired from his ministership at the Berkeley Street Synagogue, but remained that synagogue's representative on the Board of Deputies. For many years he was vice-president of the Anglo-Jewish Association.

MAGNUS, SIR PHILIP MONTEFIORE, journalist and author, b. England, 1906. He was the grandson of Sir Philip Magnus, whom he succeeded to the baronetcy in 1933, and the son of Laurie Magnus. Sir Philip Montefiore Magnus was graduated from Oxford and entered government service in 1928, becoming assistant principal of the Office of Works. He retained this post until 1930, when he was made a member of the Board of Education, where he remained until 1932. After 1932 he became a regular contributor to British journals; in 1939 his first book, *Life of Edmund Burke,* was published. He was a member of the executive committee and treasurer of the Anglo-Jewish Association, and a member of the executive committee of the Jewish Historical Society.

MAGNUS, RUDOLF, physician and pharmacologist, b. Braunschweig, Germany, 1873; d. Pontresina, Italy, 1927. He was baptized in his childhood. Magnus studied medicine at the University of Heidelberg, where he became professor of pharmacology in 1904, remaining until 1908. In 1908 he was called to the University of Utrecht, Holland, where he served as professor of pharmacology until his death, except for an interval during the first World War, when he returned to Germany for scientific service to the country whose citizenship he retained during his entire life. Magnus also worked in various British laboratories in 1900, 1905 and 1908.

In the field of pharmacology alone, Magnus specialized in the influence of certain drugs on the intestinal tract and the nervous system. Much of his investigation had to do with digitalis, and he was responsible for the international standard example of this drug. But he was also an experimental physiologist of importance, and had concentrated on investigating the functions of the central nervous system and the reflex mechanisms of body posture in relation to the earth's movement. Despite his retention of German citizenship, Magnus was a member of the Holland commission for revising pharmacopoeia, and he served in two international conferences on biological standards. Magnus died just as a laboratory, endowed by the Rockefeller Foundation, was being completed in Utrecht for his use. He was the author of many scientific papers. Among his larger works were *Vom Urtier zum Menschen* (1908) and *Wilhelm Boelsche* (1909).

Lit.: Huebner, W., "Rudolf Magnus' Gedächtnisrede," *Klinische Wochenschrift* (1927); Liljestrand, G., "Nachruf auf Rudolf Magnus," *Ergebnisse der Physiologie* (1929) 647-55; *Nature* (London), vol. 120 (1927) 414-15.

MAGOG, see Gog and Magog.

MAGYAR MAHMOUD PASHA (Fishel Freind), Turkish commander and governor, b. Brzeziny, near Lodz, Russian Poland, 1828; d. Beirut, Syria, 1885. He was apprenticed to a watchmaker, but when his father, who sold lottery tickets, won "the big prize" with one of the unsold tickets, Fishel, then fifteen, helped himself to part of the winnings and ran away. With a companion of twenty he wandered about from town to town until he found himself in Hungary, penniless. His companion went back to Brzeziny but Fishel sang in the streets for his living, learned Hungarian, became Ferdinand instead of Fishel, and finally found a job in a wine shop.

A Hungarian officer who was a patron of the wine shop took Fishel or Ferdinand for a servant and had his secular education improved somewhat. Freind was now twenty. The Hungarian revolt against Austria in 1848 found many supporters among the Jews; Freind, too, joined the Hungarians under Lajos Kossuth. He soon distinguished himself by his bravery. He was decorated and commissioned an officer. When the revolt was suppressed, Freind, like Kossuth, fled to Turkey.

In Turkey Freind, who had left Orthodox Judaism for the Reform Judaism with which he had become ac-

Gusztáv Magyar-Mannheimer

quainted in Hungary, now dropped Judaism for Mohammedanism and as Mahmoud Hamid (*hamid* is the Turkish for *freind,* which is the Yiddish for "friend") entered the Turkish army. A colonel in the war with the Slavs of Montenegro (1876), he again distinguished himself. After the Russo-Turkish war of 1877, Magyar Mahmoud, who had been raised to the rank of pasha, was exiled to Rhodes in company with the minister of war and other defeated commanders. Here he is said to have visited the chief rabbi of the island often to engage him in Biblical and Talmudic discussions. He was, afterwards, it is reported, appointed governor of Syria, where the Druses and Maronites were troublesome, and proved to be, it is added, an excellent and honest administrator.

Freind or Hamid, according to the traditions of Brzeziny, did not forget his relatives there and sent them money and gifts. When his brother-in-law, a certain Israel Krüger, visited him in Constantinople, Krüger returned to Brzeziny with many gifts and a snuff-box for the rabbi—which was considered proof among the Jews of the town that the pasha was still a Jew at heart.

Lit.: Galanté, Abraham, *Turcs et Juifs* (1932) 110-11; Kahan, Israel, "A Jewish Grand Vizier," *Jewish Chronicle Supplement* (London), Dec. 25, 1925, pp. vi-vii.

MAGYAR-MANNHEIMER, GUSZTÁV, painter, b. Pest, Hungary, 1859; d. Budapest, 1937. His adventurous years of study foreshadowed the extremes of his artistic personality and helped him acquire an almost universal skill and conception of two-dimensional art. As a schoolboy he earned his living by doing woodcuts for novel illustrations, and at the same time attended the evening course of the Graphic School, where Bertalan Székely was his master. At this time he made drawings of tramps, of the inhabitants of the slums. He was discovered by the painter

Mihály Zichy, spurned an opportunity to be taken to Paris, and studied instead at the Academy of Vienna, drawing illustrations at night in order to be able to pay his fees. Photo-retouching in the Russo-Turkish war, assisting the steel-engraver Leonhard Raab in Munich, and collaborating with Makart on the murals with which the well-known Austria painter was decorating the Museum of Art History, Vienna, marked further stages in his apprenticeship. The influence of Makart was congenial to his own romantic and heroic temperament. In such paintings as *Venus and Tannhäuser* he wanted to revive the great style of the baroque masters. He painted allegories and sketched frescoes, some of which he was subsequently allowed to execute in the Royal Palace and in the cafes New York and Bodo at Budapest.

A trip to Italy made him discover another self: an analyst of color and light. His Italian landscapes are among his greatest masterpieces, some of them rounded and organized, breathing idyllic serenity, others astorm with a grandiose passion. In 1901 he had success both in Venice and in Budapest; his painting *Spring* was then acquired for the Venice Gallery.

On his return to Hungary he painted a number of landscapes in the heroic style, among them *Storm over Lake Balaton; Landscape in the Vág Valley; Landscape in the Great Plain.* Although he had a negative attitude toward the school of impressionism then prevalent in Hungary, he could not help being influenced by it. Some of his later landscapes project the picturesque and romantic Magyar countryside.

His varied experience of technique made him an artist passionately bent on new ways of interpreting beauty.

Magyar-Mannheimer was awarded several gold medals. Twenty of his paintings are in the Museum of Fine Arts, Budapest; several were bought by Francis Joseph I and by Italian galleries. He was member and founder of art societies. Yet he did not belong to any group or school of painters, official honors bestowed on him were scarce, he had no immediate followers, and died at the age of seventy-eight, towering in his artistic and human isolation.   ANNA BETTELHEIM.

Lit.: Eisler, M. J., "Magyar-Mannheimer Gusztáv," *Magyar Müvészet,* vol. 5 (1929) 121; Pesti Futár, *Életrajzok* (1928); Rózsa, Nicolas, "Gustave Magyar-Mannheimer," *Nouvelle Revue de Hongrie* (1937) 167; *Magyar Zsidó Lexikon,* p. 552.

MAH NISHTANNAH, *see* HAGGADAH, PASSOVER.

MAH TOBU, the beginning of *Num.* 24:5, "How goodly are thy tents, O Jacob, thy dwellings, O Israel," which is applied in the Talmud to the synagogues. Hence the sentence is frequently found as an inscription over the entrance of synagogues. It is also the first of a number of loosely arranged verses from the Bible which have been placed in the beginning of the prayer-books for the German and Polish ritual ever since the first printed copies were issued. The paragraph is to be recited on entering the synagogue for the Morning Service. In modern times these verses were set to music.

Lit.: Elbogen, I., *Der jüdische Gottesdienst,* 87, 526; Singer, S., and Abrahams, I., *The Authorised Daily Prayer Book* (1922) 2, vi; Idelsohn, A. Z., *Jewish Liturgy* (1932) 73-74.

MAHAMAD (MAAMAD), a phrase meaning the leaders of the people meeting in prayer, primarily identified with the board of trustees of the Spanish and Portuguese congregations. The powers of the Mahamad were all-inclusive in the congregations of Amsterdam, and later in England. Its regulations, called the Ascamoth, governed not only the synagogal life of the Jews but their general life as well. Both in Amsterdam and in the Bevis Marks Synagogue in London, which adopted the Amsterdam code of decorum practically in its entirety, severity marked the arrangement. The Mahamad had the power to grant the right to marry and to divorce; no Hebrew book could be published without its consent; seating arrangements were under its control, and non-Sephardic Jews could pray in the synagogue only with its permission. In the 17th and 18th centuries, in England, no Jew could buy or rent a house from another Jew without the sanction of the Mahamad. The Mahamad is known to have once forced a London Jew to turn over to it evidence with which he was threatening to betray a Portuguese Marrano family to the Portuguese authorities because he could not collect a debt from the Marranos.

The Mahamad consisted of four directors and a treasurer, chosen by the Yehidim, or members of the synagogue. No near relatives could serve on the Mahamad at the same time. Those refusing to accept posts in the synagogue were subject to fine. One of the last instances of this was in the case of Isaac Disraeli, who was fined forty pounds for refusing to accept the post of warden (1813). This conflict was one of the superficial reasons offered for Disraeli's eventual desertion of Judaism. To the 19th cent., too, belongs the excommunication by the Mahamad of London of those Jews who formed the Liberal Synagogue. Thereafter, however, the power of the Mahamad decreased rapidly. Though the term is still used to describe the board of trustees of the English Spanish and Portuguese synagogues, the activities of the group are entirely synagogal and directive. In America, the term "ajunto" was used, rather than Mahamad, in early references to the board of trustees. In Continental Europe the Spanish and Portuguese congregations use the term Mahamad in conversation, but the official term for the board of trustees is usually a word from the language of the country in which the synagogue is located, and the powers are always limited.

Lit.: Gaster, Moses, *History of the Ancient Synagogue of the Spanish and Portuguese Jews* (1901); Picciotto, James, *Sketches of Anglo-Jewish History* (1875).

MAHARAM, abbreviation of the Hebrew words *Morenu Harab Rabbi M.* ("our teacher, Rabbi M."); it is used frequently in the case of famous rabbis whose names begin with that initial. Among these are Meir of Rothenburg (d. 1293); Moses Minz, rabbi in Bamberg in 1469; Moses Alsheich (16th cent.); Moses Alashkar (16th cent.); Meir Katzenellenbogen of Padua (d. 1565); Moses di Trani (d. 1585); Moses Galante (d. 1608); Meir Lublin (d. 1616); Meir Schiff of Fulda (d. about 1644); Mordecai Süsskind Rothenburg, rabbi in Witzenhausen in 1682; Moses Habib (d. 1688); Meir de Boton of Gallipoli (17th cent.); Meir Asch (d. 1744); Moses Hagiz (d. about 1750); Meir Barby of Pressburg (d. 1789); Meir Asch of Ungvar (d. 1851 or 1852); Mordecai Broda (d. 1882).

MAHARIK, see Colon, Joseph.

MAHARIL, see Jacob ben Moses Halevi.

MAHARSHA, see Edels, Samuel Eliezer ben Judah Halevi.

MAHARSHAL, see Luria, Solomon ben Jehiel.

MAHLER, ARTHUR, art historian, government official and Jewish nationalist, b. Prague, 1872; d. Vienna, 1916. After a short career in his father's machine business, Mahler turned to the study of archeology and art, and in 1902 was made lecturer in classical archeology at the German University in Prague, as well as professor at the American Archaeology Institute in Rome. His lectures, given in English, were published under the title *Paintings of the Louvre, Italian and Spanish,* and were a valuable guidebook for the Louvre. Mahler was chosen to represent the Galician electoral district of Czotkow-Trembola in the Austrian Reichstag in 1907. He remained a member of the Reichstag until 1911, all the while adhering openly to his pro-Zionist principles and belonging to the Parliamentary "Jewish Club," which had four members. Anti-Semitic agitation finally forced Mahler to relinquish his teaching position at the German University in Prague. He traveled extensively at various periods in his life, and was for some time a member of the editorial staff of the *Pester Lloyd* and of the *Illustriertes Extrablatt.* Mahler was the author of *Polyklet und seine Schule* (1902) and *Die Juden und die Freiheit der Wissenschaften* (1909).

MAHLER, EDE (EDUARD), orientalist, b. Cziffer, Pozsony county, Hungary, 1857. His father was rabbi at Cziffer and gave his son an early and thorough instruction in Hebrew, Aramaic, Bible and Talmud. At the age of twelve young Mahler was able to conduct independent studies in Talmud and rabbinic literature, but he also had to earn his living, his father being very poor. He graduated from the Gymnasium at Pozsony (Pressburg), and studied mathematics and astronomy at the Universities of Vienna and Budapest, where he also took up Semitic languages and Egyptology. After receiving his Ph.D. degree from the University of Budapest in 1880, he published, for several years, a number of original and important articles on mathematics, especially on the theory of surfaces. As assistant to Oppoltzer at the Vienna Observatory, he published (1885) the result of his research on the eclipses of the 20th cent. and was led on to research on the eclipse in ancient Egypt to which he held that the Bible refers. His "Astronomische Untersuchungen über in hebräischen Schriften erwähnte Finsternisse" appeared in the reports of the Vienna Academy of Sciences (1885), and from that time on he turned more and more to the astronomy and chronology of the ancient Orient, relinquishing the pursuit of pure mathematics and publishing *Biblische Chronologie und Zeitrechnung der Hebräer* (1887); *Maimonides' Kiddusch Hachodesch* (1889); *Anleitung zu den Grundzügen der Chronologie* (1889).

In 1895 Mahler returned to Budapest, where he served at the institute of trigonometric measurements (1896) and as custodian of the National Museum (1898). That same year he became instructor at the University of Budapest for the languages, archeology

and history of civilization of the ancient Orient. In 1909 the Hungarian Academy of Sciences elected him a member; he became assistant professor in 1910 and full professor in 1914, retiring in 1928 after thirty years of service. In 1924 he became a member of the Arabic Academy of Damascus and a member of the board of governors of the rabbinical seminary of Budapest.

He traveled in the Middle East, publishing the results of his research in Egypt in *Ethnographia* (new series, vol. 6, 1910). He also supervised the excavations at the site of an old Roman settlement at Dunapentele, where the oldest monument testifying to the presence of Jews in what is now Hungary was found.

In 1937 the university and the rabbinical seminary of Budapest jointly published a volume to celebrate his eightieth birthday. He wrote over 270 works, contributing in English, German, Hebrew, French and Hungarian to forty-six journals of science.

His published books include: *Der Kalender der Babylonier* (2 vols., 1892-93); *Adalékok az egyiptomi nyelvhez* (Notes on the Egyptian Language; 1901); *Der Pharaoh des Exodus* (1896); *Babylonien und die Bibel* (1903); *A legregibb törvénygyüjtemény* (The Oldest Collection of Laws; 1904); *Babylonien und Assyrien* (1906); *Die historische Bedeutung der aramäischen Papyrusdokumente von Assuan und Elefantine* (1911); *Ókori kronológiai kutatások* (Research on the Chronology of Antiquity; 1915); *Biblische Chronologie* (2 vols.); *Handbuch der jüdischen Chronologie* (1916); *Naptárunk ujjálakitása és a husvéti kérdés* (The Reform of Our Calendar and the Question of Easter [Passover]; 1917); *Zur Chronologie der El-Amarna Zeit* (1923); *Keleti tanulmányok* (Oriental Studies. On the Time of the Exodus of the Jews from Egypt; 1925); *Vergleichungstabellen der muhammedanischen und christlichen Zeitrechnung* (1926). In 1937 Mahler was preparing his work *Leiden und Auferstehung Christi. Zur Osterfrage.* In 1939 he was still contributing to the *Magyar Zsidó Szemle* articles on chronology and the Jewish calendar.

Anna Bettelheim.

MAHLER, FRITZ, conductor and composer, nephew of Gustav, b. Vienna, 1901. He studied music with Guido Adler, Alban Berg and Arnold Schönberg. In 1922 he made his debut as conductor at the Vienna Volksoper. From 1929 to 1932 he was director of orchestral concerts over the Berlin radio. In 1930 he served as a conductor of the Dresden Philharmonic, and from 1932 to 1936 he was principal conductor of the Copenhagen Symphony Orchestra. He came to the United States in 1936, where he has since been active as a conductor of symphony concerts and opera. Mahler composed several orchestral works, chamber music compositions, and songs.

MAHLER, GUSTAV, world-famous composer and conductor, b. Kalischt, Bohemia, 1860; d. Vienna, 1911. He was a student of Anton Bruckner and Julius Epstein at the Vienna Conservatory, winning awards for composition and piano playing.

As a composer, Mahler enriched music with nine symphonies, *Das Lied von der Erde,* the *Kindertotenlieder, Das Klagende Lied,* and a number of songs. At the bottom of Mahler's creative work lies an ele-

Gustav Mahler

mental musical instinct. While the spiritual undertone of his music was at first decidedly romantic, his subsequent development shows the conflict and blending of romantic and classic elements. To the classic attitude belongs his positive will to put the musical stream into solid forms, to curb and master his virile power, his imagination, and his emotions. Romantic—in a wider sense—was his daring and unbounded imagination, the "nocturnal" in him, the "nature sound," as was also his inclination to extremes, and to utilize even the grotesque in order to achieve the desired expression, but, above all, the intermingling of poetic and other concepts with his musical imagination. It was a violently agitated world of music, of passionate humanity, poetic imagination, philosophic thought, and religious emotion with which he wrestled. However, inasmuch as, in addition to an exuberant heart, he was gifted with the power of formulation, he succeeded in subjecting his highly individual musical language to the domination of symphonic form. This form, in turn, became regnant in his creative work. He developed it to increasingly loftier and newer expression by the firm grasp of a substance which, in its diversity, richness, and fluctuation, originally had bordered upon the chaotic.

Even when he wrote his *First Symphony* Mahler was wholly under the spell of the symphonic idea, although, in its fundamental intentions, the work may be called the creed of his heart set to music. Beginning with the *Second Symphony,* he pursued more consciously and strictly the path of the symphonic artist who develops, from a thematic core, the structure of movements, with close adherence to form, and is unswerved by emotional excess, poetic thought, or even by musical inspiration, unwilling to sacrifice the principle of organic compactness of a movement. Indeed, Mahler continued to develop symphonic forms

—but with all the audacity of modulation, of intensified treatment of motives—until their dimensions assumed gigantic proportions. His creations remained symphonic organisms in which the thought of the whole was ever present in minutest detail. Here we see him following closely in the footsteps of Beethoven. There are, however, also Schubert and Bruckner influences in the melodiously joyful flow of some of the themes and in the gaily Austrian character of certain melodies. Only by looking upon Mahler's work as the musical manifestation of a great soul can we gain a correct appraisal of him. Standards of humanity need to be added to those of art for a full appreciation of the creative work of Mahler.

His first important engagement as opera conductor was at Leipzig, where he attracted attention also with a performance of Mendelssohn's *St. Paul.* Then followed engagements at the opera houses in Prague and Budapest, and, in 1891, at the Hamburg Opera.

It was in Hamburg that the writer first worked with Mahler in the capacity of coach and director of the chorus. Youthful experience permitted him but vaguely to sense and appreciate Mahler's complex inner life: his astonishing mental range, the conflicts of his soul, the dark powers with which he wrestled, the yearning which was the leit-motif of his life and work. Mahler's work at the Budapest Opera and later in Hamburg had aroused the enthusiasm of leading European musicians. In 1897, upon the recommendation of Brahms and Guido Adler, Mahler was chosen director of the Vienna Opera. Four years later he called the writer to the same institution to serve as assistant conductor under him, thus gaining an enviable opportunity to witness Mahler's artistic activity in Vienna for six consecutive years.

The Mahler epoch at the Vienna Opera was a ten-year feast to which a great artist invited co-workers and devotees. What a stroke of good fortune in the history of music that the rich resources of a noble institution of art were, for a decade, from 1897 to 1907, placed at the disposal of a musical genius, a man of general spiritual force, passionately devoted to the stage, and that this period of activity coincided with the prime of Mahler's life and with a period of comparative political tranquillity. He was then indeed at the zenith of his career. His powers derived new vigor from the lavishness with which he expended them and from the artistic accomplishments to whose importance his own instinct and public acclaim bore witness. And there was no end to giving.

Concerning the general public's attitude toward Mahler's activity, particularly during his last years in Vienna, it may be said that, while the best remained his followers to the very day of his departure, admiring the daring spirit that penetrated beyond accepted theories into the realm of the problematic and approving the ruthless vehemence with which he pursued his artistic goals, his fanaticism, and the personal harshness of his expressions made him many enemies among the more commonplace and faint-hearted of his co-workers. His dauntlessness in the domain of art also aroused antagonism among the more conservative public and press. They looked with disfavor upon the uncomfortably new, failing to realize that the experiment of today creates the law of tomorrow.

In October, 1907, Mahler parted from the Vienna Opera with a performance of *Fidelio* and, in November, with a presentation of his *Second Symphony,* he said farewell to his Vienna friends whose expressions of love, loyalty, and sorrow, occasioned by the news of his leaving, had deeply pleased and moved him. A great epoch of operatic art had come to an end—the achievements of one man and of his inspired co-workers. Everyone had learned from him, everyone had been led to the utmost of his capacity. The achievements of his art are still looked upon as the unforgotten days of glory of the Vienna Opera.

At the bottom of Mahler's impetuous production and interpretation of music there was an inexorable exactness. As conductor he rendered strict obedience to the musical score, to the value of its notes, and to its direction concerning time, delivery, and dynamics; he demanded this also of all his co-workers. He asked for an instrumental exactness from his singers and was never satisfied until the last measure of precision had been achieved by all. His insistence upon absolute musical clearness was commensurate with the clearness of his conducting and the exemplary beat of his baton, the distinctness of which was not impaired by even the most violent emotion.

Mahler's most striking characteristic and strength as conductor, however, was his warmness of heart, a quality that infused his interpretations with the impressiveness of a personal avowal and made one forget all the painstaking rehearsals, all traces of his educational work, all virtuosity and perfection of execution, and made the music he produced into a spontaneous message from soul to soul.

In December, 1907, Mahler went to the United States for the first time. During the next year he officiated as conductor, first at the Metropolitan Opera House, then both at the Metropolitan and at Carnegie Hall with the New York Philharmonic Orchestra. Suffering from heart trouble for a long time, he collapsed in 1911 and was taken to Paris for serum treatments. In May he was carried back to Vienna, a dying man. Messages of friendship and reverence, which found their way to his sick-bed, gave him great pleasure and comfort. He died on the 18th of May.

BRUNO WALTER.

Lit.: Engel, Gabriel, *Gustav Mahler: Song-Symphonist* (1932); Ewen, David and Frederic, *Musical Vienna* (1939); Stefan, Paul, *Gustav Mahler* (1913); Walter, Bruno, *Gustav Mahler* (1941).

MAHLER, RAPHAEL, Jewish historian, b. Nowy Sacz, district of Cracow, Poland, 1899. He studied philosophy, sociology and history at the University of Vienna (Ph.D., 1922). From 1924 to 1937 he taught general and Jewish history at the Gymnasium and at the Lyceum "Ascola," in Warsaw. In 1937 he emigrated to the United States.

Mahler wrote extensively in the field of Jewish history, his special subjects being the socio-economic history of the Jews in Poland, the history of the Jewish social and religious movements, and the theory of Jewish historiography. His investigations were carried out chiefly in cooperation with the Yiddish Scientific Institute of Vilna (in 1942 in New York). He was active in the Warsaw branch of the Polish Historical Society.

From his early youth Mahler identified himself with the Jewish workers' movement. He contributed to and edited such publications as *Der Yunger Historiker* (1926-29) and *Bleter far Geshichte* (1934-39), year books of the IVO (Yiddish Scientific Institute); *Dos Virtshaftliche Lebn;* and *Fraie Yugnt* (all in Warsaw). He headed the Jewish Workers Educational Society in Poland (Geselshaft Ovent Kursn far Arbeter) until 1931, when it was dissolved by the Polish government.

About thirty of his articles on the history of Jewish communities in Poland were published in the *Encyclopaedia Judaica* (Berlin). He also contributed to the *Universal Jewish Encyclopedia.*

Among his works are: *Sources of the History of the Jews in Poland during the Middle Ages* (Polish and Yiddish; Warsaw, 1930); *Jewish Emancipation, a Selection of Documents* (New York, 1941); *Haskole Un Chsides in Galitzie* (New York, 1942); "Antisemitism in Poland," in *Essays on Antisemitism* (New York, 1942).

Lit.: A short biography of Mahler is included in the *Essays on Antisemitism* (1942); Mukdoni, A., in *Morgn Zhurnal,* March 4, 1942; Niger, S., in *Tog,* Feb. 28, 1942.

MAHOMET, *see* MOHAMMED.

MAHOZA, Babylonian city on the Tigris river. Due to its proximity to the royal canal Nehar Malka, it was known also as Mahoza-Malka. Mahoza was situated a short distance to the south of Ctesiphon, the Parthian capital; the influence of this latter city on the former was such that it became notorious for the frivolous, luxurious and dissolute life of its inhabitants, to which various caustic references in the Talmud testify (*R.H.* 17a; *Sab.* 109a; *Taan.* 26a). On the other hand, the citizens of Mahoza also bore a reputation for intelligence and charitableness (*Ber.* 59; *B.K.* 119a).

The population of the city consisted almost entirely of Jews, many of whom were descended from proselytes. About the middle of the 3rd cent. an academy was established there by Joseph bar Hama, the father of Raba. When the latter, one of the greatest of the Amoraim, became head of the academy, it attained an importance in the field of Talmudic studies which enabled it for a period to eclipse even Pumbeditha.

The city was destroyed by the army of Julian the Apostate in 363, during the war between the Romans and Persians. It was later rebuilt, and for a while in a later period was the capital of a small Jewish principality, headed by the exilarch, Mar Zutra II. This came to an end in 520, when the Persians under King Kobad defeated Mar Zutra's Jewish army. The prince himself was put to death, and the inhabitants of Mahoza were taken into captivity.

In the 6th cent. a town known as Antiocheia-Rumia was established near the former site of Mahoza by Chosroes II Anushirwan. While the population was largely recruited from war captives from Antioch, many Jews also settled there. The majority of this Jewish population was exterminated by their massacre at the hands of the Persian general Mebodes, when he took the town during a civil war at the end of the 6th cent.

MAHPACH, *see* CANTILLATION.

MÄHRISCH-OSTRAU (in Czechoslovakian, **Moravská Ostrava**), city with about 130,000 inhabitants, including the suburbs, of whom about 8,000 were Jews (1937). It is situated at the borders of three countries or provinces, Moravia, Silesia and Poland, in the center of large coal deposits and iron industries. The Jewish population is composed of emigrants from Moravia, Slovakia, Silesia, Vienna and nearby Poland. As a result, varied religious and political ideas prevail in the community. The last election showed an equality among the Jewish inhabitants between the pure "Democrats" and Zionists. Jewish community life in Mährisch-Ostrau was rich in activity up to the Nazi German occupation (1938-39). It was the seat of the congress of the Moravian Jews, whose chairman, M. Hilf, was for many years president of the community, and of the Zionist Party, whose chairman was Joseph Rufeisen.

The Jewish community has had a relatively short history, compared with the other communities of Moravia. There is record (1792) of the first Jew to settle there (Mordecai Schönhof). Simon Frankl came from Ungarisch-Brod (1832) and founded a cultural society which had the first Minyan (quorum of ten men for religious services) in the city. A cemetery was laid out in 1872, and in 1875 an independent community was established. The small communities of Hrabuvka, Marienberg, Přivoz, Vitkovice, Zábreh, Hermanice, Hrušov, Kunčičky, Michelkovice and Radvanice all formed part of the community of Mährisch-Ostrau, most of them until 1938.

In 1879 a great temple was dedicated, with Rabbi Adolf Jellinek delivering the sermon. In 1911 a temple was dedicated in Vitkovice, and in 1926 an Orthodox synagogue in Mährisch-Ostrau. The first community president was Martin Strassman (to 1903); Jacob Spira (1897 on) was the most important rabbi.

The Jewish school, established in 1863, is of interest as indicative in part of the change in the intellectual and cultural life of the Jews, since it developed from a strictly private school into a general public school of Jewish character. The language used, for the most part German, was later changed to Czech. The young community of Mährisch-Ostrau was also the first in Czechoslovakia to provide an endowment for the founding of a national home in Palestine.

From the beginning of the Nazi regime in Germany, Mährisch-Ostrau offered a place of refuge to many German emigrants. An organization of German and, later, Austrian Jews forced into Eastern Europe was formed in the city. After the Nazis' march on Vienna it received thousands of Jews. When the Nazis seized Czechoslovakia, it was one of the first of the larger cities occupied by them. The Jews were, for the most part, robbed of their possessions, Jewish establishments were taken over, and many Jews were sent to Poland (1939-41). Nevertheless, the rest maintained close connection with the Jews of Moravia and the other part of Czechoslovakia. Until just before the outbreak of the second World War thousands of Jews and later also Czechs found secret ways of going to Poland and Russia from the city, to escape Nazi persecutions. However, they were not permitted to go unpunished; in 1940 only a few Jews remained in Mährisch-Ostrau; their lives were beset with difficulties. OSCAR FRANKL.

MAHZOR, *see* PRAYER-BOOKS; MAHZOR VITRY.

MAHZOR VITRY, the best-known and most comprehensive Mahzor (prayer-book for the holidays), compiled by Simhah ben Samuel of Vitry (d. about 1105). It contains the texts of the various prayers, commentaries and explanations of the text, rules and prescriptions from all provinces of the Jewish ceremonial and religious law, formularies for all possible documents, and a large number of Piyutim (liturgical poems), both known and unknown. The Mahzor Vitry was discovered by Samuel David Luzzatto; it was published for the first time in the recension of S. Hurwitz (Berlin, 1889-93), according to a manuscript contained in the British Museum.

Lit.: Mabo Lemahzor Vitry; Elbogen, I., *Der jüdische Gottesdienst,* 363; Dembitz, L. N., *Jewish Services* (1898).

MAIBAUM, RICHARD WALTER, playwright, b. New York city, 1909. He received his M.A. degree from the University of Iowa in 1932 and taught there that same year. In 1935 he joined the staff of scenario writers of Metro-Goldwyn-Mayer. His play, *Birthright,* dealing with the sufferings of some of the Jewish refugees from Nazi Germany, was produced in New York city in 1933, and a second play, *Sweet Mystery of Life,* in 1935. In 1942 Maibaum was living in California and collaborating in the writing of motion picture scenarios.

MAIMON, ABRAHAM BEN MOSES (called also Abraham Maimuni, and Abulmeni), physician and scholar, b. Fostat, Egypt, 1186; d. Fostat, 1237. He succeeded his father Maimonides in the office of Nagid, i.e. head of the Egyptian Jews, and like him was active as a physician at the Egyptian court. The reputation he enjoyed among the Jews in Egypt and in the entire Orient he owed not merely to his father's renown, but also to his own learning, which elevated him far above the average of the Oriental savants of his time, even though he was by no means a distinguished personality. His mental and religious bent was wholly determined by his father, whom he honored exceedingly. He resolutely combatted various attacks directed against his father. With purely learned explanations he opposed the objections which an Oriental savant, Daniel ben Saadia Hababli, had raised to the Talmudic writings of Maimonides. But it was with deep indignation that he repelled the suspicions which had been cast upon the religious sentiments of Maimonides by the anti-Maimunists of Provence and Spain and had led to the passionate controversy with reference to the *Moreh Nebuchim.*

Maimuni wrote a comprehensive Halachic code, one part of which deals in a philosophic manner with questions of ethics, and an unfinished commentary on the Pentateuch, both in Arabic. The former was edited and published with an English translation under the name of *The High Ways to Perfection* by Samuel Rosenblatt (vol. 1, New York, 1927; vol. 2, New York, 1938). He wrote also a public letter, called "Sefer Milhamoth Adonai" (The book of the Wars of the Lord; cf. *Num.* 21:14), addressed to the anti-Maimunists, the opponents of his father's philosophical system. In 1938, at Jerusalem, Abraham Hayim Freimann published his responsa (Hebrew).

Lit.: Eppenstein, *Abraham Maimuni, sein Leben und*

seine Schriften (1914); Graetz, H., *History of the Jews,* vol. 3 (1927) 523; Neubauer, Adolf, *Medieval Jewish Chronicles,* vol. 1 (1887) 134.

MAIMON, SALOMON BEN JOSHUA, philosopher, b. Nieszwicz, Lithuania, 1753; d. Nieder-Siegersdorf, Silesia, 1800. His original name was Salomon ben Joshua, but he later assumed the surname Maimon by reason of his reverence for Maimonides. He was taught Hebrew and Talmud by his learned father and in the Heder of Mirz, the nearest little town. Later he spent six months in the Yeshiva of Iwenetz, where the rabbi gave him private instruction. At the age of seven he was able to study the Talmud by himself. At eleven he was married off by his father, and at the age of fourteen he was a father himself. "My life in Poland from my marriage to my emigration," Maimon said in his autobiography, "was a series of miseries with a want of all means for the promotion of culture." Dissatisfied with the Talmud and the method of teaching it, he read secretly, against his father's will, astronomical and historical books written in Hebrew. He studied Cabala, which he characterized later as "enlarged Spinozism," and one day he began to plunge into Maimonides' *Moreh Nebuchim.* He wrote a commentary on this work (*Gibeath Hamoreh*) but he could not afford to edit it as long as he lived in Lithuania. This commentary is by no means a mere interpretation of the text but the outline of his original philosophical thoughts.

In 1778 Maimon went to Königsberg to study medicine. He had learned German without teacher or grammar, having laboriously deciphered the German alphabet, but he was not yet able to pronounce German correctly when he arrived at Königsberg. Some Jewish students there provided him with small means and sent him to Berlin. But there he was repulsed as a vagabond. Desperately he wandered through Prussia for six months until Rabbi Hirsch Janower, at Posen, took care of him and provided for his maintenance for two years. Then Maimon went to Berlin, armed with recommendations, and was supported by Moses Mendelssohn, Lazarus Bendavid and Marcus Herz. In Berlin he studied German philosophers, especially Leibnitz and Wolff, and wrote critical articles which were appreciated by his protectors.

But soon Maimon scandalized Mendelssohn by his conduct of life and his radical ideas. He left Berlin and again wandered for years. He went to Holland, sojourned at Hamburg and Dessau, and at Altona supplied his long-felt want of secular education by attending a public school. It was at Hamburg that Maimon one day, despairing of his future, decided to be converted to Protestantism. But he presented to the clergyman a declaration to the effect that he considered Judaism nearer to the truth than Christianity, and that only practical reasons were influencing him to adopt the Christian religion. The clergyman therefore declined to baptize him.

Having completed his studies at Altona, Maimon went to Breslau, and was assisted by Ephraim Kuh and by the philosopher Garve, a friend of Mendelssohn. There Maimon translated Mendelssohn's *Morgenstunden* into Hebrew. After Mendelssohn's death, Maimon returned to Berlin, but he was still unable to get a secure position until, in 1790, Count Adolf

Salomon ben Joshua Maimon

Kalckreuth offered him a refuge on his estate at Nieder-Siegersdorf, where Maimon spent the last ten years of his life. Kalckreuth was interested in Maimon because of his critical remarks on Kant's philosophy, which Maimon began to study in 1788.

In 1790 Maimon published his first book, *Versuch über die Transcendentalphilosophie,* which attracted the attention of the greatest philosophers of that time. Kant acknowledged Maimon as the most acute of all his critics. Maimon's later publications, however, were criticized less favorably by Kant. In 1791 Maimon published a fragment of a dictionary of philosophical terms, *Philosophisches Wörterbuch,* which contains a collection of Maimon's articles previously printed in periodicals. In 1792 he edited his *Kommentar zur More Newuchim des Maimonides* and the treatise *Ankündigung und Aufforderung zu einer allgemeinen Revision der Wissenschaften.* In the same year the German psychologist Karl Philipp Moritz edited Maimon's autobiography, *Salomon Maimons Leben,* which was translated into several languages. It proves that Maimon, despite the fact that he once tried to be baptized, remained loyal to Judaism. He describes Jewish life in Lithuania and the doctrine of Cabala and of Maimonides, and vindicates the Jewish religion and morals, especially rabbinic morality, against misunderstanding and anti-Semitic accusations. Similarly, in the preface to his *Versuch über die Transcendentalphilosophie,* dedicated to the king of Poland, Maimon pleaded in favor of his coreligionists. In 1793 he published his treatise *Über die Progressen der Philosophie,* in 1794 *Versuch einer neuen Logik,* and in 1797 *Kritische Untersuchungen über den menschlichen Geist.* Besides, he wrote notes and commentaries on Bacon and Aristotle, and two works in Hebrew (*Taalumoth Hochmah* and *Heshek Shelomoh*) which were not published.   Hugo Bieber.

Lit.: Kuntze, Friedrich, *Die Philosophie Salomon Maimons* (1912); Cassirer, Ernst, *Das Erkenntnisproblem,* vol. 3 (1923); Rosenbaum, Curt, *Die Philosophie Salomon Maimons in seinem hebräischen Kommentar zur More Nebukim des Maimonides* (1928).

The grave of Maimonides at Tiberias (left); a hypothetical likeness (right) of Maimonides

MAIMONIDES (properly, Moses ben Maimon; often called RaMBaM, from his title of rabbi and the initials of his name; his Arabic name was Abu Imran Musa ibn Maimun ibn Abdallah), the most important Jewish philosopher and codifier of the Middle Ages, and a physician of note.

1. Life. Maimonides was born in Cordova, Spain, on Nisan 14, 1135. From his father, Maimon ben Joseph, he received his first instruction in Bible, Talmud and mathematics, and later on Arabic teachers introduced him to philosophy and the natural sciences, especially medicine. When he was thirteen, Cordova was conquered by the fanatical Almohades, who compelled non-believers to accept Islam or to emigrate. Like the majority of the members of the Cordova Jewish community, Maimon and his family left the city, and about the year 1160 arrived in Fez, Morocco. Here, too, the Jews were forced to confess Mohammed as prophet and to visit the mosques. In 1160 Maimon addressed an admonitory epistle in Arabic to the Jewish communities, in which he urged them to endure their lot to the end and to continue to practise Jewish customs.

Moses Maimonides was associated in Fez with Mohammedan physicians and philosophers, continued his studies there, and began to work on his commentary on the Mishnah. In his *Iggereth Hashemad* (Epistle on Apostasy) he defended those Jews who perforce confessed Islam with their lips, but he advised those who were able to do so to emigrate. The family of Maimon, seeing that their lives were in danger in Fez, emigrated to Palestine in 1165. But this restless country was no place of rest for them, so they left Acco, journeyed through the country and settled in Egypt, where Maimon died. Maimonides, who suffered from bodily complaints and often from the slanders of informers, finally came to the conclusion that he had to pursue a practical vocation, after his younger brother David, who had supported both of them through his trade in jewels, had perished in the Indian Ocean. He thus became a physician in Fostat (Old Cairo) and gave public lectures on philosophy. In 1168 he completed his commentary on the Mishnah, written in Arabic and called *Siraj* (Illumination).

In 1171 Sultan Saladin attained to rulership over the country, and under his sway Egypt became a refuge for the persecuted Jews. Maimonides addressed a consolatory epistle, *Iggereth Teman* (Epistle of Teman, i.e. Yemen), to the Jews of Yemen, who at that time were bitterly persecuted. Although not welcomed by the local Jewish scholars, Maimonides was already a recognized rabbinical authority, with the result that questions of religious law were referred to him from far-off communities in the West as well as the East. In the midst of his strenuous activity in communal affairs, and his continued studies in the Talmud, philosophy and the natural sciences, he completed, in 1180, his second important work, the gigantic religious code, *Mishneh Torah,* which was to summarize the entire spiritual and intellectual content of the Talmud into one organized whole. Within ten years the work was well-known to the Jews of Europe, Africa and the Near East, and the first opposition to it soon began to manifest itself. In this period, too, Maimonides suffered various misfortunes, especially sickness.

About 1185 he had become personal physician to many of the potentates of the country and was especially favored by the vizier, Al-Kadi al-Fadil al-Baisami. He soon became the head (Nagid) of all the Jewish communities of Egypt. He utilized his influence in behalf of the persecuted Jews of the Orient. His practice as physician increased greatly and occupied the greater part of his time. But his powers of labor were so highly developed that he still found time for an extensive literary activity, especially in the fields of medicine and astronomy.

About 1190 he finished his main work, *Moreh Nebuchim* (Guide to the Perplexed), his philosophical defense of Judaism. In this he attempted to establish a harmony between the teachings of Judaism and the teachings of reason which, according to him, coincided to a large extent with the teachings of Aristotle, "the prince of philosophers." The work exercised a strong influence on the thought of the contemporary and subsequent Jewish world, and became a guide even to Arabian and Christian philosophers. This book, too, was violently assailed by Maimonides' Orthodox opponents.

Meanwhile Saladin's eldest son, Alafdal, had ascended the throne, and Maimonides became his personal physician. He dedicated several short works on hygiene to his sovereign. In this period the greatest part of his time was taken up by his medical practice, but he found time to correspond with Jewish communities both near and far. In Southern France, in particular, there was marked interest in and understanding of his spiritual labors; from this region came the later defenders of his intellectual works. He died at Fostat on Tebet 20, 1204, and his body was interred in Tiberias. His fame is recorded in the saying, "From Moses to Moses there is none like unto Moses." His death was a signal for a dispute between his followers (Maimunists) and their opponents (anti-Maimunists) that split Jewry in two.

ARON SANDLER.

2. Maimonides as Philosopher. Maimonides is the central figure of the Jewish philosophy of the Middle Ages. He influenced its development as did no other thinker. Everything which preceded him became historical and antiquated after his appearance, and, with few exceptions, lost all importance in the further development of the philosophical problems. Again, all thinkers subsequent to him were influenced by him, either by taking over substantial parts of his teaching or else by reacting to it. Even those who were opposed to him in fundamental points regarded the problems in the same way as that in which he had formulated them, and attained to their own position through their study of his works or their analysis of his teachings.

Maimonides' position of preeminence was not confined to the inner development of Jewish philosophy. It becomes most manifest, perhaps, in the fact that the struggle for the very right of philosophy in Jewish life in general, a struggle which lasted for almost a century and stirred the Jewries of Spain and of the Provence to their very depths, was conducted as a struggle for or against the philosophy of Maimonides That influence which Jewish philosophy exercised on Christian scholasticism as well as on modern Christian philosophy went back primarily to Maimonides. Even Ibn Gabirol, who alone is to be compared with him in this respect, was far inferior to Maimonides in the scope and duration of his influence. Finally, the internal influence which Maimonides exerted on Judaism extended far beyond the close of the Middle Ages. To say nothing of his influence on Spinoza, in the 18th cent. he was still the guide of Moses Mendelssohn and Salomon Maimon in their philosophical development. Even in the 19th and 20th centuries he was an inspiration to Hermann Cohen.

The work from which this influence especially proceeded was his *Moreh Nebuchim* (Guide to the Perplexed; in Arabic, *Dalalat al Hairin*). This philosophical masterpiece of Maimonides, the last of the series of his larger works, was completed in 1190. A few years later, while Maimonides was still alive, and under his direction, it was translated into Hebrew by Samuel ibn Tibbon. Several years later the well-known poet Judah Alharizi undertook a new translation which was far superior to that of Samuel ibn Tibbon in facility and fluency of style, but which was not very widely disseminated in Jewish circles because of its deficiencies as regards exactitude and philosophical precision. However, it became the basis for the first Latin translation of the *Moreh Nebuchim* which was made as early as the first half of the 13th cent.

The purpose of the work is clearly indicated by its title. It aimed to be a guide to those who had become perplexed and uncertain in their faith as the result of the apparent contradictions between the teachings of philosophy and those of the Bible. It was therefore intended for a group of readers to whom the teachings of philosophy, that is, the Aristotelian doctrine as it was understood by its Islamic interpreters, were already well-known. Maimonides limits himself to discussing merely those questions concerning which a harmonization with the views of Judaism was required. Accordingly, the plan of the work conspicuously differs from the logical order of the questions discussed.

Even before he wrote the *Moreh Nebuchim*, Maimonides often treated philosophical problems in his great Talmudic works. In his commentary on the Mishnah (1168) he wrote an introduction, consisting of eight chapters, to *Aboth* (*Shemonah Perakim*), in which the fundamentals of ethics are systematically treated. Similarly, in his excursus to the commentary on the tenth chapter of the tractate *Sanhedrin,* he collated and explained the dogmas of Judaism, the thirteen "roots" or articles of faith (*sheloshah 'asar 'ikkarim*) which had to be discussed at greater length. In the first section of the *Mishneh Torah* ("Yesode Hatorah"), while explaining certain Biblical laws (such as, to love God, or to fear God), he gave a summary of metaphysics and physics, and in the second section ("Deoth") he summarized the principles of ethics. This summary is in substantial agreement with the *Moreh Nebuchim*, but in various passages in which he deviated from the traditional Jewish view he chose a form of presentation which is more suitable to it than is that of the *Moreh Nebuchim*, and which transposes the concepts in the whole from the language of philosophy to that of Jewish tradition. After the completion of the *Moreh Nebuchim*, Maimonides wrote his *Maamar Tehiyath Hamethim* (Treatise on Resurrection), in which he defended himself against the suspicion that he had denied this basic creed. Of all the philosophical writings of Maimonides there is only one which is not directly related to specifically Jewish teachings—his *Milloth Hahiggayon* (Treatise on Logic), which was composed probably in his sixteenth year and is mainly an explanation of the most important technical terms of logic.

The extraordinary significance of Maimonides' philosophy consists in the fact that it brought the Aristotelian doctrine in Jewish philosophy to predominance and provided the classical explanation of the problems of the Law (Torah) from the standpoint of Aristotelianism. Whereas, in the philosophy of Islam, the trend toward Aristotelianism occurred as early as the 9th cent. and after that became more and more pronounced, Jewish philosophy had remained loyal to Neo-Platonism even into the 12th cent., and it was only a few decades before Maimonides that Abraham ibn Daud had for the first time introduced Aristotelianism into Jewish philosophy. But Maimonides, whose work was far superior to that of Abraham ibn Daud, first marked the triumph of Aristotelianism and at the same time determined the special form of this Jewish Aristotelianism.

In his conception of the Aristotelian doctrine itself, Maimonides followed his Islamic predecessors, among

A page from the illuminated manuscript (15th cent.)
of Maimonides' "Mishneh Torah"

Facsimile of an autograph letter by Maimonides

whom he considered the most important Alfarabi, who had impregnated it with a great number of Neo-Platonic views. His originality consists merely in his application of this doctrine to the problems of Jewish religion, in other words, in his harmonization with the Biblical and Talmudic tradition. The contrast, on the one hand, between the dynamic and teleological (purposive) Aristotelianizing view of the world, which understood reality as a necessary association of teleological forces proceeding from God, and, on the other hand, the ethical and personalistic religious attitude of Judaism, with its belief in the creative spontaneity of God and in the feature of will which characterizes the relationship between human beings and God, forms the central problem of his work. His harmonization of the two conceptions consisted essentially in that he understood the relations within the universe itself in the sense of the dynamic metaphysics of Aristotelianism, but that he rejected that doctrine as far as the influence and effect of God were concerned; he subjected the dynamically conceivable sphere of the natural association of things to a conception of the world which was, in its final analysis, personalistic. This train of thought, it is true, is not always strictly adhered to with the same exactitude, and in various individual problems Maimonides yields to the Aristotelian explanation of the world more than is in accordance with this position. He is more closely attached to Aristotelianism as regards ethics. Above all, he stresses the superiority of intellectual perfection to moral perfection in particular, and proceeding from this point of view he arrives at some sort of contemplative religion, strikingly different

from the practical religion of the Bible and Talmud. Maimonides' attempt to do justice to the traditional Jewish view, significant as it is, was singularly unsuccessful.

Within the sphere of theoretical philosophy, he unconditionally followed the school tradition in his concept of God. He followed this tradition in the proofs for the existence, unity and incorporeality of God. He equally followed Islamic Aristotelianism in conceiving of God as absolutely One in the sense of Neo-Platonism, thus excluding every plurality, even that of purely logical character. This conception had been prevalent in Jewish speculation long before Maimonides, but none of his predecessors carried it out with such radical energy as he did. This energy renders likewise the contrast with the Biblical conception of God especially manifest. The absolute oneness of God makes any positive assertion about God impossible, and thus the living God of the Bible was converted into the absolutely indeterminable unity of Neo-Platonism, regarding which man knows merely the fact that God is, but in no positive way what He is. In reconciling this antithesis, Maimonides again follows his Islamic and Jewish predecessors. The manifold assertions which the Bible makes of God, says Maimonides, are by no means intended to give a positive definition of the divine being. Despite their positive form they either have a negative meaning, and purport only to exclude from God definite imperfections, or they designate not the nature, but only the effects or the actions of God. Nevertheless, Maimonides attempts to do justice to the ethical meaning of the Biblical idea of God. That which we are able to perceive of God is only His actions. But this is exactly the only thing which we need to know; for only God's actions, as distinguished from His essence, can be the pattern of human morality, and thus all moral knowledge is traced back to the knowledge of God.

While Maimonides is in broad agreement with what he considered the philosophical teaching concerning God, he is radically opposed to the philosopher's conception of the relation of God to the world. Maimonides naturally sided with the Jewish tradition which teaches that God, by His free action, created the world out of nothing (*creatio ex nihilo*). The philosophers asserted that the world is eternal (Aristotle), or that it is the product of an eternal and necessary emanation from God (Neo-Platonism). Maimonides traced the contrast between the Biblical teaching and the philosophical teaching back to the central antithesis between the assertion and the denial of divine will. Probably the most important argument adduced by Maimonides in favor of the Biblical view is this: if the world had emanated from God in an eternal and absolutely necessary way, the existence as well as the structure of this world must be deducible from God.

Following earlier critics of the theory of emanation, Maimonides first shows that not even the existence and plurality of spiritual beings intermediate between God and the material world can be deduced from the divine One. He then carried this thought further, stating that in the transition from the spiritual to the corporeal world the individuality and the accidental nature of the given constellation of the corporeal world remains undeducible. Even on the most lucid plane of the corporeal world, in the heavens, we find a manifoldness of the most varied objects and motions, which can not be derived from a single principle. From facts such as these Maimonides concludes that the world can not be the product of emanation, but must have its origin in a free action of God, in the act of creation.

This argument does not, as it might appear at first sight, go so far as to invoke the aid of the divine will in order to make up for the deficiencies of our knowledge. Rather does it, with great keenness, touch on the point by which every *a priori* construction of reality has to be tested, that is, in the derivation of the individual and the particular; and it logically sees throughout in the divine will the principle which completes the conceptually underivable "determination" of the particular. However, Maimonides does not believe that he has demonstrated the creation of the world, but merely asserts that the problem admits of no demonstrative decision, even though probability overwhelmingly favors the creation of the world. In view of this state of affairs he considers it right that religious interest shall decide the issue. But this does not mean that Maimonides appeals to the letter of the Bible, for, as he indicates, the Biblical story of creation is susceptible of being interpreted in agreement with a belief in the eternity of the world. The religious interest consists rather in the fact that the idea of the free creation by the Deity is required in order for one to be able to conceive of God as

the Lord of the World who rules over it in free sovereignty.

By establishing the creation of the world, Maimonides is enabled to speak of a purpose of divine action, a purpose which is not compatible with the assumption of a necessary sequence of the world from God. His extraordinarily profound discussion of the problem of purpose, it is true, leads to a paradoxical result. We are able to comprehend the purpose of God within the world, but the problem of the purpose of the world as a whole is incapable of solution. To the question of the purpose of the world as a whole there is only the one answer, that God willed its existence. The paradoxical feature of this conception consists in the fact that Maimonides assumes for all individual beings or creations a reasonable purpose, and regards it as incompatible with the idea of the wisdom of God to deny that the action of God has any such purposiveness, while for the world as a whole he renounces the idea of purpose or meaning. But even if likewise the purpose of the world must thus be relegated to the divine will itself, none the less its metaphysical character as a product of divine purposiveness still remains.

Proceeding from this same basic conception, Maimonides arrives at the possibility of carrying out the personalistic manner of viewing things in the problems of miracles, providence, and prophecy. Maimonides himself, at the very outset, points to the connection between the idea of miracles and the concept of the creation when he characterizes the religious interest, which renders the maintenance of the idea of creation necessary. Only when God is thought of as the free Creator of the world is the idea of miracles logically possible. But in the carrying out of the idea of miracles Maimonides remains true to the tendency which had been marked out previously, that of adhering to the explanation of nature given by Aristotelianism with regard to the connection of things within the world. He regards miracles not as a subsequent infringement of the world order, but as a component part of the original constitution of this very world order.

As regards providence, the contrast between the philosophical and the Jewish conception comes to the fore in an especially characteristic manner. According to the conception attributed to Aristotle, divine providence in the terrestrial world does not extend to the individuals, but only to the species of things; in other words, divine providence is only another term for the natural purposive connection and cohesion of the world which are based on the general purposive order of nature. Maimonides, on the contrary, firmly adheres to individual providence, but confines it to human beings, while as regards the lower realms of nature he recognizes the Aristotelian conception. The reason for this is to be seen in the fact that he wishes to relieve the problem of the justice of God from the questions which in the realm of the lower animals arise from their sufferings and pains. But he chooses this pathway primarily because he believes that he can, within these limits, give a natural explanation of the idea of providence.

According to this explanation, divine providence for individuals depends on the communion of their intelligence with God. Providence is therefore graded in accordance with the intensity and fervor of this communion. Here, then, Maimonides tries to harmonize philosophy with Judaism by justifying the idea of individual providence on the basis of an Aristotelian conception. As regards prophecy, he breaks still more sharply with Aristotelianism. The Islamic Aristotelians had attempted to understand prophecy as a natural phenomenon. According to their opinion, all knowledge depended on the actualization of the individual human intellect by the universal "active intellect" which guides the terrestrial world and from which truth streams into the intellect of the individual. The specific difference between prophetic knowledge and the knowledge attainable to the philosopher, they held, is merely this, that in the prophet's case the influence of the "active intellect" is not confined merely to the intellect, as it is in the case of the philosopher, but determines phantasy as well.

Maimonides accepted this natural explanation of prophecy, and gave it the finest, most perfected and most consistently executed form which it ever received and which is never surpassed. But he limited it in two characteristic points. First, in accordance with the belief in creation and miracles, he maintains that even if an individual meets all the conditions necessary for becoming a prophet, it none the less depends on the will of God as to whether or not a man will in fact become a prophet. Secondly, he emphasizes that the natural explanation of prophecy does not apply to the prophecy of the highest prophet, Moses, whose prophecy was absolutely unique and an utterly inexplicable phenomenon. Maimonides' first limitation of the idea of prophecy, again, expresses the metaphysical basic antithesis. Maimonides accepts the natural explanation of prophecy, but here, too, he subordinates the sphere of nature to the free action of God which makes use of the cohesion and association of nature for its purposes. Thus he understands prophecy as a mission which proceeds from the will of God.

The exceptional position which Moses occupied he bases on the statements of the Bible which lift Moses above the rank of all the other prophets. But its real reason is a different one. The natural explanation of prophecy has as its consequence that the various religions are equally referred to a prophetic origin. It abolishes the fundamental antithesis between revealed religions and those which are based on human invention, and substitutes for it the relative difference between a more and a less perfected revelation, always in accordance with the level of the various prophets. The absoluteness of the Biblical religion can be assured only by setting up as its basis a prophecy of supernatural kind which is distinguished in its principal features from all other forms of prophecy.

As has been stated at the outset, Maimonides is more closely attached to Aristotle in ethical questions than in metaphysical ones. He believed, as did Aristotle, that the highest perfection of man is the intellectual, in comparison with which the moral one forms merely a preliminary stage. Perceiving is the real goal of man's existence on earth. With this Aristotelian evaluation of perceiving and cognition, Maimonides, like the Islamic Aristotelians, associates the Neo-Platonic conception which sees the highest goal of man in union

שא גאולת עולם תהיה ללויים   ישראל שירש את אבי
אמו לוי   הרי זה גוי כלויי אעפ שאינו לוי הואיל והארי
או השרות של לויים גוי לעולם   שריך זה תלוי במקומות
לו ולא בבעלים ולוי שירש את אבי אמו ישראל גוי כישראל
ולא כלויים שלא נאמר גאולת עולם תהיה ללויים אלא בערי
הלויים   כל שבט לוי מוזהרין שלא ינחלו בארץ
כנען וכן הן מוזהרין שלא יטלו חלק בבוה בשעה שכובשין
את הערים שנאמר לא יהיה לכהני הלויי כל שבט לוי חלק
ונחלה עם ישראל חלק בבוה ונחלה בארץ   וכן הוא אומר
בארצ לא תנחל וחלק לא יהיה לך בתוכם בבוה וכן לוי
או כהן שנטל חלק בבוה לוקה   ואם נטל נחלה בארץ
מעבירין אותה ממנה יראה לי שאין הרברי אוסרין
אלא בארץ שנכרתה עליה ברית לאברהם ליצחק
וליעק וירשוה בניה ונתחלקה להם אבל שאר
כל הארצות שכובש מלך ממלכי ישראל
הרי הכהני והלויי באותן הארצו ובביתן
ככל ישראל ולמה לא זכה לוי   בנחלת
ארץ ישראל ובבותה עם אחיו מפני
שהובדל לעבור את ה ולשרתו
ולהורו דרכיו הישרי ומשפטיו
הצריקים לרבים שנא יורו
משפטי ליעקב ותורתך
לישראל לפי הובדלו
מדרכי העול לא
עורכין
מלחמה כשאר
ישראל ולא נוחלין
ולא זוכין   לעצמן
בכח גיפן אלא הם חיל
ה שנאמ ברך ה חילו והוא
ברוך הוא זוכה להם   שנ אני
חלקך ונחלתך   ולא שבט לוי
בלבר אלא כל איש ואיש מכל באי
העולם אשר נרבה רוחו אותו והבינו
מרעו להבדל לעמור לפני ה לשרתו
ולעברו לרעה את ה והלך ישר כמו שעשהו
האלהים ופרק מעל צוארו עול החשבונות הרבי
אשר בקשו בני הארם   הרי זה נתקרש קורש
קרשים ויהיה ה הלקו   ונחלתו לעולם ולעולמי
עולמים   ויזכה לו בעולם רבר המספיק לו כמו שזכה
לכהנים וללויים   הרי רוד עליו השלום אומ ה מנת חלקי
וכוסי אתה תומיך גורלי

A page from Maimonides' "Mishneh Torah," printed before 1480 by Solomon ben Judah and Obadiah ben Moses in Italy

with God. This union with God is brought about through perception. For metaphysical knowledge, or cognition, represents a real association of human intellect with the "active intellect" and through it with God. Thus cognition receives a religious meaning, since it guides the soul upwards to God. But this religiousness is not the ethical religiousness of the Bible, but a contemplative religiousness of mystical association or community with God. Maimonides attempts, it is true, to associate the ethical character of religion with this conception by defining the highest knowledge, in which the community of man with God is perfected, as a knowledge of the moral government of God, a knowledge which expresses itself in conduct patterned after the ways of God. But these restrictions are not bound up with his basic conception.

To this there corresponds also the form of Maimonides' theory of immortality, in which he followed the more radical tendency of Islamic Aristotelianism. Of man there is immortal only the cognitive part, and then, too, only when it has passed from potentiality to actuality. Only the thinker from whose activity of thought "acquired reason" proceeds has a share in immortality. In this discussion the moral aspect of personality comes into consideration only in so far as it is the condition for intellectual perfection. The statement of the *Mishneh Torah* on this point is, to be sure, closer to the traditional conception; it grants all the pious a portion in immortality, and excludes only the wicked.

Maimonides' view of knowledge as the highest value is the basis likewise for the interpretation of the meaning of the divine revelation. That which distinguishes the Torah from a human law is the fact that it is intended not only to determine man's actions, but also to enlighten him in his thinking and to make the truth accessible to him. In the divine revelation there is contained all the truth to which the thought of man can attain. But the depths of its contents are disclosed only to the thinker, who can penetrate from the literal meaning to its deeper sense. Generally speaking, the literal meanings are addressed to the "vulgar." In this respect Maimonides approached the view of his Islamic contemporary Averroes, who believed that the esoteric meaning of the divine law intended for the masses does not transcend the realm of morality, whereas its esoteric meaning embraces the realm of speculation as well. But he differs decidedly from Averroes in that he demands that certain basic truths (unity and incorporeality of God) be made accessible to all members of the community. It appears that he regards this as sufficient to enable one to attain to immortality and eternal bliss, even though in a lower degree, and that this conception forms the basis for his above-mentioned representation of the doctrine of immortality in the *Mishneh Torah*.

Maimonides understands the ceremonial laws of Judaism as the means to moral and intellectual perfection. They are intended either to assist the performance of the moral demands of the Torah or to inculcate its basic truths. Maimonides' interpretation of those laws from which such a meaning can not directly be derived evidences great originality. He believes that they were intended to oppose pagan views and forms of worship which were prevalent at the time of the divine legislation. From this Maimonides proceeds to explain the sacrificial legislation, which he regards as an adaptation to the then generally prevalent custom of worshipping God by means of sacrifices. While accepting the belief in the verbal inspiration of the document of revelation, Maimonides thus arrives at a historical conception of the Biblical legislation which in many respects touches upon the modern religious historical view.

Maimonides' conviction that immortality and eternal happiness are dependent upon the perception of definite basic truths led him to set up in his commentary on the Mishnah the thirteen doctrines of faith which every Jew had to acknowledge in order to have a share in eternal life. The occasion for this was provided by *Sanh.* 10:1, a passage in the Mishnah which declares that all Israel has a share in the world to come, but then mentions a few exceptions, in particular those that deny resurrection and the divine origin of the Torah, as well as the "Epicureans." In contrast to the unsystematic character of the Mishnaic statements, Maimonides sought to compile in systematic manner the principles which are to be recognized by every Jew and the denial of which excludes one from a share in the coming world. But it is not only his systematic presentation which distinguishes him from the Mishnah. Whatever the relation of Maimonides' principles of faith to the statements of the Mishnah may be, it is characteristic that with him philosophical intellectualism becomes religious dogmatism, which demands the recognition of definite articles of belief as a condition for bliss.

Maimonides' thirteen creeds or articles of faith are as follows: (1) The existence of God; (2) His unity; (3) His incorporeality; (4) His eternity; (5) His exclusive right to be worshipped; (6) the fact of prophecy; (7) the superiority of Moses' prophecy to that of all the other prophets; (8) the divine origin of the Torah; (9) the eternity of the Torah; (10) the omniscience of God; (11) divine reward and punishment; (12) the coming of the Messiah; (13) resurrection.

The general tendency which forms the basis for this choice of doctrines is evident. The doctrines referring to the God conception are intended to keep it free from any material or sensual coloring. The doctrines which deal with prophecy and the Torah have as their aim the guaranteeing of the eternal validity of the Torah and are manifestly directed against the claim of Islam that the Koran abrogated the Torah. The last group of doctrines is concerned with the idea of retribution. It is perhaps owing to Maimonides' regard for the Mishnah that he included in this category the belief in resurrection. However, it is apparent that this selection of doctrines is logically disputable, a fact which was often noted by the later philosophers of religion. All the later attempts to fix the basic doctrines of Judaism resulted from the criticism made of Maimonides' systematic presentations. In fact, his attempt to set up a body of Jewish dogmas became one of the most influential sections of his teachings. Maimonides' articles of belief, despite the criticism to which they were subjected, were incorporated into the religious life of Judaism. There are a great number of poetic elaborations of these creeds, one of which, the *Yigdal,* has become a component part of the Orthodox Jewish daily prayers. In addition, a brief enumeration of the thirteen articles of belief as a confession (Ani Maamin), is found in the Orthodox prayer-book at the conclusion of the morning service (Shaharith). It is found also in the evening service for holidays of the *Union Prayer Book.*   JULIUS GUTTMANN.

3. Maimonides as Codifier. A. The *Mishneh Torah* (from *Deut.* 17:18, "copy of the law," in the sense of "second teaching" or "repetition of the Law") is the chief code compiled by Maimonides. It is more generally known as the *Yad Hahazakah* ("strong hand"), because it consists of fourteen books, and the Hebrew numeral fourteen (Yod Daleth) can be read as *yad,* "hand." The work was originally composed by Maimonides for his personal use, but as it progressed it developed into a work intended for those

שעדיין לא יצא לדרך תעשה על פיהם מאחר שידעו הרי זה פטור

פרק חמשה עשר

כבר בארנו שכל שגגה שההודיוט מביא עליה חטאתו הקבוע כשבה או שעירה אם שג בה הנשיא מביא שעיר ואם שג בה כהן משיח מביא פר במה דברי אמורי שבהן משיח מביא פר על שגגתו כשהוא בהורת עצמו ועשה מעשה בשגנת ההוראתו לבדה והוא שיהיה חכם כיפלא שנאמר אם הכהן המשיח יחטא לאשמת העם הרי משיח כצבור מה הצבור שהן בית דין אינן חייבין בקרבן עד שיהיו חכמים ראוין להוראה וטעו בהוראה ועשו העושים על פיהם מחדו לבטל מקצת ולקיים מקצת כך המשיח בכל הדרכים האלו כיצד כן בשיא שטעה בהוראה לעצמו ודמה שהתורק טרשות לרשות בשבת מותר דוק מרשות לרשת ויצא ותלה בהוראתו לעצמו כשיודע לו שחטא יביא פר לחטאת אבל אם לא תלה בהוראתו אלא שג חדק בשנגה או שתלה בהוראתו ולא היה חכם מופלא או שעקר כל הגו בהוראתו לעצמו או ששנג בהוראתו לבטל מקצת ולא עשה והוא סמך על הוראתו אלא עשה בשנגה אחרת או שהדיה מזד בהודאה ושג במעשה הרי זה פטור מקרבן כלל שדינו להודאה עצמו כדין הקהל להודאת בית דין לכל דבר הורה לעצמו ושכב ומאחד טעם הורה ובשעה שעשה אמר חריני עושה על דעת הודראתי הרי זה מביא פר חטאת הורה לעצמו לבטל מקצת ולקיים מקצת בעז"ו ועשה כפי הוראתו הרי זה מביא שעידה כהדיוט שאין הכהן המשיח חייב קרבן אלא בהעלם דבר בהודאה עם שנגת דמעשה בצבור אבל אם שג

מביא שעיר שטעיר נשיא במקום כשבה או שעירה של הדיוט הזא עומד נשיא שנצטרע עבר מנשיאתו ונשא שעבר בנשיאתו הרי הוא כהדיוט, חטא כשהוא נשיא ועבר מגדולה הרי זה מביא שעיר שנא' על חטאתו אשר חטא בשעת הטאתו הוא מביא כהן משיח או מלך שחטאו עד שלא נתמנו אעפ' שלא נודע להם אלא אחר שנתמנו הרי אלו כהדיוט שנאמ' אשר נשיא יחטא אם הכהן המשיח יהטא עד שיחטא כשהוא נשיא וכשהוא משיח לפיכך אם אכל חלק חלב כשהוא הדיוט ונודע לו על ספק תאחר שנתמנה להיות כהן גדול הרי זה מביא אשם תלוי אכל חצי זית חלב כשהוא הדיוט וחצי זית כשהוא נשיא אינו אחד או שאכל חצי זית כשהוא נשיא וחצי זית אחד שעבר אינו מצטרף ופטור אכל חצי זית כשהו הדיוט ונתמנה ועבר ואכל חצי זית כשהו הדיוט הרי זה ספק' אם מצטרף' או כבר הפסיק הנשיאות

הלכות מחוסרי כפרה

יש בכללן ארבע מצות עשה והו פרטן א' שתקריב הזבה כשתטהר קרבן ב' שתקריב היולדת כשתטהר קרבן ג' שיקריב הזב כשיטהר קרבן ד' שיקריב מצורע בשיטהר קרבן' ואהר' שיקריבו קרבנותיהן תנמר טהרתן וביאור מצות אלו בפרקים אלו

פרק ראשון

Two pages from Maimonides' "Mishneh Torah," printed in 1490 at Soncino, Italy, by Gerson ben Moses Soncino

who, while not possessing a deep and comprehensive knowledge of the Talmud, were called upon to render ritual and judicial decisions. With a perfect sense of order, clarity and compelling force, Maimonides compiled all the results of earlier Halachic literature, even that part of the Halachah which referred to Palestine or the Temple and was no longer regarded as in force. The *Mishneh Torah* includes not only Jewish law in the broadest sense of the word, but also dogmatics, physics, metaphysics, ethics and dietetics. For systematic structure and logical presentation it has no equal in Jewish literature.

It was the purpose of Maimonides to summarize the Halachic research of fifteen centuries and to create a firm and fixed structure of the teachings of Judaism, a *magnum opus* of all the traditional Jewish lore. He had no intention of abolishing the study of the Talmud thereby, but only of simplifying it. It was actually his intention to publish a separate book in which all the sources would be quoted, but he never was able to complete this inspiring work. The Talmudical discussions form the basis for his decisions; he takes cognizance of the opinions of the Geonim and he gives special expression to his own decisions. In contrast to his other writings, he used the Hebrew language of the Mishnah. The concise brevity of Maimonides' juristic terminology surpasses that of the Mishnah and of Rashi; for the Mishnah has regard for beauty of style and the formulation of the ideas, while Rashi includes topics that belong to the work of the commentator—references, contradictions and peculiarities of grammar. Maimonides, however, is solely concerned with giving clear and precise definitions for the legal ideas. Similarly, Maimonides attempted to achieve brevity of presentation and unity for the entire Jewish legal field.

The introduction to the *Mishneh Toreh* was intended to demonstrate the unity prevalent within the events of history and to confirm the traditional view of revelation. Maimonides explains that legal ideas which are externally different are in reality uniform, and thus a true unity prevails. He considers human punishment a release or redemption, since a settlement is possible for the general consequences of an action; an act that is unatoned is an enduring evil. He regards religious law as an amplification of natural law; nor does he recognize a difference between norms that are purely religious and those which are both religious and legal, since both together form the basis for the perfect social cosmos. By classifying them into groups, he succeeds in securing a proper basis for the concepts, which is of fundamental importance for legal technique. The sum total of the individual details coincides with the definition of the institution dealt with.

The presentation starts with clear definitions and proceeds from the more to the less important regulations. The work is systematically divided into the fourteen most important spheres of human life, each one of which receives a separate book, as follows:

1. Book of Knowledge (unity of God, prohibition of idolatry).
2. Book of Love (love of God, prayers, phylacteries, priestly blessing, circumcision).

3. Book of Festivals (Sabbath and holidays).

4. Book of Women (marriage, divorce, levirate marriage).

5. Book of Consecration (sexual intercourse, forbidden foods).

6. Book of Separation (oaths, vows).

7. Book of Seeds (Sabbatical year, jubilee, tithes, heave offering).

8. Book of Temple Worship (building of the Temple, communal offerings).

9. Book of Sacrifices (individual offerings).

10. Book of Cleanliness (ritual purity and impurity).

11. Book of Damages (damages to property and life).

12. Book of Acquisition (sale and purchase).

13. Book of Legal Disputes (guardians, debtors, objections, denials).

14. Book of Judges (Sanhedrin, capital punishment, taking of testimony, king, war, Messiah).

Shortly after the book appeared it was attacked bitterly by Abraham ibn Daud in his notes ("Hassagoth"), but it became authoritative as a code. It was one of the three works cited as authoritative by Joseph Caro for the decisions reached in the *Shulhan Aruch*, many commentaries on it were written, and it was consistently and thoroughly studied. In some respects, however, it was harmful to Judaism, because it codified and thus gave a sanction to many a view which might better have been left in oblivion.

B. The *Sefer Hamitzvoth* (Book of Commandments) is the other code compiled by Maimonides. It deals with the 613 commandments and prohibitions in the Torah. This work was preliminary to the *Mishneh Torah* and was entirely independent of previous kindred works. The laws are classified into those referring to God and those referring to man. In many cases the reasons for the particular laws are given; ethical, technical and factual explanations are woven into the text; all is done with the greatest brevity and thoroughness. The punishment for the violation of each commandment is added; its validity as to place and time is expressly stated; those who are obligated with reference to each particular ordinance, whether men or women, priests of Levites, or Jews as a whole, are specifically mentioned. The book was originally written in Arabic and repeatedly translated into Hebrew. Like the *Mishneh Torah*, it met both attack and praise, and many commentaries on it were written.

Louis Lewin.

4. Maimonides as Physician. It is a surprising and disappointing fact that the medical achievements of Maimonides have been grossly and arbitrarily underrated by the numerous scholars who have given due weight to his achievements as philosopher and codifier. He has been portrayed as merely echoing the views of Galen, Hippocrates and the Arabian physicians, and without originality of his own. Actually he was the culmination of a whole school of Arabic-Jewish medicine which had begun about 700, and by the time of his death he was acclaimed the greatest physician of his day.

It is possible that Maimonides began the study of medicine at an early age. While at Fez, Morocco, between the ages of twenty-three and thirty (1158-65) he had the opportunity of reaching perfection in the art of healing. In his treatise on asthma he mentions

that he discussed the subject with two prominent physicians at Fez, Muhammed ibn Zuhr and Abu Yusuf. His commentary on the Mishnah, written at the age of thirty, shows a medical knowledge which is on a par with his most advanced medical works, written toward the end of his life.

Shortly after his arrival in Cairo in 1165, Maimonides was appointed physician to Abd ar-Rahim ibn al Baysani, vizier to Saladin, and later to the court of Saladin himself. That he was the favorite physician of the ruling classes at the capital is evidenced by the somewhat caustic remark of the renowned Baghdad physician Abd al-Latif (1162-1231) about him: "He was a man of exceeding worth, but very ambitious and catering to the powerful." Among his pupils were his son Abraham, physician to Sultan al Kamil, Ibn Akhnin, physician to the court of Saladin's brother, and Abu Usaibia, the medical historian.

An idea of the importance and fame of Maimonides in Egypt can be obtained from a letter which he wrote to Samuel ibn Tibbon of Lunel, a physician and translator of many Arabic works of Maimonides into Hebrew. Maimonides writes to dissuade Ibn Tibbon from coming to study under him in the following words: "Do not anticipate being able to spend even one hour alone with me, whether by day or night . . . I am in Fostat and the Sultan is in Cairo. Every day I have to go to Cairo (to the Sultan's palace) early in the morning, and even if nothing special happens I return to Fostat at noon and I am famished. All the galleries of my house are full of people, non-Jews and Jews, prominent and ordinary, judges and officials, friends and enemies, a mixed mob that knows when I return . . . and I go out to treat them and prescribe medications . . . till nightfall, and often for two hours later, so that I am completely exhausted and unable to talk. No Jew can talk to me or stay with me any day except the Sabbath . . . And I have told you but little." When the Jewish community of Lunel asked him to translate his *Guide to the Perplexed* into Hebrew, he answered that his numerous duties did not give him time "to write even a little chapter" and that he had "become aged, but not with years." All this bespeaks an immense practice and an outstanding reputation.

Maimonides did find time to compose medical treatises in Arabic, ten of which are extant. In these he quotes profusely not only from the writings of Hippocrates and Galen, but also from the writings of the Arabian physicians Mesue the Elder, ar-Razi, Ibn Juljul (10th cent.), Alfarabi, Ibn ul Wafid (997-1075), Ibn Ridwan (998-1065), Jonah ibn Janah (995-1050), Said at-Tamimi of Jerusalem (10th cent.), Ibn Zuhr, Ibn Roshd, Al Ghafigi (d. 1165) and others. Several of these works, in Latin translation, became standard texts for centuries in the chief medical schools of Europe, Asia and Africa. The works definitely known to have been written by Maimonides are:

1. *Al Mukhtasarat* (The Extracts), as the name implies, excerpts from the writings of Galen.

2. *Sharh Fusul Abugrat* (Commentary on the Aphorisms of Hippocrates); it was translated into Hebrew by Moses ibn Tibbon.

3. *Fusul Musa fit-Tibb* (Medical Aphorisms of Moses). A Hebrew translation was made by Nathan Hameati under the title *Pirke Mosheh* (Lemberg, 1850; Vilna, 1888); there is another, still in manuscript, by Zerahiah Hen. Latin translations appeared in Bologna (1489), Venice (1497, 1500) and Basel (1579). Maimonides modestly states in his preface that he gleaned these aphorisms from earlier sources, but there is not a page that does not contain his additions to and criticisms of earlier physicians. The twenty-five chapters cover the whole range of medicine.

4. *Fil Bawasir* (On Hemorrhoids), including both medication and proper diet. H. Kroner published the Arabic text in *Janus* (1911). There are in manuscript four anonymous Hebrew translations and one in Spanish (*Sobre los milgros*).

5. *Fil Jima* (On Coitus), written for Saladin's nephew Nur ad-Din, sultan of Syria. It was translated into Hebrew by Zerahiah Hen; Kroner published the original text with a German translation (1906).

6. *Maqala fir-Rabu* (Discourses on Asthma), composed in 1190. It was translated into Hebrew by Joshua Xativa under the title *Sefer Hamisadim* (Book of Nourishments). Another Hebrew translation was made by Samuel Benveniste from a Latin version in 1320; it was published, with a scholarly introduction, by S. Muntner (Jerusalem, 1940).

7. *Kitab as-Summum wal Mutaharriz min al-Adwiya al-Quttala* (On Poisons and Protections Against Deadly Remedies); it deals with hurts caused by reptiles, insects, mad dogs and humans, and was composed in 1199. It was translated into Hebrew by Moses ibn Tibbon (*Hamaamar Hanichbad*), into French by I. M. Rabbinowicz (1865) and into German by Steinschneider (1873).

8. *Fi-Tadbir as-Sihha* (On the Regulation of Health). It was translated into Hebrew by Moses ibn Tibbon under the title *Maamar Behanhagath Haberiuth* in 1244 (Prague, 1838; Jerusalem, 1885; Warsaw, 1886). The convert John of Capua made a Latin translation; German translations were made by Winternitz (1843) and Kroner (with the Arabic original, *Janus*, 1923-25).

9. *Maqala fi Bayan al Arad* (Discourses on the Explanation of Fits). It was translated into Hebrew (*Teshuboth al Sheeloth Peratioth*) and from Hebrew into Latin (Pavia, 1501). Kroner published the Arabic original and a German translation (*Janus*, 1928). An interesting note defends the prescription of wine and music as therapeutic agents, whereas Islam forbids both: "Religion prescribes all that is useful and forbids all that is harmful in the world to come, while the physician indicates what is useful and warns against what is harmful in this world."

10. *Sharh Asma al-Uqqar* (Glossary of Drug Names). The manuscript of this work was discovered in the library of Aya Sofia, Istanbul; the copy was written by no less a physician than the greatest Arabian pharmacological author, Ibn al Baytar (d. 1248). It consists of 405 paragraphs, and lists in alphabetic order the names of about 2,000 drugs in Arabic, Syriac, Greek, Persian, Berber and Spanish.

The style, approach and analyses of Maimonides in these writings are strikingly "modern." He was no subservient follower of Hippocrates and Galen, but he challenged their conclusions in many cases. He gave especial care to public health and sanitation. He anticipated modern discoveries on how psychic factors affect bodily health, and that asthma is often caused by allergies. He identified and isolated the autonomous nervous system that regulates the functions of the body apart from human volition. He stressed the study of individual constitutions, opposed "heroic" doses, and preferred in many cases to build up the patient's strength and leave the rest to nature. He ridiculed superstitious cures, but acknowledged their psychological effect. He explained epilepsy as being due to pressure on the ventricles of the brain. He laid unusual stress, for his time, upon a proper regimen of health, and his efforts were concerned as much with the prevention of disease through rational living and proper diet as with the cure of the sick.

The impression that he made upon his contemporaries is summed up in the words of the poet Ibn Sina Almulk: "Galen's art heals the body alone, but Abu Imram (Maimonides) heals both body and soul. His knowledge made him the healer of his generation. Verily, if the moon would submit to his art, he would heal her of her spots."

HIRSCH LOEB GORDON.

Lit.: Yellin, David, and Abrahams, Israel, *Maimonides* (1936); Bacher, Wilhelm, Brann, Markus, and Simonsen, David, edit., *Moses ben Maimon* (2 vols., 1908 and 1914; issued in celebration of the 700th anniversary of the death of Maimonides); Fishman, Judah Loeb, edit., *Rabbenu Mosheh ben Maimon* (1935; issued in honor of the octocentennial of Maimonides' birth); Epstein, I., edit., *Anglo-Jewish Papers* (1935; issued on the occasion of his octocentennial); Baron, Salo W., edit., *Essays of Maimonides* (1941); Friedlander, Israel, "Moses Maimonides," *Past and Present* (1919) 158-91; idem, "Maimonides as a Master of Style," *ibid.*, 429-38; idem, "Maimonides as an Exegete," *ibid.*, 193-216; Graetz, H., *History of the Jews*, vol. 3 (1927) 446-93, 522-45, 623-34; Munk, Salomon, *Le Guide des Égarés par Moïse ben Maimon* (1856-66); Joel, Manuel, *Die Religionsphilosophie des Mose ben Maimon* (1859); Lévy, Louis-Germain, *Maimonides* (1911); Scheyer, S., *Das psychologische System des Maimonides* (1845); Rosin, D., *Die Ethik des Maimonides* (1876); Diesendruck, Zevi, *Maimonides' Lehre von der Prophetie* (1927); idem, *Die Teleologie bei Maimonides* (1926); Efros, Israel, *Maimonides' Treatise on Logic* (1938); idem, *Philosophical Terms in the Moreh Nebukim* (1924); Kaufmann, David, *Geschichte der Attributenlehre in der jüdischen Religionsphilosophie* (1877); Husik, Isaac, *A History of Mediaeval Jewish Philosophy* (1916); Guttmann, Julius, *Die Philosophie des Judentums* (1933); Strauss, Leo, *Philosophie und Gesetz* (1935); *Maimonides' The Guide of the Perplexed* (1885; English trans., M. Friedlander); Efros, Israel, edit., "Maimonides' Treatise on Logic, The Original and Three Hebrew Translations," *Proceedings of the American Academy for Jewish Research*, vol. 8 (1938) 3; Finkel, Joshua, "Maimonides' Treatise on Resurrection, The Original Arabic and Samuel ibn Tibbon's Hebrew Translation, and Glossary," *ibid.*, vol. 9 (1939) 63; Baron, Salo W., "The Historical Outlook of Maimonides," *ibid.*, vol. 6 (1936) 5; Diesendruck, Zevi, "Maimonides' Theory of the Negation of Privation," *ibid.*, vol. 6 (1936) 139; Geiger, "Moses ben Maimon," *Nachgelassene Schriften*, vol. 3, pp. 34-96; Münz-Berent, *Moses ben Maimon; Moses ben Maimon, sein Leben, seine Werke und sein Einfluss* (1908-10, *Schriften der Gesellschaft zur Förderung der Wissenschaft des Judentums*); Wolfson, Harry A., "The Aristotelian Predicables and Maimonides' Division of Attributes," *Essays and Studies in Memory of Linda R. Miller* (1938) 201-34; idem, "The Amphibolous Terms in Aristotle, Arabic Philosophy and

Maimonides," *Harvard Theological Review*, vol. 31 (1938) 151-73; Diesendruck, Zevi, "On the Date of the Completion of the More Nebukim," *Hebrew Union College Annual*, vol. 12-13 (1937-38) 461-97; Blau, Ludwig, "Fustat, la residenza di Maimonide," *Annuario di studi ebraici*, vol. 16 (1938) 65-85; Zolli, Israel, "In margine a Hilkot 'Abodat Kokabim di Maimonide," *ibid.*, vol. 16 (1938) 87-97; Elbogen, Ismar, *ibid.*, vol. 16 (1938) 99-105; Sonne, I., "Maimonides' Letter to Samuel ben Tibbon according to an Unknown Text in the Archives of the Jewish Community of Verona," *Tarbitz*, vol. 10 (1938-39) 135-54, 309-32; Guttmann, Michael, "Maimonides über das biblische 'jus talionis,'" *Magyar Zsidó Szemle* (1936-38) 255-66; Ravidowicz, Simon, *Knowledge of God, A Study in Maimonides' Philosophy of Religion;* Hoffmann, Ernst, *Die Liebe zu Gott bei Mose ben Maimon* (1937); Strulovici, Josef, *Der Einfluss Moses Maimonides in der Schrift "De Veritate" des Thomas von Aquin* (1936); *Mishneh Torah* (1937; edited according to the Bodleian codex with English translation by Moses Hyamson); Strauss, Leo, "Der Ort der Vorsehungslehre nach Ansicht Maimunis," *Monatsschrift für Geschichte und Wissenschaft des Judentums*, vol. 81 (1937) 93-105; Neubauer, Jakob, "Zum ursprünglichen Titel von Maimunis Buch der Gebote und seiner Geschichte," *ibid.*, vol. 81 (1937) 105-19; Wustenfeld, F., *Geschichte der arabischen Ärzte und Naturforscher* (1840); Haeser, *Geschichte der Medizin und die epidemischen Krankheiten* (1875); Leclerc, L., *Histoire de la médecine arabe* (1876); Steinschneider, M., *Die hebräischen Übersetzungen des Mittelalters* (1893); idem, *Die arabische Literatur der Juden* (1902); Pagel, I., *Maimuni als medizinischer Schriftsteller* (1908); Sarton, G., *Introduction to the History of Science* (1931); Castiglioni, A., "Mose Maimonide," *Rassegna clinico-scientifica* (1935); Marx, A., "Texts by and about Maimonides," *Jewish Quarterly Review* (1935); Gordon, H. L., "Mabo Letorath Harefuah shel Harambam," *Hadoar*, vol. 22 (1935); Muntner, S., *Sefer Hakazereth* (1940); Meyerhof, M., "L'oeuvre médicale de Maimonide," *Archivio di storia della scienza* (1929); "The Medical Works of Maimonides," *Essays on Maimonides* (1941).

MAIMONIDES COLLEGE, 1. The first educational institution for rabbinical and other higher Hebrew learning in the United States, opened on October 25, 1867, in Philadelphia. It was established, after many years of persistent endeavor, by the Hebrew Education Society of Philadelphia and the Board of Delegates of American Israelites. Isaac Leeser was president of the college, and among the members of its faculty were Aaron S. Bettelheim, Laemlein Buttenwieser, George Jacobs, Marcus M. Jastrow and Sabato Morais. Leeser died three months after the college was opened, but the college carried on until 1873, when lack of support finally forced it to close. Five students comprised the first class, and three graduates occupied pulpits in the United States.

2. An institution for higher Jewish learning, founded in New York city in 1927 by Simon Glazer. It was a lay school, open to adults. Glazer was head of the institution until his death (1938).

Lit.: Morais, H. S., *The Jews of Philadelphia* (1894) 189-89; *Publications of the American Jewish Historical Society*, No. 29 (1925) 106-8.

MAIMUNI, MAIMUNISTS, *see* MAIMONIDES.

MAIMUNI, ABRAHAM, *see* MAIMON, ABRAHAM BEN MOSES.

MAINE, a state in the northeastern part of the United States, with a population (1940) of 847,226, of whom a little more than 9,000, or less than 1.1 per cent, were Jews.

In 1906 there were only four Jewish congregations, with a membership of 205 persons, in Maine. According to the 1936 census of religious bodies issued by the Bureau of the Census, there were then twenty-three congregations, all but two of which were in urban centers. Of the twenty-three congregations, eighteen had buildings. Their total membership was 8,386, and only fifty-eight members resided outside of urban centers.

The Jewish population of the state is largely divided between three cities: Portland, 3,650; Bangor, 1,650; and Lewiston, 1,000. Augusta, the capital of Maine, has a very small Jewish population. Portland and Bangor have fine Jewish community buildings, which are the centers of Jewish life in their respective communities. These two cities, as well as Lewiston, also have B'nai B'rith lodges. For a small Jewish community of about 800 families, the Portland Jewish center has a complete five-story building that was taken over from the Knights of Pythias in 1937. There are three congregations in Portland, all Orthodox, and directed by one rabbi. Only in the late 1930's did Portland engage an English-speaking rabbi. The entire religious community is unified under the Kehillah-like setup and is supported by the returns from Kashruth.

Bangor, with some 250 Jewish families, is another community that revolves around the Jewish Community Center. Lewiston, along with its twin city, Auburn, has about 200 Jewish families. Unlike Portland and Bangor, which are old Yankee communities, the population of Lewiston and Auburn is largely French Catholic. Small Jewish communities exist in Gardner, Biddeford, Brunswick, Waterville, Rumford Falls and Old Orchard Beach. There is a large Jewish population at Old Orchard Beach during the summer.

Maine, which was part of Massachusetts until 1820, did not have an actual Jewish community until after 1800, but before that several individual Jews were known to have traveled in the region. Susman Abrams (b. Hamburg, Germany) is known to have settled in the area during the period of the Revolutionary War. First he lived in Waldborough and Thomaston, but later he moved to Union, where he conducted a tannery for many years. The annals of Maine Masonry show no Jewish members before the year 1810.

A number of Jews throughout the state have held public office. Harry Taylor was a member of the Portland Board of Aldermen (1902-4), and a member of the state legislature (1904-6). Louis Kaplan was Portland's tax assessor in 1901. Max L. Pinanski was a justice of the Portland municipal court (1927-31), a member of the Portland school board (1932), a state senator for Cumberland County (1934-36), and a member of the State Public Utilities Commission (1936-38). Professor Albert Abrahamson of Bowdoin College, in 1942 executive director of the National Refugee Service, was state director of the W. P. A. (1935-39). Edward I. Gleszer was a justice of the Bangor city court (1926-30). Three Berman brothers, attorneys, have been active in the communal life of Lewiston: Ben Lewis Berman was state's attorney for Androscoggin County (1921-22 and 1924-26) and county probate judge (1929-33). David Victor Berman was corporation counsel of Lewiston (1930-31). Jacob Harrison Berman was state's attorney for Cumberland County (1915-17) and United States Commis-

sioner for Maine (1925-29). Simon Spill was city attorney for Biddeford (1936-40). Herman S. Gerrish
was chairman of the Board of Selectmen of Old
Orchard Beach in 1936.   HENRY W. LEVY.

MAISKY, IVAN MIKHAILOVITCH (originally Ivan Mikhailovitch Liukhovetsky), diplomat, b.
Omsk, Russia, 1884. As a student of the University of
St. Petersburg he was involved in the revolutionary
youth movement; he repeatedly suffered imprisonment
and was twice sent into exile. In 1908 he was expelled
from the university for revolutionary activities, and
soon after left Russia for Germany, where he attended the University of Munich, making economics
the object of his studies. While in Germany he was
a member of the Social Democratic Party of that
country. From 1912 to 1917 he lived in England. Although he belonged to the moderate Menshevik wing
of the Russian Social Democratic Labor Party, he returned to Russia in 1918, after the victory of the
Bolsheviki, and adhered to their program.

The Soviet government availed itself of his knowledge of the Far East by appointing him head of an
expedition for the exploration of Mongolia (1919-20),
in the course of which Maisky was instrumental in
setting up the Mongol Soviet Republic. In 1921 he
became president of the State Planning Commission
for Siberia. His experience in England was put to
profit in his appointment as counsellor of the Russian
Embassy at London (1925 to 1927). Other stages in
his diplomatic career were his counsellorship of the
Tokyo Embassy (1927-29) and his service as Minister
to Finland (1929-32) until, in 1933, he was sent to
London as ambassador, a post which he still held
in 1942.

Maisky, who for many years represented a cause
unpopular in England with much tact and dignity,
was a convinced supporter of Litvinoff's policy of
collective security and indivisible peace. In 1936 he
pronounced himself against the philosophy of the
mailed fist.

He was author of the volumes: *Contemporary Mongolia; Foreign Policy of the R.S.F.S.R. 1917-22; Trade
Union Movement in the West.*

   Lit.: Lenin, Nikolai, *Selected Works*, vol. 2 (Russian
ed., 1933); *Saturday Review*, Nov. 23, 1935, p. 497; *Time*,
April 24, 1939, p. 20.

MAISLER, BENJAMIN, archeologist, b. Grodno,
Poland, 1906. He studied at the Universities of Gies-
sen and Berlin, and received his Ph.D. degree in
1929. He went to Palestine that same year. From
1930 to 1932 Maisler was director of excavations at
Ramath Rachel; later he was associated with the
Hebrew University and also with the Institute of
Palestinology in Tel-Aviv. Maisler was on the execu-
tive committee of the Jewish Palestine Exploration
Society and director of the Sheikh Abreiq excavations.
He was the author of *Untersuchungen zur alten
Geschichte Syriens und Palästinas* (1930); *Hashemoth
Hageografiim shel Hayishubim Beeretz Yisrael* (1932);
and *Toledoth Hamehkar Haarkeologi Beeretz Yisrael*
(1936), and was joint editor of *Yedioth.*

MAIYAN, *see* COLONIES, AGRICULTURAL.

MAJOR, HENRY, painter and caricaturist, b.

Ivan Maisky

Nagyszalonta, Hungary, 1889. He was living in New
York city in 1942. Major studied painting at the Art
School of Budapest under Károly Ferenczi, and from
1928 on spent several years in Paris and at Amsterdam,
Holland, concentrating on old and modern masters. He
exhibited crayon drawings at Budapest and won an
award with his self-portrait in oil, in 1913. From 1921
to 1923 Major lived in Holland and England, contributing drawings to *Telegraaf, Graphic* and *Daily
Graphic.* From 1923 on he lived in the United States,
where his drawings and caricatures appeared in the
Hearst daily newspapers, in the *Wall Street Journal*, and
in *The New Yorker, Town and Country* and *Ken*
magazines. Exhibits of his paintings in New York city
(Reinhardt Galleries, 1938; Harriman Gallery, 1940)
revealed him as a conservative artist excelling in the
character portrait.

In 1913 Major published *Panopticum*, caricatures of
Hungarian men of letters; in 1927 an *Album* containing
the caricatures of the 180 wealthiest men of America,
and in 1938 an album entitled *Hollywood Caricatures.*
He wrought also small caricature sculptures.

MAJORITY (*rob, rubya*, in contrast to *miyut,
miyuta*, "minority"), the principle for all decisions as
to the civil and religious law in uncertain, doubtful
cases. It is based on the traditional interpretation of
Ex. 23:2, which speaks of a majority. The basic
thought of this principle is that the whole bears the
character of the majority of its members; from this
the law is derived that the doubtful individual has
the same nature as that of its kind (*kol defarish
merubba farish*, *Keth.* 15a). In this the minority receives no consideration and is treated as if it were
not present at all (*Kid.* 80a).

There are a number of regulations for the law,
in which one is directed to apply the rule of the
majority even when the latter is empirically assumed.
Thus it would not be possible to make the Passover

offering except on the basis of this norm. The law is that no bone of it should be broken; it would be manifestly impossible to make an investigation to see if it is unfit (*terefah*) for this reason, in the case of the brain that lies within the skull, and finally, this would cause an injury to the skin. It is only on the basis of the presupposition that most animals are sound and free of defects that this necessary examination can be dispensed with (*Hul.* 11ab). Or again, there is mention of a majority of women who become pregnant and give birth (*Yeb.* 119a), of a majority who do not miscarry, which is of importance for the levirate marriage, of a majority of women who marry as virgins (*Keth.* 16a; *B.B.* 92b), and of a majority of sick who recover (*Git.* 28a).

The principle of majority receives a manysided application in the most varied fields of law. The Biblical principle that a simple majority is sufficient (*had bithre batel*) is valid in civil law in that a majority of one vote is sufficient. However, in criminal cases, the procedure is different. The Biblical verse (*Ex.* 23:2), "Thou shalt not follow a multitude to do evil," was interpreted to mean that a condemnation could not result from the same majority as an acquittal; a majority of at least two was required in the former case, whereas a simple majority was sufficient for the latter (*Sanh.* 1:1). The law of majority, finally, was applied to the divisions of the Sanhedrin on Halachic matters and was effective to a very great extent. Thus the Talmud relates that two of the most important sages of the Law, Akabiah ben Mahalalel and Eliezer ben Hyrcanus, were excluded from the Sanhedrin and placed under the great ban because they strove against obeying the conclusions of the majority (*Eduy.* 5:6; *B.M.* 59b). The law of the majority also prevails over two other principles that are no less important, that of presumption (*hazakah*) and that of nearness (*karob, kureba*). If the principle of majority comes into conflict with one of these principles, the decision is according to the former (*Kid.* 80a; *B.B.* 23b). Both these rules experience all sorts of limitations in the Talmud and with the Posekim.

It is important to note that the principle of the majority has no application in money matters. Even in ritual matters, where the principle of majority is valid as a rule, it is in many cases excluded by casuistry. In this connection one should mention the *rubba dethalya bema'aseh*, the majority which is dependent on a definite action, such as the pregnancy of an animal, which is possible only through the act of copulation (*Bech.* 20a); also the cases in which the objects to be tested are regularly found at a stipulated place at a stipulated time (*Zeb.* 73b-74a). The Biblical principle, *had bithre batel,* that a forbidden thing is completely annulled by mixture with two things like it, but permitted, is often limited by the rabbis. Thus, for fluids or things well mixed by cooking a mixture of one in sixty is required (*Hul.* 97b; *Shulhan Aruch, Yoreh Deah* 106); in the case of the heave-offering, a proportion of one in a hundred; and in the case of fruits of the first three years (Orlah) and mixtures of seeds (Kile Hakerem), even a ratio of one to 200 (*Orlah* 2:1). Finally, there are many things in which the possibility of nullifying what is prohibited by mixture with what is permitted is completely excluded,

such as entire beings (*biryah*), considerable pieces which are fit for serving, a thing the prohibition of which is again recalled, living beings (*ba'ale hayyim; Yoreh Deah* 100 to 103, 110), things which are purchased by number (*Betz.* 3b), and other cases.

Whereas most of the rabbis, in their opinions about the Halachah, regard the minority as if it did not exist at all, Meir pays attention to the minority, in that he makes use of it to derive greater rigor in the law (*Yeb.* 61b, 119b); on the other hand, he gives no consideration whatsoever to the minority of a minority (*ibid.;* cf. *ibid.* 119b).

For majority in respect to age, *see* COMPETENCY, LEGAL.   JAKOB PINCHAS KOHN.

MAKAI, EMIL, poet, b. Makó, Hungary, 1870; d. Budapest, 1901. His original name was Emil Fischer; he was the son of Antal Enoch Fischer, rabbi of Makó, who destined his son for a rabbinical career. His mother fell a victim to a cholera epidemic when the son was three years old, and he was raised by one of his older sisters, a widow. She followed him to Budapest when, in 1884, he became a student in the high school of the rabbinical seminary. While he was still there, his recitation of verse was applauded by József Kiss, the Hungarian poet laureate.

Makai published *Vallásos énekek* (Religious Songs; 1888), a first slender volume of verse. It was followed, in 1892, by *Zsidó költők,* an anthology in Magyar of poems by Solomon ibn Gabirol, Judah Halevi, Samuel Hanagid and other Hebrew poets. Its nation-wide success won popularity alike for Hebrew poetry in Hungary and for Makai. From 1889 he attended the college of the seminary, but he had become engaged also in journalism, and felt more and more attracted toward a literary career. It was after a prolonged inner struggle that, in 1893, he obtained his father's consent to discontinue rabbinical studies. In 1895 there appeared his *Margit,* a volume of love poems. Others to follow were *Ujabb költemények* (New Verse; 1899) and *Poétasors* (Fate of the Poet; 1901).

From 1897 on Makai was assistant editor of József Kiss' literary journal *A Hét;* he was also a member of the dramaturgic committee of the National Theatre of Budapest. His comedies *Kaland* (Adventure; Ferenc Szécsi, co-author); *A királyné apródja* (Her Majesty's Page Boy), a comedy in verse (Jenő Heltai, co-author); and *Tudós professzor Hatvani* (The Learned Professor Hatvani) were performed during the years 1897 to 1900 at the Vigszinház, foremost comedy stage of Hungary. He also translated and adapted over one hundred plays for the Hungarian stage, many of them in verse.

His sister nursed him through his long illness to the end. When, in compliance with his wish, his body was transferred for burial to Makó, the literary world of Budapest paid homage at the farewell ceremony.

Makai possessed true lyric genius. Orphaned at a tender age and burdened with basic conflicts, his soul was surcharged with great emotional strains which he sublimated in musical lyricism. His poetry is suffused with nostalgia for the implicit faith of his boyhood, a melancholy sense of guilt for having forsaken the path traced by father and religion, yet a realization that he could not have done otherwise. His love poems were inspired by a longing for the unattainable.

ANNA BETTELHEIM.

Lit.: Kiss, Arnold, "Emlékezés," *Egyenlöség,* Aug. 11, 1901; Farkas, Gyula, *Az asszimláció kora a magyar irodalomban; Magyar Zsidó Lexikon* (1929) 569-70.

MAKAMA, name given to a sort of rhymed prose which was practised in the courts of oriental rulers. These compositions were presented in the form of a tournament, and later produced a variety of Arabic literature. In the Hebrew language and literature, the first to introduce this species of composition was Judah al-Harizi (about 1220). He took over from Hariri, the Arabian, the famous vagabond Makamas, which he translated into Hebrew and published under the title of *Mahberoth Itiel.* Later he independently composed a counter-piece to this under the name of *Tahkemoni.* The second important writer of Makamas was Immanuel ben Solomon of Rome (about 1300), who wrote *Mahberoth Immanuel.* This poetry obtained considerable charm through its use of the mosaic style.

MAKKES, *see* PHRASES, POPULAR.

MAKKOTH ("corporal punishment"), fifth tractate of Nezikin, the fourth division of the Mishnah and Talmud. It follows immediately after the tractate *Sanhedrin,* the two probably constituting originally a single tractate. Its three chapters deal partly with the offenses for which the flogging prescribed as punishment in *Deut.* 25:1-3 forms the sentence. The first chapter is concerned with false witnesses; it closes with rabbinical opinions opposed to frequent cases of capital punishment. The second chapter deals with the unintentional homicide who had to flee to a city of refuge. The third chapter is the only one that actually deals with corporal punishment as such; it enumerates the offenses for which it is a penalty, and describes the manner in which it was carried out. It is noted that one who voluntarily subjects himself to flogging becomes free from the divine punishment of excision ("being cut off from his people"). The tractate closes with the saying of Hananiah ben Akashiah: "God desired to give Israel the opportunity of acquiring much merit; therefore He gave them a great Law and many commandments."

The Tosefta to the tractate has four chapters, the last two corresponding to the third of the Mishnah. The Babylonian Gemara amounts to twenty-four pages; the Palestinian Gemara extends only over the first two chapters.

MAKKOTH MARDUTH, *see* CORPORAL PUNISHMENT.

MAKOWER, ERNEST SAMUEL, merchant and art patron, b. London, 1876. He was educated at the University College School and in France and Germany. Makower was the chairman of the silk section of the Chamber of Commerce and a member of the financial executive of the British Council of Commerce. Among his contributions to the civic art collections of England were his presentation of the Essex key to Westminster Abbey and of the Prime Minister's room to the London Museum. Makower and his wife collected portraits, autographs and various other personalia relating to the prime ministers of Great Britain from Sir Robert Walpole to modern times and then made the collection a part of the Museum, of which Makower is a trustee. He was in 1942 a director of the Royal Academy of Music.

MAKOWER, FELIX, lawyer and Jewish communal leader, b. Berlin, 1863; d. Berlin, 1933. He was the son of Hermann Makower, whom he succeeded as a spokesman of the board of the Jewish orphan asylum in Berlin-Pankow. He was a founder and the last president of the Verband der Deutschen Juden, which combined the Jewish organizations and communities in 1904, and fought for the recognition of the Jewish organizations as public institutions. When this goal was attained in 1920 Makower became a member of the Preussischer Landesverband Jüdischer Gemeinden and of the board of the Jewish community in Berlin from 1924 to 1927. Furthermore he was a member of the board of the Centralverein deutscher Staatsbürger jüdischen Glaubens in Berlin, and founded the organization which published *Die Lehren des Judentums,* a series of publications by Leo Baeck, Ismar Elbogen, S. Hochfeld, M. Holzman and A. Loewenthal (edited by Simon Bernfeld) with the purpose of popularizing among Jews and non-Jews the knowledge of Judaism.

As a lawyer Makower published *Die Verfassung der Kirche in England* and *Gezügelte Kirche im freien Staat.*

Lit.: C.-V.-Zeitung, Feb. 9, 1933.

MAKOWER, HERMANN, lawyer and communal worker, b. Santomischel, Prussian Poland, 1830; d. Berlin, 1897. When he was nine, his father sent him to Berlin, virtually without means. The boy earned his living as a chorister in a synagogue, and later by teaching. He attended the Französisches Gymnasium, the best and most exacting classical school in Berlin. In 1851 he passed his first juridical examination, and in 1856 became associate judge of the municipal courts of Berlin. In 1857 he attracted attention by his study *Die Stellung der Verteidigung im preussischen Strafverfahren,* dealing with a problem which lost none of its juridical and political importance until the beginning of the Third Reich. He gained new repute by his *Studien zur Konkursordnung* (1861) and established his authority through *Das allgemeine deutsche Handelsgesetzbuch* (1862). During his lifetime Makower was generally esteemed as a keen commentator on commercial law in Germany. After his death, another Jewish lawyer, Hermann Staub, was his successor.

In 1866, Makower retired from the bench and resumed the practice of law. That same year, he was elected to the executive board of the Jewish community of Berlin. In 1870 he became member of the directorate of the Jewish community and remained in this office until 1892. In 1873 he published *Die Gemeinde-Verhältnisse der Juden in Preussen.* Deeply interested in the promotion of the Jewish Lehranstalt, he lectured on its behalf in several German towns and supported a variety of its research endeavors. In 1875 he was appointed member of the examining board for Prussian jurists. He was regarded as one of the greatest and most successful German lawyers, and, as Eduard von Simson said, "a credit to the bar."

Ornament from the first edition of the "Makre Dardeke" printed in 1488 by Joseph ben Jacob Ashkenazi

Makower was treasurer of the general union of German lawyers. In 1884 he successfully tried the case of the Jews of Neu-Stettin who were accused of burning their synagogue, which in fact had been set afire by anti-Semites. The town of Neu-Stettin remained for many years a center of rabid anti-Semitism, and after the verdict, the Jews there were the victims of a pogrom. Makower espoused their cause and also defended the noted historian Mommsen, who was accused of having offended Bismarck personally. It was a thorny task to oppose the powerful chancellor in court, but Makower mastered it with courage, tact and humor.

For many years Makower was juridical counsellor of Prince Chlodwig of Hohenlohe-Schillingsfürst, later chancellor of the Reich. In particular, he defended the prince in connection with his inheritance of immense landed properties in Russia. In 1888 he accompanied the prince to Russia, and there met Czar Alexander III and the Russian minister of foreign affairs. The prince was highly satisfied with Makower's adroit handling of his difficult lawsuit.

Makower was at all times an ardent defender of liberalism, which he considered identical with humanitarian ideals. He was a leader of the radical liberal party, and after it split, in 1893, he joined the Freisinnige Vereinigung, led by Bamberger and Rickert, serving on its direcorate until his death.

MAKOWER, WALTER, physicist, b. London, 1879. He was educated at University College, London, and Trinity College, Cambridge, where he received his M.A. degree in 1909. From 1906 to 1917 he was a lecturer in physics at the University of Manchester, and later assistant director of the physical laboratories there. Entering military service in 1917, Makower was in both the volunteer naval reserve and the air corps until 1919. In 1925 he became a professor of science at the Woolwich Military Academy, and held this post until 1938. He became vice-president of the Institute of Physics in 1934. Makower was the author of *Radio-Active Substance* (1907) and *Practical Measurements in Radio Activity* (1913).

MAKRE DARDEKE, a name given in the Middle Ages to Hebrew glossaries. The literal translation of the phrase is "teacher of children." The first work of this type was compiled by Perez Trevot, in Italy, at the end of the 14th cent., and was published in Naples in 1488. Containing Italian and Arabic equivalents for every Hebrew word, and brief definitions in Hebrew

itself, the Makre Dardeke was intended to aid Jews in understanding their own literature and to equip them for a defense against Christian and Moslem arguments. Definitions from the French, taken from the commentaries of Rashi and David Kimhi, are also found in the Makre Dardeke. In addition to its value from the point of view of Hebrew, the first Makre Dardeke is informative as to 14th cent. Italian usage. Other glossaries of the same type were published in Germany, France and Spain in subsequent periods.

MALABAR, the southwestern region of British India, in the district of Madras, along the shore of the Arabian Sea, west of the province of Travancore. In 1942 its Jewish population was small, except in the port of Cochin and in the four adjoining towns of Ernakulam, Paroor, Chennota (or Chennanmangalum) and Malla, where there were, in all, 1,500 Jews.

These communities are of great antiquity, dating back in all probability to the 1st cent. C. E. There are no authentic records regarding the early immigration and settlement of Jews on the Malabar Coast. Tradition states that the first Jews came thither about 68 C.E., and settled chiefly in Cranganore and its environs, enjoying rulership over the place. Here, probably, these first Jewish settlers purchased slaves and converted the natives of Malabar to the Jewish faith. For centuries they dwelt at peace with their Hindu and Mohammedan neighbors. The famous Jewish traveler, Benjamin of Tudela, who visited Malabar in 1167, refers to the Jews there and speaks of their being "only about one hundred Jews, who are of black color."

However, with the Portuguese invasion of the Orient and the rivalry between the Portuguese and the Dutch, an era of persecution at the hands of the former began. The Portuguese burned the settlements of the Jews, whence they fled as exiles. Jewish records of early days which had been preserved were destroyed at this time by their fanatical assailants. It was probably at this period that the Jews of the Malabar Coast became scattered, and as times improved and the Dutch, who favored them, defeated the Portuguese, the Jews took shelter by settling in the above-mentioned five places, where they built their synagogues and homes.

The Jews of the Malabar Coast, under the influence of the Hindu caste system, are divided into three groups, the White Jews, the Brown Jews, and the Black Jews. These three groups do not intermarry, or

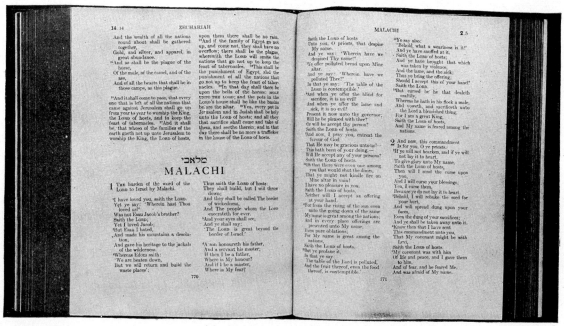

Pages from an English translation of the book of Malachi, published by the Jewish Publication Society of America

dine with one another, or hold religious services in common. All three castes observe the Orthodox Sephardic ritual.

In 1520 the Black Jews wrote to Rabbi David ben Solomon ibn Zimra of Cairo, claiming that the discrimination practised against them was not in accordance with the Jewish religious law. Ibn Zimra decided in their favor. Some years later Rabbi Jacob Castro of Alexandria (d. 1610) arrived at the same conclusion. In 1882 the Black Jews addressed the same complaint to Rabbi Phanizel, chief rabbi of Jerusalem, and he, too, agreed with Ibn Zimra. However, the White Jews refused to change their customs.

The so-called White Jews resident in Malabar in modern times are the descendants of Jews who first emigrated from Amsterdam, Holland, in 1685. This emigration was subsequently supplemented by immigrations from Palestine, Persia, Baghdad, Egypt, Poland and Germany. These White Jews, described in the public accounts and records of the native rajahs as Pardesis (an Indian word meaning "foreigners"), claim to be the offspring of the tribe of Manasseh which had been carried off into captivity and exiled by Nebuchadrezzar, king of Babylonia (after 586 B.C.E.), all the way to Cape Comorin, the southernmost tip of India. The so-called Black (non-white) Jews are considered to be the descendants of the slaves purchased by the first Jewish settlers and of other natives of Malabar converted to Judaism. However, the Black Jews themselves claim descent from the Judeo-Arabians who are still found at Sanaa in Yemen and at Aden. The Brown Jews have a tradition that they were the first to reach and settle on the Malabar Coast, in the 1st cent. C. E. Rabbi Jacob Saphir (1822-86), who traveled in India in 1854, says of the non-white Jews: "They are not black like the raven, or as the Nubians, but only as the appearance of copper" (*Eben Sappir,* vol. 1, 1866; vol. 2, 1874).

The Jews of Malabar in modern times strictly practise monogamy, evidently through the influence of the Dutch and other European Ashkenazic Jews who settled among them. Malabar Jewry is remarkable for the intensity of its religious devotion. Their synagogues are the center of all social activity, and there is probably less of an assimilationist tendency in their community than anywhere else in the Jewish world. The White Jews of Cochin have only one synagogue, built in 1568 and rebuilt in 1664. The Black Jews of Cochin have three synagogues. In addition, synagogues of the Black Jews are found in the other towns of Malabar as follows: Ernakulam, two, one built in 1300 and the second in 1600; Malla, one, built in 1400; Paroor, one, built in 750; Chennota, one, built in 1420. In 1942 there were no White Jews living in any of the towns of the Malabar Coast except Cochin.

Many scholars are of the opinion that, inasmuch as the date of the earliest tombstone of the White Jews is only 200 years old, while the earliest date of a tombstone of the Black Jews is 600 years old, the institutions of the Black Jews antedate those of the Whites.

See also: COCHIN; INDIA; JEWS' TOWN; RAHABI.

EZEKIEL MOSES EZEKIEL.

Lit.: Mandelbaum, David G., "The Jewish Way of Life in Cochin," *Jewish Social Studies,* vol. 1, No. 4, pp. 423-60; see also the literature under COCHIN; JEWS' TOWN.

MALACH HAMAVETH, *see* ANGEL OF DEATH.

MALACHI, last of the books of the twelve Minor Prophets of the Bible. The book, which contains three chapters (or four in the ancient translations and the English Version), is really anonymous, for the name Malachi is merely the Hebrew word for "my messenger," picked up from 3:1, "Behold, I send My messenger (*mal'achi*), and he shall clear the way before Me." The author appears to have written about 445 B.C.E., and may be regarded as a propagandist for the reforms introduced by Nehemiah. Indeed, his prophecies become fully intelligible only when read in the light of *Nehemiah,* for they are, in essence, a series of polemics against specific trends and ideologies mentioned in that work.

The book opens with a brief denunciation of Edom (1:2-5), a term which probably comprehends those Arabians and Ammonites who are described in *Neh.* 4:1 (cf. 13:1) as obstructing the repair of the walls of Jerusalem. The prophet then proceeds to recite the reasons why God has apparently disregarded His people, and suffered them to fall upon evil times:

1. The priests, violating His time-honored covenant with Levi, have sought to cheat Him of His dues, offering in sacrifice such blemished and inferior animals as even a mortal ruler would disdain to accept. They can therefore expect no favors from Him (1:6 to 2:9).

2. The people have offended God by divorcing their lawful wives and forming alliances with foreign women. How, then, can they expect God to grant them offspring? (2:10-16; cf. *Neh.,* 10:31; 13:23).

3. There has been an all too prevalent idea that God is not interested in justice, and that only evildoers are permitted to prosper. Defrauding Him of His tithes and tributes has therefore been viewed with complacency (2:17; 3:7-9; cf. *Neh.* 10:38; 12:44; 13:12).

These crimes will not go unpunished, according to the author. In a picture of final judgment, to take place on "the great and awful day of the Lord," the prophet portrays the future advent of God in the capacity of a refiner who will purge the gold from the dross and cleanse the tarnished House of Levi. "Then shall the offering of Judah and Jerusalem be pleasant unto the Lord, as in the days of old, and as in ancient years" (3:2-4). Judgment will be executed upon all who defect from the ancestral faith, marrying foreign women and swearing allegiance to alien gods. Described ironically as "sorcerers, adulterers and perjurers," they are regarded as of one piece with those who cheat servants of their wages, or oppress widows, orphans and guests (3:5). God will keep record both of those who "fear Him and esteem His name" (an expression which probably includes proselytes) and of those who arrogantly foreswear Him. When the Great Day comes, it will "burn like an oven," and devour like chaff all who have done wickedly. But upon the faithful there shall rise a sun "with healing in its wings" (a reference to the winged solar disk of ancient iconography), and they shall go forth and trample the wicked like ashes beneath their feet (3:16-21). Moreover, if they but pay their tithes regularly, current famine (cf. *Neh.* 5:2-3) will be removed, the sluice-gates of heaven will be opened, and produce will abound (3:10-12).

In the closing verses (cf. *Neh.* 1:7; 8:2-8) the people are counselled to "remember the law of Moses My servant, which I commanded unto him in Horeb" (3:22), and they are promised that before the Great Day dawns, the prophet Elijah will reappear to reconcile parents and children, lest the land be cursed.

The style of Malachi betrays a period of prophetic decadence. It is cumbrous, artificial and pedestrian. The meter is careless, and there is little control over the poetic medium. Nevertheless, despite inadequacies of form, the prophet is capable of rising to a fine nobility of sentiment, as in the memorable lines (2:10): "Have we not all one father? Hath not one God created us? Why do we deal treacherously every man against his brother, profaning the covenant of our fathers?"   THEODOR H. GASTER.

Lit.: Smith, J. M. Powis, *Malachi (International Critical Commentary,* 1912); Horst, *Die zwölf kleinen Propheten,* vol. 2 (1938); Junker, *Die zwölf kleinen Propheten,* vol. 2 (1938); Smith, G. A., *Book of the Twelve Prophets* (1928); Margolis, Max L., *Malachi,* in A. Kahana's Hebrew critical edition of the Old Testament (1929); Friedlaender, Michael, "Notes on Malachi," *Jews' College Jubilee Volume* (1906); Smith and Irwin, *The Prophets and their Times,* 2nd ed. (1941) 266-70.

MALAMUD, WILLIAM ZEV, psychiatrist, b. Kishinev, Russia, 1896. He studied medicine at McGill University (M.D. and C.M., 1921). He came to the United States in 1921. He was clinical director at the Foxboro (Mass.) State Hospital from 1926 to 1929, and in the latter year he became associate professor of psychiatry at the College of Medicine of the State University of Iowa. From 1931 on he was professor of psychiatry. He was also appointed clinical professor of psychiatry at Boston University School of Medicine (1941).

Malamud is the author of *Outlines of General Psychopathology* (1935), a study of abnormal mental processes "primarily from the point of view of objective observation" (Introduction).

MALAMUT, J. L., Yiddish writer, b. Snitkov, province of Podolia, Russia, 1886. His childhood was spent in a home of strong Hasidic tradition, but he was orphaned at the age of fourteen, and became a teacher in the provinces. In 1903 Malamut came to the United States. His first published work, sketches and stories, appeared in the *Arbeiter Freind* (London) in 1904. Malamut lived in London during 1906, working on the *Yiddishe Velt.*

Returning to London in 1907, Malamut was a collaborator on the *Forverts, Zeitgeist* and other papers. In 1910 he was editor of a humorous weekly, *Der Shpiegel.* From 1911 to 1916 Malamut lived in Canada, where he was associated with the *Keneder Adler,* and worked in Montreal and Winnipeg. Then he went to Chicago, where he had charge, first, of the Chicago edition of the *Forverts,* and later of the *Tog.* Subsequently he was the editor of newspapers in Detroit and Los Angeles.

In 1925 Malamut founded a literary monthly, *Zunland.* He published several volumes of children's stories in Yiddish, a novel, later made into a play, *Beim Rebben in Hoif,* and another play, *Der Egoist,* produced in Canada and Chicago. Malamut is considered a pioneer in the field of the American provincial Yiddish press.

Lit.: Reisen, Z., *Lexikon fun der Yiddisher Literatur, Presse un Filologie,* vol. 2 (1930), cols. 298-301.

MALARIA, the most widespread endemic disease in Palestine, because of the country's topography and seasonal rainfall. Other factors which favored the epidemic extension of malaria were: the low standards of living of the majority of the rural population, prior to the first World War (1914-18); the low economic status of the non-immune Jewish immigrants; the wandering of the nomadic Bedouins. The prevalence of malaria in Palestine reached a climax during the first World War, possibly because the presence of a large number of infected Turkish troops prevented control and the population was weakened by starvation.

After the War, the British government established the Medical and Health Service Department for the control of malaria. The government was aided in its

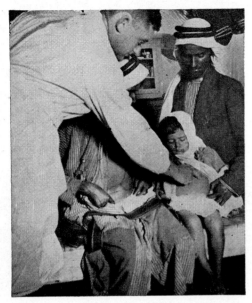

Treating Arab patients at the Hebrew University's malaria research station

task by medical groups endowed by various divisions of the Zionist movement and the Joint Distribution Committee. The Medical Research Unit for the control of malaria was established in 1922; Israel Jacob Kligler was made its chief medical officer in 1926.

The prevalence of malaria is measured by (a) the spleen-rate; (b) parasite-rate; (c) registration of returns by physicians; (d) mortality figures. The spleen-rate among Jewish children in Jerusalem ranged from 36 to 60 per cent in 1904; about 50 per cent of all outpatients were afflicted with malaria. In 1912 there was a spleen-rate of 40 to 83 per cent among children and a parasite-rate of 22 per cent among adults. It was highest among children under five years of age (53 per cent), less between the ages of six and fifteen (30 per cent) and least among persons of sixteen and older (17 to 20 per cent). In 1919 a spleen-rate of 47 per cent was recorded among school children. In 1921 the routine examination of 851 children in government schools gave a spleen-rate of 19 per cent.

While in 1919 the malaria patients in the controlled areas constituted 68 per cent of the total population, they comprised only 11 per cent of the 26,729 inhabitants in 1926. The malaria index in rural districts varies and is slightly higher than in the cities. The spleen-rate for children from 1935 to 1938 was:

	URBAN	RURAL
1935	1.7	7.4
1936	1.8	6.7
1937	1.5	4.7
1938	1.4	4.5

The methods of mosquito control which have proved of value are: (1) mechanical; (2) chemical; (3) biological. The first is the most widely-employed method, and consists of drying the swamps and damming or deflecting the streams. In the chemical method, water-surfaces are covered with mixtures of paraffine and crude oil (known as petrolization) or

are sprayed with poisons, such as copper sulphate or paris green. In the biological method fish are employed as antilarval agents.

In the Jewish sections of Palestine, the malaria problem has become one of repeating the control procedure each time new settlements are opened in swampy areas. Total drainage being impossible, the research units had to depend on the detection of carriers, mosquito control and education. Results vary according to the degree of topographical handicap and the cooperation provided. The proximity of heavily-infected Arab villages is frequently an impediment. Such handicaps made control in the new settlements around Huleh, in northern Palestine, more difficult. Yet in some of the settlements in the region there were only three cases of malaria in 1940, out of a population of 450, as against twenty-one cases in 1939, out of a population of 200. In the whole Huleh region, the proportion of malaria victims was 24 per cent in 1939 and 7 per cent in 1940. The Haifa Bay region settlements developed during the 1930's required a great deal of swamp clearance, reducing mosquito-breeding significantly. Whereas, from March to July, 1939, some 15,000 mosquitoes were caught in the official "catching" stations, only 850 were trapped during the same period in 1940. In 1942 Kligler was still in charge of the medical research unit.

NATHAN RICARDO.

Lit.: British Colonial Office Reports: Palestine and Transjordania (1935-39); Kligler, Israel Jacob, *The Epidemiology and Control of Malaria in Palestine* (1930); Schneider, *Organisation und Erfolg der Malariabekämpfung in Palästina* (1928).

MALBIM, abbreviation of the Hebrew name (later the family name) of Meir Löb ben Jehiel Michael, known under the name of "The Kempner," Talmudist and exegete, b. Volochisk, Russia, 1809; d. Kiev, Russia, 1879. He was rabbi in Wreschen, Kempen, Leczica, Bucharest and Mogilev, and later of the Russian community in Königsberg. Over Malbim's election in Kempen a long drawn out feud broke out with which the Prussian authorities were also concerned and through which the community was split into two hostile camps. After serving as rabbi in several pulpits he became chief rabbi in Bucharest, where he evoked the bitter opposition of the rich German Jews when he attempted to block their efforts to introduce reforms in the ritual. They went so far as to have him arrested and imprisoned. He was freed through the intervention of Sir Moses Montefiore, on condition that he leave the country. His efforts to secure redress in Constantinople were fruitless. He lived in Paris for half a year, following which he served successively in several pulpits in Russia. Throughout his life Malbim was embittered by his uncompromising and fearless attitude toward the wealthy German Jews. He died on his way to fill a pulpit at Kremenchug.

Despite his wandering life and incessant persecution, Malbim wrote a number of valuable books, including *Artzoth Hahayim,* a commentary on the *Shulhan Aruch; Artzoth Hashalom,* sermons; and *Mashal Umelitzah,* a book of verse. His most important works are an exhaustive commentary on the entire Bible—chiefly the commentary on the Pentateuch, *Hatorah Vehamitzvah*—and an edition of the Halachic Midrashim, *Mechilta, Sifra* and *Sifre,* in which he shows profound knowledge of the Hebrew language, a talent for fine analysis and great Talmudic acuteness. He also wrote several books of responsa, a commentary on the code of Maimonides, and a work on Hebrew syntax and synonyms (*Ayeleth Hashahar*).

ISSAK MARKON.

Lit.: Bravermann, in Rabinowitz, *Keneseth Yisrael,* vol. 3, pp. 207-12; Maggid-Steinschneider, *Ir Vilna,* p. 233, No. 3; Meisl, in *Yeshurun* (1925) 112-26; Waxman, M., *A History of Jewish Literature,* vol. 3 (1936) 550-55; Seligsohn, Max, in *Jewish Encyclopedia,* vol. 8, pp. 276-77.

MALCHUTH SHAMAYIM, *see* KINGDOM OF HEAVEN.

MALCHUYOTH ("Biblical verses about the kingdom of God"), the first of the three benedictions peculiar to the Musaf (additional) Tefillah of Rosh Hashanah. The Malchuyoth praise God as the King of the world. Originally they consisted of Biblical verses arranged in order, four of which were taken from the Torah and three apiece from the Prophets and the Hagiographa. Later an introduction was added, the well-known Alenu and the *'al ken nekavveh lecha,* two sections which proclaim the thought of the kingdom of God on earth and the union of all mankind together with the acknowledgment of One God. Abba Aricha probably composed the Malchuyoth, most likely making use of older models. The Malchuyoth idea is contained also in the prayer *ubechen ten pahdecha,* which is recited as the third portion of the Tefillah for Rosh Hashanah and Yom Kippur, since these two days are dominated by the thought of the kingdom of God. The Malchuyoth have been accompanied, from the very oldest times, by the blowing of the Shofar. About the 4th or 5th cent., a prayer was introduced after them, beginning with the words *hayom harath 'olam* ("Today is the birthday of the world"). American Reform prayer-books which omit Musaf or additional services have transferred an abridged form of the Malchuyoth (as of the Zichronoth and Shofaroth) from the Shofar service of the Musaf to the Shofar service which traditionally follows the Torah reading.

See also KINGDOM OF GOD.

Lit.: Elbogen, I., *Der jüdische Gottesdienst,* 141-44; Singer, S., and Abrahams, I., *The Authorised Daily Prayer Book* (1922) 247-49, cxcviii-cxcix; Idelsohn, A. Z., *Jewish Liturgy* (1932) 213-14.

MALECH, LEIB (Leibl Salzman), Yiddish poet and dramatist, b. Zvalin, province of Radom, Poland, 1894; d. Paris, 1936. He had a thorough Jewish schooling until the age of thirteen, when he went to Warsaw. Here, while working as a laborer in various trades, he proceeded with his self-education. Making his debut as a poet in 1915 in the *Varshever Tageblatt,* Malech later published poems and fiction in the *Haint,* the *Moment* and other journals. He specialized in children's poetry.

In 1922 Malech went to Argentina and wrote for various publications there and in other South American countries. Among his plays were *Apfalen,* set in the Warsaw underworld; *Iberguss,* dealing with prostitution in Argentina; and *Mississippi,* which was very successful. His best-known published work includes *Alters Yugendyohren,* an autobiographical novel; his

poem *Borochovzes;* and travel sketches, particularly about Palestine. Malech was active in various Jewish activities, especially as a Poale (Labor) Zionist.

Lit.: Reisen, Z., *Lexikon fun der Yiddisher Literatur, Presse un Filologie,* vol. 2 (1927), cols. 431-34; *Lexikon fun Yiddishen Teater; Proletarisher Gedank,* Aug. 1, 1941.

MALFEASANCE IN OFFICE. Jewish law mentions various offenses that can be committed in the exercise of an office, the most important office being that of judge. The Biblical law already forbids the acceptance of bribes; this was punished even when it had not influenced the decisions. Even the smallest favors might be regarded as bribes which honest judges will always seek to avoid. A judge is likely to be prejudiced not only by being related to one of the opposed parties, but also by being on particularly friendly terms with such a person; in these cases he is not allowed to serve. An error in declaring the law constitutes misfeasance on the part of the judge, because an appeal is rendered very difficult; but this applies only to cases of failure to observe the generally known rules of law, such as the decisions of the Mishnah, and the like. On the other hand, the incorrect apprehension of a question which had been left to the judge to decide according to his own judgment does not constitute malfeasance in office.

Similarly, judicial officers charged with the execution of a sentence are personally responsible for their actions, especially where they have overstepped the rights accorded to them in the court proceedings. Thus, an officer is adjudged to have committed accidental homicide and is sentenced to internment in a city of refuge should he inadvertently have given an offender, sentenced to whipping, an additional stroke beyond the prescribed number, and thereby have caused his death. There is no provision in Jewish law for the impeachment of judges, since it is provided that if a judge has deliberately erred or has been unjust in the rendering of a decision, he must pay for the loss incurred, but if it is a question of his own judgment he is not responsible for damages. In certain cases the judge was required to grant a new trial, but if such new trial was not possible he was not held responsible for monetary damages.

Guardians appointed by the court, according to the opinion of Rabbi Hai and of Nahmanides, are responsible for all losses. Guardians and executors appointed by the testator, on the other hand, are free from all liability for unintentional loss, because such an appointment to guardianship carries with it full authority. This severe liability as guardians appointed by the court had, as an indirect result, an unwillingness to accept such an office. Certain alleviations were therefore instituted. Guardians could exonerate themselves by means of an oath that they were not guilty of negligence.

The Sabbath prayer Mi Sheberach invokes a blessing upon those representatives of public interests who "faithfully discharge the duties of their office." This prayer now applies especially to the rabbis and lay leaders of congregations. MOSES HYAMSON.

Lit.: Bloch, M., *Die Vormundschaft nach mosaisch-talmudischem Rechte,* § 44.

MALISOFF, WILLIAM MARIAS, chemist, b. Ekaterinoslav, Russia, 1895. He was brought to the

United States in 1905. In 1925 Malisoff received his Ph.D. degree from New York University. He had begun to teach chemistry in 1916, serving until 1918 as instructor at Columbia University and in 1924 and 1925 at New York University. Malisoff entered the industrial chemistry field in 1925, joining the research department of the Atlantic Refining Company in Philadelphia. Working first as consultant, then as director, he remained with the firm until 1934. Numerous patents were issued to him on processes now in operation. He became associated during this period with the graduate school of the University of Pennsylvania, and in 1938 was appointed professor of biochemistry at the Graduate School of the Polytechnic Institute of Brooklyn, a position which he still held in 1942.

Malisoff was especially interested in the chemical possibilities of combatting hardening of the arteries, and in conjunction with investigations in this field he became affiliated with the laboratories of Montefiore Hospital in 1934. In 1942 he was still engaged in these investigations. He wrote: *A Calendar of Doubts* (1930); *Meet the Sciences* (1932); *The Span of Life* (1937); *The Conquest of Sex* (1942); *The Dictionary of Biochemistry* (1942). He also wrote scientific articles and book reviews for various magazines, and is editor of *Philosophy of Science* (1934-). He was, in 1942, president of the Philosophy of Science Association, and a member of the executive board of the American Committee for Democracy and Intellectual Freedom and of the Consumers Union.

MALKIN, MANFRED, pianist and teacher, b. Odessa, Russia, 1884. A student of Charles de Bériot at the Paris Conservatory, he made his debut in Paris in 1904, appearing in New York city one year later. For several years he concertized extensively, sometimes appearing in joint recitals with Eugene Ysaye. In 1914 he founded the Malkin Conservatory of Music in New York, directing it successfully until 1930. Since that time he has taught the piano privately.

His brothers, Jacques (b. Slobodka, Lithuania, 1876) and Joseph (b. Odessa, 1879), distinguished themselves as violinist and cellist respectively. Jacques Malkin was a member of the famous Société des Instruments Anciens in Paris, founded by Saint-Saëns. After coming to the United States, he served as head of the violin department in the Malkin Conservatory of Music in New York. Joseph Malkin was head of the cello department of the Malkin School in New York. In 1933 he founded (and in 1942 still directed) the Malkin Conservatory in Boston, where Jacques Malkin became head of the violin department.

Over a period of many years the Malkin Trio, consisting of the three brothers, has given excellent concerts of chamber music throughout the United States.

MALKIZEDEK, see MELCHIZEDEK.

MALKOTH, MALKUTH, see CORPORAL PUNISHMENT.

MALLER, JULIUS B., educator and sociologist, b. Lithuania, 1901. He received his higher education in New York city, securing his doctorate in Hebrew letters from the Jewish Theological Seminary of America in 1928 and his Ph.D. degree from Columbia University in 1929. An expert in the general field of edu-

cation, Maller contributed also to the special province of Jewish education. From 1929 to 1932 he was director of educational research for the Union of American Hebrew Congregations. His published contributions include achievement tests in Jewish history, and a syllabus of educational psychology which embodies an application of certain general principles to the teaching of Jewish studies. In 1933 he published the results of a survey of juvenile delinquency among Jews.

For the board of regents of the state of New York he conducted an inquiry into the the character and cost of public education in the state, making an exhaustive analysis of the relation of schools in given communities to the social and economic backgrounds of those communities. The results of this research were published in *School and Community* (1939). Character education of the child particularly interested him. He served on the board of directors of the Institute of Crime Prevention, and published *Studies in Service and Self-Control* (1929) and *Character and Personality Tests* (1934).

From the Lincoln School at Columbia University Maller went to teach at New York University, but was later called to be chief of the social research section of the United States Housing Authority in Washington.

Lit.: Maller, Julius B., *Educational Psychology Syllabus,* 19; *School and Community* (1939).

MALLINSON, HERBERT, philanthropist, b. Tyler, Texas, 1894; d. Dallas, Texas, 1941. He was educated at the Pennsylvania Military College. Although he began his business career in a dry goods firm, he soon changed to the paper trade, in which he remained until 1933. In 1934 he entered the oil and lumber business, and was a director in some of the leading oil and lumber companies in the Southwest.

Mallinson was active in civic and communal work of many kinds. He was chairman of the southwest region of the Joint Distribution Committee, and a member of the board of directors as well as Texas chairman of the National Refugee Service. He was also a director of the Council of Jewish Federations and Welfare Funds, and a member of the national board of the National Conference of Christians and Jews. Among Mallinson's secular communal activities were his membership on the Dallas County Parole Board and on the board of directors of the Dallas Community Chest. After his death the Dallas Jewish Federation for Social Service allotted a special grant of $35,000 to the United Jewish Appeal in his memory.

MALSHIN, see INFORMERS.

MALTA, an island in the Mediterranean Sea, about sixty miles south of Sicily, belonging to Great Britain. A number of catacombs bearing Jewish symbols discovered on the island are proof that Jews lived there in the early Roman period. That the language of the Jews of Malta in that period was Greek can be seen from fragments of Hellenic ornaments which were found. However, during the subsequent centuries, despite lack of positive knowledge, it is certain that a Jewish community existed there. The Abbot Gilbert reported to Emperor Frederick II that in 1240 twenty-five Jewish families lived in Malta and eight families on the neighboring island of Gozzo. The little islet of Comino, just a large rock between Malta and Gozzo, had at least one Jew.

Abraham ben Samuel Abulafia of Saragossa (b. 1240), who had tried to convert Pope Nicholas III, but was sentenced to be burned, escaped and fled to Sicily. When he was denounced as a false Messiah by Rabbi Solomon ibn Adret of Barcelona, he went to Malta, where he was not heartily welcomed and finally settled on Comino, near Malta, where in 1288 he wrote his *Sefer Haoth,* and his *Imre Shefer* in 1291.

Jews from Malta began early to settle in other communities. Bulfaracchio of Malta, one of the presiding officers (*Proti;* literally, "the first," "the heads") of the community of Messina, had close relations with the crown in the 14th cent. David Malti was authorized, in 1447, to collect donations from the Jews of Noto. Many Jews from Malta and Gozzo went to live in Syracuse. The Maltese Jews were engaged in various occupations. Most of them were peddlers, visiting the neighboring islands, while others engaged in agriculture, such as Musci (Moses) Aruverani, who possessed land. Still others traded with the mainland; many Maltese Jews did· considerable business with Palermo. Jewish physicians practised in Malta; Leone Maltese of Polizzi was authorized in 1398 to practise medicine, and in 1401 became medical assistant to the king. His son was probably Simon Maltese, who became a physician at Palermo in 1413.

The Jews of Malta had an organization called Aljama (in Spanish) or Judaica (in Latin) similar to that of the Jews of Sicily; the communities of Malta and Gozzo were regarded as one. The king's control over them was strict, and they were supervised by the captains of the islands. In 1434 Andrea Speciali was appointed to a· new office, having full jurisdiction over the Jews of Malta and Gozzo, but after long-standing protests by the citizens of Malta the viceroy returned control over Malta and Gozzo to the captains in 1466. The community was headed by the Proti, a body consisting generally of twelve persons chosen every year by four representatives who in turn were elected by the entire community. Elections took place, as everywhere in Jewish communities, after Passover. By an order of Martin I in 1397, the rich, the middle class and the poor were to have equal representation on this body. Later on the Proti retiring from office nominated the Proti for the coming year. A council of Maggiorenti (Memunim, appointed officials), elected by the community and possessed of an absolute authority, assisted the Proti in Malta. The Maggiorenti were responsible for the collection of taxes.

The synagogue, generally called either by its Arabic name of *Mechita* or by the Hebrew equivalent *Chyrusia,* was the center of religious Jewish life. The synagogue of Malta was situated at Notabile, in the "bargo di lo castello." Near the city was a place, which is still today called Kibir el Lhud (Burial Place of the Jews), where the cemetery was located. The office of rabbi was often combined with that of physician. In the second half of the 15th cent. Abraham Safaradi and Abraham Saba were known as rabbis and physicians. The office of notary of the Jews of Malta and Gozzo, called *sopher,* which required a knowledge of Hebrew and of Jewish law, was created in 1485; Raphael Cheti was appointed to this post.

The relations between Jews and Gentiles were friendly in the 13th and 14th centuries. Conditions changed, however, from the beginning of the 15th cent. on. The ecclesiastical authorities started persecutions of the communities of Malta and Gozzo. Before the expulsion, in 1492, there lived approximately 500 Jews in Malta and 350 in Gozzo. They left the two islands in 1493. Some went to Northern Africa, others to Turkey. The family name of Malti was very common in the Balkan cities, and in Sofia there was in existence a Malta Landsmannschaft which owned a synagogue.

In 1530 Malta was assigned by Emperor Charles V to the order of St. John of Malta. The knights carried on a fight against the pirates, and brought some of them as slaves to Malta. Jewish travelers were also captured by the knights, and for over two centuries the island became a place of Jewish slaves, mostly captured on the way to the Holy Land. Their treatment by the monks of Malta was cruel and evil, and Malta became in Jewish eyes a symbol of cruelty. The Hebrath Pidyon Shebuyim of Venice took a special interest in the liberation of these Jewish slaves, and for this purpose had a representative on the island. Baccio Bandinelli was the first agent who represented the society, from 1648 to 1670; he was succeeded by François Garsin, who was a judge of the Tribunal of the Consolato Del Mare. On the arrival of these slaves small sums of money were given to them by the agent, and a special amount in case of sickness. The agent notified the association at Venice of the number of new arrivals and, if enough funds were available, money was sent for their immediate ransom. Since great numbers of slaves arrived frequently, the collection of funds was difficult; furthermore, many other difficulties arose which made their redemption hard to obtain. Quite a number therefore remained in slavery, and as a result there was in Malta a strange Jewish community composed entirely of slaves.

Another strange aspect was the conscientious care of these Catholic agents, who looked not only after the general welfare of the Jewish slaves but also after their religious needs. They rented special places in the prison for religious worship, for which they paid, and gave them facilities to bake their own bread (Matzoth) for Passover. Some learned men were among the slaves of Malta, one of the most prominent being Jacob Lebeth Levi, translator of the Koran from Latin into Hebrew, who later became rabbi at Zante, wrote a volume of responsa, and died there in 1634. Not until 1800 did slavery finally cease in Malta, by official decree.

Toward the end of the 18th cent. Jews again began to settle on the island voluntarily. With the British occupation (1800) conditions changed entirely. A constitution was given to the Jewish community by General Maitland, governor of Malta from 1813 to 1824. Joseph Mazliah, a Palestinian rabbi, visited the island in 1821; Benjamin Disraeli came there in 1830. There were six Jewish families on Malta in 1838. The opening of the Suez Canal was one of the main reasons for an increase in the Jewish population thereafter (120 persons in 1892). A pamphlet was distributed in 1892 in Malta under the title *The Blood of Catholics shed by Jews* (in the Maltese language). From that

Henry Malter

period on the Jewish community decreased steadily (by 1904 it numbered seventy-five members); in 1942 it still maintained its synagogue and rabbi.

FERDINAND DANZIGER.

Lit.: Assaf, S., "Letoledoth Hayehudim Bei Malta," *Zion,* vol. 2 (1927) 67-75; Roth, Cecil, "The Jews of Malta," *Jewish Historical Society of England, Transactions,* vol. 12 (1928) 187; Wischnitzer, Mark, *Die Juden in der Welt* (1935) 88-91; *The Jewish Student Quarterly,* June, 1931, pp. 5-7, 12.

MALTER, HENRY, rabbi and scholar, b. Banse, Galicia, Poland, about 1864; d. Philadelphia, 1925. He studied Arabic and theology under Moritz Steinschneider at the Veitel Heine-Ephraimsche Lehranstalt from 1890 to 1898. He attended the University of Heidelberg (Ph.D., 1894), the University of Berlin (1889) and the Lehranstalt für die Wissenschaft des Judentums (rabbi, 1898).

In 1900 Malter accepted the invitation of the Hebrew Union College, of Cincinnati, to become instructor in medieval philosophy and Arabic, a post he held for seven years. During this time he served also as rabbi of the Shearith Israel Congregation. He resigned from the faculty of the Hebrew Union College in 1907 because of a disagreement in principle with President Kaufmann Kohler, and spent the next two years collaborating on J. D. Eisenstein's Hebrew encyclopedia *Otzar Yisrael.* When Dropsie College was founded in 1909 Malter became professor of Talmudic literature, and occupied this position until his death.

He was one of the profoundest Jewish scholars of his day. His specialty was Judeo-Arabic philosophy, and he wrote many articles on this subject for learned journals. Perhaps his most important contribution was *Saadia Gaon, His Life and Works* (1921), which is generally recognized as one of the finest biographies of a Jewish scholar in the English language.

Lit.: American Jewish Year Book, vol. 28 (1926-27) 261-72.

MALTZ, ALBERT, playwright and writer of fiction, b. Brooklyn, N.Y., 1908. He studied at Columbia University (A.B., 1930) and was a student in George Pierce Baker's playwriting course (Yale School of the Drama, 1930-32).

In 1932 *Merry-Go-Round,* Maltz's play about the effect of corrupt municipal government, written with George Sklar, was staged in New York city at the Provincetown Theatre. It was subsequently produced as a motion picture (*Afraid To Talk*). The Theatre Union, as its first production, presented in 1934 *Peace on Earth,* a play by Maltz and Sklar dealing with the makers of munitions and war. In 1935 the Theatre Union produced *Black Pit,* a play of the coal mines in West Virginia. Maltz's one-act play, *Private Hicks,* about the use of the National Guard in breaking strikes, was awarded first prize in the New Theatre League contest that year. Together with George Sklar again, he wrote *Zero Hour,* produced in 1941, a study of a liberal who, refusing to compromise, is forced into open opposition to reactionaries.

Maltz has written for the screen as well as the stage. His work on screen plays, in addition to *Afraid To Talk,* includes *The Happiest Man On Earth* (1941, "a short") and *This Gun For Hire* (1942).

A collection of Maltz's short stories, *The Way Things Are,* was published in 1938. His *Man on a Road* (a victim of silicosis), first published in the *New Masses* (January 8, 1935), was often reprinted. Maltz won first prize in the O. Henry Memorial Awards for 1938 with *The Happiest Man on Earth* (a story of unemployment). His novel *The Underground Stream* (1940) is a study of a communist among the automobile workers in Detroit. His work has appeared in *Harper's Magazine, Scribner's Magazine,* and *The New Yorker,* among other journals, and in leading anthologies, such as Edward J. O'Brien's annual *The Best Short Stories* (1936, 1939 and 1941).

One of the proletarian writers whom the hard times which followed the panic of 1929 produced in the United States, Maltz, both as playwright and as writer of fiction, devoted himself to the working class and its problems. It has been pointed out by critics that, although Maltz himself was the son of a wealthy man, he did not write of the workers with pity, as an outsider might, but that he saw them as they saw themselves.

Maltz was an instructor of playwriting at New York University from 1937 to 1941.

MALVANO, GIACOMO, Italian diplomat, b. Turin, Italy, 1841; d. Rome, 1922. He began his diplomatic career in 1862, in the ministry for foreign affairs. Later he became general secretary for foreign affairs and held the post for about ten years, until 1885. In 1887 Malvano was appointed envoy extraordinary and minister plenipotentiary to Tokyo, a post from which he resigned in 1889. Once more resuming his work as general secretary for foreign affairs, he now continued to act in this position until 1893.

In 1896 Malvano became a senator, serving until 1907. Though he left the foreign office, he continued to assist the department in the Council of State, of which he was eventually made president. At various times during his career, he was particularly active in commercial and monetary negotiations with other countries. From 1907 until his death he seems to have held no government posts. Malvano was for many years vice-president of the Italian Geographical Society.

MAMMELASHON, MAMMELOSHEN, *see* YIDDISH.

MAMMON (properly *mamon*), a Mishnaic Hebrew word, which probably is of Punic origin and is used in the sense of worldly gain, advantage, balance on hand, property. In the Sermon on the Mount (*Matt.* 6:24; there is a similar saying in *Luke* 16:13) Jesus uses the term as a scornful personification of the idol of money-grabbing, hence the expression "servants of Mammon." The Bible translations introduced the word into literary language, and it has remained there as the idea of a crassly material way of life.

MAMREM (also *mamre, mamram;* plural, *mamramoth*), designation for a special document which is something like a bill of exchange or a check. The Mamrem has been used from the 16th cent. on, on the basis of rabbinical ordinances, as a valid document which corresponds to commercial paper payable to bearer and a personal bill of exchange. The expression is used for the first time in the *Lebush* of Mordecai Jaffe (vol. 5, *Ir Shushan,* chap. 48). The legal nature of the Mamrem is that of a transferrable commercial paper payable to bearer; its form is that of the Shetar, reduced to a minimum. One side of it contains the autograph signature of the debtor or the signature of the witnesses; the reverse side contains the amount of the debt and the time-limit for payment. On the other hand, there is no mention of the reason for the contract, the name of the creditor, or the place of payment. The Mamrem approaches the character of the bill of exchange in modern law in so far as the transference of the claim it represents is accomplished without forms, needs no indorsement, and is enforced over any objection.

It is probable that the Mamrem was created by the Jewish legal teachers in order to meet the needs of commerce; but it is also certain that they consciously based the new institution on that formula for commercial paper payable to bearer that goes back to the Talmudic teacher Rabbi Huna (in *B.B.* 172a). In Poland, where the business of Jews with one another had assumed rather large proportions, there was an evident necessity of some means of furthering the flow of capital, since the old Shetaroth made it too difficult to transfer claims. They also seem to have been in the habit of discounting the bill of exchange, as is shown, for instance, by the writings of Sabbatai Hakohen (*Sifthe Kohen* to *Shulhan Aruch, Hoshen Mishpat* 50:7). Naturally it was possible that the formless Mamrem might be used for dishonest purposes, and the rabbis endeavored to meet this in various ways. An express theoretical basis for the Mamrem is given in *Ketzoth Hahoshen* (*Hoshen Mishpat* 61:3).

The blank Mamrem (*mamrem halak*) was developed later to meet the needs of commerce and above all the furthering of credit. It contained only the signature, the amount of the debt and the time limit of the payment being left blank at the time when the bill of exchange was given over to the creditor; these figures were filled in later by the latter himself. The unlimited trust of the debtor in the creditor, which is shown by such a practice, is good proof that Jewish merchants enjoyed a high measure of credit, a thing which the Polish Jews who visited the markets probably needed in countries which were foreign to them.

In any case, the Mamrem has only the significance of an acknowledgment in writing, when it came to prove the responsibility of the debtor. It was not as binding as the document (Shetar) which bore the signatures of witnesses, and hence had not the force of a general hypothecation.

There is a dispute as to the etymology of the word Mamrem. Goldschmidt thinks that it is not an abbreviation, but a corrupted form of the Latin *in memoriam,* which would have the meaning of an I.O.U. for the debt, to be given to the creditor. This would have about the same meaning as the *shetar zechirah* (*Tur Hoshen Mishpat* 61:3). The objection to this explanation is that the Mamrem has legal power as a document. David Kaufmann (*Die Memoiren der Glückel von Hameln,* p. 221, note 2) suggests with more reason that Mamrem is nothing else but the medieval *membrana,* the name given to the parchment on which a bond was written.

L'Estocq and others have considered the word to be an abbreviation, and have traced it back to the savant Meir ben Gedaliah Lublin, who may have been the first to introduce this institution into Jewish law. It is probably nearer the truth to conceive of Mamrem as an independent Hebrew word formation from *hamir* ("to change"), a derivation which would also agree with the meaning of the institution.   MARCUS COHN.

Lit.: In addition to what is given in the text, Zippfel, *Tractatus von Wechsel-Briefen* (1701); L'Estocq, *Exercitatio de . . . Mamre* (1755), printed in Beseke, *Thesaurus Iuris Cambialis* (1783) 1169; Auerbach, *Jüdisches Obligationenrecht,* 288 et seq.; Bloch, in *Festschrift für A. Berliner* (1903) 50 et seq.

MAMROTH, PAUL, financier and industrialist, b. Breslau, Germany, 1859. After serving with a banking house at Breslau, he was employed by the Darmstädter Bank in Berlin, and in 1883 was made member of the directorate of the Deutsche Edison-Gesellschaft, predecessor of the AEG (Allgemeine Electrizitäts-Gesellschaft). Mamroth thus became a valuable associate of Emil Rathenau and later of Walther Rathenau. He cooperated also with Carl Fürstenberg, president of the board of the AEG. Mamroth directed the financial affairs of the whole AEG concern, controlling nearly one hundred of the most important industrial enterprises of Germany. Remaining in the background most of the time, Mamroth was nevertheless an influential leader in German industrializations. His services to the development of the electrotechnical industry were generally acknowledged, and in 1921 he was awarded an honorary degree by the Breslau Institute of Technology.

Mamroth gave impetus to the German lignite industry, and was one of the earliest promoters of aviation in Germany. He was member of the directorate of the Berlin stock exchange, and of its board of examiners for the registration of stocks.

Lit.: Keitner, *Menschen und Menschenwerke,* vol. 3 (1925).

Manasseh ben Israel. From an etching by Rembrandt van Rijn; reproduction of photograph by courtesy of the Union of American Hebrew Congregations

would return to Palestine led him to the belief that this event would take place as soon as the Jews were scattered all over the earth. This belief was the driving force behind his effort to secure permission for the Jews to resettle in England, whence they had been expelled in 1290.

In order to achieve his purpose, Manasseh wrote a book, *Esperança de Israel* (1650; English trans., M. Wall, *Hope of Israel*), at the beginning of which he wrote a dedication addressed to the English Parliament and the state council. The book attracted the attention of the Protector, Oliver Cromwell, who ordered the English commission then negotiating a commercial treaty in Holland to confer with Manasseh concerning the readmission of the Jews into England. In 1655 he gave the latter permission to come to England, where he had already had connections with members of the Marrano community in London. Upon his arrival in England in the same year, Manasseh presented Cromwell with "a humble address to the Lord Protector"; the latter then called a conference to deliberate on the question of the return of the Jews to England, without any definitely favorable answer to Manasseh's petition. Nevertheless, Cromwell tacitly gave his consent to the resettlement of the

Jews, and henceforth they could live in England freely. As a further sign of his good-will Cromwell granted Manasseh an annual pension of one hundred pounds. In 1657 the latter returned to Amsterdam, where he died soon after.

In order to refute the objections of those who wished to debar the Jews from England, Manasseh wrote his book *Vindiciae Judaeorum* (Vindication of the Jews; 1656), which was widely circulated. His other works are on Biblical and rabbinic literature, and on theology and history; they were widely read, but are not especially profound or original and include some current errors, such as the belief that the American Indians were the Ten Lost Tribes. The most famous of these is the *Conciliador* (1632-51), a philosophical and mystical work which attempts to reconcile the contradictions in the Bible and which won him great reputation among non-Jews. Others of this type include *De creatione* (1653); *De resurrectione mortuorum* (1635); *De termino vitae* (1639); *Thesoro dos dinim* (1645); *Nishmath Hayim* (1652). He wrote a concordance to the Midrash, a bibliography of rabbinical literature, and other minor works.

WALTER DUCAT.

Lit.: Roth, Cecil, *Manasseh ben Israel* (1934); Kayserling, M., *Manasseh ben Israel* (1861); Wolf, Lucien, *Menasseh ben Israel's Mission to Cromwell* (1901); Adler, E. N., in *Jewish Quarterly Review* (1904); Abrahams, Israel, *By-Paths in Hebraic Bookland* (1920); there is considerable material in the volumes of the *Transactions of the Jewish Historical Society of England*.

MANASSEH BEN JOSEPH OF ILYE, Talmudist and forerunner of the Haskalah, b. Smorgony, Lithuania, 1767; d. Ilye, Lithuania, 1831. He was a pupil of Elijah Vilna, but was also self-educated in languages and in medieval Jewish philosophy. His liberal views drew upon him the attacks of the Orthodox, and as a result only a few of his writings in behalf of liberalism in Judaism and in Jewish customs could be printed. His *Pesher Debar* (Vilna, 1807) is a criticism of contemporary Jewish life; his other works include *Tikkun Kelali,* of which only fragments have survived, *Alfe Menasheh* (first part, 1822; 2nd part, 1905) and *Shekel Hakodesh* (1823), which attacked early marriage among the Jews and was therefore so bitterly assailed that only a few copies have survived. In order to spread his ideas about social justice and a reconciliation between the Hasidim and their opponents, Manasseh began to write in Yiddish, and to issue a book *Sama Dehayye* (Elixir of Life) in installments; but only a few of these appeared. Manasseh's ideas were ahead of his generation, but prepared the way for the spread of the Haskalah after his death.

Lit.: Plungian, M., *Ben Porat* (1858); Spalter, M., introduction to the second part of *Alfe Menasheh* (1905).

MANA-ZUCCA (original name, Zuckerman), pianist and composer, b. New York city, 1894. She studied piano, singing, and composition in New York, Berlin, London and Paris, her teachers including Alexander Lambert, Leopold Godowsky, Busoni, and von zur Mühlen. She appeared as a piano prodigy, scoring a sensation in New York at her debut which took place in 1898 with the New York Symphony Society. Subsequently she concentrated on singing, appearing in London in Lehar's *Count of Luxembourg* (1914) and in New York in a variety of musical comedies and operettas. She is best known as a composer, having produced more than 1,000 songs, some of which, like *Rachem, Nichovo,* and *I Love Life,* have become world-famous. She appeared in the United States and Europe in recitals of her own works. Besides her songs, she composed orchestral works, piano pieces, and various compositions for chamber music ensembles. She composed also two grand operas. She founded the American Music Optimists and Mana-Zucca Music Club.

MANCHESTER, city in Lancashire, England. With 33,000 Jews out of a total population of 950,000 (2.5 per cent), Manchester in 1942 was the second largest Jewish center in the British Commonwealth, being exceeded only by London. Jewish settlement dates from the end of the 18th cent., when it was concentrated mainly in the Shudehill and Long Millgate sections. A conventicle existed in the latter district about 1780, and in 1794 there was a Jewish cemetery near St. Thomas Church, Pendleton. A philanthropic society was founded in 1804, and twenty years later the first formal synagogue was erected on Halliwell Street. A Jews' School, still existent, was opened in 1838. A schism in the community led, in 1840, to the establishment of a rival congregation in Miller's Lane, but the two groups were later reconciled and joined forces as the Great Synagogue. Nevertheless, in 1856 further dissension arose over the choice of a rabbi, and a number of members seceded, subsequently to found a Reform synagogue. Meanwhile, Manchester, as a center of the clothing and textile industries, was steadily attracting Jews from Germany and Eastern Europe, and with their arrival en masse during the 1860's and 1870's the community rapidly expanded. The immigrants settled especially in Cheetham Hill, and a number of new synagogues, including one of the Sephardim (1873), were erected in that area. In 1867 a Jewish Board of Guardians was set up to care for the needy and destitute.

In 1942 Manchester was united administratively with the neighboring Salford. The community at that time possessed a complete network of religious, educational and philanthropic organizations. There were thirty-six synagogues, the more important of which were the Great (1858), the Spanish and Portuguese (1873), the Reform (1871), the Central (1871), the South Manchester (1872), the Higher Broughton and the Higher Crumpsall synagogues. A communal burial board maintained a joint cemetery at Rainsough, and there were other large graveyards at Urmston and Philips Park. Ritual baths (Mikvaoth) were operated, under rabbinical authority, in the Cheetham Hill and Broughton sections. Educational effort was represented by the central Jews' School and by three Talmud Torah schools (1,500 pupils), while study circles for adolescents were held under communal auspices. There was a Talmudical College (founded 1911) in the Crumpsall district, and from 1938 on the Manchester Central Library possessed a Jewish division. Hospitalization was provided by the highly efficient Victoria Memorial Jewish Hospital (founded 1903) and by a Home for the Aged, Needy and Incurable, and there were kosher kitchens both at the Royal Infirmary and at the Crumpsall Institute and Hospital. There

was also a Holiday Home for Mothers and Children, as well as a Fresh Air Home and School, at Delamere. Welfare services included, in addition to the Jewish Board of Guardians, a Jewish Aid Committee, a Soup Kitchen (founded 1895) and a number of smaller relief societies. Athletic organizations were affiliated in a central Maccabi Association, and there were several literary and social societies, often associated with synagogues. A Zionist Central Council coordinated the activities of some seventeen local groups, and incorporated the Manchester branches of the Jewish National Fund Commission and of the Jewish Agency. Friendly societies were especially active, the Achei Brith and Shield of Abraham (organized 1888) having four lodges, the Sons of Jacob (organized 1900) nine, the Achei Emeth (organized 1897) eight, and the Ancient Maccabaeans (organized 1891) and Grand Order of Israel and Shield of David (organized 1897) seven each. The B'nai B'rith, originally established in Manchester (1900), controlled in 1942 eleven local lodges, while the Order Achei Sholom, founded in 1928, numbered eight branches at the time of their amalgamation in 1939. Most of the Friendly Societies were associated in a central council.

The representative body of the community was (1942) the Council of Manchester and Salford Jews, constituted by delegates from all synagogues, Friendly Societies and institutions, local members of the Board of Deputies, Jewish magistrates and councillors. This body maintained a Co-ordinating Committee for Defense, and was responsible for the engagement of a communal rabbi. The latter position was, in 1942, held by Dr. Alexander Altmann (b. 1906), formerly rabbi of the Berlin Jewish Community (1931-38). The ecclesiastical supervision of the community was in the hands of a Beth Din, whose permanent officials, in 1942, were Rabbis Altmann and Rivkin. There was also a Jewish Ecclesiastical Council, of which the Communal rabbi was president. Affairs concerning Shehitah were administered by a local board; youth activities were centralized in a Jewish Youth Council.

An admirable picture of Jewish life in Manchester is painted by Louis Golding in his novel *Magnolia Street* (1932), where the Cheetham Hill section is named Doomington.

Manchester Jewry suffered severely in the air raids of 1940. The Victoria Memorial Jewish Hospital was put out of action for two months, the Reform Synagogue was demolished, and some of the Jewish schools were hit. Considerable damage was done also to private property. A communal Inquiry Office was set up to assist the destitute, and many mothers and children were evacuated to safe areas. In 1942, when "black market" operations were causing concern to the government, the Manchester Jews set up a special tribunal to exact sanctions against any of their number convicted of profiteering.

THEODOR H. GASTER.

Lit.: Jewish Year Book (London), 1941.

MANCHUKUO (MANCHURIA), a puppet state dominated by Japan, which created it out of the northeastern provinces wrested from China in 1931. Its population in 1940 was 37,000,000. Until Japan declared war on the United States and Great Britain in

December, 1941, the Jewish population of Manchukuo was variously estimated at between 10,000 and 15,000, two-thirds of whom were concentrated in Harbin. Smaller communities existed in Mukden and Dairen. The Jewish community dates from about 1900, when Russian Jews were attracted to Manchuria, as it was then known, by the construction of the Trans-Siberian Railway, by contracts for the Far Eastern Russian army and by the fur trade.

Most of these early settlers were well-to-do. But after the Russian revolution, Harbin became a mecca for impoverished Jews fleeing from the Bolsheviks. The city was also a stopping-off point for Jews bound for the United States by way of China. As other Jews found themselves stranded on the way out of European Russia, the Jewish community of Harbin grew in stability and numbers. On the eve of the Japanese conquest the Jewish community, which had been given official status by the Chinese authorities, boasted of several synagogues, a cemetery, a loan society, Zionist society and a branch of the Revisionist Youth.

From 1931 to 1942 Jewish life in Manchukuo was a long series of economic ups and downs caused by political upheavals and the arrival of large numbers of German and Austrian Jewish refugees. During this decade or more there took place several anti-Semitic outrages provoked by White Russian émigrés with the connivance of the Japanese military. Kidnappings, boycotts and even murders of Jews were frequent, despite repeated promises by the Japanese authorities to put a stop to them. Protests by Jewish organizations in the United States proved unavailing.

The organization in 1939 of a Conference of Far Eastern Jewish Communities, headed by Abraham Kaufman, of Harbin, the establishment of two Jewish weeklies, one in Russian and the other in Yiddish, the steady impoverishment of the Jewish community because of political upheavals and Japanese monopoly, and the settlement of a limited number of German refugees until the Japanese closed the doors highlighted Jewish affairs in Manchukuo between 1939 and 1942. Immediately after Japan declared war on Great Britain and the United States, all synagogues in Manchukuo were closed and Jewish leaders arrested.

MANCROFT, ARTHUR MICHAEL SAMUEL, BARON, British government official, b. Norwich, England, 1872. He was Lord Mayor of Norwich in 1912 to 1913. In 1914 he joined the War Office staff, and later was transferred to the Ministry of Munitions. Samuel was a member of Parliament for the Farnham division of Surrey from 1918 to 1937. From 1924 to 1937 he was Parliamentary Under-Secretary of State for Foreign Affairs, Parliamentary Secretary to the Board of Trade and Minister for the Department of Overseas Trade. He was Financial Secretary to His Majesty's Treasury from 1927 to 1929.

Samuel was made a baronet in 1932 and a baron in 1937, the first to bear the title Baron Mancroft. He held various official and honorary posts with economic and trade associations throughout the empire. He was the author of: *Life of Giovanni Battista Piranesi; The Working of the Bill of Exchange with an Explanation of the Overseas Trade Balance; The Herring: its Effect on the History of Britain; The Mancroft Essays.*

MANDATE FOR PALESTINE, *see* PALESTINE MANDATE.

MANDEANS, a sect of ancient origin, living in the vicinity of Bassorah, in Iraq, and in the district of Khuzistan, in Iran (Persia). In Iraq the Mandean population, according to the latest census (1931), was about 4,800, most of the adults practising the occupation of silversmiths, in which they are highly skilled.

The religion of the Mandeans, entirely peculiar to themselves, is a product of syncretism, unique in that it is the sole surviving creed of gnostic character. In addition to this gnostic element, the Mandean religion reveals tendencies ascribable to the influence of Judaism and possibly early Jewish Christianity, as well as later Christianity, Zoroastrianism, Babylonian cultism and Mohammedanism. A number of its doctrines also bear strong affinities to those of Manicheanism.

The Mandeans became known to the Western world through the activities of an Italian Carmelite missionary, Ignatius a Jesu, in the 17th cent. It was due to him that they became known as "Christians of St. John," a name he gave them because of the high reverence which they pay to John the Baptist, their insistence upon the practice of frequent ritual immersion, and certain similarities between their religious practices and those of the Christians. This, however, proved to be a misinterpretation, for not only are they not Christians, but their creed is bitterly anti-Christian. The Arabs refer to them as Sabians, a word which is believed to be derived from the Aramaic root *tzabba,* "to dip," "to immerse," applying to their practice of baptism. They often refer to themselves as Nasoreans, as well as Mandeans. The former term has interesting connotations, in view of the fact that some scholars hold that it originally applied to the followers of John the Baptist rather than those of Jesus, and that it has the signification of "the observers." The standard interpretation of "Mandeans" derives the term from their worship of Manda de Hayye, knowledge (Gnosis) of Life.

The origin and history of the Mandeans is unknown, except insofar as it may be derived from their popular traditions and from the internal evidence of their writings; the former are vague, while the latter, although containing historical treatises, are confused and overburdened with myth and allegory. A considerable body of opinion among orientalists has inclined to the belief that the Mandeans are not other than descendants of John the Baptist, being accordingly of Palestinian origin. This belief is based upon evidence such as their reverence for John, their practice of baptism in rivers, their use of the name "Nasorean," their abhorrence of Jesus as the false Messiah, their bitter strictures against the unbelieving Jews, their use of Biblical terminology, and, finally, the fact that a central feature of their theosophy is "the Jordan." At the opposite extreme lies the opinion that the Mandean origin is posterior to Mohammed. This school asserts that their present writings are not earlier than that time, that their knowledge of the Bible is derived from the Syriac *Peshitta,* that John is of secondary importance in their religion, that their antipathy to Christianity appears to be directed toward a phase of it that had a well-formed ecclesiastical organization, and that their anti-Jewish polemics really refer to Christians. Between these two lie a variety of opinions.

The majority of scholars, however, definitely hold that the origin of the sect certainly lies in pre-Mohammedan times, a view which is corroborated by the findings of pottery of an early date, and of one tablet ascribed to the beginning of the 5th cent. A contemporary observer, Mrs. E. S. Drower, reports that a tradition current among the Mandeans holds that they once occupied a mountainous area to the northwest, suggesting, in connection with other data, a possible derivation from the Madda or Manda tribes of ancient Media. This theory is supplemented by an Iranian etymology of "Manda," meaning settlement, which significance, it is suggested, may be found in the designation of "Mandi" for their cult-huts, or temples. An early reference, which some scholars believe applies to the Mandeans, is that in the Koran, wherein the Sabeans, as monotheists, were granted religious toleration. In later times Sabeans were described by Arabic writers, and also by Maimonides, as worshippers of the planets, but in the 9th cent. a distinction was drawn between the Sabeans of Babylonia and those of Harran, the latter having adopted the name to cloak their pagan beliefs.

The Mandean creed includes numerous diverse and conflicting elements. These are not the result of an accumulation of concepts stemming from popular folklore, or of the elaboration of a nature worship, but the consequence of a process, several times repeated, whereby new outside influences were artificially harmonized with existing beliefs and absorbed into their general framework. The diversity of their beliefs suggests a diverse origin; certain passages in their writings, although unreliable as history, at least make possible the supposition that at an early period an original community of pagan baptists in Babylonia was supplemented by a group of Jewish Christians, or Johannine baptists, from Palestine, this community later becoming involved either indirectly or through other group accretions, with the Gnosticism that swept through a large part of the world, while both later Christianity and Mohammedanism left a heavy impress. It was probably as a means of protection against the latter that the heterogeneous Mandean writings or teachings went through the process of redaction and compilation which left them in their present form, which is much later than the material they contain. These books are written in a peculiar script resembling Old Palmyrenian, and the language in which they are written is an Aramaic idiom very similar to that of the Babylonian Talmud.

Moses Gaster pointed out that this language has affinities also to Palestinian Aramaic, and that the Mandean writings have many points of contact, in concept and phraseology, with those of the Samaritans. This second fact suggests either the direct influence of the latter, or that both were subject to the same influences. The process of examination to which the Mandean books were subjected beginning with the early part of the 20th cent. rendered the substance of their contents available, but there are still numerous phrases and expressions that are beyond the scope of the translators.

The most important and most ancient of their writings is the *Sidra Rabba* or *Ginza;* "the treasure" is the usual interpretation of the latter name, but Gaster suggests *Book of the Mystery,* analogous to the significance of the Hebrew *Genizah.* This book is divided into a right and a left part, and consists of theological, mythological and ethical treatises interspersed with prayers and hymns. The next most important compilation is the *Sidra de Yahya,* or *Drase de Malka,* wherein legends of John are expounded; this is evidently a work of later origin. Another work, the *Qolasta,* contains liturgical matter, and may also be of later origin. There are a number of scrolls called *Divans* which treat of liturgy and of the halting-places which the soul of a dead Mandean must pass on its way to the ascent. Another work, the *Asfar Malwase,* contains astrological material of Arabic, Persian and Jewish origin.　　Sol Bernstein.

Lit.: Pallis, *Essay on Mandean Bibliography 1560-1930* (1933; containing a complete bibliography to 1930); Drower, E. S. (Mrs. Stevens), "Mandean Writings," *Iraq,* vol. 1 (1934) 171-82; Burkitt, F. C., *Church and Gnosis* (1932) 96-122; Kraeling, C. H., in *American Oriental Society Journal,* vol. 49 (1929) 195-218; Gaster, Moses, *The Astir* (1927) 127-34.

MANDEL, FRANK, playwright and producer, b. San Francisco, 1884. He received his B.L. degree from the University of California in 1904. His first play, *Miss Princess,* was produced in Chicago in 1913, and his second, *Lady We Love,* in Los Angeles in 1914. Among other plays, produced in New York city, were *Trifling with Tomorrow* (1914); *Sherman Was Right* (1915); *Bosom Friends* (1918); *Look Who's Here* (1919); *Luck* (1919); *The Five Million* (1919); and *My Lady Friends* (1919). Mandel was also the author, with various collaborators, of such theatrical successes as *No, No, Nanette* (1924); *Desert Song* (1926); *Lady Killer* (1923); *Sweet Little Devil* (1924); *Captain Jinks* (1925); and *New Moon* (1927). In conjunction with Lawrence Schwab, Mandel also engaged in the production of plays. Among their productions were several of the plays on which Mandel had collaborated. In 1942 Mandel was living in the vicinity of New York and occasionally collaborating on the motion picture scenarios of plays, such as the film version of *New Moon* (1940).

MANDEL, GEORGES, French statesman, b. Chatou, near Paris, 1885. His original name was Jerobeam Rothchild (not Rothschild). In 1903, at the age of eighteen, Mandel was introduced to Georges Clémenceau who at that time edited the newspaper *Aurore,* which fought for the rehabilitation of Alfred Dreyfus. The second day after he met Clémenceau, Mandel astonished the grim editor by the excellent execution of a difficult journalistic task, whereupon he became Clémenceau's regular collaborator. Within a few months Mandel gained his editor's full confidence. When Clémenceau, in 1906, became minister of the interior and prime minister, he appointed Mandel head of his office (chef de cabinet).

During Clémenceau's first ministry (1906-9), Mandel remained relatively unknown to the public. Only the French socialists and trade unionists accused him of severity against striking workers and officials. When Clémenceau, in 1917, assumed direction of the cabinet and governed in a quasi-dictatorial manner, with the

Georges Mandel

approval of Parliament, Mandel, who collaborated on Clémenceau's newspaper, *L'homme libre* (after the outbreak of the first World War named *L'homme enchaîné*), was again made Clémenceau's chef de cabinet. In that capacity he endeavored to crush defeatism. He prosecuted all and sundry suspected by Clémenceau of being treacherous defeatists or of hampering vigorous warfare.

Under Clémenceau's supreme direction, Mandel worked hand in hand with Edouard Ignace (b. Baccarat, 1864; d. Paris, 1924), also a Jew (the war cabinet of Clemenceau between 1917 and 1919 had three Jews: Louis L. Klotz, minister of finance; Mandel; and Ignace). The latter was a strong personality, as ruthless as Mandel, fanatically devoted to the mission assigned him by Clemenceau: to combat defeatism. Elected a deputy to the French Chamber in 1914, Ignace quickly rose to the presidency of the important commission on civil and criminal legislation, and soon afterwards, to the more pivotal position (France was then at war) of president of the military commission. In both posts he won recognition, among others, by Clemenceau, who chose intelligent, hard-working, patriotic, and courageous leaders. Thus, when he came to power, he chose Ignace as under secretary of justice. In this capacity he had to direct, together with Mandel, all prosecutions for treason, for defeatism, and for what Clemenceau then considered as pacifist defeatism. It was a very dangerous job, but Ignace, firm and fearless, performed it, with the aid of Mandel, thoroughly.

Mandel and Ignace became more hated than Clémenceau himself. Mandel especially was decried as "that grey eminence" of the government and as "the evil genius of Clemenceau." Some of his adversaries even declared that he was the real dictator of France.

Clemenceau supported Mandel with all his energy against attacks by deputies, seenators, and journalistic foes. He was extremely beholden to Mandel who, according to General Mordacq, Clemenceau's military adviser, was "best informed about all things and men." At every stage of his political activity, Mandel was so well posted that his friends and adversaries alike were puzzled about his sources of information. Some of them even supposed that he maintained a system of private espionage. Although affable in private life, often tolerant in theoretical discussions, Mandel was, as a public man, brusque, aggressive and provoking, a pitiless adversary. Even those who approved his political activities were often alarmed by his demeanor.

When the first World War ended, Mandel arranged the elections, which were a victory for the national bloc. In November, 1919, before the elections took place, Mandel left the ministry in order to contest a seat in parliament. This step was unprecedented in France. Generally a chef de cabinet who retired from office retained a post in the supreme court of accounts, or a well-paid sinecure. Mandel, despising that kind of reward, entered the political arena and openly faced his adversaries, who were seeking to wreak vengeance for years of pressure at Mandel's hands. During the electoral contest an attempt was made to assassinate Mandel. Upon his election the deputies of the socialist and radical parties assailed him frequently and attempted to shout him down when he answered their charges. Nor was there any lack of anti-Semitic attacks against Mandel, who never concealed his loyalty to Judaism, although he did not devote himself to any particular Jewish interests after his efforts in favor of the revision of the Dreyfus trial. Mandel resisted all these attacks with urbane sarcasm, and he was generally respected, though by no means on friendly terms with members of the left. In the elections of 1924, which represented a victory for the leftists, Mandel was defeated, but in 1928 he was reelected, and remained member of parliament until the overthrow (1940) of the representative system in France.

Mandel, who never was a friend of Germany and combated Briand for his attempts to reconcile France and Germany, became one of the most stirring voices against German aggression after Hitler came to power. He denounced Germany's secret arming under Hitler. He advocated resistance to Hitler's claims and the strengthening of French armament. In 1935 Mandel entered Flandin's cabinet and became minister of communications. He instituted basic reforms, particularly in his vigorous resistance to trade union demands, and became popular because of improvements he wrought. Mandel assumed the same functions in the Sarraut cabinet.

When Hitler remilitarized the Rhineland (March, 1936), Mandel advocated a strong stand against him, but was defeated by a coalition of French fascists and pacifists. The government of the Front Populaire, led by Léon Blum, ousted Mandel from office, but in 1938 Daladier assigned the ministry of colonies to Mandel, who successfully claimed a place in the committee of national defense, and prepared a plan for the enlargement of the French colonial army.

In May, 1940, Mandel entered the Reynaud cabinet as minister of the interior. Immediately he began to clean house and to arrest the real fifth columnists while he interned also the Jewish refugees.

After the military collapse of France, Mandel advocated continuance of the war in Africa. He bitterly combatted Laval, Pétain and Weygand at the meeting of the members of the government near Tours. Pétain exerted heavy pressure upon Mandel and arrested him at Bordeaux. Thee protests of the presidents of the Chamber of Deputies and Senate caused Mandel's liberation. Mandel went to Morocco to organize resistance, and was arrested there again by the governor, then was escorted to France and imprisoned by the Pétain government. He did not appear at the trial in Riom in 1942.   HUGO BIEBER.

Lit.: Buell, Raymond Leslie, *Contemporary French Politics* (1920); Mordacq, *Le ministère Clemenceau* (1930-31); Suarez, Georges, *Soixante années d'histoire française* (1932); Armstrong, Hamilton Fish, *Chronology of a Failure* (1940); *New York Herald Tribune,* April 29, 1942, p. 26.

MANDEL, PÁL, Hungarian deputy, b. Nyirbátor, Szabolcs county, Hungary, 1839; d. in the 1930's in Hungary. Having studied law at Pest and Vienna, he devoted himself to its practice in the capital of Hungary. In 1875 the constituency of his native Nyirbátor sent him to the Lower Chamber of parliament as a member of the Liberal Party. He was reelected three times, being deputy of Alsó-Lendva from 1892 to 1897. A member of the judiciary commission of the Lower Chamber from 1881 on, he collaborated on the bills of guardianship, copyright and notaries public. His most important speeches in parliament were those on behalf of the abolition of capital punishment (1878), for civil marriage and freedom of religion (1880 and 1884), and against anti-Semitic agitation (1885).

MANDELBAUM, SAMUEL, judge, b. Poland, 1886. After receiving his LL.M. degree from New York University in 1913, Mandelbaum entered the practice of law in New York city. In 1923 he was elected to the New York State Assembly, and served in this capacity until 1932, when he was elected state senator. In 1936 he was appointed to the Federal Court for the southern district of New York, and in 1942 still held this post.

MANDELKERN, SOLOMON, Hebrew poet and scholar, b. Mlynov, Volhynia, Russia, 1846; d. Vienna, 1902. In his early youth he was associated with the Hasidim, and studied Talmud, Cabala, and philosophy of religion; subsequently he identified himself with the Haskalah movement. He graduated from the rabbinical seminary of Vilna, studied Orientalia at the University of Leningrad, and was awarded a gold medal for his treatise on the parallel passages of the Old Testament in relation to the old Bible translations, the Septuagint, Vulgate and Peshitta, and the paleography of the Semitic languages. From 1873 to 1880 he was assistant rabbi at Odessa; during this period he graduated also from a law school. In 1880 Mandelkern went to Germany, obtained the Ph.D. degree at the University of Jena, and then settled in Leipzig. In 1910 he visited the United States.

Mandelkern began his literary career with *Teruath Melech Rab* (The Triumph of a Great King), an ode to Alexander II of Russia. From then on he

Solomon Mandelkern

contributed articles, poems and epigrams to many Hebrew journals and year-books, including *Hashahar* and *Haasif.* He wrote also in Russian and German. His poems *Shire Sefath Eber* (Poems of the Tongue of Eber; in two parts); *Bathsheba,* a Biblical poem; *Hitzim Shenunim* (Sharp Arrows), epigrams; and his Hebrew translations of Byron's *Hebrew Melodies* and Heine's *Jehudah ben Halevi* gained him a prominent place in Hebrew literature. Other original and translated works of his are: *Dibere Yeme Russiah* (History of Russia; Warsaw, 1875); *Tamar* (a translation of Abraham Mapu's *Ahabath Tziyyon;* 1884; without mention of the author's name); and a translation of Mapu's *Ashmath Shomron* (The Guilt of Samaria; 1890). He devoted twenty years of his life to his concordance of the Hebrew Bible. It is the most complete work of its kind in existence (1942); an abridged edition of the concordance, *Tabnith Hechal* (The Pattern of the Tabernacle), appeared later.

MANDELL, MIKE, city and county official, b. Dauendorf, Alsace, France, 1857. He arrived in the United States in 1872 and became a merchant. He was elected mayor of Albuquerque, N.M., in 1892. Upon the admission of New Mexico as a state (1912), he was elected treasurer of Bernalillo County, and served as such for five years. He was the first Jew to be elected to either office.

Mandell took a leading part in the early communal

Mike Mandell (extreme right) shown at a session of the city government of Albuquerque

life of the Jews of Albuquerque. He was a charter member, and served as president, of Temple Albert, and was also a charter member of the Albuquerque lodge of the B'nai B'rith (organized in 1890). He was still alive in 1942.

MANDELLI, DAVID, philologist, b. Pozsony (Pressburg), Hungary, about 1780; d. Paris, 1836. At the age of twelve he was sent to the Yeshiva at Rajka, but in 1799 he was already a student at the University of Prague, and in the following year he studied at that of Berlin. In 1805 he was a tutor in Offenbach on Main, Germany. Having walked to Paris, he there earned a bare means of subsistence by teaching mathematics and Arabic. In 1882 he was appointed to catalogue the rare Oriental manuscripts and books of the Bibliothèque Nationale, at an annual salary of 1,800 francs. He finished the big task in a month, received one month's salary and resigned. Thereafter he lived in the cellar of the Arsénal, feeding on plants.

He was regarded by many as the greatest linguist of his age, including Cardinal Mezzofanti. He combined Latin, Greek, Hebrew, Arabic, Persian and Chinese to form a new language of his own. His notes on mathematics were written on a slate and effaced after he solved the problem. He never published anything.

On a winter day, in 1836, he walked down barefoot to the Seine to get some water in a pitcher, slipped, fell into the river and was drowned. His eulogy was delivered at the French Academy by Notier, and the world press mourned his passing.

Lit.: Oettinger, *Moniteur des dates;* Tessedik, Sámuel, *Utazás Franciaországban* (1837); *Magyar Zsidó Lexikon* (1929) 572.

MANDELLO, KÁROLY, economist, b. Győrsziget, Hungary, 1829; d. Budapest, 1906. He studied at universities outside of Hungary, and returned to his native country as a qualified railway engineer. In 1871 he became economics editor of the *Pester Lloyd,* Hungarian German language daily. His major published works are: *Visszapillantások Magyarország közgazdasági fejlődésére* (A Glance at the Economic Development of Hungary); *Erkölcstan és mennyiségtan az értékelméletben* (Ethics and Mathematics in the Theory of Value); *Gegen Jesuitismus und Cäsarismus in der Volkswirtschaft; Studien über Ungarns Staatsvermögen und Staatsbudget; Über Ungarns Einkommensteuer; Le commerce, l'industrie et le régime des transports en Hongrie* (1891).

Mandello adopted the Christian faith.

GYULA MANDELLO, economist and educator (b. Rannersdorf, 1868; d. Budapest, 1919), son of Károly Mandello, like his father, embraced Christianity. He studied at the universities of Budapest and several other cities outside of Hungary. At first instructor at the Academy of Law at Pozsony (Pressburg), he was appointed in the same capacity at the University of Budapest and finally became professor of public economics at the Technical School of Budapest. He edited *Közgazdasági Lexikon* (Encyclopedia of Economy) and *Közgazdasági Szemle* (Economic Review). In his published works he was concerned with the history of economics and wages, with wage and criminal statistics, and social planning. He wrote a

monograph (in Hungarian) on royal jurisdiction in England from the 11th to the 14th centuries.

MANDELSHTAM, LEONID ISAAKOVICH, physicist, b. Odessa, Russia, 1879. He was professor at the University of Moscow in 1942. He graduated from the University of Strasbourg in 1902, joined its staff as an assistant and subsequently lectured there and at the University of Würzburg.

In 1914 he returned to Russia and became professor at Novorosiisk University. Subsequently he held the chair of physics at Tiflis and Odessa Polytechnical Institutes. From 1925 on he was professor at the Pokrovsky State University of Moscow. In 1929 he was elected an active member of the Academy of Sciences of the USSR.

Mandelshtam's work was mainly in the field of optics and the theory of equilibrium, his outstanding achievement in optics being on the combined dissemination of light. He also devoted a great deal of activity to technical questions and to experiments in radio. He held many patents in this and in related fields. Many of his papers appeared in German scientific publications.

Lit.: Bolshaya Entziklopedia (1931); Poggendorf, J. C., *Biographisch-literarisches Handwörterbuch zur Geschichte der exacten Wissenschaften,* vol. 5, part 2; vol. 6, part 3.

MANDELSTAMM, BENJAMIN BEN JOSEPH, Hebrew writer, b. Zhagory, province of Kovno, Russia, about 1800; d. Simferopol, Crimea, Russia, 1886. He was a leading exponent of the Haskalah movement, although he was later somewhat disappointed in its results. His chief work, *Hazon Lamoed* (Vision for the Season; Vienna, 1877), is divided into three parts; the first describes a trip to Moscow, made about 1835, the second contains letters written from Vilna about 1841 to 1843 in reference to the educational mission of Max Lilienthal, while the third describes the Crimea and efforts to improve the conditions of the Russian Jews. Mandelstamm was in the employ of the Günzburgs for about forty years. He made a trip to Paris in 1875, and gave an account of it in his *Paris* (Warsaw, 1878); his *Mishle Binyamin,* a collection of aphorisms, was published in *Haasif,* vols. 1 and 2.

Lit.: Haasif, vol. 3, p. 117.

MANDELSTAMM, LEON (ARYE LÖB), Hebraist, author, and educator, brother of Benjamin ben Joseph Mandelstamm, b. Zhagory, province of Kovno, Russia, 1809; d. St. Petersburg, Russia, 1889. He was educated at the University of Moscow and the University of St. Petersburg; here he was the first Jew to graduate with the B.A. degree in philology in 1844.

While still a student in 1843 he was secretary to the Rabbinical Commission at St. Petersburg, which had been called in order to determine the principles for the education of Russian Jews. From 1846 to 1857 he worked under the Russian ministry of public instruction as the administrator of the Rabbinical Commission's plans. These plans were unpopular with the Jewish masses, who blamed Mandelstamm for their educational and financial troubles.

From 1857 to his death he spent most of his time in Germany. He engaged in several business enterprises with but little success, and continued to write

Max Emanuel Mandelstamm

in Russian, Hebrew, and German. After his death his library was bought by the New York Public Library, where it forms part of the Jewish Division. Among his many works are: *Stikhotvoreniya* (poems; 1840); *Chinnuk Nearim* (a Hebrew-German textbook for schools; 2 vols., 1849-50); *V Zashchitu Yevreyev* (1858); *Biblische Studien* (2 vols., 1862); *Stimmen in der Wüste* (1880). He also translated the Old Testament into Russian (1862); the government insisted that the translation be published with the Hebrew text.

Lit.: Mandelstamm, B., "Alumme Arye Mandelstamm," *Hamelitz* (1892), Nos. 267 to 271; Wiernik, Peter, in *Jewish Forum*, vol. 4 (1921) 866-70.

MANDELSTAMM, MAX EMANUEL, ophthalmologist and Zionist leader, b. Zhagory, province of Kovno, Russia, 1839; d. Kiev, Russia, 1912. He studied at the Universities of Dorpat and Kharkov, receiving his medical degree from the latter in 1860. After working in various eye clinics in Germany, Mandelstamm took up the practice of ophthalmology in Kiev, and became known as one of the leading oculists in Russia. He was a lecturer at the University of Kiev and, although he headed the eye clinic from 1876 to 1880, his appointment to a professorship was three times rejected by the authorities on religious grounds. Mandelstamm resigned from his university posts, continuing ophthalmological work in private.

Mandelstamm's whole-hearted participation in Jewish nationalist movements developed in contrast to his assimilationist family environment. Two of his uncles, Leon and Benjamin Mandelstamm, had received a thorough Jewish education, but they were leading propagandists for complete assimilation. Mandelstamm himself, given a secular education from his childhood on, joined the Chovevei Zion movement in 1881 and the political Zionist movement under Theodor Herzl from its inception. At the First Zionist Congress (1897) Mandelstamm was made a member of the executive committee. Later Mandelstamm became an advocate of territorialism, and left the Zionist movement after the rejection of the Uganda project by the Seventh Zionist Congress in 1903.

Mandelstamm's position in science as well as his devotion to Jewish interests made him an influential figure among the Russian Jewish masses, particularly in the southern regions. In addition to his published work in the field of ophthalmology, he wrote several pamphlets emphasizing the significance to healthy Jewish life of a productive economic pattern and a homeland. *How Jews Live* (1900) was the translation of one of his studies; he was author also of *Zum Yiddishen Folk* (1901).

Lit.: Brainin, R., in *Ahiasaf* (1900) 336-49; Mandelstamm, Max Emanuel, *Pamyati;* Dubnow, S. M., *History of the Jews in Russia and Poland,* vols. 2 and 3.

MANDL, BERNÁT, historian and pedagogue, b. Szenic, Nyitra county, Hungary, 1852; d. Budapest, 1940. He studied at the Yeshivas of Rabbis Israel Hildesheimer at Eisenstadt and David Feuchtwang at Nikolsburg, and received teacher's diplomas from teachers' training schools (Jewish and secular) at Budapest. From 1896 on he was a teacher and subsequently titular principal of the Boys' Burgher School of the Jewish Community of Pest. He published books on the state of Jewish education in Hungary under Joseph II, on the Jewish schools of Hungary in the 19th cent., and on the life of Marcus Moses, an 18th cent. physician. His main work was *Monumenta Hungariae Judaica* (vols. 2 and 3, 1938; vol. 4, 1940), the first volume having been published by A. Frisch in 1908; it was a collection of Hungarian documents of Jewish interest, forming an important reference source for the history of the Jews in Hungary. He conducted extensive researches into the history of the Jews of Pozsony (Pressburg), Szenic, and other communities of northwestern Hungary and Bohemia. Some of this material was published in journals of Hungary and other Central European countries; the greater part remained unpublished. He was a founder and executive member of the Budapest Jewish Museum.

MANDL, EMMA B. (Mrs. Bernhard Mandl, née Adler), communal worker, b. Pilsen, Bohemia, Austria, 1842; d. Chicago, 1928. She was one of the founders of the Baron Hirsch Woman's Club (1889; originally, North Side Ladies' Aid Society, organized in 1880), and was president of the club from 1893 to 1897. In 1910 she founded the Baron Hirsch Co-Workers, an organization of young women assisting the members of the Baron Hirsch Woman's Club in their communal activities.

The Baron Hirsch Woman's Club was engaged in aiding the Home for Jewish Orphans when, in 1901, Mrs. Mandl helped organize the Chicago Home for Jewish Friendless and Working Girls. She was its first president. The purposes of the organization were to provide an emergency home for children until they could be admitted to the Home for Jewish Orphans or rejoin their parents, and to furnish living quarters for girls who had no suitable homes. The latter purpose, however, was best performed by a separate organization, the Ruth Club, of which Mrs. Mandl was the chief organizer in 1905.

In 1907 she was one of the founders of the Jewish Home Finding Society to help mothers, whose children were in orphan asylums, to establish homes of their own. Another purpose of the society was to place children, not admissible to orphanages or temporarily dependent, in private homes. This organization, in 1918, finally took over the work of the Chicago Home for Jewish Friendless and Working Girls and the latter was closed.

Through the Baron Hirsch Woman's Club, Mrs. Mandl also helped establish the Chicago-Winfield Tuberculosis Sanitarium, of which she was honorary president, and, in 1915, the Home for Convalescent Men and Boys.

In connection with her work for children and adolescent girls, she became a probation officer of the Juvenile Court.

MANDL, LOUIS, anatomist, b. Pest, Hungary, 1812; d. Paris, 1881. He studied medicine, philosophy and astronomy at the University of Vienna, and received his M.D. degree from that of Pest in 1836, and another M.D. degree in 1842 in Paris, where he had settled after having gone there to pursue further studies. He devoted himself to microscopic anatomy, and published the first volume of his *Anatomie microscopique* in 1838, the second volume following in 1857. This book, as well as his *Traité pratique du microscope et de son emploi a l'étude des corps organisés* (1839), largely contributed to popularizing the medical use of the microscope in France. Becoming a French citizen in 1849, Mandl taught at the École Pratique des Hautes Etudes, located in the Sorbonne. Later he did pioneer work in the diseases of the larynx and the respiratory organs. Some of his published works are: *Recherches médico-légales sur le sang* (1842); *Anatomie générale* (1843); *De la fatigue de la voix dans les rapports avec le mode de respiration* (1855); *Traité pratique des maladies du larynx et du pharynx* (1872). He also published minor works in the *Archives de médecine*. He gave gratuitous treatment to a great number of indigent sick.

MANES, ALFRED, one of the leading personalities in insurance matters, b. Frankfort, Germany, 1877. He studied in Frankfort, Berlin and London, and traveled extensively in the Far East, the South Seas and Australia, where he was in the service of the government from 1913 to 1914. As a result of these activities he wrote several books on workmen's insurance in New Zealand and Australia, and about his travels in Japan. After the first World War he published *Britain's Changes during the War* (1918).

From 1906 to 1925—interrupted only by his travels —Manes was professor at the commercial academy in Frankfort, and from 1926 to 1935 professor at the university and the commercial academy in Berlin. During a lecture tour through the United States in 1935 he had differences with the German government over the "Aryan" clause, and resigned. He went to South America to lecture, returned later to the United States and worked at Indiana University and the University of Chicago in 1941.

Manes was one time presiding officer of the Deutscher Verein für Versicherungswissenschaften, director of the insurance seminary and editor of the periodical *Zeitschrift für die gesamte Versicherungswissenschaft,* and from 1913 to 1933 published nine volumes of the *Versicherungs Bibliothek* and from 1903 to 1933 fifty-three volumes of the *Veröffentlichungen des deut-*

schen Vereins für Versicherungswissenschaft. He wrote articles on insurance matters in many handbooks and encyclopedias, such as *Herders Konversationslexikon, Handwörterbuch der Staatswissenschaften,* and *Brockhaus' kleines Konversationslexikon.*

His numerous works include: *Recht des Pseudonyms* (1898); *Die Diebstahlversicherung* (1899); *Haftpflichtversicherung* (1902); *Versicherungswesen* (3 vols., 1905; 5th ed., 1930-31); *Ins Land der sozialen Wunder* (1911); *Der soziale Erdteil* (1914). The latter two represent, among others, the results of his researches in Australia and New Zealand. His wide field of activity touched upon such interesting problems as the abolition of stamps and their substitution by postage meter as early as 1914. His *Versicherungslexikon* went through three editions from 1909 to 1930, and three editions of his *Staatsbankrotte* were published between 1918 and 1922. Furthermore, Manes was the author of the German scheme for the establishment of a world labor law (1919-20). *Teoria y Practica del Seguro* appeared in 1934. The following essays of his were published in 1941: "Insurable Hazards" (in *Journal of Business,* Chicago); "Ramos de seguro deconocidos en América" (in *Seguros,* Havana); "Neue amerikanische Versicherungsliteratur (in *Schweizerische Versicherungszeitschrift,* Bern).

MANETHO, an Egyptian high priest and annalist, a native of Sebennytus in the Nile Delta; he lived during the reigns of Ptolemy I and II. His history of Egypt in three volumes, written about 280 B.C.E. and based upon native records and traditions, is known only through fragments quoted by Josephus and the tables of dynasties and kings preserved in the Biblical chronographies of the Christian chronologists Julius Africanus and Eusebius. While it is difficult to judge the original from these extracts, which are undoubtedly corrupt in many places, this work has proved of inestimable value to Egyptologists; all modern histories of Egypt are still based upon the division of the dynasties, thirty-one in number, made in this work.

Of special significance for Jewish history are the excerpts quoted by Josephus in his *Against Apion* (i, 14-16, 26-27), which have a direct bearing on the story of the Exodus. According to one version (i, 14-16), the Hyksos invaded Egypt and ruled it for a long period, and were later driven out to Judah, where they built Jerusalem. Jewish apologetes viewed this account as a confirmation of the Biblical reports and as a proof of the great antiquity of Israel. The other version (i, 26-27) has it that the Jews are the descendants of a group of 80,000 lepers and untouchables who revolted against the Egyptian king Amenhotep after they had been sent by him to the quarries east of the Nile. Their leader, Osarsiphos, a priest of Heliopolis, gave them new laws and called upon the Hyksos of Jerusalem for aid. He then assumed the name Moses, and, together with the Hyksos, ruled Egypt for thirteen years until they were driven out by the Egyptians. Parallels to this story, which is attacked by Josephus, are found also in writings of Egyptian and Greek anti-Jewish authors. The story is pure fiction, and is based on the Bible and on Egyptian folk-tales. It is possible also that this account was not found in Manetho's original work, but was added later by an enemy of the Jews. In general, the references to the Hyksos dynasty contain valuable information, but the theory of their connection with the Israelites is untenable.

The fragments of Manetho's work which have been preserved are contained in C. Müller's *Fragmenta Historicorum Graecorum* (Paris, 1848, vol. 2, pp. 515-616). Several other works are attributed to Manetho.

SAMUEL RABINOWITZ.

Lit.: Christ, W. von, *Geschichte der griechischen Literatur* (6th ed., 1920), vol. 2, pp. 224-25; Meyer, Eduard, *Geschichte des Altertums* (2nd ed.), vol. 1, part 2, pp. 12 et seq., 314; Schürer, Emil, *A History of the Jewish People in the Time of Jesus Christ* (4th ed.), vol. 3, pp. 529-31.

MANGER, ITZIK, Yiddish poet, b. Czernowitz, Bucovina, 1901. At the age of fourteen he was taken to Jassy by his parents, and here he continued to work as a tailor, an occupation for which he had been trained by his father. Although Manger soon began to write, his first work was in German and Roumanian. In 1918, however, he turned to Yiddish, and his first Yiddish poems were published in *Kultur* (1921). The collections of his verse which were published subsequently show a mystical and profoundly imaginative traditionally Jewish influence, expressed with original and often grotesque fantasy. Manger continued to live in Roumania, but visited Poland frequently, and several of his books were published in Warsaw. The first collection of his poems was *Shtern Oifen Dach* (1929). This was followed by *Lamtern in Vint* (1933); *Humesh Lieder* (1936); *Megillah Lieder* (1936); *Velvel Zbaruzher Shreibt Briev zu Malkele der Sheiner* (1937); and *Noente Geshtalten* (1938).

Lit.: Reisen, Z., *Lexikon fun der Yiddisher Literatur, Presse un Filologie,* vol. 2 (1930), cols. 303-4.

MANHEIMER, MORITZ, philanthropist and community worker, b. Commern, Prussian Saxony, 1826; d. Berlin, 1916. A wealthy merchant, he retired from business in his early manhood in order to devote his resources and his time to charity, aided by his wife, Bertha Lewes Manheimer (d. 1918). During his lifetime Manheimer distributed a considerable part of his fortune, founding more than forty charitable endowments, such as the hospital of the Jewish community of Berlin, the Jewish asylum for the aged poor at Berlin, the home for Jewish apprentices at Pankow, a suburb of Berlin, and the "tolerance-professorship" at the Jewish high school at Berlin. In his last will Manheimer made provision for more than fifty charitable legacies.

From 1881 on he was member of the representative assembly of the Jewish community of Berlin, of whose financial committee he was chairman. He belonged to the Jewish liberal party. Even as an octogenarian Manheimer worked untiringly in the assembly, and presided over meetings of Jewish organizations. Emperor William II honored him by several decorations and by gifts on the occasion of his golden and diamond weddings. The latter was celebrated in the synagogue with the directorate, the whole representative assembly, and all the rabbis of the Jewish community of Berlin in attendance.

MANIEVICH, ABRAHAM ANSHELOVICH, painter, b. Mstislavl, province of Mogilev, Russia,

A self-portrait of Abraham Manievich

1883. He studied at the government art school in Kiev and then, upon a stipend from the Russian government, in Munich (1909-10). An additional allowance from the government enabled him to travel in Germany, Italy, Switzerland, and France from 1910 to 1912.

His first exhibition was at the Kiev museum in 1910, and he had exhibitions in Paris (1913), Petrograd, and Moscow. He returned to Kiev to become an instructor in the Ukrainian academy of art in 1918, and taught there until 1920. In 1922 he came to the United States where he has lived ever since. His paintings, from then on, were exhibited in various cities of the United States and Canada.

Manievich began as a painter of Ukrainian landscapes—woods, villages, and streets—canvases bright with color. In contrast to these was his somber *Destruction of the Ghetto,* commemorating the years of death by famine and pogrom that marked the civil war in Russia after the revolutions of 1917. In the United States Manievich devoted himself chiefly to scenes in the Bronx or Brooklyn, in Camden or Pittsburgh, or wherever he happened to live, showing again his bright rich coloring but a bolder design—painting, neither academic nor naturalistic, that attains, as Christian Brinton wrote in the introduction to the catalogue of one of Manievich's exhibitions, "a subjective synthesis, a vivid emotional unity—a veritable état d'âme." Other critics regarded him as almost morbidly sensitive to "moods" and as possessed of the ability to sense the "spirit" of a locality and transfer it to his canvas, at the same time preserving his own personal outlook, and as able to reproduce on his canvases the hidden color mysteries of everyday life, since he was a master of color and its faithful interpreter upon the canvas.

The paintings of Manievich are to be found in such institutions as Luxembourg Museum, Paris: *Through the Branches;* Horvatt Gallery, Geneva, Switzerland: *Rome, Italy,* and *Spring, Capri, Italy;* Folk Museum, Moscow: *Autumn Symphony;* Kiev Museum of Art: *Miestetchks* and *My Birthplace;* Brooklyn Museum of Art: *Birch* and a landscape. Other canvases of Manievich are to be found in the Government Museum and the Tretiakov Gallery in Moscow, the Academy of Art and the Kuindzi Museum in Leningrad, the Government Museum and the Tereschenko Museum in Kiev, the Museum of Art in Odessa, and the Art Gallery of Toronto, Canada.

MANILA, *see* PHILIPPINE ISLANDS.

MANIN, DANIELE, Italian patriot and dictator of Venice, descendant of a family of scientists which had embraced Christianity, b. Venice, 1804; d. Paris, 1857. He studied at the University of Padua, became a doctor of law at an early age, and served as consulting lawyer in civil cases. Well-versed in jurisprudence, political economy and languages and noted as translator into Italian of Pothier's work on Russian law, he became a leader of liberal thought in Venice. When he demanded that the Austrian government make the Lombard-Venetian kingdom independent, he was imprisoned early in 1848 on a charge of high treason. However, in March, 1848, when the revolution in Venice broke out, he was released by the populace, and was made head of the patriotic movement and president of the restored Republic of St. Mark. He organized a civic guard, drove the Austrians from the arsenal, and prevented unlawful excesses by the mob.

When Charles Albert of Sardinia invaded Lombardy, Manin resigned, but resumed his power when the Sardinian army was defeated, and became dictator of Venice in March, 1849. After Venice's capitulation to the Austrians on August 24, 1849, Manin and other leaders of the revolution went to Paris, where he labored as journalist and language teacher. Although an ardent believer in an Italian republic, he advocated a Piedmontese monarchy for the sake of Italian unity, and, together with Giorgio Pallavicini and Giuseppe La Farina, founded the Società Nazionale Italiana at Paris. In 1868 his remains were brought back to Italy and honored with a public funeral, and statues of him were erected at Turin (1861), Florence, Venice, and on the Monte Pincio in Rome. His son Giorgio, a scientist, took part in Garibaldi's struggles for Italian freedom.

Lit.: Works on the life of Daniele Manin by Henry Martin (1850), Hugh Martin (1862) and Errera and Finzi (1872); Perlbach, *Daniele Manin und Venedig* (1878); Macaulay, Trevelyan, *Manin and the Venetian Revolution of 1848* (1923); Sanderson, Edgar, *Hero Patriots of the Nineteenth Century* (1901) 270-94; Wininger, S., *Grosse Jüdische National-Biographie,* vol. 4, p. 257.

MANITOBA, the central province of Canada, bounded on the east by the province of Ontario and Hudson Bay, on the south by the states of North Dakota and Minnesota, on the west by the province of Saskatchewan, and on the north by the North West Territories. Its length from north to south is 761 miles, and its breadth from east to west 278 miles. Its present (1942) area is 251,832 square miles, of which 27,055 square miles are covered by water. Manitoba is the oldest of the three prairie provinces, having been set up as a province on July 15, 1870.

Jewish fur traders and merchants may have visited the territory which is now Manitoba in the days of the Hudson's Bay Company and the North West Company, but the earliest mention of a Jew in Manitoba is that of Max Goldstine, who came from Ontario as a trooper with the Wolseley Expedition during the Riel Rebellion of 1870. Next came Reuben Goldstein and Hyman Miller in 1879, followed by A. Beber, Philip Brown, George Frankfurter, David and Samuel Ripstein and Louis Wertheim in 1880. The first government census of 1881 showed a Jewish population of thirty-one in Manitoba, of whom twenty-one lived in Winnipeg, seven in Emerson and three in Morris.

A group of twenty-four Jewish men, women and children arrived in Winnipeg on May 26, 1882, and the men were described by the Manitoba Free Press at that time as "young, none of them over 30 years of age, stalwart looking and evidently intelligent . . . able and willing to work . . . among them are three carpenters, one blacksmith, one cabinet maker, one painter, one dyer, and the remainder farmers." Within a week they were followed by a larger group of 247 men, women and children, and others followed in successive waves. Many of the immigrants passed through Winnipeg to take up free homesteads as farmers in Western Canada. Many more found work on the Canadian Pacific Railway as track laborers, foremen and cooks in building the first transcontinental line to cross Canada.

Population. The Jewish population of Manitoba rose rapidly from thirty-one in 1881 to 791 in 1891, then to 1,514 in 1901 and 10,741 in 1911. By 1921 the Jewish population of the province had reached 16,669, increased to 19,431 in 1931 and decreased to 18,596 in 1936, according to the official government censuses. Jews formed 2.76% of the total population of the province in 1931, as compared with 2.09% in the province of Quebec, 1.81% in the province of Ontario, and 1.50% in Canada as a whole. The Jewish population in 1942 formed the seventh largest ethnic group of non-Anglo-Saxon origin in the province, being exceeded by the Ukrainians with 12.23%, Germans with 7.37%, French with 6.70%, Poles with 4.94%, Scandinavians with 4.43%, and Dutch with 3.44%.

Distribution. Winnipeg, the capital city of Manitoba, was, in 1942, the fourth largest city in Canada, and had the third largest Jewish community in the Dominion. Of the total Jewish population of Manitoba, 16,888 lived in Winnipeg in 1936, forming 90.8% of the Jewish population of the province. The only two other towns in Manitoba with a Jewish population exceeding 100 were Selkirk with 110, and Brandon with 108. Jewish communities with twenty or more persons, but less than 100, were found in 1936 in the towns and villages of St. Boniface, Portage la Prairie, Dauphin, Beausejour, Roblin, Winkler, The Pas, Transcona and Gimli. There were fifty-six towns and villages in Manitoba in 1936, and Jews were living in forty-four of them.

Occupational Distribution. Of all the Jews gainfully occupied in the province of Manitoba when the 1936 census was taken, 23.28% were engaged in the manufacturing industries, as compared with only 7.97% among the gainfully occupied of all origins. Out of every 100 Jewish men in Manitoba in 1936 gainfully occupied, twenty were retail merchants, eight were wholesale merchants, and seven were salesmen. Furriers, tailors, canvassers and unskilled laborers numbered three each. Farmers, bookkeepers, office clerks, truck drivers, teamsters, leather workers, shippers and sewing machine operators numbered two each, while lawyers, doctors, teachers, barbers, insurance agents, ironers and pressers, commercial travelers, tinsmiths, painters, carpenters, metal workers, mechanics, printers, clothing cutters and shoe repairers numbered one each.

Out of every 100 Jewish women gainfully occupied, twenty were sewing machine operators, seventeen were stenographers, sixteen were salesladies, six were teachers and four were bookkeepers. Fur workers, glovemakers, packers, retail merchants, nurses and domestic servants accounted for two each, while dressmakers, milliners, knitters, bookbinders, shippers, boarding house keepers, hairdressers and unskilled workers numbered one each.

Synagogues. The oldest existing congregation in Manitoba is the Shaarey Zedek Synagogue in Winnipeg, formed by the union of two earlier congregations in 1890, whose rabbi in 1942 was Solomon Frank. There are seven other synagogues in Winnipeg, one in Brandon, and one in Portage la Prairie. The Shaarey Zedek Synagogue follows the Conservative form of worship, and the sermon is given in English. The other synagogues follow the Orthodox form of service, and the sermon is given in Yiddish. Israel Kahanovitch in 1942 was senior rabbi in the province, having come to Winnipeg in 1909.

Jews in Civic Life. S. Hart Green, K.C., who was elected a member of the Provincial Legislative Assembly in 1910 and sat in the Legislative Assembly from 1910 to 1914 as a Liberal member, was the first Jew to be elected to a provincial or dominion legislative body from Manitoba. A. A. Heaps, who had been an alderman of the city of Winnipeg for many years, was elected Labor member of the House of Commons for the constituency of Winnipeg North, and held his seat from 1921 to 1940. Captain William Tobias was elected Conservative member of the Manitoba Legislature in 1927, and retained his seat until 1932, while Marcus Hyman, K.C., elected Labor member of the Manitoba Legislature in 1932, held his seat until his death in 1939. M. A. Gray was elected to the Manitoba Legislature in 1941.

LOUIS ROSENBERG.

Lit.: Rosenberg, Louis, *Canada's Jews, A Social and Economic Study* (1939); *The Jew in Canada,* A. D. Hart edit.; Wilder, H. D., "An Outline of the History of the Jews in Canada," *Souvenir of the 50th Anniversary of Jewish Settlement in Western Canada* (1931).

MANKIEWICZ, FRANK, professor of education, b. Berlin, 1872; d. Los Angeles, 1941. He came to New York city in 1892, and began his career as a writer for German newspapers in the United States. He studied modern languages and became a teacher of languages at different high schools. In 1927 he became associate professor at the College of the City of New York, and in 1936 professor of education. From 1930 until his death he was president of the Association of Teachers of German of New York and Vicinity. He was the author of textbooks in German and French, and a leading personality in all educational fields of the United States. From 1933 on Mankiewicz devoted a great part of his time to aiding Jewish émigrés from Germany and other European countries. He was a member of the American Friends of the Hebrew University.

MANKIEWICZ, HERMAN JACOB, writer and play producer, b. New York city, 1897. He was the son of Frank Mankiewicz. He received his A.B. degree from Columbia University in 1916. After a career as reporter in the United States and abroad, Mankiewicz became interested in the theatre. During the first World War he served with the United States Marines in the American Expeditionary Force. From 1922 to 1926 he was a member of the dramatic staff of the *New York Times;* in 1925 and 1926 he was also dramatic critic of the *New Yorker.*

The Good Fellow, a play he had written with George S. Kaufman, was produced by Mankiewicz in 1927. He also produced *The Wild Man of Borneo,* written by him in collaboration with Marc Connelly (1927), and his own play, *The Meal Ticket* (1937). Late in the 1920's Mankiewicz went to Hollywood, where he became a producer and writer for various motion picture companies. Among the outstanding motion pictures with which he was connected were *Dinner at Eight* (1933); *The Show-Off* (1934); and *Escapade* (1935). In 1942 Mankiewicz won the Academy Award for his original screen play, *Citizen Kane.*

MANKIEWICZ, JOSEPH LEO, writer and motion picture producer, b. Wilkes-Barre, Pa., 1909. He was the son of Frank Mankiewicz and the brother of Herman Jacob Mankiewicz. He received his A.B. degree from Columbia University, New York city, in 1928. After a year in newspaper work in Germany, Mankiewicz went to Hollywood when he became affiliated with the motion picture industry. He collaborated in the production of many screen plays, and was himself the producer of *Fury* (1936); *Double Wedding* (1937); *Mannequin* (1937); *Huckleberry Finn* (1939); *Strange Cargo* (1940); and *The Philadelphia Story* (1940).

MANN, JACOB, historian, b. Przemysl, Galicia, 1888; d. Cincinnati, 1940. He came to England in 1908, a youth of twenty, and prepared himself for the rabbinate at Jews' College while pursuing his secular studies at London University. In 1913 he received his B.A. degree from that university, and in the following year he qualified for the Jewish ministry at Jews' College. He received his M.A. degree in 1915, and his D.Litt. degree in 1920.

The chief rabbi of the British Empire, Joseph H. Hertz, employed Mann as his Hebrew secretary. Hertz was helpful in making possible the publication of two volumes of tremendous importance, based upon hitherto unexplored Genizah material: *The Jews in Egypt and in Palestine under the Fatimid Caliphs* (vol. 1, Oxford, 1920; vol. 2, Oxford, 1922).

Jacob Mann

In 1920 Mann came to the United States. He was engaged as instructor of Bible, Talmud and Jewish history at Baltimore Hebrew College and Teachers' Training School from 1921 to 1922. He then came to the Hebrew Union College, at Cincinnati, to occupy the chair of Jewish history, serving until his death.

In 1927 to 1928 he was honored by the Hebrew University, Jerusalem, with an invitation to teach as a visiting professor. It was during that trip abroad that he gathered much documentary material of new Gaonic and Karaitic investigations, which he later used in his *Texts and Studies in Jewish History and Literature* (vol. 1, Cincinnati, 1931; vol. 2, Karaitica, Philadelphia, 1935). His last great work was *The Bible as Read and Preached in the Old Synagogue—a Study in* the Cycles of the Reading from Torah and Prophets, as well as from Psalms and in the Structure of the Midrashic Homilies (Cincinnati, 1940), on which he was working when he was fatally stricken.

VICTOR REICHERT.

Lit.: Marcus, Jacob R., in *Central Conference of American Rabbis Year Book*, vol. 51 (1941) 247-49; Reichert, Victor E., in *American Jewish Year Book*, vol. 43 (1941-42) 407-14; Mahler, R., "Jacob Mann's Life and Works," *Yivo-Bleter*, vol. 16, No. 2 (Nov.-Dec., 1940); Waxman, Meyer, *A History of Jewish Literature*, vol. 4 (1941) 1137-40.

MANN, LOUIS, actor, b. New York city, 1865; d. New York city, 1931. He made a first appearance on the stage at three, but later parental opposition forbade a return. Then in the 1880's his career began to get under way; with various troupes he appeared in a great number and variety of roles, including that of "Page" in the early Oscar Wilde drama *Vera the Nihilist* (1883). Among the famous actors in whose repertoires Mann engaged was Edwin Booth. Personal triumph came in 1891 in a play called *Incog;* from then on his climb was rapid, until at the height of his half-century career he was acclaimed one of the country's leading comedians. He had developed and exploited the comedy type of a lovable, if erratic, German-American; it was such a character that brought him his greatest success in *Friendly Enemies,* in which he co-starred with Sam Bernard. The play opened in Washington, D. C., in 1918, and President Woodrow Wilson rose in his box to pay personal tribute to Mann. Besides acting, Mann wrote or collaborated on several pieces for the stage.

Mann was an intimate of celebrities in every profession; among those who came to pay him tribute at his death were James J. Walker, Alfred E. Smith, William Randolph Hearst and Herbert H. Lehman.

CLARA LIPMAN MANN, actress and playwright (b. Chicago, 1875), was the wife of Louis Mann. At the age of ten she was acting in Madame Modjeska's company. She met and married her husband during his engagement in *Incog,* and after that they frequently played together; they co-starred in *The Strange Adventures of Miss Brown* (1895), *Telephone Girl* (1898), *Red Kloof* (1900), *Julie Bon Bon* (1908) and *French Lady* (1927). Miss Lipman also wrote *Julie Bon Bon,* and was author of and collaborator on several other plays. She was

Louis Mann (right) and his wife (left), Clara Lipman Mann

Thomas Mann

known to theatre-goers for her exceptional personality, as much as for her style of melodramatic acting.

Lit.: *Jewish Tribune*, Feb. 20, 1931, p. 6; Feb. 27, 1931, p. 3; *New York Times* and *Herald Tribune*, Feb. 16, 1931.

MANN, LOUIS LEOPOLD, rabbi, b. Louisville, Ky., 1890. He studied at Johns Hopkins University and, after graduating from the University of Cincinnati (M.A., 1912) and the Hebrew Union College (rabbi, 1914), he became rabbi of Congregation Mishkan Israel, New Haven, Conn. In 1920 he received his Ph.D. degree from Yale University, where he was lecturer in comparative ethics for the next three years. In 1923 he became rabbi of Chicago Sinai Congregation, succeeding Emil G. Hirsch; in the following year he became a professorial lecturer in the Department of Oriental Languages at the University of Chicago, and was still serving in both these positions in 1942. In 1931 he gave a course of lectures on the evolution of the soul for the W. F. Ayres Foundation. That year he was made an officer of the French Academy.

Mann was a key figure in communal and Jewish affairs. He was one of the founders of the B'nai B'rith Hillel Foundation, playing an important part in the launching of the movement, and he served as its acting national director from 1928 to 1933. Mann was closely associated with the National Association for the Outlawry of War, the Big Brothers and Big Sisters Movement of America, and chancellor of the Jewish Chautauqua Society. He was active in the Central Conference of American Rabbis, the Jewish Publication Society of America, the Religious Education Association of America, and similar organizations. He aided in the founding of the Round Table of Jews and Christians, and was appointed by President Herbert Hoover a member of the White House Conference of Child Welfare. Mann is editor of the department of ethics of this encyclopedia. He was the first rabbi in America to introduce psychiatric supervision in the religious school course. He collaborated on the new *Thorndike Dictionary* and contributed to the *American Dictionary of Biography*. Mann was a founder of the Birth Control League and served on the advisory council of the American Library Association. He wrote *In Quest of the Blue Bird*.

MANN, THOMAS, German non-Jewish writer, b. Lübeck, Germany, 1875. In 1933 he left Germany as a voluntary exile; in 1942 he lived in America.

Besides his literary significance, Mann became especially important for Jewry as the outstanding German non-Jewish fighter against Hitlerism, hence also against the persecution of Jews. In contributions to newspapers and in public speeches he assailed the National Socialist (Nazi) system as the arch enemy of European civilization, morals and Christianity. When he was deprived of his title of honorary doctor of the University of Bonn, Germany, Mann replied in an open letter to the dean of the Philosophical Faculty of this university, dated New Year's Day, 1937. In this letter, published in the United States under the title *An Exchange of Letters*, Mann expounds his general attitude toward Hitlerism on the one hand and toward the cultural heritage of Germany on the other hand.

The literary work of Mann, which is most representative of his latest period and one of the greatest achievements of modern narrative prose, deals with a Biblical subject: the Joseph saga. Begun in an epoch of social dissolution and political despair and continued while its author was homeless, the Joseph story became the most profoundly poetic expression of Mann's belief in eternal values in those dark times in which human culture and morals seemed to be disintegrating. The legend of Israel's founder, Jacob, and of his son Joseph goes back to the earliest stage in Jewish history, to the mythical stage and mentality of the human race. In plumbing the depths of prehistoric times, Mann plumbs the depths and abysses of the human soul as well. The whole Joseph cycle demonstrates that myth is in every respect the very foundation of human history, "the legitimization of life." It is by the mythical attitude that man becomes convinced that there are spiritual values beyond time and space.

This mythical causation of the story is paralleled by the psychological. The various images from the childhood of mankind, as embodied in the old legends, demonstrate an early stage of human feeling and reasoning. This reciprocal character pervades the whole mythological sphere, so that the myths also reflect a certain human attitude towards life. In Judaism the highest reciprocal symbol is the covenant between God and man. In the idea of the covenant, says Mann, Abram became the father of God: "He perceived and brought Him forth; His mighty qualities, ascribed to Him by Abram, were probably His original possession; Abram was not their inventor, yet in a sense he was, by virtue of his recognizing them and therewith, by taking thought, making them real."

In the primitive attitude the typical governs the individual, and the myth teaches everybody how to act. In this sense, too, myth is "the legitimization of life." The whole Joseph story tells how the individual character, bound to time and space, derives from the timeless and collective character of the mythical epoch and conquers it. These are the fundamental ideas in the light of which Mann retells the Biblical stories. An early chapter of Jewish history becomes the symbolic story of human life and fate. The reader shares Jacob's life

The rain of Manna. From a 15th cent. painting by Dirk Bouts

near Hebron, watching the growing of the charming youth Joseph who is being educated in the way of the fathers and loved by Jacob with a "twofold and altogether provocative preference." In Egypt, then, he becomes an individual whose knowledge is greater than that of the people of the mythical epoch. But he can not forget his origin, neither his father nor his God.

Mann conceived the idea of writing the Joseph story as early as 1926. The author studied Jewish ethnology and the Bible, and visited Palestine and Egypt. The work as a whole was published under the title *Joseph und seine Brüder* (Joseph and His Brothers). The first volume, *Die Geschichten Jaakobs,* appeared in 1933; the English translation of this volume, by H. T. Lowe-Porter, has the general title of *Joseph and His Brothers* (1934). The second volume, *Der junge Joseph,* was published in 1934; the English translation, *Young Joseph,* in 1935. The work had not yet been completed (up to 1942) by the author. The third volume, *Joseph in Ägypten* (1936), is only the introduction to the last part. The English translation, *Joseph in Egypt* (2 vols.), was published in 1938.　　RUDOLF KAYSER.

Lit.: Slochower, Harry, *Thomas Mann's Joseph Story* (1938); Flanner, Janet, in *New Yorker,* Dec. 13, 1941, pp. 31-42; Dec. 20, 1941, pp. 22-35; *American Hebrew,* Sept. 19, 1930, p. 465; Sept. 30, 1932, p. 357; Sept. 15, 1933, p. 265; May 18, 1934, p. 13; Sept. 7, 1934, p. 289; Sept. 11, 1936, p. 280; March 26, 1937, p. 1049; Aug. 20, 1937, p. 10; April 23, 1937, p. 1138; *Opinion,* May, 1937, pp. 9-11.

MANNA, the food which, according to the Bible, miraculously sustained the Israelites in the wilderness during their journey to the Promised Land. First described in *Exodus* (chap. 16) and then in *Numbers* (chap. 11), manna is called "bread from heaven" and pictured as "a fine, scale-like thing, fine as the hoarfrost on the ground," and again like "coriander seed, white." When the Israelites saw it first, they said to each other, "What is it?" (*man hu*), and from this some derive the name, manna; but it has also been attributed to the Egyptian *mennu,* meaning "food."

After the dew fell upon the camp at night, the manna fell upon it; in the morning, when the dew was gone, the manna lay upon the face of the wilderness. The Israelites were to gather an omer (about four quarts) for each person. Whoever gathered more for those in his tent had nothing over, and he that gathered less lacked nothing. As the sun grew hot, it melted. The Israelites were also to leave nothing for the next morning. Those who did so found that the manna "bred worms, and rotted." On the sixth day of the week the Israelites were commanded to gather twice as much, that they might rest on the Sabbath, and the manna kept for that day neither spoiled nor melted.

The manna was either baked or boiled; it was ground in mills or crushed in mortars, boiled in pots and made into cakes. It tasted like wafers made with honey or, according to the narrative in *Numbers,* like a cake baked with oil. In spite of its delectable taste, many of the Israelites tired of it; when they thought of the fish which they had had in Egypt, the cucumbers and melons, the leeks, onions, and the garlic, they said bitterly, "Our soul is dried away; there is nothing at all; we have nought save this manna to look to" (*Num.* 11:6), and, later, "our soul loatheth this light bread" (*Num.* 21:5).

According to *Exodus* (chap. 16), the Israelites ate manna for forty years until they came to the borders of Canaan and camped on the plain of Jericho. After they had eaten of the food of the Promised Land, the manna ceased (*Ex.* 16:35; *Josh.* 5:12). But, as commanded (*Ex.* 16:32-34), the Israelites had kept an omer of it in a jar that the generations to come might see the bread with which their fathers had been fed in the wilderness.

Moses (*Deut.* 8:3) warned the Israelites to remember how in their wanderings God fed them with manna, and the Psalmist, recounting the marvels of the Exodus, says of the Lord, "He caused manna to rain upon them for food, and gave them of the corn of heaven. Man did eat the bread of the mighty; He sent them provisions to the full" (*Ps.* 78:24-25). The statesman Nehemiah, too, listing God's benefactions to the children of Israel, includes "bread from heaven for their hunger," and, addressing God as "ready to pardon, gracious and full of compassion," adds that, in spite of their murmurings, He withheld not His manna from their mouth (*Neh.* 9:15, 20). According to a legend about Jeremiah, when those whom he urged to study the Torah asked how they were to make a living if they did, the prophet brought out the jar in which the omer of manna had been preserved and said that God, Who had fed their fathers, would see to it that they did not starve.

In late Hebrew and in Christian writings manna came to be a symbol for spiritual nourishment (cf. *Deut.* 8:3). In the New Testament (*John* 6) Jesus likens his teachings to manna, "that bread which came down from heaven," but adds that those who did eat it are all dead, whereas those who shall follow him shall live forever. And, according to *Rev.* 2:17, "the Spirit saith unto the Churches; to him that overcometh will I give to eat of the hidden manna." Paul (*Heb.* 9:4) mentions "the golden pot" that held the manna in the sanctuary, although, according to the traditions of the rabbis, it was an earthen vessel.

The rabbis considered manna a reward to the children of Abraham for that patriarch's piety and, just as he brought bread to the angels, God gave his children

bread. Manna is still, it was said, being ground in heaven to be food for the pious (cf. *Rev.* 2:17). In the legends of the Jews, manna tasted to children like milk, to their elders like bread, and to the old like honey; to the sick it was like barley steeped in oil and honey. It was perfumed and all who ate of it were fragrant. None of it was voided because it completely dissolved in the body. And the rabbis thought the murmurings of the Israelites against manna really an expression of their dissatisfaction with the yoke of the Law.

The miraculous food of the Bible is said to have been much like the tamarisk manna found to this day in the wilderness of Sinai and sometimes gathered by the Arabs to be sold to pilgrims. It was supposed to exude from the branches of the tamarisk when they were punctured by an insect (Coccus manniparus). In 1927 an expedition, headed by Fritz S. Bodenheimer of the Hebrew University, Jerusalem, discovered that the manna, like honey, is an excretion of the insect (living on the leaves of the tamarisk). Falling in honey-like drops, the manna is found on the ground hardened in the chill of the early morning.

CHARLES REZNIKOFF.

Lit.: Ginzberg, Louis, *The Legends of the Jews* (particularly vol. 3, pp. 41-50, and, for Talmudic references, vol. 6, pp. 16-20, notes 92-118).

MANNE, MORDECAI ZEBI, Hebrew poet and painter, b. Radushkowitz, near Vilna, Lithuania, 1859; d. Radushkowitz, 1886. He received the usual traditional training, and was taught Hebrew by his father. In 1876 he became a student at the art school of Vilna, and at the same time wrote poetry. In 1880 he studied at the Academy of Fine Arts at Leningrad (St. Petersburg); in 1882 Grand Duke Vladimir awarded him a silver cross on behalf of the Academy. In 1886 his promising career was cut short when he died at the age of twenty-eight from a pulmonary disease.

Manne's collected poems, essays and letters were published posthumously by his friends, under the title of *Kol Kithebe Manne* (1 vol., in 2 parts, Warsaw, 1897). Some of his best poems are: "Massath Nafshi" (The Burden of My Soul), "Hashoshanah" (The Lily), "Halaylah" (The Night), "Atzeb Anochi" (I Am Grieved), "Zikkaron Leyom Daled Shel Hol Hamoed Pesah" (A Memorial of the Fourth Day of the Profane Days of the Passover), and "Tikvah Laobed" (Hope for the Worker); the latter poem, somewhat didactic in character, depicts the contrast between hope and despair. The subject matter of his essays is the art of painting, painters, the art of poetry, and esthetics. His most elaborate essay deals with the painter Oppenheim.

Manne may be regarded as the first modern Hebrew lyric poet. He succeeded in casting off the bonds of the so-called Melitzah style of writing Hebrew, and was the first to introduce European metre into Hebrew poetry. His lyric poems are in general imbued with profound sadness, longing and a beautifully depicted love of nature. In his last days the motive of the love of Zion assumed a place in his poetical writings. Some of his poems, for example the "Massath Nafshi," were set to music, and are still sung by the Hebrew-reading public.

Lit.: Klausner, Joseph, *A History of Modern Hebrew*

Literature, pp. 112-13; Scheinhaus, A. L., Manne's biography in *Kol Kithebe Manne* (1897); Waxman, Meyer, *A History of Jewish Literature,* vol. 4 (1941) 207-10.

MANNERS. Jewish law regulates all relationships between man and his fellows. This is why one of the minor tractates of the Talmud, *Derech Eretz* (Proper Conduct), is devoted to a discussion of the principles of good manners and etiquette, and their applications. This tractate was edited and translated by Michael Higger in 1935. Although many of the laws of this tractate are quoted in other tractates of the Talmud, it contains many dicta which are not found elsewhere in the Talmud.

Good manners were considered such an important part of one's education that Akiba invited his pupils to dine with him so that he could, personally, instruct them in proper table manners (*Derech Eretz,* edit. Higger, p. 72). Among the rules of table etiquette prescribed are the following: one should not break off and hold in his hand a piece of bread larger than an egg, nor should one drain his cup in one gulp (*ibid.,* p. 71). The older and more learned were to be served first, and the others were to wait for them to commence eating (*ibid.,* p. 72). One should neither eat nor drink standing up, nor should one lick his fingers while at the table (*ibid.,* p. 45). One should not grasp his glass or a dish if his hands are greasy, nor should he mop up the bottom of his dish with a piece of bread (*Kallah Rabbathi,* edit. Higger, 9:6-7).

The guest should honor the wishes of the host (*Pes.* 86b), and it was the custom for the guest to bring gifts to the children of his host (*Derech Eretz,* p. 74). The guest also inserted a special blessing for the host in the grace which he recited after the meal (*Ber.* 46a). A host should never gaze at the portion of food which his guest takes, for that may embarrass him. When a poor man is eating at one's table he should be treated as a member of the family (*Aboth* 1:5). If one visits another and finds him at the table, the former should be invited to join in the repast (*Derech Eretz,* p. 45). One should not eat garlic or anything which gives off an offensive odor (*Sanh.* 11a).

Good manners and politeness in Judaism are not merely courtesies extended to members of one's religion or to members of one's own social caste. Neither are they merely amenities engendered by the inescapable closenesses of social contacts, nor civilities shown to members of a lower social stratum. They are, rather, illustrations of the living principle, "Love thy neighbour as thyself," symbolizing the equality of men who were all created in the image of God (*Midrash Gen.,* chap. 24, at the end). This spirit permeates all the utterances of the rabbis on the subject of politeness and good manners.

Thus, it is related of Johanan ben Zakkai, who was the spiritual leader of his generation, that he was so prompt in greeting people that no one, even a non-Jew of slight acquaintance whom he met in the market place, was ever able to greet him first (*Ber.* 17a). One was commanded to treat a Hebrew bondsman as a full equal in matters of food, drink, clothes and comforts of residence (*Kid.* 20a). It is well known that the Jews of the Middle Ages treated their servants almost as members of the family. The aim for which one was to

strive was, "Let the honor of your friend be as dear to you as your own" (*Aboth* 2:15).

Good-breeding is nowhere so evident as in respect shown parents and elders. The Talmud details the signs of respect which a child must show a parent. Among these are that a child should not contradict his parents, nor should he sit in their place, but should be alert to serve their every wish. Similar and even greater respect was to be shown a teacher. The Biblical commandment, "Thou shalt rise up before the hoary head, and honour the face of the old man" (*Lev.* 19:32), is interpreted to mean that one should stand up when greeting a learned man or anyone who has reached the age of seventy (*Shulhan Aruch, Yoreh Deah* 244), and one should not seat himself until his elders are seated (*Derech Eretz,* p. 47).

Talebearing was forbidden, idle gossip and even garrulousness were discouraged (*ibid.,* p. 38). The sages warned against praising a man if the conversation would thus be led to a discussion of his shortcomings (*Arach.* 16a). The law regarded embarrassing a person in public or in private as equal to the shedding of his blood, and declared that one who was guilty of this crime would have no share in the world to come (*Aboth* 3:5). For this reason it was forbidden to remind a sinner of his past misdeeds, and a creditor was forbidden to pass before his debtor if he knew that he was unable to meet his debt (*B.M.* 75b). The rabbis went so far as to declare that one should not use any language which might possibly cause embarrassment. For example, one should not say to a man, "Hang up this fish for me," if any member of that man's family was ever hanged (*B.M.* 58b-59b).

This deep consideration for the feelings of another is illustrated in many other regulations. It was permitted to disregard rabbinic laws in situations where their fulfillment would cause embarrassment (*Sab.* 81b). The Talmud contains a list of changes in laws which were instituted by the rabbis to spare the poor embarrassment (*M.K.* 27ab). One of the highest forms of charity was stated to be that whereby the donor and the recipient do not know each other's identity (*B.B.* 10b). It was forbidden to speak harshly to an orphan or widow, or to hurt their feelings in any manner (*Mechilta de Rabbi Simeon ben Yohai,* p. 150). Those who were afflicted with kidney trouble and those whose illness made talking a strain were not to be visited at all, and sickroom etiquette provided that one's visit should be short, that the discussion of dismal topics be eschewed, and that the visitor should supply the needs of the sick one. It was suggested that persons between whom ill-will existed should not visit each other in their sicknesses or bereavements, and that one should not comfort a mourner before his dead had been interred (*Shulhan Aruch, Yoreh Deah* 335).

Women were to be treated with the utmost of tenderness. They were never to be spoken to in a harsh manner (*Mechilta* to *Ex.* 19:3), and the Mishnah (*Hor.* 3:7) states that a woman takes precedence over a man in being rescued from captivity and in being clothed. At the Friday evening table a special chapter of the Bible (*Prov.* 31) was recited by the husband in honor of his wife. The Talmud advises that a man spend proportionately more money on his clothes than on his food, and that he should spend proportionately more money on his wife and children than on himself (*Hul.* 84b).

Cleanliness of body and neatness of appearance are fundamental to Jewish life, for personal dignity consists in cleanliness of person, and cleanliness in speech and thought. This is the meaning of the Mishnaic statement that "cleanliness leads to holiness" (*Sotah* 9:15). A scholar who wears clothes that are not spotlessly clean or shoes that are patched disgraces himself and the Torah which he represents by his disgraceful appearance (*Sab.* 114a). In general, a scholar was supposed to be especially courteous in all his actions (*Derech Eretz*, p. 49). Cleanliness in speech consisted in not using any impolite language and in using euphemisms wherever necessary (*Pes.* 3a). Jews were among the first to use handkerchiefs in the Middle Ages.

The rabbis stated that one who acts uncouthly can not be truly sin-fearing (*Aboth* 2:6). They insisted that everyone, no matter how unexpected or unwelcome, was to be greeted and accepted cheerfully and graciously (*Aboth* 1:15; 3:16). They realized that a cheerful word often means more than actual assistance (Aboth de Rabbi Nathan, chap. 13). For this reason proselytes were to be treated with special kindness. Anger to the extent of losing one's self-control was accounted as being akin to idolatry (*Zohar, Genesis*, p. 27b). The one who keeps more silent during a quarrel is obviously the better-bred (*Kid.* 71b), and interrupting was considered a sign of impoliteness (*Sifre, Numbers*, chap. 103).

It was pointed out that one should not act differently from his fellow men in company (*Derech Eretz*, p. 47). A man should make himself liked by all, as God is pleased with one who is liked by every one (*Keth.* 17a; *Aboth* 3:13). One of the requisites of being a precentor was to be liked by all.

Among the general rules of etiquette to be found in the Talmud are the following: one should not even enter his own house without first knocking (*Midrash Lev.* 21:8; *Nid.* 16b). One should always accompany a guest a short distance when he departs (*Sotah* 46b). One should not be a fault-finder or grumbler (*Derech Eretz*, p. 15), nor should one expectorate in front of anyone (*ibid.*, p. 113). When entering, the elder precedes; when leaving, the younger precedes (*ibid.*, p. 47). When one yawns he should cover his mouth with his hand (*Ber.* 24b).

See also: DECORUM; HONOR; HOSPITALITY; PARENTS AND CHILDREN.   HIRSCHEL REVEL.

Lit.: Higger, Michael, *Derech Eretz* (1935); idem, *Masechtoth Zeiroth* (1929); Abrahams, Israel, *Studies in Pharisaism and the Gospels*, Second Series (1924) 109-19; idem, *Jewish Life in The Middle Ages*, 2nd ed. (1932); Friedmann, Joseph, *Der gesellschaftliche Verkehr und die Umgangsformen in talmudischer Zeit* (1914).

MANNES, DAVID, violinist, conductor and educator, b. New York city, 1866. He studied music in Berlin and Brussels. In 1891 he joined the violin section of the New York Symphony Society, rising to the position of concertmaster. In 1898 he was married to Clara Damrosch, daughter of Leopold Damrosch, and two years thereafter he began giving sonata recitals with his wife, continuing this practice for over two decades. In 1906 Mannes became director of the Music School Settlement in New York, beginning a long and fertile career as music educator. In 1912 he founded, and for five years directed, the Music School Settlement for Colored People. In 1915 he founded his own school, the David Mannes School, which was still in existence in 1942 and of which his wife was co-director.

Mannes was prominent also as conductor, inaugurating free concerts at the Metropolitan Museum of Art in 1912. In 1918 he received a subsidy which enabled him to continue these concerts each winter, attracting audiences as large as 17,000 to each concert.

Both David and Clara Mannes received from the French government the Rosette of the Officier de l'Instruction Publique. Mannes is the author of an autobiography, *Music Is My Faith* (1938).

LEOPOLD DAMROSCH MANNES (b. New York city, 1899) the son of David and Clara Mannes, distinguished himself both as pianist and as scientist. He won the Pulitzer Prize (1925) and the Guggenheim Scholarship (1926), both for music, following which he taught at the Mannes School. He later abandoned music professionally to turn to scientific research and, together with Leopold Godowsky (the son of the world-famous pianist), he invented the Kodachrome process of color photography.

MANNHEIM, city in the German province of Baden, with 6,402 Jews (1940), out of a total population of 250,000. In 1650 five Jewish families from Pfeddersheim, near Worms, settled there; in 1663 there were already fifteen; of these, two Portuguese families were held in especial esteem by the Elector, Karl Ludwig, who had set out to repopulate the city. From 1660 on the legal status of the Jews was regulated by a charter. Until 1672 they were exempt from the payment of a tax for their protection; however, they had to pay a tax for wood and wine. Jews could engage in all handicrafts, and could even practise medicine if approved by the University of Heidelberg.

When a new charter, based on that of 1660, was granted the Mannheim Jews by Elector Johann Wilhelm (1691), they, like the Christian population, had left the city, which had been devastated by the French, for other places within the Palatinate or abroad. In 1697 the city authorities ordered the exiled Jews to return to Mannheim, under threat of punishment. The following year the elector granted the reestablished Jewish community a new charter which required every new immigrant not only to build a house but also to bring with him the sum of 1,000 thalers. Further charters were given by the electors on January 15, 1706, in 1717, and on April 16, 1722.

The Jewish community rose from fifteen families (1663) to 264 families in 1771. The residence of Jews among the Christians aroused much displeasure among the latter, but not until 1766, after repeated pressure from the city administration, did the government decree that within three years all Jews would have to settle in a special section of the city. After a few years, however, this experiment was abandoned.

Most of the Jews traded in cattle and grain. Despite permission to engage in all handicrafts, life was made quite difficult for the Jewish craftsmen by their Christian competitors. At the end of the 17th cent., during the administration of Philipp Wilhelm (1685-90), the guild butchers unsuccessfully petitioned the elector to forbid the cattle-trade of the Jews.

In the 18th cent. Emanuel Oppenheimer was the

Two views of the synagogue at Mannheim destroyed by Nazi intolerance

first and foremost of a number of influential court Jews. Like his father, he was an army contractor and court banker; he owned a magnificent palace in Mannheim. His Mannheim representative, Lemble Moyses Rheinganum (d. 1724), was for some time lessee of the salt-monopoly. He founded the Lemble Moyses Klaus (foundation) and the synagogue attached to it (1708). Emanuel Mayer, by a loan, saved the state tobacco manufactory in Mannheim from liquidation. Elias Hayum, chief assistant to Jud Süss, supplied the army from Mannheim as a purveyor during the Seven Years' War (1756-63). The first Jewish physician in Mannheim was Hayum Jacob (d. 1682), who treated Elector Karl Ludwig in his last illness; his son, Abraham Hayum (d. 1721), and his grandson (until 1775) practised medicine in Mannheim.

Through the charter of 1660 the Jews were enabled to build up a flourishing communal life. In 1661 the cemetery was founded; in 1664 the synagogue and ritual bath were acquired; in 1674 the burial fraternity was organized; in 1711 a house was acquired for sheltering poor and foreign Jews (from 1832 on called the Israelitisches Kranken- und Pfründnerhaus). There were also very pious and charitable foundations. Among the chief rabbis were: Naphtali Herz (1657-71); David Tebele Hess (1751-68), known as a result of the "Klever Get" quarrel; Hirschel Lewin (1770-73), who went to Berlin; Michael Scheuer (1782-1809).

At the end of the 18th cent. the Jews, pointing to the Edict of Tolerance of Emperor Joseph II, endeavored to resist pressure exerted by the citizens with the intention of decreasing their number and restricting Jewish business life. In 1799 the elector appointed a commission which, in cooperation with the Jews, was to work out a scheme for the improvement of their conditions. In 1803 the city was turned over to the grand duchy of Baden. By the edict of June 4, 1808, the Jews became *Staatsbürger* (citizens of the state), and by that of January 13, 1809, a constitutionally acknowledged religious group. But the Hep! Hep! riots of 1819 affected also the Jews of Mannheim.

They shared the general fate of the Baden Jews in their struggle for full emancipation. Dr. Leopold Ladenburg (1809-89) was in the forefront in this fight. In 1805 Herz Sinzheimer received permission to arrange public lectures on commercial science. The Jewish public school, founded in the beginning of the

19th cent., was converted into a general school in 1870. In 1817 a Jewish recreation society was founded from which emerged, in 1823, an association for the cultivation of literature and art.

In 1848 Jews were elected for the first time to the community council of Mannheim. But not until 1862 did the last communal and civic barriers in Baden fall. Due to the generally favorable conditions, the Mannheim community grew, in the course of a century, from 1,456 Jews (1825) to 6,972 in 1925. The Jews of Mannheim played a prominent part in the grain trade, tobacco business, cigar-manufacturing, banking and in the stock-market. The publishing business, established by J. Bensheimer in 1838, was one of the most important in southwestern Germany. The Handelshochschule was greatly indebted to Jews for their support, as well as to Jewish teachers. Among the numerous Jewish court justices, Nathan Stein became the first German Jew to serve as president of the Landgericht in Mannheim (1914-24).

Jewish religious life was changed by the Reform Movement, which resulted in the establishment of a new synagogue, consecrated by Dr. Moses Präger, the city rabbi, with organ music (1855). Jewish institutions, such as the August Laurey Lodge (I.O.B.B.), the Israelite nurses' home (1906) and the Israelite Orphan Asylum (1907), were actively supported by the members of the congregation, but the congregational religious life came to a certain standstill and there was even a strong trend toward conversion in the upper classes.

The Zionist Movement helped improve this state of mind. In 1920 the teaching of Hebrew was introduced into the public and high schools as a compulsory part of religious instruction. In 1928 a newspaper of the congregation was founded. Increased interest was directed toward youth and Jewish knowledge. Among the rabbis of this period was Moritz Steckelmacher (1880-1919), author of philosophical works; Max Grunewald was creator of the youth congregation, in September, 1912, and of the "Klaus" Isaak Unna and Lauer.

Among the famous Jews of the city was the attorney and Socialist leader, Ludwig Frank (1874-1914), who had enlisted as a volunteer in the German army and was killed in the second month of the first World War. He was one of the 135 Mannheim Jews who died in the War. Otto Lenel (b. Mannheim, 1849) was a distinguished scholar in the field of Roman law, Max Hachenburg (b. 1860), the last scholar in the field of commercial law, was also for a time a member of the Upper Council (*Oberrat*) of the Israelites in Baden. The American statesman Henry Morgenthau, Sr. (b. 1856), was a native of Mannheim.

The Nazi regime wrought havoc with the Jewish community. In the pogroms of November, 1938, the main synagogue was completely demolished and the Klaus partly destroyed. On October 22, 1940, the end of the community was brought about. Among the 10,000 Baden Jews who were transported to the camp at Gurs, in Southern France, there were about 2,000 Mannheim Jews, including the inmates of the Home for the Aged, some of whom were over ninety. Eugen Neter, president of the congregation, who for personal reasons could have remained in the city, went with the others into their wretched exile.

ADOLF KOBER.

Lit.: Bloch, Joseph, "Le testament d'une femme juive au commencement du xviiie siècle," *Revue des études juives,* vol. 90 (1931) 146-60; *Gedenkbuch zum hundert-undzwanzigjährigen Bestehen des Oberrats der Israeliten Badens* (1934); Lewin, Adolf, *Geschichte der badischen Juden seit der Regierung Karl Friedrichs* (1909); Loewenstein, Leopold, *Geschichte der Juden in der Kurpfalz* (1895); Rosenthal, Berthold, *Heimatgeschichte der Juden Badens seit ihren geschichtlichen Anfängen bis zur Gegenwart* (1927); idem, "Oberrabbiner Michael Scheuer als Kritiker seiner Zeit," *Zeitschrift für die Geschichte der Juden in Deutschland,* vol. 3 (1931) 72-75; idem, "Briefe von Mannheimer Juden aus den Jahren 1695-1697," *ibid.,* vol. 7 (1937) 98-107; Unna, Isaak, "Oberrabbiner Scheuer als Kritiker seiner Zeit," *ibid.,* vol. 1 (1929) 322-28.

MANNHEIM, KARL, sociologist and social philosopher, b. Budapest, 1893. He studied philosophy, became lecturer at the University of Heidelberg (1926), and professor of sociology at the University of Frankfort (1930-33). In 1933 he left Germany for England, and joined the staff of the London School of Economics and Political Science, at the University of London. In 1942 he became lecturer also at the Institute of Education, University of London.

Mannheim was a leading figure in European sociology. He emphasized the interconnection of historical and social facts with the modes of thought and ideas as an approach to the inner understanding and interpretation of society. His thought exerted great influence upon university life and public opinion in Great Britain.

His first publications (*Strukturanalyse der Erkenntnistheorie,* 1922; *Zum Problem einer Klassifikation der Wissenschaften,* 1922; *Beiträge zur Theorie der Weltanschauungsinterpretation,* 1922; *Historismus,* 1924) treated philosophical subjects. *Das Problem einer Soziologie des Wissens* (1925) delved into the fundamental problems of modern sociology of knowledge. Characteristic for this method of sociological interpretation was his *Ideologie und Utopie* (1929). Enlarged by Mannheim's article, "Wissenssoziologie," which appeared in *Handwörterbuch der Soziologie* (1931), it was translated into English by Louis Wirth and Edward Shils under the title *Ideology and Utopia. An Introduction to the Sociology of Knowledge* (1936). In 1934 he published a lecture in English on "Rational and Irrational Elements in Contemporary Society." The fundamental significance of sociology for the 20th cent. was already demonstrated in the essay, "Die Gegenwartsaufgaben der Soziologie" (1932). Thereafter his outstanding articles dealing with the analysis and shaping of society were: "Present Trends in the Building of Society," in *Human Affairs* (1937); "The Sociology of Human Valuations," in *Further Papers on the Social Sciences* (1937); "Mass Education and Group Analysis," in *Educating for Democracy* (1939). His book, *Mensch und Gesellschaft im Zeitalter des Umbaus* (1935), was a collection of studies on contemporary social structure and on the crisis of culture in the age of mass-democracies and dictatorships. A revised and greatly extended version was translated into English by Edward Shils under the title of *Man and Society in the Age of Reconstruction* (1940).

Mannheim was editor of *Schriften zur Philosophie und Soziologie,* and subsequently of *International Library of Sociology and Social Reconstruction.* In 1942 he was preparing a book on the sociological approach to the study of history.

Lit.: Merton, Robert King, *Karl Mannheim and the Sociology of Knowledge* (1941).

MANNHEIM, LUCIE, actress, b. near Berlin, 1898. She made her first stage appearances when very young, and during the first World War played in Königsberg at Leopold Jessner's "New Theatre." In 1920 she made her Berlin debut as Käthie in *Old Heidelberg.* Then she played in various German cities as well as in the *Volksbühne* theatre in Berlin. Among her roles at this period was that of Cornelia in *King Lear.*

From 1924 to 1930 Miss Mannheim was the leading actress at the Berlin Staatstheater, playing Nora in *A Doll's House,* Puck in *Midsummer Night's Dream,* Juliet in *Romeo and Juliet,* and other roles. She also made occasional appearances in other Berlin theatres, and was as adept in the grace and energy required for *Possen,* or old farce comedies, as in dramatic roles. In 1935, ousted by the Hitlerian decrees, she went to London, where she acted the part of Nora in English and took other leading roles. She also played in motion pictures, became a naturalized British subject, and in 1942 was living in London.

MANNHEIM, VICTOR AMEDÉE, mathematician and French army officer, b. Paris, 1831; d. Paris, 1906. He entered the École Polytechnique in 1848, at an unusually early age for that school. Two years later he was graduated as a sub-lieutenant of artillery and stationed at Metz. While on duty there he began to write mathematical treatises. Mannheim combined this theoretical work with his service in the French army, which brought him, through various advancements, to the rank of colonel after the siege of Paris in 1870, during which he commanded a legion.

In 1859, when already a captain, he was made a quizmaster at the École Polytechnique. Later he became admission examiner and, in 1864, professor of descriptive geometry. When he retired from the faculty in 1901 a farewell ceremony, which stands alone in the annals of the school, was held in his honor. Mannheim's treatises, which were of acknowledged importance in the science of mathematics, dealt largely with kinematic and infinitesimal geometry.

Lit.: Loria, Gino, "A. Mannheim—Soldier and Mathematician," *Scripta Mathematica* (1934) 337-42.

MANNHEIMER, ISAAC NOAH, rabbi, b. Copenhagen, Denmark, 1793; d. Vienna, 1865. He was appointed Jewish catechist by the Danish government in 1816, and became head of the Danish Jewish reform party which, among other things, transferred the Sabbath services to Wednesday, a manifestation of radicalism which led to schisms in the community. In 1821 Mannheimer went to Vienna, where he gave advice in the new method for the regulation of divine service and helped to improve the political position of the Viennese Jews, who were not allowed to form any communities officially. Subsequently serving in Hamburg, he became a friend of Gabriel Riesser and of the preachers Kley and G. Salomon.

In 1824 he was called to Vienna as preacher of the

Isaac Noah Mannheimer

achten gegen die Reformpartei in Frankfurt am Main in Angelegenheit der Beschneidungsfrage (1843).

Lit.: *Mannheimer-Album.* *Ein Nachhall zur siebzig-jährigen Geburtstagsfeier,* published by Major Kohn (1864); Rosenmann, M., *I. N. Mannheimer;* Wolf, G., *Geschichte der Juden in Wien* (1876); idem, *I. N. Mannheimer* (1863).

MANNHEIMER, MICHAEL, physician, b. Mönichsroth, Bavaria, Germany, 1844; d. Chicago, 1891. He was the son of a physician. He studied at the Universities of Munich, Erlangen, Vienna, and Heidelberg. In 1865 Mannheimer came to Chicago. Four years later he was graduated from the University of Louisiana. Returning to Chicago, he became an inspector in the department of health; as such, his studies of trichinosis were published by the Illinois State Board of Health.

Mannheimer soon became one of the leading Jewish physicians of Chicago. He was chief attending physician of Michael Reese Hospital until his death, and chief attending physician at the Alexian Brothers Hospital; he was also professor of medicine in the Chicago Polyclinic and Hospital.

MANNHEIMER, SIGMUND, educator, b. Kemel, Hesse-Nassau, Germany, 1835; d. Cincinnati, 1909. He studied at the teachers' seminary at Ems and then taught at the Jewish schools of Schierstein (1853) and Hegenheim (1858). In 1861 he became a student again and entered the University of Paris (Bachelier ès Lettres, 1863).

Mannheimer came to the United States in 1865 and lived, until 1867, in Baltimore, until 1873 in New York, until 1876 in St. Louis, and then in Rochester, earning his living as a teacher. In 1884 he was appointed professor of exegesis and Aramaic, as well as librarian, at the Hebrew Union College, in Cincinnati, serving for twenty-five years until his death.

His publications include a Hebrew grammar and reader (1873), of which there were many editions. He was the author also of several translations, including: *Das Judenthum oder die Wahrheit über den Talmud* (1858; from the French of Salomon Klein); *Anti-Semitism* (1897; from the French of Henri Jean Baptiste Anatole Leroy-Beaulieu); *Iggereth Musar* (1898; from the Hebrew of Solomon Alami).

He was awarded the honorary D.D. degree by the Hebrew Union College in 1909.

LOUISE HERSCHMAN MANNHEIMER (b. Prague, Bohemia, 1845; d. New York city, 1920), wife of Sigmund Mannheimer, was a writer and communal worker. She came to the United States in 1866 with her parents. Mrs. Mannheimer wrote in prose and verse for German and English periodicals, and translated Nahida Remy's *Das jüdische Weib* into English (1895). She founded an industrial school for boys in Cincinnati.

JANE MANNER (Jennie Mannheimer), elocutionist, was the daughter of Sigmund and Louise Mannheimer. She was born in New York city. She studied at the Hebrew Union College (B.H., 1888) and at the College of Music in Cincinnati. Miss Manner taught diction and dramatics in Cincinnati and, afterwards, in New York city. From 1900 to 1907 she was director of the drama department of the College of Music in Cincinnati. From 1913 on she gave readings from Shake-

temple in Seitenstettengasse. But since the Austrian government refused to sanction either a Jewish community or a rabbi, he received the title of "director of the Vienna imperial, royally sanctioned Israelite religious public school." He prepared a new ritual for the temple, retaining Hebrew in the services, including prayers for the restoration of Zion and preventing the installation of an organ. Thus he averted the schism between Orthodox and Reform Jews which was taking place in so many European countries. His resolution (1827) that "the knowledge of the Hebrew language is most necessary" for Jewish religious instruction, was likewise of acknowledged merit. In 1826 he introduced the records of birth, marriage and death, for the keeping of which he was commissioned by the government in 1831. To his initiative was due also the establishment of many Jewish social organizations in Vienna. The moderate reform introduced by Mannheimer and the institutions created by him became models for the communities of all Austria, with the exception of Galicia.

Mannheimer fought successfully against Professor Rosas, who in 1842 wished to restrict the admittance of Jews to the study of medicine. In 1846, together with twenty-four rabbis of Austria, he obtained the abolition of the ignominious medieval Jewish oath (*more judaico*) and the acceptance of a form of oath which he considered reasonable. Sent to the Reichstag by the city of Brody, Mannheimer, together with Fischhof, Goldmark and Meisels, effected the removal of the disgraceful Jewish tax.

His most important publications were: *Gottesdienstliche Vortäge über die Wochenabschnitte des Jahres (über Genesis und Exodus)* (Vienna, 1834); the translation of the Siddur and the first translation of the *Festgebete* (1840); *Rede am Grabe der Gefallenen, Freitag, den 17. März 1848* (Vienna); *Gutachten für das Gebetbuch des Hamburger Tempels* (1841); *Gut-*

speare and modern drama, as well as readings with music, before colleges and clubs throughout the United States. She edited *The Silver Treasury* (1934), a collection of recitations, and *The Junior Silver Treasury* (1938), for high schools and colleges.

EUGENE MAX MANNHEIMER (b. Rochester, N. Y., 1880), rabbi, was the son of Sigmund and Louise Mannheimer. He studied at the University of Cincinnati (A.B., 1902), the Hebrew Union College (rabbi, 1902), and at the Universities of Chicago and Columbia. He was rabbi of Sinai Congregation, Sioux City, Iowa, from 1902 to 1905, and of Congregation B'nai Jeshurun, Des Moines, from 1905 on. In 1942 he was still serving in that capacity.

From 1928 on Mannheimer was a member of the executive committee of the School of Religion at the University of Iowa. He was a member of the board of managers of the Department of Synagog and School Extension of the Union of American Hebrew Congregations (1933-35).

In Des Moines, Mannheimer helped organize the Jewish Community Center (1907) and the United Jewish Philanthropies (1914); he was president of the Federated Jewish Charities since its organization (1908).

He was a contributor to this encyclopedia.

Lit.: Gross, Louis D., "Memorial Address—Prof. Sigmund Mannheimer," *Central Conference of American Rabbis Year Book,* vol. 20 (1910) 170-75.

MANOELLO, *see* IMMANUEL BEN SOLOMON OF ROME.

MANSH, PHILIP, communal worker and cultural leader, b. Lemberg, Galicia, 1838; d. Lemberg, 1890. He received his Ph.D. degree from the University of Lemberg, and practised law there. Mansh was the founder and director of Shomer Yisrael, a Jewish communal organization, and until his death editor of *Der Israelit,* the magazine published by the organization. He was also Parnas of the Jewish community of Lemberg. Mansh was the translator of Sholom Aleichem and a collaborator in the preparation of the philological study *Der jüdisch-polnische Jargon* (1888-90). Despite his interest in Yiddish, Mansh did not write the language himself.

Lit.: Reisen, Z., *Lexikon fun der Yiddisher Literatur, Presse un Filologie,* vol. 2 (1930), cols. 314-15; Weinreich, M., *Stapplen.*

MANTINO, JACOB, physician, b. Spain, about 1490; d. after 1549. He was brought as a child to Italy after the expulsion of the Jews from Spain in 1492, apparently from Tortosa. He studied medicine and philosophy at the Universities of Padua and Bologna, became a practising physician, and translated several works from Hebrew into Latin at the request of Christian scholars. He dedicated his rendering of Averroes' *De patribus et de generatione animalium,* together with the commentary of Gersonides (1521), to Pope Leo X. When the Imperialists invaded Rome in 1527, Mantino left the Papal States and settled first in Verona, then in Venice (1528), where the council exempted him from the necessity of wearing the hat required of other Jews. He returned to Rome a few years later.

About the same time Mantino became involved in the dispute about the proposal of Henry VIII of England to divorce his wife Catherine. Since the discussion revolved around a point in Biblical law, Mantino was approached by the English ambassador at the papal court and urged to give an opinion favorable to the king. He was at first inclined to do so, but hearing that Pope Clement VII was of the opposite opinion, withdrew from the proceedings. The consequence of this action was a violent quarrel between Mantino and Elijah Halfon. Solomon Molcho took the side of the latter, and Mantino was so embittered that he denounced Molcho as a heretic, and the latter escaped the stake only through a ruse of the pope.

Mantino was greatly favored by Pope Paul III, who made him his personal physician and in 1539 appointed him professor of medicine at the University of Rome. He remained there until 1544, enjoying a high position, and then, for some unknown reason, again settled in Venice, where he made more translations of philosophic works. In 1549 he journeyed to the East with a Venetian nobleman; nothing further is heard of him, so it is presumed that he died on the journey.

Lit.: Vogelstein, H., *The Jews of Rome* (1940) 245 et seq.; Münz, I., *Die jüdischen Ärzte im Mittelalter.*

MANTUA (Italian, Mantova), city in Northern Italy, capital of the erstwhile duchy of Mantua, with 459 Jews out of a total population of 39,600 (1938). A Jewish settlement is first mentioned in connection with the stay of Abraham ibn Ezra, who finished his grammatical work, *Tzahoth* (1153), there. The Jewish community gained major importance in the 15th cent. when, under the protection of the Gonzaga rulers, the Jews could devote themselves not only to financial enterprises, but also to the professions. Their position, however, was gravely imperiled by a quarrel between the two famous rabbis officiating in Mantua, Joseph Colon and Judah di Napoli (Messer Leon), who were expelled by the duke in 1475. In 1484 Bernardino da Feltre preached in Mantua against the Jews, and founded there a municipal pawnshop (*monte di pietà*) to break their monopoly on money-lending. The situation became worse to such an extent that in 1496 the Jews were ordered to wear the Jew badge. In 1531 Solomon Molcho, adventurer, was burnt at the stake in Mantua during the visit of Emperor Charles V.

There was an improvement by the middle of the 16th cent. A ducal decree of 1545 stated: "We desire that the Jews shall be as free and secure in pursuing their business and professions in our city and in our duchy as the Christians."

Mantua was, for a long period, the most important seat of Hebrew culture in Italy. Valuable Hebrew incunabula were printed in Mantua. It had many Talmudists and exegetes, preachers and philosophers, historians and critics, physicians and engineers, poets and writers in Italian as well as Hebrew. The most famous were Azariah dei Rossi, physician and scholar (1514-78), and Solomon Rossi who, in 1587, was a musician at the court of Vincenze I, where his sister was employed as a singer. For a long time the community was even obliged to furnish the court with a company of actors. The medical family of Portaleone furnished the Gonzagas with court physicians.

At the end of the 16th cent. the condition of the Mantua Jews again became worse. In 1577 the Jew badge was reintroduced, in 1590 all foreign Jews were

expelled, and in 1602 seven Jews charged with offending a Jew-baiting monk were condemned to death.
In the same year Jewish physicians were forbidden
to treat Christians without special permission. In 1610
a ghetto was established, the regulations of which,
Tolleranza generale, renewed every eight years on the
payment of a large sum, remained in force until 1791.

When Mantua was beleaguered, in 1628, the Jews
participated in the fortification and defense of the city.
Two years later the city was occupied by imperial
troops; 1,800 Jews were expelled and their property
confiscated. Although they were later allowed to return, the medieval treatment continued until, under
the Hapsburg rulers Empress Maria Theresa and especially Joseph II and Leopold I, in the second half of
the 18th cent., their civic status improved.

During the Napoleonic rule of Mantua which, with
a brief interlude, lasted from 1797 to 1814, the Jews
enjoyed full freedom with their coreligionists in the
French empire. Two Jews, David Pavia and Felice
Coen, were made members of the municipal council;
the latter became member also of the central administration of the district of Mincio, while Rabbi Abraham
de Cologna became a member of the cabinet of the
Cisalpine republic. He was also elected vice-president
of the Sanhedrin in Paris, and afterward president of
the consistory.

After the restoration of Austrian rule, many Mantuan Jews were active in the Italian underground
movement. In 1858 the community reached its peak,
with 2,523 persons. One of the heroes of Italy's struggle
for unity, Giuseppe Finzi, was a Mantuan Jew. Full
civic freedom was gained with the incorporation of
the duchy of Mantua into the kingdom of Italy in

Interior of the synagogue at Mantua

1870. From that year to 1942 the community played
no important part in Jewish history. The anti-Jewish
legislation of the Fascist government from 1938 on
was, of course, applied also to the Mantuan community.

ALFRED WERNER.

Lit.: Colorni, Vittore, "Fatti e figure di storia ebraica
Mantovana," *La Rassegna Mensile di Israel,* Sept.-Oct.,
1934; idem, "Note per la biografia di alcuni dotti ebrei
vissuti a Mantova nel secolo XV," *Annuario di Studi
Ebraici* (1934); Friedenthal, Harry, "Jewish Physicians in
Italy," *Publications of the American Jewish Historical Society,* No. 28 (1922) 133-211.

MANUAL ARTS, *see* ARTISANS.

MANUEL, ESTHER, Prussian war heroine who
participated in many battles against Napoleon during
the years 1813 to 1815. Disguised in man's clothing,
she entered the regiment of lancers of East Prussia,
and was wounded thrice. As a gallant cavalry soldier,
she excelled in patrols and skirmishes, and was decorated with the Iron Cross. According to Professor
Martin Philippson, the report published by Esther
Manuel in 1815 was verified almost completely by an
official account. She later married one of her Christian
companions in arms, and assumed the name Luise
Grafemus.

Lit.: Im deutschen Reich (1906) 417.

MANUEL, EUGÈNE, French poet and educator,
b. Paris, 1823; d. Paris, 1901. He attended the École
normale supérieure at Paris from 1843 to 1847, when
he graduated. Then he was professor at several colleges of Paris. Together with his brother-in-law Ernest
Lévy-Alvarès, he published *La France,* a textbook of
geographical and historical instruction in four volumes
which was highly esteemed by French pedagogues and
attained many editions. Manuel's first collection of
lyric poems, *Pages intimes* (1865), was crowned by the
French Academy. In 1870 Jules Simon, minister of
education in the government of national defense, appointed him leader of his office (chef de cabinet). In
the same year Manuel wrote a versified drama, *Les
ouvriers,* which was produced successfully at the

*A page from the Mantuan Haggadah (1564). From
a photograph by Herbert S. Sonnenfeld*

Théâtre Français, and often revived. In 1872 he published lyric poems under the title of *Poèmes populaires,* and in 1873 *Pendant la guerre.* Manuel's comedy *L'Absent* also met with great applause on the stage, in 1873. In 1878 he became inspector general in the office of education.

In all his works Manuel manifested conservative feeling, loyalty to national traditions and to the authorities of the state. He exalted the beauty of family life and the poetic qualities of home and hearth. His language was considered classical by his contemporaries and by conservative critics of later times. The literary school of French "home poetry," represented mainly by François Coppée and adopted by French nationalism, was inaugurated by Manuel. He was loyal to Judaism throughout his life. He was one of the founders of the Alliance Israélite Universelle, and composed its first proclamation. It was due to his influence that the Alliance fostered education in foreign countries.

MANUEL, ISAAC, South African merchant, b. Colmar, Alsace, d. Cape Town, South Africa, 1845. In 1804 he enlisted in Napoleon's army, and in 1805 participated in the battle of Austerlitz. After Napoleon's defeat Manuel, apparently fearing that the rights of the Jews in France would be restricted, emigrated to South Africa, where he settled in 1819. In 1823 he visited London and was married there. As a naturalized British subject, Manuel returned to Cape Town in 1833, and began to organize the collection of home products, especially hides, for export, by sending native agents to the rural districts. He was highly successful, and his example was followed by other merchants. Manuel was respected by his fellow citizens because of his great interest in public welfare. He contributed money for the founding of the South African College, and in 1834 was one of the petitioners who urged the desirability of Natal for colonization. Before a Jewish community was established at Cape Town, Manuel probably joined the English Church, but in 1841 he became a member of the society of the Jewish community Tikvath Israel, to which he donated funds regularly and liberally until his death.

Lit.: Herrman, Louis, *A History of the Jews in South Africa* (1935).

MANUEL, ROLAND (original name, Roland Alexis Manuel Lévy), composer and writer on music, b. Paris, 1891. He studied with Roussel and D'Indy at the Schola Cantorum, also privately with Maurice Ravel. For several years he distinguished himself as music critic of *L'Éclair.* He wrote biographies of Ravel (*Maurice Ravel et son oeuvre,* Paris, 1914), Honegger, and Manuel de Falla. His compositions include a two-act opera-bouffe, *Isabelle et Pantalon* (Paris, 1922), a four-act opera-comique, *Le Diable Amoureux,* and various tone poems, chamber music compositions, songs, and pieces for the piano.

MANUSCRIPTS (abbreviated, singular, **MS.;** plural, **MSS.**), term designating any document written by the human hand with the aid of quill, pen, pencil or other instrument which can be used with cursive facility, as distinguished from an inscription engraved with chisel or graver, worked laboriously. The term

The oldest manuscript on paper (831), owned by the Jewish Theological Seminary of America

manuscript has come to be employed primarily to designate a written work of the ancient world or of the Middle Ages. In brief, every text written by hand on flexible material and intended to be placed in a library, private or public, is called a manuscript. Collections of such manuscripts, especially ancient ones, are highly prized and are stored in public and private libraries. However, one must exclude from the study of manuscripts (a) texts graven on stone or bricks, (b) all public acts (diplomas, charters, and the like), the study of which constitutes the object of diplomatics, and (c) texts designed for ritualistic usage and prepared in accordance with legally prescribed regulations. Down to the time of the invention of printing and until the printed book had driven it out of the field, the manuscript was the vehicle for the conservation and dissemination of literature and discharged all the functions of the modern book. This article deals primarily with various aspects of the ancient Hebrew manuscript, bringing it down to the introduction of printing.

The principal materials successively employed in the making of Hebrew manuscripts have been papyrus, parchment or vellum, and paper. In some cases other materials have been used (for example, leather, linen

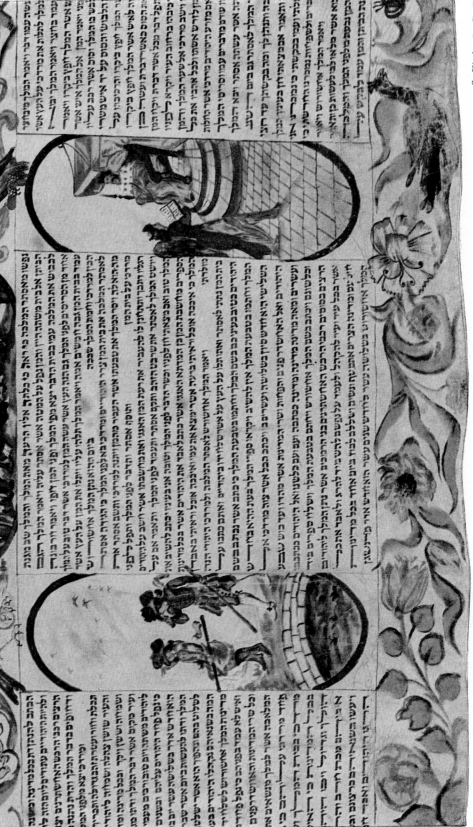

THE PURIM STORY

From a Megillah Manuscript of the 16th Century

A page from a Spanish manuscript (probably 13th cent.), containing the Pentateuch and the Haftarah. From the Mayer Sulzberger collection at Dropsie College

and silk). The earliest materials used for writing were substances such as stone, wood and metal upon which symbols were cut or engraved with a stilus. Early, too, is the use of animal substances, upon which characters were written with liquid preparations. But in considering the development of the Hebrew manuscript, one might practically confine his attention to three of the more pliant and therefore generally more convenient substances derived from vegetable growths and animal skins: papyrus, parchment or vellum, and paper, the employment of which, each in turn, as a writing material became almost universal.

Papyrus is associated in Greek and Roman literature with the roll form of the ancient manuscript, and the supersession of this material by parchment or vellum led to the change of shape to the book form. Papyrus was obtained from a long-stemmed plant terminating in a large and elegant umbrella. The stem was cut in long strips which were placed one beside the other. On the vertical strips others were placed horizontally; then, after they had been wet with the water of the Nile, they were submitted to strong pressure, dried in the sun and rubbed with shells to render them solid. To make a book, the separate pages were first written on; then they were put end to end, the left margin of each page being made to adhere to the right margin of the preceding page. A roll was thus secured, of which the dimensions were sometimes considerable. The end of the last page was fastened to a cylinder of wood or bone which gave more consistency to the roll. The page having been ruled, the writing was done with a sharpened reed on the horizontal portion of the fibres. From being almost exclusively used in Egypt, the employment of papyrus spread to Greece about the 5th cent., then to Rome and throughout the West. Egypt retained the monopoly of the manufacture, which

furthermore belonged to the state. Alexandria was the principal market. In the first centuries of the Middle Ages it was exported to the west by the "Syrians," but the conquest of Egypt by the Arabs (640) stopped the trade. The Arabs had attempted to cultivate the plant in Sicily. The number of Hebrew papyri which has come to light is not very large when compared with the vast amount of classical papyri discovered in Egypt. The most important are those which have come from Elephantine in the furthest south of Upper Egypt.

Most of the books in antiquity were, as it is known, in the form of scrolls, and the synagogue has preserved this usage for copies of Scriptural texts (especially the Pentateuch and Megilloth) even to the present day. Formerly, and in some countries even now, such texts were written on animal skins tanned into leather, but later parchment or vellum was preferred. Parchment, usually made of the skin of sheep, goats, calves, asses, and the like, provides a material thin, strong, flexible and usually smooth of surface on both faces. It replaced the use of papyrus at an early date. It was at the end of the 3rd cent. that its adoption for the making of books began. Once prepared, the parchment was cut into leaves which were folded in two; four leaves to

Two pages of Bible manuscript in the library of the Jüdisch-theologisches Seminar at Breslau

gether formed a book of eight folios; all the books formed a *codex,* the manuscript in book form composed of separate leaves stitched together. There was no paging before the 15th cent.; writers merely numbered first the books (signature), then the folios. The dimensions of the leaves varied; that most in use for literary texts was the large quarto. Parchments were written on both sides (opistographs). As parchment became rare and costly during the Middle Ages, it became the practice in some quarters to scratch or wash out the old text in order to replace it with new writing. These erased manuscripts are called palimpsests. With the aid of reacting chemicals and other means the old writing has often been made to reappear and lost texts have thus been discovered. Thus portions of the lost *Mahzor Yannai,* a liturgical work of the 7th cent., was recovered by the late Israel Davidson on a palimpsest underneath which was the text of Aquila's Greek translation of the Bible. Manuscripts thus treated have been nearly always incomplete or mutilated; a complete work has never been recovered on a palimpsest. Finally, by sewing strips of parchment together, rolls were made similar to those formed of papyrus. The famous scroll of the Hebrew Pentateuch in Brussels, written in the 9th cent., is made up of fifty-seven skins and is forty yards in length. When and where the codex form first appeared among the Jews is as yet unknown. The transition from the scroll to the codex probably began in the 7th cent. and proceeded gradually, since no distinct mention of a codex seems to be found in early rabbinical writings.

Parchment had a long career among the Jews as a writing material for literary and historical texts. For ritualistic purposes it still continues to hold its place in the religious life of the Jews. In its turn, however, parchment eventually gave place to paper, which is reputed to have been invented in China in 105 C.E. Specimens of paper of the 5th cent. have been found in Eastern Turkestan. It was after the taking of Samarkand (704) that the Arabs learned to make paper, and introduced it into Baghdad (795) and into Damascus. It was known in Europe as early as the end of the 11th cent.; in the 12th cent. it began to be used for

manuscripts. It was sold even then in quires and reams, and in the 13th cent. appeared the filigranes or watermarks. According to chemical analyses, the paper of the Middle Ages was made of hempen or linen rags. In the 15th cent., even a bit earlier, paper became the common material for the manuscript book. However, the introduction of paper for writing purposes brought no change in the form of the manuscript. It possessed exactly the same qualities as a writing material, as parchment or vellum: it could be inscribed on both sides; it could be made up into quires and bound in the codex form; and it had the further advantage of being easily manufactured in large quantities, and therefore of being comparatively cheap.

Incidentally, Jews played a leading role in the introduction and manufacture of paper in various lands. The earliest known paper mill in Spain had been established and operated in the 13th cent. by Jews at Xativa (see Blum, André, *On the Origin of Paper,* 1934, pp. 23-29).

For the writing of their manuscripts Jews, no doubt, employed the same kind of ink as that used by their non-Jewish neighbors. Only black effaceable ink, which was renewed when necessary, might be used for Biblical texts. Metallic ink was known, but was forbidden. The *Letter of Aristeas* tells of the copy of the Bible, written in gold, which had been sent by the high priest to the Egyptian King Ptolemy. The Talmud, too, speaks of gold-writing, which may have been a Jewish invention (see Blau, Ludwig, *Studien zum althebräischen Buchwesen,* 1902, pp. 13, 150 et seq.). The copyists of the Middle Ages used chiefly black ink, composed of a mixture of gall, nuts and vitriol. Red ink was reserved from ancient times for titles. It is sometimes used alternatively with the usual writing fluid. Gold ink and silver ink were used for manuscripts de luxe and especially for illuminations of the text. The ink approved by Moses Maimonides, and very likely used by himself for the writing of his own Scroll of the Torah, was, according to a responsum by him, made of oil, pitch, resin, gum arabic and other ingredients. By burning these substances, a soot was formed which was mixed with gum and honey, and the thin slices formed of ink were finally dissolved in an infusion of galls (see

A page of Hebrew Bible manuscript written (1492) for Jacob ben Samuel Aboab by Abraham Caliph.
From the collection of the Jewish Theological Seminary of America

Teshuboth Harambam, edit. A. Freimann, 1934, pp. 119-22). Vitriol is expressly excluded by Maimonides, although he does not absolutely forbid its use. He is primarily concerned with the importance of having the ink cleave firmly to the vellum and at the same time with seeing to it that there should be no difficulty in erasing it. Scrolls of the Torah are always written in black ink, although in early Samaritan scrolls ink of a reddish hue seems to have been used.

Not all Hebrew manuscripts, although written in Hebrew characters, are always those of Hebrew texts; they are of texts in other languages as well. It has been customary among the Jews to employ Hebrew script in the writing of texts in the vernacular which they used in the various countries in which they dwelt. Accordingly, the great collections of Hebrew manuscripts in well-known libraries contain numerous texts in different languages transcribed in Hebrew characters. Not only Semitic tongues like Hebrew, Arabic, Aramaic and Persian, but also Greek, Latin, English and Ger-

man, French and Provençal, Spanish and Portuguese, Russian and Italian, in addition to Turkish and Tataric, are represented in that script.

Hebrew manuscripts, unlike those in Latin and Greek, were not copied by men shut up in cloisters, but usually by sociable persons living in the world and sharing its joys and sorrows. Even women were employed in the art of copying them. Many a Hebrew manuscript contains illustrations and illuminations representing fine examples of Jewish ecclesiastical art. Although there is a popular fallacy to the effect that the Jews could not paint or draw pictures, because they had a prejudice against the semblance of the human form divine, the semblance is not always so close as to be forbidden, and whether they could draw or not, they did, and there is ample evidence of that fact in many of the attractive and often curious illustrations in Hebrew manuscripts. Some of the pictures in early Hebrew manuscripts are humorous and often grotesque. They are humorous only because they look quaint, and not intentionally so. Sometimes the illustration is intended to be funny. Such, for example, is the illustration in the Prague Haggadah (1526), certainly a reproduction of a manuscript. The head of the family at the Seder, when pointing to the bitter herbs, points to his wife instead. Grotesque illustrations are not uncommon in Hebrew manuscripts. Jewish copyists were often imitators and frequently followed the fashion of the non-Jewish scribes. Some Hebrew manuscripts, profusely illustrated, are provided with grotesque borders in the style of the familiar German illustrated books of the 15th and 16th centuries. Monkeys and elephants, queer animals, half-birds and half-fishes and like illustrations abound in their decorations. In fact, everything in a Hebrew manuscript is of interest: the arrangement of the matter—text and illustrations—the various notes on the margins and fly leaves made by its successive owners, the colophon, containing, as a rule, the signature, date of completion and other observations of the copyist in which one often finds recorded important data, historical, biographical and literary. They all set the reader thinking, and contribute many a sidelight to the history and literature of the Jews.

In addition to their own historical merits, Hebrew manuscripts are of great value for the advancement of Jewish learning because of the absence of critical editions of many an important text in Jewish literature and thought. Correctly established texts form the basis of every historical and literary investigation, and yet very little, in comparison with other literatures, has been done for the production of well-edited texts of standard works in Hebrew literature and lore. To be sure, a great many Hebrew texts not available now in printed form perhaps no longer deserve consideration for publication by the printing press, but one can not confidently assume that all the best and most interesting works have been made accessible by the printing press. Students of Hebrew literature, in whatever branch of Jewish thought they be interested, can always find in the great collections of Hebrew manuscripts some useful text requiring attention. Manuscripts of Hebrew texts, even of works well known and widely published, are not without interest. Let it be remembered that for restoring the correct reading in a given text the most acute mind is not half so good as an accurate reading in a well-copied manuscript. Many are the instances where careless misprints were the bases for ingenious constructions and fanciful hypotheses. Moreover, many a publisher of Hebrew texts derived from ancient manuscripts unfortunately was not always guided by the best literary and scholarly motives. While they issued and reissued many works of which one edition would have sufficed, many a work of great importance for Jewish history of literature is still obtainable only in manuscript form. As is often the case, some editors and publishers of important texts were careless in their choice of the manuscripts from which editions of valuable works have been prepared. Almost all the major works of the medieval Hebrew authors will have to be reedited and made available in critically prepared editions before they can properly be studied. But such editions can be prepared only with the aid of manuscripts from which their texts can be established with a reasonable amount of correctness.

Descriptive catalogues of Hebrew manuscript collections are virtually the only means of enabling one to obtain a general view of the number and nature of the manuscripts which they describe. Moritz Steinschneider was virtually the first among Jews to give serious bibliographical attention to collections of Hebrew manuscripts. He compiled a considerable number of descriptive catalogues of collections of Hebrew manuscripts in great European libraries. In them, as well as in his *Vorlesungen über die Kunde hebräischer Handschriften* (Leipzig, 1897), he described the nature and value of some of the best known of available Hebrew manuscripts, especially those which he had occasion to examine and to catalogue during the years 1875 to 1895. Some efforts have been made by others to augment his work by offering descriptions of newly accumulated collections of Hebrew manuscripts in various parts of the world. With but few exceptions, little has been done to make known the content and character of collections of Hebrew manuscripts in American libraries. Hebrew paleography has likewise been considerably neglected. This no doubt is partly responsible for the apparent lack of interest in the care, preservation and study of Hebrew manuscripts.

On the other hand, because of all kinds of dangers which threaten manuscripts, efforts have been made in recent years to reproduce in facsimile most precious manuscripts. Thus, for instance, H. Strack produced in facsimile the oldest dated manuscript of the Hebrew prophets and the only complete manuscript copy of the Babylonian Talmud which escaped the numerous efforts to destroy it. Fragments of Talmudic manuscripts are numerous.

Hebrew manuscripts, or, for that matter, even sacred texts printed in Hebrew, which can no longer be used for practical purposes, may not be destroyed. When they were worn out, Biblical and other Hebrew manuscripts were protected against profanation by being deposited in the Genizah. When worn out, Scriptural manuscripts, especially copies of the Scroll of the Torah, were often hidden in the grave of a dead scribe or pious scholar. In consequence of this custom, not a single Biblical manuscript in Hebrew has been preserved from antiquity, nor is there any hope that one will ever come to light. It is not unlikely that in ancient times there were Biblical books in Hebrew written on papyrus, although not a fragment of such papyrus is now extant. Many of them found their decay in their permanent hiding-place—the grave. "When applied to books, it means much the same thing as burial means in the case of men. When the spirit is gone, we put the corpse out of sight to protect it from abuse. In like manner, when the writing is worn out, we hide the book to preserve it from profanation. The contents of the book go up to heaven like the soul. 'I see the parchment burning, and the letters flying up in the air,' were the last words of the martyr R. Chanina ben Tradyon, when he went to the stake wrapped in the scrolls of the Law" (Schechter, Solomon, *Studies in Judaism*, vol. 2, p. 1). The practice in Jewry gradually developed that not only Bible manuscripts (in later times printed texts as well) which had become unfit for use, but all Hebrew writings or fragments of these, as soon as they were useless, were deposited in some nook or corner, not easily accessible, in the synagogue, and thus protected from profanation. Since the special aim was thus to

A page from a Bible manuscript (13th cent. ?), bearing Masoretic notes as ornamentation. From the original in the British Museum

An illuminated page of Bible manuscript (14th cent.)

protect the divine name appearing in them, they gradually assumed the designation Shemoth (Names, i.e. Divine names). From time to time such accumulated Shemoth are given a final resting-place in the cemetery. This treatment was accorded also to such Hebrew writings which never aspired to the dignity of real books, but are none the less of great importance in Jewish life. As it is known, the use of the Hebrew language was, among the Jews, not confined to sacred texts. With the Jews Hebrew was a living language. "They wrote in it their letters, kept in it their accounts, and composed in it their love-songs and wine-songs. All legal documents, such as leases, contracts, marriage settlements, and letters of divorce, and the proceedings as well as the decisions of the courts of justice, were drawn up in Hebrew, or, at least, written in Hebrew letters. As the Jews attached a certain sacredness to everything resembling the Scriptures, either in matter or in form, they were loth to treat even their secular documents as mere refuse, and when they were overtaken by old age, they disposed of them by ordering them to the Genizah, in which they found a resting-place for centuries" (Schechter, Solomon, *ibid.,* p. 3).

Often the number of Hebrew manuscripts forming a collection of literary or historical writings contain more works than the number of manuscripts which the collection comprises. This is due to the fact that a goodly number of Hebrew manuscripts contain more than one work, in some cases even three or four, so that the number of Hebrew works is far greater still. Save for some exceptions which are becoming more and more rare,

An illuminated page from the manuscript prayer-book (18th cent.) of the synagogue in Wolpa. From "Istoriia Yevreiskago Naroda" (Moscow, 1914)

A Yemenite manuscript of a page from the Pentateuch, believed to have been written in the 19th cent.
Reproduced by courtesy of the Jewish Theological Seminary of America

many of the Hebrew manuscripts copied during the Middle Ages are at present stored in great public and institutional libraries. The various private collections of Hebrew manuscripts which have been formed since the 16th cent. have eventually been fused with the great repositories of Hebrew books and manuscripts in European and American libraries. They comprise works in whole or in part or a fragment of a work representing all branches of theological and secular learning and even of human folly.

See also: ARCHEOLOGY AND THE BIBLE; ARCHEOLOGY, JEWISH; BOOKS; GENIZAH; PALEOGRAPHY.

JOSHUA BLOCH.

Lit.: The best general introduction to the study of Hebrew manuscripts is Steinschneider, Moritz, *Vorlesungen über die Kunde hebräischer Handschriften,* 2nd ed. (1937). Helpful are: Adler, Elkan N., *About Hebrew Manuscripts* (1905); Berliner, A., *Gesammelte Schriften* (1913); Procksch, O., *Der hebräischer Schreiber und sein Buch* (1928); Schechter, Solomon, *Studies in Judaism,* Second Series (1908). The number of catalogues and the descriptive lists of collections of Hebrew manuscripts is too large for inclusion in this survey of the literature. For the most important catalogues of manuscripts, see *Encyclopaedia Judaica,* vol. 7 (1931), cols. 943-44. In 1942 a catalogue of the most valuable manuscripts in the Jewish Theological Seminary of America was in preparation.

MAOZ, *see* COLONIES, AGRICULTURAL.

MAOZ TZUR ("fortress and rock," after *Isa.* 17:10), a Piyut for Hanukah, sung in the home after the kindling of the Hanukah lights, and frequently in the synagogue. It describes the various deliverances of Israel—first from Egypt, then from Babylonia, from Haman, and, finally, in the time of the Maccabees. The initial letters of the five stanzas give the name of the author, Mordecai; he is otherwise unknown, but presumably lived about the 13th cent. The tune to which Maoz Tzur is universally sung is a bright and cheerful melody which has added much to the popularity of the song; as Birnbaum has shown, it is a German folk-melody which was utilized also by Luther and others as a setting for hymns. Reform Jewish congregations have retained the musical setting for a Hanukah hymn in the vernacular, which echoes the sentiments of the Maoz Tzur but speaks more directly of Hanukah; it is known as "Rock of Ages," from its opening words.

Lit.: Idelsohn, A. Z., *Jewish Liturgy* (1932) 162; Cohen, F. L., in *Jewish Encyclopedia*, vol. 8, pp. 315-16; Singer, S., and Abrahams, I., *The Authorised Daily Prayer Book* (1922) 275.

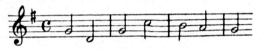

Opening bars of a melody for the "Maoz Tzur" widely used by Jews in Western Europe

MAPU, ABRAHAM BEN YEKUTHIEL, Hebrew novelist, b. Slobodka, a suburb of Kovno, Russia, 1808; d. Königsberg, Germany, 1867. His father, a teacher of Talmud, earned a meagre livelihood. Abraham was a dreamy, timid and impressionable child, who was interested in mysticism. He received his early education at Heder, and showed extraordinary talents, becoming known as an Illui (young genius). Following his marriage at the age of eighteen to the daughter of a Hasid, he intensified his study of the Cabala, and soon came completely under the influence of the Hasidic movement. At one time, it is said, he sought to become invisible by following Cabalistic prescriptions.

About this time Mapu became acquainted with Elijah Kalisher (Ragoler), rabbi of Slobodka, from whom he obtained a copy of the *Psalms* with a Latin translation, by means of which he studied Latin. At the age of twenty he embarked upon a teaching career in a rural section, and added to his knowledge of Latin with the aid of a Catholic priest. Upon returning to Kovno he undertook the study of German, French and Russian, and before long became openly associated with the Maskilim, thus breaking with Hasidism. The first to encourage him in his literary work was the scholar Shneiur (Senior) Sachs, whom he met at Rossieny, a center of the Haskalah. Later, at Vilna, he came into contact with Adam Hacohen Lebensohn, Kalman Shulman and Samuel Joseph Fünn, though they did not assist him. In 1848 Mapu was appointed teacher at the government school for boys at Vilna, a position which he held until his death.

During his early years he read Hebrew translations of some of the German and French classics and also of Eugene Sue's *Les mystères de Paris,* translated in a

Abraham Mapu

stilted manner by Kalman Shulman (1847-48). Under the influence of these works and because of dissatisfaction with his environment, he wrote his first romance, *Ahabath Tziyyon* (Love of Zion), during the year 1831. He revised and polished the manuscript over a period of twenty years, and by 1853, utilizing his savings, and together with his brother's financial aid, was enabled to publish the book. It created an immediate sensation with the Hebrew-reading public and established his reputation as a novelist. The romance deals with the times of the prophet Isaiah and King Hezekiah of Judah, and skilfully reconstructs Jewish society and atmosphere of Palestine of that period. The success of the book was due to idyllic descriptions, its romance, and the Biblical phraseology, rather than to character delineation or logical sequence of events. By 1873 the novel had gone through four editions, and was translated into English three times, by Frank Jaffe, Shapiro, and Marymont (London, 1887; New York, 1902-28; New York, 1919), seven times into Yiddish, into Judeo-Persian and into Arabic (1908). A German translation was published by Solomon Mandelkern, entitled *Tamar, Roman aus dem biblischen Altertume* (Leipzig, 1885), without mention of the author's name on the title page.

Mapu's second novel, *Ayit Tzabua* (Painted Vulture; Vilna, 1857-61), deals with contemporary life, describing the struggles of the Maskilim with fanatics and hypocrites, such as the miracle-worker, Rabbi Zadok, who exploits superstition for his own aggrandizements, and Rabbi Gaddiel, the honest but misled henchman of Rabbi Zadok. The book is not considered genuinely creative; it lacks psychological analysis and its characters are artificial. The atmosphere is militant and its moral tendency is obvious. The third novel from Mapu's pen, *Ashmath Shomron* (The Guilt of Samaria; Vilna, 1865; Warsaw, 1870), is an epic in the true sense. It reproduces vividly the conflicts between Jerusalem and Samaria in the days of Ahaz, king of

Judah, and of Pekah the son of Remaliah and Hoshea the son of Elah, kings of Israel, idealizing the men and women of Judah, and depicting as rogues and plotters those of Samaria. Again the delineation of character is poor, though in local color and Biblical life the "author's touch is even surer than in *Ahabath Tziyyon*." Mapu wrote also a novel in two parts, of the time of Sabbatai Zevi, which was destroyed in manuscript by his opponents. Only a fragment of it was published from the literary remains of the author, under the title *Hozeh Hezyonoth* (1869). Mapu wrote also two textbooks for the study of Hebrew, *Hanoch Lanaar*, and *Amon Padagog* (Vilna, 1859, and Königsberg, 1868), and also *Hausfranzose* (Vilna, 1861). In 1860 Mapu began to suffer from palsy in his right hand, and was compelled to write with his left hand. During his remaining years he suffered greatly, and died in 1867 while en route to Paris for medical treatment.

Mapu's literary heritage is not large. However, inasmuch as he was the first to introduce the novel into Hebrew literature, he is regarded as the father of the Hebrew novel. Indirectly his novels imbued the reader with a love of Zion, and he may therefore be considered an effective propagandist of Zionist sentiment.

Other editions and translations of Mapu's works include the following: *Kol Kithebe Abraham Mapu* (New York, 1918); *Beth Hanan*, edited by Joseph Klausner (Jerusalem, 1918); *Ashmath Shomron*, with an introduction by Jacob Fichman (Warsaw, 1928); *Der Tsvua*, Yiddish translation by Beilinson (1896); *Die Zind fun Shomron*, a Yiddish translation by B. Epelbaum (Warsaw, 1928); *Kol Kithebe Abraham Mapu* (Tel-Aviv, 1939).   CARL ALPERT.

Lit.: Zitron, S. L., *Yotzere Hasifruth Haibrith Hahadashah*, 36-42; Waxman, Meyer, *A History of Jewish Literature*, vol. 3 (1936) 267-78; Brainin, Reuben, *Abraham Mapu* (1900); Kleinman, M., "Abraham Mapu Vehashpaatho," *Demuyoth Vekomoth*, 51-65; Waldstein, *Modern Hebrew Literature*, 18-23; Spiegel, Shalom, *Hebrew Reborn* (1930) 225; Klausner, Joseph, in *Yotzerim Ubonim*, vol. 1, pp. 176-98; Bar Tuviah, "Bereshith Safruthenu Hahadashah," *Hashiloah*, vol. 16; Streit, S., *Baaloth Hashahar*, 54; Slouschz, Nahum, *The Renascence of Hebrew Literature* (1909) 139-51; Bloch, Joshua, in *American Hebrew*, Jan. 29, 1937, p. 840.

MAR HUNA (exilarch), *see* HUNA.

MAR SAMUEL, called also Yarhinaah ("The astronomer"), the most important Babylonian Amora of the first generation besides Abba Aricha (Rab), b. about 180; d. 257. His birth, like his name, was glorified by legend. He received his first instruction from an otherwise unknown rabbi and then from his father Abba bar Abba, himself a learned Amora and rich silk merchant who is referred to in the Babylonian Talmud as *'abuha dishemu'el* ("the father of Samuel"). Later Samuel studied under Levi ben Sisi, and then went to the academy of Judah I. For some reason, possibly because of his interest in secular studies, particularly astronomy and medicine, Samuel was not ordained by Judah, and hence was not called "rabbi." Upon his return to his native Nehardea the exilarch Mar Ukba appointed him district judge of Nehardea in view of his wide reputation as a man of learning and wisdom. He was associated with the learned

judge Karna, and the two were generally referred to as the *dayyane golah* ("judges of the Diaspora"; see *Sanh.* 17b and Rabbenu Gershom to *B.B.* 70b). After the death of Shela, head of the academy at Nehardea, Rab refused to officiate as rector of the academy in Samuel's native town, and the latter was appointed to that office.

Mar Samuel's school in Nehardea, like that founded later by Rab in Sura, reached a high pitch of prosperity and helped to raise the level of Jewish learning and the service of God in Babylonia, thus creating a center of Jewish learning and culture independent of Palestine. Rab and Mar Samuel are referred to as "our teachers in Babylonia" (*Sanh.* 17b). Their activity formed the transition from the Tannaim to the Amoraim, and their interpretations of the Mishnah and Halachic analysis served as the foundation of the Babylonian Talmud. Samuel also compiled a collection of Baraithas which was held in high esteem and is referred to as *Tanna debe Shemuel* (*Sab.* 54a and numerous other passages).

In matters of law Rab is placed above Mar Samuel and his decisions are accepted, while in matters of civil law the latter is considered superior and his decisions in this branch of the law received Halachic validity (*Bech.* 49b). Samuel introduced some very important principles into Jewish law, the most significant of which is his dictum *dina demalchutha dina* ("the law of the state is the final law"), that is, in civil matters the law of the land is legally binding upon the Jews from the religious point of view (*Git.* 10b). This principle created the theoretical basis for the existence of the Jews in the Diaspora. Samuel's positive attitude toward the surrounding world is evident also from his insistence that the Jews be as honest with non-Jews as with their own coreligionists (*Hul.* 94a).

Both Samuel and Rab contributed much to the liturgy. They modified the wording of many an old prayer, established uniformity in the order of the public services, and introduced new prayers of their own composition. Thus Samuel composed the Habinenu prayer, a short form of the Eighteen Benedictions, and very likely also the Ahabah Rabbah prayer before the Shema as well as various other prayers. It is likely that he is the author also of many benedictions, in accordance with his fundamental principle that "all religious duties must have a benediction pronounced before they are performed" (*Suk.* 39a).

After the death of Rab, whom Samuel regarded as superior to himself, the position of rector of the academy at Sura remained vacant and Samuel was recognized as the leader of Babylonian Jewry. Huna, Rab's greatest disciple and head of the academy of Sura after Samuel's death, subordinated himself to Samuel and even to Johanan. The most prominent teachers in Palestine, who at first hesitated to recognize Samuel as an authority, finally became convinced of his greatness (*Hul.* 95b).

Mar Samuel was far more versatile than his friend and colleague Rab. In this respect he was quite exceptional for that period. He pursued the study of astronomy to such an extent that he was able to say: "The paths of the heavens are as well-known to me as the streets of Nehardea, except the comets, whose nature I do not know" (Ber. 58b). He was on very friendly terms with the non-Jewish astrologer Ablat, although, unlike his friend, he repudiated all astrological superstitions. Samuel turned his knowledge of astronomy to practical account and drew up a calendar which was designed to make Babylonian Jewry independent of Palestine in determining the time of the appearance of the New Moon and the days when the holidays were to be celebrated. Samuel refrained from publishing this calendar, probably out of regard for the Patriarch and in order not to destroy the unity of Judaism, allowing the computation of the festivals to remain a secret art. It is difficult to determine the extent of his knowledge of medicine, but it must have been considerable if we are to judge by the numerous medical and dietetic rules of his scattered throughout the Talmud. He claimed to be able to cure all diseases except three, and he attributed all diseases to the influences of the atmosphere (B.M. 107b); an eyesalve of his was much in demand (Sab. 108b).

Samuel was of a very modest and gentle disposition, and moderate in his views. He favored friendly relations with non-Jews, and professed a particular affection for Persian customs. As a result he was in exceedingly good repute at the Persian court, and was on intimate terms with King Sapor I. For this reason he was called by his contemporaries "Shabur Malka" (King Sapor; B.B. 115b), probably in jest. He was loyal to the new rulers, the dynasty of the Sassanids, and it is probably for this reason that he was called Arioch (meaning probably the "Aryan," or partisan of the neo-Persians). Samuel was liberal-minded, and far from fanatical imaginings; thus he did not expect the supernatural to occur during the Messianic age, but only the political independence of the Jewish people (Ber. 34a).

Mar Samuel was one of the greatest Jewish leaders of his period, contributing not only a great deal to Jewish teaching, but also initiating the development of Babylonia as the center of Jewry. He was revered by his contemporaries and glorified by legend after his death.   SAMUEL RABINOWITZ.

Lit.: Hoffmann, D., Mar Samuel, Rektor der jüdischen Akademie zu Nehardea (1873); Fessler, S., Mar Samuel, der bedeutendste Amora (1879); Bader, G., The Jewish Spiritual Heroes, vol. 3 (1940) 78-90; Bacher, W., Agada der babylonischen Amoräer, p. 37 et seq.; the Jewish histories for the period.

MAR ZUTRA I, exilarch and Amora of the 5th cent. He was overshadowed by his great contemporary, Ashi, with whom he was on friendly terms. Ashi's influence among the Babylonian Jews of the time was so great that Mar Zutra found it necessary to remove from Nehardea to Sura, where Ashi resided, in order to hold his formal receptions. According to Lazarus ("Die Häupter der Vertriebenen," in Brüll, N., Jahrbücher für jüdische Geschichte und Literatur, 1890, pp. 113-14, which seems to be the most probable view), Mar Zutra's exilarchate was in effect about the year 441; others suggest the views that his term of office was the period from 401 to 409 (or 410) or that he died in 417. Many of his interpretations, as handed down by Rabina and other sages, are found in the Talmud. According to a tradition cited by Sherira Gaon, Mar Zutra succeeded Rab Kahana for a short

time as head of the academy at Pumbeditha; however, it is possible that this may have been another person of the same name.

Lit.: Hyman, Aaron, Toledoth Tannaim Veamoraim (1910) 382-84; Fürst, Juden in Asien (1849) 75, 256, 259; Graetz, H., History of the Jews, vol. 2 (1927) 606, 610; idem, Geschichte der Juden, vol. 4, p. 351, note 37; Heilprin, Jehial, Seder Hadoroth, vol. 1, p. 167a; Otzar Yisrael, p. 288.

MAR ZUTRA II, exilarch, b. about 495; d. about 520. There are differences of opinion about his parentage and the years of his life. Graetz makes him the son of the exilarch Huna II and gives him the period from 495 to 520, with rule as an exilarch from 512 to 520. Funk and Dubnow, however, believe him to have been the son of the exilarch Huna-Mari, who was executed in 471 during the reign of Firuz the Wicked. This is supposed to have been the reason for the revolt Mar Zutra II is known to have led. According to this reckoning, the revolt took place about 491.

The Graetz version gives Mar Zutra the exilarchate while he was still a child, left to the protection of his maternal grandfather Mar Hanina. Until his majority his brother-in-law Mar Pahda was exilarch, then Mar Hanina impressed the king with Mar Zutra's right to rule, and the exilarchate was turned over to him. He is then supposed to have led a revolt which succeeded in overcoming the Persian power and establishing an independent Jewish kingdom that lasted seven years with a capital in Mahuza. The Persians finally conquered, however, and executed Mar Zutra and Mar Hanina, decapitating them and suspending their bodies on crosses in Mahuza. Legend, which surrounds the story of Mar Zutra, says that his son, Bar Mar Zutra, was born the day of the father's death and became a famous scholar and archipherecite in Palestine.

Lit.: Graetz, H., History of the Jews, vol. 3 (1927) 3-4; Dubnow, S., Weltgeschichte des jüdischen Volkes, vol. 3 (1926) 293-4; Funk, S., Die Juden in Babylonien, vol. 2, pp. 119-21, 143-45.

MARAGOWSKY, JACOB SAMUEL (Zeidel Rowner), cantor, b. Radomishel, Kiev, Russia, 1856. In 1942 he was living in New York city. Maragowsky became one of the best-known East European cantors of the 19th and early 20th centuries. Upon the death of his father he was adopted by the local cantor, who supervised his musical and Hebrew education. With the encouragement of Jacob Isaac Twersky, rabbi of Makarow, young Zeidel began his cantorial career. For five years he officiated on High Holidays in Kiev. In 1881 he became cantor in Zaslav, the following year in Rovno, and in 1885 was engaged in Kishinev as successor of the noted cantor Nisen Belzer Spivak. In 1896 he was called to the important position of cantor in Berdichev, serving for seven years. Other great positions followed, in London and in Lemberg, and finally in Rovno, the place with which his name is associated.

Due to persecutions in Czarist Russia, Maragowsky came to the United States in 1914, making his debut at Carnegie Hall, New York, but his functions as cantor were infrequent thereafter. His great popularity may be attributed to innate melodic inventiveness which characterizes his prolific compositions. Gifted with a flexible, fine lyric tenor voice, and influenced by Hasidic as well as secular band music, he and his choirs achieved striking instrumental effects and arresting modulations. Their many tours found enthusiastic listeners throughout Eastern Europe. Among his pupils were Mordecai Hershman, David Roitman, I. Breeh, J. Rapoport and D. M. Steinberg.

Lit.: Autobiography, in *Die Chazanim Velt* (1939), vols. 51-54 (these articles were reprints from *Der Tog*, 1938-39); *The History of Hazzanuth* (1929; published by the Cantors' Association) 92; Zaludkowsky, E., *Kulturtrager fun der Yiddisher Liturgie* (1930).

MARAH ("bitter"), a place in the wilderness which the Israelites reached on the third day of their march from the Red Sea and in which they found bitter waters, whence the term "bitter" (*Ex.* 15:23). According to the Talmud (*Suk.* 56a), Moses gave his first three laws there.

MÁRAMAROSSZIGET (Sighet), city in Máramaros county, Hungary, with a Jewish community of 12,000 out of a total population of 21,000. Máramarossziget has been a stronghold of Orthodox Jewry in Hungary, due to a strong influx of Hasidic elements from the neighboring Galicia. It is generally believed that the community was founded early in the 18th cent. Its first rabbi was Judah Kahan (d. 1819), whose ministry lasted several decades. Jewish emancipation and prosperity in Hungary attracted many Jews from Galicia who were victims of politically and economically adverse conditions. The famed Yeshiva of Máramarossziget was founded about the middle of the 19th cent. by Chief Rabbi Salman Leb Teitelbaum.

In 1883 the congregation joined the national organization of Orthodox communities, which step resulted in some inner dissension. The community maintained, in addition to a Yeshiva attended regularly by about 160 students, a Talmud Torah school, an elementary school and a Talmud Torah Association for adult education. In 1928 a trade school for weaving was established. Many outstanding Talmudic works were published by members of the rabbinical collegium of Máramarossziget.

From 1918 to 1940 Máramarossziget formed a part of Roumania under the name of Sighet. It was returned to Hungary by the Vienna award (1940). The years after 1938 have been frought with discomfort and the curtailment of rights for the Jews of Máramarossziget, first under Roumanian and then under Hungarian rule, both governments receiving from Germany inspiration for their anti-Jewish policy.

MARBURG (Maribor), *see under* YUGOSLAVIA.

MARCEL-IANCU, painter and architect, b. Bucharest, Roumania (date of birth unknown). He was a disciple of Iser, Jewish painter and caricaturist, from whose classicizing influence he soon freed himself. In 1916, notwithstanding the War, he left for Switzerland where, together with another Roumanian Jewish painter, Tristan Tzara, he inspired the Dadaist school of extreme modernism. His painting, *Insurrection at Zurich,* was acclaimed by adherents of the new art. On his return to Roumania, in 1926, he was highly successful as an architect, an art he had thoroughly studied while in Switzerland. He designed a large number of buildings in Bucharest, of cubistic inspiration, his art having meanwhile evolved along that form of expression. Marcel-Iancu's paintings and theories, which he set forth also in writing, shaped the vision of a large number of Roumanian painters, sculptors and architects. In the words of the Bucharest critic, Eugene Relgis (1936): "Marcel-Iancu, a master of technique, wields crayon, pen and brush with equally consummate skill. . . . His designs stand out among hundreds. What he expresses (in painting and in design) is startling, vivid and unforgettable." Two cubistic paintings, *Abstract Transformations* and *Nature Awakened,* were particularly extolled by the critics.

When anti-Semitism in the garb of Hitlerism began to infiltrate into Roumania, it bitterly assailed Jewish painters. Marcel-Iancu, in particular, was subjected to attack for being a cubist. According to Relgis, in one of his paintings Marcel-Iancu expressed all the horror of our time.

MARCHESHVAN, *see* CALENDAR (under Heshvan).

MARCIN, MAX, playwright and producer, b. province of Posen, Germany, 1879. He came to the United States as a child, and was educated in New York city. His first work in writing was in the newspaper field. Later he wrote fiction, and from 1910 on concentrated on the theatre. Among his plays were: *See My Lawyer* (1915); *Cheating Cheaters* (1916); *The Woman in Room 13* (1917). He wrote other plays as collaborator, and was co-producer of several successes. In the 1920's Marcin joined the film colony in Hollywood, where he still lived in 1942, writing screen adaptations.

MARCKWALD, WILLY, chemist, b. Jakobskirch, Silesia, Germany, 1864. He was appointed professor at the University of Berlin in 1899, and became director of the chemical department of its physico-chemical institute. In 1910 he was awarded the title of privy councillor, and in 1924 he received the honorary degree of doctor of engineering. From 1928 to 1931 he headed the Deutsche Chemische Gesellschaft. He retired from teaching in 1930.

Marckwald did research on the constitution of the ring-system in organic chemistry as well as in the field of stereochemistry, and discovered many chemical combinations and new bodies of the pyridine series and mercaptans. He was instrumental in the discovery of radium by isolating the polonium in pitchblende; he also pointed out the phenomenon of "phototropy," as he called the change in, or loss of color of, certain rare compounds under the action of light. He did important physico-chemical research on the boiling point and melting point of chemical combinations, and contributed to such noted scientific periodicals as *Jahrbuch der Radio-Activität und Elektronie* and *Zeitschrift fur physikalische Chemie.*

In 1942 Marckwald was living in the Koch-Weser colony, near São Paulo, Brazil.

Among his works are: *Über die Beziehungen zwischen dem Siedepunkte und der Zusammensetzung chemischer Verbindungen* (1888); *Die Benzoltheorie* (1898); *Radium in Biologie und Heilkunde* (1911-12).

MARCO-BARUCH, JOSEPH, *see* BARUCH, JOSEPH MARCOU.

MARCOSSON, ISAAC FREDERICK, journalist, b. Louisville, Ky., 1876. His father, Louis Marcosson, served as major in the Confederate Army. It was in his native Louisville, under the guidance of one of

America's noted editors, Henry Watterson, that young Marcosson's reporting career got off to an auspicious start. From there he moved east, where in 1907 he became financial editor of the *Saturday Evening Post,* the journal with which his name and fame are most intimately identified. After three years of this financial editorship, during which time he published *How to Invest Your Savings* (1908), he left to become an editor of the then famous *Munsey's Magazine,* but soon returned to the *Post* to assume an association which was to last for thirty years and bring him world-wide repute as reporter of the contemporary scene.

In the course of his assignments, Marcosson ranged the globe, covering Europe, Asia and Latin America. He had earlier achieved the journalistic distinction of being the first to interview certain notable leaders of finance, the "money captains," of America, and he had vividly publicized these personalities for American readers. Now Marcosson pursued big foreign names in the same determined way. He would be the first to get at the men behind events, making them articulate, so that he could report how they looked and what they said for the stay-at-home readers of the *Saturday Evening Post.*

In this reporter's Odyssey Marcosson manoeuvered with enormous zeal, ingenuity and daring. As reward he scored many a big scoop. His were the first war interviews with Lloyd George, Haig, Kerensky. He saw Stinnes of Germany, and Kreuger, match king of Sweden. In Russia he spoke with Trotsky, and in Italy with Mussolini. And finally in Japan, on the strength of having already been received by one royal monarch, Albert of Belgium, he achieved the grand scoop of an audience with Hirohito, then prince regent.

These interviews with the world's famous, colorful, powerful personalities were gathered into two substantial volumes, first in *Adventures in Interviewing* (1919), covering experiences from Marcosson's earliest reporting days to the close of the first World War, and later in the sequel, *Turbulent Years* (1938), which begins in

Isaac Frederick Marcosson

Marcus Aurelius Antoninus

1919 and closes with the year of the author's retirement from the *Post* in 1937.

Marcosson's talents as a reporter were generally acknowledged, whatever criticism may have been made of his powers as analyst. His keen eye and ear seem to have missed nothing of either the man or the background he would present. He had a great flair for delineating characteristic detail, vivid speech, amusing sidelights, and his style never faltered or grew heavy. Thus, in the pages of Marcosson's two main works, dozens of personalities whom events of contemporary history have thrust into the limelight were further lighted up for the average American reader, made real in a homely, intimate fashion. One critic says of Marcosson: "No man has done more than he to bring Main Street into touch with the seething civilizations or barbarisms, however they be regarded, of the twentieth century."

In addition, Marcosson was author of more than a dozen volumes treating of the first World War, politics, industry, business and personalities, including: *The Autobiography of a Clown* (1910); *The War after the War* (1916); *Leonard Wood, Prophet of Preparedness* (1917); *The Rebirth of Russia* (1917); *S. O. S.—America's Miracle in France* (1919); *An African Adventure* (1921); *The Black Golconda* (1924); *David Graham Phillips and His Times* (1932).

SHERRY ABEL.

Lit.: Marcosson, Isaac F., *Adventures in Interviewing* (1919); *Turbulent Years* (1938); Wilson, "Mr. Marcosson and the Mighty," *New York Times Book Review,* Oct. 16, 1938, p. 2.

MARCUS AURELIUS ANTONINUS, Roman emperor, b. Rome, 121 C.E.; d. in the territory of the German wars, 180 C.E. Aurelius was raised to the rank of Caesar in 139, having been chosen for the line of succession by Hadrian, who had designated Titus Antoninus Pius as his own successor and demanded that Antoninus adopt Aurelius. Aurelius became consul in 140. When Antoninus died in 161, he chose Aurelius to succeed him solely. But Aurelius, whose natural superior mental endowments had been subjected to sterling training in morality and ethics, insisted on sharing his reign with Lucius Verus, who had been adopted by Antoninus with Aurelius.

The historical facts of Aurelius's reign—Verus played little part in it—give scant foundation to his suggested identity with Antoninus in the Talmud, the Roman emperor who was supposed not only to have been extraordinarily intimate with the Jews but eventually a convert to Judaism. Antoninus of the Talmud was also a friend of Judah Hanasi, or Rabbi. While it is true that the magnificent philosophy expressed by Aurelius in his *Reflections,* or *Meditations,* might indicate tolerance to all subjects, Aurelius was in practice antagonistic to Christians and unfriendly to Jews. Graetz cites one contrary instance, according to which Simeon ben Yohai is supposed to have gone to Rome (169) and obtained from Aurelius a decree abolishing anti-Jewish laws. In 175, however, Aurelius visited Judea and expressed displeasure with the reception accorded him by the Jews. Instead of paying servile respect, they demanded the abrogation of discriminatory taxes. No legislation favoring the Jews is known to have come from Aurelius.

The similarity between the ethical rules laid down in his *Reflections* and Jewish precepts is manifest, but such similarity can be found between any two moral systems chosen from any unrelated groups.

Lit.: Graetz, H., *History of the Jews,* vol. 2 (1927) 447, 449, 458, 463; Bodek, D. Arnold, *Marcus Aurelius als Zeitgenosse und Freund des Rabbi Jehuda ha-Nasi* (1868); Krauss, S., *Antoninus und Rabbi* (1910); Hastings, James, edit., *Encyclopaedia of Religion and Ethics,* vol. 8 (1922) 409-14.

MARCUS, AHRON, Hebrew etymologist and philosopher, b. Hamburg, Germany, 1843; d. Frankfort, Germany, 1916. Although by birth and early training he might have turned to the Western European Jewish tradition, Marcus chose the Eastern European tradition instead. At the Yeshiva in Boskowitz, which he attended after studying at the Hamburg Talmud Torah, Marcus concentrated on Hasidism. His knowledge of modern science did not wane, but his interest in the Cabalistic Hasidic approaches grew with it, and to them both he added Orthodoxy in personal practice. Marcus joined the political Zionist movement at its inception, but when his hopes that the movement would incorporate an ultra-Orthodox viewpoint were not fulfilled, he turned to the doctrines of the Agudath Israel.

Living in Podgorre-Cracow the greater part of his life, Marcus spent his time in quiet research and writing, though a series of travel sketches dealing with the European continent was also among his published works. Under the pseudonym "Verus" he wrote a monograph on Hasidism, *Der Chassidismus* (1901). His etymological study *Barzilai* (1905) attempted to reduce the Hebraic three-root system to original word stems with two radicals, to which the third radical was joined as a differentiation sign. Marcus was author of *Hartmanns induktive Philosophie in Chassidismus* (vol. 1, 1888;

vol. 2, 1889) and (in Hebrew) *Kadmonioth,* dealing with Babylonian-Assyrian excavations and the Holy Writ. His *Jüdische Chronologie,* part 1, was published at Frankfort in 1935.

Lit.: Frankfurter Zeitung, March 6, 1916; Möller, J., in *Yeshurun,* vol. 4 (1917) 154-60, 248-52.

MARCUS, ERNST, philosopher, b. Kamen, Germany, 1856; d. Essen, Germany, 1928. He studied law and was for many years a noted judge in the industrial center of Germany. Although his juridical profession consumed most of his time, Marcus acquired a vast knowledge in the range of science and philosophy. He concentrated on the historical and systematic interpretation of Kant, and endeavored to prove that Kant's point of view remained the leading idea of modern thinking. He published: *Die exakte Aufdeckung des Fundaments der Sittlichkeit und Religion und die Konstruktion der Welt aus den Elementen Kants* (1899); *Das Erkenntnisproblem* (1905); *Logik* (1908); *Kants Weltgebäude* (1917); *Theorie einer natürlichen Magie* (1924). Proceeding from Kantianism, Marcus criticized Einstein in 1926 in his *Kritik des Aufbaus der speciellen Relativitätstheorien,* and in 1927 opposed to Einstein's theory his *Die Zeit-und Raumlehre Kants.*

MARCUS, JACOB RADER, historian, b. Connellsville, Pa., 1896. He was educated at the University of Cincinnati (A.B., 1917), the Hebrew Union College (rabbi, 1920), the University of Kiel (1923) and the University of Berlin (Ph.D., 1925). He later pursued post-graduate studies at Paris and Jerusalem (1925-26). During the first World War Marcus served with the United States Army as a second lieutenant.

Marcus was an instructor in Bible and rabbinics at the Hebrew Union College, in Cincinnati, from 1920 to 1926, assistant professor of Jewish history from 1926 to 1929, and associate professor from 1929 to 1934. In 1934 he was appointed professor of Jewish history, a post he still held in 1942. In 1941 he lectured at the Harvard University Conference on "Religion and the World Today."

Marcus contributed greatly to the knowledge and popularization of Jewish history in the United States. His books include: *Israel Jacobson* (1928); *The Rise and Destiny of the German Jew* (1934); *An Index to Jewish Festschriften* (1937; with Albert T. Bilgray); *The Jew in the Medieval World—A Source Book* (1938). He wrote articles on religious and historical subjects for learned journals.

MARCUS, LOUIS WILLIAM, judge, b. Buffalo, N. Y., 1863; d. Buffalo, 1923. He was educated at Cornell University (LL.B., 1889), was admitted to the bar in 1889, and practised law privately for six years. In 1895 he was elected surrogate of Erie County, N. Y., on the Republican ticket, and was reelected in 1900. Marcus was appointed justice of the Supreme Court of New York State, eighth district, in 1905, and elected to the same position the following year. He was reelected for a fourteen-year term in 1920, and served until his death.

MARCUS, MICHAEL, British government official, b. Edinburgh, Scotland, 1896. He was educated at Edinburgh University, where he received his law degree and entered the practice of law. In 1926 Marcus was elected to the Edinburgh Town Council, and from 1929 to 1931 he was a member of Parliament for Dundee, representing Labor. Marcus was active in Zionist affairs, first in Edinburgh and later more generally. He was a deputy member of the World Jewish Agency Executive for Palestine from 1929 to 1931, and honorary secretary of the Parliamentary Palestine Committee during the same period. He was also a member of the council of the English Zionist Federation in 1931 and 1932, and for a time a member of the Board of Jewish Deputies. After 1932 he was inactive in communal affairs. Marcus wrote *Legal Aspects of Trade Unionism*.

MARCUS, MOSES (Mordecai Rofe), physician, b. Pozsony (Pressburg), Hungary, about 1730; d. Altstrelitz, Germany, 1786. He was a son of Mose Lwuw, chief rabbi of Pressburg, called Rabbi Moses Harif, and a grandson of Rabbi Mordecai Mochiah. Early in life Marcus married a girl of great wealth, but before he was thirty years of age he lost his wife, his two children and his fortune. He was attracted to Germany by wealthy relatives living there and by the fame of Jonathan Eybeschütz. He stayed for some time at Breslau, at Frankfort on Oder, where he completed one term at the university, and at Berlin, where he may have imbibed Mendelssohnian ideas in the home of his wealthy uncle.

One day in 1763 he arrived at the little town of Bützow in Mecklenburg. Penniless, exhausted and sick, he was taken to the house of a coreligionist, Aaron Isaak Petschirstecher (engraver of seals), who subsequently founded the Jewish community of Stockholm. Olaus Gerhart Tychsen, professor of Orientalistics at the Fridericianum, made himself Marcus' protector and director of studies. Tychsen had studied at the Gymnasium of Altona and had come under the influence of Jonathan Eybeschütz, whose Yeshiva he was said to have attended. He mastered Hebrew and Judeo-German, and had received from Rabbi Lipschütz of Kirchheim the title of "Haber" for his proficiency in rabbinics. A close friendship sprang up between the older and the younger man, to which their preoccupation with pursuits and ideas which only they had in common gave particular color and intensity. Tychsen had previously used his Jewish erudition to attempt in several cities of Germany the conversion of Jews for whom he had a great liking. It was he who obtained from the duke of Mecklenburg-Schwerin permission for Marcus to take his medical degree, the oath being slightly changed for the occasion of being pronounced by a Jew for the first time. At the inauguration ceremony, which was attended by all the Jews of Bützow and of the neighborhood, Marcus had to dispute with his professors, the disputation between Tychsen and himself being conducted in rabbinical style. The title of his inaugural dissertation was *De cura infantum recens natorum penes Ebraeos olim usitata etc.* (On the Treatment of Newly Born Infants as Practised by the Ancient Hebrews; 1766). For the occasion Tychsen had prepared a Hebrew panegyric in florid rabbinical language which has been preserved by the University of Rostock. After bidding farewell to the graduate in a humorous Judeo-German poem of his own making, Tychsen admonished him to use his knowledge to dispel among his coreligionists the prejudice against the Christian faith.

The young medical doctor married the daughter of the wealthy Feibush Meshullam of Altstrelitz and became a prosperous practitioner in that city. Frequent letters, mostly in Judeo-German, were exchanged with Tychsen. The family of his wife was apprehensive of Tychsen's influence, and there seems to have been much family dissension. The conflicting trends and emotions of his life eventually cast Marcus into a state of depressive melancholy, Tychsen endeavoring to comfort him and suggesting ill-will on the part of the family. In one letter he wrote in classical Latin: "Nigri enim sunt, hos tu, Romane, caveto! (For they are black, beware of them, thou, a Roman!). In his mental anguish Marcus once more resorted to flight, going to Breslau and thence to Lissa, where he became physician at the Jewish hospital with an annual income of 500 Reichstaler (1772). In the following year his wife and two children joined him, and thenceforth he lived with them peacefully in Lissa. In 1786 the family returned to Altstrelitz, where Marcus died several months later.

Tychsen, who survived him for several decades and whose philo-Semitism attracted many Jewish students to the Fridericianum, alleged that Marcus had adopted Christianity at Breslau, but his burial record in the book of the Hebrah Kaddisha of Altstrelitz disproves this point.

Marcus, who enjoyed the reputation of an excellent physician in his second year at the Fridericianum, published in that year: *Veterum rabbinorum placita de bestiis licitis and illicitis* (1764); *Von den Krankheiten des Alters aus Prediger des Salomon, Cap. XII. 1-7* (1764); *Disputatio de pentateucho Samaritano praes. Tychsen* (1764); He also published *Epistola gratulationis in diem natalem Frederici IX ducis Megapolitis Strelitz* (1766).   ANNA BETTELHEIM.

Lit.: Seligman, Josef, edit., *Aron Isaks sjelfbiografi* (1897); *Denkwürdigkeiten des Aron Isak, 1730-1817* (1930); Donath, *Geschichte der Juden in Mecklenburg*, 140 et seq.; Tychsen, O. G., in *Gelehrte Beiträge zu den Mecklenburg-Schwerinschen Nachrichten*, parts 6 and 7 (1766); Hartmann, T., *O. G. Tychsen, oder Wanderungen durch die mannigfaltigsten Gebiete der biblisch-asiatischen Literatur* (6 vols., 1818-23); Mandl, Bernát, *Med. Dr. Marcus Moses, Sohn des Pressburger Oberrabbiners, Arzt in Deutschland* (1928).

MARCUS, RALPH, teacher and writer, b. San Francisco, 1900. He received his M.A. degree from Columbia University in 1920, and his Ph.D. degree in 1928. Marcus' father, Moses I. Marcus, was an instructor in Talmud at the Jewish Institute of Religion, in New York city, from 1928 to 1936, and Marcus himself became associated with the Institute in 1927. He served first as instructor in Bible and Hellenistic Judaism and later as assistant professor; in 1942 he was professor of Semitic philology there. He was also (1927-) lecturer in Semitic languages at Columbia University.

Marcus wrote for various professional journals, and was the editor of vols. 5, 6 and 7 of the *Works of Josephus* for the Loeb Classical Library (1934-42). He was also author of *Law in the Apocrypha* (1927) and *Index to Journal of Bible Literature* (1942). He was consulting editor for the 1934 edition of *Webster's International Dictionary* and on the editorial board of the *Review of Religion*. He was founder of the Group

*Model of the gas-driven automobile (above) designed by
Siegfried Marcus in 1875; (right) Siegfried Marcus*

for Hamitic and Semitic Linguistics (1941), a member
of the council of the Society of Biblical Literature
(1938-40) and corresponding secretary of the American
Academy for Jewish Research (1938-41).

MARCUS, SIEGFRIED, inventor, b. Macklin,
Mecklenburg, Germany, 1831; d. Vienna, 1898. He
showed unusual aptitude in mechanics at an early age,
studied first in his native city and then in Hamburg.
In 1848 he went to Berlin and joined the newly-established engineering firm of Siemens and Halske. At this
time the firm was engaged in establishing the first telegraphic communication between Berlin and Magdeburg.
Marcus participated in the work and was responsible
for certain improvements in the development of the
telegraph.

In 1852 Marcus went to Vienna, where he worked
and taught. He established his own laboratory in 1860.
Although the most remarkable of his inventions, from
the 20th cent. point of view, was the benzine motor
car which he patented first in 1864 and again (a new
model) in 1875, there was hardly a field in the industrialization of natural resources that Marcus did not
touch on. He was creative and versatile; he worked
on the use of electricity for purposes of illumination,
patenting an electric lamp in 1877; he developed telegraphic relays, electrical fuses for submarine mines and
a loudspeaker microphone. His versatility was his misfortune; otherwise he might have foreseen the possibilities of the benzine power vehicle and concentrated on
its development. The 1875 model of his car was preserved in the Viennese Industrial Museum. Marcus held
thirty-eight patents in Austria alone, and seventy-six in
all in about a dozen countries. He received the gold
medal of the Austrian Academy of Sciences.

Lit.: Kurzel-Runtscheiner, Erich, "Siegfried Marcus,"
*Zeitschrift der Österreicher Ingenieur und Architekten
Vereines* (1928) 262-64; Skouronnek, K., "Siegfried Marcus," *Umschau* (1931) 743-44; Postal, Bernard, "'Grandfather' of the Automobile," *American Hebrew*, Sept. 25,
1931, pp. 405, 416.

MARCUSE, ADOLF, astronomer and geodesist,
b. Magdeburg, 1860; d. Berlin, 1930. The son of a
banker, Marcuse was educated in the universities of
Strasbourg and Berlin. Very early he began to go
abroad on astronomical researches, participating in 1882
in the German Venus-expedition, going to St. Petersburg in 1885 to study at the nearby Pulkova Observatory, and then, in 1886, leaving for Chile to serve as
astronomer-in-chief at the National Observatory there.

Back in the Royal Observatory in Berlin, he worked
on the problem of periodical changes in latitude and
then in 1891 headed the astronomical expedition to the
South Sea Islands to further these investigations. He
published his findings in *Die Hawaiischen Inseln*
(1894).

Returning to Germany he engaged in teaching astronomy and mathematical geography in several institutions. In 1897 he was admitted as lecturer at Berlin University; and from 1907 to the close of his career,
he was professor in the Handelshochschule in Berlin.
In addition, he was appointed instructor in the Bavarian Luftschiffbataillon. He interrupted his teaching
career in Germany for a period in 1925 to go to Japan,
where he gave a course of lectures.

Marcuse made a number of important studies bearing
on the astronomical determination of aircraft positions.
Among his other notable achievements was the development of the photographic telescope for taking polar
heights. In the more than twenty volumes he published
dealing with geography, astronomy, and aeronautics,
can be seen the wide range of his scientific accomplishments.

Lit.: Wininger, *Grosse Jüdische National Biographie,*
vol. 4, p. 266.

MARCUSE, LUDWIG, writer, b. Berlin, 1894.
He received his Ph.D. degree with a thesis on Nietzsche
from the University of Berlin (1917). In Germany
Marcuse was active as a lecturer on philosophy and literature in various institutions of higher learning, and
as a dramatic critic. Among his books are: *Georg
Büchner und seine besten Bühnenwerke* (1921); *Strindberg. Das Leben der tragischen Seele* (1922); *Die
Welt der Tragödie* (1923); *Revolutionär und Patriot*
(a biography of Ludwig Börne; 1929); *Heinrich Heine,
ein Leben zwischen gestern und morgen* (1932; English trans., 1933). He edited *Gerhardt Hauptmann und
sein Werk* (1925) and *Weltliteratur der Gegenwart*
(2 vols., 1925). After the establishment of the Nazi
regime Marcuse emigrated to France; in April, 1939, he

came to the United States; in 1942 he resided at Beverly Hills, Cal. In the United States he published *Soldier of the Church* (a biography of Ignatius Loyola, founder of the Jesuits; 1939).

In October, 1937, the Nazi government expatriated Marcuse, revoking his German citizenship. In October, 1939, he took out his first papers for American citizenship.

MARCUSE, MOSES, 18th cent. physician, b. probably in Germany. He studied medicine in Königsberg, and came to Poland in 1774. Marcuse practised medicine and also, with the aid of a Polish landowner, published *Sefer Refuoth* (1790), in Yiddish. For the first time the Jewish masses were given access to elementary instruction in hygiene and medicine. The book also had great cultural and philological value. The "Teitsh" in which it is written has been adjudged excellent by various philologists. Marcuse is considered one of the pioneers of Enlightenment in Poland, a forerunner of the Maskilim. He was alert also to the social needs of the Jewish population, agitating for a productive life as opposed to *Schnorrerei* (used not in the sense of mendicancy, but in that of an unproductive life). Noah Prilutzki called Marcuse a Yiddishist of the 18th cent.

Lit.: Reisen, Z., *Lexikon fun der Yiddisher Literatur, Presse un Filologie,* vol. 2 (1928), cols. 345-48; Prilutzki, Noah, *Zamelbicher,* vol. 2.

MARCUSE, PAUL, lawyer and tax expert, b. Berlin, 1881. He attended the Französisches Gymnasium in Berlin, studied law and political economy at the universities of Berlin and Freiburg, and won his doctorate of law at the University of Rostock.

He practiced law in Germany (1909-1936), was accredited interpreter in English and legal adviser to the American Chamber of Commerce in Berlin. As expert in the law of taxation he was on the board (1924-33) of many German organizations such as the Berliner Anwaltsverein, Berliner Anwaltskammer, Steuerausschuss des Deutschen Anwaltsvereins, Prüfungskommission für Wirtschaftsprüfer. Upon the advent of Naziism he had to relinquish all these positions as a result of the Aryan-laws in Germany.

In 1904 and in 1909, Marcuse visited the United States, where he arrived again as a refugee from Nazi Germany in 1936. Settling in New York, he has engaged in the practice of law, particularly in its international and taxation aspects.

He wrote a number of text books, and contributed to periodicals and commentaries on the law of taxation and of tax statutes. He was editor of *Die neue Steuerzeitung* (1919-1925) and published (1928) a text book on the American income tax which was the only work of its kind in German. The following of his publications are especially noteworthy: *Das amerikanische Notenbankgesetz vom 30. Mai 1908, Die Bankreform in den Vereinigten Staaten* (1915), *Betrachtungen über das Notenbankwesen in den Vereinigten Staaten* (1907), *Die Einkommensteuer in den Vereinigten Staaten* (1928).

MARCUSE, RUDOLPH, sculptor, b. Berlin, 1878; d. London, 1940. He studied at the Academy of Berlin. In 1903 Marcuse won the Michael Beer prize with his relief *The Judgment of Solomon,* and in 1910 the silver medal and the Prix de Rome, as well as a gold medal

in Brussels. During the first World War, Marcuse was commissioned by the German government to model fifty heads of prisoners in war camps. All races and varieties were represented, and the studies Marcuse made were used subsequently in ethnic studies. After the establishment of the Nazi regime in 1933, Marcuse settled in London.

MARCZALI, HENRIK, historian, b. Marcali, Hungary, 1856; d. Budapest, 1940. His original name was Morgenstern. His father, Mihály Marczali-Morgenstern, was rabbi at Marcali and fought for Jewish emancipation. Henrik Marczali graduated from high school at the age of fourteen, winning an award for distinguished achievement in mathematics and physics. He studied history at the University of Budapest, obtaining his teacher's diploma at the age of seventeen and his Ph.D. degree at nineteen. A state scholarship enabled him to do graduate work at Berlin and Paris, and on his return in 1878 he became an assistant teacher under Mór de Kármán at the Model Secondary School. The following year he was offered a full professorship at the University of Budapest on condition that he renounce his faith. Being unwilling to do so, he was promoted only to a full teaching position at the Model School. Not until sixteen years later, when his important works had been translated and published in German and other languages, did he receive the university appointment from a more liberal government (1895), having been a member of the Hungarian Academy from 1893 on.

Marczali's major works, which made him the greatest authority of his time on Hungarian history, include: *A magyar történet kutföi az Árpádok korában* (1880; in German: *Die Quellen der ungarischen Geschichte in der Arpadenzeit,* 1882); *Magyarország története II. József koraban* (3 vols., 1882-88; English trans. published by Cambridge University); *Mária Terézia* (1891); *Az Árpádok és Dalmácia* (1898); (in French: *Les relations de la Dalmatie du XIᵉ au XIIIᵉ siècles,* Paris, 1898); *A magyar történet kútföinek kézikönyve* (Handbook of the Sources of Hungarian History; 1902); *A nemzetiség története bölcsészeti szempontból* (The History of Nationality from the Philosophical Point of View; 1904); *Hungary in the Eighteenth Century* (1910); *Ungarische Verfassungsgeschichte* (Tübingen, 1910); *Ungarisches Verfassungsrecht* (Tübingen, 1911); *Italicae res* (1915); *Világpolitika és világgazdaság* (World Politics and World Economics; 1918); *Die Entwicklung des ungarischen Königtums* (1917). He contributed three volumes to the millennial history of Hungary edited by Szilágyi, and six volumes on the history of the modern age to the illustrated history of the world edited by himself. For four decades his name appeared under articles or monographs on the history of Hungary in encyclopedias and dictionaries all over the world.

His career as an educator came to an end after the first World War, when successive revolutionary and anti-revolutionary governments applied themselves to a deliberate reinterpretation of history. He was pensioned in 1924, at the age of sixty-eight, after having suffered many difficulties and tribulations for five years. He continued to write, probing into the causes and circumstances of the War: *A béke könyve* (The

Book of the Peace; 1920); *Hogyan készült a nagy háboru* (How the Great War Was Brought About; 1923). He also prepared a great work of economic history, *Az ár- és bérviszonyok története Magyarországon* (A History of Price and Wages Conditions in Hungary), and published *Erdélyország története* (History of Transylvania; 1935).

MARDUK, one of the most important gods of the Babylonians. He was originally the local god of the city of Babylon, with his festival at the spring equinox. As the city grew in power, the position of Marduk in the pantheon was advanced and he was made the hero of the creation epic, in which he vanquishes the primeval monster Tiamat (equals the Hebrew *tehom*, "abyss") and takes from her the tablets of destiny. According to this legend, he formed the heaven and earth out of the two halves of the body of Tiamat. Some of this story is perhaps reflected in the Bible account of the creation (*Gen.* 1). Marduk was known also as the Bel ("lord"), and the two names are used synonymously. The Bible contains references to both Bel and Marduk, but it is vocalized Merodach (*Isa.* 46:1; *Jer.* 50:2). The name Mordecai is likewise connected with Marduk, and some scholars have seen in the *Esther* story a reworking of a legend originally told of the votaries of Marduk.

MARÉES, HANS VON (Johann Hans Reinhard), painter, b. Elberfeld, Germany, 1837; d. Rome, 1887. The son of the jurist Adolph Marées and of a Jewish mother (née Sussmann, from Halberstadt), he studied art in Coblenz, in Berlin under Steffeck, and in Munich under Piloty. After visiting France and Spain, he finally settled in Rome in 1864; later he returned to Rome after a three-year visit in Berlin and Dresden. His works, the subjects of which are taken from mythology and the lives of the saints, exhibit great vigor and individuality. They include: *The Esperids; Saint Martin; Saint Georges; Saint Hubert; The Three Ages of Life;* the frescoes of the zoological station of Naples. Most of his paintings, exhibited at Munich in 1891, became the property of the Bavarian State, forming a collection in the Marées Gallery at Schleissheim.

Lit.: Meier-Graefe, *Hans von Marées, sein Leben und sein Werk* (3 vols., 1912); *Encyclopaedia Britannica,* vol. 14, p. 873; *Bryan's Dictionary of Painters and Engravers,* vol. 3 (1904) 284; Thieme, U., and Becker, F., *Allgemeines Lexikon der bildenden Künstler,* vol. 24, pp. 83-85.

MAREK, PETER (PESACH), historian and critic, b. Shadov, province of Kovno, Lithuania, 1862; d. Saratov, Russia, 1920. His father was a Hebrew teacher. Marek studied law at the University of Moscow. With Menachem Mendel Ussischkin and others, he was one of the founders of the Bnei Zion.

Marek's literary debut was made in 1888, in *Voskhod,* a Russian Jewish magazine, with a history of Jewish printing establishments in Russia. In collaboration with Saul Ginsburg, Marek published a large collection of Yiddish folk songs. After studying Jewish cultural history, Marek wrote *Sketches of Jewish Culture in Russia* (Russian; 1909), a book which covers the period between 1844 and 1873 and depicts the struggle between the religious and mundane systems. He wrote also for the historical periodicals *Yevreiskaya Starina* and *Perezhitoye.*

During the period of the Russian revolution, Marek lived in Saratov, suffering hunger and illness. He left many unpublished works, including a history of the Jewish intelligentsia. Though he wrote mostly in Russian, Marek did occasional articles in Yiddish.

Lit.: Reisen, Z., *Lexikon fun der Yiddisher Literatur, Presse un Filologie,* vol. 2 (1930), cols. 338-42; Marek, P., "Reminiscences," *Yevreiski Mir,* Nos. 7-9 (1910).

MARESHAH, a locality in the tribe of Judah, in the lowland—the Shefelah—of Palestine, between the mountains and the Coastal Plain (*Josh.* 15:44; *Micah* 1:15). It was fortified by Rehoboam (*II Chron.* 11:8), and the battle between Asa and Zerah the Ethiopian (*II Chron.* 14:9-14) was fought in its neighborhood. The place is mentioned in connection with the wars of Judas Maccabeus in 164 B.C.E. (*I Macc.* 5:66; *II Macc.* 12:35; Josephus, *Antiquities,* book 12, chap. 8, section 6; it is called Marisa or Marissa in Greek). It was subjugated by John Hyrcanus (Josephus, *Antiquities,* book 13, chap. 9, section 1; chap. 10, section 2), liberated by Pompey (Josephus, *Antiquities,* book 14, chap. 4, section 4), and destroyed by the Parthians (Josephus, *Antiquities,* book 14, chap. 13, section 9). The entire Hellenistic town of Mareshah was excavated by Bliss and Macalister in 1899; the present name is Tell Sandahanneh, situated one mile south of Beit Jibrin (Eleutheropolis). The excavated remains are those of a Seleucidan city which was built on top of an earlier Jewish settlement; the latter itself was not explored. In the Seleucidan period Mareshah was a colony of the Sidonians or Phoenicians, who have left tombs with extremely important fresco paintings.

Lit.: Bliss and Macalister, *Excavations in Palestine* (1902); Peters and Thiersch, *Painted Tombs in the Necropolis of Marissa* (1905); Thomsen, *Palästina und seine Kultur in fünf Jahrtausenden,* 2nd ed. (1917) 93-94.

MARETZEK, MAX, opera impresario, b. Brünn, Moravia, 1821; d. Staten Island, N. Y., 1897. Before coming to the United States he was conductor of orchestras in Germany, France and England. Shortly after arriving there he was appointed conductor at the Astor Place Opera House in New York city. In 1849 he organized his own opera company which, three years later, failed because of competition offered by the brilliant Jenny Lind visiting America under Barnum's direction.

Following this venture Maretzek became director of the Astor Place Opera House, the Academy of Music, and Niblo's Gardens. He was one of the pioneers in popularizing grand opera in the United States. He was responsible for presenting to American opera audiences the premières of such now-accepted classics as *Rigoletto, Il Trovatore, La Traviata, Le Prophète, L'Africaine, Romeo et Juliette* and *Don Pasquale.* Many brilliant singers were introduced to the United States under his direction, including Minnie Hauk. Maretzek composed two operas of his own, neither of which was successful. He was author of two books of reminiscences, *Crotchets and Quavers* (New York, 1885) and *Sharps and Flats* (New York, 1890), which give a vivid picture of the early history of opera-making in New York.

MARGARITA, ANTONIUS (Anton Margaritha), apostate enemy of the Jews, b. Ratisbon (Regensburg), Germany, about 1490; d. Vienna. The son of Rabbi Jacob Margolioth, Margarita was descended from a prominent rabbinical family. First converted to Catholicism, he left that faith, after being punished for certain calumnies, to join the Lutherans. In 1530 Emperor Charles V, having heard the denunciations of Josel of Rosheim against Margarita as an enemy of the Jews, imprisoned and banished the apostate from Augsburg. He then lived in Zellan, Leipzig and Vienna, teaching Hebrew at the universities.

It is from Margarita's chief work of calumny against the Jews, *Der Gantz Jüdisch Glaub mit Sampt Ainer Grundlichen und Wahrhafften Anzaygunge, Aller Satzungen, Ceremonien, Gebetten, Haymliche und Offentliche Gebreuch, Deren sich dye Juden Halten, Durch das Gantz Jar, Mit Schönen un Gegründten Argumenten Wyder Jren Glauben* (Augsburg, 1530; Leipzig, 1713), that Martin Luther received much of his own material for attacking Judaism. Margarita's work itself is in large measure plagiarized from similar works by the converts Pfefferkorn and Karben. The book had a wide circulation and deleterious influence.

Lit.: Mannheimer, Sigmund, in *Jewish Encyclopedia*, vol. 8, pp. 326-27; Graetz, H., *History of the Jews*, vol. 4 (1927) 551.

MARGET, ARTHUR WILLIAM, economist, b. Chelsea, Mass., 1899. The name Marget is an erroneous transliteration, by United States immigration officials, of Maggid, the surname adopted by the family after several generations of Maggidim.

Marget received his A.M. degree from Harvard in 1921 and his Ph.D. degree in 1927, and also worked in various European universities. From 1923 to 1927 he was an instructor in economics at Harvard. In 1927 he became associate professor of economics at the University of Minnesota, and in 1930 was made professor there, a post he still held in 1942. He was also a guest lecturer at the London School of Economics (1933), at Bocconi University, Milan (1934), and at the University of California summer school (1936).

In his book, *The Theory of Prices* (vol. 1, 1938; vol. 2, 1942), Marget dealt with various aspects of money circulation and at the same time sought to explain the functioning of the economic process in time under the money economy in such a way as to make it capable of analytical extension to all problems involving statistical measurement.

MARGOLIES (Margulies), BERL, *see* BRODER, BERL.

MARGOLIES, SAMUEL L., painter and etcher, b. New York city, 1897. He studied art at Cooper Union Institute, the National Academy of Design and the Beaux Arts, all in New York. Margolies exhibited at various galleries in New York and in other leading American cities, and his work is found in the permanent collections of the Society of American Etchers, the Library of Congress and many Federal and State buildings. In 1936 and 1937 Margolies was an instructor at the Queensboro Art Academy in Jamaica, N. Y., and after that he was a private instructor in etching as well as a lecturer on the subject. He was the author of *Don'ts for Etchers* and *Tricks of the Trade for Etchers,* and editor of *Highlights and Shadows,* an art monthly, in 1936 and 1937. During the first World

War Margolies served with the American Expeditionary Force.

MARGOLIN, ARNOLD, lawyer and journalist, b. Kiev, 1877. Having previously acted for Jews in pogrom trials, he was called into the famous Beilis case by the wife of Mendel Beilis. He organized a committee of influential Kiev Jews for the defense, and then directed all his own efforts to hunting down the actual murderers of the boy whom Beilis was falsely accused of having killed. Margolin was finally convinced that the woman Tcheberiak and her gang were guilty. By exposing Tcheberiak in other crimes he decisively discredited her as a witness for the prosecution; but, though he pursued his investigations long after Beilis was acquitted, he never succeeded in bringing Tcheberiak to justice, and his chance to do so ended when the Bolsheviks summarily shot her and her brother.

As a punitive measure for his activity, Margolin was disbarred when the case closed, but was restored to practice after the revolution. He then became active in Ukrainian politics; in 1918 he was appointed associate justice of the highest Ukraine court, and later was associate minister of foreign affairs in the Ukrainian Directorate, but resigned in 1919 after the Proskurov pogrom.

When the Bolsheviks assumed power in the Ukraine, Margolin fled to Paris, then went on to the United States in 1922. Here he became active as journalist, lecturer and lawyer, and was admitted to the Massachusetts bar in 1929 and in 1936 to the bar of Washington, D. C.

His writings include *The Jews of Eastern Europe* (1926). The section on the Beilis case purports to relate aspects of the affair which could not be revealed under the old Russian regime.

Lit.: Margolin, A., *The Jews of Eastern Europe* (1926); Beilis, *Story of My Sufferings* (1926).

MARGOLIOTH (also Margolis, Margoliouth, Margulies and other variations), a family widely ramified throughout Central and Eastern Europe. The name is derived from *margalith,* the Hebrew word for pearl.

JACOB MARGOLIOTH (d. Nuremberg, Germany, about 1492) was the first outstanding rabbi of that name known in Central Europe. There are many evidences of his importance, and it is assumed that he presided at the 1474 meeting of German rabbis.

Another JACOB MARGOLIOTH, also a rabbi, who lived in Ratisbon (Regensburg), Germany, about 1500, corresponded with Johann Reuchlin.

The Polish branch of the Margolioth family traced its descent from Rashi and produced many Talmudic scholars. Its first known representative was SAMUEL MARGOLIOTH, Dayan at Posen, whom Sigismund I made "senior" of the Jews of Greater Poland in 1527.

NAPHTALI MARGOLIOTH (b. Vienna, about 1562) was baptized and adopted the name Julius Conrad Otto. He became professor of Hebrew at Altdorf at the beginning of the 17th cent. He wrote several textbooks on the Hebrew language, and eventually returned to Judaism.

MEIR BEN ZEBI HIRSCH MARGOLIOTH (b. probably Galicia; d. Ostrog, Volhynia, 1790) was rabbi for the district of Lemberg (not including the city itself) for about forty years, until 1782. He was a pupil of Israel Baal Shem Tob (BESHT), and was among the first Talmudists to acknowledge Hasidic affiliation.

EPHRAIM ZALMAN MARGOLIOTH (b. Brody, Galicia, 1762; d. Brody, 1828) was a Talmudist who also a successful banker. He opened a private Yeshiva in Brody, in his own home, and was its head. Margolioth was author of various commentaries and responsa.

JUDAH LÖB BEN ASHER MARGOLIOTH (d. Frankfort, Germany, 1811) was rabbi in various Polish and German cities and author of responsa and treatises on philosophy.

Various other members of the Margolioth family achieved lesser prominence as rabbis and authors.

Lit.: Ir Hatzedek, 42; Buber, S., Kiryah Nisgabah, 8; Jewish Encyclopedia, vol. 8, pp. 327-30.

MARGOLIOUTH, DAVID SAMUEL, Arabic scholar, b. London, 1858; d. London, 1940. He was the eldest son of the missionary Ezekiel Margoliouth. He was educated at New College of Oxford University, where he received the M.A. and D.Litt. degrees. From 1881 to 1889 he held a fellowship in Arabic at New College. He was appointed Laudian professor of Arabic in 1889, and occupied that post until his retirement in 1937. He was moderator in oriental languages and Hibbert lecturer at the University of London in 1913. In 1916 and 1917 he was special lecturer in oriental history at the University of Panjab. He was a reader in Arabic historians at the University of Calcutta and Wilson lecturer at the University of Bombay in 1929.

Margoliouth was one of the outstanding orientalists of his day, and was frequently honored by learned societies. He was elected director of the Royal Asiatic Society in 1905, and served as president of that organization from 1934 to 1937. He was president of the Eastern Question Association in 1910. In 1912 he represented the British government at the Orientalist Congress at Athens, Greece. In 1931 he was president of the John Payne Society.

He was a prolific author, editor, and translator. His works include: Analecta Orientalia ad Poeticam Aristoteleam (1888); Letters of Abul 'Ala (1898); Mohammed and the Rise of Islam (1905); Mohammedanism (1911); Dictionary of Learned Men (edited in Arabic, 1907-27); Eclipse of the Abbasid Caliphate (with H. F. Amedroz, 7 vols., 1922); Lectures on Arabic Historians (1930); Mohammed (1939). In 1906 he edited W. Whiston's translation of the works of Josephus.

MARGOLIOUTH, GEORGE, scholar and writer, b. Wilkowiczky, Russian Poland, 1853; d. New Brighton, England, 1924. He was educated at Düsseldorf, at the University of Bonn, Cuddesdon College, Oxford, and Queen's College, Cambridge. Like his uncle Moses Margoliouth (1820-1881), he became a convert to Christianity and was ordained in 1881. He was a learned Biblical and Oriental scholar, and did much valuable work for the British Museum where he was in charge of the Hebrew, Syriac and Ethiopic manuscripts from 1891 until his retirement in 1914. This included a Descriptive List of the Hebrew and Samaritan MSS. in the British Museum (London, 1893); to

Max Leopold Margolis

this he added a Catalogue of the Hebrew and Samaritan MSS. in the British Museum (3 vols., London, 1899-1915), in 1899 also he had published Descriptive List of the Syriac and Karshuni MSS. in the British Museum acquired since 1873. During his service at the British Museum he founded the Text and Translation Society for the publication of Oriental works (1900), and was honorary secretary of the society until 1903. From 1909 to 1913 and from 1917 until his death Margoliouth was an examiner in Hebrew and Aramaic at the University of London. Among his other publications are: The Liturgy of the Nile (London, 1896); The Palestinian Syriac Version of the Holy Scriptures (London, 1897); The Problem of Immortality and Some Stray Leaves (London, 1904). Margoliouth also wrote for various scholarly journals, including the Jewish Quarterly Review.

Lit.: The Times (London) May 17, 1924, p. 14.

MARGOLIS, JUDAH LEIB, rabbi and a forerunner of Enlightenment (Haskalah) in Poland, b. 1747; d. Frankfort on Oder, Germany, 1811. He served as rabbi in various towns of Poland and finally in Frankfort on Oder. He wrote responsa and several works of secular content, including Or Olam Katon (Frankfort on Oder, 1877), on natural science; Beth Middoth, on moral teachings; Tal Oroth, on immortality and the essence of the soul; Atze Eden, on belief and philosophy, including a criticism of Moses Mendelssohn's Jerusalem. He was also author of a book on style and a collection of poems.

MARGOLIS, MAX LEOPOLD, philologist, Biblical exegete and historian, b. Meretz, province of Vilna, Russia, 1866; d. Philadelphia, 1932. His father was a rabbi, and imparted to his son not only a comprehensive Hebrew and Talmudic training but the rudiments of a secular education as well. This was supplemented by instruction from the village priest. Afterward Margolis studied in Berlin.

In 1889 he came to the United States, receiving his M.A. degree from Columbia University the following year and his Ph.D. degree in 1891. Though his major interest during these formative years had been the Talmud and he had written—in Latin—his thesis on a Talmudic subject, Biblical exegesis appealed to his nature, and in 1892 Margolis became professor of Hebrew and Biblical exegesis at the Hebrew Union College. He held this appointment until 1897, and returned to the college as professor in the same subject in 1905, remaining until 1907. In the interim he had taught Semitics at the University of California.

Margolis became editor-in-chief of the new translation of the Hebrew Bible under preparation by the Jewish Publication Society of America, in 1908, and retained the direction of this work until its completion in 1917. He had become professor of Biblical philology at Dropsie College in 1909, and was occupying that post when he died. Through his four decades of teaching, his insistence on leading his students always to the basic sources of knowledge helped many young minds to a grasp of fundamentals rather than to contentment with superficialities. In his orientation to contemporary life Margolis was a Zionist, and held to the belief that in the reconstruction of Palestine lies the perpetuation of the Jewish ideal, although in his work Margolis was often affiliated with men who believed otherwise.

The most unusual study that Margolis undertook was left unfinished; part 1 was published at Paris in 1931, and parts 2 to 4 at Paris from 1932 to 1938. In 1942 part 5 was still in course of publication. This was the *Book of Joshua in Greek*, which represented twenty years of work. Margolis was also author of: *An Elementary Textbook of Hebrew Accidence* (1893); *The Holy Scripture with Commentary on Micah* (1908); *A Manual of the Aramaic Language of the Babylonian Talmud* (1910); *The Story of Bible Translations* (1917); *The Hebrew Scriptures in the Making* (1922), and co-author, with Alexander Marx, of *A History of the Jewish People* (1927). Margolis was editor of the *Journal of Biblical Literature* (1914-21), and from 1922 until his death he was editor of the *Journal of the American Oriental Society*. He was an early proponent and among the planners of the *Universal Jewish Encyclopedia*.

Lit.: Marx, Alexander, "Max L. Margolis, an Estimate," *Proceedings of the Rabbinical Assembly* (1932); Adler, Cyrus, "Max Leopold Margolis," *American Jewish Year Book*, vol. 35 (1933) 139-44; Galter, David J., "Max L. Margolis," *Jewish Exponent* (Philadelphia), April 8, 1932.

MARGOLIS, YEDIDE, Yiddish writer, b. Pustiki, province of Grodno, Russia, 1884. He came from a family of Jewish colonists. Margolis spent 1904 and 1905 in the United States, then returned to Russia (1906). In 1911 and 1912 he published, in Yiddish, a collection of short stories and a novel, and in Hebrew, *Shir Hayihud*, a poem. *Sozialism in der Yiddisher Literatur* (1918) was a scientific study. In 1923 Margolis published a volume of poems and *Imchah*, a drama. *Zvishen zvei Fronten*, another collection of short stories, appeared in 1930. Most of Margolis' belletristic work depicts pogroms and civil war, and is an emotional expression of the Jewish reaction to the tragedy of Jewish life. Margolis was on the staff of

the Communist *Emes*, but despite this was considered one of the Mitloifer, writers not officially Communists.

MARGOSHES, (ELIEZER) JOSEPH, Yiddish writer, b. Lemberg, Galicia, 1866. He received a Jewish education and later, for a time, applied himself to agriculture. Margoshes came to the United States first in 1898. In 1903 he returned to settle in New York city, and served as a traveling correspondent for various Yiddish newspapers. Subsequently he was for three years affiliated with the Bureau of Jewish Education and collaborated on the *Jewish Communal Register* (1916).

Until the end of 1919 Margoshes worked with the *Tog*; in 1921 he joined the staff of the *Morgen Journal*. In 1942 he was still writing for that newspaper, devoting most of his work to Jewish history and ethnography. He wrote several series of special articles, such as *Asereth Hashebatim* and *Yidden in Veite Lender*. Margoshes was active in Jewish writers' groups. His autobiography, *Erinnerungen fun mein Leben*, appeared in 1936. He was co-founder of the Jewish Writers' Union, and for fourteen years its secretary and manager.

Lit.: Reisen, Z., *Lexikon fun der Yiddisher Literatur, Presse un Filologie*, vol. 2 (1930), cols. 325-26.

MARGOSHES, SAMUEL, Yiddish writer and editor, son of Joseph, b. Josefow, Galicia, 1887. He attended a Yeshiva and a Gymnasium in Europe, and came to the United States in 1905. In 1910 he received a rabbinical degree from the Jewish Theological Seminary of America, in New York city, and in the following year a Ph.D. degree from Columbia.

Margoshes began his career in journalism in 1906, as editor of the *Neie Shtimme*. Later he worked for the *Tog* and for various Anglo-Jewish publications. From 1910 to 1917 he was affiliated with the New York Kehillah as director of the textbook department for its educational division. Subsequently (1917-19) he was president of the American Federation of Galician and Bucovina Jews, and later was director of the Keren Hayesod in Canada. Margoshes became editor-in-chief of the *Tog* in 1926, and in 1942 still held this post.

Lit.: Reisen, Z., *Lexikon fun der Yiddisher Literatur, Presse un Filologie*, vol. 2 (1930), cols. 326-28.

MARGULIES, ADELE, pianist, b. Vienna, 1863. After studying at the Vienna Conservatory where, for three years in succession, she won first prize for piano playing, she came to New York city to make her concert debut in 1881. In 1890 she organized a trio which won great favor in American concert halls. At the same time she taught the piano at the National Conservatory of Music in New York. For a period she taught the piano in Houston, Texas, then returned to Vienna in 1936 for retirement. In 1938 she came back to the United States.

MARGULIES, JOSEPH, artist, b. Lemberg, Galicia, 1896. In 1899 his parents emigrated to the United States and settled in New York's lower east side; and there young Margulies became intimately acquainted with the ghetto types he later portrayed. He won numerous awards at various art schools in New York, then went to study in Europe's leading art centers. Exhibiting in the United States, France, Italy, Germany, he had established a reputation by the time he reached thirty. After two years under Joseph Pennell, he held his first one-man show in 1928.

Margulies is distinguished for his mastery of etching and has conducted new experiments in this medium; he has travelled throughout the United States lecturing on the etching technique. He also produced in oils, water colors and pastels and became noted for his representations of Mexican peasant and Jewish types. His portraits of celebrities include Albert Einstein, Arturo Toscanini, Lord Marley, Henrietta Szold, Herbert Hoover, Fannie Hurst, Paul Muni, Joseph Pennell, Morris R. Cohen and Jo Davidson. Examples of his works are owned by many institutions including the Metropolitan Museum and the Public Library of New York city, Brooklyn Museum, Library of Congress in Washington, Yale University Library, San Francisco Museum, and the Jewish Theological Seminary. He executed murals for the Jewish Hospital of Brooklyn. Margulies has taught at the College of the City of New York and Brooklyn Museum, and was in 1942 chairman of the art committee of the Jewish Club.

Lit.: Wallach, Sidney, "Art of Joseph Margulies," *B'nai B'rith Magazine,* October, 1926, p. 36-37.

MARGULIES, SAMUEL HIRSCH, rabbi, b. Brzczany, Galicia, 1858; d. Florence, Italy, 1922. In addition to the Biblical and Talmudic education he was given, Margulies taught himself modern languages and literature. Later, from 1878 on, he studied at the Jewish theological seminary and the University of Breslau, receiving his Ph.D. degree from the university in 1883. Two years later he became rabbi in Hamburg, and later served as rabbi in Weilberg, Hesse.

In 1890 Margulies was called to be chief rabbi of Florence, Italy, where he worked successfully toward a revival of higher Jewish education in the city. When the Collegio Rabbinico Italiano was moved to Florence from Rome, in 1898, Margulies became its director. Many of his students later occupied rabbinical posts in leading Italian cities, and he was largely responsible for reestablishing a connection between Italian and other Jewries.

Margulies contributed to various periodicals; he founded the *Rivista Israelitica* (1904-11) and was its editor, and he was editor of *La Settimana Israelitica.* He was also one of the consulting editors of the *Jewish Encyclopedia.* Margulies was active in the Alliance Israélite Universelle and the World Zionist Organization.

Lit.: Israel, March 10 and June 15, 1922; March 8, 1923.

MARHESHVAN, *see* CALENDAR (under HESHVAN).

MARIA HEBREA (Maria the Jewess), early alchemist. Although historians seem to accept the fact of her existence and are even unanimous as to some of her discoveries, there are contradictory legends about the period of her existence. By some authorities she is said to have been the sister of Moses. Others say that she was the daughter of the king of Saba, and others make her a resident of Memphis in the 1st cent., and say that she was taught alchemy by the priests of the Temple.

Maria is supposed to have discovered hydrochloric acid and the "bain-Marie" (Balneum Mariae), which is used in chemical processes. She constructed stoves and recommended the use of glass vessels. Maria also taught the impermeabilization and the joining of utensils by the use of wax and fats. The great French scientist Marcellin Berthelot (1827-1907) did much to establish the existence of this remarkable woman through *Les Origines de l'alchimie* (1885) and his translations in the *Collections des anciens alchimistes grecs.*

Lit.: Manget, J. J., *Bibliotheca Chemica Curiosa* (1705), vol. 2, plate 8, figure 6; *La Grande Encyclopédie,* vol. 2, p. 14; Berthelot, M. P. E., *La Chimie en Moyen-Âge,* vol. 3, p. 125; Lippman, *Entstehung und Ausbreitung der Alchemie* (1919).

MARIA THERESA, *see* AUSTRIA (under 3).

MARIAMNE, 1. wife of Herod the Great. She was one of the last Hasmoneans, and as much because of her beauty and heritage as because of her attitude and behavior she roused both the ambition and the anger of the Idumean monarch. Betrothed to Herod by her grandfather Hyrcanus II, who sought in the alliance security as Herod sought aristocracy, Mariamne typified and perhaps expressed all the resentment of the Hasmoneans against Idumean rule.

Between Mariamne and her mother Alexandra on the one side and Herod's family—led by his sister Salome—on the other a feud for power went on. The ferment reached such a pitch that in 34 B.C.E. Herod, leaving to defend himself before Antony for the murder of Mariamne's brother Aristobulus, commanded Salome's husband, Joseph, to kill Mariamne if he himself did not return. Joseph confided these instructions to Mariamne. When Herod returned unharmed, Salome convinced him that Mariamne and Joseph had been guilty of misconduct. Joseph was immediately executed, but Mariamne was this time spared. Several years later Herod left similar instructions for Mariamne's murder if he failed to return from a voyage. Again she discovered the truth, and again, on Herod's return, Salome had a tale to tell. This time Herod was convinced that Mariamne had schemed his murder, and she was executed on the scaffold (29 B.C.E.). Herod became temporarily insane. Her two sons, Alexander and Aristobulus, were killed by their father some twenty years later.

2. Herod's second wife of that name. She was the daughter of Simon, a lower priest of Jerusalem. Like the first Mariamne, she was beautiful, and Herod raised her father to the high priesthood to justify his marriage to her. This marriage took place several years after the death of the first Mariamne. A son of the second marriage, named Herod, was among Herod's disinherited sons.

Lit.: Graetz, H., *History of the Jews,* vol. 2 (1927) 93, 104-5, 107; Schürer, Emil, *A History of the Jewish People in the Time of Jesus Christ,* division 1, vol. 1, pp. 396, 420-23, 429; Mathews, *A History of New Testament Times in Palestine* (1921) 112, 117-21.

MARIBOR (Marburg), *see* YUGOSLAVIA.

MARINOV, JACOB, Yiddish writer and humorist, b. Sernik, province of Minsk, Russia, 1869. He attended a Heder until the age of twelve; until he was eighteen he worked as a village blacksmith. Then, moving to Odessa with his family, Marinov became a tailor. In 1890 he went to London, where he again worked as a tailor for two years, after which he came to the United States.

Settling in Boston for a short time, Marinov later moved to Denver, where he lived for thirteen years. While there he cooperated with Yehoash and others in organizing the Jewish Society for the Aid of Consumptives, and raised funds for the Society. His first published work was *Dos Hammer Lied,* which appeared in the *Arbeiter Zeitung,* and a sketch in *Emes* (1895). Later he wrote for the *Forverts, Zukunft, Yiddishe Velt* and other papers. Then he became connected with *Der Groisser Kibitzer,* and finally served as editor of the weekly *Der Groisser Kundes* (1909-27), a magazine of humor and satire which played a significant part, in the period before the first World War, in criticizing various tendencies in American Jewish life, such as assimilationist trends and political opportunism. *Der Groisser Kundes* not only attracted the best Jewish writers, but during its heyday, before the stoppage of immigration brought its decline and ultimately its disappearance, it had a circulation of 35,000.

In addition to writing his feuilletons and editing the magazine, Marinov wrote verse. He was also co-editor, with A. Voliner, of a three-volume anthology, *Humor un Satire,* and did many translations. A collection of his songs and ballads, *Spiel un Kampf,* was published in 1938. A Jewish resort, Kundesland, near Bergenfield, N. J., was named after *Der Groisser Kundes.*

I. ARONSON.

Lit.: Reisen, Z., *Lexikon fun der Yiddisher Literatur, Presse un Filologie,* vol. 2, cols. 333-37.

MARITIME PROVINCES, the name commonly given to the three maritime provinces of Canada, New Brunswick, Nova Scotia and Prince Edward Island. These three provinces, which are the smallest in Canada, occupy an area of 51,597 square miles and are situated on the Atlantic coast, bounded on the north by the St. Lawrence and the province of Quebec, on the west by Maine, on east and south by the Atlantic.

Jewish Communities and Statistics. The earliest Jews known to have settled in the Maritime Provinces of Canada were Nathan Green, Solomon Hart and Henry Levy, brothers-in-law who came to St. John in the province of New Brunswick from England in 1858. The census of 1871 showed forty-eight Jews living in the province of New Brunswick, but none in Nova Scotia or Prince Edward Island. By 1881 the number of Jews in the maritime provinces had increased to eighty-seven, and to 105 in 1891, taking a jump to 861 in 1901 and 2,419 in 1911. The Jewish population continued to increase after the first World War until it reached 3,425 in 1931, but decreased to 3,328 in 1931. The Jewish population of Nova Scotia in 1931 was 2,046, New Brunswick 1,262, Prince Edward Island 20.

The largest and oldest Jewish community in 1942 was in St. John, New Brunswick, which increased from thirty-four in 1891 to 848 in 1921, and fell to 683 in 1931. The first synagogue, known as the Ahavas Achim synagogue, was consecrated on January 11, 1899. The congregation was later known as the Shaarei Zedek. In addition to the synagogue there were, in 1942, a Talmud Torah, a Y. M. H. A., an Immigrant Aid Society which was founded in 1896, a Senior and Junior chapter of Hadassah, a Zionist Habonim lodge, and several Young Judea groups, besides a branch of the Canadian Jewish Congress.

The second largest Jewish community in the Maritime Provinces in 1942 was Halifax, in Nova Scotia, whose Jewish population increased from eighteen in 1891 to 582 in 1931, forming slightly less than 1 per cent of the total population. There were a synagogue and Talmud Torah in the city, Senior and Junior Hadassah chapters, a Young Judea group, a B'nai B'rith lodge and A. Z. A. chapter, a Y. M. H. A., Community Council and a local committee of the Canadian Jewish Congress. The Jewish Immigrant Aid Society, under the leadership of Charles Zwerling, has had a long and useful record of activity in view of the importance of Halifax as a port. Jewish communities in Nova Scotia in 1931 were Sydney (Jewish population, 425), Glace Bay (395), Yarmouth (167), New Waterford (80) and New Glasgow (53). Other Jewish communities in Nova Scotia with less than fifty Jews were Dartmouth (29), Amherst (24), Kentville (17), Bridgewater (15), Digby (15), Inverness (15), Dominion (13), Springhill (13), North Sydney (11), Stellarton (10), Sydney (10), Pictou, Westville, Antigonish, Louisburg, Port Hawkesbury, Truro, Bridgetown and Parrsboro. Jewish communities in New Brunswick according to the latest census were Moncton (164), Fredericton (125), Chatham (39), Woodstock (31), Campbellton (26), Bathurst (22), St. Stephen (19), Dalhousie (18), Newcastle (17), Edmundston (12), Grand Falls, Sackville and St. George. Of the twenty Jews in the island province of Prince Edward Island, 18 lived in the capital, Charlottetown.

The Jewish population of Nova Scotia in 1942 formed only four-tenths of 1 per cent of the total population of the province, and was exceeded by the population of French, German, Dutch, Negro and Indian origin. In New Brunswick the Jewish population formed only three-tenths of 1 per cent of the total population and was exceeded by the population of French, Dutch, German, Scandinavian and Indian origin. In Prince Edward Island the Jewish population was negligibly small, being only two-hundredths of 1 per cent of the population, and exceeded by the population of French, Dutch, German, Indian, Scandinavian, Syrian, Negro, Chinese and Italian origin.

Occupational Distribution. Out of every 100 Jews gainfully occupied in 1931 in the Maritime Provinces, seventy were engaged in merchandising, six in manufacturing industries, five in clerical occupations and five in the professions. Jewish fishermen, transport workers, unskilled laborers and insurance agents numbered two each, while farmers, construction workers and dry cleaners numbered one each out of every 100 Jews gainfully occupied. Among the total population of all origins in 1931, out of every 100 gainfully occupied twenty-eight were farmers, thirteen were unskilled laborers, eight were engaged in personal service, seven in manufacturing industries, seven in wholesale and retail trade, seven in transportation, five in the professions, five in fishing and hunting, five in mining, four in clerical occupations, four in construction trades, two in lumbering, and one each in civil service and electric power production.

See also: CANADA. LOUIS ROSENBERG.

Lit.: Rosenberg, Louis, *Canada's Jews. A Social and Economic Study* (1939); Sack, B. G., *The Jew in Canada* (1926).

Adolph Marix

MARIX, ADOLPH, American rear admiral, b. Dresden, Saxony, Germany, 1864; d. Gloucester, Mass., 1919. He was educated at the United States Naval Academy at Annapolis, Md., and entered the Navy as a midshipman in 1868. The following year he became an ensign. In 1870 he was promoted to the rank of master and assigned to special duty with an Arctic expedition. He was commissioned as a lieutenant in 1872 and assigned to the office of the judge-advocate-general.

In 1893 Marix was promoted to the captaincy of the battleship *Maine,* which he commanded till a few weeks before its mysterious explosion in the bay of Havana. Marix was recognized as the leading naval authority on maritime law of his time and hence was appointed judge-advocate of the investigation of the *Maine* disaster. It was the report of his findings, which placed all blame on the Spaniards, that directly precipitated the Spanish-American War. Later research cast doubt on the certainty of this charge but not on the honesty and efficiency of the investigation.

In 1908 President William Howard Taft appointed Marix rear admiral; he was the first Jew ever to attain that rank. He retired in 1910. He was a corresponding member of the American Jewish Historical Society, and evinced keen interest in the philanthropic and social work of the Jewish community.

MARK, GOSPEL OF, *see* GOSPELS.

MARK, AARON, journalist, b. Lomze, Poland, 1904; d. Vilna, 1938. He studied at a Yeshiva, and graduated from the University of Warsaw, where he specialized in literature, Slavic philology and history of art. In 1924 he taught at the Bialystok gymnasium; later he was editor of *Der Hammer,* a short-lived magazine published in Lomze, and a collaborator on the *Neier Leben* (Bialystok), *Literarishe Bletter* and other journals. Mark also wrote verse, and translated Romain Rolland's *Jean Christophe* into Yiddish (1927).

Lit.: Reisen, Z., *Lexikon fun der Yiddisher Literatur, Presse un Filologie,* vol. 2 (1928), col. 342.

MARK, YOODL, Yiddish philologist, b. Polonge, Lithuania, 1897. Upon graduating from the Gymnasium in Vilna, he enrolled for courses in history and philology at the University of St. Petersburg (1915-18). He also attended the Baron Günzburg courses. In 1917 Mark identified himself with the folkist movement. In 1919 he organized the Folkspartei in Libau, and was elected a member of the city council (of the Kehillah). In 1920 he took up residence in Vilkomir, Lithuania, where he helped found the Vilkomir Real Gymnasium, which remained for many years the only Yiddish Gymnasium in Lithuania. There he taught Yiddish and was director of the school. In 1923 he became general secretary of the Jewish National Council of Lithuania at Kovno. In 1927 he left for Riga, where he taught Yiddish methodology at the Yiddish Gymnasium and at the Pedagogic Courses.

In Latvia Mark was a leader of the Zisho (Central Yiddish School Organization). His first article appeared in *Nais* (1921), a Yiddish weekly published in Kovno. With Joseph Tchernichov he edited this newspaper in 1923. In 1926 he was its sole editor. From 1930 to 1932 he was co-editor of the *Folksblatt,* a Yiddish daily in Kovno; from 1932 to 1934 he edited it alone.

He emigrated to the United States in 1936, where he has continued active interest in the Yiddish schools. He has been closely associated with the Yivo (Jewish Scientific Institute), and since 1937 he has been a key member of its philological section. He contributed many articles on Yiddish grammar, language and philology to the various publications of Yivo, and in 1941 became editor of *Yiddishe Shprach,* a publication of the philological section of the Yivo. From 1939 he edited also the *Pedagogisher Buletin,* the first twenty-two issues of which were published by the Workmen's Circle; those of more recent date were issued by the Committee for Jewish Education, of which Mark is a member, as representative of the Yiddish schools.

He wrote the first Yiddish school grammar (Kovno, 1921; Berlin, 1923), and a pamphlet, *Die Einheitliche Folkshul* (1922). His translation of Thomas Mann's *Tonio Kroeger* (together with an essay on Mann) was published at Riga in 1930.

Lit.: Lehrer, L., in *Dos Neie Lebn* (1923); Kalmanovitch, Z., in *Nais,* No. 76; Zaretzki, A., in *Pedagogisher Buletin* (Kiever Lerer-Buro), No. 4; Rubin, I., in *Bicher-Velt* (1923).

MARKENS, ISAAC, historian, b. New York city, 1848; d. Newark, N. J., 1928. He was the son of Elias Markens, a linguist and orientalist. But Markens himself had little formal schooling, and entered business, acting as a commercial traveler and later doing stenographic work. In 1881 he started newspaper work by becoming assistant manager of the United Press Association. Later he was connected with the *New York Commercial Advertiser,* the *New York Star* and the *Mail and Express.*

While working for the *Mail and Express,* in the 1880's, Markens wrote a series of articles on "Hebrews in America," which were developed into book form in 1888. Several earlier studies of the subject had been made, but Markens was the first to undertake it on a comprehensive scale, and went to original newspaper material as well as entering into a great deal of personal correspondence to ascertain and substantiate his facts. Nevertheless, Markens' own untrained approach kept the book from achieving all its possible value, because he neglected to annotate it sufficiently.

Markens later became one of the country's most indefatigable researchers into Lincolniana. His *Lincoln's Masterpiece*, a study of the Gettysburg Address, appeared originally in 1913 and was later included in Emanuel Hertz's *Abraham Lincoln—the Tribute of the Synagogue* (1927). Markens became a close friend of Lincoln's son, Robert, and through him had access to usually restricted data. He also wrote *Abraham Lincoln and the Jews* (1900); *President Lincoln and the Case of John Y. Beall* (1911); *Why President Lincoln Spared Three Lives* (1911); *Manassas, an Israelite of Colonial Days* (1917); and *Origin of Famous Lincoln Sayings* (1918).

Lit.: Hertz, Emanuel, in *American Hebrew*, Sept. 14, 1928, pp. 594, 598-99; Kohler, Max J., in *Publications of the American Jewish Historical Society*, No. 32 (1931) 129-32.

MARKISH, PERETZ, Yiddish poet, b. Polonnoe, Volhynia, Russia, 1895. His father was an artisan. Markish, after a few years of study in a Heder, left home when he was eleven or twelve and joined the choir of the Berdichev Hazan (cantor). Later he lived in Odessa and took special courses at the university. After a short period of military service in 1916, he was wounded and discharged.

Markish's first poems were published in *Der Kempfer* (Ekaterinoslav, 1917), and in *Eigens*, an anthology (Kiev), in 1918. The following year a collection of his verses, *Shvellen*, appeared, and in 1920 the volumes *Stamm, Pust un Pass*, and *In Mitten Veg*. By this time he was known as one of the coterie of young Yiddish poets in Kiev whose work reflected the new tendencies in Jewish literature: themes, rhythms, experiences born out of the first World War, universal change, and pogroms.

Despite their personal familiarity with the events leading up to the Bolshevik revolution of 1917, many of these poets subsequently left Russia, Markish among them. From 1921 to 1926 Markish lived in various European countries outside of Russia, chiefly in Poland. His pogrom epic, *Die Kupe* (1921), evoked extensive and varied comment everywhere. He also collaborated in the editing of the *Khaliastre* almanacs (Warsaw, 1922; Paris, 1924).

In 1926 disappointment and chagrin at the hopeless condition of the Jews in Poland and the spread of anti-Semitism impelled Markish to return to Soviet Russia, where he soon became one of the outstanding Jewish literary personalities. His epic poem, *Brieder* (1927), combines the motives of the Russian civil war with the renascence of the toiling masses; *Farkleite Zieferblatt* (1929) is an even more candid acceptance of the Communist revolution. A series of plays was successful on both the Yiddish and Russian stages throughout the Soviet Union: *Nit Gedaiget* (1931), based on the yearning toward the soil on the part of the Jewish masses; *Finfter Horizont*, dealing with their absorption in industry; *Ver Vemen*, depicting the movement toward socialistic reconstruction among Jews; *Mishpoche Ovadis*, the only play dedicated to the intelligentsia. *Neitten Bekker*, a novel, dealt with the return of a Jewish worker from America to Russia and his assimilation in socialist constructive work.

After 1930, Markish became a more vigorous exponent of socially motivated viewpoints, and this zeal worked toward the retarding of his creative and poetical growth. He was active in Soviet public affairs, served as secretary of the Association of Jewish Writers, and was decorated by the government. In 1942 he was serving as reporter with the Soviet armies on the Russo-German front. I. Aronson.

Lit.: Reisen, Z., *Lexikon fun der Yiddisher Literatur, Presse un Filologie*, vol. 2 (1930), cols. 348-53.

MARKON, ISAAK DOW BER, scholar and author, b. Rybinsk-Volga, Russia, 1875. He studied from 1896 to 1901 in St. Petersburg and at the rabbinical seminary in Berlin. His dissertation, *Comparison of the Canonical Laws on Forbidden Marriages of Kindred of the Apostolic Church with those of the Talmud and the Karaites* (Russian), was awarded a prize by the University of Leningrad. Markon worked as librarian in the Imperial Public Library in Leningrad from 1901 to 1914, as instructor at the Academy of Oriental Lore from 1908 to 1911, as instructor in the lore of Judaism at the University of Leningrad from 1917 to 1920, and as associate professor at the White Russian University in Minsk from 1922 to 1924. From 1911 to 1917 he was member of the Learned Committee of the ministry for public instruction.

From 1926 to 1938 Markon lived in Germany, and for several semesters delivered guest lectures at the Berlin rabbinical seminary. In 1929 he became chief librarian of the library of the Deutsch-Israelitische Gemeinde in Hamburg. In the spring of 1938 he was among sixty Jewish Soviet citizens who were deported from Germany. He went to Amsterdam, Holland, where he worked until the invasion of the Low Countries in May, 1940. Markon escaped to England, and in 1942 was working at the Judith Montefiore College in Ramsgate.

Markon took an active part in the public life of Russian Judaism, serving on the board of directors of the Leningrad Jewish community and in the ORT Association. He was editor of the *Yevreiskaya Entziklopedia* for four years and for the German *Encyclopaedia Judaica* until 1937, edited the quarterly *Hakedem* from 1907 to 1912 in Hebrew and German, and the *Harkavy Jubilee Book* in collaboration with Baron Günzburg.

Of Markon's numerous publications, especially on the history of the Karaites, the following are noteworthy: *Texts and Researches in the Field of Karaite Marriage Law* (1908); "The Book of the Forbidden Degree of Relationship of the Karaite Moses Bashyatze" (in vol. 3 of the periodical *Hakedem*); "On the Mahzor according to the Ritual of Kaffa" (in the *Harkavy Jubilee Book*, 1908); "Daniel al-Kumisi" (in *Korrespondenzblätter der Akademie für die Wissenschaft des Judentums*, Berlin 1927); *Die Juden in Abessinien; Wesen, Entstehung und Entwicklung des Karäertums*.

Among many posts of honor he held the presidency of the association for the advancement of the Hebrew language, known as the Agudath Hobebe Sefath Eber.

MARKOWITZ, JACOB, physician and author, b. Bucharest, Roumania, 1901. He received his medical degree from the University of Toronto in 1923, and his Ph.D. degree from the same university in 1926. From 1927 to 1930 Markowitz worked at the Mayo Clinic in Rochester, Minn., first as assistant in experimental surgery and pathology and later as instructor in physiology. In 1930 he received the M.S. degree in experimental surgery from the University of Minnesota and became professor of physiology at Georgetown Medical School, where he remained until 1932. Then he was made research associate at Toronto University. Markowitz was the author of *Textbook on Experimental Surgery* (1937). In 1942 he was on leave from Toronto University and serving with the military forces outside of Canada.

MARKS, B. S., artist and communal worker, b. Cardiff, Wales, 1827; d. London, 1916. He studied art in his native city, and from the very first combined his interest in painting with communal activities by organizing drawing classes for artisans. Later he did portraits of King Edward VII (as Prince of Wales), of other members of the British royal family and of leading British citizens.

While in Cardiff, Marks was president of the Cardiff Hebrew Congregation and helped found the Cardiff and Ealing Public Libraries. Later, living in London, he continued his manifold activities in art and communal affairs. He was on the Committee of the Jews' Free School, of the Westminster Jews' Free School and the Bayswater Jewish Schools. He was also vice-president of the industrial committee of the Jewish Board of Guardians and was a pioneer in recommending training in drawing as a basis for technical work.

MARKS, DAVID WOOLF, rabbi and leader in Anglo-Jewish Reform Judaism, b. London, 1811; d. London, 1909. He was educated at the Jews' Free School in London, and after a period as teacher he went to Liverpool (1833) to become assistant reader and secretary of the Hebrew congregation there. In 1841 Marks was made senior rabbi of the newly-established West London synagogue of British Jews, and held this post until the end of 1895. A strong advocate of reform in Jewish ritual practice, Marks had the opportunity, during the sixty years of his administration in the West London synagogue, to effect many of the changes he urged. With his colleague, Albert Löwy, he prepared the Reform prayerbook. It was mainly as the result of his efforts that his synagogue was legalized for marriages.

Marks was Goldsmid professor of Hebrew at University College, London, from 1844 to 1898, and was dean of the college from 1875 to 1877. He was also for a time professor of Hebrew at Regent's Park Baptist College. He published three volumes of sermons (1851-54), and wrote the first half of *Memoir of Francis Henry Goldsmid* (1879). Marks was also a contributor to Smith's *Dictionary of the Bible.*

HARRY HANANEL MARKS (b. London, 1855; d. 1916) was a son of David Woolf Marks. He was the editor and publisher of *The Financial News* and also a Member of Parliament. After studying at the University College, London, and the Athénée Royale in Brussels, he lived in the United States from 1871 to 1873 as a journalist. After his return to England he served on the London County Council in 1889 and again in 1895.

Ernest Samuel Marks

From 1895 to 1900 Marks was a Member of Parliament for St. George, Tower Hamlets, and again from 1904 to 1910 for the Isle of Thanet Division of Kent. He was the author of *Leaves from a Reporter's Note-Book* (1881); *The Metropolitan Board of Works* (1888); and *The Case for Tariff Reform* (1905).

Lit.: *Jewish Year Book* (London), 1906-7, p. 374; *Central Conference of American Rabbis Year Book,* vol. 19 (1909) 66.

MARKS, EDWARD BENNETT, music publisher, b. Troy, N. Y., 1865. He studied at the College of the City of New York. In 1894 he entered the music publishing business as the organizer of the Joseph W. Stern and Company firm. He remained with the firm until 1925, when it was reorganized under his presidency and under his name. In 1942 he was still head of the firm. Marks was himself the composer of many popular songs, including *My Mother Was A Lady, December and May* and *Kaddish of My Ancestry.* In 1934 he published his memoirs, *They All Sang.* Marks served on President Franklin D. Roosevelt's council for coordination of industry in 1935 and 1936, and later on other commissions for fair trade practice.

MARKS, ERNEST SAMUEL, Lord Mayor of Sydney, b. West Maitland, New South Wales, Australia, 1872. He was educated in Sydney, and though he engaged in the wool and produce business, Marks early in his life became associated with athletic movements. From 1896 to 1933 he was honorary secretary of the Amateur Athletic Union of Australia, and for twenty-five years was president of the New South Wales Sports Club. Marks was a delegate to various Olympic games; in 1912 he served on the International Jury in the Stockholm games.

Marks also entered political life at an early age. He was one of the founders and president of the Darlinghurst Liberal and Reform Club. He was also president of the King Division of the Liberal and Reform party and director of the National Club. From 1927 to 1930 Marks represented North Sydney in the New South Wales Parliament. When the City Council was re-established in Sydney in 1930, Marks was made the first Lord Mayor. He was chairman of the United Charities of New South Wales, deputy chairman of the Australian Red Cross, chairman of the New South Wales division of the British Jewish War Memorial and honorary secretary of the New South Wales branch of the Anglo-Jewish Association. Marks wrote on municipal government, as well as on sport, for various publications. He was made a commander of the Order of the British Empire in 1938.

MARKS, SIR HENRY, public official in the Fiji Islands, b. Melbourne, Australia, 1861; d. Fiji Islands, 1938. Marks came to the Fiji Islands from Australia in 1881 and established a mercantile business. He later became interested in several other businesses in the British colony. From 1913 to 1929 he was Commissioner of Currency, served as a member of the legislative council for seven times, and was elected mayor of Suva, capital of the Fiji Islands, serving from 1926 to 1930. He was a member of the Executive Council by appointment of the Secretary of State. In 1918 King George V made him a Commander of the British Empire, and in 1933 knighted him for public services. Marks was granted the use of the prefix, Honorable, in Fiji for life, for his services while a member of the legislative council. He was Danish consul at Suva.

MARKS, HYMAN, merchant and early resident of Richmond, Va., date and place of birth unknown; d. Philadelphia, 1825. He was a well-known resident of the Virginia metropolis and is so mentioned in a petition to the Common Council of that city. Marks was among the signers of a petition to the legislature of Virginia for the incorporation of a bank in Richmond (1811). He belonged to Masonic fraternities both in Richmond and in Philadelphia, to which latter place he removed. While in Philadelphia he took an active part in the affairs of Congregation Mickve Israel, serving as its president from 1815 to 1818. An engraving of Marks, done by St. Memin in 1805, is in the possession of the American Jewish Historical Society.

Lit.: Ezekiel, H. T., and Lichtenstein, G., *The History of the Jews of Richmond from 1769 to 1917* (1917) 80, 82-83, 85, 130; *Publications of the American Jewish Historical Society,* No. 6 (1897) 110, 154; No. 19 (1910) 53, 62, 73, 93; Morais, H. S., *The Jews of Philadelphia* (1894) 45.

MARKS, JOSEPH, merchant of Philadelphia in the middle of the 18th cent. He was prominent socially and belonged to the famous City Dancing Assembly, organized in 1748, composed of the élite of Jewish society. Along with David Franks and Samson Levy, he was one of the subscribers to the first ball given by that social organization. In his capacity as merchant, Marks was the owner of at least six trading vessels, registered at the Port of Philadelphia, from 1743 to 1751. He appears to have been the largest ship owner in the Middle Atlantic States among the Jewish merchants of his time.

Lit.: Publications of the American Jewish Historical Society, No. 1 (1892) 284; No. 26 (1918) 235; Watson's Annals, vol. 1, p. 284.

MARKS, LEVY, merchant and patriot of the American Revolution. Prior to the War of Independence he resided at a place which he described in a newspaper advertisement (*Pennsylvania Packet,* March 11, 1776) as "that large convenient Inn," located on the banks of the river Schuylkill, about four miles from Philadelphia. He also owned 1,200 acres of land, divided into four tracts, situated on Wiconesco Creek in Lancaster County, which he likewise offered for rental or lease at the same time.

After his removal from his dwelling near Philadelphia (about April 1, 1776), Marks resided in Lancaster during the Revolutionary War. Together with Barnard Gratz, Joseph Simon and other prominent Jewish merchants, he subscribed, about September, 1777, to a fund for the hiring of "one or more proper persons to ride between Lancaster and General Washington's Army with and for intelligence." Another evidence of his espousal of the patriot cause is his taking of the oath of allegiance to the state of Pennsylvania, in 1779, thereby pledging himself to maintain the freedom and sovereignty of the United States.

Lit.: Publications of the American Jewish Historical Society, No. 1 (1892) 59, 88; No. 6 (1897) 56-57; No. 8 (1900) 148; No. 9 (1901) 30, 34, note; Morais, H. S., The Jews of Philadelphia (1894) 23.

MARKS, LIONEL SIMEON, engineer, b. Birmingham, England, 1871. After receiving his engineering degree in Birmingham in 1891 and his B.Sc. degree from London University in 1892, Marks came to the United States. For two years he did research at Cornell, then became instructor in mechanical engineering at Harvard. In 1900 he was made assistant professor at Harvard and in 1909 full professor; in 1942 he still held the latter post. In addition, Marks was from 1914 to 1918 professor at the Massachusetts Institute of Technology. He served on various government advisory boards. Among his published works was *The Airplane Engine* (1928). He was editor of the *Mechanical Engineer's Handbook.*

MARKS, LOUIS BENEDICT, consulting engineer and inventor, b. New York city, 1869; d. New York city, 1939. He was a brother of Marcus M. Marks. Marks received his M.A. degree from Cornell University in 1890. Three years later he invented the inclosed arc lamp, which was awarded the gold medal at the Paris Exposition of 1900. Subsequently he became internationally known as a consultant in problems of illumination. Marks designed the lighting systems for many important buildings in New York city, among them the General Post Office at Eighth Avenue and 33rd street and the guest hall at the College of the City of New York. During the first World War he served on the Navy Consulting Board. Marks was one of the founders (1905) of the Illuminating Engineering Society and its first president (1906). He also served as treasurer of the society from 1913 to 1928.

Lit.: Transactions of the Illuminating Engineering Society (1939) 1123-24.

MARKS, MARCUS M., communal leader and civic official, b. Schenectady, N. Y., 1858; d. New York city, 1934. He was the brother of Louis Benedict Marks. Marks graduated from the College of the City of New York in 1877, and entered the clothing business established by his father. He remained in the business until 1913, when interest in civic affairs prompted his retirement. In the interim he was for many years president of the National Association of Clothiers.

Marks was an arbitrator in industrial disputes, and served on President Theodore Roosevelt's Nobel Prize Committee of Nine on Industrial Peace. In 1913 Marks was elected president of the borough of Manhattan in New York city. During his incumbency, which lasted until 1917, he instituted welfare systems for civic employees and also established public markets. In 1917 Marks founded the National Daylight Saving Association, of which he was the first president. It was through the efforts of this organization that a system of daylight saving was inaugurated in the United States. Marks was a founder and first vice-president of the Educational Alliance, founder and (until 1913) president of the Tuberculosis Preventorium for Children in Farmingdale, N. J., a director of the Church Peace Union and of the Peace Congress. His communal activities during the last years of his life were centered on peace work.

MARKS, MICHAEL, early American merchant, b. London, 1761; d. Philadelphia, 1829. He came from England with his father, Henry Marks, one of the original members of Congregation Mickve Israel in Philadelphia and a contributor to its first synagogue building, in 1782. After his marriage in 1786 to Johaveth Isaacs of Newport, R. I. (whose father, Moses Isaacs, or Isaacks, served in the Continental army), Marks moved to Sing Sing (later Ossining), N. Y. According to the Marks family records, they had ten children, forty-one grandchildren and twenty-eight great-grandchildren, among whom are included the families of Allen, Mitchell, Hart, Davis and others. Marks' daughter Anna married Lewis Allen (1793-1841) and was a social worker in Philadelphia.

See also ALLEN, ANNA.

Lit.: Morais, H. S., *The Jews of Philadelphia* (1894) 242-43; *Publications of the American Jewish Historical Society*, No. 22 (1914) 182.

MARKS, MORRIS, judge, b. Prussia, 1847; d. Louisiana, 1912. He must have come to the United States in his early youth, for in 1868 he was already elected judge of the parish of Ascension, in the southern part of the State. The post-Civil War Period was a violent one in Louisiana; during the year in which Marks was elected, some 1,000 people were murdered, many of them during election conflicts between those who wanted to abide by the equality regulations of citizenship, regardless of race divisions, and those who did not. Marks, representing the Republican party, which was in favor of the equality attitude, was harassed in his town of Donaldsonville, and even warned not to return there, lest he be murdered. He testified to this effect in the post-election investigations of 1869.

In 1870 Marks was elected State Senator, but never took his seat. In 1878 President Ulysses S. Grant appointed him collector of internal revenue for the first district of Louisiana.

Lit.: Biographical and Historical Register of Louisiana, vol. 2, p. 237; *Supplemental Report of Joint Committee, General Assembly of Louisiana* (1869) 123-24.

MARKS, SAMUEL, South African mining and industrial pioneer, b. Sheffield, England, before 1850; d. Johannesburg, 1920. With Isaac Lewis, Marks entered business in Sheffield in the early 1860's. In 1868 they went to South Africa, and Marks was one of the young bloods whose introduction to the diamond industry was through work with pick and shovel. Subsequently, in partnership with Isaac and Barnett Lewis, Marks became one of the most active and wealthy mine-owners and industrialists of the developing continent. He followed the expansion of mining from Kimberley to Berberton to Witwatersrand, and aided the Transvaal with loans of £60,000 before gold was discovered. As a friend of Paul Kruger, Marks was later able to aid in the peace negotiations that ended the Boer War in 1902, and he remained a trusted adviser of the Boer people.

Marks was especially important in the industrialization of the Transvaal, where he not only owned coal, copper, gold and diamond mines, but established factories of many kinds for the utilization of natural resources in commercial products. He was interested also in scientific farming, and was the owner of model farms. Urged by General Jan Smuts and other South African leaders, Marks became a senator of the Union of South Africa; he was still serving in this post at the time of his death. Marks remained an active member of the Jewish community. He built the synagogue and Jewish school in Pretoria, and was one of the founders of an orphanage in Jerusalem.

Lit.: Herrman, Louis, *A History of the Jews in South Africa* (1935); *Jewish Chronicle* (London), Feb. 27, 1920, p. 14.

MARKS, SIMON, merchant and philanthropist, b. Leeds, England, 1888. Educated in the Manchester Grammar School, Marks entered the field of business after spending twenty-seven years in France and Germany, studying business methods. Together with his brother-in-law, Israel M. Sieff, he developed the chain store firm of Marks and Spencer which in 1942 was one of the foremost merchandising organizations in Great Britain with branches in all its principal cities. As chairman and managing director of Marks and Spencer, Marks achieved a position of preeminence in the British business world. In his career as a leader of British Jewry he devoted more than twenty-five years to the development of the Zionist Movement and every phase of the upbuilding of the Jewish homeland in Palestine.

He worked at the side of Dr. Chaim Weizmann, president of the Jewish Agency for Palestine, and was one of the most generous supporters of Palestine reconstruction. During the first World War Marks was one of the most vigorous leaders in the movement to bring about the issuance of the Balfour Declaration. Together with Sieff, Herbert Sidebotham and Harry Sacher, he organized the British Palestine Committee, which was instrumental in creating a better understanding of Zionist aims among members of the British Parliament and influential non-Jewish leaders in the government. The activities of this committee also helped to bring about a more favorable attitude among certain elements in British Jewish leadership.

In January, 1936, Marks visited the United States as a member of a three-man British delegation including Viscount Herbert Samuel and Lord Bearsted for the

Simon Marks

purpose of enlisting American Jewish cooperation in a large-scale emigration project in behalf of German Jewry. This plan called for the emigration over a period of four years of 100,000 Jews from Nazi Germany from the ages of seventeen to thirty-five. Half this number were to be settled in Palestine and the rest in other overseas countries.

Marks became a member of the World Council for German Jewry when that body was formed in 1936 to extend greater assistance to the victims of Hitlerism. In the course of his activities in behalf of Palestine, Marks served as president of the British Section of the Jewish Agency for Palestine, vice-president of the Zionist Federation of Great Britain, chairman of the Keren Hayesod of England, and president of the Emergency Jewish Colonization Association for Jewish Settlement in Palestine. In 1941 he was president of the Appeal Committee of the campaign for the Keren Hayesod in Great Britain.

In 1931, he was given the honorary D.Sc. degree by the University of London for his outstanding work in the field of marketing and distribution economics. During the second World War the government appointed him deputy chairman of the London and South Eastern Industrial Mobilization Committee.

MEIER STEINGLASS.

MÁRKUS, DEZSŐ, justice and codifier, b. Paks, Hungary, 1862; d. Budapest, 1912. He studied law at the University of Budapest and was admitted to the bar. In 1894 he was appointed to the codification division of the Hungarian ministry of justice. In 1911 he was named justice of the Hungarian Supreme Court. His numerous published works deal with problems of common and public law. Among these were: *Die ungarischen kirchenpolitischen Gesetze* (1895); *A holt-kézi törvények Magyarországon* (Laws of the mainmorte in Hungary; 1896); *A Pragmatica Sanctio lényege és annak helyzete a magyar közjogban* (The Essence of Pragmatica Sanctio and its Place in Hungarian Public Law; 1898); *A Corpus Juris Hungarici és a magyar magánjogi codificatio* (Corpus Juris Hun-garici and the Codification of Hungarian Common Law; 1899); *A választójog* (Suffrage; 1912). In addition to several law periodicals, he edited the *Magyar Jogi Lexikon,* an encyclopedia of Hungarian law in six volumes (1898-1907). Márkus was an advocate of woman's emancipation.

MARKUS, LUDWIG (LOUIS MARCUS), orientalist, b. Dessau, Germany, 1798; d. Paris, 1843. He studied medicine at the University of Berlin from 1818 to 1821, but discovered that he was more interested in philosophy and astronomy. He studied the latter subject so enthusiastically that he suffered a nervous breakdown. But he soon gave up his interest in astronomy and devoted all his time to the Society for Jewish Culture and Science. In the study of the science of Judaism and related subjects he at last found permanent intellectual satisfaction.

In 1825 Markus went to France, where he became friendly with Cuvier. Cuvier was instrumental in placing him as a teacher of German at the Royal College of Dijon in 1830, a post he held for eight years. It was about this time that he was absorbed in what was to be his life's work, a history of the foreign colonies of Abyssinia and especially of the Falashas. His flamboyant, eccentric temperament and the esoteric nature of his studies made him a well-known figure of the Parisian boulevards, and he was universally called "the King of Abyssinia," a title bestowed by his friend, Heinrich Heine. His last years were spent in an insane asylum.

Despite his erratic character Markus left a considerable body of work behind him, distinguished by scintillating style and penetrating scholarship. His books include *Storia dei Vandali* (1836) and *Géographie ancienne des Barbaresques* (1842). Unfortunately, his work on Abyssinia was never completed.

Lit.: Heine, Heinrich, *Gesammelte Werke,* vol. 14, pp. 179-202.

MÁRKUS, MIKSA, editor, b. Budapest, 1868. He was political columnist, as well as owner-publisher and chief editor, of the daily newspaper *Magyar Hirlap* until 1923, and editor of *Pesti Hirlap,* Hungarian daily of widest circulation, from 1926 on. He served faithfully the interests of his fellow newspapermen, endeavoring to raise their social status as well as improve their economic security. For distinguished public service he was made a councillor of the court by Francis Joseph I in 1908, and was awarded the Second Class Cross for Civic Merit by Regent Nicholas Horthy in 1928. He held offices, honorary and otherwise, in all associations of Hungarian newspapermen and authors. He also published the novels *Katalin asszony* (Madame Catherine); *Égszakadás-földindulás* (Cataclysm); and *Két galamb* (Two Doves). In 1940 Markus lived in retirement in the Hungarian capital.

MARLIBRUN (Meir le Brun), painter who lived in Billingsgate, London, in the latter half of the 13th cent. Marlibrun, considered the most notable artist of his time, was commissioned by Edward I to paint a picture of the Virgin for All-Hallows Church, Barking, in London ("Vade cras mane ad quendam Judaeum nomine Marlibrunum totius mundi sapientiorem picturae artificem apud Billingsgate, London, commorantem"). The picture became a great attraction for the faithful, who made pilgrimages to the shrine in order to view it, and for a long period it was regarded as one of the sights of London.

Lit.: Newcourt, *Repertorium Ecclesiasticum Parochiale Londinese* (1708), vol. 1, p. 765; Davis, Myer, in *Jewish Chronicle* (London), May 31, 1901, p. 18; Schwarz, Karl, *Die Juden in der Kunst* (1928) 114.

MARLOWE, CHRISTOPHER, non-Jewish dramatist, b. Canterbury, England, 1564; d. Deptford, England, 1593. A contemporary of Shakespeare, he has a place in the history of the Jews in Europe because of *The Famous Tragedy of the Rich Jew of Malta* which he wrote in 1589, seven years before the creation by Shakespeare of the figure Shylock. *The Jew of Malta,* as the play is commonly known, was acted first in 1592 and printed in 1633, forty years after its author's death. The name of Barabas evidently was chosen for the chief character because of the resemblance to Barabbas, the thief in the New Testament who was released in place of Jesus.

Barabas is depicted in the play the devil in human form, vengeful, cynical and unworthy of sympathy. When the Christian rulers of Malta confiscate his property and convert his house into a nunnery, Barabas persuades his daughter to become a nun in order that she may act as his tool in his personal war against the Maltese. He helps the Turks conquer the island, but afterwards betrays them to the Christians, whose gratitude Barabas wants to win in order to become master of the island. Having many murders on his conscience, the "Jew of Malta" is finally betrayed and ensnared by the Christians.

This play—one of Marlowe's inferior dramas—obviously purported to depict the Jew as the public of Elizabethan England liked to see him: a Machiavellian evildoer and atheist who is caught in his own trap at last. "It is," says Symonds, in *Shakespeare's Predecessors,* "as though Marlowe had raked the dregs and ransacked the dung and vices of humanity to justify the melodrama of the hero's cursing end." Moreover, this figure, almost inhuman in its intense lust for gold with which to acquire power, but still credible in the first act, becomes so exaggerated and unreal in the following acts, so much a mere Elizabethan stage monster, that there is some doubt whether the rest of the drama was written by Marlowe himself.

When Edward Alleyn, a noted actor of Marlowe's day, first performed the role of Barabas on the stage, he wore a long false nose to make the monster appear even more hideous. *The Jew of Malta* was a great success and the title role was often played by outstanding actors, such as Edmund Kean, who was of Jewish descent. But its success was gradually overshadowed by the more sympathetic, more genuine interpretation of the Jewish character in *The Merchant of Venice.*   ALFRED WERNER.

Lit.: Levi, Harry, *Jewish Characters in Fiction (English Literature)* (1911); Davidson, Israel, *Shylock and Barabas, A Study in Character* (reprint from *The Sewanee Review,* vol. 9, No. 3).

MARMER, HARRY AARON, tidal engineer, b. Proskurof, Ukraine, Russia, 1885. He was brought to the United States at the age of four. His early schooling was received at the agricultural school in Woodbine, N. J., and he received his B.Sc. degree from Rutgers College in 1907. After a short period as engineer in private enterprise, Marmer became a tidal computer for the United States Coast and Geodetic Survey in Washington (1907). He remained in that post until 1920, when he became assistant chief of the division of Tides and Currents of the department. In 1942 he still held this post. Marmer was the author of many professional studies and surveys of tidal problems, as well as of *The Tide* (1926) and *The Sea* (1930), both full-length books. He was also a contributing editor of the *Geographical Review.*

MARMOR, KALMEN (KARL), Yiddish journalist, scholar and critic, b. Maishagole, district of Vilna, Russia, 1879. He attended the government school affiliated with the Jewish Teachers' Institute of Vilna. For a short time he was also a student at Katzenelenbogen's School in Vilna. From 1893 to 1894, by special permission of the librarian, he made a study of the most significant works of Hebrew literature in the library of Strashun, in Vilna. Under the influence of the Hebrew prophets he became a socialist, abandoning his studies to work as a carver. He entered the underground radical movement and founded the Carvers' Union.

In 1899 Marmor resumed his education at the University of Bern, specializing in literature, art, philosophy, history and political economy. For three years he studied at the University of Freiburg (biological sciences, philosophy, Hebrew, Bible study and Assyriology). He traveled extensively in Italy, Greece, Syria, Palestine and Turkey. In protest against his assimilationist fellow students at the university, he became a Zionist and was a delegate to the Zionist congresses of 1901, 1903, 1905 and 1907. Marmor was one of the founders of the Velt-Farband Poale-Zion, lectured on Socialist Zionism throughout Europe, and was active in its congresses which were held in England, the United States and Palestine. In 1914 he became a member of the Socialist Party (in the United States), and in 1919 he formally renounced Zionism to become a communist (American Labor Alliance, which became the Worker's Party and later the Communist Party), leaving his position with the Chicago *Daily Forward.*

Marmor began his literary career in 1901 in *Der Yiddisher Arbeiter,* organ of the Jewish Bund. His translations, literary criticisms, literary-historical essays and columns have since been published in almost all the daily Yiddish newspapers, weeklies and literary magazines of England and the United States, also in numerous Hebrew periodicals. His name is closely associated with leftist Yiddish literature. He was one of the editors of the *Neie Velt,* official organ of the Yiddish section of the Communist Party; and when this weekly became a daily newspaper in April, 1922 (the *Freiheit*), he became one of its major contributors. In 1926 he was one of the editors of the *Hammer,* a leftist literary magazine.

In 1933 Marmor visited the Soviet Union, where he resided for three years as a research worker in the Kiev Institute for Yiddish Proletarian Culture.

Among his published works are: *Klasnkampfn in Altertum* (New York, 1933); *Dovid Edelshtat* (a com-

Alexander Marmorek

plete edition of his poetry, including a biography; Moscow, 1935); *Morris Wintchevsky* (the collected works of Wintchevsky, in 10 vols., with a biography; New York); a translation of Oscar Wilde's *De Profundis,* with an introduction and explanatory notes (New York, 1926).

Among the most significant series of articles by Marmor which were printed in the Freiheit was *Vegveiser der Mentshheit,* a series of biographies. He also wrote extensively on the history of the Yiddish press and literature in the United States.   N. B. MINKOFF.

Lit.: Reisen, Z., *Lexikon fun der Yiddisher Literatur, Presse un Filologie,* cols. 491-99; Maizl, N., in *Freiheit,* March 22, 1942; Rontch, I. A., *ibid.,* March 15, 1942.

MARMOREK, ALEXANDER, bacteriologist and Zionist leader, b. Mielnick, Galicia, 1865; d. Paris, 1923. He studied at the University of Vienna (M.D., 1887). At first an obstetrician, he turned to bacteriology. His investigations on the role played by the lymphatic glands in the body's defense against bacteria drew the attention of Pasteur to him. Marmorek was suggested for the post of assistant at the medical faculty of the University of Vienna, but was rejected because he was a Jew. Therefore in 1893 he went to Paris, where at the age of twenty-eight he was made research director (chef des travaux) at the laboratory of the Pasteur Institute. At thirty-three he was appointed to the Legion of Honor. Marmorek discovered a serum against streptococci with which he treated scarlet fever, and also became active in the fight against tuberculosis. After leaving the Pasteur Institute, he established his own laboratory and worked there until interrupted by the first World War.

As an Austrian he found himself an enemy alien in France in 1914. Not permitted to continue his researches, he served as physician with the Allied armies in Eastern Europe. After the armistice he returned to France, where he continued his research work, especially on typhus and diabetes.

Marmorek played a prominent role in the Zionist movement. As a student he was a member of the Kadimah, the first Zionist students' organization in Vienna. Like his brothers Oscar and Isidore an intimate friend of Theodor Herzl and Max Nordau, he participated in the Zionist congresses and was a member of the Greater Actions Committee of the Zionist Organization. He was also at the head of the French Zionist Federation, and founder of the Jewish Popular University in Paris and of the *Écho Sioniste,* organ of the French Zionists.

Marmorek was a spokesman of "political" Zionism, opposing "practical" Zionism and regarding the Balfour Declaration as politically inadequate, incapable of fulfilling the Zionist demand for the creation of a Jewish state.

Among his published works are *Versuch einer Theorie der septischen Krankheiten auf Grund experimenteller Untersuchungen* (Stuttgart, 1894) and *Le sérum antituberculeux, ses effets et son application* (Paris, 1910).

MARMOREK, OSCAR, architect and Zionist leader, b. Skala, Galicia, 1863; d. Vienna, 1909. He was a younger brother of Alexander Marmorek and, like him, a member of the Kadimah, Zionist students' organization. He constructed various exhibition buildings in Vienna and Budapest as well as synagogues. At the first Basel Zionist Congress, in 1897, he was elected to the Lesser Actions Committee of the Zionist Organization, to which he belonged for several years. In 1901, at the fifth congress, the fourth to be held in Basel, he proposed the establishment there of a Zionist Congress Home, plans for which he had prepared. In the following year he took part as an expert on colonization in the El Arish expedition which, however, after a careful survey, rejected the Anglo-Egyptian offer of Jewish mass settlement in this district. Herzl modeled (in his novel *Altneuland*) the figure of the architect Steineck after his friend Oscar Marmorek.

MARMORSTEIN, ARTHUR, theologian and historian, b. Miskolcz, Hungary, 1882. In 1912 he was appointed lecturer in Bible and Talmud at Jews' College, London. Besides numerous articles in learned periodicals, he published: *Studien zum Pseudo-Jonathan Targum* (1905); *Talmud und Neues Testament* (1908); *Religionsgeschichtliche Studien* (1910-12); *The Doctrine of Merits in Old Rabbinical Literature* (1920); *The Old Rabbinic Doctrine of God* (1927); *Tannaitische Midraschen* (Stuttgart, 1933; in collaboration with Gerhard Kittel); *Die Tosefta* (Stuttgart, 1933; in collaboration with Kittel and Karl H. Rengstorf).

MARONI, DAVID JACOB, rabbi, b. Reggio Emilia, Italy, 1810; d. 1888. He became rabbi in Florence in 1860. Under the influence of Munk's French translation of Maimonides' *Moreh Nebuchim,* Maroni wrote an Italian translation, with notes (three parts were printed from 1871 to 1876). In 1874 he published an edition of Moses Zacuto's *Yesod Olam.*

MAROR (bitter herbs), *see* SEDER.

MAROSVÁSÁRHELY, *see* TARGUL MURES.

MARR, HEINRICH, actor and stage manager, b. Hamburg, Germany, 1797; d. Hamburg, 1871. In 1813 he enlisted as a volunteer in the war against the French oppressors, and in 1815 made his debut on the stage. In the following years he played in Lübeck, Hannover and Leipzig, and from 1827 to 1837 was in Brunswick, where he was the first to play the part of Mephistopheles in Goethe's *Faust* in Germany, acquiring a mastery in character roles equalled by few actors. After a stay at the Burgtheater in Vienna, he became general stage manager in Leipzig (1844), then in Weimar, and, until his death, at the Thalia Theater of Hamburg. In 1865 he celebrated the golden jubilee of his connection with the stage.

Lit.: Merbach, *Heinrich Marr* (1926); *Allgemeine Deutsche Biographie*, vol. 20, p. 417 et seq.

MARRANOS, general term for those Jews who were compelled to renounce their religion, as well as for their descendants, who in many cases secretly practised the rites of Judaism for centuries. The term is probably derived from a Spanish word meaning "swine," which was derisively applied to the converts; there are other proposed derivations, such as Maranatha, "accursed," or the Arabic *murain*, "hypocrite," which are less likely. The Hebrew equivalent of Marranos is *'anusim*, "those compelled."

1. The Christian Marranos. a. France and Spain. The first examples of mass forced conversions of Jews occurred in Visigothic Spain in the 7th cent.; such converts, although baptized, were not regarded as having equal rights, and were zealously supervised by both church and state. Another wave of forced conversions resulted from the First (1096) and Second (1146) Crusades; but the authorities frowned upon such conversions and most of the baptized Jews returned to Judaism. On the other hand, there was an increase in forced conversions in southern France, Italy and Spain in the 13th and 14th cent.; these new converts were not permitted to return to the religion of their fathers, and were despised and suspected by the Christians because of their origin and because it was felt that their fidelity to Christianity was only slight.

The Marranos became a definite mass phenomenon in Spain as the result of the compulsory baptisms enforced in the year 1391. They were officially designated as Conversos or Cristianos Nuevos; the term Marranos arose in the 16th cent. as an expression of derision, but is never used in official documents. The renegades in Spain sought in part to assimilate themselves quickly into Christian society, obtained high posts in church and state, and occasionally persecuted their former coreligionists. Nevertheless they were hated by the Christians and repeatedly fell victim to bloody excesses.

After many generations the love for Judaism still stirred within many Marranos. The bulk of them, who were to be found in rather large numbers especially in Andalusia, in the vicinity of Toledo and in Barcelona, practised Jewish rites in secret. The Inquisition, which was newly organized in 1481, was intended to suppress the remnants of the old faith among the Marranos. However, the proceedings of the Inquisition showed clearly, for the first time, the strong attachment of the Marranos to Judaism, how

Inscription on an ancient Marrano synagogue

deeply the Jewish religion and traditions were rooted in their hearts, and with what constancy they kept alive within themselves the belief in an immediate Messianic deliverance. The expulsion of the Jews from Spain in 1492 did not accomplish its purpose of severing the connection of the Marranos with Judaism as a whole.

On the contrary, the number of the Marranos on the Pyrenean peninsula increased significantly as a result of the compulsory baptisms which took place in Portugal in 1497. The assimilation of the Marranos from the religious and social point of view was a task for whose fulfillment the Inquisition and the state in Portugal and Spain strove; it was three centuries before they finally achieved success. Moreover, during the 16th and 17th centuries groups of Marranos emigrated successively to North Africa, Italy and Turkey for the purpose of returning to Judaism there. In Bordeaux and Bayonne, France, there arose small communities of Marranos which openly professed Judaism at the end of the 17th cent. Amsterdam became the greatest Marrano center, followed by Hamburg and London. Marranos sought refuge also in the colonies of Spain, Portugal and Holland in the Americas and elsewhere.

FRITZ BAER.

b. Portugal. Whereas in Spain, in the course of the centuries, the last traces of the Marranos disappeared, considerable numbers of such secret Jews continued to live in the northern provinces of Portugal. These groups, even up to the present day, have continued to maintain a rather close connection with one another. These secret Jews, who are recognized as

A Marrano home in Villarinho, Portugal

A group of Marrano Jews and their families in 20th cent. Portugal

such by their non-Jewish neighbors, have lost every connection with the Jewish people and the Jewish faith, and have actually reached the point where they regard the customs which have been handed down among them as the entire content of Judaism, and the secret practice thereof as the essential constituent of their religion. Besides the Sabbath they still observe the Passover festival and Yom Kippur, but they celebrate these holidays on other days than those fixed by the Jewish calendar. This they do in order to divert attention from themselves. They know of no other Jewish holidays, and have only a few ritual customs which they practise. Among these Marranos the Hebrew prayers have been totally lost, but they still possess a few Portuguese prayers in which several Hebrew phrases occur in garbled form. In general, their knowledge of Judaism is extremely limited, and for the most part the practice of their religion, which has a strong admixture of superstition, is confined to the women. Although the Portuguese Marranos attained to religious freedom as a result of the revolution of 1910, they have not availed themselves of this opportunity of openly avowing their affiliation with Judaism; on the contrary, the religious freedom which has prevailed in Portugal since then has resulted in a rapid dissolution of the old limitations which had until then kept them within their Crypto-Jewish confines. Their number, which is alleged to be about 10,000 families, is not known with definiteness, since there is no longer any border line between those who still adhere to Judaism

and those who have preserved only a vague memory of their Jewish past.

The Marranos of Belmonte form a somewhat special group among the Portuguese Marranos. These pride themselves on being descended directly, and with no admixture of foreign blood, from the old Portuguese Jews. Yet it is quite possible that many cases of intermarriage with the Portuguese Christians took place, and such intermarriages occur even today, and have occurred ever since Portugal became a republic.

Despite the keen vigilance of the Inquisition among the New Christians of Belmonte (as in the neighboring New Christian communities of Covilhã, Caria, Funão, and Idanha-a-Nova), actual remnants of the Jewish services have been preserved. Thus, for example, the Sabbath candles are lighted, and Yom Kippur is observed as a fast day; on the eve of that day candles are lighted in memory of the dead. Passover is more generally observed; no kind of Hametz (leaven) is consumed as food, and only Matzoth (unleavened bread) are eaten. In particular, the Belmonte Marranos strictly refrain from eating swine flesh on the Sabbath and holidays. The Jewish form of the marriage ceremony has also been retained ("Em nome de Deus de Abrahão, Isaac e Jacob eu vós uno; cumpri vos a sua benção"; In the name of the God of Abraham, Isaac and Jacob I unite you; I commend you to His benediction). A few mourning customs likewise are preserved, such as the "Taharah," or washing of the corpse, and the burning of the light for the dead during the first week of mourning. The use of the Hebrew language has practically disappeared among the New Christians of Belmonte as the result of the prohibitions of 1497; only the sentence *'Adonai Sebaoth male (melo) kol ha'aretz kebodo* (The Lord of Hosts, the whole earth is full of His glory) has been retained in the ritual.

In recent years, as a result of the revival of Jewish consciousness in some of these Marranos and their connection with those Jews who profess their faith publicly, a certain interest in them has been manifested among world Jewry. This is due chiefly to the efforts of Samuel Schwarz, a Jewish mining engineer from Galicia who, a resident of Portugal, took steps to bring to them anew the message of historic Judaism.

An appeal from the Jewish community of Lisbon to spread Judaism among the Marranos, especially through

Modern Marranos at Villarinho, Portugal

Young Marrano couple of the Balearic Islands

the establishment of a school for their children, induced the Alliance Israélite Universelle, the Anglo-Jewish Association and the Spanish and Portuguese Community in London to make inquiries through Lucien Wolf into the religious conditions and needs of the Marranos. The result was the institution of an international committee for the Portuguese Marranos in London, which assumed as its task that of facilitating the return of the Marranos to Judaism. The first act of the Committee was the creation of a Jewish religious center, "Mekor Hayim," in Oporto, the center situated nearest to the settlement of the Marranos, under the direction of Captain Arthur Carlos de Barros Basto (Ben Rosh), the first Portuguese Marrano openly to profess Judaism in that country within the last 150 years. A Jewish community, Pidyon Shebuyim, was founded also among the Marranos in Braganza in 1928, and one in Covilhã in 1929. A Portuguese Jewish monthly, *Halapid* (The Torch), edited by Barros Basto, has been published in Oporto since April, 1927, for the purpose of spreading among the Marranos the knowledge of traditional Judaism.　PAUL GOODMAN.

c. Balearic Islands. The term Chuetas ("porkeaters") was given to the Marranos of the Balearic Islands, who were forcibly baptized in 1391 and after. They were called by this derisive name because they ate pork publicly while secretly remaining Jews. In 1488, when the Inquisition was established on Majorca, a general amnesty was granted to these Crypto-

Jews and about 700 Chuetas were taken back by the church upon the payment of a heavy fine. In 1509 several members of the community were discovered secretly practising the Jewish faith, and were burned at Palma. In 1679 a community of about 200 Jews, consisting mainly of bankers and business men, were discovered practising Judaism covertly at Palma de Majorca; their property was confiscated and many of them were imprisoned. In 1691, when most of the members of the community attempted to escape on a British vessel hired for this purpose, they were caught; more than fifty of them, including their leaders, Rabbi Raphael Valles, his pupil Rabbi Benito Terongi, and the latter's sister Catalina, were burned at the stake, while the others were imprisoned and their property confiscated.

In the 20th cent. the Chuetas, in contrast to the Marranos in Portugal, have completely lost all connection with the Jewish religion, even in secret. However they had so long been forced to live in a separate quarter and to endure the ostracism of the Christians that they remained a class apart. It was not until 1782 that the separate quarter was abolished, and not until 1785 were they declared eligible for military service and public office. Though they have increased in wealth and position, they have still been subject to social stigma and they suffered severely after the Spanish Civil War of 1936 to 1939.　NICHOLAS SARGOLOGOS.

2. The Mohammedan Marranos (Pseudo-Mohammedans). Despite the provision of the Koran that Jews were to be accorded toleration, Mohammedans of a non-orthodox trend often compelled them to embrace Islam. However, since the Moslems did not establish an Inquisition and since they observed the inviolability of the family and home, which remain strictly secluded in the Orient, the Jews, despite their compulsory profession of Islam, were able, with a

Marrano vinegrowers

little precaution, to follow the precepts of the Jewish religion and even to study Torah.

Compulsory conversion to Islam was not of long duration. The first Jewish Pseudo-Mohammedans, as far as is known, were those of Egypt during the persecutions of Caliph Hakhim (1008-20). In 1146 Abd el Mumin, the victorious leader of the fanatical sect of the Almohades, compelled the Jews of Morocco, and later those of Andalusia, to accept Islam. A similar fate overtook the Jews of Yemen about 1172. Most of these Jews returned to Judaism after the persecutions had ceased.

Jews were occasionally converted by force to the Shiite form of Islam prevalent in Iran. Thus about 1840 a number of Jews were compelled to adopt Islam in Khorasan. About 2,000 of their descendants were living in Meshed in the 20th cent. They live within their homes in accordance with Jewish customs; on the Sabbath only minor children remain within the stores, and secluded Sabbath services are held. Their Judaism is an open secret, exposing them now and then to revilings and even to menaces. About twenty-five families of these Crypto-Jews emigrated to Jerusalem, where they openly returned to Judaism.

See also: BRAZIL; CHILE; INQUISITION; SPAIN; PORTUGAL.   ABRAHAM JAKOB BRAWER.

Lit.: Roth, Cecil, *A History of the Marranos* (1932); Braunstein, *The Chuetas of Majorca* (1936); Zimmel, H. J., *Die Marranen in der rabbinischen Literatur* (1932); Schwartz, S., *Os Cristãos-Novos em Portugal no sécolo XX* (1925); Baer, F., *Die Juden im christlichen Spanien* (1929); Farinelli, A., *Marrano: storia di un vituperio;* Roth, Cecil, "The Religion of the Marranos," *Jewish Quarterly Review,* New Series (1931); *Marranos in Portugal,* report of the Portuguese Marranos Committee (1938); Wolf, Lucien, *Report on the "Marranos" or Crypto-Jews of Portugal* (1926).

MARRIAGE. Table of Contents:

I. In Bible Times. A number of Biblical scholars have maintained that originally the husband lived in the wife's community under a system known as "matriarchate" or "mother-right." The transition to father-right, where the man is the head of the household, is explained by the hypothesis of "marriage by capture." However, as E. Crawley (*The Mystic Rose,* 2nd ed., 1927, vol. 2, p. 95) says: "Few theories of primitive society have had such a vogue as that of marriage by capture, yet few theories have been built on such slender foundations. The tinge of romance belonging to the hypothesis has no doubt something to do with its popularity."

Actually there is no direct evidence in the Bible to show a condition of marriage by capture, and indeed, it is questionable whether such an institution was ever found in any society. (Jacobson, David, *Social Background of the Old Testament,* chap. 2). According to

the Bible, betrothal was legally effected by the payment on the bridegroom's part of money or goods, known as *mohar,* to the parent or guardian of the bride. The money or goods may be looked upon either as the purchase price or as the wealth which the bride brought to her new home. There is little evidence, however, that the wife was actually bought like a chattel from the family. It is true that an impecunious groom might serve the family of his wife or intended wife (cf. *Gen.* 29:19-30; *Ex.* 2:21; *Josh.* 15:16-19; *Judges* 1:12-15; *I Sam.* 17:25; 18:25-27; *II Sam.* 3:14) or that he might offer payment of goods to the custodians of the girl (*Gen.* 34:12; *Ex.* 21:7; 22:15-16; *Deut.* 22:28-29; *Ruth* 4:5, 10). However, the bride usually brought to her new home goods of such value that one is led to the conclusion that the original payment of goods or services was for the purpose of providing the bride with wealth.

In ancient Israel, the head of the family chose the bride for his son; as for his daughter, he accepted on her behalf the choice made by the bridegroom's father. It was only exceptional that the daughter was consulted. Among the Semites generally it seems to be a rule that a man has a prior right to the hand of his father's brother's daughter. In the Old Testament a number of cousin marriages are recorded. Esau married Basemath, the daughter of his father's brother Ishmael (*Gen.* 36:3). Isaac married Rebekah, the daughter of his paternal uncle's son (*Gen.* 24:15). Jacob married Rachel and Leah, his mother's brother's daughters (*Gen.* 28:2). There was a distinct desire to marry within the group. Thus, Abraham expressly enjoined his servant to seek out a wife for his son, Isaac, out of his own country and kindred (*Gen.* 24). On the other hand, marriages outside the Israelitic group were sometimes regarded as quite natural. When marriage with an alien was interdicted, it was because of religious, not ethnic, objections (cf. *Deut.* 7:4: "For he will turn away thy son from following Me, that they may serve other gods"). Even *Judges* 3:6 and *Gen.* 38:2 regard alliances with Canaanites and other foreign groups as quite natural. Ruth the Moabitess is included in the genealogy of David (*Ruth* 4:22); and David himself married a daughter of the king of the Geshurites (*II Sam.* 3:3). Nevertheless, *Deuteronomy* forbids any marital alliances with Canaanites or other heathen peoples (*Deut.* 7:1-3; 23:4; cf. also *Ex.* 34:15-16). Exceptions are made for humanitarian reasons in the case of foreign women taken in war (*Deut.* 21:10-14).

That the marriage regulations of *Deuteronomy* were not always observed in practice may be seen from *Ezra* 9 and 10; yet, according to *Ezra,* as in *Gen.* 26:34-35; 27:46; 34:22; and *Judges* 14:3, marriage with aliens was condemned for religious reasons only.

Within the group certain close marriages were sanctioned. Besides the levirate marriage, marriage between uncle and niece was permitted, but not between aunt and nephew. *Lev.* 18:18 prohibits marriage with a wife's sister during the lifetime of the wife, but Jacob (*Gen.* 29:15-30) married Leah and Rachel. The Old Testament marriage prohibitions are found in *Deut.* 23:1; 27:20, 22-23; and *Lev.* 18; 20:11-21. In addition to these forbidden marriages of close relations, there are marriage regulations applying to the divorced woman, the widow and the priest. A divorced woman who has remarried may not return to her former husband even if the second husband is dead (*Deut.* 24:4). The widow may remarry only after she has been refused in the levirate ceremony (*Gen.* 38:9-12; *Deut.* 25:5-10; *Ruth* 3:13). The priest is forbidden to marry a harlot, a profaned, or a divorced woman (*Lev.* 21:7).

In ancient times polygamy was practised, although probably the bulk of the population was monogamous. Yet this, no doubt, was due to economic considerations. The kings certainly had more than one wife (*II Sam.* 5:13; *I Kings* 11:1-3; cf., however, *Deut.* 17:17). A number of the wealthy, it seems, were monogamous. Thus Nabal (*I Sam.* 25:3) and the Shunammite woman's husband (*II Kings* 4:8-9) had but one wife. The creation story in *Gen.* 2:24 seems to imply a condition of monogamy. However, *Deut.* 21:15 assumes that a man may have at least two wives. Concubinage was much practised. The general tendency is that polygamy was replaced by monogamy as social life became more complicated and competitive, even though the desire for numerous offspring was a motive of great compulsion in early Israel.

See also: DIVORCE; FAMILY AND FAMILY LIFE; LEVIRATE MARRIAGE; MATRIARCHATE; PATRIARCHATE; WIDOW.

DAVID JACOBSON.

II. In Rabbinical Law. 1. Introduction. Since the family was and is the foundation of the Jewish social structure, it was natural that the institution of marriage should have received particular attention in Jewish law. According to Judaism, marriage is not a rite but a contract; yet as a contract it is of such supreme importance that it is given the title of "sanctification" (*kiddushin*) and is supported by the loftiest ideals and the most exact provisions and regulations. Thus the rabbinical law of marriage has not only all the safeguards surrounding a contract but also a special religious character; the formula of marriage, which is purely legal, is surrounded by benedictions that invoke the blessing and sanction of God. While the marriage contract, like any other contract, can be dissolved, this can be done only under certain special conditions which are based on due regard for the proper interests of all the parties involved.

The marriage law as stated in the Mishnah is a complete summary of rabbinic law as it existed in the time of the Jewish state. Later on, when the Jewish people lost its independence, and the application of the Jewish law was limited along certain lines, especially as to marriage, there arose the necessity for new pronouncements on the conditions of the marriage law. These are taken up in the discussions in the Talmud, which also further elaborates the rules laid down in the Mishnah. The third division of the Mishnah, Nashim, treats particularly of the regulations of the Jewish law of marriage; five tractates—*Yebamoth, Kethuboth, Sotah, Gittin* and *Kiddushin*—are solely concerned with this branch of Jewish law.

Jewish marriage law shows an explicit tendency to elevate marriage from the plane of private contract law to that of morality. Marriage is regarded as a social provision of mankind, its purpose being to discourage purely human desires and to contribute to the advancement of the family, the tribe and the nation. In contrast to the Greek and Roman conception, which saw in marriage only a valuable means of increasing the national strength, and accordingly sometimes permitted the father to expose his child, or the state to kill a monstrosity, Jewish law emphasizes the moral principle, lays stress on personal rights, and forbids the father to kill his child. The moral implications in the Jewish concept of marriage arose naturally since Judaism recognizes no separation of government and morality. The prophets regarded a marriage based on moral principles as a symbol of the close connection of God and Israel (as in *Hosea* 2:21-22). Judaism as a whole had little regard for celibacy, and the sect of the Essenes, which rejected marriage in order to lead a life of austerity and piety, failed to interest Jewry as a whole and was later absorbed into Christianity.

Since marriage means the founding of a home, it was naturally observed with great festivity and joy. Marriage was called "the building of joy"; the Talmud calls the child the staff upon which the mother can lean in her old age. Jewish tradition has handed down many injunctions regarding the choice of a life companion. Thus, one should not take a husband or wife without the consent of one's parents; in Biblical times parents were the matchmakers, although marriage without this would be legal. The married couple should, as far as possible, be of the same age. Jewish writings sharply emphasize the necessity of care in entering marriage, in order that a harmonious life may follow and that the children may be educated with proper cooperation. Especial weight was laid upon purity of blood and distinguished ancestry. At times this went so far that some, out of fear of being sullied, refused to marry. Great emphasis was laid also upon the virginity of the bride, since this was deemed a guarantee of the moral purity of marriage and to exclude any other individual interests. Virgins, therefore, received a preference, not only in regard to the wife's marriage portion (Kethubah) but also in the wedding ceremonies, where a virgin bride was distinguished by a special veil and flowing hair. Children were brought before the virgin bride, and were even permitted to testify to the fact of the wedding in later years, because the ceremonies were so impressive as to remain firmly fixed in their memories (*Keth.* 2:1).

2. Historical Development. Biblical law was at first based on polygamy, which was the usual form of marriage in the Orient. This institution was in all probability due to the economic conditions of early times, which placed an unmarried woman in a precarious position and made it necessary for her to have a protector. Thus polygamy was a counteracting influence against sexual license. Even the Levirate marriage, that of the brother of a deceased man with his childless widow, assumes this polygamy; for this duty is obligatory even on the brother who is already married. Biblical law sought to prevent many evils which might result from polygamy; thus, for instance, marriage with two sisters at the same time was forbidden (*Lev.* 18:18). The rights of the first-born of the first wife, who is very plainly called "the hated," might not be lessened in favor of the son of the second, or "the beloved" (*Deut.* 21:15-17). Polygamy became gradually less and less prevalent among Jews, and it was finally virtually abolished by Rabbi Gershom ben Judah of Worms in 1040.

The Biblical law also recognized concubinage as a special form of polygamy. The legal position of the concubine (*pilegesh*) was distinguished from that of the wife proper only in reference to the form of the marriage ceremony and her monetary claims.

3. Fitness for Marriage. As marriage takes place in the form of a contract in rabbinical law only those who possess the ability to make a contract were eligible to enter into it; therewith all are excluded who are unable, mentally or physically, to express their will, especially the deaf and dumb, the mentally incompetent, and minors (*heresh shoteh vekatan*). The deaf and dumb were, however, enabled by a regulation of the Mishnah (*Yeb.* 14:1) to contract marriage if they could make themselves understood in the sign language.

Impotence is an absolute hindrance to marriage; eunuchs and castrates could therefore not marry (*Deut.* 23:2). Tumtums, that is, those whose genitals lay so deep that their sex could not be distinguished, could marry only after the exact certification of their sex.

4. Impediments to Marriage. There were two sorts of impediments to marriage: permanent and temporary.

A. Permanent Impediments to Marriage. *a. Marriage of Relatives.* The first possible bar to marriage was close relationship. Sexual intercourse with certain blood relations or those related indirectly by marriage is forbidden in *Lev.* 18 and 20. The degrees of relationship which debar relatives from marrying are the same for everyone; in contradistinction to the law of the Catholic church, Jewish law permits no dispensations or exceptions.

The Bible gives no reasons for this ban on marriage between blood relatives or those indirectly related by marriage. Some trace the reason to natural laws; yet civilized nations of antiquity like the Egyptians, Greeks and Persians did not have this prohibition. The best reasons are those given by Saadia and Maimonides, who believe that their purpose was the maintenance of chastity and morality within the family, and thus the uniting of all the members into a close union without sexual or erotic relationships.

b. Specific Prohibitions of Marriage on the Ground of Morality. Another group of prohibitions of marriage is intended to preserve the purity of marriage and the requirement of chastity. These include the following laws:

A husband might not remarry his divorced wife, in case she had been married again and had been set free either by the death of her second husband or by divorce (*Deut.* 24:4).

A wife who had been guilty of adultery might neither continue in her marriage nor marry the adulterer after she had been divorced.

In order to avoid suspicion, a woman was not permitted to marry any one who acted as her representative in a divorce case, or who was the only witness to her husband's death (*Eben Haezer* 12:1).

c. Religious and Moral Prohibitions. According to Jewish law, some persons were forbidden to marry even before they are born. The principal example of this is the Mamzer, or child of a forbidden marriage; such a person could not contract a marriage, and the prohibition extended to the tenth generation and beyond. The same ban applied to the foundling and

to the Shethuki, a child whose father was not known. On the other hand, there was no prohibition of the marriage of children born of a union which had not been contracted according to the rabbinical ritual.

The Mosaic law forbade also intermarriage with the Canaanites. This prohibition was later extended to all foreigners, and all mixed marriages were forbidden. However, there was no objection to marriage to a proselyte from another nation. The only exception was the Gibeonites, and their descendants, the Nethinim. In the case of male Ammonites and Moabites, and both male and female Egyptians and Edomites, marriage was not permitted with Israelites until their third generation (*Deut.* 23:4-9); however, these restrictions were later annulled (*Yad.* 4:40). No marriage could take place between Israelites and Canaanite slaves, but after their manumission they were considered to be Jews in every sense.

Jewish law knows of no marriage that is prohibited because of difference of rank. On the other hand, the priests had special marriage restrictions of their own, in addition to those for all Jews.

B. Temporary Impediments to Marriage. Certain impediments were valid only for a certain period, after which they were no longer in force. Thus a widow or divorcee might not remarry within ninety days after the death of her husband or the serving of the bill of divorce (Get). The object of this law was to avoid uncertainty as to paternity. A widow or divorcee who was nursing a child might not marry until the child was twenty-four months old—a period that was based on the prevailing custom of nursing a child for two years (*Yeb.* 42a). This point was frequently discussed in the responsa literature of the last few centuries, as cases had to be handled individually, and in many cases the prohibition could be removed.

In its regulations concerning divorce, the Jewish law fixes no especial period of waiting. On the other hand, a widower may not remarry within the thirty days of mourning prescribed by the religious law, but must wait until three festivals have passed before he can take another wife (*Yoreh Deah* 392:2). However, in case he has small children who need a mother's care, he may remarry sooner.

If two successive husbands of a woman die, and their death is not a matter of accident, she may not marry a third time, because the fate of her two former husbands is an unhappy presage of what may happen (*Yeb.* 64b); in post-Talmudic times this hindrance to marriage was no longer regarded as compulsory.

A woman already married might not take a second husband. In early times, a married man could take an additional wife; in modern usage, except in countries allowing polygamy, as in Asia and Africa, he is prohibited by the ban of Rabbi Gershom. In all ages, however, a woman could be married only to one man at a time; consequently she can marry again only after divorce or the death of her husband. Since, according to Jewish law, it is the husband who must initiate the act of divorce, and since the court is not permitted to issue it without his consent, a wife abandoned by her husband is often in the pitiable condition of being neither married nor free if she strictly observes the rabbinical law. She can not remarry unless she receives a divorce from her husband or definite proof that he is dead; there is no possibility of a legal declaration of his death after a certain period of years, or of divorce for desertion. She remains an Agunah, one "bound" to the husband who has disappeared.

5. The Marriage Ceremony. The natural form of taking in marriage, and that universally practised in ancient times, was the actual sexual union of the man and the woman. Marriage by cohabitation is mentioned in the Mishnah (*Kid.* 1:1) as one of the valid forms for contracting marriage; it was probably the most usual form of marriage in the earliest times. It was only at a later period, when this form no longer comported with the moral sense of the time, that it was looked down upon as shameful. If a marriage had been entered into without form, it could be dissolved without form; but such a marriage did not accord the wife, who was in a less favorable economic position, the necessary security. The rights and obligations of the married couple were not sufficiently defined by it, nor was the care of the children regulated. Accordingly, as the laws of Jewish marriage developed, they stipulated that marriage was to be contracted only according to forms defined and enforced by law.

It is evident in Jewish laws concerned with marriage that the oldest form of matrimony was marriage by purchase, in which the husband pays for his wife. No definite cases of marriage by capture are mentioned as occurring in Bible times, but a general reference is made to them (*Deut.* 21:10-14; *Judges* 21:6-23). There is no doubt that in Bible times marriage according to the Jewish law was governed by the idea of marriage by purchase, or, more exactly, engagement by purchase, since this form really effected the development of the engagement contract and not that of the marriage proper, which was a later institution. The marriage itself was contracted in the form of an agreement which contained promises of mutual performance, and which, like every other contract, was based on the voluntary action of the parties. Naturally this did not hinder marriage from having an inherent moral content and objective, despite the fact that its form was that of a contract.

From the legal point of view, marriage began with the engagement; it was this which made the maiden one who was "betrothed" and "married," and not the marriage ceremony or the wedding itself. Therefore the infidelity or the violation of an engaged girl was punished by death, like adultery in the case of a woman who had been married (*Deut.* 22:23-27). Separation from an engaged woman required an act of divorce.

The form which Jewish marriage law gives to the Erusin, or engagement ceremony, shows that it was regarded as the beginning of marriage. In earlier times the engagement represented an interim, in which the maiden was partly independent of her father. Yet she was already regarded as married; it was merely that an interval of twelve months was given to permit the maiden time to gather her trousseau and prepare herself for wedded life. Any longer interval was censured. On the other hand, a widow did not need so much preparation, and so a month was considered enough for her (*Keth.* 2:2). During this period of waiting, and in the first year of his marriage, a bridegroom was freed from military service (*Deut.* 20:7).

In the earliest times the engagement took place when the husband paid the bride's father, in the presence of witnesses, the purchase price (*mohar*). Fifty shekels is mentioned as the minimum price (*Ex.* 22:15; *Deut.* 22:29). It was also possible for a suitor to acquire a wife by serving the bride's father, as Jacob served Laban for Leah and Rachel. The purchase price remained in the father's possession, but he would usually spend it on his daughter's outfit, as otherwise she might feel herself disgraced because she had been sold as a slave (*Gen.* 31:15). This *mohar,* which thus was turned over to the daughter, eventually developed into the dowry given by the father to the bride. In the post-Exilic period the marriage settlement had completely taken the place of the purchase price, which had previously become merely symbolic; cf. *Tobit* 8:21; *Sirach* 25:21. It is probable that in addition to his purchase price there were certain presents which the bridegroom made to the bride at the time of the engagement (*Gen.* 34:12).

The marriage ceremony occurred at the end of the engagement period. It was called Nissuin, or bringing the wife to the husband's home, and it was celebrated with great pomp. The bride was led to the bridegroom's chamber, an act which completed the ceremony; in a later age this bridal chamber was symbolized by the baldachin, or Huppah.

As the more primitive conditions which were contemplated by the Mosaic law gradually disappeared, it began more and more to be considered a disadvantage that the engagement, contrary to its real character as a promise and a contract, linked the bridal pair together, and could be dissolved only by a formal divorce. For this reason, and particularly in countries of Western Europe, the authorities of the Middle Ages united the two institutions into one ceremony; the traditional Jewish marriage ceremony now embodies both the Erusin ceremony, or engagement, and the Huppah ceremony, or wedding proper. As a result of this the preliminary promises (Shidduchin) again became more important; this developed into the betrothal in the sense in which it is normally understood—a preliminary contract settling the details of the coming marriage, such as the wedding day, the dowry, and the like. As far back as Talmudic times these preliminary promises were considered so necessary that their omission called for severe censure, and Rab (Abba Aricha), in the 3rd cent. C.E., declared them to be obligatory. Since these agreements were not binding by themselves, they were made formal legal agreements (Tenaim) by an act of acquisition (Kinyan) which was performed at the same time; they were thus guaranteed by a penalty for non-fulfillment.

Accordingly, the traditional Jewish marriage ceremony comes some time after the engagement, which is of a purely contractual character, and is a combination of the two religious ceremonies of betrothal (Erusin) and wedlock (Nissuin). The specific regulations covering the wedding ceremony are as follows:

A. The betrothal (*'erusin*) takes place by means of the espousal (*kiddushin*), in which the man acknowledges the woman as his own, she becomes consecrated to him, and thus forbidden to everyone else (*Kid.* 2b).

According to the laws laid down in the Mishnah (*Kid.* 1:1), espousal can take place in three ways:

1. By Delivery of an Article of Value (*kesef*). This method of espousal was the one commonly used. The article of value, which at the same time is symbolical of the "purchase price," was received by the maiden, or, if she was a minor, by her father or relative.

The Halachah agrees with the opinion of the school of Hillel in fixing the minimum amount of the *kesef* at a Perutah, the smallest copper coin in Talmudic times. The petty value of such an article showed that this delivery was not considered as a purchase price, but was merely the symbolization of the acquisition of the woman by a proper purchase. In ancient times the wedding ring was practically unknown; but it has been in use among Jews for several centuries, since it combines the possibility of easy safekeeping with the nature of an ornament.

2. By the Delivery of a Document (*shetar*). The marriage document (*shetar kiddushin* or *shetar 'erusin*) had to contain the formula "be thou consecrated unto me"; it had to be written for that particular purpose (*lishemah*), and with the woman's consent (*mida'atah; Kid.* 9a). The names of both the man and the woman had to be mentioned in the document (*Eben Haezer* 32:4). As the symbol of acquisition became the customary form of betrothal in post-Talmudic times, this document of betrothal went completely out of use.

3. By Marital Intercourse (*bi'ah*). Consummation of the betrothal by means of cohabitation is mentioned in the Mishnah as a possible method of espousal, and was undoubtedly in use in very ancient times. The Talmud denounces this custom as a sign of indecency, and Abba Aricha even punished by flogging those who followed it (*Kid.* 12b).

The only method employed nowadays by Jews is the first one, that of the *kesef*. The man gives the wedding ring to the woman, and at the same time pronounces the following Aramaic espousal formula: *"hare 'at mekudesheth li betabba'ath zo kedath mosheh veyisra'el"* ("Behold, thou art consecrated unto me with this ring according to the law of Moses and Israel").

This act of espousal must be performed in the presence of two unobjectionable witnesses. The declaration is followed by the delivery of the *kesef,* and the pronouncing of the betrothal blessing (*birkath 'erusin*) in the presence of ten adults (Minyan). The betrothal presupposes the consent of the two parties to the marriage. As a rule, a marriage which takes place by compulsion (*'ones*) or mistake is invalid. The mutual consent of both parties is considered as evidenced when the man sets forth purpose of his action in the words of the prescribed formula, or in any other way that is understood by the woman; while the latter expresses her consent by silent acceptance of the *kesef*.

In Talmudic times the espousal was often made conditionally. This condition had to be phrased in accordance with the Jewish regulations for the formulation and pronouncement of a condition. If this was done, the espousal became invalid if the condition was not fulfilled.

It is probable that it was customary as far back as Talmudic times for both the parties to be present at the ceremony; nevertheless, either of them could be represented by a proxy at the espousal. The regulations as to representation for this part of the marriage ceremony are especially precise; in fact, such representation for marriage and divorce forms a precedent for the entire Jewish law of agency.

B. The wedding (*nissu'in*), the actual marriage, which in ancient times had been celebrated at the end of a waiting period, followed immediately after the espousal. In ancient times the marriage was consummated by conducting (the literal meaning of the verb *nasa*) the bride to the house of the bridegroom. Later this was symbolized by the use of the Huppah, and sometimes by drawing a prayer cloak (Tallith) over the man and woman. Next came the marriage benedictions (*birchoth nissu'in*) spoken in the presence of ten men. The Kethubah, or marriage contract, was then read; it had to be signed by two witnesses, and contained the various provisions required in Jewish law for the proper care and maintenance of the wife. The last act of marriage was the "seclusion" (*yihud*) of the couple, symbolizing the consummation of the marriage.

The traditional Jewish marriage ceremony varies but little from this arrangement. The bridal pair are conducted under the Huppah. Then follows the benediction of espousal over the first cup of wine, from which the bride and groom drink. Next the groom places the ring on the left hand of the bride while reciting the espousal formula. The Kethubah is then read, and this is followed by the benediction over the second cup of wine, from which the couple also drink, and by the other marriage benedictions. These basic parts of the ceremony are accompanied by various embellishments, such as a speech, processions and similar expansions to lend pomp and dignity to the ceremony.

Jews who do not strictly observe the traditional forms usually shorten the ceremony by the omission of one of the cups of wine and some of the benedictions; the Huppah is frequently absent, and the ceremony is modeled to some extent after current wedding forms. The espousal formula and the use of the ring are common to all Jewish religious ceremonies of marriage.

6. Obligations and Rights of the Married Couple. The duties of the husband to his wife are essentially derived from *Ex.* 21:10. This verse deals with the case of the Hebrew handmaid whose master gives her as wife to his son; in case the latter takes another wife, her rights must not be diminished: "her food, her raiment, and her conjugal rights, shall he not diminish" (*she'erah kesuthah ve'onathah lo yigra*). The same rights were considered the essential rights of every married woman. They are discussed in detail in the Mishnah and the Talmud, and constitute the duties of the husband. The following regulations define his obligations throughout the continuance of the marriage.

1. Securing a Living for the Wife. The husband is bound to feed the wife, to clothe her, and to provide her with a home. All his property, even his real estate, is the security for his obligation of maintenance; in case he refuses to pay, the judicial authorities may interfere to compel him.

If the husband has been away more than three months, and the wife has no means of support, the authorities furnish her the necessary sums for maintenance, and charge it against the husband's property.

It is assumed that the husband has left her enough to provide for the first three months (*Keth.* 107a).

The husband expressly takes upon himself the duty of maintenance in the Kethubah, the final formulation of which made the bridegroom say: "Become my wife according to the laws of Moses and Israel, and I will work for you, honor you, provide your food, and take care of you, according to the existing statutes for Jewish husbands, who in good faith work for their wives, honor them, take care of them, and clothe them."

If the husband has no property and no earnings, he must even hire out as a day laborer, in order to be able to provide food for his wife (*Eben Haezer* 70:3).

In fixing the amount of the sum required for proper maintenance, due weight was first given to the means of the husband, then to the wife's former standard of living in the house of her parents. As a rule, the Talmudic principle: "The wife is raised to her husband's level, but she does not sink to his" (*Keth.* 61a), was taken as the standard. Thus it is mentioned, for instance, that a husband should not let his wife be without ornaments.

The forms of the Kethubah prevalent in Jerusalem and Galilee in Talmudic times contained the stipulation that the wife should have a claim to maintenance and a home even after the death of her husband. In Judea the clause "until the heirs pay the Kethubah to you" was added. This made the period of maintenance dependent on the will of the heirs (*Keth.* 4:13). The Talmud sharply criticized the attitude of the Judeans, saying that "the people of Judea think more of their money than of their honor" (*Yer. Keth.* 4:14). Eventually the formulation of Jerusalem came into general use, and the widow could always prefer a claim to maintenance up to the time that she herself made a claim for the payment of the Kethubah; this generally happened when she wished to remarry. Of course, as soon as she remarried the duty of maintaining her was cancelled.

It is worthy of note that the claims of the widow always had precedence over those of the heirs, and that the testator could not diminish her rights by directions in his will.

The obligation of maintenance applied also for the daughters of the testator, and this obligation was incumbent on the heirs, even if it was not expressly provided for (*Keth.* 4:11).

2. OBLIGATION OF MARITAL INTERCOURSE. From the nature of marriage and its object—to fulfill the duty of propagation (*peru urebu*)—it follows that the most important common obligation of the married couple is the performance of the marital act. Jewish law, therefore, especially emphasizes this obligation, and declares also, without false modesty, the consequences of fulfilling this duty in all details. In the Talmud the marital act is treated as the duty of the husband and the right of the wife; this interpretation arises from the originally polygamous basis of Jewish marriage. The husband is obligated to fulfill this duty in a measure corresponding to his health and his manner of living. For this reason he had no right to change his occupation or to travel, without his wife's consent. An exception was made in favor of Torah students, who might be absent from their wives for many years for the purpose of studying the Torah.

Neither husband nor wife might decline the marital act, and an agreement to this effect was not valid. If the man refrained from cohabitation in consequence of a vow, the maximum duration of his abstinence was fixed as one week. In case of the wife's refusal of marital connection, the husband had the right to a divorce, and the wife lost her claims in the Kethubah. The husband, however, could also have her Kethubah claims diminished by the court, in order to compel her acquiescence. Should the husband refuse cohabitation, the wife could have him fined by the court, in such manner that to her claims in the Kethubah a fixed sum was added for every week of his omission (*Keth.* 5:7). She had also the right to demand a divorce from him. In the Talmud (*Keth.* 63a) and in the corresponding responsa (cf. especially that of Rabbi Meir of Rothenburg, no. 1021) it is reported that the court took pains to issue a special decree to hold husband and wife to the fulfillment of their duties, and eventually compelled a divorce.

If the husband could not fulfill his marital duty because of sickness or debility, and there was no improvement in his condition in a period of six months, divorce might follow, if the wife demanded it (*Eben Haezer* 76:11).

3. MARITAL FIDELITY. The husband had the right to demand faithfulness in marriage. Even slight infractions of marital morality could give the husband a right to divorce, and to declare that the wife had lost her claim to property on the ground of the Kethubah. The wife's infraction of marital fidelity was punished as adultery.

4. MEDICAL ATTENTION FOR THE WIFE. In case of the wife's sickness, the husband was in duty bound to see that she was cured; if he died in the meantime, this obligation descended to the heirs.

The husband was regarded as especially blameworthy if he made use of his one-sided right of divorce without the consent of the wife, when his wife was sick (*Sifre* to *Deut.* 21:14).

5. RANSOM OF THE WIFE FROM CAPTIVITY (*pidyon shebuyoth*). In the early centuries of the Common Era, when the Jews had lost their independence, the captivity of wives was a frequent occurrence. For that reason the Mishnah laid especial emphasis on the ransoming of wives (*Keth.* 4:9). Even the married men belonging to the priestly families (*kohanim*) were obliged to ransom their wives, although they might not resume marital relations with them afterwards.

In most cases there was a limitation in regard to the ransoming of captives, namely, that no ransom was to be paid above the ordinary price of a slave, in order not to encourage the robbers to further crimes (*Git.* 45a). This rule was relaxed in favor of the wife, and, according to the opinion of some, the husband was permitted to sacrifice his entire wealth for her (*Eben Haezer* 78:2). If both man and wife were made captives at the same time, the authorities were to use his means to ransom the wife first, even if this was against his will (*Hor.* 13a; *Yoreh Deah* 252:10).

6. OBLIGATION TO BURY THE WIFE. The husband is obligated to provide suitable burial for his wife. The exact kind is determined by local custom (*Keth.* 4:4).

The proper management of the home is designated

in the Bible as the particular duty of the wife (*Prov.* 31:10-31); this famous encomium of the worthy wife reflects, of course, the conditions of the time. On the other hand, a quarrelsome or jealous wife is censured (*Sirach* 25:16-26; 26:1-12).

According to the Biblical law (*Num.* 30:7), the wife was obliged to recognize the husband's right to annul her vows which she made without his consent.

The Talmud obligates the wife to take charge of the household and help in earning a living. However, if she renounced her claim to maintenance, she could free herself of this duty to work. In Talmudic times, too, the wife had to give her earnings to her husband, and her money belonged to him; he had a claim to the use of her entire property during the continuance of the marriage, and was her heir when she died.

These extensive economic rights of the husband are considered in the Talmud (*Keth.* 47b) as an equivalent for the obligations undertaken by him:

1. The claim upon her earnings as equivalent for his obligation of maintenance.

2. The claim upon the use of her property as equivalent for the duty of releasing her from captivity.

3. The claim upon the property she leaves at her death as equivalent for the obligation to bury her.

In addition to these obligations, the wife always had to follow her husband to his residence. She could, however, refuse to move into the city, if she preferred the more healthful residence in the country. Palestine had the preference over other countries; Jerusalem over other cities of that country. The wife could, therefore, compel the husband (and he naturally could compel her) to move to Palestine, and when there to Jerusalem (*Keth.* 110b et seq.).

Concerning these legal mutual relations of the married couple, the principal weight is laid by the Jewish writings on the mutually sincere and moral behavior of the married couple. The prophet warned against angering and abusing the wife; God Himself appears as witness, in case she is unlovingly treated (*Mal.* 2:14). The wife is warned to avoid every kind of behavior that would excite scandal, and not to wish to domineer over the husband. The duty of the married couple is mutual, to love and honor each other (*Prov.* 5:15-20), to honor each other's parents, and to obey the precepts of the Jewish law (*Pirke de Rabbi Eliezer,* chap. 13).

7. Property Rights in Marriage. In all law there is a serious problem of finding the proper medium between the common marital interests, which call for community of property for the sake of a united family, and the interests of the wife, whose complete dependence on her husband is undesirable. In Jewish law the problem was solved by placing the husband, for the duration of the marriage, in the position of manager and beneficiary of his wife's property, and by requiring that at the time of entering the marriage relation he should undertake specified responsibilities and obligations in reference to the regulation of property rights in case of dissolution of the marriage.

The property of the wife was defined by Jewish law as that property, whether personal or real estate, which she brought into the marriage as dowry or which she had received during that state, either by inheritance or as a gift.

The marriage settlement (*nedunya*) was derived probably from the *mohar,* the original "purchase price" which was paid for the bride, as well as from the presents which the bridegroom made to the bride on contracting the marriage. In the Mishnah (*Kid.* 2:6; *B.B.* 9:5) these presents are called *siblonoth.*

At an early period it became the custom for the parents of the bride to give voluntary presents, evidence for which is found in the Bible (*Gen.* 29:24; *Judges* 1:15). At first this remained the wife's private property, and formed then, apparently, the basis of the later Kethubah, the actual marriage contract, which had as its object the securing for the wife, in case of dissolution of the marriage, of the return of her personal property, and further additions by the husband.

In this marriage contract concerning the wife's property, drawn upon entering into wedlock, the wife was insured the payment of a sum of 200 Zuz (in case of widows, 100 Zuz) by the husband. These sums were, however, manifestly only minimum amounts, and could at will be increased, in which case they were called "additions to the Kethubah."

The wife's property was divided, according to the rights and obligations which the husband had in connection with it, as follows:

1. Nichse tzon barzel ("property of iron flock"). The expression points to former times, when sheep-raising was the principal branch of industry. The "sheep" with their periodical crop of wool represents the husband's right to the enjoyment of the income; "iron" represents the safety and inconvertibility of the property. This was that part of the wife's property which was written into the Kethubah as hers, and therefore served as safe capital for her. This property of the wife passed at marriage into the husband's possession, so that he had the management thereof, and was personally responsible therefor. He was personally responsible for its return in case of dissolution of the marriage; his entire property was covered by a general mortgage in the wife's favor for this possibility. The husband had no right to sell this property or to pledge it (*B.B.* 50a). The married couple could dispose of it only in common. In post-Talmudic times this regulation was made somewhat less strict (Maimonides, *Hilchoth Mechirah* 30:5).

2. Nichse melug (*melug* is "usufruct," or "paraphernalia"). This property was not designated in the marriage contract, and the husband was not responsible for it; consequently he had only the right to use it, while the wife retained the right to dispose of it. However, the wife could not dispose of it by herself, as she had not the right to give away the use of it (ordinance made at Usha, *Keth.* 50a).

3. Private Property of the Wife (*nechasim she'en leba'al reshuth bahem,* "property to which the husband has no claim"). This was property given to the wife by the husband or a third party, with the proviso that the husband should have no rights over it. The wife then retained exclusive management and use of this property, as in the case of the wife's "separate property" in modern law. Sometimes the wife, in order to prevent her husband from having the use of it, made over her property to a third person before her marriage.

In all questions of property the difference between

the two categories is of extreme importance. Thus the Mishnah states that if a priest contracts a marriage forbidden to him, a slave who belongs to the *tzon barzel* property may eat of the heave-offering; but if he belongs to the *melug* property, this is forbidden to him (*Yeb.* 7:1).

The Talmud generally shows the tendency to unite all the wife's property which she brings into the marriage, in the interest of peaceful conditions; but it seeks to protect the wife from mistakes made by the husband through the retention of her property rights in the *melug,* and the responsibility of the husband for the *tzon barzel.* In according to the husband the right to use the entire property, Jewish law was governed by the thought that this single right of use would best protect the interests of the wife. The rights of the husband and his income from the wife's property are balanced against his obligations as detailed above, such as the furnishing of maintenance for the wife, the assumption of the costs of housekeeping, and the duty of ransoming her from captivity.

In case of the dissolution of the marriage by the husband's death or by divorce, the wife had a right to the repayment of her dowry. The *melug* property was given back to her in the condition in which it was at the time of the dissolution of the marriage; the *tzon barzel* property had to be restored in the condition in which it was at the time of the marriage. On the other hand, this had as a result that the husband received any increase in value that had taken place in the *tzon barzel* property in the meantime. If, however, the divorce took place because of the delinquency of the wife, this claim was invalid, and she could claim only as much of her dowry as was actually on hand (*Eben Haezer* 115:5).

When the wife died, her property went first to her sons, or to her other relatives. This right of inheritance seems to have been a part of the *kethubah benin dichrin* (*Keth.* 4:10). In the latter part of the Talmudic period, the husband was assured the right of inheritance of the wife's dowry, so that the other rights of the wife's kin were not valid until after his death. Later regulations limited the husband's right of inheritance in case there were no children; thus it was decreed that if the wife died in the first year of her marriage, her dowry reverted to her parents, and if it was in the second year, it was divided between her parents and her husband.

The Jewish law as to property in marriage was a combination of the German system of common property and the Roman system of separate property. The husband had the unlimited use and management of his wife's property. If the wife died, he inherited part of or all her property; if he died, or there was a divorce, the wife got back her own property. When the marriage took place the wife could indicate in the Kethubah which of her property was to be considered as *tzon barzel* and which as *melug;* in this way she could provide for a heavier or lighter responsibility and liability on the part of her husband.

8. Marital and Extra-Marital Relationships. Jewish law regarded extra-marital, or illegitimate, relationship as almost on the same level as marital, or legitimate, relationship. Relationship with the mother and the mother's family was assured by birth. The acknowledgment of the father was sufficient proof of descent from him. Licentious living with a woman, however, did not establish an illegitimate relationship, such as is formed under non-Jewish law. Thus no illegitimate relationship ensued either for the innocent third party, or even for the parties concerned. Extramarital relationship had the same results as marital in excluding relatives by affinity from acting as witnesses; in Jewish law it established a complete right of inheritance; it made a number of possible marriages incestuous, and could prohibit sexual intercourse with certain relatives. In principle, a natural relationship had the force of a real one; matrimonial sanction served only as a formal strengthening of family ties.

See also: BETROTHAL; DIVORCE; WEDDING AND WEDDING CUSTOMS.

MARCUS COHN.

Lit.: Tractates of the Mishnah and Talmud: *Yebamoth, Kethuboth, Kiddushin;* Maimonides, *Hilchoth Ishuth* 1 to 28; *Issure Biah* 1 to 22; *Eben Haezer* 1 to 118; Hamburger, J., *Realencyclopaedie für Bibel und Talmud,* vol. 1, pp. 255 et seq., 1260 et seq., 1282 et seq.; Buxtorf, *De sponsalibus et divortiis* (1652); Selden, *Uxor hebraica* (1673); Mendelssohn, *Ritualgesetze der Juden, betreffend Erbschaften, Vormundschaftssachen, Testaments und Ehesachen* (1778); Mayer, Samuel, *Die Rechte der Israeliten, Athener und Römer* (1862-76) 207 et seq.; Frankel, Z., "Grundlinien des mosaisch-talmudischen Eherechts," *Jahresbericht des jüdisch-theologischen Seminars* (1860); Buchholz, P., *Die Familie in rechtlicher und moralischer Beziehung nach mosaisch-talmudischer Lehre* (1867) 12 et seq.; Duschak, *Das mosaisch-talmudische Eherecht* (1864); Fassel, H. B., *Das mosaisch-rabbinische Civilrecht,* 44 et seq.; Lichtstein, M., *Die Ehe nach mosaisch-talmudischer Auffassung und das mosaisch-talmudische Eherecht* (1879); Bergel, J., *Die Eheverhältnisse der alten Juden im Vergleich mit den griechischen und römischen* (1881); Löw, L., "Eherechtliche Studien," *Gesammelte Schriften,* vol. 3 (1893) 13 et seq.; Mielziner, M., *The Jewish Law of Marriage and Divorce in Ancient and Modern Times* (1901); Schwartz, A., in *Monatsschrift für Geschichte und Wissenschaft des Judentums,* vol. 45 (1901) 258 et seq.; Lévy, Louis-Germain, *La famille dans l'antiquité israélite* (1905); Weill, Emmanuel, *La femme juive, sa condition légale d'après la bible et le talmud* (1907); Preuss, J., *Biblisch-talmudische Medizin* (1911) 523 et seq.; Guttmann, M., "Marriage Law in Bible and Talmud," *Publications of the Hebrew University, Jerusalem* (1925).

MARRIAGE BENEDICTIONS. The traditional Jewish marriage ceremony is a combination of what were originally two separate ceremonies: the espousal (Erusin) and the wedding (Nissuin). Each of these parts of the ceremony has its special benedictions, known as the *birchoth 'erusin* and *birchoth nissu'in,* respectively.

The *birchoth 'erusin* are two in number. The first is the customary blessing over wine: "Blessed art Thou, O Lord our God, King of the universe, Creator of the fruit of the vine." The second deals more directly with marriage: "Blessed art Thou . . . Who hast sanctified us by Thy commandments, and hast given us commandments concerning forbidden marriages; Who hast disallowed to us those which are improper, but hast sanctioned unto us such as are wedded to us by the rite of the canopy and the sanctification. Blessed art Thou, O Lord, Who sanctifiest Thy people Israel by the rite of the canopy and the sanctification."

The *birchoth nissu'in* are seven in number, and are therefore known also as the "seven benedictions" (*sheba berachoth*). The first is the customary blessing over wine. The other six run as follows: "2. Blessed art

Thou . . . Who hast created all things for His glory. 3. Blessed art Thou . . . Who hast created man. 4. Blessed art Thou . . . Who made man in His image, after His likeness, and hast prepared for him, out of his very self, a perpetual fabric. Blessed art Thou, O Lord, Creator of man. 5. May she who was barren (Zion) be exceedingly glad and rejoice, when her children are gathered within her in joy. Blessed art Thou, O Lord, Who makest Zion joyful through her children. 6. O make these loved companions greatly rejoice, even as of old Thou didst gladden Thy creation (Adam and Eve) in the Garden of Eden. Blessed art Thou, O Lord, Who makest the bridegroom and the bride to rejoice. 7. Blessed art Thou . . . Who hast created joy and gladness, bridegroom and bride, mirth and exultation, pleasure and delight, love, brotherhood, peace and friendship. Soon, O Lord our God, may there be heard in the cities of Judah and in the streets of Jerusalem the voice of joy and gladness, the voice of the bridegroom and the bride, the jubilant voice of bridegrooms from their marriage chambers and of youths from their feasts of song. Blessed art Thou, O Lord, Who makest the bridegroom to rejoice with the bride." These benedictions were in use as early as the Talmudic period (*Keth.* 8). They are incorporated into the grace after the wedding banquet.

In Reform Jewish ceremonies, the main thoughts of these benedictions are retained in the ceremony, but the traditional benedictions are not recited.

Lit.: Singer, S., and Abrahams, I., *The Authorised Daily Prayer Book* (1922) 298-99, ccxvi.

MARRIAGE-BROKER, *see* SHADCHAN.

MARSCHAK, JAKOB, economist, b. Kiev, Russia, 1898. While he was studying at the Technical College of that city, the Russian revolution and the civil war broke out, and he had to interrupt his studies several times. In 1919 he left Russia to continue his studies in mathematics, economics and statistics in Germany at the Universities of Berlin and Heidelberg, where he obtained his Ph.D. degree in 1922. From 1924 to 1926 he was a writer on economics on the *Frankfurter Zeitung*. Later he became a member of the Institut für Weltwirtschaft und Seeverkehr in Kiel, and during 1928 to 1930 he was a permanent expert for the Enquête Commission, working on statistical inquiries for the government. In 1930 he was appointed assistant professor of economic statistics at the University of Heidelberg, and by 1933 he was recognized as one of the outstanding German workers in that subject.

When he was dismissed by the Nazi regime, he was called to the University of Oxford, in England, where he became a lecturer in economics and was awarded the M.A. degree. In 1935 he organized the Institute of Statistics, and became its first director and also reader in statistics at the University of Oxford. In the studies of the Institute, the theoretical methods of economic statistics were applied to varied empirical researches on capital market, trade fluctuations, employment, and labor mobility. In 1939 he joined the staff of the Graduate Faculty of Political and Social Science in The New School for Social Research, in New York city. He contributed many articles to its journal *Social Research*, of which he was co-editor. He conducted a research project on demand analysis in 1941 to 1942.

Marschak emphasizes the importance of and the possibilities for "quantitative economics" as a scientific tool to approach the problems of statics and dynamics in economic life. Characteristic for his method are his studies and books: *Die Lohndiskussion* (1930); *Elastizität der Nachfrage* (1931); *Kapitalbildung* (with Walter Lederer; London, 1936). His "Labor Mobility in Great Britain" (with H. Makower and H. W. Robinson) was published in *Oxford Papers* (1939-40), of which he was co-editor, and his "Money and the Theory of Assets" in *Econometrica* (vol. 6, No. 4, 1938).

Until 1933 he contributed to the social economic journal *Archiv für Sozialwissenschaft und Sozialpolitik*. His study "Der neue Mittelstand" (with Emil Lederer), in *Grundriss der Sozialökonomik* (vol. 9), was translated into English under the title of *The New Middle Class* (by WPA, Columbia University, 1937).

Lit.: Oxford Magazine, Oct. 31, 1935, pp. 80-81; Oxford Institute of Statistics, annual reports, 1935 to 1939; Oxford University, *Report on the Social Studies Scheme*, 1936, pp. 3, 14.

MARSEILLE. 1. In the Middle Ages. Founded by the Greeks about 600 B.C.E., probably on the site of an earlier Phoenician settlement, Marseille on the Mediterranean is likely to have had Jewish residents since its inception. Evidence of the presence of Jews at Marseille, however, is extant only from the Frank period on. Gregory of Tours mentions the Jew Priscus, court financier and supplier of King Chilperic, who, in 582, went from Paris to Marseille, where his son was to marry a "Massiliensim Hebraeam" (a Jewish girl of Marseille). In 576 Jews from Clermont, persecuted by Bishop Avitus, had fled to Marseille. Benjamin of Tudela, having visited Marseille in 1160, reported 300 Jewish families to be living there in the two divisions of the Upper and Lower City.

The Jews of Marseille—forming a Universitas Judeorum with syndici or baylous—were subjects of the city administration and of the counts of Provence; from 1481 on they were subjects of the king of France. Until the end of the medieval period (1501) their status was regulated by the statutes and privileges of the city; to this the count of Provence had agreed in 1257. They were *cives Massilie,* and the city protected them as its subjects against the encroachments of the Church and of the counts of Provence. However, in accord with the decree of the Lateran Council (1215), Jewish men were to be distinguished by a ring-shaped badge on the breast of their garment, and Jewish women by a silk or linen veil. They were allowed to bathe in public baths only once a week; they took the Oath "More Judaico" upon the law of Moses; a Christian had the right to protest against a Jewish witness. Only four Jews were allowed to travel on board one ship; none on board ships bound for Alexandria. Jews had to abstain from work on Sundays or Christian holidays, but they were exempted from the cleaning of the streets on Saturday.

The counts of Provence also protected the Jews. Thus, in 1320, during the persecution of the shepherds (Pastoureaux), Robert, king of Naples, count of Provence (1309-43), instructed his officials to protect the life and property of the Jews and give them refuge in the royal castles and forts. The city, too, on this occasion, was zealous in remedying the grievances of the Jews. Robert, in 1322, ordered cessation of the excessive taxation of the Jews; in 1331 another decree for the safety of the Jews was issued. Their privileges were renewed by Marie, regent for Louis II, at the request of the Jew Bonjusas Bondavin (1387), her trusted adviser, and by Louis II (1384-1417) himself (1389). Both Louis II and Queen Yolanda, countess of Provence (in 1422), saw to it that the city and the royal officials did not infringe upon the rights of the Jews. King René, count of Provence, protected them, too (February 4, 1463); he had the Baptisterium of St. Martin closed on account of the illegal baptism of Jews (1481).

The Jews of Marseille paid the counts of Provence, for the protection accorded them, 300 livres in 1303, in other years 100 and 200 livres. From 1419 to 1420 the contribution of the Jews of Marseille toward the tax levied upon the Jewish community of Provence was set by the delegates at 400 florins; in 1446, out of the total of 2,745 florins, they paid, in addition to the 400 florins for the count of Provence, fifty florins to the conservateur des juifs.

The benevolence of the city and of the counts of Provence toward the Jews was well grounded in their economic importance. The Jews acted as brokers; in 1367 seventy-six Jewish brokers (courtiers) took the official oath before the city magistrate. Trading in spices, timber, textiles, colonial goods, wheat and other products, the Jews traveled across the sea to Sicily, Alexandria and Algiers. They acted as commissioners for non-Jewish merchants, and vice versa. Forty-five Jews were engaged in maritime trade in the first half of the 13th cent. Up to the 14th cent. they borrowed money from non-Jews; from the 14th cent. on they engaged in money-lending. The counts of Provence assisted them in collecting payment provided that they charged the legal rate of interest, which amounted to 15 per cent in the 13th and 14th centuries, and to 25 per cent in the 15th cent. The Jew Crescas Davin (1371-1404) introduced the manufacture of soap at Marseille; there were also Jewish butchers. A stonemason is mentioned in the 13th cent.

Many Jews were engaged in the medical profession. In the 13th cent. one Samson, son of Abraham, was the only known Jewish physician, but in the 14th cent. there were nineteen, among them a woman practicing that profession; in the 15th cent. thirty-two Jewish physicians were recorded. Their services were greatly appreciated in the frequent epidemics occurring about 1383; the city council employed the Jewish physicians Solomon Mosse (1369); Crescas (1396), Solomon Orgier (1402-3) and Vitalis (1476).

The Jews lived in a separate quarter. Its main street, the Carreria Judaeorum, was of considerable extent, and formed a sort of island, "Insula Juzatarie." The Jews, however, had the right to own real estate and, apparently for a time, to live outside of the Jewish quarter. They had several synagogues, including the Scola Major and the Scola Minor. Their cemetery was situated on the "Mont Juif." They had also a bath house for women, a hospital, slaughterhouse, meat market and pious foundations. After 1348 the Jews of the Upper and Lower City united.

From the 12th cent. on Marseille was a center of Jewish learning. Benjamin of Tudela called it a city of Geonim and sages; its scholars were in close contact with those of Spain and South Italy. On September 27, 1194, Maimonides sent his answer regarding an inquiry on astrology to the rabbis and scholars of Marseille, commending their zeal for learning. The following scholars may be mentioned: Isaac, probably Isaac ben Abba Mari, author of Sefer Haittur, written about 1170 to 1193; of the Ibn Tibbon family, residing at Marseille: Moses ben Samuel, noted translator (about 1252-53), before he went to Montpellier; his son Samuel; Jacob ben Machir ibn Tibbon, grandson of the translator Samuel ben Judah ibn Tibbon; Jacob Anatoli, a kinsman of the Tibbonides, likewise of Marseille origin. Anatoli is probably identical with the translator and philosopher who lived at the court of Frederick II; Shemtob ben Isaac de Tortosa (b. 1196), who first settled at Montpellier, then as a physician at Marseille, and who translated from Arabic into Hebrew (1254-58) Zahrawi's medical work, Kitab al Tacrit (30 books); Joseph of Marseille, Bible commentator; Moses of Marseille who, about the middle of the 13th cent., lived probably at Paris; Solomon Nasi ben Isaac Nasi Cayl, liturgical poet, who lived at Marseille about 1285; Rabbi Jonathan at Marseille and Aaron ben Abraham ben Isaac of Marseille and Shemtob Falcon of Marseille, correspondents of Solomon ibn Adret.

In the 14th cent. there lived Nissim ben Moses ben Solomon ben Moses, whose philosophical commentary on the Pentateuch, characteristic of trends of Jewish thought at Marseille, resembles the even bolder work of Levi ben Abraham of Villefranche; Samson of Chinon, who provided a supercommentary on the commentary of Ibn Ezra; Samuel ben Judah of Marseille (b. about 1294), who subsequently devoted himself to astronomy at Salon and, in 1321, among other Arabic writings, translated into Hebrew Averroes' commentary on Aristotle's Ethics; Joseph of Marseille, who in 1333 became rabbi at Jerusalem; Joseph ben Johanan, who about 1343 was rabbi at Marseille, and from 1360 to 1375 rabbi at Paris. There lived in Marseille at the end of the 14th cent.: Maestre Bonjudas Bondavi, rabbi at Cagliari, Sardinia, who in the early 15th cent. corresponded with Isaac ben Sheshet. He is probably identical with the physician Bonjusas Bondavin who, about 1390, went to Alghero, Sardinia, and who was equally devoted to Talmudic and secular learning.

To the 15th cent. belong Halafta Hasofer ben Abraham Hasofer of Marseille, who copied two medical works in Italy (1434 and 1436); Jacob ben David Provençal from Marseille, who lived at Naples in the last third of the 15th cent.

The incorporation of Provence in the kingdom of France, which had expelled its Jews as early as 1394, changed the situation of the Jews in the Provence. In 1487 a resolution was passed in Marseille to petition for the expulsion of the Jews, who allegedly were ruining the city by their credit operations. King Charles VIII cancelled all debts to the Jews on which illegal interest had been charged. In 1492 the Jews of Marseille ransomed for the sum of 1,500 écus 118 Jews driven from Aragon, Spain, who had found temporary refuge at Marseille. Royal edicts, however, from 1496 on, ordered the Jews of the various Provençal cities to be expelled, and in 1501 the community of Marseille was dissolved.

2. In the Modern Period. When, in 1669, Marseille became a free port, Jewish merchants of Livorno attempted to settle there. The merchant class of Marseille protested; Minister Colbert, however, declared at first (1676) that the spirit of enterprise of the Jews would be beneficial to the city. But in 1682 Louis XIV expelled the Jews from Marseille and the south of France; in 1710 he branded as illegal the one-month visiting permits which the parliament of Provence granted Jewish merchants. Throughout the first half of the 18th cent. the latter had great difficulty in trading with Marseille.

Not before the late 18th cent. did Jews settle at Marseille again. Of 209 Jewish families settling there between 1789 and 1808, twenty-six were of French, the rest of Levantine origin. The community of Marseille, as well as the Jews of the department of Bouches-du-Rhône, were represented in the Assembly of Notables of 1806 by Sabbaton Constantini, who lived at Marseille from 1767 on. He also demanded that exception be made in the case of the Jews of the department from Napoleon's "infamous decree" of 1808. Napoleon's decree of December 11, 1808, made Marseille capital of the consistorial district of Marseille, embracing eight departments and 2,527 Jews; in 1847 the district had 3,958 out of the total Jewish population of France of 95,910. In 1896 Marseille had 5,000 Jews in a total population of 420,300; in 1918, 5,500 Jews. After the separation of church and state (December 9, 1905), Marseille remained the capital city of the Association Cultuelle Israélite de Marseille, comprising (in 1923), with its district, 8,000 persons. Marseille alone had 2,000 Jews in 1931 out of a total population of 914,239. The synagogue of Marseille, in the Rue Bréteuil, was dedicated on September 22, 1864; the cemetery of 1783 was closed in 1855, the new cemetery was situated in the quarter of St. Pierre. A number of charitable institutions, cultural and trade associations for the Jewish youth and a Talmud Torah school were in existence. The first rabbi of the consistorial district was Mardoché Roquemartine. Others were Jonas Weyl (d. 1903); Honel Meiss (1904-20); Joseph Sachs (from 1920 on).

After the collapse of France (June, 1940) the full weight of anti-Jewish legislation, culminating on June 14, 1941, was brought to bear upon the Jews of Marseille. Two boats, carrying 172 Jewish refugees from Marseille, were stopped on October 14, 1940, by French officials. French and foreign Jews were driven from Marseille to other places. On June 2, 1941, the Vichy government approved the reestablishment of the Agudath Israel at Marseille. Several committees to assist needy Jews were formed. On July 7, 1941, 1,200 Jews of Russian nationality, including officials of the ORT and of the HIAS-ICA, were imprisoned; others were arrested as communists. According to a report of September 14, 1941, a provincial administrator was named for the "Aryanization" of Jewish business enterprises at Marseille. After June, 1940, Marseille was one of the foremost ports of emigration.   ADOLF KOBER.

Lit.: *American Jewish Year Book,* vol. 42 (1940-41); vol. 43 (1941-42); Anchel, Robert, *Napoléon et les Juifs* (1928); Aronius, J., *Regesten,* Nos. 38, 44, 46 and 52; Barthélemy, L., *Les médecins à Marseille avant et pendant le Moyen-Âge* (1883); *Contemporary Jewish Record,* vols. 3 and 4 (1940 and 1941); Crémieux, Adolphe, *Les Juifs de Marseille au Moyen-Âge* (1903); Dubnow, S., *Weltgeschichte*

des jüdischen Volkes, vols. 4, 5 and 7 (1926, 1927 and 1928); Gross, Henri, *Gallia Judaica* (1897); Juster, Jean, *Les juifs dans l'empire romain* (1914) 184; Mabilly, Philippe, *La ville de Marseille au Moyen-Âge* (1905); Masson, Paul, *Marseille depuis 1879* (1921); *Revue des études juives* (see the quoted essays and passages in the Index 1-50, p. 248); *The Jews in France. Studies and Materials,* edit. E. Tcherikower, vols. 1 and 2 (1942).

MARSHAK, SAMUIL IAKOVLEVICH, Soviet writer, b. Russia, 1887. Although his first work, which took the form of poetry, was published in 1907, it was not until 1917 that his reputation began to spread. By then he was specializing in literature for children; the first of his publications was a compilation of plays, *Theatre for Children,* which he prepared in collaboration with E. Vasileva. Later there were adaptations from the English and original work. Marshak takes toys, inanimate objects, animals and social problems for his subjects and writes about them in simple and comprehensible images. His books have been translated into many of the languages of the Soviet Union as well as into foreign languages, including English. In 1942 he was also writing verse for war posters and was, in addition, participating in other propaganda work. Marshak is one of the leaders in the Children's Writers' Section of the Union of Soviet Writers, and is the recipient of the Order of Lenin. In 1942 he was awarded a Stalin prize for his very effective verses composed for the Kukryniksy war posters.

MARSHALIK, a buffoon or jester who participated in Jewish wedding festivals in Eastern Europe. The word is a derivation from the German *marshal,* meaning the highest royal servant. The diminutive ending naturally gave the term a satirical twist.

It was the duty of the Marshalik to improvise wedding songs and riddles, to announce the wedding gifts (frequently in verse), and to tell barbed or pleasant truths about the bride and groom. Since his role was that of jester, considerable license was allowed him, and he did not always refrain from giving accurate descriptions of the bride, the groom and other members of the wedding party.

Lit.: *Mitteilungen für jüdische Volkskunde,* vol. 8, p. 157; Abrahams, Israel, *Jewish Life in the Middle Ages* (1896) 198.

MARSHALL, JAMES, lawyer and educational executive, b. New York city, 1896. After receiving his law degree from Columbia University in 1920, Marshall was admitted to the New York bar the following year. Until 1930 he was a member of the law firm of Guggenheimer, Untermyer and Marshall, then he practised alone for several years and in 1934 formed the firm of Marshall, Bratter and Seligson.

The communal life of which his father, Louis Marshall, had been an integral part early claimed the interest of the son as well. He cooperated in general and Jewish activities, and assumed responsible posts in relief campaigns and social welfare movements of many kinds. His concern with civic duties brought Marshall into a directive role in education. In 1933 he became a member of the board of the New York State Training School for Boys, and in 1934 and 1935 he was president of the school. An opportunity of greater scope was given to Marshall in 1935, when Mayor Fiorello H. LaGuardia appointed him to the

New York city Board of Education. In 1938 Marshall was elected president of the Board, a post which pays no salary, despite its full claims on the time of the incumbent. He served until 1942, when he resigned. Marshall had to defend the New York city school system against many attacks from teachers' and citizens' groups for supposed inadequacies. With the entry of the United States into the war in 1941, Marshall became chairman of the Committee of Civilian Defense in the schools, and worked out a program for the protection and care of New York city school children in the war emergency.

In shaping educational policy Marshall has had a potent instrument through which to express his own high purposes of a democratic society. His presidency marks a period of progress in the history of New York city's public school system. Through his writings, his speeches, his contacts with the professional staff, and through studies of various aspects of the school system initiated by him, Marshall has influenced educational policy throughout the country.

Some of the most far-reaching reforms in educational policy and practice have resulted directly from studies and investigations initiated and directed by Marshall during his membership on the Board of Education of New York city. He was chairman of the Joint Committee for the Study of Maladjustment and Delinquency (1935-37); a five-volume report was published on the basis of this two-year study. He was also chairman of the Committee for the Study of the Care and Education of Physically Handicapped Children, the reports of which were published in eleven volumes in 1941; chairman of the Committee for the Survey of Vocational Education (1941-42); chairman of the National Committee on the Protection of School Children and School Property (1941—), established by the Office of Civilian Defense, Washington, D. C.; and chairman of the Committee on Law of the Board of Education (1938—). Under the leadership and direction of Marshall a comprehensive revision of the by-laws of the Board of Education of New York city was undertaken.

While serving as president of the Board of Education, Marshall retained his various active posts in general and Jewish communal life. He was elected honorary vice-president of the Jewish Publication Society of America in 1940, and in 1942 was serving on the executive committee of the American Jewish Committee as well as of the Joint Distribution Committee. Marshall also wrote on legal and social welfare subjects for various magazines, and was the author of *Ordeal by Glory* (1927) and *Swords and Symbols* (1939), both expository presentations of economic and political subjects. He was awarded the Columbia University Silver Medal for 1940, for competence in philosophy or education.

ROBERT MARSHALL (b. New York city, 1901; d. 1939), brother of James Marshall, was a forester. He received his degree from the College of Forestry of Syracuse University in 1923 and his Ph.D. degree from Johns Hopkins University in 1930. Much of his time was spent in forest survey work, including a period of more than a year above the Arctic Circle in Alaska. From 1933 to 1937 Marshall was director of the forestry division of the Office of Indian Affairs for the United States Government. Then he was made chief of the division of recreation and soil conservation of the government forestry service, which post he held at the time of his death. Marshall wrote various studies on the subject of forestry, and was the author also of *Arctic Village* (1933), *The People's Forests* (1933) and *The Universe of the Wilderness is Vanishing* (1937).

BENJAMIN VEIT.

MARSHALL, LOUIS, lawyer, communal and civic leader, b. Syracuse, N. Y., 1856; d. Zurich, Switzerland, 1929. Educated in the public schools of Syracuse, Marshall for two years read law in the offices of Nathaniel B. Smith in that city and then went to New York to study at the Law School of Columbia University where he completed the two-year course in one year. In recognition of his brilliance as a student, Marshall, on the day that he was admitted to the Bar of the State of New York, was invited to become a law partner of one of the examining attorneys, William C. Ruger. Later Ruger became chief justice of the Court of Appeals, the state's highest tribunal, and the firm changed its name to Jenney, Brooks and Marshall. His growing fame, as a constitutional lawyer, brought Marshall to New York city in 1894, where he became a partner in the firm of Guggenheimer, Untermyer and Marshall, a connection he maintained until his death.

Marshall was recognized as one of the leaders of the American bar. During his thirty-five years of practice in New York city he was concerned in a great variety of cases, largely involving principles of constitutional law, both Federal and State, and of corporation law. Among the hundreds of cases he argued before the highest courts of the land were many involving the constitutionality of statutes concerning bonus payments to war veterans, inheritance and special franchise taxes, workmen's compensation for injuries received in industrial accidents, alien immigration, the ownership of real estate by Japanese, the segregation of Negroes, the naturalization of Hindus and other races, the abolition of private and parochial schools, and the conservation of the nation's forests and wild life.

Despite his eminence as an attorney and a civic leader, Marshall neither sought nor held salaried public office. Yet he had an intense interest in politics insofar as they affected the law and good government. Invariably his sympathies were with those whose legal and human rights he felt threatened.

In 1902 he was appointed by Mayor Seth Low of New York city as a member of a commission investigating slum conditions in the lower East Side. In 1909 he was named by Governor Charles Evans Hughes chairman of the Commission of Immigration of New York State, the work of the commission resulting in important reforms. His interest in immigration legislation continued for the rest of his life. Marshall was chief counsel for Governor William Sulzer of New York in the impeachment proceedings through which the latter was removed from office in 1913. At about the same time he joined with other eminent lawyers in defending the rights of five Socialists elected to the New York State Legislature when efforts were made to deny them their seats—this despite the fact that he was a lifelong Republican and opposed to Socialism.

Louis Marshall

In 1910 Marshall was called upon to act as mediator in the great clothing industry strike of that year. The protocol which he prepared not only settled the clothing strike but was the basis for adjustments in many other industrial disputes in subsequent years. He was a member of the arbitration committee which settled the New York clothing strike in 1919, and was often called upon in ensuing years for similar services. Marshall also served at three state constitutional conventions (1890, 1894, and 1915), the first New Yorker and probably the first American to serve thrice in such a capacity. During the first World War he was a member of the New York district draft board.

Marshall was both mentor and leader to his generation of American Jews. He played a major role in the relief efforts for the victims of the first World War; he was, though not a Zionist, an active figure in the upbuilding of Palestine; he was the leader in the struggle to establish the principle of minority rights at the Versailles Peace Conference. Throughout his career he fought against discriminatory immigration laws and alien-baiting legislation.

Marshall first gained prominence as a communal leader during the passport agitation which in 1911 resulted in the abrogation of Russia's commercial treaty with the United States (1832). The so-called Passport Question arose as a result of the determined policy of the Russian Government, after 1880, in violation of the terms of the commercial treaty, to deny travel visas to American Jews and to Roman Catholic and Protestant missionaries. At the turn of the century, when the State Department tended to let the matter rest, leaders of the American Jewish Committee (founded in 1906) sought to obtain a stronger government policy.

Marshall's first public address on the issue, delivered before the convention of the Union of American Hebrew Congregations on January 18, 1911, was both an impassioned appeal and a legal document. On February 10, 1911, a resolution calling for the abrogation of the treaty was introduced in the House by Representative Herbert Parsons of New York. On February 15, a day prior to the opening of hearings on the Parsons Resolution, Marshall and other Jewish leaders were invited by President Taft to discuss the issue at the White House. The President presented the view that Russia's violations of the treaty by failing to honor the American passport had, despite constant protest, continued so long that it was now too late to apply the logical remedy—abrogation of the treaty. Marshall and his colleagues refused to adopt this view. The next day Marshall appeared as the principal witness at the hearing on the Parsons Resolution. He urged immediate abrogation because further continuation of diplomatic negotiations would find the conscience of America growing weary and protest fainter "until gradually we will read into this treaty an acquiescence in the Russian doctrine of discrimination among citizens and of a discrimination against men by reason of their faith." The Parsons Resolution and one introduced by Senator Charles A. Culbertson of Texas in the Senate, on February 26, were permitted to die as the congressional session came to an end.

Substitute measures were offered at the new session of Congress in December. In the meantime public interest in the issue reached a high pitch, with a number of state legislatures memorializing Congress for abrogation of the treaty and many outstanding national leaders urging it. The major congressional hearing took place before the House Committee on Foreign Affairs (December 11, 1911) when it met to consider the new Sulzer Resolution. Marshall appeared as the principal spokesman for those seeking an end to the treaty. He called witnesses and cited facts in an unending stream. His knowledge of the law amazed the listeners. His feats of memory in connection with obscure legal points and citations were prodigious, and at the close of the hearing the Committee voted unanimously to report the resolution favorably

to the House, which then adopted it with only one dissenting vote.

At the hearing before the Senate Committee on Foreign Relations, two days later, Marshall was again the first and principal witness. The Senate Committee was so impressed with Marshall's testimony that Senator Henry Cabot Lodge of Massachusetts reported to President Taft that unless the treaty was denounced by executive action, the Senate would adopt unanimously the resolution of the House. As a result, Taft did not wait for further congressional action. Acting on powers vested in him as President, he notified the Russian government that the United States was determined to abrogate the treaty, and that, in accordance with the one year notice required by its terms, the treaty would lapse on December 31, 1912.

The successful outcome of the campaign marked Marshall's emergence in the front rank of Jewish communal leadership. It gave him national prestige and he became, shortly thereafter, president of the American Jewish Committee. His close study of the Russian issue made Marshall acutely aware of the disabilities and persecutions suffered by Jews in Russia and other East European lands, and he spent the remainder of his life endeavoring to improve the civic and political status of the Jews in those countries. In 1913, as president of the American Jewish Committee, he appealed to President Taft to employ the good offices of the government with the powers at the London Peace Conference in behalf of the minorities that would be affected by the new treaty ending the Balkan War. Marshall renewed his appeal with President Wilson after the Taft Administration left office.

The great opportunity to obtain guarantees of minority rights, however, did not arrive until after the first World War. In the meantime, the American Jewish community experienced a great internal struggle between groups of widely differing principles. The struggle developed about the efforts of Zionist groups to establish an American Jewish Congress "democratically elected" which would represent all of American Jewry at the forthcoming peace conference. Marshall and his colleagues, who rejected the Jewish nationalist ideal, opposed such a congress as an effort to erect a super-structure atop the existing communal organizations that would enable the Zionists to gain control of and dominate the American Jewish community. In the long struggle which then ensued, lasting until the end of the war, compromises were finally reached and an American Jewish Congress of limited jurisdiction and of temporary character was established. The two chief points that Marshall insisted upon were that the Congress should be limited to the task at Versailles, disbanding immediately after its completion; and that no meeting of the Congress should be held prior to the cessation of all hostilities on the European battlefront. The course of events justified and vindicated the position taken by Marshall on the major issues.

Marshall regarded the Jewish community as a religious community. He was opposed to its organization as a unit along secular lines. The secular schisms among Jews were, in his opinion, the same as the schisms among non-Jews, and the natural form of organization would be for Jews to become integrated into the general secular community. He was, therefore, opposed to the establishment of a national Jewish body, such as a Congress by general election, which was intended to be the spokesman for all Jews on all subjects. This attitude brought down upon him, and upon the American Jewish Committee which he led, the vehement criticism of Zionist groups, and faced him with the accusation that he was opposed to democratic methods and to democratic organization.

In the movement to obtain civil and religious rights for the Jews of Eastern Europe, the various groups in the community concerned differed as to the meaning of the terms. Were the Jews of Eastern Europe to seek national rights or minority rights; special status as national groups or merely equal civil and political rights with other citizens? In the democratic countries Jews neither desired nor required special status, and the efforts for such status for Jews in Eastern Europe were looked upon by some with trepidation.

Marshall saw the issue clearly. Personally and as the representative of the American Jewish Committee, he was opposed to the national minority concept. But he recognized the historical influences which motivated its adherents both in the United States and abroad. He became the great mediator among the various groups that had lost themselves in a maze of phraseology and involved meaning, yet he remained completely faithful to his own principles. More than any of his confrères, he was able to appreciate the viewpoint of the Jews of Eastern Europe which was being echoed in the United States. The role of conciliator which he assumed at this time, he continued until the establishment of the American Jewish Congress in 1918 and throughout the Peace Conference at Versailles. It made him the outstanding figure in the efforts to obtain minority rights for the Jews of Eastern Europe. It was the outstanding feat of statesmanship of his life.

At Versailles, where he arrived as a delegate of the American Jewish Congress (March 27, 1919), Marshall found himself confronted with two major tasks which, because the peace conference was already making rapid progress, had to be met simultaneously. The first was to obtain unity and a basis of cooperation among the various Jewish delegations; the second to obtain in the instruments, even then being drawn up by the major powers, the guarantees of the rights of the Jews and the establishment of a system of enforcement that would put teeth into these guarantees.

Marshall soon found that unity was even less attainable in Paris than it had been within the American Jewish community. The chief anti-nationalist group was French Jewry, represented by the Alliance Israélite Universelle; somewhat less determined in its anti-nationalist viewpoint was the British Joint Delegation. In the opposition faction were grouped the delegations from East European countries who were dominated by Zionist leadership and were almost fanatical in their zeal for national rights. These factions had practically severed relations with each other by the time Marshall arrived, and it looked as if the American delegation, which had already achieved a platform upon which both American nationalists and non-nationalists could cooperate, would not be able to heal the breach.

Realizing that some form of unity would have to be achieved among the Jewish delegations and that some common program would have to be formulated if the maximum of attention and sympathy were to be obtained for their cause from the leaders of the major powers, Marshall began to steer negotiations toward a less all-embracing agreement. Two factors led him to this line of action: first, that with time so short and the opposing factions so unyielding, no union could be achieved; secondly, that no union was really needed just so long as the conflict did not come out into the open with Jewish delegations presenting opposing memoranda to the peace conference leaders.

Under Marshall's patient but persistent leadership a formula was finally reached. As he himself reported it, it was arranged that "there should be the fullest cooperation and interchange of views as to all matters concerning which the several committees were in accord, that the Committee of Jewish Delegations was to present its views on the subject of national rights to the Peace Conference in such forms as it deemed desirable, and that the other committees, while not giving affirmative approval to the contentions of the Committee of Jewish Delegations on that subject, would abstain from acting in hostility to the proposals that might be urged in support of national rights. So far as it was possible to act in accordance with this oral understanding, it was done, save in a few instances, and even so far as the latter were concerned an open conflict, which would have been most unfortunate, was happily avoided."

The final draft of the memorandum agreed upon for submission to the Peace Conference leaders approximated the position adopted by the American delegation. In essence, the rights sought were "the rights of the most favored minority." So long drawn and exhausting were the discussions that the document was not presented to the Peace Conference until June 10th, by which time the matter had become "purely academic," except insofar as the thoughts expressed in it had been presented in the meantime to those engaged in drafting the peace treaties by Marshall and others of the American delegation.

Simultaneously, with his efforts to achieve a measure of unity among the Jewish delegations in Paris, Marshall, together with Judge Julian W. Mack, who for a time was president of the Committee of Jewish Delegations (then was succeeded by Marshall), urged the cause of minority rights with President Woodrow Wilson, Colonel House and the legal advisors of the American delegation to the Peace Conference. In accordance with his interest in all minority questions, Marshall not only acted as counsel and advisor to negroes in matters involving their race, but appeared several times before the Supreme Court to argue civil rights questions in regard to negroes. The National Association for the Advancement of Colored People honored him both during his life and after his death.

During his years as head of the American Jewish Committee (1912-1929) Marshall carried on unending war against those who attacked Jews or maligned their good name. He labored equally to destroy organized anti-Semitism and to challenge the casual defamer. Marshall spoke out eloquently on the basis of the civil liberties guaranteed by the Constitution of the United States, defending and explaining the rich culture and the tradition of Judaism in terms of the concepts of law and order, morality and American values. In the main he believed that the benighted could be enlightened and that the bigoted would listen to reason. But occasionally when bigotry was coupled with knowledge, intelligence with premeditated malice, he realized that disputation, however much logic was on his side, would be of little avail.

At the close of the first World War, with a chaotic Europe in search of a scapegoat to explain their misery to the long suffering population, anti-Semitism, long possessed of a rationale, now also acquired its bible— the fabricated, incredible document known as the "Protocols of the Elders of Zion," which imputed to Jews a conspiracy to gain domination of the world. Marshall became acquainted with the bloody history of the forgery during his stay in France for the Versailles Peace Conference. He learned then that the manuscript of such a document was "for sale," and some years later the American Jewish Committee was offered the "original" manuscript in the vain hope that a substantial sum would be paid to suppress it.

A series of articles, based on the "Protocols," was published in book form in England under the title of *The Cause of World Unrest,* and G. P. Putnam's Sons published an American edition (1920) with an introduction by H. A. Gwynne, editor of the *London Morning Post,* and a publisher's note disavowing responsibility for the contents of the book. This spread of the "Protocols" libels through reputable publications and publishing houses was alarming to American Jews. Marshall, ever a defender of free speech and the freedom of the press, was appalled at the crimes being perpetrated in their name. He wrote in this vein to Major George Haven Putnam protesting against the appearance of *The Cause of World Unrest* and also against the projected publication of the "Protocols" under the Putnam imprint as a companion volume to the former. The publisher, Marshall declared, could not rationalize his position by disclaiming responsibility for the books he published. Putnam refused to accept Marshall's reasoning, but offered to publish a refutation to *The Cause of World Unrest* if Marshall would write it. Marshall rejected this offer, contending once more that the right of free speech could not be stretched to include malicious slander such as the "Protocols." Whether Marshall's reasoning prevailed or not, Putnam shortly thereafter dropped the projected publication of the "Protocols." While he would not write the refutation sought by Putnam, Marshall felt convinced that dignified silence upon the part of American Jews as a community would not meet the "recrudescence of medieval bigotry and stupidity" which was being disseminated by means of the "Protocols" and commentaries based on them. As president of the American Jewish Committee, therefore, he asked the outstanding Jewish organizations to join with the Committee in a formal "address" to the country which would answer the various assaults being made upon the Jews. Marshall himself drafted the address which was entitled *The Protocols, Bolshevism and the Jews.* The reaction to the address from the press and from outstanding figures and organizations in the country was gratifying.

From 1920 until 1927, however, the slanders of the "Protocols" continued to be published in Henry Ford's *Dearborn Independent* in a series of articles entitled *The International Jew.* Marshall's efforts to check the *Dearborn Independent's* campaign of calumny were dictated by a sense of generalship that rejected all tactics that would serve to spotlight or publicize the slanders spewed forth by the publication. Once in 1921, by obtaining the intercession of President Warren G. Harding, Marshall succeeded in having publication of the articles stopped. But after Harding's death, the *Dearborn Independent* reverted to type and the scurrilous attacks continued. They stopped again in 1927. This time Marshall received from Henry Ford himself a public retraction of the articles and a public apology.

In June, 1927, Marshall was approached by Earl J. Davis of Detroit, and Joseph A. Palma of New York, representatives of Ford, who declared that Ford had become convinced that all of the charges made against Jews, individually and collectively, were without foundation and unjust, and that he desired to make amends. Marshall's reply to Ford's emissaries was that amends could be made only by a complete retraction of the lies, a full apology, a discontinuance of the attacks, a withdrawal of the pamphlets constituting the *International Jew,* and a pledge that such publications would never again be issued. Ford agreed to sign a statement, suggested by Marshall, incorporating these points. In order to prevent any future misunderstandings, Ford personally made the retraction public by sending a copy of it to Arthur Brisbane, editor of the Hearst newspapers, asking him to publish it.

Marshall was not too sanguine about the effect that Ford's retraction would have in stopping all further dissemination of the objectionable pamphlets. And so it proved to be. Ford withdrew from circulation such of the material as was under his direct control, but he was less successful in foreign countries where *The International Jew* was reprinted by anti-Semitic agitators. Despite considerable effort, Ford never wholly succeeded in stopping the circulation of the pamphlets.

The unique position achieved by Louis Marshall in American Jewish life has had no precedent, nor has it been matched since. His personality, his leadership and his wisdom reached out and touched every facet of Jewish life. His career is a history of the Jewish community of his time.

A non-Zionist, yet he made important contributions to Palestine, and long before the Balfour Declaration he believed in Palestine as a place for Jewish settlement. His post-war leadership brought non-Zionists into close cooperation with the World Zionist Organization, first through the establishment of a Palestine Survey Commission and later through the creation of the enlarged Jewish Agency for Palestine. The last public act of his life, before he was stricken in Zurich, was to append his name to the constitution of the enlarged Jewish Agency.

Marshall, too, was a leader in the war and post-war relief efforts in behalf of stricken Jewish communities in Europe. He was president of the American Jewish Relief Committee, organized by the American Jewish Committee in 1914, and was a prime mover in the establishment of the American Jewish Joint Distribution Committee when in the same year it became the central body for bringing relief to distressed Jewish communities overseas. Marshall remained an active

Louis Marshall. From a snapshot (the last) taken of him at Zurich in 1929

perhaps was rendered by Franklin D. Roosevelt, then governor of New York, who recommended to the State Legislature in 1930 an appropriation of $600,000 for the erection of a new building, which now bears Marshall's name, for the State College of Forestry at Syracuse University. Marshall's love of nature welled up out of his religious spirit and he regarded the preservation of the nation's forests and wild life almost as a religious matter. He was chairman of the board of trustees of the State Forestry School for many years, and it was under his leadership, as Mr. Roosevelt phrased it, that the school "became recognized as the premier institution of its kind in the United States."

See also: AMERICAN JEWISH COMMITTEE; ANTI-SEMITISM; JEWISH AGENCY FOR PALESTINE; LEAGUE OF NATIONS; MINORITY RIGHTS.

NATHAN CARO BELTH.

Lit.: Adler, Cyrus, in *American Jewish Year Book,* vol. 32 (1930-31) 21-55; Marshall, Louis, in *Judaean Addresses,* vol. 2 (1917) 52-57; *American Hebrew,* Aug. 1, 1919, p. 263; Oct. 10, 1924, p. 686; Oct. 24, 1924, p. 754; Oct. 31, 1924, p. 778; Nov. 14, 1924, p. 13; Dec. 19, 1924, p. 194; Nov. 6, 1925, p. 838; Dec. 3, 1926, p. 126; March 11, 1927, p. 599; April 20, 1928, p. 906; Nov. 9, 1928, p. 898; Nov. 23, 1928, p. 76; April 5, 1929, p. 752; June 28, 1929, p. 201; Sept. 13, 1929, pp. A, B, C and D; Sept. 20, 1929, p. 521; Sept. 27, 1929, p. 541; Oct. 4, 1929, p. 646; Nov. 22, 1929, p. 32; Sept. 7, 1934 (memorial issue); Sept. 14, 1934, pp. 325, 327, 330-35; Sept. 28, 1934, p. 369; *Jewish Tribune,* May 12, 1922, p. 5; Feb. 2, 1923, p. 2; June 29, 1923, p. 1; Aug. 24, 1923, p. 2; June 27, 1924, p. 10; Dec. 10, 1926 (special issue on the occasion of Louis Marshall's seventieth birthday); annual reports of the American Jewish Committee from the time of its organization until Marshall's death.

MARTEAU, HENRI, violinist and teacher, b. Rheims, France, 1874; d. Lichtenberg, Bavaria, Germany, 1934. A pupil at the Paris Conservatory, he won first prize in violin playing in 1892. He made his concert debut at the age of ten with the Vienna Philharmonic under Richter. A successful appearance in London followed (also under Richter), and following this a tour of the United States in 1892. His subsequent tours of America and Europe were extensive. Major composers like Massenet, Reger and Dubois wrote concertos expressly for his use.

In 1900 Marteau was appointed professor of violin at Geneva Conservatory, and in 1908 he succeeded Joachim as head of the violin department at the Berlin Hochschule. During the first World War he transferred his home to Sweden, where for several years he was active as teacher and conductor. From 1921 to 1924 he taught at the German Musical Academy in Prague, becoming its director in his last year. From 1926 to 1928 he taught at the Leipzig Conservatory, and in 1928 he joined the faculty of the Dresden Conservatory. He was also founder and leader of the Marteau String Quartet which toured Europe and was one of the major musical groups of its kind. He translated into French the violin school texts of Joachim and Moser, and he composed operas, orchestral works, two concertos for violin, chorals and chamber ensembles.

MARTI, KARL, Protestant theologian, b. Bubendorf, near Basel, Switzerland, 1855; d. Bern, Switzerland, 1925. In 1895 he left the ministry for professorships at the University of Bern, where he taught theology and Semitic philology in 1901. Many European and American rabbis were his pupils. Among his books

figure in the J. D. C. until the time of his death.

A deeply religious man, Marshall throughout his lifetime maintained an interest in a wide variety of Jewish religious institutions. He was president of the Reform Temple Emanu-El in New York and at the same time president of the Conservative Jewish Theological Seminary. He was also active in the Y.M.H.A., the Jewish Welfare Board, the Jewish Publication Society of America, and the Bureau of Jewish Education. He endowed the Florence Marshall Schools for the education of Jewish girls as a tribute to his wife, and was active in many other religious educational endeavors. In 1939, on the tenth anniversary of his death, Jewish leaders of all shades of opinion paid homage at his grave.

Under Marshall's administration as president of Temple Emanu-El, a merger was effected between that congregation and Temple Beth-El (1927), forming one of the largest Reform congregations in the world. Marshall became president of the new congregation.

So varied and active a career was difficult of appraisal even for Supreme Court Justice Benjamin Cardozo, who wrote of Marshall: "One feels that he somehow has been transformed into a great civic institution, coordinating the energies and activities of many men, so that with all his intensely human traits he has acquired, in his own life, a new and, as it were, a corporate personality. He is a great lawyer; a great champion of ordered liberty; a great leader of his people; a great lover of mankind."

A tribute that would have pleased Marshall most

are the *Kurzgefasste Grammatik der biblisch-aramä-ischen Sprache* (1896; 2nd ed., 1911) and the *Geschichte der israelitischen Religion* (1897; 3rd ed., 1907). In the *Kurzer Handkommentar zum Alten Testament* (Tübingen), edited by him, he wrote the volumes on *Isaiah* (1900), *Daniel* (1901), the Minor Prophets (1904), and the introductory volume, *Die Religion des Alten Testaments unter den Religionen des vorderen Orients* (1906; English trans., *The Religion of the Old Testament,* London, 1907). In E. Kautzsch' *Heilige Schrift des Alten Testaments* he translated *Deuteronomy, Daniel* and five books of the minor prophets. From 1907 to 1923 he was editor of the *Zeitschrift für die alttestamentliche Wissenschaft.* A list of Marti's publications may be found in the jubilee volume published by Budde on Marti's seventieth birthday, *Vom Alten Testament* (41st supplement of the *Zeitschrift,* Giessen, 1925).

MARTIAL, *see* Roman Writers on Jews.

MARTIN V, *see* Popes.

MARTIN, RAYMOND, anti-Jewish Catholic theologian, b. Subirats, Catalonia, Spain, early in the 13th cent.; d. Spain, after 1284. In 1250 he studied oriental languages at a Dominican school which was devoted to the struggle against Judaism and Mohammedanism. In 1264 he was appointed a member of a commission to examine the Talmud for anti-Christian passages. Martin recommended leniency toward the Talmud, because he found in many parts of it statements which he considered a support of the Christian doctrine.

Martin wrote two books against the Jews, *Capistrum Judaeorum* (which was never printed) and *Pugio Fidei,* written in 1270 and published in Paris in 1651. The latter work is an attack on the Jewish religion; it asserts that Jesus was announced as the Messiah in early rabbinical literature but was later renounced by the authors of the Talmud, whom Martin accused of having tampered with the text of the Bible. Solomon ben Abraham ibn Adret (RaSHBA), rabbi of Barcelona, wrote a small pamphlet in which he refuted the arguments against Judaism advanced by Martin and his followers. According to 20th cent. scholars such as Saul Lieberman, Martin was not guilty of forging Talmudic texts, as had long been thought, but derived his fanatical interpretations from Talmudic versions extant during his time.

Lit.: Graetz, H., *History of the Jews,* vol. 3 (1927) 603, 622-23; Dubnow, S., *Weltgeschichte des jüdischen Volkes,* vol. 5 (1927) 96, 119; *Jewish Encyclopedia,* vol. 8, pp. 351-52.

MARTINEZ, FERNANDO (FERRAND), archdeacon of Ecija (Andalusia), one of the most influential ecclesiastics of the archdiocese of Seville, Spain, at the end of the 14th cent. and an implacable enemy of the Jewish people. He planted the seeds of the Inquisition by preaching the doctrine that Spain had to rid herself of the Jews by forcing them into baptism through violence. Despite the repeated interventions of his superiors and of the king, Martinez continued to preach against the Jews, accusing them of greed and other vices and inciting the mob to riots.

After the death of King John I and of Archbishop Barraso, who had acted vigorously against Martinez, the latter was appointed vicar-general. Taking advantage of the unsettled political conditions in the country which were due to dissensions among the members of the regency who ruled in the name of King Henry III, then eleven years old, Martinez proceeded on a campaign of extermination of the Jews. The first riots broke out in Seville on March 15, 1391. The Jews appealed to the regency and the riots were stopped for a time. On June 6th the mob resumed its work in earnest. In Seville alone 4,000 Jews perished, while the remainder of the community of about 6,000 families, with few exceptions, allowed themselves to be baptized. Women and children were sold into slavery, and the synagogues were converted into churches or demolished. From Seville the riots spread to other cities in Castile and then to Aragon, Catalonia and the island of Majorca. In Castile alone about seventy prosperous Jewish communities were destroyed. In 1395 King Henry III ordered the imprisonment of Martinez, but he was soon released because of his great popularity among the people, who worshipped him as a saint.

Lit.: Graetz, H., *History of the Jews,* vol. 4 (1927) 167-69, 193; Dubnow, S., *Weltgeschichte des jüdischen Volkes,* vol. 5 (1927) 258-63, 346.

MARTINIQUE, an island in the West Indies, 380 square miles in area with a total population of 250,000. It was a French colonial possession (1942).

The island was wrested from the Carib natives, in 1635, in the name of the French Compagnie des Iles d'Amérique. In 1654, 300 Jews from the Dutch-held port of Recife (or Pernambuco), Brazil, who were fleeing from the Portuguese attacking that port, sought refuge on Martinique. This event is believed to mark the beginning of Jewish settlement on the island. Other opinions as to the presence of Jews on Martinique prior to 1654 (see *Revue des études juives,* vol. 2, p. 93 et seq.), or even prior to 1635, do not rest on valid authority. Although the governor of Martinique was willing to receive the refugees from Recife, all but a few, through the interposition of the Jesuits, were soon compelled to leave. Those that remained were at first greatly restricted in their occupations and in the practice of their faith. The following year these restrictions were removed. In proof, the Jewish citizens of New Amsterdam, directing a petition to the Dutch West India Company for the privilege of trade and travel, cited the privileges enjoyed by the Jews of Martinique.

Purchased by the French government after 1658, Martinique was assigned to the French West India Company and became part of the Royal French domain in 1674. In spite of machinations by the Jesuits who had almost succeeded in effecting the expulsion of the Jews in 1664, they were left undisturbed through the favorable attitude of Colbert, Louis XIV's minister of finance; and their immigration was stimulated by the tolerant French authorities. After Colbert's death in 1683, Louis XIV yielded to the Jesuits and immediately ordered the expulsion of the Jews from the island. This edict was in time relaxed. Early in the 18th cent. there were a number of Jewish-owned business establishments on Martinique. Except for brief intervals of occupation and government by the British in the late 18th and early 19th cent., Martinique remained a French possession throughout its history. In 1764 a special Jewish tax was imposed which remained in force until the French Revolution in 1789.

In 1942 Martinique's contingent in the total Jewish population of 10,706 persons of the West Indies was barely 1 per cent.

MARTOS, FERENC, author and playwright, b. Arad, Hungary, 1875; d. Budapest, 1938. His historical drama in verse, *Balassa Bálint,* and his comedies, *Simonyi obester* (Colonel Simonyi) and *Muskátli* (Geranium), were performed by the National Theatre of Budapest. His libretto, *Bob herceg* (Prince Bob), for which Jenő Huszka wrote the music, proved a great hit, and from that time on he devoted himself entirely to the writing of libretti for various composers of operettas, such as *Marriage Market* and *Sybil* (music by Victor Jacobi), both performed in New York city in the 1920's; *Pacsirta* (The Lark; 1918; music by Franz Lehár); *Zsuzsi kisasszony* (music by Emeric Kalman); *A ballerina* (1926; music by Albert Szirmai); *Rothschildok* (1932; music by Lajthai). *Princess Charming* (music by Albert Szirmai) was performed in New York city in 1930.

MARTOV, JULIUS (YULY OSIPOVICH ZEDERBAUM), Russian revolutionary and journalist, b. Constantinople, 1873; d. Schömberg, Baden, Germany, 1923. He was a grandson of Alexander Zederbaum, editor of *Hamelitz,* the first Hebrew daily in Russia. Martov became affiliated with the social revolutionary movement in 1891. He was first arrested in St. Petersburg in 1892, while a student at the university, for conducting revolutionary study circles among his fellow students and for the distribution of illegal literature. While exiled at Vilna by the czarist government (1892-95), he participated in the Jewish labor movement and founded a propaganda group from which some of the most famous agitators and revolutionaries emanated.

Upon his return to the capital in 1895 Martov, together with Lenin, founded the League for the Struggle for Liberation of the Working Classes. In the same year he advocated the organization of the Jewish proletariat which was later realized in the "Bund." He was arrested in 1896 and banished to Siberia in the following year, but returned to Russia after having served his sentence. In 1901 he went to Switzerland where, together with Lenin and Plekhanov, he edited *Iskra* (The Spark), party organ of the Russian Social Democrats.

At the Party Congress of 1903 he broke with Lenin, who represented the "majority," while Martov led the "minority." The split was motivated especially by the question of party organization. Martov upheld the Western Socialist idea of a definitely democratic party in opposition to Lenin's thesis of a party of "professional revolutionaries" controlled by a "central committee." Having participated in the ill-fated Russian revolution of 1905, he was exiled abroad in 1906, to return to Russia in 1913, taking over the editorship of the two Menshevik newspapers.

During the first World War he lived abroad again. At the Zimmerwald Conference (near Bern, Switzerland) of 1915 he subscribed to the internationalist attitude; but, unlike Lenin, he wished to avoid breaking with the Second International, in order to come to terms with the Social Democratic faction that supported the belligerent governments.

After the outbreak of the February revolution in 1917 Martov returned to Russia, where he championed the principle of democracy and proletarian unity. During the civil war he called on labor opponents of Bolshevism to fight against Denikin, Wrangel and the foreign interventionists. In the fall of 1920, after the suppression of the Social Democratic party by the Bolshevist regime, he emigrated to Berlin. There he edited the Russian organ of the Menshevists, *Sozialistichesky Vestnik* (Socialist Messenger), until he died of tuberculosis in 1923.

Martov wrote numerous works on the history of revolutionary and labor movements in Russia, including *World Bolshevism* (Russian; Berlin, 1923) and *History of the Russian Social Democracy* (Russian; German trans., Berlin, 1926). *The State and the Socialist Revolution* (New York, 1938) is a selection of Martov's writings, translated into English by Integer.

MARTYROLOGY, list or biography of martyrs. Such lists and biographies, called *memorialia,* were produced by the Church early in its history for the adoration of its saints generally and for the use of particular congregations who commemorated them on their anniversaries by the celebration of requiem masses. What is probably the oldest such list in Jewish literature is that given in *Midrash Lam.* 2:2, containing the names of the ten martyrs who died for their faith during the reigns of Trajan and Hadrian. This list, repeated with slight variations in *Midrash Ps.* 9:13, was later developed, in narrative fashion, in the Midrash *Eleh Ezkerah* (These men will I remember) or *Asarah Haruge Malkuth* (Ten Martyrs). It subsequently formed the theme of several liturgical dirges, the best-known of which are the *Eleh Ezkerah,* recited in some communities on the Day of Atonement and in others on the Fast of Ab, and the *Arze Lebanon* (Cedars of Lebanon) by Meir ben Jehiel.

During the Middle Ages, especially following the Crusade of 1096 and the Rindfleisch persecutions of 1291 to 1298, the custom grew up among German Jewish communities of incorporating a commemoration of martyrs in the traditional memorial services (Hazkarath Neshamoth) of the synagogue on the Sabbaths preceding Pentecost and the Ninth of Ab. For this purpose chronological registers were drawn up. The oldest of such lists are those of Worms (1096 and 1049), Nuremberg, Heilbronn and Krautheim. Many of these were subsequently incorporated into the *Memorbuch* of Nuremberg, begun in 1296 by Isaac ben Samuel of Meiningen and subsequently augmented by succeeding generations, especially after its transference to Mayence in 1346. The resultant corpus, published by Siegmund Salfeld in 1898, covers a period of some 250 years (1096-1349) and contains the names of martyrs in the several cities of Germany during the Crusades, the disturbances of 1298, the Armleder persecutions of 1336 to 1339 and the Black Death excesses

Adolf Bernhard Marx

of 1349. Persecutions outside of Germany (for instance, in France and England) are also mentioned, and in some cases the names of victims are recorded.

Similar to the German lists are those anciently preserved by the Amsterdam community, containing the names of its members martyred by the Inquisition.

See also: MEMORIAL SERVICES; LAMENTATIONS, LITURGICAL.

Lit.: Salfeld, S., *Das Martyrologium des Nürnberger Memorbuches* (1898; the standard work); Lowe, *The Memorbook of Nürnberg* (1881); Neubauer, A., "Le Memorbuch de Mayence," *Revue des études juives,* vol. 4, p. 1 et seq.; Zunz, L., *Die synagogale Poesie des Mittelalters,* chap. 11; Finkelstein, L., "The Ten Martyrs," *Essays and Studies in Memory of Linda R. Miller* (1938) 29-55.

MARX, ADOLF BERNHARD, educator, composer and writer on music, b. Halle, Germany, 1795; d. Berlin, 1866. He was first intended for law, but his love for music drove him to abandon the legal profession for art. In 1824 he founded (with Schlesinger) the *Berliner Allgemeine Musikalische Zeitung,* one of the pioneer music journals of the world, which fought vigorously to bring recognition to deserving German composers. In 1830 he was appointed professor of music at Berlin University, becoming music director two years later. In 1850 he helped to found the Berlin Conservatory. He retired in 1856 to devote himself to composition and literary work. He composed voluminously, including an opera, three oratorios, symphonies, and songs. His music was too academic and formal to survive. It was criticized severely even in its own day, and among its severest critics was Felix Mendelssohn, resulting in the disruption of a lifelong friendship between the two musicians. More important by far are Marx's theoretical works, including a monumental four-volume thesis on composition which was many years later reissued and reedited by Hugo Riemann. Marx also wrote studies of Beethoven and Gluck, and a volume of reminiscences. A three-volume collection of his most important essays was issued in 1912 under the title of *Über Tondichter und Tonkunst.*

Lit.: Selle, G. F., *Aus Adolf Bernhard Marx' litterarischen Nachlass* (1898).

MARX, ALEXANDER, educator and librarian, b. Elberfeld, Germany, 1878. He studied at the rabbinical seminary in Berlin, and received his Ph.D. degree from the University of Königsberg in 1903. That same year he came to the United States to serve as professor of history and librarian at the Jewish Theological Seminary of America, in New York city, both of which posts he still occupied in 1942.

Marx collated and edited material relating to many previously unstudied periods of Jewish history, from Talmudic to modern times. Among his works are: *Seder Olam* (1903); *Aims and Tasks of Jewish Historiography* (1918); *Samuel Poznanski* (1922); *Glimpses of the Life of an Italian Rabbi* (1924); *The Correspondence between the Rabbis of Southern France and Maimonides about Astrology* (1926); *A History of the Jewish People* (with Max L. Margolis; 1927); *A Jewish Cause Célèbre in Sixteenth Century Italy* (1932); *Zunz's Letters to Steinschneider* (1934); *Moses Maimonides* (1935); *The Scientific Work of Some Outstanding Medieval Jewish Scholars* (1938). A bibliography of Marx's scientific papers, published on the occasion of the twenty-fifth anniversary of his connection with the Seminary, contained 206 items.

Under his direction and largely through it, the library of the Jewish Theological Seminary became one of the largest and most valuable Jewish libraries in the world. Marx was known as a leading Jewish scholar in America and an authority in the field of Hebrew bibliography. He was on the publication committee of the Jewish Publication Society of America, a member of the executive council of the United Synagogue, of the American Jewish Historical Society and of the Academy of Jewish Research. He was also a fellow of the Medieval Academy of America. Marx was awarded an honorary D.H.L. degree by the Jewish Institute of Religion in 1938.

Lit.: Cohen, Boaz, "Professor Alexander Marx," *The United Synagogue Recorder,* vol. 8, No. 1; Rockwell, William Walker, "Alexander Marx at Sixty," *American Hebrew,* Jan. 28, 1938, pp. 9, 12; *Jewish Tribune,* March 14, 1930, p. 6.

MARX, BURLE, pianist, conductor and composer, b. São Paulo, Rio de Janeiro, Brazil, 1902. He was the son of a Jewish father. After a period of study with his mother, he toured Brazil as child prodigy. In 1921 he went to Berlin to study piano with Barth, Koch and Kwast, following which he gave recitals in Vienna, Berlin and Paris. He also studied composition with E. N. von Reznicek, and conducting with Felix Weingartner. In 1929 Marx returned to Brazil, and thereafter was an important force in developing the musical life of his country. He founded, and for several years directed, the Rio de Janeiro Symphony Orchestra. He also served as a guest of many principal orchestras of the United States and Europe, such as the Berlin Philharmonic and the Hamburg Philharmonic (1932 and 1933) and the New York Philharmonic at the World's Fair (1939 and 1940). Marx was a gifted composer who combined European classical forms with native Brazilian musical idioms and colors. His choral works *Ave Maria* and *In Memoriam* were performed by the Schola Cantorum in New York in 1939. He composed also works for orchestra (including the *Fantastic Episode,* performed in New York in 1939 under his own direction), choral pieces, and various compositions for chamber music ensembles.

MARX, JULIUS (GROUCHO), comedian, b. New York city, 1895. Although not the eldest of the three Marx brothers, who became famous for their farcical antics on the stage and the motion picture screen, Groucho's dependence on words and his general professor-like stewardship of the madness in which they all participated made him seem the dominant one of the trio.

ARTHUR (HARPO) MARX (b. 1893) never broke his silence while acting, but used an excited wig, pantomime and his facility on the harp in the creation of his character, which was that of indiscriminate wooer. LEONARD (CHICO) MARX (b. 1891), a piano-playing zany, did not, however, spurn the use of words. A fourth brother, HERBERT (ZEPPO) MARX (b. 1901), participated in the early performances, but retired in 1935.

The four brothers began their stage career in an act with their mother and aunt. Later they made up their own act, and after playing in vaudeville and revues went over to the motion pictures. In 1932 they appeared in *Animal Crackers* and *Monkey Business.* *Horsefeathers* and *Duck Soup* were produced in 1933. In subsequent years came *A Night at the Opera, A Day at the Races, At the Circus* and *Go West.* The trio broke up in 1941, each brother planning to continue with his own type of acting or musical work. Groucho was the author of *Many Happy Returns* (1941), a humorous study of the income tax.

MARX, KARL (Heinrich Karl), philosopher, economist and founder of scientific socialism, b. Trier, Germany, 1818; d. London, 1883. He was the son of Heinrich (Hirschel) Marx, a lawyer. On both paternal and maternal side Karl Marx was descended from rabbinical families. While born a Jew, Karl was baptized at the age of six when his father embraced Lutheranism, a practice prevalent at the time, when Jews in Germany found it impossible to embark upon professional careers.

Upon graduation from the Trier Gymnasium (1835), Marx entered the school of jurisprudence at Bonn University. That year he also betrothed Jenny von Westphal, said to be a descendant of the Duke of Argyle (beheaded by James II), whom he married in 1843. Following his studies at Bonn, Marx pursued historical and philosophical courses at Berlin (1836), where he joined the circle of young Hegelians. His first literary efforts (poetry) date from that year. In 1841 he obtained the Ph.D. degree from the University of Jena for his thesis on Democritus and Epicurus.

Marx was a contributor to, then editor of, the *Rheinische Zeitung* (1842-43), published at Cologne in collaboration with Arnold Ruge. This journal was suppressed (1843) for its attacks upon government policy in Prussia. Under pressure of increasing reaction, Marx moved to Paris where he resided until 1845. During these two years he studied assiduously such English and French economists as Adam Smith, David Ricardo, and Pierre Boisguillbert. He associated with refugees then resident in the French capital, among them Heine, Bakounin, and Proudhon, as well as with leading Hegelian students. It was at this time, too, that he met Frederick Engels, resulting in a lifelong friendship and collaboration in the fundamental philosophy that came to be known throughout the world as Marxism.

In 1844, Marx edited and published, with Ruge, the one issue of the double number of a magazine, the

Karl Marx

Deutsche-französische Jahrbücher, which contained two contributions by Marx, one dealing with Hegelian philosophy and the other, "Zur Judenfrage," with the Jewish question. At the instance of the Prussian government, Marx was expelled from Paris in 1845. He went to Brussels, renouncing his Prussian citizenship, and remained there until 1848. The Brussels period saw the beginning of his collaboration with Engels and publication of some of his leading works. Together with Engels, he published *The Holy Family* and *German Ideology* in 1845. Marx also contributed to four journals, in Brussels, Westphalia and Germany. *The Poverty of Philosophy* (1847) was Marx's reply to Proudhon's *The Philosophy of Poverty* (1845). In 1847 Engels joined Marx in Brussels more or less permanently, and they launched a magazine, the *Deutsche Brüsseler Zeitung.* Marx visited London as a member of the Communist League. He and Engels were directed by that League to draft the *Communist Manifesto.* This *Manifesto,* one of the classics of all time, was written by Marx and Engels and published in February, 1848. It soon was translated into most of the languages of the world. The *Communist Manifesto* concludes with: "Workers of the World, Unite!"—familiar slogan of the revolutionary workers' movement.

The members of the Communist League residing in Paris were expelled, and Marx removed to Cologne where he resumed publication of what was known as the *Neue Rheinische Zeitung,* which described itself as "organ of democracy." About this time he met Ferdinand Lacsalle and visited Vienna, where he lectured to the workers association of that city. In 1849 he was indicted, and tried by a jury at Cologne, on the charge of press offenses and incitement to armed insurrection. Although Marx was acquitted, the *Neue Rheinische Zeitung* was suppressed, and Marx was expelled from Germany. That year he visited Paris, carrying credentials as representative of German democracy to the National Assembly of Paris. However, he was soon expelled from Paris; he went to London where he continued to reside until his death in 1883.

Marx's life in London was productive in spite of sufferings from poverty and illness, and from premature deaths in his family. In a family of six only two daughters were to reach maturity; one of these married the English socialist Edward Aveling, the other the French socialist Jean Longuet. In 1850 Engels joined Marx in London. Marx continued to contribute from London to the *Neue Rheinische Zeitung,* and lectured to English workers. In 1850, too, he sustained a further blow in the death of his only son.

From 1852 to the end of 1861 Marx was regular London correspondent of the *New York Tribune.* On the reelection of President Abraham Lincoln, Marx drafted the resolution of English workers which hailed that event. President Lincoln, despite opposition by conservative elements, personally and warmly acknowledged these greetings. The year 1852 saw the publication of two of Marx's classics, *The Civil War in France* and *The Eighteenth Brumaire of Louis Bonaparte.* In 1857 he became a contributor to the *New American Encyclopedia.* His *Critique of Political Economy,* another fundamental work, was issued in 1859. Two years later he visited Germany and saw Lassalle. His outstanding work, *Value, Price and Profit,* forerunner of the monumental *Das Kapital,* known as *Capital,* was published as a result of lectures in London in 1865. And that year also saw the conference that led to the foundation of the First International. In 1866 the first congress of the International met at Geneva under the leadership of Marx. In 1867 he published the first volume of *Capital.* During all the years of his London residence Marx's financial condition was relieved by help from Engels and other friends; but during that entire period Marx was wracked by illness which interrupted his work, carried on largely at the British Museum.

While Marx's activity in journalistic polemics, and in organizational endeavor did not abate, his *Critique of the Gotha Programme* was published in 1875. In 1879 his health began to decline rapidly. In 1881 his wife died. This misfortune was followed by the death of his daughter Jenny in 1882. That year, in the hope that his health would improve, he was induced to journey to Algeria, France and Switzerland, but soon after returning, in 1883, he died. He was buried in a cemetery in London. The second and third volumes of *Capital* were published posthumously (1885 and 1894); both were edited by Engels from manuscripts and notes left in Engel's custody.

Marx made the economic development of modern Europe the study of a lifetime. The labors of few men in our times have affected the course of history as have the writings of Karl Marx. The scope of his philosophy, embracing not only historical and economic research and interpretation, but the method and approach to ideology and life itself, has given rise to a veritable army of interpreters, misinterpreters, qualifiers, apologists and enthusiasts, all of whom became known or wished to be known as Marxists. At the close of his life Marx himself stated that he hoped that he was not a "Marxist." While the collected works of Marx are voluminous, the contribution made by his followers embraces an entire library, in probably every language of the world. The words Marxism and Marxist have become commonplaces.

In the whole range of Marx's writings and utterances there are but two or three instances of his specific interest in the Jewish problem, notably in two letters and in a critique he wrote concerning Bruno Bauer's brochure *Zur Judenfrage* (1844). It was that blunt review (stressing the need for "the emancipation of the Jew as the emancipation of the state from Judaism, Christianity and from religion generally") that gave

rise to the accusation that Marx was antagonistic to the Jews. In contrast to this there is the fact that Marx wrote to Arnold Ruge (1843) of his readiness—in drafting a petition to the Landtag—to aid the Jews in the Rhineland in their struggle to remove legal and civil restrictions from which they then suffered. In that communication he spoke of the "obnoxious Jewish faith," yet branded as "too abstract" Bauer's advocacy that "Jews must free themselves from their religion before they can claim political equality." He went on to urge that "as many breaches as possible be made in the Christian state in order to smuggle in the rational view. . . . At any rate, one must try to do it—and the embitterment grows with every petition that is turned down with protest."

It is likewise a fact that Heinrich Graetz, noted Jewish historian, harbored an admiration for Marx and his family, as expressed in a letter (dated Breslau, Feb. 1, 1877) to Marx, wherein he records the pleasure derived from the reading of certain of Marx's writings.

Marx's evaluation of contemporary Jewry was neither racial nor religious. He sought to deal with it, in general terms, against a historic as well as economic background. His theory of the emancipation of the working class and of the oppressed masses under capitalism, through the establishment of a socialist society, envisioned the complete and final removal of all forms of economic, social and political oppression—of which national and racial oppression are particularly obnoxious manifestations, according to Marx.

Marx's whole life was devoted to the passionate defense of national as well as economic freedom. His teaching of international working class solidarity, urging united fraternal action by the toiling peoples of every race and nationality, sought to create a potent weapon against racial discrimination, and the hatred and oppression that go with it. One need not agree with the whole Marxist doctrine to recognize the experience of the Soviet Union, home of 6,000,000 Jews, as testimony of the Marxist position on the question of national and racial equality. Even hostile critics have come to recognize the striking fact that the one country which professes official allegiance to Marxian teachings is the one where anti-Semitism has been outlawed and its resurgence rendered impossible by the removal of social and economic inequalities.

In his eulogy at the fresh grave of Marx in London (March 17, 1883), Frederick Engels said:

"As Darwin discovered the law of evolution in organic nature, so Marx discovered the law of evolution in human history: the simple fact, previously hidden under ideological growths, that human beings must first of all eat, drink, shelter and clothe themselves before they can turn their attention to politics, science, art and religion; that therefore the production of the immediate material means of life and thereby the given stage of economic development of a people or of a period forms the basis on which the state institutions, legal principles, art, and even the religious ideas of the people in question have developed, and out of which they must be explained . . ."

In addition to the titles already mentioned, the principal works by Karl Marx accessible in English (issued largely by International Publishers, New York) include: *The Class Struggle in France—1848-1850; Founding of the First International; Letters to Kugelmann; Selected Works;* (in collaboration with Frederick Engels) *The Civil War in the United States; Revolution in Spain; Selected Correspondence of Marx and Engels.*   CHARLES RECHT.

Lit.: Mehring, Franz, *Karl Marx, Story of His Life* (1935); Yiddish Scientific Institute, "A Letter from Heinrich Graetz to Karl Marx" (Yiddish), *Historishe Shriften,* vol. 2 (1937) 658, 662-63; Nicolaievsky, Boris, and Maenchen-Helfen, Otto, *Karl Marx: Man and Fighter* (1936); Lazaron, Morris S., *Seed of Abraham* (1930); Lenin, Nikolai, *Marx, Engels, Marxism* (1934); Rühle, Otto, *Karl Marx: His Life and Work* (1929).

MARX, MODEL, court Jew to Margrave William Frederick of Ansbach at the beginning of the 18th cent.; he was descended from one of the richest and most influential families of Swabia and Franconia. His interests were at first promoted by the court; tardy debtors and those who compelled him to extend loans against his will were apprehended by the authorities and punished. In 1691 the privilege of printing the Talmud was bestowed upon him by the margrave. Under Frederick George (1695), officials were instructed to be lenient in the collection of taxes from Marx.

Due to the intervention of Marx, Jews in Ansbach were granted special consideration and were permitted to settle in restricted territories. Although he used his power to alleviate the condition of his coreligionists, he at times assumed a dictatorial tone in his demands upon them, especially upon those from the community of Fürth. Violent rivalry between Marx and Elhanan Fränkel for the position at court led first to the downfall of Fränkel and later of Marx. His reputation was so diminished through an accusation of embezzlement that he and his family were compelled to emigrate to the city of Pfalzburg, in the consistorial district of Metz. From there some members of the family returned to Ansbach later on, but never again attained their former influence.

Lit.: Haenle, *Geschichte der Juden im ehemaligen Fürstentum Ansbach* (1867) 71 et seq.

MARX, ROBERT S., lawyer, b. Cincinnati, 1889. He received his law degree from the University of Cincinnati in 1909 and was admitted to practice the following year. From 1920 to 1926 he was judge of the Superior Court of Cincinnati. After resigning to re-enter private practice, Marx became known for his work in taxation and receivership cases throughout the United States.

During the first World War Marx was wounded while in action in France, and was awarded the Distinguished Service Cross, the Order of the Purple Heart with three battle clasps and the French medal for the Defense of Verdun. From 1920 to 1926 Marx served as major, judge advocate general's department. He was the first national commander of the Disabled American Veterans of the World War (1920-21), an organization he founded. Marx was also active in Jewish communal work; he was one of the co-founders of the Wise Center, president of the Jewish Settlement and director of the board of trustees of the United Jewish Charities. Marx was the author of various technical legal papers. In 1942 he was living in Cincinnati.

MARY, name of the mother of Jesus of Nazareth. Mary is the Grecized and Latinized form of the Hebrew name Miriam, written as Mariam in the Greek text of the New Testament. According to the oldest Christian tradition, Mary had borne Jesus to Joseph, a Jewish carpenter in Nazareth, in legal marriage. A later tradition, which became the universal Christian belief and was already recorded in the Gospels of *Matthew* and *Luke,* stated that Mary had conceived Jesus through the Holy Ghost.

Like the rest of the family of Jesus, Mary does not appear among his followers during his lifetime; in fact, on one occasion, Jesus refused to see her (*Mark* 3:31-35

and parallels). After his death, however, when the belief in his resurrection had arisen, she and her other sons are found in the circle of the early Christian community in Jerusalem (*Acts* 1:14). After the deification of Jesus, steadily increasing religious veneration was bestowed on Mary in Christendom, and many festivals were dedicated to her in the medieval church. The Reformation abolished the cult of Mary among the Protestants. In the religious life of the Roman and the Greek churches and in art, Mary as the "Mother of God" is a dominant figure.

Lit.: Hasenclever, *Maria die Mutter Jesu, in Geschichte und Kunst* (1874); Lehner, F. von, *Die Marienverehrung in den ersten Jahrhunderten* (1886); Loewe, H., *Die Juden in der katholischen Legende* (1912); the Biblical dictionaries, especially Hastings, James, edit., *Dictionary of the Bible,* vol. 3 (1919) 278-93 (cf. also the additional literature cited there).

MARYLAND, one of the original states of the United States, with a population of 1,821,244 (census of 1940) including about 76,000 Jews. Of these, almost all live in Baltimore and only about 3,000 elsewhere in the state.

The early proprietors of Maryland, the Calverts, were Roman Catholics and they intended the colony (the provincial government of which was established in 1634) to be an asylum for the persecuted members of their faith. However, as subjects of England, a Protestant country, the proprietors and their officers could hardly bar Protestants, even if they wished to. But their toleration did not extend beyond believers in Trinitarian Christianity. Accordingly, the famous toleration act, passed by the Maryland assembly in 1649, provided that "no person in this province professing to believe in Jesus Christ shall be in any way troubled," but further provided that any person who denied "Jesus Christ to be the Son of God" should be punished by death and the forfeiture of lands and goods. Except for a brief period (1654-58) the act was in force until the American Revolution, somewhat modified by an act in 1723 which provided that, for the first offense, the offender was to have his tongue bored, for the second his face branded, and only for the third put to death.

However, although a Jew in colonial Maryland was liable to be punished and even executed for his faith, as a matter of fact he was generally permitted to live at peace and to acquire land and chattels. On the part of the Jews, "percolation rather than influx, and quiet exercise rather than open profession of faith, seem to distinguish the period" (*Publications of the American Jewish Historical Society,* No. 1, p. 25). Names that were possibly, or probably, those of Jews, such as Solimon Barbarah, Isaac de Barette, Isaack Bedlo, Hester Cordea, Mathias de Costa, David Ferreira, Abraham Hart, Sarah Hayes, Francis Hyems, Joseph Lazear, Jacob Leah, Daniel Mathena, Philip Salomon, and Mathias de Sousa, appear in the early 17th cent. records, as well as the name of Jacob Lumbrozo, who was certainly a Jew. He was in Maryland by 1656 and, although known to be a Jew, was not disturbed in the practice of his profession as a physician —or, it has been supposed, because of it—until 1658 when he was arrested and tried for denying the divinity of Jesus. The case seems to be the only one of its kind brought against a Jew. (Lumbrozo was soon discharged under a general amnesty in honor of Richard Cromwell, began to call himself John instead of Jacob, and acquired certain civil rights and a grant of land in 1663.) When an act of George II (1740) authorized the naturalization of Jews in the American colonies, in the interests of English trade, the following were naturalized in Maryland: Phineas Alferino (1742-43), Jacob Stern (1743-44), Jacob Frank of Frederick County (1749), and Ansell Israels (1757).

With the American Revolution and, in 1776, the adoption of a constitution by Maryland (including a broad declaration of rights), the Jews in the state could profess their religion by right as well as in fact. But they could not hold a state office, for the oath of office was administered only after the applicant had declared his belief in Christianity; in addition, there were other disabilities. Solomon Etting and his father-in-law, Barnard Gratz, began, in 1797, to petition the legislature to permit Jews to hold public office. In 1818, Thomas Kennedy of Washington County first introduced a bill, called "the Jew Bill," for that purpose. He continued to do so session after session. It finally passed the legislature in 1825 by one vote and became a law the following year when ratified in the next session. The act did not abolish a religious test but provided that an officer might profess to be a Jew and, if so, must profess his belief in a future state of rewards and punishments. This is the law in Maryland today (1942).

Among other disabilities of the Jews in Maryland, the prohibition against labor on Sunday (dating from the law of 1723) is related to the prohibition of blasphemy, and does not intend to provide merely for a day of rest but to prevent an unchristian act. It is still (1942) the law of Maryland that witness and juror must not only believe in God but believe that "under His dispensation such person will be held morally accountable for his acts and be rewarded or punished therefor in this world or in the world to come;" but there may be Jews who do not believe in such reward or punishment and who are neither atheists, agnostics, or deists. It is still an offense "to utter profane words of or concerning our Saviour, Jesus, or the Trinity."

In 1790 it was supposed by Federal officials that there were 1,243 Hebrews in the United States of whom fully 626 were in Maryland (*A Century of Population Growth,* published by the Bureau of the Census, 1909). If correct, the Jews in Maryland at that time probably included many refugees from Philadelphia and other cities that had been occupied by the British. In 1825, Solomon Etting estimated that there were about 125 Jews in Baltimore and as many in the rest of the state. Nathaniel Levy of the First Baltimore Cavalry had served under Lafayette during the Revolutionary War and Reuben Etting had been among the Colonial soldiers captured by the British at the surrender of Charleston (1780). Another Reuben Etting (1762-1848) helped suppress Loyalist uprisings in Maryland, organized the Independent Blues and was made their captain in 1797 when war with France looked likely, and in 1801 was appointed United States marshal for Maryland by President Thomas Jefferson. During the War of 1812, eight Jews of Maryland were among the defenders of Fort McHenry, near Baltimore, when

Francis Scott Key wrote *The Star Spangled Banner:* they were: Mendes I. Cohen, Philip I. Cohen, Samuel Cohen, Jr., Israel Davidson, Samuel Etting, Jacob Moses, Solomon Myers, and Samuel Solomon.

Leon Dyer, who came to Baltimore when a boy, acted as mayor of the city during the bread riots, and later fought for the independence of Texas and in the Mexican War. A number of Jewish young men of Baltimore, mostly immigrants, formed a volunteer corps in 1846, during the Mexican War, to join the army; the officers, under a non-Jew, Captain Carroll, were: Levi Benjamin, first lieutenant; Joseph Simpson, second lieutenant; Samuel G. Goldsmith, third lieutenant; S. Eytinge, first sergeant; and Doctor J. Horwitz, surgeon. At the outbreak of the Civil War, after the attack on Fort Sumter, Leopold Blumenberg organized the Fifth Regiment of Maryland Volunteers, of which he was appointed major; wounded at Antietam and disabled, he was appointed provost marshal of the Third Maryland District by President Lincoln.

At present, besides Baltimore (which is treated in a separate article), there are six communities in Maryland with one hundred Jews or more: Annapolis, Bladensburg, Cumberland, Frederick, Hagerstown, and Salisbury.

Annapolis, with a population of 13,069 (census of 1940) including about 600 Jews, has a Jewish congregation, Keneseth Israel, organized in 1906.

Cumberland (population 39,483, census of 1940) has the largest number of Jews in the state outside of Baltimore—about 850. Congregation Be'er Chayim (Reform) was established in the early 1850's. Aaron H. Lefkowitz, whose service began in 1934, was rabbi in 1942. The congregation owns a cemetery. In 1939 the Jewish Community Fund of Western Maryland was organized at Cumberland. Isaac Hirsch was president of the city council in 1895, established the municipal lighting plant in 1898, and was a member of the commission that established a new city water system in 1908. He helped inaugurate the city's commission plan of government (1910) and was chairman of the city planning commission (1915). Aaron Gorbaty of Cumberland was appointed a chaplain in the United States army in 1941.

Frederick (population 15,802, census of 1940) with about 125 Jews has a synagogue, erected by Congregation Beth Sholom (incorporated 1917).

Hagerstown (population 32,491, census of 1940) has a Jewish community of about 500. Congregation B'nai Abraham (Reform) was organized in 1891. The congregation owns a cemetery. The rabbi in 1942 was Abraham Ruderman.

Salisbury (population 13,313, census of 1940) with about 125 Jews has a Jewish religious organization, Congregation of Israel (Reform), of which Stephan Sherman was the rabbi in 1942.

There is a Hillel Foundation, under the leadership of Rabbi Samuel M. Silver, at the University of Maryland in College Park (1942).

Besides Reuben Etting who was marshal for Maryland at the beginning of the 19th cent., the Jews of Maryland in public service include: Isidor Rayner (1850-1912), member of the United States House of Representatives from 1887 until 1895 and United States Senator from 1905 until 1912; Harry B. Wolf, member of the United States House of Representatives from 1907 until 1909; Jacob H. Hollander, treasurer of Porto Rico from 1900 until 1901; Aaron Cecil Snyder, United States district attorney for Porto Rico in 1933; Simon E. Sobeloff, United States district attorney for Maryland from 1931 until 1934. Isaac L. Strauss was attorney general of Maryland in 1907, and Philip B. Perlman secretary of state from 1920 to 1923.

Mendes I. Cohen was a member of the Maryland House of Delegates from 1847 to 1848; Jacob M. Moses was a state senator from 1900 until 1904; Lewis Putzel was also a member of the state senate at about the same time; Harry Oscar Levin was a member of the state senate from 1923 until 1929; Emanuel Milton Altfeld, who had been a member of the lower house from 1914 to 1916, was a state senator from 1930 to 1934; Melvin L. Fine, who had also been a member of the lower house from 1926 to 1929, was a state senator from 1934 to 1938; Emanuel Gorfine was elected to the state senate in 1938 for a four year term after serving two terms in the House of Delegates and as speaker of the house from 1935 until 1938—the first Jew to hold the office in Maryland. Other members of the state assembly include: Martin Emereich and Henry Field (1902); Morris Hess, Emanuel Jacobi, and Martin Lehmayer (1904); Charles Newman (1911); and Abram Berman (1925).

Harry Oscar Levin was appointed a member of the State Board of Welfare in 1935 and of the Public Service Commission of Maryland in 1937; he resigned both posts to become chairman of the State Tax Commission for a six year term. Joseph Sherbow was counsel to the State Public Service Commission in 1941. Isaac H. Taylor of Ellicott City in 1941 was chairman of the Howard County Board of Education.

See also BALTIMORE.　　　CHARLES A. RUBENSTEIN.

Lit.: Altfeld, E. Milton, *The Jew's Struggle for Religious and Civil Liberty in Maryland* (1924); Hartogensis, Benjamin H., "Unequal Religious Rights in Maryland Since 1776," *Publications of the American Jewish Historical Society*, No. 25 (1917) 93-107; Hollander, J. H., "Some Unpublished Material Relating to Dr. Jacob Lumbrozo, of Maryland," *ibid.*, No. 1 (1893) 25-39; idem, "The Civil Status of the Jews in Maryland, 1634-1776," *ibid.*, No. 2 (1894) 33-34; the literature under BALTIMORE.

MASARJAWIAH (called also Maser-Djewaih Ebn Djaldal, Masarjis, and Maserdjawah Ibn Djeldjal), one of the earliest Arabic Jewish physicians. He lived in Basra around 683, when he is known to have translated the *Pandects* of the presbyter Aaron, a physician from Alexandria. The *Pandects,* a disquisition on smallpox, was rendered into Arabic by Masarjawiah from the Syriac, and supplemented by observations of his own. Masarjawiah also wrote, in Arabic, treatises on the virtues of foods and on the virtues of medical plants. None of his works has been preserved intact, but they are known through quotations. He was physician to Caliph Moavia I. His son Isa (Jesus) was also a translator and the author of several books on colors, smell and taste.

Lit.: Steinschneider, Moritz, *Die arabische Literatur der Juden* (1902) 13-15; Carmoly, E., *Histoire des médecins juifs* (1844) 17-18; Friedenwald, "Jewish Physicians," *Gratz College Publications* (1897) 119-20.

MASARYK, THOMAS GARRIGUE, first president (1918-35) of the Czechoslovak Republic, b.

Thomas Garrigue Masaryk

Hodonin, Moravia, 1850; d. Prague, 1937. His long, active and unusually fruitful life as democrat, scholar and statesman was closely bound up during several decades with the fight for political and social truth. Masaryk's motto was: "Truth Conquers."

Masaryk's quest for justice and truth determined his attitude toward the Jews. Although he considered as unfair any interference in their religious practices, he examined carefully their virtues and shortcomings and did not refrain from criticism when he believed it warranted. "The Jews lack the discretion of the Prophets; they are too well satisfied with themselves," he stated. One of Masaryk's important utterances was: "I am convinced that he who has Jesus for his guide cannot be an anti-Semite. That is clear to me because Jesus was a Jew, not because the apostles were Jews, nor because ancient Christianity, especially Catholicism, has much in itself that is essentially Jewish. No. If I accept Jesus, I cannot be an anti-Semite. I can be only one or the other. Christian or anti-Semite."

The first work of Masaryk as a young man was a sketch, *Naš pán Fuchsel* (Our Mr. Fuchsel). It is not free from criticism of the Jews. As a student in Auspice, Brno, and later at the University of Vienna, he became acquainted with many Jews. When he witnessed an attack on one of his Jewish classmates at prayer, Masaryk gave this incident serious thought. In Vienna, where he tutored the sons of a Jewish banker, he became familiar with Jewish economic and intellectual circles. Theodore Gompertz was among his teachers. Joseph Redlich, later a scientist, was among his friends. In Prague he met Professor Klein of the German University and he was well acquainted with Edvard Lederer and Hlavač. As president of the Czechoslovak Republic he made George Guth, a Jew, his master of protocol.

Masaryk's ideas about Jews and Judaism are scattered throughout most of his writings. His thesis: *Šebevražda; hromadným jevem společenským moderní osvěty* (Suicide as a Social Symptom of Modern Civilization, 1881), says: "The Jews do not care for alcohol, therefore suicide is less frequent among them. Their joy of life, clinging to the religion of their forebears, practical optimism and spirituality make them strong." In a review he wrote (1883) of Renan's book, *Judaism as a Race and Religion,* we find: "Hatred toward the Jews is based on difference of character. Mutual understanding will be the remedy of this looming social disease." In *Vědecká a filosofická krise současného marxismu* (The Factual and Philosophical Crises of Contemporary Marxism, 1898) he criticized certain of Marx' views of the Jews. According to Masaryk, the Jewish people is represented not only by usurers, but also by Jeremiah, Spinoza and Christ.

His pamphlet denouncing the accusation against and the "ritual murder" trial at Polna of twenty-two-year-old Leopold Hilsner, who was condemned to death and sentenced by the emperor to forced labor for life, effected a revision of the case. It was at this stage in his career that Masaryk resolved upon fighting for justice. In his magazine *Čas* (Time) he also took a firm stand against the false accusation of Mendel Beilis of Kishinev, Russia (1913).

On his visit to the United States in 1907 he was greeted with enthusiasm by the Jews of that country. His contact with American Jews was even closer during his trip in 1917, during his fight for the independence of his people. Everywhere in the States he was supported by Jews, he stated. He had many personal interviews with representatives of Orthodox Jewry as well as with Zionists. Among the latter were Louis D. Brandeis, Nahum Sokolow and Louis Marshall.

While he was president, one of the first laws of the Czechoslovak republic established the legal equality of the Jews. Czechoslovakia was the first state to recognize Jewish nationality. Some instances of Masaryk's official recognition of the Jews were the reception of the Jewish National Council (1918); his address to the Association of Jewish Students (1919), and his reception of the representatives of the Jewish National Fund (1930).

Masaryk regarded Zionism primarily from a moral standpoint: "I see in Zionism a drop of oil of the Prophets." He did not think that all the Jews should go to Palestine, but maintained that every individual has the right to make his own decision. When visiting the Czech colony in Palestine (1927), he said: "I hope that the Jewish people in Palestine will lead a life of freedom, and that God will bless this work of reconstruction."

The city of Tel-Aviv made him an honorary citizen during his lifetime. In 1940 a settlement of Czechoslovakian Jews, situated between Haifa and Acre on an area of 2,000 dunams, was named Kfar Masaryk in honor of him who laid the foundations of a state on truth and justice.

Masaryk's foremost disciple was Edvard Beneš, second president of the Czechoslovak Republic, and president of the Czechoslovak Government in Exile (1942), who upheld his master's teachings of assigning to the Jews a place among democratic nations and peoples.

JAN MASARYK, a son of Thomas Garrigue Masaryk, was in 1942 foreign minister of the Czechoslovak Government in Exile. He followed in the footsteps of his father. Speaking at the session of the National Conference for Palestine (New York city, 1939), he said: "The Jews are a small minority everywhere. And without tolerance and decent treatment of minorities, democracy cannot survive. . . . One of the most important pillars of hope in these dark hours is the idea of the national home: a homeland for defenceless people who for centuries were never masters of their own destiny." At a mass rally (1941), he said: "I remember the Jews of my mother country, locked in the ghetto, with the same sorrow as I remember my own mother." To him, the Jewish problem was one aspect of the general struggle of humanity for freedom.

OSCAR FRANKL.

Lit.: Beneš, Eduard, *Where Would Masaryk Stand Today?* (1940); *Liberator,* Sept., 1937 (funeral oration at Masaryk's burial); Čapek, Karel, *T. G. Masaryk, a Modern Type of Universalism* (1930); Bagger, Eugene S., *Eminent Europeans: Studies in Continental Reality* (1922); Butler, Nicholas Murray, *Doctor Masaryk* (1930); Donath, Oskar, *Masaryk und das Judentum* (1920); Hromadka, Josef L., *Nad Masaryk ceskou otazkou* (1936); Mann, Thomas, *In Memory of Masaryk* (1937); Street, Cecil J. C., *Thomas Masaryk of Czechoslovakia* (1930); *Thomas G. Masaryk and the Jews* (1941; essays collected and translated by Benjamin R. Epstein).

MASÉ, JACOB, crown rabbi and communal worker, b. Mohilev, Russia, 1860; d. Moscow, 1924. Masé received his law degree from the University of Moscow in 1886, and entered on the practice of law in that city. As early as 1879, however, he had begun to write for the *Hamelitz,* and his articles there, as well as his activities in establishing the pro-Zionist societies Berah Dodi (1881) and B'nai Zion (1884) at the University of Moscow, made his affiliation with the Jewish cause obvious.

In 1893 Masé was made crown rabbi of Moscow. The position was official and carried the imputation of collaboration with the czarist government. Masé was aware of this, and accepted the post despite it, because it provided the most effective method of speaking for the causes he chose to represent. His communal activity in Moscow and his courage before officialdom made him popular with the Russian Jews. His testimony during the Beilis trial in 1913, during which he was keen and eloquent in defense as well as attack, won him even more admiration and love.

Masé's memoirs, which he wrote in Hebrew, were published posthumously in a Yiddish translation in the New York *Jewish Morning Journal.* They appeared in Hebrew, also posthumously, under the title of *Zichronoth,* in four volumes (Tel-Aviv, 1936-37). In religious matters Masé was an advocate of reform and change in Jewish customs. At a rabbinical conference held in Leningrad, for instance, Masé suggested doing away with the ceremony of Halitzah.

Lit.: Yevreiskaya Entziklopedia, vol. 10, p. 498; Moskwin, D., "Jacob Mase, Rabbi and Leader of Russian Jewry," *The Jewish Tribune,* Jan. 11, 1924, p. 5.

MASHAL (plural, **Meshalim**). **1. In the Bible.** The word *mashal* is used in the Bible in a number of significations. The root-meaning seems to have been that of a comparison, one of the oldest forms of prov-

מ ש ל

הקדמוני

ספר סופר אמרי שפר נקרא משל הקדמוני
אותו העיר האיש מאיר בכמר יעקב פרענצוני
נם הוא אמונה אף אם חונה מאחיהו השילוני

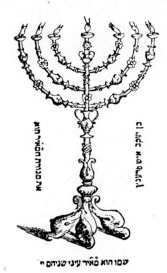

*Title page of "Mashal Haḳadmoni," by Meir Parenzo,
printed at Venice in 1546*

erb; from that it came to mean any proverbial saying or parable. Thus in *I Sam.* 24:14 David says: "As saith the proverb (*mashal*) of the ancients: Out of the wicked cometh forth wickedness." Since the fate of evil-doers would be an object of popular derision and reproach, the term is used also in the sense of byword (*Deut.* 28:37).

The Biblical book of *Proverbs* is known in Hebrew as *Mishle,* a shorter form of *Mishle Shelomoh,* "the Proverbs of Solomon." The older portions of the book, chaps. 25 to 29, contain numerous examples of the proverb that is in the form of a comparison, the comparison always preceding the type of individual who is satirized in the proverb. A typical instance is: "A continual dropping in a very rainy day and a contentious woman are alike" (*Prov.* 27:15). It should be noted, however, that the other parts of the book are not as a rule comparisons, but rather nuggets of homely wisdom, for the most part short sentences, but sometimes expanded into paragraphs.

Since figures of speech were common in prophetic utterances, the word *mashal* is occasionally used for prophetic flights of fancy. Thus the various oracles of Balaam (*Num.* 23 and 24) bear the name of *mashal,* and a song of prophetic derision against the king of Babylon is so described (*Isa.* 14:4). Ezekiel generally confines the term to prophecies in which he makes

actual use of an extended metaphor (*Ezek.* 17:2; 24:3). On the other hand, the term in some places is synonymous with poetry in general (*Num.* 21:27; *Ps.* 49:5).

There are a few parables in the Bible of the type that would be called *mashal* in Talmudic times, although no specific name is given to them. Thus Jotham gives the parable of the trees of the forest as a satire against Abimelech (*Judges* 9), and Jehoash uses a similar plant fable in his reply to Amaziah (*II Kings* 14:9). Nathan the prophet told the story of the rich and the poor man as an introduction to his rebuke of David (*II Sam.* 12:1-4), and the wise woman of Tekoa presented a similar tale in pleading for Absalom (*ibid.* 14:5-7). The most elaborate parable in prophetic writings is Isaiah's parable of the vineyard (*Isa.* 5).

2. In Post-Biblical Literature. The Talmud and the Midrash make an especially fertile use of all varieties of the Mashal. There is hardly a moral or religious thought which the rabbis have not illuminated by a comparison or an appropriate tale. It is noteworthy that while the Palestinian teachers use such figures freely the Babylonian teachers did so very seldom. The following passage from the Midrash (*Midrash Song of Songs* 1) gives the rabbinic opinion of the value of the Mashal and at the same time offers a number of good examples of such comparisons:

"'And besides that Koheleth was wise, he also taught the people knowledge, yes he pondered (*'izzen*) and sought out and set in order many proverbs.' This means that he made handles (*'oznayim*) for the Torah. . . . Rabbi Nahman gave two explanations: 1) It is like a great palace which has many entrances, and whoever went in lost his way among the entrances. A clever man came and took a coil of thread and fastened one end to the entrance; now every one could go in by way of the thread and find his way back again (cf. the Greek legend of the labyrinth and the thread of Ariadne). Thus before Solomon appeared, none could understand the words of the Torah; but after he appeared all began to comprehend the Torah. 2) It is like a thicket of reeds which no one was able to penetrate. A clever man took a sickle, made strokes this way and that, and prepared a way; after that all began to come in and go out. So it was with Solomon. Rabbi Jose said, It is like a great chest which is filled with fruits but can not be carried away, because it has no handles; a clever man made handles for it, and now it can be carried away. . . . Rabbi Shela said, It is like a great vessel full of boiling water and without handles; it is only after the handles are made for it that it can be carried away.

"Rabbi Hanina said, It is like a well of cool, pleasant and good water, from which, however, no one can drink. Then came one and bound line to line and cord to cord and so drew water from it and drank; then all began to draw water and drink. So Solomon passed on from word to word, from comparison to comparison, to the understanding of the Torah. The rabbis said, Let not the Mashal be light in thine eyes; for through the Mashal one can attain to the understanding of the Torah. It is like a king who has lost a piece of money or a precious pearl in his house. Can he not find it again by means of a wick that costs only a penny? Thus can one come to a comprehension of the Torah by means of a Mashal" (cf. *Erub.* 21b).

Of the Tannaim, Meir was especially famous as a teller of fables. His lectures consisted of one-third Halachah, one-third Haggadah, and one-third fables. He was said to know 300 fables about foxes; one has been preserved (see *Sanh.* 38b-39a and Rashi to the passage) which runs as follows:

"The fox persuaded the wolf to go to a Jewish home on Friday night and take part in the preparation of food for the Sabbath; he assured him that if he did so, he would be invited for the Sabbath meal. The wolf tried this, but received blows instead of an invitation. He wanted to kill the fox. The latter said, 'I can do nothing about it. You have been beaten because of your father. He was once invited to help in preparing the food for the Sabbath and went and ate it up himself.' 'But how do I come to be beaten on account of my father?' asked the wolf. The fox answered, 'Is it not written (*Ezek.* 18:2), "The fathers have eaten sour grapes, and the teeth of the children are set on edge?" But come, I will show you where you can eat your fill.' He went with the wolf to a well and stepped into one of the two buckets, which immediately sank while the other came up. He called up from below, 'Here is meat and cheese in plenty,' and showed the wolf the reflection of the moon, telling the wolf that it was a great cheese. Upon his advice the wolf climbed into the second bucket; this now sank into the depths, while the other bucket, with the lighter fox, rose to the surface. When the fox had gotten out of the well, he said, 'Now you see that it must be true when it is said (*Prov.* 11:8), "The righteous is delivered out of trouble, and the wicked cometh in his stead," and also (*Lev.* 19:36) "Just balances, just weights"' (an ironical allusion to the two buckets)."

The parables of Jesus are of the same category as the parables of the rabbis. In fact, the formulas used by Jesus to begin his parables are very similar to those used by the rabbis; the latter include such opening phrases as "A Mashal; what does the thing resemble?," "It is like a king (or man, etc.) who," or "As people say."

Jewish preachers made frequent use of the Mashal even after the completion of the Talmud and the Midrash. It was a favorite with preachers, philosophers and moral teachers. Thus Bahya ibn Pakuda uses such parables and comparisons in his *Hoboth Halebaboth,* and Judah Halevi in his *Kuzari.* The works of Jacob Kranz of Dubno are especially rich in well worked out comparisons.

See also: ALLEGORY; PREACHING; PROVERBS.

JOHANN KRENGEL.

Lit.: Lauterbach, Jacob Z., in *Jewish Encyclopedia,* vol. 9, pp. 512-14; Bialik, C. N., and Rabnitsky, J. H., *Sefer Ha-aggadah,* introduction and index; Strack, H. L., and Billerbeck, P., *Kommentar zum Neuen Testament aus Talmud und Midrasch,* vol. 1 (1922) 653 et seq., 664; vol. 2 (1924) 7; vol. 4 (1928).

MASHGIAH, a term used to describe the person who oversees the Kashruth of food and drink. It means superintendent. Originally the function of the Mashgiah was primarily to watch the correctness of slaughtering or of the baking of Matzoth. With the development of modern life his role expanded. Not only meat products, but victuals of all kinds, manufactured in quantity, were subjected to the super-

vision of a Mashgiah. These included, among others, canned goods, dairy products, drinks, bakery products and the many foods for Passover which became obtainable in prepared form.

MASHIAH, *see* MESSIAH.

MASHIB HARUAH ("Who causes the wind to blow [and the rain to descend]"), formula in the second paragraph of the Eighteen Benedictions (Shemoneh Esreh) describing this sign of the divine omnipotence. It is added in winter, that is, from the Additional Service (Musaf) on Shemini Atzereth to the Musaf service on the first day of Passover. The present text of this passage can be traced back as far as about 70 C.E. This particular form of the insertion was the only one known in Babylonia; in Palestine, on the other hand, there were other similar additions, which were connected with various natural occurrences. Thus the addition *morid hatal* ("Who causes the dew to descend") was inserted in the same place in Palestine during the summer months. From Palestine it passed into the Italian prayer-book, and, strikingly enough, also into the Spanish liturgy. The Reform Movement, realizing that the countries in which Jews now live have different climatic conditions from those of Palestine, does not use the formula during the winter, but on Passover and Sukkoth uses a common prayer in place of the older elaborate Tefillath Tal and Tefillath Geshem.

Lit.: Elbogen, Ismar, *Der jüdische Gottesdienst,* 44-45, 518-19; Singer, S., and Abrahams, I., *The Authorised Daily Prayer Book* (1922) lix-lx; Davidson, Israel, *Otzar Hashirah Vehapiyut,* vol. 3, p. 189.

MASHKIN, *see* MACHSHIRIN.

MASKILIM, *see* HASKALAH.

MASLIANSKY, ZEVI HIRSCH, Yiddish orator, b. Slutzk, Minsk, Russia, 1856. He studied at the Yeshiva of Mir, and from 1882 to 1890 taught at the Yeshiva of Pinsk. His early influences were Mapu, Smolenskin, Gordon and Lilienblum; during his career as teacher he was able to transmit these influences to his pupils, among whom was Chaim Weizmann.

Masliansky's devotion to Zionism started in his early manhood; in 1881 he was one of the co-founders of the first Russian Zionist Society, the B'nei Zion. His work as orator on behalf of Zionism began while he was still in Russia; after his arrival in the United States in 1895, Masliansky's talents developed until the incomparability of his power was unchallenged.

The phrase Mattif Leume, orator of the people, is the cue to the difference between him and the Maggid, or preacher. The preacher was concerned with the conduct and fate of the individual rather than with the welfare of the community; he was concerned with the individual's proper relations to God, and consequently neglected the sphere of man's relations with his fellows. Zionism called for a new type of oratory, fostered by men who emphasized the importance of the community while not neglecting the interests of the individual. These new orators had to resort to moralizing and to exhortation in order to arouse the dormant national consciousness. They had to imbue their contemporaries with enthusiasm for future tasks by inspiring them with the grandeur of the past.

Zevi Hirsch Masliansky

Masliansky became the orator in Yiddish par excellence. He came to the masses as a comforter and not as a harsh critic and reprover; but he was a critic, and he showed that all the functions of the orator could be harmoniously blended. Nor was he loathe to shed and to evoke tears. Although Masliansky had the intonation of the old-time preacher and quoted Biblical and Talmudic passages with ease, it was evident that he was unlike other preachers. His diction was crisp and precise; his sentences polished. He could put parables and metaphors to effective use, but he applied them sparingly.

Not all those who admired Masliansky's oratory realized that it was more than mere brilliant fireworks. He was a versatile Jewish scholar, mastering the Bible, Talmud and Midrashic literature with no less virtuosity than medieval and modern Hebrew literature. Above all, he understood the Bible in the light of its meaning to his own generation. He understood the eternal significance of the prophetic messages, and when he quoted them he pointed them out as lessons for the present. In addition to his unique gift for oratory, Masliansky had an imposing appearance that invariably attracted attention. Even before he began to speak, the crowd was enthralled by his noble features and majestic head. He was also a master of gesture and mimicry; every limb and every muscle shared in the effort of his oratory.

Masliansky moved and aroused Jewish audiences for more than half a century. During this period, Jewish life underwent many changes, but Masliansky went along with the trends of the day. As a result, he understood and respected the younger generations, and they, in turn, gave him their love and veneration.

Masliansky's career began in Europe, but it was in the United States that he became a tribune of his people and the voice of popular Zionism. Much of what is best in American Jewish life is due to Masliansky's labors. His efforts were devoted to practical cooperation as well as to inspiration. He was, from 1900 to 1910, vice-president of the Federation of American Zionists. From 1915 to 1920 Masliansky was president of the New York section of the Jewish Consumptives' Relief Society of Denver. He was president and co-editor, with Louis Marshall, of the *Yiddishe Velt* (1902-5). Among his published works were a two-volume edition of his sermons (Yiddish, 1909; English trans., by Edward Herbert, 1926); his memoirs (Yiddish, 1924); and a collection of articles in Hebrew (1929).   ABRAHAM GOLDBERG.

Lit.: Reisen, Z., *Lexikon fun der Yiddisher Literatur, Presse un Filologie*, vol. 2 (1930), cols. 321-23.

MASLOV, PETER PAVLOVICH, journalist and economist, b. Russia, 1867. In 1896 he was editor of the first legal Marxist paper in Russia, *Samara News.* After the split in the Russian Social Democratic Party he joined the moderate Mensheviks. Maslov wrote under the pseudonyms "X" and "John." At the time of the revolution of 1905 he was the author of a project for the municipalization of the land. At the Stockholm Congress of 1906 he defended this plan against Lenin's nationalization.

Maslov was imprisoned several times during the czarist regime, and also for some time, about 1922, by the Soviet authorities. He contributed to minor publications, voicing his disagreement with the economic policies of the Soviet government. Several years after his release from prison he was allowed to teach, and in the 1930's he was professor at the University of Kharkov.

Maslov published: *Agrarnyi vopros v Rossii* (The Agrarian Question in Russia; German ed. *Die Agrarfrage in Russland,* Stuttgart, 1907); *Teoriia razvitie narodnogo khoziaistva* (The Theory of the Development of National Economy; German version, *Die Theorie der Volkswirtschaft,* Leipzig, 1912); *Mirovaia sotsial'naia problema* (The World Social Problem); *Nauka narodnogo khoziaistva* (The Science of National Economy); *Istoriia khoziaistva byta zapodnoi Evropy* (The History of the Economy of the Manners and Customs of Western Europe); *Osnovy kooperatsii* (The Foundations of Cooperation); *Vliianie estestvennykh i sotsial'nykh uslovii na proizvoditel' nost' truda* (The Influence of Natural and Social Conditions on the Productivity of Labor); *Perenaselenie russkoi derevni; opyt morfografii* (The Over-Population of the Russian Village; an Experiment in Morphography; 1930).

MASONRY (also Freemasonry), a non-sectarian brotherhood with separate organizations functioning throughout the world. Its real origin is undetermined, but the first known modern mother lodge was established in England in 1717. The builders' symbols, as well as the Hebraic terminology attending the masonic ritual, have led to the contention that the order was first restricted to masons who had worked on the construction of the Second Temple. Other legends trace it to the Rosicrucians and the Knights Templar. Some of the words connected with the ritual are derived from terms that might have been identified with the Second Temple. The Scottish Rite system of the order also includes a Hebrew chronology.

How the Order was developed and its ritual evolved must, however, remain a mystery, despite varied suggestions and interpretations. It is likely that unconnected groups, following the brotherhood ideology later accepted by Masonry, existed throughout Europe before the foundation of the modern mother lodge in 1717. There is, for instance, an unverifiable report that in 1658 a group of Dutch settlers in Rhode Island who happened to be Jews founded a Masonic lodge in Newport.

The Masonic Order specifies that its members must be men of good repute and of that religion in which all men agree. For this reason, the theory of Masonry has always been the acceptance of men of all creeds on equal terms. The oddity of this situation in 18th cent. Europe, where Jews had not yet achieved emancipation, made those Jews who wandered into the new world enthusiastic Masons and in many cases the originators of new lodges. Although there have been theoretical and actual defections from the rule of equality regardless of creed, the basis has remained unchanged.

Europe. In England the line of development, as far as the Jew is concerned, has remained quite unchanged. Christians and Jews were members of the same lodge in London as early as 1723. Isolated evidences of hostility to the equality principle have occurred there, as everywhere. With the spread of Masonry, lodges have naturally grown up with entirely Jewish membership, but the rule of the Order is not thereby negated.

Soon after the establishment of the mother lodge in England in 1717, Masonic lodges began to appear on the European continent. France had its first one in 1725, Italy in 1733, Germany (Hamburg) in 1737, Austria in 1741, Russia at about the same time. Leading government figures and citizens in all these countries have been members of the order, and among them were frequently the outstanding Jews of the period. Ernesto Nathan, who was burgomaster (mayor) of Rome from 1907 to 1913, was for a time grand master of the Fraternity in Italy. The Masonic Order in Italy came to an end with the establishment of the Fascist regime in 1922.

In Germany, particularly in Prussia, the Masonic Order went through the most openly manifested disagreements in regard to Jewish membership. The lodge which was established in Hamburg in 1737 under the sponsorship of the English mother lodge adhered to the "ancient charges," or so-called humanist principle, based on "the religion on which all men agree." But against this system developed several lodges of the so-called Christian principle, which altered the requirements so as to make eligible for membership only Christians of good repute. Partly, the aberration from the primary rule grew out of a demand by Frederick the Great, who was himself a member of a lodge of the Hamburg System. The Christian principle was derived from old Christian orders and was allied to the principles followed by Swedish lodges. This development was not anti-Semitic in character, but designed to meet the objections of the Church to the Masonic Order because the Order did not stress the acceptance of the Christian creed. At the same time that the Christian lodges developed in Prussia, however, several others, founded on the humanist principle, were inaugurated elsewhere.

And despite the fact that the question as to whether Jews might be admitted even as visitors to Christian lodges was long discussed, there was no hostility between the members of the two systems. Mistaken interpretation of the Christian principle, leading to unpleasantness and conflict, was rare.

In 1889, however, relations deteriorated. Hermann Settegast of Berlin, the grand master of the Royal York Lodge, which accepted the humanist principle, resigned his post, charging that Jews were being rejected by the lodge because they were Jews. A new lodge, formed by Settegast, was refused a permit by the Berlin chief of police on the ground that an edict of 1798 forbade the existence of all secret organizations in Prussia except the three mother lodges (two Christian and one humanitarian) then named. Settegast, aided by Alexander Katz, a Berlin judge of Jewish birth, succeeded in having the police order set aside. Various humanitarian lodges outside of Prussia, especially those of Hamburg and Frankfort, now established auxiliaries in Prussia, and the lodge founded by Settegast affiliated itself with the Hamburg mother lodge. Many Jews joined the new organizations. From then on, until the end of the first World War in 1918, the relations between Christians and Jews in the Masonic Order throughout Germany were good. Jews were accepted equally in non-sectarian lodges, and could be honorary members of those lodges which adhered to the Christian principle.

In the disintegrating internal conditions of Germany between 1918 and 1933, rising anti-Semitism influenced the Masonic Order as well. The Royal York Lodge, which had become the Great Lodge of Prussia during the first World War, accepted the Christian principle. Except for the Frankfort Lodge, Masonic lodges in Germany forbade their members to join the B'nai B'rith, which they considered a secret order.

United States. Because the development of the Masonic Order in Europe coincided with the 18th cent. development of the American colonies, Masonry found root in almost all parts of the country. Jews were active in its transplantation.

The supposed, perhaps apocryphal, story of the establishment of a Masonic lodge in Newport, R. I., in 1658, is substantiated insofar as Mordecai Campanall and Moses Pachecho (Levi), mentioned in the story, are known to have lived there at the time. In the 18th cent. Masonic activities in Rhode Island, Jews were prominent. The first lodge, the King David's Lodge, was organized in Newport in 1780 by Moses Michael Hays.

Hays became deputy inspector general of Masonic activities in the colonies in 1768, by appointment of Stephen Morin, who was himself deputy for Frederick II of Prussia. Frederick, as grand master of Masons in Europe, had the American colonies under his jurisdiction. In 1769 Hays became grand master of King David's Lodge in New York. In 1780 he moved to Newport and established Masonry there. In 1788 he became master of the grand lodge in Massachusetts. Hays also introduced the Scottish Rite into America. In his capacity as deputy inspector general for all the colonies, Hays appointed deputies for the separate colonies.

One of these deputy inspectors was Moses Seixas, who was also active in Rhode Island. He was the first master of the lodge formed in Newport in 1790 by the merger of King David's Lodge with St. John's Lodge. Later, (1802-9) he was grand master for Rhode Island. In 1790 Seixas delivered a special address to George Washington, who was himself a Mason.

Hays' King David Lodge was probably not the first in New York, having been preceded by Trinity Lodge No. 4, founded in 1760. Jonas Phillips, grandfather of Mordecai M. Noah, and Aaron Hart were members of the earlier group.

Pennsylvania showed many Jewish names in its 18th cent. Masonic records. The Sublime Lodge of Perfection, founded in 1781 in Philadelphia, included Solomon Etting and Isaac Franks. Later Michael Gratz was mentioned. Solomon Bush, by appointment of Hays, was deputy grand inspector for Pennsylvania. Etting, in 1785, was one of the founders of a Masonic lodge in Lancaster, Pa. Haym Salomon was a member of the Philadelphia lodge. Abraham Forst, also a member, was deputy inspector general for Virginia.

In the southern colonies there was very early Jewish participation in Masonic life. Four Jews were charter members of the first lodge formed in Savannah in 1734. This lodge may have been founded by Governor James Edward Oglethorpe, and it is said that his hospitality to the Jewish settlers in Georgia was partly due to his acceptance of the Masonic tradition. In South Carolina, Isaac da Costa was a member of a Charleston lodge in 1753 and treasurer in 1759.

In Delaware, Maryland, Virginia, North Carolina, Connecticut, and New Hampshire there were also early Jewish members. The period of the greatest Jewish activity in the Masonic Order in the United States was between 1780 and 1810. As the country grew the pioneering role assumed by the Jews necessarily diminished. Jews continued to be important in the Masonic Order, however. Abraham Jonas, the friend of Abraham Lincoln, was grand master in Illinois and later in Kentucky. Isaac Mayer Wise, who was made a Master Mason in 1856, was the first rabbi in the world to reach this degree. There have been many Jewish grand masters for the various states. Increased population has brought about, in large cities, the formation of lodges which have an all-Jewish membership, but there are many groups, in large as well as small cities, where mixed membership is usual.

Twentieth Century Developments. In addition to the affiliation which the Masonic tradition has with Hebraic symbols, Masonry has been attacked on the same basis of secret conspiracy which has been used in so many canards against the Jews. Derived as it is from a disregard of creed divisions, it has become a target for movements which use creed differentiation as a method of attack. The canards, which became particularly articulate early in the 20th cent., reached their fullest ramification with the lies of the Hitlerian movement, based, in turn, on the Elders of Zion falsifications. The charges of a Masonic-Jewish conspiracy for world power were easy grist for the sluggish mill of pro-dictatorship mentalities. To this the acknowledged Biblical symbolism of the Masonic ritual provided supplementary material, as did the fact that many of the leading intellectuals and liberals of 18th and 19th cent. Europe had been Masons. The Nazis abolished the German Masonic Order in 1933. The regulations of the Order against discrimination on the basis of creed persisted, however, despite the attacks, and Jews continued to remain part of it. Among the lodges that were established throughout the world were some in the Near East, including Palestine. In Palestine a Masonic monthly, *Haboneh Hahafshi,* was published from 1935 to the outbreak of war in 1939. The bulk of its contents was in Hebrew, but there were Arabic and English supplements.   NATHAN RICARDO.

Lit.: Lennhof, Eugen, *The Freemasons* (1934); Wright, Dudley, *The Jew and Freemasonry* (1931); Shillman, Bernard, *Hebraic Influences in Masonic Symbolism* (1929); Blumenthal, Walter Hart, "Masonic Pioneers in America," *American Hebrew,* Sept. 22, 1933, pp. 302, 312; Oppenheimer, Samuel, "The Jews and Masonry in the United States Before 1810," *Publications of the American Jewish Historical Society,* No. 19 (1910) 1-94; Frankenberg, Albert M., "A List of Jews Who Were Grand Masters of Masons in Various States of the Country," *ibid.,* pp. 95-100.

MASORAH AND MASORITES. The term Masorah is a late word formation derived from the root *masar,* "to hand down," and meaning the work of preserving the traditional Bible text. The men who performed this function were known as Masorites or Masoretes (Massoretes), and the present Hebrew text of the Bible is known as the Masoretic text, in contrast to the text underlying such early translations as the Septuagint and to the emendations in the text proposed by Bible scholars. The Hebrew term for Masorites is *ba'ale hamasoreth.*

The necessity for instituting a special watch over the text was felt at an early time. In the period of the Second Temple the Torah was the source of all Jewish law, and great attention was paid to the exact wording of the text. In the Mishnaic period laws were deduced from such small points as the extra letters Vav, Yod and He, which are sometimes included in the transcription and sometimes omitted. In the course of the rise of Christianity, there were numerous disputes which turned on the question of whether a certain passage was actually a part of the Hebrew text, or how it was to be read. The Masorites met these questions by carefully comparing and annotating the texts that were in existence in their own time. As a result, whereas the Septuagint (about 300 B.C.E. on) and the Targum (perhaps as early as the 4th cent. B.C.E. on) often show deviations, the later translations, such as those of Aquila (2nd cent. C.E.) and Jerome (4th cent.), evidently used a text that was almost identical with that now found in Hebrew Bibles.

The task that lay before the Masorites was twofold, due to the peculiar nature of the Hebrew language and the way in which it was written. In all the early manuscripts only the consonants are put down, the vowels being omitted. Since the inflection of Hebrew largely consists of fitting a different set of vowels to a given group of root consonants, the same set of consonants may be used for a number of words. Thus the written letters M-L-CH may be read, according to the context, as *melech* ("king"), *malach* ("he reigned"), *molech* ("reigning"), *meloch* ("reign!"), *maloch* ("to reign") or even as *Molech* (the idol Moloch). The Masorites worked to preserve not only the correct consonantal text, but also the correct readings.

It was therefore one of the first tasks of the Maso-

A Bible manuscript with Masoretic notes known to have existed as early as 1058. From the Firkovitch collection at Leningrad

rites to indicate the irregularities, deviations and unique places found in the text. They had to decide which words had to be read (*kere*) other than they were written (*kethib*), those places where words were written but not read aloud (*kethib velo kere*), those places where words were lacking but were to be supplied in the reading (*kere velo kethib*), and finally, which words should be written full and what words defective, that is, in what cases certain letters which indicated the vowels (Aleph, Vav, Yod) should be written in the words and when they should be omitted.

The regulation that certain superfluous letters should be retained in the copies but not read was called *'ittur soferim* ("ornamentation of the scribes"; another interpretation is "separation of the scribes"); this occurs in only five places (*Gen.* 18:5; 24:55; *Num.* 31:2; *Ps.* 36:7; 68:26; cf. *Ned.* 37b). In other cases obnoxious expressions were changed, and this is called *tikkun soferim* ("improvement of the scribes"); thus in *Gen.* 18:22 they changed the reading from "but the Lord stood yet before Abraham" to "but Abraham stood yet before the Lord."

They made note of and counted the points that are occasionally to be found over words, even in the oldest Bible manuscripts (as in *Gen.* 16:5; *Num.* 3:39), and which seem to have been used to indicate dubious or variant readings. In the same way they noted anything that was unusual in Bible manuscripts, especially the large (*rabbathi*, as in *Gen.* 1:1; *Deut.* 6:4) and small (*ze'er*, as in *Deut.* 32:18) letters, letters that are suspended (*talui*), that are written above the line (as in *Judges* 18:30), or are reversed (*hafuch*, as in *Num.* 10:34, 36). They also noted other peculiarities, such as letters that are broken off (*keti'a*, as in *Num.* 25:12) or gaps in a verse (*piska*, *Gen.* 35:22).

These irregularities have led to much discussion among modern students of the Bible text. Some of them are recognized as serving a definite purpose. Thus large letters are used at the beginning of important passages and to prevent the possibility of error;

thus the letter Daleth is large in *Deut.* 6:4 to see that the last word is read as *'ehad* ("one") instead of *'aher* ("other"). The large Vav in the word *gahon* (*Lev.* 11:42) marks the middle of the Torah, according to letters. Small letters are always conjectural emendations which supply letters apparently missing. Suspended letters may be emendations to avoid offense; thus in *Judges* 18:30 Moses is changed to Manasseh, to avoid the inference that a descendant of the lawgiver was a priest at an idolatrous shrine. Reversed letters may indicate a passage out of place, while gaps in a verse hint at an omitted passage. Nevertheless there are many cases where there is no obvious explanation and the peculiarity in the text is an unsolved phenomenon.

The realm of the tradition also includes the division of the text into larger or smaller paragraphs and verses, as well as the statement of the number of these versions and paragraphs. The division into larger sections (Sidras) and smaller sections (Parashahs) as well as into verses was already known in very ancient times; on the other hand, there was no designation of verses and chapters by numbers and letters until the 13th cent. The Talmudic writings divide the text into verses and give the number of these; but their numbers are often different from those found later in the Masorah.

The Talmud traces the first regulations as to the division and counting of verses back to the Soferim in the period of the Second Temple, basing its inference on *Neh.* 8:8, and counting Ezra as the first of this group. Yet no especial signs for the division of the verses were made in the copies of the Bible, and the scrolls of the Torah still do not contain any punctuation marks. All printed Bibles contain at the end of every book the sum of the verses, as well as those of the larger and smaller sections, and the middle verse of each book; this is followed by a mnemotechnical verse, the letters of one or more words of which amount to the sum given. This work of registration was intended to place a permanent check upon the size and state of the text, and especially to prevent insertions. The Halachic tractate *Soferim,* based on earlier sources, contains a collection of Masoretic rules for the scribes who write the Bible texts.

The punctuation, or vocalization, of the Biblical text was a continuation of the Masorah. In this instance the Jews probably followed the example of the Syrians. It was not until the 8th cent. C.E. that a complete system of vowel and accent marks, such as is used nowadays, came into existence.

There are two forms of vocalization, the Tiberian and the Babylonian. The former, called the western system (*ma'arba'e*), is the one that is now generally used; the marks are usually below the line, and it originated among the sages of the Palestinian school in Tiberias. The latter, the eastern system (*madinha'e*), was created by the Babylonian Masorites. It has been preserved only in individual manuscripts and differs from the Tiberian system in that the accents are written above the line. The oldest dated manuscript of the Bible is the Petersburg codes of the Prophets of the year 916, edited by Strack in 1876.

Tiberias was the seat of a whole series of authorities who were engaged in Masoretic studies, and the family of Aaron Moses ben Asher was especially active. Ben

Asher, a contemporary of Saadia, was regarded as the supreme authority in the field of Masorah; and with him the work of the Masorah may be regarded as concluded. His codex of the Bible, provided with Masoretic notes, was hailed as the only authority. A contemporary of his was the Masorite Ben Naphtali.

After the 11th cent., the Masorites who occupied themselves with the Biblical text were called also punctuators (*nakdanim*). They were primarily writers of the Bible who at the same time placed vowels and accents in the text. Sometimes two of them participated in this work; one wrote the text, the other added the points and the accents. These men also wrote books about punctuation, and in a certain sense continued the work of the Masorites. The most noteworthy were Moses Hanakdan, or Hazan, of London (beginning of the 13th cent.), Samson Hanakdan, a connoisseur on the form of language who was familiar with the works of the Spanish Jewish grammarians, and Jekuthiel ben Judah Hakohen (13th cent.). The notations which referred to the Bible text, and which at first had been handed down orally, gradually came to be written down on the margins of the Bible. These short notations on the margins were called the little Masorah (Masorah Parva), while the express and explanatory notations on the upper and lower margins of the manuscripts were called the greater Masorah (Masorah Magna). In printed Bibles some of the Masoretic notes are placed beside or beneath the text, and the rest at the end of the individual books.

In course of time the space available in the margins and fly-leaves of the books was not sufficient for the Masoretic notes, so parts of these were gathered into independent works. Such is the collection *Ochlah Veochlah*, published by Frensdorff (1864) after a Paris manuscript. The most noteworthy of the later Maso-

A Bible manuscript written (1479) in Cordova (Spain). The geometric designs of the border consist of Masorah texts in minute characters. Reproduced by courtesy of the Jewish Theological Seminary of America

retic works is that of Meir Abulafia ben Todros, in the 12th cent. In the 16th cent. Jacob ben Hayim ibn Adonijah collected the material that was scattered in manuscripts, and it was published in the second rabbinical Bible printed by Daniel Bomberg in 1525. Elijah Levita was the first to attempt a scientific criticism of the Masorah; in the 19th cent. Christian D. Ginsburg assembled all the material about the Masorah.

See also: OCHLAH VEOCHLAH.

ALEXANDER KRISTIANPOLLER.

Lit.: Ginsburg, C. D., *Introduction to the Massoretico-Critical Edition . . .* (1897); Levias, Caspar, in *Jewish Encyclopedia*, vol. 8, pp. 365-71; Gordis, R., *The Biblical Text in the Making* (1937).

MASORETES, *see* MASORAH.

MASORETIC TEXTS, *see* BIBLE.

MASSACHUSETTS, one of the thirteen original states of the United States, with a population of 4,316,721 (1940 census), and a Jewish population of 262,945 (1937). This comprises about 6 per cent of the total population of the state and about 5½ per cent of the total Jewish population of the United States. Massachusetts ranks fifth in a listing of Jewish population by states, preceded by New York, Pennsylvania, Illinois and New Jersey.

According to the 1936 Census of Religious Bodies issued by the Bureau of the Census, there were 186 Jewish congregations in the state, 162 of which were in urban centers with populations of over 2,500 persons. Of the 186 congregations, 172 had buildings solely devoted to religious purposes. One hundred and seven

A page from Elijah Levita's "Masoreth Hamasoreth," printed by Bomberg at Venice in 1538

of these congregations reported a valuation on syna-gogue buildings of $6,493,313.

Over 68 per cent of the Jewish population of the state (1937 figures) resided in the Boston Metropolitan area: Boston, 118,000; Chelsea, 21,260; Malden, 11,170; Revere, 9,365; Brookline, 7,750; Cambridge, 4,580; Winthrop, 2,600; Somerville, 2,200; Everett, 1,920; Quincy, 1,870. Other large centers of Jewish population throughout the state are: Worcester, 13,350; Spring-field, 12,275; Lynn, 9,800; Fall River, 5,900; New Bed-ford, 4,520; Lawrence, 4,125; Haverhill, 4,100; Brock-ton, 3,900; Lowell, 2,420; Salem, 1,900; Pittsfield, 1,830; Holyoke, 1,870; Peabody, 1,250; Beverly, 1,115.

Despite the large Jewish population of Massachusetts and its leading city, Boston, the Jewish community of this state is comparatively young. Organized Jewish life dates back to 1843 and the founding of Congre-gation Ohabei Shalom, second oldest Jewish congre-gation in New England. There is a record, however, of many pre-Revolution Jews in the history of the commonwealth. In 1648 one Isaac Abrahams is re-corded as having appeared before the well-known Bos-ton notary, Aspinwall, as a witness to a bill of sale of his vessel, *Bride of Enchusen.* That Abrahams may well have been a permanent resident of Boston at the time, and that other Jews may have lived in the com-munity, is evidenced by the fact that three years earlier, in 1645, the word "Jew" appears in a letter of toler-ance written by Edward Winslow of Plymouth to Governor John Winthrop.

Despite the fact that the Puritans came to the New World in search of religious freedom, and that they had a great interest in Jewish customs, Jewish prophecy and the study of Hebrew, there existed an unfriendly atmosphere toward the Jews and there was a question as to the legal right of Jews to settle within the juris-diction of the commonwealth.

In 1649 Solomon Franco, after delivering a cargo to Major General Gibbons, attempted to settle in Boston. Though the General Court of the community declined to give him permission to do so, they allowed Franco "Six shillings p weeke out of the treasury for tenn weekes for his substance till he cann get his passage into Holland, so as he doe it within that time."

Another Jew, named Solomon, described as "ye malata Jue," was prosecuted in 1668 in the quarterly courts of Essex County for profaning the Lord's Day by traveling through Wenham on his journey toward Puscatqua.

The first Boston tax list, dated 1674, included the name of Rowland Gideon, described as "ye Jew." He was one of the Jews to whom letters of denization had been granted by the British government in 1769, which gave him permission to reside in English col-onies. He was rated at eighteen shillings.

The list of inhabitants of Boston for 1695, now in-cluded in the Massachusetts Historical Society's collec-tions, contains the names of two Jews, Raephaell Aban-dana and Samuel, the Jew. The Reverend Samuel Sewall, minister of the Second Church of Boston, wrote in 1697 that "there are two (Jews) at Boston; anno 1697, viz., Mr. Joseph Frazon and Mr. Samuel Frazon, his brother, to whom I am beholden for a sight of the Spanish Bible. Joseph Frazon was sometimes scholar to the learned Yeosuah da Sylva in London."

The Reverend Sewall further records the fact that the father and grandfather of the Frazons had lived in the Dutch plantations in Brazil where "Jews were formerly very numerous." In a later diary, Sewall records that Joseph Frazon died in 1703 or 1704 and that his body was "carried in Simson's coach to Bristow and from thence by water to Newport where there is a Jew burying-place."

Isaac Lopez and Abraham Gotatus landed in Boston in June, 1716. Lopez quietly attained eminence as a merchant and in 1720, at the annual town meeting, he was elected one of the constables. He declined office and paid a fine to be excused from service. In 1722 Lopez applied for and received permission to erect a building, thus becoming the first Jew in the state, so far as is known, to do so.

Michael Asher first appeared in 1716 as a witness on a deed for a transaction involving John Wakefield. According to the Suffolk Registry of Deeds, he lived in the South End of Boston, on Newbury Street, now part of Washington Street, and ran a snuff mill. As Asher later became guardian of his niece, Bilah Levy of New York, after she became orphaned, it is assumed that he came to Boston from New York. Asher's partner was Isaac Solomon. On February 22, 1733, the year following the birth of George Washington, Asher and Solomon, according to a document in the Suffolk Registry of Deeds, purchased a plot of land at what is now 15-17 Chambers Street, where they erected a shop after setting aside a part as a burying ground for "The Jewish Nation." This cemetery was known to be in existence as late as 1750, but all trace of it is lost after that date.

Isaac Solomon, who may or may not have been the partner of Michael Asher, is known to have later mar-ried Elizabeth Lowe of Marblehead, whence he en-listed on June 1, 1775, as a private in Captain William Bacon's Second Company of Captain Glover's 21st Regiment.

Another Jew known to have served in the Massachu-setts forces during the Revolution was Colonel Isaac Franks. Although not strictly a Massachusetts man, he was commissioned an ensign in the 7th Massachu-setts Regiment by Governor John Hancock. This is the same Isaac Franks who later served as aide-de-camp to General George Washington.

Harvard College, which as early as 1653 had an in-structor in Hebrew, Michael Wigglesworth, in 1722 hired Judah Monis, a Hebrew scholar just recently converted to Christianity. Monis (b. Italy, 1683) is known to have been admitted as a freeman by the mayor and Common Council of New York city on February 28, 1715-16. He came to Boston in 1720, where he attracted the attention of two ministers, In-crease Mather and a Mr. Leverett.

Monis, who was awarded the M.A. degree by Har-vard in 1720, the only honorary degree conferred upon a Jew by Harvard before 1800, was converted, under the influence of his ministerial friends, in 1722, after which he was made instructor of Hebrew at Harvard. A public ceremony of baptism was held in the College Hall on March 27, 1722. Monis taught Hebrew at Harvard until his retirement in 1760 at the age of seventy-seven. In 1735 Monis persuaded the college authorities to publish a Hebrew grammar that he had written as early as 1726. A font of Hebrew type was imported from England, and the Monis grammar was the first Hebrew book published in America. The book was dedicated to "His Excellency Jonathan Belcher, Esq.: Governour in Chief of His Majesty's Province of the Massachusetts Bay in New England, and the Rest of the Honourables and the Reverend Overseers of Harvard College, and the Reverend Mr. Benjamin Wadsworth, President, and the Rest of the Honourable and Reverend Corporation of Said College." A thousand copies were printed.

Two years after his appointment to the Harvard faculty, Monis married Abigail Marret, sister-in-law of John Martyn, the first minister of the Second Church in Westboro, Mass. After the death of his wife in 1760, Monis retired to Westboro, where he lived with Martyn. Monis took a great interest in the affairs of Martyn's church, and gave to the congregation three silver communion cups which are still preserved in the Boston Museum of Fine Arts as an outstanding example of old silver. Monis died in 1764, and was buried in Westboro.

A few Jews are known to have visited the Massachusetts Bay Colony only to be "warned out" in accordance with the right held by the New England towns of allowing only those persons to reside there who were chosen by the townsmen. Philip Samuel, a New York Jew, was ordered to leave Boston on April 24, 1756. A Rhode Island Jew, David Campenall, was "warned out" of Boston on June 15, 1726. In 1762 Isaac Moses, who later became a leading member of the New York Chamber of Commerce and a well-known Revolutionary patriot, was warned to leave Boston within fourteen days or to give security. Later it was the generosity of Moses that made possible the shipment of a cargo of corn from Virginia to John Hancock and Samuel Adams in order to relieve the suffering caused by the siege of Boston. Campenall, who died in Ipswich in 1732, had a son, William, who served in the French and Indian Wars and during the Revolutionary War.

In 1737 Solomon Isaac appeared before the selectmen of Boston to procure a release from quarantine of the Philadelphia sloop, *Sarah*. The Boston *Weekly Gazette* of October and November, 1754, evidenced a business dispute between Emanuel Abrams and one of his Christian competitors in the tobacco and snuff trade.

Aaron Lopez, one of the greatest pre-Revolutionary Jewish figures in New England, became a naturalized citizen of Massachusetts on October 15, 1762. Although he had resided in Newport, R. I., and Swansea, Mass., since October 13, 1752, he had been denied naturalization by the Supreme Court in Newport in March, 1762. Appearing in the Superior Court of Judicature of Taunton, Lopez became the first Jew to be naturalized in Massachusetts. Born a Marrano Jew, Lopez had been baptized a Catholic at his birth, but when this very Orthodox early American Jew took his oath of citizenship in Massachusetts, the words "upon the true faith of a Christian" were omitted.

Although the greater part of Lopez's life was spent in Newport, he was always intimately associated with the business life of Boston. From Newport, he was engaged in the manufacture of spermaceti products

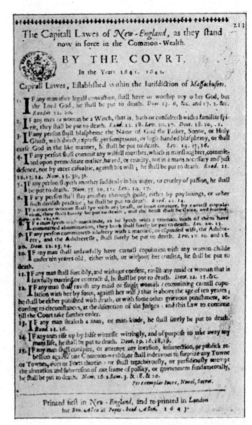

The capital laws of Massachusetts, dated 1641, containing Old Testament texts

and the carrying on of a coast-wide shipping business extending to Boston, New York, Philadelphia and Charleston, S. C. Later Lopez developed a very extensive trade with England, but this was not very successful. More profitable was his trade with the West Indies during the ten years immediately preceding the outbreak of the Revolution.

With the outbreak of the war, Lopez' ships became an important part of the Continental fleet. Just before the occupation of Newport by the British, Lopez, together with his father-in-law, Jacob Rodrigue Rivera, and his son-in-law, Abraham Pereira Mendes, and their families—all told about seventy—left Newport for Leicester, Mass. There Lopez purchased an estate and erected a large mansion which today is the site of the Leicester Academy, a gift to the community made by the Lopez family. Lopez was buried in the Newport cemetery after a eulogy delivered by the Reverend Dr. James Manning, president of Brown University. After Lopez left Leicester, the Jewish community in that town died out without leaving any appreciable trace.

In 1764 Ezra Stiles, then president of Yale University, stated that 4,000 pounds sterling had been lent to the Massachusetts treasury by a Mr. Jacobs of Newport. In 1776 Sarah, daughter of Aaron Isaacs, married William Payne of Boston. She was the mother of John Howard Payne, author of "Home, Sweet Home." Her parents conducted a school in Boston.

Abraham Jacobs was initiated into the second degree of Masonry on July 22, 1782, in St. Andrews Lodge of Boston, of which Paul Revere was then Master.

The Academy at Leicester, Massachusetts, of which the Lopez mansion is a part

Another Mason, one of the highest ranking in Colonial history, was Moses Michael Hays. He was Grand Master of the Grand Lodge of Masons of Massachusetts, and serving under him as Deputy Grand Master was Paul Revere. Hays, for many years one of the most prominent residents of Boston, was born in Lisbon in 1739, and migrated to New York with his father in 1763. After some years in Jamaica he settled in Newport, where he married Reyna Touro, sister of Rabbi Isaac Touro, and became a leading merchant. He came to Boston from Newport before the outbreak of the Revolution and lived first on Hanover Street and later on State Street. In Boston he was an insurance broker. In 1784 he was one of the organizers of the first bank in the city of Boston, a precursor of the First National Bank of Boston.

Moses Michael Hays had one son, Judah Hays, and five daughters. The daughters, except one who died in 1802, moved to Richmond, Va., but the son remained a prominent citizen of Boston. On May 9, 1805, Judah Hays was elected Fire Ward of the city for the coming year, being in all likelihood the first Jew elected to public office in Boston. He was also one of the founders of the Boston Athenaeum, the first library association in the United States.

Judah and Abraham Touro, nephews of Moses Michael Hays, were brought up in his Boston household. Abraham Touro, like his cousin, Judah Hays, continued as a Boston merchant, while Judah Touro moved to New Orleans in 1803. That he never forgot his many years in Boston is indicated by the fact that he contributed the $10,000 necessary for the completion of the Bunker Hill Monument.

These Colonial Jews, and others not mentioned, are recalled only as individual Jews who lived in Boston. No real Jewish community emerged until a small group of recent immigrants met in 1842 for religious services, the group which in 1843 organized Congregation Ohabei Shalom, later located in Brookline. This group lived, with few exceptions, within the limits of Boylston, Washington and Church streets.

On March 22, 1845, the congregation, then having forty members, procured its charter of incorporation. Four years later the first Jewish Sunday school in Boston was organized. By September, 1852, a synagogue was erected on Warren street, later called Warrenton street. This was accomplished through the benevolence of Alexander S. Saroni, who advanced the sum of $3,417.23 necessary to purchase the land. In 1854, when a new rabbi was to be elected, dissen-

sion arose among the members of the congregation. It was thus that Congregation Adath Israel, commonly known as Temple Israel, was founded. The first home of Temple Israel, now the largest Reform Jewish temple in New England, was a 250-seat house of worship on Pleasant street that was dedicated in September, 1854. A second split away from Congregation Ohabei Shalom resulted in the formation of Congregation Mishkan Tefila (1858), the third oldest congregation in the state.

In 1864 the Jewish community organized the United Hebrew Benevolent Society, the precursor of the later Associated Jewish Philanthropies of Boston. Then some $4,000 or $5,000 was spent in helping the poor. In 1941 the Associated Jewish Philanthropies had an annual budget of $620,000. The Philanthropies, through its sister organization, the United Jewish Campaign, engages in a combined appeal for local, national and overseas relief which in 1941 raised $1,229,000.

Another philanthropic organization, the Ladies Sewing Circle, was organized in 1869. About thirty-five years later it merged with the United Hebrew Benevolent Society as the Federation of Jewish Charities of Boston. In the first year of this new organization, 1895, the budget was $27,628. In 1930 another merger took place and nineteen organizations in all were incorporated as the Associated Jewish Philanthropies.

Boston's first Jewish Community Center was established in 1890 by Miss Lina Hecht, under the name of the Hebrew Industrial School for Girls. It has since become known as the Hecht House. In 1890 the Jewish population of the United States was 400,000 and the Jewish population of Boston was about 6,000. The establishment of the Hecht House, a counterpart of New York's Henry Street Settlement, coincides with the birth of Boston as a great Jewish community. In 1942 located in the populous Dorchester section, the Hecht House was originally housed in the South End at Hanover street. It was later housed at Chambers, Allen, and Charles streets in the West End, and then in Dorchester, always following the center of Jewish population. In the late 1930's the Jewish population trend was from the Dorchester, Roxbury, Mattapan district toward Brookline and Newton.

Massachusetts Jews, among the earliest and most active of American Zionists, played a large part in the popularization of Zionism in the United States. In 1919 the Massachusetts Zionists were successful in having the House of Representatives of the Commonwealth pass a resolution urging the President of the United States to take steps to "assure the development of Palestine into a Jewish Commonwealth" and to urge "the American Representatives at the Peace Conference to use their best endeavors to accomplish this object." Three years later, under the leadership of Elihu D. Stone, a group of Massachusetts Zionists were largely responsible for the introduction of a resolution into the United States Senate by Senator Henry Cabot Lodge, placing the United States on record as urging "the establishment in Palestine of the National Home for the Jewish people." The New England Zionist Region, of which Stone was president for the first thirteen years, was the first Zionist Region to be organized in the United States.

Chelsea, Malden, Everett, Somerville, Brookline, Newton and Quincy are all separate towns or cities

Design of a memorial, by Maurice Sterne, at Worcester, Mass., depicting the struggle of the Puritans with the wilderness

having Jewish communities of over 1,000, but must be considered part of Greater Boston. (The larger cities in the state are treated in separate articles.)

One of the most populous Jewish communities in the United States is Chelsea, a neighboring municipality only ten or fifteen minutes removed from the center of Boston. Over 40 per cent of the population of Chelsea is Jewish. Chelsea had, in 1942, a Conservative synagogue, Temple Emanuel, founded in 1935 and led by Rabbi Sidney Guthman, as well as fourteen Orthodox congregations.

Lynn, with a Jewish population of 9,800, is a community more removed from Boston than Chelsea. Lynn has its own local charities and conducts its own United Jewish Appeal campaign for local and overseas needs, which raised over $40,000 in 1941. The leading synagogue, Temple Beth El, is a Conservative congregation. Founded in 1927, it was headed by Rabbi Israel Harburg in 1942. In addition, Lynn had four Orthodox congregations, two over forty years old, and two smaller ones.

Brookline and Newton are completely a part of Boston Jewish communal life, even though they are separate corporate towns. Brookline contained Boston's three leading synagogues: Temple Ohabei Shalom and Temple Israel, Reform; and Kehillath Israel, Conservative. Joshua L. Liebman was rabbi of Temple Israel, Samuel J. Abrams of Temple Ohabei Shalom and Louis M. Epstein of Kehillath Israel in 1942. Rabbi Samuel N. Sherman, in 1942, headed Temple Emanuel of Newton (Conservative), and Beryl Cohon was rabbi of Temple Sinai (Reform).

Neighboring communities, Cambridge, Somerville, Everett and Malden, all have local charitable groups but cooperate with Boston in the United Jewish Campaign. The leading congregations in 1942 were: Cam-

bridge, Temple Beth Israel, Conservative, Rabbi Benjamin H. Gorrelick; Somerville, Temple B'nai B'rith, Conservative, Rabbi Hyman J. Routtenberg; Everett, Jewish Center, Orthodox, Rabbi S. H. Gordon; and Malden, Temple Tifereth Israel, Conservative, Rabbi Joseph H. Margolies.

Outside the Boston area there were, in 1942, many active Jewish communities. In North Adams, which had about 725 Jews, the United House of Israel (Orthodox) was founded in 1890, and its rabbi in 1942 was Moses Mescheloff. In Pittsfield, Anshe Amonim (Reform) was organized in 1867, and its rabbi in 1942 was Saul Habas. Also in Pittsfield was Israel Synagogue (Orthodox), whose rabbi was M. Furman. Temple Emanu-El (Reform) of Haverhill had Abraham I. Jacobson as rabbi, while Israel Harburg was rabbi of Temple Beth El (Reform) of that city. In Lawrence Morris A. Frank was rabbi of Temple Emanuel (Conservative), while in the comparatively recent Jewish community of Roxbury Benjamin L. Grossman was rabbi of Temple Beth Hamidrash Hagadol (Conservative). Roxbury is also the site of the first Jewish hospital in New England. Beth Israel Hospital was dedicated there on October 22, 1916.

Many Massachusetts Jews have been active in public life. Justice Louis Dembitz Brandeis (1916-39) and Justice Felix Frankfurter (1939-) were appointed to the United States Supreme Court from this commonwealth. Charles E. Wynanski, Jr., was named to the Federal Court for Massachusetts in 1942. On the State Superior Court have been David A. Lourie (1924-30), who served on the city court (1922-24); Abraham E. Pinanski (1930-); and Lewis Goldberg (1932-).

There have been many Jewish judges in the lower courts and among the prosecuting attorneys of the state. Those who have been assistant United States attorneys for Massachusetts are: Judge Goldberg (1921-26); Elihu D. Stone (1922-34); Charles Rome (1934-37); Jackson J. Holtz (1937-).

Among those who have served as assistants in the office of the Massachusetts Attorney General have been: Jacob Lewiton (1941-); Harry Greenblatt (1941-); Harold Seidenberg (1941-); Louis Novins (1938-40); Maurice Goldman (1936-40); Jacob J. Weisman (1928); Albert Hurwitz (1926-27); Leon Eyges (1918-20); Max Levinson.

Philip Rubinstein was in 1942 justice of the Juvenile Court. Associate justices of the Boston Municipal Court are Elijah Adlow (1931-) and Jennie Loitman Barron (1936-). Israel Ruby has been chief justice of the Williamstown District Court since 1938, and Philip Sherman associate justice of the Somerville Court since 1940. A large number of Jews are also special justices (part time) of various district courts throughout the state. Among them are: Abraham K. Cohen (1912-), Boston; Jacob Spiegel (1939-), Boston; Jacob Asher, Worcester; Samuel Barnett, Bristol; Mrs. Golda R. Walters, Northern Middlesex; Harry C. Mamber, Williamstown; Nyman H. Kolodney, district court of Williamstown; David A. Rose, Dorchester (1936-); Francis S. Wyner, Brookline (1933-); Jacob J. Kaplan, Dorchester (1932-35); Sadie Lipner Shulman, Dorchester; Samuel Eisentadt, Roxbury; Frank Kopelman, Barnstable; Israel Cherry, Southern Essex; Samuel Blassberg, Eastern Franklin.

Leopold Morse of Boston served five terms as a Congressman from Massachusetts (1877-85 and 1887-89). Abraham C. Ratshesky was minister to Czecho-slovakia from January, 1930, to June, 1932. Sarah Wambaugh was a member of the secretariate of the League of Nations during the time of the Danzig Plebiscite and a member of the Committee on the Saar of the League of Nations at the time of the Saar Plebiscite.

Holding various state positions have been Reuben L. Lurie, chairman of the Parole Commission (1940-); Abraham C. Webber, member of the State Board of Tax Appeals (1936); Abraham I. Zimon, deputy state income tax commissioner; David Brackman, public utilities commissioner (1940-), member of the State Senate (1936-40) and a member of the Boston city council (1931-35); Lincoln Filene (1912-22) and Alexander Brin (1922-), members of the State Advisory Board of Education; Joseph B. Grossman, member of the Governor's Council (1936-40); Esther M. Andrews, member of the Governor's Council (1932-36); Herbert B. Ehrmann, member of the State Civil Service Commission (1941-); and David A. Ellis, commissioner of public utilities.

Members of the state legislature have been Isaac Rosnosky, Boston (1883), the first Jew to be elected; Abraham C. Ratshesky, Boston (1888-90); Bernard Wolf, Boston (1892-94); Daniel England, Pittsfield (1898); Samuel Silverman, Boston (1915-16); Samuel Borofsky, Boston (1900-2); Simon Swig, Boston (1916); Jacob Wasserman, Boston (1916); David Brackman, Boston (1936-40); Philip Barnett, New Bedford (1934-); David A. Rose, Boston (1934-36); Philip Sherman, Somerville (1936-40); Albert Rubin, Fall River (1938-); William R. Gilman, Malden (1936-); Charles Miller, Boston (1936-); Morris Kritzman, Boston (1938-40); Charles Kaplan, Boston (1938-40); Edward Bromberg, Boston (1906-8); Jackson Holtz, Boston (1936); Max Ulin, Boston; Elihu D. Stone, Boston (1917-20); Samuel Benjamin Finkel, Boston (1918-20).

In 1892 the Massachusetts legislature passed an act granting to rabbis the right to perform the marriage ceremony. On February 13, 1919, the legislature passed a resolution endorsing the Jewish homeland in Palestine, and on March 10, 1919, Benzion Mossinson addressed the legislature on the aims of Zionism. In 1941 a bill was passed by the legislature and signed by Governor Leverett Saltonstall which compelled the dissolution of the Industrial Defense League, a leading anti-Semitic organization.

A number of Jews have been prominent in municipal affairs throughout the state. Leopold Morse was a member of the Boston School Board (1875) before he was elected to Congress. Louis E. Kirstein is president of the Boston Public Library and was the chairman of the Boston Port Authority. Samuel Silverman was corporation council of Boston (1930-34). In 1942 there were six Jewish assistant corporation counsels in Boston: Nathan Moger, Hirsh Freed, Herman Carp, Edward S. Gerber, Rudolph Robinson and Louis Weinstein. David Lasker was chairman of the Boston Finance Commission (1937), and Max Ulin was commissioner of the Metropolitan District Commission (1941-). Nathan A. Heller was chairman of the

Overseers of Public Welfare of Boston (1926-30) and a member of the Transit Commission (1926-34). Herman L. Bush is the Soldiers' Relief Commissioner of Boston (1938-).

Godfrey Morse was president of the Boston City Council (1880-83). Other Jews who served on the council include Abraham C. Ratshesky (1884-88), Isaac Rosnosky (1878-90), William Berwin (1893-1908), Samuel Borofsky (1898-1900). In 1907 William Berwin was acting mayor.

Henry Lasker was a member of the city council of Springfield (1908-12), and president of the city council (1912-16). Henry M. Lewis was president of the Malden city council (1930). Daniel England was mayor of Pittsfield (1902). Elihu A. Hershenson was city solicitor of Peabody (1935-37). Morris Silverstein was city solicitor of Everett (1942). Max Wise was city solicitor of Chelsea (1937-41), and Joseph Israelite succeeded him in that position (1942). Maurice Garber was chairman of the Chelsea School Board (1936-38). Mrs. Abraham E. Pinanski was a member of the Brookline School Committee (1936-), and Simon Kuhn was commissioner of recreation of Worcester (1936). Also of Worcester is Jacob Asher, associate justice of the district court (1917-). Serving as county district attorneys were: George L. Rabb, Norfolk and Plymouth; Hyman F. Goldman, Suffolk; and Benjamin Hurvitz, Bristol.

Jews have been prominent throughout the state in the mercantile field and the shoe and textile industries. Edward A. Filene, Lincoln Filene, and Louis E. Kirstein were associated with the Filene Department Store, the Vorenberg family with the Gilchrist store in Boston, and the England brothers with the England department store in Pittsfield.   HENRY W. LEVY.

Lit.: Publications of the American Jewish Historical Society; Friedman, Lee M., Early American Jews (1934) 3-45.

MASSAD, MASSADA, see COLONIES, AGRICULTURAL.

MASSARANI, TULLO, author, senator, and painter, b. Mantua, Italy, 1826; d. Milan, Italy, 1905. He was educated at the University of Pavia, but he had to flee that city at the age of twenty-two because of his participation in the unsuccessful Italian revolution of 1848. He lived in Germany, France, and Switzerland for many years, and later returned to Milan, where he was elected to parliament in 1860, a post he held for seven years. In 1876 he was appointed senator. He anticipated future events by advocating the then unpopular cause of Italian reconciliation with Germany.

His critical paper on Heine in the magazine *Crepo-scolo* (1867) and his translation of Heine's poetry and prose into Italian were largely responsible for Heine's popularity in Italy. He wrote many volumes on politics, history, literature, and art in French, German, and Italian. His works include: *Quelques mots sur la défense de Venise* (1849); *Deutschland und die italienische Frage* (1859); *Studii di letteratura e di arte* (1873); *L'arte a Parigi* (1879); *Storia e fisiologie dell' arte di ridere* (1900-2). His collected works were published in twenty-two volumes in Florence (1906-9).

Massarani enjoyed a considerable reputation as an

artist in Italy, although in other countries his criticism of art was more highly appreciated than his painting. His pictures were in the romantic manner of Delacroix, and his most successful work was *The Warm Baths of Alexandria.* In 1878 he was president of the international jury of art at the Paris Exposition.

MASSARY, FRITZI, actress, b. Vienna, 1882. She made her debut in Vienna at the age of sixteen, appearing in a revue, and was launched on her career by the director of the Berlin Metropol Theater where she was a star from 1904 to 1933. Establishing her reputation in the title role of Leo Fall's operetta *The Empress,* she subsequently enacted leading parts in *Madame Pompadour, The Rose of Stamboul* and *The Spanish Nightingale.* Other triumphs followed with her appearances in *Cleopatra, Carnival Fairy, The Merry Widow* and *The Last Waltz.* Such outstanding composers of musical comedies as Leo Fall, Imre (Emmerich) Kálmán, Franz Lehár and Oscar Straus wrote operettas for her special talents. Touring throughout Central Europe with immense success, she was called "Berlin's most winsome soubrette." The most popular operetta star of pre-Nazi Germany, she delighted audiences with her charm, verve and versatility.

Equally brilliant as actress and singer, Fritzi Massary aspired to grand opera and was successful in the higher class comedy, especially in St. John Ervine's *The First Mrs. Fraser* and in Bruno Frank's *Nina.* She married the comedian Max Pallenberg in 1918, and retired from the stage on the death of her husband, who was killed in an aeroplane accident in 1934. In March, 1938, however, she appeared on the stage again, playing at His Majesty's Theater, London, in *Operetta* by Noel Coward. The following year she emigrated to the United States, where she was living (in Los Angeles) in 1942 with her daughter and son-in-law, Bruno Frank, playwright and novelist.

MASSECHETH, MASSECHTA, see MISHNAH; TALMUD.

MASSEMATTEN, see PHRASES, POPULAR.

MASSÉNA, ANDRÉ (ANDREA), Duke of Rivoli, Prince of Essling, marshal of France, b. Nice, 1758; d. 1817. Although the fact cannot be authenticated, most of Masséna's biographers are convinced that he was of Jewish ancestry, originally named Manasse. His father was a tanner who, together with his brother, also manufactured soap. Orphaned in his early years, Masséna was cabin-boy on a merchant vessel. At the age of seventeen he became a soldier but left the army, after twelve years of service, in disgust at failing to obtain a sub-lieutenancy. Then he joined his cousin Bavastro, who was a famous corsair.

After the outbreak of the French Revolution, Masséna became a soldier in the republican army, and in 1793 was appointed general. In 1794 he campaigned successfully against the Austrians, and obtained strategic control of the Maritime Alps. In 1795 he was victorious at Loano, but his severity toward his soldiers caused a mutiny.

When Bonaparte took command of the French

Fritzi Massary

"Italian Army," Masséna was his best second in command. Masséna distinguished himself at Rivoli and Lodi, and Bonaparte praised him as "enfant chéri de la victoire." But Masséna remained unpopular with the privates, who reproached him for avarice and severity. In 1797, Masséna was offered a seat in the directorate, but he declined. He consistently refused to enter politics. When Bonaparte went to Egypt, Masséna assumed supreme command. He was victorious in the battle of Zurich, thus averting the invasion of France. In 1800 he won further glory in his defense of Genoa, thus allowing Bonaparte to prepare his campaign, which was crowned by victory at Marengo. In 1804, Bonaparte, who became Emperor Napoleon I, named Masséna marshal.

The following year, Masséna held command in Italy, and prevented the Austrians from reinforcing their army for the battle of Austerlitz. He excelled in Poland (1807), and Napoleon named him duke of Rivoli. In the campaign of 1809, Masséna effected the decisive victory at Wagram, and was named prince of Essling by Napoleon. In 1810 and 1811, he directed operations of the French army in Portugal and Spain. He was unsuccessful in attacking Wellington, but his retreat is recorded as a masterly feat although it was also disgraceful in consequence of excesses by the French soldiers against the population of Portugal and Spain. Masséna was prevented by illness from participating in the Russian campaign (1812). In 1814 he directed the defense of France in the wake of Napoleon's final defeat.

After Napoleon's return from Elba, Masséna, who had sworn allegiance to Louis XVIII, sided with the emperor again but was too cautious to expose himself as fully as other generals did. Nevertheless, he fell into disfavor with the returned king. Although Masséna risked his life in numerous battles, he never was wounded, but his health was shattered after 1810. He was regarded as Napoleon's best general, the only one capable of commanding an army on his own. He was no learned theorist; on the contrary, he disliked reading.   HUGO BIEBER.

Lit.: Memoires du Maréchel Masséna, edited by General Koch (1848-50); Journal of the Royal United Service Institution (1913).

MASSIAS, ABRAHAM A., United States army officer, b. Charleston, S. C., 1772; d. Charleston, 1848. The Massias family evidently came from Barbados and settled in Charleston, for the most part. Massias is noted as having been a Mason in Newport in 1800. In 1802 he was an ensign and in 1804 a lieutenant in the New York militia. In 1809 he resigned his post as captain in the New York State militia to become a captain in the United States army. During the War of 1812 Massias, in charge of a garrison of sixty men, repelled and defeated British attempts to land at Cumberland Island, Ga. He was made a major in 1814. In 1818, during discussions in the Maryland legislature for the removal of Jewish disabilities in the state, the services offered by Massias to his country were cited as evidence that such a change was desirable. He was an active member of the Charleston synagogue.

Lit.: Publications of the American Jewish Historical Society, No. 19 (1910) 19-20; No. 26 (1918) 192-93.

MASSIG GEBUL, see BOUNDARIES, REMOVAL OF.

MASTBAUM, JULES E., theatre owner and philanthropist, b. Philadelphia, 1872; d. Philadelphia, 1926. With his brother Stanley (b. Philadelphia, 1875; d. Philadelphia, 1918) he was among the first to enter the motion picture theatre field (1913), opening a chain of theatres from New York to West Virginia. The chain was subsequently named the Stanley Theatre Corporation in memory of Stanley Mastbaum.

Mastbaum served on the executive committee of the Sesquicentennial exhibition in Philadelphia in 1926. In conjunction with the exhibition he founded at his own expense a permanent museum of Rodin sculpture. Containing ninety-eight pieces of Rodin originals and copies, the collection is the largest outside of Paris. The museum was dedicated to the city of Philadelphia in 1929. Mastbaum was active in general and Jewish philanthropies. He was on the executive board of various local Jewish institutions, and in 1925 headed the Federation Building Fund campaign in Philadelphia.

Lit.: Jewish Tribune, July 2, 1926, p. 10; American Hebrew, Dec. 4, 1925, p. 105; Dec. 10, 1926, p. 221; Publications of the American Jewish Historical Society, No. 28 (1922) 292.

MASTBOIM, YOIEL (JOEL), Yiddish writer, b. Meseritz, province of Shedletz, Russia, 1882. He received a secular education and in his early childhood displayed an interest in painting. Later he turned to literature and made his debut in Veg in 1906 with a sketch, Yerachmialke dem Shochets. Other short stories were published in Unser Leben and Moment.

The first collection of Mastboim's work, Skizzen un Bilder, appeared in 1912 in Warsaw, where Mastboim belonged to a group of young Yiddish writers who were followers of David Frischman.

On a Melodie, a dramatic poem, was published in 1917; in 1920 Mastboim was one of the contributors to an anthology, Poilens Klangen, for which he wrote a series of études, Stett un Stettlech. Though Mastboim later spent some time in London, where he worked on the Zeit, most of his writing deals with the Jews of Poland. Fun ro:ten Leben, a novel describing the 1905 revolution, was published in 1921; it was followed by Drei Doires (1923); Maritas Glick (1923); and Halutzim (1926). Mastboim was considered one of the most original Yiddish writers of his time.

In 1935 Mastboim settled in Palestine where a number of his works were translated into Hebrew.

Lit.: Reisen, Z., Lexikon fun der Yiddisher Literatur, Presse un Filologie, vol. 2 (1930), cols. 316-21.

MASTER OF THE NAME, see BAAL SHEM; BAAL SHEM, THE.

MATHEMATICS, JEWS IN. 1. The Ancient Period. The ancient Jewish mathematicians were not interested in the development of mathematics as a science per se, but rather for practical purposes, such as the fixing of festivals in the lunar month, which depended upon exact astronomical calculations, the surveying of land, and the duration of the twilight, which required meticulous mensuration. The extreme piety of the majority of the Jewish logicians of this period compelled them to delve into various geometrical constants for ritual measurements, such as Sabbath distances, since Jews were permitted to walk on a public road only a specified distance (2,000 cubits, or 3,000 feet) in order that they might adhere to the Biblical injunction of remaining within limits on the seventh day, as related in Ex. 16:29. Moreover, the determination of agricultural limitations and sound legislation calling for the sowing of the fields, in which (as stated in Lev. 19:19) two kinds of seeds might not be sown within a certain distance of each other, demanded a basic knowledge of mathematics. Their chief interest lay in multiplication (Hebrew, daraba, then called geometric multiplication), division and fractions; they entirely disregarded addition and subtraction. This geometric procedure was derived from the Hebrew term saraf, based upon Babylonian and Egyptian derivations, which represented multiplication as a process of plaiting of rushes or weaving.

Frequent allusions to mathematical propositions are made in the Mishnah and Talmud by the early sages Judah, Joshua, Samuel, and the eminent astronomer Gamaliel. The Talmud also mentions (Erub. 43b) certain surveying methods for calculating distances which, as Maimonides observed in his commentary on Erub. 41b, necessitated a knowledge of similar triangles, and their trigonometric solution. The value of a prism was correctly computed in the Talmud, but in calculating the volume of a cylinder the Mishnah and Gemara erroneously suggested the value of the Greek letter π as being equal to three (I Kings 7:23). This deduction was fallaciously based upon the Roman school of logic.

The oldest Hebrew mathematical treatise known is

the *Mishnath Hamiddoth,* written in pre-Arabian times (150 C.E.) and at the time of the Mishnah (about 100 to 200 C.E.). It was originally discovered in 1862 by Moritz Steinschneider and published in 1864. This was an abbreviated geometrical work, originally compiled by Nehemiah (150 C.E.), famous teacher of the Mishnah, and it contained forty-two paragraphs in five chapters dealing specifically with definitions, terms and practical rules of plane and solid geometry, without offering, however, either proofs or demonstrations. This volume was intended to be a guide for surveyors. His most significant contribution to Jewish knowledge of mathematics was his enunciation of the fact that the value of the Greek letter π is approximately equal to 3 1/7.

2. The Medieval Period. Jewish scholars, through the encouragement received from the Moors, came to enjoy an enviable reputation in mathematics in the 11th cent. in Spain. It was they who did most to encourage the translation of the Arabic works into Latin, as witness the contributions of Abraham ibn Ezra (1092-1167) and of his older contemporary, the renowned interpreter Abraham bar Hiyya Hanasi, better known as Savasorda (about 1065-1136), who derived most of his sources from Plato of Tivoli. Ibn Ezra wrote voluminous works on the Cabala, the theory of numbers, the calendar and astronomy. He is more popularly known to modern scholars for his *Sefer Haehad,* dealing primarily with elementary mathematics, the latter being based on Arabic and Hindu sources.

Until the 12th cent. Jewish mathematicians regarded mathematics solely as a science introductory to philosophy. It was the gradual interest in and development of the physical world about them by the Greek and Arab scientists which led the Jews to participate actively in mathematical pursuits, gradually deviating from their elementary mathematical conceptions (based upon the Talmudic tractates *Kilayim, Erubin, Middoth* and *Ohaloth,* and in the *Silluk* of the Payetan Eleazar Hakalir to Shabbath Shekalim) pertaining to astronomical calculations, the fixing of the calendar, and certain ritual regulations that required measurement.

Very few Hebrew contributions were known to have been made before the 12th cent., for until this period the comparatively insignificant writings composed by Jews were neglected in favor of astronomy and astrology. Mashullah, the eminent astrologer and astronomer, who lived about 900 C.E., was the accepted mathematical authority of his day. He explained and elaborated on Euclid's *Elements,* which was regarded as an authoritative basis for further investigation. His contemporary, Sahl Rabban al Tabari, who was regarded as the outstanding geometrician of his era, wrote several treatises on both algebra and geometry, and translated many mathematical works from Arabic into Latin.

The 13th cent. witnessed a gradual discovery of the works of ancient thinkers and writers. Notable among them were the writings of Greek and Arabic mathematicians, and of such eminent scholars as Abraham bar Hiyya Hanasi, who wrote the *Hibbur Hameshihah Vehatishoreth* (Treatise on Areas and Measurements; published by Jehiel Michael Guttmann, Berlin, 1913), expounding the elements of geometry, and Levi ben

Gershon (Gersonides, 1288-1344; known also as Leo de Balneolis), in his *Sefer Hamispar* (published by Gershon Lange, Frankfort, 1909), and in his *Maaseh Hosheb* (edit. Lange, Frankfort, 1909), dealing with elementary algebra. Gersonides translated mathematical treatises from a philosophical as well as a scientific point of view, and in his works was concerned chiefly with the development of "plane surfaces" and "plane numbers," which led him to coin the Hebrew word *shetah,* a word which has that meaning.

Moses ben Maimon, better known as Moses Maimonides, laid a strong foundation for the furtherance of astronomy by means of mathematical calculations. In his monumental *Hilchoth Kiddush Hahodesh* (Laws for the Sanctification of the Month; published in 1178), he enumerates a vast number of working rules, as well as an abundance of numerical data, whereby the exact position of the sun could be found at any moment. This had been important during the Talmudic period, when the commencement of a new month had been determined by the accredited evidence of witnesses, and the reliability of their testimony as to the position and visibility of the moon had been ascertained by mathematical computations. Euclid's geometrical principles served as an accepted basis for all mathematical disputations in the 13th cent. In 1278 Euclid's entire work was translated from Arabic into Hebrew by Moses ibn Tibbon. Judah ben Samuel Cohen of Toledo (1238), his famed contemporary, who wrote an encyclopedia in Arabic, translated extracts from Euclid's *Elements* from Arabic into Hebrew under the title of *Midrash Hahochmah.* Numberless commentaries on it soon appeared, written by Arabian mathematicians, more particularly by Alfarabi and Ibn Haitham, which were translated by Kalonymus ben Kalonymus (1286-1328). There are still other commentaries on the *Elements* extant in manuscript form in various European libraries, for example Bonn, written by such distinguished logicians as Jacob ben Machir (1230-1307), on the introduction to book one, by Levi ben Gershon, on the propositions of books 1, 3, 4 and 5, and by Elijah Mizrahi. Three new authoritative translations of Euclid's *Data* were rendered into Hebrew from the Arabic version of Hunain ibn Ishab and Jacob ben Machir's translation, entitled *Sefer Hamattanah,* and were published between 1775 and 1875 by Abraham Joseph ben Simon Minz with annotations by Meir and Fürth, called *Reshith Limmudim Hasefer Iklides.*

The Alexandrian mathematician had a profound influence on the Jewish mathematicians. Well-known writers and translators, such as Jacob ben Machir, translated most of his works on spherical figures into Hebrew. This translation served as a focal point for future discussion among Jewish mathematicians. It inspired Kalonymus to translate Archimedes' works on conoids and spheroids, one on algebraic propositions, a work on geometry entitled *Al Shakel al Katta,* and a treatise on cones and cylinders by Asba ben Mohammed.

3. The Modern Period. Until the 16th cent., however, no real contributions to mathematics were made, for its study was maintained at universities in a half-hearted manner. No great mathematicians appeared to inspire students to further study. Moreover, the persistent feudal conflicts and clerical timidity hampered the free growth of thought. The Church clung tenaciously to the enforcement of beliefs on grounds of supernatural truth, not to be discovered, they reasoned, by observation of the world around them and the unbridled use of individual thought.

However, with the arrival of the 16th cent., a period of increased intellectual activity was ushered in. In this era men's minds became clearer, stronger and less servile. The indistinctness of thought, so characteristic of medieval learning, began to be remedied chiefly by the steady cultivation of pure mathematics and astronomy. Dogmatism was bitterly attacked. The Copernican system was set in opposition to the time-honored Ptolemaic system. Thus, by slow degrees, the servile minds of men were cut adrift from their old scholastic moorings, and sent forth to judge freely and independently in matters of science. Men like David Gans (1541-1613), the famous Jewish historian and author of *Migdal David, Prozdor,* and *Maor Hakatan,* based his works chiefly on those of the Italian algebraists, notably Ferrar and Bombelli. He solved completely the cubic and biquadratic equations, improved the symbolism of algebra and generalized the use of letters to an extent whereby it placed algebra substantially upon its present strong foundation. At about this time, when elementary algebra was becoming crystallized, a revival in geometry took place. On the side of pure geometry were men like the non-Jew Johann Kepler (1571-1630) and the Jew Joseph Solomon Delmedigo (1591-1655), who based their works primarily on Descartes' invention of the method of analytic geometry. It was Delmedigo whose epoch-making books, *Maayan Gannim* and *Basmath Bath Shelomoh,* brought the Jewish position in the mathematical world to the zenith of its fame. In his book he incorporated a lucid survey on algebra, trigonometry and geometry.

The 18th cent. was devoted largely to the investigations of the foundations of the new analysis, to a consideration of its applications, to the study of the infinite series, and to the understanding of the nature of the complex numbers. Many of these investigations were incorporated into the works of the noted Gaon and Talmudist, Elijah Vilna (d. 1729), who wrote treatises on trigonometry, geometry, algebra and astronomy.

Jews began to make more solid contributions in the 19th and 20th centuries. The industry of Carl Gustav Jacobi (1804-51) had become proverbial in the world of mathematics. His unique and huge contribution to the development of elliptic functions to the theory of numbers made him one of the mathematical glories of his day. By means of this theory Jacobi provided a testing ground for the discovery and improvement of general theorems in the theory of functions of a complex variable. This was to become a favorite discussion with some of the greatest mathematicians who followed him. Almost every branch of mathematics was favored with vital fundamental contributions from him. His chief works related to partial fractions, functional determinants, the calculus of variations and the transformation of homogeneous functions.

It was the subtle difficulties of the Fourier series of trigonometric functions which inspired the brilliant Georg Cantor (1845-1918), one of the foremost rationalists that the mathematical world has ever known,

to penetrate more deeply to the foundations of analysis than any of his contemporaries had cared to look, and he was led to his renowned attack on the mathematics of the infinite itself, which is the basis for all questions concerning continuity, limits and convergence. His revolutionary theory of the infinite, which led to the aggregate theory (*Mengenlehre*), was one of the most disturbingly original contributions to mathematics in the past 2,500 years, and finally came to be accepted as a fundamental contribution to all mathematics, and more particularly to the foundations of analysis. In 1874 he successfully demonstrated the existence of an infinite number of transcendental numbers within an interval of real numbers. The transition from the unidimensional continuum to the multidimensional one, which Cantor had previously deemed unachievable, was unexpectedly discovered by him (1877).

During the same period a brilliant group of mathematical physicists, led by the eminent Heinrich Hertz (1857-94), transformed applied mathematics by systematically basing their deductions upon the law of the conservation of energy and the hypothesis of the ether which pervades space. It was well known, as a necessity of James Clark Maxwell's mathematical electromagnetic theory, that the polarization and depolarization of an insulator must give rise to the same electromagnetic effects in the neighborhood as a voltaic current in a conductor. Experimental proof, however, was still lacking, and although several experiments had come very near its discovery, Hertz was the first who actually succeeded in supplying it (1887). Continuing his inquiries for the next few years, he was able to discover the progressive propagation of electromagnetic action through space, to measure the length and velocity of electromagnetic waves, and to show that in the transverse nature of their vibration and susceptibility to reflection, refraction and polarization they are in complete correspondence with the waves of heat and light. This led him to believe without doubt that ordinary light consists of electrical vibrations in an all-pervading ether which possesses the properties of an insulator and of a magnetic medium. This served as a medium for further mathematical discoveries, and led to the detection of the existence of electric waves in addition to the spark-gap which he originally employed, and the results of his observations, the earliest interest of which was simply that they afforded a confirmation of an abstruse mathematical theory, have been applied to the practical purpose of signalling over considerable distances (wireless telegraphy).

It was not long thereafter, however, that a feeling began to emerge in scientific circles that the fundamental notions upon which science is based were by no means satisfactory. It was Mach (1836-1916) who first suggested that they be revised and redefined in the hope that scientific theory might become less complex and more intelligible. This work was left to Albert Einstein (1879-   ), who, following in Mach's wake, had at once revised the notions of space and time and the law of gravity. It was the singular experiments of the eminent physicist Albert A. Michelson (1852-1931) which gave rise to the movement for scientific reform. It was he who paved the way for Einstein's unique revelations. His treatise *The Law of Emission and Absorption of Light* indicated the retreat of scientific thought from the "wave theory" of light back again to the "corpuscular" theory, and rapidly paved the way for the explanation of the theory of rays which has since held a vital position in theory and practice. The basis of Einstein's theory of relativity, which maintained that "nature is such that it is impossible to determine absolute motion by any experiment whatever," and that the laws of nature will hold good, regardless of what coordinates are used to represent the distances and time involved, was the fact that all measurement is relative and may, at least in specific instances, be affected by the fact that it is made from a moving body, such as the earth. The laws thus deduced contain a factor which does not appear in the law as stated by Newton or any other physicist thus far. It is on the ground of precisely this new factor, which takes account of contraction effects due to motion, that Einstein is able to explain certain variations in the orbit of the planet Mercury, which have hitherto been regarded as inexplicable. Basing his assumptions on Kepler's theory that there is a variation of eight minutes in the arc of the planet Mars, he declared that there is a difference of forty-three seconds in the motion of Mercury, completely revolutionizing 19th cent. conceptions not only of purely astronomical mechanism but also of the nature of time, space and the basic tenets of science.

Among the exponents of modern mathematics, the following Jews are especially noteworthy: M. Abraham (mathematical theory of electricity); Moritz Cantor (historian of mathematics); F. M. Eisenstein (theory of numbers and functions); Gordon (basal principles of theory of invariants); J. Hadamard (theory of numbers and functions); Halphen (reduction of linear equations to integrable form, and investigations on spatial curves); Hamburger (differential equations); Felix Klein (algebra, geometry and analysis); Leo Königsberger (differential equations and elliptic functions); Lebesque (integration and Fourier Series); Maurice Levi (well-known for his researches in mathematical physics); Tullio Levi-Civita (absolute calculus); Hirsch Meyer (properties of symmetrical functions); Herman Minkowski (geometrical number theory); Arthur Moritz (geometry and the theory of aggregates); Emmy Noether (modern algebra); Pasch (geometrical experiments on the theory of complexes); Pringsheim (infinite process and analysis); Rosanes (geometrical transformation and apolarity); Schapiro (algebraic iterations and cofunctions); Ludwig Schlesinger (original investigations on differential equations); Schwarzschild (authority on mathematical astronomy); Weingarten (foremost authority on the theory of surfaces); Wolfskehl (development of the theory of numbers).

SOLOMON BALSAM.

Lit.: Sutter, Geschichte der mathematischen Wissenschaften (1873); Zuckermann, Das Mathematische im Talmud (1878); Cantor, Vorlesungen über Geschichte der Mathematik (1880); Hankel, Zur Geschichte der Mathematik im Altertum und Mittelalter (1886); Marx, Alexander, Scientific Work of Outstanding Medieval Jewish Scholars, vol. 3; Smith, Eugene, History of Mathematics, vol. 2 (1925); Feldman, William M., Rabbinical Mathematics and Astronomy (1931); Gandz, Solomon, Mishnath Hamiddoth (1932); Steinschneider, Moritz, Die Mathematik bei den Juden (1901); Bell, E. T., Men of Mathematics (1937); Cajori, Florian, A History of Mathematics (1919); Prasad, Ganesh, Some Great Mathematicians of the Nineteenth Century (3 vols., 1933); Rosenhead, L., "Jewish Mathematicians of the Middle Ages," Jewish Chronicle (London), Aug. 21, 1928.

MATHMID, see STUDENTS, TYPES OF.

MATRIARCHATE, or mother-right, a system of social organization by which descent, kinship and all social relations are reckoned after the mother, and in which the women have a considerable share in the activities of the group. A number of Semitic scholars have suggested that originally the form of Hebrew social organization was matriarchic. G. A. Wilken in 1884 and W. Robertson Smith in 1885 declared that there were Biblical indications validating this assumption. Smith maintained that there were two types of matriarchal marriages. One he called *beena* marriage, a regulated union "in which the woman remained with her kin and chose and dismissed her partners at will, the children belonging to the mother's kin and growing up under their protection" (*Kinship and Marriage in Early Arabia*, 2nd ed., 1903, p. 86). *Mot'a* marriage is the name he applied to a temporary, unregulated union. "The *mot'a* marriage was a purely personal contract, founded on consent between a man and a woman, without any intervention on the part of the woman's kin. In *mot'a* marriage the woman did not leave her home, her people gave up no rights which they had over her, and the children of the marriage did not belong to the husband" (*ibid.*, p. 84). Marriages based on a system of male kinship that developed later, Smith called *ba'al* marriages. This type of marriage, he declared, was one of domination, in which the wife lost her freedom and was a subject of her husband. The theory of an original matriarchate has been contested by a number of writers, although the majority of modern Biblical scholars probably accept this hypothesis.

Lit.: Jacobson, David, Social Background of the Old Testament (1942); Malinowski, B., The Father in Primitive Society (1927); Westermarck, E., History of Human Marriage, 5th ed. (1921).

MATRIMONY, see MARRIAGE; SHADHAN; WEDDING AND WEDDING CUSTOMS.

MATTAN TORAH, see REVELATION; SHABUOTH.

MATTATHIAS, author and organizer of the Maccabean revolt against the Syrians and Hellenists, d. 166 B.C.E. He is described in *I Maccabees* as the son of John, the son of Simon, whom Josephus identifies as the son of Asamoneus (Hashmonai). Mattathias was a priest of the order of Joiarib, and lived in Modin, north of Jerusalem, from which paganized city he may have fled. When Antiochus Epiphanes of Syria resolved to uproot Judaism entirely, many of its adherents sought protection in hidden mountain passes.

Mattathias, however, though already an old man (*I Maccabees* makes him 146 at the time of his death), realized the ineffectuality of meeting the sword only with prayer, and took upon himself the organization of the resistance which was to have such far-reaching historical significance. When a band of the king's soldiers appeared in Modin, in 168 B.C.E., set up an altar to Zeus, and commanded Mattathias to sacrifice upon it, he not only defied them on behalf of himself and his sons, but slew a renegade Jew and destroyed the

Boris Schatz' conception of "Mattathias Slaying the Defiler." From the collection of the Hebrew Union College, Cincinnati

altar, while his sons killed the captain of the troops. Then Mattathias issued a call to all who were "zealous for the Law and maintain the covenant" to follow him in battle. They soon became a formidable body, particularly when, at their leader's command, they abandoned their scruples against fighting on the Sabbath—scruples which had cost a thousand Hasideans (Hasidim, "pious") their lives. Mattathias and his followers now went through the land, destroying the heathen altars, killing the apostates, circumcising male children, and inspiring the people throughout the country to join the uprising. When Mattathias died the following year he left his five sons, Judas, Simon, John, Eleazar and Jonathan, to carry on his work.

See also HASMONEANS.

Lit.: Graetz, H., *History of the Jews,* vol. 1 (1927) 458-61, and other Jewish histories for the period.

MATTERSBURG (known also as **Mattersdorf;** in Hungarian, **Nagymarton**), a town in Western Hungary which was incorporated into Austria in 1921 and annexed by Germany in 1938. The greater part of the Jews expelled by the city of Sopron (Ödenburg), in 1526, settled in Mattersburg, where they weathered the Turkish wars, religious and civil (16th and 17th centuries), under the protection of the mightiest lords of Hungary, the Esterházys. In 1749 there were one hundred Jewish families in Mattersburg who paid the

Princes Esterházy annually, for protection, 400 gulden, and a tax of 100 gulden to the magistrate of the town. Abraham Leeb and Moses Joseph supplied the imperial mint at Vienna with gold and silver. In 1770 the number of Jewish families was 179; in 1848 the total population of 4,500 included 1,500 Jews. Between 1785 and 1800 Peter Beer, famous pedagogue and author, taught at the German school of Mattersburg.

Mattersburg was noted for a succession of outstanding spiritual leaders, including Rabbi Mose (about 1660); Judah Leb Frankfurter (1730-37); Aryeh Leb Schotten; Gerson Abraham Chayes (about 1770); Jeremiah Mattersdorf (about 1780); Issachar Beer Bloch (d. 1789). The Yeshiva of Mattersburg was founded by Rabbi Moses Sofer (Hatham Sofer, 1789-1806), subsequently of Pressburg, and it was carried on by his successors Eger Bunem, Meier Popper, by his own son Simon Sofer (1842-60), subsequently rabbi of Cracow, reaching its zenith under his grandson Samuel Ehrenfeld (1877-83), called Hathan Sofer after his work. He was succeeded by his son Simche Bunem Ehrenfeld (1883-1920), author of *Maneh Simhah,* published by his son, Rabbi Samuel Ehrenfeld (1921-).

In 1938, after the Nazi occupation of Austria, the Jews of Nagymarton, approximately 1,000 persons, were driven across the border to the neighboring Hungary, whence they proceeded to France, Palestine and the United States. Rabbi Samuel Ehrenfeld, in New York city, reestablished the Yeshivath Hatham Sofer which, in 1942, had seventy students.

MATTERSDORF, JEREMIAH BEN ISAAC EISIK, rabbi and author, who lived in the second half of the 18th cent. He derived his surname from Mattersdorf (Nagymarton), a town in Western Hungary, where he was rabbi, probably up to 1801, when he was called to Abaujszántó, Hungary. Among his pupils was Aaron Chorin. He was one of the great authorities on Jewish civil law. His work *Modaah Rabbah,* commentaries on Hayim Sabbatai's *Torath Hayim (Modaah Veones)* was published by his son Joab in the work *Modaa Zutta* (1798).

JOAB BEN JEREMIAH MATTERSDORF, rabbi and author, son of Jeremiah (place and date of birth unknown; d. 1807, probably at Abaujszántó), was rabbi at Zsarnóc, for a prolonged period at Deutschkreuz, subsequently at Hunsdorf (Hunkovce), and in 1806 succeeded his father in the rabbinate of Abaujszántó. He published *Shaare Binah* (1792), notes to the *Shaare Shebuoth* of Rabbi Isaac ben Reuben; *Modaah Zuta* (1798), including also *Modaah Rabbah,* the work of his father, notes to Hayim Sabbatai's *Torah Hayim* and *Hen Tob* (1806), commentaries on *Shulhan Aruch, Eben Haezer.* His responsa on *Shulhan Aruch, Orah Hayim* and *Yoreh Deah, Imre Noam,* were published posthumously, in 1885, as were his homilies under the title of *Imre Yoab* (1895). He was considered one of the greatest Halachists of his time.

MATTES, L. (pseudonym of Mattes Lunianky), Yiddish writer, b. Bialystok, Russia, 1897; d. Los Angeles, 1929. He came to the United States at the age of fourteen and settled in Chicago, where he worked in a cigar factory during the day and studied in the evenings. His first poem appeared in 1918 in the local Yiddish daily, *Velt,* and after that in numer-

Israel Isidor Mattuck

ous periodicals. His poems are mostly short, lyrical pieces which are delicate, tuneful and adorned with colorful images. Mattes fell an early victim to tuberculosis, and soon after he began to publish became an inmate of a sanatorium in Colorado; a great deal of his poetry deals with his illness and his life in the sanatorium. He wrote the following books: *Ofene Toirn* (Open Portals; Denver, 1923); *Momentn* (Moments; Chicago, 1926); *A Yiddishe Tragedie* (Los Angeles, 1927); *In Karahod* (Los Angeles, 1929), poems for children; *Veise Trit* (White Steps; Los Angeles, 1929); *Der Veiser Printz fun der Veiser Plog* (The White Prince of the White Plague; Los Angeles, 1927).

Lit.: Olgin, M., in *Freiheit,* Nov. 1, 1923; Marmor, K., *ibid.,* April 5, 1927, and Nov. 18, 1929.

MATTHEW, GOSPEL OF, *see* GOSPELS.

MATTUCK, ISRAEL ISIDOR, rabbi, b. Lithuania, 1883. He graduated from Harvard College in 1905, and received his rabbinical degree from the Hebrew Union College in 1910. Before 1912, when he was called to London, Mattuck served as minister of the Reform congregations at Lincoln, Neb., and at Far Rockaway, N. Y. In London Mattuck became minister of the Liberal Jewish Synagogue, which post he still held in 1942. He was instrumental in organizing the World Union for Progressive Judaism in 1926 and has since then played an influential role in liberal Judaism in England. In 1927 Mattuck visited the United States at the invitation of the Central Conference of American Rabbis. He was the author of *What Are The Jews* (1939).

MATZ, ISRAEL, merchant and philanthropist, b. Kalvaria, Lithuania, 1869. He came to the United States in 1890. In 1907 Matz established a firm manufacturing Ex-Lax, a type of laxative. Matz was a large contributor to various undertakings having to do with the development of Palestine and the advancement of

Hebrew language and literature. From 1922 to 1926 he was publisher of *Hatoren,* a Hebrew monthly edited by Reuben Brainin. The Israel Matz Foundation, established in 1925, allows for an annual income of $15,000 to be distributed to the families of Hebrew writers and scholars in the United States and other countries. In 1942 Matz was living in Brooklyn, N. Y., and was still president of the Ex-Lax firm.

MATZ, JULIUS, plant pathologist, b. Kaunas, Lithuania, 1886. He came to the United States in 1905, and received his B.S. degree from the Massachusetts State College in 1913. His Ph.D. degree was received from Johns Hopkins in 1932. From 1913 to 1918 Matz was assistant plant pathologist at the Florida experimental station in Gainesville, and from 1918 to 1922 he was engaged in various directive capacities in the experimental station in Puerto Rico. Matz remained in Puerto Rico until 1930, mostly in charge of agricultural research for the private sugar industry. Returning to the United States in 1930, he became a pathologist for the Bureau of Plant Industry in Washington, which position he still held in 1942.

MATZEBAH, an upright stone pillar, generally used with some religious significance. Among those mentioned in the Bible are the pillow-stone of Jacob, upon which he later poured oil after receiving a divine revelation (*Gen.* 28:18, 22), those of Moses at the altar at Sinai (*Ex.* 24:4), that of Joshua at Gilgal (*Josh.* 4:20), which is connected with a mass circumcision, and the two pillars, Jachin and Boaz, placed by Solomon at the entrance of the Temple (*I Kings* 7:15-22). On the other hand, certain passages in the Bible regard the Matzebah as an idolatrous symbol and order its destruction (*Lev.* 26:1; *Deut.* 16:22; *II Kings* 18:4 and other places).

Bible scholars see in the Matzebahs a landmark in the development of the religion of Israel. Originally the Israelites, like other ancient peoples, believed in sacred stones which were given reverence; the Caaba of Islam at Mecca is an example that has endured to modern times. In other cases they are regarded as fitting altars, witnesses of the confirmation of the covenant, or even as phallic symbols. As the religion of the Israelites advanced, and their god-conception became more spiritual, these pillar stones, once regarded as sacred, came to be contemned as idolatrous and were discarded.

In the Middle Ages the word Matzebah came to mean a tombstone, perhaps from the shape of the latter, and it is still employed in this sense in modern times.

Lit.: Handcock, *The Archaeology of the Holy Land* (1916); Nowack, W., *Hebräische Archäologie,* vol. 2, p. 18 et seq.

MATZOTH (singular, **Matzah**), unleavened bread, particularly that unleavened bread which is eaten during the week of Passover. Such unleavened bread was used regularly in the sacrificial ritual of the Temple at Jerusalem; for nothing leavened could be offered up upon the altar (*Lev.* 2:11). The Bible connects the commandment to eat Matzoth on Passover with the story of the Exodus; the people left in such haste that they did not have time to leaven their bread and so baked unleavened cakes (*Ex.* 12:34, 39). Bible scholars, however, think that the eating of the Matzoth goes back to an old agricultural spring festival, in which unleavened cakes were prepared from the new produce and eaten as part of the ritual, and only later, they hold, was the practice given a historical basis. The Bible gives no details as to how Matzoth are prepared, but the Talmud (*Pes.* 35a-38b) gives details as to the materials used, the proper thickness of the cakes, and similar directions.

Ordinary Matzoth are made from a dough of flour and water, which is kneaded and rolled out thin; the separate cakes are then perforated in order to keep it from rising in baking, and then put immediately into the oven and baked. When finished they are white in appearance, with a few brown spots, about one-fourth of an inch or less in thickness, and of the consistency of a cracker. It is usual to take cold water for the mixing and to make the process as rapid as possible, in order to prevent any possibility of fermentation. Matzoth are made also from dough to which honey, fruit-juices, or eggs have been added; but since these are richer in taste and hence not literally the "bread of affliction" prescribed in the Bible (*Deut.* 16:3), they may not be eaten on the first night of the festival (*Pes.* 36a).

Matzoth were originally made in the home, but even as far back as ancient times they were prepared by professional bakers as well. During the Middle Ages there were community ovens which were used for the baking of Matzoth. The perforation was at first done with any convenient instrument, but later a special wheel with sharp teeth (*reidel*) was employed for the purpose. In modern times, Matzoth are generally prepared in Western countries by professional bakers, with the aid of special machinery.

Matzoth can be made in any shape desired; they were generally round, but illustrations in medieval manuscripts show them in triangular and other forms. In modern times the square form has proved most convenient for machine-baked Matzoth and is the predominant form in the United States. In 1942 special V-shaped Matzoth were baked as a part of the "V for Victory" movement.

Small pieces of Matzoth left over from baking are ground up into Matzah meal (*Matzomehl*), which is used in preparing a variety of Passover dishes.

A special form of Matzoth is the Matzah Shemurah ("guarded Matzah") or Matzah Shemirah ("Matzah of watching"). For this every process must be under the supervision of the strictly Orthodox. The grain for the purpose must be grown on land which is owned by the Orthodox, it must be reaped and ground by them, and they must perform all the operations of baking. Such specially prepared Matzoth are used by the extremely pious throughout the entire festival, although others use them only for the Seder.

The commandment to eat Matzoth on Passover is considered fulfilled if one eats them on the first night; for the rest of the festival it is a voluntary, though meritorious act (*Pes.* 120a). They may be eaten throughout the entire year, except on the day before Passover, when one should refrain from them in order to heighten the joy of the festive observance.

Matzoth are not sacred in the sense that they are reserved especially for those who keep the commandment of Passover. They are frequently eaten by non-Jews; in

the 20th cent. polar expeditions have taken along special supplies of Matzoth, since they do not deteriorate over long periods of time. Nevertheless, Matzoth have acquired a certain sanctity among Jews. Many synagogues in Eastern Europe and the Orient keep a piece of Matzah hanging in one of its walls, as a remembrance of the Exodus; there are also instances in which a piece of Matzah, especially one from the Afikomen (the piece hidden during the Seder), is regarded as possessing talismanic properties.   SIMON COHEN.

Lit.: Maimonides, *Hilchoth Hametz Umatzah* 5 and 6; *Shulhan Aruch, Orah Hayim* 453 to 462, 471 to 482; Eisenstein, J. D., in *Jewish Encyclopedia*, vol. 8, pp. 393-96.

MAUCLAIR, CAMILLE, writer, b. Paris, 1872. He was originally named Faust. His parents migrated to France from Denmark. They were probably converted to Christianity before Mauclair was born. In his memoirs, *Servitude et grandeur littéraires* (1922), he sought to conceal his Jewish origin by emphasizing the fact that he had been baptized immediately upon birth. He did this in order to explain his opposition to anti-Semitism on grounds of free will rather than because of his antecedents. He was educated at the Lycée Louis le Grand, and was a fellow pupil of Edouard Herriot. Devoted to literature from his early youth, he was influenced by Mallarmé, Barrès, and Maeterlinck.

Mauclair was on intimate terms with representatives of French symbolism, and in 1893 was one of the founders of the theatre L'Oeuvre, pioneering in modern arts. In 1898 he became a contributor to Clemenceau's *L'Aurore.* He assisted the latter in his campaign on behalf of Alfred Dreyfus, but he was a technical aide rather than a fighter in the Dreyfus case.

Mauclair distinguished himself in literary criticism as well as in the history of arts and music, displaying considerable originality in thought and approach. Occasionally he yielded too readily to paradox, but nearly always prepared his publications by means of authentic research. He wrote numerous studies on artists, including *Rodin* (1905), *Watteau* (1926), *Corot* (1930) and *Degas* (1939). His musical absorptions were those of the historian (*Histoire de la musique européenne,* 1914) and of the philosopher (*La religion de la musique,* 1909). Many of his studies pertaining to poets were based upon personal recollections, such as *Maeterlinck* (1900) and *Mallarmé chez lui* (1935). Mauclair published also novels which give evidence of his psychological insight and metaphysical ideas, especially in *L'amour tragique* (1908).

MAURETANIA, EASTERN, see ALGERIA.

MAUREY, MAX, dramatist and stage director, b. Paris, 1868. His one-act plays, portraying the French petit bourgeoisie in satirical yet sympathetic presentations, were frequently in the repertory of Parisian theatres. He founded the Théâtre des Capucines in Paris, and for several years successfully directed the Théâtre du Grand Guignol in the French Capital.

His best-known comedies—mostly one-act plays—are: *Asile de nuit* (1904; reprinted 1936); *La fiole* (1904); *L'aventure* (1904); *Depuis six mois* (1909); *Le chauffeur* (1909); *Rosalie* (1913); *Le Stradivarius* (1921); *Monsieur Lambert, marchand de tableaux* (1922); *La délaissée* (1926); *Le bonheur retrouvé* (1928); *Pour tuer le temps* (1931); *Un ami d'Argentine* (a four-act

André Maurois

play, together with Tristan Bernard; 1931); *Le faiseur de monstres* (a two-act drama, 1935). In 1913 he dramatized Charles Dickens' *David Copperfield* in a five-act play for the French stage. The Vichy government deprived him of his citizenship, but restored him in 1942 in recognition of Maurey's services to French letters. He was living at Cannes in 1942.

MAURICE, CHERI (CHARLES), stage director, b. Agen, France, 1805; d. Hamburg, Germany, 1896. He was son of the Jewish merchant Maurice Schwartzenberger (b. Metz, 1780; d. Hamburg, 1853). In 1826 the family removed to Hamburg where the son, prevented by his father from becoming a French actor, entered the Schwartzenberger distillery of French liquors. In 1827 they rented "Tivoli," a famous place of amusement. There the son directed an open-air theatre, and in 1831 he became co-director of the Theater an der Steinstrasse.

Maurice excelled at first in staging shows of local interest. In 1843 he founded the Thalia-Theater of Hamburg, and became one of the most reputable stage managers in Germany. Now and then he shocked the orthodox taste of critics by including performances of acrobats, jugglers, and even trained animals. Maurice admitted frankly that he aimed also to make money. On the other hand, he was an adroit manager who skillfully directed his ensembles and great actors. Most of the star players of Germany began their careers under the direction of Maurice, who was especially canny in discovering unknown talents. In 1853 Maurice gave the first presentation of the complete *Faust* of Goethe, regarded up to that time as an impossible task. He introduced great foreign actors to Germany, among them Aldridge, Rachel, and Ristori. He attained his greatest fame between 1840 and 1880.

MAURITIUS, *see* REFUGEES.

MAUROIS, ANDRÉ (HERZOG), writer, b. Elbeuf, France, 1885. He was educated at the Lycée de Rouen, where he studied philosophy. At the age of twenty-one he became manager of his father's textile plant at Elbeuf, a post he held for ten years.

His first book, *Les Silences du Colonel Bramble*

(1916), was a fictionalized account of his experiences as a translator for the British Military Intelligence during the first World War; *Les Discours du Docteur O'Grady* (1920) contained more material on the same subject. These two works were very popular in France, and were the beginning of his role as interpreter of English culture in France and of French culture in England and the United States. Among his most successful efforts in this field were: *Ariel, ou la vie de Shelley* (1924); *Disraeli* (1927); *Eduard VII et son temps* (1930); *Byron* (1930); *Dickens* (1934). His books attained even greater popularity in the English-speaking world than in France, and several of his later works, for example *Voltaire* (1932) and *Chateaubriand* (1938), were especially designed to deepen the appreciation of the French genius in England and the United States.

Maurois' writing was popular rather than scholarly, and some critics accused him of sensationalism and superficiality; but his brilliance and facility were unquestioned. He was generally considered one of the best biographers writing in French. In 1931 and 1932 he was invited to the United States to lecture on French literature at Princeton University and at the New School for Social Research, in New York city. He was elected to the French Academy in 1938, and in 1939 he was made a Knight Commander of the Order of the British Empire for his services as an "unsurpassed liaison officer between French and English letters."

In 1939, during the second World War, Maurois resumed his old post as translator with the British armies in France. The following year, after France's capitulation to the Nazis, Maurois came to the United States, where he published *The Tragedy of France: An Eyewitness Account* (New York; Denver Lindley, translator). The thesis of this book is that the débâcle was caused by the middle-class fear of communism rather than by any active fifth column. Although his textile business was confiscated by the Pétain government (1941), Maurois was accused of sympathy with Pétain.

The tragedy of France and his personal misfortunes did not dim Maurois' literary faculties, and in 1942 he published a novel, *A Time for Silence* (New York; Edith Johannsen, translator). He also lectured and contributed articles extensively to the American press.

Lit.: Bakeless, *André Maurois* (1930); Larg, David Glass, *André Maurois* (1932); *American Hebrew*, Nov. 25, 1927, p. 88.

MAUSOLEUM, a sumptuous tomb; in modern usage, a structure of stone, or of stone and metal, erected above the ground for the interment of a family group. The usual form is that of a small house, the door of which leads directly into a hall, along the sides of which are placed shelves where the bodies are to be laid, each shelf being covered in front by a slab or metal plate that serves as a tombstone. Mausoleums were comparatively rare down to modern times, being reserved for rulers and for the very wealthy.

The Jews of ancient and medieval times universally followed the custom of interring the dead beneath the ground, either in caves or catacombs hewn out of the rock, or in graves dug in the soil. The so-called Absalom's Tomb, near Jerusalem, is the only possible exception; but it is doubtful if this was intended as a sepulchre, being probably a memorial for a burial place. Such memorials bore the name of *nefesh* (literally, "soul") as early as the time of the Mishnah. Many graves of distinguished Jews of the Middle Ages and after are decorated by such raised structures upon which epitaphs are written; but the body is always interred beneath the ground, and accordingly these structures can not be classified as mausoleums.

Interment beneath the ground became such a fixed custom among the Jews that the *Shulhan Aruch* considers it the only proper form of Jewish burial. However, in modern times, various individuals, especially those who were wealthy and in close contact with the rulers, erected mausoleums in imitation of non-Jewish practices. In the United States, in the latter half of the 19th cent., numerous individuals in Reform Jewish congregations erected mausoleums upon family plots, as was also a growing custom among non-Jews. They held that it was a dignified and honorable way of burial and in no way incompatible with the spirit of the Jewish religion. The innovation, however, was bitterly opposed by more conservative groups, who insisted that burial beneath the ground was the only proper form of interment. Orthodox rabbis have refused to conduct services for interments that are made in mausoleums.

In the 20th cent. the use of mausoleums for Jewish burials slowly increased. In some cemeteries designed for the more conservative, mausoleums were erected with earth heaped about them in such a way that the interment could be regarded as technically underground. The *Rabbi's Manual* (1928), issued by the Central Conference of American Rabbis, contained a special prayer written by Simon Cohen for use in connection with interment in a mausoleum.

MAUTHNER, FRITZ, writer and philosopher, b. Horsitz, near Königgrätz, Bohemia, 1849; d. Meersburg, on Lake Constance, Germany, 1923. He studied law at the University of Prague, but later devoted himself exclusively to literature, gaining public renown chiefly through one of his earliest works, *Nach berühmten Mustern* (1878), parodies in prose which ridicule Berthold Auerbach and other contemporary writers. A dramatic critic of the *Berliner Tageblatt,* Mauthner was author also of numerous novels, short stories, sketches and poems. The most interesting of his larger prose works are: *Der arme Franischko* (1879; with a chapter "Wie der Franischko einen Juden bekehren wollte"); *Der neue Ahasver* (1882), on the Jewish problem in Berlin; *Xantippe* (1884; English trans., *Mrs. Socrates,* 1926), which ridiculed the conventional form of the historical novel; *Der letzte Deutsche von Blatna* (1887), on the struggle between Germans and Czechs; *Hypatia* (1892), which stirred indignation in the Catholic press because it defended pagan philosophy against the Christian saints (while the figure of the intolerant orthodox archbishop Cyrill of Alexandria was modelled after the anti-Semitic Protestant court preacher, Adolf Stöcker). On the occasion of Mauthner's seventieth birthday a selection from his fictional writings were issued in six volumes (1919).

Mauthner's importance rests, however, on his achievements as a critic of his epoch and as philosopher. In his *Aturenbriefe* (1885) he charged, like Max Nordau, that the civilization of modern Europe was founded upon falsehoods. His semi-philosophical works, such

Fritz Mauthner

as *Totengespräche* and *Der letzte Tod des Gauthama Buddha,* as well as his biographical essays on Aristotle, Schopenhauer and Spinoza, were held in high esteem by connoisseurs. Mauthner's principal philosophical works, however, are: *Beiträge zur Kritik der Sprache* (3 vols., 1901-2); *Wörterbuch der Philosophie* (2nd, enlarged ed., 3 vols., 1923-24); *Der Atheismus und seine Geschichte im Abendlande* (4 vols., 1920-23); *Gottlose Mystik* (1925). There he developed, in a brilliant Voltairian style, his original ideas on language —which he discarded as a means of perception and considered only an esthetic phenomenon—and his sceptical philosophy, an "agnostic mysticism."

Through his scholarly works he exposed himself to violent attacks by the conservative school. He never held a post at a university, nor was his work accorded official recognition in the world of scholarship. This was due partly to the radicalism of his thought (he was a pioneer in his special field of Sprachphilosophie), partly to his political views, since, like Maximilian Harden, he was a champion of Bismarck's policy in sharp opposition to Emperor Wilhelm II.

Mauthner was entirely estranged from Judaism. In his *Erinnerungen* (1919), of which only the first volume, covering his youth in Prague, was published, he explained why, as a son of a completely dejudaized family, settling in bilingual Bohemia, he had "keine Muttersprache, keine Mutterreligion." Despite his many Jewish friends, such as the writers Gustav Landauer and Auguste Hauschner, he remained persistently aloof from Jewish affairs.   ALFRED WERNER.

Lit.: Landauer, Gustav, *Skepsis und Mystik* (1902); *Neue Österreichische Biographie,* vol. 3.

MAUTNER, EDUARD, author and playwright, b. Pest, Hungary, 1824; d. Baden, near Vienna, 1889. He studied at the Universities of Prague, Vienna and Leipzig, and was a friend of Moritz Hartmann. He was a mercurial student of philosophy, medicine, law and literature, at the same time contributing poems, short stories and critical and literary articles to the leading magazines in Austria and Germany. During the revolution of 1848 he wrote political articles for Frankl's *Sonntagsblatt* in Vienna. In 1851 his comedy *Das Preislustspiel* won second prize of the Hofburg theater. Mautner was successively connected with the State Railway Society, Vienna (1855-64), assistant at the Imperial Library (1865), and an official in the press bureau of the Austrian Foreign Ministry. His works include: *Gedichte* (1847); *Gräfin Aurora* (1852); *Kleine Erzählungen* (1858); *In Catilinam* (sonnets against Napoleon III; 1859); *Während der Börse* (performed at the Hoftheater, Berlin, 1863); *Eine Frau die an der Börse spielt* (1863); *Eglantine* (1863); *Die Sanduhr* (1871); *Eine Mutter vor Gericht* (1872); *Eine Kriegslist* (1878); *Im Augarten* (1880); *Von der Aar zur Donau* (1881); *Ausgewählte Gedichte* (1889).

MAVAMBU, MAWUMBU, see NEGRO JEWS.

MAX, EDOUARD-ALEXANDRE (DE), tragedian, b. Jassy, Roumania, 1869; d. Paris, 1924. His father, a physician, on discovering the boy's leanings for the theatre, sent him to study at the Conservatoire in Paris. He graduated from that school in 1891, winning the first two prizes for enacting tragic roles. He appeared in turn on all the great stages of Paris, beginning at the Odeon. Later he joined Sarah Bernhardt's theatre, and played with her in many roles for three years, from 1893 to 1896. His career culminated in his appointment to the Comédie Française, where he remained until his death.

The auditorium of the Comédie was filled to capacity whenever de Max was announced to appear. His unique style of playing was that of the lyric tragedian. His fine voice carried far and, in parts like that of Nero in Racine's *Britannicus,* and also in other plays, he kept his audience spellbound to a point where his accent, which was not absolutely pure French, passed unnoticed. He acted the great roles of French classical tragedy, especially those of Racine.

During the first World War de Max appeared on the Roumanian stage and was favorably received. At that time Roumania was an ally of the Western democracies. Subsequently, when he tried to arrange another appearance in his native country, in response to invitations, the Roumanian anti-Jewish press assailed him for being a Jew; disheartened, he gave up the attempt.

Shortly before his death de Max completed the translation into French of Schiller's drama, *Die Räuber.*

MAY LAWS, see RUSSIA.

MAY, family of merchants which flourished in the 16th, 17th and 18th centuries in the Tyrol. Its founder was Salomon, who went to Austria from Bassano and in 1509 received from Emperor Maximilian I permission to trade everywhere in the empire and in the countries of the House of Habsburg, as well as to reside everywhere "except the duchies of Austria, Styria and Carinthia."

Emperor Charles V renewed Salomon's privilege in 1538, and in 1544 and 1548 he granted Salomon's son Maggius the same privileges. Maggius Germanized his name, calling himself May.

A branch of the May family went to Poland, and a Jewish physician named May is mentioned as court physician of Duke Albrecht, grand master of the Teutonic Order, at Königsberg. There were other descendants of Salomon who remained at Bassano or resided in other Italian towns, among them the Grassini family which prospered in the first decades of the 17th cent.

There is no definite evidence that Samuel May was a son or a nephew of the former Maggius. At any rate, Samuel May continued to play an important part in the economic history of the Habsburg monarchy which was inaugurated by Salomon and Maggius. Samuel May was protected by the ducal court at Innsbruck, capital of the Tyrol, from 1577 on. In 1578 he was a member of the princely household of Duke Ferdinand of Tyrol. In 1581 he was accused by Christian citizens of Innsbruck of having offended against the Christian religion on Corpus Christi day. The ducal court, after an inquiry, extended its protection to May.

In 1584 Samuel May, together with his sons Abraham, Marx and Ferdinand, received the privilege of residing in Innsbruck, and the city council of Innsbruck was pledged by the ducal court to protect the May family. In 1587 Abraham May, notwithstanding protestations by the citizens of Innsbruck, acquired a mansion, which was in the possession of his family until 1673. Samuel May and his son Marx acquired two great storehouses, and dealt in arms, cloth, grocery and jewels. In 1598 Samuel May was allowed by Duchess Anne Catherine of Tyrol to found a family mausoleum. In 1630 Archduke Leopold permitted the sons of Marx May (d. 1618) to found another family tomb.

Although the Christian merchants of Innsbruck continued to combat the May family, its wealth and importance increased steadily. During the Thirty Years' War Samuel and Abraham May supplied the armies of the emperor with arms and corn. Therefore they were granted special privileges in 1630. In 1631 Abraham May lent Count Nicholas Fugger 30,000 florins, and became mortgagee of the dominions of Enn and Caldit. Abraham May and his family were exempted (1638) from the *Leibzoll* and the yellow Jew badge under a privilege granted by Archduke Leopold. All their privileges were renewed (1667) by Emperor Leopold I. In 1675 Jacon Bözel from Mayence, Abraham May's brother-in-law, was granted the same privileges.

While the May family was prosperous and united in coping with non-Jewish adversaries, it was a house divided against itself. For long years Abraham May conducted a bitter lawsuit against his stepmother Gentilia Donati, mother of Leon Bassevi, in which he was finally defeated. There were also litigations carried on by one brother against the other. In 1649 Abraham's son Samuel fled from home and was baptized. Later on other members of the May family became converted to Catholicism, but the majority remained loyal to Judaism. They lodged many Jews in their mansion until, in 1663, the government ordered the city to find a place of refuge for the Jewish newcomers. Johann Ferdinand May was farmer of the excise levied upon tobacco until 1677 when the government yielded to pressure by Christian merchants. In 1714 the city petitioned the government to expel the Jews from Innsbruck, but the May family was expressly exempted.

HUGO BIEBER.

Lit.: Hirn, Josef, *Kanzler Biener und sein Prozess* (1898); Scherer, J. E., *Die Rechtsverhältnisse der Juden in den deutsch-österreichischen Ländern* (1901); *Chronik der Stadt Innsbruck* (1929).

Mitchell May

MAY, CHARLES HENRY, ophthalmologist, b. Baltimore, 1861. He received his medical degree from the College of Physicians and Surgeons of Columbia University in 1883. Later he studied in Europe. In 1887 May was made lecturer in diseases of the eye at New York Polyclinic. Three years later he went to Columbia University as instructor in ophthalmology and chief of its ophthalmological clinic; he held this post until 1903. May was director and visiting surgeon of the eye department at Bellevue Hospital from 1915 to 1925, and was consulting ophthalmologist for many other hospitals in New York city. He was known particularly for the improved electric ophthalmoscope which he invented in 1914, and which subsequently came to be generally used. May was the author of *Manual of the Diseases of the Eye* (1900), which had sixteen editions and was translated into many foreign languages. He was also a contributor to medical encyclopedias and journals.

Lit.: Kagan, Solomon R., *Jewish Contributions to Medicine in America* (1939) 704-5.

MAY, HENRIETTE (née Lövinson), social worker, b. Berlin, 1862; d. Berlin, 1928. Active in welfare and social movements, she was one of the founders, in 1890, of the Jewish Women's movement, a member of the Gesellschaft für Ethische Kultur, and instrumental in founding the Jüdischer Frauenbund. She was a co-worker in the Zentralwohlfahrtsstelle der Deutschen Juden. In 1916 she made a journey of inspection to Lodz and Warsaw in behalf of the Hilfsverein der Deutschen Juden and the Jüdischer Frauenbund; her report was of service in the amelioration of the condition of the Jews there.

Lit.: Henriette May zum Gedächtnis (1929).

MAY, LEWIS, merchant and communal leader, b. Worms, Germany, 1823; d. New York city, 1897. He came to the United States at the age of seventeen, and after working for a few years in Pennsylvania and Alabama, he established an independent business at Shreveport, La. In the years of the gold rush he went to California with the early prospectors and established a business in San Francisco and Portland, Ore., where he became prominently identified with Jewish and Masonic activities. He was also one of the founders of the Oregon Grand Lodge. After his return to New York, in 1856, May became a leading figure in Jewish communal, educational and philanthropic work, and was elected president of Congregation Emanu-El, a position which he retained until his death. In 1869 he retired from mercantile life to found the banking firm of May and King. He served as treasurer and director of Mount Sinai Hospital in New York for nineteen years, and was an organizer and first president of the Young Men's Hebrew Association. In recognition of his services, Congregation Emanu-El placed a memorial window in its temple, which was retained also in the new temple in 1928.

MAY, MAX BENJAMIN, judge, b. Cincinnati, 1866; d. Cincinnati, 1929. From 1901 to 1907 he served on the board of governors of the Hebrew Union College. In 1912 he was elected judge of the court of common appeals in Hamilton County, Ohio. May was the author of a biography of his grandfather, Isaac Mayer Wise (1916), and of various historical papers.

MAY, MITCHELL, judge, b. Brooklyn, N. Y., 1870. He was educated at the Brooklyn Polytechnic Institute and the Columbia University Law School (LL.B., 1892). He was admitted to the bar in 1892 and practised law privately for seven years.

From 1899 to 1901 he was a Republican member of the House of Representatives. He served as a member of the New York city Board of Education from 1901 to 1910. In 1910 he was counsel to the clerk of Kings County, and in 1910 and 1911 he acted as assistant district attorney of Kings County, in which capacity he investigated the failure of the Union Bank and successfully prosecuted its president. As secretary of state of New York State (1913 and 1914) he was responsible for many reforms in traffic legislation. He was elected county judge of Kings County in 1916 for a five-year term. In 1922 he was elected judge of the New York State Supreme Court, a post he held until 1940, when he retired. After his retirement he entered private practice again with the firm of Weisman, Celler, Quinn, Allan and Spett, with whom he was still connected in 1942.

May engaged also in Jewish and general philanthropic work. He was particularly interested in the Brooklyn Federation of Jewish Charities, of which he was president eight times. After his retirement from the bench he devoted most of his time to the Federation, and was appointed director.

MAY, PAUL, Belgian diplomat, b. Belgium, 1872; d. Washington, D. C., 1934. His early education was acquired in Belgium under private tutors, then he studied at Oxford and at the University of Brussels, where he received the degree of Doctor of Civil Laws and Political Science. In 1895 May entered the Belgian diplomatic service and, having passed the examination with distinction, was attached to the Foreign Office at Brussels. In the following year he was sent to Washington as attaché of the Belgian Legation there, and was eventually promoted to secretary to the Legation.

Paul May

Subsequently, May served in the Far East—in China and Japan. In 1901 he was appointed secretary to the Legation at London. Three years later he was placed in charge of the Belgian Legation at Lisbon, and in 1908 was made Counselor of the Legation at Constantinople. May returned to London in 1911 as Counselor of the Belgian Legation to the Court of St. James. In the following year he was again promoted and sent as Belgian Minister to Mexico, where he rendered most active and efficient service, at the risk of his own life, in protecting the interests of his country during the troubled period of the Mexican revolution.

During the early years of the first World War May served on a special mission to England, where he worked in behalf of Belgian refugees. In 1917 he was appointed Minister to Pekin. After several years at that post he was appointed Belgian Envoy Extraordinary and Minister Plenipotentiary to Sweden and Finland, and in 1925 he was sent to Rio de Janeiro as Ambassador Extraordinary and Plenipotentiary to the republic of Brazil. In 1931 his government selected May as Belgian Ambassador to Washington. During his mission in the United States the Ambassador was accompanied by his family; his wife was the daughter of Raphael Georges Lévy, who was a member of the French Senate and also president of the Institut de France.

May was a man of great culture, broad sympathies and engaging personality, and was the recipient of numerous honors from Belgium and other countries. He remained throughout his life a faithful adherent of the Jewish faith. On his death the United States government accorded him the honor of a military funeral and transported his remains, by a United States warship, to his native land.

Lit.: *American Hebrew*, Sept. 7, 1934, pp. 291, 306-7.

MAY, RAPHAEL ERNST, economist, b. Hamburg, Germany, 1858; d. Hamburg, 1933. He was the son of Simon May, then chairman of the Jewish community in Hamburg. Although a merchant, he pursued intensive private studies in economic and statistical problems. He visited several countries in the course of his research. His work on German economy, *Die wirtschaftliche Entwicklung* (1896-97), and numerous pamphlets attacking Marxism were violently criticized. When the Prussian ministry of war published its ill-famed denominational statistics concerning the Jewish combatants during the first World War, May wrote (1917) his *Konfessionelle Militärstatistik*, which invalidated the anti-Semitic claims of the government's pamphlet. His essay was published by the *Archiv für Sozialwissenschaft und Sozialpolitik*, whose editors at that time were such noted men as Werner Sombart, Max Weber and Emil Lederer. His other works include: *Die Wirtschaft in Vergangenheit, Gegenwart und Zukunft* (1901); *Das Grundgesetz der Wirtschaftskrisen und ihr Vorbeugungsmittel im Zeitalter des Monopols* (1902); *Die deutsche Volksernährung* (1917); *Verstaatlichung,* an essay (1919); *Mischehen und Ehescheidungen,* an essay (1929).

From 1906 to 1923 May served as president of the united Jewish communities of Altona, Hamburg and Wandsbeck.

MAYBAUM, SIGMUND, rabbi, b. Miskolc, Hungary, 1844; d. Berlin, 1919. He studied at the Yeshivas of Eisenstadt, where he was a pupil of Israel Hildesheimer, of Pozsony (Pressburg), and of the Breslau theological seminary, graduating from the latter. After serving as rabbi in Alsó-Kubin (Hungary) and Saaz (Bohemia), he was called in 1881 to Berlin where, because of his oratorical prowess, he quickly achieved a position of leadership. He founded the association of rabbis in Germany; the first rabbinical congress met at Berlin in 1884. In 1888 he was appointed instructor in homiletics at the Hochschule für die Wissenschaft des Judentums. He was not active in Jewish political life except as one of the rabbis protesting against the convening of the first Zionist Congress in Germany in

Sigmund Maybaum

Ancient Jewish cemetery at Mayence

1879. Maybaum adopted the critical approach to the Bible and accepted the idea of evolution. In 1903 Emperor William II bestowed on him the title of professor.

A jubilee volume was issued in honor of Maybaum's seventieth birthday in 1914. His major works are: *Die Anthropomorphien und Anthropopathien bei Onkelos und den späteren Targumim* (1870); *Die Entwicklung des alt-israelitischen Priestertums* (1880); *Die Entwicklung des israelitischen Prophetentums* (1883); *Jüdische Homiletik* (1894); *Methodik des jüdischen Religionsunterrichts* (1895); *Die Anfänge der jüdischen Predigt* (1901). His sermons were published in several volumes.

MAYENCE (MAINZ), city in Germany, capital of the province of Rhine Hesse. Mayence, founded as a castle by Drusus (14-9 B.C.E.) and later a city, probably had a settlement of Jews in the days of the Roman Empire. The first documentary evidence of Jews at Mayence dates from an ecclesiastical council held there about the year 900. Whether the German branch of the Kalonymus family settled there in the 10th cent., whether the Kalonymus family was under imperial protection by reason of the fact that a Jew, Kalonymus, saved the life of Emperor Otto II at the battle of Cotrone (982), and whether the window with the image of a protecting eagle (dating from the year 1000) which was found in 1904 belonged to the "Kalonymus house," are moot questions. Discoveries at the site of the oldest Jewish settlement indicate Jews to have traded with the Near East and Italy, importing rare commodities from those parts.

The Jews were expelled from Mayence in 1012, but there were Jews in Mayence again in 1013. Part of the community left Mayence for Speyer due to a conflagration in 1084. When they heard about the Jews in France being threatened by the Crusaders in January, 1096, they still felt secure. Nevertheless, their doom was impending despite the fact that they sought and were granted protection by Emperor Henry IV, by the archbishop, and by the Burgrave of Mayence, and despite the promise of security pledged them on receipt of money by the leader of the Crusade, Godfrey of Bouillon. When, however, Crusaders were admitted into the city, the Jews were massacred notwithstanding their desperate efforts to defend themselves in the very palace of the archbishop and in the castle of the Burgrave. The number of those slaughtered, judging from the lists given in the so-called Nuremberg (but actually the Mayence) *Memorbuch,* was from 700 to 1,300, including women who killed themselves and their children to escape baptism. Only a few Jews were compelled to accept baptism; in 1097 Emperor Henry IV allowed them to return to Judaism.

The reorganized Jewish community of Mayence escaped destruction on the occasion of the Second Crusade only through the appearance in the city of Bernard of Clairvaux. When, in February, 1188, the Third Crusade was launched, the Jews of Mayence took refuge for several months at Münzenberg; they were safeguarded by the imperial edict threatening with the loss of a hand anyone who dared attack or hurt a Jew, and with loss of life those who killed one.

On November 20, 1209, King Otto IV renounced all claims of the empire to the Jews of the archbishopric in favor of Archbishop Siegfried III of Mayence. In the 13th cent. the archbishops had sole power to impose taxes upon the Jews, but in general the emperors shared with the archbishops in taxing them; also during the following period. Notwithstanding this protection, persecution of the Jews of Mayence continued throughout the centuries. In 1281 Rabbi Meir ben Abraham was slain, the synagogue set on fire and the scrolls of the Torah destroyed. In 1187 the community had succeeded, by making an oath and through the payment of a substantial sum, in averting a blood accusation. Ten innocent Jews fell victim to a blood libel in 1283, before an investigation ordered by the archbishop was completed. It was probably as a result of this that the Jews had to appear before the tribunal of King Rudolf of Hapsburg in 1286 and that the latter ordered expropriation of all property owned by the Jews who had fled from Mayence, Worms, Speyer and other places. In 1295 the archbishop was granted only an annual sum of 112 marks denarii and he ceded to the city the right of taxing the Jews, of which the city availed itself until 1462. At the same time the archbishops and the electors of Mayence continued to impose taxes upon Jews, but also to admit them to the city. The ecclesiastical councils in Mayence of 1310 and 1451 ordered the Jews to wear a badge.

In the years 1348 to 1349 the Jews of Mayence fought in the streets for several days in defense of their lives. Finally they set fire to their own homes and threw themselves into the flames. As early as 1355, however, Archbishop Gerlach of Nassau again admitted a Jew to the city. In the 15th cent. the Jews were shunted about between the archbishops and the city. In 1438 the guilds prevailed upon the city council to expel the Jews and to confiscate their synagogue and cemetery. Another expulsion occurred in 1462; in the years 1470 to 1471 Archbishop Adolph II expelled the Jews from the city of Mayence, tolerating them only in his archbishopric. Thus the merchants of Mayence were rid of their competitors.

During the 10th and 11th centuries the Jews engaged in foreign trade, as well as in domestic business; they visited the Cologne fairs. From the 12th cent. on money lending became the practice; there were Jews engaged also in medicine and in the trades.

The first synagogue was mentioned in 1093; the second, destroyed by fire in 1281, was first referred to in 1188; a ritual bath existed in 1248. The Jews also owned a cemetery, bakery, abattoir, hospital, and house of as-

Interior of the synagogue of the Israelitische Religionsgesell-schaft at Mayence

sembly (referred to also as the Jewish ballroom). The cemetery, in the Mombacherstrasse, enlarged gradually, was not closed until 1880. When medieval fortifications were demolished in the 19th cent. and in 1921, several revealing tombstones were unearthed.

From the middle of the 12th cent. on the Jewish communities of Speyer, Worms and Mayence (in Jewish sources referred to by the contracted initials ShUM) formed an alliance, and the decisions made by the synods held at Mayence (1150, 1220, 1245 or 1250, and 1381) subsequently served as models for every communal organization in Germany. The secular head of this community was first called "Jewish Bishop" in a document dated 1286; he was referred to also as "Magister Judaeorum" or (in the 15th cent.) "Hochmeister." Funds and inspiration from Jews in Italy and France influenced Jewish culture at Mayence, which flourished as early as the 10th cent. Judah ben Meir Hakohen (about 980), coming from Italy, inaugurated the searching study of the Talmud in France and Germany; his contemporaries were Moses ben Kalonymus, first writer of Piyutim in Germany; Meshullam ben Kalonymus, synagogal poet and interpreter of the law; Simon the Great ben Isaac ben Abun, poet; Gershom ben Judah, surnamed the "Light of the Exile" (Meor Hagolah; 960 to 1028 or 1040), who reestablished the authentic text of the Talmud and wrote commentaries on it, and whose decisions included the prohibition of polygamy. The 11th cent. saw Jacob ben Jakar (d. 1064), Rashi's teacher; Eliezer ben Isaac the Great, author of *Orehoth Hayim;* and Benjamin (Zerah) of Mayence, a prolific poet. Eliezer ben Nathan (Raben), a rabbinical authority, poet and chronicler, lived in the 12th cent.; Eliezer ben Samuel, author of *Sefer Yereim,* flourished about 1195. Baruch ben Samuel, eminent Talmudist and poet, took part in the synod of 1220. Legendary figures of Mayence were Elhanan, son of Simon the Great, who was said to have become pope; Rabbi Amnon, to whom the "Unethanneh Tokef" is attributed; and Rabbi Amram. Rabbi Jacob of Nordhausen was mentioned at Mayence in 1365; Rabbi Jacob ben Moses Halevi (Maharil) lived there in the late 14th cent. and until 1425. He was the greatest authority in the field of religious customs, liturgies and melodies as practised in the Rhineland; they were recorded by his pupil, Zalman of St. Goar. About 1458 Moses ben Isaac Halevi Menz was rabbi at Mayence; his

cousin, Judah ben Eliezer Menz (Maharam), was rabbi at Padua (1462-1509).

In 1583 the Jewish community at Mayence, which had been dissolved for more than a century, was reorganized. Refugees from Hanau under the leadership of Rabbi Elijah Loans were the new settlers. Their status was governed by means of letters of protection and ordinances. On December 8, 1662, a decree was issued by the elector Johann Wilhelm of Schönborn, compelling the twenty Jewish families tolerated at Mayence to remove their quarters to an unhealthful section of the city called "Schweinemisten." As late as 1775 a new regulation was issued as regards the Jewish poll-tax. From 1630 on there were again rabbis at Mayence; in 1685 a new synagogue was erected and richly endowed with devotional objects; charitable foundations were also established.

At the end of the 17th cent. a hundred Jewish families lived at Mayence. David ben Aryeh Loeb of Lida (1679-83), Moses Brandeis (Charif; 1733-67) and David Tevele Scheuer (1768-82) were among its noted rabbis.

The archbishop elector Karl Joseph of Erthal (1774-1802) opened a new era for the Jews. Under the influence of Joseph II he improved the situation of his protected Jews by extending them equal right with non-Jews before the law and by admitting them to schools, to the university and to agricultural occupations. In 1787 Joseph Hamburg received his doctor's degree from the University of Mayence. When Mayence was taken by the French in 1792, the Jews obtained citizenship rights. They sent four delegates to the Great Sanhedrin at Paris in 1807. Mayence was the capital city of the consistory (its first rabbi was Samuel Wolf Levi), but the infamous decree of Napoleon (1808) remained in force until 1847, long after Mayence had been incorporated into the grand duchy of Hesse.

The first result of the effort to acquire modern culture was the establishment of an elementary school by Michael Creizenach (1814). From 1831 the institutions of the Jewish community were modernized; in 1840 Dr. Charles B. Cahen held the first confirmation of children. Dedication of an organ synagogue (1853) and adoption of a revised (Reform) prayer-book (1856) led to the founding of a Religionsgesellschaft (Orthodox) in 1858, which in turn founded a school, Beth Hamidrash and Talmud Torah. From 1926 on Mayence was the seat of the national union of Hessian Israelite congregations, comprising eighty-five communities with 14,000 members. Simultaneously with the founding of a society for Jewish antiquities (1925) and of a Jewish museum (1926), restitution of the old cemetery on the Judensand took place.

The rabbis of Mayence in the 19th cent. included Herz Scheuer (1800-10, 1814-22), Loeb Ellinger (1823-47), Joseph Aub (1852-60), Elias Caan (1866-80), and Sigmund Salfeld (1880-1918). Sali Levi served as rabbi in Mayence from 1918 to 1941. The rabbis of the Religionsgesellschaft included Markus Lehmann (1858-90) and Jonas Bondi.

The orientalist Joseph Naphtali Derenbourg (1811-95) as well as Friedrich and Heinrich Derenburg stemmed from Mayence.

The slow growth and decline of the Jewish population of Mayence from the early part of the 19th cent. to the year 1934 may be illustrated by the following figures:

Year	Jewish Population	Per Cent of Total Population
1828	1,620	5.3
1861	2,665	5.8
1871	2,998	5.6
1910	2,931	2.5
1913	2,926	about 3
1925	2,738	2.5
1934	about 2,500	1.75

From 1933 on every persecution and disability imposed upon the Jews of Germany by the Third Reich were brought to bear also upon the community of Mayence.   Adolf Kober.

Lit.: Carlebach, Ephraim, Die rechtlichen und sozialen Verhältnisse der jüdischen Gemeinden Speyer, Worms, und Mainz von ihren Anfängen bis zur Mitte des 14. Jahrhunderts (1901); Germania Judaica, vols. 1 and 2 (1934) 174-223; Kober, Adolf, Aus der Geschichte der Juden im Rheinland (1931) 202-9; Levi, Sali, Beiträge zur Geschichte der ältesten jüdischen Grabsteine in Mainz (1926); "Magenza," special number of the Menorah (Vienna, 1927; cf. also the literature given on pp. 102-7); Menzel, I. S., Beiträge zur Geschichte der Juden von Mainz im 15. Jahrhundert; Rothschild, Leopold, Die Judengemeinde zu Mainz, Speyer und Worms von 1349-1438 (1904); Salfeld, Sigmund, Das Martyrologium des Nürnberger Memorbuches (1898); idem, Bilder aus der Vergangenheit der jüdischen Gemeinde Mainz (1903); Schaab, K. A., Diplomatische Geschichte der Juden zu Mainz (1855).

MAYER, ADOLPH A., American army major during the Civil War, b. Philadelphia, 1827; d. Texas, 1869. Mayer, who was a brother-in-law of Abraham Jonas, was living in Peoria, Ill., early in the 1850's. Then he went to New Mexico on a mining venture. The Civil War broke out while he was there, and he organized the first New Mexican cavalry as the Fourth New Mexico Volunteers. Mayer became major and Kit Carson colonel. During the period when the regiment was stationed in Pennsylvania, Mayer took a message from the governor of Pennsylvania to Abraham Lincoln, with whom he had already had some

political communication while living in Peoria. Lincoln appointed Mayer inspector general of volunteers. He died as a result of wounds received in the Civil War.

Lit.: Publications of the American Jewish Historical Society, No. 17 (1909) 157; No. 20 (1911) 151; Morais, Henry S., The Jews of Philadelphia (1894) 532.

MAYER, AUGUST LIEBMANN, art historian, b. Darmstadt, Germany, 1885. An expert on Spanish paintings, he was professor at the University of Munich, chief conservator of the Bayrische Staatsgemeinde-Sammlung in the Bavarian capital, and editor of the periodical Pantheon in Munich until 1933. In 1927 he edited, together with Bruno Italiener and Aron Freimann, a facsimile printing of the famous Darmstädter Haggadah, originating around 1420. After the Nazis came to power he went first to Paris and from there escaped to Cannes in 1940, where he was working (1942) as a free-lance writer.

The following of Mayer's numerous works are noteworthy: Die Meisterlieder des Hans Foltz (1908); Jusepe de Rivera (1908; 2nd ed., 1922); Toledo (1910); Die Sevillaer Malerschule (1911); El Greco (1911; 3rd ed., 1920); Geschichte der spanischen Malerei (1913; 2nd ed., 1922); Avila, Segovia, El Escorial (1913); Murillo (1913); Spanische Handzeichnungen (1918); Expressionistische Miniaturen des deutschen Mittelalters (1918); Goya (1922); Mittelalterliche Plastik in Spanien (1922); Spanische Barokplastik (1923); Velazquez (1925); Historia de la pintura española (1926); Die Gotik in Spanien (1928); El Estilo Romanico en Espana (1931). Most of his works were translated into Spanish, and several into English. In the period between 1932 and 1942 Mayer published many essays in French, English and American periodicals, the subjects including Velasquez, Goya, Rubens and the late 15th cent. Castilian paintings.

MAYER, CONSTANT, artist, b. Besançon, France, 1832; d. New York city, 1911. He studied in Paris under Léon Cogniet and at the École des Beaux-Arts. In 1857 Mayer came to the United States and settled in New York city, although he continued to exhibit frequently at the Paris salon and was made a chevalier of the Légion d'Honneur in 1869. In the United States Mayer painted portraits of General Ulysses S. Grant and General William T. Sherman. Other well-known paintings by him were Beggar-Girl (1863); Maud Muller (1867); Song of the Shirt (1875); Mandolin Player (1884); and First Grief (1885). Mayer was elected to the National Academy of Art in 1866, and also belonged to the American Art Union.

MAYER, DAVID, chief governmental privy councillor, b. Mühlheim, Baden, Germany, 1854; d. Karlsruhe, Germany, 1931. He was the first Jew to serve in the Baden ministry in Karlsruhe (1871), and became an official in the administrative court of Baden. The establishment of the Friedrich-Luisen-Hospiz for children at Bad Dürrheim in 1910 was due to Mayer's efforts and those of his wife, Marie Mayer. Besides his activity as a political leader in his home state, Mayer devoted time to the improvement of the conditions of the Jewish communities in Baden. He was spiritual leader, a member and for many years president of the supreme council of the Jews of Baden from 1880 to 1920, when he retired.

Mayer's wife, who shared his social and humane activities, was deported by the Gestapo to France in 1940, and died in Camp de Gurs in the autumn of 1941.

MAYER, EDGAR, physician, b. New York city, 1890. He received his medical degree from the College of Physicians and Surgeons of Columbia University in 1913. As a specialist in pulmonary diseases, Mayer was a member of the faculty of the Trudeau School of Tuberculosis at Saranac Lake, N. Y., and also associate professor of medicine at the Cornell University Medical College. He was consultant with various hospitals and sanatoriums. Mayer was the author of *Clinical Application of Sunlight* (1926) and *Curative Value of Light* (1932).

MAYER, EDWARD EVERETT, psychiatrist, b. Allegheny, Pa., 1876. He received his medical degree from the University of Pittsburgh, and spent the following two years in Europe doing post-graduate work. Mayer entered practice in Pittsburgh in 1900. He occupied various posts with hospitals, and in 1910 was made assistant professor of psychiatry at the University of Pittsburgh, which post he still held in 1942. He was also supervising psychiatrist at the behavior clinic of the Allegheny County criminal courts, and psychiatrist with the federal courts of western Pennsylvania. Mayer was the first president of the Pennsylvania Penal Society. Among his published works was a translation of *Oppenheim's Diseases of the Nervous System* (1900). Mayer was active in local Jewish communal affairs, and was also a member of the board of governors of the Union of American Hebrew Congregations. In 1942 he was living in Pittsburgh.

MAYER, EMIL, physician, b. New York city, 1854; d. New York city, 1931. He was educated at the College of the City of New York (1868-70), the New York College of Pharmacy (Pharm.G., 1873), and the medical department of New York University (M.D., 1877).

From 1893 to 1904 Mayer was chief of the clinic of the throat department of the New York Eye Infirmary. In 1895 he lectured on diseases of the nose and throat at the New York Polyclinic Hospital. He was chief of the clinic of the throat and ear department of Mount Sinai Hospital from 1904 to 1916, and consulting laryngologist at that institution from 1916 to the time of his death.

Mayer was one of the leading authorities on laryngology in the United States. Among his most important contributions to medical science were the invention of tubes for use in nasal operations and his experimentation with cocaine, which proved that it was an unreliable anesthetic. He was elected to many positions of honor by his medical colleagues, including the presidency of the American Laryngological Association in 1922 and the chairmanship of the permanent committee of the American Medical Association from 1920 to 1931. Mayer wrote many articles for medical journals.

MAYER, GUSTAV, German historian, b. Prenzlau, Brandenburg, 1871. He was the descendant of a Jewish family which had resided in his native town since the 17th cent. He was educated at the Gymnasium of Prenzlau, and studied at the Universities of Berlin, Freiburg and Göttingen. Mayer was the first German historian to specialize in the history of German socialism, and surpassed his socialist predecessors because of his incontestable critical methods. Although he did not adhere to any political party, he never concealed his sympathy with the personalities of the founders of German socialism and with their cause. He thus won the confidence of leaders of the socialist party, who allowed him access to their archives, and Mayer made non-socialist historians appreciate, with decreasing prejudice, the historical significance of Lassalle, Marx and Engels.

In 1908 Mayer published *Johann Baptist von Schweitzer und die Sozialdemokratie,* in which he endeavored to defend the successor of Lassalle against aspersions by Marx's disciples. In *Die Trennung der proletarischen und der bürgerlichen Demokratie in Deutschland* (1911), he dealt with the problem of the formation of an independent German proletarian party independent of bourgeois democracy. He edited *Lassalles nachgelassene Briefe und Schriften* (1921-25), and published *Lassalles Weg zum Sozialismus* (1925).

Some of Mayer's briefer articles on the history of socialism were collected (1927) in *Aus der Welt des Sozialismus.* He was particularly interested in the personality of Friedrich Engels, Marx's friend, companion and protector. Prior to Mayer's great biography, *Friedrich Engels* (1919), the true relationship between Marx and Engels had not been sufficiently clear. His biography, published as part of an edition of Engels' writings, accomplished this important task and contributed to a balancing of the historical function of socialism as a force in German history. Mayer, who became professor at the University of Berlin relatively late, completed the enlarged second edition of his biography of Engels just four weeks before the Nazis came to power and turned him out of office. He emigrated to Holland, and there published this second edition. An English translation appeared in 1936. At the end of the book Mayer expressed the conviction that the tide of nationalism would hamper but not definitely bar the progress of humanitarian civilization.   Hugo Bieber.

MAYER, HENRY (HY), caricaturist, b. Worms on Rhine, Germany, 1868. The son of a wealthy London merchant, he received an excellent education, and after graduation from the Gymnasium at Worms he trained for a commercial career in London. In 1886, however, he emigrated to the United States. He spent a year in Mexico, began as artist at Cincinnati in 1887, and lived in New York city from 1893 on. He did illustrations for the foremost magazines and newspapers in the world, including *Black and White, Pall-Mall Magazine, Life, Harper's, Collier's, Le Rire* (Paris) and *Fliegende Blätter* (Munich). He edited *Punch* in 1914, and from 1915 on was a contributing editor. From 1904 to 1914 he was a cartoonist for the New York *Times.*

Mayer was the author of numerous books of illustrations, including *Autobiography of a Monkey* (1896); *Fantasies in Ha-Ha* (1899); and *Adventures of a Japanese Doll* (1901). He illustrated such books as *The Tumble Man* (1913) and *Puck Album of Caricatures* (1915). Well known for his pen-and-ink drawings, he was also an etcher and painter. He was the first artist to draw for the motion pictures. The emperor of Japan presented him with two Japanese vases in appreciation of his cartoons during the Russo-Japanese war.

Mayer's caricatures had no sting and his levity was benign. He was admired for his inventiveness and his mirth-inspiring humor. Differing from his unpolitical drawings, however, was his famous mordant cartoon "Vive l'Armée!" which, with others, appeared during the Dreyfus agitation in France. It showed a senile general on a pedestal, surrounded by an excited crowd, one hand resting on his sword, the other triumphantly holding aloft the scalp of Truth. "The entire episode of French history is depicted in this cartoon as it could not be done in columns upon columns of editorial writing," a contemporary critic said of this cartoon.

MAYER, ISAAC, rabbi, b. Alsace, 1809; d. New York city, 1898. After losing a great deal of property in the German revolution of 1848, Mayer came to the United States, where he was first a teacher and rabbi in Cincinnati (1849-56). From 1856 to 1859 Mayer was rabbi in Rochester, N. Y., and from 1859 until his retirement about 1869 he served in Hartford, Conn. He was the author of a Hebrew grammar (1854), one of the first to be published in the United States. At approximately the same time he issued also a German translation of *Sirach. The Source of Salvation,* a book of instruction for Hebrew and Sabbath schools, appeared in 1874. Mayer was a Conservative in religious practice, and at odds with the Reform elements of his day.

    Lit.: The American Israelite, Jan. 13, 1898, pp. 2, 7.

MAYER, JULIUS M., judge, b. New York city, 1865; d. New York city, 1925. He received his law degree from Columbia University in 1886, and entered practice in New York city. As counsel to the state legislative committee investigating the condition of women and children in workshops (1894), Mayer was instrumental in effecting important reforms in factory laws. In 1902 he was made justice of the court of Special Sessions, in which position he served two years. From 1905 to 1907 Mayer was attorney general for the state of New York. President William Howard Taft appointed him judge of the district court of the southern district of New York in 1912, and President Warren G. Harding made him United States circuit judge in 1921. Mayer was president of the Columbia Law Alumni.

MAYER, LEVY, lawyer, b. Richmond, Va., 1858; d. Chicago, 1922. He was brought to Chicago as a child and educated in the public schools there. In 1876 he studied at Yale College and at the Yale Law School. For the next five years he served as librarian of the Chicago Law Institute, and during this period edited and revised the works of David Rorer on private international law and other aspects of legal procedure. In 1881 Mayer entered the practice of law and finally became one of the leading corporation lawyers in the United States and a recognized authority in other countries as well. During the first World War Mayer served on the State Council of Defense for Illinois, and later (1920-22) he was a member of the Constitutional Convention of Illinois. From his youth on Mayer was unofficially active in civic and Jewish com-

munal affairs. After his death his widow gave $500,000 to Northwestern University for the erection of a law school building dedicated to his memory.

    Lit.: Masters, Edgar Lee, *Levy Mayer* (1925); Meites, Hyman L., *History of the Jews of Chicago,* p. 403; Kraus, Adolf, *Reminiscences and Comments.*

MAYER, LIPPMAN, rabbi, b. Mulhouse, Baden, Germany, 1841; d. Latrobe, Pa., 1904. He studied in Karlsruhe, then in Würzburg, where he received his Ph.D. degree, and attended the Yeshiva. Later he received the Ph.D. degree also from the University of Berlin. Coming to the United States, about 1868, Mayer became rabbi of the French congregation in New York city. In 1869 he was called to the Jewish Congregation in Selma, Ala., and in 1870 to Rodeph Sholom Congregation in Pittsburgh, with which he remained until his death.

Mayer was an early advocate of the German Reform Movement in the United States. He was secretary of the Philadelphia conference in 1869 and was one of the prime movers in the calling of the important Pittsburgh conference in 1885. He was active in the promotion of interfaith amity, particularly in regard to the German churches throughout Pennsylvania. Mayer was one of the founders of the Central Conference of American Rabbis. Among his accomplishments in the communal life of Pittsburgh was his establishment of the first public kindergarten in Allegheny county and of a school for Russian immigrants. In 1880 Mayer founded a Young Men's Hebrew Association in Pittsburgh. He was for many years a trustee of the Western University of Pennsylvania.

    Lit.: Levy, J. Leonard, in *Publications of the American Jewish Historical Society,* No. 13 (1905) 147-49; *Central Conference of American Rabbis Year Book,* vol. 15 (1905) 269.

MAYER, LOUIS BURT, motion picture producer, b. Minsk, Russia, 1885. He was brought to Canada as a child, and was educated in the schools of St. John, New Brunswick. For a time he worked with his father in the ship salvaging business in Canada, but at the age of eighteen he came to the United States, settling in Massachusetts.

Mayer began his film career in 1907, by opening a store show in Haverhill, Mass., serving also as his own janitor. Eventually, with Nat Gordon, he succeeded in establishing a chain of theatres throughout New England—the Gordon-Mayer chain. Later he embarked on distribution and finally entered the producing field, forming the Louis B. Mayer Pictures Corporation. In 1924 this corporation was merged with the Metro Pictures Corporation and subsequently with the Goldwyn firm, becoming the Metro-Goldwyn-Mayer Corporation. Mayer became first-vice-president in charge of production, a post he still held in 1942.

In his direction of the production activities of the large Metro-Goldwyn-Mayer firm, he was a pioneer in introducing new techniques and acquiring new performers. Among his first productions was *Ben Hur,* one of the earliest spectacular films; later came *The Student Prince* and *The Big Parade.* His search for new performers brought Luise Rainer to *The Great Ziegfeld* and later gave her a leading role in *The Good Earth,* both performances winning an Academy award. Other leading actors developed under Mayer's tutelage

Louis B. Mayer

include Robert Montgomery, Robert Taylor, Mickey Rooney and Norma Shearer, who in *The Trial of Mary Dugan* appeared in the first talking picture Mayer produced. Notable among his films were *Trader Horn, Anna Christie, Grand Hotel, Dinner at Eight, Thin Man, Mutiny on the Bounty, San Francisco, Romeo and Juliet, Boys Town* and *The Citadel*.

Mayer was a delegate to the Republican National Convention in 1928. In 1929 he was offered, by President Hoover, the post of ambassador to Turkey, which he declined. He was president of the Motion Pictures Producers Association from 1931 to 1936, and a member of the Los Angeles Chamber of Commerce. He also served as trustee of the Los Angeles Jewish Orphans Home. Mayer was made an officer of the French Legion of Honor in 1937 and was awarded the Cross of the White Lion by Czechoslovakia in 1938. He received an honorary LL.D. degree from the University of New Brunswick in 1939.

Lit.: *American Hebrew,* July 20, 1928, p. 318; *idem,* August 9, 1929, p. 359; *Jewish Tribune,* March 16, 1928, p. 3; *idem,* Feb. 8, 1929, p. 8.

MAYER, LUCIUS W., mining engineer, b. New York city, 1882. He received his degree in mining engineering from Columbia University in 1904, and subsequently served as engineer with various mining companies in Colorado and Missouri and also in Europe. Afterward he was associated with other companies as construction engineer. In 1917 he became a partner in the engineering firm of Rogers, Mayer and Ball, and in 1942 was still functioning with this firm. Mayer was the author of *Mining Methods in Europe* (1907) and *Financing of Mines* (1916).

MAYER, MARCUS R., theatrical producer, b. New Orleans, La., 1843; d. Amityville, L. I., 1918. He was educated at Fordham College in New York city and went out to California while still a very young man. There he first became a printer, then a journalist, working on the *Territorial Enterprise* and the *Scientific American.* In 1869 he was a state senator in California.

Mayer became a theatrical manager in 1872. Among the performers who appeared under his management were Julia Dean Hayne, Edwin Booth, Lawrence Barrett, Adelaide Neilson, Rose Eytinge, Sir Henry Irving, Sarah Bernhardt, Monet Sully, Mary Anderson and Adelaide Patti.

Lit.: Markens, Isaac, *The Hebrews in America* (1888) 230.

MAYER, MARUM (MAX) SAMUEL VON, law teacher, one of the foremost authorities on Roman law, b. Freudenthal, Germany, 1797; d. Stuttgart, Germany, 1862. A scholarship awarded him by Frederick I of Württemberg enabled him to study at the state university; he was one of the few Jewish scholars in Germany who obtained an academic teaching position at the beginning of the 19th cent. without having to be baptized first, like Eduard Gans. In 1829 he became instructor and in 1831 assistant professor of law at the University of Tübingen; in 1833 he became assistant professor at the University of Leipzig. After a long inner struggle which impaired his health, Mayer embraced Christianity and married a pastor's daughter. He then became professor (1839) and rector (1849-50) at the University of Tübingen. He wrote: *Die öffentlichen Verhältnisse der Juden* (1827); *Legaten und Fideikommissen* (1834); *Über römisches Recht und neue Gesetzgebung* (1839).

Lit.: Wininger, S., *Grosse Jüdische National-Biographie,* vol. 4 (1930) 306; *Allgemeine Deutsche Biographie,* vol. 22, p. 128 et seq.

MAYER, NATHAN, physician, b. Germany, 1838; d. Hartford, Conn., 1912. He was the son of Isaac Mayer, and with him came to the United States in 1849, settling in Cincinnati. During the French war against Austria (1859) Mayer was in Europe, and served as a surgeon with the French army. He returned to the United States in time to serve as surgeon in the sixteenth Connecticut infantry during the Civil War. Taken prisoner, he was for a time kept in Libby Prison. After his release he acted as medical purveyor for the Union troops in North Carolina, with the rank of brigadier general.

At the close of the Civil War, Mayer settled in Hartford, where he practised for the rest of his life. He was also surgeon general for the state of Connecticut, and in this capacity wrote a report on the state's prisons and county jails (1873). Besides contributing musical criticism to the general press and writing for the Jewish press, Mayer was the author of a novel, *Differences* (1867), dealing with the problems of the Civil War.

Lit.: Morrison, Hyman, *Early Jewish Physicians in America* (1929); *Boston Medical and Surgical Journal,* vol. 67 (1912) 108; Kagan, Solomon R., *Jewish Contributions to Medicine in America* (1939) 41.

MAYER, SAMUEL, rabbi, jurist and author, b. Hechingen, Germany, 1807; d. Hechingen, 1875. After studying law at the University of Würzburg, he became rabbi in Hechingen in 1830 and practised law at the same time. His main work, embracing public, civil and penal law, on which he labored for twelve years, was the three-volume *Die Rechte der Israeliten, Athener* *und Römer* (1862-76), in which he set three codes side by side, as a contribution to a system and history of universal law. Mayer edited the *Israelitisches Samstagsblatt* and the *Israelitischer Musenalmanach* (1840).

Lit.: Wininger, S., *Grosse Jüdische National-Biographie,* vol. 4 (1930) 305-6.

MAYER, SIGMUND, physiologist, b. Bechtheim, Hesse, Germany, 1842; d. Prague, 1910. He was educated at the Universities of Giessen, Heidelberg and Tübingen, graduating from the latter in 1865. Up to 1869 he was assistant to the illustrious Hermann Helmholtz in Berlin, and lectured at the University of Vienna from 1869 to 1878, when he was appointed assistant director of the Psychological Institute at the University in Prague. He became director of the Institute of Histology at the same university in 1880, and associate professor in 1884.

Together with Von Basch, Mayer wrote *Untersuchungen über Darmbewegungen, Zur Physiologie des Herzens und der Blutgefässe* and *Histologisches Taschenbuch* (1887). The results of his extensive researches were printed mostly in essays which appeared in *Sitzungsberichte der Wiener Akademie der Wissenschaften, Strickers Handbuch der Lehre von den Geweben, Hermanns Handbuch der Physiologie, Archiv für Psychologie und Nervenkrankheiten* and *Zeitschrift für wissenschaftliche Mikroskopie.*

Mayer's close connection with Jewish life and Jewish problems is documented in his earlier publications. He translated from French into German Israel Michel Rabbinowicz's studies on medical problems in the Talmud. In 1881 there appeared *Die thalmudischen Principien des Schächtens und die Medicin des Thalmud,* a comparison with the principles of Hippocrates and of modern science, and in 1883 *Einleitung in die Gesetzgebung und die Medicin des Thalmud.*

MAYER, SYLVAIN, writer, b. England, 1863. He received his B.A. degree from London University in 1882 and his Ph.D. degree from the University of Heidelberg in 1884. Mayer entered the practice of law and became a King's Counsel in 1913. His writing ranges from theatre comedies to discussions on law that have gone into several editions; it includes: *Papa's Honeymoon* and *A Gay Widower,* plays; *Captured in Court,* a novel; *Code of Law of Rating; Law of Agricultural Holdings; Law of Compensation; French Code of Commerce; The Representation of the People Act* (1918); *Reminiscences of a K.C., Theatrical and Legal* (1924); *Funeral Oration of Pericles* (1926). In 1942 he lived in comparative retirement at the British capital.

MAYER, TEODORO, Italian senator and economist, b. Trieste (then Austria), 1860. One of the leading figures in the "irredenta" movement in the former Austrian provinces of Trieste and Trento he founded (1881) the Italian language paper *Il Piccolo* in Trieste which became the chief tribune for Italy's cultural and territorial claims. *Il Piccolo* was suppressed by the Austrian authorities in 1915, but reappeared in 1919, after the formal annexation of Trieste to Italy.

Mayer acted as secret emissary of the Italian patriotic society Dante Alighieri in the Trieste province, and carried out important confidential missions in behalf of the Italian government. He founded and promoted various cultural institutions in Trieste aimed at keeping alive Italian culture and the "irredenta" spirit, and for his patriotic services was nominated (1920) member of the Italian Senate, where he achieved prominence as rapporteur of the financial budget and for pointing out many deficiencies of Fascist financial policy and administration. In 1925 he became chairman of the central commission for direct taxation and in 1931 was nominated Minister of the State. He was president of the Istituto Mobiliare Italiano, a government-controlled organization which aimed at supervising and protecting Italian industrial corporations.

As a result of the new anti-Semitic policy of the Fascist government, Mayer was discharged from all his positions and compelled to yield up ownership of *Il Piccolo.*

ALDO MAYER (b. Trieste, 1882; d. 1939), author and publicist, was the son of Teodoro Mayer. He, too, founded patriotic circles in the province of Trieste, and was one of the most fervent propagandists for the annexation of the provinces of Trieste and Trento to Italy. In 1919 he assumed the directorship of *Il Piccolo.* Together with the Duchess of Aosta, he founded at Rome the Association for the Redeemed Provinces of Italy. He was author of several novels and books on patriotic themes.

MAYER, WOLF BEN HAYIM (also Maier Wolf), pedagogical author and exegete, b. Klattall, Bohemia, 1776; d. Prague, 1850. At the age of thirteen he was well-versed in the Talmud, which he studied at the same time as the famous preacher, Veith. As a young man, Mayer went to Prague, where he studied under Ezekiel Landau, who was then active as the last chief rabbi of Bohemia. After teaching Hebrew at the Jewish Free School in Berlin, he joined the faculty of the largest Jewish school in Prague, where he was active for forty years.

Mayer was both an author and a Hebrew poet. His widely circulated textbooks had a favorable influence on the development of religious instruction, especially instruction in the Hebrew language. He edited liturgical publications and Moses Mendelssohn's Hebrew editions of the Bible with translation and commentary. Some of his outstanding works are: *Torath Leshon Ibrith* (1827, 1832 and 1880); *Sifethe Yeshurun* (1828), dealing with the language and expressions of Rashi, Kimhi, Ibn Ezra and other Hebrew grammarians and commentators; *Leshon Limmudim,* children's fables and stories in Hebrew and German; *Toledoth Yeshurun,* the history of the world to the time of the Second Temple (1841); *Tehinoth,* a prayer-book for educated women. He wrote essays and poems in Hebrew periodicals.

Lit.: Wininger, S., *Grosse Jüdische National-Biographie,* vol. 4 (1930) 307.

MAYERSOHN, LAZAR, physician and Zionist, b. Bucharest, Roumania, 1879. He studied medicine at Paris where, in 1905, he received the M.D. degree, his thesis, *De la circoncision et spécialement de la circoncision rituelle, envisagée du point de vue rituel, hygiénique et prophylactique,* being awarded a prize. Later he published a work on the subject of Jews in medicine (1914), and one on Roumanian Jews in medicine. In 1938 he added another kindred work to his early thesis on the hygienic aspects of circumcision.

His scientific papers were published at Paris, Bucharest and Jerusalem.

In 1907 Mayersohn founded at Bucharest the Society of Oto-Laryngology, of which he became president in 1934. He fought in the first World War (1916-18) and received a military decoration. In 1940, when the Jews were removed from the ranks of the Roumanian army, he held the rank of colonel.

He associated himself with Zionism from the very inception of the movement. At Paris he was a member of the Zionist Student Association, and at Bucharest of the organization Chovevei Zion. Ardently devoted to the Zionist cause, he was a leader or member of all the central Zionist committees, and collaborated on all Zionist publications until the Roumanian government ordered Jewish political parties and associations to be dissolved and all Jewish press activities discontinued. He fought for the civic rights of the Roumanian Jews.

MAZAL. The original meaning of Mazal was star, constellation, planet, or, in particular, sign of the zodiac. Mazaloth is still the term for the twelve signs of the zodiac in the astronomy of modern Hebrew, just as it was in ancient times. Ancient peoples—the Egyptians, the Babylonians, and later on the Jews, believed that the stars had special powers and could influence the fate of man; hence the word Mazal in Jewish literature received the figurative meaning of fortune and fate (as in *Yeb.* 64b). In Hebrew literature as well as in the Yiddish vernacular, Mazal (or Mazel) is used in the sense of fortune, good luck, or a fortunate occurrence. The greeting *mazel tob* ("Good Luck!") is used on joyful family occasions or at the beginning of an enterprise fraught with great expectation. If one desires to indicate that another is lucky, he says, "He has Mazal," or "He is a Bar-Mazel" ("son of fortune").

The expressions derived from Mazal are Mazeldig (lucky), Shlimmazel (bad luck), and Shlimmazeldig (unlucky).

See also: PHRASES, POPULAR; ASTROLOGY.

MAZAR PASHA (originally Stephen Lakeman), British and Turkish soldier, b. London, 1812; d. London, 1897. He was a picturesque figure and led an unusual life. His father, a wealthy banker, wanted him to follow in his own footsteps and gave him a thorough education. Young Stephen, however, felt attracted toward a military career and entered a British school for officers. He was appointed lieutenant at the age of twenty-five and served in South Africa and India. Here he suppressed a revolt, and displayed such bravery and humanity that he became very popular in India. Due to his military aptitude he advanced rapidly, being the youngest colonel in the British army.

When Turkey sought the aid of Great Britain to secure good officers to reorganize its army, Colonel Lakeman was chosen for the mission. He entered the ranks of the Turkish army and was soon promoted to general, assuming the name of Mazar Pasha, under which he was known for the rest of his life. He was barely forty-seven when the Turkish government sent him to Roumania at the head of a military mission. Since Turkey at that time exercised a protectorate over Roumania, he was received with great deference. His position as a Jew in Roumanian aristocracy was a unique one; he was not only received by that very ex-clusive class, but married one of its members, Maria Filipescu. After his marriage Mazar Pasha renounced his military rank in the Turkish army and settled in Roumania, where he remained for twenty years. He manifested concern over the fate of the Jewish population and intervened on its behalf. After his wife's death, he refused to accept her estate, and returned to England, where he wrote his memoirs.

MAZE, IDA, Yiddish poet, b. Ugol, province of Minsk, Russia, 1893. She came to America with her family in 1908, settling in Montreal. In the 1930's her first volume of poems, *A Mame,* appeared. This was followed by *Lieder far Kinder* and *Neie Lieder* (1941). Critics consider her work the typical poetry of a woman, serious and lyrical, simple and profound. It has been described as "the poetry of a girl in love, of a young woman, of a happy mother and a mother sorrowing over her child's death." Ida Maze was active in Jewish cultural activities in Montreal, particularly in propaganda for Yiddish poetry.

Lit.: Presse, Aug. 27, 1941; *Keneder Adler,* Dec. 12, 1941.

MAZELDIG, MAZELIG, see PHRASES, POPULAR.

MAZELTOV, *see under* MAZAL; GREETING AND WISH FORMULAS.

MAZER, CHARLES, physician, b. Kiev, Russia, 1881. He came to the United States in 1893. Mazer received his medical degree from the Medico-Chirurgical College of Philadelphia in 1908. Specializing in gynecology, he became associated with various hospitals in Philadelphia. In 1922 he was made assistant professor of gynecology and obstetrics of the University of Pennsylvania Graduate School of Medicine, a post he still held in 1942. In collaboration with other physicians, Mazer originated and evolved many tests and treatments for women's ailments. With Leopold Goldstein, he was author of *Clinical Endocrinology of the Female* (1922) and *The Diagnosis and Treatment of Menstrual Disorders and Sterility* (1941). Mazer was active in civic and communal affairs. In 1935 he was Socialist candidate for mayor in Philadelphia. He was president of the Philadelphia Jewish Physicians Organization (1935-　　).

Lit.: Kagan, Solomon R., *Jewish Contributions to Medicine in America* (1939) 260-61, 689, 714.

MAZLIACH EFFENDI, NISSIM, deputy in the Young Turk Parliament, b. Magnesia, near Smyrna, Turkey; d. Beirut, Syria, 1931. One of the most active leaders of the Young Turk movement, he was the only one of the four Jewish deputies who was courageous enough to represent Jewish interests in the Turkish Chamber. When Zionism and Turkish Jewry were violently attacked in Parliament by the Palestinian delegates in 1911, Mazliach Effendi conducted their defense. After the first World War he retired from political life and devoted himself to his profession as lawyer, without, however, losing contact with the government, especially as regards Jewish interests.

MAZUR, PAUL MYER, banker and author, b. Boston, 1892. He received his A.B. degree from Harvard in 1914, and entered the merchandising field in Boston. In 1917 Mazur joined the United States Army; in 1918 and during part of 1919 he was stationed in

France and England. On his return to the United
States in 1919 Mazur entered the Lehman Bros. banking firm. He became a partner in the firm in 1927, and
in 1942 was still functioning in this capacity. He wrote:
*Principles of Organization Applied to Modern Retail-
ing* (1927); *American Prosperity* (1928); *America
Looks Abroad* (1930); *New Roads to Prosperity* (1931).

MEAL-OFFERING, *see* SACRIFICE.

MEALS, FESTAL (Hebrew, *se'udah* or *mishteh*).
In addition to the normal occasions in the lives of individuals or families, such as births, weddings or the
celebration of happy events, there were, in both ancient
and medieval times, numerous festal meals of a more
or less religious nature. Probably the oldest meal of
this type is the Seder on Passover eve which, as ushering in the festival of freedom, was given an especially
joyous nature. The festival meal at every New Moon
is mentioned in the historical books of the Bible (*I
Sam.* 20; *Amos* 8:5). In the period of the Second
Temple, the observance of the New Moon as a holiday
declined, but that of Shabuoth and Sukkoth increased,
especially the latter. In the Talmudic period the third
meal of the Sabbath (*shalosh se'udoth,* corrupted into
Shalashudos), which marked the distinct character of
the day, became an especially festive meal.

The Talmudic rabbis laid special emphasis on the
meals that came under the category of a "meal honoring the commandment" (*se'udath mitzvah*), in which
they included the festal meal on Purim, or that given
at the conclusion of the study of a Talmudic tractate
(Siyum). Banquets were given on the occasion of rabbinical assemblies to discuss the problems of the day,
and the Midrash has an interesting transcription of the
speeches delivered at such a banquet which was held
at the conclusion of the synod of Usha toward the
middle of the 2nd cent. C.E. (*Midrash Song of Songs*
2). Formal invitations were sent out for these religious
banquets, and whole companies participated in them.
Indeed, it was the duty, as well as the privilege, of
such distinguished persons as officials and scribes to
partake in these ritual banquets. The guests came
garbed in gala attire; they were anointed in the home
with sweet-scented oil, and their hair was adorned with
wreaths. Lavish entertainments were prepared for them
and, if it were possible, they were served by the master
of the house himself, otherwise by an attendant (*sham-
mash*). While there is no reference to professional
entertainment, there was music, singing, dancing and
games; guests entertained one another with jokes and
riddles, or with clever sayings. The departing guests
were given gifts. Women participated in these banquets, and the inviting of impecunious students was
especially recommended. It was said by way of praise
of the noble-minded in Jerusalem that they never partook of unless they knew all their table companions.

In modern times, special festal meals of a religious
nature are held to celebrate the achievements of an
individual in communal endeavor, for various festivals,
as a congregational Seder, or for the celebration of a
communal or congregational anniversary. With the
institution of Bar Mitzvah the custom arose, and is
still prevalent today, of having a festal meal, which is
often held within the precincts of the synagogue.
Simhath Torah is frequently observed by the distribution of cakes and drinks to those present at the services.

See also: MELAVVEH MALKAH; SEDER; SIYUM.

Lit.: Rosenzweig, *Geselligkeit und Geselligkeitsfreuden
in Bibel und Talmud;* Bible dictionaries, under Banquet.

MEARS, OTTO, pioneer, b. Courland, Russia,
1840; d. Pasadena, Cal., 1931. To him goes historic
credit for the development of the San Juan district in
Colorado. After three years of voluntary service in the
Civil War in New Mexico (partly under Kit Carson
against the Navajos), young Mears settled in Conejos,
Col., where he set up a sawmill and gristmill and soon
began to grow wheat. Then, to reach the newly opening markets over Poncho Pass, he built the first of his
more than 300 toll roads over the hills and across the
plains of Colorado, which came to be known as the
Mears system and are his distinctive contribution to
the state. His enterprises multiplied and culminated
in the construction of the Silverton Northern Railroad
and the Rio Grande Southern in southwest Colorado.
In the difficult deal with the Utes, Mears, negotiating
for the government, was instrumental in getting the
Indians to give up their vast Colorado reservations, so
that the land could be exploited.

Mears served in the state legislature and helped con-
struct the famed capitol building, in the dome of which
his portrait appears. At Bear Creek Falls, on the Ouray-
Silverton highway, is a granite memorial tablet to him.

The panic of 1893 wiped out his ownership of the
Rio Grande Southern; he then went east and built the
railroad between Washington, D. C., and Chesapeake
Beach.

Lit.: Jocknick, Sidney, *Early Days on the Western
Slopes of Colorado; Dictionary of American Biography,*
vol. 12, p. 485.

MEASSEFIM, a group of Hebrew writers, mostly
from Germany, so called from their periodical,
Hameassef (The Collector). Inspired by Moses Mendelssohn, this group endeavored to resurrect and develop the use of Hebrew as a literary medium, and as
a means of introducing European culture to the Jewish masses. They were therefore the founders of modern Hebrew literature. In 1783 Isaac Abraham Euchel
and Mendel Bresselau issued a proclamation at Königsberg, calling for the formation of a society to develop
the Hebrew language. In the following year *Hameassef* was established to that end, and it continued publication until 1811. Its first editor was Euchel; among
its subsequent editors were Joel Löwe and Aron Wolfsohn. Its contributors included both such older leaders
as Mendelssohn, Wessely and David Friedländer, and
such younger writers as Ben Zeeb, Bresselau, Euchel,
Herz, Lindau and Lewisohn. Its policy was that of
introducing European culture and rejuvenating the
Jewish spirit; in religious matters it wavered between
Orthodoxy and proposals for reform. The first three
volumes appeared monthly in Königsberg; others were
published there and at Berlin, Breslau, Altona and
Dessau. It paved the way for the spread of Haskalah in
Galicia, Poland and Russia in the next generation.

Lit.: Waxman, M., *A History of Jewish Literature,*
vol. 3 (1936) 119-29; Bernfeld, S., *Dor Tahpuchoth;*
Spiegel, S., *Hebrew Reborn* (1930).

MEASURES, *see* WEIGHTS AND MEASURES.

MEAT, INSPECTION OF, *see* SLAUGHTERING.

MEAT TAX, *see* TAXATION.

MECHILTA (more correctly, Mechilata), name usually employed to designate the Tannaitic Midrash on *Exodus*. The word *mechilta* is the Aramaic equivalent of the Hebrew *middah* ("treatise") and was used originally to designate any arranged collection of laws. In the Middle Ages, however, the word was so frequently applied to the Halachic Midrash on *Exodus,* beginning with Nissim of Kairwan (11th cent.), who used it as a specific title for the book, that three centuries afterwards it had completely replaced the old name of Sifre Debe Rab, and today Mechilta alone is universally used to indicate the Midrash on *Exodus.*

The Mechilta is called also by the fuller name Mechilta Debe Rabbi Ishmael, indicating that it comes from the school of the Tanna Ishmael of the 2nd cent. C.E. However, this does not apply to the entire Mechilta; it merely means that there is an original core of teachings from Ishmael or his disciples, which formed the basis for later accretions and additions.

Because it derives from the school of Ishmael, the Mechilta is of utmost importance to all students of rabbinic Judaism. It contains a number of decisions and rules which are opposed to the seemingly universally accepted teachings found in many of the Talmudic sources. This is due to the fact that the Mishnah and other standard rabbinic codes were based almost completely on the school of Akiba and have ignored the opinions of the rival school of Ishmael. Thus the Mechilta variations from the usually accepted norms of rabbinic Judaism furnish new insights into the issues which were being discussed by the leaders of the various schools of thought in Judaism as late as the 2nd cent. C.E.

In its present form, the Mechilta is a continuous commentary on *Ex.* 12 to 23. It seems that either its first compiler or one of the later editors intended it to be a Halachic Midrash and therefore began it with the rabbinic comments on *Ex.* 12, which contains the first law in the book. Whether the Mechilta ever extended beyond these chapters is extremely difficult to determine. However, there are statements in the *Aruch* of Nathan ben Jehiel and the *Hamafteah* of Nissim which show that as early as the 11th cent. the Mechilta was contained within its present limits.

Although the original intention of the editor was to compile a Halachic Midrash on *Exodus,* the Mechilta in its present form contains more material that is homiletic than that which is legalistic. Lauterbach (*Mechilta,* p. xix) estimates that only two-fifths of its contents are of a Halachic nature. It has now been established that the combination of the Haggadic and Halachic sections dates from a comparatively late period, probably no earlier than the 3rd cent. C.E.; before that time, the Haggadic sections formed a series of separate works. For this reason a great deal of the Haggadic material is also found, with only minor textual variations, in the Mechilta of Rabbi Simeon ben Yohai, a parallel work from the school of Akiba.

The Mechilta is divided into nine Masechtoth ("tractates"), each of which has an individual name. The first, covering part of the Sidra *Bo* (12:1 to 13:16), is called the Tractate of the Passover; the second, covering the first part of *Beshallah* (13:17 to 14:31), is called the Tractate of *Beshallah;* the third, covering the Song of Moses (15:1-21), is called the Tractate of the Song;

the fourth, covering *Ex.* 15:22 to 17:7, is known as the Tractate of *Vayassa,* from its first word; the fifth, covering the end of *Beshallah* and the beginning of *Yithro* (17:8 to 18:27), is called the Tractate of Amalek, because the opening verses deal with the story of Amalek's attack on Israel; the sixth, covering the Ten Commandments (19:1 to 20:23), is called the Tractate of the Commandments; the seventh, dealing with the civil code (22:1 to 22:23), is known as the Tractate of the Civil Law; the eighth, covering *Ex.* 22:24 to 23:19, is known as the Tractate of Kaspa because of the opening words of this section; the ninth deals with two portions which refer to the Sabbath (31:12-17; 35:1-3), and is therefore called the Tractate of the Sabbath.

During the 1930's two editions of the Mechilta appeared, both based on a number of manuscripts: that of Horovitz-Rabin, published in 1931 by the Gesellschaft zur Förderung der Wissenschaft des Judentums; that of Jacob Z. Lauterbach, published in 1933 in the Jewish Classics Series of the Jewish Publication Society of America. The latter is furnished with a lucid translation. EPHRAIM I. BENNETT.

Lit.: Weiss, I. H., edit., *Mechilta* (1865); Friedmann, M., edit., *Mechilta* (1870); Hoffmann, D., *Zur Einleitung in die halachischen Midraschim* (1887); Albeck, C., *Untersuchungen über die halachischen Midraschim* (1927); Strack, H. L., *Introduction to the Talmud and Midrash* (1931); Lauterbach, J. Z., "The Name of Mechilta," *Jewish Quarterly Review,* New Series, vol. 11 (1920); idem, "The Arrangement and the Divisions of the Mechilta," *Hebrew Union College Annual,* vol. 1 (1924); Finkelstein, L., "The Mechilta and Its Text," *Proceedings of the American Academy for Jewish Research,* vol. 5 (1933-34); idem, "Studies in the Tannaitic Midrashim," *ibid.,* vol. 6 (1934-35).

MECHILTA LESEFER DEBARIM, a lost Halachic Midrash on *Deuteronomy,* which was compiled either by Ishmael (2nd cent.) or by his disciples. It seems to be the same as the Tanna debe Rabbi Ishmael mentioned in the Talmud as the source for many external legal opinions (Baraithoth). It disappeared at an early date and is not quoted by medieval authors, with the exception of the author of the *Midrash Hagadol,* who cited many passages that are extremely valuable for a knowledge of the old exegetic material. They were collected and published by David Hoffmann (1897); other fragments of this Mechilta, from the Genizah, were published by Solomon Schechter in the *Jewish Quarterly Review.*

Lit.: Hoffmann, David, in *Hildesheimer Festschrift,* German section, 83-98; Hebrew section, 3-22.

MECHILTA OF RABBI SIMEON BEN YOHAI, a collection of Halachic Midrashim to *Exodus,* frequently cited, especially by Nahmanides in his commentary on the Bible. The work as a whole has disappeared, but numerous fragments, incorporated into the *Midrash Hagadol,* were collected and published by David Hoffmann in *Hapeles,* vols. 1 to 4. They contain much valuable material not found in other compilations of Halachic Midrashim. The Midrash follows the methods of Akiba, and it was edited by his disciple, Simeon ben Yohai. J. N. Epstein published fragments of a manuscript of this Mechilta in *Tarbitz,* vol. 1 (1929).

Lit.: Hoffmann, David, *Zur Einleitung in die halachischen Midraschim* (1887) 45-51; Lewy, *Ein Wort über die "Midrasch des R. Simon"* (1889).

MECHULLEH, see PHRASES, POPULAR.

MECHUTTAN, see PHRASES, POPULAR.

MECKLENBURG, a province of the German Reich. Originally one duchy, it was, in 1701, divided into two grand duchies, Mecklenburg-Schwerin, which in 1900 had 1,163 Jews among 607,770 inhabitants, and Mecklenburg-Strelitz, with 102,602 inhabitants of whom 331 were Jews. In 1925 the former had 1,125 Jews, the latter 182. Reunited under the Nazi regime, Mecklenburg had about a thousand Jews in 1933.

Jews are first mentioned in this North German district in a decree of 1266, granted to the city of Wismar. There they are classed with the private servants and officials of Prince Henry I. Wismar, where the ghetto was situated on the present Altböterstrasse, then called Platea Judaeorum, with its synagogue, the Domus Judaeorum, seems to have been the oldest Jewish settlement in Mecklenburg. The settlement in Schwerin which, in modern times, was to become the center of Jewish activities Mecklenburg, was founded about 1340.

Jewish life in the Middle Ages was more or less the same in the various parts of Germany, although the general living conditions of the Jews were perhaps worse in backward Mecklenburg than in more developed parts of the country. A mass expulsion of Jews took place in 1350, the time of the Black Death, after the Mecklenburg Jews had been accused of poisoning the wells. While in Wismar there was no trace of Jewish residence for the five following centuries, some Jews returned to their old places after a few decades. But in 1492 twenty-five men and two women were burned on a hill ("Judenberg") near the city of Sternberg, in connection with the usual charge of host desecration, the rest of the Jews were forced to leave the country, and the rabbis declared a ban against any Jews who should return to Mecklenburg.

Jews settled there again not earlier than the second half of the 17th cent. In 1676 Duke Christian I called Abraham Haym and Nathan Benedix of Hamburg to his court, granting them the first tobacco monopoly in Mecklenburg. A hundred years later there were already about 200 Jewish families in Mecklenburg-Schwerin and about one hundred families in the other duchy, after the rabbinical ban against the country had been lifted. A distinguished Mecklenburg Jew of the 18th cent. was Doctor Marcus Moses, the first Jew to practise medicine in this part of Germany, while two Jewish traders started the export of wool from Mecklenburg.

In their fight for emancipation the Jews were strongly supported by the Christian Hebraist and Orientalist Olaus Gerhart Tychsen (1734-1815), who taught at Mecklenburg universities and claimed a speaking knowledge of "the Talmudic language." In 1812 Duke Frederick Francis granted equal rights to the Jews, but under the influence of the Junkers the law was suspended as early as 1817. The Jews were again deprived of their right to practise handicrafts and forbidden to settle in such trade centers as Rostock and Wismar. A thorn in the side of the Junkers, however, was Israel Jacobson (1768-1828), the philanthropist and reformer who, having bought an estate in Mecklenburg, was entitled to a seat and vote in the diet. In 1848 the emancipation of the Mecklenburg Jews was reestablished through the adoption of the constitution of the Frankfort Parliament

by the two duchies, but this freedom lasted for only two years. During the 1860's while their almost medieval oppression continued, the Jews found strong advocates of their rights in the persons of the Mecklenburg deputies Wiggers and Prosch. Only the union of Mecklenburg with the North German Federation (1869) and, subsequently, the adoption of the Constitution of the German Empire (1871), put the Mecklenburg Jews on the same level with the rest of German Jewry.

Although small in number, Mecklenburg Jewry played a certain role in the history of Jewish assimilation. When, in 1772, the duke of Mecklenburg ordered his Jews not to bury their dead before the third day, contrary to the Jewish usage, the Jews requested Rabbi Jacob Emden of Altona to explain to the authorities that this exposure of the corpse would be against the law. Emden referred them to Moses Mendelssohn, who was well-known in Christian circles, but the philosopher agreed with the ducal order. More widespread were the controversies between Orthodoxy and the Reform Movement, when Samuel Holdheim championed the reformist views as the chief rabbi of Mecklenburg (1840-47). He was followed by an even more radical reformer, David Einhorn, whose views regarding Hebrew and circumcision were opposed so strongly by Orthodoxy that, in 1851, the government had to appoint an Orthodox rabbi.

A well-known scholar was Jacob Hamburger, who served as chief rabbi of Mecklenburg-Strelitz from 1859 until his death in 1911. He was author of the *Realencyclopaedie für Bibel und Talmud* (Strelitz, 1862 et seq.) The most famous Jew of Mecklenburg, however, was the German lexicographer, Daniel Sanders (1819-97), who from 1842 to 1852 was principal of the Jewish school at his native Alt-Strelitz, where he had studied in his youth.

When the Nazis came to power, the Jews in the provinces suffered even more than their coreligionists in the large cities under the anti-Jewish legislation and at the hands of the mob. Yet despite the flight of some Mecklenburg Jews to Berlin and other cities with large Jewish communities and the emigration of others to foreign countries, small Jewish communities existed up to November, 1938. During the pogroms of that month the synagogues in Mecklenburg were destroyed, scrolls of the Law publicly burned and many Jewish men interned in concentration camps. A few Jews were still living in Mecklenburg in 1939, but by 1942 practically all had left the province.   ALFRED WERNER.

Lit.: Donath, L., *Geschichte der Juden in Mecklenburg* (1874); Silberstein, S., "Familiennamen der Juden unter Berücksichtigung der gesetzlichen Festlegung in Mecklenburg," *Festschrift zum 75 jährigen Bestehen des Jüdisch-Theologischen Seminars,* vol. 2 (1929); idem, "Die Stellung Preussens und Mecklenburgs zum Artikel XIV der Deutschen Bundesakte," *Festschrift zum 70. Geburtstage Martin Philippsons* (1916).

MECKLER, DAVID L., editor, b. Vilna, Lithuania, 1891. He came to the United States in 1907 and was educated in Boston. Later he studied journalism at Columbia University. Meckler's first literary work was published in the *Yiddisher Advokat* (Boston); in 1911 and 1912 he was editor of the *Jewish Weekly* in Boston, a publication which appeared in both Yiddish and English. Coming to New York city in 1913, Meckler joined the staff of the *Varheit,* where he remained until

Medal of Rabbi Eliezer ben Samuel Schmelka struck on the occasion of his installation at Amsterdam in 1735

Medal of Moses and Judith Montefiore engraved (1864) by Hayim Wiener

Medal of Joseph von Werth-eimer issued (1867) upon his retirement from the presidency of the Kultusgemeinde, Vienna

1918. In 1918 he became affiliated with the *Morning Journal,* of which he later became editor, still holding that post in 1942.

Meckler, who is known also under the pseudonym Ben Shloima, was the author of *Miracle Men,* Hasidic tales in English (1936); *Fun Rebens Hoif,* Hasidic tales in Yiddish (2 vols., 1932); *The Truth About Henry Ford* (Yiddish; 1924); and *Machine and Men in Soviet Russia* (Yiddish; 1935).

MEDALIE, GEORGE ZERDIN, lawyer and civic worker, b. New York city, 1883. He received his LL.B. degree from Columbia University in 1907, and established himself in the practice of law in New York city the same year. From 1910 to 1915 he was assistant district attorney of New York county; from 1931 to 1933 he was United States attorney for the southern district of New York. At various other times he served gratuitously in special and important legal capacities; he was, for instance, a special assistant attorney general in election fraud investigations (1926-28) and in census prosecutions (1928). In 1932 Medalie was a candidate for the United States Senate on the Republican ticket.

Medalie was one of the most active members of the New York community in Jewish affairs. He was for many years a trustee of the Federation of Jewish Philanthropic Societies of New York city; in 1941 he was elected its president, and was reelected in 1942. He was also a member of the executive committee of the American Jewish Committee, and (in 1931) president of the Jewish Board of Guardians. Medalie was co-chairman of the United Palestine Appeal for Greater New York in 1941. He was president of the New York County Lawyers' Association and of the Columbia Law Association.

CARRIE K. MEDALIE (b. New York city), wife of George Zerdin Medalie, was in 1938 appointed by Mayor Fiorello H. LaGuardia to the Board of Higher Education of New York city.

Lit.: *American Hebrew,* Sept. 30, 1932, p. 388; *New Palestine,* Jan. 23, 1942, pp. 22-23.

MEDALS. The earliest medals coined by or for Jews were probably struck in the 15th cent. One of the first known is the great brass medal struck in 1504 by the Jews of Rome in honor of Pope Julius II, who immediately on his accession imposed restrictions on the Spanish Inquisition. This medal, now in the Bibliothèque Nationale at Paris, was discovered in Lyon in 1654 and, owing to its peculiar Hebrew text, was,

Medal of the Glockengasse synagogue at Cologne, wrought upon its dedication

Medal issued to commemorate the opening of the Jewish orphan asylum for boys at Amsterdam in 1865

until comparatively recently, a diversely interpreted riddle. More recent researches have shown that Benjamin ben Beer, whose name is mentioned on the medal, was not its author; it was rather dedicated to him because he had rendered some services in connection with the pope's edict. The image on the medal is not that of the pope, but the laurel-crowned head of a Roman emperor, possibly Augustus. The Eli Romi mentioned in the text is probably that of the Jewish artist; this is doubtful, since the numerous errors found in the inscription suggest that the medal may not have been struck by Jews.

The portrait medals of Elijah and Rica Delatas (Lattes), dated in 1552, and one of Gracia Mendesia, engraved in 1556 by Paolo Poggini of Ferrara, have also been preserved. Three medals of the 17th cent.

memorializing events of Jewish interest are extant. The number of such medals increased rapidly in the 18th cent. and in the 19th many medals were struck to commemorate events affecting the Jews, or the consecration of synagogues and philanthropic institutions, or to celebrate the installation or jubilee of a ruler. Other medals are in the nature of amulets, containing Cabalistic charms, the Tashlich prayer or a prayer for a safe journey; there are medals for circumcision and Bar Mitzvah.

Fewer medals have been struck in the 20th cent. On the other hand, Jewish organizations, periodicals and fraternities have adopted the custom of awarding medals to individuals for meritorious services to Jews or to Jews who have shed luster on the name Jew during a current year.

Among the Jews who coined such medals or were important as engravers and designers were Jean Henri Simon, Abraham Heilbut, Jacob Abraham and his son Abraham Abrahamson, Jacob, Leopold and Charles Wiener, Stern, the two Griliches, Ascher Wappenstein, J. Elion, Arthur Soldi, Victor David Brenner, Benno Elkan and Arnold Zadikow.

Samuel Friedenberg, of New York city, was in 1942 the outstanding collector of Jewish medals in the United States.

Lit.: Hoffmann, C. Tassilo, *55 Jahre Berliner Medaillenkunst (1755-1810)* (1928); Wolf, Albert, in *Jewish Encyclopedia,* vol. 8, pp. 401-5 (giving a list of medals up to 1904).

MEDEBA, Transjordanian city, now Madeba, south of Heshbon, in Palestine. Originally settled by the tribe of Reuben (*Num.* 21:30; *Josh.* 13:9, 16), it was subjugated in Omri's reign by Mesha, king of Moab (Moabite Stone 7, 29; cf. *Isa.* 15:2). The city is mentioned in *I Chron.* 19:7 as the camp of the Ammonites and Arameans in the war against David. John Hyrcanus (135-104 B.C.E.) regained possession of the city for the Jews (*I Macc.* 9:36; Josephus, *Antiquities,* book 13, chap. 9, section 1), although many of the original Arabian (or Nabatean) inhabitants probably remained there. The history of the city thereafter is almost totally unknown. Some 300 years later the Jewish inhabitants of Medeba brought a question of religious law to Rabbi Ishmael in Judea for solution (*Mik.* 7:1). Christianity took root quickly in the city, as is evidenced by the remains of basilicas of the Byzantine period. In one of the churches in 1896 a portion of a remarkable map of Palestine in the form of a floor-mosaic was discovered. The map, based partly on the Onomasticon (Palestinian index of place-names) of the church father Eusebius, nevertheless reveals independent knowledge of the country and of Egypt on the southern border. Of particular interest are the mosaic vignettes adjoining the Greek names of the towns, vignettes which attempt to portray the localities in question.

Lit.: Musil, *Moab,* 123; Jacoby, *Das geographische Mosaik von Madeba;* Klein, *Eber Hayarden Hayehudi,* 6, 34.

MEDEM, VLADIMIR, Socialist leader and author, b. Libau, Latvia, 1879; d. New York city, 1923. His father was a Russian army doctor, and although his parents had not yet officially abandoned the Jewish faith at the time of his birth, Medem was baptized at once. In

Minsk, however, which was the family's home city, Medem became attracted to the Jewish tradition and languages. While studying at the University of Kiev he was converted to Socialism. In 1900 he combined this new belief with his return to Jewishness, and joined the Bund, the Jewish Socialist organization. When he was arrested for Socialist activities in Minsk (1901), he classified himself as a Jew.

Sentenced to Siberia for five years, Medem escaped to Bern, Switzerland, where he soon became involved in the workers' movement, particularly in its Jewish aspects. In 1903 he was made a member of the foreign committee of the Bund, and moved to Geneva, its headquarters. He attended several congresses of the Bund, and was chairman for most of the sixth congress (Zurich, 1905). During this period, also, he wrote a lengthy brochure on Social Democracy and Nationalism which eventually appeared (1906) in both Yiddish and Russian.

Returning to Russia in 1905, Medem settled in Vilna, where he became co-editor of *Nashe Slovo,* Russian organ of the Bund. In his articles for this publication, and in speeches and literary work elsewhere, he defended the pro-nationalist group within the Bund ranks. His affiliation with Jewish life had in the meantime grown deeper. He had started to learn Yiddish several years before. In 1910 he made his first speech in Yiddish; in 1913 he wrote his first article in that language. Eventually he became a splendid Yiddish stylist and a master orator; he was also, because of his charm, one of the most beloved leaders in the Jewish Socialist movement.

In 1913 he was sentenced, in Warsaw, to four years in prison. Ill health forced his transfer to the prison hospital, from which he was freed in 1915, after the evacuation of Warsaw by the Russians. During the German occupation Medem devoted himself to the cause of Socialist agitation and to the propagation of Jewish culture. He sponsored petitions to the German government for making Yiddish the official language of the Jews, and was active in the maintenance of Jewish schools. Medem came to the United States in 1921, and remained there until his death, writing and speaking on behalf of the Bund. He wrote regularly for the *Forverts.* Among his published works were his memoirs, *Zichroines un Artikeln* (1917); *Fun Mein Notizbuch* (1920) and *Fun Mein Leben,* an autobiography in two volumes (1923). Many cultural and welfare institutions were named after Medem, including a preventorium for tuberculous children in Poland—destroyed by the Germans with heavy loss of life during the first days of the war in 1939.   NATHAN RICARDO.

Lit.: Reisen, Z., *Lexikon fun der Yiddisher Literatur, Presse un Filologie,* vol. 2 (1930), cols. 441-50; *Encyclopaedia of the Social Sciences,* vol. 10 (1933) 271.

MEDGYES, LADISLAS (LÁSZLÓ), painter, stage designer and art critic, b. Budapest, 1892. He first exhibited at Budapest in 1917, and published a map of figures and book illustrations. After 1919 he traveled and painted in Tunisia and Italy, and finally made Paris his home. He exhibited in the Salon of 1924 and subsequently in several private showings. In 1925 he was art director of the Beriza Theatre, where he employed partly painted and partly plastic stage designs. He founded and directed a school of stagecraft. An analytic and speculative tendency is revealed in his paintings, landscapes, sports and street scenes by decomposition of space as well as by graphic handling of form. His later work, such as *Boats* (1932), is rendered more complete and satisfying by pictorial and compositional qualities. His paintings were shown in the United States in 1925 (New York Gallery) and 1927 (Sterner Galleries, New York city), and in 1925 the Theatre Guild exhibited his stage and theatre models. Medgyes was art editor of *International Studio* and the *American Hebrew,* and in 1927 was a guest lecturer at American universities.

Lit.: Reproductions of Medgyes' paintings in *Revue de l'Art antique et moderne, Bulletin de l'Art,* July 29, 1927, p. 295; Jan., 1933, p. 22; *Magyar müvészet* (1926) 149; Waldemar, G., "Ladislas Medgyes, Versatile Artist," *American Hebrew,* Aug. 27, 1926, p. 427; Rittenberg, Louis, "A Poet in Glass," *ibid.,* Nov. 4, 1927, pp. 900-22.

MEDIA, an extensive district in northern Iran, formerly either an independent kingdom or an Assyrian tributary; its capital was Ecbatana (Hamadan). It is mentioned as one of the places to which the Assyrians transported the Israelites after the fall of Samaria (721 B.C.E.). About the middle of the next century the Medians threw off the Assyrian yoke, and it is probable that the Israelites there were augmented by Judeans who drifted eastward from Babylonia after the destruction of the First Temple and exile to Mesopotamia. About 550 B.C.E. Cyrus the Great incorporated Media into the Persian Empire, of which it was a leading province. The cities of Ecbatana and Rhagae (now Teheran) were flourishing and had large Jewish communities; the story of *Tobit* is laid in Media. Many Jews remained in the region as late as the Middle Ages. There is a report of the "free Jews" who lived in the mountainous regions to the north of the country and were unwilling to pay taxes to their rulers. These mountain Jews seem to have taken part in the Messianic movements of Abu Isa Isfahani (about 685) and David Alroy (about 1160).

MEDIATION and MEDIATOR. Mediation is the doctrine that the will of God is effected in the world and that God is approached by man, not directly, but through an agent or agents. This doctrine derives from the concept of God as so transcendent in His nature that the gap between Him and man and between Him and the created world can not be bridged except through an intermediary or intermediaries.

In Judaism, the strict monotheism which was the keystone of the Mosaic religion found no contradiction between the concept of a deity who was at once the sovereign of the universe and at the same time near to the individual (*Deut.* 10:17-18; *Isa.* 57:15; *Ps.* 68:5-7). This resolution is expressed in rabbinic writings in the statement in *Meg.* 31a: "Wherever you find God's power mentioned there, too, do you find His humility mentioned."

At the same time, man's ability to approach God through prayer is considered an essential part of Jewish doctrine (*1 Kings* 8:27-53). The finest rabbinical formulation of this idea is found in *Yer. Ber.* 13a, at the bottom: "If a man has a patron, when a time of trouble comes upon him, he does not at once enter into his patron's presence, but comes and stands at the door of his house and calls one of the servants or a member of the family, who brings word to him, 'So and so is standing at the entrance of court.' Perhaps the patron will let him in, perhaps he will make him wait. Not so God. If trouble comes upon a man, let him not cry to Michael or to Gabriel; but let him cry unto Me, and I will answer him forthwith, as the Scripture says: 'Whosoever shall call on the name of the Lord shall be delivered (*Joel* 3:5).'"

It is evident, however, from this last statement that there was a system of angelology in Judaism and that a place was found for intermediaries between God and man. In some cases the agent was merely a favored human being, such as Moses and the prophets. Thus Abraham acted as mediator between God and Abimelech (*Gen.* 20:7, 17; 18:23-33), Moses between God and Pharaoh and the Egyptians (*Ex.* 8:5-8, 24-26; 9:28-33) and also between God and Israel (*Ex.* 17:11; 32:10; *Deut.* 9:18). The prophets, too, acted as mediators or messengers of God to Israel and to the nations. In other cases the agent was a subordinate member of the celestial court, a *mal'ach* or messenger. Thus the *mal'ach* of God leads Israel (*Ex.* 23:20, 23; 33:15), appears to the parents of Samson (*Judges* 13:3-5), and speaks to the prophets (*Zech.* 1:9-17). In Biblical times, these latter agents were not invested with proper names or special functions, but merely acted as God's messengers or envoys who executed God's will in the world. In later times they assume more specific roles, for not only are God's revelations communicated through them, and not only do they act providentially and in history, but also the forces of nature are controlled by them. The Hellenistic period was the golden age of this angelology. But even these *angeloi* are at first only messengers or watchmen. It is in this period, however, that they become for the first time personified angels instead of impersonal messengers. In spite of this development no "'doctrine of angels" was evolved and "the religious importance of Jewish notions and imaginations about the angelic hierarchy, its occupation in heaven, and its commissions on earth, is in small proportion to their abundance" (Moore, George Foote, *Judaism,* vol. 1, p. 410). "The angel mythology of Judaism is a naive way of imagining the mediation of God's word and will in the universe by personal agents. They are not, like the good demons in the later phases of Neoplatonism, the product of an abstract or transcendent idea of God, but of one naively personal, and they do not consciously infringe upon the belief in His omnipresence or omniscience" (*ibid.,* vol. 1, pp. 404-5).

Still another development of the idea of mediation is to be found in Jewish thinking. The separation between the transcendent deity and the material world was especially emphasized in Hellenistic thought. Under this Neo-Platonic influence which required a necessary intermediary between God and the world, Philo of Alexandria introduced the concept of the logos, which was in a sense a "secondary deity," or divine intermediary. This new development was accepted to a degree in Hellenistic Jewish circles and became the foundation of certain Christian doctrines, at a later date. However, the main stream of rabbinic Judaism never took over this philosophic interpretation, this in spite of the fact that a persistent effort has been made to read such a doctrine into the Targumic use of such words as *memra, yekara, shechinta, pithgam,* and the like, which were nothing more than circumlocutions that sought to avoid literal rendition of phrases detracting from the dignity of God.

In Christianity this doctrine of the divine mediator was transformed into that of "the first-created Son of God" who, in the further development of Christian thought, became the second member of the trinity, the incarnate word of God (*John* 1:1 et seq.; cf. also *Hebrews* and *Colossians*). Judaism, with its strict and uncompromising monotheism, rejected any attempt either to separate God from the world or to infringe upon His simple unity, and thus the Hellenistic philosophizing about the nature of Jesus helped to make the breach between Judaism and its daughter religion complete. Further, for Judaism the Messiah might be "a wiser and better and greater king than was ever seen, but he was not a supernatural being"; he was a man, not a divine mediator.

In summary the words of George Foote Moore are definitive: "The agencies which God employs to manifest his presence or convey his revelation, or execute his will, whether personal or impersonal, may in this function be called intermediaries, as Moses is called an intermediary in the giving of the Law; but not 'mediator' in the sense which we commonly attach to the word" (*Judaism,* vol. 1, p. 438). While the Cabala contains many indications of a doctrine of mediation such did not become dominant in Jewish thought.

Modern Judaism has been true to the pure stream of rabbinic tradition and has consistently refused to acknowledge any doctrine in which mediation or a mediator between God and man is necessary (Kohler, Kaufmann, *Jewish Theology,* pp. 204-5; Schechter, Solomon, *Some Aspects of Rabbinic Theology,* chap. 2).

See also: ANGELS; LOGOS.   LOU H. SILBERMAN, JR.

Lit.: Kohler, Kaufmann, *Jewish Theology* (1928) 180-88, 197-205; Moore, George Foote, *Judaism in the First Centuries of the Christian Era,* vol. 1 (1932) 364-65, 401-42; Schechter, Solomon, *Some Aspects of Rabbinic Theology* (1909) 21-45.

MEDICI, PAOLO (known also as Paolo Sebastiano), convert. He was baptized in Livorno at the age of sixteen. Before his conversion his name was Israel Meir Leon. In 1692 he was appointed professor of Hebrew at the University of Florence. In his travels through Italy Medici preached Christianity to the Jews and succeeded in converting the two rabbis, Nicolo Stratto and Sabbatai Nahum of Ancona. He wrote a book on the rites and customs of the Jews, the publication of which the Jewish community of Rome (under the leadership of the energetic Rabbi Tranquillo Vito Corcos) managed to prevent (1697). It appeared, however, in Florence in 1736 (*Riti e costumi degli ebrei descritti e confutati dal dott. Paolo Medici*), had a wide circulation and was often reprinted.

MEDICINE. 1. In the Bible. The occasional references to health and to disease found in the Bible are hardly sufficient to form a satisfactory conception of the state of medical knowledge and practice among the Jews in the first thousand years of their existence. They neither warrant sweeping claims of advanced medical knowledge among the Jews of ancient times nor support the assertions of critics that the Israelites of old were a rude, uncultured people with no medical science whatsoever. The Bible is a book of law, history, prophetic utterances, hymns and the like, and seldom goes into explicit details as to the life and customs to which it alludes. Its references to medicine, scattered and fragmentary as they are, must be studied carefully and evaluated both in the light of contemporary civilizations and of modern medical knowledge.

The very earliest texts of the Hebrew Bible mention the activities of professional physicians, dressers of wounds, midwives and pharmacists, pointing to an advanced state of culture. It is not surprising that Joseph, as viceroy of Egypt, had physicians in attendance (*Gen.* 50:2), as Egyptian medicine was of high repute from time immemorial. Yet even the earliest legislation contains the explicit direction that among the damages to be paid for an assault is medical treatment (*verappo yerappe; Ex.* 21:19), which would indicate the presence of professional physicians able to treat ordinary injuries. King Asa of Judah (915-875 B.C.E.) is recorded in the Bible as being "diseased in his feet until higher up" (was his disease): "yet in his disease he sought not to the Lord, but to the physicians" (*II Chron.* 16:12). This ailment, which spread from the feet upward, may have been a form of gangrene: senile (he lived to a high old age), traumatic (he participated in many battles), diabetic, thrombotic, a spreading infection (cellulitis, erysipelas) or, as the Talmud states (*Sótah* 10a), podagra (gout). The outstanding implications of the statement are that about 450 years before Hippocrates the people of Judah had professional physicians who practised rational therapeutics and were so detached from magic and religion that they are mentioned in direct contrast to God. Jeremiah, in the 6th cent. C.E., describing the distress of the people, bursts out with the exclamation: "Is there no balm in Gilead? Is there no physician there? Why then is not the health of the daughter of my people recovered?" (*Jer.* 8:22). Job compares his false friends to worthless physicians (13:4).

Isaiah's advice to apply "a cake of figs" to the "boil" of the dying King Hezekiah (*II Kings* 20:7) and the subsequent success of this treatment appear quite rational, as the boil was probably a furuncle on the face, threatening an invasion of the cavernous sinus, or a carbuncle on the neck, causing excruciating pain and liable to develop into septicemia. A poultice or hot fomentation of figs would be likely to diminish the pain, bring the boil to a head and cause evacuation of pus.

A great help to the secularization of medical practice in ancient Israel was the unusually severe legislation against the practice of magic, sorcery, witchcraft and divination, either by the consulting of the dead, or any other form. Professional midwives are mentioned on more than one occasion in the Bible. The art of the compounder (*rokeah*), which includes that of the pharmacist, is mentioned on more than one occasion (as in *Ex.* 30:25, 35). There are frequent references to spices such as balm of Gilead, ladanum, myrrh, cinnamon, calamus, cassia, aloes and henna, many of which are still in use in medical preparations.

The acquaintance of the ancient Hebrews with the fundamentals of animal and human anatomy is evidenced by the numerous references in the Bible to the internal and external organs of the body. The animal sacrifices in the Temple required a preliminary inspection, since blemishes (*Lev.* 22:22-24) disqualified the offering. Similarly, the priests could not serve if they had certain blemishes (*Lev.* 21:18-20; the rabbis expand this list by subdivision until the total number of blemishes is 140). The human corpse was regarded as the chief cause of uncleanliness by contagion, and hence to be dreaded and avoided. As bones last longer, particularly in the dry desert climate, they were considered a continuous menace to cleanliness (*Num.* 19:16).

The chief diseases mentioned in the Bible are those of the skin and the sexual organs. The references to skin diseases are chiefly in *Leviticus* (13:2-46), to which is appended a list of appearances (probably fungoid growths) on garments (*Lev.* 13:47-49) and on the walls of houses (14:34-53). Many hold that the *tzara'ath* of the Bible is not leprosy but psoriasis; in fact the Greek word *lepra* really denoted psoriasis.

The diseases of the sexual organs are described as discharges and secretions from the genital organs, such as the menstrual flow (*niddah*), hemorrhage between periods, gonorrheal issue (*zob*) and spermatorrhea (*shichebath zera*). The Biblical regulations about menstruation and childbirth have been praised by many modern hygienists. The other running issues are clearly venereal, and the isolation of such patients was a remarkable measure of preventive medicine.

Most of the dietary regulations of the Bible can stand the scrutiny of modern dietetics, if considered in the light of the times in which they were promulgated. The danger of trichinosis is greatest in the flesh of swine (forbidden in *Lev.* 11:7). Aquatic animals unendowed with means of locomotion (such as those mentioned in *Lev.* 11:10) are apt to be dangerous if they inhabit stagnant, contaminated waters.

Though circumcision acquired a religious significance as a sign of the covenant between God and Israel, it likewise possesses a great medical value in preventing phimosis, paraphimosis, balanoposthitis, adherent and redundant prepuces and the serious, even fatal, diseases that often develop from them (balanitis, calculi, epithelioma, gangrene, priapism and papillomata). In most modern hospitals, including those which are non-Jewish, circumcision is performed as routine on newborn boys.

There are two interesting lists of maladies in the Bible, both of which occur in denunciations—an example of the accidental way in which medical items appear in the Bible. The description of the calamities that will befall Israel if they are disobedient, as given in *Lev.* 26:14-41, contains both physical and mental ailments: consumption, fever, pestilence, terror, languish, delusions of persecution and nervous exhaustion. The parallel denunciation in *Deut.* 28:15-68 repeats these and adds inflammation, burns, jaundice, Egyptian rash, scab, eczema, psoriasis, blindness, angina pectoris, confusion, insanity and depression.

From these gleanings in the Bible it can be clearly seen that the ancient Jews observed rational and effective sanitary laws, and that their health was watched over by professional physicians whose methods were exclusively rational.

2. In Talmudic Literature. The extensive literature that developed in the centuries following the closing of the Bible canon contains even more medical detail, proportionately, than does the Bible, and shows a still more advanced state of medical knowledge. As in the case of the Bible, the references to medicine in the

Talmud are scattered in a mass of literature and are by no means a complete picture. However, enough can be gathered to show that the Jews of Talmudic times were fully abreast of and in some cases ahead of the medical knowledge of the day.

There is abundant evidence to show that the profession of physician was widely followed and was held in high esteem. There are references to general practitioners, internists, psychiatrists (*Sanh.* 75a), oculists (*B.M.* 89b), dentists (*Kid.* 24b), gynecologists (*Nid.* 47a), obstetricians and surgeons (*Arach.* 7b and other passages). Physicians were consulted in questions of damage sustained by assault, and to determine the amount of flagellation a culprit could bear. There was a physician in the Temple to treat the ailments of the priests (*Shek.* 5:1-2). Simeon ben Halafta experimented on fowls (*Hul.* 57b), Assi on ravens (*Midrash Lev.* 19:1), and Simeon on the hoopoe (*Yer. Ber.* v, 9b). Mar Samuel was a noted physician and devised methods of examining the contents of his own stomach (*Ned.* 50b). The pupils of Ishmael are recorded to have boiled the body of a dead prostitute to determine the number of bones (*Bech.* 45a). In addition, the various regulations as to defilement from corpses, leprosy, menstruation and the like called for medical knowledge on the part of those who interpreted the Law.

The following is a summary of some of the teachings of the Talmudic rabbis in various fields of medicine:

Anatomy: The Skeletal System. The human body was said to consist of 613 parts, of which 248 were "limbs" (*'ebarim*) and 365 sinews (*gidim*; *Targum Pseudo-Jonathan* to *Gen.* 1:27). Limbs were defined as a part of the body containing a bone covered by flesh; an enumeration is made in *Ohal.* 1:8, which compares favorably with the medical knowledge of the time, while the excess in number is probably due to a separate enumeration of what modern anatomy regards as parts of the same bone. The exact meaning of *gidim* is not clear, but it probably refers to sinews, nerves and blood-vessels.

The Digestive System. The Talmud mentions various types of teeth, such as molars (*metale'oth*), canines (*kakim*) and bicuspids (*mat'imoth*). The pharynx (*beth habeli'ah*) passes into the esophagus (*veshet*), consisting of two layers (*'oroth*), the external, reddish one containing elastic fibres (*Hul.* 43b). The teachers even noticed the minute internal papillae (*melath*, "down"). Other parts mentioned are the stomach, small intestine, ileum, colon, rectum and anus. The Talmudic teachers were acquainted with salivary action (*Midrash Ex.* 29).

Respiratory System. The Talmud shows a good knowledge of the parts of the respiratory system, such as the larynx (*garon*), the trachea (*gargereth, kaneh*), the thyroid cartilage (*koba'*) and its parts. The trachea was noted as consisting of rings (*hulyoth*) held together by muscular fibres. The lungs are called *re'ah*, and their parts are described. In the pleura (*keruma*) the Talmudical teachers distinguish between a visceral (*tata'ah*) and a costal (*'ila'ah*) layer. They describe the diaphragm (*tarpeshta*); the term is also used for the pericardium.

Circulatory System. The Talmud dwells at length on the functions of the heart and describes its structure. The organ is correctly placed toward the left of the body (*Men.* 37a); larger and smaller cavities, i.e. auricles and ventricles, are distinguished (*Hul.* 45b), and Nahman speaks of "tubes" connecting the heart with the lungs, liver and other parts of the body. The aorta is called the "tube of the heart." The terms used for blood vessels are *'orek* and *verid*, meaning "vein" and "artery," respectively. The spleen (*tehol*) is mentioned frequently, and it is described with its convex part (*dad*), its capsule (*kerum*) and its hylus vessels (*huttin*; *Hul.* 23a). Splenectomy was known (*Sanh.* 21b).

Blood, as in the Bible, was regarded as the seat of the soul. It keeps man warm while he is asleep (*Midrash Gen.* 13). Abba Saul makes the observation that the amount of blood (one-fourth of a *log*) from a corpse considered as defiling is precisely enough to maintain life in a viable foetus of seven months' gestation (*Tos. Ohal.* 3). According to one statement, blood is composed of "water" and blood proper (*Midrash Lev.* 15), a division similar to the modern division into plasma and solid parts. An enumeration is made of the various shades of menstrual blood, and of seven reagents to determine whether a stain is that of human blood or a dye (*Nid.* 19ab; 9:6; 62a-63a).

Nervous System. The Talmud refers to the brain (*moah*) and the spinal cord (*hut hashidrah*). The parting between the cerebrum and the spinal cord was known as the "two beans," i.e. the occipital condyles (*Hul.* 45ab). Of the membranes of the brain, the Talmud speaks of the dura (*keruma 'ila'ah*) and pia mater (*tata'ah*); the arachnoid was not distinguished. The fontanel (in infants) was described as the place where the brain "pulsates and is compressible" (*Men.* 37a). The brain was regarded as the seat of the intelligence (*Men.* 80b), and the brain and the spinal cord as interdependent (*Midrash de Rabbi Nehunya* 9:10). What might be the earliest connection of paralysis with a spinal lesion is mentioned in the Talmud when the hind legs of a calf were paralyzed and Rabina suggested a lesion in the spinal cord subsequently verified by an autopsy (*Hul.* 51a).

Genito-Urinary System. The kidneys were regarded as controlling the emotions. The Talmud distinguished in them the hilum (*haritz*) and the pelvis (*hivra detoti*), as well as "dense" and "soft" parts. Cases of solitary and supernumerary kidneys are mentioned (*Bech.* 39ab).

The genitalia are referred to by many expressions, mainly euphemisms or metaphors. The Talmud states that there are separate canals for the sperm and the urine, separated by a membrane as thin as the skin of an onion (*Yeb.* 75b-76a), a notion which survived in European anatomies until the time of Vesalius (16th cent.). Many anomalies are described, such as the hermaphrodite ('*androginos*) and the cryptorchitic (*tumtum*); the latter could be made normal by an operation (*Yeb.* 83b). Mar Samuel decided that a man with only one testicle could still propagate (*Yeb.* 75a). The Talmud distinguished between surgical and congenital castrates (*Yeb.* 8:4), and describes such malformations as hypospadia and epispadia, or unusual conditions in regard to the prepuce. There are references to the testicles, the scrotum, and the spermatic cords. Each testicle is described as having its proper tunics, the albuginea and vaginalis (*Hul.* 45a). The method of determining whether a substance noted was semen or the white of an egg was that of heating (*Git.* 57a). The Jewish teachers, with Aristotle, thought that the sperm emanates from the brain (*Midrash de Rabbi Nehunya* 51a).

The Talmud uses euphemistic terms in speaking of the female genitalia: "chamber," "anti-chamber" and "upper chamber," which probably refer to the vagina, the external genitalia and the womb, respectively. The Talmudic teachers' knowledge of female anatomy was very confused.

Embryology: The Talmud is well aware that all human beings are the product of the union of male and female (*Midrash Gen.* 8). The male is credited with giving the foundation to the nerves and the skeletal tissues, while all the rest comes from the female (*Nid.* 31b). It is noted that blind and crippled parents produce normal children (*Hul.* 69a), i.e. that acquired characteristics are not inherited. Conception is held to take place either just before or after menstruation (*Nid.* 31a). The role of the umbilical vessels in the nourishment of the foetus is indicated by Abba Saul, who states that the foetus develops from the umbilicus in both directions (*Yoma* 85a). The bones are held to be the last part of the body to develop (*Midrash Gen.* 14); until the fortieth day of gestation the embryo is in fluid form (*Yeb.* 69b). The human embryo is described as being at first like a locust, its two eyes wide apart and like two dots, its extremities like threads, and its shape oval like a lentil (*Nid.* 25a). Another description is that the embryo lies folded, with its hands on its temples, its elbows touching its thighs, its heels touching its buttocks, and its head between its knees. It derives all nourishment from the umbilicus and all the orifices are closed (*Nid.* 30b-31a; *Midrash Song of Songs* 7).

Pathology: The dominating view in the Talmud is that a disease involves changes in structure and that its immedi-

ate cause is a physical agent. There is emphasis on dietetics and sound mental and physical habits to guard against disease. Headache is related to poor sight (*Midrash Lev.* 6), exposure (*ibid.* 19), alcoholism (*Yalkut Shimeoni* 873) and menstruation (*Nid.* 63a). Eye diseases may be caused by the touch of unclean hands (*Sab.* 108b). Heavy meals may be injurious in a cardiac condition (*Hul.* 59a). It is noted that the eating of unclean fruits or drinking of impure water may introduce parasites into the body (*Sab.* 90a). These are but a few examples of seeking rational rather than mystical explanations of disease.

Therapeutics: The Talmud contains a great deal of folk medicine, but a far greater number of rational remedies. A noteworthy statement is to the effect that a remedy which is good for one man is not necessarily beneficial to another (*Pes.* 113a). Special diets, bathing, exercise, fresh air and sunshine, change of environment, avoidance of excitement and worry, and similar rational means of combatting disease and regaining health are described in great detail; herbs and potions play only a minor role.

Surgery: Operative procedures were widely resorted to by the Jews during the Talmudic period. Circumcision was of course universally practised; there were safeguards against possible danger to the child, and in certain cases it was postponed or dispensed with (*Sab.* 134a; *Yeb.* 64b). Amputations were performed to prevent the spread of a malignant tumor, or infections due to wounds (*A.Z.* 10b; *Yer. Nazir* 7:1; *Ker.* 15a). Septic areas in the body were excised (*Hul.* 77a, 121a). Cranial bones were raised to relieve pressure (*Yer. A.Z.* 2:2), and craniectomies were performed to remove cerebral growths (*Keth.* 77b). There is a mention of plastic surgery on the cranium (*Hul.* 77b; *Tos. Ohal.* 2). Operations on the eye were also practised (*Tos. Bech.* 4:2; *Pes.* 65b; *Erub.* 103b). Laparatomies, preceded by a sleeping potion, were successfully performed; the abdominal incisions were sutured (*Hul.* 56b, 57a). Among the surgeons' instruments mentioned are the scalpel, scissors, haemostat and drill (*Aboth de Rabbi Nathan* 23; *Bech.* 38a).

Surgical intervention was also employed in obstetrics and gynecology. There is reference to *yotze dafan* ("going out from the side"), apparently a Caesarean section after the mother had died in childbirth. In other cases, if it was a question of saving either mother or child, the life of the former was considered more important and the child was dissected in the womb and brought out piecemeal.

Nervous and Mental Diseases: The Talmud associates paralysis with nerve injury (*Hul.* 51a). It distinguishes between congenital feeble-mindedness and insanity which develops in a normal person, and notes that certain insane persons have periods of normalcy. Descriptions of the behavior of the insane show keen observation, the characteristics noted including rambling, seclusiveness, destructiveness, inability to take care of one's self, lack of insight, incapacity to concentrate and the like. A disease called *kardiakos* is mentioned, a sort of temporary seizure, as well as *ruah tezazith*, a sort of shaking; these may be forms of epilepsy. During such a seizure a convulsion involves the arms and legs, the mind is confused, there may be an impulse to arson, destructiveness or assault (possibly an epileptoid seizure or a temporary mania). Epilepsy was considered a hereditary disease (*Yeb.* 64a), and was observed in some cases to occur at regular intervals (*Keth.* 77a). The possible causes given for it are only folk medicine. The progress of senile deterioration is likewise observed and described, and study is said to preserve the mind in old age (*Sab.* 152a).

See also: EUGENICS; HYGIENE; PHYSICIANS.

HIRSCH LOEB GORDON.

Lit.: Preuss, Julius, *Biblisch-talmudische Medizin* (1923; second printing, with extensive bibliography); Kazenelenson, J. L., *Hatalmud Vehochmath Harefuah* (1928); Hyrtl, J., *Das Arabische und Hebräische in der Anatomie* (1879); Perlman, M., *Midrash Harefuah* (1928); Masie, A. M., *Dictionary of Medicine and Allied Sciences*, S. Tchernichowsky edit. (1934; with extensive bibliography); Gordon, H. L., *L'anatomia e la fisiologia nella Bibbia, Talmud e la Cabbala* (1934); Meyerhoff, M., articles in *Isis* (1929 and 1938) and *Medical Leaves* (1939); *Harefuah* (Tel-Aviv, 1922 et seq.); *Harofe Haibri* (New York, 1928 et seq.); *Medical Leaves* (1939 et seq.).

MEDIGO, DEL, see Delmedigo.

MEDINA, after Mecca the second holiest city of Islam, situated north of Mecca. Originally named Yathrib, it was later known as Medinat Annabi ("City of the prophet," that is, Mohammed). In the age of Mohammed there were many Jews in Medina, whose ancestors had probably settled there after the first destruction of Jerusalem (586 B.C.E.). It was also probable that, in all later persecutions which the Jewish people suffered, refugees found a haven in Medina. The Jews played a prominent part in the public life of the city. The best-known and most prominent of these were the Banu Kainuka, the Banu Kuraiza and the Banu al-Nadir; the genealogies of the last two indicate them as descendants of Aaron. On his arrival in Medina Mohammed showed himself friendly toward the Jews in the hope of finding followers of his teachings among them. Thus he designated the tenth day of the seventh Jewish month (the 10th of Tishri), on which day he came to Medina, as it is asserted, as a holiday. He ordered worshippers to face Jerusalem in praying. The Jews, however, derided him and his teachings. They entered into discussions with him and showed him the misunderstanding of the Jewish traditions involved in his religious system. This explains the later policy of Mohammed in persecuting the Jews.

Lit.: Wellhausen, J., *Mohammed in Medina (Wakidi)* (1882); Horovitz, J., in *Islamic Culture*, vol. 3, No. 2; Graetz, H., *History of the Jews*, vol. 3 (1927) 59, 67-81.

MEDINA, SAMUEL DI (called RaSHDaM), Talmudic author and scholar, b. 1505; d. Salonika, 1589. He was the head of the Talmudic school of Salonika, from which many distinguished scholars graduated. Medina's works include *Ben Shemuel* (Mantua, 1622), comprising thirty sermons, and *Piske Rashdam* (4 vols., Constantinople, 1550, and Salonika, 1594-97), a compilation of 956 responsa published in its entirety by his son Moses. The latter gave large subsidies for the printing of Hebrew books, and imported typesetters from Venice, some of whom became converted to Judaism.

Lit.: Conforte, D., *Kore Hadoroth* (1846) 34b, 38ab, 39b, 52a; Azulai, H. J. D., *Shem Hagedolim,* vol. 1, p. 79b; Cassel, D., *Lehrbuch der jüdischen Geschichte und Literatur* (1879) 408.

MEDINA, SIR SOLOMON DE ("the Jew Medina"), Anglo-Jewish financier of the first half of the 18th cent. A man of vision and enterprise, he followed William III to England and became one of the greatest army contractors of his day. Medina was the first professing Jew to be knighted. In 1711 he came into prominence on charges preferred against the duke of Marlborough, more or less proved, of having received about £6,000 per annum from Medina during the period that he held the contract for supplying the army with bread and bread wagons. Medina accompanied the duke of Marlborough on all his campaigns, advancing him money, but it was said that he amply repaid himself by his system of expresses, which surpassed those of the government and bore intelligence of victorious battles. He was one of the largest contributors to the Bevis Marks Synagogue.

Lit.: Picciotto, James, *Sketches of Anglo-Jewish History* (1875) 58-59; *Report of Commissioners for Taking,*

Examining and Stating Public Accounts of the Kingdom (1711).

MEDINI, HAYIM HEZEKIAH, rabbi and Talmudist, b. Jerusalem, 1833; d. Hebron, Palestine, 1905. Medini was ordained for the rabbinate in Jerusalem in 1852, and almost at once went to Constantinople, where he was a member of the rabbinical court until 1865. Called to Karasubazar, in the Crimea, he served there for twenty-three years, officiating as rabbi for the native-born Crimean Jews. His achievements in raising their cultural standards were so great that his reputation spread even among the Russian and Tatar populations.

In 1889 Medini returned to Palestine, and from 1891 until his death he was Hacham Bashi of Hebron. Once again his spiritual leadership influenced those outside his immediate sphere; the Mohammedans were so impressed by his piety that they made an effort to have his body transferred from the Jewish to the Mohammedan cemetery. Medini wrote *Michtab Lehizkiyahu* (1863); *Or Li* (1874); and *Pakkuoth Sadeh* (1900). His most important work was *Sede Hemed,* an encyclopedia in eighteen volumes of Jewish laws and ritual responsa, published between 1890 and 1911. The last five volumes appeared after his death.

Lit.: Sokolow, N., *Sefer Hashanah* (Warsaw, 1900); Goldenstein, in *Hatoren*, vol. 11, No. 6, pp. 13-20; *Jewish Encyclopedia*, vol. 8, p. 425; *Yevreiskaya Entziklopedia*, vol. 10, p. 742.

MEGAS, JOSEPH IBN, see Ibn Migas, Joseph ben Meir Halevi.

MEGASTHENES, see Greek Writers on Jews.

MEGIDDO, an ancient Canaanite city at the southwestern edge of the Plain of Jezreel, now represented by the large mound of Tell el-Mutesellim. Although captured by Joshua, according to late Hebrew tradition (*Josh.* 12:21), it was able to maintain its independence

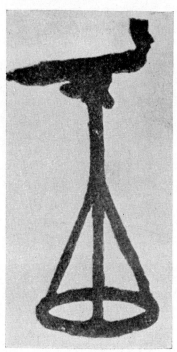

A lamp upon a bronze stand found at Megiddo

Reconstruction of a large building in Solomonic Megiddo

Ruins of one of the Solomonic stables at Megiddo. Reproduced by courtesy of "The Biblical Archaeologist"

of Israel during the period of the Judges (*Judges* 1:27). The Song of Deborah celebrates an Israelite victory over the confederated Canaanites near Megiddo (*Judges* 5). Its last appearance in Biblical history is in connection with the death of Josiah in battle against Pharaoh-necho (*II Kings* 23:29; *II Chron.* 35:22), a catastrophe which made a profound impression on the Jewish people, and which seems to underlie the myth of the great battle of Armageddon at the end of the world.

Excavations were carried on at Tell el-Mutesellim by the German Palestine Society under the direction of Schumacher, from 1903 to 1905. The University of Chicago excavated here from 1925 to 1939 under the successive direction of Fisher, Guy and Loud.

The foundation of the city goes back to the earliest times, probably around 3500 B.C.E., but its greatest importance was in the Middle and Late Canaanite periods. About 1470 B.C.E. it was captured by Pharaoh Thutmose III, after a general Canaanite revolt in which Megiddo played a leading role. It seems to have fallen into Israelite hands in the time of David, whose successor, Solomon, made it capital of one of his twelve administrative districts (*I Kings* 4:12). The excavations have uncovered the ruins of remarkably well-built and arranged stables for horses and chariots, confirming the Biblical statements (*I Kings* 9:15-19). It continued to be a provincial capital after the Assyrian conquest (735 B.C.E.), but lost its importance in the 7th cent. B.C.E. and was abandoned in the 4th cent. B.C.E.

Lit.: Schumacher and Watzinger, *Tell el-Mutesellim,* vols. 1 and 2 (1908 and 1929); Fisher, *The Excavation of Armageddon* (1929); Guy and Engberg, *Megiddo Tombs* (1938); Lamon and Shipton, *Megiddo I* (1939); May and Engberg, *Material Remains of the Megiddo Cult* (1935); Loud, *Megiddo Ivories* (1939).

MEGILLAH ("scroll"), designation for the Biblical book of *Esther*. The term was originally applied to any book written on a roll of animal skin or parchment, and as such it appears in several passages in the Bible (*Jer.* 36:2; *Ezek.* 2:9 and others). Later on a distinction was made between the larger book, *sefer,* and the smaller scroll, *megillah;* the difference being that the *megillah* was formed in a single roll and spread out like a letter. Five books of the Bible are known as Megillahs: *Song of Songs, Ruth, Lamentations, Ecclesiastes* and *Esther;* but as early as the time of the Mishnah the term Megillah, without any other qualification, specifically denoted *Esther*.

Like other Biblical books, *Esther* was read in the synagogue from a special handwritten manuscript, which is also called Megillah. This Megillah is written in the same manner as the scroll of the Torah, in columns of equal width and height and with neither vowels nor punctuation. The directions for writing the Megillah (*Orah Hayim* 691) are for the most part the same as those for writing the Torah; in certain details they are less rigorous, since the scroll was not considered as holy as the Sefer Torah. It differs in appearance from the Sefer Torah in that it is smaller, not mounted upon rollers, and is kept in a single rather than a double roll when not being read.

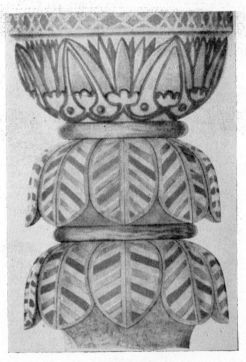

Incense column found during the excavations at Tell el-Mutesellim (1903-05) by the German Palestine Society

Three ornate Megillah containers: (top) from the Ignaz Friedmann collection, Budapest; (center) from the art collection of the Berlin Jewish community; (above) from the Russian Ethnographic Museum, Leningrad

An Augsburg Megillah (below) owned by Ignaz Friedmann, Budapest; (right) page from a Megillah in a Pentateuch manuscript, dated 1238, in the Stadtbibliothek, Breslau

A page from an illustrated Megillah, showing the gallows upon which Haman was hanged. Reproduced by courtesy of the Union of American Hebrew Congregations

The Megillah is read in Orthodox Jewish synagogues on the evening and morning of Purim, in a special mode of cantillation (Niggun). *Esther* 2:5; 8:15-16 and 10:3 are chanted by the congregation and repeated by the reader; 2:6 and 3:15b are chanted in the mode of the elegies (the Echah Niggun); the names of the ten sons of Haman (9:7-9) are recited in a single breath. In many congregations the children are allowed to make a noise with rattles (Hamandreher or Greger) at every mention of the name of Haman. Reform Jewish congregations have modified these customs considerably, frequently omitting all reading of the Megillah, but giving an extract in the vernacular in the Sabbath service preceding Purim. In former times the reading of the Megillah and the blowing of the Shofar on Rosh Hashanah were the only occasions when young girls came to the synagogue; in the former case, this was because of the important role of Esther in the story.

The copies of the Megillah used in the synagogue, like the scrolls of the Torah, were permitted no decorations or pictures in addition to the text. However,

Megillahs intended for private use were frequently illustrated and decorated. The earliest extant examples are from the 16th cent. The roll is sometimes attached to a rod upon which it is wound, and some Megillahs are kept in cases of carved wood, embossed silver or filigree work.

The number of columns into which the text of a Megillah is divided varies, as does the size of the roll and the arrangement of the decorations. These decorations usually consist of a number of frame-shaped openings (portals) enclosing the columns of the text, with figures in between that portray the main protagonists of the Esther story, as well as floral designs and allegorical devices above the portals and a kind of predella with small narrative scenes from the story, at the bottom of the roll. The right hand border of the scroll occasionally bears the signature of the artist and the date of the work, mounted on a decorative shield. Megillahs are extant which are decorated with pen and ink illustrations, wash drawings and engravings, especially with the latter.

The signed Megillahs that are extant include the fragmentary scroll of Andrea Marelli, an engraver known to have worked in 1567-72 in Rome, scrolls by Shalom d'Italia, son of Mordecai, in Amsterdam, one with engravings, and another in pen and ink, dated 1649, in the museum of the Gesellschaft zur Erforschung Jüdischer Kunstdenkmäler. There is a Megillah illustrated with engravings, some of which are copied by Haggadah woodcuts of the 16th cent., executed by J. Franck in Prague about 1700. Another Megillah with engravings is signed by Griselini. There are two Megillahs signed by Aryeh Loeb ben Daniel of Poland, who worked in Venice; one, dated 1745, is in the collection of the Jewish Theological Seminary in New York city, while the other, dated 1748, is at the Hebrew Union College in Cincinnati.

RACHEL BERNSTEIN WISCHNITZER.

Lit.: Kaufmann, D., "Zur Geschichte der jüdischen Handschrift-illustration," in Müller and Schlosser, *Die Haggadah von Sarajewo* (1898); Wolf, A., in *Mitteilungen für jüdische Volkskunde*, vol. 15 (1905); Frauberger, H., in *Mitteilungen der Gesellschaft zur Erforschung jüdischer Kunstdenkmäler*, vols. 5-6 (1909); Kirschstein, S., *Jüdische Graphiker* (1918); Stern, M., "Illustrierte Estherrollen," *Jüdisches Gemeindeblatt, Berlin*, March 4, 1927; Wischnitzer-Bernstein, R., in *Monatsschrift für Geschichte und Wissenschaft des Judentums*, vols. 9 and 10 (1930); Fooner, M., in *Opinion*, March, 1936; Landsberger, F., "Jewish Artists Before the Period of Emancipation," *Hebrew Union College Annual*, vol. 16 (1941).

Silver Megillah container in the collection of Ignaz Friedmann, Budapest

MEGILLATH ANTIOCHUS, *see* Antiochus, Scroll of.

MEGILLATH ECHAH (RABBAH), *see* Midrash Lamentations.

MEGILLATH SETHARIM ("secret roll"). Abba Aricha (3rd cent. C.E.) quotes two Halachic precepts of Ise ben Judah, contemporary of Rabbi, which he found in a Megillath Setharim in the school of Hiyya (*Sab.* 6b; 96b; *B.M.* 92a). Originally there existed a prohibition against writing down oral traditions in order to avoid giving them the finality of written law. According to Rashi, scholars would record in rolls such sentences and precepts of Tannaim as were seldom repeated in the schools in order to preserve them from oblivion. Another view is that Hiyya kept these rolls secret only during the lifetime of Judah Hanasi, who had omitted these opinions from his Mishnah compilation, in order not to offend him.

It is also suggested that Setharim refers to the cryptic style employed in the scroll. According to Zunz, it is identical with another lost work, Megillath Hasidim ("roll of the pious"), which contained not only Halachic but also ethical precepts.

Lit.: Kaplan, J., *Redaction of the Babylonian Talmud,* 277.

MEGILLATH TAANITH ("scroll of fasting"), a sort of calendar which enumerates thirty-six days which mark joyful occasions in Jewish history from the 2nd cent. B.C.E. to the 2nd cent. C.E.; public fasting is forbidden on all of them, and on some of the more important ones, which were regarded as semi-holidays, even mourning was forbidden. The text consists of two parts: an Aramaic text, written in brief style, often giving directions as to observance without recording the reason for rejoicing; a Hebrew commentary, which explains the obscure allusions in the Aramaic or supplies them. The book is divided into twelve chapters, one for each month of the Jewish calendar; there is an appendix which lists a number of days which are observed as anniversaries of events that were detrimental to the Jews.

A book of this name was known in the time of the Mishnah, as it is mentioned and regarded as an authority (*Taan.* 2:8). It was apparently limited to the Aramaic text, and was said to have been drawn up by Hananiah ben Hezekiah of the Garon family (*Sab.* 13b) or his son Eleazar, a general in the War against Rome (66 C.E.; *Megillath Taanith* 12). If this is correct, Hananiah may have begun to compile the work, and Eleazar made further additions; still others were made some seventy years later, as there are references to the cessation of persecutions under Trajan and Hadrian. The Hebrew commentary is much later, probably not earlier than the 7th cent.

The Megillath Taanith seems to have been highly regarded in the time of the Mishnah, but after that it gradually fell into disuse and its prescriptions were no longer regarded.

Lit.: Zeitlin, S., *Megillat Taanit* (1922); Lichtenstein, H., *Die Fastenrolle* (1931).

MEHRING, WALTER, poet, b. Berlin, 1896. He was the son of Sigmar Mehring (1856-1915), editor of the comic magazine *Ulk,* and a translator from the French. Active in the revolutionary literary movement

Ludwig Meidner (left) in his studio

of post-War Germany, Walter Mehring was noted for his political songs (*chansons*) that appeared in leftist weeklies and were recited in progressive literary cabarets. Aggressive in tone and strongly marked in rhythm, they were collected in *Das Ketzerbrevier* (1921), *Arche Noah S.O.S.* (1931), and other works. Mehring lived in Paris for several years and there wrote novels, including *Algier* and *Paris in Brand*. He also translated Balzac's *Contes Drolatiques* into 16th cent. German.

Presentation of his play, *Der Kaufmann von Berlin* (1929), on the Piscator stage was received with indignation by Jews as well as anti-Semites. It relates the tragedy of Simon Hayim Kaftan, an Eastern European Jew who arrived in Berlin in the inflation year of 1923 with one hundred dollars which he had stolen. Kaftan made an enormous fortune with the aid of an unscrupulous Pan-German lawyer named Müller, but lost his money when the mark was stabilized. After his emigration Mehring wrote, among other works, *Müller, Die Chronik einer Sippe* (1935), the genealogy of a typical Teutonic family. In 1942 he was living in Los Angeles.

MEIDNER, LUDWIG, painter, etcher and writer, b. Bernstadt, Silesia, Germany, 1884. In 1942 he was living in London. He first became a mason's apprentice, but in 1905 went to Berlin, where he drew fashion figures for periodicals. His studies in Paris from 1906 to 1907 exerted a decisive influence on his future. He changed from naturalism to impressionism. His landscapes and portraits (1905 to 1910) were executed in vivid colors. His final awakening occurred shortly before the first World War, when together with friends he founded the society *Die Pathetiker* whose members were all represented in the famous *Sturm* exhibition in 1912. Meidner worked under severe hardships until 1914. His paintings, especially his portraits, were vibrant with emotion.

During the War he developed his poetry and wrote ecstatic hymns which later were published in several

Julius L. Meier

volumes: *Im Nacken das Sternenmeer* (1918); *Septemberschrei* (1920); *Einkehr* (1923); *Gang in die Stille* (1927), reflected confessions of a highly emotional soul. His *Autobiographische Plauderei* appeared in 1923. After the War he nearly abandoned color painting and became a master in black and white drawings, etchings and engravings. His religious convictions changed, too. At one time an atheist, he later was stirred by Christian ideas, but eventually returned to the Jewish faith with increasingly mystical thoughts. Drawings of praying Jews, of Hasidim at study, portraits of Jewish personages, among them the famous portrait of Chief Rabbi Leo Baeck in Berlin, were among his final works in Berlin.

Meidner fled to Prague, after the Nazis' rise to power, and thence to London (1938), where he worked in a Camden Town studio in poverty and forgotten, surrounded by his paintings which he had saved from Hitler's storm troops. When war broke out in 1939 his case suddenly came to public notice because of his internment by the British government, but subsequently he was released.

Lit.: Brieger, Lothar, *Junge Kunst* (1914); *C.-V.-Zeitung; Allgemeine Zeitung des Judentums,* No. 15 (1934); Meidner, Ludwig, *Autobiographische Plauderei* (1923).

MEIER, JULIUS L., governor of Oregon, b. Portland, Ore., 1874; d. near Corbett, Ore., 1937. His father was Abraham Meier, immigrant from Bavaria, and Oregon pioneer; in 1857, in the settlement which was to become the city of Portland, he started the small business that his son Julius later built into the Meier and Frank Company, one of the West's greatest department stores.

Before entering his father's business, young Meier practised law for four years (1895-99) as partner of the late Senator George W. Joseph; thus began an intimacy which, in future, was destined suddenly and dramatically to turn Meier's career into channels of high public life. Leaving the law, Meier devoted his acute business talents to the department store; in 1911 he was made general manager, and later president. At the same time he was becoming one of Oregon's foremost patriots and publicists. For years he served on the chamber of commerce; vigorously he promulgated the state's famous highway system, promoted its aviation, agriculture, industry. He acted as director of "On to Oregon, Inc.," and conceived the idea of publicizing Oregon's attractions by radio and motion pictures. In 1915 he was Oregon state commissioner of the Panama-Pacific exposition in San Francisco.

During the first World War he was appointed northwest regional director of the Council of National Defense, and chairman of the Liberty Loan drives in Portland. He spent several months in Washington, D. C. Afterwards he was an early champion of relief for veterans.

Similarly, Meier's role in Jewish life was on the concrete side: his was the driving power that successfully carried through major organizational campaigns. Director of B'nai B'rith, member of the National Council of the Joint Distribution Committee, president of the Federated Jewish Societies of Portland, and president of his own congregation, Beth Israel, he became publicly identified as Oregon's leading Jewish citizen.

The year 1930 marked the unexpected turn of this busy private career to that of the first Jew to become governor of a state in which the Jewish population rated a small 1½ per cent. Meier's friend and one-time partner, George Joseph, a political liberal in the early tradition of the West and a great people's favorite, had been nominated for governor by the Progressives in the Republican party; but when he suddenly died, the state Republican committee discarded his platform, which included the too radical plank of state control of water rights. Thereupon Joseph's adherents turned to Meier and persuaded him to run in place of his friend. At an unprecedently dramatic mass meeting Meier was nominated independent candidate for governor, to run against the two old-line Republican and Democratic candidates. Without a day's experience in career politics, a millionaire running on a platform to benefit the poor, he was hailed as a modern Moses who would lead the people out of the wilderness of machine politics, and was elected by a record plurality.

His four years of administration (1931-34) were fraught with excitement, distinguished above all, for the injection of sound business methods into state government. Inefficient employes were weeded out, budgets in every institution and department were streamlined to save taxpayers' money. Accused of czarism, but admitted to be scrupulously honorable in motive and method, Meier cleaned house in the colleges, the state police force, the prison system. By the end of his first year in office he had effected savings of $6,000,000.

Among his progressive measures, Meier prided himself on legislation for relief funds, a bill to protect the rivers of Oregon for the people, a bill to safeguard the fish and game of the state, and one to supply free texts to school children. He appeared before a special session of the legislature to advocate state ownership and development of water-power projects. By the time he retired from this four-year political fray, he had been branded by his reactionary opponents a dangerous radical; by those who had looked to him to perform great feats of legislative liberalism, he was, on the contrary, regarded with great disappointment. But it was acknowledged generally that in the last period of his administration Meier proved himself a better governor than any who had preceded him in the previous quarter of a century.   SHERRY ABEL.

Lit.: Neuberger, Richard, "Julius L. Meier," *Opinion,* July, 1934, pp. 10-12; *American Hebrew,* Oct. 23, 1931, p. 509 et seq.

MEIEROVICS (MIEROVITZ), ZIGFRIDS, Latvian statesman, b. Durben, near Libau, Latvia, 1887; d. in a motor accident near Riga, Latvia, 1925. The son of a Jewish physician and a German mother, he was educated at the Riga Polytechnic. In 1918 he became foreign minister, which office he held almost continuously until his death. Participating as Latvian delegate in the Peace Conference, he secured Latvia's de jure recognition by the Powers and, later, her admission to the League of Nations. He was twice prime minister (1921-23 and 1923-24), and took part in the Genoa Conference of 1922 as one of Latvia's six delegates. Considered one of the most influential Baltic statesmen, he favored close cooperation among the Baltic States.

MEILAH ("trespass"), eighth tractate of Kodashim, the fifth division of the Talmud; it contains six chapters and deals with the improper use of sacred property and the necessary sacrifices that must be brought by way of atonement (*Lev.* 5:15-16; *Num.* 5:6-10). It enumerates the cases in which such trespass can occur, gives a list of the sacred things one should not use, but the use of which does not incur the guilt of trespass, establishes the amount of the trespass in order to calculate the amount of the atoning sacrifice, and discusses cases where it is necessary to fix responsibility for a trespass on one or more of the individuals involved.

The Tosefta to the tractate has three chapters and parallels the Mishnah. The Babylonian Gemara consists of twenty-two pages and is almost entirely legalistic; the only Haggadah is the story of Ben Temalion (17ab). There is no Palestinian Gemara.

MEINHARD, CARL, theatrical director, b. Zchlava, Czechoslovakia, 1875. He began his career in the Brahms Ensemble at the Lessing Theatre in Berlin, then was director in various theatres there, and attracted attention through the presentation of Strindberg's and Wedekind's plays. He developed the Königgrätzerstrasse Theatre to the height of prominence. *Einer von Unsere Leute,* a play dealing with Viennese environment, with a kindly attitude toward Jews, attained a number of performances through him. When the Nazis came to power in Germany, Meinhard went to Prague; from there, as stage manager, he joined Leopold Kramer, theatre director at Brünn. Subsequently he was on the staff of the Reinhardt Seminary in Vienna, and, after Austria's Anschluss, returned to Prague. In 1942 he was living in Continental Europe.

MEIR (often with the surname Baal Hanes, "miracle-worker"), Tanna of the third generation, one of the foremost exponents of Jewish learning in the 2nd cent. C.E. His original name was possibly Measha; Meir is a title that was bestowed upon him in the meaning of "enlightener," because of his brilliant

expositions of the Scriptures (*Erub.* 13b). He studied under Akiba and Ishmael and was a friend of the heretic Elisha ben Abuyah, to whom he remained faithful long after the latter's apostasy. Meir's wife was Beruriah, the scholarly daughter of Hananiah ben Teradyon. He had to leave Palestine at the time of the Bar Kochba revolt (132-35 C.E.), and returned only after the end of the Hadrianic persecution. He was one of the main organizers of the synod at Usha, which reestablished the patriarchate and the Sanhedrin. He received the position of Hacham in the latter but later, together with the vice-president Nathan, came into conflict with the patriarch, Simeon ben Gamaliel II; he refused to bend to the latter and was eventually placed under the ban (*Hor.* 13a). He later conducted a school of his own in Hamath (Ammaus), near Tiberias.

In his interpretation of the laws, Meir made use of an ingenious, dialectical method, which he took over from Akiba and further developed. This enabled him to advance a number of proofs both for and against an interpretation of the law, and insured his legal opinions a speedy recognition. At the same time Meir's formulations of the individual sentences of the Mishnah were so excellent for their brevity and clarity that they became the chief source for Judah Hanasi, who made the final compilation of the Mishnah. Meir is quoted more than 300 times in the Mishnah; in addition, Johanan declared that any anonymous Mishnah was derived from Meir (*Sanh.* 86a).

Meir used to make his Halachic discourses interesting to his audience by clever interpretations and the use of parables and fables. He was famous as a teller of fables, and was reputed to know 300 about the fox alone (*Sanh.* 38b). His moral greatness, his love for his fellowmen and for the Torah finds expression in his opinions and Haggadic sayings, of which a quantity have been preserved. His favorite saying was: "Lessen thy toil for worldly goods, and be busy in the Torah; be humble of spirit before all men" (*Aboth* 4:12). He was well acquainted with Stoic philosophy, and frequently entered into discussions with non-Jews (*Hag.* 15a); he declared that a heathen who studied the Torah and sought to fulfill it was as worthy as a high priest (*B.K.* 38a). Meir died in Asia Minor and was buried in Tiberias, where his reputed grave is still shown.

Numerous stories are told of his charm and skill, some of which may be overcolored, but nevertheless give a picture of his character. One relates how he rescued his sister-in-law from a house of prostitution by his adroitness; another how he wrote the entire scroll of *Esther* from memory. He was so attractive to women that they thronged his lecture-hall, and he was even compelled to allay the jealousy of husbands. The latter part of his life was darkened by the loss of two of his sons through a sudden illness (an occasion on which Beruriah consoled him by the story of the loan of the jewels) and by some misfortune connected with Beruriah of which the Talmud only hints (*A.Z.* 18a; cf. Rashi to the passage).

The Talmud mentions nothing of Meir as a miracleworker. It is only from the latter part of the Middle Ages that the custom arose of making collections in the homes in the name of Meir Baal Hanes. Such

The Meir Baal Hanes (Meir) Synagogue at Tiberias. From a photograph by H. S. Sonnenfeld

boxes are used for the Halukkah and for various philanthropies, as well as to buy candles to burn at the reputed tomb of Meir. Since all these customs are of recent origin, it is possible that the grave at Tiberias which is ascribed to Meir is not that of the Tanna, but of another Meir of much later time, who was famous as a wonder-worker.   SAMUEL ATLAS.

Lit.: Bader, G., *The Jewish Spiritual Heroes,* vol. 1 (1940) 362-77; Bacher, W., *Die Agada der Tannaiten,* vol. 2; Blumenthal, *Rabbi Meir, Leben und Wirken* (1888).

MEIR BAAL HANES, *see* MEIR.

MEIR BEN BARUCH OF ROTHENBURG, Talmudist and poet, b. Worms, Germany, about 1220; d. in the fortress of Ensisheim, Alsace, 1293. In his youth he studied at Würzburg under Isaac ben Moses of Vienna and at Mayence under Judah Hakohen. His riper years were spent in France in the Yeshivas of Samuel ben Solomon of Falaise and Jehiel ben Joseph of Paris, who defended the Talmud in the reign of Louis IX. In Paris Meir was an eyewitness to the public burning of twenty-four cartloads of Tal-

mudic manuscripts on Friday, June 17, 1244. He lamented this act of desecration in the elegy *Sha'ali Serufah,* a verse of which reads:

> "Lo, I weep for thee until my tears
>   Swell as a stream and flow
> Unto the graves where thy two princely seers
>   Sleep calm below:
> Moses and Aaron in the Mountain Hor;
>   I will of them inquire:
> Is there another to replace this Law
>   Devoured by fire?"
>   (trans. Nina Davis, *Songs of Exile,* p. 82)

In 1245 Meir returned to Germany, where he held temporary rabbinical posts in several large communities. The center of his activity, however, was Rothenburg ob Tauber, where he maintained, at his own cost, a Talmudical academy, gathering about him a number of disciples, who later carried his teaching to Austria, Spain and Portugal. The most famous of these were the codifiers Asher ben Jehiel and Mordecai ben Hillel. Meir's method of instruction was a synthesis of the dialectics of the Tosafists and the systematic method of Maimonides. His authority was universally acknowledged. Communities in France and Italy frequently sought his opinion, addressing him as "father of rabbis," "Gaon" and "light of the exile," the latter title having been conferred only upon Rashi and Gershom ben Judah among his predecessors.

Meir's responsa, of which about 1,500 have been preserved, are of the utmost importance in the study of the inner life of the German Jews, their social, occupational, educational, political and communal organization. He wrote no large work, but displayed his erudition in numerous expositions, decisions, exegetic notes and responsa, the greater part of which are extant only in manuscript. He wrote Tosafoth and notes to various Talmudic tractates; a commentary to the first and sixth divisions of the Talmud (printed in modern editions); *Piske Erubin,* on the regulations of the Erub; *Halachoth Pesukoth,* a collection of deci-

Tombstone (left) of Rabbi Meir ben Baruch of Rothenburg

Jacob Meir

sions; *Hilchoth Berachoth,* giving the proper forms of benedictions; *Hilchoth Abeluth,* on mourning customs; *Hilchoth Shehitah,* on ritual slaughtering; a treatise on the duties of husband and wife; Masoretic notes; a book on synagogue customs and liturgical poetry.

Owing to repeated persecutions, Meir in 1286 took his entire family and set out for Palestine, together with a group of well-to-do members of his community. While passing through Lombardy he was recognized by an apostate Jew who was accompanying the archbishop of Mayence. The archbishop had Meir seized and taken back to Germany where, upon the order of Emperor Rudolph, he was confined in the fortress of Ensisheim. His friends offered the emperor 20,000 marks in silver for the release of their leader. The rabbi, however, refused the freedom thus offered, fearing to create a precedent for the extortion of money from the Jews by the imprisonment of their rabbis. His disciples were permitted to meet with him, and he was even able to compose several of his works within the prison walls. He remained in confinement for seven years until his death. His body was not surrendered until fourteen years later, when a heavy ransom was paid by Alexander Süskind Wimpfen, a generous Jew of Frankfort. Wimpfen in return asked that after his own death his body should be laid to rest in Worms by the side of the saintly rabbi. His wish was carried out.

Meir was not only a man of profound erudition and noble character, but also played a large part in the organization of Jewish communal life. He was one of the greatest rabbinical authorities of his day, and, after Rabbenu Gershom, the most characteristic personality of German Jewry.

JOSEPH MARCUS.

Lit.: Back, S., *Rabbi Meir ben Baruch aus Rothenburg* (1895); Zimmels, H. J., *Beiträge zur Geschichte der Juden in Deutschland* (1926); Graetz, H., *History of the Jews,* vol. 3 (1927) 625-40.

MEIR BEN GEDALIAH, *see* LUBLIN, MEIR.

MEIR BEN SAMUEL HAZAKEN (RaM), called also "Hayashish" ("The ancient"), b. Ramerupt, France, about 1060; d. after 1135. He came from the school of Lorraine, married Rashi's second daughter Jochebed, and had four distinguished sons. Meir was one of the founders of the Northern France school of exegetes, known as the Tosafists, who supplemented (Tosafoth) to Rashi's commentary on the Talmud. Some of his decisions and a part of his commentary on the Talmud were printed in the works of other authors, as well as a penitential prayer (Selihah).

See also: RABBENU TAM; RASHBAM.

Lit.: Berliner, A., *Beiträge zur Geschichte der Raschi-Kommentare* (1903) 16, 46; Gross, H., *Gallia Judaica* (1897) 304, 542, and 635; Graetz, H., *History of the Jews,* vol. 3 (1927) 289, 345.

MEIR LÖB BEN JEHIEL MICHAEL, *see* MALBIM.

MEIR PRZEMYSLANI, Hasidic master and scholar in Poland, b. 1787; d. 1858. He served for a time as rabbi in Przemysl, and was reputed to have a grim sense of humor, and to have the ability to foretell events and miraculous occurrences. He is said to have predicted the terrors of 1848, which in Poland were accompanied by pestilence. Much of his humor consisted in his reinterpretations of Biblical verses which he would then announce as truths to those who came to visit him. Extremely punctilious in ritual matters, he lived a life bordering on utter asceticism, and was so charitable that he never had a single penny in his possession over night.

Lit.: Verus (A. Markus), *Der Chassidismus,* 344-48; Berger, Israel, *Eser Ataroth* (1910).

MEIR OF ROTHENBURG, *see* MEIR BEN BARUCH OF ROTHENBURG.

MEIR SHEFAYA, *see* COLONIES, AGRICULTURAL.

MEIR, JACOB, chief rabbi of the Sephardic Jews of Palestine, b. Jerusalem, 1856; d. Jerusalem, 1939. During 1882 to 1885 he traveled in Bokhara, Tunisia, Algeria and other countries as representative of the Sephardic communities of Palestine. In 1887 he became a colleague of Chief Rabbi Jacob Saul Elyashar in Jerusalem. When the latter died (1906) Meir was elected as successor; but he was regarded by some as too advanced in ideas, the Sultan refused to ratify the appointment, so Meir accepted instead the chief rabbinate in Salonika, where he served from 1907 to 1919. He joined the Zionist movement at an early period, represented the Palestinian Yishub at the colonial ministry in London and was a delegate to the Thirteenth Zionist Congress. In 1920 he became chief rabbi of the Sephardic Jews in Palestine, and in 1925 honorary president of the World Federation of Sephardic Jews; he held both positions until his death. He conducted the Porath Yosef Yeshiva, and the Ohel Yaakob Yeshiva was named after him.

He received many honors and decorations from such countries as Turkey, Arabia, Greece and Serbia, and was a Commander of the British Empire (1922) and a chevalier of the Legion of Honor. In 1936 his eightieth birthday received a public celebration, and a jubilee volume, *Zichron Meir,* was published.

MEIRI, MENAHEM BEN SOLOMON, known also as Don Vidal Solomon, Talmudist and commentator, b. Perpignan, Provence, France, 1249; d. Perpignan, 1306. He was a pupil of Hayim of Narbonne. His keen grasp of the intricacies of the Talmud and his classic and concise style of writing made him one of the outstanding commentators of the Middle Ages. His main work is *Beth Habehirah,* commentaries on most of the tractates of the Talmud, of which the following were published: *Megillah* (Amsterdam, 1769); *Yebamoth* (Salonika, 1794); *Yoma* (Livorno, 1760); *Sabbath* (Livorno, 1794); *Nedarim, Nazir, Sotah* (Livorno, 1795); *Aboth* (Vienna, 1854); *Hullin* (Jerusalem, 1936); *Rosh Hashanah* (Vienna, 1936). Meiri also wrote commentaries on the Bible, of which those pertaining to *Proverbs* (Leiria, 1492) and *Psalms* (Jerusalem, 1936) are extant. He was also the author of *Hibbur Hateshubah* (manuscript de Rossi, No. 1313) and of *Kiryath Sefer,* a Masoretic work (on the method of writing scrolls of the Law; two parts, Smyrna, 1863 and 1881). Other works of Meiri, no longer extant, were mentioned by Azulai (*Beth Yad, Magen Aboth* and *Ohel Moed*) and by Meiri himself (*Kethab Dath*).

Meiri took part in the controversy between Barcelona and Montpellier about the permissibility of applying to the Holy Scripture the allegorizing tendencies of contemporary philosophy. In a letter addressed to Abba Mari he pronounced himself in favor of the study of secular philosophy provided the student had a sound Talmudic foundation. On his death Abba Mari dedicated an elegy to his memory.

MEISEL (also **Meisels** and **Meisl**), a family well-known in Bohemia, Russia, Hungary and other East European countries. The family seems to have originated in Cracow, where ABRAHAM MEISEL, one of the elders of Kazimierz, lived at about the end of the 16th cent., and the typographer MENAHEM BEN MOSES SAMSON (called NAHUM) MEISEL worked in the first half of the 17th cent. JUDAH LÖB BEN SIMHAH BUNEM MEISEL (17th cent.) was also a typographer and the son-in-law of Nahum Meisel. He reopened his father-in-law's printing establishment in 1663. It remained open until 1670. He was himself the author of *Taame Hamassoreth,* a commentary on the Masorah (Amsterdam, 1728).

MEISEL, ELIAS HAYIM, rabbi, b. Gorodka, Poland, 1821; d. Lodz, Poland, 1912. He served as rabbi in various Polish communities and engaged in welfare activities. In Lodz, where he was rabbi from 1873 on, he founded a Talmud Torah in which the Pilpulistic method of studying the Talmud was no longer followed. He endeavored to aid Jewish laborers who had become unemployed as a result of the introduction of machinery into the textile factories of Lodz; he even built a factory for this purpose, but his attempt finally failed. He advocated the creation of a Jewish colonization project in Poland which, however, was not realized.

Lit.: Eisenstadt, *Dor Rabbanav Vesoferav* (1900) 28 et seq.; *Yevreiskaya Entziklopedia,* vol. 10.

MEISEL, MOSES BEN MORDECAI, scholar and author, b. Vilna, about 1760; d. Hebron, Palestine, after 1838. He was a pupil of Elijah Gaon of Vilna.

Later, under the influence of Shneor Zalman, the Hasidic leader, he joined the Hasidim but never entered into the local religious controversies of the period. On the contrary, he approved the work of Moses Mendelssohn and other Haskalah representatives.

Meisel seems to have gone to Germany, where his name is connected with Napoleon—Shneor Zalman, an opponent of Napoleon's, evidently tried to win Meisel over to the Russian cause and thus aroused Napoleon's suspicions. In 1813 Meisel went to Hebron and did not return to Russia until after Napoleon's defeat. He stayed only a short time, however, and went back to Palestine. Meisel's poem, *Shirath Mosheh* (1788), is on the 613 precepts, each line beginning with a letter from the Ten Commandments.

ARYEH LÖB MEISEL (d. 1835), a Vilna Hasidic leader, was a son of Meisel.

Lit.: Fünn, S. J., *Kiryah Neemanah,* 246-47; *Beth Rabbi,* 93-103; Teitelbaum, *Harab Miladi,* 156-58.

MEISEL, NACHMAN, critic, journalist and editor, b. Russia, 1887. He was reared in Kiev, and received his early education, both religious and secular, from private tutors.

He began his literary career in Hebrew with an article in the *Hazeman,* a Vilna daily (1908), and contributed also to other literary publications. In 1910 he turned to Yiddish as his literary medium, and began with an essay on the Yiddish prose writer David Bergelson. Together with Bergelson, he edited and published the *Yiddisher Almanach* (1910) and its anthologies, *Fun Tzeit tzu Tzeit* (From Time to Time). In collaboration with Bergelson, Litvakov and Dobrushin, Meisel was one of the founders of the *Kiever Literarishe Gruppe,* whose program it was to broaden the scope of Yiddish literature and to combat the tone of futility and resignation then prevalent therein.

In 1924 Meisel (together with I. J. Singer, Meilech Ravitch and Peretz Markish) edited the weekly *Die Literarishe Bletter,* but from 1925 on he was sole editor of this journal of letters. In 1936 Meisel visited Palestine, and published his impressions in a book called *Teg un Necht in Emek* (Days and Nights in the Emek, 1938). He conducted extensive research into the life and letters of the famous classic writer Isaac Loeb Peretz, which resulted in two volumes: *Peretzes Briv un Redes* ('Peretz' Letters and Speeches; Warsaw, 1929) and *I. L. Peretz, Lebn un Shafn* (I. L. Peretz, his Life and Works; Warsaw, 1931).

In 1937 Meisel migrated to the United States, where he became secretary and member of the executive committee of the Yiddisher Kultur Farband, New York city, and editor of its monthly magazine, *Yiddishe Kultur,* published from 1938 on. He also lectured on Yiddish literature. Meisel was a member of the Yiddish Pen Club and one of the founders of the "Yivo" (Yiddish Scientific Institute) of Vilna.

He was also author of the following works: *Sholom Asch, sein Lebn un Shafn* (1929); *Noente un Veite* (Far and Near, 2 vols. 1924-26); *Ahron Liberman* (1934); *Chaim Nachman Bialik* (1934); *Mendele Mocher Sforim* (1936); *Oif Undser Kultur Front* (On our Cultural Front, 1936); *Joseph Opatoshu, sein Lebn un Shafn* (1937); *Abraham Goldfaden* (1939); *Der Koach fun Yiddish* (1939); *Sholem Aleichem* (1939); *David*

Wolf Alois Meisel

Bergelson (1940); *Uriel Acosta* (1940); *Peretz Markish, D`chtcr un Prosaiker* (1942); *Doires un Tkufes in der Yiddisher Literatur* (Generations and Centuries in Yiddish Literature, 1942).

MEISEL, WOLF ALOIS (BENJAMIN ZEEB), rabbi and author, b. Roth-Janowitz, Bohemia, 1815; d. Budapest, 1867. Following an early Talmudic education in Bohemia, he studied at a Gymnasium at Hamburg and at the Universities of Berlin and Breslau, continuing also the study of the Talmud. He proved himself a master of the sermon as a guest preacher at Gleiwitz, and in 1843 was called to the rabbinate of Stettin. He refused an invitation to Prague (1845), and accepted one to Pest, Hungary (1859). He found that community in the throes of religious and constitutional rebirth, a state of affairs by which his position was rendered extremely difficult. In his periodical, *Hakarmel,* Meisel strove to bridge the gap separating Conservatives from Progressives, but he could not avoid being bitterly denounced as a reformer by Israel David Schlesinger, the uncompromising rabbi of Bazin, in his work *Har Tabor.* Meisel also created several charitable institutions (Meiselverein), and founded a Talmud Torah where Alexander Kohut was among his pupils. He met with sudden death while delivering a sermon.

His *Homilien über die Sprüche der Väter* (Stettin, 1851; in Hungarian, 1862) contains models of synagogue oratory. He published also *Leben und Wirken Hartwig Naphtali Wesselys* (1841) and *Wörterbuch zu den fünf Büchern Mose* (1860), and translated two volumes of poems, *Prinz und Derwisch* (from Abraham ibn Hasdai's *Ben Hamelech Vehanazir;* several editions) and *Der Prüfstein* (from Kalonymus ben Kalonymus' *Eben Bohan,* 1878).

MEISEL-HESS, GRETE, writer, b. Prague, 1879; d. Berlin, 1922. She was first a novelist, but later turned to the problems of women. Her earlier writings were: *Generationen und ihre Bildner* (1900); *In der modernen Weltanschauung* (1903); *Die sexuelle Krise* (1909). After she settled in Berlin she published the novel *Geister* (1912), the sharply attacked *Die Intellektuellen* (1913), and the larger works *Das Wesen der Geschlechtlichkeit* (2 vols., 1916) and *Die Ehe als Erlebnis* (1921).

MEISELS, DOB BERUSH, rabbi, b. Szczekoeiny, Poland, 1798; d. Warsaw, 1870. In Poland Meisels played a unique role. As spiritual head of Polish Orthodox Jewry, he worked toward one goal: Poles should recognize Jews as equals and brothers, and Jews should become an integral part of Polish life, so that, united, they could fight for a free and independent fatherland. Toward that end he advocated that all distinctions between Jews and Poles in customs, dress and language be abolished. He urged Jews to engage in agriculture and handicrafts.

Meisels was descended from an old family of Cracow, and in that city he became rabbi in 1832. In 1846, recognized as a leader in the liberation movement, he was elected to represent his city in the senate of the new Cracow republic. Two years later, when the great revolutionary wave sweeping Europe was at its crest, he was sitting in the provisional Austrian senate, helping to reorganize Austria.

When, in 1856, he became rabbi of Warsaw, he soon agitated in the very forefront of the second Polish insurrection against Russia. Using his influence as rabbi, he rallied the Jews of Warsaw around the cause of freedom. Jews participated in all revolutionary activities, and several were killed in the fatal street demonstration of February 27, 1861. Meisels was on the protest delegation to the Warsaw viceroy, and in the funeral procession of the martyrs he headed the Jewish clergy marching alongside the Catholics. Jews and Poles fraternized in churches and synagogues; the Polish national anthem was sung during the Jewish New Year services; finally Jews and Catholics both closed their houses of worship in protest against invading Russians, and Meisels, together with the Reform rabbi Jastrow and the Catholic Kramshtyk, was imprisoned in the Warsaw citadel for three months. Meisels was then banished, but soon permitted to return.

With the final suppression of the rebellion in 1863, political reaction and a wave of Russification set in, and Meisels accordingly lost much of his former influence.

Meisels' chief scholarly contribution is *Hiddushe Mahardam,* notes to Maimonides' *Sefer Hamitzvoth.*

Lit.: Dubnow, S., *History of the Jews in Russia and Poland,* vol. 2 (1918) 177-83.

MEISL, JOSEF, historian, b. Brünn, Moravia, 1883. In addition to articles for the Zionist publication *Unsere Hoffnung* (1904-6), he wrote numerous historical articles in the *Monatsschrift für die Geschichte und Wissenschaft des Judentums* and other periodicals, and was co-editor of the *Jüdisches Lexikon* and *Dubnow Festschrift* (1930); he compiled the bibliography to the latter work. His works include: *Die Juden im Zartum Polen* (1916); *Heinrich Graetz* (1917); *Haskalah* (1919); *Geschichte der Juden in Polen und Russland* (Berlin, vol. 1, 1921; vol. 2, 1922; vols. 3-4, 1925); *Die Durchführung des Artikel 44 des Berliner Vertrages in Rumänien und die europäische Diplomatie* (1925). From 1915 to 1934 Meisl was general secretary of and held other offices with the Jewish Community of Berlin, after which he settled in Haifa, Palestine. In 1936 he published a work on the Pinkas of the Berlin Jewish community, and in 1939 (at Jerusalem) a history of the Sir Moses Montefiore Testimonial Fund, entitled *Eleh Toledoth Keren Maz-kereth Hasar Mosheh Montefiore.*

Lit.: Wininger, S., *Grosse Jüdische National-Biographie,* vol. 4 (1930) 322; *Kürschners Deutscher Gelehrten-Kalender* (1928-29, 1935).

MEISSES, *see* PHRASES, POPULAR (under Maases).

MEISSNER, ALFRED, Czechoslovakian political leader and lawyer, b. Jungbunzlau, Bohemia, 1871. One of the key figures in the Czechoslovakian Social Democratic Party before the first World War, he was a member of the Austrian parliament. During the War he was elected to the Czechoslovakian National Council, and in 1918 president of the Czechoslovakian Constitutional Committee. From 1920 to 1929 he was minister of justice, and in 1934 became minister of social welfare.

Meissner later retired from the administration, devoting himself to research on social security and the cultural rights of minorities. He remained in Czechoslovakia after the occupation of that country by Germany in 1939, and was believed to be not among the living in 1942. He wrote for daily and periodical publications, and published political and legal works, including a handbook on industrial law.

MEISTER, MORRIS, teacher and author, b. Gonietz, Poland, 1895. He was brought to the United States at the age of seven. Meister received his M.A. degree in 1917 and his Ph.D. degree in 1921 from Columbia University. In 1936, after occupying teaching posts in various colleges and schools in New York city, he was made director of science instruction in the public schools of New York city. Two years later he was made principal of the High School of Science, one of New York's new educational institutions designed for the schooling of children with special capacities and interests. In 1942 he still held this post.

Meister was a member of various scientific organizations; he was president of the American Science Teachers Association (1942) and on the board of managers of the American Institute (1935-). He was also the founder of the Educator's Lodge of the B'nai B'rith.

Among Meister's published works were: *Living with Science* (6 vols., 1929); *The Wonderworld of Science* (6 vols., 1939); *Teacher's Guide for the Smithsonian Scientific Series* (1936). He was editor of *The Science Classroom,* contributing editor of *Science Education,* and the author of various articles for educational publications. During the first World War he was a war instructor in physics.

MEISTERLIN (or MEISTERI), Jewish family of the 14th and 15th centuries, residing in Styria and at Vienna. The name is probably a translation of Hayim into German. A member of this family, Meisterlin of Perchtoldsdorf, who owned a house at Vienna, was the first victim of the Vienna Gezerah (1421). He was martyrized, together with his sons Jacob and Schmerl. To their last breath Meisterlin and his sons refused conversion. Meisterlin, a son of the martyrized Jacob, was saved. His Hebrew name was probably Samuel Hayim (1416-78). In 1467 he was allowed by Emperor Frederick III to rent the emperor's house at Bruck. The document confirming the lease expressed the

emperor's extraordinary good will toward Meisterlin, and in 1468 the emperor took special care to protect him. Meisterlin was entrusted with the collection of the Jewish taxes, and was granted the privilege to acquire real estate. A cousin of Meisterlin of Perchtoldsdorf, also named Meisterlin, resided at Wiener Neustadt, and was martyrized in 1421. His son Meisterlin (1390-1461) was a fellow student of Israel Isserlein when he studied under Aron Blumlein.

After 1421 Meisterlin was an official of the rabbinate at Wiener Neustadt. Later on he engaged in a violent conflict with Isserlein who, notwithstanding the fact that he was right and deeply offended, continued to have high regard for Meisterlin's scholarship. Meisterlin, who directed the Jewish school of Wiener Neustadt, was also at odds with the Jewish community there, in consequence of which a rival school was founded. Apparently Meisterlin was an irascible character. He corresponded extensively with many learned rabbis.

Lit.: Krauss, S., *Die Wiener Geserah* (1920); Herzog, in *Monatsschrift für Geschichte und Wissenschaft des Judentums* (1935).

MEITNER, LISE, physicist, b. Vienna, 1878. She was lecturer at the University of Berlin (1922) and assistant professor from 1926 until 1933, when she was dismissed in consequence of the "non-Aryan" edicts. However, she continued her researches as a member of the Kaiser Wilhelm Institut für Chemie in Berlin-Dahlem until she found a new field of activity in Stockholm, Sweden, where she was living in 1942. Her main studies were concentrated on thorium and actinium, two emanations of radium. She discovered, together with Otto Hahn, the element protactinium (1918). She wrote *Beiträge zur Physik der Atomkerne, Atomvorgänge und ihre Sichtbarmachung* (1926) and *Der Aufbau der Atomkerne* (1935; together with Max Delbrück).

MEKHLIS, LEV ZAKHAROVICH, Soviet military and political commissar, b. Russia, 1889. Joining the Bolshevik party in 1918, he became a Red Army commissar, and fought on several fronts throughout the civil war. His most glorious engagement, celebrated in Soviet history, took place at Kakhovka, which the Red soldiers captured by crossing the Dnieper river under fire of the Whites. There Mekhlis was wounded; for his achievements he was awarded the Order of the Red Banner.

After the civil war, Mekhlis rose rapidly in government administration. By 1930 he had assumed charge of *Pravda,* and in 1937 he was given direction of the press and publishing of the central committee of the Communist party. The Order of Lenin was bestowed on him for his press services.

In 1937 he was elected to the Supreme Soviet of the USSR; in 1939, having already been a member of the central committee of the Communist party for many years, he was elected to the organizational bureau of that committee. With the progress of the second World War, Mekhlis became one of the country's leaders in defense efforts. In 1937 he was appointed vice-commissar of defense and chief of the political department of the Red Army; then in 1940 he was given the post of People's Commissar of State Control in the commissariat newly created to supervise the general finances, labor and production of all state organizations. At the same time he was appointed vice-chairman of the Council of People's Commissars of the USSR.

Lit.: Pravda, May 1, 1937; Dec. 31, 1937; Feb. 10, 1939; *Moscow News,* Jan. 12, 1938; March 27, 1939; Sept. 12, 1940; *New York Times,* Sept. 8, 1940.

MEKIZE NIRDAMIM ("Awakers of Those Asleep"), society for the publication of Hebrew manuscripts and rare books of ancient literature, founded in 1864 at Lyck, Germany, and directed by Eliezer Lippmann Silbermann, editor of the *Hamaggid.* Its first board consisted of prominent Hebrew scholars and philanthropists such as Rabbi Nathan Marcus Adler, Sir Moses Montefiore and Joseph Zedner of London, Albert Cohn of Paris, Michael Jehiel Sachs of Berlin, Samuel David Luzzatto of Padua, and Mathias Straschun of Vilna. After Silbermann's death in 1882, the society was revived under the leadership of Abraham Berliner at Berlin; the new board consisted of Moses Ehrenreich, Joseph Derenbourg, David Günzburg, Solomon Zalman Halberstam, Abraham Harkavy, and others. During this period of great activity the society published forty-two works. In 1909, through the efforts of Samuel Abraham Poznanski, the society was again revived; David Simonsen was chairman, and Aron Freimann vice-chairman. After Simonsen's death in 1932, Freimann became chairman, and still held this post in 1942. Altogether, more than ninety books were published by the society up to 1942.

Lit.: Verzeichnis der Schriften des Vereins Mekize Nirdamim (1885-95) 96, 98; Lippe, H. D., *Bibliographisches Lexikon,* New Series, vol. 1, pp. 391-92; *Jewish Encyclopedia,* vol. 8, pp. 447-48; Rabinowitz, Michael, *Reshimah Bibliografith shel Sifre Hebrath "Mekitze Nirdamim"* (1938).

MEKLENBURG, JAKOB ZEBI, rabbi, b. Hohensalza (now Inowroclaw), Poland, 1785; d. Königsberg, Germany, 1865. In 1830 he became rabbi in Königsberg, where he remained the rest of his life. He wrote decisions and interpretations of the prayer-book and the Passover Haggadah, and biographical data on Elijah Vilna. His most important work was his Hebrew Pentateuchal commentary *Hakethab Vehakabbalah* (Leipzig, 1839), reprinted in several editions. In his exegesis, which followed closely Samuel David Luzzatto and Elijah Vilna, he endeavored to prove the inner connection of Jewish tradition with the text of Scripture.

Lit.: Druck, David, in *Horeb,* vol. 4 (1937) 171-79.

MEKOR HAYIM, *see* IBN GABIROL, SOLOMON.

MELACHIM, *see* KINGS, BOOKS OF.

MELAMED, SAMUEL MAX, writer and editor, b. Vilkovski, Lithuania, 1885; d. New York city, 1938. He studied at various European universities and received his Ph.D. degree from the University of Bern in 1908. He soon began to write for Hebrew periodicals, and in 1909, with his departure for London as a representative of a German newspaper syndicate, Melamed began his polylingual career in journalism and literature.

In 1914 Melamed came to the United States, and until 1933 was an editorial writer for the *New York Staats Zeitung.* Meanwhile his participation in Jewish literary life continued and developed. From 1914 to 1918 he was editor of the *American Jewish Chronicle,* and from

1928 to 1936 of *The Reflex,* a monthly review. He lived for some time in Chicago, where he was active in Jewish organizational work and (1921-24) president of the Chicago branch of the Zionist Organization of America.

Among Melamed's longer published works were: *Theory, Origin and History of the Idea of Peace* (1909), which was awarded first prize by the International Peace Bureau; *Der Staat im Wandel der Jahrtausende* (1911), which was translated into Japanese and used as a college textbook in Japan and in European countries; *Psychologie des jüdischen Geistes* (1914); *Schatten und Gestalten,* short stories; with David Neumark, *Mahuth Hayahaduth* (1915); *On the Eve of Redemption* (1917); *Breaking the Tablets* (1930); the first volume of a planned trilogy, *Spinoza and Buddha.* Many of his books were translated into other languages.

MELAMMED, *see* TEACHERS.

MELAVVEH MALKAH, the meal and festivities attending the end of the Sabbath. The words mean "escort of the queen" and refer to the honor due the "queen" (Sabbath) on her departure.

The Talmud obligates Jews to three meals on the Sabbath, but Hidka believed that a fourth meal, at the end of the holiday, was also commanded, and Hanina agreed. Although the Sabbath restrictions come to an end with the evening prayer and Habdalah, and weekday labors are thenceforth permitted, the practical end of the Sabbath was considered as arriving only with the finish of the Melavveh Malkah collation. Isaac Luria believed that not until the Melavveh Malkah was over did the sinful dead return to hell from their Sabbath rest, for now the protective "over-soul" resumed its place in heaven.

This post-Sabbath meal is also called Seudath David, or King David's feast. This identification grew out of the belief that David had been warned that he would die at the expiration of a Sabbath and celebrated his survival into each new week with special joy. The Melavveh Malkah service is introduced with the sentence: "This is the feast of King David." In fact, the name is sometimes interpreted to mean "escort of the king," that is, David, on his return to supervise purgatory at the conclusion of the Sabbath holiday.

In Eastern Europe the Melavveh Malkah was frequently the occasion for protracted gayety, not only in family groups, but in larger assemblages. The Hasidim, in particular, utilized it as an opportunity for feasting and dancing far into the night.

MELBOURNE, capital of the Australian province of Victoria, with a Jewish population of about 6,000 out of a general population of 1,016,500. Nearly all the Jews of Victoria reside in Melbourne and its suburbs.

Divine service was held for the first time in Melbourne in 1839 at the residence of M. Lazarus, on Collins Street. The Jewish residents of Melbourne then were not sufficient in numbers to form even a Minyan. Melbourne was then a city of new buildings, of white tents and of bush. In 1840, several newcomers having meanwhile arrived in the colony, the first Minyan was held at the residence of Solomon Benjamin and prayers

The Great Synagogue at Melbourne, Australia

were read on that occasion by Edward Hart, Michael Cashmore, S. H. Harris and Isaac Lincoln. The names of Benjamin, Hart and Cashmore became linked with the fortunes of the Melbourne Hebrew Congregation. A grandson of Solomon Benjamin, Louis Benjamin, was in the 1920's president of the Melbourne Hebrew Congregation.

In 1841 Asher Hyman Hart called a meeting of Jews to consider the erection of a synagogue; twenty-five persons attended. In 1844 the government granted land in Bourke Street as a site for the building; in 1853 the synagogue was erected; up to this time services had been held in the home of Solomon Benjamin. In 1858 the consecration service was conducted by E. M. Myers. Moses Rintel was the first minister (1853), and was followed by A. F. Ornstein, Raphael Benjamin, D. D. Jacobson, Joseph Abraham (appointed in 1904) and Israel Brodie, who succeeded Jacobson in 1923. H. Freedman was rabbi in 1941, when the congregation celebrated its centenary.

In 1873 the congregation established a Jewish daily school, where both Hebrew and Jewish religion as well as English, mathematics and other secular studies were taught. This school existed for twenty-six years, and its closing was due chiefly to the introduction by the Victorian state government of compulsory secular education. Its headmaster, Joel Fredman, became head of the newly opened school at St. Kilda.

In 1858, due to a schism caused by internal and social conditions, a second Jewish congregation was founded in Melbourne, the East Melbourne Synagogue, with Solomon Solomon as its first president and Moses Rintel as minister. The congregation obtained a grant of land in Stephen Street, and in 1860 a small building was opened for services. In 1877 the foundation-stone of a new and more commodious synagogue was laid in Albert Street; it was first used for services on the New Year of 1877. Henri J. Hart was then president and Marks Herman treasurer. M. Grünbaum succeeded Rintel several years later; subsequent ministers were D. Wolinski, Isadore Myers and Jacob Lenzer (1888-1921). With Lenzer's death in 1921 and the drift of former members to the St. Kilda congregation, the East Melbourne Hebrew Congregation began to lose

its prominence in the affairs of the community. Lenzer was succeeded eventually by Solomon Mestel, a graduate of Jews' College, London. Owing to the serious financial depression of 1930, the East Melbourne Hebrew Congregation became temporarily unable to support a minister, and Mestel returned to England. But shortly before 1938 W. Rechter became its rabbi.

The third large congregation, the St. Kilda Hebrew Congregation, was founded in 1871, with Moritz Michaelis, Israel Bloomington and Hyam E. Hart as the first executive officers. In 1872 a synagogue was erected and in 1873 Elias Blaubaum was called from Germany to be its rabbi. Blaubaum remained minister until his death in 1904, and in the following year Jacob Danglow succeeded him. Danglow was still rabbi in 1941. In 1929 a new synagogue costing about £40,000 was erected. Hebrew and Sabbath schools provided for about 200 children in 1942. General Sir John Monash was one of the active members of the board of management of the St. Kilda Hebrew Congregation.

Beth Israel, the first Liberal congregation in the Melbourne Community, was established in 1930. H. M. Saenger was the rabbi in 1941. In addition to the larger synagogues, there are smaller United Hebrew congregations in Melbourne, the members of which are mostly Jewish immigrants from Eastern Europe. There are also smaller Minyanim, all of which are in Carlton, Melbourne's northern suburb. Even a Hasidic Stiebel thrived (in the 1930's) amid Australian surroundings. All the Melbourne congregations subscribe to the funds of the office of the chief rabbi of the British Empire and recognize the jurisdiction of the holder of that position.

Melbourne Jewry's communal activities are well organized. The Melbourne Jewish Advisory Board, representing the congregation, deals with general communal matters and ensures cooperation between the various institutions. The Jewish Philanthropic Society (established in 1840 by the Benjamin brothers and A. H. Hart and M. Cashmore as the Society for the Relief of Indigent Jews) attends to philanthropic work in Melbourne; it disburses direct relief and also controls the Moses Montefiore Home for the Aged and Infirm, established in 1870 and situated in St. Kilda. There are also the Hebrew Ladies' Benevolent Society, the Jewish Women's Guild (hospital work and the provision of clothing for the sick and poor), Council of Jewish Women of Victoria, Jewish Aid Society (founded in 1888 by Philip Blashki, Isadore Myers and Nahum Levinson for the purpose of lending various sums without interest), Judean League (a social organization controlling a Jewish gymnasium and a number of sports and athletic clubs and a well-equipped Jewish communal center in Carlton), and the Victorian Jewish Immigration Questions Committee and Victorian Jewish Welcome Society, which aids immigrants to secure suitable employment.

Jewish education in Melbourne is under the direction of the United Jewish Education Board, established in 1904 and endowed by Jacob Kronheimer. Daily tuition is provided for some 300 Jewish children. The scattered nature of the Jewish population presents a considerable difficulty, and many centers accordingly have to be conducted, although the average attendance at each may be extremely small. Hebrew is a subject for matriculation at the University of Melbourne. The Council of Victorian Zionists and the Victorian Zionist Association Hatchia are affiliated with the Australian Zionist Federation.

Melbourne has had many outstanding Jewish citizens, in civic life as well as in communal affairs. Harold Cohen, Henry Isaac Cohen and Archie Michaelis were at various times members of Parliament for Victoria. Edward Cohen was mayor of Melbourne in 1862; Sir Benjamin Benjamin occupied this post for two terms (1887-89). Henry Isaac Cohen served as minister of education. An outstanding publisher of Australia was Theodor Fink. Isador Smith (d. 1940) was a Melbourne resident who was awarded a Victoria Cross in the first World War. Jews have at various times been connected with the University of Melbourne. Among the leading women of the community were Isabel Phillips, a pathologist and executive in hospital work, Frances Barkman, an examiner at the university and Julia Rapke, a special magistrate at the Children's Court.

In the years between 1933 and 1939, Melbourne Jewry participated in refugee aid, although immigration into Australia was limited. A Refugee Council was formed in 1938 and the Jews of the community raised £17,000. With the entry of the British Empire into the second World War, the Jews of the city entered fully into the war activities, both in the military and home services. The spread of the war to the Pacific in 1942 imposed additional tasks of war organization on the Jewish community, including that of hospitality for the Jewish soldiers from other countries coming to Australia.   N. H. ROSENTHAL.

Lit.: American Hebrew, Jan. 30, 1931, p. 291; Jewish Chronicle (London), Dec. 23, 1938, p. 28; Hertz, J. H., The First Pastoral Tour to the Jewish Communities of the British Overseas Dominions (1924) 25.

MELCHETT, LORD ALFRED (Sir Alfred Moritz Mond), industrialist and statesman, b. Farnworth, Lancashire, England, 1868; d. London, 1930. The son of Ludwig Mond, chemist and industrialist, he studied law at the Universities of Cambridge and Edinburgh, and practised as a barrister for a while (1894). But, entering the firm of Brunner, Mond and Co., which had been founded by his father, Sir Alfred became director in 1895 and subsequently chairman of the

Lord Alfred Melchett

board. A "field marshal of industry," as he was to be called in New York city shortly before his death, he organized and headed the International Nickel Company, Ltd., and the Imperial Chemical Industries, Ltd., regarded one of the most powerful trusts in the world. Considered the wealthiest man in England, he served his country as a resourceful industrial organizer, especially during the first World War when, according to outstanding British statesmen, it would have been impossible for Great Britain to carry on the war successfully save for the research work done by Lord Melchett's firms and the output maintained by them.

Although opposed to Socialism and trade unionism, Melchett recognized the necessity for cooperation between capital and labor and organized the Mond-Turner conference (1928), attended by representatives of the trade unions which endeavored to promote mass production and improve relations between employers and employees. Melchett who, in a poll of "The Best Brains of England," conducted by the Spectator, was seventh, came to be regarded as the man who saved England after the War by his promulgation of a wise industrial policy.

He was a member of parliament from 1906 to 1928, having been elected on the liberal ticket for Chester, Swansea and Carmarthen, consecutively. He was created a baronet in 1910, made a Privy Councillor in 1913, and he served in Lloyd George's cabinet as First Commissioner of Works (1916-21) and as Minister of Health (1921-22). There his great organizing talents came into play, but he met with much opposition not only because of his anti-Socialistic viewpoint, but also because of his German Jewish origin. In 1926 he broke with the Liberal Party, disagreeing with the principles embodied in Lloyd George's land policy, and joined the Conservative Party. Two years later he was raised to peerage, becoming one of the three Jewish members of the House of Lords.

Melchett expounded his political and economic ideas in several books, including: Questions of To-Day and To-Morrow (1912); Why Socialism Must Fail (1923); Industry and Politics (1927); Imperial Economic Unity (1930).

Melchett received many academic honors, such as honorary degrees from several universities, including the Sorbonne, Paris, and the gold medal of the British Institute of Mining and Metallurgy. He was a fellow of the Royal Society.

Brought up as a Christian and married to a non-Jewess, he publicly manifested interest in Jewish affairs for the first time in April, 1917, when, "trembling with passion," he addressed a meeting at Queens Hall, London, protesting against the persecution of the Jews in Russia. In November of the same year, shortly after the publication of the Balfour Declaration, he sent an encouraging message to a Zionist meeting in Swansea, the borough he represented in Parliament. This letter was quoted in a Zionist memorandum to the British government which set out to disprove the assertions of certain anti-Zionist sections of British Jewry that Melchett was opposed to the principles involved in the Balfour Declaration.

In 1918 he became a member of Lord Herbert Samuel's advisory committee for the economic development of Palestine. In 1921 he met Chaim Weizmann in London, and in the same year made a journey to Palestine. "I have never lived so intensely as a Jew before," he reported. Chairman of the British Economic Board for Palestine, president of the English Keren Hayesod Committee as well as honorary president, from 1928 on president of the Zionist Federation of Great Britain, he donated large sums for the reconstruction of Palestine and founded the orange plantation known as Tel Mond. In 1929 he was elected chairman of the Council of the Jewish Agency, together with Louis Marshall, but he resigned in 1930 in protest against the Passfield White Paper which imputed to the Jews part of the blame for the riots of 1929.

Although he never formally returned to Judaism, Lord Melchett was an ardent Jewish nationalist. "I do not consider myself as an Englishman," he said. "I am a Palestinian. My heart is in Eretz Israel. This is my electorate. These are my people." He was buried in a Jewish cemetery and his son recited Kaddish in Hebrew.

LORD HENRY MELCHETT (b. London, 1898), son of Lord Alfred Melchett succeeded his father as chairman of the industrial trusts. He served in the first World War and became a Conservative Member of Parliament in 1929. Of partly Jewish blood, he returned to Judaism in 1933, as a protest against Hitlerism; in the same year his sister, EVA VIOLET MELCHETT, married to Gerald Rufus Isaacs, Marquess of Reading, embraced Judaism. In 1940 Lord Henry Melchett's wife, Lady Gwendolyn Melchett, was received into the Jewish community. The two sons of the Melchetts were brought up as Jews. Lord Melchett was in 1942 chairman of the Council of the Jewish Agency, while that same year his sister was president of the British section of the World Jewish Congress. Lord Melchett is the author of *Thy Neighbor* (1936), an eloquent affirmation of his new-found faith and a challenge to anti-Semitism.   ALFRED WERNER.

See also MOND.

Lit.: Bolitho, Henry Hector, *Alfred Mond, First Lord Melchett* (1933); Stone, Robert, "Melchett: Titan of British Industry," *Jewish Tribune*, Jan. 1, 1931; Zukerman, William, "The Young Lord Melchett," *Opinion*, Feb., 1933; Caiserman, H. M., "The Rt. Hon. Sir Herbert Samuel and Sir Alfred Moritz Mond," *Canadian Jewish Magazine*, Sept., 1941; *New York Times*, Dec. 28, 1930.

Lord Henry Melchett

MELCHIOR, Jewish family of merchants, physicians and lawyers, originally residing in Hamburg, Germany. While one of its branches remained there, three Melchior brothers went to Copenhagen, Denmark, and there founded a widely ramified branch. Other members of the Melchior family went to England, and became related by marriage to the Danish Melchiors. In 1760 MOSES MELCHIOR (b. Hamburg, 1736; d. Copenhagen, 1817) emigrated from Hamburg to Denmark. He married Rachel Zippora (1743-92), daughter of Nathan Rosbach, and had fourteen children. He was followed, in 1765, by his brother, SAMSON MELCHIOR (b. Hamburg, 1744; d. Copenhagen, 1808), who married Rachel Fürth (1741-88). In 1783 their brother, WULFF MELCHIOR (b. Hamburg, 1742; d. Copenhagen, 1808), went to Copenhagen, and married Esther Unna (1752-1818). The descendants of the three brothers married into the Ballin, Heckscher and Trier families. Among them were reputable artists, such as the painters David Jacob Jacobsen and F. M. H. Ballin, and the illustrious mathematicians Harald August Bohr and Niels Bohr. Moses Melchior founded at Copenhagen (1795) the firm Moses Melchior, which prospered for a century and a half. His son, GERSON MELCHIOR (b. Copenhagen, 1771; d. Copenhagen, 1845), became his partner and successor.

NATHAN GERSON MELCHIOR, ophthalmologist, eldest son of Gerson Melchior (b. Copenhagen, 1811; d. Copenhagen, 1872), studied medicine at the University of Copenhagen, and was graduated in 1835. Mainly interested in ophthalmology, he visited the ophthalmologic institutes of Berlin, Leipzig, Dresden, and Prague from 1836 to 1837. Because of his contributions to scientific journals in his special field, he was elected (1842) member of the Medical Society of Brussels. During the war against Germany of 1848 and 1849,

Melchior was army surgeon in a lazaretto at Copenhagen. In 1853 he received the honorary title of professor. In 1855 Melchior became lecturer on ophthalmology at the University of Copenhagen. In 1857 he became member of the directory of the Ophthalmologic Institute of Copenhagen, after he was sent (1856) by the Danish king abroad to study the Egyptian eye-disease. Melchior was interested in the promotion of charitable institutions for the blind.

MORITZ GERSON MELCHIOR (b. Copenhagen, 1816; d. Copenhagen, 1884), second son of Gerson Melchior, entered his father's business in 1840. After his father's death, in 1845, he was the principal director of the firm, having admitted his younger brother Moses as partner. Moritz Melchior augmented the firm considerably, and in 1853 founded a branch in Melbourne, Australia, which was dissolved in 1862. From 1851 to 1869 he was a member of the town council of Copenhagen, and from 1866 to 1874 he was a member of the Landsthing (Upper House). His fellow citizens respected Melchior because of his patriotism, and he was considered as disinterested in party politics. Melchior was the first Jew to become member and later leader of the Danish Chamber of Commerce (1849) and of the commercial court. He was also a trustee of the Jewish community of Copenhagen (1849 to 1852) and during the final year president of the Jewish community. In 1855 he was appointed member of the directorate of the harbor committee of Copenhagen, and in 1857 was a founder of the Privatbank.

An ardent foe of protectionism, Melchior participated (1861) in the founding of the Danish Free Trade Society, collaborating with Cobden. Melchior was interested also in the development of telegraphic communication in Scandinavia, and was a member of the directory of the Northern Telegraphic Society. He and his wife, Dorothy Henriquez, were generous patrons of literature and the arts. The poet Hans Christian Andersen, who was received hospitably for many years in Melchior's home, glorified the noblemindedness of the Melchiors in his letters, diaries, and some of his poems.

Lit.: Reumert, E., Hans Christian Andersen, og det Melchiorske Hjem (1924).

MOSES MELCHIOR (b. Copenhagen, 1825; d. Copenhagen, 1912), third son of Gerson Melchior, became (1845) a partner in the firm established by his grandfather. After his brother Moritz' death, Moses was the principal director of that firm. He often went abroad. He was in Australia from 1853 to 1855, and organized a branch of the firm Moses Melchior & Son at Melbourne. He visited the Danish West Indies several times, and in 1898 founded a branch of his firm at New York. Melchior was member of the town council of Copenhagen from 1869 to 1884, and from 1885 to 1904 member of the Chamber of Commerce. He was also member (1883 to 1905) of the Commercial and Maritime Court. He was a generous philanthropist, and supported Jewish and other charitable organizations.

CARL HENRIQUEZ MELCHIOR (b. Copenhagen, 1855; d. Copenhagen, 1938), son of Moritz Gerson Melchior, was educated at Copenhagen, and, from 1872, in England. Thence he went to Vevey, Switzerland. Upon returning to Denmark, Melchior entered business in Aarhus, and (1883) became partner of the firm of Moses Melchior & Son. He visited the Danish West Indies and the United States more than once. In 1898 he organized at New York the associated firm Armstrong and Dessau. Although Melchior was a successful and high-principled merchant, he was mainly interested in sports, and he considered it one of the most important tasks of his life to introduce into his native Denmark as many kinds of athletics as possible. When Melchior began his efforts in that direction, modern sport was almost unknown in Denmark. It is due to Melchior's intensive propaganda that the Danish people excelled later on in many athletic contests. Melchior himself was an excellent sportsman, and imparted to his fellow citizens the results of his studies and observations in England and Switzerland. Thus the Danish people's habits of life were changed decisively because of Melchior's example and teaching. Melchior not only patronized all Danish athletic organizations, but also inaugurated several institutions for the open-air life of children. Melchior was member of the directory of the union of Danish shipowners, and, from 1911 to 1929 president of the Jewish community of Copenhagen. Together with his wife, Clara Raphael, he published (1915) family memoirs entitled Familieminder.

MAX JOSEPH MELCHIOR (b. Copenhagen, 1862), son of Joseph Melchior (1818-86), was a physician and professor of dental surgery. He studied medicine at Copenhagen from 1880, and passed his medical examination in 1886. Then he was assistant surgeon at the Frederik Hospital under Oscar Bloch and C. J. Salomonsen, excelling in surgical operations. His thesis Om Cystetis og Urininfection (1883) was based on clinical, experimental and bacteriological studies, and was crowned with the Prix Godard of the French Academy of Sciences. In 1887 Melchior became surgeon in the Danish army, and in 1900 chief physician of the army corps. From 1896 on Melchior practised on civilian patients, and specialized in surgery of the urinary organs. Later he became interested in the application of modern surgery to dentistry. Melchior became an influence in modern dental surgery because of his methods of narcosis and local anesthesia. In 1927 he received an honorary degree from the University of Rostock, which had been the only home of scientific dentistry in Germany for a long time. From 1919 to 1933 Melchior was professor and chief of the clinic of dental surgery at the University of Copenhagen. Many generations of Danish dentists were educated by Melchior, who untiringly advocated improvement of the education of dental surgeons.

CARL MELCHIOR (b. Hamburg, 1871; d. Hamburg, 1933), jurist and statesman, was a descendant of the German branch of the Melchior family. He studied law at the Universities of Berlin, Bonn and Jena, and became a judge in his native town. In 1902 he was offered the post of syndic by the owners of the banking house of M. M. Warburg at Hamburg. Melchior accepted, and became a partner of the firm in 1917. After the outbreak of the first World War in 1914, Melchior went to the front as lieutenant in the Bavarian artillery. Having been injured in an accident, he collaborated in the Zentral-Einkaufs-Gesellschaft (ZEG), the largest supply house in Germany. Presently he was made member of its directorate and he

Carl Melchior

reorganized the firm. When the treaty of Brest-Litovsk was ratified by the Bolshevist government, Melchior accompanied the German Ambassador von Mirbach to Moscow, and later he accompanied Minister von Mumm to Kiev.

In November, 1918, Melchior became financial adviser of the German delegation for the armistice and peace treaty. He was also one of the six members of the German delegation at Versailles. He joined the opposition to the treaty and advocated its rejection at the risk of a large invasion into Germany. In 1920 Melchior published a pamphlet dealing with Germany's obligations assumed by the Treaty of Versailles, *Deutschlands finanzielle Verpflichtungen aus dem Friedensvertrage*. He participated in the conferences at Spa, Geneva, and Brussels, and accompanied Walther Rathenau to the conference at Genoa. He declined the post of secretary of the treasury in 1919, that of minister of economy in 1920, and that of minister of finance in 1921.

Meanwhile his opposition to the peace terms diminished, as he realized that the German point of view, originally shared by him, was not defensible. In 1922 Melchior became chairman of the German editorial board of the economic and social history of the World War whose editor-in-chief was Professor James T. Shotwell. According to Shotwell, Melchior "combined long experience in international finance with an intuitive perception of political realities." In 1926 the German government, after Germany's admission to the League of Nations, sent Melchior as commissioner of finance to Geneva. In 1931 Melchior was appointed member of the directorate of the Bank for International Settlements at Basel. He also labored indefatigably for the realization of the reconstructive arrangements inaugurated by Owen Young.

After the Nazis came to power, Melchior entered the central committee of German Jews, and sought to organize assistance to the persecuted Jews. But his health was already shattered, and he died in the fall of 1933. His early death was a severe blow to the German Jews.   HUGO BIEBER.

MELCHIZEDEK ("Zedek is my king"), king of Salem and priest of El Elyon (perhaps meaning "God the Most High"), who, after the defeat of Chedorlaomer and his Babylonian allies by Abraham, met the patriarch on his return to Canaan, offered him bread and wine, blessed him and received tithes from him (*Gen.* 14:18-20). The Tel-el-Amarna tablets (about 1400 B.C.E.) designate Uru-salim as one of the chief cities of Canaan (*uru* is equivalent to the Assyrian *alu*, "city"); whereas in the inscriptions of Rameses II and Rameses III, Jerusalem is called Sholam or Salem. In the letters, Ebed-tob, the king of Uru-salim, begs the Amenhoteps to send help against his enemies. He received his crown from *sarru dannu*, which is parallel to El Elyon (Most High), according to Hommel. The mountain of Uru-salim is called Bit-Ninip, thus identifying El Elyon with Ninip, Babylonia's warrior sun-god. Ebed-tob, as priest-king, offers a striking parellel to Melchizedek. Uru-salim was clearly the city of Salim, the god of peace and security. The action of Melchizedek in welcoming the peaceful return of Abraham and the acceptance of the tithe is derived from long established Babylonian custom, persisting in Jewish tradition (cf. *Ps.* 110 and *Hebrews* 7:1-6). Melchizedek's formula for blessing Abraham is found also in Egyptian sources. Because Melchizedek united the royalty with the priesthood, like the kings of the ancient Near East, he became the prototype for the priestly rulers of the Hasmonean dynasty (cf. *Ps.* 110:4). In order to claim the priesthood for Jesus, early Christianity designated him as after the order of Melchizedek (*Hebrews* 6:20).

Rabbinic tradition assigned to Melchizedek supernatural origin, along with Elijah, the Messiah ben Joseph, and the Messiah ben David (*Suk.* 52b). Abraham is alleged to have learned the practise of charity from Melchizedek (*Midrash Ps.* 37). Philo regards Melchizedek as "the logos, the priest whose inheritance is the true God." Melchizedek assisted David in writing the *Psalms* (*Ps.* 110; cf. *B.B.* 14b et seq.). Melchizedek is associated also with Shem, the son of Noah (*Ned.* 32b; *Targum to Gen.* 14:4; *Pirke de Rabbi Eliezer* 23). In the Ethiopian *Book of Adam and Eve*,

Melchizedek blesses Abraham. From a painting by Hippolyte Flandrin (1809-1864)

tradition supplies the events of Melchizedek's life before he welcomed Abraham. He was taken by Shem, at Noah's instruction, and by the angel Gabriel to Jerusalem to minister at the altar at "the center of the earth." Melchizedek offered bread and wine upon the altar near the place where Shem and the angel had deposited the body of Adam. There Melchizedek lived and worshipped under the guidance of Gabriel and unknown to men until he was met by Abraham. So great was the influence of this tradition that it led to a heretical Christian sect of Melchizedekites who regarded Melchizedek as a heavenly being, superior to Jesus.   ADOLPH J. FEINBERG.

Lit.: Sayce, Driver and Hommel, "Melchizedek," *Expository Times,* vols. 7 and 8; Hastings, James, edit., *Dictionary of the Bible,* vol. 3, p. 335; Skinner, *Genesis,* and other commentaries on *Gen.* 14:18-20; Kohler, Kaufmann, in *Jewish Encyclopedia,* vol. 8, p. 450.

MELDOLA, eminent Sephardic family of rabbis, scholars and physicians. David Israel Meldola married into the Montalto family, outstanding members of which were Elijah Montalto, physician to Marie de Medici, wife of Henry IV of France, and councilor to Louis XIII of France, and G. S. D. Montalto, painter.

ISAIAH MELDOLA, rabbi (b. Toledo, Spain, 1282; d. Mantua, Italy, 1340), the first known member of the family, was at first Dayan and then Haham of the Jewish community of Toledo. Later he emigrated to Italy, where he served as chief rabbi of Mantua and head of the Mantua Yeshiva.

ISAIAH MELDOLA, physician (b. Mantua, date of birth unknown; d. 1475, place of death unknown), occupied in Mantua the same positions as had been held by the earlier Isaiah Meldola. He wrote a commentary on *Isaiah* and a work on physiology, and practised medicine.

SAMUEL MELDOLA, physician and author, lived in Verona, Italy, early in the 17th cent. He was a court physician to the duke of Mantua, and wrote, beside a medical book, *Refuoth Tesaleh,* two religious works, *Keriath Shema* and *Debar Shemuel* (responsa).

RAPHAEL MELDOLA, rabbi and author (b. Livorno, Italy, 1685; d. Livorno, 1748), became (1710) Dayan of Livorno; from 1712 to 1729 he served as rabbi in Pisa, Italy, then was appointed rabbi of Bayonne, France. From 1742 to his birth he served again as rabbi of the Livorno community. He was the author of several theological works, among them *Mayim Rabbim* (responsa; 1737).

ABRAHAM MELDOLA, author and printer (b. Livorno, 1705; d. 1755), a son of Raphael Meldola, printed a large number of Hebrew theological works.

DAVID MELDOLA, rabbi (b. Livorno, 1714; d. Amsterdam, 1800), another son of Raphael Meldola, published his father's works in Amsterdam, where he served as a rabbi. Among his numerous works are *Moed David* (1741; a work on astronomy and mathematics); *Dibre David* (responsa; 1753), *Dareche Yesod Halimmud* (a work on the methodology of the Talmud; 1754); and many others in Hebrew and Portuguese.

MOSES HEZEKIAH MELDOLA, proofreader, merchant and philologist (b. Livorno, 1725; d. Livorno, 1791), was the youngest son of Raphael Meldola. It is said that for a time he taught oriental languages in the University of Paris.

ABRAHAM MELDOLA, philologist (b. Amsterdam, 1754; d. Altona, Germany, date of death unknown), was a son of David Meldola and lived in Altona. He was the author of many works, including *Traduccion de las cartas mercantines y manuales* (1784); *Nova grammatica portuguesa* (1785); *Kol Hazirim Tahath Hashir* (1805); *Tulpen und Staatspapiere* (1830).

RAPHAEL MELDOLA, rabbi and author (b. Livorno, 1756; d. London, 1828), first a Hebrew printer, then a rabbi in Livorno, was elected Haham of the Spanish and Portuguese Jews of London in 1804. A great scholar, he was the friend of Isaac Disraeli and his son, Benjamin, who later became Earl of Beaconsfield. His works include *Korban Minhah,* a commentary on the Abodah, or description of the sacrificial services of the Day of Atonement; *Huppath Hathanim,* on the marriage ritual (frequently republished); and *Derech Emunah,* published by his son David after the author's death (1848).

DAVID MELDOLA, rabbi (b. Livorno, 1796; d. London, 1853), a son of Raphael Meldola, was, as an officer of the Beth Din of the London Sephardic community and as acting chief rabbi (1828-53) opposed to the Reform Movement, using his office to prevent the formation of Reform congregations. A founder of the *Jewish Chronicle,* he left Hebrew writings in manuscript.

RAPHAEL MELDOLA, chemist and naturalist (b. London, 1849; d. London, 1915), a son of Samuel Meldola, was appointed (1873) lecturer at the Royal College of Sciences, and (1885) professor of chemistry at the Finsbury Technical College. He headed an expedition of the Royal Society to the Nicobar Islands for the study of the eclipse of the sun (1875). He was the discoverer of several coal-tar dyes.

MELLER, ROSE (pseudonym, Frank Mahr), author and playwright, b. Budapest, 1902. In the years following 1920 she lived in Vienna and attracted notice with her novel *Frau auf der Flucht.* The title has a suggestion of autobiography; like so many other Jewish intellectuals, she was an exile from her native Hungary. The motives of persecution and a sense of guilt were taken up again both in the life and other works of the author. She had achieved great success with her original and imaginative play, *Leutnant Komma* (1933), which made her name well-known in Central Europe and upon which American producers held options. In 1933 the sensational case of attempted murder against her by Nazis was tried in a Vienna court. She was sentenced to six months' imprisonment, charged with inflicting the wound upon herself.

Another play by Rose Meller, *Ich hab's getan,* the story of a guilty woman, was a great stage success and provided a role of many colors for great actresses. Miss Meller, who used the pseudonym Frank Mahr, was author of the novels *Anka* and *Erde,* and of the plays *Die Weiber von Zoinsdorf* and *Kamerad.*

In 1942 she was living in Budapest where, in accordance with the special Hungarian legislation, the work of Jewish stage authors could not be produced.

MELLER, SIMON, art historian, b. Györ, Hungary, 1875. He studied in Budapest and Berlin, receiving his Ph.D. degree in 1898. In 1901 he joined the staff of the National Gallery, Budapest, and in 1910 became head of the graphic division of the Museum of Fine Arts there. He enlarged the graphic as well as the sculpture collection of the museum. In 1919 he became professor at the University of Budapest, an appointment which was as short-lived as the communist government to which he owed it. He continued to serve at the Museum of Fine Arts until 1924, when he left for Munich.

Meller published works in Hungarian on the architecture of ancient Rome, Michelangelo, Goya, the Esterházy Gallery, and the Palazzo Farnese at Rome. He created violent controversy by attributing a horseman's statuette on the estate of the sculptor István Ferenczy to Leonardo da Vinci. His works attest keen judgment and originality. He also published in German *Peter Vischer der Ältere und seine Werkstatt* and *Die deutschen Bronzestatuetten der Renaissance* (1926). Some of his minor essays touch upon Jewish subjects.

MELO, DAVID ABENATAR, *see* IBN ATTAR, DAVID MELO.

MELTZER, SAMUEL JAMES, physician, b. Trape, near Kovno, Russia, 1851; d. New York city, 1920. Of an Orthodox family and originally intended for the rabbinate, he studied physiology and medicine at the University of Berlin (M.D., 1882). He came to the United States in 1883. Among his many important discoveries are a new method of artificial respiration (1912) and one of treating lockjaw, which resulted from his special studies of wounded soldiers in 1914, as well as his application of magnesium sulphate as an anesthetic.

Meltzer was head of the Department of Physiology and Pharmacology at the Rockefeller Institute from 1906 to his death. He was founder and first president of the American Society for the Advancement of Clinical Investigation, of the Society for Experimental Biology and Medicine, and of the Medical Brotherhood for the Furtherance of International Morality, a pacifist organization. Holding the rank of major in the Medical Officers Reserve Corps, he was made honorary doctor of three American and European universities. He published more than 200 monographs on biology, physiology and allied topics.

MELVILLE, LEWIS (pseudonym), *see* BENJAMIN, LEWIS SAUL.

MEM, *see* ALPHABET.

MEMEL (Lithuanian, **Klaipeda**), Baltic port and district (Memelland), with a population of 140,000, of whom 5,000 to 6,000 were Jews (estimated before the Munich crisis, in the fall of 1938). Belonging until the Versailles treaty to the district of Königsberg, East Prussia, the city itself had, in 1900, a population of 19,796, including 1,214 Jews.

The Jews of Memel were mentioned for the first time in 1567, in connection with an expulsion decree. Only a hundred years later, the Great Elector, Frederick William of Brandenburg, permitted the Dutch merchant, Moses Jacobsohn de Jonge, to settle there (1664). De Jonge, however, was compelled by financial difficulties to leave, and in the following period Jews were allowed to enter Memel only during the fairs. The Prussian edict of 1812, granting citizenship to the Jews of Prussia, enabled the Jews to settle in Memel, too, and the city's flourishing wood trade with Russia attracted many Polish and Russian Jews. The community

was organized in 1862; its first rabbi was Dr. Isaac Rülf (1865-98), writer and Zionist, who founded a parochial school and hospital and aided Russian refugees.

Under the Treaty of Versailles (1919) the city of Memel and the Memelland were detached from Germany and placed under the control of the Conference of Ambassadors, but they were seized by the Lithuanians in 1923. The following year the League of Nations recognized Memel as being under the sovereignty of Lithuania. For the next sixteen years the Jews of Memel shared the fate of the entire Lithuanian Jewry. According to a statement made by M. Bertulait, former president of Memel, in March, 1939, the Memel Jews owned 330 factories and industrial enterprises (among them tobacco, textile and chocolate factories), employing 70 per cent of Memel's German workers. But there were many Jewish professional men and craftsmen.

Their situation, already jeopardized by the constant clashes between the Lithuanian rulers and the German majority, took a turn for the worse in 1933, when the German agitation for Memel's return to the Reich was directed into anti-Semitic channels in order to disguise the immediate objective of the Nazi foreign policy. The Memel Nazis, under the leadership of Ernst Neumann, who had been imprisoned (1935) for attempting an armed insurrection, but was amnestied some time later, organized the anti-Jewish terror. A bill of February 26, 1937, aimed at depriving Jewish artisans of work, adopted by the German majority in the Memel diet, was vetoed by the Lithuanian governor. In March of the same year Hitler youth attacked Jewish visitors to the seaside resort of Schwarzort, and the autonomous German police refused to protect them. In June the Lithuanian police confiscated large numbers of anti-Jewish pamphlets calling on the German population to boycott the Jews, while the windows of a synagogue were smashed during a riot between Germans and Lithuanians. In October, 1938, a conference of German leaders demanded introduction of the Nuremberg laws.

After the Munich crisis, in September, 1938, an ever-increasing exodus of Jews who feared a Nazi coup d'état took place, and Jewish-owned capital estimated at nearly $10,000,000 was exported to the interior of Lithuania. In the December, 1938, elections, when the Memel Nazis won twenty-six out of twenty-nine diet seats, Memelland became practically part of the Reich. Anticipating the unavoidable annexation of Memel by the Reich, about half of the Jewish population (which included a number of refugees from Germany) had left Memel by the early months of 1939. On March 22, 1939, Memel was occupied by the German army, and the rest of the Jews left for Lithuania. A number of Jewish merchants and doctors, however, were caught by the Nazis and thrown into concentration camps; the Jewish-owned property that fell into Nazi hands in Memelland was valued at $17,000,000. All synagogues were destroyed, and Jewish communal institutions taken over by the Nazis. In 1942 there were no Jews left in Memel. ALFRED WERNER.

Lit.: Rülf, Isaac, "Zur Geschichte der Juden in Memel," in the first *Bericht der israelitischen Religionsschule* (1900); Rönne-Simon, *Die früheren und gegenwärtigen Verhältnisse der Juden in den sämtlichen Landesteilen des preussischen Staates* (1843); Kollenscher, *Rechtsverhältnisse der Juden in Preussen; Bericht der jüdischen Sejmfraktion* (1923-26).

MEMOIRS. The earliest memoirs in Jewish literature are the reminiscences of Ezra and Nehemiah in the Biblical books of the same name and the autobiography of Josephus. There were a large number of autobiographical writings in the Middle Ages, which may be grouped according to country and place, and furnish valuable insight into the history of the times. Into this category there fall, in addition to elegies and occasional pieces, the accounts of such travelers as Benjamin of Tudela, Pethahiah of Regensburg, Judah Alharizi, Menahem ben Zerah (*Tzedah Laderech;* Spain, 14th cent.) and Asher ben Jehiel in the collection *Minhath Kenaoth* (13th to 14th centuries). After the 15th cent. the number of autobiographical writings increased; in the 16th cent. they were written by such men as Joseph Hakohen, David ben Judah and Josel of Rosheim; on the other hand, the memoirs of David Reubeni are of doubtful historicity. Since the middle of the 19th cent. they have constituted a significant group. The value of these memoirs for the writing of history is easily discernible from the following arrangement by countries:

Germany: The most important memoirs of the 17th cent. are those of Glückel of Hameln, which not only give a true picture of the family life, customs and traditions of the Jews of Germany but also furnish important information on economic conditions in Hamburg and other cities of Northern Germany and Lorraine. Similarly the memoirs of Asher Levi, who lived in Central Europe and Alsace, for the period 1598-1635 (edit. M. Ginsburger, Berlin, 1913), throw light upon the history of the Jews of Lorraine, Alsace and Western Germany during the Thirty Years' War.

Jacob Emden is as important for the 18th cent. as Glückel of Hameln is for the 17th. His autobiography (*Megillath Sefer,* edit. David Kahana, Warsaw, 1896) takes one over most of Northern Europe, from Altona to Holland, Emden, Berlin, Breslau, Hamburg, Ungarisch-Brod, Lemberg, Hannover, Frankfort, London, Prague, Brünn, Dresden and Amsterdam, where the Jewish jewelry trade was flourishing. Then one returns again to Altona where the controversy about amulets between Jacob Emden and Jonathan Eybeschütz broke out; all of Jewry became involved in this affair. This autobiography sheds light upon the conditions affecting the Jews in these places. Conditions in the triple community of Altona, Hamburg and Wandsbeck are touched upon in the defense of Ebyeschütz, *Luhoth Eduth* (1750).

According to his travel diary (edit. David Kaufmann, *Aus H. Heines Ahnensaal;* Breslau, 1896), Simon van Geldern was making trips out of Düsseldorf, after 1750, about the same time as Jacob Emden. He visited the most important cities of Germany, England, Holland, Austria, Italy, Egypt, Palestine as well as European and Asiatic Turkey, Hungary, Moravia, Bohemia, France and Denmark. The family Megillah of Isaak Behrendt of Hannover shows how a Jewish merchant was despised and treated in those days. The activities of the Frankists in Offenbach are described from first hand experience by Moses Porges of Prague (edit. Gelber, in *Historishe Shriften des Yiddishen Vissenshaftlichen Instituts,* Vilna, 1929); it contains reports also of Jewish life in South Germany and of the war between Austria and France. Itzig Behrend tells of the Frankists in Hannover at the beginning of the 19th cent. in his *Unsere Familienchronik.*

Valuable contributions to the study of the last part of the 18th cent. and the beginning of the 19th are furnished by Aron Isak, the founder of the Jewish community at Stockholm. His memoirs tell of the Jews and Jewish communities in the provinces of Brandenburg, Pomerania and Mecklenburg; they are also important source material for Swedish history. In this connection mention must be made also of Henriette Herz (*Jugenderinnerungen;* Berlin, 1897) who was part of the circle of Moses Mendelssohn; Salomon Maimon (edit. Moritz, Berlin, 1792-1793 and Munich, 1916) who came from Poland to Hamburg and Berlin; and Therese Devrient whose *Jugenderinnerungen* (1803-1844) touch upon Hamburg (Salomon Heine), Upper Silesia (Ratibor), Berlin (the Mendelssohns), Herz, Rahel Varnhagen, Gans and Moritz Veit.

There were relationships between Goethe and Bendavid (*Selbstbiographie,* which tells about Berlin and Vienna; Berlin, 1804), Rahel Varnhagen (*Rahel, Ein Buch des Andenkens;* Berlin, 1833), Heinrich Heine, Moritz Oppenheim, the artist (*Aus dem Leben eines Glücklichen,* which tells also about the Jews of Rome; 1927), and Salomon Munk. The names of Schelling and Molitor are found on a subscribers' list of Moses Koerner who describes in *Rishpe Kesheth* (Hannover, 1831) his wanderings through Germany, Austria and Holland and the system of begging in his times.

The desire for education and the educational development of a poor Jew of those times are reflected in the autobiographical sketch by Heymann Arnheim (edit. Grunwald, in *Lewy-Festschrift*), who came to Glogau from Wengerow by way of Berlin. Thuringia, especially the Franz School in Dessau, is described in the autobiography of Gotthold Salomon (*Schriften zur Förderung der jüdischen Literatur*), by M. Jost (*Sippurim;* vol. 3; Prag, 1855), and by H. Steinthal (*Über Juden und Judentum;* Berlin, 1906). The circle around Leopold Zunz is depicted by Judah Leon Gordon (*Reshumoth,* vol. 5). Fanny Lewald's autobiography (1861-1863) tells of Königsberg, Berlin, Breslau and the emancipation of the Jews. German musical life (Beethoven, Felix Mendelssohn-Bartholdy, Meyerbeer) is treated in Ferdinand Hiller's *Erinnerungsblätter* (Berlin, 1884). The same period is described by Moritz Lazarus in his collection of essays, *Treu und Frei,* by D. Honigmann in the memoirs of his student days, and by E. Bernstein in his memoirs, *Von 1850-1872, Kindheit und Jugendjahre* (1926).

The following writers in professional circles contributed to this literature: the Metz Hazan, Solomon Lifschütz, who tells of cantors in *Teudath Shelomoh* (1718); A. Geiger, *Die letzten 2 Jahre* (Breslau 1840); Leopold Stein, *Meine Verteidigung in Zweibrücken* (Frankfort, 1860) and *Mein Dienstverhältnis* (Frankfort, 1817); I. Kley, preface to the second volume of sermons given in the Hamburg Synagogue and *Blätter der Erinnerung* (1844); the Talmudist, S. S. Landsberg, *Toar Pene Shelomoh* (Krotoschin, 1870); Heinrich Graetz' diary; Ludwig Barnay, *Erinnerungen* (1903); Ignaz Moschele's diary, *Aus Moscheles Leben* (Leipzig, 1872; in English, 1873); A. J. Paperna, *Das erste jüdische Drama . . . Meine Erinnerungen an A. Goldfaden* (Warsaw, 1923); the opera singer Paul

Kalisch, *Lebende Geschichten* (Berlin, 1916); the violin virtuoso Heinrich Grünfeld, *In Dur und Moll* (Leipzig, 1923); Siegfried Ochs, *Geschehenes, Gesehenes* (1922); Angelo Neumann, *Erinnerungen an R. Wagner;* the clinician K. F. Cannstatt, *Klinische Rückblicke und Abhandlungen* (1848-1851); the physiologist Julius Bernstein; the ophthalmologists, Hermann Cohen, *30 Jahre ärztliche und akademische Lehrtätigkeit* (Bresl..u, 1897) and Julius Hirschberg, *Erlebnisse und Erinnerungen* (1923); the lexicogr..pher Daniel Sanders, *Aus der Werkstatt eines Wörterbuchschreibers* (Berlin, 1889); the authors Johann K. August Lewald, *Aquarelle aus dem Leben* (1836-1837), *Neue Aquarelle aus dem Leben* (1840), *Ein Menschenleben* (12 vols., 1843-1846), A. Halbert, *Die Katastrophe unserer Kultur* (1912), Max Ring, *Erinnerungen,* Julius Rodenberg, *Erinnerungen aus der Jugendzeit* (1899) and *Aus seinen Tagebüchern* (1919), Alexander Moszkowski, *Das Panorama meines Lebens* (1924), and Jakob Wassermann, *Mein Weg als Deutscher und Jude* (1928); as theologian, the convert Paulus Cassel, *Aus guten Stunden* (Berlin, 1874); the statesman of the Bismarckian era, Ludwig Bamberger (edit. P. Nathan, Berlin, 1927); Ferdinand Lassalle, *Tagebuch* (Berlin, 1927); Eduard Lasker, *Erlebnisse einer Mannesseele* (anonymous, edit. Berthold Auerbach, Stuttgart, 1873); the lawyer Max Hachenburg, *Lebenserinnerungen eines Rechtsanwaltes* (Düsseldorf, 1924); *Unser Vaterhaus* (anonymous, about the family of the physicist Heinrich Hertz); the cantor A. Friedmann, *50 Jahre in Berlin* (Berlin, 1929); the chess player Emanuel Lasker, *Mein Wettkampf mit Capablanca* (Berlin, 1922). Jewish family and community life is described by the following: I. Kastan, *Altkempen, Breslauer Erinnerungen* and *Berliner Erinnerungen;* A. Berliner, *Aus meiner Knabenzeit;* Rosalie Perles, *Unsere Grossväter; Unsere Grossmütter;* Ludwig Kalisch, *Bilder aus meiner Knabenzeit* (Leipzig, 1872); Felix Holländer, *Unser Haus* (1911); Samuel Blach, *Kindertage* (Halberstadt, 1924); Lion Wolff, *50 Jahre Lebenserfahrungen eines jüdischen Lehrers und Schriftstellers* (Leipzig, 1919); Mosenthal, *Tante Gutraud* (Hesse); Ulla Frank's memoirs about Upper Silesia, in short story form; Lina Morgenstern's memoirs of A. Geiger, the revolution of 1848 and her *Erinnerungsblätter aus dem Kriegsjahre 1870-71* (Berlin, 1895); Emil Lehmann, *Ein Halbjahrhundert in der israelitischen Religionsgemeinde Dresden* (1890); Reinstein, *Die Stadt der Originale* (about Friedrichstadt, in *Die Wahrheit,* Vienna 1929). In 1927 S. Rosenberg published, in Frankfort, *Familienchronik der Familie Rosenberg.*

Alsace. The Alsatian contributors to this field of literature are Alexander Weil, *Ma jeunesse;* M. Schuhl, *Nos usages religieux, souvenirs d'enfance* (Paris, 1896); Louis Halévy's memoirs; Alfred Dreyfus, *Cinq années de ma vie, 1894-99* (Paris, 1901); Sarah Bernhardt's memoirs (edit. by A. Kohut; Leipzig, 1908); Honel Meiss, *Moshelisch* and *Traditions populaires alsaciennes* (Nice, 1928).

France. The most important are Ernest Blum, *Les mémoires d'un vieux beau* (1896); E. Fleg, *The Boy Prophet* and *Why I Am a Jew;* Pallière, *The Unknown Sanctuary;* Israel Roukhomovsky, *Mein lebn un mein arbet* (Yiddish; Paris, 1928).

Austria. The *Privatbriefe* published by Landau-Wachstein provide important data on the period of the Thirty Years' War; in addition there is Yom Tob Lipmann Heller's *Megillath Ebah* (edit. M. Körner with a German translation, Breslau, 1836). A classical sourcebook on the economic development of Vienna is Siegmund Mayer's *Ein jüdischer Kaufmann* (Berlin, 1911); in the field of political activity it is Joseph Bloch's *Erinnerungen aus meinem Leben* (3 vols., Vienna, 1922) in which there is an authentic presentation of the high water mark of Luegerian anti-Semitism and the defense against Rohling, Deckert and others, as well as the internal politics of Austrian Jewry.

The Revolution of 1848 and other events are described by L. A. Frankl in *Erinnerungen* (edit. Hock, Prague, 1910) and in his essays which for a time appeared every year on March 18 in the *Neue Freie Presse.* In this connection must be mentioned Berthold Auerbach, *Tagebuch aus Wien* (Breslau, 1849); Moritz Hartmann, *Erzählungen eines Unstäten* (Berlin, 1858; he also published *Tagebuch aus Languedoc und Provence,* 1852); and the autobiography of the mathematician Spitzer. The difficulties placed in the path of the Jew who wanted to pursue an academic career are described by the neuropathologist Moritz Benedikt in *Aus meinem Leben* (1906; it describes also Jewish life in the Carpathian region), the chemist Adolf Lieben (in the preface to the *Festschrift* on his seventieth birthday, Vienna, 1906), and Sigmund Freud in his autobiography (Leipzig, 1927). *Essays und Erinnerungen* (Stuttgart, 1905) of the philolo..ist Theodor von Gomperz may be considered memoirs in part. Wilhelm von Gutmann's autobiography (privately printed) tells the history of the house of Gutmann Brothers. The eminent Auspitz family is treated in the autobiographical work, *50 Jahre eines Wiener Hauses,* by J. Winter (Vienna, 1928). The influence of a Jewish lecturer on a Protestant faculty is described by Albert Cohn, who later became the administrator of charities for the Rothschilds of Paris ("Lettres juives," in *L'univers Israélite,* 1864-1865). Mention must also be made of the works of the following Austrians: the outstanding jurist and confidant of the imperial family, Adolf Bachrach, *Aus meiner Werkstatt* and his autobiographical sketch in Grunwald's *Die Juden und Judengemeinden Mährens* (Brünn, 1929); the anonymous Viennese author (Friedmann) of *40 Jahre Journalist;* Alfred Meissner, *Schattentanz* (Zurich, 1881) and *Geschichte meines Lebens* (2 vols., 3rd ed., Teschen, 1884); Wilhelm Goldbaum's memoirs; Peter Altenberg's *Tagebuch-Notizen und Skizzen* and *Mein Lebensabend;* Fleischner's *Parlementsbilder* (Vienna, 1918); Lola Kirschner (Ossip Schubin), *Die Flucht aus dem Alltag.* Musical life is treated by Josef Sulzer in *Erinnerungen eines Philharmonikers* and by S. Bachrich in *Aus verklungenen Zeiten* (Vienna, 1914). A part of the autobiography of Popper-Lynkeus together with other biographical sketches appeared in Grunwald's *Juden als Erfinder und Entdecker* and deals also with Bohemian Jewry. *Zichronothai* by I. H. Weiss (Warsaw, 1895) deals with Jewish spiritual life in Hungary and Moravia. The life of the Jews in the Carpathian region (Eisenstadt) is described in Alfred Fürst's *Sitten und Gebräuche einer Judengasse* (Székesfehérvár, 1908).

Bohemia and Moravia. Jewish memoirs from these localities include "Milhamah Beshalom" in *Bikkure Haittim* (5584) by Judah Löb ben Joshua, which tells of the siege of Prague by the Swedes in 1648; and the sermons *Or Layesharim* of Zerah Eidlitz published by his son in Prague in 1795, recalling his youth and the religious life before the expulsion from Prague in 1740 in contrast to later periods; they tell of the activities in the cafes, dancing and the various sieges of Prague. The physician Jonas Jeitteles published *Mitteilungen aus den Tagebüchern des Dr. Jonas Jeitteles im Jahre 1783 mit Zusätzen seines Sohnes Isak Jeitteles;* the educator Peter Beer wrote his *Selbstbiographie* (Prague, 1834); and one of the earliest protagonists of better understanding between Jews and Czechs, S. Kapper, described *Die ersten Schmerzen* (Bohemia, 1849). H. J. Landau, grandson of Ezekiel Landau, published his *Albumblätter* in manuscript, in which were entries by most of the famous personalities of his time, such as Sulzer, L. A. Frankl, Mosenthal, Meyerbeer, J. and S. Heller, M. J. Landau and David Popper; he also tells of his father and his audience with Emperor Francis. The following authors described Jewish life in Prague during the first half of the 19th cent.: Fritz Mauthner, *Jugenderinnerungen* (Munich, 1918); E. H. Kisch, the physician at Marienbad, *Erlebtes und Erstrebtes* (Stuttgart, 1914); G. L. Weisel, *Aus dem Neumarker Landestor.* Moravia is the locale of *Jugenderinnerungen* of Julius Gomperz (2nd ed., 1903); *Tagesereignisse 1836-37* of Pollack (Trebitsch); *Erlebtes und Erstrebtes* of Gotthard Deutsch; *Schilderungen aus dem Prerauer Ghettoleben* of Ignaz Briess (2nd ed., Brünn, 1912); "Die mährische Judengasse in vormärzlicher Zeit" of M. Hrdlitschka (*Juden in Mähren,* 1929); and *Mährische Dorfjuden* of M. Grünfeld (Brünn, 1928). Moses Sofer, in his *Sefer Zikkaron,* describes events in Pressburg at the beginning of the 19th cent. and especially the siege by the French. Pressburg life is represented in *Autobiographische Blätter* by Leopold Dukes (edit. David Kaufmann). The widely travelled Leopold Katscher, like Kisch, wrote about Marienbad (1872) and a diary of the Russian Revolution (1906); he also wrote *50 Jahre Gräfenberger Erinnerungen* (1906). An interesting series of recollections of a sleeping-car conductor were published by Husserl in the *Jüdische Volksstimme* (Brünn, 1927-1929).

Hungary. Jews and Jewish life are depicted by the Komorn Rabbi Schnitzer in *Kulturskizzen,* which tell of the joys and sorrows of the Bachur; and by Rebekah Kohut in her autobiography, *My Portion* (New York, 1925). Religious struggles are found in Aaron Chorin's *Yeled Zekunim* (Vienna, 1839). Julius Schulhof was an eye-witness of the siege of Ofen in 1688 which he describes in *Megillath Ofen* (edit. David Kaufmann, Trèves, 1894). A part of the youth of each of the following was spent in Budapest and is described in their memoirs: Theodor Herzl, autobiography in the *Jewish Chronicle* (1895) and in *Die Welt* (commemorative issue, 1904); Max Nordau, *Erinnerungen* (Leipzig 1928); the violin virtuoso, Leopold Auer, *My Long Life in Music* (New York, 1924); Arthur Holitscher, *Erinnerungen eines Rebellen* (1926) and *Mein Leben in dieser Zeit* (1928).

Holland. Mention must be made of M. B. Mendes da Costa, *Tooneelherinneringen* (Amsterdam, 1900) and Uriel Acosta, *Exemplar humanae vitae* (published repeatedly since 1687).

Switzerland. Nahida Lazarus wrote *Ein deutscher Professor in der Schweiz* (Berlin, 1910).

Roumania. Some of the representative Roumanian writers of memoirs are Goldfaden, whose recollections appeared in the form of an autobiography (1928); Dobrogeanu; Gerea (Katz), *Actul meu de nastere,* and *Amintiri din trecutul indepartat* (1908); and Psanter, *Sefer Zichronoth* (Bucharest, 1889), which deals with the inmates of the Bucharest home for the aged but contains a preface on the personal history of the author.

England. Included here are Moses Montefiore's diaries for 1812-1883 (London, 1890) and travels in Palestine (1870), as well as I. Abrahams' childhood memories in *Jewish Festivals.*

Italy. Examples of this type of literature are found in Leon da Modena, *Hayye Yehudah* (17th cent.) and his letters and articles (edit. Blau, Budapest, 1903); Azulai's diary, *Maagal Tob* (edit. Liber-Freimann, Berlin, 1922); S. D. Luzzatto's childhood memories (in *Hamaggid,* 1858, 1859, 1862) as well as his autobiography; the family Megillah of Meldola; Giuseppe Levi, *Autobiografia di un padre di famiglia* (1868); Elijah Benamozegh, the rabbi of Livorno who became famous through Pallière and whose autobiography appeared in the *Sefer Zikkaron* (Warsaw, 1889); and the notes of Judah Gonzago concerning Rome in particular.

Russia, Poland and Lithuania. Memoirs from these countries are of a broader scope. Beer of Bolechow (1723-1805) gives in his *Zichronoth* (Berlin, 1922) a faithful picture of the economic condition of Poland in the 18th cent. and life in the Jewish community which came into its own with the Hasidic movement. Salomon Maimon, mentioned above, also describes Polish Jewish life. M. Letteris (1807-1861) surveys the entire cultural life of the Jews during the first half of the 19th cent. in *Zikkaron Basefer* (1869); the second half of the century is treated by Markus Landau, a part of whose manuscript appeared in the *Deutsch-Österreichische Wochenschrift.* Eliakim Zunser described in his Yiddish autobiography (English trans. S. Hirshdansky, 1905) the pitiful conditions in Russia under Nicholas I, the kidnapping of children for the army and the Kahal tyranny. G. J. Bogrov, a fanatic on the Russification of the Jews, later became baptized and published *Zapiski Yevreya* (1871-1873). *Meine Zichroines* (Berlin, 1929) by Yehezkel Kotik depicts the political situation of the Jews and their cultural, vocational and personal lives from Nicholas I to the assassination of Alexander II. Pauline Wengeroff is credited with having written the Jewish *Buddenbrooks,* the rise and decline of a house, in *Memoiren einer Grossmutter* (Berlin, 1908-1910). Perez Smolenskin describes his own life in the orphan Joseph, hero of his *Hatoeh Bedarche Hahayim* (2nd ed., 1876). R. Brainin wrote the biography of his brother Leon (d. 1929) who narrated it to him (the manuscript is in possession of his family). M. L. Lilienblum sponsored greater freedom in Jewish spiritual life and was a protagonist of emigration to Palestine in his *Hattoth Neurim* (1876). Moreover, the following authors wrote memoirs in essay or other literary form: Ahad Haam, *Pirke Zichronoth;* S. Bernfeld, *Zichron-*

oth; Sholem Alechem, *Das Leben eines Menschen;* Mendele Mocher Sforim (Abramowitsch), *Schloimele;* Zmirinski, *Ajarati Motele* which describes life in a Lithuanian village; Ish Naami, *Mitehom Haneshiah;* K. E. Franzos, *Pojaz* and foreword to *Die Geschichte des Erstlingswerkes.*

The entire spiritual development of the Jews during the 19th cent. is described by the following authors: Isaac Joel Linetzki, opponent of Hasidism, *Arob funem yerid* (1909, on his 70th birthday); Jacob Dinesohn tells of childhood in *Der Jid* (1900) and *Meine ersten Kinderjahre;* J. L. Lewin, who changed from Social Democrat to Zionist, in *Zikkaron Basefer* (1910); Abraham Cahan writes of himself from Bahur to editor and Socialist leader, of the Nihilist persecutions in Russia, the mass emigration after the pogrom, Socialism in America, the Jewish question at the Socialist Congresses, and Yiddish newspaper and theatrical life in New York, in his four-volume work *Bletter fun mein Leben* (New York, 1926-1928); Mark Lidzbarski, *Auf rauhem Wege;* Jehudo Epstein, *Mein Weg von Ost nach West* (Vienna, 1929); Shemarya Levin, *Childhood in Exile* (vol. 1, of his memoirs, in English and in Yiddish, New York, 1929); Jakob Teitel, *Aus meiner Lebensarbeit, Erinnerungen eines jüdischen Richters aus dem alten Russland* (Frankfort, 1929); Judah Loeb Gordon, *Al Nehar Kevar;* P. Minkowski, *Misefer Hayyai* (on the history of Hazanuth); Jacob Mase (memoirs in the *Jewish Morning Journal,* 1926); Israel Bunemowicz; memoirs (edit. Lewin, Vilna, 1928); Dubnow, *Fun Jargon bis Yiddish* (Vilna, 1929).

United States. There are comparatively few memoirs of importance in the United States. There is no diary of any early settler, though that of the Christian divine Ezra Stiles furnishes some information. A number of individuals have written autobiographies which are largely personal in tone and interest, but shed interesting sidelights on contemporary Jewish life. The *Reminiscences* of Isaac Mayer Wise are important for the history of the early Reform Movement in Judaism in America. The American writers of memoirs include Cyrus Adler (*I Have Considered the Days*), Boris D. Bogen (*Born a Jew*), Henry Morgenthau, who wrote of his experiences as ambassador, Simon Wolf, Mary Antin (*The Promised Land*), A. S. Sachs (*Worlds That Passed*), Nathan S. Jonas (*Through the Years*), Philip Cowen (*Memoirs of an American Jew*), Rebekah Kohut (*My Portion* and *As I Know Them*), Toby E. Rosenthal, Ludwig Lewisohn (*Upstream* and *Mid-Channel*), Oscar S. Straus, (*Under Four Administrations*), David Philipson (*My Life as an American Jew*), Esther Bengis (*I Am a Rabbi's Wife*), Frances Nathan Wolff (*Four Generations*), and Gotthard Deutsch (in *Scrolls,* vol. 1). American Yiddish authors of memoirs include Goldfaden, Cahan, Kobrin, Kopielow and Moishe Nadir. The memoirs of Lorenzo da Ponte contain a section on his career in the United States.

South America. One of the outstanding examples of memoirs from this part of the globe is *30 Johr in Argentinien* by Mordecai Alperson (Buenos Aires, 1928).

Palestine. The following authors include Palestine as the locale of their writings: Moses Montefiore; Judith Montefiore, travel diaries for 1827 and 1840 (privately printed); Joshua Yellin, *Zichronoth Leben Yerushala-* *yim* (Jerusalem, 1924) which describes the beginnings of the reconstruction of Palestine, the differences between the Sephardim and the Ashkenazim, the Sassoons, Baghdad, India and other topics; Trumpeldor's diaries and letters tell of the battles during the first World War and later in Palestine; Eliezer Ben Jehudah's memoirs; Jehiel Eisenstadt's diary covering the years from 1887 to 1914 and describing his service in the founding of colonies; Mordecai ben Hillel Hakohen, *Olami;* Moses Smilanski, *Zichronoth* (Tel Aviv, 1928-1929).

On the other hand this type of literature frequently throws light upon special topics and situations which are historically important. The following works are arranged accordingly:

Hasidism: M. Buber, *Mein Weg zum Chassidismus* and *Erinnerungen* (1911).

Zionism: Herzl, *Tagebücher* (Berlin, 1922-1923); N. Sokolow, *Sefer Zikkaron;* R. Brainin, *Bene Dori.*

Socialism: Lassalle; Cahan cites the memoirs of Jochelmann and J. Rosenberg; B. Michalewitsch, *Zichroines fun a Yiddishen Sotzialist;* Helfand, *Studien und Erinnerungen;* L. Grigorovich Deutsch, *16 Jahre in Sibirien;* L. Benedikt (Morris Wintschewesky), *Journalistische Erinnerungen;* Dobrogeanu; Eduard Bernstein, *Entwicklungsgang eines Sozialisten* (1930).

Communism: Erich Mühsam, *Weltanarchist* (an autobiography published on his 50th birthday, Berlin, 1928); Leon Trotzky, *My Life;* J. Steinberg, *Als ich Volkskommissar war* (Munich, 1929).

War Experiences: Memoirs from Germany revolving about Napoleon by Zach. Zaudy of Wesel (in Grunwald's *Feldzüge Napoleons*); Jacob Meyer of Dransfeld who fought in Spain and Russia; Gabriel Schramek of Isenheim who fought in Saxony and Austria; Isador Lehmann who supplied the armies in Spain and Russia; Emil Neumann, captain in Russia (*Jüdisches Volksblatt,* 1860); on the Prussian side, Meno Berg, *Aus meinem Dienstleben* (1789-1853; edit. L. Geiger, Leipzig, 1916); on the Austrian side, Josef Kraus of Bohemia, with the Schwarzenberg Uhlans; on the Mecklenburg side, Löser Cohen, sculptor, who was a volunteer, *Die Wahrheit* (Vienna, 1928); Mosche Wasserzug (edit. H. Loewe, Berlin, 1911) deals with the effects of the war in East Prussia; A. H. Heymann (edit. H. Loewe, Berlin, 1909) treats especially the Jews in Berlin during the 19th cent.

Travel Experiences: Mordecai Manuel Noah, of Ararat fame, *Travels in England, France, Spain and the Barbary States from 1813 to 1815* (New York, 1820); S. Cerfberr, *Mémoires sur la Grèce et l'Albanie* (1826); many travel reports of Benjamin II; Krauskopf on Spain; M. Lewin, *Iberia* (Berlin, 1892); M. Ehrenpreis, *Das Land Zwischen Orient und Okzident* (about Spain, Berlin, 1927); Ephraim Deinard, *Massa Krim* (about the Jews in the Crimea, Warsaw, 1878); Romanelli, *Marokko;* the Austro-Hungarian rear admiral, T. L. Oesterreicher, *Aus fernem Osten und Westen* (Vienna, 1879).   MAX GRUNWALD.

METZKER, YUD (Itzchok), Yiddish story writer, b. Kozaczyzna, near Borszczow, Galicia, 1901. After attending the high school of Borszczow, he left home when eighteen years old to study at the

Memorbuch of the Jewish community of Frankfort, containing entry in memory of Jacob Joshua (1756)

Humboldt Hochschule in Berlin, Germany. Coming to the United States three years later, he made his home in New York city, working in a fur factory during the day and attending evening sessions of the Jewish Teachers Seminary. In 1932 he was appointed a teacher at the Workmen's Circle Schools.

In 1927 Metzker published his first poem in the *Amerikaner*, a Yiddish weekly. From then on he published many short stories and novelettes in the foremost Yiddish periodicals on two continents. He was a romantic realist, at his best in mirroring the peasantry of his native Galicia and in poetic descriptions of nature; his works won the acclaim of Jewish critics, who considered him one of the most talented of the younger Yiddish prose writers in America.

Among Metzker's books are: *Toly un Toby* (1936); *Zun und Erd*, a collection of stories (1936) and *Don Yitzchok Abarbanel*. In 1942 his novel, *Die aibike Stime*, was being serially published in issues of the Yiddish daily *Forverts*.

Lit.: Nadir, Moishe, *Morning Freiheit*, May 31, 1937; Rabinowits, S., *Zukunft*, Jan., 1938; Niger, S., *Tog*, Apr. 24, 1938.

MEMORBUCH (derived from the Latin *memoria*, but taken from the Book of Remembrance, *sefer zikkaron*, Mal. 3:16), a book used by many of the Jewish communities, beginning with the late Middle Ages, containing lists of martyred Jewish dead. These books were read in the synagogue on specific occasions. Since the purpose of the first Memorbuch seems to have been to honor the victims of the First Crusade (1096), and the Crusade swept over certain parts of Germany at about the time of the Feast of Weeks (Shabuoth), the reading of the Memorbuch took place on the Sabbath before that holiday. Later it was read also on other Sabbaths and holidays, whenever possible in conjunction with the memorial service (Hazkarath Neshamoth).

The names of the martyrs of later persecutions were incorporated into the books, and eventually the meaning of the term martyr came to include all those who had died violent deaths. Finally, the books enumerated those who were renowned in the country or the community for reasons other than martyrdom. The perpetuation of one's name in the Memorbuch came to be sought after as an honor, and the members of the Jewish community depended on notable philanthropies to achieve it.

The earliest Memorbuch extant was begun by Isaac ben Samuel of Meiningen in 1296, and was so thoroughly compiled that it was probably the model for others. Since its editing by Siegmund Salfeld (1896 and 1898) there have been differing opinions about its locale. Salfeld concluded that despite its possession by the community of Mayence, it was actually the Nuremberg Memorbuch, but Magnus Weinberg decided that its contents applied to Mayence. In it are a summary of the persecutions of 1096 to 1298, the names of the martyred who died between 1096 and 1349, and a list of cities and villages in which massacres took place under Rindfleisch (1298) and Armleder (1336-39) and at the time of the Black Death (1348-49). Salfeld also enumerates fifty-nine other such books, of which fifty-two seem to have come from Bavaria alone. The Memorbuch of Worms offers a list of the communities which suffered during the Chmielnicki pogroms (1648-49).

The books contain a liturgical section, with prayers and blessings for the sick and sometimes other living persons, a necrological section, naming those of general as well as local renown, and a martyrology, also general and local. The old names and records were copied into later versions of the books, but with decreasing fidelity as time went on. New names were added, but after 1850 the Memorbuch was in general disuse.

NATHAN RICARDO.

Lit.: Salfeld, S., *Das Martyrologium des Nürnberger Memorbuches* (1896-98); Zunz, L., *Nachtrag zur Literaturgeschichte*, 670-71; Weinberg, Magnus, *Die Memorbücher der jüdischen Gemeinden in Bayern* (1937-38).

MEMORIAL LIGHT, *see* YAHRZEIT.

MEMORIAL SERVICE (Hazkarath Nesha-moth), a service containing prayers for the souls of the departed, often with the accompaniment of offerings made in memory of the departed. The service is known also by the Hebrew names Mazkir and Yizkor; the first is derived from the fact that all religious ordinances on the subject begin with the word *mazkirin* ("they bring to remembrance"), while the latter is the name of the principal memorial prayer. All groups of Jews agree in having a memorial service on Yom Kippur, but most of them have memorial services on other occasions in the year.

The earliest reference to the custom is in *Il Macc.* 12:39-45, which states that Judas Maccabeus and his army uttered prayers and offered sacrifices in order to obtain forgiveness of sin for the souls of those who had fallen in battle. Inasmuch, however, as the passage in which this occurs speaks of Judas' having found heathen amulets on the bodies of the slain Jewish soldiers, it is possible that this was not yet a regular custom, but merely a special occasion. Yet the idea of praying for the dead rose very naturally out of the feeling that if the soul was immortal, death made no difference, and that God would not refuse to hear petitions in behalf of a sinner. Hence the Halachic Midrash *Sifre* (on *Deut.* 21:8; edit. Friedmann, 112b) states that there is an atonement for the dead as well as for the living (cf. *Hor.* 6a). The *Midrash Tanhuma* (on *Deut.* 32), written in the 6th cent., cites this passage in the *Sifre* and *Pesikta Rabbathi* 20 as the reason for the current custom of memorializing the dead and giving charity for them on the Sabbath and on Yom Kippur. On the other hand, Hai Gaon and his pupil Nissim ben Jacob, in the 11th cent., considered this custom justified only in a very limited degree, since only the real merit of the deceased can be of any avail before God.

During the Middle Ages memorial services became extremely widespread among the Jews of Central and Eastern Europe. The custom first arose in the Rhine country as a result of the great persecutions of the Jews at the time of the First Crusade (1096). The names of the martyrs were entered in the memorial book of the community, together with an account of their sufferings. These were read in the synagogues on the Sabbaths between Passover and Shabuoth, when the massacres occurred, and on Yom Kippur, which lent itself to memorial services since the traditional Scriptural portion for the day began with the words *'ahare moth* ("after the death"; *Lev.* 16:1). A special prayer was said for the repose of the souls of the martyrs; in certain congregations this led to prayers for all pious persons, and eventually to prayers by individuals for their deceased parents and relatives. The practice of giving alms as an atonement for the departed at the time that prayers were uttered for them seems to have spread from the Rhine countries to Italy; there it was extended to every Sabbath.

As the Jews from Germany migrated to Eastern Europe in the 14th cent. and after, they introduced the memorial service into their new communities. It consisted of mentioning the names of the dead, prayer for them and giving alms; but the extension of the custom to every Sabbath must have come thither from Italy. In course of time the memorial services among the Ashkenazic Jews acquired a certain established prac-

tice. A general memorial prayer, the Ab Harahamim, recalling the souls of the martyrs, is recited on every Sabbath immediately after the reading from the Scriptures, except certain special Sabbaths. Memorial services in which individuals utter personal prayers for the souls of departed parents are held four times a year, on Yom Kippur and the last days of the three pilgrimage festivals, that is, the eighth day of Passover, the second day of Shabuoth, and on Shemini Atzereth.

The exact form of the memorial service varies among Jews of different countries and even of individual communities. Among the more usual of the prayers incorporated are the Ab Harahamim, phrased to include parents, the El Male Rahamim, and the Yizkor prayer, which is said by the individual as a silent devotion. Appropriate passages are recited from the *Psalms* and other parts of the Bible, or more general prayers to God for blessing. The Yizkor prayer is unknown in Italy and the Orient. In Northern Africa it is the custom in many congregations, either every week or every month, to mention in the synagogue the names of those who have died in the period just elapsed, or to say a silent Hashkabah, or prayer for the welfare of the soul. Such a memorial prayer is always recited in Sephardic congregations at the request of anyone who is called up to the Torah.

In the 19th cent. the memorial service was broadened and given a wider application. Reform Jews began to limit the memorial service to Yom Kippur and to elaborate on it by setting some of the prayers to music, adding meditations and silent devotions, and introducing poems by Bahya, Ibn Gabirol and Judah Halevi. The place of the service was shifted from after the morning prayer to just before the concluding (Neilah) service, and has been invested with great solemnity. Memorial prayers are said for all near relatives, instead of for parents alone. The service is closed by a Kaddish recited by the entire congregation. Even Conservative congregations have adopted the custom of the annual memorial service. In 1940 some of the Reform Jewish congregations in America returned to the custom of having four memorial services a year in order to come nearer to the general practice, the four days being Yom Kippur, the seventh day of Passover, Shabuoth, and Shemini Atzereth.

See also: El Male Rahamim; Kaddish; Yizkor.

SIMON COHEN.

Lit.: Singer, S., and Abrahams, I., *The Authorised Daily Prayer Book* (1922) 326-27, ccxxxiii-ccxxxiv; Dembitz, L. N., in *Jewish Encyclopedia*, vol. 6, pp. 283-84; Kohler, Kaufmann, *ibid.*, vol. 8, p. 463.

MEMORIAL VOLUMES, *see* Jubilee, Memorial and Tribute Volumes.

MEMPHIS, the largest city of Tennessee, with a population of 292,942 (census of 1940), including about 6,500 Jewish residents. Jews were living in Memphis in the 1840's. In 1847 Joseph J. Andrews, formerly a resident of Charleston, S. C., and Philadelphia, who had married Haym Salomon's daughter, Sallie, gave his fellow Jews of Memphis several acres for a cemetery on the occasion of his brother's death. Joseph J. Andrews' son, Joseph G. Andrews (d. 1920), was the first Jew born in Memphis (*American Israelite,* Sept. 9, 1920).

In 1850 a Hebrew benevolent society was formed in Memphis. By 1853 the Jewish community had become

Christian-Jewish amity at Memphis. Scene shows formal presentation (1936) to St. Agnes College of a building by three sons and a daughter of Jacob Goldsmith, an erstwhile citizen of Memphis, whose home the house had been

numerous enough to organize the first congregation, Children of Israel. The act of incorporation (1854) lists the names of Joseph J. Andrews, M. Bamberger, M. Bloom, R. Folz, Solomon Hess, D. Levy, H. Reinach, Julius Sandec, Moses Simons, Joseph Strauss, and John Walker. Simons was president and Hess secretary.

Judah Touro of New Orleans (d. 1854) left the new congregation $2,000 in his will. The members used the bequest to purchase a lot on which to build a synagogue and, in the meantime, worshipped in a hall on Front Street. Jonas Levy had come from Little Rock to be the Hazan and Shohet. The Hebrew school was under the guidance of L. Sternheimer. In 1858 a building, formerly occupied by a bank, was acquired as a place of worship, and Jacob Joseph Peres, a native of Holland, was elected Hazan.

Simon Tuska, who had been a rabbi in Rochester, N. Y., became rabbi of Children of Israel in 1860. Tuska added the music of an organ to the services, girls sang in the choir, and he rearranged the seating to have men and women sit together in family pews. Dissatisfied with these innovations, the Orthodox members of the congregation, under the leadership of Jacob Joseph Peres, the Hazan, in 1862 withdrew from the congregation to form another, Beth El Emeth. Joel Alexander was the rabbi in 1865. In 1882 the members of Congregation Beth El Emeth rejoined Children of Israel.

During the Civil War, it is recorded, a number of Confederate soldiers attended in a body one of the Sabbath services of Children of Israel. The group included Major Abraham S. Levy, Captain Maurice A. Freeman, Lieutenant Isaac Strauss, Corporal M. A. Kuhn, Privates Lou Leubrie, Samuel Jackson, Harry Cohen, Julius Nathan, Emil Gross, Harry Jeessel and several others. Upon the death of President Abraham Lincoln, the two Hebrew congregations in Memphis (then under federal control) joined those of other denominations in a memorial service held in the city park.

From 1863 to 1868, Congregation Children of Israel maintained the Hebrew Educational Institute, a non-sectarian school, under the supervision of L. Kremer, with Andrew J. Hale as principal. English, Hebrew, German, French and music were taught, but the project had to be abandoned for lack of funds.

Rabbi Tuska of Children of Israel died in 1870. His successor (1871) was Max Samfield, who was to serve the congregation for forty-four years. On the very day of his death in 1915 he was to have preached his last sermon before retiring. At the time of his funeral most

places of business in Memphis closed out of respect, and every street car stopped running for a while. In 1870 the members of Children of Israel decided to hold services on Friday evening in English, and in 1875 the trustees requested men and boys to take their hats off during the services and the rabbi to preach his sermon without cap and gown. The first Sabbath school building of the congregation was erected in 1876.

When the members of Beth El Emeth rejoined the Children of Israel congregation, a lot was purchased on Poplar Street and a new temple built in 1884. In 1910 William H. Fineshriber, of Davenport, Iowa, became an associate rabbi and in 1915, on the death of Rabbi Samfield, rabbi. He served until 1924, and was succeeded by Harry W. Ettelson, who was still serving in that capacity in 1942. Morton J. Cohn was associate rabbi from 1938 to 1940. Dudley Weinberg was assistant rabbi in 1942. In 1916 the present temple of Children of Israel, modeled upon the mosque of Saint Sophia in Istanbul but without its minarets, was erected; in 1926 the Joy and Mary Newburger Annex was donated by Joseph Newburger, president of the congregation. In 1942 Congregation Children of Israel had an active Temple Sisterhood, a Temple Men's Club, a Junior Congregation, a Temple League, and a Young Couples Club as constituent organizations.

Some members of Children of Israel who preferred the Orthodox ritual formed a new congregation in 1916, using the old name of Beth El Emeth. They bought the Poplar Street Temple from Congregation Children of Israel. This was remodeled in 1927 and an annex added in 1940. The first religious leader, Rabbi Hyman, served from 1925 to 1930. Morris Shimony was the cantor in 1942.

The first permanent Orthodox congregation in Memphis is named after Baron Maurice de Hirsch (1831-96), the philanthropist. It was organized in 1891. The members of the congregation had been worshipping together at least from 1884 on (from 1886 until 1890 on the second floor of Isaac's Bookstore). The Baron Hirsch Congregation bought a negro church in 1891 and remodeled it into a synagogue. Its present synagogue was built in 1914 on the same site. The Menorah Institute, a three-story building, was erected by the congregation in 1928 to serve as a community center. Their first rabbi was Benjamin Mayerowitz, who served from 1891 to 1893; later, Morris N. Taxon was rabbi from 1930 until his death in 1942.

In addition to the Baron Hirsch Congregation and

Congregation Beth El Emeth, there were in 1942 three other Orthodox congregations in Memphis: Congregation Anshei Sphard, organized in 1898; Congregation Anshei Mischne, organized in 1900; Congregation Galicia, organized in 1912. Congregation Anshei Sphard first met in the home of Samuel Barnchman. In 1904 a residence was bought and remodeled into a synagogue. The synagogue which it used in 1942 was built on this site in 1925. The first rabbi was L. Cohen, who served from 1898 to 1903; the rabbi in 1942 was Mose Turetsky. Congregation Anshei Mischne was organized by former members of Congregation Baron Hirsch. The synagogue used in 1942 was built in 1927. The first rabbi was Ignatz Isaac, who was still serving in that capacity in 1942. Congregation Anshei Galicia was formed by members of Anshei Sphard who wished to follow their own ritual.

Congregations Children of Israel, Baron Hirsch, Anshei Sphard, and Beth El Emeth had their own cemeteries (1942).

The first Jewish welfare agency was organized in Memphis as early as 1864. A number of others, subsequently, functioned more or less until 1906, when they were united in the Federation of Jewish Charities. From 1923 on the Federation—its name was changed in 1924 to the Federation of Jewish Welfare Agencies —has been supported solely by the Memphis Community Fund. There is also a Jewish Welfare Fund, organized in 1934. In 1911 Rabbi Fineshriber, assisted by Mrs. Alexander Bloch, Mrs. Henry Gluck, and Arthur Jacobs, organized the Jewish Neighborhood House to care for immigrants and assist them in becoming citizens. The B'nai B'rith Home for the Aged, long a cherished project of Rabbi Samfield, was opened in 1927.

There is a lodge of the B'nai B'rith in Memphis and a chapter of the Hadassah. The Salon Circle, a cultural organization, was founded in 1891 by Mrs. Mark Davis and Mrs. William Katzenberg. The Young Men's Hebrew Association, organized in 1881, erected its own building in 1911, but went out of existence in 1920, although it had a membership of more than 400. Other organizations in 1942 included branches of the Aleph Zadik Aleph, Sons of Israel, and Progressive Order of the West.

William Bailey Rosenfield of Memphis was a member of the legislature of Tennessee from 1917 to 1919. Joseph Hanover was a member of the Tennessee House of Representatives from 1918 until 1919, and as Democratic floor leader aided in securing the eventual adoption of the 19th amendment of the Federal constitution granting women the right to vote. Fletcher Gans Cohn was a member of the Tennessee House of Representatives for three terms, from 1929 to 1933, and Democratic floor leader in 1933; from 1935 on he was a master of the federal court in Memphis. Sam Taubenblatt was acting judge of the courts of Shelby county from 1933 to 1937. Sophie Goldberger Friedman was vice-president of the Tennessee National Association of Women Lawyers. Israel H. Peres, son of Jacob Joseph Peres, was a member of the Memphis Board of Education and served as its president. Milton Samuel Binswanger was chairman of the Industrial Division of the Chamber of Commerce from 1927 to 1930. Abe Goodman was chairman of the board of directors of the Tuberculosis Association of Shelby County and Memphis from 1933 on. David Asher Levy was chairman of the Board of Mendicants (the municipal organization regulating the solicitation of alms). For many years Israel David Michelson, the bacteriologist, was on the faculty of the University of Tennessee College of Medicine: he was appointed associate professor in 1923. In 1927 he was awarded first prize by the Southern Medical Association for scientific exhibits. William Gerber, who served as city attorney, was in 1942 attorney general of Shelby County. In 1932 Rabbi Harry W. Ettelson was given the Newburger Cup Award for civic achievements.

The children of Jacob Goldsmith in 1936 presented his home, after his death, to the nuns of St. Agnes College to be used as a library.

The Jewish Spectator, a weekly, was edited by Rabbi Samfield from 1885 until his death in 1915, and publication was then terminated. In 1942 a weekly, *The Hebrew Watchman,* founded in 1925 by Leo I. Goldberger as *The Memphis Hebrew,* was edited by his brother, Milton Goldberger.

MILTON W. GOLDBERGER.

Lit.: The Tennessee Historical Records Survey, Work Projects Administration, *Inventory of the Church and Synagogue Archives of Tennessee: Jewish Congregations* (1941); Malamut, Joseph L., and Goldberger, Milton W., edit., *Southern Jewry* (1933).

MEMRA, see LOGOS.

MENACHEM (pseudonym of Menachem Boraisha Goldberg), poet and journalist, b. Brest-Litovsk, Poland, 1888. He was the brother of Abram Goldberg. Menachem moved to Warsaw in 1905 and arrived in the United States in 1915. He had begun to write poetry at an early age, nearly all of it in Yiddish. His work was published in magazines and collections edited by Isaac Loeb Peretz, Weiter, Gorelick, Niger and others. His first poem appeared in 1906 in the *Veg,* edited by Peretz in Warsaw.

A poetic work in book form, *Poilen* (Poland), was published in Warsaw in 1913, and translated into Polish and Hebrew. In the United States Menachem published several long poems: *A Ring in der Keit* (A Ring in the Chain; 1915); *Zamd* (Sand; 1920); *Savel Rimmer* (1924); *Der Gilgul* (The Transformation; 1927); *Der Pastuch Dovid* (The Shepherd David; 1931); and *Der Gayer* (The Traveler; 1933).

Menachem's work as journalist began in 1909, on the *Haint* (Warsaw). He remained there until his departure for the United States. In New York he worked on the *Day,* the *Firer,* and when the latter suspended publication, on the *Day* again. For ten years he was in charge of press work in Yiddish at the Joint Distribution Committee. Later he took over similar work for the American Jewish Congress, and was also an editorial writer (in English) for the *Congress Weekly.* In the interim Menachem had dropped the family name of Goldberg and taken his mother's name: Boraisha. All of his later work appeared under the name of M. Boraisha.

Menachem is recognized as one of the leading poets in Yiddish literature, taking his place with Leivik and other modern classics. He is a disciple of Peretz, who sought in literature not merely a portrayal of life but the discovery of ethical and spiritual principles. Like Peretz, Menachem also seeks the specifically Jewish spirituality, and goes to the Jewish past as well as to the Jewish present in search for his material. His writing combines the realistic with the symbolic, and often contains enunciations of faith that approach the mystical. His later work, especially, returns to esoteric influences.　　MOSES Z. R. FRANK.

MENAHAMIYA, *see* COLONIES, AGRICULTURAL.

MENAHEM, king of Israel from about 741 to 736 B.C.E.; his history is recorded in *II Kings* 15:14-22. He seized the throne during the anarchy which followed after the death of Jeroboam II, and is reported to have practised great cruelties in the course of the civil war that raged. He was compelled to pay a heavy tribute of 1,000 talents to the king of Assyria, which he raised by confiscatory levies on the people. It is probable that he had to struggle against an anti-Assyrian faction in the people, headed by Pekah, who claimed rulership and eventually became king after Menahem was succeeded by his son. The prophet Hosea, a contemporary, gives a graphic depiction of the conditions of the time (*Hosea* 4 to 14).

MENAHEM ABELIM, *see* MOURNING AND MOURNING CUSTOMS.

MENAHEM AZARIAH DA FANO, *see* FANO, MENAHEM AZARIAH DA.

MENAHEM BEN AARON BEN ZERAH, rabbi, b. Estella, Navarre, 1310; d. Toledo, Spain, 1385. His parents and four brothers were killed in the massacre of March 5, 1328, in which 6,000 Jews of Navarre lost their lives. Menahem was saved through the help of a knight who was a friend of his father's. Though he planned to go to Toledo at once, he remained in Navarre for two more years, studying. In 1331 he finally went to Toledo, where he studied and wrote until 1350, when he went to Alcala to become head of a seminary. The civil war of 1368, during which he lost his entire fortune, sent Menahem back to Toledo. Here he found a patron in Don Samuel Abravanel, to whom *Tzedah Laderech* is dedicated.

Tzedah Laderech (Provision for the Way), which consists of five volumes containing 372 chapters, is a compilation of canonical and ethical rules, written primarily for those who came in contact with non-Jews. The quality of the chosen people, according to Menahem, is to live according to the word of God; a non-Jew who does so is of more value than a Jew who does not. Much of Menahem's work remained in manuscript. Among his pupils were Hayim de Brivisia, Joseph ben Israel and Samuel ibn Shoshan.

Lit.: Freimann, Alfredo, "Menachem ben Zerach," *Annuario di studi ebraici,* vol. 1 (1934) 247-67; Kayserling, M., *Geschichte der Juden in Spanien und Portugal* (1861) 39 et seq.; Wininger, S., *Grosse Jüdische National-Biographie.*

MENAHEM BEN JACOB BEN SOLOMON, synagogal poet, d. Worms, Germany, 1203; the place and date of his birth are unknown. His great-grandfather, Simson (Hadarshan) of Worms, was quoted by Rashi on *Isa.* 58:14 and *Amos* 6:3. Menahem's synagogal poetry evidences the gloom and despondency characteristic of the Jews during this period. Among the thirty-one liturgical poems which Zunz attributes to him and only ten of which have been published

are Maarib, Yotzer, Ofan, Ahabah, and Zulath poems. De Rossi identifies him with Menahem ben Jacob de Lutra, also a synagogal poet, because of an unproved belief that he was born in Kaiserslautern.

Lit.: Zunz, L., *Synagogale Poesie* (2nd ed.) 263; idem, *Literaturgeschichte der synagogalen Poesie,* 294 et seq.

MENAHEM BEN SARUK (Menahem ben Jacob ibn Saruk Hasefardi), Hebrew lexicographer and grammarian, b. Tortosa, Spain, 910; d. 970. He used the earlier work of Judah Ibn Kuraish, Saadia and the Karaite grammarians in his own study of the Hebrew language. Menahem lived in great poverty until he was called to Cordova by Hasdai ibn Sharprut. He worked as Hasdai's secretary and was the scribe who wrote Hasdai's letter to the Khazars. Hasdai also helped Menahem by his financial patronage, but later, as the result of attacks on Menahem's work, Hasdai's friendship cooled.

Menahem's Hebrew lexicon, *Mahbereth,* based more on empirical observations than on a strict scientific and linguistic knowledge, was criticized by Dunash ibn Labrat and his pupils, and defended by Menahem's own pupils. It was the first complete Hebrew dictionary of its kind, giving the differentiation of the words according to their roots, and was used for many centuries. It was preserved in the libraries of Berlin, Florence, Hamburg, Leyden, Oxford, Paris, Palma, Rome and Vienna. The disputes which followed the appearance of the dictionary led Judah Hayyuj to the basic discovery of the three-lettered root.

Lit.: Filipowski, *Machberos* (1854); Backer, W., *Hebräische Sprachwissenschaft,* 23 et seq., Stern, *Teshuboth Talmide Menahem Vedunash* (1870); Graetz, H., *History of the Jews,* vol. 3 (1927); Gross, *Menachem ben Saruk* (1873); Wininger, S., *Grosse Jüdische National-Biographie.*

MENAHEM THE ESSENE, one of the important leaders of the Herodian period, about the middle of the 1st cent. B.C.E. He appears to have excelled in those qualities of saintliness and prophetic ability which the Essenes cultivated. According to Josephus (*Antiquities,* book 15, chap. 5), Menahem once met Herod when the latter, then a boy, was on his way to school, and clapping him on the back, foretold that he would become king and be great, but lacking in piety and justice. In later years Herod remembered the occasion and paid special favor to the Essenes. Menahem is probably identical with the figure of like name who is mentioned in the Mishnah as Ab Beth Din while Hillel was the president of the Sanhedrin. It appears, however, that he found this post uncongenial, and resigned in favor of Shammai. According to legends found in the Talmud, he later became a Gnostic, or a heretic (*Yer. Hag.* ii, 77d).

Lit.: Graetz, H., *History of the Jews,* vol. 2 (1927) 100; Dubnow, S., *Neuste Geschichte des jüdischen Volkes,* vol. 2, p. 310.

MENAHEM MENDEL OF KOCK (family name, Morgenstern), Hasidic leader and scholar, d. 1859. He was a pupil of Bunem, in Przysucha, and of Jacob Isaac, in Lublin. After spending some time in Tomaszow, he moved to Kock. Menahem possessed vast Talmudic knowledge, and made his study of the Talmud an almost exclusively religious exercise. He had a large following in younger circles, and the large gatherings held by his followers were said, by outsiders, to have contributed to the extremism of Polish Hasidism.

Menahem was known as a miracle-worker. For the last twenty years of his life he lived in seclusion, spending his nights in the study of the Talmud and the Cabala. One reputed explanation of his ascetic life speaks of insanity, and says that he was held prisoner by his neighbors. Another attributes it to atheism. Menahem's son and disciple, David, was unable to hold his father's adherents together, and many of the Hasidim of Kock joined the group attached to David's pupil, the Gerer Rebbe.

Lit.: Wininger, S., Grosse Jüdische National-Biographie, vol. 4 (1930) 330; Verus (Aaron Markus), Der Chassidismus (1901) 177-82, 304-9; Walden, Shem Hagedolim Hehadash; Sokolow Festschrift (1904) 340; Bergman, L., Kotzker Maisses (1924).

MENAHEM MENDEL OF LIUBAVICH

(Shneerson dynasty), Hasidic leader of the Habad school, b. 1789; d. 1866. He spent his early childhood in the home of Shneor Zalman, and began the study of the Cabala at the age of thirteen. After he succeeded Shneor's son, Baer of Ladi, the reverence he commanded was so great that he was called a "soul out of the world of the Word." Menahem claimed to have received Shneor's teachings in dreams, after the latter's death, and put them into writing, as well as his own thoughts. In 1843 Menahem was summoned to St. Petersburg, to a meeting of rabbis convoked by the minister of education. The free practice of Hasidism was to be considered; it was in danger because of the hostility of the other rabbis. A prayer uttered by Menahem, it is said, so stirred the minister of education that he altered his previous negative decision.

Menahem's collection of Shneor's teachings, together with his original work, was issued in a book, Likkute Torah. His grandson published some of his voluminous writings posthumously, in Tzemah Tzedek, but much of the work was burned in a fire which destroyed his house.

Lit.: Heilmann, Beth Rabbi; Dubnow, S., Weltgeschichte des jüdischen Volkes, vol. 9 (1929); Wininger, S., Grosse Jüdische National-Biographie, vol. 4 (1930) 330.

MENAHEM MENDEL OF RYMANOW, Ha-

sidic leader and wonder-worker, b. Neustadt, Germany, 1745; d. 1815. A legend is told of him that Isaac Alfasi, into whose writings he had delved, appeared to him in a dream, urging him to go to Rabbi Elimelech, whose disciple he ultimately became. Numerous stories tell of his miraculous cures of the sick, which won him fame among non-Jews as well as Jews, his powers of clairvoyance, his incessant stories which were seldom interrupted even by sleep, and his strict religious guidance of his community. Legend has it that his form appeared to Napoleon in his dreams as long as the latter was under divine protection. By order of Menahem Mendel himself, he was succeeded by his faithful servant, Hersch Rymanower, who was accordingly given the title Meshareth ("servant"). His Cabalistic interpretations of the Bible were published after his death by his disciple Ezekiel Paneth, in Kralsburg.

Lit.: Verus (Aaron Markus), Der Chassidismus (1901) 161-63, 278, 294.

MENAHEM MENDEL OF VITEBSK, Hasidic

leader and disciple of Baer of Meseritz, d. Tiberias,

Palestine, 1788. Together with Shneor Zalman, he attempted to become reconciled with the Gaon of Vilna, who unfortunately declined to grant them an audience. When Baer of Meseritz died in 1772, the development of the Hasidic movement was stifled; Menahem Mendel, accompanied by 300 Hasidim, emigrated to Palestine and settled at Safed in 1777; later he moved to Tiberias. From Palestine he corresponded with the Hasidic leaders of the Diaspora and greatly influenced the progress of the movement. Although he poignantly felt the persecutions of the Mithnaggedim who attempted to discredit him even in the Holy Land, he admonished his Hasidim to refrain from antagonizing them.

Lit.: Horodezky, S. A., Hahasiduth Vehahasidim, vol. 2, pp. 15-35; Kahana, Sefer Hahasiduth (1922) 171-72; Minkin, Jacob S., The Romance of Hassidism (1935).

MENAHEM NAHUM OF TCHERNOBYL,

known as the "Great Rabbi Nahum," one of the earliest leaders of Hasidism in southern Russia, b. 1730; d. 1797. He was reared by his uncle, who sent him to a Lithuanian Yeshiva where he became one of the outstanding students. He married young and became a teacher. Caring little about earning a livelihood, he delved into the study of the Cabala and the works of Isaac Luria. As a result he became a follower of the teachings of practical Cabala, stopped eating meat and drinking wine on weekdays, fasted twice a week and rose at midnight to mourn the destruction of the Temple.

At this time word of the popularity of Israel Baal Shem Tob, the founder of Hasidism, reached Nahum, and he decided to go to see him. Various legends are told by Hasidim about their meeting; it left a profound impression on Nahum. After the death of the Baal Shem, Nahum became a disciple of the "great Maggid" of Meseritz. The teaching of the Baal Shem that God manifests himself everywhere and that man must serve God through every act changed Nahum's outlook. A new world, free of the asceticism of the Lurian Cabala and its attendant morbidity and pain, opened up before him. He became aware of God's presence in all things, and felt that man's objective should be to draw near to the holy spirit that resides within him and thus become part of the infinite. He taught that man can serve God in everything he does, even in eating and drinking, but that the highest service is right thinking, which leads to understanding God and to fear and love of Him. Nahum, himself a Talmudist, knew the importance of that study, but derided those who indulged in it only to display their prowess, without perceiving the inner meaning of the Torah. He felt that the men of learning of his day could not meet the needs of the people; the "Zaddik," he believed, should be an inspiration to the masses and their intermediary with God.

Nahum did not contribute much that is original to Hasidic theory, but his modesty, simplicity, natural piety and moral fervor made him a fit medium for the dissemination of its teachings. His reputation spread among Hasidim, and he was called to Tchernobyl to serve as "Maggid." He lived there in poverty, going about from village to village to teach the new doctrine and to bring the wayward back into the fold. Such money as he collected he devoted to charity, especially to dowries for poor brides and to securing the release of imprisoned Jews. His Meor Enayim, homilies on the Pentateuch, and *Yismah Leb,* on the Haggadoth of the Talmud, were published posthumously (1798) in Slawuta. Nahum was the founder of a Hasidic dynasty.

Lit.: Horodezky, S. A., *Rabbi Nahum of Tchernobyl and His Descendants* (Hebrew; 1902); idem, *Hahasiduth Vehahasidim;* idem, *Leaders of Hassidism* (1928) 39-41; Dubnow, S., in *Voskhod* (1890).

MENAHOTH ("meal-offerings"), second tractate of Kodashim, the fifth division of the Talmud. It contains thirteen chapters and discusses the regulations applying to the sacrificial offerings that were made of cakes baked from grain. It deals with such topics as a definition of the various ways in which such an offering can be made unfit, the preparation of such offerings, the manner of their being burnt upon the altar, and the like. A special section discusses the way in which the Israelites performed sacrificial rites in the wilderness. The tractate discusses a number of other offerings not contained under its title, such as the thank-offering, the offering of the Nazirites, the Omer and the showbread. A section is devoted to enumerating the weights and measures used in the Temple; another contains the discussion of whether the one who brought the sacrifice should lay his hands on the animal offered. Altogether Menahoth contains an unusual variety of subjects, linked together by the fact that they are all concerned with the Temple ritual.

The Tosefta to the tractate has some interesting details about the rapacity of the chief priests in the time of the Second Temple. The Babylonian Gemara (there is no Palestinian) consists of 110 double pages; of these the section 29 to 44 is important, as it includes the regulations about the writing of the scrolls of the Torah, as well as about the Tefillin, Mezuzah and fringes (Tzitzith). Toward the end there is a history of the founding of the Temple of Onias in Egypt.

Lit.: Lauterbach, Jacob Z., in *Jewish Encyclopedia,* vol. 8, pp. 472-73; Danby, Herbert, *The Mishnah* (1933) 491-513.

MENANDER, 1. putative author, presumably during the period of Roman rule. In 1862 Land discovered and edited, under the title of *Anecdota Syriaca,* a Syriac manuscript now in the British Museum. Its original title is: "The Sage Menander Said." Little attention was given it before Frankenberg sought to prove that these sentences are of Jewish origin. Spiritually they belong to *Sirach* and *Proverbs,* as there is hardly a theme in Menander that was not treated there. Similarly, the duties of humanity and divine punishment are emphasized, but the Jewish ritual is hardly mentioned. Altogether, the sentences are the expression of a Judaism that has already become diluted with paganism, but the fact that they do not allude to Christianity at all seems to exclude the possibility that the author was a Christian.

There are differing opinions as to whether the proverbs were originally written in Hebrew or were translated from Greek into Syriac. Moreover, it is unknown whether Menander is the Hellenized name of the Jewish author or simply fictitious, as the Greek dramatist of that name who was noted for his moral maxims used to be credited with the authorship of epigrams of doubtful authenticity. The allusion to gladiators and crucifixion seems to give evidence that the proverbs were written in the period of Roman rule.

2. historian (b. Ephesus, Asia Minor), who lived in the second half of the 3rd cent. B.C.E. He was also called "the Pergamene," after the kingdom of Pergamum, which reached its cultural zenith in his time. A history of Phoenicia, for which he used the original documents of the archives at Tyre, is the only work of his that has been preserved. Josephus cites him as a witness for the historicity of the Bible, as Menander mentioned the fact that King Hiram of Tyre supplied King Solomon with trees from the Lebanon for the building of the Temple in Jerusalem. There is in Menander's work a strange reference to the younger son of a certain Abdemon reported to have vanquished Solomon in guessing riddles.

Lit.: Krauss, Samuel, in *Jewish Encyclopedia,* vol. 8, pp. 473-74.

MENASHEH BEN JOSEPH OF ILYE (ben Porat), *see* MANASSEH BEN JOSEPH OF ILYE.

MENASSEH, *see* MANASSEH.

MENDEL (name of several Hasidic leaders), *see* MENAHEM MENDEL.

MENDEL, prominent family in Hungary (15th and 16th centuries) whose members held the office of Jewish prefect. About 1477 King Mátyás (Matthias) created this office, entrusting a Jew with jurisdiction over the Jews, collection of taxes, and representation before the crown. Thus the king appointed Jacobus Mendel, head of the Jewish community of Buda, who held the office of prefect until 1502. He succeeded in collecting five times the amount in taxes that had been previously collected from Jews. At the coronation of King Ulászló II (1490) he appeared in shining armor, with a suite of twenty-four horsemen. Ulászló, puppet king of the Magyar overlords, made ample use of the services of the prefect in order to supplement the income which the lords denied him from the money-bags of the Jews. However the royal passport granted Judah Mendel (1502-12) was of little avail when, during the anti-Jewish riots in Buda (1505), the prefect fled to Pozsony (Pressburg), for he met with violence in the former city.

His son and successor, Jacobus II Mendel (1512-23), turned to other protectors to ensure the security of the Jews in a country where public safety was very inadequate after the peasant uprising of 1514. In 1515 he prevailed upon Emperor Maximilian to take under his wing the prefect, his family and all the Jews of Hungary. In 1520 Jacobus assigned, by contract, an annuity of 400 gulden to the Palatine István Báthori for the protection he would grant to the Jews. Both King Ulászló II and the Palatine Báthori exempted Jacobus from the wearing of the Jewish garb, and saw to it that he and his family were allowed to dispense with it in their travels inside and outside the country.

Israel Mendel, who was prefect from 1523 to 1526, probably went to Pressburg in 1525 when bloody anti-Jewish riots raged in Buda. He died in the year of the battle of Mohács (1526), and was succeeded by Isaac Mendel, who was the last prefect, the office being abolished by the Habsburg kings. The family appears

Lafayette Benedict Mendel

to have been allowed to stay in Pressburg when, after the battle of Mohács, the Jews were expelled from the inner city. In 1548 Tobias Mendel asked for permission to sell his house in Pressburg.

Lit.: Bettelheim, S., "Akten und Urkunden," *Juden und Judengemeinde Bratislava; Magyar Zsidó Lexikon* (1929) 586.

MENDEL, EMANUEL, psychiatrist, b. Bunzlau, Silesia, Germany, 1839; d. Berlin, 1907. In 1861 he began to practise medicine in Pankow, near Berlin, and in 1868 he overcame tremendous difficulties to establish a sanitorium for mental cases, which ultimately became a model for the entire world. In 1875 he was given the right of lecturing and in 1884 he became assistant professor at the University of Berlin. He was famous both as a teacher and a physician, and made numerous contributions to the knowledge of paralysis, tabes, mania, paranoia and epilepsy; he also contributed much to forensic medicine in matters affected by mental diseases. He was founder and editor of the *Neurologisches Centralblatt.*

MENDEL, LAFAYETTE BENEDICT, physiological chemist, b. Delhi, N. Y., 1872; d. New Haven, Conn., 1935. To him, together with the chemist Osborne, belongs the credit, in the United States, for pioneer work in vitamins, particularly vitamin A.

Mendel became professor in the Yale Sheffield Scientific School in 1903, and in 1921 was appointed Sterling professor of physical chemistry of Yale University. He attracted and inspired great numbers of students, with many of whom he collaborated on studies in nutrition.

From the beginning Mendel pursued two general lines of research: study of the relationship between the chemical constituents of foods, especially proteins, and growth and nutrition of young and adults; and the study of accessory factors in growth and nutrition. The latter opened up the whole field of vitamins. His forty years' research (1894-1934) contributed brilliantly to the new science of nutrition and made him a world authority.

Mendel was active in numerous private and govern-

mental projects in science, serving as executive, advisor, educator, editor. In 1913 he was elected member of the National Academy of Sciences; he was first president of the American Institute of Nutrition; and in 1935 was awarded the Conne Medal by the Chemical Club of New York for his contributions to medicine.

Lit.: Chittenden, Russell, "Lafayette Benedict Mendel," *Biographical Memoirs of the National Academy of Sciences,* vol. 18, pp. 123-55.

MENDELE MOCHER SFORIM, *see* ABRAMOWITSCH, SHALOM JACOB.

MENDELSOHN, ERICH, architect and engineer, b. Allenstein, East Prussia, Germany, 1887. He studied at the University of Berlin and later (1907-11) with Theodor Fischer in Munich. In 1915 he returned to Berlin, where he became located permanently except for trips to the United States, Russia, other countries of continental Europe, and Palestine. With the coming of the Nazi regime to power in Germany, he emigrated to England and later to Palestine (1936-38); in 1941 he settled in the United States. In 1940 he completed the Rothschild-Hadassah-University Hospital and Medical School. In 1941 his projected plans and original sketches were exhibited at the Museum of Modern Art in New York city.

Mendelsohn has been a genius possessed of musical temperament which he disciplined through architecture. There is no architectural problem with which he has not dealt. The number, importance and influence of his completed works alone merit serious attention. Badovici called him the prophet of modern architecture who understands the problems of the times. Mendelsohn, philosophical in a deep social sense, was convinced that architecture cannot avoid the simultaneity of effect brought on by revolutionary political phenomena and changes in human relations in economics, science, religion or art. To him architecture was an experience. The architect must subordinate his personality to the laws of responsibility of a new social order. He must overcome habit, tradition and history.

Mendelsohn possessed great ability in engineering and architecture, coupled with social insight involving problems of communication, transportation, lighting, housing and industrial plants. His works are plastic and dynamic, and the result has been often described as scientific architecture of tensions. By utilizing reinforced concrete, Mendelsohn freed the unity of the structure from the limitations of material. Materials become the means for freedom and for mastery over purpose. The Einsteinturm in Potsdam (1920-21) is a fine example of the wholeness of structure.

Mendelsohn has also a sense of the dramatic, and his structures are bold and exciting. He has attempted to create new spatial sense and relationships. An impression of perfect proportions, light and dark, space and form, design and movement, are created.

Mendelsohn made effective use of glass, and delved deep into the question of proper light supply. His commercial and industrial buildings follow the collective impulse with large halls, maximum light and a maximum use of wall space, as in the case of the factories in Lueckenwalde and in Leningrad, or the department stores in Cologne and Berlin. The ever increasing speed of traffic was an important factor for

Mendelsohn. He emphasized the horizontal, for as one moves in traffic, the eye must be able to travel along restfully and unhindered; the Schocken department stores in Chemnitz (1928), Nuremberg (1926) and Stuttgart (1926-28) are good examples of Mendelsohn's horizontalism.

Mendelsohn devoted much of his time and energy to housing (Woga Bauten, 1927). In this connection, price and utility as well as terrain and livability were major considerations. For Mendelsohn, the geography and climate have been especially important in architecture. His home at Rupenhorn is, in an exaggerated sense, an example of the combination of art and mechanics adapted to the geography of the land.

Mendelsohn believed that America and Russia are antipodal, and that the solution will come in a harmonious meeting of these two extremes. He demonstrated this theory through architecture in his two books, *Russland, Europa, Amerika: Ein architektonischer Querschnitt* (Berlin, 1929) and *Amerika, Bilderbuch eines Architekten* (Berlin, 1928).

EMANUEL K. SCHWARTZ.

Lit.: Badovici, Jean, "Erich Mendelsohn," *L'Architecture Vivante*, No. 38 (Winter, 1932) 33-47; "Erich Mendelsohn," *Architect and Building News*, vol. 130 (May, 1930) 629-31; *Hadassah Newsletter*, May-June, 1940; *Aufbau*, Dec. 19, 1941.

MENDELSOHN, JOSÉ, Yiddish journalist and author, b. Ukraine, Russia, 1891. He was educated in the local Yeshiva and Gymnasium. In 1912 he emigrated to Argentina, where he first engaged in teaching in the schools of the Jewish Colonization Association; then, turning to journalism, he joined the staff of the Buenos Aires *Yiddishe Zeitung* (1917); in 1920 he became its editor-in-chief. His essays and translations appeared in Yiddish, Hebrew, Russian and Spanish. In 1941 he published a volume on Rashi in Yiddish. In 1942 Mendelsohn was teaching at the Seminary for Jewish Teachers. He was a member of the Central Committee of the Zionist Federation of South America.

MENDELSON, SHLOIME (SOLOMON), Yiddish writer and educator, b. Warsaw, Poland, 1896. Up to the age of fourteen he received an Orthodox Jewish education. In 1913 he was graduated from the Gymnasium and entered the University of Warsaw as a medical student. After the outbreak of the first World War he studied in the Polish University in Warsaw, which was founded during the German occupation. He left the medical school to study law (in the same university), which course he had almost completed when he was expelled (1920) for his opposition to the war between Poland and Soviet Russia. For a short time he studied at the University of Cracow, then for five years taught history and literature in Polish Gymnasiums. Mendelson's name is closely associated with the Yiddish school movement in Poland. In 1921 he was one of the organizers of the first conference on Yiddish secular education, and was elected by that body director of the Yiddish secular schools, a post which he held until 1939. For ten years he was general secretary of the Zisho (Central Yiddish School Organization) in Poland. His numerous articles on the theory and methods of education were published in *Naie Shul, Shul un Lebn* and *Shulvezn*, magazines of which he

was co-editor. He wrote a brochure, written in Polish, on the Yiddish schools. He was a member of the central committee of the Jewish Bund of Poland, also a member of the Warsaw city council and of the Jewish Community (Kehillah) as a representative of the Bund.

Mendelson began his writing career in 1917. For two years he was editor of *Dos Folk* (organ of the Folkspartei), to which he contributed many political and literary articles. He was also editor of the first Yiddish magazine published by manual workers in Poland, *Der Hantverker*. During the last two years before the second World War he was editor of the literary magazine *Forois* (Warsaw). He was a steady contributor to the *Folkstzeitung* (Warsaw), *Vochnshrift* and *Bicher-Velt*. Articles of his appeared in the Vilna *Tog*.

In 1921 he edited Shloime Ettinger's *Mesholim* (then published for the first time). His preface was in the form of a critical essay on Ettinger. He wrote critical essays on Sholem Aleichem, Isaac Loeb Peretz, I. M. Weissenberg, H. D. Nomberg, M. Kulbak, M. L. Halpern, S. Horontchik, I. A. Trunk, Mendele, Sholem Asch, Ernst Toller, and others.   N. B. MINKOFF.

Lit.: Reisen, Z., *Lexikon fun der Yiddisher Literatur, Presse un Filologie*, cols. 455-58; Koverov, Sigfried, in *Die Evige Revolution* (1923).

MENDELSON, YOISEF (JOSEPH), Yiddish journalist and scholar, b. Tcherkas, district of Kiev, Russia, 1889. He received both an Orthodox Jewish and a secular education. From 1904 to 1905 he studied at the Yeshiva in Kremenchug. Although he had completed his examinations for eight classes of the Gymnasium, he could not enter the university because of the numerus clausus. In 1912 he emigrated to Argentina, where he soon learned Spanish and studied chemistry at the University of La Plata. For a period of six years he was teacher and director of an ICA school in the Jewish colony, Moisesville. Subsequently he devoted himself entirely to journalism.

Mendelson's literary career was begun in Europe as a correspondent for the Russian provincial press. He made his debut in Yiddish (1916) in the weekly *Kolonist*, published in Domingos, center of the Jewish colony Entre Rios. He wrote journalistic and political articles, also essays on Yiddish and Spanish authors. In 1917 he became a steady contributor to the *Yiddishe Zeitung* in Buenos Aires, and later one of the editors. Among the works which he translated into Yiddish are: Mordovtzev, *Hurdus* and *Undzere Piramidn*; Kasanova, Sofia, *Die Russishe Revolutzie in Bilder un Figurn*; Zola, Émile, *Der Emes*; Dickens, Charles, *Tzvei Shtet*; also works by Vicente Blasco Ibañez and Adolfo Gustavo Becker. In 1933 he translated Alberto Gershunov's *Boruch Spinoza's Liebe*.

Mendelson contributed greatly to progress in Yiddish letters in Argentina. He was editor of its first chapbook, *Af die Bregn fun Plata* (1919), and of the monthly, *Argentina*. In 1940 he wrote a research paper, "Fuftzik Yur Yiddish Lebn in Argentina," which was published in the jubilee book of the *Yiddishe Zeitung*. He edited the *Rashi Buch* commemorating the 900th birthday of Rashi (1941), which includes an essay by Mendelson on his life, spirit and influence.

Lit.: Reisen, Z., *Lexikon fun der Yiddisher Literatur, Presse un Filologie*, vol. 2 (1927), cols. 452-55; Ginzburg, M., in *Keneder Adler*, May 5, 1941; Twersky, J., in *Zukunft*, Jan., 1942.

MENDELSSOHN, ABRAHAM, banker, second son of Moses, b. Berlin, 1776; d. Berlin, 1835. In 1803 he became cashier of the banking house of Fould, Oppenheim and Co. at Paris. A year later he married Lea Salomon and went to Hamburg, where he became partner of his elder brother Joseph. He fell from grace with the leader of the French army which occupied Hamburg, and the brothers fled secretly to Berlin. Although Abraham Mendelssohn remained an ardent Francophile, he was impressed by the anti-French spirit of Germany, and participated in the patriotic movement which arose in 1813. He was rewarded for his patriotic efforts and named city councillor of Berlin.

Mendelssohn displayed an analogous spirit of assimilation with the majority surrounding him when he had his children baptized immediately after their birth. He professed in a letter to his eldest daughter Fanny, who later married the artist Wilhelm Hensel: "We, your mother and I, were born and educated by our parents in Judaism, and we have followed God without changing this form. We reared you, your brother and sister in the Christian faith because that is the form of religion of most cultivated men." Mendelssohn used to jest about the fact that at one time he had been called the son of Moses Mendelssohn, but later was referred to as the father of his son, Felix Mendelssohn-Bartholdy. He preferred to be known as the father of his children. He guided especially the education of his son Felix, the composer, and the whole family was convinced that Mendelssohn-Bartholdy owed much of his success to his father, who accompanied him when he traveled and selected his teachers.

In 1819 Abraham Mendelssohn was sent to Paris by the Prussian government in order to negotiate the war debts. Just as his father had been troubled by a feud in defense of Lessing in the days before he died, so his own last days were disturbed by a bitter discussion with Varnhagen who, according to Mendelssohn, had offended against the memory of Lessing.

Lit.: Hensel, Sebastian, *Die Familie Mendelssohn* (1886).

MENDELSSOHN, ARNOLD, composer and teacher, cousin of Felix Mendelssohn-Bartholdy, b. Ratibor, Germany, 1855; d. Darmstadt, Germany, 1933. After studying at the Berlin Hochschule, he served as organist and instructor at the University of Bonn (1880-83). In 1883 he became conductor of the Musikverein in Bielefeld, and from 1885 to 1890 was professor at the Cologne Conservatory. After 1912 he was also professor at the Hoch Conservatory in Frankfort. In 1919 he was made a member of the Berlin Academy, and in 1927 received an honorary doctorate from the University of Tübingen. He composed prolifically, including operas, secular and church choral works, three symphonies, various smaller works for orchestra, chamber music and songs. He edited several volumes of Heinrich Schütz's oratorios, and a volume of madrigals by Monteverde.

Lit.: *Monographien Moderne Musiker,* vol. 1 (1906).

MENDELSSOHN, DOROTHEA (Yiddish, **BRENDEL**), society leader and writer, b. Berlin, 1763; d. Frankfort, Germany, 1839. The eldest daughter of Moses Mendelssohn, she was also the most brilliant and adventurous of the philosopher's children. She re-

ceived a careful education in her father's home, where she met outstanding philosophers and writers. Together with Joseph, her eldest brother, and the two Humboldt brothers, she attended her father's philosophical lectures. A vibrant girl, she took part in theatrical performances at the homes of wealthy Berlin Jews, and organized reading circles which were attended by Marcus and Henriette Herz, among others. Although not beautiful, she was "cheerful and strong, noble and mild, as passionate as a man, tender as a woman," as she was described by the writer Helmina von Chezy.

In 1783 she married the banker Simon Veit, by whom she had two children, Johannes and Philipp, who became noted as painters. Intellectually superior to her uncultured husband, and unhappy in her marriage, she left Veit after making the acquaintance of the non-Jew Friedrich Schlegel at the Herz salon. The brilliant writer, who was seven years younger than she, and whom she was to follow "from one folly to another," unfortunately was "a chameleon in sentiments and views" (Graetz). Having accompanied him to Paris, she turned Protestant in order to marry him (1802). Six years later, on their return to Germany, the Schlegels embraced the Roman Catholic faith in Cologne.

For many years Dorothea led a destitute life with her moody and unstable husband, and frequently had to depend on what she earned by her writings. When Schlegel was appointed imperial court secretary at the headquarters of the Austrian archduke Charles, the couple moved to Vienna (1809). After her husband's death (1829) Dorothea went to Frankfort, where she lived on a small pension.

The "child of enlightenment," she became a follower of romanticism; her "god" was Goethe, his *Faust* her favorite work of literature. She was a gifted writer. Her unfinished romantic novel, *Florentine,* published anonymously (1801) and highly praised by Friedrich Schiller, was compared by critics to Goethe's novels. She made several translations from old and modern French, among the latter Madame de Stael's *Corinne* (1807). But credit for her masterly translations was given entirely to her husband, under whose name they appeared. Dorothea also contributed articles, signed only "D," to Schlegel's literary magazine, *Europa.* In her later years she occupied herself with needlework. "There are," she explained to a friend, "too many books in the world; but I have never heard that there are too many shirts."

Shortly before his death Mendelssohn had expressed concern over the attitude to be adopted by his children in the future. By renouncing Judaism, Dorothea acted like three of her six brothers and sisters. But in certain points, in her attitude toward Judaism, she differed from the two other great lights of the Berlin salons. While Dorothea was converted publicly, her friend Henriette Herz received baptism secretly to avoid hurting her Jewish friends, and Rahel Varnhagen realized the importance of Judaism at least at the end of her life. Dorothea kept on loathing "the old Judaism," as she had expressed herself in a letter to the Protestant preacher, Friedrich Schleiermacher.

ALFRED WERNER.

Lit.: Hensel, Sebastian, *The Mendelssohn Family* (no date); Kayserling, M., *Die jüdischen Frauen in der Ge-*

schichte, Literatur und Kunst (1879); Meyer, Bertha, *Salon Sketches* (1938); Zeydel, Edwin H., "An Unpublished Letter of Dorothea Schlegel to Ludwig Tieck," *The Germanic Review*, vol. 17 (1942) 56-61.

MENDELSSOHN, FELIX ROBERT, cellist, b. Berlin, 1896. He was a descendant of Felix Mendelssohn-Bartholdy. He studied at the Stern Conservatory, later teaching the cello there for several years. He toured Europe as cellist with marked success. In 1936 Mendelssohn came to the United States, settled there permanently, and joined the faculty of New York University as professor of the cello and instructor in chamber music.

MENDELSSOHN, HENRIETTE, educator, daughter of Moses, b. Berlin, 1775; d. Berlin, 1831. Henriette, who outwardly resembled her father far more than did her brothers and sisters, in her early years renounced marriage. In 1799 she went to Vienna, and there became tutor in a Jewish family. Later she occupied a similar position in the household of the banker Fould, at Paris, and a few years thereafter she established, at Paris, a boarding school for young ladies which was in vogue until, because of her delicate health, she disposed of it in 1811.

Soon after her arrival at Paris she became popular with literary and political circles of the French capital. Many German visitors frequented her home in the Rue Richer; Madame de Staël, Benjamin Constant, Wilhelm von Humboldt and Varnhagen von Ense became her friends or revived their friendship. She was also a thoughtful and ingenious correspondent. Her letters are as full of life and wit as those of Rahel Varnhagen, who was fond of her and often mentioned her in her own letters. Both of them were aware of their intellectual kinship. They were admired and enjoyed being admired. Both were kindhearted and capricious, sensitive and ironical. They were patient and humble when they met men considered great, and they were intolerant toward average men and toward almost all women.

Henriette Mendelssohn was for a long time an adherent of rationalism.

When, in 1811, she learned that her sister Dorothea had embraced Christianity, she resentfully severed relations with her. But in 1814 Henriette herself embraced Catholicism when she entered the home of General Sebastiani in order to educate his daughter Fanny. Henriette was highly esteemed by Sebastiani, and indeed was a devoted and conscientious tutor who replaced Fanny's deceased mother. Henriette did not leave Sebastiani's house until Fanny was married to the duke of Choiseul-Praslin, who murdered his wife in 1847. Henriette Mendelssohn was on friendly terms also with Marshal Davoust and other generals of Napoleon.

When she became a convert to Christianity she did not yet believe in the Catholic faith. But she became orthodox, and in her last will expressed regret at not having converted her relatives to Catholicism. After her death Henriette's conversion caused a bitter discussion between her sister Dorothea and the musician Zelter, a friend of Goethe and teacher of Felix Mendelssohn-Bartholdy. Zelter, in a letter to Goethe, had used strong words about the conversion of Henriette,

a daughter of Moses Mendelssohn. Dorothea protested when Goethe's correspondence with Zelter was edited (1835), and Zelter replied with great candor.

Hugo Bieber.

Lit.: Hensel, Sebastian, *Die Familie Mendelssohn* (1886).

MENDELSSOHN, JOSEPH, banker, eldest son of Moses, b. Berlin, 1770; d. Berlin, 1848. Moses Mendelssohn was greatly interested in his eldest son's education, but preferred the indirect method in guiding his progress and the development of his children. In a letter to Herz Homberg (Oct. 4, 1783) Mendelssohn said that his son Joseph "is reasoning rightly and profoundly," but he was concerned about Joseph's "inflexibility" and "unkindness." Indeed Joseph Mendelssohn retained a blunt frankness during his lifetime. He studied Hebrew, but in 1784 gave up these studies, and his father allowed him to study "whatever he liked." In 1795 he founded a banking house in Berlin under the firm name of J. A. Mendelssohn, which became one of the greatest financial institutions of Germany.

Until 1804 Mendelssohn's business was on a modest scale, with only two employees. Upon admittance (1804) of his younger brother Abraham to partnership, the seat of the firm was moved to Hamburg. When the French army occupied that city, Joseph and Abraham Mendelssohn were forced to flee from the city, disguised and under the cover of night. They returned to Berlin, and Abraham retired from the business. Back in Berlin Joseph Mendelssohn saw his firm thrive; in 1828 its name was changed to Mendelssohn & Co., and this remained unchanged until the firm was abolished when the Nazis came to power.

Mendelssohn was keenly interested in scholarship throughout his life. He was an intimate and generous friend of Alexander von Humboldt. He acquired the house where Humboldt was living when that man of learning became involved in a conflict with the landlord, in order that Humboldt might be relieved of his trouble. Mendelssohn wrote an unpretentious but excellent biography of his father which was printed (1843) in the edition of Moses Mendelssohn's works. In 1845 he participated in the discussions concerning the founding of a bank of issue which began to agitate public opinion in Germany. In the preface to his pamphlet *Über Zettelbanken,* Mendelssohn declared with his usual frankness: "I am advocating an institution which will yield a profit to me." This small book, a condensation of Mendelssohn's experiences, presents definitions of the banking business which were not surpassed by later specialists.

Lit.: *Jahrbuch für judische Geschichte und Literatur* (1931).

MENDELSSOHN, MOSES (in Hebrew and Yiddish Moses ben Menahem Mendel, or Moses Dessau), philosopher, critic, translator of the Bible, b. Dessau, Germany, 1729; d. Berlin, 1786. In his native town he received the traditional Jewish education from his father, a writer of Torah scrolls, and from the rabbi of Dessau, David Hirschel Fränkel, whom he followed to Berlin in 1743. There he acquired an extensive secular knowledge, first from books which he secured quite haphazardly, later instructed by Jewish university grad-

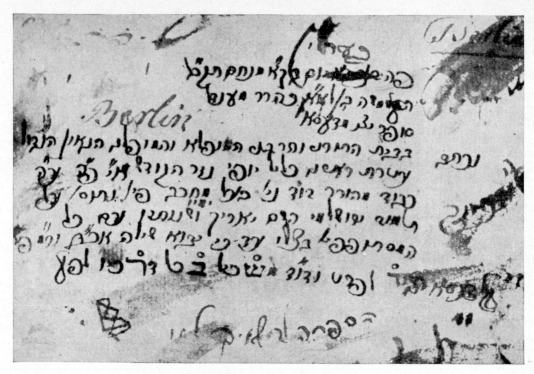

Moses Mendelssohn's Hebrew handwriting at the age of thirteen

uates, such as Israel Samosz, Dr. Abraham Kisch, and Dr. Aaron Solomon Gumpertz. In 1750 Mendelssohn became the tutor of the children of Isaac Bernhard, owner of a silk factory. When Gumpertz, in 1754, introduced him to Gotthold Ephraim Lessing and other littérateurs of Berlin, Mendelssohn's learned interests had already clearly crystallized around philosophy and literary criticism.

The discussions with Lessing and Lessing's friends, Friedrich Nicolai in particular, provided the stimulus for Mendelssohn's first philosophic and esthetic writings. *Koheleth Musar,* two installments of discussions in Hebrew about general moral problems, published in 1754, was shaped after the model of the contemporaneous "moral weeklies." But it was not until his first German book appeared, in 1755, that he became known to the larger public. This first publication, *Philosophische Gespräche,* which Lessing had given to the press without Mendelssohn's knowledge, dealt with problems of Leibnitzian philosophy in a rather school-philosophic manner. A second booklet, *Über die Empfindungen,* published in the same year, opened wider perspectives. It laid the ground for a new understanding of the character of beauty. Its views were elaborated in some later essays (collected in 1761 as *Philosophische Schriften;* revised editions, 1771 and 1777), and led to a new psychological theory stressing the genuine character of esthetics.

As a critic and contributor to the outstanding literary magazines of his time, Mendelssohn found ample opportunities for proving and illustrating his esthetic theories. He was an industrious collaborator on Nicolai's *Bibliothek der schönen Wissenschaften und freien Künste.* The part which he took in the famous *Briefe, die neueste Literatur betreffend* made him known all over Germany. He became the literary arbiter of Ger-

many. In thorough reviews of new publications he advocated the ideals of enlightenment, sometimes using a sharp tongue which did not spare even the Prussian king. Frederick the Great took revenge by twice vetoing the election of Mendelssohn as a member of the Prussian Academy.

Apart from Mendelssohn's growing fame as a writer, his economic position improved. From 1754 on Bernhard had employed him as a bookkeeper in his factory. Although this position limited the time available for his studies and did not satisfy him at all, it permitted him to stay as a Jew in Berlin and provided him with the means for making a decent living. In 1761 he became engaged to Fromet Gugenheim of Hamburg. A large number of letters written before and some written after his marriage reflect the happiness of the couple. In 1763 the authorities granted Mendelssohn the privileged status of a "protected Jew"; the Jewish community of Berlin honored him by exempting him from all Jewish taxes and fees.

The same year brought new laurels to Mendelssohn. The Prussian Academy had announced a contest on an epistemological problem. Mendelssohn's writing *Über die Evidenz in metaphysischen Wissenschaften* was awarded the prize against such competitors as Kant and Thomas Abbt. In the following years the character of Mendelssohn's philosophical works changed. Esthetic problems were no longer dealt with as extensively as before. A correspondence with Thomas Abbt on the destination of man resulted eventually in Mendelssohn's most famous book, *Phaedon,* which was first published in 1767, reprinted very often and translated into many languages. The book proved the immortality of the human soul out of the very concepts of the soul, God, and God's relation to man. Its success was enormous. It was regarded as the finest expression of 18th cent.

By A. Graff

MOSES MENDELSSOHN

From the Mendelssohn Family Collection

Exhibition of Mendelssohniana at the New York Public Library (1929) on the 200th anniversary of Moses Mendelssohn's birth

enlightenment, as a flawless synthesis of antique form and modern *Weltanschauung,* as the most convincing refutation of mechanistic and naturalistic philosophy. The noble teachings and the classic style of the *Phaedon* impressed the contemporaries. Mendelssohn had become a European celebrity. The élite of society and the literary world regarded it as a distinction to meet him. The leading German writers, among them Herder, Wieland, Gleim, Hamann, and Kant, consulted him.

The *Phaedon* was also one of the causes that led to Mendelssohn's disputations with the Swiss theologian Johann Caspar Lavater in which for the first time Mendelssohn publicly discussed his Jewish belief in a philosophic manner. In 1769 Lavater dedicated to Mendelssohn his German translation of Bonnet's French book on the proofs of the Christian dogmas. He asked him to refute Bonnet's proofs or to accept the consequences of his philosophic views such as expressed in *Phaedon* and to renounce the Jewish religion. Mendelssohn answered, unwillingly, with the *Schreiben an den Herrn Diakonus Lavater in Zürich* (1770). He stressed his reluctance to becoming involved in a public discussion of matters of personal belief. He declared patently that his philosophic views had never moved him to doubt his religious beliefs. On the contrary, his philosophy had reaffirmed his religious views. Lavater wrote in reply a pamphlet to which Mendelssohn again answered. Finally, Lavater apologized. However, the good will of both men immediately concerned was no longer sufficient to bring the discussion to an end. A long series of pamphlets continued the discussion, and such men of fame as Michaelis, Semler and Lichtenberg rose to defend Mendelssohn's sincerity against his attackers' bigotry.

The public confession of Judaism by Mendelssohn introduced a new period in his life. His purely philosophic interests receded, whereas his activities in behalf of Jews increased. Where law or administration abrogated Jewish rights, Mendelssohn used his name and reputation to intervene. When the judicial functions of the rabbis or a part of them were to be conferred upon civil authorities, Mendelssohn composed a book, *Ritualgesetze der Juden,* designed to convey to non-Jewish judges a basic knowledge of Jewish law (1778). For Ernst Ferdinand Klein, a Breslau jurist, who had to report on the Jewish oath, Mendelssohn wrote an expert opinion.

There had been, at an earlier time, writings in the Jewish field which had not been motivated by such practical necessities. In 1761 Mendelssohn had published a Hebrew commentary on *Milloth Hahiggayon,* a work on logic by Maimonides, and in 1771 a commentary on *Ecclesiastes.* However, these books never gained the importance of Mendelssohn's German translation of the Bible. Originally it was designed only for Mendelssohn's children, but Solomon Dubno, a teacher in Mendelssohn's house, persuaded Mendelssohn to publish it. In 1778 a specimen (*Alim Literufah*) was printed. Two years later the first book of the Pentateuch appeared, with a commentary by Solomon Dubno. The commentary on the second book (1781) was composed by Mendelssohn himself; later Hartwig Wessely and others helped him. In 1783 the translation of the Pentateuch was completed. In the same year a separate German translation of *Psalms* came out. The progressive elements of the public greeted the translations with enthusiasm, others rejected and some rabbis even banned them.

In 1781 Christian Wilhelm Dohm, a Christian, had advocated the emancipation of the Jews in his book *Über die bürgerliche Verbesserung der Juden.* To support its thesis Mendelssohn, in 1782, wrote an introduction to Markus Herz' German translation of Manasseh ben Israel's *Vindiciae Judaeorum.* Both Dohm's book and Mendelssohn's introduction were discussed and accused extensively. One of the polemic pamphlets reproached Mendelssohn for having expressed in his introduction opinions contradictory to the basic views of Judaism. Mendelssohn replied with his book *Jerusalem oder über religiöse Macht und Judentum* (1783). In this work he expressed systematically his views on church law, the ban, and the like, which he had thitherto mentioned only occasionally. In a broad philosophical analysis he defined state law and church law and their mutual limits. The state is not allowed to request particular convictions, and the latter should not be made compulsory by a church order. The state can interfere in matters of thinking only when certain teachings endanger its very existence. Judaism does not know of any compulsory belief. What it commands and asks for are no dogmatic opinions, no truths of salvation, no sentences conveying any knowledge. Judaism never experienced the conflict between religion and thinking. It can not become an obstacle to a religion of reason because it is not a religion in the strict sense of the word at all. It is revealed law. It contains prescriptions for the life of the Jews, not prescriptions for a certain way of thinking. The commandments of Judaism are ceremonial law, a sort of constitution for the Jewish community. The ceremonial law is designed to bind the Jews together, and is valid only for Jews. Besides the law, Jewish teachings are of a general philosophic nature and in complete harmony with a general religion of reason.

After the publication of the *Jerusalem* Mendelssohn became once more involved in a controversy which affected him more than any other one before. In 1781 Lessing had died. A few years later Mendelssohn learned from his friend, Elise Reimarus, that Lessing, when he had been visited by F. H. Jacobi, a romanticizing philosopher, had confessed to being a "determined Spinozist." Mendelssohn, perplexed and horrified by the assertion that Lessing, with whom he had believed himself to be in complete harmony, should have been a Spinozist and an atheist, was unwilling to believe it. He used the publication, *Morgenstunden oder Vorlesungen über das Dasein Gottes* (1785), a book containing philosophic lectures which he had held in his house, to state his position concerning Spinoza and his views on rational religion. Jacobi did not wait for the publication of this book. In a work, *Über die Lehre des Spinoza in Briefen an den Herrn Moses Mendelssohn,* he gave his version of the case. Now Mendelssohn deemed it necessary to protect Lessing against what he thought was infamous discrimination. In December, 1785, he wrote his reply, which appeared in the following year, after his death, under the title *An die Freunde Lessings. Ein Anhang zu Herrn Jacobis Briefwechsel über die Lehre Spinozas.* The emotion connected with the polemic had shattered his frail health. On June 31st he himself had taken the manuscript of his last book to the printer; on January 4, 1786, he died. His death was mourned by Jews and Christians. Once again it became evident what an influential position Mendelssohn had held in his time.

Mendelssohn's achievements, for which he became famous in the literature and philosophy of his time, have been dimmed by the greater achievements of greater men who followed him. In Jewish history, however, a new epoch begins with him. This is not due to his theory of Judaism. In its original form this theory has had no far-reaching influence. The main impact Mendelssohn made resulted from the fact that he was the first Jew in modern times who in his personality combined Judaism and modern culture and was recognized as such by the non-Jewish world. The advocates of Jewish emancipation could point to him as striking evidence for their assertion that the Jew can become an equal member of modern civilization. Mendelssohn was vitally and practically interested in an education of the Jews designed to raise them to the level of general culture. However, he was not the protagonist of Jewish religious reform. His disciple David Friedländer accepted only half of Mendelssohn's theory of Judaism when he developed the idea of a rational Jewish religion. The reformers who laid the theoretic foundations for Reform Judaism, men such as Holdheim, Stern, Ritter and Einhorn, were well aware of the "orthodox" tendencies in Mendelssohn's theory of Judaism. In popular opinion, however, Mendelssohn lives as the man from whom, somehow, the modernistic tendencies of 19th cent. Judaism originated.

Mendelssohn's writings were reprinted very often, legitimately and illegitimately. The first systematic collection of his works was published by a descendant, G. B. Mendelssohn (*Gesammelte Schriften,* 7 vols., Leipzig, 1843-45). The work on the comprehensive critical edition planned on the occasion of the 200th anniversary of Mendelssohn's birth could not be completed; seven volumes appeared from 1929 to 1938 (*Gesammelte Schriften, Jubiläumsausgabe,* edited by Ismar Elbogen, Eugen Mittwoch, Fritz Bamberger and others, Berlin). Some of Mendelssohn's books were translated into English (*Memoirs,* London, 1825 and 1827; *Jerusalem,* London, 1838).   FRITZ BAMBERGER.

Lit.: Kayserling, M., *Moses Mendelssohn. Sein Leben und Wirken* (2nd ed., 1888); idem, *Moses Mendelssohns philosophische und religiöse Grundsätze* (1856); Bamberger, Fritz, *Die geistige Gestalt Moses Mendelssohns* (1929); *Moses Mendelssohn, Zur 200jährigen Wiederkehr seines Geburtstages* (published by the *Encyclopaedia Judaica,* 1929); papers by Walter Rothman, Felix A. Levy, and Louis J. Kopald, in *Central Conference of American Rabbis Year Book,* vol. 39 (1929) 305-401; Walter, H., *Moses Mendelssohn* (1930); Zarek, Otto, *Moses Mendelssohn, ein jüdisches Schicksal in Deutschland* (1936); *Jewish Encyclopedia,* vol. 8, pp. 479-85; Goldstein, Ludwig, *Moses Mendelssohn und die deutsche Ästhetik* (1904); Braitmaier, Friedrich, *Geschichte der poetischen Theorie und Kritik,* vol. 2 (1889) 72-279; Auerbach, Jakob, *Lessing und Mendelssohn* (1867); Schmidt, Erich, *Lessing* (4th ed., 1923); Cohen, B., *Über die Erkenntnislehre Moses Mendelssohns* (1921); Cahn, N., *Moses Mendelssohns Moralphilosophie* (1921); Pinkuss, Fritz, *Moses Mendelssohns Verhältnis zur englischen Philosophie* (1929); Scholz, H., edit., *Die Hauptschriften zum Pantheismusstreit;* Cassirer, Ernst, "Die Idee der Religion bei Lessing und Mendelssohn," *Festgabe zum zehnjährigen Bestehen der Akademie für die Wissenschaft des Judentums* (1929); Ritter, J. H., *Geschichte der jüdischen Reformation* (1858 et seq.); Spiegel, Shalom, *Hebrew Reborn* (1930) 47-72; *Lessing-Mendelssohn Gedenkbuch* (1879); *Gedenkbuch für Moses Mendelssohn* (1929).

MENDELSSOHN, SIDNEY, bibliographer, b. Bristol, England, 1861; d. London, 1917. He was the son of the Reverend Meyer Mendelssohn, the first permanent Jewish minister on the Kimberley Diamond Fields. Mendelssohn came to South Africa at an early age and settled at Kimberley, where he became a successful diamond dealer. He was chairman of the New Vaal River Diamond and Exploration Company. Sidney on Vaal, a village near Kimberley, was named in his honor.

He lived the last twelve years of his life in London. He was for some years prior to his death treasurer of the Liberal Synagogue, London, for whose services he wrote a number of hymns. He was also a member of the Council of the Jewish Historical Society of England, contributing to its *Transactions* (vol. 7, 1911-14, pp. 180-205) a study, "Jewish Pioneers of South Africa." Another essay of his, "Judaic or Semitic Legends and Customs amongst the South African Natives," appeared in the *Journal of the African Society* (1913-14).

He is, however, best remembered by his two-volume book entitled *Mendelssohn's South African Bibliography* (London, 1910), generally regarded as an invaluable sourcework on South Africa's history. He bequeathed to the Union of South Africa his far-famed private collection of Africana, together with sums of money for its extension by the purchase of new works and of such earlier publications as he himself had not been able to procure. His collection was later housed at Parliament House, Cape Town.

Mendelssohn wrote two other books (published posthumously, London, 1920): *The Jews of Africa, especially in the Sixteenth and Seventeenth Centuries* and *The Jews of Asia.*

In July, 1902, he instituted a memorial at the Kimberley Synagogue in honor of the Jewish soldiers killed in the Anglo-Boer war of 1899 to 1902.

Lit.: *Jewish Chronicle* (London), Aug. 29, 1902; Abrahams, Israel, *ibid.,* Oct. 5, 1917, p. 6; Rochlin, S. A., in *Hasholom* (Durban), Sept., 1933, pp. 14-15; *South Africa* (London), Sept. 29, 1917, p. 465; Oct. 13, 1917, p. 59.

MENDELSSOHN-BARTHOLDY, ALBRECHT VON

jurist and historian, b. Karlsruhe, Germany, 1874; d. Oxford, England, 1936. He was the son of the historian Karl Mendelssohn-Bartholdy and the grandson of the composer Felix Mendelssohn-Bartholdy. He studied law, and became professor of law at the University of Würzburg in 1905; professor and director of the Institut für auswärtige Politik at Hamburg in 1920. In 1922 Mendelssohn-Bartholdy became executive secretary of the German editorial board of the *Economic and Social History of the War* whose editor-in-chief was the American James T. Shotwell. He represented Germany at the Permanent Court of Arbitration at The Hague, and received the honorary LL.D. degree from Harvard University. In 1933, when he was forced to look for an asylum abroad, Balliol College at Oxford created a lectureship for him.

Mendelssohn-Bartholdy began with studies on the theory of law which won the admiration of experts. In 1900 he published his penetrating study *Grenzen der Rechtskraft*, which was continued in the equally illuminating study *Räumliches Herrschaftsgebiet des Strafrechts*, dealing with the problems of sovereignty

Felix Mendelssohn-Bartholdy

and juridical competence (1907). Proceeding from studies on English juridical institutions, Mendelssohn-Bartholdy published *Das Imperium des Richters* (1910), comparing the status of English and German judges. From 1914 on he was more interested in modern history and diplomacy than in the science of law. He participated moderately in German war propaganda by writing a pamphlet on Ireland, but he was converted to the idea of the League of Nations, and in 1918 published a pamphlet, *Völkerbund als Arbeitsgemeinschaft.*

Nevertheless, he stubbornly defended the official German assertion that Germany was free from war guilt, and in consequence, he was made co-editor of the official collection of documents concerning the genesis of the first World War, *Die grosse Politik der europäischen Kabinette.*

From 1922 to the beginning of the Nazi regime Mendelssohn-Bartholdy edited the periodical *Europäische Gespräche,* devoted to the fostering of mutual understanding among nations and to interpreting contemporary events with a view toward promoting the League of Nations idea. In 1927 he published a study, *Diplomatie,* which contrasts existing diplomacy with its ideal, and in the same year an account of the European situation, addressed to American readers. His last work, *The War and German Society: The Testament of a Liberal* (New Haven, 1937), was edited after his death; reviewing the effects of the war, Mendelssohn-Bartholdy dealt also with the situation of the Jews in Germany, but his views on German Jews and anti-Semitism are considered its weakest part.

HUGO BIEBER.

Lit.: *Social Research,* vol. 7, No. 1 (1940) 102-5.

MENDELSSOHN-BARTHOLDY, FELIX

composer, grandson of Moses and son of Abraham Mendelssohn, b. Hamburg, Germany, 1809; d. Leipzig, Germany, 1847. It is a singular fact that there were two Mendelssohns: one who was an immediate hit with the "people" and remains so; another who made his way slowly with a handful of connoisseurs who have grown in proportion to the increasing availability of musical education. Combined they do not make for one universal genius whose *best* works appeal equally

Felix Mendelssohn's Birthplace in Hamburg

to layman and musician, but remain two separate entities—a lesser and greater Mendelssohn.

The popularity of the lesser Mendelssohn—he of the countless *Songs Without Words,* with their faint odor of cliché; of the songs *with* words, vague and mildly melancholy; of the turgid oratorios, church services and hymns—rose to such legendary proportions before his death in 1847 that the adoring German masses wondered if the master were not being recalled from heaven to be meted out a mortal end.

The Mendelssohn of the *Midsummer Night's Dream* suite (1826), the three sets of *Variations* for piano, the Octet, Quintet and Quartets for strings, the violin concerto, the *Scotch* and *Italian* symphonies and the *Hebrides* (1831) and *Meeresstille* overtures is a composer of a far different stripe. His recognition was slow and embattled, coming from the *avant garde* of his time: the very opposite of the masses. His works passed from the alembic of one generation of the musically acute to the next. Each time their discourse became clearer and more impressive until modern ears, basing comparison on the established landmarks, have been able to evaluate them properly.

The place of this Mendelssohn among the hierarchy of musical genius is undisputed. He sits alongside his fellow classic Romanticists, Weber and Schubert, not at the head of the table with the more heroic titans, Bach, Beethoven and Brahms, it is true, but definitely

in their company. As such, he is Jewry's greatest contribution in the realm of creative music.

Oddly enough, it was the greater Mendelssohn who was first to develop. Unlike most composers who try their wings with minor compositions (Beethoven did not write his first symphony until the age of thirty, Brahms until forty-three), Mendelssohn, the most astonishing musical prodigy since the boy Mozart, essayed the symphonic form before he was fifteen. A grandson of the Platonist Moses Mendelssohn, and son of a woman who read Homer in the original Greek, he was, so to speak, born to the classical tradition. However, Beethoven's *Pastoral Symphony* had already touched off the first sparks of romanticism; and it must be remembered that Mendelssohn's youth coincided with the last years of the Bonn master. It was, therefore, only natural that the young fledgling, whose veneration of Beethoven was enormous, should absorb some of the new spirit.

When Mendelssohn-Bartholdy's father acquired a sumptuous residence in Berlin, with a seven-acre park equipped with picturesque huts and a concert hall capable of seating several hundred guests, the Romantic mood was full upon the sixteen-year-old lad. He could sit in his study and from the window view the fairy loveliness of the surrounding terrain. A closed world of imaginary woodland creatures held him by skeins of poetic rapture. Here, before the winter was out, was written his first mature work to hold its ground against time, the Octet in E flat for strings.

A year later, in 1826, the German translations of Shakespeare became available. The ecstasy of the Mendelssohn coterie knew no bounds. They went about the garden enacting scenes from the comedies and addressing each other in the manner of Shakespearean characters. This, also, had its inevitable effect on the gifted, sensitive composer. That summer he conceived and completed the *Midsummer Night's Dream* overture. (It was not until another seventeen years had rolled by that the twelve additional numbers comprising the suite were composed.) This is music which must be included among the world's imperishable masterpieces. It is romantic, descriptive writing, peopled with all the twinkling, legendary folk of Shakespeare's and Felix Mendelssohn's imagination.

Thus the real Mendelssohn reached his full stature at an incredibly early age. But aside from the large circle of intimates, he made no headway in Berlin until he had been proclaimed elsewhere. In fact, the failure of a previously written opera the following year created such ill-feeling between the composer and Berlin that he waged a war against it for nearly twenty years. His first substantial successes were achieved abroad, principally in England, where he visited ten times and became the personal friend of Queen Victoria and her music-loving consort. The host of meretricious compositions, the sops to the masses alternating with the gold, came into being, in the main, at the request of choral groups, churches and publishers who sought material salable in volume. These works, curiously, epitomized the moral and earnest Protestantism of the Victorian Era more than the productions of any of his contemporaries.

Mendelssohn's especial niche is as a dash joining two great styles in music. He was a product of his heredity as well as of his time. For, like his grandfather who brought together the old and new Judaisms, and his father, a self-characterized "dash uniting Moses and Felix Mendelssohn," Felix Mendelssohn was a dash uniting classicism and romanticism.

To say that one does not think Mendelssohn great because he is no Beethoven is analagous to saying that ultramarine is a mediocre color because it is not red, or that Barrie is lacking in merit because he does not attain the same epic sweep as Shakespeare. Each has his place in the scheme of things, and in his own poetic field Mendelssohn ranks beside his fellow classic romanticists, Schubert and Weber.

It is to be hoped that the romantic renaissance will not bring upon us an indiscriminate avalanche of Mendelssohnism, but will cast out the multitude of animalculae, whose unimportance no one realized more than the composer, and will let us revalue him in the concert hall through the still impressive amount of his first-rate music: the three sets of masterly *Variations* for piano (1841), the *E-major Sonata* (1826), the *Octet* (1825), the *Violin Concerto* (1844), the *Scotch* (1842) and *Italian* (1833) symphonies, the *Hebrides* (1832), *Meeresstille* (1828), *Ruy Blas* (1839), and *Melusina* (1833) overtures; and the insuperable *Midsummer Night's Dream* music (1826; 1842).

SCHIMA KAUFMAN.

Lit.: Hadden, J. Cuthbert, *Life of Mendelssohn* (1900); Kaufman, Schima, *Mendelssohn* (1934); Mendelssohn, Felix, *Letters* (1863); Polko, E., *Reminiscences of Mendelssohn* (1869).

MENDES, 1. prominent Sephardic family of Spain. After the expulsion of the Jews from Spain in 1492, a few members of the family remained in Spain as Marranos; however, the majority emigrated to Holland, England and France; others went to America. They married into the Pereira, Da Costa, De Sola and other famous families, and distinguished themselves as scholars and communal leaders.

Outstanding members of the French branch, which settled chiefly in Bordeaux and Bayonne, were the communal leaders Edouard Mendes and Elysée Mendes, and especially the poet Catulle Mendes. The Holland branch produced such notable writers as the Hebrew poet David Franco-Mendes and the ritualists Samuel Rodrigues Mendes and Samuel da Silva Mendes. Rodrigo Mendes da Silva, royal historiographer at the court of Spain, emigrated to Venice. Here he became a Jew openly and adopted the name of Jacob. The vast number of his historical works earned him the name of the "Spanish Livy." João Mendes da Silva, an eminent lawyer and poet, lived in Brazil.

2. an American family of Sephardic (Spanish-Portuguese) origin, several members of which became distinguished as rabbis, authors and educators during the 19th cent., both in the United States and in England. David Pereira Mendes, a fugitive of Spain, was the first of the family to reach America, arriving at Jamaica in 1786. There he died during the same year, leaving a son, Samuel Mendes (1775-1838), who remained in the West Indies and brought up a large family. One of Samuel Mendes' grandsons, Abraham Pereira Mendes, was an outstanding English rabbi. Abraham Pereira Mendes' sons were noted American rabbis, Frederick de Sola Mendes and Henry Pereira Mendes.

MENDES, ABRAHAM PEREIRA, minister and educator, b. Kingston, Jamaica, 1825; d. New York city, 1893. He was the son of Isaac Mendes. His great-grandfather, David Pereira Mendes (1740-86), was the first of the West Indian or American branch of the Mendes family, having arrived at Jamaica as a fugitive from Spain in 1786, the year in which he died.

After serving as an instructor in the Beth Limud School in Jamaica, one of the first institutions of its kind in America, Abraham Pereira Mendes crossed over to England, where he studied under the learned rabbi, Dr. David Meldola, and also under the Reverend D. A. de Sola, whose daughter Eliza became his wife. In 1845 Mendes began his rabbinical career by delivering a series of sermons in English in the London Portuguese Synagogue. Returning to Jamaica, he served for a time as assistant to the Reverend Isaac Lopez and as preacher in the Portuguese congregation. Soon after, the Montego Bay congregation elected him its spiritual head.

In 1851 Mendes was compelled to leave Jamaica for England, and was, for a brief period, instructor at the Hebrew National School in Birmingham, but early in 1852 he became preacher of the congregation in that city. He received a call to a larger communal institution in London, the Neveh Zedek, and from 1858 to 1864 occupied the pulpit of that congregation. He thereupon established Northwick College, an educational institution for Jewish youth. He organized courses of lectures which served to spread Jewish culture in London. However, he continued to deliver sermons, succeeding Benjamin Artom as rabbi of the Sephardic congregations of England, and on occasion served as ecclesiastical chief.

In 1883 Mendes accepted a call to the ministry of the old Newport congregation, in Rhode Island, where he spent the last decade of his life. Thus his career ended in America, where it had begun. Among his literary achievements was a volume of his sermons (1854). He made a translation of the *Daily Prayer Book of the German Jewish Ritual with Dinim.* He also aided his father-in-law in the translation of the *Mahzor* (holy day prayer-book), taking full charge of the work upon his death. Among his other works are a post-Biblical history of the Jews to the period of the Second Temple, and the *Interlinear Translation* of the prayer-book (published by Vallentine). He was author also of "The Jewish Cemetery at Newport" (*Rhode Island Historical Magazine,* vol. 6, pp. 81-105).

Lit.: Mendes, H. P., in *Publications of the American Jewish Historical Society,* No. 11 (1903) 207-11.

MENDÈS, CATULLE, poet, novelist and dramatist, b. Bordeaux, France, 1841; d. St. Germain, France, 1909. The son of a banker, he left Bordeaux and settled in Paris in 1859, shortly thereafter founding the periodical *Revue fantaisiste,* where there appeared his erotic poem "Roman d'une nuit," which won him general notoriety, and a fine of 500 francs and a month's imprisonment. Mendès was one of the group of contemporary poets who launched the classical "Parnassian" movement; when his first volume, *Philoméla,* appeared in 1863, it won great acclaim for its extraordinary technical command of poetics. Later, to judge by his numerous further collections, he was generally considered a dexterous rather than a highly original poet.

Besides poetry, Mendès' more than fifty volumes included drama, critical writings, novels and short stories, the latter in the tradition of the erotic tale. The dramatic pieces were favorably received on the Paris stage, and included: *La part du roi* (1872); *Justice* (1877); *Le fils de l'étoile* (1904), which dramatizes the story of Bar Kochba. Among his better-known novels was *Le roi vierge* (1880), dealing with Ludwig II of Bavaria and Richard Wagner; Mendès was an early follower of Richard Wagner, and published a critical work on the composer in 1886. Other critical writings included the three volumes of *L'art au théâtre*, an annual collection of the pieces he wrote for the press. In 1894 Mendès received the cross of the Legion of Honor.

Mendès was first married to Judith Gautier, younger daughter of the poet, and later to the poetess Jane Primitive Mette.

Through some undetermined accident he was found dead in the railway tunnel of St. Germain. He seemed to have stepped out of the compartment, unaware that his train had not yet reached the station.

Lit.: Bertrand, A., *Catulle Mendès* (1908); Nordau, Max, *Degeneration* (1895) 266-71; *The Bookman*, vol. 29 (1909) 174-78.

MENDES, FRANCISCO, Marrano banker, d. Lisbon, Portugal, about 1535. He was a member of the wealthy Nasi family who had adopted the name Mendes, and the husband of Beatrice de Luna, better known as Gracia Mendesia. Mendes was the founder of one of the greatest banking houses of Europe, which he established in Lisbon with branches in Flanders and France; it had extensive business relations with Charles V, the French king Francis I, and other monarchs.

Upon his premature death, when unsuccessful attempts were made by the crown to confiscate the family fortune on the ground that they were Jews, Mendes' widow fled from the Inquisition. She was accompanied by her daughter, Reyna, her sister-in-law, the widow of Dr. Micas (Miguez), erstwhile physician of the king of Portugal, and the widow's young son, John Micas (Miguez), who later became Joseph Nasi, Duke of Naxos. In London she met business agents of her late husband, while in Antwerp, where she settled, his younger brother, Diogo, directed the local banking branch which was opened in 1512. After Diogo's death, about 1545, Gracia moved to Venice.

Lit.: Graetz, H., *History of the Jews*, vol. 4 (1927) 571-72; Wolf, Lucien, *Essays in Jewish History* (1934) 75-76 et seq.; Kayserling, Moritz, *Geschichte der Juden in Portugal* (1867) 211, 266 et seq.

MENDES, FRANCISCO (ISAAC MEDEIROS), one of the earliest leaders of the first Sephardic community in Holland. About 1598 he emigrated, with his parents and his brother Christoval (Franco Mordecai), from Oporto, Portugal, to Amsterdam. Here he distinguished himself by his literary accomplishments, and was highly esteemed by the senate. Together with other members of his family, he founded at Amsterdam in 1608 the second Jewish synagogue, Neveh Shalom. He died at an early age.

Catulle Mendès

Lit.: Kayserling, M., *Sephardim*, 168; idem, *Geschichte der Juden in Portugal* (1867) 211.

MENDES, FREDERICK DE SOLA, rabbi, author and editor, b. Montego Bay, Jamaica, British West Indies, 1850; d. New Rochelle, N. Y., 1927. He was the son of Abraham Pereira and Eliza de Sola Mendes. Inspired by the example of his father, he pursued various studies in preparing himself for a rabbinical career. His education began in the Northwick College, which his father had founded in London. He subsequently attended London University, graduating with honors in 1869. Thereupon followed further studies at the University of Breslau and the Jewish theological seminary of that city. In 1871 he received the Ph.D. degree from the University of Jena.

Having acquired a broad educational equipment, Mendes returned to London, where he was appointed preacher in the New Synagogue, Great St. Helen's, London (1873). After serving a few months, he received a call from Congregation Shaaray Tefilla (later the West End Synagogue) of New York city as assistant minister to Rabbi Samuel M. Isaacs. In 1877 Mendes was elected rabbi of the congregation, this election being confirmed for life in 1904. He officiated as rabbi until 1920, when he retired as rabbi emeritus.

From the pen of Mendes appeared several books and numerous essays on topics of Jewish interest. He was author of *Outlines of Jewish History; Child's First Bible; Synagogue and School; Jewish Home Prayer Book;* and *A Hebrew's Reply to the Missionaries;* also of several translations, including *Life of Manasseh ben Israel* (translated from Kayserling). Mendes was one of the founders of *The American Hebrew,* and one of its editors (1879-85); he was for a time an editor of the *Menorah Monthly.* He served on the editorial staff of the *Jewish Encyclopedia* as head of the bureau of translations and revisions, and contributed, among other important articles, the one on "America, Judaism in." He was one of the editors of the new Bible translation and the Jewish classics, both issued by the Jewish Publication Society of America. Mendes contributed important articles to *Johnson's Encyclopedia* and the *Encyclopedia Americana,* and also to various other periodicals.

Mendes was a champion of Jewish ideals and active in social welfare movements. In 1890 he founded the Shaaray Tefilla Sisterhood for personal service. He also aided the Alliance Colony of Russian Jews in Vineland, N. J. He was a founder and secretary of the Jewish Ministers' Association.   CLARENCE I. FREED.

Lit.: Markens, Isaac, *The Hebrews in America* (1888) 296-97; *American Hebrew,* Oct. 28, 1927, p. 865.

MENDES, GRACIA (MENDES-) NASI, *see* MENDESIA, GRACIA.

MENDES, HENRY (CHAIM) PEREIRA, rabbi, b. Birmingham, England, 1852; d. Mt. Vernon, N. Y., 1937. Mendes received his education from the age of twelve at Northwick College, London. This school, founded and directed by his father, trained an unusual number of boys who attained high distinction in later life, among them Lord Reading, lord chief justice of England and viceroy of India, and Professor Raphael Meldola, father of the British coal tar industry. From 1870 to 1872 Mendes attended University College, London, while continuing his Hebrew studies under his father and the Reverend H. L. Harris, father of Rabbi Maurice H. Harris of New York city. During his early ministry in New York, Mendes took up the study of medicine, graduating from the medical school of New York University on June 8, 1884. In 1904 the Jewish Theological Seminary of America bestowed upon him the honorary D.D. degree, and in 1937 the Jewish Institute of Religion honored him with the D.H.L. degree.

Mendes served as Hazan and minister in Manchester, England, from 1875 to 1877, then accepted a call to Congregation Shearith Israel in New York. Besides carrying out his exacting duties as Hazan, preacher and teacher, and as superintendent of the Polonies Talmud Torah School, Mendes always found time to work for every Jewish cause, frequently intervening with city authorities to prevent the introduction of sectarian exercises into public schools, organizing Jewish schools and societies to counteract the excessive ardor of those missionaries who did not scruple to lure Jewish children away from their parents, safeguarding the religious interests of Jewish patients in city and state institutions and having examination dates in colleges and universities set on some day other than a Jewish holy day.

Mendes was one of the first Zionists in America. Theodor Herzl asked his cooperation in organizing the movement in the United States, and he was elected vice-president of the Federation of American Zionists, and a member of the Actions Committee of the World Zionist Organization at the Second Zionist Congress in Vienna (1898), and again in Basel (1899). All his life he remained an eloquent, albeit at times the sole, exponent of what he called "Bible Zionism" or "spiritual Zionism."

From the moment of Mendes' arrival in the United States, he threw himself heart and soul into the activities of the Jewish community of New York. The birth of the Montefiore Hospital is due to the fact that, early in 1884, at the instance of Mendes, representatives of the synagogues of the city were called together to plan a fitting celebration of Sir Moses Montefiore's forthcoming hundredth birthday.

Similarly, it was Mendes who gave first impetus to the Sabato Morais' proposal for the founding of an Orthodox Jewish theological seminary. The preparatory meetings were held in the rooms of Mendes' synagogue, and the Jewish Theological Seminary of America was formally opened there (1887). For many years, Mendes was president of the Seminary's advisory board, and professor of Jewish history in the Seminary. On the death of Morais in 1897, Mendes served as its acting president until Professor Solomon Schechter was called from Cambridge University in 1902.

In 1896, at the invitation of Bishop Henry Potter of the Protestant Episcopal diocese of New York, Mendes became chairman of a committee which organized the Crippled Children's East Side Free School, New York, opened in 1901. He founded the Horeb Home for Jewish Deaf-Mutes, of which he was made the president. While he was engaged in this work, the large school for deaf-mutes on 67th Street and Lexington Avenue was acquired for the comparatively small sum of $30,000, which Mendes raised; he was able (1908) to take over the whole institution. He set up in it a Jewish regime. This school, with 250 pupils, became one of the leading schools for the handicapped in America.

With their Sephardic background of enlightened Orthodoxy, Mendes and his cousin, Meldola de Sola, minister of the Spanish and Portuguese Congregation in Montreal, called into existence the Union of Orthodox Jewish Congregations of the United States and Canada, its first convention being held in June, 1898, in the assembly hall of Mendes' synagogue. He became its first president, and held that office for fifteen years.

In 1885 he organized a branch of the Alliance Israélite Universelle in his synagogue, becoming its president. Later he was vice-president of the New York branch of the Alliance. He gave up days and weary nights as a member of the executive committee of the New York Kehillah, organized in 1909, helping to organize and unite all the Jews of New York city into one coherent body. He was one of the founders of the New York Board of Jewish Ministers in 1882, and its first secretary, a position which he filled for a quarter of a century. Later he became its president. At the beginning of the 20th cent., Mendes and his wife interested Mrs. Israel Unterberg, a member of Shearith Israel Congregation, in planning and organizing the Young Women's Hebrew Association.

Notwithstanding these multifarious communal and public activities, Mendes was continuously engaged in literary work. Many of his editorials, articles, poems and translations from Hebrew are to be found in the early pages of *The American Hebrew,* of which he was a founder. Many sermons, essays and articles from his pen were republished in pamphlet form, notably: *The Position of Woman in Jewish Law and Custom*

(1884); *The Sphere of Congregational Work* (1885); *The Lifting of the Veil* (1888); *Why I Am a Jew; The Solution of War; Peace Anthem;* his *Farewell Message* (1920); *Fiftieth Anniversary Sermon* (1927).

In 1897 he published *England and America, The Dream of Peace,* a poetic, impassioned appeal for an Anglo-Saxon union between England and America. In 1899 there issued from his versatile pen a remarkable study in anticipations entitled *Looking Ahead.* He published a volume for children called *In Old Egypt.* In more serious mood he was one of the American board of consulting editors of the *Jewish Encyclopedia.* In 1895 he was invited by the Jewish Publication Society of America to prepare the translation of the book of *Amos* for the new English translation of the Bible which the Society was planning. To meetings of the American Jewish Historical Society he contributed papers dealing with the history of his own congregation (1887), the Jews of Newport (1899), and notes (1898 and 1901), a glossary to the twenty-seventh volume of its *Publications,* as well as a memorial tribute to his father (1902) and one to the Reverend Abraham H. Nieto (1902). He wrote an article included in the brochure *Early Religious Leaders of Newport,* published by the Newport Historical Society in 1918.

Among his numerous publications in verse were: *A Ballad of Purim;* his Purim drama, *Esther and Harbonah* (1917); a Hanukah play published in the *American Hebrew;* and a number of hymns included in the *Jewish Hymns for Jewish Schools,* which he published. Mendes was keenly musical and, in connection with his Purim plays, he wrote the melodies for the incidental songs. Some of his compositions found their place in the services of his congregation alongside of melodies composed by his grandfather, D. A. de Sola, "the learned Hazan," and other members of his family.

In the field of liturgy Mendes issued, jointly with David de Sola Pool, *The Burial Service as Used in the Congregation Shearith Israel of New York* (1910) and *Mekor Hayim, the Mourner's Hand-Book* (1915). In the evening of his days, in commemoration of the completion of sixty years of ministry, he compiled and published *Derech Hayim, The Way of Life* (1934), a collection of prayers and meditations for home use.

DAVID DE SOLA POOL.

Lit.: Pool, David de Sola, "Henry Pereira Mendes," *American Jewish Year Book,* vol. 40 (1938-39) 41-60; idem, in *Publications of the American Jewish Historical Society,* No. 35 (1939) 316-19; idem, *H. Pereira Mendes,* a biography (1938).

MENDES, ISAAC P., rabbi, b. Kingston, Jamaica, British West Indies, 1853; d. Savannah, Ga., 1904. He studied first at Northwick College, London, and later he was educated by his uncle, rabbi A. P. Mendes. In 1870 he officiated at the Bevis Marks Synagogue in London. Mendes was rabbi and preacher of the Beth Shalome Congregation in Richmond, Va. Thereafter he occupied the pulpit of the Mickve Israel Congregation of Savannah, Ga., until 1903, when he retired as rabbi emeritus. Mendes was the author of *Pure Words,* a collection of special prayers, and of *First Lessons in Hebrew.*

Henry Pereira Mendes

MENDES, MOSES, poet and dramatist, b. London, date unknown; d. Old Buckenham, Norfolk, England, 1758. He was the son of a stockbroker and a grandson of the physician Moses (Fernando) Mendes. Notable among his dramatic works was *The Double Disappointment,* a ballad opera, first performed in 1746. *The Chaplet,* a "musical entertainment" (score by William Boyce), was first produced in 1749. Both were immensely popular. *The Chaplet* was revived on the New York stage in 1942.

Among Mendes' other works were *Henry and Blanch,* a tale taken from the French (1746), poems written in imitation of Edmund Spenser, and a translation of Mapphaeus' sequel to Vergil's *Aeneid.* Mendes was a friend of the poet James Thomson. His two sons changed their name to "Head," and Mendes' grandson, Francis Bond Head, was created a baronet in 1838.

MENDES, MOSES (FERNANDO), physician, place and date of birth unknown; d. London, 1724. A Portuguese Marrano, he studied medicine at Montpellier, France (M.D., 1667). He was a professor of medicine at the University of Coimbra, Portugal, and physician to King John IV of Portugal. When the king's daughter, Catherine of Braganza, became seriously ill on her way to England where she was to marry King Charles II of England, Mendes was summoned to treat her. A favorite of hers, he accompanied Catherine to England where, in 1669, he was appointed physician ordinary to the queen. He was one of the physicians in regular attendance on Charles II in his last illness. Mendes, who like his wife openly professed Judaism in London (taking the name of Moses), was created, by the charter of James II, a member of the Royal College of Physicians (1687), but at the accession of William and Mary (1689) his name was removed from the rolls. His only published work was his M.D. thesis (Lyon, 1668). Moses Mendes, the dramatist, was his grandson.

MENDES DA COSTA, JOSEPH, *see* COSTA, JOSEPH MENDES DA.

MENDES DA COSTA, MAURITS BENJAMIN, philologist and writer, b. Amsterdam, Holland, 1851. He published an *Index etymologicus dictionis homericae* and an edition of the *Iliad* and *Odyssey* with critical notations, as well as other works on Homer and other Greek poets. In 1891 he became curator of manuscripts at the library of the University of Amsterdam, in which capacity he issued a catalogue of manuscripts, *De Handschriften der Stedelijke Bibliotheek met Latere Aanwinsten.* In 1898 the University of Amsterdam made him an honorary doctor. Mendes da Costa loved the stage; he wrote a number of comedies and plays, and translated others. Among his writings are *Tooneel Herinneringen,* a work in three volumes, and his plays *Tehuis Gebleven* and *Zijn Model.*

MENDÈS-FRANCE, PIERRE, French deputy, jurist and politician, b. Paris, 1907. He studied law at the Sorbonne, finished his studies at the age of eighteen, and was admitted to the bar of Paris. His thesis, *Le redressement financier français en 1926 et 1927* (1928), attracted wide attention among French jurists, economists, and politicians. In the same year Mendès-France published a penetrating study, *L'oeuvre financier du gouvernement Poincaré.* Acknowledging Poincaré's soundness and technical dexterity, Mendès-France reproached him for having been unfair in placing the blame and of having favored vested interests. This statement by Mendès-France became the slogan of French leftists who had been much troubled by the failure of their financial reform in 1924, and he became one of the financial authorities of the radical party.

In 1930 he published *La Banque internationale,* and in 1932 *Le mouvement des cartels et la crise.* That same year he was elected member of the Chambre des Députés, becoming the youngest French deputy, as he had been the youngest lawyer in Paris for many years. Mendès-France at once outlined an economic program for the radical party which was accepted at its congress at Toulouse in the summer of 1932. He became member of the tax committee of the Chambre, and professor at the École des Hautes Études Sociales; he was re-elected in 1936. He strongly advocated the formation and maintenance of the Front populaire. He also advocated resistance to the Nazis.

After the collapse of France (June, 1940) he attempted to organize the opposition to Pétain's policy of "collaboration" with Germany. He was persecuted, then arrested by the Pétain government and sentenced to prison, but at the end of 1941 he succeeded in escaping to England, joining the Free French movement under General Charles de Gaulle.

MENDESIA, GRACIA, Marrano champion of Jewish rights, b. probably in Portugal, about 1510; d. Constantinople, 1568. She was a member of the wealthy Benvenisti family. Under her Christian name of Beatrice de Luna she married a fellow Marrano, her cousin Francisco Mendes (Nasi). After his premature death (1535) the young widow eluded the Inquisition by going with her daughter, Reyna, and several relatives to Antwerp to join her brother-in-law, Diogo Mendes, taking over the directorship of the Mendes banking house after Diogo's death (1545). In 1549, however, after Emperor Charles V had attempted to confiscate her fortune, she fled with her daughter, her widowed sister and the latter's daughter to Venice.

Denounced as a secret Jewess to the Venetian authorities by her sister, who loathed her guardianship, Donna Gracia was imprisoned and her property confiscated. Owing to the intervention of the Sultan, protector of her nephew Don Joseph Nasi, she was freed and her possessions restored after two years of effort. She then moved to Ferrara where, under the protection of the liberal-minded d'Este ruler, she was able publicly to profess Judaism. The Marrano poet Samuel Usque dedicated to her his work, *Consolaçam ás tribulaçoens de Israel* (Consolation for the Tribulations of Israel), which appeared there in 1552. In 1553 she went to Constantinople, where she remained for the rest of her life.

Donna Gracia contributed most liberally to Jewish charity, supported scholars and founded synagogues and institutions of learning. Hundreds of exiled Marranos were resettled with her financial aid, while others captured by pirates were ransomed by the "Grand Widow of Kusta."

Memorable among her political acts was her intercession on behalf of the Marranos of Ancona, who had been arrested by the fanatical Pope Paul IV with the intention of burning them. On Sultan Suleiman's demand, the Turkish Marranos were released. In order to punish the inhuman pope, Donna Gracia made an effort to organize a Jewish boycott of the port of Ancona and the banning of the pope by the rabbis, but her efforts were unsuccessful due to the lack of unanimous support by her coreligionists.

MENDICANCY. There is practically no reference to mendicants in Biblical times; there are frequent allusions to the poor and needy, who are to be helped through gifts and through certain portions of the harvest, but these are rather the poor agriculturists and laborers than beggars as such. The reason for this absence of a class of mendicants is partly the result of an agricultural economy in which practically every family took care of its own, and partly due to the fact that a poor man could sell himself into slavery and thus receive support from his master. In addition to these factors, the social legislation of the Bible, with its insistence on certain rights of the poor, must have materially reduced the number of those in actual penury.

Social conditions in the period of the Second Temple were far less favorable. The comparatively few Jewish pioneer settlers had to work hard to wrest a living from the soil; Palestine was again and again devastated by wars and bled white by excessive taxation imposed upon it by its rulers. The families could no longer provide for their needy members. Hence in course of time a class of beggars arose, consisting mainly of the lame, halt and blind, or of widows, orphans and the aged, to which there are references in *Psalms, Sirach* and the New Testament. When Jews were taken captive into other lands, many of them found it difficult to secure a livelihood, especially in the larger cities; the satirists of Rome uttered gibes against the Jewish beggars. The Talmud and the Midrash note the rise of a class of professional beggars, who would feign diseases or deformities to arouse the sympathy of the passersby; yet at the same time they recognized the fact that many Jews were beggars merely because of misfortune and poverty.

The Jewish communities set about solving the problem of Jewish mendicancy by organizing their own system of philanthropy. They made loans to needy coreligionists to set them up in business; they ransomed Jewish slaves and captives and gave them employment; they made collections for the poor, administered by special committees and with the greatest amount of privacy. The needy became guests on Sabbaths and festivals; the community assisted in cases of marriage, sickness and death. As a result, for a good part of the Middle Ages Jewish beggars were practically non-existent in Europe, though they remained in the less well-organized communities in the East.

The persecutions of the Jews from the 12th cent. on broke up the community system and increased the number of Jewish mendicants. Refugees from countries of persecution streamed over Europe and taxed the resources of the communities; the fact that Jews were shut up in ghettos facilitated the rise of permanent mendicants, who could not go from door to door without being seen by non-Jews. At first begging was restricted to Fridays, the middle days of Passover, and Shabuoth, but it gradually spread throughout the year. By the 17th cent. there were even swarms of mendicants, known as Schnorrers or Kabtzanim, who became even an imposition upon the community, but who were protected by the generous instincts of the Jews who could afford to give alms. Another class of professional mendicants was that of the Jews who had emigrated to Palestine and who lived on the proceeds of the Halukkah collections.

In the latter part of the 19th cent. Jewish communities began to meet the question of persistent house-to-house begging with the creation of central offices, staffed by trained social workers, to which all mendicants were referred. In the United States an agreement between social welfare organizations, making each community responsible for the transient beggars that originated from it, did much to check the practice of professional Jewish mendicants who would live from the bounty of one community after another. As a result of these social endeavors, the number of Jewish mendicants has diminished and the worthy needy have been aided. An additional factor in this connection is the recognition on the part of governments of a social responsibility toward the dependent.

SIMON COHEN.

Lit.: Bogen, Boris D., *Jewish Philanthropy* (1917); Frisch, E., *A Historical Survey of Jewish Philanthropy* (1924); Abrahams, I., *Jewish Life in the Middle Ages,* chaps. 17 and 18; Malter, H., in *Jewish Encyclopedia*, vol. 2, pp. 639-40.

MENDL, ARTHUR, writer on music and conductor, b. Boston, 1905. He studied at Harvard University, and music at the École Normale in Paris. For a period he taught at the Dalcroze School of Music in New York city. From 1930 to 1933 he was music

critic of the *Nation,* and from 1930 to 1938 he was literary editor of the music-publishing house of G. Schirmer. He founded and directed the Cantata Society of New York, which has given seasonal concerts of great choral music.

MENDL, SIR SIGISMUND FERDINAND, British merchant and Member of Parliament, b. England, 1866. He received his B.A. degree from Oxford in 1887 and his M.A. degree in 1890, after which he entered the practice of law. From 1898 to 1900 Mendl was a member of Parliament for Plymouth. Later he held various directive posts in trade associations and also served on government advisory committees and commissions. He was knighted in 1918. In 1942 he was living in London.

SIR CHARLES MENDL (b. 1871), a brother of Sir Sigismund Ferdinand Mendl, was connected with the press department of the British Foreign Office for many years, after having been invalided out of the army in 1915 during the first World War. From 1926 to 1940 he was press attaché of the British Embassy in Paris. He was knighted in 1924. In 1942 he was living in the United States.

MENDONÇA, HYPOLITO JOSÉ DA COSTA PEREIRA FURTADO DE, Brazilian patriot and journalist, b. Sacramento, La Plata, Argentina, 1774; d. Kensington, England, 1823. Mendonça was either of Marrano or avowed Jewish descent. He studied law at the University of Coimbra, in Portugal.

From 1798 to 1800 Mendonça was chargé d'affaires for Portugal in Philadelphia, then capital of the United States. After returning to Portugal he was soon arrested by the Inquisition on the charge of freemasonry. He spent three years in prison, suffering various tortures. Finally he escaped, carrying with him copies of the rules of the Inquisition, which he later published in full, together with the story of his sufferings. He succeeded in fleeing from Portugal to Spain disguised as a servant, then going to Gibraltar and from there to England.

In England, Mendonça carried on a fight for Brazilian independence, editing *Correio Brasiliense,* a magazine of which twenty-nine volumes appeared before its publication was forbidden by the Portuguese government in 1817. When Brazil was declared an independent kingdom in 1822, Dom Pedro I made Mendonça the representative of the government to the English court.

Mendonça was author of *Nova grammatica portugueza e ingleza* and of several diaries of various periods of his life; he translated Sir Benjamin Thompson Rumford's essays into Portuguese. During the periods of his diplomatic service he made studies of tobacco, hemp and sugar cane, on which he wrote reports. The centenary of Mendonça's death was observed by literary and journalistic circles in Brazil, who looked on Mendonça as the first Brazilian journalist.

Lit.: Galeria Nacional, *Vultos Preeminentes da Historia Brasiliera,* vol. 8; Peregrino da Silva, Manoel Cicero, *O patriarcha dos jornalistas brasilieros* (1923); "Centenario de Hypolito da Costa," *Revista da Academia Brasiliera de letras,* vol. 14 (1923) 53-58.

MENDOZA, DANIEL, champion pugilist, b. London, 1763; d. London, 1836. Mendoza is historically famed for having revolutionized the technique of fighting in England, substituting for its more blatant brutalities a science of new blows and footwork, of quick thinking and precise sparring to outmatch the then fashionable heavy slugging. His general influence and contribution came to be known as the school of Mendoza, and his three sensational bouts with the gentleman boxer Richard Humphries aroused a new interest in the sport, which had been on the decline for several years.

It was after he beat Martin, the Bath butcher, in 1787, that the fight fans began to take notice of the new "Star of Israel," who stood five feet seven inches, with remarkable chest development, unusually good wind, and a quick, neat style. Then followed the three fights with Humphries, whom he decisively bested the last time in 1790. From there Mendoza passed to new triumphs, beating Fitzgerald of Ireland and Warr of Bristol, until in 1795, matched against the physically superior John Jackson, teacher of the poet Byron, Mendoza went down to defeat. This was accounted the hardest fought bout in the short space of ten and one-half minutes in the ring's history, and is famous for Jackson's having grabbed Mendoza's hair.

At the too advanced age of fifty-seven Mendoza returned to fight against one Owen, six years younger, and was beaten. Thereafter he devoted himself exclusively to his public house, the Admiral Nelson, in Whitechapel, and to his very successful tours and exhibits which, he claimed, were largely instrumental in propagandizing in favor of boxing instead of knifing or shooting as a general method of self-defense.

See illustration in vol. 1, p. 581.

Lit.: Boulton, William, *Amusements of Old London*, vol. 2, pp. 71-121; Miles, Henry, *Pugilistica*, vol. 1 (1906) 71-83; *American Hebrew*, Sept. 18, 1936, p. 337.

MENE, MENE, TEKEL UPHARSIN, the words of the handwriting on the wall at Belshazzar's feast (*Dan.* 5:25). According to Daniel (*Dan.* 5), Belshazzar, the last king of Babylon, at a banquet in his court, insolently and sacrilegiously ordered that the vessels of the Temple of Jerusalem, which Nebuchadnezzar his father had confiscated, be brought to him and used for heathen devotions. "In the same hour came forth fingers of a man's hand, and wrote over against the candlestick upon the plaster of the wall of the king's palace" (*Dan.* 5:5). In his panic the king summoned all the wise men to interpret the cryptic handwriting, but they were unable to decipher it.

Daniel, known for his earlier prophecies to Nebuchadnezzar, was brought before the king and was offered royal gifts if he could read the mystic characters. Daniel disdained the gifts and interpreted the Aramaic words as follows: "Mene, God hath numbered thy kingdom, and brought it to an end. Tekel, thou art weighed in the balances, and art found wanting. Peres, thy kingdom is divided, and given to the Medes and Persians." (*Dan.* 5:26-28). Thereupon Daniel received the promised reward and was elevated to the third highest rank in the kingdom. "In that night Belshazzar the Chaldean king was slain" (*Dan.* 5:30).

Why the script, if it was in Aramaic signs, could not immediately be read by the wise men of the land, who were experts in the art of writing (*Dan.* 5:8), has puzzled many commentators. Modern exegetes surmised, therefore, that the mystic message had been transmitted in picture writing which Daniel ingeniously combined, while the exposition of the words as given in the Bible is considered a secondary play on their meaning.

The phrase has come to be used as a symbol of pronounced judgment, and the scene at Belshazzar's banquet has served as subject matter for several famous poems. Heinrich Heine wrote a ballad, *Belshazzar,* and Lord Byron was the author of *Vision of Belshazzar.*

Lit.: Montgomery, *Book of Daniel* (1927) 249-66; Hastings, James, edit., *Dictionary of the Bible*, vol. 3, pp. 340-41; Kohut, George A., *Hebrew Anthology*, vol. 1, pp. 424-37; vol. 2, pp. 1035-53.

MENELAUS (or **Onias**), renegade high priest, from 171 B.C.E. to the 160's B.C.E.; d. about 162 B.C.E. He represented the extreme pro-Hellenist element in the conflict over the paganizing of Judea.

Menelaus was not of priestly descent, but was, according to *II Macc.* 4:23, a Benjaminite. He achieved the high priesthood by means of bribery. As deputy for the high priest Jason, delegated to deliver the annual contribution to Antiochus Epiphanes, the Syrian king, Menelaus promised the king 300 additional talents and obtained the post of high priest for himself. Antiochus despatched a body of troops to Jerusalem to impose Menelaus' usurpation of office.

Menelaus, however, was soon embarrassed by his difficulty in raising the 300 talents he had promised Antiochus. On being summoned to appear before the king, he seized a number of sacred vessels from the Temple, intending to sell them, and left Jerusalem to answer the royal command. His brother Lysimachus was left in charge of the Temple. Menelaus' sacrilege was exposed by the former high priest Onias III, but before Onias could denounce Menelaus to the king, Menelaus induced the royal officer Andronicus, with whom he had shared the plunder, to murder Onias (171 B.C.E.).

The pilfering from the Temple evoked a popular uprising, in which the high priest's soldiers were put to flight and Lysimachus killed. Menelaus then accused his anti-Hellenist opponents of plotting with Egypt against Antiochus. Three delegates were sent from Jerusalem to deny this charge, but although they succeeded in exposing Menelaus' sacrilege, Menelaus had again bribed his way to preference and the delegates were executed. Menelaus proceeded with his slander and made Antiochus believe that in his campaign against Egypt the Jews would be a subversive element. While Antiochus was engaged in the Egyptian war, the displaced high priest Jason, aided by an armed force, succeeded in capturing Jerusalem, and Menelaus was compelled to retire to the fortress of Acre (170).

Antiochus, temporarily leaving his Egyptian triumphs, marched on Jerusalem, massacred its inhabitants, and with the help of Menelaus despoiled the Temple. In the religious persecutions which followed as the result of the Roman prohibition against Antiochus' warring further against Egypt (he used up his energy in pillaging Jerusalem), Menelaus was probably a leading instrument of Antiochus' tyranny and a participant in the desecration of the Temple (168 B.C.E.). But the scales reversed at last. Menelaus was finally executed by order of Lysias or Antiochus V Eupator, as a conciliatory gesture to the Jews, who had in the meantime become victorious under the leadership of the Maccabeans. The charge against Menelaus was that his miscalculated urging of a ruthless program on the Syrian kings had precipitated the successful revolt of the Maccabees. LIBBY BENEDICT.

Lit.: Josephus, *Antiquities,* book 12, chap. 15; *Jewish War,* book 1; Graetz, H., *History of the Jews,* vol. 1 (1927) 437-80; Hastings, James, edit., *Dictionary of the Bible,* vol. 1, pp. 105-7; vol. 3, pp. 341-42.

MENES, AVROHOM (ABRAHAM), Yiddish historian, b. Grodno, Poland, 1897. He received a traditional Jewish education, and from 1921 to 1926 studied history in Berlin. His earliest work was published in Berlin (1923) under the title "Sotziale un Virtshaftliche Farheltenishn bei die Yiddn in Altertum" in *Bletter far Yiddishe Demografie, Statistik un Ekonomik.* Two years later he published "Die sozialpolitische Analyse der Urgeschichte" (in German) in *Zeitschrift für die alttestamentliche Wissenschaft.* This essay discussed the utopian elements in the stories contained in *Genesis. Die vorexilischen Gesetze Israels* (Giessen, 1928) is a treatise on the laws of the Pentateuch in relation to the general political and economic development of Israel.

Several of Menes's essays on Jewish economic and social problems were published by the Yivo (Yiddish Scientific Institute) in *Virtshaft un Lebn* (Berlin, 1928-31) and in the *Encyclopaedia Judaica.* The most significant among these were: "The Impact of Economic Conjuncture on Conditions of the Jewish Population" (*Yivo-Bletter,* vol. 3) and "The Prophets and the Congregation of the People" (*ibid.,* vol. 9).

Menes emigrated to Paris in 1933 where he became one of the editors of a general Yiddish encyclopedia, to which he contributed articles on Bible literature, Jewish history and the history of the Jewish religion. Together with A. Tcherikover and several others, he edited a special issue of the *Yivo-Shriftn* (in Paris) devoted to the history of the Jewish labor movement. He published articles on Jewish cultural problems and on religious socialism in the *Zukunft, Freie Shriftn* and *Afn Sheidveg.* Believing, like Rudolph Otto and others, that religion is an independent factor of man's life ("Religion is religion and must be explained by itself"), Menes attempts to point out in his social and historical analyses the interrelationships of religion, economics and society, and their mutual influence upon each other.

In 1940 Menes settled in New York city, where he continued his work with the general Yiddish encyclopedia. His latest articles appeared in *Zukunft.*

N. B. MINKOFF.

MENGS, ANTON RAPHAEL, painter, son of Ismael Israel Mengs, b. Aussig, Bohemia, 1728; d. Rome, 1779. His father, a severe and systematic teacher, taught him his art and brought him to Rome, where he studied and copied the old masters, and became a skilled artist. In 1744 he was appointed court painter to August III of Poland and Saxony, who helped him to continue his studies in the Academy of Rome. While

Anton Raphael Mengs

painting his first large canvas, *The Holy Family* (1748), he fell in love with his model, a peasant girl, became a Catholic and married her. On his return from a visit to Dresden in 1752 he was appointed director of the Art Academy at the Vatican. Charles III of Spain, who invited him to Madrid, named him first court painter in 1761, adopting also his five daughters and granting pensions to his two sons. Mengs finally returned to Rome from Dresden and Madrid because of his impaired health.

The themes of his paintings which adorn the museums of several cities as well as famous palaces and churches in Rome, Dresden, and Madrid were chosen from the New Testament, history, and mythology. They include: *The Ascension of Christ,* an altar-piece at Dresden; *Saint Eusebius,* a ceiling at the Celestine Monastery in Rome; *Apollo and the Muses on Parnassus,* a ceiling at the Villa Albani, Rome; *Maria Magdalena; Jesus and St. John; The Nativity; Cleopatra; St. Peter; Apotheosis of Trajan; Temple of Fame;* also portraits of himself, his children, princes, kings, princesses and many noted personages. Mengs wrote also a few works on art, which were published in Parma, Italy, in 1780 and were translated into English in 1796. He was interred in St. Peter's, Rome, where a monument was erected in his memory by Empress Catherine II of Russia. His valuable collection of objects of art was bequeathed to the academies of Dresden and Madrid, together with a large sum of money for the aid of destitute art students.

Lit.: Bryan's Dictionary of Painters and Engravers, vol. 3, p. 322; Spooner, *Biographical History of the Fine Arts,* vol. 2, pp. 549-51; Champlin, *Cyclopedia of Painters and Paintings,* vol. 3, pp. 243-44; Woermann, "Ismael und Rafael Mengs," *Zeitschrift für bildende Kunst,* New Series, vol. 5 (1893); Thieme, U., and Becker, F., *Allgemeines Lexikon der bildenden Künstler,* vol. 24, pp. 390-92; Hoare, Richard Colt, "Memoirs and Letters of Raphael Mengs,"

Annals of Fine Arts, vol. 2, pp. 492-506; Schwarz, K., *Die Juden in der Kunst* (1928) 118.

MENGS, ISMAEL ISRAEL, painter, b. Copenhagen, Denmark, 1688; d. Dresden, Germany, 1764. A pupil of B. Coffre and P. Jochumsen in Copenhagen, of J. Harper and P. Heinecke in Lübeck, and of an English painter named Cooper, he painted miniatures on enamel and also some historical subjects. Thanks to the great fame gained by his son Anton Raphael Mengs, to whom he was an' art mentor, his works acquired an extra value. They include his own portrait (Dresden Gallery), sixteen religious miniatures, the *Portrait of a Merchant* (Leipzig Museum), a portrait of August III of Poland and Saxony, who named him his court painter, and the miniatures of *A Lady* and *Diogenes.* Mengs taught his art also to his daughters Julia (d. 1789) and Theresa Concordia von Maron (1725-1808). He traveled through Germany, Austria and Italy, and became director of the Art Academy of Dresden. He was baptized as a Protestant.

Lit.: Champlin, *Cyclopedia of Painters,* vol. 3, p. 244; Thieme, U., and Becker, F., *Allgemeines Lexikon der bildenden Künstler,* vol. 24, pp. 392-93.

MENKEN, ADAH ISAACS, actress and poetess, b. Milneburg, suburb of New Orleans, La., 1835; d. Paris, 1868. As a young girl, she apparently received an excellent education: she astonished people by her knowledge of the Bible, literature, and languages, including Latin and Hebrew. At one time she taught in a girls' school.

A woman of "peerless" beauty, brilliant and unconventional mind, and an insatiable if forever frustrated passion for a perfect romantic destiny, she flashed violently across a decade of the mid-nineteenth century, blazing on two continents a trail of glamor and gossip. Critics constantly disagreed about her factual, moral, and psychological biography; but the disputed fact of her origin appears to have been finally settled by the researches of Allen Lesser, who published the study "La Belle Menken" in his volume *Weave a*

Ismael Israel Mengs

Adah Isaacs Menken

Wreath of Laurel (1938). He asserted that she was born neither Dolores Adios Fuertes, daughter of a Spanish Jew, nor Adelaide McCord, an Irishman's daughter, who later became a convert to Judaism. Her father was one Theodore, and she was named Adah, Hebrew for "beauty." Lesser adduced as evidence her own declaration of Jewish birth, made in answer to a piece published in a New York paper, and cited the fact that in the theatre she never performed on the High Holy Days.

The first major event in her life was her meeting and elopement in Texas, in 1856, with Alexander Isaac Menken, handsome musician son of a wealthy Cincinnati Jewish family. Thereafter, changing Isaac to Isaacs, she kept his name. The young couple lived for a while in New Orleans, where, when the panic of 1857 affected her husband's fortune, Adah Menken went on the professional stage. But they soon left to live with the Menkens in Cincinnati.

Here began the period of the young poetess' mystical and audacious protagonism of the Jewish destiny. She had already published poems in Isaac M. Wise's Cincinnati *Israelite.* Among others, there appeared the poems "At Spes Non Fracta," "The Kingdom of the Mind" and "Light for the Soul"; they called on Jews to awake to the sufferings of their fellows and the glory of their historic role, and to act. Now she announced herself the herald of the Messiah. Militantly she engaged in the struggle (1857-58) of Baron Lionel Nathan de Rothschild of England to be given his rightful seat in Parliament, which he had been denied. Rothschild in turn acclaimed her a "Deborah," and it was he who erected the monument on her grave in Montparnasse.

This career of intense Judaism ended with her disillusioned separation, by rabbinical divorce, from her husband. She left for New York, the stage, and a series of unsuccessful marriages with the Irish prize fighter John Heenan, the satirist Robert Newell, the Wall street business man James Barclay. Particularly did her relations with Heenan arouse nation-wide gossip, and when he disclaimed the marriage and the short-lived child born of it, Adah Menken wrote a suicide note in her room in Jersey City in December, 1860.

But she lived to pursue a reckless career as the famous Mazeppa in the adaptation of the Byron play, given first in Albany, N. Y., in 1861. Clad in tights, she allowed herself to be tied to the horse and actually carried (up to that time a dummy had been used in the climbing scene) up the papier mâché mountains. She became the sensation of a dozen American cities, and particularly of San Francisco. Literary men gathered around her; one of her great admirers was Mark Twain. In 1864 she left for London, where her personality dazzled Charles Dickens and Charles Reade, while her performances as Mazeppa called down the moralizing anathema of the press.

In Paris, during the great Exposition, her triumph as a theatrical performer rose to new heights: she became the darling and the rumored mistress of kings and princes; and she cultivated her intimate and ambiguous friendship with the elderly Alexandre Dumas. She returned to London and was involved with the poet Swinburne. In 1868 she left for Paris again, to appear in a new production; but very soon the ailments that had set in years before brought on her death, in an attic room opposite the theatre. Among others, Henry Wadsworth Longfellow visited her; and the poet Thomas Buchanan Read was with her to the end. A rabbi attended her last hours.

In the theatre her beauty, charm and daring, rather than ability to act, constituted her triumph. Her poetry, of which she published two volumes, the more important *Infelicia* (1868) appearing a week after her death, aroused critical controversy. *Memoirs* had appeared in 1856. The poet Dante Gabriel Rossetti praised *Infelicia*, and his brother William included examples in an anthology; later the critic Clement Wood rated it highly. But others judged most of it inferior. Lesser pointed out that she was the first to follow daringly the free verse patterns of her friend Walt Whitman. An example in this style is her famous "Hear O Israel."

The contradictions between the idealistic aspirations of her poetry and the chaotic public life she led were summed up by the American writer Edgar Lee Masters in his *Doomsday Book:* "My body and my soul are in a scramble and do not fit each other."

SHERRY ABEL.

Lit.: Lesser, Allen, *Weave a Wreath of Laurel* (1938); Kendall, John S., *Louisiana Historical Quarterly,* July, 1938, pp. 846-68; Otis, Joseph, in *Opinion,* Feb., 1936, pp. 17-20; Falk, Bernard, *The Naked Lady* (1934).

MENKEN, ALICE DAVIS, social worker, b. New York city, 1870; d. New York city, 1936. The wife of the late Mortimer M. Menken, New York attorney, she was a descendant of colonial American Jewish stock, and through her mother, Miriam Peixotto Davis, a member of the Daughters of the American Revolution.

Beginning about the end of the 19th cent., Mrs. Menken engaged for thirty years as voluntary worker in the rehabilitation of youthful delinquents; she became a recognized, scientific authority in this field, famed for her advocacy of personal guidance in each instance of crime or delinquency, and equally noted for her outstanding success in her many "case histories." She was especially concerned with the reeducation of young Jewish women discharged from penal institutions, and helped organize the Big Sister movement to further such work. In 1920 Governor Alfred E. Smith appointed her to the board of managers of the New York State Reformatory for Women, and shortly afterward she was made the board's secretary, serving until 1932.

Throughout her career Mrs. Menken was connected with the sisterhood of the Spanish and Portuguese Synagogue, serving the organization as president for almost three decades. A prolific writer of pamphlets and periodical pieces on her work, Mrs. Menken summed up her sociological experience with youthful "criminals" in the book *On the Side of Mercy,* published in 1933, with an introduction by Governor Herbert H. Lehman; the central thesis of the book was that therapy, not punishment, is the corrective for the young misdoer.

Lit.: American Hebrew, March 26, 1926, p. 651; April 27, 1934, p. 498.

MENKEN, HELEN, actress, b. New York city, 1901. Her long career in the theatre began when she appeared as one of the fairies in *Midsummer Night's Dream,* the play that opened the Astor Theatre in New York in 1906. Later she played with such famous actors as DeWolf Hopper, Eddie Foy and John Drew. In 1918 came her first personal triumph, as Miss Fairchild in *Three Wise Fools.* She followed up in the role of Diane in *Seventh Heaven,* in 1922, and five years later starred in the same play in London. Playing the name part of Bourdet's French import, *The Captive,* in New York in 1926, she became involved in the moral controversy and police action which the drama aroused.

Later triumphs came when she played Elizabeth in *Mary of Scotland* (1933), and in 1935, when she co-starred in the Pulitzer Prize play, *The Old Maid.* Her talents in various Shakespearean roles added to her reputation as one of the country's leading emotional actresses. In 1934 she engaged successfully in radio drama. Miss Menken was twice married, the first time to the actor Humphrey Bogart.

Lit.: Who's Who in the Theatre (1939) 1088-89.

MENKEN, JACOB STANWOOD, merchant and philanthropist, b. Cincinnati, Ohio, 1838; d. Memphis, Tennessee. The youngest son of Solomon Menken, he was the business genius of the family. When the Civil War broke out, he enlisted and served in Missouri until he fell victim to malaria. Then he settled in Memphis in 1863 and began to build the business which later grew into the large department store of Menken and Co. and made him and his brothers leading merchants in the city.

Menken's social and philanthropic activities were numerous and distinguished. He organized the famous Children's Christmas Club, opened the first free kindergarten in Memphis in 1886, and some years later instituted the first kindergarten in the south for Negro children. In 1897 he was one of the Memphis citizens who went to Washington and persuaded Congress to grant the city an appropriation of $200,000 for relief of flood sufferers.

MENKEN, NATHAN DAVIS, merchant and soldier, b. Cincinnati, 1837; d. Memphis, Tenn., 1878. The second son of Solomon Menken, he was the family's most distinguished soldier in the Civil War, cited for exceptional bravery as a cavalry captain and commander of General Pope's bodyguard. He engaged in some thirty skirmishes and battles, including the second Battle of Bull Run.

Afterwards he joined his brothers, Jules and Jacob, in their business in Memphis, where he became a leading citizen, fighting particularly for honest administration in municipal affairs. When the yellow fever struck the city in 1878, Menken, though giving money to numerous fellow Jews to enable them to flee, himself chose to remain as a leader in the work of the Howard Society, which had been organized for the relief of the sick, poor and dying. He carried on until he was stricken by the plague and died.

Lit.: Markens, Isaac, *The Hebrews in America* (1888) 172-73; Morais, H. S., *The Jews of Philadelphia* (1894) 510-11.

MENKEN, S. STANWOOD, lawyer and publicist, son of Nathan Davis Menken, b. Memphis, Tenn., 1870. After being educated at Cornell University and Columbia, he was admitted to the New York bar in 1894, thereafter appearing in numerous cases for leading corporations. He was attorney in a suit involving management of the New York city street railways, and likewise in a noted suit concerning fixing of drug prices.

Politically active, he organized the Hall of Records association in 1896, enrolling 10,000 members and getting the city to build a $7,000,000 structure for its records. In 1908 he formed the Democratic League with 32,000 members, and in 1915 he organized the National Security League of America. As member and active president until 1933, he took a foremost part, through lecture and press, in agitating for the League's principles of Americanism.

MENKEN, SOLOMON, Cincinnati pioneer, b. Westphalia, Prussia, 1787; d. Cincinnati, 1853. He was married to the daughter of Benjamin Morange, French ambassador to Spain under Napoleon. Arriving from Holland, he settled in Cincinnati in 1820, one of the first Jews to take up residence in that city, and the first known member of his family in the United States. About 1825 he established his wholesale drygoods business, into which his three sons were eventually drawn. His eldest son, Jules (b. 1836; d. 1890), was a lieutenant in the Cincinnati Home Guards during the Civil War. The war forced the business into bankruptcy, but in later years the three sons completely redeemed its debts.

Lit.: Philipson, David, "Jewish Pioneers of the Ohio Valley," *Publications of American Jewish Historical Society,* No. 8 (1900) 43-57.

MENORAH, originally the seven-branched golden candlestick of the Tabernacle, as depicted in *Ex.* 25:31; 37:17-24; *Lev.* 24:4. In the Temple of Solomon there were ten golden Menorahs (*1 Kings* 7:49), which are not described in detail. *1. Chron.* 28:15 mentions, in

Representation of a Menorah (found in the ruins of Gadara) in the possession of the Louvre, Paris

addition, silver Menorahs in the Temple. The Menorah in private use is referred to in *II Kings* 4:10.

According to the description in *Exodus,* the Menorah of the Tabernacle was a pedestal lamp with three arms on either side of the columnar stand and a central arm which was a prolongation of the shaft. The seven lamps carried by the arms were fuelled with olive oil and were apparently of the type of open bowls furnished with floating wicks. The Menorah was set on the south side of the Tabernacle. The tree-like shape of the Menorah with its shaft and arms molded like almond flowers may suggest a derivation from the tree of life. *Zech.* 4:2-3, 11-12 uses the Menorah, which apparently was an important appurtenance also in the Second Temple, as a cosmological, political symbol.

The golden Menorah played a part in the religious ideology of the Maccabean revolt. After Antiochus Epiphanes had despoiled the candlestick and other Temple appurtenances of their gold revetment, Judas Maccabeus rededicated the Temple (165 B.C.E.) and restored, among the other utensils, the Menorah (*I Macc.* 1:21; 4:49). Josephus interprets the seven lamps of the Menorah (Jewish War, book 5, chap. 55, section 7) as the seven planets.

Carried away from the Herodian Temple by Titus in the Jewish War (70 C.E.), the Menorah was reproduced with the other spoils of the Temple at Jerusalem on a relief on the Arch of Titus in Rome built by Domitian. This representation is still the earliest preserved and most authentic of the seven-branched candlestick.

The seven-branched candlestick of the synagogue is an imitation of the Temple Menorah. An early example is the candlestick cut out of a block of limestone discovered in the synagogue of Hammath—near Tiberias—dating back to the early centuries of the Common Era. It measures 60 centimeters in width by 46 centimeters in height and 13 centimeters in thickness. This candlestick was in actual use in the synagogue. It shows the traditional flower decoration; the seven lamps, however, are not separately set on the branches of the candlestick, but are placed in a trough supported by these branches. Either form is to be found on representations of the seven-branched candlestick on gilded glasses and sarcophagi, and in catacomb and

An artist's sketch of the remarkable house Menorah owned by Judge Irving Lehman of New York

synagogue decoration. The primitive bowls with floating wicks appear to be replaced by the lamp bowls of the shoe-shape type provided with spouts and special grooves for the wicks. These changes, due to the technical advance in the means of illumination, reflect the evolution of the candlestick of the synagogue.

The Menorah with eight lamps, used in the eight-day festival of Hanukah established in commemoration of the rededication of the Temple by Judas Maccabeus, appears in two different forms. The candlestick-form shaped after the seven-branched candlestick is the later one. The Menorah of this type has four lamps on either side of the stand and an extra ninth lamp, the kindling light, called the Shammes (servant), placed on an arm projecting at a right angle from the shaft. There are some examples showing the ninth light set on the top of the shaft, for example the Hanukah Menorah of the synagogue at Padua. The pedestal type of the Hanukah Menorah has occasionally replaced the seven-branched candlestick in the synagogue. It is set usually at the right side of the Ark. There is one particularly elaborate type of Hanukah Menorah in silver, made in Frankfort about 1680, formerly in the possession of Georg Speyer. Another version of this Menorah is in the Musée de Cluny in Paris. They are all marked with initials of Christian silversmiths. These candlesticks have the figure of Judith with the head of Holophernes at the top of the stand and animal decoration at the back panels of the oil burners. Another type, cast in brass, presumably of East European origin, existing also in several versions, is represented in the Jewish Museum of Berlin and Budapest;

two specimens were in private possession in Vienna. The larger one in Vienna was 1.58 meters high and dated 1770. These Menorahs are crowned with the one-headed eagle.

The Menorah for Hanukah, as used mostly for the family celebration, exhibits a row of eight small spoon-shaped or rectangular oil lamps provided with a groove for the wick, and backed by a sconce-like panel. Occasionally it has a narrow trough as a drop-catcher beneath. The "Shammes" light is set, in the earlier examples, within the row of burners at the left end and is slightly larger than the others. Later on it becomes fixed to the panel, above, sidewise or in the center. In the examples from Poland and Eastern Germany the "Shammes" oil burner is frequently substituted by a candleholder or a pair of candleholders set on either side of the back panel. The candles are meant to be used for reading and working, as the Hanukah lights are not allowed to be used for profane (non-religious) purposes. The Hanukah lamps with a back panel are meant to be suspended on the wall, especially the Italian and oriental specimens, or else they have four short legs. Occasionally they are provided with a lid for the trough; some lamps of this box-type have no rear panel. The house Menorahs are executed in bronze, brass, pewter, silver, earthenware and lead. There are some modern examples in glass.

The earliest Menorah of this type which has been preserved is believed to be the lamp of the Albert Figdor collection, of Vienna, in brass; this lamp in 1942 was in the possession of Judge Irving Lehman, of New York city. It shows on the back panel a blind arcade and medallions with a salamander and two lions. Above the arcade runs the verse, "For the commandment is a lamp, and the law is light" (*Prov.* 6:23).

The particular type of panel composition translated in terms of Moorish architectural decoration and executed in open work is found in Hanukah lamps from Morocco and Tunis. A marble Menorah of Italian origin once exhibited in Frankfort is said to belong to the 15th cent. A feature of the Italian Hanukah lamps in bronze is the back panel, mostly in open work decorated with tritons, centaurs, vases, sometimes merely with a burning lamp flanked with lions. Although ex-

Combination Menorah and Sabbath candlestick, owned by Ignatz Friedmann, Budapest

A collection of Italian
Menorahs privately
owned by a Venetian
citizen

Menorah, made in 1367, owned by the Sephardic community of Sarajevo

hibiting Renaissance decoration, these lamps are hardly earlier than the 17th cent. Several silver Menorahs of Frankfort make were identified as pieces of the 16th and 17th centuries. A Dutch Hanukah lamp with an embossed heart-shaped motif on the panel, in the Nauheim collection in Frankfort, is dated 1693. The Great Portuguese Synagogue at Amsterdam possesses a Hanukah lamp of the house Menorah type dated 1638.

Among the Menorahs in silver filigree with bird decoration and occasionally vases instead of saucers for the lights, of Russian origin, there may be mentioned the lamp said to have belonged to Rabbi Israel Baal Shem Tob, the founder of the Hasidic movement (in the Bezalel Museum in Jerusalem). Russian and Polish specimens in silver and brass show the stags and tree of life motif in their panel decoration. In Poland earthenware Menorahs also were produced. A Hanukah lamp in pottery in the Museum of the Jewish community in Worms, dated 1790, was manufactured probably in Hesse.

Oriental lamps, from Palestine and neighboring countries, frequently exhibit in their decoration the crescent and star, birds, the hand amulet. They often have glass vases as burners. The tracing of the different types of decoration of the Menorah and the establishing of the dated specimens will help to determine the history of this lamp.

The candlestick type is related to the tripod bronze lamps and the clay lamp with seven radiating nozzles from Megiddo as well as the clay stands from Gezer and Megiddo of the 10th and 9th centuries B.C.E. The lamp with the back panel can be traced back to the ancient open bowl-shaped oil lamp with a nozzle for the wick. The vertical panel has developed out of the projecting knob or handle of the oil lamp of the late Roman and Byzantine period. At this period the lamps with their chamber for the oil covered in frequently show several wick holes in one range. Some of them exhibiting eight holes at the foreridge for the wicks and one at the rear for pouring in the oil were identified as Hanukah lamps. This type of lamp has been found in Jerusalem. The motif of the niche or arcade in the upper surface decoration is not confined to the lamp with eight burners, but occurs also on lamps with fewer wick holes than eight. It is therefore hard to tell whether there existed in earlier times a particular lamp for the Hanukah festival, although the existence of lamps with eight burners may suggest this assumption.   RACHEL BERNSTEIN WISCHNITZER.

Lit.: Frauberger, H., in *Mitteilungen zur Erforschung jüdischer Kunstdenkmäler,* vols. 3-4 (1903); Toeplitz, E., "Die Menorah des Chanukkafestes," *Beiträge zur jüdischen Kulturgeschichte,* Gesellschaft zur Erforschung jüdischer Kunstdenkmäler, vol. 1 (1924); Bronner, J., "Vier ostjüdische Chanukahmenoroth," *Menorah* (Vienna, 1926); Reifenberg, A., *Palästinensische Kleinkunst* (1927); Hintze, E., *Katalog der Ausstellung Das Judentum in der Geschichte*

Schlesiens (1929); Sukenik, E., *Ancient Synagogues in Palestine and Greece* (1930); Wischnitzer-Bernstein, R., "Chanukkaleuchter," *Encyclopaedia Judaica,* vol. 5 (1930); idem, "L'origine de la lampe de Hanouka," *Revue des études juives* (1930); idem, *Symbole und Gestalten der jüdischen Kunst* (1935); Hallo, R., *Judaica* (1932); Watzinger, C., *Denkmäler Palästinas,* vol. 1 (1933); Zwarts, J., *De zevenarmige Kandelaar in de romeinse Diaspora* (1935); Stern, M., *Aus dem Berliner jüdischen Museum* (1937); Gundersheimer, H., and Schönberger, G., "Frankfurter Chanukkahleuchter," *Notizblatt der Gesellschaft zur Erforschung jüdischer Kunstdenkmäler,* No. 34 (1937); Schönberger, G., *Die Sammlung Siegmund Nauheim im Museum jüdischer Altertümer in Frankfurt am Main,* published by the Gesellschaft zur Erforschung Jüdischer Kunstdenkmäler (1937); Robins, F. W., *The Story of the Lamp* (1939).

MENORATH HAMAOR, *see* ABOAB, ISAAC, THE ELDER; AL-NAKAWA, ISRAEL BEN JOSEPH.

MENSTRUATION. 1. In Religious Law. The Bible and Talmud contain a number of detailed regulations as to the period of menstruation. The menstruous woman (Niddah) is regarded as ritually unclean for the entire period, and this uncleanliness extends to objects with which she comes into contact. Originally the period of impurity was reckoned as seven days and was ended with the taking of a ritual bath (Mikveh). About 250 C.E., in the time of Zera, it became the rule to postpone the ritual bath until seven days after the cessation of menstruation, thus prolonging the period of ritual impurity. The Talmud deals extensively with menstruation and similar physical conditions of women in the tractate *Niddah* and other places. Sexual intercourse is entirely forbidden during the period; it is punished, according to the Bible, by excision (Kareth), but in later times, corporal punishment was inflicted by order of the court. A wife who violates the regulation either openly or by means of fraud was to be divorced with the loss of her marriage portion.

2. Statistics. According to the Talmud, the onset of menstruation occurred in Palestine as a rule in the twelfth year of life, and earlier among the urban than among the rural population. It also noted a number of causes that might bring on the menses, such as excitement, physical exertion or sickness. A number of investigators, such as F. Weber, Weissenberg, Oppenheim, Fishberg, A. Theilhaber and F. A. Theilhaber, studied the time of the first menstruation of Jewish girls. The fact that it appears earlier in Jewesses than among other women of the same environment has not been satisfactorily explained; the influence of occupation, diet, mode of life, internal secretions and hereditary factors have all been suggested. According to A. Theilhaber, menstruation with Jewesses begins earlier and lasts longer, predisposes to benevolent tumors and is the cause of a lesser mortality from portiocarcinomas. The fact that the first menstruation among non-Jewesses occurs earlier among the well-to-do and the city population suggests that the environmental factor is important. The American Maurice Fishberg found that the daughters of immigrants in New York city had an earlier beginning of the menses (twelve years as against thirteen) than their mothers; he found little difference between the time for native Jewesses and non-Jewesses. Weissenberg examined 2,000 cases in Elisavetgrad, and found that for Jewesses the average time for the beginning of menstruation was fourteen

Yehudi Menuhin (right) with his sister Hephzibah and their intimate friend Arturo Toscanini

years and two months as against fourteen years and eleven months for the non-Jewish women in cities and fifteen years and three months for those in the country. F. E. Herstein showed that in a period of famine there was a delay in the onset of menstruation, as follows:

	BEFORE 1917	1917-23
Ukranian girls	14 years 7 months	
Russian girls	14 years 2 months	15 years 4 months
Jewish girls	13 years 6 months	14 years 9 months.

FELIX A. THEILHABER.

Lit.: Glogner, "Über den Eintritt der Menstruation bei den Europäerinnen in den Tropen," *Archiv für Schiffs- und Tropen-Hygiene* (1905); Weissenberg, S., "Menorrhoë und Menopause bei Jüdinnen und Russinnen in Südrussland," *Centralblatt für Gynäkologie* (1909); Fishberg, M., *The Jews;* Herstein, F. E., in *Ose-Rundschau* (1927), No. 4.

MENTAL DISEASES, *see* HEALTH OF THE JEWS; MEDICINE.

MENUBBEL, *see* PHRASES, POPULAR.

MENUCHAH, MENUCHE, *see* PHRASES, POPULAR.

MENUHIN, YEHUDI, violinist, b. New York city, 1916. He studied in San Francisco with Louis Persinger, and later in Europe with Georges Enesco and Adolf Busch. Internationally noted as a concert artist for the last fifteen years, he was in 1942, at twenty-six, generally considered the foremost member of the younger generation of musicians in his field.

Less than a year after his birth his parents, Moshe and Marutha Menuhin, moved to San Francisco, where, at the age of four, he began his studies with Persinger. At seven he appeared as soloist with the San Francisco Symphony Orchestra under Alfred Hertz, and at nine, on January 17, 1926, he gave his first New York recital at the Manhattan Opera House. But his sensational success as a child musician dates from the following year, when he made his Paris debut with the Lamoureux Orchestra on February 2nd, and was heard with the New York Symphony Orchestra under Fritz Busch on November 25th and 27th, playing the Beethoven concerto. This, as Lawrence Gilman wrote in the New York *Herald Tribune,* was played with "a ripeness and dignity of style, a sensitive beauty of conception, an easeful brilliance of technique, which brought great names involuntarily to the tip of the listener's tongue." Olin Downes, writing in the New York *Times* about his recital of December 12th, found a "superb responsiveness to music, intuitively felt, when it is not intellectually comprehended; and a big nature, an uncommon intelligence, already in a child."

Other critics wrote in a similar vein, and it was generally recognized that the musical world had acquired not a child prodigy who skilfully parroted what his teachers told him, but a young artist of rare promise whose intellectual gifts, taste and musical sensitivity matched his remarkable technical career. In the spring of 1929 he made his first appearances in Germany, where the critical acclaim matched that which he had received in the United States and France; Vienna and London first heard him in the fall. In 1931 several of the principal orchestras of continental Europe, departing from their usual practice, collaborated with him in special programs entirely devoted to concertos.

During the next few years he carried out a gradually increasing concert schedule in America and Europe. In September, 1933, he declined an invitation from Wilhelm Furtwaengler, conductor of the Berlin Philharmonic Orchestra and a member of the Prussian State Council, to play in Germany, saying that he could not do so until the policy which had driven noted Jewish musicians from the country and banned Mendelssohn's music should be changed.

He gave his first recital of violin and piano sonatas with his sister Hephzibah, in December, 1934. In March, 1935, he began a round-the-world tour of 110 concerts in seventy-five cities and thirteen countries. In March, 1936, he retired from the concert stage for eighteen months devoted to rest and study, except for a few radio concerts, resuming his regular schedule in the fall of 1937.

In December, 1937, he gave the first American performances of Robert Schumann's violin concerto, which had been published over eighty years after its composer's death, and played it in most of the principal American cities during the next few months. He refused to admit any editing of the score for the sake of playability, and has always been strongly in favor of presenting what he performs, so far as is possible, exactly as written by the composers.

A child virtuoso scoring such a success as Menuhin won at the outset of his career runs the risk of the exploitation of his talents at the expense of their future development, but fortunately this was avoided, thanks to the vision and judgment of his parents, who carefully limited his annual quota of concerts and took care that he should have a comprehensive, well rounded general education. For the fact that his artistic perspective was not lost in the widespread and early acclaim which he received in childhood and adolescence one can credit both the influence of his parents and his own modesty and strong spirit of self-criticism.

At times, during his adolescent years, critics occasionally thought that his style was undergoing a certain transition and changing in its character, but on the whole his playing as a young mature artist represents a continuance and development of the characteristics and indications which marked it when his work first became widely known. His technical mastery and fundamental musicianship are unsurpassed; his tone is particularly distinguished for its purity and clarity; his phrasing and his general interpretation reflect his discerning taste and thorough understanding of his music.

In his playing, Menuhin has seemed to place lucidity of medium above pronounced opulence of tone, fineness of shading above boldness of color, although his art has reflected largeness as well as a fundamental seriousness of interpretative outlook. While wholly individual, it has been essentially objective, seeking a complete revelation of the music rather than a focussing of attention upon the performer's talents and personality; this impression extends even to his deftly wrought and amazingly skilful performances of bravura passages featuring technical display. In avoiding an emotionalism of an obvious sort, Menuhin sometimes gave an impression, during the early 1940's of a certain expressive reserve, suggesting, however, an aristocracy of interpretation rather than a non-realization of the expressive significance of the music. In 1942 the greater part of his career was still before him, but most critics and musical observers would certainly have ranked Menuhin among the first half dozen in any list of pre-eminent violinists of their day.

HEPHZIBAH MENUHIN, sister of Yehudi Menuhin, (b. San Francisco, 1920), distinguished herself as a concert pianist. She made her debut in her eighth year, then went into temporary retirement to devote herself to intensive study. She later appeared in sonata recitals with Yehudi, and in performances of trio music with Yehudi and Maurice Eisenberg. She showed great promise, but because her parents discouraged a concert career for her, she abandoned the stage for domesticity.

FRANCIS D. PERKINS.

MEPHIBOSHETH, the lame son of Jonathan, the son of Saul and friend of David. His real name was apparently Merib-baal (*I Chron.* 8:34; 9:40); later scribes changed the name in order to avoid the inclusion of the opprobrious name of the idol Baal. David provided for Mephibosheth after the death of Jonathan (*II Sam.* 4:4); but at the time of Absalom's revolt Mephibosheth's servant Ziba accused his master of plotting to secure the throne. David accordingly gave the property of Mephibosheth to Ziba. When David was restored to the throne, Mephibosheth appeared before him with apologies, which David accepted, but he did not restore his property to Mephibosheth; the Bible gives no reason for this failure to act (*II Sam.* 16:1-4; 19:25-31).

The name Mephibosheth was borne also by a son of Saul, one of the seven who were surrendered to the Gibeonites in recompense for the wrong that Saul had done to them in the past (*II Sam.* 21:1-11); his mother was the greathearted Rizpah.

MERCADO, CHARLES ERNEST DE, communal leader, b. Kingston, Jamaica, British West Indies, 1863; d. 1909. He was a partner in Lascelles de Mercado and Co. of Kingston, E. A. de Pass and Co., of London, and Lascelles and Co., of New York, New Orleans, Porto Rico and Barcelona, and a director of many companies. A member of the board of governors of the Institute of Jamaica and of the Board of Agriculture, and one of the vice-presidents of the Jamaica Chamber of Commerce, he was elected (1899) member of the Legislative Council. After the earthquake of 1907 he did splendid work as a member of the Relief Committee. Mercado was one of the leaders of the movement which led to the appointment of Baron Glivier as governor. For many years he was lay head of the Jewish community, and served as president of the United Congregation of Israelites.

Lit.: Files of the *Gleaner*, Feb. 15, 1909.

MERCHA KEFULAH, *see* CANTILLATION.

MERCHAVYA, *see* COLONIES, AGRICULTURAL.

MERCY (*rahamim, hesed*), the beneficence of God, especially His pardoning kindness to him who is pardoned without merit on his own part; it represents the highest degree of good will and forgiveness in human relations. In the broadest sense, every gift of life which contributes to human welfare, all the favorable decrees of fate, all the successes achieved and the abilities possessed by man, may be regarded from the religious point of view as due to the mercy of God. But the especial expression of that mercy is God's clemency toward human transgressions, His support and enlightenment of erring mankind that leads them to the way of salvation.

In pre-prophetic Israel the divine mercy, like the divine wrath, was regarded as often an impenetrable mystery. But the prophets and the rabbis after them taught that such mercy was no mere caprice but the result of the infinite love of God for man. Yet this love was to a certain extent conditioned by human conduct; it was more readily granted to the repentant sinner than to him who persisted in his evil ways. The divine love, aware of the frailties and shortcomings of mankind, greatly desires to show mercy to the penitent. It does not desire the death of the sinner, but that he return to God and live (*Ezek.* 33:11).

God's mercy is therefore necessarily limited by God's justice, for unless there is punishment of evil man can not be led along the right way. Both are necessary for man's salvation and for the salvation of Israel and mankind as a whole. Rabbinic literature speaks of two attributes of God, the attribute of justice (*middath hadin*) and the attribute of mercy (*middath harahamim*), which are in perpetual conflict. Yet the attribute of justice is always subordinate to the attribute of mercy. Punitive justice is employed only for the purpose of securing the fulfillment of man's moral mission. Once this has been assured by the penitent return of the sinner, justice is replaced by love, which is given the higher rank. The preponderance of love over justice is expressed in the Decalogue (*Ex.* 20:5-6), in the theophany of God to Moses (*Ex.* 34:6-7) and in *Jonah,* where the author deliberately emphasizes the mercy of God to all humanity (cf. *Sirach* 18:13). The mercy of God is especially granted to those who forgive their fellow men (*Sirach* 28:2, 5; *Sab.* 151b) and to those who study the Law (*Hag.* 12b). The meritorious acts of the fathers also secure divine mercy for their children.

In return for the mercy of God, man is expected to do His will and to show mercy to his fellow men and all creatures. As the rabbis have pointed out, the world can not endure on strict justice; justice must be supplemented by unstinting beneficence and forgiveness on the part of God and man.

See also: ALTRUISM; FORGIVENESS; LOVE; MERIT OF THE FATHERS.

Lit.: Kohler, K., *Jewish Theology,* chaps. 17 to 20; Koller, A. H., *Foundations of Jewish Ethics,* and the literature cited there.

MERESHIN (MERESHENI), ABRAHAM, Yiddish writer, b. Mereshani, province of Kherson, Russia, about 1880. After receiving a well-grounded Jewish education, Mereshin became a teacher in Odessa. He was at first a Hebraist, later a fervent Yiddishist. He aided in the preparation of Yiddish literature for children, and was co-founder of the journal *Blimelech* (Odessa).

Mereshin was one of the teachers for the Hebrah Mefitze Haskalah, where he continued his agitation on behalf of Yiddish. After the revolution of 1917 he joined the Socialist Bund, and wrote a brochure, *Bund un Zionism.* He was affiliated also with several Socialist and Bundist undertakings. When the Russian Socialist parties split (1918-20), Mereshin allied himself with the Communists. During the occupation of the Ukraine by the Denikin armies, Mereshin went to Moscow, where, between 1919 and 1930, he became one of the leaders of the Yevsektsia (Jewish Communist Group). From 1925 to 1926 he was associated with Jewish colonization in the Crimea. He also wrote for the *Emes,* and was author of several pamphlets on colonization. Between 1936 and 1938 Mereshin incurred the displeasure of the Soviet government and was ousted from all his posts.

Lit.: Reisen, Z., *Lexikon fun der Yiddisher Literatur, Presse un Filologie,* vol. 2 (1930), cols. 471-73.

MERIB-BAAL, *see* MEPHIBOSHETH.

MERIDEN, a city in Connecticut having a total population of 39,494 (census of 1940), including about 1,300 Jews. Jews from the countries of Eastern Europe began to settle in Meriden in 1882. The great majority were peddlers, tailors, cobblers and blacksmiths. Others worked in the town's woollen mill, long since defunct.

Congregation Chevra B'nai Abraham (Orthodox) was established in 1888. The first rabbi was Simon D. Silverman and the rabbi in 1942 was Hyman Friedman. In 1910 a new building was built under the active leadership of Hoscar Frank, Esedor Derektor, Samuel White, Hyman Arinofsky, Samuel Loitz and Benjamin Krentzman. The old building served as the Hebrew school. Beginning with 1920 the Hebrew school was supported by community funds.

Hoscar Frank was founder of the Meriden Hebrew Loan company, where many Jewish merchants obtained finances for their enterprises. He also directed the war relief drive in 1918. Samuel Umansky was president of the Meriden Zionist district since its organization in 1922. Fred S. Harris was national commander of the Jewish War Veterans (1940-41). Among the Jewish national agencies that had branches in Meriden in 1942 were Hadassah, the American Zionist Organization, Young Judea, N.F.T. Sisterhoods, Jewish National Workers' Alliance, the Arbeiter Ring, the American Jewish Congress, the National Refugee Service, Aleph Zadik Aleph, and a post of the Jewish War Veterans.

MERIT OF THE FATHERS (*zechuth 'aboth*), a concept in Jewish theology expressive of the idea that each individual profits in his life time by the meritorious acts of his ancestors, which constitute as it were a permanent and inalienable store of benediction. The earliest expression of this idea occurs in the Torah, where the Israelites are promised possession of Canaan because of the merits of the three patriarchs Abraham, Isaac and Jacob, and in the Second Commandment, which speaks of God as punishing the descendants for the sins of their immediate ancestors, but showing kindness to the progeny of the righteous even to the thousandth generation. The earliest use of the expression is in *Aboth* 2:2, where Gamaliel II warns the leaders of the community not to account themselves righteous because of their success in life, but rather to attribute it to the merit of their ancestors. The liturgy also contains references to the merit of the fathers, especially the Patriarchs, and in particular the sacrifice of Isaac (Akedah). In more recent times, if a person is exceptionally lucky or escapes misfortune, he is apt to hear the expression, "The merit of his fathers came to his aid."

For the development of the idea, *see* PARENTS AND CHILDREN; ZECHUTH ABOTH.

MERKABAH ("divine chariot"). The prophet Ezekiel describes in a vision (*Ezek.* 1 and 10) how he saw God riding upon a chariot composed of marvelous creatures (*hayyoth*), accompanied by other attendants, wondrous movements and divine manifestations. This led to a series of mystical speculations which culminated in the activity of the mystics in the 2nd cent. C.E. and was known as the Maaseh Merkabah ("lore of the divine chariot").

There are many references to this lore of the Merkabah in the Talmud, but it was regarded as so secret that the details are scanty and by no means clear. It appears from these, however, that Maaseh Merkabah centered about the essence of the Deity, His attributes, revelation and manifestation to man, and His relation to the world.

To the early Jewish mystics the mysteries of Maaseh Merkabah were best left alone (*Sirach* 3:21-22). It was "an important matter" (*Suk.* 28a), beset with many difficulties. It was to be confided only to the Tzenuim ("chaste ones"), an esoteric order, who were able to understand them by reason of their age, saintliness, self-discipline, and unusual mental qualifications. According to an old Mishnah, the Maaseh Merkabah was to be explained only to one who possessed exceptional understanding (*Hag.* 2:1). When Johanan offered to instruct Eleazar on the subject, the latter declined on the ground that he was not old enough; the belief was that one who studied such mysteries too soon in life or without proper preparation would die suddenly.

The Talmud mentions a number of scholars who studied the mysteries of the Merkabah, such as Johanan ben Zakkai, Joshua ben Hananiah, and others. The story of the four who entered Paradise (*Hag.* 14b)— Akiba, Ben Zoma, Ben Azzai and Elisha ben Abuyah —of whom only Akiba remained unaffected, illustrates the mysteriousness surrounding the esoteric doctrine and the danger attached to it.

Many of the ancient mystics sought a more ambitious goal than that of mere knowledge. They believed that by training themselves to a life of untarnished holiness they might ascend to actual contact with God while they were still living. They called themselves *yorede merkabah* ("riders on the divine chariot") since they believed that they might be able actually to mount the divine chariot, like Elijah, and ascend to heaven, where they would behold the innermost secrets of the universe. Such ascensions were actually claimed to have been made by Persian, Arabian and Egyptian mystics, who undoubtedly influenced Jewish esoteric doctrine.

See also: APOCALYPSE; ASCENSION; MYSTICISM.

JACOB S. MINKIN.

Lit.: Abelson, J., *Jewish Mysticism* (1913) 33-51; Waxman, M., *A History of Jewish Literature*, vol. 1 (1930) 379-80.

MERNEPTAH, king of Egypt, the fourth of the nineteenth dynasty (1225-15 B.C.E.), the son of and successor to Rameses II; he is supposed to have been the Pharaoh of the Exodus. His name is perhaps preserved in Me Nephtoah (*Josh.* 15:9), a fountain near Jerusalem. In the fifth year of his reign Libyan and other tribes invaded and harassed the land. While suppressing the invasion he came into contact with Israel. In the stele of victory which he set up in his mortuary temple at Thebes he gave an account of his wars and victories. The Hymn of Victory concludes with the following description of the conquest of certain peoples in Palestine:

"The kings are overthrown, saying: 'Peace!'
Not one holds up his head among the foreign nations.
Wasted is Libya,
Hittite land is at peace,

An excavated bust of
Merneptah

Plundered is the Canaan with every evil,
Carried off is Ashkelon,
Seized upon is Gezer,
Yanoam (near Damascus) is made as a thing not
existing.
Israel is desolated, her seed is not.
Kharu (Palestine) has become a (defenseless) widow
for Egypt."

This is the first reference to Israel in an Egyptian document. The inscription was discovered by W. M. Flinders Petrie in 1896.

It is assumed on the basis of this inscription that already at the time of the "Egyptian bondage" there were Hebrew tribes settled in Palestine, who were called by the name Israel. These are regarded as Palestine (= Israel) tribes, in contrast with the Goshen (= Jacob) tribes. The Hebrews, leaving Egypt and arriving in Palestine, coalesced with them, adopting their name and identifying their eponymous ancestor with Jacob.

See also ISRAEL STELE.

Lit.: Barton, G. A., *Archaeology and the Bible* (1925) 31, 129-30, 338; Olmstead, A. T., *History of Palestine and Syria* (1931) 227 et seq.; Oesterley, W. O. E., and Robinson, T. H., *History of Israel*, vol. 1 (1932) 75.

MERODACH-BALADAN (more properly, Marduk-apil-iddina), ruler of Babylonia from about 721 to 701 B.C.E. He enlisted the aid of the Elamites and seized the throne of Babylonia in defiance of its Assyrian overlords while the Assyrian empire was in disturbance after the death of Shalmaneser IV. Sargon, the new king, immediately proceeded against Babylonia as soon as he had secured the throne, while Merodach-baladan sought allies from the countries that had felt the Assyrian scourge. It was probably for this reason that Merodach-baladan sent envoys to Hezekiah (*Isa.* 39), who showed him his resources but apparently lent no aid. Sargon eventually recovered rule over Babylonia.

The form Merodach for Marduk in the Bible is a vocalization based on the word *bosheth* ("shame") which was later read for the name of idols. Similarly, Astarte was changed to Ashtoreth, and Melech to Molech.

MEROM, WATERS OF, the common but incorrect name given to a lake situated in the northern part of Palestine and known to the Arabs as Bahrat el Huleh (Lake Huleh). The latter, according to Josephus, was called Semachonitis in ancient times; the term used in rabbinic writings is Subcho or Sumcho. The reason that this body of waters is often called Merom is that it has been incorrectly identified with the "waters of Merom" (*me merom;* Merom is the same as Meron) where Joshua defeated the northern group of Canaanite kings (*Josh.* 11:5, 7). Lake Huleh has but a shallow depth, and is surrounded by great swamps which make it impossible to establish a larger settlement in this region.

Lit.: Hastings, James, *Dictionary of the Bible* (1927) 606.

MERON, city in Upper Galilee, Palestine, apparently identical with the Merom of the Bible, where Joshua defeated the Canaanites (*Josh.* 11:5, 7). Some scholars hold that Meroz, cursed in the Song of Deborah because its inhabitants "came not to the help of the Lord" (*Judges* 5:23) was actually Meron, and that the text of the song was later changed to avoid giving offense to the city. Meron is mentioned in the Mishnah, which praises the quality of the olives grown in that neighborhood. Simeon ben Yohai settled there in the 2nd cent. and founded an academy. His grave and that of his son are still shown there today, and on the 18th of Iyyar (Lag Baomer), their memorial day, thousands of persons stream thither from all parts of the country. Not far from the village are the remains of a very old synagogue; the side-posts of its door are monoliths ten feet high. A short distance from the synagogue are the traditional sites of the graves of

Leonard Merrick

Johanan Hasandalar, of Hillel and thirty-six of his disciples, and of Shammai. The latter are situated in caves under a hillock. (*See illustration in vol. 5, p. 362.*)

Lit.: Klein, Samuel, *Beiträge zur Geographie und Geschichte Galiläas* (1909) 22 et seq.; idem, *Jüdisch-Palästinisches Corpus Inscriptionum* (1920) 80.

MERRICK, LEONARD, author and actor, b. London, 1864; d. London, 1939. Merrick was descended from a Jewish family named Miller. He was educated at Brighton College, but because of his father's financial reverses he was suddenly compelled to earn his own living, and turned to the stage. After several vain attempts to obtain an engagement in England, Merrick, at the age of twenty, went to New York city. But he was no more fortunate in the United States; discouraged and practically penniless, he returned to London. Even then his theatrical career was not a brilliant one, but it enriched Merrick's later literary career. His stage experiences inspired Merrick to create certain characters theretofore unknown in English literature, particularly in portraying frustrated ambitions, splendid misery, and disillusionment. Nevertheless, when Merrick began to write, he refrained from utilizing this advantage.

In 1891 Merrick published his first novel, *Violet Moses,* the story of a Christian girl who married a Jewish broker while in love with a Jewish author. Jewish characters are represented by Merrick in this novel without any special sympathy, but he projected a great variety of traits. However, he did not excel in the psychological analysis he sought to develop in his first novel; even his novel *Cynthia* (1897) was devoid of the artistic qualities which later became his virtues. It was the novel *The Actor-Manager* (1898) that first gave evidence of Merrick's originality. William Dean Howells compared the author of this novel

Ruins of the synagogue of Rabbi Simeon ben Yohai at Meron

with such great Russian creators of fiction as Turgenev and Tolstoi. Even he who cannot share Howell's appreciation must acknowledge Merrick's keen observation, his faculty for whetting the reader's curiosity and holding his interest. *The Quaint Companions* (1903), another novel, combined psychological analysis with abundant facts of a picturesque life, relating the story of a negro tenor who married a white woman, and of his mulatto son, a poet. At the same time, Merrick wrote a modern "sentimental journey" in the charming novel *Conrad in Quest of His Youth*. He obtained his relatively greatest success in publishing (1907) a collection of stories, *The Man Who Understood Women*.

As a literary artist, however, Merrick was most successful in *The Position of Peggy Harper* (1912). Depicting a character conceived as a blend of enthusiasm and ineptitude, Merrick created an original literary type, and displayed rare finesse and humor in delineating his figures. He continued to perfect a concise and easy style, a seemingly casual but actually most conscious manner in linking situations with dialogue. From the very outset Merrick cultivated a moralistic vein disguised by cynical observations, as in *When Love Flies Out o' the Window* (1919) and *A Chair on the Boulevard* (1921). Most of his novels and stories have their settings in the world of actors, artists and writers. Evidently Merrick was conscious of being more familiar in that milieu than in middle-class or aristocratic society.

Merrick often sojourned in France, and loved Paris. The influence of French life and literature is evident in almost all his later works. He was by no means an "insular" Briton, nor was he as keenly appreciated by English critics as he deserved. In 1918 a great number of world-renowned British and American authors—among them H. G. Wells, G. K. Chesterton, J. M. Barrie, Arthur Pinero and William Dean Howells—resolved to render justice to Merrick. They reedited his works, and each of them wrote a preface to one of his novels or collections of stories. This act of esprit de corps was crowned with success. Merrick was thenceforth generally acknowledged as a great British author.   HUGO BIEBER.

Lit.: Weygandt, Cornelius, *A Century of the English Novel* (1925); Salomon, Sidney, *The Jews of Britain* (1938); *The Bookman*, Nov., 1932.

MERTON, WILHELM, financier, industrialist and philanthropist, b. Frankfort, Germany, 1848; d. Berlin, 1916. His father, originally named Moses, went to Frankfort from England, and married into the family which owned the old banking house of L. A. and H. Cohen, whose principal seat was at Hannover. The Cohens were on intimate terms with the Hanoverian government, and in that way they enjoyed a preferential treatment on the part of the Hanoverian administration of mines. Merton entered his father's business, and then went to England, where his elder brother, who had returned some years before, owned several enterprises. In 1876 Merton returned to Frankfort, and became his father's partner. In 1881 he founded the Metallgesellschaft, dealing in lead, copper, tin and zinc. A few years later he expanded his interests in metallurgy and chemical industry, and it is due principally to his efforts that Frankfort became one of the most important markets for metals and

that German metal traders drove their English competitors from the world market. In 1911 Merton founded the Berg-und-Metallbank and the Metallurgische Gesellschaft.

As he studied the mines of almost all countries, especially those of Australia, where his own concern owned or controlled the principal mines, Merton's conscience was troubled by the unsanitary conditions under which the miners worked. He instituted social reforms and his inventive spirit did not stop at improving the situation of a single class. Opposed to traditional poor-law systems, Merton attempted to organize social welfare scientifically. In 1890 he founded the Institut für Gemeinwohl at Frankfort, in 1899 the Centrale für private Fürsorge, in 1901 the Soziales Museum, and in 1904 the Bureau für Sozialpolitik in Berlin. From 1893 on he financed the journal *Soziale Praxis,* which pioneered in social ideas in Germany.

By 1900 Merton became a German citizen, and at the same time he embraced Christianity. He was devoted to Emperor William II, whom he considered a protector of social reforms because of his conflict with Bismarck. During the first World War Merton was attached to the German general staff.

Lit.: Stein, Philipp, *Wilhelm Merton* (1917); Fürstenberg, Carl, *Lebensgeschichte eines deutschen Bankiers* (1931).

MERZBACHER, ABRAHAM, banker, numismatist and philanthropist, b. Baiersdorf, near Erlangen, Bavaria, Germany, 1812; d. Munich, Germany, 1885. He was educated at the Talmudic schools of Erlangen and Fürth and at the classical schools of Fürth and Munich, and studied philosophy at the University of Munich. After ordination, Merzbacher was for a short time rabbi in Ansbach, but in 1840 entered the banking house of J. N. Oberndoerffer at Munich, which was at the same time the leading German numismatic concern, and before 1860 the only great trader in medals in Germany. Merzbacher became a learned numismatist at Paris, where he entered the numismatic firm of Rollin and Fenardent, and was taught by Rollin, one of the leading authorities of the 19th cent. Merzbacher studied especially the famous "Becker's counterfeits," and exposed their methods and results.

Merzbacher often sojourned at Vienna, where there was a branch establishment of Oberndoerffer, and traveled in Poland and Russia, being equally interested in scholarship and in trade. Thus he became an authority on Polish medals, but studied especially Jewish coins and medals and all kinds of specimens pertaining to Jewish life and history. He owned a precious collection of such items. In 1873 he retired from business, and devoted his time to the promotion of Jewish learning by supporting Hebrew authors or by supplying learned Jewish men and organizations with rare books, manuscripts and coins which he unearthed at a sacrifice of much time and money. Merzbacher's important library was preserved at Frankfort.

Lit.: *Mitteilungen der Bayerischen numismatischen Gesellschaft,* fascicle 4 (1885).

MERZBACHER, EUGEN, numismatist, son of Abraham, b. Munich, Germany, 1845; d. Munich, 1903. He studied classical philology and archeology at the Universities of Munich and Berlin, where he was a disciple of Mommsen and Curtius, but decisive in his life was the influence of Julius Friedlaender, director of the royal numismatic collection at Berlin. Merzbacher idolized him as his real teacher, while his first teacher in numismatics was his father. He was influenced also by M. A. Levy of Breslau, author of a valuable monograph, *Altjüdische Münzen*. Friedlaender and Levy inspired Merzbacher to study the oldest Jewish coin, the shekel, and Merzbacher was graduated from the University of Berlin because of his thesis *De siclis, nummis antiquissimis Judaeorum* (1873). Then he founded the numismatic firm of Dr. Eugen Merzbacher at Munich, from which he retired in 1902, after having gained an international reputation. Merzbacher contributed numerous studies to the journal of the Bavarian numismatic society, which elected him member of its directory. He contributed often also to the *Numismatic Circular*. Merzbacher had a vast knowledge of Greek, Roman and modern coins, but was interested mainly in ancient Jewish history, Jewish folklore and religion. His catalogues, especially *Medals* (1900), were highly esteemed.

Lit.: Mitteilungen der Bayerischen numismatischen Gesellschaft (1903).

MERZBACHER, GOTTFRIED, explorer, b. Baiersdorf, near Erlangen, Bavaria, Germany, 1843; d. Munich, Germany, 1926. He was educated in the secondary school for modern subjects at Erlangen, and was a merchant in Paris, London and St. Petersburg. In 1868 he founded a fur trade in Munich, which made him reputable and prosperous. After gaining financial independence, Merzbacher developed an interest in science and mountain climbing. Excellently trained, he had been a well-known alpinist before retiring (1888) from the fur business in order to devote his leisure to mountain tours. Thus he explored the mountains of Africa and North America, and from 1898 on reported on his journeys in scientific publications. Together with Purgsteller, greatest German alpinist of his time, Merzbacher explored the Northern Caucasus in 1891. From 1892 on he spent several years in Arabia, Persia and the Indies.

In 1902, Merzbacher began his great exploration of the Central Tian Shan Mountains which, after interruptions, he resumed in 1907. His reports, published in the transactions of the Bavarian Academy of Sciences, were commended for their thoroughness and accuracy. Merzbacher greatly enhanced the knowledge of geology, botany, zoology, ethnography and meteorology. A chain of the Tian Shan Mountains was named the Merzbacher range, in his honor. In 1901 he published *In den Hochregionen des Kaukasus,* which became classical in German literature by virtue of its scientific approach and artistic descriptions. Merzbacher's book, *The Central Tian Shan Mountains* (1905), was likewise esteemed by English readers. In the closing years of his life Merzbacher prepared a great scientific atlas of the Tian Shan Mountains on the scale of 1:100,000. His remarkable collection of skeletons, unique in Europe, and his valuable library were preserved in the Ethnological Museum of Munich.

Lit.: Zeitschrift der Gesellschaft für Erdkunde (1919); *Geographische Zeitschrift* (1926); *Mitteilungen der geographischen Gesellschaft München* (1926).

MERZBACHER, LEO, rabbi, b. Germany; d. New York city, 1856. As rabbi of the first Reform congregation of New York city he became a spiritual and organizational leader in the spread of the Reform Movement in the United States. By 1845 he had begun to preach a moderate Reform Judaism in the New York congregation Anshe Chesed, but when, one Sabbath morning, he denounced the wearing of the Sheitel by the women of the congregation, he aroused so much opposition that he was not reappointed at the expiration of his term. His partisans in the congregation, including its president, Isaac Dittenhoefer, then combined forces with the members of the Cultus Verein, a society of young German Jews unrelated to any congregation, and in April, 1845, this Verein organized itself into the first Reform congregation of the city under the name of Temple Emanu-El, and called in Merzbacher to be rabbi and lecturer, at a salary of $200 per annum.

Merzbacher delivered his discourses in German, organized a religious school, had an organ installed, and prepared a new prayer-book; most significant, he introduced, in 1848, confirmation of both boys and girls. In general, he followed a program of making the congregation a center of intellectual as well as religious culture. At his death he was succeeded by Samuel Adler.

Merzbacher was active in the earliest days of the Independent Order of B'nai B'rith, and the name was his suggestion.

Lit.: American Hebrew, April 16, 1920, p. 719 et seq.; Oct. 4, 1929, p. 591; Stern, Myer, *History of Temple Emanu-El* (1895).

MESA, ISAIAH (or **ISAAC**), known also as Meza and probably as Mera, first known Jewish trader in Pennsylvania. His name appears several times in a lawsuit on a tobacco transaction during the first half of 1657. The record identifies him as "a Jew." There was also a person of the same name resident in the Jewish community of Surinam in 1677, and there is some likelihood that the two records refer to the same person.

Lit.: Publications of the American Jewish Historical Society, No. 5 (1897) 192-94; No. 18 (1909) 66; *Annals of Pennsylvania,* p. 237; *Albany Records,* vol. 15, p. 202.

MESCHA, *see* COLONIES, AGRICULTURAL (under KFAR TAVOR).

MESERITZ, BAER OF, *see* BAER OF MESERITZ.

MESHA, *see* MOABITE STONE.

MESHUGGA, MESHUGGE, *see* PHRASES, POPULAR.

MESHULLACH, MESHULLAH, *see* FUNCTIONARIES, RELIGIOUS AND COMMUNAL.

MESHULLAM BEN JACOB OF LUNEL, a patron of learning and literature in the 12th cent., d. after 1170. Because of his own knowledge of the sciences and law he was called "Prince" Meshullam. At his urging, Judah ibn Tibbon translated the *Duties of the Heart* into Hebrew from the Arabic of Bahya ibn Pakuda. Meshullam ben Jacob's influence encouraged the extensive translation into Hebrew, during the Middle Ages, of literature from other languages and also the philosophical studies of the Jews in southern France.

Lit.: Steinschneider, M., *Die hebräischen Übersetzungen des Mittelalters* (1893); Gollancz, Hermann, *The Ethical Treatises of Berachyah* (1902).

MESHULLAM BEN KALONYMUS III (called "The Great"), liturgical poet and author, who lived at the end of the 10th cent. He was the son of Kalonymus II of Lucca, a liturgical poet whom the German Emperor Otto II is supposed to have permitted to move to Mayence from Italy in return for services rendered to his army by the Kalonymus family during the war against the Saracens (982). Meshullam ben Kalonymus is known as the author of Piyutim, including *Emecha Nasati* and *Moreh Hattaim* for the morning service, of the Abodah for the Yom Kippur afternoon service, and of a commentary on the *Sayings of the Fathers* (*Pirke Aboth*). Meshullam also wrote polemics against the Karaites. His tombstone was discovered in Mayence in 1859.

Lit.: Müller, *Responsen des Rabbi Meschullam, Sohn des Kalonymus* (1893); Freimann, A., "Meschullam ben Kalonymos' Polemik gegen die Karäer," *Judaica. Festschrift zu Hermann Cohens 70. Geburtstage* (1912) 569-78.

MESHUMMAD, *see* APOSTATES; PHRASES, POPULAR.

MESILOTH, *see* COLONIES, AGRICULTURAL.

MESOPOTAMIA, name given in ancient times to the region between the Euphrates and the Tigris rivers, in Asia. Its history is treated under the following separate articles:

1. Ancient History, see ARAM; ASSYRIA; BABYLONIA.
2. Middle Ages, see ARABIA; BAGHDAD; PERSIA.
3. Modern Times, see TURKEY.
4. Recent Times, see IRAQ.

MESQUITA, BENJAMIN BUENO DE, Portuguese merchant, who resided in the island of Jamaica, apparently prior to 1660, and possibly even before Jamaica was captured by the British. In 1664 he prayed the king of England for relief from the provisions of the Navigation Act, which prevented him, a foreigner, from trading with his majesty's plantations, where he had all of his estate. He therefore desired to be granted letters of denization, so drawn, however, that he might take the oath of allegiance there. Permission for this had scarcely been given when, moved by the failure of some Jews in Barbados to find certain promised gold mines, the wrath of the king was aroused, and Mesquita and his two sons were banished from the island, but not before they paid certain customs dues and made sundry other restitutions. They evidently repaired to New York, for Benjamin was buried there in 1683. His tombstone is probably the oldest memorial stone extant marking any Jewish grave in New York city, and is in the cemetery, originally situated in New Bowery, of the Spanish and Portuguese Congregation Shearith Israel. He himself is not mentioned in the records of the congregation, which are not extant for the period preceding 1728, but other members of his family were members of the synagogue for many years after the above date and were persons of position and influence.

There are scattered records of members of the family in the West Indies throughout the 17th and 18th centuries. Mention is made of one named Abraham Bueno de Mesquita in Barbados in 1694, possibly the brother mentioned in Joseph Bueno's will (1708) as a resident of the island of Nevis; of another of the same name who left Amsterdam for Surinam in 1731, and of the banishment of still another from Surinam in 1792 at the request of the Portuguese deputies. Luis de Mesquita, alias de Amesquita Sarmiento, originally of Segovia, Castile, is mentioned in the records of the Inquisition of Mexico, where he was a citizen and merchant, as a "Hebrew new Christian, Judaizing heretic, reconciled 1646." The name of the family disappears in America in the 19th cent., but the family Bueno de Mesquita still exists in England.

Lit.: *Publications of the American Jewish Historical Society,* index volume (1914) 349-50.

MESQUITA, JOSEPH BUENO DE, merchant, probably the son of Benjamin Bueno de Mesquita. It is recorded that in 1680 John Foster went forty pounds security that Joseph Bueno, as he was generally known, would not become chargeable on the town of Boston. This was probably the same Joseph Bueno who was given permission in 1683 "to trade and traffic within the city of New York," and was a leading Jew in the colony of New York in the period from 1682 to his death in 1708. Although the records of Congregation Shearith Israel before 1728 are not extant, it is also probable that he was president of the congregation for a time. In 1682 he purchased the congregational cemetery, originally situated in New Bowery, from William and Mary Merrett, in trust for the "Jewish Nation." A history of the transaction and a record of his will are printed in the *Publications of the American Jewish Historical Society.* That he was financially prominent is proved by the fact that Lord Bellamont, governor of the colony, made use of his services in pecuniary matters about 1700.

Lit.: *Publications of the American Jewish Historical Society,* index volume (1914), under Bueno; Friedman, *ibid.,* No. 23 (1915); Oppenheim, *ibid.,* No. 31 (1928) 99-103; Daly, Charles P., *The Settlement of the Jews in North America* (1893) 27.

MESSEL, ALFRED, architect, b. Darmstadt, Germany, 1853; d. Berlin, 1909. He studied at the Art Academy in Cassel, Germany, and later on at the Architects' Academy in Berlin. During the decade from 1878 to 1888 he was in the service of the German government, and traveled through Italy, France and Spain. In the 1890's he renounced Judaism and became associate professor and finally Geheimrat, as well as a member of the Prussian Academy of Art in Berlin.

Messel's epoch-making buildings were erected mainly in Berlin, where he built the Volkskaffeehallen in 1890 and several apartment houses from 1892 to 1895. World-famous was the Wertheim department store at the Leipzigerstrasse, erected in 1897 (the extension in the Leipziger Platz was opened in 1904). This large building combines architectural beauty with practical efficiency. It was the first building totally constructed of steel and stone. Noteworthy also is the bank building of the Berliner Handelsgesellschaft at the Gendarmenmarkt, the Nationalbank on the Behrenstrasse, and the villa of Eduard Simon. Realization of his plan for the Deutsches Museum at the Museumsinsel was prevented by the first World War,

Alfred Messel

but was finally carried out in 1933, after Ludwig Hoffmann had made many changes on Messel's original design.

Many striking buildings in other German cities were erected by Messel. Foremost among them are the Hessisches Landesmuseum in Darmstadt (1906) and the palace of Baron Cohn in Dessau. His works in interior decoration are very impressive by reason of their simplicity. Conspicuous among them was the Minister's Conference Chamber in the new building of the Preussischer Landtag in Berlin, and the interior of the Palazzo Cafarelli in Rome. His efforts in the improvement of workers' homes is worth recording. Messel's creations were mostly in the style of the early Renaissance in Italy; however, the Wertheim department store and the museum in Darmstadt are related to baroque, and his last creation, the Pergamon museum, is classical. Each of those styles was but the basis for his own imagination which gave all his works a distinctiveness of clarity and simplicity. Messel was the teacher of Peter Behrens, who in turn taught Walter Gropius, indicating clearly the direct line connecting Messel with modern architecture.

Lit.: Ruckwaldt, *Alfred Messels Berliner Bauten* (1896); *Alfred Messel,* fifth special number of the *Berliner Architekturwelt* (1905); Osborn, Max, *Baukünstler und Bauten, C.-V. Zeitung,* vol. 10 (1931) 338-39; Schwarz, Karl, *Die Juden in der Kunst* (1928).

MESSEL, RUDOLPH, chemist, b. Darmstadt, Germany, 1848; d. Silvertown, Essex, England, 1920. Messel was of Jewish lineage, but was born into a banker's family that had been converted to Lutheranism. He studied at the Universities of Zurich, Heidelberg and Tübingen, and received his D.Sc. degree from the last-named institution.

Shortly before the outbreak of the Franco-Prussian War, Messel went to England. He returned to Germany to enter the army when the war began, and was invalided out after being wounded. On his return to England Messel engaged in experiments for the preparation of fuming sulphuric acid, which was becoming an increasingly necessary ingredient for the growing dye industry. He joined the firm of Squire, Chapman and Company, later known as Spencer, Chapman and Messel. The laboratories at Silvertown, where sulphuric anhydride was made by the catalytic process, which Messel and Squire had evolved, were headed by Messel. He was also an engineer and was known for his versatility as well as his ability to maintain good relations with his workmen.

Messel was made a fellow of the Royal Society in 1912. In 1910 to 1911 and again from 1914 to 1920 he was honorary foreign secretary of the Society of Chemical Industry; in 1911 to 1912 he was president and in 1912 to 1913 vice-president. Messel bequeathed most of his fortune to the Royal Society and the Society of Chemical Industry.

Lit.: Nature (London), vol. 105 (1920) 270-71; *Journal of the Society of Chemical Industry, Jubilee Number,* July, 1931, p. 79; Jan. 16, 1937, p. 51.

MESSENGER. In contradistinction to the agent, who may undertake a legal matter for his principal with direct effect, the messenger is but a tool in the latter's hand, a bearer of another's will. He acts as a representative only in regard to the declaration of purpose, and not when it is necessary to come to a decision. Therefore any action undertaken by a messenger is purely a matter of actual facts. The Mishnah and the Talmud use the same expression, *shaliah,* for both messenger and agent; in these cases the context must show whether it refers to the real action of a messenger or the legal action of an agent. However, the functions of a messenger, especially in post-Talmudic writings, are described by the striking term "only the actions of a monkey" (*ma'aseh kof be'alema*). This is derived from a discussion in the Talmud (*Erub.* 31b; *Meil.* 21a), where it is explained that the real actions of a representative could be executed even by persons not capable of being agents, such as minors, since all these could be performed by a trained ape. This terminology shows that even in Talmudic times a distinction was made between the actions of an agent and those of a messenger.

Lit.: see under AGENCY, LEGAL.

MESSER LEON, *see* LEON, DAVID MESSER.

MESSIAH. Out of the belief, held by Jews, in a future Messianic period which will bring salvation to the Jewish people and to the whole world there gradually emerged the idea of an individual, the person designated to lead this movement and to assume responsibility for the moral and social changes hoped for by the Jews. The term Messiah comes from the Hebrew word *mashiah,* meaning "anointed," and was applied in the Bible to persons who were appointed to specific high offices and anointed with the sacred oil. The name was given to Saul, the first king of Israel (*I Sam.* 12:3, 5; 24:7), to David (*Ps.* 132:17), and to the high priest (*Lev.* 4:3, 5, 16; 6:15). The term is used also figuratively to designate persons especially favored by God (*Ps.* 105:15; *I Chron.* 16:22), and in one instance (*Isa.* 45:1) the heathen king, Cyrus of Persia, is called God's anointed.

The hope for a future king who will redeem Israel and establish the kingdom of God upon earth is not expressly found either in the Biblical or in the Apoc-

"Messiah" by Enrico Glicenstein

ryphal writings. The various passages in the Prophets which speak of such a person, notably those of *Isaiah* (11:1-9; 9:5), have been interpreted by Bible scholars to refer rather to contemporaneous events than to the hope for the remote future (cf. also *Jer.* 23:5-6; 33:15-16; *Ezek.* 34:23-24; 37:24). However, the idea of the future righteous king was present even in the earlier periods, though not so designated. The association of the figure of the Messiah with King David (*Ezek.* 34:23-24; 37:24) or with a descendant of David (*Jer.* 23:5-6; 33:15-16) is explained by the idealized picture of the personality of David current among the people as the one who organized the nation on a firm political level, who ruled in accordance with the ideals of justice and righteousness, and to whom the promise was made that his dynasty would endure forever (*II Sam.* 7:8-17; *I Chron.* 17:7-15; cf. *Gen.* 49:10). The idealized David gradually became the prototype of the expected redeemer although the delineation of his functions and characteristics remained vague and undefined.

The proclamation issued by Cyrus for the return of the Babylonian exiles to Palestine was hailed as the fulfilment of the Messianic prophecies, and the Second Isaiah beheld him as the Messiah of God. However, the prophet did not intend to imply that Cyrus was the awaited Messiah but rather the agent through whom the era of peace and good-will would be inaugurated. Haggai (2:23) and Zechariah (3:8; 6:12), in the 6th cent. B.C.E., apparently regarded Zerubbabel, a scion of the Davidic family, as the Messiah, although Joshua the high priest was associated with him. On the other hand, Malachi, the last of the prophets, makes no mention of a personal Messiah, but he does look forward to a future revival in the spirit of the Torah. In *Malachi* (3:23) is found the first mention of Elijah as the forerunner of the glorious period, an idea that played an important role in the later conception of the Messiah.

The Messianic hope received a new complexion in the apocalyptic literature of the last two centuries B.C.E. The revolution which came about in the world through the conquests of Alexander the Great may have stirred hopes in the hearts of many Jews, and some may have regarded him as the Messiah who would bring about the period of peace and happiness foretold by the prophets. In *Daniel,* which is to a large extent Messianic, there is hardly any reference to the person of the Messiah. *Sirach* often refers to the eternity of the Davidic dynasty and to the hope for its restoration, but adds nothing definite as to the person of the Messiah.

Mystical features relating to the person of the Messiah were added in the apocalyptic books, most of which were composed during the period of Roman domination when the hope for a natural redemption was dimmed and replaced by the expectation of miraculous events that would be inaugurated to bring about the lifting of the detested yoke of Rome. In the Ethiopic *Enoch* the Messiah is represented as coming after the world has become regenerated, while in some of the other books, such as the *Testament of the Twelve Patriarchs* and the *Sybilline Oracles,* it is the Messiah who will inaugurate the era of peace. In the *Psalms of Solomon* he is represented as purging Jerusalem of all its sins, apportioning the land to Israel while permitting the stranger to dwell in its midst. In the entire range of this literature, in which many new elements are added to the notion of the Messianic period, the figure of the Messiah is often represented as a great and powerful warrior and ruler and then again as a supernatural being, existing from the beginning of days, close to God, designated as the "son of man" or as "My son." He is sometimes described as an angelic being whose existence antedated the creation of the world, waiting for the proper time to reveal himself and to assume the seat of glory whence he will dispense justice to all the inhabitants of the earth.

The belief in a personal Messiah reached its highest tension during that period of the 1st cent. when Rome sent her despotic procurators to rule over Judea. The yoke was most oppressive, and the Jews awaited a leader whom God would send to articulate their latent spirit of rebellion and free them from the Roman tyranny. Several outbreaks of a Messianic nature are recorded as having occurred during the period of the Herodian dynasty, but all of them were ruthlessly suppressed by the Roman legions.

A more spiritual note was struck by the movement inaugurated by John the Baptist, who appealed for repentance and good deeds whereby the generation might become worthy to enter the kingdom of God upon earth. Jesus of Nazareth, a disciple and admirer of John, continued the agitation initiated by John and left with his immediate followers the impression that he regarded himself as the long-awaited Messiah although he warned them "to tell no man that he was the Christ" (Christ being the Greek rendering of the Hebrew *Mashiah*). He even hinted that John the Baptist was Elijah, and had foretold the appearance of the Messiah. The early writings of the New Testament adduce proof of the advent of the Messiah in the personality of Jesus from prophetic and other writings of the Old Testament. These passages may have been familiar to the Jewish apostles because of their frequent use in the synagogue and the houses of study, and the fact that out of them comfort was extracted for the heartening of the despairing people in those days of misery and oppression.

The double concept of the nature of the Messiah, that of a military leader and that of a spiritual being, is reflected also in Tannaitic literature and in the later beliefs centering around the Messianic ideal. The idea of the pre-existence of the Messiah is reduced in a Baraitha merely to the name of the Messiah which is one of the seven things that existed before the world was created (*Pes.* 54b; *Ned.* 39b; cf. *Midrash Gen.* 1). As Meir Friedmann rightly explained, the idea conveyed by the Baraitha is that the belief that Israel will produce a redeemer who will bring about a world regeneration had been part of God's plan of Creation. (Introduction to *Seder Eliyahu Rabbah,* p. 114). On the other hand, the double function of the Messiah, that of a great warrior who would bring about the defeat of the enemies of Israel and the restoration of Israel to their land, and that of a moral and spiritual regenerator of the world, was separated and apportioned to two distinct individuals—Messiah, son of Joseph, and Messiah, son of David. The former will wage war against Gog and Magog and will be killed while defending Jerusalem but will be resurrected by Messiah, son of David. This new concept was probably introduced after the fall of Bar Kochba, but opinions differ greatly as to its origin.

The rabbis of the Talmud introduced greater emphasis and stronger lineaments to the previously accepted concept of the Messiah. One Amora, indeed, dared to announce that there would be no Messiah for Israel (Rab Hillel, *Sanh.* 98b); for this pronouncement he was mildly rebuked by Joseph. The idea of a personal Messiah had become so deeply rooted in the consciousness of the people that it is taken for granted throughout rabbinic literature. What the rabbis did was merely to add a few details to the belief. These details helped to enhance the nature of the Messiah as a spiritual reformer, one who would reestablish the Jewish commonwealth on the basis of the exalted principles of the Torah. His military prowess is toned down or given a fanciful and exotic direction. The figure of Elijah is used merely as the one who will

announce the Messiah's coming and then anoint him with the sacred oil. The stress laid on the supernatural features of the person of the Messiah varied with the conditions under which Jews lived at different times. The more difficult the conditions were and the more hopeless their lot appeared, the more tenaciously did they cling to the idealized person of a redeemer who would bring redemption by means of miracles and wonders.

During the Middle Ages the twofold aspect of the Messiah was followed by Jews everywhere and the emphasis laid on one or the other aspect depended on whether mysticism or rationalism held sway. Saadia Gaon (10th cent.) speaks of the Messiah who will lead all the Jews to Palestine and even mentions Elijah in his usual role, but neither of them plays a very important part in the Messianic picture when God will bring about the redemption of His people. A mystical apocalypse of that period, however, *The Book of Zerubbabel,* contains all the details of the belief, including the Messiah, son of Joseph, named here Nehemiah ben Hushiel, and the Messiah, son of David, named Menahem ben Amiel, whose mother Hephzibah will appear five years before the appearance of Messiah, son of Joseph, and slay two mighty kings with the staff of Aaron.

A purely rationalistic conception of the Messiah is presented by Maimonides (12th cent.). The belief in the coming of the Messiah is asserted by him and even made into an article of religious dogma, but the Messiah will be an ordinary human being, wiser than Solomon and almost as great a prophet as Moses, who will teach the word of God to all peoples; he will eventually die, however, and his son will succeed him as king. Under the rule of the Messiah men will be relieved of much of their current trouble and will be able to devote themselves more thoroughly to spiritual matters. "And do not imagine for a moment that the king Messiah will have to perform wonders and miracles, create new phenomena in nature and cause the resurrection of the dead . . . but the world will go on in its usual course" (*Mishneh Torah, Hilchoth Melachim* 11 and 12).

While Maimonides' rational ideas, with some minor exceptions, were adopted by many of his followers among the medieval Jewish philosophers, the many difficulties that befell the Jewish people in various lands caused the great mass of them to follow rather the mystical ideas about the Messiah in which they found solace and comfort. The *Zohar,* the premier book of the Cabalists, added other bizarre features to the person of the Messiah and to the time of his appearance. The Messiah's pre-existence is assumed and his abode is placed in Paradise, whence he will arise and proceed to earth in a pillar of fire. There are also many references in the *Zohar* to the sufferings sustained by the Messiah, wherewith he effects atonement for the sins of Israel. Fantasy and speculation about this cherished hope were given free rein, and many extravagant pictures were developed in the popular mind which make an interesting chapter in Jewish folklore.

The misfortunes which came upon the Jews in the wake of the various false Messiahs who made their appearance from time to time, and especially the excitement caused by the exploits of Sabbatai Zebi (1666) and Jacob Frank (18th cent.), induced the rabbis to regard with disfavor the mystical speculations about the

A Venetian woodcut (1740) depicting the future entrance of the Messiah into the Temple, preceded by the prophet Elijah

Messiah that were rampant. Belief in the coming of the Messiah was maintained with all intensity, but calculation regarding the time of his appearance was discouraged because it led to extravagant hopes and to grave disappointments.

The period of the Enlightenment inaugurated in Germany by the end of the 18th cent. brought many changes in the traditional Messianic hope and especially in the belief in a personal Messiah. The Reform Movement in Judaism discarded the belief in a Messiah and interpreted the ancient Messianic hope to refer to a period of peace and human regeneration, omitting all reference to the restoration of the Jewish nationhood on the soil of Palestine. While at first the main impetus toward the denial of Jewish nationalism was the desire for emancipation, it later assumed a scientific basis, whereby the Messianic ideal was stripped of all its par-

A Haggadah page illustrating the coming of the Messiah

ticularistic and national elements. All references to the Messiah and to the hope for a return to Palestine were removed from the Reform prayer-books, and at the various conferences, held in Germany and in the United States, this new interpretation of the Messianic belief was given prominence.

With the rise of Zionism toward the end of the 19th cent., this belief again underwent revision and reinterpretation. The early protagonists of the Zionist movement, with its practical attitude toward the settlement of Jews on the soil of Palestine, had to reconcile their views with the tradition that one should not "force" the arrival of the Messiah. A new theory was evolved by Rabbi Hirsch Kalischer and was followed by other rabbis who espoused the new movement. This was that the beginning of the redemption would be brought to pass in a natural way, by the desire of the Jews to settle in Palestine and by the willingness of the nations to help them in this work. The Messiah would make his appearance, it was asserted, and all the promised miracles and wonders would occur only after a goodly number of Jews should have established their home in the Holy Land and after Jerusalem should have been rebuilt and the Temple again erected. To live in Palestine and to help rebuild its ruins were in themselves considered meritorious acts, since according to tradition, many of the commandments of the Torah can be fulfilled only on the sacred soil. Some of the rabbis even went so far as to dissociate the movement for the colonization of Palestine from the Messianic hope, while others hoped to see Palestine become the spiritual center for the Jews of the world.

With the establishment of political Zionism under the leadership of Theodor Herzl and Max Nordau, the question of the old belief was again raised and the latter found it necessary to disclaim all pretensions of Messiahship either for himself or for his colleague. The movement, however, met with violent opposition from both the Orthodox and the Reform camps. Güdemann, one of the chief opponents of Herzl, speaks of the belief in a personal Messiah as "the fancy of homilists," but emphasizes the universalistic elements of the Messianic ideal. The Orthodox Jews continued to cling to the hope for the appearance of a personal Messiah, a scion of the house of David, and opposed the methods of the movement as well as its ideals. Zionism, however, in its later development counted its votaries in both the Orthodox and the Reform camps. Many Zionists have abandoned belief in a personal Messiah, retaining, however, the hope for a national revival on the land of Palestine. Others find it possible to reconcile Zionism with the Messianic hope in all its details, including the personal Messiah, without doing violence to either. The prayers for the restoration of the land and the coming of the Messiah son of David have been retained among the prayers recited by many Zionists, although the significance given to them may vary with different persons.

JULIUS H. GREENSTONE.

Lit.: The various Bible dictionaries and encyclopedias, especially under Eschatology, Jesus, Messianic Movements and Messianic Era. Greenstone, Julius H., *The Messiah Idea in Jewish History* (1906); Silver, Abba Hillel, *A History of Messianic Speculation in Israel* (1927); Sarachek, Joseph, *The Doctrine of the Messiah in Medieval Jewish Literature* (1932).

MESSIAHS, FALSE, *see* MESSIANIC MOVEMENTS.

MESSIANIC ERA (*yemoth hamashiah,* literally, "days of the Messiah"), the hoped for period of redemption to be ushered in and ruled over by the Messiah. In traditional and in modern Judaism the phrase, which is sometimes confused with the phrase Kingdom of Heaven, indicates that utopian period of peace and justice on earth for whose establishment mankind ceaselessly yearns.

The term "days of the Messiah" has at various times been filled with varying content. To some, they were to be a golden age of unmeasured duration (*Pesikta Rabbathi* 1; cf. *Testament of Levi* 18); to others, an interim period preceding the last judgment and the ushering in of the "world to come" (*Sab.* 113b). Some authorities conceived them as the era of perfect human felicity foretold in Biblical prophecy; others held that the "days of the Messiah" would differ from "this world" only in the fact that the people of Israel would have attained political independence (*Sanh.* 99a, *Ber.* 34b). There is even a statement that we need look for no Messiah, and thus by implication that one need look for no messianic age (*Sanh.* 98b, 99a; *Sab.* 63a, 151b). But where the coming of a messianic era in this limited sense may be specifically denied, the coming of a blessed era of divine kingship and redemption by the hand of God is specifically affirmed (as in *Sanh.* 99a and *Rashi ad loc.*). Thus when the messianic hope is excluded from the company of the fundamental doctrines of Judaism, as it is by some post-rabbinic thinkers (for instance, Albo, *Ikkarim,* edit. Husik, p. 413 et seq.), the reference is to the hope for a personal redeemer but not to the hope for the establishment of God's kingdom of perfect righteousness and happiness on earth.

One of the important elements of the Jewish conception of the Messianic era both in Biblical and post-Biblical literature is the return of the people of Israel to the land of Israel (*II Esdras* 13:25-49; *Isa.* 11:11-12). The yoke of the foreign tyrant was to be broken. Other nations were either to be conquered (*Isa.* 11:14) or annihilated (*Isa.* 11:15) or converted (*A.Z.* 3b), but whatever their destiny, they were no longer to be a source of pain and suffering for Israel.

The prophetic picture of the messianic era is one which is characterized by universal peace, by national security and justice, and by pastoral harmony and prosperity. The hope for divine intervention which would bring political redemption in the affairs of the nation often expressed in Biblical prophecy (*Nahum* 1-2:2; *Jer.* 3:17-18) is probably the foundation stone on which the messianic idea is built. *Amos* 9:1-4, 7-9 pictures the future golden age as a re-establishment of the national state under a scion of David. It is to be an era of blessedness and righteousness and great agricultural fertility (*Amos* 9:13-14; cf. *Lev.* 25:5; *Sybilline Books* 3:652, 741-758).

In apocalyptic literature the idea of the Messianic era deepens and develops. There are statements that the Messiah will bring deliverance from Rome, initiate the messianic era and rule until the last judgment (*II Esdras* 12:31-33; 7:26-44, *Syriac Baruch* 36-40, 72-74, 29). *Enoch* 90:20-42 describes a new Jerusalem under the rule of the Messiah which is to be established *after* the last judgment, thus placing the concept definitely in the realm of eschatology.

There is no clear definition of the messianic era in rabbinic literature. Even the terminology is often confused and the phrase "world to come" or "future" seems to be applied in some instances to the messianic times (as in *B.B.* 74b, 122a, *Keth.* 111b, *Yalkut Shimeoni* to *Isa.* 25:8). The rabbis in general conceive the messianic era to be an interim period between this world and the "world to come," that is, of the Kingdom of Heaven. Its advent will be accompanied by the breaking of the Roman yoke and the political liberation of the people of Israel. According to one opinion all the nations of the world, with the sole exception of the Roman empire, will be able to make amends for their wrongdoings and will be forgiven (*Pes.* 118b). The nations will flock to Israel and non-Jews will seek to become converts to Judaism, but there are conflicting opinions as to whether or not these proselytes will be received. According to some authorities their motives will be suspect, since self-interest may well direct their desire for conversion; others on the contrary indicate that they will be welcomed into the Jewish fold (*A.Z.* 3b; *Yeb.* 24b). But the particularistic aspects of the messianic hope serve as a foundation for the hope of universal redemption in which all the children of men will share the blessing of an era of universal peace and brotherhood (*Midrash Song of Songs* to 7:1).

The messianic era will be characterized by a deepened devotion to Torah, which will be studied and observed more scrupulously than ever before (*Sifre Deut.* 317). The "days of the Messiah" are transitory and distinct from the "world to come," which will usher in the resurrection, the judgment, and the reign of God (*Sanh.* 99a; *Yalkut Shimeoni* to *Isa.* 25:8, *Midrash Ex.* 15:21).

Popular fancy ran riot during the rabbinic period, picturing the material blessings of the messianic time. The land of Israel will be fabulously fertile (*Sab.* 30b, *Keth.* 111b), each grain of wheat the size of a large bullock's two kidneys, each grape will yield at least 30 jars of wine, and the like. Jerusalem will be marvelously extended and rebuilt (*Midrash Song of Songs* to 7:5, *Sifre* to *Deut.* 1:1). There will be a messianic banquet at which the chief delicacy will be the flesh of Leviathan and Behemoth and the banqueters will drink wine which has been preserved in the grape since creation (*B.B.* 74ab, *Midrash Lev.* 22:7, *Ber.* 34b, *Sanh.* 99a).

The messianic era will be immediately preceded by an intensification of social and political woes and by a period of extreme poverty, misfortune and heresy and wars (*heblo shel mashiah,* "the travail of the Messiah," *Sotah* 9:15, *Sanh.* 97a-98a). Just before it is ushered in, the wicked will meet their doom in a great pestilence (*Midrash Song of Songs* to 2:13). It will begin when all are worthy. Sin postpones the advent of the messianic era (*A.Z.* 9a; *Seder Eliyahu Rabbah* 2). Rabbinic literature testifies to innumerable attempts to calculate the time of the coming of the Messiah and the initiation of the messianic era, but it is also filled with warnings against such calculations (*Sanh.* 97a).

Messianic speculation includes prediction of the catastrophic wars of Gog and Magog (*A.Z.* 3b) variously placed by different teachers at the beginning or at the end of the messianic era. The duration of the messianic era is also the subject of much speculation. The idea of a thousand-year period which gave rise to the Christian doctrine of the "millennium" as well as the idea, probably Zoroastrian in origin, of six millennia of strife between good and evil which are to be climaxed by the seventh millennium of messianic peace and the reign of God, are both found in rabbinic literature. One scheme has it that this world is to endure six millennia in all and that the last two thousand years will constitute the messianic era.

Among other varying estimates of the duration of the messianic period are these: 40 years, 70 years, three generations, 365 years, 400 years, six hundred years, 7000 years, and one view that the years of the messianic period are uncountable (*Sanh.* 99a, *Yalkut Shimeoni* to *Ps.* 72:5 par. 806, *Pesikta Rabbathi* 1, edit. Friedmann, 4ab).

These Messianic speculations had an important part in the history of Israel in the first two centuries of the Christian Era. The final submission to Rome after the deposition of Archelaus (6 C.E.) and the hated rule of the Roman procurators was regarded by fanatics as tokens of the "birth-pangs of the Messiah" and the Zealots began to anticipate the inauguration of the kingdom of God. The procuratorship of Pontius Pilate was marked by revolts, and the teachings of Jesus show traces of anticipation of an immediate Messianic era —though whether these traces are a part of the original message of Jesus or an interpretation placed upon them by his disciples is a moot question. Certainly the gospels contain more than one statement that the present generation shall not taste death until the coming of the kingdom (*Matt.* 16:28 and parallels; cf. *Matt.* 24). Under the procuratorship of Felix two Messianic pretenders arose; the fanatic zeal of the Jews in the Great War against Rome (66-73 C.E.) was strengthened by their belief that the Messianic era was near at hand. The loss of the Temple only increased the speculations as to the coming of the Messiah; the Jews of Egypt revolted a few years later, and those of Mesopotamia flew to arms when a near disaster to the Roman army raised the false hope that a great deliverance was at hand. The futile Bar Kochba revolt (132-35 C.E.) gained adherents even among the most sober of the rabbis. The last spark of such movements in Mediterranean countries flared in Crete in the 5th cent., but as

late as the early Middle Ages Messianic pretenders were reviving hopes of the Messianic era in Western Asia.

Jewish philosophical speculation of the Middle Ages conceived the messianic era to be a future perfect society which God would establish on earth. For Saadia the messianic age was to bring perfection not only to society but also to the lives of individuals, who would each be filled with the Divine Glory (*Emunoth Vedeoth* 8). Maimonides conceived of a messianic kingdom which would bring political independence to Israel reconstituted as a nation on its own soil in Palestine. This was not merely to insure physical security and material well-being but to enable Israel to devote itself "without care or anxiety to the study of the Torah and universal wisdom, so that by their teachings they may guide all mankind to the knowledge of God and enable them also to share in the everlasting joy of the world to come." The material descriptions of fertility, of the new Jerusalem, and of banquets found in rabbinic writings were, according to Maimonides, meant only figuratively. What they intend to indicate is that in time to come man will be able to gain a livelihood without hardship and the expenditure of painful energy. The gradual climb of man away from those primitive instincts which lead him into ways of violence or disrespect for his neighbor will after thousands of years produce the brotherhood and peace which will characterize the messianic era. (Introduction to Commentary on *Sanh.* 10; *Perek Helek;* also *Hilchoth Melachim* 11).

That aspect of messianic aspiration which dealt with the return of the people of Israel to the land of Israel has led many modern Jewish thinkers to claim that Zionism is the "modern garb of the old Messianic hope . . . it aims through a regenerated Israel to help bring about the regeneration of all mankind" (Levinthal, *Judaism,* p. 204; cf. Greenstone, *Messiah Idea in Jewish History,* p. 243 et seq.) Others (see Philipson, *Reform Movement in Judaism,* p. 246 et seq. and p. 492) have sought to divorce the messianic hope from all particularistic implications, with mankind itself as the messiah and a universal order as the messianic era. But modern Jewish thought would be unanimous in saying with one teacher that ". . . at the very bottom of our souls there still persists the saving belief in a messianic future when the earth will no more be full of injustice, and when humanity will be governed by the ideals of justice and righteousness." (Israel Friedlaender, *Past and Present,* p. 158). Thus the platform adopted by American liberal rabbis in 1937 proclaims: "We regard it as our historic task to cooperate with all men in the establishment of the kingdom of God, of universal brotherhood, justice, truth and peace on earth. This is our messianic goal" (*Central Conference of American Rabbis Year Book,* vol. 47, p. 99).

ARTHUR J. LELYVELD.

See also: BEHEMOTH; FUTURE LIFE; GOG AND MAGOG; KINGDOM OF HEAVEN; LEVIATHAN; MILLENNIUM; RESURRECTION.

Lit.: Moore, G. F., *Judaism in the First Centuries of the Christian Era,* vol. 2 (1932) 323 et seq.; Higger, Michael, *The Jewish Utopia* (1932); Greenstone, Julius H., *The Messiah Idea in Jewish History* (1906); Silver, Abba Hillel, *A History of Messianic Speculation in Israel* (1927); Kohler, Kaufmann, *Jewish Theology* (1928) 378 et seq.; Sarachek, Joseph, *The Doctrine of the Messiah in Medieval Jewish Literature* (1932).

MESSIANIC MOVEMENTS. Recurrent efforts to usher in the millennium and to resurrect the kingdom of David in miraculous fashion occurred again and again in Jewish history. During the last years of the Second Commonwealth (1st cent. C.E.) the Roman oppression intensified Messianic hopes, as exemplified by the preaching of John the Baptist and Jesus. About 44 C.E. an obscure, self-styled prophet named Theudas attracted a following on the strength of a promise to lead them across the Jordan dry-shod, but his party was massacred by the Romans. Similar treatment was accorded two other pretenders of the same generation, one of whom was an Egyptian Jew. After the fall of the Jewish state in 70 C.E., the Messianic hope was again kindled during the persecution by Emperor Hadrian. The leader of this rebellion, Bar Kochba, was proclaimed king in 132 C.E., and his Messiahship is said to have been acknowledged not only by the Jewish population of Palestine but even by Akiba and other rabbis.

After this rebellion was crushed, no claimant to Messiahship is known to have arisen for three centuries. During the first half of the 5th cent., one (whose real name is unknown) presented himself on the island of Crete and, as a self-styled Moses, persuaded a group of Jews that he would lead them dry-shod to Palestine. Some of them are said to have leaped into the sea with him, with disastrous results. Disillusioned, those who were rescued adopted Christianity. Thereafter, similar minor manifestations are recorded during the following two centuries in Mesopotamia.

During the early period of Moslem rule, of the four known Messianic pretenders three led sectarian movements in opposition to Orthodox Judaism, heralding the emergence of Karaism. Abu Isa al-Isfahani, who flourished about 700 in Persia, claimed to be a prophet and the final precursor of the Messiah. He introduced a number of ascetic practices, such as abstinence from wine and meat, and founded a sect which survived his death by two centuries or more. According to later accounts, he led an army against Almansur and died in battle near Teheran. His disciple, Yudghan of Hamadan, called "the shepherd," continued his master's departures from orthodoxy and was believed by some to be the Messiah. His followers formed another sect, which was likewise still in existence in the 10th cent. A similar figure named Shirini (or Sirini) is mentioned in a responsum of the Gaon Natronai II (about 860). About the year 720 there appeared in or around Mardin (in Mesopotamia) a false Messiah, named Severus, said to have been converted from Christianity. He persuaded his followers to turn over their wealth to him in preparation for the return to Palestine, but he was stopped short by the caliph. (This Severus has been erroneously identified with the Sirini or Serene of the aforementioned responsum, chiefly because his name appears as Serenus in a late Latin passage.)

A decade or two before the First Crusade (1096) an unnamed false Messiah appeared in France, and during the ensuing century the Jewish population in various countries was repeatedly aroused by such visionaries. While the Franco-German communities were a prey to the depredations of the Crusaders, the distant Salonika community and other groups viewed the oncoming struggle for the Holy Land as the signal for the imminent appearance of the Messiah. During the two decades which followed, apparently in reaction to the Almohades' harsh policy, Messiahs arose in Cordova and Fez. At the other extremity of the Jewish world, about 1160, a Persian Jew, David Alroy, summoned the Jews to arise and throw off the Moslem yoke. The Jews of Baghdad promptly responded, turning over their wealth to Alroy's agents for distribution among the poor, and gathering on the roof-tops to watch the Messiah's miraculous flight to Jerusalem. Alroy found military support among the Jews of Azerbaijan, and steps were taken to get possession of the fortified town of Amadia. Threatening retaliation against Persian Jewry, the Sultan brought pressure to bear on the exilarch at Baghdad to stop Alroy, who, however, disregarded the Jewish leaders. Before his plans could be put into effect, he met his death by assassination. His followers, the Menahemite sect, continued to exist in Persia for several centuries.

The sufferings of the Jews of Yemen during the same period gave rise to a pretender in their midst, but the Yemenite ruler had him executed (about 1170). The local Jewish leader applied to Maimonides for guidance during this episode, and the famous philosopher took a stand against calculations as to the date of the beginning of the Messianic era and against movements led by pretenders. Nevertheless, Maimonides' own family had a tradition that the Messiah was expected in the year 1216. In the decade following Maimonides' epistle to Yemen, the tension caused by the Third Crusade again aroused widespread Messianic expectations. Half a century later the advance of the Mongol horde into Eastern Europe (1240) again kindled millennial hopes among the Jews.

The development of the Cabala lent fresh impetus to the Messianic hope, as evidenced by the career of Abraham ben Samuel Abulafia (1240-92). In the course of his travels he sought an audience with Pope Nicholas III (1277-80), intending, at the risk of his life, to convert him to Judaism. Escaping, he proceeded to Messina in Sicily, where he proclaimed himself Messiah until exposed by Solomon ibn Adret of Barcelona.

During the century preceding the expulsion of the Spanish Jews, Messianic hopes prevailed among many of them, and following the catastrophe of 1492 the chief pretenders were products of Spanish Jewish mysticism and scions of exiles from the Iberian peninsula. The career of the Marrano pretender, Solomon Molcho (flourished 1525-32), was stimulated by David Reubeni, who arrived in Italy from the East, posing as a prince and general of a Jewish kingdom in Arabia. He was received in audience by Pope Clement VII at Rome (1525) and proposed an alliance for the purpose of defeating the Turks. He was encouraged to proceed to Portugal to solicit the aid of John III, and Reubeni took advantage of his visit to establish contact with the Marranos in that kingdom. One of them, Diogo Pires, gave up a government post in order to return to Judaism and fled to Turkey, where he embraced his ancestral faith and changed his name to Solomon Molcho. Feeling inspired to assume Messianic leadership, Molcho came to Rome, where he created a sensation by foretelling the overflowing of the Tiber and an earthquake (1530-31) before their actual occurrence. However, he aroused opposition as well as enthusiasm, and after having been denounced to and condemned by the Inquisition escaped from Rome with the connivance of the pope. After he had rejoined Reuben, the two enthusiasts went to Regensburg to obtain an interview with Emperor Charles V. Whether or not Molcho attempted to convert the emperor, he was sent back to Italy to be tried again by the Inquisition. He was again condemned to death and was never heard of thereafter.

The famous Cabalist, Isaac Luria (1534-72), developed his Messianic delusions while leading a solitary ascetic life in Egypt. After settling in Safed, Palestine, then the great center of Jewish mysticism, he gathered a following which acknowledged him to be the Messiah of Joseph's line and the immediate precursor of the Davidic Messiah. During the closing years of his life his closest disciple was Hayim Vital, who was Luria's successor as leader of his circle in Safed and in the role of Messianic precursor.

The intensive cultivation of the mystic life, particularly among oriental Jews, brought the Messianic hope to a climax during the 17th cent. Millennial calculations were rife, and in far-off Mexico the Marranos awaited the advent in 1642 to 1643, fixing their attention on a youth named Gaspar Vaez Sevilla.

The most famous of all false Messiahs, Sabbatai Zevi (1626-76), was born in Smyrna and in his 'teens became a devotee of Luria's system of mysticism. He gave the first overt indication of his ambition in 1648, the year to which Cabalists had looked forward as that of the Messiah's advent, when he pronounced the ineffable name YHVH. For this offense he was excommunicated, and thereafter spent some years in Constantinople and Salonika. While his attempt to gain recognition did not show immediate results, the mood of the Jewish world was becoming more receptive to his propaganda as a result of the harrowing decade 1648 to 1658 ushered in by the Chmielnicki massacres in Poland. After a sojourn in Egypt and in Jerusalem, Sabbatai acquired a wealthy sponsor, a "prophet" in the person of Nathan of Gaza, and a helpmate, Sarah, a young Jewess who had become unbalanced because of her experiences during the massacres in Poland.

So rapidly did the movement spread that when the "Messiah" returned to his native Smyrna (1665) he was given a great ovation, and the majority of Jews throughout the world acknowledged the pretender's claims. The first setback came when Sabbatai journeyed to Constantinople to receive the Sultan's homage, and was instead imprisoned at Abydos. The pretender maintained his role in prison, but was forced into a more difficult position by a "prophet" from Poland, Nehemiah Cohen. This visitor rejected Sabbatai's claims, and after turning Moslem denounced him to the authorities as a conspirator. To save his life, Sabbatai accepted Islam, on September 16, 1666, thereby losing all but a small part of his following.

The Sabbatian movement continued under various forms down to the end of the 19th cent. and later. Abraham (Miguel) Cardoso presented himself as a reincarnation of Sabbatai, while Mordecai of Eisenstadt, an eloquent preacher, asserted that the deceased hero was his own precursor. Those disciples who had followed the master's example in adopting Islam founded a sect known as the Dönmeh, which numbered thousands of adherents in Turkey, some of whom have undoubtedly continued faithful to Sabbatai's memory. During the second half of the 18th cent., Polish Jewry was seriously menaced by the adventurer Jacob Leibovicz Frank (1726-91), founder of the Frankist sect which acknowledged him as Messiah.

See also: FRANK, JACOB LEIBOVICZ, AND THE FRANKIST MOVEMENT; SABBATAI ZEVI.   JOSHUA STARR.

Lit.: Hyamson, A. M., in *Encyclopaedia of Religion and Ethics,* vol. 8, pp. 581-88; Greenstone, J. H., *The Messiah Idea in Jewish History* (1906); Silver, A. H., *Messianic Speculation in Israel* (1927); "A Letter by Maimonides to the Jews of South Arabia," in *Jewish Quarterly Review,* new series, vol. 25 (1934) 330-69; Dubnow, S. M., *History of the Jews in Russia and Poland* (1916), vol. 1, pp. 207, 211-22; Baron, S. W., *Social and Religious History of the Jews* (1937), vol. 1, pp. 345-46; vol. 2, pp. 78-85; vol. 3, pp. 114-15; Vogelstein, H., *History of the Jews in Rome* (1941) 177-79, 247-52; Roth, C., *History of the Marranos* (1932 and 1941) 146-49, 172, 249-51; Friedlaender, I., "Jewish Arabic Studies," *Jewish Quarterly Review,* new series, vol. 1 (1910-11) 183-215; vol. 2, pp. 481-516; vol. 3, pp. 235-300; Baer, *Die Juden im christlichen Spanien* (1929-36), vol. 1, part 1, pp. 718-20; part 2, pp. 437-43, 468-72, 513-15, 528-42; Scholem, G., in *Zion* (quarterly), vol. 6 (1941) 119-47, 85-100; Epstein, J. N., and Aescoly, A. Z., in *Tarbiz, vol.* 2 (1940) 207-19; Heller, B., in *Revue des études juives,* vol. 84 (1927) 1-137; vol. 85 (1928) 56-62; Starr, J., *The Jews in the Byzantine Empire* (1939) 73-75, 92, 203-8; Mann, J., *Texts and Studies in Jewish History and Literature* (1931), vol. 1, pp. 34-44.

MESSINA, *see* SICILY.

MESSING, a rabbinical family which originated in Prussia and came to the United States in the 19th cent.

JOSEPH MESSING (b. Argenau, Prussia, 1812; d. London, 1880) occupied several pulpits in various parts of Germany. He was well-known as a Talmudist, and was author of twelve homilies and works on Bible exegesis.

AARON J. MESSING (b. Argenau, Prussia, 1840; d. Chicago, 1916), son of Joseph Messing, was rabbi in Mecklenburg, Germany from 1859 to 1867, when he was called to New York, where he served as rabbi until 1870. Later he was rabbi in San Francisco (1871-91), and from 1891 until his death at B'nai Sholom Temple, Chicago. During his two decades in San Francisco, he founded twelve congregations and twenty-three Sunday schools in various Western states. He was author of several Sunday school textbooks. ABRAHAM JOSEPH MESSING (b. Chicago, 1873), son of Aaron J. Messing, was ordained a rabbi at the Hebrew Union College in 1897, and occupied several posts in Alabama and Illinois.

MAYER MESSING (b. Genivkovo, Prussia, 1843; d. Indianapolis, Ind., 1930) was the second son of Joseph Messing. In 1867 he became rabbi of the Indianapolis Hebrew Congregation, and held this post until his retirement in 1907.

HENRY J. MESSING (b. Gostyn, Posen, 1848; d. St. Louis, 1913) was the third son of Joseph Messing. In 1878, after serving as rabbi in several other American cities, he became rabbi of the United Hebrew Congregation of St. Louis, where he remained for the rest of his life.

ALFRED HENRY MESSING (b. Williamsport, Pa., 1875), the son of Henry J. Messing, was a newspaper editor and advertising executive. He was connected with the St. Louis *Star* from 1900, when he became city editor, until 1904, when he was managing editor; in 1904 he became news editor of the Chicago *Examiner,* and on his retirement in 1919 was its publisher. He came to New York city in 1919, entering various advertising and commercial fields. In 1942 he was living in New York. He was a director of the Federation of Jewish Philanthropic Societies.

MESTEL, YANKEV (JACOB), Yiddish poet and actor, b. Zlotshov, Galicia, 1884. Up to the age of thirteen he attended Heder. In 1905 he completed his course at the Lemberg high school and entered the teachers' seminary and rabbinical school under Professors M. Schur and M. Balaban. He was a teacher at the Lemberg folk school for a period of three years. In 1907 he left for Vienna, where he studied philosophy, graduated from the military school (for officers) and from the state college for acting and directing. His career as an actor and director began in 1910, when he identified himself with the Yiddish theatre of Vienna, a troupe which played in the various cities of Austria, Germany, and Roumania. During the first World War (1914-18) he was a first lieutenant in the Austrian Army, was three times wounded, and received several medals and honors. He became director of the Vienner Freie Yiddisher Folksbiene in 1919.

In 1920 Mestel emigrated to the United States, where he still resided in 1942. His name was closely associated with the Yiddish Art Theatre and the Ben-Ami Repertory Group. He was one of the founders and the first director of the Artef Theatre, also teacher and director of the Artef Studios and of other theatre groups. He was director of the Yiddish division of the Federal Theatre Project. He acted in and directed Yiddish plays in many cities in the United States, Canada, South America, London, Paris and Vienna.

Mestel began his literary career in 1903, when his first critical essays and articles were published in Lemberg. His articles appeared in various publications in Europe and the United States, in the *General Yiddish Encyclopedia* (articles on the theatre), in the *Yung Galitzianer Almanach* (of which he was one of the editors), and in the *Lexikon fun Yiddishn Teater* (of which he was an editor).

His earliest verse was published in 1906, and thereafter his poetry was printed in various newspapers and magazines of Europe and the United States. Among his books of verse and prose are: *Farcholemte Shoen* (Lemberg, 1909); *A Liebes Lied* (Cracow, 1911); *Vita Haizad* (Cracow, 1913); *Dimioines,* a dramatic trilogy in verse form (New York and Vienna, 1921); *Milchome Notitzn fun a Yiddishn Offitzier* (2 vols., Warsaw, 1924), fragments of which were translated into German and Hungarian; *Soldatn un Paiatzn Lieder,* an anthology (Warsaw, 1928); the novel in letter-form *Lukretzias Toit* (Warsaw, 1936).

Mestel translated many plays from German, Polish and English, and wrote scenarios for films which he directed and in which he acted.

Lit.: Reisen, Z., *Lexikon fun der Yiddisher Literatur, Presse un Filologie,* vol. 2 (1927), cols. 458-61; *Lexikon fun Yiddishn Teater* (1931); Niger, S., in *Tog,* Aug. 31, 1924; Balaban, M., in *Literarishe Bletter* (1924), No. 45; Mukdoni, A., in *Morgn-Journal,* May 29, 1925; Zhitnitzki, L., in *Die Presse* (Buenos Aires), June, 1931; Bienenstock, M., in *Nasz Przeglad,* Oct. 30, 1923; Holder, Josef, in *Mult es Jövő,* Feb., 1926.

METAPHYSICS. The term metaphysics originally designated, not a discipline, but a book, or rather a collection of treatises of Aristotle which was called in post-Aristotelian times "metaphysics" ("after the physics") because of its place in the body of the Aristotelian writings. Aristotle himself called the discipline to which the subject matter of that book belongs "First Philosophy" or "First Science" or "Theology." He ascribed to it three functions: knowledge of being as such; investigation of the principles of all sciences dealing with a specific class of "beings" or things; and knowledge of the highest being. As far as the highest being or the highest beings are the incorporeal beings, "metaphysics" came to mean primarily the doctrine, independent of revelation, concerning God and the angels. It is in this sense that metaphysics was conceived of by the Jewish medieval thinkers in general and by Maimonides in particular; the latter identified metaphysics with *ma'aseh merkabah.*

In the modern period the study of the first principles of human knowledge became more and more divorced from metaphysics as the doctrine of incorporeal beings. Since Kant, "metaphysics" frequently means knowledge of the "thing in itself," or of "absolute reality," as distinguished from the "world of phenomena," which is the subject of the sciences. Only when using the term "metaphysics" in this sense can one speak of a materialist metaphysics. Another characteristic implication of that modern view is that metaphysical knowledge is not considered scientific knowledge, but of an either supra-scientific or non-scientific character.

Lit.: For the ancient and medieval concept of metaphysics, see Falaquera, *Reshith Hochmah,* edit. David, pp. 53-55 (translations of important passages from Alfarabi and Avicenna); Maimonides, *Treatise on Logic,* chap. 14. For the modern concept, see Bergson, Henri, *Introduction to Metaphysics.* The most easily accessible summary of medieval metaphysics is to be found in Maimonides, *Mishneh Torah, Hilchoth Yesode Hatorah* 1 and 2.

METATRON, a term for the highest angel, found only in ancient times in Haggadic and Cabalistic literature. He is occasionally identified with the "prince of the presence," with the archangel Michael, and with Enoch after the latter was transformed into a heavenly being. There are many legends and interpretations of Biblical passages (for instance, *Ex.* 24:1) about Metatron, in which he sometimes appears as "recorder" of the merits and sins of mankind, sometimes as the highest godlike mediator, but with a warning against the recognition of two divine powers. He is by far the mightiest angel, the confidant of his Lord, the "prince of the presence" (*sar hapanim*). The numerical value of his name (in its shorter form) is equal to that of Shaddai. In the older Cabala, Metatron appears occasionally (as does Raziel) as the one who inspires higher wisdom; in the *Zohar* he is the archetype of man and even identical with Shaddai.

The name, which, according to Samuel Krauss, is found also among the Druses in the Lebanon, may come from the Latin *metator,* "marker of the boundaries," from the Greek *meta thronon,* "after (or nearest) the divine throne," or from the Persian god Mithra.

Lit.: Schwab, M., *Vocabulaire de l'angélologie* (1897); Krauss, Samuel, *Griechische und lateinische Lehnwörter in Talmud, Midrasch und Targum;* Blau, L., in *Jewish Encyclopedia,* vol. 8, p. 519.

METCHNIKOFF, ÉLIE, biologist, b. province of Kharkov, Russia, 1845; d. Paris, 1916. His mother was the daughter of a rich and cultured Polish Jew who had turned Lutheran. Metchnikoff inherited his mother's cast of mind, and ascribed his love for science to his Jewish descent.

Science appeared early in childhood as his true vocation; and when, in the lycée in Kharkov, he read Buckle's *History of Civilization,* he passionately absorbed the idea that the progress of man depends on science and this creed became his life's religion. On a brief trip to Germany he discovered Darwin's *Origin of Species,* became a fanatical convert to evolutionism and soon began to be absorbed in comparative embryology, choosing to work with the lowest orders of animal life. Eventually this work led to his famous theory of immunity from disease in man.

His early manhood was spent traveling, experimenting, theorizing, meeting and impressing some of Europe's most distinguished scientists. But though he finally received appointments to teach in St. Petersburg, and then in Odessa, where he became professor of zoology in 1870, he was restless, unhappy and deeply pessimistic. He suffered from violent headaches and poor eyesight. Marriage to a young woman in failing health made matters worse, and the struggle against disease and poverty intensified. When this wife died (1873), Metchnikoff made an unsuccessful attempt at suicide.

He then returned to Odessa, and there in 1875 married a young student of his. This second wife, Olga, became the devoted companion of the rest of his life. He settled down to teaching, but in 1882 his relations with the reactionary authorities of the university had become overstrained and he and his wife left for the island of Sicily.

Here, observing through his microscope the englobing action of the moving cells in a starfish larva, Metchnikoff almost instantly formulated his theory of "phagocytosis," and proclaimed it to the scholars of Europe. He had discovered, he said, what makes man immune to invading hostile bacteria. The white blood corpuscles are wandering cells, "phagocytes," and when threatening bacilli get into the body, these cells hasten to the spot to engulf, digest and destroy the bacteria, and thus protect the body.

The next decade or more of Metchnikoff's life was a fierce battle to establish the validity of this theory against the then prevalent opposing idea that it was the chemical action of the blood itself which immunized men from disease. Today the science of immunity, still in its infancy despite these important early researches, takes both theories into account.

In 1888 Metchnikoff accepted Pasteur's offer of a laboratory in his Paris institute; here he spent the rest of his life in research. The laboratory became a great rallying point of young scientists; experiments in numerous infectious diseases were constantly under way.

By the beginning of the 20th cent. Metchnikoff's theory, first so violently repudiated (especially in Germany), was generally accepted, and Metchnikoff was honored everywhere, including his native Russia. In 1908 he shared the Nobel Prize for medicine with Paul Ehrlich.

Among the notable contributions of his laboratory

Élie Metchnikoff

was the discovery that syphilis could receive effective early treatment at the immediate source of infection by means of calomel ointment. Subsequently Metchnikoff began to publicize his ideas on neutralization of the putrefying bacteria in the large intestine with Bulgarian sour milk; and the whole movement of drinking Bulgarian sour milk for the prolongation of life had a great vogue, despite serious criticism by the medical profession.

In his declining years a confirmed optimist, Metchnikoff looked to science to dispel the disharmonies of life, maintaining that man's span of life is naturally much longer than we now see it, and that after such a long, fully-lived existence death would be painless and welcome. The social and ethical problem was to allow the majority to reach this whole cycle of their natural existence.

Metchnikoff himself died after a long and painful illness, observing to the end his own reactions. He was cremated, and the urn holding his ashes put in the library of the Pasteur Institute.

Included in the long list of publications put out from 1865 to 1916 are his great work, *Immunity in Infectious Diseases* (English trans., 1905), and *Nature of Man* (English trans., 1904).   SHERRY ABEL.

Lit.: Metchnikoff, Olga, *Life of Élie Metchnikoff* (1921).

METEMPSYCHOSIS, *see* SOULS, TRANSMIGRATION OF.

METHIBTA, *see* ACADEMIES.

METHUSELAH, son of Enoch, and eighth in the list of ten names of antediluvians from Adam to Noah (*Gen.* 5:25-27). He is said to have lived 969 years, the longest age recorded in the Bible; hence Methuselah became famous as the oldest man, and a proverbial figure. According to the chronology of *Genesis,* he either died just before or perished in the Flood. The Samaritan Pentateuch assigns him 720 years of life, which terminate at the time of the Flood. The similarity between Methuselah and Methusael in the Cainite genealogy (*Gen.* 4:18) has caused Bible scholars to suggest that the name and story are borrowed from that source.

METRE, *see* POETRY, HEBREW.

METULLA, *see* COLONIES, AGRICULTURAL.

METURGEMAN, *see* BIBLE EXEGESIS; BIBLE TRANSLATIONS; TARGUM.

METZ, *see* LORRAINE.

METZENBAUM, MYRON FIRTH, physician, b. Cleveland, 1876. He received his B.S. degree from Adalbert College in Cleveland in 1897, and his M.D. degree from Western Reserve University in 1900, following this at various times with graduate study in European medical centers. From 1902 to 1905 Metzenbaum was a lecturer in anatomy at Western Reserve University.

Metzenbaum was awarded the United States Government medal for research in radium at the St. Louis Exposition of 1904. He had previously (1900) introduced drop-ether anesthesia; later he pioneered in adapting scopolamin, commonly known as twilight sleep, to general surgery, and he evolved new methods for treating nasal injuries and infections in children. In 1909 he established in Cleveland an ambulance system under the control of the police department; this system was later adopted throughout the country. Metzenbaum was living in Cleveland in 1942.

Lit.: Kagan, Solomon R., *Jewish Contributions to Medicine in America* (1939) 697.

METZIA, METZIE, *see* PHRASES, POPULAR.

METZKER, YUD (Itzchok), Yiddish short story writer, b. Kozaczyzna, near Borszczow, Galicia, 1901. After attending the high school of Borszczow, he left home when eighteen years old to study at the Humboldt Hochschule in Berlin, Germany. Coming to the United States three years later, he made his home in New York city, working in a fur factory during the day and attending evening sessions of the Jewish Teachers Seminary. In 1932 he was appointed a teacher at the Workmen's Circle Schools.

In 1927 Metzker published his first poem in the *Amerikaner*, a Yiddish weekly. From then on he published many short stories and novelettes in the foremost Yiddish periodicals on two continents. A romantic realist, at his best in mirroring the peasantry of his native Galicia and in poetic descriptions of nature, his works have won the acclaim of Jewish critics who consider him one of the most talented of the younger Yiddish prose writers in America.

Among Metzker's books are: *Toly un Toby* (1936); *Zun und Erd,* a collection of stories (1936) and *Don Yitzchok Abarbanel.* In 1942 his novel, *Die aibike Stime,* was being serially published in issues of the Yiddish daily *Forverts.*

Lit.: Nadir, Moishe, *Morning Freiheit,* May 31, 1937; Rabinowits, S., *Zukunft,* Jan., 1938; Niger, S., *Tog,* Apr. 24, 1938.

METZUDATH USSISHKIN, *see* COLONIES, AGRICULTURAL.

Señor Carvajal, choir leader, and his daughters in front of the Indian synagogue at Mexico City

MEXICO, a federal republic of North America, with about 20,000 Jews (1942) in a total population of 16,000,000. While this Jewish community is comparatively small, Mexico occupies an important place in the history of the Jews in the New World. The period of the conquest of Mexico coincided with the expulsion of the Jews from Spain (1492) and the compulsory general conversion of the Jews in Portugal (1497). Until this compulsory baptism, Portugal was the refuge for the largest group of Spanish Jewish exiles. By royal decree these new converts, frequently referred to as Portuguese New Christians, were not permitted to emigrate without a license. Because of the Bull of Pope Paul III (1537) forbidding any apostate to go to the Indies, the faith of an applicant for an overseas license was carefully scrutinized. However, in order to free themselves of the suspicion and constant surveillance of the Inquisition, many Conversos tried to secure the privilege of sailing to New Spain, as Mexico was then called.

Among the first of these was Hernando Alonso, who accompanied Cortes as a shipbuilder, and as a reward for participating in the conquest of Mexico City in 1521 was granted an encomienda (land grant) whereon he raised cattle and supplied meat to Mexico City. He was followed by other Portuguese New Christians—overseers, doctors, tailors, shoemakers, silversmiths, merchants and traders in Chinese products. Soon they were found in every town in Mexico, where the Castilians resented their commercial competition. The 16th and 17th cent. records of the Mexican Inquisition reveal more than 900 cases against converted Jews. Add the thousands not brought before the ecclesiastical court, and the settlement of Marranos in colonial Mexico reaches large proportions.

The most notable colonizer of Portuguese Jewish origin was the famous conquistador, Luis de Carvajal y de la Cueva. Leaving in Seville his wife, who secretly practised Judaism, Carvajal came to Mexico in 1567, and on June 14, 1579, he received patents from King Philip II of Spain to explore and govern a huge area, extending from the present Tampico, Mexico, to north of San Antonio, Texas. This territory Carvajal called Nuevo Reino de Leon. The communities and mining enterprises around present-day Monterrey are the result of his able administration. Because of his capture of Hawkins' buccaneers, his pacification of the Indians, his explorations and successful government, the viceroy, Conte de Coruña, was advised by his predecessor to rely on the counsel of Carvajal.

The king gave Carvajal the special privilege of inviting to his province one hundred persons, including members of his family, without requiring them to establish proof of their zeal for Christianity. A conflict over political jurisdiction arose between Carvajal and the Conte de Coruña, who used the Inquisition to eliminate his rival by accusing him of secretly practising Judaism. Although this charge was not established, Governor Carvajal was exiled in 1590 for six years because he failed to denounce to the Office of the Inquisition those members of his family who were "living by the law of Moses." At this trial his family was reconciled to the Church, but five years later 120 persons of this group were accused a second time of *judaizante* (judaizing themselves and others), and a number were burned at the auto da fé of 1596. Among these was the Jewish mystic and poet—one of the first Jewish writers in America—Luis Rodriguez de Carvajal, nephew of the governor. He is called "el mozo," the the younger, to distinguish him from the governor, "el viejo," the elder.

Many converted Jews imagined that by going to the New World they could escape the vigilance of the Spanish Inquisition, but even before that Inquisition was officially extended to Mexico, the Mexican Dominican Order assumed inquisitorial powers which later the first bishop, Fray Juan de Zumarago, incorporated into an established episcopal court to try apostates (1538). Before the arrival of the official Inquisition, some twenty-four persons had already been tried for Judaism, the first being Hernando Alonso himself, who was burned at the stake in 1528. It should be understood that the Spanish crown extended the Inquisition to control the colonies politically as well as religiously. With the appointment of Dr. Pedro Moya de Contreras in 1571 as the first Inquisitor to Mexico, many corrupt officials and unprincipled priests were called to account, but considerable time was devoted to hunting out Jews who had lapsed in their loyalty to Catholicism. The extent of this activity is indicated by the fact that Mexico City averaged thirty-four such cases every year from 1574 to 1600 in comparison to the parent tribunal at Toledo, which averaged only one case more per year during the same period. Several autos da fé in Mexico were notorious. In 1574 eighty Judaizers died at the stake. There were sixty and one hundred "sambenitos" (a special garb worn by the forgiven) in 1596 and 1602 respectively, and seventy suits in 1646. The official records of all these cases are preserved in the National Archives of Mexico. In addition, eyewitness accounts of autos da fé in Mexico City may be found in *De origine et progressu officii sanctae Inquisitionis, eiusque dignitate et utilitate,* by Paramus (Madrid, 1598), and *Relacion historiada de las exequias funerales de la Magestad del Rey D. Philippo II, Neustro Senor,* by Ribera Florez (Mexico, 1600).

Of special interest among those acquitted of the charge of judaizing and of limpieza (impurity of blood) were Gregorio Lopez, a prominent monk, and Dr. Cristobal Miranda, Dean of the Cathedral of Yucatan. One Dominican, Fray Hernando de Ojea, disturbed by the apostasy of the Jewish converts, hoped

to persuade them to remain faithful by writing a book for their reading, entitled *La Venida de Christo y Su Vida y Milagros: en que se concuerdan los dos testamentos divinos Viejo y Nuevo* (The Coming of Christ, His Life and Miracles: In Which the Two Divine Testaments Old and New Agree; Medina del Campo, 1602). However, many Inquisitors were more interested in the confiscation of Jewish property than in the conversion of Jewish souls, as is indicated in the condemnation of the prominent merchant, Thomas Tremiño de Sobremonte, in 1638.

The Inquisition had done its work so well that by the time it was suppressed in 1820 it had succeeded in stamping out all but faint memories of Jewish ancestry in the minds of hundreds of Mexican Marranos. Although in the anti-clerical days of 19th cent. liberalism it was popular to attribute Jewish ancestry to such Mexican leaders as Porfirio Diaz or Madero, most Jews as such had disappeared. Some Mexicans today—among them the famous artist, Diego Rivera—speak of their colonial Jewish descent, and there exists a group of about 3,000 Indian Jews who claim Spanish Jewish ancestry. The latter have a synagogue in Mexico City and are led by a Mexican Indian lawyer, B. Ramirez.

It was not the bitter memory of the Inquisition, now suppressed, but rather the greater economic attraction of the United States, which accounted for the small immigration of Jews to Mexico in the second half of the 19th cent. Despite the favor which Diaz showed to European immigration, only 10,000 Jews had arrived in Mexico by 1910. More than half of these were Ashkenazim who came in connection with German, Austrian and American business enterprises. The remainder were Spanish-speaking Levantine Jews, most of whom were peddlers. The latter established a synagogue and relief society, and were encouraged by Professor Francisco Rivas, probably the last surviving descendant of Marrano Jews from Yucatan. This beloved Mexican scholar published a Jewish newspaper, *El Sabado Secreto,* in 1889, at a time when there was little Jewish community life. To aid the indigent Jewish immigrants, Rabbi Martin Zielonka, of El Paso, Texas, helped to found (1908) the Sociedad de Beneficencia Aliance Monte Sinai.

A new chapter in the history of the Jews in Mexico opened after the first World War. Quota restrictions in the United States compelled European Jews driven from their homes by the War to seek refuge elsewhere. Many thousands of Polish Jews, several thousand Arabic-speaking Jews from Syria, and Sephardim from Salonika and Turkey, expelled by the population exchange, entered the open door of Mexico. The American B'nai B'rith rendered them valuable assistance. Mexico became even more inviting when the president, General Plutarco Elias Calles, in a public statement on October 28, 1924, extended "a friendly invitation for immigration into Mexico of Jews who are prepared to join with the Mexican nation in the up-building of the national industries of the country as law-abiding citizens. . . . The government of Mexico in so far as its good offices are needed will help these people to adapt themselves and prosper as citizens of Mexico."

This first official welcome, considered a Jewish Bill of Rights, stimulated for a time the immigration of from 300 to 500 Jews a month. About 6,000 East

Interior of the synagogue at Mexico City

European Jews arrived before immigration quotas were imposed in 1937, because of a combination of economic problems and the rise of Mexican anti-Semitism. The feelings of local shopkeepers against Jewish peddlers were exploited by a few politicians and ex-generals who were supported by Nazi fifth-column activity. These anti-Semitic fascists organized the Gold Shirts in 1934, but an anti-Jewish outbreak in 1939 stirred the labor parties, the public and the government under Cardenas to curb their influence. The break in relations with the Axis powers in 1942 further diminished the anti-Semitic movement.

The modern Jewish community grew apace. At first it was necessary for the B'nai B'rith to establish a bureau in 1924 to assist the new Jewish immigrants with funds, a program of Mexicanization, and placement in industry to eliminate peddling. However, by 1930, the settlement was sufficiently stabilized to show the beginnings of a self-sustaining Jewish community. Peddlers had by 1942 almost disappeared. There were a good number of Jewish shopkeepers, but there were also small textile and leather manufacturers, watchmakers, artisans, workers, and a small percentage of professionals. Some recent Jewish immigrants, such as the builder of the famous Pan-American highway from Laredo to Mexico City (financed by Leon Sourasky), several professors at the National University, engineers, musicians, and art collectors, made notable contributions to Mexican life.

While Jewish families were to be found, in 1942, in almost all the cities and considerable numbers in Monterrey and Guadalajara, 80 per cent of the Jewish population resided in Mexico City. Beginning with 1939, a Central Jewish Committee attempted to coordinate community work, advise immigrants, deal with the government, and fight anti-Semitism. Members of its executive committee were elected in proportion to the number in the various groups; the Yiddish community was represented by nine, the Spanish Sephardim by three, Arabic Sephardim, two, Germans, two, Hungarians, one, French, one, Anglo-American, one. To help place Jews in industry, a Jewish bank was established with a capitalization of 500,000 pesos. There were two credit loan societies in 1942, the larger called Nidchei Israel, and a Jewish Chamber of Commerce. A decided cultural and religious advance came with the growth of the Yiddish-speaking community. A Yiddish newspaper, *Der Veg,* was published three times a week from 1929 on. (A Spanish language weekly, *La Verdad,* was short-lived.) A young men's Hebrew association, renamed Centro Cultural de Jovenes Israelitas de Mexico, sponsored an active program.

An incident of American Jewish interest in the religious history of Mexico occurred in 1927. At that time an American good-will mission composed of Protestant clergymen and several rabbis visited Mexico to ascertain for itself the circumstances surrounding the persecution of the Catholic Church by the Calles government. At a historic conference in the palace of the bishop of Tobasco in Mexico City, where this mission met with three bishops of the Catholic Church, Rabbi Isaac Landman was requested by representatives of the bishops and of the good-will mission to preside. The Americans then had an interview with President Plutarco Elias Calles which proved to be instrumental in easing up the government's persecution of the church.

Members of an inter-American good-will meeting held in the patio of the Bishop of Tobasco, Mexico, on January 7, 1927. (l. to r.) Dr. Leopoldo Ruiz, Archbishop of Michoacan; Dr. Pascuel Diaz, Bishop of Tobasco; Rabbi Isaac Landman; Dr. Miguel de la Mora, Bishop of San Luis Potosi

Jewish children attended public schools, but there were in 1942 several parochial schools, and two notable private Jewish schools incorporated into the Mexican federal school system. One was in Monterrey, but a larger one, called Colegio Israelita de Mexico, was in Mexico City. This school, which extends through high school, opened in 1925, and was (1942) housed in splendid buildings; it had (1939) 534 students. Its courses are given in Spanish, Yiddish and Hebrew. Because of its high academic standing, some non-Jews attend. There were a number of religious congregations, but until recently only the Arabic community had a synagogue. In 1942 both the Nidchei Israel and the Spanish Sephardim were building synagogues. All types of philanthropic, Zionist, B'nai B'rith and women's organizations functioned. A Jewish historical and statistical society, recently organized by the prominent citizen, Leon Sourasky, estimated that the Mexican Jewish community in the year 1940 raised 400,000 pesos for local and overseas charity campaigns.

It is obvious that this modern Mexican Jewish community, though less than twenty-five years old, has made notable progress. Its bright future has led many to believe that Mexico might become a refuge for German Jews. Approximately 700 have been admitted since 1933, but several poorly planned agricultural projects failed. A competent study made by a joint commission of the American Jewish Joint Distribution Committee and the American Friends Society in 1939 came to the conclusion that with proper financing and guidance and sympathetic encouragement from the government, a Jewish agricultural colonization in Mexico offers great possibilities for the mutual advantage of the Jewish settler and the economy of Mexico.   HENRY E. KAGAN.

Lit.: Publicaciones del archivo general de la nacion: 1. *Los judíos en la Nueva España, Seleccion de documentos del siglo XVI* (1932) 2. *Proceso de Luis de Carvajal (el mozo)* (1935); Medina, José Toribio, *Historia del Tribunal del Santo Oficio de la Inquisicion en Mexico* (1905); Palaccio, D. Vincente Rivo, *Mexico a traves los siglos,* vol. 2 (republished, 1940); Robles, Vito Alessio, *Coahuila y Texas en la epoca colonial* (1928); Amador de los Rios, José, *Historia de los judíos de España y Portugal* (1875); idem, *Estudios historicos, politicos y literarios sobre los judíos de España* (1848); Lea, Henry Charles, *The Inquisition in Spanish America* (1888); Roth, Cecil, *A History of the Marranos* (1932); Adler, Cyrus, "Trial of Jorge de Almeida by the Inquisition in Mexico," *Publications of the American Jewish Historical Society,* No. 4 (1896) 27-79; Kohut,

George Alexander, "Jewish Martyrs of the Inquisition in South America," *ibid.* (1896) 101-87; *ibid.,* No. 7 (1899); Ricard, Robert, "Pour une étude du Judaisme portugais au Mexique pendant la période coloniale," *Revue d'histoire moderne,* Aug., 1939; Hexter, M. B., "The Jews in Mexico," *Jewish Social Service Quarterly,* March and June, 1926; *Der Veg,* edit. M. Rosenberg, Jubilee number, Jan. 1940; Kahan, Solomon, "The Jewish Community in Mexico," *Contemporary Jewish Record,* May-June, 1940, pp. 253-63; Zielonka, Martin, in *Central Conference of American Rabbis Year Book,* vol. 33 (1923) 425-43; Weinfeld, Eduardo, "Los judíos en Mexico," *Judaica* (Buenos Aires), July, 1940, vol. 15, pp. 3-14.

MEYER, ADOLF CHARLES, socialist agitator and author, b. Copenhagen, Denmark, 1858; d. Skodsborg, near Copenhagen, 1938. The son of a Jewish father and a Christian mother, Meyer grew up in a freethinking atmosphere. When he became an apprentice in a sewing-machine factory he attracted attention by his speeches, poems, and contributions to Pio's *Social-Democraten.* In 1876 he entered the directorate of the Danish trade unions, and in 1878 was one of the founders of the Danish Social Democratic Party; in 1885 he was elected member of its directorate. In 1886 he founded the Karl Marx Club, whose president he was for many years. Meyer participated in the international workers' congress at Paris (1889). In the electoral contests of 1887, 1890 and 1892 Meyer was defeated, but from 1895 to 1932 he was member of the Folkething, the Danish lower house.

Meyer was a powerful agitator rather than a political leader, and became more and more interested in the cultural reform of the working classes, winning the sobriquet "labor's troubadour." He became a pioneer in the workers' sports movement, and supervised workers' choral societies as well as public high schools. Meyer published his political poems *Frie Sange* in 1894, and *Under rød Flag* in 1892. His poem on the first of May became popular among Danish socialists. He adapted Pottier's *Internationale* to the Danish language. He published non-political poems, *Nattern Sange* (Songs of the Night; 1906) and *Minde digte* (Memorial poems; 1920). Creating popular novels and plays, Meyer became stage manager of the Thalia Theater in Copenhagen from 1907 to 1915. He published his memoirs under the title of *En agitators Erindringer* (1929-33).

MEYER, ADOLPH, American Congressman, b. Natchez, Miss., 1842; d. New Orleans, 1908. While a student at the University of Virginia he enlisted in the Confederate Army and served until the close of the Civil War, attaining the rank of assistant adjutant general. Later he engaged in banking in New Orleans. In 1881 he was appointed brigadier general of the First Brigade of the Louisiana State National Guard, embracing all the uniformed militia in the state. He was elected as a Democrat to Congress in 1890, and served from 1891 until his death.

Lit.: *Biographical Dictionary of the American Congress* (1928) 1309; *American Jewish Year Book* (1904-5) 154.

MEYER, ALFRED, physician, b. New York city, 1854. He received his A.B. degree from Columbia University in 1874 and his M.D. degree from the same university in 1877. In 1880 Meyer entered the practice of medicine in New York city. He was clinical professor of medicine at New York University and Bellevue Medical College from 1910 to 1919.

In addition to occupying several consultative posts in New York city hospitals, Meyer was active in antituberculosis work throughout the country. He was, in 1942, honorary director of the National Tuberculosis Association, of which he had been vice-president in 1918 to 1919; he was also, for thirty-five years, a director of the New York Tuberculosis and Health Association, and for a long period chairman of the research advisory board of the National Jewish Hospital for Consumptives. As chairman of the New York State Committee for the International Tuberculosis meeting in Washington in 1908, he raised the funds necessary to bring to New York city the exhibit attached to the meeting. In 1942 Meyer was living in New York city, though he had retired from active work some years earlier.

Lit.: Kagan, Solomon R., *Jewish Contributions to Medicine in America* (1939) 55, 764.

MEYER, ANNIE NATHAN, author and lecturer, b. New York city, 1867. She was the wife of Dr. Alfred Meyer, prominent New York physician. Her great achievement as a pioneer advocate of women's higher education was the founding of Barnard College, the women's school of Columbia University. She herself, after being privately educated, took examinations at Columbia, where at that time women were excluded as students. Then in 1888 she obtained the sanction of the university trustees for the establishment of a women's school, and in the following year it was opened. Serving continuously on the board of trustees since its inception, Mrs. Meyer was the most powerful single propagandist for Barnard's expansion, and was in turn honored by the institution. In 1937 the Annie Nathan Meyer Drama Library was established at the school; to it Mrs. Meyer donated her own large collection of books on the drama, a subject in which she was especially interested.

Her writings include a number of plays of her own, among them: *The District Attorney* (produced 1920); *The Advertising of Kate* (produced 1921); *Black Souls* (produced and published, 1932). The latter is a study of miscegenation in the South. Mrs. Meyer published also *Woman's Work in America* (1891); *Robert Annys* (1901); *The Dominant Sex* (1911); *The Dreamer* (1912); *Barnard Beginnings* (1935).

Mrs. Meyer was a prominent lecturer on art and education, and appeared in other public capacities. During the first World War she was chairman of the emergency committee of the American Home Economics Association, and later cooperated with Herbert Hoover in his food savings plan. She was active in the National Conference of Christians and Jews.

She was a member of the Daughters of the American Revolution.

Lit.: *American Hebrew,* Feb. 19, 1937, p. 906; Askowith, Dora, *Three Outstanding Women* (1941).

MEYER, ARTHUR, journalist, b. Le Havre, France, 1844; d. Paris, 1924. He studied law, and became an officer in a French prefecture until he was dismissed in 1870 when the empire of Napoleon III ended. He then became a broker and frequented the bourse of Paris. One of his customers was Esterhazy, who became famous in the Dreyfus case. In the early 1870's Meyer and Esterhazy joined in many speculations at the bourse of Paris. Even before Meyer was dismissed from his office at the prefecture he was engaged in the newspaper business. In 1865 he acquired the *Gaulois,* sold it in 1866, acquired the *Paris-Journal* (1867), and sold it a few years later.

In 1879, Meyer again acquired the *Gaulois,* which became the official paper of the prince imperial, son of Napoleon III, but after the prince's death Meyer sold it, abandoning Bonapartism, and reacquired (1881) the *Paris-Journal.* But a few months thereafter he acquired for the third time the *Gaulois,* then devoted to royalism. Until his death he remained an ardent royalist. He supported General Boulanger because he expected that the general, when victorious, would restore the monarchy of the house of Bourbon.

In the Dreyfus Case Meyer was a rabid anti-Dreyfusard, although he immediately recognized Esterhazy's handwriting when the notorious "bordereau" (memorandum) was published. Meyer was unconcerned about the anti-Semitic attitude of the anti-Dreyfusards; on the contrary, he supported anti-Semitism as a weapon in the struggle for royalism. Nevertheless, radical anti-Semites scorned Meyer, who was forced into a duel with Drumont. He became a convert to Catholicism shortly before the end of the Dreyfus trial.

In his memoirs Meyer attempted to justify his attitude. He claimed to be fair towards the Jews. He was ready to acknowledge their virtues as well as their sins. He even detested anti-Semitism, but he characterized it as "a poisonous plant grown up from the Third Republic." He made republicanism responsible for anti-Semitism, and contended that the Jews in France would have been untroubled had the old monarchy continued to exist. Although Meyer was an unscrupulous polemist, his political adversaries did not hate him personally. He was a "boulevardier," and as an "old Parisien of Paris" he had no enemies. He published his memoirs under the titles of *Ce que mes yeux ont vu* (1911), *Ce que je peux dire* (1912), and *Ce qu'il faut faire* (1914). The author of these memoirs was no longer the polemist of his earlier days; he was a prattler, ready to captivate dissenting readers, although he remained a champion of conservatism. He related interesting details of his life and the history of modern France, but he jumbled them up with gossip and false statements and sought to establish facts which his eyes never saw and his ears never heard.

MEYER, SIR CARL, banker and industrialist, b. Hamburg, Germany, 1851; d. London, 1922. He went to England in his early manhood, and was naturalized there in 1877. He entered the banking house of N. M. Rothschild and Sons, and in 1880 was sent to South Africa, where he became chief representative of the Rothschilds. When Cecil Rhodes turned for financial assistance to the Rothschilds, Meyer prepared the decisive transactions and acted as intermediary in the arrangement which enabled Rhodes to acquire the majority of the shares in De Beers Mines. From 1888 to 1921 Meyer was member of the board of De Beers, and subsequently chairman of the London Committee of De Beers. Throughout his stay in South Africa he looked after also the Rothschilds' interests in the Rhodes concern, even after his outward connections with the Rothschilds had been severed and he himself owned several important mining enterprises. Meyer often collaborated with Sir Alfred Beit and Sir Ernest Cassel. After he left South Africa he was for several years director of the National Bank of Egypt. In 1911 he was knighted because of his ardent support of the Shakespeare Memorial.

LADY ADELE LEVIS MEYER, his wife, was interested in social reform. In 1909 she published, together with C. Black, *Makers of Our Clothes,* the result of a year's investigation into the work of women in the tailoring, dressmaking and underclothing trades at London. Together with her son, Sir Frank Cecil, and her daughter, Marjorie, she became converted to Catholicism.

MEYER, CHARLES HARRISON, lawyer, b. New York city, 1892. Admitted to the New York bar in 1914, he practised with several firms, and in 1938 became a member of Skutch, Meyer and Burton. An authority on financial law, he contributed articles dealing with stock brokerage and economic problems of securities markets to business and legal journals. His publications include: *The Law of Stock Brokers and Stock Exchanges* (1931); supplements, 1932, 1933 and 1936); *The Securities Exchange Act of 1934 Analyzed and Explained* (1934); *Legal Pitfalls of the Stock Brokerage Business* (1936).

During the first World War, Meyer served on the legal advisory board of the Selective Draft Service, and was government appeal agent from 1917 to 1918. From 1916 to 1922 he was a trustee and secretary of the Corner House.

MEYER, DAVID AMSEL, financier, b. Copenhagen, Denmark, 1755; d. Copenhagen, 1813. He was a son of Amsel Jacob Meyer (1728-98), who went from Altona to Copenhagen, and the younger brother of Moses Amsel Meyer (1755-82), the first Jew admitted to citizenship in Copenhagen. Meyer was interested in overseas trade, and in 1780 was the first Jew who, against the bitter opposition of Christian wholesalers, became a wholesale trader-citizen. In 1793 he founded the firm of Meyer and Trier, and succeeded in surviving many grave crises caused by the revolutionary wars.

The political situation of Denmark led Meyer to an absorption in state finances, and for many years he was on friendly terms with the outstanding Danish Min-

Eduard Meyer

ister, Count Schimmelmann. From 1806 on Meyer collaborated officially with the Danish government. He criticized the issuance and circulation of non-consolidated Danish public funds, and he evolved the idea of 5 per cent treasury bonds which won public confidence. Supported by King Frederick VI of Denmark, who was persuaded in audience with Meyer, he succeeded in counteracting Denmark's financial panic. But by combatting speculators he gained many influential enemies.

In 1811 Meyer retired from his firm of Meyer and Trier to become an official agent of the Danish government. While Danish public funds were about 33 1/3 per cent below par before Meyer managed them, they rose to about 20 per cent above par in 1812. Meyer's influence caused a "literary Jewish feud," yet even his adversaries were forced to acknowledge his financial genius. Nor could they gainsay his patriotism. Meyer bequeathed his fortune to Jewish schools, to Jewish charitable institutions, and to the general promotion of science in Denmark.

MEYER, EDUARD, non-Jewish historian and Bible exegete, b. Hamburg, Germany, 1855; d. Berlin, 1930. He was professor of ancient history at the Universities of Breslau (from 1855 on), Halle (from 1889 on) and Berlin (1903-27). In 1927, as professor emeritus, he visited Palestine and delivered a lecture at the Hebrew University, Jerusalem.

He was noted as an authority on the civilizations of ancient Egypt and the Near East. He explored the origins of the great religions as powerful factors in the history of the peoples professing them. Of especial Jewish interest are his works: *Die Entstehung des Judentums* (1896); *Die Israeliten und ihre Nachbarstämme* (1906; B. Luther, co-author); *Der Papyrusfund von Elephantine* (1912); *Reich und Kultur der Chetiter* (1914). He had a controversy with Julius Wellhausen concerning the authenticity of the documents referred to in *Ezra* and of the list of names in *Nehemiah.* His essay "Die Gemeinde des neuen Bundes im Lande Damaskus" (in *Abhandlungen der preussischen Akademie der Wissenschaften,* philosophisch-

Eugene Meyer, Jr.

historische Klasse, 1919, No. 9) interpreted in the light of religious ferment under the Seleucides two manuscripts published by Solomon Schechter (in *Documents of Jewish Sectaries*, vol. 1). His *Geschichte des Altertums* (5 vols., 1884-1905; new edition, 4 vols., 1925-39), which has become a classic, includes a history of the Jewish state and evaluates the influence of social and economic factors on the evolution of Judaism. In *Ursprung und Anfänge des Christentums* (3 vols., 1921-23), he dealt with the relation between Judaism and early Christianity.

Meyer looked upon Judaism only as a forerunner of Christianity. While he appreciated prophetism, he censured Talmudic and rabbinic Judaism for what he termed its sterility and for its forcing of mystic thought into the straightjacket of a logical formalism. In general he was rather unsympathetic toward Jews and Judaism.

MEYER, ERICH, physician, b. Berlin, 1874; d. in the Alps, 1927. He was educated at the Universities of Heidelberg and Munich, lecturer in 1905. His fruitful activities at the University of Strasbourg, where he was appointed associate professor (1914), were interrupted by the first World War. He served at the front and later as medical head of an army hospital in Strasbourg. His experiences during the War were published posthumously (Munich, 1929) under the title *Der unbekannte Soldat, Erlebnis und Gedanken eines Truppenarztes an der Westfront*. The French expelled Meyer from Strasbourg in 1918. Thereafter he lectured at the Universities of Frankfort and Göttingen. In September, 1927, he met with an accidental death in the Alps.

His most important works are *Zur Pathologie und Physiologie des Durstes* (1918) and *Mikroskopie und Chemie am Krankenbett* (10th ed., 1922). He was co-editor of the periodical *Ergebnisse der inneren Medizin und Kinderheilkunde*, and published in other periodi-

cals important essays on heart diseases and diseases of the kidneys.

MEYER, ERNST (AHRON), painter, b. Altona, Schleswig-Holstein, 1797; d. Rome, 1861. He studied at the Copenhagen Art Academy under C. A. Lerentzen and Eckersberg, and as a pupil of the Model School received a silver medal in 1816 and 1818. In 1819 he went to Munich, where he studied for three years under Cornelius. In 1824 Meyer went to Naples and Amalfi, and finally settled at Rome in 1833. Meyer had close relations with the sculptor Thorwaldsen. In 1843 he became a member of the Copenhagen Academy, and was awarded the Danebrog order. Many of his pictures were placed in the Copenhagen Museum, in the Thorwaldsen Museum, in the Berlin National Gallery, and in the Hamburg Kunsthalle. His painting *Fishermen Landing the Tourists at Capri*, which was exhibited by the Copenhagen Academy in 1837, became very popular. Other paintings of his are: *Scene at a Well near a Capuchin Monastery* (1827); *A Neapolitan Fisher Family* (1833); *A Fisherman Observing the Wind; Parents Leading Their Son to the Cloister.* He made copies of several of his works.

Lit.: Thieme, U., and Becker, F., *Allgemeines Lexikon der bildenden Künstler*, vol. 24, p. 470; Bryan's *Dictionary of Painters and Engravers*, vol. 3, p. 331; *Salmonsens Konversations Leksikon*, vol. 16, p. 1056.

MEYER, EUGENE, JR., financial expert and publisher, b. Los Angeles, 1875.

The son of the late Eugene Meyer, international banker, young Meyer went abroad after his graduation from Yale University to study languages and European banking. On his return he entered his father's business, but shortly thereafter, in 1901, organized his own firm of Eugene Meyer Jr. and Company. He became a power in numerous corporations. He dissolved his business in 1917.

Considered one of the keenest financial minds in the United States, he gained exceptional repute as creator and administrator of projects designed to link government finance to private industry and agriculture. Democratic and Republican presidents alike enlisted his talents, and publicly acclaimed them.

The year 1917 marked his entrance into government service. Sponsored by Bernard Baruch, he went to Washington, D. C., and there stepped from one war job into another with spectacular success. As adviser on non-ferrous metals, he immediately was able to save the government millions. As assistant to the Secretary of War on aircraft production, he inspired reorganization of that department; he was also a member of the War Savings Committee. Finally President Woodrow Wilson appointed him director (1918), then manager of the War Finance Corporation, which was to help finance business needed for the war effort. Here serving under three presidents, he remained until the corporation's final dissolution in 1925; his record achievement: back into the United States treasury went all the capital loaned out by the corporation, and a substantial profit as well.

Then in 1927 President Calvin Coolidge called Meyer in as a "trouble-shooter" to reorganize the Federal Farm Loan Board. Meyer was an expert in farm problems, and he was needed to give relief to western farmers without antagonizing Eastern bankers. For Herbert

Hoover, in the years of the depression, Meyer became a one-man brain trust. Hoover appointed him, in 1930, governor of the Federal Reserve Board; again he was expected to solve the farm problem. Meyer then conceived and organized the Reconstruction Finance Corporation (1932), to prime the country's dying business; he served as chairman for six months, reputedly resigning over difficulties with Secretary of the Treasury Ogden Mills. Thereafter he devoted his attention to the Federal Reserve Board, until his resignation in 1933, when Franklin D. Roosevelt took office.

Meyer then bought the Washington *Post* (1933), declaring that he would run it as an independent newspaper. By 1941 he had increased its circulation 173 per cent, and reduced its reputed million dollar a year deficit to about $300,000. An opponent of Roosevelt's domestic measures, he backed the president's foreign policy; in 1941 Roosevelt selected Meyer to serve on the National Defense Mediation Board, set up to speed the war effort.

Meyer believed the future of good government to lie in efficient administration, and in 1904 he established the Yale University Public Service Fund, to train men for government service. He engaged in a number of philanthropies, non-sectarian and Jewish. He was onetime director of the Protectory for Jewish boys at Hawthorne, N. Y., and for nine years a director of Mt. Sinai Hospital. In 1915 he became interested in the University Zionist Society, and served on the Provisional Committee for Zionist affairs.

Meyer's wife, the former Agnes Elizabeth Ernst, was prominently identified with the social and cultural development of Westchester County, where the Meyers had a palatial home in Mt. Kisco. She helped found (1923) and was chairman until 1942 of the Westchester County Recreation Commission.   SHERRY ABEL.

Lit.: Pearson, D., and Allen, R. S., *More Merry-Go-Round* (1932); *American Hebrew,* Jan. 21, 1921, p. 302 et seq.; Sept. 12, 1930, p. 427; *Jewish Tribune,* April 29, 1927, p. 3 et seq.; Sept. 12, 1930, p. 1.

MEYER, JOHN D. (Jonas Daniel), lawyer, b. Arnhem, Holland, 1780; d. Amsterdam, Holland, 1834. Louis Napoleon, upon his accession to the throne of Holland (1806), appointed him director of the *Koninklijke Courant* and bestowed upon him the order of The Lions of Holland, an honor which no Jew had thitherto obtained. Meyer became editor of the official gazette in 1808, and in 1814 took a prominent part in the drafting of the constitution of The Netherlands. Together with Carel Asser, he was the first official in the ministry of justice and a member of the state council. He was a courageous champion of Jewish interests; from 1808 to 1814 he was president of the Dutch consistory of Jewish communities. When, in 1814, self-government of the Jewish communities was substituted for the consistory, and a high commission was appointed by the ministry to supervise and represent their interests, Meyer became president of this commission. His works include: *Esprit, origine et progrès des institutions judiciaires; Principes sur les questions transitoires; Verhandelingen in Geleerode Genootschappen; Mémoire couronné par l'Académie du Gard sur cette question: Déterminez le principe fondamental de l'intérêt, les causes de ses variations et ses rappórts avec la morale."*

MEYER, LEON, French public official, b. Le Havre, France, 1868. A relative of Arthur Meyer, he remained loyal to Judaism. He was elected to the general council of the department of Seine Inférieure (1907) and to the city council of Le Havre in 1912. In 1919, Meyer was elected mayor of Le Havre, and in 1921 became a member of the Chamber of Deputies. He adhered to the Radical party, and was for many years a member of its directorate. In 1925 Premier Herriot appointed Meyer under-secretary of state. He was also under-secretary of state (1929) in the Steeg cabinet. In 1932, he became minister of the mercantile marine in the second Herriot cabinet, and retained this post under the premiership of Paul-Boncour in 1933.

Meyer was opposed to the policy of the Front Populaire, and constantly advocated political moderation and the independence of the Radical party. While this attitude met with violent opposition in his own party, Meyer was generally respected as an authority on mercantile shipping. Under his mayoralty Le Havre became second in importance as a thriving seaport of France and one of the most modern in Europe. Meyer also stimulated shipowners of Le Havre to new construction. He was especially interested in the planning of the subsequently ill-fated (1942) *Normandie.*

In 1940, after the collapse of France, Meyer was forced to retire from office.

MEYER, LOTHAR JULIUS, biological chemist, b. Oldenburg, Germany, 1830; d. Tübingen, Germany, 1895. The son of a physician, he first studied medicine at the Universities of Zurich and Würzburg, and then went to the University of Heidelberg to study under Bunsen and Kirchoff. As a teacher, he was stationed at the Karlsruhe Polytechnic when that institution was turned into a hospital in the Franco-Prussian War (1870-71); Meyer then was active in caring for the wounded. In 1876 he was appointed professor at the University of Tübingen, where he remained until his death.

By his experiments on the blood's absorption of oxygen, nitrogen, carbon monoxide and carbon dioxide he placed the whole problem of this branch of physiological chemistry on a sound scientific basis. His fame chiefly rests, however, on his work with chemical elements; in his famous atomic volume curve he achieved a graphic and significant summary of the relations between the properties of the elements and their atomic weights, and thus contributed to the formulation of the law which states that the properties of the elements are periodic functions of their atomic weights. This is a fundamental law in chemistry.

Similar work was being carried on at the same time by the Russian chemist Mendeleeff, and in 1882 the Royal Society of England awarded the Davy Medal to both scientists. Among Meyer's further contributions to his science was the introduction of the various valency terms to describe the combining power of the elements.

Lit.: Encyclopaedia Britannica, 11th ed., vol. 18, p. 348.

MEYER, SIR MANASSEH, oriental Jewish leader, b. Baghdad, Iraq, 1846; d. Singapore, 1930. He was descended from Haham Sasson ibn Hajmili, and was given a well-grounded Jewish education. As a young boy he went to Calcutta to work in a business owned

Manasseh Meyer

by an uncle of his. But the desire for English schooling impelled him to go to Singapore in 1861. In 1867 Meyer entered business in Rangoon, but soon returned to Singapore, where he spent the rest of his life. He became a leading merchant and a dominant figure in the growing Eastern community, collaborating with the various racial groups, all of whose languages he spoke.

Meyer was for many years on the municipal commission of Singapore, and he founded the science department of Raffles College. His role in the Jewish life of the city was that of uncrowned potentate. He built the Jewish School for Boys and the Singapore synagogue, to which he provided special transportation. He founded the first Zionist society in Singapore—the first Zionist society in the whole Far East. A Yeshiva in Jerusalem was built and maintained by Meyer. He was knighted in 1929.

Lit.: *Jewish Tribune*, Jan. 10, 1930, pp. 2, 4-5.

MEYER, MARIANNE, friend of Goethe, sister of Sarah, b. Berlin, about 1770; d. Vienna, 1812. After disagreeing with her father, who was Orthodox, Marianne severed relations with her family when she came of age, and embraced Protestantism. She was pampered by Berlin society because of her extraordinary beauty and keen intellect. Many noblemen became enamored of her, and even jealous women would not deny Marianne's attractiveness. Count Gessler, minister of Saxony to the court of Prussia, asked her hand in marriage, as did Count Bernstorff, son of then powerful minister of Denmark. But Marianne married Prince Henry XIV of Reuss, an aged and ugly man of keen wit. The marriage was kept secret, but when the prince died (1799) the dynasty of Reuss and the government of the small principality had to consider Marianne's claim to the title Princess of Reuss. Through the intercession of emperor Francis II, a compromise was reached and Marianne became Baroness of

Eybenberg. Subsequently she resided at Vienna, where her home was frequented by princes, ministers and illustrious foreigners.

But Marianne's most illustrious friend did not visit her home at Vienna, preferring to meet her at various times at Karlsbad and elsewhere. This was the poet Goethe, who had met Marianne in 1793 at Frankfort, having been previously acquainted with Prince Henry of Reuss during the campaign in France (1792). Goethe fell in love with Marianne and became her ardent friend. She was his confidante in literary affairs, the first to read his manuscript of *Die Wahlverwandtschaften,* and many minor poems. Goethe also appreciated her epistolary talent; even when his ardor had cooled, he awaited her missives impatiently. Goethe utilized some of Marianne's sayings in his writings; in particular, her comments on women were perpetuated in Goethe's *Maximen und Reflexionen.* At times, however, Goethe was disconcerted by the boldness of her ideas and the trenchancy of her judgment. Goethe said that she had "sweet lips and a sharp tongue."

Lit.: Sauer, August, *Goethe und Osterreich* (1903).

MEYER, MARTIN A., rabbi, b. San Francisco, 1879; d. San Francisco, 1923. He was graduated from the Hebrew Union College in 1901, obtained a fellowship at the American School in Jerusalem as the result of a competitive examination (1901-2), and received his Ph.D. degree from Columbia University (1906). He was rabbi of Temple Beth Emeth of Albany, N. Y. (1902-6), Temple Israel of Brooklyn, N. Y. (1906-10) and Temple Emanu-El of San Francisco from 1910 to his death. Here he occupied a notable position as one of the leading rabbis of the Pacific Coast. He was president of the California Conference of Social Work, the Big Brother Movement of San Francisco, the Pacific Coast branch of the Jewish Chautauqua and the Young Men's Hebrew Association, a member of the California Commission of Charities and Corrections (1911-20), of which he was president for eight years, and a vice-president of the Jewish Publication Society of America. During the first World War he served with the overseas American Red Cross in France (1918-19). He was also a member of many national Jewish committees, including the American Jewish Congress, the Zionist Organization of America, and the Palestine Restoration Fund. He wrote: *The History of the City of Gaza* (1906); *Jew and Non-Jew* (1913); *Methods of Teaching Post-Biblical History and Literature* (1915); historical sketches of the Jews of California. He was a contributor to the *Jewish Encyclopedia,* editor of the periodical *Emanu-El* (1910-11), and a member of the board of consulting editors of the *Menorah Journal* when it was first launched.

Lit.: *Publications of the American Jewish Historical Society,* No. 29 (1925) 179-81; *American Jewish Year Book,* vol. 27 (1925-26) 246-59.

MEYER, RAPHAEL LUDWIG, Danish philologist, b. Copenhagen, Denmark, 1869; d. Copenhagen, 1925. He studied German philology at Copenhagen from 1887, and in 1893 began to teach German and to translate into Danish. From 1897 to 1899 he was assistant librarian at the University of Copenhagen. In 1899 he was granted a scholarship by the Carlsberg Foundation, and went to Rome to study manuscripts of the library of the Vatican. After his return to Denmark, Meyer was appointed director of the library of the agricultural university, and became well-known because of the new organization of this library. Taking into account the fact that agriculture is Denmark's principal industry and that the success of Danish agriculture depends on the scientific training of farmers, the organization, planned and developed by Meyer, was generally acknowledged as an important aid in the promotion of national welfare.

Meyer published several textbooks for schools. In 1904 he rendered significant service to the history of Danish literature and to modern philosophy by editing *Kierkegaards Papirer,* which proved to be a source of stimulation to many great thinkers of many European nations. In 1906 Meyer completed Peter Hansen's biography of Goethe, and in the following years contributed to the knowledge of classical literature through articles in periodicals. In 1918 he published a study on Yiddish, and became the official authority on Yiddish in Denmark.

MEYER, RICHARD MORITZ, historian of literature, b. Berlin, 1860; d. Berlin, 1914. He studied under Wilhelm Scherer, historian of German literature, became lecturer at the University of Berlin in 1886, and was appointed assistant professor in 1903. Having begun his career as a scholar in the field of Old German and Germanic literature, he achieved fame through his prize-winning biography of Goethe (1895; 4th ed., 1913), which was followed by *Geschichte der deutschen Literatur im neunzehnten Jahrhundert* (1899; 7th ed., 1923; revised and enlarged by Hugo Bieber, this edition covering also the first decades of the 20th cent.). Although a brilliant author, Meyer, being a Jew, was on many occasions denied recognition and never became a full professor. To spare his children the handicaps of Jewish life, he had them baptized, endeavoring to justify this act in a public statement.

Among Meyer's many other writings are: *Jonathan Swift und Georg Christian Lichtenberg* (1886); *Die altgermanische Poesie* (1889); *Nietzsche* (1913); *Die Weltliteratur im zwanzigsten Jahrhundert vom deutschen Standpunkt betrachtet* (1913).

MEYER, SAMUEL, French war hero, b. Beaucour, department of Haut-Rhin, France, 1901. He entered the army in 1918, was made a second lieutenant in 1926, a first lieutenant in 1928 and a captain in 1936. During the fighting against the Germans on May 20, 1940, Meyer led a counter-attack directly against the enemy's artillery fire. He remained at the head of his troops, giving orders to the chiefs of his sections, until very seriously wounded. In 1941, despite the pressure of anti-Jewish doctrines imposed by the then victorious German armies, Meyer was cited by General Huntziger for the Legion of Honor and other military awards.

MEYER, SARAH, pupil of Moses Mendelssohn and friend of Goethe, b. Berlin, about 1760; d. Oranienburg, near Berlin, 1828. She was the eldest daughter of a wealthy merchant who was a friend of Lessing and Mendelssohn. The latter guided her education. He taught her philosophy, and when she was twelve read with her some works of Shaftesbury. But she was by no means a grateful disciple. She disliked the philosophy of the Enlightenment period, and preferred Goethe's *Werther.* When Mendelssohn, the following year, came upon her unawares reading *Werther* and writing love-letters to a gentleman friend at Hamburg, the indignant philosopher flung the book into the blazing stove. Sarah came down with a fever, that illness being the first symptom of the excessive irritability with which she was afflicted during her life. Some months later Lessing, visiting Berlin, sought to soothe her by presenting another copy of *Werther.*

At the age of fifteen, Sarah was married to Lipman Wulff. It was an unhappy union and Sarah reproached Mendelssohn for having insisted upon it. After Wulff's death, she married (1799) Baron von Grotthuss, a Prussian officer. In 1795, she became afflicted with a grave neurotic malady. She was nursed in a Jewish home at Berlin. After her convalescence she made the acquaintance of Goethe at Karlsbad, and thenceforth until her death corresponded with Goethe, who became her confidant through his devotion to her sister Marianne. Although Goethe was sometimes troubled about Sarah's irritability, he enjoyed her appreciation of his poetry and esteemed her intellect. He made many references to her in his diaries. Some of his shorter poems were dedicated to Sarah, who often sent him books, objets d'art, caviar, smoked fish, smoked goose, and home-made cakes. From 1806 on her pecuniary circumstances grew wore because of her husband's financial incompetency. In her final years she was forced to earn her living by writing articles and novels. But she never succeeded in editing her novel *Sophie ou la différence de l'éducation.*

Lit.: *Goethe-Jahrbuch,* vol. 14; Goethe, *Tagebücher* and *Briefe.*

MEYER, SELIGMANN, rabbi and author, b. Reichelsheim, Hesse, Germany, 1853; d. Regensburg, Germany, 1925. In 1873 he became preacher at Wetzlar and editor of the *Jüdischer Bote,* appearing at Bonn. From 1876 on he was editor of the *Jüdische Presse* (Berlin), and at the same time studied for a rabbinical diploma at the Hildesheimer seminary and for his Ph.D. degree at the University of Berlin, receiving the latter in 1878 from the University of Leipzig. In 1882 he became municipal rabbi, in 1887 district rabbi at Regensburg. In 1884 he founded a Jewish magazine, *Laubhütte* (later *Deutsche Israelitische Zeitung*), which he edited until his death and which became very popular in South Germany.

Meyer, who in his ministry championed Orthodoxy, was the author of several books and numerous articles in the campaign against the anti-Semitic movement of 1870 to 1880. He also wrote against the Prussian law which was to regulate withdrawal from the Jewish community (1876), and published *Contra Delitzsch,* a protest against Friedrich Delitzsch's biased presentation of the primacy of Babylonian culture over Biblical ethics. Meyer advocated the colonization of Palestine. He was a noted preacher and wielded great influence with the authorities. After the death of C. Werner, he became president of the Bavarian Rabbinical Conference (1918-23).

MEYER, VICTOR, chemist, b. Berlin, 1848; d. Heidelberg, Germany, 1897. His imaginative intellect

Victor Meyer

and ceaseless activity made him an outstanding pioneer in organic chemistry. He entered the University of Heidelberg in 1865, and became Bunsen's most promising pupil. He then studied under the great Baeyer in Berlin, and when he was twenty-four received appointment as director of the chemical laboratory in the Zurich Polytechnic. Here, employing his unusual gift of language, he gained a European reputation as lecturer. The thirteen years at Zurich were fruitful of significant contributions by himself and his pupils, including about 130 papers which enriched the literature of chemistry. To crown his career, he was called to take Bunsen's place at the University of Heidelberg, and thus, at forty, became head of the world's most famous school.

Among his numerous chemical achievements were the discovery of oximes, the determination of the properties of the halogens, and, most brilliant of all, the discovery of thiophene, which he obtained from coal-tar in 1882, thus adding a whole new section to organic chemistry.

Meyer's name is associated also with various forms of laboratory apparatus, notably the device for determining vapor densities. In 1891 the Royal Society awarded him the Davy Medal. Ill-health plagued him through many years; finally, in despair, he committed suicide at Heidelberg.

RICHARD EMIL MEYER (b. Berlin, 1846; d. 1926), chemist, was the brother of Victor Meyer. In 1886 he became instructor at the University of Munich, and in 1889 assistant professor at the Technische Hochschule of Brunswick. He published the *Jahrbuch der Chemie* (vols. 1-28, 1891-1918) and *Vorlesungen über Geschichte der Chemie* (Leipzig, 1922), and wrote a large biography of his brother, *Victor Meyer, Leben und Wirken eines deutschen Chemikers und Naturforschers.*

Lit.: Thorpe, T. E., "Victor Meyer Memorial Lecture," *Journal of the Chemical Society of London* (1900) 169-206.

MEYER, WILLIAM, lawyer and public official, b. Germany, 1883. He was brought to Butte, Mont., at the age of two. In 1902 he received his law degree from New York University, and the following year he was admitted to the bar. Returning to Butte, Meyer became active in political affairs. He was a member of the Montana Legislative Assembly in 1919 and 1920, and subsequently was many times chairman of the Democratic Committee of his county. From 1930 to 1934 he was a member of the Montana State Board of Education. Meyer was also active in Jewish communal affairs and was a director of the National Farm School. He was president of District Grand Lodge No. 4 of the B'nai B'rith (1941-42), and a director of the Western States Region of the Council of Jewish Federations and Welfare Funds, Inc. In 1942 he was living in Butte.

MEYER, SIR WILLIAM STEVENSON, High Commissioner for India, b. London, 1860; d. London, 1922. He was of Jewish descent but a practising Christian. Meyer entered the Indian Civil Service in 1881. From 1886 to 1889 he was assistant secretary to the Madras government. Later he occupied various posts in the Indian government, including that of financial secretary from 1905 to 1909. He retired from the Indian Civil Service in 1918, but was made first High Commissioner for India in 1920. Meyer was knighted in 1909.

MEYER, WILLY, surgeon, b. Minden, Westphalia, Germany, 1858; d. New York city, 1932. He received his medical degree from the University of Bonn in 1880, and until 1884 worked as an assistant in the surgical clinic of the university. In 1884 he came to the United States. Meyer was a professor in clinical surgery at the Women's Medical College in New York from 1886 to 1893. In 1887 he became also an instructor at the New York Post-Graduate School and Hospital. Later he was made a professor, retaining this post until 1918. From 1919 until his death he was professor emeritus.

Meyer's originality and pioneering in the field of surgery made him one of the outstanding practitioners in America. In cystoscopy, hypertrophy of the prostate, gastrostomy, appendectomy and radical excision of breast cancers he evolved new approaches and new techniques, and the breast operation he advocated bears his name. Meyer also presented the theory that malignancy involves chemical changes in the entire organism. He was the author of *Cancer, Its Origin and Development* (1931).

Lit.: Kagan, Solomon R., *Jewish Contributions to Medicine in America* (1939) 206-8, 454.

MEYER-COHN, ALEXANDER, banker, art collector and philanthropist (brother of Heinrich), b. Berlin, 1853; d. Berlin, 1904. He was the eldest son of Meyer Cohn, who rose from a modest start as typesetter to the ownership of a banking house which was called the "trustee of the Junkers" because most of the patrician families of Brandenburg, as well as many Hohenzollerns, entrusted Meyer Cohn with the administration of their fortunes.

Alexander Meyer-Cohn was educated at the Französisches Gymnasium of Berlin, then worked in various positions in Frankfort, Basel, Brussels and London. Upon returning to Berlin, he entered his father's business, although he would have preferred a literary

Giacomo Meyerbeer

career. Assisted by his younger brother Heinrich, he enjoyed the trust of his father's customers until, after his death, the firm of Meyer Cohn passed into the hands of a joint-stock bank.

Meyer-Cohn was at no time absorbed completely by his business. He cultivated various scholarly pursuits, and was well-grounded in the subjects he studied, especially German literature of the 18th cent. He was also a leading collector of and authority on autographs in Germany. The catalogue of his collection, published in 1884, was treasured by students of German literature. It is due to Meyer-Cohn's sagacity and generosity that important letters and manuscripts of Goethe and of Kleist were saved for posterity. He prepared a second edition of his autograph collection, which in later years was considerably enlarged, and he was greatly grieved because of the impossibility of bequeathing the collection of first editions of German literature to the Goethe-Archiv at Weimar. He also donated precious manuscripts to public libraries especially interested in them.

Meyer-Cohn was a profound scholar in the folklore and history of Berlin, and a member of a committee of experts appointed by the prehistoric department of the ethnographic museum of Berlin. In 1897 he published the letters of William I to his brother, Prince Charles of Prussia. He edited several curiosities and rarities of German literature, and distributed them without cost among his numerous learned friends and scientific institutions.

Meyer-Cohn also was a philanthropist. He supported many young artists and scholars, and rendered assistance to poor but respectable persons who were ashamed to seek alms. As his friend, Professor Erich Schmidt, said in his obituary: "He liked to give, much and in friendly manner, but he liked most to give secretly."

Lit.: Biographisches Jahrbuch (1904).

MEYER-COHN, HEINRICH, lawyer and communal worker, brother of Alexander, b. Berlin, 1855;

d. Berlin, 1905. He studied law, and became a reputable jurist. Named councillor of justice, he was the attorney for prominent industrial societies and many Jewish organizations. As a partner of the banking house of Meyer Cohn, he arranged with his brother Alexander for the distribution of that part of their surplus which was devoted to benefactions. While Alexander Meyer-Cohn was interested mainly in the promotion of science and the arts, Heinrich fostered Jewish welfare causes. He offered a helping hand whenever called upon, and often supported individuals and organizations spontaneously. He was intensely interested in the improvement of the political, economic and cultural conditions of Jewish life in Germany, and was at the head of well-nigh all important Jewish charitable institutions of Berlin. He was especially helpful to the Lehranstalt für die Wissenschaft des Judentums, the Verband für die Vereine für Jüdische Geschichte und Literatur, the Central-Verein deutscher Staatsbürger jüdischen Glaubens, and several educational institutions. He held numerous offices in the Jewish community of Berlin.

But he regarded the struggle against anti-Semitism as his main task. He was one of the founders of the Verein zur Abwehr des Antisemitismus, which included many of the illustrious personages of Germany. Heinrich Meyer-Cohn inspired its founding, and personally directed its difficult preparatory work. He contributed anonymously to almost every issue of the *Mitteilungen des Vereins zur Abwehr des Antisemitismus* and to numerous pamphlets and encyclopedias combatting anti-Semitism. He was a regular collaborator on the *Allgemeine Zeitung des Judentums*.

Lit.: Allgemeine Zeitung des Judentums, Nov. 7, 1905; *Mitteilungen des Vereins zur Abwehr des Antisemitismus,* Nov. 1905.

MEYERBEER, GIACOMO (Jakob Liebmann Beer), composer, b. Berlin, 1791; d. Paris, 1864. He studied piano with Muzio Clementi, theory and composition with Bernhard Anselm Weber and Georg Josef (Abbé) Vogler. Jakob Liebmann Beer was the son of a Jewish banker of Berlin. When he received an inheritance from a relative named Meyer, he prefaced his last name with that of his benefactor, also Italianizing Jakob into Giacomo. At the age of seven he was first noticed musically as a pianist. His contemporaries believed that if he had persisted at the keyboard he would have become the foremost virtuoso of his time. However, he soon abandoned interpretation for composition. He wrote in many forms—his incidental music for his brother Michael Beer's play *Struensee,* for example, was long considered his finest composition —but he is remembered chiefly as the leading practitioner of 19th cent. spectacle opera.

Meyerbeer's first operas were composed to inferior German texts, and brought him little success. His musical erudition was so enormous that *Jephthas Gelübde,* an oratorio-like opera he composed before he was twenty-one, brought him approving nods from critical pundits. Nothing about the later style (or styles) of his music, however, indicates that he would be remembered at all had he followed his friend Carl Maria von Weber's advice and remained a German composer. Instead, he accepted the suggestion made by Mozart's famed rival Antonio Salieri, and went to Italy to study techniques of singing and writing for the voice.

In Venice, then as ever a capital of song, Meyerbeer met the Rossini mania. The great Italian's *Tancredi* was holding the boards. Its hit song, "Di tanti palpiti," had achieved and maintained such epidemic popularity as to receive notice from the police as a public menace. Meyerbeer, whose assimilative powers have been exceeded in music only by Handel's, was not slow to learn what Rossini's operas had to teach. Between 1818 and 1824 he composed six imitative scores to Italian texts. They were mildly successful in Italy itself, and von Weber staged one of them at Dresden, hoping thus to please his errant colleague and win him back to the sacred cause of German opera. Meyerbeer obliged with another try with a German libretto, but when that failed of performance in Berlin, returned to Venice and produced his last Italian—and first "Meyerbeerian"—opera, *Il Crociato in Egitto* (1824), composed to a text by Gaëtano Rossi, responsible also for Rossini's *Semiramide*. This spectacle of the Crusades, preceding by a few years both Auber's *La Muette de Portici* and Rossini's *Guillaume Tell*, clearly foretold that the immediate future of the lyric stage was grand opera of the most elaborate sort.

In 1826 Meyerbeer took the step which proved decisive in the shaping of his career, and that of opera in general, for half a century. He visited Paris, and set out earnestly, with the full powers of a brilliant eclectic mind, to become a French composer. With unerring instinct for the theatrically useful, he selected a book by Eugène Scribe, librettist extraordinary to the France of Louis Philippe and Louis Napoleon. The result was *Robert le diable* (1831), a monstrous five-act pageant opera that overnight established Meyerbeer as the monarch of the Opéra, Rossini having retired from active competition. Elaborately scored for large orchestra, full of pictorially effective tableaux, giving every opportunity to star singers, taking full advantage of every superficial theatrical effect, *Robert le diable* had an instant and continuing appeal to Meyerbeer's contemporaries, though today it would probably not survive restaging.

Five years after *Robert le diable*, Meyerbeer presented Paris with *Les Huguenots* (1836). This masterly mélange of fact and fiction built around the massacre of St. Bartholomew's became the favorite opera of all managers who could provide seven or eight star singers for its gigantic cast. Although Meyerbeer is often admirable as an entertainer, it is usually difficult to rate him highly as a dramatic composer. But in Act IV of *Les Huguenots* he produced a dramatic unit of such compelling power as to squeeze grudging words of praise from his archenemy Richard Wagner. On the basis of this dazzling scene alone it is possible to judge what music lost because Meyerbeer aimed at glitter and success rather than at deepening and intensifying his natural dramatic genius.

Germany recognized Meyerbeer's preeminence in 1842, when Frederick William IV of Prussia appointed him general music director at Berlin. Valiantly Meyerbeer tried once more, and for the last time failed, to create a good German opera. *Der Feldlager in Schlesien* (1840) is remembered today only for the fact that Jenny Lind scored one of her early successes in it. But even while producing it in Berlin, Meyerbeer was preparing another musical extravaganza for Paris. *Le Prophète* (1849) is a hodgepodge of borrowed styles. Yet out of it there arises one of the notable characters of mid-19th cent. opera, the heroic mother, Fidès. By making an older person a central figure in a successful opera Meyerbeer paved the way for Halévy to do the same with Eléazar in *La Juive* and for Verdi to do it with Azucena in *Il Trovatore*.

After *Le Prophète*, perhaps tiring of his own jewelled and brocaded confections, Meyerbeer stepped out of his field to compose two light works for the Opéra-Comique. *L'Étoile du nord* (1854) was a recast version of *Der Feldlager in Schlesien*, and was a circus staged for the most lightheaded type of coloratura soprano pyrotechnics. *Le Pardon de Ploërmel* (1859), better known under its Italian title *Dinorah*, has survived somewhat longer because it contains that favorite showpiece, "*Ombre légère*." Neither of these opéras-comiques represents Meyerbeer at either his best or his most characteristic.

From 1838 on Meyerbeer was intermittently at work on the setting of a much worked over Scribe libretto. It was in rehearsal, and he had completed what for the moment he regarded as the final corrections, when he died on May 2, 1864. Not quite a year later *L'Africaine* was produced. It had been further tampered with by several of the composer's friends, and clearly did not represent the opera Meyerbeer might finally have evolved from his materials had he lived. So disparate are the styles of its various sections, composed over a period of twenty-six years, that it is all but impossible to think of it as a unit. Among its sections, however, are several that for sheer musical beauty stand above everything else Meyerbeer composed.

Meyerbeer's operas have been dropped all but completely from the regularly performed repertoire. This makes it unusually difficult to judge them, for performance—and sumptuously mounted performance—was in a very particular sense their only life. Nor does Meyerbeer survive in concert repertoire excerpts. His very considerable talents, exquisitely ordered to provide the second half of his century with the sage entertainments it wanted, created almost nothing that can hold a modern listener. Meyerbeer lacked a clearly defined musical personality and failed to evolve profound convictions. In the process of creating a meticulously polyglot international style, he lost himself. It may be that another era will properly revive *Les Huguenots, Le Prophète,* and *L'Africaine,* making them the glittering stage spectacles they were designed to be.

HERBERT WEINSTOCK.

Lit.: (there is no modern biography of Meyerbeer in English) Brockway, Wallace, and Weinstock, Herbert, *The Opera, a History of its Creation and Performance,1600-1941* (1942); Lang, Paul Henry, *Music in Western Civilization* (1942); Van Dieren, Bernard, *Down Among the Dead Men*.

MEYERHOF, OTTO, physiologist, b. Hannover, Germany, 1884. His contribution to science may be indicated by the title of his first important publication, *The Dynamics of Living Phenomena*, in which he investigated the chemistry of the muscles. Together with the English physiologist, A. B. Hill (London), he received the Nobel Prize in recognition of their researches in this special field of science in 1922. The chemistry of the muscles, which both discovered, works somewhat as follows: sugar is shifted to the muscle, the carbohydrate, into which the sugar has changed, is burned and lactic acid is formed and is transformed again into carbohydrate when the muscle relaxes. The explanation of this process shows the cause of fatigue in the human body.

Meyerhof was appointed director of the Physiologische Forschungsanstalt am Kaiser Wilhelm Institut in Berlin-Dahlem (1924), and associate professor and director of the Institut für Physiologie im Kaiser Wilhelm Institut für medizinische Forschung in Heidelberg. He came to the United States in 1940 to teach biochemistry at the University of Pennsylvania, in Philadelphia.

Of his numerous works, the following may be mentioned: *Beiträge zur psychologischen Theorie der Geistesstörungen* (1910); *Über Goethes Methode der Naturforschung* (1910); *Zur Energetik der Zellvorgänge* (1913); *Chemical Dynamics of Life Phenomena* (1924); *Die chemischen Vorgänge im Muskel* (1930). More than one hundred of his important essays were printed in scientific periodicals, especially his "Die Energieumwandlungen im Muskel" (1923), representing the results of those researches for which the Nobel Prize was awarded him.

MEYEROWITZ, WILLIAM, painter and etcher, b. Ukraine, 1898. He was a modernist, known especially for his etchings, colored as well as black and white. In his oils, he was noted for his skillful drawing and vibrant color. He came to New York city in 1906, and studied at the National Academy of Design. His work, which includes many Jewish subjects, was shown in group exhibits as well as in several one-man shows. Examples of it are to be found in private collections and in numerous art galleries and institutions throughout the United States, including the Phillips Memorial Gallery (Washington, D. C.), the Chicago Art Institute and the United States National Museum. He was represented also in art galleries of London and Paris.

Meyerowitz' portraits of famous persons included those of the late Supreme Court Justices Oliver Wendell Holmes and Louis D. Brandeis, of Albert Einstein and Chaim Weizmann.

Lit.: *Who's Who in American Art* (1940-41) 443; *American Art Annual*, vol. 26 (1929); *American Hebrew*, March 30, 1928, p. 725; *Current Biography*, vol. 3, No. 5 (1942) 63-65.

MEYERS, CHARLES B., architect, b. New York city, 1875. Educated at Pratt Institute in New York, he started his private architectural practice in 1900, and soon became active in public building. His New York State building at the Panama Pacific Exposition in San Francisco (1915) won the gold medal.

Meyers was particularly active in New York city's architectural and building problems, serving from 1926 to 1928 as an important member of a joint committee composed of representatives of city departments. From 1916 to 1929 he worked on a group of buildings for the New York city reformatory, and in 1929 surveyed and reported on the need for a comprehensive prison system for Greater New York.

Examples of his work include several hospitals, the new building for the Yeshiva College, and the synagogue and community center of Rodeph Sholom, of which congregation he was a trustee. In 1934 he was

Otto Meyerhof

engaged on the new buildings for Hunter College, New York.

MEYERS, EDUARD MAURITS, attorney and jurist, b. Den Helder, Holland, 1880. He studied at the University of Amsterdam, was admitted to the bar in 1903, and practiced law in Amsterdam from 1903 to 1910, when he became professor of civil and international law at the University of Leyden. From 1928 on he was also a substitute councillor in the High Court of Justice, at The Hague.

Beginning with 1905 Meyers wrote a large number of articles and books on various legal subjects, but more particularly those concerning various phases of civil law, seen in the light of history. Between 1905 and 1910 he devoted the bulk of his writings to the legal relationships of labor. In 1908 he published *The Labor Contract*, which has been the standard legal treatise on this subject published in The Netherlands. He was editor of the influential *Sociaal Weekblad* from 1906 until it ceased publication (Sept., 1911). In 1909 he wrote his *Legal Decisions Regarding the Law on Labor Contracts*, rewrote and greatly expanded it in 1934. He was, simultaneously, deeply interested in the economic side of all labor problems, and kept close contact with the Bureau for Social Advice.

As university professor Meyers concentrated upon international civil law and succession law, particularly on the history of law-giving. He illuminated international law in *Bijdrage tot de geschiedenis van het internationaal privaat- en strafrecht in Frankrijk en de Nederlanden* (1914), followed (1934) by *L'histoire des principes fondamentaux du droit international privé, à partir du moyen âge*. Meyers' book on succession laws (1915) and his subsequent publications on the Ligurian laws of succession were hailed as remarkable achievements.

He published also a multitude of legal contributions. Thus he succeeded in unearthing the long-lost "Observationes tumultuariae," reissuing them in collaboration with De Blécourt and Bodenstein (2 vols., vol. 1,

1926; vol. 2, 1934). With De Blécourt he also published the *Memorials of the Court of Zeeland and West Frisia,* by its secretary, Jan Rosa, and in 1932 issued *Le droit coutumier de Cambrai,* followed in 1934 by *Les lois et coutumes de Saint-Amand* (in collaboration with the philologist, Salverda de Grave). He encouraged students to share in the authorship of some of his works.

Meyers wrote and published many contributions regarding civil law. Especially known are his essays on "short causes" (*Het kort geding*), which virtually stabilized this rather puny branch of law-making, and did much to further its development.

The total of his writings, by the middle of July, 1935, had become so large that an index and bibliography, prepared by a number of his former pupils, was presented to Meyers, on the occasion of his silver jubilee.

In Nov., 1940, the German occupation authorities ordered the peremptory dismissal of all Jewish professors. This led to an impressive demonstration in the auditorium of the University of Leyden, where hundreds of students were addressed by their dean, Professor R. P. Cleveringa, who himself had been a pupil of Meyers. Cleveringa, describing Meyers as "one of the greatest lawyers of many countries and many periods . . . an excellent citizen . . . a faithful, honest child of his people . . . a noble and true son of our nation," denounced the German invaders for ousting from his post "this man, this father of his students, this scholar." "In our thoughts the image and figure, the full personality of Dr. Meyers will continue to live, because we can not cease believing that he should be here and that, if fate will it, return he shall." Cleveringa was immediately imprisoned, and remained in a German concentration camp until Jan., 1942, when he was reported back in The Netherlands.

Of Meyers' fate nothing was known in 1942.

J. F. W. STOPPELMAN.

MEYERS, MILTON KAYTON, neurologist, b. Philadelphia, 1882. He received his medical degree in 1902 from the University of Pennsylvania. From 1904 to 1912 he was affiliated with various laboratories at the University of Pennsylvania, and from 1919 to 1921 he was consulting neurologist with the United States Public Health Service. Meyers held many hospital posts, among them that of chief of the nerve clinic of St. Agnes Hospital. He was editor of Lang's *German-English Medical Dictionary* (1913), translator and editor of Falta's *Endocrine Diseases, Including Their Treatment,* and author of the chapter on nervous diseases in Loewenberg's *Diagnostic Methods in Internal Medicine.* (?)

Lit.: Kagan, Solomon R., *Jewish Contributions to Medicine in America* (1939) 628.

MEYERSON, ÉMILE, philosopher, b. Lublin, Poland, 1859; d. Paris, 1933. His early education in Germany stressed science, particularly chemistry, and when, in 1882, he settled permanently in France (of which country he became a citizen), he went into business as a practical chemist. But he soon abandoned this to devote himself to the study of the history of natural science in all its branches, and in this field he became the outstanding authority of his time. While thus engaged he worked as translator and editor for the Havas news agency.

As he investigated the history of scientists from the very beginning, their thought processes, their psychology in their struggle to understand and master the world of nature, became for him the summary of all human thinking, and he was thus led into an examination of human reason itself, and of the relation of scientific thinking to common sense thinking.

Meyerson's intellectual temperament has been attributed to his descent from a line of Talmudic scholars; one of his ancestors was said to have been the chief rabbi of Prague, Ezekiel Landau, whose own lineage, in turn, is linked with that of the great Rashi.

In 1908 he published his historic *Identity and Reality* (English trans., 1930), in which his main ideas were expounded, buttressed throughout by unprecedented detail of research, yet in lucid and trenchant style. His theory is that of causalism, though not theological or anthropomorphic. Scientists, he maintained, do not seek for laws alone, laws by which they can predict and control; they seek explanation, cause. The human mind has an inborn urge to *identify,* and it strives always to reduce the vast and diverse world of reality to its own unity. True, reality resists this effort of the mind, and the irrational remains in nature. So we can only arrive at the *plausible:* to the extent to which the innate and indomitable craving of the mind for rationality is satisfied, to that extent are real phenomena explicable. But a total explanation is illusory. Further, common-sense thinking is like scientific thinking; only its action is unconscious in the great majority of men. It was Einstein who said that the work of Meyerson, unlike that of other natural scientists, reflects a spirit of faith in the uniformity of nature and its accessibility to the speculative intellect.

Following his first volume, Meyerson's ideas were further developed in several succeeding works, the last important one being *Le cheminement de la pensée* (1931). He gained a reputation among scholars of the whole world and among the general European public as well. Just before his death, a committee was formed to do him homage on his approaching seventy-fifth birthday.

With all this intensive intellectual occupation, Meyerson was also a contributor to Jewish life. He took an active part in the French Zionist movement from the beginning, at one time going to Russia to organize the work of the Jewish Colonization Association. Together with over a thousand co-workers he published a report on the conditions of Jews in Russia. Poor health forced him to retire from further active participation.

SHERRY ABEL.

Lit.: Meyerson, Émile, *Identity and Reality* (English trans., 1930); Serouya, Henri, "Émile Meyerson," *Menorah,* 1932, pp. 84-86; Boas, George, *A Critical Analysis of Émile Meyerson* (1930); Kelly, Thomas, *Explanation and Reality in the Philosophy of Émile Meyerson* (1937).

MEYERSON, MALVINA (née Horowicz), writer, mother of Émile, b. Lublin, Poland, 1839; d. Lublin, 1922. She came from a family of learned Talmudists; together with Eliza Orzeszko, she launched Polish Jewish literature. She "discovered" the well-to-do Polish Jew; it was through her endeavors that his romanticism found expression in Polish literature. Her novels —appearing in the age of Victor Hugo, George Eliot and Berthold Auerbach—are infused with the lofty humanitarian ideas which held sway in Poland during the liberation of the serfs. She wrote *David* and *Aus engem Kreise*. For a long time her contributions were a feature of the publication *Izraelita*.

MEYERSTEIN, EDWARD HARRY WILLIAM, writer, b. London, 1889. He was educated at Oxford. From 1913 to 1918 he was connected with the manuscript department of the British Museum, although in 1914 he served with the Royal Dublin Fusiliers. Meyerstein's published work includes: *The Door* (1911); *Selected Poems* (1935); *New Odes* (1936); *Boy of Clare* (1937); *Briancourt* (1937); *Sonnets* (1939); and *Eclogues* (1940), all volumes of poetry. He was author of several novels, collections of short stories, plays and of *A Life of Thomas Chatterton* (1930). In 1942 he was living in London.

Sir Edward William Meyerstein (b. 1863) was the father of Edward Harry William Meyerstein. He was twice high sheriff of Kent (1937-38 and 1941-42), and was knighted in 1938.

MEYERSTEIN, MORITZ, physicist and inventor, b. Göttingen, Germany, 1808; d. Göttingen, 1882. He was university mechanic at Göttingen, and was given an honorary doctorate. He invented a spectroscope for the determination of the coefficients of refraction and dispersion of various media (1856), a caliper-spherometer, and various other optical, mechanical, and electromagnetic instruments.

Lit.: Poggendorf, J. C., *Biographisch-literarisches Handwörterbuch zur Geschichte der exacten Wissenschaften* (1898) 910.

MEYROWITZ, SELMAR, conductor, b. Bartenstein, Prussia, Germany, 1875. He was a pupil of Reinecke and Jadassohn at the Leipzig Conservatory, and of Max Bruch at the Berlin Meisterschule. He attracted the attention of Felix Mottl, famous Wagnerian conductor, who appointed him assistant at Karlsruhe in 1897. When Mottl came to the United States in 1903 to conduct at the Metropolitan Opera House, he brought Meyrowitz with him as assistant. In 1915 Meyrowitz was appointed first conductor of the National Theatre in Prague. This was followed by several important conductorial engagements, including one with the Berlin Philharmonic in 1917. In 1920 Meyrowitz became conductor of the Blüthner Orchestra, and in 1924 he was appointed first conductor of the Berlin State Opera. For a while he was also musical director of the Radio in Berlin. After the advent of the Nazi government, Meyrowitz discontinued all musical activity.

MEYSL, MORDECAI MARCUS, communal leader and philanthropist, b. Prague, 1528; d. Prague, 1601. Records of the Bohemian chancellery give his name as Miska Marek, while a number of documents made public by the imperial chancellery refer to him also as Meussl or Meusel. His name appeared first in a document dated 1569 pertaining to his business relations with one Isaac Rofe who became (1581) Meysl's father-in-law. Meysl seems to have played a vital role in the history of the Jews of Prague in the early 1560's. Prior to that they had been twice expelled, but by 1566 the German emperor (who was also king of Bohemia) evidenced a change of heart toward the Jews presum-

Tombstone of Mordecai Marcus Meysl in the Jewish cemetery at Prague

ably in appreciation of their offer of financial aid in his war against the Turks.

Meysl is believed to have been author of the idea in order to restore the Jews to the favor of the emperor, who had been long harassed by the Turks. A man of wealth even before 1566, Meysl's fortune grew rapidly during the ensuing years through financial favors he rendered the emperor, the Diet of Bohemia, many members of the nobility, and to sundry others. Transactions in goods on credit also yielded him a substantial income. Non-Jewish chroniclers of that period acknowledged Meysl's signal services to king and country. Yet in 1579 certain envious officials sought to discredit him before the Bohemian chancellery by accusing him of irregularities in connection with mortgage transactions. But Meysl was thoroughly exonerated. Indeed, in 1592 he was granted an imperial charter guaranteeing his safety, even in the face of denunciations by non-Jews. This document of immunity stipulated that any charges against Meysl must be referred forthwith to the emperor for personal consideration. In 1598 another imperial charter granted him important privileges in recognition of his meritorious services in the war against the Turks.

Meysl dedicated a large portion of his wealth to the welfare of his co-religionists. David Gans, contemporary Jewish chronicler, called him "the Maecenas of learning, hero of benevolence, father of the poor, indefatigable friend of his fellow-Jews."

Meysl acquired a large tract of land in Prague, and erected there a Mikveh, a Beth Hamidrash, a hospital which existed until modern times, and a bath-house. He enlarged the cemetery of Prague, had the streets of the ghetto paved, extended free loans to poor deserving Jews, and annually furnished the dowry for two Jewish brides. Meysl also built the Meysl Synagogue, and he is said to have erected also the Great Synagogue and the Jewish town hall. He donated frequently to the Jewish communities of Posen and Cracow, sent money to Jerusalem, and contributed toward the erection of a Christian church at Prague. In all probability, Meysl was consulted as to the distribution of charity abroad by Rabbi Judah Löw ben Bezalel. The chief rabbi of Prague was venerated by Meysl, and he did his utmost to grant Löw's requests. As president of the Jewish community of Prague Meysl succeeded in obtaining for it autonomy in the appointment of its officials and the administration of its cultural affairs.

At Meysl's funeral Emperor Rudolph II was represented by a royal emissary. Nevertheless, a few days later Meysl's property was seized in the name of the emperor, and his last will was declared void despite the official privilege granting Meysl free disposition of his property by will. Meysl's nephews, his legal heirs, prosecuted a lawsuit which continued for almost a century. It was not Lang, the baptized Jew (as almost all historians alleged) but his predecessor Matkowsky, groom of the emperor's chamber, who was ringleader of those who attempted to steal Meysl's fortune.

HUGO BIEBER.

Lit.: Lieben, Koppelmann, *Gal-Ed* (1856); Kisch, Alexander, *Das Testament Mardochai Meisels* (1893); Stein, A., *Die Juden in Böhmen* (1904).

MEYUHAS, JOSEPH, pedagogue and author, b. Jerusalem, 1868. He came of a Sephardic family which had provided rabbis for the Jerusalem community for more than 250 years, but his own father was one of the first Sephardic Jews in Palestine to take up agriculture. Meyuhas studied at various Yeshivas in Jerusalem, and from 1885 on was a teacher in both Yeshivas and secular schools. For twenty-eight years he taught Hebrew, French and Arabic in the Anglo-Jewish Society School in Jerusalem, and for twenty-five years was director of the Ezra Seminary. In 1918 he became director of the City School for Boys in Jerusalem.

Meyuhas was a participant in cultural and communal activities in Jerusalem and throughout Palestine. He was founder of several libraries and of the Sephardic Union. From 1920 to 1931 he was president of the Vaad Kehillath Yerushalayim. He was a member of the Vaad Leumi from the time of its establishment, and was one of the founders of the Vaad Halashon. Extending his communal work outside of Palestine, Meyuhas was instrumental in establishing B'nai B'rith lodges in Greece and Bulgaria.

Among Meyuhas' published works were: *Mishle Yishmael; Sihoth Yishmael; Almon Haobel; Halashon Vehahinnuch; Torath Em O Bath Hayil; Halichoth Olam; Eretz Yisrael Hayom Ulefanim; Yalede Arab.* Meyuhas contributed to various periodicals in Hebrew and Ladino, and was editor of a Ladino periodical, *Gan Perahim.*

MEZEI, ERNŐ, Hungarian deputy and publicist (younger brother of Mór Mezei), b. Sátoraljaujhely, Hungary, 1851; d. Budapest, 1932. A graduate of the law school of the University of Budapest, he became a political columnist at the age of twenty (1871). When he was candidate for the Lower Chamber (1878) Kossuth (in exile) coined a campaign slogan for him:

"Ernő Mezei is a deputy in whom Lajos Kossuth delights." He failed in that election, but won in 1881. In parliament he fought for an independent Hungary and for the rights of the Jews, taking an active part in the debates for a separate Magyar army and civil marriage, denouncing anti-Semitic machinations in the blood accusation of Tisza-eszlár (1882), and speaking in favor of placing the Jewish religion on an equal footing with other denominations. He was a columnist of the *Egyetértés* for thirty-five years, and contributed to the Jewish press. He published: *Tisza Kálmán pálfordulása* (Kálmán Tisza's Change of Front, 1875); *A polgári házasság története* (History of Civil Marriage; 1876); *Tisza Kálmán 1877-ben* (Kálmán Tisza in 1877; 1877); *Bolyongások az olasz ég alatt* (Roving Under Italian Skies, 1877).

MEZEI, MÓR, communal leader and publicist (brother of Ernő Mezei), b. Sátoraljaujhely, Hungary, 1835; d. Budapest, 1925. He was educated in Budapest, where he studied jurisprudence, and in 1861 he founded the Omike (National Association of Hungarian Jews), becoming its secretary and subsequently president. He also edited the *Magyar Izraelita,* and advocated the convening of a national Jewish congress in order to effect religious reform and obtain civic rights. For his strongly Magyar nationalistic tendencies he was court martialed by the dictatorial Austrian government and had to resign his editorship in 1862. In 1864 he was allowed to practice law only by special permission of the king.

Mezei played a leading part at the national Jewish congress convoked in 1868, and became president of the Israelite chancery, an administrative body created by the Congress. In this capacity he became also chairman of a non-partisan committee working to achieve "reception," an act by which Judaism was recognized as a state religion equal to other denominations (1896). From 1893 to 1901 Mezei was deputy in the Lower Chamber and delivered several major addresses. He was one of the leading practitioners of commercial law in Hungary, and contributed many articles to law journals.

MEZEY, FERENC, philanthropist and communal leader, b. Nyiracsád, Hungary, 1860; d. Budapest, 1927. He was destined for a rabbinical career and pursued advanced religious studies, but became a lawyer after studying at the University of Budapest. While still a student he joined the staff of the Israelite chancery, national organization of Hungarian Jewish communities (1880), becoming its secretary (1902), vice-president under Mór Mezei and president, then acting president, after the latter's death (1925). He was vice-president (until 1916) of the Hebra Kaddisha of Pest, which he reorganized and which, by securing large donations, he enabled to found and maintain a home for the aged, a home of charity and a free hospital which became institutions of great importance. As a high official of the chancery he advocated confessional rights and the development of cultural and humanitarian institutions among Hungarian Jewry. He also fought for the improvement of civic conditions of Roumanian Jews and for the development of the cultural level of Galician Jews.

During the difficult revolutionary era of 1919 to 1925 Mezey displayed much tact and fortitude in safeguarding the rights of Hungarian Jewry. He served for forty years on the board of governors of the rabbinical seminary of Budapest, being its chairman for fourteen years. He secured endowments for dormitories connected with the seminary as well as with the Jewish teachers' training school and obtained an increase of government subsidies for the seminary. As co-editor (1884-91) of its journal, *Magyar Zsidó Szemle,* he advocated improvement of the social standing and material security of Hungarian rabbis. He was responsible for the establishment of a Hungarian Jewish public fund, which subsidized cultural endeavors and individual artists, of the Imit (Hungarian Jewish Literary Society) and of the Jewish museum (founded in 1916). In 1910 he was made royal councillor in recognition of distinguished public service. In addition to articles on law and matters of general public interest contributed to periodical and daily publications, he was author of a volume, *Rajzok a magyar zsidó életből* (Sketches of Hungarian Jewish Life; 1925).

MEZŐ, FERENC, pedagogue, athlete and sports writer, b. Pölöskefő, Hungary, 1885. He was living in Budapest in 1942. He received his Ph.D. degree in classical philology from the University of Budapest, and was principal of the public school at Zalaszentgrót. He took part in the first World War, and published two books on his War experiences. From 1918 on he was a teacher, and subsequently titular principal, at the King Mathias state Gymnasium at Budapest. A teacher of Latin and Greek, Mező endeavored to revive the athletic spirit of ancient Greece. In his younger years he had won several prizes in athletics, and devoted himself to research on the history of sports in ancient Greece and modern Hungary. His main work is a history of the Olympic Games, which was published in Hungarian (1928) and in German (1930 and 1936), and with which he won the literary world championship at the Amsterdam Olympic Games (1928). This was followed by a dozen other works in Hungarian dealing with sports in Greece, the history of sports in Hungary, the history of marathon races, a survey of the Olympic Games of 1932 and monographs on Hungarian sportsmen. Mező was awarded by Regent Nicholas Horthy the First Class medal of the citizen's Signum Laudis. He wrote for sports journals abroad.

MEZŐFI, VILMOS, political and communal leader, and Hungarian deputy, b. Debrecen, Hungary, 1870. He attended commercial high school at Budapest, but circumstances prevented completion of his studies there and Mezőfi became a watchmaker's apprentice. He educated himself by reading, and became a journalist, at first as columnist for various liberal newspapers. Later he became associated with the Social Democratic daily newspaper *Népszava,* which he edited for some time together with a number of trade union journals. In 1896 he became editor of *Népolvasótábor,* a literary magazine for workmen. He had a leading part in the endeavor of the Hungarian Social Democratic Party to organize the masses of agricultural workers in 1905, a movement which the government held dangerous and suppressed.

Mezőfi, however, was elected deputy and represented the party in the Lower Chamber from 1905 to 1910, fighting for universal suffrage in and outside of parliament. His interest was focussed on the agrarian problem; he severed relations with the Social Democratic Party, and when, after the first World War, a democratic small landowners' party was organized, Mezőfi served as editor of its organ *Szabad Szó* (Free Word). Thus he was one of the very few Jews who retained a degree of public influence in post-War Hungary in non-Jewish affairs. When, in 1938, legislative action was taken to deprive the Jews of their civic rights and means of livelihood, Mezőfi, who was then sixty-eight, vigorously championed the Jewish cause, devoting much effort to the organization of Jewish self-aid within Hungary. For distinguished service he was elected president of the tenth synagogue district of Pest (1941).

Mezőfi published a great number of books, especially in his earlier, socialist period. Some of them are: *A szociáldemokrácia evangéliuma* (The Gospel of Social Democracy); *Weitling Vilmos, a legelső német kommunista élete és tanitása* (The Life and Doctrines of Wilhelm Weitling, First German Communist); *A munkabérek Magyarországon az 1896-98 években* (Wages in Hungary during the Years 1896-98); *Kik a hazaárulók?* (Who are the Traitors?); *Évezredek története* (History of the Millennia; 10 vols.).

In 1937 he published, for the benefit of the agricultural population, the pamphlet *Irás a zsidókról* (Script on the Jews), to counteract Nazi propaganda by German agents among that class.

MEZUZAH (literal meaning, "doorpost"), in the religious terminology of the Jews, the designation for the parchment scroll placed upon the doorpost of a house. It contains, in a metal or wooden box, two portions of the Pentateuch, consisting of *Deut.* 6:4-9 (the Shema) and *Deut.* 11:13-21. The first passage, *Deut.* 6:4-9, treats of the unconditional love of the One God and devotion to Him; the second passage, *Deut.* 11:13-21, treats of divine retribution and the responsibility of man for the observance of the commandments, as well as the rewards and material blessings which man will receive for obeying them. The Mezuzah thus admonishes one to take both these Biblical passages to heart and to fulfill them. Traditionally, the Mezuzah is placed on the doorposts of all houses and courts, and on the doors of every room in the house that is occupied by persons. Exceptions to this rule are storerooms, barns, sheds, stables, cellars, schoolhouses and houses of worship.

The Mezuzah is attached to the right doorpost as one enters the house. Among Orthodox Jews it is the custom, as one enters the house or room or leaves it, to touch the Mezuzah with the fingers and then to kiss the fingers. At a later period, perhaps from the 3rd cent. on, the originally purely ethical and religious significance of the Mezuzah inscription was interpreted and given an additional meaning along superstitious lines in many places, and its purely spiritual nature was diminished to such an extent that the Mezuzah was expected to ward off evil spirits, as was the amulet, and to protect men from demons of all kinds; for this reason, the names of angels, names of God, and cor-

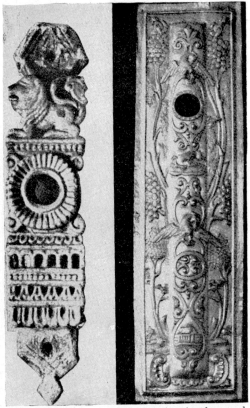

(left) Mezuzah of wood (14th cent.), privately owned in Ansbach (photographed by Theodor Harburger, of Munich); (right) Mezuzah of metal, from Poland, in the possession of Dr. Ignaz Friedmann, of Budapest.

responding verses from the Bible were placed in the Mezuzah box, in addition to the original two Biblical passages. The misuse of the Mezuzah and the abuse of its basic idea were bitterly and resolutely opposed by Maimonides in his great religious work *Yad Hahaza-kah* (Hilchoth Mezuzah 5:5).

Among the lowest strata of the Jewish people (the so-called Am Haaretz), the Mezuzah custom had ceased to be observed even in the Talmudic period. The Karaites did not practise it, and hence it is doubtful whether the Sadducees observed it. On the other hand, however, the custom of putting inscriptions on doorposts was practised by the ancient Egyptians, and the Mohammedans still practise it today by putting verses from Koran and the like on house entrances.

This Jewish custom, which has today been elevated to the status of a religious commandment, is based on the identical words found in *Deut.* 6:9 and 11:20: "And thou shalt write them (i.e. the words dealing with God's love and retribution, as well as with His commandments) upon the door-posts of thy house, and upon thy gates." It is still a subject of dispute as to whether these words were originally intended figuratively or literally, and whether, in the latter event, they were intended to reinterpret in an ethical and religious sense an already existent pagan custom or rite intended to protect the house from the entrance of demons and evil spirits by means of placing amulets on the door-post.   MAX JOSEPH.

Lit.: Shulhan Aruch, Yoreh Deah 285-91; Hirsch, S. R., *Horeb*, chap. 40.

MEZUZAH, one of the seven minor tractates of the Talmud, consisting of two chapters. It deals with the regulations connected with the Mezuzah, such as the parchment used, the manner of writing, the buildings on which it should be placed, the exact spot on the door-post to which it is affixed, and differences in regulations for houses within and outside of Palestine.

Lit.: Higger, M., *Seven Minor Treatises* (1930).

MI ADDIR ("Who Is Mighty?"), the beginning words of an alphabetical hymn telling of the greatness of God. It is employed as an introductory song at betrothals, and is for this reason chanted as invoking a blessing upon bridegroom and bride. The author of the Mi Addir is unknown, but the hymn can hardly be very old. The beginning and end of *Ps.* 8 (verses 2 and 10), *mah 'addir shimecha* ("How glorious is Thy name"), may be compared with it. The melody of the Mi Addir is not traditional. An "ancient" melody is cited in Baer, Abraham, *Baal Tefillah,* p. 79.

The Mi Addir has been the subject of many musical compositions, mostly for cantor with organ accompaniment; Kirschner (seven melodies), Lewandowski (with choir), Naumbourg, Weintraub, Birnbaum (with orchestra), and Sulzer (with harp) cite many of these musical compositions. In many places, where the bride and the bridegroom do not appear at the same time, the Mi Addir is customarily sung only when the bridegroom makes his appearance, whereas the usual song sung at the bride's appearance is the blessing *Addir Elohenu,* which resembles it to an extent (for the melody, see Baer, *Baal Tefillah,* No. 283).

MI CHAMOCHA ("Who is like unto Thee"), a verse from the Song of Moses (the Song of the Sea, *Ex.* 15:11), which, together with verse 19, "the Lord shall reign for ever and ever," is recited in the Geullah prayer in both the morning and the evening services. In addition, a Piyut (liturgical poem) which is inserted into the morning service before this Biblical verse is called Mi Chamocha.

There is also a second Mi Chamocha (but not written, as is the first, with a He at the end) based on *Ps.* 35:10, "All my bones shall say: 'Lord, who is like unto Thee.'" This verse is cited in the Nishmath prayer. In connection with this Mi Chamocha, too, a Piyut was written bearing this same name. Finally, Mi Chamocha is an interpolation in the second benediction of the Tefillah during the Ten Days of Penitence; it reads as follows: "Who is like unto Thee, Father of mercies, who remembereth His creatures unto life?" This interpolation, like the others at the beginning and at the end of the Tefillah, were not written until the post-Talmudic period.

The Biblical verse which forms a part of the congregational responses is chanted, in the simple recitative form of divine services (for example, on weekdays), in the usual and traditional manner. For the more elaborate divine service on the Sabbath there are numerous Mi Chamocha compositions written for the Mi Chamocha prayer by the synagogal musicians. For holidays and for the Sabbaths occurring during the festivals, the traditional festival melody is used, thus for Pesach (Addir Hu) and for Hanukah (Maoz Tzur); cf. also the grouping in Baer, Abraham, *Baal*

Tefillah, where in part other traditional motives of the individual festivals are given, as in Lewandowski, Louis, *Todah W'simrah,* vol. 2).

The Mi Chamocha Ab Harahamim . . . found in the Eighteen Benedictions recited on the Ten Penitential Days derives its melody from the neighboring portions of the service, or is a free composition.

Lit.: Elbogen, Ismar, *Der jüdische Gottesdienst,* 45, 210; Singer, S., and Abrahams, I., *The Authorised Daily Prayer Book* (1922) 43-44, 113d.

MI SHEBERACH, *see* TORAH, READING OF.

MIAMI, a city on the southeast coast of Florida. Greater Miami (comprising Miami, Miami Beach, and Coral Gables), according to the 1940 census, had a population of 250,537, including approximately 25,000 Jews. All Jewish activities in 1942 were sponsored in the Greater Miami area.

Jews began to settle in the city of Miami in 1896. Isidor Cohen, who came to Miami on February 6, 1896, was the first Jew to establish residence. He was followed by Philip Ullendorff a few months later.

There were a few scattered Jewish families from 1896 to 1912 whose members met in various homes and halls to observe the holidays. In 1912 the first Jewish synagogue, B'nai Zion, was founded. Among the early members were Louis Fein, M. Zion, H. Schneidman, Samuel Cohen, J. Engler, M. Plant, S. Abenson, A. Engler, Max Shaff, Max Dubler and Isidor Cohen. In 1917 the name of the congregation was changed to Beth David, and a synagogue bearing that name was erected in 1920. Max Shapiro was rabbi of the congregation in 1942.

In 1922 Temple Israel (Reform) was organized in the home of Harry V. Simons of Miami, who was elected its first president. Dr. Sali Stein was the first rabbi. The synagogue of Temple Israel was dedicated on February 17, 1928, and Jacob Kaplan was its first rabbi. Coleman A. Zwitman was rabbi in 1942.

In 1930 the Miami Jewish Orthodox Congregation was organized by members who formerly belonged to the Beth David Congregation. Abraham A. Kellner was rabbi of the congregation in 1942.

The Jewish community of Miami Beach was organized in 1925 and established Beth Jacob Congregation, an Orthodox religious institution with a Talmud Torah. This synagogue served primarily the influx of winter tourists in Miami Beach. The rabbi in 1942 was Moses Mescheloff.

The Miami Beach Jewish Center, a Conservative religious institution maintaining a Talmud Torah and a synagogue for local and transient parents and children, was established in July, 1941. Samuel Bension was rabbi in 1942.

There was no organized Jewish community in Coral Gables in 1942.

A Miami Jewish Cemetery Association, organized in 1930, was composed of representatives of the Beth David Synagogue, the Miami Jewish Orthodox Congregation and the Beth Jacob Synagogue at Miami Beach. The association owned and controlled the cemetery lots of these congregations.

In 1938 the Greater Miami Federation of Jewish Welfare Funds was organized; Stanley C. Myers was its first president. In 1940 the name was changed to the Greater Miami Jewish Federation. Thus a multiplicity of drives for finances were consolidated into a single fund-raising agency.

Baron de Hirsch Meyer was a member of the Miami Beach city council from 1931 to 1937. Abe Arnovitz was city solicitor of Miami from 1935 to 1940. Isidore Zukernick was municipal court judge of Miami Beach in 1940, and E. Albert Pallot was deputy district attorney of Miami in 1941.

There was one English-Jewish newspaper in Miami in 1942, *The Jewish Floridian,* published every Friday. J. Louis Shochet was its founder and editor, and after his death Fred K. Shochet became its editor. Earlier Jewish newspapers were the *Jewish Standard, Jewish Weekly,* and *Jacobean.* MAURICE GROSSMAN.

MIBASHAN, *see* BRAUNSTEIN, MENAHEM MENDEL.

MICAH, sixth book of the Minor Prophets, consisting of seven chapters. The author was a younger contemporary of Isaiah, and the period of his preaching was from about 735 to 691 B.C.E. He is described in both the superscription of the book (1:1) and in *Jer.* 26:18 as a native of Moresheth, which is probably to be identified with Moresheth-gath in Judah, against which he inveighs in one of his utterances (1:14). He was thus a product of the countryside, and from the fact that his father's name is not mentioned it may be assumed that he was of humble birth.

Micah's prophecies are directed against Judah and Jerusalem; the title of the book mentions Samaria as well, but there is only one passing reference (1:5-6) to that region.

Micah is essentially a teacher of ethics. His message is directed toward the moral regeneration of his people rather than toward the maintenance of prescribed forms of worship. His anger is aroused not so much by laxity in the cult as by moral turpitude. The crimes for which he lashes the leaders of Israel are oppression and extortion (2:2), perversion of justice (3:9, 11; 7:3), and violence and despotism (3:2-3, 10; 7:2). Similarly, the official court prophets are castigated not because they are the advocates of apostasy or the spokesmen of pagan deities, but because they are dishonest, trimming their sails to the winds of political expediency (3:5; 7:4). To Micah the religious ideal is not the meticulous performance of standard rites, nor the soulless offering of "thousands of rams, myriads of rivers of oil" (6:7). It lies rather in the observance of ethical principles: "What doth the Lord require of thee, save to do justice, and to love mercy, and to walk humbly with thy God?" (6:8).

The Book of Micah may be divided into three major sections:

Chaps. 1 to 3. This part of the book is written mainly in a vein of denunciation. The first chapter is a series of short oracles delivered against the cities of Jerusalem, making use of puns which give an unfavorable interpretation to their names. Thus Achzib is destined to be *'achzab,* the wady that suddenly dries up; they that dwell in Lachish are to harness the *rechesh,* or steed, to the chariot in preparation for flight. It is possible that some of the original puns have been lost by editorial replacement of rare terms by more familiar ones. Chap. 2 is a forceful diatribe against the violence and ruthlessness of corrupt leaders and the mercenary opportunism of officially approved prophets, the latter being contemptuously termed "babblers." At the close there is a note of hope (verses 12-13) in that the remnant of Israel will ultimately be gathered "like sheep in a fold, like a flock in the midst of their pasture." Many scholars, however, regard this message of comfort as a later addition. Chap. 3 continues the harangue; it denounces the political bosses for "devouring the flesh of My people, flaying their skin and crushing their bones" (verse 3) and the so-called prophets for lulling their hearers into a sense of false security (verse 5).

Chaps. 4 and 5. The tone of this section is one of hope, and it envisions a Golden Age in which all nations will stream to Mount Zion to receive the teaching of God. Idolatry will be uprooted and a theocracy established upon earth. Assyria, whose powerful monarchs had but lately been invading Israel and Judah, will be vanquished, and a Davidic king, born in Bethlehem, will reign over Judah. In words which recur in *Isa.* 2:2-4 there is a vision of a time when men "shall beat their swords into plowshares, and their spears into pruning-hooks; nation shall not lift up sword against nation, neither shall they learn war any more."

Chaps. 6 and 7. In this final section the thunder of prophetic fury is blended with the softer tones of a singularly tender compassion. God will enter suit against His people because of their apostasy. His case will be that He has fulfilled His covenant with them, while they have betrayed it. He will cite as evidence His deliverance of them from Egypt, how He sent them Moses, Aaron and Miriam; they have sought merely to appease Him with mechanically proffered oblations. Because of their corruption the people of Israel will suffer a day of reckoning. They will eat, but not be satisfied, sow, but not reap (6:14-15). The prophet, however, will wait patiently for the God of his salvation (7:7). At the end there is a note of buoyant hope: "Though I have fallen, I yet shall rise; though I sit in darkness, the Lord is a light unto me" (7:8). Israel's foes will yet be vanquished, and their boundaries will be restored and expanded, while nations will humble themselves before them (7:11). The poem closes with a hitherto unnoticed allusion to time-honored mythological lore. Like the fabled deities of Canaan and Assyria (Baal or Marduk) who cast their monstrous foe (Mot or Tiamat) into the sea, so will God "vanquish our iniquities and cast our sins upon the ocean bed" (7:18-19).

Some modern scholars regard only the first section of the book (except 2:12-13) as the genuine work of Micah, the rest being later additions, but this verdict rests upon the assumption that eschatological prophecy was unknown before the Babylonian Exile, an assumption which is by no means certain, and doubtful in view of what the increasing knowledge of ancient Semitic literature reveals. Certainly the forceful, picturesque style of the author appears in every chapter of the book.

Several passages from Micah are used in the liturgy. 5:6 to 6:8 is the Haftarah to Balak, because of its reference to the events of the Pentateuchal story. The closing verses of the book, with their promise of forgiveness, are read at the end of *Jonah* in the afternoon service of Yom Kippur, and are used in the Tashlich ceremony. 7:19 is quoted daily in the Orthodox morning service.   THEODOR H. GASTER.

Lit.: Smith, J. M. P., *Book of Micah, International Critical Commentary* (1911); Smith, G. A., *Book of the Twelve Prophets* (1928); Haupt, Paul, "Notes on Micah," *American Journal of Semitic Languages*, vol. 26, pp. 201-52; vol. 27, pp. 1-63; Margolis, Max L., *Micah* (1908); Cheyne, T. K., *Micah, Cambridge Bible* (1891); Wynkoop, J., *Micah*, in A. Kahana's Hebrew critical edition of the Hebrew Bible; Robinson, T. H., *Die Zwölf Kleinen Propheten*, vol. 1 (1936); Smith, J. M. P., and Irwin, W. A., *The Prophets and their Times* (2nd ed., 1941) 122-25.

MICAH JOSEPH BIN GORION (pseudonym), *see* BERDYCZEWSKI, MICAH JOSEPH.

MICHAEL ("Who is like God?"), one of the most important figures in Jewish angelology. According to these mystical speculations, he is the viceroy of God, and the special defender of Israel. According to *Dan.* 10:13, he fought against the princes of the other nations, and in *Dan.* 12:1 he is to stand up and defend Israel in time of great trouble. There are numerous references to his place and functions in apocalyptic and Midrashic literature. At the end of the world he will avenge the Jews on their enemies. He is the heavenly scribe who records the actions of nations and men, and at the same time he is the medium for the transmission of the Law to Moses and Israel.

Michael is occasionally called "epitropos" ("guardian"), and he is the most important of the four great angels who sit at the right hand of God. He is identified with the angel who wrestled with Jacob and later blessed him. He was regarded as the angel of mercy, and some mystics envisioned him as serving as a heavenly high priest.

Michael's adversary is Samael, the enemy of God and Israel. When the latter was hurled from heaven, he sought to drag Michael down with him, and the latter was saved only by the power of God. Michael and Samael debated the merits of Israel before God on the occasion of the passage of the Red Sea, and they continue to struggle until the final deliverance. The Christian legend of Michael overcoming the dragon is probably derived from Jewish sources.

Michael is credited also with having guided Israel safely through the wilderness, annihilating the army of Sennacherib, and saving the three Hebrew youths from the fiery furnace of Nebuchadnezzar. These are all identifications, such as were indulged in by Jewish mystics, of the angels mentioned anonymously in the Bible.

According to Jewish legend, Michael and his aides stand at the portal of the Heavenly Jerusalem to admit the souls of the just. Even David was refused admission there until Solomon had built the Temple (*Yalkut Hadash, David* 13). When the Messiah comes, Michael and Gabriel will be stationed at the entrance of Paradise, holding the keys of both heaven and hell. The trumpet of resurrection, which will be followed by the opening of the graves and the rising of the dead, is to be blown by Michael (*Othoth Hamashiah*, in Jellinek, *Beth Hamidrash*, vol. 2, pp. 61-62).

Lit.: Lüken, W., *Michael* (1898); Kohut, Alexander, *Über die jüdische Angelologie und Dämonologie* (1866); Schwab, Moïse, *Vocabulaire de l'angélologie* (1897).

MICHAEL, HEIMANN JOSEPH, bibliophile, b. Hamburg, Germany, 1792; d. Hamburg, 1846. Beginning to collect at the age of twelve, he accumulated, in the course of a lifetime, over 5,400 books and 860 manuscripts covering all branches of Hebrew literature, now among the Bodleiana collection in Oxford. The catalogue of the library, *Ozaroth Hayyim, Katalog der Michael'schen Bibliothek,* appeared in Hamburg in 1848. The only printed work by Michael was his rabbinical bibliographical dictionary *Or Hahayim* (Frankfort, 1891), comprising only a few letters of the alphabet. His voluminous correspondence with such men as Franz Delitzsch, Rabbi Akiba Eger, Wilhelm Gesenius, Wolf Heidenheim, Samuel David Luzzatto and Leopold Zunz is of great bibliographical value.

Lit.: Allgemeine Deutsche Biographie, vol. 21, p. 673.

MICHAEL, JEROME, law professor, b. Athens, Ga., 1890. He first entered practice in his native town, where he was city attorney from 1913 to 1916. He then settled in New York city, and was law professor at Columbia University from 1927 on.

A lieutenant in the first World War, he served as director of the war transactions section of the Department of Justice, and from 1924 to 1926 he was special assistant to the United States attorney general.

In 1942 he was chosen, together with Horace M. Kallen, to head the Board of Trustees of the Institute of Jewish Affairs, established by the American Jewish Congress and the World Jewish Congress.

Michael is co-author, with Mortimer J. Adler, of *Crime, Law and Social Science* (1933).

MICHAEL, MAX (originally Meyer Isaac), painter, b. Hamburg, Germany, 1823; d. Berlin, 1891. He studied first under Hardorff in Hamburg and afterward at the Dresden Academy of Arts, and then under Lehman and Couture in Paris (1846-51). From Paris he went to Italy, where he lived mostly in Venice and Rome, painting scenes from Italian popular life and the monasteries. He was awarded the Michael Beer prize in 1850. In 1870 he returned to Berlin, where, in 1875, he was appointed professor at the Academy of Arts, a post which he held until his death.

Michael's paintings include: a portrait of Julius Opperts (1848); *Girls' School in the Sabine Mountains; A Visit of the Cardinal to the Monastery; Job Disputing with His Friends; Bertini Painting an Altar-Piece in the Monastery of the Camaldolites; Neapolitan Fishermen.* Some of his works were placed in the Hamburg Kunsthalle, in the Wallraf-Richartz Museum at Cologne, and in the Ravené collection in Berlin.

Lit.: Thieme, U., and Becker, F., *Allgemeines Lexikon der bildenden Künstler,* vol. 24, p. 506; *Jewish Chronicle* (London), April 3, 1891, p. 9.

MICHAELEVICH, BENISCH, see ISBITZKI, JOSEPH.

MICHAELIS, JOHANN DAVID, orientalist and scholar, b. Halle, Germany, 1717; d. Göttingen, Germany, 1791. For nearly fifty years he lectured on Bible and Semitic languages at the University of Göttingen. His works covered all fields of linguistic and literary research, and were especially influential in the revival of investigations on Biblical antiquity. He wrote *Ehegesetze Mosis* (1755) and *Mosaisches Recht* (6 vols., 1769-75), a systematic presentation of Biblical law, and from 1771 to 1791 edited *Orientalische Bibliothek.*

Lit.: Allgemeine Deutsche Biographie, vol. 21, pp. 685-90.

MICHAELIS, LEONOR, biochemist, b. Berlin, 1875. Educated in Freiburg and Berlin, he rose to prominence in Berlin's medical research circles, working in several institutions of the city. From 1898 to 1899 he was assistant to Professor Paul Ehrlich, and in 1908 he was appointed professor of medicine at the University of Berlin. He was made professor of physical chemistry in 1920. But he left Germany for Japan where, in 1922 to 1926, he served as professor of biochemistry in the medical school of Nagoya.

Michaelis then went to the United States and lectured for three years at Johns Hopkins University. In 1929 he was given life membership in the Rockefeller Institute for Medical Research, in New York city, where in 1942 he was still head of the department of physicochemistry. He was noted for attainments in the field of physical chemistry as applied to biology and medicine, and contributed a notable number of publications to the research literature of this field.

MICHAELIS, SIR MAX, philanthropist, b. Eisfeld, Saxe-Meinigem, Germany; d. Zürich, Switzerland, 1932. The son of a German privy councillor, he was educated in a commercial school at Nuremberg, followed by a period of service in a great banking-house at Frankfort. He migrated to South Africa in 1876. Two years later he was attracted to Kimberley, center of the diamond industry, where he was instrumental in forming the Cape Diamond Company, which was later taken over by de Beers. It was at this time that Michaelis came into close contact with Cecil Rhodes, Alfred Beit and Julius Wernher. In 1896 he proceeded to London, where he remained in connection with the business of Wernher, Beit and Company until 1919.

A wealthy man by the time he reached London, Michaelis throughout his residence in England constantly showed the deepest interest in hospital work, education and art. It was in those years that he gathered a magnificent art collection of the English, Dutch and other schools, as well as of Italian bronzes of the Renaissance era. He also became a most generous benefactor to University College, London, to the Imperial College of Science and Technology, of which he was one of the founders, to the Jewish War Memorial Oxford scholarships, and to the Goldman Institute for Medical Research in Berlin. But he never forgot South Africa. One of his first donations was the establishment of a scholarship for the Christian Brothers School at Kimberley, followed by a bursary to St. Andrews College, Grahamstown. Both these benefactions were made on Cecil Rhodes' personal suggestion. In 1912 Michaelis purchased, for presentation to the Union of South Africa, a collection of pictures by Dutch and Flemish masters belonging to Sir Hugh Lane. It comprised many examples of Dutch and Flemish art at the period of its greatest achievement. The collection, housed in the Old Town House, Cape Town, was transferred to the Union Government in 1916. At the instance of Lady Phillips, wife of Sir Lionel Phillips, the interior of the Old Town House was carefully reconstructed by J. M. Solomon, a young South African Jewish artist of genius, in consonance with the period in which the pictures were painted.

After his return to South Africa in 1919, Michaelis made further benefactions to local art and education.

He made generous gifts to the Johannesburg Art Gallery and the Johannesburg Public Library. He gave £20,000 to the University of Cape Town, with which the Michaelis School of Fine Art was founded.

The University of Cape Town honored him with the LL.D. degree in 1923. He was created K.C.M.G. in 1924.   S. A. ROCHLIN.

Lit.: London Times, Jan. 27, 1932, p. 12; Jan. 30, 1932, p. 14; *Cape Times* (Cape Town), Jan. 27, 1932, p. 9; Jan. 28, 1932, p. 11.

MICHAELSEN, JOSEPH, government official and political writer, b. Naestved, Denmark, 1826; d. Copenhagen, Denmark, 1908. The son of Judah Michaelsen (1797-1852) and Rebecca Israel Levin (1791-1864), he was educated at Vordingborg. From 1845 on he studied at the University of Copenhagen. From 1846 to 1851 he contributed to the newspaper *Faedrelandet,* the most important journal of the Danish national party. In 1853 he was appointed an official in the ministry of finance, but continued to contribute to political papers, and for some years collaborated closely with Meyer Aron Goldschmidt.

In 1858 Michaelsen became assistant to the general director of the Danish postal system and immediately tackled the problems of the postal service. In 1859 he wrote a study, *Om Transitportoens og den internationale Portos Afskaffelse og Afløsning.* His recommendation to abolish international frankage and to substitute a general reciprocal account was not published, but the Danish government communicated the suggestion to foreign governments and postal authorities. Although Michaelsen's proposal for free communication was not accepted, he contributed in other ways to the solution of the complicated problem of international accounts in postal conventions. In 1879 he retired from office and devoted his time entirely to politics. Michaelsen became an opponent of the ruling national liberal party and advocated a political program that was adopted many years later by the farmers' party. He was a founder of the Landmandsbank (1871). In 1890 and 1893 Michaelsen published his memoirs, *Fra min Samtid,* which was hailed as a significant and reliable record of contemporary Danish history.

MICHAL, younger of the two daughters of King Saul. The king consented to David's marrying Michal, who had fallen in love with the young hero, on condition that David kill one hundred Philistines; David killed 200 (*1 Sam.* 18:17-28). When Saul sent messengers to slay David, Michal saved her husband's life by lowering him through a window and placing in his bed a household image (*1 Sam.* 19:11-17). Thereupon Michal was given in marriage to Palti, the son of Laish (*1 Sam.* 25:44). Yet David, on ascending the throne, claimed her from her second husband (*II Sam.* 3:14-16).

Michal was childless, as punishment for severely criticising and mocking David for leaping and dancing when the ark was brought to Zion (*II Sam.* 6:16, 20-23). Hence the name Michal in the verse "the five sons of Michal, the daughter of Saul" (*II Sam.* 21:8) should read Merab, the name of Saul's elder daughter. However, the rabbis say that Michal spent her remaining years in bringing up Merab's children, for which reason they are called her sons (*Sanh.* 19b, 21a).

MICHEL JUD (known also as "Rich Michel"), a merchant influential in Germany during the fifth decade of the 16th cent.; d. Berlin, 1549. Contemporary chronicles and correspondence relate fabulous tales concerning the origin and death of Michel Jud. He was described as a tall, powerful and impressive man, and an eloquent speaker. Some of the German princes esteemed him not only for his wealth but also for his wisdom. When out walking or touring the country he was usually accompanied by a retinue of well-armed and accoutred Jewish servants.

In 1548 Michel Jud negotiated with German princes assembled at Augsburg; his appearance caused a greater stir than the deliberations of the Reichstag there. Elector Joachim II of Brandenburg was especially intimate with him. Joachim was an ambitious sovereign, always in financial difficulties, who needed an experienced and solvent confidant like Michel Jud. He rewarded the latter's services in 1544 when Michel Jud married Merle, daughter of a Jew of Schleusingen, and the elector granted her a life annuity of 6,000 gold florins.

In the following year Michel Jud, who owned two houses at Berlin and one at Frankfort on Oder, was accused by several citizens of the latter city of having poisoned a well. The elector, disregarding details of the charge, arrested and heavily fined the informers, and published a proclamation branding the denunciation as calumny. In 1549, Michel was attacked and captured on the highway near Wittenberg by a squad of disguised and heavily armed patricians of Magdeburg. Saxon gendarmes arrested the robbers together with the captured Michel at Torgau. Immediately after learning of Michel's capture, Joachim II sent two special envoys to the Elector of Saxony, demanding his release. Thereupon Michel was returned with all his goods to Berlin, and Joachim II, through pressure exerted on Saxony and Magdeburg, secured the execution of the robbers.

A few weeks after his rescue, Michel Jud died, probably as the result of an accident. His death created as great a sensation as had his life. Johannes Lichtenberger, in the same year, published a pamphlet, *Von Michel Judens todt,* replete with legendary, superstitious and slanderous tales. It was the source of Jobus Fincelius, who dealt with Michel's death in *Wunderzeichen* (1556). Mathias Dresser's *Sächsisches Chronikon* (1596) and A. Angelus' *Annales Marchiae* (1598) drew freely upon Fincelius. Michel's widow continued to receive for many years the annuity granted her by Joachim II, probably until her death.

Lit.: Heise, Werner, *Die Juden in der Mark Brandenburg* (1932).

MICHEL, SIMON (known also as Simon Pressburg), financier, ancestor of Heinrich Heine, d. Vienna, 1719. He was active on behalf of the imperial court chancery (ministry of finance) of Vienna, probably from 1687 on, as purveyor to the mint of Pressburg (Pozsony) and as an assistant to the court factor Samuel Oppenheimer. Subsequently he provided funds to finance the civil war against the Kurucz insurgents and for the War of the Spanish Succession. He provided also food supplies for the armies, and maintained communication with beleaguered fortresses often under extremely difficult conditions. From 1693 on

Michel lived at Pressburg; in 1705 funds secured for the empress mother obtained for him from Emperor Joseph I the privilege of residing at Vienna. After he had heavily contributed toward the cost of the coronation of Charles VI as emperor of Germany, a loan of 75,000 gulden to the court chancery effected the renewal of his privilege for ten more years (1716-26). In 1717 he had to sign a war loan of another 75,000 gulden.

Michel was prefect of the Jews of Pressburg from 1699 on. In his capacity as prefect of the Jews of Transdanubia he represented the cause of the Jews against the city of Nagyszombat (Trnava) before the Royal Hungarian Chancery, obtaining for them free passage through the city, which had been prohibited for 200 years. His plan for establishing the first banking house in Hungary was frustrated by opposition on the part of the city of Pressburg. His estate was valued at 204,-000 gulden, from which bequests were made for houses of study at Pressburg, Ungarisch-Brod and Fürth.

Among Michel's sons, Marcus (d. 1752) was Jewish judge at Pressburg in 1714; Samuel Simon Pressburg became an agent of the Russian Imperial Chamber and took part in the Russian campaign of 1735 as intendant of the army treasury; Jehiel Pressburg (known also as Michel Simon) became court factor of the Margrave of Ansbach and head of the Ansbach community; Abraham (d. 1759) became head of the community of Prague in 1725. His daughter, Sarah Lea, married Lazarus von Geldern of Düsseldorf, and was the great-grandmother of Heinrich Heine.

MICHELSON, ALBERT ABRAHAM, physicist, b. Strelno (near Poland), Germany, 1852; d. Pasadena, Cal., 1931. His mother, Rosalie Przlubska, was the daughter of a well-known physician, and was left motherless in early youth. She met, fell in love with, and married the proprietor of a dry goods shop, a man of forty years, Samuel Michelson. She was then but eighteen years of age. In 1855 they decided to come to the United States, where Samuel Michelson had a sister living in California. They first settled in a little mountain town in Calaveras County called Murphy's Camp, and there Albert's early childhood was spent.

As the young Michelson grew older he was sent to San Francisco to school, where he lived for several years with the family of the principal of the high school, who later paid him three dollars a month—his first earnings—to keep the physical instruments in order. When Albert was sixteen he went back to the home of his father, who by that time had moved his dry goods business to Virginia City, Nev. The elder Michelson wanted his son Albert to enter the Navy, so when, the next year, there was a vacancy in Nevada's quota, Albert took the examination for congressional appointment to Annapolis. He tied with another boy, who through influence got the appointment while Michelson was made alternate. After he had waited at Annapolis for the chance of a vacancy through the failure of one of the new appointees who had not yet passed his examination, this hope failed, and Michelson was just starting back for Washington when the commandant sent a messenger after him and informed him that President Ulysses S. Grant had given him "an appointment at large." Since this was the eleventh such appointment—the president had informed him that he had al-ready exhausted his ten appointments at large—Michelson always maintained that his career was started by an illegal act.

He was graduated from the United States Naval Academy in 1873 and commissioned a midshipman of the United States Navy. From 1875 to 1879 he was an instructor in physics and chemistry at the United States Naval Academy. In 1877, while he was studying for the purposes of a lecture the three purely terrestrial determinations of the velocity of light that had thus far been made—one by Fizeau in 1849, one by Cornu in 1872, both by Fizeau's toothed-wheel method, and one in 1862 by Foucault—a slight but, for accuracy, very vital modification of the Foucault method suggested itself to Michelson which, to quote his own words, "dispenses with Foucault's concave mirror and permits the use of any distance." Between November, 1877, and March, 1878, he built at an expense of ten dollars a rotating mirror, and, using with it a lens which he found in the physics lecture equipment at Annapolis, he obtained a displacement of the indicating spot of light six times as great as that of Foucault; he therefore was able to measure the velocity of light with six times more accuracy than Foucault had done. Michelson wrote his results to the editor of the *American Journal of Science*. This letter takes up half a page of the May issue of 1878, and is Michelson's first publication. (This problem, with which his career began, was also the one with which it closed. The introduction to his last paper was written by Michelson but ten days before he lost consciousness. As he wrote it, it had the same title as the paper with which he began his career, "On a Method of Measuring the Velocity of Light.")

By the measurement made in 1878 at Annapolis, Michelson had sprung at the age of twenty-six into international repute as a physicist. But, however important his work on the velocity of light may have been, the permanence of Michelson's place in physics undoubtedly rests in largest measure upon his invention of the Michelson interferometer and what he accomplished with it. Early in 1879 Michelson left the Naval Academy, and was employed for a year at the office of the Nautical Almanac in Washington. He then spent two years studying at Berlin, at Heidelberg, and at the Collège de France (1880-82). It is probable that it was his careful study in Paris of Fizeau's work which got him started on his main lifework in interferometry. Michelson's first use of his interferometer was for testing the relative velocity of the earth and the ether. It was while he was still in Europe, at the age of twenty-eight, that he made his first try at this epoch-making experiment. But it was not until 1886 and 1887 that this experiment, repeated at the Case School of Applied Science with great care and refinement by Michelson and Edward Williams Morley, begins to take its place as the most famous and in many ways the most fundamentally significant experiment since the discovery of electromagnetic induction by Faraday in 1831. The special theory of relativity may be looked upon as essentially a generalization from it. (Michelson was professor of physics at the Case School of Applied Science in Cleveland from 1883 to 1889, at Clark University from 1889 to 1892, and at the University of Chicago from 1892 to 1929.)

Only second to his use of the interferometer for test-

Albert A. Michelson

ing the relative velocity of the earth and the ether is the use which Michelson made of his interferometer, especially in the years 1887 to 1897, in proving, through his penetrating and very skillful study of the so-called visibility curves characteristic of different spectral lines, the great complexity of all save a very few of such lines. Interferometry was applied also to the measurement of the diameters of stars—a measurement which, for the first time, made possible the direct determination of a stellar diameter, and, to take but one example, fixed the diameter of Betelgeuse at 240,000,000 miles—about 280 times that of the sun. The essentials of the method had been published by Michelson as early as 1890.

No event in Michelson's career showed the originality of his mind better than the echelon spectroscope, which appeared in 1898. By 1900 the attainment of high spectroscopic resolution had become a major objective with Michelson, and it was perhaps because he thought he had about exhausted the possibilities of the interferometer and the echelon for this purpose that he turned his attention to the problem which gave him more trouble and at the same time filled his associates with more admiration for him than any of its predecessors had done, namely, the problem of ruling very high resolution gratings. He often said he regretted that he ever got "this bear by the tail," but he would not let go, and, in spite of endless discouragements, at the end of about eight years of struggle he had produced a good six-inch grating containing 110,000 lines (resolving power is measured by the number of lines times the order of the spectrum), which was fifty per cent better than the best otherwise produced at that time, and in 1915 he produced both an eight-inch and a ten-inch grating, still among the most powerful instruments of diffraction. (However, with the extraordinary developments of quantum and nuclear physics, the subject has become so important for physics, astronomy, chemistry and even biology that a considerable number of in-

stitutions are now hard at work on the grating problem.)

The problem of the rigidity of the earth which Michelson, in collaboration with Henry Gordon Gale, solved so magnificently in 1919 is unlike most of Michelson's work in that it was undertaken at the request of others. The results, published in the *Astrophysical Journal* for 1919 by Michelson and Gale, undoubtedly give the best values yet obtained of the earth's rigidity, as well as its viscosity.

In 1907 Michelson was awarded the Nobel Prize for Physics by the Swedish Academy of Sciences.

The total volume of Michelson's published work is very small. In an active life as a physicist, extending from the age of twenty-five to that of seventy-nine, he wrote two small books that are found in all libraries. The first is entitled *Light Waves and Their Uses* (University of Chicago Press, 1903). It represents his Lowell Lectures delivered in 1899. The second is *Studies in Optics* (University of Chicago Press, 1927), and consists of a condensed summary of his major researches.

His bibliography of scientific papers contains but seventy-eight titles all told, and many of these are abstracts and most of them are quite short articles. Not a few of them are reprintings of the same article in different journals and different languages. One's knowledge of Michelson must be gained, then, more from what he did than from what he said. Also, one must call upon the testimony of those who lived and worked side by side with him for a quarter-century and more. That testimony will, most likely be unanimous in the judgment that his most outstanding characteristic was his extraordinary honesty, his abhorrence alike of careless, inexact, ambiguous statement, as well as of all deception and misstatement. His was a remarkably clean-cut mind, which left little room for adjustment and compromise.

If his most outstanding characteristic was his honesty, his second most notable characteristic was the singleness, simplicity and clarity of his objective—an objective from which he let nothing divert him, however great the pressure. He was an intense individualist, he knew what he wanted to do, he had confidence in his ability to do it, and he refused to let anything divert him from it, no matter what other interests had to be sacrificed or who stood in the way.

It will probably be generally agreed that the three American physicists whose work has been most epoch-making and whose names are most certain to be frequently heard wherever and whenever in future years the story of physics is told are Benjamin Franklin, Josiah Willard Gibbs and Albert A. Michelson. Michelson, pure experimentalist, designer of instruments, refiner of techniques, lives as a physicist because in the field of optics he drove the refinement of measurement to its limits and by so doing showed a skeptical world what far-reaching consequences can follow from that sort of process and what new vistas of knowledge can be opened up by it. It was a lesson the world had to learn. The results of learning it are reflected today in the extraordinary recent discoveries—among others—in the field of electronics, of radio-activity, of vitamins, of hormones, and of nuclear structure. All these fields owe a large debt to Michelson, the pioneer in the art of measurement of extraordinary minute quantities and effects.

Michelson received no religious training, had no interest in Judaism, and took no part in Jewish communal activities.   ROBERT A. MILLIKAN.

Lit.: Halc, *Astronomical Society of the Pacific,* vol. 43 (1931) 175; Lemon, H. B., *The American Physics Teacher,* vol. 4 (1936) 1; Lodge, Oliver, *Nature,* Jan. 2, 1926, pp. 1-6; Millikan, Robert A., "Albert Abraham Michelson: The First American Nobel Laureate," *The Scientific Monthly,* vol. 48 (Jan., 1939) 16-27; idem, "Biographical Memoir of Albert Abraham Michelson," *National Academy of Sciences, Washington: Biographical Memoirs,* vol. 19 (1939) 121-46 (bibliography of Michelson's publications, pp. 142-46); idem, in *American Hebrew,* Oct. 4, 1929, pp. 585, 652, 667.

MICHELSON, CHARLES, journalist and public relations expert, b. Virginia City, Nev., 1869. Unlike his elder brother, the great physicist Albert A. Michelson, he ran away from a formal education and turned to newspaper work. In the late 1880's he joined William Randolph Hearst's San Francisco *Examiner,* and he stayed with Hearst for thirty years, becoming one of that publisher's favorites, working in San Francisco, Chicago, New York, and Washington, D. C. His rise with Hearst was rapid and spectacular, but in 1919 he deserted to join the old New York *World* as chief of their Washington Bureau. There he worked until 1928, when John J. Raskob called him to take over publicity for the National Democratic Committee at the unprecedented yearly salary of $20,800.

To this job of press agent for the Democrats, and with the objective of winning the next presidential election, Michelson brought an intimate knowledge of the country's politics for two decades, a skill in maneuvering and showmanship, and great literary flair. Almost immediately he became the miracle man of the Democrats and the bête noire of the Republicans. Given a free hand, he became ghost writer of many a Congressman's speech, and the skillful manipulator of attack and counter-attack in the country's press. Two of his great press triumphs were his steady barrage against Herbert Hoover and his combat with the Liberty League. In 1932 Michelson broke with the anti-New Dealers in the Democratic Party and went with Franklin D. Roosevelt, in time becoming one of the president's close assistants. He directed public relations for the NRA in 1933 to 1934.

Lit.: Johnston, Alva, "Hundred-Tongued Charley, the Great Silent Orator," *Saturday Evening Post,* May 30, 1930, p. 5 et seq.

MICHELSON, LEO, painter and etcher, b. Riga, Latvia, 1887. He studied at the academy in St. Petersburg, continued to work in Dorpat, and settled down in Berlin in 1911. Educational trips through Italy, Spain and France and a short return to his homeland interrupted his stay in Berlin, where he became a close friend of the famous painter Lovis Corinth.

Michelson's paintings depict the landscape and people of the Baltic. They are in oil and water colors and illustrate the melancholy mood of the country. However, his Italian paintings are full of color, as are his many paintings of Berlin's waterfront. In addition he portrayed and etched Jewish personages and lowly characters, as well as general Jewish motives. His woodcuts for Jewish books, such as those for the *Mishle*

Shualim of *Berechiah ben Natronai Hanakdan* (Berlin, 1921) and to the *Sefer Hayashar* (Berlin, 1923), rank with those of Lilien, Steinhardt and Budko.

After the Nazis' rise to power Michelson went first to Italy, and then (1941) to the United States.

MICHELSON, MIRIAM, author, sister of Charles and Albert A. Michelson, b. Caleveras, Cal., 1870. As a newspaper woman she did drama criticism and special features for various Philadelphia and California newspapers. Besides contributing numerous short stories to leading magazines, she wrote a number of popular novels. Best-known among them are: *In the Bishop's Carriage* (1904); *A Yellow Journalist* (1905); *Superwoman* (1912); *Country of Two Kings* (1921). In 1934 she published *Wonderlode of Silver and Gold.*

MICHIGAN, one of the east north central states of the United States, with a population of 5,256,106 (census of 1940) including about 95,000 Jews (1942). Most of these, about 85,000, live in Detroit and about 1,800 in Flint and 1,700 in Grand Rapids (the three cities are the subject of special articles in this encyclopedia); the rest, about 6,500, live in the other cities and elsewhere in the state.

Jewish traders were probably among the first arrivals at the trading posts along the Great Lakes. At the time of Pontiac's conspiracy (1763), two Jews, Levy and Chapman, were captured by the Indians. Ezekiel Solomon of Montreal is listed among the traders at Fort Michilimackinac (Mackinac) from 1763 until 1816. He was one of the few who escaped the massacre of the British garrison by the Indians in 1763. The jurat to his affidavit for use before the military court of inquiry into the massacre omits the phrase "Sworn before me on the Holy Evangelist," used in the other affidavits taken before the same officer; it reads merely "Sworn, etc." Although he did not sign the two petitions to the governor of Canada asking that a Roman Catholic missionary be sent to the post, his name is among those who volunteered to contribute to the support of the missionary. Levy Solomons of Montreal, who may have been related to Ezekiel Solomon, was also a trader at Mackinac. William Solomons, supposed to have been the son of Ezekiel Solomon by an Indian woman, is listed as an official interpreter at the post until 1816.

During the War of 1812, Jacob Franks, one of the Franks of Montreal, was a resident of Mackinac. With three others, he was appointed in 1814 to inventory two captured schooners. When the English surrendered Mackinac, after the war, his house was among several pillaged. His nephew, John Lawe, was a lieutenant in the force defending the fort against the Americans.

Jews began to settle in Michigan during the late 1840's together with other immigrants from Germany, Austria, and Hungary. Washtenaw County was then the best county of the state for farm stock, wool and hides. Many of the farmers, also recent immigrants, were German, and here the German and Austrian Jews found the language of their native land and a place where they could earn a living as peddlers or craftsmen until they could establish themselves as merchants and manufacturers. Many of the Jews who settled later in Detroit came from Ann Arbor and Ypsilanti in Washtenaw County. In the 1870's, Jewish communities were established in Grand Rapids and Bay City, and, in the next decade, in Alpena, Benton Harbor, and Traverse City. All five cities were flourishing centers of the lumbering business.

At the end of the 19th cent. and the beginning of the 20th most of the Jewish immigrants to the United States were from Eastern Europe. Not all of these turned to trade or manufacture on the eastern border. Several attempts were made to organize agricultural colonies in Michigan. The first, called the Palestine Colony, was established at Bad Ax in 1891. The colony, although assisted by the Hebrew Relief Society of Detroit and other organizations, disbanded after four years. In 1933 Sunrise Colony was established in Alicia near Saginaw but after three years this, too, was disbanded. Many of the later immigrants were Orthodox (as indeed most of the earlier immigrants had been at first) and established Orthodox congregations. In 1939, the Michigan Synagogue Conference of Orthodox Congregations was formed at Detroit.

About seventy of the cities or townships of Michigan had more than ten Jews in 1942 and about ninety places less than ten.

ADRIAN (population 14,230, census of 1940) with about twenty-five Jews had two Jewish residents before 1850, Solomon and Andrew Freedman. They removed afterwards to Detroit.

ALPENA (population 12,808, census of 1940) with about thirty-five Jews has a Reform congregation, Temple Beth El, organized in 1884. The synagogue was dedicated in 1888 and remodeled in 1926. The first resident rabbi was J. Buchalter (1888).

ANN ARBOR (population 29,815, census of 1940) with about 200 Jews had a number of Jewish residents before 1850. Among the first were five brothers, Solomon, Moses, Leopold, Marcus, and Jacob Weil from Bohemia. Solomon settled in Ann Arbor in 1843 and the others afterwards. Leopold Weil and Judah Sittig tried farming and so did Moses Weil and another Bohemian Jew, Woodel, but all gave it up after a year or so. Charles Fantle came to Ann Arbor from Bohemia in 1848. Other Jewish residents in Ann Arbor or the neighboring city of Ypsilanti (population 12,121, census of 1940, including about fifty Jews) before 1850 were: Isaac Altman, Solomon Bendit, Charles, Adolph, and Louis Bresler, with their father, Leo Bresler, the Fantes brothers, one Feder, one Hayman, Adam Hersch, and Moses Rindskopf. Goodkind, the Guiterman brothers, and Solomon Sondheim probably came after 1850. Charles Bresler lived in Ypsilanti where he bought horses for shipment east. Like many others of the Ann Arbor-Ypsilanti community, he later settled in Detroit.

The Weil brothers were Orthodox Jews and conducted religious services—said to be the first Minyans held in Michigan—from 1845 on. A burial ground was acquired in 1848 or 1849. But it was not until 1920 that a congregation was organized. In that year Beth Israel (Orthodox) was formed. A synagogue was dedicated in 1927. The first resident rabbi was Pincus Gropstein (1915-18). In 1940 the rabbi was Isaac J. Goldman.

The University of Michigan is at Ann Arbor and a number of Jews were members of the faculty in 1942; among others: Moses Gomberg, professor emeritus of chemistry; Isaiah L. Scharfman, chairman of the department of economics; Samuel A. Goudsmit, physicist;

Reuben L. Kahn, bacteriologist; and Nathan Sinai, professor of hygiene and public health.

William Haber of Ann Arbor was state emergency relief administrator in 1936. In 1939 he became executive director of the National Refugee Service and served until 1941. He was special assistant to United States Director of the Budget (1942), on leave from the University of Michigan, where he was professor of economics.

AU SABLE township (population 309, census of 1940) had an Orthodox congregation from 1874 on. A Presbyterian church was bought and remodeled in 1885 for a synagogue. But a fire which destroyed the synagogue caused the congregation to disband in 1911. Selig Solomon (d. 1935) was mayor of Au Sable city (annexed to Au Sable township in 1931).

BATTLE CREEK (population 43,453, census of 1940) with about 250 Jews has two congregations, the Jewish Center of Battle Creek (Orthodox) and Congregation Beth-El (Reform). The Jewish Center was organized in 1935. The first resident rabbi was Manuel Greenstein (1935-38); the rabbi in 1942 was William B. Silverman. Memorial Park Cemetery for the Jewish community was organized in 1939.

BAY CITY (population 47,956, census of 1940) has about 800 Jews (1942). Congregation Anshe Chesed (Reform) was organized in the 1870's. Its synagogue, dedicated in 1892, was remodeled in 1922. The first resident rabbi was Wolf Landau who served from 1878 until 1903. Congregation Shaary Zedek (Orthodox) was organized in 1899. Its synagogue, dedicated in 1899, was remodeled in 1915 and again in 1934. The first rabbi was Joseph Taub who served from 1899 until 1914. In 1940 the rabbi was Mendel Glancz. Another Orthodox congregation, Temple Abraham, was organized in 1914. The first resident rabbi was Samuel Lite (1914-15). The rabbi in 1940 was Pierce Ames. Bay City has several Jewish cemeteries: B'nai Brith, organized in 1878 by Anshe Chesed Congregation; Shaary Zedek, organized in 1884; and Chevra Kadisha, organized in 1890. The Northeastern Michigan Jewish Welfare Federation (including Alpena and other communities), organized in 1940, has its offices in Bay City. William Hellerman was attorney of Bay County in 1936. In 1942 Louis B. Harrison, nationally recognized as an authority on water purification, was chief water chemist.

BENTON HARBOR (population 16,668, census of 1940) has about 900 Jews (1942). Congregation B'nai Israel (Conservative) was organized in 1882. Its third synagogue was dedicated in 1923. The first resident rabbi was Abraham Schmidt (1889-92). The rabbi in 1940 was Moses A. Schwab. Congregation Ahavath Shalom (Orthodox) was organized in 1912. The first resident rabbi was Simon Hyman, who served from 1912 to 1919. The rabbi in 1940 was Abraham J. Tuckman. B'nai Israel Cemetery was organized in 1900. Shaarey Shalom Cemetery was organized in 1919.

HANCOCK (population 5,554, census of 1940) with about forty Jews (1942) has an Orthodox body, Congregation of Israel, organized in 1913. The synagogue was dedicated that year.

IRON MOUNTAIN (population 11,080, census of 1940) with about ninety Jews (1942) also has an Orthodox congregation, Anshai Knesseth, organized in 1908. Its synagogue was dedicated in 1910. The first rabbi was

J. Pasten who served from 1907 until 1915. The rabbi in 1940 was Lawrence Dain.

JACKSON (population 49,656, census of 1940), has a Jewish community of about 200. Temple Beth El (Reform) was originally an Orthodox congregation, organized in 1859 as Beth Israel. It was reorganized as a Reform congregation under its present name in 1909. Services of the old Orthodox congregation were first held in the homes of Jacob Hirsch and Henry Lang. Both, and perhaps Joseph Hanau, were residents of Jackson before 1850. The first synagogue, a church purchased from the Congregationalists, was dedicated in 1864. In 1905 a Lutheran church was purchased, moved to the present site and dedicated as a synagogue. The first resident rabbi was M. Wetterhahn (1864). The rabbi of Beth El in 1942 was Bernard Zeiger. Temple Beth Israel Cemetery was organized in 1860. The first interment, however, had taken place the year before. The Jewish Federation in Jackson, supporting local social services as well as national and overseas welfare programs, was organized in 1937. Harry Hirschman was city treasurer of Jackson (1933).

KALAMAZOO (population of 54,097, census of 1940) has a Jewish community of about 400. Mannes Israel who had been born in Pyrmont, Germany, settled in Kalamazoo about 1846. Another early Jewish resident of Kalamazoo was Emil Friedman from Bavaria. Israel's son, Edward, lost his life as a member of Lieutenant Adolphus W. Greely's polar expedition (1881-84) of which he was mathematician and astronomer. Congregation Bene Israel (Reform) was organized in 1865. The first services were held in the home of a Mr. Rosenberg. The first synagogue was dedicated in 1872, and a second in 1911. The first resident rabbi of Bene Israel was Jacob Epstein who served from 1872 to 1875; the rabbi in 1942 was Philip F. Waterman.

Congregation of Moses (Orthodox) was organized in 1886. Services were held at first in the home of H. Goldstein. Its synagogue was dedicated in 1906 and enlarged in 1939. The first resident religious leader was Rabbi Rosnick who served from 1886 until 1904; the rabbi in 1940 was Herman Price. Congregation of Moses Cemetery was organized in 1891.

Samuel Folz was mayor of Kalamazoo in 1903. He was afterwards appointed postmaster (1916).

LANSING (population of 78,753, census of 1940), capital of the state, has a Jewish community of about 500. Henry and Emanuel Lederer, who came from Bohemia and had first settled at Ann Arbor in 1847, moved to Lansing after two years and established a general store, a tannery, and a soap factory. Congregation Shaarey Zedek (Conservative) was organized in 1918. Its synagogue, the second belonging to the congregation, was dedicated in 1932. The first resident rabbi was Herman Price (1932-34); the rabbi in 1940 was Arthur Zuckerman; in 1942 Morris Applebaum was rabbi. In 1898 Mount Hope Cemetery was organized. The Federated Jewish Charities of Lansing was organized in 1939. Alex Cohen of Lansing was elected to the state legislature.

LUDINGTON (population 8,701, census of 1940) has about sixty Jews. An Orthodox congregation, Sons of Israel, was established in Ludington in 1893 and continued until 1900. Israel Rotenborsky (1893-94) was the first resident rabbi. William Zeiv was mayor of Ludington in 1917.

MACKINAC was one of the places where Jews first settled in Michigan during the 19th cent. as well as in the 18th. In 1845 Lewis F. Leopold (whose name had been Freudenthaler), a native of Baden, Germany, with his wife, Babette, who was a member of the Austrian (Österreicher) family, their infant son, Lewis' sister, Hannah, and Lewis' brother, Samuel, were on the island. The brothers became pioneers in the fishery business and were soon shipping a thousand barrels of salted fish to Cleveland every season. Samuel Leopold left Mackinac in 1853 to become one of the first white men to settle at Fond du Lac, Wisconsin. Edward Kanter, who worked for the Leopolds and Austrians at Mackinac in 1846, left the island in 1852 and became a resident of Detroit. He was a member of the state legislature from 1866 until 1870.

MARSHALL (population 5,253, census of 1940) has very few Jews. As early as 1848, Samuel and Marx Hart, who came from southern Germany, had settled there.

MOUNT CLEMENS (population 14,389, census of 1940) has about 300 Jewish residents. Congregation Beth Tefilath Moses (Orthodox) was organized in 1912. The synagogue was dedicated in 1920. The first resident rabbi was Meyer Davis who served from 1912 until 1920; the rabbi in 1940 was David Winchester.

MUSKEGON (population 47,697, census of 1940) has about 300 Jews. Sons of Israel (Conservative) was organized in 1911 as an Orthodox congregation. It became Conservative in 1937. Services were held, at first, in the home of Henry Rubinsky. The synagogue was dedicated in 1917. Benjamin Cohen (1934-36) was the first resident rabbi; Aaron Cohen was rabbi in 1940.

PETOSKEY (population 6,019, census of 1940) with a Jewish population of about seventy-five, has an Orthodox congregation, B'nai Israel, organized in 1894. The synagogue, dedicated in 1911, was originally a Baptist church. The first resident rabbi was I. Koplowitz (1911-15). B'nai Israel Cemetery was organized in 1895.

PONTIAC (population 66,626, census of 1940) has about 550 Jews. Temple Beth Jacob (Reform) was first organized as the Jewish Community Center of Pontiac in 1923. The synagogue was dedicated the following year and the present name adopted in 1933. The first resident rabbi was Elmer Berger, who served from 1932 to 1936. The rabbi in 1942 was Eric Friedland. Congregation B'nai Israel (Orthodox) was organized in 1934. Its synagogue was purchased and remodeled in 1937. The first resident rabbi was A. E. Miller (1937-38); in 1940 the rabbi was Isidore Strauss. The Federated Jewish Charities of Pontiac was organized in 1936.

PORT HURON (population 32,759, census of 1940) with a Jewish community of about 220 has an Orthodox congregation, Mt. Sinai, organized in 1898. Its synagogue was dedicated in 1924. The first resident rabbi was Leon Gerstein (1898). Mt. Sinai Cemetery was organized in 1898.

RIVER ROUGE (population 17,008 census of 1940) has an Orthodox congregation, River Rouge Jewish Congregation, organized in 1929. The synagogue was dedicated in 1938.

SAGINAW (population 82,794, census of 1940) has about 475 Jews. Congregation B'nai Israel (Orthodox) was organized in 1890. The synagogue, dedicated in

1913, was remodeled in 1928. The first resident rabbi was William Reiches (1890-2); the rabbi in 1940 was Israel T. Notis. Temple Beth El (Reform) was organized in 1903. Services were first held in the home of Samuel Seitner. Beth El's synagogue was purchased, remodeled, and dedicated in 1921. The first resident rabbi was Moses Abraham (1903-4). The Saginaw Hebrew Cemetery was organized in 1898. The Jewish Welfare Federation was organized in 1939.

SOUTH HAVEN (population 4,745, census of 1940) with about 300 Jewish residents has an Orthodox Hebrew congregation, organized in 1920. Its synagogue was dedicated in 1928. The first resident rabbi was David Rosenbloom (1928-30).

TRAVERSE CITY (population 14,455, census of 1940) with about twenty-five Jews has an Orthodox congregation, Beth El, organized in 1883. Oakwood Cemetery was organized in 1884.

WYANDOTTE (population 30,618, census of 1940) has about 200 Jews. Beth El Congregation (Orthodox) was organized in 1926. The first resident rabbi was A. Davis (1926-28). In 1940 Abraham Danzig was rabbi.

Besides the Jews of Michigan in public service already mentioned, the following from Detroit were members of the state legislature: Adam Bloom (1881-83); Joseph Weiss (1887-93, state senate 1891-93); David E. Heineman (1891-93); Charles C. Simons (state senate 1903-4); Henry Marks (1908); Joseph Maas and Nathan Nagel (1912 and 1920); Henry Glass (1934); and Charles Blondy (state senate 1940). Charles C. Simons was afterwards a United States District Judge (1923-32) and a member of the United States Circuit Court of Appeals for the Sixth Circuit (from 1932 on). Henry M. Butzel of Detroit was a member of the Supreme Court of Michigan from 1929 on (chief justice 1931-39). Julius Houseman, who was the first Jewish resident of Grand Rapids, after serving as mayor of the city (1872-76) was a representative in the United States Congress from 1881 until 1883. Other Jewish mayors, besides those mentioned, include: Norman Henry Wiener (member of Albion city council 1928-30), mayor of Albion (population 8,345, census of 1940) from 1931 on; Edward Frensdorf, in 1907 mayor of Hudson (population 2,426, census of 1940); Benjamin Bloomrosen, in 1907 the first mayor of Manistique (population 5,399, census of 1940); William Saulson, in 1911 mayor of St. Ignace (population 2,669, census of 1940); and Jack Greenberg, in 1940 mayor of Vassar (population 2,154, census of 1940). State officials include: Mrs. Schmarya Kleinman, unemployment commission, 1931; A. C. Lappin, labor relations board, 1939 to 1941; Samuel Metzger, commissioner of agriculture, 1933; Thom George Sternberg (city attorney of Harrisville, 1931; municipal justice, Harrisville, 1932), assistant attorney general of Michigan, 1937. County officials include: Henry Behrend, sheriff of Wayne county, 1931; Jack Korn, prosecutor of Wexford county, 1941. Nate S. Shapero was, in 1942, president of the Detroit Fire Commission.

In March, 1942, *The Jewish News,* a weekly of statewide interests, and the first community-sponsored Jewish periodical in Michigan, was founded in Detroit. Philip Slomovitz was its editor.

See also: DETROIT; FLINT; GRAND RAPIDS.

PHILIP SLOMOVITZ.

Lit.: Heineman, David E., "Jewish Beginnings in Michigan before 1850," *American Jewish Historical Society Publications,* No 13 (1905) 47-70; idem, "The Startling Experience of a Jewish Trader During Pontiac's Siege of Detroit in 1763," *ibid.* (1915) 31-35; *Inventory of the Church and Synagogue Archives of Michigan: Jewish Bodies* (prepared by The Michigan Historical Records Survey Project, Work Projects Administration, 1940); Wolf, Simon, *The American Jew as Patriot, Soldier, and Citizen* (1895, list of 130 soldiers from Michigan who served in the Civil War, pp. 209-14).

MICKIEWICZ, ADAM, non-Jewish Polish poet, b. near Nowogrodek, Russia, 1798; d. Constantinople, 1855. In *Pan Tadeusz* (1834), his masterpiece (rendered into Hebrew by J. Lichtenbaum and into Yiddish by D. Königsberg), Mickiewicz depicted the ideal type of Jewish patriot, a musician named Jankiel, who, loyal to Poland and deeply religious, aroused the Polish patriots to fight for freedom against Russian oppressors.

At a time when the Polish government still abhorred the idea of granting civic rights to the Jews, Mickiewicz already advocated their full emancipation. Inclined toward mysticism and Messianic ideas, he strongly believed in the lofty mission of the Jewish people whose task, like that of the Poles, he believed to be the liberation of all oppressed nations. The poet, who lived for many years in exile in France, attempted during the Crimean War (shortly before his death), together with the French army physician Levy, to organize Jewish legions to fight against Russia. He once delivered a sermon in a Paris synagogue in which he expounded his ideas regarding Judaism.

Polish anti-Semites asserted that he was of Jewish origin, while liberals charged that he was poisoned by Polish reactionaries.

MICROCOCCUS PRODIGIOSUS (also **Bacillus Prodigiosus**), *see* HOST DESECRATION.

MIDDLE DAYS OF HOLIDAYS (Hol Hamoed), *see* HOLIDAYS.

MIDDOTH ("measurements"), tenth tractate of Kodashim, the fifth division of the Mishnah; there is no corresponding Tosefta or Gemara. It consists of five chapters and deals with the measurements and institutions of the Temple in Jerusalem. The tractate is almost purely descriptive; there is a minimum of discussion. The first chapter treats of the night watches, the Temple gates, and the chamber of the hearth; the second gives the dimensions of the Temple; the third deals with the altar of burnt-offering, the place of slaughtering, the laver and the porch. The fourth is devoted to the sanctuary (Hechal), while the fifth describes the Temple court and its chambers, including the chamber of hewn stone (*lishkath hagazith*) where the Sanhedrin used to meet.

Lit.: Danby, Herbert, *The Mishnah* (1933) 589-98.

MIDIAN, MIDIANITES, an ancient people, frequently mentioned in the Bible. The Midianites lived in northwestern Arabia. Some of them were merchants who participated in the gold and incense trade from Yemen, and in the trade between Egypt and Syria; others were wild warriors who, in the days of the judges, made destructive inroads into Central Palestine, but were decisively defeated by Gideon (*Judges* 6 to 8). One clan, the Kenites, which dwelt near

Mount Sinai and to which Moses fled from Pharaoh (*Ex.* 2:15), is described as consisting of peaceful shepherds. Jethro, Moses' father-in-law, was a priest of Midian. Whenever Midian is mentioned by later Jewish writers, the name is used with reference to Israel's triumph over its foes (*Isa.* 9:3; *Hab.* 3:7). Aside from this, the Midianites are not mentioned again in the Scripture.

MIDLOURSKY, J. F., physician, b. Russia. He practiced medicine in Russia and earned various Czarist decorations. Moving to England, he became active in general and Jewish communal activities, as well as in medical work. Midloursky was made a life governor of Queen Mary's Hospital, the Royal Chest Hospitals and the Royal Ophthalmic Hospitals, in acknowledgment of his work as president of the Mutual Friendly Aid Hospital Society. He occupied executive posts in London County Council schools as well as in Jewish educational undertakings, and was president of the Hackney Hostel for Refugee Children. In 1942 Midloursky was reported to be still a resident of London.

MIDRASH (from the Hebrew root *darash*, "to search," "to investigate"), that type of Biblical exegesis which attempts, by a minute examination and broad interpretation of the text, to penetrate more deeply into the spirit of the Bible. At times the purpose of the Midrash is to define more clearly the meaning, or explain more fully the operation, of a Biblical law; it is known then as Midrash Halachah, the word Halachah denoting that rule of life which takes the form of law and ritual. More often, however, it is the purpose of the Midrash to interpret the Biblical text from the ethical or devotional point of view; it is known then as Midrash Haggadah, the word Haggadah signifying a form of teaching that seeks to admonish and edify rather than to legislate. In either case, the chief object of the Midrash is to search after the inner content of the Bible, whether it deals with questions of law or with aspects of the purely ethical and spiritual life.

The need of such a method of interpretation as the Midrash represents made itself felt very early in the religious history of the Jew. No sooner was the Law, as embodied in the Torah, definitely formulated than the aid of trained interpreters had to be invoked. For no law can be so framed as to apply to all possible questions and situations. It became necessary, therefore, to expound the deeper meaning of the Law in order to make it answer the problems and needs which arose during later centuries. Thus the rabbis, accepting the Bible as the sole guide of life, endeavored to find expressed or implied in Biblical statement everything that would meet the exigencies of an increasingly complex life.

There was yet another factor which proved effective in promoting the search after the deeper meaning of the Biblical text. There were those who, like the Sadducees, wished to apply the Law literally and insisted that the Oral Law could not be held as absolutely binding, since it lacked divine sanction. This opposition to the Oral Law gave rise to an even greater effort on the part of the rabbis, the zealous guardians of Jewish tradition, to discover a firm basis in Scripture for the transmitted customs and practices associated with the religious life. Animated by this motive, the rabbis sought so to interpret every word of the Bible as to find in it support for all the accumulated teachings and traditions of the past.

As the ethical thought and legendary lore of the Midrash are largely based on luminous interpretations of the Biblical texts, it was but natural for the Darshan (preacher) of later centuries to make use of the Midrashic material in the development of his own religious message. The Midrash thus became for the Jewish preachers of subsequent ages an inexhaustible source of thought and inspiration.

The methods employed by the rabbis in their search after the hidden possibilities of Biblical texts were in most instances simple and effective. In commenting, for instance, on the verse: "It is a tree of life to them that lay hold of it" (*Prov.* 3:18), the Midrash deduces a most significant spiritual truth. "Scripture does not say," it observes, "that the Torah is a source of life to those who *study* it; for then the world would soon become lifeless. To *lay hold of it* must mean to support it and strengthen it, or to conform one's conduct to its teachings—an accomplishment which is within the reach of all men."

Frequently no new idea is discovered in the text. The teacher is merely bent on making the truth of the text more pointed and vivid. Thus, in elucidating the text: "Now the Lord said unto Abraham, Get thee out of thy country, and from thy kindred" (*Gen.* 12:1), the teacher says that Abraham may be compared to a flask of balsam. When the flask lies in an obscure corner, tightly sealed, it keeps its fragrance and sweetness to itself. But when it is opened and carried from place to place, its sweet fragrance is diffused, bringing delight to many people who inhale its aroma. It was thus that God spoke to Abraham our father: "Go forth and wander from place to place that thy name may become great and through thee all the nations may be blessed."

The best known and most important of the Midrashic collections were compiled by various unknown editors during a period of approximately 1,000 years. These are: the *Mechilta*, to *Exodus*, the *Sifra*, to *Leviticus*, and the *Sifre*, to *Numbers* and *Deuteronomy*, all from the period of the Tannaim (up to about 200 C.E.); the Midrash Rabboth to the entire Pentateuch and the five Scrolls: *Song of Songs*, *Ruth*, *Lamentations*, *Ecclesiastes*, and *Esther*, proceeding from various centuries; the *Tanhuma*, homilies to the whole Pentateuch, of which there are two different compilations; and the *Pesikta* homilies, comprising two separate volumes, and revolving around holy days and other special occasions.

All this wealth of Midrashic material has long formed an integral part of the Jewish literary heritage. From it Jews of all lands have drawn comfort and strength; in it they have found the inspiration for living a worthier and nobler life.

See also: The individual articles below; MECHILTA; PESIKTA; SIFRA; SIFRE; TANHUMA; YALKUT.

ISRAEL BETTAN.

Lit.: Bettan, Israel, *Studies in Jewish Preaching;* Friedlander, Gerald, *Rabbinic Philosophy and Ethics;* Ginzberg, Louis, *The Legends of the Jews;* Lazarus, M., *The Ethics of Judaism;* Strack, H. L., *Introduction to the Talmud and Midrash.*

MIDRASH DEUTERONOMY (DEBARIM RABBAH), homiletic Midrash to *Deuteronomy*. In its printed form it is divided into eleven sections, corresponding to the eleven Parashahs of the Biblical book; but Zunz detected that there were originally twenty-seven homilies, all of which began with the word *halachah* ("religious law"). Each has the same pattern: a legal exposition (a feature peculiar to this Midrash), interpretations based on passages from other books, and in conclusion an expression of consolation or hope in the Messianic future. The book was probably composed about 900, which would make it the latest of the Midrashic works on the Pentateuch; Weiss, basing his conclusions on the number of Greek loan words, held that it was composed in the Byzantine Empire. The manner of interpretation is very witty; there are occasional plays on words, and some fine psychological observations. The part that deals with the death of Moses is especially beautiful.

The tractate has been translated into English in H. Freedman and Maurice Simon's edition of the Midrash Rabbah (London, 1939).

Lit.: Zunz, L., *Gottesdienstliche Vorträge;* Weiss, I. H., *Dor Dor Vedoreshav,* vol. 3.

MIDRASH ECCLESIASTES (KOHELETH RABBAH),

an exegetical Midrash to *Ecclesiastes.* The interpretation follows the text verse by verse, only a few verses being left without comment. It is divided into four sections, beginning with 1:1, 3:13, 7:1 and 9:7, respectively. The compiler drew largely from the older Midrashim and the Babylonian and Palestinian Talmuds. Since this Midrash refers by name to the tractate *Aboth* and even to several of the minor Talmudic tractates, it has been designated "a work of a later epoch" (Zunz, L., *Gottesdienstliche Vorträge,* 2nd ed., p. 277). This Midrash combines allegorical with simple exposition. The former is chiefly called into use in explaining away the skeptical and hedonistic views of the Biblical book; it does this by taking the pleasures of the senses encouraged there as really meaning the pleasure derived from the study of the Law and the performance of good deeds.

There is an English translation of the Midrash in H. Freedman and Maurice Simon's edition of the Midrash Rabbah (London, 1939).

MIDRASH ESTHER (ESTHER RABBAH),

exegetic Midrash to *Esther.* It is divided into ten parts, corresponding to the chapters of the Biblical book, but the material is much more elaborate at the beginning; the first six parts expound the first two chapters of *Esther,* while the last four deal with all the remaining chapters. The material is rich and variegated, and appears to come from a number of sources, some very early; there is a citation, for instance, from the Bible translation of Aquila (2nd cent.). There are several other Midrash collections to the Biblical or Apocryphal *Esther,* and in the Talmud *Meg.* 10b to 16a is such a Midrash.

Midrash Esther has been translated into English in the edition of the Midrash Rabbah by H. Freedman and Maurice Simon (London, 1939).

Lit.: Weiss, I. H., *Dor Dor Vedoreshav,* vol. 3, p. 274.

MIDRASH EXODUS (SHEMOTH RABBAH),

homiletic Midrash to *Exodus.* It consists of fifty-two chapters; the first fourteen of these may be called exegetic since they consist of a running exposition of the

individual verses. There are nine sections that begin with, "Thus began Rabbi Tanhuma bar Abba," which is characteristic of *Midrash Tanhuma.* The work was compiled about the 11th or 12th cent., but contains much older material, as the Tosafists cite from it, and there are passages borrowed from the *Mechilta* as well as from *Tanhuma;* the latter appear especially in the first fifteen chapters, the former in the subsequent chapters.

Lit.: Epstein, A., *Beiträge zur jüdischen Altertumskunde,* vol. 1, p. 67 et seq.

MIDRASH GALUTH

("Midrash of the Exile"), known also as *Midrash Eser Galliyoth* ("Midrash of the Ten Exiles"), a Midrash which enumerates and describes ten exiles suffered by the Jewish people: four each under Sennacherib and Nebuchadnezzar, the other two under Vespasian and Hadrian. It is similar in style and content to *Seder Olam,* and may possibly have formed a part of the latter. It has been published by Adolf Jellinek (in *Beth Hamidrash*), by Grünhut (in *Sefer Halikkutim*) and by Eisenstein (in *Otzar Hamidrashim*).

Lit.: Jellinek, Adolf, *Beth Hamidrash,* vols. 4 and 5.

MIDRASH GENESIS (BERESHITH RABBAH),

a homiletic Midrash to *Genesis.* In the printed editions it is divided into 100 chapters; the last few chapters repeat the exposition of the last verses of the Biblical book and may therefore be a later edition. A characteristic form of discourse to be found in the Midrash is that which begins with a verse taken from another part of the Bible and leads up to the verse in *Genesis* to which the Midrash is attached; according to Bacher, this is characteristic of the post-Tannaitic period, and places the date of the compilation of Midrash Genesis at a comparatively early period, estimated as from the 4th to the 6th cent. There are numerous loan words from Greek; the language is generally Mishnaic Hebrew, but Aramaic is used for narratives and popular stories. Since *Genesis* is narrative in nature, the Midrash is entirely homiletic and didactic.

In 1903 Judah Theodor began a critical edition of Midrash Genesis, based on a manuscript in the British Museum; the work was continued by Chanoch Albeck and was completed in 1937 (*Bereschit Rabba mit kritischem Apparat und Kommentar*). There is an English translation of the Midrash in the edition of the Midrash Rabbah by H. Freedman and Maurice Simon (London, 1939).

Lit.: Theodor, Judah, in *Festschrift zum 70. Geburtstag Jakob Guttmanns,* 148-71; Moore, George Foot, *Judaism in the First Centuries of the Christian Era,* vol. 1 (1927) 163-66.

MIDRASH HAGADOL

("The Great Midrash"), a Midrashic compilation to the entire Torah, discovered at the end of the 19th cent. in Yemen. It includes both Halachic and Haggadic Midrashim, excerpts from old Midrash collections and late rabbinical works, such as the *Aruch* of Nathan ben Jehiel and the writings of Rashi, Abraham Ibn Ezra and Maimonides. The compiler is unidentified, but the work was apparently completed in the 14th cent. It is put together without critical appraisal; the compiler seems to have incorporated every Midrash that he could find. This enhances the value of the work, however, since some extremely old sources have been preserved which would otherwise have been lost. Unlike the compiler of the Midrash collection *Yalkut Shimeoni,* the editor of Midrash Hagadol does not give his sources. Modern scholars such as Hoffmann and Horovitz have endeavored to reconstruct some of the older Midrashim from the information given in Midrash Hagadol. In many instances the legends and expositions in the text are very similar to those recorded in Mohammedan sources.

Of the work, the part to *Genesis* was issued by Schechter (Cambridge, 1902), a fragment of the section on *Exodus* by Hoffmann (Berlin, 1913) and the section on *Leviticus* by E. N. Rabinowitz (New York, 1932).

Lit.: Heller, B., in *Encyclopaedia Judaica,* vol. 1 (1928), cols. 1032-33.

MIDRASH LAMENTATIONS (ECHAH RABBATHI), expository Midrash to *Lamentations;* it is sometimes called Megillath Echah (Rabbah). Its method of interpretation resembles that of *Midrash Genesis;* the homilies begin with a verse from a different part of the Bible and lead up to the text in *Lamentations* as a sort of summary. Thirty-four of these constitute an introduction (*pethihah*) leading up to the first verse of the book; there is much material dealing with *Lam.* 1 and very little with *Lam.* 5. The central object of contemplation is naturally the description of the destruction of the First and Second Temples, as well as of the subsequent persecutions of the Jews; these are balanced by promises of consolation in the Messianic period. Apparently much of the material in the book is taken from discourses delivered on the Ninth of Ab (Tishah Beab). None of the rabbis quoted is later than the completion of the Palestinian Talmud; there are many Greek loan words and much praise of Palestine and Jerusalem. From this it may be inferred that Midrash Lamentations was one of the earliest Midrash compilations, that it arose in Palestine, and received its final editing about the 7th cent.

A critical edition was made by Salomon Buber (*Midrasch Echa Rabba,* Vilna, 1899). A German translation was made by A. Wünsche (Leipzig, 1881), and there is an English rendition in H. Freedman and Maurice Simon's edition of the Midrash Rabbah (London, 1939).

Lit.: Zunz, L., *Gottesdienstliche Vorträge* (2nd ed.) 189-91.

MIDRASH LEKAH TOB, *see* PESIKTA.

MIDRASH LEVITICUS (VAYIKRA RABBAH), a homiletic Midrash to *Leviticus;* it contains thirty-seven sections, each of them apparently for a weekly portion of the Biblical book in a three-year cycle of the Torah. The passages in *Leviticus* are frequently connected with verses from the Hagiographa, and emphasis is laid upon the spiritual meaning behind the ritual laws. The style of the Midrash is close to that of the *Pesikta de Rab Kahana;* there are many proverbs and parables. The time of compilation is probably the 7th cent.

Lit.: Zunz, L., *Gottesdienstliche Vorträge* (2nd ed.) 191-94; Weiszburg, Gyula, *A Midrás Leviticus Rabba* (1890).

MIDRASH NUMBERS (BEMIDBAR RABBAH, sometimes called Bemidbar Sinai Rabbah), Midrash to *Numbers,* consisting of twenty-three chapters. The first fourteen are essentially different from

the following nine; the former are concerned only with the first two Sidras (*Num.* 1 to 8), the latter with the following eight (*Num.* 9 to 36). From this disproportion it may safely be concluded that there were two authors. In both parts many Halachic passages have been inserted, which, like the Haggadic passages, have been taken from older Midrashim. The first part echoes Kalir's Piyutim and Cabalistic views, and displays an acquaintance with the works of later, especially French, rabbis. It therefore seems to be the work of an author later than that of the more concise second part. The second part is, as Benveniste showed in 1565, almost a word-for-word repetition of *Midrash Tanhuma. Midrash Numbers* is first mentioned in the 13th cent., so that its completion can not antedate the 12th cent.

Lit.: Zunz, L., *Gottesdienstliche Vorträge,* 261.

MIDRASH PROVERBS (MIDRASH MISHLE), exegetic Midrash to *Proverbs.* It is in the form of a running commentary on the text, giving explanations and interpretations of the proverbs. Some chapters are missing; either they were passed over or the extant text is defective. There is now and then a wealth of Haggadic material, as in the riddles of the queen of Sheba, the stories of Akiba and Gamaliel, and the application of the passage about the virtuous woman (*Prov.* 31:10-31) to twenty women of the Bible. A good part of the Midrash is of a pseudepigraphic nature, as sayings which certainly are not original are put into the mouths of various famous Tannaim. Zunz holds that this Midrash was composed in the 11th cent. A critical edition was made by Buber (Vilna, 1893).

Lit.: Zunz, L., *Gottesdienstliche Vorträge* (2nd ed.) 280-81.

MIDRASH PSALMS (MIDRASH TEHILLIM), exegetic Midrash to *Psalms.* It is known also as Midrash Shoher Tob ("He that diligently seeketh good"), from the opening words of *Prov.* 11:27, with which the Midrash begins. Midrash collections dealing with the *Psalms* are mentioned in the Talmud (*Yer. Kil.* 32b), and some of them seem to have furnished the older portions of this Midrash. It falls into two distinctly different parts: *Ps.* 1 to 118, and 119 to 150. The place and time of the compilation of the Midrash is in dispute; the fact that it pays attention to such Masoretic points as Kere and Kethib, full and defective writing, and the Hebrew vowels, as well as Gematria and Notarikon, point to a rather late date. The second part reveals borrowings from other Midrash collections.

Lit.: Strack, H. L., *Introduction to the Talmud and Midrash.*

MIDRASH RABBAH, collective term for the standard homiletic Midrash collections to the five books of the Torah and the five Megilloth (*Song of Songs, Ruth, Lamentations, Ecclesiastes* and *Esther*). The title is actually a misnomer and is derived from the fact that *Midrash Genesis* begins with a saying of Hoshaiah Rabbah ("Hoshaiah the Elder"). As a result, that Midrash became known as *Bereshith Rabbah,* and the latter word, being interpreted in the sense of "great," was applied to all the other Midrash collections. By a still further extension of the mistake, they are sometimes known as the Rabboth.

The entire Midrash Rabbah was translated and published under the editorship of H. Freedman and Maurice Simon (London, 1939).

See the articles to the individual Midrash collections.

MIDRASH RUTH, exegetic Midrash to *Ruth,* consisting of an introduction and eight sections. The introduction is devoted to the idea that wherever the words "and it came to pass in the days of" occur in the Bible they indicate portentous times. The passage to *Ruth* 3:13 contains the story of Meir and Elisha ben Abuyah. The style is similar to the Palestine Midrash collections; there are borrowings from the Palestinian Talmud, *Pesikta de Rab Kahana, Midrash Genesis* and *Midrash Leviticus,* and this points to a time of compilation later than these works.

There is an English translation of Midrash Ruth in the edition of the Midrash Rabbah by H. Freedman and Maurice Simon (London, 1939).

Lit.: Weiss, I. H., *Dor Dor Vedoreshav,* vol. 3, pp. 273-74.

MIDRASH SAMUEL, a Haggadic commentary to parts of *I* and *II Samuel;* it consists of thirty-two sections, and takes up such portions of the narrative as the stories of Hannah, Eli, the Ark of the Covenant, Samuel, Saul, and the life of David up to the purchase of the site of the Temple. Most of its content has been derived from the Palestinian Talmud and the older Midrash collections. Since Babylonian Amoraim are not mentioned and there are a number of Greek loan words, this compilation was made in Palestine; its time is probably the 11th cent., as it is often cited by Rashi and Maimonides. The manner of exposition is often acute but at the same time artificial and far-fetched. It was first published at Constantinople (1517) and Venice (1546); Buber made a critical edition in 1893.

MIDRASH SONG OF SONGS (SHIR HA-SHIRIM RABBAH), exegetical Midrash to *Song of Songs;* it is known also as Midrash Hazitha ("Seest thou?"), from the opening words of *Prov.* 22:29 with which it begins. The love passages in the Biblical book are interpreted as symbolic of the relations of God and Israel. The interpretations and parables in the Midrash are clever and full of plays on words; there are numerous grammatical and lexicographical notes. Interpretation of *Song of Songs* began at an early period, so that the nucleus of the book, especially those parts which resemble the Palestinian Talmud and the earlier Midrash collections, may go back to the 6th cent. The final redaction of the work was apparently in the 9th cent.

There is an English translation of Midrash Song of Songs in the edition of the Midrash Rabbah by H. Freedman and Maurice Simon (London, 1939).

Lit.: Weiss, I. H., *Dor Dor Vedoreshav,* vol. 3, p. 263 et seq.

MIDRASHIM, MINOR. In addition to the main Midrashim which have been discussed separately, there are hundreds of smaller Midrashim, usually of a later date, which have been assembled by Jewish scholars in the 19th and 20th centuries. The two chief collections of these are the six-volume *Beth Hamidrash* of Adolf Jellinek and the two-volume *Otzar Midrashim* of Judah David Eisenstein. The chief of these Minor Midrashim are: Midrash Abkir, so called from the abbreviation of the formula *'amen beyamenu ken yehi ratzon* ("Amen, in our days! May it please God!"), which conclude its

Leo Mielziner

separate sections; Midrash Asereth Hadibroth, devoted to Shabuoth and the Ten Commandments; Dibre Hayamim shel Mosheh, on the life of Moses; Midrash Eser Galiyyoth, on the ten exiles of the Jews; Midrash Petirath Aharon and Midrash Petirath Mosheh, on the deaths of Moses and Aaron; Midrash Taame Haseroth Veyetheroth, Haggadic expositions of peculiarities in the Masoretic text of the Bible; Midrash Eleh Ezkerah, dealing with the ten martyrs in the time of Hadrian; Midrash Leolam, of a didactic nature; Midrash Tadshe, known also as the Baraitha of Phinehas ben Jair.

Lit.: Eisenstein, J. D., *Otzar Midrashim* (1915); Theodor, Judah, in *Jewish Encyclopedia,* vol. 8, pp. 572-80.

MIELZINER, LEO, portrait painter, b. New York city, 1869; d. Truro, Mass., 1935. He was the son of Moses Mielziner. Mielziner studied at the Cincinnati Art Museum Academy, and in 1890 he went to Paris. In Paris he studied at the Beaux Arts under Gêrome, at l'Académie Julian under Bouguereau, and at Colorossi's under Courtois. In 1919 he became a professor at the Art Students League in New York.

Mielziner was a man of many talents. He gave lectures on art, among them one entitled *Beauty,* appearing in the 1906 *Year Book* of the American Club of Paris. His address to Louis Loeb was published in *Judaean Address, 1900-1917.* He wrote verses, including the *Ballad of Queen Esther,* delivered at Coblenz before the Jewish soldiers of the Army of Occupation in 1919. He engaged in amateur theatricals. He was a sculptor. But he is best remembered as a portraitist.

Mielziner's portrait work falls into many classes. His miniatures, pastels, pencil and charcoal drawings, bas reliefs and small busts (including one of Zangwill) are perhaps less widely known than his paintings, lithographs and silverpoints. Over 150 paintings include portraits of Woodrow Wilson, Harlan F. Stone, Louis Loeb, Solomon Schechter, Theodor Herzl and many other distinguished personages. His drawings of Mark Twain, Herbert Hoover, John J. Pershing, Theodore Roosevelt, Oscar Straus, Thomas A. Edison, J. P. Morgan, etc. form a contemporary portrait gallery notable for the excellence in likeness. In the field of lithography portraits of Felix Adler, George Bellows, Julius Rosenwald, Isaac N. Seligman, Ernest Haskell, Calvin Coolidge, William H. Taft and other American presidents attest Mielziner's skill on stone. But he was at his happiest in silver points. His portraits in this medium of various members of the Schiff and Warburg families, and notably the picture of his wife, *Meditation,* have a delicacy and charm peculiarly their own.

Mielziner was a founder of the Painter-Gravers of America, and an organizer of the New York League of Artists. His work is included in the Metropolitan Art Museum, Boston Art Museum, Worcester Art Museum, Brooklyn Art Museum, and other representative collections in the United States.   GEORGE S. HELLMAN.

MIELZINER, MOSES, educator, rabbi and writer, b. Czerniejewo-Schubin, province of Posen, 1828; d. Cincinnati, 1903. His father, Rabbi Benjamin Leib Mielziner (b. 1797; d. 1849)—first of Mielczyn (hence the name), then of Czerniejewo, and finally of Schubin—was the son of Rabbi Meir. His mother was Rosa Rachel Caro, daughter of Löb, called "Morenu," of Kleczewo, a descendant of Joseph Caro of Toledo and Safed. Educated first by his father, then at Exin, Moses Mielziner at sixteen received from Rabbi Wolf Klausner his Haber and Morenu degrees. He entered the Werder Gymnasium, Berlin, 1844; and matriculated at Berlin University, 1848, receiving his degree in philosophy and philology in 1851. His Hebrew theological studies continued in Berlin under Rabbi Joseph Oettinger, who endorsed his Hebrew diploma. He was a favorite disciple of Samuel Holdheim, Reform pioneer, who gave him authorization to preach in 1852.

Mielziner occupied his first pulpit at Waren, Mecklenburg, for two and a half years. His first published sermon was delivered there and republished in the *Allgemeine Zeitung des Judentums* (Oct., 1854). From 1855 to 1865 he was principal of a Jewish religious school at Copenhagen, organizing there Denmark's first rabbinical preparatory school. A commencement day address on a practical method of Jewish religious instruction was published, and reprinted in *Ben Chananja* (July 26, 1861). In 1858 Mielziner received authorization to preach from Chief Rabbi A. A. Wolff of Denmark and from Chief Rabbi Leopold Löw of Hungary. The Ph.D. degree was bestowed on him (1859) by the University of Giessen. His thesis, "Die Verhältnisse der Sklaven bei den alten Hebräern, nach biblischen und talmudischen Quellen dargestellt" (Copenhagen and Leipzig, 1859), established his reputation for learning and lucid literary style throughout Europe. It was translated into English under the title of *Slavery Amongst the Ancient Hebrews* (1st ed., 1861; several other editions were printed subsequently) for propaganda purposes and widely used in the American abolitionist movement (1861-62). This work was quoted by Herbert Spencer in *Descriptive Sociology.*

In 1865, with his wife Rosette Levald (great-granddaughter of Jacob Teixere of Elsinore) of Copenhagen, he went to New York to occupy the pulpit of Anshe Chesed Congregation (1865-73). He then opened a private school for boys, and was also principal (1875) of Temple Emanu-El Preparatory School for Rabbinical Students, which in 1877 became one of the preparatory schools for the newly organized theological seminary

Moses Mielziner

in Cincinnati, later known as the Hebrew Union College. When its first collegiate faculty was assembled, Mielziner was appointed professor of Talmud and rabbinical disciplines, was given its degree of D.D. in 1898, and became its acting president (1900) on the death of its founder, Isaac M. Wise.

Mielziner as interpreter of rabbinic law for the Reform Movement was preeminent. He did brilliant work in establishing at the Hebrew Union College methods of teaching Hebrew and rabbinical learning for the first time in the English tongue, which resulted in his magnum opus, *Introduction to the Talmud* (1894; 2nd ed., 1903; 3rd ed., 1925). Others of his works include the first Jewish almanac in the Danish language (Copenhagen, 1861); sermons in German and a number of Hebrew poems of lyric beauty; articles in English in *The Hebrew Review,* published by the Rabbinical Literary Association of America (1880-82); *Jewish Law of Marriage and Divorce* (1884; 2nd ed., 1901); *A Selection from the Book of Psalms* (1888); *Legal Maxims from the Talmud* (1898); *Rabbinical Law of Hereditary Succession* (1900).

Mielziner was chairman (1892-94) of the committee on revision of the prayer-book of the Central Conference of American Rabbis. He was consulting editor and contributor to the *Jewish Encyclopedia* (1901), and translated parts 1 and 2 of *Chronicles* (published posthumously, 1917), for the Jewish Publication Society of America.

He was a member of the first Rabbinical Conference in America (1869), and was on the curriculum committee of the Union of American Hebrew Congregations (1881). He was also president of the Hebrew Sabbath Union (1888-89), and that year was on the organizing body and the first executive committee of the Central Conference of American Rabbis. He became its vice-president in 1894, its honorary president in 1901.   ELLA McKENNA FRIEND MIELZINER.

Lit.: Kohler, Max J., *Publications of the American Jewish Historical Society,* No. 5, pp. 137-155; No. 9, pp. 45-53; *American Hebrew,* Feb. 20, 1903, p. 467; Aug. 3, 1928, p. 361; Rosenau, William, "A Tribute to Moses Mielziner" in *Reform Advocate* (Chicago), April, 1928; Mielziner, Ella Friend, *Moses Mielziner* (1931; containing a complete bibliography of his writings, pp. 192-203).

MIESES, well known Jewish family name, widespread especially in Galicia and Austria. It is derived from the personal name Miese, which is a variant of Mina. As early as the middle of the 18th cent. two bearers of this name, Solomon and Leib Mieses, were heads of the Jewish community in Lemberg. Another, who attained some prominence in America, was Abraham Isaac Mieses, rabbi and preacher. He had migrated to the United States from Milisch, Silesia, where he had been a preacher, and from 1868 on served as a rabbi in New York, Chicago and San Francisco. In the course of a few years he established eight Jewish communities and twenty-three Hebrew schools in the state of Nevada.

Lit.: Wininger, S., *Grosse Jüdische National-Biographie,* vol. 4, p. 385.

MIESES, FABIUS, philosopher and author, b. Brody, Galicia, 1824; d. Leipzig, 1898. Though his early education and interest were entirely in the field of Hebrew literature, the influence of M. Schöngut, whom he met in Dresden, led him to philosophy and other secular subjects. Under the direction of Schöngut, Mieses studied German, French, Italian, Latin, mathematics and astronomy simultaneously; his brilliance gained for him the reputation of being a genius.

"Gegenwart und Vergangenheit im Judenthume," an essay, appeared in Fürst's *Orient* in 1846, and after its publication, Mieses became assistant editor of the periodical, as well as a regular contributor. In 1878 a poem, "Haemunah Vehatebunah," dealing with the controversy about Darwinism, was published, and Mieses won his reputation as a Hebrew poet. Articles in German and Hebrew appeared throughout his lifetime, and Mieses was the author also of *Hakabbalah Vehahasiduth, Betrachtungen eines Beobachters* (1866); *Koroth Hafilosofiah Hahadashah,* a history of the philosophy of his time, of which the first volume, devoted to the period between Kant and Hegel, appeared in 1887; *Geschichte der Philosophie von Baco v. Verulam bis auf die neueste Zeit in fasslicher Darstellung* (1878); *Shirim,* a collection of poems (Cracow, 1891); and *Die Bibel der Vernunft* (1895).

Lit.: Wininger, S., *Grosse Jüdische National-Biographie,* vol. 4, p. 385; *Jewish Encyclopedia,* vol. 8, p. 582.

MIESES, ISAAC, writer, b. Lemberg, Poland, 1802; d. Thorn, Poland, 1883. As a child he received a thorough Talmudic education, but later devoted himself to philosophy and Cabala. He published *Beitrag zur Würdigung der Wirren im Judentum* (Leipzig, 1845); *Zofnath Paneah, Darstellung und kritische Beleuchtung der jüdischen Geheimlehre* (2 parts, 1862); "Benedict Spinoza und sein Verhältnis zum Kritizismus" in *Zeitschrift für exakte Philosophie* (vol. 3, 1869).

MIESES, JACQUES, chess master, b. Leipzig, 1865. He received his education at the Universities of Leipzig and Berlin. He learned to play chess when fourteen years old, at seventeen was a member of the Leipzig Chess Club, one of the best in Germany, and in the same year won first prize in the Club tournament. He obtained third prize at the international tournaments (1889; 1907) in Breslau and Ostend. Soon thereafter he gained first prize at Vienna (1907), first prize at Liverpool (1923), first prize at the Margate Premier Reserves in 1937 and again in 1939. Mieses has been especially proficient in solving problems and in blind-fold play. At the age of 73, upon expulsion from Germany by the Nazi authorities, he gave a blindfold exhibition against six boards simultaneously in Holland. On his 75th birthday he faced twenty-two players in simultaneous display, won fifteen games, drew five, and lost two. He has written a number of works on problems and theory of chess.

MIESES, JUDAH LÖB, author and champion of Haskalah, b. Lemberg, Galicia, at the beginning of the 19th cent.; d. Lemberg, 1831, a victim of cholera. The rapid spread of the Haskalah movement in Lemberg and in Brody, two strongholds of the Mendelssohnian school, gained enthusiastic devotees among the rich and noble Jewish families. Mieses, as the son of one of those distinguished families, received a careful education in rabbinics and in the modern literatures. He associated with the leading Maskilim of his time, such as Rapoport, Bloch, and Erter; being financially independent, he was fearless in the struggle against religious fanaticism and Hasidism.

At an early age he published a revised and enlarged edition of the book *Techunath Harabbanim* (Vienna, 1823). Although he did not mention the name of the real author, David Caro, he cannot be accused of plagiarism, as in his introductory remarks he distinctly asserted that it was not his work, but that he merely revised its language and enlarged it by means of copious quotations and lengthy footnotes. In 1828 he published *Kinath Haemeth,* a spirited and learned defence of the more enlightened and rational conception of Judaism, basing his arguments on eminent Jewish authorities from Saadia Gaon, Maimonides, and other leading rabbis and scholars down to his own century, seeking to prove the folly and the un-Jewish sources of all the superstitious customs accepted and revered by certain Jewish sections as inviolable religious law. His book was warmly applauded by his own friends and by men like David Friedländer, Herz Homberg, Jeitteles, and others. His early death removed from the small band of fighters of the battle of Haskalah a man of considerable ability and undaunted courage.

Juda Leo Landau.

Lit.: Kerem Hemed, vol. 1; *Bikkure Haittim,* vol. 11; *Monatsschrift für Geschichte und Wissenschaft des Judentums* (1928) 77.

MIGAS, JOSEPH BEN MEIR HALEVI IBN, see Ibn Migas, Joseph ben Meir Halevi.

MIGDAL, see Colonies, Agricultural.

MIGRATIONS OF THE JEWS. Table of Contents:

1. Beginnings of Organizational Work in Europe and America.
2. The Hebrew Sheltering and Immigrant Aid Society (HIAS).
3. The Period After the First World War.

I. Introductory Survey. The history of the Jewish people, from its remotest beginnings, forms an almost uninterrupted chain of migrations. There were periods of settlement which lasted for centuries; but these were often merely stages of a migration process which materially affected the development of the Jewish people and its individuals. For generations the history of the Jews was a history of Jewish migration. In many cases the migration was directly compulsory; in other cases, the Jews sought to migrate because of the wretched state in which they were compelled to live. Thus the legend of the Wandering Jew became a reality in the life of the Jewish people; and the uncertainty of his

existence, the scattering of his family groups, and the constant change from one form of society to another, had a profound effect upon the character, occupations and social institutions of the Jews.

The various types of Jewish migrations can be differentiated as follows: deportations, such as those from Palestine to Mesopotamia, Egypt and Rome; expulsions, as from England, France, Spain, Portugal and Germany; migrations to improved economic conditions, such as the colonization of the Mediterranean area in ancient times and the movement from Eastern Europe to the United States in modern times; religious migrations, such as the Exodus from Egypt and the returns to Palestine; nationalist migration, as in the Zionist resettlement of Palestine.

As a result of these migrations there has been a constant shifting of the dynamic centers of Jewry. The principal migrations, as well as the centers created by them, are illustrated in the table below.

PERIOD	FROM	TO	TYPE	DYNAMIC CENTER OR CENTERS
Before 1300 B.C.E.	Babylonia Palestine	Palestine Egypt	Nomadic	
around 1300	Egypt	Palestine	Conquest	
1300 to 800				Palestine
8th cent. B.C.E. to 1st cent. C.E.	Palestine	Assyria Babylonia Egypt Rome	Deportation	Palestine
about the 4th cent. B.C.E. to about 200 C.E.	Palestine	Arabia Mediterranean countries	Commerce	Palestine Egypt
200 to 1000 C.E.	Palestine Babylonia Egypt	Central Asia and Western Europe	Commerce	Babylonia
1000-1500				Western Europe: France to 1300 Italy to 1400 Spain to 1500
1300-1750	Western Europe Central Europe	Holland Turkey Slavic countries	Expulsions	Holland Poland Lithuania Turkey
1750-1880	Eastern Europe	Central and Western Europe; America; South Africa	Escape from economic need	Germany Poland Russia
1880-1933	Eastern Europe	England America South Africa Palestine Far East	Escape from political and religious persecutions and from economic need	Germany Russia Poland United States Palestine
1933-1941	All Europe	America Palestine British Empire	Escape from political and racial persecutions and from war	United States Palestine British Empire

II. Ancient Times. Both the beginning and the end of the Biblical period are marked by migrations. True Jewish history begins with the migration of Abraham and his family from Mesopotamia through the Aramean countries into Canaan (*Gen.* 12). It is noteworthy that the confession to be recited over the offerings (*Deut.* 26:5) contains the historical reminiscence, "A wandering Syrian was my father." This is apparently based on an old tradition, which does not appear in the Bible. Further instances of migration have been furnished by archeology. Wandering tribes of Habiri, who may have been the same as the Hebrews, are mentioned in the Tell el Amarna letters of the 15th cent. B.C.E.

The Bible next declares that the descendants of Abraham, the patriarch Jacob and his family, migrated to Egypt in order to escape from famine—an economic motivation. Then, according to the narrative, their descendants, grown to millions, eventually migrated from Egypt, and after a period of forty years wandering in the wilderness, conquered Canaan and settled there. According to Bible scholars, this narrative is merely a fusion of various traditions; they agree, however, that the process of Israelite settlement in Canaan was one of constant infiltration from the very countries mentioned in the Bible, Aram (Syria), Egypt and the regions east of Palestine.

The conquest of Canaan was followed by about 500 years of permanent settlement during which time the separate tribes consolidated, exterminated or absorbed the remainder of the aborigines, and became a nation (later divided) under rulers of its own. But in the 8th cent. world powers began to invade the land. In 734 and again in 722 tens of thousands of Israelites were transported to places in Mesopotamia; in 597 and 586 B.C.E. the greater part of the population of Judea was transplanted to Babylonia. In 537 a small part of them, probably those of the humbler classes, returned with Zerubbabel after Cyrus had issued an edict allowing them to return, while the remainder preferred to stay in Babylonia, where they developed a new Jewish center. In the following centuries the settlement in Palestine gradually grew and acquired strength, but at the same time there was a gradual dispersion (Diaspora) of the Jews along the shores of the Mediterranean. Beginning in the 4th cent. B.C.E. there was a steady migration to Egypt, partly forced, partly voluntary, so that by the time of Philo (1st cent. C.E.) that country had a Jewish population of at least several hundred thousand souls (estimates run to as high as a million and a half).

At the same time new Jewish communities arose in Asia Minor, Greece and Northern Africa, as is evidenced by the fact that the New Testament book *Acts* tells of visits by the early Christian apostles of the 1st cent. C.E. It is not clear just when the Jewish settlement in Rome began, but by the middle of the 1st cent. B.C.E. it had reached such proportions that Cicero could speak of the Jews as a not inconsiderable element in the voting population. The conquest of Palestine by Titus in 70 C.E. and the resulting captives no doubt enormously increased the Roman Jewish population. The fact that Paul proposed to journey to Spain (*Rom.* 15:24,28) suggests that there were Jewish communities in that country in the 1st cent. C.E.; this is not surprising in view of the importance of that country in commerce.

In the East, the Jewish community in Babylonia, Media, Armenia and Persia became more and more a dynamic center as Palestine was devastated, first by the destruction of the Second Temple and the unsuccessful revolt of Bar Kochba, then by persecutions under the Christians in the 4th cent. and after. On other occasions, when Mesopotamia became the seat of war between Rome and the Parthians or Persians, Jews migrated still further east and southeastward.

III. The Middle Ages. Jews had come into Arabia from Palestine, in some places at a very early period. A near kinship of race, language and culture made immigration and friendly neighborhood easier. Jewish religious conceptions and practices influenced the rise of Islam, and with the Arab conquests numbers of Arabic Jews settled in the countries that had been conquered by Islam.

On the other hand, Palestine was always the goal for the immigration of pious Jews, especially those who wished to be buried there. However, this was a migration of individuals and never reached large proportions in the Middle Ages, except in the case of the Karaites. The conquest of Palestine by the Crusaders in the 12th cent. reduced the Jewish population, but new immigration set in after the Mohammedans recovered it in the 13th cent. Thus in 1211 more than 300 French and English rabbis moved there. The chief settlements were at Jerusalem and at Safed, the latter a center of Cabala in the 16th cent. and after.

Babylonia, which probably had the majority of Jews in the world in the 7th and 8th centuries, sent many of its Jews to India, Arabia and Europe. This was particularly true after the gradual decay of the caliphate had brought ruin and devastation to the once flourishing centers of Mesopotamia.

Of the Mediterranean countries Spain, during the time it was under the dominion of the Arabs (especially from 700 to 1150) offered most favorable conditions for the Jewish immigrants. There were also streams of Jewish migrants into Provence, where Jews had probably settled as early as Roman times, into Portugal, where Jews settled as early as the 12th cent. and into Western and Southern Germany, where there had been Jews along the Rhine since the time of the Roman empire. Up to about the end of the 11th cent. conditions were favorable for Jewish settlement in all of these countries and it is probable that they attracted many settlers from the lands to the east and the south.

From the 11th to the 16th centuries, however, persecutions and expulsions began in these countries. The economic position of the Jews began to be shaken by the change from a natural economy to a mercantile economy, by the growing commerce of the towns and the increase in non-Jewish traders. Prior to that time the Jews had been almost the sole traders and bankers; now a new middle class arose which usurped the part they had played in the economy of the countries. At the same time there was a drive against the Jews on the part of such religious leaders as Gregory VII (around 1070) and Innocent III (about 1200) who strove to isolate the Jews and make them objects of contempt by Jew badges, ghettoes, the Inquisition, and discriminatory legislation, while encouraging mobs to assault them and slay or baptize by force, and governments to expel them from their districts. Religious fanaticism and personal gain worked together against the Jews; they were unbelievers, they were rivals in business, they were creditors. Whenever there was a breakdown in the financial system or a relaxation in the power of the authorities, it was easy to divert the wrath of the penniless classes and bankrupt nobility by expelling the Jews and seizing their property.

The Jews who were expelled from England in 1290 fled for the most part to France. Expulsions in France had already begun in the 13th cent.; in 1306 about 100,000 Jews and in 1394 those still remaining were forced to leave the country. They settled in Savoy, Germany, Italy and Spain. In 1492 from 300,000 to 500,-000 Jews were expelled from Spain, and migrated chiefly to Northern Africa, Italy and Turkey, as well as the kingdom of Naples and the Netherlands. More than 100,000 fled to Portugal, but that country expelled all its Jews in 1497. These emigrants from the Iberian Peninsula, known as the Sephardic or Spaniolish Jews, formed their own communities all over the world. Sicily, which had a number of old Jewish settlements, expelled its Jews in 1492; most of them settled in Turkey.

Thus from about 1500 on Turkey and the Levant became one of the chief goals of Jewish migration. In addition to the Jews of Western Europe, a stream of Jewish migrants, beginning with the 15th cent., flowed there from Central Europe, especially from Germany and Italy. Constantinople (Istanbul), Adrianople and Salonika became important Jewish settlements.

The same period saw the first Jewish migration to America. Jews had played a part in the financing, the scientific equipment and the personnel of the early explorations; many of the secret Jews of Spain and Portugal found their way, first to the countries of South America, then to the West Indies, and finally to North America.

The same movement to the East that is characteristic of the Jews of Western and Southern Europe is found among the German Jews. The Crusades (1096-1320) and Black Death (1348-49), false charges of ritual murder, host desecration and the poisoning of wells, the increasing discriminations and open attacks, the crowding into ghettos and the constant restrictions, all contributed to turning the eyes of the Jews to countries where they would be more favorably received. The movement was not a mass one, because in many cases the free movement of the Jews was hindered by the powers; on the other hand, it was furthered by frequent local expulsions. Thus the Jews were expelled from Austria in 1349 and again in 1421, from the Palatinate in 1390, from Cologne in 1426, from Styria in 1496, from Nuremberg in 1499, from Regensburg in 1519, from Berlin and Brandenburg in 1573, from Vienna in 1670, and from Prague and Bohemia in 1745.

From the barbaric Germany of the Middle Ages, where Jews were seldom free from the threat of death and ruin, hundreds of thousands of Jews of every age, class and occupation made their way to the Slavic countries. There they found a ready reception and favorable economic conditions, as they supplied an important missing element—a middle class of tradesmen, artisans, tax collectors, lease holders, merchants and the like. The middle of the 14th cent. was the period in which Poland, including Lithuania, Galicia and the Ukraine, countries to which there had been a small Jewish migration as early as the time of the Byzantine Empire (4th to 11th centuries), began to develop large Jewish communities. Under the protection of economically progressive rulers, they flourished and grew, until they became the largest Jewish group and the reservoir of future Jewish migration.

As the Polish kingdom declined, misfortunes set in for the Jews, the worst being the Chmielnicki massacres in 1648 and after. A return movement set in, especially to Germany, where Jewish settlements grew in Prussia, Hamburg, Frankfort and other cities, and in Austria, where the Jewish community of Vienna, even after the expulsion of 1670, grew into one of the largest Jewish communities in the continent.

The return to Western Europe began in the 17th cent. when the Netherlands, which had finally won their independence in 1609 from the Spaniards, enunciated the principle of toleration. Jewish migrants came thither from Spain and Portugal (Marranos) and later from Poland, and a flourishing community arose in Amsterdam, which later furnished Jewish immigrants to North and Central America. The resettlement of the Jews in England in the same century was largely effected from Holland. Other countries of Europe gradually opened their doors to the Jews in the course of the 18th and early 19th cent.

The results of these continuous forced migrations upon the Jews of the 11th to 16th centuries were profound. It was not that the expulsions were always permanent; in many cases cities and states, experiencing financial ruin as a result of their action, more than once recalled the Jews. But the whirlpool of constant movement prevented the Jews from taking root in any country. They were compelled to take up occupations which they could liquidate quickly or could take with them. Thus instead of engaging in agriculture, industry or warehousing, they turned to the professions, commerce, banking, agencies, tax collecting and the like—all occupations which were not so seriously affected by forced migrations.

The various countries of Europe were likewise affected by the migration of the Jews. The economic problems of communities could not be settled by driving out the Jews and replacing them by a new set of traders and financiers who were inexperienced, intolerant and greedy. The international trade fostered by the Jews was replaced by local rivalries, economically unprofitable. Northern Italy, Holland, England, Northern Germany and such cities as Amsterdam, Hamburg and Frankfort flourished in the 16th to 18th centuries as Jews came there, while Spain and Portugal as well as cities such as Augsburg, Nuremberg, Ulm and Antwerp sank into decay after they had expelled the Jews. For the Jews had been the vehicle of the exchange of money which had fostered commerce, overcoming the obstacles of space and time, and it was only after long and painful experiences that they could be replaced, if they were not recalled.

Kaplun-Kogan has summed up the migrations of the Jews up to the end of the 16th cent. in the following tendencies: In the first half of the Middle Ages they migrated from countries of backward economy to those of a more advanced economy: in the latter half, they did just the reverse, moving from countries of advanced economy to those of backward economy or those just beginning to develop, such as Northern and Eastern Europe and America. In the 19th cent. there was a renewal of the tendency to go from economically backward sections to industrial regions, as from Eastern Europe to Western Europe and the United States, as well as internal migration in Germany from the eastern part to Berlin and to the western part, and in Russia in the direction of Poland.

Lit.: The general Jewish histories; Baron, S., *A Social and Religious History of the Jews,* and the literature cited there; Kaplun-Kogan, V. W., *Die Wanderbewegungen der Juden* (1913).

IV. Modern Times. 1. The Period of Unrestricted Migration (up to 1924).

Modern Jewish migration began in the 1820's and came to an end in 1924, when the United States Immigration Act of that year placed drastic restrictions on the number of those who were permitted to enter the country. During this period approximately three million Jews emigrated: over half a million to Western Europe, over two million to the United States, and about a quarter of a million to Africa, Asia and Australia.

From 1820 to 1870 the Jewish immigrants came chiefly from Germany, Bohemia and Austria; from 1870 the overwhelming majority of them came from Eastern Europe.

The political reaction and economic crisis after the Napoleonic Wars caused the Jews of Germany, Bohemia and Austria to emigrate to France, England, the United States, Australia and South Africa. This migration, however, was small in number compared to the migration from Galicia, Russia and Roumania from 1881 to 1924. The Jewish mass emigration from these countries was a consequence of the political oppression under which Jews lived in the latter two countries, as well as the general poor economic condition of the Jewish masses in all three countries. About 80 to 85% of this emigration went to the United States. Accurate figures are only possible from 1899, when the American immigration reports began to differentiate as to countries of origin. During sixteen years about 1,300,000 Jews emigrated from Russia to the United States, amounting to about 40% of the entire Russian migration thither, and about ten times the proportion of the Russian Jewish population. During the pogrom years of 1903 to 1906 this migration was especially large: 77,544 in 1903-4; 92,388 in 1904-5; 125,234 in 1905-6; 114,932 in 1906-7. From 1899 to 1914 about 300,000 Jews migrated from Austria-Hungary to the United States, the larger part from Galicia, a much smaller one from the other Austrian lands, and only about 25% from Hungary.

Jewish emigration from Roumania to the United States increased before the World War because of the consistent disenfranchisement and the systematic exclusion of the Jews from many occupations. From 1899 to 1914 this emigration was 62,813. At the same time there was a steady migration of Roumanian Jews to other countries, so that between 1899 and 1912 the excess of emigration over the natural increase of the Jewish population amounted to 27,000 persons.

The territorial regrouping that ensued after the World War resulted in a considerable shift in the center of Jewish emigration from Europe. Poland replaced Russia as the chief source of Jewish immigration to the

United States; thus over 40% of the Jewish immigrants in 1920-23 originated from Poland, six and a half times their proportion to the general population. On the other hand, Jewish emigration from Russia decreased considerably, partly because there was a smaller Jewish population in Russia after the War and partly because of the difficulties connected with a departure from the Soviet Union. Only 14% of the Jews who emigrated to the United States in the post-War years came from the Soviet Union.

Jewish emigration from Roumania to the United States increased greatly immediately after the War as a result of the annexation to Roumania of Bessarabia (which incidentally received a large immigration from Russia in the first years after the War); from 1920-24 it comprised 13.73% of all the Jewish immigration into the United States. In those years the relative proportion of Jewish immigrants was fourteen times that of their number in the population of Roumania.

The following are the chief countries of Jewish immigration:

ENGLAND. Before the World War, and particularly before the Aliens Act of 1906, England absorbed a large part of Jewish immigration to Western Europe. Since English immigration statistics do not record the religion of immigrants but merely their places of origin, it is impossible to obtain exact figures as to Jewish immigration. However, it is known that the greater part of those who came to England from Russia were Jewish and therefore the number of Jews can be stated approximately from the number of those giving Russia (including Poland) as place of origin. From 1891 to 1906 about 300,000 Jews landed in England.

According to an inquiry made by a governmental commission in 1902 most of the Jewish immigrants, though weakly in appearance, were organically healthy. As a rule they had but little money; about 60% were artisans and handworkers, others were traders, and only a small number were without occupation. Many of those who had reported themselves as tradesmen turned to manual labor after they reached England. Thus, according to the census of 1901, of 29,522 Russian and Polish immigrants about 85% were workingmen and only about 7% traders. The greater part of the Jews were working in the needle trades, 61% of the men and 69% of the women were thus employed; of these 42% of all the men and 57% of all the women were tailors. Smaller numbers of Jewish immigrants were employed in the manufacture of shoes and of furniture, and in the tobacco industry. The Jewish tailors were for the most part superior workers and as a result the production costs for clothing were reduced and became an article that could be cheaply manufactured and distributed within the country, whereas before there had been considerable importation from abroad. At the same time there was no competition with the native English laborers; for the piece-work system and the sweat-shop conditions under which clothing was manufactured did not attract the British workers to the industry.

One of the results of the seasonal nature of the garment trade was that after a time Jewish immigrants began to move from the overcrowded East End of London to Manchester, Leeds, Liverpool, Glasgow and other cities where working and living conditions were more favorable, or else they went on again to the United States. For a large part of the migrants England was only a way station. English Jewish organizations systematically aided such further migration. From 1882 to 1904 they assisted about 43,000 immigrants in proceeding to America or returning to their native countries; during the same period many left England at their own expense. From 1899 to 1907 about 29,000 Jews emigrated from England to the United States. According to a report made by the Royal Statistical Commission in 1905, only about 105,000 of the approximately 300,000 Russian immigrants since 1891 were still in England.

Despite the proportionately small number of Jewish immigrants, the ability of the country to absorb them, and their contributions to the national economy, agitation for a restriction of their immigration began in the 1890's. The movement became especially strong at the beginning of the 20th cent. because of a period of unemployment after the Boer War. The Jewish immigrants were charged with being sharp competitors, a burden on the population and to have caused an increase in criminality and overcrowding. An investigation by a commission in 1902 found no grounds for these charges, but the agitation grew so strong that an act to restrict immigration was passed in 1904 and became law on January 1, 1906. One of its provisions that was especially severe on Jewish immigrants was the requirement that each immigrant had to possess five pounds of money for himself and two pounds additional for each member of his family. As a result of this and of the panic that affected the Jews of Eastern Europe on hearing of the passage of the law, the immigration from Russia and Poland decreased from 37,922 in 1905 to 12,800 in 1906. In the last years before the first World War the Jewish immigration to England never reached its earlier figures.

UNITED STATES. After the year 1881 the United States was the most important country of refuge for the Jews. Between that time and the first World War more than two million Jews landed in North American ports; one and a half million of these came in the years between 1899 and 1914. In no other country in the world has Jewish population increased as much by immigration as in the United States; from 3,000 in 1812 it grew to 230,000 in 1880 and to about three million in 1914, a thousandfold increase in a century.

Next to the Italians, the Jews were the second largest group of immigrants in the period between 1899 and 1914. It did not, as did those of other groups, diminish in times of depressions in America, but retained a fairly constant character. This may be seen from the accompanying table:

Year	Jewish Immigrants
1899	37,415
1900	60,764
1901	58,098
1902	57,688
1903	76,203
1904	106,236
1905	129,910
1906	153,748
1907	149,182
1908	103,387
1909	57,551
1910	84,260

Year	Jewish Immigrants
1911	91,223
1912	80,595
1913	101,330
1914	138,051

Total from 1899 to 1914: 1,485,641.

The largest Jewish immigration was in the pogrom year 1906; the average immigration yearly was about 93,000. Nearly all these immigrants settled permanently in the United States; the percentage of returning Jewish immigrants amounted to only 7.14% as against a general 30.76%.

A significant feature of Jewish immigration was the very large number of women and children among them. From 1899 to 1914 there were forty-four Jewish women to every fifty-six Jewish men, and twenty-four children under fourteen to every seventy-six adults. Over a million Jews (654,080 women and 362,073 children)—more than any other immigration group—accompanied or followed their relatives to the United States. Due to the limited provisions for education in Russia the number of illiterates (24.86%) was relatively high. Most of the immigrants were poor; only 6.07% possessed fifty dollars or more on their arrival, 38.6% had less than fifty dollars, and 55.33% had no money at all. The average money possessed by Jewish immigrants was $15.50, as against a general average of $22. This low figure was partly due, however, to the greater number of Jewish women and children. 67.24% of the Jewish immigrants made the trip on money furnished by relatives, as against 35.81% in the general group.

The division into occupations among Jewish immigrants was entirely in keeping with the social structure of the Jewish population of Eastern Europe. There was a relatively high proportion of those reported as being without occupation, due to the large number of women and children. During the last five years before the first World War the number of Jewish immigrants with occupations was much higher, rising to 63% in 1914. Of the Jews with occupations 68.19% were skilled workers, while there were relatively small proportions of unskilled laborers, traders and domestics. The proportion of skilled workers was the largest of any immigration group. 57.8% of the Jews with occupations were workers in the needle trades and the making of shoes, hats, furs and the like; of these 48.6% were tailors.

The mass immigration of Jewish skilled workers was primarily due to the increase in competition along these lines and the increasingly poorer condition of the Jewish workers in Eastern Europe. As in England, their immigration to the United States stimulated the clothing industry to a remarkable degree, and made possible the sale of ready-made clothing in large quantities and at greatly reduced prices. Thanks to Jewish immigration, production of clothing in the United States increased in value from $241,000,000 in 1880 to $1,100,000,000 in 1914. Jews participated to a considerable extent in other trades; in 1914, out of forty-nine trades in America, Jews were relatively more engaged in nineteen, and numerically more engaged in eleven.

The first World War practically stopped Jewish immigration to the United States from 1914 to 1918; from July 1, 1914 to June 30, 1919 the total number of Jewish immigrants was only 65,764; of these 19,414 came from Canada between 1915 and 1919. In 1920 Jewish immigration began to grow and reached a new height in 1921. This can be seen from the following table:

Year	Jewish Immigrants
1915	26,497
1916	15,108
1917	17,342
1918	3,672
1919	3,055
1920	14,292
1921	119,036
1922	53,524
1923	49,719
1924	49,989

Total from 1915 to 1924: 352,234.

The lowered numbers of the last three years were due to the restrictions passed upon immigration in 1921, with the introduction of the first quota system.

CANADA. Jewish immigration into Canada from Eastern Europe, as in the United States, was largely increased by the persecutions in Russia from 1881 on. The first groups of any size arrived in 1882; in 1884 a colony of about thirty families was founded in Moosomin with the aid of the Mansion House Committee, but was not successful. The Oxbow (1891) and Hirsch (1892) colonies, on the other hand, flourished, but the majority of the Jewish immigrants settled in the cities. The yearly average Jewish immigration to Canada from 1901 to 1914 was about 5,000, the last year before the first World War showing the greatest (11,252). The proportion of Jewish immigrants among all those who migrated to Canada was less than a fourth of that for the United States.

In Canada the number of Jewish women and children among the immigrants was high, amounting to 28.36 children out of every hundred, and 28.25 women out of every hundred adults. The classification from 1905 to 1914 was as follows: skilled workers, 52.89%; unskilled workers, 16.78%; various occupations, 11.72%; trade, 9.47%; agriculture, 5.88%; domestics, 2.99%; mining, 0.18%.

The first World War brought an almost complete cessation of Jewish immigration into Canada. From 1916 to 1920 there were only 371 Jews who settled in Canada. In 1921 there was an increase to 2,763 and in 1922 to 8,404, a rise from 1.86% of the total immigration in 1921 to 9.34% in 1922. This increase was due to the fact that the Jews of Eastern Europe, knowing of the restrictions on migration to the United States from 1921 on, turned to Canada. However, the Canadian immigration law of 1923, designed to favor agricultural immigration and to restrict all others, reduced the Jewish immigration of that year to 2,793.

ARGENTINE. Jewish immigration to Argentine was more of an agricultural and colonizing character. As early as 1889 attempts had been made by Russian Jewish immigrants to establish farms in Argentine, but without success. In 1890 a larger group, amounting to 800, arrived in Buenos Aires, and in the same year the oldest Jewish colony, Moisesville, was founded. New impetus was given to the movement by the work of the Jewish Colonization Association, which aided the work of the colonies. Nevertheless, there were discouragements and removals and by 1893 there were less

than 3,000 Jewish immigrants in the colonies. In consequence of the increasing oppressions suffered by the Jews of Eastern Europe and various reforms introduced by the officials of the Association, the Jewish population of Argentine grew to about 40,000 in 1903. The figures for 1904 to 1914 are as follows:

Year	Jewish Immigrants
1904	4,000
1905	7,516
1906	13,500
1907	2,518
1908	5,444
1909	8,557
1910	6,581
1911	6,378
1912	13,416
1913	10,860
1914	3,693

The chief point of origin of the Jewish immigrants was Southern Russia, and the high point before the first World War was reached in the pogrom year of 1906. During the first World War there was very little Jewish immigration; none at all was registered from 1916 to 1918 and only 280 in 1919. In 1920 the stream of immigrants had begun to flow again; it reached its height in 1923, with 13,700 persons.

OTHER COUNTRIES: Immigration to BRAZIL was comparatively insignificant before 1924. The same applied to other countries of Latin America, such as CHILE, URUGUAY, CUBA, and MEXICO, which received greater numbers of Jewish immigrants beginning from the 1920's.

The SOUTH AFRICAN UNION played an important role in the history of Jewish migration in the 19th cent. The pioneers of the immigration movement came in the first decades of that century from St. Helena, Great Britain and Germany. In the 1870's Russian Jews arrived in South Africa from England and in the eighties the number of East European immigrants, particularly those from Lithuania, grew in size. They formed the overwhelming majority of the Jewish population of the Union which in 1926 amounted to 71,816 persons. Until 1930 immigration to the Union was practically unrestricted.

The pioneers of Jewish immigration to AUSTRALIA were British Jews, and Polish Jews mostly from Posen. They were single and married non-Jewish women, but the children remained Jews. In the first years of the 20th cent. Russian Jews immigrated and in the 1920's again Polish Jews arrived, especially with increased difficulties of immigration to the United States.

Jewish immigration in NEW ZEALAND started in 1840 but it never was large. The Jewish community in that dominion is small. The first immigrants came from England; later other Jews, including those from Eastern Europe, arrived.

The British colonies of Southern and Northern Rhodesia, as well as Kenya and Tanganyika received Jewish immigrants beginning with the last decade of the 19th cent. or even later. The majority of the immigrants came from Eastern Europe.

Lit.: *Annual Report of the Commissioner General of Immigration to the Secretary of Labor,* 1899 et seq.; Fairchild, Henry Pratt, *Immigration a World Problem and its American Significance* (1913); Stephenson, G. Malcolm, *A History of American Immigration, 1820-1924* (1926); Wittke,

Carl, *We Who Built America; the Saga of the Immigrants* (1940); Taft, Donald R., *Human Migration* (1936); Kaplun-Kogan, V. W., *Die jüdischen Wanderungen in der neuen Zeit* (1919); idem, *Jüdische Wanderbewegungen vor und nach dem Weltkriege* (1930); Lestschinsky, Jacob, *Idische Wanderung far di Lezte 25 Yor* (1927); idem, *Di Onhoiben fun der Emigrazie un Kolonisazie bai Iden* (1929); *Report of the Royal Commission on Alien-Immigration with Minutes of Evidence* (4 vols., 1903-4); Sack, B. G., "A Quarter Century of Canadian Jewish Immigration," *Neuland* (1926); Kohler, Max J., "The German-Jewish Migration to America," *Publications of the American Jewish Historical Society*, No. 9; Bernheimer, C. S., *The Russian Jew in the United States* (1905); Herrman, Louis, *A History of the Jews in South Africa* (2nd ed., 1935); Wischnitzer, Mark, *Die Juden in der Welt* (1935); Linfield, Harry S., *Jewish Migration as a Part of World Migration Movements, 1920-1930* (1933).

2. Reversed Migration Movements in 1925-1933.

UNITED STATES OF AMERICA. Anti-immigration tendencies existed in the United States already in the 19th cent. They originated from two sources. Labor circles were afraid of the influx of foreign, cheap workers while adherents of racial trends and hysterical patriotism raised their voices against arrivals not belonging to the so-called Nordic race. The post-War atmosphere proved favorable to both trends of opinion. Labor strongly demanded immigration restriction, claiming in 1919 that two million men were idle. Conservatives pointed to the dangers on the part of radical immigrants from the South and East of Europe while the racialists appealed for the preservation of the native American type. The bill of 1921 was the first serious breach in the liberal immigration policy of the United States but it was greatly overshadowed by the Immigration Act of 1924 called after its author the Johnson Bill. According to it only 2% of a national group living in 1890 in the United States were admitted for immigration. Nationality was determined by place of birth. The new Immigration Act caused a very considerable decrease of immigration of people from Eastern Europe. When the Immigration Act came into force 10,000 emigrants from East Europe, provided with American visas and shipping cards, were on their way in various European ports to the States. The plight of these stranded people caused united action by European and American organizations to help their settlement in other countries or to repatriate them to their countries of origin. A United Evacuation Committee was formed in the summer of 1924, to cope with this emergency. The drastic results of the Immigration Act of 1924 are visible in the immigration figures of the years following its adoption:

Years	Persons
1925	10,292
1926	10,267
1927	11,483
1928	11,639
1929	12,479
1930	11,526
1931	5,692
1932	2,755
1933	2,372

The further decline noticeable in 1931-33 was the result of the economic crisis in the United States and all over the world, and also of special powers granted to the United States consuls to investigate more rigorously into each case. The quotas of the main East European countries of emigration were fixed as follows; Poland, 6,542; Russia, 2,784; Roumania, 295; Lithuania, 386;

Latvia, 256; Esthonia, 116; altogether, 10,341 persons.

After the War return migration from the United States to East Europe was still less than before 1914. The Jewish return migration percentage fell from 7.14 in 1908-14 to 1.66 in 1915-28. Another characteristic feature of post-War immigration to the United States was the substantial increase of the percentage of Jewish women and children among the Jewish immigrants. The number of illiterates among Jewish immigrants substantially decreased after the War; of 100 Jewish adult immigrants only 7.41 were illiterates. The chief causes for this decrease were the Immigration Law of 1917 which barred entrance to adult immigrants who could neither read nor write and the improvement of education in East European countries after the War. Post-War Jewish immigration to the United States bore still more a marked family character. On the other hand the workers' group since the War has decreased in percentage by a third. The decline of the workers element among the Jewish immigrants in post War years as compared with 1900-1914 is particularly striking in the group of workers engaged in the clothing industry.

CANADA. Jewish immigration to Canada in 1924 and after was fairly large despite the restrictive law of 1923. This was partly due to the efforts of the Jewish organizations which obtained special concessions from the Canadian government. In 1924-1930 33,810 Jews immigrated to Canada; the percentage in the total immigration was over 3.5%. 40% were artisans and industrial workers, 12% traders, 12% agriculturists, 8.8% unqualified workers and 27.2% domestics. In 1930 a new immigration law was adopted by which nearly all immigration to Canada was stopped with the exception of that coming from England but the English quota was heavily limited. Later on each Canadian province was permitted to promulgate its own immigration law. In consequence of the law of 1930 immigration to Canada fell considerably; in 1936 there were only 391 immigrants.

ARGENTINE. The decline in immigration beginning from 1924 in comparison with the top year of 1923 was caused by the selective immigration policy of the Argentinian Government which favored entrance of Romanic peoples and also by the adverse state of the labor market. However, considering the low figures of Jewish immigration to the United States in 1924-1933 those of Argentine appear quite respectable, but from the figures quoted below is to be seen that 1931 marked a decline in immigration which was caused by new restrictive rules. Farmers with a capital of 1,500 pesos and close relatives of people already residing in Argentine were admitted.

The table below gives the figures:

Year	Jewish Immigrants
1924	7,800
1925	6,920
1926	7,534
1927	9,681
1928	6,852
1929	5,986
1930	7,805
1931	3,553
1932	1,747
1933	1,962
Total	59,840

BRAZIL. In the same years Jewish immigration to Brazil assumed a growing importance. Approximately 35,-000 Jews immigrated to that republic in 1925-1933, more than twice as many as the Jewish population of Brazil in 1922. The Brazilian Jewish immigration is noteworthy for the fact that the immigrants have spread over 100 localities.

URUGUAY. The republic of Uruguay, which at the beginning of the 1920's had still fewer Jews than Brazil, received in 1925-1933 about 10,000 Jewish immigrants.

OTHER SOUTH AMERICAN COUNTRIES. Immigration to Chile, Colombia and Peru developed in 1924-1933 on a moderate scale while other South American countries were entered by Jews only sporadically.

CUBA. Cuba had a large influx in 1924, about 8,500, but most of them emigrated to the United States or other American countries while some returned to their European homes. A small but consistent immigration set in in the following years. In 1933 there were about 8,000 Jews in Cuba.

MEXICO. Great hopes were attached in the 1920's to large scale immigration of Jews to Mexico. The presidents then in office offered land for Jewish settlements but an investigation on the spot by a Jewish delegation was not encouraging and the plan of mass settlement had to be given up. However immigration of individuals developed consistently and in 1934 Mexico had about 35,000 Jewish residents.

SOUTH AFRICA. In the first years following the War, Jewish immigration to the South African Union was insignificant. In 1924 not more than 774 came in as immigrants. But immigration figures went up beginning with 1925, as follows:

YEAR	JEWISH IMMIGRANTS
1925	1,282
1926	1,479
1927	1,752
1928	2,293
1929	2,788
1930	1,881

Immigration was thus unrestricted in those years but a drastic change took place in 1930. On May 1 of that year a Quota Immigration Act came into force. Under the provisions of this act a person born in any country except the territories of the British Commonwealth, Austria, Belgium, Denmark, France, Germany, Italy, Norway, Portugal, Spain, Switzerland, Sweden and the United States was forbidden to enter the Union for permanent residence, unless he was in possession of a permit issued by the Secretary of the Interior. From non-scheduled countries, such as the East European states, from which Jews mainly hail, not more than fifty persons were allowed to immigrate to the Union in any one calendar year. In addition to this quota of fifty persons any person of a non-scheduled country could immigrate provided that the number additionally admitted did not in the aggregate exceed 1,000. The results of the restrictive Act of 1930 were visible in the following years: 1931, 885; 1932, 676; 1933, 745. Only in 1934 did immigration rise somewhat in connection with the arrival of German Jewish immigrants, Germany belonging, as indicated, to the scheduled countries.

Lit.: Gillman, Joseph M., "The Two-Fold Treatment of the Immigration Problem," *Jewish Social Service Quarterly,* vol. 4, No. 1, Sept., 1927; *Tzen Yor Idische Emigratzie, 1927-1936,* mimeographed report of the Hicem (1936); reports of the Jewish Colonization Association for 1924 to 1933; reports of the Hilfsverein der Deutschen Juden for 1926-1932; Kreinin, M., *Einwanderungsmeglichkeiten kein Sidamerike* (1928); *American Jewish Year Book,* section "Statistics of Jews," containing figures on migrations, for the years 1924-1933; Linfield, Harry S., *Jewish Migration as a Part of World Migration Movements, 1920-30* (1933).

3. Migration Movements under Nazi Pressure (1933-1941).

The Nazi upheaval in 1933 marked the beginning of a new phase in the history of Jewish migration. The problem of finding outlets for the Jewish emigrants from Germany was very complicated. The economic world crisis which in the late 1920's had shattered the prosperity of the overseas countries was still in its full swing in the early 1930's. The fall in prices of raw materials and growing unemployment caused severe restrictions of immigration. Unemployment increased to such an extent that a return movement from America to Europe had taken place. The countries which had encouraged immigration in the 19th cent. were now imbued with hostile feelings toward newcomers. This attitude remained in force even after the crisis was overcome, unemployment decreased and a certain shortage of labor was felt. Under these circumstances it was very hard for the Jews of Germany to find new homes overseas, in those standard countries of immigration where, thanks to liberal immigration policy, large Jewish communities had grown up in the last decades of the 19th and in the beginning of the 20th cent. And still new outlets had to be found under the growing Nazi pressure. In addition to Palestine which in 1933-36 absorbed the largest portion of German-Jewish migrants the United States, South Africa, Argentina, and to a lesser degree Canada, Brazil and Australia, the following countries became the goals of emigration: Mexico, Costa Rica, Guatemala, Nicaragua, Honduras, Salvador, Dominican Republic, Haiti, Curacao, Venezuela, Colombia, Ecuador, Peru, Chile, Uruguay, Paraguay, Egypt, Algeria, Tunis, Morocco, Angola, Kenya, Tanganyika, Southern Rhodesia, Asiatic Turkey, Syria, Iraq, Iran, India, Thailand, China, Japan, Manchukuo, the Philippines, Netherland India, New Zealand. Never before had Jewish migration assumed the character of such widely spread dispersion.

In the nine years of emigration from Germany and Nazi-dominated countries five stages may be established: the first, from the spring of 1933 to the fall of 1935 when the Nuremberg Laws were promulgated; the second, from the winter of 1935-36 until February, 1938, marked by an increase of emigration; the third, the period starting with the annexation of Austria to the Reich and ending early in November, 1938; the fourth, the period beginning with the pogroms of November, 1938, which gave a new impetus to the migration movement; the fifth, which started with the outbreak of the War, September 1939.

The first stage was marked by a panic flight to Western European countries—France, Holland, Belgium, Switzerland, Czechoslovakia, England. Among the 80,000 persons who sought refuge there and in a number of other European countries about 80% were Jews. Emigration to Palestine was considerable in that period but only a few thousand went overseas. The majority of the refugees remained in Europe, while some were repatriated to their native lands, for instance, Poles, Lithuanians, and Roumanians who lived in Germany for many years and fled together with German Jews to save their lives from the Nazi oppressors. Some of the refugees returned to Germany in the expectation that things there would be arranged in one or another way and that the Jews would be able to make a living under modified conditions. Emigration markedly slowed down in 1934 and in the first part of 1935.

The Nuremberg Laws issued on September 15, 1935 brought home to the German Jews that their sole chance lay in emigration. The second stage, ushered in by this enactment, was characterized by a continuous decline of European migrations, by the diminishing of the absorptive capacity of Palestine and by a consistent increase of emigration overseas. The main goals were the Western Hemisphere and the Union of South Africa. This British dominion received in 1936 3,330 emigrants from Germany but on February 1, 1937, further immigration was practically stopped by the South African Aliens' Act which stipulated that only those immigrants capable of assimilation to the European population of the Union were to be admitted. Meanwhile emigration to the United States began to increase and Argentina admitted in 1937 more people than in 1936. Emigration in 1936 and 1937 amounted to about 25,000 yearly, and the Jewish agencies calculated that at this rate a quarter of a million of the younger German Jews could migrate in the course of ten years.

In March, 1938, Austria was occupied. To the 360,-000 Jews left in Germany—out of 500,000 listed in June, 1933—180,000 Austrian Jews were added, making a total of 540,000 in Greater Germany. The Jews both in Germany and Austria were ordered by the Gestapo organs to make speedy arrangements for emigration. But as the possibilities for orderly immigration in most of the overseas countries slackened during 1938—despite the efforts made at the Evian Conference in July, 1938—the Gestapo agents started organizing illegal transportation (to Palestine, Shanghai and other parts of the world). The persecutions of the Austrian Jews who were treated in a more brutal way than the Jews of Germany, and the pogroms of November, 1938 throughout the whole of Greater Germany necessitated precipitated departures without proper preparations. Panic flight ensued. According to conservative estimates at least 100,000 Jews emigrated from Greater Germany in 1938 (the greater part came from Austria).

Emigration proceeded in 1939 in a still more precipitous way. It was forced by the Nazi officials, particularly in Austria. After the occupation of Czechoslovakia in March, 1939, a new contingent of migrants was added. The outbreak of the War in September at first did not interrupt emigration from Germany and the lands dominated by the Nazis, an emigration which had already assumed a mass character. Exact figures for this period cannot be given, as uncontrolled, illegal migration steadily increased.

It has been estimated that from 1933 to the beginning of 1940 a total of 260,000 Jews left Germany proper, 124,000 migrated from Austria, and 43,000 fled from Czechoslovakia. An estimate made by the Joint Distribution Committee of the Jews who embarked for overseas countries, including Palestine, in 1940 and the first five months of 1941, gave a total of 75,000. Of these only 36,000 came direct from Germany, Austria and Czechoslovakia; the remainder were refugees who had spent some time in other countries in Europe. Adding this sum of 36,000 to the Jewish emigrants of the previous years, one finds a total of about 460,000 Jews who emigrated from Germany, Austria and Czechoslovakia in 1933-1941.

Emigration of Jews continued in those years from other lands, particularly from Eastern Europe. The figures for this emigration can also be given only approximately. Poland provided most of the emigrants. From 1933-1937 94,444 Jews left Poland, according to official emigration data. In 1938-1941 at least 50,000 must have left (deportations to Soviet Russia not included). 50,000 probably emigrated in 1933-1941 from Lithuania, Latvia and Roumania. This gives a figure of 200,000 Jewish emigrants from Eastern Europe in that period, which is a rather conservative estimate. Altogether 660,000 or possibly 700,000 Jews left their European native lands in 1933-1941. Official statistics for those years show much lower figures of overseas immigrants. Many of the immigration countries have not published statistical data of entrance, while those countries which keep regular records of immigration have not as yet revealed the figures from 1939 on. The fact of illegal infiltration should also be borne in mind. Finally there are still many potential overseas migrants waiting in Europe for opportunities, both legal and technical, to move away from Europe.

Following are statistical data of Jewish immigration:

IMMIGRATION TO THE UNITED STATES FROM 1933 TO 1940

YEAR	JEWISH IMMIGRANTS	PERCENTAGE OF TOTAL IMMIGRATION
1933	2,372	10.28
1934	4,134	14.3
1935	4,837	13.84
1936	6,252	17.21
1937	11,352	22.59
1938	19,736	29.07
1939	43,450	52.35
1940	36,945	52.21
TOTAL	129,078	

IMMIGRATION TO CANADA FROM 1933 TO 1940

YEAR	JEWISH IMMIGRANTS	PERCENTAGE OF TOTAL IMMIGRATION
1933	772	3.90
1934	943	6.06
1935	624	5.14
1936	880	7.93
1937	619	5.15
1938	584	3.73
1939	890	5.20
1940	1,623	10.02
TOTAL	6,915	

IMMIGRATION TO ARGENTINA FROM 1933 TO 1939

YEAR	JEWISH IMMIGRANTS	PERCENTAGE OF TOTAL IMMIGRATION
1933	1,962	8.06
1934	2,215	8.04
1935	3,169	7.06
1936	4,261	8.95
1937	5,178	12.49
1938	1,050	2.78
1939	4,300	73.62
TOTAL	22,133	

IMMIGRATION TO BRAZIL FROM 1933 TO 1939
(ACCORDING TO HICEM)

YEAR	JEWISH IMMIGRANTS	PERCENTAGE OF TOTAL IMMIGRATION
1933	3,317	6.80
1934	4,010	7.96
1935	1,759	4.90
1936	3,450	27.01
1937	2,004	5.78
1938	530	2.73
1939	4,600	12.00
TOTAL	19,670	

Immigration to Uruguay amounted according to estimated figures available from 1933 to 1939 to 9,732.

Immigration to Chile amounted to a figure estimated at 12,000. Immigration to Bolivia reached according to estimates of the organizations about 10,000, to Colombia at least 1,200, to Ecuador 1,400, to Paraguay 1,000, to Peru 2,000, to Venezuela about 500, (all these estimates are rather conservative).

Immigration to Central America was comparatively small. The largest number was to Cuba, whither nearly 3,000 immigrated in the period under review, then followed Mexico, where roughly 1,000 have entered and Santo Domingo with a total of 600-700, Panama with about 1,200, while the other republics—Guatemala, Nicaragua, Honduras, Salvador, Costa Rica and Haiti—have received 1,000 immigrants.

Immigration to the Western Hemisphere thus amounted to some 212,500, but since figures for 1939-1940 are not fully available, it can be assumed that about 225,000 immigrated to the American countries.

Among the Asiatic countries PALESTINE absorbed about 230,000 immigrants in 1933-1941. Shanghai had a great influx of refugees beginning from the second half of 1938. Some have since emigrated to the UNITED STATES, PALESTINE and other lands but about 20,000 were reported to be still there in 1942. About 2,000 reached JAPAN and some 1,300 entered the PHILIPPINES. The majority of the latter group landed there as participants in a program of selected immigration started in the fall of 1938 at the instance of the Economic Refugee Corporation. In the middle of the 1930's Manchukuo had absorbed a certain number of emigrants from Central Europe. India, Iran, Burma and Thailand were goals of migration, but even estimates are not available.

The chief goal of immigration in Africa was the SOUTH AFRICAN UNION. Some 8,000 Jews, mainly from Germany, came there in 1933-38. Kenya, Southern Rhodesia, South West Africa, and other African territories have probably absorbed a maximum of 1,000 immigrants.

Immigration to Australia was insignificant in the earlier 1930's. A total of 7,280 refugees from Europe entered in 1937-1939; about 3,000 of these were from Germany, 2,000 from Austria, and about 2,000 from Czechoslovakia, Poland and Roumania. With the outbreak of the second World War, immigration was stopped. A few hundred entered NEW ZEALAND in the period under review.

Lit.: Annual reports of the Hilfsverein der Deutschen Juden (1933-1937); reports of the Jewish Colonization Association (1933-1937); reports of the Reichsvertretung der Juden in Deutschland, Berlin (1935-1938; mimeographed); reports of the Vienna Jewish Community (1938-1939; mimeographed); annual reports of the Hias (1933-1941); *Aid to Jews Overseas,* reports of the Activities of the American Jewish Joint Distribution Committee for the years 1936, 1937, 1938, 1939, and for 1940 and the first five months of 1941; Bentwich, Norman, *The Refugees from Germany* (1936); Bernstein, John L., "The Migration of Jews in Recent Years," *American Jewish Year Book* (1936-37); Wischnitzer, Mark, "Jewish Emigration from Germany 1933-1938," *Jewish Social Studies* (1940) No. 1.

4. Immigration to Palestine (1882-1941). Modern Jewish immigration to Palestine started in 1882. Toward the end of the 19th cent. about 4,500 Jews were settled on the land, and in 1907 this number reached 7,000. In 1914 about 12,000 persons lived in colonies and farms. The Turkish government opposed any large scale Jewish immigration. Economic backwardness, diseases and the chicanery of the local authorities made difficult any intensive colonization. But immigration to the cities was also rather slow in the years before the first World War. The following approximate data show the increase of the Jewish population in six cities from 1882 to 1914.

CITIES	JEWISH POPULATION 1882	1914
Jerusalem	18,000	58,000 (according to Ruppin 45-50,000)
Jaffa	2,000	15,000
Safed	6,000	7,000
Tiberias	5,000	5,000
Haifa	1,000	3,000
Hebron	3,000	1,000
TOTAL	35,000	89,000

This rise in the population of the cities was, however, due mainly to natural increase. Total immigration to Palestine amounted to about 20,000 in 1882-1900 and to about 16,000 in 1901-1914.

During the War many Jews, especially those originating from countries engaged in war with Turkey, had to leave the country. On account of this emigration and the considerable mortality in that time there were in 1918 only about 55,000 Jews in Palestine. Thanks to the new situation created by the Balfour Declaration it soon became a center of Jewish immigration efforts. A stream of immigrants influenced by nationalist motives poured into the country shortly after the War. Simultaneously numerous Jews who had become uprooted on account of the War and the Bolshevik revolution in Russia tried to get to Palestine. With the establishment of civil administration the Zionist organization obtained in 1920 permission to transport a certain number of immigrants to Palestine provided that their support or occupation would be guaranteed for one year. After the Arabic riots Jewish immigration was stopped in the spring of 1921, but a month later it was resumed. Restrictions were introduced against an influx of immigrants whose economic progress seemed doubtful. Despite interventions of the Zionist Executive the immigration policy of the Palestinian government remained restrictive.

Between October, 1919 and September, 1921, an aggregate of 14,532 immigrants arrived in Palestine—according to other information only 12,000. But in the same period about 3,000 emigrated. The following table contains figures of the annual Jewish immigration from October, 1921, to September, 1940, according to the statistics issued by the Jewish Agency for Palestine, which however differ from the figures of the Immigration Department of the Palestinian government:

Year	Jewish Immigrants
1922	7,844
1923	7,421
1924	12,856
1925	33,801
1926	13,081
1927	2,713
1928	2,178
1929	5,249
1930	4,944
1931	4,075
1932	9,553
1933	30,327
1934	42,359
1935	61,854
1936	29,727
1937	10,536
1938	12,868
1939	16,405
1940	4,547
Total	312,338

To the above-given total figure of immigrants there must be added those persons who entered the country illegally and remained there—in 1939, for instance, 11,156, according to governmental data, entered Palestine illegally and in 1940 the number of illegal arrivals amounted to 5,898. Up to 1932 the Immigration Department of the Palestinian government published the figures of emigration from Palestine, which were in some years extraordinarily high, having reached in 1928 186.9% of the figure of immigration and in 1929 99.5% of that figure. In the years 1920 to 1932 31,350 persons emigrated from Palestine, or 26% of those who immigrated.

No emigration figures are available for 1933 to 1935. In 1936 to 1940, emigration was comparatively small; it amounted altogether to 4,469.

Of the total number of Jewish immigrants about 50% came on labor certificates, 17% were capitalists, 18% were dependents of Palestine residents and the rest belonged to other categories. 70% of the immigrants originated from Poland, Russia, Germany and Roumania, the chief countries of emigration to Palestine, while the remaining 30% accounted for the Baltic States, the East and various other parts of the world.

Lit.: Palestine Zionist Office, *Sefirath Yehude Eretz Yisrael* (1918); Ulitzur, A., *Two Decades of the Keren Hayesod* (1940); *General Monthly Bulletin of Current Statistics,* Sept., 1941, published by the Office of Statistics, Jerusalem; "The National Home in 1940. Statement on the work of the Jewish Agency and the development of the Yishuv," *New Judea,* Sept., 1941; chapters "Statistics of Jews," *American Jewish Yearbook; An Interim Report on the Civil Administration of Palestine during the Period July 1, 1920, to June 30, 1921* (1921); *Palestine Royal Commission Report* (1937), chap. 10, Immigration.

5. Internal Migration. During the 19th and 20th centuries there was a considerable movement of the Jewish population within the various countries of Europe and the United States, due to political and economic conditions. This movement was primarily from the smaller provincial localities to the larger cities. When the Jews of Central and Western Europe attained civil and political rights in the course of the 19th cent. they began to move to the larger commercial and industrial centers where there were greater opportunities. The same economic factor caused the Jews of

the United States to tend to move to larger cities in common with a large part of the general population.

During this period there was a steady growth of such Jewish communities as Paris, Berlin, Vienna, Budapest and Prague, each of which drew from the smaller cities and towns of their respective countries. As a rule the migration was chiefly from the less prosperous parts of the countries; thus the migration to Paris was chiefly from Alsace, and that to Berlin from the eastern part of Germany.

The first World War saw an internal migration of refugees. Tens of thousands of Jews fled from Galicia and Bucovina before the invading Russians and settled permanently in Vienna.

The situation in Russia was somewhat different. In the early part of the 19th cent. Jews were not allowed to settle in the larger cities, but they flocked to the south of Russia and Siberia as long as colonization areas were open to them. Under the milder reign of Alexander II (1855-81), when restrictions to settlement were less rigorously enforced, numbers of Jews moved to the larger cities; they were forced to migrate from these during the reactionary reigns of Alexander III and Nicholas II. After 1920, when all restrictions upon Jewish residence were abolished, there was a steady internal migration of Jews to regions outside of the Pale of Settlement. Thus from 1920 to 1939 about 600,-000 Jews migrated from the Ukraine and White Russia to the Great Russian Republic, to the Ural region, Central Asia and the Far East, including Birobidjan. The growing industrialization of Russia, at the same time, attracted thousands of Jews to the larger cities. Thus about 1939 there were about 1,280,000 Jews, or about 42% of all the Jews in Russia, concentrated in the following cities:

Moscow	400,000
Leningrad	275,000
Odessa	180,000
Kiev	175,000
Kharkov	150,000
Dnepropetrovsk	100,000

In the United States, the migration was chiefly to such centers as New York, Detroit, Chicago and Los Angeles; there was also a movement from the crowded ghetto of New York into the surrounding states, particularly New England.

Lit.: Rotholz, *Die deutschen Juden in Zahl und Bild* (1925); Lestschinsky, J., *Dos Sovyetishe Identum* (1941).

V. The Care of the Migrants Through Jewish Organizations. 1. Beginnings of Organizational Work in Europe and America. In 1846 Ludwig Philippson, editor of the *Allgemeine Zeitung des Judentums,* issued an appeal for the creation of an organization to aid in assisting the plight of the Russian Jews by providing means of emigration. Similar movements were started in Vienna, Prague and Budapest about 1848. In 1869 the Alliance Israélite Universelle called a conference of Jewish leaders at Berlin to form committees to aid Jewish emigrants who were crossing the border between Russia and Prussia in large numbers. When Jewish emigration from Russia grew to a flood after 1881, national committees for the aid of these refugees were set up in London, Paris, Amsterdam, Berlin and Vienna. The German and Austrian committees undertook the task of sheltering the refugees in the border towns and en route, while the British Mansion House Committee undertook to provide transportation overseas. The first meeting for international coopera.ion among Jews in aid to migrants took place in Berlin in 1882.

In 1891 a new flood of Russian emigration called for the organization of relief organizations. Among these were the Central Russian Refugees Committee, the United Hebrew Charities of New York, the Baron de Hirsch Fund, the Russian Transportation Fund, the Jewish Alliance of America, and the American Committee for Ameliorating the Conditions of the Russian Exiles. The need for more permanent organizations was felt and this was met by the creation of the Jewish Colonization Association in 1891 and the Hilfsverein der Deutschen Juden in 1901, the latter taking as one main object the care of the Russian migrants. In 1904 an international conference at Frankfort entrusted the Hilfsverein with the establishment of a Central Bureau for Jewish Migration. In Russia hundreds of branch offices were established by the ICA. In the United States the Hebrew Sheltering and Immigrants Aid Society (Hias), founded in 1898, received and protected the immigrants, and the National Council of Jewish Women took especial care of girls and women. In 1901 the Industrial Removal Office was created to help in relieving the congestion in New York and other cities, and in 1907 the Jewish Immigrants' Information Bureau was established at Galveston.   MARK WISCHNITZER.

2. The Hebrew Sheltering and Immigrant Aid Society (HIAS).

This organization was American Jewry's principal instrument in the field of immigrant aid and Americanization services since the 1880's. The institution represents a merger of two societies: (a) the Hebrew Sheltering House (Hachnosas Orchim), established in the early 1880's in New York city to render first-aid and shelter to the refugees from Czarist Russia; and (b) the Hebrew Immigrant Aid Society, founded on a wider scope program in pursuit of a similar purpose in 1902. The merger was effected in 1909, and the institution was named the Hebrew Sheltering and Immigrant Aid Society. It operates from its own building in Lafayette Street, New York city, and is popularly known by its abbreviated name: HIAS. The overwhelming majority of the nearly three million Jewish immigrants who came to the United States during the past half-century benefited from one or the other sort of services being rendered by HIAS.

The purposes of the Society, as formulated by the founders and pursued during the past five decades, are:

To facilitate the lawful entry of Jewish immigrants at the various ports of the United States; to provide Jewish aliens with temporary shelter, food, clothing and such other aid as they may require; to help the newcomers in reaching their destination and joining their relatives or friends; to encourage the settlement of the newcomers in uncongested areas; to foster American ideals among the new arrivals and to help them in their culture and economic adjustment; to prevent the newly arrived immigrants from becoming a public charge by facilitating their integration into the economical fabric of the country; to disseminate accurate information regarding the United States immigration laws and to foster compliance with these laws by advising and helping American relatives or friends or sponsors of prospective immigrants in the preparation and filing of the required

"Affidavits of Support" and other legal and technical documents to be submitted to the Department of State, Washington, D.C., and/or to the United States Consular Service abroad.

To carry on its service, HIAS maintains, in addition to its national headquarters in New York city, a bureau at Ellis Island, a legal office in Washington, D. C., and branch offices in Boston, Baltimore, Philadelphia, Chicago, San Francisco and Seattle.

For its American services, the organization maintains the following special departments: 1. pier work and guide service, which meets incoming steamers and ministers to the needs of Jewish aliens upon arrival; 2. a personal service department, which receives and answers inquiries in person or by mail regarding immigration questions; 3. an affidavit department, which helps American relatives and friends of prospective immigrants in the preparation and filing of the required affidavits and petitions; 4. a correspondence department, which handles numerous inquiries from all parts of the world regarding the whereabouts of Americans being sought by their relatives or friends who seek to invoke their cooperation with a view to emigrating overseas; 5. a transportation department which facilitates and in some instances (when this is not contrary to prevailing regulations) covers all or a part of the transportation costs; 6. an Americanization and citizenship bureau, which helps the new arrivals in learning English and the principles of Americanism and in obtaining their naturalization; 7. an employment department; 8. a shelter department, which maintains modern dormitory facilities to provide lodging and food for the new arrivals prior to their departure for their destinations; 9. a special service department, which ministers to emergency needs and provides medical care for the inmates of the HIAS dormitories when the need arises.

The Society's activities assumed international proportions in 1915, when a commission was sent to Japan to assist Jewish immigrants who were making their way to the United States from Russia through the Far East. Offices were opened in Yokohama, Harbin, Irkutsk and Vladivostok, and since then a permanent office has been maintained in Shanghai. In 1916, with the consent and cooperation of the United States government and the Central European powers, HIAS was empowered to send a commission to Eastern Europe for the purpose of locating those relatives of American residents in Eastern Europe of whom all trace had been lost, due to war conditions.

In 1920 the Society inaugurated its activities in connection with the reunion of families, sending a commission to Eastern Europe for that purpose. The European activity of HIAS has become a permanent part of its work. It maintains offices in Poland, Latvia, Lithuania, Roumania, Danzig, Belgium, Holland, Soviet Russia and Harbin. As a result of this work, tens of thousands of wives and children, parents, brothers and sisters, and orphaned children have been saved and reunited with their families. In 1920 it inaugurated the activities for the transmission of funds by American residents to their relatives abroad for relief and transportation purposes.

With the passage of the 1924 Immigration Quota Law by Congress and the necessity of exploring the possibilities for immigration to other parts of the world,

HIAS sought to strengthen and enlarge its activities abroad. In 1927, it entered into an agreement with the Jewish Colonization Association (ICA) of Paris, France, for the purpose of forming what has since become known as HICEM, the abbreviated name for the HIAS-ICA Emigration Association. This association, with headquarters in Paris, and branch offices in thirty-two countries of emigration, transit and immigration, became the European arm for a world-wide immigrant and refugee service. In the period between 1925 and 1939, an average of 100,000 Jewish men, women and children emigrated from the area of Jewish misery in Europe each year. In consequence of this effort, hundreds of thousands of Jews had been helped to settle not only in the United States, but in the dominions of the British Empire, in the Far East, in South and Central America, and in Palestine. Notable was the program of rescue carried out by HIAS-ICA for the benefit of the refugees from Germany since the advent of the Nazis in 1933. After the invasion of France by the German forces in 1940, the HIAS-ICA headquarters moved to Lisbon, Portugal.

The Society derives its financial support from (a) a nation-wide dues-paying membership; (b) allocations from Jewish federations and welfare funds in all parts of the United States. The affairs of HIAS are governed by a board of directors of thirty-six members. Since the merger in 1909, the society was presided over by the following presidents: Judge Leon Sanders, John L. Bernstein and Abraham Herman. Isaac L. Asofsky was the executive director (1941). In 1909, the Society's annual budget called for an expenditure of $10,000; in 1941 the budgetary needs of HIAS were $1,000,000.

A notable contribution toward ameliorating the suffering of the refugees and victims of the second World War was made by the Society since September 1, 1939. With the beginning of the War, the activities of HIAS at home and abroad have been considerably augmented and carried on under the slogan "Rescue Through Emigration."   ISAAC L. ASOFSKY.

Lit.: HIAS, annual, published in March, 1941; HIAS Activities in the United States and Overseas (1940); reports and documents in the archives of the Hebrew Sheltering and Immigrant Aid Society.

3. The Period After the First World War.

The dislocations resulting from the War and the peace treaties that followed, the internal disturbances and pogroms that were frequent in 1920 and after, brought new problems to the organizations. In addition to the work done by the HIAS and its associate organizations, societies for emigration in Roumania, Poland, Lithuania and Russia lent their aid. Two international conferences were held in 1921, at Brussels and Prague, to centralize the work of the organizations; the result was the creation of the Emigdirect. In July, 1924, forty-two American Jewish organizations formed an Emergency Committee to work with the Jewish Colonization Association and the Emigdirect to take care of stranded migrants. Hicem was established in 1927; the Hilfsverein was in close cooperation with it.

A new emergency arose in 1933, when the Nazis came to power, and new measures were taken by the organizations. The Hilfsverein was made responsible for the emigration of German Jews to all parts of the world except Palestine, in which case migrants were advised

and assisted by the Palestine Office of the Jewish Agency, in Berlin. The repatriation of foreign Jews residing in Germany to their native countries was undertaken by the Hauptstelle für jüdische Wanderfürsorge. These three central organizations were in close contact with the Reichsvertretung der Juden. Special refugee committees were created in other countries whither Jews were likely to migrate permanently or temporarily. The most important of these were at Paris, Amsterdam, Brussels, Antwerp, Zurich and London; the latter acted also as a clearing station for the refugees to emigrate from England to various parts of the British Empire.

In the United States the care of the immigrants was at first assumed by the HIAS and the Council of Jewish Women. In 1934 the Coordinating Committee for Jewish Refugees was established; it was later reorganized as the National Refugee Service. The Hicem took care of immigration to South America, aided by local committees. In South Africa there was a special organization in Johannesburg, and aid was furnished by the South African Jewish Board of Deputies and Board of Guardians. In the Far East, the Harbin committee of the Hicem rendered important aid to Jewish refugees; it was later removed to Shanghai, which became an important center for Jewish refugees from Europe. In Australia the chief work of aiding immigrants was done by the Australian Jewish Welfare Society at Sydney.

The following organizations also dealt with the needs of the immigrants in the United States: American Committee to Save Refugees; American Jewish Congress, Women's Division; Emergency Committee in Aid of Displaced Foreign Scholars; Emergency Rescue Committee; Exiled Writers Committee; German Jewish Children's Aid; Jewish Agricultural Society; Musicians Emergency Fund; President's Advisory Committee on Political Refugees; Refugee Economic Corporation; Self-Help of Émigrés from Central Europe; United States Committee for the Care of European Children. The work carried on by these organizations was financed, up to the outbreak of war in 1939, chiefly by the Joint Distribution Committee, the Council for German Jewry, in Great Britain, and the Jewish Colonization Association.

The governments of various countries also paid some attention to the problems of thousands of refugees from the Nazi terror. The League of Nations set up a High Commissioner for Refugees, with a liaison committee made of representatives of the principal philanthropic organizations. In July, 1938 representatives of thirty-two governments met at Evian, at the suggestion of President Franklin D. Roosevelt of the United States, to discuss problems of Jewish emigration from Germany; it decided to appoint an intergovernmental committee to deal with the problems of migration. This endeavor came to an end with the outbreak of the second World War in 1939.   MARK WISCHNITZER.

Lit.: See the literature on the individual organizations mentioned above; American Jewish Year Book, reports of organizations from 1928 on; Contemporary Jewish Record, Sept., 1938; Nov.-Dec., 1939.

MIKHOELS (stage name of Solomon Mikhailovich Vovsy), actor, b. 1890. He studied law at the University of St. Petersburg, and at the age of twenty-eight entered the Petrograd Jewish Dramatic Studio school. The following year (1919) he became a professional actor. After the Studio moved to Moscow, where it changed its name to the State Jewish Theatre, Mikhoels became its leading actor. Later he was also a director. In 1929 he became the art director of the Theatre and in 1931 he began to teach in the Jewish Theatrical School.

Mikhoels' first role was Uriel Acosta, and from the very beginning, the vividness of his character portrayals, marked by profound inner meaning, was evident. Mikhoels was a student of Jewish history, its trends and significance, and this knowledge of his added to the depth of his art. He played Shimele Soroker in Sholom Aleichem's *200,000*, Notsmakh in Goldfaden's *The Witch*, Benjamin in Moicher Sforim's *The Travels of Benjamin the Third;* later he took the title role in Shakespeare's *King Lear* and was Tevye in Sholom Aleichem's *Tevye der Milchiger*. The Soviet Government honored Mikhoels with the title of People's Artist, and on the occasion of the 20th anniversary (1931) of the State Jewish Theatre Mikhoels was awarded the Order of Lenin.

Lit.: Bolshaia Entsiklopedia (1938); *Malaia Entsiklopedia* (1937); *Sovetskoe Iskusstvo*, April 2, 1939; *Tass*, April 9, 1939; *Pravda*, April 1, 1939; *Soviet Embassy Bulletin*, Aug. 24, 1941.

MIKLÓS, ANDOR, editor and publisher, b. Budapest, 1880; d. Budapest, 1913. He made his journalistic debut in 1901 and, after serving as financial editor of the daily newspaper *Pesti Napló* (1902 to 1910), he founded (1910) *Az Est* (Evening), the first boulevard newspaper in Hungary. Miklós introduced in Hungary American methods of newspaper writing and distribution, providing for his paper an international news service of its own and claiming for his newspapermen the right of enquiring into the way executive, economic and social power was exerted inside Hungary. He subsequently acquired the late evening paper *Magyarország* and the morning paper *Pesti Napló*, becoming an influential exponent of Liberal-capitalistic ideas and securing the collaboration of the best contemporary Hungarian authors. As owner of the Athenaeum publishing house, he also published collected editions of the works of many of these writers. In 1927 he cooperated with Viscount Rothermere in an endeavor to bring about a revision of the Trianon Peace Treaty of 1920.

He was succeeded in the presidency of the newspaper concern by his widow, the actress Frida Gombaszögi. When Jewish influence in the Hungarian press was eliminated by legislative action (from 1938 on), the *Est* chain of newspapers passed into different hands.

MIKVAOTH ("ritual baths"), sixth tractate of Toharoth, the sixth division of the Mishnah; it is placed seventh in the Babylonian Talmud, and was given the first place in the division in the 1559 and 1606 editions of the Mishnah. The tractate consists of ten chapters, and discusses the rules and regulations in reference to the ritual bath required of persons cured from leprosy (*Lev.* 14 and 15). According to rabbinic tradition, such a ritual bath had to contain at least forty seahs (about sixty gallons) and had to be of running water, not water which was drawn. The tractate discusses the various sources of water and their respective merits and demerits, whether the addition of drawn water in certain amounts makes the ritual bath unfit, the proper construction and maintenance of ritual baths, the manner of bathing, and the ritual immersion of vessels. The Tosefta to the tractate has eight chapters (seven in the Codex Erfurt); there is no Gemara.

Lit.: Danby, H., *The Mishnah* (1933) 732-45.

MIKVEH, a Hebrew word meaning "gathering of water," later used chiefly in the sense of a plunge or ritual bath. Biblical law requires a purifying bath to remove uncleanliness after venereal discharges, sexual emissions, contact with the dead, or after menstruation (*Lev.* 12:2; 15:5-13; *Num.* 19:19; *Deut.* 23:12). Also, the high priest had to bathe before officiating at the Yom Kippur services (*Lev.* 16:4; *Yoma* 7:4). All these ritualistic ablutions had to take place in running (river) water, or in rainwater accumulated in pits or cavities. The water entirely loses its effectiveness if poured into a vessel; in this proscription lay the origin of the baptisms performed by John the Baptist in the Jordan.

Although the regulations about priestly bathing lost their significance after the destruction of the Temple, those pertaining to the post-menstrual and post-confinement bathing of women, with whom sexual intercourse is forbidden until after the ritual bath has been taken, are still in force even in the 20th cent. From ancient times until the present day there has always been in every Jewish community a Mikveh, or public ritual bath, conforming to the requirements of Jewish law. It must hold a minimum of about two cubic yards, or about 200 gallons, of water, enough to cover the entire human body (*Hag.* 11a). The Mikveh was used also for dipping new dishes, which must receive a cleansing bath before they are used.

In the 19th cent. there were discovered along the Rhine baths of architectonic and artistic interest which were first regarded as Roman baths but which later proved to have belonged to ancient Jewish communities in the region. The baths had been built by the same architects as those responsible for the local romanesque churches and cathedrals. They are set checkerwise into the ground to a depth of about eighty feet and are well-like structures, with artistic winding staircases, underground niches for purifying baths and plunge baths generally laid at what was calculated to be the average height of the Rhine. The decorations of the pillars and consoles are carefully carried out in romanesque style; illumination is furnished through a rather large opening in the upper ceiling. Mikvehs of this sort were preserved in Worms (mentioned in documents, 1557; discovered, 1896; presumably built, 1034), Speyer (from the beginning or middle of the 12th cent., used until 1534); Deutz (probably dating from the middle of the 15th cent.); Andernach (erected about 1220, with the city hall built over it), and Friedberg, in Hesse (erected about 1260).

The modern interpretation has been to consider the Mikveh regulations as part of other Jewish laws of hygiene, and therefore subject to different interpretations in a civilization where baths are common. In places where there are no regular bathing facilities, however, the Mikveh still has an inestimable value.

JAKOB PINCHAS KOHN.

(See illustrations in vol. 2, pp. 109-11.)

Lit.: Levy, Benas, *Die Juden im Worms* (1914); Hildenbrandt, F. J., *Das romanische Judenbad in Speyer* (1920).

MIKVEH ISRAEL, *see* COLONIES, AGRICULTURAL.

MILAH, *see* CIRCUMCISION.

MILAN, a city in the north of Italy. Of a population of 992,000, there were, before introduction of anti-Semitic laws in Italy (1939) some 4,500 Jewish residents and a number of Jewish refugees from Central Europe. Old inscriptions give evidence of the presence of Jews in Milan about the end of the 4th cent. During the early Christian period, the Jews suffered persecution. Ambrose, Bishop of Milan, was especially inimical; in 388, when Emperor Theodosius ordered a bishop to rebuild a synagogue which had been destroyed by some monks, Ambrose called the emperor a Jew. In the following centuries, however, Jews became extensive land owners. Theodoric (d. 526) confirmed the protection of the synagogue. A master of the mint named Gedeone Azzo is mentioned for the year 923, but it has not been established whether he was a Jew. In 1025 the Jews are said to have been expelled from Milan, but they must have returned after that, since it is certain that they were expelled in 1320. In 1387 Duke Gian Galeazzo Visconti permitted their return and gave them privileges which were later confirmed by the House of Sforza. In 1475 a monk who preached against the Jews in Milan, playing up the blood accusation in Trent, was driven out of the city. However, a short time afterwards, Jews were permitted to take up only temporary sojourn of two or three days in the city of Milan, but until 1597 they were allowed to settle in the other cities of the duchy of Milan. In 1597 all the Jews were expelled, and all their belongings confiscated.

During the War of the Spanish Succession, Prince Eugene of Savoy, who occupied Milan as the Austrian generalissimo, permitted the Jews (1707) to settle in the city and territory of Milan. With this period begins the history of a new Jewish community of Milan. Since through the Treaty of Rastatt (1714) Milan was left to Austria, the Jewish community was able to consolidate. In the last years of the Austrian rule and after the union of Milan (1859) with the kingdom of Piedmont, which became part of the kingdom of Italy in 1861, the great economic development of the city drew many Jews to Milan. In 1857 about 500 Jews lived there, 3,012 in 1891, and 2,000 in 1900, including many Ashkenazim who came from the other side of the Alps. The growing influx of Jews from the smaller communities of Lombardy, Piedmont, Tuscany and other provinces of Italy was fostered by the rapid growth of Milan as one of Italy's major industrial and commercial centers. In 1931, according to official sources, the Jewish population of Milan was 5,865.

For the religious, cultural and educational interests of the Milan Jewish community the appointment, in 1892, of Alessandro da Fano, formerly of Corfu, to succeed Prospero Moise Ariani as rabbi of Milan was of great importance. In 1892 the erection of the Jewish Temple on the Via Guastalla was also completed. Alessandro da Fano held his post as chief rabbi of Milan for forty-three years, until his death in 1935, and during this long period he promoted and organized the principal cultural and educational institutions of that community. Da Fano founded the Asilo Infantile Israelitico and the Jewish Elementary School which, shortly before his death, had 250 pupils and was transferred from modest premises to much larger ones on the Via Eupili.

Da Fano was also among the founders of the Milanese Zionist Circle, which was headed for many years by the famous Italian-Jewish playwright and literary critic, Sabatino Lopez. This Circle organized a lively activity of Zionist and general Jewish cultural interest among Italian Jews and the numerous new emigrés.

The Fascist racial laws paralyzed and later completely cut off the various Jewish educational and cultural organizations in Milan. The large colony of Levantine Jews, mostly from Turkey and Salonica, which settled in Milan in the post-war years, as well as German, Austrian and Eastern European Jews there, fell under the provisions of the law of September 12, 1939, which fixed a six months deadline for their departure from Italy. Hundreds of commercial and industrial enterprises established by these Jews had to be sold within the specified period, bringing heavy losses to their owners.

The chief rabbinate of Milan, after the death of Da Fano in 1935, was assumed by Gustavo Castelbolognesi, formerly chief rabbi of Padua and Tripoli. The president of the Milan Jewish community, in 1942, was the former naval commander, Federigo Jarach.

DAVID KLEINLERER.

Lit.: *Educatore Israelita,* vol. 3, p. 106 et seq.; Rota, "Gli Ebrei e la Politica Spagnuola in Lombardia," *Bollettino della Societa Paverse di Storia Patria,* vol. 6, p. 349 et seq.; Canetta, "Gli Ebrei del Ducato Milanese," *Archivio Storico Lombardo,* vol. 8, 1881, p. 632 et seq.; Lewinsky, *Revista Israelitica,* vol. 6, pp. 54-55; Ferorelli, *Vessillo Israelitico,* 1914, pp. 237, 357; Schaerf, *Appunti Storici Sugli Ebrei della Lombardia,* 1926 (special reprint from *Rassegna Mensile di Israel*); *Revue des études juives,* vol. 20 (1890) 34-72.

MILAN, GABRIEL, soldier of fortune, b. Hamburg, Germany, 1631; d. Copenhagen, Denmark, 1689. He went to France, and entered the French army under Cardinal Mazarin. After eventful years, Milan went to Amsterdam, where he became a merchant. He was prosperous as long as he managed his affairs jointly with his wealthy brother-in-law, Joshua Abensour, but after Abensour's death Milan's financial situation became difficult. In 1667 he entered into relations with the Danish court, becoming the banker of Prince Jørgen of Denmark, who traveled across Europe from 1667 to 1670. He was also a secret agent of the Danish government in Holland. The government was highly satisfied with Milan's services, but the Danish minister to The Hague was on bad terms with him. In a justificatory letter to the Danish government Milan talked proudly of his loyalty to Judaism, of his loyalty to the king of Denmark, and of his family "which occupied, and is still occupying responsible positions in Spain, Flanders, and Italy."

In 1670 Milan visited Copenhagen and there married a daughter of Benjamin Musaffia, physician of the Danish king and a descendant of the De Castro family. Milan was named "residerende Commissarius" of the Danish court in Holland. In 1675, after his wife's death, Milan married Juliane Sophie von Breitenbach, a widow. In 1678 he went to Copenhagen for a second time, and was granted permission to coin 300,000 riksdollars. Yet his financial situation became more and more desperate, and in 1682 he bewailed the lack of bread in his house.

After being baptized, Milan applied for the post of governor of the Danish West Indies. In 1684 he was elected governor by the Danish West Indian Company, and the appointment was confirmed by the king on April 24, 1684. Milan obtained this post, despite his prominent competitors, because he was master of the Spanish, French, Portuguese, German and Dutch languages. The company also acknowledged Milan's "better training in commercial matters" and his "common sense."

But the Danish Company and the government of Denmark were soon disappointed. In May, 1684, Milan, together with his wife, five children, a governess, three lackeys, three men servants and three servant girls, embarked for St. Thomas on the sailing vessel *Fortuna.* On board, he engaged in violent conflict with the captain. After arrival at St. Thomas, he acted contrary to instructions. He arrested his predecessor instead of sending him to Denmark, and extorted money from him. He terrorized the planters, and neglected the sending of sugar and tobacco to Denmark, as he was obliged to do in accordance with his duties as governor. He even exposed the colony to danger by means of inconsiderate reprisals made on Spain. The government of Copenhagen, soon burdened with complaints by the colonists, sent a commissioner, Mikkel Mikkelsen, to St. Thomas. When he arrived, on February 24, 1686, Milan tried to mobilize the colonists, and after failing to recruit them took shelter behind the citadel. After resistance lasting three days, Milan was forced to surrender, and was sent, together with his predecessor, to Copenhagen. He was sentenced to death and, upon rejection of his appeal, was executed in March, 1689, on Kongens Nytorv, the largest square of Copenhagen. His estate and plantation were confiscated in settlement of the claims which the Danish West India Company had against him.   HUGO BIEBER.

Lit.: Publications of the American Jewish Historical Society, No. 28 (1922) 213-21; Larsen, Kay, *Dansk Vestindien 1666-1917* (1928).

MILCH, JACOB, Yiddish publicist, b. Warsaw, 1866. Until the age of twelve, he received a Talmudic education. At fifteen, under the influence of the Warsaw Maskilim, he became interested in Hebrew literature. Economic pressure forced him to learn a trade, and Milch became a wood-carver and was employed in a furniture factory.

In 1886, Milch was drafted into the Russian army and served the full four years. His literary and communal activities began in 1891, when he came to the United States. That same year his first published work appeared in the *Arbeiter Zeitung*—a satire on anarchism, *Gvald, lozt machen a revolutzie.* Later Milch was a collaborator on the *Ovent-Blatt* and the *Zukunft* and for a time (1907) edited the latter journal.

Milch was secretary of the United Hebrew Trades in 1893. After working as a wood-carver, he became a successful candy manufacturer and issued, at his own expense, a magazine called *Neie Velt* (1909). He was author of many articles on publicistic, cultural and historical matters, and published *Zichronot,* his memoirs of the origin of the *Forverts* (1936), and of the *Zukunft* in the *Penkess* (Vilna, 1913). Milch also wrote a three-volume study, *Yiddishe Problemen* (1920) and translated works by Perez Smolenskin and Gerhart Haupt-

mann into Yiddish, as well as Plato's *Dialogues* (1928). He was a collaborator on the *Morgen-Freiheit.*

Lit.: Reisen, Z., *Lexikon fun der Yiddisher Literatur, Presse un Filologie,* vol. 2 (1930), cols. 402-6; *Morgen-Freiheit,* Dec. 14, 1941; Milch, Jacob, "Autobiographishe Skizzen," *Morgen-Djurnal* (1942).

MILCH, LUDWIG, professor of mineralogy and geology at the University of Breslau, b. Breslau, Germany, 1867; d. Breslau, 1928. Some of his works are: *Die Grundlagen der Bodenkunde* (Vienna, 1899); *Möglicher Zusammenhang zwischen Festigkeitsverminderung (Massendefekten) in der Erdrinde und der Entstehung von Tiefengesteinsmassiven* (1903); *Lehre von der Regional-Metamorphose; Klassifikation der Anorganogenen Gesteine* (1894); *Die Zusammensetzung der festen Erdrinde als Grundlage der Bodenkunde* (Leipzig, 1926).

Milch was baptized. His grandfather, Lobel, his father, Hugo, and his brother, Friedrich, were all members of the consulting board of the Fraenckel Foundation.

MILCHDIG or **MILCHIG,** *see* DIETARY LAWS.

MILCOM, *see* MOLOCH.

MILHAUD, ALBERT, historian and secretary general of the Radical and Radical Socialist Party of France, b. Paris, 1876. Milhaud, who was descended from a Jewish family of scholars and artists, studied history at the Sorbonne. In 1897 he published a contribution to the social history of Flanders in the Middle Ages, *La lutte des classes en Flandre au moyen âge,* which attracted the attention of the ministry of public education. From 1900 to 1906 he published several summaries of modern history which were used in French classroom teaching by order of the minister of public education. In 1910 Milhaud was appointed chef du cabinet in the ministry of commerce. In 1916 he published *La question d'occident* and in 1917 *La guerre qui venait.* From 1920 to 1921 he directed a department of the French ministry of foreign affairs. He then became secretary general of the Radical and Radical Socialist Party, for many years being actually the directing head of that party and one of the most influential men in the political life of France. Milhaud also directed *L'ère nouvelle,* official organ of the Radical Party. He adhered rather to the right wing of French radicalism, and was opposed to the Popular Front. His influence began to wane in the 1930's, and after the Radical Party accepted the program of the Popular Front (1936) Milhaud retired to private life.

MILHAUD, DARIUS, composer, b. Aix, France, 1892. A student at the Paris Conservatory, the pupil of D'Indy, Gédalge and Widor, he won prizes in violin playing, counterpoint and fugue. During the first World War, he was an attaché of the French Legation in Rio de Janeiro. It was during this period that Milhaud became acquainted with South American music, an idiom and style which he has employed in several of his works. When the war ended, Milhaud returned to Paris and associated himself with a group of young French composers who, guided by Erik Satie, became known throughout the world of music as the famous school of the "French Six." This school was determined to free French music from the bondage of impressionism, through the employment of simplicity, feeling, and satire. It exerted a profound influence on the direction of French music, and for many years enjoyed great prestige. When the "Six" dissolved—largely because of clashes of temperament—Milhaud went his own way, continuing to grow as artist until, when Maurice Ravel died, he was generally conceded to be the foremost living French composer. He was appointed a member of the superior council for radio broadcasts in Paris, and served as a member of the advisory boards of the Opéra Comique and the Paris Conservatory.

In 1922, Milhaud visited the United States for the first time, touring the country as conductor, pianist, and lecturer. He abandoned Paris in 1940 (his opera *Médée* was the last work performed at the Paris Opera before the entrance of the Nazi troops), joining the music faculty at Mills College in Oakland, California.

Though Milhaud's fecundity in every field of composition is perhaps without parallel in modern music, there is rarely a sign of haste in his writing. He commands an extraordinary technique, and what he has written is generally well formulated and in good taste, frequently with a beautiful sense of symmetry in the construction. That there is also superficiality in his music is to be expected in a man who composes so much for the cinema and the radio. At his best, he is an imaginative creator, with a warm and human melodic vein, a bent for brilliant satire, and an inexhaustible inventiveness in harmonic and rhythmic constructions. Milhaud is probably best in his operas, of which are *Le Pauvre Matelot, Christophe Colomb,* and *Maximilien,* all three of which have been produced successfully, are notable examples. He has also written copiously for orchestra (including two piano concertos), chamber music ensembles, voice, piano, two pianos, violin, and chorus. He employed many different styles with equal dexterity. He was one of the first European composers to treat the jazz idiom seriously; his jazz ballet, *La Creation du Monde,* may be said to have been the direct precursor of Gershwin's *Rhapsody in Blue.* DAVID EWEN.

Lit.: Copland, Aaron, *Our New Music* (1941); Rosenfeld, Paul, *Discoveries of a Music Critic* (1936).

MILHAUD, EDGARD, political and social economist, b. Paris, 1873. In his early years he joined the French Socialist Party, and became its authority in dealing with problems of public utilities. He was especially interested in efforts to nationalize the French railways. In addition to various studies on railway management, Milhaud published (1903) *La démocratie socialiste allemande.*

In 1914 he was appointed professor of economics at the University of Geneva. After the outbreak of the first World War, Milhaud combatted German propaganda in Switzerland, and became one of the earliest advocates of the League of Nations idea. He published (1915) *Du droit de la force à la force du droit* and (1917) *La société des nations.* In 1919 he published a study, *La neutralité suisse.* After the founding of the League of Nations, the International Labor Department charged Milhaud with an inquiry about the possibilities of increasing production. During the years 1920 and

Darius Milhaud

1921 he visited almost all the countries of Europe for special studies on forty-seven important branches of economical activity. His reports were published from 1923 to 1925. Milhaud became director of the unemployment department and chief of section in the research division of the International Labor Department.

In 1929 Milhaud became editor of the *Annals of Collective Economy.* Proceeding from the problem of unemployment, he became interested mainly in the problems of international barter arrangements and currency. Almost all Milhaud's studies concerning these problems were published at the same time in French and English. In 1933 he wrote *A Gold Truce* and *Fresh Work, Fresh Markets,* and in the following years several treatises on organized compensation.

In 1934, on the thirtieth anniversary of Milhaud's professorship, many economists of almost all European nations edited *Mélanges d'économie politique et sociale.*

MILHAUD, GASTON SAMUEL, mathematician and philosopher, b. Nîmes, France, 1858; d. Paris, 1918. He was educated at the École normale supérieure and the École polytechnique at Paris. Graduating in 1898, he was appointed professor of mathematics at the college of Le Havre. In 1900 he became professor of philosophy at the University of Montpellier and in 1905 professor at the Sorbonne.

As a disciple of Paul Tannery Milhaud concentrated his studies, on the one hand, upon the history of science and, on the other, upon clarifying the character and value of scientific knowledge. He stressed the inventive spontaneity of human reason, as did Bergson; but Milhaud, unlike Bergson, sought to detach his concepts of truth from all qualitative determinations and to establish philosophical truth according to mathematical methods. Milhaud was a firm Hellenist and Latinist as well as a mathematician. He published *Leçons sur les origines de la science grècque* (1893); *Essai sur les conditions et les limites de la certitude logique,* completed by an essay, *Le rationel,* published in the same year

(1898); *Les philosophes-géomètres de la Grèce* (1900); *Le positivisme et le progrès de l'esprit* (1902); *Nouvelles études sur l'histoire de la pensée scientifique* (1911).

Milhaud's disciples and friends edited his important study *Descartes savant* in 1921, and in 1934 the complete edition of Descartes's letters, prepared by Milhaud. The knowledge of Descartes owes more than one important discovery to Milhaud. He demonstrated especially that Descartes discovered on his own the law of the sine, and thus rediscovered analytic geometry.

MILK (Hebrew *halab*) 1. In the Bible. Milk was evidently regarded as a highly desirable food by the nomads, since Palestine is more than once praised as the "land of milk and honey." Goats' as well as cows' milk was used, especially the former, as cattle can be raised only in certain parts of Palestine. Jerusalem had a street of cheese-makers, but there the milk had to be imported, as it still is in modern times. Fresh milk was a favorite drink; it was usually kept in leathern bags for the refreshment of the family and the wayfarer (*Judges* 4:19). There are references to a substance called *hemah*, which may be either butter or curds, and was regarded as a delicacy. There is no reference to sour milk, though it has always been a popular refreshment in the East and may well have been prepared and drunk in Bible times. The *haritze hehalab* which David took to his brothers (*1 Sam.* 17:18) apparently means slices of cheese.

2. In the Talmud. The Talmud speaks of the use of goat's milk as a remedy for illness (*B.K.* 80a) and notes that it was necessary to milk an animal at least once a day. There are numerous regulations as to the use of milk for food; the milk of unclean animals was forbidden, and meat products and milk products might not be eaten together.

There is considerable information on the way in which milk was prepared to make various products. Milk was curdled by the use of rennet, and there are references to preparations such as "milkwater" and *kem*, possibly curdled milk. Milk was used in cooking cereal foods, in pastry and with vegetables, in fact with all other foods but meat. Like all liquids, it had to be kept covered for fear of pollution by an insect or a reptile; the blessing said over milk was to be "Blessed art Thou, O God . . . by Whose word all things came into being."

Lit.: Dalman, *Arbeit und Sitte in Palästina;* Greenstone, J. H., in *Jewish Encyclopedia,* vol. 8, pp. 590-92.

MILLAUD, ARTHUR PAUL DAVID ALBERT, playwright and journalist, son of Moïse, b. Paris, 1844; d. Paris, 1892. He joined the editorial staff of the journal *Figaro* in 1869, and published there sarcastic small tales which were collected under the title *La petite Nemesis*. Married to the renowned actress Judic (Anna Damiens-Israel, 1850-1911), Millaud wrote many dramatic pieces which offered his wife a great opportunity of displaying her special talent. Millaud's plays met with great applause, especially *Madame Archiduc* (1874), *Niniche* (1878), and *Mam'zell Nitouche,* which did not disappear from the French stage until 1940. Millaud was generally esteemed as one of the best representatives of the "esprit gaulois" and "verve parisienne." He published *Physiologies parisiennes* in 1886.

MILLAUD, EDOUARD, French jurist and parliamentarian, b. Tarascon, France, 1834; d. Paris, 1912. He was educated at Lyon and admitted to the bar of that city in 1856. He was opposed to the government of Napoleon III, and became renowned because he courageously vindicated the right of prosecuted republicans. In 1869 he founded a law school at Lyon which eventually became the law faculty of the University of Lyon.

In 1870, after Napoleon's fall, Millaud was appointed attorney general of Lyon by the government of national defense, and rendered vigorous assistance to Gambetta. In 1871 Millaud retired from office when he was asked by Gambetta's successor to prosecute radical republicans. That same year Millaud, together with Gambetta and others, founded the French republican party, and was elected member of the Chamber of Deputies. Reelected in 1876 and 1877, he combatted the government of Marshal MacMahon, and in 1880 was elected senator. Never defeated, Millaud was, as deputy or senator, a representative of the Rhone department from 1871 until his death. He was highly esteemed, by political friends and adversaries, because of his sincerity and unselfish patriotism, and was considered one of the most powerful orators in the French parliament. Millaud was president or vice-president of several important parliamentary committees, such as those on financial and military affairs. In 1886 he was minister of public works in the Freycinet cabinet, and held the same post in the Goblet cabinet in 1887.

Millaud published (1859) a study on Cicero's rival, *Études sur l'orateur Hortensius,* and a study on *Daniel Manin* (1867). He also issued (1867) a notable pamphlet, *De la réorganisation de l'armée.* His diaries were published posthumously (1914 and 1920) under the title *Le journal d'un parlementaire.* Millaud's notes (1864 to 1896) are an important source of French political history, especially from 1870 to 1890.

Although Millaud remained loyal to Judaism, he did not assume representative posts in Jewish organizations.

MILLAUD, MOÏSE POLYDORE, banker and publisher, b. Bordeaux, France, 1813; d. Paris, 1871. Millaud, descendant of a family of Jewish small traders, was successively clerk in a bailiff's office, in a banking house, and in a bookseller's shop. In 1833, at the age of twenty, he founded *Le lutin* (The Imp), which was published in Nantes. In 1836 he went to Paris, and there founded *Le glaneur.* Millaud intended to devote this journal to industrial subjects, but, failing, transformed it into a theatrical review. Undaunted, he founded another journal, *Le gamin de Paris,* and a banking house (1838), although he owned only 200 francs. That same year he launched *Le négociant,* and enlisted the most prominent leaders of several political parties to serve on its board of administration. Crémieux became Millaud's legal adviser and remained his confidant until the latter's death. Millaud established (1839) *L'audience,* a magazine devoted to juridical affairs. In 1840 he created the "Office général des actionnaires" and an insurance company. Then he founded the *Journal des familles* (1845) and transformed *L'audience* into *La nation.*

Upon the heels of the revolution of 1848, Millaud launched *Le pamphlet,* an illustrated daily, and *La liberté,* the first French newspaper sold for five centimes. He then acquired *Le journal des chemins de fer* and, associated with his coreligionist Mirès, founded (1849) *Le conseiller du peuple,* which yielded a million francs in three years. Millaud's fortune increased even after the foundation of *Le Pays* (1850), and he was called by the boulevardiers Millaud-million. In 1856 he founded *La presse,* but in the same year lost most of his fortune and was forced to sell his house and his horses. Millaud, however, recovered rapidly because he had acquired a large number of building sites near the new railway terminals of Paris, and he soon found reward in the development of the city.

In 1863 he ventured upon his greatest enterprise by founding *Le petit journal,* which revolutionized the French press. Creating a selling organization of 1,200 agents, Millaud precipitated a violent, competitive battle which ruined more than one publishing house.

In 1869 Millaud's victory was decisive. *Le petit journal* became one of the four representatives of the French "grande presse," and existed until 1940. He is recognized as one of the three great creators in the history of the French press. He is especially credited with having initiated the French popular newspaper by means of resourcefully attractive headlines, discovery and training of young journalistic talent. Millaud evidenced rare imperturbability in both hard times and prosperous days. He was a great patron of learning and a philanthropist. His brilliant fêtes were the talk of Paris. At his funeral Rabbi Zadoc Kahn extolled his piety, Crémieux his beneficence, and Gaboriau his daring courage.   HUGO BIEBER.

Lit.: Morienval, Jean, *Les créateurs de la grande presse en France* (1934).

MILLENNIUM, a general term for a period of future happiness, conceived as lasting either a thousand years, or an indefinite period, and occurring at the end of time. While the idea is most definitely emphasized in Christian theology, it first arose among the Jewish apocalyptists of the time of the Second Temple. They conceived of world history as a week of seven divine days; each day was to be a thousand years (*Ps.* 90:4). The seventh period, the equivalent of the Sabbath, was the reign of righteousness. This idea was never fully accepted in Judaism, where various numbers were proposed for the duration of the Messianic kingdom, but it was taken over into Christianity as the period during which Jesus and his disciples would reign on earth. This form of belief, often called chiliasm (the Greek equivalent of millennialism), appeared again and again in the form of various movements in both Judaism and Christianity, especially in the 17th cent. In modern times the idea of a "kingdom of a thousand years" persists as a phrase implying permanence.

MILLER, EMANUEL, psychiatrist and author, b. London, 1893. He was educated at Cambridge and at the London Hospital Medical School. Miller served as honorary psychiatrist for various London hospitals, as honorary director for child guidance clinics and was the co-director of the Institute for Scientific Treatment of Delinquency. He was also sometime lecturer to the medical postgraduates in psychology at Cambridge University and chairman of the medical section of the British Psychological Society.

Among Miller's published works were: *Types of Mind and Body; The Mind as Organism; Modern Psychotherapy* and *Insomnia and Disorders of Sleep.* He was the editor and co-author of *Neurosis in War* (1940). In 1940 Miller was made a major in the Royal Army Medical Corps. He was living in London in 1942.

MILLER, GEORGE JULIUS, lawyer and historian, b. Perth Amboy, N. J., 1895. He entered private law practice in 1915 and since 1935 has been assistant attorney general of New Jersey. Several times he has stood as candidate for the state legislature. Miller is an expert in local New Jersey history, having been appointed director of the New Jersey historical records survey of the Works Progress Administration in 1936. Among his publications are *Ye Old Middlesex Courts* (1932), and *Court of Chancery of New Jersey, 1648-98* (1934). He also wrote *David A. Borrenstein: Study of a Princeton Printer* (1935).

As a student of Jewish history, he is a member of the Jewish Historical Society of England and the American Jewish Historical Society. In the publications of the latter appears his "James Alexander and the Jews, Especially Isaac Emanuel" (1939).

MILLER, ISAIAH (Shin), Yiddish writer, b. Philipovich, province of Volhynia, Russia, 1895. He came to the United States at the age of eighteen. In 1917 Miller's first stories were published in the *Freie Arbeiter Shtimme, Yiddisher Kempfer* and other magazines. He also wrote feuilletons and verse. *Dertzehlungen* (Cleveland, 1921) was his first book; among others which appeared subsequently were: *Bletter Fallen* (1926), *A Bliask oif Tog* (1933), and *Motiven. Motiven* (Los Angeles, 1937) was awarded a prize by Ikuf. Miller belongs to the neo-realist school of Yiddish writers, and according to critics, is one of the most profound of the 20th cent. Yiddish story-writers.

Lit.: Reisen, Z., *Lexikon fun der Yiddisher Literatur, Presse un Filologie,* vol. 2 (1930), col. 418.

MILLER, JESSE ISIDOR, lawyer, b. Lexington, Ky., 1891. Educated in his native city, he there began his law practice, but has been pursuing his career in Washington, D. C., since 1920. He served as assistant solicitor in the Bureau of Internal Revenue in 1920; and in 1921 he was sent by the United States government officially to observe the presidential elections in the Nicaragua. He held the important post of executive director of the National Labor Board in 1933-34, and is author of articles on labor relations and federal taxation. During the first World War he rose to the rank of major, judge advocate (1919-20), becoming aide-de-camp to Major General E. H. Crowder, with whom he collaborated on the book *The Spirit of Selective Service* (1919). In 1942 he was civilian advisory representative of the Department of Justice and War Department in matters pertaining to enemy aliens.

MILLER, JOSEPH, Canadian revenue officer, b. Vobolnik, Russia, 1872. He was educated at a Yeshiva in Russia and at Hamilton College of Law, from which he received the degree of LL.B. He served the Province of Quebec as naturalization commissioner (1904-18); was named justice of peace, commissioner of the Supreme Court of Quebec for life (1908) and revenue officer for the Province of Quebec in 1932. He helped to naturalize more than 12,000 Jewish citizens in the Province of Quebec. Miller served in the South-African War; he was sergeant instructor in the Canadian Heavy Artillery (1913 to 1921) and the first Jew in Canada to be awarded the Long Service and Good Conduct Medal.

Soon after his immigration to Canada, Miller dedicated himself to civic and beneficial endeavors. He organized the Montreal tailors under the banner of the Knights of Labor and subsequently was president of the United Garment Workers (1896-1908). He also organized and was president of the Independent Hebrew Sick Benefit Association (1901), subsequently known as Canadian Hebrew Sick Benefit Association.

MILLER, JULIUS, judge, b. New York, 1880. As a student he won the Jacob Schiff prize for Jewish history. He worked his way through college and was admitted to the Bar in 1901. He practised law for several years before entering politics. In 1919 he was elected state senator from New York city; many bills introduced by him became state laws. Elected president of the borough of Manhattan in 1921, he was reelected in 1925 and 1929; he distinguished himself particularly for important, wide-scale municipal improvements, such as the West Side Express Highway to facilitate traffic movement, and large building projects for modern housing for citizens of moderate means. In 1930 he was elected for a term of fourteen years a justice of the first judicial district of the Supreme Court of New York State. He was still in office in 1942.

MILLER, LOUIS, Yiddish writer, b. Lanovitz, province of Volhynia, Russia, 1887. He received a Jewish education under the tutelage of his father, who was a rabbi and the author of several books. He also studied Russian. In 1906 Miller came to the United States, where he worked at various trades and lived in Philadelphia, Chicago and Detroit. Finally he became a marble and granite salesman.

Miller's first published work appeared in the *Freie Arbeiter Stimme* in 1910; later he wrote for other magazines and anthologies. Considered one of the most talented representatives of the new school of Yiddish poetry, Miller was co-editor of the anthology, *Shriften,* where he also published a novel, *Abba. Oif Gotts Velt* (1919), a volume of verse, displayed Miller's lyric-idyllic characteristics. A selection of his poems, *Do iz mein Haim* (1939) indicated that Miller was freeing himself from the influence of individualism. A volume of translations from the works of Walt Whitman (1940) won a great deal of praise.

Miller also participated in Jewish cultural movements, with an orientation that leaned toward the radical and communist cultural organizations. In 1925 Miller published, in Chicago, several issues of *Kultur,* a magazine dealing with Jewish cultural problems in the United States.

Lit.: Reisen, Z., *Lexikon fun der Yiddisher Literatur, Presse un Filologie,* vol. 2 (1930), cols. 414-16; *Morgen Freiheit,* Nov. 5, 1939.

MILLER, LOUIS E., *see* BANDES, LOUIS E.

MILLER, NATHAN J., banker and philanthropist, b. Baltimore, 1873; d. Paris, 1927. President of the firm of Miller and Company, he was a prominent member of the New York stock exchange for twenty-two years, until 1924. He took an active role in Jewish affairs, serving as chairman of the New York committee of the Union of American Hebrew Congregations, and engaging in Jewish relief work during the first World War. He was a noted patron of Jewish culture.

His wife, LINDA MILLER (b. 1877; d. 1936) has been designated one of the great patronesses of learning and literature. Among her numerous gifts to the Jewish Theological Seminary of New York was a collection of rare manuscripts. Israel Davidson's *Thesaurus of Mediaeval Hebrew Poetry* was made possible through her generosity. Her greatest single contribution, given in memory of her husband, was a quarter-million-dollar endowment to Columbia University for a chair in Jewish literature, history, and institutions.

Lit.: Hurwitz, Ruth Sapin, "Linda R. Miller: An Appreciation," *Essays and Studies in Memory of Linda R. Miller,* 1938, pp. 3-8.

MILLIN, PHILIP, jurist, b. Cape Town, South Africa, 1888. He graduated from the South African College, Cape Town, in 1906, with honours in mental and moral science. After working as a journalist in Cape Town, Bloemfontein and Johannesburg, he qualified as an advocate and was admitted to the Transvaal Bar in 1913. He was created a K.C. in 1927. In 1936 Millin acted as judicial commissioner for Basutoland and president of the Special Courts of Bechuanaland and Swaziland. He is the co-author, with G. Willie, of *Mercantile Law of South Africa* (tenth edit. 1941). In 1937 he was appointed judge of the South African Supreme Court (Transvaal Provincial Division).

Millin was the husband of Sarah Gertrude Millin, South Africa's foremost authoress. He was a member of the Hebrew University Council of South Africa.

S. A. ROCHLIN.

Lit.: The Zionist Record, Sept. 3, 1937; *South African Law Journal,* Aug., 1938, pp. 265-67.

MILLIN, SARAH GERTRUDE, writer, b. Lithuania, 1892. She was taken to South Africa as an infant, and has lived there ever since. Her husband, Philip Millin, judge of the South African Supreme Court, is described above.

At nineteen she published her first short story, and ten years later her first novel, *The Dark River* (1920), appeared. In the intervening years she contributed to various South African journals. Following *The Dark River,* which was already distinguished by her particular gifts of observation, insight and style, Mrs. Millin produced a number of works in steady succession. She had been bred in a part of South Africa sparsely populated by whites, and in her stories she dealt with those racial antagonisms which she had come intimately to know. She likewise presented the problems of the minority groups: Germans, Jews, Indians. Her *God's Stepchildren* (1924) treated the conflicts of miscegenation in the Transvaal country with such force and brilliance that it established her international reputation as the foremost South African writer who, as Francis Brett Young pointed out, was the first to make use of the vast literary material that lay in the gold-reef. Young characterized Mrs. Millin as a woman of keen observation, inquisitive intellect, and genuine literary gift.

Besides the two mentioned above, Mrs. Millin's novels include: *Middleclass* (1921); *Adam's Rest* (1922); *The Jordans* (1923); *Mary Glenn* (1925); *An Artist in The Family* (1927); *The Coming of the Lord* (1928); *The Fiddler* (1929); *The Sons of Mrs. Aab* (1931); *Three Men Die* (1934); *What Hath a Man?* (1938); *The Herr Witch Doctor* (1941). In addition she wrote the biographies *Rhodes: A Life* (1933), upon which a film produced in 1936 was based; and *General Smuts* (1936). Others of her books are: *The South Africans* (1926, 1934), which discusses the country's life and politics during the past century, and includes an analysis of the role of the Jew in South African society; *Men on a Voyage* (1930); *South Africa* (1941, British Commonwealth series); and her autobiography, *The Night Is Long* (1941). In 1929 Mrs. Millin made a lecture tour in the United States.

Lit.: Tante, Dilly, *Living Authors* (1931) 269-70; Lewis, Ethelreda, *The Bookman* (New York, Oct., 1925) 190-92; Bernstein, Edgar, *The Zionist Record* (Johannesburg, Sept. 7, 1934) 71-73; Young, Francis Brett, *London Mercury* (March, 1929) 512-13.

MILSTEIN, NATHAN, violinist, b. Odessa, 1904. He was a pupil of Eugene Ysaÿe and Leopold Auer. He concertized throughout Russia during the years of the revolution, frequently in joint recitals with Vladimir Horowitz. In 1925 he went to Paris where a patron financed his Paris debut. This proved so successful that engagements followed throughout all of Europe. In 1928 his American debut took place with the Philadelphia Orchestra. His extraordinary technique first attracted the attention of American music lovers, but since his debut it has become apparent that he has musical maturity, interpretive insight, and a musical style of depth and immaculate taste.

MILTON, JOHN, non-Jewish English poet, b. London, 1608; d. London, 1674. He was interested in Hebrew learning and wrote religious poetry based on Biblical subjects. His father recognized the latent talents in his son and was very ambitious for his future. He had the boy taught Hebrew as well as classical and modern languages, the boy's tutor being Thomas Young, who later was pastor of an English congregation in Hamburg. In 1620 Milton began attendance at St. Paul's School in London, where Hebrew was part of the school curriculum. At Cambridge, where Milton spent seven years, one of his tutors was Joseph Meade, an outstanding Hebrew scholar. Milton's devotion to Hebrew learning was caused by his early intention to become a clergyman, but he abandoned this idea and decided to devote his talents to literature. His interest in religious problems, however, continued throughout his life, and most of his literary work shows his intense and deep devotion to religious ideals.

When civil war broke out in England between the Parliamentary forces and King Charles, Milton decided to devote himself to the Puritan struggle for freedom from the domination of the Stuarts. Much of Milton's writing in the middle years of his life was given up to ecclesiastical and political controversy in the service of the Puritan Commonwealth. In his *Defense of the English People* Milton often cites Biblical precedent for the overthrow of tyrants. He contends that the Hebrews were free to have what government they would when they rejected their judges and chose a king, and

Sarah Gertrude Millin

that therefore the supreme power was in the people and all nations and peoples possess this free choice. Moreover, the king of the Hebrews was "bound by God's ordinance to all the laws even as were the people, and no exemptions from the law are found in Scripture." Milton draws many parallels between the children of Israel and the English Puritans. "The children of Israel cried unto the Lord; so did we. The Lord raised them up a saviour; so did he for us."

Not only does Milton refer to Biblical authority in his controversial prose writings, but he often quotes the rabbis to substantiate his contentions. He cites Rabbis Jose and Judah for the interpretation of the passage in the book of *Samuel* on the abuse of power of kings, and Maimonides on the distinction between the kings of Judah and Israel. He quotes Maimonides, Kimhi, and Gersonides on divorce. He appeals to the works of Philo Judaeus and Josephus who justify a curb on tyrannical rulers. There are many other references to Philo and to Josephus in Milton's prose, and several references to Rabban Gamaliel.

In his tractate on *Education* Milton encourages the study of Hebrew. This publication grew out of Milton's experiment in teaching his young nephews and the sons of a few acquaintances. His nephew Edward Phillips wrote of this instruction, which included Hebrew "so far as to go through the Pentateuch or Five Books of Moses in Hebrew, and to make a good entrance into the Targum, or Chaldee Paraphrase." The writing of his ideas on education was urged upon Milton by some friends interested in his theories of teaching young Englishmen. In his course of study Milton includes Hebrew, "that the Scriptures may be now read in their own original, whereto it would be no impossibility to add the Chaldee and the Syrian dialect."

In the same year Milton wrote his noble defense of the freedom of the press, his *Areopagitica*. In it he warns the Parliament of the Commonwealth not to fall into the same tyrannies against which they rebelled to gain their freedom. His love of learning and truth makes him zealous to save good books from an inefficient censor, for a good book, Milton says, "is the precious life-blood of a master-spirit, embalmed and treasured up on purpose to a life beyond life; . . . he who destroys a good book, kills reason itself." Milton urges perfect freedom of discussion and expression of opinion; he believes that the liberty to argue freely according to conscience is above all other liberties. He pleads for the expression of truth frankly and openly, and he asks: "Who ever knew truth put to the worse in a free and open encounter?"

In the *Christian Doctrine* Milton declares that "there is in reality but one true independent and supreme God . . . and the Jews, the people of God, have always considered Him as one." The moot question in Milton's theology is whether or not he accepted the orthodox idea of the Trinity. Some scholars believe that Milton was not a Trinitarian, but an Arian. A great concession for a Christian of his day is made by Milton in the *Christian Doctrine* when he says that many, both Jews and others, would be saved by faith in God alone. In spite of his Arian leanings, however, Milton expressed the attitude toward the Jews of the conventional Puritan of his day. In 1649 he wrote: "And yet while we detest Judaism, we know ourselves commanded by St. Paul to respect the Jews, and by all means to endeavor their conversion." It will be remembered that at this time there were no Jews in England, and that it was in 1655 when a petition was sent to Cromwell by the Jews of Holland for permission to settle in England. There was much opposition to this proposal among Puritan divines, although Cromwell himself was in favor of it. The Puritan ministers who were willing to grant this permission hoped by this means to convert the Jews. There is no evidence that Milton took any part in this controversy, or that he had any contact with the Manasseh ben Israel delegation which came to England to confer with Cromwell. Milton's blindness in 1652 and the consequent reduction of his duties in the Puritan government may account for this.

In the last years of his life Milton had time to devote to the writing of poetry, and he created his greatest work in this period: *Paradise Lost, Paradise Regained,* and *Samson Agonistes.* All these are based on Biblical materials. *Paradise Lost* is drawn largely from the book of *Genesis,* but Milton's vast learning and many-sidedness enabled him to include much of Jewish traditional lore found in Hebraic myth and legend and in the commentaries of the rabbis, some of whom Milton mentions by name in his prose works. Much of Milton's angelology and demonology was drawn indirectly or directly from Hebrew sources. Recent studies by Professors Denis Saurat and Harris F. Fletcher have demonstrated the extent of Milton's indebtedness to the *Zohar,* to the commentaries of Rashi, and to pseudepigraphic and Midrashic literature.

LEAH R. C. YOFFIE.

Lit.: Fletcher, Harris F., *Milton's Semitic Studies* (1926); idem, *Milton's Rabbinical Readings* (1930); idem, *The Use of the Bible in Milton's Prose* (1929); Saurat, Denis, *Milton, Man and Thinker* (1925); Jung, Leo, *Fallen Angels in Jewish, Christian, and Mohammedan Literature* (1926); Gehman, Henry Snyder, "Milton's Use of Hebrew in the De Doctrina Christiana," *Jewish Quarterly Review,* New Series, vol. 29 (1938-39) 37-44.

MILWAUKEE, the largest city, and seat of a county of the same name, in the state of Wisconsin,

situated on the shores of Lake Michigan, about ninety miles north of Chicago. It grew from a village of 1,712 in 1840 to a metropolis (Greater Milwaukee) of 765,-480 in 1940. The earliest records show Shoyer and Bros. opening a clothing store, and Henry Newhouse arriving, in 1836, a dozen years before the city was incorporated and the territory admitted to statehood. The collapse of the European revolutionary movement in the 1840's brought a considerable German immigration to Milwaukee, and by 1850 the population exceeded 20,000, including about a hundred Jews. In 1940 the estimated number of Jews in the community was 29,600.

Jews contributed greatly to the economic and cultural growth of Milwaukee. They were among the pioneers and founders of many of the city's leading commercial and industrial establishments, and were represented in the manufacture of engines, elevators, agricultural implements, mining machinery, as well as in tanning, clothing, knitting, packing, grain and feed, malt and flour enterprises and department store operation. They were prominent among the patrons of the fine arts and among the leaders in movements for social reform.

Thus, to cite a few examples, Jacob Elias Friend (1857-1912), one of the founders and president of the Nordberg Manufacturing Co., was a member of the state legislature in 1885, when he introduced in the House the bill which took the Milwaukee fire and police departments out of politics and placed them under civil service rule. Henry M. Mendel (1839-1905), another prominent merchant, was for many years president of the Milwaukee Conservatory of Music; early in the 1860's he was instrumental in building the first large hall in the city, which subsequently became known as the Academy of Music. Victor L. Berger (1860-1929), editor of a daily newspaper, *The Milwaukee Leader,* was the first Socialist Congressman (House of Representatives, 1911-13 and 1923-29) and head of the Socialist Party of America. Samuel Becker (1903-) served as executive counsel to Governor Philip F. La Follette from 1931 to 1933. Some believe that General Frederick Salomon, who served in the Civil War, and Edward Salomon, who was governor of Wisconsin in 1865, were both of Jewish stock although they did not profess the faith.

While a number of the early Jewish settlers intermarried, and their stock blended with that of the non-Jews in Milwaukee, including some of the socially most prominent families, many of those pioneers remained observant Jews and founded religious institutions which have weathered the storms of a century. The first congregation, Emanu-El, was established in 1847, with Gabriel Shoyer as president, and the Rosh Hashanah service that year, attended by a Minyan of twelve men, was held at the home of Isaac Neustadtl. In 1852 Congregation Ahavath Emunah was formed, with J. M. Hardt as president, and on October 26, 1856, the two congregations merged under the name of B'ne Jeshurun, with Nathan Pereles as president. That year the first synagogue was acquired, on Fourth between State and Prairie streets. At the same time, a third congregation, Anshe Emet, came into being, but in 1859 it amalgamated with B'ne Jeshurun, and the enlarged congregation erected a new synagogue, on Fifth between Wells and Cedar streets.

The first salaried official (at $300 per annum) of

B'ne Jeshurun was Raphael Lasker, who acted as Hazan, Shohet and collector. The rabbis were, in succession, I. Kalisch (1856-63), S. Falk (1863-66), Elias Eppstein (1869-80), Emanuel Gerechter (1880-92), Victor Caro (1892-1912), and Charles S. Levi (1913-27). The congregation prospered under these leaders, and found it necessary to build a new synagogue on the same site in 1872, to erect a still larger temple, on Tenth and Cedar streets, in 1886, and to reconstruct that edifice on the occasion of its fiftieth anniversary, in 1906.

In 1869 thirty-five of the eighty-five members of B'ne Jeshurun seceded from the older congregation, and founded the first Reform temple in Wisconsin, reviving the original name of Emanu-El. Under the leadership of its first president, David Adler, the new congregation substituted English for German as its official language, followed the call of Isaac M. Wise for the promotion of American Reform Judaism, and erected a temple in 1872. The rabbis of Emanu-El were E. B. M. Browne (1870), M. Spitz (1872-79), I. S. Moses (1879-87), Sigmund Hecht (1888-89), Julius H. Meyer (1900-4), Samuel Hirshberg (1904-), and Joseph L. Baron (1926-). In 1922 the congregation erected one of the most beautiful religious edifices in the city, Temple Emanu-El, on Kenwood Boulevard.

After the arrival of Rabbi Baron, and under the presidency of A. L. Saltzstein, Emanu-El made rapid progress. More than a hundred new members joined the congregation in that year (1926), and the religious school facilities of the new temple soon became overtaxed. Week-day instruction in Hebrew and a high school department were immediately added to the curriculum, leading the Reform temples of the country in these innovations, and a splendid collection of Judaica, comprising 10,000 items, was launched as the Temple Library for the free use of the general community. In 1927 the temple absorbed the older congregation through consolidation, and the new temple, Emanu-El B'ne Jeshurun, soon changed from an organization of about 400 families to one of nearly a thousand. In recent years it has followed an extension program, aiding in the establishment of synagogues throughout the state. The congregation in 1942 was under the leadership of its president, George P. Ettenheim, and three rabbis, Hirshberg, Baron, and Mordecai I. Soloff.

The wave of East European immigration reached Milwaukee in 1881, and led to the organization of a number of new congregations: Beth Israel (1884), B'ne Israel (1886), Anshe Sfard (1893), and Anshe Lebowich (1906). These synagogues, and six more, differentiated chiefly by the national origin of their respective members, were, in 1942, served by a number of rabbis, chief among whom were Solomon I. Scheinfeld, a Lithuanian rabbi who began his ministry in Milwaukee in 1892, and J. Twerski, a Hasidic rabbi, who came to the city in 1930. A Conservative congregation, Beth El, was founded in 1923; its successive rabbis were Eugene Kohn, Philip Kleinman and Louis J. Swichkow.

There was a Hebrew Relief Society in Milwaukee as early as 1867, and before that a Hevra Bikkur Holim, assisted by the Treue Schwestern and subsequently by the Ladies Relief Sewing Society. The year 1903 was perhaps the most fruitful in the history of Milwaukee Jewish philanthropy, for it was then that A. W. Rich and Louis Gimbel organized the project to settle Russian Jewish refugees on Wisconsin farm land, that Mt. Sinai Hospital was founded, and the Federated Jewish Charities launched. Among the directors of the last-named agency for many years were Jacob Billikopf, Maurice Hexter, Kurt Peiser and Benjamin Glassberg. The Hospital erected a fine building in 1914, and an extension in 1932, and was, in 1942, regarded as one of the best Jewish institutions of its kind in the land, rendering a particularly valuable service to the city through its free dispensary, and performing all its functions on a non-sectarian basis. A Settlement House had been opened in 1900, and in 1911 it was reorganized as the Abraham Lincoln House, maintained largely by funds from the *Settlement Cook Book*, a project, developed by Mrs. Lizzie Kander, which has financed many valuable educational and philanthropic enterprises in Milwaukee. In 1930 the Lincoln House was abandoned, and the Milwaukee Jewish Center, under the direction of George M. Peizer, was organized in its place with an altogether new program.

In 1942 the Federated Jewish Charities was no longer active, three of its constituent agencies having been taken over by the Milwaukee County Community Fund, a non-sectarian body. These agencies were the Jewish Social Service Association, the Children's Outing Society (providing summer recreation to the needy at Camp Sidney Cohen), and the Jewish Center. An excellent Home for Aged Jews, supported by the entire community, and the Home for Dependent Jewish Children and the Hebrew Sheltering Home, supported chiefly by Orthodox Jews, were independent institutions. In 1938 the Milwaukee Jewish Welfare Fund was organized, in an attempt to unite in one annual campaign the various appeals for overseas relief, national agencies, the Mt. Sinai Hospital, and other local institutions of Jewish education, vocational service, and refugee aid not otherwise provided for. In 1941 the Fund collected about $210,000, and in 1942 the budget set for the support of its forty-three beneficiaries was $344,538.

All the national Jewish organizations had active branches and representatives in Milwaukee: B'nai B'rith (four lodges), Council of Jewish Women, Hadassah, Zionist Organization, American Jewish Committee, American Jewish Congress, National Workers Alliance, Workingmen's Circle, and Histadruth Ivrith. Thus the community presented a cross-section of the American Jewish scene, embracing all its varied ideals and intense struggles and movements, ranging from the ultra-conservative to the ultra-radical. There were, in 1942, two local periodicals devoted to Jewish affairs: *Milwauker Wochenblat-Jewish Press,* a weekly in Yiddish and English, established in 1906, edited by Isador Horwitz, and the *Wisconsin Jewish Chronicle,* founded in 1920, edited by A. J. Margolis. The *Milwaukee Sentinel,* founded in 1929 but no longer in existence, was edited by Julius Liebman.

The original Congregation Emanu-El purchased an acre of land for a Jewish cemetery on Hopkins Road in 1848. That cemetery was still in existence in 1942, although it was closed for interments in 1872, when the Greenwood Cemetery was established. Since then, five cemeteries were added, Mt. Zion, Second Home, Agudath Ahim, Everest, and Spring Hill, the last one administered by the B'nai B'rith.

Among Milwaukee Jews who attained particular distinction, in addition to those already referred to, the following may be mentioned: Marcus Otterbourg (1827-93), United States Consul in Mexico City (1861-67) and Minister to Mexico (1867); Philip Stein (1844-1922), who moved to Chicago in 1868 and subsequently became presiding judge of the Appellate Court of Illinois; Alexander Wetzel, one of the 331 Wisconsin Jews who served in the Civil War, who was promoted to corporal, sergeant and major for special bravery at Chancellorsville and was mortally wounded at Gettysburg; Charles L. Aarons (1872-), president of the Milwaukee School Board (1909-10), and judge of the Circuit Court of Wisconsin from 1925; Benjamin Poss (1877-), president of the State Bar Association (1937-38); Nathan Krass (1880-), rabbi of the New York Temple Emanu-El and professor of homiletics at the Jewish Institute of Religion; Louis Schapiro (1886-1931), field worker for the Rockefeller Foundation, specializing in tropical diseases, and serving the government of Siam at the time of his death; Harry V. Meissner (1890-), president of the Milwaukee School Board (1930 and 1935); Joseph A. Padway (1891-), member of the state senate (1925), and the national counsel for the American Federation of Labor from 1938; Joseph H. Seidelman (1895-), vice-president of Paramount Productions in charge of foreign activities; and Max Raskin (1902-), city attorney (1932-36), and member of the national executive committees of the Socialist Party of America and of the Farmer Labor Federation.

JOSEPH L. BARON.

MINCHAH, *see* AFTERNOON SERVICE.

MINHAG, MINHAGIM BOOKS, *see* CUSTOM.

MINHAH, *see* AFTERNOON SERVICE.

MINIATURE PAINTERS, *see* ARTISTS.

MINIKES, CHONON YANKOV, writer and publisher, b. Vilna, 1867; d. New York city, 1932. He studied at the Yeshiva in Volozhin, then went to Germany, where he was associated with the Jewish leaders of the time: Israel Hildesheimer, Israel Salanter and others. Minikes was one of the founders of the Ahavath Zion organization. His first appearance as a writer was in *Hashahar,* edited by Peretz Smolenskin.

In 1888 Minikes had to leave Germany and came to the United States, where he was active as a teacher and also participated in the Jewish labor union movement. He was one of the first delegates to the United Hebrew Trades. At the same time, Minikes worked for various Jewish cultural institutions. In 1897 he began the publication of anthologies, usually on the occasion of Jewish holidays, called the *Minikes Yomtob Bletter.* These volumes were popular and reached a circulation of 35,000. He also published *Minikes Illustrierte Monat Bletter* and *Minikes Illustrierte Zammelbletter. Die Yiddishe Biehne,* the first book to be published in New York on the subject of the Yiddish theatre, was published by Minikes in 1897. The volumes published by Minikes included articles, feuilletons and stories written by himself.

Lit.: Reisen, Z., *Lexikon fun der Yiddisher Literatur, Presse un Filologie,* vol. 2 (1930), cols. 418-20; Zylbercwajg, Z., *Lexikon fun Yiddishen Theater,* vol. 2 (1934), cols. 1323-25.

MINIM, the name applied in the Talmud and cognate literature to certain persons of Jewish origin who were regarded with severe disapproval as being false in their profession of Judaism. The references to the Minim amount to more than eighty passages, and for the most part these belong to the period extending from the end of the 1st to the beginning or middle of the 3rd cent. C.E. The etymology of the word is not quite certain, but the best explanation is that given by Bacher, according to which "Min" is the usual Hebrew word for "sort" or "kind" (*Gen.* 1:11). In the Greek translation, known as the Septuagint, this word is rendered by "genos"; and Josephus writes of the "genos" and also of the "haeresis" of the Sadducees. This indicates that "Min" is related to "haeresis," and is, in short, a heretic. "Haeresis" means "choice," and more particularly the act of one who "chooses" to go his own way in matters of religion instead of following that prescribed by the recognized authority. A definition of "minuth," the principle according to which a "Min" acts, is given in *Sifre,* §115, where, quoting the text *Num.* 15:39, "and that ye go not about after your own heart," it says "This is Minuth."

The Min, accordingly, was some kind of heretic, and the term is always applied to persons of Jewish origin. A Gentile is never called a Min, unless by inadvertence. But not every unfaithful Jew was called a Min. In *Tos. Sanh.* 13:4 there is given a list of no less than ten different classes of persons of whom an especially severe judgment is passed; and of these the Minim come first. The passage indicates that the Minim were not merely wicked but were in some way secret enemies, traitors in the camp. They were to be met with in the common contacts of Jews, in the synagogue, on the street, in the market and the home. A passage, *Tos. Hul.* 2:20-21, lays down the general rule that the Minim are to be boycotted as far as possible; "One does not sell to them or receive from them, or take from them or give to them; one does not teach their sons trades, and one does not obtain healing from them, either of property or of life."

Precautions were taken for detecting Minim if they were present in the synagogue or recited the prayers there. The so-called formula against the Minim, Birkath Haminim (*Ber.* 28b-29a), was devised presumably for this purpose. It was drawn up by official authority, and the date of it is probably 80 C.E., or thereabouts. The formula is still found in the Eighteen Benedictions (Shemoneh Esreh), but with the word *malshinim,* slanderers, in place of the word *minim.* It has been held that the original word was *notzerim,* Nazarenes; but there is no manuscript authority for this, though Christians were no doubt intended. The Mishnah does not refer to the Birkath Haminim, but it mentions (*Meg.* 4:8-9) several liturgical variations which were to be regarded as signs of Minuth in the person who used them. The Minim had a literature of some kind, and their books were severely denounced by two eminent teachers, Tarphon and Ishmael, both of whom lived at the end of the 1st and the beginning of the 2nd cent. C.E.

The question as to who exactly the Minim were resolves itself into a choice between Jewish Christians and Jewish Gnostics. Most scholars decide in favor of Jewish Christians. Many of the passages which refer to

Minim would allow of either interpretation; but in a few the close association of Minuth with Christianity is beyond question. A story is told (*A.Z.* 16b and in three other places) of how Rabbi Eliezer was once arrested for "Minuth," and how a certain Min had imparted to him a piece of Midrash, with the words, "Thus hath Jesus the Nazarene taught me." Also, in the same tractate (*A.Z.* 27a), it is told how a certain Min offered to cure a sick man "in the name of Joshua ben Pandira." In the light of these instances, neutral passages must be taken to refer to Jewish Christians unless evidence equally strong can be brought against such reference. In one or two passages, Min denotes Sadducee or Zealot; but these can easily be distinguished. But no crucial passage has so far been produced to show that Min denotes a Gnostic and not a Christian. The leading passage in which Gnosticism is dealt with is *Hag.* 15a; not even Elisha ben Abuyah, who became an apostate through meddling with Gnostic doctrines, is called a Min.

It may be taken as practically certain that in most cases the Minim are Jewish Christians, and are not Jewish Gnostics. It is true that the subjects in dispute, in the very numerous polemical encounters between Minim and rabbis, were not specifically Christian, in the sense that Jesus is hardly ever referred to by name. No mention is made of any Messianic claim made by him or on his behalf. The question most often raised is whether there were two powers in heaven or only one. The explanation is that by the end of the 1st cent. the Christian church, under Gentile influence, had greatly modified its original belief about Jesus, and had come to regard him as a being hardly if at all lower than God. That this belief reacted on the Jewish Christians is shown by the *Epistle to the Hebrews,* which speaks of Christ "through whom (God) made the worlds." The original followers of Jesus had remained Jews in all respects except their belief that he was the Messiah. But the change just indicated, in the raising of Christ almost to the level of God, was not compatible with adherence to Judaism, which was founded on the sole unity of God. Hence, the new type of Jewish Christian became a source of grave danger, all the more because those who held the new view still professed to be Jews. The situation fits exactly the allusions to the Minim, and it does not fit the case of the Gnostics. The doctrine of two powers is expressly associated with Christianity, in *Pesiḳta Rabbathi* 100b. The main subjects of Gnostic speculation were known to and studied by rabbis of such unimpeachable soundness as Johanan ben Zakkai and Eliezer ben Hyrcanus, who were never blamed for such study. It began to be considered dangerous only in the time of Akiba, whose escape from the danger is expressly noted. And this is just the period when the new doctrine about Christ was affecting the original simplicity of Jewish Christian belief. This is the period when the Minim were most prominent in rabbinical literature, and the hostility against them was most acute. In the 3rd cent. and onwards, the danger decreased, as it was seen that the Jewish Christians were a weak and discredited element in the church, and the relations between Jews and Minim became accordingly less strained.

The conclusion remains, therefore, that the term Minim denotes Jewish sectaries, and that the particular

kind of sectary is to be inferred from the passage where they are mentioned, in this or that case. Usually the reference is to Jewish Christians holding a doctrine of Christ which tended to place him on a level with God.

The Minim, as Jewish Christians, are mentioned by Jerome (5th cent. C.E.), who says that they were to be found "in all the synagogues of the East." No further trace of them occurs in Christian literature. In rabbinical literature, the later references show that only a vague notion remained of what a Min was, and why he had been dangerous.   R. TRAVERS HERFORD.

Lit.: Herford, R. Travers, *Christianity in Talmud and Midrash,* part 2 (1903); idem, "Problem of the Minim further Considered," *Studies in Memory of G. A. Kohut* (1935) 359-69; Broydé, Isaac, in *Jewish Encyclopedia,* vol. 8, pp. 594-95; Elbogen, Ismar, *Der jüdische Gottesdienst,* 36 et seq., 51; Kellermann, *Das Minäerproblem;* Büchler, Adolf, "Über die Minim von Sepphoris und Tiberias im zweiten und dritten Jahrhundert," *Judaica, Festschrift zum 70. Geburtstage Hermann Cohens* (1912) 271-95; Hahn, Stephen, "Siphre Minim," *Magyar Zsidó Szemle* (1936-38) 267-75.

MINIS, a distinguished family in the early history of Georgia.

ABRAHAM MINIS (b. 1696; d. 1797) was one of the earliest settlers in the colony. He arrived in Savannah on the ship bearing forty Jews of Spanish and Portuguese descent which landed soon after the founding of the colony. He was accompanied by his wife, Abigail, two daughters, Leah and Esther, and a brother, Simeon. Minis was a man of means, being one of those few Jews to whom land was granted by the General Conveyance of the Town Lots executed on December 21, 1733. While in Georgia he followed the mercantile pursuit and seemed successful in his business undertakings. When, in 1740, many Jews left Savannah on account of a crisis that arose in the colony, Minis remained there. His brother, Simeon, was also one of the grantees of lots, and was also engaged in business.

PHILIP MINIS (b. Savannah, 1743; d. 1789), son of Abraham Minis, was the first white child born in Savannah. Like his father, he was engaged in business. At the outbreak of the Revolutionary War Minis, then a young man, embraced the patriotic cause and gave of himself and his money to the Revolution. As evidence of his monetary contributions to the Revolutionary cause there may serve the order of Congress (1778) that he be paid $7,000 for money advanced by him to the acting paymaster of the troops of Virginia and South Carolina in Georgia. Another congressional order ordered the payment of $5,000 to Minis and Cohen for their contributions. When the French troops landed in Savannah in 1779, General D'Estaing entrusted Minis with the following task, "to conduct the force of men whenever ordered to do so." Minis was mentioned in the Disqualifying Act issued by the British in 1786. He was actively associated with the civic and communal life of Savannah, and was prominently identified with the Jewish community, serving as president of Mikveh Israel Congregation of Savannah.

Other members of the Minis family, WILLIAM MINIS and JAMES MINIS, participated actively in the battles "in the Georgia Line."

MRS. PHILIP MINIS and her daughter, JUDITH, brought food to Mordecai Sheftall when the latter was in captivity. Both women were known in the early history of Georgia as "Great Whigs." After Savannah was captured by the British they were confined to their dwelling and subsequently were ordered to leave town.

The rest of the Minis family consisted of: DAVID MINIS, who was prominently identified with the Masonic Order of that city; ISAAC MINIS, son of Philip, who served as a private in the War of 1812; ABRAHAM MINIS, son of Isaac; and ISAAC MINIS, son of Abraham, all of whom took an active part in the civic and communal life of Savannah.

MINISTRY FOR JEWISH AFFAIRS, *see* LITHUANIA; MINORITY RIGHTS; UKRAINE.

MINKIN, JACOB SAMUEL, rabbi and author, b. Swieciany, Poland, 1885. He studied at Talmudic academies in Poland and, after graduating from the gymnasium in Prague, he came to the United States in 1904. Studying at Columbia University, he took his M.A. in 1909. Minkin served as a rabbi in Hamilton, Ontario (1910-1917), Temple Beth El, Rochester, N. Y. (1919-1929) and at the Inwood Hebrew Congregation, New York City (1929-1933). After 1933 he retired from the rabbinate to devote himself exclusively to writing.

Author of a syndicated weekly column, *News of the Jewish World* (1922-1930), Minkin also reviewed books, mainly on religious and philosophical topics, for the magazine *Isis* and wrote articles for numerous Jewish publications. In 1935 he published *The Romance of Hasidism*, the first complete history and analysis in English of the Hasidic movement from its beginnings to its present decline—an unbiased, though fervidly written, treatise for which he was awarded the degree of Doctor of Hebrew Letters by the Jewish Theological Seminary. This book, which made a strong impression also on the non-Jewish world, was followed by a biography of *Herod* (1936), which appeared also in French and Swedish. A psycho-pathological study of political tyranny in the ancient world, the book undertook to show the "gorgeous criminal" of history as a victim of monstrous circumstances rather than as a monster, giving without moralizing a vivid picture of a time not unlike ours. *Abarbanel and the Expulsion of the Jews from Spain* (1938) endeavors to describe the close of the "golden age" of Spanish Jewry. Around the thinker, scholar and political leader appear the other romantic figures of contemporary Christianity and Judaism, furnishing a dramatic background for his meteoric career. Minkin was a contributor to this encyclopedia.

MINKOFF, NOCHUM BORUCH, Yiddish poet and essayist, b. Warsaw, 1893. He was graduated from a Russian Gymnasium in 1914 and emigrated to the United States immediately thereafter, shortly before the outbreak of the first World War, and has resided there ever since. He received the LL.B. degree from the New York Law School, and studied also at Columbia University, the College of the City of New York, and New York University.

Minkoff's first Yiddish verse was published in *Neie Velt* (1918). Since then his poetry and essays have appeared in numerous periodicals, among them *Yiddishe Folk*, *Freie Arbeter Shtimme*, *Tog*, *Undzer Buch*, *Kern*, *Bodn*, *Kempfer* and *Tzukunft*. With A. Leyeless and Yankev Gladstein he wrote the "Insichist" manifesto, introducing the introspectivist movement in Yiddish

literature. He was one of the editors of the *In Sich* anthology (1920) and the In Sich magazines. With Michl Licht as co-editor, he published and wrote for the magazines, *1925* and *1926* in an attempt to break away from the cliché and stereotyped forms of "Insichism" and to create a school of modern classicism in poetry and prose. He was also editor of *Bodn*.

Minkoff's poetry symbolizes the spirit of contemporary civilization. In concise lines and formula-like phrases he paints a grim picture of a declining world. An "objectivist" in verse as in criticism, he is nevertheless intensely emotional. His images are often phantasmagoric, sordid and real. His books of verse include: *Lieder* (1924); *Undzer Pierrot* (1927); *Masoes Fun Letztn Shotn* (1936). All these were published in New York city.

His book of criticism, *Yiddishe Klassiker Poetn* (New York, 1937), contains a revaluation of the Yiddish poets, Frug, Peretz, Liessin, Yehoash, Rosenfeld, and A. Reisen. He has also written numerous essays on American-Yiddish poets and is the author of an extensive article on the history of Yiddish literature printed in the *General Yiddish Encyclopedia*, as well as of articles for *Universal Jewish Encyclopedia*, of which he was a contributing editor. Minkoff's analytical essays have made him one of the keenest critics of Yiddish literature.

Lit.: Licht, M., in *Chicago* (Dec. 4, 1925); Kurtz, A., in *Undzer Buch* (Nov.-Dec., 1926); Cooperman, Hasye, in *In Sich* (Jan.-Feb., 1930); Haimovitch, M. I., in *Freie Arbeter Shtimme* (March 13, 1936); Tutchinsky, A., in *Freie Arbeter Shtimme* (May 6, 1938); Bickl, S., in *Tog* (Feb. 28, 1942).

MINKOWSKI, HERMANN, mathematician, b. Alexoten, Russia, 1864; d. Göttingen, Germany, 1909. As a student at the University of Königsberg, from which he graduated in 1885, he was awarded the international prize by the Paris Academy. He was lecturer at the University of Bonn (1887), associate professor (1893), and on the faculty of the University of Königsberg (1894). In 1896 Minkowski was appointed professor at the Zürich Polytechnic, and went to the University of Göttingen in 1902. He was a prominent expounder of the theory of numbers. The most important of his works are: *Geometrie der Zahlen* (1896); *Diophantische Approximationen* (1907), an introduction to the theory of numbers. In his early introduction to the formulae of the special theory of relativity, he couched the physical laws in such mathematical forms as to give the time-coordinate the same importance as the three space-coordinates. Minkowski was baptized.

Lit.: Wininger, S., *Grosse jüdische National-Biographie*, vol. 4, p. 391.

MINKOWSKI, MAURICE, painter, b. Warsaw, Poland, 1881. At five, due to an accident, he became deaf and dumb. He displayed aptitude in art and at the age of eleven painted the portrait of the governor of Warsaw. This was so successful that he was commissioned to paint the prince of Ineritinsky. From 1900 to 1904 Minkowski studied at the Cracow Academy, where he won one gold and two silver medals. The experience of a pogrom in Bialystok (1905) caused him to abandon landscape painting for the depiction of Jewish suffering. Thus he became the artist of the persecuted and downhearted. His paint-

Hermann Minkowski

Oscar Minkowski

ings are replete with detail, and his large aquarelles have striking themes. In 1908 he exhibited at the Salon des Artistes Français, Paris, and received honorable mention. He also participated in exhibitions at Antwerp, Brussels, Düsseldorf, and Berlin, gaining great renown. In 1936 Minkowski was living in Berlin.

His major works include: *The Emigrant, In the Waiting Room, After the Pogrom, God of Abraham, Esther, The Synagogue of Tolna, Women in the Synagogue,* and *The Talmudist.*

Lit.: Wininger, S., *Grosse jüdische National-Biographie,* vol. 4, p. 392; Salon Henri Brendlé, Zürich, *Jüdische Künstler unserer Zeit,* p. 21; *Dictionnaire Critique et Documentaire des Peintres, Sculpteurs, Dessinateurs et Graveurs,* vol. 3, p. 282.

MINKOWSKI, MIRCZYSLAW, professor and cerebral anatomist, b. Warsaw, Poland, 1884. He was graduated in 1907 from the University of Breslau, became lecturer at the University of Zurich in 1913, titular professor in 1926, and assistant professor in 1928. Minkowski was one of the foremost cerebral anatomists and physiologists, the author of many illuminating works on physiology and pathologic anatomy of the central nervous system. He investigated especially the central optic pathways as well as the anatomical connections within the cerebrum and advanced the knowledge of reflexes, automatic and involuntary movements, and idiomuscular phenomena. Minkowski contributed to the comprehension of athetosis and aphasia. Of special interest are his neurobiological investigations of human fetuses.

His works include *Experimentelle Untersuchungen der Beziehungen der Grosshirnrinde und der Netzhaut zu den primären optischen Zentren* (Wiesbaden, 1913) and "Experimental and Anatomic Research on Athetosis," in *Zeitschrift für die gesamte Neurologie und Psychologie,* vol. 102 (1925) 650-718.

Minkowski lived at Zurich in 1942, and was editor of the *Schweizer Archiv für Neurologie und Psychiatrie.* There he was also director of the cerebral-anatomical institute and neuropolyclinic at the University of Zurich.

Lit.: *Kürschners Deutscher Gelehrten Kalender* (1935), col. 914; *Quarterly Cumulative Index Medicus.*

MINKOWSKI, OSCAR, endocrinologist, b. near Kovno, Lithuania, 1858; d. Wiesbaden, Germany, 1931. A brother of Hermann Minkowski, he received his M.D. degree from the University of Königsberg (1881). He was professor of medicine at the University of Strasbourg from 1891 to 1900, director of the City Hospital in Cologne (1900-3) and Greifswald (1904-9), and associate professor of internal medicine at the University of Breslau from 1909 to 1926. Minkowski was baptized.

Together with Joseph von Mering, he discovered the relation between diabetes and the pancreas; by removing the pancreas from dogs they produced the disease artificially. Thus they made possible the discovery of the universally employed remedy, insulin, from the islands of Langerhans in the pancreas.

Among Minkowski's works are: *Vorkommen von Axibuttersäure im Harn bei Diabetes mellitus* (1884); *Einfluss der Leberextirpation auf den Stoffwechsel* (1885); *Untersuchungen über den Diabetes mellitus nach Extirpation des Pankreas* (1893); *Untersuchungen zur Physiologie und Pathologie der Harnsäure* (1898); *Die Gicht* (1903); *Pathologie der Atmung* (1912); *Erkrankungen durch Einwirkung giftiger Gase* (1921). He contributed to various medical reference works and encyclopedias.

MINKOWSKY, PINCHOS, b. Belaya Tzerkov, Russia, 1859; d. Boston, 1924. Son of the local cantor, young Pinchos was foretold a promising career in the rabbinate, but his musical talent led him instead to follow in his father's footsteps. After his marriage at the age of sixteen, he was engaged by a local synagogue. Desiring, however, first to master all the musical requirements of a Hazan, he left his family to sing in the choir of the renowned Nisi Belzer at Kishinev, and when the latter moved to Berditchev, Pinchos was in his retinue. At the age of eighteen, Minkowsky was engaged as cantor in Kishinev, succeeding his teacher, Nisi Belzer.

After the holidays, Minkowsky went to Odessa to hear the well known cantors Piche Abras and Nisen Blumenthal, and to study harmony with the latter's choir leader, the gifted composer David Nowakowsky. Four years in Kishinev were followed by an identical period in Cherson. By this time his fame reached far and wide. Offers came from the Chor Shul of Lemberg, from the great synagogue in Odessa (whence the great Bachman had left for Budapest), from Wilna to succeed Cantor Israel Cooper (who left for America), but he finally accepted an invitation from the Eldridge Street Synagogue in New York. There he served for five years.

At this time the Broder Synagogue in Odessa celebrated the fiftieth jubilee of their cantor Nisen Blumenthal and, upon the latter's recommendation, Minkowsky was chosen as his successor. Here Minkowsky and Nowakowsky modernized the synagogue service and introduced the organ. Divested of all operatic trills and cabaret songs, executed by such an earnest scholar and esthetic singer as Minkowsky (accompanied by a choir of about forty adults under the masterful guidance of Nowakowsky), that service attracted musicians of all nationalities and races eager to hear a truly sublime rendition of the ancient Hebrew liturgy. The post-war upheavals in Russia (1918-23), as well as family difficulties, impelled his return to the United States where he spent the last year of his life.

Minkowsky wrote much in Hebrew, German, and Yiddish, lectured before musical societies, was professor of music in the Jewish conservatory in Odessa, contributed articles to *Hatoren, Hatzefirah, Reshumoth, Hashiloah, Hatekufah, Wahrheit* (Vienna) *Hamburger Familienblatt, Haolam,* and *Hamelitz.* He also wrote the articles on music for *Otzar Yisrael* and for the Russian *Yevreiskaya Entziklopedia.* Minkowsky was also author of *Die Entwicklung der synagogalen Liturgie* (Odessa, 1902); *Der Sulzerismus* (Vienna, 1905).

MAX WOHLBERG.

Lit.: *The History of Hazzanuth* (New York, 1924); *Hazzanuth* (Jewish Ministers and Cantors' Association, New York, 1937) 20; *Die Hazzanim Welt* (Warsaw, March, 1934).

MINNEAPOLIS, the largest city of Minnesota with a population of 492,370 (census of 1940) including about 21,000 Jewish residents. Jews of German and Bohemian origin came to Minneapolis shortly after the Civil War. Among the first Jewish settlers were Samuel Alexander, Jacob Cohen, A. Krutzkoff, Samuel Laucheim, B. H. Plechner, Ralph, Theodore, and Gustave Rees, and Jacob Skoll. At this time (1865-1870), Minneapolis, still a frontier community, was a center of the lumber industry. Jewish merchants supplied lumbermen who came to the city from surrounding camps with clothing and other goods.

The first Jewish organization in Minneapolis was the Montefiore Burial Association, formed in 1876 with Ralph Rees as the first president. Another early Jewish society was a B'nai Brith lodge whose charter was issued in 1877. Ralph Rees was also president of the lodge. A year later, in 1878, the first Jewish congregation, Shaari Tov, now Temple Israel (Reform), was incorporated. Among the charter members were Max Benson, Edward Bernstein, Lewis Brin, K. Brin, Jacob Cohen, Jacob Deutsch, Isaac Faller, George Jacoby, Emanuel Kayser, A. Krutzkoff, Louis Metzger, Gustave Rees, Ralph Rees, Herman Rothschild, Max Segelbaum, Sander Segelbaum, Jacob Skoll, Harry Weixelbaum,

Louis Werth, H. Wilk, and Morris Wilk. Leopold Ehrlich was the first president. The first synagogue was built in 1880. In 1903 it was destroyed by fire and another synagogue was erected on the same site. The present temple (1942) was completed in 1928. The rabbis of the congregation were Henry Illiowizi (1880-8), Samuel Marks (1888-93), Aaron Friedman (1893-1900), and Samuel N. Deinard (1902-21). The rabbi of Temple Israel (1942) was Albert Greenberg Minda whose service began in 1922.

There are two Conservative synagogues in Minneapolis: Adath Jeshurun, organized in 1885, and Beth El, organized in 1921. Albert Isaac Gordon was rabbi of Congregation Adath Jeshurun in 1942. He was preceded in that position by Calman David Matt who served as rabbi from 1912 to 1927. The synagogue of Adath Jeshurun was built in 1927. Abraham Meyer Heller, first rabbi of Beth El, served from 1921 to 1923; the rabbi in 1942 was David Aronson whose service began in 1924. The synagogue of Beth El was built in 1926.

The large number of Jewish immigrants from the countries of eastern Europe after 1881 contributed to the growth of Orthodox congregations in Minneapolis. B'nai Abraham was organized in 1889, Keneseth Israel in 1890, Agudas Achim in 1903; other Orthodox congregations include Mikro Kodesh, Tifereth B'nai Jacob, and Shaarei Zedek. S. M. Silber was rabbi of Keneseth Israel from 1902 until 1925. Hirsch Heiman was rabbi in 1942. The rabbi of Mikro Kodesh (1942) was S. T. Swirsky; of Tifereth B'nai Jacob, Israel Friedman; and of Shaarei Zedek, S. I. Levin.

In addition to the religious organizations, there are a number of Jewish communal institutions. The Minneapolis Talmud Torah, organized in 1894, sponsors a city-wide program of Jewish education. The Emanuel Cohen Center was founded in 1924; its present building (1942) was erected in 1940. The Jewish Sheltering Home for Children, to provide temporary care, was founded in 1919. The Minneapolis Federation for Jewish Service, organized in 1929, serves as a central body for the co-ordination of local social service and the collection and distribution of welfare funds. In 1938, the Minnesota Jewish Anti-Defamation Council was organized with headquarters in Minneapolis, and here, too, the Minnesota area of the National Conference of Christians and Jews (organized in 1939) has its offices. Almost all the Jewish national organizations have branches in the city. Mrs. Arthur Brin (Fanny Fligelman) was president of the National Council of Jewish Women.

The Jews of Minneapolis have participated fully in the communal life of the city, state, and nation. Simon Meyers, in 1892, and Samuel H. Bellman, from 1935 until 1939, served in the state legislature. Henry H. Bank was a member of the City Council from 1933 on. Robert S. Kelliner was appointed a judge of Hennepin County District Court in 1924. I. S. Joseph was a member, from 1933 on, of the Minneapolis Public Welfare Board. Ira Weil Jeffery of Minneapolis, a member of the American naval forces, was killed when the Japanese attacked Pearl Harbor on December 7, 1941.

There were (in 1942) about 950 Jewish students at the University of Minnesota in Minneapolis (total enrollment in 1941 was 13,500). The B'nai Brith Hillel

Foundation was established at the university in 1940 with Abraham Millgram as the first director. In 1942 the following were members of the faculty: Eugen Altschul, professor of economics; A. B. Baker, assistant professor of pathology and of nervous and mental diseases; Moses Barron, professor of medicine; T. L. Birnberg, associate professor of pediatrics; Lillian Cohen, associate professor of inorganic chemistry; Herbert Feigl, professor of philosophy; Harriet Goldstein, associate professor of home economics; Vetta Goldstein, associate professor of home economics; Isaac Maurits Kolthoff, professor of chemistry and head of the analytical chemistry division since 1927; Alex M. Levens, assistant professor of drawing and descriptive geometry; Hyman S. Lippman, associate professor of nervous and mental diseases; Arthur W. Maget, professor of economics; Abe Pepinsky, professor of musical education and music; Stefan A. Riesenfeld, assistant professor of law; Leo G. Rigler, professor of radiology since 1929; Lawrence D. Steefel, assistant professor of history; and Samuel Arthur Weisman, professor of medicine.

The American Jewish World, a weekly established in 1912 by Rabbi Samuel N. Deinard, is published in Minneapolis. Leo H. Frisch was the editor in 1942.

See also: DULUTH; MINNESOTA; ST. PAUL.

ALBERT G. MINDA.

Lit.: *Archives of Minnesota State Historical Society;* Linfield, Harry S., *Statistics of Jews in the United States.*

MINNESINGERS, see TROUBADORS.

MINNESOTA, a north central state of the United States, having a population of 2,792,300 (census of 1940), including about 37,500 Jews. The Jewish population, approximately 1.5 per cent of the total, was, in 1942, distributed for the most part among three major cities: Minneapolis (18,000), St. Paul (12,200), Duluth (3,500). Hibbing had a Jewish community of about 285, and Chisholm, Eveleth, St. Cloud and Virginia had Jewish communities of between 100 and 150. Rochester had about ninety Jews. In 1942 there were about thirty-five Jewish congregations in Minnesota.

Among the early Jewish settlers in Minnesota were the Samuels brothers, who emigrated from England and ran an Indian trading post at Taylor Falls on the St. Croix River about 1852. One of these brothers, Morris Samuels, served as a captain in the Civil War. Julian Austrian was another early settler, who had a trading post which was situated at the bend of the Fond De Luck River. His claim probably included part of the present site of the city of Duluth. Isaac Marks established himself in Mankato. St. Paul, however, was the first large Jewish settlement in Minnesota. S. E. Becket, Henry Cali, T. N. Cardozo, Abram Greenwald, Joseph Oppenheimer, S. Josephs, Henry Marks and Julius Mendelsohn were among the early Jewish settlers in that locality. T. N. Cardozo served as United States district commissioner at St. Paul (1855-60). The first Jew to be elected to the state legislature after Minnesota was incorporated into the Union in 1858 was Jacob Abraham (1859-63).

The first Jewish community in Minnesota was organized in St. Paul. A Jewish congregation was formed there in 1855 and officially chartered by the Minnesota territorial legislature in 1857. This was originally called Mount Zion Hebrew Association, but by special act of the state legislature (1872) the name was changed to Mount Zion Hebrew Congregation. Henry Cali was first president of the temple, and in 1862 E. Marcuson was chosen Hazan, Shohet and teacher. In 1872 Leopold Winter became its first rabbi.

Minnesota's first Orthodox congregation was also organized in St. Paul. In 1873 the Sons of Jacob was founded (B'nai Yaakov Society—Polish), and its building dedicated in 1879. The first Jewish cemetery in Minnesota was half an acre of land purchased by Mount Zion Hebrew Congregation. A Sabbath school existed in St. Paul as early as 1862.

Beginning in the 1880's additional congregations were established both in St. Paul and in other sections of the state. In 1907, Minnesota with a Jewish population of about 13,000, had congregations in Chisholm, Duluth, Eveleth, Hibbing, Minneapolis, St. Paul and Tower. In 1942 rabbis were located in St. Paul, Duluth, Hibbing, Minneapolis, Rochester and St. Paul.

In some of the outlying districts of the state, Jews were engaged in farming and dairying. However, as the Jewish population was chiefly urban, Jews engaged mainly in industrial and professional occupations. Many of them were in mercantile businesses, but a still greater proportion were in manufacturing enterprises. Within limits, Jewish occupational trends paralleled those of the rest of the community. When the jobbing business was an important phase of the business life of the Northwest, many Jews were jobbers. With the decline of jobbing in recent years, Jews went into retail merchandising and manufacturing. In the medical and legal professions Jews were well represented in 1942.

Moses D. Winthrop was a member of the state senate from 1906 to 1910, Henry Weiss from 1911 to 1913, and Henry Horvitz was elected in 1940. Other members of the state legislature were Joseph Oppenheimer (1882), Joseph Freidman (1909), J. F. Rosenwald (1909), Charles Herzberg (1911), Samuel H. Bellman (1934-40). Edward Haas was chairman of the state securities commission (1919-25).

See also: DULUTH; MINNEAPOLIS; ST. PAUL.

HARRY S. MARGOLIS.

Lit.: *Archives of Minnesota State Historical Association; Reform Advocate,* Nov. 15, 1907; *American Jewish World,* Sept. 22, 1922; Linfield, Harry S., *Statistics of Jews in the United States.*

MINOR PROPHETS, see PROPHETS, THE TWELVE.

MINOR TRACTATES OF THE TALMUD, see TALMUD TRACTATES, MINOR.

MINOR, SALOMO SALKIND, rabbi, b. Vilna, Russia, 1827; d. Vilna 1900. One of the first graduates of the rabbinical seminary of Vilna, he became instructor (1854) in Talmudic and rabbinic literature at that institution; adviser on Jewish affairs to the governor-general in 1856; government rabbi in Minsk (1859-69). In 1869 he was called to Moscow and obtained permission from the government to form for the first time an independent Jewish religious organization in that city, to which were attached a synagogue, Hebrew school, orphan asylum and other community institutions. In 1891 his efforts in behalf of the members of his community who were expelled, and of the synagogue which

had been closed by the authorities, caused him to be deposed from office; he was sent back to Vilna.

An outstanding preacher, Minor was the first to deliver sermons at the synagogue in Russian. Leo Tolstoi was guided by Minor in his studies of the Old Testament and the Hebrew language. Minor also corresponded with the outstanding Maskilim of his time. Painstakingly he collected material for the history of the Jews in Lithuania and White Russia. In addition to articles contributed to the Russian supplement of *Hakarmel* and to *Yevreiskaya Biblioteka,* he published many pamphlets. One of them, *Rabbi Ippolit Lutosanski* (1879), was directed against the slanderer Lutosanski, author of the grossly ignorant broadside (in Russian) *Concerning the Use of Christian Blood by the Jews* and of *The Jews and The Talmud.* Minor also published *Poslye Pogromov* (1882) on the pogroms in Russia, and *Biblia ob utotrbleniye vina* (1889) on the partaking of wine according to the Bible.

LAZAR MINOR (b. 1855), a son of Salomo Salkind Minor, was professor of neurology at the Moscow University.

JOSEPH MINOR (b. 1861), a second son of Salomo Salkind Minor, social revolutionary, was several times condemned to forced labor. In 1917 he was chairman of the Moscow city duma.

Lit.: Kazenelson, A., *Is Martyrologa Moskovskoi Obshtshiny, Yevreiskaya Starina* (1909), vol. 2; *Yevreiskaya Enziklopedia,* vol. 11, p. 77; Dubnow, Simon, *Weltgeschichte des jüdischen Volkes,* vol. 2 (1925).

MINORITY RIGHTS.

The problem of the presence of minority groups distinguished by reason of religion, race or nationality began to play an important part in both national and international affairs toward the end of the 18th cent. During the period of absolutism all the subjects of a monarch were subject to his will, and hence no question of rights arose. But after the American Revolution of 1776 and the French Revolution of 1789 had established the principle of the rights of man, and had put those rights into application in the form of republican government, the peoples of Europe were stirred to demand new freedoms for themselves. At first, under the influence of the French Revolution, the demands were for the rights of man; later, under the growing nationalism that prevailed during the 19th cent., many groups began to demand rights based on race and nationality.

The end of the Napoleonic Wars and the lines drawn by the Congress of Vienna (1815) found the world apportioned among a number of kingdoms and empires that were far from being unified in language, culture or race. Russia had incorporated a large part of the Polish nation; Austria-Hungary was a congeries of diverse peoples; Catholic, French- and Walloon-speaking Belgium had been combined with Protestant, Dutch-speaking Holland; Turkey was suzerain over the Roumanians, Serbs, Bulgarians and Greeks—peoples different in both race and religion. The political map of Europe was superimposed upon a racial and national map—a condition which led to intense struggles within many countries, and occasionally to intervention on the part of the Great Powers.

For about seventy years after the Congress of Vienna the struggles of the minorities were mainly directed toward securing independence. There were a few interventions in behalf of persecuted minorities. Thus the British and French protested against the treatment meted out by Russia to the Poles after the unsuccessful revolts of 1830 and 1863, and the major Powers intervened with Turkey in behalf of the Christian groups in the Balkan States. The Berlin Treaty of 1878 provided that the new states carved out of Turkey should grant equal rites to the Jews living there. On the whole, however, the chief political changes were in the direction of creating new states based on nationality rather than hereditary rulership. In 1821 Greece won its independence, largely because of the backing of the Great Powers; in 1830 Belgium separated from the Kingdom of the Netherlands. Germany achieved unity by wresting Schleswig-Holstein from Denmark (1864) and Alsace-Lorraine from France (1870); Italy, after decades of struggle, finally freed itself almost entirely of the Austrian yoke (1861) and became a united nation in 1871. The Balkan States won independence or autonomy in 1878. The last change of this type prior to the first World War was the peaceful separation of Norway from Sweden in 1905.

While these changes removed some of the friction caused by the presence of minorities, it by no means ended the discontent and the agitation. Some of the changes, such as the annexation of Alsace-Lorraine and Schleswig-Holstein by Germany, and of Savoy by France, produced other minorities; Russia and Austria-Hungary added new minority groups to their empires. All over Europe there were sore spots in which various racial and religious groups were so intermingled that each could claim special rights for itself: Transylvania, with Hungarians and Roumanians; Macedonia, with Greeks, Bulgars and Albanians; Eastern Galicia and Western Russia, with Poles, Ruthenians and Ukrainians. Encouraged by the rising tide of nationalism in Europe, minorities began to demand more and more governmental rights for themselves, while at the same time the imperial governments strove for unity by trying to impose a single language and a single culture upon all their subjects. In Austria-Hungary the language question threaten to shake the foundations of the empire; Russia struggled to suppress the aspirations of the Poles, the Ukrainians and the Finns. The larger nations, especially Russia as representative of the Slavs, and Germany as representative of the Teutons, used these discontented minorities very often as pawns in the larger game of the struggle for power.

In many instances the minorities did not so much desire complete independence as special language and cultural rights within the countries in which they lived. Thus the struggle for independence was to some extent altered into a struggle for minority rights in the form of autonomy.

The situation at the beginning of the first World War was as follows: in the countries of the greatest democracy, such as the United States, France and the Scandinavian countries, there were almost no minorities and no agitation; but Central and Eastern Europe were beset by seething, restless minorities, amounting to some 100,000,000 persons. Some of these minorities sought complete independence; others desired to be united with their own nationals who were already established as an adjacent sovereign state; still others desired some form of autonomy within the state in which they resided.

During the first World War each side endeavored to foment the revolutionary spirit among the minorities under the control of their enemies. Germany encouraged the Poles to hope for independence; the Allies had even greater success with the minorities in the Austria-Hungarian empire. At first purely a war measure, these promises began to take the form of a world program when President Woodrow Wilson enunciated the principle of self-determination for all peoples. It was but natural, therefore, that the new map of Europe created by the Versailles Peace Conference should follow ethnic lines more closely than had ever been done before in world history and that, where it was impossible to separate the interlocked racial groups, an effort should have been made to create a system of minority rights within the new states.

It was against this background of minority rights in general that the discussion of minority rights for the Jews took place. Up to the end of the 19th cent. the chief desire of the Jews had been that of civic and political equality within the countries in which they lived, and this they had achieved in Western and Central Europe. Later, however, the rise of Jewish nationalism, especially after the First Zionist Congress of 1897, the disappointment over the pogroms in Russia and the rise of anti-Semitism, as well as the increasing tension between Jews and other groups in Eastern Europe, led many Jews to hope that the problems of the Jews could be settled by granting them minority rights in the countries where the Jewish population was the largest and most separated from non-Jews by language and culture.

Looking back, therefore, upon the ineffectual efforts of the 19th cent. to protect minorities by treaty, upon the failure of these treaties to set up adequate machinery which would enforce the pledge of new states and upon the evasions and broken promises of these states, the men fighting for minority rights hopefully embraced President Wilson's plan for a League of Nations. They saw that the crux of the problem lay in the system of enforcement which was to be established and believed that the success of all efforts in behalf of minorities would depend almost wholly upon the effectiveness of this enforcement system. Those who came to Versailles in 1919 to work for the protection of Europe's minorities sought not only the establishment of minority guarantees, but the creation of a strong power which would be able to enforce the treaty rights of minorities. The League, they hoped, would be the instrument whereby the enforcement of minority rights in the new states would be achieved.

The Great Powers and the special groups working for minority rights approached the problem with the promise that the presence of a minority within a nation did not necessarily indicate the existence of a minority problem or the need for international protection of its rights. Thus ethnic and religious minorities in the Western democracies saw no need for a protection system for themselves nor did they wish to be included within the scope of any system that might be set up, since they already enjoyed full equality of citizenship within their own lands.

This attitude was most strongly represented in the Jewish delegations from the United States, England and France which came to Versailles in 1919 to aid Jews of Eastern Europe in pleading the cause of minority rights. Their goal was to obtain for the suppressed Jewish populations of Eastern Europe some of the benefits of democracy for which the Allies had ostensibly fought. In the United States the possibility that an opportunity would present itself at the close of the War for the improvement of the condition of the Jewish communities of Eastern Europe had led to the American Jewish Congress movement, while in Eastern Europe itself and in England and France Jewish leaders organized themselves for the effort to obtain civil and political equality for Jews in Eastern Europe.

The Jewish delegations which came to Paris, however, did not see eye to eye as to the kind of minority rights to be sought. The viewpoint of any delegation was naturally colored by the political experience and the political thinking to which each group had been subject at home. The delegations from Eastern Europe, dominated by a Zionist leadership, zealously sought "national" rights, while French Jewry as represented by the Alliance Israélite Universelle was just as zealously opposed to the nationalist ideal. A more moderate opposition toward the nationalist view was adopted by the British Joint Delegation. It was fairly obvious to those who had come to plead the Jewish cause in Paris that some common platform would have to be formulated, if the maximum support were to be obtained for their cause from the leaders of the major powers. This task of acting as a healing agent was undertaken by the American delegation, which had already achieved a platform upon which both American nationalists and non-nationalists could cooperate.

The chasm that separated the political thinking of the various Jewish groups, however, was too deep and too wide to be bridged. While the Eastern European delegations and the delegates from the American Jewish Congress formed themselves into a Committee of Jewish Delegations, the French and the British Jewish representatives refused to join such an over-all group which might necessitate a recession from their stand on "national" rights. In view of this, the American delegation, led by Louis Marshall, sought a more modest agreement. Marshall felt that the chief problem was to prevent the internal conflict from injuring the cause as a whole. He therefore proposed that the differing Jewish delegations refrain from presenting to the Powers at the Peace Conference opposing memorandums upon those points on which they could not agree.

The position of the nationalists was cogently argued by Nahum Sokolow, the Polish Zionist leader, who later became president of the World Zionist Organization. He felt that Jews in Eastern Europe required more than a guarantee of civil, political and religious rights, as was proposed by the non-nationalists. As a result of the disruption of the Russian and Austro-Hungarian empires, he argued, Jews had already been forced to declare themselves Jews by nationality, even as the Lithuanians, the Estonians and the Poles had set themselves up as national groups. The situation was such, he asserted, that a declaration of nationality was the only course which Jews could follow. They could not call themselves Poles without inviting attack from the Lithuanians and Germans, or vice versa. Nor were the Poles willing to accept them as Poles. He found something ridiculous in asking the Jews of Prague to declare themselves Czechs when their language was German, and yet neither could they consider themselves German. For their survival, he felt, the Jews of Eastern Europe must achieve the status of national groups even as the German, Lithuanian and other minorities in the newly constituted states had acquired it.

But if the word "national" was open to misinterpretation and was obnoxious to the representatives of Western European communities, he was willing to forego the term, so long as the rights implied by the term could be obtained, and these rights included linguistic autonomy, the right of Jews to control their own educational system and their own philanthropic and communal organizations, and the right to proportional representation in the parliaments.

Sokolow, however, did not carry along with him the support of the extreme nationalists for such a definition of "nationalism," and he himself wavered from it under pressure. The extremists asserted that the "Jews are a nation and not a religious sect" and demanded the establishment of a world Jewish parliament, representation in the League of Nations, a share in war indemnities and indemnities for pogrom damage, national curiae in some of the new states, government departments of Jewish affairs, and compulsory membership for Jews in the national minority.

These extreme demands were never presented to the leaders of the Peace Conference, for the nationalist delegations, having affiliated themselves with the Committee of Jewish Delegations, were bound by the platform finally adopted by this joint body. This platform was an approximation of the stand taken by the American delegation. Minority autonomy was defined as essentially the right of the minority to control its own educational, religious and social institutions; political rights were limited to a request for proportional representation by means of electoral colleges. In essence the political and civil rights sought were those of the "most favored minority."

The British and French groups, while not joining in the memorandum submitted to the Peace Conference by the Committee of Jewish Delegations, refrained, by agreement, from acting in opposition to it. The effectiveness of the formal memorandum, however, was probably negligible, for it was not officially presented to the Peace Conference until June 10, 1919. By that time the fate of the minority rights treaties had practically been settled.

Nevertheless, the contribution made by the Jewish representatives toward the inclusion of the minority protective clauses in the peace treaties is not to be underestimated. Long before submission of the memorandum of the Committee of Jewish Delegations, Louis Marshall and Julian W. Mack had communicated its views to President Wilson and his aides, Colonel House, David Hunter Miller and Manley O. Hudson, and were in frequent consultation with them in the drafting of the minority rights clauses. These clauses were adopted by the Peace Conference largely through the efforts of Wilson and his advisers who gained for them the support of the other members of the Council of Four at Versailles, Lloyd George, Georges Clemenceau and Vittorio Emanuele Orlando of Italy. British and French

Jews were also able to enlist the interest of their governments in the minority clauses.

The task of drafting the treaties setting up the new states and giving protection to minority groups within them was assigned on May 1, 1919, to a Commission on New States composed of representatives of the United States, France, Great Britain and later Italy and Japan. The Committee drafted five treaties, the first of which was that with Poland, which served as the pattern for the others. Poland and the Allied Powers signed the instrument at Versailles on June 28, 1919. Yugoslavia and Czechoslovakia agreed to the same general minority rights terms upon signing their treaties with the Allied Powers at St. Germain on September 10, 1919; Roumania signed at Paris on December 9, 1919; and Greece at Sèvres on August 10, 1920. Minority rights protection clauses were also incorporated by the Allies into the peace treaties signed with Austria at St. Germain on September 10, 1919; with Bulgaria at Neuilly on November 27, 1919; with Hungary at Trianon on June 4, 1920; and with Turkey at Lausanne on July 24, 1920.

The Polish treaty, which provided the pattern, gave minorities civil and political equality together with religious and linguistic guarantees under the protection of the League of Nations. Article 1 of the treaty recognized these rights "as fundamental laws," and declared "that no law, regulation or official action shall conflict or interfere with these stipulations, nor shall any law, regulation or official action prevail over them." Poland then undertook, in Article 2, to protect "life and liberty to all inhabitants of Poland without distinction of birth, nationality, language race or religion," and guaranteed "to all inhabitants . . . the free exercise of any creed, religion or belief, whose practices were not inconsistent with public order or public morals."

Articles 6, 7 and 8 in the treaty guaranteed Polish citizenship to all those born in Polish territory, provided that all Polish nationals "shall be equal before the law and shall enjoy the same civil and political rights," including admission to public employment, exercise of the professions, use of any language other than Polish in private intercourse, the press, public meetings or in the courts, and the rights of racial, linguistic or religious minorities to establish and control their own schools and charitable, religious and social institutions. The only direct mention of Jews was made in Article 11, which guaranteed to them the sanctity of the Sabbath and provided that no elections might be held on a Saturday.

The binding clause was inserted in Article 12 which declared that "Poland agrees that the stipulations in the foregoing articles so far as they affect . . . minorities, constitute obligations of international concern and shall be placed under the League of Nations." The Article further provided that none of the minority protective clauses could be modified without the assent of a majority of the Council of the League and that any member of the Council could ask for action in case of an infraction of the agreement. The Permanent Court of International Justice was set up as the arbiter in any dispute arising out of such an infraction.

The new states which were required to accept these minority clauses were restive under what they considered infringement of their sovereignty. When the clauses were submitted to the Polish delegation, Ignace Paderewski transmitted a letter of criticism, which stressed chiefly the alleged international interference with Polish internal affairs. The letter was referred back to the Commission on New States, which found that the difference between the Polish position and the proposed treaty was "fundamental."

The delegates of the new states, however, smarted under alleged "discrimination," declaring that they would not object to the minority clauses if the other members of the League accepted similar clauses. Under this type of argument, the League Assembly in 1922 adopted a resolution expressing the hope that states "not bound by the any legal obligations to the League with respect to minorities will, nevertheless, observe in the treatment of their own minorities, at least as high a standard of justice and toleration as is required by any of the treaties. . . ."

Such declarations were made before the Council of the League by Albania on October 2, 1921, by Finland in connection with the Aland Islands on June 27, 1921, by Lithuania on May 12, 1922, by Latvia on July 7, 1923, and by Estonia on September 21, 1923. In addition, a special German-Polish Convention provided for the minorities in Upper Silesia on May 15, 1922, while the Memel Territory Convention was signed on May 8, 1924.

The minorities rights treaties, while they form a significant chapter in the struggle of small ethnic, religious and national groups for civil and political equality, failed of their purpose. They failed not because the basic principle—international enforcement of minority guarantees—was in error, but because the instrument of enforcement, the League of Nations, proved to be too weak. The treaties could be no stronger than their protective arm. As the League weakened, minority rights were whittled away in Eastern European countries. In Poland and Roumania, Jews never in fact achieved more than a fraction of these rights. Appeal to the League was difficult, and by 1934 the minority rights clauses had become a deadletter. On September 13th of that year the Polish foreign minister, taking unilateral action in violation of the Polish treaty, repudiated the entire system which had been written into the treaty. He was following in the wake of a new wave of minority suppression coming out of Germany, where Nazism had risen to power in 1933. The creation of a refugee problem by Germany, however, served to emphasize again to democratic governments the need for an effective minority rights protective system, and the fact that suppression of minorities in any country is a matter of international concern.

See also: AMERICAN JEWISH CONGRESS; COMITÉ DES DÉLÉGATIONS JUIVES; MACK, JULIAN W.; MARSHALL, LOUIS; VERSAILLES PEACE CONFERENCE.

NATHAN CARO BELTH.

Lit.: Janowsky, O., The Jews and Minority Rights (1933); Judaean Addresses, vol. 3 (1927) 168-206; Kohler, Max J., in American Jewish Year Book, vol. 19 (1917-18) 106-60; Baron, Salo W., A Social and Economic History of the Jews, vol. 2 (1937) 311-15, 322-25, 376-77; vol. 3 (1937) 166-67; Robinson, J., Das Minoritätenproblem und seine Literatur (1928); Chasanowitsch, L., and Motzkin, L., Die Judenfrage der Gegenwart.

MINSK, capital of the White Russian Soviet Republic, with a Jewish population of about 55,000 (1935). As far back as the 15th cent. Jews were named tax-farmers. Following their return to Minsk in 1503, after their expulsion from Lithuania (1495), a converted Jew, later Lithuanian finance minister, Abraham Josefowicz, took possession of the customs, and at his death was succeeded by his unconverted brother Michael Josefowicz. King Stephen Bátory, in 1579, granted to the Jews of Minsk a charter which determined their legal position. The non-Jewish merchants, however, in 1606, obtained from King Sigismund III privileges by which Jewish commerce and trade were handicapped. In 1609 the king liberated the Jews from special taxes, donated to them "for eternity" the place on which the synagogue and the cemetery were, and permitted them to enlarge the cemetery by the purchase of land (1629). Nevertheless, the Jews were not allowed to buy real estate or build houses in the city limits.

During the Chmielnicki uprising (1648-50) and the persecutions connected with it, the position of the Jews became unbearable. From 1654 on they were several times expelled from Minsk by the Russians. They returned when the Poles took the town in 1658, and began to rebuild their houses, but as early as 1671 they were attacked and plundered by the city militia under orders of the Orthodox burgomaster.

King John III Sobieski took the Jews under his protection and in 1679 granted them a privilege which formed the basis of their rights: they were to occupy their houses and synagogues, cemeteries and schools, in safety, and were allowed free trading and commerce. In 1722 King August II confirmed this basic privilege. At the end of the 17th and the beginning of the 18th centuries the Jews were nearly the only merchants in Minsk and played an important part at the great fairs in Mir. In 1766 there were 1,322 Jews in Minsk.

The following were some of the noted Minsk Jews in the 17th and 18th centuries: Rabbi Moses, son of Mordecai, who founded a Yeshiva in 1685; in 1696 Leibele was elected rabbi, and he acted also as head of the Yeshiva; in 1712 he was followed by the historiographer and Cabalist Jehiel ben Solomon Heilprin; a younger contemporary of Heilprin was Aryeh Löb ben Asher, author of the famous work *Shaagath Aryeh,* who organized his own Yeshiva. Minsk at that time became a popular center of Talmudic learning which attracted many students from Poland and Lithuania. Israel Liflender, who became rabbi in 1733, was appointed rabbi also of the district of Minsk. In the later decades of the 18th cent. the rabbinical office was filled by Samuel, author of the responsa *Teshuboth Shemuel,* and by Israel Mirkish, who enjoyed wide authority outside of the city.

In 1793, in the second partition of Poland, Minsk was allotted to Russia. The controversy between the Hasidim and Mithnaggedim and, later, between the Mithnaggedim and the Maskilim, as in all Russia, raged also in Minsk. The Haskalah was represented by such men as Jekuthiel Rapoport, Jacob Hillel Ettinger, Jacob Aaron Lurie, and Isaiah Zachary Jolles of Lemberg. The reform plans of the Russian government in 1840 were greeted with joy in Minsk. Zionism also found many adherents. In August, 1902, the second conference of the Russian Zionists was held in Minsk. Beginning with the 1890's Minsk became one of the most important centers of the Jewish labor and revolutionary movements.

By the middle of the 19th cent. the number of Jewish residents of Minsk had reached 13,000. The population of the city was 90,900 in 1897, including 47,500 Jews; 102,000 in 1904, including 53,000 Jews; and 152,600 in 1917, including 67,000 Jews. The Jews had almost complete control of the lumber and export trades. They were strongly represented also in the retail trade and in various crafts. However, 17 per cent of the Minsk Jewish population lived on public charity in 1898. There were the following schools in Minsk before 1914: a private Jewish high school; four public schools, each with two classes; a Talmud Torah school; two dental schools; two trade schools; English night classes. There were also a public library and a model farm. However, about 63 per cent of the children received no education.

During the first World War thousands of fugitives and exiles from Courland and Latvia looked for refuge and aid in Minsk, but the funds of the relief committee (Jekopo) were quickly exhausted. With the Kerenski era (1917) better times seemed to have come for the Jews. In 1918, following the German occupation, Minsk was cut off from the rest of Russia. At that time a united administration of eighty-five members was formed; it was composed of twenty-five Orthodox Jews, twenty-three Zionists, six non-affiliated Jews, two members of the People's party, seventeen Federalists, eight Poale Zionists, two United and two left-wing Poale Zionists. However, its accession to office was prevented by the Bolshevik occupation of Minsk (December, 1918, to August, 1919).

During the Polish rule which followed, the Orthodox and Zionists obtained an overwhelming majority in the new Jewish local administration. In 1920 Minsk finally became a Russian possession. As in the rest of Russia, the Jewish middle class was entirely annihilated. With it perished nearly all the Jewish institutions (the great synagogue, for instance, was transformed into a public hall). In the Minsk Institute for White Russian Culture a Jewish section with a number of scientific departments which issued their works in Yiddish existed for several years. In 1926 to 1928 there appeared three volumes of the *Journal,* a scientific collection of Jewish history, literature and folklore. The University of Minsk established in the pedagogic faculty a Jewish section for the instruction of students of the Jewish high schools. In 1928 to 1929 there were in this section two professors, seven lecturers and six assistants; the students numbered 201. In 1930 the White Russian Commissariat for Education decided to suppress this Jewish section, and in its stead established a section of anti-religious propaganda.

The official census of 1926 showed a Jewish population in Minsk of 53,686 persons, constituting 40.8 per cent of the total population. According to the census of 1939, the city's population reached 238,772, nearly 107,000 more than in 1926, but the number of Jews in 1939 was not revealed.

Documents from the archives of the Kahal of Minsk were published in a partly distorted way by the renegade J. Brafman in his book *Kniga Kahala* (1869-71).

The Nazi attack on Soviet Russia (June, 1941) marked the beginning of a tragic chapter in the history of the Jews of Minsk. Some of them were evacuated or fled to the inner districts of the Soviet Union. The Yiddish National Theater of Minsk was transferred to Novosibirsk, in Siberia. According to reports published in the press in March, 1942, the Jews who remained in Minsk were massacred by order of the Gestapo. In the Minsk area the number of the victims was reported to have reached 80,000.

MARK WISCHNITZER.

Lit.: Eisenstadt, Benzion, *Rabbane Minsk Vahachameha* (1899); *Sefer Toledoth Hayamim Ureshumoth Mipinkasim Yeshanim shel Hebrah Kaddisha Shiba Keruim Ubeth Hamidrash Hagadol Asher Beir Minsk* (2 vols.); *Jewish Encyclopedia,* vol. 8, pp. 600-2; *Yevreiskaya Enziklopedia,* vol. 11 (see also the literature cited there); Rudenski, M., "Minsk Amol un Haint," *Zukunft* (1920); *Annals of the White Russian University* (1929, No. 23, Jewish Section of the Pedagogic Faculty); Lestschinsky, Jacob, *Dos Sovetishe Identum* (1941).

MINTERS. In the Middle Ages the Jews were commissioned to buy gold and silver for the mints of various sovereigns and occasionally the mints were leased to them. A Jew named Priscus made coins at Châlons in 555. About 1063 Queen Anastasia of Hungary authorized certain Jewish merchants to coin their own silver money. In the 10th cent. there was a Jewish mintmaster named Gideon in Milan; in 1170 David Hakohen minted coins in Hesse, Germany. Three Jews are said to have coined money at Winchester in 1181, and in the 12th cent. coins appeared in England with markings of David of London, Isaac of York, and Samuel, Simon and Salomon of Canterbury, but the Jewishness of these minters has not been definitely confirmed. The Babenberg dukes of Austria committed the administration of the mint to Jews. There was one Schlom, a mintmaster to Leopold V (1177-94) of Austria.

At the end of the 12th cent. and in the beginning of the 13th cent., the Polish kings Mieczyslav III and Casimir IV retained Jews as mintmasters. On the coins struck by these Jews the names of the rulers were inscribed in Hebrew letters. The mintmaster Jehiel of Bishop Otto (1207-23) of Würzburg issued coins bearing his own name. The silver coins of the Hungarian king, Béla IV (1235-70), are marked with the first letter of the Hebrew alphabet. Jews were mintmasters also under the Hungarian kings István V (1270-72) and Lajos II (1516-26). In Prussia, Hertz Gumpertz, Daniel Itzig and Veitel Heine Ephraim of Berlin, and Joseph Süss Oppenheimer, known as Jud Süss, in Württemberg, were all well-known Jewish minters. Many Jews were employed in supplying gold and silver to the mint of the Hapsburg emperors in the 17th and 18th centuries.

Lit.: Jacobs, Joseph, *The Jews of Angevin England* (1893) 392-96; Dubnow, Simon, *History of the Jews in Russia and Poland,* vol. 1 (1916) 42; idem, *Weltgeschichte des jüdischen Volkes,* vol. 7 (1928) 229, 309; *Revue des études juives,* vol. 7, col. 237; Madden, *Coins of the Jews* (1903).

MINYAN ("number"), term used especially as a designation for the least number of persons, i.e. ten, who are required for the holding of congregational services. The Minyan consists of ten men who are at least thirteen years of age. The number ten is derived from the Biblical *'edah* ("congregation"); in *Num.* 14:27 ten men are understood by the term "congregation" (cf. also *Gen.* 18:23-32). A public divine service containing the Kaddish, Kedushah, Priestly Blessing and the reading of the Torah can not be held without a Minyan (*Meg.* 4:4). However, where ten Jewish men are assembled, any kind of Jewish divine service, even on Yom Kippur, can be held in its complete form, without there being required the services of a rabbi or the ministrations of a priest. In cases where there are nine men present for services, and it is impossible to secure another man, a minor may be counted as the tenth for the Minyan.

Even in ancient Palestine it was not always easy to obtain a Minyan, since the settlements were small and the inhabitants were all engaged in occupations. According to *Meg.* 1:6, a place in which there were ten "Batlanim," i.e. ten men who were free from their occupations and trades to the extent that they voluntarily went to the house of prayer at the times designated for the various services, was regarded as a great city. Beginning with the Diaspora it became a difficult matter to secure a Minyan. Hence the custom developed of hiring Jewish men for this purpose; these hired Minyan members came to the synagogue, especially on weekdays, and made it possible to hold divine services. Such a person, in popular speech, is called a Minyanmann. Reform congregations, on the basis of the general principle of the full religio-legal equality of men and women, permit the inclusion of women in the counting of a Minyan.

See also: BAR MITZVAH; DIVINE SERVICE; KADDISH; TORAH, READING OF.

Lit.: Elbogen, Ismar, *Der jüdische Gottesdienst*, 493-94; Krauss, S., in *Festschrift zum vierzigjährigen Bestehen der israelitisch-theologischen Lehranstalt in Wien* (1933) 51-74.

MINYAN SHETAROTH, *see* ERAS.

MINZ (family), *see* MÜNZ.

MIRABEAU, HONORÉ GABRIEL RIQUETTI, COUNT, French non-Jewish political leader, b. Bignon, France, 1749; d. Paris, 1791. The most powerful orator of the French revolutionary movement, Mirabeau professed liberal ideas long before the outbreak of the French Revolution. While most of the other French liberals and representatives of the "esprit philosophique" ignored the Jewish question, or directly excepted the Jews from the political emancipation and equality of rights claimed for all Christian Frenchmen, Mirabeau not only expressed in private letters his sympathy toward the Jews but became convinced of the right of Jews to citizenship and of the general interest in their emancipation. This conviction resulted from his observation of Jewish life in England, Holland, and Prussia, where the Jews played a far more important part than in France. Especially when Mirabeau sojourned at Berlin in the last year of the reign of Frederick the Great did he realize that humanitarian principles as well as sound policy demanded improvement of the conditions of Jewish life.

At Berlin Mirabeau was acquainted with Marcus and Henriette Herz; he attended a lecture on experimental physics in Herz' home. He was influenced, too, by Christian Wilhelm von Dohm, Prussian champion of Jewish rights, and by Mauvillon, one of the keenest critics of German civilization of that time. Mirabeau

Gabriel Riquetti Mirabeau

published his views on the Jewish question in his book *Sur la réforme politique des juifs* (1788), which dealt with Moses Mendelssohn, the British Act of Naturalization of 1753, and the special question of the situation of the Jews and its improvement, and defended the Jewish religion against accusations.

After the outbreak of the French Revolution in 1789, Mirabeau was ready to put in force his principles concerning the Jews in favor of the Jews of France. In his paper *Courrier de Provence* he sought to win public sentiment in favor of equality of rights for the Jews. At the sessions of the Constituante (October 10, December 23 and 24, 1789) Mirabeau supported Abbé Grégoire and Stanislaus Clermont-Tonnerre, who advocated the granting of equal rights to the Jews. Although Mirabeau was firm in his principles in behalf of the Jews, he nevertheless was aware of the practical difficulties, especially concerning the Jews of Alsace, and of the crucial question of timing and method while the population of Alsace was rabidly anti-Semitic and menaced by riots the safety of the Jews. Mirabeau, therefore, supported the duke of Broglie, who proposed transitory measures. Thus the Jews of Alsace were granted equality of rights later than the Jews of Southern France. But it was due mainly to Mirabeau's defense of the Jews that the idea of justice to them, although not originating in France, ran a speedier course there than in other countries.

Lit.: *Revue d'histoire économique et sociale* (1928).

MIRACLE, an extraordinary occurrence, in which the believer, who is convinced of the divine omnipotence, believes that he recognizes the visible intervention of God. It is considered a direct revelation of the divine will, which appears for the purpose of accomplishing a special intention: God's communication with chosen individuals, especially with Moses and the other prophets. The basis for the belief in miracles is the acceptance of a relative regularity of events, a certain obedience of nature to laws, from which the miracle stands out as supernatural; it is therefore dependent upon a definite amount of knowledge. In addition to this, Biblical religion regards God as strictly separated from and independent of the world. In the beginning

He created it out of nothing, endowed it with the laws of inner formation and germs of preservation and natural development, but at the same time reserved for Himself the possibility of new creation and radical transformation.

The Bible, therefore, differentiates between God's miraculous creation (*bara*, "create") and the ordinary form (*'asah*, "make"; *yatzar*, "form"). Later Jewish philosophers believed that special value was to be assigned to creation at a definite time, because this miracle of all miracles warrants the possibility of all later ones within the world so called into existence. These are indispensable both for the Biblical and Talmudic religious consciousness, because the latter has its foundation in the revelation of the Torah. This revelation which God has bestowed upon His chosen people, presents itself as an extraordinary and supernatural thing, as the distinctive great beneficence which God has conferred upon His first-born. Tradition in the Jewish religion has regarded the gift of the Torah as a real miracle, the greatest in the created world, even though it teaches that the divine wisdom is something entirely evident, comprehensible to the human mind, which the latter can acquire inwardly. All other miracles are always conceived in connection with this fact, decisive for the religion. The miracles of phantasy and of mythology, of fabulous and bizarre nature, are therefore put into the background in Jewish religious feeling, as far as the latter has its center of gravity in the Mosaic-Talmudic law, in contrast to the mystical and Cabalistic frame of mind. The Torah and the fact of the divine legislation are miracles; but in ordinary life, in human affairs and decisions, one must never, as is expressly forbidden in Talmudic law, "rely upon a miracle."

Following the position taken by the medieval philosophers that miracles may not be offered as proof of doctrines in Judaism, modern Judaism rejects belief in the miraculous altogether, including the miracles of the Bible narratives. The miracles there related, according to this thesis, are records of natural phenomena which the observers could not understand or interpret.

This proposition simplified the attitude of modern Jewish thought during the 19th cent. conflict between religion and science. If the miracles associated with the Creation as described in the early chapters of *Genesis* have no bearing on the problem of the existence of God and on the religious doctrines that follow therefrom, then Judaism can accept the conclusions of science, such, for example, as the theory of evolution; whether man was created as the author of *Genesis* reports it, or not, in no way modifies or destroys the ethical doctrines of Judaism as these were propounded by the Jewish prophets and rabbis, and philosophers of human behavior. The stories that Elijah breathed life into a child that was presumably dead, for example, or that Ezekiel in a vision beheld a whole valley of dry bones click together, come alive "and stood upon their feet, an exceeding host," regarded once as miracles that proved the doctrine of the bodily resurrection of the dead, were dismissed by Jewish theologians in the face of the proof of science to the contrary.

On the question of miracles, then, modern Judaism returns to the literary prophets who performed no seemingly supernatural acts to prove their "call" to proph-ecy, or to confirm their authority to speak the word of God as they received it, or to substantiate the ethical doctrines they taught. For the modern Jew, what may seem miraculous in the field of natural phenomena is proof that, not only in Bible times but in the days of the greatest achievements of science, man has by no means discerned the ways of God in the universe.

MAX WIENER.

Lit.: Kohler, *Jewish Theology*, sections 24 to 28; Wiener, Max, "Zur Geschichte des Offenbarungsbegriffs," *Festschrift für Hermann Cohen*, pp. 1-24.

MIRANDA, ISAAC, one of the earliest Jewish settlers of Philadelphia and the first known Jew in Lancaster, where he died in 1733. The date and place of his birth are unknown. James Logan, secretary of the Province of Pennsylvania, refers to him in a letter, in 1723, as "an apostate Jew or fashionable Christian proselyte," who had official business to transact relative to a mine beyond the Susquehanna. In 1727 Miranda was an "Agent to Receive and Collect the Perquisites and Rights of Admiralty" in Philadelphia County. Later in the same year he was appointed deputy judge of the Court of Vice-Admiralty of the Province of Pennsylvania.

The year 1730 found Miranda in Lancaster, where a complaint was lodged against him by two Indians who petitioned the justices of the county to investigate the case and compel Miranda to make restitution of the goods which they alleged he had taken from them. But nothing further was heard about the case. Isaac Miranda appears to have been a wealthy landowner and his name was frequently mentioned in the records of the colony. His will (signed June 30, 1732) appears in the testamentary records of Philadelphia.

Lit.: Publications of the American Jewish Historical Society, No. 5, pp. 196-97; No. 22, pp. 149-50; *Philadelphia Wills* (Book E) 320; *Pennsylvania Archives* (Second Series), vol. 7, p. 77; vol. 9, pp. 587, 632 and 738.

MIRIAM, eldest sister of Moses and Aaron, mentioned frequently in *Exodus* and *Numbers*. According to the Biblical account she watched over the infant Moses when he was exposed on the river Nile, and had her own mother serve as nurse for him for the daughter of Pharaoh. She sang a song of praise after the crossing of the Red Sea (*Ex.* 15:20-21). At a later period she and Aaron criticized Moses for marrying a Cushite woman; for this she was punished by temporary leprosy (*Num.* 12). She died at Kadesh (*Num.* 20:1), before either Aaron or Moses.

According to Josephus, Miriam was the wife of Hur and the grandmother of Bezalel; the rabbis make her the wife of Caleb and the mother of Hur. According to the legends, she gave her father wise advice by counselling him to have children even in time of persecution, was one of the midwives mentioned in *Ex.* 1, and prophesied the birth of a deliverer. The well which accompanied the Israelites on their journeys through the wilderness was due to her merits, and disappeared at her death.

Lit.: The Bible dictionaries; Ginzberg, Louis, *Legends of the Jews.*

MISCH, GEORG, philosopher, b. Berlin, 1878. He attended the Leibniz Gymnasium, Berlin, and studied law, economics and philosophy from 1896 on. In 1899 he was graduated and baptized. He married Clara Dilthey, daughter of the great philosopher Wilhelm Dilthey, and considered it the major aim of his life to explain and defend the philosophic ideas of his father-in-law which he adopted and enriched. In 1905 Misch became lecturer in philosophy at the University of Berlin, in 1911 professor of philosophy at the University of Marburg, where he opposed Hermann Cohen and his school of philosophy. From 1916 to 1933 he was professor of philosophy at the University of Göttingen.

Misch published his enlarged thesis, *Zur Entstehung des französischen Positivismus* (1901). He also issued the first volume of his *Geschichte der Autobiographie* (1907), which was crowned by the Akademie der Wissenschaften of Berlin. In 1912 he edited Lotze's *System der Philosophie,* with an introduction which was generally recognized as a valuable appraisal of the influence of Lotze. In 1924 Misch published *Diltheys Lebensphilosophie,* and in 1926 he outlined his own philosophical position in *Der Weg in die Philosophie.* In 1931 he discussed the philosophy of Husserl in *Lebensphilosophie und Phänomenologie.* Misch edited several volumes of Dilthey's collected works, and assisted his wife (1933) in editing the history of her father's youth, *Der junge Dilthey.*

MISCH, MARION L., civic worker, b. Newark, N. J., 1869; d. Providence, R. I., 1941. She began a long career as educator and community worker by organizing the first Jewish sabbath school in Pittsfield, Mass., when she was only fourteen; and by the time of her death she had been acclaimed one of Rhode Island's leading civic workers. In Providence she was known for her work both in Jewish activities and in the city's educational and communal life. Music was one cf her main interests; as mcmber of the Providence school board, she effected the extension of music education in the schools.

Traveling all over the world, Marion Misch lectured on music, education, womanhood and Judaism. She held a score of executive offices in national and local organizations: as president of the National Council of Jewish Women, director of the Providence Society for Organizing Charity, and president of the Rhode Island State Federation of Women's Clubs. She engaged prominently in various types of public service during the World War. She published *Selections for Homes and Schools,* a collection of Jewish prose and poetry, (1911), and a "Children's Service" for the Day of Atonement.

Lit.: Schwarz, Arthur, "Marion L. Misch," *B'nai B'rith,* March 1930.

MISCHAKOFF, MISCHA, violinist, b. Proskouroff, Russia, 1895. He studied at the St. Petersburg Conservatory under Leopold Auer, graduating in 1914 with a gold medal and the Rubinstein prize. For a while he served as concertmaster with the St. Petersburg symphony orchestra, then with the Warsaw philharmonic. In 1922 he came to America, making his debut as concert violinist after winning first prize in a contest held by the Stadium Concerts in New York. Following an extensive concert tour of the country, Mischakoff was appointed concertmaster of the New York Symphony Society. In 1927, he held a similar post with the Philadelphia Orchestra; then he transferred his activity to the Chicago Symphony for seven years. When the N.B.C. Orchestra was founded (1937)

Mischakoff became its concertmaster. He has also appeared as soloist with most of the major American orchestras, and has assisted in performances of chamber music.

MISES, LUDWIG EDLER VON, economist and sociologist, brother of Richard Martin Mises, b. Lemberg, Galicia (then Austria-Hungary), 1881. Descendant of a prominent Jewish family, he was educated in Vienna, where he received his doctor's degree (1913) and became assistant professor (1918). He was also secretary of the chamber of trade, commerce and industry in Vienna, and in 1926 created the Austrian institute of research into economic cycles. Mises, an expert in monetary matters, lived in Switzerland from 1934 on, and in 1942 was working at the Institut universitaire des hautes études internationales in Geneva.

His numerous works include: *Entwicklung der gutsherrlich-bäuerlichen Verhältnisse in Galizien 1772-1848* (1902); *Theorie des Geldes und der Umlaufsmittel* (Munich, 1912; 2nd ed., 1924; English trans., H. E. Batson, London, 1934); *Nation, Staat und Wirtschaft* (1919); *Die Gemeinwirtschaft* (Jena, 1922; 2nd ed., 1932; English translation by J. Kahane, London, 1936); *Geldwertstabilisierung und Konjunkturpolitik* (Jena, 1928); *Kritik des Interventionismus* (Jena, 1929); *Die Ursachen der Wirtschaftskrisen* (Tübingen, 1931); *Grundprobleme der Nationalökonomie* (Jena, 1933); *Les illusions du protectionisme et de l'autarchie* (Paris, 1938); *Nationalökonomie, Theorie des Handelns und Wirtschaftens* (Geneva, 1940).

MISES, RICHARD MARTIN EDLER VON, mathematician, b. Lemberg, Galicia (then Austria-Hungary), 1883. He studied in Vienna and at the technical high school in Brünn, became assistant professor at the University of Strasbourg in 1909, associate professor at the University of Dresden in 1919, and director of the Institut für angewandte Mathematik at the University of Berlin in 1920. He was an active pilot in the German Army during the first World War.

Mises was a member of the Prussian Akademie der Wissenschaften and editor of the *Zeitschrift für angewandte Mathematik.* Shortly after the Nazis' rise to power he left Germany for Turkey, where he was appointed professor of mathematics at the University of Istanbul. In 1940 he came to the United States, where in 1942 he was teaching at the Graduate School of Engineering at Harvard University, in Cambridge, Mass.

Mises' main field of research was problems of dynamics. Only a few of his works may be mentioned: *Theorie der Wasserräder* (1908); *Dynamische Probleme der Maschinenlehre* (1911); *Elemente der technischen Hydromechanik* (1914); *Fluglehre* (1918; 3rd ed., 1926); *Naturwissenschaft und Technik der Gegenwart* (1922); *Die Differential- und Integralgleichungen der Mechanik und Physik* (1925; 3rd ed., 1930); *Wahrscheinlichkeit, Statistik und Wahrheit* (1928; English ed., London, 1939), *Vorlesungen über angewandte Mathematik* (1931); *Ernst Mach und die empiristische Wissenschaftsauffassung* (The Hague, 1938).

MISHLE, see PROVERBS, BOOK OF.

MISHLE MIDRASH, see MIDRASH PROVERBS.

MISHLOAH MANOTH, see PURIM.

MISHMAR HA'EMEK, MISHMAR HA'-SHARON, MISHMAR HA'SHLOSHA, MISHMAR HA'YARDEN, MISHMAR ZEBULUN, *see* Colonies, Agricultural.

MISHMAROTH, *see* Colonies, Agricultural.

MISHNAH. The name Mishnah is applied in particular to the collection of Halachoth or laws made by Judah Hanasi (generally known as Rabbi) and his colleagues at the beginning of the 3rd cent. C.E. The word Mishnah is derived from the Hebrew verb *shanah,* meaning "to repeat" or, in its later development, "to study or teach by means of repetition," and was used in this broader sense to refer to: (1) the entire content of the oral tradition until the beginning of the 3rd cent. C.E.; (2) the sum of the teaching of a single Tanna or teacher; (3) a single statement of law; (4) any collection of laws. Thus, for example, mention is made in the Talmud of the Mishnah of Eliezer ben Jacob, or the Mishnah of Rabbi Akiba. Today, however, the name Mishnah, applied without any qualifications, has become synonymous with the Mishnah of Judah Hanasi. The association has resulted from the fact that this Mishnah, due to Judah's great prestige and authority and his thoroughness in gathering and sifting traditions, gained immediate recognition and became the standard text for study and comment in all the academies of Palestine and Babylonia.

The Mishnah represents the culmination of a series of attempts to bring order into the vast mass of traditions that had been transmitted orally for many centuries. The Law, as embodied in the Pentateuch, is extremely general and can not be applied to daily living without further amplification. Thus it is reasonable to assume that from the very beginning there must have existed, together with the written Law, a body of explanations, interpretations, and applications, which was handed down orally. As the life of the nation developed and became more complex, conditions arose which necessitated the creation of new institutions and the expansion of old laws. Many problems confronted the people which could not have been foreseen and which could be solved only by the formulation of new laws. In order to give proper sanction to these new practices, customs, and laws, the Soferim, the teachers during the period beginning with Ezra (about 450 B.C.E.) and ending with Simon the Just (about 300 B.C.E. or, according to some, about 200 B.C.E.), interpreted the written text in such a way as to show clearly that these customs and practices were implied therein. Later, in either the 2nd or 1st cent. B.C.E., the laws were transmitted in the Mishnah form independently of the Biblical text. (For a more detailed study of the relationship between the Midrash form and the Mishnah form and the various theories as to when and why the latter was adopted, see Lauterbach, Jacob Z., *Midrash and Mishnah.*) Gradually the Halachoth, or abstract legal statements, became so numerous that only a prodigious memory could retain them all, and a great need arose to bring the laws together in a logical order, to resolve their contradictions, and to remove all extraneous material. This need led ultimately to the Mishnah.

The compilation of the Mishnah is not, however, the work of one man, or even of the scholars of one age, but rather the result of a long process extending over a period of two centuries. A close study of the text of the Mishnah and of the statements of the early Amoraim sheds much light on the various stages in this process. Thus it is possible to state: (1) the Mishnah contains traces of collections of Halachoth which date from the early part of the 1st cent. C.E.; (2) there was a concerted effort on the part of the sages of Jabneh (about 90 C.E.) to assemble and harmonize the Halachah. The result of this activity is incorporated in the Mishnah in the tractate *Eduyoth;* (3) Akiba (d. about 135 C.E.) arranged the Halachoth in a logical order and probably constructed the framework of the present-day Mishnah; (4) the collection of Akiba was enlarged and brought up to date by his disciple, Meir; (5) it became the custom, after the time of Akiba, for every head of an academy to compile his own Mishnah, so that the confusion which resulted from this multiplication of collections motivated Judah Hanasi to compile a standard, authoritative Mishnah; (6) although it is reported that Judah made use of thirteen different collections of Halachoth in his work, his Mishnah is based largely upon the collection of Meir and indirectly, therefore, upon that of Akiba.

Although the Mishnah is primarily a collection of Halachoth or laws, it is not a code in the strict sense of the word. Although it tries to indicate the authoritative norm by devices such as an anonymously stated opinion, or the quoting of a decision in the name of the sages, the Mishnah nevertheless includes the different opinions held on each subject, and thus allows for further study and discussion. Moreover, the Mishnah differs from modern codes in that it contains Haggadic, or homiletical, material. There are sixty-five Haggadic Mishnayoth (individual paragraphs) besides the special tractate (*Pirke Aboth*) which deal with the basic beliefs of Judaism, the value of religious and social ideals, and the importance of ethical conduct.

The Mishnah in its present form is not identical with the redaction of Judah. A great many statements are found in the text which could not have been included by Judah, such as, "When Rabbi died, humility and the fear of sin ceased" (*Sotah* 9:15), or those passages in which authorities who lived after Judah are mentioned (cf., for example, *Mak.* 3:15, where Rabbi's son is cited). Most of these additions were probably incorporated into the Mishnah during the generation following Judah.

Although one of the reasons which led to the compilation of the Mishnah was the desire to facilitate the remembrance of the Halachoth, it is a much disputed point whether or not Judah committed his Mishnah to writing. There have been two schools of thought on this question. On the one hand, Samuel Hanagid, Judah Halevi, Maimonides and Isaac Abravanel among the medieval Talmudists, and Zacharias Frankel, Isaac Hirsch Weiss and Jakob Brüll among the modern scholars, maintain that the Mishnah was recorded in writing by Judah; on the other hand, the medieval scholars Rashi, Moses of Coucy and Simon Duran, and the modern scholars Samuel David Luzzatto, Graetz and Löw maintain that the Mishnah was not committed to writing until the beginning of the 6th cent. C.E. It is possible that though no official copy of the Mishnah was written down before the 6th cent., there were many unofficial copies in existence which the scholar consulted privately to refresh his memory.

The Mishnah is divided into six main divisions, termed "orders" (*sedarim*). Each order, in turn, is divided into a number of tractates (*massechtoth;* singular, *massecheth*). The tractates are divided into chapters (*perek*), and the chapter into paragraphs (*mishnah*). The six divisions are as follows:

1. Zeraim (Seeds)—the laws relating to the cultivation of the soil and the produce thereof.
2. Moed (Festivals)—the laws concerning the observance of the Sabbath and the holidays.
3. Nashim (Women)—the laws concerning marriage, divorce, and problems connected with the family.
4. Nezikin (Damages)—contains most of the civil and criminal laws, including the intricate details of court procedure.
5. Kodashim (Holy Things)—laws pertaining to sacrifices and the Temple service.
6. Toharoth (Purities)—the laws of purity and impurity.

For details, see the separate articles on the divisions and the separate tractates.   EPHRAIM BENNETT.

Lit.: Danby, Herbert, *The Mishnah* (1933; introduction and English translation); Strack, H. L., *Introduction to the Talmud and Midrash;* Kassovsky, Hayim Joshua, *Otzar Leshon Hamishnah* (1927; a concordance of the Mishnah).

MISHPACHAH, *see* PHRASES, POPULAR (under MISHPOCHE).

MISHPAT HASHALOM, *see* ARBITRATION.

MISHPOCHE, *see* PHRASES, POPULAR.

MISKOLC, capital of Borsod county, Hungary, with 10,800 Jewish inhabitants in a total population of 62,000 (1930). During and before the first half of the 18th cent. Jews were living in the villages surrounding Miskolc, and were visiting the fairs of that city, being debarred from residing there. Subsequently some Jews were permitted to settle in the city in houses or domains of noblemen who found the protection of Jews a profitable business, although they had to contend with opposition on the part of the city burghers and of the monastic order of the Minorities.

The Jewish community of Borsod county, with Miskolc as the seat of its rabbi, was founded in 1765 under the auspices of the royal crown domain of Diósgyőr. The crown domain supervised the election of the community board, but gave it and the rabbi sweeping judicial powers. The county rabbinate was in existence up to 1850 when its jurisdiction was limited to the city of Miskolc. At first the Jews of Miskolc busied themselves in trades, commerce being in the hands of Greek merchants. Presently the Jews succeeded the Greeks who retired from business and returned to their fatherland. As the business activities of the Jews grew, so the city gained in importance as a commercial center of northeastern Hungary. The Jewish tradesmen constituted a guild of their own (1836), again under the auspices of the crown domain. The guild, converted in 1864 into a trade association, was still in existence in 1936. In 1835 the 215 Jews of Miskolc were paying 700 gulden, in 1847 361 Jews were paying 1,900 gulden as toleration tax. In 1848 the city council, anxious to stop the influx of more Jews, in-structed the board of the community to prevent by every means the settlement or marriage of outsiders into the community. In the same year, a Jewish teacher, Móric Strausz, founded the first commercial school at Miskolc.

A marked change of attitude is revealed in a letter of the city council to the Jewish community in 1861, expressing the esteem and appreciation of the citizens for the Jews who at that time still had no citizenship rights. The synagogue of the community was enlarged in 1843, and new synagogues were built in 1863 and 1900. Dissension concerning the synagogue ritual repeatedly led to division within the community from 1863 practically to the end of the 19th cent., resulting in the excommunication of the rabbi and the community board by a conference of Orthodox rabbis in 1864. The community eventually accepted the Orthodox statutes. In 1929 it had thirteen committees attending to various matters of self-government.

In addition to several charitable institutions, the community maintained a Jewish Hospital for Upper Hungary, founded in 1929; several elementary schools, one with 1,000 pupils being among the largest and best housed parochial schools of all denominations in Hungary; a women teachers' training school, founded in 1928; boys' and girls' high schools; three Yeshivas, and three Talmud Torahs. A Mishnayoth and Talmud Torah Association enabled adults to pursue Jewish studies.

A history of the community, *A miskolci hitközség története,* was written by Rabbi Salamon Spira. During the decade from 1920 to 1930, the Jewish inhabitants of Miskolc decreased by 5% in marked contrast to a steady increase prior to the first World War. In 1942 twelve Jewish members of the city council were removed in accordance with a national law debarring from municipal councils all persons falling under the Jew laws.   ANNA BETTELHEIM.

Lit.: Magyar zsidó lexikon, pp. 606-8; Szendrey, J., *Miskolc város története; Egyenlőség,* July 30, 1936, p. 13.

MISSEMESHUNNA, *see* PHRASES, POPULAR (under MITHAH MESHUNNAH).

MISSION OF ISRAEL, the conviction of the Jew that his people has received a mandate from the Universal God to bear witness to His truth and that it has been endowed with unique spiritual capacity to perform its task. As it has appeared and reappeared in Jewish thought since exilic days, this doctrine may be understood only in the light of the doctrines of (1) Israel's election; (2) his performance of the task; and (3) the Divine Kingdom, which is the goal of Jewish striving and the end-aim of missionary activity.

1. The Election of Israel. It has frequently been pointed out that every racial or national group has its own peculiar aptitude, its own special capacity of soul or intellect which enables the historian to speak of its mission to the world and of its contribution to civilization. Geiger refers to the capacities of the Greek and Roman and to their contribution to art and law. However, this is purely a retrospective evaluation. Israel, on the other hand, became aware of its election, even before its contribution had been made. In fact, the modern Jew realizes that his work as missionary has not been completed.

This awareness of mission has been the result of Israel's awareness of his own individuality. When the monotheistic idea took hold of the Jewish heart, Israel began to realize its universal significance. By virtue of its having attained the only possible truth of Divinity, Israel realized that it had an obligation to bring this truth to the rest of mankind. For, if God is the Father of all men, the truth in Israel's possession belongs to all His children. Israel is the "first-born" (*Ex.* 4:22). By virtue of this special endowment, this precious knowledge of the Divine, Israel is a "kingdom of priests and a holy nation." According to *Deut.* 7:6-8 the reason for this election is the love of God. "Because the Lord loved you and because He would keep His oath." In prophetic literature (*Isa.* 49:1-6) the election of Israel is regarded as pre-natal. "The Lord hath called me from the womb; from the bowels of my mother hath He made mention of my name—and He said unto me, 'Thou art My servant, Israel in whom I will be glorified!' "

The rabbis reconstructed the history of their people to prove that Israel was selected by God to perform His divinely appointed task. Abraham is pictured in rabbinic literature as an itinerant missionary who attracts converts to monotheism (*Midrash Gen.* to *Gen.* 12:5). Furthermore, the Decalogue was offered to all the seventy nations but only Israel accepted it with the words, "We will do and obey," for at that time only Israel had the innate capacity to respond to the appeal of the Commandments. The medieval Jewish philosophers saw in the people of Israel, rather than in the individual Israelites alone, the capacity to serve God and to bear witness to His truth. In the eyes of Judah Halevi, Moses attained his high estate only because of Israel whom he led.

This awareness of one's election is at first a centripetal force but it becomes centrifugal the moment its full implications are realized. It does not eventuate in racial pride or in national arrogance, but rather in the blessed realization that "what is distinctively Jewish is at bottom distinctively human." Election implies duties. It is indeed *noblesse oblige*. Said the Lord to his people, "You only have I known of the families of the earth; therefore will I visit upon you all your iniquities" (*Amos* 3:2).

2. The Performance of the Task. By virtue of its innate vision, granted it by its Creator, Israel is consecrated to the task of being the servant of the Lord, the witness to the nations (*Isa.* 43:10). The performance of this task entails suffering (*Isa.* 42:18 et seq.). The sorrows of Israel thus lose their adventitious quality, becoming truly purposive. At times, Israel has been blind; the prophet rebukes the people for it (*Isa.* 42:18). But the long sweep of history shows that Israel has remained true to its sacred mission. The universalistic passages of Scripture are our first evidence. *Jonah* is a defense of missionary activity. The prophet is required to bring to the people of Nineveh the message of the one and only God. *Ruth* reflects the Jewish conviction that proselytes are worth the effort. Indeed, these proselytes shall glory in their newly accepted truth (*Isa.* 44:5): "One shall say, 'I am the Lord's'; and another shall call himself by the name of Jacob; and another shall subscribe with his hand unto the Lord, and surname himself by the name of Israel."

In the rabbinic period the sincerity of individual con-

verts justified the mission-idea. Aquila, Shemaiah and Abtalion were proselytes (*Git.* 56b). Many non-Jews were accepted into Judaism by Hillel (*Midrash Lev.* 2:8). The Greek translation of the Bible made the treasures of Judaism available for the non-Jewish world. It was indeed a "Septuagint," a book for the seventy nations. The existence of conversion manuals—such as the *Didache* and the *Didascalia,* Christian adaptations of earlier Jewish handbooks—shows with what thoroughness Israel undertook the task of preparing converts. The reference in the New Testament (*Matt.* 23:15) to the conversion activities of the Pharisees is most significant. It reflects what might have been a world-wide missionary program. It was only with the change in the external circumstances of the Christian group that one rabbi permitted himself to speak disparagingly of the practice of accepting converts (*Yeb.* 42a). However, a contemporary insisted that the only reason for the dispersion was Israel's greater opportunity to make proselytes (*Pes.* 82b). Indeed, Israel lost no opportunity to win souls for the Universal God. An instance of mass conversion is that of the Khazars.

Not only through its own activities did Israel bear witness to the Divine but also through the activities of its daughter-religions, Christianity and Islam. Israel transmitted to these religions certain qualities which enabled the daughter-religions to help Israel to prepare the world for Jewish monotheism and the Messianic Kingdom. Also in a cultural sense, by keeping learning alive in the Dark Ages, by translating important books and by serving as intermediary, did Israel help to bring enlightenment to the world and thus served in the capacity of missionary.

3. The Kingdom of God. What then is the goal of Jewish striving? Because the Divine Kingdom was not near at hand, but afar off, there is no clear delineation of it. It is always described poetically (*Isa.* 2:2-5; *Micah* 4:2-5). It shall come in the end of days. All nations will flow unto God's house. They will seek instruction in Israel's truth. War will be no more; weapons will be refashioned into instruments of peace. Every man will dwell securely within his own home (*Isa.* 11:1-9). The messianic king will rule in justice and in right, destroying evil and establishing goodness. Even the antagonisms in nature will be forgotten. "The earth will be filled with the knowledge of the Lord as the waters cover the sea" (*Hab.* 2:14). The prophets foresaw the time when, as the result of Israel's activities, the Temple on Zion would become a "house of prayer for all people" (*Isa.* 56:6-7).

Following rabbinic ideas of universalism as reflected in the Noahide laws (*Sanh.* 56b), Kohler pictures the kingdom in this wise: "Not a church universal, nor a uniform religion for all, but the Divine truth reflected in many systems of belief and thought—a religion ever progressive on lines of historic continuity, but never finished or final—leading all nations and classes to the mountain of God—this is Judaism's aim."

Ahad Haam takes exception to this mission-ideal of the Jewish people on the ground that it is of Western European origin. In his opinion, the Western European Jews have no rich Jewish message to bring to the world, while the Eastern European masses would never be accepted as a pattern of inspiration by those who reject them and rob them of all human rights. Ahad Haam regards the mission-ideal as spirit without body, a logical contradiction. Furthermore, he objects to the theory that the dispersion is Israel's missionary opportunity. He ignores the undeniable fact that, while adopted by Western European Jews, the mission-idea was not invented by them. It is as old as Jewish life, appearing not only in the Bible and rabbinic writings but also in the liturgy itself, as in the *Alenu* prayer.

Israel is sometimes spoken of as a "barometer" people, the political and social status of which in any country is an indication of the health or degeneracy of the country itself. When Israel suffers, according to this view, it is a sign that the nation or civilization which permits it to suffer is afflicted with an illness. Spain's illness was reflected in medieval Jewish suffering; it led to the decline of the Spanish empire. Germany's treatment of the Jews presaged an illness of world-wide significance. This theory may be correct, but it is inadequate. Israel's status is not that of a passive "barometer" of events but of an active agent, an aggressive missionary. Even as the prophets realized that their message would fall on deaf ears and would have to be saved for the generation that would understand, so Israel, in spite of suffering and disappointment, must continue to regard itself as the "light of the nations, the witness of the Divine truth."   ABRAHAM SHUSTERMAN.

Lit.: Joseph, Morris, *Judaism as Creed and Life;* Kohler, Kaufmann, *Jewish Theology;* Baeck, Leo, *The Essence of Judaism;* Ahad Haam, *Selected Essays;* Cohon, Samuel S., in *Christianity and Judaism Compare Notes;* Geiger, Abraham, *Judaism and Its History;* Kohler, Kaufmann, "Mission of Israel," *Central Conference of American Rabbis Year Book,* vol. 29 (1919) 265-88.

MISSIONS TO THE JEWS. Saul of Tarsus, a Jew, the founder of Pauline Christianity, tried to convert his co-religionists to his point of view, failed, turned his attention to proselyting non-Jews, became a successful "apostle to the Gentiles," established many Pauline churches, and created the schism between primitive Christianity and Pauline Christianity, a schism which has continued to the present day. Pauline Christianity grew by leaps and bounds until, finally, a three-cornered fight developed between Pauline Christianity, Judaism, and the so-called mystery-religions of the East for domination of the religious life of the Roman Empire. Pauline Christianity won out and, in 325, was recognized as the official religion of Rome.

Until this time, the efforts of the Christians to win over the Jews were mainly literary and argumentative. As early as the post-Bar Kochba period, Christian tracts, designed to gain Jewish converts for Christianity, were written.

In an era when the only learned men in Christian countries were the Christian clergy and the despised Jews, many of the clergy made determined efforts to bring the Jews down to the cultural level of the ignorant and superstitious peasantry among whom they dwelt. The treatment accorded the Jews by the Crusaders, the fanatic preaching friars, and the professional, Jew-baiting controversialists forms one of the saddest pages in all of Jewish history. A few Jews, motivated by misguided zeal or by material desires, deserted the Jewish religion and became willing tools in the hands of those who warred against Judaism. The actions of these renegades are chiefly responsible for the bitter hatred which many Jews feel toward one of their number who becomes a Christian.

The liberal spirit engendered by the Renaissance and the Reformation ended this thousand-year reign of terror. Although centuries more had to elapse before the Jew was granted full civil and religious freedom, Christian conversionists ceased to use force as their main weapon and once again resorted to the use of persuasion.

In the latter half of the 17th cent., a new type of approach to the Jew made its appearance in Christian missionary circles, a type of approach which, until the 20th cent., was accepted as the norm in Christian efforts to convert the Jews. Until this time the Jew had been classified with Moslem, heretic, and infidel under the general heading of "unbelievers" or "heathen." He was regarded as merely a part of the great mass of unregenerate humanity which would have to be won over before Christianity would dominate the world. But the great revival of interest in the Hebrew language and in Hebrew culture, which was one of the outstanding characteristics of the Renaissance and the Reformation, led, gradually, to a determination to convert the Jews, not as part of the task of world-wide redemption of all unbelievers but as a necessary prelude to that larger work.

The ancient Pauline injunction, "to the Jews first," received renewed emphasis and Protestant theologians deemed it their sacred duty to devise special ways and means of bringing their religious propaganda to the Jews. They believed ardently that the conversion of the Jewish people would lead to the Christianization of the entire world, and that this, in turn, would result in the coming of the millennial age. It has taken more than two and a half centuries of feebly rewarded toil, bitter experiences with thousands of worthless scoundrels, and millions of wasted dollars to convince the majority of Christendom that this method of bringing about the millennium holds little promise of success.

The first organized missionary effort designed to attract only Jews dates from the year 1658 and the city of Hamburg, Germany. In that the Rev. Esdras Edzard, a disciple of John Buxtorf, was filled with a desire to convert the Jews of Hamburg and he labored toward that end for almost fifty years. In 1667, he founded the Esdras Edzard Institute for the conversion of the Jews, the first missionary society formed for the specific purpose of reaching the Jews. The society was still functioning as late as 1888, but it has since ceased to exist.

The next major effort in this field was that made by the Moravian brethren in the eighteenth century. Through the efforts of this sect, the Institutum Judaicum was established in Halle, Germany, in 1728, by Professor John Henry Callenberg (1699-1760). The Halle Institute printed much literature and trained many missionaries. The most famed of these was Stephen Schultz (1714-1776), who travelled all over Europe and Asia in search of Jews who would listen to the gospel-message. During one of his journeys, he came into the presence of Johann Wolfgang von Goethe, famed author of *Faust,* who paid his respects to this 18th cent. apostle with these words:

Mr. Schultz is one of the worst missionaries who have ever disturbed the nations. The conversion of the Jews is his purpose, and the talent which directs him to that end is his ability to speak Hebrew and what belongs to that.

. . . He runs through the world, barks at the Jews, who, at least, are cleverer than he, occupies himself with them, accomplishes nothing, and gratifies the good people who refresh him with eating, drinking, etc. (quoted in *Jewish Messenger,* Oct. 5, 1888, p. 4).

The rationalist spirit, which played such havoc with traditional religion toward the end of the eighteenth century, was responsible for the death of the Halle effort in 1792.

The high-water-mark of modern Christian attempts to convert the Jews was reached in the 19th cent. During this century, hundreds of Christian missionary societies for Jews were founded and labored in every section of the world. Only a small number of these societies outlived their founders. Most flourished for a few years, some for a few decades. Less than twenty passed their fiftieth birthdays. Those which managed to exist to 1942 are the London Society for Promoting Christianity amongst the Jews (founded 1809), the Basle Society of Friends of Israel (1830), the Jewish Work of the Church of Scotland (1841), the British Society for the Propagation of the Gospel among Jews (1842), the Zion Society for Israel (United States, 1878), and a number of others which were organized in the closing years of the 19th cent.

The 20th cent. has been marked by an ever-decreasing interest in separate missions to the Jews and an ever-increasing tendency on the part of evangelical Christian denominations to regard the conversion of the Jew as merely a part of the general scheme of world-wide Christianization. In other words, that part of the Christian world which still clings to the "old-time religion" is abandoning its special efforts to reach the Jews as Jews and is once again assuming the attitude that the Jews are to be converted through general missionary efforts, directed toward unbelievers of all nationalities and all non-Christian religions.

United States and Canada. The few Jews who lived in North America during the colonial period were subjected to the usual well-meant but futile efforts to convert them to Christianity. As early as 1667, the eminent Puritan divine, Increase Mather, wrote a series of proselytizing sermons titled *The Mystery of Israel's Salvation, Explained and Applyed.* The first recorded attempt to convert an American Jew dates from about 1692, when it was noted by a non-Jewish chronicler that "that Jew whom Mather the Elder has taken great Pains to Convert to the Xtn Faith . . . went over to Jamaica and dyed a hardned wrech." Increase and Cotton Mather and Ezra Stiles, president of Yale College (1778-1795), were among the colonial clergymen who made vigorous attempts to Christianize their Jewish neighbors.

The first conversionist organization in the United States was the Female Society of Boston and Vicinity for Promoting Christianity among the Jews, established June 5, 1816. Its prime mover was a frail, middleaged, bookish Episcopalian spinster, Hannah Adams, one of "the" Massachusetts Adamses. The Boston Female Society lasted until about 1843.

The American Society for Meliorating the Condition of the Jews (1820-1870), organized by Joseph Samuel Christian Frederick Frey (born Joseph Samuel Levy), was the most important 19th cent. society of its kind. John Quincy Adams, Elias Boudinot, General Stephen

Van Rensselaer, DeWitt Clinton, and many other prominent Americans interested themselves in the Society. For the first twenty years of its existence, the Society attempted, unsuccessfully, to colonize foreign Christian Jews in America. Then, for another thirty years, the Society endeavored, also unsuccessfully, to convert the Jews who were already here.

The first Canadian missionary society for the conversion of Canadian Jews dates from 1840.

The rapid influx of East European Jews, beginning about 1880, gave a tremendous impetus to Christian missionary work among the Jews of the United States and Canada.

The more important of the North American conversionist agencies of recent times include:

1. Church Society for Promoting Christianity amongst the Jews (Episcopalian), 1878-1904.
2. Zion Society for Israel (Norwegian Lutheran), 1878 to the present.
3. First Hebrew Christian Church (Jacob Freshman), New York, 1883-1892.
4. Chicago Hebrew Mission (William E. Blackstone), 1887 to the present.
5. American Mission to the Jews (Hermann Warszawiak), New York, 1890-1903.
6. American Board of Missions to the Jews, Inc. (Leopold Cohn), Brooklyn, 1893 to the present.
7. Department of Jewish Evangelization (Northern Presbyterians), 1908 to the present.
8. Christian Approach to the Jews (International Missionary Council), 1922 to the present.

Missionary programs specifically designed to reach American Jews cost in 1942 about $600,000 a year. On the basis of mission reports, the average annual harvest does not amount to more than four hundred individual Jews. Excluding Jewish Christian Scientists, the number of Christian Jews in the United States and Canada is quite insignificant. The Hebrew Christian Alliance of America, which is more than a quarter-century old, has about two hundred members, mostly professional missionaries.

At the present time, there is a definite tendency in American Christian religious circles to abandon all direct attempts to persuade American Jews to accept Christianity.   DAVID MAX EICHHORN.

Lit.: An exhaustive history of this subject titled *A History of Christian Attempts to Convert the Jews of the United States and Canada* by D. M. Eichhorn is to be found, in manuscript form, in the Hebrew Union College Library, Cincinnati.

British Empire. British missions to the Jews are the product of long-standing evangelical tendencies. During the reign of Edward I Jews of London were compelled to attend Dominican conversion services, while in the era of the Resettlement the argument was frequently advanced that Jews should not be admitted to a Christian country unless they adopted the Christian faith.

Formal missions, however, developed only at the beginning of the 19th cent., when the belief grew up that the millennium was at hand. Zealous evangelists therefore sought to save the Jews from impending doom by establishing societies for their conversion. Of those which still survive the most prominent is the London Society for Promoting Christianity amongst the Jews. Founded in 1809, it originally concentrated on the capital, but later spread to the provinces and to the Near East. Boys' and girls' schools were opened in 1819 and

1821 respectively, and were followed by a network of medical missions (1891 and 1897) and a labor home (1894). The Society operates mainly through local "stations," usually manned by converts, and also grants subsidies to "promising" parishes. Its publications have included Hebrew and Yiddish translations of the New Testament (1817 and 1821) and a Hebrew version of the Anglican prayerbook (1836). Since 1841, its patron has been the Archbishop of Canterbury. The results of its work have been poor, only 2,150 baptisms being recorded between 1809 and 1910, and this despite the fact that between 1863 and 1894 the Society was said to have been paying sums between £600 and £3,000 for a conversion.

Scarcely less important is the British Society for the Propagation of the Gospel, founded in 1842, while missions to the Jews are also maintained by the Presbyterian Churches of England (1870), Scotland (1841) and Ireland (1841). Among more local organizations, operating in the metropolis, mention may be made of the London City Mission (1874) and the Barbican Mission to the Jews (1878). The latter has been particularly active among the immigrant population of the East End of London; it was partly to combat its efforts that the Jewish Free Reading Room was established almost opposite.

Another branch of missionary endeavor is represented by the Hebrew Christian movement which seeks to provide a medium whereby converted Jews may yet retain something of their traditional heritage. A Hebrew Christian Prayer Union and Alliance, claiming 650 members, was established in 1882. It was later succeeded by a Hebrew Christian Union which concentrated upon bringing Christianity into Jewish movements, especially Zionism. The leading spirit in the Hebrew Christian movement in 1942 was the Reverend Paul Levertoff, a distinguished rabbinical scholar and himself a convert. The Hebrew Christians meet regularly at a church in Hart Street, London, and celebrate Mass in Hebrew, the officiant wearing a Tallith.

A Pan-Anglican Conference of Missions to the Jews was held under Church auspices in 1897 and resolved that "a more prominent position be assigned to the evangelization of the Jews in the intercessions and almsgiving of the Church." A Committee of the Convocation of Canterbury later reported (1903) that missionary work of this type would be more effectively prosecuted through individual parishes, and in 1911 the London Society for Promoting Christianity among the Jews allocated special grants to East London pastors for this purpose.   THEODOR H. GASTER.

Lit.: Gidney, W. T., *Missions to Jews* (11th ed., 1914).

MISSISSIPPI, one of the southern states of the United States, with a population of 2,183,796 (census of 1940), including about 4,600 Jews. Before becoming part of the United States, the land that is now the state of Mississippi was under French (1699-1763), English (1763-81), and Spanish (1781-98) rule. There probably were Jews in the territory under all three governments. In 1724, Jean Baptiste le Moyne, Sieur de Bienville, the founder of New Orleans and governor of Louisiana (which included what is now Mississippi), as the first provision of his laws known as the "Black Code," ordered all Jews expelled from the colony. The English, when the territory of British West Florida included the southern half of the present state, issued an order merely forbidding Jews to vote. In 1789 Samuel S. Forman, who left a record of his journey down the Mississippi, wrote "in the village of Natchez resided Monsier (Monsieur) and Madam Masantee (Monsanto in the Spanish records of Natchez)—Spanish Jews, I think—who were the most kind and hospitable of people."

Three years after it became a state (1817), there were probably not more than one hundred Jews in Mississippi. The first Jews to settle there came north from New Orleans, south from Cincinnati and Louisville, or west from Montgomery, Alabama. Most of the settlers in the 1850's were immigrants from Germany. They made their living peddling or as owners of small stores. By 1861 Jews had settled in most of the cities of the state, and in a number, including Natchez, Vicksburg, Port Gibson, Columbus, Jackson, and Woodville, they had established congregations.

When the Civil War broke out, many Jews, although recent immigrants or from the North, enlisted with their neighbors in the Confederate armies. The number of Jewish Confederate soldiers from Mississippi can never be ascertained now; Simon Wolf recorded the names of more than 150 but other Jews are known to have served, and others were certainly never known as Jews. Most distinguished of the Jewish soldiers from Mississippi were Major Isaac Scherck, Major Charles H. Jonas (one of five brothers in the war, three of whom, including Charles H. Jonas, were in Barksdale's Mississippi Regiment), and Max Frauenthal, a private, whose bravery became proverbial.

In the latter part of the 19th and in the beginning of the 20th centuries a number of the migrants to the United States from Eastern Europe settled in Mississippi, particularly in the cities and towns between the Mississippi and Yazoo rivers in what is known as the Delta section. Here many became not only merchants and professional men but owners of farms and plantations. About fifty communities of Mississippi had ten Jews or more in 1942.

There were eighteen Jewish congregations in the state in 1942, with a membership approximating 3,000; fifteen of the congregations owned their places of worship. In several cases, as instances of the vitality of Judaism in Mississippi, a synagogue serves, and is supported by, the surrounding Jewish communities as well as its own. In Cleveland (population 4,189, census of 1940) with a Jewish community of about 50, Congregation Adath Israel (Reform, organized in 1923, temple built in 1927) had in 1940 seventy contributing families, drawn, for the most part, from the neighboring towns and villages, including Benoit, Boyle, Buelah, Drew, Merigold, Pace, Rosedale, Ruleville, Shaw and Sunflower. The first resident rabbi was Jacob Halevi, who served from 1928 to 1931; Newton J. Friedman was rabbi from 1939 to 1941; in 1942 the rabbi was Louis A. Josephson. And in Indianola (population 3,604 in 1940) with a Jewish community of about 50, Congregation Beth El, organized in 1940 by Newton Jerome Friedman, rabbi of Adath Israel of Cleveland, had that year a membership of 40 families, resident not only in the place itself but in the neighboring towns and villages, including Belzoni, Inverness, Isola and Moorhead.

Greenville (population 20,892 in 1940) had the largest Jewish community of Mississippi, numbering about 450. It is the state's fifth largest city. There were a number of Jewish families there in 1869. Until 1879, Charles Rawitzer was the rabbi of a small congregation, known as B'nai Israel. This was reorganized in 1880 as the Hebrew Union Congregation (Reform). A church, remodeled in 1884, served as its synagogue until 1900, when a new building was erected on the site. This was twice damaged by Mississippi floods (1927 and 1939). Joseph Bogen served as rabbi from 1881 until 1901; Abram Brill from 1901 until 1910; Harry Abram Merfeld from 1915 until 1919; the congregation had 130 contributing members in 1942, and Samuel A. Rabinowitz was rabbi. The Hebrew Union Congregation owns a cemetery.

Clarksdale (population 12,168, census of 1940) had a Jewish community of more than 400, the second largest in the state. Congregation Beth Israel was organized in 1896. The first synagogue was built in 1910; in 1942 it was used as a B'nai Brith Home. A new synagogue was built and dedicated in 1929. Orthodox Conservative, and Reform services are now conducted in the synagogue. M. Lupchansky was the rabbi from 1907 to 1912; A. H. Freyman from 1912 to 1932. Jerome Gerson Tolochko was the first resident rabbi (1932-40). Benjamin Kelson was the rabbi in 1942. Congregation Kahelas Jakef was organized about 1905 and went out of existence about 1915, most of its members joining Beth Israel.

Beth Israel of Clarksdale had a membership (1942) of only fourteen families but its Sunday school enrollment was almost 150. As part of the system of instruction, the Mississippi Institute of Jewish and Cognate Studies was chartered in 1938; its purpose, among others, the training of Sunday school teachers. The institute is authorized to confer the degree of Bachelor of Hebrew History and Literature, and the faculty includes non-Jewish clergymen who teach other than the Jewish religion.

Vicksburg had a Hebrew congregation as early as 1841. Congregation Anshe Chesed (Reform) was then organized. Its temple was built in 1868 and, in that year, Bernard Harold Gotthelf became the first resident rabbi. The original temple was remodeled in 1893. For thirty-three years, Sol L. Kory was the rabbi until his death in 1937. Stanley Rosenbaum Brav succeeded him. The congregation owns its own cemetery. There were almost four hundred Jews in Vicksburg (population 24,460 in 1940), of whom 118 were contributing members of the congregation. An Orthodox congregation, Ahavas Achim, was organized in 1900 but went out of existence about 1906. In 1937 the Jewish Welfare Federation was organized. Among the distinguished Jews of Vicksburg, Henry Mayer was treasurer of the city in 1884. Herman Bien (1831-95), rabbi and writer, spent the last ten years of his life in Vicksburg.

Meridian (population 35,481 in 1940), the second largest city of the state, had about 350 Jews. Congregation Beth Israel was organized in 1868. For a long time, the congregation worshipped above a grocery store. In 1906, a synagogue was built and dedicated. The first rabbi, Dave Bergman, began his service soon after the congregation was organized and continued until 1874. In that year, the congregation adopted the Reform service of the Union of American Hebrew Congregations. Wolff Willner was rabbi from 1895 until 1905; Max Raisin from 1905 to 1913; Abram Brill from 1913 until 1920. William Ackerman, rabbi in 1942, began his service in 1924. The congregation had 108 contributing members in 1939. Congregation Ohel Jacob was organized in 1880. The first rabbi was Samuel Goldstein. The rabbi was Hirsch Zissman in 1942. Both the Orthodox (Sephardic) and the Reform ritual are used. Beth Israel and Ohel Jacob each has its own cemetery. In 1906 the Meridian Jewish Orphans' Home and Benevolent Association was organized.

Of the distinguished Jews of Meridian, Nahum Enoch Katz was consulting chemist for the Meridian water department from 1933 on; Gabriel Jacobson, who had been a first lieutenant of the Mississippi Volunteer Infantry in the Spanish American War, was a referee in bankruptcy from 1910 to 1912, president of the Mississippi Bar Association in 1921, and a member of the Mississippi Board of Law Examiners.

Greenwood (population 14,767 in 1940) had a Jewish community of about 300. Congregation Ahavath Rayim (Orthodox) was organized in 1893. Dave Schapperstein, who served from 1914 to 1923, was the first resident rabbi. The synagogue was built in 1922, and Philip Danziger served as rabbi in 1942. In 1940, there were thirty-five members. Congregation Beth Israel (Reform) was organized in 1897. The congregation bought a church building for a synagogue in 1902. It was destroyed by fire in 1914 and the temple used in 1942 was dedicated in 1918. Samuel A. Rabinowitz of the Hebrew Union Temple in Greenville conducted services in 1942. There were twenty-three members in 1940.

Jackson (population 62,107, census of 1940, of whom 250 are Jews), is the largest city of the state. Jews are supposed to have bought a cemetery as early as 1854. Congregation Beth Israel (Reform) was organized in 1861. Its first synagogue, a wooden building, was burned by the Federal troops in 1863 at the capture of the city. A new synagogue of brick and stone was built and dedicated in 1874. When it was sold in 1940, it was the oldest building used for religious purposes in Jackson. In 1940, the congregation erected the present synagogue. Meyer Lovitt, rabbi of Beth Israel in 1942, began his service in 1929. In 1939, the congregation had seventy-two members. The Jewish Community Fund was organized in 1935.

Gladys Ascher King of Jackson was a member of the State Board of Administration (in charge of eleven eleemosynary institutions) from 1934 to 1938; from 1931 on, she was treasurer of the State and Hinds County Maternity Centers. She was also president of the Mississippi Federation of Temple Sisterhoods (1932-34). Lehman Engel, conductor and composer, was born in Jackson (1910).

Hattiesburg (population 21,026 in 1940) had a Jewish community of about 215. One of the first Jews to settle there was Maurice Dreyfus of Brookhaven who, in 1901, came to run a saw and planing mill. Congregation B'nai Israel was organized in 1915. Its synagogue was built in 1920; some of the material came from the hut of the Jewish Welfare Board at Camp Shelby. Although the congregation joined the Union of American

Hebrew Congregations (Reform) in 1934, both Reform and Orthodox services are held. Arthur Brodey (Reform), whose ministry began in 1935, was rabbi in 1942. The Orthodox services are conducted by a layman. The congregation bought a cemetery in 1935. B'nai Israel had a membership of 36 families (140 persons) in 1940. In 1937, the Jewish Welfare Fund was organized.

Natchez, the oldest Jewish community in the state, had (1942) about 125 Jews out of a population of 15,296 (1940 census). Jewish services were held in Natchez about the beginning of the 19th cent., although Jews had settled there before that. These services were Orthodox, held in homes, in a loft over a store and, by 1880, in an engine-house of the fire department. About 1910, these were discontinued. There is a tradition of an early Orthodox cemetery.

Congregation B'nai Israel (Reform) of Natchez was organized in 1840. A cemetery, a narrow walled-in strip of the city cemetery, was bought by the congregation the same year. A temple was built in 1867 (dedicated 1872). It was destroyed by fire in 1904 and the synagogue still in use, dedicated in 1905, was built on the same site. Meyer H. Marx was rabbi in 1942. In 1939, B'nai Israel had fifty-four contributing members from Natchez and about thirty-five from the near-by towns of Lorman, Bude, Fayette, and Ferriday (La.).

The Jewish Appeal of Natchez, which also serves the surrounding communities in Mississippi and Louisiana, was organized in 1938. Isaac Lowenburg was mayor of Natchez from 1882 to 1886. Samuel Ullman was a member of the city council for more than twenty-five years (1861-88).

Canton (population 6,011, census of 1940, including about eighty-five Jews), organized its Congregation B'nai Israel in 1877 and built its synagogue the same year. In 1878, the yellow fever epidemic caused a suspension of the services. The first resident rabbi was Joseph Sophor (1879-80). In 1942 Max Lewinthal was rabbi. The congregation is Reform and had 35 members in 1939. The Jewish community has its own cemetery (purchased in 1870).

Laurel (population 20,598, census of 1940) has a Jewish community of about sixty-five. Congregation Kenneseth Israel was organized in 1906. Its temple was completed in 1932. Services were conducted (1942) by Arthur Brodey, rabbi of B'nai Israel in Hattiesburg. In 1940, the congregation, which had been a member of the Union of Orthodox Hebrew Congregations of America, joined the Union of American Hebrew Congregations (Reform).

Columbus (population 13,645, census of 1940) has a community of about sixty Jews. German and French (Alsatian) Jews settled in Columbus as early as 1836. Congregation B'nai Israel (Reform) was organized in 1845. The congregation purchased a cemetery in 1850. The first resident rabbi was Joseph Herz, who served from 1881 until his death in 1909. While he was still rabbi, a building that had served as a church was bought and remodeled for a synagogue (1908). The rabbi in 1942 was Bernard Adler.

Lexington (population 2,930, census of 1940) also has about sixty Jews. Congregation Beth-El (Reform) of Lexington was organized in 1904. Its temple was built in 1905. The first rabbi was Abram Brill of the Hebrew

Union Congregation in Greenville who conducted services from 1905 until 1910; Stanley R. Brav, rabbi of Congregation Anshe Chesed of Vicksburg, was in charge in 1942. In 1940, Congregation Beth-El had about thirty members.

Brookhaven (population 6,232, census of 1940) has a Jewish community of about fifty. Jews had settled in Brookhaven by 1852. In 1861 they bought land for a cemetery. Congregation B'nai Sholom (Reform) was organized in 1894; its temple was dedicated in 1896. Meyer H. Marx, rabbi of B'nai Israel of Natchez, conducts services twice a month (1942). B'nai Sholom had twenty-six members in 1940.

Port Gibson (population 2,748, census of 1940), like Brookhaven, has a Jewish community of about fifty. Among the early Jewish settlers in Mississippi, some had settled at Grand Gulf, where they bought a cemetery, but, when the encroaching waters of the Mississippi led to the abandonment of that town, the Jews, among others, moved to Port Gibson. Here, in 1859, Congregation Gemiluth Chassed (Reform since 1874) was organized, and in 1871 the congregation purchased a cemetery. The synagogue was built in 1892. The first resident rabbi was Nathan Michnik. Gemiluth Chassed had eleven contributing members in 1939. In 1942 services were conducted by laymen. Simon Unger was mayor of Port Gibson from 1891 to 1898.

One of the earliest settlements of Jews in Mississippi was at Woodville (population 1,433, census of 1940) in the southwest corner of the state. In 1849 two peddlers, Jacob Cohen and Jacob Schwarz, bought some land in Woodville for fifty dollars to bury a fellow peddler, Henry Burgance, who had died there. The cemetery is still in use. Congregation Beth Israel was organized in 1878, as an outgrowth of the Woodville Hebrew Educational Association (established 1876). The services were at first Orthodox but, in time, became Reform. The synagogue, built soon after the organization of the congregation, was destroyed by fire in 1896 and the corner-stone for a new synagogue was laid the same year at the same site. Henry Cohen was rabbi from 1885 to 1888. The congregation, because of deaths and removals, went out of existence about 1910. The synagogue was sold and moved to Main Street where, until it was destroyed by fire, it was first a school and then a theatre. Woodville had only a few Jews in 1942.

About 1870 there was a Jewish community in Summit (population 1,254, census of 1940); a congregation, Ohaveh Scholem, was organized and a synagogue built. In the 1890's about twenty families attended services but when, in 1924, a tornado destroyed the building the congregation disintegrated. Other Jewish congregations, at Clinton (1852), at Starkville (B'nai Israel, organized 1906), and at West Point (Congregation Emanuel, organized 1905), have also been recorded. Summit had very few Jews in 1942; there were probably none at Clinton; Starkville had about 35; West Point about 15.

B'nai Brith had, in 1942, thirteen lodges in Mississippi and more than six hundred members. The first lodge was organized at Vicksburg in 1867; others are in Natchez (1870), Columbus (1871), Greenville (1871), Jackson (1873), Meridian (1877), Greenwood (1894), Hattiesburg (1908), Laurel (1910), Lexington (1926), Clarksdale (1927), Cleveland (1928), and Tupelo

(1938). The last draws its membership not only from Tupelo but from more than ten other towns in the neighborhood. The lodges at Canton (1868) and Brookhaven (1898) have been inactive for some time. Hadassah, the women's Zionist organization of America, has three chapters in Mississippi, all organized in 1939; these are at Clarksdale, Hattiesburg, and Jackson.

Among distinguished Jews of Mississippi, Moses Emanuel was a member of the state senate in 1846; and other Jewish members of the state legislature include: Leopold Marks (1877-85); Morris Levy (1882-86); Israel N. Moses (1906-10); Isaac Friedman (1912-14); and Barney Semmelman of Clay County (1917-21). Jacob Cohen was mayor of Shaw from 1892 to 1897. John Champenois, one of the first Jews to settle in Clarke County in the 1890's, became a member of the board of supervisors. Isidore Loeb was treasurer of the town of Hazlehurst, Copiah County, in the 1880's. Henry Loeb was town clerk of Hazlehurst from 1887 to 1919; Paul Kemp alderman in 1940; and Carroll Kemp attorney for Hazlehurst in 1940. Morris Cohn, who settled in Belzoni, Humphreys County, in 1880, became an alderman. N. Pickard was the first circuit and chancery clerk in Sharkey County (1876); C. Blum was treasurer of the county in 1898 and S. Dover was county treasurer in 1900. Dave Wolerstein, who died in 1936, was secretary of commerce of Yazoo City, Yazoo County.

Kahnville, in Amite County, was named for Louis Kahn, a merchant, but by 1884 there was no population listed for it, although still a post office, and it does not appear in subsequent census reports.

Rabbi Newton J. Friedman, of Temple Adath Israel, in Cleveland (1939-41), organized a counselorship of the B'nai B'rith Hillel Foundation at the University of Mississippi.

CHARLES REZNIKOFF.

Lit.: Inventory of the Church and Synagogue Archives of Mississippi: Jewish Congregations and Organizations (1940, The Mississippi Historical Records Survey Project, Division of Professional and Service Projects, Work Projects Administration); Cohen, Henry, "A Modern Maccabean," *Publications of the American Jewish Historical Society*, No. 6, pp. 31-37; Wolf, Simon, "The American Jew as Soldier and Patriot," *Publications of the American Jewish Historical Society*, No. 3, pp. 24, 26, 38; idem, *The American Jew as Patriot, Soldier, and Citizen* (1895) pp. 214-220.

MISSOURI, one of the central states of the United States, with a Jewish population of over 87,600 in a total population of 3,784,664 (1940). As much as 75 per cent of the Jewish population lived in the two principal cities of St. Louis and Kansas City; the remainder, distributed in virtually all the other urban centers and the rural areas, comprised the communities of St. Joseph, with over 3,000 Jewish residents in a total of 80,835; University City, with about 3,000 in a total of 25,809; Joplin, with about 300 in 33,454; Springfield, with about 260 in 57,257; Sedalia, with 249 in 20,806; Columbia, with 123 in 14,967; Maplewood, with 117 in 12,657; Jefferson City, with about 100 in 21,596; Hannibal, with about 100 in 21,596. The increase graph for the number of the state's Jewish population since 1900 shows an average gain per annum in excess of the general population's annual increase percentage; responsible for this ratio was the accelerated pace of the Jewish mass migrations from Eastern Europe.

Authentic information regarding the pioneer Jewish settlers dates as far back as 1807 to 1808, when the Philipson brothers—John, Jacob and Simon—arrived from Philadelphia and soon became prominent merchants at St. Louis. Wolf Bloch, a native of Schwihau, Bohemia, is shown by family records to have established himself in the little frontier town of St. Louis before 1816. At Weston, near Kansas City, there lived in 1846 the families of David Bowman, Isaac Goldstein, Jacob Mayer and Abraham Wise. The Philipson-Valle house, one of the landmarks of the oldest Missouri town, Sainte Genevieve, is thought to have been built by Jacob Philipson and used for his home during 1811 to 1814, when he is known to have resided at Sainte Genevieve.

In 1837 the United Hebrew Congregation of St. Louis was formed. Like this earliest congregation, a second one, B'nai El, founded in St. Louis in 1840 and reorganized in 1852, was still active in 1942. The United Hebrew Benevolent Society, instituted in 1842 at St. Louis, was legally incorporated in 1847. The first Hebrah Kaddisha (burial society) was also in St. Louis; its cemetery, on Pratt Avenue, purchased in 1844, was used until 1856. The St. Louis Bikkur Holim, a volunteer visiting nurse society, in existence before 1837, visited and took care of the ill, whether needy or well-to-do, its membership, whenever necessary, dividing into relays, one individual or squad, in turn, replacing another in the sick-room all through the day and night.

In St. Joseph the Adath Joseph congregation was organized in 1857 with seven members. The Kansas City Jewish community of the same era had become accustomed in some measure to depend on Leavenworth, Kan., to furnish them the ministrations of organized religion. All congregations until the formation of Shaarai Emeth at St. Louis in 1866 were at first Orthodox in ritual, although most of the members were lax in the observance of the other Orthodox Jewish practices. Pioneer congregations, in addition to those already enumerated here, include the Kansas City B'nai Jehudah, organized in April, 1870; the Joplin United Hebrew Congregation, organized in 1891; the Sedalia Temple Beth El, reorganized in the summer of 1931; the Springfield Temple Israel, organized in 1892.

In the eleven larger communities of the state there were, in 1942, about sixty-five synagogues. The rabbis in charge of these in the principal smaller communities included: at Joplin, Joseph Leiser, Garry J. August, Abraham I. Shinedling, Isaac L. Rypins, and the incumbent in 1942, Phineas Smoller; at Sedalia, Newton J. Friedman, Samuel H. Baron, Nathan E. Barasch, and the 1942 incumbent, Harry S. May; at Springfield, the incumbent in 1942, Karl Richter. For the Reform synagogues Rabbis Samuel Sale, Leon Harrison and Harry H. Mayer acted in the capacity of state supervisors under appointment by the Union of American Hebrew congregations, but the office of state supervising rabbi, nationally coordinated, was after a number of years allowed to lapse in Missouri as in all other sections of the United States. Supplementary Sunday services with weekly sermons by the rabbi were held by Temple Israel, St. Louis, regularly for forty-one years and by Congregation B'nai Jehudah, Kansas City, regularly for sixteen years.

There were in 1942 two Jewish hospitals, two country

clubs, two homes for aged and infirm, two Young Men's and Women's Hebrew Associations (now usually known as Jewish Community Centers), one Yeshiva (Kansas City), one Jewish Students Council (Columbia), one American Legion Post, two federations of welfare funds, two foster home societies for the care of indigent children, ten B'nai B'rith lodges, ninety or more Zionist societies of varied type, and numerous other societies for charity, education or recreation. The state association of B'nai B'rith lodges held its twenty-first annual convention on October 25 to 26, 1941, in St. Louis. State or regional associations were likewise established by the Temple brotherhoods, the Temple sisterhoods, the B'nai B'rith women's auxiliaries, the Zionist societies and the Hadassah. The Jewish Students' Foundation, formed in 1929 by Rabbi Samuel S. Mayerberg, maintained a professorship at the Bible school connected with the University of Missouri at Columbia; Dr. Isadore Keyfetz, the Foundation's appointee to this chair, served continuously from its beginning.

The foremost Jewish leaders before 1900 were Isidor Busch and Jacob Furth. Contemporary with them, or nearly so, were A. J. Latz, J. B. Greensfelder, B. A. Feineman, Benjamin Altheimer, Marcus Bernheimer, Alfred Benjamin, Leon Bloch, Samuel Bowman, Moses Fraley, Aaron Fuller, J. D. Goldman, Samuel Hasenbush, Elias Michaels, Jonathan Rice, Moses Sale, Isaac Schwab, Charles A. Stix, Aaron Waldheim, Jacob J. Wertheimer.

During 1910-1912 Jacob A. Harzfeld was president of the Missouri Public Service Commission. Max Zach was conductor of the St. Louis Symphony orchestra. Abe Rosenthal was, in 1942, music director of the Sedalia Little Symphony Orchestra. Henry Boernstein and Joseph Pulitzer were distinguished newspaper publishers. Edward Platt and Walter H. Negbaur were, in 1942, the rationing administrators respectively for St. Louis and for Kansas City and Jackson County. Louis H. Ehrlich in that year was president of the American Red Cross Society for the Kansas City area. Herman Zuzak was acting president of the Red Cross for Boonville and Cooper County.

Missouri had a practical farmer of some note in the person of Samuel Kahn. Living on the 1,600-acre grain and livestock farm developed by him on Big Lake, four miles west of Bigelow in Holt County, where he arrived in 1880, a sturdy, young Russian immigrant untrained in American agricultural methods, he soon added to his other crops the cultivation and marketing of onions of such excellent quality, on a scale so large and for so many years, that he came to be affectionately known far and wide in the northern midwest as the onion king. His two sons remained on the farm after his death, and ran it successfully, raising corn, alfalfa, oats and wheat, hogs, cattle, horses and mules, until they sold the farm ten years later.

The acting president of the University of Missouri during 1923 was Isidor Loeb. The executive director of the Near East Relief of the Western Missouri District in 1921 was Rabbi Harry H. Mayer. I. E. Bernheimer was on the state utility commission; Rabbi S. H. Sonneschein and Rabbi Louis Bernstein were on the state board of charities. Benjamin Altheimer originated and promoted Bundle Day and the patriotic and re-

ligious observance of Flag Day as now nationally celebrated by the American public.

Authors who gained national recognition for the books they wrote include Garry J. August, novel; Henry Berkowitz, Judaism and the social order; A. B. Frey, textbook on law; Leslie B. Hohman, psychiatry and child training; Fannie Hurst, "best seller" novels; Joseph Krauskopf, Jewish history and Jewish apologetics; Oscar Leonard, novel (translation); Hanau W. Loeb, surgery; Isidor Loeb, political science; Virgil Loeb, dentistry; Harry H. Mayer, Bible poetry; Jane Rothschild Mayer, novel; David Morantz, Talmudic tales; Gabe Neuburger, Ozark dialect narrative free verse; Abraham Sachar, Jewish history; Herbert Bayard Swope, current political and diplomatic affairs; Frank William Taussig, tariff and political economy; Martha Wolfenstein, fiction.

Music for the synagogue was composed by Moyssaye Boguslawski, Abraham I. Eppstein, Arthur Lieber, Rabbi Harry H. Mayer and Arnold Volpe.

Edward David Taussig, of Jewish parentage but brought up in the Unitarian faith, was made a lieutenant-commander in the United States Navy in 1892; his son, Joseph K. Taussig, was in 1942 a rear-admiral in the United States Navy.

Max Judd was United States consul general at Vienna, Austria. Jacob A. Harzfeld was an assistant military attaché to Russia and military observer with the allied forces, also American member of the military commission to exchange prisoners with the Soviet Republic's commission (1918-19).

Louis Sulzbacher was a justice of the Porto Rico Supreme Court (1900-4), also judge of the United States District Court, Indiana Territory (1904-9). Cusil Lechtman was commander-in-chief of the Missouri national guard. Nathan Frank was a United States Congressman from St. Louis for the term of 1889-1891. Jerome Joffee was a state senator (1933-36); Lee D. Seelig was a state senator (1936-39).

There were more than seven circuit judges, including Robert L. Aronson, Max G. Baron, Irving Barth, Abraham B. Frey, Moses Hartman, Moses Sale and Ben Terte; more than nine members of the state assembly, including Max Asotsky, Louis Becker, Jules Brinkman, David Hess, Jerome Joffee, Alfred Metzger, David Porlers, Joseph Pulitzer and Julius Rakovsky; five or more municipal judges or justices, including Harry Raskin, St. Louis, Alex Sapir, Kansas City, Ben Spitz, Kansas City. Of aldermen and councilmen, best known have been: at Sedalia, Henry Laupheimer, Lawrence Laupheimer; at Kansas City, B. A. Feineman, Charles Neil, Isaac Taylor, Isaac Reicher, Arthur Fels, George Goldman; at St. Louis, Louis P. Aloe, Albert Arnstein, Moses Fralay; at Liberty, Manheim Goldman.

Moses Alexander, governor of Idaho for two terms (1915-19), was mayor of Chillicothe, Mo., in 1887; Louis P. Aloe was acting mayor of St. Louis during the first World War; George Goldman was acting mayor of Kansas City (1925); Manheim Goldman was mayor of Liberty (1894-95); Isaac Hirsch was mayor of Chillicothe (1903); J. Lowenheim was mayor of Bridgeton (1931); Otto Stein was mayor of Trenton (1923). Reuben S. Crohn was public administrator of Jackson County. R. Robert Cohn was, in 1942, chairman of the Missouri Workman's Compensation Commission. Alexander J. Sachs was county surveyor and highway engineer of Jackson County.

Jacob Billikopf and Oscar Leonard were presidents of the Missouri State Conference of Charities. Isidor Loeb served as president of the State Historical Society of Missouri. Nathan Frank was publisher of the old *St. Louis Star.*

The governor of Missouri in 1871 to 1873, B. Gratz Brown, was the namesake of Benjamin, brother of the famous Rebecca Gratz.

There were, in 1942, three newspapers, appearing weekly and catering primarily to the local clientele: the *Modern View,* St. Louis, founded in 1900; the *Jewish Record* (Yiddish and English), St. Louis, founded in 1913; the Kansas City *Jewish Chronicle,* founded in 1920.

See also: KANSAS CITY; ST. JOSEPH; ST. LOUIS.

HARRY H. MAYER.

Lit.: Bowman, Samuel, *Tribute to Isidor Busch* (pamphlet, 1920); Isserman, Ferdinand M., and Keyfitz, Isadore, *Jewish Students at the University of Missouri and at Stephens College* (pamphlet, 1941); Jenkins, Burris A., Torrent (1932) 262-63; *Missouri, A Guide to the "Show-Me" State,* compiled by Workers of the Writers' Program under the federal Work Projects Administration, American Guide Series (1941) 125, 278.

MISTAKE, see ERROR.

MITHAH MESHUNNAH, see PHRASES, POPULAR.

MITTWOCH, EUGEN, orientalist, b. Schrimm, Germany, 1876. A descendant of an old Jewish family, many of whose members possessed a profound knowledge of Bible and Talmud, he studied in Berlin at the rabbinical seminary and at the university, where he won his doctor's degree in 1905. In 1907 he accompanied Paul Nathan on his travels to the Orient.

Mittwoch became assistant professor at the University of Berlin in 1915, associate professor at the University of Greifswald in 1917, and returned to Berlin in 1919. When Eduard Sachau retired, Mittwoch was appointed (1928) director of the seminary for oriental languages at the University of Berlin. In 1935, he was dismissed by the Nazi government. In 1942 Mittwoch was living in London, where he worked with the British Library, assisting the Ministry of Information on Arabian and Persian problems.

Mittwoch's high repute in the world of scholarship had its foundation in his deep knowledge not only in the sphere of linguistics but also in the history of art, literature and religion. This enabled him to depict the richness of Arabic culture. His numerous works include: *Proelia Arabum paganorum* (1899); *Die arabischen Augenärzte nach den Quellen bearbeitet* (together with J. Hirschberg and J. Lippert; 1905); *Ibn Saad* (1905 and 1918); *Die literarische Tätigkeit Hamza al-Isbahanis* (1909); *Zur Entstehungsgeschichte des islamischen Gebets und Kultus* (1913); *Deutschland, die Türkei und der Heilige Krieg* (1915); *Die Verbreitung des Islam in Togo und Kamerun* (together with Diedrich Westermann; 1914); *Die traditionelle Aussprache des Äthiopischen* (1925); *Der deutsch-ethiopische Freundschafts- und Handelsvertrag* (1926); *Aus dem Jemen* (1926); *Untersuchungen über die Gise Pyramide und deren Inschriften* (together with Ludwig Borchardt and Ernst Sittig; 1926); *Literaturdenkmäler*

aus Ungarns Türkenzeit (1927). He was editor of the *Mitteilungen des Seminars für orientalische Sprache* and co-editor of the jubilee edition of the works of Moses Mendelssohn published by the Akademie Verlag in Berlin (6 vols., 1929-38).

Lit.: Elbogen, Ismar, "Eugen Mittwoch, zum 60. Geburtstag," *C.-V.-Zeitung; Allgemeine Zeitung des Judentums,* vol. 15, No. 49 (1936); Gottschalk, Walter, "Die Schriften Eugen Mittwochs," *Monatsschrift für Geschichte und Wissenschaft des Judentums,* vol. 81 (1937) 243-50.

MITZVAH (plural, Mitzvoth), a commandment, precept or charge, opposed to *'aberah,* transgression or sin. The term is derived from the Hebrew root *tzavah* ("to set up," "to mark," "to direct," "to join together," "to establish," "to strengthen," "to confirm"; cf. Gesenius and Fürst, under *tzavah* and *mitzvah*), and thus upholds the accepted traditional view of Judaism that the Mitzvoth form the true bond of union between God and Israel. This conception of the Mitzvoth permeates Jewish literature, both Biblical and rabbinic. In the former, God's fulfillment of the covenant is conditioned by Israel's performance of the Mitzvoth (*Lev.* 26:3-13); in the latter, adherence to the Mitzvoth is deemed to be identical with adherence to God, the source of life (*Midrash Num.* 17:7). Judah Halevi states this opinion without equivocation (*Kuzari* 2:46), notwithstanding the fact that he, like many other philosophers and exegetes who shared this opinion, labored zealously to interpret and to establish a basis in reason for all the Mitzvoth of the Torah.

According to the higher critics, Mitzvah came late into the Biblical writings. The Pentateuch draws no line between *mitzvah* ("commandment"), *hukkah* "statute"), *mishpat* ("ordinance"), *'eduth* ("testimony"). *mishmereth* ("observance"), and *torah* ("teaching"), although there is no doubt whatsoever that each of these terms represented a distinct category of precepts or injunctions in pre-Exilic Israel (*II Chron.* 19:10). Frequently they are grouped together or used interchangeably (*Gen.* 26:5; *Deut.* 5:28; 6:1; 7:11), and in due time *mitzvah* and *torah* become synonymous (*Deut.* 8:1; 11:8, 22), the entire Torah thereby emerging ultimately as one divinely ordained Mitzvah. In the Prophets, and particularly in the wisdom literature and the *Psalms,* Mitzvah designates the ethical and moral life in its totality (*Jer.* 7:23; *Mal.* 2:1; *Prov.* 4:4; 6:20, 23; 7:2; *Eccl.* 8:5; *Ps.* 119). Later, during the Talmudic period and the Middle Ages, this unique conception of Mitzvah as a divine principle of conduct and duty is raised to most picturesque and inspiring heights in the voluminous writings of these respective periods.

It is probable that the men who earned the title of Soferim (scribes), because they counted all the letters of the Torah (*Kid.* 30a), also counted the Mitzvoth which it contained. Simlai, a Palestinian Haggadist and controversialist of some renown, thus transmits a current tradition that "613 Mitzvoth were spoken to Moses, 365 negative precepts corresponding to the solar year and 248 positive precepts corresponding to the parts of the body" (*Mak.* 23b). Attempts were made also to group the Mitzvoth into specified units, lighter commandments, *mitzvoth kalloth,* and weightier commandments, *mitzvoth hamuroth,* with some of which all proselytes to Judaism had to be familiarized (*Yeb.*

47b). With but very rare exceptions, however, rabbinic literature does not define or identify these commandments. It seems that they were so designated because of the ease or difficulty with which they could be performed or the degree of personal sacrifice which they entailed (*Hul.* 142a; *A.Z.* 3a). It was therefore to be expected that laxity in their observance would become prevalent. This condition called forth the famous exhortation of the rabbis to be mindful of all the Mitzvoth, light and weighty, for no one knows the reward attached to them (*Aboth* 2:1).

With the development of the Halachah, the religious tradition of the Jews was separated into two main bodies or divisions of law, *mitzvoth de'oraitha,* the Biblical commandments, and *mitzvoth derabbanan,* the rabbinic commandments (*Pes.* 10a; *Suk.* 44a). In addition to the 613 Mitzvoth committed to Moses, which were designed for Israel alone, the Torah contained seven more precepts entrusted to the sons of Noah, *sheba mitzvoth bene Noah,* charging them (1) to erect courts of justice, (2) to abstain from idolatry, (3) to abstain from blasphemy, (4) to abstain from incest, (5) to abstain from murder, (6) to abstain from robbery, and (7) to abstain from eating flesh cut from living animals (*Tos. A.Z.* 8:4; *Sanh.* 56ab). Special consideration was given also to seven rabbinical precepts: (1) recitation of the Hallel liturgy on certain festivals, (2) reading the Esther scroll on Purim, (3) kindling the Hanukah candles, (4) kindling the Sabbath candles, (5) washing the hands before meals, (6) benedictions for all occasions of thanksgiving, and (7) the preparation of the Erub (*Sefer Hahinnuch*). These precepts were treated on the same level with all Biblical commandments. They were added to the 613 *Mitzvoth,* thereby bringing the total to 620, the numerical value of *kether* (crown), the Mitzvoth thus being represented as Israel's crown of glory.

Basing themselves on the tradition of Simlai (the binding authority of which has been disputed by Nahmanides), theologians during the Middle Ages set out to identify and enumerate the 613 *Mitzvoth* of the Torah. Simeon Kayyara (9th cent.) was the first to complete this task. His *Halachoth Gedoloth,* which reveals unmistakable traces of its dependence upon the *Sheeltoth* of Ahai Gaon, served as the model for many subsequent enumerators. However, not being able to discover 613 in the Pentateuch, he included many rabbinical precepts to round out this number, a procedure which later prompted Maimonides to write the *Sefer Hamitzvoth,* in which he lists the Biblical precepts according to fourteen fixed rules of enumeration. Kayyara was followed by the Azharists, who recorded their enumerations in special liturgical poems, the Azharoth. Saadia, Isaac Gikatilla, Solomon ibn Gabirol, Isaac of Barcelona (Albargeloni), Elijah Hazaken, Eliezer ben Nathan, Isaac Kimhi, Krespia Hanakdan, Elijah Hakohen Zelebi, Menahem Tamar, Menahem Egozi and Joshua Benveniste are among those Payetanim who composed such Azharoth for the synagogue service of Shabuoth, the festival historically associated with the giving of the Torah. The Azharoth were not always favorably received. Abraham ibn Ezra, Maimonides, the Tosafists and others criticized some of their authors for the chaotic and illogical manner in which they treated the Mitzvoth.

From this philosophical premise Maimonides proceeds to classify all the 613 Mitzvoth of the Torah (and, in the *Mishneh Torah,* of the entire Jewish tradition) into fourteen distinct categories.

Even in the *Sefer Hamitzvoth,* where the precepts of the Torah are grouped into positive and negative Mitzvoth, along the lines of the *Halachoth Gedoloth,* the above-mentioned categorical classification is implicitly followed. Although Nahmanides and others took issue with Maimonides about specific details or individual items of his work, and notwithstanding the fact that he was not always consistent, no subsequent writer added much of significance to his contribution in this field. The *Sefer Hahinnuch* by Aaron Halevi of Barcelona, the *Sefer Mitzvoth Gadol* by Moses of Coucy, and the *Sefer Mitzvoth Katon* by Isaac of Corbeil are the most important for additional study of this subject.

Jewish religious genius has imbued the concept of Mitzvah with characteristic uniqueness. It added spiritual flavor to the routine performance of religious ceremonies. Mitzvah is every "opportunity to fulfill the comprehensive duty of men to their fellows," and thus it describes an attitude of mind that attaches divine pleasure to every meritorious thought and act, to the whole boundless sphere of human relationships. God clothed every thing in this world with a Mitzvah for Israel (*Midrash Num.* 17:7). If the door of the Jewish home is not opened for the Mitzvoth it will be opened for the doctor (*Midrash Song of Songs* 6:17). Mitzvah denotes alms or charity (*Midrash Lev.* 34:4). To bury the dead is a Mitzvah (*Hor.* 13a). Obedience is a Mitzvah (*Hul.* 106a). To pray at sunrise is a Mitzvah (*Ber.* 29b). To bring about a reconciliation between men is a Mitzvah (*Sanh.* 6b). Keeping the body clean is a Mitzvah (*Midrash Lev.* 34:3). To hearken to the words of the wise is a Mitzvah (*Sanh.* 53b). To feed crippled servants is a Mitzvah (*Yer. B.K.* v, 4). To treat all comers with kindness is a Mitzvah (*Midrash Ps.* 52). Israel has submitted to martyrdom for the sake of the Mitzvoth (*Mechilta, Yithro*). It is therefore no wonder that even the emptiest of virtues among them yet abounds in Mitzvoth as the pomegranate abounds in seeds (*Midrash Song of Songs* 4:3).

The Mitzvoth were not given to Israel for the purpose of material gain (*R.H.* 28a), and the final reward for their performance is not of this world (*Kid.* 39b), but real happiness and true sanctification can be achieved only through them (*Sab.* 30b; *Sifre to Lev.* 20:7). Man should therefore not even look forward to any material reward in performing the Mitzvoth. The improvement of the moral character that results from such performance is in itself adequate reward, for one Mitzvah invariably brings another in its wake (*Aboth* 1:3; 4:2). And since the Mitzvoth were designed to perfect the moral character of man, one Mitzvah must not be performed at the cost of violating another (*Suk.* 30a). The performance of the Mitzvoth must be invested with absolute sincerity of heart and mind (*Ber.* 13a et seq.), for they are the visible manifestations of man's love for God, a love that must flow directly from both heart and mind (*Yoma* 86a). The Torah contains 248 positive precepts corresponding to the 248 parts of the human body; each part pleads with man to perform some Mitzvah with it. Again, the Torah contains 365 negative precepts corresponding to the number of the days of the year; each day pleads with man not to commit any transgression in it (*Tanhuma* to *Ki Thetze* 2). God was lavish with Israel and showered them with Mitzvoth even as one uncorks a flask and pours forth its contents without stint (*Tanhuma* to *Yithro* 3). Hence the religious life is no burden, for God so desired to confer merit upon Israel that He multiplied for their sake the Torah and the Mitzvoth (*Mak.* 23b). These are but a few concepts of Mitzvah, taken at random from the boundless sea of rabbinic lore.

Of supreme interest and importance is the conclusion of the tradition transmitted by Simlai to the effect that David comprehended the 613 Mitzvoth in eleven (*Ps.* 15), Isaiah comprehended them in six (*Isa.* 33:15), Micah comprehended them in three (*Micah* 6:8), Isaiah further comprehended them in two (*Isa.* 56:1), Amos comprehended them in one, "Seek ye Me, and live" (*Amos* 5:4), and, according to another teacher, Habakkuk also comprehended them in one, the summa summarum of prophetic religion: "The righteous shall live by his faith" (Hab. 2:4). Similarly, Bar Kappara, in seeking a comprehensive principle for the entire Torah, found one in the utterance of the Proverbialist (*Prov.* 3:6): "In all thy ways acknowledge Him, and He will direct thy paths" (*Ber.* 63a). In Jewish tradition, God-consciousness is the beginning and end of the Mitzvoth.

See also: COMMANDMENTS, THE TEN; DECALOGUE; LAW, JEWISH: CLASSIFICATION OF; LAWS, JEWISH: SOURCES AND DEVELOPMENT OF; NOAHIDE LAWS; PRECEPTS, THE 613; TORAH.   IRVING M. LEVEY.

Lit.: Schechter, Solomon, *Studies in Judaism* (1896); Montefiore, Claude G., *Hibbert Lectures* (1898); Kohler, Kaufmann, *Jewish Theology* (1918); Moore, George Foote, *Judaism in the First Centuries of the Christian Era* (3 vols., 1927-30); Weiss, I. H., *Dor Dor Vedoreshav* (1924); Greenstone, Julius H., *The Jewish Religion* (1925); Koller, Armin H., *Foundations of Jewish Ethics* (1929); Baeck, Leo, *Essence of Judaism* (1936); Cohen, Abraham, *Everyman's Talmud* (1932); Joseph, Morris, *Judaism as Creed and Life*, 5th ed. (1925); Bloch, M., "Les 613 lois," *Revue des études juives*, vol. 1, p. 197 et seq.; vol. 5, p. 25 et seq.; Rosin, D., *Ein Kompendium der jüdischen Gesetzeskunde* (1871); Creizenach, Michael, *Thariag* (1833); Jellinek, Adolf, *Konteres Thariag* (1878).

MITZVAH DANCE, see WEDDING AND WEDDING CUSTOMS.

MITZVOTH, see PRECEPTS, THE 613.

MIXED MARRIAGE. Mixed marriage between Jews and members of other religions, particularly Christians, is a manifestation of the emancipation and assimilation era. It first took place among Jews of the upper economic strata who actually achieved emancipation earlier than the others and thus had the chance to mingle socially with non-Jews in the same economic and cultural milieu. Salons in the homes of Jewish bankers in Berlin and Vienna offered the first common meeting-places for free-thinking Christians and Jews, and it was from this association that the first mixed marriages resulted.

Religion was the most powerful and the most important barrier between Jews and non-Jews. It had kept them apart for centuries. Emancipation, however, not only weakened Jewish religiosity; the whole basis of Jewish particularism and exclusiveness began to lose its force; ambition to assimilate and take root in the newer surroundings outside the ghetto assumed broader scope.

In the Americas and in Soviet Russia, mixed marriages are prevalent even in the lowest classes. Nevertheless, the dense Jewish populations of these countries and the inertia inherent in non-Jewish contacts have prevented mixed marriages from reaching the percentages they attained in countries where the Jewish population was smaller and comprised a larger proportion of upper bourgeois and intellectual groups.

Statistics are not available for mixed marriages in all countries where they were common. As for England, Ignaz Zollschan wrote: "During the 19th cent. numerous marriages took place between Jewish families who had been long settled in England and non-Jewish families of high social standing." The same might be said of France, with even more truth, because French Jewry was more assimilated than English Jewry.

Denmark, despite the fact that much of its Jewish population is of immigrant stock, provides the following astonishing figures. Between 1880 and 1905, in Copenhagen, there were 395 all-Jewish marriages and 272 mixed marriages, so that the proportion of mixed marriages to Jewish marriages was 68.9%. The chronological development is even more interesting. Between 1880 and 1889 there were ninety mixed marriages and 161 Jewish marriages. Between 1900 and 1905, however, there were eighty-one mixed marriages and eighty-seven all-Jewish marriages or almost an equal number.

These percentage figures cannot tell the whole story because, while there are two Jewish partners to a Jewish marriage, there is only one in a mixed marriage. Later statistics did not consider the number of marriages in their entirety, but kept records for men and women.

In Trieste, another small Jewish settlement, there were between 1869 and 1922 1,568 all-Jewish marriages and 721 mixed marriages, or half as many. Between 1923 and 1927 there were seventy-three all-Jewish marriages and seventy-nine mixed marriages—an excess of mixed marriages. In a Catholic community like Trieste, it is natural that seventy-three of the seventy-nine mixed marriages were with Catholic partners.

What is true of Copenhagen and Trieste is true also of most countries in which there are small Jewish settlements: Sweden, Norway and other countries. Reports from South America show that the situation is repeating itself there. The smaller the Jewish population, the less resistance there is against assimilation through mixed marriages. In the remote communities where there are only a handful of Jewish families, mixed marriages—even when they are not accompanied by conversion of the Jewish partner—mean that the children are taken away from the Jewish community because they usually have a Christian upbringing.

In a small Jewish community resistance is weak because Jews and Christians live in social amity and equality; boys and girls fall in love and marry. This was proved by the Sephardic settlements in South America.

The larger the Jewish settlement, the lower the percentage of mixed marriages, no matter what the degree of assimilation. But until 1933 mixed marriage was on the rise everywhere, except in the heavily-populated Jewish settlements in Eastern Europe, where it remained a rarity.

Germany. In Germany mixed marriages had the longest tradition, and were frequent even in the middle

TABLE 1. STATISTICS OF MIXED MARRIAGES IN GERMANY

Years	Number of Jewish Men Marrying	Number of Jewish Men Marrying Non-Jewish Women		Number of Jewish Women Marrying	Number of Jewish Women Marrying Non-Jewish Men		Number of Marriages With Both Parties Jewish
			Percent			Percent	
1901–1905*	4,299	381	8.8	4,241	323	7.6	3,918
1906–1910*	4,473	513	11.3	4,384	424	9.6	3,960
1911–1915*	3,690	692	18.9	3,469	471	13.6	2,998
1916–1920*	4,507	775	17.2	4,221	489	14.2	3,732
1921–1925*	5,487	1,129	20.6	5,008	650	13.0	4,358
1926–1930*	3,793	974	25.7	3,379	560	16.6	2,819
1931	3,384	900	26.6	2,989	505	16.9	2,484
1932	3,182	875	27.5	2,810	503	17.8	2,307
1933	3,368	1,194	35.5	2,673	499*	18.6	2,174
1934	3,079	557	18.1	2,757	235	8.5	2,522
1935	3,104	353	11.4	2,901	150	5.2	2,751
1936	2,723	58	2.1	2,697	32	1.2	2,665

* Yearly Average.

of the 19th cent. During the last quarter of the 19th cent. there were about one-fourth as many mixed marriages as all-Jewish marriages. Only in the 20th cent., when assimilation spread from the upper classes and the intellectual groups to the lower classes, did mixed marriages become a mass manifestation and assume serious proportions.

Table 1 presents a clear picture of the development of mixed marriages in Germany, and shows both its peak and its sudden end. The table is constructed precisely: men and women are considered separately. At the beginning of the 20th cent. only 8.8% of the Jewish men married non-Jewish women. But the percentage grew steadily; at the outbreak of the first World War it was 18.9%. During the war it fell somewhat but rose again sharply until, in 1930, more than a quarter of the Jewish men married non-Jewish women. As the Hitler catastrophe approached, the percentage rose still higher, evidently because many pairs hastened to legalize already existing relationships. In 1933, with Hitler ruling, more than one-third (35.5%) of the Jewish men married non-Jewish wives. This was the peak of the development. In 1934 the percentage fell by half: in the Hitlerian atmosphere it was hard to effect mixed

relationships. On September 15, 1935, a decree for the "protection of German blood and honor" made marriage to a Jew heavily punishable. Even in 1936, however, there were mixed marriages, but the women were Jewesses who had previously been converted to Christianity. Religiously, they were mixed marriages, but according to the Nazi racial theories, they were not. Nevertheless, only 2.1% of the Jewish men marrying that year took Christian wives of Jewish descent.

The history of mixed marriages between Jewish women and non-Jewish men was the same, except that the percentages were lower straight through. This is true everywhere. Jewish men always marry non-Jewish women in higher percentages than Jewish women marry non-Jewish men. The number of marriages in which both partners were Jews is given in the last column of the table, enabling further comparisons.

In the larger cities of Germany, where assimilation was more widespread, the percentage of mixed marriages was greater than in the provinces.

Table 2 shows the mixed marriage statistics in Berlin from 1921 to 1937. The figures are much higher than for Germany as a whole.

In Frankfort, where Jewish religious and communal

TABLE 2. STATISTICS OF MIXED MARRIAGES IN BERLIN

Years	Number of Jewish Men Marrying	Number of Jewish Men Marrying Non-Jewish Women		Number of Jewish Women Marrying	Number of Jewish Women Marrying Non-Jewish Men		Number of Marriages With Both Parties Jewish
			Percent			Percent	
1921–1925*	1,792	502	28.0	1,543	253	16.4	1,290
1926–1930*	1,377	449	32.6	1,174	246	21.0	928
1931	1,310	397	30.3	1,105	192	17.4	913
1932	1,243	420	33.8	1,035	212	20.5	823
1933	1,265	463	36.6	1,006	204	20.3	802
1934	1,281	256	20.0	1,140	115	10.1	1,025
1935	1,201	170	14.1	1,112	81	7.3	1,031
1936	1,075	27	2.5	1,066	18	1.7	1,048
1937	1,094	27	2.4	1,082	15	1.4	1,067

* Yearly Average.

TABLE 3. STATISTICS OF MIXED MARRIAGES IN HUNGARY

Years	Number of Jewish Men Marrying	Number of Jewish Men Marrying Non-Jewish Women		Number of Jewish Women Marrying	Number of Jewish Women Marrying Non-Jewish Men		Number of Marriages With Both Parties Jewish
			Percent			Percent	
1913–1917*	4,725	502	10.6	4,611	388	8.4	4,223
1918–1922*	5,440	614	11.3	5,311	485	9.1	4,826
1923–1927*	4,208	495	11.8	4,182	469	11.2	3,713
1928	4,240	530	12.5	4,197	487	11.6	3,710
1929	3,839	457	11.9	3,845	463	12.0	3,382
1930	3,960	531	13.4	3,948	519	13.1	3,429
1931	3,735	550	14.9	3,667	482	13.1	3,185
1932	3,584	512	14.3	3,576	504	14.1	3,072

* Yearly Average.

life was more intense, the figures were always lower than in Berlin. The statistics on Jewish men marrying non-Jewish women was:

Year	Per Cent
1910-14	13.7
1915-18	19.5
1919-22	13.1
1923-27	17.1
1928-29	20.9
1933	20.5
1934	10.5

In general, the percentage of Jewish men marrying non-Jewish women was half as large in Frankfort as in Berlin. The same was true of the Jewish women.

Among the 170 Jewish men (in Berlin) who married non-Jewish women in 1935, marriage occurred with various non-Jewish creeds in the following proportions:

Protestant Women	115	67.6%
Catholic Women	25	14.7%
Without Affiliation	30	17.7%

Two-thirds of the men married Protestant women and only one-seventh married Catholics. Those without affiliation were mostly baptized Jewish women. Among the 81 Berlin Jewish women who contracted mixed marriages in 1935, the division was as follows:

Protestant Men	48	59.3%
Catholic Men	10	12.3%
Without Affiliation	23	28.2%

The "without affiliation" percentage is higher among the Jewish women than among the Jewish men. Since "without affiliation" non-Jews are usually baptized Jews, Jewish women enter on mixed marriages even less frequently than the actual statistics show.

The percentage figures as to creeds cited for Berlin are generally typical for all of Germany.

It cannot be said that all children of mixed marriages are lost to the Jewish people. In Prussia, in one given year, 25.8% of the children born to a Jewish father and non-Jewish mother were given a Jewish up-bringing. In marriages where the mother was Jewish, in the same given year, only 23.7% of the children were brought up as Jews. For Germany as a whole it may be said that 20 to 25% of the children of mixed marriages were brought up as Jews; 60 to 65% were brought up as Christians and the rest were reared without any confession.

Hungary. The differences between the big cities and the provinces can be seen by comparing the statistics for all of Hungary (Table 3) with those of Budapest (Table 4).

By the end of the 19th cent. the percentage of mixed marriages in Budapest was three times as great as in the whole of Hungary, one and a half times as great among the men and also among the women. The percentage for the provinces alone is obviously smaller than for all of Hungary, since the statistics for Budapest are included in the general figure. In the Hungarian provinces, a high degree of Orthodoxy prevails.

TABLE 4. STATISTICS OF MIXED MARRIAGES IN BUDAPEST

Years	Number of Jewish Men Marrying	Number of Jewish Men Marrying Non-Jewish Women		Number of Jewish Women Marrying	Number of Jewish Women Marrying Non-Jewish Men		Number of Marriages With Both Parties Jewish
			Percent			Percent	
1921–1925*	2,265	359	15.8	2,221	315	14.2	1,906
1926–1930*	2,047	356	17.4	2,008	317	15.7	1,691
1931	2,016	393	19.5	1,943	320	16.4	1,623
1932	1,928	378	19.6	1,888	338	17.9	1,550
1933	2,039	379	18.6	1,987	327	16.5	1,660
1934	2,192	438	20.0	2,085	331	15.8	1,754
1935	2,219	419	18.9	2,152	352	16.3	1,800
1936	2,205	456	20.7	2,070	321	15.5	1,749

* Yearly Average.

TABLE 5. STATISTICS OF MIXED MARRIAGES IN AMSTERDAM

Years	Number of Jewish Men Marrying	Number of Jewish Men Marrying Non-Jewish Women		Number of Jewish Women Marrying	Number of Jewish Women Marrying Non-Jewish Men		Number of Marriages With Both Parties Jewish
			Percent			Percent	
1918–1922*	646	82	12.7	614	50	8.1	564
1923–1927*	593	77	12.9	578	62	10.8	516
1928–1932*	545	97	17.8	515	67	13.0	448
1933	617	116	18.8	578	77	13.3	501
1934	683	150	21.9	611	78	12.8	533
1935	686	137	20.0	632	83	13.1	549
1936	678	95	14.0	670	87	13.0	583
1937	696	133	19.1	676	113	16.7	563

* Yearly Average.

Hungarian statistics for the upbringing of the children of mixed marriages are especially interesting, for the Hungarian law provides that the partners to a marriage may make a written agreement as to the upbringing of the children.

MARRIAGE WITH		MARRIAGES	AGREE-MENTS	JEWISH No.	UPBRINGING PER CENT
1934	Jewish father	439	96	22	22.9%
1934	Jewish mother	332	85	8	9.4%
1935	Jewish father	419	88	15	17.0%
1935	Jewish mother	352	76	4	5.3%
1936	Jewish father	456	104	12	11.5%
1936	Jewish mother	321	95	4	4.2%

Agreements are made in only a small number of cases and it may be assumed that where no agreement was made, the Jewish partner renounced rights to the Jewish upbringing of the children. And even where there are agreements the percentage of Jewish women who insist on a Jewish upbringing for their children is nominal; it is never more than 10% and in several instances considerably smaller. Among the marriages where the men are Jewish, the percentage is higher; in 1934 it covered 22% of all the agreements, but it fell to 11.5% in 1936.

Czechoslovakia. Still further evidence that mixed marriages are less prevalent in the provinces than in large cities is shown by certain sections in Czechoslovakia. The percentage (per hundred Jews) of mixed marriages in 1933, was:

COUNTRY	MEN	WOMEN
Bohemia	30.73%	25.25
Carpatho-Russia	0.72%	1.25

In Bohemia, where the Jews were no less assimilated than in Germany, Jewish men married non-Jewish women 43 times as frequently as in the orthodox communities of Carpatho-Russia, and Jewish women married non-Jewish men 21 times as frequently. This provides a clear picture of the difference, as regards mixed marriage, between a Jewish community that has remained practically in the ghetto, in the cadre of strict religiosity, segregated from the surrounding world, and a Jewish community which has separated itself considerably from its Jewish traditions and has become affiliated with the German and the Czech milieu.

Holland. Table 5 deals with Amsterdam where, while Orthodoxy is still strong, mixed marriages were nevertheless widespread.

Here there was also a marked increase of mixed marriages. Within fifteen years, the number of Jewish men contracting such marriages increased one and a half-fold and the number among women was doubled.

Eastern Europe. Table 6, for Latvia, offers statistics on a typical Eastern European settlement during the period from 1929 to 1938. The number of Jewish men marrying non-Jewish women rarely exceeds 2%, and the number of Jewish women entering mixed marriage is still smaller.

TABLE 6. STATISTICS OF MIXED MARRIAGES IN LATVIA

Years	Number of Jewish Men Marrying	Number of Jewish Men Marrying Non-Jewish Women		Number of Jewish Women Marrying	Number of Jewish Women Marrying Non-Jewish Men		Number of Marriages With Both Parties Jewish
			Percent			Percent	
1929	845	16	1.9	844	15	1.8	829
1930	867	17	1.9	867	17	1.9	850
1931	812	10	1.2	817	15	1.8	802
1932	703	12	1.7	702	11	1.6	691
1933	881	14	1.6	900	33	3.7	867
1934	1,115	26	2.3	1,101	12	1.1	1,089
1935	1,008	21	2.1	999	12	1.1	987
1936	893	20	2.3	885	12	1.4	873
1937	857	18	2.1	859	20	2.3	839
1938	892	19	2.1	885	12	1.4	873

TABLE 7. STATISTICS OF MIXED MARRIAGES IN CANADA

Years	Number of Jewish Men Marrying	Number of Jewish Men Marrying Non-Jewish Women		Number of Jewish Women Marrying	Number of Jewish Women Marrying Non-Jewish Men		Number of Marriages With Both Parties Jewish
			Percent			Percent	
1926	1,122	35	3.1	1,105	18	1.6	1,087
1927	1,180	56	4.7	1,138	14	1.2	1,124
1928	1,393	42	3.0	1,362	11	0.7	1,351
1929	1,545	67	4.4	1,494	16	1.1	1,478
1930	1,509	50	3.3	1,488	29	1.9	1,459
1931	1,420	39	2.8	1,404	23	1.6	1,381
1932	1,494	55	3.7	1,466	27	1.8	1,439
1933	1,567	41	2.6	1,571	45	2.9	1,526
1934	1,523	56	3.7	1,486	19	1.3	1,467
1935	1,517	46	3.0	1,510	39	2.6	1,471
1936	1,700	69	4.1	1,657	26	1.6	1,631
Total: (1926-1936)	15,970	556	3.5	15,681	267	1.7	15,414

In the more conservative Polish Jewish community the percentages of mixed marriages were even smaller than in Latvia. During the year 1927 there were in Poland, which then had about 3,000,000 Jews, or 30 times as many as Latvia and 6 times as many as Germany, only 16 Jewish men who married non-Jewish women and 9 Jewish women who married non-Jewish men. This was about 0.1% of the Jewish men marrying and about 0.06% of the women. During 1928, Warsaw, with 350,000 Jews, had only two mixed marriages. Cracow also had only two mixed marriages that year. But in Posen, which had once belonged to Germany, there were seven mixed marriages that year in a Jewish population 1/150 of Warsaw.

Russia. Russian Jewry, prior to the first World War, was similar to Polish Jewry, though less pious. The same conditions that existed in Poland tended to unify the Russian Jewish communities as well. The 1917 revolution brought about not only a geographical and economic upheaval in the life of Russian Jews, but also a profound spiritual change. This is shown clearly in the record of mixed marriages. Before the first World War they were very rare, and usually occurred in St. Petersburg and Moscow, where the upper intellectual classes of Jews were assimilated. Post-revolution statistics for Leningrad are as follows:

Year	Jewish Grooms	Non-Jewish Brides	Jewish Brides	Non-Jewish Grooms
1925	1,013	252	930	169
1926	1,253	314	1,118	170
1927	1,241	331	1,142	232

Thus by 1927 the percentage of mixed marriages for Jewish men was 26.6, and for Jewish women 20.

Mixed marriages were therefore rapidly on the increase. After a decade of emancipation, the Jews of Leningrad reached the same percentage as the Jews of Berlin after a century.

In Moscow the situation was the same. In the older Jewish settlements of White Russia and the Ukraine, the percentages are not so high, though much higher than in Poland. Between 1924 and 1926, out of every hundred Jews marrying, the percentages entering mixed marriage were:

Area	Men	Women
Central Russia	20.7	12.5
Ukraine	4.2	4.9
White Russia	1.9	3.7

In Central Russia, where the Jewish population came from other sections and is largely concentrated in the cities of Moscow and Leningrad, the percentage of mixed marriages for Jewish men is ten times that of White Russia; for women three as great. Ukraine stands between, because here there are larger cities and the Jewish population always had a more assimilationist attitude.

Of 4,579 children born in Leningrad between 1925 and 1927, of all-Jewish or mixed marriages, 1,280 or 28% were of mixed marriages; 689 had a Jewish father and 591 had a Jewish mother. Those children were given no religious upbringing at all.

Canada. Statistics for Canada show that the Jewish settlement there resembles South America more than the United States. It is a comparatively young settlement—scarcely fifty years old. It was neither of Sephardic nor of German origin, but Eastern-European. And it was part of a country in which there was a conflict between cultures and two languages. All these factors contributed toward weakening the assimilationist tendencies. Nevertheless, the record was far different from that of Poland and even Latvia. Table 7 covers the period from 1926 to 1936 for Canada.

Of the 556 Jewish men who married non-Jewish women during the eleven years cited, 382, or 70%, married Protestants; 150 married Catholics and twenty-three married members of the Greek Orthodox or Greek Catholic faiths. Two-thirds of the mixed marriages seem therefore to have been with English women, more than one-fourth with French women and very few with Slavic elements. Of 267 Jewish women who married non-Jewish men 174, or 65%, married Protestants; fifty-six, or 20.9%, married Catholics; thirty married Slavs.

United States. In the United States no records are kept of mixed marriages. Neither religious nor racial statistics regarding the parties contracting marriages are registered in any state of the Union. Private studies are rare.

Walter Laidlaw, in the *American Hebrew* of May 19, 1905, wrote that between 1895 and 1904, in New York, there were only eighty-five mixed marriages as compared to 8,627 all-Jewish marriages, or 1 per cent. Joseph Jacobs, in the *Jewish Encyclopedia,* gave an even smaller figure—seventy-eight mixed marriages, and 9,668 all-Jewish marriages. Donald Taft, in *World Migration* (1936, p. 255) states that only 1.8% of marriages in which Jews participate are mixed marriages, while the ratio among Italians is 7.1%, among Slavs 7.2% and among the Irish 21.8%. The same figures are cited by Bessie Bloom Wessel (*An Ethnic Survey of Woonsocket, Rhode Island,* 1931, p. 109).

Samuel Koenig, in a study of the Jewish community of Stamford, Conn., shows that, in 1938, there were in Stamford 823 all-Jewish couples and fifty-nine mixed couples, or 7.2%. He believes that the percentage is even higher, since it was impossible to include those couples of whom one partner was Jewish that had broken away entirely from the Jewish community. Such severance takes place particularly when a Jewish woman marries a non-Jewish man. Of the fifty-nine mixed pairs noted, forty were Jewish husbands with non-Jewish wives, and nineteen Jewish wives with non-Jewish husbands. In most of the mixed marriages, Italians provided the second partner; the Irish came next, Yankee stock was third, and Poles and Germans shared fourth place. Most of the Jews who had entered on mixed marriages were native Americans.

It is especially interesting that out of thirty-one Jews who had entered on mixed marriages, twenty-six came from Orthodox households, and 5 from Conservative backgrounds. Most of those studied, particularly among the men, remained within the Jewish community; some even retained their membership in a synagogue. Of fourteen families married for an average of nine years, the children of five families were known to have received no religious training at all, in five cases they were known to have been given a Jewish education, and in three cases the children were brought up as Christians. The remaining seventeen couples were childless. These figures are probably typical for most American communities.

Ray Baber, an American sociologist, in a study on mixed marriages, has presented some interesting material on the subject. He made a study of 130 cases, of which fifty-four were Jewish men with Catholic wives, twenty-nine Catholic men with Jewish wives, thirty-one Jewish men with Protestant wives and sixteen Protestant men with Jewish wives. Baber's deductions are; 1) Jewish men marry non-Jewish women with twice as much frequency as Jewish women marry non-Jewish men. 2) There is a greater frequency of marriage between Jews and Catholics than between Jews and Protestants. The second deduction supports the Stamford data on the frequency of marriages with Italians and Irish as compared to marriages with Yankees. It may perhaps be said that in the United States, unlike Europe, mixed marriages occur more frequently in the lower economic classes than in the upper ones. This is further supported by the fact that almost all the mixed marriages were of the children of immigrant parents.

Baber discovered that a high percentage of the mixed marriages turned out to be happy. The marriages with Catholics turned out to be 70% happy, those with Protestants 79%. In both instances, happiness was more frequent in the cases where the husband was Jewish. There were more children among the unhappily married couples than among the happy ones. Twice as many children were brought up as Jews in Jewish-Protestant marriages as in Jewish-Catholic marriages.

JACOB LESTSCHINSKY.

Lit.: Bachi, Roberto, *Dei problemi della popolazione;* Roma, *Istituto poligrafico dello stato* (1931); Engelman, Uriah Zevi, "Intermarriage among Jews in Germany, U.S.S.R. and Switzerland," Jewish *Social Studies,* vol. 2 (1940) 157-78; Bergman, A., *Jewish Trials For Racial Offenses in Germany* (Yiddish); *Die Yiddishe Ekonomik* (1937); Bienstock, W., and Novozelski, S., *The Jews of Leningrad* (Russian); *Biology and Pathology of the Jews* (1926); Goldhammer, L., *Die Juden Wiens* (1927); Gorin, M., "Jews in Magdeburg," *Die Yiddishe Ekonomik* (Yiddish), April and June, 1939; Isaev, B., "Die Sfardim in Buenos Aires," *Argentiner Yivo Shriftn,* March, 1941; Rosenberg, Louis, *Canada's Jews* (1939); Ruppin, Arthur, *The Jewish Fate and Future* (1940); Tartakover, A., "Jews in the New Poland" (Polish), *Number and Natural Movement of Polish Jews* (1935); Theilhaber, Felix A., *Der Untergang des deutschen Judentums* (2nd ed., 1921); idem, "Die Genealogie einer jüdischen Familie in Deutschland," *Archiv für Rassen- und Gesellschaftsbiologie* (1912, fascicle 2; 1913, fascicle 1-2); Zollschan, I., *Das Rassenproblem* (1920); Zoller, I., *La communità israelitica di Trieste;* Metron, in *Rivista internazionale di statistica;* Ferrara, in *Italia,* vol. 3, March 3, 1924; *Zeitschrift für Demographie und Statistik der Juden* (1930); *Jüdische Wohlfahrtspflege und Sozialpolitik* (1931 and 1935); *Statistisches Jahrbuch der Stadt Berlin* (1930-37); *Statistisches Jahrbuch für das deutsche Reich* (1929-36); *Statistischer Archiv fun di Yiddishe Ekonomik* (1939); for Hungary: *Publications statistiques* (1924, 1929, 1937); *Budapest Székesfőváros statisztikai es közigazgatási évkönyve* (1935-37); *Statistisch Jaarboek der Gemeente Amsterdam* (1921-38); for Latvia: *Valsts Statistika Parvalde* (1930-38); *American Hebrew,* May, 1905; Taft, Donald D., *World Migration* (1936); Koenig, Samuel, "The Socio-Economic Structure of an American Jewish Community" (Stamford, Conn.), *Jews in a Gentile World* (1942).

MIXTURES, PROHIBITED (Kilayim). Three classes of mixtures are regarded as prohibited in traditional Jewish law: mixtures of plants (*kil'e zera'im*), mixtures of animals (*kil'e behemah*), and cloth made of wool and linen (*sha'atnez*).

Two passages in the Bible refer to prohibited mixtures. *Lev.* 19:19 runs: "Thou shalt not let thy cattle gender with a diverse kind, thou shalt not sow thy field with two kinds of seeds, neither shall there come upon thee a garment of two kinds of stuff mingled together"; *Deut.* 22:9-11 states more specifically: "Thou shalt not sow thy vineyard with two kinds of seed; lest the fulness of the seed thou hast sown be forfeited, together with the increase of the vineyard. Thou shalt not plow with an ox and ass together. Thou shalt not wear a mingled stuff, wool and linen together."

Summing up these commandments, there result four sorts of forbidden mixtures: 1) in sowing, including the prohibition of the grafting of trees; 2) in the vineyard; 3) of cattle; 4) of clothing. The prohibition of mixtures in sowing and in vineyards was held to apply only to Palestine, while the other prohibitions were observed everywhere. However, the rabbis ruled that the prohibition of mixtures in vineyards applied also outside of Palestine (*Kid.* 39a; *Tur Yoreh Deah* 295; *Yoreh Deah* 295:1; 296:1; 297:1-2). In any case the hybridization of animals was forbidden, by which was meant the breeding of clean animals, such as are permitted for food, with unclean ones, or the breeding of different species of unclean animals, such as wolves, dogs and foxes, with one another (*Kil.* 1:6; *B.K.* 54b). Ploughing with two animals of a different species was forbidden (*ibid.* 54b); but a man could draw a plough together with an animal (*Kil.* 8:6). The only mixture in clothing that is forbidden is that of linen and wool; the Mishnah explains the term Shaatnez as a condensation of the three words, *shu'a* ("combed"), *tavui* ("spun") and *nuz* ("twisted"). The prohibition extends only to garments; Shaatnez cloth may be used for all other purposes (*Yoreh Deah* 298 to 304).

The medieval rabbis disagreed as to the purpose of the Biblical prohibition of such mixtures. Bahya ibn Pakuda, in the introduction to *Hoboth Halebaboth,* declared that the reason was beyond human comprehension. Maimonides (*Moreh Nebuchim,* vol. 3, chap. 37) supposed that hybridization was forbidden because the heathens used such mixtures for immoral purposes. Rashi (to *Lev.* 19:19) does not believe they were instituted for any reason, but for disciplinary purposes. Nahmanides, anticipated by the Amora Samuel, holds that they were intended to remind man that he should not arbitrarily change the normal order of things. However, modern scholars point out that the Israelites did use certain hybrid animals, such as the mule, and they suggest analogies between the Biblical laws and certain similar prohibitions found to be the custom among the Hittites.

In modern industrial society, the only one of these prohibitions that has concerned the orthodox Jew is that of Shaatnez. In 1941 the Union of Orthodox Jewish Congregations of America announced the institution of a special laboratory to test clothing and to stamp clothing that was free from a mixture of wool and linen and could therefore be worn by orthodox Jews.

SCHULIM ABI TODOS.

Lit.: The Bible dictionaries on the topics mentioned; Lifschütz, *Tifereth Yisrael* (1886).

MIZMOR SHIR LEYOM HASHABBATH, *see* PSALMS, LITURGICAL.

MIZPA, *see* COLONIES, AGRICULTURAL.

MIZPAH or **MIZPEH** (literally, "watch"), the name of several Jewish towns in Palestine. Mizpeh in Gilead was the home of Jephthah (*Judges* 11:34), but the site is not known. By far the most important town of this name was Mizpah of Benjamin (also Mizpeh), often mentioned in narratives of the 11th cent. B.C.E. (*Judges* 20 to 21; *1 Sam.* 7 and 10). In the time of Samuel it was the meeting-place of Israel and its base against the Philistines; it was also Samuel's favorite place of worship. After several centuries of obscurity it suddenly emerged as the capital of Judah after the fall of Jerusalem; Gedaliah, regent of Judah after Nebuchadrezzar's conquest of the land, resided and was assassinated there by Ishmael (*Jer.* 41). Finally, Judas Maccabeus assembled his troops and worshipped there before attacking the Syrian army. One of the oldest Tannaim, Simon, is said to have been a man of Mizpah. The modern identification is not certain, but the majority of scholars accept the identification with Nebi Sam-

wil, a very ancient shrine of Samuel, northwest of Jerusalem. Nebi Samwil is the highest point in Benjamin. An alternative site is Tell en-Nasbeh, on the road from Jerusalem to Ramallah, where excavations were carried on in 1926 to 1935 by W. F. Badè for the Pacific School of Religion. Mizpah is also the name of an agricultural colony in Palestine.

WILLIAM F. ALBRIGHT.

Lit.: American Schools of Oriental Research Annual, vol. 4, p. 90 et seq.; *Zeitschrift für Alttestamentliche Wissenschaft* (1929) 161 et seq.

MIZRA, *see* COLONIES, AGRICULTURAL.

MIZRACHI (or **MIZRAHI**), a Zionist organization of religious Jews which aims at the realization of two objectives: the upbuilding of Palestine as a Jewish state in the spirit of the Written and Oral Torah, and the strengthening of traditional Judaism and its influence in the Diaspora. The Mizrachi popular motto is: *'Eretz Yisra'el le'am Yisra'el 'al pi torath Yisra'el* ("The land of Israel for the people of Israel on the basis of the Torah of Israel"). Briefly, Mizrachi strives for the achievement of the Zionist aim as laid down by the first Basel Congress on the basis and in the spirit of traditional Judaism. The name "Mizrachi" consists of the first and last letters of the term *Mercaz Ruchani,* "spiritual center," which summarizes the Mizrachi ideal.

As a religious party, though a distinct and separate faction within the Zionist movement, the Mizrachi came into being in 1902, five years after the convocation by Theodor Herzl of the First Zionist Congress. Among the famous spiritual leaders of those days, such leaders of the Chovevei Zion movement as Rabbi Samuel Mohilever of Bialystok, Rabbi Isaac Jacob Reines of Lida, Rabbi Jonathan Eliasberg, and Rabbi Naphtali Zvi Judah Berlin, venerable head of the Volozhin Yeshiva, thought that in spite of differences which existed between them and the secularist nationalists in matters of religion, they could find common ground in the political and economic phases of Zionism and Yishub Eretz Yisrael. These leaders were the forerunners of the Mizrachi movement, which took organizational shape at its first conference convened by Rabbi Isaac Jacob Reines in Vilna on the 25th and 26th of Adar, 5662 (March 4 and 5, 1902). Reines took this step after the Fifth Congress in 1901, which endangered the movement on account of the so-called Kulter Kampf, which disrupted the forces of the movement. The establishment of a religious faction within the Zionist movement not only prevented religious members from leaving it, but made it possible for them to combat the secularistic tendencies within.

Central bodies of the Mizrachi were set up for Eastern Europe in Vilna and Lida; for Western Europe, in Frankfort, and in Altona, near Hamburg. As the years went by, the organization spread in many parts of Europe, especially in Poland, where it became a stronghold.

The World Mizrachi Organization, as a constituent of the World Zionist Organization, participates in all branches of its economic and colonization activities and is represented on its governing bodies (the General Council and Executive) as well as on the governing bodies of the funds created by the Congress—the Keren Hayesod (Palestine Foundation Fund) and the Keren

Kayemeth Leyisrael (Jewish National Fund). Besides engaging in Zionist activities in political, economic and colonization spheres, the Mizrachi strives for the furtherance of Traditional Judaism in Eretz Yisrael and in the Diaspora by: (a) the setting up of national and traditional Jewish school systems (20,000 pupils in 1942 attended the ninety schools in Palestine, from kindergarten and elementary high school); (b) the promotion of Traditional Jewish cultural works; (c) the founding of financial institutions facilitating middle-class agricultural and industrial settlement in Eretz Yisrael; (d) providing for religious needs in towns and settlements in Eretz Israel; (e) defraying or subsidizing the salaries of rabbis and Shohetim in Eretz Yisrael towns and settlements; (f) assisting in the consolidation of the Eretz Yisrael chief rabbinate and district rabbinical councils; (g) subsidizing and defraying the cost of synagogues and similar buildings in Eretz Yisrael settlements; (h) the maintenance of teachers' training seminaries and Yeshivas in Eretz Yisrael and in the Diaspora; (i) the founding and maintenance of an Agricultural Yeshiva in Eretz Yisrael; and (j) political activities to secure the return of representatives of national religious Jewry in Eretz Yisrael to the legislative bodies and municipal councils to safeguard the interests of Traditional Jews and Traditional Judaism.

The financial instruments of Mizrachi are: (1) Keren Eretz-Yisrael Shel Hamizrachi (The Mizrachi Palestine Fund), recognized by the Zionist Congress; (2) the Mizrachi Bank, Ltd. (with its main office in Jerusalem and branch offices in Tel-Aviv and Haifa). Its share capital at the outbreak of the second World War, in September, 1939, was 100,000 Palestinian pounds. Heshel Farbstein, veteran Mizrachi leader, was president of the Mizrachi Bank in 1942. The head office of the Mizrachi World Organization is in Jerusalem. Rabbi Meyer Berlin, founder and head of the American branch for many years, was its president in 1942, Rabbi Wolf Gold, former president of Mizrachi in America, was the chairman of the executive committee.

The Mizrachi Organization of America came into being in 1911. At that time groups already existed in New York city and St. Louis; the latter became the seat of the central bureau when Mizrachi in America was established as a national organization at its first convention held at Cincinnati in 1914. This took place after the arrival in the United States of Rabbi Meyer Berlin, who toured the country. It was through his initiative that the movement in America developed and Mizrachi groups were organized on the American continent. Rabbi Dov Ber Abramowitz of St. Louis was the first president of the American Mizrachi Organization. In later years many of the outstanding Orthodox rabbis and lay leaders became its champions. One who helped the movement in its early stages was Professor Hermann Struck, the famous painter who in 1942 resided in Haifa. Later Rabbi J. L. Fishman of Jerusalem, together with Rabbi Meyer Berlin, were at the helm of the American Mizrachi, while Dr. Meyer Waxman was its general secretary. At the same time, Rabbi Berlin, who edited the Mizrachi literary weekly, *Haibri,* transferred the publication from Berlin to New York, where he continued to edit it for many years.

Former presidents of the organization include Rabbi Jacob Levinson, Gedaliah Bublick and Rabbi Wolf Gold. Leon Gellman was elected president in 1935, and still held that office in 1942. Affiliated organizations are the Hapoel Hamizrachi, the religious youth pioneer movement, whose guiding spirit is embodied in the motto *Torah Va'abodah* (Torah and Labor); the youth affiliate *Hashomer Hadathi,* religious scout groups who train themselves as pioneers for Palestine, where they become part of the Bnei Akiba, religious scout movement; the Mizrachi Women's Organization of America, which has established technical training schools, farms and cultural centers for girls in Palestine, and consists of senior and junior chapters throughout the United States.

From 1936 on the Mizrachi Palestine Fund was a part of the United Palestine Appeal, which included the Keren Hayesod and the Keren Kayemeth Leyisrael. With the Jewish population of Palestine increasing daily, and particularly with the influx of refugees from Germany, Poland, and Austria, the Mizrachi had to augment its educational as well as its colonizing activities for those newcomers who desired a truly Jewish education and traditional background. New trades and possibilities for the many religious-minded pioneers entering the country also had to be provided.

Hatzofeh, the first religious Hebrew daily in the world, was founded in Tel-Aviv by the Mizrachi late in 1937. The American organization provided two new model linotype machines, both for newspaper uses and to create a printing business that will offer a livelihood to over a hundred families. In America, the Mizrachi maintains two monthly publications, the *Mizrachi Veg* (Yiddish) and *The Jewish Outlook* (English).

Mizrachi in America steadily participated in all efforts designed to strengthen Orthodox Judaism in that country, including the furtherance of Sabbath observance, religious education, Yeshivas and Talmud Torahs, and all activities conducive to the general welfare of the Jewish people. The Mizrachi Organization of America secured its annual budget through membership dues and voluntary contributions, through its branches in the United States and Canada.

Mizrachi groups on the American continent were rapidly established from 1939 on in the larger Jewish communities of Argentina, Brazil, Uruguay and Mexico. These new branches were the result of visits during 1940 and 1941 by the Mizrachi leaders Rabbi Wolf Gold and Gedaliah Bublick. The Mizrachi's unique achievement in 1942, pertaining to Orthodox Jewry in America, was the convening of the first "Sabbath Congress" in the United States, under the auspices of Mizrachi's Rabbinical Committee, known as Vaad Lehizzuk Hatorah Vehayahaduth.

The officers of the Mizrachi Organization of America in 1942 were: honorary presidents: Rabbi Meyer Berlin, Gedaliah Bublick; honorary vice-president: Rabbi A. M. Ashinsky, Pittsburgh; chairman, Mizrachi World Executive: Rabbi Wolf Gold; president: Leon Gellman; vice-presidents: Rabbi Jacob Hoffman, Dr. Pinkhos Churgin; honorary secretary: Rabbi Bezalel Cohen; executive secretary: Rabbi Max Kirshblum; treasurer: Max Nadler; chairman, Rabbinical Committee: Rabbi Jacob Levinson; chairman, National Executive: Rabbi Joseph H. Lookstein; chairman, National Mizrachi Council: M. Morton Rubenstein.

SOLOMON KERSTEIN.

A Mizrah of modern times, with typical illustrations, owned by Maurice Herrmann, of New York city

MIZRAH (originally "the rising of the sun," then "the east"), the direction in which most Jews face during prayer. During the Biblical period those who were in the Temple at Jerusalem faced the Holy of Holies; those in Jerusalem turned toward the Temple court; those in the rest of Palestine faced in the direction of Jerusalem; those living outside of Palestine turned toward the east.

The Bible (*Dan.* 6:11) states that Daniel prayed three times a day in the upper chamber of his house, the windows of which were open toward Jerusalem. While there are no regulations in the Talmud regarding the orientation of synagogues, nevertheless the Talmud occasionally recommends placing the entrance door in the east and having the structure itself face toward the west, i.e. toward Jerusalem. The most varied directions are recommended for the prayer of the individual, most frequently, however, the east. But one must not face directly toward the east, but rather slightly toward the southeast, in order to avoid even the appearance of sun worship. He who does not know which direction is the east is required to direct his thoughts at least toward Jerusalem. With one exception, the extant ruins of the synagogues in Galilee are all orientated from south to north. The Christian churches early adopted the direction toward the east, and this practice gradually became the usual procedure among the Jews likewise. Mohammed took over the "Kibla," "the facing in prayer," from the Jews, originally requiring his followers to face toward Jerusalem, but later changed it to a "facing" ("Kibla") toward Mecca.

In order to indicate the direction of prayer for services in the home, in many homes of pious Jews a drawing, frequently with artistic adornments, and in one or many colors, is attached to the easterly wall of the room on parchment or on paper, and either in original or a printed copy. This wall-drawing also is called "Mizrah." The Mizrah drawing always shows the name of God, representations of the Temple at Jerusalem, of the temple mount Moriah or of the city of Jerusalem, and also, in most cases, a Menorah, which usually is illustrated with figured script. Some of these Mizrah leaflets are artistically adorned with illustrations and texts; of especial interest are the Mizrahs with Cabalistic signs and illustrations. These Mizrahs are seldom found in the synagogues; however, two silver Mizrahs in the form of mural candelabra dating from the 18th cent. and found in the synagogue at Frankfort on Oder are of unusual beauty and value.

Long before the rise of the Zionist movement Mizrahs with pictures of the Temple site were widely distributed in Palestine. Inasmuch as these contained also the picture of the Mosque of Omar, they were, in the late 1920's and early 1930's, employed by the Grand Mufti at Jerusalem as a means of incitement against the Jews.

ALFRED GROTTE.

MNEMONICS. The Jews of Bible times, in common with many of the peoples of antiquity, transmitted much of their law and literature not only through writing but also through the memory of generation after generation. It was frequently after the lapse of many years, and only when there was danger of their being forgotten, that tales centuries old were written down. At first it was not the whole story or speech that was written down, but enough to refresh the memory; thus various narratives, especially in the Torah, and some of the earlier books of the prophets, read more like summaries than complete accounts. In the latest books of the Bible, however, the stories and narratives are recorded in great detail, indicating that literary composition had replaced oral transmission.

The problem of remembering teachings arose again in the latter part of the pre-Christian era, with the rise of the sect of the Pharisees. These promulgated the doctrine that there was not one Law but two: a Written Law which was embodied in the Torah, and an Oral Law, likewise promulgated to Moses, but to be handed down by word of mouth from generation to generation (*Aboth* 1:1). Thus every teacher of the Oral Law had to commit to memory all the regulations and the discussions about them. In course of time, due to the additions and supplements made by generation after generation of rabbis, this Oral Law grew to such an enormous amount that it was difficult for any ordinary student to hold it all. Accordingly, various methods were employed to aid in memorizing.

One of the earliest of these methods was grouping by numbers, that is, by announcing that there were so and so many cases that came under the same category, and then proceeding to enumerate them. The tractate *Eduyoth* is full of such number mnemonics. Another was to group various laws according to similarities and differences (*Meg.* 1:4-11), the day on which they were promulgated (*Sotah* 5:2-5; *Yad.* 4:1-4), or other connections (examples are found in *Men.* 3:5-7; 4:1-4; *Hul.* 1:4-7; *Arach.* 2:1-6; *Nid.* 6:2-10; *Parah* 8:2-7).

The chief need for aids to the memory, however, arose in the Amoraic period, when the mass of oral tradition became a veritable "sea of the Talmud." For this purpose various indicators were employed known as *simmanim,* or "signs" (singular, *simman*). The Babylonian teachers laid especial emphasis on such aids to the memory and held that the knowledge of the Torah had been better preserved in Judea than in Galilee because the students in the former country paid attention to such signs and those of the latter did not. Such aids to memory occur often in the Babylonian Talmud. They usually consist of short sentences or abbreviations. The sentences may be verses from the Bible, proverbs, or, less frequently, well-known names; the abbreviations are made by combining the initial letters of various words that go to make up the essence of the passage to be remembered.

A few examples may be given of the numerous mnemonic phrases and abbreviations that occur in the Talmud. The fact that the heathen festival of the calends comes eight days after the winter solstice and that of the Saturnalia eight days before the solstice is recalled by the Bible verse (*Ps.* 139:5), "Thou hast beset me behind and before" (*A.Z.* 139b). The fact that the poor Hiyya would throw away the oil of unripe olives, while the rich Simeon bar Rabbi would use it as a sauce, is recalled by the sentence, "The rich are thrifty" (*Men.* 86a). The alphabet is sometimes used for mnemonic purposes. Thus Samuel's recommendation of a fish diet as an aid to the eyes is expressed by three successive letters of the alphabet, Nun Samech Ayin, which can be interpreted in the sense of "fish supports eye" (*Ned.* 54b). The difference between truth (*'emeth*), and falsehood (*sheker*) is recalled by the position of their consonants in the alphabet: the letters of truth (Aleph, Mem, Tav) are widely dispersed, so truth is hard to attain; the letters of lie (Shin, Kof, Resh) are close together, so falsehood is always near at hand (*Sab.* 104a).

Sometimes a number of words, each of which formed the beginning of a series of passages, were combined into a mnemonic sentence. Thus the following are the opening words of the passages read from the Torah in the morning service for the eight days of Passover: *mishchu* (*Ex.* 12:21-51); *shor* (*Lev.* 22:26 to 23:44); *kaddesh* (*Ex.* 13:1-16); *'im kesef* (*Ex.* 22:24 to 23:19); *pesal* (*Ex.* 34:1-26); *bemidbar* (*Num.* 9:1-14); *beshallah* (*Ex.* 13:17 to 15:26); *kol habechor* (*Deut.* 15:19 to 16:17). These opening words were made into a sentence, "Lead the ox, betroth with money, carve in the wilderness, send away the firstborn" (*Meg.* 31a). Or words might be made from initials as an aid to memory. Thus there are four blessings to be said at the close of the Sabbath followed by a holiday: over the wine (*yayin*); over the light (*ner*), over the separation (*habdalah*) and for the sanctification of the festival (*kiddush*). One teacher declares that they are to be in the order expressed by the word YiNHaK ("he will groan"); the other, in the order expressed by the word YiKNeH ("he will buy"; *Pes.* 102b).

In addition to these forms of mnemonic signs, the Talmud contains others based on the initials of the teachers mentioned or words giving a list of the subjects treated. These signs are found frequently in the course of the Talmudic text and were retained even after the old prohibition of writing down the Oral Law had been generally disregarded. They occur much more often in manuscripts than in the printed editions, since those who used the printed editions had but little need for them.

In the period after the writing down of the Talmud, the chief use of mnemonics in Jewish literature was for the purpose of remembering numbers. Since every Hebrew letter has a numerical value, it was easy to translate a number into a word which served as an aid to memory. Every Masoretic number was given its corresponding key-word. For example, the number of verses in *Daniel* is 357; the key-word (*simman*) is *nashbah* (*Isa.* 40:7), as the sum of its letters (Nun, 50; Shin, 300; Beth, 2; He, 5) is 357. The date of the

death of Moses Maimonides (Monday, Tebeth 20, 4965) is remembered by the words *yeme bechi 'ebel mosheh* ("the days of the mourning of Moses"); for the Beth of *bechi* recalls the second day of the week, the Kaf, the 20th day, the Yod, the tenth month, and the sum of the numerical values of the letters of *bechi 'ebel* is 65.

                 EDUARD BANETH.

Lit.: Brüll, J., *Doresh Letzion* (1864); Brüll, N., in *Brülls Jahrbuch*, vol. 2, p. 59 et seq.

MOAB, MOABITES, a country and people in the southern part of Transjordan. Moab consisted of slopes and a plateau elevated about 3,000 feet above sea level. It was watered by the rivers Arnon and Zered and by numerous wadis. The territory lay opposite the Jericho region of Palestine, and it was there that the Israelites encamped after they had passed through the wilderness. At a later period part of this territory was wrested from Moab by the Ammonites to the north. The chief products of the country were wheat, wine, fruits and cattle. The Bible speaks of the capital of Moab as Ar Moab or Rabbath Moab (the present-day Rabba); these names may refer to the same city or to two. There is also a reference to the fort of Kir Moab (modern Kerak) and to Luchith and Zoar. The country abounds in stone monuments, especially dolmens.

According to the Bible, the original inhabitants of the country were the gigantic Emim who were dispossessed by the Moabites. The latter are traced to the incest of Lot, which indicates the hate felt for them by the Israelites. The deity of Moab was Chemosh; the language of the Moabites was very close to Hebrew. The Bible genealogies make them closely related to Ammon and less closely to the Israelites.

There are references to the early history of Moab in *Gen.* 36 and *Num.* 21:28-29, and more detailed accounts in the later books. The Moabites allowed the Israelites free passage on their way to attack Canaan; but Balak, king of Moab, was so fearful of Israel that he hired Balaam to curse them, only to have the curse turn into a blessing. During the period of the Judges, the tribe of Benjamin was subject to Eglon of Moab for eighteen years and was finally delivered by Ehud. Saul won a victory over them, but they did not become tributary to Israel until they were conquered by David, himself the descendant of the Moabitess Ruth. After the division of the kingdom of Solomon, the exact status of Moab is uncertain; there are indications that it became independent for a time and was reconquered by Omri.

As indicated in the Moabite Stone and in the Bible, although they do not agree in all particulars, Moab revolted and gained its independence in the reign or after the death of Omri's successor, Ahab. It was never recovered by the Israelites and remained more or less hostile, at times harrying the Israelites (*II Kings* 13:20). Many of the prophetic books contain denunciations against Moab and predictions of its fall. The Moabites may have been subdued by Jeroboam II, who is said to have restored the boundaries of the kingdom of Solomon. Moab evidently was subdued by the Assyrians as Israel was, and its name disappeared from history, being replaced by that of the Nabatean Arabs.

According to *Deut.* 23:4 (cf. *Neh.* 13:1), the Israelites

*The Moabite Stone as reconstructed and exhibited in the
Louvre at Paris*

were forbidden to intermarry with the Moabites, although the rabbis later lifted the ban in regard to Moabite women (*Yeb.* 8:3).

In the 20th cent. much work was accomplished in the exploration of sites in Moab, especially by Nelson Glueck.   SAMUEL KRAUSS.

Lit.: The Bible dictionaries; Tristram, H. B., *The Land of Moab;* Glueck, Nelson, *The Other Side of the Jordan* (1940).

MOABITE STONE, an inscribed slab of black basalt, measuring about three and a half by two feet, the only surviving inscription from the kingdom of Moab. It was first discovered at Dibon, east of the Dead Sea, in 1868 by a Prussian missionary, F. A. Klein. In the following year Clermont-Ganneau attempted to purchase it, and the Arabs, hoping to obtain more money for it through a sale to various parties, broke it into a number of pieces. Of these only about twenty were recovered; but fortunately, the inscription had been preserved through a squeeze (pressing wet paper into the engraved lines) and by a copy, so that the stone could be reassembled and the missing parts replaced (the difference between the darker original and the lighter replacements can be seen in the illustration). The original stone is in the Louvre at Paris, and a replica is in the British Museum.

The inscription, which is written in a language almost identical with Hebrew, comes from Mesha, a king of Moab who was a contemporary of Ahab (middle of the 9th cent. B.C.E.). He relates how his country had been subdued by Omri and Ahab of Israel, but that it was delivered because his god, Chemosh, had bidden him go and fight against Israel. It recalls the various cities that were recaptured by Mesha and his rebuilding of the waste cities. The closing part of the inscription is illegible.

The inscription is of great interest as confirming and at the same time enlarging on the Biblical narrative in *II Kings* 1 and 3. It was apparently written after the revolt and before the punitive invasion of Ahab and his allies, which did not, however, succeed in recovering the country; another possibility is that the revolt took place at the end of the reign of Ahab. Many of the place names mentioned in the text occur in passages of the Bible.

Lit.: Barton, George A., *Archaeology and the Bible,* 4th ed. (1925) 421-23; Hastings, James, edit., *Dictionary of the Bible,* vol. 3, pp. 403-8 (text and translation); Smend and Socin, *Die Inschrift des Königs Mesa von Moab.*

MOBILE, the second largest city and the only seaport of the state of Alabama, with a population of 78,720 (1940 census), including about 1,050 Jews. Mobile was founded in 1702 by Sieur de Bienville, serving under Louis XIV of France. There are evidences of Jewish settlement during the French period of Mobile's history, but no definite data are available. In 1724, Bienville promulgated the "Black Code" which ordered all Jews to leave the settlement and asserted that Roman Catholicism would be the only religion tolerated.

Mobile was the first capital of the Province of Louisiana, later Louisiana territory, and came under British rule in 1763. In the period of British control occurred the first distinct reference to Jewish residents. The Probate Records of Mobile County reveal that certain property had been sold on July 9, 1765 to Samuel Israel, Alexander Solomon and Joseph Depalacios, merchants and co-partners in Mobile. In 1783, Spain succeeded Britain in the control of Mobile and ruled the territory until 1813, when it was seized by General Wilkinson for the United States.

In 1824 there settled in Mobile Solomon Mordecai, one of the earliest Jewish physicians in the southern states. The following names of Jewish residents appear in state and county records between 1820 and 1830: E. L. Andrews, Solomon Andrews, George Davis, Isaac Davis, Solomon Jones, Isaac Lazarus, Ben Newhouse, Simon Oppenheim and David Salomon. In 1841, E. Salomon was a member of the committee appointed by the Whig party formally to notify William Henry Harrison of his nomination for the presidency.

The most prominent Jewish resident of Mobile in this early period was Philip Philipps. He came to Mobile from Charleston, South Carolina, in 1834, was admitted to the bar and elected a member of the Alabama legislature from Mobile in 1844. Elected to Congress in 1853, he became the first Jew to serve as Congressman in the United States. He remained in Washington after his first term in Congress and practised law. In 1859, he succeeded in having Congress establish the first Court of Claims in the United States.

Synagogue of Congregation Ahavas Chesed at Mobile, Alabama

After the Civil War, he wrote an authoritative study entitled: *Statutory Jurisdiction and Practise of the United States Supreme Court.*

The first Jewish congregation in Alabama was organized (1844) in Mobile under the name of Congregation Shaarai Shomayim u-Maskil el Dol. At the time of its founding the congregation had fifty-two members and by 1854 there were eighty-eight names on the congregational roster. In 1861, the congregation reported having 117 members, a Hebrew School with 90 pupils enrolled, a Hebrew Relief Association, and a Ladies Hebrew Benevolent Society. The congregation has had a continuous existence for almost a century. Mendes Da Silva was its first rabbi, and Sidney M. Berkowitz and Alfred G. Moses were its rabbis in 1942. The latest temple was built and dedicated in 1908. The Orthodox congregation, Ahavas Chesed, was organized in 1900 by a group of Russian Jews who, in 1911, built and dedicated the synagogue now used by the congregation. In 1938, an elaborate social center building was constructed directly opposite the synagogue. In 1942, Louis Cassel was rabbi of Ahavas Chesed congregation.

A local B'nai B'rith lodge was organized in Mobile as early as 1856. The National Council of Jewish Women established a Mobile section in 1899, and in 1912 a local unit of the Federation of Jewish Charities was introduced.

In 1861 almost an entire company of Jewish young men marched from the Jackson Street synagogue to join the Fourth Alabama Regiment of the Confederate Army under the leadership of Major Adolph Proskauer, later member of the Alabama legislature and president of Congregation Shaarai Shomayim.

Many Jews were active in the civic life of Mobile. A. Baerman, Max Michael, and Lazarus Schwarz were members of the Board of Aldermen. A number of Jews have been public school commissioners, including H. A. Forchheimer, Heyman Gabriel, Herman W. Leinkauf, and William H. Leinkauf. Lazarus Schwarz was one of the first three commissioners of the new type of commission government introduced into Mo-

bile. Dr. Henry Hirshfield served as coroner of Mobile County for almost twenty years.

See also ALABAMA.   LOUIS CASSEL.

Lit.: Moses, A. G., "A History of the Jews of Mobile," *Jewish Historical Society Proceedings* No. 12 (1904) 113-25; Smolkin, W., *History of Congregation Ahavas Chesed.*

MOCATTA, Anglo-Jewish family, originally named Lumbrozo. When the Jews were driven from Spain in 1492, one branch of the Lumbrozo family migrated to Italy; the other, after a period in Holland, moved to England about 1670. In 1790, ABRAHAM LUMBROZO DE MATTOS was allowed by King George III to change the family name to Mocatta, after a maternal ancestor, possibly Haham Hanaalah Moseh Mocatta who died before 1695.

In 1790, Abraham Lumbrozo-Mocatta also founded the firm Mocatta & Goldsmid, bullion brokers to the Bank of England. His daughter Rachel Mocatta was the mother of Sir Moses Montefiore. Abraham's son Moses Mocatta (1806-82) continued the firm Mocatta & Goldsmid. So did Moses' son Frederick David Mocatta (1828-1905) who left no issue.

The Lumbrozo-Mocatta family is also related by marriage to the families Ximenez, Lousada, Mendes da Costa and Brandon. Owen Mocatta, a relative of Frederick David Mocatta, was chairman of the Mocatta Library Committee.

MOCATTA, FREDERICK DAVID, philanthropist, communal worker and historian, b. London, 1828; d. there, 1905. Educated at home by excellent private tutors, Mocatta entered (1843) his father's firm Mocatta & Goldsmid which he directed from 1857 on when his father died. In 1874 he retired from business to devote himself to Jewish studies and to questions of public and private benevolence. He was especially interested in the improvement of housing for the working classes, and supported nearly every hospital of London.

Mocatta also endeavored to reform philanthropy in general by means of technical organization and by seeking to imbue charitable workers with progressive

Frederick David Mocatta

social ideas. As vice-president of the Anglo-Jewish Association, as member of the Rumanian and Russo-Jewish Committee and of the Alliance Israélite, Mocatta played an active part in the amelioration of the plight of persecuted Jews in Eastern Europe. The tradition of his family led Mocatta to the study of the Jews in Spain and Portugal. In 1877 he published *The Jews of Spain and Portugal and the Inquisition* (re-edited by David Bortin, 1928). This work, describing the methods of the Inquisition in full detail, was highly esteemed by Jewish and non-Jewish historians because of its style and scholarship; it was translated into several languages and utilized by many later historians, often without crediting Mocatta.

In 1888 Mocatta delivered a lecture on *The Jews at the Present Age in their Various Habitation* which was printed and translated into several languages. Mocatta also was a patron of Jewish learning. He subventioned Zunz to edit two important works, as well as Abraham Berliner and the English translation of Graetz's *History of the Jews*. The great exhibition of Jewish historical and ceremonial objects in London (1887) which led to the foundation of the Jewish Historical Society of England, owed its inception to Mocatta who was its president from 1900 to 1902. On his seventieth birthday, 8,000 persons, including members of the royal family, the chief rabbi, the archbishops of Canterbury, Westminster and Armagh, signed a testimonial of gratitude for Mocatta's social services. Mocatta founded a great Jewish art collection and a library whose catalogue (a volume of more than 700 pages) was printed in 1904. He wished these collections to become a guide to the study of Judaism, and bequeathed them to the University College of London. The Mocatta Library was also the home of the Jewish Historical Society of England.   HUGO BIEBER.

Lit.: Levine, Ephraim, *The Origin and Growth of the Mocatta Library* (1933).

MOCATTA, MOSES, communal worker and author, b. London, 1768; d. London, 1867. After having directed the firm of Mocatta & Goldsmid founded by his father (Abraham), Mocatta retired from business in middle life in order to devote himself to Jewish scholarship and communal work. He patronized the *Hebrew Review* and the Jewish authoress Grace Aguilar.

In 1834 he edited *The Wisdom of Solomon,* a selection (in Hebrew and English) from *Proverbs* and *Ecclesiastes.* In 1845 he wrote *The Inquisition and Judaism,* containing the translation of a sermon by Diogo de Annunciao (addressed to the Jewish martyrs of the auto da fé at Lisbon in 1705) and of the reply by C. Vero. In 1851, Mocatta edited his own translation of *Hizzuk Emunah* (by Isaak ben Abraham of Troki) under the title *Faith Strengthened.* Mocatta was deeply devoted to the organization and support of Jewish schools and teachers in London. In 1841 he helped establish the West London Synagogue, whose supporters seceded from the Bevis Marks Synagogue, and rendered great service to the young congregation through his energy and vast knowledge of Hebrew.

MOCH, GASTON, French army officer and writer (son of Jules), b. Paris, 1859. He entered the French army in 1880 and became lieutenant of artillery. After advancing to captaincy in the artillery, Moch became an officer in the reserves until he reentered the army (1914) upon the outbreak of the first World War, and was promoted to commandant (major). In 1885 he published *Sedan,* a vivid description of the catastrophe of Napoleon III's army, glorifying his father's exploits. The following years he published several studies on problems of military techniques. Then he was attracted to political questions. In 1894 he published *L'Alsace-Lorraine devant l'Europe,* demanding the restitution of the provinces which France lost in 1871 as pre-requisite to lasting peace in Europe. He endeavored in vain to convert German pacifists to that program.

Notwithstanding this failure, Moch continued to advocate pacifism and international conciliation. In 1910 he published *Histoire sommaire de l'arbitrage permanent.* He also advocated, in *L'armée de la démocratie* (1900), disarmament and the substitution of militias for standing armies, holding up Switzerland as a pattern. In 1935 he wrote *Comment se fera le désarmement.* He sought to promote the use of an international language (Esperanto). He was interested in scientific problems, and published (1922) *Initiation aux théories d'Einstein* and *La relativité des phénomènes.*

MOCH, JULES, French army officer, b. Sarrelouis, France, 1829; d. Paris, 1881. He was educated at the classical school of Metz, and entered the military school of Saint-Cyr in 1849. Two years later he was commissioned as sub-lieutenant of infantry. He participated in the Crimean War (1855-56), and because of his feats was appointed tutor at Saint-Cyr after the war. In 1860 he took part in the French military expedition to Syria. Upon returning to France (1861) he was examiner at Saint-Cyr until he participated in the French occupation of Rome during the years 1863 to 1867.

In the Franco-Prussian War (1870-71), Moch commanded a battalion of the third regiment of infantry. He distinguished himself in the battle of Sedan, and succeeded in escaping when the French army was forced to surrender. Then he placed himself at the disposal of the government of national defense, and continued to fight until the last shot was fired. After the war, Moch published many articles on the reorganization of the French army. He was one of the founders and vice-president of the Club Militaire, an association of former French officers, which issued *Le Bulletin,* later superseded by the *Revue du cercle militaire.* Moch retired from service after he rose to colonelcy. He was regarded as a gallant officer and as one of the few modern theorists in the French army under Napoleon III.

MOCH, JULES SALVADOR, French deputy and socialist leader, b. Paris, 1893. He was educated at the École normale supérieure and the École polytechnique, Paris, passing all his examinations with high honors. Converted to socialism when still a collegian, he became an intimate friend of Léon Blum, who esteemed him highly because of his scientific gifts and his wide experience in industrial business management which Moch acquired in his early years as an engineer and industrial manager at Brussels. Moch was also esteemed or hated, according to the different points of view of party politics, because he represented a blend of "esprit juif" and "esprit normalien," as Blum did.

At the end of the first World War, Moch participated in discussions of the problem of European reconstruction by publishing *Restitution et réparation* (1921) and *La Russie des Soviets* (1925). After visiting the leading industrial countries in Europe to study attempts to modernize and rationalize industry, Moch published (1927) *Socialisme et rationalisation,* with a preface by Léon Blum. In the same year he contributed to the ideology of socialism by publishing *Jean Jaurès et les problèmes du temps présent.* In 1928 Moch defined the position of his party as regards financial problems through his *Le parti socialiste et la politique financière,* and the French socialist party issued his *Socialisme, crise, nationalisation* (1932) as a handbook for the use of its officials.

When Moch was elected deputy in 1932, he became keenly interested in the defense of the republican regime in Spain; together with his wife, Germaine Moch-Picard, he published (1933) *L'oeuvre de la révolution,* treating of the revolution in that country. Subsequently he was active in combatting Fascism within France, as well as the Fascist powers of Spain, Italy and Hitlerism.

MODENA, city in Northern Italy, with about 500 Jews out of a total population of 60,000. The first Jews who resided in Modena seem to have been bankers, to whom Margrave Alberto d'Este extended the privilege of trading in exchange (1393). The number of Jews increased when the Duke of Este ceded Ferrara to the Papal State (1597), and many Jews from Ferrara moved to Reggio and Modena which still remained under the rule of the duke. In 1638 the Jews were forced into a ghetto.

Commerce and industry occupied the Jews of that period, but the study of the Talmud also flourished in Modena to the end of the 18th cent. There was also a strong Cabalistic movement. A distinguished Jewish scholar of Modena was Joseph Solomon Graziano (d. 1685).

Under French rule (1796-1814) the Jews of Modena enjoyed a period of full equality. After restoration of the duchy (1814), the Jews took an active part in the patriotic movement. The ducal regime terminated in 1859, and in the same year the municipal administration granted the Jews complete equality. In 1921 the community consisted of about 650 Jews.

The first Italian-Jewish periodical, *Rivista Israelitica* (1845-48), published at Parma, was edited by Cesare Rovighi of Modena. At the beginning of the 20th cent. a Zionist weekly, *L'Idea Sionista,* was published in Modena by Carlo Conigliani, who taught law at the university of the city. In 1882 a congress of the Jewish communities in Italy was held at Modena, appointing a commission which in the following year decided upon the establishment of the Collegio Rabbinico in Rome.

MODENA, GUSTAVO, actor and patriot, b. Venice 1803; d. Turin, 1861. Son of the Jewish actor Giacomo Modena (1766-1841), Gustavo Modena was educated at Venice and Verona. He studied law at Verona and became a lawyer at the age of 19. But that same year (1820) Modena participated in a revolutionary riot against Austria, and was forced to flee to Bologna where he began to recite publicly. In 1824 he appeared as David in Alfieri's *Saul.* In 1831, he joined the secret league Giovine Italia, and when the Italian revolution broke out afresh, he fought against the Austrian troops by force of arms. Modena then successively emigrated to Switzerland, France, Belgium, and England. As a refugee, Modena earned a meager livelihood as a macaroni-vendor until he began to recite parts from Dante's plays and met with great success in England.

In 1839, being granted amnesty, he returned to Milan, but in 1841 Metternich ordered Modena's prosecution. He became director of a touring company of actors and he trained many young colleagues who became renowned thespians—among them Rossi and Salvini. In 1848 Modena participated anew in the revolutionary movement and in the defense of Rome, collaborating through fiery speeches with Mazzini and Garibaldi. After the conquest of Rome by the French expeditionary forces, Modena managed to escape and found refuge in Sardinia.

At the end of his life Modena was pleased with the news of Austria's defeat but he did not live to see the liberation of his native town.

Lit.: Rassegna storica del Risorgimento, vol. 26 (1939).

MODENA, LEON JUDAH (ARYEH), *see* LEON OF MODENA.

MODERN HEBREW LITERATURE, *see* LITERATURE, HEBREW.

MODIGLIANI, AMEDEO, artist, b. Livorno, Italy, 1884; d. Paris, 1920. Although his career was tragically cut short at the age of thirty-six, he has left an imperishable mark on the art of the 20th cent. Incidentally, he has become the hero of the last great romantic legend of "bohemian" Paris.

Modigliani was descended from two distinguished Jewish families. His father's forebears were bankers to the cardinals in Rome; his mother, of the Garsino family, traced her descent from Spinoza. His brother, Emmanuele, was a socialist deputy until after the rise of Mussolini.

In 1906, after two years' study in Venice and in Florence, his mother made it possible for Modigliani to open a studio in Paris. Settled in Montmartre, he made friends of and exchanged ideas with men of

Amedeo Modigliani

revolutionary artistic ideas such as Picasso, Max Jacob, Derain, Vlaminck and Utrillo—all of whom at that time were living in penniless misery. Sculpture was ever to be Modigliani's chief love; but the bad effects of stone dust on his weak lungs forced him to abandon it in favor of painting. His first picture to gain a measure of recognition was the *Violincellist,* exhibited at the Salon des Indépendants in 1910.

During the first World War Modigliani painted under conditions of great poverty, which he shared from 1916 to 1918 with the English poetess Beatrice Hastings, of whom he made numerous portraits. Like many another Montmartre artist, rising rents in that quarter drove him to the cheaper Montparnasse, where he began to haunt the cafés in search of the price of a drink or a block of drawing-paper to barter for one of his drawings. Although Modigliani had sold a few canvases for tiny sums to such admirers as the author Francis Carco, the dealer Paul Guillaume and the American collector Dr. Albert C. Barnes, it was not until he met the poet Leopold Zborowski and his wife that his fortunes began to improve. These two became so convinced of Modigliani's ultimate fame that they sacrificed all their possessions in order that he might be able to continue to paint. But by the time that Zborowski's enthusiasm had begun to persuade the dealers to buy, the painter's health was completely undermined. Although he now had a devoted wife (Jeanne Hébuterne) who had borne him a daughter, he did not cease to use drink and even drugs, while feverishly producing some of his finest works, as if in expectation of imminent death. One day in his cold studio Modigliani was found stricken with influenza and was rushed to the Charité hospital, where he died a few days later, on January 25, 1920. The funeral procession to the Père Lachaise cemetery was followed by thousands of persons paying tribute to this proud, eccentric, yet always generous and lovable figure of the cafés. Hearing of his death, his widow threw herself from a window, killing herself and her unborn son. Ironically, a sensational rise in the prices of the painter's work immediately followed news of his death.

When one appraises Modigliani's work, his innate love of pure sculptural form is the dominating factor in his personal conception of art. The elongations and distortions, characteristic of both his portraits and nude studies, are basically derived from the soaring verticals of medieval Gothic sculpture, but more directly from that of the Congo, Gabun and the Ivory Coast of Africa, which was already admired by certain painters at the time of Modigliani's first arrival in Paris. However, despite this influence, and that of a few contemporaries such as Picasso and Matisse, his own personality emerges clearly, and actually he is never far removed in his spirit and in his use of color from the Italian painers of the 14th and 15th centuries —from Duccio to Botticelli. While he continually sought abstract beauty in line, form, color and design, Modigliani's paintings and drawings are never cold or remote. Somehow his eye penetrated the outer shell of his subjects: their personalities are fully revealed— sometimes with almost brutal clarity, though always with an elusive, melancholy charm. The student of fine painting will always admire Modigliani's economy and his technical subtleties. But rather because he managed to suggest this intangible inwardness of his sitters his work reaches the rare level of universal appeal.

Works by Modigliani are included in important collections, such as the Museum of Antwerp, the Chicago Art Institute, the Detroit Institute of Arts, the Museum of Grenoble (France), the Los Angeles Museum, the National Gallery, Millbank ("Tate Gallery," London); the Museum of Western Art (Moscow), the Museum of Modern Art (New York city), the Museum of Non-Objective Paintings (New York), the Phillips Memorial Gallery (Washington, D.C.), the Kunsthaus (Zurich), and the Barnes Foundation (Merion, Pa.), as well as in the private collections of Stephen C. Clark (New York), Ralph M. Coe (Cleveland), Samuel Courtauld (London), Chester Dale (New York), Sam A. Lewisohn (New York), and S. Wright Ludington (Santa Barbara, Cal.). Works of his were included in such important exhibitions as the International Art Exhibition (Venice, Italy, 1922), the exhibition of the Paul Guillaume Collection (Galerie Bernheim-Jeune, Paris, 1929), that at the Basel Kunsthalle (January, 1934) and that of Pierre Matisse (New York, January-February, 1942). In March, 1940, Mrs. John D. Rockefeller, Jr., presented to the Museum of Modern Art, in New York, a head in stone by Modigliani, considered by the museum "possibly the finest of Modigliani's stone heads."   M. DONALD WHYTE.

Lit.: Basler, Adolphe, *Modigliani* (1931); Brielle, Roger, "Les peintres juifs, I: Modigliani," *L'amour de l'art,* June, 1933; Carco, Francis, *De Montmartre au Quartier Latin* (1927); Cendrars, Blaise, *Modigliani* (1927); Cingria, C. A., preface to the catalogue of the Modigliani exhibition at the Basel Kunsthalle, Jan.-Feb., 1934; Coquiot, Gustave, *Des peintres maudits: Modigliani* (1924); Dale, Maud, *Modigliani* (1929); Earp, T. W., "The Modern Movement in Painting," special spring number of *The Studio* (London, 1935); Faure, Élie, in *Histoire de l'art,* vol. 4 (1924); George, Waldemar, in *Amour de l'art,* vol. 6 (1925); Georges-Michel, Michel, *Les Montparnos* (1929); McBride, Henry, in *The Arts* (New York), vol. 3 (1923); Pfannstiel, Arthur, *Modigliani* (1929); Rutter, Frank, in *Apollo* (London), vol. 9, No. 52 (1929); Salmon, André, "Le vagabond de Montparnasse," *Les oeuvres libres* (1929); Scheiwiller, Giovanni, *Amedeo Modigliani* (1936); Wilenski, R. H., in *Modern French Painters* (1940); Vlaminck, Maurice, "Souvenir de Modigliani," *L'art vivant,* Nov., 1925.

MOED ("festivals"), second division of the Mishnah and Tosefta, treating in twelve tractates the regulations for the Sabbath, festivals and fast days. The order of the tractates is as follows: Sabbath, Erubin, Pesahim, Shekalim, Yoma, Sukkah, Betzah, Rosh Hashanah, Taanith, Megillah, Moed Katan and Hagigah. In the editions of the Babylonian Talmud the Palestinian Gemara to Shekalim is printed together with that tractate, no Babylonian Gemara being now extant, and none, in all probability, having ever existed. To Sabbath 21 to 28, no Palestinian Gemara is extant.

Lit.: Strack, H. L., *Introduction to Talmud and Midrash,* p. 34.

MOED KATAN ("minor festivals"), eleventh tractate of Moed, the second division of the Mishnah. It consists of four chapters, and discusses the regulations as to the types of labor permitted and prohibited during the days between the first and the last day of Passover and Sukkoth; these days were later known as Hol Hamoed. The general principle is that while work may be done on the intervening days of the festivals, it should be limited to work that is vitally necessary and cannot be put off to a later date, such as the repair of agricultural canals. Marriages may not be contracted, except the remarriage of a divorced wife, and the cutting of hair and washing of clothes are limited to those for whom they are absolutely necessary; mourning customs are abrogated if the period of mourning falls within this time. The tractate, incidentally, gives a good deal of information on the occupations, methods of work, public institutions and mourning customs of the Mishnaic and Talmudic period.

The Tosefta to the tractate is divided into two chapters and parallels the Mishnah. There are Gemaras to Moed Katan in both Talmuds, which contain numerous tales and proverbs, and an especially interesting account of funeral and mourning customs.

Lit.: Danby, H., *The Mishnah* (1933) 207-11; Lauterbach, J. Z., in *Jewish Encyclopedia,* vol. 8, p. 640.

MOGEN DOVID, *see* SHIELD OF DAVID.

MOHÁCS, city in Baranya county, Hungary, with 784 Jewish inhabitants in a total population (1920) of 15,800. Mohács, a royal privileged city, did not admit any Jews until 1839. The Jewish community and Hebrah Kaddisha of Mohács were founded in 1848 as a branch of the county rabbinate of Pécs. Although of comparatively recent origin and numerically small, the community prospered as a result of being organized (1860) in a modern spirit and due to the successful handling of its financial problems. The synagogue, for which land was acquired in 1854, was dedicated in 1864, the members of the community contributing towards the cost by buying perpetual seats. Land to provide salaries for rabbi and teachers was donated by the bishopric of Pécs. The first rabbi, Jakab Grünwald (d. 1880), was succeeded by Dr. Ármin Flesch, author of several works, including a Hebrew Haggadah with commentaries in Magyar. A school was founded in 1893; the community also maintained a Talmud Torah and library. Up to the enactment of the anti-Jewish laws (1938-42) numerous members of the community held important city and county offices.

MOHÁCSI, JENŐ, author, Magyar and German poet, b. Mohács, Hungary, 1886. In 1942 he lived in Budapest. Mohácsi started as a newspaperman, contributing to various publications in Magyar and German. He published his first volume of poems, *Crescens* (1904), at the age of eighteen and his play *Hamu* (Ashes) was performed by the Thalia Society, Budapest, in 1908. His principal work is an impeccable translation into German of *Az ember tragédiája* (The Tragedy of Man), a classical dramatic poem by Imre Madách (first German ed., 1927; second ed., 1934).

Mohácsi, who rendered into German two other classics of Hungarian dramatic literature (Katona's historical play *Bánk bán* and Vörösmarty's fairy play *Csongor és Tünde*), was recipient of many honors and distinctions in his own country. He also published (in German, with G. Voinovich co-author) *Madách und die Tragödie des Menschen* (1935) and (in Hungarian) *Lidércke,* a romantic biography of Madách's wife. In addition to several volumes of poems, short stories and dramas, he wrote texts for several original Hungarian operas and many radio plays in Magyar and German. Some of his poems in German were published in German anthologies.

MOHAMMED (more correctly, Muhammad; wrongly Mahomet), the founder of the Muhammadan religion, b. Mecca, about 570; d. Syria, 632. He was a member of the Hashim family of the tribe of Kuraish. According to none too reliable traditional accounts, he was still at an early age when he lost both his father, 'Abd Allah, and his mother, Amina; he was taken in first by his wealthy grandfather, 'Abd al-Muttalib, and later by his uncle, Abu Talib, the father of 'Ali, his cousin and future son-in-law. He was apparently well treated and was given employment with the commercial caravans sponsored by his relatives for trade with Syria, South Arabia, Mesopotamia, perhaps also Egypt and Abyssinia. The young man's circumstances were much improved by his first marriage, at the age of twenty-five, to the forty-year-old Khadija bint Khuwailid, a widow possessed of considerable property. Undoubtedly a marriage of convenience (Khadija on her part needed an energetic and experienced businessman to manage her mercantile interests), it developed, however, into a nearly ideal companionship of affection and mutual respect; Mohammed took no other wives during Khadija's lifetime and ever thought of her in terms of deep gratitude enhanced by his sorrow over the loss of the two sons whom she had borne to him.

The beginning of Mohammed's prophetic mission is shrouded in clouds of legends. The pagan Arab worship of tribal gods and holy objects had long ceased to satisfy the more thoughtful elements of Arab society, and both Jewish and Christian monotheistic ideas were current, especially in Yathrib which had a large Jewish population, and in both North and South Arabia where Christianity had won over a large number of converts. With these converts and their sympathizers Mohammed must have come into frequent contact, both at home in Mecca and on his commercial journeys, and while he misunderstood much of what he heard from them, its impress on his mind was nevertheless powerful. In any case, the first revelations found expression in his short, clipped utterances in rhyme, surcharged with powerful feeling and accompanied by great bursts of emotion and physical exaltation. Their central point was the call to belief in Allah, the one and only God, and in the future life, and to the abjuration of the native Meccan paganism; to this may have been added ordinances relating to ritual ablutions and periodical assembly for common worship.

The earliest converts were Khadija, 'Ali, and Abu Bakr (later the first caliph)—their unflinching devotion and Abu Bakr's wisdom played no small part in the ultimate victory of the new faith. Great skill was employed by Mohammed in choosing further converts among such able men as 'Umar ibn al-Khattab and 'Uthman ibn 'Affan, both of whom later became caliphs. But this progress necessarily aroused the enmity of the ruling Meccan oligarchy, and Mohammed quickly realized that he had no immediate future in his native city. A delegation sent to negotiate with the Negus of Abyssinia, the age-old enemy of the Arabs, aroused the ire of the Meccans still further, and Mohammed's position became so acute that he eagerly accepted an invitation from the inhabitants of Yathrib (subsequently renamed *Madinat al-Nabi*, "the Prophet's city," or for short Madina or Medina) to settle among them as their ruler. The migration (622 C.E.) thither is called by the Mohammedans a flight (*hijra*, Hegira), but was in all probability rather a gradual and well-planned movement, as a result of which Mohammed became dictator of a population largely converted to his faith and owing him complete obedience. The Jewish tribes resident in the city and its environs (the Banu Kainuka, the Banu Nadir, and the Banu Kuraiza) refused to acknowledge his mission and were ruthlessly exterminated, and modifications were introduced into the new faith in order to lead it farther away from Judaism and bring it nearer to Arab paganism, so as to exert a greater appeal to prospective converts.

With Mohammed's power consolidated in Madina and harmony established between the Meccan immigrants (*muhajirun*) and the Madinese converts (*ansar*), there began a series of forays against Meccan caravans. A victory over the Meccans at Badr (624 C.E.) was counterbalanced by a crushing reverse at Uhud, followed by a siege of Madina, which, however, was beaten back by Mohammed's disposing his forces in a fortified trench—a most unsporting stratagem to the mind of his Meccan opponents. Soon after a treaty of peace was signed at Hudaibiya, and the Meccan leaders, especially their two best strategists, Khalid ibn al-Walid and 'Amr ibn al-'Asi, becoming converted to Islam, the city itself quickly and peaceably came under Mohammed's power. He knew enough, however, to exploit his victory to the full by foregoing all thought of reprisal for past wrongs and treated the Meccans not only with generosity but also with marked benevolence, even though he kept Madina as his permanent residence. Even the Meccan sanctuary, the Caaba, though cleansed of idols, was left in the custody of its Meccan keepers, but henceforth only Moslems were permitted to take part in the pilgrimage ritual. One more serious battle (at Hunain) had to be fought with a confederation of pagan tribes, but after this

the submission of the whole of Central Arabia was obtained with comparatively little difficulty. Old gods were discarded with no regrets, and the only dangerous fly in the ointment remained the obligation to pay the alms-tax, which irked the unruly Arab spirit of independence greatly and was one of the prime causes of the general revolt which flared up immediately after the Prophet's death. Letters were sent also to neighboring lands demanding the conversion of their rulers and brought varying responses, some favorable and some hostile, but none of any dependable value, and Mohammed himself seems to have realized that the new faith would have to embark upon a career of conquest by the sword, for he was organizing an expeditionary force for Syria when death overtook him in June of 632.

To the medieval Christian writers Mohammed appeared to be the spawn of Antichrist, while to the medieval Jews he was an impostor (*pasul*), a pun on his Arabic title, *rasul Allah*, "the Messenger of Allah"). An impartial examination of the historical evidence supports neither of these views, nor the view of some modern writers who regard Mohammed's call as the manifestation of epileptic seizures. There is no valid ground for suspecting his sincerity, and if the spiritual exaltation and physical exhaustion which accompanied Mohammed's revelations be taken for pathological phenomena, then the Hebrew prophets and Jesus must come under the same general classification. To his credit belong his abolition of such features of Arab paganism as polytheism, blood-feuds and infanticide; his insistence on social equality and kindness to the weak and dependent; and his consistent emphasis of his mortality and rejection of any worship of his person.

That in the latter part of his career, as a powerful dictator, he fell into serious moral lapses both in his personal conduct and his official behavior, only emphasizes the fact that although seared with the divine flame he was after all human. His frequent marriages (some of which were pure political alliances) and his barbarous treatment of the inoffensive Jewish tribes are, no doubt, unworthy of one claiming to be the "seal" of the Jewish prophetic succession from Abraham to Jesus, but neither Abraham nor Jesus ever found himself in the position of a dictator of a warlike people driven by economic suffocation to world conquest. His adoption of several features of Arab paganism, subsequent to his realization that there was no hope of Jewish acceptance of his mission, was an act of political expedience, but so were Paul's reforms.

Mohammed's personal appearance, according to traditional accounts which need not be distrusted, was that of a rugged and healthy man of simple habits and tastes, a good and generous friend and a formidable enemy, and an engaging personality given to whole-hearted expressions of both rage and mirth. Of his several wives and concubines whom he acquired after Khadija's death, the favorite was 'Aisha, the daughter of Abu Bakr, who was many years his junior; his two sons by Khadija died young, and of his daughters he favored most Fatima, later the wife of 'Ali.

For the essence and later history of Mohammed's teaching, *see* ISLAM; KORAN. LEON NEMOY.

Lit.: Muir, W., *The Life of Mohammad, New and Revised Edition* (1912; a scholarly work, but marred by anti-

Mohammedan bias); Margoliouth, D. S., *Mohammed and the Rise of Islam* (1931); Chauvin, V. C., *Bibliographie des ouvrages arabes,* vol. 11, *Mahomet* (1909); Leszynsky, R., *Die Juden in Arabien zur Zeit Mohammeds* (1910); Wolfensohn, I. (Ben Zeeb), *Hayehudim Baarab* (1931).

MOHAMMEDANISM, *see* ISLAM.

MOHEL, *see* CIRCUMCISION; FUNCTIONARIES, RELIGIOUS AND COMMUNAL.

MOHILEV on the Dnieper, city in White Russia. Belonging at first to the princes of Lithuania, it subsequently formed part of the Kingdom of Poland; it was occupied by Russia in 1694 and incorporated definitely into that empire as capital city of the government of Mohilev after the first partition of Poland (1772). Mohilev was first mentioned in documents of the 14th cent.; it received the status of a city in 1561. The mode of life and security of the considerable Jewish community of Mohilev were precarious in a country ruled by the bigoted, anti-Jewish Polish nobility. At the request of the burghers of Mohilev, King Sigismund III confirmed (1633) an earlier order relegating the Jews to the outskirts of the city; subsequently they were forbidden to rent houses in non-Jewish neighborhoods. The Russians invading Mohilev in 1654 ordered expulsion of the Jews and distribution of their property among local and occupying authorities. Nearly all the Jews who lingered on, waiting for the termination of the war, were massacred with their wives and children by the Russians in the following year.

Sabbatianism deeply stirred the Jews of Mohilev, who were stricken by the horror of massacres. A monastic chronicler of the 17th cent. recorded that the inscription "Sapsai" and proclamation of the imminent arrival of the Messiah appeared on the walls of the churches at Mohilev. The Russians took many Jewish prisoners with them from the region around Mohilev (later the province of Mohilev) whom they allowed to remain at Moscow. These Jews, who attracted others of their coreligionists to Moscow, became the nucleus of a Jewish community there.

In 1772 Mohilev, as capital city of the government of Mohilev, became a part of the Russian Empire. The Russians imposed a head tax of one ruble on every Jew. Mohilev became also gubernatorial Kahal, with authority over smaller communities of the government. In the 18th cent., the communities of what became the government of Mohilev were united in the White Russian Synagogue. They held conventions (*Vaade Medinah*) which deliberated on matters of internal government (education, rabbinate) as well as on matters touching upon relationships with the Polish authorities, such as taxes and the selection of deputies to the Polish diet. The White Russian Synagogue held joint conferences also with the Lithuanian Synagogue (a union of Lithuanian communities). When both Lithuania and White Russia were united under Czarist rule, these associations became even closer. Elijah Vilna directed one of his letters to the gubernatorial Kahal of Mohilev, enjoining upon it the duty to eliminate Hasidism from its sphere of authority. Previously a rabbinical conference had been held at Mohilev which resolved to persecute the movement of Hasidism.

Early in the 19th cent., when village Jews were herded into the towns, those of the government of

Samuel Mohilewer

Mohilev applied for agricultural settlement in New Russia (governments of Bessarabia and Kherson). Mohilev sent its delegate to the conference of Jewish notables which assembled at St. Petersburg after the pogroms of 1882. The deputy, one Shmerling, after delivering his heartrending account, collapsed and died. In 1904 the smoldering discontent of reservists called up for the unpopular Russo-Japanese War was, in Mohilev as in other cities, diverted against the Jews. In the resultant pogrom the families of Jews fighting in the war were not spared. In the revolution of January, 1905, a Jewish youth of Mohilev made an unsuccessful attempt to wreak vengeance upon the chief of police who was credited with having instigated the pogrom.

Under Soviet rule, in the 20th cent., Mohilev had a total population of 50,000, of whom 34 per cent were Jews.

MOHILEWER, SAMUEL, rabbi and Zionist leader, b. Glubokoje, near Vilna, 1824; d. Bialystok, Poland, 1898. He studied at the Yeshiva of Bialystok and graduated as rabbi at the age of eighteen. For a time he followed a business career, but in 1848 he became rabbi in his native town. Here he remained until 1856, when he was called to Schakin, then to Suwalki, then to Radom, and finally to Bialystok. After the Russian persecutions of the Jews in 1881, Mohilewer personally accompanied the refugees to Lemberg and succeeded in diverting part of the emigration to Palestine.

These experiences interested him in the problem of Jewish emigration. He joined the Hibbath Zion movement and went to Paris to interest Edmond Rothschild in Jewish colonization in Palestine (1882). As a result of his efforts the colonies of Ekron and Rishon Le Zion were founded, and the consolidation of the Petach Tikvah colony, then in a difficult position, was also effected. Later on he helped found the Rehovoth colony (1890). With the growth of Zionism, he devoted time and effort to the movement and helped untiringly toward its popularization. He became the recognized leader of the Russian Zionists, before the

discusses the religious development of Judaism during the Persian, Greek and Roman periods. The 3rd volume treats extensively of the influence of Jews in the Roman empire.   GEORGE WRIGHT.

Lit.: Vogelstein, H., "Die Juden in Mommsens römischer Geschichte," *Allgemeine Zeitung des Judentums* (1904) 103-6; Gudeman, A., *Grundriss der Geschichte der klassischen Philologie* (2nd ed., 1909) 240-42; *Mitteilungen aus dem Verein zur Abwehr des Antisemitismus* (1893) 177; 1894, p. 55; 1897, p. 387; 1903, pp. 345 and 381; Gooch, G. P., *History and Historians in the Nineteenth Century* (2nd ed., 1920) 454-65; Fowler, W. W., "Theodor Mommsen: His Life and Works," *Roman Essays and Interpretation* (1920) 250-68; *Abwehr-ABC* (published by the Verein zur Abwehr des Antisemitismus) 40 et seq.

MONASH, SIR JOHN, general and engineer, b. Melbourne, Australia, 1865; d. Melbourne, 1931. Although not a career soldier, Monash was the first Australian to command his country's army corps in France (during the first World War), and the first Jew to attain the rank of general in England.

Monash's grandparents were printers of Hebrew books in Vienna; and he was related to the historian Heinrich Graetz. His father, Louis Monash, settled in Melbourne and at the university there young Monash took degrees in arts, law, and civil engineering. He then embarked on a conspicuously brilliant engineering career, becoming a pioneer and an expert in the use of reinforced concrete in construction.

Joining the Victoria militia, he rose rapidly; and, after reorganization of the armed forces of the Commonwealth (1912), he was made colonel. Upon the outbreak of the World War, he served for a while as chief censor, but soon was placed in command, with rank of brigadier general, of the 4th Infantry Brigade, and left with his troops for Gallipoli. Here "Monash Valley" commemorated his service. He was then called from the Suez Canal to England.

There he organized the 3rd Infantry Division, which he took to France in 1916. Finally in May, 1918, with the rank of lieutenant general, he was named to succeed General Birdwood as commander of all Australian expeditionary forces on the Western front. It was in the crucial last months of the war that Monash's corps figured decisively, participating in the important engagements that led to final Allied victory. On August 8, 1918, the Australian corps launched the great sixty-day counter-offensive which hastened the enemy's ultimate collapse. Monash wrote of these engagements in his *Australian Victories in France in 1918* (1920).

Monash was an intense Australian chauvinist, proud of his democratic army, which he called the "finest" in France. As a general he was famous for his brilliant organizing ability, which he claimed was based on "common sense." Both Lloyd George and Liddell Hart refer to him as the man who might have been commander-in-chief of the British forces, had the war lasted longer. No serious military mistake has ever been held against Monash in post-war analyses. After the armistice he had charge of the demobilization of his forces, and in London on Anzac day (1919) he led the march of 5,000 picked Australian troops. He returned to civil life and engineering, and was appointed director of the electrical project in the coal fields at Yallourn. In 1929 he was given general's rank.

John Monash

A man of diverse interests, Monash was a member and officer of numerous learned and engineering societies. He became active in the Jewish life of Australia, and in 1928 was elected president of that country's Zionist Federation. He expressed great admiration for the fighting qualities of the American soldiers in France, and his many foreign military honors included the Distinguished Service Medal conferred upon him by the United States government.

SHERRY ABEL.

Lit.: Monash, J., *War Letters of General Monash* (edit. F. M. Cutlack, 1934); Miles, "Le Général Monash," *Le Correspondant,* Oct., 1918, pp. 29-43; *Jewish Chronicle,* Oct. 16, 1931, pp. 10-11; *American Hebrew,* Oct. 16, 1931; *Australian Jewish Herald,* Oct. 15, 1931.

MONASTIR, see BITOLJ.

MOND, ALFRED, see MELCHETT.

MOND, EMILE, industrialist and philanthropist, d. London, 1938. He was educated in Paris and Zurich, then went to London to work with his famous uncle, Ludwig Mond, in the latter's chemical plant known as Brunner, Mond and Company. Shortly thereafter he became a member of that firm's board, and of the board of the Mond Nickel Company. He was likewise chairman of the South Staffordshire Mond Gas Company and of the Power-Gas Corporation Limited.

Mond was an officer of the Chemical Society and of the Faraday Society. He had a close interest in the affairs of the Institut Français de Royaume Uni, and was chairman of its finance committee; he was made an officer of the French Legion of Honor.

In 1919 he established the Francis Mond professorship in aeronautical engineering at Cambridge University, in memory of an aviator son killed in France in the first World War.

Lit.: Jewish Chronicle (London), Jan. 6, 1939, p. 12.

MOND, LUDWIG, manufacturing chemist, b. Cassel, Germany, 1839; d. London, 1909. Through his talent for solving the technical problems of production by applying the principles of science, he rose to be one of the world's foremost chemical industrialists.

After studying in Germany, under Kolbe at Marburg and under Bunsen at Heidelberg, young Mond (employed in a Leblanc soda works) discovered a process of recovering the sulphur from calcium sulphide in alkali waste. In 1862 he went to England to patent his process and secured a job there with the chemical works of Hutchinson and Company. He left to establish his own Leblanc manufactory at Utrecht; but in 1867 he crossed the channel once more, this time to become a citizen of England. He rejoined Hutchinson and perfected his sulphur process.

Several years later Mond made a trip to Belgium to investigate the new process of producing carbonate of soda which had been developed by the chemist Ernest Solvay. Convinced of the commercial superiority of the process, he obtained Solvay's option to exploit it in England.

In partnership with John T. Brunner, a fellow-employe at Hutchinson's, Mond opened (1873) his own ammonia soda works at Winnington, near the Cheshire salt beds. A long struggle to perfect production technique followed, and ended in triumph when in 1880 the partners reorganized into Brunner, Mond and Company, world's largest alkali makers. During this period Mond commercialized many new discoveries; most important among them his method of obtaining a valuable power gas, devised while trying to produce ammonia from the nitrogen of air. Thereafter his great gas factory supplied more than one hundred fifty works with Mond power gas.

Mond spent the period of 1884-1909 in further research, now assisted by Carl Langer, one time pupil of Victor Meyer. Working on chlorine by-products, Mond and Langer stumbled on their discovery of volatile metal carbonyls. This distinguished contribution to pure science Lord Kelvin characterized as "giving wings to the heavy metals." Discovery of the nickel carbonyl led to a new process of extracting nickel from ore. Mond and his sons developed extensive nickel mines in Canada and set up the great smelting and refining works in South Wales. In time the Mond process was producing one-third the world's nickel.

Mond acquired a vast fortune and in his magnificent London home gathered a priceless collection of Italian paintings, which were finally given to the National Gallery. His outstanding gift to scientific research was a quarter of a million pounds for the Davy-Faraday Laboratory, which became the Royal Institute's nucleus of creative scientific activities.

Lit.: Donnan, F. G., "Ludwig Mond Memorial Lecture," *Proceedings of the Royal Institute of Great Britain* (1938-39) 709-36.

MOND, SIR ROBERT LUDWIG, industrialist, b. Farnworth, Lancashire, England, 1867; d. Paris, France, 1938. He was educated at the universities of Cambridge, Edinburgh and Glasgow, and at the Zurich Polytechnicum. Mond was the eldest son of Ludwig Mond, and the brother of Lord Melchett. Entering the chemical manufacturing business which Ludwig Mond

had established, Robert L. Mond developed his own interests and renown, not only in many branches of scientific discovery and endeavor, but by aiding scientific research and in philanthropy in general. He had assisted his father in the discovery of carbonyls; later Mond carried out his own research in pure and applied chemistry, electro-chemistry and colorphotography. A fellow of the Royal Society, honorary secretary of the Davy-Faraday Research Laboratory of the Royal Institute, and a member in many other scientific societies in Great Britain and other countries, Mond was the recipient of honors and awards from various governments. He was a commander of the Legion of Honor, and an officer of the Order of Leopold. Knighthood was conferred on him (1932) in recognition of his public services.

Among the scientific interests outside his own field, archeology won a great part of Mond's attention. A series of excavations in Thebes, Palestine and Brittany was carried out by him; he was founder of the Mond expedition to Egypt, president of the Egypt Exploration Society, treasurer of the Palestine Exploration Fund, vice-president of the Archaeological Institute at the University of London, and honorary treasurer of the British School of Archaeology at Jerusalem.

To hospitals, Mond's benefactions totalled about £800,000. The Infants Hospital in Westminster (London) had been founded by Mond in memory of his first wife, Helen Levis Mond (d. 1905), and he was treasurer of the institution. He remained identified with Jewish interests all his life, but became particularly active after the rise of the Nazi regime in Germany, when he was made president of the Jewish Representative Council for the Boycott of German Goods and Services. In 1934 he visited the United States on behalf of the boycott movement. Prior to these events, however, Mond had been one of the honorary vice-presidents of the Society of Friends of the Hebrew University, and had also served as honorary president of the World Jewish Economic Federation. Mond wrote a great deal on chemical subjects. The universities of Liverpool and Toronto awarded him honorary LL.D. degrees.

LIBBY BENEDICT.

Lit.: Jewish Chronicle (London), Oct. 28, 1938, p. 12; *New York Times,* Oct. 23, 1938.

MONEY-CHANGERS IN THE TEMPLE, *see* PHRASES, BIBLICAL.

MONEY LENDING. According to many modern historians, it was not religious fanaticism that caused persecutions of the Jews in the Middle Ages, but economic reasons. It was the reaction of desperate peoples allegedly exploited by Jewish usurers. Since the close of the 10th cent., the Jews, who had been mercantile traders considerably earlier, engaged in money lending, which was forbidden to Christians by canonical law. In the course of a few decades almost the whole population everywhere in Christian Europe was indebted to the Jews, who, it was claimed, became owners or holders of pawned villages, towns, and even sanctuaries of the Church. This state of things was intolerable, and was altered by violence.

Money lending has been common to Western civilization since its development led to the formation of states even on a small scale. It reached a high status in

Greece long before the Jews came into contact with the Greeks, in Rome where mighty organizations of money lenders existed, and in the clearing houses of Egypt. But money lending in the ancient world did not aim so much to increase and accelerate the production of goods as to provide the population with means for paying taxes and tribute, and there was a constant tendency to sink accumulated wealth in palaces and temples instead of investing it for economic production. Hence money became rare, expensive, and its lack contributed to the decay of ancient civilization.

Contemporary public opinion, however, was inclined to treat all lenders and brokers as rascals whom it was just to pillage when opportunity arose. This attitude of the common people, lasting up to modern times, was formed long before the Jews were occupied with money lending.

The Jews of Biblical times, on the other hand, were scarcely interested in financial operations. Their commercial progress was rather slow compared with that of the neighboring peoples. In the times of Nehemiah, Jewish landowners, requiring money to pay their share of the tribute, were called upon to face difficulties similar to those confronting them in Greece and Rome. Philo declaimed against usury, and even many sages of the Talmud regarded all commercial gains with suspicion and were opposed to loans at interest. They relied on *Ex.* 22:24; *Lev.* 25:36-37; *Deut.* 23:20-21. The Jews of the Diaspora were mainly landowners or farmers without fortune. The situation of the Jews of Alexandria, where some Jews were money lenders, was exceptional. No pagan polemist accused the Jews of being greedy for money, nor characterized them as traders. Neither did any Christian polemist before the 4th cent.

The lack of money which impaired the economy of the ancient world became a calamity injurious to the economy of medieval Europe, which was by no means a pure barter economy. The Jews, who were the principal agents in mercantile transactions in Northern Europe during the 9th and 10th centuries, and educated Christian merchants until these displaced their teachers, attempted to remedy this drawback even before they were forbidden to deal in goods. Sporadic Jewish money lenders were active in the Frankish kingdom beginning with the 6th cent. When the Jews were prohibited to deal in goods, the need of money lending became by far more urgent in Northern Europe. For the Jews, thanks to their international relations, founded upon mutual confidence between coreligionists, were dependent on payment in currency in far lesser degree than were the Christian merchants. By carrying on the money trade the Jews of the Middle Ages rendered great services to the development especially of Northern Europe that gained predominance in Europe in the ensuing centuries.

But this activity of the Jews in the later Middle Ages was fatally influenced by their legal status and the attitude of the Church toward money lending.

The canonical law forbade lending money at interest. The attitude of the Church was altogether adverse to commerce, and especially to money trade, although it was steadily forced to compromise. The doctrine of the Church relied on the above-mentioned verses of the Old Testament in addition to a misinterpreted verse

from the Gospel according to Luke. Money lending at interest was stigmatized by the Church as usury. This stigmatization influenced the mental attitude even of thinkers who were adversaries of Christianity, and led to an erroneous criticism of Jewish money lending in the Middle Ages by confounding it with usury as it is defined by modern law. But the operations of the Jews in the Middle Ages were quite different from those defind by modern law as usury. The Jews lent money at a rate fixed by law or by decree of the government. Usury in modern times means overstepping the rate of interest fixed by law or custom. Moreover, the Jews did not conduct business on their own account; the princes were their partners.

The Jews were exempted from canonical law. They were expressly allowed to lend money. But this fact did not mean their monopoly of money lending. There were many ways for Christians to evade the law, whether by naming the expected gain *damnum, consideratio,* premium, reward, gratuity, finance, *frais, bene, civanza,* or the like, or by means of juridical fictions, such as the participation of the creditor in the debtor's business. In the Mediterranean countries, money lending was in practice, generally allowed because the law of the Church expressly exempted the *foenus nauticum,* corresponding to the risk of maritime trade, and it was impossible to determine whether or not a loan directly or indirectly concerned maritime risks. In Spain, Italy and Southern France, therefore, Jewish money lending activity was not very different from that of their Christian colleagues, and the importance of Jewish finance did not become manifest before the discovery of the maritime routes to Asia and America.

In Northern Europe, however, a sharp competition arose between Jewish money lenders and Christian merchants coming from Southern Europe, who were called Lombards and Cahorsins and were supported by the popes. The Church, too, lent money, and not without gain, but against a land gage whose revenues were bestowed upon it until the loan was paid back. Thus the prohibition of usury was respected, since the money originally lent did not by itself produce any interest. The Church, too, invested much of its capital in the business of Italian merchants. But the vigor of the Lombards and Cahorsins was by far greater than their technical efficiency. They carried on money lending in the same way as their Greek and Roman predecessors, and did not alter the conditions. Money was lent against pledges, for short periods and at a high rate of interest. No money market existed. Every credit operation was an isolated agreement, determined by consideration of particular circumstances. There was no difference between commercial and consumptive loans, nor between public and private loans.

Although the Jews took many more risks than their Christian competitors, because they were forced at all times to expect confiscation of their fortunes, arbitrary remission of debts on the part of the ruler, and ill-will on the part of powerful debtors, they were generally able to lend at a lower rate of interest than the Lombards. In Southern Europe the price of money in general was indicated by a rate of interest between 20 and 33 1/3 per cent for short period loans; in Northern Europe the discount was generally about 43 per cent, and occasionally it increased considerably when great loans accumulated. The Jews alone, at this time, voluntarily or forcibly, observed the conventional rate of interest, while the Lombards took every opportunity of raising the price of money. Thus the township of Brindisi, Italy, hailed the first Jew who entered the community as their deliverer from tyrannization by Christian creditors, as did the town of Lindau, in Germany, where the Lombards demanded more than 200 per cent. Almost everywhere in Northern Europe debtors expressed their fear of being treated worse by Christian creditors when a ruler intended, or was pressed by the clergy, to expel the Jews. This fear was expressly mentioned as the reason for the privilege granted Jews in 1470 by Emperor Frederick III. Besides, there are many evidences in the responsa literature to the effect that Jews were indebted to Christians.

But in general the Jews carried on money lending with the exclusive aid of their coreligionists. The Jewish communities took care of the observance of the decrees concerning the rate of interest and of the regulation of the engagements of Jews who changed their residences. The Jews furnished bail for each other. Because of their wide dispersion and their ability to maintain relationships in the Diaspora they became relatively independent of local difficulties. They introduced, if they did not invent, the bill and letter of credit, and they inaugurated two important reforms which, when they became general, later revolutionized the economic life of the world. Modern trade balances its indebtedness, in the main at least, not by each debtor's paying his creditor, but through the joint regulation of their engagements by the debtors of all countries. This innovation was practised to a certain degree by the Jews of the Middle Ages within their relationship. Furthermore, the Jews used their credit to provide themselves with money to lend out beyond their actual fortune, while the Lombards lent only the bullion which was in their cellars. In the course of the 17th cent. the new Jewish practice was adopted by Christian bankers in Holland and Sweden, and then by the Bank of England. This revolution in banking practice made it possible to finance the rapid growth of 18th cent. commerce and the huge industrial development which followed it.

The principal wants satisfied by Jewish money lenders of the Middle Ages were warfare and building. The Jews of Würzburg financed Emperor Rudolf of Hapsburg, those of Augsburg and Überlingen Emperor Louis of Bavaria. Even the Crusades were in part financed by Jews. They lent money to German, French and English townships to fortify the inhabited places and in that way to secure their economic development which was menaced by feuds.

The great epoch of Jewish money lending in the Middle Ages coincides with that of the erection of the churches, cathedrals and monasteries, many of which were built with the aid of Jews. Commercial credit was given by the Jews also to private merchants and craftsmen as well as to guilds and communities. The occasional purchase played an important part in medieval trade, and generally the debts could be paid back easily. The Jews who survived the persecutions of the first crusades owed their escape partly to the possibility of taking refuge in the castles whose owners

were their debtors and had no cause to hate their creditors.

Even when the Jews were not expropriated by the princes, they were a source of wealth because of the heavy taxes which they paid and the loans which they contracted for them. The striking disproportion between the financial power of the Jews and their juridical and political helplessness made them the puppets of political parties everywhere. They were considered great assets of the rulers who owned them. Adversaries of the latter, both neighboring states and diets within their territory, attempted to deprive their respective adversaries of this asset mainly by means of stirring up religious fanaticism. In 1385 the towns of Swabia purchased the Jews living there from the emperor in order themselves to exploit them. In 1434 their rival, the duke of Württemberg, lured away the Jews of Swabia by granting them civil rights which he later withdrew. The archbishops of Trèves remained mighty as long as they were served by Jewish money lenders who were at the same time their financial administrators. Muskin, the Jew, directed the finances of Trèves from 1323 to 1336, Jacob ben Daniel from 1336 to 1341, his son-in-law Michael from 1341 to 1350. They contracted important loans for the archbishop, often a million dollars a year, with the aid of the Jews of Metz and Strasbourg. In 1350 some knights opposed to the archbishop instigated persecutions of the Jews which led to their expulsion at the end of the century and their replacement by the Lombards. The result was a financial catastrophe which plunged the archbishop into debt and increased the power of the diet. Trèves, once the mightiest state of Germany, never recovered, and its disintegration contributed to the weakening of the other ecclesiastical principalities. Contrary-wise the rising territorial states of Germany utilized the court Jews to strengthen their power. The court Jews played a considerable role in the formation of the states which constituted the modern German empire.

The doctrine according to which the Jews were the property of the Christian ruler was applied practically by the Angevin kings of England with unrivalled ruthlessness. They adopted the canonical law, as did the king of France, contrary to most of the continental rulers, and they utilized the Jews as sponges to absorb the resources of their Christian subjects. Repeatedly impoverished because of royal confiscation of their property, the Jews in 1254 petitioned to be permitted to leave England, saying that the Lombards would be their substitutes (*usurarii Papae nos supplantaverunt*). But they were not allowed to emigrate. King Henry III proclaimed Jewish money lending as "king's service."

No Jew was allowed to pursue another profession. The king was even opposed to the baptism of Jews who should be prevented from money lending after their conversion. Jewish money lending meant indirect taxation of the king's Christian subjects. Notwithstanding their always precarious situation, the English Jews rendered great services to the country. They contributed one-twelfth of the king's resources. Their money was wanted by the clergy, the nobility and gentry, by guilds and townships, while the vast masses lived by barter. The money was employed to build monasteries and castles, to equip the retainers of the vassals and to finance wars. During the reign of King

Stephen alone 1,115 castles were erected in England with the financial aid of the Jews. Josce of Gloucester financed the conquest of Ireland. Aaron of Lincoln (1166) was the leading banker of his time. He employed loan agents in Paris and perhaps in Germany. When Aaron's fortune, after his death, escheated to the king, it was necessary to organize a special department of the exchequer for the purpose of winding up his affairs. Aaron financed the archbishop of Canterbury, the earl of Leicester, and the towns of Winchester and Southampton. Nine monasteries, the Abbey of St. Albans and many public buildings were erected from the sums advanced by him.

In order to control Jewish money lending and, on the other hand, to protect lenders against any attempt by mobs to burn their papers, King Richard I founded (1194) the Exchequer of the Jews. This office registered all money-lending operations of the Jews and provided them with copies. The British parliament recognized the fact that the Jews were the source of the king's financial independence. The great battle between crown and parliament was fought at the expense of the Jews. Pressed by parliament, Edward I forbade the Jews to lend money (1275), and in 1290 he was forced to expel them from England after parliament and clergy promised to give him one-fifteenth of the parliament's and one-tenth of the clergy's fortune. The expulsion of the Jews represented a serious defeat for the crown and caused the financial difficulties which led to the *confirmatio cartarum*. The Lombards were incapable of acting the positive part of the Jews, although in 1305 they secured dominating influence over the whole of the English administration. They raised the rate of interest to 60 per cent and more, and extorted from the people more than the Jews ever did; but they could not satisfy the economic wants of the country. Their regime in England ended with the ruin (1345) of their leading banking houses, Bardi and Perruzzi. The Lombards were replaced by the Hansards, who were equally hated, and expelled after a rule of about two centuries.

While in England the crown was deprived of its Jewish assets by parliament, in France the barons were deprived of them by the crown, which slowly gained power. The French barons claimed sovereignty. They possessed the right of coinage and of owning Jews. As long as the barons were in power the Jews were prosperous. They served both king and nobles by money lending, but in order to subordinate the nobles the kings were eager to suppress the Jews. The royal house of Capet evinced an anti-Jewish attitude which was unparalleled by other dynasties in Europe until the crown of Spain became the champion of the persecution of the Jews. In 1219 the Jews were forbidden by royal ordinance to grant productive loans to workmen. In 1230 the statute of Melun forbade the Jews to extend loans against written obligations and allowed them to make loans only against dead pledges.

Thus the important progress effected by the Jews was sacrificed to political domination and religious fanaticism. King Louis IX avowedly neglected economic reasons in order to realize his religious ideas. King Philip the Fair, who suppressed and persecuted the Templars in 1305, ordered expulsion of the Jews from France in 1306 and confiscated their fortune after his famous debasement of the currency. In France, too, the

expulsion of the Jews caused a financial crisis; for a long time no credit was available.

The Jews expelled from England and France began a partly new activity in Burgundy. But there they met with quite different conditions. It was a wealthy land, and there was sharp competition in money lending. Princes, knights, merchants, individuals and corporations lent money. Nevertheless, the Jews played an important part in the money trade during the 14th and 15th centuries, especially in their centers of Arras and the towns of Hainaut. In the 16th cent. most of them went to Holland, which also was a part of Burgundy. There they met their coreligionists who were refugees from Spain.

In Germany the Jews were generally excluded from great transactions in money lending from the end of the 14th cent. on. Some of them, however, continued to function on a large scale. The Jew Joseph, who owned the house "at the golden swan" at Frankfort, was a partner of the Fuggers.

In the 16th cent. Lisbon was the main center of Jewish money lending. Then the Jews went to Amsterdam, and there developed the banking business. Portuguese Jews were welcomed also at Hamburg, which city recognized the importance of money lending and thus became the leading commercial city of Germany. Jews took an active part in the issuing of the first regulations relating to exchange in 1605, and in the founding of the deposit bank of Hamburg in 1619. At the same time Abraham del Banco participated in the founding of the Banco Giro of Venice.

In Italy some of the governments had recourse to Jewish money lenders in order to cope with foreign competition. In 1389 the senate of Venice challenged the Roman Curia by giving a concession to a Jewish banker. In 1456 Duke Francesco Sforza of Milan solicited papal protection for some Jewish bankers at Novara. Even the pope himself, in 1483, exempted the Jews of Toscanelli, who founded a banking house at Lusignano, from all juridical consequences of their possible transgressions. The Jews, however, were not of great importance to Italy until the discovery of maritime routes to Asia and America endangered Italian trade, which was unable to compete with the countries along the Atlantic coast. The Medici were the first Italian princes to recognize the necessity of reforming finance with the aid of the Jews. In 1493 the Medici opened Livorno to Jewish money lenders, who remained there until modern times and developed vital activity.

The popes of the Renaissance were generally friends of the Jews, but the popes of the Counter-Reformation persecuted them and suppressed money lending. Realizing the decay of Italy, Pope Sixtus V, although adhering to the principles of the Counter-Reformation, radically shifted his policy concerning Jewish money lending. His bull of Oct. 22, 1586, fixed the status of Jewish lending bankers. They were allowed to reside outside of the ghetto. Their firms were registered in the *Liber Diversorum*. Three volumes of this register are preserved. From 1587 to 1669 the popes gave 1,003 patents to Jewish lending bankers in their states, i.e. twelve a year. This important development of the Jewish banking business in the Papal States by no means caused anti-Jewish feeling on the part of the population. The measures of Pope Sixtus V, maintained by his successors, saved the pontifical countries from the financial ruin which the neighboring kingdom of Naples suffered after the expulsion of the Jews, caused by its Spanish sovereign.

The 17th cent. shows the beginning of the regeneration of Jewish money lending which led to the development of the modern banking business. Modern banking, however, is quite different from medieval money lending because it is no longer founded upon odious privileges but, at least in principle, upon general economic and juridical laws and general insight into the legality of rewarding loans which are necessary for production by payment of interest. Any reason for economy and any reason for saving would be untenable without this insight.

See also: CAPITALISM; FINANCE.   HUGO BIEBER.

Lit.: Hoffmann, Moses, *Der Geldhandel der deutschen Juden* (1910); Juster, Jean, *Les juifs dans l'empire romain* (1914); Jacobs, Joseph, *The Jews of Angevin England* (1893); Lamprecht, Karl, *Deutsches Wirtschaftsleben im Mittelalter* (1885); Roth, Cecil, in *The Cambridge Medieval History,* vol. 7; Gonsiorowski, Herbert, *Die Berufe der Juden Hamburgs* (1927); Quilici, Brunetto, *L'evoluzione finanziaria del popolo ebraico* (1927); Loevinson, Ermanno, "La concession de banques de prêts aux Juifs par les papes," *Revue des études juives,* vol. 92-95 (1932-33).

MONGRÉ, PAUL (pseudonym for Felix Hausdorff), mathematician and philosopher, b. Breslau, 1868, d. 1932. He was professor of mathematics at the universities of Leipzig, Bonn, and Greifswald; in 1921 he was appointed associate professor at the University of Bonn. He was the founder of the *Bürger-und Bauern-Kalender,* which he issued annually from 1897 on. He published numerous philosophical papers, all of them reflecting the influence of Nietzsche: *Sant-Ilario: Gedanken aus der Landschaft Zarathustras* (Leipzig, 1897); *Das Chaos in kosmischer Auslese* (1898); and *Versuch einer positivistischen, ethisch-biologischen, kritischen Erkenntnistheorie; Ekstasen* (1900). Mongré's main mathematical work is *Grundzüge der Mengenlehre* (2nd ed., 1927); other works of his are *Analytische Beiträge zur nichteuklidischen Geometrie* (1899), and *Theorie der Systeme complexer Zahlen* (1900). He published in *Puck* a series of Jewish humoresques entitled "Briefe von Dobbljef Zussesbeusser." He also wrote brilliant theatre plays, one of which, *Der Arzt seiner Ehre,* a voluminous one-act play, a spiritual satire on duelling, had a great success.

Lit.: Heinze-Überweg, *Grundriss der Geschichte der Philosophie* (12th ed.), vol. 4, pp. 527, 549; *Poggendorffs biographisch-literarisches Wörterbuch für Mathematik,* vol. 5 (1925), part 1, p. 507; Wininger, S., *Grosse jüdische National-Biographie,* vol. 3, pp. 15-16.

MONIN, JOSÉ, writer and educator, b. Kazanka, Ukraine, 1895. After an early education in the agricultural colonies at Kherson, Monin went to Argentina, and graduated from the department of philosophy at the University of Buenos Aires in 1924. Subsequently he became a Zionist leader in Argentina. From 1924 to 1926 he was director of the cultural department of the Zionist Federation; in 1933 he founded the Zionist Youth Federation and in 1935 the Histadruth Ivrith. Monin was made president of the Vaad Hahinuch in 1936; he was also director of the Seminary for Jewish Teachers. Among his published works are *Sionismo renacentista* (1937); *Historia de los Judíos de la*

A broadside advertisement of Judah Monis' "Hebrew Grammar" issued in 1726

América Contemporánea (1939) and *Figuras de Renacimiento Judío* (1942).

MONIS, JUDAH, convert and Hebrew scholar, b. 1683; d. 1764. He prepared a Hebrew grammar for Harvard students (*Dickdook Leshon Gnebreet*), published in 1735 and distinguished as the first work of its kind in America. Little is known of his career prior to his coming to America and becoming an instructor at Harvard in 1722. He is said to have been an Italian Jew. In 1720 Harvard bestowed upon him the honorary degree of Master of Arts. Two years later, Monis became instructor of Hebrew in the University, but this was contingent upon his acceptance of the Christian faith. He professed the new belief in a discourse which he delivered on the day of his baptism, March 27, 1722. This address was printed the same year, "dedicated to the Jewish Nation." Monis also wrote two essays dealing with his belief in Christianity.

Whether Judah Monis was sincere in his conversion or not remains a matter of doubt; but, he continued until his death to observe the seventh day as his Sabbath. For about forty years Monis filled the position of Hebrew teacher at the University where he was popular with his students. Upon the death of his wife in 1759, he resigned his instructorship, and retired to Westboro, to live with his wife's relatives. The inscription in verse on his tombstone in Westboro refers to his Jewish origin. Judah Monis was the first to hold the title of Instructor in Hebrew at Harvard University and also the first to bring out a Hebrew grammar in this country (Boston, 1735).

Lit.: Publications of the American Jewish Historical Society, No. 3, pp. 112-14; No. 11, p. 80-81; No. 19, p. 110; No. 22, pp. 1-24; *Jewish Encyclopedia,* vol. 8, p. 657; Adams, Hannah, *History of the Jews* (1818); Kohut, G. A., in *American Journal of Semitic Languages,* vol. 14, p. 217 et seq.; vol. 15, p. 56 et seq.; idem, *Ezra Stiles and the Jews* (1902), pp. 22-23, 39-43, 137.

MONNICKENDAM, MARTIN, painter, etcher and lithographer, b. Amsterdam, 1874. Pupil of the Dutch State Academy of Arts from 1891 to 1894, he worked in Bruges (Belgium) and Paris from 1895 to 1897. In France he made twelve well-known etchings of "Old Paris." Afterwards he settled in Amsterdam where he became one of the better known painters of figures and landscape. His preferred medium was painting in oils but in later years many of his town scenes were done in water colors.

Monnickendam was a romantic painter of colorful scenes; through a very personal technique his canvases are often reminiscent of enamel work. He liked a multitude of figures and, therefore, chose theatrical scenes, or scenes in variety shows or concert halls. He also had a leaning toward figures surrounded by birds. Monnickendam painted many large canvases, but his small, simple Dutch town views and landscapes—particularly those of later date—achieved a higher degree of artistic merit. His better known works include *Boas and Ruth, Auction, Salome,* and many others. Nothing was known of his fate in 1942, after occupation of the Netherlands (May, 1940).

Lit.: Ost und West, April, 1911, cols. 327-44.

MONOBAZES II, king of Adiabene, a province on the banks of the Tigris, who succeeded his younger brother Izates to the throne about 55 C.E.; his reign was of short duration. Like his predecessor, Monobazes abandoned heathen worship for Judaism, and is said to have submitted secretly to circumcision. He emulated his mother, Queen Helena, in sending provisions to Jerusalem during a famine. He maintained a palace in the Holy City, and presented to the Temple golden vessels to be used on the Day of Atonement. When his mother and brother died, he had their remains removed to Jerusalem and buried in a magnificent tomb. The ruins of this mausoleum, erroneously called the Tombs of the Kings, are still in existence. Monobazes and other members of his family are honorably mentioned in the Talmud because of his adherence to Judaism in a time of stress. In 66 and 67 C.E. kinsmen of Monobazes fought against the Romans in the ranks of the Jews.

Lit.: Graetz, Heinrich, *History of the Jews,* vol. 2, p. 216 et seq.; Dubnow, Simon, *Weltgeschichte des jüdischen Volkes,* vol. 2, pp. 505-6.

MONOGAMY. Monogamy is a social condition that limits the marriage of a person to only one other person during their joint life. In the Bible it is assumed as the normal domestic state that can alone lay the firm foundation of a home in which peace and tranquility may dwell and children be properly reared. The idea of monogamy is easily traced in the Biblical account of the creation in which Adam is given only one mate. As in the Hebrew language the specific term for wife in relation to her husband is *'ishah,* the feminine form of *'ish,* the man, there is a direct indication that the man and the woman, united in marriage, form an equal partnership in the promulgation of the best purposes of life.

If language registers correctly the genius of a people,

the monogamous union thus reflects the true spirit of ancient Israel in the field of domestic relations. It is, indeed, lifted to a spiritual level and becomes symbolic, in the prophetical writings, of the close spiritual relation between God and Israel, in which God is represented as the husband and Israel as the spouse. It becomes a holy covenant. In such a sanctified union, perhaps the most eloquent tribute to the wife in any literature is found in the last chapter of *Proverbs.*

While in the Bible monogamy is assumed as an ideal in marriage, there are nevertheless many examples of polygamy. But the polygamous state is only tolerated. This phase of it is best illustrated in the life of the patriarchs. Abraham took Hagar as a wife only on the insistence of Sarah, who thought that she would always remain childless. Isaac had only one wife. Jacob had two wives only because of the trickery of Laban. And Moses, the law-giver, had only one wife, as did the high priest Aaron and his son Eliezer. There was apparently no need of legally enacting monogamy in the Mosaic code. It was assumed as the norm in domestic life. The levirate marriage which would seem to be an invasion of monogamy is sanctioned only by special dispensation.

In the post-exilic period monogamy became not alone the ideal but the all prevailing custom among the Jewish people. In fact it was this quality of marriage, ensuring the stability and religious character of the home, which formed one of the greatest factors in the development of Judaism after the exile. This is reflected in the Apocrypha, notably in *Tobit* and in *Sirach.*

The Talmudic period reveals monogamy as the ideal marriage state. Only in exceptional cases, owing chiefly to Oriental influence, is the monogamous ideal ignored.

In the Middle Ages Maimonides in his letter to the Provençal rabbis severely rebukes them for not insisting on monogamy in their respective communities. While polygamous unions among Jewish people dwelling in Islamic countries and even in Western Europe were not infrequent, Jews as a whole during all that period regarded monogamy as the ideal. Where that was disregarded it was the case of childlessness that was always the determining factor. Hence it was easy for Rabbi Gershom in the 11th century to make monogamy a mandatory statute in Jewish domestic life; and his rabbinical writ ran throughout the Jewish communities in Western Europe. Even in Islamic Spain, towards the close of the Middle Ages, it had full force. Since then monogamy has remained the fixed and invariable rule among the Jews, the exceptions, relatively few in number, being noted only in the Orient.

It is a historical fact that monogamy was first instituted in Europe by Jews and not by the Church. When Rabbi Gershom (960-1028) established the monogamous principle, the Church was still permitting simultaneous marriage with two persons—even as late as the time of Martin Luther.

CHARLES A. RUBENSTEIN.

Lit.: Lindo, E. H., *The Jews of Spain and Portugal;* Abrahams, I., *Jewish Life in the Middle Ages;* Lazarus, M., *Ethics of Judaism;* Amram, D. W., *The Jewish Law of Divorce;* Lecky, W. E., *History of European Morals* (1894); Graetz, H., *History of the Jews.*

MONOTHEISM. Monotheism, the belief in one God, is a distinguishing characteristic of the Jewish religion. While it is true that this concept of Divine Unity has appeared among other religious and philosophic groups, Hebrew monotheism is unique. It is not the outgrowth of philosophic reasoning as it was among the Greek philosophers, but it is the flowering of the ethical spirit of the Jewish people. "Monotheism came into being as the result of the realization of the absolute character of the moral law" (Baeck, Leo, *The Essence of Judaism,* 52). Hence the basic difference between Jewish monotheism and other religious theories is not in the number of gods but in the essence and nature of the Deity whom Israel worships.

Even before absolute monotheism reached its highest development in prophetic teachings, Israel's recognition of the moral nature of the Deity and, by implication, His absolute perfection presaged the lofty concepts of ethical monotheism and of universalism. The pagan gods strove for mastery; the God of Israel demanded that the people obey the moral law. While there is a difference between the theology of the Decalogue, in which idolatry is forbidden but the existence of other gods is not denied, and the absolute denial of other deities in the teachings of the prophets (*Zech.* 14:9; *Isa.* 45:5-7), the jealousy of God and His insistence on obedience to the law of the Decalogue point unmistakably in the direction of later monotheism.

According to Jewish tradition, monotheism began with Abraham (*Midrash Gen.* 38), but it is unquestionable that monotheism did not come into being fully developed. The several strata of Scripture reveal conclusively that there were many preliminary steps. Significant Biblical statements show that monolatry preceded monotheism (*Ex.* 15:11; *I Sam.* 26:19). Yahveh was Israel's God, but the existence of the gods of other nations was not categorically denied. Rather it was affirmed by David's statement: "for they have driven me out this day that I should not cleave unto the inheritance of the Lord, saying: Go, serve other gods." Even Elijah's attempt to eliminate other gods from Israel's land (*I Kings* 18:21) may be regarded as his zeal for Yahveh in a universe of competing deities.

However, the great literary prophets, realizing the full implications of the belief in the moral nature of God, were true universalists. They proclaimed that their own people, Israel, had no monopoly on God's favor. They knew Him to be the one and only God of all mankind. The first of the literary prophets, Amos of Tekoa (*Amos* 1 and 2), held that the universal God had established a moral law which applied to all peoples, to Tyre, Edom and Ammon as well as to Israel and Judah. Indeed, God would punish all who broke the moral law. With the same impartiality God led the Philistines from Caphtor, Aram from Kir, and Israel from Egypt (*Amos* 9:7). This pre-Exilic monotheism of Amos and of later prophets (for example, *Isa.* 6:3) became even more explicit in the sermons of Jeremiah (*Jer.* 10:10). The post-Exilic struggle with Persian dualism made it even more imperative that the monotheistic message be proclaimed vigorously. In answer to the Zoroastrians, who held to the belief in two universal powers, the god of light and the god of darkness, Deutero-Isaiah (*Isa.* 45:5-7) declared in the name of the One and Only God: "I form the light, and create darkness; I make peace, and create evil; I am the Lord, that doeth all these things." While the appearance of Satan

in the book of *Job* reflects Persian influence, it is evident that Satan is not co-equal with God but completely subordinate to Him (*Job* 1 and 2). Morris Joseph (*Judaism as Creed and Life,* 66) speaks of Satan in Jewish literature as the "personification of evil," rather than as an independent power. Thus, in the face of the challenge of Persian dualism, Israel retained its monotheism.

In Talmudic times and in later periods of contact with Christian and other religious philosophies the Jewish people adhered to the belief in one, unique God. Rabbinical utterances reflect the controversies which demanded a vigorous restatement of Jewish principles. Speaking in God's name, the rabbis declared that everything has a mate but God, who is alone and unique in the world He has fashioned (*Midrash Deut.* 2). God is called *Makom* because the entire universe exists in Him, who is greater than all creation (*Midrash Gen.* 68). "He who denies the existence of other gods is a Jew" (*Meg.* 13a).

In the creedal statements of Jewish philosophers and in their general writings the monotheistic principle is stressed (*Emunoth Vdoth* 1:7; *Moreh Nebuchim* II:1). The philosophers are aware of the challenge to monotheism of the Christian doctrine of incarnation, and they respond with the reaffirmation of the Jewish point of view (*Hoboth Halebaboth* 10). In Jewish liturgy, traditional and revised, the Divine Unity is proclaimed vigorously and repeatedly (the Shema, Adon Olam, Yigdal, Alenu, and other prayers). A declaration that God is one is the death-bed statement of every loyal Jew. The most recent formulation of Jewish principles contains this declaration: "The heart of Judaism and its chief contribution to religion is the doctrine of the One, living God" (*Central Conference of American Rabbis Year Book,* vol. 47, p. 97).

ABRAHAM SHUSTERMAN.

Lit.: Kohler, Kaufmann, *Jewish Theology;* Joseph, Morris, *Judaism as Creed and Life;* Baeck, Leo, *The Essence of Judaism;* Cohon, Samuel S., *Judaism and Christianity Compare Notes;* Schechter, Solomon, *Some Aspects of Rabbinic Theology.*

MONSKY, HENRY, lawyer and welfare leader, b. Omaha, Nebraska, 1890. The first Nebraskan to attain national stature in Jewish affairs, Monsky was the son of a synagogue cantor who hoped his son would be a rabbi. Although thoroughly grounded in Jewish religious affairs (on occasion he still conducts a religious service in Omaha) Monsky chose law and received his degree (1912) from Creighton University, a Jesuit institution in Omaha. He was only thirty-one when elected president of B'nai B'rith's District Grand Lodge No. 6, largest in the Order. In 1923 he was chosen a member of the B'nai B'rith executive committee, and in 1938 he was elected national president, an office to which he was reelected in 1941.

Monsky was an organizer and in 1942 vice-president of the General Jewish Council. Since 1939 he has been an honorary national chairman of the United Jewish Appeal and of the United Palestine Appeal at whose annual conferences (1939, 1940, 1941 and 1942) he was a principal speaker. He also served on the executive committees of the National Refugee Service, the Joint Distribution Committee, the Council of Jewish Federations and Welfare Funds, the National Conference of

Christians and Jews and the American Association for Jewish Education.

Monsky was also on the honorary advisory committee of Youth Aliyah, honorary vice-president of the Jewish Publication Society of America, a member of the honorary board of trustees of the Jewish Chautauqua Society, a member of the Army and Navy Committee of the Jewish Welfare Board and a member of the Jewish Committee on Boy Scouting.

Long identified with social welfare organizations, Monsky has been president of the Omaha Community Chest, the Omaha Boy Scout Council, the Nebraska Conference of Social Work, the Plains States Association of the Council of Jewish Welfare Funds, and a member of the boards of the Family Welfare Association of America, the National Council for Naturalization and Citizenship and the American Forum for Democracy.

Under his presidency, the B'nai B'rith membership has doubled and its program has been streamlined. Travelling extensively over the country, he has kept in close touch with all aspects of B'nai B'rith activity. Since the beginning of the second World War he has been devoting himself to mobilizing B'nai B'rith manpower and resources for war service. In 1941 President Roosevelt appointed him a member of the National Voluntary Participation Committee of the Office of Civilian Defense. In 1942 Monsky was awarded the honorary degree of Doctor of Hebrew Letters by Dropsie College for Hebrew and Cognate Learning.

(*See illustration in vol. 2, p. 425*)

BERNARD POSTAL.

Lit.: Current Biography, vol. 2, Nov., 1942.

MONTAGU, EDWIN SAMUEL, English statesman, second son of Sir Samuel Montagu, the first Lord Swaythling, b. 1879; d. London, 1924. He entered Parliament in 1906 as Liberal member for the Chesterton division of Cambridgeshire; Asquith, then chancellor of the exchequer, chose him as his parliamentary secretary. From 1910-14 he served as under-secretary of state for India under Lord Morley and Lord Crewe, and made a journey to India. During the first World War, as financial secretary of the treasury, he originated the proposal to issue War Savings Certificates.

In 1915 Montagu entered the cabinet as chancellor of the Duchy of Lancaster, but soon resumed his post in the treasury department; through his suggestion an arrangement was made with J. P. Morgan & Co. whereby the Allies were assured of a large and continuous supply of munitions and war material. In 1916 he was made minister of munitions. In 1917, as secretary of state for India, he visited India again; he and the viceroy, Lord Chelmsford, issued a joint report recommending various constitutional reforms which formed the basis for the Government of India Bill passed in 1919. In 1922 he was forced to resign his position as secretary of state for India because his policies conflicted with the anti-Turkish policies of Lloyd George and his cabinet, and withdrew from political life following a defeat in the general elections. Montagu took no part in Jewish life, and during the negotiations between the Zionist Organization and the British government he sharply opposed the plan of creating a Jewish national homeland in Palestine.

EWEN EDWARD SAMUEL MONTAGU, barrister and naval

Edwin Samuel Montagu

officer (b. 1901). He was the second son of the second Lord Swaythling (Montagu) and was educated at Harvard University and at Trinity College, Cambridge, where he received his B.A. and LL.D. degrees. In 1924 he was called to the bar and in 1939 was made King's Counsel. Montagu was a lieutenant-commander in the Royal Naval Volunteer Reserve. Among his activities in the Jewish community was his post as treasurer of the United Synagogue of England.

LIONEL SAMUEL MONTAGU, army officer and banker (b. 1883), youngest son of the first Lord Swaythling (Montagu). He was educated at Oxford. During the first World War, Montagu served with the British armies from 1914 to 1919, and was awarded the Distinguished Service Order. In 1940 he was commissioned a temporary major in the Royal Marines.

IVOR GOLDSMID SAMUEL MONTAGU, film producer and author (b. London, 1904). He was the youngest son of the second Lord Swaythling (Montagu) and was active in the left-wing labor movement in England. He also wrote film surveys and reviews, particularly on the Russian cinema. He was president of the International Table Tennis Federation, and chairman of the English Table Tennis Association. Montagu was the author of *Table Tennis Today* (1923) and of *Table Tennis* (1936).

MONTAGU, LILIAN HELEN, social worker and religious leader, b. London, 1874. She was the daughter of the first Lord Swaythling. After completing her education under private tuition, Miss Montagu entered social work. In 1900 she became affiliated with the National Council of Women in the United Kingdom and in 1908 with the Women's Industrial Council. She was also chairman of the West Central Jewish Club.

Miss Montagu was regarded as the dominant spiritual figure in social work in England, but more especially in Jewish social work. Having seen the value of Jewish piety in her own home, she early became concerned with the difficulties of adapting the ritual of Jewish tradition to modern life. In July, 1899, an article she wrote for the *Jewish Quarterly Review,* on "The Spiritual Possibilities of Judaism Today" suggested that the tenets of Judaism could be so practiced as to make them suitable for the demands of the time. The ideological ground for action had been prepared in the writings of Claude G. Montefiore, and it was with Montefiore and several others that Miss Montagu, in 1902, started the series of meetings which were to result in the establishment of the Liberal Synagogue of England, or the Jewish Religious Union.

Miss Montagu was made a lay preacher by the Jewish Religious Union, the first woman to perform this function. She spoke, not only as preacher, but as advocate of liberal Judaism, throughout Great Britain, the United States, and other countries. In 1926 she was instrumental in calling the first international conference of Liberal Judaism and was made honorary secretary of the World Union for Progressive Judaism. She was also, in 1942, president of the Jewish Religious Union of England.

Among Miss Montagu's books were *Naomi's Exodus*; *Broken Stalks*; *What Can a Mother Do?*; and *Thoughts on Judaism.* Miss Montagu was awarded an honorary D.H.L. degree by the Hebrew Union College in 1929. Her communal and civic work in other fields included the co-chairmanship of the Westminster Juvenile Court and service as a justice of the peace. She was given the Order of the British Empire in 1937.

REBEKAH KOHUT.

Lit.: Montagu, Lily H., "The History of Liberal Judaism in England," *The Judaeans,* vol. 4 (1933) 152-62; *American Hebrew,* June 25, 1926, p. 199.

MONTAGU, LOUIS SAMUEL, *see* SWAYTHLING, SECOND BARON.

MONTAGU, SAMUEL, *see* SWAYTHLING, FIRST BARON.

MONTAGU, SIR SAMUEL STUART, Member of Parliament, b. Liverpool, 1856; d. London, 1926. He was the brother of Sir Herbert Samuel Montagu and the nephew and business partner of Sir Samuel Montagu, the first Baron Swaythling, whom, upon his retirement in 1900, he succeeded in the House of Commons as representative from Whitechapel, a district with a large Jewish population. In 1912 he was made a baronet. In 1919 the British government delegated him to go to Poland to gather information on excesses committed against the Jews. An active member of the London Jewish community, he was president of the Association of Friendly Societies, of the Home and Hospital for Jews, and vice-president of the Mizrahi in England.

MONTAGU, STUART ALBERT SAMUEL, *see* SWAYTHLING, THIRD BARON.

MONTAIGNE, MICHEL DE, essayist, b. in the château of Montaigne near Bordeaux, 1533; d. there, 1592. An attempt was made (by Henri Bertreux) in the 1930's to prove that Montaigne's ancestry on his father's side is traceable to a family of Jewish merchants established in Portugal, and that Eyquem (or Ayquem), the patronymic of the Montaignes, is of Hebrew derivation. This theory is doubtful. On the other hand, it is certain that his mother was of Jewish descent. Her maiden name was Antoinette de Louppes, as she

Lilian Helen Montagu

signed herself. She was the daughter of a wealthy merchant of Toulouse, Pierre de Lopez, a descendant in the fifth generation of one Mayer Paçagon, who was a member of a prominent Jewish family of the city of Calatayud, Spain. Mayer seems to have embraced Christianity early in the fifteenth century and assumed the name of Juan Lopez de Villanueva. The family removed to Saragossa and at the end of the fifteenth century some of its members settled north of the Pyrenees, at Toulouse and Bordeaux, while others went to Holland, both branches prospering greatly.

A few of the members of the Paçagon clan seem to have remained within the fold; certain of the others are known to have perished at the hands of the Inquisition. One of Mayer's sons and two grandsons died on the scaffold because of their secret attachment to Judaism. For the rest, his descendants seem to have been faithful Christians, several of them marrying into old Christian families. Among Montaigne's maternal relatives, then, there were both devoted Catholics and zealous Protestants, and doubtless kinsmen of his could also have been found in the Jewish quarters of the cities of the Levant. But it is not likely that he knew of the latter.

Antoinette de Louppes was married to Pierre d'Eyquem in 1528 and bore him at least eight children, of whom Michel was the eldest. She survived both her husband and her first-born, dying in 1601, apparently a nonagenarian. She seems to have been an energetic, shrewd, capable matriarch who, by her own account, helped her husband to build up his large fortune. She does not appear to have lavished much affection on her studious son and at least toward the end she may even have resented the fact that through no merit of his own he was, as his father's sole heir, enjoying the fruits of her labors. She is said to have been a Protestant, but this is not certain. The one reference to her in Montaigne's writings is to the effect that she learned enough Latin to converse with him in those early years when he was kept ignorant of any other language.

Various opinions have been put forward as to the effect of Montaigne's Jewish ancestry upon his temperament and mentality. Such speculations, however, remain of necessity in the realm of conjecture. His only mention of the Jews in the *Essays* is a reflection on the tenacity with which they hold to their faith in the face of suffering. When he observes in this passage that they seldom make sincere converts, one wonders whether he had any knowledge of his Marrano relatives. In his diary of his journey to Italy (1580-81) he notes, among the pleasures Rome afforded him, a sermon by a renegade rabbi who preached every Saturday to a group of his former co-religionists, compelled to listen to his discourse. Montaigne's sensibilities do not seem to have been offended by this act of intolerance. That his curiosity extended to Jewish practices is evident from the fact that he had a long talk with the Verona Jews about their ceremonies, and set down a careful account of a circumcision that he witnessed in Rome, but his seems to have been the curiosity of a stranger.

AVRAHM YARMOLINSKY.

Lit.: Bertreux, Henri, "Les véritables ascendances de Montaigne," *La revue hébdomadaire,* Feb. 12, 1938; Nicolai, Alexandre, "À propos des ascendances de Montaigne," *Revue bleue,* Sept. and Dec., 1938; idem, "Les ascendants de Montaigne," *Revue philomathique,* Oct./Dec., 1938; Roth, Cecil, "L'ascendance juive de Michel de Montaigne," *La revue des cours et conférences,* Dec. 30, 1937; idem, *The Jewish Contribution to Civilisation* (1938) 98-99; Courteault, Paul, "La mère de Montaigne," *La revue historique de Bordeaux,* vol. 27 (1934), and *Mélanges de littérature, d'histoire et de philologie offerts à Paul Laumonier* (1935); Ginsburger, Ernest, "La mère de Montaigne," *La revue juive de Genève,* Nov., 1935; Corraze, Raymond, "Les Lopez, ancêtres maternels de Michel de Montaigne," *Bulletin philologique et historique du Comité des travaux historiques et scientifiques, Années 1932-3* (1935); Vischer, W., "Der Prediger Salomo im Spiegel M. de Montaignes," *Jahrbuch der theologischen Schule Bethel,* vol. 4.

MONTANA, the third largest state of the United States with respect to territory, but with a population of only 559,456 (census of 1940), including about 1,800 Jews. The Jewish population decreased in the two decades from 1920 to 1940. In 1917 there were about 2,500 Jews in Montana, whose population was then about 473,000.

Jews were among the first to settle in Montana. They were members of the Virginia City vigilante organization formed to suppress outlawry before the territorial organization of Montana in 1864. Jacob Feldberg was elected to the first Virginia City Council in 1865, and Henry Jacobs was chosen the first mayor of Butte in 1879. From 1885 to 1889 Henry Lupin served as mayor of that city. Ben Ezekiels was a member of the territorial legislature in 1873, and Albert J. Seligman from 1889 to 1890. Sol Starr was made territorial auditor in 1874. The names Kaufman, Sands, Gans and Klein were prominent among Montana cattlemen of this early period. The rancher Kaufman employed Charlie Russell, the celebrated cowboy artist. Jews were among the early Montana storekeepers and bankers. The firm of Herschfeld Brothers was one of the first banks in Montana. Albert J. Seligman was in the banking business in Helena.

Temple B'nai Israel of Butte, Montana

Butte, the largest city in Montana, also had the largest Jewish population in 1942. In that year the population of Butte was 37,081 (census of 1940), including about 550 Jews. It had two congregations, Adath Yisroel (Orthodox) and B'nai Israel (Reform). The latter was founded in 1897. The first rabbi of Temple B'nai Israel was M. Eisenberg (1897-99). The rabbi in 1942 was Joseph Gitin, whose service began in 1935. He was the only rabbi in the state of Montana (1942). Jewish organizations in Butte included a Baron de Hirsch Lodge, a B'nai B'rith Lodge, and the Butte Jewish Welfare Chest.

Sam Jacobs was city treasurer of Butte in 1908, and Herman Strassburger occupied this position in 1910. William Meyer served as police commissioner from 1917 to 1918 and as chairman of the Silver Bow County Democratic Committee for ten years.

Helena, the capital city of Montana, had the state's oldest Jewish community; in 1942 this numbered about sixty-five out of a total city population of 15,056 (census of 1940). As early as 1870 there was a benevolent society, a social club and a ladies auxiliary. Temple Emanu-El was founded in 1887 and its synagogue built in 1891. The first rabbi was Samuel Schulman, later of New York city. With the decline in Jewish population the building was no longer used and was subsequently given to the state of Montana as a gift from the Jewish community. Among the Jews of Helena prominent in civic activities were Lester Noble, Isaac Boyer, and Norman Winestine, who were presidents of the Helena Chamber of Commerce. Sol Hepner was county attorney for Helena in 1897, and Lester Noble in 1917. Emanuel Fischer was city treasurer in 1910.

Billings, with a population of 23,261 (census of 1940), had about seventy-five Jews. Among the early Jewish settlers were Samuel Wolfson (1895), Morris Slomowitz (1897), Morris Gittleson (1901) and Louis Herron (1903).

Great Falls had a Jewish community of about one hundred. There were about thirty Jews residing in Lewistown. Other cities that had between ten and twenty Jewish residents in 1942 were Anaconda, Bozeman, Livingston, Miles City, and Missoula. Adolphus N. Veit was mayor of Livingston in 1913; Louis Newman was mayor of Great Falls. Meyer Henry Wolf of Missoula was, in 1923, made assistant regional forester of the United States Department of Agriculture Forest Service for Montana, northern Idaho, and eastern Washington. Robert Lloyd Housman of Missoula was head of the school of journalism of the University of Montana in 1936.

Harry Meyer was member of the state senate from 1935 to 1939 and Democratic floor leader from 1938 to 1939. Other Jews who were members of the state legislature included Sol Hepner (1897), James Lessner (1910), Frank Eliel (1911), Joseph Binnard (1911), H. S. Hepner (1913), Mark Ezekiels (1913), William Meyer (1919), Lester Noble (1919) and A. B. Cohen (1940). William Meyer was on the state board of education from 1932 to 1936. Dr. L. H. Fligman, who was president of the Montana Medical Association, was a member of the Montana state board of health. Meyer Henry Wolf served on the Montana state planning board.

Dr. Samuel Steinberger was a member of the American Board of Radiology. Earl Genzberger was a state commander of the American Legion. Joseph Gitin was president of the Montana branch of the Volunteers of America from 1940 to 1941. He was also fraternal delegate to the Silver Bow County Trades and Labor Council in 1937. Among the Jewish Grand Masters of the Montana Grand Lodge of Masons were Sol Starr, Moses Morris, Sol Hepner and Henry L. Frank.

JOSEPH GITIN.

MONTEFIORE, Italian-English family, many members of which distinguished themselves in public life and letters. The family traces its origin from one of several small Italian towns of the same name. In the 17th cent. there were merchants bearing this name in Ancona, and since the beginning of the 18th cent. in Livorno. In 1752 Moses Hayim Montefiore (1712-89) married the daughter of a Moorish merchant and moved from Livorno to London. His fourth son, Joseph Elias Montefiore, married Rahel, a daughter of Abraham Mocatta and became the father of Sir Moses Montefiore. His seventh son, Eliezer Montefiore, married a granddaughter of Simon Barrow of Amsterdam and emigrated to the West Indies.

Outstanding members of the Montefiore family beside those who are given separate articles below are: Abraham Montefiore, stockbroker (b. London, 1788; d. Lyons, France, 1824), a brother of Sir Moses Montefiore; Charlotte Montefiore, authoress and philanthropist (b. London, 1818; d. London, 1854); Joseph Barrow Montefiore, merchant (b. London, 1803; d. Brighton, England, 1893) who, like his brother Jacob Montefiore, was among the early pioneers of Australia; Joseph Mayer Montefiore, communal worker (b. London, 1816; d. London, 1880), a nephew of Sir Moses Montefiore; Nathaniel Montefiore, communal worker

and leading member of the Sephardic congregation in London (b. London, 1819; d. London, 1883).

MONTEFIORE, CLAUDE JOSEPH GOLDSMID, theological scholar and philanthropist, grand-nephew of Sir Moses Montefiore, b. London, 1858; d. London, 1938. Montefiore was educated at Oxford University. Of strong religious leanings, he was greatly influenced by the teachings and personality of Benjamin Jowett. He studied theology for a time at the Hochschule für die Wissenschaft des Judentums in Berlin, in order to prepare himself for the ministry of the West London Reform Synagogue, of which his mother's family, the Goldsmids, were among the founders. However, he found himself out of sympathy with what appeared to him to be the inadequacy of German Reform, and for this reason did not accept this position.

Although he never became a professional preacher, religion continued to be the center of his studies and absorptions, especially through his close relationship with Israel Abrahams and Solomon Schechter, then the foremost English Jewish scholars. In conjunction with Abrahams, Montefiore founded the scholarly *Jewish Quarterly Review* at London in 1888. While still a young man, he established his reputation as a Biblical scholar of the first rank. He was called upon to deliver the Hibbert Lectures for the year 1892 on the subject of "The Religion of the Ancient Hebrews" (published at London in the same year under the title of *Lectures on the Origin and Growth of Religion as Illustrated in the Religion of the Ancient Hebrews*), and wrote and lectured considerably on both the Old and New Testament and on kindred subjects, in the spirit of the words of Benjamin Jowett, which Montefiore often quoted: "The facts of an ancient or religious history are amongst the most important of all facts; but they are frequently uncertain, and we only learn the true lesson which is to be gathered from them when we place ourselves above them."

Through his impartial attitude, Montefiore, in several of his works, aimed to give to Christians a better understanding of the rabbis, and to Jews a better knowledge of the teachings of Jesus. This very detachment, however, made him the target of bitter reproaches on the part of his fellow-Jews, many of them claiming to see in his writings a leaning toward Christianity.

Montefiore championed the cause of Liberal Judaism in England. It was due largely to his efforts that there was established in England (1902) the Liberal Jewish Union, as well as the synagogues connected with it and the exposition of its thought. He was for years president of the Liberal Jewish Synagogue in London, founded in 1911. Recognized by his contributions to Liberal Judaism as the world leader, he was elected president of the first World Union for Progressive Judaism in 1926, and served in this position until his death. Maintaining that Liberal Judaism aims to diminish the racial and national elements in Judaism and that it must be free to move along the path of universalism, Montefiore was always a sturdy and consistent opponent of Zionism.

Montefiore took an active part in religious, philanthropic and educational organizations of British Jewry.

Claude Joseph G. Montefiore

A few of these were the Jewish Religious Union, the Jewish Colonization Association, the Jews' Infant Schools, the Westminster Jews' Free School, and the University College, Southampton. He was president of the Anglo-Jewish Association for twenty-five years (1895-1920). Oxford University awarded him the honorary D.Litt. degree, Manchester University the honorary D.D. degree, and the Jewish Institute of Religion (New York city) the honorary D.H.L. degree.

Montefiore was distinguished for thorough scholarship and broad tolerance. Though storms of controversy raged about him, and he was often the target of abuse and attack, he himself was always a pattern of respect for his opponents. Stephen Wise testified to this when he declared in 1926: "His anti-Zionist position is most significant, after all, and most potent because we know that his words are not a pretense, not a pose, not a bit of ecclesiastical humbuggery. They represent the deep convictions of a deep soul." His intense universalism did not in any way weaken his intense Jewishness. "I cannot bear," he once said, "that a single life should be lost to Judaism or that a single Jewish soul lose the fullness and possibilities of the religious life."

Montefiore's sense of humor and his deep humanity have been testified to again and again by his associates. His ability as a preacher has been recognized by all who heard or read his sermons. But more important, he was a magnificent preacher even according to the difficult standard which he, a layman, set up for the Jewish ministry, when he said, "The good life of a clergyman is his best sermon."

Montefiore was the author of the following works: *Aspects of Judaism* (jointly with Israel Abrahams; 1895); *Bible for Home Reading* (2 vols., 1899-1900); *The Synoptic Gospels* (1909; 2nd, rev. ed., 1927);

Liberal Judaism (1903); *Some Elements of the Religious Teaching of Jesus* (1910; Jowett lectures for 1910); *Outlines of Liberal Judaism*, (1912; 2nd ed., 1923); *Judaism and St. Paul* (1915); *Liberal Judaism and Hellenism* (1918); *The Old Testament and After* (1923); *Rabbinic Literature and Gospel Teaching* (1930); *A Short Devotional Introduction to the Hebrew Bible for the Use of Jews and Jewesses* (1936); *A Rabbinic Anthology* (1938).   PAUL GOODMAN.

Lit.: Reichert, Victor E., "The Contribution of Claude G. Montefiore to the Advancement of Judaism on the Commemoration of His Seventieth Birthday," in *Central Conference of American Rabbis Year Book*, vol. 38 (1928) 499-520; Burkitt, F. C., "Claude Montefiore: an Appreciation," in *Speculum Religionis* (1929) 1-17; *Festgabe für Claude G. Montefiore* (1928); Wolfs, J., "Claude Montefiore: Sa Vie et ses Idées," in *La Question d'Israël*, vol. 17 (1939) 503-16, 561-72; Cohen, Lucy, *Some Recollections of Claude Goldsmid Montefiore* (1940).

LEONARD GOLDSMID MONTEFIORE, communal leader (b. London, 1899). He was a son of Claude Goldsmid Montefiore and became president of the Anglo Jewish Association (1926). He was also a member of the council of the Jewish Colonization Association. In 1934 he wrote a pamphlet exposing the Nazi falsehoods about the Jews in Germany.

MONTEFIORE, SIR FRANCIS ABRAHAM, communal leader, b. London, 1860; d. London, 1935. A grand-nephew of Sir Moses Montefiore, he inherited the baronetcy in 1886. In 1894 he became high sheriff of the county of Kent, and of Sussex in 1895. In 1904 he was elected chairman of the council of elders of the Spanish Portuguese community of London. He was one of the leading adherents of Theodore Herzl and rendered the Zionist movement valuable services by his efforts in higher English circles for Zionist recognition. For a number of years he headed the Zionist Federation of Great Britain. In 1900 he published a volume on the history of the French court prior to the revolution. He married a daughter of Moritz von Guttmann, coal baron of Austria.

MONTEFIORE, GEORGES LEVI, engineer and industrialist, b. Strijthem, near Brussels, 1832; d. Brussels, 1906. By birth his name was George Levi, but he adopted the name of his mother, Esther Hanna Montefiore, and was known under the name of Georges Levi Montefiore. He studied at the École des Mines at Liége and graduated as engineer in 1852. Within a few years Montefiore became one of the important Belgian industrialists. He owned the phosphorous bronze foundry at Anderlecht, Belgium, and another foundry at St. Denis near Paris. Montefiore's methods of using phosphorous bronze, invented by himself, were keenly appreciated, especially by the war offices of several European countries. In 1872 the United States Navy Department commissioned its chief clerk, John D. Brandt, to translate Montefiore's essay on the founding of cannon, and published it, as an official paper, under the title *Essay on the Use of Various Alloys, Especially of Phosphorous Bronze, for the Founding of Cannon.* Montefiore also was president of the Grand Central Railroad Company of Belgium. From 1882 to 1902 he was senator of the kingdom. He founded the Montefiore Electro-Technical Institute in Liége, which became part of the University of Liége and where thousands of electrical engineers from all parts of the world were trained. He founded also a home for convalescent children at Esneux, Belgium.

Montefiore became interested in politics, and was nominated senator by the Liberal Party. He was especially interested in the economic problems of Belgium. He also granted numerous fellowships to foreign students, especially from Russia and Roumania.

MONTEFIORE, JACOB ISAAC LEVI, merchant and pioneer, b. Bridgetown, Barbados, British West Indies, 1819; d. London, 1885. In 1837 he emigrated to Sydney where his uncle Jacob Montefiore was influential and very active in the various schemes of colonization of Australia. A leading merchant of Sydney, Jacob Isaac Levi Montefiore was elected to the New South Wales legislature in 1857. He acted as president of the Chamber of Commerce and was for many years a director of the Bank of Australasia. In 1876 he left Australia and settled in England, where he became a director of several banks and of other large commercial undertakings. His brother, George Levi Montefiore, was a Belgian senator.

MONTEFIORE, JOSHUA, English attorney, soldier and author, b. London, 1762; d. St. Albans, Vt., 1843. He was the sixth son of Moses Vita Montefiore (1712-89) and uncle of Sir Moses Montefiore. In 1784 he became a barrister, and late in 1791, as military leader, he joined a group of 275 adventurers, consisting of naval officers and London merchants, who formed a society for the colonization of the island of Bulama, on the west African coast near Sierra Leone. Owing to the strong resistance of the natives the expedition failed.

Montefiore traveled for a time among the tribes in Sierra Leone and then returned to London. In 1794 he published his experiences in a tract entitled *An Authentic Account of the Late Expedition to Bulama on the Coast of Africa, with a Description of the Present Settlement of Sierra Leone and the Adjacent Country.* He was offered and declined the order of knighthood, but accepted a commission as captain in the British army; he was the first English Jew thus commissioned as an officer in the British army.

Following service in the West Indies and various parts of the Empire, he resigned in 1812 and emigrated to the United States, settling in New York city, where he practised law and edited a weekly political journal called *Men and Measures.* Subsequently he settled in St. Albans, Vt., where he remained until his death. He attained considerable success as an author. His *Commercial Dictionary* (London, 1803; two editions were published in the United States) was considered a standard work, and his published writings, chiefly legal, included compendiums of mercantile and commercial law and copyright law.

MONTEFIORE, MOSES, British communal leader and philanthropist, b. Leghorn, Italy, 1784; d. Ramsgate, England, 1885. He was the son of Joseph Elias Montefiore and Rachel de Mattos Mocatta. Moses Montefiore was taken to England in infancy. His early manhood was spent in business partnership with his brother Abraham, but this association terminated in 1816. Although himself a staunch Sephardi and a prominent member of the Bevis Marks Synagogue in London, in 1812 Montefiore braved current prejudices by marrying an Ashkenazi in the person of Judith, daughter of Levi Barent Cohen and a sister of Mrs. Nathan Meyer Rothschild (1784-1862). Establishing himself as a neighbor of the Rothschilds in New Court, he became one of the city's most successful financiers, and in 1821 was able to retire from the Stock Exchange, turning his attention to the development of new business enterprises. In 1824 he founded the Alliance Assurance Company, and in the following year became a director of the newly-established Imperial and Continental Gas Association, a body which pioneered in the introduction of gas lighting in English homes. He also helped to establish the Provincial Bank of Ireland. In 1832 Montefiore purchased East Cliff Lodge, Ramsgate, which subsequently became his seat, and in 1833 he established a small, but singularly beautiful synagogue adjoining that property. In 1836 he was created a fellow of the Royal Society, and thereafter civic honors fell to him in rapid succession. In 1837 he was elected Sheriff of London and Middlesex, and in this capacity was privileged to welcome Queen Victoria on her first visit to the City. In 1846 he received a baronetcy, and in the following year was appointed High Sheriff of Kent, the county in which his estate was situated.

Nor was it only in commercial and civic life that Montefiore earned distinction. Following its formal establishment in 1836, he became first president of the London Committee of Deputies of British Jews, and was six times elected parnas presidente (chief warden) of the Spanish and Portuguese Congregation.

Montefiore's place in Jewish history is due, however, to his tireless exertions on behalf of his oppressed brethren abroad. These took the form of repeated missions to foreign lands, including no less than seven visits to Palestine (1827, 1838, 1849, 1855, 1857, 1866, 1875). In 1838 he submitted to Mohammed Ali, Pasha of Egypt, a plan for Jewish colonization in the Holy Land. Two years later he joined Adolphe Crémieux and Salomon Munk in making personal representations to the same authority concerning the notorious bloodlibel and massacre at Damascus, securing an official repudiation of the charge and the release of Jews wrongfully accused. In 1846, and again in 1872, he visited Russia and on both occasions obtained from the Czars assurances of fair treatment for Jews. In 1859 he journeyed to Rome to intercede in the famous Mortara case of forced baptism. In 1863 he visited Morocco and interviewed the Sultan concerning the persecution of the Jews. Four years later, he embarked on a similar mission to Roumania, receiving from Prince Carol (later Carol I) a formal statement repudiating charges of oppression.

Montefiore was likewise renowned for his benefactions. During his several visits to Palestine he endowed a number of hospitals, settlements and charitable institutions, and also administered the fund bequeathed by Judah Touro for the development of Jewish life in the Holy Land. Besides his public charities, Montefiore gained an enviable reputation for personal benevolence. It is recorded in his diary that on a single evening he responded to as many as sixty requests for aid from indigent Jewish widows, while

Moses Montefiore

his support of impoverished Jewish scholars was constant throughout his long life. It was his habit to give to public institutions, on his birthdays, sums of money corresponding with the years of his age, and on Saturdays, when his religious scruples prevented him from handling money, he would relieve the distress of the needy by distributing meal-tickets. In all of his benefactions Montefiore was insistent that the traditional discrimination between Sephardim and Ashkenazim should be broken down, and throughout his career spared no effort to bring about unity between the two wings of the community.

In matters of religion, Montefiore was a man of staunch Orthodox principles and of deep, almost naive, piety. Although himself no scholar, he took a keen and practical interest in the advancement of Jewish learning. As a memorial to his wife, he established, in 1866, the Judith Montefiore College in Ramsgate, with the orientalist Louis Loewe (his own amanuensis) as first principal. This endowment, together with the synagogue, was administered after his death by the Spanish and Portuguese Congregation of London. Designed originally as a Yeshiva of the old type, the institution later developed, under Haham Moses Gaster, into a westernized rabbinical seminary. Difficulties, however, subsequently arose, and in 1901 it was closed, the bulk of its library, which included valuable books and manuscripts from the Zunz and Halberstamm collections, being transferred to Jews' College, London. During the second World War the institution served as a retreat for lay scholars, and since 1933 has provided sanctuary for a few emigrés from Germany.

Lit.: Loewe, L., *Diaries of Sir Moses and Lady Montefiore;* Wolf, Lucien, *Sir Moses Montefiore, A Centennial Biography* (1884); Wolbe, Eugen, *Sir Moses Montefiore, Ein Lebensbild für jung und alt* (1909); Goodman, Paul, *Moses Montefiore* (1925); *Anglo-Jewish Historical Exhibition Catalogue* (1887), Nos. 650-698 (Montefioriana); Goodman, Paul, and Cardozo, D. A., *Think and Thank* (Centenary Volume of the Ramsgate Synagogue, 1933).

MONTEFIORE, TOMMASO MOSE, Italian composer and musical critic, b. Livorno, 1855; d. Rome, 1933. He studied in Florence under Ernesto Bocucci and Teodoro Mabellini. His first musical opera, *Un bacio al portatore,* was performed in Florence (1884).

Encouraged by its success, Montefiore composed many musical works, most noteworthy among which was *Cecila,* staged in Ravenna, in 1905.

He wrote prolifically for Italian musical publications and periodicals on problems of the Italian opera and on the musical traditions of Italy. He published also various articles and studies on Italian copyright law. His proposals, aimed at the introduction of necessary modifications in the existing copyright regulations, were adopted and found expression in the new copyright law of Italy (Sept. 7, 1925). He was member of the Santa Cecilia Musical Academy of Rome.

Montefiore was active in Jewish communal and social life in Italy and bequeathed his entire patrimony to Jewish charitable institutions in Rome.

MONTEGO BAY, principal town of the parish of St. James in Jamaica, British West Indies, ranking next to Kingston in size, population and commerce. It is one of the outstanding health resorts of the West Indies with a regular American winter colony.

Jews gathered here in small numbers in the closing decades of the 18th cent. The early settlers included the Delvailles, Rodrigues, Isaacs, Da Costa, Solomon, Phillips, Nunes, Pereira, Gedelia, Alberga, Corinaldi, Melhado, Millinger, De Pass, Delgado, Simon, De Lisser, Feurtado, and Mesquita.

Early in the 19th cent. there were sufficient Jews to form a congregation, which was called United Brethren of the Jewish Faith. Services were held in private homes. Sir John Simon presented the first cemetery to the Jewish community in Union Street. The oldest tombstones decipherable are those of Moses Fernandes Mesquita (d. 1773) and Leah Gedelia (d. 1791). In the latter part of the 19th cent. another cemetery was acquired on the road to Falmouth. Charles Levy (d. 1900) was the first person interred there.

In 1844 the residence of Esther Nunes on King and Market streets was purchased for £540. The House of Assembly voted the sum of £300. The residence was remodeled and converted into a synagogue which was designated as K. K. Beth Yaakob (House of Jacob). An advertisement appeared on January 31, 1845 in *The Voice of Jacob* of London for "a gentleman (an unmarried Englishman would be preferred) qualified to officiate as Chazan, Lecturer, Mohel, Baal Kore, Baal Tokea, Shochet—the latter to be only temporary. The salary £200 sterling per annum with a fine residence. . . . He will be required to superintend instruction—Hebrew and English—which will yield an additional yearly sum of about £100."

On April 2, 1845, the synagogue, which could accommodate 250 persons, was consecrated by Rabbi B. C. Carillon, then minister of the Spanish Town Synagogue. The membership was just over 130. The Parnasim (board of trustees) were Barnet Isaacs (president), Cecil L. Isaacs (vice-president) and George L. Phillips (treasurer). The latter, in 1861, was appointed by the governor of Jamaica as a member of the Privy Council of the island and a member of the Legislative Council, and in the following year Custos Rotulorum for St. James. The Portuguese Minhag was used in the synagogue. The old register of births, marriages and deaths of the synagogue records the first marriage of "Alexander, son of Emanuel Levy and Miriam the proselyte, intermarried on Wednesday: 11th Iyar (May 6, 1846), 5606. Rabbi B. C. Carillon officiated."

Carillon served the community until 1847. Gradually the reforms in the service which he introduced met with a great deal of opposition on the part of some of the leaders of the community. A protest against his innovations was signed by seventeen members of the congregation. His cause, however, was espoused by one of the Parnasim, Aaron Isaacs. Correspondence on the subject may be seen in *The Voice of Jacob* of that time.

The second minister was Rabbi Abraham Pereira Mendes (1847-51), whose sons Frederick De Sola and Henry Pereira Mendes later ministered to New York city congregations. Other ministers were the Reverends I. Jacob, M. De Sola (who was rabbi of the Sephardic synagogue Beth Israel of Baltimore in 1857) and Aaron C. Henriques. For over a quarter of a century Samah Corinaldi acted as lay reader.

Owing to the fact that the majority of the Jews moved to Kingston or emigrated to the United States, the funds of the congregation had become so attenuated that it was found impossible to engage a minister. From 1869 to 1900 the synagogue was opened only on Passover, New Year and the Day of Atonement. On these occasions Jews from the neighboring towns, for example from Falmouth, Lucea, St. Ann's Bay, Sav-La-Mar, Black River and Brown's Town, would gather for divine worship and the synagogue would be filled.

In 1900, with the removal to Kingston of Samah Corinaldi, the lay reader, the synagogue was permanently closed and the Scrolls of the Law were removed to the Duke Street synagogue of Kingston. The building was made uninhabitable in 1912, the year of the hurricane.

In 1942 only a few Jews remained in Montego Bay, including Edmund Hart, J.P. (a great-great-grandson of Aaron Hart, the first chief rabbi of the Ashkenazic Jews of England).

Jews were prominent in the Masonic Friendly Lodge of Montego from its inception in 1818. Five out of six of its founders were Jews, i.e. Daniel Levy, Barnet Isaacs, Cecil Isaacs, Moses Gedaliah and Jacob Corinaldi. The first worshipful master was Moses Gedaliah. Edmund Hart, J.P., was worshipful master seven times, at various dates from 1914 on, and in 1942 was extremely active in civic affairs.

One of the most prominent Jews born in Montego Bay was Sir John Simon, son of Isaac and Rebecca Simon. In 1864 he was created a sergeant-at-law, and was a member of the British House of Commons from 1868 to 1888.   HENRY P. SILVERMAN.

Lit.: *The Gleaner Geography and History of Jamaica* (12th ed.); the record book of births, marriages and deaths of the old Montego Bay Synagogue; files of *The Voice of Jacob* (London); files of *The First Fruits of the West* (Kingston, Jamaica); *The Falmouth Post*, April 3, 1845; *The Jamaica Almanac* (1869 et seq.); Andrade, J. A. P. M., *A Record of the Jews in Jamaica*, 93-95; *Votes of Assembly of Jamaica*, Oct. 30, 1844, p. 85.

MONTEUX, PIERRE, conductor, b. Paris, 1875. He was graduated from the Paris Conservatory where he was a pupil of Lavignac and Berthelier. After serving as chorus master and assistant conductor of the Colonne Orchestra, he rose to the post of principal conductor in 1911. For the next two seasons, he was also one of the principal conductors of Diaghilev's Ballet Russe, directing the world premières of Stravinsky's *Rites of Spring* and Ravel's *Daphnis and Chloe.*

In 1914, Monteux founded the Société des Concerts Populaires in Paris, and at the same time officiated as conductor at the Paris Opéra and as a guest conductor of opera houses in England, Germany, Hungary and Austria. During the first World War he served in the 35th Territorial Infantry, seeing action at Rheims, Verdun, Soissons, and the Argonne. He was released from the army in order to go to America to conduct the Diaghilev Ballet. In 1917, he directed French opera at the Metropolitan Opera House, and in 1919 he became principal conductor of the Boston Symphony Orchestra. When, in 1924, Monteux yielded his baton in Boston to Koussevitzky, he returned to Europe to become conductor of the Paris Symphony Orchestra, holding this post until 1928. Since then he has directed most of the major orchestras in Europe and America.

In 1935 Monteux became permanent conductor of the San Francisco Symphony Orchestra, a post he still held in 1942. He was called upon to direct the first concerts of the newly founded N.B.C. Symphony in 1937. A self-effacing and conscientious musician, Monteux has been a penetrating interpreter of French music and the modern repertory. His performances have been characterized by sincerity, complete command of the score, and devotion to high ideals.

Lit.: Ewen, David, *The Man With the Baton* (New York, 1936).

MONTEVIDEO, see URUGUAY.

MONTEZINOS, DAVID, librarian, b. Amsterdam, 1828; d. Amsterdam, 1916. He was a noted bibliophile who possessed one of the largest private libraries of his time. In 1866 the Portuguese Jewish seminary "Etz Haim" appointed him its librarian, which post he held until his death. His valuable collection, which consisted of more than 20,000 books, portraits, pamphlets, rare editions and manuscripts, he bequeathed to the above seminary in 1889. In 1891, when new wings were added to the seminary's library, they were dedicated in Montezinos' name.

See LIBRARIES, under Holland.

Lit.: Da Silva, Rosa, J. S., *De Stichter der Livraria D. Montezinos* (1914); idem, *Het Boek* (1917) 49-54.

MONTGOMERY, capital and third largest city in the state of Alabama, having a population of 93,697 (census of 1940), including about 1,200 Jews. The first Jew to settle in the vicinity of Montgomery was Abram Mordecai of Pennsylvania, who established a trading post in 1789.

In 1846 the Jews of Montgomery formed an association for the relief of the sick, which later was expanded to meet the religious needs of the Jewish citizens. Services were conducted by laymen in various temporary meeting places. In 1852 this organization was incorporated as Kahl Montgomery. The congregation was originally Orthodox, but later became Reform. In 1862 a synagogue was dedicated, and in the following year James K. Gutheim became the first

Temple Beth-Or of Montgomery, Alabama

ordained rabbi of Kahl Montgomery. In 1942 the rabbi of Temple Beth-Or (Reform), originally Kahl Montgomery, was Eugene Blachschleger, whose service began in 1933. The congregation had in 1942 about 270 members.

In the late 19th cent. Jews from Russia, Poland, Galicia and Roumania arrived in Montgomery. In 1902 Congregation Agudath Israel was organized, and in 1928 its new temple was dedicated. Benjamin G. Eisenberg served the congregation from 1938 on. In 1942 it had a membership of about sixty.

Unlike Mobile, Montgomery had practically no Sephardic or Portuguese Jewish element preceding the incoming of German and Polish Jews. In 1906 Ralph Coen, a Sephardic Jew, came to Montgomery from the island of Rhodes. He was followed by other Sephardim, and in 1912 Etz Ahyim Congregation was organized. In 1942 there was in Montgomery a Sephardic community of about forty families.

The following organizations played an active part in Jewish life in Montgomery: B'nai B'rith (1873); Council of Jewish Women (1897); Hadassah (1916); Jewish Federation (1930); Montgomery Jewish Welfare Board Committee (1941). The Standard Club (1871) served as the scene of much of the social life of Montgomery Jewry.

There were two Jewish cemeteries in Montgomery in 1942, Oakwood, maintained by Temple Beth-Or, and Greenwood, by Agudath Israel and Etz Ahyim.

Judah P. Benjamin was a resident of Montgomery from 1862 to 1865. Albert Strassburger, Henry E. Faber and M. L. Moses were mayors of Montgomery. Julius Sternfield was an assistant district attorney, and during the crusade against peonage acted as a special agent of the administration.

See also ALABAMA.　　　EUGENE BLACHSCHLEGER.

Lit.: Moritz, Charles F., *History of Kahl Montgomery;* Moses, A. G., "The History of the Jews of Montgomery," *Publications of the American Jewish Historical Society,* No. 13 (1905) 83-88.

MONTH, BLESSING OF THE, *see* BENEDICTIONS.

MONTHS. From the earliest times the Hebrews calculated months by the moon. Nevertheless, they accommodated them to the solar year. In the ancient Canaanite calendar, adopted by the Israelites in pre-Exilic times, the months bore names associated with specific agricultural or climatic conditions, implying that their variability had been stabilized and that they had somehow been harmonized with the static solar year.

The Canaanite year began at the new moon preceding the autumn harvest. Four of its months are mentioned in the Bible: Ethanim, or "constant waters," in reference to the replenishment of the dried-up wadys, and corresponding to September-October (*1 Kings* 8:2); Bul, i.e. "produce" or "moisture," corresponding to October-November (*1 Kings* 6:38); Abib, or "ripe ears," corresponding to March-April (*Ex.* 13:4; 23:15; 34:18), and Ziv, or "Blossom-time," corresponding to April-May (*1 Kings* 6:1, 37). The month was reckoned as a round thirty days (cf. *Num.* 20:29 and *Deut.* 21:13).

New moon and full moon were festive days. The former is mentioned already in the 16th cent. B.C.E. in the Canaanite documents from Ras Shamra, where a sacrifice of two sheep to Ashtoreth is prescribed (R.S. 1929, III.48). The latter is implied by later allusions in *Ps.* 81:4 ("blow the horn at the new moon, at the full moon for our feast-day") and *Prov.* 7:20 ("He hath taken the bag of money with him; he will come home at the full moon"). Moreover, from the fact that Sabbath is often associated in the Bible with new moon (for example, *II Kings* 4:23; *Isa.* 66:23), many scholars are of the opinion that this term also originally denoted the plenilunar festival, when the moon, so to speak, comes to a full stop (cf. Hebrew, *shabath,* "to stop"), and that it was only later applied to the lunar quarters. There is evidence, however, in the Ras Shamra texts that the seven-day week was indeed known in early Canaan.

During the Exile the Babylonian system was adopted, the names of the months being derived from the common Babylonian calendar, itself based on the earlier Sumerian system in use at Nippur. These names refer, for the most part, to ancient Sumerian myths associated with the respective seasons. Thus, Tammuz is the month dedicated to the worship of the fertility-spirit of that name; Elul is the month when he was bewailed (cf. Hebrew, *'alal,* "wail") after vanishing from the earth; Tebeth is the month when he sank (Hebrew, *taba*) into the netherworld, and so forth. On the other hand, Tishri is simply the "opening" month of the year (cf. Hebrew *sharah*), and Marheshvan is a distortion of the Assyrian Arahsamna, "eighth month." Other names, like Sivan, Nisan, Kislev and Ab, still defy elucidation. Of these new names only the following are mentioned in the Bible: Tebeth (*Esther* 2:16), Shebat (*Zech.* 1:7), Adar (*Esther* 3:7; 9:17, 19, 21), Nisan (*Esther* 3:7; *Neh.* 2:1), Sivan (*Esther* 8:9) and Elul (*Neh.* 6:15). The occurrence of others, however, in the Aramaic papyri from Assuan, Egypt, shows that they were fully adopted in Jewish circles by the 5th cent. B.C.E.

The following list gives the names of the Jewish months, in consecutive order, together with the number of days which each comprehends, its principal festival and fast days, and the leading ideas associated with it in Jewish folklore.

1. TISHRI (September-October). Thirty days. New Moon is reckoned as one day. 1 to 2: New Year. 3: Fast of Gedaliah. 10: Day of Atonement. 15 to 21: Feast of Tabernacles. 22 to 23: Eighth Day of Solemn Assembly. 23: Rejoicing of the Law.

The ten days between New Year and the Day of Atonement constitute a period of penitence.

The New Moon of Tishri is not blessed, as are those of other months. This is due to a fanciful interpretation of *Ps.* 81:4, "Blow the horn at new moon, at the full moon, for our feast-day," the Hebrew word *kese*, properly meaning "full moon," being associated with the similar *kissvi*, "secret," as if to imply that the new moon of the festival-month must be proclaimed in secret. Tishri is regarded as the birth-month of the three patriarchs, Abraham, Isaac and Jacob. It is customary to dedicate new synagogues in this month. The zodiacal sign of Tishri is the Scales, thought to symbolize the weighing of man's deeds between New Year and Atonement. The sign is the emblem of the tribe of Ephraim.

2. MARHESHVAN or HESHVAN (October-November). Twenty-nine or thirty days. New Moon is reckoned as two days (i.e. the last of Tishri and the first of Heshvan). The zodiacal sign is the Scorpion, emblem of Manasseh.

3. KISLEV (November-December). Twenty-nine or thirty days. New Moon is irregular, being either one or two days, in different years. 25th of Kislev to 2nd (or 3rd) of Tebeth: Feast of Dedication (Hanukah). The zodiacal sign is the Archer (Sagittarius), emblem of Benjamin.

4. TEBETH (December-January). Twenty-nine days. New Moon is irregular. 10: Fast of Tebeth. It is customary to refrain from slaughtering geese during Tebeth and the following Shebat. The zodiacal sign is Capricorn, emblem of Dan.

5. SHEBAT (January-February). Thirty days. New Moon is reckoned as one day. 15: "New Year for Trees." It is believed that demons are abroad in this month. The zodiacal sign is the Waterman (Aquarius), emblem of Asher.

6. ADAR (February-March). Twenty-nine days. New Moon is two days. (In a leap year, Adar has thirty days, and New Moon is one day.) 7: Day of the birth and death of Moses. 13: Fast of Esther. 14: Purim. 15: "Shushan Purim." During the 17th cent. it was customary to fast on Adar 7th in Turkey, Italy and southern Europe, and this usage was later adopted by the Hasidim. The zodiacal sign is Pisces (The Fishes), emblem of Naphtali.

6a. SECOND ADAR. Occurs only in leap year. Twenty-nine days. New Moon is two days. In leap year the Fast of Esther and Purim are postponed to the Second Adar. Anniversaries (Yahrzeits) of deaths occurring in the First Adar are commemorated by the Sephardim in the Second Adar. Among the Ashkenazim the practice varies.

7. NISAN (March-April). Thirty days. New Moon is one day. 14: Fast of the first-born. 15 to 22: Passover. 16: Beginning of the "counting of the Omer," or Sefirah, i.e. the seven weeks until Pentecost (Shabuoth). The entire month is regarded as a prolonged festival, and as one in which it is blessed to die. Every twenty-five years the sun is especially blessed in Nisan. The zodiacal sign is the Ram, emblem of Judah.

8. IYAR (April-May). Twenty-nine days. New Moon is two days. 14: "Second Passover," for those unable to celebrate the proper date in Nisan (cf. *Num.* 9:9-14). 18: The thirty-third day of the Omer (Lag Beomer), a "scholar's holiday." Until the 18th of Iyar there is a period in which no marriages are celebrated by the Orthodox. The zodiacal sign is the Bull, emblem of Issachar. It is taken to symbolize the calf offered by Abraham to his angelic guests (*Gen.* 18:7).

9. SIVAN (May-June). Thirty days. New Moon is one day. 6 to 7: Shabuoth (Pentecost). The zodiacal sign is the Twins, emblem of Zebulun. It is taken to symbolize Jacob and Esau.

10. TAMMUZ (June-July). Twenty-nine days. New Moon is two days. 17: Fast of Tammuz, commemorating the first breach in the walls of Jerusalem and also, according to one tradition, the breaking of the tablets of the Law. Actually the fast is a reinterpretation of a Babylonian festival. The zodiacal sign is the Crab, emblem of Reuben. Since the crab lives in water, it is taken to symbolize Moses, drawn out of the waters of the Nile.

11. AB (July-August). Thirty days. New Moon is one day. 9: Fast of Ab, commemorating the destruction of the First and Second Temple. The Expulsion from Spain (1492) also fell on this date. The zodiacal sign is the Lion, emblem of Simeon. It is taken to symbolize the assailant lion of *Jer.* 4:7. Moreover, since a name of Jerusalem is Ariel (*Isa.* 29:1), which may be connected with Hebrew 'ari, "lion," a further allusion to the destruction of Jerusalem is seen.

12. ELUL (August-September). Twenty-nine days. New Moon is two days. The month is devoted to Selihoth, or propitiatory (penitential) prayers, recited daily in preparation for the solemn season of New Year and Atonement. The zodiacal sign is the Virgin, emblem of Gad.

THEODOR H. GASTER.

Lit.: Langdon, S., *Babylonian Menologies and the Semitic Calendars* (the Schweich Lectures of the British Academy, 1933) (1935); Dillmann, C. F., "Über das Kalenderwesen der Israeliten vor dem babylonischen Exil," *Monatsbericht der königlichen preussischen Akademie* (1881) 987; Nowack, W., *Lehrbuch der hebräischen Archäologie,* vol. 1 (1894) 215-18; Morgenstern, Julian, "The Three Calendars of Ancient Israel," *Hebrew Union College Annual,* vol. 1 (1924); vol. 3 (1926); vol. 10 (1935); Rappoport, A. S., *The Folklore of the Jews* (1937) 18; Friedländer, Michael, *Text-Book of the Jewish Religion* (1890) 83-87.

MONTICELLO, summer resort in Sullivan County, New York, having a population of 3,737 (census of 1940), including about 1,200 Jews. During the summer months the Jewish population increased greatly due to the influx of vacationers from New York city. The bulk of the Jewish population went to Monticello between 1914-18 and was engaged as merchants and hotel keepers. Among the first Jewish settlers were Max and Joe Fleishman, Philip Goldstein, and Rabbi Harris Bercowsky.

The Synagogue of Congregation Tefereth Yisroel was built in 1912, the first to be constructed in Sullivan county. Harris Bercowsky was rabbi of the congregation from its inception until his death in 1940. The first Talmud Torah was established in this synagogue in 1914. Congregation Chesed Shel Emes was founded in 1928 and a synagogue building was purchased in 1930. After a period of independent existence, the Talmud Torah of this synagogue was merged with that of Tefereth Yisroel. In 1923 the Cold Spring Road Synagogue was built to accommodate the Jews who lived on the outskirts of the town. The Jewish Community Center was established and incorporated in 1936. Its rabbi in 1942 was Aaron Walden.

Nathan Leffler was mayor of Monticello (1936-37).

The Jewish community maintained the Hebrew Hospital Association of Monticello and chapters of the Zionist Organization of America, Hadassah, and other national organizations. AARON WALDEN.

MONTORO, ANTON DE (El Ropero), Marrano poet, b. Montoro, province of Cordova, Spain, 1404; d. about 1480. A relative of the troubadour Juan Alfonso de Baena, Montoro was a second-hand clothing dealer and devoted part of his time to poetry, in which he excelled. Men like the Marquis de Santillana and Juan de Mena held him in high esteem, and he enjoyed the protection of Don Pedro de Aguilar and his son Alfonso, the protector of the New Christians. However, the converso poet remained inwardly faithful to Judaism during his entire life.

When the persecution of Jews and Marranos broke out in Spain, the poet untiringly but vainly appealed on their behalf to the Spanish grandees. In 1473, following riots against the Marranos in Cordova, Montoro lost all his possessions. In 1474 he addressed a poem to Queen Isabella, painting a terrible picture of the deplorable condition of his brethren. Montoro is considered the last of the great troubadours, and his writings, collected and published in Madrid, 1900, under the title *Cancionero de Anton Montoro (El Ropero de Cordova)*, show him to be a master of epigram and a writer of mordant satirical poetry.

Lit.: Kayserling, M., *Sephardim*, p. 85 et seq.; Graetz, Heinrich, *History of the Jews*, vol. 8, p. 306; Roth, *A History of the Marranos* (1932), pp. 26, 37.

MONTPELLIER, capital of the department of Hérault in southern France, formerly a part of the old French province of Languedoc, and seat of the famous Jewish community in the Middle Ages which was established during the second half of the 11th cent. The Jews of the city contributed greatly to the development of Montpellier's commerce and to the advancement of the University of Montpellier's faculty of medicine.

The testament of Guilham V, king of Majorca and ruler of Montpellier, first mentions the Jews in 1121, and forbids his heirs to appoint a Jew as bayle (steward or administrator) of Montpellier. This document proves that even at that time the Jewish community of the city was an important one. As early as 1180 the Jews of the city were allowed to teach and to practice medicine, and even before this period, some Jews had been farmers of the taxes and tolls. In 1176 a Jew named Eleazar of Castres was a toll-collector, and a Jew named Saltel was collector of taxes in 1201. At about that time the Jews lived in an assigned district of the city, and had their own slaughter-house and water-supply.

In 1293 Montpellier was ceded to France, and in 1306 the Jews were expelled. They came back to the city in 1319, however, and enjoyed a temporary period of peace which was terminated in 1348 when the city was again acquired by France. Restrictions and humiliations were imposed upon them from that time on, such as the wearing of the Jew-badge, ordered in 1363, and the prohibition against Jews' drinking the water of any other well than of the one assigned specifically to them. In 1387 a new synagogue was built, but in 1394 the Jews were permanently expelled from Montpellier at the same time that all the Jews were expelled from France. All their efforts to return proved unavailing.

In the 16th cent., a number of Marranos who had fled from Spain and Portugal were allowed to settle in Montpellier; these established a modest Jewish community. In 1705 many other Jews returned to the city, especially from the county of Venaissin, but the Jews of the city never again regained the cultural or commercial importance which they had enjoyed in the Middle Ages. At present (1940) the city of Montpellier has very few Jews; in 1902 there were no more than thirty-five Jewish families in the city, and the present population is not believed to be any larger, out of a total population of 82,820 (1931 census).

In the medieval period several Jewish physicians taught in the faculty of medicine of the University of Montpellier; in 1300 a Jew named Jacob ben Machir ibn Tibbon (Profatius Judaeus) was dean of this faculty. The famous physician Bonet ben Meshullam ben Solomon Abigdor was a member of this school. In the 16th cent. the Marrano physician Antoine Saporta became dean of the faculty.

Benjamin of Tudela, the famous Jewish traveler, who visited Montpellier in 1165, wrote in his memoirs that the Jews of Montpellier were wealthy and that Judaism was thriving there. He mentions Reuben ben Todros, Nathan ben Zakariah, Salamieh, Mordecai and especially Samuel, rabbi of the community, as the "most famous disciples of our sages." The Jewish seminary of the city was held in such high esteem that it was sometimes compared to the great Sanhedrin of early rabbinic times; Montpellier itself was, in the Hebrew literature and source-books of later times, referred to as *'Em Beyisra'el* (Mother in Israel) and *Har Hakodesh* (Holy Mountain). The attack on the religious philosophy of Maimonides began at Montpellier in 1232 with the suppression of his book *Moreh Nebuchim* (Guide to the Perplexed), and the work was even declared to be hostile to Christianity.

At the beginning of the 14th cent. a controversy sprang up between those who favored philosophical studies, such as Jacob ben Machir ibn Tibbon, Judah ibn Tibbon, and Jedaiah Bedaresi, and those who were opposed to them; the latter group was headed by Abba Mari ben Moses of Lunel. Other noted Jewish scholars of Montpellier were Abraham ben David of Posquières, Moses ibn Tibbon, Aaron ben Joseph Halevi, Abraham Avigdor, and Simeon ben Joseph (En Duran of Lunel). GEORG HERLITZ.

Lit.: Kahn, S., *Les Écoles Juives et la Faculté de Médecine de Montpellier* (1890); Gross, H., *Gallia Judaica* (1897) 322-35; Kahn, S., in *Revue des études juives*, vol. 19 (1889) 259-81; vol. 22 (1891) 264-79; vol. 28 (1894) 118-41; vol. 33 (1896) 283-303; Germain, A., *Histoire du Commerce de Montpellier*, vol. 1 (1861) 2-6; Azémard, Émile, *Étude sur les Israélites de Montpellier au moyen âge* (1924).

MONTREAL, the largest city in Canada and the second largest port on the North American continent, situated on the Island of Montreal at the confluence of the Ottawa and St. Lawrence rivers, in the province of Quebec. It grew out of a missionary settlement founded by the Sieur de Maisonneuve in 1642. It contains the largest Jewish community in Canada.

The first Jews to enter Montreal were officers in the British Army under General Amherst in 1760. The earliest Jewish settlers were importers and fur traders of Sephardic origin, who came originally from England and Germany and had spent many years in the American colonies. By 1768 there were sufficient Jewish residents to form a congregation, but although they took an active part in commercial, political and military life in the latter part of the 19th cent., their numbers increased very slowly, so that there were less than one hundred Jews in Montreal in 1831.

The first Jewish families from Poland arrived in 1846 and were soon followed by others fleeing from persecution in Russia and Roumania. The Jewish population of Montreal numbered 181 at the census in 1851, increased to 2,473 in 1891, to 6,941 in 1901, and jumped to 28,807 in 1911, when it formed 5.33 per cent of the total population of the city. By 1921 the Jewish population of Greater Montreal had increased to 45,802, and the 1931 census showed 57,997 Jews living in Montreal and the surrounding towns and cities which form part of the metropolitan area of Montreal. Of these, 48,724 lived in Montreal itself, 6,783 lived in the city of Outremont, and 1,780 in Westmount, while the remainder lived in the eleven other satellite towns and villages on the island.

Although the Jewish population of Montreal increased numerically during the decade from 1930 to 1940, the proportion of Jews to the total population decreased from 6.13 per cent in 1921 to 5.79 per cent in 1931. The situation of the Jewish community in Montreal is unique, since it is the only community with more than 1,000 Jews on the American continent resident in a city in which the majority of the population is French-speaking and of French origin. Jews form the third largest ethnic group in the city of Montreal, being exceeded only by those of French origin, with 64 per cent, and those of Anglo-Saxon origin, with 21.8 per cent.

Jews engaged in industry formed the largest group of Jews gainfully occupied in the city of Montreal in 1931, constituting 35 per cent of all gainfully occupied Jews as compared with 19 per cent engaged in industry among the total population of all origins. Out of every hundred Jews gainfully occupied in Montreal, twenty-four were clothing workers, fourteen were retail merchants and twelve were salesmen. Office workers numbered five, while building and construction workers and cleaners and pressers numbered four each. Fur workers, leather workers and shippers numbered two each, while truck drivers, chauffeurs, teamsters, printers, butchers, restaurant keepers, metal product workers, wood product workers, doctors, rabbis and Shohetim and musicians numbered one each and other professional men totalled three.

On the other hand, out of every 100 Jewish women gainfully occupied, thirty-four were clothing workers, eighteen were saleswomen, sixteen were stenographers, eight were bookkeepers and cashiers, five were office clerks, three were domestic servants, and two were retail merchants, while teachers, textile workers, tobacco workers, music teachers, boarding house keepers and cleaners and pressers numbered one each.

The first Jewish congregation to be established in Canada was that of Shearith Israel, which was founded in Montreal in 1768 by the early Jewish settlers who were of Sephardic origin. The first synagogue was erected in 1777 at the corner of Notre Dame and St. James Street; a second synagogue, on Chenneville Street, was erected in 1838; and this in turn was replaced by the Stanley Street synagogue, erected in 1890.

The second congregation to be established in Montreal was that of the English, German and Polish Jews, now known as the Shaar Hashomayim, established in 1858, whose first synagogue was erected in 1860 on St. Constant Street, now known as Cadieux Street. This building was replaced by a new synagogue on McGill College Avenue in 1886, and was followed by the synagogue on Cote St. Antoine Road which was erected in 1922. This congregation follows the Conservative form of worship.

Interior of the Chenneville Street synagogue at Montreal

The only Reform congregation in Montreal in 1942 was that of Temple Emanu-El, founded in 1882. The first temple was erected on Stanley Street in 1892, and was subsequently replaced by the present building on St. Catherine Street, erected in 1911.

There were, in 1942, forty Orthodox congregations in Montreal, in addition to the three older congregations. The oldest Jewish cemetery in Montreal was that on St. Janvier Street, consecrated in 1755, and the oldest grave that of Lazarus David, one of the earliest settlers, who, born in Wales, died in Montreal in 1776.

Jewish settlers in Montreal prior to 1848 were mainly men of considerable means. With the influx of immigrants fleeing from persecution, the need for organized assistance became evident, and in 1848 the Hebrew Philanthropic Society was founded by the Reverend Dr. Abraham de Sola and Moses Judah Hayes. After a more or less active existence it was reorganized in 1863 as the Young Men's Hebrew Benevolent Society, adding the name Baron de Hirsch Institute in 1890 in recognition of the munificent gifts of the Baroness de Hirsch.

During the following quarter of a century the number of Jewish social service organizations in the city increased with the growth of the Jewish population, and it was suggested by Lyon Cohen, then president of the Baron de Hirsch Institute, that the work of these organizations be coordinated by setting up a Federation of Jewish Philanthropies. The task was not an easy one and five years elapsed before the Federation was actually organized in 1917. Among its first constituent organizations were the Baron de Hirsch Institute, Mount Sinai Sanitorium, Herzl Dispensary, Hebrew Orphans Home, Beth Israel Day Nursery and Ladies Hebrew Benevolent Society. The Hebrew Free Loan Association was founded in 1911 by Zigmond Fineberg for the purpose of advancing loans free of interest to needy persons, and in addition there were (1942) some eighteen sick benefit and mutual loan societies. The Montreal Jewish General Hospital was erected in 1934; in 1942 it had a modern hospital building with accommodations for more than 185 patients.

There was in 1942 no undenominational public school system in Montreal, but a dual system of Protestant and Catholic schools maintained by taxation. Jewish children attended the Protestant schools under an arrangement whereby taxes on Jewish property were paid over to the Protestant school board. The provincial government had the right to establish a Jewish school system parallel with the Catholic and Protestant systems and maintained by taxes on Jewish property owners, but the possibility of such enabling legislation was remote in view of the attitude of the French Roman Catholic majority.

The first Talmud Torah in Montreal was established in 1896. The number of Talmud Torahs increased, and in 1919 they were amalgamated under the name of the United Talmud Torahs. A modern school building was erected in 1931, and in addition there were (1942) six branches in various parts of the city. The Peretz School, founded in 1912, and the Jewish Folk School, founded in 1914, were secular supplementary Jewish schools in which Yiddish was the language of instruction and Hebrew also was taught.

Among the other Jewish educational institutions in Montreal in 1942 were the Young Men's Hebrew Association, founded in 1910 and housed in a modern building erected in 1929 on Mount Royal Avenue, the Young Women's Hebrew Association, and the Jewish Public Library, founded in 1914.

Montreal in 1942 was the home of the national office of the Zionist Organization of Canada and of the Canadian Jewish Congress. The head offices of the Jewish Colonization Association of Canada and the Jewish Immigrant Aid Society were also situated in Montreal. There was also a B'nai B'rith Lodge (founded in 1881), a section of the Council of Jewish Women (1918), Habonim Lodge and numerous Senior and Junior Hadassah chapters, Poale Zion and Pioneer Women's Groups and Young Judaea Clubs. In 1941 the Jewish Writers Association, consisting of forty Jewish journalists, was founded in Montreal.

Samuel W. Jacobs, K.C., was elected Member of Parliament for a Montreal constituency in 1917, and was reelected repeatedly until his death in 1938. Peter Bercovitch, K.C., was elected a member of the Quebec Provincial Legislature in 1918, resigning in 1938 to stand for election as Member of the Dominion Parliament, to which he was elected the same year. Louis K. Fitch, K.C., was elected a member of the Provincial Legislature for Montreal in 1938, but was defeated and replaced by Maurice Hart in 1939. The first Jew to be elected an alderman of the city of Montreal was Samuel Benjamin (1849); the next alderman was Abraham Blumenthal (1912), followed by Louis Rubenstein (1914) and Lyon W. Jacobs (1918). There were two Jewish aldermen on the Montreal City council in 1942, Joseph Schubert and Max Seigler. In 1941 Rabbi S. Gershon Levi, of Montreal, was appointed chaplain of the Jewish troops in Canada, with the rank of honorary captain.

Montreal Jews were prominent in the early industrial and commercial history of Canada. David David was one of the founders of the Bank of Montreal (1817) and was elected a member of its first board of directors (1818). Moses Judah Hays organized and managed the first water works system in Montreal. Jesse Joseph organized and was president of the Montreal Gas Company and the City Passenger Railway of Montreal. He was largely responsible for the building of the St. Lawrence and Champlain Railway, the first railway ever built in Canada. He was also a director of the Banque

George Foot Moore

Nationale, the Great North Western Telegraph Company, and founder of the People's Telegraph Company. Edgar M. Berliner, head of the Victor Talking Machine Company of Canada, was a member of the Jewish School Commission of Montreal (1930), one of the five founders of the Montreal Symphony Orchestra, and instrumental in the organization of the Federation of Jewish Philanthropies of Montreal. He was a generous supporter of Canada's George the Fifth Fund for cancer research and of ethnological and anthropological research in Palestine and neighboring countries conducted by the Hebrew University, Jerusalem. In 1942 Berliner resided in California.

LOUIS ROSENBERG.

See also: CANADA; QUEBEC.

Lit.: Rosenberg, Louis, *Canada's Jews, A Social and Economic Study* (1939); Sack, B. G., "History of the Jews in Canada," *The Jew in Canada* (1926); Da Silva, Saruco, "The Sephardic Jew in Canada," *Jewish Standard*, Sept. 19, 1930, p. 305.

MONUMENTS, *see* ARCHEOLOGY.

MOON, *see* CALENDAR; NEW MOON.

MOON, BLESSING OF THE, *see* BENEDICTIONS.

MOORE, GEORGE FOOT, non-Jewish Biblical scholar, b. West Chester, Pa., 1851; d. Cambridge, Mass., 1931. A graduate of Yale University, the Union Theological Seminary and several other American and European universities, he was professor of the history of religion at Harvard University from 1902 until his retirement in 1928. He edited the Journal of the American Oriental Society (1896-1900) of which society he was president from 1911 to 1913.

Moore, who was in close contact with Jewish scholars, is the author of numerous valuable works, such as a translation of and a commentary and treatise on the book of *Judges*. Other works of his include *The Literature of the Old Testament* (1913), *History of Religion* (vol. I, 1913, rev. edition, 1920, vol. II, 1919), *Christian Writers on Judaism* (1921), *Intermediaries in Jewish Theology* (1922) and *The Rise of Normative Judaism* (1924-25).

His monumental work is *Judaism in the First Centuries of the Christian Era* (3 vols., 1927-30). It deals with the age of the Tannaim (teachers of the Oral Law) and is the fruit of a critical knowledge of rabbinical sources unique among Christian scholars of any age. With reference to *Judaism,* Moore was one of the two Christians, cited for notable achievement during the year in behalf of America and the Jewish people in the 1927 Who's Who issue of the *American Hebrew*. The book, the outcome of studies extending over more than thirty years, would, according to the editor of this magazine, tend to break down and destroy many current prejudices and misinterpretations regarding Judaism.

Moore was an honorary member of the Jewish Academy of Arts and Sciences, and was awarded honorary degrees by the Hebrew Union College and the Jewish Theological Seminary of America.

MOOSOMIN, see Colonies, Agricultural.

MORAIS, HENRY SAMUEL, minister and author, b. Philadelphia, 1860; d. New York city, 1935. He was the son of Sabato Morais, under whose tutelage he was educated. After more than a decade of teaching in various religious schools in Philadelphia, Morais went to Syracuse in 1899 to become rabbi of the Adath Yeshurun Congregation. The next year he went to Newport to serve as rabbi, then returned to Syracuse, remaining until 1903. Later he founded the Congregation Mickveh Israel in New York city, of which he was for some time rabbi, and subsequently he became rabbi of Congregation Sons of Israel in Brooklyn.

While living in Philadelphia, Morais was on the special staff of the Philadelphia *Public Ledger*. He was also editor of the *Musical and Dramatic Standard* in that city and of the *Hebrew Watchword and Instructor*. The *Jewish Exponent,* which Morais established in 1879, was under his editorship for the first two years of its existence. Morais was the author of *Eminent Israelites of the Nineteenth Century* (1880) and of *The Jews of Philadelphia* (1894).

MORAIS, SABATO, Sephardic rabbi and one of the founders of Conservative Judaism in the United States, b. Livorno, Italy, 1823; d. Philadelphia, 1897. The Morais family, of Portuguese origin, was settled in Italy for several centuries. Sabato Morais' immediate forebears were ardent champions of Italian freedom and national unification. They belonged to the secret Masonic order which was then identified with liberal movements, and for this reason suppressed. Samuel Morais, his father, was an ardent patriot who suffered persecution for his political views. His political creed was best described in his exclamation: "Even the boards of my bed are Republican."

In this atmosphere Sabato Morais, the oldest son and the third of nine children, was reared. His early Hebrew studies were carried on under the instruction of the local rabbis, Funaro and Ourait. In the more advanced stage he studied Talmud under Chief Rabbi Abraham Baruch Piperno, and Semitics with Professor Salvatore de Benedetti. Through arduous self-application he mastered the Hebrew and Italian literatures, besides studying Aramaic, French and Spanish.

Morais carried on his studies largely through his own endeavors, while contributing to his own support and that of the family by teaching and tutoring. In 1845, when a vacancy arose in the Spanish Portuguese Congregation in London, Morais applied for the post of assistant Hazan; owing to his unfamiliarity with English, however, his application was not successful. Nevertheless, he was recalled from Livorno to London a year later for the post of Hebrew master of the orphans' school in the same congregation.

During the years he spent in London (1846-51) he acquired a remarkable mastery of the English language and cultivated such friendships as those with Sir Moses Montefiore and with the famous Italian patriot and refugee Giuseppe Mazzini. A love of Italy and a passionate desire to work for its liberation from a foreign yoke united both men.

His experience in London seemed to be preparatory for his true life work in the United States. In 1850 Isaac Leeser resigned as rabbi of the historic Mikveh Israel Congregation of Philadelphia, the pulpit of which he had made one of the most famous in America. Morais was one of a number of applicants for this post. He arrived in Philadelphia on March 17, 1851, and instantly created a profound impression upon the congregation. On April 13th, following, he was elected minister, and retained this position until his death.

Morais' ministry was a landmark in the history of the American rabbinate. It revealed the gradual transfer of congregational leadership from the laity to the rabbinate. Leeser before him had fought bitterly to this end, and created powerful enemies, which led finally to his retirement. Morais fought similar battles with courage and prophetic zeal; but it was his humility and saintly character which gained for him universal love and reverence, and spiritual leadership.

Morais' striking physical appearance harmonized with deep mental and spiritual qualities to stamp his presence with an aura of a Biblical or prophetic character —a tall figure with an ascetic face and patriarchal beard, with silken hair that showed tender curls, and deep set dark eyes that accentuated the fervor of his preaching voice.

The congregation prospered under his ministry, and in 1860 the old synagogue on Cherry Street, which had served Mikveh Israel for about eighty years, was vacated for a new and handsome edifice on Seventh Street above Arch. The vision and interest of his ministry were world-wide. His influence extended to the whole of American Israel.

Morais felt keenly the religious perplexities of his age, even as he championed unswerving loyalty to the ancient traditions. Passionately he preached anti-slavery sermons from his pulpit in defiance of those who sought to silence him. For this breach the congregation penalized him by seriously curtailing his right to preach, but the Union League Club of Philadelphia acclaimed him, electing him honorary member.

When his indignation was aroused in a just cause he was fearless. The secret baptism and abduction of the child Edgar Mortara (the notorious Mortara case), Morais hoped, would lead to the intercession of the United States government. When President James Buchanan refused to intercede, Morais omitted the recital of the prayer for the government the following Sabbath, much to the consternation and protest of the lay authorities of the congregation.

Morais labored assiduously in behalf of the Russian immigrants of 1881 and 1882, despite his linguistic handicap, as he spoke neither Yiddish nor German. He worked zealously to help them adjust themselves in the new environment, and they rewarded him with trust and confidence. He arbitrated and settled many a bitter feud between employers and laborers in the days of sweat-shop tyranny. He secured loans for the Jewish colonists in the Baron de Hirsch settlements of New Jersey, and visited them frequently.

It was as an educator—as a religious guide to a perplexed generation—that Morais' greatest contribution to American Judaism was made. He did not overlook the need of elementary education. The Hebrew Sunday School Society, the Hebrew Education Society of Philadelphia and the Young Men's Hebrew Association were served by him devotedly. His house was a miniature academy, and by personal instruction he influenced a corps of students who became leaders of the rising generation of American Jews. Cyrus Adler, Isaac Husik, David Werner Amram and Gerson B. Levi were representative disciples. He also exerted a strong influence upon such men as Hyman Gratz (founder of Gratz College), Moses Aaron Dropsie (founder of the Dropsie College for Hebrew and Cognate Learning) and Mayer Sulzberger. His enduring contribution was as a founder of the Conservative Movement in American Judaism. This role he exercised through the founding of institutions of higher Jewish learning and, principally, through the formation of the Jewish Theological Seminary of America.

In 1867 he joined forces with Isaac Leeser in the establishment of the first Jewish college in America, the Maimonides College. During the six years of its existence he held the professorship of Bible and Biblical literature. When this institution was suspended for lack of support, he hailed with satisfaction the establishment of the Hebrew Union College in Cincinnati, and gave this institution his moral support. He accepted the office of official examiner at the College, hoping that the College might develop as a rabbinical seminary for all groups of American Jewry. Despite growing theological differences and religious misgivings, he continued to cling to this hope as late as July, 1885. But when, toward the end of that year, at the Pittsburgh Conference of Reform Rabbis, resolutions were adopted renouncing the binding authority of the Bible and the Talmud, and introducing bold innovations in the theory and practice of Judaism, Morais abandoned all hope of attaining theological unity with his Reform colleagues and decided that the time had come for Conservative Jews to establish a seminary for the training of rabbis according to the

Sabato Morais. Reproduced by courtesy of the Jewish Theological Seminary of America

principles of Jewish tradition and adherence to the practices of historic Judaism.

In January, 1886, he issued a call, signed by himself and six other rabbis, declaring that "it is imperative to make a strong effort for the perpetuation of Judaism in America," and that "it is proposed to form an institution in which Bible and Talmud shall be studied to a religious purpose." On January 2, 1887, the formal opening of the Seminary took place in New York city in the vestry room of the Shearith Israel Congregation, with Morais presiding at the ceremonies. For the remaining days of his life Morais served the Seminary as president of the faculty and professor of Bible.

Morais was not a professional theologian nor given to philosophical speculation. His approach to Judaism was historical and pragmatic. This lack of theological definition continued to characterize the institution which truly expresses the spirit of its founder.

In 1887 the University of Pennsylvania conferred upon him the honorary degree of Doctor of Laws—a signal honor, as he was the first Jew upon whom this university conferred this distinction.

Morais wrote prolifically both in a popular and scholarly vein. He was a frequent contributor to the *Occident, Asmonean, Menorah, Jewish Record* (Philadelphia), *American Hebrew* (New York), and *Jewish Exponent* (Philadelphia). He wrote a brief work on the *Book of Esther*; a *Biography of S. D. Luzzatto,* translated into Italian by J. Luzzatto, and into German by M. Gruenwald; a translation of Samuel David Luzzatto's *Prolegomena to a Grammar of the Hebrew Language* (in the *Fifth Biennial Report of the Jewish Theological Seminary*); and various essays on the history and literature of the Jews in Italy. Many of these were collected and published on the occasion of the one hundredth anniversary of his birth in a volume entitled *Italian Hebrew Literature,* edited by Julius H. Greenstone (New York, 1926). Morais also wrote Hebrew verse and sonnets. Shortly before his death he completed the translation of the *Book of Jeremiah* for the Jewish Publication Society of America.

ABRAHAM A. NEUMAN.

Lit.: Morais, H. S., *The Jews of Philadelphia* (1894); idem, "Sabato Morais, a Memoir," *Sixth Biennial Report of the Jewish Theological Seminary* (1896; reprinted separately, 1898); Rosenau, William, "Sabato Morais—An Appreciation on the Centenary of His Birth," *Central Conference of American Rabbis Year Book,* vol. 33 (1923) 356-74 (reprinted separately 1923); *Commemoration of the One Hundredth Anniversary of the Birth of the Reverend Doctor Sabato Morais by the Congregation Mikveh Israel in the City of Philadelphia* (1924); Morais, Sabato, *Italian Hebrew Literature,* Julius H. Greenstone edit., with foreword by Henry S. Morais (1926).

MORALIST MOVEMENT, *see* MUSAR MOVEMENT.

MORALITY.

Morality may be described as a recognition of duties leading to good conduct. It is distinguishable only in a most general manner from ethics which likewise has for its province the nature and grounds for proper conduct. Ethics as a science is all inclusive and deals with such broad principles as are applicable to mankind as a whole; while morality is, in a sense, concerned chiefly with the personal relations of an individual to particular fellow-individuals or to a collective group. Thus the general principles of justice, truth and honor, universally considered, belong properly to the province of ethical philosophy, while the same principles involving the personal relations between individuals are subject matter for morality. The two coalesce at numerous points, and the line of demarcation cannot easily be traced. In general, ethics may be said to lay the philosophical foundation for conduct while morality is concerned with their practical application. Ethics and morality, often used synonymously, stand in mutual relation as science to art.

It is with respect to the origin and nature of moral laws that the conception of morality of the Hebrew people in the days of the prophets made such a great departure. With the prophets laws of morality are not arbitrary or variable, subject to individual or collective caprice, but remain absolute and immutable because they come from God "Who changeth not." They are not imposed by men from a love of power or self interest but by a God of righteousness, the Father of all mankind. In this conception of morality lay enfolded all that men, with advancing civilization, have since learned of justice, liberty and the rights of man.

The difference between these moral systems and the Jewish conception of morality is thoroughgoing. In the Jewish code the material benefit from upright conduct is secondary. To put it plainly, a good life is mandatory because it is the will of God. That is the sole reason. It answers the question why we should deal justly, respect the rights of our fellow-men and love our neighbor as ourselves. That we are obeying God's command is of importance rather than the practical good which exemplary moral conduct may bring about. The only and exclusive incentive for a moral life lies in the will of God. "Ye shall be holy because I, the Lord your God, am holy." Here there is no implication of securing individual happiness or the greatest good of the greatest number; there is no special faculty in the individual that enables him to distinguish right from wrong; there is no intimation that the moral life is to be pursued purely for its own sake without reference to God or man.

That is the distinctive and epochmaking contribution the Jewish people have made to the development of the moral consciousness in the world: the moral Law as an expression of the will of God. For no other reason are we to follow the path of virtue in our own personal life and in our relations to fellow-men. If individual or communal benefits follow such a course they are simply a happy concomitant of it. The real meaning of the command "Righteousness, righteousness ye shall pursue in order that your days may be prolonged in the land" becomes clear when instead of the words "in order that" we use the words "with the result that". That would be in strict accord with the spirit of the moral law. It is in perfect harmony with the spirit of the Law that we find in the Mishnah (*Aboth* 1:3), "Be not like servants who serve their master for the sake of reward," and (*ibid.* 4:2), "The reward for fulfilling a precept is the opportunity for fulfilling another precept, while the commission of a sin leads only to the commission of another sin."

In other words, according to the Jewish conception of morality, we are to practice righteousness unconditionally. That we may prosper through such a course is more or less of a coincident; the all-absorbing end is to fulfill the command of God.

This idea of morality was not developed in Israel until the time of the prophets. The early Hebrews, like all other primitive communities, were guided only by self-interest and self-preservation; and right and wrong were determined accordingly and proportionally appraised. As the community widened the ideas necessary for the promotion of communal welfare grew wider in content and became more general. By degrees the ideas of justice, right, honor, loyalty to the tribe, and the like, emerge in the form of moral obligations. Then such ideas, to give them greater force, were gradually associated with a belief in a god or gods, and a breach of the moral convention was in the nature of a sin which could be expiated only by sacrifice, and the wrath of the deity was averted.

The sense of individual responsibility had not yet wholly developed, as it was social righteousness rather than individual that necessitated moral commands or taboos. Not until the rise of the prophets were the Hebrew people taught the source and scope of morality with its implications for the individual as well as for the people. They were taught that the moral Law expressive of the will of God, was imperative and compelling in its commands and that its violation was equivalent to the denial of God's very existence. No breach of this Law could be atoned for directly or vicariously by sacrifices, but by a radical change in thought and character, in a creation of a "new heart"— in fine, in a fundamental moral conversion. The numerous passages from *Amos, Isaiah,* and the other earlier prophets give ample proof of the fact that the group morality of the ancient Hebrews was to be replaced by a law of morality that would fix moral responsibility on every individual and, through the individual, embrace all mankind. That was the universalism, under moral law, taught especially by the later prophets: as God is to be universally acknowledged so is the moral law to be universally observed.

God's will is henceforth the sole source of moral obligation. It follows, therefore, that the revelation of God in the Torah is the practical rule of human conduct.

Morality and religion thus form an indissoluble union. To recognize the existence of God means also the recognition of the compelling force of the moral law. Hence it is that throughout the history of Israel since the prophetic era Judaism has been so full of moral content.

The prophetic teaching is the key to all that is Jewish life and thought. In the post-Exilic period, in the Second Commonwealth and in the Middle Ages down to modern times Judaism maintains that the affirmation of God means a recognition of the imperativeness of a moral life. This combination of religion and morality with its implications forms the subject matter of the vast rabbinic literature beginning with the Mishnah to the latest Responsa. Every minutia of human conduct is prescribed. Duties to God, to one's self, to our neighbors, to the State, not to speak of filial duty, chastity, truthfulness and honesty, charity, mercy, hospitality and personal honor—every phase of human conduct in everyday life is brought under the divinely inspired moral law. Even worship in the synagogue and prayers recited by the individual have, according to the rabbis, the chief if not the only merit in that they help to withstand the temptation to break the law.

This conception of morality is thus inclusive. It is the inspiration of religious worship, it colors every phase of domestic life, it informs every act and thought of the individual. Nothing better shows the all-embracing domain of the moral law than the passage in Deuteronomy: "And these words which I command thee this day shall be on thy heart. Thou shalt teach them diligently unto thy children; and shalt talk of them when thou sittest in thy house, and when thou walkest by the way, and when thou liest down and when thou risest up" (*Deut.* 6:5).

CHARLES A. RUBENSTEIN.

Lit.: Hobhouse, L. T., *Morals in Evolution* (1915); Kaplan, Mordecai M., *Judaism as a Civilization* (1934); Abrahams, Israel, *Jewish Life in the Middle Ages* (1917); Joseph, Morris, *Judaism as Creed and Life* (1903).

MORAVIA, one of the most fertile provinces in Central Europe, and possessed of important industries, such as those at Brünn (Brno) and Mährisch Ostrau (Morava Ostrava). It belonged to the Austro-Hungarian monarchy until 1918; from the end of the first World War to March, 1939, it formed a part of the Czechoslovakian republic, when it was occupied by Nazi Germany. According to the census of 1935, there were about 38,000 Jews in Moravia, about 1.4 per cent of the whole population. In 1921 the Jewish population numbered 37,989, and in 1930 it was 41,155.

Despite the relatively low number of Jews in Moravia, they were important culturally, scientifically and commercially for many centuries. The Jewish community, though small and for a long time confined to a ghetto, was known the world over, and many Jews famous in both Jewish and general fields of art and science are known to have come from or lived there. The first or oldest document in the history of the Jews is the so-called ordinance of "Raffelstetten," at the beginning of the 10th cent., dealing, among other things, with the taxes payable by Jews attending fairs in Mo-

ravia and with ship privileges. In 1096 Crusaders marching through Bohemia and Moravia forced the Jews living in small villages to submit to baptism. In 1097 Henry IV permitted them to return to Judaism.

At that time there were already larger Jewish colonies in Moravia, the largest being in Brno. In 1229 this community led an independent life. King Přemysl Ottokar, a very tolerant sovereign, granted the Jews of his country, Moravia, special privileges (1254), and these were granted to the Jews of Brno in particular (1268). He compassionately admitted the Jews of other countries, sympathizing with them in their persecution by other sovereigns. The "safe-conduct" was still valid at the beginning of the 14th cent. under Wenceslaus (Venceslav) II. It must have been at this time that the Jews of Brno became wealthy. In 1311 Jan of Prague was welcomed by the Jews when he entered the city for the first time.

Jews are found for the first time in Kroměříž (Kremsier) in 1322, and in Jihlava in 1345; however, they were expelled from the latter place in 1426. One of the oldest communities is Austerlice (Austerlitz), where RaSHBA (Rabbi Solomon ibn Adret) pronounced his historic verdict (1300). The fight between the Taborites and the Orthodox also brought much trouble to the Moravian Jews. The Vienna Gezerah (1421) and the expulsion of the Jews from Jihlava are connected with the Hussite war.

The fate of the Moravian Jews became still worse when Pope Nicholas V brought the French Franciscan monk Johann Capistrano to Bohemia and Moravia to strengthen the Catholic Church. Hatred against Jews became boundless, and they were forced to emigrate from Znojmo (Znaim), Brno and Olomouc (Olmütz) in the 1450's. Only the Jews of Uherské Hradiště were successful in their opposition to him.

In 1551 Emperor Ferdinand I commanded the Jews to wear a small wheel of yellow cloth on their clothes. In 1642 they were invaded by the Swedes (Lípník, Ungarisch Brod, Kroměříž and Tobičov). The Chmielnicki uprising and the Russian-Polish war (1648-55) brought about Jewish emigration from Poland into Moravia. Viennese emigrants came to Mikulov (Nikolsburg) and Kroměříž in great numbers. In 1657 Jews were permitted to attend the fairs. In 1681 a dispensation of the National Guard ordered that the Jews maintain the same force as in 1657. As a result, only one son in every Jewish family was permitted to marry (1726). The Jews were driven from the trades into business, and had to pay high protection and taxes. Because of these decrees, the Jews of Moravia were compelled to live in their own houses and streets (ghettos). They were not permitted to live near a church, and had to give up their houses in those neighborhoods to Christians.

Their position became even more deplorable from 1740 on, under Empress Maria Theresa. The Prussian invasion of Moravia and Silesia brought them increased suffering. They were accused of high treason and had to pay high taxes. In 1745 they were to be expelled from all Moravia, but this law was recalled the same year. However, only a small number of families remained in Moravia. In 1754 a law was passed to change the unbearable situation of the Jews.

A better era for the Jews was inaugurated with the

Edict of Toleration of Emperor Joseph II (1782). They were allowed to attend the schools and also the university, and Jewish physicians were permitted to practice their profession. But the changes progressed slowly; the cities and their inhabitants resisted the dispersion of the Jews of the ghettos and their participation in the economic life of their cities. It was the Austrian Parliament of Kroměříž (1848-49) which established the civil and religious freedom of the Jews (two historic messages from the chief rabbi of Moravia, Samson Raphael Hirsch, were delivered on this occasion). The student Heinrich Spitzer, of Bsenec, was one of the first victims of Vienna during the revolution.

Under Emperor Francis Joseph (1848-1916) many Moravian Jews came to Vienna, and took an admirable part in the intellectual, political and economic life of the monarchy. Professor Redlich, the last old-Austrian secretary of the exchequer, was born in Hodonin; the minister Eisler in Boskovice (Boskowitz); the government councillor Bachrach in Steinberg; the first secretary of the body of merchants, Dr. Otto Müller, in Hulin; and the general manager of the Anker Assurance, Dr. B. Schwoner, in Kroměříž.

In the free Czechoslovakian republic of Thomas G. Masaryk and Eduard Beneš, the Jews of Moravia, because of their fairness and authority and their wide knowledge and understanding (which they and their parents had acquired in the ghettos), were active in all offices of state. The "Kehillah" (Jewish community organization) was maintained in many cities, with its Jewish self-governing bodies. Here were to be found all the expressions of national and religious life, until the occupation of the Czechoslovakian republic by the Nazis. A great number of Jews freely declared their allegiance to Judaism and thus evaded the fight between the Czechs and the Germans. One of the regulations which prevailed in Moravia for centuries and which continued in practice up to 1939 was the so-called "Landesmassa-Fund," started in the time of Emperor Joseph II. Five gulden per year were collected as the family tax from the 5,400 Jewish families. This was newly reinstated, and 40 per cent of the collections was set aside for educational purposes. In the last years of the republic the interest brought this fund to about 100,000 Czech kronen yearly. The Zemský Svaz of Jewish communities was reinstated under the republic (1924).

The Jews of Moravia, the home of Masaryk, made it their mission to effect a bond between the west (Bohemia) and the east (Slovakia) of the republic, and to bring them together. Towns like Brno, Olomouc and Morava Ostrava became stronger through the addition of smaller communities. However, there was also a vigorous Jewish community life prevailing in the east: in Jihlava (1,355 Jews), Břeclav (1,500 Jews), Znojmo (890), Mikulov (755), Hodonin (800), Ungarisch Brod (800), Kroměříž (750), Boskovice (580).

When the Nazis came to power in Germany, Morava Ostrava acted as a reservoir for the Prussian-Silesian Jews. From 1934 on political refugees from Vienna were admitted into Brno. In 1942, under the German "protectorate," there were only a remnant of Jews in Moravia. They had to quit the small towns, leaving all their possessions behind, for Prague, and from 1941 on a large part of the Jews were sent to Poland. Their possessions were, for the most part, transferred to Germans from southern Tyrol and Galicia.   Oscar Frankl.

Lit.: Haas, Theodor, *Die Juden in Mähren* (1918); Bondy-Dvorsky, *Zur Geschichte der Juden in Böhmen, Mähren und Schlesien* (1906); D'Elvert, *Zur Geschichte der Juden in Mähren* (1895); Gold, Hugo, *Die Juden und Judengemeinden Mährens in Vergangenheit und Gegenwart* (1929); Frankl-Grün, Adolf, *Geschichte der Juden in Kremsier und Ungarisch Brod* (1900-6); Ložek, J., *Židě na Moravě;* Müller, Willibald, *Beiträge zur Geschichte der mährischen Judenschaft* (1903); Löw, "Das mährische Landesrabbinat seit 100 Jahren," *Gesammelte Schriften,* vol. 2 (1890) 165 et seq.; Moskowitz, Moses, "The Jewish Situation in the Protectorate of Bohemia-Moravia," *Jewish Social Studies,* vol. 4 (1942) 17-44.

MORDECAI, hero of the story told in *Esther* of the deliverance of the Jews in the reign of Ahasuerus of Persia. His name is probably connected with that of the Babylonian deity Marduk. He was a Benjaminite by descent and the uncle or cousin (the Hebrew *dod* can mean either) of Esther, whom he reared in his house. His unrewarded revealing of a conspiracy against the king paved the way for his future elevation to prime minister; his refusal to bow down to Haman led the latter to assail the Jews; his firmness of faith inspired Esther to risk her life and accomplish the rescue of her people. The additions to *Esther* in the Apocrypha represent Mordecai as a prophet and a composer of prayers. Bible critics have doubted the historicity of the entire narrative and suggest that the character of Mordecai is drawn as the type of the unselfish, unflinching and wise Jewish sage.

Rabbinical sources enlarge on the story of Mordecai. They explain his name as meaning "pure myrrh" (*mor dechaya*) and identify him with one or more of the other characters in *Esther* or with the prophet Malachi. He had been a member of the Sanhedrin and it was through his knowledge of the seventy languages that he was able to detect the plans of the conspirators against the king. Mordecai and Esther are credited with the composition of the Hallel Psalms.

See also Esther.

Lit.: The literature cited under Esther; Ginzberg, *Legends of the Jews,* vols. 4 and 6.

MORDECAI BEN HILLEL ASHKENAZI, codifier of halacha, died a martyr with his wife and five children at Nuremberg in 1298. He was descendant of a prominent family of scholars and a pupil of Rabbi Meir of Rothenburg. His principle work was a comprehensive legal code published posthumously as *Sefer Hamordecai,* popularly called *The Mordecai.* This compilation is usually printed in the form of a newspaper or an appendix to Alfasi's *Halachot,* but this is merely a superficial correction, the various passages following rather the order of the Talmud. The interpretations, responsa, and decisions of a great number of post-Talmudic authorities bearing upon the particular problem involved are given, including Mordecai's own analysis. Probably due to the fact that the work was edited by his pupils after his death, the larger part of the work bears a minimum of systematic arrangement. *The Mordecai* performed a most useful service by rendering accessible to widely scattered scholars and rabbis the intellectual products of over three hundred and fifty of the leading Jewish thinkers up to that time.

After Mordecai ben Hillel Ashkenazi's tragic death (he, his wife and five children were killed during the

*Alfred Mordecai, Sr. From a painting (1836) by
Thomas Sully*

massacres instigated by Rindfleisch), his pupils disagreed over the manner in which the manuscript should be edited. This resulted in two different editions, known as Rhenish and Austrian versions respectively. The former attained the greater popularity, perhaps because of its conciseness, and was the one to be printed. It became widely known throughout all of Europe, while in Germany and adjoining lands it was considered highly authoritative. The Austrian version, which sometimes quotes different authorities, is more flexible in its interpretations and more detailed, but is perhaps closer to Mordecai's original design.

About sixty years after Mordecai's death, Samuel ben Aaron of Schlettstadt made extracts from the Austrian views which he applied as glosses to the Rhenish text, this being known as the *Hagganot Mordecai,* or *Mordecai Haḳaton.* The importance conceded to Mordecai's work resulted in its inclusion in the first printed treatise of the Talmud (Soncino, 1482). Leading scholars and codifiers drew upon *The Mordecai* extensively and a great number of commentaries and glosses were written upon it. Mordecai also wrote in Hebrew, a *Selicha* on the martyrdom of a proselyte, a poem on the Hebrew vowels, and a treatise (also in verse) on Shechita and Kashruth.

Lit.: Cat. Bodleiana; Daiches, Samuel, *Jewish Codes and Codifiers in Aspects of Hebrew Genius* (1910) 106; Grayzel, Solomon, *The Church and the Jews in the Thirteenth Century* (1938) 25; Graetz, Heinrich, *History of the Jews,* vol. 4, p. 36.

MORDECAI, ABRAM, pioneer in Alabama, b. Pennsylvania, 1775; d. Alabama (almost a century later). His father was a Jew, and his mother was German. He served for three years in the American army during the Revolutionary War and fought in most of the engagements in Delaware and New Jersey. In 1783, he settled among the Cusseta Indians of Georgia and became a trader. He often acted as an agent for the government in its dealings with the Indians. In 1789, he removed to Montgomery county, Alabama, established himself as a trader among the Curvalla Indians and became the first American citizen to settle in that locality. For many years, he dealt in skins and furs, pink root, and other medicinal barks. These he conveyed to Augusta and Pensacola on pack horses, and to New Orleans and Mobile by boat.

In 1804, a little below the junction of the Coosa and Tallapoosa rivers, Mordecai established the first cotton gin in the state of Alabama. The construction was done by Lyons and Barnett of Georgia, reported to be Jews, "who brought their tools, gin saws, and other materials from that State on pack-horses." Mordecai planned that the Indians in the neighboring territory should bring their cotton crop to him for ginning. He, in turn, would sell it at New Orleans. In 1805, however, the project was destroyed by the Indians and Mordecai was almost killed in the attack.

Ruined financially, he returned to Georgia and joined the forces of General Floyd at the outbreak of the War of 1812. In 1814, when General Jackson assigned the Indians their territory, Mordecai, with his wife (part Negro and part Indian) and his family, settled there. He lived the last years of his life in an Indian hut, in the outskirts of Dudleyville, Tallapoosa county, Alabama.

Lit.: Messing, A. J., "Old Mordecai"—The Founder of the City of Montgomery," *Publications of the American Jewish Historical Society,* No. 13, pp. 71-81.

MORDECAI, ALFRED (SR.), army officer and engineer, b. Warrenton, N. C., 1804; d. Philadelphia, 1887. He was the fifth son of the pioneer educator Jacob Mordecai and added to the family's public esteem by a distinguished career in the United States army, where for more than two decades he served as an ordnance expert attached to the staff corps.

After being graduated from West Point at the head of his class in 1823, he first taught in the Academy, but left shortly to assist in the construction of several forts. In 1839 he was appointed to the ordnance board and held that post until his resignation from the army in 1861. He saw service in the Mexican war, and was brevetted major in 1848. About ten years later, together with Capt. George B. McClellan (later general), and Maj. Richard Delafield, he was sent abroad to report on the Crimean war. His observations were published by order of Congress in 1860. It was on this visit that Mordecai had an audience with the Czar of Russia.

During his career Mordecai was in charge of a number of important arsenals, including Watervliet in New York (1857 to 1861). On resigning from the army he entered private life as an engineer and business executive. Famed in both the United States and Europe as a scientific investigator, he published several works, including *Experiments on Gunpowder* (1845).

Lit.: *Publications of American Jewish Historical Society,* No. 1, p. 124; No. 3, p. 40; No. 6, p. 47; Morais, H. S., *Jews of Philadelphia,* pp. 461-63.

MORDECAI, ALFRED (JR.), army officer and engineer, b. Philadelphia, 1840; d. Washington, D. C., 1920. He was the son of Alfred Mordecai; his career was patterned after that of his father and was in some respects no less distinguished. On graduation from the West Point Military Academy in 1861, he was brevetted second lieutenant of topographical engineers and served in the Manassas campaign, taking part in the Battle of Bull Run (July 21, 1861). His services during the Civil War, both in the field and as ordnance officer at arsenals, received due recognition when he was made lieutenant-colonel (1865).

After the war Mordecai was instructor of ordnance and gunnery at West Point, holding this post from 1865 to 1869 and again from 1874 to 1881. In subsequent years he rose to the rank of brigadier-general and occupied several important positions with the United States Army, chiefly as ordnance officer and inspector of arsenals. His last post was with the Ordnance Department in Washington, D. C., from which he resigned in 1904 to go into retirement.

Lit.: Morais, H. S., *Jews of Philadelphia* (1894) 464-66.

MORDECAI, JACOB, educator, son of Moses Mordecai and Elizabeth Whitlock, b. Philadelphia, 1762; d. Richmond, Va., 1838. He began his business career in the office of David Franks, distinguished merchant. Later Mordecai lived for a time in New York, then in Richmond and in Petersburg, Va., and finally settled at Warrenton, N. C., about 1787, where he became a "country merchant." Since he was obviously a scholar rather than a man of commercial interests, he was persuaded by influential friends to establish a boarding-school for young ladies, the first of its kind in the South. The Warrenton Seminary (opened Jan., 1809) proved a successful venture. Many young ladies of prominent families were educated there. The school was strictly non-sectarian, and flourished for ten years. Rachel, Mordecai's eldest daughter, who became the wife of Aaron Lazarus, was an important factor in maintaining the high standard of this institution.

Mordecai was twice married. His first wife was Judith Myers of New York; on her death, in 1796, he married her younger half-sister Rebecca Myers. Of his many children six sons and seven daughters grew to maturity. His eldest son, MOSES MORDECAI (b. 1785), became a leading member of the North Carolina bar. His second son, SAMUEL MORDECAI, was a successful merchant of Richmond, Va., and wrote a clever history, *Richmond in Byegone Days.* Then came SOLOMON MORDECAI, who studied medicine in Philadelphia and became a popular physician in Mobile, Ala. His fourth son, GEORGE WASHINGTON MORDECAI (b. 1801), settled in Raleigh and rose to distinction as a lawyer, railroad president and president of the Bank of North Carolina. The fifth son was the distinguished officer of the United States Army, Major ALFRED MORDECAI; the sixth and youngest, AUGUSTUS MORDECAI, took to farming near Richmond, Va., where he married and settled. EMMA MORDECAI (1812-1906), the youngest of Jacob Mordecai's seven daughters, devoted her long life to various educational and religious activities in which she played a prominent part.

Lit.: Gratz, Mordecai, *Publications of the American Jewish Historical Society,* No. 6, pp. 39-48; Ezekiel and Lichtenstein, *Jews of Richmond,* pp. 23-5; *American Jewish Year Book,* vol. 6, pp. 156-7.

MORDELL, ALBERT, writer and lawyer, b. Philadelphia, 1885. The eldest son of the Hebrew grammarian Phineas Mordell, he manifested an early interest in literature, and in 1906, after a period at Jewish journalism, he was admitted to the bar (1910) in Philadelphia. His first literary pamphlet was *Shifting of Literary Values,* in 1912; his thesis, much debated in contemporary periodicals: past literary productions must be judged in the light of modern values.

Mordell's career was thenceforth divided between law and literature. In the latter field he produced several original works and performed a number of editing jobs. In 1915 he published *Dante and Other Waning Classics,* a book of literary opinions from which William Dean Howells dissented in *Harper's Magazine.* In 1918 appeared *Karma,* first of his collections of Lafcadio Hearn's writings, followed by others published in Japan as well as in the United States, and including *Essays in European and Oriental Literature* (1923), *An American Miscellany* (1924), and *Occidental Gleanings* (1925). Mordell also collected and edited writings from Henry James, Pierre Loti and Guy de Maupassant.

Mordell's study of Sigmund Freud's ideas resulted in his volume *The Erotic Motive in Literature* (1919), an application of psychoanalysis to literature which aroused both protest and praise. In 1921 appeared *The Literature of Ecstasy.* His *Quaker Militant: John Greenleaf Whittier* (1933) portrayed a new Whittier, with much novel material, some controversial, and was favorably received by such critics as William Lyon Phelps and Hervey Allen. His later publications included: Lafcadio Hearn's translations, *Sketches and Tales from the French* (1935) and *Stories from Émile Zola* (1936); *The Federal Constitution Celebration 1937-1938* (co-author; 1938); *History of the Jews in Vienna,* by Max Grunwald (1936; co-editor). In addition, his prolific contributions appeared in the Jewish and non-Jewish press. He was appointed to the editorial boards of the Jewish Publication Society of America and the *Jewish Quarterly Review.*

MORDELL, LOUIS JOEL, professor of mathematics, b. Philadelphia, 1888. Son of the grammarian Phineas Mordell, he was educated at Cambridge, and received several academic awards; in 1912 he published the first of an extensive series of mathematical papers appearing in various scientific journals, English, American and others. In 1916 he became lecturer at Birkbeck College in London, but five years later went to the College of Technology at the University of Manchester where he was made Fielden Professor of Pure Mathematics. In the summer of 1923 he was visiting professor at the University of Chicago, and in 1930 he lectured at various institutions in Germany.

Mordell's writings include *Three Lectures on Fermat's Last Theorem* (1921) and *On Rational Solutions of the Indeterminate Equations of the Third and Fourth Degrees* (1922). In 1941 he was awarded the De Morgan Medal by the Council of the London Mathematical Society, in recognition of his contributions to the theory of numbers. He became a British subject.

MORDELL, PHINEAS, Hebrew grammarian and philologist, b. Kovno, Lithuania, 1861; d. Philadelphia, 1934. He was educated in the Kovno Yeshiva and taught Hebrew for several years. In 1881 he emigrated to the United States, where he earned his living in a Philadelphia factory. First becoming interested in Hebrew grammar through the work of Lerner, he was encouraged in his researches by Marcus Jastrow, and in 1895 published a pamphlet of a new Hebrew text for the *Sefer Yetzirah*. There followed several articles in *Hashiloah*, dealing with various disputed grammatical questions, and in 1905 Mordell began his life's work of teaching Hebrew.

Continuing his researches in *Sefer Yetzirah*, he made a restored text, and published, in English, theories he had formulated on the origin of letters and numerals, in the *Jewish Quarterly Review* (1912 and 1913); the work later appeared in pamphlet form in 1922. At the same time he was creating the nucleus of a new grammar in articles appearing in *Ha-ivri*, and later in revised form in *Leshonenu* (1929 and 1930). He died before the grammar could be published.

Most important of the articles Mordell contributed to the *Jewish Quarterly Review* between 1925 and 1934 was "The Beginning and Development of Hebrew Punctuation" (Oct., 1933). He maintained that Hebrew was not a purely consonantal language, and that the Jews, not the Phoenicians, had invented the alphabet. A summary of Mordell's correspondence with other scholars was published in *Ramah* (1938).

In political philosophy, Mordell was a follower of Henry George. He was also a Zionist. He was the father of Albert and Louis Joel Mordell.

Lit.: Haolom, June 17, July 1, July 8, 1937.

MOREELL, BEN, engineer and naval officer, b. Salt Lake City, Utah, 1892. After serving the city of St. Louis, Mo., as civil engineer, he entered the engineering corps of the United States navy in 1917, and shortly thereafter was appointed staff aide to the commander of the Atlantic fleet, Azores detachment. He acted as public works officer in the Azores (1918-1919), and was awarded a World War medal with star. Moreell was then sent to Haiti to be public works officer (1920-24), and received from the Republic of Haiti a medal of honor and merit. He was again honored by Haiti in 1937.

From 1926 to 1930 Moreell was in the Bureau of Yards and Docks, and served as public works officer in the Puget Sound navy yard. Commissioned rear admiral (1937), he was appointed chief of the Bureau of Docks and Yards and Chief of Navy Civil Engineers.

Moreell, an expert in the use of concrete, spent 1933-34 in the École Nationale des Ponts et Chaussées in Paris. He published *Standards of Design for Concrete* (1929), and in 1935 was awarded the Wason medal for research by the American Concrete Institute. He was elected president of the Army and Navy club in 1939.

MOREH NEBUCHE HAZEMAN, *see* KROCHMAL, NACHMAN.

MOREH NEBUCHIM, *see* MAIMONIDES.

MORGENSTERN, JULIAN, rabbi and Biblical scholar, president of the Hebrew Union College, b. St. Francisville, Ill., 1881. After graduating from the University of Cincinnati (1901) and receiving his rabbinical degree from the Hebrew Union College (1902), he went to Germany for two years of post-graduate work. He studied Semitics at the Universities of Berlin and Heidelberg, and received the Ph.D. degree from the latter (1904). His doctoral dissertation was *The Doctrine of Sin in the Babylonian Religion* (1905).

Returning to the United States, Morgenstern became rabbi of Congregation Ahaveth Achim (later Temple

Julian Morgenstern

Israel) of LaFayette, Ind., where he served for three years. But despite a most happy experience in the ministry, he soon found himself drawn back to academic life. He became professor of Biblical and Semitic languages at the Hebrew Union College, where his systematic and thorough methods made him a successful teacher. In 1921, on the retirement of Kaufmann Kohler, he became acting president, and in 1922 was elected president of the College. He continued, however, to give Bible courses both to rabbinical and post-graduate students.

During his presidency many important changes occurred in the life of the Hebrew Union College. The faculty was enlarged to include departments of education, social studies and Jewish music; three buildings were completed—a dormitory, gymnasium, and new library; the separate chartering of the College (which had previously been included in the charter of the Union of American Hebrew Congregations) and the creation of an endowment fund were achieved; several lectureships and publication funds were established; and the *Hebrew Union College Annual*, which became an outstanding journal of Jewish scholarship, was founded.

After his return to the Hebrew Union College, Morgenstern resumed intensive study of the Bible. He permitted his conclusions in Biblical research to mature slowly; six years elapsed after the publication of his doctoral thesis before his article "Biblical Theophanies" began to appear (in the *Zeitschrift für Assyriologie*, 1911 and 1913). As his ideas ripened and were tested in classroom and seminar teaching, his tempo of publication steadily increased. His articles appeared in the *Journal of the American Oriental Society, Jewish Quarterly Review, Journal of Biblical Literature* and many other American and German publications.

His scholarly output continued despite the inroads on his time by administrative duties and by the emergency tasks that fell upon Jewish leaders during the period of his presidency of the College. Notably, every volume of the *Hebrew Union College Annual* contained a contribution from his pen, some of considerable magnitude.

Despite trends toward conservatism in Biblical science, Morgenstern adhered in a general way to the approach associated with the names of Graf and Wellhausen. But he was not a slavish follower of the German school. He did not rely on linguistic criteria for the analysis of the Pentateuchal documents, but distinguished the sources by their varying social and cultural backgrounds, and divergences of theological viewpoint. In the field of source-analysis, his most original contribution is perhaps "The Oldest Document of the Hexateuch" (*Hebrew Union College Annual*, 1927), which incidentally gave substance to the so-called "Kenite hypothesis," which had previously been little more than a guess—the view, namely, that the religion of Moses was derived in some measure from that of his wife's tribe, the Kenites. Morgenstern made also a detailed investigation entitled "The Book of the Covenant" (*ibid.*, 1928 and 1932). He gave full weight to economic and social factors in the history of the Israelite people and religion. This is well illustrated in his *Amos Studies* (1941), which is a complete treatise on the book of *Amos,* including reconstruction and translation of the text.

His contributions to the history of Jewish observance include: "The Origin of Maṣṣoth and the Maṣṣoth Festival" (*American Journal of Theology,* 1917); "Two Ancient Israelite Agricultural Festivals" (*Jewish Quarterly Review,* 1917); and the series, "The Three Calendars of Ancient Israel" (*Hebrew Union College Annual,* 1924, 1926 and 1935). In these and other studies his varied knowledge of ancient and modern Semitic customs and folklore proved most useful. In 1942 he was preparing an exhaustive treatise on ceremonies at birth, marriage, and death among the Semites.

Significant for the history of religion are his researches showing that the Israelites retained many ceremonies and even concepts derived originally from solar worship as demonstrated in his "Biblical Theophanies" and "The Gates of Righteousness" (*Hebrew Union College Annual,* 1929). Mythological survivals in the Bible are illustrated in "Moses with the Shining Face" (*ibid.,* 1925) and in more recent studies of *Ps.* 82 and 48 (*ibid.,* 1939 and 1941). Morgenstern conducted some highly original inquiries into the history of post-Exilic Judaism; his findings appear in part in some of the articles previously mentioned, and in "A Chapter in the History of the High-Priesthood" (*American Journal of Semitic Languages,* 1938). He was the Biblical specialist on the Board of Editors of the *Universal Jewish Encyclopedia,* and his method and outlook may be seen from his numerous articles on Biblical topics. Designed for general readers and religious school teachers is his *A Jewish Interpretation of the Book of Genesis* (1920).

Morgenstern was associated with many learned endeavors, and served as president of the American Oriental Society. He received honorary degrees from the University of Cincinnati and the Jewish Theological Seminary of America.

Lina Morgenstern

His philosophy of Judaism is organically related to his scholarly research. He sees in the Jewish religion a growing and evolving entity, constantly modified in expression by social and intellectual currents in the world without, yet retaining its fundamental principles and essential character, impressed upon it by the prophets of Israel.   BERNARD J. BAMBERGER.

MORGENSTERN, LINA, communal worker and writer on pedagogy, b. Breslau, Germany, 1830; d. Berlin, 1909. She organized the first Fröbel kindergarten (1859) and established the first seminary for kindergarten teachers in Germany (1863). During the Prussian-Austrian war of 1866, she established in Berlin and Breslau the first free kitchens for the needy, in recognition of which she was nicknamed "Suppenlina." Among the many other charitable institutions founded by her are the Kinderschutzverein for the care of underprivileged babies (1869) and a society for the salvation and education of paroled girl prisoners (1881).

Lina Morgenstern was also a pioneer in the emancipation and education of women. In 1873 she founded the first union of Berlin housewives (Berliner Hausfrauenverein) which aimed at the spiritual welfare of women, the organization of a mutual credit fund for domestic workers, a campaign against the increase in the cost of living, and the founding of cooking schools. At the first International Women's Congress, convoked by her at Berlin (1896), 1,800 representatives of women's organizations from all parts of the world were present. She was active also in the peace movement.

Her numerous books dealt chiefly with women's problems, notably the education of children. She wrote, besides, many stories for children. *Das Paradies der Kindheit* (1860) was the first German textbook for the Fröbel kindergarten. Lina Morgenstern was editor of the *Deutsche Hausfrauenzeitung* and of a monthly magazine for young girls. In recognition of her achievements she received many royal honors.

MORGENTHAU, HENRY, diplomat and financier, b. Mannheim, Germany, 1856. He came to the United States at the age of nine and was educated in the public schools of New York city and at the College of the City of New York. Graduating from the law school of Columbia University in 1877, he established a law firm in partnership with Samson Lachman and Abraham Goldsmith. Morgenthau, however, was more interested in the real estate business than in the prac-

tice of law. Sufficiently farsighted to realize that New
York city was growing rapidly, he purchased numerous
land parcels along the main arteries of expansion in
Harlem, Washington Heights and the Bronx. In 1899,
he was a leading figure in the organization of the
Central Realty Bond and Trust Company founded for
the purpose of dealing in real estate on a large scale.
Although this corporation was absorbed in 1905 by
the Lawyers' Title Insurance Company, its real estate
holdings were purchased by Morgenthau and administered by the Henry Morgenthau Company. Morgenthau was a director of the Underwood Typewriter
Company, the Equitable Life Assurance Society of the
United States, and headed the Herald Square Realty Co.

In 1912 he entered the sphere of national politics.
Attracted to the progressive democracy of Woodrow
Wilson, he became one of Wilson's most ardent supporters. Wilson, in turn, recognizing Morgenthau's
valuable service as chairman of the finance committee
of the Democratic National Committee and as a campaign strategist, nominated him ambassador to Turkey.
The appointment was confirmed in the Senate on September 4, 1913. At Constantinople, in addition to the
administration of the routine affairs of the embassy,
he showed particular interest in Christian missionary
activities and in the problems of Turkish Jewry. Morgenthau well remembered the parting injunction of
President Wilson, "that anything you can do to improve the lot of your co-religionists is an act that will
reflect credit upon America." With the outbreak of the
first World War, however, Morgenthau had less time
for these pursuits. From 1914-16, in addition to the
regular business of the American embassy, he was in
charge of the interests in Turkey of Great Britain,
France, Italy, Russia, Belgium, Montenegro, San Mar-
ino, Serbia, and Switzerland.

In 1916, Morgenthau was once again in the United
States, actively campaigning for the re-election of
Woodrow Wilson. In June, 1917, Wilson sent him to
Europe on a secret diplomatic errand and on his return
to America Morgenthau advised him to appoint a spe-
cial advisory commission to be stationed in Europe.

Morgenthau strongly supported Wilson's plans for
the post war reconstruction of Europe. Early in 1919,
with William H. Taft, A. Lawrence Lowell, and Henry
Van Dyke, he signed an "appeal to our fellow citizens,"
calling for the support of the covenant of the League
of Nations. In March of that year he was in Europe
assisting Henry P. Davison in the organization of the
International Red Cross. While in Paris, it was suggested by the American peace commissioners that he
make a careful study of the Turkish question. It was
Morgenthau's idea to send the Harbord Commission
to Armenia for the purpose of resolving the conflicting
claims of the French and Armenians in that area and
to report on the advisability of an American mandate.

Also in 1919, President Wilson named Morgenthau
head of a commission to investigate the treatment of
the Jews in the newly created Polish republic. After
an intensive and impartial investigation, Morgenthau
concluded that the conflict of peoples in Poland was
in some measure caused by the impoverished condition
of the nation. Therefore, he proposed the creation of
a giant corporation with stock subscription on a national and international scale, with provision for the

Henry Morgenthau, Sr.

eventual transfer of all of the stock to the Poles. What
would eventually become a "Polish people's institution," according to Morgenthau's plan, would have restored the credit of Poland. However, this far-sighted
proposal was vetoed by the Polish leaders, whose nationalism would permit of no compromise.

In 1920 Morgenthau was nominated ambassador to
Mexico by Wilson, but the Senate Foreign Relations
Committee deemed it unwise to send a new envoy in
view of the political unrest prevalent there. However,
with the creation by the League of Nations of the
Refugee Settlement Commission in 1923, Morgenthau
accepted its chairmanship.

The problem which confronted the commission was a
gigantic one. Over a million Greek refugees from
Ionia, who fled their Turkish conquerors in 1923, had
to be settled in European Greece. At the same time
350,000 Moslems were to leave their homes in Greece
for resettlement in Turkey. The solution of the many
problems incidental to the interchange of populations
was Morgenthau's crowning achievement. Honorary
citizenship was conferred upon him by Athens and by
Salonika. In 1930 Governor Franklin D. Roosevelt of
New York appointed him to the Saratoga Commission.

In 1933 Morgenthau was appointed delegate to the
Wheat Conference at Geneva, and served as technical expert at the London Monetary and Economic Conference.

Morgenthau was active in religious and philanthropic
work. He was a member of the Board of Directors
of Mt. Sinai Hospital in New York. He and his wife
founded Bronx House, a settlement which they fostered
and financed until it was taken over by the New York
Federation of Jewish Philanthropic Societies. He secured large contributions for the Federation, and on a
cross-country tour with Adolph S. Ochs, for the endowment fund of the Hebrew Union College in Cincinnati. He was a member of the executive committee
of B'nai B'rith. He was president of the Free Synagogue
in New York city, but resigned this position in 1919,
because of his differences with Stephen S. Wise on the
Zionist movement. "Zionism," wrote Morgenthau, "is a

surrender, not a solution of the Jewish question." At the Paris Peace Conference (1919) Morgenthau was chairman of an American Jewish Commission that attempted the introduction into the Covenant of the League of Nations of a Universal Religious Liberty clause.

Among the decorations awarded him were that of Grand Officer of the Legion of Honor of France, Honorary Grand Knight of the British Empire, and Knight of the Saint Saveur of Greece. Morgenthau received the honorary degree of LL.D. from the Constantinople College for Women, Oberlin College, Temple University of Philadelphia, Syracuse University, and the University of Athens, Greece. He was a director of the Institute of International Education, president of the Economic Club, and voted Chairman of the Near East Relief Inc., by act of Congress (1919-21). He was author of an account of his activities in Turkey entitled *Ambassador Morgenthau's Story* published in New York (1918) and in England under the title *Secrets of Bosphorus.* His autobiography, *All in a Life-Time,* was published in 1922; *My Trip Around the World* in 1928, and his experiences in Greece, *I Was Sent to Athens,* in 1930.

Henry Morgenthau's life has been of peculiarly American proportions. Beginning with an absorption in material pursuits, his evolution as humanitarian, diplomat and statesman proved to be of service to his country, to his co-religionists, and to his fellow-men in many lands.

ISAAC LANDMAN.

Lit.: American Hebrew, vol. 106, pp. 455, 503, 530, 556, 562, 616; vol. 111, p. 651; vol. 116, p. 387; Morgenthau, H., *I Was Sent to Athens* (1930); idem, *All in a Life-Time* (1922); idem, *Ambassador Morgenthau's Story* (1918).

MORGENTHAU, HENRY JR., farmer, publisher, financier and public official, b. New York city, 1891. He was educated in private schools, at the Phillips Exeter Academy, and at Cornell University.

Upon leaving Cornell University, where he studied agriculture (1913), Morgenthau made a careful study of farming opportunities in the United States. The outcome was his purchase of adjoining farms in Dutchess County that were expanded into the 1500-acre diversified farm which he still operated in 1942. Here in 1916 he took his bride, Elinor Fatman of New York, and here they not only worked together to build a successful modern farm on a pattern suitable to the productive capacities of the region, but joined with their neighbors in projects to improve community life and living conditions. He had gained insight into social problems prior to his college days as a resident and volunteer worker at the Henry Street Settlement in New York and as one of the supporters and directors of the Surprise Lake Camp for boys from the streets of New York. His experience had been enriched through knowledge of international affairs gained by serving for a time as secretary to his father, who was United States Ambassador to Turkey from 1913 to 1916.

When the United States entered the first World War, Morgenthau, working under the Food Administration, inaugurated a system of cooperative activities in Dutchess County to increase home-produced food. Then he conceived the idea of a tractor regiment for France which would increase France's food production at home and, what was at the time even more important, release United States food-carrying ships. Upon request of the Food Administration to carry the idea into practice, Morgenthau organized the tractor regiment and sailed to France to put it into operation. When he returned home, early in 1918, he enlisted in and was assigned to Naval Overseas Transport Service as lieutenant (junior

grade). At the end of the War he returned to the farm and devoted considerable time and energy with groups urging America's entry into the League of Nations as a measure to prevent future wars.

In the elections of 1920 his friend and Dutchess County neighbor, Franklin Delano Roosevelt, was the Democratic candidate for the vice-presidency, but was defeated as the nation turned in reaction against Woodrow Wilson's idealism and the League of Nations. Though industrial America seemed to rise on a spiral of prosperity, the farmers were in a precarious condition. Farm income was declining and farm mortgage indebtedness had risen from \$3,000,000,000 in 1910 to nearly \$11,000,000,000 in 1923. In 1922 Morgenthau acquired the *American Agriculturalist,* which he used as an outlet to plead the case of the American farmer, and he became active in national farm problems as a director of the Jewish Agricultural Society.

Morgenthau's opportunity to carry out some of his ideas came when Governor-elect Roosevelt appointed him chairman of the Agricultural Advisory Commission, which was to study agricultural problems in New York state. Within three months the commission, including leaders of farm organizations and legislators, brought in recommendations ranging from methods for improving farm-to-market roads to an adjustment in taxation for the benefit of agricultural cooperatives, which were written into law substantially as submitted. They have been regarded as the most constructive legislation for farmers ever put on the statute books of New York state.

In December, 1930, Morgenthau was appointed conservation commissioner of the state of New York and took office on January 1, 1931, at the beginning of Governor Roosevelt's second term. By that time the state, as well as the nation, was rapidly sliding into the trough of depression. Commissioner Morgenthau reorganized his department completely, brought in efficient and well-trained men, established each division on a business-like basis, and eliminated political patronage. During his administration a vast reforestation and soil conservation program was inaugurated in New York state. Long before any relief funds became available in the state Morgenthau devised a number of work projects, organized county by county on a non-partisan basis, to employ needy heads of families. As soon as the Temporary Emergency Relief Administration was established, his projects were ready to absorb many unemployed persons in useful work, designed to increase and improve all state park and public recreation facilities. These projects later served as a pattern on a national scale both for the Civilian Conservation Corps and the Works Progress Administration.

Morgenthau resigned as commissioner of conservation when Roosevelt became president, and he went to Washington as chairman of the Federal Farm Board but charged by the president with the responsibility of consolidating farm credit agencies to save debt-burdened farmers from bankruptcy. When the Farm Credit Administration was established (May, 1933), the president appointed Morgenthau its first governor. The reorganization of cooperatives bankrupted by speculation induced by prior Federal Farm Board policies and the liquidation of vast stocks of farm products held by them were among his responsibilities. Washington soon began to know him as a skillful and aggressive administrator with a broad knowledge of farm finance and the problems of cooperatives.

Due to the grave illness of Secretary William Woodin, who died in 1934, the Treasury Department lacked vigorous direction, and in November, 1933, the presi-

dent appointed Morgenthau under secretary of the
Treasury, to be acting secretary during Secretary
Woodin's illness. Finding that the state of his health
would not permit him to return to active duty, Secretary Woodin resigned and Morgenthau, at the age of
forty-two, became secretary of the Treasury (January 1,
1934), one of the youngest men ever to hold the second-
ranking place in the cabinet of an American President.

The provision of funds to operate the government in
the face of a disorganized market and great timidity on
the part of investors was an immediate and urgent concern. Morgenthau called in experts in the government
bond market, economists of high rank, the executives
of the Federal Reserve system and leading bankers. He
received their advice but made his own decisions. The
market received with approval the price and terms of
his first issue and it was a success. To avoid market
disturbance, a quarterly program of financing was
adopted and the same careful procedure of analysis and
preparation was followed with succeeding issues. Confidence in government securities was restored to the
same degree if less dramatically than confidence in the
banking system had earlier been restored by the Roosevelt administration. Competition intensified in bidding
for later issues to the degree that many were oversub-
scribed ten to fourteen times and the interest rates sank.

Outstanding issues of liberty loans, remaining from
the first World War, were called for redemption along
with other higher-rate bonds and refunded at sharply
lower rates. To provide a safe repository for savings in
relatively small amounts and to stimulate popular interest in government finance, Morgenthau obtained authority from Congress (1935) to sell directly to the
public United States savings bonds, which later, as war
savings bonds, became an important auxiliary means of
financing expenditures in the second World War.

In 1933 the markets of the world were practically
closed to American products because of monetary disparities. Morgenthau, then governor of the Farm Credit
Administration, was called on to assist the President of
the United States in administering a program of gold
purchases to counteract these disparities, with resultant
benefit both to American agriculture and to American
industry. Through the provisions of the Gold Reserve
Act (1934), the dollar was stabilized and the creation of
the stabilization fund, managed by the Secretary of the
Treasury, together with other provisions of the Gold
Reserve Act, put the dollar in a dominant position with
respect to all internal and external needs and gave it
unquestioned standing as the soundest currency in the
world. The effectiveness of the fund was demonstrated
through operations of the Tripartite Monetary Pact,
negotiated by Morgenthau with Great Britain and
France in 1936 and adhered to by The Netherlands,
Belgium and Switzerland. Other monetary measures
initiated by Secretary Morgenthau included the retirement of National Bank notes and the making of all
United States currency legal tender.

Changes in tax laws, coupled with business recovery,
increased federal revenues from $2,000,000,000 in the
fiscal year 1933 to $7,600,000,000 in 1941, with further
great increases to result from changes in the law already
made or in prospect in 1942. In recommending tax
law changes, Morgenthau was a consistent advocate of
taxation according to ability to pay and sought to
lighten rather than to increase the burden on low-income groups. He fought relentlessly for closing loop-
holes in the law that favored privileged classes, and
prosecuted tax evaders vigorously irrespective of their
influence or position. As a result of Morgenthau's ag-

Henry Morgenthau, Jr.

gressive action under the leadership of President Roosevelt in the securities, monetary and tax fields it has
become a common saying that "the financial capital has
been moved from Wall Street to Washington."

The Treasury is not alone a financial institution, but
a great business and law enforcement organization. As
the head of it, Morgenthau brought about a coordination of half a dozen Treasury police agencies, greatly
adding to their efficiency. Bootlegging and rum-run-
ning gangs were smashed after the repeal of prohibition,
narcotics smuggling practically wiped out, counterfeit-
ing reduced to the vanishing point. Systems of federal
purchasing were reorganized and, through competition
among architects under the direction of an advisory
board, new freshness, simplicity and vigor of design
were introduced into public buildings. His keen interest in projects of social value found expression in his
close attention to the work and the financing of all relief projects and agencies. Studies independently made
by his direction were a guide and a check on expenditures. The Public Health Service, then a part of the
Treasury, made under his direction a survey of nutrition
in low-income groups out of which grew, in cooperation
with the Department of Agriculture, the food stamp
plan for supplementing the diets of low-paid workers
and persons on relief.

The United States Coast Guard, a maritime police,
safety and rescue agency under military organization,
which operates under the Treasury in times of peace
and under the Navy in war, was brought to a high state
of preparedness through additions to its fleet and equipment and improvement of its training methods.

Foreseeing the probability of United States involve-
ment in world war, Morgenthau exerted his influence
for better preparation. Acting in a liaison capacity for
the president, he assisted representatives of the British

and French governments in placing orders for American airplanes and other military equipment both before and after the outbreak of the war, a work which he continued until the lease-lend organization was set up as a separate government agency. In this capacity he brought expert advisers from important industries to Washington and induced manufacturers to add to their stocks of materials and to make great plant extensions.

A special organization created (May, 1941) under his close personal supervision for defense financing became the war savings staff, which, devoted primarily to the sale of war savings bonds and stamps, conducted in every state a campaign for self-denial and whole-hearted participation in the war effort.

Besides administrative ability of high quality and financial expertness, Morgenthau, as fiftieth Secretary of the United States Treasury, displayed profound interest in projects for the relief of distress and improvement of the conditions of the underprivileged, a factor in his character reflecting in part, no doubt, early experience as a voluntary social worker. His training in finance shows a logical progression. Concerned first with farm production, he devoted increasing attention to farm management, then to the broader fiscal and organizational problems of the farmer and their place in the general economy, then to public finance and monetary problems on a national and, finally, an international scale.

Henry Morgenthau, Jr. was in 1942 a member of the Foreign Service Buildings Commission; member of the board of trustees of the Smithsonian Institution; chairman of the board of trustees, Endowment Fund, American Red Cross; member of the board of trustees, Postal Service System; member of the National Archives Council; member of the National Park Trust Fund Board; chairman, Library of Congress Trust Fund Board; member, board of trustees of the National Gallery of Art; member, Foreign-Trade Zones Board; member, National Munitions Control Board; trustee, board of trustees of the Federal Old-Age and Survivors Insurance Trust Fund; member, Jewish Welfare Board. He was formerly a director of Mt. Sinai Hospital, New York city. His fraternal affiliations included membership in the Masons and in B'nai B'rith.

Morgenthau received the honorary degree of Doctor of Laws from Temple University in 1938, and the honorary degree of Doctor of Laws from Amherst in 1942.

JOSEPH GAER.

Lit.: Literary Digest, April 8, 1933; Jan. 13, 1934; Feb. 17, 1934; *New York Times,* June 4, 1939, Magazine Section, p. 3; *ibid.,* June 22, 1941, p. 10; *New York Times,* May 20, 1940, p. 9; May 28, 1940, p. 15; *Newsweek,* June 24, 1933; May 13, 1940; *Time,* Nov. 20, 1939; *Saturday Evening Post,* April 1, 8 and 15, 1939; *American Hebrew,* May 25, 1934; June 18, 1934; Dec. 25, 1936.

MORGULIS, MENASHE (MIKHAIL GRIGORYEVICH), Russian jurist and publicist, b. Berditchev, 1837; d. Odessa, 1913. After graduation, he had, by official regulation, to become a government rabbi, but he finally succeeded in entering the University of Kiev, where he studied law.

In 1869 Morgulis moved permanently to Odessa. In his student days he had organized a Sabbath school, founded a Jewish club, published educational writings and translations into the Yiddish. In Odessa he continued this type of active communal life. He was prominently associated with the society for the promotion of culture, the rabbinical commission, and the Palestinian Society. He was for many years head of the Jewish industrial school Tzud, and associated with the agricultural fund. Morgulis opposed Zionism.

His writings, begun in his university days, dealt with every phase of Russian Jewish life. The major

Albert Moritz

collection of his articles was issued in 1889. Especially noteworthy was his study of education among the Jews in Russia. A catalogue of his works was in the "systematic register" of the literature on Jews in Russian (St. Petersburg, 1892). Morgulis also wrote on questions of Mosaic-Talmudic law.

MORIAH, name of the mountain on which the Temple was built (*II Chron.* 3:1), otherwise called Har Habayith, "Mount of the Temple," or Zion, a name originally belonging to the Jebusite acropolis south of the Temple. The origin of the name is obscure, and it is perhaps non-Semitic. Moriah appears in *Gen.* 22:2 as the name of a land, on one of the mountains of which Abraham was commanded to sacrifice Isaac. There can be little doubt that the proper reading is "Land of the Amorites," with the Syriac version.

MORINI, ERICA, violinist, b. Vienna, 1908. She studied the violin with Sevčik at the Vienna Conservatory, making her debut at the age of eight. A concert tour of Europe followed, in which she was acclaimed one of the most sensational musical prodigies of the period. She grew into a mature and sensitive artist, and was generally recognized in Europe as the leading woman violinist. Her high position was proved in 1920 when she was engaged as the only soloist to participate with the Vienna Philharmonic during its one-week festival. In 1921, she made a successful debut in America. Since then, she has appeared extensively in this country and in Europe. Her recitals throughout the United States in 1942 evoked great critical praise.

MORITZ, ALBERT, engineer and navy commander, b. Cincinnati, 1860; d. New York, 1941. He was graduated from the Naval Academy in 1881, and for years thereafter served on several ships and on shore duty. In 1898, during the Spanish-American war, he took part in the engagement off Cienfuegos, Cuba. In the Philippine Insurrection (1899) he was chief engineer of the *Newark* and present when Capt. B. H. McCalla received the surrender of the Northern Luzon provinces. As chief engineer of the *Yosemite,* he took a leading part in rescue work when that cruiser was wrecked off Guam (Nov., 1900), and was cited by the Navy Department. In the same year he erected the first ice plant in Guam.

Voluntarily retired in 1905, Moritz returned to duty during the first World War as machinery inspector in the building plants of Camden and Brooklyn navy yards, retiring again in 1919. He was author of *Hints on the Inspection of Steel.*

He was active in communal and civic affairs, becoming involved in a long struggle against discrimination in electricity rates by the power companies. The Post Office Department adopted (1937) Moritz's proposal to issue stamps commemorating American territorial acquisitions, and a series of presidential likenesses.

MORLEY, EDITH JULIA, professor and author, b. London, 1875. She took final honors at Oxford in the school of English language and literature in 1899. After lecturing in these subjects at several institutions, she was appointed (1908) professor of English language at the University of Reading, England (emeritus, 1940).

Among her books of literary research and criticism are: *Hurd's Letters on Chivalry and Romance* (1911); *Young's Conjectures on Original Composition* (1917); *Blake, Coleridge and Wordsworth* (1922); *Correspondence of Crabb Robinson with the Wordsworth Circle* (1927); *The Life and Times of Henry Crabb Robinson* (1935); *Henry Crabb Robinson on Books and Their Writers* (1938).

MORNING SERVICE (Shaharith), more properly *tefillath shaharith,* "the morning prayer," the daily prayers recited early every morning. Jewish tradition traces the introduction of the morning service back to Abraham in connection with *Gen.* 22:3, which states "And Abraham rose early in the morning." In actuality, however, a morning prayer is entirely in keeping with a natural impulse on the part of a religious person. For this reason, it is older than the sacrifice which it was later explained as having replaced. As a morning prayer it was connected with the sacrifice to the extent that the priests in the Temple at Jerusalem interrupted the sacrifice in the morning by means of a prayer containing the principal contents of the morning service. These are the Keriath Shema (the reading of the Shema) and the Tefillah.

In addition there are, as introduction, the Birchoth Hashahar (the morning blessings) and the Pesuke Dezimra (the verses of songs), and the conclusion is formed by the Tahanunim (supplications). The latter are omitted on the festive days. There are no basic variations in the text of the various prayers composing the Morning Service, with the exception of the Tefillah for the Sabbath and the holidays.

MOROCCO (in Arabic, El-Maghrib el-Aksa), a sultanate in Northern Africa, divided in 1912 into a French protectorate, a Spanish protectorate and the international zone of Tangiers. The number of Jews in Morocco in the 1940's was about 300,000.

To the Beginning of the 20th Cent. There were numerous Jewish colonies in Northern Africa long before it became a Roman province (42). After the suppression of the Jewish uprising against the Romans in Cirenaica (115-18), the vanquished Jews may have fled to Morocco (Mauretania), a territory not yet entirely under the influence of the Roman Empire. The Council of Elvira (313), in which a number of bishops from Mauretania participated, forbade the faithful servants of the church to ask for the benedictions of the rabbis. Jerome (331-420) asserted that the Jewish communities formed an unbroken chain from Maure-

tania to Egypt and India. These communities seem to have waged a severe struggle against Christian proselytism, for in Carthage (336) and elsewhere edicts of protection had to be issued in favor of the New Christians of Jewish origin, who were being persecuted by their former coreligionists. At the same time, Jewish Christian mixed marriages and the circumcision of slaves belonging to Jews were forbidden.

In 429 the Vandal king, Genserich (428-77), defeated the Romans and conquered Mauretania with the aid of the Jews, whom he freed from all the restrictions imposed upon them. The Jews devoted themselves thenceforth to navigation, maritime commerce, vine-growing and agriculture. In 534 Belisarius reconquered Mauretania for the Eastern Roman emperor, and the Jews fled into the high mountains of Mauretania. Later many Spanish Jews emigrated to Morocco in order to escape persecutions under the Visigoth kings; they brought with them the Latin language and culture, industry and commerce.

From about the 7th cent. on, according to the reports of the Arabian historians, many Berber tribes professing Judaism came into power. In 696 Hassan ibn al-Nu'man, general of Caliph Abdalmelek, attacked Mauretania with 40,000 warriors and did away for ever with Byzantinian dominion, but he was defeated by the heroic priestess Kahinah of the Jewish Berber tribe of Jerua (Djarwa), under whose leadership most of the Berber tribes united. Subsequently, however, the Arabs returned, vanquishing Kahinah, who fell in battle.

Under the rule of Rashid (794-804) and Idris II (804-28) the Jews lived in peace, and many Andalusian Jews, who were fleeing from the persecutions of the Omaiyad Caliph Chakam ibn Hisham, settled in Morocco. The Jews' residential quarter was called the "Mellah" (salted place, i.e. marsh). However, the Jews were not obliged to live in this quarter; they could settle in any part of the Moroccan empire.

In the 13th cent., in order to avoid persecutions of the Jews, the sultans were obliged to assign special quarters to them. But these quarters put the Jews more in evidence, and besides being an easy target for Mohammedan fanaticism, brought considerable moral and material decline to Moroccan Jewry. The "Mellah" paid the sultan yearly tribute of 30,000 denares.

Abu al-Kamil Tamin of the dynasty of the Zeinites seized Fez in 1032, ordered 6,000 Jews slaughtered, and dragged their women off into slavery. The liberal Almoravids finally came into power in 1062, first in Fez, then in Marrakesh, which they made the capital, and finally in Spain. All these districts, especially Kairwan and Fez, were centers of Jewish learning.

The Almoravids were conquered by the Almohades in 1147. Jews and Christians were now confronted with the alternative of emigrating or embracing Islam. The third ruler of this dynasty, Abu Yusuf Yakub al-Mansur, compelled the new Mussulmen of Jewish origin, many of whom still lived as Jews in secret, to wear a special costume—prototype of the Jew-badge.

In the middle of the 13th cent., when the Almohade rule was broken, Morocco was a nest of Mussulman fanaticism, and the Jewish communities suffered greatly. Many Jews migrated to Spain and Egypt.

The massacres in Seville and the destruction of the famous Jewish quarter there (1391), and the expulsion of the Jews from Spain (1492) and from Portugal (1497) brought many thousands of fugitives to Morocco; here they were very badly received by the Mussulmen and even by the Moroccan Jews themselves. In Alcazar-Quivir they were robbed of their property.

The Spanish and Portuguese Jews brought art and industry, European culture and international commerce to Morocco. Despite this, however, their situation did not improve until the middle of the 16th cent. Of the Spanish Jewish scholars who lived in Morocco at that time the most noteworthy were: Abraham Azulai (1570-1643), Hayim ben Moses ibn Atar (Abenatar) (1696-1743), whose relative, Moses de Avila, built a special Yeshiva for him in Meknes, Jacob ibn Zur, Samuel ibn Abbas, Menahem Athias, Jacob ben Malka, Judah Koriat and Abraham Koriat.

The appearance of Sabbatai Zevi aroused much Messianic agitation in Morocco in 1666, despite the warnings issued by Jacob Sasportas, rabbi of Salé. This agitation was continued until 1672, and caused numerous persecutions of Jews. Mulai Rashid, who seized power in Morocco (about 1666), persecuted the Jews cruelly. His brother Mulai Ismail, "the bloodthirsty," repeatedly ravaged the Jews, but permitted them to erect their synagogues anew on the ruins of the old. During his reign a Jew, Daniel Toledano, was raised to the rank of minister; Toledano's son Joseph concluded and signed the treaty of peace with the Netherlands in the name of the sultan. In 1721 another Jew, Moses Abenatar, represented the sultan in London and signed a treaty with Great Britain.

The wars with France and Spain (1844-59) led to new persecutions in Mogador (1844) and Tetuan (1859). After the persecutions were repeated (1863-64), the Jews appealed to the Board of Deputies in London, which intervened through Sir Moses Montefiore. Montefiore came to Morocco in 1864 and demanded from the sultan an emancipation edict; this was authorized in 1873 by Mulei El Hasan and in 1880 by the Conference at Madrid. But the situation of the Jews continued to be a miserable one. They were cooped up in their "Mellahs," dirty, narrow, dark, stuffy and unhealthful residential quarters, were continually mistreated, and were occasionally massacred. They were not permitted to acquire land outside of their quarter, and they were allowed to dress only in black. They could visit the Mohammedan residential quarters only barefooted and with bowed head, never on horseback, and had to make way reverently for every Mussulman they met, who, as reward, insulted and mistreated them. They were compelled to do all the servile tasks possible, even on the Sabbath and on holy days; they did not have the right to defend themselves from the attacks of the Mussulmen, except when the latter penetrated into their houses; they were not permitted to appear as witnesses before the court. Their beasts of burden, their houses, furniture and beds always had to stand at the disposal of the governors and their guests; even their women were compelled to render service. They had to exchange good money for false coins, to sell their wares to the governors at half price, to buy their wares when prices were falling, and to pay in advance. This situation lasted till the last years of Moroccan independence.

From 1868 to 1906 epidemics, starvation, fevers and privations decimated the populations of the "Mellahs." In 1899 about 2,500 Jewish children died in Marrakesh alone of smallpox, and in 1901 an epidemic of typhus claimed 3,000 victims in four months. The inhabitants of the "Mellahs" were the continual prey of epidemics as well as of moral and material misery. Girls married at the age of from six to nine years, boys at thirteen. Only the Talmud Torah school was accessible to Jewish youths, so that the latter grew up in the deepest ignorance of secular and general knowledge. During the late 19th cent. and at the beginning of the 20th cent. the Jews of Morocco were mere pawns of Europe in the hands of the Moroccans; frequently the "Mellahs" were attacked merely as a protest against the European powers. SAUL MEZAN.

2. **Modern Period.** Beginning with the Franco-Spanish occupation, the situation changed. Compulsory service and the bastinado were abolished in 1907; the Sabbath was recognized, and all other ignominious special rules for the Jews were eliminated. Damages were paid by the government to the families of murdered Jews.

The Jews of Morocco of the 20th cent. might be divided into five classes: (1) Berbers or Mountain Jews; (2) town and village Jews; (3) Sephardic Jews; (4) European Jews; (5) refugees from the second World War.

There were, in 1942, at least 30,000 Berber or Mountain Jews in Morocco, in the mountainous regions or in the desert. The men were tall, healthy, swarthy and thoroughly free of urban influence. Living impoverished and isolated lives, they remained attached to inherited modes of worship and belief. Although ritually observant, they knew little about Judaism, except for the tales of Jerusalem and Palestine that came down to them. Some of them spoke a little Hebrew. Both men and women married early, the women at the age of eight, ten or twelve, and the men at twelve or fifteen. Polygamy was permitted. The numerous children resulting from their early marriages and their fecundity had no source of education but the Heder, where several hundred children, Jews and Arabs, were crowded together. While an Arab read the Koran a Jewish teacher read the Bible, at the same time, in the same voice, and with the same gestures.

The town Jews, who filled the "Mellahs," were for the most part mountaineers who had moved into urban centers. These constituted the bulk of Moroccan Jewry, numbering about 160,000. They lived in crowded houses, packed into dirty ghettos. In addition to the large ghettos in Casablanca and Fez, there was a settlement of some 20,000 Jews in Marrakesh and one of about 10,000 in Meknes. Tangiers, in Spanish Morocco, had about 15,000 Moroccan and 3,000 European Jews.

The languages spoken by the older urbanized Mountain Jews were Berber, Arabic and a little Hebrew; the younger generation knew some French. The most rigid piety prevailed amid surroundings ridden with filth. Trade, handicraft and begging provided the means of livelihood and were practiced indiscriminately in the variegated and colorful background. About 50 per cent of the Jews living in Moroccan ghettos were engaged in handicrafts.

The Sephardic Jews, who are the descendants of the immigrants from Spain and Portugal, were represented by several thousand families in Morocco. They lived in the European quarters of the larger cities, and many were wealthy tradesmen. Although they were assimilated with the Moroccan Jews, the Sephardic Jews had their own synagogues and their own cultural life. Jewish life outside their own sphere was strange to them, but they were pious and Zionistically inclined; they were also very hospitable and charitable.

European Jewry was represented, among Moroccan settlers, by no more than several hundred families throughout the whole country. Their contribution to the life of Moroccan Jewry was not very great, except that they fostered cultural and Zionist work.

Refugees from Western Europe came to Morocco in the middle of 1940, after the Nazis had occupied Belgium and Holland and defeated France. Many of them sought Morocco as a temporary haven, hoping to leave for the American continent. Some succeeded in doing so, but most of the refugees were put into work camps and concentration camps.

The adoption of anti-Jewish laws by the Vichy government, following the signing of the armistice with Germany in 1940, soon had its effect in Morocco. There were some anti-Jewish demonstrations in the leading cities; Jews were ordered back into the ghetto and ousted from all government and professional posts.

M. DLUZNOWSKI.

Lit.: Ortega, M., "Los Hebreos en Marruecos," Revista de la Raza (1927-28); Bulletin de l'Alliance Israélite Universelle (1884-85, 1910), Semach, "L'avenir des Israélites marocains," Paix et droit, No. 6 (1927); Saisset, "Les juifs marocains et la culture française," Palestine, No. 5 (1928); Bauer-Landauer, Ignacio, Apuntes para una bibliografía de Marruecos (1922); Nahon, M., "Les Israélites du Maroc," Revue des études ethnographiques et sociologiques, vol. 2 (1909) 258-79; Dubnow, Simon, Weltgeschichte des jüdischen Volkes; Revue des études juives, vol. 37, pp. 120-26; Aubin, Le Maroc d'aujourd'hui (1912) 356-82; Graetz, H., History of the Jews, vol. 6 (1927); Schloessinger, Max, in Jewish Encyclopedia, vol. 9, pp. 18-29.

MOROR, see SEDER.

MORPURGO, Austrian-Italian Jewish family whose ancestors, according to family tradition, resided in Ratisbon during the 13th century, and moved to Vienna and Marburg in Styria about the middle of the 14th century. According to the same tradition, the learned rabbi Israel Isserlein, who went from Marburg to Vienna in 1457, was one of their ancestors. In 1509 Aron de Marburg was granted a privilege by Emperor Maximilian I. In 1560 Isaak Marburg was expelled from Vienna by Emperor Ferdinand I. The main branch of the Marburg family settled then in Gradisca (Istria) which became an important emporium because it was the main stopping place of the emperor's armies in wars against Turks and the republic of Venice.

In 1624 Moses and Jacob Marburger at Gradisca were granted a privilege by Ferdinand II, allowing them to move of their own free will to and from Vienna, certainly to supply the army with arms and food. Proceeding from Gradisca, the family formed branches in Vienna, Trieste, Venice, Padua, Ancona, Salonika, Cairo, Tripoli, Tunisia, and Amsterdam. Other branches of the family settled since the end of the 16th century in Moravia and Cracow (Galicia). Moses ben Uria Marburg, who had resided in Vienna since 1659, went to Berlin after the expulsion of the Jews of Vienna in 1670. His descendants, among them the composer Friedrich Wilhelm Marpurg (1718-1795), embraced Protestantism. Apart from this Prussian branch, very few apostasies from Judaism occurred in the history of the family. Many of their members contributed to

the knowledge of Judaism or fought for the rights of their co-religionists.

Many members of the family were excellent physicians. In 1615, Scemarja Marpurch (who died in 1631 of the plague) was elected chief of the Hebrew University of Padua where Simon Marpurg Cracoviensis had already studied and lectured on medicine from 1444 to 1466. Scemarja's son David was graduated as a doctor of medicine (1623). According to the Schedario degli studenti Ebrei in Padova, compiled by A. K. Modena, ten members of the family (named Marhuc, Marpurg, Marpuch, Morpurgo) were students of medicine at the Ateneo of Padua. In the 19th cent. Victoro and Benedetto Morpurgo were renowned physicians. Giulio Morpurgo excelled in chemistry. Gerolamo Morpurgo (b. Friuli, 1847; d. Rome, 1920) was president of the disciplinary council of the Milan bar association; of patriotic and philanthropic associations; and he effected reforms in taxation in Milan.

Another renowned jurist was Carlo Morpurgo (d. 1939) acknowledged as a leader of European barristers. Caliman Morpurgo (b. Trieste, 1823; d. there, 1885) was a philanthropist. He published in 1854 Storia sacra, a manual of Biblical history for the use of Jewish children. Other philanthropists were Giuseppe Morpurgo (b. Trieste, 1815; d. there, 1896); Marco Morpurgo, president of the Osterreich-Ungarisches Lloyd (1838-96), and Benjamin Morpurgo (b. Venice, 1838; d. there, 1906). In 1902 the Jewish community of Trieste was composed of 541 families. Among them twenty-five families were named Morpurgo. This form corresponded to the Venetian pronunciation of the name Marburg. Attilio Morpurgo, vice-president of the Jewish community of Gorizia, participated in the meeting of Jewish representatives of Italy (March 30, 1937), the last effort of the Italian Jews to counteract publicly the rising anti-Semitism in Italy. The Morpurgo family, although living in Italy, adhered to the German Jewish rite.

HUGO BIEBER.

Lit.: Morpurgo, Edgardo, La famiglia Morpurgo di Gradisca sull' Isonzo 1585-1885 (1909); Morpurgo, Edgardo, Notizie sulle Famiglie Ebree esistiti a Padova nel XVI. secolo (1909); Vessillo Israelitico (1877-1879 and 1885).

MORPURGO, EDGARDO, physician and historian, b. Padua, Italy, 1872. He studied medicine at the university of his native town, and after graduation he concentrated upon psycho-pathology. In 1897 he published an important study on the restriction of the pupil of mentally diseased patients, in 1903 Sulle condizioni somatiche e psichiche degli Israeliti in Europa, and in 1905 Psicologia e psicopatologia degli Ebrei. In the same year he published Le origini del movimento Sionista. He wrote the history of his own family, La famiglia Morpurgo di Gradisca sull'Isonzo 1585-1885 (1909); the study, L'Università degli Ebrei in Padova nel XVI. secolo, and Notizie sulle famiglie Ebree esistiti a Padova nel XVI. secolo. That year Morpurgo took the initiative in the foundation of Jewish cultural committees in Florence, Bologna, Padua, and Milan.

With the approval of the Italian government, Morpurgo incorporated the collection of Judaica and Semitica belonging to his family into the library of Padua University, as a special division named "Raccolta Morpurgo di letteratura e storia dei popoli semitici" whose Catalogo generale he published in 1924.

MORPURGO, ELIA, president of the Jewish community of Gradisca and author, b. Gradisca, 1740; d. Padua, 1830. In 1781 Morpurgo was appointed "capo della nazione Ebrea di Gradisca." In this post he was granted four audiences by Emperor Joseph II, who was interested in the emancipation of the Jews. Morpurgo also was honored by Grand Duke Leopold of Toscana, who allowed him to copy manuscripts of the Bibliotheca Laurentiana at Florence.

Morpurgo published *Orazione funebre all' Imperatrice Maria Theresia* (1781), and *Discorso alla nazione Ebrea* (1782), a lecture on enlightenment and tolerance. He translated the letters of Wessely into Italian. He corresponded with Wessely, Moses Mendelssohn and Herz Homberg. His writings in Hebrew were edited by the Gesellschaft hebräischer Literaturfreunde at Berlin (1809-12). Morpurgo had a vast knowledge of Oriental languages, and excelled in Biblical exegesis. He translated into Italian Jedaiah Bedaresi's *Behinath Olam,* which inspired Pope's *Essay on Man.*

MORPURGO, BARON ELIO, banker, deputy, and senator, b. Udine, Italy, 1858. The son of Abraham Morpurgo and Caroline Luzzatto, he directed almost all the principal financial and industrial enterprises of Friuli, and entered public life as a member of the town council of Udine, capital of Friuli. From 1885 to 1888, Morpurgo was assessor of the Corporation of Udine, and from 1889 to 1895 mayor of the town. At the same time he represented Friuli in the Italian Chamber of Deputies, participating mainly in agricultural, industrial and commercial debates.

The Chamber of Deputies appointed Morpurgo a member of its military and viticultural committees. He was also president of the Banca cooperativa, the Teatro sociale, and the chamber of commerce of Udine. In 1906 Morpurgo became a member of the Sonnino cabinet, as secretary of the post office department. He also was member of Sonnino's second cabinet in 1910, and assistant secretary of the ministry of industry and commerce in Boselli's cabinet (1916-18). In 1920 King Victor Emmanuel appointed him senator of the kingdom.

MORPURGO, EMILIO, economist and deputy, b. Venice, 1836; d. Padua, Italy, 1885. The son of Abraham Vita Morpurgo, he was one of the first Italian scholars to study agrarian and labor questions from a modern scientific standpoint. In 1859 Morpurgo published *Il proletariato e la società di mutuo soccorso.* At the same time he rendered great service to the organization of agrarian associations, especially to the organization of associated dairy farmers of the province of Belluno which has been integrated into the new kingdom of Italy since 1859. Morpurgo was elected member of the provincial council of Belluno.

When the province of Venice was absorbed by Italy in 1866, Morpurgo was appointed professor at the University of Padua, and later its rector. He represented Padua in the Italian Chamber of Deputies. The great Italian statesman Minghetto appointed Morpurgo secretary of the ministry of agriculture in his last cabinet. In 1865 Morpurgo published a study on the history of money lending, *I prestatori di danaro al tempo di Dante;* in 1868 a collection of essays, *Saggi statistici e economici;* in 1875 the Italian government edited his treatise, *L'Istruzione tecnica in Italia.* Morpurgo's manual, *La Finanza,* published in 1877, was translated into several languages. His last publication, written in the year of his death, was entitled *La Democrazia e la Scuola* and generally esteemed as the formulation of the tenets of Italian liberalism.

Lit.: Luzzatti, Luigi, *Commemorazione di Emilio Morpurgo* (1885).

MORPURGO, GIUSEPPE LAZZARO, economist and poet, b. Trieste, 1762; d. Venice, Italy, 1835. Educated in an elementary school at Trieste, he was sent to Verona (1774) where he pursued rabbinical and secular studies with the aid of private teachers. Returning to Trieste (1780), Morpurgo found employment with a maritime insurance office. In 1807 he founded his own maritime insurance agency. From 1809 to 1815 Morpurgo, an Austrian patriot, was disturbed in his occupations by the Napoleonic wars because he was opposed to the French government which occupied his native town. His patriotism won recognition from Emperor Francis II when he reconquered Trieste; Morpurgo was thenceforth patronized by the Austrian government.

Morpurgo was appointed arbitrator of disputes in maritime trade. In 1823 Morpurgo, at the behest of the government, introduced fire insurance protection throughout the Hapsburg monarchy, and in 1832 he founded the Assicurazione Generale, the first life insurance company in Austria. Morpurgo was repeatedly elected president of the Jewish community of Trieste. Deeply interested in the religious education of Jewish children, he wrote *Della Educazione e Istruzione della Gioventù Israelitica,* which was edited and issued (1846) after his death. Morpurgo also furnished funds for the printing of a German and Italian translation of the Siddur. He translated many English poems into Hebrew, among them Pope's *Essay on Man.* A selection of his original Hebrew poems was edited under the title *Zimrath Eretz* in 1827.

JOSEPH MORPURGO (1816-98), his son, continued the administration of the Assicurazione Generale, and founded the banking house Morpurgo & Parente at Trieste which formed international branches but was liquidated in 1890. Joseph Morpurgo was knighted by Emperor Francis Joseph.

Lit.: Jost, *Israelitische Annalen,* 1840, No. 12; Zeitlin, William, *Bibliotheca Hebraica Post-Mendelssohniana; La Rassegna mensile di Israel,* vol. 5 (1931).

MORPURGO, RAHEL, nee Luzzatto, poetess, b. Trieste, Austria, 1790; d. Trieste, 1871. She was a daughter of Baruch (Benedetto) Luzzatto and Berakha, sister of Samuel David Luzzatto's father. Under the tutelage of her uncles, Hezekiah and David Luzzatto, she studied the Pentateuch until the age of twelve. At the age of 14 she was able to read the Talmud, Bahya's *Hoboth Halebaboth,* and the commentaries of Rashi. She was extraordinarily skilled in needlework, made her own clothes as well as those of her mother, and later on those of her daughter.

Rahel Morpurgo also learned the art of lithography and assisted kinsmen in their handicraft. At the age of twenty-nine she married Jacob Morpurgo, but was unhappy since her husband was interested only in business.

Rahel had begun to write poems in Hebrew at the age of eighteen. Her style had an ingratiating purity. She also wrote occasional verses as philosophical meditations.

When in 1848 the revolution broke out, Rahel contrasted in a sonnet the political aspiration for liberty, uttered "by sage and madman," with the eternal liberty of the reign of God. Belief in the coming of the Messiah was the keynote of her poetry. It was expressed with great force in her last poem, "Emek Achor," which she wrote in her seventy-seventh year. A selection of Rahel's poems, *Ugab Rahel* (Rahel's Lyre; 1890), was edited by Vittorio Castiglione on the centenary of her birth. Some of Rahel's poems were printed during her lifetime in various Hebrew periodicals. Samuel David Luzzatto, her cousin, a very severe critic, held her poems in high esteem and sent her manuscripts to M. E. Stern in Vienna, who edited *Kochebe Yitzhak*. Luzzatto mentioned Rahel in his autobiography as "a rare example in the present century."

Lit.: Luzzatto, Isaïe, *Index raisonné des livres de correspondance de feu Samuel David Luzzatto* (1878); Luzzatto, Samuel David, *Epistolario* (1890); Slouschz, Nahum, *La renaissance de la littérature Hébraique* (1903); Salaman, Nina, *Rahel Morpurgo* (1924).

MORPURGO, SALOMONE, philologist and librarian, b. Trieste, then Austria, 1860; d. Bologna, Italy, 193?. As a student he participated in a disturbance against the Austrian government, for which he was arrested and prosecuted. Soon thereafter he went to Rome and continued to profess and support Italian Irredentism. Together with Allino Veratti, he directed the *Archivio Storico per Trieste l'Istria e il Trentino* (1881-93), devoted to the history of the "unredeemed countries." From 1884 to 1891 he was co-director of the *Rivista critica della letteratura Italiana.*

As a disciple of Carducci, Morpurgo contributed to the knowledge of Dante and Petrarch through philological inquiries. He rendered signal services to the history of the Italian language by editing the vulgate Latin texts which reveal the genesis of the Italian language and the transition from Latin to Italian. In 1891 he published *L'Ebreo errante in Italia.* He was appointed director of the Bibliotheca Riccardiana whose Italian manuscripts he described scientifically (1893 to 1897). Then he was placed in charge of the Marciana library of San Marco in Venice, and published a description of this library (1906). From 1905 to 1923 he was director of the Bibliotheca Nazionale in Florence, and became professor of Italian literature at the University of Bologna. His edition of the *Breviarium Grimani* (1903-10) made accessible one of the most important documents of the fine arts of the Middle Ages.

MORPURGO, SAMSON BEN JOSHUA MOSES, rabbi, physician and author, b. Gradisca, Austria, 1681; d. Ancona, Italy, 1740. He completed a course in medicine at the University of Padua, but upon returning to Gradisca, he was not allowed to practise because he did not belong to the "ruling nation" and because his diploma was acquired at a foreign university. He went to Ancona and published there *Confutazioni alle Saette del Gionata del Benetelli* (1703), a polemical treatise directed against the learned monk Benetelli who had attempted to discredit Judaism. Morpurgo was therefore stigmatized as anti-Christian by De Rossi in his *Bibliotheca anti-Christiana* (1703), being defended by Simone Luzzatto and Leon da Modena. In 1709 Morpurgo received his rabbinical diploma

from Leon Briel, rabbi of Mantua, and officiated together with his father-in-law, Joseph Fiammetta, in the rabbinate of Ancona until Fiammetta's death (1721), when he became chief rabbi of Ancona. Notwithstanding the papal restrictions imposed upon Jewish physicians, Morpurgo practised medicine with great success, especially during the plague of 1730; he rendered great services which were highly esteemed by Archbishop Lambertini of Ancona, later Pope Benedict XIV. Morpurgo tried to help Moses Hayim Luzzatto in his tribulations resulting from his Cabalistic ideas, but Luzzatto did not heed Morpurgo's advice. Morpurgo published various theological and philosophical works, among them *Etz Hadaath* (1704), a commentary on Jedaiah Bedaresi's *Behinath Olam.* He also composed a number of theological responses on the *Shulhan Aruch* which were edited by his son Marco Morpurgo (1742-43). Samson Morpurgo and his children were granted various privileges by the popes, such as exemption from wearing the Jew badge.

Lit.: Morpurgo, Edgardo, *La famiglia Morpurgo* (1909); *Vessillo Israelitico,* Anni 1877 and 1878.

MORPURGO, VICTOR, physician and diplomat, b. Trieste, Austria; d. Paris, 1856. He studied medicine at the University of Pisa where he was graduated in 1828. Later he practised medicine for several years at Smyrna and Cairo, and established friendly relations with many Turkish Pashas. In 1838 Morpurgo went to Paris, and there was attached to the Turkish legation; the minister entrusted Morpurgo with supervision of all Turkish subjects sojourning in Paris and with various other secret missions.

Morpurgo wrote political as well as medical studies, the former mainly on commission by and with the sponsorship of the Turkish government. He published *Considerazione mediche sull'Egitto* (1831); *Considérations sur la question d'Orient* (1839); a biography of *Vincenzo Gioberti* (1852); and *La politique de la Russie en Orient* (1854).

MORRIS, IRA NELSON, diplomat, b. Chicago, 1875; d. Chicago, 1942. He was the son of Nelson Morris, wealthy Chicago meat packer. Upon retirement from active financial affairs, though extensively interested in many corporations, Morris was a writer, traveler, diplomat and patron of the arts.

Having successfully discharged a special diplomatic mission to Italy (1913), he was named United States Minister to Sweden by President Wilson in 1914, a post for which he was fitted by training in business and international law. From neutral Sweden, where he enjoyed the intimate friendship of King Gustav, he was in a good position to observe the rest of Europe at war. He published his impressions in *From an American Legation* (1923), and continued to serve as Swedish minister (under President Harding), remaining in that post until 1923. In the years following his retirement from Stockholm, Morris was at various times mentioned for similar posts in Turkey, Germany, Mexico, and other countries.

Morris held decorations from numerous governments of Europe and Asia, including one from Marie of Roumania, with whom he and his wife (Constance Lily Rothschild) were on terms of intimate friendship. They accompanied Marie on her American tour. In 1897 he published *With the Trade Winds.* He was founder of the International Radio Forum.

Lit.: Morris, I. N., *From an American Legation* (1923); *New York Times,* Jan. 18, 1942.

MORRIS, NELSON, meat packer, b. Schwarzwald, Germany, 1839; d. Chicago, Ill., 1907. At twelve he came to the United States. In the new country, one of his first jobs was heaving coal in Lakeville, Conn., at a wage of five dollars a month. It was to seek greater opportunity that he worked his way by cattle boat to Buffalo, N. Y., and thence on foot to Chicago, Ill. There he secured another five-dollar-a-month job, this time driving sheep and tending hogs in the city's fast developing stockyards.

In time, Nelson Morris, a pioneer industrialist who developed the meat business from butchering to packing ten years ahead of any important rival, came to be known as the dean of meat packers; and the history of his vast personal enterprise coincided with the history and expansion of the unique American industry of meat packing. Though his first corporate organization was the Fairbanks Canning company, he conducted his business as a partnership with his sons, until in 1903, Morris and Company, of Maine, was incorporated with a capital stock of $3,000,000. Morris packing centers rose not only in Chicago, but in East St. Louis, Ill., Kansas City, Kan., and St. Joseph, Mo. In the great meat strike of 1904 Morris and his company appeared prominently in the country's press, and some years later, after Morris' death, when his grandson Edward Morris was president, the company, together with its numerous subsidiaries, was one of the big five meat packing houses to be defendants in government litigation. Finally, in 1923, Morris and Company came to the end of its independent existence, merging with Armour and Company.

Morris' wife, Sarah (née Vogel, d. Fontainebleau, France, 1909), left a bequest of $450,000 to charity; of that sum $300,000 went to Chicago's Michael Reese Hospital, and $10,000 each was given to the Home for Aged Jews and Home for Jewish Friendless and Working Girls.

Lit.: The New York Daily Tribune, August 28, 1907.

MORROS, BORIS, motion picture producer and music director, b. St. Petersburg, Russia, 1895. He received his musical education in his native city and conducted at the opera house there from 1913 to 1918. Afterwards, he directed at the Baku conservatory and opera house, and at various times directed opera in France, Italy and Egypt. In 1922 he came to the United States. Entering the theatre and motion picture field, he served in numerous executive posts. From 1926 to 1934 he was general music director of the Paramount Publix chain of motion picture houses, and he then became associate producer and general music director of Paramount Productions in Hollywood. He left Paramount in 1939 to form his own producing company. He also made army training films for the Academy of Motion Picture Arts and Sciences (1942).

As composer, Morros was well-known to the American public for his successful Russian musical revue *Chauve Souris,* and particularly for its hit piece, "Parade of the Wooden Soldiers." In St. Petersburg he had published eighteen string quartets and forty-eight songs. Morros was appointed a Kentucky colonel in 1935. In 1937 he was elected honorary member of the American Institute of Cinematography.

MORSE, LEOPOLD, American Congressman, b. Wachenheim, Bavaria, 1831; d. Boston, 1892. He emigrated to the United States in 1849, and first lived in New Hampshire. Moving to New Bedford, Mass., he opened a clothing store. In 1851 he settled in Boston, where he built his business into a large organization.

About 1870 he entered on an active political career; in 1876 he was a delegate to the Democratic National Convention at St. Louis, and the following year he took his seat as Representative in the Forty-Fifth Congress of the United States. He served three more terms consecutively, and then was elected for the last time in 1887. Each time he won his election as a Democrat from a district which was supposedly Republican.

In a suburb of Boston, Morse founded the Boston Home for Infirm Hebrews and Orphanage; the name was later changed by act of the state legislature to the Leopold Morse Home for Infirm Hebrews and Orphanage. This was the first institution of its kind in New England.

GODFREY MORSE (b. Wachenheim, 1846; d. Dresden, 1911), lawyer, was a brother of Leopold Morse. From 1882 to 1885 he was assistant counsel of the United States in the Court of Commissioners of Alabama Claims. In 1883 he served as president of the Boston Common Council.

Lit.: Biographical Directory of the American Congress, 1774-1927 (1928) 1339-40; *Publications of the American Jewish Historical Society,* No. 22 (1914) 228-30.

MORTAL SIN, a term used in the Roman Catholic Church to designate those sins which are so grave as to entail spiritual death and loss of the divine grace, in contrast to the lighter, or venial sin. There is no exact equivalent of this in Jewish theology, although it was taken over by Abraham Jagel in his *Lekah Tob* (1587). However, Judaism has a category of crimes which must not be permitted in any event, even in the greatest need; one may even prevent a person from committing them by killing him, if he can be stopped in no other way, according to traditional Jewish law. These crimes are 1. idolatry; 2. crimes against morality: a) incest; b) adultery; c) bestiality; d) pederasty; 3. murder (*Sanh.* 74a).

MORTALITY OF THE JEWS, *see* HEALTH OF THE JEWS.

MORTARA CASE. In 1858 Edgar Mortara, the six year old child of a Jewish family of Bologna, Italy, was abducted by Papal Guards and placed in a monastery. The child had previously been secretly baptized through the efforts of Anna Morisi, a servant in the employ of the Mortara family. When her confessor reported the matter to the Papal authorities, who at that time held temporal sway over the Papal States, the child was forcibly removed from the custody of his parents to be reared in the Catholic faith.

The parents attempted in vain to regain possession of their child. Several governments protested this infringement of religious freedom and parental rights, and even Napoleon III, guardian of the Holy See, protested against this act as one likely to affect the prestige of the papacy. In 1860, after Bologna had been annexed to the Kingdom of Italy, the parents made another effort for the return of their child, but in vain, for he had been removed to Rome where he was brought up as a ward of the pope, Pius IX. Nor could the Italian government prosecute Anna Morisi who enjoyed the protection of a nunnery.

The case had world wide repercussions; a large number of German rabbis under the leadership of Ludwig Philippson sent a petition to Pius IX; Sir Moses Montefiore made a futile attempt to petition the pope in person for the release of the child; mass meetings of protest were held in England and in the United States. But against all representations Pius IX maintained that while the Church deprecated abductions, the baptism of the child had made him a Christian, a spiritual condition against which no temporal considerations could prevail. In 1870, when the temporal power of the Papacy was abolished, Edgar Mortara was free to re-adopt the faith of his fathers which he refused to do. He became a prominent member of the Augustine order, adopting the name of Pius. He preached before the Vatican Council, was often sent as a missionary to cities in Germany and also preached before Italian congregations in Catholic churches in New York city. Mortara died at Liége, Belgium, in 1940.

The Mortara case was one of the compelling causes for the formation of the Alliance Israélite Universelle "for the defense of Jewish rights wheresoever attacked," in 1860, and of the Board of Delegates of American Israelites, in 1859, the latter organization later merging into the Union of American Hebrew Congregations.

Lit.: Publications of the American Jewish Historical Society; "Report of a meeting held at San Francisco, Jan. 15, 1859," Occident, vol. 17, p. 10; Graetz, H., History of the Jews, vol. 5 (1927) 701.

MORTARA, LODOVICO, jurist and senator, b. Mantua, Italy, 1855; d. Rome, 1937. He was recognized as Italy's outstanding authority on civil law and procedure, and taught at the University of Pisa (1896). Later he assumed the same chair at the University of Naples (1903). He embarked upon a judiciary career, achieving great prominence and rising to the position of first president of the Supreme Court of Appeals in Rome. His juridical works, particularly in the field of civil law and procedure, deeply influenced Italian juridical thought and practice.

In 1920 Mortara became a member of the Italian Senate. In the same year he was offered the portfolio of justice and public education in the government of Francesco Nitti. From 1891 on he was managing editor of La Giurisprudenza Italiana, Italy's leading juridical publication. Mortara was an opponent of Fascism and criticized the constitutional changes wrought by the Fascist government as well as the juridical value of the Fascist decree-laws. He was awarded the title of honorary professor by the universities of Pisa and Naples. Among his best known works are: Lo Stato Moderno e la giustizia (1885); Principi di procedura civile (1890; 7th ed., 1922); Manuale della procedura civile (9th ed., 1921).

Lit.: Rotondi, M., L. Mortara (1937); Calamandrei, P., L. Mortara (1937).

MORTGAGE ('ipotiki, from the Greek hypotheke). There was no place for a mortgage in Biblical law, as all real estate was hereditary and could be pledged only for a period until the jubilee, and never permanently transferred. During the period of the Second Temple, however, when the law of the jubilee no longer was enforced, Jewish law began to recognize the mortgaging of real estate and adopted the rule that "the property of a man is security for him" (B.B. 174a). A mortgage document covering real estate is mentioned in the Mishnah (Shebi. 10:5).

The chief use of the mortgage was in marriage law, since all the husband's property is regarded as under a tacit mortgage for the wife's marriage portion (Kethubah). Similarly, every assumption of a debt creates a general mortgage upon all the property of the debtor, under Jewish law, provided that this property is in possession of the debtor at the time he assumes the responsibility for payment. The creditor has a claim on such property even if it has been subsequently sold or given away. This is a legal pledge of all existing assets of the debtor. However, there is also in Jewish law a limited sort of mortgage, known as 'ipotiki, which, as the Greek nature of the word indicates, found its way into Jewish jurisprudence through Greek legal influence. In this case the real estate is retained by the debtor and serves only as security to the creditor. A distinction is made between the following two classes of mortgage:

a) the general mortgage, which has the following formula in the deed: "out of this property you shall satisfy your debt." In this case the creditor is to look primarily to this property for payment, so that the general property liability for the debt is converted into a special mortgage. A third party who purchases the property can either raise the mortgage by paying the indebtedness to the creditor or can shift it, by agreement, to other property of the debtor.

b) the special mortgage, with the formula: "only out of this property can you collect your claim." The liability of the debtor is thus limited solely to the mortgage. In this case a purchaser would have to surrender the property to the creditor if the mortgage is foreclosed; the latter can not be transferred to property of the debtor.

In another form of mortgage of real estate, accomplished by the shetar mashkanta ("document of pledge"), the mortgaged property is placed in the possession of the creditor, who has the right to use it as he sees fit. Since Jewish law prohibits the taking of interest, this type of mortgage is permitted only when such a mortgage is based on the amortization of the debt within a given time (B.M. 67b). During the period when Jews owned slaves, the latter were considered property on which a mortgage might be given.

See also: LOAN; PLEDGE.   MARCUS COHN.

Lit.: Dembitz, L. N., in Jewish Encyclopedia, vol. 9, pp. 37-38; Maimonides, Hilchoth Malveh Veloveh 18; Shulhan Aruch, Hoshen Mishpat 117 to 120.

MORTON, LEAH (pseudonym), see STERN, ELIZABETH GERTRUDE.

MORTON, MARTHA, playwright, b. New York, 1865; d. New York, 1925. In the decades from 1890 to 1910 she became rich and famous through her prolific contributions to the New York theatre. At one period she was considered the country's most successful woman playwright; and, though her plays did not win superior critical approval, they were almost always hits and money-makers.

Her first play was *The Refugee's Daughter,* produced in 1888; shortly thereafter she won a $1,500 prize from the *New York Herald* for a play entered in a competition. There followed a play almost every year including: *The Fool of Fortune* (1896); *A Bachelor's Romance* (1897); *On the Eve* (1909, adapted from the German); *The Three of Hearts* (1915). Some of her successes were produced abroad, several in London.

Martha Morton was adept at full character drawing; she fashioned her plays particularly for some of the famous actors of her day, including Sol Smith Russell and William H. Crane. Several of her plays were published as books. She wrote a novel, *Val Sinestra* (1924).

MOSCHCOWITZ, ALEXIS VICTOR, surgeon, b. Giralt, Hungary, 1865; d. New York city, 1933. He emigrated to the United States at fifteen and received his medical education at Columbia University; there he was appointed professor of clinical surgery (1913) at the College of Physicians and Surgeons. In 1899 he had entered on his career-long connection with Mount Sinai hospital; was up to 1914 associate surgeon, and from then on consulting surgeon. He was attached to other hospitals, including Beth David and Israel-Zion.

As a practical surgeon of long and versatile experience, Moschcowitz made important contributions to surgical knowledge of various subjects. Outstanding and fundamental was his work in hernia, carried on over a quarter of a century. His operation on femoral hernia, reported in 1907, is called the "Moschcowitz" operation, and his paper in *Johnson's Surgery* (1913) is considered a classic. A method of operating for rectal prolapse is also identified with his name. Moschcowitz wrote of numerous other operations. His final contribution, before his death, was a report to the American Surgical Association on the hitherto unknown disease of the male breast, vestigial mastitis. During the first World War Moschcowitz was a consultant chief in the Surgeon General's office in Washington, D. C. His researches, as a member of the Empyema Commission, resulted in a markedly lower mortality rate from empyema in the army. He was retired as a colonel.

MOSCHELES, IGNAZ, pianist, composer and teacher, b. Prague, 1794; d. Leipzig, 1870. At the age of fourteen he appeared in a concert in Prague performing his own concerto. He then went to Vienna where his teachers included Salieri and Albrechtsberger. His professional music career was launched when he began teaching the piano in Vienna, and appearing in public concerts. In Vienna, he became a personal friend of Beethoven who regarded him highly. Under Beethoven's personal supervision, Moscheles prepared the piano arrangement of *Fidelio.*

Subsequently his tours as pianist—to Munich, Dresden, Leipzig and other German music centres—made him one of the renowned concert pianists of the time. In 1821, he settled in London where he achieved great success as pianist and teacher. In 1837 he was a guest conductor of the London Philharmonic, becoming permanent conductor of that organization in 1845. He was a teacher of Felix Mendelssohn-Bartholdy, soon becoming one of his closest friends. After Mendelssohn founded the Leipzig Conservatory, Moscheles joined the faculty and enjoyed there a brilliant career as professor of the piano.

Moscheles composed prolifically for the piano, but few of his works have stood the test of time. Among his compositions, about one hundred and forty in all, are concertos, etudes, chamber music works, and several volumes of excellent exercises for piano students. He translated into English Anton Schindler's biography of Beethoven (London, 1841). His own correspondence with Mendelssohn was edited by his son.

DAVID EWEN.

Lit.: Moscheles, C. M., *Aus Moscheles Leben* (1872).

MOSCOVITCH, MAURICE, actor, b. Odessa, Russia, 1871; d. Hollywood, 1940. His first role was at the National Theatre in Odessa, at the age of fourteen. His choice of a profession displeased his Orthodox parents, and in 1890 he came to New York with Jacob Adler's company. He toured many European countries in 1897-99, and with his own company of Yiddish actors travelled through America, Canada, Brazil, Argentina and Europe in 1900-04. His Yiddish repertoire included all the best known classics of Jewish authors, as well as plays by Tolstoi, Turgeniev, Andreev and Strindberg. At the Gaiety Theatre in Manchester, England, he made his English-speaking debut (1919) as Shylock in *The Merchant of Venice.* Additional world tours took him to South Africa and Australia with a varied repertoire which included Shakespeare, Shaw, and (Edgar) Wallace.

He returned to New York in 1930 and appeared in *Josef Suss.* Moscovitch made his motion picture debut in 1936 and enacted roles in *Winterset, Suez, Gateway, Love Affair, Lancer Spy,* and *In Name Only,* establishing a reputation for dignified characterizations.

MOSCOW, capital of the Soviet Union and the Russian Soviet Republic, with 430,000 Jews at the beginning of 1941. It is the third largest Jewish community in the world, exceeded only by New York and Warsaw. The first evidence of the presence of Jews in Moscow comes from the time of Ivan III (1462-1505). The prohibition of 1490 notwithstanding, Jewish tradesmen came singly from Poland, Lithuania and more remote points to Moscow. In 1550 a new immigration ban was issued. However, the Jewish war prisoners were obliged to remain in Moscow after the peace of Andrussov (1667). But later Czar Feodor Alexievitch (1676-82) again forbade the immigration of Jewish merchants. This ban was renewed in the peace treaties with Poland of 1678 and 1686.

When White Russia was incorporated into the Russian Empire (1772), the Jews of this and other parts of the Russian Empire endeavored to obtain the right to settle in Moscow, and as early as at the end of the 18th cent. many tradesmen were allowed to settle there. The Jews had charge of the foreign trade. But at the suggestion of Moscovite merchants, the admission of Jews to the guild was forbidden in 1791. From then on they were allowed to come to Moscow only for business purposes. An exception was made for the Jewish soldiers, especially the Cantonists who, on being discharged from military service, could reside in the city together with their families. The Glyebov Trade Hotel was the dwelling place for transient Jews. The Moscow ghetto was built in the center of the commercial section. The Jews were permitted to unload their wares and array their shops only in this section (1826).

The residential rights of the Jewish tradesmen, which had granted them a stay of six months outside the Pale of Settlement, were revised in 1828, forbidding a residence beyond one month's time to the Jewish merchants of the first and second guilds. Only after many difficulties did they succeed in obtaining an extension of this residence period to six months and also exemption from the necessity of securing the authorization of the government officials each and every time. This facilitation increased the Jewish population of Moscow to such an extent as to make the ghetto inadequate to harbor them all. In 1856, the Jews were permitted to reside in any part of the town. Nevertheless, not only the general limitation of rights of the Jews in Russia existed in Moscow, but also some special exceptional rules, such as the 1867 regulations concerning Jewish physicians, were enacted there. During the Ignatiev administration, after the issuing of the May Laws (1882), their expulsion from Moscow was ordered, but not strictly enforced.

In 1890 the community consisted of about 26,000 persons, who formed 3 per cent of the entire population. Burgomaster Alexiev, who, due to some dispute with the Jewish industrialist Lazar Poliakoff, had a strong prejudice against the Jews, advocated their expulsion. On March 28, 1891, Jewish artisans and laborers were forbidden entry to the city and government of Moscow, and, at the same time instructions were issued for gradually clearing Moscow of Jews. This evacuation took place in the dead of winter, combined with the most arbitrary vexations by the police. Artisans, merchants, employes and teachers who had to leave the city in three relays (at intervals of three to six, six to nine and nine to twelve months, respectively), were the worst hit. After the evacuation of part of the Jewish population from the city, the governor general, Grand Duke Sergei Alexandrovitch, took energetic steps against the existence of the Moscow Jewish community. The dome of the synagogue had to be removed, and since Rabbi Solomon S. Minor and the president of the congregation presented a plea against this, the rabbi was deprived of his office and banished to the Pale of Settlement, and the president of the congregation was compelled to leave the city. Finally the congregation was asked either to sell the synagogue or to transform it into a charitable institution. The congregation then attempted to establish a handicraft school and later a Talmud Torah there. But the authorities objected to this, too, and demanded that the building be transformed into a hospital. The building was eventually adapted to permit the restoration of the synagogue to its original purpose. This, however, was not granted until after the 1905 revolution, the fourteen Minyanim that had at one time existed in the city having meanwhile been reduced to five by the authorities.

The Jewish tradesmen who had stayed in Moscow, and especially the temporary immigrants from the provinces, underwent agonies of persecution. An ukase of 1899 made the sojourning in Moscow by even the Jewish tradesmen of the first guild dependent upon the approval of the minister of the interior, which was tantamount to a prohibition.   JOSEF MEISL.

Moscow Jewry played a conspicuous part in the cultural life of the Jews of Russia. In the 1880's a group of Jewish intellectuals, mostly students at the University of Moscow, were engaged in historical research work. The activities centered around the Moscow branch of the Society for the Advancement of Enlightenment among the Russian Jews. Rabbi Minor was succeeded in 1893 by Jacob Mase, prominent orator, Hebrew writer and noted Palestinophile. In the first decade of the 20th cent. W. O. Harkavy founded, in 1906, together with others, the Society for the Diffusion of True Information on the Jews, against the defamation campaign of the anti-Semites. S. Wermel and the historian P. Marek were among the Jewish intellectuals of those years. In 1914 there appeared a comprehensive volume, *History of the Jews in Poland and Lithuania,* in the Mir publishing house, owned by Jews.

The Hebrew theatre Habimah attained its high artistic standard in Moscow (1918-25) under Bolshevik rule. In 1920 another Yiddish theatre was organized there by Alexander Granowsky, which was elevated to the rank of the Moscow Jewish State Theatre and in 1942 was under the management of the popular artist Mikhoels. A Yiddish communist paper, *Emes,* began to appear in Moscow (1918); it was discontinued in the 1930's.

The headquarters of the Agro-Joint, of the Russian branch of the Jewish Colonization Association, and of the ORT, which carried on reconstructive work among the Jews, were located for several years in Moscow.

After the expulsion in 1891 a few thousand Jews were left behind. According to the census of 1897, there lived in Moscow 8,473 Jews (1 per cent of the total population); in 1926 the number of the Jews was 131,000 (6 per cent of the total); and in 1940 they were estimated to number 400,000 (10 per cent of the total). The influx of Jews to Moscow had begun already during the first World War.

The Moscow synagogue remained intact under the Bolshevik regime and was administered by a private committee. With the approach of the Nazis to Moscow in the fall of 1941 many Jews were evacuated from the city. The synagogue committee was evacuated to Tashkent and, according to press information, was there assigned the rights of the representative organ of the evacuated Jews in that part of the Soviet Union. In August, 1941, a meeting of Jewish intellectuals in Moscow issued an appeal to the Jews of the world for an active fight for the destruction of Nazism. After the Nazi troops had been routed before Moscow, in December, 1941, thanksgiving services were held in the synagogue which were attended by thousands of Jews, including many soldiers.   MARK WISCHNITZER.

Lit.: Regesti i nadpisi, vols. 1 to 3; Marek, P., "K istorii Yevreyev v Moskve," *Voskhod* (1893), Nos. 2, 3 and 6; idem, "Moskovskoye getto," *ibid.,* (1895), No. 9; (1896), No. 10; Goldowski, in *Byloye* (1907), No. 9; Hessen, *Istoria yevreyskaya naroda v Rossii,* vol. 1 (1925); vol. 2 (1927); idem, in *Yevreiskaya Starina* (1915) 1-19, 153-72; idem, "Moskovskoye getto," *Perezhitoye,* vol. 1, pp. 51-65; *Yevreiskaya Entziklopedia,* vol. 11; Kaznelsohn, A. S., "Is martirologa moskovskoy obchtchini," *Yevreiskaya Starina,* vol. 1 (1909) 175-88; Frederic, Harold, *The New Exodus. A Study of Israel in Russia* (1892); *Yevrei v Moskve* (1904); *Jewish Affairs,* vol. 1, No. 1 (published by the Institute of Jewish Affairs, Aug., 1941); *American Jewish Year Book,* vol. 43 (1941-42) 314-21.

MOSCOWITZ, GROVER M., judge, b. Hot Springs, Ark., 1886. He received his law degree from the New York University Law School (1906) and was admitted to the bar the following year, entering practice in Brooklyn. In 1909-10, and again in 1922 and 1925, Moscowitz was special deputy attorney general in charge of prosecution of election frauds in Brooklyn.

In 1925 President Calvin Coolidge appointed Moscowitz United States District Judge for the Eastern District of New York. Subsequently he held court not only in the chief cities of New York State, but also in Connecticut, and in 1937 and 1941, by designation of Chief Justice Charles Evans Hughes, in Mississippi. During his incumbency Moscowitz handed down many opinions which marked departures in the legal interpretation of new problems, and also sat in many spectacular cases. Among the trials over which he presided were the Hazeltine radio patent trial (1926) and the Schick electric razor patent trial (1936), which gave added enforcement to patent rights; the McKesson and Robbins fraud trial (1939) and the trial of Joseph Schenck, motion picture magnate, for tax fraud. In 1936, by legalizing the importation of contraceptive material that a physician might desire to use to save a human life, Moscowitz established a progressive precedent in the long-standing fight to have birth control information made public. In naturalization proceedings, Moscowitz introduced the practice of denying citizenship to Communists, Fascists and Nazis.

As an active member of the Brooklyn Jewish community, Moscowitz held many directive posts. He was, from 1914 to 1921, president of the Young Men's Hebrew Association; he was also the organizer (1923) and first president of the Brooklyn Jewish Social Service Bureau, the centralized merger of the Brooklyn agencies doing Jewish delinquency work. In 1926 he was chairman of the United Jewish Campaign in Brooklyn and in 1928 chairman of the United Palestine Appeal. During the first World War, Moscowitz was a member of the Legal Advisory Board.

MOSENTHAL, ADOLF, South African pioneer, b. Cassel, Germany; d. Cape Town. By 1840 Mosenthal went to South Africa, and settled at Graaf Reinet. In 1850 he was authorized by the Cape Town congregation to represent its interests in Graaf Reinet. Associated with his brother Julius, Mosenthal succeeded in establishing a chain of trading houses that extended over all the eastern and midland farming districts of the Cape colony and well into the Orange Free State.

The Mosenthals caused, directly or indirectly, a regular flow of immigration of Jewish families with their kinsmen. These Hessian Jews became managers or sub-managers for the Mosenthals, or carried on the same type of enterprise on their own account, supported by the same firm. In 1851 the Mosenthals engaged an agent in Constantinople to export Angoras to South Africa, but this enterprise failed.

Immediately after the Crimean war, Adolf Mosenthal proceeded to Asia Minor and, with the assistance of the British government, he succeeded in purchasing a number of rams and ewes. Notwithstanding the reluctance of the Turkish government, and the outbreak of the cholera which forced Mosenthal to remain in a port of the Black Sea, he brought approximately thirty of the purest bred Angora goats to South Africa and sold them to the farmers around Graaf Reinet. Mosenthal continued to import fresh stocks, still frequently having to meet great difficulties and great risks. Due to

his efforts the production of mohair of superior quality became an established industry of the Cape colony.

Lit.: Theal, G. M-C., *History of South Africa,* vol. 4; Herrman, L., *A History of the Jews in South Africa* (1935).

MOSENTHAL, HARRY, South African banker and pioneer (son of Adolf Mosenthal), b. Cape Town, 1850; d. Cape Town, 1915. He entered his father's business early. When diamonds were first heard of in South Africa (1867), young Harry, immediately recognizing the importance of staking out in the diamond fields, induced his father's firm to engage in mining. By 1870 Mosenthal, at the age of twenty, founded the London and South Africa Exploration Company, cooperating with Lord Farquhar and Sigmund Ochs. The company purchased the two first farms whose surface soils were recognized to be diamond yielding fields, and within a few years Mosenthal became the owner of many mines and surrounding land including the township of Beaconsfield and a part of Kimberley.

In the 1880's Mosenthal collaborated with Rhodes, Barnato and Beit, and rendered them valuable assistance. He participated especially in the negotiations (Paris, 1887) for the purchase of property of the French mining company. In 1888 the De Beers Consolidated Mines Limited was incorporated. It took over assets representing the whole of De Beers mine, three fourths of the Kimberley mine, and controlled interests in Bultfontain and Dutoitspan mines. While Rhodes, Beit, Barnato and Philipson-Star were elected life-governors, Mosenthal was only one of the directors of the company. Mosenthal participated also in the consolidation of the Rand mine, and in the organizing of the Diamond Committee at London in 1890. He was not only a daring and keen pioneer; he also was a careful trainer of his young employees. Many of Mosenthal's former agents became important diamond traders.

Lit.: Mendelssohn, Sidney, *Jewish Pioneers in South Africa* (1915); Herrman, Louis, *A History of the Jews in South Africa* (1935); Chilvers, H. A., *Story of De Beers* (1939).

MOSENTHAL, JULIUS, South African pioneer, b. Cassel, Germany, 1818; d. Cape Town, 1880. Son of the merchant Herz Mosenthal who suddenly lost his fortune, Julius Mosenthal followed his brother Joseph to Africa in 1839, and was followed by his brother Adolf, while the fourth brother Salomon remained in Germany and became there a renowned dramatist. In 1842, the brothers Mosenthal founded a firm at Graaf Reinet which was at that time one of the important centres of South African trade. While Adolf Mosenthal was mainly interested in wool and hides, and Joseph in banking, Julius chose ostrich breeding and developed it to a flourishing industry. Nevertheless Julius also had expert knowledge of the wool trade, and contributed articles on the subject to the *Cape Monthly Magazine.* In 1857, Mosenthal was elected member of the legislative Council of the Cape Colony. He was the first professing Jew in the Cape parliament. Mosenthal was appointed French consul-general at Cape Town. He published *On Ostrich and Ostrich Farming* (1877). His brother Joseph was elected a member of the Legislative Council in 1861. HUGO BIEBER.

MOSERIM (singular, Moser), term used in Hebrew literature for informers. It was first used in the 2nd cent. for informers to the Roman government. *See* INFORMERS.